ST/ESA/STAT/SER.G/43

DEPARTMENT FOR ECONOMIC AND SOCIAL INFORMATION AND POLICY ANALYSIS
STATISTICS DIVISION

DÉPARTEMENT DE L'INFORMATION ÉCONOMIQUE ET SOCIALE ET DE L'ANALYSE DES POLITIQUES
DIVISION DE STATISTIQUE

1994
INTERNATIONAL TRADE STATISTICS YEARBOOK
ANNUAIRE STATISTIQUE DU COMMERCE INTERNATIONAL

VOLUME II

TRADE BY COMMODITY

COMMERCE PAR PRODUIT

UNITED NATIONS/NATIONS UNIES
New York, 1995

NOTE

Symbols of United Nations documents are composed of capital letters combined with figures.

General disclaimer

The designations employed and the presentation of material in this publication do not imply the expression of any opinion whatsoever on the part of the Secretariat of the United Nations concerning the legal status of any country, territory, city or area, or of its authorities, or concerning the delimitation of its frontiers or boundaries.

Where the designation "country or area" appears in this publication, it covers countries, territories, cities or areas. In previous issues of this publication, where the designation "country" appears in this headings of tables, it should be interpreted to cover countries, territories, cities or areas.

In some tables, the designation "developed" or "developing" economies is intended for statistical convenience and does not necessarily express a judgment about the stage reached by a particular country or area in the development process.

NOTE

Les cotes des documents de l'Organisation des Nations Unies se composent de lettres majuscules et de chiffres.

Déni de responsabilité

Les appellations employées dans cette publication et la présentation des données qui y figurent n'impliquent de la part du Secrétariat de l'Organisation des Nations Unies aucune prise de position quant au statut juridique des pays, territoires, villes ou zones, ou de leurs autorités, ni quant au tracé de leurs frontières ou limites.

L'appellation "pays ou zone", figurant dans cette publication, désigne des pays, des territoires, des villes ou des zones. L'appellation "pays" figurant dans certaines rubriques des tableaux de numéros antérieurs de cette publication doit être interprétée comme désignant des pays, des territoires, des villes ou des zones.

L'appellation économie "développée" ou économie "en voie de développement" qui figure dans certains tableaux est utilisée pour plus de commodité dans la présentation des statistiques et n'implique pas nécessairement un jugement quant au stade de développement auquel est parvenu un pays ou une zone donné.

ST/ESA/STAT/SER.G/43

UNITED NATIONS PUBLICATION
Sales No. E/F.96.XVII.2, vol. II

PUBLICATION DES NATIONS UNIES
Numéro de vente : E/F.96.XVII.2, vol. II

ISBN 92-1-061164-0

Inquiries should be directed to:
PUBLISHING DIVISION
UNITED NATIONS
NEW YORK, N.Y. 10017

Adresser toutes demandes de renseignements à la :
DIVISION DES PUBLICATIONS
NATIONS UNIES
NEW YORK, N.Y. 10017

Printed by the United Nations Reproduction Section, New York
Imprimé par la Section de la reproduction des Nations Unies, New York

TABLE OF CONTENTS

Volume II

SPECIAL TABLES

TABLE DES MATIERES

Volume II

TABLEAUX SPECIAUX

ABBREVIATIONS AND COUNTRY NOMENCLATURE

Names of some countries or groups of countries and of some commodities or groups of commodities have been abbreviated. Exact titles will be found in the following publications referred to in the introduction:

(i) United Nations Standard Country Code (Annex II, Country classification for international trade statistics),

(ii) United Nations Standard Country or Area Code for Statistical Use,

(iii) Standard Country or Area Codes for Statistical Use,

(iv) Standard Country or Area Codes for Statistical Use, Interim List

(v) Standard International Trade Classification, Revised (SITC, Revised),

(vi) Standard International Trade Classification, Revision 2, (SITC, Revision 2),

(vii) Classification by Broad Economic Categories (BEC),

(viii) Classification of Commodities by Industrial Origin and

(ix) International Standard Industrial Classification of all Economic Activities (ISIC).

1. Data relating to the People's Republic of China generally include those for Taiwan Province in the field of statistics relating to population, area, natural resources, natural conditions such as climate, etc. In other fields of statistics, they do not include Taiwan Province unless otherwise stated. Therefore, in this publication the data published under the heading China exclude those for Taiwan Province. Figures representing the trade with Taiwan Province which may have been reported by any reporting country or area are included in the grouping Asia.

2. On 22 May 1990 Democratic Yemen and Yemen merged to form a single State. Since that date they have been represented as one Member with the name "Yemen". All data shown in this publication relating to the period prior to 1990 refer to the former Democratic Yemen and the former Yemen.

3. Through accession of the German Democratic Republic to the Federal Republic of Germany with effect from 3 October 1990, the two German States have united to form one sovereign State. As from the date of unification, the Federal Republic of Germany acts in the United Nations under the designation of "Germany". All data shown which pertain to Germany prior to 3 October 1990 are indicated separately for the Federal Republic of Germany and the former German Democratic Republic based on their respective territories at the time indicated. Where data for united Germany (subsequent to 3 October 1990) are not available, they are shown separately and pertain to the territorial boundaries prior to 3 October 1990.

4. Unless otherwise indicated, data provided for Yugoslavia prior to 1 January 1992 refer to the Socialist Federal Republic of Yugoslavia which was composed of six republics, whereas data provided for Yugoslavia after that date refer to the Federal Republic of Yugoslavia which is composed of two republics (Serbia and Montenegro).

5. Data for the Czech Republic and Slovakia, where available, are shown separately under the appropriate country name. For periods prior to 1 January 1993, where no separate data are available for the Czech Republic and Slovakia, unless otherwise indicated, data for the former Czechoslovakia are shown under the country name "former Czechoslovakia".

6. In 1991, the Union of Soviet Socialist Republics formally dissolved into fifteen independent republics (Armenia, Azerbaijan, Belarus, Estonia, Georgia, Kazakstan, Kyrgyzstan, Latvia, Lithuania, Republic of Moldova, Russian Federation, Tajikistan, Turkmenistan, Ukraine and Uzbekistan). From 1992 onwards data are shown for the individual republics. Prior to 1992 data are shown for the former USSR.

ABREVIATIONS ET CODES PAYS.

Les noms de certains pays ou groupes de pays et de certains produits ou groupes de produits ont dû être abrégés. On trouvera les intitulés exacts de ces noms dans les publications suivantes qui figurent dans l'Introduction:

(i) United Nations Standard Country Code (Annex V, 'Standardized Abbreviated French Country Names'),
(ii) United Nations Standard Country or Area Code for Statistical Use,
(iii) Standard Country or Area Codes for Statistical Use
(iv) Standard Country or Area Codes for Statistical Use, Interim List
(v) Classification type pour le commerce international révisée, (CTCI révisée),
(vi) Classification type pour le commerce international (deuxième version révisée) (CTCI, Révision 2),
(vii) Classification par grandes catégories economiques (CGCE)
(viii) Classification des marchandises par origine industrielle et
(ix) Classification internationale type, par industrie, de toutes les branches d'activité économique (CITI).

1. Les données relatives à la République populaire de Chine comprennent en général les données relatives à la province de Taïwan lorsqu'il s'agit de statistiques concernant la population, la superficie, les ressources naturelles, les conditions naturelles tel que le climat, etc. Dans les statistiques relevant d'autres domaines, la province de Taïwan n'est pas comprise, sauf indication contraire. C'est le cas dans cet Annuaire où les données pour la Chine ne comprennent pas celles de la province de Taïwan. Lorsque des pays partenaires ont déclaré des échanges avec Taïwan ceux-ci sont inclus dans Asie.

2. Le Yémen et le Yémen démocratique ont fusionné le 22 mai 1990 pour ne plus former qu'un seul Etat, qui est depuis lors représenté comme tel à l'Organisation, sous le nom 'Yémen'. Toutes les données présentées dans cet Annuaire qui se rapportent à la période antérieure à l'année 1990 se réfèrent aux anciens Yémen démocratique et Yémen.

3. En vertu de l'adhésion de la République démocratique allemande à la République fédérale d'Allemagne, prenant effet le 3 octobre 1990, les deux Etats allemands se sont unis pour former un seul Etat souverain. A compter de la date de l'unification, la République fédérale d'Allemagne est désignée à l'ONU sous le nom 'Allemagne'. Toutes les données se rapportant à l'Allemagne avant le 3 octobre 1990 figurent dans deux rubriques séparées, basées sur les territoires respectifs de la République fédérale d'Allemagne et l'ancienne République démocratique allemande selon la période

indiquée. En l'absence de données pour l'Allemagne unifiée (à compter du 3 octobre 1990), les données sont fournies séparément sous les rubriques Allemagne (République fédérale d') et Allemagne (ancienne République démocratique) et se rapportent aux limites territoriales antérieures au 3 octobre 1990 lorsqu'elles sont disponibles.

4. Sauf indication contraire, les données fournies pour la Yougoslavie avant le 1er janvier 1992 se rapportent à la République fédérative socialiste de Yougoslavie, qui était composée de six républiques; les données fournies pour la Yousgoslavie après cette date se rapportent à la République fédérative de Yougoslavie, qui est composée de deux républiques (Serbie et Monténégro).

5. Les données relatives à la République tchèque, et à la Slovaquie, lorsqu'elles sont disponibles, sont présentées séparément sous le nom de chacun des pays. En ce qui concerne la période antérieure au 1er janvier 1993, pour laquelle on ne possède pas de données séparées pour les deux Républiques, les données relatives à l'ancienne Tchécoslovaquie sont, sauf indication contraire, présentées sous le titre 'ancienne Tchécoslovaquie'.

6. En 1991, l'ex Union Soviétique a été scindée officiellement en quinze républiques indépendantes (Arménie, Azerbaïdjan, Bélarus, Estonie, Fédération de Russie, Géorgie, Kazakstan, Kirghizistan, Lettonie, Lituanie, Ouzbékistan, République de Moldova, Tadjikistan, Turkménistan et Ukraine). A partir de 1992 les données sont indiquées pour chaque république individuellement. Avant 1992, les données sont indiquées pour l'ancienne URSS.

EXPLANATION OF SYMBOLS
EXPLICATION DES SIGNES

Category not applicable .... Ne s'applique pas	.or..
Not available................................... Aucune donnée disponible	blank or...
Magnitude of less than half the unit used............. Grandeur inférieure à la moitié de l'unité utilisée	0 or 0.0
Provisional or estimated figures..................... Donnée provisoire ou estimation	X
Area (1,000 square metres)............................ Superficie (1,000 mètres carrés)	A
1,000 kilowatt-hours.................................. 1,000 kilowatts-heures	H
Weight (kilograms).................................... Poids (kilogrammes)	K
Length (1,000 metres)................................. Longeur (1,000 mètres)	L
1,000 times unit shown................................ 1,000 fois l'unité indiquée	M
Number.. Nombre	N
Other... Autres	O
Number of pairs....................................... Paires	P
Volume (cubic metres)................................. Volume (mètre cube)	V
Weight (metric tons).................................. Poids (tonnes métriques)	W
1,000,000 times unit shown............................ 1 million de fois l'unité indiquée	Y
Decimal figures are always preceded by a period except for the Country Notes in French where they are preceded by a comma............................. Les décimales sont toujours précédées d'un point, a l'exception des notes de pays en français où elles sont précédées par une virgule.	(.)

MAGNETIC TAPES AND DISKETTES

External trade data, for the majority of countries from 1962 to the latest year, are available in machine readable form. Detailed information on coverage and price is available, on request, from the United Nations Statistical Division, New York, N.Y. 10017, USA. The data cover annual periods but, for certain countries, cumulative quarterly data are available in the SITC Classification supplied by the reporting country.

BANDES MAGNETIQUES ET DISQUES

Les données du commerce extérieur pour la majorité des pays de 1962 à la dernière année écoulée sont disponibles sous forme de supports magnétiques. Les informations détaillées sur la nature, le volume, les dates et les prix de ces supports magnétiques peuvent être obtenues auprès Division de Statistique des Nations Unies, New York, N.Y. 10017, Etats Unis. Les données sont annuelles mais, pour certains pays, seules les données trimestrielles cumulées sont disponibles dans la classification CTCI soumise par le pays concerné.

INTRODUCTION

The forty-third edition of the International Trade Statistics Yearbook provides the basic information for individual countries' external trade performances in terms of the overall trends in current value, as well as in volume and price, the importance of trading partners and the significance of individual commodities imported and exported. This edition shows annual statistics for 182 countries or reporting customs areas. It is published in two volumes.

VOLUME I

Volume I contains detailed data for individual countries. For each country the following tables usually appear:

(a) Table 1, showing ten series, five for imports and five for exports. The five are: total merchandise trade and trade in gold (generally in national currency, but in US dollars for some countries), conversion factors for converting total merchandise trade from national currency into United States dollars, quantum index numbers and unit value index numbers for total imports and exports.

(b) Table 2, showing for the years 1988 to the latest year available, percentage breakdowns of imports by broad economic categories of end use and of exports by industrial origin. Data for the years 1970 to 1987 were shown in previous issues of this Yearbook. The analysis for imports is based on the Classification by Broad Economic Categories 1/ and for exports on the Classification of Commodities by Industrial Origin 2/. Reclassification of foreign trade according to broad economic categories or industrial origin requires statistical information at the five-digit level of the Standard International Trade Classification, Revised. (For history and background of the SITC, see pages xxi-xxiii). When such details are not available, approximate allocations are made, using the three-digit level of the SITC Revised. In comparing statistics of international trade with statistics of production, problems of limitation exist in addition to those of classification. Exports of products which are obviously not produced in the reporting countries (e.g., exports of tea and cocoa from the Netherlands or the United Kingdom) have been allocated to the industrial origin in which they would have been classified in the producing countries; in the case of tea and cocoa: Agriculture. The industrial origin in the reporting country of these exports is, in fact, the wholesale trade. In the Classification of Commodities by Industrial Origin, SITC, Revised headings are subdivided to correspond, roughly, to groups of the <u>International Standard Industrial Classification of All Economic Activities</u>, (Revision 1) <u>3</u>/. The breakdown of exports by industrial origin is derived as much as possible from national or special exports.

(c) Table 3, showing up to the most recent five years available, the value in United States dollars of import and export trade analyzed by the principal countries or areas and regions of provenance and destination. The analysis is made according to the United Nations <u>Standard Country or Area Codes for Statistical Use</u> <u>4</u>/. In some instances, owing to the nature of the national country classification, the conversion to the United Nations country classification could not be done precisely. A maximum of 50 trading partners are shown in order of magnitude, based on the sum of the values over the years included in the table, with imports and exports ranked separately. Below the value table is a listing showing the percentage breakdown of trade by regions and the percent of trade accounted for by each of the first ten trading partners for the latest available ten years.

(d) Tables 4 and 5, showing up to the most recent four years available, the quantity and the value in United States dollars of imports and exports analyzed by commodities. Data for a commodity will appear if the value in any year is greater than or equal to 0.3 per cent of the total trade for that year. The commodities are shown in terms of SITC headings (abbreviated). An <u>asterisk</u> (*) preceding the description indicates that these are the only codes belonging to the next higher level of the SITC, and the next higher level is therefore not shown.

In some instances the figures shown in United States dollars in the tables indicated under (c) and (d) above may not correspond to those in United States dollars in the table described under (a) above or to those in national currency in that table after the application of the currency conversion factors. These discrepancies arise in large part from revisions to the more recent data at the total level where such revisions were not broken down for the more detailed data by commodity and partner; it was felt that a partial revision of the tables referred to under (c) and (d) above to make the totals consistent with those in (a) should not be made.

For all countries, the analysis of imports and exports by commodity is made according to the Standard International Trade Classification (SITC) <u>5</u>/ as follows:

i) SITC, Revised for countries reporting according to that revision or according to the original SITC for the latest four years.

ii) SITC, Revised for countries that have begun reporting according to the SITC, Revision 2, but with less than four years of data in that nomenclature.

iii) SITC, Revision 2 for countries reporting according to that revision for the latest four years.

iv) SITC, Revision 2 for countries reporting data according to the SITC, Revision 3 or the Harmonized Commodity Description and Coding System (HS). The data so reported for these countries, in volumes I and II, were converted from SITC, Revision 3 to SITC Revision 2 and are footnoted in the tables. In a few cases because of the difficulties of converting data from SITC, Revision 3 to SITC, Revision 2 this resulted in data which are not comparable with data for earlier years reported in terms of SITC, Revision 2 to a very significant extent.

In a few cases, the conversion to SITC from the national commodity classification system could not be done precisely and, therefore, some of the SITC codes are not exact in their coverage.

When available, more detailed data by commodity and partner country are published according to the SITC, Revised, Revision 2 or Revision 3 in Commodity Trade Statistics 6/ and are also available on microfiches.

VOLUME II

Volume II contains commodity tables showing the total trade of certain commodities analyzed by regions and countries.

Commodity tables. These tables show imports and exports of commodities at the group (3-digit) level of the SITC, Revision 2 (all groups except for 351 and 688). The years covered are the five years 1990 to 1994. The values are in U.S. dollars and both imports and exports are analyzed by regions and principal trading countries. A maximum of 50 countries are shown in order of magnitude, based on the sum of the values over the years 1991, 1992 and 1993 included in the table, with imports and exports ranked separately. The systems of trade applicable to these countries are the same as those indicated under tables 4 and 5 in the country tables section of this publication. No quantity data are shown. In preparing these tables, in many cases estimates were made for countries whose data were not yet available. Notes on these estimates appear on pages 1 of Volume II.

Volume II also contains special tables showing, inter alia, (a) the contribution of the trade of each country to the trade of its region and of the world, (b) the flow of trade between countries and regions and (c) the fluctuations of the prices at which goods moved internationally. The special tables are:

(a) Total imports and exports by regions and countries or areas;
(b) World exports by commodity classes and by regions;
(c) Growth of world exports by commodity classes and by regions;
(d) Structure of world exports by commodity classes and by regions;
(e) Total imports and exports: index numbers by countries or areas;
(f) Total exports and imports: index numbers of quantum, unit value and terms of trade by regions;
(g) Manufactured goods exports;
(h) Fuel imports: developed economies;
(i) Some indicators on fuel imports: developed economies;
(j) Export price index of machinery and transport equipment for selected countries;
(k) Export price index numbers of primary commodities and non-ferrous base metals.

Special Tables

The economic and geographic groupings in all the special tables are in accordance with those of Special Table A in this issue, although Special Table A sometimes includes more detailed geographic sub-groups. (See Special Table A for the details).

(A) Total imports and exports by regions and countries or areas. The regional, economic and world totals have been adjusted: (a) to include estimates for countries or areas for which full data are not available; (b) to include insurance and freight for imports valued f.o.b.; (c) to include countries or areas not listed separately; (d) to approximate special trade; (e) to approximate calendar years; and (f) where possible, to eliminate incomparabilities owing to geographical changes, by adjusting the figures for periods before the change to be comparable to those for periods after the change, for example, the European Community and the European Free Trade Association. The figures shown for individual countries correspond to the national currency figures which appear and are described in table 1 of the country tables. The letters in the first and last columns of the table indicate the system of trade used: G: General trade; S: Special trade. For footnotes see the end of the table.

Monthly and quarterly data appear in the Monthly Bulletin of Statistics.

(B) World exports by commodity classes and by regions. For the general note and footnotes, see the end of the table.

(C) Growth of world exports by commodity classes and by regions.

The annual average rates of change in percentage terms given in this table have been uniformly calculated by the use of the compound interest formula:

$$r = \left(\sqrt[t]{\frac{Vn}{Vo}} - 1 \right) 100$$

r = Annual average rate of change in percentage terms
Vn = Value of exports during the last year of the period
Vo = Value of exports during the first year of the period
t = Number of years in period

For the general note and footnotes, see the end of Special Table D.

(D) Structure of world exports by commodity classes and by regions. The figures shown under the heading 'Origin of Exports' refer to the exports of the region or country appearing in the 'Area' column; those shown under the heading 'Destination of Exports' refer to the exports of the world to the region or country appearing in the 'Area' column. For the general note and footnotes, see the end of the table.

(E) Total imports and exports: index numbers by countries or areas. Unless otherwise stated in the footnotes, the unit value indices are in terms of national currencies. For the general note and footnotes, see the end of the table.

Monthly and quarterly data appear in the *Monthly Bulletin of Statistics*.

(F) Total exports and imports: index numbers of quantum, unit value and terms of trade by regions. For the footnotes, see the end of the table.

Quarterly data appear in the *Monthly Bulletin of Statistics*.

(G) Manufactured goods exports. For the general note and footnotes, see the end of the table.

Quarterly data appear in the *Monthly Bulletin of Statistics*.

(H) Fuel imports: developed economies. For the general note and footnotes, see the end of the table.

Quarterly data appear in the Monthly Bulletin of Statistics.

(I) Some indicators on fuel imports: developed economies. This table shows the share of fuel imports in the total value of imports and in the total value of exports, and the ratio of unit value indices of manufactured goods exports to those of fuel imports. For the general note and footnotes, see the end of the table.

Quarterly data appear in the Monthly Bulletin of Statistics.

(J) Export price index of machinery and transport equipment for selected countries. For general note, see the end of the table.

Quarterly data appear in the Monthly Bulletin of Statistics.

(K) Export price index numbers of primary commodities and non-ferrous base metals. For the general note and footnote, see the end of the table.

Monthly and quarterly data appear in the Monthly Bulletin of Statistics.

SOURCES AND PRESENTATION

The figures for Volumes I and II are obtained from national published sources, from data supplied by the Governments for use in this publication and the following United Nations publications: Commodity Trade Statistics, Monthly Bulletin of Statistics and Statistical Yearbook, and from publications specially prepared by other United Nations agencies. Estimates for some missing data are made by the United Nations Statistics Division.

The country and regional names used by various countries are not uniform for their trade statistics. Also, where former geographical entities commonly referred to in national statistics have changed, countries may introduce the corresponding changes in their statistics at different times. Wherever possible, however, parts of the world have been designated by the names they currently bear.

The country aggregates shown throughout this publication are based on those set forth in the United Nations Standard Country or Area Codes for Statistical Use 4/, except where indicated.

NATIONAL INDEX NUMBERS

National index numbers of unit value in national currencies or United States dollars and of quantum are shown in table 1. They are the official indices which show the changes in the volume, (quantum index) and the average price (unit value index) of the aggregate merchandise imports or exports. Each index number represents a change between the period to which the number refers, called the current period, and a fixed period, called the publication base, in which the index is represented by the percentage 100. In order to facilitate comparison, the indices shown have been adjusted, where possible, so that the calendar year 1990 is the publication base. When changes are made in the coverage, formula or base period of an index, the two series are linked together if they have an overlapping period and are sufficiently comparable.

Quarterly and monthly figures in these index series appear in the United Nations Monthly Bulletin of Statistics and a more detailed description of their compilation is given in the 1977 Supplement to the Statistical Yearbook and the Monthly Bulletin of Statistics 7/.

TRANSITION COUNTRIES

For the period covered by this Yearbook, countries formerly classified for statistical purposes as centrally planned economies had systems of official rates between their currencies and other currencies, all consistent with rates of 0.90 new roubles to the United States dollar prior to 24 December 1971 and 0.829 new roubles to the United States dollar until February 1973; since then these rates have been fluctuating. They generally used these rates when it was necessary to convert foreign into domestic currencies for the purpose of compiling external trade statistics. The resulting data are for comparison with the external transactions of the rest of the world rather than with domestic monetary transactions.

The trade statistics of these countries had definitions somewhat different from those which exist in other countries. Differences in definition contribute to the discrepancies which can be observed between statistical records referring to the same flow of goods but kept by two trading partners having different economic systems. The trade among these countries was carried out on a basis not comparable to that governing trade with other countries. The concept of transaction value, for instance, as applied outside those countries is based on the existence of a market between exporters and importers in which the interaction of supply and demand has more effect than it can be assumed to have had in those countries; in the absence of data on the unit values of specific commodities entering the trade of those countries with one another, it is difficult to assess the possible effects on the trade statistics of this kind of incomparability.

GENERAL STATEMENTS 8/

1. Territory. The statistics reported by a country refer to the customs area of the country. In most cases this coincides with the geographical area of the country. Where it does not, the fact is indicated in country notes. Changes in customs areas are also noted in country notes. Unless otherwise stated, the combination of two territories, formerly separate, results in the elimination from the statistics of their trade with each other. The separation of two territories, formerly together, results in the appearance of their trade with each other in the statistics for each territory.

2. System of trade. Two systems of recording trade are in common use, differing mainly in the way warehoused and re-exported goods are recorded:

(a) Special trade: special imports are the combined total of imports for direct domestic consumption (including transformation and repair) and withdrawals from bonded warehouses or free zones for domestic consumption. Special exports comprise exports of national merchandise, namely, goods wholly or partly produced or manufactured in the country, together with exports of nationalized goods (nationalized goods are goods which, having been included in special imports, are then exported without transformation).

(b) General trade: general imports are the combined total of imports for direct domestic consumption and imports into bonded warehouses or free zones. General exports are the combined total of national exports and re-exports. Re-exports, in the general trade system, consist of the outward movement of nationalized goods plus goods which, after importation, move outward from bonded warehouses or free zones without having been transformed.

Direct transit trade, i.e., goods merely being trans-shipped or moving through the country for purposes of transport only, is excluded from the statistics of both special and general trade.

Each of the tables indicates in its heading the system of trade to which the figures relate. More details are, where necessary, available in country notes.

3. Valuation. At its fifteenth session, in 1953, the Economic and Social Council, taking the view that trade statistics must reflect economic realities, recommended that the Governments of Member States of the United Nations, wherever possible, use transaction values in the compilation of their national statistics of external trade or, when national practices are based on other values, endeavour to provide supplementary statistical data based on transaction values (Economic and Social Council resolution 469 B (XV)). In the case of imports, the transaction value is the value at which the goods were purchased by the importer plus the cost of

transportation and insurance to the frontier of the importing country (a c.i.f. valuation). In the case of exports, the transaction value is the value at which the goods were sold by the exporter, including the cost of transportation and insurance, to bring the goods onto the transporting vehicle at the frontier of the exporting country (a f.o.b. valuation).

4. Currency conversion. For data in this publication, conversion of values from national currencies into United States dollars is done by means of currency conversion factors based on official exchange rates. Values in currencies subject to fluctuation (such currencies increased in number beginning December 1971) are converted into United States dollars using weighted average exchange rates specially calculated for this purpose. The weighted average exchange rate for a given currency for a given year is the component monthly factors, mostly furnished by the International Monetary Fund, weighted by the value of the relevant trade in each month. A monthly factor is the exchange rate (or the simple average rate) in effect during that month. These factors are applicable to total imports and exports respectively, but not necessarily to trade in individual commodities or with individual countries.

5. Merchandise. In order that external trade statistics shall be suited to the measurement of the influence of national economies upon one another, merchandise trade is defined to include, as far as possible, all goods which add to or subtract from the material resources of a country as a result of their movements into or out of the country. Unless, therefore, statements to the contrary are made in country notes or in footnotes to the country tables, the treatment of the classes of goods listed below are as indicated:

(a) Gold. Gold traded internationally is usually defined as encompassing the three following types:

i) Gold coins (issued and unissued) and bullion, including banking and monetary gold;
ii) Unrefined gold, including gold ores and concentrates;
iii) Partly-worked gold in which the value of the gold is 80 per cent or more of the total value, including scrap, jewellers' sweepings, dust, primary shapes (such as rods, wire and gold leaf) and gold alloys (crude or in primary shapes).

Of the types of gold listed above, those belonging to the category of monetary gold are excluded from merchandise trade, and those classified as non-monetary gold are included, except as indicated below. Any gold shipment received by the central monetary authority of a country is treated as monetary gold. All other gold shipments (whether to commercial banks or to individuals), on the other hand, are considered non-monetary. SITC, Revised, treated all types of gold as non-merchandise trade. In compliance with the SITC, Revised, as well as for practical reasons, all types of gold listed above are in general excluded from the merchandise trade statistics compiled under this version of the classification. However, data compiled under SITC, Revision 2 and Revision 3, include non-monetary gold.

(b) Silver ore, concentrates, bullion, unissued coin (see (c) below), scrap and partly-worked and manufactured silver are all included in merchandise trade statistics.

(c) Currency and titles of ownership which have been issued into circulation, e.g., issued silver and base metal coins, bank notes, other paper currency and securities, are excluded from merchandise trade statistics. Unissued currency and titles of ownership are included at their intrinsic value as stamped metal or printed paper rather than at face value.

(d) Trade on government account is included as merchandise trade. Movements under government foreign aid programmes (civil and military), war reparations and restitutions and military goods 9/ moving internationally are therefore included. When goods are destined for use of national agencies (including embassies and military forces) stationed abroad they are, however, not considered to have moved in external trade and are excluded.

(e) Temporary imports and exports. Tourists' and travellers' effects not acquired abroad (including vehicles), goods for exhibitions or study, animals admitted to a country temporarily, merely for racing or breeding, returnable containers, etc., the movements of all of which are expected to be reversed within a limited time, are excluded.

(f) Improvement and repair trade. Countries sending goods abroad for improvement or repair and return are said to be engaging in the passive improvement and repair trade; countries receiving goods from other countries for improvement or repair and eventual return engage in the active improvement and repair trade. Inward and outward movement in this trade are generally excluded from imports and exports.

(g) Postal trade is included in merchandise trade.

(h) Trade in fish, etc. Fish and salvage sold abroad or to foreign vessels off national vessels, and fish and salvage landed from foreign vessels in national ports are excluded from merchandise trade statistics.

(i) Trade in ships and aircraft. New ships and aircraft bought and sold are included. Second-hand ships and aircraft entering or leaving the registers of the reporting country as a result of transfer of ownership are excluded.

(j) Bunkers and stores for ships and aircraft. In general, bunkers and stores should be included in aggregate merchandise exports.

6. Partner country. The following terms describe methods that may be used by reporting countries in determining, for each shipment of goods, the partner country under whose name it should be recorded: (a) for imports: country of origin or production, country of consignment, country of purchase or country of provenance; (b) for exports: country of consumption or consignment, or country of sale.

7. Trade analyzed by commodity. Analysis is according to the Standard International Trade Classification.

THE STANDARD INTERNATIONAL TRADE CLASSIFICATION (SITC)

In July 1950, the United Nations Economic and Social Council, on the advice of its Statistical Commission, recommended that Governments compile trade by commodity statistics according to the original SITC 5/ in order to have available data in internationally comparable categories suitable for the economic analysis of trade. The original SITC had been prepared by the United Nations Secretariat with the assistance of expert consultants and in co-operation with Member Governments and interested international organizations.

In May 1960, the Statistical Commission approved a revision, similarly prepared, of the original SITC, known as the SITC, Revised, designed to take account of the changes in the pattern of trade since 1950 and to simplify the relation between the SITC and internationally agreed customs tariff nomenclatures 5/. The SITC, Revised, is a rearrangement into statistical order of the items of the 1955 Tariff Nomenclature (CCCN) of the Customs Co-operation Council.

The relation between the original SITC and the SITC, Revised is discussed in the introductions to certain issues of Commodity Trade Statistics, notably those for January-December 1960 and 1961.

The SITC, Revised, is based on 625 subgroups (identified by code numbers of four digits), most of which correspond to items of the original SITC. A number of subgroups are further subdivided either to distinguish commodities of statistical importance or to permit exact correspondence with the CCCN; this results in a basic (5-digit code) level for the SITC, Revised, consisting of 1,312 items. The subgroups are combined, progressively, into 177 groups, 56 divisions and 10 sections.

The headings of the SITC, Revised, are fully determined by their code numbers. The precise composition of each number is defined in the SITC, Revised, itself. In comparing data according to the SITC, Revised, with data according to a national commodity classification it must be remembered that the same brief description may refer to aggregates differing somewhat in composition.

Although the SITC, Revised, of 1960 represented a great improvement on the original SITC, basically the same reasons which led to the creation of the SITC and its first revision were found, in the late nineteen-sixties, to be once more valid. Since 1960 the volume of trade had increased rapidly and its geographic and commodity patterns had changed fundamentally. Consequently, a second revision of the SITC was undertaken. In October 1974 the Statistical Commission approved of this revision, known as SITC, Revision 2 5/, and in May 1975 the Economic and Social Council recommended that Member States of the United Nations should report data on external trade according to the SITC, Revision 2, as far and as soon as possible. Starting with data for 1976, some countries began reporting trade statistics based on the SITC, Revision 2.

The basic headings of the SITC, Revision 2 had a one-to-one correspondence with the subdivisions of the Customs Co-operation Council Nomenclature (CCCN). However, there were a number of users who found the subdivisions of CCCN (and thus SITC, Revision 2) insufficient for their needs 10/. There was also an expressed need for the harmonization of economic classifications 11/. Partly to satisfy these needs, the Customs Co-operation Council in May 1973 undertook responsibility for the development and completion of the Harmonized Commodity Description and Coding System (HS). The work resulted in the revision of CCCN and the expansion of its four-digit categories into HS comprising 5,019 six-digit headings 12/.

At its twenty-first session, in January 1981, the Statistical Commission had taken note of the fact that a third revision of SITC would have to be made available when both the revised CCCN and HS came into force 13/. Accordingly, later that year, the United Nations Secretariat commenced work on the revision of SITC, Revision 2, based on the principle that every effort should be made to maintain its general character and structure but taking into account the need for its harmonization with the revised CCCN, the International Standard Industrial Classification (ISIC) Revision 3 14/ and a Central Product Classification 15/ which was developed jointly by the United Nations Statistics Division and the Statistical Office of the European Communities.

The final draft was revised and approved by the Statistical Commission at its twenty-third session, in February 1985, and a resolution was adopted by the Economic and Social Council on 28 May 1985 (resolution 1985/7) which, inter alia, recommended that Member States should report internationally data on external trade statistics according to the Standard International Trade Classification, Revision 3, as far and as soon as possible, it being understood that Member States may not wish to make the change until they would in any case be reviewing their customs nomenclature.

1/ Classification by Broad Economic Categories (in terms of the SITC Revised), Statistical Papers, Series M No.53, (United Nations publication, Sales No. 71.XVII.12).

2/ Classification of Commodities by Industrial Origin (Relationship of the Standard International Trade Classification Revised to the International Standard Industrial Classification of All Economic Activities, Revision 1), Statistical Papers, Series M No.43, (United Nations publication, Sales No. 66.XVII.7).

3/ International Standard Industrial Classification of All Economic Activities (Revision 1), Statistical Papers, Series M No. 4, Rev. 1, (United Nations publication, Sales No. 58.XVII.7).

4/ United Nations Standard Country Codes, Statistical Papers, Series M No. 49 (United Nations publication, Sales No. E.70.XVII.13).

United Nations Standard Country or Area Codes for Statistical Use, Statistical Papers, Series M No. 49, Rev. 1, (United Nations publication, Sales No. E.75.XVII.8).

Standard Country or Area Codes for Statistical Use, Statistical Papers, Series M No. 49, Rev.2, (United Nations publication, Sales No. E.82.XVII.8).

Standard Country or Area Codes for Statistical Use, Interim List (United Nations Statistical Division).

5/ Standard International Trade Classification, Statistical Papers, Series M No.10 Second edition, (United Nations publication, Sales No. 51.XVII.1).

Standard International Trade Classification Revised, Statistical Papers, Series M No. 34, (United Nations publication, Sales No. 61.XVII.6).

Standard International Trade Classification Revision 2, Statistical Papers, Series M No.34/Rev.2, (United Nations publication, Sales No. E.75.XVII.6).

Standard International Trade Classification Revision 3, Statistical Papers, Series M No.34/Rev.3, (United Nations publication, Sales No. E.86.XVII.12).

6/ Commodity Trade Statistics, Statistical Papers, Series D, carries annual figures showing the provenance and destination of trade for a large number of headings of the SITC, Revised, SITC, Revision 2, and SITC, Revision 3. Quarterly and annual figures are available on microfiches.

7/ 1977 Supplement to the Statistical Yearbook and Monthly Bulletin of Statistics, ST/ESA/STAT/SER.S/SUPPL.2, ST/ESA/STAT/SER.Q/SUPPL.2, (United Nations publication, Sales No. E.78.XVII.10).

8/ The treatment of items 1 to 7 is drawn mainly from International Trade Statistics Concepts and Definitions, Statistical Papers, Series M No. 52, Rev.1, (United Nations publication, Sales No. E.82.XVII.14).

9/ Countries excluding military goods from imports or exports use varying definitions of this category of merchandise, but for most countries concerned, weapons and their ammunition constitute a major part of the military goods excluded.

10/ United Nations Statistical Division and Statistical Office of the European Communities Joint Working Group on World Level Classifications, "A Harmonized Commodity Description and Coding System for Use in International Trade" (UNSO/SOEC/1/2).

11/ United Nations Secretariat, "The Harmonization of Statistical Classifications: report of an expert group meeting". (ST/ESA/STAT/78).

12/ Customs Co-operation Council, The Harmonized Commodity Description and Coding System, Brussels, 1985.

13/ Official Records of the Economic and Social Council, 1981, Supplement No. 2 (E/1981/12).

14/ International Standard Industrial Classification of All Economic Activities, Statistical Papers, Series M No.4, Rev.3 (United Nations publication, Sales No.E.90.XVII.11).

15/ Provisional Central Product Classification, Statistical Papers, Series M No.77 (United Nations publication, Sales No.E.91.XVII.7).

INTRODUCTION

La quarante troisième édition de l' annuaire statistique du commerce international présente les informations nécessaires à l'étude des échanges de chaque pays, en termes de valeur courante, de volume et de prix ainsi que l'importance des différents pays partenaires et des principaux produits importés et exportés. Cette édition présente des données annuelles pour 182 pays ou zones douanières déclarants. L'annuaire est publié en deux volumes.

Volume I

Le Volume I fournit des renseignements détaillés sur chaque pays au sujet duquel on trouvera généralement les tableaux suivants:

a) Tableau 1, donnant 10 séries, 5 à l'importation, 5 à l'exportation. Ces cinq séries sont: échanges de marchandises et échanges portant sur l'or (généralement en monnaie nationale mais pour quelques pays, en dollars des Etats-Unis), facteurs pour convertir les monnaies nationales en dollars des Etats-Unis, indices du quantum et de la valeur unitaire pour les importations et exportations totales.

b) Tableau 2, présentant de l'année 1988 jusqu'à la dernière année disponible, les pourcentages par rapport au commerce total des importations par grandes catégories économiques et les exportations par branches d'origine. Les pourcentages pour 1970 à 1987 ont été publiés dans les éditions précédentes de cet Annuaire. L'analyse pour les importations est basée sur la Classification par grandes catégories économiques 1/; pour les exportations sur la Classification des marchandises par origine industrielle.2/ Toute reclassification du commerce extérieur par grandes catégories économiques ou par origine industrielle nécessite le détail au niveau des 5 chiffres de la CTCI, révisée. (Se référer aux pages xxxv à xxxvi pour l'histoire et le fond de la CTCI). Lorsque les statistiques n'étaient pas disponibles à ce niveau on a utilisé les données au niveau des trois chiffres de la CTCI, révisée. En comparant des statistiques du commerce extérieur avec des statistiques de production on se heurte à certaines incohérences qui s'ajoutent aux problèmes de classification. Les exportations de marchandises qui de toute évidence n'ont pas été produites dans les pays exportateurs (exportation de thé et de cacao des Pays-Bas ou du Royaume-Uni) ont été classées dans la branche où elles auraient été classées dans le pays d'origine; dans le cas du thé et du cacao : l'agriculture. La branche dans le pays déclarant est en fait dans ce cas le commerce de gros.

Pour obtenir la Classification des marchandises par origine industrielle, les postes de la CTCI, révisée sont regroupés afin de correspondre approximativement aux groupes de la Classification international type, par industrie, de toutes les branches d'activité économique (révisée) (CITI, Révision 1) 3/. Dans toute la mesure du possible les exportations nationales ou spéciales ont été utilisées.

c) Tableau 3, présentant jusqu'aux cinq années les plus récentes la valeur en dollars des Etats-Unis des importations et des exportations selon les principaux pays ou zones et régions d'origine et de destination. La distribution géographique est faite selon le Standard Country or Area Codes for Statistical Use 4/ des Nations Unies. Parfois, étant donné la nature des codes géographiques nationaux, la conversion des données selon le code des Nations Unies n'a pu être effectuée que moyennant quelques imprécisions. Dans ces tableaux figurent les 50 pays partenaires les plus importants classés par ordre d'importance selon la somme des valeurs sur les années comprises dans le tableau. Une classification différente est effectuée pour les importations et les exportations. La ventilation en pourcentage est également indiquée pour les zones d'origine et de destination et pour les 10 premiers pays partenaires pour les dix plus récentes années.

d) Tableaux 4 et 5, présentant les quantités et les valeurs en dollars des Etats-Unis des importations et des exportations par marchandises jusqu'aux quatre plus récentes années. Les chiffres sont publiés pour une marchandise donnée si sa valeur pour une année donnée est égale ou supérieure à 0,3 pour cent de la valeur totale pour ladite année. Les marchandises sont présentées selon les titres de la CTCI (en abrégé); lorsque les descriptions sont précédées d'un astérique (*) cela indique que les chiffres donnés sont égaux à ceux du niveau de la CTCI immédiatement supérieur qui dans ce cas n'est pas publié.

Parfois les données en dollars des tableaux décrits en (c) et (d) ci-dessus peuvent ne pas correspondre à celles en dollars des Etats Unis du tableau décrit en (a) ou à celles en monnaies nationales de ce tableau après l'application des facteurs de conversion. Les différences sont dues pour la plupart à des révisions au niveau du total du commerce qui parfois ne sont pas disponibles à un plus grand niveau de détail par produit et partenaire et qui n'ont donc pas été apportées aux tableaux décrits en (c) et (d).

Les importations et les exportations par produit sont présentés pour tous les pays selon la Classification type pour le commerce international (CTCI) 5/ de la façon suivante:

i) En CTCI, révisée pour les pays qui ont utilisé cette révision ou la CTCI originale pour les quatre dernières années;

ii) En CTCI, révisée pour les pays qui ont commencé à utiliser la CTCI, Révision 2 mais pour lesquels les quatre dernières années ne sont pas disponibles en CTCI, Révision 2;

iii) En CTCI, Révision 2 pour les pays qui ont utilisé cette révision pour les quatre dernières années disponibles;

iv) En CTCI, Révision 2 pour les pays qui rapportent les données en Révision 3 ou selon le système harmonisé de désignation et de codification des marchandises (SH). Dans les Volumes I et II, les données ainsi rapportées par ces pays ont été converties, de CTCI, Révision 3 en CTCI, Révision 2 et font l'objet d'une note en fin de tableau. Dans certains cas, à cause de difficultés de conversion des données de CTCI, Révision 3 en CTCI, Révision 2, on obtient des données qui, de façon très substantielle, ne sont pas comparables à celles des années précédantes rapportées sous forme de CTCI, Révision 2.

Dans quelques cas, la conversion en CTCI à partir des nomenclatures nationales n'ayant pu se faire avec suffisante précision, certains codes de la CTCI ne couvrent pas exactement les échanges qui devraient leur être imputables.

Lorsqu'elles sont disponibles, des données plus détaillées par produit et pays partenaire du commerce extérieur, en CTCI, révisée, en CTCI, Révision 2 ou en CTCI, Révision 3 sont publiées dans Commodity Trade Statistics 6/ et le sont également sous forme de microfiches.

Volume II

Le Volume II présente un chapitre sur le commerce de certains produits analysé par pays et par régions ainsi que des matrices des échanges.

Tableaux par produits. Ces tableaux comprennent les importations et les exportations au niveau du groupe à 3 chiffres de la CTCI, Révision 2, (tous les groupes à l'exception de 351 et 688). Les années couvertes sont les cinq années de 1990 à 1994. Les valeurs sont exprimées en dollars des Etats-Unis et les échanges sont analysés par pays et régions. Dans ces tableaux figurent les 50 pays les plus importants classés selon la somme des valeurs sur les années 1991, 1992 et 1993 inclus dans la tableau. Une classification différente est effectuée pour les importations et les exportations. Le système du commerce appliqué par les pays déclarants est le même que celui indiqué aux tableaux 4 et 5 des chapitres par pays de cet Annuaire. Les quantités ne figurent pas dans ces tableaux. Dans bien des cas des estimations ont été effectuées pour compléter les données non encore disponibles. On trouvera à la page 1 du Volume II des notes explicatives sur ces estimations.

Le Volume II aussi fournit des tableaux spéciaux où est indiquée la contribution des échanges de chaque pays et région dans le commerce international. Les titres des tableaux spéciaux sont:

(a) Importations et exportations totales par régions et pays ou zones;

(b) Exportations mondiales par classes de marchandises et par régions;
(c) Croissance des exportations mondiales par catégories de marchandises et par régions;
(d) Structure des exportations mondiales par catégories de marchandises et par régions;
(e) Importations et exportations totales: indices par pays ou zones;
(f) Exportations et importations totales: indices du quantum, de la valeur unitaire et des termes de l'échange par régions;
(g) Exportations des produits manufacturés;
(h) Importations des produits énergétiques: pays à économies développées;
(i) Quelques indicateurs sur les importations des produits énergétiques: pays à économies développées;
(j) Indices des prix des exportations de machines et materiel de transport pour certains pays;
(k) Indices des prix des exportations des matières premières et des métaux non-ferreux;

Tableaux spéciaux.

Les groupes économiques et géographiques dans tous les tableaux spéciaux sont conformes aux groupes de pays ou zones sont présentés dans le Tableau Special A de ce numéro, bien que le Tableau Special A comprenne quelquefois plus de details en ce qui concerne les sous-groupes géographiques. (Voir le Tableau Special A pour les détails).

(A) Importations et exportations totales par régions et pays ou zones. Les totaux régionaux, économiques et mondiaux, ont été ajustés: a) pour y inclure des estimations pour les données non disponibles; b) pour transformer le cas échéant les importations f.o.b. en importations c.a.f.; c) pour y inclure les pays ou zones pour lesquels il n'existe pas de liste séparée; d) pour ramener les données au commerce spécial; e) pour ramener les données à l'année civile; et f) autant que possible, éliminer les incompatibilités dues à des modifications géographiques pour obtenir des séries comparables par example, la Communauté économique éuropéenne et l'Association européenne de libre-échange. Les données pour chaque pays correspondent aux données en monnaie nationale sont présentés dans le tableau 1 des tableaux par pays. Les lettres des premières et dernières colonnes de ce tableau indiquent le système du commerce utilisé: G: Commerce général; S: Commerce spécial; Voir la fin du tableau pour les notes.

Le Bulletin Mensuel de Statistique présente des données mensuelles et trimestrielles.

(B) Exportations mondiales par classes de marchandises et par régions. Voir la fin du tableau pour la remarque générale et les notes.

(C) Croissance des exportations mondiales par catégories de marchandises et par régions. Les taux annuels de croissance ont tous été calculés à l'aide de la formule des intérêts composés:

$$r = \left(\sqrt[t]{\frac{Vn}{Vo}} - 1 \right) 100$$

r = Le taux annuel de croissance en pourcentage.
Vn = La valeur des exportations durant la dernière année de la période.
Vo = La valeur des exportations durant la première année de la période.
t = Le nombre d'années.

Voir la fin du Tableau Special D pour la remarque générale et les notes.

(D) Structure des exportations mondiales par catégories de marchandises et par régions. Les chiffres publiés sous le titre 'Origine des exportations' se réfèrent aux exportations de la région ou du pays indiqués dans la colonne zone. Il en est de même pour les 'Destinations des exportations'. Voir la fin du tableau pour la remarque générale et les notes.

(E) Importations et exportations totales: indices par pays ou zones. Sauf indication contraire, les indices de la valeur unitaire sont exprimés en monnaie nationale. Voir la fin du tableau pour la remarque générale et les notes.

Le Bulletin Mensuel de Statistique présente des données mensuelles et trimestrielles.

(F) Exportations et importations totales: indices du quantum, de la valeur unitaire et des termes de l'échange par régions. Voir la fin du tableau pour les notes.

Le Bulletin Mensuel de Statistique présente des données trimestrielles.

(G) Exportations des produits manufacturés. Voir la fin du tableau pour la remarque gènèrale et les notes.

Le Bulletin Mensuel de Statistique présente des données trimestrielles.

(H) Importations des produits énergétiques: pays à économies développées. Voir la fin du tableau pour la remarque générale et les notes.

Le Bulletin Mensuel de Statistique présente des données trimestrielles.

(I) Quelques indicateurs sur les importations des produits énergétiques: pays à économies développées. Ce tableau indique la part des importations de combustibles dans la valeur totale des importations et des exportations ainsi que le rapport de l'indice de la valeur unitaire des produits manufacturés qu'ils exportent et de l'indice de la valeur unitaire des combustibles qu'ils importent. Voir la fin du tableau pour la remarque générale et les notes.

(J) Indices des prix des exportations de machines et matériel de transport pour certain pays. Voir la fin du tableau pour la remarque générale.

Le Bulletin Mensuel de Statistique présente des données trimestrielles.

(K) Indices des prix des exportations des matières et des métaux non-ferreux: économies de marché. Voir la fin du tableau pour la remarque générale et les notes.

Le Bulletin Mensuel de Statistique présente des données mensuelles et trimestrielles.

SOURCE ET PRESENTATION

Les données pour les Volumes I et II sont obtenues à partir de publications nationales, d'états soumis par les gouvernements pour cet ouvrage et autres publications des Nations Unies telles que: Commodity Trade Statistics, Bulletin Mensuel de Statistique et parfois de publications préparées par certaines agences spécialisées des Nations Unies. Des estimations pour quelques données faisant défaut sont préparées par la Division de Statistique des Nations Unies.

Les noms de pays et régions utilisés par divers pays pour leurs statistiques du commerce extérieur ne sont pas uniformes. Aussi, lorsque d'anciennes entités geographiques généralement indiquées dans les statistiques nationales ont changé, les pays peuvent avoir introduit les changements correspondants dans leurs statistiques à différentes époques. Dans la mesure du possible toutefois, les pays ou zones ont été désignés par leur nom actuel.

Sauf indication contraire, les groupements de pays sont conformes à ceux du Standard Country or Area Code for Statistical Use 4/ des Nations Unies.

INDICES NATIONAUX

Les indices nationaux, exprimés en monnaies nationales, ou en dollars des Etat Unis sont présentés dans le tableau 1. Ils indiquent les modifications dans le quantum et dans les prix (valeur unitaire) des agrégats des importations et des exportations. Chaque indice représente une modification entre la période à laquelle l'indice se réfère, la période courante, et une période fixe, la base de publication pour laquelle l'indice est représenté par 100. Pour faciliter les comparaisons, chaque fois qu'il était possible de le faire, les indices ont été ramenés à la base de publication 1990. Lorsque des modifications sont faites dans la couverture, la formule ou la période de base d'un indice, si cela est techniquement possible les deux séries s'enchaînent.

Les indices mensuels et trimestriels sont publiés dans le Bulletin Mensuel de Statistique des Nations Unies. On trouvera également dans le Supplément de 1977 à l'Annuaire Statistique et au Bulletin Mensuel de Statistique 7/ des notes plus détaillées sur les méthodes de calcul des indices nationaux.

PAYS EN TRANSITION

Pour la période couverte par l'Annuaire les pays classifiés antérieurement pour des raisons statistiques à économies planifiées centralement avaient un système de taux de change officiel entre leurs monnaies et celles des pays extérieurs consistant avec le taux de 0,90 nouveau roubles pour 1 dollar des Etats-Unis avant le 24 décembre 1971 et 0,829 jusqu'à février 1973; depuis cette date le taux a fluctué. Les pays d'Europe orientale utilisaient généralement ces taux lorsqu'il était nécessaire de convertir des devises en monnaie nationale pour préparer les statistiques du commerce extérieur. Les données qui en résultent permettent davantage une comparaison avec les transactions des autres pays qu'une comparaison avec les transactions monétaires intérieures.

Les statistiques du commerce extérieur de ces pays ont des définitions différentes de celles qui peuvent exister dans les autres pays. Les différentes définitions peuvent être la source des divergences observées pour le même flux de marchandise enregistré par deux pays partenaires ayant un système économique différent. Les échanges entre ces pays peuvent être conduits sur une base différente de celle qui régit les échanges entre autres pays. Le concept de la valeur de transaction, par example, est basé sur l'existence d'un prix de marché entre l'importateur et l'exportateur sur lequel les variations de l'offre et de la demande ont plus d'influence qu'ils ne peuvent en avoir dans les échanges de ces pays. Faute de données précises sur les valeurs unitaires des produits de base échangés entre ces pays, il est difficile de connaître les effets possibles de ces différences sur les statistiques du commerce extérieur.

NOTE GENERALE 8/

1. Territoire. Les statistiques rapportées par un pays s'appliquent au territoire douanier de cet état. Généralement territoire douanier et territoire statistique coïncident, le cas contraire étant indiqué dans les notes par pays. Les modifications dans le territoire douanier sont également

indiquées dans les notes par pays. Sauf information contraire, l'unification de deux territoires séparés auparavant donne lieu à l'élimination des échanges entre ces deux territoires. Dans le cas d'une séparation d'un territoire en deux, les échanges entre ces deux territoires viennent à apparaître.

2. Système du commerce. Deux systèmes sont généralement utilisés ne différant que par la façon dont le commerce d'entrepôt et les réexportations sont enregistrés.

a) Commerce spécial. Les importations spéciales comprennent les marchandises entrées directement pour la consommation (y compris les transformations et réparations) et les marchandises sorties des entrepôts douaniers ou des zones franches pour être mises à la consommation. Les exportations spéciales comprennent les exportations de produits nationaux, c'est-à-dire les marchandises entièrement ou partiellement produites ou fabriquées dans le pays, ainsi que les exportations nationalisées (ces dernières sont des biens qui ayant été inclus dans les importations spéciales sont réexportés en l'état.)

b) Commerce général. Les importations générales comprennent les importations pour la consommation et les importations en entrepôt douanier ou en zone franche. Les exportations générales comprennent les exportations de produits nationaux et les réexportations. Ces dernières, dans le système du commerce général, comprennent les exportations nationalisées et les marchandises exportées des entrepôts douaniers et des zones franches sans avoir été transformées depuis leur importation.

Le transit direct, c'est-à-dire les marchandises uniquement transbordées ou traversant le pays pour des raisons de transport, est exclu du commerce général aussi bien que du commerce spécial.

Les titres de chaque tableau indiquent le système du commerce auquel se réfèrent les données. Des notes plus détaillées figurent, si nécessaire dans les notes par pays.

3. Evaluation. Lors de sa quinzième session en 1953, le Conseil Economique et Social, tenant compte du fait que les statistiques du commerce extérieur doivent refléter la réalité économique, a recommandé que les gouvernements des pays membres des Nations Unies utilisent, dans la mesure du possible, les valeurs de transaction en préparant leurs statistiques du commerce international ou qu'ils fournissent des informations supplémentaires basées sur les valeurs de transaction quand les politiques nationales font état d'autres valeurs (Résolution 469 B (XV) du Conseil Economique et Social). La valeur de transaction à l'importation est la valeur à laquelle les marchandises ont été achetées par l'importateur plus le coût de l'assurance et du frêt jusqu'à la frontière des pays importateurs (valeur c.a.f.). A l'exportation, la valeur de transaction représente la valeur à laquelle les marchandises ont été vendues

par l'exportateur y compris le coût de l'assurance du transport pour amener les marchandises à la frontière des pays exportateurs (valeur f.o.b.).

4. Conversion des monnaies. Pour les données dans cet Annuaire la conversion des valeurs nationales en dollars des Etats-Unis est effectuée au moyen de taux de conversion basés sur les taux de change officiels. Pour les monnaies sujettes à de larges marges de fluctuations par rapport au dollar, dont le nombre s'est accru considérablement depuis 1971, on utilise des moyennes pondérées des taux de change calculées spécialement dans ce but. La moyenne pondérée est le résultat des taux de change mensuels, généralement fournis par le Fonds Monétaire International, pondérés par les valeurs des importations et des exportations correspondantes. Les facteurs de conversion s'appliquent aux totaux des échanges mais pas nécessairement aux importations ou à l'exportation d'une marchandise donnée.

5. Marchandises. Dans la définition du commerce extérieur on entend par marchandises tous les biens dont l'importation ou l'exportation contribue à l'accroissement ou à la diminution du stock des ressources matérielles dans un pays. Sauf information contraire dans les notes par pays, le traitement des catégories de marchandises suit les règles énoncées ci-dessous:

a) Or. L'or dans le commerce international se présente sous trois formes:

i) Pièces d'or et lingots y compris l'or monétaire;
ii) Or non raffiné y compris les minerais et les concentrés;
iii) Or semi ouvré dont la valeur de l'or représente au moins 80% de la valeur totale, y compris la limaille et les poussières et les formes primaires telles que feuilles et barres et les alliages d'or.

De ces différents types d'or, l'or monétaire est exclu du commerce des marchandises tandis que les autres types sont inclus, à l'exception de ceux indiqués ci-dessous. Tout transfert d'or entre les autorités monétaires doit être traité comme échange d'or monétaire, les autres échanges portant sur l'or sont classés comme or non-monétaire. A la différence de la CTCI, révisée, la CTCI, Révision 2 et Révision 3 incluent l'or non- monétaire.

b) Minerai d'argent. Concentrés, lingots, pièces non émises, limailles et argent ouvré ou semi ouvré sont tous inclus dans les échanges de marchandises.

c) Monnaie et titres de propriété. Pièces de monnaie d'argent et de métal, billets de banque et titres en circulation sont exclus du commerce. Les pièces, billets et titres non en circulation sont inclus à la valeur intrinsèque du papier ou du métal frappé.

d) Le commerce pour le compte de l'Etat. Il est inclus dans le commerce des marchandises. Les échanges au titre des programmes d'aide civile et militaire, les réparations de guerre et les équipements militaires 9/ sont donc inclus. Quand les marchandises sont destinées à des institutions nationales (ambassades ou forces armées) stationnées à l'étranger, elles ne sont pas comprises dans les statistiques.

e) Importations et exportations temporaires. Les effets des touristes et des voyageurs (y compris les véhicules) qui n'ont pas été acquis à l'étranger, les objets pour expositions ou études, les animaux pour la course ou la reproduction, les échantillons et les emballages en retour qui sont considérés comme devant être retournés dans un intervalle de temps assez court sont exclus.

f) Trafic de perfectionnement et de réparation. Les pays qui envoient à l'étranger temporairement des marchandises pour réparation ou complément d'ouvraison effectuent un trafic passif de réparation. Les pays recevant des marchandises dans les mêmes conditions effectuent un trafic actif de réparation. Les mouvements d'entrée et de sortie sont généralement exclus des importations et des exportations.

g) Commerce par poste. Il est inclus dans le commerce des marchandises.

h) Poisson. Le poisson et les épaves débarqués dans des ports étrangers par des navires nationaux et ceux débarqués dans des ports du pays par des navires étrangers sont exclus des statistiques.

i) Vente et achat de navires et d'aéronefs. La vente et l'achat de navires et d'aéronefs neufs sont inclus. Les navires et les aéronefs d'occasion inscrits sur le registre d'immatriculation du pays ou radiés de ce registre sont exclus du commerce quand ces mouvements sont dûs à un transfert de propriété.

j) Avitaillement des navires et des avions. Ils doivent etre généralement inclus dans les exportations de marchandises.

6. Pays Partenaire. Les pays partenaires peuvent être distingués : a) à l'importation, suivant : l'origine ou la production, la consignation ou la provenance ou l'achat; b) à l'exportation, suivant : la consommation, la dernière destination connue ou la vente.

7. Echanges par produits. L'analyse est selon la Classification Type pour le Commerce International.

CLASSIFICATION TYPE POUR LE COMMERCE INTERNATIONAL (CTCI)

En juillet 1950, le Conseil Economique et Social des Nations Unies, sur avis de la Commission de Statistique, a recommandé aux pays de rassembler leurs statistiques des échanges par produits selon la CTCI originale 5/ afin de disposer au niveau mondial de données comparables pour l'analyse du commerce extérieur. La CTCI originale a été préparée par le Secrétariat des Nations Unies avec l'aide d'experts et en coopération avec les gouvernements et les organisations internationales concernées.

En mai 1960 la Commission de Statistique a approuvé une révision de la CTCI appelée la CTCI, révisée, qui tenait compte des modifications dans les courants commerciaux intervenus depuis 1950 et qui permettait un passage plus facile entre la CTCI et les nomenclatures internationales. 5/ La CTCI, révisée présentait selon une classification statistique les positions de la nomenclature tarifaire NCCD du Conseil de Coopération Douanière.

La relation entre la CTCI originale et la CTCI, révisée est décrite dans l'introduction de certains fascicules de Commodity Trade Statistics en particulier ceux de janvier - décembre 1960 et 1961.

La CTCI, révisée comprend 625 sous-groupes (identifiés par un code à quatre chiffres) qui correspondent pour l'essentiel aux postes de la CTCI originale. Un certain nombre de sous-groupes ont été subdivisés soit pour obtenir des détails supplémentaires soit pour assurer une concordance exacte avec la NCCD. La CTCI, révisée comporte donc 1312 rubriques de base (niveau des 5 chiffres de la CTCI). Les sous-groupes sont rassemblés en 177 groupes, 56 divisions et 10 sections.

Les positions de la CTCI sont individualisées par leur numéro de code. Le contenu précis de chaque code est défini dans la CTCI, révisée. Si l'on compare les données selon la CTCI, révisée avec des données classées selon une nomenclature nationale, il faut tenir compte de ce que la même description, généralement abrégée, peut s'appliquer à des groupes de marchandises légèrement différents.

La révision de 1960 représentait par rapport à la CTCI initiale une amélioration considérable. Néanmoins vers la fin des années 1960 on a constaté que, pour l'essentiel, les raisons qui avaient conduit à l'établissement de la CTCI puis à sa première révision, se retrouvaient à nouveau valables. Depuis 1960 le volume des échanges commerciaux s'est accru rapidement tandis que leur répartition géographique et leur composition par produits se modifiaient radicalement. Une nouvelle révision de la CTCI fut donc entreprise. En octobre 1974, la Commission

Statistique a approuvé cette révision, la désignation de la nouvelle révision est CTCI, Révision 2. 5/ En mai 1975 le Conseil Economique et Social a recommandé aux Etats membres des Nations Unies de communiquer les données sur les statistiques du commerce extérieur en se conformant autant que possible et le plus tôt possible à la CTCI, Révision 2. A partir des données pour 1976, certains pays ont commencé à communiquer leurs données selon la CTCI, Révision 2.

Il y avait entre les titres de base de la Classification type pour le commerce international, Révision 2 et les subdivisions de la Nomenclature du Conseil de Coopération Douanière une correspondance biunivoque. Toutefois, un certain nombre d'utilisateurs ont estimé que les subdivisions des positions de la NCCD (et par conséquent celles de la CTCI, Révision 2) ne suffisaient pas à leurs besoins 10/. La nécessité d'une harmonisation des classifications économiques a également été signalée 11/. En partie pour répondre à ces besoins, le Conseil de coopération douanière a assumé en mai 1973 la responsabilité d'élaborer et de mettre au point un système harmonisé de désignation et de codification des marchandises (SH). Ce travail a abouti à la révision de la NCCD et à l'extension de ses numéros de position (à 4 chiffres) en 5019 codes à 6 chiffres qui constituent le SH 12/.

A sa vingt et unième session, en janvier 1981, la Commission de statistique a pris note du fait qu'une troisième révision de la CTCI devait être disponible lorsque la NCCD révisée et le SH entreraient tous deux en vigueur 13/. En conséquence, dans le courant de la même année, le Secrétariat de l'ONU a commencé à travailler à la révision de la CTCI, Révision 2 en partant du principe que le maximum devait être fait pour en conserver le caractère général et la structure, tout en tenant compte de la nécessité de son harmonisation avec la NCCD révisée, avec la Classification internationale type, par industrie, de toutes les branches d'activité économique (CITI), Révision 3 14/ et avec une Classification des produits centrale (CPC) 15/ dont l'élaboration était menée conjointement par la Division de statistique des Nations Unies et l'Office statistique des Communautés européennes.

Le projet final a été révisé et approuvé par la Commission de statistique à sa vingt-troisième session, en février 1985, et une résolution a été adoptée par le Conseil économique et social le 28 mai 1985 (résolution 1985/7) qui, inter-alia, a recommandé aux Etats Membres de communiquer des données sur les statistiques du commerce extérieur aux institutions internationales en se conformant autant que possible et le plus rapidement possible à la Classification type pour le commerce international (troisième version révisée) étant entendu que les Etats Membres peuvent juger bon de ne faire cette substitution qu'au moment où il leur faudra, de toute façon, réviser leur nomenclature douanière.

1/ Classification par grandes catégories économiques, (selon les définitions de la CTCI, révisée), Etudes statistiques, série M No. 53, (publication des Nations Unies, numéro de vente 71.XVII.12).

2/ Classification des marchandises par origine industrielle (Relation entre la Classification type pour le commerce international et la Classification internationale type, par industrie, de toutes les branches d'activité économique), Etudes statistiques, série M No. 43, (publication des Nations Unies, numéro de vente 66.XVII.7).

3/ Classification internationale type, par industrie, de toutes les branches d'activité économique (révisée), Etudes statistiques, série M No. 4, Rév. 1. (publication des Nations Unies, numéro de vente 58.XVII.7).

4/ United Nations Standard Country Code, Statistical Papers, Series M No. 49, (United Nations publication, Sales No. E.70.XVII.13).

5/ United Nations Standard Country or Area Code for Statistical Use, Statistical Papers, Series M No. 49, Rev. 1, (United Nations publication, Sales No. E.75.XVII.8).

Standard Country or Area Codes for Statistical Use, Statistical Papers Series M No. 49, Rev.2, (United Nations publication, Sales No. E.82.XVII.8).

Standard Country or Area Codes for Statistical Use, Interim List (United Nations Statistical Division).

5/ Classification type pour le commerce international, Etudes statistiques, série M No. 10, 2ème édition, (publication des Nations Unies, numéro de vente 51.XVII.1).

Classification type pour le commerce international révisée, Etudes statistiques, série M. No. 34, (publication des Nations Unies, numéro de vente 61.XVII.6).

Classification type pour le commerce international, (deuxième version revisée), Etudes statistiques, série M No. 34/Rév. 2, (publication des Nations Unies, numéro de vente F.75.XVII.6).

Classification type pour le commerce international (troisième version révisée), Etudes statistiques, serie M No.34/Rév. 3, (publication des Nations Unies, numéro de vente F.86.XVII.12).

6/ Commodity Trade Statistics, Statistical papers, Séries D, présentent annuellement les échanges par origine et destination pour un grand nombre de positions de la CTCI, révisée, de la CTCI, Révision 2 et CTCI, Révision 3. Les données annuelles sont disponibles sur microfiches.

7/ Supplément de 1977 à l'Annuaire Statistique et au Bulletin mensuel de statistique, ST/ESA/STAT/SER.S/SUPPL.2, ST/ESA/STAT/SER.Q/SUPPL.2, (publication des Nations Unies, numéro de vente F.78.XVII.10).

8/ Le traitement des articles 1 à 7 est dérivé principalement de Statistiques du commerce international concepts et définitions, Etudes statistiques, série M No. 52 Révision 1, (publication des Nations Unies, numéro de vente F.82.XVII.14).

9/ Les pays qui excluent l'équipement militaire utilisent des définitions différentes pour cette catégorie de marchandise, pour la majorité des pays cependant, armes et munitions constituent la plupart de l'équipement militaire exclu des statistiques.

10/ Groupe de travail commun Division de statistique de l'ONU - Office statistique des Communautés européennes sur les nomenclatures au niveau mondial, "Système harmonisé de désignation et de codification des marchandises pour les besoins du commerce international" (UNSO/SOEC/1/2).

11/ Secrétariat de l'ONU, "L'harmonisation des classifications statistiques : compte rendu d'une réunion d'un groupe d'experts" (ST/ESA/STAT/78).

12/ Conseil de coopération douanière, "Système harmonisé de désignation et de codification des marchandises", 1985.

13/ Documents officiels du Conseil économique et social, 1981, Supplément No. 2. (E/1981/12).

14/ Classification International Type, par industrie, de toutes les branches d'activité économique, Etudes statistiques, série M No. 4, Révision 3 (publication des Nations Unies, numéro de vente F.90.XVII.11).

15/ Classification centrale de produits (CPC) provisoire, Etudes statistiques, série M No. 77 (publication des Nations Unies, numéro de vente F.91.XVII.7).

TOTAL TRADE

COMMODITY TABLES

GROUP (3-DIGIT) LEVEL OF THE SITC, REVISION 2

351, 675 and 688 are excluded

NOTES ON ESTIMATES

In preparing these tables, a number of estimates are made for countries whose data are not yet available. At the country level these estimates are shown with a sign 'x' for all years. They are included in the regional and world totals.

COMMERCE TOTAL

TABLEAUX PAR PRODUITS

NIVEAU DES GROUPES (3-CHIFFRES) DE LA CTCI REVISION 2

A l'exclusion des groupes 351, 675 et 688

NOTES SUR LES ESTIMATIONS

Pour la préparation de ces tableaux, un nombre des estimations ont été effectuées pour les pays dont les données n'étaient pas disponibles. Ces estimations au niveau des pays apparaissent avec le signe 'x' pour toutes les années.

TRADE BY COMMODITY IN THOUSAND U.S. DOLLARS – COMMERCE PAR PRODUIT EN MILLIERS DE DOLLARS E.U

COUNTRIES–PAYS	IMPORTS – IMPORTATIONS				
	1990	1991	1992	1993	1994
Total	8786899	8665003	9716640	8098291	8577480
Africa	x240810	x243192	x155577	x187609	287165
Northern Africa	112102	136581	x130709	x162752	258832
Americas	1474589	1606121	1912010	1895293	1965067
LAIA	206863	333780	370481	232112	424995
CACM	4954	8806	16604	x22728	x23022
Asia	1714914	1827454	1979782	x1895696	x1867411
Middle East	897412	930910	1001387	x927841	x832891
Europe	5007168	4850077	5540715	3987298	4277213
EEC	4789479	4789657	5391417	3915202	4198861
EFTA	37621	33149	32018	29917	38814
Oceania	x105719	x66480	x60110	x61278	x76387
Italy/Italie	1962486	1945448	2060031	1573254	1512644
USA/Etats–Unis d'Amer	1167636	1149644	1413478	1518838	1371760
France, Monac	544501	611455	582661	452991	536785
Netherlands/Pays–Bas	385946	426171	552572	495608	529109
Germany/Allemagne	381487	399203	689476	331551	369700
Belgium–Luxembourg	418166	416853	469150	351803	407628
Saudi Arabia	402883	453797	387321	x374901	x307275
Hong Kong	332255	361786	432683	403057	413067
Spain/Espagne	314395	354118	396107	335102	448335
United Kingdom	507557	349839	362017	213117	192225
Singapore/Singapour	160487	192511	213688	250789	249327
Mexico/Mexique	104239	252753	261546	141888	198804
Japan/Japon	168611	167469	129303	126919	127687
Turkey/Turquie	109138	107986	108976	102801	22702
Canada	74098	102602	100134	111923	135078
Kuwait/ Koweït	67256	47469	119635	132053	137117
Ireland/Irlande	90687	106807	120103	48810	55653
Syrian Arab Republic	41656	x74505	121654	x50454	x47919
Greece/Grèce	68455	82411	71123	57651	53046
Libyan Arab Jamahiriya	44862	81780	x38385	x53250	x23964
United Arab Emirates	62963	44082	38416	x70320	x85648
Jordan/Jordanie	32049	54970	38069	40081	43798
Qatar	48042	61157	40201	30915	x15929
Australia/Australie	84125	42862	41760	41696	55490
Portugal	45236	43683	51800	30366	61276
Lebanon/Liban	x25784	x27294	x29803	x68686	x125713
Brazil/Brésil	73459	38763	30313	45036	122902
Thailand/Thaïlande	27683	43439	30656	22408	20846
Algeria/Algérie	28367	28297	45572	22168	26558
Malaysia/Malaisie	23737	24186	33271	29049	36902
Cote d'Ivoire	x111074	x84190	x772	x771	x981
Switz.Liecht	34196	30105	28028	26022	32757
Philippines	17324	14087	25409	43671	53526
Egypt/Egypte	16944	6358	13821	60665	146846
Poland/Pologne	3693	10106	40115	30618	57148
Croatia/Croatie			67326	9127	x12304
Macau/Macao	17749	23695	24724	26072	28242
Yemen/Yémen	71753	9353	56441	x7300	x5401
Argentina/Argentine	5607	9229	36880	15214	11821
Iran (Islamic Rp. of)		x21541	x23765	x13946	x1349
Oman	16718	17273	19030	20619	26782
Indonesia/Indonésie	16443	8597	18424	27617	56037
New Zealand	19346	21176	16089	16320	19082
China/Chine	13619	19685	17978	13367	11600
Sweden/Suède	31499	28657	13553	8722	9590
Morocco/Maroc	7762	12897	21078	16110	53561
Venezuela	2261	18550	17943	4397	2122
Korea, Republic of	11884	14992	12822	11777	16157
Slovenia/Slovénia			23997	12163	20388
Bahrain/Bahreïn	x16364	x9716	x13848	x10761	x9797

COUNTRIES–PAYS	EXPORTS – EXPORTATIONS				
	1990	1991	1992	1993	1994
Totale	8599338	8821898	9521465	8237287	8735769
Afrique	x219258	x106699	x115275	x72242	x19350
Afrique du Nord	x52922	x54356	x77034	40812	11966
Amériques	1669834	1875256	2074847	2077735	2052116
ALAI	436104	442267	406981	504007	515808
MCAC	6376	8052	14439	20345	18210
Asie	1073772	1027625	971412	1051719	1019960
Moyen–Orient	463995	x400891	283972	x382822	x317389
Europe	4483775	4669791	5276108	4262450	4776882
CEE	4321992	4539701	5131869	4205778	4740760
AELE	27606	25234	24310	23738	22898
Océanie	x254834	x214679	x259513	x288727	x356320
France, Monac	1543113	1581833	1778297	1672811	1812415
Canada	733644	762913	1041253	1058749	953452
Netherlands/Pays–Bas	867594	804003	1079356	714715	797867
Germany/Allemagne	584627	791312	670470	508914	574330
USA/Etats–Unis d'Amer	486869	661349	611406	493632	563191
United Kingdom	447081	495057	579818	402776	447608
Belgium–Luxembourg	350742	450311	512264	394476	459022
China/Chine	429731	439146	459078	434165	445157
Mexico/Mexique	349821	360350	331572	450591	362307
Poland/Pologne	248017	378672	224866	166094	175307
Ireland/Irlande	329144	217344	219880	226632	269637
Turkey/Turquie	201663	201779	125994	281701	221722
Malaysia/Malaisie	141007	150084	188762	195003	207389
Hungary/Hongrie	x197191	x173397	x205193	x112437	x118433
Australia/Australie	133155	138998	161709	190072	255934
Bulgaria/Bulgarie	x345706	x182864	118351	39408	49161
Syrian Arab Republic	230246	x123257	116092	x58155	x25290
New Zealand	121428	75505	97685	98596	100284
Czechoslovakia		x80375	x160221		
Austria/Autriche	78204	63704	90604	81856	x86566
Spain/Espagne	40489	41862	70274	99642	170520
Denmark/Danemark	35131	54619	83599	64102	70071
Romania/Roumanie	16424	61327	74401	55266	85081
Yugoslavia SFR	131810	x102960			
Sudan/Soudan	x36782	x38650	x43176		
Former GDR	x90014	x40778	x40778		
Croatia/Croatie			55407	22390	x8784
Czech Republic				77424	56125
Somalia/Somalie	x35398	x30006	x26577	x15396	x885
Egypt/Egypte	6000	11591	28513	30600	1378
Jordan/Jordanie	2973	13740	22452	26802	18850
Italy/Italie	17671	17601	21382	22304	34650
Switz.Liecht	23440	21229	20322	19260	18521
Saudi Arabia	16611	40787	13190		
Colombia/Colombie	450	29481	21410	3386	1588
Uruguay	13847	13980	25984	13436	46393
Lithuania/Lituanie				x48735	26661
Indonesia/Indonésie	13561	14820	14414	16774	15007
Slovakia				x33780	x27026
Portugal	14861	13880	13727	3075	7860
Brazil/Brésil	3704	5771	13275	10501	4710
Argentina/Argentine	7768	7696	8200	13102	50628
Sweden/Suède	7366	6980	7771	12267	8917
Slovenia/Slovénia			15930	4351	2119
Nicaragua	2273	1716	4969	13512	11440
Bolivia/Bolivie	49500	17867	18	630	4351
Tunisia/Tunisie	8921	3612	4786	9318	9994
Yugoslavia/Yougoslavie			x14890	x103	x195
Burkina Faso	10006	10553	x1829	x1834	
Chile/Chili	5103	6119	4540	3275	8225

(VALUE AS % OF TOTAL)(VALEUR EN % DU TOTAL)

	1985	1986	1987	1988	1989	1990	1991	1992	1993	1994
Africa	7.0	4.4	5.5	4.5	2.8	x2.7	x2.8	x1.6	x2.3	3.3
Northern Africa	6.5	3.9	4.8	3.8	2.5	1.3	1.6	x1.3	x2.0	3.0
Americas	17.3	14.6	11.5	15.5	14.8	16.8	18.6	19.7	23.4	22.9
LAIA	4.0	2.2	2.1	4.6	2.9	2.4	3.9	3.8	2.9	5.0
CACM	0.3	0.1	x0.1	0.1	0.1	0.1	0.1	0.2	x0.3	x0.3
Asia	21.8	21.2	21.4	19.8	19.1	19.5	21.1	20.4	x23.4	x21.8
Middle East	13.2	13.1	12.6	10.4	x10.0	10.2	10.7	10.3	x11.5	x9.7
Europe	50.1	55.6	56.9	55.7	59.6	57.0	56.0	57.0	49.2	49.9
EEC	49.3	54.3	55.6	53.8	56.6	54.5	55.3	55.5	48.3	49.0
EFTA	0.6	0.8	1.0	1.3	1.2	0.4	0.4	0.3	0.4	0.5
Oceania	1.5	1.9	x2.0	x2.0	x1.7	x1.2	x0.7	x0.6	x0.7	x0.9
Italy/Italie	22.2	24.2	24.5	23.8	24.5	22.3	22.5	21.2	19.4	17.6
USA/Etats–Unis d'Amer	11.7	10.5	7.7	9.7	10.5	13.3	13.3	14.5	18.8	16.0
France, Monac	6.1	6.8	7.0	6.0	6.0	6.2	7.1	6.0	5.6	6.3
Netherlands/Pays–Bas	1.8	2.9	3.6	3.3	3.9	4.4	4.9	5.7	6.1	6.2
Germany/Allemagne	4.5	3.8	4.9	5.0	4.6	4.3	4.6	7.1	4.1	4.3
Belgium–Luxembourg	4.1	4.8	4.9	4.1	4.6	4.8	4.8	4.8	4.3	4.8
Saudi Arabia	8.5	6.7	5.8	5.0	5.2	4.6	5.2	4.0	x4.6	x3.6
Hong Kong	5.6	4.5	4.0	3.8	3.8	3.8	4.2	4.5	5.0	4.8
Spain/Espagne	1.1	2.5	2.1	2.1	3.7	3.6	4.1	4.1	4.1	5.2
United Kingdom	5.8	6.6	5.4	6.4	5.7	5.8	4.0	3.7	2.6	2.2

	1985	1986	1987	1988	1989	1990	1991	1992	1993	1994
Afrique	2.3	x2.3	x1.8	x1.9	x2.5	x2.5	x1.2	x1.2	x0.8	x0.2
Afrique du Nord	1.4	0.7	0.3	0.6	x0.8	x0.6	x0.6	x0.8	0.5	0.1
Amériques	18.7	15.3	12.6	17.3	15.5	19.4	21.2	21.8	25.2	23.5
ALAI	3.3	4.8	3.1	3.0	3.5	5.1	5.0	4.3	6.1	5.9
MCAC	0.1	0.0	0.0	0.1	0.1	0.1	0.1	0.2	0.2	0.2
Asie	10.7	10.8	11.1	11.0	12.7	12.4	11.6	10.2	12.7	11.7
Moyen–Orient	4.7	5.1	4.6	4.4	5.9	5.4	x4.5	3.0	x4.6	x3.6
Europe	57.1	62.1	59.1	54.1	54.6	52.1	52.9	55.4	51.7	54.7
CEE	54.0	59.4	55.2	50.5	51.5	50.3	51.5	53.9	51.1	54.3
AELE	1.4	1.4	1.6	1.5	1.5	0.3	0.3	0.3	0.3	0.3
Océanie	5.0	4.4	x4.3	4.7	x3.9	x3.0	x2.4	x2.7	x3.5	x4.1
France, Monac	17.3	19.5	19.1	18.6	18.3	17.9	17.9	18.7	20.3	20.7
Canada	6.9	3.9	3.6	6.3	5.9	8.5	8.6	10.9	12.9	10.9
Netherlands/Pays–Bas	11.5	12.1	11.6	9.4	9.6	10.1	9.1	11.3	8.7	9.1
Germany/Allemagne	6.2	7.5	6.2	5.2	6.9	6.8	9.0	7.0	6.2	6.6
USA/Etats–Unis d'Amer	8.3	6.4	5.8	7.8	5.9	5.7	7.5	6.4	6.0	6.4
United Kingdom	7.1	7.3	7.6	5.7	5.3	5.2	5.6	6.1	4.9	5.1
Belgium–Luxembourg	4.2	5.3	4.9	5.1	5.8	4.1	5.1	5.4	4.8	5.3
China/Chine	4.6	4.4	4.9	4.9	5.0	5.0	5.0	4.8	5.3	5.1
Mexico/Mexique	3.0	4.3	2.7	2.6	2.7	4.1	4.1	3.5	5.5	4.1
Poland/Pologne	2.3	2.2	2.4	2.6	2.6	2.9	4.3	2.4	2.0	2.0

TRADE BY COMMODITY IN THOUSAND U.S. DOLLARS – COMMERCE PAR PRODUIT EN MILLIERS DE DOLLARS E.U

COUNTRIES–PAYS	IMPORTS – IMPORTATIONS				
	1990	1991	1992	1993	1994
Total	30709158	31798066	34548570	31572505	33866108
Africa	x520741	x417565	x524083	x517200	x630076
Northern Africa	280223	188066	203306	227197	257755
Americas	4206409	4497661	4536147	4406408	4515346
LAIA	708858	899445	1124946	942473	1241552
CACM	2125	10586	23509	17616	19030
Asia	7005519	8062883	x9009689	x9520336	x10779248
Middle East	x945364	x1234125	x1166827	x1497147	x1217855
Europe	17034781	17377204	20057198	16604549	17303220
EEC	16389645	16955326	19531062	16082976	16755123
EFTA	324026	301692	309428	305064	344599
Oceania	151803	x177637	x190894	x202200	x182063
Japan/Japon	4805425	5240363	6158741	6477220	7381660
Germany/Allemagne	3807847	4381235	5468537	4196564	4214627
Italy/Italie	3957761	4191402	4342549	3325280	3389405
France,Monac	3461256	3421801	3712449	3217686	3502987
USA/Etats–Unis d'Amer	2458180	2434266	2379706	2406854	2240344
United Kingdom	1616130	1510586	1772907	1676561	1535308
Greece/Grèce	825197	622898	919000	758119	756982
Netherlands/Pays–Bas	602229	651396	841149	785794	891512
Mexico/Mexique	360227	678275	768716	634769	825221
Spain/Espagne	628889	698188	749752	623296	690608
Belgium–Luxembourg	683353	647459	734716	683660	747270
Canada	614675	696477	662642	699318	724931
Hong Kong	471262	529146	562410	601557	840774
Korea, Republic of	338890	540908	543950	385534	572571
Saudi Arabia	385114	490747	368044	x513728	x519436
Russian Federation			x744328	x496996	x875913
Former USSR/Anc. URSS	1552493	x1058117			
Iran (Islamic Rp. of)		x303576	x276805	x380416	x157940
Portugal	278008	259044	356215	315135	414742
Switz.Liecht	312153	290056	296637	287956	319993
Denmark/Danemark	229019	236995	274358	259999	284844
Singapore/Singapour	148793	154751	157884	161561	201080
Egypt/Egypte	208864	137169	119978	166954	177351
Poland/Pologne	23451	128645	124749	162732	203054
United Arab Emirates	185403	105723	117087	x163574	x172724
Sweden/Suède	107452	130398	158287	93666	134389
Brazil/Brésil	307313	132836	132834	53080	143666
Israel/Israël	72580	121833	85874	100822	146609
Austria/Autriche	111663	105472	99113	91030	94367
Malaysia/Malaisie	78926	92249	89000	97757	117825
Argentina/Argentine	6138	29393	116957	127960	125088
Ireland/Irlande	71599	94140	96122	52003	83357
Jordan/Jordanie	53104	81682	73926	84901	61846
Kuwait/ Koweït	41881	38279	90642	105032	93697
Cuba	x98944	x136550	x50036	x30091	x10982
Oman	54952	62820	63787	68045	71314
China/Chine	53253	59891	56148	68117	85025
Reunion/Réunion	59180	51822	61082	56666	57079
Chile/Chili	5344	21074	65662	77135	91393
Martinique	50412	48814	53863	55597	54603
Papua New Guinea	36447	x49064	x51067	x54845	x49040
So. Africa Customs Un	25494	34524	75968	43604	149839
Guadeloupe	43108	42941	44784	44557	46226
Bahrain/Bahreïn	x33398	x39777	x40650	x43081	x27811
French Polynesia	40258	38911	39887	x38023	x29596
Slovenia/Slovénia			60300	56029	73286
Croatia/Croatie			61859	40208	x39484
Turkey/Turquie	16072	32720	33060	31436	10245
Hungary/Hongrie	x4458	1867	x24618	x66270	x97436
Yugoslavia/Yougoslavie			x37501	x49051	x19793

COUNTRIES–PAYS	EXPORTS – EXPORTATIONS				
	1990	1991	1992	1993	1994
Totale	28428706	29669798	32838162	30760585	33603204
Afrique	78130	x91201	112390	107031	x113973
Afrique du Nord	16019	9164	24096	21042	12961
Amériques	5524367	5786152	6579824	6928984	7998037
ALAI	1531472	1504907	1659921	1760370	2026524
MCAC	170646	157591	138083	x169961	x173174
Asie	1209566	1394873	1278499	1283873	1684364
Moyen–Orient	58369	69045	69906	x96770	x105341
Europe	16338209	17293425	19440849	17381395	18646434
CEE	16156547	17188778	19244467	17279688	18566973
AELE	23367	9404	20349	10257	7465
Océanie	x3850156	4084105	4261224	x4296696	x4411882
Netherlands/Pays–Bas	4204290	4301065	4830608	4241879	4428309
USA/Etats–Unis d'Amer	2989723	3383196	3920593	4001352	4795079
France,Monac	2664604	2866142	3452744	3308876	3551131
Australia/Australie	2364422	2543519	2661764	2662489	2746442
Denmark/Danemark	2190464	2303952	2779567	2445494	2878269
Germany/Allemagne	2385048	2633007	2146915	1742254	1578340
Belgium–Luxembourg	1637208	1896200	2130339	1919965	1938715
New Zealand	1478561	1537222	1595727	1632350	1660779
Ireland/Irlande	1225053	1268974	1554053	1501943	1568025
United Kingdom	1016393	1091565	1334008	1214936	1561698
Canada	817077	720563	851454	976624	983233
Brazil/Brésil	475432	635823	861610	994109	1008660
Hungary/Hongrie	x831407	x625351	x758068	x449074	x418436
Argentina/Argentine	563383	505845	463615	472591	627906
China/Chine	522655	557706	367057	344950	630582
Thailand/Thaïlande	306334	415661	427289	370162	408691
Italy/Italie	255543	364612	440160	354088	381001
Spain/Espagne	258791	194436	299396	287193	389785
Uruguay	264773	171530	183911	174565	243273
Austria/Autriche	205470	164343	166158	141280	x166646
Poland/Pologne	208686	149396	155860	114360	123663
Hong Kong	83439	100777	115332	166570	211364
India/Inde	76568	93335	98794	109494	125396
Romania/Roumanie	3424	64241	84870	93884	118269
So. Africa Customs Un	53187	71743	76258	68831	38983
Korea, Republic of	54808	42246	68317	81776	79686
Czechoslovakia		x112722	x76240		
Bulgaria/Bulgarie	x355269	x54806	80629	32419	43528
Costa Rica	49333	60506	41966	x46565	x59898
Paraguay	133369	54283	47061	46211	52744
Nicaragua	68029	38664	41639	61944	64726
Slovenia/Slovénia			74473	47463	36724
Sweden/Suède	81097	43392	31375	40870	36759
Mexico/Mexique	35471	31459	45109	35597	39427
Finland/Finlande	18871	38274	40035	32337	47830
Honduras	24863	28963	37275	42898	39466
Croatia/Croatie			67125	28154	x24844
Yugoslavia SFR	158204	x94751			
Israel/Israël	25093	27028	29101	30243	34167
Indonesia/Indonésie	16354	24501	31872	24867	22482
Chile/Chili	20326	31463	27098	21908	33147
Singapore/Singapour	25029	23074	26495	26743	31230
Portugal	4421	14397	29350	31847	16693
Turkey/Turquie	24691	15833	26230	26535	42763
Guatemala	26744	29406	17062	18374	8881
Colombia/Colombie	17120	41589	14531	4726	5157
Venezuela	19013	29818	16447	10160	13713
Lithuania/Lituanie			44986	x7554	30372
Czech Republic				50535	29851
Saudi Arabia	3028	24180	16315	x8864	x11978

(VALUE AS % OF TOTAL)(VALEUR EN % DU TOTAL)

	1985	1986	1987	1988	1989	1990	1991	1992	1993	1994
Africa	2.9	x3.1	x2.6	x2.5	x1.9	x1.7	x1.3	x1.5	x1.6	x1.8
Northern Africa	2.5	1.8	1.3	1.2	0.9	0.9	0.6	0.6	0.7	0.8
Americas	16.3	15.7	14.2	13.6	13.6	13.7	14.1	13.1	13.9	13.4
LAIA	1.4	3.4	1.9	1.6	2.7	2.3	2.8	3.3	3.0	3.7
CACM	0.0	0.0	0.0	0.0	0.0	0.0	0.0	0.1	0.1	0.1
Asia	20.9	x21.3	x23.3	x26.2	x25.6	22.8	25.4	x26.1	x30.1	x31.8
Middle East	4.5	x5.6	x6.1	x6.3	x4.6	x3.1	x3.9	x3.4	x4.7	x3.6
Europe	55.0	54.1	54.6	53.1	54.5	55.5	54.6	58.1	52.6	51.1
EEC	53.1	52.0	52.2	50.4	52.0	53.4	53.3	56.5	50.9	49.5
EFTA	1.6	1.7	1.9	2.0	1.8	1.1	0.9	0.9	1.0	1.0
Oceania	0.3	x0.5	x0.5	0.5	x0.5	0.5	x0.6	x0.6	x0.6	x0.5
Japan/Japon	12.8	13.1	14.0	16.4	17.1	15.6	16.5	17.8	20.5	21.8
Germany/Allemagne	12.0	11.3	11.6	11.4	11.4	12.4	13.8	15.8	13.3	12.4
Italy/Italie	15.0	14.2	13.6	12.1	13.1	12.9	13.2	12.6	10.5	10.0
France,Monac	11.8	11.7	11.1	11.0	11.2	11.3	10.8	10.7	10.2	10.3
USA/Etats–Unis d'Amer	11.8	9.7	9.6	8.9	7.8	8.0	7.7	6.9	7.6	6.6
United Kingdom	5.7	5.5	5.5	6.0	5.4	5.3	4.8	5.1	5.3	4.5
Greece/Grèce	2.9	2.9	3.3	2.1	2.8	2.7	2.0	2.7	2.4	2.2
Netherlands/Pays–Bas	1.7	1.7	1.8	2.0	1.8	2.0	2.0	2.4	2.5	2.6
Mexico/Mexique	0.9	0.4	0.3	1.3	1.3	1.2	2.1	2.2	2.0	2.4
Spain/Espagne	0.7	1.3	1.3	1.5	1.8	2.0	2.2	2.2	2.0	2.0

	1985	1986	1987	1988	1989	1990	1991	1992	1993	1994
Afrique	0.5	x0.3	0.4	0.3	x0.3	0.3	x0.3	0.3	0.3	x0.3
Afrique du Nord	0.0	0.0	0.0	x0.0	0.0	0.1	0.0	0.1	0.1	0.0
Amériques	20.1	18.7	16.8	18.7	19.4	19.4	19.5	20.0	22.5	23.8
ALAI	7.0	5.8	4.8	5.4	5.2	5.4	5.1	5.1	5.7	6.0
MCAC	0.7	0.6	0.5	0.5	0.6	0.6	0.5	0.4	x0.6	x0.5
Asie	4.0	4.0	x6.9	x6.5	4.0	4.2	4.7	3.9	4.1	5.0
Moyen–Orient	0.7	0.6	x0.4	0.4	x0.2	0.2	0.2	0.2	x0.3	x0.3
Europe	58.2	61.8	56.9	55.5	57.4	57.5	58.3	59.2	56.5	55.5
CEE	54.8	59.6	55.0	53.9	55.9	56.8	57.9	58.6	56.2	55.3
AELE	2.2	1.6	1.3	1.0	1.1	0.1	0.0	0.1	0.0	0.0
Océanie	15.8	x13.7	x13.3	x13.4	x13.4	x13.5	13.8	13.0	x14.0	x13.1
Netherlands/Pays–Bas	14.6	15.9	14.4	14.0	14.4	14.8	14.5	14.7	13.8	13.2
USA/Etats–Unis d'Amer	8.0	8.2	7.9	9.8	10.7	10.5	11.4	11.9	13.0	14.3
France,Monac	7.8	8.6	8.2	8.8	9.1	9.4	9.7	10.5	10.8	10.6
Australia/Australie	7.7	7.6	7.6	7.8	7.7	8.3	8.6	8.1	8.7	8.2
Denmark/Danemark	8.1	8.8	7.9	7.7	7.6	7.7	7.8	8.5	8.0	8.6
Germany/Allemagne	7.1	8.7	7.2	6.7	7.5	8.4	8.9	6.5	5.7	4.7
Belgium–Luxembourg	4.5	5.4	5.1	5.2	5.7	5.8	6.4	6.5	6.2	5.8
New Zealand	8.1	6.0	5.8	5.7	5.7	5.2	5.2	4.9	5.3	4.9
Ireland/Irlande	4.5	5.0	5.0	4.5	4.5	4.3	4.3	4.7	4.9	4.7
United Kingdom	4.5	4.3	4.5	4.2	4.3	3.6	3.7	4.1	3.9	4.6

TRADE BY COMMODITY IN THOUSAND U.S. DOLLARS – COMMERCE PAR PRODUIT EN MILLIERS DE DOLLARS E.U

COUNTRIES–PAYS	IMPORTS – IMPORTATIONS 1990	1991	1992	1993	1994
Total	1530441	1480476	1527726	1225027	1216936
Africa	x12422	x5458	x6108	x9882	x5873
Northern Africa	119	42	x130	248	54
Americas	79326	96115	94744	109327	122733
LAIA	4827	13682	22176	31002	39983
CACM	727	27	360	115	167
Asia	45620	42328	30866	26833	32041
Middle East	x2217	x2224	x1721	x1372	x1444
Europe	1367011	1327008	1392194	1077004	1054518
EEC	1327073	1304496	1368400	1055664	1024269
EFTA	13783	14201	14826	12701	13455
Oceania	x25091	x2815	x2961	x1312	x1135
United Kingdom	960966	901193	899603	696247	624189
France,Monac	163417	167785	191271	141426	139001
Germany/Allemagne	86083	106759	130524	101324	116322
USA/Etats–Unis d'Amer	42156	50500	49465	54555	60345
Belgium–Luxembourg	27525	32735	38183	34933	39846
Ireland/Irlande	32511	29550	32066	16354	20222
Netherlands/Pays–Bas	28036	27934	27904	22114	32504
Mexico/Mexique	4091	11639	17445	22533	21759
Hong Kong	20901	20029	11975	11333	13841
Switz.Liecht	13275	13670	14338	12513	13208
Italy/Italie	9255	11451	13861	14613	19692
Spain/Espagne	5175	10329	14075	12351	11430
Japan/Japon	17411	13910	11009	8095	6868
Sweden/Suède	9775	9689	10339	6336	6071
Portugal	1150	3410	5768	4499	6686
Argentina/Argentine	8	1537	4085	7778	15819
Guadeloupe	3729	3851	4233	4649	4637
Andorra/Andorre	x3629	x3779	x3776	x2971	x3015
Singapore/Singapour	3743	2819	3513	3797	5645
Netherlands Antilles	3776	3625	3361	x2512	x1510
Canada	4530	2997	2074	3464	4207
Angola	x3193	x1281	x973	x5525	x2351
Panama	1937	2128	2142	2269	2216
Denmark/Danemark	1527	1312	2255	2870	5193
Martinique	2039	1775	2157	2427	2527
Bahamas	4589	4962	x574	x675	x313
Trinidad and Tobago	2154	2565	2035	1607	1238
Russian Federation			x659	x5370	x21397
Greece/Grèce	828	1575	2096	1883	1821
Croatia/Croatie			2841	2585	x4620
Bulgaria/Bulgarie	x24		50	x52	x114
French Polynesia	x2106	x1770	x2345	x554	x410
Yugoslavia SFR	21993	x4062			
Barbados/Barbade	1617	1383	1292	1192	x498
Reunion/Réunion	1259	1101	1272	1080	1365
China/Chine	325	1865	764	665	1619
United Arab Emirates	1125	1115	795	x802	x517
French Guiana	931	892	1105	641	744
Mozambique	x2634	x1718	x653	x94	x102
Aruba	1470	2032	x188	x191	x278
Belize/Bélize	x703	x790	756	733	774
Ghana	x257	123	1802	x257	x384
Greenland/Groenland	839	748	750	666	x163
Austria/Autriche	825	774	455	707	1264
Yugoslavia/Yougoslavie			x1627	x118	x1621
Former USSR/Anc. URSS		x1606			
Bermuda/Bermudes	x837	x264	x652	x675	x314
Suriname/Suriname	98	1366	20	x202	x261
Indonesia/Indonésie	17	489	923	81	66
Grenada/Grenade	810	764	x297	x359	x139

COUNTRIES–PAYS	EXPORTS – EXPORTATIONS 1990	1991	1992	1993	1994
Totale	1524701	1477389	1545424	1248769	1360410
Afrique	213	126	x209	962	x20
Afrique du Nord	82	44	53	72	3
Amériques	71590	77976	96079	90744	118374
ALAI	6911	6950	6994	6946	9139
MCAC	45	52	142	185	243
Asie	19037	17974	9986	7995	15188
Moyen–Orient	400	x126	157	x304	x140
Europe	1417687	1367175	1423090	1141664	1218472
CEE	1403299	1354012	1402272	1122847	1196326
AELE	13147	12837	13858	13108	14117
Océanie	5902	6697	7010	5415	4597
Denmark/Danemark	437345	464813	458844	319597	359401
Netherlands/Pays–Bas	460221	382494	389814	262251	262753
Italy/Italie	188081	191194	207800	217144	233035
Belgium–Luxembourg	127798	122975	118510	108122	103586
Germany/Allemagne	74983	69329	73303	65335	60899
France,Monac	47164	53426	58516	72474	80948
Canada	30246	37581	46778	42419	48416
USA/Etats–Unis d'Amer	34269	33158	41972	41167	60522
Ireland/Irlande	35443	34105	48247	32071	33221
Spain/Espagne	8112	14590	23317	23798	35611
United Kingdom	19543	17248	20425	16340	22085
Switz.Liecht	13037	12616	13537	12915	13913
China/Chine	14637	14213	7891	5851	11184
Hungary/Hongrie	x6889	x5349	x8187	x1321	x926
Brazil/Brésil	4132	4054	3787	4726	5137
Slovenia/Slovénia			6745	5502	8000
Australia/Australie	1522	2148	4180	3537	3446
New Zealand	4345	4528	2761	1838	1151
Uruguay	2357	2778	3071	1151	1533
Portugal	1281	1156	1506	3134	2148
Sweden/Suède	2341	1995	971	757	941
Austria/Autriche	427	557	891	1542	x1180
Hong Kong	1777	1848	452	372	398
Poland/Pologne	2956	1622	74	71	2369
Thailand/Thaïlande	48	31	735	654	375
Mexico/Mexique	0	12	3	970	2198
Singapore/Singapour	209	268	367	333	1137
Viet Nam	x1343	x853	x27	x7	
Former GDR	x428	x426	x426		
Malaysia/Malaisie	7	210	218	369	1072
Norway,SVD,JM	110	220	321	192	203
Romania/Roumanie		8	273	327	128
So. Africa Customs Un	23	9	66	511	
Cyprus/Chypre	116	94	149	238	82
Martinique	45	214	142		
Finland/Finlande	527	63	109	152	431
Yugoslavia SFR	1223	x325			
Croatia/Croatie			124	191	
Korea Dem People's Rp	x302	x299			
Kenya	7	29	19	219	
Czech Republic				216	323
Greece/Grèce	28	62	17	128	87
Zimbabwe	62	30	25	145	
Indonesia/Indonésie	8	44	57	66	83
Costa Rica	24	47	83	x21	
Egypt/Egypte	73	44	30	71	
Venezuela	22	65	29	34	35
Papua New Guinea	16	17	67	39	
Honduras	7			115	
Guatemala	13	5	59	38	

(VALUE AS % OF TOTAL)(VALEUR EN % DU TOTAL)

	1985	1986	1987	1988	1989	1990	1991	1992	1993	1994
Africa	0.2	x1.6	x1.8	x0.7	x1.7	x0.8	x0.4	x0.4	x0.8	x0.5
Northern Africa	0.0	x0.0	0.0	x0.0	0.1	0.0	0.0	x0.0	0.0	0.0
Americas	15.6	6.1	6.3	4.9	4.9	5.2	6.5	6.2	8.9	10.1
LAIA	0.1	0.2	0.1	x0.4	0.5	0.3	0.9	1.5	2.5	3.3
CACM	0.1	0.0	0.1	0.1	0.0	0.0	0.0	0.0	0.0	0.0
Asia	4.8	5.0	5.4	x6.0	4.3	2.9	2.8	2.0	2.2	2.7
Middle East	0.1	x0.3	x0.4	x0.8	x0.1	x0.1	x0.2	x0.1	x0.1	x0.1
Europe	77.1	85.7	86.0	86.6	88.6	89.3	89.6	91.1	87.9	86.7
EEC	75.8	83.6	83.7	84.7	85.9	86.7	88.1	89.6	86.2	84.2
EFTA	1.3	1.9	2.0	1.6	1.5	0.9	1.0	1.0	1.0	1.1
Oceania	1.9	1.5	x0.4	x1.4	0.4	x1.6	x0.2	x0.2	x0.1	x0.1
United Kingdom	60.2	62.7	60.5	62.4	63.5	62.8	60.9	58.9	56.8	51.3
France,Monac	8.0	10.5	10.9	10.7	10.5	10.7	11.3	12.5	11.5	11.4
Germany/Allemagne	2.9	4.0	5.0	5.1	4.7	5.6	7.2	8.5	8.3	9.6
USA/Etats–Unis d'Amer	1.9	2.1	2.2	2.0	2.0	2.8	3.4	3.2	4.5	5.0
Belgium–Luxembourg	1.3	1.8	2.0	1.8	1.7	1.8	2.2	2.5	2.9	3.3
Ireland/Irlande	1.1	1.3	1.5	1.8	2.2	2.1	2.0	2.1	1.3	1.7
Netherlands/Pays–Bas	1.4	1.8	2.0	1.6	1.7	1.8	1.9	1.8	1.8	2.7
Mexico/Mexique	0.1	0.1	0.0	0.1	0.3	0.3	0.8	1.1	1.8	1.8
Hong Kong	2.5	2.1	1.5	1.8	1.7	1.4	1.4	0.8	0.9	1.1
Switz.Liecht	0.7	1.0	1.1	1.0	0.9	0.9	0.9	0.9	1.0	1.1

	1985	1986	1987	1988	1989	1990	1991	1992	1993	1994
Afrique		x0.0	x0.1	x0.0	x0.0			x0.0		x0.0
Afrique du Nord	0.0	0.0	0.0	x0.0	0.0	0.0	0.0	0.0	0.0	0.0
Amériques	9.9	9.2	x7.7	7.0	5.5	4.7	5.3	6.2	7.3	8.7
ALAI	5.6	4.5	x1.1	0.3	0.7	0.5	0.5	0.5	0.6	0.7
MCAC	0.1	0.0	0.0	0.0	0.0	0.0	0.0	0.0	0.0	0.0
Asie	13.3	13.2	x3.0	3.3	1.5	1.2	1.2	0.6	0.6	1.2
Moyen–Orient	0.0	0.0	x0.0	x0.0	0.0	0.0	x0.0	0.0	x0.0	x0.0
Europe	66.2	76.7	87.8	88.6	92.2	93.0	92.5	92.1	91.4	89.6
CEE	65.4	75.7	86.5	87.6	91.2	92.0	91.6	90.7	89.9	87.9
AELE	0.7	1.0	1.1	0.9	0.9	0.9	0.9	0.9	1.0	1.0
Océanie	0.4	x0.5	x0.7	x0.3	x0.3	0.4	0.5	0.4	0.4	0.3
Denmark/Danemark	28.4	28.5	30.4	28.0	29.7	28.7	31.5	29.7	25.6	26.4
Netherlands/Pays–Bas	16.1	19.5	23.5	27.3	28.2	30.2	25.9	25.2	21.0	19.3
Italy/Italie	8.3	11.3	13.0	12.8	12.8	12.3	12.9	13.4	17.4	17.1
Belgium–Luxembourg	5.1	7.0	8.8	8.4	9.0	8.4	8.3	7.7	8.7	7.6
Germany/Allemagne	2.8	3.8	4.2	5.0	5.1	4.9	4.7	4.7	5.2	4.5
France,Monac	1.2	1.8	2.1	2.1	2.2	3.1	3.6	3.8	5.8	6.0
Canada	1.3	1.8	3.0	2.3	2.1	2.0	2.5	3.0	3.4	3.6
USA/Etats–Unis d'Amer	2.8	2.8	3.5	4.4	2.6	2.2	2.2	2.7	3.3	4.4
Ireland/Irlande	1.8	2.0	2.6	2.3	2.2	2.3	2.3	3.1	2.6	2.4
Spain/Espagne	0.2	0.2	0.2	0.2	0.3	0.5	1.0	1.5	1.9	2.6

TRADE BY COMMODITY IN THOUSAND U.S. DOLLARS – COMMERCE PAR PRODUIT EN MILLIERS DE DOLLARS E.U

COUNTRIES–PAYS	IMPORTS – IMPORTATIONS 1990	1991	1992	1993	1994
Total	4559550	5029027	4846788	4249982	4558729
Africa	x98123	x79347	x88663	x76479	x137275
Northern Africa	12262	10466	14448	4206	5702
Americas	x1038779	x1005613	x844945	x928393	x937626
LAIA	37274	67088	106794	141360	172555
CACM	4828	5125	4722	x7430	6580
Asia	444749	x530845	619711	x648400	x735554
Middle East	x77062	x90438	x73265	x68541	x79834
Europe	2468724	2796953	3182505	2491054	2654463
EEC	2355609	2689685	3015597	2315845	2472829
EFTA	72139	72838	79198	66459	70459
Oceania	x64998	x71711	x77599	x58626	x47027
United Kingdom	788698	847837	908131	703183	698848
Germany/Allemagne	584886	756503	842774	587500	623678
USA/Etats–Unis d'Amer	697895	644546	501551	522942	511987
Russian Federation			x450021	x484319	x521476
France,Monac	273321	289225	324062	263997	280112
Japan/Japon	190262	228520	295416	314816	375730
Netherlands/Pays–Bas	185142	223121	250961	181584	244225
Former USSR/Anc. URSS	346450	x499138			
Italy/Italie	118979	142501	165363	138284	142554
Belgium–Luxembourg	135375	142538	154164	139578	155511
Canada	112929	114453	124282	148081	147425
Hong Kong	91631	98898	123068	123290	149178
Spain/Espagne	88464	88637	112130	93380	96274
Mexico/Mexique	34661	59032	93481	125930	145498
Switz.Liecht	68201	68847	74533	62349	67053
Sweden/Suède	49571	52280	71936	51910	49237
Singapore/Singapour	46223	52494	61857	60502	59634
Ireland/Irlande	39996	47653	62281	48872	62319
Greece/Grèce	44958	45009	50035	44234	40389
Denmark/Danemark	23618	26753	29722	29971	37253
Cuba	x82310	x60819	x8611	x8605	x7824
Reunion/Réunion	18676	18552	23208	19812	21071
Martinique	18447	20049	20915	20351	20256
Korea, Republic of	12855	17844	19515	22699	22089
Yugoslavia/Yougoslavie			x16644	x43071	x9360
Croatia/Croatie			40394	18195	x42340
Austria/Autriche	13876	16307	23786	16227	19898
Saudi Arabia	22058	31537	9649	x13934	x13572
Ukraine			x2323	x47689	x6180
Guadeloupe	16008	17616	15910	16112	18278
Lebanon/Liban	x14636	x20116	x15107	x12437	x26191
Portugal	8218	10842	19476	16625	22129
French Polynesia	x21051	x16077	x18442	x5447	x3471
Malaysia/Malaisie	13848	11727	13552	14393	13521
Australia/Australie	11473	14002	12559	11082	9388
Korea Dem People's Rp	x1673	x18743	x7047	x10564	x563
New Caledonia	6444	x11122	x12595	x12014	x7241
Poland/Pologne	18076	20296	8817	4516	3646
American Samoa	x11186	x10550	x11883	x9547	x2241
United Arab Emirates	9935	11595	9689	x9401	x10131
Angola	x18619	x6377	x7365	x16370	x27925
Malta/Malte	6074	11648	9564	8465	x6785
Kuwait/ Koweït	2569	4222	12294	10913	12061
Jamaica/Jamaïque	9184	8561	x6329	x12326	x8604
Egypt/Egypte	11800	10117	13410	3130	3923
Bahamas	10749	11890	x5620	x5062	x2879
Romania/Roumanie	53990	9688	7655	4691	6578
Jordan/Jordanie	6783	6465	9101	6367	5702
Hungary/Hongrie	x3242	5225	x9420	x7121	x4973
Papua New Guinea	2915	x6779	x7836	x6704	x6838

COUNTRIES–PAYS	EXPORTS – EXPORTATIONS 1990	1991	1992	1993	1994
Totale	4164879	4636122	4902286	4685000	4975080
Afrique	11334	18440	x18354	27404	x23796
Afrique du Nord	194	306	721	533	626
Amériques	754418	983906	1031776	1053179	1082711
ALAI	485269	678950	704877	641958	639647
MCAC	1301	2041	3334	x6204	x2748
Asie	349785	439192	322845	454687	454670
Moyen–Orient	13322	9171	15701	x13686	x18773
Europe	2614536	2883135	3233878	2873123	3114575
CEE	2520643	2842162	3160853	2816587	3049773
AELE	12138	5998	8242	6291	7431
Océanie	50564	50878	42167	44155	x61513
Denmark/Danemark	698007	689787	678378	612494	638596
Belgium–Luxembourg	400527	455031	522444	476420	506512
Netherlands/Pays–Bas	441210	479183	520823	414041	412723
Germany/Allemagne	254911	394633	365525	331100	315843
France,Monac	281429	326253	362603	363964	457614
Argentina/Argentine	309440	386231	304026	275593	289991
Brazil/Brésil	144166	251785	357431	333323	319200
China/Chine	254183	334203	202534	310587	268278
USA/Etats–Unis d'Amer	195329	238855	267302	334524	356285
Italy/Italie	169312	187173	351525	239810	219847
Hungary/Hongrie	x187861	x166034	x168812	x129425	x107489
Ireland/Irlande	105332	129106	146514	126766	170232
United Kingdom	56443	79498	96987	111926	140927
Poland/Pologne	118597	62705	60504	63564	89192
Canada	68528	59283	50678	66324	77647
Thailand/Thaïlande	7791	20094	38664	63415	89435
Spain/Espagne	16786	24269	36699	48449	74163
Uruguay	29609	37924	38178	23825	20822
Australia/Australie	36462	34729	23401	23748	29920
Hong Kong	20619	22575	21183	21178	28324
Slovenia/Slovénia			35667	27863	42657
Greece/Grèce	14132	25273	21312	16660	30605
Austria/Autriche	10542	11661	15853	26577	x14714
Finland/Finlande	44680	12928	14944	25951	23981
New Zealand	12902	14913	16249	18990	29332
Portugal	19240	20183	17319	12051	18742
Croatia/Croatie			22730	21057	x14561
Singapore/Singapour	19974	19616	11787	11091	12684
Israel/Israël	15858	15773	12684	13105	15204
Romania/Roumanie	2543	11695	13962	13358	13558
Yugoslavia SFR	81709	x34886			
Japan/Japon	8438	10174	8715	10134	9087
Zimbabwe	3267	6607	7945	13524	x10704
Sweden/Suède	7766	6859	9926	10380	25274
Czechoslovakia		x18406	x8191		
Czech Republic				19173	15237
So. Africa Customs Un	4172	8262	4148	5643	
Malaysia/Malaisie	6092	4508	6386	6945	7539
United Arab Emirates	1259	4518	9957	x2298	x4333
Saudi Arabia	1130	1980	3483	x6281	x7736
Norway,SVD,JM	2943	3106	4577	4039	4731
Mauritius/Maurice	270	432	2604	6799	12089
Switz.Liecht	9183	2877	3637	2214	2641
Yugoslavia/Yougoslavie			x6353	x326	x95
Guatemala	290	408	603	4798	1072
Costa Rica	1011	1631	2675	x1276	x1503
Bulgaria/Bulgarie	x29496	x1716	x1798	x1694	10263
Slovakia				x5206	x2065
Korea, Republic of	1194	1464	1555	1983	3090
Chile/Chili	64	1069	1938	1994	2940

(VALUE AS % OF TOTAL)(VALEUR EN % DU TOTAL)

	1985	1986	1987	1988	1989	1990	1991	1992	1993	1994
Africa	2.4	x3.3	x2.5	x3.0	x2.4	x2.1	x1.6	x1.8	x1.8	x3.0
Northern Africa	1.1	1.1	0.6	0.5	0.3	0.3	0.2	0.3	0.1	0.1
Americas	33.7	x28.7	x27.5	24.9	24.0	x22.8	x20.0	x17.4	x21.9	x20.6
LAIA	0.3	0.2	0.2	0.4	0.6	0.8	1.3	2.2	3.3	3.8
CACM	0.5	0.2	x0.1	0.1	0.1	0.1	0.1	0.1	x0.2	0.1
Asia	8.9	x8.9	x8.7	x11.0	x11.6	9.8	x10.5	12.8	x15.2	x16.1
Middle East	1.8	x2.3	x1.9	x2.7	x1.8	x1.7	x1.8	x1.5	x1.6	x1.8
Europe	44.8	46.7	49.7	50.5	52.4	54.1	55.6	65.7	58.6	58.2
EEC	42.4	43.9	46.6	47.3	48.9	51.7	53.5	62.2	54.5	54.2
EFTA	2.1	2.4	2.6	2.8	2.9	1.6	1.4	1.6	1.6	1.5
Oceania	0.6	x1.2	x0.9	x1.1	x1.3	x1.4	x1.5	x1.6	x1.3	x1.0
United Kingdom	17.5	16.3	16.8	17.4	18.3	17.3	16.9	18.7	16.5	15.3
Germany/Allemagne	9.5	10.5	10.6	10.9	10.6	12.8	15.0	17.4	13.8	13.7
USA/Etats–Unis d'Amer	29.5	24.4	22.9	19.4	16.7	15.3	12.8	10.3	12.3	11.2
Russian Federation								x9.3	x11.4	x11.4
France,Monac	3.8	4.5	5.0	5.2	5.5	6.0	5.8	6.7	6.2	6.1
Japan/Japon	2.8	3.0	3.3	4.2	5.4	4.2	4.5	6.1	7.4	8.2
Netherlands/Pays–Bas	2.8	3.1	3.6	3.7	3.6	4.1	4.4	5.2	4.3	5.4
Former USSR/Anc. URSS	8.2	9.7	9.2	8.1	7.1	7.6	x9.9			
Italy/Italie	3.3	3.0	3.3	2.9	2.8	2.6	2.8	3.4	3.3	3.1
Belgium–Luxembourg	2.2	2.4	2.8	2.6	2.8	3.0	2.8	3.2	3.3	3.4

	1985	1986	1987	1988	1989	1990	1991	1992	1993	1994
Afrique	1.0	x0.8	x1.8	x1.2	x0.3	0.3	0.4	x0.4	0.6	x0.5
Afrique du Nord	0.0	0.0	0.0	0.0	0.0	0.0	0.0	0.0	0.0	0.0
Amériques	24.1	19.9	17.4	18.4	18.3	18.1	21.2	21.1	22.5	21.7
ALAI	20.8	17.7	15.7	15.7	14.1	11.7	14.6	14.4	13.7	12.9
MCAC	0.8	0.1	0.1	0.0	0.0	0.0	0.0	0.1	x0.1	x0.1
Asie	2.5	2.8	8.6	9.8	10.2	8.4	9.5	6.5	9.7	9.2
Moyen–Orient	0.1	x0.2	0.5	0.4	0.5	0.3	0.2	0.3	x0.3	x0.4
Europe	68.4	67.3	58.6	58.3	59.9	62.8	62.2	66.0	61.3	62.6
CEE	60.7	63.3	55.2	55.5	56.9	60.5	61.3	64.5	60.1	61.3
AELE	3.3	1.9	1.6	1.4	1.3	0.3	0.1	0.2	0.1	0.1
Océanie	2.1	x1.8	1.6	1.7	x1.9	1.2	1.1	0.9	0.9	x1.2
Denmark/Danemark	24.3	23.3	18.6	17.5	16.8	16.8	14.9	13.8	13.1	12.8
Belgium–Luxembourg	7.7	9.5	8.5	8.8	8.9	9.6	9.8	10.7	10.2	10.2
Netherlands/Pays–Bas	10.1	10.5	9.5	9.1	9.6	10.6	10.3	10.6	8.8	8.3
Germany/Allemagne	3.8	4.7	4.6	5.0	5.5	6.1	8.5	7.5	7.1	6.3
France,Monac	5.4	6.5	6.0	6.0	6.8	6.8	7.0	7.4	7.8	9.2
Argentina/Argentine	7.3	7.1	7.8	6.7	7.3	7.4	8.3	6.2	5.9	5.8
Brazil/Brésil	12.9	9.6	7.4	8.5	6.0	3.5	5.4	7.3	7.1	6.4
China/Chine			5.4	6.5	7.1	6.1	7.2	4.1	6.6	5.4
USA/Etats–Unis d'Amer	1.6	1.2	1.0	1.5	2.9	4.7	5.2	5.5	7.1	7.2
Italy/Italie	3.3	3.8	3.3	4.0	3.5	4.1	4.0	7.2	5.1	4.4

TRADE BY COMMODITY IN THOUSAND U.S. DOLLARS – COMMERCE PAR PRODUIT EN MILLIERS DE DOLLARS E.U

COUNTRIES–PAYS	IMPORTS – IMPORTATIONS 1990	1991	1992	1993	1994
Total	8941222	9172363	10827319	10564075	10783930
Africa	x959582	x901630	x1186448	x1225053	x962662
Northern Africa	571607	520223	755244	737801	630073
Americas	1230809	x1043253	1275657	x1366708	x1300678
LAIA	822626	612969	858454	890000	838195
CACM	53401	59002	87192	95102	92563
Asia	x2042173	1988956	2092366	x2301999	x2489838
Middle East	x796996	581564	x469249	x664220	x641355
Europe	4487599	4846742	6117940	5499471	5898258
EEC	4396929	4794578	6029687	5394540	5801897
EFTA	24685	24530	30329	27086	25618
Oceania	x52493	x70014	x83290	x81484	x73244
Netherlands/Pays–Bas	1230883	1300439	1701597	1253423	1348873
Italy/Italie	1124693	1197633	1378464	1248912	1336194
Belgium–Luxembourg	388567	570769	681674	782839	805931
France,Monac	293801	467573	719823	607502	670871
Algeria/Algérie	392475	379061	558721	569404	493657
Germany/Allemagne	555633	388969	434386	421092	452984
Mexico/Mexique	605507	168269	461228	490145	371792
Spain/Espagne	202130	262257	321130	374602	459191
United Kingdom	209902	251803	345718	278372	249983
Greece/Grèce	277718	223847	271273	259887	269444
Malaysia/Malaisie	175777	181948	228156	247659	240356
Saudi Arabia	266269	283526	118452	x250580	x260210
Philippines	232535	188614	227056	230339	278886
Japan/Japon	162485	212959	205167	179095	185194
Hong Kong	129824	154914	183623	200800	280367
Thailand/Thaïlande	139083	132221	188012	177390	209114
Singapore/Singapour	124619	144292	158877	155937	164751
Russian Federation			x251302	x104650	x60164
Venezuela	38789	151763	105147	79334	114716
Brazil/Brésil	105522	150736	59253	116149	156990
Cuba	x109078	x131266	x73698	x110977	x59362
Indonesia/Indonésie	55964	74482	90243	96517	97014
Former USSR/Anc. URSS	127941	x256241			
Nigeria/Nigéria	21038	72737	x62457	x73190	x36011
Bangladesh		72210	65221	68201	x34486
United Arab Emirates	102673	60190	59444	x81126	x84387
Sri Lanka	55303	62919	63959	71408	81423
Peru/Pérou	37465	38797	74326	76301	88623
Argentina/Argentine	1791	54428	81665	42645	35118
Libyan Arab Jamahiriya	65752	47628	x59281	x56527	x24383
China/Chine	68262	59981	57018	45659	72251
Kuwait/Koweït	28653	30531	49472	79654	81125
Ireland/Irlande	39088	41019	56156	60356	78050
Oman	43631	48057	49152	52083	57458
Yemen/Yémen	x56285	28563	x62169	x44151	x37775
Senegal/Sénégal	38088	35941	x43640	x54197	x28237
Egypt/Egypte	29566	33535	48732	37197	x36788
Chile/Chili	20940	24094	44408	50506	29151
Korea, Republic of	13381	37613	32028	47637	59017
Tunisia/Tunisie	29299	23050	46698	41878	29743
Jordan/Jordanie	28046	32531	34456	42583	24601
Denmark/Danemark	28809	33436	41840	29723	36635
USA/Etats–Unis d'Amer	33942	28387	34093	41670	56983
Cote d'Ivoire	x44570	x27245	x33091	x43367	x19841
Mali	24094	x28769	x29409	x38501	x9201
Mauritius/Maurice	27925	26679	29557	32355	32048
Trinidad and Tobago	27418	26859	25678	28011	21588
Guatemala	19266	20807	29915	29791	33365
Martinique	27674	26614	25726	25264	24308
Dominican Republic	x18478	x21501	x26288	x27835	x59001

COUNTRIES–PAYS	EXPORTS – EXPORTATIONS 1990	1991	1992	1993	1994
Totale	8622815	9119948	11122511	10620091	10739947
Afrique	26038	x37376	25196	x47587	x8633
Afrique du Nord	110	x3458	1133	7096	2710
Amériques	317818	362588	477752	575248	564989
ALAI	87121	72836	68529	144072	181483
MCAC	4464	3773	12187	x9715	x5271
Asie	231575	294419	323422	329697	438003
Moyen–Orient	41658	70617	68763	x50710	x51545
Europe	6908920	7088248	8844585	8112516	7998728
CEE	6883221	7061006	8780240	8065062	7966338
AELE	22850	23093	24452	25755	9444
Océanie	x984904	x1023222	x1103669	x1221863	x1442939
Germany/Allemagne	1890873	2389466	2989854	2688985	2427413
France,Monac	1463926	1361648	1586955	1420536	1678259
Netherlands/Pays–Bas	1410188	1191557	1340373	1435989	1277290
Belgium–Luxembourg	680048	822270	1000291	1010128	1020780
New Zealand	658835	691616	701185	794032	844909
United Kingdom	481363	460461	535598	511033	572413
Ireland/Irlande	302960	275301	751367	442551	401945
Australia/Australie	325707	331163	402123	427541	597821
Denmark/Danemark	352762	326613	344011	348050	376128
USA/Etats–Unis d'Amer	95004	187390	298607	343969	293280
Poland/Pologne	70620	123871	193890	181777	158746
Czechoslovakia		x149589	x112387		
Canada	122982	88555	89608	65641	66107
Spain/Espagne	106442	77390	98372	63174	72088
Hong Kong	39564	60032	77367	93227	175365
Singapore/Singapour	68467	66673	74588	69779	73958
Malaysia/Malaisie	32526	39844	47785	52794	56636
Czech Republic				137996	117756
Saudi Arabia	26259	51665	49879	x26381	x28822
Austria/Autriche	51409	38818	38443	50053	x22477
Lithuania/Lituanie			37316	x89311	68328
Argentina/Argentine	64187	31882	21333	53061	87266
Uruguay	16557	29640	26730	43743	51726
Portugal	18775	32829	28112	29047	46421
Finland/Finlande	45773	31762	26851	19686	26251
So. Africa Customs Un	14590	27809	17531	25611	
Hungary/Hongrie	x39032	x25209	x36070	x4888	x4247
China/Chine	13004	15188	22000	27023	22470
Switz.Liecht	21172	21335	21536	20828	8025
Slovenia/Slovénia			33746	18483	22147
Thailand/Thaïlande	11558	12021	14129	20797	33528
Italy/Italie	10021	13821	16486	16383	18034
Sweden/Suède	51877	23330	8283	15023	10823
Greece/Grèce	16450	15388	15243	14422	16018
Russian Federation			x16610	x19524	x16037
Brazil/Brésil	458	846	7957	21426	1855
Indonesia/Indonésie	16076	14196	8592	4696	3361
Chile/Chili	5291	6333	7636	12525	19175
United Arab Emirates	5444	6552	7775	x10319	x10339
Costa Rica	4209	3530	11720	x8597	x4554
Latvia/Lettonie			x1420	x21619	5684
Estonia/Estonie			x1360	x17928	x16470
Zimbabwe	4265	3035	3950	7423	x4076
Former USSR/Anc. URSS	27172	x13849			
Israel/Israël	2878	7545	3404	2744	3847
Panama	4701	4021	3725	5261	5552
Mexico/Mexique	8	2082	1373	7390	11901
Norway,SVD,JM	1673	1751	2714	4893	1365
Ukraine			x3143	x5427	x10095
Trinidad and Tobago	828	1878	2169	4045	6857

(VALUE AS % OF TOTAL)(VALEUR EN % DU TOTAL)

	1985	1986	1987	1988	1989	1990	1991	1992	1993	1994
Africa	16.7	x12.9	x11.3	x9.3	x11.4	x10.8	x9.9	x11.0	x11.6	x8.9
Northern Africa	9.8	6.8	5.8	4.8	7.0	6.4	5.7	7.0	7.0	5.8
Americas	9.5	11.4	10.3	9.9	14.4	13.8	x11.4	11.8	x12.9	x12.1
LAIA	5.6	7.2	6.1	6.6	10.3	9.2	6.7	7.9	8.4	7.8
CACM	0.9	0.7	x1.0	0.6	0.8	0.6	0.6	0.8	0.9	0.9
Asia	23.1	x20.9	x23.0	x23.4	x22.8	x22.8	21.7	19.3	x21.8	x23.1
Middle East	8.1	x9.0	x8.8	x7.3	x7.6	x8.9	6.3	x4.3	x6.3	x5.9
Europe	49.1	52.8	53.5	54.0	48.9	50.2	52.8	56.5	52.1	54.7
EEC	48.3	51.6	52.5	52.9	47.8	49.2	52.3	55.7	51.1	53.8
EFTA	0.5	0.7	0.6	0.7	0.7	0.3	0.3	0.3	0.3	0.2
Oceania	0.3	x0.5	x0.5	x0.4	x0.5	x0.6	x0.8	x0.7	x0.7	x0.7
Netherlands/Pays–Bas	13.2	12.4	19.9	20.0	15.1	13.8	14.2	15.7	11.9	12.5
Italy/Italie	17.6	14.8	15.5	14.4	13.4	12.6	13.1	12.7	11.8	12.4
Belgium–Luxembourg	2.8	2.6	2.8	2.9	3.4	4.3	6.2	6.3	7.4	7.5
France,Monac	1.7	1.6	3.0	3.9	3.3	3.3	5.1	6.6	5.8	6.2
Algeria/Algérie	6.1	4.1	3.6	3.4	5.0	4.4	4.1	5.2	5.4	4.6
Germany/Allemagne	6.2	12.1	4.3	3.9	4.2	6.2	4.2	4.0	4.0	4.2
Mexico/Mexique	2.9	2.2	2.2	3.0	5.8	6.8	1.8	4.3	4.6	3.4
Spain/Espagne	1.4	2.3	1.7	2.3	2.3	2.3	2.9	3.0	3.5	4.3
United Kingdom	1.1	0.9	1.0	1.7	2.0	2.3	2.7	3.2	2.6	2.3
Greece/Grèce	3.3	3.7	3.5	2.6	2.9	3.1	2.4	2.5	2.5	2.5

	1985	1986	1987	1988	1989	1990	1991	1992	1993	1994
Afrique	0.2	x0.1	x0.1	x0.1	x0.2	0.3	x0.4	0.3	x0.4	x0.1
Afrique du Nord	0.0	0.0	x0.0	0.0	x0.0	0.0	x0.0	0.0	0.1	0.0
Amériques	8.2	7.0	5.2	5.7	5.6	3.7	4.0	4.3	5.5	5.2
ALAI	0.1	0.1	0.2	0.5	1.2	1.0	0.8	0.6	1.4	1.7
MCAC	0.0	x0.0	0.0	0.0	0.0	0.1	0.0	0.1	x0.1	x0.0
Asie	1.3	1.5	2.0	2.0	2.3	2.6	3.2	2.9	3.1	4.0
Moyen–Orient	0.1	0.1	x0.1	0.3	0.4	0.5	0.8	0.6	x0.5	x0.5
Europe	79.2	81.8	83.3	81.7	79.4	80.1	77.7	79.5	76.4	74.5
CEE	76.8	79.5	81.4	80.4	77.8	79.8	77.4	78.9	75.9	74.2
AELE	2.4	2.3	1.8	1.3	1.6	0.3	0.3	0.2	0.2	0.1
Océanie	9.0	x7.9	x7.5	x8.1	x9.7	x11.4	x11.2	x9.9	x11.5	x13.4
Germany/Allemagne	21.6	20.5	28.1	31.4	24.8	21.9	26.2	26.9	25.3	22.6
France,Monac	14.0	16.5	13.8	13.6	14.1	17.0	14.9	14.3	13.4	15.6
Netherlands/Pays–Bas	18.9	19.0	16.9	16.6	16.3	16.4	13.1	12.1	13.5	11.9
Belgium–Luxembourg	6.2	7.6	8.0	6.6	7.9	7.9	9.0	9.0	9.5	9.5
New Zealand	6.2	5.6	5.0	5.6	6.4	7.6	7.6	6.3	7.5	7.9
United Kingdom	4.9	5.4	4.4	4.3	4.8	5.6	5.0	4.8	4.8	5.3
Ireland/Irlande	4.6	4.0	4.0	3.0	4.3	3.5	3.0	6.8	4.2	3.7
Australia/Australie	2.8	2.3	2.4	2.4	3.3	3.8	3.6	3.6	4.0	5.6
Denmark/Danemark	4.1	4.0	3.7	2.6	3.2	4.1	3.6	3.1	3.3	3.5
USA/Etats–Unis d'Amer	5.1	4.7	3.7	3.7	3.0	1.1	2.1	2.7	3.2	2.7

TRADE BY COMMODITY IN THOUSAND U.S. DOLLARS – COMMERCE PAR PRODUIT EN MILLIERS DE DOLLARS E.U

COUNTRIES–PAYS	IMPORTS – IMPORTATIONS 1990	1991	1992	1993	1994
Total	3331067	x3370522	3238197	x3282257	2899156
Africa	348926	186322	254365	259592	211462
Northern Africa	287059	157034	210031	222362	172915
Americas	114327	x171180	152294	x149050	140159
LAIA	74739	103714	115234	99845	100624
CACM	933	2032	3304	2202	4636
Asia	x330301	x374002	x330511	x574301	x382122
Middle East	x181647	x176129	x127726	x262664	x161585
Europe	1974811	2171867	2419487	2238420	2129840
EEC	1944383	2155808	2398340	2219253	2105593
EFTA	7264	5478	8896	9619	5213
Oceania	x19897	x17004	x18768	x17107	x16350
United Kingdom	440787	391152	500545	408728	405257
Germany/Allemagne	399943	392704	472672	387008	415328
Belgium–Luxembourg	328557	423273	402464	367691	362854
Netherlands/Pays–Bas	314543	389104	380684	406501	233011
France, Monac	239767	328801	411841	414677	436799
Russian Federation			x276661	x235207	x132381
Italy/Italie	139855	141638	146100	123501	132919
Former USSR/Anc. URSS	456153	x383900			
Mexico/Mexique	48617	62645	70885	69404	63245
Egypt/Egypte	125772	48985	71878	79068	75448
Algeria/Algérie	94804	54998	63868	74010	37343
Iran (Islamic Rp. of)	x49198	x62197	x31103	x81966	x17602
Mongolia/Mongolie	x12807	x2082		x142480	x3008
Morocco/Maroc	36441	36752	56966	48002	53369
Saudi Arabia	59024	54553	20941	x53480	x65312
Denmark/Danemark	28434	44132	30785	45055	39679
Singapore/Singapour	24215	28807	31071	29519	29712
Poland/Pologne	5896	31959	33671	16410	4828
Greece/Grèce	25898	24164	26055	26226	27906
Thailand/Thaïlande	21291	21915	27128	22781	31806
Malaysia/Malaisie	13934	18945	18992	18621	18986
Indonesia/Indonésie	8577	17506	17403	19019	16328
Philippines	16620	17673	16083	17792	22837
Spain/Espagne	16319	14319	16756	19076	24777
Japan/Japon	13401	38546	5541	5021	5252
Hong Kong	13335	13125	16836	18996	27768
Cuba	x5590	x32730	x2214	x13925	x6381
Brazil/Brésil	15612	20726	9565	15286	23147
Iraq	x9829	x2527	x4327	x35040	
Pakistan	5603	9568	28712	2009	2958
United Arab Emirates	13781	11612	12092	x16271	x15900
Argentina/Argentine	220	13467	21654	3357	3484
Syrian Arab Republic	3980	x4477	9593	x23059	x11798
Oman	9975	11652	11960	12714	10649
Bulgaria/Bulgarie	x40462	x20584	2641	x9814	x2361
Libyan Arab Jamahiriya	18706	11335	x8845	x12030	x2086
Romania/Roumanie	13826	8893	15935	3026	6306
Viet Nam	x3624	x7362	x7588	x10802	x8454
Switz.Liecht	7117	5404	8799	9568	5137
Reunion/Réunion	6756	6506	9028	7470	8715
Tunisia/Tunisie	11169	4926	8271	9132	3524
Lebanon/Liban	x7881	x8232	x6004	x7964	x11670
Andorra/Andorre	x8444	x6573	x6970	x6137	x5585
Turkey/Turquie	3003	4672	6860	6863	5155
Ireland/Irlande	7061	4024	5794	8440	8698
Kuwait/Koweït	6746	2047	7832	7959	10104
Senegal/Sénégal	6252	4269	x7364	x5887	x2540
Ukraine			x239	x17125	x1630
Lithuania/Lituanie			600	x16698	310
Albania/Albanie		x4020	x8800	x4302	x473

COUNTRIES–PAYS	EXPORTS – EXPORTATIONS 1990	1991	1992	1993	1994
Totale	2986117	3456810	3426897	3427213	3037066
Afrique	5774	x3451	x4948	x7209	x1284
Afrique du Nord	71	257	426	x199	119
Amériques	146139	71488	179994	186282	130663
ALAI	28225	12040	3280	7853	19414
MCAC	228	300	174	x172	x244
Asie	23000	27698	36023	81053	31553
Moyen–Orient	3422	8528	13980	55945	x4131
Europe	2236495	2777613	2731246	2511904	2233527
CEE	2216357	2767881	2720704	2500692	2228451
AELE	19794	9264	8533	10078	4420
Océanie	x479638	527947	448272	572810	x600982
Netherlands/Pays–Bas	541061	623004	702677	734703	524049
Ireland/Irlande	252475	460775	556395	398716	387479
New Zealand	389271	429485	364152	448922	469472
Belgium–Luxembourg	359871	439327	421482	362827	349486
Germany/Allemagne	220729	447971	224041	216308	153983
France, Monac	330369	327462	259521	267825	265743
Denmark/Danemark	186064	184377	191225	155677	169986
United Kingdom	140255	121195	172738	182863	182543
USA/Etats–Unis d'Amer	111255	45505	158330	170102	108133
Australia/Australie	81896	98450	84108	123868	131375
Italy/Italie	45716	54894	71994	69807	72769
Spain/Espagne	12226	22580	53180	45770	67525
Finland/Finlande	57381	31894	26908	22322	29341
Sweden/Suède	47658	28203	23559	25978	12659
Jordan/Jordanie	257	6069	11058	49128	343
Czechoslovakia		x34463	x20820		
Portugal	18186	22410	15058	16448	10860
Czech Republic				44029	27319
Singapore/Singapour	12305	12202	13262	15094	11158
Lithuania/Lituanie			37093	x2476	21741
Canada	6056	13230	17878	7907	2729
Poland/Pologne	20994	8885	1715	22323	11474
Norway,SVD,JM	19792	9257	8510	10026	3924
Uruguay	19532	7749	2648	5136	16863
Hong Kong	2285	3723	4800	6544	12698
So. Africa Customs Un	3878	2254	3305	5107	
Hungary/Hongrie	x8422	x4240	x3724	x587	x121
Argentina/Argentine	8581	4154	212	2521	2331
Austria/Autriche	3984	3523	1458	868	x1866
Estonia/Estonie			x656	x4026	x736
India/Inde	730	917	1759	1147	2098
Turkey/Turquie	434	498	1354	1539	325
Cyprus/Chypre	562	411	93	2050	141
Cote d'Ivoire		x797	x885	x851	x774
United Arab Emirates	787			x2243	x1868
Malaysia/Malaisie	604	376	1097	769	263
Slovenia/Slovénia			1391	714	638
Nepal/Népal	612	737	529	277	x233
Latvia/Lettonie			x1009	x297	3103
Greece/Grèce	211	94	469	580	162
Syrian Arab Republic		x249	640	x189	x76
Saudi Arabia	145	668	240	x168	x452
Zimbabwe	310	28	151	736	x329
Former USSR/Anc. URSS	21869	x883			
Slovakia				x778	x91
Turkmenistan/Turkménistn				x756	x222
Egypt/Egypte	71	255	291	122	64
Belize/Bélize	x215	x271	319	48	1
Former Yemen	x300	x300	x300		
Israel/Israël	1998	455	72	43	58

(VALUE AS % OF TOTAL)(VALEUR EN % DU TOTAL)

	1985	1986	1987	1988	1989	1990	1991	1992	1993	1994
Africa	12.3	10.6	x8.4	x7.6	6.8	10.4	5.5	7.9	7.9	7.3
Northern Africa	11.4	9.0	5.8	6.1	5.6	8.6	4.7	6.5	6.8	6.0
Americas	4.9	5.3	3.7	3.1	4.8	3.4	x5.1	4.7	x4.6	4.8
LAIA	1.8	2.4	1.6	1.4	2.8	2.2	3.1	3.6	3.0	3.5
CACM	0.3	0.1	x0.0	0.1	0.2	0.0	0.1	0.1	0.1	0.2
Asia	12.1	x9.6	x12.5	x9.9	x10.0	x9.9	x11.1	x10.2	x17.5	x13.2
Middle East	7.0	x6.1	x7.1	x4.6	x4.6	x5.5	x5.2	x3.9	x8.0	x5.6
Europe	59.4	66.1	66.9	68.5	64.6	59.3	64.4	74.7	68.2	73.5
EEC	58.7	65.2	66.0	67.9	63.9	58.4	64.0	74.1	67.6	72.6
EFTA	0.6	0.5	0.5	0.3	0.2	0.2	0.2	0.3	0.3	0.2
Oceania	0.2	x0.5	x0.4	x0.3	x0.4	x0.6	x0.5	x0.6	x0.5	x0.6
United Kingdom	14.6	15.8	12.7	11.3	11.1	13.2	11.6	15.5	12.5	14.0
Germany/Allemagne	10.8	11.7	11.9	12.4	11.8	12.0	11.7	14.6	11.8	14.3
Belgium–Luxembourg	12.5	11.5	11.6	11.5	12.6	9.9	12.6	12.4	11.2	12.5
Netherlands/Pays–Bas	8.7	11.7	16.2	19.2	13.6	9.4	11.5	11.8	12.4	8.0
France, Monac	4.4	6.3	5.7	7.0	7.5	7.2	9.8	12.7	12.6	15.1
Russian Federation								x8.5	x7.2	x4.6
Italy/Italie	5.8	5.8	5.6	3.9	4.2	4.2	4.2	4.5	3.8	4.6
Former USSR/Anc. URSS	11.1	6.1	7.0	8.9	11.9	13.7	x11.4			
Mexico/Mexique	1.1	0.5	0.5	0.9	1.6	1.5	1.9	2.2	2.1	2.2
Egypt/Egypte	4.3	3.7	3.1	3.6	1.8	3.8	1.5	2.2	2.4	2.6

	1985	1986	1987	1988	1989	1990	1991	1992	1993	1994
Afrique	0.1	x0.1	x0.1			0.2	x0.1	x0.1	x0.2	x0.0
Afrique du Nord	0.0	0.0	x0.0	0.0	0.0	0.0	0.0	0.0	x0.0	0.0
Amériques	3.9	1.7	1.0	0.7	2.3	4.9	2.1	5.2	5.4	4.4
ALAI	0.5	0.5	0.3	0.4	0.6	0.9	0.3	0.1	0.2	0.6
MCAC	0.0	0.0	0.0	0.0	0.0	0.0	0.0	0.0	x0.0	x0.0
Asie	0.6	0.6	0.5	0.6	0.8	0.8	0.8	1.0	2.4	1.0
Moyen–Orient	0.1	0.0	x0.1	0.1	x0.1	0.1	0.2	0.4	1.6	x0.1
Europe	76.0	81.3	82.9	82.9	83.5	74.9	80.4	79.7	73.3	73.5
CEE	74.0	79.8	81.4	81.8	81.4	74.2	80.1	79.4	73.0	73.4
AELE	2.0	1.5	1.5	1.1	2.0	0.7	0.3	0.2	0.3	0.1
Océanie	18.0	14.1	10.9	11.2	10.9	x16.1	15.3	13.1	16.7	x19.8
Netherlands/Pays–Bas	20.4	21.0	18.6	21.1	21.0	18.1	18.0	20.5	21.4	17.3
Ireland/Irlande	10.2	9.9	15.3	13.8	14.3	8.5	13.3	16.2	11.6	12.8
New Zealand	15.2	11.7	9.8	9.8	9.2	13.0	12.4	10.6	13.1	15.5
Belgium–Luxembourg	12.4	15.8	15.5	13.3	11.8	12.1	12.7	12.3	10.6	11.5
Germany/Allemagne	7.0	12.0	9.1	8.2	7.4	7.4	13.0	6.5	6.3	5.1
France, Monac	12.8	8.4	11.8	12.2	10.2	11.1	9.5	7.6	7.8	8.8
Denmark/Danemark	6.3	7.6	5.9	5.0	5.1	6.2	5.3	5.6	4.5	5.6
United Kingdom	2.5	3.2	3.3	4.6	6.0	4.7	3.5	5.0	5.3	6.0
USA/Etats–Unis d'Amer	3.3	1.2	0.5	0.3	1.5	3.7	1.3	4.6	5.0	3.6
Australia/Australie	2.7	2.4	1.2	1.4	1.8	2.7	2.8	2.5	3.6	4.3

024 CHEESE AND CURD

FROMAGE ET CAILLEBOTTE 024

TRADE BY COMMODITY IN THOUSAND U.S. DOLLARS – COMMERCE PAR PRODUIT EN MILLIERS DE DOLLARS E.U

IMPORTS – IMPORTATIONS

COUNTRIES–PAYS	1990	1991	1992	1993	1994
Total	8212152	8352332	9279702	8714190	9143668
Africa	128521	109723	x121717	x125689	x134607
Northern Africa	83415	70069	x70993	x74718	x83835
Americas	756457	727976	801646	x856095	963230
LAIA	82184	99140	115933	146536	229102
CACM	3731	4708	6897	x7760	x9815
Asia	x776928	x855153	x722266	x903129	x899597
Middle East	x416978	x469820	x301855	x455516	x397426
Europe	6377731	6500748	7469849	6653229	6976600
EEC	6068610	6255596	7190618	6356040	6697030
EFTA	179872	187312	202243	189279	206342
Oceania	x92343	x97423	x99717	x93323	x99749
Germany/Allemagne	1851583	1989863	2297709	1834460	1962525
Italy/Italie	1322165	1276298	1380754	1233803	1273154
United Kingdom	817773	768909	977148	795972	803450
Belgium–Luxembourg	658357	673422	751316	740332	757360
France,Monac	501656	518304	602022	565116	585491
USA/Etats–Unis d'Amer	477046	431412	471777	496661	528962
Netherlands/Pays–Bas	271039	323451	369436	347577	362392
Japan/Japon	294302	316496	336633	356903	383620
Greece/Grèce	192880	224649	230853	261628	269827
Spain/Espagne	192741	200693	255688	259029	303759
Switz.Liecht	164488	171161	184775	172795	190096
Iran (Islamic Rp. of)	x99251	x180541	x97295	x155059	x43100
Saudi Arabia	137980	164868	61578	x137067	x175082
Canada	101940	102532	106357	102107	101891
Austria/Autriche	70559	71269	90671	103442	119998
Sweden/Suède	79489	80102	83133	79532	90053
Australia/Australie	73267	78984	79952	73942	82938
Mexico/Mexique	29335	37566	63087	76046	92754
Denmark/Danemark	51673	58390	61955	56125	73462
Ireland/Irlande	31626	39970	46983	38454	46498
Egypt/Egypte	49168	44828	36804	33064	38296
Russian Federation			x49276	x62926	x168476
Poland/Pologne	642	34406	38914	32771	20249
United Arab Emirates	27237	29193	25607	x34938	x31603
Andorra/Andorre	x29873	x30452	x31182	x26865	x25510
Kuwait/ Koweït	21199	15014	34468	36611	41101
Brazil/Brésil	47570	46245	8133	25115	89971
Portugal	13337	16244	25702	24707	28430
Lebanon/Liban	x26895	x24999	x17395	x23439	x46737
Philippines	17259	16909	21477	23256	28944
Libyan Arab Jamahiriya	28194	21343	x13992	x25740	x26297
Reunion/Réunion	15515	16303	21967	22423	22753
Hong Kong	14945	15393	17588	19290	23155
Norway,SVD,JM	15327	16037	17360	16385	16108
Singapore/Singapour	13138	13988	16998	16578	19580
Finland/Finlande	13731	14032	17248	15863	20631
Martinique	12886	13743	15075	16302	x16546
Malta/Malte	14055	12953	15869	14851	x14880
Argentina/Argentine	444	7952	20537	14653	20962
Yugoslavia/Yougoslavie			x6400	x36217	x2134
Venezuela	3918	4532	18986	18507	6588
Guadeloupe	12498	13672	10345	15074	15348
Bahrain/Bahreïn	x13275	x12402	x10504	x13101	x9006
Jordan/Jordanie	8362	11315	12267	12117	14713
Cyprus/Chypre	9153	8441	11745	10951	11082
Oman	7007	8238	8749	10315	10575
Jamaica/Jamaïque	10288	5686	x10227	x10278	x6138
Trinidad and Tobago	7765	8131	10635	7024	8173
Indonesia/Indonésie	6625	7553	9738	7844	8883
Croatia/Croatie			11816	12093	x14904

EXPORTS – EXPORTATIONS

COUNTRIES–PAYS	1990	1991	1992	1993	1994
Totale	8107120	8214260	9341924	9016803	9668964
Afrique	5458	5273	5247	6639	6512
Afrique du Nord	3703	4135	4193	4809	6259
Amériques	160717	149860	153278	162507	207742
ALAI	74411	54770	38143	50994	81968
MCAC	568	406	850	x767	x2962
Asie	29792	30549	29551	x32955	35954
Moyen–Orient	21891	x23326	20298	x22272	x23926
Europe	7335577	7522300	8557818	8193107	8663319
CEE	6850126	7056079	8035496	7724059	8198467
AELE	481560	464777	505469	454125	458344
Océanie	x357794	x390135	x457704	x507943	x628476
Netherlands/Pays–Bas	1783179	1930052	2159485	1928794	2028500
France,Monac	1604032	1645501	1853239	1845287	1972303
Germany/Allemagne	1243907	1192568	1402196	1344755	1410869
Denmark/Danemark	690065	700940	743483	813146	808466
Italy/Italie	465757	531874	582181	589702	644572
Switz.Liecht	407318	397240	428513	387845	393303
Belgium–Luxembourg	311154	339042	428465	426943	429096
Ireland/Irlande	287756	255955	388961	271294	321490
New Zealand	209063	222078	251910	276267	345439
Australia/Australie	148705	167983	205760	231383	282593
United Kingdom	152330	166818	178725	184146	191528
Austria/Autriche	125608	104392	101761	118186	x124940
Finland/Finlande	87136	80464	72407	74011	84768
Norway,SVD,JM	73874	66449	75965	66277	65038
Greece/Grèce	49217	54678	64019	62835	76594
USA/Etats–Unis d'Amer	44258	44509	59697	66916	81852
Bulgaria/Bulgarie	x136269	x39572	53546	32307	36628
Canada	34332	43262	44963	36019	32445
Spain/Espagne	31780	34742	42626	44644	66979
Hungary/Hongrie	x55104	x44207	x51399	x17041	x9774
Uruguay	21836	23315	21915	27394	33337
Argentina/Argentine	50832	29797	12911	19794	45292
Czechoslovakia		x21305	x20542		
Poland/Pologne	11066	8016	9266	13745	37274
Czech Republic				29471	28030
Portugal	7577	8590	9158	11387	13007
Sweden/Suède	10345	10181	8789	8929	25357
Cyprus/Chypre	5397	6074	6254	7924	9288
Turkey/Turquie	7325	5336	6100	7505	8872
Lithuania/Lituanie			9708	x8951	18899
Slovakia				x17977	x13151
Croatia/Croatie			10225	6878	x2685
Saudi Arabia	540	6330	4633	x2169	x1697
Egypt/Egypte	3679	4095	4048	4330	5695
Latvia/Lettonie			x827	x9066	3429
Singapore/Singapour	2176	2562	3320	3350	3912
Romania/Roumanie		2422	3479	3061	2093
Israel/Israël	2961	1999	2791	4120	3505
Belize/Bélize	x2408	x1466	4692	2743	967
Slovenia/Slovénia			5317	2696	3130
Panama	1285	1658	2175	2781	2727
Hong Kong	1622	1771	2072	2216	3178
Jordan/Jordanie	1191	1369	1568	1439	1137
Syrian Arab Republic	3848	x3196	678	x358	x390
Brazil/Brésil	77	710	1848	1224	870
Jamaica/Jamaïque	1937	1741	x814	x766	x1017
Martinique	847	994	817	852	1181
So. Africa Customs Un	1018	800	722	1022	
Estonia/Estonie			x460	x1710	x719
Iceland/Islande	368	1089	991	4	2

(VALUE AS % OF TOTAL)(VALEUR EN % DU TOTAL)

	1985	1986	1987	1988	1989	1990	1991	1992	1993	1994
Africa	3.5	2.1	x2.2	x2.1	2.0	1.5	1.3	x1.3	x1.4	x1.5
Northern Africa	3.1	1.4	1.4	1.4	1.5	1.0	0.8	x0.8	x0.9	x0.9
Americas	14.1	12.2	10.2	8.9	9.7	9.3	8.7	8.6	x9.9	10.5
LAIA	0.7	1.6	0.5	0.5	0.9	1.0	1.2	1.2	1.7	2.5
CACM	0.1	0.0	0.0	0.0	0.0	0.0	0.1	0.1	x0.1	x0.1
Asia	7.7	x9.0	x9.1	x9.6	x9.5	x9.5	x10.2	x7.7	x10.4	x9.8
Middle East	3.9	x5.8	x5.9	x5.3	x4.7	x5.1	x5.6	x3.3	x5.2	x4.3
Europe	72.7	74.9	76.2	77.3	76.7	77.7	77.8	80.5	76.3	76.3
EEC	69.0	70.5	71.7	72.9	72.1	73.9	74.9	77.5	72.9	73.2
EFTA	3.5	3.8	3.9	3.8	3.8	2.2	2.2	2.2	2.2	2.3
Oceania	1.2	x1.2	x1.1	1.1	x1.1	x1.1	x1.2	x1.1	x1.1	x1.1
Germany/Allemagne	19.3	20.3	21.4	20.9	20.8	22.5	23.8	24.8	21.1	21.5
Italy/Italie	19.6	18.3	18.4	17.8	17.5	16.1	15.3	14.9	14.2	13.9
United Kingdom	10.0	9.6	8.5	10.7	9.3	10.0	9.2	10.5	9.1	8.8
Belgium–Luxembourg	7.0	7.5	7.8	7.7	7.6	8.0	8.1	8.1	8.5	8.3
France,Monac	5.3	5.8	6.1	6.4	6.3	6.1	6.2	6.5	6.5	6.4
USA/Etats–Unis d'Amer	10.2	7.8	7.1	5.7	5.9	5.8	5.2	5.1	5.7	5.8
Netherlands/Pays–Bas	1.9	2.3	2.6	2.9	3.1	3.3	3.9	4.0	4.0	4.0
Japan/Japon	3.1	2.6	2.7	3.5	4.0	3.6	3.8	3.6	4.1	4.2
Greece/Grèce	2.1	2.5	2.3	1.8	2.4	2.3	2.7	2.5	3.0	3.0
Spain/Espagne	1.3	1.5	1.7	1.8	2.1	2.3	2.4	2.8	3.0	3.3

	1985	1986	1987	1988	1989	1990	1991	1992	1993	1994
Afrique		x0.1	x0.1		0.1	0.1	0.1		0.1	0.1
Afrique du Nord	0.0	0.1	x0.1	0.0	0.1	0.0	0.1	0.0	0.1	0.1
Amériques	2.1	2.0	1.6	1.9	1.9	2.0	1.9	1.6	1.8	2.2
ALAI	0.6	0.8	0.5	0.6	0.9	0.9	0.7	0.4	0.6	0.8
MCAC	0.0	0.0	0.0	0.0	0.0	0.0	0.0	0.0	x0.0	x0.0
Asie	0.3	0.3	0.3	0.3	0.4	0.3	0.3	0.3	x0.4	0.3
Moyen–Orient	0.3	0.2	0.2	0.2	0.2	0.3	x0.3	0.2	x0.2	x0.2
Europe	90.7	92.0	90.9	90.1	89.9	90.5	91.6	91.6	90.9	89.6
CEE	79.5	81.1	80.6	80.9	80.8	84.5	85.9	86.0	85.7	84.8
AELE	11.1	10.8	10.3	9.2	8.9	5.9	5.7	5.4	5.0	4.7
Océanie	6.3	x5.0	x4.6	x4.7	x5.0	x4.4	x4.7	x4.9	x5.6	x6.5
Netherlands/Pays–Bas	18.7	20.5	21.6	22.1	21.9	22.0	23.5	23.1	21.4	21.0
France,Monac	19.0	18.9	18.6	18.1	18.2	19.8	20.0	19.8	20.5	20.4
Germany/Allemagne	15.8	16.6	15.8	16.1	15.7	15.3	14.5	15.0	14.9	14.6
Denmark/Danemark	9.1	8.7	8.5	7.8	7.9	8.5	8.5	8.0	9.0	8.4
Italy/Italie	4.4	4.4	4.7	4.8	5.4	5.7	6.5	6.2	6.5	6.7
Switz.Liecht	5.9	6.4	6.0	5.5	5.3	5.0	4.8	4.6	4.3	4.1
Belgium–Luxembourg	2.7	2.9	3.1	3.2	3.2	3.8	4.1	4.6	4.7	4.4
Ireland/Irlande	3.5	3.5	2.8	3.7	3.0	3.5	3.1	4.2	3.0	3.3
New Zealand	3.3	2.9	2.7	2.7	2.8	2.6	2.7	2.7	3.1	3.6
Australia/Australie	3.1	2.1	1.9	2.0	2.2	1.8	2.0	2.2	2.6	2.9

TRADE BY COMMODITY IN THOUSAND U.S. DOLLARS – COMMERCE PAR PRODUIT EN MILLIERS DE DOLLARS E.U

COUNTRIES–PAYS	IMPORTS – IMPORTATIONS 1990	1991	1992	1993	1994
Total	1288364	1343717	1317520	1140426	1148143
Africa	x26365	x28335	x23813	x27389	x29643
Northern Africa	20205	21818	x15792	x17770	x17139
Americas	99197	108492	114837	x128733	x133132
LAIA	16612	30041	34973	35158	40539
CACM	2697	4770	4616	x6241	7261
Asia	x262904	262542	271983	x271940	x253765
Middle East	x90211	x47781	x81071	x71625	x57141
Europe	874460	911174	872266	673798	695320
EEC	821374	857997	812846	621639	638216
EFTA	43312	48800	47802	41612	44951
Oceania	x9408	x2524	x1678	x2504	x6141
Germany/Allemagne	398248	454837	404810	263344	275539
Hong Kong	90230	99511	91023	84326	87537
France,Monac	87558	78834	84872	71080	66146
Belgium–Luxembourg	69637	70764	75523	56775	64239
Italy/Italie	66976	72110	70831	50030	51655
Singapore/Singapour	35221	48148	46902	64299	48372
Netherlands/Pays–Bas	38832	46720	51646	60355	59916
Switz.Liecht	42417	47843	47035	40994	44474
Japan/Japon	31750	49739	35035	37901	40147
United Kingdom	71185	48247	38927	30159	39812
Spain/Espagne	39492	35201	32515	44102	25054
Canada	27824	27298	25425	31199	36265
USA/Etats–Unis d'Amer	24535	19941	27888	35379	31045
Poland/Pologne	3492	19073	25958	27792	14592
Austria/Autriche	18073	16620	19367	17625	19057
Kuwait/ Koweït	9243	4765	21085	22788	15422
United Arab Emirates	17166	14851	16440	x12597	x15904
Mexico/Mexique	7014	9452	11732	13795	17231
Denmark/Danemark	9083	9170	10540	8012	9132
Oman	7942	8332	8368	8419	9125
Algeria/Algérie	17381	18429	4968	945	1555
Greece/Grèce	6347	8395	8017	7447	8007
Sweden/Suède	5994	7181	7199	6995	10653
Jamaica/Jamaïque	7738	8506	x5588	x6405	x6381
Ireland/Irlande	6433	8050	6822	3279	4207
Saudi Arabia	4216	4929	6071	x6866	x7207
Argentina/Argentine	227	3486	7169	6104	6678
Yemen/Yémen	x9445	41	x11060	x5181	x3847
Venezuela	806	3733	8773	3763	2761
Libyan Arab Jamahiriya	828	490	x6808	x7457	x8226
Iran (Islamic Rp. of)	x385	x2171	x5782	x5351	x133
Brazil/Brésil	6572	7336	2431	3260	2307
Tunisia/Tunisie	548	2015	2981	7634	5171
Korea, Republic of	4527	4915	4406	2751	6284
Iraq	x34196	x4330	x3826	x2763	x252
Former USSR/Anc. URSS	2540	x9681			
Martinique	3151	3228	3072	2862	2992
Qatar	3054	3034	2610	2772	x296
Macau/Macao	2846	3016	2893	2504	2551
Colombia/Colombie	285	202	2756	4757	3638
Hungary/Hongrie	x1434	993	x3779	x2853	x6714
Croatia/Croatie			4628	2873	x1710
Peru/Pérou	837	4262	1020	1386	3951
Turkey/Turquie	763	2287	2486	1438	956
Guadeloupe	2140	1947	2140	1918	1785
Portugal	3473	1807	1721	2368	4723
Barbados/Barbade	2041	1955	1984	1858	x308
Nicaragua	253	1027	1756	2953	3109
Malaysia/Malaisie	2094	1870	1828	1942	2813
Malta/Malte	1433	1517	1861	1950	x851

COUNTRIES–PAYS	EXPORTS – EXPORTATIONS 1990	1991	1992	1993	1994
Totale	1266021	1338362	1261093	1148647	1157409
Afrique	7423	8256	4935	x12024	4733
Afrique du Nord	3240	2387	x881	x4577	4209
Amériques	118592	159348	157217	165982	191011
ALAI	8847	12455	13767	12374	14761
MCAC	2204	3032	3069	2609	4537
Asie	139738	146600	142184	x123251	x127200
Moyen–Orient	33977	30091	32048	x23146	x22475
Europe	923242	960186	909561	819205	814322
CEE	920805	955555	900377	810611	807507
AELE	1373	2403	1791	1953	2056
Océanie	1216	1729	x1622	2209	2846
Netherlands/Pays–Bas	581272	582371	533985	495302	439997
USA/Etats–Unis d'Amer	83789	119331	117150	124011	145464
Belgium–Luxembourg	116032	120118	125887	100484	121201
France,Monac	76482	84762	94045	93125	93620
Germany/Allemagne	78193	88493	77713	59858	72951
China/Chine	41675	41856	38249	29098	31933
United Kingdom	26543	35412	30953	27178	36379
Malaysia/Malaisie	23624	29452	31708	30447	32204
Canada	22636	24266	23036	26617	25269
Saudi Arabia	11250	15400	15604	x9613	x6115
Hungary/Hongrie	x16552	x18799	x12048	x6822	x5032
Denmark/Danemark	14302	14057	11590	10712	7667
Viet Nam	x9194	x11480	x12095	x11334	x12547
Czechoslovakia		x18849	x14216		
Israel/Israël	8919	10534	7196	15106	15684
Thailand/Thaïlande	13732	13585	9155	6333	4962
Ukraine			x12317	x14732	x3175
Jordan/Jordanie	13003	9674	10624	5712	3438
Bulgaria/Bulgarie	x35120	x9637	x12451	x3672	x1716
Finland/Finlande	10535	8031	6256	7866	10237
Spain/Espagne	3018	9444	4458	6216	11949
Russian Federation			x9643	x9777	x4849
Brazil/Brésil	2411	4619	6697	5049	3260
So. Africa Customs Un	3947	4968	3072	5736	
India/Inde	1157	3657	6169	2893	2072
Romania/Roumanie	851	3766	6206	1925	2872
Italy/Italie	4015	3153	3475	4877	6918
Czech Republic				11322	6105
Former USSR/Anc. URSS	x15272	x11108			
Portugal	2520	4562	4281	2040	3744
Hong Kong	4419	3068	3213	2747	3479
Slovenia/Slovénia			5372	3273	3241
Sweden/Suède	5007	2092	3363	1953	1393
Chile/Chili	658	1337	2119	3785	7318
Colombia/Colombie	886	3448	2100	1577	1729
Belarus/Bélarus			x4510	x1894	x1273
Syrian Arab Republic	4444	x2050	3155	x1095	x1008
Norway,SVD,JM	1368	2396	1788	1944	1998
Guatemala	1875	2053	1806	1780	1902
Latvia/Lettonie			x1048	x4000	210
Greece/Grèce	590	1596	2462	750	891
Singapore/Singapour	1524	1589	1402	975	921
Turkey/Turquie	4062	1833	479	1287	7107
Tunisia/Tunisie		227	370	2989	4167
Libyan Arab Jamahiriya	3179	1868	x134	x1547	
Lebanon/Liban	x22	x19	x1389	x1844	x1241
Estonia/Estonie			x510	x2488	x492
Ireland/Irlande	2116	1281	1603	55	289
Argentina/Argentine	1555	1683	763	462	440
Croatia/Croatie			1370	1364	x985

(VALUE AS % OF TOTAL)(VALEUR EN % DU TOTAL)

	1985	1986	1987	1988	1989	1990	1991	1992	1993	1994
Africa	11.5	5.7	4.8	2.8	3.7	x2.0	x2.1	x1.8	x2.4	x2.6
Northern Africa	11.1	5.2	4.4	2.4	3.2	1.6	1.6	x1.2	x1.6	x1.5
Americas	7.7	7.5	6.4	7.4	9.2	7.7	8.1	8.7	x11.3	x11.6
LAIA	0.5	1.1	0.8	1.2	1.3	1.3	2.2	2.7	3.1	3.5
CACM	0.2	0.2	0.1	0.3	0.2	0.2	0.4	0.4	x0.5	0.6
Asia	19.9	x24.8	x23.5	x25.7	x21.9	x20.4	19.5	20.7	x23.9	x22.1
Middle East	6.0	x11.0	x12.2	x11.6	x8.4	x7.0	x3.6	x6.2	x6.3	x5.0
Europe	59.1	59.5	64.1	62.4	64.5	67.9	67.8	66.2	59.1	60.6
EEC	54.2	54.2	59.0	57.6	60.1	63.8	63.9	61.7	54.5	55.6
EFTA	4.8	5.0	4.7	4.5	3.9	3.4	3.6	3.6	3.6	3.9
Oceania	0.1	x0.1	x0.1	x0.7	x0.1	x0.7	x0.2	x0.1	x0.3	x0.6
Germany/Allemagne	31.0	31.3	33.0	32.2	29.7	30.9	33.8	30.7	23.1	24.0
Hong Kong	7.8	6.9	6.1	7.5	7.2	7.0	7.4	6.9	7.4	7.6
France,Monac	3.9	4.1	6.1	6.6	6.6	6.8	5.9	6.4	6.2	5.8
Belgium–Luxembourg	3.5	4.1	4.8	5.2	5.0	5.4	5.3	5.7	5.0	5.6
Italy/Italie	6.5	6.5	7.7	5.1	6.6	5.2	5.4	5.4	4.4	4.5
Singapore/Singapour	2.3	2.0	2.0	3.0	2.6	2.7	3.6	3.6	5.6	4.2
Netherlands/Pays–Bas	1.6	1.5	1.1	1.6	2.3	3.0	3.5	3.9	5.3	5.2
Switz.Liecht	3.2	3.1	2.9	2.8	2.5	3.3	3.6	3.6	3.6	3.9
Japan/Japon	2.7	4.2	2.0	2.4	2.5	2.5	3.7	2.7	3.3	3.5
United Kingdom	3.8	2.8	2.2	2.6	3.7	5.5	3.6	3.0	2.6	3.5

	1985	1986	1987	1988	1989	1990	1991	1992	1993	1994
Afrique	0.6	x0.4	x0.3	x0.2	x0.3	0.6	0.6	0.3	x1.0	0.4
Afrique du Nord	0.1	0.0	0.0	0.0	0.0	0.3	0.2	x0.1	x0.4	0.4
Amériques	8.9	9.7	7.9	10.9	9.4	9.4	11.9	12.5	14.4	16.6
ALAI	1.0	1.1	0.6	0.3	0.6	0.7	0.9	1.1	1.1	1.3
MCAC	0.1	0.2	0.1	0.1	0.1	0.2	0.2	0.2	0.2	0.4
Asie	16.5	13.0	x14.9	14.5	11.5	11.0	11.0	11.3	x10.7	x11.0
Moyen–Orient	8.7	6.0	x6.2	4.6	3.3	2.7	2.2	2.5	x2.0	x1.9
Europe	71.7	74.9	71.2	67.9	66.9	72.9	71.7	72.1	71.3	70.4
CEE	67.8	71.7	69.5	66.6	65.7	72.7	71.4	71.4	70.6	69.8
AELE	2.6	2.2	1.3	1.0	1.1	0.1	0.2	0.1	0.2	0.2
Océanie	0.8	x0.6	0.4	0.3	x0.1	0.1	0.1	x0.1	0.2	0.2
Netherlands/Pays–Bas	45.9	47.8	47.2	44.7	41.5	45.9	43.5	42.3	43.1	38.0
USA/Etats–Unis d'Amer	5.5	6.6	5.5	9.0	6.5	6.6	8.9	9.3	10.8	12.6
Belgium–Luxembourg	5.8	7.4	7.8	8.0	8.1	9.2	9.0	10.0	8.7	10.5
France,Monac	4.6	4.6	3.6	3.7	4.9	6.0	6.3	7.5	8.1	8.1
Germany/Allemagne	4.9	5.7	5.7	5.0	5.2	6.2	6.6	6.2	5.2	6.3
China/Chine	4.4	4.2	4.9	5.2	3.7	3.3	3.1	3.0	2.5	2.8
United Kingdom	3.2	2.7	2.4	3.0	3.4	2.1	2.6	2.5	2.4	3.1
Malaysia/Malaisie	0.8	0.7	0.8	1.5	1.5	1.9	2.2	2.5	2.7	2.8
Canada	2.3	1.7	1.7	1.5	2.1	1.8	1.8	1.8	2.3	2.2
Saudi Arabia	1.3	x0.3	x1.4	1.0	0.9	0.9	1.2	1.2	x0.8	x0.5

TRADE BY COMMODITY IN THOUSAND U.S. DOLLARS – COMMERCE PAR PRODUIT EN MILLIERS DE DOLLARS E.U

COUNTRIES–PAYS	IMPORTS – IMPORTATIONS 1990	1991	1992	1993	1994
Total	16743334	18882649	19426359	18529579	20100645
Africa	x321004	x392900	x323062	x311072	x308768
Northern Africa	71114	52795	63326	45086	64241
Americas	2553070	2658782	x2478526	x2648708	x2795267
LAIA	118353	110791	89452	127828	181909
CACM	14471	12037	16577	x8752	x7046
Asia	6107848	7244329	8006254	8316209	9204431
Middle East	63722	x90599	x101950	x135286	x123706
Europe	7456195	8210946	8249571	6863861	7398495
EEC	7135021	7726611	7827640	6497057	7005441
EFTA	276207	336749	359821	324012	352735
Oceania	x209145	x216217	x264744	x253453	x191311
Japan/Japon	4378962	4981330	5655878	6074412	6746101
USA/Etats–Unis d'Amer	2197346	2290329	2111573	2175584	2250674
France,Monac	1335266	1391780	1412299	1155318	1208358
Spain/Espagne	1076445	1254775	1293614	1078471	1169897
Germany/Allemagne	1023557	1157589	1174352	1057888	1246993
Italy/Italie	1110027	1167296	1130970	898813	884441
Thailand/Thaïlande	737824	962013	816503	644045	554964
United Kingdom	851136	815464	820552	690063	660339
Denmark/Danemark	591443	663573	669060	508616	549776
Netherlands/Pays–Bas	370157	431855	453354	364662	425482
Korea, Republic of	246186	396711	340228	360338	431803
Hong Kong	258227	307394	347712	352346	414710
Belgium–Luxembourg	277578	294581	308927	259629	277919
Canada	182937	206602	208746	271655	304465
Singapore/Singapour	150402	188010	231188	234045	234645
Portugal	146273	197477	208966	199050	239227
Switz.Liecht	173291	174942	174681	160096	175579
China/Chine	76821	81608	206733	212419	368533
Norway,SVD,JM	102699	160020	182283	152038	159005
Sweden/Suède	154307	154730	175576	139991	171872
Malaysia/Malaisie	78060	88880	150961	159489	180829
Nigeria/Nigéria	676	128125	x106478	x103787	x61611
Australia/Australie	91199	98175	102929	105294	115337
American Samoa	x69833	x59615	x111633	x97732	x25321
Poland/Pologne	11650	57856	83452	92057	136367
Brazil/Brésil	100940	87916	52814	90492	117077
Israel/Israël	51362	65681	69874	67348	68140
Philippines	50176	67591	63887	51517	53786
Austria/Autriche	57132	62683	62424	53727	59411
Greece/Grèce	69733	63776	59492	48280	48937
Cote d'Ivoire	x74827	x54110	x44399	x64102	x93884
Egypt/Egypte	62050	46379	58903	39123	56530
Andorra/Andorre	x7713	x120324	x8999	x7572	x7626
Russian Federation			x90621	x33489	x78198
Finland/Finlande	35603	38014	32764	27380	44117
Saudi Arabia	27003	32181	26103	x16227	x17045
Former USSR/Anc. URSS	31652	x73585			
Guam	x19190	x18909	x22131	x32331	x23054
Cameroon/Cameroun	47760	51091	x7049	x12905	x1184
Ireland/Irlande	30371	27025	25289	15168	18671
Mauritius/Maurice	17957	19665	19474	13590	17428
United Arab Emirates	5817	3287	4504	x44784	x46800
Iran (Islamic Rp. of)		x17243	x18295	x15176	x3004
Turkey/Turquie	7351	9491	17389	20365	22226
So. Africa Customs Un	18126	16115	13803	13261	15321
Faeroe Islds/Is Féroé	2930	12293	23397	7468	9259
Ghana	x6379	2382	29272	x8638	x5773
Cuba		x1041	x15590	x23030	x13171
Costa Rica	14171	11929	16080	x8211	x6520
Senegal/Sénégal	43202	23214	x3777	x6875	x9831

COUNTRIES–PAYS	EXPORTS – EXPORTATIONS 1990	1991	1992	1993	1994
Totale	13599280	15232724	14965019	14229297	15911625
Afrique	x527158	x444357	x498456	x441339	x578756
Afrique du Nord	225221	195014	132060	116148	112332
Amériques	4001907	4211949	4295574	3927210	x4186535
ALAI	845038	1078376	1103632	1126935	1310723
MCAC	43944	35010	34850	x28781	x53332
Asie	2306831	2677963	2807860	3052870	3449739
Moyen–Orient	81105	x75541	x69976	x77917	x80337
Europe	6202113	6658204	6633429	6064359	6857561
CEE	3900872	4168587	4112922	3731186	4161310
AELE	2056925	2192801	2208391	2083483	2470752
Océanie	x435489	x550905	x649707	x689919	x762097
USA/Etats–Unis d'Amer	1788206	1857197	2123918	1782285	1842558
Norway,SVD,JM	1291157	1377643	1460605	1419655	1751602
Denmark/Danemark	1023727	1081921	1058986	1054124	1104321
Canada	1153465	1091322	919285	875506	827614
Netherlands/Pays–Bas	752657	811711	808102	694022	695237
Iceland/Islande	761766	812264	745629	662334	717406
Russian Federation			x1019215	x1134108	x1204614
Korea, Republic of	659355	745957	666311	636054	697363
France,Monac	590403	594133	606461	493006	540613
United Kingdom	432892	509687	533507	406388	457483
Chile/Chili	323941	406960	510230	502075	571468
New Zealand	295522	387923	446017	437644	418999
China/Chine	296118	311291	381884	424911	660904
Thailand/Thaïlande	184349	325515	328829	335509	348605
Japan/Japon	259896	307189	330862	321124	318735
Spain/Espagne	336866	322521	283429	323180	449681
Indonesia/Indonésie	177369	253548	281892	391619	369378
Argentina/Argentine	230785	302015	279526	302256	365653
Faeroe Islds/Is Féroé	227958	283690	275454	217547	199356
Germany/Allemagne	200543	245195	223262	214667	262066
Singapore/Singapour	216589	229578	225267	225261	253171
Former USSR/Anc. URSS		x617014			
Hong Kong	193682	180884	186335	173824	231045
Ireland/Irlande	151278	174265	189917	165901	178157
Morocco/Maroc	164500	132870	100102	78574	79500
Portugal	120530	124906	104262	79856	80080
So. Africa Customs Un	47347	71514	95131	113972	159129
Italy/Italie	74395	81242	93137	102797	129975
India/Inde	53310	63506	92540	102543	172685
Uruguay	60865	100048	91175	66879	73403
Australia/Australie	81933	74467	93986	79903	87640
Belgium–Luxembourg	81774	88522	79955	69125	77402
Senegal/Sénégal	86928	45065	x123034	48569	x72065
Sweden/Suède	95963	88961	64810	42565	70912
Greece/Grèce	24581	35719	53862	75680	101984
Ecuador/Equateur	51986	50835	56413	53100	x90092
Colombia/Colombie	35020	58155	51383	47801	62555
Malaysia/Malaisie	32940	35219	52360	62979	55639
Mexico/Mexique	55362	73896	40091	33198	28711
Pakistan	12213	12917	45919	86684	31710
Greenland/Groenland	73729	47882	51571	43042	x54659
Korea Dem People's Rp	x48942	x45209	x46603	x41730	x17452
Brazil/Brésil	26858	33686	41873	57899	41313
Mauritania/Mauritanie	x36502	x42882	x46651	x41406	x33782
Philippines	35790	32093	29081	58351	66736
Oman	30476	27625	25924	45759	43674
Poland/Pologne	24304	28760	47784	20593	40040
Viet Nam	x7557	x16453	x24019	x49332	x61682
Peru/Pérou	27511	27577	14988	43864	51834
Federated States of Micronesia			x20760	x63751	x108363

(VALUE AS % OF TOTAL)(VALEUR EN % DU TOTAL)

	1985	1986	1987	1988	1989	1990	1991	1992	1993	1994
Africa	3.3	x2.6	x1.9	x1.7	x2.0	x1.9	x2.1	x1.7	x1.7	x1.6
Northern Africa	0.6	0.6	0.4	0.4	0.5	0.4	0.3	0.3	0.2	0.3
Americas	24.9	22.5	22.3	16.5	18.2	15.2	14.1	x12.7	x14.3	x13.9
LAIA	0.2	0.7	0.7	0.3	0.6	0.7	0.6	0.5	0.7	0.9
CACM	0.1	0.0	0.1	0.1	0.1	0.1	0.1	0.1	x0.0	x0.0
Asia	32.8	34.7	33.2	40.2	39.1	36.5	38.3	41.2	44.8	45.8
Middle East	0.7	0.6	x0.7	x0.5	x0.6	0.4	x0.5	x0.5	x0.7	x0.6
Europe	36.9	38.3	40.3	38.4	38.2	44.5	43.5	42.5	37.0	36.8
EEC	33.7	35.0	37.1	35.3	35.1	42.6	40.9	40.3	35.1	34.9
EFTA	3.0	3.0	3.0	2.8	2.8	1.6	1.8	1.9	1.7	1.8
Oceania	1.1	x1.1	x1.1	x2.2	x1.7	x1.3	x1.1	x1.3	x1.4	x1.0
Japan/Japon	25.5	26.8	25.3	29.6	28.0	26.2	26.4	29.1	32.8	33.6
USA/Etats–Unis d'Amer	22.8	20.1	19.9	14.8	15.9	13.1	12.1	10.9	11.7	11.2
France,Monac	6.5	6.8	7.2	6.8	6.5	8.0	7.4	7.3	6.2	6.0
Spain/Espagne	2.5	2.9	4.2	5.1	5.2	6.4	6.6	6.7	5.8	5.8
Germany/Allemagne	5.3	5.7	5.2	4.9	5.0	6.1	6.1	6.0	5.7	6.2
Italy/Italie	6.5	5.7	6.3	5.6	5.7	6.6	6.2	5.8	4.9	4.4
Thailand/Thaïlande	1.8	2.8	2.0	3.7	4.6	4.4	5.1	4.2	3.5	2.8
United Kingdom	5.0	5.0	4.6	4.2	4.1	5.1	4.3	4.2	3.7	3.3
Denmark/Danemark	2.5	3.0	3.2	2.9	2.7	3.5	3.5	3.4	2.7	2.7
Netherlands/Pays–Bas	1.5	1.7	1.8	1.7	1.8	2.2	2.3	2.3	2.0	2.1

	1985	1986	1987	1988	1989	1990	1991	1992	1993	1994
Afrique	2.4	x4.0	x3.4	x2.6	x2.7	x3.8	x2.9	x3.3	x3.1	x3.6
Afrique du Nord	0.9	1.3	1.0	0.9	1.2	1.7	1.3	0.9	0.8	0.7
Amériques	31.7	31.0	25.6	26.5	28.4	29.4	27.7	28.7	27.6	x26.3
ALAI	6.5	5.6	4.9	4.5	5.5	6.2	7.1	7.4	7.9	8.2
MCAC	0.1	0.2	0.2	0.2	0.4	0.3	0.2	0.2	x0.2	x0.3
Asie	19.3	17.2	x22.5	x23.3	18.1	17.0	17.6	18.8	21.5	21.7
Moyen–Orient	0.5	0.6	x0.4	0.6	x0.6	0.6	x0.5	x0.5	x0.5	x0.5
Europe	41.7	44.0	39.9	37.8	41.0	45.6	43.7	44.3	42.6	43.1
CEE	27.3	28.8	25.7	24.0	26.4	28.7	27.4	27.5	26.2	26.2
AELE	12.6	13.4	12.8	12.6	13.1	15.1	14.4	14.8	14.6	15.5
Océanie	3.2	3.6	x3.1	x3.4	x3.5	x3.2	x3.6	x4.3	x4.8	x4.8
USA/Etats–Unis d'Amer	11.1	10.8	9.1	11.0	11.8	13.1	12.2	14.2	12.5	11.6
Norway,SVD,JM	6.0	7.0	7.1	7.4	7.5	9.5	9.0	9.8	10.0	11.0
Denmark/Danemark	7.6	8.7	7.7	6.6	6.3	7.5	7.1	7.1	7.4	6.9
Canada	11.5	11.9	9.5	9.0	8.6	8.5	7.2	6.1	6.2	5.2
Netherlands/Pays–Bas	5.9	6.4	5.4	4.6	4.7	5.5	5.3	5.4	4.9	4.4
Iceland/Islande	5.5	5.7	5.0	4.2	4.8	5.6	5.3	5.0	4.7	4.5
Russian Federation								x6.8	x8.0	x7.6
Korea, Republic of	6.7	7.5	6.7	6.7	6.4	4.8	4.9	4.5	4.5	4.4
France,Monac	3.8	3.8	3.4	3.4	3.9	4.3	3.9	4.1	3.5	3.4
United Kingdom	2.5	2.8	2.8	2.6	2.9	3.2	3.3	3.6	2.9	2.9

TRADE BY COMMODITY IN THOUSAND U.S. DOLLARS – COMMERCE PAR PRODUIT EN MILLIERS DE DOLLARS E.U

COUNTRIES–PAYS	IMPORTS – IMPORTATIONS					COUNTRIES–PAYS	EXPORTS – EXPORTATIONS				
	1990	1991	1992	1993	1994		1990	1991	1992	1993	1994
Total	2486329	2488666	2554413	2261558	2446341	Totale	2207218	2335493	2374670	2175403	2541791
Africa	x92463	x38416	x54059	x55027	x39932	Afrique	x24511	x29361	x33805	x32831	x29642
Northern Africa	3310	1863	x2126	x1650	2921	Afrique du Nord	4303	6154	2482	1837	2049
Americas	277745	301670	x296873	x312386	x362760	Amériques	503080	512528	520027	x469135	x403976
LAIA	89414	105871	83090	110928	143674	ALAI	28626	41568	68787	55393	68807
CACM	107	220	404	x475	x381	MCAC	2054	2961	7724	x5614	x6245
Asia	614988	640657	774412	776498	806628	Asie	317745	273153	343005	367401	x499169
Middle East	5846	6051	6380	x7533	x9200	Moyen–Orient	x7915	9043	x14026	x17533	x31037
Europe	1362357	1478198	1409199	1098567	1216176	Europe	1353226	1496014	1458216	1288285	1582559
EEC	1310844	1431951	1378449	1067897	1186344	CEE	594117	614810	596864	542682	672537
EFTA	46593	43449	27620	26959	25694	AELE	699512	815758	799748	715139	867924
Oceania	x15960	x14213	x13805	x15313	x15895	Océanie	x8428	x14530	x15260	x11854	x14047
Portugal	378542	416776	381294	278071	281497	Norway,SVD,JM	433310	538814	574922	537049	659569
Japan/Japon	363088	328736	350267	380359	387197	Canada	372850	337795	319304	275051	215038
Italy/Italie	314041	358330	306883	239809	266060	Denmark/Danemark	245935	256958	276042	252283	359143
Hong Kong	164982	197909	270764	244906	262639	Iceland/Islande	264602	275687	223708	176919	207355
Spain/Espagne	179779	185785	195736	150009	156867	USA/Etats–Unis d'Amer	87286	117291	111885	120891	104448
Germany/Allemagne	143724	162945	182027	132602	171065	United Kingdom	59606	63279	67797	68687	81386
USA/Etats–Unis d'Amer	119283	125743	135038	123319	123603	Netherlands/Pays–Bas	67036	71521	65064	61768	59274
France,Monac	94419	109825	108634	84097	102944	Hong Kong	46710	57956	63359	64850	72663
Brazil/Brésil	80306	94193	69401	93557	123511	Spain/Espagne	85506	88026	41652	38061	42945
Singapore/Singapour	28642	39204	51024	46787	46622	France,Monac	47755	55851	61123	45104	54641
Denmark/Danemark	52788	45798	48322	37893	60558	Faeroe Islds/Is Féroé	59462	65116	61254	30373	41992
Sri Lanka	32728	40624	41823	39838	42341	China/Chine	94406	25917	54213	62717	133192
Greece/Grèce	33149	31551	33289	29631	26613	Indonesia/Indonésie	27764	34380	44904	53269	83550
Belgium–Luxembourg	25814	28139	28178	31696	36181	Singapore/Singapour	22495	29010	44056	40669	55364
Netherlands/Pays–Bas	21768	25233	28979	31658	24136	Thailand/Thaïlande	20154	26228	26302	36398	23723
Sweden/Suède	30130	33186	27556	23430	25295	Japan/Japon	21386	22153	24494	19996	20622
China/Chine	6836	8403	33024	35475	32584	Colombia/Colombie	2964	12738	28939	15761	20994
Switz.Liecht	19048	19693	18964	17585	19664	Korea, Republic of	29474	21567	17109	17246	13476
Canada	10834	9580	14798	18249	31875	Germany/Allemagne	17572	14970	22890	16136	18500
Congo	x11055	x9942	x12600	x17082	x7306	Ireland/Irlande	19609	18238	17798	16468	12582
Norway,SVD,JM	27378	22564	7972	8656	5632	Pakistan	13270	14922	18069	15024	10708
Dominican Republic	x9756	x9663	x15775	x12111	x23537	Argentina/Argentine	10140	12084	17618	16335	14836
United Kingdom	14221	13094	14634	9623	14263	Greece/Grèce	18263	13573	13041	17377	12851
Australia/Australie	12711	11488	11825	13275	14504	Belgium–Luxembourg	12412	14616	10935	10846	13598
Nigeria/Nigéria	x47791	2852	x16801	x16609	x10315	So. Africa Customs Un	8357	11756	11246	12030	
Martinique	9648	12282	11962	11003	9495	Russian Federation			x13360	x18715	x26005
Austria/Autriche	9414	9788	12125	11468	12957	United Arab Emirates	3799	5051	8471	x15390	x21911
Malaysia/Malaisie	5810	10811	9656	10187	8925	Portugal	12023	8910	8198	6595	6732
Jamaica/Jamaïque	15715	9153	x7334	x13125	x8474	Bangladesh	5429	4984	9572	8945	x10289
Mexico/Mexique	7870	8547	8969	11671	13804	Chile/Chili	6081	4626	7902	9052	18488
Guadeloupe	6836	7043	8669	6684	6697	Maldives	x4389	x7879	x4083	x4896	x12936
Poland/Pologne	5675	14575	4706	2147	2824	St Pierre & Miquelon	3573	5173	5478	x4639	x243
Reunion/Réunion	4893	5569	8491	5785	6260	Mexico/Mexique	5980	6707	3957	4496	4672
Finland/Finlande	5354	4975	7626	4910	4996	Korea Dem People's Rp	x12056	x5302	x4814	x4955	x8049
Zaire/Zaïre	x5546	x4314	x3590	x3347	x3198	Italy/Italie	5350	5627	5760	3388	4939
Ireland/Irlande	5530	4356	3167	2999	2912	New Zealand	4215	5635	3947	5073	5245
Angola	x5774	x2448	x1783	x3808	x3635	Senegal/Sénégal	3663	3825	x5868	3399	x3496
Israel/Israël	2614	2996	2880	2053	2378	Sweden/Suède	2754	2799	5744	4142	2305
Russian Federation			x2731	x4617	x16747	Myanmar	x2281	3073	x3592	x5399	x2886
Gabon	x3331	x2482	x2559	x2296	x902	Poland/Pologne	180	2740	4078	5164	12124
Haiti/Haïti	x1976	x1687	x2821	x2201	x2171	Viet Nam	x2418	x2469	x2934	x6317	x9249
Venezuela	540	1436	2245	2802	2059	Greenland/Groenland	6836	5660	3345	636	x882
Macau/Macao	1167	1513	1830	2380	2137	Australia/Australie	1551	2100	3527	3886	4767
Cameroon/Cameroun	2804	3634	x1016	x923	x304	Costa Rica	920	1353	5235	x2481	x2604
Argentina/Argentine	475	1308	2171	2008	2803	Sri Lanka	1314	1689	3877	3066	2694
So. Africa Customs Un	1720	1688	2223	1549	1767	Peru/Pérou	949	1378	3516	3651	2094
Netherlands Antilles	x1955	1872	1961	x1383	x872	Morocco/Maroc	4077	5696	1868	819	1375
Saint Lucia/St. Lucie	1114	1277	x1929	x1864	x1218	Brazil/Brésil	1582	1659	3053	3199	2422
Antigua and Barbuda	x898	x1337	x1796	x1844	x1237	Former USSR/Anc. URSS		x6944			
Barbados/Barbade	1741	1641	1901	1370	x1255	Guam	x682	x1902	x2676	x1700	x2158

(VALUE AS % OF TOTAL)(VALEUR EN % DU TOTAL)

	1985	1986	1987	1988	1989	1990	1991	1992	1993	1994		1985	1986	1987	1988	1989	1990	1991	1992	1993	1994
Africa	1.9	x4.3	x3.3	x2.5	x2.6	x3.7	x1.6	x2.1	x2.5	x1.7	Afrique	0.8	x1.1	x1.3	x1.3	x1.2	x1.1	x1.3	x1.4	x1.6	x1.2
Northern Africa	0.3	x0.2	x0.2	x0.2	x0.1	0.1	0.1	x0.1	x0.1	0.1	Afrique du Nord	0.2	x0.1	0.1	0.3	0.3	0.2	0.3	0.1	0.1	0.1
Americas	14.0	15.2	10.4	9.9	13.5	11.1	12.1	x11.7	x13.9	x14.9	Amériques	25.8	19.9	x17.3	27.7	25.0	22.7	22.0	21.9	x21.6	x15.9
LAIA	3.6	5.7	2.9	2.5	4.4	3.6	4.3	3.3	4.9	5.9	ALAI	1.8	1.2	1.0	1.2	1.7	1.3	1.8	2.9	2.5	2.7
CACM	0.0	0.0	0.0	0.0	0.0	0.0	0.0	0.0	x0.0	x0.0	MCAC	0.0	0.0	0.0	0.1	0.1	0.1	0.1	0.3	x0.3	x0.2
Asia	32.7	26.5	27.0	29.6	27.9	24.7	25.7	30.3	34.3	32.9	Asie	12.3	9.9	x12.6	x11.9	12.3	14.4	11.6	14.4	16.9	x19.6
Middle East	0.8	x0.5	x0.3	0.3	x0.3	0.2	0.2	0.2	x0.3	x0.4	Moyen–Orient	0.1	x0.1	x0.5	x0.3	x0.4	x0.4	0.4	x0.6	x0.8	x1.2
Europe	50.3	52.8	55.9	54.1	52.4	54.8	59.4	55.2	48.6	49.7	Europe	60.9	68.6	66.9	57.1	60.3	61.3	64.1	61.4	59.2	62.3
EEC	47.5	48.7	52.0	50.7	48.7	52.7	57.5	54.0	47.2	48.5	CEE	23.8	24.3	25.6	23.1	25.1	26.9	26.3	25.1	24.9	26.5
EFTA	2.7	3.9	3.8	3.3	3.5	1.9	1.7	1.1	1.2	1.1	AELE	33.4	40.2	37.3	30.9	31.9	31.7	34.9	33.7	32.9	34.1
Oceania	1.1	x0.9	x0.8	x0.8	x0.8	x0.6	x0.5	x0.6	x0.7	x0.6	Océanie	0.2	x0.4	x0.8	x1.1	x0.6	x0.4	x0.6	x0.6	x0.5	x0.6
Portugal	14.1	13.0	15.5	15.8	12.6	15.2	16.7	14.9	12.3	11.5	Norway,SVD,JM	20.2	24.5	20.1	17.2	19.1	19.6	23.1	24.2	24.7	25.9
Japan/Japon	22.1	16.9	16.2	17.0	16.1	14.6	13.2	13.7	16.8	15.8	Canada	9.5	9.3	8.7	16.7	16.9	16.9	14.5	13.4	12.6	8.5
Italy/Italie	13.4	12.4	14.0	13.2	13.5	12.6	14.4	12.0	10.6	10.9	Denmark/Danemark	8.7	9.4	10.6	9.9	10.3	11.1	11.0	11.6	11.6	14.1
Hong Kong	5.9	5.8	6.2	7.4	7.3	6.6	8.0	10.6	10.8	10.7	Iceland/Islande	12.9	15.3	17.0	13.2	12.6	12.0	11.8	9.4	8.1	8.2
Spain/Espagne	3.6	5.4	5.4	6.1	6.1	7.2	7.5	7.7	6.6	6.4	USA/Etats–Unis d'Amer	13.9	8.7	7.0	9.1	5.6	4.0	5.0	4.7	5.6	4.1
Germany/Allemagne	4.5	5.0	4.7	4.8	4.8	5.8	6.5	7.1	5.9	7.0	United Kingdom	2.6	2.6	2.4	2.4	2.7	2.7	2.7	2.9	3.2	3.2
USA/Etats–Unis d'Amer	6.6	5.8	4.8	4.4	5.3	4.8	5.1	5.3	5.5	5.1	Netherlands/Pays–Bas	2.8	2.6	2.3	2.1	2.5	3.0	3.1	2.7	2.8	2.3
France,Monac	3.7	4.2	4.1	4.0	4.2	3.8	4.4	4.3	3.7	4.2	Hong Kong	2.8	2.0	2.1	2.2	2.5	2.1	2.5	2.7	3.0	2.9
Brazil/Brésil	3.1	5.6	2.8	2.3	4.2	3.2	3.8	2.7	4.1	5.0	Spain/Espagne	4.5	3.6	3.6	2.9	3.1	3.9	3.8	1.8	1.7	1.7
Singapore/Singapour	1.4	1.1	1.2	1.4	1.4	1.2	1.6	2.0	2.1	1.9	France,Monac	1.9	2.5	2.8	2.3	2.1	2.2	2.4	2.6	2.1	2.1

TRADE BY COMMODITY IN THOUSAND U.S. DOLLARS – COMMERCE PAR PRODUIT EN MILLIERS DE DOLLARS E.U

COUNTRIES–PAYS	IMPORTS – IMPORTATIONS				
	1990	1991	1992	1993	1994
Total	12072646	13231302	13561847	14134197	16749073
Africa	28015	38105	33702	x28927	x33442
Northern Africa	1480	1482	x1479	x966	x1980
Americas	x2669888	2862210	3177905	x3373779	x4015675
LAIA	8847	12112	52434	48745	54923
CACM	1002	1553	3313	x5429	x4401
Asia	5754249	6322129	6376471	7044253	8427192
Middle East	12563	17064	27697	x42074	x43622
Europe	3491756	3891480	3870853	3559127	4099880
EEC	3373493	3782644	3753599	3444934	3990410
EFTA	95326	94798	104804	101296	92883
Oceania	x114511	x110629	x97241	x107941	x152005
Japan/Japon	4849354	5282904	5189579	5782817	6773075
USA/Etats–Unis d'Amer	2395055	2562099	2830586	3005727	3613010
Spain/Espagne	934808	1080326	1135366	969490	1084677
France,Monac	712250	781204	748729	693458	790668
Italy/Italie	639128	723230	701770	591610	671995
Hong Kong	585419	605006	640764	641371	799393
Canada	237738	258227	252550	278094	307059
Denmark/Danemark	242283	253920	201124	219460	236058
Belgium–Luxembourg	190607	206271	219248	220087	287632
Singapore/Singapour	136187	176978	196548	208418	244065
Germany/Allemagne	151799	169230	178724	173021	216924
United Kingdom	191654	180881	153722	165342	236434
Netherlands/Pays–Bas	85494	128929	134683	158963	178018
Portugal	78927	123630	134345	123783	138089
Korea, Republic of	85202	116559	105644	105079	190164
Australia/Australie	99577	92621	79813	89909	131766
Sweden/Suède	86420	83214	86146	74056	86548
China/Chine	17834	31093	82720	115353	171113
Thailand/Thaïlande	21767	42484	63481	80380	116789
Switz.Liecht	47779	48544	48498	44942	51092
Malaysia/Malaisie	30222	35710	52572	53271	67048
Norway,SVD,JM	32363	36414	46859	46937	37015
Greece/Grèce	34860	26137	34137	34168	35999
Mexico/Mexique	1830	1986	39161	32952	30142
So. Africa Customs Un	9541	13940	11892	9570	11923
Ireland/Irlande	13797	13675	12259	8571	9463
United Arab Emirates	1701	2674	5458	x25796	x24775
Reunion/Réunion	9769	9436	13121	10842	12217
Austria/Autriche	7642	8721	10549	9982	14267
Iceland/Islande	15185	9840	9447	9416	4775
Cyprus/Chypre	6052	7130	8810	6288	8289
Martinique	5134	6348	7530	7758	9537
New Zealand	5607	7464	5770	5869	8908
Poland/Pologne		1303	709	15523	14868
Argentina/Argentine	1515	3939	6251	6625	8509
Guadeloupe	3287	5351	5416	5421	6819
Macau/Macao	10577	7123	4601	4325	5824
Russian Federation			x4815	x9546	x13969
Greenland/Groenland	715	3207	9733	387	x1310
Saudi Arabia	1157	3648	6552	x2324	x2891
Mauritius/Maurice	3056	3130	4079	3655	3108
Netherlands Antilles	x1053	2189	2587	x5891	x1688
Bermuda/Bermudes	x3746	x1560	x4461	x4241	x2624
Faeroe Islds/Is Féroé	6396	4343	2875	2741	2507
Guam	x3254	x2861	x3187	x3720	x3218
French Polynesia	x3129	x4328	x3637	x1796	x1838
Indonesia/Indonésie	809	879	6280	2414	2841
Finland/Finlande	3815	3266	2798	2944	3639
Slovenia/Slovénia			3552	4728	6310
Brunei Darussalam	3229	3675	x1663	x1703	x4524

COUNTRIES–PAYS	EXPORTS – EXPORTATIONS				
	1990	1991	1992	1993	1994
Totale	11291805	12174496	12581225	13098372	x15975305
Afrique	x640836	x735679	x873339	x808560	x1118388
Afrique du Nord	292223	374284	349061	372727	438795
Amériques	x2904085	3195913	x3516780	x3778227	x4406687
ALAI	932708	1174034	1294967	1475750	x1837685
MCAC	75527	105475	149199	138699	195304
Asie	5103847	5521377	5789358	6189999	7724366
Moyen–Orient	x79048	x50626	x39936	x43253	x61990
Europe	1699792	1753952	1714174	1613278	1856737
CEE	1479494	1515665	1481781	1457566	1695192
AELE	167083	200905	205037	119076	121360
Océanie	528713	x580392	x673111	x701686	x862155
Thailand/Thaïlande	1060778	1354737	1565949	1825695	2322494
USA/Etats–Unis d'Amer	724587	836898	852458	844892	874493
Indonesia/Indonésie	710199	796093	788500	906843	1050850
China/Chine	925574	758538	920501	758227	1002223
India/Inde	468041	513365	570710	700258	938703
Canada	496891	468489	586676	677863	886025
Ecuador/Equateur	341227	492554	529194	468211	x722735
Australia/Australie	389382	424783	496985	538872	623272
Korea, Republic of	366035	410709	372864	327842	327256
Morocco/Maroc	213270	313837	292881	312938	381844
United Kingdom	315461	337416	293150	251692	301753
Denmark/Danemark	309764	315860	281353	284458	313514
Philippines	256749	319419	258399	282196	310306
Viet Nam	x218841	x250889	x257409	x346844	x448007
Mexico/Mexique	241065	258671	239727	325711	376406
Hong Kong	358271	284106	263322	211820	242427
Russian Federation			x298556	x391426	x622736
Argentina/Argentine	68882	99961	218711	330842	291977
Spain/Espagne	180478	195045	213470	238162	323718
Singapore/Singapour	149451	208027	193354	179300	215193
France,Monac	216087	197217	193487	182676	184122
Netherlands/Pays–Bas	173309	163709	194372	206900	231887
Cuba	x307890	x238497	x155648	x152545	x76922
Mauritania/Mauritanie	x130481	x134580	x198806	x151819	x178490
Bangladesh	134271	155111	143606	181135	x277355
Greenland/Groenland	176819	179553	155053	142387	x252537
New Zealand	125305	131856	151456	149368	213500
Malaysia/Malaisie	114823	140240	141512	123273	144002
Bahamas	43902	49515	x154809	x165033	x65723
Brazil/Brésil	110737	118862	117373	122526	124305
Iceland/Islande	103010	136508	150585	63076	64302
Italy/Italie	75915	86095	87336	87040	97453
Colombia/Colombie	79508	96204	76670	83629	124462
Former USSR/Anc. URSS	238322	x251320			
Pakistan	77850	78191	67148	94117	97294
Japan/Japon	73524	78730	70311	78287	93297
Ireland/Irlande	76677	79515	76131	49075	56058
Korea Dem People's Rp	x68284	x78533	x66821	x57817	x34433
Panama	50048	56178	64095	65512	77410
Belgium–Luxembourg	48993	48971	51343	74239	100187
Norway,SVD,JM	63768	63785	53036	55494	56278
Tunisia/Tunisie	78443	59178	53836	58220	54033
So. Africa Customs Un	48729	48897	53856	52485	58784
Madagascar	39388	49058	46456	46789	98726
Honduras	32189	45860	41335	54830	73191
Senegal/Sénégal	34738	30209	x88255	12054	x68094
Peru/Pérou	32239	35643	43133	48031	83622
Venezuela	37864	48139	36013	40789	42163
Germany/Allemagne	28369	40237	31831	39101	46534
Poland/Pologne	44706	99575	5318	3416	3465

(VALUE AS % OF TOTAL)(VALEUR EN % DU TOTAL)

	1985	1986	1987	1988	1989	1990	1991	1992	1993	1994
Africa	0.3	x0.2	x0.2	x0.2	0.2	0.3	0.3	0.3	x0.2	x0.2
Northern Africa	0.0	0.0	x0.0	0.0	0.0	0.0	0.0	x0.0	x0.0	x0.0
Americas	35.0	x30.3	x27.6	x24.2	x24.1	x22.1	21.6	23.4	x23.8	x24.0
LAIA	0.2	0.1	0.1	0.1	0.1	0.1	0.1	0.4	0.3	0.3
CACM	0.0	0.0	x0.0	0.0	0.0	0.0	0.0	0.0	x0.0	x0.0
Asia	43.9	45.3	45.2	49.7	47.4	47.7	47.8	47.0	49.8	50.3
Middle East	0.2	0.2	x0.2	0.1	x0.1	0.1	0.1	0.2	x0.3	x0.3
Europe	19.9	23.4	26.0	25.2	27.4	28.9	29.4	28.5	25.2	24.5
EEC	18.4	21.7	24.3	23.5	25.7	27.9	28.6	27.7	24.4	23.8
EFTA	1.5	1.6	1.7	1.5	1.6	0.8	0.7	0.8	0.7	0.6
Oceania	0.8	x0.8	x0.9	x0.8	x0.8	x1.0	x0.9	x0.7	x0.8	x0.9
Japan/Japon	37.9	39.2	38.5	42.0	40.4	40.2	39.9	38.3	40.9	40.4
USA/Etats–Unis d'Amer	31.8	27.5	25.1	21.9	21.8	19.8	19.4	20.9	21.3	21.6
Spain/Espagne	2.7	3.9	5.8	5.4	6.9	7.7	8.2	8.4	6.9	6.5
France,Monac	4.8	5.6	5.5	5.2	5.3	5.9	5.9	5.5	4.9	4.7
Italy/Italie	4.1	4.4	4.5	4.7	5.1	5.3	5.5	5.2	4.2	4.0
Hong Kong	4.0	4.2	4.2	5.0	4.6	4.8	4.6	4.7	4.5	4.8
Canada	2.7	2.4	2.1	1.9	2.0	2.0	2.0	1.9	2.0	1.8
Denmark/Danemark	1.6	1.8	2.2	2.0	2.0	2.0	1.9	1.5	1.6	1.4
Belgium–Luxembourg	1.0	1.3	1.3	1.3	1.4	1.6	1.6	1.6	1.6	1.7
Singapore/Singapour	1.1	1.1	1.2	1.1	1.1	1.1	1.3	1.4	1.5	1.5

	1985	1986	1987	1988	1989	1990	1991	1992	1993	1994
Afrique	5.7	x8.5	x7.5	x7.1	x6.5	x5.6	x6.0	x6.9	x6.2	x7.0
Afrique du Nord	2.8	2.6	2.4	2.7	2.5	2.6	3.1	2.8	2.8	2.7
Amériques	32.9	x31.4	26.3	23.9	23.4	x25.7	26.2	x27.9	x28.8	x27.6
ALAI	15.4	x15.0	12.0	10.6	10.2	8.3	9.6	10.3	11.3	x11.5
MCAC	2.3	1.5	1.1	0.9	0.6	0.7	0.9	1.2	1.1	1.2
Asie	35.2	37.1	x43.4	x46.9	47.3	45.2	45.3	46.1	47.3	48.4
Moyen–Orient	0.4	x0.5	x0.6	x0.7	x0.9	x0.7	x0.4	x0.3	x0.3	x0.4
Europe	16.2	15.8	14.0	13.5	14.4	15.1	14.4	13.6	12.3	11.6
CEE	13.5	12.9	11.7	11.2	12.3	13.1	12.4	11.8	11.1	10.6
AELE	2.2	2.5	1.9	1.9	1.5	1.5	1.7	1.6	0.9	0.8
Océanie	8.7	6.0	5.5	5.1	5.1	4.7	x4.8	x5.4	x5.4	x5.4
Thailand/Thaïlande	5.9	5.9	5.3	6.0	9.0	9.4	11.1	12.4	13.9	14.5
USA/Etats–Unis d'Amer	3.5	3.7	3.9	4.4	5.2	6.4	6.9	6.8	6.5	5.5
Indonesia/Indonésie	4.5	4.4	3.8	4.9	5.6	6.3	6.5	6.3	6.9	6.6
China/Chine		2.8	4.9	6.6	7.2	8.2	6.2	7.3	5.8	6.3
India/Inde	6.7	5.7	4.0	3.7	3.7	4.1	4.2	4.5	5.3	5.9
Canada	7.5	6.3	5.0	4.6	4.2	4.4	3.8	4.7	5.2	5.5
Ecuador/Equateur		x4.5	4.0	3.6	3.2	3.0	4.0	4.2	3.6	x4.5
Australia/Australie	6.3	4.3	3.9	4.0	3.6	3.4	3.5	4.0	4.1	3.9
Korea, Republic of	4.9	4.9	4.7	5.0	4.1	3.2	3.4	3.0	2.5	2.0
Morocco/Maroc	2.1	1.7	1.6	1.8	1.8	1.9	2.6	2.3	2.4	2.4

TRADE BY COMMODITY IN THOUSAND U.S. DOLLARS – COMMERCE PAR PRODUIT EN MILLIERS DE DOLLARS E.U

COUNTRIES–PAYS	IMPORTS – IMPORTATIONS				
	1990	1991	1992	1993	1994
Total	6042966	6780741	7102001	7029077	7777703
Africa	x164714	x160425	x128383	x139381	x128127
Northern Africa	36582	59231	x27211	x24844	x33662
Americas	1110085	1280202	1242200	1256582	1417228
LAIA	64835	57924	103082	125148	179354
CACM	7137	6747	10509	8439	9787
Asia	1168067	1548525	1722301	x2074980	x2466477
Middle East	x54432	x84669	x56067	x71134	x89478
Europe	3340570	3513444	3735189	3263348	3467031
EEC	3168314	3334949	3539019	3078514	3273356
EFTA	155156	160756	167158	150336	159785
Oceania	x217678	x235639	x238550	x242360	x242193
Japan/Japon	915954	1226443	1369902	1679506	1960355
USA/Etats–Unis d'Amer	810035	972322	897861	851408	951972
United Kingdom	670374	720076	765044	715342	623036
France, Monac	656240	624999	625417	546470	603661
Germany/Allemagne	416423	490714	500405	404930	500734
Italy/Italie	304318	370043	426589	348009	359735
Belgium–Luxembourg	223138	216006	222159	191529	207447
Spain/Espagne	167592	197495	245006	170276	177911
Canada	174021	188430	188999	228747	236943
Denmark/Danemark	205305	165289	204973	191623	229227
Netherlands/Pays–Bas	177167	183948	168710	172100	159179
Australia/Australie	138480	150345	158687	157231	165626
Sweden/Suède	145665	143959	151375	121864	154953
Switz.Liecht	119408	125597	121969	113647	118039
Hong Kong	84136	102208	126831	131289	161403
Austria/Autriche	61908	66248	71895	70651	95901
Singapore/Singapour	39189	48877	59082	69286	87224
Finland/Finlande	58709	60130	56124	47984	63635
Papua New Guinea	34970	x41609	x39374	x42826	x35933
Ireland/Irlande	38064	39205	42163	36438	29790
Norway, SVD, JM	34928	34052	44106	35678	40586
Greece/Grèce	36311	36863	37575	38449	37463
Saudi Arabia	24236	39269	19391	x31421	x30649
Malaysia/Malaisie	21836	28200	26876	31221	34037
So. Africa Customs Un	35503	26459	23692	32622	28086
Colombia/Colombie	21832	19135	27869	33973	44097
Korea, Republic of	4012	15080	21298	40479	54886
New Zealand	24402	22982	23056	23557	26192
Portugal	7098	19973	21584	22848	30683
Mexico/Mexique	23024	13949	20570	28901	50579
Russian Federation			x30034	x31935	x51383
Libyan Arab Jamahiriya	12908	33022	x9199	x17158	x15716
Argentina/Argentine	1401	5978	23321	28400	44961
Egypt/Egypte	22893	23612	16057	7087	15178
Poland/Pologne	6961	16727	11295	16254	14959
Israel/Israël	15848	14057	13984	16043	16702
Sri Lanka	10554	9388	14310	10074	16480
Brazil/Brésil	10536	8102	9235	14392	16138
Chile/Chili	4233	6004	13881	10478	10533
Panama	8289	8841	11439	10076	9109
Reunion/Réunion	8285	7565	9288	9947	10092
Ukraine			x5167	x21332	x8169
Thailand/Thaïlande	8973	6576	9320	8631	13010
Malta/Malte	7116	9954	8640	5766	x5932
United Arab Emirates	5516	10893	4456	x8587	x8009
Jamaica/Jamaïque	12416	13126	x4675	x5849	x4417
Cyprus/Chypre	5560	7140	8883	6964	7364
Mozambique	x9879	x14680	x5265	x2230	x4411
Lebanon/Liban	x6330	x11053	x5217	x5653	x11265
Czechoslovakia	15746	x7806	x13933		

COUNTRIES–PAYS	EXPORTS – EXPORTATIONS				
	1990	1991	1992	1993	1994
Totale	5748947	6152139	6188474	6463973	7367842
Afrique	x397448	x449557	x381429	x383703	x402212
Afrique du Nord	142493	156658	160399	146489	159383
Amériques	x993761	x1101403	1156989	1162149	x1220009
ALAI	242843	285888	339897	422964	x498620
MCAC	9030	14446	21487	x16006	x22888
Aṣie	2041818	2363336	2405164	2651087	3266851
Moyen–Orient	x61179	x57020	x59480	x47890	x67840
Europe	1923464	1958432	2069971	2038089	2239058
CEE	1609954	1687248	1752440	1679773	1823714
AELE	272320	242716	265345	315244	381711
Océanie	108186	148049	x147963	x180231	x168077
Thailand/Thaïlande	993146	1188052	1150728	1204729	1486827
Denmark/Danemark	460144	464293	487746	469979	482647
USA/Etats–Unis d'Amer	303688	369655	397669	350557	331615
Korea, Republic of	304901	306398	294523	344140	362326
Japan/Japon	309177	316410	312629	302482	285280
Netherlands/Pays–Bas	269529	274239	298240	296145	322271
Germany/Allemagne	226801	276918	294225	256769	268176
Canada	222314	244108	234228	209794	222371
Norway, SVD, JM	238823	217604	238974	198186	211279
China/Chine	53688	85417	202031	295857	523103
Morocco/Maroc	141934	154904	159341	146002	157724
Chile/Chili	117005	138583	146459	173867	147016
Spain/Espagne	126017	144514	145559	152630	185563
Philippines	101480	117040	102385	133899	153219
Cote d'Ivoire	x135374	x104153	x105976	x118288	x125065
United Kingdom	96434	104397	102309	119155	140597
Portugal	115501	118986	110347	90062	108875
Greenland/Groenland	118352	91212	105038	102810	x115478
Malaysia/Malaisie	75266	81857	96103	115952	122405
France, Monac	92397	90557	93476	85511	105028
Senegal/Sénégal	90712	136157	x62626	57086	x57441
Russian Federation			x119414	x130132	x112470
Australia/Australie	56412	71397	75099	97311	83267
Belgium–Luxembourg	80107	74434	72906	67651	68441
Indonesia/Indonésie	55325	89325	54550	64406	77743
Cuba	x96131	x94327	x53811	x59477	x28597
Italy/Italie	66725	62943	58085	57244	50775
Iceland/Islande	29332	22989	24321	114804	168565
Ecuador/Equateur	30958	28942	44169	71682	x134633
Mexico/Mexique	35689	44526	49638	44026	47260
Hong Kong	23967	45497	42098	50003	69168
Argentina/Argentine	5286	31898	41691	57165	52703
New Zealand	17893	32388	44652	48876	49042
Former USSR/Anc. URSS	274343	x120472			
Sweden/Suède	40051	38986	42837	36467	41897
Iran (Islamic Rp. of)	x37316	x36160	x39250	x24666	x36987
Singapore/Singapour	23945	29438	28823	33435	37865
Greece/Grèce	28411	23092	26772	27051	23369
Poland/Pologne	1876	6709	22380	39734	61011
Fiji/Fidji	26602	30923	19167	17509	27052
Viet Nam	x10284	x15589	x23338	x24707	x35060
Peru/Pérou	26624	19522	18910	24043	31177
Mauritius/Maurice	9271	18679	18717	24151	28007
Faeroe Islds/Is Féroé	22503	17947	23637	18209	17299
Venezuela	24382	13877	18838	26141	20530
Turkey/Turquie	16662	17018	18268	21170	28933
So. Africa Customs Un	8197	19584	18461	17896	
Costa Rica	8817	14255	21074	x15687	x22842
Ireland/Irlande	5269	10776	15482	15722	18796
Croatia/Croatie			20073	18503	x11094

(VALUE AS % OF TOTAL)(VALEUR EN % DU TOTAL)

	1985	1986	1987	1988	1989	1990	1991	1992	1993	1994
Africa	2.4	x3.4	x2.7	x2.8	x2.9	x2.7	x2.4	x1.8	x2.0	x1.7
Northern Africa	0.8	0.5	x0.2	x0.3	0.4	0.6	0.9	x0.4	x0.4	x0.4
Americas	26.3	x22.5	20.2	19.7	19.4	18.4	18.9	17.5	17.9	18.2
LAIA	1.0	0.8	0.9	0.7	1.0	1.1	0.9	1.5	1.8	2.3
CACM	0.2	0.1	0.1	0.1	0.2	0.1	0.1	0.1	0.1	0.1
Asia	16.6	16.4	x17.8	x22.5	21.0	19.3	22.8	24.3	x29.5	x31.7
Middle East	2.2	x1.5	x1.0	0.9	x1.1	x0.9	x1.2	x0.8	x1.0	x1.2
Europe	47.9	51.9	53.7	49.9	51.8	55.3	51.8	52.6	46.4	44.6
EEC	41.4	44.7	46.2	43.4	45.3	52.4	49.2	49.8	43.8	42.1
EFTA	6.4	7.1	7.3	6.3	6.2	2.6	2.4	2.4	2.1	2.1
Oceania	5.0	x4.5	x4.1	x4.0	x4.0	x3.6	x3.5	x3.4	x3.5	x3.1
Japan/Japon	10.4	11.2	12.3	16.9	16.4	15.2	18.1	19.3	23.9	25.2
USA/Etats–Unis d'Amer	20.6	17.4	15.2	14.6	13.3	13.4	14.3	12.6	12.1	12.2
United Kingdom	11.2	11.8	10.0	10.3	11.3	11.1	10.6	10.8	10.2	8.0
France, Monac	8.4	8.7	10.2	9.5	9.2	10.9	9.2	8.8	7.8	7.8
Germany/Allemagne	5.4	5.5	5.5	4.9	5.0	6.9	7.2	7.0	5.8	6.4
Italy/Italie	3.2	3.6	4.2	3.9	4.0	5.0	5.5	6.0	5.0	4.6
Belgium–Luxembourg	2.9	3.2	3.2	2.8	3.1	3.7	3.2	3.1	2.7	2.7
Spain/Espagne	0.8	1.1	1.6	2.0	2.0	2.8	2.9	3.4	2.4	2.3
Canada	3.4	2.9	3.2	3.5	3.7	2.9	2.8	2.7	3.3	3.0
Denmark/Danemark	2.2	3.1	3.3	2.7	3.0	3.4	2.4	2.9	2.7	2.9

	1985	1986	1987	1988	1989	1990	1991	1992	1993	1994
Afrique	5.7	5.6	x5.1	4.9	6.3	x6.9	x7.3	x6.2	x6.0	x5.5
Afrique du Nord	2.4	2.3	1.9	1.9	2.3	2.5	2.5	2.6	2.3	2.2
Amériques	22.4	x26.8	x20.5	12.9	16.9	x17.2	x17.9	18.7	18.0	x16.5
ALAI	9.0	9.9	4.2	3.3	4.4	4.2	4.6	5.5	6.5	x6.8
MCAC	0.0	0.0	0.0	0.1	0.2	0.2	0.2	0.3	x0.2	x0.3
Asie	34.4	32.0	x37.7	x42.6	37.7	35.5	38.4	38.9	41.0	44.4
Moyen–Orient	1.5	2.6	x2.2	x1.6	1.2	x1.1	x0.9	x1.0	x0.7	x0.9
Europe	31.6	29.3	30.1	26.4	31.6	33.5	31.8	33.4	31.5	30.4
CEE	23.4	22.4	23.4	21.3	25.4	28.0	27.4	28.3	26.0	24.8
AELE	7.5	6.4	6.0	4.4	5.5	4.7	3.9	4.3	4.9	5.2
Océanie	1.9	1.7	1.8	8.3	2.3	1.9	2.4	x2.4	x2.8	x2.3
Thailand/Thaïlande	9.7	10.4	11.1	14.2	16.3	17.3	19.3	18.6	18.6	20.2
Denmark/Danemark	6.1	6.6	6.5	6.3	6.8	8.0	7.5	7.9	7.3	6.6
USA/Etats–Unis d'Amer	3.8	3.3	2.7	3.3	5.9	5.3	6.0	6.4	5.4	4.5
Korea, Republic of	4.6	5.4	5.3	6.3	5.8	5.3	5.0	4.8	5.3	4.9
Japan/Japon	14.4	10.3	7.6	6.1	6.5	5.4	5.1	5.1	4.7	3.9
Netherlands/Pays–Bas	2.9	3.0	3.5	3.0	3.8	4.7	4.5	4.8	4.6	4.4
Germany/Allemagne	3.1	3.1	3.4	3.2	3.5	3.9	4.5	4.8	4.0	3.6
Canada	8.0	7.0	8.4	4.3	4.8	3.9	4.0	3.8	3.2	3.0
Norway, SVD, JM	6.2	5.2	4.6	3.2	4.2	4.2	3.5	3.9	3.1	2.9
China/Chine			0.4	0.6	0.9	0.9	1.4	3.3	4.6	7.1

TRADE BY COMMODITY IN THOUSAND U.S. DOLLARS – COMMERCE PAR PRODUIT EN MILLIERS DE DOLLARS E.U

COUNTRIES–PAYS	IMPORTS – IMPORTATIONS					COUNTRIES–PAYS	EXPORTS – EXPORTATIONS				
	1990	1991	1992	1993	1994		1990	1991	1992	1993	1994
Total	16085219	x14317777	14609266	13218847	x13332295	Totale	15436347	13642357	16643045	14617546	11787303
Africa	2082834	1438446	x1939855	x1884124	x2244859	Afrique	24971	x5218	x1414	x5408	4524
Northern Africa	1604270	1130126	1544646	1251097	1740622	Afrique du Nord	47	630	x17	8	3948
Americas	x1229935	x1357340	1744994	x1533533	x1591743	Amériques	7663075	7155216	9105072	7599906	7332764
LAIA	541453	798883	1140635	896178	887558	ALAI	912220	490219	716116	734991	699978
CACM	86301	123606	125712	x134143	x180024	MCAC	3		15	36	26
Asia	x7065300	x5271396	x6572171	x5635518	x6066402	Asie	206950	357566	501265	x354385	x412700
Middle East	x2035348	x890848	x885304	x752237	x566625	Moyen–Orient	183651	293558	493437	x338387	x373988
Europe	3114164	3912450	4034647	3718995	3310275	Europe	5445611	4898368	5850671	5112187	3994078
EEC	3015522	3844067	3923083	3595153	3185753	CEE	5382624	4890907	5829019	5107323	3991520
EFTA	89169	61595	89657	80850	100890	AELE	25	1	1981	2357	1501
Oceania	56826	x67937	46643	53842	59909	Océanie	1792121	1160748	x1081423	x1511403	1027
Italy/Italie	1204951	1685759	1647553	1142626	962340	USA/Etats–Unis d'Amer	3887012	3350183	4498631	4667808	4061192
China/Chine	2156528	1459542	1503726	834076	960577	Canada	2863430	3314752	3890187	2196672	2571557
Russian Federation			x2769636	x809616	x80349	France,Monac	3297187	2792977	3290320	3060843	1998774
Japan/Japon	1006263	917767	1175283	1136399	1352460	Australia/Australie	1791942	1160735	1081293	1511210	1020
Former USSR/Anc. URSS	2480904	x2172680				United Kingdom	790314	757282	773230	654597	516516
Korea, Republic of	419438	577380	543690	673929	783446	Germany/Allemagne	497757	462853	878038	619105	799334
Egypt/Egypte	789088	506800	704657	335521	766647	Argentina/Argentine	870937	478739	715788	734865	669979
Belgium–Luxembourg	379471	502575	532025	441286	366310	Greece/Grèce	156270	309030	268628	160008	167133
Iran (Islamic Rp. of)	x826944	x533172	x437370	x247096	x221783	Turkey/Turquie	4384	204270	340853	75494	88470
Indonesia/Indonésie	281883	366361	403853	442005	579681	Denmark/Danemark	228764	210442	157562	174312	103149
Spain/Espagne	167332	460445	344755	382675	404288	Saudi Arabia	169560	84986	141017	x256517	x274934
Netherlands/Pays–Bas	328839	357926	363642	439198	451452	Belgium–Luxembourg	104952	103744	148523	132147	116587
Pakistan	320207	150222	445159	344732	282958	Spain/Espagne	60618	72878	91461	63831	75809
Algeria/Algérie	417250	247525	320911	353785	602387	Netherlands/Pays–Bas	59776	31284	25083	106347	59876
Germany/Allemagne	426791	297584	270676	319236	249890	Italy/Italie	29793	42338	45352	70702	107284
United Kingdom	193919	170020	320841	387350	248720	Austria/Autriche	54564	25031	38166	37084	x15602
Morocco/Maroc	171110	151289	320483	351517	162584	Poland/Pologne	1058	39800	57837	294	
Philippines	260441	218442	271826	297757	368859	Sweden/Suède	77188	55862	35341	5014	20707
Brazil/Brésil		304804	390313	783	1532	India/Inde	17158	58681	3939	66	13484
Portugal	96015	175315	239888	210391	202545	Bulgaria/Bulgarie		x7048	41960	5025	1394
Uzbekistan/Ouzbékistan			x356834	x202796	x164172	Ireland/Irlande	21594	17839	22545	12456	4352
Cuba	x383601	x255377	x137571	x141351	x87343	Finland/Finlande	3847	3257	22404	8417	5406
Venezuela	167629	162609	179773	186969	183067	Czech Republic				16132	3605
Malaysia/Malaisie	144387	181860	162256	184666	214773	Oman	4742	4158	5345	6087	6916
USA/Etats–Unis d'Amer	84123	69619	200107	226664	300536	Portugal	1	6091	6817	2461	991
Mexico/Mexique	46295	67029	163539	232807	189255	Croatia/Croatie			9957	2491	x1035
Ukraine			x93486	x316411	x20766	Romania/Roumanie		11820		0	32
Romania/Roumanie	22752	44742	157800	205115	53	Uruguay	21469	11461			
Israel/Israël	110624	112804	133067	144574	173345	Yugoslavia/Yougoslavie			x9452		
Colombia/Colombie	118604	71735	140600	132807	134802	China/Chine	558	265	296	8238	10055
Peru/Pérou	102434	71925	101506	166773	175364	Hungary/Hongrie	x3350	x1852	x2466	x4230	x34266
India/Inde	12272		273971	40056	122	Slovakia				x7942	x2882
So. Africa Customs Un	88365	79866	69263	145396	72782	Yugoslavia SFR	62961	x7460			
Jordan/Jordanie	110257	86664	78890	110450	74236	Singapore/Singapour	4684	3581	2235	480	1038
Thailand/Thaïlande	57337	72580	91368	110877	134266	Syrian Arab Republic	4490	31	6098		x3335
Tunisia/Tunisie	140843	69396	90574	90020	98693	Kazakstan				x4863	x13191
Libyan Arab Jamahiriya	54590	79880	x74206	x89816	x64723	Gabon				x4796	
Yemen/Yémen	x152661	27458	x120018	x83222	x82255	Lithuania/Lituanie				x4346	5980
Greece/Grèce	85088	79882	76665	60887	76686	Norway,SVD,JM	21		1966	2339	1381
Turkey/Turquie	386900	22151	13913	178894	75945	Former USSR/Anc. URSS	128815	x4252			
Korea Dem People's Rp	x106257	x164889	x29859	x8978	x2080	Malaysia/Malaisie	703	979	485	797	816
Chile/Chili	8550	21676	85593	77297	109091	Togo	353	2237			
Nigeria/Nigéria	25	13	x36432	x137733	x50829	So. Africa Customs Un	22450	954	708	80	
Poland/Pologne	10489	2288	66937	104021	35617	Equatorial Guinea		x1094			
Tajikistan/Tadjikistan			x45397	x118592	x15606	Albania/Albanie		x433	x15	x634	x30
France,Monac	56691	35876	40009	80125	100345	Hong Kong	157	463	559	6	125
Sri Lanka	87933	81012	66090	1027	120692	Pakistan				961	
Switz.Liecht	51143	46166	49582	51271	46264	Czechoslovakia		x35	x924		
Ethiopia/Ethiopie	76311	10059	69133	62576	x86697	Morocco/Maroc	47	630	11		2922
Sudan/Soudan	x31389	x75235	x33815	x30439	x45587	Uganda/Ouganda			x635		

(VALUE AS % OF TOTAL)(VALEUR EN % DU TOTAL)

	1985	1986	1987	1988	1989	1990	1991	1992	1993	1994		1985	1986	1987	1988	1989	1990	1991	1992	1993	1994
Africa	15.6	14.4	10.3	10.3	12.8	12.9	10.1	x13.3	x14.3	x16.2	Afrique	0.1	x0.0	x0.0	x0.3	x1.0	0.1	x0.0	x0.0	x0.0	
Northern Africa	11.0	10.1	7.9	8.0	10.7	10.0	7.9	10.6	9.5	13.1	Afrique du Nord	0.0	x0.0	x0.0	x0.0	x0.0	0.0	0.0	x0.0	0.0	0.0
Americas	13.0	9.7	9.7	7.3	6.9	x7.6	x9.5	12.0	x11.6	x12.0	Amériques	56.9	47.7	51.0	58.5	52.0	49.6	52.5	54.7	52.0	62.2
LAIA	9.6	6.4	6.5	4.8	4.3	3.4	5.6	7.8	6.8	6.7	ALAI	8.6	3.5	3.1	2.5	4.2	5.9	3.6	4.3	5.0	5.9
CACM	0.7	0.7	0.6	0.6	0.6	0.5	0.9	0.9	x1.0	x1.4	MCAC	0.0	0.0	0.0	x0.0	0.0	0.0		0.0	0.0	0.0
Asia	30.3	x33.5	x38.3	x41.9	x47.8	x43.9	x36.8	x45.0	x42.6	x45.8	Asie	0.8	x0.6	x1.8	x2.8	x2.0	1.3	2.6	3.0	x2.4	x3.5
Middle East	3.3	x7.5	x8.1	x9.4	x13.0	x12.7	x6.2	x6.1	x5.7	x4.3	Moyen–Orient	0.4	x0.4	x1.5	2.7	1.9	1.2	2.2	3.0	x2.3	x3.2
Europe	19.4	26.2	25.9	21.9	18.1	19.4	27.3	27.6	28.1	25.0	Europe	26.8	33.8	33.2	29.3	30.6	35.3	35.9	35.2	35.0	33.9
EEC	18.6	24.8	24.7	21.1	17.2	18.7	26.8	26.9	27.2	24.1	CEE	25.5	32.8	32.3	27.9	29.5	34.9	35.9	35.0	34.9	33.9
EFTA	0.7	0.8	0.8	0.7	0.8	0.6	0.4	0.6	0.6	0.8	AELE	1.3	1.0	0.8	0.8	0.7	0.0	0.0	0.0	0.0	0.0
Oceania	0.2	0.1	0.2	0.4	0.5	0.4	x0.4	0.3	0.4	0.4	Océanie	14.0	16.7	12.4	7.4	12.2	11.6	8.5	x6.5	x10.3	
Italy/Italie	6.1	9.1	8.8	7.5	8.2	7.5	11.8	11.3	8.6	7.3	USA/Etats–Unis d'Amer	27.3	26.3	26.6	32.1	34.9	25.2	24.6	27.0	31.9	34.5
China/Chine	6.3	6.6	11.1	10.9	14.9	13.4	10.2	10.3	6.3	7.3	Canada	21.0	17.8	21.2	23.9	12.9	18.5	24.3	23.4	15.0	21.8
Russian Federation								x19.0	x6.1	x0.6	France,Monac	17.8	19.4	19.3	17.9	16.5	21.4	20.5	19.8	20.9	17.0
Japan/Japon	7.6	7.3	6.4	6.5	6.8	6.3	6.4	8.0	8.6	10.2	Australia/Australie	14.0	16.7	12.4	7.4	12.2	11.6	8.5	6.5	10.3	0.0
Former USSR/Anc. URSS	19.3	14.5	12.7	15.2	13.0	15.4	x15.2				United Kingdom	2.1	5.8	4.5	1.9	3.1	5.1	5.6	4.6	4.5	4.4
Korea, Republic of	3.4	3.5	3.5	3.4	2.5	2.6	4.0	3.7	5.1	5.9	Germany/Allemagne	1.2	3.1	2.9	3.0	4.3	3.2	3.4	5.3	4.2	6.8
Egypt/Egypte	3.8	4.1	3.1	2.8	3.4	4.9	3.5	4.8	2.5	5.8	Argentina/Argentine	8.6	3.5	3.1	2.3	3.9	5.6	3.5	4.3	5.0	5.7
Belgium–Luxembourg	1.8	1.9	2.3	2.3	1.4	2.4	3.5	3.6	3.3	2.8	Greece/Grèce	0.5	1.1	1.2	0.9	1.9	1.0	2.3	1.6	1.1	1.4
Iran (Islamic Rp. of)		x1.9	x4.0	x4.1	x4.1	x5.1	x3.7	x3.0	x1.9	x1.7	Turkey/Turquie	0.4	0.0	0.2	1.3	0.4	0.0	1.5	2.0	0.5	0.8
Indonesia/Indonésie	2.0	2.2	2.0	1.4	1.7	1.8	2.6	2.8	3.3	4.4	Denmark/Danemark	0.5	0.6	0.8	0.9	0.7	1.5	1.5	0.9	1.2	0.9

TRADE BY COMMODITY IN THOUSAND U.S. DOLLARS – COMMERCE PAR PRODUIT EN MILLIERS DE DOLLARS E.U

COUNTRIES–PAYS	IMPORTS – IMPORTATIONS 1990	1991	1992	1993	1994
Total	x4137686	x4287283	x4795388	x4709004	x6417686
Africa	x633077	x694357	x696138	x596194	x696570
Northern Africa	65870	89093	x91110	x89787	x150770
Americas	x701236	x951202	x788765	x827662	1007682
LAIA	316851	534449	384660	416974	605676
CACM	36443	37563	40636	37503	x58865
Asia	x1437413	x1332922	x1978774	x2068863	x3286074
Middle East	x830144	x743664	x1182166	x1316464	x1023749
Europe	1087210	1081654	1190795	1092732	1334816
EEC	1033568	1041141	1143368	1052391	1286023
EFTA	35260	32469	38846	31886	33731
Oceania	82699	43163	x45893	x40378	x37561
Iran (Islamic Rp. of)	x142830	x249330	x362603	x393977	x157983
Saudi Arabia	152441	153116	295860	x377587	x371689
Brazil/Brésil	144011	372332	156111	214999	323429
France,Monac	215784	230719	255671	197514	212422
United Kingdom	209630	208403	241772	190214	221732
Germany/Allemagne	164684	194907	205726	142466	166734
Hong Kong	150054	160406	169295	157059	174002
United Arab Emirates	132420	88857	135113	x202371	x187145
Malaysia/Malaisie	99769	127216	135998	110030	112613
USA/Etats–Unis d'Amer	83653	93600	106548	124191	150070
Belgium–Luxembourg	101124	110444	111041	101694	117841
So. Africa Customs Un	86742	116939	105880	99444	126999
Netherlands/Pays–Bas	94846	92297	102149	105648	189807
Peru/Pérou	102621	87159	91305	98539	76141
Singapore/Singapour	81840	80224	91903	96682	108671
Russian Federation			x205163	x52100	x33962
Cuba	x99538	x118565	x54412	x68089	x13751
Indonesia/Indonésie	14131	53065	172611	7196	157322
Turkey/Turquie	66578	41470	100049	85799	56256
Canada	62447	68134	74966	73618	81624
Mexico/Mexique	45706	35949	103105	72134	104074
Portugal	50224	41623	67281	93445	80375
Senegal/Sénégal	92384	71254	x54609	x60431	x39215
Benin/Bénin	x35215	x48181	x58284	x49984	x44976
Sri Lanka	32320	38325	66112	49179	13261
Spain/Espagne	74738	35808	32066	78657	114758
Cote d'Ivoire	x44237	x48156	x44887	x52982	x29218
Syrian Arab Republic	36263	x36632	43360	x50249	x56989
Oman	47363	41269	35136	50373	37520
Kuwait/ Koweït	15064	12073	57330	55332	66496
China/Chine	11594	39842	39053	34969	141488
Libyan Arab Jamahiriya	42641	56160	x56524	x438	x38337
Yemen/Yémen	x39800	26968	x60412	x21478	x22962
Jordan/Jordanie	42060	39565	30797	29750	22852
Mozambique	x57473	x58212	x24792	x14980	x8702
Former USSR/Anc. URSS	118318	x97703			
Mongolia/Mongolie	x19	x2133	x1924	x91210	x377
Sudan/Soudan	x8255	x9018	x12547	x72576	x82665
Haiti/Haïti	x16599	x20347	x42510	x30226	x31652
Ghana	x12177	3364	73352	x15390	x14337
Sweden/Suède	22310	23585	26684	37012	52338
Austria/Autriche	31746	27701	29151	30410	48955
Israel/Israël	27847	25416	30194	28965	29662
Switz.Liecht	27276	24690	30205	24418	23734
Italy/Italie	23176	31010	21467	26506	26560
Bahrain/Bahreïn	x22911	x16846	x22890	x30263	x12804
Mauritius/Maurice	27057	20241	17773	29372	21864
Reunion/Réunion	6185	22578	24240	18482	22944
Cameroon/Cameroun	26514	47252	x12635	x845	x16352
Poland/Pologne	8277	18211	20041	21509	20603

COUNTRIES–PAYS	EXPORTS – EXPORTATIONS 1990	1991	1992	1993	1994
Totale	3994602	4275226	4882022	4790207	5779855
Afrique	31054	47790	63624	44580	81995
Afrique du Nord	20408	38751	57319	39993	79241
Amériques	993539	968231	1031863	x1187978	x1527403
ALAI	155733	179377	176863	252901	282933
MCAC	943	434	2353	x3190	2878
Asie	x2104999	2357769	2785268	2539813	3230571
Moyen–Orient	79390	8988	x7405	x16593	x18117
Europe	807507	891600	986499	849002	931654
CEE	807212	891197	985034	846940	929772
AELE	274	248	367	569	1109
Océanie	2896	x3096	x5303	x166054	x3397
Thailand/Thaïlande	1086122	1195536	1426098	1301963	1555893
USA/Etats–Unis d'Amer	803776	756272	734983	770319	1015176
Italy/Italie	353043	360554	450966	374086	430858
India/Inde	254373	307068	376358	410207	384019
Pakistan	242389	414020	394406	270024	317048
Viet Nam	x302893	x209825	x276418	x168023	x346994
China/Chine	84135	151834	217854	252760	514608
Belgium–Luxembourg	168075	152813	158088	134604	161311
Spain/Espagne	108232	171510	160755	100034	61312
Uruguay	102258	115813	105652	150057	152135
Netherlands/Pays–Bas	78921	78422	76915	85900	108738
Australia/Australie	2256	2980	5083	165902	3328
Argentina/Argentine	27373	36068	53105	75846	79840
France,Monac	37082	45486	55245	60340	50299
Egypt/Egypte	20395	38710	57313	39989	79156
Germany/Allemagne	32506	47361	39292	38491	40956
Myanmar	27440	39801	40830	43395	x32342
Netherlands Antilles	139	154	39366	x74067	x132897
Guyana	13000	18600	35000	32667	x33892
Indonesia/Indonésie	175	36	8490	57844	27879
Suriname/Suriname	1777	1041	26492	x38093	x31685
Hong Kong	9885	21436	24560	14811	17212
United Kingdom	7611	12972	20237	22016	27498
Greece/Grèce	1833	9310	8140	24400	37292
Venezuela		5	14000	19397	23881
Colombia/Colombie	19141	25044	333	1477	928
Portugal	17815	10226	11205	4085	6603
French Guiana	13666	5575	10144	9424	7161
United Arab Emirates	67287			x12842	x11054
So. Africa Customs Un	2488	5432	3444	2405	
Philippines	2	2342	8517	1	
Brazil/Brésil	778	1087	2379	5431	1434
Bulgaria/Bulgarie	x709	x578	x7609	x89	x1832
Martinique	3148	2760	2537	2719	2655
Saudi Arabia	234	4508	2568	x100	x107
Former USSR/Anc. URSS	x53800	x4968			
Denmark/Danemark	654	1138	1795	2000	3609
St Vincent & Grenadines	x694	x1362	x1754	x1516	x1063
Turkey/Turquie	798	2104	986	1400	628
Korea Dem People's Rp	x14631	x3098	x1283	x55	x225
Korea, Republic of	1220	1450	828	1265	627
Ukraine			x847	x1964	x1182
Russian Federation			x1729	x887	x4182
Canada	299	246	557	1471	1328
Oman	952	529	1304	401	4318
Guadeloupe	47	136	852	1162	277
Guatemala		142	210	1763	1351
Czech Republic				1942	2729
Czechoslovakia		x1007	x935		
Sweden/Suède	242	327	1179	413	779

(VALUE AS % OF TOTAL)(VALEUR EN % DU TOTAL)

	1985	1986	1987	1988	1989	1990	1991	1992	1993	1994
Africa	16.3	x16.5	x15.4	x16.0	x14.1	x15.3	x16.2	x14.5	x12.6	x10.9
Northern Africa	1.6	1.6	0.8	x1.0	2.2	1.6	2.1	x1.9	x1.9	x2.3
Americas	14.2	19.4	x8.8	9.3	11.8	x16.9	x22.2	x16.5	x17.6	15.7
LAIA	4.8	12.5	2.3	2.2	4.7	7.7	12.5	8.0	8.9	9.4
CACM	0.6	0.5	x0.7	0.7	1.0	0.9	0.9	0.8	0.8	x0.9
Asia	36.8	x31.5	x40.7	x41.2	x45.3	x34.8	x31.1	x41.2	x43.9	x51.2
Middle East	15.7	x21.2	x25.2	x22.2	x21.6	x20.1	x17.3	x24.7	x28.0	x16.0
Europe	28.1	26.7	25.5	25.1	21.3	26.3	25.2	24.8	23.2	20.8
EEC	25.7	23.7	23.4	23.2	19.3	25.0	24.3	23.8	22.3	20.0
EFTA	2.1	2.7	2.0	1.8	1.7	0.9	0.8	0.8	0.7	0.5
Oceania	1.6	1.6	1.8	1.8	1.6	2.0	1.0	x0.9	x0.9	x0.6
Iran (Islamic Rp. of)		x2.4	x8.5	x3.4	x5.8	x3.5	x5.8	x7.6	x8.4	x2.5
Saudi Arabia	7.7	6.0	5.2	4.5	3.0	3.7	3.6	6.2	x8.0	x5.8
Brazil/Brésil	3.1	10.8	0.8	0.9	1.2	3.5	8.7	3.3	4.6	5.0
France,Monac	5.4	5.8	5.6	5.2	4.1	5.2	5.4	5.3	4.2	3.3
United Kingdom	4.7	5.3	5.1	5.0	3.8	5.1	4.9	5.0	4.0	3.5
Germany/Allemagne	3.4	3.6	3.6	3.4	2.7	4.0	4.5	4.3	3.0	2.6
Hong Kong	4.2	3.7	3.1	3.5	3.3	3.6	3.7	3.5	3.3	2.7
United Arab Emirates	2.4	2.8	x2.8	2.6	x2.7	3.2	2.1	2.8	x4.3	x2.9
Malaysia/Malaisie	3.9	1.5	1.2	2.0	2.6	2.4	3.0	2.8	2.3	1.8
USA/Etats–Unis d'Amer	1.1	1.3	1.3	1.7	1.5	2.0	2.2	2.2	2.6	2.3

	1985	1986	1987	1988	1989	1990	1991	1992	1993	1994
Afrique	0.2	x0.5	x0.7	0.4	0.2	0.8	1.1	1.3	1.0	1.4
Afrique du Nord	0.2	0.4	0.6	0.3	0.2	0.5	0.9	1.2	0.8	1.4
Amériques	26.6	26.6	21.7	25.2	24.9	24.8	22.7	21.2	x24.8	x26.4
ALAI	4.3	3.9	2.2	2.8	3.1	3.9	4.2	3.6	5.3	4.9
MCAC	0.0	0.2	0.0	x0.0	x0.1	0.0	0.0	0.0	x0.1	0.0
Asie	53.0	51.0	54.5	56.7	57.0	x52.7	55.1	57.0	53.0	55.9
Moyen–Orient	1.4	1.7	x1.0	0.9	x0.3	2.0	0.2	x0.2	x0.3	x0.3
Europe	18.1	19.9	20.8	17.2	15.3	20.2	20.9	20.2	17.7	16.1
CEE	18.1	19.9	20.8	17.2	15.3	20.2	20.8	20.2	17.7	16.1
AELE	0.0	0.0	0.0	0.0	0.0	0.0	0.0	0.0	0.0	0.0
Océanie	2.1	1.9	x1.1		x0.0	0.1	x0.1	x0.1	x3.5	x0.1
Thailand/Thaïlande	27.3	25.8	27.1	35.5	38.2	27.2	28.0	29.2	27.2	26.9
USA/Etats–Unis d'Amer	21.9	20.8	17.7	20.8	21.2	20.1	17.7	15.1	16.1	17.6
Italy/Italie	10.0	9.4	9.5	7.7	6.6	8.8	8.4	9.2	7.8	7.5
India/Inde	5.3	5.2	8.0	5.9	5.7	6.4	7.2	7.7	8.6	6.6
Pakistan	9.0	10.1	9.4	8.6	6.7	6.1	9.7	8.1	5.6	5.5
Viet Nam			x0.1	x0.3	x2.2	x7.6	x4.9	x5.7	x3.5	x6.0
China/Chine	7.0	6.3	5.7	4.7	2.0	2.1	3.6	4.5	5.3	8.9
Belgium–Luxembourg	3.7	4.3	4.7	3.9	3.4	4.2	3.6	3.2	2.8	2.8
Spain/Espagne	1.1	0.7	2.3	1.7	1.9	2.7	4.0	3.3	2.1	1.1
Uruguay	2.7	2.7	1.6	2.3	1.9	2.6	2.7	2.2	3.1	2.6

TRADE BY COMMODITY IN THOUSAND U.S. DOLLARS – COMMERCE PAR PRODUIT EN MILLIERS DE DOLLARS E.U

COUNTRIES–PAYS	IMPORTS – IMPORTATIONS					COUNTRIES–PAYS	EXPORTS – EXPORTATIONS				
	1990	1991	1992	1993	1994		1990	1991	1992	1993	1994
Total	2573858	x2584943	2677424	x2220160	x2380646	Totale	3082283	2897697	3162314	2250784	2001302
Africa	225070	114685	x114687	x246317	x234085	Afrique	1157	x123	6670	269	8542
Northern Africa	222185	109981	x92802	x241108	x228372	Afrique du Nord	1055	55	6576	180	8520
Americas	119456	134831	147734	139502	278287	Amériques	701037	563773	489775	490441	521693
LAIA	72695	72486	97013	79940	78508	ALAI	19971	15207	23522	37689	13133
CACM	42	52	116	57	637	MCAC	5	4	36	x6	x6
Asia	x674548	618527	1248202	x778365	x1020184	Asie	7843	70708	68402	x44208	x81971
Middle East	x331203	x240844	825191	x351666	x524152	Moyen–Orient	7431	69120	67864	x43233	x81252
Europe	1039351	1186028	1139123	840671	774120	Europe	1988355	1982768	2276220	1477539	1375664
EEC	992943	1171913	1121988	813420	738466	CEE	1988195	1982644	2273310	1476001	1375357
EFTA	13614	7466	6057	10166	19402	AELE	152	123	3	128	46
Oceania	x1048	x730	x4882	x2113	3617	Océanie	353544	256000	277975	221883	942
Belgium–Luxembourg	355725	468019	404408	285068	239602	France, Monac	759948	708252	926638	758988	533310
Saudi Arabia	88934	72129	686687	x197704	x381725	Germany/Allemagne	244387	323501	437512	220498	261738
Japan/Japon	184289	210359	225842	221779	228880	Canada	433753	393184	269510	297893	354821
Russian Federation			x538085	x59878	x3281	United Kingdom	333936	339381	310305	175998	188139
Netherlands/Pays–Bas	168777	186579	200860	146881	186762	Australia/Australie	347410	249623	273048	217557	921
Former USSR/Anc. URSS	439919	x422116				Denmark/Danemark	255473	260679	234867	117496	112696
Italy/Italie	146153	164459	112317	113750	90498	USA/Etats–Unis d'Amer	247308	155376	196706	154853	153734
China/Chine	109091	110236	134258	127941	178855	Belgium–Luxembourg	108169	131721	109797	60925	62103
Germany/Allemagne	138585	117872	126470	86265	86724	Spain/Espagne	147864	69645	94276	55936	136557
Libyan Arab Jamahiriya	149703	80358	x33976	x101617	x62697	Turkey/Turquie	2556	68977	67850	23366	48590
Romania/Roumanie	16010	87566	11178	103365	35758	Ireland/Irlande	70858	49860	48607	23904	10619
USA/Etats–Unis d'Amer	36475	57153	48728	56421	197424	Finland/Finlande	5029	37730	28941	15590	23043
France, Monac	43795	69822	48036	27123	12840	Sweden/Suède	11339	39182	35698	1608	13625
United Kingdom	64442	47399	57939	39186	31220	Netherlands/Pays–Bas	19021	16292	13932	25453	25993
Israel/Israël	39967	45498	46474	52098	71713	Austria/Autriche	31992	6313	28164	18337	x6642
Morocco/Maroc	1854	17206	41047	65370	9722	Argentina/Argentine	9796	7452	22479	17156	12394
Jordan/Jordanie	30360	30673	33076	51659	43750	Bulgaria/Bulgarie	x5412	x2024	x19649	x5488	x9
Denmark/Danemark	8168	9363	58432	41886	21310	Uruguay	10070	6090	211	19763	524
Greece/Grèce	33562	64437	18158	26266	20352	Poland/Pologne	11567	10793	12335	36	
Algeria/Algérie	51605	8616	16981	70273	113557	Syrian Arab Republic	1243			x17382	x32372
Iran (Islamic Rp. of)	x57630	x47594	x6532	x40492	x20408	New Zealand	6134	6377	4928	4326	21
Cyprus/Chypre	40512	33662	24202	25702	26395	Hungary/Hongrie	x1260	x1043	x11004	x3061	x3835
Poland/Pologne	107	109	6489	76658	7359	Former USSR/Anc. URSS	11454	x9606			
Ukraine			x3669	x78041		Slovakia				x7251	x4705
Portugal	25151	16461	40658	23623	26608	Tunisia/Tunisie		55	6172	162	3733
Spain/Espagne	6505	23056	42386	11160	7391	Croatia/Croatie			2857	1244	x101
Brazil/Brésil	14846	24453	30670	21407	25612	Chile/Chili	69	1659	824	754	209
Colombia/Colombie	19866	16323	19150	25291	26649	United Arab Emirates	1707			x2413	x284
Latvia/Lettonie			x53944	x15		Mongolia/Mongolie	x153	x1241	x291	x166	
United Arab Emirates	6215	333	35398	x6757	x88	Italy/Italie	179	82	581	1024	771
Mexico/Mexique	22516	10423	17373	13497	6736	Czechoslovakia		x807	x285		
Peru/Pérou	12780	13065	11792	12112	9268	Kazakstan				x617	x504
Syrian Arab Republic	18757	28296	5791			Czech Republic				609	3898
Korea, Republic of	6229	8683	12489	7767	8634	Egypt/Egypte			404	18	
Belarus/Bélarus			x18460	x9837	x1200	Russian Federation			x8	x348	x2214
Turkey/Turquie	36194	10927	5271	11972	17943	Hong Kong	123	178	101	16	
Hungary/Hongrie	x17130	15572		x9598	x17556	Portugal	2	7	8	241	103
Oman	5641	9469	8999	5782	12899	Oman	5	135	8	55	
Kuwait/Koweït	14480	700	12847	6997	16593	Switz.Liecht	143	107		86	5
Czech Republic				20294	7252	China/Chine		55	62	65	28
Ecuador/Equateur	2204	4257	12369	2988	x605	Zambia/Zambie	x75	x49	x92	x28	x20
Switz.Liecht	5281	7374	5884	5275	2661	Bosnia and Herzegovina				x161	x16
Slovenia/Slovénia			6649	11497	10710	Singapore/Singapour	47	48	31	46	71
So. Africa Customs Un			14040	15	24	Korea, Republic of	69	25	17	29	15
Uzbekistan/Ouzbékistan			x158	x12852	x1324	Norway,SVD,JM	9	15	3	42	41
Malta/Malte	4313	3423	3954	4543	x4510	So. Africa Customs Un			1	58	
Lithuania/Lituanie			4686	x6141	79	Slovenia/Slovénia			50	5	145
Qatar	4308	2673	4615	3006		Malaysia/Malaisie		26		27	47
Estonia/Estonie			x6465	x3329		Romania/Roumanie		53			42
Zimbabwe	2700	2794	4531	2298		Afghanistan	x17	x16	x33		

(VALUE AS % OF TOTAL)(VALEUR EN % DU TOTAL)

	1985	1986	1987	1988	1989	1990	1991	1992	1993	1994		1985	1986	1987	1988	1989	1990	1991	1992	1993	1994
Africa	6.2	4.6	x3.3	7.2	6.1	8.7	4.4	x4.3	x11.1	x9.8	Afrique	0.2	x0.1	x0.0	0.9	x0.1		x0.0	0.2		0.4
Northern Africa	6.2	4.2	2.9	7.2	5.6	8.6	4.3	x3.5	x10.9	x9.6	Afrique du Nord		0.0		0.8	x0.0	0.0	0.0	0.2	0.0	0.4
Americas	4.6	3.3	2.8	3.2	4.9	4.7	5.2	5.5	6.3	11.7	Amériques	12.5	20.4	x26.4	16.3	24.0	22.7	19.4	15.4	21.8	26.1
LAIA	3.3	2.2	1.9	2.1	3.2	2.8	2.8	3.6	3.6	3.3	ALAI	0.6	0.3	0.2	0.9	1.2	0.6	0.5	0.7	1.7	0.7
CACM	0.0	0.0	0.0	0.0	0.0	0.0	0.0	0.0	0.0	0.0	MCAC	0.0	0.0	0.0	x0.0	0.0	0.0	0.0	0.0	x0.0	x0.0
Asia	36.3	31.8	30.8	x21.9	x32.0	x26.2	23.9	46.6	x35.0	x42.8	Asie	1.2	x0.6	x0.3	2.9	x1.3	0.3	2.4	2.2	x2.0	x4.1
Middle East	23.4	21.8	20.3	12.7	x21.1	x12.9	x9.3	30.8	x15.8	x22.0	Moyen–Orient	0.6	x0.6	x0.3	2.9	1.2	0.2	2.4	2.1	x1.9	x4.1
Europe	34.3	47.2	50.9	41.5	31.7	40.4	45.9	42.5	37.9	32.5	Europe	62.8	67.9	65.2	73.2	67.7	64.5	68.4	72.0	65.6	68.7
EEC	32.6	45.3	48.8	39.4	30.2	38.6	45.3	41.9	36.6	31.0	CEE	59.4	65.2	63.8	72.6	66.4	64.5	68.4	71.9	65.6	68.7
EFTA	1.4	1.7	1.9	1.8	1.1	0.5	0.3	0.2	0.5	0.8	AELE	3.4	2.8	1.4	0.7	1.3	0.0	0.0	0.0	0.0	0.0
Oceania		x0.0	x0.0	x0.0		x0.0	x0.0	x0.2	x0.1	0.1	Océanie	22.8	10.9	7.8	6.4	6.5	11.5	8.8	8.8	9.9	
Belgium–Luxembourg	10.2	9.2	11.9	9.4	9.0	13.8	18.1	15.1	12.8	10.1	France, Monac	23.2	20.1	24.4	27.8	22.3	24.7	24.4	29.3	33.7	26.6
Saudi Arabia	18.2	16.7	17.4	8.1	10.8	3.5	2.8	25.6	x8.9	x16.0	Germany/Allemagne	3.3	4.8	4.0	4.5	6.2	7.9	11.2	13.8	9.8	13.1
Japan/Japon	10.4	7.2	6.0	6.0	7.0	7.2	8.1	8.4	10.0	9.6	Canada	8.9	15.2	15.0	8.5	15.9	14.1	13.6	8.5	13.2	17.7
Russian Federation								x20.1	x2.7	x0.1	United Kingdom	15.7	23.2	15.1	12.2	13.3	10.8	11.7	9.8	7.8	9.4
Netherlands/Pays–Bas	4.5	5.8	7.1	9.5	4.8	6.6	7.2	7.5	6.6	7.8	Australia/Australie	22.1	10.1	7.4	6.1	6.3	11.3	8.6	8.6	9.7	0.0
Former USSR/Anc. URSS	16.8	12.5	7.5	7.6	15.5	17.1	x16.3				Denmark/Danemark	5.3	6.6	9.3	9.2	7.9	8.3	9.0	7.4	5.2	5.6
Italy/Italie	6.0	8.4	10.8	6.0	6.5	5.7	6.4	4.2	5.1	3.8	USA/Etats–Unis d'Amer	3.0	4.9	11.1	6.9	6.9	8.0	5.4	6.2	6.9	7.7
China/Chine	0.2	0.9	1.0	0.3	1.6	4.2	4.3	5.0	5.8	7.5	Belgium–Luxembourg	3.6	2.8	3.1	3.2	2.6	3.5	4.5	3.5	2.7	3.1
Germany/Allemagne	8.6	9.4	9.8	7.1	5.3	5.4	4.6	4.7	3.9	3.6	Spain/Espagne	3.2	3.3	2.4	8.9	10.0	4.8	2.4	3.0	2.5	6.8
Libyan Arab Jamahiriya	2.5	3.7	2.5	2.9	1.9	5.8	3.1	x1.3	x4.6	x2.6	Turkey/Turquie	0.5	0.0	0.1	1.5	0.4	0.1	2.4	2.1	1.0	2.4

TRADE BY COMMODITY IN THOUSAND U.S. DOLLARS – COMMERCE PAR PRODUIT EN MILLIERS DE DOLLARS E.U

COUNTRIES–PAYS	IMPORTS – IMPORTATIONS 1990	1991	1992	1993	1994
Total	10431742	x9061924	9194384	8373595	8319359
Africa	x619056	x485553	x1395548	x819174	x684769
Northern Africa	431502	351063	395889	486539	549033
Americas	x1138445	704699	940391	x984988	1449005
LAIA	710335	450033	582610	626313	1029184
CACM	70550	75630	64547	x77280	x102970
Asia	x4033681	x3616540	x4071935	x3953757	x3750761
Middle East	x453090	x324922	x412488	x491496	x307920
Europe	2749058	2587066	2702607	2402860	2380194
EEC	2567198	2545751	2639974	2334017	2322276
EFTA	23340	22732	16718	14601	19490
Oceania	x7784	x4413	x4584	x7030	x5282
Japan/Japon	2276640	2234702	2248044	2132765	2261863
Korea, Republic of	836504	697234	847018	702320	696179
Former USSR/Anc. URSS	1684419	x1531026			
Netherlands/Pays–Bas	533917	536187	515862	346572	410269
United Kingdom	395199	397474	423735	360136	329305
Russian Federation			x637041	x524199	x83989
Germany/Allemagne	371498	397019	397178	341135	285089
Spain/Espagne	295875	255840	288283	397754	404898
Belgium–Luxembourg	295338	287831	272796	310470	350031
Italy/Italie	359005	290565	279389	135302	137075
Portugal	133505	157033	254316	211594	194869
Malaysia/Malaisie	178939	174537	204941	222811	226512
Iran (Islamic Rp. of)	x123500	x171826	x174763	x215860	x47389
Egypt/Egypte	190424	134489	177788	239490	263812
So. Africa Customs Un	2236	20208	411943	103240	11571
Mexico/Mexique	436081	178966	185563	69727	369528
Korea Dem People's Rp	x86118	x51060	x147896	x194138	x22358
Algeria/Algérie	121684	111538	136956	142493	186099
Brazil/Brésil	96141	110371	72057	176009	198716
Ukraine			x115769	x208699	x13306
Zimbabwe	13	67	237438	70001	x687
Venezuela	73435	44073	100066	155446	106896
France, Monac	71102	108280	78965	105287	94888
Peru/Pérou	77407	66930	89806	86272	118269
Canada	80728	38798	93385	92877	89537
Greece/Grèce	50486	63912	72373	61492	43028
Mozambique	x48188	x36790	x99421	x50559	x30912
USA/Etats–Unis d'Amer	25138	42359	74925	66581	90811
Israel/Israël	49613	44797	64795	66555	51605
Jordan/Jordanie	66361	40239	78161	50391	40795
Saudi Arabia	34046	16704	51231	x94613	x111435
Colombia/Colombie	5289	2386	70918	79041	143127
Poland/Pologne	3302	5968	18174	118652	13611
Romania/Roumanie	73185	34843	48954	52486	2768
Chile/Chili	13739	38498	49507	46316	66840
Zambia/Zambie	x29663	x26542	x88977	x11628	x1055
Indonesia/Indonésie	1701	45951	8324	68037	153510
Tunisia/Tunisie	40421	32743	42665	36504	32218
Syrian Arab Republic	60140	43636	16747	x48861	x34746
Dominican Republic	x34367	x30440	x38575	x39751	x68858
Costa Rica	26473	34001	32079	x40006	x47408
Morocco/Maroc	19920	23767	31156	45055	46344
Kenya	4093		70104	13355	x16660
Denmark/Danemark	22782	25094	26346	29820	29644
Libyan Arab Jamahiriya	54495	47355	x6934	x22422	x19861
Thailand/Thaïlande	513	1497	70684	2173	3488
Reunion/Réunion	16201	13244	22860	28076	13121
Slovenia/Slovénia			35195	28240	28788
Guatemala	18372	21437	15009	23991	22933
Singapore/Singapour	25727	20705	19938	19712	6672

COUNTRIES–PAYS	EXPORTS – EXPORTATIONS 1990	1991	1992	1993	1994
Totale	9798348	8690593	9500839	8557389	8333880
Afrique	370010	113506	106520	102890	x485391
Afrique du Nord	110	1	718	x2633	x834
Amériques	6584356	5671402	5681250	5089008	4804309
ALAI	348735	431134	675763	563138	552542
MCAC	513	269	2060	1020	2447
Asie	612102	1057829	1261863	1233319	1016768
Moyen–Orient	x4336	4730	6374	x14722	14328
Europe	2120340	1804063	2337992	2048190	1962124
CEE	2097168	1793254	2292495	2007046	1953584
AELE	114	45	96	49	116
Océanie	2975	x7085	4482	x5000	3181
USA/Etats–Unis d'Amer	6205803	5146694	4951007	4473932	4187101
France, Monac	1854284	1421220	1907133	1740816	1654845
China/Chine	403561	864469	1187200	1153992	944270
Argentina/Argentine	329098	409614	636604	525341	491845
Greece/Grèce	31564	93720	156334	21659	39826
Germany/Allemagne	73224	89916	79034	66693	77819
Thailand/Thaïlande	161973	153311	20916	28402	23181
Canada	27568	92909	52083	49117	62097
So. Africa Customs Un	235116	51756	91779	41037	455297
Spain/Espagne	41921	86511	38930	26041	11151
Hungary/Hongrie	x31844	x31290	x68504	x46897	x35269
Belgium–Luxembourg	21415	44767	32826	52511	59666
Zimbabwe	108600	50130	9089	31275	x21521
Italy/Italie	21798	8326	33472	41133	6954
Chile/Chili	12701	13901	32171	22468	30252
Austria/Autriche	35549	29486	25474	13577	x41765
Netherlands/Pays–Bas	12116	12929	14103	39069	57194
Croatia/Croatie			23652	23954	x4758
Bulgaria/Bulgarie	x36929	x3978	x33406	x4302	x1742
Viet Nam	x10398	x12451	x14479	x7566	x12816
Uganda/Ouganda	3318	4188	3894	23319	x2543
Indonesia/Indonésie	16780	3873	19000	7944	5617
Singapore/Singapour	10843	9825	7077	11367	6695
Yugoslavia/Yougoslavie			x16918	x5664	x2687
Slovakia				x21495	x14791
Turkey/Turquie	3104	4498	5632	9274	13250
Myanmar	2053	4486	4919	4515	x4466
Mexico/Mexique	89	3678	2812	6221	4626
United Kingdom	4571	4355	3662	3647	3836
Bosnia and Herzegovina			x3711	x7731	
Australia/Australie	2889	3304	2807	4549	1637
Yugoslavia SFR	22769	x10335			
Romania/Roumanie	121	351	3271	3352	7312
Peru/Pérou	2355	2476	987	3082	4997
Madagascar	4438	2011	140	3087	3278
Republic of Moldova			x5103	x51	30974
Lebanon/Liban	x660	x200	x683	x3832	x11
Philippines	927	3409	736	495	1586
Kenya	11156	3501	464	107	x16
Portugal	203	1560	900	1470	144
Venezuela	184	135	1692	1862	2132
Pacific Isld (Tr Terr.)		x3182			
India/Inde			90	3079	2643
Czechoslovakia		x736	x2421		
Czech Republic				2938	1907
Egypt/Egypte	73		717	2175	427
New Zealand	86	595	1674	442	1544
Ecuador/Equateur	68	107	185	2172	x7067
Brazil/Brésil	221	302	515	1587	2068
Malaysia/Malaisie	468	514	508	756	821

(VALUE AS % OF TOTAL)(VALEUR EN % DU TOTAL)

	1985	1986	1987	1988	1989	1990	1991	1992	1993	1994
Africa	6.7	6.8	5.9	5.1	6.0	x5.9	x5.3	x15.2	x9.7	x8.2
Northern Africa	4.6	5.2	4.5	3.5	4.9	4.1	3.9	4.3	5.8	6.6
Americas	8.0	10.4	8.8	8.6	9.0	x10.9	7.8	10.2	x11.8	17.4
LAIA	5.0	6.9	6.3	5.7	5.0	6.8	5.0	6.3	7.5	12.4
CACM	0.4	0.2	0.3	0.5	0.5	0.7	0.8	0.7	x0.9	x1.2
Asia	33.5	x36.6	x38.9	x40.1	37.6	x38.7	x40.0	x44.3	x47.3	x45.1
Middle East	2.7	x4.3	x3.7	x3.4	x3.9	x4.3	x3.6	x4.5	x5.9	x3.7
Europe	28.4	33.5	32.8	27.4	19.6	26.4	28.5	29.4	28.7	28.6
EEC	27.4	32.6	31.6	26.6	19.1	24.6	28.1	28.7	27.9	27.9
EFTA	0.9	0.7	0.7	0.5	0.4	0.2	0.3	0.2	0.2	0.2
Oceania	0.1	x0.2	x0.1		x0.1	x0.0	x0.0	x0.0	x0.1	x0.0
Japan/Japon	22.3	23.3	20.5	22.1	21.7	21.8	24.7	24.5	25.5	27.2
Korea, Republic of	4.9	5.2	5.6	6.1	8.2	8.0	7.7	9.2	8.4	8.4
Former USSR/Anc. URSS	22.7	11.8	10.0	13.3	21.6	16.1	x16.9			
Netherlands/Pays–Bas	4.8	6.5	6.5	5.6	4.3	5.1	5.9	5.6	4.1	4.9
United Kingdom	3.1	4.5	4.5	3.4	3.0	3.8	4.4	4.6	4.3	4.0
Russian Federation								x6.9	x6.3	x1.0
Germany/Allemagne	3.8	4.8	5.1	3.7	3.1	3.6	4.4	4.3	4.1	3.4
Spain/Espagne	5.8	3.4	2.1	3.1	2.3	2.8	2.8	3.1	4.8	4.9
Belgium–Luxembourg	3.1	4.6	4.5	4.1	2.6	2.8	3.2	3.0	3.7	4.2
Italy/Italie	2.5	3.0	4.3	4.1	2.0	3.4	3.2	3.0	1.6	1.6

	1985	1986	1987	1988	1989	1990	1991	1992	1993	1994
Afrique	1.1	x3.2	x3.7	1.6	x3.6	3.8	1.3	1.2	1.2	x5.9
Afrique du Nord		x0.0	x0.1	x0.0	x0.0	0.0	0.0	0.0	x0.0	x0.0
Amériques	71.9	51.9	54.1	65.7	68.4	67.2	65.3	59.8	59.5	57.7
ALAI	9.0	9.9	4.5	4.6	2.6	3.6	5.0	7.1	6.6	6.6
MCAC	0.1	0.0	0.0	0.0	0.0	0.0	0.0	0.0	0.0	0.0
Asie	11.7	14.6	7.4	x7.1	6.8	6.2	12.2	13.3	14.4	12.2
Moyen–Orient	0.0	0.0	x0.1	x0.1	x0.0	x0.0	0.1	0.1	x0.2	0.2
Europe	14.8	29.8	32.6	23.9	19.9	21.6	20.8	24.6	23.9	23.5
CEE	13.0	25.9	30.6	23.3	18.7	21.4	20.6	24.1	23.5	23.4
AELE	0.1	0.4	0.5	0.4	0.4	0.0	0.0	0.0	0.0	0.0
Océanie	0.2	0.2	x0.1	x0.0			x0.0		x0.1	
USA/Etats–Unis d'Amer	62.3	41.1	49.3	60.8	65.7	63.3	59.2	52.1	52.3	50.2
France, Monac	9.5	19.9	22.7	17.1	15.6	18.9	16.4	20.1	20.3	19.9
China/Chine	8.2	9.1	4.8	4.6	4.3	4.1	9.9	12.5	13.5	11.3
Argentina/Argentine	8.9	9.9	4.4	4.5	2.3	3.4	4.7	6.7	6.1	5.9
Greece/Grèce	0.4	2.0	1.7	0.2	0.4	0.3	1.1	1.6	0.3	0.5
Germany/Allemagne	0.3	0.4	0.5	0.8	0.4	0.7	1.0	0.8	0.8	0.9
Thailand/Thaïlande	3.3	5.3	2.2	1.8	1.6	1.7	1.8	0.2	0.3	0.3
Canada	0.6	0.8	0.4	0.4	0.1	0.3	1.1	0.5	0.6	0.7
So. Africa Customs Un	0.6	x1.9	x2.5	0.5	3.3	2.4	0.6	1.0	0.5	5.5
Spain/Espagne	0.0	0.2	1.7	2.1	1.1	0.4	1.0	0.4	0.3	0.1

TRADE BY COMMODITY IN THOUSAND U.S. DOLLARS – COMMERCE PAR PRODUIT EN MILLIERS DE DOLLARS E.U

COUNTRIES–PAYS	IMPORTS – IMPORTATIONS 1990	1991	1992	1993	1994
Total	1644884	1587345	1765344	1614022	1573363
Africa	55911	x90220	x57312	x29143	x55171
Northern Africa	43791	x42768	x16364	x6585	x45746
Americas	543467	545837	758209	645191	680059
LAIA	374632	400127	594009	454752	458402
CACM	3964	3524	4170	4102	6479
Asia	712192	621194	616736	x574772	x518820
Middle East	8829	22547	23222	53766	x4827
Europe	308239	284067	307355	305570	307677
EEC	275522	267101	285518	285324	283175
EFTA	25993	14899	17544	16269	19700
Oceania	8211	x2678	x5186	x3907	x8866
Japan/Japon	590402	520877	499680	460531	471037
Mexico/Mexique	334567	368555	555939	399908	416958
USA/Etats–Unis d'Amer	120202	132444	140340	173956	207029
Spain/Espagne	58055	45961	54740	65979	73026
Russian Federation			x124322	x41825	x399
Netherlands/Pays–Bas	40716	44635	49687	41489	45458
Belgium–Luxembourg	47708	53161	43609	37455	36762
Germany/Allemagne	44145	32552	52593	48673	37203
Italy/Italie	38500	42717	44313	43981	37036
Turkey/Turquie	3228	16977	17282	50049	1154
Poland/Pologne		5370	17811	49915	647
Israel/Israël	50505	24319	25562	23156	12011
Korea, Republic of	53582	14502	37867	10607	10273
Lithuania/Lituanie			789	x50995	638
Bangladesh		30060	14616		
Latvia/Lettonie			x39287	x5212	487
Brazil/Brésil	18671	12744	13504	18183	22622
Sudan/Soudan	x1717	x29534	x11643	x537	x13907
United Kingdom	14913	13543	13454	14355	11595
Switz.Liecht	14210	12415	14406	12962	13806
Belarus/Bélarus			x37289	x311	x463
France, Monac	14532	12329	10053	14207	18597
So. Africa Customs Un	1538	2910	27576	5244	3009
Colombia/Colombie	6329	5029	9439	11840	8594
Denmark/Danemark	4452	9120	7689	5798	7029
Romania/Roumanie	8892	19378	1598	63	9
Ecuador/Equateur	7154	7296	7640	4217	x68
Former USSR/Anc. URSS		x16684			
Portugal	2726	5763	4897	3868	6183
Algeria/Algérie	24132	7476	3225	3042	27962
Chile/Chili	215	961	2120	10106	3190
Ukraine			x5076	x7437	x1102
Canada	3842	3478	3160	4582	5794
Mongolia/Mongolie			x23	x11183	x12
Bahamas	56	38	x5522	x5152	x342
Niger		x5654	x2551	x1888	x193
Nigeria/Nigéria	x8	8063	x849	x236	
Kenya	14	8	1049	8016	
Philippines	882	576	7680	794	1228
Senegal/Sénégal	4219	7251	x195	x1550	
Norway, SVD, JM	11402	2034	2935	3193	5777
Venezuela	1706	1647	2816	3406	2622
Peru/Pérou	2101	1534	650	5303	804
Mali	1237	x6852	x617		
Netherlands Antilles	3205	2735	3801		
Libyan Arab Jamahiriya	3158	4962	x764	x801	x304
Thailand/Thaïlande	1909	2536	1765	2092	1953
Guatemala	2311	2248	2331	1786	1682
Cuba	x32665	x989	x4835	x208	
Mozambique	x421	x469	x3248	x2171	x1603

COUNTRIES–PAYS	EXPORTS – EXPORTATIONS 1990	1991	1992	1993	1994
Totale	1554918	1417159	1789294	1607977	1429793
Afrique	x22874	12279	x4902	x140113	x38808
Afrique du Nord	x18441	1684	x1845	x136898	x38522
Amériques	1085563	932917	1126648	946651	949894
ALAI	139403	142558	125113	109003	85745
MCAC	677	287	410	x789	3687
Asie	71199	86580	95479	75829	77021
Moyen–Orient	x2948	x328	x270	1413	x852
Europe	275630	283963	428065	380513	305866
CEE	275346	283217	421133	379274	305480
AELE	106	11	5274	397	46
Océanie	44429	46558	63064	x41130	x43066
USA/Etats–Unis d'Amer	811176	701284	896248	683799	695087
Argentina/Argentine	136902	134847	119773	100412	78659
Canada	133738	88653	104866	153031	165239
Germany/Allemagne	12932	36163	122272	141898	64993
France, Monac	111088	98768	102223	83643	96611
China/Chine	55717	58470	79554	58207	62997
Australia/Australie	44327	46337	62960	40913	42867
Finland/Finlande	42453	50716	27513	59095	46289
Sudan/Soudan	x16786			x135115	x37874
Sweden/Suède	39113	39079	45040	13721	26978
Denmark/Danemark	26687	5183	52020	17150	8567
Poland/Pologne	9160	20323	50557	560	766
Netherlands/Pays–Bas	15235	16297	18859	22676	25638
Hungary/Hongrie	x15085	x23274	x15990	x9378	x9291
United Kingdom	3449	4938	19643	12436	4177
Thailand/Thaïlande	7572	21295	8617	5635	5105
Spain/Espagne	3849	10873	5871	7712	13775
Belgium–Luxembourg	7603	7381	6680	9492	10818
Austria/Autriche	8810	6976	8117	5257	x2508
Ireland/Irlande	3324	5851	10645	1178	3116
India/Inde	1527	2851	3830	7767	6255
Venezuela	3	300	3593	6992	4957
Former USSR/Anc. URSS	883	x9872			
Albania/Albanie				x8347	x3013
Kenya	630	5371	1150	625	x2
Zimbabwe	972	4540	304	1751	x41
Norway, SVD, JM	10	4	5182	7	11
Czechoslovakia		x1219	x3918		
Mexico/Mexique	87	5006	21	24	61
Hong Kong	1313	1490	1873	1605	774
Czech Republic				4286	1475
Portugal	15	16	37	4209	385
So. Africa Customs Un	1064	327	1332	597	
Italy/Italie	789	662	945	578	1614
Bolivia/Bolivie	309	642	586	716	1443
Greece/Grèce		314	1268	228	10
Egypt/Egypte			876	907	103
Turkey/Turquie	340	195	181	1213	263
Tunisia/Tunisie	331	681	420	387	4
Chile/Chili	1168	695	292	384	112
Bulgaria/Bulgarie	x30062	x150	x649	x565	x212
Croatia/Croatie			641	677	x303
Libyan Arab Jamahiriya	1240	480	x203	x453	x48
Guatemala	526	214	395	497	596
Brazil/Brésil	506	284	467	313	96
Mongolia/Mongolie	x760	x1061			
Yugoslavia/Yougoslavie			x910		
Russian Federation			x474	x290	x4186
Belarus/Bélarus			x277	x459	x1248
Kazakstan			x217	x493	

(VALUE AS % OF TOTAL)(VALEUR EN % DU TOTAL)

	1985	1986	1987	1988	1989	1990	1991	1992	1993	1994
Africa	1.9	x1.6	x1.6	x3.6	2.8	3.4	x5.7	x3.3	x1.8	x3.5
Northern Africa	0.4	x0.2	0.2	x2.1	2.4	2.7	x2.7	x0.9	x0.4	x2.9
Americas	30.9	21.5	21.2	29.7	30.6	33.0	34.4	42.9	40.0	43.2
LAIA	26.1	16.5	14.2	21.6	21.4	22.8	25.2	33.6	28.2	29.1
CACM	0.3	0.3	x1.1	0.3	0.2	0.2	0.2	0.2	0.3	0.4
Asia	51.0	55.3	x43.1	x37.0	36.8	43.3	39.1	35.0	x35.6	x33.0
Middle East	0.7	1.0	x0.6	x0.5	x0.7	0.5	1.4	1.3	3.3	x0.3
Europe	15.1	20.0	28.1	19.9	15.9	18.7	17.9	17.4	18.9	19.6
EEC	12.4	16.7	23.9	16.7	13.3	16.8	16.8	16.2	17.7	18.0
EFTA	2.3	3.1	3.4	2.8	2.3	1.6	0.9	1.0	1.0	1.3
Oceania	0.3	0.2	0.3	x0.1	0.7	0.5	x0.2	x0.3	x0.3	x0.5
Japan/Japon	42.1	47.3	34.3	30.6	28.6	35.9	32.8	28.3	28.5	29.9
Mexico/Mexique	18.6	6.7	5.7	8.6	14.7	20.3	23.2	31.5	24.8	26.5
USA/Etats–Unis d'Amer	4.1	4.3	4.5	6.8	7.7	7.3	8.3	7.9	10.8	13.2
Spain/Espagne	0.4	0.7	1.4	2.2	2.9	3.5	2.9	3.1	4.1	4.6
Russian Federation								x7.0	x2.6	x0.0
Netherlands/Pays–Bas	2.2	2.7	4.7	2.4	1.7	2.5	2.8	2.8	2.6	2.9
Belgium–Luxembourg	2.4	3.3	5.5	2.4	2.3	2.9	3.3	2.5	2.3	2.3
Germany/Allemagne	3.3	3.9	4.7	3.2	1.9	2.7	2.1	3.0	3.0	2.4
Italy/Italie	1.5	2.1	3.0	2.5	2.3	2.3	2.7	2.5	2.7	2.4
Turkey/Turquie		0.0	0.0	0.0	0.1	0.2	1.1	1.0	3.1	0.1

	1985	1986	1987	1988	1989	1990	1991	1992	1993	1994
Afrique	0.5	x1.3	x8.2	2.1	x2.6	x1.5	0.8	x0.3	x8.7	x2.7
Afrique du Nord	0.1	0.6	7.8	1.8	x2.3	x1.2	0.1	x0.1	x8.5	x2.7
Amériques	68.0	59.1	53.1	64.7	65.8	69.8	65.8	63.0	58.8	66.5
ALAI	19.7	16.0	8.1	11.1	3.8	9.0	10.1	7.0	6.8	6.0
MCAC	0.0	0.2	0.1	0.1	0.0	0.0	0.0	0.0	x0.0	0.3
Asie	2.7	2.9	4.8	5.3	7.1	4.6	6.1	5.3	4.7	5.4
Moyen–Orient	0.0	0.2	0.5	0.5	0.3	x0.2	x0.0	x0.0	0.1	x0.1
Europe	16.7	24.4	24.5	18.0	17.6	17.7	20.0	23.9	23.7	21.4
CEE	11.7	19.2	21.7	15.8	14.1	17.7	20.0	23.5	23.6	21.4
AELE	5.0	5.1	2.7	2.2	3.5	0.0	0.0	0.3	0.0	0.0
Océanie	9.0	11.1	x6.0	6.6	3.8	2.9	3.3	3.5	x2.5	x3.0
USA/Etats–Unis d'Amer	46.0	39.0	39.5	47.4	52.4	52.2	49.5	50.1	42.5	48.6
Argentina/Argentine	19.2	15.5	7.6	10.6	3.5	8.8	9.5	6.7	6.2	5.5
Canada	2.2	3.9	5.4	6.1	9.6	8.6	6.3	5.9	9.5	11.6
Germany/Allemagne	0.1	2.4	4.0	2.4	1.4	0.8	2.6	6.8	8.8	4.5
France, Monac	4.4	7.0	5.7	5.4	3.9	7.1	7.0	5.7	5.2	6.8
China/Chine			2.5	3.9	6.1	3.6	4.1	4.4	3.6	4.4
Australia/Australie	9.0	11.1	6.0	6.6	3.8	2.9	3.3	3.5	2.5	3.0
Finland/Finlande	1.0	1.5	0.7	0.0	1.3	2.7	3.6	1.5	3.7	3.2
Sudan/Soudan		0.5	7.7	1.6	x2.3	x1.1	x0.0	x0.0	x8.4	x2.6
Sweden/Suède	3.7	3.0	1.8	1.6	1.6	2.5	2.8	2.5	0.9	1.9

TRADE BY COMMODITY IN THOUSAND U.S. DOLLARS – COMMERCE PAR PRODUIT EN MILLIERS DE DOLLARS E.U

COUNTRIES–PAYS	IMPORTS – IMPORTATIONS				
	1990	1991	1992	1993	1994
Total	x1700323	x1592834	x1837913	x2104397	x2016750
Africa	x720233	x655429	x684930	x807142	x880936
Northern Africa	490865	407711	x447239	x579566	x626843
Americas	x265976	x165327	x208249	x187523	x214612
LAIA	82156	55134	64203	54630	66221
CACM	5069	3017	5514	x2180	3707
Asia	x391498	x319321	x552337	x724602	x483295
Middle East	x194887	x120074	x231221	x205003	x219233
Europe	248927	268333	335766	321825	x378570
EEC	241812	260443	310619	274956	295235
EFTA	2288	2363	3017	2965	3290
Oceania	x15505	x13650	x13331	x14365	x15543
Algeria/Algérie	76180	115902	231814	281254	323197
Libyan Arab Jamahiriya	164964	151687	x133803	x131546	x145443
Egypt/Egypte	235071	104912	58193	144439	70775
Mongolia/Mongolie		x15005	x12367	x257520	x4314
Netherlands/Pays–Bas	67724	76754	97752	91244	97427
Syrian Arab Republic	113948	x58759	92921	x103152	x48140
Russian Federation			x235013	x17364	x5638
Yemen/Yémen	x47672	19238	x99081	x63813	x109802
Viet Nam	x46998	x50763	x63573	x66905	x65777
Former USSR/Anc. URSS	56083	x167159			
France, Monac	46003	49671	57827	50039	57759
Cuba	x126448	x50451	x50930	x36287	x25140
Germany/Allemagne	45375	51092	49538	34151	28242
Belgium–Luxembourg	33393	37129	42697	37912	36340
Hong Kong	32076	35600	35884	29256	37259
Singapore/Singapour	25576	27463	30032	36791	34881
Cameroon/Cameroun	50165	56368	x29578	x5404	x35081
Haiti/Haïti	x7186	x13166	x38603	x28877	x30136
Sudan/Soudan	x14388	x35209	x23254	x22019	x86017
Ireland/Irlande	25846	26188	29712	23254	25142
Iraq	x1653	x19728	x24957	x17367	x41182
Peru/Pérou	60394	24466	13383	23804	12361
China/Chine	18668	25030	26588	7104	8447
Mozambique	x11720	x13440	x19117	x25342	x19765
Bolivia/Bolivie	17284	19326	25579	10126	8006
Azerbaijan			x38985	x13097	x17379
USA/Etats–Unis d'Amer	9625	7913	13712	25663	47969
Georgia/Géorgie			x27624	x17545	x27461
Equatorial Guinea		x17463	x14234	x9963	x720
Niger	x8850	x15863	x20310	x4099	x1552
Chad/Tchad	x7039	x17452	x9940	x12585	x10186
Korea Dem People's Rp	x186	x869	x27798	x11170	x1634
Albania/Albanie		x2264	x14956	x22125	x26038
Malawi	x10779	9487	x14651	x12523	x10136
United Kingdom	7843	10397	13177	11485	18961
Un. Rep. of Tanzania	x1800	x13181	x11996	x8995	x3669
Mexico/Mexique	3187	9995	15715	7358	5752
Yugoslavia/Yougoslavie			x6832	x25390	x3500
Martinique	10022	10080	10334	10990	12295
Angola	x16909	x4558	x6749	x19245	x38192
Poland/Pologne			17606	12463	5251
Turkmenistan/Turkménistn			x7562	x22033	x1112
Guinea/Guinée	x10639	x9125	x8270	x11916	x15075
Mauritania/Mauritanie	x8650	x9823	x9888	x8446	x13278
Denmark/Danemark	3332	3191	12122	12431	12128
Zaire/Zaïre	x9594	x9364	x8695	x9385	x8255
Thailand/Thaïlande	10595	9416	8799	7601	7619
Indonesia/Indonésie	6597	9185	8424	7551	5717
Philippines	13238	11189	7361	5855	12128
Congo	x5442	x6237	x11051	x5771	x2232

COUNTRIES–PAYS	EXPORTS – EXPORTATIONS				
	1990	1991	1992	1993	1994
Totale	1721567	1763664	2045503	1965691	1961773
Afrique	44056	53436	42565	57096	16933
Afrique du Nord	6543	672	5159	7307	13157
Amériques	288419	277277	278167	304833	360474
ALAI	49527	34526	30286	42884	68263
MCAC	275	113	184	633	795
Asie	173461	269772	272165	248505	280571
Moyen–Orient	x50640	126168	108540	86158	111773
Europe	1144669	1145225	1384372	1317950	1273326
CEE	1125453	1140343	1374444	1306284	1269953
AELE	340	335	273	371	583
Océanie	18059	17924	18912	19025	18946
France, Monac	367819	351064	394730	398984	364418
Italy/Italie	300967	336500	381693	251632	214329
USA/Etats–Unis d'Amer	187238	189944	191455	211287	215914
Belgium–Luxembourg	164119	154073	193951	192350	207056
Germany/Allemagne	126990	149028	215332	150368	144733
Turkey/Turquie	27471	116053	106004	82040	107629
Spain/Espagne	45936	39367	67124	173855	173779
Japan/Japon	71953	68997	70620	77597	75841
Netherlands/Pays–Bas	62897	54033	65133	74129	80494
Canada	42346	41128	43811	39174	65146
United Kingdom	34452	34406	38605	35805	39850
Argentina/Argentine	31814	31890	27996	36971	59176
So. Africa Customs Un	18402	20864	34839	40327	
Singapore/Singapour	20967	26759	25993	18196	27627
China/Chine	418	5559	25153	37893	27638
Australia/Australie	17803	17582	18057	18051	17458
Hong Kong	14562	21736	19627	9426	8013
Malaysia/Malaisie	11956	16969	16810	15091	19761
Greece/Grèce	5331	5976	6008	15948	12959
Guadeloupe	4732	7053	8778	8223	9865
Cameroon/Cameroun	1790	23654			
Poland/Pologne			23307		1207
Sweden/Suède	11164	9303	4737	2381	8031
Croatia/Croatie			5980	10343	x283
Czechoslovakia			x13071		
Tunisia/Tunisie	6530		5128	7252	10977
Hungary/Hongrie			x9260	x2637	x6781
Czech Republic				11711	1704
Denmark/Danemark	1455	1558	1927	5459	13301
Jordan/Jordanie	1614	7805	42	66	64
Thailand/Thaïlande	817	1694	3826	2281	3372
Togo	12306	6826			
St Vincent & Grenadines	x2351	x2325	x2275	x1731	
Ireland/Irlande	1387	2295	1572	2376	6734
Zimbabwe	570	373	32	5355	
Mauritius/Maurice	341	13	1776	3512	3634
Austria/Autriche	1894	1448	1576	1859	x2072
Yugoslavia SFR	18876	x4547			
Portugal	1033	1286	1841	979	332
Bulgaria/Bulgarie			x3684	x234	x1516
United Arab Emirates	12410	540	1288	x1820	x1854
Slovakia				x3640	x301
Bahrain/Bahreïn	x771	x1347	x450	x1115	x122
Korea, Republic of	384	764	1083	776	1188
Venezuela	111	433	564	1491	440
Chile/Chili	16332	1533	449	477	383
Slovenia/Slovénia			1573	815	2473
Grenada/Grenade	755	1322	x454	x491	
Peru/Pérou		2	7	2253	5571
Uruguay	1044	653	729	510	25

(VALUE AS % OF TOTAL)(VALEUR EN % DU TOTAL)

	1985	1986	1987	1988	1989	1990	1991	1992	1993	1994
Africa	64.1	x51.5	x44.3	x46.7	x39.9	x42.3	x41.2	x37.2	x38.3	x43.7
Northern Africa	49.9	34.2	29.7	x27.2	29.6	28.9	25.6	x24.3	x27.5	x31.1
Americas	8.5	x12.8	x11.4	x7.0	12.6	x15.6	x10.4	x11.3	x8.9	x10.6
LAIA	4.3	2.1	x1.9	0.9	5.7	4.8	3.5	3.5	2.6	3.3
CACM	0.1	0.7	0.2	0.2	0.4	0.3	0.2	0.3	x0.1	0.2
Asia	10.6	x18.2	x22.6	x24.7	x31.0	x23.0	x20.1	x30.0	x34.4	x24.0
Middle East	4.8	x12.0	x10.6	x6.1	x12.4	x11.5	x7.5	x12.6	x9.7	x10.9
Europe	12.3	13.5	17.8	17.8	13.0	14.6	16.8	18.3	15.3	x18.8
EEC	11.7	12.9	17.1	17.2	12.5	14.2	16.4	16.9	13.1	14.6
EFTA	0.5	0.5	0.5	0.4	0.2	0.1	0.1	0.2	0.1	0.2
Oceania	0.3	x1.1	x0.9	x1.2	x0.7	x0.9	x0.8	x0.7	x0.7	x0.8
Algeria/Algérie	6.0	7.6	7.4	5.0	7.0	4.5	7.3	12.6	13.4	16.0
Libyan Arab Jamahiriya	7.9	6.1	5.7	5.4	6.6	9.7	9.5	x7.3	x6.3	x7.2
Egypt/Egypte	33.4	16.6	13.6	12.3	12.9	13.8	6.6	3.2	6.9	3.5
Mongolia/Mongolie			x0.0				x0.9	x0.7	x12.2	x0.2
Netherlands/Pays–Bas	3.1	3.7	5.1	5.0	3.6	4.0	4.8	5.3	4.3	4.8
Syrian Arab Republic	0.7	1.9	4.1	3.4	3.8	6.7	x3.7	5.1	x4.9	x2.4
Russian Federation								x12.8	x0.8	x0.3
Yemen/Yémen					0.5	x2.8	1.2	x5.4	x3.0	x5.4
Viet Nam			x1.0	x9.6	x7.4	x2.8	x3.2	x3.5	x3.2	x3.3
Former USSR/Anc. URSS	4.0	3.0	3.0	2.6	2.6	3.3	x10.5			

	1985	1986	1987	1988	1989	1990	1991	1992	1993	1994
Afrique	0.6	x0.7	x0.4	1.1	x1.7	2.6	3.0	2.1	3.0	0.9
Afrique du Nord	0.0	x0.3	x0.2	x0.0	x0.1	0.4	0.0	0.3	0.4	0.7
Amériques	19.9	x23.1	x22.2	x20.5	21.6	16.7	15.7	13.6	15.5	18.3
ALAI	1.0	0.6	0.4	0.4	1.4	2.9	2.0	1.5	2.2	3.5
MCAC	0.0	0.1	x0.0	x0.1	x0.0	0.0	0.0	0.0	0.0	0.0
Asie	9.4	9.3	x9.6	x9.4	10.6	10.1	15.3	13.4	12.7	14.3
Moyen–Orient	5.5	3.9	x3.4	x2.1	3.5	x2.9	7.2	5.3	4.4	5.7
Europe	66.3	61.7	62.8	63.2	61.2	66.5	64.9	67.7	67.0	64.9
CEE	65.3	61.2	62.1	62.6	59.6	65.4	64.7	67.2	66.5	64.7
AELE	0.9	0.6	0.7	0.6	0.7	0.0	0.0	0.0	0.0	0.0
Océanie	0.7	x1.0	1.0	x1.8	1.4	1.0	1.0	0.9	0.9	0.9
France, Monac	22.7	22.9	22.3	23.9	21.3	21.4	19.9	19.3	20.3	18.6
Italy/Italie	18.4	18.2	15.6	15.0	15.8	17.5	19.1	18.7	12.8	10.9
USA/Etats–Unis d'Amer	13.7	17.2	17.3	15.6	16.3	10.9	10.8	9.4	10.7	11.0
Belgium–Luxembourg	4.6	4.8	6.7	6.4	6.9	9.5	8.7	9.5	9.8	10.6
Germany/Allemagne	7.4	6.3	6.6	8.2	7.5	7.4	8.4	10.5	7.6	7.4
Turkey/Turquie	3.3	2.3	2.1	x1.1	2.8	1.6	6.6	5.2	4.2	5.5
Spain/Espagne	1.9	1.3	1.9	1.8	1.5	2.7	2.2	3.3	8.8	8.9
Japan/Japon	2.8	4.1	4.4	4.3	4.0	4.2	3.9	3.5	3.9	3.9
Netherlands/Pays–Bas	3.8	3.3	4.5	3.6	3.4	3.7	3.1	3.2	3.8	4.1
Canada	4.7	4.2	3.5	3.4	3.1	2.5	2.3	2.1	2.0	3.3

TRADE BY COMMODITY IN THOUSAND U.S. DOLLARS – COMMERCE PAR PRODUIT EN MILLIERS DE DOLLARS E.U

COUNTRIES–PAYS	IMPORTS – IMPORTATIONS 1990	1991	1992	1993	1994
Total	363742	358968	314012	293758	x337430
Africa	162998	x132482	x80685	x62470	x73896
Northern Africa	125885	82719	44504	x30239	x28796
Americas	37368	45808	51776	77389	100048
LAIA	4672	9715	15603	29459	34215
CACM	741	3818	1502	5416	16986
Asia	55017	67032	62765	54299	54166
Middle East	x6672	14995	10149	x7833	x6073
Europe	98370	98929	113312	92467	100569
EEC	87921	93736	105076	85589	92125
EFTA	4134	2910	3394	3099	3850
Oceania	x2935	x4065	x2899	x3050	x5101
Algeria/Algérie	122959	79253	40943	22247	11187
Canada	17873	18890	21183	23917	25178
Netherlands/Pays–Bas	19326	17140	19361	15939	15259
United Kingdom	11268	13858	17805	13983	15526
Denmark/Danemark	14328	14718	16574	10600	9944
Russian Federation			x24863	x15193	x362
Israel/Israël	13323	9801	14576	11984	12947
France, Monac	10099	9713	12508	11471	15264
Hong Kong	10580	11968	11474	9102	10427
Malaysia/Malaisie	7373	9403	10740	10826	10977
Belgium–Luxembourg	5550	10468	9761	8689	8162
Germany/Allemagne	11010	9879	10140	7269	7622
Mexico/Mexique	1519	4101	5842	15314	17873
USA/Etats–Unis d'Amer	8078	4701	7331	12234	15445
Burkina Faso	x2199	x8939	x5436	x7538	x1062
Spain/Espagne	5986	7364	8113	5798	6493
Singapore/Singapour	5006	6882	6497	6472	5639
Saudi Arabia	829	9741	5351	x1818	x1784
Cameroon/Cameroun	3222	14873	x899	x1027	x2942
Indonesia/Indonésie	7577	7452	4474	3843	2064
Bolivia/Bolivie	2951	2656	4169	6226	1434
Mozambique	x4718	x5676	x3878	x3022	x1502
Zimbabwe		120	9522	1395	x121
Sudan/Soudan		x1826	x2065	x7028	x12012
Former USSR/Anc. URSS		x10364			
Peru/Pérou	29	2371	3819	4087	4880
Sweden/Suède	3352	2922	3535	3672	5001
Angola	x1491	x805	x1600	x6875	x14420
Italy/Italie	1893	2443	2824	2650	1998
Ireland/Irlande	2690	2972	1842	2112	2418
Japan/Japon	1716	2095	2211	1793	1729
Chad/Tchad	x941	x5447	x368		x1469
Poland/Pologne			2431	3139	2523
So. Africa Customs Un	1514	1313	1755	2314	2527
Australia/Australie	1077	2357	1274	1263	2188
Jordan/Jordanie	857	1706	1710	1073	989
Trinidad and Tobago	1170	1475	1422	1398	1580
Slovenia/Slovénia			2119	2172	2777
Madagascar	278	1322	900	1768	1262
Portugal	346	629	1244	2071	3146
Norway, SVD, JM	1210	571	1668	1685	1912
Iceland/Islande	2474	1694	1120	922	1296
Oman	349	312	505	2675	477
Rwanda	x2695	x134	x746	x2566	x6465
Philippines	469	2955	210	266	207
Mali	912	x2719	x294	x190	x111
Haiti/Haïti	x821	x717	x740	x1656	x1836
El Salvador		2179	271	605	1844
Egypt/Egypte	2597	1320	813	859	1656
Guatemala	158	597	170	2221	3418

COUNTRIES–PAYS	EXPORTS – EXPORTATIONS 1990	1991	1992	1993	1994
Totale	243332	289062	323648	353967	427674
Afrique	6885	19177	8137	5049	2988
Afrique du Nord	1970	25	521	129	2842
Amériques	81218	93408	90169	133412	177274
ALAI	22744	15359	17789	38106	51596
MCAC	603	859	1083	x1919	x3140
Asie	37968	44912	55152	64030	88588
Moyen–Orient	x921	x1943	x542	x373	x432
Europe	111746	128831	163999	146156	151286
CEE	111150	128194	161888	144567	150730
AELE	227	238	151	124	229
Océanie	2238	2589	x2988	x3422	6161
USA/Etats–Unis d'Amer	55443	74150	65331	82203	107115
Thailand/Thaïlande	28341	34865	45185	52991	61342
France, Monac	34010	38609	48500	41493	47825
Italy/Italie	26399	26131	42442	47997	37952
Germany/Allemagne	30173	37964	36716	27202	26898
Bolivia/Bolivie	9241	12236	9946	26755	23999
Netherlands/Pays–Bas	6896	8682	10194	7091	7635
United Kingdom	7047	7672	10315	6948	7821
So. Africa Customs Un	2499	13633	6751	4268	
Belgium–Luxembourg	3782	4691	6890	8715	9336
Canada	2189	2663	5660	9786	15222
China/Chine	2162	2938	3924	3798	12881
Venezuela	310	913	2249	6813	10540
Australia/Australie	1850	2172	2347	2899	4923
Malaysia/Malaisie	854	1271	2018	2144	1306
Zimbabwe	1404	5035	70	142	x11
Mexico/Mexique	11939	639	2840	672	13995
Hong Kong	1350	1698	1139	1235	1646
Portugal	262	647	1946	1228	2081
Brazil/Brésil	37	92	1606	2009	675
Greece/Grèce	749	1343	1756	248	4386
Spain/Espagne	364	484	783	1962	5284
Denmark/Danemark	476	1045	999	905	668
Indonesia/Indonésie	569	594	812	1163	1867
Poland/Pologne			2247	204	303
Ireland/Irlande	583	620	735	342	164
Guatemala	359	377	469	839	1109
Chile/Chili	143	887	347	398	798
Russian Federation			x340	x1279	x1301
Croatia/Croatie			706	788	x75
Singapore/Singapour	554	513	610	333	1197
Syrian Arab Republic		x1321			
Netherlands Antilles	13	75	36	x1160	x21
New Zealand	383	410	386	476	1228
Slovenia/Slovénia			858	343	251
Sweden/Suède	350	274	567	324	423
Colombia/Colombie	907	327	424	366	327
Sri Lanka	80	268	335	424	401
Mauritius/Maurice	20	20	672	334	9
Malta/Malte	305	324	350	331	
Korea, Republic of	218	485	104	405	323
India/Inde	58	56	170	762	216
Argentina/Argentine	155	124	150	701	488
Costa Rica	60	125	310	x512	x1222
Hungary/Hongrie	x197	x112	x316	x511	x809
El Salvador		282	300	280	590
Turkey/Turquie	366	300	216	203	341
Czech Republic				595	148
Slovakia				x588	x86
Barbados/Barbade	95	166	189	194	x44

(VALUE AS % OF TOTAL)(VALEUR EN % DU TOTAL)

	1985	1986	1987	1988	1989	1990	1991	1992	1993	1994
Africa	45.7	x43.8	33.7	x32.5	42.9	44.8	x36.9	x25.7	x21.3	x21.9
Northern Africa	31.9	24.4	25.9	21.7	36.6	34.6	23.0	14.2	x10.3	x8.5
Americas	10.9	x18.4	x21.6	9.3	x15.4	10.2	12.8	16.5	26.3	29.6
LAIA	1.8	1.8	1.8	0.5	0.7	1.3	2.7	5.0	10.0	10.1
CACM	0.8	x0.8	x0.6	0.9	0.7	0.2	1.1	0.5	1.8	5.0
Asia	21.5	15.3	x19.2	x27.0	15.3	15.1	18.7	19.9	18.5	16.0
Middle East	7.1	x3.2	x3.1	x8.9	x5.3	x1.8	4.2	3.2	x2.7	x1.8
Europe	21.5	22.0	24.6	29.0	24.0	27.0	27.6	36.1	31.5	29.8
EEC	17.2	19.1	22.3	26.2	21.1	24.2	26.1	33.5	29.1	27.3
EFTA	4.3	2.9	2.3	2.3	2.6	1.1	0.8	1.1	1.1	1.1
Oceania	0.3	x0.4	0.8	0.7	0.7	x0.8	x1.1	x1.0	x1.0	x1.5
Algeria/Algérie	31.5	23.0	24.7	19.6	36.3	33.8	22.1	13.0	7.6	3.3
Canada	4.7	3.7	3.2	4.5	4.9	4.9	5.3	6.7	8.1	7.5
Netherlands/Pays–Bas	3.2	4.1	5.6	6.0	4.3	5.3	4.8	6.2	5.4	4.5
United Kingdom	1.4	1.8	2.3	2.7	2.5	3.1	3.9	5.7	4.8	4.6
Denmark/Danemark	3.3	3.8	4.3	5.3	3.8	3.9	4.1	5.3	3.6	2.9
Russian Federation								x7.9	x5.2	x0.1
Israel/Israël	0.5	1.4	4.1	1.3	0.9	3.7	2.7	4.6	4.1	3.8
France, Monac	3.1	3.4	2.7	3.1	2.7	2.8	2.7	4.0	3.9	4.5
Hong Kong	4.4	4.2	4.3	4.2	2.9	2.9	3.3	3.7	3.1	3.1
Malaysia/Malaisie	4.2	2.0	2.1	2.4	2.1	2.0	2.6	3.4	3.7	3.3

	1985	1986	1987	1988	1989	1990	1991	1992	1993	1994
Afrique	0.9	x2.0	x3.2	x2.9	x1.5	2.8	6.6	2.5	1.4	0.7
Afrique du Nord	0.1	0.0	0.0	0.0	0.1	0.8	0.0	0.2	0.0	0.7
Amériques	43.9	36.5	38.7	27.7	40.0	33.4	32.3	27.8	37.7	41.4
ALAI	2.1	1.3	3.1	4.9	10.1	9.3	5.3	5.5	10.8	12.1
MCAC	0.1	x0.1	0.2	0.2	0.1	0.2	0.3	0.3	x0.5	x0.7
Asie	8.1	8.2	8.2	30.9	x16.8	15.6	15.6	17.1	18.1	20.7
Moyen–Orient	0.1	x0.4	0.0	17.0	x3.4	x0.4	x0.7	x0.2	x0.1	x0.1
Europe	22.9	24.3	24.5	36.2	39.4	45.9	44.6	50.7	41.3	35.4
CEE	22.6	24.1	24.3	35.8	38.9	45.7	44.3	50.0	40.8	35.2
AELE	0.1	0.1	0.1	0.2	0.3	0.1	0.1	0.0	0.0	0.1
Océanie	4.5	0.3	0.2	0.9	x1.3	0.9	0.9	x0.9	x1.0	1.4
USA/Etats–Unis d'Amer	19.9	13.9	10.5	19.7	28.4	22.8	25.7	20.2	23.2	25.0
Thailand/Thaïlande	7.2	6.9	6.7	10.9	10.7	11.6	12.1	14.0	15.0	14.3
France, Monac	3.4	3.7	4.6	8.3	13.2	14.0	13.4	15.0	11.7	11.2
Italy/Italie	3.9	3.9	3.5	6.6	7.3	10.8	9.0	13.1	13.6	8.9
Germany/Allemagne	7.6	8.2	8.0	13.2	11.3	12.4	13.1	11.3	7.7	6.3
Bolivia/Bolivie	0.5	0.8	2.5	4.1	8.0	3.8	4.2	3.1	7.6	5.6
Netherlands/Pays–Bas	4.4	4.1	5.4	3.1	2.6	2.8	3.0	3.1	2.0	1.8
United Kingdom	0.6	0.5	0.9	2.0	2.6	2.9	2.7	3.2	2.0	1.8
So. Africa Customs Un	0.1	x1.1	x3.2	2.7	0.5	1.0	4.7	2.1	1.2	
Belgium–Luxembourg	2.3	3.2	1.5	1.7	1.1	1.6	1.6	2.1	2.5	2.2

TRADE BY COMMODITY IN THOUSAND U.S. DOLLARS – COMMERCE PAR PRODUIT EN MILLIERS DE DOLLARS E.U

COUNTRIES–PAYS	IMPORTS – IMPORTATIONS				
	1990	1991	1992	1993	1994
Total	9727868	10807665	11969231	12341020	13569368
Africa	x369055	x332324	x358944	x363611	x400329
Northern Africa	42697	55121	x63690	x62852	x80525
Americas	1831273	1981441	2259125	3055390	3469874
LAIA	648261	624505	736188	1390135	1522656
CACM	33147	50153	60405	x82345	x96869
Asia	x1721684	x1875155	1931525	x2180803	x2376012
Middle East	x436878	x481594	x340752	x459468	x386310
Europe	5533012	6166547	7098937	6355404	6915495
EEC	5185515	5804823	6671163	5927562	6434179
EFTA	287663	314490	340786	333728	350883
Oceania	x177913	x190821	x205964	x205091	x209158
Germany/Allemagne	1100060	1303783	1522373	1245000	1321448
France, Monac	1092222	1177401	1306076	1175559	1273274
United Kingdom	656272	747654	862185	821739	856056
USA/Etats–Unis d'Amer	651536	718920	809823	884918	1055966
Japan/Japon	570279	567749	635321	653739	772703
Brazil/Brésil	482628	426101	372942	959347	998211
Belgium–Luxembourg	472810	530151	568993	542732	610029
Netherlands/Pays–Bas	449691	461931	549471	479660	540160
Canada	316007	384429	452336	495823	560990
Italy/Italie	353650	389128	439676	388977	405317
Ireland/Irlande	220033	254016	290049	243794	260300
Spain/Espagne	172819	213747	302598	253067	295748
Russian Federation			x383936	x243933	x380570
Switz.Liecht	163852	186504	202996	203877	212238
Hong Kong	142463	167081	199117	200341	247374
Austria/Autriche	150526	161551	185890	185618	214833
Mexico/Mexique	54332	83564	195863	240743	308746
Sweden/Suède	155650	167822	185937	161218	181150
Denmark/Danemark	145055	152676	169619	161653	169165
Saudi Arabia	122427	168413	93792	x156169	x150088
Malaysia/Malaisie	113824	124381	142858	142515	158242
Greece/Grèce	110193	118949	137349	138801	146826
Singapore/Singapour	87638	103723	123002	151104	171244
Norway, SVD, JM	106655	108516	116031	110497	118856
Australia/Australie	76936	81992	98503	98967	102630
Iran (Islamic Rp. of)	x88167	x134857	x61955	x81401	x20602
Thailand/Thaïlande	61220	77047	89913	110075	121353
Portugal	61242	79624	104134	89390	109800
Philippines	83258	80715	89317	82760	132021
Venezuela	50023	60862	69077	61385	47088
Korea, Republic of	35577	55221	67308	63244	76397
Israel/Israël	42639	60216	59346	59167	68929
India/Inde	66582	66163	70324	34892	26445
Former USSR/Anc. URSS	25619	x171003			
So. Africa Customs Un	49453	51786	44473	38899	41645
Finland/Finlande	45292	46392	46810	40354	50072
United Arab Emirates	41385	38510	36792	x53914	x55945
Poland/Pologne	5069	43857	45304	36749	39342
New Zealand	34068	39155	39018	42846	50050
Cameroon/Cameroun	52218	45531	x30194	x22626	x29588
Reunion/Réunion	26391	27523	36340	33971	38720
Peru/Pérou	16571	18728	30006	37072	37208
Libyan Arab Jamahiriya	9753	18515	x34702	x24993	x9474
Bangladesh		5677	5195	66648	x7612
Kuwait/ Koweït	13096	10106	31265	32743	36548
Hungary/Hongrie	x3881	13831	x20744	x34492	x45018
Martinique	16808	22542	24257	21848	22251
Nigeria/Nigéria	x25012	6558	x31891	x29995	x25067
Lebanon/Liban	x25083	x29677	x15401	x20130	x35600
Argentina/Argentine	771	3323	26719	33980	43134

COUNTRIES–PAYS	EXPORTS – EXPORTATIONS				
	1990	1991	1992	1993	1994
Totale	9483029	10572486	11992759	12154229	13457722
Afrique	42694	51734	51289	44269	27039
Afrique du Nord	14780	26360	23845	17411	22878
Amériques	1055710	1318230	1512508	1822293	x2071477
ALAI	139607	186339	205251	254906	323996
MCAC	21050	25791	33587	x44905	x59614
Asie	772323	889468	1072884	1179150	1444149
Moyen–Orient	105050	123845	126956	124930	x169368
Europe	7364637	7979445	9044675	8765203	9487087
CEE	7219511	7825803	8842067	8517667	9257587
AELE	134876	145941	161180	184162	192993
Océanie	216355	223776	203759	211369	270866
Germany/Allemagne	1315802	1442181	1574321	1460854	1552297
France, Monac	1143198	1205791	1390099	1285113	1382226
Italy/Italie	960918	1115462	1363679	1279026	1429514
Netherlands/Pays–Bas	988443	1072239	1195280	1155291	1204835
United Kingdom	838552	927622	1079976	1044164	1072951
USA/Etats–Unis d'Amer	580323	761661	882214	1058762	1134713
Belgium–Luxembourg	802877	873914	912576	906833	999740
Denmark/Danemark	385670	438473	493050	490541	512420
Canada	285962	320215	365419	414921	469879
Ireland/Irlande	336981	295603	343283	356633	461582
Japan/Japon	175810	180528	205526	245102	214165
Australia/Australie	190871	196579	169366	172558	209911
Switz.Liecht	112831	121145	134315	161506	162102
Sweden/Suède	141242	134123	143112	133130	157602
Spain/Espagne	57250	99294	124223	144262	203141
Singapore/Singapour	87902	108425	123229	134451	173469
Austria/Autriche	123286	120943	123505	112855	x123384
China/Chine	67074	85113	129321	122191	166967
Hong Kong	78686	95927	114087	112487	138168
Korea, Republic of	88523	95518	99686	118937	175307
Malaysia/Malaisie	63275	77159	102321	114649	159884
Turkey/Turquie	36410	76390	75023	91650	123886
Thailand/Thaïlande	49429	56357	73501	98360	126138
Mexico/Mexique	21257	41100	57055	69846	96030
Czechoslovakia		x93228	x73859		
Finland/Finlande	92782	51425	44282	67805	67795
Argentina/Argentine	46706	55738	38623	45337	63952
Greece/Grèce	22347	28237	38312	60451	54653
Uruguay	26632	38856	30145	42229	45025
Chile/Chili	24095	27512	32331	42932	43971
Indonesia/Indonésie	16828	22181	27384	33185	34921
New Zealand	20402	21224	26971	33250	53953
Czech Republic				74859	73313
Norway, SVD, JM	21964	24778	26825	22605	30715
Israel/Israël	12544	13752	29116	24068	24190
Croatia/Croatie			22468	37187	x15999
Portugal	9800	20131	16367	20710	35446
Guatemala	13805	15847	18040	22593	27564
India/Inde	12266	14933	15945	19213	21759
So. Africa Customs Un	11944	15148	17260	15070	
Saudi Arabia	6424	17560	18668	x10554	x21155
Colombia/Colombie	8068	10791	23606	11966	20437
Tunisia/Tunisie	10749	15113	16326	12512	15695
Poland/Pologne	6907	7074	18033	18686	42390
Brazil/Brésil	5046	7068	14211	21870	26645
Trinidad and Tobago	12503	13236	14566	13831	19684
Philippines	9249	9508	9562	17496	20371
Hungary/Hongrie	x9212	x7902	x14652	x10715	x11509
Venezuela	4897	4274	6903	17980	22389
Slovenia/Slovénia			14349	12791	13209

(VALUE AS % OF TOTAL)(VALEUR EN % DU TOTAL)

	1985	1986	1987	1988	1989	1990	1991	1992	1993	1994
Africa	9.5	x6.1	x4.8	x4.5	x4.1	x3.8	x3.1	x3.0	x2.9	x2.9
Northern Africa	4.7	0.5	0.4	x0.5	0.4	0.4	0.5	x0.5	x0.5	x0.6
Americas	20.2	17.8	16.7	13.8	17.1	18.8	18.3	18.8	24.8	25.6
LAIA	3.3	2.7	2.7	2.4	3.5	6.7	5.8	6.2	11.3	11.2
CACM	1.0	0.4	x0.6	0.4	0.5	0.3	0.5	0.5	x0.7	x0.7
Asia	17.8	16.9	x16.2	x20.0	x19.7	x17.7	x17.3	16.1	x17.7	x17.5
Middle East	4.8	x5.5	x4.4	x6.0	x4.6	x4.5	x4.5	x2.8	x3.7	x2.8
Europe	50.2	57.1	60.2	58.3	56.4	56.9	57.1	59.3	51.5	51.0
EEC	43.5	49.4	52.5	51.6	49.9	53.3	53.7	55.7	48.0	47.4
EFTA	6.5	7.4	7.5	6.4	6.2	3.0	2.9	2.8	2.7	2.6
Oceania	1.3	x1.6	x1.6	x1.6	x1.8	x1.8	x1.7	x1.7	x1.6	x1.5
Germany/Allemagne	8.7	10.1	10.7	10.2	9.6	11.3	12.1	12.7	10.1	9.7
France, Monac	9.3	11.7	12.2	11.0	10.7	11.2	10.9	10.9	9.5	9.4
United Kingdom	4.9	4.9	4.8	6.1	6.5	6.7	6.9	7.2	6.7	6.3
USA/Etats–Unis d'Amer	10.2	9.3	8.6	6.5	7.7	6.7	6.7	6.8	7.2	7.8
Japan/Japon	5.2	5.2	5.3	5.8	6.8	5.9	5.3	5.3	5.3	5.7
Brazil/Brésil	1.3	1.3	1.2	1.1	1.6	5.0	3.9	3.1	7.8	7.4
Belgium–Luxembourg	4.9	5.4	5.7	5.4	4.7	4.9	4.9	4.8	4.4	4.5
Netherlands/Pays–Bas	4.2	4.6	5.0	4.9	4.6	4.6	4.3	4.6	3.9	4.0
Canada	3.4	3.1	2.8	2.6	3.1	3.2	3.6	3.8	4.0	4.1
Italy/Italie	3.7	3.7	3.9	4.1	3.7	3.6	3.6	3.7	3.2	3.0

	1985	1986	1987	1988	1989	1990	1991	1992	1993	1994
Afrique	0.5	0.4	x0.4	0.4	x0.6	0.4	0.4	0.4	0.3	0.2
Afrique du Nord	0.1	0.1	0.2	0.2	0.2	0.2	0.2	0.2	0.1	0.2
Amériques	13.8	9.7	8.4	8.1	9.5	11.1	12.4	12.6	15.0	x15.4
ALAI	1.8	1.2	1.2	1.1	1.4	1.5	1.8	1.7	2.1	2.4
MCAC	0.4	0.3	0.3	0.3	0.2	0.2	0.2	0.3	x0.4	x0.4
Asie	6.3	5.7	x7.7	8.5	8.8	8.2	8.4	9.0	9.7	10.8
Moyen–Orient	1.1	x0.9	x1.8	1.3	1.3	1.1	1.2	1.1	1.0	x1.3
Europe	75.1	79.9	78.8	78.8	76.9	77.7	75.5	75.4	72.1	70.5
CEE	69.8	74.2	73.1	73.7	71.7	76.1	74.0	73.7	70.1	68.8
AELE	4.4	5.3	5.5	5.1	5.0	1.4	1.4	1.3	1.5	1.4
Océanie	2.8	2.7	2.6	2.5	2.9	2.3	2.2	1.7	1.7	2.1
Germany/Allemagne	10.8	13.1	13.9	13.0	12.6	13.9	13.6	13.1	12.0	11.5
France, Monac	13.2	12.6	11.5	11.4	11.2	12.1	11.4	11.6	10.6	10.3
Italy/Italie	9.0	9.9	10.4	9.4	9.7	10.1	10.6	11.4	10.5	10.6
Netherlands/Pays–Bas	8.2	9.3	9.0	11.2	10.0	10.4	10.1	10.0	9.5	9.0
United Kingdom	9.9	8.8	8.9	8.9	8.4	8.8	8.8	9.0	8.6	8.0
USA/Etats–Unis d'Amer	7.8	4.8	3.6	3.4	4.8	6.1	7.2	7.4	8.7	8.4
Belgium–Luxembourg	8.3	9.2	8.9	8.1	8.0	8.5	8.3	7.6	7.5	7.4
Denmark/Danemark	5.6	5.8	5.0	3.9	3.9	4.1	4.1	4.1	4.0	3.8
Canada	3.5	3.2	3.1	3.0	2.9	3.0	3.0	3.0	3.4	3.5
Ireland/Irlande	0.9	0.9	0.7	3.6	3.4	3.6	2.8	2.9	2.9	3.4

TRADE BY COMMODITY IN THOUSAND U.S. DOLLARS – COMMERCE PAR PRODUIT EN MILLIERS DE DOLLARS E.U

COUNTRIES–PAYS	IMPORTS – IMPORTATIONS 1990	1991	1992	1993	1994	COUNTRIES–PAYS	EXPORTS – EXPORTATIONS 1990	1991	1992	1993	1994
Total	19164520	20389607	20638210	19297090	21566950	Totale	17645064	18717104	18856709	18086433	20412943
Africa	x439145	x439548	x581803	x432080	x630100	Afrique	379342	419166	x441346	x378906	x389035
Northern Africa	255539	275081	x363497	x200608	x376294	Afrique du Nord	250434	315355	297383	251026	237562
Americas	x3263543	x2907375	x2903913	x3344992	x3686149	Amériques	3397020	3328223	3428102	3886790	4518460
LAIA	621846	423993	470136	529464	744887	ALAI	1386970	1304368	1359978	1663291	1878709
CACM	29027	23199	33584	29729	38347	MCAC	67840	71841	79214	x83903	x117100
Asia	2911500	x2981053	3318041	x3545423	x4204325	Asie	3271708	3451379	3742449	3297426	3571519
Middle East	x707246	x625778	x621540	x630213	x648210	Moyen–Orient	856967	x944146	x900692	x716889	x732398
Europe	12210979	13549830	13532841	11617251	12673903	Europe	9504858	10531612	10274222	9690032	10950797
EEC	11640142	13016128	12967544	11055093	12042724	CEE	9439741	10466721	10192038	9629673	10877289
EFTA	459630	483772	481147	437134	507755	AELE	8315	8387	5701	4818	4904
Oceania	x125143	x117467	x120204	x140911	x132984	Océanie	299257	x318339	374436	x394699	x505028
Germany/Allemagne	3517079	4108014	4201484	3349426	3499745	Netherlands/Pays–Bas	3277428	3632874	3587583	3211543	3840252
United Kingdom	1814033	1833466	1758386	1545832	1752654	Spain/Espagne	1139628	1431830	1608531	1737183	1947310
France, Monac	1650307	1712366	1665847	1428635	1596829	USA/Etats–Unis d'Amer	1488498	1508012	1523003	1660139	1872280
Netherlands/Pays–Bas	1314050	1479751	1601644	1476381	1490425	Italy/Italie	1405971	1441762	1298318	1332202	1394988
USA/Etats–Unis d'Amer	1575651	1438001	1341521	1692309	1861513	France, Monac	1343083	1449281	1282709	1190521	1149151
Japan/Japon	1118758	1261207	1371766	1587931	2015514	Belgium–Luxembourg	964621	1089825	1084633	1041402	1246640
Italy/Italie	771809	943084	874807	746231	848558	Mexico/Mexique	1009748	897875	929975	1250985	1340959
Canada	771460	782963	805126	874180	837128	China/Chine	723096	883440	960229	1001316	1361670
Belgium–Luxembourg	793972	842376	815374	718964	813217	Thailand/Thaïlande	900329	885549	1058289	799415	611617
Spain/Espagne	532071	681054	695881	601617	712164	Turkey/Turquie	521204	559823	463974	444748	452688
Switz.Liecht	371915	393247	376844	350050	398505	Germany/Allemagne	398436	515556	454205	365435	425262
Sweden/Suède	296836	328695	325559	276730	306688	Canada	395592	390647	430084	440919	599318
Hong Kong	214038	233436	281531	272398	300298	United Kingdom	223464	257795	288528	201773	275067
Austria/Autriche	225872	254896	243632	235184	245563	Australia/Australie	169616	185313	226936	248585	296301
Portugal	216507	264091	236705	182109	196917	Greece/Grèce	280995	235812	220113	197833	211706
Brazil/Brésil	217103	203693	178138	206537	347991	Poland/Pologne	118426	254535	226773	144707	164790
Singapore/Singapour	126742	178102	179702	202392	229584	Argentina/Argentine	177998	201820	172594	187102	262618
Denmark/Danemark	151495	168517	168564	160284	172748	Morocco/Maroc	132554	172317	148451	127305	136415
Ireland/Irlande	147972	158887	169909	145148	167703	Indonesia/Indonésie	164462	134658	147476	140241	111372
Saudi Arabia	150841	150816	153424	x150925	x149211	Hungary/Hongrie	x189401	x137814	x173039	x109343	x107567
India/Inde	299221	122108	133677	190744	199928	Denmark/Danemark	169711	165170	118522	114605	104334
Malaysia/Malaisie	119521	132479	145468	167926	179129	Chile/Chili	139159	130263	133660	125082	152359
Greece/Grèce	96915	131939	101481	89658	120021	New Zealand	119109	118795	137631	132511	188738
Finland/Finlande	111223	108992	108270	98892	119491	Portugal	106877	118733	128590	115180	132299
Egypt/Egypte	66479	75508	156062	66735	93432	Syrian Arab Republic	121843	x164083	133788	x37752	x43672
Korea, Republic of	80153	82824	106231	105764	149383	Hong Kong	70256	78850	116613	97460	116489
Mexico/Mexique	300080	87058	100657	97067	162980	Myanmar	x70878	81283	x108717	x93581	x125648
Lebanon/Liban	x103185	x123121	x75420	x77209	x136107	India/Inde	77332	90047	83232	95272	118016
Algeria/Algérie	135940	133767	103722	37326	133534	Egypt/Egypte	62500	87154	91364	87620	75544
United Arab Emirates	151815	77555	86797	x98992	x109816	Israel/Israël	115448	98240	72529	82560	85501
Former USSR/Anc. URSS	87957	x261952				Czechoslovakia		x110376	x116430		
Norway,SVD,JM	79870	82584	96494	79303	100528	Ireland/Irlande	73677	66311	67284	72758	74936
Cuba	x114619	x81321	x93148	x67407	x52857	Korea, Republic of	60079	69281	93201	37619	36224
Venezuela	42843	66842	81270	91820	80795	Bulgaria/Bulgarie	x392984	x117863	58333	20759	46094
Kuwait/Koweït	61309	26851	106228	97604	105587	Jordan/Jordanie	56798	64304	58720	69026	63205
Russian Federation			x158283	x70036	x193698	Cyprus/Chypre	75322	71928	57885	50330	57704
Australia/Australie	74213	63077	67142	84154	80233	Singapore/Singapour	44152	52712	47307	60422	93026
Pakistan	34643	52244	79554	82573	58704	Iran (Islamic Rp. of)		x22296	x106233	x26043	x35000
Indonesia/Indonésie	43953	48977	53496	60100	102166	Korea Dem People's Rp	x93318	x48639	x38913	x36791	x69159
Poland/Pologne	1865	41786	47450	65901	64916	Guatemala	38518	34846	37571	40606	43524
Sri Lanka	29811	53713	49315	43880	66571	Peru/Pérou	16701	19272	57442	35284	48647
Thailand/Thaïlande	26682	38283	49110	48717	64809	Costa Rica	24708	29839	33941	x33894	x53361
Libyan Arab Jamahiriya	6704	16814	x72288	x32608	x56270	Czech Republic				91234	91165
Oman	35581	39863	35099	34698	34123	Malaysia/Malaisie	29102	16864	25131	43541	37644
Colombia/Colombie	34385	30512	47219	29460	58736	Saudi Arabia	5310	33193	39085	x11539	x6846
Iraq	x62729	x40529	x25197	x36940	x13439	Sudan/Soudan	x23190	x21729	x36498	x24364	x12703
China/Chine	47842	29810	42996	27050	18481	So. Africa Customs Un	33889	29091	26491	25715	
So. Africa Customs Un	10116	9027	57124	33346	35674	Kenya	31056	27780	27885	25512	x72884
Romania/Roumanie	28214	13796	69118	11767	9775	Austria/Autriche	25227	30652	25292	22259	x27383
Turkey/Turquie	35858	21946	27942	42614	12608	Colombia/Colombie	16710	22323	30801	24071	29065

(VALUE AS % OF TOTAL)(VALEUR EN % DU TOTAL)

	1985	1986	1987	1988	1989	1990	1991	1992	1993	1994		1985	1986	1987	1988	1989	1990	1991	1992	1993	1994
Africa	2.5	x3.3	x2.1	x2.4	x2.4	x2.3	x2.1	x2.8	x2.3	x3.0	Afrique	2.8	x3.1	2.7	2.4	x2.3	2.2	2.3	x2.3	x2.1	x1.9
Northern Africa	1.7	2.3	1.2	1.1	1.3	1.3	1.3	x1.8	x1.0	x1.7	Afrique du Nord	1.9	1.9	1.6	1.5	1.3	1.4	1.7	1.6	1.4	1.2
Americas	18.1	x17.3	x13.5	x12.1	16.2	x17.0	x14.3	x14.1	x17.3	x17.1	Amériques	21.5	20.1	14.9	14.2	15.3	19.3	17.7	18.2	21.5	22.1
LAIA	2.7	2.8	1.5	1.3	2.0	3.2	2.1	2.3	2.7	3.5	ALAI	8.6	8.8	5.7	5.4	5.4	7.9	7.0	7.2	9.2	9.2
CACM	0.4	0.2	x0.2	0.2	0.2	0.2	0.1	0.2	0.2	0.2	MCAC	1.3	0.4	0.3	0.3	0.3	0.4	0.4	0.4	x0.5	x0.6
Asia	16.4	15.6	x14.5	16.9	x16.3	15.2	x14.6	16.1	x18.3	x19.5	Asie	20.4	20.8	21.7	21.9	20.1	18.5	18.5	19.8	18.2	17.5
Middle East	3.6	x4.0	x3.5	x3.8	x3.5	x3.7	x3.1	x3.0	x3.3	x3.0	Moyen–Orient	5.1	6.0	x4.4	4.7	5.1	4.9	x5.0	x4.8	x4.0	x3.6
Europe	60.8	61.1	67.1	66.1	63.1	63.7	66.5	65.6	60.2	58.8	Europe	51.7	52.7	53.6	54.3	55.5	53.9	56.3	54.5	53.6	53.6
EEC	55.6	55.7	61.0	60.1	57.4	60.7	63.8	62.8	57.3	55.8	CEE	50.5	51.6	52.5	53.2	54.5	53.5	55.9	54.0	53.2	53.3
EFTA	5.1	5.3	6.0	5.7	5.4	2.4	2.4	2.3	2.3	2.4	AELE	0.5	0.5	0.5	0.4	0.4	0.0	0.0	0.0	0.0	0.0
Oceania	0.4	x0.5	x0.4	0.6	x0.6	x0.7	x0.6	x0.6	x0.7	x0.6	Océanie	1.6	x1.7	x1.8	2.0	1.9	1.7	x1.7	2.0	x2.2	x2.5
Germany/Allemagne	17.6	17.7	19.0	18.5	17.1	18.4	20.1	20.4	17.4	16.2	Netherlands/Pays–Bas	18.9	20.2	20.6	18.1	18.0	18.6	19.4	19.0	17.8	18.8
United Kingdom	8.3	8.1	8.4	9.3	9.5	9.5	9.0	8.5	8.0	8.1	Spain/Espagne	6.5	6.3	7.4	7.6	7.3	6.5	7.6	8.5	9.6	9.5
France, Monac	8.2	8.3	9.3	8.5	8.2	8.6	8.4	8.1	7.4	7.4	USA/Etats–Unis d'Amer	8.0	7.5	6.0	5.9	6.8	8.4	8.1	8.1	9.2	9.2
Netherlands/Pays–Bas	8.4	8.0	7.9	7.3	6.0	6.9	7.3	7.8	7.7	6.9	Italy/Italie	5.5	5.4	5.4	8.9	8.9	8.0	7.7	6.9	7.4	6.8
USA/Etats–Unis d'Amer	8.8	8.1	6.1	5.3	8.1	8.2	7.1	6.5	8.8	8.6	France, Monac	7.3	6.9	7.1	7.1	6.9	7.6	7.7	6.8	6.6	5.6
Japan/Japon	5.6	5.2	5.3	6.4	6.8	5.8	6.2	6.6	8.2	9.3	Belgium–Luxembourg	4.6	5.1	5.1	4.6	5.1	5.5	5.8	5.8	5.8	6.1
Italy/Italie	3.8	3.1	3.7	3.8	4.2	4.0	4.6	4.2	3.9	3.9	Mexico/Mexique	5.8	6.5	4.4	4.3	3.8	5.7	4.8	4.9	6.9	6.6
Canada	5.0	4.1	3.9	4.1	4.5	4.0	3.8	3.9	4.5	3.9	China/Chine	1.4	1.1	3.7	4.4	4.2	4.1	4.7	5.1	5.5	6.7
Belgium–Luxembourg	3.5	3.6	3.9	4.1	3.9	4.1	4.1	4.0	3.7	3.8	Thailand/Thaïlande	8.4	8.0	6.9	6.3	6.6	5.1	4.7	5.6	4.4	3.0
Spain/Espagne	0.8	1.3	2.0	2.2	2.4	2.8	3.3	3.4	3.1	3.3	Turkey/Turquie	3.8	4.2	2.8	3.3	3.2	3.0	3.0	2.5	2.5	2.2

TRADE BY COMMODITY IN THOUSAND U.S. DOLLARS – COMMERCE PAR PRODUIT EN MILLIERS DE DOLLARS E.U

COUNTRIES–PAYS	IMPORTS – IMPORTATIONS				
	1990	1991	1992	1993	1994
Total	5099865	5234496	5475544	4927668	5402986
Africa	161957	139693	x58151	x43632	x46511
Northern Africa	118386	109132	x18350	x6475	x8873
Americas	x856037	883852	x973831	x914025	x1064061
LAIA	43819	49570	89152	92873	139531
CACM	8484	7753	11884	x8855	x9977
Asia	988640	1136122	1181627	1207267	1308045
Middle East	134674	157930	123133	x104310	x100579
Europe	2664149	2922174	3136927	2615724	2828636
EEC	2512672	2789659	2986084	2462727	2677359
EFTA	106755	112141	117872	114801	119144
Oceania	x86874	x92834	x90347	x91230	x92536
Germany/Allemagne	1003564	1163592	1206663	869015	936897
USA/Etats–Unis d'Amer	618179	627779	659943	604243	698112
Japan/Japon	346070	428329	513500	599861	691797
France,Monac	392732	402510	415688	375293	421419
Hong Kong	285785	322276	287737	257901	269023
United Kingdom	233167	262922	303843	298309	279045
Italy/Italie	269419	302577	302697	234819	249051
Netherlands/Pays–Bas	187024	202386	236684	246470	235409
Belgium–Luxembourg	169126	165795	188020	141228	208296
Canada	124337	148766	156939	151299	163181
Singapore/Singapour	100263	105893	112907	100466	78791
Switz.Liecht	82153	85028	86721	83482	86269
Sweden/Suède	74636	82776	83711	72676	81394
Australia/Australie	65810	70340	68282	67720	69668
Spain/Espagne	43297	51589	73137	67732	93259
Saudi Arabia	66419	85590	45289	x37814	x36403
Denmark/Danemark	38169	41687	54035	47903	52971
Korea, Republic of	34585	42445	51170	48994	52765
Austria/Autriche	38790	41906	47434	41472	42580
Mexico/Mexique	21716	26745	45681	39709	62434
Israel/Israël	36603	28706	35250	31205	26885
United Arab Emirates	26059	29968	33819	x24343	x21050
Norway,SVD,JM	21260	23272	27052	27801	29260
Ireland/Irlande	24736	25201	27004	23856	23502
Libyan Arab Jamahiriya	73760	59368	x3813	x2791	x5006
Malaysia/Malaisie	15757	16352	19696	24030	32620
Argentina/Argentine	1638	4885	21674	21773	20621
Greece/Grèce	9921	14934	16484	16740	21123
Finland/Finlande	16095	16860	14933	13846	14904
Russian Federation			x14167	x30870	x68354
Portugal	11997	14925	15750	13369	17510
Algeria/Algérie	37001	42019	210	27	97
Former USSR/Anc. URSS	268567	x39750			
Poland/Pologne	1592	1313	12735	19977	19479
Oman	7163	7621	10158	13170	13765
New Zealand	7348	8505	8763	9928	12872
Reunion/Réunion	7722	6886	9420	9608	9650
Croatia/Croatie			11112	13991	x9820
Bahamas	3666	4313	x8516	x10875	x7047
So. Africa Customs Un	6004	5587	9293	8751	9543
Romania/Roumanie	11365	8994	9143	5186	5054
Martinique	6782	7114	7887	7684	7608
Egypt/Egypte	6671	7236	12946	1980	848
Thailand/Thaïlande	5940	7926	7080	6667	8435
Indonesia/Indonésie	4150	5668	6239	9541	17359
Venezuela	2529	5818	6304	7769	4785
Bahrain/Bahreïn	x5861	x8281	x5361	x6049	x3878
Brazil/Brésil	13545	5715	4722	8958	32151
Hungary/Hongrie	x4981	5014	x4957	x8939	x6721
Kuwait/ Koweït	3160	3167	7916	7237	7984

COUNTRIES–PAYS	EXPORTS – EXPORTATIONS				
	1990	1991	1992	1993	1994
Totale	4636242	4977453	5228228	5003574	5674875
Afrique	148746	164378	152690	126003	139150
Afrique du Nord	132361	142581	130561	100360	121705
Amériques	440930	525022	566500	677884	803516
ALAI	152886	175331	174925	238180	258219
MCAC	10623	11693	14070	x6345	x7120
Asie	1364549	1530280	1494958	1468690	1790668
Moyen–Orient	122962	158965	157660	157966	212682
Europe	2439085	2583772	2787065	2575581	2780149
CEE	2381004	2530193	2726562	2529571	2727347
AELE	23789	20729	28988	24594	28353
Océanie	20530	x23552	x26022	x22089	x23127
Netherlands/Pays–Bas	687467	740310	785976	801039	823134
China/Chine	591717	612794	603714	633846	848677
France,Monac	386678	447279	503510	454868	451172
Spain/Espagne	499347	475488	511411	417474	489263
USA/Etats–Unis d'Amer	250257	312566	354474	404866	494341
Belgium–Luxembourg	242721	242062	260631	252941	296436
Germany/Allemagne	227658	256212	256123	209779	228759
Hong Kong	229213	262791	228815	209749	193098
Thailand/Thaïlande	158823	215212	201054	183545	221832
Turkey/Turquie	104796	129458	136903	134369	187011
Greece/Grèce	133718	127300	147386	120921	124734
Italy/Italie	89287	110617	127555	139843	159197
Morocco/Maroc	119261	123790	111386	82853	99917
Hungary/Hongrie	x75091	x81875	x107662	x60879	x52630
Mexico/Mexique	41773	59002	73307	74362	75328
United Kingdom	60428	62962	65087	62422	72230
Japan/Japon	74697	64110	58533	49639	58021
Korea, Republic of	55958	54435	52371	57758	66050
Peru/Pérou	31448	52229	24004	66784	70753
Indonesia/Indonésie	34328	47260	48756	35760	41770
Argentina/Argentine	64054	42043	31750	45774	49681
Singapore/Singapour	30304	35617	39721	41070	39528
Denmark/Danemark	23788	32560	32102	31238	29317
Bulgaria/Bulgarie	x130818	x42527	x32350	x17186	x6431
Chile/Chili	11838	16004	36657	38972	43228
Poland/Pologne	6441	6016	47089	34063	63305
India/Inde	12845	21763	28557	23946	33533
Malaysia/Malaisie	17247	20160	22575	21960	20877
Canada	22749	21910	18597	23395	28469
Israel/Israël	19077	18430	20714	19121	20307
Switz.Liecht	19735	15838	19936	14886	17298
Ireland/Irlande	9948	15387	13762	17839	18004
New Zealand	13004	14176	15684	14241	14199
Egypt/Egypte	11310	12325	16550	14281	19095
Yugoslavia SFR	34202	x32663			
So. Africa Customs Un	10902	10509	11333	9172	
Portugal	9683	9125	10586	9942	20461
Kenya	3382	8136	6757	12372	x12049
Pakistan	9144	8260	10150	8300	8108
Australia/Australie	7315	8077	9341	7800	8784
Norway,SVD,JM	4054	4891	9051	9706	11055
Philippines	965	1365	8229	11520	9806
Syrian Arab Republic	6530	x9086	3208	x5057	x5258
Sri Lanka	1583	3086	5752	8356	6602
Czechoslovakia		x9432	x7523		
Costa Rica	5721	7029	8664	x1177	x1622
Slovenia/Slovénia			11166	5466	6064
Austria/Autriche	3690	4344	5378	4610	x5132
Yugoslavia/Yougoslavie			x13304	x958	x268
Croatia/Croatie			6146	7421	x4515

(VALUE AS % OF TOTAL)(VALEUR EN % DU TOTAL)

	1985	1986	1987	1988	1989	1990	1991	1992	1993	1994
Africa	3.5	x3.8	x2.7	3.0	4.3	3.2	2.7	x1.1	x0.9	x0.9
Northern Africa	2.8	2.1	1.2	2.2	3.4	2.3	2.1	x0.3	x0.1	x0.2
Americas	21.2	x17.6	x15.9	x17.9	x17.6	x16.8	16.9	x17.8	x18.5	x19.7
LAIA	0.5	0.3	0.3	0.3	0.6	0.9	0.9	1.6	1.9	2.6
CACM	0.3	0.1	0.1	0.1	0.2	0.2	0.1	0.2	x0.2	x0.2
Asia	16.9	17.0	x18.0	20.3	20.7	19.4	21.7	21.6	24.5	24.2
Middle East	3.3	x3.8	x3.8	x2.3	x3.3	2.6	3.0	2.2	x2.1	x1.9
Europe	46.9	49.6	51.0	43.8	47.7	52.2	55.8	57.3	53.1	52.4
EEC	42.0	44.6	45.8	39.1	42.2	49.3	53.3	54.5	50.0	49.6
EFTA	4.8	4.9	5.0	4.4	4.8	2.1	2.1	2.2	2.3	2.2
Oceania	1.8	x1.6	x1.3	x1.5	x1.8	x1.7	x1.8	x1.6	x1.9	x1.7
Germany/Allemagne	15.8	17.3	17.2	15.6	15.7	19.7	22.2	22.0	17.6	17.3
USA/Etats–Unis d'Amer	16.7	14.0	12.6	14.2	13.1	12.1	12.0	12.1	12.3	12.9
Japan/Japon	6.0	6.1	6.9	8.2	7.5	6.8	8.2	9.4	12.2	12.8
France,Monac	5.9	5.9	6.4	6.1	7.0	7.7	7.7	7.6	7.6	7.8
Hong Kong	3.9	3.8	4.0	5.4	6.0	5.6	6.2	5.3	5.2	5.0
United Kingdom	6.5	6.9	6.8	3.6	4.0	4.6	5.0	5.5	6.1	5.2
Italy/Italie	3.6	3.7	4.0	4.3	5.0	5.3	5.8	5.5	4.8	4.6
Netherlands/Pays–Bas	3.0	3.4	3.4	2.7	3.0	3.7	3.9	4.3	5.0	4.4
Belgium–Luxembourg	3.0	3.2	3.3	2.6	2.9	3.3	3.2	3.4	2.9	3.9
Canada	3.1	2.4	2.1	2.1	2.6	2.4	2.8	2.9	3.1	3.0

	1985	1986	1987	1988	1989	1990	1991	1992	1993	1994
Afrique	2.6	x2.5	x2.0	2.6	3.0	3.2	3.3	2.9	2.5	2.5
Afrique du Nord	2.2	2.0	1.7	2.3	2.6	2.9	2.9	2.5	2.0	2.1
Amériques	9.0	7.2	5.7	7.5	10.5	9.5	10.5	10.8	13.6	14.1
ALAI	2.7	2.5	2.4	3.2	4.8	3.3	3.5	3.3	4.8	4.6
MCAC	0.4	0.1	0.1	0.2	0.2	0.2	0.2	0.3	x0.1	x0.1
Asie	22.8	23.5	x32.9	x37.8	30.5	29.4	30.8	28.6	29.4	31.6
Moyen–Orient	2.5	3.1	6.7	5.5	x1.5	2.7	3.2	3.0	3.2	3.7
Europe	64.5	65.8	54.6	46.0	50.7	52.6	51.9	53.3	51.5	49.0
CEE	62.7	64.3	53.2	43.8	48.5	51.4	50.8	52.2	50.6	48.1
AELE	0.6	0.6	0.6	0.7	0.7	0.5	0.4	0.6	0.5	0.5
Océanie	0.3	x0.4	x0.3	0.4	x0.4	0.4	x0.4	x0.5	x0.4	x0.4
Netherlands/Pays–Bas	9.8	11.2	9.6	10.9	13.1	14.8	14.9	15.0	16.0	14.5
China/Chine	7.1	7.5	8.9	13.3	14.2	12.8	12.3	11.5	12.7	15.0
France,Monac	8.1	8.8	6.7	8.0	8.0	8.3	9.0	9.6	9.1	8.0
Spain/Espagne	12.2	11.2	9.3	10.3	11.4	10.8	9.6	9.8	8.3	8.6
USA/Etats–Unis d'Amer	3.9	3.5	2.5	3.5	4.8	5.4	6.3	6.8	8.1	8.7
Belgium–Luxembourg	3.9	4.9	4.1	4.6	4.8	5.2	4.9	5.0	5.1	5.2
Germany/Allemagne	3.1	3.9	3.5	4.4	4.8	4.9	5.1	4.9	4.2	4.0
Hong Kong	3.3	3.2	2.9	4.8	5.4	4.9	5.3	4.4	4.2	3.4
Thailand/Thaïlande	3.2	3.6	2.7	3.1	3.7	3.4	4.3	3.8	3.7	3.9
Turkey/Turquie	2.1	2.7	6.3	5.1	0.9	2.3	2.6	2.6	2.7	3.3

TRADE BY COMMODITY IN THOUSAND U.S. DOLLARS – COMMERCE PAR PRODUIT EN MILLIERS DE DOLLARS E.U

COUNTRIES–PAYS	IMPORTS – IMPORTATIONS 1990	1991	1992	1993	1994
Total	23708113	25553651	26288616	23838394	26881282
Africa	x96371	106781	x102080	x101372	x133587
Northern Africa	32953	48851	x49079	x39545	x71266
Americas	4232403	4570351	4676946	4794206	5170797
LAIA	335132	429831	453593	592652	860602
CACM	13008	15783	20961	x23623	x23745
Asia	3554017	4024564	4333081	x4446253	x4785743
Middle East	784701	x707567	x795953	x782739	x744983
Europe	14735539	16063450	16522575	13804264	16022183
EEC	13692596	15099354	15576154	12930452	15047339
EFTA	787136	826175	822846	759832	846469
Oceania	x189541	x202640	x209977	x199227	x212741
Germany/Allemagne	4240692	4981625	4951216	3899597	4558197
USA/Etats–Unis d'Amer	2650740	2781206	2940602	2887575	3043961
France,Monac	2374805	2558718	2546699	2125135	2374732
United Kingdom	2293801	2310958	2442663	2160112	2235829
Japan/Japon	1477117	1646113	1754384	1727377	1844164
Netherlands/Pays–Bas	1177736	1248295	1350568	1239994	1511270
Canada	1158234	1267038	1194888	1222549	1156851
Italy/Italie	842103	1076547	1217143	856978	1090099
Belgium–Luxembourg	728281	727328	752747	651444	825981
Hong Kong	544276	644779	700908	745210	812296
Switz.Liecht	573963	608149	590984	555604	626478
Austria/Autriche	466066	467681	490067	446299	477097
Sweden/Suède	471267	516054	484938	394245	452613
Spain/Espagne	346735	400528	510838	367604	513059
Singapore/Singapour	275436	324963	345936	358980	358447
Saudi Arabia	237202	261098	250821	x222731	x244334
Finland/Finlande	241745	238047	234203	203204	295023
Denmark/Danemark	203274	231668	226098	186116	225533
Norway,SVD,JM	199216	201467	216257	190043	205501
India/Inde	132292	149536	218096	223338	319936
Poland/Pologne	26749	230827	189534	168615	189786
Korea, Republic of	48436	249687	131044	111609	116880
Portugal	115440	142183	146610	201566	236060
Brazil/Brésil	173952	189869	119340	138517	223906
Mexico/Mexique	59002	84548	144502	207466	331481
Russian Federation			x165843	x265768	x506042
United Arab Emirates	267219	141126	146387	x133506	x119262
Ireland/Irlande	129051	136075	140006	124001	136781
Australia/Australie	98456	108501	109455	104228	115288
Malaysia/Malaisie	80545	80251	99312	118952	135163
Argentina/Argentine	32097	62441	77735	111529	121075
Hungary/Hongrie	x51310	85320	x89958	x68498	x58361
New Zealand	77063	76834	81916	81243	86626
Greece/Grèce	61599	63647	82359	74158	115065
Lebanon/Liban	x39036	x95689	x56520	x56933	x98755
Kuwait/ Koweït	69704	24707	82969	97904	109508
Czechoslovakia	141193	x93131	x107978		
Oman	55857	60005	68758	67976	62274
Israel/Israël	48479	47946	53239	52909	63884
Thailand/Thaïlande	32139	28426	45334	77970	97198
Czech Republic				142200	179946
Former USSR/Anc. URSS	558024	x129336			
Yugoslavia SFR	232682	x113403			
China/Chine	23649	26587	40439	44848	66020
Bahrain/Bahreïn	x33625	x35496	x32785	x43225	x29035
Indonesia/Indonésie	6577	16291	36703	57262	69631
Turkey/Turquie	16916	18964	34999	53502	29535
Romania/Roumanie	24344	35822	38199	31664	31505
Venezuela	18357	35205	32658	33865	31589
Pakistan	27660	26353	30445	31875	39550

COUNTRIES–PAYS	EXPORTS – EXPORTATIONS 1990	1991	1992	1993	1994
Totale	19059801	20980081	21819722	21110155	x24803201
Afrique	x1060079	x1190728	x1370947	x1420672	x1388855
Afrique du Nord	333785	367967	360936	326362	275235
Amériques	6358375	7254609	7906528	x7667952	x9258410
ALAI	2223781	2914991	3015466	2777474	x3595443
MCAC	693188	814209	1043241	x1018464	x1378587
Asie	3539422	3510505	3625723	x3655744	x4141035
Moyen–Orient	1740896	1540026	1568050	x1446596	x1700780
Europe	7161314	8028718	7991113	7483027	9063846
CEE	7142849	8008508	7969212	7465865	9042495
AELE	5623	4953	4779	5132	7147
Océanie	x703981	x681846	x707722	x675686	x686837
USA/Etats–Unis d'Amer	2835740	2945759	3097246	3181081	3549810
Spain/Espagne	2195039	2548153	2819439	2754282	3026734
Italy/Italie	1878506	2079757	1989355	1702206	2026296
France,Monac	1087904	1242003	1006639	940122	1189857
Turkey/Turquie	977364	876162	808098	897590	1079878
Netherlands/Pays–Bas	748137	834906	833204	849184	1166589
Chile/Chili	684436	720435	803009	734699	819615
Ecuador/Equateur	472905	721682	678959	560732	x1135706
Costa Rica	371799	466950	568743	x623553	x1085548
So. Africa Customs Un	392607	485812	562011	556057	545315
Greece/Grèce	444870	499905	488788	388772	447915
New Zealand	519855	466662	456205	411602	442025
Iran (Islamic Rp. of)	333000	477896	503498	x350781	x429948
Colombia/Colombie	327953	444417	423724	438619	501072
Mexico/Mexique	248257	451845	426012	415115	477038
India/Inde	284089	324868	345337	393537	459223
Belgium–Luxembourg	344596	266349	299541	419561	591549
Philippines	258189	301848	307813	370114	348103
Germany/Allemagne	272353	309402	291862	232579	287556
Argentina/Argentine	222987	283593	308278	237191	275728
China/Chine	258677	224256	268313	331614	396530
Honduras	203456	224365	329871	263334	145367
Brazil/Brésil	187371	211356	270341	273201	266697
Australia/Australie	178337	212479	248045	259854	239871
Israel/Israël	281582	282460	211308	216968	214842
Cote d'Ivoire	x213506	x196488	x228922	x268486	x266285
Morocco/Maroc	176961	217232	179797	170184	170998
Panama	92631	92825	222578	214956	212807
Hong Kong	108839	156019	173785	177287	204093
Korea, Republic of	118421	122989	127786	99359	147993
Guatemala	88026	93034	125228	118487	135004
Singapore/Singapour	81706	97360	89106	114854	142895
Martinique	118406	89514	114815	71832	63471
Malaysia/Malaisie	74430	75686	85415	106282	101314
Cameroon/Cameroun	26543	37070	x84645	x134357	x108111
United Kingdom	70543	86638	99102	60218	85821
Poland/Pologne	7568	67068	78190	91830	101254
Hungary/Hongrie	x66480	x102748	x81161	x48312	x50855
Canada	66133	76472	80309	67304	78607
Viet Nam	x56244	x65161	x77264	x53947	x62638
Tunisia/Tunisie	64320	67914	62614	62379	66719
Thailand/Thaïlande	58379	46892	67768	75686	110611
Saint Lucia/St. Lucie	74527	60760	x69650	x59664	x64675
Jamaica/Jamaïque	41461	46165	x63490	x63023	x73536
Sri Lanka	48913	52003	68018	46570	51911
Indonesia/Indonésie	21077	48331	53198	62156	92698
Cuba	x49977	x64736	x37443	x55064	x17749
Guadeloupe	41145	56733	58408	40449	39463
Japan/Japon	42127	54324	51883	42742	38321
Afghanistan	x47382	x31757	x50896	x63352	x14005

(VALUE AS % OF TOTAL)(VALEUR EN % DU TOTAL)

	1985	1986	1987	1988	1989	1990	1991	1992	1993	1994
Africa	0.5	x0.5	x0.4	x0.4	0.5	x0.4	0.4	x0.4	x0.5	x0.5
Northern Africa	0.3	0.1	0.1	0.1	0.2	0.1	0.2	x0.2	x0.2	x0.3
Americas	22.0	18.8	16.9	16.6	18.1	17.9	17.8	17.8	20.1	19.2
LAIA	1.1	1.2	1.0	1.0	1.4	1.4	1.7	1.7	2.5	3.2
CACM	0.0	0.1	0.1	0.0	0.1	0.1	0.1	0.1	x0.1	x0.1
Asia	16.3	16.1	x15.3	17.0	16.5	15.0	15.7	16.5	x18.7	x17.8
Middle East	4.3	x3.6	x3.1	3.8	x3.0	3.3	x2.8	x3.0	x3.3	x2.8
Europe	55.2	58.2	60.9	59.8	59.9	62.2	62.9	62.9	57.9	59.6
EEC	47.3	49.7	52.0	51.4	51.5	57.8	59.1	59.3	54.2	56.0
EFTA	7.4	8.1	8.4	7.9	7.7	3.3	3.2	3.1	3.2	3.1
Oceania	0.9	x0.9	x0.8	0.8	x0.9	x0.8	x0.8	x0.8	x0.9	x0.8
Germany/Allemagne	13.9	14.8	16.0	14.7	14.6	17.9	19.5	18.8	16.4	17.0
USA/Etats–Unis d'Amer	14.8	12.0	11.1	10.4	11.2	11.2	10.9	11.2	12.1	11.3
France,Monac	9.0	9.9	9.5	9.4	9.4	10.0	10.0	9.7	8.9	8.8
United Kingdom	8.7	8.8	8.6	8.9	9.2	9.7	9.0	9.3	9.1	8.3
Japan/Japon	6.5	7.3	6.7	7.3	7.8	6.2	6.4	6.7	7.2	6.9
Netherlands/Pays–Bas	4.1	4.3	4.2	4.5	4.3	5.0	4.9	5.1	5.2	5.6
Canada	5.7	5.1	4.6	4.8	5.1	4.9	5.0	4.5	5.1	4.3
Italy/Italie	3.0	2.6	3.4	3.9	3.4	3.6	4.2	4.6	3.6	4.1
Belgium–Luxembourg	2.6	2.7	2.9	2.7	3.2	3.1	2.8	2.9	2.7	3.1
Hong Kong	2.4	2.2	2.1	2.3	2.5	2.3	2.5	2.7	3.1	3.0

	1985	1986	1987	1988	1989	1990	1991	1992	1993	1994
Afrique	6.3	x7.0	x6.8	x6.1	x4.7	x5.6	x5.7	x6.3	x6.7	x5.6
Afrique du Nord	3.1	2.4	2.4	2.1	1.9	1.8	1.8	1.7	1.5	1.1
Amériques	36.5	33.3	31.1	32.1	33.5	33.3	34.6	36.3	x36.3	x37.3
ALAI	13.2	11.1	9.7	10.8	11.8	11.7	13.9	13.8	13.2	x14.5
MCAC	5.4	4.8	5.0	4.0	3.9	3.6	3.9	4.8	x4.8	x5.6
Asie	19.2	20.9	x20.4	20.2	19.0	18.6	16.7	16.6	x17.3	x16.7
Moyen–Orient	7.2	9.2	x8.4	8.6	8.4	9.1	7.3	7.2	x6.9	x6.9
Europe	34.3	35.2	35.5	35.5	37.6	37.6	38.3	36.6	35.4	36.5
CEE	33.8	34.8	35.2	35.2	37.3	37.5	38.2	36.5	35.4	36.5
AELE	0.1	0.2	0.1	0.2	0.2	0.0	0.0	0.0	0.0	0.0
Océanie	3.1	x3.3	x3.7	x4.0	x3.6	x3.7	x3.2	x3.2	x3.2	x2.7
USA/Etats–Unis d'Amer	14.7	12.2	11.8	13.5	14.0	14.9	14.0	14.2	15.1	14.3
Spain/Espagne	8.8	11.3	11.7	12.2	12.3	11.5	12.1	12.9	13.0	12.2
Italy/Italie	10.9	9.8	9.4	9.5	9.3	9.9	9.9	9.1	8.1	8.2
France,Monac	4.7	4.7	5.4	5.0	5.5	5.7	5.9	4.6	4.5	4.8
Turkey/Turquie	5.4	5.3	4.6	4.9	4.4	5.1	4.2	3.7	4.3	4.4
Netherlands/Pays–Bas	2.7	2.7	2.8	3.4	3.2	3.9	4.0	3.8	4.0	4.7
Chile/Chili	3.8	3.9	3.1	3.5	3.6	3.6	3.4	3.7	3.5	3.3
Ecuador/Equateur	2.3	2.1	1.8	1.9	2.4	2.5	3.4	3.1	2.7	x4.6
Costa Rica	2.2	1.9	1.8	1.9	2.2	2.0	2.2	2.6	x3.0	x4.4
So. Africa Customs Un	2.0	2.2	2.1	1.9	2.0	2.1	2.3	2.6	2.6	2.2

TRADE BY COMMODITY IN THOUSAND U.S. DOLLARS – COMMERCE PAR PRODUIT EN MILLIERS DE DOLLARS E.U

COUNTRIES–PAYS	IMPORTS – IMPORTATIONS 1990	1991	1992	1993	1994
Total	10083458	10222562	11202788	9660546	10722533
Africa	x44918	x46382	x66975	x61516	x70824
Northern Africa	7064	9092	x21338	x12524	x17802
Americas	2428118	2048564	2392115	x2126571	x2238041
LAIA	61685	91166	158476	196603	266684
CACM	10672	12602	18341	x23468	x25264
Asia	1325846	1530911	1721561	x1634202	x2005468
Middle East	x174584	186778	x162485	x148559	x139316
Europe	5757775	6334637	6791319	5601830	6099272
EEC	5470154	6066056	6477715	5326414	5798187
EFTA	223934	235774	254784	216445	245799
Oceania	x116041	x138536	x151567	x133900	x154489
Germany/Allemagne	1767714	2036609	2156295	1570030	1656956
USA/Etats–Unis d'Amer	1835146	1391975	1641453	1386746	1416472
France,Monac	883367	939944	1053572	895349	1037953
Japan/Japon	747785	848379	969992	931900	1223696
United Kingdom	913014	864880	951355	804846	764054
Netherlands/Pays–Bas	552146	643624	675262	729375	802066
Canada	423938	453042	478802	426513	438093
Belgium–Luxembourg	330915	364848	382678	322320	372834
Italy/Italie	252269	333805	309766	227861	240626
Sweden/Suède	177573	186135	212504	177193	213581
Austria/Autriche	157262	171953	170472	152310	193131
Switz.Liecht	147847	153124	163298	139879	154593
Spain/Espagne	116041	171451	165628	109809	139070
Korea, Republic of	95155	130706	166157	129732	174591
Hong Kong	99545	127256	152323	140830	149801
Singapore/Singapour	117512	132461	136592	140614	151621
Denmark/Danemark	99795	117194	119935	88221	89015
Finland/Finlande	89351	93335	99917	90273	125879
Australia/Australie	59391	86682	94884	78242	99023
Saudi Arabia	98059	116832	65386	x49541	x49039
Norway,SVD,JM	68630	74101	83161	69465	83699
Ireland/Irlande	60464	62783	77090	67536	66607
Russian Federation			x50721	x120337	x218082
Mexico/Mexique	32340	36924	64484	66206	104096
Greece/Grèce	46737	42633	58414	55023	48191
Israel/Israël	35357	47429	55266	48622	54982
Argentina/Argentine	3146	15399	41161	70115	62636
Portugal	23505	36862	44827	36267	48225
New Zealand	30417	31368	33331	35887	39679
Poland/Pologne	11110	38710	26106	23970	34231
Malaysia/Malaisie	17672	19893	27361	23192	30740
United Arab Emirates	21048	16015	18619	x33478	x25903
Hungary/Hongrie	x11320	21577	x18054	x17018	x20700
Kuwait/ Koweït	7050	7927	23225	16888	18662
China/Chine	7633	6801	12551	24014	15561
Brazil/Brésil	12312	13030	10576	17673	42655
Panama	12661	12847	13325	14204	15483
Croatia/Croatie			20346	19387	x15526
Former USSR/Anc. URSS	308612	x35718			
Slovenia/Slovénia			18594	16510	22271
Reunion/Réunion	9897	8844	13408	12105	13874
Czech Republic				34323	67525
Romania/Roumanie	6112	14372	11858	7634	10721
Bahamas	11583	12765	x10054	x10895	x7366
Philippines	7160	6850	9926	13626	19684
Chile/Chili	5820	8643	10267	9652	12433
Martinique	8446	9200	9299	9466	10481
Venezuela	1329	5591	12797	9480	5821
Oman	7933	7621	9530	10332	7991
Guadeloupe	9793	8455	9888	8623	11075

COUNTRIES–PAYS	EXPORTS – EXPORTATIONS 1990	1991	1992	1993	1994
Totale	8884243	9346575	10135315	9267521	10461756
Afrique	312080	357611	343947	334432	x361374
Afrique du Nord	82472	65056	35060	57503	58209
Amériques	2990367	2663115	3085819	2750746	3053362
ALAI	1981387	1462209	1729012	1370634	1562497
MCAC	32578	40688	46990	x49021	x71166
Asie	1589470	1842918	1967815	1779969	1978408
Moyen–Orient	229424	x302622	x328929	238867	346738
Europe	3465050	3859143	4114344	3825599	4351249
CEE	3290824	3668384	3959210	3685149	4121300
AELE	46638	51766	55512	55804	76650
Océanie	x125517	x160176	x176461	x149071	187942
USA/Etats–Unis d'Amer	830734	1019529	1149047	1154729	1222324
Brazil/Brésil	1543191	972189	1148491	923717	1070708
Germany/Allemagne	665411	718977	762507	690620	830269
Italy/Italie	595913	668160	717349	572638	614958
Netherlands/Pays–Bas	509793	543506	555546	688925	821467
Thailand/Thaïlande	402986	550619	583969	550293	545249
Spain/Espagne	356823	424309	451062	426701	446267
Greece/Grèce	294713	323925	395496	341757	307163
France,Monac	259275	294020	327166	298417	354818
Belgium–Luxembourg	242038	277323	311858	249935	279845
China/Chine	186032	225621	270974	249768	328938
Israel/Israël	355679	268834	256358	197929	195519
So. Africa Customs Un	179815	227951	246281	217338	215502
Poland/Pologne	141337	178777	247727	261865	316759
Philippines	155027	179925	175518	200120	192591
Turkey/Turquie	132971	183749	161332	194301	283764
Argentina/Argentine	154850	152858	229212	124420	111211
Chile/Chili	65375	120750	163805	143438	155545
United Kingdom	119326	126582	134264	119293	142017
Hungary/Hongrie	x134574	x141543	x140044	x94874	x105729
Australia/Australie	93022	117700	127260	108242	136496
Mexico/Mexique	164096	134836	100045	115904	162126
Austria/Autriche	106533	119482	105143	108826	x144435
Denmark/Danemark	74248	88183	98722	85555	84274
Canada	75175	78587	85787	108006	119940
Hong Kong	49931	72509	83668	78376	78929
Singapore/Singapour	64095	72276	72904	74135	93579
Iran (Islamic Rp. of)		x60104	x114907	x8290	x19609
Indonesia/Indonésie	28170	52509	55702	58111	58029
Switz.Liecht	42385	44438	48564	51120	68892
Sweden/Suède	34322	38414	50201	54654	37843
Malaysia/Malaisie	39952	47922	49457	43532	45336
Kenya	36744	49863	46979	43366	x69137
Yugoslavia SFR	123713	x135046			
New Zealand	29992	40720	45311	38620	48899
Morocco/Maroc	71106	55133	29253	26061	45154
Bulgaria/Bulgarie	x92211	x43429	x26143	x32637	63434
Costa Rica	18620	27147	33756	x36509	x59018
Colombia/Colombie	16347	41542	37976	17788	9667
India/Inde	25378	23733	30576	32853	38253
Korea, Republic of	39492	29760	25858	27456	28584
Czechoslovakia		x44973	x24248		
Ireland/Irlande	16065	23689	20348	16866	17152
Belize/Bélize	x24709	x17819	27673	14136	17614
Ecuador/Equateur	4827	7654	23602	21525	x22741
Cuba	x11331	x13665	x15074	x23851	x14905
Finland/Finlande	8616	12734	18324	21136	34595
Yugoslavia/Yougoslavie			x43800	x7310	x869
Former USSR/Anc. URSS	27939	x48988			
Russian Federation			x27952	x19152	x20128

(VALUE AS % OF TOTAL)(VALEUR EN % DU TOTAL)

	1985	1986	1987	1988	1989	1990	1991	1992	1993	1994
Africa	0.5	x0.6	x0.5	x0.5	x0.4	x0.5	x0.5	x0.6	x0.7	x0.7
Northern Africa	0.1	x0.1	0.1	0.1	0.1	0.1	0.1	x0.2	x0.1	x0.2
Americas	31.4	27.7	25.1	23.7	22.8	24.1	20.0	21.3	x22.0	x20.9
LAIA	0.8	0.4	0.4	0.4	0.5	0.6	0.9	1.4	2.0	2.5
CACM	0.2	0.1	0.1	0.1	0.1	0.1	0.1	0.2	x0.2	x0.2
Asia	11.7	11.4	x11.5	12.8	13.7	13.2	15.0	15.4	x16.9	x18.7
Middle East	3.3	x2.9	x2.5	2.0	x2.0	x1.7	1.8	x1.5	x1.5	x1.3
Europe	50.5	53.2	55.8	56.1	56.9	57.1	62.0	60.6	58.0	56.9
EEC	44.6	47.0	49.1	49.6	50.5	54.2	59.3	57.8	55.1	54.1
EFTA	5.8	6.0	6.6	6.4	6.2	2.2	2.3	2.3	2.2	2.3
Oceania	1.4	x1.2	x1.2	x1.4	x1.5	x1.2	x1.4	x1.3	x1.4	x1.4
Germany/Allemagne	13.7	15.3	15.6	15.2	14.8	17.5	19.9	19.2	16.3	15.5
USA/Etats–Unis d'Amer	23.2	21.2	18.9	17.8	16.7	18.2	13.6	14.7	14.4	13.2
France,Monac	6.0	6.6	6.8	7.1	8.1	8.8	9.2	9.4	9.3	9.7
Japan/Japon	4.8	5.1	5.5	6.6	7.7	7.4	8.3	8.7	9.6	11.4
United Kingdom	9.5	8.7	9.5	9.3	9.3	9.1	8.5	8.5	8.3	7.1
Netherlands/Pays–Bas	5.2	5.4	5.5	5.8	5.8	5.5	6.3	6.0	7.6	7.5
Canada	6.3	5.0	4.7	4.4	4.5	4.2	4.4	4.3	4.4	4.1
Belgium–Luxembourg	2.7	3.2	3.0	3.0	3.0	3.3	3.6	3.4	3.3	3.5
Italy/Italie	1.7	1.7	2.1	2.2	2.4	2.5	3.3	2.8	2.4	2.2
Sweden/Suède	1.6	1.6	1.7	1.7	1.6	1.8	1.8	1.9	1.8	2.0

	1985	1986	1987	1988	1989	1990	1991	1992	1993	1994
Afrique	4.8	x4.6	x3.9	3.7	x3.8	3.5	3.8	3.4	3.6	x3.5
Afrique du Nord	0.8	0.6	0.4	0.8	0.9	0.9	0.7	0.3	0.6	0.6
Amériques	32.3	29.2	27.7	30.9	30.2	33.7	28.4	30.5	29.7	29.2
ALAI	21.6	17.9	17.9	20.5	19.4	22.3	15.6	17.1	14.8	14.9
MCAC	0.4	0.4	0.3	0.2	0.3	0.4	0.4	0.5	x0.5	x0.7
Asie	18.9	16.9	19.3	20.3	19.6	17.9	19.8	19.4	19.2	18.9
Moyen–Orient	2.5	2.6	x2.8	3.0	2.9	2.6	x3.2	x3.2	2.6	3.3
Europe	39.2	43.8	41.5	38.2	39.7	39.0	41.3	40.6	41.3	41.6
CEE	35.5	39.7	37.4	34.7	36.1	37.0	39.2	39.1	39.8	39.4
AELE	2.1	2.6	2.2	1.9	2.1	0.5	0.6	0.5	0.6	0.7
Océanie	1.7	x1.9	x1.9	1.8	1.5	x1.4	x1.7	x1.7	x1.6	1.8
USA/Etats–Unis d'Amer	8.7	8.4	7.6	8.2	8.6	9.4	10.9	11.3	12.5	11.7
Brazil/Brésil	18.3	14.8	14.0	16.3	15.2	17.4	10.4	11.3	10.0	10.2
Germany/Allemagne	5.4	7.0	6.6	6.8	7.2	7.5	7.7	7.5	7.5	7.9
Italy/Italie	8.4	8.5	7.4	6.4	6.3	6.7	7.1	7.1	6.2	5.9
Netherlands/Pays–Bas	5.9	6.3	6.3	6.2	6.3	5.7	5.8	5.5	7.4	7.9
Thailand/Thaïlande	3.7	3.4	3.2	4.0	4.3	4.5	5.9	5.8	5.9	5.2
Spain/Espagne	4.2	3.9	4.1	3.7	3.7	4.0	4.5	4.5	4.6	4.3
Greece/Grèce	3.0	3.6	3.6	2.3	3.2	3.3	3.5	3.9	3.7	2.9
France,Monac	2.3	2.7	2.8	2.6	2.7	2.9	3.1	3.2	3.2	3.4
Belgium–Luxembourg	2.4	3.2	2.7	2.6	2.8	2.7	3.0	3.1	2.7	2.7

TRADE BY COMMODITY IN THOUSAND U.S. DOLLARS – COMMERCE PAR PRODUIT EN MILLIERS DE DOLLARS E.U

COUNTRIES–PAYS	IMPORTS – IMPORTATIONS 1990	1991	1992	1993	1994
Total	16932129	10299477	10617621	x9361830	11320203
Africa	1400925	x1095629	x1023918	x1002583	x1192247
Northern Africa	940652	702821	501884	533865	694807
Americas	2443714	1965654	x1781763	x1666836	x1941250
LAIA	734278	501765	314795	269833	495073
CACM	16451	8934	27596	16818	14552
Asia	x4081349	x2860735	x3199348	x2912644	x4134260
Middle East	x1541089	x763669	x868482	x747035	x920954
Europe	3506209	3897930	4289295	3519967	3805419
EEC	3279335	3716770	4047407	3299758	3551815
EFTA	164318	155769	161042	144382	162169
Oceania	x87180	x92626	x89187	x83128	x97858
United Kingdom	985273	1021643	1128785	1078609	1049328
USA/Etats-Unis d'Amer	1197823	1057077	1036472	958933	964885
Japan/Japon	703310	621480	632161	609298	643240
Germany/Allemagne	526682	586590	614818	496806	545350
Russian Federation			x877187	x744087	x132299
France,Monac	446138	460583	482234	458986	474351
Korea, Republic of	402846	340226	357151	362922	425304
Netherlands/Pays-Bas	280943	309075	328202	300408	291355
Canada	411247	308889	287852	325328	364663
Spain/Espagne	218971	254025	379823	287655	191475
Italy/Italie	259150	382874	317673	180473	264398
Iran (Islamic Rp. of)	x350375	x304041	x291918	x214787	x183118
Algeria/Algérie	314808	293097	177322	253291	297283
Belgium-Luxembourg	170937	252481	349618	106478	329683
Malaysia/Malaisie	228022	231079	225735	225530	266223
China/Chine	379974	257401	257507	114528	411279
Nigeria/Nigéria	120831	120039	x188466	x174201	x85185
Portugal	136424	197449	151714	90350	110092
Egypt/Egypte	354854	180687	132474	68596	129722
Mexico/Mexique	565054	274447	57894	47435	77095
Sri Lanka	131593	126380	117786	118313	182555
Israel/Israël	142502	118453	117869	124990	134770
Syrian Arab Republic	149923	x139471	105463	x100143	x104171
Indonesia/Indonésie	129477	117153	122158	81361	55984
Denmark/Danemark	81686	93922	113708	110578	86201
Saudi Arabia	64008	47337	88957	x131147	x176129
Romania/Roumanie	99865	79062	117810	66456	72742
United Arab Emirates	139639	86476	93996	x79044	x111833
Morocco/Maroc	81812	68972	95256	93783	127823
Singapore/Singapour	79722	71203	83210	88811	103311
Peru/Pérou	61188	69578	75253	93164	107836
Former USSR/Anc. URSS	5075634	x233430			
Switz.Liecht	74253	72530	78461	76130	82574
Yemen/Yémen	x94629	11169	x138115	x69941	x106817
Norway,SVD,JM	81867	76382	76055	62743	72603
Hong Kong	85969	76255	68210	65457	81143
Venezuela	23112	46101	88146	66621	81046
Ireland/Irlande	58133	60075	73771	64427	60644
Libyan Arab Jamahiriya	99972	107010	x29976	x54125	x44396
Tunisia/Tunisie	82902	48350	66023	59958	90266
New Zealand	53159	60163	49980	56246	69479
Lithuania/Lituanie			1894		1829
Jordan/Jordanie	82969	68358	44135	49921	83446
Mongolia/Mongolie	x20	x3107	x14055		x6038
Pakistan	159836	73401	49890	19421	6224
Austria/Autriche	35203	38637	33724	39699	53426
Kazakstan			x92913	x15624	x20647
Chile/Chili	50966	70410	29990	7326	26970
Bulgaria/Bulgarie	x160636	x24672	70760	6021	9889
Hungary/Hongrie	x17205	20032	x12099	x67317	x29621

COUNTRIES–PAYS	EXPORTS – EXPORTATIONS 1990	1991	1992	1993	1994
Totale	x12181502	x10430495	10670651	10468796	10142535
Afrique	1010640	846834	741098	661667	x774637
Afrique du Nord	x33107	x43893	x35552	x32290	x29697
Amériques	x5247663	x4046885	x3347958	x3212205	x3188554
ALAI	1018418	838507	943857	1133917	1409243
MCAC	226912	253625	282709	241454	260940
Asie	1621883	1342150	2241013	1844203	1837591
Moyen–Orient	83599	46123	152352	169235	187240
Europe	3817431	3694546	3925818	3657718	3900560
CEE	3790596	3663785	3889704	3635565	3885424
AELE	3091	3554	5159	4815	6166
Océanie	205740	274256	225596	913447	277124
France,Monac	1730357	1581647	1665337	1453936	1653196
Cuba	x3018099	x1965471	x1180775	x893702	x490708
Germany/Allemagne	687728	808794	797447	751370	770173
Thailand/Thaïlande	739639	638849	795675	507747	731550
Brazil/Brésil	534517	445781	602500	791896	996923
China/Chine	305009	185217	709746	674162	402665
Belgium–Luxembourg	330626	405162	425381	358237	437850
Mauritius/Maurice	358689	344386	370585	376895	322283
Netherlands/Pays–Bas	382374	260181	302324	357088	321934
USA/Etats–Unis d'Amer	352497	352197	287747	229347	291544
Australia/Australie	29032	29737	39885	794107	66380
United Kingdom	186639	176679	237279	239406	247383
Guatemala	130733	149556	169100	154271	169970
Dominican Republic	158222	157356	142974	158059	x205080
Fiji/Fidji	156016	197559	155962	94986	180793
Italy/Italie	114123	96825	131260	173422	111237
Canada	124141	125440	136075	135678	148657
So. Africa Customs Un	288023	228621	109286	56602	134512
Philippines	133795	135914	109955	128096	75704
Colombia/Colombie	142983	74231	124804	162580	162835
Reunion/Réunion	138603	100196	145479	113626	104186
Denmark/Danemark	150666	129625	118816	109162	108171
Guyana	81500	92800	134100	118079	x118033
Turkey/Turquie	4310	36804	141047	153734	171483
Korea, Republic of	128917	94214	100578	87037	110675
Argentina/Argentine	165404	100676	98864	71746	76484
Poland/Pologne	116953	103988	80095	86148	98171
Spain/Espagne	66282	87761	87988	88803	147220
India/Inde	20938	64343	138371	57992	21679
Jamaica/Jamaïque	74940	87004	x73865	x85123	x101396
Mexico/Mexique	48748	121718	55253	47668	53473
Malaysia/Malaisie	89678	72347	78530	56380	67331
Pakistan	43893	34263	58643	67019	135588
Ireland/Irlande	50270	46076	52650	38948	37308
Belize/Bélize	x48961	45400	40876	46283	45543
El Salvador	16913	23517	48440	39721	35894
Hungary/Hongrie	x44969	x31994	x55520	x22990	x19681
Indonesia/Indonésie	33793	24688	47974	35518	48474
Trinidad and Tobago	30537	32365	33013	27540	30709
Austria/Autriche	42037	24711	30856	33072	x25324
Guadeloupe	34772	28705	22884	33979	31984
Barbados/Barbade	33293	30905	30645	23707	x23633
Nicaragua	40021	34704	30226	19102	17854
Costa Rica	25422	21464	28118	x22419	x31171
Bolivia/Bolivie	31613	30747	25360	15727	45486
New Zealand	15725	20166	26644	24313	29925
Panama	36899	24632	21400	21959	17073
Malawi	28677	26286	25231	15571	x16776
Peru/Pérou	41237	33031	18448	14476	31005
Sudan/Soudan	x16875	x20807	x22179	x20293	x12917

(VALUE AS % OF TOTAL)(VALEUR EN % DU TOTAL)

	1985	1986	1987	1988	1989	1990	1991	1992	1993	1994
Africa	5.2	6.1	x5.9	6.4	7.5	8.3	x10.6	x9.7	x10.7	x10.5
Northern Africa	3.0	3.6	3.8	4.4	5.6	5.6	6.8	4.7	5.7	6.1
Americas	16.8	x12.3	x9.6	9.5	11.5	14.4	19.1	x16.8	x17.8	x17.1
LAIA	0.6	0.6	1.0	1.3	2.4	4.3	4.9	3.0	2.9	4.4
CACM	0.0	0.1	0.1	0.0	0.0	0.1	0.1	0.3	0.2	0.1
Asia	18.4	x18.3	x20.1	22.6	x22.5	x24.1	x27.8	x30.2	x31.1	x36.5
Middle East	2.1	x4.0	x5.9	x3.6	x4.2	x9.1	x7.4	x8.2	x8.0	x8.1
Europe	20.2	20.8	21.9	23.6	22.0	20.7	37.8	40.4	37.6	33.6
EEC	18.5	19.1	20.1	21.6	19.9	19.4	36.1	38.1	35.2	31.4
EFTA	1.5	1.6	1.6	1.6	1.6	1.0	1.5	1.5	1.5	1.4
Oceania	0.6	x0.4	x0.4	x0.5	x0.6	x0.5	x0.9	x0.8	x0.9	x0.9
United Kingdom	6.6	6.3	6.3	6.9	6.3	5.8	9.9	10.6	11.5	9.3
USA/Etats-Unis d'Amer	14.0	8.9	5.8	5.6	6.5	7.1	10.3	9.8	10.2	8.5
Japan/Japon	3.6	3.8	3.7	4.8	5.1	4.2	6.0	6.0	6.5	5.7
Germany/Allemagne	2.9	3.2	3.0	3.1	3.2	3.1	5.7	5.8	5.3	4.8
Russian Federation								x8.3	x7.9	x1.2
France,Monac	2.0	2.4	2.7	2.9	2.6	2.6	4.5	4.5	4.9	4.2
Korea, Republic of	1.8	1.7	1.7	2.2	2.7	2.4	3.3	3.4	3.9	3.8
Netherlands/Pays-Bas	1.6	1.7	1.9	1.8	1.8	1.7	3.0	3.1	3.2	2.6
Canada	1.8	1.9	1.6	2.0	1.9	2.4	3.0	2.7	3.5	3.2
Spain/Espagne	0.2	0.5	1.0	0.9	1.1	1.3	2.5	3.6	3.1	1.7

	1985	1986	1987	1988	1989	1990	1991	1992	1993	1994
Afrique	5.7	6.5	7.5	7.6	7.5	8.3	8.1	6.9	6.3	x7.6
Afrique du Nord	0.1	x0.3	x0.2	x0.3	0.1	x0.3	x0.4	x0.3	x0.3	x0.3
Amériques	65.7	60.8	51.2	52.2	47.6	x43.1	x38.8	x31.4	x30.7	x31.4
ALAI	6.3	6.3	5.8	7.0	5.9	8.4	8.0	8.8	10.8	13.9
MCAC	1.3	1.2	0.9	1.9	1.2	1.9	2.4	2.6	2.3	2.6
Asie	7.8	6.9	8.3	8.0	12.5	13.3	12.9	21.0	17.6	18.1
Moyen–Orient	0.8	x0.3	x0.8	0.4	x0.2	0.7	0.4	1.4	1.6	1.8
Europe	16.6	18.4	22.6	26.5	27.6	31.3	35.4	36.8	34.9	38.5
CEE	16.2	17.9	22.3	25.8	26.9	31.1	35.1	36.5	34.7	38.3
AELE	0.2	0.3	0.3	0.4	0.5	0.0	0.0	0.0	0.0	0.1
Océanie	3.0	5.7	6.1	1.8	1.8	1.7	2.7	2.1	8.7	2.7
France,Monac	6.0	6.0	6.6	13.3	14.4	14.2	15.2	15.6	13.9	16.3
Cuba	51.5	46.1	37.4	36.4	33.0	x24.8	x18.8	x11.1	x8.5	x4.8
Germany/Allemagne	2.9	3.7	4.0	3.8	4.1	5.6	7.8	7.5	7.2	7.6
Thailand/Thaïlande	2.8	3.0	3.4	3.6	6.5	6.1	6.1	7.5	4.9	7.2
Brazil/Brésil	4.3	4.1	3.4	3.4	2.8	4.4	4.3	5.6	7.6	9.8
China/Chine	0.7	1.1	1.4	0.9	1.9	2.5	1.8	6.7	6.4	4.0
Belgium–Luxembourg	1.9	2.5	3.3	1.1	1.9	2.7	3.9	4.0	3.4	4.3
Mauritius/Maurice	2.0	2.6	3.2	3.0	2.7	2.9	3.3	3.5	3.6	3.2
Netherlands/Pays–Bas	1.9	2.3	3.3	2.1	2.1	3.1	2.5	2.8	3.4	3.2
USA/Etats–Unis d'Amer	1.3	1.5	1.8	1.8	2.3	2.9	3.4	2.7	2.2	2.9

TRADE BY COMMODITY IN THOUSAND U.S. DOLLARS – COMMERCE PAR PRODUIT EN MILLIERS DE DOLLARS E.U

COUNTRIES–PAYS	IMPORTS – IMPORTATIONS 1990	1991	1992	1993	1994
Total	2093720	2293625	2609965	2575120	2883748
Africa	x31118	x33245	x39267	x44722	x46482
Northern Africa	1938	1129	x4858	x6757	x7226
Americas	406803	472507	594877	616304	705968
LAIA	41278	63854	91656	123321	162406
CACM	9176	12579	17950	x20038	x23500
Asia	281397	331989	389354	x415925	x510652
Middle East	x79682	x99753	x108708	x93264	x95157
Europe	1146314	1271365	1419352	1279974	1430368
EEC	1035716	1156917	1297153	1155845	1292022
EFTA	81108	94564	96111	93462	101415
Oceania	x57516	x54352	x62700	x66922	x70296
USA/Etats–Unis d'Amer	251525	283605	358935	335448	368799
Germany/Allemagne	234051	248271	261382	209187	265941
United Kingdom	113599	139759	168166	153897	151885
France,Monac	109390	130567	145686	149800	165519
Netherlands/Pays–Bas	108000	107875	153976	117918	135455
Hong Kong	65173	89487	116071	121912	158045
Italy/Italie	95968	109472	113356	89000	91950
Canada	77648	84732	97826	109169	117009
Belgium–Luxembourg	72669	84017	88014	83904	89755
Sweden/Suède	73878	75134	78852	79407	87534
Russian Federation			x62168	x148868	x279244
Spain/Espagne	42540	55449	65028	59584	72164
Poland/Pologne	44470	79332	60025	37295	41467
Ireland/Irlande	52425	56063	57581	52655	56053
Norway,SVD,JM	45389	54939	54271	51150	56930
Japan/Japon	46521	44412	48562	67027	67801
Austria/Autriche	49018	47964	51305	51559	50223
Mexico/Mexique	25418	32151	39526	58177	65729
Denmark/Danemark	29020	36493	40265	45216	50499
Switz.Liecht	32341	35650	38224	39327	41381
Australia/Australie	32537	28562	36124	36452	40951
Finland/Finlande	34831	35292	31584	28453	27474
United Arab Emirates	21393	27835	33880	x25342	x24679
Saudi Arabia	23064	31019	22693	x25981	x29268
Bulgaria/Bulgarie	x3756	x2101	3375	x66329	x15572
Singapore/Singapour	20656	21961	22468	25762	30086
Korea, Republic of	21318	19601	17929	23992	27132
Portugal	8700	15424	20090	19349	22115
Israel/Israël	15773	14791	18304	21532	30595
Greece/Grèce	11626	15138	21865	15918	25457
Argentina/Argentine	441	5407	23482	20462	17998
China/Chine	9501	12235	14928	18086	34881
New Zealand	12529	13349	12165	16564	19949
Romania/Roumanie	6391	14654	15173	6951	13737
Kuwait/Koweït	6526	5978	18709	11987	13913
Czechoslovakia	14255	x12775	x18148		
Ukraine			x3503	x18593	x18241
Malaysia/Malaisie	4937	5262	6530	10133	12901
Lebanon/Liban	x7908	x9798	x4952	x5623	x8317
Korea Dem People's Rp	x1693	x5278	x12594	x2087	x846
Venezuela	1055	2054	5911	11924	7382
Hungary/Hongrie	x4690	1903	x7350	x10491	x16756
Former USSR/Anc. URSS	93413	x19328			
Latvia/Lettonie			x1049	x17708	2005
Slovenia/Slovénia			7144	9140	12660
Slovakia				x15402	x9849
Reunion/Réunion	4508	4459	5006	5452	6506
Brazil/Brésil	5498	7943	3229	3503	7933
Chile/Chili	2672	3213	3764	7663	9634
Bahrain/Bahreïn	x3735	x5030	x3591	x5596	x2286

COUNTRIES–PAYS	EXPORTS – EXPORTATIONS 1990	1991	1992	1993	1994
Totale	2054082	2351527	2757983	2835797	3339703
Afrique	24411	32505	30429	35507	x12758
Afrique du Nord	3970	9209	6803	12716	10497
Amériques	254402	310006	435134	513785	587576
ALAI	86372	109553	151103	197272	241049
MCAC	11750	16103	20079	x21055	x25303
Asie	207453	285716	361214	404631	544540
Moyen–Orient	42621	54803	57925	73332	155300
Europe	1489040	1664374	1875723	1796433	2081699
CEE	1390257	1567752	1758904	1678071	1959836
AELE	86674	90412	97172	95284	102124
Océanie	21385	23172	26899	29169	36334
Germany/Allemagne	216197	262355	323611	288321	343027
Netherlands/Pays–Bas	231780	268607	306109	277459	275128
United Kingdom	241845	259066	288377	256363	322810
Belgium–Luxembourg	138601	158109	183857	205892	232341
USA/Etats–Unis d'Amer	112145	131643	174386	213055	229430
France,Monac	133593	138337	146589	147895	169669
Denmark/Danemark	113936	120124	131508	139958	170159
Spain/Espagne	109158	123071	128241	139065	218995
Switz.Liecht	77768	80069	85005	82894	88716
Italy/Italie	53544	67430	72050	63480	62151
Hong Kong	40104	54407	75439	68725	99972
Canada	35435	48209	69047	75356	85708
Brazil/Brésil	42305	46367	61769	83245	70722
Ireland/Irlande	57461	60678	65274	56798	56554
Korea, Republic of	24350	38915	54938	71258	82896
Sweden/Suède	49488	48613	47460	38449	42886
Japan/Japon	30384	37947	43247	44778	45595
Turkey/Turquie	20898	30269	33979	60498	143408
China/Chine	12506	17070	41532	50441	35263
Mexico/Mexique	8339	15517	30347	43499	67502
Austria/Autriche	8424	23481	28645	32056	x27687
Australia/Australie	12897	16643	21109	23894	27661
Thailand/Thaïlande	9368	14963	19920	22458	32843
Argentina/Argentine	16326	16380	18321	21697	35995
Poland/Pologne	40620	18006	14678	22235	47354
Chile/Chili	7701	14971	18784	19649	26957
Malaysia/Malaisie	13961	19451	15944	16882	24643
Indonesia/Indonésie	6506	16688	17949	17106	24148
Greece/Grèce	17309	17750	18281	13351	15225
Finland/Finlande	16771	16523	15993	16810	16587
So. Africa Customs Un	10904	15790	17761	13097	
Colombia/Colombie	6445	9858	14519	20358	23429
Norway,SVD,JM	8776	10142	11861	12136	12986
Philippines	8471	10491	11824	9645	9397
Guatemala	8526	10372	10383	10377	11581
Singapore/Singapour	8497	11170	6722	8883	14061
Slovenia/Slovénia			12927	12440	15670
Egypt/Egypte	1780	7105	5111	11636	7646
Czech Republic				22081	21025
Pakistan	1833	3444	7558	8878	7913
Hungary/Hongrie	x5270	x7126	x6972	x5711	x2852
Israel/Israël	3520	4082	5311	10155	9326
Saudi Arabia	4386	8309	7415	x1440	x2005
Guyana			x14690	x2286	
Czechoslovakia		x10018	x6553		
New Zealand	7844	5728	4921	4505	5961
Syrian Arab Republic	7583	6162	5575	x1845	x1775
El Salvador	1296	2112	4745	6697	8164
Costa Rica	1903	3455	4792	x3243	x5178
Zimbabwe	5246	3424	3598	4249	x1715

(VALUE AS % OF TOTAL)(VALEUR EN % DU TOTAL)

	1985	1986	1987	1988	1989	1990	1991	1992	1993	1994
Africa	0.9	x1.9	x1.4	x1.3	x1.1	x1.5	x1.5	x1.5	x1.8	x1.6
Northern Africa	0.0	0.1	0.0	0.1	x0.1	0.1	0.0	x0.2	x0.3	x0.3
Americas	27.4	23.4	x19.9	18.3	19.9	19.4	20.6	22.8	24.0	24.4
LAIA	0.6	0.4	0.5	0.6	1.4	2.0	2.8	3.5	4.8	5.6
CACM	0.6	0.4	0.6	0.7	0.6	0.4	0.5	0.7	x0.8	x0.8
Asia	13.4	x12.5	x11.7	x14.1	14.2	13.5	14.5	15.0	x16.1	x17.7
Middle East	6.4	x5.3	x4.3	4.4	x4.2	x3.8	x4.3	x4.2	x3.6	x3.3
Europe	52.7	55.5	59.8	58.1	56.1	54.8	55.4	54.4	49.7	49.6
EEC	42.9	44.6	48.1	46.8	44.9	49.5	50.4	49.7	44.9	44.8
EFTA	9.6	10.5	11.2	10.9	10.6	3.9	4.1	3.7	3.6	3.5
Oceania	1.7	x1.8	x2.0	x2.5	x2.6	x2.8	x2.3	x2.5	x2.6	x2.4
USA/Etats–Unis d'Amer	19.9	17.8	14.2	12.5	13.0	12.0	12.4	13.8	13.0	12.8
Germany/Allemagne	7.9	8.5	8.8	9.0	8.5	11.2	10.8	10.0	8.1	9.2
United Kingdom	5.7	5.6	5.7	5.6	5.5	5.4	6.1	6.4	6.0	5.3
France,Monac	5.5	6.1	6.3	5.6	4.9	5.2	5.7	5.6	5.8	5.7
Netherlands/Pays–Bas	4.5	4.6	5.1	4.9	4.6	5.2	4.7	5.9	4.6	4.7
Hong Kong	2.9	2.6	2.5	3.0	3.7	3.1	3.9	4.4	4.7	5.5
Italy/Italie	5.1	4.8	5.7	5.3	4.9	4.6	4.8	4.3	3.5	3.2
Canada	5.4	3.7	3.6	3.4	3.5	3.7	3.7	3.7	4.2	4.1
Belgium–Luxembourg	3.5	3.6	4.1	3.9	3.8	3.5	3.7	3.4	3.3	3.1
Sweden/Suède	2.8	2.9	3.1	3.1	3.2	3.5	3.3	3.0	3.1	3.0

	1985	1986	1987	1988	1989	1990	1991	1992	1993	1994
Afrique	1.3	x1.0	x1.6	x1.2	x0.8	1.2	1.4	1.1	1.3	x0.4
Afrique du Nord	0.0	0.1	0.1	0.1	0.2	0.2	0.4	0.2	0.4	0.3
Amériques	10.7	9.4	9.7	9.9	11.8	12.4	13.1	15.8	18.1	17.6
ALAI	3.8	4.0	4.2	4.3	5.3	4.2	4.7	5.5	7.0	7.2
MCAC	0.7	0.5	0.7	1.0	0.7	0.6	0.7	0.7	x0.7	x0.8
Asie	6.9	6.2	x7.4	9.1	10.0	10.1	12.2	13.1	14.2	16.3
Moyen–Orient	0.9	x0.8	x1.0	1.3	x1.4	2.1	2.3	2.1	2.6	4.7
Europe	78.2	80.6	77.2	75.5	74.8	72.5	70.8	68.0	63.3	62.3
CEE	69.3	70.1	67.3	65.9	65.5	67.7	66.7	63.8	59.2	58.7
AELE	8.1	9.7	9.3	8.9	8.5	4.2	3.8	3.5	3.4	3.1
Océanie	0.8	0.7	0.8	x1.0	1.2	1.0	1.0	0.9	1.0	1.1
Germany/Allemagne	10.6	11.0	9.6	9.5	10.1	10.5	11.2	11.7	10.2	10.3
Netherlands/Pays–Bas	11.0	11.8	11.2	11.9	11.7	11.3	11.4	11.1	9.8	8.2
United Kingdom	14.0	12.5	12.7	13.1	12.4	11.8	11.0	10.5	9.0	9.7
Belgium–Luxembourg	4.9	5.6	5.7	5.9	6.1	6.7	6.7	6.7	7.3	7.0
USA/Etats–Unis d'Amer	4.1	2.4	2.4	2.8	4.1	5.5	5.6	6.3	7.5	6.9
France,Monac	7.4	6.9	6.3	5.9	5.9	6.5	5.9	5.3	5.2	5.1
Denmark/Danemark	5.0	5.5	5.3	4.8	5.1	5.5	5.1	4.8	4.9	5.1
Spain/Espagne	4.1	4.2	4.8	4.6	4.7	5.3	5.2	4.6	4.9	6.6
Switz.Liecht	3.3	4.1	4.2	4.1	3.8	3.8	3.4	3.1	2.9	2.7
Italy/Italie	4.0	3.7	3.4	2.9	2.3	2.6	2.9	2.6	2.2	1.9

TRADE BY COMMODITY IN THOUSAND U.S. DOLLARS – COMMERCE PAR PRODUIT EN MILLIERS DE DOLLARS E.U

COUNTRIES–PAYS	IMPORTS – IMPORTATIONS 1990	1991	1992	1993	1994
Total	9646606	9365296	8437427	8478670	13592719
Africa	258919	253671	x153241	187404	482268
Northern Africa	141287	201685	106105	151767	406195
Americas	x2416758	2360113	2181706	1982854	3232794
LAIA	50233	62030	71739	78235	170565
CACM	247	641	2087	2733	x3601
Asia	992503	1110785	1018291	x1061687	x1780674
Middle East	x113902	x147355	x135119	x122139	x187374
Europe	5415205	5180554	4746473	4837583	7421220
EEC	5009982	4855561	4465077	4519702	7016969
EFTA	280714	263682	224458	202962	329718
Oceania	x110579	x112675	x109694	x113487	x174765
USA/Etats–Unis d'Amer	2070907	1998672	1848448	1634691	2571866
Germany/Allemagne	1492477	1540708	1399668	1365631	2037853
France,Monac	691223	695439	643819	639678	1051839
Japan/Japon	643318	694277	573261	624388	1064805
Italy/Italie	551068	469804	397567	467940	744587
Netherlands/Pays–Bas	421492	414881	410711	367499	493481
United Kingdom	396818	387071	367560	409771	602080
Spain/Espagne	298546	293867	265757	252107	441818
Belgium–Luxembourg	288164	240483	249788	281805	422229
Canada	265392	273802	237689	254824	459368
Sweden/Suède	227689	223016	182768	208328	357337
Austria/Autriche	204592	201950	190142	158826	237914
Switz.Liecht	180189	160906	141502	123988	179049
Finland/Finlande	138264	129961	105776	133266	238769
Poland/Pologne	31906	121303	111732	134881	255948
Russian Federation			x153589	x178770	x224847
Denmark/Danemark	104754	108341	101939	97391	168885
Algeria/Algérie	84691	144214	56914	105822	308163
Korea, Republic of	81099	89957	89082	93729	172097
Australia/Australie	90516	92204	90132	89541	138031
Norway,SVD,JM	93927	95279	76092	72239	142205
Singapore/Singapour	65541	58825	73846	82931	198635
Greece/Grèce	116105	70500	68248	54375	90736
Portugal	57020	57367	58490	64567	101762
Argentina/Argentine	37631	43554	45119	51130	95550
Saudi Arabia	43218	57202	41314	x33343	x45165
Hungary/Hongrie	x59910	48834	x42164	x34660	x42481
Israel/Israël	35118	37373	39368	40973	64621
Romania/Roumanie	44974	30474	37736	30701	23600
Yugoslavia/Yougoslavie			x20583	x63941	x13524
Hong Kong	24571	28547	29878	25210	32875
Czechoslovakia	64694	x51714	x25743		
Former USSR/Anc. URSS	121024	x76505			
Morocco/Maroc	27066	25400	27092	23657	38516
Bangladesh		18967	29877	23922	x605
Ireland/Irlande	21770	22172	22846	18519	27679
So. Africa Customs Un	17700	17412	16666	21557	45707
Turkey/Turquie	15192	16559	15135	22522	24878
Yugoslavia SFR	115729	x52043			
Bulgaria/Bulgarie	x51296	x18446	10351	x23018	x38606
Czech Republic				49459	81779
Syrian Arab Republic	2047	x14362	14490	x20327	x27839
Malaysia/Malaisie	14014	16163	16328	16589	29857
Lebanon/Liban	x13402	x20393	x12999	x9840	x38649
New Zealand	14223	13830	13082	16315	27661
Korea Dem People's Rp	x1277	x4377	x14593	x17174	x11950
Chile/Chili	8792	10551	12634	12812	25774
Ukraine			x5666	x26193	x8125
United Arab Emirates	9736	10474	10308	x9051	x12384
Croatia/Croatie			14946	13169	x9489

COUNTRIES–PAYS	EXPORTS – EXPORTATIONS 1990	1991	1992	1993	1994
Totale	8658559	8413770	7622320	7907308	x13854061
Afrique	x1349575	x1111401	x996817	x1075533	x1707604
Afrique du Nord	2337	1386	2856	x1284	7923
Amériques	4804384	4821157	4039180	4253833	7600184
ALAI	3423600	3571836	2921162	3030816	5761532
MCAC	975060	874111	771298	x821084	x1222309
Asie	811974	767614	x707507	x884697	x2020573
Moyen–Orient	x28992	x19643	x42258	x3668	x20881
Europe	1556405	1599698	1748056	1554411	2303902
CEE	1494647	1543154	1682475	1496091	2228462
AELE	60894	55393	57462	51274	72401
Océanie	124512	108386	x114191	111892	x192378
Brazil/Brésil	1282906	1507205	1135378	1306395	2585417
Colombia/Colombie	1472870	1398651	1324495	1209398	2102925
Germany/Allemagne	614134	589942	625499	605293	811412
Mexico/Mexique	376003	413922	295272	299710	436675
Indonesia/Indonésie	378979	375921	242037	351861	753634
Cote d'Ivoire	x275331	x278858	x274559	x271804	x294696
Guatemala	323712	286760	249249	267802	318556
France,Monac	256792	279669	291156	154950	368109
Costa Rica	245625	263799	202733	x164835	x366633
USA/Etats–Unis d'Amer	183326	174753	189597	234090	408449
Belgium–Luxembourg	172231	180986	198258	205986	293748
El Salvador	180021	131622	136241	223195	267767
Kenya	143555	159381	126329	194830	x313568
India/Inde	148432	135280	145602	174054	335496
Honduras	145112	152576	135801	128917	192119
Netherlands/Pays–Bas	121601	120763	133790	98368	149631
Ethiopia/Ethiopie	131508	116233	107310	129177	x197724
Italy/Italie	89478	99053	115464	128826	194940
Uganda/Ouganda	140384	117641	95372	106775	x334579
Cameroon/Cameroun	174643	86508	x120543	x106020	x121557
United Kingdom	87436	86491	93994	110092	155605
Ecuador/Equateur	129890	109953	71816	107368	x371568
Viet Nam	x76662	x61022	x86683	x136794	x401129
Papua New Guinea	108531	80082	70558	94523	x173154
Peru/Pérou	98577	113019	70724	60075	206791
Austria/Autriche	56650	82221	101889	50438	x15357
Singapore/Singapour	70362	74980	68105	82411	317650
Un. Rep. of Tanzania	82123	75536	x72925	x67661	x97156
Burundi	56022	74149	49665	43262	x57745
Cuba	x93033	x75508	x42155	x49396	x15271
Switz.Liecht	59550	54926	57005	50877	71210
Canada	48427	48239	54978	50210	72939
Spain/Espagne	44908	48121	53231	40937	82342
Thailand/Thaïlande	50699	29338	51652	51789	88527
Rwanda	80780	x61352	x32519	x32160	x27163
Nicaragua	80591	39354	47274	36335	77235
Madagascar	38896	28339	31783	40511	131883
Dominican Republic	46626	43534	26055	26419	x68271
Zaire/Zaïre	x95287	x44583	x21321	x25265	x24950
Sweden/Suède	18563	26160	30826	27267	49916
Venezuela	26065	13761	11591	34891	31539
Hong Kong	16636	21361	18551	15471	20549
Japan/Japon	10259	17157	14440	19604	15845
Denmark/Danemark	16351	13480	17987	17492	26693
Jamaica/Jamaïque	9530	12221	x14532	x21132	x17715
Australia/Australie	15445	18297	15591	12747	17896
Togo	17809	9050	x19114	x18050	x23358
American Samoa		x9689	x27451	x4131	
Zimbabwe	60033	22195	11713	4906	x11330
Panama	13958	13190	10904	11951	13588

(VALUE AS % OF TOTAL)(VALEUR EN % DU TOTAL)

	1985	1986	1987	1988	1989	1990	1991	1992	1993	1994
Africa	1.6	x1.7	3.1	1.7	x2.5	2.7	2.7	x1.8	2.3	3.5
Northern Africa	1.5	1.0	2.6	1.2	1.9	1.5	2.2	1.3	1.8	3.0
Americas	30.4	28.9	x25.2	22.4	23.5	x25.0	25.2	25.8	23.4	23.8
LAIA	0.6	0.9	0.6	0.6	0.5	0.5	0.7	0.9	0.9	1.3
CACM	0.0	0.0	x0.0	0.0	0.0	0.0	0.0	0.0	0.0	x0.0
Asia	8.6	9.5	x9.3	x10.3	x9.9	10.3	11.8	12.1	x12.5	x13.1
Middle East	0.8	x1.1	x1.3	x1.3	x1.2	x1.2	x1.6	x1.6	x1.4	x1.4
Europe	56.5	56.5	55.7	57.0	57.7	56.1	55.3	56.3	57.1	54.6
EEC	48.3	46.9	46.3	47.7	48.4	51.9	51.8	52.9	53.3	51.6
EFTA	7.9	8.2	7.9	7.8	8.1	2.9	2.8	2.7	2.4	2.4
Oceania	1.0	x1.0	x1.0	x1.1	x1.1	x1.2	x1.2	x1.3	x1.3	x1.3
USA/Etats–Unis d'Amer	27.0	25.4	21.8	19.0	20.3	21.5	21.3	21.9	19.3	18.9
Germany/Allemagne	12.9	13.5	13.3	14.3	14.9	15.5	16.5	16.6	16.1	15.0
France,Monac	7.7	6.9	6.9	6.9	6.9	7.2	7.4	7.6	7.5	7.7
Japan/Japon	5.8	6.1	6.0	6.5	7.0	6.7	7.4	6.8	7.4	7.8
Italy/Italie	6.6	5.3	5.6	5.1	5.3	5.7	5.0	4.7	5.5	5.5
Netherlands/Pays–Bas	3.9	3.8	3.8	4.0	3.7	4.4	4.4	4.9	4.3	3.6
United Kingdom	3.6	3.5	3.6	3.8	3.6	4.1	4.1	4.4	4.8	4.4
Spain/Espagne	2.8	3.1	2.7	2.8	2.8	3.1	3.1	3.1	3.0	3.3
Belgium–Luxembourg	3.2	2.8	2.8	2.8	2.8	3.0	2.6	3.0	3.3	3.1
Canada	2.7	2.5	2.5	2.6	2.5	2.8	2.9	2.8	3.0	3.4

	1985	1986	1987	1988	1989	1990	1991	1992	1993	1994
Afrique	15.1	x19.4	x17.9	17.3	x18.0	x15.6	x13.2	x13.1	x13.6	x11.1
Afrique du Nord	0.0	x0.0	x0.0	0.0	0.0	0.0	0.0	0.0	x0.0	0.1
Amériques	63.3	59.6	59.2	57.1	54.7	55.5	57.4	53.0	53.8	55.6
ALAI	48.4	42.6	41.9	41.3	41.1	39.5	42.5	38.3	38.3	42.2
MCAC	11.9	11.3	11.7	11.8	9.8	11.3	10.4	10.1	x10.4	x9.0
Asie	9.8	9.6	9.0	9.9	9.8	9.4	9.1	x9.3	x11.2	x14.8
Moyen–Orient	0.1	x0.1	x0.1	x0.1	0.2	x0.3	x0.2	x0.6	x0.0	x0.2
Europe	10.5	9.9	12.4	14.3	15.4	18.0	19.0	22.9	19.7	16.9
CEE	9.5	9.0	11.3	13.1	14.2	17.3	18.3	22.1	18.9	16.3
AELE	1.0	0.9	1.1	1.2	1.2	0.7	0.7	0.8	0.6	0.5
Océanie	1.2	1.4	1.4	1.3	1.7	1.5	1.3	x1.5	1.5	x1.4
Brazil/Brésil	23.6	14.4	19.1	19.4	16.9	14.8	17.9	14.9	16.5	18.9
Colombia/Colombie	16.0	18.8	14.9	14.8	14.9	17.0	16.6	17.4	15.3	15.4
Germany/Allemagne	4.2	4.4	5.3	5.8	6.3	7.1	7.0	8.2	7.7	5.9
Mexico/Mexique	4.8	5.3	4.6	4.2	5.5	4.3	4.9	3.9	3.8	3.2
Indonesia/Indonésie	5.0	5.0	4.7	4.8	4.6	4.4	4.5	3.2	4.4	5.5
Cote d'Ivoire	5.9	4.5	4.0	4.3	3.0	x3.2	x3.3	x3.6	x3.4	x2.2
Guatemala	3.5	3.2	2.7	3.7	2.3	3.7	3.4	3.3	3.4	2.3
France,Monac	1.2	1.1	1.4	2.2	2.5	3.0	3.3	3.8	2.0	2.7
Costa Rica	2.8	2.4	2.9	2.8	2.7	2.8	3.1	2.7	x2.1	x2.7
USA/Etats–Unis d'Amer	1.9	2.2	2.2	2.3	1.9	2.1	2.1	2.5	3.0	3.0

TRADE BY COMMODITY IN THOUSAND U.S. DOLLARS – COMMERCE PAR PRODUIT EN MILLIERS DE DOLLARS E.U

COUNTRIES–PAYS	IMPORTS – IMPORTATIONS 1990	1991	1992	1993	1994
Total	4231143	4088614	4137711	3934380	4687580
Africa	32594	34427	x105313	x93969	x134315
Northern Africa	9198	10157	18452	9320	14118
Americas	1006506	1056865	1010883	975726	962224
LAIA	44333	59345	60665	57342	90863
CACM	1348	2474	3508	x1703	x1793
Asia	350487	383095	384549	334016	382980
Middle East	26176	x32174	30759	x33519	x38866
Europe	2544631	2433986	2496277	2363722	2999043
EEC	2388045	2306918	2357587	2227002	2868253
EFTA	129635	119454	125462	111082	123277
Oceania	x70870	x58809	x54414	x60008	x76846
USA/Etats–Unis d'Amer	863804	902319	844865	813426	757339
Germany/Allemagne	652043	641913	638861	554759	700987
Netherlands/Pays–Bas	494829	481745	498937	504288	678160
United Kingdom	338557	314213	299145	296987	348900
France, Monac	294330	299691	296177	289120	383684
Belgium–Luxembourg	183682	178287	210394	220722	332062
Italy/Italie	144352	136718	149853	128635	151120
Japan/Japon	143963	147691	139900	120508	130191
Canada	93030	89303	97667	100020	109070
Switz.Liecht	107499	95811	101811	88632	100983
Singapore/Singapour	107024	93909	109844	77863	87229
Spain/Espagne	87460	79623	80881	70331	93405
Poland/Pologne	19629	46210	52944	63720	83406
Australia/Australie	55779	48630	45472	49334	63946
Austria/Autriche	49512	43071	44068	38747	48798
Sweden/Suède	41138	39479	38803	38985	42811
Argentina/Argentine	21983	37719	38101	36112	48443
China/Chine	12103	35652	33428	31872	34233
Ireland/Irlande	32951	33597	35505	18879	22086
Korea, Republic of	21039	24116	22760	24592	23592
Finland/Finlande	20611	17749	22683	26841	28144
Russian Federation			x30227	x35482	x25091
Norway, SVD, JM	20724	22038	21779	20844	20588
Greece/Grèce	27264	19307	20078	18805	18022
Turkey/Turquie	14572	17678	17486	20790	25352
So. Africa Customs Un	19815	20805	16433	15279	23068
Israel/Israël	12444	16483	17030	17468	21701
Nigeria/Nigéria		191	x23849	x25988	x22550
Cote d'Ivoire			x22159	x24134	x30808
Hungary/Hongrie	x19280	20313	x10913	x12442	x13550
Former USSR/Anc. URSS	118112	x41881			
Denmark/Danemark	13638	13590	13905	14255	14255
Togo	39	26	x20863	x15164	x40481
Philippines	15315	14989	9090	10607	15083
Chile/Chili	6605	7941	11852	10189	15244
New Zealand	14546	9609	8315	9804	12440
Yugoslavia/Yougoslavie			x5217	x19253	x4160
Romania/Roumanie	16375	10025	8335	5815	9395
Portugal	7678	7936	8296	5647	5820
Mexico/Mexique	11868	7680	6934	6656	12264
Thailand/Thaïlande	5997	7064	7400	5945	8789
Czech Republic				20215	22811
Korea Dem People's Rp	x4508	x3997	x6963	x4329	x3546
Egypt/Egypte	4704	5680	4797	4028	4669
Algeria/Algérie	873	1213	9561	1871	3786
Syrian Arab Republic	2098	x3960	3747	x4515	x2687
Saudi Arabia	3576	4858	2870	x3938	x4746
Croatia/Croatie			6036	4307	x322
Czechoslovakia	36295	x2825	x6959		
Bulgaria/Bulgarie	x15303	x150	7090	x1463	x1936

COUNTRIES–PAYS	EXPORTS – EXPORTATIONS 1990	1991	1992	1993	1994
Totale	x4186423	x3931052	x3953332	x3955319	x4808642
Afrique	x1808098	x1674016	x1633592	x1655740	x2006441
Afrique du Nord	308	x487	72	30	60
Amériques	710372	578052	520902	543638	x672936
ALAI	535341	433757	387171	406338	x476067
MCAC	8417	6363	7053	x5860	x7678
Asie	592514	636947	665604	671271	758211
Moyen–Orient	114	x51	285	222	x600
Europe	1019247	991212	1086906	1041765	1313698
CEE	1017852	988721	1083931	1037022	1306211
AELE	1353	2299	2264	4396	7344
Océanie	42567	45695	41559	38398	x53791
Cote d'Ivoire	x974540	x929517	x1073941	x959800	x1134481
Netherlands/Pays–Bas	575793	560051	622021	671692	819778
Ghana	472004	180096	300564	x374801	x527000
Brazil/Brésil	340777	271689	257366	265010	295215
Malaysia/Malaisie	269457	247167	234014	242667	250939
Germany/Allemagne	259560	237144	262958	161300	204182
Cameroon/Cameroun	168519	361272	x133604	x141052	x92563
Singapore/Singapour	150913	191498	222690	163751	172051
Indonesia/Indonésie	119859	143253	152802	204755	273166
Nigeria/Nigéria	141238	143824	x89012	x145078	x215516
Ecuador/Equateur	125278	107070	68741	78448	x127601
France, Monac	67440	79180	67180	83510	144132
USA/Etats–Unis d'Amer	88102	64212	72219	73283	93207
United Kingdom	40439	39480	44438	50834	49011
Dominican Republic	43717	43717	35224	33325	x69318
Papua New Guinea	34178	36746	35695	34889	x48375
Spain/Espagne	29764	32634	35724	28257	42178
China/Chine	20944	22970	28466	32934	27200
Italy/Italie	15129	15914	25489	19830	18599
Belgium–Luxembourg	27576	20284	20996	18932	24663
Mexico/Mexique	16982	6367	26767	24450	11760
Philippines	20289	18796	12844	13314	17831
Colombia/Colombie	23064	17318	10833	15100	16312
Venezuela	12300	16358	12022	11051	10303
Peru/Pérou	13048	13754	10511	11233	14050
Equatorial Guinea	6372	x19133	x5047	x6675	x4639
Sao Tome and Principe	x11151	x10911	x9769	x9465	x4866
Canada	6904	7456	6306	9208	9016
Togo	15185	10966	x8236	x2057	x8575
Japan/Japon	7040	6585	6724	7403	8347
Cuba	x13274	x9641	x1871	x3960	x1465
Thailand/Thaïlande	1724	4102	5063	4334	5662
Trinidad and Tobago	5573	5003	2704	3929	3348
Costa Rica	4526	3875	3974	x3569	x5969
Sierra Leone	6266	x6998	x1518	x2178	x4019
Solomon Isls	4366	4946	x3454	x2030	x2398
Jamaica/Jamaïque	4329	3225	x4169	x2993	x4025
Madagascar	2449	3972	2508	3595	5645
Switz.Liecht	1174	1999	1918	4298	7154
Grenada/Grenade	2621	3065	x1943	x2377	x3481
Poland/Pologne	6182	2333	2894	1470	2115
Honduras	3089	1973	2070	2041	1379
Hungary/Hongrie	x7389	x2529	x1604	x1218	x1025
Gabon	x2082	x1115	x2853	x998	x1103
Vanuatu	2114	2312	1457	x915	x2518
Guinea/Guinée	x1125	x1072	x1515	x1966	x3314
Un. Rep. of Tanzania		x233	x2018	x1747	x2370
Zaire/Zaïre	x2632	x1614	x1203	x1045	x721
Sweden/Suède	20	137	3232	324	217
Haiti/Haïti	x956	x981	x1457	x1059	x3896

(VALUE AS % OF TOTAL)(VALEUR EN % DU TOTAL)

	1985	1986	1987	1988	1989	1990	1991	1992	1993	1994
Africa	0.8	1.0	x1.0	x0.9	0.8	0.8	0.8	x2.5	x2.4	x2.9
Northern Africa	0.4	0.3	0.3	0.2	0.3	0.2	0.2	0.4	0.2	0.3
Americas	23.6	20.3	22.7	20.8	21.9	23.8	25.9	24.5	24.8	20.5
LAIA	1.0	1.0	0.8	0.7	0.7	1.0	1.5	1.5	1.5	1.9
CACM	0.1	0.0	0.0	0.0	0.0	0.0	0.1	0.1	x0.0	x0.0
Asia	6.3	7.6	7.7	9.6	8.9	8.3	9.4	9.3	8.5	8.1
Middle East	0.2	x0.4	x0.4	0.4	x0.5	0.6	x0.8	0.7	x0.9	x0.8
Europe	59.2	60.3	57.0	58.0	57.0	60.1	59.5	60.3	60.1	64.0
EEC	53.2	53.6	51.1	51.8	50.7	56.4	56.4	57.0	56.6	61.2
EFTA	5.1	5.7	5.4	5.5	5.5	3.1	2.9	3.0	2.8	2.6
Oceania	1.7	x1.7	x1.8	x2.0	x1.9	x1.7	x1.4	x1.3	x1.5	x1.6
USA/Etats–Unis d'Amer	20.5	17.2	19.5	17.9	18.8	20.4	22.1	20.4	20.7	16.2
Germany/Allemagne	14.2	13.9	13.1	13.0	13.2	15.4	15.7	15.4	14.1	15.0
Netherlands/Pays–Bas	12.3	11.4	10.9	11.3	10.3	11.7	11.8	12.1	12.8	14.5
United Kingdom	8.0	8.6	7.9	7.9	7.8	8.0	7.7	7.2	7.5	7.4
France, Monac	6.0	6.5	6.6	6.4	6.3	7.0	7.3	7.2	7.3	8.2
Belgium–Luxembourg	3.5	3.8	3.5	3.4	3.8	4.3	4.4	5.1	5.6	7.1
Italy/Italie	3.1	3.0	3.1	3.3	3.2	3.4	3.3	3.6	3.3	3.2
Japan/Japon	2.9	3.0	3.0	3.4	3.5	3.4	3.6	3.4	3.1	2.8
Canada	2.0	2.1	2.2	2.1	2.1	2.2	2.2	2.4	2.5	2.3
Switz.Liecht	2.3	2.5	2.4	2.4	2.5	2.5	2.3	2.5	2.3	2.2

	1985	1986	1987	1988	1989	1990	1991	1992	1993	1994
Afrique	36.8	x48.0	x42.8	40.8	46.8	x43.1	x42.6	x41.3	x41.9	x41.7
Afrique du Nord	0.0	0.0	x0.0	x0.0	0.0	0.0	x0.0	0.0	0.0	0.0
Amériques	27.1	19.0	20.1	19.3	14.8	17.0	14.7	13.2	13.8	x14.0
ALAI	24.1	15.9	16.0	16.0	11.6	12.8	11.0	9.8	10.3	x9.9
MCAC	0.3	0.3	0.3	0.2	0.2	0.2	0.2	0.2	x0.1	x0.2
Asie	9.9	9.2	12.9	15.8	13.5	14.2	16.2	16.8	17.0	15.8
Moyen–Orient	0.0	x0.0	x0.2	x0.0	0.0	0.0	x0.0	0.0	0.0	x0.0
Europe	24.6	22.4	22.1	22.2	23.1	24.3	25.2	27.5	26.3	27.3
CEE	24.5	22.3	22.0	22.1	23.1	24.3	25.2	27.4	26.2	27.2
AELE	0.0	0.1	0.0	0.1	0.1	0.0	0.1	0.1	0.1	0.2
Océanie	1.6	1.3	1.4	1.3	1.4	1.0	1.1	1.0	1.0	x1.1
Cote d'Ivoire	19.5	26.4	24.7	18.2	28.0	x23.3	x23.6	x27.2	x24.3	x23.6
Netherlands/Pays–Bas	13.7	12.5	12.5	12.3	11.8	13.8	14.2	15.7	17.0	17.0
Ghana	9.3	10.0	9.3	10.1	9.5	11.3	4.6	7.6	x9.5	x11.0
Brazil/Brésil	17.9	12.6	11.7	11.4	7.8	8.1	6.9	6.5	6.7	6.1
Malaysia/Malaisie	5.2	5.0	6.9	7.5	6.1	6.4	6.3	5.9	6.1	5.2
Germany/Allemagne	6.5	6.0	5.2	5.6	5.6	6.2	6.0	6.7	4.1	4.2
Cameroon/Cameroun		3.5	3.3	x3.1	4.6	4.0	9.2	x3.4	x3.6	x1.9
Singapore/Singapour	2.8	2.8	3.4	5.1	4.3	3.6	4.9	5.6	4.1	3.6
Indonesia/Indonésie	1.5	1.2	1.3	1.8	1.9	2.9	3.6	3.9	5.2	5.7
Nigeria/Nigéria	6.2	5.5	x3.3	7.5	3.4	3.4	3.7	x2.3	x3.7	x4.5

TRADE BY COMMODITY IN THOUSAND U.S. DOLLARS – COMMERCE PAR PRODUIT EN MILLIERS DE DOLLARS E.U

COUNTRIES–PAYS	IMPORTS – IMPORTATIONS 1990	1991	1992	1993	1994
Total	4291575	4475225	5104869	4803913	5611931
Africa	x30438	x26791	x39095	x40738	x46278
Northern Africa	6342	4716	x8262	x8213	x11077
Americas	554746	572001	682139	722352	802006
LAIA	52566	86406	119847	140597	206789
CACM	1972	3969	6394	x6928	x9136
Asia	549959	556168	626836	x651597	x769448
Middle East	x129030	151288	142694	x159021	x167417
Europe	2978960	3109246	3542795	3126463	3721615
EEC	2709600	2935368	3362569	2938007	3500945
EFTA	115246	110824	123324	120852	136923
Oceania	x79045	x76285	x82960	x83198	x91343
Germany/Allemagne	557471	643999	716849	627532	811452
France,Monac	507035	550980	633469	568569	770760
United Kingdom	440861	448109	506844	443957	509184
USA/Etats–Unis d'Amer	305759	272799	305017	321372	332519
Netherlands/Pays–Bas	259057	276325	374648	241760	269522
Japan/Japon	233908	209125	231258	230572	257322
Russian Federation			x166196	x499568	x681336
Canada	157453	172489	211730	215117	212398
Belgium–Luxembourg	170054	186493	207021	188933	169343
Italy/Italie	151749	156942	164433	151042	181855
Spain/Espagne	123934	125063	162587	141113	154371
Denmark/Danemark	88059	106534	127054	137528	139564
Austria/Autriche	102622	101111	106788	117506	126052
Ireland/Irlande	88898	98559	104420	95467	112893
Sweden/Suède	83183	84026	96988	85930	110750
Hong Kong	75215	79385	91945	82689	96807
Portugal	54701	61621	71127	67051	65454
Mexico/Mexique	41413	58562	68211	72433	90422
Norway,SVD,JM	57360	55247	60918	60337	74694
Switz.Liecht	51653	49151	56120	55346	56759
Saudi Arabia	42533	69407	29002	x45927	x54152
Korea, Republic of	29972	36058	50058	56496	56578
Greece/Grèce	31137	48989	51407	40381	43345
Australia/Australie	45578	41969	49253	48030	57520
Finland/Finlande	50838	46616	38932	31236	36399
Singapore/Singapour	28915	32033	38582	37364	48309
Hungary/Hongrie	x12801	16655	x34834	x50957	x43148
Poland/Pologne	18549	39187	33362	29615	35628
Argentina/Argentine	1159	11223	32761	42288	54929
Kuwait/ Koweït	23449	11444	36533	37799	33406
United Arab Emirates	21905	23891	25543	x26478	x26741
New Zealand	21949	23449	21652	23173	23376
Romania/Roumanie	16834	21986	24434	20156	27281
Slovenia/Slovénia			20052	28868	31291
Philippines	5977	8236	17095	21116	29029
Israel/Israël	12744	13126	17259	14578	24806
Ukraine			x10884	x33087	x25030
Yugoslavia SFR	138349	x42858			
Slovakia				x39949	x27013
Czechoslovakia	8428	x12136	x23929		
Bulgaria/Bulgarie	x37234	x14247	13061	7211	3849
Oman	5123	9479	13527	9517	11909
Lithuania/Lituanie			662	x31434	5653
Reunion/Réunion	9107	9132	12318	9978	10809
Former USSR/Anc. URSS		x30415			
Malaysia/Malaisie	6923	6714	12167	11227	14846
Thailand/Thaïlande	7759	7493	11072	11156	16008
Czech Republic				28640	40350
Lebanon/Liban	x12415	x12277	x7362	x7623	x14218
Malta/Malte	4439	8584	9776	8657	x7021

COUNTRIES–PAYS	EXPORTS – EXPORTATIONS 1990	1991	1992	1993	1994
Totale	4220569	4419107	5135633	5459407	6470828
Afrique	x18778	x22858	x20633	x15319	x2839
Afrique du Nord	2347	5224	1397	869	1652
Amériques	368964	421023	510925	628273	652267
ALAI	43909	65226	80792	84259	103323
MCAC	1911	3536	4836	x2779	x3721
Asie	163540	167817	207366	237296	274088
Moyen–Orient	48067	30653	41829	x53156	x65411
Europe	3582352	3706359	4283942	4381793	5304991
CEE	3328177	3457608	3993061	4081648	4980888
AELE	236631	244831	260038	270365	307578
Océanie	x76338	x74797	x77600	101795	x125754
Germany/Allemagne	569689	584368	707792	735307	1126145
Belgium–Luxembourg	525450	588292	675850	714212	828565
Netherlands/Pays–Bas	548589	547743	638857	639607	648236
France,Monac	414366	418233	483901	514083	734025
United Kingdom	393914	435689	492798	464265	558062
Italy/Italie	285724	301865	342710	367673	337042
USA/Etats–Unis d'Amer	201333	219868	267900	363229	353345
Switz.Liecht	220742	223515	230506	231524	267482
Ireland/Irlande	241325	214782	234286	181900	215023
Canada	114569	125436	151829	171902	185509
Sweden/Suède	116364	135716	135066	114294	137040
Austria/Autriche	68376	62012	73083	96971	x88512
Denmark/Danemark	61478	68928	73820	83878	82538
Finland/Finlande	58820	55035	67601	89788	102106
Australia/Australie	40213	44556	58108	77253	96110
Singapore/Singapour	43865	47671	51808	47436	48560
Spain/Espagne	27060	31898	50911	58868	96852
Brazil/Brésil	23239	34642	40239	41983	43865
Norway,SVD,JM	15889	21303	29509	38783	40011
Hong Kong	14426	18862	29951	34224	47314
Turkey/Turquie	5848	13040	27431	37915	48501
New Zealand	35278	30045	19372	24504	29479
Israel/Israël	12661	13001	19181	32564	32949
Malaysia/Malaisie	10065	14788	18401	23873	25391
Chile/Chili	4331	12731	19842	18038	19708
Korea, Republic of	11737	13628	18397	16695	26208
Czech Republic				46978	43638
Greece/Grèce	15186	11360	14675	18707	23385
Hungary/Hongrie	x7682	x13637	x15171	x13010	x16901
Croatia/Croatie			22921	17301	x7829
Poland/Pologne	2133	2475	9463	17803	36188
So. Africa Customs Un	5024	7009	6259	12287	
China/Chine	6150	6067	7673	11680	8186
Mexico/Mexique	4043	5828	7275	11271	12536
Japan/Japon	5113	8845	8177	6467	6844
Indonesia/Indonésie	8224	9462	6031	6185	6845
Czechoslovakia		x9794	x9860		
Slovakia				x16767	x13728
Ecuador/Equateur	4890	5065	5116	2628	
Slovenia/Slovénia			6114	6691	6644
Ghana		1780	9823	x35	x53
Syrian Arab Republic	22820	6696	3556	x1272	x1474
Cote d'Ivoire	x9990	x7652	x2475	x925	x773
Colombia/Colombie	2738	3022	3784	3536	4795
Cyprus/Chypre	1901	2808	3504	3318	3755
Trinidad and Tobago	2909	2671	2695	3926	3836
Saudi Arabia	610	4340	2391	x1725	x2148
Argentina/Argentine	1668	2088	2267	3479	19111
Costa Rica	1190	2486	2856	x1444	x2450
Jamaica/Jamaïque	2013	2286	x2318	x1883	x1675

(VALUE AS % OF TOTAL)(VALEUR EN % DU TOTAL)

	1985	1986	1987	1988	1989	1990	1991	1992	1993	1994
Africa	0.5	x0.8	x0.6	x0.7	x0.6	x0.7	x0.6	x0.8	x0.9	x0.8
Northern Africa	0.1	x0.1	x0.0	x0.1	x0.1	0.1	0.1	x0.2	x0.2	x0.2
Americas	22.8	18.5	x14.0	13.5	12.6	12.9	12.8	13.3	15.1	14.3
LAIA	0.2	0.2	0.2	0.3	0.9	1.2	1.9	2.3	2.9	3.7
CACM	0.1	0.0	0.1	0.0	0.1	0.0	0.1	0.1	x0.1	x0.2
Asia	10.1	x10.0	x11.1	13.8	x14.3	12.8	12.5	12.3	x13.6	x13.7
Middle East	3.0	x3.0	x3.5	3.5	x3.8	x3.0	3.4	2.8	x3.3	x3.0
Europe	65.0	69.1	69.2	67.5	67.0	69.4	69.5	69.4	65.1	66.3
EEC	56.9	60.1	60.5	59.0	57.9	63.1	65.6	65.9	61.2	62.4
EFTA	8.1	8.6	8.3	8.1	8.1	2.7	2.5	2.4	2.5	2.4
Oceania	1.1	x1.1	x1.1	x1.5	x2.3	x1.9	x1.7	x1.6	x1.7	x1.6
Germany/Allemagne	12.7	13.3	13.0	13.0	10.8	13.0	14.4	14.0	13.1	14.5
France,Monac	9.4	10.7	10.9	10.1	10.5	11.8	12.3	12.4	11.8	13.7
United Kingdom	10.1	10.5	10.1	10.0	10.0	10.3	10.0	9.9	9.2	9.1
USA/Etats–Unis d'Amer	18.3	14.3	10.5	8.6	7.1	7.1	6.1	6.0	6.7	5.9
Netherlands/Pays–Bas	4.8	4.8	5.2	4.5	4.9	6.0	6.2	7.3	5.0	4.8
Japan/Japon	4.2	4.3	4.6	6.4	6.6	5.5	4.7	4.5	4.8	4.6
Russian Federation								x3.3	x10.4	x12.1
Canada	3.6	3.1	2.5	3.6	3.6	3.7	3.9	4.1	4.5	3.8
Belgium–Luxembourg	4.1	4.5	4.7	4.7	4.2	4.0	4.2	4.1	3.9	3.0
Italy/Italie	4.5	4.2	3.7	3.5	3.7	3.5	3.5	3.2	3.1	3.2

	1985	1986	1987	1988	1989	1990	1991	1992	1993	1994
Afrique	0.7	x1.8	x1.2	x0.3	0.3	x0.4	x0.6	x0.4	x0.3	x0.0
Afrique du Nord	0.0	0.0	0.0	0.0	0.0	0.1	0.1	0.0	0.0	0.0
Amériques	10.9	9.8	7.5	8.5	8.6	8.8	9.5	10.0	11.5	10.1
ALAI	5.1	3.8	2.0	1.7	1.3	1.0	1.5	1.6	1.5	1.6
MCAC	0.2	0.1	0.1	0.1	0.1	0.0	0.1	0.1	x0.1	x0.1
Asie	2.0	2.2	x3.7	3.8	3.4	3.9	3.8	4.0	4.3	4.2
Moyen–Orient	0.3	0.6	x1.3	1.1	x0.6	1.1	0.7	0.8	x1.0	x1.0
Europe	84.7	85.1	85.8	85.4	85.3	84.9	83.9	83.4	80.3	82.0
CEE	72.9	73.1	73.6	73.2	73.1	78.9	78.2	77.8	74.8	77.0
AELE	11.3	11.4	11.6	11.9	11.4	5.6	5.5	5.1	5.0	4.8
Océanie	1.4	x1.1	x1.4	x1.7	x2.0	x1.8	x1.7	x1.5	1.9	x1.9
Germany/Allemagne	12.4	12.6	12.6	12.4	12.1	13.5	13.2	13.8	13.5	17.4
Belgium–Luxembourg	10.9	11.7	12.2	11.4	12.0	12.4	13.3	13.2	13.1	12.8
Netherlands/Pays–Bas	13.3	14.0	12.9	13.9	13.2	13.0	12.4	12.4	11.7	10.0
France,Monac	8.0	7.8	7.9	7.6	7.9	9.8	9.5	9.4	9.4	11.3
United Kingdom	9.8	8.2	8.5	8.8	8.5	9.3	9.9	9.6	8.5	8.6
Italy/Italie	5.6	5.7	6.2	6.0	6.3	6.8	6.8	6.7	6.7	5.2
USA/Etats–Unis d'Amer	2.8	2.9	2.7	4.2	4.9	4.8	5.0	5.2	6.7	5.5
Switz.Liecht	5.1	5.3	5.4	5.2	5.1	5.2	5.1	4.5	4.2	4.1
Ireland/Irlande	4.8	5.1	5.0	5.1	5.0	5.7	4.9	4.6	3.3	3.3
Canada	2.7	2.8	2.5	2.3	2.1	2.7	2.8	3.0	3.1	2.9

TRADE BY COMMODITY IN THOUSAND U.S. DOLLARS – COMMERCE PAR PRODUIT EN MILLIERS DE DOLLARS E.U

IMPORTS – IMPORTATIONS

COUNTRIES–PAYS	1990	1991	1992	1993	1994
Total	3158071	x2679934	2413169	x2408202	x2234354
Africa	408577	321751	x492690	x318627	x325659
Northern Africa	316085	275363	409203	x246994	x260440
Americas	261002	262346	277273	268232	289862
LAIA	50785	52946	59001	60319	67199
CACM	1160	1326	1572	x1773	x1730
Asia	x930414	x920621	x846588	x940908	x783337
Middle East	x441783	x479855	x332846	x315592	x285851
Europe	757803	702329	711546	748900	702741
EEC	720338	672638	681750	722239	676462
EFTA	23072	24494	24402	22673	23043
Oceania	x34695	x36621	x43439	x55809	x57813
United Kingdom	380801	332495	329864	367849	324463
Pakistan	179165	175252	185482	217456	174642
Iran (Islamic Rp. of)	x130512	x240098	x147575	x59171	x21330
Japan/Japon	131951	138341	160147	145522	162751
Egypt/Egypte	153983	155296	168459	106977	89954
USA/Etats–Unis d'Amer	142205	139784	146619	139130	152323
Russian Federation			x186936	x225467	x193849
Former USSR/Anc. URSS	722886	x376287			
Germany/Allemagne	81742	86229	88476	115972	111291
Morocco/Maroc	70984	60558	73871	70958	74248
Hong Kong	57699	60533	73538	55756	58926
United Arab Emirates	49544	52441	33038	x102487	x95921
France, Monac	68036	63286	63718	60106	58320
Canada	58568	60475	62339	59300	60529
Netherlands/Pays–Bas	53440	53355	57879	54291	50794
Poland/Pologne	29944	50958	36708	60504	60091
Saudi Arabia	75866	74546	38048	x32031	x48226
Syrian Arab Republic	35795	x44243	38043	x56123	x47394
Italy/Italie	31242	37013	41250	30708	31791
Libyan Arab Jamahiriya	51421	30086	x43833	x28129	x29866
Algeria/Algérie	16454	743	94937	1955	20096
Australia/Australie	19684	23072	29530	42523	43536
Ukraine			x1527	x93256	x29060
Chile/Chili	24161	27308	26763	26896	27882
Ireland/Irlande	34341	28829	25534	23531	24142
Afghanistan	x32708	x21482	x22517	x33282	x21827
Uruguay	23240	22224	27181	26180	29956
Mongolia/Mongolie	x23162	x446	x3303	x57727	x388
Tunisia/Tunisie	17754	19814	21641	17242	18790
Singapore/Singapour	22291	17261	16497	24792	22336
Sweden/Suède	18952	18740	18157	16636	19875
Uzbekistan/Ouzbékistan			x11419	x39380	x19385
Belgium–Luxembourg	14848	15079	17209	17225	17998
So. Africa Customs Un	14767	11822	17253	17608	16173
Senegal/Sénégal	12776	4125	x20341	x22079	x12808
Yemen/Yémen	x14234	10514	x22739	x10013	x12939
Kuwait/ Koweït	11093	7256	14146	16521	22743
Jordan/Jordanie	15349	14666	11744	11173	13787
Sudan/Soudan	x5489	x8865	x6461	x21733	x27485
Switz.Liecht	11165	11345	12174	11646	11486
Norway,SVD,JM	11254	12320	11663	10377	10912
Denmark/Danemark	9563	10612	10334	8929	9728
New Zealand	10413	9408	9502	9463	11004
Malaysia/Malaisie	8194	8383	9572	9060	11083
Oman	7059	8372	8146	8912	9876
Spain/Espagne	7601	7852	9098	7540	7097
Finland/Finlande	8643	8051	8033	7740	9530
Austria/Autriche	7646	6061	7057	6488	7871
Israel/Israël	7814	6831	6530	5636	7441
Nigeria/Nigéria	x5745	5498	x8390	x4787	x4987

EXPORTS – EXPORTATIONS

COUNTRIES–PAYS	1990	1991	1992	1993	1994
Totale	2650492	2420469	2278082	2397033	x2262693
Afrique	297789	366241	387382	447380	x467585
Afrique du Nord	x117	x264	97	771	x1996
Amériques	103217	100237	110539	133169	136084
ALAI	86809	83256	89726	110985	109976
MCAC	235	418	2340	774	x820
Asie	1843970	1567012	1373309	1437563	1262214
Moyen–Orient	67801	9722	8867	54047	x16069
Europe	389610	377664	392286	358889	370666
CEE	382268	368962	382471	350383	362333
AELE	7185	8575	9235	7909	8138
Océanie	8955	6655	9219	11131	x14126
India/Inde	584749	486024	366414	330604	306934
Sri Lanka	493045	428795	341554	403857	416774
China/Chine	412710	376058	361895	355678	294359
Kenya	195761	278366	289721	336871	x376700
United Kingdom	245683	242421	240579	207110	196258
Indonesia/Indonésie	181013	143130	140828	155696	96181
Hong Kong	30776	45785	63929	47789	49987
Argentina/Argentine	49490	42926	46185	60781	59993
Germany/Allemagne	49929	42561	43846	57577	61356
Bangladesh	33437	40248	48901	37681	x17626
Brazil/Brésil	32820	36180	39908	46150	44844
Netherlands/Pays–Bas	37331	34355	44125	36512	38860
Malawi	46287	35577	27543	35465	x39180
Singapore/Singapour	27063	24128	20196	27469	26405
Belgium–Luxembourg	15190	18366	24613	24320	28980
Turkey/Turquie	43255	3089	6200	45875	5529
France, Monac	17921	14340	16548	15632	24330
USA/Etats–Unis d'Amer	12661	13442	14528	17453	18077
Un. Rep. of Tanzania		x2151	x23477	x17423	x14581
Uganda/Ouganda	3566	6780	7721	x16124	x1881
Rwanda	9725	x12101	x10612	x7336	x9421
Zimbabwe	12962	11915	7332	9988	x8723
Viet Nam	x5919	x4373	x10554	x11699	x10435
Burundi	7810	8328	9400	8674	x7495
Switz.Liecht	7003	8456	9118	7806	7836
Papua New Guinea	7022	4407	6755	7343	x7353
Mauritius/Maurice	5733	5270	6203	6557	4549
Japan/Japon	2991	3664	3883	4972	5489
Poland/Pologne		906	5003	5643	4371
Italy/Italie	4852	5734	3657	908	1436
Ireland/Irlande	4907	5548	2986	1028	849
Austria/Autriche	3547	2108	2318	3535	x2033
So. Africa Customs Un	1800	2387	2432	2725	
Canada	1363	1932	2556	2512	2757
Australia/Australie	1530	1528	1788	3286	6332
Ecuador/Equateur	1477	1623	1605	2041	x2022
Denmark/Danemark	1517	1703	1696	1519	1668
Myanmar	x42	201	x1523	x3045	x338
United Arab Emirates	21220			x4467	x5511
Jordan/Jordanie	490	3037	655	213	1006
Malaysia/Malaisie	1526	1080	1178	1106	1389
Democratic Kampuchea	x8	x2048	x729	x490	
Chile/Chili	613	1046	1046	1007	1734
Panama	1358	852	1095	1030	894
Korea, Republic of	977	666	917	951	1719
Oman	839	381	566	1351	1100
Cote d'Ivoire	x689	x615	x853	x797	
Qatar	746	697	657	584	
Costa Rica	15	23	1834	x57	x139
Sweden/Suède	484	512	793	584	2264

(VALUE AS % OF TOTAL)(VALEUR EN % DU TOTAL)

	1985	1986	1987	1988	1989	1990	1991	1992	1993	1994
Africa	14.8	13.4	12.6	15.1	x12.4	13.0	12.0	x20.4	x13.2	x14.6
Northern Africa	13.0	11.0	9.4	12.1	10.2	10.0	10.3	17.0	x10.3	x11.7
Americas	12.3	11.3	9.1	11.1	10.2	8.3	9.8	11.5	11.1	12.9
LAIA	1.5	1.6	1.6	2.6	1.9	1.6	2.0	2.4	2.5	3.0
CACM	0.0	0.1	0.0	0.1	0.1	0.0	0.0	0.1	x0.1	x0.1
Asia	24.6	x27.5	x31.4	x29.6	x28.2	x29.4	x34.3	x35.1	x39.1	x35.0
Middle East	9.5	x12.2	x16.9	x14.1	x11.1	x14.0	x17.9	x13.8	x13.1	x12.8
Europe	31.7	30.6	26.8	27.5	25.9	24.0	26.2	29.5	31.1	31.5
EEC	29.3	28.0	24.1	24.9	23.7	22.8	25.1	28.3	30.0	30.3
EFTA	2.0	2.2	2.4	1.9	1.8	0.7	0.9	1.0	0.9	1.0
Oceania	2.7	x2.1	x1.9	x1.2	x1.5	x1.1	x1.4	x1.8	x2.4	x2.5
United Kingdom	18.5	17.0	13.4	14.7	13.8	12.1	12.4	13.7	15.3	14.5
Pakistan	8.1	6.3	5.5	4.9	7.0	5.7	6.5	7.7	9.0	7.8
Iran (Islamic Rp. of)		x2.0	x6.4	x3.8	x2.6	x4.1	x9.0	x6.1	x2.5	x1.0
Japan/Japon	3.7	4.8	4.3	4.4	4.7	4.2	5.2	6.6	6.0	7.3
Egypt/Egypte	5.7	5.0	4.7	5.9	4.1	4.9	5.8	7.0	4.4	4.0
USA/Etats–Unis d'Amer	7.9	6.8	5.0	5.8	5.7	4.5	5.2	6.1	5.8	6.8
Russian Federation								x7.7	x9.4	x8.7
Former USSR/Anc. URSS	10.1	11.4	13.6	11.6	19.1	22.9	x14.0			
Germany/Allemagne	2.8	2.7	2.7	2.4	2.4	2.6	3.2	3.7	4.8	5.0
Morocco/Maroc	2.4	2.3	2.3	2.8	2.9	2.2	2.3	3.1	2.9	3.3

	1985	1986	1987	1988	1989	1990	1991	1992	1993	1994
Afrique	16.3	x16.4	x14.1	14.1	x13.7	11.3	15.1	17.0	18.7	x20.7
Afrique du Nord	0.1	x0.0	x0.0	x0.0	0.0	x0.0	x0.0	0.0	0.0	x0.1
Amériques	4.7	4.9	4.2	5.2	4.1	3.9	4.1	4.8	5.5	6.0
ALAI	3.3	3.1	2.9	4.2	3.5	3.3	3.4	3.9	4.6	4.9
MCAC	0.0	0.0	x0.0	0.0	x0.0	0.0	0.0	0.1	0.0	x0.0
Asie	65.8	65.4	67.3	66.9	69.4	69.6	64.8	60.3	59.9	55.8
Moyen–Orient	0.6	1.1	x0.2	0.8	1.8	2.6	0.4	0.4	2.3	x0.7
Europe	11.6	12.7	13.5	13.3	12.3	14.7	15.6	17.2	15.0	16.4
CEE	11.2	12.2	13.0	12.8	11.9	14.4	15.2	16.8	14.6	16.0
AELE	0.4	0.5	0.5	0.5	0.4	0.3	0.4	0.4	0.3	0.4
Océanie	0.6	0.4	0.4	0.4	0.4	0.4	0.3	0.4	0.5	x0.6
India/Inde	22.7	22.4	21.4	18.6	23.3	22.1	20.1	16.1	13.8	13.6
Sri Lanka	19.1	16.0	16.8	17.4	15.6	18.6	17.7	15.0	16.8	18.4
China/Chine	12.4	16.4	16.9	18.1	17.6	15.6	15.5	15.9	14.8	13.0
Kenya	10.9	11.5	10.1	10.2	x9.4	7.4	11.5	12.7	14.1	x16.6
United Kingdom	8.0	8.7	9.4	8.7	8.1	9.3	10.0	10.6	8.6	8.7
Indonesia/Indonésie	6.5	4.9	5.5	5.6	6.6	6.8	5.9	6.2	6.5	4.3
Hong Kong	1.0	1.5	1.5	1.8	1.2	1.2	1.9	2.8	2.0	2.2
Argentina/Argentine	2.1	1.6	1.4	1.5	1.7	1.9	1.8	2.0	2.5	2.7
Germany/Allemagne	1.0	1.0	1.2	1.4	1.4	1.9	1.8	1.9	2.4	2.7
Bangladesh	1.9	1.7	1.5	1.7	1.8	1.3	1.7	2.1	1.6	x0.8

TRADE BY COMMODITY IN THOUSAND U.S. DOLLARS – COMMERCE PAR PRODUIT EN MILLIERS DE DOLLARS E.U

IMPORTS – IMPORTATIONS

COUNTRIES–PAYS	1990	1991	1992	1993	1994
Total	1516305	1534198	1613212	1517464	1657263
Africa	53838	70330	x59728	x53630	x57249
Northern Africa	29134	43357	x32516	28592	x31480
Americas	364483	401553	436384	418539	471631
LAIA	52480	64516	83248	74749	78601
CACM	2947	2623	4426	4534	4739
Asia	513855	538025	605689	x541192	x557461
Middle East	148609	140976	159665	x99543	x117276
Europe	474864	450069	476876	453701	510561
EEC	435746	422798	443301	424268	479947
EFTA	24082	23588	24222	22039	23654
Oceania	x16225	x18730	x17381	x18316	x20894
USA/Etats–Unis d'Amer	256772	285537	298635	283437	331010
Japan/Japon	96933	108305	133212	135779	137250
Germany/Allemagne	124493	123147	122336	113709	126118
Singapore/Singapour	128909	112177	105708	105804	103562
France, Monac	65955	61755	62438	64328	66309
Saudi Arabia	63750	63658	60783	x34391	x40611
Hong Kong	37729	49799	52879	51905	57066
United Kingdom	48168	44375	50193	55747	54258
Spain/Espagne	36303	46620	55728	45192	53666
Netherlands/Pays–Bas	57869	48426	50352	48434	67377
United Arab Emirates	47724	46473	60796	x28255	x36293
Canada	35624	35308	38628	45185	46141
Mexico/Mexique	26642	33450	45274	34928	36753
Malaysia/Malaisie	23398	29405	34637	37343	34123
Belgium–Luxembourg	24343	23927	24112	23050	26832
Italy/Italie	28595	24950	24011	20396	23322
Korea, Republic of	11570	16409	21076	12635	16835
Switz.Liecht	17182	16490	16642	14934	16037
Sri Lanka	9191	18516	19114	10195	13686
India/Inde	11226	11229	13014	16816	11953
Pakistan	16716	14778	13266	12533	12244
Sweden/Suède	12542	12452	13441	13326	15360
So. Africa Customs Un	11115	12864	14014	11295	13987
Australia/Australie	10986	12925	11860	12988	15326
Morocco/Maroc	10903	12064	13227	11545	7561
Austria/Autriche	11746	11313	11325	11411	13976
Brazil/Brésil	8378	9195	10130	11775	12132
Denmark/Danemark	8621	9500	10798	9446	11645
China/Chine	2574	6575	14699	7878	7000
Former USSR/Anc. URSS	63136	x26623			
Egypt/Egypte	7108	9546	7102	6179	11110
Argentina/Argentine	4535	6703	8618	7105	9365
Indonesia/Indonésie	5534	6303	7830	7825	8248
Kuwait/Koweït	7992	2107	9444	10266	10899
Algeria/Algérie	1812	13132	3622	4259	4672
Bangladesh				x20702	x14146
Myanmar	1432	4493	12734	2976	x1236
Norway,SVD,JM	6253	6513	7087	6590	7043
Russian Federation			x7987	x10867	x13009
Colombia/Colombie	5155	3522	6738	7552	6638
Poland/Pologne	3528	6821	3239	7383	12669
Hungary/Hongrie	x11736	7611	x4270	x5355	x5268
Israel/Israël	5137	5158	5514	5692	6637
Czechoslovakia	7384	x9911	x6349		
Greece/Grèce	4091	4876	4819	5868	4663
Oman	4666	4769	4556	5864	5608
Nepal/Népal	7651	5585	4846	4405	x3297
Finland/Finlande	4793	4275	4737	4943	6162
Peru/Pérou	2832	4612	4470	4257	6060
Portugal	4090	3644	5032	4467	4778

EXPORTS – EXPORTATIONS

COUNTRIES–PAYS	1990	1991	1992	1993	1994
Totale	1415073	1369931	1460930	1413484	1630369
Afrique	131665	142615	130961	119387	x176819
Afrique du Nord	28519	32893	25555	22377	29223
Amériques	158693	159607	143885	167375	188202
ALAI	63254	72745	51484	54602	67148
MCAC	38858	33858	37402	44209	48722
Asie	771454	779118	x831408	814263	947786
Moyen–Orient	x99061	x94395	x143916	x99447	x100408
Europe	246588	232127	293924	254996	272484
CEE	238904	225535	284568	237076	265106
AELE	1786	1973	2343	2716	2791
Océanie	11308	11414	x11573	x10416	x10898
Indonesia/Indonésie	152372	154127	141891	139800	167092
Singapore/Singapour	137698	129479	124815	128529	142960
India/Inde	109260	121180	112241	142095	149167
China/Chine	91058	84688	100004	107797	153949
Spain/Espagne	67805	68090	118988	54368	58023
Germany/Allemagne	59717	60392	64168	58439	61624
Madagascar	79887	72943	63619	44365	113059
Iran (Islamic Rp. of)	x19352	x48716	x90924	x29301	x30029
Hong Kong	36224	47124	50048	50302	56971
USA/Etats–Unis d'Amer	37653	38615	44093	50717	52269
Sri Lanka	39487	40922	41514	45550	42432
Brazil/Brésil	50688	56305	32147	35344	49525
Netherlands/Pays–Bas	43559	34093	39897	41198	60061
Turkey/Turquie	31247	32193	37772	44167	41203
Guatemala	34947	29742	32477	39799	42734
Malaysia/Malaisie	48503	35888	26225	27128	50085
France, Monac	32679	25685	21451	35878	34877
Hungary/Hongrie	x25000	x20892	x26356	x19009	x17085
Viet Nam	x13439	x14260	x15144	x28174	x41229
Comoros/Comores	10725	19761	15996	20504	x15500
Pakistan	13056	21543	19230	9867	12334
Thailand/Thaïlande	13786	12765	21735	14480	9669
United Kingdom	14288	13836	14929	20209	18797
Bulgaria/Bulgarie	x68648	x20016	x15438	x12551	x6125
Morocco/Maroc	14365	16698	12991	9121	10476
Syrian Arab Republic	6649	x9999	12843	x12462	x17606
Mexico/Mexique	5350	7052	11905	10432	10064
So. Africa Customs Un	3814	7146	8696	10509	
Myanmar		5076	x16345	x3169	x4274
Belgium–Luxembourg	7942	7711	7880	7431	7967
Tunisia/Tunisie	6687	9222	6804	6736	8055
Egypt/Egypte	7428	5641	5171	5798	9567
Canada	1759	3394	2416	10030	7571
Australia/Australie	3144	3911	5522	6068	5761
Nepal/Népal	3530	5384	5326	4147	x4104
Un. Rep. of Tanzania		x804	x8775	x4850	x2292
Chile/Chili	3887	5520	3837	4128	4227
Jamaica/Jamaïque	6432	4183	x4952	x3696	x5174
Italy/Italie	3701	3814	4302	4312	6084
Greece/Grèce	2200	4023	2963	4359	3960
United Arab Emirates	37759	140	1	x9882	x8569
Japan/Japon	1424	2966	2811	4182	5415
Costa Rica	3202	3107	3906	x2929	x4483
Korea, Republic of	2875	2708	4132	2815	3132
Austria/Autriche	1850	2159	3020	4311	x5922
Grenada/Grenade	8052	4633	x2267	x2486	x4653
Denmark/Danemark	2693	3016	3218	2845	3101
Fiji/Fidji	3985	3822	2866	950	1249
Albania/Albanie	x782	x1862	x2334	x3258	x1556
Israel/Israël	2661	1485	2951	2595	3404

(VALUE AS % OF TOTAL)(VALEUR EN % DU TOTAL)

	1985	1986	1987	1988	1989	1990	1991	1992	1993	1994
Africa	3.9	4.2	3.7	x4.9	3.9	3.5	4.5	x3.7	x3.5	x3.4
Northern Africa	2.9	2.9	2.2	3.3	2.7	1.9	2.8	x2.0	1.9	x1.9
Americas	22.5	25.3	26.1	22.4	24.9	24.1	26.2	27.0	27.6	28.5
LAIA	2.4	2.3	2.8	2.8	3.1	3.5	4.2	5.2	4.9	4.7
CACM	0.3	0.2	0.2	0.3	0.2	0.2	0.2	0.3	0.3	0.3
Asia	42.5	33.8	29.1	33.0	31.9	33.9	35.1	37.5	x35.6	x33.7
Middle East	12.7	x11.1	x7.9	7.9	x6.7	9.8	9.2	9.9	x6.6	x7.1
Europe	25.0	29.3	30.0	29.5	29.7	31.3	29.3	29.6	29.9	30.8
EEC	21.8	25.5	26.5	25.9	26.1	28.7	27.6	27.5	28.0	29.0
EFTA	2.7	3.0	3.0	3.0	3.0	1.6	1.5	1.5	1.5	1.4
Oceania	0.9	x1.0	x1.0	x1.1	x1.3	x1.1	x1.2	x1.1	x1.2	x1.2
USA/Etats–Unis d'Amer	17.4	20.0	20.4	16.4	18.8	16.9	18.6	18.5	18.7	20.0
Japan/Japon	5.0	5.4	5.7	6.3	6.6	6.4	7.1	8.3	8.9	8.3
Germany/Allemagne	6.3	7.2	7.7	7.1	7.0	8.2	8.0	7.6	7.5	7.6
Singapore/Singapour	9.6	7.4	6.4	6.6	8.2	8.5	7.3	6.6	7.0	6.2
France, Monac	4.3	4.8	5.2	5.0	4.8	4.3	4.0	3.9	4.2	4.0
Saudi Arabia	9.3	6.2	4.3	3.3	2.5	4.2	4.1	3.8	x2.3	x2.5
Hong Kong	3.9	3.2	2.4	3.1	3.1	2.5	3.2	3.3	3.4	3.4
United Kingdom	2.9	2.8	2.6	2.7	2.9	3.2	2.9	3.1	3.7	3.3
Spain/Espagne	0.6	0.9	0.9	1.3	1.6	2.4	3.0	3.5	3.0	3.2
Netherlands/Pays–Bas	2.2	3.2	3.4	3.2	3.7	3.8	3.2	3.1	3.2	4.1

	1985	1986	1987	1988	1989	1990	1991	1992	1993	1994
Afrique	12.8	x10.0	x9.3	7.2	x9.9	9.3	10.4	9.0	8.4	x10.8
Afrique du Nord	1.2	1.2	1.1	1.4	1.8	2.0	2.4	1.7	1.6	1.8
Amériques	12.1	14.7	14.2	11.5	9.2	11.2	11.7	9.9	11.8	11.6
ALAI	8.3	7.3	8.0	5.2	4.4	4.5	5.3	3.5	3.9	4.1
MCAC	0.3	3.3	2.7	2.8	1.6	2.7	2.5	2.6	3.1	3.0
Asie	60.6	60.7	59.5	63.1	60.7	54.5	56.8	x56.9	57.6	58.1
Moyen–Orient	2.8	x3.2	x5.4	x5.9	3.8	x7.0	x6.9	x9.9	x7.0	x6.2
Europe	14.0	14.1	13.7	14.9	15.3	17.4	16.9	20.1	18.0	16.7
CEE	13.3	13.7	13.2	14.2	14.7	16.9	16.5	19.5	16.8	16.3
AELE	0.2	0.2	0.2	0.3	0.3	0.1	0.1	0.2	0.2	0.2
Océanie	0.5	x0.5	x0.6	0.5	0.6	0.8	0.8	x0.8	x0.7	x0.7
Indonesia/Indonésie	10.5	14.6	13.7	13.9	12.2	10.8	11.3	9.7	9.9	10.2
Singapore/Singapour	11.6	12.9	10.4	12.1	12.3	9.7	9.5	8.5	9.1	8.8
India/Inde	19.1	15.3	13.8	10.8	10.3	7.7	8.8	7.7	10.1	9.1
China/Chine	2.5	1.6	4.1	5.0	7.3	6.4	6.2	6.8	7.6	9.4
Spain/Espagne	4.5	3.9	3.6	3.9	3.6	4.8	5.0	8.1	3.8	3.6
Germany/Allemagne	2.0	2.2	2.3	2.8	2.9	4.2	4.4	4.4	4.1	3.8
Madagascar	7.2	5.6	x5.5	3.8	x4.8	5.6	5.3	4.4	3.1	6.9
Iran (Islamic Rp. of)		x0.5	x1.6	x1.7	0.8	x1.4	x3.6	x6.2	x2.1	x1.8
Hong Kong	4.4	3.5	2.3	3.1	3.4	2.6	3.4	3.4	3.6	3.5
USA/Etats–Unis d'Amer	1.9	1.8	1.6	1.8	1.8	2.7	2.8	3.0	3.6	3.2

TRADE BY COMMODITY IN THOUSAND U.S. DOLLARS – COMMERCE PAR PRODUIT EN MILLIERS DE DOLLARS E.U

COUNTRIES–PAYS	IMPORTS – IMPORTATIONS 1990	1991	1992	1993	1994
Total	16849895	17931886	19146498	18934899	19775601
Africa	633331	558374	x557570	x568625	x663647
Northern Africa	465745	384039	x386447	x438913	x477383
Americas	x1372154	x1473841	1702214	x1886860	x2038310
LAIA	355913	445489	625236	624359	688154
CACM	30204	51026	57645	59256	73937
Asia	3132404	3937758	4376106	x4733214	4713405
Middle East	291132	x476543	x637576	x720900	x484791
Europe	10649891	10653068	11808824	11053551	11586736
EEC	10109520	10193980	11245861	10488461	11071998
EFTA	339785	322491	367470	348041	377595
Oceania	x100441	x112656	x109207	x113937	x142295
Germany/Allemagne	1651462	1756136	1988812	1557405	1515809
Japan/Japon	1286834	1523396	1729190	1817974	1851672
France, Monac	1442097	1476324	1537935	1414523	1531388
Netherlands/Pays-Bas	1411132	1242741	1366919	1433933	1830942
United Kingdom	1116099	1094815	1263940	1307229	1167536
Italy/Italie	1124577	1166426	1203006	1078117	1124705
Belgium–Luxembourg	946856	942847	1002511	909181	984357
Spain/Espagne	668066	757415	833841	809793	836006
Denmark/Danemark	589602	569560	690398	688362	669437
China/Chine	304655	599830	461517	308164	349213
Canada	345030	402527	439154	489087	513152
USA/Etats-Unis d'Amer	354610	376623	408830	517189	561477
Ireland/Irlande	351968	356391	388616	363704	435577
Korea, Republic of	286934	286770	344752	396350	391310
Thailand/Thaïlande	193109	243733	335726	413221	482675
Portugal	252194	287085	332766	284489	270376
Indonesia/Indonésie	192365	225565	213757	334011	416584
Mexico/Mexique	150409	193573	292777	257712	327743
Russian Federation			x515352	x220841	x143236
Former USSR/Anc. URSS		x724316			
Philippines	199949	187255	216158	276255	227380
Switz.Liecht	214768	207249	240174	224939	237564
Iran (Islamic Rp. of)		x132870	x242795	x254778	x55625
Sweden/Suède	179979	183384	221299	221295	258180
Austria/Autriche	205800	179011	202760	187319	189210
Poland/Pologne	77188	107348	195922	196079	269663
Malaysia/Malaisie	111302	118332	174259	175741	207013
Greece/Grèce	101821	115231	138364	162209	156834
Hungary/Hongrie	x243821	127452	x167736	x118178	x115893
Venezuela	94938	118496	134918	148394	82239
Libyan Arab Jamahiriya	188817	141747	x131038	x110350	x168752
Egypt/Egypte	129185	112576	119099	143204	184274
Norway, SVD, JM	117377	109378	121523	117727	134356
Hong Kong	128711	132658	112442	98205	84556
Czechoslovakia	116517	x164332	x142091		
Turkey/Turquie	52604	75940	105002	110766	85052
So. Africa Customs Un	101435	103737	103682	58588	116359
Saudi Arabia	30331	41275	84086	x123596	x115716
Algeria/Algérie	107204	92490	66083	89324	65394
Finland/Finlande	67866	66614	74694	70901	101641
Cuba	x176059	x83678	x52339	x65291	x44675
Romania/Roumanie	136155	47619	56153	86204	68502
Singapore/Singapour	46086	53394	76822	53142	46162
Australia/Australie	53100	64949	56912	60064	77649
Colombia/Colombie	29798	35860	63666	75046	108791
Syrian Arab Republic	38054	x44699	48886	x55020	x49996
Yugoslavia/Yougoslavie			x42522	x92834	x20033
Jordan/Jordanie	38728	37951	50651	45254	50836
Chile/Chili	23132	29644	45790	46512	56575
Peru/Pérou	39779	32599	42718	45890	49253

COUNTRIES–PAYS	EXPORTS – EXPORTATIONS 1990	1991	1992	1993	1994
Totale	15602786	16428945	18219190	17981515	18497015
Afrique	x163710	x129777	x156292	x154385	x127351
Afrique du Nord	x24485	x19077	x27485	x39533	x33631
Amériques	7114393	7530705	8337314	8608629	8844587
ALAI	3815669	3818611	4263192	4538381	4846346
MCAC	7725	7118	9615	x10197	x15104
Asie	1841136	2082866	1961029	2009617	1936804
Moyen-Orient	27991	42913	44875	x35456	x40000
Europe	5809914	6003846	7082185	6589904	7097903
CEE	5522891	5740069	6735747	6315363	6795632
AELE	223365	225887	289534	238597	265505
Océanie	x476690	x465558	x537793	x481721	x334849
USA/Etats-Unis d'Amer	2923809	3280940	3635326	3583441	3458686
Brazil/Brésil	1774367	1518757	1775960	2001510	2152135
Netherlands/Pays-Bas	1509825	1476985	1735146	1718695	2042885
Argentina/Argentine	1199809	1270119	1459439	1451123	1348966
Germany/Allemagne	1246937	1206368	1448204	1357607	1348345
France, Monac	1041308	1127451	1313926	1171668	1175673
Belgium–Luxembourg	642879	609070	704599	684826	683180
China/Chine	758206	854874	502788	455841	466439
India/Inde	336007	376495	597594	748185	582380
United Kingdom	427603	535228	592251	470987	554523
Chile/Chili	401718	483943	560104	386810	472836
Peru/Pérou	372521	457963	347004	582754	766211
Canada	346827	352495	410632	454014	498821
Denmark/Danemark	259078	336955	396769	375939	446660
Australia/Australie	195801	228327	297600	291921	294854
Italy/Italie	146652	173441	238647	223121	194900
Thailand/Thaïlande	150663	190831	189782	202889	204589
American Samoa	x238890	x192891	x203145	x159739	
Indonesia/Indonésie	93190	116754	115755	126060	157223
Japan/Japon	149173	144522	106646	91638	86680
Malaysia/Malaisie	103984	98026	114642	111412	123661
Norway, SVD, JM	62995	99203	124369	80391	98718
Ireland/Irlande	78459	80980	93936	74457	94130
Switz.Liecht	87772	84663	82561	78313	87159
Spain/Espagne	55881	68624	77612	83327	125064
Hong Kong	85484	89759	74972	55493	50758
Iceland/Islande	72598	42021	82603	79893	79628
Singapore/Singapour	42588	46816	83337	69071	71309
Philippines	56796	59654	57948	55328	63040
Hungary/Hongrie	x55144	x56222	x66878	x40199	x31536
Paraguay	21053	32363	60048	58628	28975
Austria/Autriche	39974	42249	47779	60835	x67505
Greece/Grèce	20915	21697	38583	53462	14758
So, Africa Customs Un	50494	49847	38460	18982	
New Zealand	38944	38605	32586	25015	31579
Poland/Pologne	29011	48517	12039	27234	39542
Russian Federation			x46526	x40142	x43666
Czechoslovakia		x32101	x51589		
Korea, Republic of	16370	26439	30686	24658	23766
Bolivia/Bolivie	16082	25170	26099	24958	31046
Portugal	24153	34025	19791	12665	14423
Sweden/Suède	22704	21369	22959	18925	21251
Senegal/Sénégal	36933	18824	x29637	13033	x16971
Bulgaria/Bulgarie	x107156	x34896	13167	7782	x17268
Saudi Arabia	12799	20793	21031	x9695	x18366
Cuba		x49291			
Cote d'Ivoire	x19376	x17355	x16053	x13543	x12005
Czech Republic				46620	43626
Former USSR/Anc. URSS	3889	x43566			
Korea Dem People's Rp	x4805	x13006	x14039	x13974	x31409

(VALUE AS % OF TOTAL)(VALEUR EN % DU TOTAL)

	1985	1986	1987	1988	1989	1990	1991	1992	1993	1994
Africa	3.9	4.1	3.0	2.7	3.0	3.8	3.1	x2.9	x3.0	x3.4
Northern Africa	3.0	3.3	2.3	2.2	2.1	2.8	2.1	x2.0	x2.3	x2.4
Americas	7.6	6.9	5.9	7.2	6.6	x8.2	x8.2	8.9	x10.0	x10.3
LAIA	1.8	1.7	1.6	2.8	1.8	2.1	2.5	3.3	3.3	3.5
CACM	0.5	0.3	0.3	0.2	0.2	0.2	0.3	0.3	0.3	0.4
Asia	12.7	x14.9	x15.3	x17.9	x18.3	18.6	22.0	22.8	x25.0	23.8
Middle East	2.7	x3.6	x2.8	x2.8	x2.8	1.7	x2.7	x3.3	x3.8	x2.5
Europe	70.5	69.2	57.2	53.1	54.5	63.2	59.4	61.7	58.4	58.6
EEC	64.5	63.5	52.3	48.5	49.5	60.0	56.8	58.7	55.4	56.0
EFTA	5.1	4.8	4.1	3.9	4.1	2.0	1.8	1.9	1.8	1.9
Oceania	0.4	0.4	x0.4	x0.4	x0.7	x0.6	x0.6	x0.5	x0.6	x0.7
Germany/Allemagne	12.2	11.3	9.2	8.3	8.3	9.8	9.8	10.4	8.2	7.7
Japan/Japon	5.0	5.7	4.9	6.0	6.4	7.6	8.5	9.0	9.6	9.4
France, Monac	8.5	9.2	7.4	6.8	7.2	8.6	8.2	8.0	7.5	7.7
Netherlands/Pays-Bas	12.6	11.3	8.4	7.6	7.0	8.4	6.9	7.1	7.6	9.3
United Kingdom	6.7	6.6	5.3	4.9	4.9	6.6	6.1	6.6	6.9	5.9
Italy/Italie	6.9	6.4	6.1	5.2	5.6	6.7	6.5	6.3	5.7	5.7
Belgium–Luxembourg	5.7	5.8	4.6	4.3	4.7	5.6	5.3	5.2	4.8	5.0
Spain/Espagne	2.2	2.5	2.2	3.0	3.1	4.0	4.2	4.4	4.3	4.2
Denmark/Danemark	3.9	4.0	3.4	2.9	3.1	3.5	3.2	3.6	3.6	3.4
China/Chine			1.2	1.9	2.3	1.8	3.3	2.4	1.6	1.8

	1985	1986	1987	1988	1989	1990	1991	1992	1993	1994
Afrique	0.7	x1.1	x1.3	x1.1	x1.3	x1.0	x0.8	x0.8	x0.9	x0.7
Afrique du Nord	0.1	0.1	0.2	0.2	x0.2	x0.2	x0.1	x0.2	x0.2	x0.2
Amériques	50.8	52.1	47.9	51.4	49.3	45.6	45.8	45.8	47.9	47.8
ALAI	26.5	25.5	24.6	28.2	28.5	24.5	23.2	23.4	25.2	26.2
MCAC	0.1	0.0	0.0	0.0	0.0	0.0	0.0	0.1	x0.1	x0.1
Asie	6.9	7.5	11.8	13.0	12.7	11.8	12.7	10.8	11.2	10.5
Moyen-Orient	0.7	0.8	0.6	x0.3	x0.2	0.2	0.3	0.2	x0.2	x0.2
Europe	39.4	37.3	35.9	31.5	32.3	37.2	36.5	38.9	36.6	38.4
CEE	36.6	34.7	33.5	29.2	30.2	35.4	34.9	37.0	35.1	36.7
AELE	2.3	2.2	2.0	1.9	1.7	1.4	1.4	1.6	1.3	1.4
Océanie	1.8	x1.6	x1.7	x1.6	x3.3	x3.1	x2.8	x2.9	x2.7	x1.8
USA/Etats-Unis d'Amer	22.2	24.7	21.2	21.1	18.6	18.7	20.0	20.0	19.9	18.7
Brazil/Brésil	15.3	12.8	12.5	13.5	14.1	11.4	9.2	9.7	11.1	11.6
Netherlands/Pays-Bas	8.4	8.2	8.4	7.7	7.9	9.7	9.0	9.5	9.6	11.0
Argentina/Argentine	6.0	7.7	6.9	8.9	8.2	7.7	7.7	8.0	8.1	7.3
Germany/Allemagne	9.1	8.8	9.1	7.0	6.8	8.0	7.3	7.9	7.6	7.3
France, Monac	6.2	6.0	5.9	5.2	5.5	6.7	6.9	7.2	6.5	6.4
Belgium–Luxembourg	5.2	4.8	4.0	3.4	3.8	4.1	3.7	3.9	3.8	3.7
China/Chine			4.6	5.6	5.3	4.9	5.2	2.8	2.5	2.5
India/Inde	1.5	1.7	1.3	1.7	2.3	2.2	2.3	3.3	4.2	3.1
United Kingdom	1.8	1.9	2.0	1.9	2.3	2.7	3.3	3.3	2.6	3.0

TRADE BY COMMODITY IN THOUSAND U.S. DOLLARS – COMMERCE PAR PRODUIT EN MILLIERS DE DOLLARS E.U

COUNTRIES–PAYS	IMPORTS – IMPORTATIONS 1990	1991	1992	1993	1994
Total	x855614	x828699	x1012890	x981152	x1083681
Africa	x63126	x55598	x79398	x75116	x90212
Northern Africa	21936	24248	x30278	26932	43576
Americas	x88564	x91084	x86908	x89112	x105589
LAIA	15940	25186	27322	34366	48160
CACM	1151	2453	5562	5271	x5787
Asia	x206802	x164590	x232138	x267884	x253389
Middle East	x117864	x81142	x102801	x133576	x108821
Europe	465956	474769	506903	468836	573765
EEC	448720	460162	478998	446799	550291
EFTA	7383	7946	9398	7851	7009
Oceania	16359	x14502	x32749	x17203	x15667
United Kingdom	119301	126940	121398	73115	87768
France,Monac	107974	96132	100560	103011	136592
Germany/Allemagne	31751	41504	46884	45371	47431
Netherlands/Pays-Bas	37195	35494	42983	54327	78447
Iran (Islamic Rp. of)	x62007	x44666	x51548	x35251	x10992
Belgium–Luxembourg	29400	31201	28057	49370	79693
Italy/Italie	32780	33330	38970	28719	29379
Russian Federation			x40845	x56351	x71163
Spain/Espagne	30447	35137	26775	33129	25331
Syrian Arab Republic	27530	x5006	27412	x53932	x36691
Mexico/Mexique	14985	22898	25010	27858	35048
Afghanistan	x38691	x17361	x40544	x16767	x3000
Algeria/Algérie	21301	23692	19754	25929	39745
Ireland/Irlande	24733	25450	24511	12533	9277
Hong Kong	17631	20104	20192	21143	27561
Singapore/Singapour	11999	15445	15709	28559	28375
Denmark/Danemark	10961	9780	17647	17425	22373
Poland/Pologne		37	20769	21293	9942
Czechoslovakia	151	x14534	x26138		
Canada	6966	10474	12872	14121	15205
China/Chine	8614	9766	14069	9227	11498
Sweden/Suède	7763	8886	12565	11449	10488
Cuba	x35281	x23136	x6505	x280	x546
Hungary/Hongrie	x6118	5508	x13961	x9428	x6269
Greece/Grèce	5292	7944	10041	9075	11382
New Caledonia	1288	x2201	x20069	x2117	x1279
Viet Nam	x195	x4942	x9268	x10155	x7389
So. Africa Customs Un	5139	5717	10205	8244	10899
Iraq	x509	x2773	x5694	x11410	x16215
United Arab Emirates	4120	5349	3340	x10706	x19374
Austria/Autriche	9311	6563	6104	6416	7717
Saudi Arabia	5479	5934	2832	x9637	x11124
Romania/Roumanie	7873	1505	8742	7066	11156
Korea, Republic of	2493	4980	3818	8416	10434
Japan/Japon	4013	4659	5690	6554	10042
Slovenia/Slovénia			9130	7271	8523
Switz.Liecht	5532	5355	5880	4733	3774
Papua New Guinea	6719	x4475	x4705	x5257	x3993
Azerbaijan			x5429	x8493	x16178
Lebanon/Liban	x9587	x8026	x2597	x3021	x4567
Ukraine			x6800	x5978	x2986
Slovakia				x12531	x5207
Australia/Australie	3667	3355	3185	4465	4391
USA/Etats-Unis d'Amer	5980	3167	3290	4367	5500
Jamaica/Jamaïque	1396	1492	x3963	x5313	x3854
Cameroon/Cameroun	3732	1211	x4103	x5331	x4017
Lithuania/Lituanie			41	x10325	6727
Bulgaria/Bulgarie		x671	4925	x4495	x7667
Congo	x2529	x1585	x4327	x3262	x1529
Norway,SVD,JM	1706	2426	3326	3007	3130

COUNTRIES–PAYS	EXPORTS – EXPORTATIONS 1990	1991	1992	1993	1994
Totale	988515	969054	1132282	1121087	1254629
Afrique	14442	23552	23187	26320	x6354
Afrique du Nord	4179	8607	9241	8571	3742
Amériques	74097	104478	147543	148045	180359
ALAI	721	3876	12991	18503	19276
MCAC	961	3111	4853	3738	4034
Asie	142411	204047	245111	215997	237981
Moyen-Orient	66322	81319	92978	82266	90893
Europe	555864	591963	665529	670567	772866
CEE	548853	585766	654851	658015	765131
AELE	6899	5987	5046	4567	5068
Océanie	x26442	x26106	x29244	x31706	x39365
Netherlands/Pays-Bas	149931	154152	161415	177406	189548
Belgium–Luxembourg	139525	141216	148214	166855	198159
Germany/Allemagne	123503	128569	177516	134811	135049
USA/Etats-Unis d'Amer	62010	88917	117121	115528	147301
Turkey/Turquie	61051	79910	89146	80939	89638
Singapore/Singapour	38930	70510	84941	52969	43793
Denmark/Danemark	48155	40291	40132	33793	41503
United Kingdom	21038	43213	42597	27544	28859
Malaysia/Malaisie	16096	24735	40123	46868	57616
Australia/Australie	22388	22628	25977	28200	35580
Ireland/Irlande	20079	29833	26600	19116	23077
France,Monac	21000	18704	18238	36719	60799
Sweden/Suède	6898	9064	15142	28527	32228
Hong Kong	9169	10711	11993	14644	17241
Italy/Italie	9843	8378	10282	12242	21595
Hungary/Hongrie	x12827	x12681	x9574	x8080	x5771
So. Africa Customs Un	6065	10601	8487	10422	
Argentina/Argentine	347	3557	9006	15249	13906
Japan/Japon	5310	6219	6726	11894	16783
Morocco/Maroc	4028	5093	6830	7192	2701
Portugal	4493	7753	4831	3976	4306
Canada	5891	3590	7087	4920	6401
Bulgaria/Bulgarie	x72045	x1805	x6987	x4780	x301
Austria/Autriche	3660	2208	5752	4970	x4130
Norway,SVD,JM	5647	4791	4365	3495	4143
Croatia/Croatie			4577	7604	x2336
Zimbabwe	2193	2684	4333	5080	x2319
India/Inde	1016	4488	4747	2766	3586
Spain/Espagne	262	1182	2745	7419	5050
Czech Republic				10902	6556
New Zealand	3928	3322	3209	3420	3746
Poland/Pologne		1996	4028	3874	4371
Barbados/Barbade	1952	2193	3286	3068	x1262
Guatemala	880	2171	3170	3104	3512
Egypt/Egypte	132	3140	2051	1086	190
United Arab Emirates	4704	932	3344	x689	x698
China/Chine	7	3043	967	697	3594
Trinidad and Tobago	1202	1560	1316	1653	1817
Finland/Finlande	106	309	476	2902	19337
Indonesia/Indonésie	3889	1188	559	1862	1812
Greece/Grèce	354	886	910	1736	1491
Mexico/Mexique	5	2	2742	400	1049
Kenya	297	491	810	1733	x1
Costa Rica	81	935	1632	x434	x73
Switz.Liecht	1252	1196	681	1070	922
Brazil/Brésil	27	84	777	2059	3046
Czechoslovakia		x2125	x495		
Macau/Macao	145	420	873	928	776
Philippines	1069	968	471	428	772
Russian Federation			x746	x789	x718

(VALUE AS % OF TOTAL)(VALEUR EN % DU TOTAL)

	1985	1986	1987	1988	1989	1990	1991	1992	1993	1994
Africa	11.0	x4.3	x5.5	x6.1	x5.1	x7.4	x6.7	x7.8	x7.6	x8.3
Northern Africa	9.0	0.3	1.1	2.3	1.9	2.6	2.9	x3.0	2.7	4.0
Americas	9.0	x13.5	x10.1	x8.0	12.0	x10.3	x10.9	x8.6	x9.1	x9.7
LAIA	5.3	5.1	4.4	3.1	2.5	1.9	3.0	2.7	3.5	4.4
CACM	0.3	0.5	x0.1	x0.2	0.1	0.1	0.3	0.5	0.5	x0.5
Asia	8.0	x15.9	x17.5	x16.3	x24.9	x24.2	x19.9	x22.9	x27.3	x23.4
Middle East	2.7	x8.0	x7.4	x4.9	x9.5	x13.8	x9.8	x10.1	x13.6	x10.0
Europe	68.7	64.5	64.3	56.3	49.8	54.5	57.3	50.0	47.8	52.9
EEC	66.6	62.1	61.6	53.2	46.4	52.4	55.5	47.3	45.5	50.8
EFTA	1.9	2.2	2.4	2.9	2.8	0.9	1.0	0.9	0.8	0.6
Oceania	1.3	x1.7	x2.1	1.7	x2.0	1.9	x1.7	x3.3	x1.8	x1.5
United Kingdom	23.8	22.3	20.7	16.5	13.9	13.9	15.3	12.0	7.5	8.1
France,Monac	11.3	12.2	14.1	11.8	10.6	12.6	11.6	9.9	10.5	12.6
Germany/Allemagne	5.4	5.0	3.7	2.7	2.8	3.7	5.0	4.6	4.6	4.4
Netherlands/Pays-Bas	10.5	8.3	6.3	5.5	4.3	4.3	4.3	4.2	5.5	7.2
Iran (Islamic Rp. of)		x0.1	x0.1	x0.1	x2.8	x7.2	x5.4	x5.1	x3.6	x1.0
Belgium–Luxembourg	5.6	5.6	4.7	3.8	3.4	3.4	3.8	2.8	5.0	7.4
Italy/Italie	3.2	3.3	4.7	4.0	3.7	3.8	4.0	3.8	2.9	2.7
Russian Federation								x4.0	x5.7	x6.6
Spain/Espagne	0.4	1.9	3.8	3.6	2.7	3.6	4.2	2.6	3.4	2.3
Syrian Arab Republic	0.0	0.2	0.3	0.0	1.9	3.2	x0.6	2.7	x5.5	x3.4

	1985	1986	1987	1988	1989	1990	1991	1992	1993	1994
Afrique	0.3	x0.2	x0.1	x0.2	x0.6	1.4	2.4	2.0	2.3	x0.5
Afrique du Nord	0.0	0.0	0.0	0.0	0.2	0.4	0.9	0.8	0.8	0.3
Amériques	8.3	9.6	8.7	8.9	x8.9	7.5	10.7	13.1	13.2	14.4
ALAI	0.6	0.5	0.6	0.6	0.3	0.1	0.4	1.1	1.7	1.5
MCAC	0.0	x0.0	0.1	0.1	0.0	0.1	0.3	0.4	0.3	0.3
Asie	8.9	11.6	13.6	14.8	17.2	14.4	21.1	21.6	19.3	19.0
Moyen-Orient	2.8	4.3	5.4	6.5	6.3	6.7	8.4	8.2	7.3	7.2
Europe	71.5	64.0	56.4	55.7	51.7	56.2	61.1	58.8	59.8	61.6
CEE	68.7	62.1	54.8	54.1	50.1	55.5	60.4	57.8	58.7	61.0
AELE	2.4	1.8	1.5	1.3	1.6	0.7	0.6	0.4	0.4	0.4
Océanie	3.3	4.1	x5.1	x2.8	x2.6	x2.7	x2.7	x2.6	x2.8	x3.1
Netherlands/Pays-Bas	21.3	20.2	16.4	18.1	15.4	15.2	15.9	14.3	15.8	15.1
Belgium–Luxembourg	15.2	14.8	13.7	13.4	12.4	14.1	14.6	13.1	14.9	15.8
Germany/Allemagne	16.2	13.9	13.4	12.2	10.8	12.5	13.3	15.7	12.0	10.8
USA/Etats-Unis d'Amer	7.3	8.0	7.1	7.0	7.6	6.3	9.2	10.3	10.3	11.7
Turkey/Turquie	2.4	3.2	5.3	5.9	6.2	6.2	8.2	7.9	7.2	7.1
Singapore/Singapour	0.9	1.6	2.7	4.6	6.6	3.9	7.3	7.5	4.7	3.5
Denmark/Danemark	4.7	4.4	4.0	4.1	4.5	4.9	4.2	3.5	3.0	3.3
United Kingdom	4.7	3.8	1.5	1.3	1.1	2.1	4.5	3.8	2.5	2.3
Malaysia/Malaisie	1.7	2.0	1.5	1.6	1.6	1.6	2.6	3.5	4.2	4.6
Australia/Australie	1.0	1.6	2.4	2.4	2.2	2.3	2.3	2.3	2.5	2.8

TRADE BY COMMODITY IN THOUSAND U.S. DOLLARS – COMMERCE PAR PRODUIT EN MILLIERS DE DOLLARS E.U

COUNTRIES–PAYS	IMPORTS – IMPORTATIONS 1990	1991	1992	1993	1994
Total	7807811	8941691	10250273	11041082	12605524
Africa	x361422	x343712	x445806	x388505	x358901
Northern Africa	115538	116013	163002	x107795	x105525
Americas	1022248	1255084	x1558168	x1738503	x2133538
LAIA	136529	204757	335930	423339	571322
CACM	87335	111696	150690	142894	167044
Asia	x1569666	1631144	1707137	x2078192	x2543358
Middle East	x522619	326479	315343	x385548	x431896
Europe	4425599	5038371	5892810	6055232	6638968
EEC	4112109	4727266	5495687	5608003	6158269
EFTA	249518	258774	285376	332786	350437
Oceania	x304894	x357512	x354483	x416185	x474028
Germany/Allemagne	821372	1015977	1204870	1339227	1491377
United Kingdom	689995	783399	898211	1078302	1041221
France,Monac	500695	542527	604916	576193	655323
USA/Etats–Unis d'Amer	381120	458645	521376	568033	624939
Japan/Japon	328590	391588	443828	547044	702463
Netherlands/Pays–Bas	373094	435354	518301	411663	472677
Belgium–Luxembourg	369957	405456	461453	470706	507737
Spain/Espagne	367592	397693	444809	433157	532993
Italy/Italie	278154	348343	395024	389462	442583
Hong Kong	305100	368060	340105	383956	456690
Canada	253739	315083	353203	362895	550911
Australia/Australie	208295	249380	243761	278871	316261
Sweden/Suède	156330	171268	205530	208828	232020
Switz.Liecht	161229	169129	181637	197755	226664
Mexico/Mexique	74109	108857	186891	227851	274043
Austria/Autriche	130358	137478	173975	168096	190278
Saudi Arabia	171136	171075	108332	x148845	x172057
Poland/Pologne	34251	140925	121660	143974	177230
Korea, Republic of	53332	95267	135223	175058	188057
Denmark/Danemark	96967	113947	143760	136876	151947
Singapore/Singapour	84763	100755	109523	140475	174169
Ireland/Irlande	92872	101135	135970	96455	109986
Russian Federation			x129554	x192310	x418710
Finland/Finlande	106723	107765	112533	96915	118307
Greece/Grèce	73067	90332	100612	119855	129068
Norway,SVD,JM	75232	74506	87470	118513	106030
Portugal	54934	76592	95723	82269	82752
Malaysia/Malaisie	65651	77689	83506	89389	119029
New Zealand	49668	58338	64059	74505	104814
Hungary/Hongrie	x20470	39547	x69509	x76324	x76008
China/Chine	37560	44496	49868	65721	74284
Israel/Israël	31716	38390	51015	59990	81839
Thailand/Thaïlande	29957	34545	46684	55788	72226
United Arab Emirates	56394	37822	43526	x52725	x59098
Egypt/Egypte	50257	48167	46060	31897	23321
Guatemala	21172	33379	47819	44842	52522
Algeria/Algérie	15276	21482	72572	28348	38115
Nigeria/Nigéria	x44594	27782	x48502	x45091	x25151
Bahamas	24390	23446	x36287	x59231	x43253
Kuwait/ Koweït	19044	25262	42877	48587	51213
Indonesia/Indonésie	22926	25361	37105	42645	53371
Argentina/Argentine	6282	16032	39555	44195	63015
Czechoslovakia	18528	x30598	x67049		
India/Inde	10411	12223	27540	46537	67056
Honduras	23807	25649	26848	31770	39202
Former USSR/Anc. URSS		x80810			
So. Africa Customs Un	18909	20539	27232	28241	35763
Romania/Roumanie	22918	14554	21479	35806	57334
El Salvador	15418	13898	26828	28877	34397
Libyan Arab Jamahiriya	24998	24603	x19783	x23159	x15984

COUNTRIES–PAYS	EXPORTS – EXPORTATIONS 1990	1991	1992	1993	1994
Totale	7511313	8725840	10441240	11357575	12995720
Afrique	x50821	60401	x43261	x51312	x28424
Afrique du Nord	20564	20263	13465	20896	18580
Amériques	1251394	1659775	2008023	2315950	2797488
ALAI	91917	124501	176783	211110	277233
MCAC	42395	52977	72681	x60227	x81306
Asie	883807	1035314	1173906	1325027	1585687
Moyen–Orient	50619	x33964	x55201	x78265	x88327
Europe	5153482	5792181	7000871	7400687	8211281
CEE	4839503	5458648	6561123	6945813	7740555
AELE	263957	300522	336745	340446	388630
Océanie	67881	x95626	x117320	x131889	x201471
USA/Etats–Unis d'Amer	989184	1298407	1505491	1758262	2135969
France,Monac	904324	1096157	1359573	1521597	1617159
Ireland/Irlande	938138	1029062	1251606	1527661	1780575
Germany/Allemagne	667588	767663	964367	941912	976590
Netherlands/Pays–Bas	680011	759510	827138	853375	924297
Belgium–Luxembourg	460613	505088	552619	507803	559214
United Kingdom	359038	381787	433330	442200	518064
Italy/Italie	278692	301446	355771	369513	425078
Denmark/Danemark	252817	287406	358531	335000	377393
Switz.Liecht	246085	277513	312747	317066	355133
Japan/Japon	162748	203094	236838	265729	296212
Hong Kong	178737	208691	218567	228922	262353
Canada	104018	158129	221172	250146	259121
Spain/Espagne	127405	143265	176238	170342	194319
China/Chine	106674	138006	132296	141353	189641
Thailand/Thaïlande	72495	98701	138229	167818	227688
Singapore/Singapour	75510	104803	118074	132782	175191
Israel/Israël	100455	88018	83972	95313	115089
Sweden/Suède	76412	72784	87677	81567	150987
Austria/Autriche	48118	57894	76090	77032	x62709
Australia/Australie	38471	54200	61867	71245	110067
Korea, Republic of	41984	48888	60938	70434	77274
Mexico/Mexique	27512	42575	62438	74880	87798
Malaysia/Malaisie	40525	47123	57085	60919	69815
New Zealand	28640	38671	53816	59923	89140
Hungary/Hongrie	x35386	x34594	x59892	x51978	x58037
Croatia/Croatie			59611	69956	x46790
Portugal	14164	20555	61408	22367	29227
Greece/Grèce	17759	23995	37257	36884	39251
Argentina/Argentine	17762	24555	31716	38055	43852
Guatemala	24044	27926	33278	30278	40647
Finland/Finlande	14179	11792	19518	58559	85692
Turkey/Turquie	10176	16095	33676	38550	51003
Poland/Pologne	25232	31646	23431	28202	68299
Brazil/Brésil	14029	19741	27978	32587	42037
Chile/Chili	6287	10782	24388	37679	71767
Norway,SVD,JM	17826	22971	23937	23345	33462
Philippines	15712	15913	18203	21696	24036
Indonesia/Indonésie	13000	15114	15378	22884	25060
So. Africa Customs Un	13788	14399	19440	19219	
Costa Rica	12429	16156	19555	x10912	x19928
El Salvador	5186	8422	17140	16313	19901
India/Inde	8602	10965	16297	14163	10748
Slovenia/Slovénia			21764	17886	26371
Malta/Malte	6517	9286	11792	13413	x2316
Venezuela	7531	6080	10352	16337	16744
Bulgaria/Bulgarie	x42171	x4881	x9018	x18827	x3541
Egypt/Egypte	14778	11248	7330	10501	7522
Panama	6610	6784	9374	11949	13789
Czech Republic				26199	36993

(VALUE AS % OF TOTAL)(VALEUR EN % DU TOTAL)

	1985	1986	1987	1988	1989	1990	1991	1992	1993	1994
Africa	4.1	x7.5	x6.0	x6.9	x5.0	x4.6	x3.8	x4.4	x3.6	x2.9
Northern Africa	2.1	1.9	1.5	2.2	1.6	1.5	1.3	1.6	x1.0	x0.8
Americas	20.4	17.5	x13.8	x15.7	13.8	13.1	14.1	x15.2	x15.7	x16.9
LAIA	2.4	1.3	1.4	1.4	1.5	1.7	2.3	3.3	3.8	4.5
CACM	0.9	1.4	1.0	1.4	1.4	1.1	1.2	1.5	1.3	1.3
Asia	23.1	x22.0	x22.1	x19.8	18.4	x20.1	18.2	16.6	x18.8	x20.2
Middle East	6.2	x7.4	x6.4	5.0	x4.4	x6.7	3.7	3.1	x3.5	x3.4
Europe	49.5	49.8	50.6	51.0	54.6	56.7	56.3	57.5	54.8	52.7
EEC	41.2	41.5	43.0	42.8	46.2	52.7	52.9	53.6	50.8	48.9
EFTA	7.6	7.6	7.1	7.7	7.9	3.2	2.9	2.8	3.0	2.8
Oceania	2.3	x2.9	x2.8	x3.5	x4.9	x3.9	x4.0	x3.5	x3.8	x3.7
Germany/Allemagne	7.4	7.3	9.4	8.6	8.7	10.5	11.4	11.8	12.1	11.8
United Kingdom	8.0	7.8	8.3	7.6	8.6	8.8	8.8	8.8	9.8	8.3
France,Monac	5.3	5.6	5.6	5.9	6.3	6.4	6.1	5.9	5.2	5.2
USA/Etats–Unis d'Amer	11.4	9.3	6.7	7.3	5.2	4.9	5.1	5.1	5.1	5.0
Japan/Japon	6.9	6.7	6.2	4.4	4.8	4.2	4.4	4.3	5.0	5.6
Netherlands/Pays–Bas	4.5	4.3	3.9	4.1	4.3	4.8	4.9	5.1	3.7	3.7
Belgium–Luxembourg	4.4	4.9	4.5	4.5	4.6	4.7	4.5	4.5	4.3	4.0
Spain/Espagne	1.2	1.2	1.7	2.1	2.3	4.7	4.4	4.3	3.9	4.2
Italy/Italie	2.6	2.3	2.3	2.2	3.2	3.6	3.9	3.9	3.5	3.5
Hong Kong	3.8	3.1	3.3	3.5	3.5	3.9	4.1	3.3	3.5	3.6

	1985	1986	1987	1988	1989	1990	1991	1992	1993	1994
Afrique	0.6	x0.5	x0.3	x0.5	x0.9	x0.7	0.7	x0.4	x0.5	x0.2
Afrique du Nord	0.1	0.1	0.1	0.1	0.4	0.3	0.2	0.1	0.2	0.1
Amériques	18.7	17.3	15.6	19.1	16.4	16.7	19.0	19.2	20.4	21.5
ALAI	1.4	1.5	1.4	1.9	1.4	1.2	1.4	1.7	1.9	2.1
MCAC	0.4	0.5	0.5	0.8	0.6	0.6	0.6	0.7	x0.5	x0.6
Asie	11.8	10.8	x12.5	13.2	12.7	11.8	11.8	11.3	11.7	12.2
Moyen–Orient	0.6	0.6	x0.7	0.9	x0.7	0.7	x0.4	x0.5	x0.7	x0.7
Europe	67.5	70.0	69.9	65.1	66.5	68.6	66.4	67.1	65.2	63.2
CEE	59.5	61.8	63.2	58.7	60.3	64.4	62.6	62.8	61.2	59.6
AELE	7.0	7.1	6.2	5.6	5.4	3.5	3.4	3.2	3.0	3.0
Océanie	0.7	x0.7	x0.6	0.8	x0.9	0.9	x1.1	x1.1	x1.2	x1.5
USA/Etats–Unis d'Amer	14.6	13.4	12.2	14.3	12.4	13.2	14.9	14.4	15.5	16.4
France,Monac	6.7	7.5	7.5	5.1	7.1	12.0	12.6	13.0	13.4	12.4
Ireland/Irlande	11.9	11.9	15.8	15.5	15.0	12.5	11.8	12.0	13.5	13.7
Germany/Allemagne	7.6	8.2	8.1	7.9	8.3	8.9	8.8	9.2	8.3	7.5
Netherlands/Pays–Bas	13.2	13.2	12.2	9.2	8.8	9.1	8.7	7.9	7.5	7.1
Belgium–Luxembourg	4.4	4.8	4.5	5.9	6.0	6.1	5.8	5.3	4.5	4.3
United Kingdom	5.5	4.7	4.6	4.6	4.7	4.8	4.4	4.2	3.9	4.0
Italy/Italie	3.0	3.5	3.3	3.2	3.5	3.7	3.5	3.4	3.3	3.3
Denmark/Danemark	3.4	3.8	3.5	4.0	3.2	3.4	3.3	3.4	2.9	2.9
Switz.Liecht	4.5	4.3	3.8	3.6	3.3	3.3	3.2	3.0	2.8	2.7

TRADE BY COMMODITY IN THOUSAND U.S. DOLLARS – COMMERCE PAR PRODUIT EN MILLIERS DE DOLLARS E.U

COUNTRIES–PAYS	IMPORTS – IMPORTATIONS 1990	1991	1992	1993	1994
Total	2405593	2618468	3141088	2920797	3638016
Africa	x85510	x62570	x76110	x91393	x113821
Northern Africa	2769	1186	x6255	x7606	x13498
Americas	x440293	503137	x573929	x602286	x787659
LAIA	11171	53241	122871	115222	183319
CACM	597	3023	8668	x9133	x10702
Asia	455423	536805	575405	x666036	x874172
Middle East	x82655	x86777	x95235	x133491	x143641
Europe	1371868	1436214	1773073	1452675	1749327
EEC	1239592	1301037	1652174	1351590	1606807
EFTA	82698	81791	82409	75808	95373
Oceania	x38468	x43219	x40726	x37925	x40383
Germany/Allemagne	259103	333157	390994	292423	407379
USA/Etats–Unis d'Amer	269003	279347	287203	319779	399982
Belgium–Luxembourg	219601	241204	284520	289202	337302
Netherlands/Pays–Bas	183694	210080	334276	197437	213475
Hong Kong	169542	220019	245766	245760	303549
France, Monac	191940	161120	179913	146800	186307
United Kingdom	165178	129798	163850	174201	175774
Japan/Japon	115160	114232	115295	132632	244755
Canada	70395	77848	67938	74095	92556
Switz.Liecht	76814	74664	71534	64700	79930
Mexico/Mexique	10330	35102	70067	85175	141230
Russian Federation			x45695	x137182	x277973
Ireland/Irlande	42391	49962	68802	51687	60300
Spain/Espagne	38908	46959	60243	45823	53592
Italy/Italie	44796	40834	46677	40738	35555
Singapore/Singapour	28438	30770	38730	43732	49277
Oman	20777	25484	33762	38235	41209
Portugal	18320	19341	34265	39167	48945
China/Chine	18229	27000	26026	27665	25161
Argentina/Argentine	126	15723	42441	20054	11900
Kuwait/Koweït	8851	18439	25532	26258	31339
Guadeloupe	22712	21160	24101	23111	26082
Greece/Grèce	26418	16659	25603	22454	21448
Saudi Arabia	9729	14928	4757	x40957	x47523
Austria/Autriche	18150	17927	21313	18063	29026
Poland/Pologne			45242	11135	7097
Sweden/Suède	14973	12091	21698	15192	18403
Czechoslovakia	1547	x16533	x28312		
Yugoslavia SFR	40545	x43551			
Reunion/Réunion	12055	12503	14639	15025	17055
Denmark/Danemark	8466	14736	11390	12760	13682
Macau/Macao	8799	10271	11985	12904	16022
Australia/Australie	11118	14273	8583	11091	12484
Romania/Roumanie	4308	6682	18104	9120	3700
Mozambique	x9051	x9728	x9054	x15030	x12766
Brunei Darussalam	13412	17009	x8150	x7969	x14880
Martinique	9903	11172	10465	10274	x11110
Korea, Republic of	3687	6506	8507	14731	7585
Angola	x19898	x5221	x9102	x14555	x26663
Norway, SVD, JM	5728	6947	10762	10912	15171
French Guiana	6723	8740	9701	8560	9927
Croatia/Croatie			18212	8031	x19890
Ukraine			x4244	x20267	x17030
Finland/Finlande	7653	7167	8632	5643	5618
Papua New Guinea	5969	x8542	x8204	x3249	x3478
Qatar	5573	5366	6714	7456	x1980
French Polynesia	x6032	x6623	x7724	x4718	x3611
Andorra/Andorre	x6061	x6757	x6734	x5466	x5802
Cuba	x2944	x7320	x4183	x7173	x6809
Slovakia				x18417	x13850

COUNTRIES–PAYS	EXPORTS – EXPORTATIONS 1990	1991	1992	1993	1994
Totale	2338380	2750390	3059410	3089803	3921519
Afrique	32413	37165	42114	47293	5644
Afrique du Nord	5801	7503	6026	6686	5010
Amériques	210637	320626	381076	420865	618012
ALAI	24988	39829	45093	53598	71035
MCAC	187	2163	5766	x7036	8108
Asie	414049	496235	552311	557400	691540
Moyen–Orient	59122	x84469	60179	x70446	x91812
Europe	1652801	1873928	2050087	1977496	2444897
CEE	1608121	1829172	1975583	1900635	2348152
AELE	38123	39200	43887	57350	75362
Océanie	x25897	x19395	x11246	12605	x17990
France, Monac	592818	630888	702021	648203	747056
Netherlands/Pays–Bas	236248	348489	343230	308991	343532
Germany/Allemagne	218007	258424	271994	226525	247729
Belgium–Luxembourg	208585	219709	232930	256504	303832
USA/Etats–Unis d'Amer	117581	154262	191771	224153	346455
China/Chine	117440	149081	167553	147111	201705
United Kingdom	85021	90857	114228	131112	184811
Austria/Autriche	97857	113475	124220	94179	x185284
Singapore/Singapour	92658	92774	117561	105034	101158
Canada	38728	98598	107759	104446	157864
Hong Kong	60929	90825	106076	108796	121547
Italy/Italie	59713	66386	60811	95369	129930
Switz.Liecht	33890	33838	37031	48814	61745
Ireland/Irlande	29525	30577	36163	27380	36584
Korea, Republic of	27875	27315	32493	33232	51126
So. Africa Customs Un	14536	25829	34773	29007	
Spain/Espagne	31861	15606	28200	35927	74640
United Arab Emirates	22289	17222	17073	x42554	x48685
Denmark/Danemark	19307	22420	27167	24149	26043
Saudi Arabia	18789	33469	20761	x12247	x15692
Poland/Pologne			11970	51838	120196
Mexico/Mexique	15872	19328	19777	21954	26675
Malaysia/Malaisie	14081	16924	21007	21695	26585
Greece/Grèce	5848	11645	10678	29813	35084
Thailand/Thaïlande	4825	6168	12789	29939	54619
Brazil/Brésil	6055	13984	15088	16232	15787
Japan/Japon	8999	9868	15415	15741	19454
Australia/Australie	23427	16814	9519	10518	12539
Slovenia/Slovénia			23893	12317	17042
Martinique	7572	9450	11866	12513	14051
Sweden/Suède	9710	9015	11418	10186	12055
Portugal	12457	10598	11593	8283	11166
Indonesia/Indonésie	9301	6450	10111	13661	8655
Trinidad and Tobago	9796	7241	9009	12240	14819
Syrian Arab Republic	951	x17190	3174	x931	x507
Turkey/Turquie	3525	4447	7135	6569	16569
Hungary/Hongrie	x2139	x2367	x8347	x7305	x5734
Venezuela	2429	3525	4239	6504	10574
Chile/Chili	250	1206	5258	6108	4803
Egypt/Egypte	2815	5230	2519	4221	2675
Czech Republic				11797	12762
Norway, SVD, JM	2157	2318	3413	5124	6672
Zimbabwe	47	45	145	10368	x7
Macau/Macao	2667	3216	3831	3191	3548
El Salvador	47	730	4827	4659	5982
Philippines	1315	5005	2749	2447	3841
Iceland/Islande	2076	3044	3443	3411	6946
Oman	3373	2960	3620	3118	2758
Israel/Israël	13819	2316	1824	4982	5703
Andorra/Andorre	x3715	x2956	x2651	x3401	x2609

(VALUE AS % OF TOTAL)(VALEUR EN % DU TOTAL)

	1985	1986	1987	1988	1989	1990	1991	1992	1993	1994
Africa	1.5	x2.8	x2.2	x2.0	x1.9	x3.5	x2.4	x2.4	x3.1	x3.2
Northern Africa	0.0	x0.0	x0.1	0.0	x0.0	0.1	0.0	x0.2	x0.3	x0.4
Americas	27.4	20.6	x18.9	x19.1	18.7	x18.3	19.2	x18.3	x20.6	x21.6
LAIA	0.1	0.1	0.1	0.1	0.7	0.5	2.0	3.9	3.9	5.0
CACM	0.0	0.0	0.0	0.0	0.0	0.0	0.1	0.3	x0.3	x0.3
Asia	22.5	17.9	19.5	23.0	22.9	19.0	20.5	18.3	x22.8	x24.1
Middle East	8.5	x6.4	x3.5	3.0	x3.5	x3.4	x3.3	x3.0	x4.6	x3.9
Europe	47.8	56.6	55.1	52.4	53.7	57.0	54.8	56.4	49.7	48.1
EEC	41.6	48.2	48.1	46.2	48.3	51.5	49.7	52.6	46.3	44.2
EFTA	5.9	7.7	6.4	5.7	5.0	3.4	3.1	2.6	2.6	2.6
Oceania	0.9	x1.9	x2.0	x2.2	x1.7	x1.6	x1.7	x1.2	x1.3	x1.1
Germany/Allemagne	7.2	8.5	8.5	7.9	7.4	10.8	12.7	12.4	10.0	11.2
USA/Etats–Unis d'Amer	20.9	14.0	12.6	12.7	12.3	11.2	10.7	9.1	10.9	11.0
Belgium–Luxembourg	8.5	10.1	9.7	9.3	8.4	9.1	9.2	9.1	9.9	9.3
Netherlands/Pays–Bas	7.2	8.0	7.6	7.0	6.8	7.6	8.0	10.6	6.8	5.9
Hong Kong	7.5	6.0	6.5	6.5	7.3	7.0	8.4	7.8	8.4	8.3
France, Monac	7.4	8.7	7.7	7.4	8.6	8.0	6.2	5.7	5.0	5.1
United Kingdom	5.0	6.0	7.7	6.7	7.9	6.9	5.0	5.2	6.0	4.8
Japan/Japon	1.1	1.7	5.2	9.1	8.0	4.8	4.4	3.7	4.5	6.7
Canada	2.3	2.0	1.6	1.9	2.0	2.9	3.0	2.2	2.5	2.5
Switz.Liecht	3.4	4.2	4.1	3.7	3.0	3.2	2.9	2.3	2.2	2.2

	1985	1986	1987	1988	1989	1990	1991	1992	1993	1994
Afrique	0.2	x0.5	x0.7	x0.6	0.6	1.4	1.3	1.3	1.5	0.1
Afrique du Nord	0.0	x0.0	0.1	x0.1	x0.1	0.2	0.3	0.2	0.2	0.1
Amériques	5.0	4.5	4.9	7.8	8.4	9.0	11.7	12.5	13.6	15.8
ALAI	0.5	0.5	0.7	0.9	1.4	1.1	1.4	1.5	1.7	1.8
MCAC	0.0	x0.0	0.0	x0.0	0.0	0.0	0.1	0.2	x0.2	0.2
Asie	21.0	16.6	x20.8	19.9	20.7	17.7	18.0	18.1	18.1	17.6
Moyen–Orient	3.9	x2.8	x3.3	2.4	x3.6	2.5	x3.1	2.0	x2.3	x2.3
Europe	73.1	77.4	71.5	69.2	69.0	70.7	68.1	67.0	64.0	62.3
CEE	65.3	69.4	65.0	63.8	63.6	68.8	66.5	64.6	61.5	59.9
AELE	7.6	7.5	6.2	5.1	5.1	1.6	1.4	1.4	1.9	1.9
Océanie	0.7	x1.1	x2.0	x2.5	x1.2	x1.1	x0.7	x0.4	0.4	x0.5
France, Monac	18.6	20.6	20.8	21.1	20.9	25.4	22.9	22.9	21.0	19.1
Netherlands/Pays–Bas	12.2	12.8	12.5	10.6	10.3	10.1	12.7	11.2	10.0	8.8
Germany/Allemagne	9.7	9.3	8.3	8.2	8.6	9.3	9.4	8.9	7.3	6.3
Belgium–Luxembourg	11.1	12.6	11.6	12.4	11.9	8.9	8.0	7.6	8.3	7.7
USA/Etats–Unis d'Amer	2.8	2.2	2.8	5.0	5.3	5.0	5.6	6.3	7.3	8.8
China/Chine			5.2	5.3	5.7	5.0	5.4	5.5	4.8	5.1
United Kingdom	3.6	3.4	2.7	2.9	2.8	3.6	3.3	3.7	4.2	4.7
Austria/Autriche	2.7	2.7	2.5	2.9	3.2	4.2	4.1	4.1	3.0	x4.7
Singapore/Singapour	3.9	3.7	4.3	4.8	4.5	4.0	3.4	3.8	3.4	2.6
Canada	1.0	0.9	0.6	0.7	0.8	1.7	3.6	3.5	3.4	4.0

TRADE BY COMMODITY IN THOUSAND U.S. DOLLARS – COMMERCE PAR PRODUIT EN MILLIERS DE DOLLARS E.U

COUNTRIES–PAYS	IMPORTS – IMPORTATIONS 1990	1991	1992	1993	1994
Total	19965652	20147923	21776869	20396656	22327634
Africa	x377490	x306299	x374564	x372139	x438424
Northern Africa	15556	12760	21685	20173	29763
Americas	x4997901	4787778	x5470482	x5325687	x5790746
LAIA	311554	419261	560994	607361	665939
CACM	18716	20936	26869	x26979	x28606
Asia	2939712	3202771	3326243	x3300583	x3984976
Middle East	x185801	x189768	x181207	x175227	x178793
Europe	10549417	11134444	12027348	10848765	11491131
EEC	9699917	10310395	11174256	10111679	10669107
EFTA	733868	712878	702763	636782	696551
Oceania	x371797	x350406	x360678	x344172	x394951
USA/Etats–Unis d'Amer	3848194	3589774	4056196	3914488	4210960
United Kingdom	2562038	2458100	2592269	2487228	2570490
Germany/Allemagne	2184653	2580972	2682588	2228389	2235552
Japan/Japon	1715435	1850898	1851026	1672177	1948213
France, Monac	1075898	1083829	1167394	985416	1096295
Belgium–Luxembourg	775818	790012	898751	939228	900784
Spain/Espagne	530759	668309	843590	815031	866213
Netherlands/Pays–Bas	668805	730542	828580	697777	763692
Italy/Italie	684983	712407	719238	592081	661487
Switz.Liecht	633407	605839	580248	525184	569951
Canada	538643	508816	528341	493450	540857
Hong Kong	367041	422400	505432	564839	648930
Singapore/Singapour	266430	368316	387547	356113	458523
Sweden/Suède	286009	293768	332070	336333	473414
Denmark/Danemark	269172	280282	333971	316528	326958
Russian Federation			x298198	x568513	x921316
Greece/Grèce	187597	206891	245952	265766	221070
Australia/Australie	222235	208576	215769	206409	234775
Ireland/Irlande	160686	180156	204512	162205	182705
Mexico/Mexique	105887	118393	187002	180969	183484
Thailand/Thaïlande	147568	153253	131089	150761	147169
Venezuela	57176	100419	131029	164090	89869
Portugal	127463	125070	146273	119243	184342
Austria/Autriche	117019	128970	114343	109311	115453
Norway,SVD,JM	85475	90822	105606	98447	112790
So. Africa Customs Un	90907	81018	86405	78022	95060
New Zealand	79645	75532	72399	82122	101241
Malaysia/Malaisie	54343	67433	65798	76087	95521
Paraguay	48914	68914	69225	62372	101418
Finland/Finlande	69018	71087	64725	57145	70652
United Arab Emirates	51413	48990	63112	x75093	x73399
Argentina/Argentine	7914	31121	71571	61396	75954
Korea, Republic of	43479	45453	55239	58976	95784
Poland/Pologne	55202	94478	28948	25899	36527
Hungary/Hongrie	x36837	42543	x50046	x47146	x39769
Andorra/Andorre	x50211	x45943	x48787	x38972	x43091
Brazil/Brésil	49242	46036	36728	49906	95744
Romania/Roumanie	16000	45254	49970	29060	18328
Aruba	14235	17031	x48690	x54408	x80291
Former USSR/Anc. URSS	405370	x110566			
Guadeloupe	37161	33175	34227	36900	36820
Angola	x59765	x19756	x40269	x39556	x73548
Ukraine			x8651	x90005	x54387
Czechoslovakia	54034	x43049	x55139		
Martinique	28982	27297	30448	29524	27830
Macau/Macao	13985	20051	29016	37003	58106
Philippines	21675	22912	26179	33280	48509
Reunion/Réunion	28263	23233	31278	25104	27512
Bahrain/Bahreïn	x19666	x21366	x29553	x27079	x15260
Un. Rep. of Tanzania	x12655	x23628	x17379	x36581	x30932

COUNTRIES–PAYS	EXPORTS – EXPORTATIONS 1990	1991	1992	1993	1994
Totale	19564505	20182673	22062560	21030568	23506299
Afrique	110912	157594	142252	x157006	168200
Afrique du Nord	40037	46880	27850	23876	32591
Amériques	1690914	1820654	x2100017	x2235688	x2471077
ALAI	393541	469742	518913	542027	727231
MCAC	3163	2948	5398	4858	6707
Asie	625712	1018922	1117620	1159301	1411887
Moyen–Orient	x60081	x63637	65635	x60857	76777
Europe	16297275	16534025	18119404	16771097	18755919
CEE	16189159	16438826	17940187	16594701	18626583
AELE	37730	37677	41177	50839	63702
Océanie	217987	x258838	x296014	x345711	x362696
France, Monac	6482867	6326867	6629215	5823572	6397465
United Kingdom	3696315	3887197	4182544	3783040	4105612
Italy/Italie	1769692	1815886	1883581	1789559	2156880
Germany/Allemagne	1075719	1037232	1275222	1258357	1612243
Spain/Espagne	759441	863643	1046657	928149	1024051
Netherlands/Pays–Bas	783897	798731	940064	1007213	1127999
USA/Etats–Unis d'Amer	561952	657437	773345	788962	928265
Canada	554771	527959	562155	582465	592381
Ireland/Irlande	464252	487428	542044	549500	507295
Portugal	450241	458347	565329	469551	495130
Singapore/Singapour	204450	463939	444826	390063	465190
Hong Kong	180133	277789	333993	396014	511654
Belgium–Luxembourg	229216	250905	283463	377187	461082
Mexico/Mexique	249001	281140	284984	275444	400750
Australia/Australie	179015	224462	249288	299503	309076
Denmark/Danemark	225804	245933	263246	251666	259760
Chile/Chili	52891	86753	121697	131273	147345
Bulgaria/Bulgarie	x358208	x112650	x113821	x111382	x74867
Bahamas	x29274	34720	x117122	x182190	x49616
Greece/Grèce	101430	88813	130585	114216	134220
China/Chine	53966	68547	111227	113993	113600
Austria/Autriche	63980	88676	88828	87575	x57171
So. Africa Customs Un	49839	89225	91833	83991	125375
Japan/Japon	57592	68663	67581	70736	78587
Sweden/Suède	50218	51016	62601	92027	205647
Hungary/Hongrie	x49320	x57064	x77512	x65174	x57663
Brazil/Brésil	43863	51092	49311	64666	77368
Czechoslovakia		x92969	x57030		
Finland/Finlande	34833	36898	46807	63091	82029
New Zealand	37941	33524	45338	44728	52299
Croatia/Croatie			67603	53859	x17761
Russian Federation			x57180	x62182	x74755
Czech Republic				116953	102223
Argentina/Argentine	32543	29511	39927	42090	47418
Ukraine			x16010	x94807	x31714
Switz.Liecht	28872	28504	28860	40000	52862
Cyprus/Chypre	34178	29618	36397	28468	35428
Jamaica/Jamaïque	29374	25998	x31482	x36311	x61810
Poland/Pologne	32334	28257	21691	35936	65735
Former USSR/Anc. URSS	166913	x82947			
Korea, Republic of	14268	16309	23393	29924	41708
Martinique	25662	22569	20931	20506	21449
Slovenia/Slovénia			35067	24334	21035
Yugoslavia SFR	64297	x51261			
Turkey/Turquie	9540	16526	16672	17992	30932
Trinidad and Tobago	14249	15441	15304	19484	24732
Cuba	x21671	x21941	x10830	x15497	x8826
Romania/Roumanie	11412	16060	14453	16264	20155
Malaysia/Malaisie	13176	14868	15292	16160	25861
Tunisia/Tunisie	10599	19668	12994	12813	22174

(VALUE AS % OF TOTAL)(VALEUR EN % DU TOTAL)

	1985	1986	1987	1988	1989	1990	1991	1992	1993	1994
Africa	1.4	x2.1	x2.0	x1.9	x2.0	x1.9	x1.5	x1.7	x1.8	x1.9
Northern Africa	0.0	0.0	0.0	x0.1	0.1	0.1	0.1	0.1	0.1	0.1
Americas	39.0	33.9	x30.4	28.3	27.4	x25.1	23.7	x25.2	x26.1	x26.0
LAIA	1.7	1.4	1.3	1.4	1.3	1.6	2.1	2.6	3.0	3.0
CACM	0.1	0.1	0.1	0.1	0.1	0.1	0.1	0.1	x0.1	x0.1
Asia	6.7	7.3	x9.0	x10.7	x13.2	14.7	15.9	15.3	x16.2	x17.8
Middle Eust	0.7	x1.1	x1.0	x1.1	x1.0	x0.9	x0.9	x0.8	x0.9	x0.8
Europe	43.5	49.4	51.4	51.9	51.1	52.8	55.3	55.2	53.2	51.5
EEC	38.4	43.1	44.9	45.7	44.9	48.6	51.2	51.3	49.6	47.8
EFTA	4.9	5.8	6.1	5.8	5.8	3.7	3.5	3.2	3.1	3.1
Oceania	1.6	x1.9	x1.7	x2.0	x2.0	x1.9	x1.7	x1.6	x1.7	x1.8
USA/Etats–Unis d'Amer	33.0	28.2	24.9	22.9	21.5	19.3	17.8	18.6	19.2	18.9
United Kingdom	10.5	11.9	12.0	12.5	11.8	12.8	12.2	11.9	12.2	11.5
Germany/Allemagne	8.6	9.8	10.3	10.2	9.7	10.9	12.8	12.3	10.9	10.0
Japan/Japon	2.9	3.1	4.0	5.3	7.8	8.6	9.2	8.5	8.2	8.7
France, Monac	4.8	4.7	4.6	4.9	5.0	5.4	5.4	5.4	4.8	4.9
Belgium–Luxembourg	3.3	3.7	4.1	3.8	3.5	3.9	3.9	4.1	4.6	4.0
Spain/Espagne	0.9	1.5	1.9	2.2	2.3	2.7	3.3	3.9	4.0	3.9
Netherlands/Pays–Bas	3.0	3.5	3.6	3.6	3.3	3.3	3.6	3.8	3.4	3.4
Italy/Italie	3.2	3.4	3.5	3.3	3.3	3.4	3.5	3.3	2.9	3.0
Switz.Liecht	2.7	3.1	3.3	3.2	3.1	3.2	3.0	2.7	2.6	2.6

	1985	1986	1987	1988	1989	1990	1991	1992	1993	1994
Afrique	0.9	0.8	x0.7	x0.5	0.5	0.6	0.7	0.6	x0.7	0.7
Afrique du Nord	0.7	0.3	0.2	0.2	0.2	0.2	0.2	0.1	0.1	0.1
Amériques	9.2	8.2	8.1	7.9	8.7	8.6	9.0	x9.6	x10.6	x10.5
ALAI	1.7	1.9	2.4	2.0	2.1	2.0	2.3	2.4	2.6	3.1
MCAC	0.0	0.0	0.1	0.0	0.0	0.0	0.0	0.0	0.0	0.0
Asie	1.8	1.7	2.0	2.5	2.7	3.2	5.1	5.1	5.5	6.0
Moyen–Orient	0.3	0.2	x0.2	0.2	x0.3	x0.3	x0.3	0.3	x0.3	0.3
Europe	85.1	86.0	82.2	82.2	83.2	83.3	81.9	82.1	79.7	79.8
CEE	83.5	84.7	81.0	81.1	82.0	82.7	81.5	81.3	78.9	79.2
AELE	0.9	0.8	0.7	0.7	0.9	0.2	0.2	0.2	0.2	0.3
Océanie	0.5	x0.6	x0.9	x0.8	x0.8	1.1	x1.3	x1.3	x1.6	x1.5
France, Monac	31.7	34.4	33.6	33.0	33.6	33.1	31.3	30.0	27.7	27.2
United Kingdom	17.8	17.4	16.5	18.0	18.1	18.9	19.3	19.0	18.0	17.5
Italy/Italie	10.9	8.8	8.5	8.4	8.9	9.0	9.0	8.5	8.5	9.2
Germany/Allemagne	7.1	6.9	6.1	5.8	5.8	5.5	5.1	5.8	6.0	6.9
Spain/Espagne	4.1	4.3	4.0	4.0	3.9	3.9	4.3	4.7	4.4	4.4
Netherlands/Pays–Bas	4.0	4.7	4.4	4.1	3.8	4.0	4.0	4.3	4.8	4.8
USA/Etats–Unis d'Amer	1.9	1.7	1.8	2.2	3.0	2.9	3.3	3.5	3.8	3.9
Canada	4.4	3.5	3.1	2.7	2.5	2.8	2.6	2.5	2.8	2.5
Ireland/Irlande	2.2	2.2	2.0	2.1	2.2	2.4	2.4	2.5	2.6	2.2
Portugal	2.1	2.3	2.3	2.4	2.3	2.3	2.3	2.6	2.2	2.1

TRADE BY COMMODITY IN THOUSAND U.S. DOLLARS – COMMERCE PAR PRODUIT EN MILLIERS DE DOLLARS E.U

COUNTRIES–PAYS	IMPORTS – IMPORTATIONS 1990	1991	1992	1993	1994
Total	5328742	6205229	6627691	5762359	5726237
Africa	x256561	308664	x353351	x311281	x343473
Northern Africa	140456	199691	219520	218660	245662
Americas	x856026	x1226575	x1215182	x1183890	x925670
LAIA	54452	120058	125524	111307	83091
CACM	7770	7445	9399	7792	10798
Asia	1055415	1207724	1462168	1262506	1395416
Middle East	x77643	92560	152979	110344	106961
Europe	2828933	3208284	3363735	2728037	2737105
EEC	2613073	2993026	3136375	2516984	2513467
EFTA	172708	193740	175955	169426	182172
Oceania	68943	x70759	x65517	x76608	x97060
USA/Etats–Unis d'Amer	731389	1033695	1002708	1001825	739612
Germany/Allemagne	653283	759063	916511	680383	719228
Japan/Japon	441237	536891	623624	607377	685869
United Kingdom	447422	570356	555212	438601	307486
Netherlands/Pays–Bas	435577	493679	489137	427784	433397
Spain/Espagne	315196	362023	309484	224086	281446
Belgium–Luxembourg	159441	153752	174049	163546	155276
Switz.Liecht	147592	166221	148512	144049	161456
Italy/Italie	179962	185599	141660	115942	111991
Egypt/Egypte	100830	119055	134016	128024	142306
Hong Kong	161532	127871	131178	101916	96359
France,Monac	100309	106600	138096	113449	132138
Turkey/Turquie	21429	68635	134255	93666	86442
Greece/Grèce	51100	77429	102859	86185	74712
Denmark/Danemark	89881	85470	88074	87784	93203
Philippines	60715	76051	94908	57215	93512
Poland/Pologne	32384	51267	74368	98310	125670
Indonesia/Indonésie	41964	58430	64546	76997	100216
China/Chine	40696	55323	87476	50501	28442
So. Africa Customs Un	40805	62438	83155	40731	45013
Korea, Republic of	36891	55389	68350	45816	53519
Singapore/Singapour	57335	61258	61327	42595	64204
Mexico/Mexique	39126	65133	57508	39976	15778
Austria/Autriche	41215	58311	55574	47371	56723
Australia/Australie	50038	51609	48612	60040	78997
Thailand/Thaïlande	56008	49391	51531	51184	60503
Russian Federation			x54095	x97246	x90398
Sweden/Suède	50870	42785	54881	41907	47059
Finland/Finlande	42262	40999	38039	37588	44746
Malaysia/Malaisie	30039	40871	36224	34671	36474
Portugal	27862	33797	39935	32466	38554
Dominican Republic	x34433	x38617	x35060	x26965	x51696
Algeria/Algérie	10597	15750	33276	44867	69324
Czechoslovakia	34585	x49927	x38708		
Hungary/Hongrie	x16702	29828	x29203	x28774	x28033
Brazil/Brésil	138	22636	35930	26070	28198
Norway,SVD,JM	25041	27419	27442	25378	20709
Ireland/Irlande	18694	23164	32864	19892	17509
Sri Lanka	3094	14115	27182	26677	24900
Israel/Israël	23144	18292	23227	21408	18784
Morocco/Maroc	13165	31624	16519	14054	16587
Tunisia/Tunisie	10853	15532	23683	20116	13634
Canada	6754	7643	22211	22793	24180
Bulgaria/Bulgarie	x14026	x14360	24486	x10699	x5963
New Zealand	13870	14818	13507	12922	13688
Libyan Arab Jamahiriya	4956	17731	x12026	x11413	x3586
Former USSR/Anc. URSS	140430	x34611			
Czech Republic				32458	46412
Korea Dem People's Rp	x2183	x2084	x18740	x8532	
Croatia/Croatie			13457	12957	x8222

COUNTRIES–PAYS	EXPORTS – EXPORTATIONS 1990	1991	1992	1993	1994
Totale	5186543	5807110	5828408	5028798	x4830234
Afrique	670437	863547	771065	654827	x767600
Afrique du Nord	1760	2233	x4608	x4200	x10215
Amériques	x2484038	2629726	2935940	2435445	2343493
ALAI	726315	914294	1025443	896344	862621
MCAC	37630	36736	58175	48356	30201
Asie	849932	1174436	941738	929289	789530
Moyen–Orient	439350	607221	315232	411642	403763
Europe	807561	1006558	1029223	911713	862297
CEE	719260	876387	916330	789306	775628
AELE	48590	62507	72837	41632	42687
Océanie	x21994	x3983	1562	x16475	x3595
USA/Etats–Unis d'Amer	1469802	1439921	1659553	1321626	1317062
Brazil/Brésil	565516	680615	803589	697002	693896
Turkey/Turquie	418491	563461	309424	395561	395166
Zimbabwe	339710	437187	434381	371257	x422566
Greece/Grèce	312070	344735	394152	349609	283767
Malawi	289070	362883	265766	212294	x274668
Italy/Italie	129258	200718	192189	169596	153958
China/Chine	58144	140428	140795	134842	93817
Argentina/Argentine	94950	136569	142686	116980	87413
India/Inde	106600	127665	137169	117401	58641
Thailand/Thaïlande	72033	112209	141726	104338	87621
Canada	56594	85237	115378	91243	65081
Bulgaria/Bulgarie	x311536	x110052	123456	53120	51015
Cuba	x169072	x131191	x59801	x63855	x25884
Netherlands/Pays–Bas	92560	100338	94558	54755	58280
Indonesia/Indonésie	58614	57861	80950	66238	53262
Germany/Allemagne	53991	66533	73533	63637	92276
Switz.Liecht	47091	62184	72221	41507	42550
France,Monac	37707	43217	48667	56732	55840
Philippines	20426	42519	33829	25666	23455
Mexico/Mexique	21431	44451	13867	39762	25112
Guatemala	23072	20265	38265	39375	24525
United Kingdom	31719	30106	44223	15147	19996
Spain/Espagne	20898	45145	22177	19808	35701
Korea, Republic of	77289	65227	17947	2130	1258
Belgium–Luxembourg	20719	20274	23403	40089	55104
Sri Lanka	3787	5878	39680	36397	32629
Colombia/Colombie	23337	25484	34221	19972	25287
Yugoslavia SFR	35815	x63604			
Un. Rep. of Tanzania	x3954	x12943	x22344	x15717	x22765
Syrian Arab Republic	11952	x40247	1851	x7649	x4308
So. Africa Customs Un	14218	21450	14480	13100	
Chile/Chili	10952	14505	19487	13453	21144
Dominican Republic	19448	16204	x11295	x12536	x40637
Albania/Albanie	x6600	x8400	x11659	x14676	x5949
Honduras	11331	11457	12124	6347	2856
Yugoslavia/Yougoslavie			x25599	x4078	x3089
Zambia/Zambie	x4760	x8996	x9431	x10118	x7153
Portugal	5221	12632	8515	3817	3743
Hong Kong	7654	5356	12157	6639	7744
Denmark/Danemark	5238	5451	7590	10643	12340
Paraguay	5685	7654	6893	7011	6943
Hungary/Hongrie	x10554	x5922	x6269	x6779	x2178
Singapore/Singapour	1908	3370	7207	6999	7692
Croatia/Croatie			11439	5836	x7133
Australia/Australie	1029	2471	1562	12419	3286
Uganda/Ouganda	2821	4533	x4372	6943	x4858
Japan/Japon	84	8	3350	12198	15741
Poland/Pologne	19352	3234	5497	4539	2308
Panama	3502	5415	5294	1018	1348

(VALUE AS % OF TOTAL)(VALEUR EN % DU TOTAL)

	1985	1986	1987	1988	1989	1990	1991	1992	1993	1994
Africa	7.0	7.1	x5.4	x5.7	x5.4	x4.8	5.0	x5.4	x5.4	x6.0
Northern Africa	5.7	4.9	3.2	3.2	2.9	2.6	3.2	3.3	3.8	4.3
Americas	14.3	x15.6	x13.2	x11.3	x15.6	x16.1	x19.8	x18.4	x20.6	x16.1
LAIA	0.5	0.5	0.4	0.5	0.5	1.0	1.9	1.9	1.9	1.5
CACM	0.0	x0.0	x0.1	0.1	0.2	0.1	0.1	0.1	0.1	0.2
Asia	15.4	14.6	17.6	x18.9	x20.0	19.8	19.4	22.1	21.9	24.4
Middle East	0.3	x0.9	x1.1	x1.1	x3.1	x1.5	1.5	2.3	1.9	1.9
Europe	56.1	55.2	53.3	51.4	50.8	53.1	51.7	50.8	47.3	47.8
EEC	50.0	49.7	47.9	45.4	45.1	49.0	48.2	47.3	43.7	43.9
EFTA	5.4	4.9	4.8	5.4	5.0	3.2	3.1	2.7	2.9	3.2
Oceania	1.4	x1.6	1.4	1.6	1.2	1.3	x1.2	x1.0	x1.4	x1.7
USA/Etats–Unis d'Amer	13.3	13.6	12.0	9.6	13.6	13.7	16.7	15.1	17.4	12.9
Germany/Allemagne	12.0	13.7	13.3	10.0	9.6	12.3	12.2	13.8	11.8	12.6
Japan/Japon	8.3	7.9	9.3	8.0	9.0	8.3	8.7	9.4	10.5	12.0
United Kingdom	8.2	7.0	6.8	7.8	7.7	8.4	9.2	8.4	7.6	5.4
Netherlands/Pays–Bas	7.0	7.4	7.7	7.1	6.8	8.2	8.0	7.4	7.4	7.6
Spain/Espagne	7.0	6.2	5.3	6.1	6.1	5.9	5.8	4.7	3.9	4.9
Belgium–Luxembourg	3.1	3.7	3.1	2.8	2.8	3.0	2.5	2.6	2.8	2.7
Switz.Liecht	2.0	2.1	2.0	2.4	2.3	2.8	2.7	2.2	2.5	2.8
Italy/Italie	3.9	3.2	3.8	4.0	4.5	3.4	3.0	2.1	2.0	2.0
Egypt/Egypte	3.9	3.1	2.0	1.9	1.6	1.9	1.9	2.0	2.2	2.5

	1985	1986	1987	1988	1989	1990	1991	1992	1993	1994
Afrique	9.3	x11.9	x12.2	12.1	x10.0	13.0	14.9	13.2	13.1	x15.9
Afrique du Nord	0.0	x0.1	x0.0	x0.0	x0.1	0.0	0.0	x0.1	x0.1	x0.2
Amériques	59.4	52.3	43.6	49.6	46.9	x47.9	45.3	50.4	48.4	48.5
ALAI	14.8	13.9	12.5	15.3	14.0	14.0	15.7	17.6	17.8	17.9
MCAC	0.6	x0.5	x0.4	0.8	0.8	0.7	0.6	1.0	1.0	0.6
Asie	18.7	18.0	16.5	15.3	18.1	16.4	20.2	16.2	18.4	16.3
Moyen–Orient	8.7	7.8	8.1	6.7	10.6	8.5	10.5	5.4	8.2	8.4
Europe	12.1	16.7	18.2	15.5	15.0	15.6	17.3	17.7	18.1	17.9
CEE	9.8	14.3	15.6	12.9	12.5	13.9	15.1	15.7	15.7	16.1
AELE	0.8	1.1	1.2	1.3	0.9	0.9	1.1	1.2	0.8	0.9
Océanie			x0.0		x0.5	x0.4	x0.0		x0.3	x0.1
USA/Etats–Unis d'Amer	39.8	33.7	27.4	30.6	29.9	28.3	24.8	28.5	26.3	27.3
Brazil/Brésil	11.7	11.1	10.3	12.7	11.5	10.9	11.7	13.8	13.9	14.4
Turkey/Turquie	8.6	7.4	7.8	6.5	10.5	8.1	9.7	5.3	7.9	8.2
Zimbabwe	5.8	6.9	6.3	6.7	x5.2	6.5	7.5	7.5	7.4	x8.7
Greece/Grèce	3.9	5.9	6.8	5.4	5.6	6.0	5.9	6.8	7.0	5.9
Malawi	2.8	3.6	4.2	4.3	3.6	5.6	6.2	4.6	4.2	x5.7
Italy/Italie	2.4	3.1	2.5	2.5	2.4	2.5	3.5	3.3	3.4	3.2
China/Chine	0.8	0.8	1.0	1.1	1.2	1.1	2.4	2.4	2.7	1.9
Argentina/Argentine	1.5	1.1	0.9	1.1	1.2	1.8	2.4	2.4	2.3	1.8
India/Inde	2.9	3.1	2.1	1.7	2.0	2.1	2.2	2.4	2.3	1.2

TRADE BY COMMODITY IN THOUSAND U.S. DOLLARS – COMMERCE PAR PRODUIT EN MILLIERS DE DOLLARS E.U

COUNTRIES–PAYS	IMPORTS – IMPORTATIONS 1990	1991	1992	1993	1994
Total	8789586	9397110	10225083	x11543644	x12675465
Africa	x216919	x248021	x249469	x267785	x279481
Northern Africa	59240	77424	107649	117460	131328
Americas	x257929	x413584	x615459	x851079	x489834
LAIA	30628	57264	59191	61120	104299
CACM	1161			3871	5417
Asia	3956493	4682237	5206135	x6296548	x6941969
Middle East	x983119	x1260071	x1193797	x1667912	x1565191
Europe	3255008	3584068	3907309	3812304	4617837
EEC	3097698	3371345	3711438	3621451	4380383
EFTA	92790	94510	94409	90783	93394
Oceania	x55141	x56107	x61602	x53831	x71584
Hong Kong	1049410	1300931	1598654	1428414	1432776
Japan/Japon	1051451	1231236	1339788	1504832	1912077
France,Monac	925813	1045397	1097567	1181888	1296767
Italy/Italie	929137	973584	1078901	777957	994591
Singapore/Singapour	436992	440541	526590	842186	832612
USA/Etats–Unis d'Amer	124650	225437	366507	618480	167479
Netherlands/Pays–Bas	313968	308943	396580	362560	438838
Germany/Allemagne	291621	297140	320834	417864	520312
Russian Federation			x557514	x342379	x492374
United Kingdom	225476	262139	255679	243650	267347
Saudi Arabia	274029	344266	98602	x312159	x339534
Turkey/Turquie	315766	298414	184718	233618	53377
Iran (Islamic Rp. of)	x38919	x175848	x211263	x273006	x133471
Belgium–Luxembourg	149437	156973	187650	192933	237837
Cyprus/Chypre	76560	142797	204331	152804	224346
Oman	21594	94249	185847	195465	201937
China/Chine	89317	108165	116795	149761	3901
Korea, Republic of	104170	119898	111296	143218	191724
Spain/Espagne	54696	100625	93476	148629	285904
United Arab Emirates	62272	43508	47072	x233145	x203186
Lebanon/Liban	x61023	x82502	x123199	x108443	x213725
Greece/Grèce	58563	63869	89705	118992	121262
Sweden/Suède	78161	81088	93930	66786	83172
Former USSR/Anc. URSS	877724	x239337			
Anguilla	x37567	x67194	x88883	x52530	x53533
Romania/Roumanie	23416	64726	54333	54277	36485
Viet Nam	x7784	x5850	x55408	x109803	x288136
Bulgaria/Bulgarie	x34689	x11441	58909	x92610	x93779
Morocco/Maroc	30545	45921	49644	63977	73769
Israel/Israël	40128	40757	52229	54988	66051
Kuwait/ Koweït	36831	29618	47130	70315	75536
Paraguay	23712	47786	47604	46731	84238
Norway,SVD,JM	48676	44777	48326	42431	43459
Ireland/Irlande	34605	41598	45673	43744	45498
Malaysia/Malaisie	20582	42004	51220	36559	27255
Switz.Liecht	32780	36910	32361	35585	36718
Macau/Macao	41621	26864	29607	46268	63015
Afghanistan	x34394	x20888	x32391	x45823	x18628
Andorra/Andorre	x24952	x28398	x35463	x34163	x22524
Poland/Pologne	36936	74154	11989	9172	15484
Australia/Australie	29611	27481	31083	30429	39797
Thailand/Thaïlande	10360	16713	28225	38253	31238
Bahrain/Bahreïn	x24726	x27587	x26724	x27096	x14156
Yugoslavia SFR	30126	x78887			
Tunisia/Tunisie	18187	18726	29104	29458	33205
Myanmar		485	x61	x73008	x125760
Canada	16273	20871	27854	23758	27410
Yemen/Yémen	x35062	1698	x44113	x21060	x30772
Philippines	6625	10606	10449	41382	89488
Lithuania/Lituanie			386	x58880	15125

COUNTRIES–PAYS	EXPORTS – EXPORTATIONS 1990	1991	1992	1993	1994
Totale	12673542	13408215	15457683	14896296	16643687
Afrique	35378	48191	x92573	60258	38597
Afrique du Nord	17873	25356	22939	21798	36788
Amériques	x5360462	x5179651	x5253075	x5285529	x6073153
ALAI	111804	261813	334234	325499	440244
MCAC	139			15890	12830
Asie	2289060	2607991	3294541	3903866	4180481
Moyen–Orient	224269	203473	308245	x474884	x532919
Europe	4941790	5515075	6522334	5346142	6166286
CEE	4659550	5243321	6166552	5024187	5794572
AELE	252439	262187	292034	267909	359066
Océanie	17550	x15010	16965	19731	x28450
USA/Etats–Unis d'Amer	5044890	4587670	4517863	4262026	5423635
Netherlands/Pays–Bas	1806291	1923547	2192365	2012127	2259047
Hong Kong	1229882	1391439	1617034	1491787	1585004
United Kingdom	1144998	1349124	1658057	951109	1320835
Germany/Allemagne	972159	1182391	1376869	1177251	1302349
Singapore/Singapour	469649	505342	639703	977989	1033193
Belgium–Luxembourg	327780	322448	335437	396885	411324
China/Chine	112315	170946	300461	505511	592543
Canada	42526	145619	279573	540337	78729
Switz.Liecht	241669	252416	277614	257792	346095
Japan/Japon	97420	136511	187769	232245	257564
Brazil/Brésil	58090	137748	178011	203780	336812
France,Monac	133455	163494	190766	141222	164541
Cyprus/Chypre	74002	126042	185197	162994	224985
Bulgaria/Bulgarie	x11615	x18376	x240236	166988	x4367
Cuba	x141588	x172512	x109371	x122814	x54215
Denmark/Danemark	118850	116529	125442	125574	132487
Indonesia/Indonésie	66187	88073	125468	110415	73160
Oman	919	36799	79285	120427	116311
Greece/Grèce	24234	47135	115397	56523	48205
Venezuela	37767	69043	91497	56114	56216
Ireland/Irlande	46522	53937	63757	61835	71130
United Arab Emirates	83329		3	x138426	x160497
Malaysia/Malaisie	8001	29627	39306	32961	31440
India/Inde	38557	25574	45701	29632	22493
Poland/Pologne	108	19843	33169	41490	51188
Austria/Autriche	20166	21218	33464	35150	x6627
Turkey/Turquie	23868	8563	23193	45465	28509
Croatia/Croatie			29843	38194	
Mexico/Mexique	6165	9526	17227	40212	31248
Tunisia/Tunisie	15895	23142	21236	20594	31935
Sweden/Suède	22039	20689	20585	19492	22188
Colombia/Colombie	3263	13712	30180	15854	428
Spain/Espagne	15655	14521	21357	22397	25639
Finland/Finlande	16934	17936	16091	13413	18573
Philippines	28554	27115	9228	9142	9171
Australia/Australie	14342	12979	14847	17526	24906
So. Africa Customs Un	2834	7230	18541	14823	
Malawi		326	x34635		
Czech Republic				34516	58617
Slovenia/Slovénia			25903	8464	10850
Norway,SVD,JM	10770	9771	14420	10117	12971
Italy/Italie	8297	8064	14182	7878	8239
Argentina/Argentine	3683	21165	5783	611	12344
Slovakia				x24689	x24893
Macau/Macao	297	373	995	21536	19089
Kenya	3136	4548	7035	9868	x229
Zimbabwe	6015	5647	5899	9241	x838
Malta/Malte	6278	8291	5610	5224	x344
Ecuador/Equateur	2027	8298	4895	5244	x65

(VALUE AS % OF TOTAL)(VALEUR EN % DU TOTAL)

	1985	1986	1987	1988	1989	1990	1991	1992	1993	1994
Africa	3.7	x3.6	x3.1	x3.1	x2.3	x2.5	x2.6	x2.4	x2.3	x2.2
Northern Africa	2.3	x1.2	0.9	x1.0	0.9	0.7	0.8	1.1	1.0	1.0
Americas	3.8	x3.4	x2.9	x2.7	x3.1	x2.9	x4.4	x6.1	x7.4	x3.8
LAIA	0.3	0.3	0.3	0.3	0.4	0.3	0.6	0.6	0.5	0.8
CACM	0.0	0.0	x0.0	x0.0	x0.0	0.0			0.0	0.0
Asia	26.6	x29.8	x36.3	x41.8	x45.9	45.0	49.8	50.9	x54.5	x54.8
Middle East	12.0	x14.6	x12.3	10.3	x12.5	x11.2	x13.4	x11.7	x14.4	x12.3
Europe	48.7	45.1	42.0	39.0	36.9	37.0	38.1	38.2	33.0	36.4
EEC	46.1	41.9	39.1	36.3	34.1	35.2	35.9	36.3	31.4	34.6
EFTA	2.4	2.8	2.5	2.2	2.2	1.1	1.0	0.9	0.8	0.7
Oceania	0.7	x0.9	x0.7	x0.7	x0.5	x0.7	x0.6	x0.6	x0.5	x0.5
Hong Kong	6.9	5.4	5.8	8.0	9.9	11.9	13.8	15.6	12.4	11.3
Japan/Japon	3.1	4.1	8.8	11.1	12.9	12.0	13.1	13.1	13.0	15.1
France,Monac	15.0	11.5	11.3	11.2	10.5	10.5	11.1	10.7	10.2	10.2
Italy/Italie	11.4	10.8	10.1	10.3	10.2	10.6	10.4	10.6	6.7	7.8
Singapore/Singapour	3.1	2.7	2.2	2.4	3.9	5.0	4.7	5.1	7.3	6.6
USA/Etats–Unis d'Amer	2.5	2.1	1.8	1.5	1.6	1.4	2.4	3.6	5.4	1.3
Netherlands/Pays–Bas	5.3	5.2	4.5	3.7	3.5	3.6	3.3	3.9	3.1	3.5
Germany/Allemagne	4.1	4.5	3.9	3.3	3.1	3.3	3.2	3.1	3.6	4.1
Russian Federation								x5.5	x3.0	x3.9
United Kingdom	4.1	3.9	3.2	2.8	2.4	2.6	2.8	2.5	2.1	2.1

	1985	1986	1987	1988	1989	1990	1991	1992	1993	1994
Afrique	0.6	x0.7	x0.6	x0.2	x0.3	0.3	0.4	x0.6	0.4	0.2
Afrique du Nord	0.2	x0.2	x0.1	0.0	0.1	0.1	0.2	0.1	0.1	0.2
Amériques	34.8	33.0	34.9	37.5	x42.2	x42.3	x38.6	x33.9	x35.4	x36.5
ALAI	0.9	0.6	0.5	0.6	0.9	0.9	2.0	2.2	2.2	2.6
MCAC	0.2	0.2	0.1	x0.1	x0.1	0.0			0.1	0.1
Asie	9.5	9.1	9.0	11.8	14.7	18.1	19.4	21.3	26.2	25.2
Moyen–Orient	0.8	0.8	x1.1	0.9	x0.6	1.8	1.5	2.0	x3.2	x3.2
Europe	54.7	56.8	48.4	43.9	41.0	39.0	41.1	42.2	35.9	37.0
CEE	51.7	53.5	45.6	41.1	38.2	36.8	39.1	39.9	33.7	34.8
AELE	2.6	3.0	2.6	2.6	2.5	2.0	2.0	1.9	1.8	2.2
Océanie	0.2	x0.2	x0.2	x0.2	0.2	0.1	x0.1	0.1	0.1	x0.2
USA/Etats–Unis d'Amer	31.2	30.5	32.9	35.5	40.1	39.8	34.2	29.2	28.6	32.6
Netherlands/Pays–Bas	15.8	18.3	16.2	13.8	13.6	14.3	14.3	14.2	13.5	13.6
Hong Kong	5.9	5.3	5.2	7.2	8.2	9.7	10.4	10.5	10.0	9.5
United Kingdom	14.5	11.5	10.1	10.5	9.2	9.0	10.1	10.7	6.4	7.9
Germany/Allemagne	11.5	13.4	10.2	9.6	8.6	7.7	8.8	8.9	7.9	7.8
Singapore/Singapour	1.4	1.5	1.0	1.5	3.0	3.7	3.8	4.1	6.6	6.2
Belgium–Luxembourg	5.0	5.2	4.3	3.4	3.0	2.6	2.4	2.2	2.7	2.5
China/Chine			0.3	0.6	0.9	0.9	1.3	1.9	3.4	3.6
Canada	0.2	0.3	0.4	0.3	0.3	0.3	1.1	1.8	3.6	0.5
Switz.Liecht	1.7	2.1	1.8	2.0	1.9	1.9	1.9	1.8	1.7	2.1

TRADE BY COMMODITY IN THOUSAND U.S. DOLLARS – COMMERCE PAR PRODUIT EN MILLIERS DE DOLLARS E.U

COUNTRIES–PAYS	IMPORTS – IMPORTATIONS				
	1990	1991	1992	1993	1994
Total	5672487	4264712	4416015	4307966	5318020
Africa	54793	31921	17179	13444	20299
Northern Africa	43234	26992	12605	9211	14809
Americas	279910	321966	357320	329054	338894
LAIA	115707	161811	173359	147232	140175
CACM	7981	10896	9846	3469	2019
Asia	2355854	1980588	2021402	2049090	2291108
Middle East	135998	128779	177351	217764	285027
Europe	2687796	1816919	1952886	1807068	2489638
EEC	2557830	1780036	1895824	1753016	2435164
EFTA	22460	16582	21104	22044	27510
Oceania	23504	x14935	16055	x18525	x24867
Italy/Italie	1295852	941811	952607	983439	1385652
Korea, Republic of	1192743	1004329	903157	881049	921954
Japan/Japon	770741	520314	500428	452423	410689
Thailand/Thaïlande	107460	167311	166748	183519	156174
Netherlands/Pays–Bas	197167	156654	194003	150591	163309
Turkey/Turquie	128539	115568	165946	214426	281237
Spain/Espagne	235175	156732	137872	116799	210527
Mexico/Mexique	95594	136193	148925	117768	114816
France,Monac	220870	129404	147768	90536	143684
USA/Etats–Unis d'Amer	97466	113210	127612	122448	129487
Germany/Allemagne	153046	102986	125354	96809	119726
United Kingdom	149284	97192	109196	113373	142933
Hong Kong	52285	74678	89904	96790	163548
China/Chine	15740	26103	105941	114841	223261
Portugal	79864	53050	62422	45984	64867
Belgium–Luxembourg	80936	46142	57450	56721	77681
Canada	53176	34750	41397	54155	64379
Austria/Autriche	44770	24406	38532	35085	51454
Sweden/Suède	35583	26332	29322	29231	30883
Czechoslovakia	97374	x65257	x15519		
India/Inde	36211	18824	24325	30923	46206
Pakistan	12163	14413	21620	34324	41265
Greece/Grèce	34155	21437	18153	19098	20948
Romania/Roumanie	86166	9332	12931	22112	16745
Hungary/Hongrie	x22644	17153	x11073	x14381	x16941
Slovenia/Slovénia			18760	18838	23138
New Zealand	13434	8068	13969	14535	22796
Indonesia/Indonésie	4374	5643	14537	15791	18709
Finland/Finlande	19094	10506	12865	11350	16055
Norway,SVD,JM	10697	8376	11765	14435	18018
Brazil/Brésil	13696	10128	9719	13880	11356
Singapore/Singapour	10388	8991	9762	13163	15713
Poland/Pologne	15235	2543	8452	19934	37425
Switz.Liecht	11479	7758	8721	7288	9111
Denmark/Danemark	7672	10249	8563	2888	3518
Yugoslavia SFR	106767	x19477			
Algeria/Algérie	33388	15633	1162	2530	5628
Morocco/Maroc	3554	6833	7190	3625	4488
Czech Republic				16359	28603
Venezuela	1181	8982	5055	395	48
Slovakia				x14295	x15420
Yugoslavia/Yougoslavie			x10447	x3294	x265
Australia/Australie	9676	6607	1863	3571	1941
Syrian Arab Republic	3667	x5188	5676	x759	x192
Chile/Chili	524	2768	3668	4499	1451
Colombia/Colombie	750	744	2482	7632	4991
Croatia/Croatie			5837	2943	x1687
El Salvador	636	4715	1953	1787	1112
Costa Rica	6034	3180	4875	x329	x245
Bulgaria/Bulgarie	x34024	x1457	3126	x3701	38079

COUNTRIES–PAYS	EXPORTS – EXPORTATIONS				
	1990	1991	1992	1993	1994
Totale	5759799	4283641	4364561	4193565	4949714
Afrique	x265312	x170465	x181342	x205729	x194695
Afrique du Nord	x45438	x24558	x28496	x32839	x43663
Amériques	1944632	1504746	1485981	1441448	1683256
ALAI	56288	20632	27992	46616	77531
MCAC	16316	14620	13599	4220	6171
Asie	x595441	x365220	x399140	x415198	x546843
Moyen–Orient	x155862	x107083	x148440	x121383	x183570
Europe	2041946	1616166	1771749	1585015	1958427
CEE	1934131	1519429	1666855	1492323	1841611
AELE	93198	77916	82844	73634	85118
Océanie	663366	x438841	x435938	458350	x452667
USA/Etats–Unis d'Amer	1621475	1281121	1275079	1207815	1417570
France,Monac	426855	314002	349281	319829	418769
Netherlands/Pays–Bas	304587	274758	301716	270907	279549
Germany/Allemagne	290036	254932	260367	236356	283998
Australia/Australie	395398	225810	239286	256079	184257
United Kingdom	322930	228270	218513	200351	281921
New Zealand	266450	208867	194137	200066	264676
Canada	248131	182450	167730	180277	176565
Ireland/Irlande	116750	96384	109707	88180	106298
Belgium–Luxembourg	103295	77393	95452	79894	103582
Russian Federation			x83129	x136050	x275110
So. Africa Customs Un	95481	65493	73672	79606	76435
Iran (Islamic Rp. of)	x56799	x64412	x82067	x67592	x106477
Spain/Espagne	65252	53180	85113	70357	95218
Hong Kong	56812	62750	67975	70444	106202
Japan/Japon	80385	61072	62940	57761	93862
Italy/Italie	85654	57045	61888	57699	80596
Denmark/Danemark	63482	52618	53898	47900	52353
Switz.Liecht	64295	52139	56062	45817	50506
Former USSR/Anc. URSS	193835	x138384			
Sweden/Suède	59707	43832	42727	48388	45262
China/Chine	123686	61105	36305	24310	59149
Austria/Autriche	37846	25167	35545	29644	x35882
Mongolia/Mongolie	x50526	x3225	x15353	x71741	x15588
Ethiopia/Ethiopie	60775	25068	32288	32697	
Norway,SVD,JM	28040	25260	26225	26513	33499
Poland/Pologne	18626	21413	36331	11353	7177
Greece/Grèce	28235	18936	28912	20542	27617
Ukraine			x33207	x26207	x38676
Sudan/Soudan	x21540	x17382	x20780	x16432	x11067
Finland/Finlande	23528	17024	18514	18110	25151
Syrian Arab Republic	10732	4417	17076	x26310	x31477
Saudi Arabia	8453	16655	16611	x8441	x13595
Hungary/Hongrie	x5486	x6329	x16793	x16844	x19160
Lithuania/Lituanie			14123	x22565	5062
Bulgaria/Bulgarie	x25000	x9239	x15671	x7935	25303
Uganda/Ouganda	x12823	x8155	x7634	x16721	x16198
Singapore/Singapour	18591	13549	8209	8451	11329
Mexico/Mexique	4681	1888	8430	17166	22499
Bangladesh	68471	26486	585	x223	x251
Czech Republic				26955	28902
Latvia/Lettonie			x9445	x17094	1371
Libyan Arab Jamahiriya	17197	6338	x6414	x13156	x26528
Kazakstan			x12778	x12897	x22234
Czechoslovakia		x9786	x15414		
Viet Nam	x23209	x14355	x4334	x5359	x6987
Zimbabwe	6511	6637	8990	8181	x1932
Lebanon/Liban	x27764	x12421	x4948	x6278	x7822
Slovenia/Slovénia			10773	9886	11281
Uruguay	10020	5707	6741	8160	11226

(VALUE AS % OF TOTAL)(VALEUR EN % DU TOTAL)

	1985	1986	1987	1988	1989	1990	1991	1992	1993	1994
Africa	0.6	0.6	0.5	0.6	0.6	0.9	0.7	0.3	0.3	0.4
Northern Africa	0.5	0.6	0.5	0.5	0.6	0.8	0.6	0.3	0.2	0.3
Americas	7.4	5.4	5.0	5.5	6.0	5.0	7.6	8.1	7.6	6.3
LAIA	4.2	2.6	2.3	2.6	2.9	2.0	3.8	3.9	3.4	2.6
CACM	0.0	0.1	0.1	0.1	0.2	0.1	0.3	0.2	0.1	0.0
Asia	23.1	29.1	x36.9	x37.6	36.6	41.5	46.4	45.8	47.6	43.1
Middle East	1.1	2.0	2.6	1.4	1.9	2.4	3.0	4.0	5.1	5.4
Europe	63.9	60.8	50.7	48.4	49.6	47.4	42.6	44.2	41.9	46.8
EEC	57.5	55.1	46.7	44.5	45.9	45.1	41.7	42.9	40.7	45.8
EFTA	3.0	3.4	2.7	2.3	2.2	0.4	0.4	0.5	0.5	0.5
Oceania	0.2	x0.1	x0.2	x0.3	0.3	0.4	x0.3	0.4	x0.4	x0.5
Italy/Italie	28.7	26.8	20.5	20.9	22.1	22.8	22.1	21.6	22.8	26.1
Korea, Republic of	8.8	13.4	14.7	15.6	18.7	21.0	23.5	20.5	20.5	17.3
Japan/Japon	12.1	12.1	10.7	12.1	12.4	13.6	12.2	11.3	10.5	7.7
Thailand/Thaïlande	0.2	0.4	0.9	1.0	1.3	1.9	3.9	3.8	4.3	2.9
Netherlands/Pays–Bas	3.2	3.1	2.7	2.8	3.0	3.5	3.7	4.4	3.5	3.1
Turkey/Turquie	0.9	1.8	2.5	1.2	1.8	2.3	2.7	3.8	5.0	5.3
Spain/Espagne	6.6	6.8	7.5	6.0	5.8	4.1	3.7	3.1	2.7	4.0
Mexico/Mexique	3.5	1.3	1.5	1.9	1.7	1.7	3.2	3.4	2.7	2.2
France,Monac	4.8	4.3	4.5	4.4	4.8	3.9	3.0	3.3	2.1	2.7
USA/Etats–Unis d'Amer	2.2	1.7	1.6	1.7	1.8	1.7	2.7	2.9	2.8	2.4

	1985	1986	1987	1988	1989	1990	1991	1992	1993	1994
Afrique	5.3	x5.9	x5.7	x5.5	x5.1	x4.6	x4.0	x4.2	x4.9	x3.9
Afrique du Nord	0.3	0.3	0.2	0.3	x0.6	x0.8	x0.6	x0.7	x0.8	x0.9
Amériques	35.6	35.3	x31.5	x32.4	33.6	33.8	35.2	34.1	34.4	34.0
ALAI	0.8	0.7	0.5	0.7	0.7	1.0	0.5	0.6	1.1	1.6
MCAC	0.0	x0.0	0.0	0.2	0.3	0.3	0.3	0.3	0.1	0.1
Asie	4.6	x7.9	x8.9	x10.0	x9.0	x10.3	x8.5	x9.2	x9.9	x11.0
Moyen–Orient	0.4	x3.5	x3.9	x3.1	x2.6	x2.7	x2.5	x3.4	x2.9	x3.7
Europe	40.8	38.0	36.5	34.3	36.7	35.5	37.7	40.6	37.8	39.6
CEE	37.2	34.5	33.0	30.9	32.9	33.6	35.5	38.2	35.6	37.2
AELE	3.6	3.5	3.5	3.4	3.6	1.6	1.8	1.9	1.8	1.7
Océanie	12.6	x11.1	x14.4	x13.6	12.7	11.5	x10.2	x10.0	11.0	x9.2
USA/Etats–Unis d'Amer	31.3	31.0	27.4	27.6	28.7	28.2	29.9	29.2	28.8	28.6
France,Monac	9.1	8.0	7.8	7.2	7.2	7.4	7.3	8.0	7.6	8.5
Netherlands/Pays–Bas	5.9	5.4	4.9	4.6	5.0	5.3	6.4	6.9	6.5	5.6
Germany/Allemagne	5.4	5.6	4.9	4.5	4.6	5.0	6.0	6.0	5.6	5.7
Australia/Australie	7.0	6.9	8.1	7.9	7.0	6.9	5.3	5.5	6.1	3.7
United Kingdom	6.3	5.5	5.5	4.9	5.9	5.6	5.3	5.0	4.8	5.7
New Zealand	5.5	4.2	6.2	5.7	5.7	4.6	4.9	4.4	4.8	5.3
Canada	3.5	3.7	3.4	3.6	3.9	4.3	4.3	3.8	4.3	3.6
Ireland/Irlande	1.7	2.1	2.1	1.8	2.0	2.0	2.3	2.5	2.1	2.1
Belgium–Luxembourg	2.2	2.0	1.7	1.7	1.8	1.8	1.8	2.2	1.9	2.1

TRADE BY COMMODITY IN THOUSAND U.S. DOLLARS – COMMERCE PAR PRODUIT EN MILLIERS DE DOLLARS E.U

COUNTRIES–PAYS	IMPORTS – IMPORTATIONS				
	1990	1991	1992	1993	1994
Total	970134	861637	926009	826907	1109193
Africa	213	122	x42	x45	825
Northern Africa	202	78	4		654
Americas	x169059	95417	x98836	96752	134310
LAIA	4452	5424	2694	1729	2929
CACM	25	18		x4	9
Asia	308195	302537	323328	412659	552240
Middle East	366	166	451	452	x1106
Europe	474760	458476	501319	308673	403337
EEC	448655	441116	481457	300121	389643
EFTA	25490	17078	19411	8079	13172
Oceania	727	134	48	x31	1039
Hong Kong	142527	138891	158183	198104	273530
Denmark/Danemark	141731	102650	119055	64033	78681
Italy/Italie	86988	102808	108912	67233	77093
Germany/Allemagne	78114	99696	92856	70969	101870
Korea, Republic of	89868	89370	61287	92271	170118
USA/Etats–Unis d'Amer	79017	57234	61964	59796	78418
China/Chine	5095	6386	45927	74531	44980
Canada	84154	32092	33477	34950	52529
Japan/Japon	47655	47325	31432	20225	33776
United Kingdom	29893	24319	26056	28707	34044
Macau/Macao	21981	19855	24997	25784	26837
France, Monac	21280	25207	26055	15521	18963
Greece/Grèce	6503	12502	28070	18515	31655
Spain/Espagne	11590	21983	22489	5418	11525
Belgium–Luxembourg	18140	15666	15903	11593	14859
Sweden/Suède	31663	16632	20497	2117	182
Finland/Finlande	12016	11374	12905	14323	16151
Norway, SVD, JM	9179	10463	14440	7630	13036
Netherlands/Pays–Bas	9290	6427	7411	1174	3392
Switz.Liecht	16311	6614	4971	448	136
Poland/Pologne	1509	1546	106	5493	13265
Lithuania/Lituanie			1016	x6002	917
Brazil/Brésil	1236	1163	1820	1307	2307
Russian Federation			x2016	x1248	x2257
Argentina/Argentine	1860	2481	500	217	369
Czechoslovakia	4651	x1536	x1581		
Austria/Autriche	1134	1394	374	274	298
Hungary/Hongrie	x1078	350	x529	x1130	x1061
Uruguay	1292	1701	44	95	204
Czech Republic				1584	2929
Portugal	311	457	874	196	915
Dominican Republic	x1356	x617	x601	x121	x272
Turkey/Turquie	279	153	422	447	280
Korea Dem People's Rp			x161	x851	
Former USSR/Anc. URSS	8408	x967			
India/Inde	125	102	442	326	860
Slovenia/Slovénia			340	472	509
Ukraine				x800	x1355
Romania/Roumanie	219	541	78	174	26
Estonia/Estonie			x25	x522	x421
Slovakia				x366	x160
Colombia/Colombie	1		308		
Thailand/Thaïlande	27	127	169		2
Yugoslavia SFR	558	x216			
Viet Nam			x195	x13	x155
Philippines		203			
Latvia/Lettonie				x179	218
Australia/Australie	699	133	12	10	1029
Bulgaria/Bulgarie		x12	142		
Haiti/Haïti	x3	x2	x50	x97	x128

COUNTRIES–PAYS	EXPORTS – EXPORTATIONS				
	1990	1991	1992	1993	1994
Totale	1017524	932851	901319	813746	1096371
Afrique	x371	x330	x547	x358	x451
Afrique du Nord	18	x67	x2		86
Amériques	236150	183623	161510	164839	206592
ALAI	487	404	1094	2354	3332
MCAC	30	29	10		
Asie	80275	x51568	x65302	102382	122175
Moyen–Orient	156	x103	332	x393	x355
Europe	610779	644157	660342	530962	752607
CEE	557026	601913	619892	498350	704340
AELE	53741	42215	40306	32592	48155
Océanie	4038	2962	2618	2685	3864
Denmark/Danemark	268093	354231	366814	278708	344089
Finland/Finlande	113533	115691	90073	104205	209821
USA/Etats–Unis d'Amer	147305	107755	97462	102041	133579
Canada	88273	75140	62663	60096	69504
Netherlands/Pays–Bas	53662	41533	54308	33920	44833
Sweden/Suède	75537	47260	51633	22740	36854
Hong Kong	36740	23429	36790	60799	86663
Norway, SVD, JM	43054	36025	36638	29814	42239
Russian Federation			x48059	x25879	x49506
Germany/Allemagne	9510	14423	18849	28073	36751
Former USSR/Anc. URSS	78312	x42786			
United Kingdom	15003	10503	11353	13167	13123
China/Chine	29671	15400	7492	11790	3822
Macau/Macao	1847	1735	7361	20305	25716
Belgium–Luxembourg	6800	6955	10293	5809	7772
France, Monac	7893	5302	9868	5026	4141
Poland/Pologne	3427	3972	7063	9046	6379
Afghanistan	x2365	x3517	x6344	x6600	x2407
Iceland/Islande	2940	3606	3154	2576	5639
Italy/Italie	3682	2684	3187	2764	2711
Japan/Japon	1608	2056	3066	1469	1534
Ireland/Irlande	2099	1514	2115	2013	2179
Mongolia/Mongolie	x7164	x4978		x588	
Latvia/Lettonie			x1045	x3600	1255
Australia/Australie	946	1684	1548	1243	1201
Syrian Arab Republic			61	x69	x86
Hungary/Hongrie	x1743	x1230	x1651	x1003	x513
New Zealand	3092	1278	1070	1442	2663
Spain/Espagne	938	1464	735	1152	1248
Switz.Liecht	7747	2584	514	202	276
Czechoslovakia		x1321	x1948		
Kazakstan			x2593	x352	x571
Argentina/Argentine	125	208	515	1948	3027
Estonia/Estonie			x542	x1520	x758
Czech Republic				1910	2557
Korea Dem People's Rp	x489	x512	x663	x22	x707
Ukraine			x940	x199	x616
Uruguay	295	140	550	291	294
Austria/Autriche	176	248	286	444	x239
Greenland/Groenland	17	292	276	347	x176
Turkey/Turquie	90	100	270	324	224
Greece/Grèce	101	50	358	247	433
Bulgaria/Bulgarie	x26	x182	x189	x275	x49
Kyrgyzstan/Kirghizistan			x511		x8
Romania/Roumanie		395	112	1	308
Belarus/Bélarus			x109	x312	x1455
Central African Rep.	x297	x175	x121	x52	x50
Slovakia				x286	x878
Un. Rep. of Tanzania	x3	x14	x203	x65	x199
Lithuania/Lituanie				x254	1084

(VALUE AS % OF TOTAL)(VALEUR EN % DU TOTAL)

	1985	1986	1987	1988	1989	1990	1991	1992	1993	1994
Africa		x0.0	x0.0	x0.0	x0.1			x0.0	x0.0	0.1
Northern Africa	0.0	x0.0	x0.0	x0.0	0.0	0.0	0.0	0.0		0.1
Americas	20.6	x16.9	x16.6	x13.9	x14.8	x17.4	11.1	x10.7	11.7	12.1
LAIA	0.1	x0.4	x0.3	x0.3	0.5	0.5	0.6	0.3	0.2	0.3
CACM			0.0	x0.0	0.0	0.0	0.0	0.0	x0.0	0.0
Asia	17.2	21.0	25.8	24.7	27.0	31.7	35.1	34.9	49.9	49.8
Middle East	0.0	x0.0	x0.0	x0.0	x0.0	0.0	0.0	0.0	0.1	x0.1
Europe	60.6	60.0	55.4	58.4	56.3	48.9	53.2	54.1	37.3	36.4
EEC	56.1	55.3	49.5	51.1	48.9	46.2	51.2	52.0	36.3	35.1
EFTA	4.4	4.6	5.8	7.3	7.4	2.6	2.0	2.1	1.0	1.2
Oceania	0.1	0.1	0.1	0.1		0.1			x0.0	0.1
Hong Kong	5.6	8.2	10.5	10.5	12.1	14.7	16.1	17.1	24.0	24.7
Denmark/Danemark	6.4	8.1	7.6	11.5	12.5	14.6	11.9	12.9	7.7	7.1
Italy/Italie	10.6	10.6	9.3	9.4	10.0	9.0	11.9	11.8	8.1	7.0
Germany/Allemagne	15.3	14.5	12.0	11.3	9.0	8.1	11.6	10.0	8.6	9.2
Korea, Republic of	6.1	6.9	8.0	8.0	8.7	9.3	10.4	6.6	11.2	15.3
USA/Etats–Unis d'Amer	11.2	8.5	8.9	7.4	8.2	8.1	6.6	6.7	7.2	7.1
China/Chine			0.7	1.1	0.5	0.5	0.7	5.0	9.0	4.1
Canada	9.3	7.7	7.1	6.0	6.0	8.7	3.7	3.6	4.2	4.7
Japan/Japon	5.0	4.8	4.7	3.0	3.3	4.9	5.5	3.4	2.4	3.0
United Kingdom	12.2	11.1	10.2	8.8	5.8	3.1	2.8	2.8	3.5	3.1

	1985	1986	1987	1988	1989	1990	1991	1992	1993	1994
Afrique	0.7	x0.4	x0.6	x0.7	x0.3	x0.0	x0.0	x0.1	x0.0	x0.0
Afrique du Nord		x0.0	x0.0	x0.0		0.0	x0.0	x0.0		0.0
Amériques	16.5	x13.5	x14.2	x13.1	x13.8	23.3	19.7	18.0	20.2	18.8
ALAI	0.1	x0.1	x0.1	x0.0	x0.0	0.0	0.0	0.1	0.3	0.3
MCAC		0.0	x0.0	x0.0	0.0	0.0	0.0	0.0		
Asie	4.0	x9.8	x5.2	x7.5	5.3	7.9	x5.5	x7.2	12.6	11.1
Moyen–Orient	0.0	x3.6	x0.1	x0.1	x0.0	0.0	x0.0	0.0	x0.0	x0.0
Europe	70.7	68.1	68.9	69.1	73.8	60.0	69.1	73.3	65.2	68.6
CEE	48.6	47.1	47.7	48.5	50.4	54.7	64.4	68.8	61.2	64.2
AELE	22.1	21.0	21.2	20.6	23.4	5.3	4.5	4.5	4.0	4.4
Océanie	0.6	x0.8	x0.7	x0.4	0.2	0.4	0.3	0.3	0.3	0.4
Denmark/Danemark	17.0	17.4	20.3	21.9	21.9	26.3	37.9	40.7	34.2	31.4
Finland/Finlande	14.2	13.6	13.2	9.5	11.8	11.2	12.3	10.0	12.8	19.1
USA/Etats–Unis d'Amer	11.9	9.9	9.4	8.0	8.6	14.5	11.5	10.8	12.5	12.2
Canada	4.5	3.4	4.7	4.9	5.1	8.7	8.0	7.0	7.4	6.3
Netherlands/Pays–Bas	1.9	2.4	1.9	2.8	2.8	5.3	4.4	6.0	4.2	4.1
Sweden/Suède	3.6	4.2	2.9	5.3	6.9	7.4	5.0	5.7	2.8	3.4
Hong Kong	1.0	1.2	1.1	2.3	2.4	3.6	2.5	4.1	7.5	7.9
Norway, SVD, JM	3.6	2.4	4.3	4.7	4.0	4.2	3.8	4.1	3.7	3.9
Russian Federation								x5.3	x3.2	x4.5
Germany/Allemagne	0.8	1.0	0.8	0.9	0.8	0.9	1.5	2.1	3.4	3.4

TRADE BY COMMODITY IN THOUSAND U.S. DOLLARS – COMMERCE PAR PRODUIT EN MILLIERS DE DOLLARS E.U

COUNTRIES–PAYS	IMPORTS – IMPORTATIONS 1990	1991	1992	1993	1994
Total	10505663	10108041	10486500	9809091	11865179
Africa	x69461	x80776	x158797	155081	186937
Northern Africa	43347	41953	55218	75081	132705
Americas	723748	968123	1199683	1217544	1608197
LAIA	366277	640795	895179	832436	1149625
CACM	28144	28350	31460	x43116	x40429
Asia	3080293	2992013	3205889	3322288	3672344
Middle East	122278	x85023	114336	x106429	x106934
Europe	6201844	5631160	5804979	4995094	6249079
EEC	5968049	5480592	5668795	4941528	6127203
EFTA	137097	111939	110237	42972	110108
Oceania	x45018	x40576	x32802	x31671	x40796
Japan/Japon	2010245	1857667	1925027	2057486	2211812
Netherlands/Pays–Bas	1482702	1320944	1431158	1135961	1853902
Germany/Allemagne	1459546	1337383	1257956	1187791	1217161
Spain/Espagne	737275	672304	742758	635185	673536
Mexico/Mexique	320258	517472	687525	706329	862211
Belgium–Luxembourg	681969	681214	694881	443952	587922
Italy/Italie	356523	354285	400610	450459	432026
United Kingdom	435288	367904	375032	402102	436873
Korea, Republic of	274608	324849	372045	331940	429019
Portugal	389372	358982	279109	217085	243301
Indonesia/Indonésie	171689	220088	221702	269672	336273
France,Monac	222054	199828	237208	219028	394709
Malaysia/Malaisie	134709	154240	149280	149627	160099
Israel/Israël	138878	142483	145971	148367	132541
Canada	156934	140619	118017	159222	111967
Greece/Grèce	106179	95407	113534	113948	115998
USA/Etats–Unis d'Amer	109496	92145	80879	112334	223147
Former USSR/Anc. URSS	184050	x255917			
Brazil/Brésil	7038	71255	112786	33870	194079
Singapore/Singapour	80004	82913	52825	69694	77432
Turkey/Turquie	32569	31976	57323	71525	75041
Norway,SVD,JM	84817	63772	67417	10084	65190
Romania/Roumanie	112322	81095	36301	23131	21089
Hong Kong	60988	56108	40172	39683	32604
So. Africa Customs Un	6504	22408	48377	59778	41570
Finland/Finlande	39280	39637	46560	39163	41626
Switz.Liecht	51995	47914	42571	32666	44667
Denmark/Danemark	24112	20680	44925	54672	69936
Colombia/Colombie	15270	18594	35861	41657	41788
Venezuela	15149	23421	37653	28439	31202
Trinidad and Tobago	30569	32004	27078	29950	32619
Poland/Pologne	1900	27177	32335	29480	49839
Bangladesh			47255	38415	x22166
Russian Federation			x65622	x19243	x32673
Costa Rica	20886	21399	24621	x35936	x36188
Australia/Australie	37762	30248	24305	22131	31296
China/Chine	18475	18636	29902	27672	60800
Philippines	18244	24587	20082	31398	57643
Korea Dem People's Rp	x47016	x18762	x24459	x26733	x7981
Egypt/Egypte	23683	19278	14722	30249	31250
Austria/Autriche	15289	15784	18676	22343	23134
Thailand/Thaïlande	311	504	39604	13752	29029
Morocco/Maroc	1584	10026	21746	20887	70386
Jamaica/Jamaïque	15968	14479	x19005	x16437	x15808
Zimbabwe	249	88	37377	8325	x221
Sweden/Suède	12696	9348	19147	11553	30318
Yugoslavia SFR	91840	x33348			
Jordan/Jordanie	15137	11452	10090	10719	7932
Algeria/Algérie	8	354	13367	18006	23028
Mozambique	x4237	x8152	x15086	x5704	x2818

COUNTRIES–PAYS	EXPORTS – EXPORTATIONS 1990	1991	1992	1993	1994
Totale	9938095	9682402	9605560	9562091	10963243
Afrique	x143790	x109379	x141858	x164740	x181399
Afrique du Nord	x61869	x45887	x61523	x91267	x92140
Amériques	6576706	6589642	7094792	7491831	8439977
ALAI	2078973	1770243	1807611	1912540	2571773
MCAC	46639	45721	37143	39621	47383
Asie	934188	1038138	669835	x710050	x986036
Moyen–Orient	x35191	x11652	11223	x32743	x28642
Europe	1986394	1635791	1512247	933375	1130366
CEE	1983281	1628593	1506719	929558	1128403
AELE	518	481	2369	2928	851
Océanie	x31461	x37975	x32560	x124434	x77304
USA/Etats–Unis d'Amer	3867408	4254874	4751288	4916699	4669078
Argentina/Argentine	821610	1075105	784498	687216	943123
France,Monac	1189951	977325	885376	426476	412483
Brazil/Brésil	912351	450353	811745	948394	1320199
Canada	583561	518672	498139	620067	1148850
China/Chine	580499	710677	439227	407368	635318
Germany/Allemagne	195797	198681	272928	200500	166795
Paraguay	270992	160302	138119	225620	223965
Netherlands/Pays–Bas	136343	171713	159707	184124	415966
Denmark/Danemark	218216	113356	60035	30334	20777
Poland/Pologne	141791	138317	51164	7423	1583
Hungary/Hongrie	x41910	x39475	x51260	x83856	x95685
Viet Nam	x46188	x69800	x22748	x68783	x95474
Sudan/Soudan	x49262	x32694	x54040	x72623	x79706
Russian Federation			x75120	x80095	x181207
India/Inde	75109	35126	36814	72159	73795
United Kingdom	111306	73237	40745	18380	30559
Australia/Australie	29795	37610	32007	44049	70764
Hong Kong	52674	49538	31549	26962	21377
Mexico/Mexique	37635	44448	39694	21832	22449
Israel/Israël	21615	27568	45457	31999	30342
Singapore/Singapour	35817	42193	27782	26503	26902
Bulgaria/Bulgarie	x72559	x32558	x33682	x22138	x22316
Spain/Espagne	66103	22041	42433	16317	19649
American Samoa			x95	x80211	x601
Myanmar	x31916	42357	x11519	x14386	x38078
Guatemala	28185	23242	19823	18589	23693
Ukraine			x17333	x42939	x110415
Bolivia/Bolivie	14976	25045	15875	18852	43972
Former USSR/Anc. URSS		x58445			
So. Africa Customs Un	19553	17631	13317	14161	29144
Uganda/Ouganda	x5126	x10780	x21958	x5799	x3541
Belgium–Luxembourg	13274	14746	8234	15116	14928
Austria/Autriche	12730	10645	9848	17176	x21639
Italy/Italie	12345	22318	8943	3424	5719
Thailand/Thaïlande	18495	14790	11792	6597	13289
Nicaragua	10018	11183	7741	12539	17153
Pakistan	16031	14771	10798	5558	10760
El Salvador	8427	11292	9559	7043	5074
Greece/Grèce	2925	2715	11196	10973	15873
Turkey/Turquie	3675	6140	8569	7559	9709
Venezuela	9644	8306	8970	4863	5655
Senegal/Sénégal	12137	10112	x9665	1907	x4873
Syrian Arab Republic	3053	x358	108	x20389	x13570
Czechoslovakia		x2503	x18121		
Egypt/Egypte	5413	3715	5368	11385	8812
Sweden/Suède	13030	12576	2795	4415	2503
Libyan Arab Jamahiriya	6364	9338	x2002	x6777	x2675
Zimbabwe	10788	4315	263	13125	x11463
Japan/Japon	6627	7901	6199	2166	1479

(VALUE AS % OF TOTAL)(VALEUR EN % DU TOTAL)

	1985	1986	1987	1988	1989	1990	1991	1992	1993	1994
Africa	0.5	x0.6	0.5	x0.6	x0.7	x0.7	x0.8	x1.6	1.6	1.6
Northern Africa	0.4	0.4	0.5	0.4	0.5	0.4	0.4	0.5	0.8	1.1
Americas	9.5	6.8	6.6	6.9	8.6	6.9	9.6	11.4	12.4	13.5
LAIA	7.4	4.8	4.6	5.0	4.9	3.5	6.3	8.5	8.5	9.7
CACM	0.1	0.1	x0.2	0.2	0.2	0.3	0.3	0.3	x0.4	x0.3
Asia	29.0	27.4	x27.8	x32.2	30.2	29.4	29.6	30.5	33.9	31.0
Middle East	0.9	0.8	1.0	1.1	1.4	1.2	x0.8	1.1	x1.1	x0.9
Europe	58.2	58.8	57.3	54.6	56.2	59.0	55.7	55.4	50.9	52.7
EEC	55.2	55.9	54.8	51.8	53.2	56.8	54.2	54.1	50.4	51.6
EFTA	2.0	2.0	1.8	1.9	2.0	1.3	1.1	1.1	0.4	0.9
Oceania	0.2	x0.1	x0.1	x0.3	0.3	x0.4	x0.4	x0.3	x0.3	x0.3
Japan/Japon	21.1	18.2	15.5	18.2	19.8	19.1	18.4	18.4	21.0	18.6
Netherlands/Pays–Bas	11.8	11.3	12.6	12.9	12.2	14.1	13.1	13.6	11.6	15.6
Germany/Allemagne	16.1	16.9	15.9	14.8	14.5	13.9	13.2	12.0	12.1	10.3
Spain/Espagne	5.6	6.3	6.3	5.2	6.7	7.0	6.7	7.1	6.5	5.7
Mexico/Mexique	6.0	3.5	2.8	3.6	4.2	3.0	5.1	6.6	7.2	7.3
Belgium–Luxembourg	6.3	6.6	7.0	6.4	6.7	6.5	6.7	6.6	4.5	5.0
Italy/Italie	5.3	4.4	2.8	2.5	3.2	3.4	3.5	3.8	4.6	3.6
United Kingdom	2.9	4.3	3.8	3.2	3.5	4.1	3.6	3.6	4.1	3.7
Korea, Republic of	2.6	2.8	2.5	2.6	3.2	2.6	3.2	3.5	3.4	3.6
Portugal	3.0	2.4	3.3	3.4	3.2	3.7	3.6	2.7	2.2	2.1

	1985	1986	1987	1988	1989	1990	1991	1992	1993	1994
Afrique	0.9	x0.9	x0.8	x0.9	x1.6	x1.5	x1.1	x1.4	x1.7	x1.7
Afrique du Nord	0.6	x0.2	x0.3	x0.4	x0.9	x0.6	x0.5	x0.6	x1.0	x0.8
Amériques	78.6	71.9	66.2	70.1	67.7	66.2	68.1	73.8	78.3	77.0
ALAI	20.7	11.8	10.3	14.8	18.4	20.9	18.3	18.8	20.0	23.5
MCAC	0.3	0.3	x0.1	0.3	0.2	0.5	0.5	0.4	0.4	0.4
Asie	6.7	9.7	8.6	8.3	8.9	9.4	10.8	6.9	x7.5	x9.0
Moyen–Orient	0.1	x0.1	x0.1	0.1	0.1	x0.4	x0.1	0.1	x0.3	x0.3
Europe	12.7	16.1	21.8	18.5	18.1	20.0	16.9	15.7	9.8	10.3
CEE	12.3	15.8	21.7	18.3	17.7	20.0	16.8	15.7	9.7	10.3
AELE	0.3	0.2	0.1	0.2	0.3	0.0	0.0	0.0	0.0	0.0
Océanie	0.3	x0.3	x0.2	x0.4	x0.2	x0.3	x0.4	x0.3	x1.3	x0.8
USA/Etats–Unis d'Amer	52.1	55.6	51.3	49.6	43.0	38.9	43.9	49.5	51.4	42.6
Argentina/Argentine	9.2	7.7	3.6	6.0	2.1	8.3	11.1	8.2	7.2	8.6
France,Monac	7.1	8.2	14.5	13.8	12.9	12.0	10.1	9.2	4.5	3.8
Brazil/Brésil	9.8	3.0	6.3	7.0	11.7	9.2	4.7	8.5	9.9	12.0
Canada	5.4	4.2	4.5	5.4	6.1	5.9	5.4	5.2	6.5	10.5
China/Chine	5.5	8.2	7.0	6.1	6.2	5.8	7.3	4.6	4.3	5.8
Germany/Allemagne	0.6	1.0	2.5	0.8	1.5	2.0	2.1	2.8	2.1	1.5
Paraguay	1.3	0.5	0.0	1.5	3.9	2.7	1.7	1.4	2.4	2.0
Netherlands/Pays–Bas	0.5	0.7	1.0	1.2	1.0	1.4	1.8	1.7	1.9	3.8
Denmark/Danemark	2.2	2.3	1.5	1.1	1.2	2.2	1.2	0.6	0.3	0.2

TRADE BY COMMODITY IN THOUSAND U.S. DOLLARS – COMMERCE PAR PRODUIT EN MILLIERS DE DOLLARS E.U

COUNTRIES–PAYS	IMPORTS – IMPORTATIONS 1990	1991	1992	1993	1994
Total	608386	566403	588648	663315	794305
Africa	x16434	13486	x13515	x6019	x9307
Northern Africa	7845	5976	2850	2586	5088
Americas	134205	83574	102045	133541	145636
LAIA	21195	14161	26107	46571	41876
CACM	2990	2468	2301	7608	16093
Asia	141536	172930	174982	x180148	x196971
Middle East	2829	x26605	35094	14770	x10364
Europe	296938	257221	267331	302364	372765
EEC	283842	247500	255589	290148	362250
EFTA	10898	8849	7504	8634	8826
Oceania	x11796	x26092	x23379	x31588	x55256
Germany/Allemagne	104031	96614	103493	104742	130858
Japan/Japon	76742	71301	67160	70244	70741
USA/Etats–Unis d'Amer	97423	57887	65032	67192	79059
Belgium–Luxembourg	26233	29652	35119	40301	62722
Netherlands/Pays–Bas	19489	20763	25213	52815	55413
United Kingdom	51513	27895	27422	25395	36460
France, Monac	22993	19830	17820	22561	24860
Australia/Australie	4132	14708	12629	22635	45443
Korea, Republic of	17536	16212	19574	14170	17991
Pakistan	15107	10440	15111	22196	26712
Saudi Arabia	1207	18341	25158	x718	x1530
Bangladesh		17878		x23644	x26111
Colombia/Colombie	49	363	9613	28366	23811
Singapore/Singapour	5990	5778	10215	11374	13178
Spain/Espagne	9832	7553	9001	9497	10867
Sweden/Suède	13343	8691	9096	7950	9717
Austria/Autriche	7235	8343	7745	7854	9761
New Zealand	5951	8316	8338	6769	6276
Mexico/Mexique	4804	5885	7019	10080	8075
Malaysia/Malaisie	2902	6590	9204	4698	6448
Denmark/Danemark	5781	10797	2216	7175	7427
Switz.Liecht	7077	6181	6256	7466	7571
Cyprus/Chypre	335	1145	5293	12719	7243
Thailand/Thaïlande	11345	7748	4699	6333	5941
Italy/Italie	10331	5266	5270	5295	6064
Brazil/Brésil	14874	5461	6154	4180	2587
Canada	4135	4267	4434	6889	7077
India/Inde	2872	5122	5251	3547	3195
Ireland/Irlande	2975	3685	5891	2386	3971
Former USSR/Anc. URSS		x10297			
Portugal	7270	3868	4462	1004	955
Poland/Pologne			4468	4773	7007
So. Africa Customs Un	2806	2696	2704	2403	2788
Greece/Grèce	1636	2916	1543	1753	1517
Zimbabwe	24	34	6108	10	x9
Cuba			x2773	x2554	x622
United Arab Emirates	525	2701	2033	x498	x628
Hong Kong	1333	1645	2289	1144	6364
Nigeria/Nigéria	x2806	3886	x1161		
Papua New Guinea	80	x1500	x1692	x1785	x2614
Nepal/Népal	149		1423	3529	x2200
Norway, SVD, JM	3727	2599	1166	1086	1172
Morocco/Maroc	908	1188	1604	1916	1410
El Salvador	1423	290	794	3352	9151
Finland/Finlande	1180	1628	1298	1420	1657
Hungary/Hongrie	x1072	1927	x1101	x1309	x1995
Egypt/Egypte	5426	3841	142	99	3109
China/Chine	2249	1589	1293	1142	1575
Lebanon/Liban	x44	x3781	x56	x73	x135
Indonesia/Indonésie	560	481	1871	1453	3286

COUNTRIES–PAYS	EXPORTS – EXPORTATIONS 1990	1991	1992	1993	1994
Totale	538695	485225	506302	513794	x672734
Afrique	x37388	x15276	x16355	x11716	x22853
Afrique du Nord	x1228	x1907	x1661	x2874	x3061
Amériques	241857	204741	179836	204939	278696
ALAI	2659	3414	11039	24348	15091
MCAC	3686	11020	10247	x10002	x7809
Asie	116815	119640	119730	106960	x140712
Moyen–Orient	x5848	x6108	x7226	x10398	12527
Europe	82834	89429	109708	111407	136374
CEE	77751	87399	108061	109821	135283
AELE	377	225	284	184	228
Océanie	31958	26431	x43144	x47306	x63516
Canada	186327	125300	106087	107679	199820
USA/Etats–Unis d'Amer	49062	64883	52442	62820	55691
Netherlands/Pays–Bas	21080	21605	29686	35718	48265
China/Chine	38270	30398	29498	26980	30699
Hungary/Hongrie	x21514	x17434	x26957	x18986	x11633
United Kingdom	9083	19719	23527	18132	14382
Belgium–Luxembourg	15083	13733	15617	21391	27269
Papua New Guinea	10351	7438	14542	16646	x26867
Philippines	21676	18730	11296	7314	8674
Germany/Allemagne	11889	12447	12296	10770	15192
Singapore/Singapour	6652	12099	12650	10423	14191
India/Inde	8284	10459	12059	12416	9294
Malaysia/Malaisie	18511	11337	14147	8159	8589
Australia/Australie	9726	7988	11597	12677	22859
France, Monac	8560	7346	11183	11268	17757
Indonesia/Indonésie	3514	10948	9454	5202	18775
Venezuela	69	59	6333	18387	11605
Nepal/Népal	504	8523	7137	8101	x3574
Guatemala	2156	7321	8462	6173	4542
Turkey/Turquie	3744	3864	4725	7823	10193
Austria/Autriche	3923	4562	6323	4484	x4820
Vanuatu	5128	4619	7366	x2003	x4426
Solomon Isls	4869	4316	x5763	x3686	x7342
Sri Lanka	3058	4576	4387	3634	4221
American Samoa				x10813	x285
Italy/Italie	2949	4202	4416	1325	1562
Czech Republic				9863	14227
Pakistan	6467	2432	1480	4393	7224
Czechoslovakia		x2864	x5022		
Former USSR/Anc. URSS		x7243			
Myanmar	x1127	56	x1542	x5538	x13154
Russian Federation			x3898	x3171	x1826
Greece/Grèce	1433	1309	2406	2336	2280
Cote d'Ivoire	x18579	x2757	x2606	x518	x2847
Kiribati	799	1628	3162	x1014	x563
Romania/Roumanie	106	1890	3253	637	2809
Ukraine			x1387	x4364	x2167
Nigeria/Nigéria	5309	1887	x2502	x1184	x2808
Mozambique	x684	x1251	x2439	x1596	x4030
Ghana	x999	905	1877	x2394	x7180
Viet Nam	x96	x130	x4637	x103	x1478
Hong Kong	1542	1878	1927	988	5007
Lebanon/Liban	x1638	x1233	x882	x2442	x779
Honduras	1031	2874	1294	361	168
Sudan/Soudan	x688	x1762	x1068	x1545	x971
Mexico/Mexique	510	270	1799	1841	359
Costa Rica	378	350	365	x2920	x2242
Spain/Espagne	1565	663	961	1843	1317
Paraguay	1354	1290	1082	1036	813
Brazil/Brésil	174	1009	1016	1025	690

(VALUE AS % OF TOTAL)(VALEUR EN % DU TOTAL)

	1985	1986	1987	1988	1989	1990	1991	1992	1993	1994
Africa	1.3	x1.5	1.2	x1.0	x0.9	x2.7	2.4	x2.3	x0.9	x1.2
Northern Africa	0.8	0.7	0.6	0.2	0.4	1.3	1.1	0.5	0.4	0.6
Americas	14.7	13.1	21.8	24.9	x20.2	22.1	14.8	17.3	20.2	18.3
LAIA	4.7	6.8	17.0	15.8	2.8	3.5	2.5	4.4	7.0	5.3
CACM	0.0	0.3	0.2	0.7	1.1	0.5	0.4	0.4	1.1	2.0
Asia	25.9	22.9	22.7	x25.4	27.5	23.2	30.5	29.7	x27.1	x24.8
Middle East	1.4	2.0	x2.0	1.9	0.7	0.5	x4.7	6.0	2.2	x1.3
Europe	54.0	58.0	48.7	42.3	47.2	48.8	45.4	45.4	45.6	46.9
EEC	49.0	53.7	45.4	37.7	42.4	46.7	43.7	43.4	43.7	45.6
EFTA	5.0	4.3	3.2	4.5	4.6	1.8	1.6	1.3	1.3	1.1
Oceania	0.3	x0.8	x0.3	x0.8	x1.4	x2.0	x4.6	x4.0	x4.7	x6.9
Germany/Allemagne	20.7	23.3	16.6	13.9	17.8	17.1	17.1	17.6	15.8	16.5
Japan/Japon	14.8	12.3	9.7	12.2	13.9	12.6	12.6	11.4	10.6	8.9
USA/Etats–Unis d'Amer	7.5	5.1	3.4	6.3	13.6	16.0	10.2	11.0	10.1	10.0
Belgium–Luxembourg	2.7	4.0	3.1	3.7	4.7	4.3	5.2	6.0	6.1	7.9
Netherlands/Pays–Bas	2.6	3.4	3.1	4.3	3.1	3.2	3.7	4.3	8.0	7.0
United Kingdom	9.0	7.0	5.9	5.2	5.0	8.5	4.9	4.7	3.8	4.6
France, Monac	3.5	4.5	5.4	3.2	3.6	3.8	3.5	3.0	3.4	3.1
Australia/Australie	0.1	0.1	0.1	0.4	0.3	0.7	2.6	2.1	3.4	5.7
Korea, Republic of	1.1	1.5	1.8	2.7	3.8	2.9	2.9	3.3	2.1	2.3
Pakistan	2.2	1.0	0.8	1.0	1.4	2.5	1.8	2.6	3.3	3.4

	1985	1986	1987	1988	1989	1990	1991	1992	1993	1994
Afrique	9.4	x9.3	x5.7	x5.7	x5.6	x6.9	x3.1	x3.2	x2.3	x3.4
Afrique du Nord	0.0	x0.0	x0.1	x0.5	x0.2	x0.2	x0.4	x0.3	x0.6	x0.5
Amériques	47.6	x50.9	50.3	x57.9	53.2	44.9	42.2	35.5	39.9	41.4
ALAI	1.0	0.8	20.8	0.3	1.1	0.5	0.7	2.2	4.7	2.2
MCAC	0.4	1.4	2.8	1.1	0.7	0.7	2.3	2.0	x1.9	x1.2
Asie	13.0	15.4	21.6	16.8	15.8	21.6	24.6	23.7	20.9	x20.9
Moyen–Orient	0.3	x0.8	x1.1	x1.0	x0.9	x1.1	x1.3	x1.4	x2.0	1.9
Europe	13.5	15.5	11.1	10.0	12.8	15.4	18.4	21.7	21.7	20.3
CEE	12.3	14.6	10.5	8.9	11.6	14.4	18.0	21.3	21.4	20.1
AELE	1.1	0.9	0.4	0.6	0.8	0.1	0.0	0.1	0.0	0.0
Océanie	16.5	x8.8	6.4	x7.0	7.9	6.0	5.5	x8.6	x9.2	x9.4
Canada	41.3	42.3	23.5	22.3	31.1	34.6	25.8	21.0	21.0	29.7
USA/Etats–Unis d'Amer	4.7	6.1	3.1	2.7	20.2	9.1	13.4	10.4	12.2	8.3
Netherlands/Pays–Bas	2.6	3.6	2.8	2.8	3.2	3.9	4.5	5.9	7.0	7.2
China/Chine			5.5	5.5	4.7	7.1	6.3	5.8	5.3	4.6
Hungary/Hongrie			x3.1	x1.7	x2.6	x4.0	x3.6	x5.3	x3.7	x1.7
United Kingdom	0.7	1.1	0.7	0.6	1.1	1.7	4.1	4.6	3.5	2.1
Belgium–Luxembourg	2.9	3.4	1.6	1.7	2.6	2.8	2.8	3.1	4.2	4.1
Papua New Guinea	8.1	2.9	2.8	3.2	3.1	1.9	1.5	2.9	3.2	x4.0
Philippines	1.4	4.9	5.4	3.9	4.0	4.0	3.9	2.2	1.4	1.3
Germany/Allemagne	1.3	1.8	1.3	1.3	1.6	2.2	2.6	2.4	2.1	2.3

TRADE BY COMMODITY IN THOUSAND U.S. DOLLARS – COMMERCE PAR PRODUIT EN MILLIERS DE DOLLARS E.U

COUNTRIES–PAYS	IMPORTS – IMPORTATIONS 1990	1991	1992	1993	1994	COUNTRIES–PAYS	EXPORTS – EXPORTATIONS 1990	1991	1992	1993	1994
Total	4524711	4171893	4119007	4053598	4878506	Totale	4109984	4006210	4186658	3962470	5277257
Africa	x96879	83237	x92653	x91080	x106828	Afrique	x135382	x141905	x183238	x206719	x233227
Northern Africa	32639	25020	27614	x26922	x37285	Afrique du Nord	x977	x112	x118	x442	79
Americas	1151684	1092312	1197306	1309967	1491518	Amériques	97475	79810	72089	65133	85984
LAIA	247630	268176	246902	262505	303693	ALAI	6166	4476	5236	2725	3733
CACM	3716	3204	3961	x4278	x4764	MCAC	12844	14921	17637	19721	27276
Asia	1966159	1887591	1767925	1683226	2071203	Asie	3814106	3716415	3860248	3610934	4859862
Middle East	151910	x127929	x128000	x123803	x114491	Moyen–Orient	184	x55	x115	x467	x428
Europe	1005701	921582	943398	863116	1076515	Europe	56886	62252	66680	62155	76276
EEC	961159	880701	908634	835638	1052765	CEE	56654	62139	65752	62007	76051
EFTA	6184	4413	3464	2823	4195	AELE	232	113	182	95	74
Oceania	36940	x36869	x41108	x45429	x60754	Océanie	5072	4623	3885	4207	x4024
USA/Etats–Unis d'Amer	813648	745603	859681	949448	1058995	Thailand/Thaïlande	921371	977609	1139055	1152836	1660583
Japan/Japon	591590	606398	593574	571952	666687	Indonesia/Indonésie	854741	971890	1042185	979086	1273081
Singapore/Singapour	521460	419157	334144	280750	303579	Malaysia/Malaisie	1120399	977866	928651	829981	1120543
Korea, Republic of	225605	236821	253332	251732	332304	Singapore/Singapour	778414	630372	593535	482612	515548
China/Chine	288721	270972	232749	222162	332769	Cote d'Ivoire	x72615	x62406	x76140	x63070	x74177
Germany/Allemagne	218957	211775	224403	183975	231943	Sri Lanka	76846	63777	68541	63597	72468
France,Monac	186525	169806	180106	167040	210222	Nigeria/Nigéria	11457	35122	x46375	x69152	x90481
United Kingdom	143733	127036	132110	134864	153859	USA/Etats–Unis d'Amer	55854	56241	47140	40812	52722
Italy/Italie	145630	133474	127159	115222	148963	Hong Kong	14948	57241	45854	33290	72841
Spain/Espagne	117065	108158	108948	98457	137737	Cameroon/Cameroun	24628	27880	x41739	x59148	x44862
Brazil/Brésil	97335	97123	87364	92665	112536	United Kingdom	20308	25748	26332	16652	21034
Canada	84471	71325	81856	90396	120050	Guatemala	12819	14813	17391	19559	27245
Malaysia/Malaisie	80097	53197	59025	98035	159025	Viet Nam	x26581	x8878	x7143	x28369	x50043
Turkey/Turquie	44762	63502	66454	74046	68907	Philippines	11768	13018	9346	12050	13599
Mexico/Mexique	62209	73090	64197	60237	74893	Germany/Allemagne	10632	7624	13054	13730	20068
Iran (Islamic Rp. of)	102000	x56410	x54388	x41556	x39588	Myanmar	479	5412	11642	14763	x26287
Hong Kong	17982	63257	50141	37712	89756	France,Monac	8407	7599	6655	8664	6429
Belgium–Luxembourg	46840	45960	52407	49311	63795	Italy/Italie	6548	8350	6120	8072	8878
So. Africa Customs Un	40032	38306	45988	45450	56114	Liberia/Libéria	x12078	x9830	x10364	x1906	x5407
Australia/Australie	32551	31815	36047	39046	52360	Netherlands/Pays–Bas	5318	4876	4471	8035	9694
Argentina/Argentine	29399	30162	28144	31906	34941	Democratic Kampuchea	x6342	x6688	x4933	x5049	x40422
Former USSR/Anc. URSS	178144	x89353				Ghana	x3105	1754	4545	x6890	x11161
Venezuela	15188	24365	22322	24774	22440	Czech Republic				12436	16581
Colombia/Colombie	24113	21165	23855	25595	25705	Mexico/Mexique	3521	2958	3841	1771	2815
Viet Nam		x46882	x22863		x14859	Spain/Espagne	1512	3326	3346	1071	2237
Bangladesh		18644	23948	25175	x2136	China/Chine	259	61	1692	5457	5073
Austria/Autriche	28598	23514	24254	19232	24922	Papua New Guinea	1877	2057	1998	2623	x3381
Pakistan	19157	16697	23671	22517	26318	Belgium–Luxembourg	1240	1502	2389	2550	1748
Czechoslovakia	30312	x34181	x24415			India/Inde	20	1931	4142	177	2333
Poland/Pologne	13677	10920	20199	19298	30054	Canada	21885	3836	791	1433	1894
Romania/Roumanie	21001	10836	23575	15424	13371	Australia/Australie	3185	2433	1781	1490	325
India/Inde	42708	12098	18036	17502	8739	Sweden/Suède	1837	1886	2166	1575	2761
Netherlands/Pays–Bas	19499	14542	13743	18323	16477	Zaire/Zaïre	x4627	x2624	x1498	x1427	x1528
Russian Federation			x21602	x24535	x26024	Korea, Republic of	303	563	1379	1940	5004
Korea Dem People's Rp	x13940	x5214	x12489	x20374	x5665	Malawi	x3577	889	x623	x1568	x1707
Yugoslavia SFR	38324	x36453				Niger	x213	x274	x423	x1765	x674
Chile/Chili	9353	10633	11822	12462	15258	Korea Dem People's Rp	x377	x175	x1239	x486	x394
Sweden/Suède	11003	9061	10741	9510	14999	Gabon		x120	x656	x846	x2562
Yugoslavia/Yougoslavie			x17910	x10995	x3372	Bolivia/Bolivie	1992	1038	327	148	115
Ukraine			x4831	x23997	x2611	Russian Federation			x583	x805	x256
Israel/Israël	7633	8105	11125	9542	10020	Japan/Japon	349	281	409	449	550
Ireland/Irlande	9614	9691	9239	8316	8990	Greece/Grèce	49	473	513	57	205
Greece/Grèce	10490	10998	6933	8314	9534	Austria/Autriche	534	194	329	505	x1355
Portugal	12132	8765	8044	7708	11445	Uruguay	520	330	544	87	113
Egypt/Egypte	11893	7292	9435	7729	14705	Jamaica/Jamaïque			x868		
Slovenia/Slovénia			12155	11784	14542	Portugal	48	238	136	484	387
Morocco/Maroc	8077	7418	7676	7396	9458	So. Africa Customs Un	507	317	223	236	
Zimbabwe	8216	7777	8199	5329	x2047	Denmark/Danemark	61	173	28	557	975
Finland/Finlande	8593	5863	7185	8067	11742	Slovenia/Slovénia			655	17	136
Peru/Pérou	5032	4858	5294	7847	8146	Sudan/Soudan	x939	x112	x110	x422	

(VALUE AS % OF TOTAL)(VALEUR EN % DU TOTAL)

Imports	1985	1986	1987	1988	1989	1990	1991	1992	1993	1994
Africa	1.5	x2.0	x1.6	x1.6	x1.7	x2.2	2.0	x2.2	x2.2	x2.2
Northern Africa	0.6	x0.6	x0.6	x0.6	0.6	0.7	0.6	0.7	x0.7	x0.8
Americas	29.8	27.8	25.3	24.1	27.3	25.4	26.2	29.1	32.4	30.6
LAIA	5.4	5.6	5.4	5.2	5.6	5.5	6.4	6.0	6.5	6.2
CACM	0.3	0.1	0.1	0.1	0.1	0.1	0.1	0.1	x0.1	x0.1
Asia	35.9	37.9	41.5	47.3	42.2	43.4	45.2	42.9	41.5	42.5
Middle East	1.3	2.6	2.3	2.2	2.7	3.4	x3.1	x3.1	x3.1	x2.3
Europe	25.8	25.3	22.5	21.0	22.2	22.2	22.1	22.9	21.3	22.1
EEC	23.1	22.9	20.5	19.1	20.2	21.2	21.1	22.1	20.6	21.6
EFTA	1.4	1.3	1.2	1.1	1.1	0.1	0.1	0.1	0.1	0.1
Oceania	1.0	x1.0	0.9	0.9	x0.9	0.8	x0.9	x1.0	x1.1	x1.2
USA/Etats–Unis d'Amer	21.5	19.8	17.7	17.1	19.6	18.0	17.9	20.9	23.4	21.7
Japan/Japon	12.3	12.4	11.3	12.3	12.5	13.1	14.5	14.4	14.1	13.7
Singapore/Singapour	12.8	11.4	11.3	12.6	11.4	11.5	10.0	8.1	6.9	6.2
Korea, Republic of	3.7	4.3	4.2	4.5	4.3	5.0	5.7	6.2	6.2	6.8
China/Chine	3.5	4.7	7.1	8.0	7.6	6.4	6.5	5.7	5.5	6.8
Germany/Allemagne	5.3	5.2	4.5	4.2	4.7	4.8	5.1	5.4	4.5	4.8
France,Monac	4.4	4.3	4.1	3.7	3.9	4.1	4.1	4.4	4.1	4.3
United Kingdom	3.3	3.2	2.9	2.8	2.8	3.2	3.0	3.2	3.3	3.2
Italy/Italie	3.8	3.8	3.3	3.1	3.3	3.2	3.2	3.1	2.8	3.1
Spain/Espagne	2.9	2.8	2.5	2.4	2.5	2.6	2.6	2.6	2.4	2.8

Exports	1985	1986	1987	1988	1989	1990	1991	1992	1993	1994
Afrique	3.7	4.5	x4.5	3.6	x2.9	x3.3	x3.5	x4.4	x5.2	x4.4
Afrique du Nord	0.0	x0.0	x0.0	x0.0	x0.0	x0.0	x0.0	x0.0	x0.0	0.0
Amériques	1.7	1.7	1.6	1.7	2.4	2.4	2.0	1.7	1.7	1.6
ALAI	0.1	0.2	x0.1	x0.1	0.2	0.2	0.1	0.1	0.1	0.1
MCAC	0.3	0.2	0.3	0.3	0.2	0.3	0.4	0.4	0.5	0.5
Asie	93.5	x92.8	x93.0	93.4	93.3	92.8	92.8	92.2	91.1	92.1
Moyen–Orient	0.0	0.1	x0.0	x0.0	x0.0	0.0	x0.0	x0.0	x0.0	x0.0
Europe	0.7	0.8	0.9	1.1	1.1	1.4	1.6	1.6	1.6	1.4
CEE	0.7	0.7	0.8	1.0	1.0	1.4	1.6	1.6	1.6	1.4
AELE	0.0	0.0	0.0	0.1	0.1	0.0	0.0	0.0	0.0	0.0
Océanie	0.1	0.2	0.1	0.1	0.2	0.1	0.2		0.1	x0.1
Thailand/Thaïlande	14.6	16.3	17.8	17.7	20.7	22.4	24.4	27.2	29.1	31.5
Indonesia/Indonésie	21.0	20.4	21.4	20.5	20.3	20.8	24.3	24.9	24.7	24.1
Malaysia/Malaisie	34.9	35.2	34.7	33.1	29.5	27.3	24.4	22.2	20.9	21.2
Singapore/Singapour	19.9	17.5	16.3	18.6	19.5	18.9	15.7	14.2	12.2	9.8
Cote d'Ivoire	0.9	1.1	1.2	1.1	1.2	x1.8	x1.6	x1.8	x1.6	x1.4
Sri Lanka	2.7	2.6	2.2	1.9	1.7	1.9	1.6	1.6	1.6	1.4
Nigeria/Nigéria	0.1	0.6	x0.7	0.1	0.5	0.3	0.9	x1.1	x1.7	x1.7
USA/Etats–Unis d'Amer	1.4	1.3	1.1	1.3	1.9	1.4	1.4	1.1	1.1	1.0
Hong Kong	0.1	0.1	0.1	0.8	0.6	0.4	1.4	1.1	0.8	1.4
Cameroon/Cameroun		0.4	0.4	x0.4	0.4	0.6	0.7	x1.0	x1.5	x0.9

TRADE BY COMMODITY IN THOUSAND U.S. DOLLARS – COMMERCE PAR PRODUIT EN MILLIERS DE DOLLARS E.U

COUNTRIES–PAYS	IMPORTS – IMPORTATIONS				
	1990	1991	1992	1993	1994
Total	4906552	4783766	5091540	4747283	5542958
Africa	x92988	76752	x90302	x76639	x82065
Northern Africa	37158	28605	x29114	x24722	32396
Americas	1005381	991600	1071503	1118344	1279196
LAIA	302623	329537	335145	347037	395518
CACM	13611	12064	12603	x18779	x14245
Asia	867820	1010502	1162126	1292551	1481507
Middle East	54536	x99581	x122493	x117981	x97467
Europe	2733041	2499932	2619385	2084752	2497250
EEC	2580204	2412589	2510340	2006749	2412081
EFTA	59462	50130	57819	45096	50157
Oceania	x44878	x40968	x43425	x50026	x57176
Germany/Allemagne	594869	566750	609184	460433	525397
USA/Etats–Unis d'Amer	487097	456838	513879	533937	605256
France,Monac	407175	381922	417918	336547	391996
Belgium–Luxembourg	304950	309859	292435	320950	320320
Italy/Italie	340465	318522	330202	258171	316767
United Kingdom	292891	267961	270985	129591	254344
Korea, Republic of	202837	198052	212370	195515	219434
Canada	194130	185252	204033	213315	258096
Spain/Espagne	219444	186040	194791	158125	186948
China/Chine	76511	140364	179156	201537	253953
Japan/Japon	143967	174500	159825	176847	202725
Netherlands/Pays–Bas	125266	120351	138111	123692	156346
Indonesia/Indonésie	80806	86380	97873	114446	134707
Brazil/Brésil	91038	96016	87770	111093	136981
Hong Kong	41036	64919	81945	126854	172977
Mexico/Mexique	65720	73241	88413	81281	102264
India/Inde	82025	62083	82538	91514	109590
Thailand/Thaïlande	64065	63847	75629	86197	95585
Austria/Autriche	87447	82772	75623	61925	72099
Turkey/Turquie	45887	45521	65044	71435	61829
Malaysia/Malaisie	27437	28129	48503	73958	68678
Sweden/Suède	56650	49235	51141	48043	61874
Venezuela	39206	51869	47279	41392	32126
Colombia/Colombie	47087	41605	43917	44140	44724
Switz.Liecht	46314	37783	48209	38013	42469
Portugal	46048	42291	40311	34590	45620
Iran (Islamic Rp. of)		x37145	x41838	x28815	x16117
Singapore/Singapour	27832	31484	31597	33683	45939
Australia/Australie	28505	27311	29308	35666	41315
Poland/Pologne	19850	27752	34131	29014	51633
Denmark/Danemark	39233	30986	31433	20582	20219
Argentina/Argentine	24784	27551	27982	27248	29938
Finland/Finlande	32541	23714	28107	29790	31314
Czechoslovakia	79905	x52516	x28026		
So. Africa Customs Un	27997	26856	27568	25177	28695
Philippines	25193	22328	26155	26885	30291
Israel/Israël	22083	21102	21860	18096	22333
Chile/Chili	16552	19169	20142	20044	19177
Former USSR/Anc. URSS		x56681			
Slovenia/Slovénia			29945	22757	26613
Greece/Grèce	19731	18971	16353	16357	16784
Hungary/Hongrie	x13166	20200	x16692	x13772	x13256
Pakistan	12110	13780	14617	13251	15130
Romania/Roumanie	30092	4128	11855	25574	22469
New Zealand	15604	12862	13616	14188	15562
Yugoslavia SFR	92081	x35760			
Ireland/Irlande	13495	13216	13746	7954	12053
Czech Republic				34613	36776
Uruguay	9099	8852	11067	9574	13894
Morocco/Maroc	11451	11337	9363	8770	9950

COUNTRIES–PAYS	EXPORTS – EXPORTATIONS				
	1990	1991	1992	1993	1994
Totale	4418986	4270749	4298040	4156391	4956869
Afrique	41501	27780	x7029	x5069	x2699
Afrique du Nord	x155	342	x290	10	102
Amériques	1218589	1197463	1336314	1254332	1451345
ALAI	106582	94119	102330	101474	143732
MCAC	313	151	79	x253	x199
Asie	639911	676163	734864	834964	1022925
Moyen–Orient	7901	1735	3396	x6790	x20057
Europe	2394642	2183071	2128329	1998192	2368869
CEE	2377311	2168979	2116144	1986893	2357610
AELE	8374	8496	9880	8723	9216
Océanie	5668	x4527	6764	x6351	x8029
USA/Etats–Unis d'Amer	873792	881184	968592	896486	1029174
France,Monac	695591	636542	621200	568073	643118
Japan/Japon	503857	523118	534650	572260	681320
Germany/Allemagne	551271	522422	512057	445556	541900
Belgium–Luxembourg	336833	321891	342495	380097	467612
United Kingdom	376773	324160	340475	306899	383577
Canada	237798	221959	265125	255955	277877
Netherlands/Pays–Bas	228771	211170	199935	199936	212462
Korea, Republic of	72999	75659	93533	103247	119262
Russian Federation			x125153	x142401	x179309
Hong Kong	18348	38398	57834	104764	132434
Italy/Italie	67763	63405	63373	55752	70364
Mexico/Mexique	57205	50303	58412	56791	71625
Former USSR/Anc. URSS		x105203			
Poland/Pologne	49894	36714	40482	24980	34484
Brazil/Brésil	22352	25849	28889	28584	52415
Spain/Espagne	67288	59284	9231	8357	12959
China/Chine	19536	13256	13222	17782	25145
Singapore/Singapour	10989	11838	12173	17563	22338
Argentina/Argentine	25706	17014	11404	12956	15030
Czechoslovakia		x17338	x22303		
Austria/Autriche	20625	13988	11562	7354	x9187
Sweden/Suède	20388	9462	8749	10888	10392
Czech Republic				27133	46616
Switz.Liecht	7991	8122	9664	8546	9071
Bulgaria/Bulgarie	x42437	x11780	x12972		x17371
Nigeria/Nigéria	36515	20841	x206	x144	x673
Australia/Australie	4433	3755	6116	5870	7735
So. Africa Customs Un	4588	4812	5549	4356	
Former GDR	x15366	x6324	x6324		
Malaysia/Malaisie	2061	3626	4529	4330	5199
India/Inde	1393	2413	4310	3133	6116
Indonesia/Indonésie	205	2571	5078	1188	1560
Turkey/Turquie	6579	822	2349	4053	13813
Hungary/Hongrie	x7105	x3166	x2019	x1668	x1022
Ireland/Irlande	1597	2103	3404	733	1174
Ukraine			x3117	x2845	x1643
Venezuela	1123	832	1681	2889	3819
Yugoslavia SFR	8835	x5286			
Korea Dem People's Rp	x644	x1396	x2033	x1352	x863
Denmark/Danemark	6948	1422	2250	704	719
Thailand/Thaïlande	1569	1079	1214	1697	5950
Finland/Finlande	2783	837	403	1859	2876
Portugal	408	1813	656	375	530
Romania/Roumanie	3873	1221	640	837	590
Saudi Arabia	925	666	266	x1690	x2888
Yugoslavia/Yougoslavie			x965	x1266	x585
Slovenia/Slovénia			1236	984	1125
Sri Lanka	44	812	1229	102	594
Colombia/Colombie	170	95	1801	145	327

(VALUE AS % OF TOTAL)(VALEUR EN % DU TOTAL)

	1985	1986	1987	1988	1989	1990	1991	1992	1993	1994
Africa	1.7	x1.9	x1.7	x1.9	x1.7	x1.9	1.6	x1.7	x1.6	x1.5
Northern Africa	0.6	0.7	0.6	0.7	0.6	0.8	0.6	x0.6	x0.5	0.6
Americas	22.2	20.2	19.3	19.6	20.7	20.5	20.7	21.0	23.5	23.1
LAIA	7.1	6.8	6.2	6.5	5.6	6.2	6.9	6.6	7.3	7.1
CACM	0.0	0.2	0.2	0.2	0.3	0.3	0.3	0.2	x0.4	x0.3
Asia	14.6	15.3	x15.2	x16.4	15.2	17.7	21.1	22.9	27.2	26.8
Middle East	1.1	x1.3	x1.5	x1.5	x1.3	1.1	x2.1	x2.4	x2.5	x1.8
Europe	55.8	57.0	54.0	51.5	50.9	55.7	52.3	51.4	43.9	45.1
EEC	47.2	49.3	46.7	44.5	44.5	52.6	50.4	49.3	42.3	43.5
EFTA	5.3	5.5	5.0	4.9	4.6	1.2	1.0	1.1	0.9	0.9
Oceania	1.2	x1.0	x1.0	x0.9	x1.0	x0.9	x0.8	x0.8	x1.1	x1.0
Germany/Allemagne	10.8	12.1	10.9	10.6	10.0	12.1	11.8	12.0	9.7	9.5
USA/Etats–Unis d'Amer	10.2	8.6	8.4	8.6	10.2	9.9	9.5	10.1	11.2	10.9
France,Monac	6.1	7.0	6.8	6.2	6.7	8.3	8.0	8.2	7.1	7.1
Belgium–Luxembourg	5.8	5.0	4.8	5.0	5.3	6.2	6.5	5.7	6.8	5.8
Italy/Italie	6.1	6.7	6.6	6.1	6.1	6.9	6.7	6.5	5.4	5.7
United Kingdom	5.6	5.1	5.2	4.7	5.1	6.0	5.6	5.3	2.7	4.6
Korea, Republic of	2.7	3.0	3.3	3.5	3.6	4.1	4.1	4.2	4.1	4.0
Canada	4.8	4.4	4.3	4.1	4.0	4.0	3.9	4.0	4.5	4.7
Spain/Espagne	3.5	4.1	3.8	3.7	3.5	4.5	3.9	3.8	3.3	3.4
China/Chine	2.4	2.5	1.2	1.3	1.3	1.6	2.9	3.5	4.2	4.6

	1985	1986	1987	1988	1989	1990	1991	1992	1993	1994
Afrique	0.1	0.2	x0.1	0.9	1.3	0.9	0.6	x0.1	x0.1	x0.1
Afrique du Nord	0.0	0.0	0.0	x0.0	x0.0	x0.0	0.0	x0.0	0.0	0.0
Amériques	32.9	30.1	28.5	24.3	24.5	27.6	28.0	31.1	30.2	29.3
ALAI	2.8	1.8	2.4	2.4	2.4	2.4	2.2	2.4	2.4	2.9
MCAC	0.0	0.0	0.0	0.0	x0.0	0.0	0.0	0.0	x0.0	x0.0
Asie	11.5	11.0	x10.5	x11.7	12.0	14.5	15.9	17.1	20.1	20.7
Moyen–Orient	0.1	x0.1	x0.1	0.1	0.2	0.2	0.0	0.1	x0.2	x0.4
Europe	54.1	57.3	47.6	49.4	50.0	54.2	51.1	49.5	48.1	47.8
CEE	53.1	56.2	46.6	48.3	48.8	53.8	50.8	49.2	47.8	47.6
AELE	0.9	1.0	0.9	1.0	1.1	0.2	0.2	0.2	0.2	0.2
Océanie	0.1	x0.1	x0.1	x0.1	0.1	0.1	x0.1	0.2	x0.1	x0.2
USA/Etats–Unis d'Amer	18.5	18.4	16.7	17.2	16.6	19.8	20.6	22.5	21.6	20.8
France,Monac	15.6	16.2	13.7	13.5	13.7	15.7	14.9	14.5	13.7	13.0
Japan/Japon	10.7	10.2	8.6	9.2	10.1	11.4	12.2	12.4	13.8	13.7
Germany/Allemagne	11.5	11.4	9.7	9.8	10.6	12.5	12.2	11.9	10.7	10.9
Belgium–Luxembourg	7.1	6.8	6.0	5.4	6.1	7.6	7.5	8.0	9.1	9.4
United Kingdom	6.9	7.4	6.3	6.3	7.2	8.5	7.6	7.9	7.4	7.7
Canada	11.6	9.9	9.4	4.7	5.4	5.4	5.2	6.2	6.2	5.6
Netherlands/Pays–Bas	7.2	7.4	6.3	6.3	7.0	5.2	4.9	4.7	4.8	4.3
Korea, Republic of	0.4	0.5	0.4	0.5	0.9	1.7	1.8	2.2	2.5	2.4
Russian Federation								x2.9	x3.4	x3.6

TRADE BY COMMODITY IN THOUSAND U.S. DOLLARS – COMMERCE PAR PRODUIT EN MILLIERS DE DOLLARS E.U

IMPORTS – IMPORTATIONS

COUNTRIES–PAYS	1990	1991	1992	1993	1994
Total	147355	131346	131124	110093	107828
Africa	x858	979	x487	669	x395
Northern Africa	75	538	66	x137	x136
Americas	22580	19837	20510	15091	14426
LAIA	12066	12905	11067	9996	10274
CACM	76	22	65	21	12
Asia	12273	11269	10599	11196	10318
Middle East	907	x842	955	x521	x641
Europe	93945	95644	98499	80952	81418
EEC	92542	94876	98003	80462	80842
EFTA	705	536	315	341	501
Oceania	x398	x478	x323	x344	x318
Portugal	45047	52144	51949	34898	35051
Italy/Italie	12891	12647	13307	14497	17341
France,Monac	12063	9304	8882	13260	12127
Germany/Allemagne	7410	8875	11469	5866	5118
USA/Etats–Unis d'Amer	9391	6282	8920	4501	3569
Argentina/Argentine	6956	7501	7160	5040	4348
Spain/Espagne	5885	4661	5333	6260	5814
Japan/Japon	6033	4932	4193	4165	3227
United Kingdom	4057	3368	3741	1839	2054
Brazil/Brésil	3261	3107	2061	2579	2212
China/Chine	1109	2107	2440	2718	2796
Netherlands/Pays–Bas	1686	1426	1463	2191	1379
India/Inde	2357	795	1222	1044	1292
Mexico/Mexique	846	1185	845	1009	2842
Russian Federation			x2217	x157	x335
Korea, Republic of	814	924	675	581	806
Austria/Autriche	927	522	605	647	704
Belgium–Luxembourg	599	631	510	406	437
Czechoslovakia	1738	x1132	x339		
Canada	876	560	355	499	551
Chile/Chili	396	539	381	391	322
Former USSR/Anc. URSS	13932	x1273			
Poland/Pologne	105	260	298	534	243
Australia/Australie	362	448	286	328	298
Turkey/Turquie	496	326	287	417	217
Hong Kong	95	27	421	581	311
Denmark/Danemark	1322	766	157	70	242
Venezuela	202	173	241	547	191
Switz.Liecht	494	332	282	288	397
Saudi Arabia	385	297	528	x42	x37
Singapore/Singapour	389	143	205	512	266
Colombia/Colombie	166	178	250	285	281
Viet Nam		x682	x4	x11	x8
So. Africa Customs Un	200	252	237	193	177
Greece/Grèce	222	165	169	322	176
Slovakia				x569	x78
Thailand/Thaïlande	133	194	149	224	388
Hungary/Hongrie	x1331	472	x32	x44	x36
Ethiopia/Ethiopie	373	112	118	293	x2
Libyan Arab Jamahiriya		484	x2	x5	x29
Sweden/Suède	182	156	190	109	215
Czech Republic				453	335
Bangladesh				395	x19
Uruguay	230	201	114	79	63
Indonesia/Indonésie	77	152	97	97	233
Finland/Finlande	204	138	102	58	98
Norway,SVD,JM	211	204	30	52	103
Malaysia/Malaisie	188	75	122	66	157
Pakistan	27	74	31	145	20
Romania/Roumanie				239	250

EXPORTS – EXPORTATIONS

COUNTRIES–PAYS	1990	1991	1992	1993	1994
Totale	122407	118631	118167	98556	93324
Afrique	5886	5904	7325	7661	7589
Afrique du Nord	5713	5885	7299	7638	7589
Amériques	1614	1465	1317	4339	1793
ALAI	41	11	25	65	121
MCAC		1	22	1	
Asie	911	566	669	768	917
Moyen–Orient	52	1	2	11	5
Europe	113811	110477	108606	85306	82926
CEE	113765	110434	108538	85253	82903
AELE	23	43	26	28	23
Océanie	142	87	218	428	90
Spain/Espagne	59427	63801	63718	44893	46235
Portugal	48495	39250	39475	37115	33485
Morocco/Maroc	4772	4083	5120	5330	5418
France,Monac	2711	4043	3395	1112	1229
Tunisia/Tunisie	942	1790	2097	2145	1477
USA/Etats–Unis d'Amer	1238	1117	860	3869	1381
Italy/Italie	1116	1864	873	1115	1066
United Kingdom	841	471	426	351	324
Canada	335	336	408	400	291
Germany/Allemagne	354	426	330	351	173
Hong Kong	162	292	285	185	166
Australia/Australie	141	85	199	426	89
Netherlands/Pays–Bas	645	368	134	30	66
Japan/Japon	95	112	101	214	141
China/Chine	47	29	187	203	482
Austria/Autriche	26	21	75	212	x184
Algeria/Algérie		13	82	138	695
Belgium–Luxembourg	129	117	62	37	20
Hungary/Hongrie	x44	x27	x32	x49	
Korea, Republic of	312	75	3	27	11
Singapore/Singapour	142	40	26	39	52
Bulgaria/Bulgarie		x99			
Switz.Liecht	23	42	26	11	14
Malaysia/Malaisie	88	16	52	7	11
Denmark/Danemark	8	29	37	7	12
Sweden/Suède	13	28	9	20	90
Colombia/Colombie	37	9	21	23	27
So. Africa Customs Un	3	19	16	17	
Russian Federation				x52	
Myanmar				x40	x3
India/Inde	3		11	22	26
Slovenia/Slovénia			25	2	1
Finland/Finlande		15	5	5	16
Egypt/Egypte				25	
New Zealand	1	2	20	2	1
Andorra/Andorre				x23	
Venezuela	1			23	
Guatemala			22		
Argentina/Argentine			1	18	9
Ukraine				x19	
Yugoslavia/Yougoslavie			x18		
Bhutan/Bhoutan				x18	
Norway,SVD,JM				17	10
Turkey/Turquie		1		11	2
Ghana			10		
Kenya				6	
Mexico/Mexique	2	1	3	1	61
Poland/Pologne		5			
Ireland/Irlande				4	
Czech Republic				3	8

(VALUE AS % OF TOTAL)(VALEUR EN % DU TOTAL)

IMPORTS – IMPORTATIONS

	1985	1986	1987	1988	1989	1990	1991	1992	1993	1994
Africa	1.7	0.9	x1.0	x0.5	0.6	x0.5	0.8	x0.4	0.6	x0.4
Northern Africa	0.3	x0.1	x0.1	0.1	0.1	0.1	0.4	0.1	x0.1	x0.1
Americas	22.2	22.1	16.8	x24.7	21.4	15.4	15.1	15.7	13.7	13.4
LAIA	10.4	11.8	8.0	7.0	11.1	8.2	9.8	8.4	9.1	9.5
CACM	0.0	0.0	x0.0	0.0	0.0	0.1	0.0	0.0	0.0	0.0
Asia	14.2	8.8	x9.3	10.4	8.6	8.4	8.6	8.1	10.2	9.5
Middle East	1.3	x0.8	0.5	x0.6	0.6	0.6	x0.6	0.7	x0.5	x0.6
Europe	44.7	51.4	52.6	48.1	56.4	63.8	72.8	75.1	73.5	75.5
EEC	42.5	49.0	50.3	45.8	54.8	62.8	72.2	74.7	73.1	75.0
EFTA	1.1	0.9	1.1	1.7	1.2	0.5	0.4	0.2	0.3	0.5
Oceania	0.7	x0.7	x0.4	0.3	0.6	x0.3	x0.3	x0.2	x0.3	x0.3
Portugal	11.4	14.9	20.7	22.8	27.0	30.6	39.7	39.6	31.7	32.5
Italy/Italie	11.6	15.4	12.6	7.8	7.7	8.7	9.6	10.1	13.2	16.1
France,Monac	4.5	4.4	5.2	5.5	6.0	8.2	7.1	6.8	12.0	11.2
Germany/Allemagne	6.5	6.8	5.9	4.0	5.5	5.0	6.8	8.7	5.3	4.7
USA/Etats–Unis d'Amer	11.7	10.0	8.1	7.8	9.1	6.4	4.8	6.8	4.1	3.3
Argentina/Argentine	4.9	6.4	3.7	3.7	5.0	4.7	5.7	5.5	4.6	4.0
Spain/Espagne	0.4	0.7	0.7	1.2	3.2	4.0	3.5	4.1	5.7	5.4
Japan/Japon	6.2	4.5	4.1	3.9	3.8	4.1	3.8	3.2	3.8	3.0
United Kingdom	2.9	2.0	2.4	2.1	2.9	2.8	2.6	2.9	1.7	1.9
Brazil/Brésil	3.1	4.1	2.9	1.4	4.2	2.2	2.4	1.6	2.3	2.1

EXPORTS – EXPORTATIONS

	1985	1986	1987	1988	1989	1990	1991	1992	1993	1994
Afrique	4.7	3.6	4.3	5.5	8.0	4.8	5.0	6.2	7.8	8.1
Afrique du Nord	4.6	3.6	4.2	5.5	8.0	4.7	5.0	6.2	7.7	8.1
Amériques	1.5	x1.6	1.7	1.5	x1.2	1.3	1.2	1.1	4.4	1.9
ALAI	0.1	0.0	0.1	0.0	0.0	0.0	0.0	0.0	0.1	0.1
MCAC			0.0	0.0	0.0	0.0	0.0	0.0	0.0	0.0
Asie	1.2	1.8	x1.2	x1.9	0.8	0.8	0.5	0.6	0.8	1.0
Moyen–Orient	0.0	0.0	x0.1	x0.6	0.1	0.0	0.0	0.0	0.0	0.0
Europe	92.6	92.8	92.6	90.5	89.7	93.0	93.1	91.9	86.6	88.9
CEE	92.5	92.6	92.5	90.4	89.6	92.9	93.1	91.9	86.5	88.8
AELE	0.1	0.1	0.1	0.1	0.0	0.0	0.0	0.0	0.0	0.0
Océanie	0.1	0.1	0.2	x0.2	x0.1	0.1	0.1	0.2	0.4	0.1
Spain/Espagne	34.6	38.8	46.3	46.6	44.4	48.5	53.8	53.9	45.6	49.5
Portugal	54.0	49.6	41.9	39.4	40.8	39.6	33.1	33.4	37.7	35.9
Morocco/Maroc	3.3	1.9	2.3	3.4	6.4	3.9	3.4	4.3	5.4	5.8
France,Monac	1.4	1.6	1.6	2.0	2.4	2.2	3.4	2.9	1.1	1.3
Tunisia/Tunisie	1.3	1.6	1.5	1.8	1.5	0.8	1.5	1.8	2.2	1.6
USA/Etats–Unis d'Amer	1.4	1.6	1.5	1.2	1.0	1.0	0.9	0.7	3.9	1.5
Italy/Italie	0.3	0.4	0.8	0.6	1.2	0.9	1.6	0.7	1.1	1.1
United Kingdom	0.9	1.3	0.9	0.8	0.3	0.7	0.4	0.4	0.4	0.3
Canada		x0.0	x0.1	0.3	0.1	0.3	0.3	0.3	0.4	0.3
Germany/Allemagne	0.5	0.4	0.5	0.4	0.2	0.3	0.4	0.3	0.4	0.2

TRADE BY COMMODITY IN THOUSAND U.S. DOLLARS – COMMERCE PAR PRODUIT EN MILLIERS DE DOLLARS E.U

COUNTRIES–PAYS	IMPORTS – IMPORTATIONS 1990	1991	1992	1993	1994
Total	199317	213992	253950	251761	235284
Africa	x766	757	3666	5107	3276
Northern Africa	64	31	2406	3654	2089
Americas	19217	19110	18701	x25596	x32134
LAIA	196	328	738	655	1205
CACM	13	12	15	33	64
Asia	42296	57548	76253	81058	x73409
Middle East	6934	15567	26812	x17448	x9746
Europe	136230	134665	154684	138240	125122
EEC	119687	120950	136727	123217	107184
EFTA	14503	12990	16905	14544	17140
Oceania	x764	x407	x381	x261	x212
Germany/Allemagne	26128	24614	35982	34138	28330
Italy/Italie	29732	38539	30753	18364	17073
Japan/Japon	19709	20804	28817	34919	38348
USA/Etats–Unis d'Amer	14605	13441	14505	20808	25284
United Kingdom	19655	16023	16995	13498	11234
Austria/Autriche	10701	12834	13176	12743	10491
Saudi Arabia	2949	10789	16264	x2791	x2639
Korea, Republic of	5690	7413	8719	10917	13659
Norway,SVD,JM	7264	5798	9077	7828	10865
Belgium–Luxembourg	6433	5669	7184	9693	7946
Netherlands/Pays–Bas	5464	4856	8848	7592	6022
Switz.Liecht	6894	6822	7516	6521	6006
France,Monac	8292	4457	5823	7195	6530
Denmark/Danemark	3740	4258	6675	5376	5200
Sweden/Suède	4010	4789	4292	4774	5022
Hong Kong	3695	3704	4232	3747	3437
Canada	3488	4528	2868	3403	4415
Spain/Espagne	2829	1703	3193	3577	2598
Turkey/Turquie	7	50	783	7390	312
Kuwait/ Koweït	1203	359	3740	3529	3095
Greece/Grèce	246	496	1801	4805	4978
Singapore/Singapour	1536	1497	2223	2627	2753
United Arab Emirates	1328	1936	2567	x1554	x1362
Egypt/Egypte	51	19	2357	3483	2037
Bangladesh				5527	
Maldives	x3	4897	x12	x27	x18
Finland/Finlande	1649	2284	1499	964	1100
Thailand/Thaïlande	1850	1003	1582	1789	1671
Malaysia/Malaisie	1384	1309	1594	1093	991
So. Africa Customs Un	479	592	1056	1180	864
Qatar	730	721	1601	486	x307
China/Chine	236	573	1060	557	475
Bahrain/Bahreïn	x340	x926	x462	x253	x408
Romania/Roumanie		1433	26	71	10
Cyprus/Chypre	58	117	633	741	782
Israel/Israël	438	304	435	611	533
Mexico/Mexique	161	274	508	446	646
Sri Lanka			339	672	1030
Macau/Macao	238	273	323	289	348
Iceland/Islande	345	370	312	195	269
Ireland/Irlande	537	275	382	207	97
Poland/Pologne		48	77	680	240
Jordan/Jordanie	58	211	329	264	227
Panama	377	273	217	307	318
Bhutan/Bhoutan	x175	x43		x725	x249
Oman	190	254	244	252	389
Ukraine			x140	x477	x28
Australia/Australie	662	293	153	159	97
Portugal	272	152	123	291	564
Slovenia/Slovénia			351	199	502

COUNTRIES–PAYS	EXPORTS – EXPORTATIONS 1990	1991	1992	1993	1994
Totale	x188542	x195073	x225025	x309409	226739
Afrique	x9244	13438	x13353	x18601	x8306
Afrique du Nord	323	4211	x1030	1325	3050
Amériques	31266	35209	32867	39918	48580
ALAI	12399	14059	10491	11889	14123
MCAC	89	14	1	x21	127
Asie	47771	48391	x77822	x160998	82563
Moyen–Orient	576	1003	1256	x573	x417
Europe	59270	x44788	54448	40376	46985
CEE	39826	34359	43737	32228	39699
AELE	669	1285	1895	764	676
Océanie	x4473	x12820	25	x654	x787
Myanmar	x3	5	x9905	x86389	x3635
Indonesia/Indonésie	17266	15594	20386	27255	31146
Hungary/Hongrie	x28544	x22561	x21070	x13982	x9516
France,Monac	9214	12157	15890	13766	20895
USA/Etats–Unis d'Amer	8170	12084	12329	11622	13061
Canada	10490	8975	9999	16372	21234
Philippines	10550	9920	10915	12078	10204
Singapore/Singapour	8021	9811	12237	9635	9613
So. Africa Customs Un	6717	7579	8733	13328	
Poland/Pologne	3540	5056	10491	13335	14915
Spain/Espagne	14457	8240	8582	4596	4461
Malaysia/Malaisie	2867	4116	7631	8494	8063
Argentina/Argentine	3762	4674	5669	6002	9648
Czechoslovakia		x6257	x9950		
Netherlands/Pays–Bas	4705	3490	7386	3325	4039
Bulgaria/Bulgarie	x3261	x1494	x3688	x8815	x5018
Mexico/Mexique	7734	7693	3200	2737	2133
China/Chine	323	875	4652	7351	9356
Solomon Isls	x4403	x12791			x23
Thailand/Thaïlande	2774	2921	3921	4354	3490
Russian Federation			x1638	x8768	x2227
Germany/Allemagne	3563	3479	4120	2626	2986
Yugoslavia SFR	18768	x9134			
Croatia/Croatie			4301	4658	x3433
Viet Nam	x2027	x1143	x3767	x2837	x2208
Czech Republic				6438	5243
Portugal	2603	2504	2031	1577	779
Belgium–Luxembourg	1941	1106	1122	3531	3125
Brazil/Brésil	823	1321	1477	2815	2020
Slovenia/Slovénia			2825	2572	3162
Sri Lanka	2416	2513	1929	830	1585
Slovakia				x4519	x2738
Libyan Arab Jamahiriya	265	4095	x218		x20
Romania/Roumanie	1102	1108	1218	1753	2081
Former USSR/Anc. URSS		x3888			
Nigeria/Nigéria	x392	112	x1030	x2167	x2332
United Kingdom	1207	928	1118	1221	1188
Switz.Liecht	391	1145	1007	590	607
Zimbabwe	448	764	1248	502	x1074
Egypt/Egypte	58	115	787	1317	3011
Italy/Italie	546	590	1078	467	302
Sweden/Suède	630	576	639	681	1159
Cote d'Ivoire	x844	x528	x629	x565	x1066
Yugoslavia/Yougoslavie			x1631		
Latvia/Lettonie			x233	x1297	2186
Saudi Arabia	198	516	642	x82	x60
Norway,SVD,JM	278	140	888	174	70
Hong Kong	510	236	589	267	316
Austria/Autriche	230	546	337	123	x154
Ireland/Irlande	197	234	577	57	110

(VALUE AS % OF TOTAL)(VALEUR EN % DU TOTAL)

	1985	1986	1987	1988	1989	1990	1991	1992	1993	1994
Africa	0.2	0.2	x0.2	0.3	x0.4	x0.3	0.4	1.4	2.1	1.4
Northern Africa	0.2	0.0	x0.0	0.1	x0.1	0.0	0.0	0.9	1.5	0.9
Americas	7.4	5.5	x6.8	6.9	x7.8	9.7	8.9	7.3	x10.2	x13.6
LAIA	0.1	0.1	x0.2	0.2	0.1	0.1	0.2	0.3	0.3	0.5
CACM		0.0	0.0	0.0	0.0	0.0	0.0	0.0	0.0	0.0
Asia	23.6	21.4	x22.0	20.2	25.3	21.2	26.9	30.0	32.2	x31.2
Middle East	4.4	x4.8	x4.6	5.3	x5.9	3.5	7.3	10.6	x6.9	x4.1
Europe	68.8	72.9	71.0	72.5	66.2	68.3	62.9	60.9	54.9	53.2
EEC	56.8	57.8	55.4	56.8	52.4	60.0	56.5	53.8	48.9	45.6
EFTA	11.3	14.8	15.3	14.9	13.2	7.3	6.1	6.7	5.8	7.3
Oceania	0.1	x0.0	x0.0	x0.1	x0.3	x0.3	x0.2	x0.2	x0.1	x0.1
Germany/Allemagne	9.8	11.2	10.3	10.4	8.9	13.1	11.5	14.2	13.6	12.0
Italy/Italie	16.8	17.4	14.1	16.8	14.4	14.9	18.0	12.1	7.3	7.3
Japan/Japon	10.1	7.3	9.1	7.7	10.4	9.9	9.7	11.3	13.9	16.3
USA/Etats–Unis d'Amer	5.2	3.9	5.4	5.3	6.1	7.3	6.3	5.7	8.3	10.7
United Kingdom	8.3	5.8	7.3	7.2	9.2	9.9	7.5	6.7	5.4	4.8
Austria/Autriche	3.9	6.1	7.3	6.3	4.9	5.4	6.0	5.2	5.1	4.5
Saudi Arabia	2.8	2.6	1.9	1.4	2.1	1.5	5.0	6.4	x1.1	x1.1
Korea, Republic of	0.5	0.8	0.8	1.2	1.8	2.9	3.5	3.4	4.3	5.8
Norway,SVD,JM	2.9	2.7	1.5	2.1	2.8	3.6	2.7	3.6	3.1	4.6
Belgium–Luxembourg	3.0	3.9	3.6	3.8	2.9	3.2	2.6	2.8	3.9	3.4

	1985	1986	1987	1988	1989	1990	1991	1992	1993	1994
Afrique	4.0	x6.6	x3.1	x3.2	x3.3	x4.9	6.9	x6.0	x6.0	x3.7
Afrique du Nord	0.0	0.1	0.0	0.1	0.1	0.2	2.2	x0.5	0.4	1.3
Amériques	10.9	8.1	6.2	9.7	11.5	16.6	18.1	14.6	12.9	21.4
ALAI	6.3	4.1	2.8	4.9	6.6	6.6	7.2	4.7	3.8	6.2
MCAC		0.1	0.0	x0.0	0.0	0.0	0.0	0.0	x0.0	0.1
Asie	36.7	31.3	26.0	20.2	28.6	25.3	24.8	x34.6	x52.0	36.4
Moyen–Orient	0.7	x0.6	x0.5	x0.9	x0.4	0.3	0.5	0.6	x0.2	x0.2
Europe	45.3	50.2	35.2	31.3	27.5	31.4	x23.0	24.2	13.0	20.7
CEE	39.0	44.0	31.2	24.8	21.2	21.1	17.6	19.4	10.4	17.5
AELE	1.4	1.9	1.3	1.6	1.0	0.4	0.7	0.8	0.2	0.3
Océanie		0.1		x0.1	x0.1	x2.3	x6.6		x0.2	x0.3
Myanmar		x1.6	x0.5	x0.4	x0.7	x0.0	0.0	x4.4	x27.9	x1.6
Indonesia/Indonésie	3.6	3.7	2.5	2.1	3.7	9.2	8.0	9.1	8.8	13.7
Hungary/Hongrie			x14.4	x12.9	x11.2	x15.1	x11.6	x9.4	x4.5	x4.2
France,Monac	5.0	7.0	4.8	4.5	4.5	4.9	6.2	7.1	4.4	9.2
USA/Etats–Unis d'Amer	3.9	3.4	2.3	2.9	4.1	4.3	6.2	5.5	3.8	5.8
Canada	0.7	0.4	1.1	1.9	0.8	5.6	4.6	4.4	5.3	9.4
Philippines	12.0	7.4	7.2	5.5	9.8	5.6	5.1	4.9	3.9	4.5
Singapore/Singapour	7.4	7.2	5.3	5.0	5.7	4.3	5.0	5.4	3.1	4.2
So. Africa Customs Un	3.3	5.5	2.9	2.8	3.0	3.6	3.9	3.9	4.3	
Poland/Pologne	2.7	3.4	2.5	2.1	2.0	1.9	2.6	4.7	4.3	6.6

TRADE BY COMMODITY IN THOUSAND U.S. DOLLARS – COMMERCE PAR PRODUIT EN MILLIERS DE DOLLARS E.U

COUNTRIES–PAYS	IMPORTS – IMPORTATIONS				
	1990	1991	1992	1993	1994
Total	1941724	2150294	2233749	2169926	2450423
Africa	8716	1040	2275	x364	x361
Northern Africa	8091	843	272	x36	87
Americas	65183	78513	79714	x82776	86354
LAIA	5065	3834	3548	675	795
CACM	3	23	34	340	312
Asia	1453064	1719149	1679224	1713957	1884748
Middle East	633	703	1513	x5729	x678
Europe	412000	347056	468457	370055	477551
EEC	373893	316182	434238	341651	441114
EFTA	34961	28690	32007	27335	34357
Oceania	x284	x396	x346	x498	x328
Japan/Japon	1433802	1700411	1638198	1629802	1795580
Finland/Finlande	171420	125323	214219	169330	194865
USA/Etats–Unis d'Amer	47566	58095	52672	59575	46490
France,Monac	28331	33221	43124	36192	47430
Korea, Republic of	11796	12173	27181	67915	81577
Sweden/Suède	59615	39710	35073	20108	37261
Italy/Italie	15628	25580	31940	24079	37641
Belgium–Luxembourg	29179	25201	27005	25730	30438
Austria/Autriche	19075	21677	28080	26156	43220
Germany/Allemagne	26742	22296	24743	15800	16882
Canada	12262	15589	23329	21922	38572
Switz.Liecht	14791	14716	16809	15885	17643
Netherlands/Pays–Bas	12768	13645	15227	11054	13254
Norway,SVD,JM	18766	12859	14496	11317	16563
China/Chine	5367	4058	11024	4678	2225
Spain/Espagne	2405	3123	6763	5229	4746
Denmark/Danemark	2881	3357	4369	3669	4055
United Kingdom	3958	2659	3008	3849	5364
Mexico/Mexique	4491	3525	3353	416	535
Czechoslovakia	51	x2906	x2594		
Turkey/Turquie	10	460	144	4267	76
Korea Dem People's Rp				x4086	
Hong Kong	983	1073	784	1048	980
Slovenia/Slovénia			1459	748	1857
Yugoslavia SFR	2947	x2021			
Iceland/Islande	1403	1115	702	133	150
Hungary/Hongrie	x406	410	x910	x369	x232
Zimbabwe			1645	3	x3
Bulgaria/Bulgarie	x16	x136	70	x1072	x63
Syrian Arab Republic		x2	1113	x3	x3
Australia/Australie	271	327	283	445	267
Lebanon/Liban	x5	x3	x23	x1004	x7
Singapore/Singapour	120	226	299	362	552
Bahamas		765	x17	x101	x21
Poland/Pologne	2004	642	64	149	69
Libyan Arab Jamahiriya	10	622	x22	x13	x11
Ireland/Irlande	605	231	336	75	232
Malta/Malte	194	155	283	164	x81
Portugal	1241	49	255	268	5617
Israel/Israël	152	192	103	146	187
Romania/Roumanie			96	298	337
Croatia/Croatie			237	129	x49
Brazil/Brésil	274	143	74	135	53
Greece/Grèce	44	111	95	113	109
El Salvador		10	25	278	282
Morocco/Maroc	214	199	109	2	5
Russian Federation			x147	x118	x141
Jordan/Jordanie	53	112	96	46	76
Cote d'Ivoire	x6		x117	x135	x15
Oman	34	96	35	102	85

COUNTRIES–PAYS	EXPORTS – EXPORTATIONS				
	1990	1991	1992	1993	1994
Totale	1518170	1320221	1204552	1366283	1503537
Afrique	x89144	x425	x857	x20068	x1355
Afrique du Nord	x86			13	11
Amériques	703187	781825	781802	690689	730533
ALAI	144736	172675	192014	162299	178496
MCAC	75	337	46	x127	x204
Asie	65631	79337	82937	x114797	117410
Moyen–Orient	44	x8	3	x33	x436
Europe	224607	244642	278961	184036	213794
CEE	218442	235998	270040	176777	204271
AELE	5801	8581	8053	6471	8930
Océanie	40571	55814	48175	346777	x394403
USA/Etats–Unis d'Amer	416508	494501	481503	428613	464486
Chile/Chili	110437	153391	164016	137326	163514
Canada	141860	113744	108169	99595	87315
Australia/Australie	299	120	673	314693	350099
Russian Federation			x135938	x167463	x172498
Germany/Allemagne	77914	100210	126828	69474	72083
China/Chine	28171	45168	43923	63367	83212
Former USSR/Anc. URSS	372224	x124365			
France,Monac	34692	35518	38319	28432	32763
New Zealand	22190	37303	26009	21820	23044
Belgium–Luxembourg	18544	18608	18769	19532	24512
Mexico/Mexique	1098	13439	20584	21018	14970
Netherlands/Pays–Bas	17270	17149	18077	14608	16489
Austria/Autriche	15432	16269	16507	11801	x22210
Indonesia/Indonésie	19480	15912	11715	14415	11507
Sweden/Suède	14271	14229	13953	9855	8904
Finland/Finlande	14091	14448	13953	9374	9535
Poland/Pologne	21106	28215	3563	2023	2193
Fiji/Fidji	10651	12657	15221	3232	11606
Thailand/Thaïlande	5815	5333	13023	6813	7832
Ireland/Irlande	5748	5684	9241	7243	7805
So. Africa Customs Un	306	351	69	19990	
Myanmar			x232	x19046	
Papua New Guinea	7432	5732	6272	7032	x9653
Denmark/Danemark	11634	6950	7355	3472	5452
Latvia/Lettonie			x7583	x9927	1693
Uruguay	3460	5838	7346		
Viet Nam		x1358	x6643	x5001	x10479
Norway,SVD,JM	4564	6107	4379	2188	2599
Czechoslovakia		x4506	x6730		
Estonia/Estonie			x2978	x7636	x10661
Switz.Liecht	1237	2474	3673	4283	6332
Malaysia/Malaisie	3889	5007	2768	1897	1039
United Kingdom	4674	4734	3815	739	1480
Hong Kong	1862	4144	2710	1663	1356
Czech Republic				5628	42174
Portugal	2651	1532	2409	1645	2354
Singapore/Singapour	2203	1378	1015	1682	309
Argentina/Argentine	29717	1	2	3940	4
Hungary/Hongrie	x1647	x1093	x1391	x1113	x697
Italy/Italie	382	561	762	529	464
Philippines	3541	513	642	654	629
Lithuania/Lituanie					4
Slovakia				x1007	x939
Belarus/Bélarus			x553	x380	x539
Croatia/Croatie			493	376	x330
Slovenia/Slovénia			324	410	264
Zimbabwe	5		562	6	x2
Belize/Bélize		x546			30
Honduras	21	326	35	90	156

(VALUE AS % OF TOTAL)(VALEUR EN % DU TOTAL)

	1985	1986	1987	1988	1989	1990	1991	1992	1993	1994
Africa	0.4	0.4	0.4	0.7	x0.5	0.4		0.1	x0.0	x0.0
Northern Africa	0.4	0.4	0.4	0.7	x0.5	0.4	0.0	0.0	x0.0	0.0
Americas	3.2	x3.7	x1.9	x3.6	3.2	3.4	3.6	3.6	x3.9	3.6
LAIA	0.0	0.0	x0.0	0.2	0.4	0.3	0.2	0.2	0.0	0.0
CACM		0.0	x0.0	0.0	0.0	0.0	0.0	0.0	0.0	0.0
Asia	38.2	33.7	x33.2	x61.4	65.1	74.8	80.0	75.1	79.0	76.9
Middle East	0.6	0.3	0.1	0.4	0.0	0.0	0.0	0.1	x0.3	x0.0
Europe	58.0	62.1	64.4	34.1	31.0	21.2	16.1	21.0	17.1	19.5
EEC	30.5	32.7	33.9	18.3	17.0	19.3	14.7	19.4	15.7	18.0
EFTA	23.8	27.6	29.1	15.8	13.9	1.8	1.3	1.4	1.3	1.4
Oceania		x0.0	x0.0	x0.0		x0.0	x0.0	x0.0	x0.0	x0.0
Japan/Japon	37.1	32.9	31.5	57.8	63.5	73.8	79.1	73.3	75.1	73.3
Finland/Finlande	8.1	6.1	6.4	8.1	8.1	8.8	5.8	9.6	7.8	8.0
USA/Etats–Unis d'Amer	1.8	1.5	0.9	2.8	2.4	2.4	2.7	2.4	2.7	1.9
France,Monac	0.7	0.6	0.8	1.0	0.9	1.5	1.5	1.9	1.7	1.9
Korea, Republic of	0.5	0.3	0.1	0.4	1.0	0.6	0.6	1.2	3.1	3.3
Sweden/Suède	8.7	12.6	14.4	3.3	3.3	3.1	1.8	1.6	0.9	1.5
Italy/Italie	3.8	3.8	3.4	0.7	0.6	0.8	1.2	1.4	1.1	1.5
Belgium–Luxembourg	3.2	3.2	3.3	1.3	1.1	1.5	1.2	1.2	1.2	1.2
Austria/Autriche	3.2	3.8	2.6	1.4	0.9	1.0	1.0	1.3	1.2	1.8
Germany/Allemagne	1.3	1.4	1.5	1.4	1.2	1.4	1.0	1.1	0.7	0.7

	1985	1986	1987	1988	1989	1990	1991	1992	1993	1994
Afrique	1.7	x2.1	x1.9	x0.1	x0.2	x5.9	x0.0	x0.1	x1.5	x0.1
Afrique du Nord	0.0	0.0	0.0	0.0	0.0	x0.0			0.0	0.0
Amériques	24.0	x19.2	16.4	38.2	46.4	46.3	59.2	65.0	50.6	48.6
ALAI	0.1	0.4	1.3	6.3	6.1	9.5	13.1	15.9	11.9	11.9
MCAC	0.0	x0.3	0.0	0.0	x0.0	0.0	0.0	0.0	x0.0	x0.0
Asie	2.2	1.6	1.3	2.1	x3.9	4.3	6.0	6.9	x8.4	7.8
Moyen–Orient	0.0	x0.0	x0.0	x0.1	0.0	0.0	x0.0	0.0	x0.0	x0.0
Europe	34.3	39.5	35.7	20.0	17.0	14.8	18.5	23.2	13.5	14.2
CEE	28.2	31.8	28.0	15.3	13.5	14.4	17.9	22.4	12.9	13.6
AELE	6.1	7.7	7.7	4.6	3.4	0.4	0.6	0.7	0.5	0.6
Océanie	14.8	14.3	14.6	2.6	3.0	2.7	4.2	4.0	25.4	x26.2
USA/Etats–Unis d'Amer	16.7	13.0	10.5	23.9	28.8	27.4	37.5	40.0	31.4	30.9
Chile/Chili	0.0	0.3	1.0	3.6	2.9	7.3	11.6	13.6	10.1	10.9
Canada	7.2	5.5	4.6	8.0	11.5	9.3	8.6	9.0	7.3	5.8
Australia/Australie	14.4	13.8	14.0	0.0	0.0	0.0	0.0	0.1	23.0	23.3
Russian Federation								x11.3	x12.3	x11.5
Germany/Allemagne	8.3	8.7	7.1	4.1	3.9	5.1	7.6	10.5	5.1	4.8
China/Chine			0.0	0.5	1.2	1.9	3.4	3.6	4.6	5.5
Former USSR/Anc. URSS	15.8	18.1	16.3	31.5	27.0	24.5	x9.4			
France,Monac	7.1	8.8	6.7	2.5	2.2	2.3	2.7	3.2	2.1	2.2
New Zealand	0.1	0.1	0.1	1.7	1.9	1.5	2.8	2.2	1.6	1.5

TRADE BY COMMODITY IN THOUSAND U.S. DOLLARS – COMMERCE PAR PRODUIT EN MILLIERS DE DOLLARS E.U

COUNTRIES–PAYS	IMPORTS – IMPORTATIONS 1990	1991	1992	1993	1994
Total	10262553	9701779	10034400	10861018	10889816
Africa	152556	107323	134509	99734	130331
Northern Africa	131135	88536	119458	88917	120580
Americas	x270538	x281903	x290553	x339049	x425645
LAIA	14457	17974	26863	24834	32130
CACM	161	514	873	x1227	x2177
Asia	6757881	6420290	6807003	8290883	7423169
Middle East	154728	168236	177637	329408	179724
Europe	2968409	2755076	2746321	2072455	2870931
EEC	2774713	2630145	2606029	1969279	2676014
EFTA	110586	107277	118608	92365	175941
Oceania	x5060	x3258	x3611	x4362	x4411
Japan/Japon	4499206	4132619	4492821	5652293	4990606
Korea, Republic of	990474	1040754	918516	1182563	1011575
Italy/Italie	706519	701574	648723	500779	633668
China/Chine	466354	470222	495071	459041	430371
Austria/Autriche	292180	359682	327880	247569	303459
Germany/Allemagne	344114	288011	318538	219409	248543
Thailand/Thaïlande	220995	267022	285402	233369	294048
France,Monac	276294	275932	270877	220194	337531
Sweden/Suède	224468	213034	272144	169503	318966
Canada	186271	200878	185979	202778	258183
Turkey/Turquie	123912	131445	142038	304864	148095
Spain/Espagne	299906	231310	209414	128793	166355
India/Inde	232440	162531	206836	134425	204134
Belgium–Luxembourg	167378	141248	138254	131320	179474
Portugal	146805	123094	147963	99072	150551
Hong Kong	60051	67657	68212	98065	102095
Norway,SVD,JM	74648	76099	82491	59508	137048
United Kingdom	60842	56830	56222	91680	104197
Finland/Finlande	92538	78292	77740	35545	76058
USA/Etats–Unis d'Amer	47874	40334	58153	89550	116075
Netherlands/Pays–Bas	68442	64587	59135	53866	58333
Philippines	41409	30087	61409	82451	56216
Morocco/Maroc	57662	43277	67373	44910	60827
Greece/Grèce	62333	64400	45248	39168	47131
Israel/Israël	42665	40895	39991	41465	51686
Switz.Liecht	35453	30714	35822	32464	38360
Czechoslovakia	12715	x54298	x25560		
Denmark/Danemark	28089	23703	26890	21486	37294
Hungary/Hongrie	x33693	58419	x4051	x6471	x3639
Indonesia/Indonésie	18198	11290	27112	22066	27583
Algeria/Algérie	44390	19748	19503	14932	14361
Mexico/Mexique	6936	15543	21847	16408	21270
Egypt/Egypte	13783	14230	18048	17879	30467
Saudi Arabia	16423	17776	16083	x13010	x9134
Singapore/Singapour	24037	15133	15489	15384	31536
Romania/Roumanie	28780	11841	15389	7318	2193
Tunisia/Tunisie	11357	9287	10477	7726	13654
Ireland/Irlande	4806	8448	7001	10896	14454
Malaysia/Malaisie	1723	4707	8729	12453	20442
Czech Republic				23785	15154
Slovenia/Slovénia			13841	6944	16470
Iran (Islamic Rp. of)		x12777	x7507		
Pakistan	3775	4107	6242	7890	8127
Yugoslavia SFR	78636	x14875			
So. Africa Customs Un	6092	3607	6787	3855	3350
Bangladesh				x13495	x10988
Mauritius/Maurice	4550	4013	4518	3913	3035
Libyan Arab Jamahiriya	3848	1985	x4058	x3469	x1270
Bulgaria/Bulgarie	x18	x61	5684	x3665	x326
Kuwait/ Koweït	4884	408	3975	4882	1359

COUNTRIES–PAYS	EXPORTS – EXPORTATIONS 1990	1991	1992	1993	1994
Totale	7923654	x7811259	7349747	7618340	x8217529
Afrique	x677250	x830636	x765259	x900104	x1187296
Afrique du Nord	329	416	242	140	x267
Amériques	2765675	2472812	2626316	3043142	2808392
ALAI	96929	107526	131339	175212	193879
MCAC	11240	11834	14588	13336	12737
Asie	1812498	1813511	1798239	1411502	x1501506
Moyen–Orient	3692	3082	5699	5501	7162
Europe	1479652	1521488	1429003	1039819	1217661
CEE	1288074	1347338	1228415	895350	1070463
AELE	135267	134978	143884	123702	113155
Océanie	289695	335651	x440510	960127	x1206415
USA/Etats–Unis d'Amer	2524539	2232500	2297350	2670617	2445916
Malaysia/Malaisie	1502042	1494446	1520125	1137867	977050
Russian Federation			x622800	x847374	x791484
Germany/Allemagne	343177	517454	389192	272667	276910
France,Monac	432073	378555	382088	238210	272774
New Zealand	181425	209331	232969	440970	427567
Gabon	x271895	x220531	x262949	x325941	x501305
Former USSR/Anc. URSS	750856	x672652			
Papua New Guinea	80845	93825	146591	423735	x643566
Cameroon/Cameroun	132691	156564	x212244	x275757	x294740
Canada	129268	118573	179066	179436	146409
Myanmar	118057	137505	103140	97753	x282502
Belgium–Luxembourg	139200	129413	111873	95498	115346
Chile/Chili	93758	81568	72651	149890	125224
Switz.Liecht	96238	96781	102819	90519	94104
Congo	43901	x110327	x106146	x68555	x101196
Cote d'Ivoire	x118638	x101468	x68890	x71499	x89908
Ghana	x33173	138273	28534	x70137	x115986
Poland/Pologne	5124	33936	116933	70237	65166
Hungary/Hongrie	x74420	x71136	x95305	x53757	x53907
Austria/Autriche	122891	80396	70478	60112	x75774
China/Chine	40640	61558	56738	70900	43181
Finland/Finlande	52512	39726	52252	78560	129999
Sweden/Suède	61867	59038	56408	50278	67658
Solomon Isls	22329	18757	x50343	x66128	x113174
Portugal	36647	36204	50778	28910	31729
Czechoslovakia		x46635	x68096		
Equatorial Guinea	12839	x48643	x25020	x40260	x48277
Norway,SVD,JM	39030	38198	41066	33183	19051
Latvia/Lettonie			x27905	x51971	60066
Hong Kong	24794	23765	20109	34303	63316
Czech Republic				77220	134483
Viet Nam	x79531	x48048	x21254	x7126	x4283
Argentina/Argentine	821	24238	42029	8354	27507
Netherlands/Pays–Bas	24324	23135	24669	19769	19241
Denmark/Danemark	24359	26146	23301	11298	20380
Democratic Kampuchea	x2412	x13980	x29466	x14874	x70796
Liberia/Libéria	x24512	x22135	x28066	x1878	x1020
Ireland/Irlande	12224	17442	21949	11739	15864
Australia/Australie	3395	13260	9030	28806	20017
United Kingdom	17853	19936	18148	11721	17158
Bulgaria/Bulgarie	x48588	x12681	x9883	x21160	x7001
Slovakia				x39493	x35676
Honduras	11211	11820	14525	13102	12543
Yugoslavia SFR	56297	x39155			
Estonia/Estonie			x5538	x33262	x57316
Zaire/Zaïre	x19788	x17579	x9684	x9312	x9719
Greece/Grèce	7768	9922	16422	7547	6254
Korea Dem People's Rp	x8135	x10008	x10187	x12926	x6378
Singapore/Singapour	12569	10262	14575	8139	12185

(VALUE AS % OF TOTAL)(VALEUR EN % DU TOTAL)

	1985	1986	1987	1988	1989	1990	1991	1992	1993	1994
Africa	2.0	1.8	1.5	1.3	1.1	1.5	1.1	1.4	0.9	1.2
Northern Africa	1.8	1.6	1.3	1.1	1.0	1.3	0.9	1.2	0.8	1.1
Americas	3.0	2.6	2.2	x2.2	x2.4	x2.7	x2.9	x2.9	x3.1	x3.9
LAIA	0.3	0.2	0.1	0.1	0.1	0.1	0.2	0.3	0.2	0.3
CACM	0.0	x0.0	x0.0	0.0	0.0	0.0	0.0	0.0	x0.0	x0.0
Asia	72.3	69.4	73.8	66.2	65.6	65.9	66.2	67.9	76.3	68.2
Middle East	1.1	1.6	1.8	1.1	0.8	1.5	1.7	1.8	3.0	1.7
Europe	22.2	25.5	21.8	29.7	30.2	28.9	28.4	27.4	19.1	26.4
EEC	19.0	21.9	18.2	21.9	22.6	27.0	27.1	26.0	18.1	24.6
EFTA	3.0	3.5	3.5	7.4	7.0	1.1	1.1	1.2	0.9	1.6
Oceania		x0.0	x0.0	x0.1	x0.1	x0.0	x0.0	x0.0	x0.0	x0.0
Japan/Japon	47.0	46.5	50.9	40.9	45.8	43.8	42.6	44.8	52.0	45.8
Korea, Republic of	8.4	7.9	7.8	8.1	8.7	9.7	10.7	9.2	10.9	9.3
Italy/Italie	4.9	5.2	4.6	4.6	4.8	6.9	7.2	6.5	4.6	5.8
China/Chine	13.1	9.8	6.3	9.7	5.5	4.5	4.8	4.9	4.2	4.0
Austria/Autriche	1.6	1.8	1.9	2.1	2.0	2.8	3.7	3.3	2.3	2:8
Germany/Allemagne	3.4	4.1	3.2	2.8	3.0	3.4	3.0	3.2	2.0	2.3
Thailand/Thaïlande	0.7	0.6	0.6	0.7	1.5	2.2	2.8	2.8	2.1	2.7
France,Monac	2.9	3.3	2.4	1.9	1.8	2.7	2.8	2.7	2.0	3.1
Sweden/Suède	0.4	0.6	0.7	3.7	3.3	2.2	2.2	2.7	1.6	2.9
Canada	1.9	1.9	1.5	1.6	1.6	1.8	2.1	1.9	1.9	2.4

	1985	1986	1987	1988	1989	1990	1991	1992	1993	1994
Afrique	4.3	x10.2	x8.6	x7.5	x7.4	x8.5	x10.6	x10.4	x11.8	x14.4
Afrique du Nord	0.0	x0.0	x0.0	x0.0	x0.0	0.0	0.0	0.0	0.0	x0.0
Amériques	36.9	30.7	33.0	35.1	35.1	34.9	31.7	35.7	39.9	34.1
ALAI	1.3	1.0	0.9	1.0	0.5	1.2	1.4	1.8	2.3	2.4
MCAC	0.0	0.1	0.1	0.3	0.2	0.1	0.2	0.2	0.2	0.2
Asie	31.0	27.1	30.9	24.6	25.5	22.9	23.2	24.4	18.5	x18.2
Moyen–Orient	0.2	0.2	x0.1	0.1	0.1	0.0	0.0	0.1	0.1	0.1
Europe	15.6	15.6	14.8	17.1	18.4	18.7	19.5	19.4	13.6	14.8
CEE	10.8	10.9	10.3	13.0	13.9	16.3	17.2	16.7	11.8	13.0
AELE	4.4	4.3	3.8	3.6	3.9	1.7	1.7	2.0	1.6	1.4
Océanie	2.4	2.3	2.9	2.7	2.8	3.6	4.2	x6.0	12.6	x14.6
USA/Etats–Unis d'Amer	32.3	26.4	27.6	30.0	31.9	31.9	28.6	31.3	35.1	29.8
Malaysia/Malaisie	29.0	23.6	28.2	20.4	21.2	19.0	19.1	20.7	14.9	11.9
Russian Federation								x8.5	x11.1	x9.6
Germany/Allemagne	2.4	2.4	2.2	2.9	3.2	4.3	6.6	5.3	3.6	3.4
France,Monac	3.3	3.5	3.4	4.6	4.9	5.5	4.8	5.2	3.1	3.3
New Zealand	0.5	0.4	0.6	0.9	1.2	2.3	2.7	3.2	5.8	5.2
Gabon		x3.5	x3.1	x2.7	x2.8	x3.4	x2.8	x3.6	x4.3	x6.1
Former USSR/Anc. URSS	9.0	13.5	8.7	9.6	8.5	9.5	x8.6			
Papua New Guinea	1.4	1.4	1.9	1.4	1.4	1.0	1.2	2.0	5.6	x7.8
Cameroon/Cameroun		1.1	1.0	x1.1	1.4	1.7	2.0	x2.9	x3.6	x3.6

TRADE BY COMMODITY IN THOUSAND U.S. DOLLARS – COMMERCE PAR PRODUIT EN MILLIERS DE DOLLARS E.U

COUNTRIES–PAYS	IMPORTS – IMPORTATIONS				
	1990	1991	1992	1993	1994
Total	20669066	19184394	21070941	23148555	27118225
Africa	1070831	811730	754453	535338	919990
Northern Africa	930741	669456	615097	367404	757219
Americas	4096573	4036357	x5155793	x6882198	x7971391
LAIA	161820	228844	376858	394655	383887
CACM	4480	3861	5346	7566	12984
Asia	4062584	4321120	4735904	x6488735	x6992261
Middle East	x314426	x413908	x471720	x474092	x467823
Europe	10916494	9533070	9949569	8670247	10677762
EEC	10370798	9090631	9495214	8236832	10068796
EFTA	490909	387681	379325	363391	511657
Oceania	x408317	x385545	x434777	x486507	x490178
USA/Etats–Unis d'Amer	3293944	3223613	4156329	5824373	6878594
Japan/Japon	2845185	2860395	2999227	4279951	4573938
Italy/Italie	1811470	1821677	1888345	1512637	1785796
United Kingdom	2425179	1764898	1724489	1671750	1990247
Germany/Allemagne	1743131	1636870	1879931	1598359	1957474
Netherlands/Pays–Bas	1063363	856427	941809	938271	1092266
France,Monac	826732	759370	703966	573939	747898
Belgium–Luxembourg	651662	602210	591215	534981	601869
Spain/Espagne	636500	560446	594797	400589	510446
Canada	477678	426509	469525	505557	507091
Thailand/Thaïlande	318105	362836	435832	509479	647864
Denmark/Danemark	459994	416354	464550	395287	587575
Australia/Australie	353887	338788	378468	441507	441452
Korea, Republic of	182092	252305	287861	515020	462631
Mexico/Mexique	108283	165331	289832	289362	277929
Austria/Autriche	244968	231624	253948	239079	297560
Egypt/Egypte	403680	329828	305314	1502	344820
Switz.Liecht	289926	205273	190197	187288	238754
Singapore/Singapour	169327	179697	169402	177467	190645
Norway,SVD,JM	181520	162548	169230	158972	256530
Saudi Arabia	89403	130879	152349	x203107	x206403
Greece/Grèce	188136	187663	149984	118405	141310
Morocco/Maroc	125585	111640	128135	105282	127715
Algeria/Algérie	245746	83782	74063	157484	154559
Hong Kong	52811	71975	104846	138303	183151
China/Chine	35467	32540	106214	167033	159898
Ireland/Irlande	139321	98867	116991	87047	136694
Israel/Israël	98103	104715	93356	100648	125583
So. Africa Customs Un	78204	85644	85578	109793	110483
Sweden/Suède	99174	77590	74920	69691	98517
Tunisia/Tunisie	89182	58317	82517	66456	90609
United Arab Emirates	61471	54724	66328	x63487	x66097
Portugal	40712	46757	70989	54589	63384
Iran (Islamic Rp. of)		x98864	x46885	x6192	x2661
Argentina/Argentine	18230	33828	50177	56429	63898
Libyan Arab Jamahiriya	58322	78135	x17345	x26508	x27554
Hungary/Hongrie	x33506	68310	x19181	x31109	x26482
Finland/Finlande	40457	29878	39280	42206	57760
Syrian Arab Republic	27919	x21442	42523	x40789	x31031
Yemen/Yémen	x31628	3376	x63617	x27725	x9695
Malaysia/Malaisie	14199	19069	25257	48812	68282
Reunion/Réunion	26774	27055	26266	22891	25873
Jamaica/Jamaïque	11798	19980	x26474	x28122	x24052
Slovenia/Slovénia			33603	34040	42440
Cyprus/Chypre	21595	20626	22124	18875	23080
Brazil/Brésil	25103	17149	16038	27737	23382
Dominican Republic	x12691	x13989	x22210	x23880	x56601
New Zealand	25082	18686	17760	23436	24448
Philippines	2392	2219	11350	45256	66690
Oman	15291	16573	18116	23982	17390

COUNTRIES–PAYS	EXPORTS – EXPORTATIONS				
	1990	1991	1992	1993	1994
Totale	18808876	17622792	18829633	21249460	24445439
Afrique	x536297	x398880	x501297	x516236	x673280
Afrique du Nord	643	282	657	2088	1944
Amériques	7671715	7664570	8797634	11022802	12162300
ALAI	504921	527557	593731	751999	903359
MCAC	13676	12051	13875	19292	24547
Asie	2237472	2321351	2685780	3200131	3201729
Moyen–Orient	32457	16489	12840	x20392	x39788
Europe	6476570	5703830	6080301	5649793	x7280618
CEE	5969572	5314710	5588904	5216382	6849551
AELE	205948	190924	230467	204825	218496
Océanie	149120	x174547	x211374	x306723	x362840
Canada	4850946	4725115	5642457	7557685	8565902
USA/Etats–Unis d'Amer	2292056	2391295	2538514	2684084	2655939
Sweden/Suède	1867763	1720433	1934021	1843535	2434166
Malaysia/Malaisie	1325823	1276268	1583422	2011826	1934545
Finland/Finlande	1176978	1015629	1031889	1086453	1565659
Austria/Autriche	1113037	919170	916251	748205	x962147
Germany/Allemagne	486410	438716	438010	367086	512233
France,Monac	444522	422764	442446	354429	421771
Russian Federation			x601572	x540100	x692803
Indonesia/Indonésie	242622	354281	342777	358299	346125
Former USSR/Anc. URSS	1432150	x883457			
Cote d'Ivoire	x318997	x230439	x261339	x226892	x296193
Netherlands/Pays–Bas	228230	236876	243945	208903	223168
Singapore/Singapour	249046	238729	225022	212316	187102
New Zealand	123701	153743	188965	282644	323447
Poland/Pologne	99712	192094	189704	194522	252368
Brazil/Brésil	147527	146629	172327	248180	353457
Chile/Chili	174523	179683	156244	192180	230237
Norway,SVD,JM	176069	157440	190085	168701	180178
Belgium–Luxembourg	177033	162749	176863	156657	200082
Mexico/Mexique	89786	99106	165297	189601	162792
Italy/Italie	110937	115668	112578	171634	221333
Czechoslovakia		x153428	x171412		
Viet Nam	x44942	x124951	x109136	x82537	x70792
Portugal	189198	119930	111940	80227	80465
China/Chine	42966	49650	103302	143069	182572
Croatia/Croatie			138735	154893	x130237
Cameroon/Cameroun	57440	74568	x92745	x101159	x102923
Romania/Roumanie	97580	55223	91692	108501	154249
Hong Kong	44780	60337	83094	104020	129060
Denmark/Danemark	69531	61492	72834	78524	86622
Ghana	x87834	26594	70983	x106278	x185955
Yugoslavia SFR	300848	x198134			
Hungary/Hongrie	x49833	x47765	x72567	x48390	x50889
Thailand/Thaïlande	47473	52447	49004	55709	71128
Bolivia/Bolivie	42576	42338	46330	49649	78548
Czech Republic				128384	219309
Myanmar	41320	11017	52472	61357	x79583
Spain/Espagne	43260	41701	38011	37226	44089
Paraguay	29411	35441	39956	41383	47844
Slovenia/Slovénia			61428	53938	60673
Lao People's Dem. Rp.	x37227	x44154	x32658	x37009	x63513
Switz.Liecht	29879	33480	40382	35954	38038
Ireland/Irlande	30462	23884	30957	39341	42728
Korea, Republic of	50992	34764	26987	27003	18088
Latvia/Lettonie			x9593	x73326	97723
Bulgaria/Bulgarie	x56943	x27348	x27578	x21096	x29141
United Kingdom	25030	23198	28673	18077	38598
Philippines	19424	20091	18612	26099	9607
Mongolia/Mongolie	x31584	x14382	x13720	x30644	x3961

(VALUE AS % OF TOTAL)(VALEUR EN % DU TOTAL)

	1985	1986	1987	1988	1989	1990	1991	1992	1993	1994
Africa	7.2	5.2	4.1	4.2	4.8	5.2	4.2	3.6	2.3	3.4
Northern Africa	6.7	4.6	3.4	3.5	4.1	4.5	3.5	2.9	1.6	2.8
Americas	34.1	30.5	25.8	22.4	22.7	19.8	21.0	x24.5	x29.7	x29.4
LAIA	0.9	0.8	0.6	0.5	0.8	0.8	1.2	1.8	1.7	1.4
CACM	0.0	0.0	0.0	0.0	0.0	0.0	0.0	0.0	0.0	0.0
Asia	13.1	13.3	x18.0	x20.6	x21.3	19.6	22.6	22.5	x28.0	x25.8
Middle East	2.3	x2.1	x1.9	x2.1	x1.9	x1.5	x2.2	x2.2	x2.0	x1.7
Europe	42.6	48.5	49.9	49.8	48.3	52.8	49.7	47.2	37.5	39.4
EEC	38.9	43.8	45.3	45.3	44.4	50.2	47.4	45.1	35.6	37.1
EFTA	3.5	4.3	4.4	4.4	3.8	2.4	2.0	1.8	1.6	1.9
Oceania	2.3	x1.8	x1.7	x2.3	x2.3	x1.9	x2.0	x2.1	x2.1	x1.8
USA/Etats–Unis d'Amer	29.2	25.7	21.7	18.1	18.2	15.9	16.8	19.7	25.2	25.4
Japan/Japon	8.4	8.7	11.9	13.8	15.4	13.8	14.9	14.2	18.5	16.9
Italy/Italie	6.6	7.0	7.8	7.6	7.6	8.8	9.5	9.0	6.5	6.6
United Kingdom	10.3	11.3	12.1	13.0	11.4	11.7	9.2	8.2	7.2	7.3
Germany/Allemagne	5.9	7.1	7.1	6.6	6.9	8.4	8.5	8.9	6.9	7.2
Netherlands/Pays–Bas	4.1	4.7	4.7	4.2	4.6	5.1	4.5	4.5	4.1	4.0
France,Monac	3.4	3.8	3.9	3.9	3.5	4.0	4.0	3.3	2.5	2.8
Belgium–Luxembourg	2.3	2.5	2.7	2.7	2.8	3.2	3.1	2.8	2.3	2.2
Spain/Espagne	1.8	2.0	2.2	2.5	2.7	3.1	2.9	2.8	1.7	1.9
Canada	2.1	2.2	2.2	2.7	2.6	2.3	2.2	2.2	2.2	1.9

	1985	1986	1987	1988	1989	1990	1991	1992	1993	1994
Afrique	0.9	x1.8	x1.7	x1.6	x0.4	x2.8	x2.3	x2.7	x2.5	x2.7
Afrique du Nord	0.0	x0.0	x0.0	x0.0	x0.0	0.0	0.0	0.0	0.0	0.0
Amériques	38.4	36.1	36.1	35.2	35.4	40.8	43.5	46.7	51.9	49.7
ALAI	1.7	1.8	2.0	2.0	2.1	2.7	3.0	3.2	3.5	3.7
MCAC	0.3	0.2	0.2	0.1	0.1	0.1	0.1	0.1	0.1	0.1
Asie	8.7	8.7	10.0	11.3	13.8	11.9	13.2	14.3	15.1	13.1
Moyen–Orient	0.2	0.2	x0.1	0.1	0.1	0.2	0.1	0.1	x0.1	x0.2
Europe	43.7	44.1	42.4	42.4	41.3	34.4	32.4	32.3	26.6	x29.8
CEE	23.8	24.6	23.6	23.9	23.2	31.7	30.2	29.7	24.5	28.0
AELE	18.4	18.5	17.7	17.3	17.0	1.1	1.1	1.2	1.0	0.9
Océanie	0.6	0.4	0.4	x0.7	0.7	0.8	x1.0	x1.1	x1.4	x1.5
Canada	29.8	26.8	26.1	23.7	23.1	25.8	26.8	30.0	35.6	35.0
USA/Etats–Unis d'Amer	6.6	7.2	7.7	9.3	10.1	12.2	13.6	13.5	12.6	10.9
Sweden/Suède	9.2	9.2	8.4	7.8	7.7	9.9	9.8	10.3	8.7	10.0
Malaysia/Malaisie	4.0	3.6	4.0	4.4	6.0	7.0	7.2	8.4	9.5	7.9
Finland/Finlande	5.5	5.3	5.3	5.4	4.7	6.3	5.8	5.5	5.1	6.4
Austria/Autriche	3.3	3.7	3.5	3.6	3.9	5.9	5.2	4.9	3.5	x3.9
Germany/Allemagne	1.7	2.0	1.9	2.1	2.0	2.6	2.5	2.3	1.7	2.1
France,Monac	1.4	1.6	1.6	1.6	1.6	2.4	2.4	2.3	1.7	1.7
Russian Federation								x3.2	x2.5	x2.8
Indonesia/Indonésie	2.0	2.0	2.3	3.0	4.1	1.3	2.0	1.8	1.7	1.4

TRADE BY COMMODITY IN THOUSAND U.S. DOLLARS – COMMERCE PAR PRODUIT EN MILLIERS DE DOLLARS E.U

COUNTRIES–PAYS	IMPORTS – IMPORTATIONS 1990	1991	1992	1993	1994
Total	19125500	15822907	16257591	13427581	17512562
Africa	205750	143252	147062	123810	175994
Northern Africa	145971	110467	113942	87475	117845
Americas	3991614	3194173	3231318	2994863	3682136
LAIA	668406	644312	674328	674883	838751
CACM	18099	14042	14011	x15971	x13519
Asia	4371098	4093476	4328317	4018970	5071568
Middle East	x126968	x132933	x157643	x175666	x179661
Europe	10032682	8103512	8273476	6034252	8282646
EEC	9533515	7737790	7868215	5738510	7878199
EFTA	359985	287323	285709	216708	296966
Oceania	172232	x107942	x125873	x101705	x104343
USA/Etats–Unis d'Amer	3005532	2301208	2257077	2018895	2453177
Germany/Allemagne	2860010	2384387	2378580	1679247	2298060
Japan/Japon	2048882	1784954	1736116	1572670	1963231
Italy/Italie	1594968	1370481	1366780	1040625	1460215
France,Monac	1446108	1132837	1174266	835469	1170127
United Kingdom	1385702	1074066	1108710	859887	967927
Korea, Republic of	1005813	890477	982611	839494	1044037
Indonesia/Indonésie	267455	286078	446363	479007	614179
Netherlands/Pays–Bas	563015	427372	437445	324888	547429
China/Chine	286532	453231	413469	294053	494431
Mexico/Mexique	392181	339203	367212	372371	483773
Spain/Espagne	423421	351827	338669	269195	371655
Austria/Autriche	376022	298550	326808	244612	348656
Canada	288812	223497	274519	276725	367305
Belgium–Luxembourg	391152	279960	276056	195316	295905
Switz.Liecht	300047	246931	254521	187082	242880
Thailand/Thaïlande	153898	195181	208336	225879	290381
India/Inde	252350	121789	157817	158544	202352
Venezuela	128891	140502	141199	123126	129483
Sweden/Suède	161423	121366	151830	98317	157846
Australia/Australie	161809	100104	111955	95290	95455
Finland/Finlande	67317	67679	136607	73848	94647
Turkey/Turquie	80166	71994	101813	103589	102242
Philippines	61092	63359	64030	80920	79308
Brazil/Brésil	66287	62556	55495	76404	83164
Greece/Grèce	111369	96675	55262	40244	57090
Denmark/Danemark	92641	77407	64581	37777	51313
Israel/Israël	72844	62183	58918	52577	55580
Hungary/Hongrie	x50689	66747	x55358	x24357	x31537
Slovenia/Slovénia			83775	61614	95536
Poland/Pologne	36413	42601	45372	37486	58320
Colombia/Colombie	38699	39093	48163	38031	57254
Argentina/Argentine	10790	30673	43708	47160	54357
Portugal	43832	38998	38473	25654	41625
Norway,SVD,JM	59933	40392	31170	29601	54075
Iran (Islamic Rp. of)		x40481	x35944	x18730	x6601
Egypt/Egypte	53426	32815	39376	20957	30459
Algeria/Algérie	44587	28044	26809	30183	50019
Pakistan	18498	23934	26470	27077	23328
Yugoslavia SFR	135873	x77144			
Malaysia/Malaisie	23291	24254	23796	26955	39379
Tunisia/Tunisie	24657	22975	28858	17989	19458
Hong Kong	23471	28466	22629	15693	17409
Morocco/Maroc	23291	25258	17242	16146	15688
Romania/Roumanie	21877	11977	27084	17157	11946
Singapore/Singapour	20884	17995	19840	16467	23276
Czech Republic				53316	71359
So. Africa Customs Un	23879	16084	14594	19921	38350
Ireland/Irlande	16535	16186	14146	13431	15704
Czechoslovakia	36262	x22793	x14743		

COUNTRIES–PAYS	EXPORTS – EXPORTATIONS 1990	1991	1992	1993	1994
Totale	17704451	14345094	14601535	11807871	16233289
Afrique	388610	327000	404823	x332430	x455088
Afrique du Nord	59970	42224	47125	28368	62571
Amériques	10363849	8910203	9448880	7875272	10476989
ALAI	1001590	931261	1341712	1256517	1666345
MCAC	1420	1545	1709	x2832	x3031
Asie	224364	216772	197901	182551	361574
Moyen–Orient	9932	5785	7280	x16851	x21800
Europe	5885048	4320617	4182077	3074118	4486504
CEE	5354167	4240179	4087694	2996809	4210729
AELE	459933	55487	60349	44011	244264
Océanie	x270823	241407	200001	200018	x257837
Canada	5288661	4348837	4229476	3607913	4963871
USA/Etats–Unis d'Amer	4069342	3626701	3873668	3006155	3838819
Sweden/Suède	1956209	1549289	1462634	1133467	1346348
Brazil/Brésil	599623	586200	742126	718439	851333
Finland/Finlande	1026385	698589	636377	515672	723858
Portugal	681800	550287	552161	362063	508461
Chile/Chili	322373	309328	535040	468894	720056
So. Africa Customs Un	324888	281421	350884	294964	370947
France,Monac	381513	311620	315366	213671	340668
Spain/Espagne	358310	320140	307500	206803	318609
Germany/Allemagne	285851	278523	328623	205860	350769
New Zealand	253686	225156	194008	189841	238002
Russian Federation			x206299	x288299	x361423
Belgium–Luxembourg	190392	148478	144930	79556	114272
Netherlands/Pays–Bas	105356	103095	110030	98665	218312
Austria/Autriche	162350	114831	107484	88484	x144988
Former USSR/Anc. URSS	451800	x207139			
Czechoslovakia		x78355	x110354		
United Kingdom	94998	68606	68300	35247	67736
Hong Kong	64072	72210	58914	39941	49590
Switz.Liecht	59235	55376	60101	43854	71056
Indonesia/Indonésie	77707	61632	51538	42396	137715
Denmark/Danemark	49876	49492	41183	35797	50459
Argentina/Argentine	70397	31111	42305	42827	63480
Morocco/Maroc	49933	33080	37606	21248	54889
Philippines	20937	25218	30916	28386	30491
Singapore/Singapour	30767	28717	21121	26937	39164
Poland/Pologne	15025	17306	28069	28704	36370
Czech Republic				66137	91273
Italy/Italie	51916	39988	6538	15731	19041
Bulgaria/Bulgarie	x99738	x22243	22540	10827	26406
Mexico/Mexique	8096	4196	21134	23583	28785
Croatia/Croatie			14540	24421	x11457
Thailand/Thaïlande	1863	11459	10723	12865	30628
Slovakia				x34487	x37716
Australia/Australie	17045	16085	5866	10102	19531
Yugoslavia SFR	69133	x24346			
Tunisia/Tunisie	9256	8673	7625	6604	6864
Slovenia/Slovénia			12108	8646	19519
Japan/Japon	13027	5911	6103	5861	19114
Saudi Arabia	5654	2764	5204	x7902	x9111
Ireland/Irlande	8324	5840	5417	3279	4471
Hungary/Hongrie	x4709	x3678	x6452	x3217	x2853
Ukraine			x1494	x11310	x2311
Malaysia/Malaisie	2582	3178	4383	2102	3253
United Arab Emirates	1945	1240	665	x7598	x8013
Lithuania/Lituanie			133	x7684	555
Mozambique	x1548	x1539	x4156	x2012	x4943
China/Chine	2072	799	2222	3965	6183
Yugoslavia/Yougoslavie			x6650		

(VALUE AS % OF TOTAL)(VALEUR EN % DU TOTAL)

	1985	1986	1987	1988	1989	1990	1991	1992	1993	1994
Africa	1.4	1.0	0.8	0.9	x1.0	1.1	0.9	0.9	0.9	1.0
Northern Africa	0.9	0.7	0.5	0.7	0.7	0.8	0.7	0.7	0.7	0.7
Americas	22.8	20.4	20.3	20.0	20.0	20.8	20.2	19.9	22.3	21.0
LAIA	4.6	3.4	5.1	4.4	3.5	3.5	4.1	4.1	5.0	4.8
CACM	0.1	0.1	0.1	0.1	0.1	0.1	0.1	0.1	x0.1	x0.1
Asia	20.8	21.5	x23.8	x26.0	24.1	22.9	25.9	26.6	29.9	28.9
Middle East	0.5	x0.6	x0.8	x1.3	x1.0	x0.7	x0.8	x1.0	x1.3	x1.0
Europe	52.0	54.0	50.6	48.9	51.4	52.5	51.2	50.9	44.9	47.3
EEC	46.2	48.1	45.3	44.0	46.3	49.8	48.9	48.4	42.7	45.0
EFTA	4.6	4.8	4.4	4.2	4.4	1.9	1.8	1.8	1.6	1.7
Oceania	0.7	x0.8	x1.0	x1.0	x0.9	0.9	x0.7	x0.8	x0.8	x0.6
USA/Etats–Unis d'Amer	16.1	15.1	13.7	14.0	15.0	15.7	14.5	13.9	15.0	14.0
Germany/Allemagne	13.2	13.8	12.8	12.8	13.7	15.0	15.1	14.6	12.5	13.1
Japan/Japon	9.9	10.4	10.2	11.0	12.3	10.7	11.3	10.7	11.7	11.2
Italy/Italie	8.1	8.2	8.0	7.9	8.2	8.3	8.7	8.4	7.7	8.3
France,Monac	7.2	7.6	7.0	6.7	6.9	7.6	7.2	7.2	6.2	6.7
United Kingdom	6.8	7.1	7.0	6.7	7.0	7.2	6.8	6.8	6.4	5.5
Korea, Republic of	3.5	3.7	3.9	4.4	4.6	5.3	5.6	6.0	6.3	6.0
Indonesia/Indonésie	1.0	1.4	1.3	1.3	1.5	1.4	1.8	2.7	3.6	3.5
Netherlands/Pays–Bas	3.0	3.0	2.6	2.6	2.7	2.9	2.7	2.7	2.4	3.1
China/Chine	2.0	1.9	2.6	3.0	2.0	1.5	2.9	2.5	2.2	2.8

	1985	1986	1987	1988	1989	1990	1991	1992	1993	1994
Afrique	1.8	2.1	1.7	1.7	1.8	2.2	2.3	2.8	x2.8	x2.8
Afrique du Nord	0.2	0.3	0.3	0.4	0.3	0.3	0.3	0.3	0.2	0.4
Amériques	46.3	46.5	46.7	48.1	49.4	58.6	62.1	64.7	66.7	64.5
ALAI	4.5	4.5	4.2	4.8	4.7	5.7	6.5	9.2	10.6	10.3
MCAC	0.0	0.0	0.0	0.0	0.0	0.0	0.0	0.0	x0.0	x0.0
Asie	0.8	0.9	x1.0	x1.2	1.0	1.3	1.5	1.4	1.6	2.3
Moyen–Orient	0.0	0.0	0.0	0.0	x0.1	0.1	0.0	0.0	x0.1	x0.1
Europe	46.2	44.8	45.0	43.7	42.8	33.2	30.1	28.6	26.0	27.6
CEE	26.3	25.7	26.2	25.7	25.1	30.2	29.6	28.0	25.4	25.9
AELE	19.5	18.7	18.5	17.7	17.3	2.6	0.4	0.4	0.4	1.5
Océanie	1.1	x1.1	x1.2	x1.3	x1.1	x1.5	1.7	1.4	1.7	x1.6
Canada	24.5	24.2	25.0	25.5	25.8	29.9	30.3	29.0	30.6	30.6
USA/Etats–Unis d'Amer	17.3	17.6	17.3	17.7	18.9	23.0	25.3	26.5	25.5	23.6
Sweden/Suède	10.9	10.0	9.9	9.5	9.0	11.0	10.8	10.0	9.6	8.3
Brazil/Brésil	2.7	2.7	2.4	3.0	3.0	3.4	4.1	5.1	6.1	5.2
Finland/Finlande	5.4	5.2	5.5	5.3	5.3	5.8	4.9	4.4	4.4	4.5
Portugal	2.8	2.8	3.2	3.2	3.1	3.9	3.8	3.8	3.1	3.1
Chile/Chili	1.4	1.6	1.6	1.5	1.4	1.8	2.2	3.7	4.0	4.4
So. Africa Customs Un	1.6	1.8	1.4	1.3	1.5	1.8	2.0	2.4	2.5	2.3
France,Monac	1.7	1.8	1.8	1.7	1.6	2.2	2.2	2.2	1.8	2.1
Spain/Espagne	1.1	1.5	1.7	1.7	1.9	2.0	2.2	2.1	1.8	2.0

TRADE BY COMMODITY IN THOUSAND U.S. DOLLARS – COMMERCE PAR PRODUIT EN MILLIERS DE DOLLARS E.U

COUNTRIES–PAYS	IMPORTS – IMPORTATIONS				
	1990	1991	1992	1993	1994
Total	879181	800989	676979	563043	739065
Africa	1236	2021	x2790	1573	1631
Northern Africa	1202	1948	x2766	1400	1141
Americas	x10018	8491	x7145	6273	7325
LAIA	75	755	656	246	861
CACM	30	55	13		82
Asia	540738	525328	455484	409624	499340
Middle East	4636	3113	2281	x4248	x2389
Europe	325281	245144	210946	144259	230092
EEC	309009	231467	201900	140491	224472
EFTA	16264	13654	8922	3714	5506
Oceania	34	17	x16	2	146
Japan/Japon	209477	186792	117626	108057	144438
Italy/Italie	211674	160696	133000	96625	153912
Hong Kong	114995	128003	111094	88205	113174
Korea, Republic of	116823	113897	105466	90856	93019
India/Inde	56653	60739	86789	86277	107408
Germany/Allemagne	55913	47942	44996	23961	39306
Thailand/Thaïlande	25811	14667	16030	16644	10154
France,Monac	32549	16085	17497	13060	19640
Switz.Liecht	16242	13646	8897	3708	5441
Former USSR/Anc. URSS	x1082	x19687			
USA/Etats–Unis d'Amer	9714	7522	6065	5920	6122
Bangladesh		6191	4069	4672	x3014
Singapore/Singapour	3928	4101	4838	4358	8080
United Kingdom	5879	4159	4067	4334	5871
China/Chine	4447	4166	2880	1676	9190
Macau/Macao	430	3034	1759	2616	3413
United Arab Emirates	1248	1376	1455	x1941	x752
Turkey/Turquie	3388	1372	723	2197	1479
Egypt/Egypte	782	443	1734	961	498
Spain/Espagne	774	805	722	1266	3354
Russian Federation			x2154	x104	x4
Korea Dem People's Rp	x2653	x16	x1659	x450	x91
Belgium–Luxembourg	672	974	707	354	553
Tunisia/Tunisie	366	715	430	406	614
Austria/Autriche	461	487	449	499	447
Indonesia/Indonésie	253	181	601	371	1307
Libyan Arab Jamahiriya		660	x448	x25	
Romania/Roumanie		105	456	536	66
Viet Nam	x37	x309		x532	x901
Venezuela	8	687	1	46	10
Bulgaria/Bulgarie	x11	x3	133	564	412
Colombia/Colombie	2	8	426	126	140
Saudi Arabia		338	x6	x107	x9
Denmark/Danemark	92	23	281	63	375
Myanmar	x144	4	x67	x269	x470
Philippines	50	9	239	70	600
Greece/Grèce	428	224	73	8	134
Morocco/Maroc	54	129	154		29
Netherlands/Pays–Bas	540	10	42	190	753
Sri Lanka	60	19	44	179	49
Dominican Republic	x37	x8	x222		
Hungary/Hongrie		160		x63	x49
Canada	53	46	109	61	237
Argentina/Argentine			126	36	105
Sweden/Suède	20	54	51	44	43
Malaysia/Malaisie		12	6	128	353
Poland/Pologne				142	
Ethiopia/Ethiopie				125	
Pakistan	11	69	35		37
Malta/Malte			79		x19

COUNTRIES–PAYS	EXPORTS – EXPORTATIONS				
	1990	1991	1992	1993	1994
Totale	742433	678765	542612	468570	624663
Afrique	x222	1209	x171	x6810	x36
Afrique du Nord	33	55			
Amériques	19995	14678	15630	14448	12780
ALAI	17894	13755	13926	13340	11107
MCAC		1		1	1
Asie	653822	594099	480982	416386	570758
Moyen–Orient	7474	229	1076	x12	x576
Europe	51006	43471	42319	30070	39677
CEE	48202	39622	39592	28385	38222
AELE	2802	3849	2727	1686	1455
Océanie	23	x19	10	22	2
China/Chine	452704	419014	324553	244704	404547
Hong Kong	126384	124344	115830	132090	121459
Germany/Allemagne	41440	34126	33254	22535	28979
Korea Dem People's Rp	x48873	x25375	x16782	x13283	x9806
Brazil/Brésil	17578	12606	11981	12302	9666
Former USSR/Anc. URSS	13066	x23225			
Thailand/Thaïlande	4955	7666	5993	7105	3635
Viet Nam	x4143	x7809	x3995	x4416	x4107
Japan/Japon	4516	5869	5541	3745	6319
Russian Federation			x6692	x5247	x8944
Switz.Liecht	2802	3843	2696	1679	1455
Singapore/Singapour	1036	1879	2890	3216	8668
Uganda/Ouganda				x6778	x29
Bulgaria/Bulgarie	x4279	x1940	3490	783	1254
Italy/Italie	2214	1796	2221	1923	2448
United Kingdom	987	1132	1740	1902	2447
USA/Etats–Unis d'Amer	2088	844	1702	1105	1668
Colombia/Colombie	316	1050	1461	573	410
Indonesia/Indonésie	52	102	1107	1646	52
Korea, Republic of	1359	472	476	1451	1533
India/Inde	836	849	574	935	4594
Spain/Espagne	1048	674	910	584	2086
Azerbaijan			x1616	x507	x119
France,Monac	1182	1036	667	372	1486
Latvia/Lettonie			x1740	x186	191
Belgium–Luxembourg	218	791	546	527	502
Uzbekistan/Ouzbékistan				x1572	x3068
Turkey/Turquie	411	213	1076	10	381
Tajikistan/Tadjikistan				x1020	x65
Paraguay		89	369	344	947
Pakistan	652	314	285	185	370
Cameroon/Cameroun	2	518			
Malawi		478			
Denmark/Danemark	20	7	4	319	34
Greece/Grèce			228	20	3
Macau/Macao	453	97	110	13	48
Malaysia/Malaisie	23	38	57	121	102
Kazakstan				x173	x29
So. Africa Customs Un	162	152	2	10	
Philippines	96	25	76	58	
Chad/Tchad			x152		
Ukraine				x148	x93
Bolivia/Bolivie			95	48	41
Netherlands/Pays–Bas	1088		3	116	77
Hungary/Hongrie		x77		x11	x20
Peru/Pérou			15	72	
Kyrgyzstan/Kirghizistan				x87	x1032
Austria/Autriche	6	12	6	59	x10
Belize/Bélize	x1	x72			
Ireland/Irlande		37	13	22	

(VALUE AS % OF TOTAL)(VALEUR EN % DU TOTAL)

	1985	1986	1987	1988	1989	1990	1991	1992	1993	1994
Africa	0.1	0.1	x0.2	0.1	0.2	0.1	0.3	x0.4	0.3	0.2
Northern Africa	0.1	0.1	x0.2	0.1	0.1	0.1	0.2	x0.4	0.2	0.2
Americas	2.5	1.6	1.6	0.9	x1.2	x1.1	1.0	x1.0	1.2	1.0
LAIA	0.0	0.0	0.0	0.0	0.0	0.0	0.1	0.1	0.0	0.1
CACM		x0.0	0.0	0.0	x0.0	0.0	0.0	0.0	0.0	0.0
Asia	52.2	52.3	55.6	61.1	55.3	61.5	65.6	67.3	72.8	67.5
Middle East	0.5	0.2	1.2	x0.4	x0.7	0.5	0.4	0.3	x0.8	x0.3
Europe	45.1	45.9	35.6	31.2	38.8	37.0	30.6	31.2	25.6	31.1
EEC	42.4	44.1	33.9	29.8	37.3	35.1	28.9	29.8	25.0	30.4
EFTA	2.6	1.7	1.8	1.3	1.5	1.8	1.7	1.3	0.7	0.7
Oceania				x0.0	x0.0			x0.0		
Japan/Japon	21.4	20.4	14.1	18.0	18.3	23.8	23.3	17.4	19.2	19.5
Italy/Italie	33.4	37.6	27.1	24.1	25.3	24.1	20.1	19.6	17.2	20.8
Hong Kong	11.3	10.4	16.3	19.3	16.6	13.1	16.0	16.4	15.7	15.3
Korea, Republic of	9.8	12.4	13.9	15.0	12.2	13.3	14.2	15.6	16.1	12.6
India/Inde	7.3	6.8	6.7	4.2	4.6	6.4	7.6	12.8	15.3	14.5
Germany/Allemagne	2.1	2.0	2.1	2.1	7.3	6.4	6.0	6.6	4.3	5.3
Thailand/Thaïlande	1.0	1.2	1.7	2.0	2.0	2.9	1.8	2.4	3.0	1.4
France,Monac	5.2	3.3	3.2	2.6	3.8	3.7	2.0	2.6	2.3	2.7
Switz.Liecht	2.6	1.7	1.7	1.3	1.4	1.8	1.7	1.3	0.7	0.7
Former USSR/Anc. URSS			x6.8	x6.6	x4.3	x0.1	x2.5			

	1985	1986	1987	1988	1989	1990	1991	1992	1993	1994
Afrique		x0.0	x0.0	x0.0	x0.1	x0.0	0.2	x0.0	x1.5	x0.0
Afrique du Nord	0.0	0.0	0.0	0.0	x0.1	0.0	0.0			
Amériques	0.6	0.7	x0.5	0.8	0.8	2.7	2.1	2.9	3.0	2.1
ALAI	0.5	0.6	0.4	0.7	0.5	2.4	2.0	2.6	2.8	1.8
MCAC	0.0	0.0	x0.0		0.0		0.0		0.0	0.0
Asie	93.6	93.8	94.4	94.8	90.0	88.1	87.6	88.6	88.9	91.4
Moyen–Orient	0.1	0.0	0.0	x0.5	x0.1	1.0	0.0	0.2	x0.0	x0.1
Europe	2.8	2.9	3.0	3.2	7.2	6.9	6.4	7.8	6.4	6.4
CEE	2.0	2.2	2.6	2.8	6.9	6.5	5.8	7.3	6.1	6.1
AELE	0.7	0.7	0.4	x0.4	0.2	0.4	0.6	0.5	0.4	0.2
Océanie		x0.0		x0.0	x0.0		x0.0			
China/Chine	72.4	70.2	62.2	53.3	61.1	61.0	61.7	59.8	52.2	64.8
Hong Kong	17.7	21.2	24.3	31.7	23.8	17.0	18.3	21.3	28.2	19.4
Germany/Allemagne	1.1	1.4	1.5	1.4	6.2	5.6	5.0	6.1	4.8	4.6
Korea Dem People's Rp			x1.9	x3.4	x2.3	x6.6	x3.7	x3.1	x2.8	x1.6
Brazil/Brésil	0.5	0.5	0.3	0.6	0.4	2.4	1.9	2.2	2.6	1.5
Former USSR/Anc. URSS	2.9	2.4	1.7	0.9	1.7	1.8	x3.4			
Thailand/Thaïlande	0.0	0.0	0.0	0.0	0.4	0.7	1.1	1.1	1.5	0.6
Viet Nam			x0.1	x0.5	x0.5	x0.6	x1.2	x0.7	x0.9	x0.7
Japan/Japon	2.5	1.5	1.8	1.1	0.8	0.6	0.9	1.0	0.8	1.0
Russian Federation								x1.2	x1.1	x1.4

TRADE BY COMMODITY IN THOUSAND U.S. DOLLARS – COMMERCE PAR PRODUIT EN MILLIERS DE DOLLARS E.U

COUNTRIES–PAYS	IMPORTS – IMPORTATIONS 1990	1991	1992	1993	1994
Total	8716786	8744852	7502259	6720415	8659981
Africa	x333367	x392081	274674	246626	234776
Northern Africa	197927	274124	182433	162291	158277
Americas	458902	511345	607837	1192065	1148620
LAIA	339069	378724	490902	1076804	1006557
CACM	14633	24195	23143	20065	33019
Asia	4527286	4966547	4372104	3373519	4754989
Middle East	152809	92493	208111	258536	250692
Europe	2705160	2412895	2000559	1685224	2164943
EEC	2370165	2240093	1837628	1545725	2024991
EFTA	159083	140292	120975	97211	98573
Oceania	x3120	3092	x2766	x3231	x3620
Japan/Japon	1204620	1249946	888779	683700	659802
Korea, Republic of	786962	824121	639575	539456	593059
Indonesia/Indonésie	485048	634349	667626	556975	701332
Italy/Italie	687950	678837	524153	482449	615928
Thailand/Thaïlande	502302	637411	567640	462782	567412
China/Chine	717815	643101	457585	25199	936140
Brazil/Brésil	163798	182041	219877	689131	592958
Germany/Allemagne	450596	439630	355858	241310	326571
Bangladesh		230563	302363	412930	x49750
Hong Kong	330801	338959	274427	185843	310399
Portugal	346406	293156	261156	212309	252056
France, Monac	260013	242922	212927	195359	279078
Turkey/Turquie	137447	80527	194321	247694	240000
Spain/Espagne	199510	189313	153299	128145	189460
Mexico/Mexique	65388	74871	148595	226861	231165
Switz.Liecht	154260	135623	117256	94351	94549
United Kingdom	121046	95155	92484	90289	101706
Poland/Pologne	72283	104967	89164	70640	125390
Philippines	79635	85986	83376	72286	113913
Romania/Roumanie	127331	86713	80629	59325	45861
Canada	79046	82683	66210	67122	73931
Malaysia/Malaisie	70860	74438	74636	59749	86576
Belgium–Luxembourg	76277	81105	66896	58685	94728
Czechoslovakia	173494	x161578	x34779		
Morocco/Maroc	67434	77015	63131	54774	76843
Austria/Autriche	52275	63603	58037	51809	63036
Algeria/Algérie	18580	57477	48168	59647	35697
Egypt/Egypte	61808	108835	30801	15061	634
So. Africa Customs Un	23710	31693	50665	52324	63331
Chile/Chili	38368	53334	33842	32367	37595
Venezuela	30788	44007	42129	26400	28595
Tunisia/Tunisie	50020	30123	39701	32382	44944
Ireland/Irlande	42143	47690	27346	26936	30104
Greece/Grèce	69901	54097	32399	14174	12715
Singapore/Singapour	33610	38201	32901	22546	29325
India/Inde	306	1888	84282	5905	161580
Bulgaria/Bulgarie	x120824	x36376	30473	x21480	90965
Korea Dem People's Rp	x64766	x44996	x25039	x16786	x1416
Hungary/Hongrie	x31221	65009	x5865	x3979	x3805
Netherlands/Pays–Bas	29281	25786	25012	21453	26235
Sri Lanka	13726	21748	22467	24642	33715
Israel/Israël	27617	21370	25370	17187	15196
Czech Republic				60329	84255
Colombia/Colombie	10999	1201	17044	39301	55378
Cote d'Ivoire	x73793	x56105			
USA/Etats–Unis d'Amer	23554	19837	15606	18355	27833
Sweden/Suède	20635	16381	15843	11739	18440
El Salvador	10917	15245	16281	11656	24540
Argentina/Argentine	11768	5679	10128	20136	8691
Slovenia/Slovénia			17485	16950	23382

COUNTRIES–PAYS	EXPORTS – EXPORTATIONS 1990	1991	1992	1993	1994
Totale	9008879	x8270439	x8020587	x6611236	x7683538
Afrique	x1442347	x1270324	x1089668	x1149738	x1110722
Afrique du Nord	x466182	x296269	x235323	x186267	x423410
Amériques	3761264	3522809	2531877	1823940	3211466
ALAI	845712	894563	430781	223199	411133
MCAC	73374	70375	42835	5904	8839
Asie	1836072	1592230	x3337379	x2704076	x2246141
Moyen–Orient	362442	x372692	244543	x353424	x302543
Europe	426111	450321	378386	409138	520784
CEE	412115	431558	362861	398099	507152
AELE	12829	15545	12459	9561	11069
Océanie	502662	x678609	x664098	x465676	x491758
USA/Etats–Unis d'Amer	2838939	2554766	2053955	1581354	2723954
Australia/Australie	502489	677457	663747	462729	491168
Turkmenistan/Turkménistn			x735495	x854571	x314353
Pakistan	482250	491792	629459	237131	85095
Uzbekistan/Ouzbékistan			x758135	x398288	x856986
Russian Federation			x638282	x462579	x554611
China/Chine	318296	373724	219951	226739	162829
Mali	204350	x203485	x211901	x351617	x118136
Former USSR/Anc. URSS	1017583	x746221			
Paraguay	330392	315233	201339	156766	153910
Azerbaijan			x414043	x158349	x32458
Sudan/Soudan	x250774	x226957	x178890	x137587	x179891
Syrian Arab Republic	162760	x178494	176970	x183784	x233991
Greece/Grèce	135763	165140	110706	204868	274797
Chad/Tchad	x159662	x174220	x155076	x112623	x93930
Turkey/Turquie	190840	192505	62138	159993	56552
India/Inde	466151	123916	70126	208365	44515
Cote d'Ivoire	x170568	x132496	x103513	x130901	x114310
Argentina/Argentine	165917	204503	77650	26509	179153
Burkina Faso	85699	x67284	x104650	x103249	x59063
Germany/Allemagne	117435	97980	92470	61653	76221
Cameroon/Cameroun	69523	109998	x43948	x63357	x42405
Brazil/Brésil	131255	151470	33116	7048	6781
Un. Rep. of Tanzania	75799	62198	x69891	x53881	x90681
Tajikistan/Tadjikistan			x44458	x137762	x136110
Egypt/Egypte	208925	60705	52699	43529	237554
Israel/Israël	86504	72384	43354	27539	53661
Colombia/Colombie	48857	72315	56538	9847	3211
Hong Kong	50213	58933	48958	28235	90382
Spain/Espagne	43913	57245	44203	29707	9977
Togo	55586	55447	x50544	x21212	x29004
Mexico/Mexique	93461	79984	32837	9991	43135
Zimbabwe	86292	60057	27305	24228	x42632
France, Monac	25848	31528	33259	38038	52287
United Kingdom	35595	35864	35018	25391	28151
Singapore/Singapour	23950	34370	27417	20343	28560
Peru/Pérou	44495	55328	18583	4577	5040
Benin/Bénin	x17451	x24035	x23720	x25223	x23193
Nicaragua	37725	44888	26262	421	4225
Senegal/Sénégal	9533	20248	x22022	27210	x7475
Ukraine			x25522	x40606	x30284
Italy/Italie	21085	16456	21480	14528	25859
Kazakstan			x33949	x15204	x43340
Guatemala	34395	23688	14636	4628	1068
Korea, Republic of	14671	16695	15729	10509	19441
Japan/Japon	16739	16885	16842	7402	13349
Switz.Liecht	12776	15528	12433	9557	11043
Czech Republic				37506	45314
Belgium–Luxembourg	15432	12529	11577	10726	16750
Bolivia/Bolivie	4888	11864	7510	8257	13954

(VALUE AS % OF TOTAL)(VALEUR EN % DU TOTAL)

	1985	1986	1987	1988	1989	1990	1991	1992	1993	1994
Africa	4.3	2.7	2.6	2.7	2.4	x3.9	x4.5	3.7	3.7	2.7
Northern Africa	2.7	1.4	1.8	2.1	2.0	2.3	3.1	2.4	2.4	1.8
Americas	3.2	5.4	5.1	4.6	6.4	5.3	5.9	8.1	17.8	13.3
LAIA	1.6	3.8	3.8	3.5	4.3	3.9	4.3	6.5	16.0	11.6
CACM	0.1	0.1	0.1	0.1	0.1	0.2	0.3	0.3	0.3	0.4
Asia	39.3	41.1	x47.6	x49.4	52.5	51.9	56.8	58.3	50.2	54.9
Middle East	0.1	x1.2	2.7	x1.5	x1.7	1.8	1.1	2.8	3.8	2.9
Europe	42.1	40.7	34.4	32.0	30.2	31.0	27.6	26.7	25.1	25.0
EEC	33.8	32.7	29.2	26.9	25.5	27.2	25.6	24.5	23.0	23.4
EFTA	3.7	3.6	2.9	2.7	2.5	1.8	1.6	1.6	1.4	1.1
Oceania	0.1	x0.0	x0.0	x0.1	x0.0	x0.0		x0.0	x0.0	x0.0
Japan/Japon	17.4	17.1	16.6	17.1	16.6	13.8	14.3	11.8	10.2	7.6
Korea, Republic of	8.8	8.4	7.5	9.3	8.7	9.0	9.4	8.5	8.0	6.8
Indonesia/Indonésie	3.0	3.6	3.9	3.9	4.5	5.6	7.3	8.9	8.3	8.1
Italy/Italie	8.3	8.4	7.5	7.5	7.3	7.9	7.8	7.0	7.2	7.1
Thailand/Thaïlande	2.9	3.6	4.0	4.2	4.6	5.8	7.3	7.6	6.9	6.6
China/Chine	0.0	0.0	0.2	0.8	8.6	8.2	7.4	6.1	0.4	10.8
Brazil/Brésil	0.4	1.5	0.6	1.5	2.5	1.9	2.1	2.9	10.3	6.8
Germany/Allemagne	6.8	6.4	6.2	4.6	5.1	5.2	5.0	4.7	3.6	3.8
Bangladesh	1.3	0.9	0.6	x0.7	x0.6		2.6	4.0	6.1	x0.6
Hong Kong	3.6	4.2	4.9	4.1	4.5	3.8	3.9	3.7	2.8	3.6

	1985	1986	1987	1988	1989	1990	1991	1992	1993	1994
Afrique	14.4	x19.0	x13.8	14.5	x15.9	x16.0	x15.4	x13.6	x17.4	x14.5
Afrique du Nord	8.9	8.8	5.0	5.1	x6.9	x5.2	x3.6	x2.9	x2.8	x5.5
Amériques	39.5	21.3	31.6	34.5	36.6	41.7	42.6	31.5	27.6	41.8
ALAI	8.6	4.6	6.1	7.6	9.2	9.4	10.8	5.4	3.4	5.4
MCAC	3.0	1.6	x1.4	1.3	0.6	0.8	0.9	0.5	0.1	0.1
Asie	23.7	30.0	25.6	24.5	20.1	20.3	19.3	x41.7	x40.9	x29.3
Moyen–Orient	5.7	5.1	2.0	2.7	3.0	4.0	x4.5	3.0	x5.3	x3.9
Europe	4.4	3.6	4.6	3.7	5.1	4.7	5.4	4.7	6.2	6.8
CEE	4.1	3.3	4.3	3.5	4.8	4.6	5.2	4.5	6.0	6.6
AELE	0.3	0.2	0.2	0.2	0.2	0.1	0.2	0.2	0.1	0.1
Océanie	3.8	x4.9	3.4	x3.9	4.8	5.6	x8.2	x8.3	x7.0	x6.4
USA/Etats–Unis d'Amer	28.0	15.0	24.1	25.5	26.7	31.5	30.9	25.6	23.9	35.5
Australia/Australie	3.8	4.9	3.4	3.9	4.8	5.6	8.2	8.3	7.0	6.4
Turkmenistan/Turkménistn								x9.2	x12.9	x4.1
Pakistan	7.2	8.8	6.8	9.4	8.3	5.4	5.9	7.8	3.6	1.1
Uzbekistan/Ouzbékistan								x9.5	x6.0	x11.2
Russian Federation								x8.0	x7.0	x7.2
China/Chine	6.8	9.4	11.3	9.3	5.1	3.5	4.5	2.7	3.4	2.1
Mali		x2.4	1.5	1.6	1.6	2.3	x2.5	x2.6	x5.3	x1.5
Former USSR/Anc. URSS	14.1	21.1	20.0	18.3	17.0	11.3	x9.0			
Paraguay	2.4	1.5	1.5	2.7	3.5	3.7	3.8	2.5	2.4	2.0

TRADE BY COMMODITY IN THOUSAND U.S. DOLLARS – COMMERCE PAR PRODUIT EN MILLIERS DE DOLLARS E.U

COUNTRIES–PAYS	IMPORTS – IMPORTATIONS 1990	1991	1992	1993	1994
Total	x180619	x147850	x132236	92433	93378
Africa	19552	19243	x19049	6878	x12954
Northern Africa	15727	16368	12814	6204	4703
Americas	x13316	x17358	x15617	x10735	9606
LAIA	5140	5665	7773	4784	4023
CACM	1696	508	803	177	1328
Asia	73362	64600	75350	59558	50231
Middle East	x8433	x9551	x8626	x12175	3136
Europe	27762	x18794	16361	11857	15568
EEC	22576	14972	13951	11646	14815
EFTA	124	52	36	139	66
Oceania	x1130	x1095	780	696	648
Pakistan	37147	33114	34422	20027	18231
Indonesia/Indonésie	11644	7594	9250	7115	4409
Thailand/Thaïlande	32	3231	13082	6817	14
United Kingdom	12806	7512	6839	4975	5140
Egypt/Egypte	9070	7679	6836	3382	2420
Iran (Islamic Rp. of)	x3043	x5124	x4137	x8267	x350
India/Inde	13159	2877	4135	10383	19653
Brazil/Brésil	4719	5085	7160	4106	3740
Former USSR/Anc. URSS	17673	x13672			
Cuba	x4404	x7017	x3693	x2089	
Turkey/Turquie	4772	3201	3598	3790	2719
Russian Federation			x9726	x126	x3306
Czechoslovakia	1476	x6819	x2972		
USA/Etats–Unis d'Amer	1709	3412	3050	3286	3744
Morocco/Maroc	4548	4390	2253	2018	2004
Japan/Japon	2310	2105	2268	2079	1899
Poland/Pologne	4349	3606	1811	977	2283
Belgium–Luxembourg	2755	1843	1892	2222	4038
Algeria/Algérie	1198	2825	2532	4	
France,Monac	1852	1893	1607	1230	1586
China/Chine	105	2285	1835	380	1037
Germany/Allemagne	1976	1496	1512	1024	1204
Korea Dem People's Rp	x69	x2640	x1211		
Yugoslavia SFR	5054	x3746			
Nigeria/Nigéria		1033	x2584		x6
Tunisia/Tunisie	890	1452	1193	792	279
Bulgaria/Bulgarie	x14341	x2663	1	x113	x20
Australia/Australie	1099	1061	760	692	642
Cote d'Ivoire	x290		x2315	x3	x5372
Portugal	1573	772	707	523	196
Yugoslavia/Yougoslavie			x1956		x199
Saudi Arabia	154	829	734	x24	
Italy/Italie	164	360	462	446	599
Netherlands/Pays–Bas	777	460	377	342	353
Uruguay	249	286	335	343	
Canada	324	444	224	293	430
Romania/Roumanie	1129		24	877	1574
Ukraine				x855	x287
Senegal/Sénégal	1		x816		x454
Ireland/Irlande	498	283	170	340	385
Un. Rep. of Tanzania		x731	x42		x107
Nicaragua	519	130	480	115	722
Czech Republic				707	340
Mozambique	x456	x495	x129		
Kenya	691	2	183	387	x303
Myanmar	x254	559			x71
Guatemala	1143	258	239	46	11
Spain/Espagne	26	55	227	235	997
Singapore/Singapour	80	310	60	84	51
Slovenia/Slovénia			373	65	366

COUNTRIES–PAYS	EXPORTS – EXPORTATIONS 1990	1991	1992	1993	1994
Totale	158593	148870	129113	93618	x72982
Afrique	980	170	x448	x412	75
Afrique du Nord				x72	75
Amériques	x1819	2177	2050	1360	x2179
ALAI	35	20	767	186	41
MCAC	37			20	259
Asie	137977	140616	120157	86933	x64855
Moyen–Orient	64	x32		x25	x23
Europe	5588	5845	6199	4066	5551
CEE	5536	5812	6047	3999	5501
AELE	13	2	9	6	26
Océanie	15	38	204	144	100
Bangladesh	106912	120255	105570	74337	x52911
China/Chine	16537	13680	8649	8040	4321
Belgium–Luxembourg	2836	2624	3220	2441	2501
India/Inde	6811	1517	2983	729	465
Thailand/Thaïlande	1628	1563	1697	1582	1346
USA/Etats–Unis d'Amer	1618	1932	1139	1050	1667
Viet Nam	x398	x1481	x665	x953	x2408
Netherlands/Pays–Bas	621	709	1008	612	749
France,Monac	402	715	766	222	574
Nepal/Népal	4849	219	12	871	x2044
Italy/Italie	420	433	401	245	672
United Kingdom	913	576	273	144	195
Germany/Allemagne	284	446	248	295	590
Lao People's Dem. Rp.	x457	x371	x310	x225	
Democratic Kampuchea	x127	x865			
Peru/Pérou		13	713	15	1
Zimbabwe	355	136	314	248	
Romania/Roumanie				590	18
Canada	80	210	104	94	116
Australia/Australie	7	38	204	144	100
Singapore/Singapour	45	259	78	41	49
Hong Kong	79	153	147	31	102
Mali			x119	x91	
Bhutan/Bhoutan		x204			
Croatia/Croatie			133	62	x22
Portugal	2	170			102
Russian Federation			x1	x155	x139
Hungary/Hongrie	x2	x24	x56	x35	x3
Argentina/Argentine			20	86	
Spain/Espagne	11	53	27	4	39
Sweden/Suède	1	4	57	20	43
Colombia/Colombie			34	45	4
Czech Republic				72	56
Panama	21	15	41	10	1
Sudan/Soudan				x65	
Austria/Autriche	6	21	30	5	x10
Indonesia/Indonésie			5	43	21
Japan/Japon	36		35		7
Syrian Arab Republic		x31			
Yugoslavia SFR	15	x30			
Finland/Finlande	1	24	2	4	1
Mexico/Mexique	33	1		29	26
Sri Lanka	18	5	3	21	23
Kenya	620	22	4		
Ireland/Irlande	27	22	4		10
Denmark/Danemark	6	6	12	3	2
Iran (Islamic Rp. of)				x19	
Brunei Darussalam				x18	
Nicaragua	37			17	
Switz.Liecht	13	2	9	5	8

(VALUE AS % OF TOTAL)(VALEUR EN % DU TOTAL)

	1985	1986	1987	1988	1989	1990	1991	1992	1993	1994		1985	1986	1987	1988	1989	1990	1991	1992	1993	1994
Africa	25.9	x20.3	x13.5	x17.5	x13.5	10.8	13.0	x14.4	7.4	x13.9	Afrique			x27.9	0.4	x0.0	0.6	0.1	x0.3	x0.4	0.1
Northern Africa	12.3	7.8	5.8	8.4	6.9	8.7	11.1	9.7	6.7	5.0	Afrique du Nord		0.0	x27.9		0.0		0.0		x0.1	0.1
Americas	4.0	11.9	x14.6	10.7	5.7	x7.3	x11.7	x11.8	x11.6	10.3	Amériques	0.9	x2.3	x0.1	x1.0	x2.8	x1.2	1.4	1.6	1.4	x2.9
LAIA	0.2	8.4	9.8	6.7	0.8	2.8	3.8	5.9	5.2	4.3	ALAI	0.9	x1.5	0.0	x0.1	0.0	0.0	0.0	0.6	0.2	0.1
CACM	0.9	1.1	0.6	0.4	0.5	0.9	0.3	0.6	0.2	1.4	MCAC	0.0	x0.0		0.0	x0.8	0.0			0.0	0.4
Asia	35.6	37.6	35.6	26.0	48.3	40.6	43.7	56.9	64.4	53.8	Asie	95.0	x93.4	65.4	93.0	89.0	87.0	94.5	93.0	92.9	x88.9
Middle East	0.7	x1.7	x4.7	x5.4	x5.6	x4.7	x6.5	x6.5	x13.2	3.4	Moyen–Orient	0.0	0.0	0.0	0.1	0.0	0.0	x0.0		x0.0	x0.0
Europe	17.9	17.1	12.2	17.0	16.6	15.4	x12.7	12.4	12.8	16.7	Europe	3.4	4.3	2.5	5.1	4.0	3.5	3.9	4.8	4.3	7.6
EEC	13.1	12.5	10.2	13.3	13.8	12.5	10.1	10.5	12.6	15.9	CEE	3.4	4.2	2.4	5.0	4.0	3.5	3.9	4.7	4.3	7.5
EFTA	0.1	0.2	0.1	0.1	0.2	0.1	0.0	0.0	0.2	0.1	AELE	0.1	0.1	x0.0	x0.0	0.0	0.0	0.0	0.0	0.0	0.0
Oceania	1.0	0.8	0.6	x1.0	x0.7	x0.6	x0.7	0.6	0.8	0.7	Océanie	0.6							0.2	0.2	0.1
Pakistan	22.6	19.9	19.6	13.5	23.2	20.6	22.4	26.0	21.7	19.5	Bangladesh	87.8	86.0	52.9	72.0	66.1	67.4	80.8	81.8	79.4	x72.5
Indonesia/Indonésie	4.5	2.3	2.9	1.0	5.5	6.4	5.1	7.0	7.7	4.7	China/Chine			7.9	10.8	12.7	10.4	9.2	6.7	8.6	5.9
Thailand/Thaïlande		1.4	0.3	0.1	0.6	0.0	2.2	9.9	7.4	0.0	Belgium–Luxembourg	1.4	2.0	1.5	2.6	2.4	1.8	1.8	2.5	2.6	3.4
United Kingdom	6.0	5.8	5.5	7.0	7.4	7.1	5.1	5.2	5.4	5.5	India/Inde	2.6	4.2	2.5	3.1	2.7	4.3	1.0	2.3	0.8	0.6
Egypt/Egypte	6.0	4.1	1.5	4.5	2.1	5.0	5.2	5.2	3.7	2.6	Thailand/Thaïlande	0.4	0.7	0.5	0.6	1.1	1.0	1.0	1.3	1.7	1.8
Iran (Islamic Rp. of)		x0.8	x3.6	x2.7	x2.5	x1.7	x3.5	x3.1	x8.9	x0.4	USA/Etats–Unis d'Amer		x0.5	x0.0	x0.5	2.0	1.0	1.3	0.9	1.1	2.3
India/Inde	2.7	1.2	1.9	3.0	4.9	7.3	1.9	3.1	11.2	21.0	Viet Nam			x0.1	x0.4	x1.5	x0.3	x1.0	x0.5	x1.0	x3.3
Brazil/Brésil		8.2	8.8	6.2	0.1	2.6	3.4	5.4	4.4	4.0	Netherlands/Pays–Bas	0.5	0.9	0.4	0.6	0.5	0.4	0.5	0.8	0.7	1.0
Former USSR/Anc. URSS	9.5	8.8	12.9	11.4	3.3	9.8	x9.2				France,Monac	0.1	0.1	0.0	0.1	0.2	0.3	0.5	0.6	0.2	0.8
Cuba			x2.4	x0.0	2.7	x2.4	x4.7	x2.8	x2.3		Nepal/Népal	1.7	1.6	1.0	3.2	2.0	3.1	0.1	0.0	0.9	x2.8

TRADE BY COMMODITY IN THOUSAND U.S. DOLLARS – COMMERCE PAR PRODUIT EN MILLIERS DE DOLLARS E.U

COUNTRIES–PAYS	IMPORTS – IMPORTATIONS 1990	1991	1992	1993	1994
Total	416202	360225	326320	436915	671689
Africa	x9382	x8510	x6192	6704	13528
Northern Africa	4768	5062	4040	4533	11835
Americas	59227	58984	63487	67714	97105
LAIA	17391	19508	24262	29990	43132
CACM	400	825	921	x821	792
Asia	75442	67967	66081	102178	133773
Middle East	3553	2145	3124	x6372	12006
Europe	240039	197466	177828	240867	390947
EEC	231827	195285	172980	236916	384243
EFTA	1022	808	655	953	2301
Oceania	2624	x2032	x2089	x2543	x2500
Belgium–Luxembourg	55224	43839	36915	62253	113233
United Kingdom	49763	37032	40492	41302	57821
USA/Etats–Unis d'Amer	40667	37748	35473	35902	52153
Japan/Japon	37231	34310	32120	40933	37988
Italy/Italie	33987	33003	28742	45340	67890
France, Monac	30328	22206	19599	33469	58753
Brazil/Brésil	10788	13773	20120	25381	33980
Germany/Allemagne	14415	16318	15867	12833	20400
Portugal	18111	16303	9311	12969	16985
Korea, Republic of	17333	14110	10339	13627	21086
Spain/Espagne	14825	10450	11024	11256	20912
China/Chine	1389	2765	4508	13569	36221
Hong Kong	9246	7394	6057	6999	5601
Austria/Autriche	7927	4948	5079	6757	10233
Former USSR/Anc. URSS	6644	x15698			
India/Inde	1909	1821	1699	11700	11838
Netherlands/Pays–Bas	1780	5931	1895	2988	5725
Hungary/Hongrie	x4382	2019	x3437	x5066	x7566
Poland/Pologne	3691	1511	1483	5766	10308
Ireland/Irlande	1031	1838	1292	5349	8420
Turkey/Turquie	2538	1377	2359	4358	9970
Morocco/Maroc	2743	2788	1961	2259	2486
Bangladesh		1056	3266	2580	x29
Romania/Roumanie	8136	3535	1493	1260	5836
Czechoslovakia	3510	x2167	x3874		
Slovenia/Slovénia			2406	2600	3671
Egypt/Egypte	1164	1491	1802	674	3121
Czech Republic				3956	9476
Mexico/Mexique	3112	1330	911	1610	5051
Colombia/Colombie	900	1623	1076	1041	1219
New Zealand	1537	1160	941	1547	1257
So. Africa Customs Un	1305	1047	1325	1216	922
Canada	440	789	1736	810	793
Malaysia/Malaisie	825	695	2091	548	780
Indonesia/Indonésie	277	1147	429	1612	2954
Denmark/Danemark	1619	1512	1108	519	1404
Pakistan	1121	894	1050	1032	1121
Australia/Australie	803	859	865	968	1194
Finland/Finlande	1402	822	819	847	1300
Venezuela	400	1197	1072	214	392
Russian Federation			x1732	x674	x428
Chile/Chili	1792	917	456	1024	1451
Greece/Grèce	879	823	601	706	757
Switz.Liecht	855	589	517	794	2115
Philippines	127	20	386	1390	1188
Tunisia/Tunisie	74	171	238	1336	4781
Yugoslavia/Yougoslavie			x1053	x290	
Yugoslavia SFR	7126	x1333			
Singapore/Singapour	1247	342	435	526	481
Cote d'Ivoire	x1706	x953	x55	x156	x195

COUNTRIES–PAYS	EXPORTS – EXPORTATIONS 1990	1991	1992	1993	1994
Totale	376298	323768	287776	406993	630843
Afrique	22911	20751	19974	22269	x37093
Afrique du Nord	4994	4402	5424	4936	10141
Amériques	65656	48579	36937	36070	x50448
ALAI	45906	31423	21145	23074	x36180
MCAC	12	54	33	x52	20
Asie	82966	74243	71529	72283	83676
Moyen–Orient	424	177	460	x126	178
Europe	192277	174555	154889	271774	449110
CEE	191254	173730	153762	270994	447145
AELE	730	533	787	722	1925
Océanie	237	62	319	58	x65
Belgium–Luxembourg	94770	78149	74274	143506	232103
France, Monac	76097	73350	67068	102871	169895
China/Chine	23838	26072	21571	26261	30811
Philippines	21797	19671	22683	19681	21898
Brazil/Brésil	37291	21917	12888	13651	19981
Sri Lanka	17435	13887	16305	14861	19498
Canada	17758	14893	12345	11085	13132
Kenya	12670	12881	10676	12794	x18557
Ecuador/Equateur	7772	9020	7124	8096	x15524
Hong Kong	10476	8832	6587	7151	4875
Netherlands/Pays–Bas	5930	11276	3458	5916	10619
Egypt/Egypte	4962	4383	5414	4807	10114
United Kingdom	4116	3737	2558	5088	9780
Ukraine			x305	x11049	x12875
Italy/Italie	4561	3063	2479	5061	9615
Germany/Allemagne	2755	2345	2030	3464	5067
Madagascar	4720	3147	1829	2631	3888
USA/Etats–Unis d'Amer	1805	2158	3302	1852	1098
Thailand/Thaïlande	3541	2587	2157	2457	2439
Czechoslovakia		x2421	x2616		
Ireland/Irlande	208	239	254	3328	5482
Un. Rep. of Tanzania			x1922	x1605	x4228
Belarus/Bélarus			x265	x2896	x11994
Lithuania/Lituanie			330	x1676	5128
Switz.Liecht	729	516	782	707	1806
Russian Federation			x864	x1138	x5063
Hungary/Hongrie	x1509	x635	x835	x508	x414
Czech Republic				1956	4149
Austria/Autriche	608	528	574	834	x1356
Mexico/Mexique	244	347	540	854	562
Poland/Pologne	287	856	104	748	2704
Former USSR/Anc. URSS	9571	x1500			
Malaysia/Malaisie	246	304	264	646	449
Portugal	513	441	446	193	467
Greece/Grèce	468	243	499	271	178
Romania/Roumanie		166	276	561	1564
India/Inde	96	70	566	287	856
Indonesia/Indonésie	1209	472	276	172	345
Viet Nam	x2188	x484	x202	x83	x345
Venezuela	529	72	387	187	68
Spain/Espagne	849	227	74	336	2391
Singapore/Singapour	313	159	180	268	339
Slovakia				x563	x1079
Myanmar		523			
Bulgaria/Bulgarie	x878		x296	x203	x543
Saudi Arabia	334	127	332		
Korea, Republic of	80	200	104	111	1256
Peru/Pérou		3	136	241	
Korea Dem People's Rp		x360	x12		x27
Australia/Australie	70	33	289	46	34

(VALUE AS % OF TOTAL)(VALEUR EN % DU TOTAL)

	1985	1986	1987	1988	1989	1990	1991	1992	1993	1994
Africa	3.2	x1.7	x1.6	x1.7	x2.7	x2.2	x2.4	x1.9	1.6	2.0
Northern Africa	1.2	0.9	0.9	0.8	1.3	1.1	1.4	1.2	1.0	1.8
Americas	10.8	10.1	8.6	11.6	13.5	14.3	16.4	19.5	15.5	14.5
LAIA	2.1	1.9	2.3	3.8	4.4	4.2	5.4	7.4	6.9	6.4
CACM	0.4	0.5	0.2	0.1	0.3	0.1	0.2	0.3	x0.2	0.1
Asia	31.5	37.9	x37.1	25.7	19.5	18.1	18.9	20.3	23.4	19.9
Middle East	0.3	x0.4	x0.3	x0.5	0.6	0.9	0.6	1.0	x1.5	1.8
Europe	49.5	46.1	44.4	52.2	58.0	57.7	54.8	54.5	55.1	58.2
EEC	45.2	42.7	41.7	48.6	52.4	55.7	54.2	53.0	54.2	57.2
EFTA	2.0	1.9	1.9	2.4	2.4	0.2	0.2	0.2	0.2	0.3
Oceania	0.6	x0.4	0.3	x0.3	0.5	0.7	x0.6	x0.7	x0.6	x0.4
Belgium–Luxembourg	11.4	13.1	12.8	13.5	14.0	13.3	12.2	11.3	14.2	16.9
United Kingdom	8.0	7.3	7.4	9.5	9.1	12.0	10.3	12.4	9.5	8.6
USA/Etats–Unis d'Amer	8.1	7.4	6.1	7.4	8.6	9.8	10.5	10.9	8.2	7.8
Japan/Japon	17.7	22.2	25.3	16.5	9.5	8.9	9.5	9.8	9.4	5.7
Italy/Italie	8.4	5.9	7.7	8.3	9.8	8.2	9.2	8.8	10.4	10.1
France, Monac	5.7	5.3	4.8	6.0	6.6	7.3	6.2	6.0	7.7	8.7
Brazil/Brésil	1.5	1.3	1.6	1.7	2.7	2.6	3.8	6.2	5.8	5.1
Germany/Allemagne	2.8	2.7	1.8	2.4	3.1	3.5	4.5	4.9	2.9	3.0
Portugal	3.5	2.8	2.3	2.9	4.0	4.4	4.5	2.9	3.0	2.5
Korea, Republic of	4.9	6.8	3.5	3.7	4.1	4.2	3.9	3.2	3.1	3.1

	1985	1986	1987	1988	1989	1990	1991	1992	1993	1994
Afrique	7.2	6.4	x4.3	x5.8	x5.5	6.0	6.4	6.9	5.5	x5.9
Afrique du Nord	0.6	1.0	0.6	0.9	1.0	1.3	1.4	1.9	1.2	1.6
Amériques	17.9	15.1	10.9	13.5	14.5	17.4	15.0	12.8	8.9	x8.0
ALAI	13.1	10.7	7.2	8.9	10.8	12.2	9.7	7.3	5.7	x5.7
MCAC	0.0	0.0	0.0	x0.0	0.0	0.0	0.0	0.0	x0.0	0.0
Asie	21.3	22.9	34.5	26.0	22.8	22.0	22.9	24.8	17.8	13.2
Moyen–Orient	0.0	0.0	x0.0	0.0	0.1	0.1	0.1	0.2	x0.0	0.0
Europe	48.3	48.7	44.6	46.4	51.3	51.1	53.9	53.8	66.8	71.2
CEE	48.0	48.4	44.4	46.2	50.9	50.8	53.7	53.4	66.6	70.9
AELE	0.3	0.3	0.2	0.2	0.4	0.2	0.2	0.3	0.2	0.3
Océanie		x0.0						0.1		x0.0
Belgium–Luxembourg	23.3	23.3	21.7	21.3	23.5	25.2	24.1	25.8	35.3	36.8
France, Monac	20.6	21.3	19.1	20.1	22.7	20.2	22.7	23.3	25.3	26.9
China/Chine			15.3	9.8	7.5	6.3	8.1	7.5	6.5	4.9
Philippines	8.4	8.7	7.9	7.3	5.9	5.8	6.1	7.9	4.8	3.5
Brazil/Brésil	10.7	8.6	5.7	7.4	8.8	9.9	6.8	4.5	3.4	3.2
Sri Lanka	4.5	4.1	2.7	2.9	4.3	4.6	4.3	5.7	3.7	3.1
Canada	4.5	4.0	3.4	4.3	3.1	4.7	4.6	4.3	2.7	2.1
Kenya	4.8	3.3	2.0	2.4	x3.0	3.4	4.0	3.7	3.1	x2.9
Ecuador/Equateur	2.4	2.0	1.5	1.4	1.8	2.1	2.8	2.5	2.0	x2.5
Hong Kong	7.8	9.5	3.4	3.1	3.7	2.8	2.7	2.3	1.8	0.8

TRADE BY COMMODITY IN THOUSAND U.S. DOLLARS – COMMERCE PAR PRODUIT EN MILLIERS DE DOLLARS E.U

COUNTRIES–PAYS	IMPORTS – IMPORTATIONS				
	1990	1991	1992	1993	1994
Total	4535454	4688622	5062078	4669295	5518016
Africa	239628	232013	270917	247240	261865
Northern Africa	130266	129833	186781	157748	185767
Americas	485015	521584	642987	763657	880599
LAIA	200088	213313	243623	255354	268327
CACM	20575	19077	22281	x21353	x18757
Asia	1468635	1872030	2061816	2065573	2269984
Middle East	x248355	x325603	x370386	x341547	x223699
Europe	1967840	1880846	1955860	1459212	1818534
EEC	1885452	1821337	1890001	1405092	1765993
EFTA	38753	37551	35806	29859	31354
Oceania	47706	x49995	x56806	x53632	x65104
China/Chine	554424	798680	793620	721503	972214
Italy/Italie	358578	374570	383608	295941	380482
Germany/Allemagne	347499	340531	358029	270471	335944
USA/Etats–Unis d'Amer	187767	214834	301902	380963	458942
France,Monac	261651	249845	261026	181452	204509
United Kingdom	263605	242120	259370	174697	253064
Belgium–Luxembourg	229647	210327	202585	155248	198212
Iran (Islamic Rp. of)	x117601	x177947	x169627	x182325	x113992
Indonesia/Indonésie	86853	119763	172346	177387	197700
Hong Kong	116094	153711	163779	142794	237808
Spain/Espagne	124659	136438	147791	99217	136699
Turkey/Turquie	123019	80076	98370	139181	84677
Bangladesh			56746	197686	x21860
Korea, Republic of	102587	94209	85580	73467	76880
Canada	67873	71860	73209	104497	133405
Pakistan	46956	73611	76188	87857	96569
Thailand/Thaïlande	48547	52734	90524	70749	70247
Netherlands/Pays–Bas	68329	65705	66922	61909	67537
Austria/Autriche	69499	61042	65931	54910	59734
Morocco/Maroc	62405	60494	60489	54048	64271
Mexico/Mexique	50711	39657	80195	51238	61080
Saudi Arabia	872	63052	95520		
Philippines	71425	50904	56581	47716	73192
So. Africa Customs Un	49399	54942	47151	48522	41454
Egypt/Egypte	36060	40814	51780	50039	64888
Australia/Australie	38957	42482	47306	45690	54835
Chile/Chili	36086	42763	48433	43485	35045
Japan/Japon	46696	43687	41824	38119	40319
Malaysia/Malaisie	27768	34906	38777	44369	59815
Poland/Pologne	35711	49355	33003	35536	46137
Greece/Grèce	46188	36146	41776	30949	30987
Portugal	37250	39973	42129	24961	32882
Algeria/Algérie	18018	12782	50388	36038	37922
Israel/Israël	26481	29072	33949	32158	32499
Switz.Liecht	31062	29874	28221	22967	23997
Colombia/Colombie	33377	22615	29114	28290	28439
India/Inde	28056	17407	24365	35652	100387
Argentina/Argentine	11604	20537	20711	35784	33300
Brazil/Brésil	20453	20109	16265	40047	45479
Viet Nam	x18108	x34690	x18822	x17935	x29274
Ecuador/Equateur	22077	28192	16602	17663	x26187
Sweden/Suède	25508	20596	19311	16774	20655
Tunisia/Tunisie	11135	14253	19049	14975	17511
Ireland/Irlande	17578	16712	14228	16752	15532
Singapore/Singapour	11464	16950	16275	13288	12640
Finland/Finlande	20756	15488	13762	12491	20118
Venezuela	7316	15597	12198	11287	9538
Czechoslovakia	35034	x25760	x11488		
Hungary/Hongrie	x19432	16042	x10286	x9038	x8331
Denmark/Danemark	14704	11844	13532	9321	9637

COUNTRIES–PAYS	EXPORTS – EXPORTATIONS				
	1990	1991	1992	1993	1994
Totale	3556826	3583796	3797097	3595649	4618029
Afrique	4743	6994	7925	5373	x2777
Afrique du Nord	661	420	3758	1518	1447
Amériques	429843	507166	517293	557581	755219
ALAI	107455	150643	191685	185395	292719
MCAC	526	584	60	x784	431
Asie	1041897	1160556	1301810	1412551	1909533
Moyen–Orient	76670	69032	44472	33383	83109
Europe	1912703	1823288	1888345	1555883	1784318
CEE	1807521	1740533	1764341	1478600	1710674
AELE	82460	67388	63007	47457	50439
Océanie	799	x3749	4082	x1577	x1439
Germany/Allemagne	754543	741345	797032	652907	758947
Japan/Japon	483874	521308	581596	624061	728114
Korea, Republic of	285943	353318	416764	521064	718334
USA/Etats–Unis d'Amer	291556	329162	279668	317620	387608
United Kingdom	48550	223696	233188	184044	192319
Italy/Italie	260294	199624	177453	131725	138590
Hong Kong	88979	120142	139060	124782	213876
France,Monac	148042	108418	122637	101911	126508
Ireland/Irlande	103235	90181	107329	121314	111878
Mexico/Mexique	45222	82060	110495	112387	214439
Spain/Espagne	181961	144067	79898	55049	104128
Belgium–Luxembourg	62055	59060	73726	83124	114309
Netherlands/Pays–Bas	89065	74425	68182	50830	53021
Austria/Autriche	84101	67392	67711	56793	x64757
Switz.Liecht	82414	67306	62945	47380	50312
Turkey/Turquie	76502	68832	43790	30697	78404
Canada	30003	26777	45665	53729	74377
Malaysia/Malaisie	27610	29102	40628	39198	44164
Peru/Pérou	35842	37089	34786	32194	36778
Portugal	20773	30135	34667	38834	44161
Thailand/Thaïlande	27348	29397	20600	28725	55653
Belarus/Bélarus			x24075	x39352	x71915
Croatia/Croatie			51645	4511	x3738
Romania/Roumanie	20741	11886	21594	18884	26393
Hungary/Hongrie	x14640	x16058	x19637	x15756	x19784
Brazil/Brésil	7891	15507	18828	12940	10012
India/Inde	30126	16299	20567	9943	21052
Poland/Pologne	29228	22995	10572	9480	20804
Colombia/Colombie	3374	6617	16595	18280	18773
Russian Federation			x19816	x19702	x18448
Indonesia/Indonésie	7725	7164	15876	14461	12146
Bulgaria/Bulgarie	x14640	x5043	x13683	x6228	81892
Czechoslovakia		x11004	x9845		
Yugoslavia/Yougoslavie			x8968	x8641	x4289
Singapore/Singapour	2503	6739	5303	3598	8001
China/Chine	7452	2725	5716	6936	15167
Yugoslavia SFR	22639	x15326			
Uruguay	5920	4200	4757	4563	4270
Argentina/Argentine	5297	3895	4786	4084	7177
Former USSR/Anc. URSS	x80122	x12748			
Pakistan	2037	4483	5090	1452	1716
So. Africa Customs Un	2978	2116	3695	3512	
Australia/Australie	573	2448	3850	1325	1369
Slovakia				x6356	x6241
Czech Republic				5979	9629
Korea Dem People's Rp	x1008	x657	x3115	x1255	x3340
Former GDR	x7470	x2309	x2309		
Philippines		5	2234	2044	3470
Sweden/Suède	1207	1351	880	1032	941
Egypt/Egypte	235	82	2830	143	187

(VALUE AS % OF TOTAL)(VALEUR EN % DU TOTAL)

	1985	1986	1987	1988	1989	1990	1991	1992	1993	1994
Africa	4.5	5.2	4.7	4.3	x4.8	5.3	5.0	5.3	5.3	4.8
Northern Africa	2.0	1.9	1.8	2.1	2.4	2.9	2.8	3.7	3.4	3.4
Americas	11.7	12.0	12.0	11.3	10.6	10.7	11.1	12.7	16.4	15.9
LAIA	3.7	3.4	4.3	3.9	4.1	4.4	4.5	4.8	5.5	4.9
CACM		0.5	0.4	0.4	0.4	0.5	0.4	0.4	x0.5	x0.3
Asia	34.0	28.4	x28.9	35.5	34.6	32.4	40.0	40.7	44.2	41.1
Middle East	1.8	x4.1	x3.0	x3.6	x3.3	x5.5	x6.9	x7.3	x7.3	x4.1
Europe	42.3	48.4	46.0	40.3	41.9	43.4	40.1	38.6	31.3	33.0
EEC	37.4	43.3	41.4	36.3	37.7	41.6	38.8	37.3	30.1	32.0
EFTA	3.8	4.2	3.8	3.2	3.3	0.9	0.8	0.7	0.6	0.6
Oceania	1.3	x1.2	x1.2	x1.2	1.3	1.0	x1.1	x1.1	x1.1	x1.2
China/Chine	20.5	11.7	8.7	16.7	15.3	12.2	17.0	15.7	15.5	17.6
Italy/Italie	8.0	8.6	7.7	6.8	6.9	7.9	8.0	7.6	6.3	6.9
Germany/Allemagne	6.4	7.4	6.9	6.0	6.7	7.7	7.3	7.1	5.8	6.1
USA/Etats–Unis d'Amer	5.4	6.0	5.2	5.4	4.2	4.1	4.6	6.0	8.2	8.3
France,Monac	5.8	6.8	6.0	5.1	5.2	5.8	5.3	5.2	3.9	3.7
United Kingdom	4.5	5.2	5.9	5.5	5.5	5.8	5.2	5.1	3.7	4.6
Belgium–Luxembourg	4.7	5.3	5.1	4.5	4.7	5.1	4.5	4.0	3.3	3.6
Iran (Islamic Rp. of)		x1.3	x1.3	x1.3	x1.3	x2.6	x3.8	x3.4	x3.9	x2.1
Indonesia/Indonésie	1.6	1.5	1.8	1.4	1.8	1.9	2.6	3.4	3.8	3.6
Hong Kong	1.7	1.7	2.1	2.5	3.0	2.6	3.3	3.2	3.1	4.3

	1985	1986	1987	1988	1989	1990	1991	1992	1993	1994
Afrique	0.1	0.1	0.1	x0.0	0.1	0.1	0.2	0.2	0.2	x0.1
Afrique du Nord	0.0	0.0	0.0	0.0	0.0	0.0	0.0	0.1	0.0	0.0
Amériques	15.2	10.8	11.3	11.8	13.0	12.0	14.1	13.7	15.5	16.3
ALAI	2.5	2.3	2.2	2.8	3.6	3.0	4.2	5.0	5.2	6.3
MCAC		0.0	0.0	0.0	x0.0	0.0	0.0	0.0	x0.0	0.0
Asie	20.9	19.0	x22.0	x28.9	29.5	29.3	32.3	34.3	39.3	41.4
Moyen–Orient	2.4	2.4	1.9	1.7	2.8	2.2	1.9	1.2	0.9	1.8
Europe	60.7	67.9	56.9	49.7	53.0	53.8	50.9	49.7	43.3	38.6
CEE	52.9	60.2	49.0	45.5	48.4	50.8	48.6	46.5	41.1	37.0
AELE	7.2	7.1	7.1	3.6	4.2	2.3	1.9	1.7	1.3	1.1
Océanie			x0.0	x0.0			x0.1	0.1	x0.0	x0.0
Germany/Allemagne	16.5	16.4	16.5	15.6	18.0	21.2	20.7	21.0	18.2	16.4
Japan/Japon	13.7	13.0	11.0	12.1	13.3	13.6	14.5	15.3	17.4	15.8
Korea, Republic of	2.5	1.5	2.2	4.1	6.9	8.0	9.9	11.0	14.5	15.6
USA/Etats–Unis d'Amer	10.3	6.6	7.2	8.6	9.1	8.2	9.2	7.4	8.8	8.4
United Kingdom	4.9	4.2	3.7	0.9	1.0	1.4	6.2	6.1	5.1	4.2
Italy/Italie	13.3	22.2	11.3	14.0	12.0	7.3	5.6	4.7	3.7	3.0
Hong Kong	1.0	0.9	1.2	1.9	2.6	2.5	3.4	3.7	3.5	4.6
France,Monac	4.9	4.3	3.7	3.4	3.7	4.2	3.0	3.2	2.8	2.7
Ireland/Irlande	1.4	1.5	1.5	1.8	2.8	2.9	2.5	2.8	3.4	2.4
Mexico/Mexique	0.6	1.0	1.3	1.3	1.8	1.3	2.3	2.9	3.1	4.6

TRADE BY COMMODITY IN THOUSAND U.S. DOLLARS – COMMERCE PAR PRODUIT EN MILLIERS DE DOLLARS E.U

COUNTRIES–PAYS	IMPORTS – IMPORTATIONS				
	1990	1991	1992	1993	1994
Total	2171773	2278655	2004103	1610315	1931822
Africa	x85567	95700	x91423	x77308	x76794
Northern Africa	26323	35429	32738	30496	24587
Americas	240115	234683	217382	231822	190193
LAIA	80094	104445	85184	94695	83769
CACM	965	1029	1283	x6891	x6167
Asia	825750	1073043	724547	529632	767012
Middle East	137928	x178795	x150933	104024	100273
Europe	906622	785022	846617	663186	794268
EEC	837423	744761	737432	606216	744088
EFTA	31563	33443	29426	27530	30941
Oceania	x27719	x25291	x20809	x21896	x21906
China/Chine	412952	392708	113846	45063	187850
Germany/Allemagne	188800	153317	145324	116420	135206
Italy/Italie	164458	142317	141320	124553	167902
USA/Etats–Unis d'Amer	145806	113172	113449	102208	73110
Turkey/Turquie	111545	95830	96862	87539	85535
France,Monac	99449	89043	90476	76390	85238
Hong Kong	16814	171854	49587	28504	119384
Korea, Republic of	103099	76623	65908	102713	92729
Netherlands/Pays–Bas	70322	66518	73010	66829	71216
Spain/Espagne	62344	64832	59346	65932	76698
Belgium–Luxembourg	72628	64146	62112	49811	61394
United Kingdom	70950	69388	72409	32480	62572
Pakistan	42113	50900	59453	48103	40435
Philippines	14838	43825	50013	32587	48388
Bangladesh			108080	x6330	x6636
Iran (Islamic Rp. of)	x18684	x74928	x30243	x6062	x4726
So. Africa Customs Un	36176	40373	33830	29339	28658
Indonesia/Indonésie	27178	22788	30716	35815	19274
Thailand/Thaïlande	22214	25801	28154	28213	22721
Switz.Liecht	27947	30098	26080	25497	28588
Croatia/Croatie			64630	15453	x5699
Viet Nam	x4431	x59341	x7186	x12618	x11463
Bulgaria/Bulgarie	x45920	x13624	37945	x25185	x15195
Argentina/Argentine	19507	24570	21514	24031	18900
Portugal	31137	26174	24455	18317	16302
Poland/Pologne	83	626	30005	35765	36234
Mexico/Mexique	30086	25608	17886	19463	19781
Australia/Australie	24267	22765	18205	19520	18906
Greece/Grèce	20206	21261	22561	15575	17435
Canada	10558	13406	14604	24791	22610
Japan/Japon	6525	5322	10639	36066	27634
Brazil/Brésil	7848	17968	9070	17288	14703
Morocco/Maroc	14913	16620	16252	10777	14623
Ireland/Irlande	20338	18397	15996	7086	10490
Chile/Chili	10787	13053	11806	12512	10066
Czechoslovakia	13967	x21537	x13096		
Hungary/Hongrie	x12563	12359	x12991	x9188	x8222
Singapore/Singapour	7146	8773	10454	13845	15840
Malaysia/Malaisie	11791	11591	9883	10306	11120
Finland/Finlande	9090	9312	9380	11985	15735
Colombia/Colombie	25	9829	11921	8753	5816
Egypt/Egypte	577	7542	10602	11822	4521
Sri Lanka	3635	11290	8441	7549	8519
Sweden/Suède	9025	7493	9895	8279	9213
India/Inde	4533	4485	9517	9135	44657
Saudi Arabia	2353	3131	17523	x682	x3333
Israel/Israël	4831	5926	6941	6333	8563
Denmark/Danemark	6370	5978	6600	5867	6712
Austria/Autriche	12306	6585	4549	6692	7974
Slovenia/Slovénia			8292	7398	7741

COUNTRIES–PAYS	EXPORTS – EXPORTATIONS				
	1990	1991	1992	1993	1994
Totale	2628544	2383381	2137206	1832244	2060433
Afrique	6150	6088	x3550	3752	1015
Afrique du Nord	2175	890	x60	587	696
Amériques	716199	750882	644909	577738	601022
ALAI	72610	70726	70050	47904	34661
MCAC	10	3	5	148	339
Asie	382293	516517	409326	337040	442792
Moyen–Orient	x3458	x1123	x1231	x1013	x2686
Europe	1325760	1052214	967721	848347	x942768
CEE	1230193	1011770	951648	839629	x937556
AELE	9279	9675	4607	3821	3682
Océanie	1384	688	494	853	944
USA/Etats–Unis d'Amer	504822	553602	437990	438932	490845
Germany/Allemagne	277883	276319	270486	253354	293403
Japan/Japon	248740	283665	268789	226831	253911
United Kingdom	396981	244203	230456	181679	215560
Austria/Autriche	245450	240051	199909	215970	x201885
Canada	138682	126481	136857	90550	75040
Finland/Finlande	151792	105291	101696	88516	95118
Hong Kong	16471	122189	44744	15982	50944
Thailand/Thaïlande	43963	56019	54846	50395	52020
Mexico/Mexique	29403	42016	43473	34281	16877
Sweden/Suède	45066	36911	35709	31033	36637
Czechoslovakia		x16033	x81656		
Spain/Espagne	34469	35443	26435	5731	23163
Belgium–Luxembourg	20859	22253	23175	19268	23393
Russian Federation			x27089	x29877	x48110
Italy/Italie	18341	15640	27575	10206	9140
Netherlands/Pays–Bas	17562	16629	17303	15442	19577
France,Monac	18477	15534	14551	16384	17382
Korea, Republic of	38650	21088	10919	10936	11198
Brazil/Brésil	24606	11967	21202	8005	8375
Indonesia/Indonésie	2463	16857	9666	12609	51748
Czech Republic				35042	36836
Romania/Roumanie	10437	8809	14227	8799	10879
Yugoslavia SFR	86075	x30605			
Poland/Pologne	879	661	10404	15976	18523
Former USSR/Anc. URSS	x159647	x24400			
Ukraine			x3244	x14416	x6720
Switz.Liecht	8580	8729	3587	2963	2784
India/Inde	2658	5189	4666	3425	4656
Venezuela	12336	8391	848	3568	8204
Colombia/Colombie	5627	6824	3828	1471	683
So. Africa Customs Un	3735	4587	3274	3045	
Hungary/Hongrie	x12951	x5792	x3235	x1808	x1735
Yugoslavia/Yougoslavie			x8569	x1977	x389
Philippines	316	256	2115	7348	4318
Singapore/Singapour	3660	3027	2898	2891	5137
China/Chine	13420	3013	1915	2578	3514
Ireland/Irlande	2532	2643	2104	630	1024
Belarus/Bélarus			x925	x3235	x4423
Sri Lanka	6	2200	950	755	676
Korea Dem People's Rp	x53	x78	x2953	x726	x311
Latvia/Lettonie			x1400	x2191	1018
Norway,SVD,JM	700	946	1020	858	898
Bulgaria/Bulgarie	x6581	x610	x912	x1187	x1943
Greece/Grèce	221	235	1289	743	422
Turkey/Turquie	1127	659	859	695	777
Australia/Australie	1338	670	478	770	707
Israel/Israël	4312	588	676	577	592
Bhutan/Bhoutan	x3201		x1837		
Slovenia/Slovénia			1153	644	598

(VALUE AS % OF TOTAL)(VALEUR EN % DU TOTAL)

	1985	1986	1987	1988	1989	1990	1991	1992	1993	1994
Africa	4.1	x4.5	x3.2	x4.7	x5.3	x4.0	4.2	x4.6	x4.8	x4.0
Northern Africa	2.9	x3.0	2.0	2.1	1.6	1.2	1.6	1.6	1.9	1.3
Americas	11.2	9.2	7.3	6.9	8.2	11.1	10.3	10.9	14.4	9.9
LAIA	7.6	5.5	4.2	4.0	3.4	3.7	4.6	4.3	5.9	4.3
CACM		0.1	0.1	0.0	0.1	0.0	0.0	0.1	x0.4	x0.3
Asia	22.9	27.1	31.9	27.8	33.7	38.0	47.1	36.2	32.9	39.7
Middle East	3.1	x3.7	x3.4	x3.3	x4.8	6.4	x7.8	x7.5	6.5	5.2
Europe	57.0	55.4	49.3	47.4	42.5	41.7	34.5	42.2	41.2	41.1
EEC	51.0	49.4	43.7	42.8	38.6	38.6	32.7	36.8	37.6	38.5
EFTA	3.3	x4.0	x4.0	2.9	2.4	1.5	1.5	1.5	1.7	1.6
Oceania	2.1	1.6	x1.3	1.2	x1.3	x1.3	x1.1	x1.0	x1.4	x1.1
China/Chine	5.5	11.6	14.5	11.5	16.3	19.0	17.2	5.7	2.8	9.7
Germany/Allemagne	10.0	9.8	8.3	8.6	8.1	8.7	6.7	7.3	7.2	7.0
Italy/Italie	12.7	10.7	9.1	9.5	8.0	7.6	6.2	7.1	7.7	8.7
USA/Etats–Unis d'Amer	2.7	2.5	2.1	1.8	3.4	6.7	5.0	5.7	6.3	3.8
Turkey/Turquie	2.7	2.8	2.6	2.2	3.6	5.1	4.2	4.8	5.4	4.4
France,Monac	4.6	4.5	4.0	4.3	4.4	4.6	3.9	4.5	4.7	4.4
Hong Kong	0.6	0.9	2.7	0.9	1.2	0.8	7.5	2.5	1.8	6.2
Korea, Republic of	3.9	5.1	4.7	4.6	5.1	4.7	3.4	3.3	6.4	4.8
Netherlands/Pays–Bas	4.4	4.4	3.9	3.2	3.0	3.2	2.9	3.6	4.2	3.7
Spain/Espagne	3.3	4.1	3.8	4.4	3.9	2.9	2.8	3.0	4.1	4.0

	1985	1986	1987	1988	1989	1990	1991	1992	1993	1994
Afrique	0.2	x0.1	0.1	x0.1	0.2	0.2	0.3	x0.2	0.2	
Afrique du Nord	0.0	0.0	0.0	0.0	0.1	0.1	0.0	x0.0	0.0	0.0
Amériques	29.5	x30.4	25.9	23.9	23.9	27.3	31.5	30.2	31.5	29.2
ALAI	1.5	x1.1	1.4	1.5	1.9	2.8	3.0	3.3	2.6	1.7
MCAC		0.0	0.0	x0.0	x0.0	0.0	0.0	0.0	0.0	0.0
Asie	14.8	12.5	x13.9	x12.4	13.6	14.5	21.6	19.1	18.4	21.5
Moyen–Orient	0.2	x0.2	0.0	0.0	0.1	x0.1	x0.0	x0.1	x0.1	x0.1
Europe	55.0	x56.5	x48.8	55.1	56.7	50.4	44.1	45.3	46.3	x45.8
CEE	41.7	34.8	29.9	38.6	39.2	46.8	42.5	44.5	45.8	x45.5
AELE	10.4	x18.7	x16.5	14.4	14.6	0.4	0.4	0.2	0.2	0.2
Océanie				0.1	x0.0	0.1				
USA/Etats–Unis d'Amer	28.0	26.1	21.6	18.6	17.6	19.2	23.2	20.5	24.0	23.8
Germany/Allemagne	13.1	11.3	10.0	8.3	9.0	10.6	11.6	12.7	13.8	14.2
Japan/Japon	13.9	11.2	9.6	8.7	9.3	9.5	11.9	12.6	12.4	12.3
United Kingdom	11.7	8.5	7.1	11.6	11.8	15.1	10.2	10.8	9.9	10.5
Austria/Autriche				8.6	8.2	9.3	10.1	9.4	11.8	x9.8
Canada		x3.2	x2.8	3.8	4.4	5.3	5.3	6.4	4.9	3.6
Finland/Finlande	6.4	5.8	5.1	4.3	5.0	5.8	4.4	4.8	4.8	4.6
Hong Kong	0.2	0.6	1.4	0.5	1.1	0.6	5.1	2.1	0.9	2.5
Thailand/Thaïlande	0.0	0.2	0.3	0.3	1.6	1.7	2.4	2.6	2.8	2.5
Mexico/Mexique	0.7	0.1	0.8	0.7	0.8	1.1	1.8	2.0	1.9	0.8

TRADE BY COMMODITY IN THOUSAND U.S. DOLLARS – COMMERCE PAR PRODUIT EN MILLIERS DE DOLLARS E.U

COUNTRIES–PAYS	IMPORTS – IMPORTATIONS				
	1990	1991	1992	1993	1994
Total	5761044	4968815	5004395	3850230	5083894
Africa	61693	45751	41882	36312	45781
Northern Africa	37134	25753	23250	15730	21152
Americas	256545	242828	259125	263272	274057
LAIA	40260	45018	51470	48012	58211
CACM	15	29	40	644	294
Asia	1858328	1808484	2125449	1810255	2155620
Middle East	x142449	x110918	x125919	x130281	x86665
Europe	2941764	2508840	2506921	1647504	2460335
EEC	2854168	2457289	2476337	1622981	2425552
EFTA	31333	26309	18802	14592	27756
Oceania	x45572	x36431	x35257	x34734	x51138
Italy/Italie	966620	861258	852169	582548	903738
Japan/Japon	926027	716498	677833	448091	684509
China/Chine	148223	359829	575622	550597	634245
Germany/Allemagne	574365	550250	541070	325044	491086
France,Monac	418210	371062	390163	224469	330591
United Kingdom	394530	290484	308967	259197	398892
Korea, Republic of	253901	240466	243563	221041	264709
USA/Etats–Unis d'Amer	206245	187247	198365	203692	201064
Belgium–Luxembourg	302772	211067	208880	114417	153132
Hong Kong	72570	102411	159570	143729	162440
India/Inde	113215	89772	128790	128441	127375
Former USSR/Anc. URSS	419146	x269482			
Turkey/Turquie	99823	71537	90050	93189	65004
Spain/Espagne	56159	67616	72433	35317	55121
Malaysia/Malaisie	53513	47229	41311	49182	72358
Nepal/Népal	35103	33217	47337	54694	x26589
Iran (Islamic Rp. of)	x40510	x35230	x32599	x30595	x14414
Australia/Australie	40574	33192	30739	30418	43537
Thailand/Thaïlande	38514	30614	25037	27258	40610
Macau/Macao	22486	31894	26721	17734	14873
Mexico/Mexique	25212	24347	22960	21582	22132
Netherlands/Pays–Bas	38870	24449	23714	18340	20509
Portugal	32219	21772	23570	12690	18453
Czechoslovakia	95714	x37267	x20368		
Viet Nam	x350	x8601	x35039	x7882	x9807
Switz.Liecht	26622	22651	14721	12347	25014
Ireland/Irlande	19069	15462	15899	13334	13543
Pakistan	22272	18401	15528	10068	10649
Israel/Israël	16651	13643	18403	10220	14075
Greece/Grèce	20488	17050	11713	13095	9287
Mauritius/Maurice	16651	12588	11903	15477	15495
Egypt/Egypte	17782	17123	15523	6669	12349
Austria/Autriche	13987	12459	12218	12373	12793
Poland/Pologne	18364	7489	7855	20356	25538
Colombia/Colombie	9529	9647	11750	11230	9428
Denmark/Danemark	12596	10019	11660	8812	12571
Canada	9702	10065	8889	10659	13668
Czech Republic				26979	27725
Russian Federation			x14481	x11479	x1139
Yugoslavia SFR	56085	x24986			
Romania/Roumanie	13658	8040	4906	4460	3462
So. Africa Customs Un	6421	5702	6072	4751	8419
Morocco/Maroc	6727	5916	5183	5330	7361
Uruguay	1470	5575	5043	4596	18911
Lithuania/Lituanie			9120	x3029	9334
New Zealand	3504	3155	4405	4222	7348
Bangladesh		1405	3138	4557	x50
Argentina/Argentine	484	2283	3714	2714	1789
Brazil/Brésil	1622	1238	4282	2400	3315
Slovenia/Slovénia			3322	3598	4178

COUNTRIES–PAYS	EXPORTS – EXPORTATIONS				
	1990	1991	1992	1993	1994
Totale	5722193	5256889	4994065	4047325	5290974
Afrique	288946	257849	x192480	x132362	x163211
Afrique du Nord	6446	1410	x2058	x4644	x2008
Amériques	581011	424067	231018	223866	303252
ALAI	519616	388864	193262	192962	242003
MCAC	2		53	508	30
Asie	x769109	x622904	x738323	x772843	x909833
Moyen–Orient	x30360	x25610	x16484	x18681	x53643
Europe	902182	723623	717374	531487	747963
CEE	878543	708005	697443	512591	716999
AELE	23346	15222	15579	14963	29935
Océanie	x3153551	x3191495	x3080381	x2358900	x3123493
Australia/Australie	2476001	2584168	2533270	1848767	2410916
New Zealand	677364	606655	546047	506614	711523
China/Chine	262383	285805	314000	293402	447825
So. Africa Customs Un	281496	255393	187824	127024	160338
United Kingdom	258305	186355	196143	161396	250504
France,Monac	301050	216179	163278	105689	134935
Hong Kong	90187	126301	173435	172029	171115
Uruguay	317187	256309	69666	60833	63930
Mongolia/Mongolie	x268682	x88597	x101334	x166131	x49651
Argentina/Argentine	159414	98627	90411	99462	132305
Germany/Allemagne	69635	85655	127976	68478	93897
Belgium–Luxembourg	107544	85255	72776	54446	88241
Afghanistan	x57235	x45390	x48574	x46346	x47588
Spain/Espagne	39600	43283	50293	39152	41536
USA/Etats–Unis d'Amer	57302	32731	34346	27909	56214
Italy/Italie	32924	31710	32200	22201	38083
Netherlands/Pays–Bas	36872	29823	24578	28034	30600
Ireland/Irlande	20861	19949	18876	23204	25273
Israel/Israël	18913	14741	16719	12171	16885
Hungary/Hongrie	x12749	x15862	x17218	x7818	x6867
Peru/Pérou	12527	10207	12688	16459	24565
Malaysia/Malaisie	11019	7861	14074	15725	16050
Switz.Liecht	15111	10412	11624	11357	24913
Pakistan	13979	10786	11652	9706	11845
Russian Federation			x19390	x11496	x48149
Chile/Chili	19048	12007	10375	6720	9937
Macau/Macao	7161	7528	10536	10774	14542
Brazil/Brésil	3392	7807	8360	6506	7243
Kazakstan			x6937	x13337	x55029
Iran (Islamic Rp. of)		x11445	x4940	x3559	x31491
Bulgaria/Bulgarie	x3836	x1616	x9741	x7128	21327
Former USSR/Anc. URSS	7665	x16795			
Japan/Japon	5381	6656	5938	3187	2722
Greece/Grèce	5537	3230	6000	5927	6503
Turkey/Turquie	3885	7195	2764	1820	7567
Norway,SVD,JM	6523	3958	2740	2639	3803
Syrian Arab Republic	2313	x3200	2663	x3246	x4887
Kyrgyzstan/Kirghizistan			x6755	x2242	x16618
Romania/Roumanie	332	131	3128	5654	7040
Saudi Arabia	3140	1948	1623	x4933	x5887
Korea, Republic of	1439	1108	3875	1962	1394
Libyan Arab Jamahiriya	5769	942	x1731	x4251	x1572
Canada	2233	1842	2667	1948	2199
Portugal	2121	2336	1993	1472	3353
Ukraine			x3517	x2173	x2502
Azerbaijan			x3060	x2297	x948
Malta/Malte		1	2090	2918	x79
Austria/Autriche	1974	1618	1381	1639	x2279
Czechoslovakia		x1985	x2620		
Jordan/Jordanie	1466	716	1464	2264	899

(VALUE AS % OF TOTAL)(VALEUR EN % DU TOTAL)

	1985	1986	1987	1988	1989	1990	1991	1992	1993	1994
Africa	1.2	1.1	0.8	0.9	0.8	1.1	0.9	0.8	0.9	0.9
Northern Africa	0.8	0.7	0.4	0.6	0.5	0.6	0.5	0.5	0.4	0.4
Americas	4.4	5.0	4.7	x5.0	5.2	4.4	4.9	5.1	6.9	5.4
LAIA	0.5	0.7	0.6	0.7	0.8	0.7	0.9	1.0	1.2	1.1
CACM	0.0	x0.0	0.0	x0.0	0.0	0.0	0.0	0.0	0.0	0.0
Asia	31.9	33.9	37.6	38.4	34.6	32.3	36.4	42.5	47.0	42.4
Middle East	1.5	x1.7	x1.8	x1.6	x2.0	x2.5	x2.2	x2.5	x3.4	x1.7
Europe	51.0	47.6	42.7	40.7	43.9	51.1	50.5	50.1	42.8	48.4
EEC	47.5	44.1	40.4	39.4	42.7	49.5	49.5	49.5	42.2	47.7
EFTA	1.6	1.7	1.4	0.7	0.6	0.5	0.5	0.4	0.4	0.5
Oceania	0.8	x0.8	x0.8	x0.8	x0.6	x0.8	x0.7	x0.7	x0.9	x1.0
Italy/Italie	13.6	11.8	11.2	11.4	12.3	16.8	17.3	17.0	15.1	17.8
Japan/Japon	15.6	14.4	16.2	15.6	16.5	16.1	14.4	13.5	11.6	13.5
China/Chine	6.6	9.9	8.1	10.0	6.6	2.6	7.2	11.5	14.3	12.5
Germany/Allemagne	6.3	5.9	5.9	6.9	7.5	10.0	11.1	10.8	8.4	9.7
France,Monac	8.2	7.7	6.4	6.7	7.6	7.3	7.5	7.8	5.8	6.5
United Kingdom	9.6	8.2	7.9	7.1	6.9	6.8	5.8	6.2	6.7	7.8
Korea, Republic of	3.1	3.5	4.0	3.9	3.9	4.4	4.8	4.9	5.7	5.2
USA/Etats–Unis d'Amer	3.6	3.9	3.9	3.8	4.3	3.6	3.8	4.0	5.3	4.0
Belgium–Luxembourg	4.7	4.9	4.7	4.3	5.0	5.3	4.2	4.2	3.0	3.0
Hong Kong	2.0	1.6	1.7	1.7	1.7	1.3	2.1	3.2	3.7	3.2

	1985	1986	1987	1988	1989	1990	1991	1992	1993	1994
Afrique	5.4	x5.8	x5.1	5.2	x4.1	5.0	4.9	x3.9	x3.2	x3.1
Afrique du Nord	0.0	x0.0	0.0	0.0	0.0	0.1	0.0	x0.0	x0.1	x0.0
Amériques	8.5	8.6	6.7	8.5	7.2	10.1	8.1	4.6	5.5	5.7
ALAI	6.9	6.8	5.5	7.6	6.2	9.1	7.4	3.9	4.8	4.6
MCAC	0.0	x0.0	0.0	x0.0	x0.0	0.0		0.0	0.0	0.0
Asie	9.8	8.5	x10.9	x9.7	x9.8	x13.4	x11.8	x14.8	x19.1	x17.2
Moyen–Orient	0.7	x0.8	x1.2	x0.6	x0.6	x0.5	x0.5	x0.3	x0.5	x1.0
Europe	16.3	15.8	15.4	13.6	14.5	15.8	13.8	14.4	13.1	14.1
CEE	15.9	15.3	14.9	13.1	14.1	15.4	13.5	14.0	12.7	13.6
AELE	0.4	0.5	0.4	0.4	0.4	0.4	0.3	0.3	0.4	0.6
Océanie	59.7	x61.0	x60.4	x62.0	x63.7	x55.1	x60.7	x61.7	x58.3	x59.0
Australia/Australie	44.0	43.7	46.1	48.8	51.3	43.3	49.2	50.7	45.7	45.6
New Zealand	15.7	17.3	14.3	13.2	12.4	11.8	11.5	10.9	12.5	13.4
China/Chine	5.5	4.3	4.8	5.0	4.6	4.6	5.4	6.3	7.2	8.5
So. Africa Customs Un	5.3	5.7	5.0	5.1	4.0	4.9	4.9	3.8	3.1	3.0
United Kingdom	5.0	5.0	4.8	3.3	4.0	4.5	3.5	3.9	4.0	4.7
France,Monac	4.7	4.3	4.1	4.8	4.5	5.3	4.1	3.3	2.6	2.6
Hong Kong	2.4	1.9	2.1	1.8	2.0	1.6	2.4	3.5	4.3	3.2
Uruguay	1.7	2.1	1.8	4.1	3.9	5.5	4.9	1.4	1.5	1.2
Mongolia/Mongolie			x0.6	x0.4	x0.6	x4.7	x1.7	x2.0	x4.1	x0.9
Argentina/Argentine	3.3	3.0	2.2	2.0	1.6	2.8	1.9	1.8	2.5	2.5

TRADE BY COMMODITY IN THOUSAND U.S. DOLLARS – COMMERCE PAR PRODUIT EN MILLIERS DE DOLLARS E.U

COUNTRIES–PAYS	IMPORTS – IMPORTATIONS				
	1990	1991	1992	1993	1994
Total	x724547	x788435	x1003778	x947961	x1150129
Africa	x177022	x174629	x275851	x238172	x311166
Northern Africa	28423	27678	34158	31283	34478
Americas	55768	74735	83564	106073	122481
LAIA	17710	34058	40232	66141	77120
CACM	10578	11807	12297	12517	13765
Asia	180493	196380	241229	277012	337694
Middle East	x21044	x19605	x24126	x25638	x26875
Europe	287760	294153	342210	263200	306646
EEC	281512	286843	335141	253600	300225
EFTA	5831	5997	4996	4273	3541
Oceania	8033	x10612	x12997	x13581	x13812
Italy/Italie	45498	48020	61880	60256	72815
France,Monac	55383	51847	61308	44467	45110
Belgium–Luxembourg	43759	38955	54278	35844	37473
Spain/Espagne	44107	53014	44379	29570	52096
Hong Kong	24513	30350	40526	50802	58288
Japan/Japon	16155	26244	34244	48327	66701
Netherlands/Pays–Bas	35972	34522	43715	27541	34317
Singapore/Singapour	23103	27330	36380	41512	44991
India/Inde	33500	21343	33868	26807	41851
Tunisia/Tunisie	21408	22224	28464	27273	30171
Pakistan	28885	27867	24086	23146	20656
Germany/Allemagne	18636	22365	27246	23587	20619
Un. Rep. of Tanzania	x2286	x21744	x26669	x21138	x20422
Chile/Chili	11096	17845	23743	26464	26003
Benin/Bénin	x19020	x21055	x19604	x18190	x9775
Malaysia/Malaisie	11483	14310	18760	25452	25570
United Kingdom	18623	18319	20894	16880	22052
Hungary/Hongrie	x14528	17552	x17370	x17719	x15867
Nigeria/Nigéria	x23589	50	x37799	x13401	x14065
Indonesia/Indonésie	9134	14706	15229	16157	20174
Mexico/Mexique	1828	3390	8260	32322	43724
Poland/Pologne			20975	17569	23784
USA/Etats–Unis d'Amer	12628	12907	12501	12393	13650
Russian Federation			x25141	x11483	x7360
Ghana	x10329	1578	16635	x18044	x21830
Zaire/Zaïre	x12616	x12241	x10708	x10258	x9799
Canada	8988	9860	11994	10946	10698
Jordan/Jordanie	9158	8423	11215	12928	12111
Uganda/Ouganda	x5367	x7864	x12329	x11916	x15807
Cameroon/Cameroun	110	179	x13910	x16118	x56079
So. Africa Customs Un	10837	12253	10529	7114	6523
Rwanda	4851	x8321	x8718	x9644	x2085
Senegal/Sénégal	6497	4839	x10349	x7685	x6423
Papua New Guinea	3654	x5593	x7813	x8292	x7279
Djibouti	5406	7787	5126	x7131	x3871
Sweden/Suède	6070	6242	8138	5310	3474
Czechoslovakia	459	x8902	x6985		
Mozambique	x4546	x5200	x3827	x6569	x3859
Burkina Faso	x3369	x4495	x6014	x4205	x2353
Saudi Arabia	4299	5154	4711	x4345	x3441
Togo	4997	3233	x7541	x3156	x9428
Guinea/Guinée	x4307	x3872	x3941	x5327	x7098
Zambia/Zambie	x1181	x1682	x4562	x6881	x6393
Morocco/Maroc	3539	4345	5116	2931	3729
Lebanon/Liban	x5757	x4089	x3976	x4140	x6331
Nicaragua	5060	4825	3493	3514	4224
Niger	x1137	x2347	x5456	x3706	x5259
Angola	x2550	x1448	x7776	x2207	x8198
Mali	1915	x2830	x3829	x4733	x2418
Guatemala	1499	2927	4004	4203	4841

COUNTRIES–PAYS	EXPORTS – EXPORTATIONS				
	1990	1991	1992	1993	1994
Totale	845677	820756	1058270	1085625	1161423
Afrique	26000	10298	9420	x9714	x10410
Afrique du Nord	9011	6852	7343	5235	7374
Amériques	x190686	212012	310347	389230	392886
ALAI	536	2445	25095	72111	72150
MCAC	178	644	216	x60	x148
Asie	166151	116379	128220	131960	167715
Moyen–Orient	67647	7629	8976	x6352	10437
Europe	446013	466255	587882	525602	557023
CEE	434714	455863	575573	512205	540237
AELE	10170	9704	11086	12715	16017
Océanie	x9304	x12035	14977	x18202	20395
USA/Etats–Unis d'Amer	174269	188570	258577	292287	290335
Germany/Allemagne	118495	128041	161848	149307	157356
Netherlands/Pays–Bas	91488	94129	102787	87158	93320
Belgium–Luxembourg	84422	85199	105438	86375	85928
United Kingdom	34203	38830	63410	60929	69442
Italy/Italie	41148	47005	60696	52751	55203
Japan/Japon	46730	45073	45567	42810	45751
France,Monac	35626	34810	42531	39165	44235
Mexico/Mexique	270	1059	24585	71658	71680
Singapore/Singapour	16207	21216	25833	32109	47716
Canada	12988	18199	23827	24710	29950
Hong Kong	13628	20333	21972	12646	14861
Australia/Australie	8729	11269	14069	17138	19134
Korea, Republic of	11667	9459	11739	19247	20428
Switz.Liecht	9533	9139	10104	10999	14068
Portugal	5929	5964	8617	11095	5900
Sweden/Suède	5798	6377	10419	6199	6542
Tunisia/Tunisie	8454	5257	6152	4303	5476
Malaysia/Malaisie	3319	3929	3640	7666	11113
Austria/Autriche	4432	4850	4983	5294	x4704
Turkey/Turquie	3756	4936	4890	5133	9148
Denmark/Danemark	5395	3901	4647	4447	5186
Greece/Grèce	4041	3873	4029	3571	4798
Pakistan	2079	3495	3629	3597	4720
China/Chine	966	1398	3514	4466	7458
Poland/Pologne			3478	4994	7492
Ireland/Irlande	432	1373	3254	2712	4446
Saudi Arabia	17659	1696	3465	x375	x358
Spain/Espagne	1025	1198	1611	1677	1601
Hungary/Hongrie	x1576	x1619	x1594	x1099	x1305
Czech Republic				4273	3541
Egypt/Egypte	531	1572	1170	889	1897
Norway,SVD,JM	599	558	962	1710	1949
Finland/Finlande	2214	247	1302	1522	1575
Czechoslovakia		x1117	x1893		
Thailand/Thaïlande	661	991	855	677	733
Panama	1673		2465		
So. Africa Customs Un	357	354	951	1057	
New Zealand	483	663	816	853	1044
Togo	66	1964	x45	x81	x32
Djibouti	12	38	298	x1668	x2106
Philippines	90	458	723	808	2479
Bahamas		1764			
Zimbabwe	6	15	418	1108	x21
Syrian Arab Republic	81	x678	182	x599	x604
Chile/Chili	103	1058	127	208	7
Macau/Macao	342	644	531	168	70
Croatia/Croatie			821	454	x537
India/Inde	741	259	371	249	689
Ethiopia/Ethiopie	41	851		x15	x83

(VALUE AS % OF TOTAL)(VALEUR EN % DU TOTAL)

	1985	1986	1987	1988	1989	1990	1991	1992	1993	1994
Africa	10.2	x23.1	x23.1	x27.9	x24.6	x24.4	x22.2	x27.4	x25.2	x27.1
Northern Africa	2.0	2.1	2.6	2.6	2.6	3.9	3.5	3.4	3.3	3.0
Americas	7.0	x6.4	x7.2	x7.1	x9.7	7.7	9.5	8.3	11.2	10.6
LAIA	1.2	1.4	1.6	1.8	2.4	2.4	4.3	4.0	7.0	6.7
CACM	0.3	x0.3	x0.6	1.1	2.3	1.5	1.5	1.2	1.3	1.2
Asia	29.7	24.0	23.0	22.5	23.8	24.9	25.0	24.0	29.2	29.3
Middle East	3.4	x2.7	x2.6	x2.3	x2.9	x2.9	x2.5	x2.4	x2.7	x2.3
Europe	51.2	45.0	43.2	39.0	38.1	39.7	37.3	34.1	27.8	26.7
EEC	48.5	42.3	40.3	36.5	35.9	38.9	36.4	33.4	26.8	26.1
EFTA	2.7	2.6	2.9	2.5	2.2	0.8	0.8	0.5	0.5	0.3
Oceania	1.0	1.0	1.2	x1.3	1.2	1.1	x1.3	x1.3	x1.5	x1.2
Italy/Italie	14.7	10.7	8.2	6.6	6.2	6.3	6.1	6.2	6.4	6.3
France,Monac	6.9	7.0	7.6	7.0	6.8	7.6	6.6	6.1	4.7	3.9
Belgium–Luxembourg	5.8	5.7	4.6	4.5	4.9	6.0	4.9	5.4	3.8	3.3
Spain/Espagne	8.9	7.2	7.4	6.8	6.0	6.1	6.7	4.4	3.1	4.5
Hong Kong	3.8	1.6	2.7	1.8	2.7	3.4	3.8	4.0	5.4	5.1
Japan/Japon	1.4	0.9	1.0	1.0	1.2	2.2	3.3	3.4	5.1	5.8
Netherlands/Pays–Bas	5.0	5.0	4.5	4.0	4.3	5.0	4.4	4.4	2.9	3.0
Singapore/Singapour	1.8	1.8	1.6	2.4	2.9	3.2	3.5	3.6	4.4	3.9
India/Inde	5.5	4.5	3.7	4.8	4.6	4.6	2.7	3.4	2.8	3.6
Tunisia/Tunisie	1.6	1.6	2.0	2.2	2.0	3.0	2.8	2.8	2.9	2.6

	1985	1986	1987	1988	1989	1990	1991	1992	1993	1994
Afrique	0.6	1.0	1.4	1.9	1.9	3.0	1.2	0.9	x0.9	x0.9
Afrique du Nord	0.5	0.7	x0.8	0.8	0.8	1.1	0.8	0.7	0.5	0.6
Amériques	30.0	x30.3	x29.8	x28.3	x25.2	x22.5	25.8	29.3	35.9	33.9
ALAI	0.2	x0.1	0.2	0.1	0.1	0.1	0.3	2.4	6.6	6.2
MCAC	0.0	0.0	x0.0	x0.0	0.0	0.0	0.1	0.0	x0.0	x0.0
Asie	14.8	9.8	10.3	15.4	16.3	19.6	14.2	12.1	12.2	14.5
Moyen–Orient	3.5	x0.6	0.7	2.6	3.7	8.0	0.9	0.8	x0.6	0.9
Europe	52.5	56.9	54.6	51.4	54.4	52.7	56.8	55.6	48.4	48.0
CEE	48.9	53.3	51.5	48.7	51.7	51.4	55.5	54.4	47.2	46.5
AELE	3.2	3.4	2.8	2.4	2.4	1.2	1.2	1.0	1.2	1.4
Océanie	1.8	x1.6	x1.6	x1.4	x1.2	x1.1	x1.5	1.4	x1.7	1.7
USA/Etats–Unis d'Amer	28.1	27.8	27.3	25.4	23.0	20.6	23.0	24.4	26.9	25.0
Germany/Allemagne	14.1	15.0	13.8	13.4	13.3	14.0	15.6	15.3	13.8	13.5
Netherlands/Pays–Bas	10.5	12.1	12.3	11.0	11.4	10.8	11.5	9.7	8.0	8.0
Belgium–Luxembourg	9.4	10.6	9.3	8.6	10.0	10.0	10.4	10.0	8.0	7.4
United Kingdom	4.0	3.7	4.1	4.1	4.4	4.0	4.7	6.0	5.6	6.0
Italy/Italie	3.3	3.5	4.1	4.4	4.9	4.9	5.7	5.7	4.9	4.8
Japan/Japon	7.6	6.2	5.8	7.0	6.6	5.5	5.5	4.3	3.9	3.9
France,Monac	4.0	4.5	3.9	4.0	4.1	4.2	4.2	4.0	3.6	3.8
Mexico/Mexique	0.1	0.0	0.1	0.1	0.1	0.0	0.1	2.3	6.6	6.2
Singapore/Singapour	1.1	1.0	1.2	1.5	1.9	1.9	2.6	2.4	3.0	4.1

TRADE BY COMMODITY IN THOUSAND U.S. DOLLARS – COMMERCE PAR PRODUIT EN MILLIERS DE DOLLARS E.U

COUNTRIES–PAYS	IMPORTS – IMPORTATIONS 1990	1991	1992	1993	1994
Total	2120885	1987818	1871609	1400605	1429882
Africa	x23782	x20040	x36974	x22731	x20494
Northern Africa	5505	1226	x2549	x941	839
Americas	226784	215280	x229632	167883	191700
LAIA	111875	99829	60797	55448	95363
CACM	16515	4665	8402	2551	x542
Asia	690955	704743	x711594	525411	538998
Middle East	x75996	x67658	x124142	x68739	x51894
Europe	912805	768960	667683	490180	479590
EEC	811881	698398	587109	408194	425111
EFTA	42747	46659	37269	39892	37439
Oceania	102621	x60350	x101536	x88487	x93437
India/Inde	190986	185496	176989	121992	152617
Japan/Japon	132197	126479	127539	125383	110869
France, Monac	179223	166310	118296	67004	73158
Belgium–Luxembourg	131485	127688	119640	88473	90407
Netherlands/Pays–Bas	111854	104528	98229	89933	81442
Korea, Republic of	97057	83174	105454	96435	92870
Spain/Espagne	120095	106777	96405	67984	93496
Indonesia/Indonésie	78961	112117	77347	14431	35471
USA/Etats–Unis d'Amer	46535	45459	84506	55062	49290
New Zealand	44378	40073	58553	57298	53777
Former USSR/Anc. URSS		x154827			
Canada	50950	48117	52503	51266	42851
Poland/Pologne	41820	20581	71413	45027	54746
Mexico/Mexique	85959	72067	27118	22044	49311
Germany/Allemagne	57834	46610	41678	28380	21589
Norway, SVD, JM	38518	43376	34137	37605	35307
Romania/Roumanie	60188	28027	42004	39286	34618
Iran (Islamic Rp. of)	x27521	x11346	x77108	x16230	x2424
Philippines	41330	47006	35453	21183	21689
Australia/Australie	57857	19874	42642	30993	39340
Turkey/Turquie	33188	31897	29333	29581	22304
Italy/Italie	49507	35721	34260	17046	16492
Malaysia/Malaisie	28360	23953	27919	32904	28347
Greece/Grèce	37796	34665	18270	12944	10593
China/Chine	18017	26517	13379	16155	20824
United Kingdom	33383	23949	20261	9406	7538
Pakistan	18413	18985	17282	17247	14557
Brazil/Brésil	12538	13203	16176	21105	31665
Austria/Autriche	27355	18926	16992	13250	12683
Lebanon/Liban	x3865	x18158	x10951	x10482	x17874
Croatia/Croatie			23845	15679	x10184
Yugoslavia/Yougoslavie			x16235	x17966	x2716
Bulgaria/Bulgarie	x23115	x9425	7310	x14795	x9580
Sweden/Suède	36176	19390	7536	4452	6025
So. Africa Customs Un	5609	8646	9746	9873	18314
Yugoslavia SFR	57993	x23684			
Dominican Republic		x11880	x11401		
Portugal	9114	8288	6527	4549	6872
Russian Federation			x16962	x988	x669
Nigeria/Nigéria	x127	190	x10304	x6361	x12
Korea Dem People's Rp	x4184	x9366	x2384	x3609	x1617
Venezuela	3989	4898	6242	2904	2886
Br. Indian Ocean Terr	x3207	x4591	x4591	x4591	
Colombia/Colombie	2802	3512	5043	4690	3506
Honduras	787	4142	6102	414	158
Guyana		x1967	x4466	x2720	x2250
United Arab Emirates	5913	1180	685	x6986	x5549
Finland/Finlande	6020	2657	3582	2583	3002
Switz.Liecht	4191	3279	3126	2256	2132
Ireland/Irlande	1151	2025	4548	1787	1256

COUNTRIES–PAYS	EXPORTS – EXPORTATIONS 1990	1991	1992	1993	1994
Totale	1370064	x1357256	x1285041	x1046563	x1023690
Afrique	681363	587891	x553009	377647	x431554
Afrique du Nord	465335	389236	359493	313885	331363
Amériques	44997	39506	53114	58003	34287
ALAI	41260	37936	50162	52077	33193
MCAC	45	11	140	242	160
Asie	470583	458305	458740	411454	416477
Moyen–Orient	386353	357797	357622	291372	302136
Europe	83509	88533	100478	82220	99171
CEE	81936	85977	98668	80100	96868
AELE	1569	2508	1447	1841	1917
Océanie	x87259	x100776	x116296	x112961	x39555
Morocco/Maroc	437004	346734	306966	259954	281673
Jordan/Jordanie	342055	322780	307089	267093	276180
Nauru	x83645	x96136	x108239	x111275	x31958
Togo	119145	122790	x119635	x50906	x62506
Israel/Israël	64158	75250	70747	79287	73557
Chile/Chili	39985	37143	49759	51588	31428
Russian Federation			x55207	x76992	x67276
Senegal/Sénégal	56962	43926	x56321	4145	x33469
Syrian Arab Republic	39021	x34344	43472	x15478	x20586
Former USSR/Anc. URSS		x79264			
Tunisia/Tunisie	19676	15150	31510	32318	32113
Netherlands/Pays–Bas	24268	23892	27942	22398	21754
Algeria/Algérie	8490	27258	19994	20120	15059
China/Chine	11864	17957	18114	26434	30043
So. Africa Customs Un	34513	29597	13720	8482	3974
Germany/Allemagne	14587	17992	19849	12746	14655
Belgium–Luxembourg	13958	15347	18849	15604	26014
France, Monac	9941	9182	10661	8618	9390
Italy/Italie	8321	8026	6889	6719	8577
Belarus/Bélarus			x14043	x4906	x162
United Kingdom	4477	4441	7973	4391	7251
Pakistan	3811	3608	4383	5677	3143
Christmas Island	x2893	x3986	x7171	x530	x6063
Saudi Arabia	5034	645	7017	x2353	x144
Malaysia/Malaisie	332	910	3185	2723	1820
Spain/Espagne	1109	1757	2468	2589	3909
Mozambique		x2018	x3664		
Lebanon/Liban				x5594	x3505
Norway, SVD, JM	1371	2295	1320	1705	1720
Indonesia/Indonésie	1677	990	2314	1741	2382
Bahamas				x4781	
Austria/Autriche	1096	683	1636	1637	x2447
Albania/Albanie	x219	x2053	x1111	x574	
Denmark/Danemark	1823	1271	864	1326	1144
Sweden/Suède	881	2774	302	202	128
Poland/Pologne		3	1167	2035	1697
Ireland/Irlande	81	499	1172	1207	1392
Netherlands Antilles	127	537	2250		
Egypt/Egypte	3	94	1022	1494	2518
Greece/Grèce	19	1	16	2553	170
Canada	3557	1017	534	884	885
Singapore/Singapour	1357	586	859	570	517
Australia/Australie	619	506	470	796	1071
Korea, Republic of	135	256	401	1104	873
Ukraine			x1165	x477	x5496
Japan/Japon	159	398	565	620	1195
Philippines	365	229	107	1191	150
Czech Republic				1008	587
New Zealand	102	147	416	354	430
Czechoslovakia		x305	x519		

(VALUE AS % OF TOTAL)(VALEUR EN % DU TOTAL)

	1985	1986	1987	1988	1989	1990	1991	1992	1993	1994
Africa	2.2	1.4	x0.5	x0.7	x1.0	x1.2	x1.0	x2.0	x1.6	x1.5
Northern Africa	0.2	0.1	x0.0	0.0	0.2	0.3	0.1	x0.1	x0.1	0.1
Americas	8.7	12.8	8.8	9.7	9.6	10.7	10.8	x12.2	12.0	13.4
LAIA	2.6	3.0	2.9	3.8	3.9	5.3	5.0	3.2	4.0	6.7
CACM	0.1	2.9	0.6	0.1	0.3	0.8	0.2	0.4	0.2	x0.0
Asia	26.0	24.8	25.9	24.6	24.9	32.5	35.5	x38.0	37.5	37.7
Middle East	2.5	2.0	1.9	2.2	x2.3	x3.6	x3.4	x6.6	x4.9	x3.6
Europe	51.6	50.8	46.6	44.4	46.0	43.0	38.7	35.7	35.0	33.5
EEC	42.9	42.3	38.6	35.1	35.1	38.3	35.1	31.4	29.1	29.7
EFTA	4.9	4.4	4.2	3.8	4.6	2.0	2.3	2.0	2.8	2.6
Oceania	5.3	4.1	x4.7	x5.5	5.3	4.8	x3.0	x5.4	x6.3	x6.5
India/Inde	6.5	5.8	5.2	5.6	6.8	9.0	9.3	9.5	8.7	10.7
Japan/Japon	7.3	6.5	6.4	5.8	5.4	6.2	6.4	6.8	9.0	7.8
France, Monac	9.2	8.0	8.0	7.4	8.0	8.5	8.4	6.3	4.8	5.1
Belgium–Luxembourg	6.0	5.9	6.0	5.5	5.3	6.2	6.4	6.4	6.3	6.3
Netherlands/Pays–Bas	5.1	4.7	4.4	4.7	4.6	5.3	5.3	5.2	6.4	5.7
Korea, Republic of	3.9	3.8	3.6	3.7	3.8	4.6	4.2	5.6	6.9	6.5
Spain/Espagne	6.3	8.7	6.3	6.1	5.5	5.7	5.4	5.2	4.9	6.5
Indonesia/Indonésie	2.9	2.2	3.2	2.5	2.3	3.7	5.6	4.1	1.0	2.5
USA/Etats–Unis d'Amer	1.5	2.7	2.0	2.3	2.4	2.2	2.3	4.5	3.9	3.4
New Zealand	2.1	0.8	1.3	1.3	1.8	2.1	2.0	3.1	4.1	3.8

	1985	1986	1987	1988	1989	1990	1991	1992	1993	1994
Afrique	52.9	39.7	33.4	37.6	36.4	49.7	43.3	x43.1	36.1	x42.2
Afrique du Nord	39.9	28.3	23.1	25.7	24.9	34.0	28.7	28.0	30.0	32.4
Amériques	17.1	x26.0	x22.8	x19.5	x20.7	3.3	2.9	4.1	5.6	3.4
ALAI	2.5	2.2	1.9	1.8	1.7	3.0	2.8	3.9	5.0	3.2
MCAC		0.0	x0.0	x0.0	0.0	0.0	0.0	0.0	0.0	0.0
Asie	27.2	24.7	22.3	24.0	24.6	34.4	33.8	35.6	39.3	40.7
Moyen–Orient	19.9	19.0	17.3	20.4	20.1	28.2	26.4	27.8	27.8	29.5
Europe	2.8	2.6	3.0	4.3	3.9	6.1	6.5	7.8	7.9	9.7
CEE	2.2	2.1	2.6	4.0	3.5	6.0	6.3	7.7	7.7	9.5
AELE	0.5	0.4	0.4	0.3	0.4	0.1	0.2	0.1	0.2	0.2
Océanie		x6.9	x6.6	x4.2	x3.7	x6.4	x7.4	x9.1	x10.8	x3.8
Morocco/Maroc	35.9	24.9	20.1	23.2	22.9	31.9	25.5	23.9	24.8	27.5
Jordan/Jordanie	18.4	16.7	14.3	17.9	17.7	25.0	23.8	23.9	25.5	27.0
Nauru		x5.2	x4.8	x3.8	x3.5	x6.1	x7.1	x8.4	x10.6	x3.1
Togo	7.1	6.0	6.1	5.5	6.1	8.7	9.0	x9.3	x4.9	x6.1
Israel/Israël	6.8	5.3	4.2	2.8	3.7	4.7	5.5	5.5	7.6	7.2
Chile/Chili	2.5	2.2	1.8	1.7	1.6	2.9	2.7	3.9	4.9	3.1
Russian Federation								x4.3	x7.4	x6.6
Senegal/Sénégal	3.7	3.2	1.9	3.3	3.0	4.2	3.2	x4.4	0.4	x3.3
Syrian Arab Republic	1.4	2.3	3.0	2.2	2.1	2.8	x2.5	3.4	x1.5	x2.0
Former USSR/Anc. URSS			x10.3	x8.6	x8.9		x5.8			

TRADE BY COMMODITY IN THOUSAND U.S. DOLLARS – COMMERCE PAR PRODUIT EN MILLIERS DE DOLLARS E.U

COUNTRIES–PAYS	IMPORTS – IMPORTATIONS 1990	1991	1992	1993	1994
Total	3234273	3390673	3623703	3605613	3806871
Africa	x37563	44918	x44983	x43968	x45500
Northern Africa	17649	18896	x17010	x26393	x25861
Americas	323970	301177	334844	355264	391813
LAIA	25667	36102	51445	53927	68797
CACM	2896	3373	4060	x2957	x5181
Asia	770658	832266	823806	1100833	1046026
Middle East	51590	x46695	59076	x115095	x104152
Europe	2057504	2150487	2348807	2018826	2236001
EEC	1857814	1967222	2164384	1852106	2046549
EFTA	177491	161446	147319	135338	158306
Oceania	x28771	x27700	x30957	x29485	x32745
Japan/Japon	492111	509376	468427	445938	479721
Italy/Italie	465135	491659	473701	423580	477855
Germany/Allemagne	286335	369895	505929	451811	484384
Netherlands/Pays–Bas	336543	327709	366098	304217	311218
Belgium–Luxembourg	210437	217014	243422	216772	241032
USA/Etats–Unis d'Amer	206052	178618	193654	211641	231878
France,Monac	176404	186119	197630	149570	172503
Switz.Liecht	147949	136452	121751	112221	131787
Spain/Espagne	116804	120734	116788	86183	98163
Hong Kong	55497	61099	61307	78901	97833
Canada	70377	62679	65428	72960	71220
United Kingdom	82084	75436	65022	56886	82770
Korea, Republic of	39977	59018	57498	60909	73933
Denmark/Danemark	52382	49093	61179	50370	45274
Singapore/Singapour	27279	36627	46533	61256	77940
Bangladesh				122406	x5258
Indonesia/Indonésie	28747	40072	34235	36347	54263
Sweden/Suède	36208	41122	37705	29738	40396
Macau/Macao	9563	9841	10938	78893	16946
Austria/Autriche	27654	26660	31506	29997	30720
Finland/Finlande	30613	26206	24586	22179	25991
Norway,SVD,JM	28022	23651	24228	21844	25263
Australia/Australie	21227	19675	21325	22497	23956
Malaysia/Malaisie	9099	14512	18435	26883	35314
Mexico/Mexique	8621	12408	24780	18300	22663
Saudi Arabia	11109	9421	12826	x32214	x20333
Portugal	14680	14939	20488	15667	16282
Poland/Pologne	54	4944	17756	20271	23793
Ireland/Irlande	15088	13729	14881	9802	12910
Philippines	11473	13550	12837	11365	15140
Israel/Israël	9673	10631	13412	13695	15769
Hungary/Hongrie	x6820	16340	x12189	x9066	x6831
Kuwait/Koweït	10156	1073	8187	21523	26794
India/Inde	11014	7433	13509	9235	14526
Qatar	3912	3255	8264	17743	x590
Thailand/Thaïlande	2918	4761	9420	13032	15829
United Arab Emirates	7149	5072	6083	x12984	x16081
Venezuela	2831	6526	7469	10020	9009
Slovenia/Slovénia			11519	11369	12928
Libyan Arab Jamahiriya	7019	5221	x4552	x12836	x7029
Colombia/Colombie	7007	6792	6552	9257	14006
China/Chine	902	1292	8082	13125	20311
Lebanon/Liban	x3381	x8094	x5490	x8351	x18478
Cyprus/Chypre	6974	7677	8163	6052	6682
Argentina/Argentine	1937	4508	6168	8731	12705
Tunisia/Tunisie	6304	7173	5598	6339	8793
Malta/Malte	4887	6604	6301	6071	x7258
Czechoslovakia	5960	x9904	x9030		
Greece/Grèce	7446	6907	5451	5333	7051
Croatia/Croatie			9590	7597	x5181

COUNTRIES–PAYS	EXPORTS – EXPORTATIONS 1990	1991	1992	1993	1994
Totale	2553420	2706911	2964518	2936781	3206768
Afrique	121850	x95797	86214	79854	x89139
Afrique du Nord	x9004	16969	22598	16368	25389
Amériques	347905	373464	x390183	x411022	x411641
ALAI	80723	83968	68515	59275	66376
MCAC	2515	2292	2466	3524	2695
Asie	406617	450396	522154	612049	737986
Moyen–Orient	x25388	x22503	x29867	x59798	x88156
Europe	1647395	1700938	1859193	1659903	1863455
CEE	1486208	1549124	1669798	1501107	1683474
AELE	146636	141237	172912	142710	164517
Océanie	x7815	29273	x9492	x49575	x11666
Germany/Allemagne	296930	290759	320707	240069	262608
Italy/Italie	243251	253933	256861	265595	270326
France,Monac	245701	257507	269258	231658	261471
Belgium–Luxembourg	202485	210977	229639	223209	257048
USA/Etats–Unis d'Amer	165980	198341	211644	219273	228502
India/Inde	118710	119851	148469	154244	197210
Norway,SVD,JM	135907	130050	160601	124968	143305
Netherlands/Pays–Bas	84396	96277	108632	112398	121981
Spain/Espagne	104532	109062	108943	88966	112874
China/Chine	66867	92655	101700	108972	120893
Canada	83211	78345	78870	86154	95327
United Kingdom	45026	53789	82298	77357	91039
Thailand/Thaïlande	56644	63816	67647	80033	89923
Austria/Autriche	55448	57810	65024	65605	x84034
Portugal	59720	63369	68173	46940	48350
Sweden/Suède	60555	61418	61570	48178	59670
So. Africa Customs Un	95747	65498	52274	46794	49383
Indonesia/Indonésie	19379	32915	49970	73612	78024
Korea, Republic of	54150	50319	43738	39195	36570
Poland/Pologne	2087	29011	48523	49735	54847
Finland/Finlande	35882	37267	35574	36759	44906
Mexico/Mexique	17615	26784	35410	40906	50299
Japan/Japon	22047	27743	32319	39400	45262
Australia/Australie	7115	27042	7846	48546	11048
Brazil/Brésil	54771	49392	22420	6594	4447
Greece/Grèce	18011	22468	25710	27860	26591
Denmark/Danemark	17531	19590	18834	24417	28443
Bahamas	x8091	4845	x21144	x35564	x9704
Czech Republic				58875	26590
Malaysia/Malaisie	13700	15210	17364	17916	26446
Czechoslovakia		x13479	x36298		
Ireland/Irlande	16739	14898	18574	12094	14135
Switz.Liecht	10544	11091	12189	17582	20950
Morocco/Maroc	5358	11831	14040	11086	16585
Turkey/Turquie	10115	10163	10751	11699	13164
Zimbabwe	14683	9238	9458	11412	x5560
United Arab Emirates	3552	630	509	x25199	x47983
Saudi Arabia	4244	4989	6152	x13624	x10158
Hong Kong	4921	3522	5667	12184	25747
Philippines	5831	6778	6047	7555	8466
Iran (Islamic Rp. of)		x3576	x8872	x5680	x10462
Croatia/Croatie			8342	9459	x8140
Korea Dem People's Rp	x4805	x4760	x5401	x4713	x3367
Singapore/Singapour	2575	3767	5140	5836	8303
Bulgaria/Bulgarie	x9815	x3805	x4030	x4418	x2028
Hungary/Hongrie	x2987	x2722	x5539	x3185	x2914
Egypt/Egypte	1151	916	6563	3314	6923
Yugoslavia SFR	14292	x10552			
Pakistan	3553	3537	3883	2302	3228
Uruguay	3205	2748	3109	2879	3123

(VALUE AS % OF TOTAL)(VALEUR EN % DU TOTAL)

	1985	1986	1987	1988	1989	1990	1991	1992	1993	1994
Africa	2.3	2.1	x1.5	x1.7	x1.1	x1.2	1.3	x1.2	x1.2	x1.2
Northern Africa	1.4	1.2	0.7	0.4	0.5	0.5	0.6	x0.5	x0.7	x0.7
Americas	24.3	28.5	11.9	10.6	11.7	10.0	8.9	9.2	9.9	10.3
LAIA	1.4	0.7	0.9	1.0	0.8	0.8	1.1	1.4	1.5	1.8
CACM	0.2	0.1	0.1	0.1	0.1	0.1	0.1	0.1	x0.1	x0.1
Asia	20.1	16.6	x21.9	x24.4	24.5	23.8	24.5	22.7	30.5	27.5
Middle East	3.5	x2.6	x2.5	2.5	x1.9	1.6	x1.4	1.6	x3.2	x2.7
Europe	51.2	51.0	62.3	61.1	61.0	63.6	63.4	64.8	56.0	58.7
EEC	43.9	43.5	52.8	52.7	52.4	57.4	58.0	59.7	51.4	53.8
EFTA	7.0	7.0	8.9	7.9	7.9	5.5	4.8	4.1	3.8	4.2
Oceania	1.6	x1.2	x1.4	x1.2	x1.1	x0.8	x0.8	x0.8	x0.8	x0.9
Japan/Japon	9.7	8.9	12.3	14.3	16.0	15.2	15.0	12.9	12.4	12.6
Italy/Italie	10.8	9.4	11.8	13.4	13.8	14.4	14.5	13.1	11.7	12.6
Germany/Allemagne	7.9	8.3	9.2	9.1	8.6	8.9	10.9	14.0	12.5	12.7
Netherlands/Pays–Bas	8.7	9.3	10.9	9.6	9.1	10.4	9.7	10.1	8.4	8.2
Belgium–Luxembourg	4.2	4.6	5.6	5.8	5.8	6.5	6.4	6.7	6.0	6.3
USA/Etats–Unis d'Amer	19.3	25.0	7.9	6.7	8.1	6.4	5.3	5.3	5.9	6.1
France,Monac	4.7	4.5	5.5	5.1	4.9	5.5	5.5	5.5	4.1	4.5
Switz.Liecht	3.4	3.8	4.8	4.4	4.4	4.6	4.0	3.4	3.1	3.5
Spain/Espagne	1.5	1.6	2.3	2.5	3.0	3.6	3.6	3.2	2.4	2.6
Hong Kong	2.0	1.9	2.1	1.9	1.8	1.7	1.8	1.7	2.2	2.6

	1985	1986	1987	1988	1989	1990	1991	1992	1993	1994
Afrique	2.7	x2.9	x3.3	3.9	x4.2	4.7	x3.5	2.9	2.7	x2.7
Afrique du Nord	0.1	0.1	0.2	x0.2	0.3	x0.4	0.6	0.8	0.6	0.8
Amériques	16.7	12.7	11.5	12.7	14.3	13.7	13.8	x13.2	x14.0	x12.8
ALAI	5.6	3.0	2.8	3.4	3.1	3.2	3.1	2.3	2.0	2.1
MCAC	0.1	0.1	0.1	0.1	0.0	0.1	0.1	0.1	0.1	0.1
Asie	12.9	13.0	16.0	17.0	17.8	16.0	16.6	17.6	20.9	23.0
Moyen–Orient	1.2	x1.4	x0.9	2.7	x2.4	x1.0	x0.8	x1.0	x2.0	x2.7
Europe	66.0	70.0	65.7	63.5	62.2	64.5	62.8	62.7	56.5	58.1
CEE	55.4	59.0	55.4	53.2	52.2	58.2	57.2	56.3	51.1	52.5
AELE	9.9	10.6	9.8	9.7	9.5	5.7	5.2	5.8	4.9	5.1
Océanie	1.3	1.2	x0.7	x0.2	0.2	x0.3	1.1	x0.3	x1.7	x0.4
Germany/Allemagne	8.6	11.3	10.6	10.0	10.0	11.6	10.7	10.8	8.2	8.2
Italy/Italie	13.7	11.3	10.7	9.2	10.2	9.5	9.4	8.7	9.0	8.4
France,Monac	8.6	9.8	9.0	9.0	8.1	9.6	9.5	9.1	7.9	8.2
Belgium–Luxembourg	7.4	8.5	7.8	7.3	6.9	7.9	7.8	7.7	7.6	8.0
USA/Etats–Unis d'Amer	6.7	5.4	4.5	4.7	6.8	6.5	7.3	7.1	7.5	7.1
India/Inde	4.4	4.2	5.0	4.2	5.0	4.6	4.4	5.0	5.3	6.1
Norway,SVD,JM	3.2	3.8	3.7	3.6	3.8	5.3	4.8	5.4	4.3	4.5
Netherlands/Pays–Bas	3.0	3.4	3.2	3.5	3.1	3.3	3.6	3.7	3.8	3.8
Spain/Espagne	2.9	3.1	3.2	3.6	3.6	4.1	4.0	3.7	3.0	3.5
China/Chine			2.5	2.2	2.5	2.6	3.4	3.4	3.7	3.8

TRADE BY COMMODITY IN THOUSAND U.S. DOLLARS – COMMERCE PAR PRODUIT EN MILLIERS DE DOLLARS E.U

IMPORTS – IMPORTATIONS

COUNTRIES–PAYS	1990	1991	1992	1993	1994
Total	1665079	1848585	1323870	673006	826402
Africa	508594	438163	394411	215690	236617
Northern Africa	442057	400226	344757	188512	211911
Americas	444555	500746	280129	150761	184125
LAIA	175082	179891	95956	71939	96915
CACM	1028	1299	1349	x1582	1479
Asia	316392	438289	394045	169243	258188
Middle East	24492	41481	19792	21216	30480
Europe	276182	303552	199551	107059	120407
EEC	243708	282638	172310	90256	103664
EFTA	11142	9186	5624	7482	10911
Oceania	x45490	x18693	x20134	x14601	x16874
Morocco/Maroc	288239	252349	214443	115419	123060
USA/Etats–Unis d'Amer	255764	295983	173903	70734	82223
India/Inde	153384	125029	135066	72183	135838
Tunisia/Tunisie	137064	126209	101415	63818	81370
Brazil/Brésil	101663	117109	66431	53412	72147
Bangladesh		118284	111627	x30	x1619
United Kingdom		60022	37420	21744	20936
Belgium–Luxembourg	57693	56515	42493	13803	16991
France,Monac	72301	63569	28456	14465	11297
Korea, Republic of	51270	48329	39945	17391	20819
Indonesia/Indonésie	17692	39292	27539	13756	25088
Former USSR/Anc. URSS		x70503			
Czechoslovakia	25830	x49111	x18986		
Mexico/Mexique	49874	38362	16328	7377	11020
Israel/Israël	32310	22940	22503	15326	11418
So. Africa Customs Un	28853	23769	18820	14588	12197
Japan/Japon	18126	18841	19174	9654	10029
Italy/Italie	23536	24732	12430	5356	12303
Jordan/Jordanie	4455	24634	4670	9692	20477
Turkey/Turquie	18209	14805	13259	10651	8649
Romania/Roumanie	36218	21107	10360	7091	2465
Egypt/Egypte	7019	10527	21861	5020	3396
New Zealand	17162	11406	13986	11342	11422
Cuba	x9977	x21575	x6593	x4212	x2653
Netherlands/Pays–Bas	24751	15533	12408	3984	2197
Greece/Grèce	9754	20023	6621	4971	5349
Senegal/Sénégal	25773	1470	x21740	x7335	x9011
Thailand/Thaïlande	11369	12356	8894	8939	6971
Germany/Allemagne	17265	13674	8813	7051	9791
Russian Federation			x26291	x497	x31
Spain/Espagne	9689	8700	7574	7549	11901
Argentina/Argentine	9718	12648	5095	4662	6087
Algeria/Algérie	9715	11141	7012	3998	4032
Sweden/Suède	9298	6701	5907	5414	5797
Switz.Liecht	9733	8493	4878	3979	3966
Australia/Australie	27841	6876	6138	3184	5085
Croatia/Croatie			11359	3171	x2267
Austria/Autriche	7794	6133	5414	2179	1509
Yugoslavia SFR	21279	x11718			
Zimbabwe	3669	5379	2912	2147	x646
Chile/Chili	7157	4606	2900	2457	2895
Malaysia/Malaisie	1744	3300	3099	3010	2501
Yugoslavia/Yougoslavie			x5674	x3602	
Colombia/Colombie	3684	3599	3035	1943	2498
Bulgaria/Bulgarie	x7327	x5015	3291	x199	
Niger	x4547	x3206	x2358	x2126	x1053
Denmark/Danemark	6654	3412	2663	1450	1869
Pakistan	3130	1655	3493	2116	858
Slovenia/Slovénia			4576	2443	3497
Canada	2615	1897	2278	2164	706

EXPORTS – EXPORTATIONS

COUNTRIES–PAYS	1990	1991	1992	1993	1994
Totale	1492055	1305851	897781	x501908	x620185
Afrique	3640	x4287	2693	1542	x2387
Afrique du Nord	6	2	30	228	106
Amériques	792037	746807	452373	190602	x266726
ALAI	148086	151059	81489	28815	25249
MCAC	15	66		x14	53
Asie	x220209	x123696	x120828	x141651	x169452
Moyen–Orient	x176287	x77837	x90665	x118490	x143581
Europe	199126	164783	145574	89093	105973
CEE	192037	156878	143511	88680	105040
AELE	6079	7145	1978	355	868
Océanie	287	2674	456	668	1071
Canada	549536	488099	312897	129006	199106
Poland/Pologne	268315	256999	171678	77179	73431
Mexico/Mexique	146612	149501	80077	27343	23559
USA/Etats–Unis d'Amer	90957	107582	57982	32427	36429
Saudi Arabia	79683	40952	52309	x86283	x109732
Germany/Allemagne	82340	74842	65161	38800	39128
France,Monac	60974	40104	35470	23563	32895
Iran (Islamic Rp. of)		x31312	x33092	x19298	x16739
Japan/Japon	27884	25238	17262	12012	15974
Netherlands/Pays–Bas	15604	12271	13126	8342	7496
Finland/Finlande	10673	8707	8152	6743	8704
Italy/Italie	5963	5977	7506	6026	10463
Spain/Espagne	5327	7213	4932	2731	2820
China/Chine	7977	7719	5817	864	1576
Bhutan/Bhoutan		x7068	x4029		
United Arab Emirates	x13685			x9805	x10743
Qatar	4582	2728	4028	2070	x2367
So. Africa Customs Un	3607	4186	2601	1313	2170
Switz.Liecht	4926	5565	1978	334	641
Belgium–Luxembourg	4521	2026	3282	1251	709
Singapore/Singapour	5648	3463	560	1775	2722
United Kingdom	2499	1897	3002	469	1328
Sweden/Suède	3727	2712	1997	381	40
Korea, Republic of	1509	1358	1274	2309	3147
Former USSR/Anc. URSS	4571	x4916			
Australia/Australie	287	2674	452	668	693
Ukraine			x2892	x423	x1351
Hungary/Hongrie	x2999	x1031	x1430	x382	x313
Bahrain/Bahreïn	x430	x1001	x672	x952	x3132
Russian Federation			x932	x1372	x15773
Czechoslovakia		x626	x1671		
Peru/Pérou	548	593	565	920	1003
Iraq	x77584	x1594	x328		
Norway,SVD,JM	1153	1580		21	226
Uzbekistan/Ouzbékistan				x1564	x1578
Afghanistan	x54	x212	x584	x676	x9
Bangladesh				1371	
Bulgaria/Bulgarie	x48		x770	x391	x267
Turkmenistan/Turkménistn				x1150	x106
Colombia/Colombie	602	495	352	303	349
Kazakstan				x1084	x191
Greece/Grèce	62	642	376	47	58
Denmark/Danemark	230	345	341	247	239
Yugoslavia SFR	1010	x761			
Venezuela	100	128	420	82	42
Albania/Albanie	x794	x31	x309	x55	x5
Thailand/Thaïlande	446	171	82	92	120
Indonesia/Indonésie	15	177	144	6	24
Netherlands Antilles				x312	x1172
Bolivia/Bolivie	178	244	5		15

(VALUE AS % OF TOTAL)(VALEUR EN % DU TOTAL)

Imports

	1985	1986	1987	1988	1989	1990	1991	1992	1993	1994
Africa	21.1	25.8	23.1	27.4	18.8	30.5	23.7	29.8	32.1	28.7
Northern Africa	18.0	22.0	19.9	23.4	16.0	26.5	21.7	26.0	28.0	25.6
Americas	21.1	22.1	22.2	20.3	23.8	26.7	27.1	21.2	22.4	22.2
LAIA	10.4	12.5	13.3	10.9	10.2	10.5	9.7	7.2	10.7	11.7
CACM	0.0	0.1	0.1	0.1	0.0	0.1	0.1	0.1	x0.2	0.2
Asia	20.0	17.3	16.6	18.7	19.2	19.0	23.7	29.7	25.1	31.2
Middle East	2.7	3.2	2.8	2.9	1.6	1.5	2.2	1.5	3.2	3.7
Europe	31.0	28.0	21.9	20.3	x20.1	16.6	16.4	15.1	15.9	14.6
EEC	27.4	24.8	19.6	17.2	x16.9	14.6	15.3	13.0	13.4	12.5
EFTA	1.9	1.6	1.4	1.5	2.0	0.7	0.5	0.4	1.1	1.3
Oceania	4.0	3.2	2.4	x3.0	2.9	x2.7	x1.0	x1.5	x2.2	x2.0
Morocco/Maroc	11.4	12.7	12.1	15.2	6.4	17.3	13.7	16.2	17.1	14.9
USA/Etats–Unis d'Amer	10.6	7.8	7.8	9.0	12.4	15.4	16.0	13.1	10.5	9.9
India/Inde	9.2	8.0	6.7	7.8	9.6	9.2	6.8	10.2	10.7	16.4
Tunisia/Tunisie	4.4	8.0	6.3	6.7	7.6	8.2	6.8	7.7	9.5	9.8
Brazil/Brésil	8.6	9.2	7.5	6.4	7.1	6.1	6.3	5.0	7.9	8.7
Bangladesh	0.3	0.1	0.2	x0.1	x0.0		6.4	8.4	x0.0	x0.2
United Kingdom	6.7	5.9	4.6	4.2	x3.0		3.2	2.8	3.2	2.5
Belgium–Luxembourg	4.3	3.9	3.3	2.8	3.1	3.5	3.1	3.2	2.1	2.1
France,Monac	4.8	4.2	3.9	3.9	4.0	4.3	3.4	2.1	2.1	1.4
Korea, Republic of	4.0	3.7	2.8	2.8	3.3	3.1	2.6	3.0	2.6	2.5

Exports

	1985	1986	1987	1988	1989	1990	1991	1992	1993	1994
Afrique	0.4	0.1		x0.3	x0.3	0.2	x0.3	0.3	0.3	x0.3
Afrique du Nord	0.1	x0.0	0.0	x0.0	x0.0	0.0	0.0	0.0	0.0	0.0
Amériques	66.5	59.9	60.6	58.3	52.4	53.1	57.2	50.4	38.0	x43.0
ALAI	6.1	6.9	10.1	10.5	10.4	9.9	11.6	9.1	5.7	4.1
MCAC	0.0	x0.0	0.2	0.0	0.0	0.0	0.0	0.0	x0.0	0.0
Asie	1.1	x10.2	x6.6	x11.9	x13.6	x14.8	x9.4	x13.4	x28.2	x27.3
Moyen–Orient	0.1	x9.2	x4.9	x10.0	x11.0	x11.8	x6.0	x10.1	x23.6	x23.2
Europe	11.2	10.1	12.7	10.9	13.8	13.3	12.6	16.2	17.8	17.1
CEE	10.7	9.5	11.7	10.0	12.6	12.9	12.0	16.0	17.7	16.9
AELE	0.3	0.5	0.8	0.8	1.2	0.4	0.5	0.2	0.1	0.1
Océanie		x0.0	0.1				0.2	0.1	0.1	0.2
Canada	50.1	40.1	41.7	40.2	35.6	36.8	37.4	34.9	25.7	32.1
Poland/Pologne	20.7	19.4	19.1	17.4	19.3	18.0	19.7	19.1	15.4	11.8
Mexico/Mexique	6.0	6.7	9.9	10.4	10.3	9.8	11.4	8.9	5.4	3.8
USA/Etats–Unis d'Amer	10.2	12.9	8.5	7.5	6.3	6.1	8.2	6.5	6.5	5.9
Saudi Arabia	0.0	x4.7	x2.4	2.3	5.1	5.3	3.1	5.8	x17.2	x17.7
Germany/Allemagne	5.5	5.5	6.0	4.5	5.4	5.5	5.7	7.3	7.7	6.3
France,Monac	4.4	2.9	3.6	3.6	3.9	4.1	3.1	4.0	4.7	5.3
Iran (Islamic Rp. of)		x0.1	x0.8	x1.5	x2.8		x2.4	x3.7	x3.8	x2.7
Japan/Japon	0.9	0.5	0.8	0.9	1.6	1.9	1.9	1.9	2.4	2.6
Netherlands/Pays–Bas	0.1	0.2	0.8	0.6	1.1	1.0	0.9	1.5	1.7	1.2

TRADE BY COMMODITY IN THOUSAND U.S. DOLLARS – COMMERCE PAR PRODUIT EN MILLIERS DE DOLLARS E.U

COUNTRIES–PAYS	IMPORTS – IMPORTATIONS				
	1990	1991	1992	1993	1994
Total	1216804	1067069	1109763	1559366	1339727
Africa	23887	19170	20303	21519	x24881
Northern Africa	6148	5338	5265	5443	5032
Americas	225586	180635	180618	175475	176981
LAIA	15475	21960	15594	20207	22380
CACM	422	428	333	145	259
Asia	351595	340646	369853	452845	395821
Middle East	x14665	x13766	x14771	x10073	x11419
Europe	579923	495987	520822	894477	724766
EEC	499713	436101	448136	811895	644185
EFTA	77225	57820	70952	79345	79686
Oceania	x8506	x21022	x12195	x7920	x8701
United Kingdom	106125	57921	46525	434083	116208
USA/Etats–Unis d'Amer	193697	144144	151418	141118	138396
Japan/Japon	145936	145100	136409	129025	139292
Belgium–Luxembourg	108618	110090	131038	136711	199468
Germany/Allemagne	86551	89266	93463	69886	113591
Korea, Republic of	71949	80472	71095	72670	80035
Italy/Italie	87109	77288	77875	67702	79149
Switz.Liecht	75954	56935	69506	78113	78049
Singapore/Singapour	15372	5775	46983	144659	61994
Thailand/Thaïlande	40726	35942	32137	19343	9184
Hong Kong	14494	15970	26245	30972	32945
Israel/Israël	28222	20373	15298	21407	29791
France,Monac	21214	18352	18141	17516	18400
Spain/Espagne	18438	17897	17549	14315	16358
Netherlands/Pays–Bas	20263	15531	16189	11757	8607
Austria/Autriche	13603	13810	14252	14327	13172
Australia/Australie	7928	20613	11590	7058	7952
Canada	15075	13138	12822	13218	15341
So. Africa Customs Un	13857	10890	13569	14365	18042
Ireland/Irlande	9884	7201	6784	21479	51335
Brazil/Brésil	8314	14355	6966	13261	8869
China/Chine	6204	9389	15051	8694	6259
Greece/Grèce	8775	9310	8880	8477	9738
Portugal	6674	8459	8448	6725	7665
Sweden/Suède	9486	8359	6632	7248	8204
Iran (Islamic Rp. of)	x5923	x7030	x4360	x4617	x2808
Turkey/Turquie	3080	3440	3832	3493	2208
India/Inde	2284	2386	2282	5759	6171
Sri Lanka	6006	2913	4043	2540	3161
Mexico/Mexique	2668	2867	3339	2621	3113
Malaysia/Malaisie	2065	1696	2037	4587	12466
Tunisia/Tunisie	3127	2521	2801	2041	2192
Poland/Pologne	7965	3877	1408	1690	2240
Morocco/Maroc	1842	2071	1582	2074	1971
Denmark/Danemark	2038	1973	1822	1193	1580
Hungary/Hongrie	x2064	1497	x1613	x1442	x1092
Indonesia/Indonésie	1015	1345	1739	1140	414
Philippines	655	3402	333	435	752
Venezuela	1487	1548	1528	935	892
Mauritius/Maurice	3118	2002	823	1124	1165
Saudi Arabia	1294	1615	1891	x350	x2137
Norway,SVD,JM	1195	795	1388	1194	1604
Czechoslovakia	2248	x2231	x848		
Cyprus/Chypre	154	138	2767	133	2450
Chile/Chili	836	898	1064	926	820
Malta/Malte	268	261	383	2236	x354
Czech Republic				2814	2638
Romania/Roumanie	4130	1102	1065	388	1990
Bulgaria/Bulgarie	x10089	x691	1039	x667	x504
Argentina/Argentine	497	631	701	765	835

COUNTRIES–PAYS	EXPORTS – EXPORTATIONS				
	1990	1991	1992	1993	1994
Totale	978602	870959	1019884	813079	924178
Afrique	341043	242819	366737	x63038	x29775
Afrique du Nord	3613	957	970	24	58
Amériques	178341	199916	205990	x227703	x269164
ALAI	5397	6753	4501	1941	x2172
MCAC	282	154	169	29	16
Asie	93500	91879	118649	188220	216788
Moyen–Orient	15578	12652	13174	11603	11430
Europe	351352	319501	311583	316336	393267
CEE	280525	259449	236953	239896	309434
AELE	70744	59373	74352	76399	83809
Océanie	x2121	3669	x10550	12599	x8814
USA/Etats–Unis d'Amer	169199	189095	198029	222648	263804
Angola	242762	165270	270000	x1884	x1620
Belgium–Luxembourg	112453	92402	87951	84251	84424
Switz.Liecht	69717	58235	72966	75006	76870
Germany/Allemagne	36081	52560	52756	67200	121644
So. Africa Customs Un	53451	59102	58366	46017	
United Kingdom	79446	72279	55144	25732	50041
Singapore/Singapour	1657	2158	21345	86840	73778
Hong Kong	13861	20441	27963	23385	45315
Russian Federation			x12283	x32330	x64579
Netherlands/Pays–Bas	24049	16633	11514	14719	11627
Ghana	x14516	6655	24272	x10472	x23367
Turkey/Turquie	15346	12457	12949	11443	11204
China/Chine	14316	7606	15709	12490	14261
Italy/Italie	12826	12610	12299	10656	12413
Japan/Japon	12202	10872	11589	12319	14508
Indonesia/Indonésie	12483	15543	8809	9250	8666
Australia/Australie	1994	3642	10484	12543	8723
Ireland/Irlande	966	1129	1775	21967	8996
Greece/Grèce	8516	5248	9250	6714	8376
India/Inde	6224	5661	6375	8398	10279
Thailand/Thaïlande	8772	9752	1850	3855	5849
Sri Lanka	2732	2847	6259	4811	2103
Korea, Republic of	160	116	1869	11718	22393
Zaire/Zaïre	x10643	x7113	x3031	x3380	x2590
France,Monac	4110	4220	4752	4548	4712
Israel/Israël	5303	3976	2746	3208	7798
Zimbabwe	96	44	9195	377	x270
Canada	3141	3753	3268	2358	2563
Romania/Roumanie	3686	557	5196	3179	3830
Ukraine			x3907	x4452	x1346
Former USSR/Anc. URSS		x7724			
Ecuador/Equateur	2912	2697	2749	890	x1003
Mexico/Mexique	1674	3571	1385	533	491
Spain/Espagne	1257	1233	1005	3084	5330
Poland/Pologne	6190	4337	155	31	62
Iceland/Islande	983	1113	1364	1342	6926
Un. Rep. of Tanzania	x11786	x2482			x2
Hungary/Hongrie	x451	x281	x363	x1488	x2353
Tunisia/Tunisie	3604	900	966	11	52
Austria/Autriche	389	588	267	480	x1301
Liberia/Libéria	x5	x160	x523	x433	x348
Argentina/Argentine	424	432	302	333	327
Sweden/Suède	284	400	145	403	246
Central African Rep.	x189	x449	x229	x152	x16
Philippines	2	9	740	16	18
Bulgaria/Bulgarie	x1850	x225	x463	x38	x18
Yugoslavia SFR	83	x667			
Sierra Leone	x73	x287	x62	x86	x851
Czech Republic				430	98

(VALUE AS % OF TOTAL)(VALEUR EN % DU TOTAL)

	1985	1986	1987	1988	1989	1990	1991	1992	1993	1994
Africa	1.0	1.0	0.9	x1.4	1.3	1.9	1.8	1.8	1.4	x1.8
Northern Africa	0.8	0.5	0.5	0.4	0.3	0.5	0.5	0.5	0.3	0.4
Americas	22.0	18.8	16.3	14.6	16.3	18.6	16.9	16.3	11.3	13.2
LAIA	1.5	1.4	1.2	1.0	1.3	1.3	2.1	1.4	1.3	1.7
CACM	0.0	0.1	0.1	0.0	0.0	0.0	0.0	0.0	0.0	0.0
Asia	21.5	23.5	26.3	34.9	27.7	28.9	31.9	33.4	29.0	29.5
Middle East	0.5	x0.7	x0.8	x0.7	x0.7	x1.2	x1.3	x1.3	x0.6	x0.9
Europe	53.4	54.5	51.0	43.6	51.3	47.7	46.5	46.9	57.4	54.1
EEC	45.8	46.4	43.6	36.7	43.2	41.1	40.9	40.4	52.1	48.1
EFTA	7.2	7.6	7.0	6.6	7.8	6.3	5.4	6.4	5.1	5.9
Oceania	0.9	x0.9	x1.1	0.8	x0.8	x0.7	x2.0	x1.1	x0.5	x0.6
United Kingdom	6.5	7.3	6.5	11.4	11.1	8.7	5.4	4.2	27.8	8.7
USA/Etats–Unis d'Amer	18.8	15.9	13.0	12.1	13.7	15.9	13.5	13.6	9.0	10.3
Japan/Japon	13.0	13.2	12.8	11.0	12.5	12.0	13.6	12.3	8.3	10.4
Belgium–Luxembourg	13.1	11.6	12.6	7.6	9.5	8.9	10.3	11.8	8.8	14.9
Germany/Allemagne	7.6	7.8	7.4	5.5	7.2	7.1	8.4	8.4	4.5	8.5
Korea, Republic of	2.9	3.5	4.5	4.5	5.2	5.9	7.5	6.4	4.7	6.0
Italy/Italie	4.6	5.2	6.4	4.7	6.4	7.2	7.2	7.0	4.3	5.9
Switz.Liecht	5.3	5.7	4.9	4.8	5.8	6.2	5.3	6.3	5.0	5.8
Singapore/Singapour	0.2	0.2	0.1	0.2	0.6	1.3	0.5	4.2	9.3	4.6
Thailand/Thaïlande	0.1	0.1	0.3	13.4	3.8	3.3	3.4	2.9	1.2	0.7

	1985	1986	1987	1988	1989	1990	1991	1992	1993	1994
Afrique	4.0	x3.9	x3.5	x26.3	x10.4	34.9	27.9	35.9	x7.8	x3.2
Afrique du Nord	0.0	x0.0	x0.0	x0.0	x0.0	0.4	0.1	0.1	0.0	0.0
Amériques	29.3	x28.3	x23.4	18.1	x24.7	18.2	22.9	20.2	x28.0	x29.1
ALAI	0.0	x0.3	0.6	0.6	0.8	0.6	0.8	0.4	0.2	x0.2
MCAC	0.0	0.0	0.1	0.0	0.0	0.0	0.0	0.0	0.0	0.0
Asie	3.0	x4.3	9.5	12.3	16.2	9.6	10.5	11.6	23.1	23.4
Moyen–Orient	0.4	x0.7	3.2	1.7	2.2	1.6	1.5	1.3	1.4	1.2
Europe	62.7	61.1	59.0	36.3	45.0	35.9	36.7	30.6	38.9	42.6
CEE	53.1	51.3	51.5	31.0	36.6	28.7	29.8	23.2	29.5	33.5
AELE	9.6	9.8	7.5	5.3	8.4	7.2	6.8	7.3	9.4	9.1
Océanie	0.9	x1.5	x0.4	x3.3	0.5	x0.2	0.4	x1.0	1.5	x1.0
USA/Etats–Unis d'Amer	29.0	27.8	22.3	16.6	23.1	17.3	21.7	19.4	27.4	28.5
Angola				x0.0		24.8	19.0	26.5	x0.2	x0.2
Belgium–Luxembourg	19.1	16.2	12.8	9.5	15.9	11.5	10.6	8.6	10.4	9.1
Switz.Liecht	9.2	9.4	6.8	5.0	8.1	7.1	6.7	7.2	9.2	8.3
Germany/Allemagne	5.5	5.4	4.7	3.4	5.3	3.7	6.0	5.2	8.3	13.2
So. Africa Customs Un	2.8	0.5	0.5	22.7	6.7	5.5	6.8	5.7	5.7	
United Kingdom	5.4	5.2	13.8	4.2	8.6	8.1	8.3	5.4	3.2	5.4
Singapore/Singapour	0.1	0.1	0.1	0.1	1.7	0.2	0.2	2.1	10.7	8.0
Hong Kong	0.5	1.0	0.9	0.6	2.0	1.4	2.3	2.7	2.9	4.9
Russian Federation								x1.2	x4.0	x7.0

TRADE BY COMMODITY IN THOUSAND U.S. DOLLARS – COMMERCE PAR PRODUIT EN MILLIERS DE DOLLARS E.U

COUNTRIES–PAYS	IMPORTS – IMPORTATIONS 1990	1991	1992	1993	1994
Total	7942880	7182089	7253853	6933372	7568054
Africa	x258377	x258328	x238523	x217720	x193685
Northern Africa	91983	84491	92877	82533	88873
Americas	1254375	1096035	1098022	1259900	1404015
LAIA	258780	302765	312586	326078	335077
CACM	19483	14591	19321	x15634	x12026
Asia	1980605	2019665	1991993	1983000	2113248
Middle East	x183703	x134841	x148470	x125955	x116928
Europe	3785539	3547031	3729443	3234334	3608776
EEC	3513274	3336249	3466875	2973041	3368837
EFTA	184761	177947	183762	171422	183444
Oceania	x48509	x50354	x54268	x53699	x67439
Japan/Japon	1077373	1116675	1016106	1016988	1057656
Germany/Allemagne	793177	774058	838572	635224	707900
USA/Etats–Unis d'Amer	708922	553511	542534	696788	803132
Italy/Italie	503144	495387	488678	414359	443468
France,Monac	410985	424957	414056	364011	411418
United Kingdom	392980	287589	295672	277048	317406
Belgium–Luxembourg	274426	261660	285057	258475	317914
Netherlands/Pays–Bas	252988	251038	263312	240274	275764
Korea, Republic of	191564	226691	236488	240224	255536
Finland/Finlande	209521	196151	204999	207223	237617
Canada	229492	195781	196960	200704	231133
Sweden/Suède	173382	168430	171208	158833	174087
Spain/Espagne	184014	170707	166342	136978	156065
Austria/Autriche	152010	146055	179596	142460	164947
Mexico/Mexique	102180	118284	127572	119801	130414
Thailand/Thaïlande	85696	107588	109478	119647	130692
Norway,SVD,JM	104106	103962	109544	104850	114648
Indonesia/Indonésie	98926	91268	101476	111345	127027
India/Inde	99821	86118	83336	71887	93841
Malaysia/Malaisie	65927	69773	81674	80879	82336
Switz.Liecht	70458	64547	65951	58941	58951
Venezuela	43340	57144	51194	50052	42823
Denmark/Danemark	52042	51166	52260	47497	61774
So. Africa Customs Un	50820	48490	43799	49674	43972
Poland/Pologne	47888	29873	56915	54882	66039
Portugal	48710	46661	51239	39969	44284
Singapore/Singapour	38394	38822	46516	44574	45969
Brazil/Brésil	36028	32641	37106	50397	50442
Turkey/Turquie	37811	40974	38800	40287	44355
Philippines	28304	42803	36598	39351	58075
Hong Kong	34853	32573	39352	41649	41643
Ukraine			x21990	x79509	x6337
Nigeria/Nigéria	x41445	43343	x39467	x18404	x10726
Colombia/Colombie	25517	26153	32745	40071	38073
Ireland/Irlande	32237	32596	30438	28535	36515
Hungary/Hongrie	x31259	35576	x22482	x32111	x23878
Czechoslovakia	45050	x57044	x32249		
Australia/Australie	27831	27431	29604	30714	42355
Greece/Grèce	33655	29793	25446	22154	19677
Israel/Israël	27532	27454	23069	21780	24608
Romania/Roumanie	42672	29551	19944	20654	22178
Saudi Arabia	19706	26366	23590	x19067	x21847
Argentina/Argentine	17635	23391	21695	23722	24564
Chile/Chili	16173	21054	24062	22030	23322
China/Chine	8345	13332	25443	27840	40312
Iran (Islamic Rp. of)	x73361	x19539	x25862	x21105	x7345
Tunisia/Tunisie	21015	18126	22023	23489	20493
Slovenia/Slovénia			37797	24808	31850
Egypt/Egypte	25700	20626	25135	16844	24811
Algeria/Algérie	23747	21034	19201	18695	20330

COUNTRIES–PAYS	EXPORTS – EXPORTATIONS 1990	1991	1992	1993	1994
Totale	7611474	6043521	5977597	6150121	5982305
Afrique	503416	x462620	371292	390974	x239221
Afrique du Nord	43904	47301	40869	32963	37347
Amériques	1751159	1763167	1712697	x1730155	x1903540
ALAI	268734	262704	259056	299824	347495
MCAC	1598	1585	3363	2658	2952
Asie	1058751	1022369	1053056	1062590	1135293
Moyen–Orient	228004	212513	209396	189670	206424
Europe	2507073	2430676	2508374	2289257	2479450
CEE	2399999	2332030	2391159	2175780	2351027
AELE	98148	92738	106586	104850	120961
Océanie	x154889	x188015	x205061	x525014	x92511
USA/Etats–Unis d'Amer	888762	937995	963195	934328	1024570
Germany/Allemagne	521154	525263	567142	462129	503885
United Kingdom	530568	513306	494879	521081	500027
Canada	548219	519828	431746	417746	449726
China/Chine	414749	385579	427972	451757	529922
Australia/Australie	144787	175115	191294	509069	76361
France,Monac	309524	296244	306165	270555	312543
Netherlands/Pays–Bas	262511	277632	280911	224955	272511
So. Africa Customs Un	320966	256785	209283	234609	109687
Turkey/Turquie	215981	204405	193936	178111	189811
Belgium–Luxembourg	181315	175255	177557	175417	184450
Spain/Espagne	151082	150827	168895	149433	168870
Mexico/Mexique	153029	154356	134402	123186	164637
Japan/Japon	107387	123577	125380	124346	124348
Austria/Autriche	125422	113389	117500	100842	x119262
Brazil/Brésil	86744	84430	95323	128192	121467
Italy/Italie	114072	104772	105575	82923	99161
Norway,SVD,JM	81023	77483	89478	86683	101743
Greece/Grèce	81379	65121	57957	58770	68788
Zimbabwe	72117	55894	63856	61967	x56470
Korea Dem People's Rp	x68833	x62096	x54572	x41365	x19312
Denmark/Danemark	56941	50983	54032	51812	58696
Czechoslovakia		x67270	x76647		
Korea, Republic of	48737	45569	40512	44315	50500
Russian Federation			x52973	x63329	x52887
Bahamas	x22307	20112	x34880	x60241	x26065
Hong Kong	28620	31482	34170	44693	40659
India/Inde	50292	45176	30409	31833	41324
Finland/Finlande	29916	29724	31863	34613	39571
Thailand/Thaïlande	29503	27483	30432	33643	31840
Kenya	24641	32392	24716	31628	x6786
Singapore/Singapour	21669	27018	26002	34900	26811
Morocco/Maroc	31240	33974	27082	19803	23844
Israel/Israël	28556	26368	24578	21960	20163
Former USSR/Anc. URSS	1503380	x66350			
Czech Republic				56151	45982
Sweden/Suède	22427	19611	20774	15178	19172
Indonesia/Indonésie	11537	16341	17685	19055	18794
Poland/Pologne	11785	8892	12163	23317	28336
New Zealand	10076	12371	13059	14426	16139
Romania/Roumanie	20438	14625	13195	10857	10251
Bulgaria/Bulgarie	x66327	x8479	x14143	x15862	x9923
Senegal/Sénégal	12952	11898	x15209	11230	x10049
Ireland/Irlande	7720	7284	5020	25703	1686
Slovakia				x37500	x30948
Un. Rep. of Tanzania	x2589	x34788	x53	x28	
Chile/Chili	17444	10667	10198	13342	31886
Switz.Liecht	8524	7669	10072	11857	11256
Ukraine			x4845	x24305	x15951
Madagascar	17411	11025	8908	8035	12614

(VALUE AS % OF TOTAL)(VALEUR EN % DU TOTAL)

	1985	1986	1987	1988	1989	1990	1991	1992	1993	1994
Africa	3.9	x2.9	x3.0	x2.8	x2.7	x3.2	x3.6	x3.3	x3.1	x2.6
Northern Africa	1.4	0.8	0.9	1.0	1.0	1.2	1.2	1.3	1.2	1.2
Americas	19.0	14.6	14.0	13.9	15.4	15.8	15.2	15.1	18.1	18.6
LAIA	7.2	4.4	4.3	3.9	3.4	3.3	4.2	4.3	4.7	4.4
CACM	0.3	0.3	x0.2	0.2	0.2	0.2	0.2	0.3	x0.2	x0.2
Asia	21.5	19.5	x19.6	x22.2	23.3	24.9	28.1	27.4	28.6	27.9
Middle East	1.4	x1.4	x1.2	x1.3	x1.6	x2.3	x1.9	x2.0	x1.8	x1.5
Europe	45.7	50.1	50.9	51.3	49.7	47.7	49.4	51.4	46.6	47.7
EEC	36.3	40.3	40.6	40.7	40.2	44.2	46.5	47.8	42.9	44.5
EFTA	7.8	8.5	8.9	9.3	8.3	2.3	2.5	2.5	2.5	2.4
Oceania	0.9	x0.8	x0.7	x0.7	0.7	x0.6	x0.7	x0.7	x0.8	x0.9
Japan/Japon	13.1	11.5	10.8	12.0	13.1	13.6	15.5	14.0	14.7	14.0
Germany/Allemagne	9.0	10.6	9.9	9.4	9.5	10.0	10.8	11.6	9.2	9.4
USA/Etats–Unis d'Amer	8.7	6.9	6.1	6.6	8.5	8.9	7.7	7.5	10.0	10.6
Italy/Italie	4.8	5.2	5.5	5.4	5.4	6.3	6.9	6.7	6.0	5.9
France,Monac	4.5	4.8	5.0	5.1	4.8	5.2	5.9	5.7	5.3	5.4
United Kingdom	3.6	3.7	3.7	3.9	4.6	4.9	4.0	4.1	4.0	4.2
Belgium–Luxembourg	2.6	3.0	3.2	3.4	3.1	3.5	3.6	3.9	3.7	4.2
Netherlands/Pays–Bas	2.6	2.8	3.0	3.0	2.8	3.2	3.5	3.6	3.5	3.6
Korea, Republic of	1.6	1.9	1.9	2.1	2.3	2.4	3.2	3.3	3.5	3.4
Finland/Finlande	1.7	2.0	2.4	2.6	2.4	2.6	2.7	2.8	3.0	3.1

	1985	1986	1987	1988	1989	1990	1991	1992	1993	1994
Afrique	7.2	6.6	x5.6	x6.2	x6.9	6.6	x7.6	6.2	6.3	x4.0
Afrique du Nord	0.6	0.5	0.5	0.5	0.6	0.6	0.8	0.7	0.5	0.6
Amériques	29.1	25.9	22.9	21.9	23.6	23.0	29.2	28.6	x28.1	x31.8
ALAI	6.9	4.8	3.5	3.3	3.5	3.5	4.3	4.3	4.9	5.8
MCAC	0.1	0.1	0.0	0.0	0.0	0.0	0.0	0.1	0.0	0.0
Asie	12.4	10.8	12.6	14.1	14.0	13.9	16.9	17.6	17.3	19.0
Moyen–Orient	4.0	3.6	3.4	3.6	3.4	3.0	3.5	3.5	3.1	3.5
Europe	31.2	33.1	33.3	31.1	31.5	32.9	40.2	42.0	37.2	41.4
CEE	28.5	30.2	30.3	28.2	28.5	31.5	38.6	40.0	35.4	39.3
AELE	2.5	2.8	2.9	2.8	2.8	1.3	1.5	1.8	1.7	2.0
Océanie	1.8	x1.6	x1.0	x1.7	x1.8	x2.0	x3.1	x3.4	x8.5	x1.5
USA/Etats–Unis d'Amer	10.7	10.4	10.5	10.0	10.6	11.7	15.5	16.1	15.2	17.1
Germany/Allemagne	4.8	5.5	5.7	5.3	5.8	6.8	8.7	9.5	7.5	8.4
United Kingdom	6.5	6.5	7.0	6.9	6.4	7.0	8.5	8.3	8.5	8.4
Canada	11.0	9.8	8.2	8.2	8.8	7.2	8.6	7.2	6.8	7.5
China/Chine	3.0	2.7	4.6	4.9	5.6	5.4	6.4	7.2	7.3	8.9
Australia/Australie	1.7	1.6	0.9	1.6	1.7	1.9	2.9	3.2	8.3	1.3
France,Monac	3.5	3.8	3.7	3.6	3.3	4.1	4.9	5.1	4.4	5.2
Netherlands/Pays–Bas	3.6	3.8	3.8	3.1	3.0	3.4	4.6	4.7	3.7	4.6
So. Africa Customs Un	4.7	4.0	3.1	3.3	5.0	4.2	4.2	3.5	3.8	1.8
Turkey/Turquie	3.8	3.4	3.1	3.4	3.2	2.8	3.4	3.2	2.9	3.2

TRADE BY COMMODITY IN THOUSAND U.S. DOLLARS – COMMERCE PAR PRODUIT EN MILLIERS DE DOLLARS E.U

COUNTRIES–PAYS	IMPORTS – IMPORTATIONS 1990	1991	1992	1993	1994
Total	10584770	11252551	10562434	9991067	10356396
Africa	65336	85712	x132684	x101159	x109739
Northern Africa	57015	74599	x121456	x97167	x107729
Americas	968287	807597	814271	766955	928073
LAIA	131025	119081	146522	114228	123197
CACM	8			5	x1
Asia	4808394	5662736	5324989	5388506	5241620
Middle East	206639	x300424	x278923	x263967	x242534
Europe	4221947	4157193	3962494	3225862	3532169
EEC	4178781	4148410	3956029	3208602	3529748
EFTA	2205	2634	4859	17101	2252
Oceania	47536	43951	51469	47323	x51442
Japan/Japon	3374087	3640499	3192779	3033994	2904132
Germany/Allemagne	1473773	1455487	1425650	1018646	1249529
Korea, Republic of	560385	828420	880078	887528	796904
China/Chine	394135	565859	766282	926981	1025483
United Kingdom	591361	512707	478498	443609	421449
France,Monac	511967	522875	490925	414752	462920
USA/Etats–Unis d'Amer	645638	492287	449386	468073	581981
Italy/Italie	466437	502304	433649	401292	377738
Belgium–Luxembourg	484804	499309	473726	340028	395834
Spain/Espagne	206987	233176	204615	173092	185288
Poland/Pologne	96736	196293	188204	191578	192547
Canada	146616	159769	184790	169261	164608
Netherlands/Pays–Bas	174087	160979	171249	172092	176965
Austria/Autriche	152932	134841	147731	122763	136376
Argentina/Argentine	126487	99730	138704	110082	117583
Indonesia/Indonésie	109290	102697	119136	111551	84818
Romania/Roumanie	153060	188680	47969	90876	128530
Finland/Finlande	89988	92405	97422	84979	90366
Saudi Arabia	84398	67292	108777	x69309	x82276
Turkey/Turquie	69673	101615	73924	57002	46608
Iran (Islamic Rp. of)		x88458	x44247	x91897	x52409
Egypt/Egypte	54529	72106	78099	49572	44683
Malaysia/Malaisie	58689	51934	32388	77489	53290
Pakistan	36887	53642	47737	55938	49392
Czech Republic				148938	155608
Australia/Australie	47522	43946	51443	47318	51426
Philippines	1201	89468	1959		95
Libyan Arab Jamahiriya	281	135	x40748	x44583	x60408
Trinidad and Tobago	44544	36427	33555	15280	55090
Czechoslovakia	167243	x56034	x25942		
Qatar	36303	32586	32315	9168	x16198
Hungary/Hongrie	x33018	53814			
Bahrain/Bahreïn	x13690	x10459	x17806	x28265	x34614
Portugal	14887	16826	16986	17084	16721
Sweden/Suède	10091	15689	13673	17980	12774
Bulgaria/Bulgarie			10114	29789	16593
Korea Dem People's Rp	x41618	x24508		x15331	x13231
India/Inde	6342	4641	5126	13964	68168
Nigeria/Nigéria	x3711	10997	x10313	x2131	x168
Norway,SVD,JM	943	1147	3609	15750	375
Paraguay	1460	4681	3588	2852	1398
Mexico/Mexique	157	4105	3833	697	2236
Brazil/Brésil	2342	6912	145	48	590
Tunisia/Tunisie	2205	2275	2153	2052	2550
Yugoslavia SFR	40958	x6140			
United Arab Emirates	1453	12	530	x5277	x10343
Denmark/Danemark	1109	1005	1181	1585	2480
Venezuela	65	2217	139	450	578
Iceland/Islande	933	917	790	968	797
Jordan/Jordanie	19		776	1748	

COUNTRIES–PAYS	EXPORTS – EXPORTATIONS 1990	1991	1992	1993	1994
Totale	7652768	8515726	7231998	6814150	6885069
Afrique	x590730	x572984	x514079	x467671	x475655
Afrique du Nord	1679	3917	3998	3542	2034
Amériques	3765990	4117449	3619361	3243710	3520092
ALAI	2919473	3158317	2766383	2454091	2669737
MCAC					1
Asie	614799	714055	480147	471945	453310
Moyen–Orient	x7173	x6470	x8562	x8894	x23768
Europe	579079	523151	589092	634529	496866
CEE	513255	458714	522144	566269	439432
AELE	62086	63914	66820	68213	54209
Océanie	1457082	x2195673	x2016159	x1980223	x1934659
Brazil/Brésil	2406931	2599533	2381352	2256905	2293992
Australia/Australie	1446593	2154095	1979979	1966333	1890029
Canada	722429	777732	665416	621932	687551
India/Inde	578179	583384	425923	437932	413270
Sweden/Suède	453137	390571	461036	421960	387511
Ukraine			x300507	x559051	x303189
So. Africa Customs Un	298891	293529	273009	283751	257407
Mauritania/Mauritanie	x255702	x255522	x215432	x173915	x216214
Venezuela	325714	353061	227956	0	139072
USA/Etats–Unis d'Amer	124088	181132	186869	167687	162718
Chile/Chili	138434	158072	137598	114732	125827
Former USSR/Anc. URSS	642262	x391644			
Russian Federation			x163619	x214239	x212355
Norway,SVD,JM	62077	63899	66819	68213	54207
Peru/Pérou	47522	43822	17354	81175	108812
Netherlands/Pays–Bas	5396	4853	2964	98006	3107
Korea Dem People's Rp	x27901	x43854	x32321	x19934	x5515
France,Monac	31076	29626	28791	25540	23610
Philippines	956	78491	396	525	454
Spain/Espagne	18724	27810	23934	16457	14243
New Caledonia		x26465	x20867		x28743
New Zealand	10489	11294	15314	13876	14497
Liberia/Libéria	x28838	x13622	x16329	x4553	
Bahrain/Bahreïn	x4907	x2899	x5631	x8816	x23753
Slovakia				x13615	x2681
Poland/Pologne			9657	2451	1720
Kazakstan			x8144	x3215	x3422
Mozambique	x3032	x4636	x5211		
Morocco/Maroc	1431	3386	2999	2730	1180
Germany/Allemagne	755	2657	2636	2228	1915
Mexico/Mexique	85	3062	1445	708	1999
Malaysia/Malaisie	276	240	3871	681	90
Belgium–Luxembourg	2471	1613	1397	745	2441
Lebanon/Liban	x2186	x3398	x332		
Czechoslovakia			x3253		
Nauru		x2632		x14	
Iran (Islamic Rp. of)		x9	x2527		
Italy/Italie	987	965	708	288	518
Bolivia/Bolivie	787	702	634	570	35
United Kingdom	526	414	539	788	510
Gabon		x1694			
Algeria/Algérie	53	267	706	533	574
Congo				x1341	
Afghanistan		x1288			
Samoa		x1188			x1391
Bulgaria/Bulgarie	x2827	x769	249		
China/Chine	107	165	727	36	104
Tunisia/Tunisie	130	264	292	280	280
Bahamas			x692		
Nigeria/Nigéria		37		x569	

(VALUE AS % OF TOTAL)(VALEUR EN % DU TOTAL)

	1985	1986	1987	1988	1989	1990	1991	1992	1993	1994
Africa	0.2	x0.1	x0.3	0.5	x0.4	0.6	0.8	x1.3	x1.0	x1.1
Northern Africa	0.0	0.1	0.3	0.5	0.3	0.5	0.7	x1.1	x1.0	x1.0
Americas	10.5	10.5	9.5	9.9	9.8	9.2	7.2	7.7	7.7	9.0
LAIA	0.9	1.4	1.2	1.3	1.4	1.2	1.1	1.4	1.1	1.2
CACM	0.0	0.0	0.0	x0.0	x0.0	0.0			0.0	x0.0
Asia	44.6	43.8	42.9	42.8	43.7	45.4	50.4	50.4	54.0	50.7
Middle East	1.1	x1.8	x1.5	1.5	2.2	2.0	x2.7	x2.6	x2.6	x2.3
Europe	38.4	38.8	38.1	39.0	40.6	39.9	36.9	37.5	32.3	34.1
EEC	35.9	36.7	35.7	36.0	37.6	39.5	36.9	37.5	32.1	34.1
EFTA	1.8	1.8	2.0	2.3	2.3	0.0	0.0	0.0	0.2	0.0
Oceania				0.1	0.3	0.4	0.4	0.5	0.5	x0.5
Japan/Japon	35.6	32.6	31.1	31.4	31.4	31.9	32.4	30.2	30.4	28.0
Germany/Allemagne	13.1	15.0	13.3	12.9	13.3	13.9	12.9	13.5	10.2	12.1
Korea, Republic of	3.7	3.5	4.7	4.7	4.9	5.3	7.4	8.3	8.9	7.7
China/Chine	2.8	4.0	3.2	2.9	3.3	3.7	5.0	7.3	9.3	9.9
United Kingdom	4.4	4.1	5.2	5.2	5.0	5.6	4.6	4.5	4.4	4.1
France,Monac	4.2	4.1	3.6	4.2	4.7	4.8	4.6	4.6	4.2	4.5
USA/Etats–Unis d'Amer	6.5	6.4	5.7	6.3	6.1	6.1	4.4	4.3	4.7	5.6
Italy/Italie	4.8	4.6	4.2	3.9	4.6	4.4	4.5	4.1	4.0	3.6
Belgium–Luxembourg	4.0	4.0	4.1	4.3	4.1	4.6	4.4	4.5	3.4	3.8
Spain/Espagne	1.5	1.2	1.5	1.6	1.9	2.0	2.1	1.9	1.7	1.8

	1985	1986	1987	1988	1989	1990	1991	1992	1993	1994
Afrique	7.0	x8.3	x7.9	x8.2	x6.9	x7.7	x6.7	x7.1	x6.9	x6.9
Afrique du Nord	0.0	x0.1	0.0	0.0	x0.1	0.0	0.0	0.1	0.1	0.0
Amériques	43.9	42.6	43.3	49.0	49.9	49.2	48.4	50.1	47.6	51.1
ALAI	27.3	27.9	29.4	33.9	35.9	38.1	37.1	38.3	36.0	38.8
MCAC	0.0	0.0	x0.0	x0.0		0.0			0.0	0.0
Asie	7.3	6.9	6.8	7.9	x8.0	8.0	8.4	6.6	6.9	6.6
Moyen–Orient	0.0	x0.6	x0.0	x0.0	x0.0	x0.1	x0.1	x0.1	x0.1	x0.3
Europe	12.3	11.7	11.7	13.2	12.6	7.6	6.1	8.1	9.3	7.2
CEE	6.1	5.8	5.8	6.8	6.3	6.7	5.4	7.2	8.3	6.4
AELE	6.2	5.9	5.8	6.4	6.3	0.8	0.8	0.9	1.0	0.8
Océanie	21.6	19.2	18.0	x10.2	x14.0	19.0	x25.8	x27.9	x29.1	x28.1
Brazil/Brésil	25.1	23.5	24.2	28.9	30.3	31.5	30.5	32.9	33.1	33.3
Australia/Australie	21.3	18.9	17.7	10.0	13.8	18.9	25.3	27.4	28.9	27.5
Canada	13.0	11.6	10.9	12.1	10.8	9.4	9.1	9.2	9.1	10.0
India/Inde	7.2	6.3	6.4	7.1	7.8	7.6	6.9	5.9	6.4	6.0
Sweden/Suède	5.4	5.1	5.0	5.7	5.6	5.9	4.6	6.4	6.2	5.6
Ukraine								x4.2	x8.2	x4.4
So. Africa Customs Un	2.9	2.4	2.1	2.6	3.1	3.9	3.4	3.8	4.2	3.7
Mauritania/Mauritanie		x2.1	x2.4	x2.2	x3.0	x3.3	x3.0	x3.0	x2.6	x3.1
Venezuela		x2.9	x3.0	3.1	3.9	4.3	4.1	3.2	0.0	2.0
USA/Etats–Unis d'Amer	3.6	3.0	3.0	3.0	2.6	1.6	2.1	2.6	2.5	2.4

TRADE BY COMMODITY IN THOUSAND U.S. DOLLARS – COMMERCE PAR PRODUIT EN MILLIERS DE DOLLARS E.U

COUNTRIES–PAYS	IMPORTS – IMPORTATIONS 1990	1991	1992	1993	1994
Total	6106513	5270690	5240895	6737788	7536724
Africa	32648	17531	17292	x24731	x18618
Northern Africa	30394	17032	14812	18354	15663
Americas	400621	320758	384267	486918	612338
LAIA	124964	93011	134084	158717	190854
CACM	5305	2759	3088	4602	3502
Asia	2868760	2460385	2452119	3540392	3343629
Middle East	578037	646235	584813	839044	855634
Europe	2795241	2452634	2354159	2646527	3537274
EEC	2715368	2412860	2271965	2553568	3447379
EFTA	22122	36358	45179	69434	43224
Oceania	1315	1064	x959	x13784	x6264
Italy/Italie	848180	704874	673875	714214	908690
Turkey/Turquie	520732	578234	561080	819657	848850
Korea, Republic of	639276	617857	457790	775724	846833
Spain/Espagne	654778	551105	544083	537689	750123
India/Inde	547169	268065	517629	223901	428406
Belgium–Luxembourg	369205	294450	338114	319082	521208
Netherlands/Pays–Bas	190546	255907	221878	407642	424544
Japan/Japon	327318	290595	162405	252339	272492
Thailand/Thaïlande	325746	126635	200169	361464	256758
Indonesia/Indonésie	176969	167884	156164	292153	175255
China/Chine	29128	33165	142287	422408	273027
Germany/Allemagne	203078	167675	151352	147591	223761
Malaysia/Malaisie	117684	153549	91049	219242	143760
USA/Etats–Unis d'Amer	169605	136964	126152	158618	214269
Sweden/Suède	126255	120312	129393	132647	186887
Canada	98997	86234	119672	163703	202557
France, Monac	151106	122011	114127	114728	186512
Mexico/Mexique	81005	64012	78481	103230	112217
Pakistan	68549	86447	81554	51139	28632
Greece/Grèce	77491	118590	30113	44074	44127
Hong Kong	15983	27554	32718	64343	38295
Switz.Liecht	19484	26248	32892	43784	18047
Ireland/Irlande	28712	22600	15622	49440	28085
Austria/Autriche	13436	8673	20052	42800	55335
Saudi Arabia	50015	57898	2470	x2001	x731
Singapore/Singapour	31219	18865	16920	20858	17063
Slovenia/Slovénia			30876	22886	46618
Colombia/Colombie	8802	11938	19283	21311	22997
Brazil/Brésil	17629	10253	23734	16700	29895
Norway, SVD, JM	2600	10109	12276	25631	25176
Egypt/Egypte	29607	16238	14229	16884	15365
United Kingdom	24985	23246	13861	7718	43277
Philippines	10358	21219	7367	8936	5023
Finland/Finlande	8589	6204	10888	19307	53330
Czechoslovakia	764	x15421	x17616		
Denmark/Danemark	9019	10968	6532	13143	16734
United Arab Emirates	2620	2932	5942	x10795	x5150
Hungary/Hongrie	x334	1843	x14264	x3205	
Syrian Arab Republic	2075	x4725	12295	x1349	x431
Czech Republic				15850	13387
Venezuela	6228	256	5325	9881	19660
Peru/Pérou	9002	4437	4532	6449	5546
New Zealand	122	18	22	12653	1813
Portugal	9988	6244	2076	3492	4767
Belarus/Bélarus			x6180	x1427	x106
Slovakia				x6225	x5152
Korea Dem People's Rp	x144	x1194	x25	x4955	x11
Argentina/Argentine	1901	1915	2561	861	412
El Salvador	776	514	1543	2849	2428
Yugoslavia/Yougoslavie			x4552	x23	x4

COUNTRIES–PAYS	EXPORTS – EXPORTATIONS 1990	1991	1992	1993	1994
Totale	5184895	4608676	4353174	5619719	5613361
Afrique	x38597	x29084	x31753	x60696	x29019
Afrique du Nord	11433	7583	x5717	14642	14726
Amériques	x1859608	x1430442	x1305194	x1554980	x1558061
ALAI	12513	16917	44356	60850	68228
MCAC	1994	1562	878	x1748	x2194
Asie	x408972	x320712	x427166	x526167	x524303
Moyen–Orient	x69727	x48265	x48422	x97500	x115764
Europe	2542623	2415797	2257954	3029330	3189019
CEE	2475194	2363694	2212237	2986532	3126379
AELE	39583	35068	34209	31944	48013
Océanie	x29434	x44292	x46588	x97123	x13671
USA/Etats–Unis d'Amer	1630069	1226337	1101564	1319250	1269482
Germany/Allemagne	795594	839183	879780	928274	1009623
Netherlands/Pays–Bas	431434	493799	438000	768031	608607
France, Monac	503235	383318	362422	490777	557496
United Kingdom	476228	379048	293269	466243	496935
Russian Federation			x152194	x311546	x380402
Japan/Japon	74439	62064	190716	190513	160486
Canada	188735	133433	123758	148792	204268
Belgium–Luxembourg	120009	113912	116946	174205	198990
Hong Kong	83430	84841	80046	100063	100768
Poland/Pologne	42635	72570	93657	83766	48533
Former USSR/Anc. URSS	173254	x187345			
Czechoslovakia		x66417	x98997		
Hungary/Hongrie	x43991	x31726	x60287	x71723	x85629
Australia/Australie	21810	29051	39885	92081	5471
Czech Republic				149521	126304
Austria/Autriche	50343	56134	39717	50631	x83290
Denmark/Danemark	51682	40310	47304	48242	55182
Singapore/Singapour	41544	38379	40115	34327	51069
Mexico/Mexique	7660	8427	34466	48330	47635
Switz.Liecht	35058	31065	29155	26691	33929
Cuba	x20679	x47818	x7215	x13678	x5463
So. Africa Customs Un	18415	15135	20660	25060	
United Arab Emirates	16752	16096	16421	x22425	x21995
Sweden/Suède	12746	22357	5557	24212	48237
Bulgaria/Bulgarie	x38677	x9863	x21371	x15933	x12302
Mongolia/Mongolie	x2906	x1479	x4877	x36907	x5610
Lithuania/Lituanie			448	x37757	25796
Viet Nam	x59294	x25365	x7318	x2816	x1572
Lebanon/Liban	x11000	x12941	x8212	x13775	x15428
Korea, Republic of	15970	16082	11075	6632	6283
Guyana		x2847	x26176	x3366	x485
Thailand/Thaïlande	8393	9311	9806	11448	20204
Slovakia				x29331	x26282
Italy/Italie	17669	11215	10784	6384	7229
Kuwait/Koweït	5235	655	5454	21250	20970
Ukraine			x5879	x18725	x15748
Portugal	5112	8190	5556	10209	18363
Turkey/Turquie	5628	7519	7846	8498	24117
Morocco/Maroc	8551	4608	3272	12746	10879
New Zealand	6124	10709	4880	3469	6265
Estonia/Estonie			x1503	x17295	x23357
Venezuela	2730	4883	6566	7236	9710
Iran (Islamic Rp. of)	x2925	x137	x749	x17500	x14180
Malaysia/Malaisie	6471	6890	6680	4658	15025
Korea Dem People's Rp	x6191	x4880	x5433	x7638	x6834
China/Chine	11415	7003	6200	3701	2764
Latvia/Lettonie			x1954	x14581	745
Yugoslavia SFR	25388	x15502			
Spain/Espagne	5205	6363	4654	4048	4950

(VALUE AS % OF TOTAL)(VALEUR EN % DU TOTAL)

	1985	1986	1987	1988	1989	1990	1991	1992	1993	1994
Africa					x0.1	0.5	0.3	0.3	x0.3	x0.2
Northern Africa	0.0	0.0	0.0	0.0	0.1	0.5	0.3	0.3	0.3	0.2
Americas	6.5	7.4	6.8	7.2	7.5	6.6	6.1	7.3	7.2	8.1
LAIA	3.6	4.3	3.1	3.1	2.7	2.0	1.8	2.6	2.4	2.5
CACM	0.0	0.0	0.0	0.0	0.0	0.1	0.1	0.1	0.1	0.0
Asia	31.1	39.3	43.7	42.3	42.8	47.0	46.7	46.8	52.5	44.3
Middle East	3.5	5.4	7.8	7.7	10.5	9.5	12.3	11.2	12.5	11.4
Europe	62.3	53.1	47.6	49.3	49.3	45.8	46.5	44.9	39.3	46.9
EEC	54.3	45.7	41.6	43.1	43.9	44.5	45.8	43.4	37.9	45.7
EFTA	5.8	5.3	4.3	5.0	4.5	0.4	0.7	0.9	1.0	0.6
Oceania		x0.0	x0.0					x0.0	x0.2	x0.1
Italy/Italie	16.9	14.5	12.3	11.2	12.6	13.9	13.4	12.9	10.6	12.1
Turkey/Turquie	3.3	5.2	7.3	6.9	9.8	8.5	11.0	10.7	12.2	11.3
Korea, Republic of	7.1	9.4	9.3	9.3	10.3	10.5	11.7	8.7	11.5	11.2
Spain/Espagne	17.1	11.6	10.2	11.2	10.2	10.7	10.5	10.4	8.0	10.0
India/Inde	5.4	7.6	6.7	6.0	6.3	9.0	5.1	9.9	3.3	5.7
Belgium–Luxembourg	4.4	4.2	4.3	5.0	5.5	6.0	5.6	6.5	4.7	6.9
Netherlands/Pays–Bas	2.4	2.9	3.0	2.4	2.8	3.1	4.9	4.2	6.1	5.6
Japan/Japon	10.4	10.7	7.8	7.0	5.7	5.4	5.5	3.1	3.7	3.6
Thailand/Thaïlande	3.3	3.1	4.3	5.0	4.5	5.3	2.4	3.8	5.4	3.4
Indonesia/Indonésie	0.7	1.6	1.4	1.5	1.6	2.9	3.2	3.0	4.3	2.3

	1985	1986	1987	1988	1989	1990	1991	1992	1993	1994
Afrique	1.0	x1.0	x1.0	x0.6	x0.9	x0.8	x0.6	x0.8	x1.0	x0.5
Afrique du Nord	0.4	0.4	0.4	0.5	0.3	0.2	0.2	x0.1	0.3	0.3
Amériques	32.3	x39.3	x35.5	x31.0	x33.9	x35.9	x31.0	x29.9	x27.6	x27.8
ALAI	0.1	x0.4	x0.3	x0.4	0.2	0.2	0.4	1.0	1.1	1.2
MCAC	0.0	0.0	x0.0	x0.0	0.0	0.0	0.0	0.0	x0.0	x0.0
Asie	4.2	x5.4	x6.7	x9.4	x8.6	x7.9	x7.0	x9.8	x9.4	x9.3
Moyen–Orient	0.7	x1.1	x1.3	x1.2	x1.0	x1.3	x1.0	x1.1	x1.7	x2.1
Europe	53.0	42.4	43.2	48.2	46.9	49.0	52.4	51.9	53.9	56.8
CEE	51.3	41.3	41.2	46.1	45.1	47.7	51.3	50.8	53.1	55.7
AELE	1.0	0.7	1.1	1.4	1.3	0.8	0.8	0.8	0.6	0.9
Océanie	1.3	x1.4	x2.1	x0.1	x0.3	x0.5	x1.0	x1.0	x1.7	x0.2
USA/Etats–Unis d'Amer	29.3	32.8	27.6	26.7	29.6	31.4	26.6	25.3	23.5	22.6
Germany/Allemagne	13.2	11.4	12.7	14.2	14.2	15.3	18.2	20.2	16.5	18.0
Netherlands/Pays–Bas	7.3	7.0	7.1	8.4	7.7	8.3	10.7	10.1	13.7	10.8
France, Monac	12.8	9.3	8.9	9.6	10.4	9.7	8.3	8.3	8.7	9.9
United Kingdom	14.1	10.6	8.8	9.1	7.8	9.2	8.2	6.7	8.3	8.9
Russian Federation								x3.5	x5.5	x6.8
Japan/Japon	1.0	2.1	1.7	1.6	1.9	1.4	1.3	4.4	3.4	2.9
Canada	2.8	2.5	3.3	3.4	2.8	3.6	2.9	2.8	2.6	3.6
Belgium–Luxembourg	2.4	2.0	2.0	2.3	2.6	2.3	2.5	2.7	3.1	3.5
Hong Kong	1.0	1.0	1.1	1.5	1.6	1.6	1.8	1.8	1.8	1.8

TRADE BY COMMODITY IN THOUSAND U.S. DOLLARS – COMMERCE PAR PRODUIT EN MILLIERS DE DOLLARS E.U

COUNTRIES–PAYS	IMPORTS – IMPORTATIONS 1990	1991	1992	1993	1994
Total	73718	213167	142797	144257	119645
Africa		71		2	49
Northern Africa				2	49
Americas	59937	30336	417	1187	7219
LAIA	21	11	23	9	165
CACM					
Asia	463	x533	56	17	x73
Middle East	1	x195		12	
Europe	13318	182216	142323	142909	112290
EEC	13317	182210	142320	142909	112289
EFTA	1	6	4		
Oceania		1	1	1	
United Kingdom		179043	139991	140282	110786
USA/Etats–Unis d'Amer	59576	28312			
France,Monac	13299	3158	2303	2066	1387
Canada	340	2014	394	1177	7054
Malaysia/Malaisie	436	331	56	4	15
Italy/Italie	9	5		296	2
Iran (Islamic Rp. of)		x195			
Hungary/Hongrie		10		x122	
Ireland/Irlande				102	104
Sweden/Suède			14	65	
Nigeria/Nigéria		71			
Belgium–Luxembourg				67	10
Spain/Espagne	6	3	12	31	
Mexico/Mexique	21	11	10	1	
Venezuela			13	8	
Czech Republic				19	15
Cyprus/Chypre				12	
Norway,SVD,JM		5	3		
Japan/Japon	20	5			
Australia/Australie		1	1	1	
Myanmar		2			
Switz.Liecht	1	1	1		
Algeria/Algérie				2	
China/Chine				1	
Thailand/Thaïlande			1		3
Argentina/Argentine			1		3
Guatemala					
Portugal					
Belize/Bélize					
Singapore/Singapour	6				

COUNTRIES–PAYS	EXPORTS – EXPORTATIONS 1990	1991	1992	1993	1994
Totale	x489735	x66986	4044	151515	11822
Afrique	x1939	x2496	x4		
Afrique du Nord					
Amériques	331	3	309		5841
ALAI		1	7		4274
MCAC					
Asie	945	117	133	x1439	x1027
Moyen–Orient					
Europe	13630	12864	2340	21717	4367
CEE	13630	12864	2340	21621	4367
AELE					
Océanie	7133	2547	1258	128344	572
Australia/Australie	7133	2547	1258	128344	572
Russian Federation			x41001	x90955	x37029
Former USSR/Anc. URSS	x465757	x48960			
Spain/Espagne		10578	2333	18003	
Portugal	8967	2231		3266	886
Niger	x11	x2461	x4		
Kazakstan				x1394	
USA/Etats–Unis d'Amer	331	2	302		1567
China/Chine	10	117	133		56
United Kingdom	4600		3	238	3474
Slovenia/Slovénia				96	
Sweden/Suède				72	
Germany/Allemagne	22	55	1	1	
Malaysia/Malaisie	294			45	49
France,Monac				41	5
Zaire/Zaïre	x348	x29			
Slovakia				x15	x15
Colombia/Colombie		1	7		
Central African Rep.		x5			
Finland/Finlande			3	1	

(VALUE AS % OF TOTAL)(VALEUR EN % DU TOTAL)

	1985	1986	1987	1988	1989	1990	1991	1992	1993	1994
Africa					x0.0					
Northern Africa					x0.0				0.0	0.0
Americas	86.4	x36.6	27.8	x1.3	55.0	81.3	14.2	0.3	0.8	6.0
LAIA		x0.0		0.0		0.0	0.0	0.0	0.0	0.1
CACM									0.0	
Asia	1.6	x0.3	0.3	x2.5	x3.6	0.6	x0.2			x0.1
Middle East		0.0				0.0	x0.1		0.0	
Europe	12.0	x63.0	x42.2	x68.7	x25.1	18.1	85.5	99.7	99.1	93.9
EEC	12.0	x62.7	x42.2	x68.6	x25.1	18.1	85.5	99.7	99.1	93.9
EFTA		x0.3	x0.0	x0.1	x0.0	0.0	0.0	0.0		0.0
Oceania										
United Kingdom		x33.0	x16.6	x33.6	x13.2		84.0	98.0	97.2	92.6
USA/Etats–Unis d'Amer	3.9	0.8	0.3	1.3	53.5	80.8	13.3			
France,Monac	11.9	4.8	4.3	7.3	8.9	18.0	1.5	1.6	1.4	1.2
Canada	82.5	35.8	27.5	0.0	1.5	0.5	0.9	0.3	0.8	5.9
Malaysia/Malaisie	1.3	0.1	0.2	0.1	0.0	0.6	0.2	0.0	0.0	0.0
Italy/Italie	0.0	0.0	0.0	x0.0		0.0	0.0		0.2	0.0
Iran (Islamic Rp. of)							x0.1			
Hungary/Hongrie							0.0		x0.1	
Ireland/Irlande	0.0	0.0			x0.0				0.1	0.1
Sweden/Suède								0.0	0.0	

	1985	1986	1987	1988	1989	1990	1991	1992	1993	1994
Afrique	29.2	x8.3	x36.7	x43.6	x0.8	x0.4	x3.7	x0.1		
Afrique du Nord		x0.0								
Amériques	30.4	x30.3	x27.1	0.4	16.0	0.1		7.7		49.5
ALAI		x1.8	x0.6				0.0	0.2		36.2
MCAC										
Asie	0.3	x0.4	x0.6	x0.4	x0.9	0.2	0.2	3.3	x0.9	x8.7
Moyen–Orient	0.0									
Europe	0.0	0.7	4.7	4.4	20.9	2.8	19.2	57.9	14.3	36.9
CEE	0.0	0.7	4.7	4.4	19.2	2.8	19.2	57.9	14.3	36.9
AELE		x0.0			0.0					
Océanie	40.1	60.3	30.8	51.4	61.5	1.5	3.8	31.1	84.7	4.8
Australia/Australie	40.1	60.3	30.8	51.4	61.5	1.5	3.8	31.1	84.7	4.8
Russian Federation								*****	x60.0	*****
Former USSR/Anc. URSS						x95.1	x73.1			
Spain/Espagne		0.7	4.7	2.8	7.8	0.0	15.8	57.7	11.9	
Portugal				1.3	4.5	1.8	3.3		2.2	7.5
Niger	29.2		35.8	43.4	x0.0	x0.0	x3.7	x0.1		
Kazakstan									x0.9	
USA/Etats–Unis d'Amer	0.1	0.1	0.1	0.2	0.0	0.1	0.0	7.5		13.3
China/Chine			0.3	x0.0		0.0	0.2	3.3		0.5
United Kingdom		x0.0	x0.0	0.2	6.8	0.9		0.1	0.2	29.4

TRADE BY COMMODITY IN THOUSAND U.S. DOLLARS – COMMERCE PAR PRODUIT EN MILLIERS DE DOLLARS E.U

IMPORTS – IMPORTATIONS

COUNTRIES–PAYS	1990	1991	1992	1993	1994
Total	19919959	17599864	15892467	13511943	15043086
Africa	x314654	x339731	x259504	x245721	x226275
Northern Africa	42954	28102	59294	68622	55796
Americas	4334128	4058673	3763187	3431568	3448154
LAIA	799770	786162	680428	665631	703635
CACM	223	162	193	x1455	x1747
Asia	6300737	5984704	5448122	4801414	5581378
Middle East	131192	186824	132538	x113611	x115422
Europe	8241717	6338180	6024155	4697508	5429759
EEC	6672099	5071452	4892812	3686323	4354491
EFTA	1384376	1193379	1037416	930030	1020438
Oceania	x191245	x184515	x171423	x173937	x184878
Japan/Japon	4281049	3874249	3513332	2929350	3417835
USA/Etats–Unis d'Amer	2563492	2279241	2064978	1705741	1557459
Germany/Allemagne	1497341	1202306	1159798	868520	918870
Canada	958161	991021	1016858	1047776	1169125
Norway,SVD,JM	1305356	1110143	971857	882666	974710
France,Monac	880278	690031	713681	508629	588387
Korea, Republic of	709021	684009	531831	630514	661895
United Kingdom	1203670	717034	636474	491159	470759
China/Chine	496983	540144	512276	453216	572910
Spain/Espagne	453384	421026	494834	418716	632567
Belgium–Luxembourg	696275	550499	446435	324849	470148
Brazil/Brésil	475339	473926	429473	403041	438470
Italy/Italie	595896	476910	439696	313514	381101
Netherlands/Pays–Bas	554606	378576	390548	301262	334331
Finland/Finlande	360919	267651	302345	236829	304653
Philippines	158892	204404	186564	233977	312274
Malaysia/Malaisie	125598	146748	178045	127608	178242
Sweden/Suède	174300	154326	150423	82834	100098
New Zealand	142927	147326	108419	118254	126326
Russian Federation			x254527	x108970	x180406
Former USSR/Anc. URSS		x347860			
Indonesia/Indonésie	160417	130479	115502	86220	73788
Mexico/Mexique	136710	100815	116070	91174	89572
Ireland/Irlande	80447	89191	84263	81078	79234
United Arab Emirates	104447	135011	78851	x22659	x32054
Venezuela	88543	109011	60476	62525	16608
So. Africa Customs Un	90901	90153	68203	71858	77614
Austria/Autriche	150908	104700	61294	49269	65934
Argentina/Argentine	88473	89503	59754	62249	75607
Poland/Pologne	76814	59822	67134	68592	84172
Bulgaria/Bulgarie	x216007	x68054	72441	x37511	x22315
India/Inde	93038	60910	70211	40063	75539
Czechoslovakia	139266	x136832	x31180		
Romania/Roumanie	91166	77027	51034	32362	38591
Cameroon/Cameroun	49652	129719	x1325	x6608	x16148
Ghana	x58727	28299	66744	x33093	
Iceland/Islande	42665	50711	42009	32029	·31559
Singapore/Singapour	58781	52369	38120	32663	44577
Zambia/Zambie	x59738	x46294	x45933	x29752	x30995
Korea Dem People's Rp	x24552	x28382	x39503	x54057	x23824
Australia/Australie	47531	31284	57922	28912	55244
Hong Kong	37150	30306	53907	31726	36704
Thailand/Thaïlande	18763	22885	29522	36162	45362
Slovenia/Slovénia			41922	34423	39552
Yugoslavia SFR	185175	x73316			
Switz.Liecht	36355	32525	23549	15335	14170
Saudi Arabia	11561	27884	28514	x14458	x5807
Egypt/Egypte	6304	5978	8216	46267	39503
Algeria/Algérie	12741	3173	37451	18805	9837
Croatia/Croatie			28944	28889	x2913

EXPORTS – EXPORTATIONS

COUNTRIES–PAYS	1990	1991	1992	1993	1994
Totale	14997139	13225502	12878725	12690738	x11866425
Afrique	x1644733	x1335576	x1342380	x1078028	x1115566
Afrique du Nord	131736	61327	63560	60722	109446
Amériques	6959263	6393709	x6275125	x5381204	x5745657
ALAI	2055975	2149040	2144965	1858355	2351908
MCAC	84	2027	18467	6257	5393
Asie	1768657	1693243	1820427	1674863	2002794
Moyen–Orient	x144013	x94706	x91423	x77338	x125280
Europe	2412446	1750109	1638690	1354454	1474910
CEE	2004283	1652303	1564498	1288831	1407369
AELE	106991	81812	68385	50991	61391
Océanie	2020252	1743625	x1690125	3126157	x1418825
Canada	2402598	1854072	1771164	1320108	1161961
Australia/Australie	1302417	1001856	1021704	2491853	794504
USA/Etats–Unis d'Amer	1553211	1388731	1244785	943221	1127475
Chile/Chili	639477	968437	1106425	953120	1262525
Indonesia/Indonésie	618019	771189	933430	892428	1133225
So. Africa Customs Un	832490	697921	671585	526546	344781
Jamaica/Jamaïque	728267	656030	x557213	x524003	x671152
Papua New Guinea	582656	595032	541188	510302	x525623
Peru/Pérou	589841	427182	470538	379246	540296
Ireland/Irlande	351099	329582	295275	267428	294615
Guinea/Guinée	x263384	x271384	x264689	x258799	x314675
Cuba	x136110	x259701	x240003	x254943	x109617
Portugal	308846	253984	244465	204307	218259
Brazil/Brésil	289311	280742	178120	240251	226502
Suriname/Suriname			241484	x382450	x225486
Bolivia/Bolivie	202999	184351	211515	141058	132709
Gabon	x232731	x199044	x218059	x117000	x204373
Philippines	251459	221908	175622	132076	135606
Sweden/Suède	239079	203594	176506	146772	143680
Germany/Allemagne	190281	168204	166073	121259	136815
Mexico/Mexique	280703	224023	135872	93155	141865
Netherlands/Pays–Bas	204461	172581	149530	118203	122798
India/Inde	174855	121118	121518	143584	148630
New Caledonia	135049	146032	x115928	122918	x98434
China/Chine	195072	143069	104579	73319	94767
Greece/Grèce	124247	112393	104073	92933	70226
Italy/Italie	140618	112140	113590	71819	66270
Mongolia/Mongolie	x85090	x96567	x88335	x90933	x58610
Belgium–Luxembourg	113349	81048	86761	89635	134078
France,Monac	101231	83295	92057	71809	88291
Russian Federation			x139010	x100913	x213603
Malaysia/Malaisie	90216	82317	82502	67820	73351
Spain/Espagne	160737	90869	79747	57383	71592
Guyana	80300	79300	56600	91027	x85072
Norway,SVD,JM	106327	81274	67611	50100	60393
Japan/Japon	66149	54882	51110	75430	108819
Morocco/Maroc	73390	57792	59570	58820	99012
Former USSR/Anc. URSS	75138	x170586			
Turkey/Turquie	99063	61901	55689	40880	54142
Sierra Leone	108099	x53527	x36125	x41926	x68699
Venezuela	35177	44851	33810	49448	43326
Hong Kong	40437	37893	51320	33272	36098
Poland/Pologne	23862	53840	42331	25176	22857
Ghana	x35492	14401	51084	x44984	x39199
United Kingdom	47442	25061	39777	36947	35974
Iran (Islamic Rp. of)	x27915	x31590	x34326	x22877	x65409
Kazakstan			x53225	x28065	x8636
Albania/Albanie	x28534	x40472	x28143	x9990	x3792
Singapore/Singapour	33569	25325	22963	15642	18547
Bulgaria/Bulgarie	x20002	x11360	x14317	x21763	x50110

(VALUE AS % OF TOTAL)(VALEUR EN % DU TOTAL)

	1985	1986	1987	1988	1989	1990	1991	1992	1993	1994
Africa	0.3	x1.8	x0.7	x0.9	x1.4	x1.6	x1.9	x1.6	x1.8	x1.5
Northern Africa	0.1	0.4	0.3	0.1	0.3	0.2	0.2	0.4	0.5	0.4
Americas	22.3	20.7	19.9	18.9	19.0	21.8	23.1	23.7	25.4	22.9
LAIA	4.7	3.9	4.2	4.2	3.9	4.0	4.5	4.3	4.9	4.7
CACM	0.0	0.0	0.0	0.0	0.0	0.0	0.0	0.0	x0.0	x0.0
Asia	26.7	27.0	28.6	32.9	30.9	31.6	34.0	34.3	35.5	37.1
Middle East	0.8	1.0	x0.4	0.6	x0.2	0.7	1.1	0.8	x0.8	x0.8
Europe	47.8	47.2	42.5	41.3	41.3	41.4	36.0	37.9	34.8	36.1
EEC	37.9	37.3	34.0	32.1	32.1	33.5	28.8	30.8	27.3	28.9
EFTA	9.0	9.1	7.9	8.5	8.4	6.9	6.8	6.5	6.9	6.8
Oceania	1.0	0.9	1.0	x1.0	0.8	x1.0	x1.0	x1.0	x1.3	x1.2
Japan/Japon	20.6	20.8	19.5	23.4	21.0	21.5	22.0	22.1	21.7	22.7
USA/Etats–Unis d'Amer	13.8	12.1	11.5	10.7	11.0	12.9	13.0	13.0	12.6	10.4
Germany/Allemagne	8.6	9.3	7.8	7.6	8.0	7.5	6.8	7.3	6.4	6.1
Canada	3.9	4.6	4.0	4.0	4.0	4.8	5.6	6.4	7.8	7.8
Norway,SVD,JM	4.6	4.7	4.2	4.8	5.0	6.6	6.3	6.1	6.5	6.5
France,Monac	4.2	4.1	3.8	3.9	3.9	4.4	3.9	4.5	3.8	3.9
Korea, Republic of	2.4	2.7	4.0	3.3	3.9	3.6	3.9	3.3	4.7	4.4
United Kingdom	7.4	6.7	6.6	6.2	5.6	6.0	4.1	4.0	3.6	3.1
China/Chine	0.4	0.5	1.5	1.4	1.9	2.5	3.1	3.2	3.4	3.8
Spain/Espagne	2.2	2.5	2.4	2.1	2.0	2.3	2.4	3.1	3.1	4.2

	1985	1986	1987	1988	1989	1990	1991	1992	1993	1994
Afrique	4.9	x9.4	x6.9	x10.1	x8.9	x11.0	x10.1	x10.4	x8.4	x9.4
Afrique du Nord	0.6	0.5	0.5	0.6	0.5	0.9	0.5	0.5	0.5	0.9
Amériques	42.9	41.4	42.9	46.4	46.9	46.4	48.3	x48.7	x42.4	x48.4
ALAI	17.1	13.5	14.2	14.7	13.2	13.7	16.2	16.7	14.6	19.8
MCAC	0.2	0.1	0.1	0.0	x0.0	0.0	0.0	0.1	0.0	0.0
Asie	10.5	10.0	10.4	14.5	13.6	11.8	12.8	14.1	13.2	16.9
Moyen–Orient	0.6	0.6	x0.6	x1.0	1.3	x1.0	x0.7	x0.7	x0.6	x1.1
Europe	16.0	15.5	14.3	13.2	15.3	16.1	13.2	12.7	10.7	12.4
CEE	12.2	11.4	10.9	10.4	11.7	13.4	12.5	12.1	10.2	11.9
AELE	2.3	2.5	2.7	2.0	2.1	0.7	0.6	0.5	0.4	0.5
Océanie	25.0	22.7	23.0	13.4	13.8	13.5	13.2	x13.1	24.6	x12.0
Canada	11.6	11.3	12.2	13.6	13.2	16.0	14.0	13.8	10.4	9.8
Australia/Australie	19.4	18.0	17.1	6.1	7.6	8.7	7.6	7.9	19.6	6.7
USA/Etats–Unis d'Amer	5.8	5.4	6.3	7.6	9.7	10.4	10.5	9.7	7.4	9.5
Chile/Chili	4.4	4.1	4.8	5.3	5.4	4.3	7.3	8.6	7.5	10.6
Indonesia/Indonésie	2.9	3.3	2.9	4.7	4.2	4.1	5.8	7.2	7.0	9.5
So. Africa Customs Un	3.8	2.6	1.9	5.5	4.7	5.6	5.3	5.2	4.1	2.9
Jamaica/Jamaïque	3.2	3.2	3.2	3.1	3.5	4.9	5.0	x4.3	x4.1	x5.7
Papua New Guinea	3.3	4.0	5.7	6.4	5.0	3.9	4.5	4.2	4.0	x4.4
Peru/Pérou	6.3	4.0	4.7	4.9	3.1	3.9	3.2	3.7	3.0	4.6
Ireland/Irlande	1.9	1.8	1.9	2.3	2.5	2.3	2.5	2.3	2.1	2.5

TRADE BY COMMODITY IN THOUSAND U.S. DOLLARS – COMMERCE PAR PRODUIT EN MILLIERS DE DOLLARS E.U

COUNTRIES–PAYS	IMPORTS – IMPORTATIONS				
	1990	1991	1992	1993	1994
Total	7310233	6576733	7133044	6473715	7568503
Africa	19264	29993	x24612	363174	x8793
Northern Africa	1719	3391	4666	349478	1318
Americas	1093508	935696	1107909	1096026	1400044
LAIA	104424	68576	62509	48023	60268
CACM	35	47	36	x1439	x747
Asia	1838263	1763885	1735952	1675731	1875207
Middle East	21955	x12439	13629	x24592	x24204
Europe	4333465	3819522	4230610	3286919	4231408
EEC	4220599	3712923	4115161	3193382	4063597
EFTA	108681	104391	101364	85965	152480
Oceania	x19212	x17475	x20004	x17155	x25383
Germany/Allemagne	1241668	1034397	1317519	959043	1196413
USA/Etats–Unis d'Amer	736118	636171	812516	825558	1007782
Japan/Japon	1065554	897775	660698	691353	825535
Belgium–Luxembourg	866138	798858	736280	547954	672991
Italy/Italie	629748	508513	563664	468446	700314
Korea, Republic of	377257	441222	297119	278033	279967
France, Monac	337242	325785	324690	199716	283064
United Kingdom	335749	254775	280993	307728	343699
Netherlands/Pays–Bas	328953	296493	305596	236094	298178
Canada	248513	226853	228604	216326	325258
China/Chine	30012	80980	281944	255889	278965
Austria/Autriche	131468	173317	175200	111851	173678
India/Inde	195541	145407	148603	164356	176007
Hong Kong	54879	80458	205608	139206	166596
Sweden/Suède	132989	129969	143021	116947	143191
Finland/Finlande	42948	70660	167577	138442	124364
Egypt/Egypte	985	2163	1155	348241	917
Norway, SVD, JM	86164	81086	77785	70178	128503
Spain/Espagne	134647	85789	61202	57100	85700
Singapore/Singapour	34255	35922	40743	37065	37876
Mexico/Mexique	58218	39088	34198	23304	32834
Pakistan	14646	20930	29371	30334	30043
Denmark/Danemark	16686	16926	24592	23463	28541
Switz.Liecht	22516	23304	23569	15766	23956
Indonesia/Indonésie	12794	18488	21388	13641	10703
Brazil/Brésil	37102	20542	13614	13962	22389
So. Africa Customs Un	11130	15451	13817	11097	5737
Malaysia/Malaisie	12856	12488	11176	15555	30585
Australia/Australie	15282	12489	14529	8837	12279
Thailand/Thaïlande	7301	8551	12293	14021	3904
Greece/Grèce	5422	3415	1998	17279	1968
Ireland/Irlande	11747	8677	7859	5350	7931
United Arab Emirates	15481	3081	3261	x12109	x14637
Nepal/Népal	2758	4776	8546	4694	x504
Slovenia/Slovénia			11553	6231	14721
New Zealand	3851	4574	5074	8091	12885
Portugal	5195	5348	4971	3969	3564
Bolivia/Bolivie	4	44	6023	7769	54
Hungary/Hongrie	x2900	4078	x3460	x5093	x3545
Czechoslovakia	966	x4819	x7768		
Slovakia				x12564	x7293
Czech Republic				12170	14569
Turkey/Turquie	1313	2907	4602	4111	2782
Jordan/Jordanie	2488	2692	3581	3832	1947
Russian Federation			x3282	x6123	x9934
Kenya	2695	3314	3950	1096	x60
Nigeria/Nigéria	x207	6392	x974	x503	x208
Panama	1830	1891	1810	3008	3755
Korea Dem People's Rp	x565	x1758	x1981	x2418	x3666
Ecuador/Equateur	691	802	4890	23	x380

COUNTRIES–PAYS	EXPORTS – EXPORTATIONS				
	1990	1991	1992	1993	1994
Totale	6135052	5538867	5577828	4445049	5798230
Afrique	x76032	x71027	x101768	x76849	x78480
Afrique du Nord	23430	30010	33033	21840	26503
Amériques	x2079080	x1649465	1432079	1218814	1714725
ALAI	76106	96474	163201	144369	253369
MCAC	6		35	x2781	x4370
Asie	546543	461920	635729	x623181	x767662
Moyen–Orient	x119143	x60275	x82613	x144474	x226881
Europe	3139905	2953207	2970673	2259663	2913076
CEE	2959507	2802559	2901442	2176167	2729209
AELE	172582	137446	130169	121133	164281
Océanie	x153748	x151449	x124723	x107013	x151216
USA/Etats–Unis d'Amer	1397882	1086745	750837	611203	914219
Germany/Allemagne	686257	760505	808735	597920	744001
Canada	568893	433128	494681	443801	526038
France, Monac	620136	517391	495749	331332	437871
United Kingdom	545425	487144	419449	352441	415243
Netherlands/Pays–Bas	398858	361490	387261	277116	356895
Russian Federation			x264554	x432641	x415895
Belgium–Luxembourg	231927	200384	216978	157269	203238
Hong Kong	155341	136278	206732	160015	173240
Australia/Australie	135540	133285	109942	92664	132273
Spain/Espagne	83117	113287	123705	92612	104596
Singapore/Singapour	111557	109867	109017	98172	129924
Mexico/Mexique	38963	49079	124428	113065	168275
Switz.Liecht	93858	84003	91649	91529	125224
Italy/Italie	81421	79982	82402	67389	93488
Sweden/Suède	57410	57226	102214	63907	85571
Denmark/Danemark	90129	74758	75621	67137	98407
Austria/Autriche	76371	62606	67808	53862	x70335
Latvia/Lettonie					1459
Hungary/Hongrie	x80313	x47185	x69617	x48240	x62477
Poland/Pologne	1168	1691	130069	25292	9515
Former USSR/Anc. URSS	3169	x126757			
Japan/Japon	43108	40009	50626	34547	42928
Finland/Finlande	18157	20739	48870	55514	42158
Malaysia/Malaisie	39554	44737	43910	31216	46447
Norway, SVD, JM	77725	52486	37765	28621	36262
Czechoslovakia		x35191	x77212		
Saudi Arabia	42307	18636	21834	x63109	x92929
Estonia/Estonie			x29834	x67628	x21457
Bulgaria/Bulgarie	x45368	x39242	x31890	x12616	x16391
Ireland/Irlande	35235	29009	28839	24922	32077
Portugal	24380	28153	29777	23813	24626
Venezuela	23532	24827	24955	23889	35477
So. Africa Customs Un	21818	18860	27769	23680	
United Arab Emirates	36951	13959	17134	x39145	x58418
Lithuania/Lituanie			1908	x66999	501
Korea, Republic of	12460	13209	23825	22406	21914
China/Chine	3303	4191	24313	23349	20980
Mongolia/Mongolie	x13700	x16895	x14195	x19675	x1022
Morocco/Maroc	10800	15580	18962	11091	14768
Philippines	18434	18765	11532	11838	19170
Czech Republic				41177	51821
Azerbaijan			x20867	x19927	x1179
New Zealand	15687	14728	12888	11070	15821
Greece/Grèce	10685	9882	14033	10932	20702
Yugoslavia/Yougoslavie			x4611	x30008	x911
Cuba	x29306	x20733	x5309	x5021	x3708
Kuwait/Koweït	4760	1791	11092	11108	19640
Israel/Israël	7838	8534	6874	8293	24524
Belarus/Bélarus			x14777	x8424	x6884

(VALUE AS % OF TOTAL)(VALEUR EN % DU TOTAL)

	1985	1986	1987	1988	1989	1990	1991	1992	1993	1994
Africa	0.2	0.3	x0.2		x0.2	0.3	0.4	x0.4	5.6	x0.1
Northern Africa	0.0	0.0	x0.0	0.0	0.0	0.0	0.1	0.1	5.4	0.0
Americas	13.2	14.2	14.6	14.8	15.1	15.0	14.2	15.5	16.9	18.5
LAIA	1.2	1.1	1.8	1.6	1.4	1.4	1.0	0.9	0.7	0.8
CACM		x0.0	0.0	0.0	x0.0	0.0	0.0	0.0	x0.0	x0.0
Asia	18.0	18.8	x24.1	x24.6	21.2	25.2	26.9	24.4	25.9	24.8
Middle East	0.1	0.1	x0.7	x0.2	x0.2	0.3	x0.2	0.2	x0.4	x0.3
Europe	68.4	66.5	59.8	59.5	63.0	59.3	58.1	59.3	50.8	55.9
EEC	62.5	60.8	54.5	53.7	57.4	57.7	56.5	57.7	49.3	53.7
EFTA	5.9	5.7	5.3	5.8	5.5	1.5	1.6	1.4	1.3	2.0
Oceania	0.2	x0.1	x0.2	x0.3	x0.2	x0.3	x0.3	x0.3	x0.3	x0.3
Germany/Allemagne	19.2	17.1	14.3	15.5	17.3	17.0	15.7	18.5	14.8	15.8
USA/Etats–Unis d'Amer	8.1	9.0	9.6	9.5	9.2	10.1	9.7	11.4	12.8	13.3
Japan/Japon	14.1	13.8	15.1	14.1	12.7	14.6	13.7	9.3	10.7	10.9
Belgium–Luxembourg	14.1	12.0	11.8	10.8	11.1	11.8	12.1	10.3	8.5	8.9
Italy/Italie	7.8	9.0	6.8	7.1	8.2	8.6	7.7	7.9	7.2	9.3
Korea, Republic of	1.4	2.1	2.7	4.1	4.4	5.2	6.7	4.2	4.3	3.7
France, Monac	3.2	3.4	3.3	3.8	4.5	4.6	5.0	4.6	3.1	3.7
United Kingdom	6.6	8.3	8.5	5.5	4.6	4.6	3.9	3.9	4.8	4.5
Netherlands/Pays–Bas	4.3	4.0	3.3	3.7	4.4	4.5	4.5	4.3	3.6	3.9
Canada	3.9	4.1	3.3	3.7	4.4	3.4	3.4	3.2	3.3	4.3

	1985	1986	1987	1988	1989	1990	1991	1992	1993	1994
Afrique	1.6	x2.0	x1.9	x1.3	x1.5	x1.3	x1.2	x1.8	x1.7	x1.4
Afrique du Nord	0.3	0.3	0.3	0.5	0.5	0.4	0.5	0.6	0.5	0.5
Amériques	40.5	42.8	38.8	38.0	35.6	x33.9	x29.7	25.3	26.9	29.5
ALAI	7.9	8.6	6.2	5.7	5.8	1.2	1.7	2.9	3.2	4.4
MCAC		x0.0	x0.0	x0.0	x0.0	0.0		0.0	x0.1	x0.1
Asie	5.3	x6.8	x7.6	x8.3	7.7	8.9	8.4	11.2	x13.7	x13.3
Moyen–Orient	1.1	x2.5	x1.8	x1.5	x1.6	x1.9	x1.1	x1.5	x3.2	x3.9
Europe	50.8	46.5	46.6	47.3	51.3	51.2	53.3	53.9	51.8	50.2
CEE	44.6	40.5	40.5	41.9	46.3	48.2	50.6	51.3	48.0	47.1
AELE	6.0	5.9	5.3	5.2	4.9	2.8	2.5	2.3	2.7	2.8
Océanie	1.1	x1.9	x1.8	x1.7	x1.8	x2.5	x2.8	x2.2	x2.4	x2.7
USA/Etats–Unis d'Amer	26.5	27.1	25.5	25.1	21.9	22.8	19.6	13.3	13.5	15.8
Germany/Allemagne	7.1	7.0	7.4	8.0	9.5	11.2	13.7	14.3	13.2	12.8
Canada	6.1	6.9	6.9	6.9	7.1	9.3	7.8	8.7	9.8	9.1
France, Monac	12.4	7.9	8.2	9.0	10.0	10.1	9.3	8.8	7.3	7.6
United Kingdom	9.6	9.8	8.4	7.9	8.5	8.9	8.8	7.4	7.8	7.2
Netherlands/Pays–Bas	5.7	5.6	5.7	6.6	7.2	6.5	6.5	6.8	6.1	6.2
Russian Federation								x4.7	x9.5	x7.2
Belgium–Luxembourg	3.1	3.2	3.0	3.4	3.8	3.8	3.6	3.8	3.5	3.5
Hong Kong	1.2	1.4	1.8	2.1	2.1	2.5	2.5	3.7	3.5	3.0
Australia/Australie	0.9	1.5	1.5	1.4	1.6	2.2	2.4	1.9	2.0	2.3

TRADE BY COMMODITY IN THOUSAND U.S. DOLLARS – COMMERCE PAR PRODUIT EN MILLIERS DE DOLLARS E.U

COUNTRIES–PAYS	IMPORTS – IMPORTATIONS				
	1990	1991	1992	1993	1994
Total	1447191	1698254	1500388	1515075	1640207
Africa	x323	x894	x1950	x2962	x2059
Northern Africa			1	10	46
Americas	231767	348547	219416	x199983	x227570
LAIA	7218	32	521	81	70
CACM				2	29
Asia	91786	100234	x95346	102581	76171
Middle East	x17	x392	x477	2505	x58
Europe	1119601	1155009	1183006	1207453	1332184
EEC	1083734	1122833	1150138	1167233	1284742
EFTA	35866	32142	32817	40219	47396
Oceania	3706	239	657	513	x485
United Kingdom	480901	490767	498982	468399	370417
Germany/Allemagne	292319	357952	336646	455500	556252
USA/Etats–Unis d'Amer	142025	269407	134454	118490	153280
Belgium–Luxembourg	48519	87158	166223	131434	201777
Japan/Japon	87452	94722	91853	96732	71742
Canada	82498	79019	84408	81357	74152
Italy/Italie	93693	60663	51152	36371	36349
France,Monac	92656	69047	52495	22514	26808
Hungary/Hongrie	x6	93209	x10	x1	x921
Sweden/Suède	43971	27811	21214	19307	30811
Spain/Espagne	18941	23574	15737	27195	56552
Switz.Liecht	24200	17892	18721	28764	30226
Norway,SVD,JM	11658	14247	14096	11455	17170
Netherlands/Pays–Bas	7565	2251	5201	4353	1874
Russian Federation			x4294	x1129	x662
Denmark/Danemark	2637	1693	1871	1301	2326
So. Africa Customs Un	310	535	1570	2414	1430
Korea, Republic of	723	1680	23	506	165
Oman				2188	
Pakistan	1079	1851	32		8
Portugal	995	1530	46	8	5
Hong Kong	1769	220	532	665	178
Australia/Australie	3692	237	656	495	274
Austria/Autriche	1400	323	370	650	1398
Mongolia/Mongolie			x1327		
Singapore/Singapour	308	165	104	843	1060
Czech Republic				984	472
China/Chine	35	176	588	197	330
Malaysia/Malaisie	325	95	189	540	2069
Saudi Arabia		303	393	x65	x29
Philippines	9	645			
Benin/Bénin			x235	x390	x353
Bulgaria/Bulgarie				x565	x46
Venezuela	1	1	448	32	5
Indonesia/Indonésie	8	230	33	19	52
Estonia/Estonie			x24	x247	x222
Korea Dem People's Rp				x270	x131
Mauritius/Maurice	2	9	102	131	183
Ireland/Irlande	128	50	102	79	102
Nigeria/Nigéria	x2	204	x25		
Thailand/Thaïlande		7	46	173	68
Finland/Finlande	8	9	94	121	51
Cyprus/Chypre		16		118	15
United Arab Emirates	x2			x133	x7
India/Inde	15	15	64	53	46
Central African Rep.		x127			
Former USSR/Anc. URSS		x110			
Israel/Israël	36	7	42	59	216
Jamaica/Jamaïque		71		x18	x8
Syrian Arab Republic		x73			

COUNTRIES–PAYS	EXPORTS – EXPORTATIONS				
	1990	1991	1992	1993	1994
Totale	1274644	1133263	1306500	1024146	1050074
Afrique	x11016	x10168	13712	x62057	x57251
Afrique du Nord	x15			15	
Amériques	809013	627252	649553	522399	509997
ALAI	192636	155231	180840	103433	128148
MCAC	4	554	1692	x1846	x1998
Asie	127353	92104	182073	x124894	x159497
Moyen–Orient	x7422	x1447	x3050	x22255	x29947
Europe	298710	358970	382445	270954	291487
CEE	254851	314377	347628	234091	257644
AELE	36335	37401	33122	34036	32187
Océanie	x10506	x10919	x9515	x8064	x6457
USA/Etats–Unis d'Amer	374291	273901	315761	300689	296199
Canada	232689	186749	139053	111388	77228
Philippines	89813	66811	129978	53444	67322
France,Monac	44083	55547	74348	49336	55002
Chile/Chili	83201	56747	74828	42787	59353
Bolivia/Bolivie	61498	55377	58796	47759	48011
Germany/Allemagne	17454	51014	70024	26564	47390
United Kingdom	58017	38642	47855	42444	44337
Netherlands/Pays–Bas	47377	47120	40143	30135	27607
Sweden/Suède	36393	35732	32837	26760	37167
Switz.Liecht	27940	33387	31720	28547	27718
Belgium–Luxembourg	10908	14331	38070	28017	12119
So. Africa Customs Un	7508	7524	6879	56517	54276
Peru/Pérou	44786	35531	26047	7767	13234
Spain/Espagne	4135	41339	11043	5625	6611
Korea, Republic of	6408	10151	18234	18242	18707
Bulgaria/Bulgarie	x11721	x11936	x24349	x6325	x8767
Poland/Pologne			20623	20359	7723
Austria/Autriche	9108	6735	17976	15325	x13609
Czechoslovakia		x11901	x18218		
Russian Federation			x7307	x19239	x11904
Australia/Australie	10078	9451	8102	4579	6074
Saudi Arabia	4403	x3	1499	x19201	x29228
Japan/Japon	3100	4601	6931	6896	6491
Hong Kong	13795	5347	4046	8723	29382
Denmark/Danemark	12390	7712	5904	3508	5143
Estonia/Estonie			x310	x15879	x12100
Italy/Italie	7947	7934	3749	4296	795
Cuba	x8841	x7683	x4603	x3211	x6092
Ecuador/Equateur			14301	27	x13
Finland/Finlande	3523	7240	4614	2071	7345
Indonesia/Indonésie	114	30	13566	49	4382
Hungary/Hongrie	x5747	x4893	x6012	x2182	x2674
Singapore/Singapour	3886	1960	4243	6823	381
Guyana		x3098	x7257	x1780	
Mexico/Mexique	2475	5644	3601	2355	1878
Norway,SVD,JM	8396	4014	1402	5490	4468
Zimbabwe	1143	2030	5877		x1785
Lithuania/Lituanie				x7244	1489
Yugoslavia SFR	x7524	x6788			
Colombia/Colombie	637	1932	2717	1913	4245
Latvia/Lettonie				x5783	509
New Zealand	409	1237	1114	3371	237
Former USSR/Anc. URSS	x108	x4830			
Czech Republic				4597	2409
Ghana	x1343	1		x4475	x888
Ukraine			x4427		x7470
Iran (Islamic Rp. of)	x47	x1281	x1551	x790	x8
Honduras		554	1692	1020	1486
Tajikistan/Tadjikistan				x3230	

(VALUE AS % OF TOTAL)(VALEUR EN % DU TOTAL)

	1985	1986	1987	1988	1989	1990	1991	1992	1993	1994
Africa	6.2	x0.3	x1.0		x0.0	x0.0	x0.0	x0.1	x0.2	x0.1
Northern Africa		x0.0	x0.1	x0.0	x0.0			0.0	0.0	0.0
Americas	31.0	x43.5	x31.8	x18.2	x18.7	16.0	20.5	14.6	x13.2	x13.9
LAIA	0.0	x0.1	x0.2	0.0	0.3	0.5	0.0	0.0	0.0	0.0
CACM			x0.0	x0.0		0.0	0.0		0.0	0.0
Asia	0.6	2.3	x5.5	x6.4	6.3	6.3	5.9	x6.3	6.8	4.7
Middle East	0.0	x0.0	x0.0	x0.0	x0.0	x0.0	x0.0	x0.0	0.2	x0.0
Europe	62.2	53.9	61.3	74.0	74.3	77.4	68.0	78.8	79.7	81.2
EEC	58.2	49.7	57.4	70.3	68.5	74.9	66.1	76.7	77.0	78.3
EFTA	4.0	4.2	3.9	3.8	5.8	2.5	1.9	2.2	2.7	2.9
Oceania			0.1	x0.5	0.3	0.3				x0.0
United Kingdom	28.2	23.6	23.7	35.8	30.3	33.2	28.9	33.3	30.9	22.6
Germany/Allemagne	14.3	13.0	19.1	18.5	19.9	20.2	21.1	22.4	30.1	33.9
USA/Etats–Unis d'Amer	6.8	8.5	10.9	9.0	12.5	9.8	15.9	9.0	7.8	9.3
Belgium–Luxembourg	3.5	2.7	1.7	2.7	2.7	3.4	5.1	11.1	8.7	12.3
Japan/Japon	0.5	2.1	3.9	5.7	5.9	6.0	5.6	6.1	6.4	4.4
Canada	24.1	34.9	20.7	9.2	5.9	5.7	4.7	5.6	5.4	4.5
Italy/Italie	0.7	1.2	3.4	3.4	3.2	6.5	3.6	3.4	2.4	2.2
France,Monac	2.7	3.1	3.6	3.7	5.8	6.4	4.1	3.5	1.5	1.6
Hungary/Hongrie				x0.0	x0.0	x0.0	5.5	x0.0	x0.0	x0.1
Sweden/Suède	3.1	2.9	1.8	0.8	3.3	3.0	1.6	1.4	1.3	1.9

	1985	1986	1987	1988	1989	1990	1991	1992	1993	1994
Afrique	0.2	x9.0	x9.0	x2.5	x2.3	x0.9	x0.9	1.0	x6.0	x5.5
Afrique du Nord	0.0	x0.7	x1.0	x1.3	x1.6	x0.0			0.0	
Amériques	57.7	x60.0	56.4	56.1	x61.1	63.5	55.3	49.7	51.0	48.6
ALAI	10.5	9.7	5.4	8.6	9.4	15.1	13.7	13.8	10.1	12.2
MCAC	1.1	x0.6	0.6	x0.1	x0.2	0.0	0.0	0.1	x0.2	x0.2
Asie	21.3	14.6	13.0	x17.3	12.5	10.0	8.2	14.0	x12.2	x15.2
Moyen–Orient	0.0	x0.6	x0.7	x1.6	x1.2	x0.6	x0.1	x0.2	x2.2	x2.9
Europe	20.4	13.7	16.7	21.0	21.7	23.4	31.7	29.3	26.5	27.8
CEE	14.8	9.5	12.2	14.3	15.0	20.0	27.7	26.6	22.9	24.5
AELE	5.5	4.2	3.9	5.8	6.2	2.9	3.3	2.5	3.3	3.1
Océanie	0.4	x2.6	x3.5	x1.6	x1.5	x0.8	x0.9	x0.7	x0.8	x0.6
USA/Etats–Unis d'Amer	19.9	15.3	16.5	22.2	25.0	29.4	24.2	24.2	29.4	28.2
Canada	26.1	21.0	24.7	15.0	16.5	18.3	16.5	10.6	10.9	7.4
Philippines	12.1	11.0	6.6	9.7	8.9	7.0	5.9	9.9	5.2	6.4
France,Monac	3.5	1.0	0.9	1.1	1.8	3.5	4.9	5.7	4.8	5.2
Chile/Chili	6.8	6.1	0.0	0.0	0.0	6.5	5.0	5.7	4.2	5.7
Bolivia/Bolivie	1.4	2.4	3.0	4.8	5.5	4.8	4.9	4.5	4.7	4.6
Germany/Allemagne	0.6	0.5	0.6	1.0	1.2	1.4	4.5	5.4	2.6	4.5
United Kingdom	3.1	1.1	2.6	2.2	2.1	4.6	3.4	3.7	4.1	4.2
Netherlands/Pays–Bas	3.1	2.8	3.7	3.5	2.7	3.7	4.2	3.1	2.9	2.6
Sweden/Suède	1.9	1.5	1.4	1.8	2.7	2.9	3.2	2.5	2.6	3.5

TRADE BY COMMODITY IN THOUSAND U.S. DOLLARS – COMMERCE PAR PRODUIT EN MILLIERS DE DOLLARS E.U

COUNTRIES–PAYS	IMPORTS – IMPORTATIONS 1990	1991	1992	1993	1994
Total	3053061	3010220	3351958	3050828	3361512
Africa	x29390	44656	x28890	x35657	x31078
Northern Africa	2798	2733	2433	1768	1894
Americas	319934	345408	384077	369575	438602
LAIA	68590	86109	99290	103295	119174
CACM	2673	3383	4015	5930	x4366
Asia	x1005594	983925	1048462	976154	1004135
Middle East	x71286	x17707	x17530	x20264	x13837
Europe	1606603	1540936	1769220	1535610	1736852
EEC	1514699	1459884	1680438	1457983	1647999
EFTA	80774	68533	68954	61845	70968
Oceania	x42977	x37781	x40681	x48491	x57099
Japan/Japon	575450	580630	602337	609238	618709
Germany/Allemagne	505025	516088	596774	520408	569605
France,Monac	276524	252836	286671	247856	289230
USA/Etats–Unis d'Amer	196352	211264	235858	215438	261539
Hong Kong	153239	166376	163922	128917	128649
United Kingdom	167835	136558	166570	150238	161555
Italy/Italie	170266	152713	148346	124359	141607
Korea, Republic of	128038	135423	159085	126679	132712
Netherlands/Pays–Bas	84841	80387	92725	83388	108163
Denmark/Danemark	45384	58787	98859	73129	77770
Spain/Espagne	67347	67472	69457	61811	70796
Belgium–Luxembourg	63077	55995	67409	59876	71677
Switz.Liecht	67134	56267	56029	50736	57854
Austria/Autriche	47921	48536	51855	48885	54412
Mexico/Mexique	25421	35195	48973	49706	55485
Poland/Pologne	8511	26235	48908	49457	58230
Canada	44686	40145	42182	39769	51371
Sweden/Suède	34896	33363	37739	32607	34344
Australia/Australie	31468	25930	30370	33872	40458
Portugal	17977	27044	30574	29918	30732
China/Chine	18458	14672	36443	35459	45674
Brazil/Brésil	25145	26357	23638	23273	28686
So. Africa Customs Un	18400	17761	17549	21266	23323
Singapore/Singapour	19916	28043	18333	9695	9239
Finland/Finlande	19820	17221	19023	13989	21188
Thailand/Thaïlande	13317	13526	15118	15326	18619
Hungary/Hongrie	x8061	8253	x12636	x16531	x14799
Indonesia/Indonésie	8307	10869	15878	10123	8692
Norway,SVD,JM	13283	11903	12457	10868	12935
New Zealand	10384	9633	8370	12611	14464
Czechoslovakia	11478	x17440	x11792		
Nigeria/Nigéria	x2226	18914	x4148	x2332	x1416
Greece/Grèce	9197	7373	8368	7394	10059
Chile/Chili	4484	6534	7986	7979	8903
Turkey/Turquie	5162	6200	8257	6540	6023
Malaysia/Malaisie	4217	5014	6375	6863	7380
Peru/Pérou	6568	6161	5568	5460	6535
Croatia/Croatie			8519	8506	x8983
Ireland/Irlande	4588	5510	6068	4125	6861
Colombia/Colombie	1893	3683	4445	6715	4873
Argentina/Argentine	2021	3323	5121	5728	11068
Iran (Islamic Rp. of)	x60383	x3185	x3813	x7020	x995
Czech Republic				12130	12863
Russian Federation			x5115	x6416	x14772
Yugoslavia SFR	9666	x10961			
Israel/Israël	5288	3870	3366	3443	4465
Romania/Roumanie	1216	2725	5586	1786	3113
Honduras	1152	2052	2375	4784	2720
India/Inde	2011	3005	2242	3464	6031
Slovenia/Slovénia			3515	3817	4343

COUNTRIES–PAYS	EXPORTS – EXPORTATIONS 1990	1991	1992	1993	1994
Totale	2629889	2616060	2689585	2442798	2820619
Afrique	x26840	x25479	x25754	x24409	x21368
Afrique du Nord	x14773	12804	x12229	x10218	13147
Amériques	x511537	483124	494940	495472	542934
ALAI	74576	71533	105184	114888	145431
MCAC	1379	2469	2020	x2018	x7776
Asie	815263	786971	829393	748835	907312
Moyen–Orient	x62227	x82290	x85346	x98544	x110490
Europe	895073	893613	959836	843282	990707
CEE	859049	852430	908409	806321	957757
AELE	26441	29145	35492	28033	27416
Océanie	x195040	x209789	x237030	x219970	x241236
China/Chine	414572	349367	399451	354419	520817
USA/Etats–Unis d'Amer	345602	339298	312753	299759	321164
Germany/Allemagne	238727	238360	263560	232111	259650
Netherlands/Pays–Bas	151220	153707	162086	159019	190251
New Zealand	114223	134300	152464	145311	158683
Hong Kong	116627	149879	144087	115611	110582
France,Monac	114105	117044	124940	104950	138128
Denmark/Danemark	100243	94690	96559	91255	107922
Hungary/Hongrie	x109347	x88712	x82680	x68585	x69973
Australia/Australie	64842	65482	74103	67886	75048
Canada	64769	54622	60721	63773	61494
United Kingdom	61557	59235	60677	48267	66720
Belgium–Luxembourg	48637	46919	50932	42097	47489
Brazil/Brésil	24617	26787	45073	50616	60256
India/Inde	40528	36426	41441	38604	38526
Italy/Italie	41272	39089	41211	34831	37793
Turkey/Turquie	40758	37173	37928	35900	36184
Poland/Pologne	24039	32058	37705	29654	35378
Spain/Espagne	35350	31900	36478	28795	33246
Russian Federation			x52376	x42793	x32442
Iran (Islamic Rp. of)	x1813	x24556	x35734	x30204	x40877
Former USSR/Anc. URSS	43295	x69375			
Singapore/Singapour	32367	32772	24516	11214	10486
Thailand/Thaïlande	18693	21364	24336	21893	22378
Ireland/Irlande	20616	20392	20119	20287	20412
Japan/Japon	21461	18833	19738	22224	24661
Mongolia/Mongolie	x23837	x22995	x16642	x20558	x4915
Korea, Republic of	16784	16857	18122	17596	19160
Pakistan	19574	18915	16934	14441	13851
Sweden/Suède	14975	15962	15820	13601	16054
Portugal	12014	16057	16419	12898	19887
Switz.Liecht	18234	14861	15624	14456	15413
Norway,SVD,JM	5505	12916	18448	12322	10559
Uruguay	14334	12824	13739	13455	15861
Mexico/Mexique	3828	4997	16851	14882	13185
Austria/Autriche	12943	11206	12487	11923	x12626
Argentina/Argentine	8347	8527	9242	12037	16948
Syrian Arab Republic	1668	x7539	733	x20240	x19525
Romania/Roumanie	878	12473	8859	3841	4407
Cuba	x19208	x11888	x6601	x4332	x1805
Indonesia/Indonésie	12718	7522	8457	6841	7446
Lebanon/Liban	x7077	x8173	x6403	x6608	x7605
So. Africa Customs Un	5750	6856	6918	7133	
Afghanistan	x6065	x5973	x6771	x7538	x355
Viet Nam	x13888	x7816	x3762	x6976	x8434
Colombia/Colombie	2467	4183	6198	7957	26370
Bahamas	x3685	1160	x6330	x9285	x4006
Venezuela	8485	3308	4931	8011	2100
Czechoslovakia		x7395	x8630		
Greece/Grèce	4734	5504	5320	4571	5455

(VALUE AS % OF TOTAL)(VALEUR EN % DU TOTAL)

	1985	1986	1987	1988	1989	1990	1991	1992	1993	1994
Africa	0.9	1.4	x0.9	x0.8	x0.8	x1.0	1.5	x0.8	x1.2	x0.9
Northern Africa	0.2	0.1	0.1	x0.1	x0.0	0.1	0.1	0.1	0.1	0.1
Americas	14.0	13.0	11.3	x11.0	11.4	10.5	11.5	11.5	12.1	13.0
LAIA	2.1	2.1	1.8	2.0	1.9	2.2	2.9	3.0	3.4	3.5
CACM	0.0	0.1	0.1	0.0	0.0	0.1	0.1	0.1	0.2	x0.1
Asia	25.8	24.5	x30.7	x32.5	33.2	x32.9	32.7	31.3	32.0	29.8
Middle East	0.3	x0.5	x0.7	x0.5	x0.4	x2.3	x0.6	x0.5	x0.7	x0.4
Europe	57.4	58.7	52.7	51.4	51.1	52.6	51.2	52.8	50.3	51.7
EEC	49.1	50.8	45.6	45.1	45.3	49.6	48.5	50.1	47.8	49.0
EFTA	8.0	7.6	6.9	6.2	5.4	2.6	2.3	2.1	2.0	2.1
Oceania	1.2	x1.2	x1.1	x1.2	1.4	x1.4	x1.3	x1.3	x1.6	x1.7
Japan/Japon	17.2	15.6	16.6	18.1	20.1	18.8	19.3	18.0	20.0	18.4
Germany/Allemagne	14.3	15.9	15.0	14.7	15.0	16.5	17.1	17.8	17.1	16.9
France,Monac	8.3	8.4	7.7	7.5	8.0	9.1	8.4	8.6	8.1	8.6
USA/Etats–Unis d'Amer	10.0	9.0	7.7	7.0	7.4	6.4	7.0	7.0	7.1	7.8
Hong Kong	3.2	3.1	4.8	5.5	5.8	5.0	5.5	4.9	4.2	3.8
United Kingdom	5.6	6.4	4.8	5.2	5.1	5.5	4.5	5.0	4.9	4.8
Italy/Italie	4.9	4.9	5.1	4.8	4.9	5.6	5.1	4.4	4.1	4.2
Korea, Republic of	2.7	3.0	2.9	3.0	3.9	4.2	4.5	4.7	4.2	3.9
Netherlands/Pays–Bas	3.1	3.3	2.7	2.8	2.7	2.8	2.7	2.8	2.7	3.2
Denmark/Danemark	2.9	2.4	1.9	2.0	1.7	1.5	2.0	2.9	2.4	2.3

	1985	1986	1987	1988	1989	1990	1991	1992	1993	1994
Afrique	1.2	x2.2	x1.9	x1.5	x1.6	x1.0	x1.0	x1.0	x1.0	x0.8
Afrique du Nord	0.4	x0.6	x0.7	0.4	x0.6	x0.6	0.5	x0.5	x0.4	0.5
Amériques	17.4	x17.9	x13.2	13.5	x16.8	x19.4	18.5	18.4	20.3	19.3
ALAI	3.8	2.8	2.1	2.6	2.8	2.8	2.7	3.9	4.7	5.2
MCAC	0.0	0.0	x0.0	0.0	0.1	0.1	0.1	0.1	x0.1	x0.3
Asie	29.0	29.3	x39.2	x39.4	35.7	31.0	30.1	30.8	30.6	32.2
Moyen–Orient	1.0	x2.9	x3.4	x3.3	x2.9	x2.4	x3.1	x3.2	x4.0	x3.9
Europe	43.7	43.3	34.2	33.2	33.5	34.0	34.2	35.7	34.5	35.1
CEE	38.7	39.4	31.3	30.2	30.6	32.7	32.6	33.8	33.0	34.0
AELE	3.6	3.2	2.3	2.3	2.2	1.0	1.1	1.3	1.1	1.0
Océanie	5.9	x5.1	x5.0	x6.4	6.7	x7.4	x8.0	x8.8	x9.0	x8.6
China/Chine	14.1	14.4	16.5	15.4	17.5	15.8	13.4	14.9	14.5	18.5
USA/Etats–Unis d'Amer	9.7	10.5	7.4	8.2	9.9	13.1	13.0	11.6	12.3	11.4
Germany/Allemagne	9.4	9.8	8.4	7.9	8.5	9.1	9.1	9.8	9.5	9.2
Netherlands/Pays–Bas	6.9	6.7	5.2	5.2	5.3	5.8	5.9	6.0	6.5	6.7
New Zealand	4.1	3.3	3.1	4.0	4.3	4.3	5.1	5.7	5.9	5.6
Hong Kong	4.5	3.0	4.9	6.2	7.0	4.4	5.7	5.4	4.7	3.9
France,Monac	5.8	5.5	4.2	4.4	4.7	4.3	4.5	4.6	4.3	4.9
Denmark/Danemark	5.5	5.4	4.2	4.0	3.4	3.8	3.6	3.6	3.7	3.8
Hungary/Hongrie			x3.3	x3.1	x3.2	x4.2	x3.4	x3.1	x2.8	x2.5
Australia/Australie	1.5	1.5	1.6	1.9	2.0	2.5	2.5	2.8	2.8	2.7

TRADE BY COMMODITY IN THOUSAND U.S. DOLLARS – COMMERCE PAR PRODUIT EN MILLIERS DE DOLLARS E.U

COUNTRIES–PAYS	IMPORTS – IMPORTATIONS 1990	1991	1992	1993	1994
Total	12544545	12841304	13782658	11818100	12854144
Africa	x196593	186930	x195295	x174831	x194260
Northern Africa	88245	77753	x82609	77508	x82901
Americas	1713156	1781772	1974297	2086592	2271287
LAIA	231160	268789	358017	371307	423751
CACM	11621	15453	20418	x19833	x20302
Asia	x2352324	2147159	2408878	2346176	2539717
Middle East	x444330	x140745	194869	x183736	x190132
Europe	7863951	8472832	8950519	6948940	7560259
EEC	7328381	7938183	8394904	6425135	6976391
EFTA	479506	485854	509601	479686	523623
Oceania	x72983	x78427	x90907	x96499	x116098
Germany/Allemagne	2411742	2773638	3040942	1982502	2146368
USA/Etats–Unis d'Amer	1189165	1227097	1307461	1399490	1525206
France,Monac	1189891	1219199	1205420	931236	1011513
Japan/Japon	840643	918922	977192	986830	1126748
United Kingdom	799662	817594	840160	716549	795510
Netherlands/Pays–Bas	684877	721924	851895	679199	784912
Italy/Italie	677902	748602	736926	647676	652668
Hong Kong	505301	506958	543136	440971	438008
Switz.Liecht	383554	391257	408194	388825	426068
Belgium–Luxembourg	325214	355114	364467	291719	336519
Sweden/Suède	284581	302495	320084	264871	265262
Spain/Espagne	252808	278036	293159	228999	255482
Canada	244982	239572	259091	268025	274395
Austria/Autriche	232151	236671	255001	244059	271089
Denmark/Danemark	181054	191559	187302	183285	185820
Mexico/Mexique	109177	122172	157262	174728	190121
Korea, Republic of	99344	128067	155974	158839	179533
Singapore/Singapour	140246	132753	139474	142871	158875
China/Chine	62172	77616	129482	134910	121314
Finland/Finlande	118568	111413	103603	82604	90851
Norway,SVD,JM	91955	90474	97405	87346	93874
Greece/Grèce	57779	64799	69224	64269	64253
Australia/Australie	55935	57383	68880	71792	85851
Malaysia/Malaisie	52861	58759	65978	64592	75068
Ireland/Irlande	61539	62094	61378	58066	65225
Portugal	50613	55045	65343	50100	50918
Argentina/Argentine	22873	38460	60446	63311	82655
Poland/Pologne	14386	30263	55519	55325	64170
Thailand/Thaïlande	38351	38517	43836	53500	59080
Hungary/Hongrie	x27433	29510	x46450	x49846	x41698
So. Africa Customs Un	46878	44275	44910	36446	38633
Brazil/Brésil	33008	40542	36227	44564	50136
Saudi Arabia	39510	34535	47535	x38565	x53237
Turkey/Turquie	26554	25393	35141	41847	36840
Pakistan	38253	34529	31614	35860	31775
Czechoslovakia	19150	x43410	x45872		
Colombia/Colombie	24288	19593	36165	26097	'27441
Israel/Israël	35396	25422	26080	29377	33291
United Arab Emirates	22791	24756	29021	x25539	x27234
India/Inde	31834	19553	24995	30303	36253
Morocco/Maroc	20975	22572	22397	26931	25147
Indonesia/Indonésie	19406	20661	22669	26245	30174
Philippines	16119	16935	18409	30180	23399
Venezuela	12970	17164	23638	20757	20157
Russian Federation			x39774	x21492	x47769
Former USSR/Anc. URSS	237211	x60482			
Egypt/Egypte	16150	15381	17157	22279	22232
New Zealand	12747	15060	17223	20498	24403
Chile/Chili	11678	12026	16533	18237	22651
Kuwait/Koweït	9265	7948	17811	20675	19296

COUNTRIES–PAYS	EXPORTS – EXPORTATIONS 1990	1991	1992	1993	1994
Totale	11454035	12021925	12942094	11683723	13182071
Afrique	x300720	x361073	x387863	x415638	x548787
Afrique du Nord	x159866	x186735	x184167	x165891	x250611
Amériques	1431070	1589478	1816937	1862157	x2067012
ALAI	448766	552423	651069	689068	800096
MCAC	89035	89652	107185	x110616	x168502
Asie	2189007	2198677	2300546	2191775	2417553
Moyen–Orient	91639	x82365	x85680	x63962	x68678
Europe	7089764	7533367	8159272	6949667	7865069
CEE	6987376	7456211	8071465	6867796	7775492
AELE	64630	63997	66941	65556	74515
Océanie	x109046	x123416	x130730	x137447	x160387
Netherlands/Pays–Bas	4194189	4456204	4863680	4077456	4740753
USA/Etats–Unis d'Amer	720675	788380	870263	869311	879924
Germany/Allemagne	573317	650107	687816	595377	620426
Denmark/Danemark	531912	580989	600237	507605	511575
France,Monac	414245	443278	490280	462925	502565
Italy/Italie	439526	433148	492110	440915	508793
Hong Kong	383875	446160	457624	377559	338553
China/Chine	394723	350350	391729	390209	596568
Belgium–Luxembourg	358851	371039	378912	337569	366140
Colombia/Colombie	230410	282888	342925	385034	434607
Korea, Republic of	318203	296693	306794	281653	296356
Israel/Israël	193588	216984	206115	213007	229380
Spain/Espagne	197454	209319	207184	189538	240397
India/Inde	171175	165604	176090	168896	186096
Canada	156023	143647	174821	179392	199874
Japan/Japon	131994	137396	175650	152623	154364
Singapore/Singapour	156653	147236	147682	152420	180374
United Kingdom	127935	132624	153945	120068	135324
Sudan/Soudan	x73506	x103521	x99501	x92580	x161929
Chile/Chili	79410	91650	97828	103989	124734
Mexico/Mexique	62621	85689	115899	89436	98457
Thailand/Thaïlande	83779	92526	99665	97054	96100
Ireland/Irlande	66675	77249	103136	62617	70031
Costa Rica	68118	66601	77321	x87374	x138375
Australia/Australie	55584	66151	67799	72210	80634
Indonesia/Indonésie	55359	60385	64488	76594	69487
Switz.Liecht	57981	57615	61559	60329	68561
New Zealand	50147	53015	60835	63531	76586
Kenya	31116	48517	58540	64000	x148982
Morocco/Maroc	50639	48920	52380	51224	64662
Poland/Pologne	75427	81936	31813	36489	39890
Philippines	57618	48193	42170	50698	59532
Hungary/Hongrie	x48816	x38626	x49325	x32691	x33762
Brazil/Brésil	32926	38074	40501	40331	47040
So. Africa Customs Un	33615	36022	37879	40813	
Turkey/Turquie	50726	43947	32558	32156	37700
Pakistan	42902	33693	33686	35218	41541
Ecuador/Equateur	18167	26071	27019	39085	x65437
Sweden/Suède	33011	41192	29829	16799	17732
Malaysia/Malaisie	21045	24515	34761	26163	35068
Viet Nam	x30862	x29642	x18321	x33854	x22372
Egypt/Egypte	28124	27223	27844	17940	20427
Portugal	16797	25708	26081	21059	24495
Korea Dem People's Rp	x20302	x27266	x20069	x18654	x8953
Austria/Autriche	20945	21224	23555	20561	x23529
Bulgaria/Bulgarie	x78184	x32834	x23122	x7982	x14488
Iran (Islamic Rp. of)	x1787	x17806	x29950	x15947	x13210
Albania/Albanie	x4745	x19117	x20058	x23084	x8619
Guatemala	15927	18563	23652	18482	24814
Zimbabwe	7074	10410	13545	31873	x39396

(VALUE AS % OF TOTAL)(VALEUR EN % DU TOTAL)

	1985	1986	1987	1988	1989	1990	1991	1992	1993	1994
Africa	2.2	2.2	x1.6	x1.5	x1.5	x1.6	1.4	x1.4	x1.5	x1.5
Northern Africa	1.2	1.1	0.7	0.8	0.7	0.7	0.6	x0.6	0.7	x0.6
Americas	18.8	16.1	14.1	14.2	14.9	13.6	13.9	14.4	17.6	17.7
LAIA	2.8	2.4	2.0	2.2	1.9	1.8	2.1	2.6	3.1	3.3
CACM	0.2	0.2	0.1	0.1	0.1	0.1	0.1	0.1	x0.2	x0.2
Asia	15.8	14.5	x16.9	x18.8	17.5	x18.8	16.8	17.5	19.9	19.7
Middle East	1.7	x1.8	x1.6	x1.3	x1.4	x3.5	x1.1	1.4	x1.6	x1.5
Europe	59.2	63.5	63.6	61.6	63.3	62.7	66.0	64.9	58.8	58.8
EEC	50.9	54.5	54.5	52.9	54.5	58.4	61.8	60.9	54.4	54.3
EFTA	8.0	8.7	8.8	8.4	8.6	3.8	3.8	3.7	4.1	4.1
Oceania	0.7	x0.7	x0.6	x0.7	x0.7	x0.5	x0.6	x0.6	x0.8	x0.9
Germany/Allemagne	16.9	18.6	18.3	17.5	17.4	19.2	21.6	22.1	16.8	16.7
USA/Etats–Unis d'Amer	13.2	11.1	9.8	9.8	10.4	9.5	9.6	9.5	11.8	11.9
France,Monac	8.0	8.9	8.9	8.4	8.9	9.5	9.5	8.7	7.9	7.9
Japan/Japon	5.3	4.8	4.7	6.3	7.3	6.7	7.2	7.1	8.4	8.8
United Kingdom	5.8	5.7	5.8	6.0	6.3	6.4	6.4	6.1	6.1	6.2
Netherlands/Pays–Bas	4.6	5.1	5.0	4.8	5.0	5.5	5.6	6.2	5.7	6.1
Italy/Italie	5.1	5.0	5.2	5.1	5.2	5.4	5.8	5.3	5.5	5.1
Hong Kong	4.3	4.1	4.2	4.2	4.0	4.0	3.9	3.9	3.7	3.4
Switz.Liecht	2.7	3.0	3.1	3.0	2.9	3.1	3.0	3.0	3.3	3.3
Belgium–Luxembourg	2.0	2.2	2.3	2.3	2.4	2.6	2.8	2.6	2.5	2.6

	1985	1986	1987	1988	1989	1990	1991	1992	1993	1994
Afrique	2.2	x3.5	x3.5	x2.7	x3.2	x2.6	x3.0	x3.0	x3.5	x4.2
Afrique du Nord	1.0	1.6	1.7	1.3	x1.4	x1.4	x1.6	x1.4	x1.4	x1.9
Amériques	15.3	12.2	10.4	11.1	12.8	12.5	13.3	14.1	16.0	x15.7
ALAI	4.6	3.8	3.1	3.6	4.2	3.9	4.6	5.0	5.9	6.1
MCAC	1.8	0.6	0.6	0.7	0.7	0.8	0.7	0.8	x0.9	x1.3
Asie	22.1	19.8	20.9	22.9	20.8	19.1	18.2	17.7	18.7	18.3
Moyen–Orient	0.8	x1.0	x0.8	x0.9	0.6	0.8	x0.7	x0.7	x0.5	x0.5
Europe	57.6	62.2	60.3	58.9	59.5	61.9	62.7	63.0	59.5	59.7
CEE	55.8	60.5	58.8	57.1	57.7	61.0	62.0	62.4	58.8	59.0
AELE	1.0	1.1	1.0	1.1	1.1	0.6	0.5	0.5	0.6	0.6
Océanie	0.8	x0.8	x0.8	0.9	x0.9	x0.9	x1.0	x1.0	x1.2	x1.2
Netherlands/Pays–Bas	31.4	34.7	33.7	34.1	34.3	36.6	37.1	37.6	34.9	36.0
USA/Etats–Unis d'Amer	7.0	5.8	4.9	5.3	6.0	6.3	6.6	6.7	7.4	6.7
Germany/Allemagne	4.9	5.4	4.8	4.7	4.8	5.0	5.4	5.3	5.1	4.7
Denmark/Danemark	4.2	4.5	4.5	4.4	4.4	4.6	4.8	4.6	4.3	3.9
France,Monac	3.9	4.2	3.8	3.4	3.4	3.6	3.7	3.8	4.0	3.8
Italy/Italie	3.9	4.0	5.0	3.3	3.6	3.8	3.6	3.8	3.8	3.9
Hong Kong	4.5	3.5	3.6	4.0	3.8	3.4	3.7	3.5	3.2	2.6
China/Chine	2.4	2.5	2.7	3.1	3.7	3.4	2.9	3.0	3.3	4.5
Belgium–Luxembourg	2.8	2.9	2.7	2.8	2.8	3.1	3.1	2.9	2.9	2.8
Colombia/Colombie	2.6	2.2	1.6	2.0	2.3	2.0	2.4	2.6	3.3	3.3

TRADE BY COMMODITY IN THOUSAND U.S. DOLLARS – COMMERCE PAR PRODUIT EN MILLIERS DE DOLLARS E.U

COUNTRIES–PAYS	IMPORTS – IMPORTATIONS 1990	1991	1992	1993	1994
Total	20178862	22446369	20796182	18577015	18362258
Africa	299023	276701	246400	261049	231592
Northern Africa	252970	220122	183315	212242	187056
Americas	1494637	1461909	1588982	1522571	1549150
LAIA	754913	801242	814215	800007	803747
CACM	88	27	26	x71	x1069
Asia	9067237	9630018	9416327	9460658	9245489
Middle East	349155	357017	x370799	x399433	418379
Europe	8869650	8690647	8927606	6573200	6630063
EEC	8517622	8526916	8769529	6371539	6482259
EFTA	132228	105223	87751	84197	98319
Oceania	11126	10304	9505	13746	x21120
Japan/Japon	6214806	6425084	6110767	5965043	5752136
Korea, Republic of	1270570	1580804	1596543	1712140	1753169
United Kingdom	1114964	1271789	1273539	1014003	870533
France,Monac	1230450	1310556	1324247	805444	772479
Italy/Italie	1137789	1153406	997355	762944	839741
Netherlands/Pays–Bas	1024605	941182	887407	781178	833249
Germany/Allemagne	705743	936106	964258	681216	790418
Belgium–Luxembourg	966345	945223	934286	693583	743187
Czechoslovakia	96419	x1892835	x141999		
Spain/Espagne	564950	710158	736590	582468	537362
Brazil/Brésil	582433	668544	669226	648479	618936
India/Inde	416822	367240	505262	451287	648350
Canada	523989	412712	490083	318564	317507
Hong Kong	339620	380410	405118	432110	304192
USA/Etats–Unis d'Amer	206791	238230	275393	393875	417117
Turkey/Turquie	309278	333825	248317	306510	377819
Austria/Autriche	269903	278561	274827	202949	186139
Romania/Roumanie	292009	232021	328679	188788	229857
Finland/Finlande	310952	259400	188800	219943	305170
Ireland/Irlande	231015	227148	224997	194753	168194
Portugal	249439	221234	208842	187098	203848
Denmark/Danemark	462110	11727	519248	27395	23574
Sweden/Suède	203010	185473	170809	165484	151927
Korea Dem People's Rp	x190604	x165941	x137228	x152436	x67423
Slovakia				x310197	x203559
Hungary/Hongrie	x6075	174471	x30852	x90899	x79744
Malaysia/Malaisie	78357	93657	102973	89771	80546
Egypt/Egypte	115702	80325	74725	92359	106532
Bulgaria/Bulgarie	x28774	x55432	98524	x92144	x73372
Ukraine			x59977	x159951	x97838
Chile/Chili	93950	80279	48312	76752	82878
Pakistan	47080	68324	58408	76066	56635
Greece/Grèce	46348	74952	64322	53081	56438
Algeria/Algérie	65169	64524	51991	70509	23085
Norway,SVD,JM	74628	63611	57279	57525	67792
Morocco/Maroc	68956	74832	54950	47675	56442
Argentina/Argentine	62880	46560	66541	52658	63814
Philippines	35267	79462	30103	51626	38137
China/Chine	74148	47199	43301	41626	33731
Iran (Islamic Rp. of)	x29469	x10122	x47267	x68601	x24207
So. Africa Customs Un	27800	37999	40596	23803	28841
Switz.Liecht	52272	36446	26079	22310	24957
Indonesia/Indonésie	32550	35302	25051	22379	13047
Croatia/Croatie			34959	45919	x6258
Thailand/Thaïlande	14047	18921	18964	36582	53937
Yemen/Yémen			x61478		
Yugoslavia/Yougoslavie			x16996	x41840	x10747
Czech Republic				57750	55672
Yugoslavia SFR	206401	x46305			
Lithuania/Lituanie			30584		18320

COUNTRIES–PAYS	EXPORTS – EXPORTATIONS 1990	1991	1992	1993	1994
Totale	18032919	18270452	16862682	15989776	15493567
Afrique	x1408342	x1415920	x1413558	x1613346	x1292263
Afrique du Nord	910	6	x175	x8564	x220
Amériques	7059636	7300423	6402419	5362123	5176439
ALAI	606446	713813	630742	687111	662310
MCAC	43	1257		11	14
Asie	x978257	x1264288	1607235	1536627	1738912
Moyen–Orient	x1472	x8712	x139	x1691	x3654
Europe	1286764	1155870	966062	784005	850331
CEE	1284128	1153739	960888	781322	846461
AELE	385	323	573	348	2285
Océanie	4429519	x4919028	5329833	5283566	4954755
Australia/Australie	4409652	4884901	5289498	5240985	4904860
USA/Etats–Unis d'Amer	4514194	4682750	4242774	3092612	2861602
Canada	1919829	1902447	1520834	1582327	1652497
So. Africa Customs Un	1400330	1409737	1408694	1601848	1289876
Poland/Pologne	970803	939045	925968	978865	1057217
China/Chine	654148	748480	742802	702238	770982
Colombia/Colombie	536972	624185	545126	557393	545575
Russian Federation			836300	x780981	x684925
Indonesia/Indonésie	165046	263846	600042	642141	819264
Germany/Allemagne	760388	637501	488044	334014	346335
Former USSR/Anc. URSS	1894682	x1062888			
Netherlands/Pays–Bas	170021	168953	175836	147812	191022
Czech Republic				426341	418394
Czechoslovakia		x208339	x204274		
Ukraine			x151166	x180202	x135504
Viet Nam	x25621	x116933	x103286	x84306	x83906
Venezuela	68953	88932	85308	129478	116301
United Kingdom	153441	126898	81218	79545	70930
France,Monac	69587	78356	79646	64613	66934
Korea Dem People's Rp	x123947	x110237	x58546	x38652	x17419
Belgium–Luxembourg	62899	67868	54835	73765	96090
Ireland/Irlande	39115	45128	54179	56306	40907
New Zealand	19867	34016	40336	42581	49895
Kazakstan			x73860	x28072	x8399
India/Inde	4792	6179	19360	20974	28150
Sweden/Suède	8053	9238	9264	11077	12297
Finland/Finlande	9183	8953	10023	8198	10840
Lithuania/Lituanie				x21632	34121
Estonia/Estonie			x2748	x17510	x23091
Singapore/Singapour	720	7820	4404	4523	1075
Latvia/Lettonie			x9275	x1709	6405
Afghanistan				x10892	
Denmark/Danemark	4661	3945	3851	2459	3774
Hungary/Hongrie	x320	x651	x7675	x1105	x3447
Italy/Italie	4863	5646	1449	832	2946
Saudi Arabia	10	x6216	x116	x994	x2442
Libyan Arab Jamahiriya				x6581	x106
Bulgaria/Bulgarie		x1537	x4245		
Bahamas	x19123		x5315		
Albania/Albanie	x2397	x2448	x929	x1742	x629
Slovenia/Slovénia			2897	1695	964
Mozambique	x4786	x2172	x1020	x1382	
Republic of Moldova			x2939	x608	12
Austria/Autriche	1405	873	1308	807	x2080
Belarus/Bélarus			x1333	x1547	x3461
Malaysia/Malaisie	649	1050	960	864	1692
Japan/Japon	686	444	1059	1028	984
Georgia/Géorgie			x2246	x210	
Zimbabwe	1498	1033	613	646	x78
Central African Rep.		x2240			x1194

(VALUE AS % OF TOTAL)(VALEUR EN % DU TOTAL)

	1985	1986	1987	1988	1989	1990	1991	1992	1993	1994
Africa	1.1	1.2	1.5	1.2	1.1	1.4	1.3	1.2	1.4	1.3
Northern Africa	1.1	1.2	1.3	1.1	1.1	1.3	1.0	0.9	1.1	1.0
Americas	8.5	8.3	7.9	7.7	7.9	7.4	6.5	7.7	8.2	8.4
LAIA	3.7	3.9	3.8	3.7	3.9	3.7	3.6	3.9	4.3	4.4
CACM	0.0	0.0	0.0	x0.0	0.0	0.0	0.0	0.0	x0.0	x0.0
Asia	41.0	41.2	x41.0	x44.6	44.2	44.9	42.9	45.3	50.9	50.3
Middle East	0.9	1.2	1.3	1.5	1.4	1.7	1.6	x1.8	x2.2	2.3
Europe	47.8	48.5	42.0	38.6	41.7	44.0	38.7	42.9	35.4	36.1
EEC	41.2	41.7	36.2	33.3	36.0	42.2	38.0	42.2	34.3	35.3
EFTA	4.9	5.3	4.5	3.9	4.1	0.7	0.5	0.4	0.5	0.5
Oceania		x0.0	x0.0		0.1					x0.1
Japan/Japon	30.5	30.0	27.0	28.6	30.4	30.8	28.6	29.4	32.1	31.3
Korea, Republic of	6.0	6.2	5.7	6.1	6.6	6.3	7.0	7.7	9.2	9.5
United Kingdom	5.2	4.1	3.7	4.1	4.2	5.5	5.7	6.1	5.5	4.7
France,Monac	5.9	6.3	4.6	4.0	4.8	6.1	5.8	6.4	4.3	4.2
Italy/Italie	7.1	7.0	6.5	5.1	5.8	5.6	5.1	4.8	4.1	4.6
Netherlands/Pays–Bas	4.0	4.3	3.9	4.1	4.2	5.1	4.2	4.3	4.2	4.5
Germany/Allemagne	3.3	3.6	2.8	2.2	2.0	3.5	4.2	4.6	3.7	4.3
Belgium–Luxembourg	3.8	4.1	4.0	3.8	4.0	4.8	4.2	4.5	3.7	4.0
Czechoslovakia	1.4	0.6	0.4	0.6	0.6	0.5	x8.4	x0.7		
Spain/Espagne	2.6	2.4	2.1	2.1	2.8	2.8	3.2	3.5	3.1	2.9

	1985	1986	1987	1988	1989	1990	1991	1992	1993	1994
Afrique	9.9	8.7	x7.8	x6.8	x7.1	x7.8	x7.7	x8.4	x10.1	x8.3
Afrique du Nord	0.0	0.0	0.0	x0.0	x0.0	0.0	0.0	x0.0	x0.1	x0.0
Amériques	42.5	35.1	33.5	37.1	40.2	39.2	39.9	38.0	33.5	33.4
ALAI	0.9	1.2	1.8	2.0	3.1	3.4	3.9	3.7	4.3	4.3
MCAC		x0.0	x0.0	0.0		0.0	0.0		0.0	0.0
Asie	2.4	2.8	4.1	x4.5	x4.6	x5.4	x6.9	9.5	9.6	11.2
Moyen–Orient	0.0	x0.0	x0.0	x0.0	x0.0	x0.0	x0.0	x0.0	x0.0	x0.0
Europe	8.5	8.5	8.6	7.6	6.7	7.1	6.3	5.7	4.9	5.5
CEE	8.4	8.4	8.4	7.5	6.6	7.1	6.3	5.7	4.9	5.5
AELE	0.2	0.1	0.2	0.1	0.1	0.0	0.0	0.0	0.0	0.0
Océanie	24.8	x22.7	23.8	22.5	23.2	24.6	x26.9	31.6	33.0	32.0
Australia/Australie	24.7	22.6	23.7	22.3	23.0	24.5	26.7	31.4	32.8	31.7
USA/Etats–Unis d'Amer	31.0	24.9	22.7	24.8	26.0	25.0	25.6	25.2	19.3	18.5
Canada	10.6	9.0	9.0	10.3	11.1	10.6	10.4	9.0	9.9	10.7
So. Africa Customs Un	9.8	8.6	7.7	6.8	7.1	7.8	7.7	8.4	10.0	8.3
Poland/Pologne	10.4	8.5	7.4	6.9	5.4	5.4	5.1	5.5	6.1	6.8
China/Chine	2.0	2.5	3.2	3.2	3.4	3.6	4.1	4.4	4.4	5.0
Colombia/Colombie	0.9	1.2	1.7	1.8	2.7	3.0	3.4	3.2	3.5	3.5
Russian Federation								5.0	x4.9	x4.4
Indonesia/Indonésie	0.2	0.2	0.2	0.3	0.5	0.9	1.4	3.6	4.0	5.3
Germany/Allemagne	5.2	5.3	5.3	4.4	4.2	4.2	3.5	2.9	2.1	2.2

TRADE BY COMMODITY IN THOUSAND U.S. DOLLARS – COMMERCE PAR PRODUIT EN MILLIERS DE DOLLARS E.U

COUNTRIES–PAYS	IMPORTS – IMPORTATIONS 1990	1991	1992	1993	1994	COUNTRIES–PAYS	EXPORTS – EXPORTATIONS 1990	1991	1992	1993	1994
Total	2016575	2121943	1933912	1760576	2064553	Totale	1995798	1950376	1812952	1544906	1773821
Africa	57682	32962	27147	x27683	21434	Afrique	24106	25513	18635	31148	x44134
Northern Africa	40701	23112	19579	20903	19031	Afrique du Nord	12664	17977	10507	22301	35129
Americas	335688	365951	447151	452141	640331	Amériques	138320	119803	x143112	137179	133701
LAIA	136882	190831	186691	194206	240705	ALAI	10267	9466	14689	8724	11432
CACM	706	606	701	657	800	MCAC	40	1	1		
Asia	x286572	189768	x239087	161031	207260	Asie	290208	342576	383192	450538	620999
Middle East	x151083	x6458	x114873	x39598	30115	Moyen–Orient	139	x464	x485	x255	1893
Europe	1211277	1288750	1144802	1007975	1103820	Europe	973271	895808	848238	550805	505261
EEC	1108566	1089757	1033985	926172	1018426	CEE	962040	889620	805700	512545	477894
EFTA	92305	82205	74779	58195	69707	AELE	651	555	19		3
Oceania	x3515	x3871	x17776	x7699	9170	Océanie	56018	80872	68116	59262	38474
Belgium–Luxembourg	299861	267497	230171	201641	223364	Germany/Allemagne	585290	552683	457164	193208	191149
Germany/Allemagne	108864	173144	225779	221054	232856	Japan/Japon	177888	241360	276173	266571	299102
USA/Etats–Unis d'Amer	127534	120197	203927	197818	330146	Poland/Pologne	157264	316513	244814	147610	266950
Brazil/Brésil	77989	142115	140939	112778	164954	China/Chine	100837	80898	97171	172201	283007
France,Monac	178656	124256	123032	123664	158954	Netherlands/Pays–Bas	94048	105136	128574	100004	89848
Austria/Autriche	147581	146130	121363	96420	90390	USA/Etats–Unis d'Amer	95788	98249	83099	108085	102150
Italy/Italie	63266	108221	69357	69029	53045	France,Monac	69803	69255	71364	75416	66332
United Kingdom	52860	61946	75530	85166	57607	Belgium–Luxembourg	105573	73425	67461	69213	48714
Finland/Finlande	105756	80874	75887	41802	42365	Australia/Australie	56018	80872	68116	59262	38474
Norway,SVD,JM	78828	67236	60857	48226	56989	Czechoslovakia		x93849	x80087		
Canada	61706	43589	43616	56736	64839	Czech Republic				139512	140072
Romania/Roumanie	111144	85024	19666	28438	11675	Russian Federation			x104361	x33296	x30472
Mexico/Mexique	22365	27669	36600	54782	48288	United Kingdom	65451	51168	34715	28424	42472
Yugoslavia SFR	10379	x116741				Croatia/Croatie			39212	36620	x26326
Netherlands/Pays–Bas	45584	41118	39339	30950	53332	Italy/Italie	26669	21661	28825	23795	19892
Sweden/Suède	48037	41612	39960	27866	65377	Hungary/Hongrie	x33535	x21946	x18437	x14741	x16054
India/Inde	18148	55356	28397	15214	60040	Egypt/Egypte	12350	17951	10490	22298	34381
Yemen/Yémen	x135378		x95105	x7		Canada	25133	12086	18980	19536	20108
Japan/Japon	36730	38557	21989	28679	43111	Former USSR/Anc. URSS	251464	x45705			
Russian Federation			x85647	x97	x2275	Spain/Espagne	9672	9242	10527	12807	12152
Hungary/Hongrie	x4249	36287	x8105	x23070	x22644	Ukraine			x9311	x16471	x5363
Former USSR/Anc. URSS		x65664				Colombia/Colombie	7782	6003	10304	7021	7346
Korea, Republic of	17688	19125	19432	20700	23408	Bahamas			x21705		
Turkey/Turquie	12645	3329	13319	30008	24069	Indonesia/Indonésie	3066	10796	2628	2934	10383
Czechoslovakia	5109	x43124	x3002			So. Africa Customs Un	3218	3458	5374	7049	
Slovakia				x45450	x22851	Singapore/Singapour	3236	5472	3670	4412	4844
Bulgaria/Bulgarie	x1336	x10518	26564	x2481	x6375	Romania/Roumanie		238	2648	6342	5370
Spain/Espagne	30314	16168	12421	10640	25209	Sweden/Suède	3762	3088	2683	3056	2489
Philippines	10276	25664	6364	6061	6559	Zimbabwe	8215	4058	2753	1721	x7775
Tunisia/Tunisie	17943	11716	11984	13715	12077	Former GDR	x27518	x3567	x3567		
Korea Dem People's Rp	x14860	x9194	x17135	x10484	x2592	Yugoslavia SFR	10580	x5632			
Malaysia/Malaisie	9845	12976	10970	11991	13019	Portugal	1212	2491	3062		12
Thailand/Thaïlande	11224	12274	11011	11991	14669	Slovakia				x5523	x2772
Peru/Pérou	13748	16598	823	17693	15626	Suriname/Suriname	7091		4639		
Switz.Liecht	9153	10626	11144	8288	9276	Bulgaria/Bulgarie	x44093	x34	x2102	x2246	x34
Denmark/Danemark	8759	11299	8739	7762	5612	Ireland/Irlande	126	1011	842	2507	2019
Yugoslavia/Yougoslavie			x18808	x5519	x109	Albania/Albanie		x3953	x3		
Ireland/Irlande	7675	8812	6481	5439	5349	Greece/Grèce				3691	
Venezuela	11888	2416	8014	8821	8095	Venezuela		8	2860	743	4
Indonesia/Indonésie	6691	5578	4102	9561	5403	Argentina/Argentine	2156	2295	980	62	3372
Morocco/Maroc	5504	6554	5812	5502	6681	Viet Nam			x100	x3005	x2502
Slovenia/Slovénia			9426	7204	8022	Slovenia/Slovénia			2171	635	513
New Caledonia			x13627	x645		Malaysia/Malaisie	26	612	1020	351	100
Suriname/Suriname	6284	6768	7354	x52		Yugoslavia/Yougoslavie			x782	x986	x464
Greece/Grèce	7880	6115	3738	3275	2702	Pakistan	3384	1728			
Australia/Australie	2085	2530	2851	6081	7904	Korea, Republic of	1334	1033	424	94	13266
Singapore/Singapour	5251	3042	3221	3551	4161	Mexico/Mexique	323	1087	8	235	41
Ukraine			x6623	x3163	x5	Chile/Chili	5	6	536	663	668
Croatia/Croatie			7625	1316	x1915	Georgia/Géorgie			x923	x224	
Iceland/Islande	4325	4344	2777	1680	3442	Lithuania/Lituanie				x634	

(VALUE AS % OF TOTAL)(VALEUR EN % DU TOTAL)

	1985	1986	1987	1988	1989	1990	1991	1992	1993	1994
Africa	1.0	x2.0	x1.2	x1.0	x1.3	2.9	1.5	1.4	x1.6	1.1
Northern Africa	0.8	0.9	0.7	0.6	0.8	2.0	1.1	1.0	1.2	0.9
Americas	10.0	8.1	9.3	17.2	21.7	16.7	17.2	23.1	25.7	31.0
LAIA	3.0	2.4	4.0	5.8	8.1	6.8	9.0	9.7	11.0	11.7
CACM	0.0	0.0	x0.0	0.0	0.0	0.0	0.0	0.0	0.0	0.0
Asia	4.6	4.5	x4.2	x5.0	5.4	x14.2	8.9	x12.4	9.2	10.0
Middle East	1.4	0.6	x0.5	0.4	0.7	x7.5	x0.3	x5.9	x2.2	1.5
Europe	82.0	83.1	54.9	50.3	54.0	60.1	60.7	59.2	57.3	53.5
EEC	59.3	59.1	39.4	38.0	40.0	55.0	51.4	53.5	52.6	49.3
EFTA	22.2	23.0	14.9	11.9	13.5	4.6	3.9	3.9	3.3	3.4
Oceania	0.2				x0.1	x0.2	x0.2	x0.9	x0.4	0.4
Belgium–Luxembourg	12.4	13.9	9.5	10.4	10.3	14.9	12.6	11.9	11.5	10.8
Germany/Allemagne	4.3	5.4	3.5	3.3	3.4	5.4	8.2	11.7	12.6	11.3
USA/Etats–Unis d'Amer	2.8	1.5	2.7	8.2	10.2	6.3	5.7	10.5	11.2	16.0
Brazil/Brésil	0.6	0.7	2.4	3.6	5.2	3.9	6.7	7.3	6.4	8.0
France,Monac	14.2	10.6	6.8	7.1	7.7	8.9	5.9	6.4	7.0	7.7
Austria/Autriche	9.1	9.4	6.3	4.8	4.3	7.3	6.9	6.3	5.5	4.4
Italy/Italie	1.5	2.3	2.5	1.6	2.8	3.1	5.1	3.6	3.9	2.6
United Kingdom	3.3	1.7	1.8	3.5	2.7	2.6	2.9	3.9	4.8	2.8
Finland/Finlande	6.6	6.6	4.3	2.8	3.5	5.2	3.8	3.9	2.4	2.1
Norway,SVD,JM	3.3	3.6	2.3	2.1	2.8	3.9	3.2	3.1	2.7	2.8

	1985	1986	1987	1988	1989	1990	1991	1992	1993	1994
Afrique	1.2	1.3	0.7	0.7	1.2	1.2	1.3	1.0	2.1	x2.5
Afrique du Nord	0.3	0.6	0.4	0.3	0.8	0.6	0.9	0.6	1.4	2.0
Amériques	6.1	x4.8	3.3	4.1	6.0	7.0	6.2	x7.9	8.9	7.5
ALAI	0.5	0.7	0.4	0.5	0.7	0.5	0.5	0.8	0.6	0.6
MCAC		x0.0	0.0	0.0	0.0	0.0	0.0	0.0		
Asie	13.3	12.8	11.8	11.6	16.0	14.5	17.6	21.1	29.2	35.0
Moyen–Orient	0.0	0.1	x0.0	x0.0	x0.0	0.0	x0.0	x0.0	x0.0	0.1
Europe	66.6	54.0	40.4	43.0	45.4	48.8	45.9	46.8	35.7	28.5
CEE	63.6	51.2	37.5	41.5	44.0	48.2	45.6	44.4	33.2	26.9
AELE	1.1	1.5	1.3	x0.7	0.3	0.0	0.0	0.0		0.0
Océanie	0.8	1.5	1.3	2.2	2.9	2.8	4.1	3.8	3.8	2.2
Germany/Allemagne	41.0	32.1	23.9	27.0	29.5	29.3	28.3	25.2	12.5	10.8
Japan/Japon	11.0	9.7	9.1	8.4	10.7	8.9	12.4	15.2	17.3	16.9
Poland/Pologne	5.1	4.0	4.3	4.9	6.0	7.9	16.2	13.5	9.6	15.0
China/Chine	1.9	2.7	2.4	2.8	4.9	5.1	4.1	5.4	11.1	16.0
Netherlands/Pays–Bas	4.6	3.8	3.5	3.3	3.2	4.7	5.4	7.1	6.5	5.1
USA/Etats–Unis d'Amer	5.0	3.6	2.5	2.9	4.1	4.8	5.0	4.6	7.0	5.8
France,Monac	4.5	3.8	2.9	3.1	2.7	3.5	3.6	3.9	4.9	3.7
Belgium–Luxembourg	4.2	3.4	3.4	4.0	4.3	5.3	3.8	3.7	4.5	2.7
Australia/Australie	0.8	1.5	1.3	2.2	2.9	2.8	4.1	3.8	3.8	2.2
Czechoslovakia	6.9	6.2	6.8	6.4	x2.8		x4.8	x4.4		

TRADE BY COMMODITY IN THOUSAND U.S. DOLLARS – COMMERCE PAR PRODUIT EN MILLIERS DE DOLLARS E.U

COUNTRIES–PAYS	IMPORTS – IMPORTATIONS 1990	1991	1992	1993	1994
Total	209080346	189584544	191806451	180251549	172619704
Africa	x2262928	x1479580	x1998644	x1711242	909451
Northern Africa	x1237186	x916109	x1152268	x985736	827721
Americas	62303562	51437300	51644611	x49985394	x49950822
LAIA	6072782	5078161	4712802	3423203	3529465
CACM	383040	329949	491693	x384239	x369118
Asia	60801143	59933428	63313170	60511055	56834290
Middle East	5794874	4630819	4619940	4538920	3178943
Europe	75349742	71162813	69952437	61885930	59234985
EEC	72335804	69608848	68545154	60432242	58333779
EFTA	810164	1001488	799597	787685	703425
Oceania	x1581707	x1675048	x1831614	x2093517	x2040517
USA/Etats–Unis d'Amer	46578989	39894284	41200411	41001607	40930163
Japan/Japon	30995477	29743443	29621069	27771439	27233288
Germany/Allemagne	12670429	13779514	14227417	12673848	12840788
Italy/Italie	12033239	10765333	10208797	8872737	8584436
France, Monac	11617236	10624112	9727500	8949245	8783568
Korea, Republic of	6385929	8133535	9548437	9150936	8878269
Netherlands/Pays–Bas	8113313	7539308	7687255	6496436	6400463
United Kingdom	7190881	6960769	6641403	6598443	4588125
Spain/Espagne	7402590	6846669	7135930	5564187	5875900
Singapore/Singapour	6922361	6635758	6339384	6418672	5857114
Belgium–Luxembourg	3607438	4162867	3882887	3090931	3035761
Canada	4541352	3919129	3431079	3477862	3483426
India/Inde	3342728	3184589	4080417	3407425	3285560
Brazil/Brésil	4839539	3785662	3491956	2414492	2560468
Turkey/Turquie	3494658	2456232	2632090	2550340	2432133
Sweden/Suède	2868962	2431614	2336386	2185981	2113445
Thailand/Thaïlande	1523164	1479265	1744977	1804610	2141760
Poland/Pologne	1195342	1714926	1642117	1625161	1442321
China/Chine	423806	926381	1724249	2323412	1573387
Greece/Grèce	997182	1362702	1718286	1732969	1424321
Bahrain/Bahreïn	1787249	1717834	1511981	1370482	
Philippines	1650328	1479030	1684001	1366326	1350606
Portugal	1857553	1404256	1544296	1330574	1581536
Australia/Australie	1039489	1188794	1379105	1628944	1567447
Finland/Finlande	1645880	1548955	1305009	1080477	1267229
Israel/Israël	1073664	1045384	1327143	1349332	1242030
Austria/Autriche	1292760	1146731	1124890	979824	970358
Indonesia/Indonésie	1171596	1143524	1037912	917241	1073171
Netherlands Antilles	1440915	1402558	976524	x635948	x899938
Romania/Roumanie	2288632	1144523	809996	832563	895794
Chile/Chili	818289	814890	832893	779692	747950
Morocco/Maroc	988312	757401	937819	720029	752734
Denmark/Danemark	661958	758893	715913	634916	601449
Switz.Liecht	568505	761145	641464	630080	595503
Bulgaria/Bulgarie	x1406206	x245594	573108	994658	636922
Pakistan	591134	492876	556566	490261	454846
New Zealand	542105	477099	448201	464571	473015
Jordan/Jordanie	356025	284421	336603	343654	332602
Bangladesh	267755	348986	313376	259453	
Korea Dem People's Rp	x172422	x289594	x326643	x288793	x87438
Cote d'Ivoire	x330351	x271541	x269843	x301993	x3437
Hungary/Hongrie		775170	x33804	x4985	
Ireland/Irlande	376382	277125	289186	241673	266400
Sri Lanka	282273	259370	161470	206881	211765
Czech Republic				606317	672753
Panama	184870	144977	225795	191952	125475
Trinidad and Tobago	120152	214426	117108	226015	8
Norway, SVD, JM	241659	240343	158133	157605	107922
Croatia/Croatie			280862	273743	x112860
Sudan/Soudan	x188401	x142137	x177614	x216362	

COUNTRIES–PAYS	EXPORTS – EXPORTATIONS 1990	1991	1992	1993	1994
Totale	x195669538	x183123755	x178158758	x153759126	x160562556
Afrique	35041610	36109672	x33286090	x29527923	x30864531
Afrique du Nord	17817439	16683013	x15192294	x14729168	x14259203
Amériques	33767571	23294146	23507126	22355598	24036751
ALAI	26253156	17228294	17359792	16544888	18103390
MCAC	20838	19593	20139	22292	22200
Asie	x85200306	x93449911	x96502605	x78808909	x80616159
Moyen–Orient	x69862641	x79256495	x81893195	x66111364	x68902633
Europe	22186281	21091184	22207754	21032953	23007682
CEE	10223514	8666720	8752356	8186003	9798701
AELE	11962768	12424442	13305361	12590552	13168553
Océanie	1427618	x1399706	1445625	2019498	x2030021
Saudi Arabia	32918811	37336667	39602635	x32428034	x32974788
Iran (Islamic Rp. of)	x16255126	x16496429	x16909538	x10525958	x12010194
Norway, SVD, JM	11962718	12424415	13304863	12590487	13168552
Nigeria/Nigéria	9820751	12375923	x11261119	x9003647	x10897024
Libyan Arab Jamahiriya	11431668	9483481	x8716282	x8597679	x9189149
United Kingdom	9414223	7784016	7898092	7509689	9086761
Venezuela	14377535	7607986	7189504	7318833	8004330
Mexico/Mexique	8918705	7264834	7419545	6485314	6761985
Russian Federation			8544800	x8480730	x8566470
Canada	4741352	5274059	5529704	5357674	5429684
Indonesia/Indonésie	6219911	5695657	5397703	4778357	5071565
Algeria/Algérie	5385389	5060041	4806712	4448707	3924450
United Arab Emirates	x11637164	x13964480	x13105617	x11747452	x11695282
Malaysia/Malaisie	3947158	3712593	3640354	3166122	2541505
Angola	3598837	3120909	3424000	x2621197	x2555488
Oman	4756567	x4640000	4540436	4147979	4107703
China/Chine	3401861	2889153	2774490	2408801	2000305
Bahrain/Bahreïn	x20582	2725287	2604542	2439101	x2400000
Former USSR/Anc. URSS	18046151	x7687798			
Qatar	2782801	2235079	2486932	2116521	x2297985
Syrian Arab Republic	1469821	x1608724	1850645	x2285707	x1663334
Gabon	x1854733	x1756554	x1712657	x1661263	x2051021
Egypt/Egypte	478986	1697931	1157748	1314628	793405
Australia/Australie	1291541	1223060	1298404	1055314	1131956
Ecuador/Equateur	1258401	1058982	1251002	1149022	x1268011
Colombia/Colombie	1539689	1137741	1149486	1058570	936914
Brunei Darussalam	1126165	1272600	x1172691	x870837	x974081
Cameroon/Cameroun	1034769	1371891	x891398	x813392	x478828
Viet Nam	x518884	x503624	x822949	x923461	x902145
Congo	796092	x668551	x724721	x589527	x592394
Denmark/Danemark	482787	603969	630007	395362	338189
Trinidad and Tobago	757579	609704	441384	361868	353893
Tunisia/Tunisie	521396	441561	511552	368138	352195
Argentina/Argentine	146792	147617	348815	527361	1125573
Iraq	x1845	x248630	x286243	x293416	x356331
Papua New Guinea	15	10	x400000	802020	x738643
Kazakstan			x382993	x230105	
Ukraine			x210555	x268736	
New Zealand	136027	168764	147221	162163	150719
Netherlands/Pays–Bas	202915	164712	133914	126128	143785
Slovenia/Slovénia			111355	230174	9116
Turkmenistan/Turkménistn			x200598	x88101	x2438
Netherlands Antilles	246500	118895	90303	x40150	x57581
Israel/Israël	75022	62920	69233	84147	85337
Albania/Albanie		x70481	x124030		x366
Zaire/Zaïre	x99804	x91645	x46522	x47587	x27829
Pakistan	48485	54042	64800	56195	36494
Greece/Grèce	53453	61339	53103	59077	25715
Neutral Zone/Zone Neutre	x8045		x102906	x36962	x21809
Latvia/Lettonie			x86676	x12653	575

(VALUE AS % OF TOTAL)(VALEUR EN % DU TOTAL)

	1985	1986	1987	1988	1989	1990	1991	1992	1993	1994
Africa	1.1	1.2	1.2	1.2	x1.2	x1.1	x0.8	x1.0	x0.9	0.5
Northern Africa	0.6	0.5	0.5	0.4	0.5	x0.6	x0.5	x0.6	x0.5	0.5
Americas	23.3	24.5	26.3	27.3	30.1	29.8	27.1	27.0	x27.8	x28.9
LAIA	3.4	2.7	3.0	3.0	2.8	2.9	2.7	2.5	1.9	2.0
CACM		0.3	0.2	0.2	x0.2	0.2	0.2	0.3	x0.2	x0.2
Asia	30.2	24.4	24.3	25.8	25.7	29.0	31.6	33.0	33.6	32.9
Middle East	3.1	2.5	2.9	2.9	2.6	2.8	2.4	2.4	2.5	1.8
Europe	42.8	36.2	36.3	34.8	36.1	36.0	37.5	36.5	34.3	34.3
EEC	38.3	32.0	32.3	31.0	32.2	34.6	36.7	35.7	33.5	33.8
EFTA	3.6	3.1	3.2	2.6	2.7	0.4	0.5	0.4	0.4	0.4
Oceania	0.4	x0.4	0.5	0.7	0.8	x0.8	x0.9	x1.0	x1.2	x1.2
USA/Etats–Unis d'Amer	16.7	16.6	18.4	19.3	22.4	22.3	21.0	21.5	22.7	23.7
Japan/Japon	16.7	13.0	12.0	12.8	12.6	14.8	15.7	15.4	15.4	15.8
Germany/Allemagne	6.6	5.3	5.3	5.9	5.4	6.1	7.3	7.4	7.0	7.4
Italy/Italie	6.5	5.7	5.3	4.9	5.2	5.8	5.7	5.3	4.9	5.0
France, Monac	6.9	5.1	5.0	5.0	5.2	5.6	5.6	5.1	5.0	5.1
Korea, Republic of	2.7	2.3	2.2	2.6	2.9	3.1	4.3	5.0	5.1	5.1
Netherlands/Pays–Bas	4.1	3.5	3.8	3.9	4.0	3.9	4.0	4.0	3.6	3.7
United Kingdom	2.7	2.5	2.7	2.5	2.8	3.4	3.7	3.5	3.7	2.7
Spain/Espagne	4.2	3.4	3.6	3.4	3.6	3.5	3.6	3.7	3.1	3.4
Singapore/Singapour	2.9	2.6	2.4	2.9	2.8	3.3	3.5	3.3	3.6	3.4

	1985	1986	1987	1988	1989	1990	1991	1992	1993	1994
Afrique	15.1	x19.1	x15.0	x16.0	x15.2	17.9	19.6	x18.6	x19.2	x19.2
Afrique du Nord	14.2	9.4	7.9	7.6	7.5	9.1	9.1	x8.5	x9.6	x8.8
Amériques	27.0	13.2	14.4	14.0	13.6	17.2	12.7	13.2	14.5	15.0
ALAI	20.4	8.4	10.2	9.7	9.5	13.4	9.4	9.7	10.8	11.2
MCAC		0.0	0.0	x0.0	0.0	0.0	0.0	0.0	0.0	0.0
Asie	35.8	x36.2	41.1	x40.0	47.5	x43.5	x51.0	x54.2	x51.3	x50.2
Moyen–Orient	19.3	28.0	33.4	31.9	40.0	x35.7	x43.3	x45.9	x43.0	x42.9
Europe	21.0	11.3	11.4	10.2	9.9	11.3	11.5	12.4	13.7	14.2
CEE	15.6	8.1	7.7	6.1	4.5	5.2	4.7	4.8	5.3	6.1
AELE	5.5	3.3	3.7	4.1	5.4	6.1	6.8	7.5	8.2	8.2
Océanie	1.1	0.4	x0.5	x0.5	0.3	0.7	x0.6	0.8	1.3	x1.3
Saudi Arabia	18.6	13.0	10.2	11.7	11.8	16.8	20.3	22.3	x21.1	x20.4
Iran (Islamic Rp. of)		5.2	7.0	6.6	7.4	x8.3	x8.9	x9.5	x6.8	x7.5
Norway, SVD, JM	5.4	3.2	3.7	4.1	5.4	6.1	6.8	7.4	8.2	8.2
Nigeria/Nigéria		x7.3	x4.8	5.0	4.7	5.0	6.7	x6.2	x5.9	x6.7
Libyan Arab Jamahiriya	9.6	5.7	4.8	4.3	4.2	5.8	5.2	x4.8	x5.6	x5.7
United Kingdom	15.0	7.7	7.4	5.8	4.1	4.8	4.3	4.4	4.9	5.6
Venezuela	6.6	3.3	3.9	3.6	3.6	7.3	4.1	4.1	4.8	5.0
Mexico/Mexique	11.9	4.1	5.2	4.7	4.6	4.6	3.9	4.2	4.2	4.2
Russian Federation							0.0	4.8	x5.5	x5.3
Canada	3.9	2.3	2.4	2.6	2.3	2.4	3.0	2.9	3.5	3.3

TRADE BY COMMODITY IN THOUSAND U.S. DOLLARS – COMMERCE PAR PRODUIT EN MILLIERS DE DOLLARS E.U

COUNTRIES–PAYS	IMPORTS – IMPORTATIONS 1990	1991	1992	1993	1994
Total	94028784	87359985	81919513	82179936	79694106
Africa	x2110047	x2224554	x2161435	x2201688	x1943703
Northern Africa	483793	605319	x698386	x662379	x729340
Americas	x23472352	19013671	x18478150	x19151052	x19283395
LAIA	2040285	2453858	2865246	3412066	3449520
CACM	468095	421735	513817	x550598	x578692
Asia	26552380	25321478	24821891	27267498	26481177
Middle East	x1730195	x2161762	x1616636	x2037205	x1375364
Europe	38440056	37221400	33473725	30504940	29460832
EEC	35057945	34347032	30567307	28064436	26527542
EFTA	2914900	2509142	2281250	1805286	1748657
Oceania	x1783963	x1802457	x1679368	x1671049	x1341753
USA/Etats–Unis d'Amer	17455149	13629390	12369096	11889631	11408750
Germany/Allemagne	8734415	9627513	8128124	6844527	5793916
Japan/Japon	9983337	7785765	6551443	5330811	5125802
France,Monac	5120502	5348434	5145766	4266857	4064086
Italy/Italie	4861873	4271620	4090898	3481999	3618160
Belgium–Luxembourg	3143960	3001875	2802094	2507579	2796733
Singapore/Singapour	2671968	2630839	2827261	2808673	3184212
United Kingdom	3873027	3235731	2571313	2180333	2322445
Korea, Republic of	2448334	2053473	2283663	2752735	3140724
India/Inde	2594246	2137517	2544801	2359158	2656556
Netherlands/Pays–Bas	2569970	2052058	1670816	2536700	2179232
Hong Kong	1587173	1649551	1955768	2017858	2343295
China/Chine	610221	901175	1433201	3023361	2001883
Switz.Liecht	2207955	1923161	1771121	1352595	1253962
Thailand/Thaïlande	1476503	1927601	1536492	1564415	1425523
Spain/Espagne	1567753	1592132	1220484	1576190	1178567
Sweden/Suède	1487245	1386419	1428714	1234370	1246733
Malaysia/Malaisie	1158309	1225717	1320760	1252247	1149313
Mexico/Mexique	838369	1036615	1202147	1091734	1015733
Canada	1392290	1071533	1069270	1082208	1001557
Indonesia/Indonésie	672304	1066788	977764	1163677	1290525
Pakistan	892492	954076	912381	1084292	943607
Australia/Australie	981776	933933	903114	881257	623094
Denmark/Danemark	844475	809596	708973	751701	768702
Brazil/Brésil	218473	444372	471989	1047934	838122
Ireland/Irlande	671584	646118	600572	556733	498844
Austria/Autriche	652907	688549	560923	533309	562437
Iran (Islamic Rp. of)	x344267	x657449	x547319	x449482	x111885
Greece/Grèce	422066	587909	461273	595253	532801
Portugal	510982	596469	567735	477976	387089
Finland/Finlande	597185	502608	609621	520909	577797
Poland/Pologne	420855	578678	534261	378132	396520
Norway,SVD,JM	556829	453005	380530	337693	384298
Philippines	166000	260137	293594	549164	567097
Turkey/Turquie	332520	396197	254684	421150	302105
Colombia/Colombie	327312	287650	324752	332672	301836
Kenya	212004	296964	328468	234346	x23415
Tunisia/Tunisie	290008	280540	271130	294892	257635
Czechoslovakia	120937	x717612	x120766		
Viet Nam	x64546	x74173	x145051	x589059	x571205
Bahamas	500151	110793	x350417	x344351	x272499
Bulgaria/Bulgarie	x129060	x83097	378524	x284315	x134261
Zimbabwe	262085	238261	247790	256844	x1954
Netherlands Antilles	61956	139327	111165	x475954	x347265
Guam	x202154	x185254	x200540	x205297	x188074
Argentina/Argentine	21260	137836	210360	230181	382372
Jamaica/Jamaïque	358958	181577	x150485	x218595	x210239
Guatemala	150680	167313	183250	184885	162080
United Arab Emirates	332907	187377	158627	x187819	x178241
Cuba	x329195	x123887	x225048	x173835	x124279

COUNTRIES–PAYS	EXPORTS – EXPORTATIONS 1990	1991	1992	1993	1994
Totale	87498689	85484801	76174525	75884632	74776873
Afrique	4917879	4395927	x4447849	x4151985	x4336495
Afrique du Nord	4305546	3762437	x3885019	x3363582	x3811619
Amériques	13467824	16895139	15852618	x16125150	x14867249
ALAI	2987500	6546942	6368749	6881158	6727646
MCAC	30545	21301	22842	7856	13294
Asie	24008650	21600542	21871365	x22055351	x23336555
Moyen–Orient	x9302203	5665394	6274690	x5636526	x6544497
Europe	33075133	33397565	31687419	30977159	29846841
CEE	31198109	31873193	29761318	29192957	28063388
AELE	1640940	1390126	1548514	1416895	1535697
Océanie	1139235	1259331	x1093291	x1068715	x1006820
Singapore/Singapour	9244224	9839484	8090707	8813624	8911854
Netherlands/Pays–Bas	8686677	8274081	7399068	7499445	7043805
USA/Etats–Unis d'Amer	5136769	5582994	5104965	5103788	4265437
Venezuela	19	4535699	4099284	4467017	4523685
Saudi Arabia	5130930	4219384	4664734	x3376373	x3939824
United Kingdom	4033529	4037112	3645234	3857777	3569794
Belgium–Luxembourg	3495599	4083201	3823871	3515413	3529401
Italy/Italie	3681726	3736025	3807569	3511312	2872043
Germany/Allemagne	2572610	2647742	3137703	2998638	3116334
Russian Federation			x3091952	x4237627	x3640785
France,Monac	2589390	2593002	2279907	2314500	2328135
Former USSR/Anc. URSS	8739969	x6688855			
Algeria/Algérie	2270378	2345792	2161214	1828798	1617020
Canada	2216380	2245501	1845975	1965931	1786862
Spain/Espagne	2585913	2523227	1652526	1470306	1306021
Korea, Republic of	606769	1399192	1629520	1738926	1618628
Sweden/Suède	1425479	1514986	1465577	1468240	1293300
Japan/Japon	1051500	1051478	1313000	1749864	2066404
Norway,SVD,JM	1573881	1282660	1458115	1317243	1428610
Netherlands Antilles	1482586	1350373	1285566	x1128055	x761453
Libyan Arab Jamahiriya	1546700	1065195	x1349878	x1169073	x1524964
Indonesia/Indonésie	1170747	1009833	1210273	905533	923317
Australia/Australie	877141	1104102	993217	956349	913050
China/Chine	877367	822931	867721	632346	624411
Hong Kong	397671	533623	664625	935782	1070409
Finland/Finlande	369149	673960	737454	619702	635948
Trinidad and Tobago	630998	657551	701222	553750	571563
Argentina/Argentine	773589	535167	635031	606179	413556
Denmark/Danemark	520186	544842	615329	598612	548430
Greece/Grèce	517227	678641	453526	610639	905052
Brazil/Brésil	675450	422651	542151	615528	742995
Mexico/Mexique	620744	428926	513134	605540	416853
Romania/Roumanie	1030929	526948	473904	474093	598483
Iran (Islamic Rp. of)	x359558	x371165	x585520	x454752	x347248
Malaysia/Malaisie	430227	372730	475506	503070	667338
India/Inde	517024	415809	532755	398684	418415
Portugal	484130	370039	492849	472184	652952
Ukraine			x590964	x701870	x198886
United Arab Emirates	56641	33737	48567	x1012271	x893803
Colombia/Colombie	410152	322787	263357	264166	295750
Hungary/Hongrie	x294784	x274625	x275338	x299859	x233946
Lithuania/Lituanie			25062	x795851	270335
Qatar	87044	286658	316746	211433	x167980
Bahamas	x362350	36069	x397639	x347307	x93512
Bulgaria/Bulgarie	x508910	x165461	x263668	x274781	x136415
Syrian Arab Republic	420459	x215231	294753	x190800	x146847
Turkey/Turquie	261996	267730	219807	160951	226222
Thailand/Thaïlande	88109	122104	180506	286666	221500
Croatia/Croatie			278752	299158	x148102
Peru/Pérou	313558	164274	199066	199468	177010

(VALUE AS % OF TOTAL)(VALEUR EN % DU TOTAL)

	1985	1986	1987	1988	1989	1990	1991	1992	1993	1994
Africa	1.9	x2.7	x2.0	x2.0	x2.3	x2.2	x2.5	x2.6	x2.7	x2.4
Northern Africa	0.8	0.7	0.6	0.8	0.5	0.5	0.7	x0.9	x0.8	x0.9
Americas	25.0	25.5	20.6	24.0	25.9	x24.9	21.7	x22.6	x23.3	x24.2
LAIA	1.2	1.3	1.5	1.9	2.3	2.2	2.8	3.5	4.2	4.3
CACM	0.5	0.4	0.3	0.3	0.3	0.5	0.5	0.6	x0.7	x0.7
Asia	17.2	18.5	19.4	22.8	26.3	28.2	29.0	30.3	33.2	33.3
Middle East	1.2	x2.2	x1.5	x1.4	x1.6	x1.8	x2.5	x2.0	x2.5	x1.7
Europe	53.2	49.0	39.1	38.3	41.8	40.9	42.6	40.9	37.1	37.0
EEC	45.9	41.4	33.8	32.5	35.7	37.3	39.3	37.3	34.1	33.3
EFTA	6.9	7.1	5.0	5.4	5.7	3.1	2.9	2.8	2.2	2.2
Oceania	2.1	x2.3	x1.5	x1.6	x2.0	x1.9	x2.0	x2.1	x2.0	x1.7
USA/Etats–Unis d'Amer	19.4	18.8	15.1	18.0	18.8	18.6	15.6	15.1	14.5	14.3
Germany/Allemagne	11.5	11.4	8.8	7.9	8.5	9.3	11.0	9.9	8.3	7.3
Japan/Japon	7.1	7.8	8.4	9.9	11.0	10.6	8.9	8.0	6.5	6.4
France,Monac	5.2	5.5	5.3	4.8	5.3	5.4	6.1	6.3	5.2	5.1
Italy/Italie	6.5	5.3	5.1	4.4	5.4	5.2	4.9	5.0	4.2	4.5
Belgium–Luxembourg	3.9	3.5	2.6	2.8	2.9	3.3	3.4	3.4	3.1	3.5
Singapore/Singapour	2.2	2.0	2.2	2.8	2.9	2.8	3.0	3.5	3.4	4.0
United Kingdom	5.8	4.5	3.3	3.4	3.7	4.1	3.7	3.1	2.7	2.9
Korea, Republic of	0.7	0.8	1.0	0.9	1.0	2.6	2.4	2.8	3.3	3.9
India/Inde	1.2	0.8	0.9	1.5	1.9	2.8	2.4	3.1	2.9	3.3

	1985	1986	1987	1988	1989	1990	1991	1992	1993	1994
Afrique	8.9	5.7	x6.0	x8.8	5.0	5.6	5.1	x5.8	x5.5	x5.8
Afrique du Nord	8.1	4.8	4.5	4.0	4.2	4.9	4.4	x5.1	x4.4	x5.1
Amériques	23.0	x17.4	16.0	16.2	18.0	15.4	19.8	20.8	x21.2	x19.9
ALAI	13.6	8.3	7.7	7.3	8.1	3.4	7.7	8.4	9.1	9.0
MCAC	0.0	0.0	0.0	0.0	0.0	0.0	0.0	0.0	0.0	0.0
Asie	20.1	x22.1	x23.1	x25.2	x25.2	27.4	25.2	28.7	x29.1	x31.2
Moyen–Orient	5.9	x9.3	x11.4	x14.2	x10.8	x10.6	6.6	8.2	x7.4	x8.8
Europe	46.4	40.1	33.3	30.7	34.2	37.8	39.1	41.6	40.8	39.9
CEE	42.4	37.2	30.1	28.0	31.2	35.7	37.3	39.1	38.5	37.5
AELE	3.7	2.7	3.0	2.5	2.8	1.9	1.6	2.0	1.9	2.1
Océanie	1.3	1.1	1.0	x1.2	x1.2	1.3	1.5	x1.5	x1.4	x1.4
Singapore/Singapour	8.3	7.4	6.0	6.3	8.6	10.6	11.5	10.6	11.6	11.9
Netherlands/Pays–Bas	13.8	12.5	9.5	8.4	9.0	9.9	9.7	9.7	9.9	9.4
USA/Etats–Unis d'Amer	5.3	4.4	4.2	3.8	4.6	5.9	6.5	6.7	6.7	5.7
Venezuela	7.7	5.4	4.5	4.6	5.3	0.0	5.3	5.4	5.9	6.0
Saudi Arabia	4.7	x3.4	x6.9	5.7	5.4	5.9	4.9	6.1	x4.4	x5.3
United Kingdom	5.4	4.3	3.5	3.6	4.0	4.6	4.7	4.8	5.1	4.8
Belgium–Luxembourg	4.3	4.7	3.6	3.7	3.8	4.0	4.8	5.0	4.6	4.7
Italy/Italie	4.9	4.3	3.7	2.7	3.5	4.2	4.4	5.0	4.6	3.8
Germany/Allemagne	2.7	2.2	1.9	2.2	2.5	2.9	3.1	4.1	4.0	4.2
Russian Federation								x4.1	x5.6	x4.9

TRADE BY COMMODITY IN THOUSAND U.S. DOLLARS – COMMERCE PAR PRODUIT EN MILLIERS DE DOLLARS E.U

COUNTRIES–PAYS	IMPORTS – IMPORTATIONS 1990	1991	1992	1993	1994
Total	6527748	6033564	5732376	6067853	6221695
Africa	x235864	271041	x272362	x175527	x162338
Northern Africa	37338	97013	38935	40975	48549
Americas	910810	874853	1129326	1872015	1732631
LAIA	254575	381533	661667	1417381	1084543
CACM	13011	13846	15106	20639	x17676
Asia	1698878	1493433	1342323	x1332285	1515239
Middle East	x157611	x190730	194663	x193023	x165171
Europe	3389482	3043949	2813980	2473819	2569316
EEC	3125293	2822200	2583066	2264698	2361317
EFTA	205013	187154	168333	156213	169937
Oceania	x240444	x157399	x118027	x133779	x151808
Japan/Japon	1044904	771885	615962	522073	623758
Germany/Allemagne	804192	711793	665881	466279	523044
Brazil/Brésil	92173	180942	440661	1180160	849453
Netherlands/Pays–Bas	618434	577301	523190	460756	426171
France,Monac	394989	363221	321268	279316	318056
Italy/Italie	407561	356995	275409	279781	313222
USA/Etats–Unis d'Amer	440822	298550	282069	252604	426417
United Kingdom	185183	175233	217351	195926	159906
Spain/Espagne	223175	196489	159934	152289	171454
Canada	181209	153856	141387	158344	167710
Belgium–Luxembourg	134422	121000	114659	164655	173999
Korea, Republic of	124461	114349	125336	136184	175131
Norway,SVD,JM	128513	116545	102322	99148	115809
Australia/Australie	153467	117285	93075	103125	109802
Indonesia/Indonésie	76534	99825	95850	89315	98144
Mexico/Mexique	60569	68976	79744	92136	104814
Turkey/Turquie	56126	51378	73926	94341	73245
Venezuela	58328	73953	69570	71780	34291
Austria/Autriche	88788	68300	62910	54323	55528
Sweden/Suède	70964	64857	63886	55813	57289
Switz.Liecht	72847	67879	62766	53765	51140
Denmark/Danemark	77720	59505	62100	51160	49513
Thailand/Thaïlande	32580	41569	56046	57894	82389
So. Africa Customs Un	60167	51765	50605	48649	37399
United Arab Emirates	32718	61108	57719	x14123	x15085
Kenya	10916	12493	106948	7476	x4763
Czechoslovakia	15700	x107459	x18539		
China/Chine	19804	18266	41053	66108	66134
Malaysia/Malaisie	37176	33557	42760	48370	52828
India/Inde	55352	54826	18928	50024	94892
Russian Federation			x82050	x37912	x40357
Singapore/Singapour	46050	35958	46251	26176	26594
Portugal	26955	39605	34640	33737	33551
Hong Kong	33625	28912	35629	34631	28098
Algeria/Algérie	16718	68360	16044	11728	8737
Philippines	14009	22359	32464	36636	24470
Ireland/Irlande	30075	34237	29214	23628	26610
Slovenia/Slovénia			43591	41755	32234
Greece/Grèce	33994	32993	29487	16705	16848
Israel/Israël	26797	54287	12232	12513	13366
New Zealand	40879	31122	20217	26075	37158
Finland/Finlande	28840	20670	23139	30330	36126
Former USSR/Anc. URSS		x67013			
Poland/Pologne	7932	8518	25507	29940	36231
Argentina/Argentine	14824	18079	19075	24388	39320
Bahrain/Bahreïn		x15823	x10716	x31797	x25698
Saudi Arabia	4503	22885	16516	x9043	x9811
Iran (Islamic Rp. of)	x38887	x18630	x13683	x15801	x6312
Cameroon/Cameroun	13494	34540	x5375	x6517	x10154
Colombia/Colombie	8089	13550	17776	10012	13152

COUNTRIES–PAYS	EXPORTS – EXPORTATIONS 1990	1991	1992	1993	1994
Totale	5447036	4783351	4562215	4444717	5050952
Afrique	x73070	54534	x175847	x290756	x271338
Afrique du Nord	23024	8049	x113589	x118604	x103070
Amériques	1776546	1552900	1381801	x1261245	x1651453
ALAI	62087	76383	107849	83150	106427
MCAC	43	77	74	1084	1077
Asie	938803	781310	823280	x857602	x932428
Moyen–Orient	186921	185027	148107	x245101	x233388
Europe	2184053	2172474	1981561	1834537	2009959
CEE	2072605	2127441	1920412	1775634	1959920
AELE	51453	37939	35678	42663	29421
Océanie	x32111	x33056	x24443	x16557	x15848
USA/Etats–Unis d'Amer	1532514	1320013	1125744	1025088	1350628
Germany/Allemagne	531698	508673	491253	407215	429502
Netherlands/Pays–Bas	381566	375615	343336	242522	314507
Spain/Espagne	278616	263918	208375	233595	243763
United Kingdom	127469	246545	223812	220672	222291
Belgium–Luxembourg	217254	234412	204576	232949	293196
France,Monac	191411	198240	209094	219850	212686
China/Chine	192878	195724	200396	184951	175092
Saudi Arabia	140606	142392	134810	x193864	x157888
Japan/Japon	138932	122545	142732	128836	146193
Singapore/Singapour	265386	120149	126096	133372	200379
Canada	170795	107281	98677	95901	158806
Korea, Republic of	75585	85428	106719	99343	105008
Italy/Italie	78837	113651	61008	60802	58946
Sweden/Suède	84721	81277	80853	70899	87890
Hungary/Hongrie	x84927	x57060	x88977	x74207	x56924
Portugal	91384	55989	48479	48510	55571
Argentina/Argentine	48137	52887	55093	41198	41835
Algeria/Algérie	15863	1847	84005	62165	44041
So. Africa Customs Un	40600	40146	45071	42405	
Netherlands Antilles	x10126	38499	34194	x50564	x15341
Nigeria/Nigéria		1083	x3171	x109631	x157299
Norway,SVD,JM	45726	31028	28517	35762	21542
Poland/Pologne	47982	27124	31674	30397	45375
Russian Federation			x30957	x53165	x30514
Austria/Autriche	34027	32886	26389	23580	x24396
Brazil/Brésil	6311	13984	35862	29489	49397
Australia/Australie	30325	32262	23940	15639	15478
Libyan Arab Jamahiriya			x20386	x46571	x35037
Hong Kong	22957	19228	24191	22181	16123
Czechoslovakia		x31638	x33273		
Former USSR/Anc. URSS	241900	x59658			
Sri Lanka	14681	19169	13286	16670	15264
Czech Republic				48844	40656
Malaysia/Malaisie	9589	17077	21350	4174	9737
Croatia/Croatie			23690	13757	x18236
Yemen/Yémen		30997			
United Arab Emirates	2953	899	927		
Trinidad and Tobago	837	8954	15157	5209	3982
Indonesia/Indonésie	13212	8875	10930	9191	9813
Bulgaria/Bulgarie	x47763	x7882	x13070	x6299	x2395
Egypt/Egypte	7152	6202	9139	9817	23989
Ukraine			x4302	x18495	x8619
Denmark/Danemark	39052	3456	15487	3781	3621
Cote d'Ivoire	x4923	x1083	x10944	x10528	x10267
Mexico/Mexique	6065	5754	6858	8923	9300
Finland/Finlande	10433	8196	5628	5951	9034
Romania/Roumanie	9615	5442	8081	6201	9170
Switz.Liecht	5726	6138	6106	6186	6678
Slovakia				x18042	x15396

(VALUE AS % OF TOTAL)(VALEUR EN % DU TOTAL)

	1985	1986	1987	1988	1989	1990	1991	1992	1993	1994
Africa	3.6	6.4	x2.4	x3.7	x3.4	x3.6	4.5	x4.8	x2.9	x2.6
Northern Africa	1.6	3.6	0.7	x1.5	1.0	0.6	1.6	0.7	0.7	0.8
Americas	19.8	16.9	10.7	11.0	14.3	13.9	14.5	19.7	30.9	27.8
LAIA	3.0	4.0	2.6	3.0	3.7	3.9	6.3	11.5	23.4	17.4
CACM	0.4	0.4	0.2	0.2	0.2	0.2	0.2	0.3	0.3	x0.3
Asia	14.5	19.2	x16.3	x21.1	27.0	26.0	24.8	23.5	x21.9	24.3
Middle East	1.5	x2.4	x1.9	x1.8	x1.5	x2.4	x3.2	3.4	x3.2	x2.7
Europe	59.6	54.5	41.9	41.0	49.4	51.9	50.5	49.1	40.8	41.3
EEC	52.0	47.0	36.9	35.6	43.1	47.9	46.8	45.1	37.3	38.0
EFTA	6.9	6.7	4.5	4.8	5.6	3.1	3.1	2.9	2.6	2.7
Oceania	2.1	x2.4	x1.7	x2.2	x2.8	x3.7	x2.6	x2.1	x2.2	x2.5
Japan/Japon	7.1	10.3	9.0	13.1	18.3	16.0	12.8	10.7	8.6	10.0
Germany/Allemagne	13.6	12.7	8.5	8.8	10.5	12.3	11.8	11.6	7.7	8.4
Brazil/Brésil	0.4	0.9	0.5	0.5	1.0	1.4	3.0	7.7	19.4	13.7
Netherlands/Pays–Bas	8.8	8.1	6.0	6.3	8.7	9.5	9.6	9.1	7.6	6.8
France,Monac	6.3	6.3	4.4	4.8	5.3	6.1	6.0	5.6	4.6	5.1
Italy/Italie	9.4	6.3	8.4	4.9	6.0	6.2	5.9	4.8	4.6	5.0
USA/Etats–Unis d'Amer	13.4	9.2	5.7	5.7	6.9	6.8	4.9	4.9	4.2	6.9
United Kingdom	2.9	2.4	2.0	2.3	2.5	2.8	2.9	3.8	3.2	2.6
Spain/Espagne	2.1	2.5	1.8	2.4	3.2	3.4	3.3	2.8	2.5	2.8
Canada	2.7	2.9	1.9	1.8	3.1	2.8	2.5	2.5	2.6	2.7

	1985	1986	1987	1988	1989	1990	1991	1992	1993	1994
Afrique	1.2	x1.7	x2.0	x2.9	x2.2	x1.3	1.1	x3.9	x6.6	x5.4
Afrique du Nord	0.2	0.3	x0.8	x1.5	x1.4	0.4	0.2	x2.5	x2.7	x2.0
Amériques	28.0	x32.7	x26.7	24.5	32.4	32.6	32.4	30.2	x28.4	x32.7
ALAI	1.9	x5.4	x4.1	1.1	1.1	1.1	1.6	2.4	1.9	2.1
MCAC	0.0	0.0	x0.0	0.0	0.0	0.0	0.0	0.0	0.0	0.0
Asie	20.3	17.2	20.1	24.9	x18.0	17.3	16.3	18.1	x19.3	x18.4
Moyen–Orient	0.7	x1.1	x1.5	x4.5	x5.8	3.4	3.9	3.2	x5.5	x4.6
Europe	45.9	43.6	42.0	38.3	37.2	40.1	45.4	43.4	41.3	39.8
CEE	41.0	39.5	38.0	34.6	33.9	38.1	44.5	42.1	39.9	38.8
AELE	3.3	3.1	3.0	2.9	2.7	0.9	0.8	0.8	1.0	0.6
Océanie	0.2	x0.2	0.3	x0.3	0.5	x0.6	x0.7	x0.5	x0.4	x0.3
USA/Etats–Unis d'Amer	18.6	23.9	18.3	20.3	29.0	28.1	27.6	24.7	23.1	26.7
Germany/Allemagne	9.5	9.8	9.1	9.5	9.3	9.8	10.6	10.8	9.2	8.5
Netherlands/Pays–Bas	8.1	7.4	7.1	5.6	5.6	7.0	7.9	7.5	5.5	6.2
Spain/Espagne	5.8	2.9	4.6	4.5	4.8	5.1	5.5	4.6	5.3	4.8
United Kingdom	5.5	5.8	5.1	2.5	2.2	2.3	5.2	4.9	5.0	4.4
Belgium–Luxembourg	3.7	4.6	3.8	4.1	3.8	4.0	4.9	4.5	5.2	5.8
France,Monac	3.8	4.3	4.0	3.6	3.2	3.5	4.1	4.6	4.9	4.2
China/Chine	1.1	1.3	2.1	2.5	2.5	3.5	4.1	4.4	4.2	3.5
Saudi Arabia	0.0	x0.1	x0.3	3.2	1.7	2.6	3.0	3.0	x4.4	x3.1
Japan/Japon	3.1	3.8	3.2	3.2	2.8	2.6	2.6	3.1	2.9	2.9

TRADE BY COMMODITY IN THOUSAND U.S. DOLLARS – COMMERCE PAR PRODUIT EN MILLIERS DE DOLLARS E.U

COUNTRIES–PAYS	IMPORTS – IMPORTATIONS 1990	1991	1992	1993	1994
Total	30635285	35800117	34060736	34407436	34614581
Africa	259058	268181	267418	258808	297079
Northern Africa	202077	215795	222141	211610	253309
Americas	4455014	4692635	5008316	5957005	6754372
LAIA	721123	818538	967454	795509	750110
CACM	42496	44809	51302	50758	64056
Asia	10932207	12391383	12385991	12331986	12549028
Middle East	488618	615991	628649	630786	667351
Europe	14296821	16984396	15180504	14348956	13854852
EEC	13453703	16562774	14548090	13634453	13307812
EFTA	369561	415171	440989	427643	425673
Oceania	x19651	x11462	x20517	x25449	x28230
Japan/Japon	9226826	10478970	10159008	9766112	9417669
Germany/Allemagne	4712305	6361564	5500751	5576332	5519651
USA/Etats–Unis d'Amer	3487900	3609318	3761671	4874858	5677878
France,Monac	3446039	4350214	3821729	3248890	3301614
Belgium–Luxembourg	1341556	1507923	1395973	1343961	1233405
Korea, Republic of	848997	933929	1158123	1382528	1561557
United Kingdom	1238176	1119357	965860	676239	459581
Spain/Espagne	567208	886145	783646	799084	853867
Netherlands/Pays–Bas	651024	654624	583245	612127	576427
Turkey/Turquie	435946	531549	559544	587208	628568
Austria/Autriche	556563	568789	517644	514798	469874
Poland/Pologne	142301	593947	468604	313469	351021
Italy/Italie	399471	514349	414265	344345	321631
Romania/Roumanie	487366	438768	378421	408741	367235
Switz.Liecht	268565	305094	325717	332352	330358
Mexico/Mexique	183912	194099	380510	304006	271357
Brazil/Brésil	245902	285255	316458	268312	258937
Finland/Finlande	274821	277779	271217	252386	312056
Bulgaria/Bulgarie			347389	358816	
Argentina/Argentine	225089	228298	136364	79556	92325
Czech Republic				402194	411933
Portugal	103428	151258	120393	122930	111383
Tunisia/Tunisie	120431	112188	156746	120808	142480
Canada	115221	131880	126294	128496	140218
Sweden/Suède	130638	128757	138189	116622	124942
Hungary/Hongrie		362347			
Philippines	70091	80761	117062	157125	179086
Norway,SVD,JM	100372	109324	114610	94796	94870
China/Chine	27191	48555	84187	157018	296305
Malaysia/Malaisie	52175	65283	84000	98098	85058
Morocco/Maroc	66236	90255	58982	80523	109290
Slovenia/Slovénia			105891	105604	92109
Lithuania/Lituanie			177220		150513
Croatia/Croatie			66007	103361	x526
Hong Kong	48788	52551	62068	43906	32375
Chile/Chili	34989	51647	49674	54027	64730
India/Inde	78966	47424	50521	55651	87337
Latvia/Lettonie				87082	85871
Guatemala	26942	29144	29795	28156	29889
Yugoslavia/Yougoslavie			x7896	x72257	x23871
Ireland/Irlande	24224	33286	26141	19328	18072
Bahamas	3517	4464	x22943	x46370	x59416
Syrian Arab Republic	22151	x33061	33514	x5246	x3965
Venezuela	1126	20389	36851	11785	173
Peru/Pérou	15998	22165	20999	17354	22901
Czechoslovakia	42150	x56851	x3010		
Panama	22008	21167	19326	17376	18100
Korea Dem People's Rp	x22785	x34389	x12350	x14	x6
Paraguay	11782	14042	16204	14613	11120
Reunion/Réunion	10099	10426	12489	10291	11759

COUNTRIES–PAYS	EXPORTS – EXPORTATIONS 1990	1991	1992	1993	1994
Totale	33304484	x33894735	26624686	x27373201	x26113952
Afrique	3124037	4358568	3872386	3563924	2951540
Afrique du Nord	3081406	4301614	3857750	3542637	2947703
Amériques	4184053	4838104	5630123	6451604	6985123
ALAI	503702	462085	275672	256883	304913
MCAC	15	1	61	19	11
Asie	7888873	9100337	9175758	x9072201	x8803991
Moyen–Orient	2059515	2144112	2737069	x2608288	x2683564
Europe	6943082	8350704	7899947	7413604	7245885
CEE	4389744	5578425	5314578	5100523	4697001
AELE	2542457	2763742	2553012	2292191	2531202
Océanie	1862	4563	x6069	831713	90434
Canada	3138660	3626200	4534771	5511047	6060907
Indonesia/Indonésie	3667293	4180495	4051987	4052729	3689124
Russian Federation			7479400	x4387389	x5676777
Netherlands/Pays–Bas	3361391	4201309	3932799	3691530	3351205
Algeria/Algérie	2951466	4016794	3643596	3329871	2677562
Norway,SVD,JM	2535326	2751246	2546776	2285192	2522733
Former USSR/Anc. URSS	11128461	x7201426			
Saudi Arabia	1937949	1910555	2126006	x2205096	x2282427
Malaysia/Malaisie	1010309	1218864	1140289	1174318	1041062
Brunei Darussalam	886077	1192342	x866098	x801386	x924187
USA/Etats–Unis d'Amer	524965	692201	742830	597152	547522
United Kingdom	316094	444782	422597	526637	479014
United Arab Emirates	1128	790	2503	x3500	x3000
Germany/Allemagne	299170	367008	397075	378006	393327
France,Monac	203803	325985	355088	279243	223247
Qatar	97403	125952	396906	313716	x203371
Australia/Australie	180	262	1537	827928	87122
Libyan Arab Jamahiriya	119592	149061	x203420	x210164	x264456
Bolivia/Bolivie	226701	234406	124668	90621	91621
Thailand/Thaïlande	104293	161571	139312	109424	128897
Mexico/Mexique	255270	198778	104312	99220	130868
Singapore/Singapour	72925	90805	83754	107507	136363
Philippines	49384	57524	76184	92323	95817
Belgium–Luxembourg	72612	66585	49751	89295	113188
Italy/Italie	60157	78881	67794	56282	48149
Iran (Islamic Rp. of)		x26132	x83814	x71088	x109148
Bahrain/Bahreïn		x66611	x113556		x62055
Argentina/Argentine	13950	28695	44300	65852	71806
Egypt/Egypte	3492	128724	5075	670	5231
India/Inde	33	81	29032	75189	55591
Trinidad and Tobago	6348	19431	42079	36677	34287
Spain/Espagne	22127	24846	18037	35282	29278
Sweden/Suède	21996	17298	39973	20161	28779
Netherlands Antilles	5986	26823	11777	x26483	x27305
Angola	7412	51102		x13471	x3311
Hong Kong	15371	16422	23230	23155	17212
Korea, Republic of	14942	26441	11343	20409	19423
Hungary/Hongrie	x25437	x14697	x17797	x14950	x10226
Greece/Grèce	13092	28527	8890	9454	8772
Bahamas		1	x20780	x20494	x5047
Croatia/Croatie			17302	17953	x17071
Czechoslovakia		x17308	x13431		
Denmark/Danemark	10731	12765	10261	7671	4550
Turkey/Turquie	22938	8464	11197	9375	8213
Switz.Liecht	7131	12496	6236	6999	8470
Ukraine			x13700	x2247	x134
Japan/Japon	3955	5072	7065	3182	5155
Albania/Albanie	x400	x4694	x4356	x5744	
Tunisia/Tunisie	6856	7035	5660	1933	454
Ireland/Irlande	5183	4948	5147	3510	3585

(VALUE AS % OF TOTAL)(VALEUR EN % DU TOTAL)

	1985	1986	1987	1988	1989	1990	1991	1992	1993	1994
Africa	0.6	0.4	0.7	0.6	0.8	0.8	0.7	0.8	0.8	0.9
Northern Africa	0.6	0.4	0.6	0.5	0.6	0.7	0.6	0.7	0.6	0.7
Americas	13.1	12.1	12.7	15.0	14.1	14.6	13.2	14.7	17.3	19.5
LAIA	2.2	2.0	2.1	2.5	2.3	2.4	2.3	2.8	2.3	2.2
CACM	0.1	0.1	0.1	0.1	0.1	0.1	0.1	0.2	0.1	0.2
Asia	27.0	25.1	29.6	35.6	35.0	35.7	34.6	36.3	35.9	36.2
Middle East	0.4	0.4	0.7	1.3	1.3	1.6	1.7	1.8	1.8	1.9
Europe	53.8	59.9	54.3	47.3	45.0	46.7	47.4	44.6	41.7	40.0
EEC	49.2	55.2	49.3	42.1	39.8	43.9	46.3	42.7	39.6	38.4
EFTA	2.9	3.2	3.6	3.7	3.7	1.2	1.2	1.3	1.2	1.2
Oceania						x0.0	x0.0	x0.0	x0.0	x0.1
Japan/Japon	25.9	24.1	26.9	31.3	30.4	30.1	29.3	29.8	28.4	27.2
Germany/Allemagne	15.9	15.6	14.7	14.5	13.5	15.4	17.8	16.1	16.2	15.9
USA/Etats–Unis d'Amer	10.5	9.4	9.8	11.7	11.0	11.4	10.1	11.0	14.2	16.4
France,Monac	9.6	11.0	10.0	10.5	10.3	11.2	12.2	11.2	9.4	9.5
Belgium–Luxembourg	4.2	4.1	4.4	3.7	3.8	4.4	4.2	4.1	3.9	3.6
Korea, Republic of	0.3	0.4	1.6	2.2	2.3	2.8	2.6	3.4	4.0	4.5
United Kingdom	5.4	6.2	6.1	6.2	4.9	4.0	3.1	2.8	2.0	1.3
Spain/Espagne	1.5	1.3	1.3	1.5	1.7	1.9	2.5	2.3	2.3	2.5
Netherlands/Pays–Bas	2.0	1.6	1.9	2.0	1.7	2.1	1.8	1.7	1.8	1.7
Turkey/Turquie	0.3	0.2	0.4	0.8	1.1	1.4	1.5	1.6	1.7	1.8

	1985	1986	1987	1988	1989	1990	1991	1992	1993	1994
Afrique	10.5	8.7	8.9	9.7	9.4	9.4	12.9	14.5	13.0	11.2
Afrique du Nord	10.5	8.6	8.8	9.5	9.4	9.3	12.7	14.5	12.9	11.2
Amériques	13.9	x10.5	x11.5	x14.1	x13.8	12.6	14.2	21.1	23.6	26.7
ALAI	1.5	x1.7	x1.6	x1.7	x1.6	1.5	1.4	1.0	0.8	1.1
MCAC	0.0	0.0	x0.0	x0.0	0.0	0.0	0.0	0.0	0.0	0.0
Asie	22.1	19.1	20.7	21.0	22.9	23.7	26.8	34.4	x33.1	x37.1
Moyen–Orient	5.4	x4.6	x6.2	x5.5	x7.0	6.2	6.3	10.3	x9.5	x10.2
Europe	30.5	28.0	22.3	20.0	18.6	20.8	24.6	29.7	27.1	27.7
CEE	21.2	16.7	13.1	10.7	11.1	13.2	16.5	20.0	18.7	17.9
AELE	9.3	11.3	9.2	9.3	7.5	7.6	8.2	9.6	8.3	9.7
Océanie	1.0	0.6	0.6		x0.2			x0.0	3.0	0.2
Canada	10.4	7.3	8.5	10.7	10.5	9.4	10.7	17.0	20.0	23.1
Indonesia/Indonésie	10.3	8.8	8.5	9.1	9.4	11.0	12.3	15.2	14.8	14.1
Russian Federation								28.1	x16.1	x21.7
Netherlands/Pays–Bas	14.9	13.1	9.5	8.0	8.4	10.1	12.4	14.8	13.4	12.8
Algeria/Algérie	10.0	8.3	8.5	9.2	8.9	8.9	11.9	13.7	12.2	10.2
Norway,SVD,JM	9.2	11.2	9.1	9.2	7.4	7.6	8.1	9.6	8.3	8.6
Former USSR/Anc. URSS	21.9	33.1	35.8	35.0	34.8	33.4	x21.2			
Saudi Arabia	5.0	3.6	4.3	4.3	3.7	5.8	5.6	8.0	x8.0	x8.8
Malaysia/Malaisie	2.4	2.4	2.6	2.7	2.8	3.0	3.6	4.3	4.2	3.9
Brunei Darussalam	3.6	3.0	2.9	3.1	3.0	2.7	3.5	x3.3	x2.9	x3.5

TRADE BY COMMODITY IN THOUSAND U.S. DOLLARS – COMMERCE PAR PRODUIT EN MILLIERS DE DOLLARS E.U

COUNTRIES–PAYS	IMPORTS – IMPORTATIONS 1990	1991	1992	1993	1994
Total	1282310	1287118	1360925	1433103	1478358
Africa	x153483	135176	x127017	x111589	x116837
Northern Africa	65368	29487	44152	40314	48457
Americas	244644	276302	273482	293969	336333
LAIA	153105	177380	171056	183698	210027
CACM	28606	29035	37815	38628	45439
Asia	254556	x279866	273346	404857	309560
Middle East	34929	x65033	x41226	x46159	47589
Europe	604830	578032	674119	604445	690906
EEC	559919	544536	633979	551691	629873
EFTA	27099	31025	33673	47476	55151
Oceania	4931	x8035	x6329	x7424	x9008
Netherlands/Pays–Bas	126428	120536	149064	100615	132003
Germany/Allemagne	86079	91011	102382	81642	84356
United Kingdom	85201	83498	92702	98561	98200
Mexico/Mexique	73982	86664	85482	99064	123161
Japan/Japon	65430	75374	88774	72672	74957
Belgium–Luxembourg	64454	63607	84119	73960	96908
Spain/Espagne	73962	66228	60693	57851	56323
Korea, Republic of	47838	52851	61358	54244	62269
France,Monac	57902	53195	61444	48908	62999
Bangladesh				146523	x10677
Italy/Italie	32385	29517	39309	42790	54536
Norway,SVD,JM	23428	28129	30272	44255	49317
USA/Etats–Unis d'Amer	22145	30116	31747	38312	37485
Turkey/Turquie	31052	24537	28430	37254	38072
Pakistan	43788	28686	28688	22702	32625
China/Chine	32770	25438	21020	33254	45876
Venezuela	21444	22286	25566	26209	21374
Colombia/Colombie	21376	27441	22936	20896	21000
So. Africa Customs Un	21020	24092	21465	23439	32323
Algeria/Algérie	24446	12641	23884	23269	27333
Brazil/Brésil	25010	22474	13821	21590	30673
Denmark/Danemark	12115	14687	18420	20649	16365
Nigeria/Nigéria	x18066	28927	x11419	x12517	x8487
Canada	10228	12058	14536	17860	24952
Zimbabwe	17350	15669	12833	15360	x9121
Guatemala	10759	13177	13202	14163	13387
El Salvador	12607	8696	14155	12405	23128
Syrian Arab Republic	313		299	x130	x150
Egypt/Egypte	33714	11023	9965	7020	11021
Iran (Islamic Rp. of)		x8595	x9969	x6398	x4976
Thailand/Thaïlande	7772	7584	7591	8745	9336
Russian Federation			x19944	x3384	x14617
Sweden/Suède	5956	7947	7388	7812	8386
Morocco/Maroc	4094	5159	6669	9229	6694
Un. Rep. of Tanzania	x1035	x5869	x7199	x5793	x1752
Uganda/Ouganda	6937	6005	10215	x2564	x6064
Portugal	4111	4631	6025	6990	3950
Nicaragua	3408	3908	5846	7353	6383
Singapore/Singapour	5055	8330	5236	2385	2711
Ecuador/Equateur	6757	9722	2836	2541	x4173
Philippines	4157	3845	6135	4949	5305
Argentina/Argentine	461	3611	7276	3790	3662
Jamaica/Jamaïque	4372	3846	x4985	x4915	x2337
Cuba	x12264	x10667	x2849	x169	x442
Chile/Chili	1646	2418	5872	4424	2334
Dominican Republic	x5077	x3847	x4033	x4758	x7795
Indonesia/Indonésie	4852	4299	4463	3457	3248
Honduras	1437	3092	4493	4494	2314
Ireland/Irlande	4614	3842	4251	3553	4368
Peru/Pérou	1377	1562	6032	3358	2006

COUNTRIES–PAYS	EXPORTS – EXPORTATIONS 1990	1991	1992	1993	1994
Totale	1106511	1099650	1244977	1220042	1450425
Afrique	10545	x9163	8937	x7252	x1287
Afrique du Nord	1151	1113	775	199	754
Amériques	505400	512586	555682	572421	721627
ALAI	36224	53168	32756	69460	133575
MCAC	20	176	60	x291	x239
Asie	80089	68798	50299	39512	39335
Moyen–Orient	7871	3560	3976	4168	5389
Europe	422591	413089	499349	431242	484345
CEE	379359	371849	435946	352706	414594
AELE	39427	38920	55283	70128	63730
Océanie	x74704	x56654	110881	x157077	x182405
USA/Etats–Unis d'Amer	400141	396863	449334	436527	516553
Germany/Allemagne	86613	80634	76407	60266	74597
Australia/Australie	41349	20871	74150	117717	134753
Canada	67655	60753	71024	63684	68780
France,Monac	68256	61486	66683	61285	71465
Netherlands/Pays–Bas	51930	49797	58183	38326	49523
Denmark/Danemark	29839	39722	57000	39422	46155
Belgium–Luxembourg	35149	38501	38789	37603	46678
New Zealand	33312	35372	35814	38037	47569
Italy/Italie	33957	30187	42542	29583	32929
Norway,SVD,JM	17991	25560	27558	28270	31887
Iceland/Islande	17921	12082	26936	41488	31651
Japan/Japon	50055	36301	23141	20334	19010
United Kingdom	26559	23758	28650	26973	30002
Ireland/Irlande	16212	16831	22082	24055	26242
Chile/Chili	14401	26351	15076	19483	44810
Peru/Pérou	7022	12022	4656	35509	67490
Spain/Espagne	5642	7396	15129	15675	16206
Portugal	6634	8514	16894	8094	5415
Indonesia/Indonésie	7964	12441	8427	3127	1790
Hungary/Hongrie	x9953	x7384	x12148	x4398	x4289
Poland/Pologne	1467	14358	2278	2972	3551
Austria/Autriche	10965	8008	6629	4905	x7221
Singapore/Singapour	3904	7392	6123	5311	1173
Sweden/Suède	6598	5640	6559	6230	7733
So. Africa Customs Un	5917	6222	5916	6225	
Uruguay	5568	6159	7171	4289	6967
Argentina/Argentine	8151	7268	2280	6924	10773
Russian Federation			x11063	x4480	x1974
Former USSR/Anc. URSS		x13650			
Hong Kong	6996	3951	4283	3544	5501
Faeroe Islds/Is Féroé	696	780	3306	5430	2918
Turkey/Turquie	6363	2710	2476	1673	2184
Panama	1111	1589	2349	2062	2461
Slovenia/Slovénia			2255	2255	2850
Czechoslovakia		x2333	x2162		
Bulgaria/Bulgarie	x1185	x1024	2303	953	x8816
Philippines	653	1499	1721	846	437
Mexico/Mexique	837	1030	1317	1580	2106
Zimbabwe	1248	1123	1821	356	
Brazil/Brésil	155	164	1838	1244	929
China/Chine	519	1075	1094	582	1192
Switz.Liecht	3515	1278	789	370	192
Finland/Finlande	982	1360	392	259	420
Morocco/Maroc	1130	1073	704	175	207
Slovakia				x1849	x1027
Czech Republic				1810	3363
Kuwait/ Koweït	1075	73	422	1301	1896
Romania/Roumanie	70	456	780	557	380
Papua New Guinea	1	178	848	723	

(VALUE AS % OF TOTAL)(VALEUR EN % DU TOTAL)

	1985	1986	1987	1988	1989	1990	1991	1992	1993	1994
Africa	7.4	19.3	x8.9	x12.2	x13.4	x11.9	10.5	x9.4	x7.8	x7.9
Northern Africa	3.1	12.7	3.6	5.3	7.1	5.1	2.3	3.2	2.8	3.3
Americas	15.4	16.7	18.5	16.2	19.7	19.1	21.5	20.1	20.5	22.7
LAIA	9.3	9.6	10.6	11.1	11.8	11.9	13.8	12.6	12.8	14.2
CACM	3.4	3.5	2.7	2.0	2.7	2.2	2.3	2.8	2.7	3.1
Asia	19.3	16.5	x20.8	x20.9	18.2	19.8	x21.8	20.0	28.3	20.9
Middle East	1.6	x2.0	x3.9	x3.5	x3.0	2.7	x5.1	x3.0	x3.2	3.2
Europe	56.6	46.5	46.1	44.9	43.5	47.2	44.9	49.5	42.2	46.7
EEC	53.9	43.5	43.3	40.5	39.6	43.7	42.3	46.6	38.5	42.6
EFTA	2.5	2.7	2.5	4.1	3.2	2.1	2.4	2.5	3.3	3.7
Oceania	0.3	0.3	0.3	0.3	0.4	0.3	x0.6	x0.5	x0.5	x0.6
Netherlands/Pays–Bas	14.5	11.0	9.4	9.8	9.0	9.9	9.4	11.0	7.0	8.9
Germany/Allemagne	13.7	9.8	8.1	8.0	7.6	6.7	7.1	7.5	5.7	5.7
United Kingdom	10.6	6.8	7.8	6.6	5.4	6.6	6.5	6.8	6.9	6.6
Mexico/Mexique	3.9	2.7	5.0	5.1	5.4	5.8	6.7	6.3	6.9	8.3
Japan/Japon	4.8	4.9	4.2	4.2	4.3	5.1	5.9	6.5	5.1	5.1
Belgium–Luxembourg	5.3	4.1	4.7	4.6	4.8	5.0	4.9	6.2	5.2	6.6
Spain/Espagne	2.7	4.9	6.0	4.5	4.8	5.8	5.1	4.5	4.0	3.8
Korea, Republic of	4.5	3.0	3.9	3.8	3.7	3.7	4.1	4.5	3.8	4.2
France,Monac	3.2	3.2	3.2	2.9	3.4	4.5	4.1	4.5	3.4	4.3
Bangladesh	1.0	0.6	0.5	x0.3	x0.3				10.2	x0.7

	1985	1986	1987	1988	1989	1990	1991	1992	1993	1994
Afrique	0.3	x0.6	x0.9	x0.8	x0.6	0.9	x0.9	0.7	x0.6	x0.1
Afrique du Nord	0.0	0.1	0.0	0.0	0.0	0.1	0.1	0.1	0.0	0.1
Amériques	51.2	47.7	44.9	46.6	48.0	45.7	46.6	44.6	46.9	49.8
ALAI	3.7	4.0	2.5	2.9	4.9	3.3	4.8	2.6	5.7	9.2
MCAC	0.0	0.0	0.0	0.0	0.0	0.0	0.0	0.0	x0.0	x0.0
Asie	5.6	6.1	5.1	9.0	5.0	7.2	6.2	4.1	3.3	2.7
Moyen–Orient	0.5	0.3	0.7	0.8	0.6	0.7	0.3	0.3	0.3	0.4
Europe	32.6	35.4	34.7	31.7	33.0	38.2	37.6	40.1	35.3	33.4
CEE	25.0	29.1	28.5	25.6	28.0	34.3	33.8	35.0	28.9	28.6
AELE	6.9	6.0	5.8	5.6	4.7	3.6	3.5	4.4	5.7	4.4
Océanie	9.4	x9.2	x9.9	x7.3	6.5	x6.7	x5.1	8.9	x12.9	x12.6
USA/Etats–Unis d'Amer	42.2	38.3	37.4	38.5	37.7	36.2	36.1	36.1	35.8	35.6
Germany/Allemagne	5.9	7.2	7.0	6.7	6.9	7.8	7.3	6.1	4.9	5.1
Australia/Australie	5.4	6.3	6.2	4.1	3.4	3.7	1.9	6.0	9.6	9.3
Canada	4.9	5.2	4.8	5.1	5.3	6.1	5.5	5.7	5.2	4.7
France,Monac	4.0	4.2	4.6	4.3	4.6	6.2	5.6	5.4	5.0	4.9
Netherlands/Pays–Bas	2.9	3.8	3.8	3.1	3.8	4.7	4.5	4.7	3.1	3.4
Denmark/Danemark	3.0	3.3	2.4	2.7	2.5	2.7	3.6	4.6	3.2	3.2
Belgium–Luxembourg	1.8	2.6	2.9	2.3	2.6	3.2	3.5	3.1	3.1	3.2
New Zealand	4.0	2.8	3.7	3.3	3.2	3.0	3.2	2.9	3.1	3.3
Italy/Italie	1.9	2.2	2.3	1.9	2.6	3.1	2.7	3.4	2.4	2.3

TRADE BY COMMODITY IN THOUSAND U.S. DOLLARS – COMMERCE PAR PRODUIT EN MILLIERS DE DOLLARS E.U

COUNTRIES–PAYS	IMPORTS – IMPORTATIONS				
	1990	1991	1992	1993	1994
Total	6112597	6726286	6208707	x6106547	8669368
Africa	x572422	x575682	x817567	x622184	x870196
Northern Africa	386089	383897	575494	370991	515553
Americas	x1157057	1199648	1286292	1360629	1768304
LAIA	457773	519623	541197	604618	829393
CACM	44509	36393	59039	62442	68552
Asia	1446128	x1531409	x1441825	x1473624	x2641261
Middle East	264777	x724354	x703255	x739277	x727980
Europe	2571027	3106266	2441127	2420672	3122438
EEC	2483353	3041279	2336668	2302196	2996976
EFTA	41280	38718	49652	68988	68971
Oceania	x82700	x90437	x102654	x106642	x113854
Italy/Italie	1029790	1308294	776481	798963	1005790
USA/Etats–Unis d'Amer	424624	480479	512668	544366	661265
Iran (Islamic Rp. of)		x381773	x353461	x440032	x320650
France, Monac	377842	370071	344173	364075	454140
Germany/Allemagne	262177	273284	275099	226644	258855
United Kingdom	197510	238654	237779	234755	217855
Turkey/Turquie	168388	229147	223839	181493	253908
China/Chine	528274	289093	194348	117439	984391
Mexico/Mexique	192893	204932	185574	199725	228555
Netherlands/Pays–Bas	135580	145953	152083	197552	302539
Belgium–Luxembourg	169035	184454	152779	139013	213226
Spain/Espagne	64974	161374	168253	89366	231517
Russian Federation			x305156	x71959	x73633
Venezuela	99569	127411	125848	118401	108127
Algeria/Algérie	3524	5201	227217	115190	176946
Hong Kong	112969	111049	96611	103831	222048
Pakistan	208103	91708	110942	104438	125421
Morocco/Maroc	76117	86781	92165	108995	135346
Brazil/Brésil	43347	72964	82706	113024	222453
Egypt/Egypte	134892	64881	115072	69528	75159
Libyan Arab Jamahiriya	102956	160981	x78760	x5092	x24857
Japan/Japon	73149	70473	70118	84944	101658
Greece/Grèce	41426	148674	29635	23151	42847
Australia/Australie	49070	55516	65058	70154	68468
Portugal	35870	54384	41532	91854	108328
Singapore/Singapour	50065	58982	58744	61945	91677
Tunisia/Tunisie	60365	57713	56030	61625	83762
Poland/Pologne	19504	42956	63308	64851	84985
Canada	44157	43427	54995	61378	66587
Chile/Chili	44027	37244	50621	70168	88822
Former USSR/Anc. URSS	203263	x151010			
Cuba	x118039	x49978	x49174	x24577	x20381
Sweden/Suède	52597	45002	39541	35780	40182
Denmark/Danemark	35866	38795	45404	30188	35373
So. Africa Customs Un	40377	13947	45443	52187	127922
Korea, Republic of	30618	57196	27051	25807	44071
Austria/Autriche	46420	36889	36897	34817	39073
Peru/Pérou	32768	31720	35516	41200	89798
Switz.Liecht	35692	32486	37705	37611	52086
Ireland/Irlande	29402	31188	31468	31789	39805
India/Inde	23712	25199	44616	21554	39602
Senegal/Sénégal	7127	31965	x22524	x35059	x44440
Malaysia/Malaisie	53240	33046	26778	25075	63614
Bangladesh				x83871	x132051
Colombia/Colombie	20175	14342	25083	43406	49691
Dominican Republic	x19019	x24331	x26263	x19440	x54877
New Zealand	18098	20858	23461	24338	29879
Syrian Arab Republic	4727	x22016	17074	x24883	x22578
Korea Dem People's Rp	x16254	x11645	x26408	x25398	x10319
Guatemala	17609	19756	17640	22259	24662

COUNTRIES–PAYS	EXPORTS – EXPORTATIONS				
	1990	1991	1992	1993	1994
Totale	6272169	6477981	6419676	6074113	8689338
Afrique	352532	422679	x269532	254019	x430222
Afrique du Nord	x192603	315932	176135	190735	340679
Amériques	2041936	1976716	2234528	2259082	3616243
ALAI	1443277	1442429	1435871	1430653	2465492
MCAC	3071	1382	3258	x8359	x12577
Asie	391428	349821	359489	318115	603953
Moyen–Orient	103352	120576	154788	59296	83864
Europe	3330536	3606952	3440243	3082338	3903638
CEE	3313182	3575859	3415255	3068642	3892161
AELE	12085	13327	11635	9157	8988
Océanie	1525	x2979	x2399	1985	4350
Argentina/Argentine	1024280	1144078	1044101	1024445	1481141
Spain/Espagne	902293	1136812	560081	688739	863629
USA/Etats–Unis d'Amer	496880	408781	627222	599421	845343
Italy/Italie	465321	537959	599983	445410	499403
Netherlands/Pays–Bas	408887	422590	463271	499601	635828
Germany/Allemagne	426764	440583	429030	451853	579876
Greece/Grèce	301367	220876	548756	312745	333648
France, Monac	323071	318330	350455	292606	411512
Brazil/Brésil	383213	250083	323454	334173	867883
Belgium–Luxembourg	295849	304636	302472	215013	321437
Tunisia/Tunisie	121166	290717	158396	179140	301765
Canada	95263	119538	164685	216250	287281
Turkey/Turquie	87509	104051	141502	40880	63247
China/Chine	95423	76519	45921	89539	207629
Hungary/Hongrie	x54604	x45697	x81029	x60606	x56555
Senegal/Sénégal	130084	72154	x63907	34138	x78350
Portugal	65933	67371	55987	38048	60141
Singapore/Singapour	60616	49248	51485	48614	87376
United Kingdom	33971	41745	34016	55651	106558
Malaysia/Malaisie	55936	39278	30580	41937	72052
Hong Kong	45827	35802	38798	35529	111426
Denmark/Danemark	35944	31529	33406	34922	48899
Sweden/Suède	41355	41630	26868	26825	23982
Paraguay	5602	13293	33519	33881	55499
So. Africa Customs Un	18073	25878	26819	25998	
Romania/Roumanie		5059	5114	60518	45032
Mexico/Mexique	9497	20107	23225	26854	33445
Russian Federation			x30568	x19359	x50408
Ukraine			x9474	x40437	x80121
Japan/Japon	12831	14789	13816	14275	13841
Former USSR/Anc. URSS	68123	x41944			
Indonesia/Indonésie	14117	10372	11767	18015	17006
Sudan/Soudan	x29632	x17810	x8075	x10666	x35786
Bulgaria/Bulgarie	x1789		x13720	x22361	x7330
Switz.Liecht	9956	10948	9565	7237	5981
Cyprus/Chypre	9042	10831	3777	7653	10523
Finland/Finlande	9723	9782	8518	3427	2560
Poland/Pologne	24426	13527	4112	1130	3187
Bolivia/Bolivie	7279	7735	5140	5858	21561
Yugoslavia SFR	5139	x17764			
Czechoslovakia		x9089	x8431		
Morocco/Maroc	41169	4996	9330	751	2785
Venezuela	13180	6751	4394	3893	1951
Czech Republic				12727	15668
Lebanon/Liban	x1545	x2847	x2347	x3191	x3182
Azerbaijan			x7314		x169
Guatemala	2740	1266	2100	3937	5199
Slovenia/Slovénia			4675	2507	1039
Jordan/Jordanie	952	1873	2968	2311	733
Trinidad and Tobago	2798	2211	2141	2520	4110

(VALUE AS % OF TOTAL)(VALEUR EN % DU TOTAL)

	1985	1986	1987	1988	1989	1990	1991	1992	1993	1994
Africa	16.2	18.7	x11.8	x10.7	x10.6	x9.4	x8.6	x13.1	x10.2	x10.1
Northern Africa	12.4	14.5	8.6	7.0	7.4	6.3	5.7	9.3	6.1	5.9
Americas	14.4	x16.2	x13.3	17.9	16.6	x19.0	17.8	20.7	22.3	20.4
LAIA	9.2	6.5	4.6	7.5	7.6	7.5	7.7	8.7	9.9	9.6
CACM	0.7	1.2	x1.0	0.8	0.7	0.7	0.5	1.0	1.0	0.8
Asia	22.1	x21.1	x28.7	x30.4	x28.8	23.7	x22.8	x23.3	x24.1	x30.5
Middle East	6.4	x7.5	x8.7	x9.4	x8.3	4.3	x10.8	x11.3	x12.1	x8.4
Europe	41.0	38.6	39.9	35.7	35.7	42.1	46.2	39.3	39.6	36.0
EEC	35.9	34.7	37.7	33.1	32.6	40.6	45.2	37.6	37.7	34.6
EFTA	3.1	2.7	2.1	2.4	2.2	0.7	0.6	0.8	1.1	0.8
Oceania	1.0	x0.9	x1.0	x1.3	1.1	x1.4	x1.3	x1.6	x1.7	x1.3
Italy/Italie	9.2	12.0	15.8	11.5	10.3	16.8	19.5	12.5	13.1	11.6
USA/Etats–Unis d'Amer	2.5	3.0	3.5	7.6	5.4	6.9	7.1	8.3	8.9	7.6
Iran (Islamic Rp. of)		x3.3	x5.1	x3.7	x3.0		x5.7	x5.7	x7.2	x3.7
France, Monac	7.9	6.3	4.9	5.8	5.4	6.2	5.5	5.5	6.0	5.2
Germany/Allemagne	4.7	3.8	3.0	4.1	4.0	4.3	4.1	4.4	3.7	3.0
United Kingdom	3.9	4.3	6.5	3.3	2.8	3.2	3.5	3.8	3.8	2.5
Turkey/Turquie	3.0	1.6	1.6	3.0	3.2	2.8	3.4	3.6	3.0	2.9
China/Chine	0.4	1.9	3.8	1.9	8.5	8.6	4.3	3.1	1.9	11.4
Mexico/Mexique	0.6	0.5	0.2	2.5	3.1	3.2	3.0	3.0	3.3	2.6
Netherlands/Pays–Bas	3.5	2.5	1.9	2.2	2.3	2.2	2.2	2.4	3.2	3.5

	1985	1986	1987	1988	1989	1990	1991	1992	1993	1994
Afrique	2.4	x3.6	x3.6	3.8	4.5	5.6	6.5	x4.2	4.2	x5.0
Afrique du Nord	0.9	1.8	1.9	x1.9	x2.0	x3.1	4.9	2.7	3.1	3.9
Amériques	46.2	35.1	30.1	39.9	34.6	32.5	30.6	34.8	37.2	41.6
ALAI	30.8	20.3	18.9	23.2	21.8	23.0	22.3	22.4	23.6	28.4
MCAC	0.0	x0.0	x0.0	x0.1	0.1	0.0	0.0	0.1	x0.1	x0.1
Asie	4.4	5.6	6.0	4.5	6.7	6.2	5.4	5.6	5.2	7.0
Moyen–Orient	1.0	1.6	1.7	1.1	2.5	1.6	1.9	2.4	1.0	1.0
Europe	45.1	53.0	55.1	48.0	49.8	53.1	55.7	53.6	50.7	44.9
CEE	44.1	51.6	53.5	46.0	48.7	52.8	55.2	53.2	50.5	44.8
AELE	1.0	1.2	1.3	1.4	0.9	0.2	0.2	0.2	0.2	0.1
Océanie	0.1	0.1	0.3	0.2			x0.0	x0.0		
Argentina/Argentine	16.6	15.4	10.8	16.3	14.0	16.3	17.7	16.3	16.9	17.0
Spain/Espagne	8.7	8.6	11.4	12.9	7.1	14.4	17.5	8.7	11.3	9.9
USA/Etats–Unis d'Amer	12.4	12.2	9.0	13.5	11.0	7.9	6.3	9.8	9.9	9.7
Italy/Italie	4.0	6.6	6.0	5.4	6.5	7.4	8.3	9.3	7.3	5.7
Netherlands/Pays–Bas	8.2	8.3	6.5	6.0	6.8	6.5	6.5	7.2	8.2	7.3
Germany/Allemagne	8.6	8.5	7.1	7.9	8.1	6.8	6.8	6.7	7.4	6.7
Greece/Grèce	1.8	5.4	4.7	1.4	6.4	4.8	3.4	8.5	5.1	3.8
France, Monac	5.1	4.7	3.9	4.8	5.7	5.2	4.9	5.5	4.8	4.7
Brazil/Brésil	14.0	4.8	7.8	6.7	7.1	6.1	3.9	5.0	5.5	10.0
Belgium–Luxembourg	5.1	5.6	4.4	4.6	5.4	4.7	4.7	4.7	3.5	3.7

TRADE BY COMMODITY IN THOUSAND U.S. DOLLARS – COMMERCE PAR PRODUIT EN MILLIERS DE DOLLARS E.U

COUNTRIES–PAYS	IMPORTS – IMPORTATIONS				
	1990	1991	1992	1993	1994
Total	4184559	4378158	5026935	5071969	6602063
Africa	353451	x329614	x472891	x449025	x333950
Northern Africa	192700	158092	x226768	x197871	x192086
Americas	491501	502374	x732817	628902	780771
LAIA	76259	117807	136193	160634	200595
CACM	5653	8233	13577	15239	30613
Asia	1636171	1937351	2029794	x2274896	x3263720
Middle East	x287317	357825	x410623	x516426	x566781
Europe	1504795	1459717	1697632	1610055	2086015
EEC	1475193	1433101	1662303	1571879	2044722
EFTA	22749	21962	30065	28497	34382
Oceania	50179	x54780	x65813	x65256	x77957
USA/Etats–Unis d'Amer	353464	314642	511062	389565	467492
Germany/Allemagne	379661	356590	419066	355083	468759
Pakistan	193920	323820	350593	444312	599599
China/Chine	419045	401144	291796	339127	759898
Netherlands/Pays–Bas	249456	206955	296638	279169	396148
United Kingdom	218181	212347	236671	272948	307789
Japan/Japon	161374	198586	267443	241641	302115
Italy/Italie	191370	188059	205734	182911	225762
Singapore/Singapour	173120	211196	166749	142605	119682
France,Monac	167305	161237	154463	136421	156999
Turkey/Turquie	90717	132534	113221	173392	150131
Korea, Republic of	75573	101370	123972	121651	156753
Malaysia/Malaisie	21948	103067	95384	123946	139946
Belgium–Luxembourg	82134	92096	105275	117876	157445
Saudi Arabia	77196	94442	113112	x86005	x134954
Egypt/Egypte	41214	44034	123515	86734	97263
Indonesia/Indonésie	10262	26910	134621	84334	82768
Mexico/Mexique	50439	62038	80705	76205	108920
Kenya	40729	68618	90498	59437	x30271
Spain/Espagne	40873	57070	64504	68063	105490
Myanmar	x63833	55464	x54292	x44420	x100431
So. Africa Customs Un	35392	30506	57950	59077	65244
Algeria/Algérie	132027	86742	21682	37899	11716
India/Inde	158689	77882	30570	35651	167991
Australia/Australie	37614	41354	48876	50597	61664
Denmark/Danemark	39373	42638	50001	40949	63319
Libyan Arab Jamahiriya	1722	1522	x62133	x60885	x63966
Canada	30542	35844	41143	38622	51090
Hong Kong	28330	34403	35901	37615	139622
Brazil/Brésil	4302	26289	25703	51518	61347
Jordan/Jordanie	16318	24610	26599	48523	91942
Sweden/Suède	22474	31433	33308	29712	49627
Yemen/Yémen	x31799	4170	x48322	x38480	x31835
United Arab Emirates	25559	27361	22428	x40617	x64467
Greece/Grèce	24991	27848	30126	20222	29420
Nigeria/Nigéria	x956	761	x22130	x51446	x13464
Sri Lanka	9382	12858	17948	39446	21157
Iran (Islamic Rp. of)		x5200	x11199	x47643	x18066
Bahrain/Bahreïn	x5802	x15045	x21308	x26803	x17942
Austria/Autriche	20232	18833	22430	21753	25052
Former USSR/Anc. URSS	106717	x61517			
Poland/Pologne	12539	14091	20182	23763	34728
Bangladesh				x56683	x43042
Equatorial Guinea		x22023	x18014	x12554	
Portugal	14898	13977	16771	20581	22910
Kuwait/Koweït	9157	9843	21224	18850	19513
Ireland/Irlande	13997	16436	17520	15805	20416
Haiti/Haïti	x6122	x8518	x19627	x16413	x20232
Switz.Liecht	13449	11173	14839	17395	19950
Oman	8057	11154	13790	17987	23799

COUNTRIES–PAYS	EXPORTS – EXPORTATIONS				
	1990	1991	1992	1993	1994
Totale	3603512	3963956	4738469	4753056	6660395
Afrique	x112409	x130123	x132532	x100453	x112076
Afrique du Nord	991	1197	1049	817	1315
Amériques	357936	310629	316013	313691	x372439
ALAI	171945	108069	91567	54849	66160
MCAC	7841	4084	14087	x15229	x21999
Asie	2618847	2994915	3708547	3726317	5408917
Moyen–Orient	57670	131551	x118032	x117281	x73345
Europe	444663	449289	467217	489810	612365
CEE	435769	439540	458552	480574	602524
AELE	7580	7205	7584	8367	7989
Océanie	62119	76831	x109614	112605	x147940
Malaysia/Malaisie	1611731	1819365	2145007	2227292	3105967
Indonesia/Indonésie	316477	457944	657771	690429	1115354
Philippines	362207	300173	482833	358832	475802
USA/Etats–Unis d'Amer	171290	192644	203820	236692	274885
Netherlands/Pays–Bas	128533	133782	139649	165146	194774
Singapore/Singapour	132781	127430	119418	87347	75038
China/Chine	59580	67434	84638	106949	277503
Papua New Guinea	43716	61115	87780	95871	x123620
Cote d'Ivoire	x73159	x62250	x94763	x78549	x72530
Belgium–Luxembourg	77111	75684	74550	73090	91612
Germany/Allemagne	79682	70540	71796	70263	93407
Turkey/Turquie	35679	84903	60194	57010	34200
India/Inde	40136	54419	46018	89100	125903
Italy/Italie	41472	45158	53943	58091	54868
France,Monac	42620	45065	49389	41938	40697
Argentina/Argentine	113605	61764	46463	23600	17400
United Kingdom	40061	45530	41550	39050	55512
Hong Kong	18419	24861	30075	32847	125403
Bahrain/Bahreïn		x10895	x25129	x33830	x6141
Cameroon/Cameroun	11510	51150	x9645	x8730	x12606
Brazil/Brésil	41446	26887	24381	11982	14371
Saudi Arabia	13742	23163	20611	x8647	x9200
Denmark/Danemark	15281	15358	13382	12513	20469
Oman	2018	6196	8574	11828	16846
Paraguay	7613	11069	8586	6544	7666
So. Africa Customs Un	14659	9228	8100	6220	
Solomon Isls	8057	6691	x9233	x6818	x13760
Sweden/Suède	5492	4876	8126	9549	11457
Switz.Liecht	7457	6738	7197	8010	7700
Costa Rica	6008	2754	8218	x7923	x15051
French Polynesia	x3725	x6075	x5954	x4994	x3740
Viet Nam	x323		x8793	x4832	x7171
Japan/Japon	4996	4586	4173	4698	5720
Thailand/Thaïlande	5345	4742	4172	3678	13475
Spain/Espagne	1377	1639	3139	7604	34026
Honduras	1336	654	4770	6384	4612
Ecuador/Equateur	2355	2535	1768	6944	x7207
Canada	1878	1968	4022	4860	5664
Togo	1314	153	x8759	x471	x1362
Mexico/Mexique	1626	1800	4494	2913	2417
Hungary/Hongrie	x6797	x1851	x3483	x2706	x3799
Fiji/Fidji	3368	1604	3835	2266	2617
Colombia/Colombie	876	1128	3851	1446	9531
Sri Lanka	7393	912	2475	2430	3896
Austria/Autriche	905	1276	2078	2217	x3726
United Arab Emirates	5294	567	1242	x3525	x4140
Saint Lucia/St. Lucie	3431	1530	x2217	x1523	
Jordan/Jordanie	17	3576	980	298	592
Bulgaria/Bulgarie				x4805	
Korea, Republic of	80	127	4362	100	704

(VALUE AS % OF TOTAL)(VALEUR EN % DU TOTAL)

	1985	1986	1987	1988	1989	1990	1991	1992	1993	1994
Africa	4.8	x9.0	5.4	7.3	x10.7	8.4	x7.5	x9.5	x8.9	x5.1
Northern Africa	1.6	2.8	2.0	3.5	6.4	4.6	3.6	x4.5	x3.9	x2.9
Americas	16.6	15.1	14.9	15.5	11.7	11.8	11.5	x14.6	12.4	11.9
LAIA	0.4	0.6	1.4	2.1	1.3	1.8	2.7	2.7	3.2	3.0
CACM	0.1	0.3	x0.2	0.3	0.3	0.1	0.2	0.3	0.3	0.5
Asia	32.1	36.7	40.9	x40.1	37.3	39.1	44.2	40.3	x44.9	x49.5
Middle East	2.7	x7.6	x6.6	x7.4	x7.7	x6.9	8.2	x8.2	x10.2	x8.6
Europe	37.5	34.9	32.6	32.0	33.2	36.0	33.3	33.8	31.7	31.6
EEC	35.6	32.9	30.9	30.4	31.5	35.3	32.7	33.1	31.0	31.0
EFTA	1.7	1.8	1.6	1.5	1.5	0.5	0.5	0.6	0.6	0.5
Oceania	0.8	x0.8	1.2	1.3	1.3	1.2	x1.2	x1.3	x1.3	x1.2
USA/Etats–Unis d'Amer	14.4	12.3	11.5	11.3	8.7	8.4	7.2	10.2	7.7	7.1
Germany/Allemagne	7.8	7.4	6.8	6.9	7.9	9.1	8.1	8.3	7.0	7.1
Pakistan	6.9	5.0	4.4	5.6	4.3	4.6	7.4	7.0	8.8	9.1
China/Chine	1.6	3.0	3.6	5.3	7.6	10.0	9.2	5.8	6.7	11.5
Netherlands/Pays–Bas	6.8	5.5	5.2	5.5	5.6	6.0	4.7	5.9	5.5	6.0
United Kingdom	6.1	5.4	5.2	5.0	4.9	5.2	4.9	4.7	5.4	4.7
Japan/Japon	4.1	3.3	3.8	4.2	4.0	3.9	4.5	5.3	4.8	4.6
Italy/Italie	4.5	4.1	3.8	3.6	3.7	4.6	4.3	4.1	3.6	3.4
Singapore/Singapour	2.8	1.6	1.7	2.4	3.7	4.1	4.8	3.3	2.8	1.8
France,Monac	5.2	4.6	4.1	3.6	3.6	4.0	3.7	3.1	2.7	2.4

	1985	1986	1987	1988	1989	1990	1991	1992	1993	1994
Afrique	1.7	x3.2	x3.1	x2.4	x2.5	x3.1	x3.2	x2.8	x2.1	x1.7
Afrique du Nord	0.0	x0.1	x0.1	0.0	0.0	0.0	0.0	0.0	0.0	0.0
Amériques	8.1	9.8	9.4	8.7	8.9	9.9	7.8	6.7	6.6	x5.6
ALAI	3.9	4.4	4.3	3.4	4.5	4.8	2.7	1.9	1.2	1.0
MCAC	0.2	0.3	0.3	0.4	0.2	0.2	0.1	0.3	x0.3	x0.3
Asie	76.0	70.2	70.9	75.3	75.0	72.7	75.5	78.3	78.4	81.2
Moyen–Orient	0.3	0.8	x0.6	0.6	x0.8	1.6	3.3	x2.5	x2.5	x1.1
Europe	11.5	14.4	13.2	10.8	10.8	12.3	11.3	9.9	10.3	9.2
CEE	11.3	14.1	12.9	10.3	10.5	12.1	11.1	9.7	10.1	9.0
AELE	0.2	0.3	0.3	0.4	0.3	0.2	0.2	0.2	0.2	0.1
Océanie	2.8	2.3	x2.3	2.2	2.2	1.7	1.9	x2.3	2.3	x2.2
Malaysia/Malaisie	44.8	45.4	43.8	45.9	46.6	44.7	45.9	45.3	46.9	46.6
Indonesia/Indonésie	8.3	4.3	7.6	11.6	10.2	8.8	11.6	13.9	14.5	16.7
Philippines	8.2	11.6	12.5	10.6	9.8	10.1	7.6	10.2	7.5	7.1
USA/Etats–Unis d'Amer	3.6	4.7	4.5	4.7	4.0	4.8	4.9	4.3	5.0	4.1
Netherlands/Pays–Bas	3.8	4.4	3.8	3.3	3.2	3.6	3.4	2.9	3.5	2.9
Singapore/Singapour	11.5	4.7	3.2	4.0	4.1	3.7	3.2	2.5	1.8	1.1
China/Chine	0.3	0.6	1.6	1.4	1.1	1.7	1.7	1.8	2.3	4.2
Papua New Guinea	2.0	1.5	1.4	1.5	1.6	1.2	1.5	1.9	2.0	x1.9
Cote d'Ivoire	1.5	x1.9	x1.9	x1.3	x1.5	x2.0	x1.6	x2.0	x1.7	x1.1
Belgium–Luxembourg	1.8	2.2	2.1	1.5	1.8	2.1	1.9	1.6	1.5	1.4

TRADE BY COMMODITY IN THOUSAND U.S. DOLLARS – COMMERCE PAR PRODUIT EN MILLIERS DE DOLLARS E.U

COUNTRIES–PAYS	IMPORTS – IMPORTATIONS				
	1990	1991	1992	1993	1994
Total	2008439	1968053	2370288	2415903	2905993
Africa	x113170	x125444	x151165	x219232	x219367
Northern Africa	x53333	x62065	x73026	x111837	x105598
Americas	149425	174686	200899	262332	303229
LAIA	41331	45335	74063	97423	107991
CACM	4966	4110	5979	x8668	10829
Asia	722278	645838	789178	x757249	x825715
Middle East	328093	x56544	x86732	x123568	x208829
Europe	960372	962888	1174521	1092471	1444170
EEC	921275	934169	1136953	1059888	1404241
EFTA	23697	22532	25425	23524	27228
Oceania	x12814	x15690	x19415	x25257	x19547
Singapore/Singapour	188596	212765	308093	309415	223574
Germany/Allemagne	212348	241068	309439	248261	317048
Netherlands/Pays–Bas	113448	113793	142664	201825	258488
France,Monac	151752	138836	163673	144006	175226
United Kingdom	125475	109044	132495	91048	174704
Belgium–Luxembourg	77449	92878	106883	97926	139590
Bangladesh		146629	119109	x18789	x13680
USA/Etats–Unis d'Amer	69575	92362	90737	98632	118461
Japan/Japon	62903	78385	70479	70814	85451
Spain/Espagne	27674	51950	72061	72561	98063
Denmark/Danemark	58360	47163	59203	60457	55860
Italy/Italie	54279	47555	49585	41199	58000
Korea, Republic of	29890	32881	55711	41255	42330
India/Inde	10129	24937	31693	46774	56214
Mexico/Mexique	23512	21752	30850	42902	35625
Canada	19453	20302	20801	45510	54410
Austria/Autriche	28864	26771	29798	26954	32180
Israel/Israël	15731	20681	26542	29349	31478
Pakistan	25335	23761	20021	29862	33228
Sweden/Suède	21941	23584	26181	22906	32319
Syrian Arab Republic	24493	x8472	33363	x25064	x20930
Russian Federation			x13275	x53334	x41092
Iran (Islamic Rp. of)	279000	x17958	x13339	x30481	x16604
So. Africa Customs Un	16789	18091	19259	21770	42140
Ireland/Irlande	17886	14501	16727	26646	31142
Un. Rep. of Tanzania	x1721	x13946	x22860	x20368	x14313
Sudan/Soudan	x11532	x14112	x16856	x23741	x28104
Libyan Arab Jamahiriya	1453	1850	x435	x49487	x35944
Switz.Liecht	15403	15675	17230	17367	18630
Saudi Arabia	4894	9294	11693	x28415	x31539
Egypt/Egypte	13966	15987	15837	12249	9929
Brazil/Brésil	2493	1913	15630	26191	31311
Thailand/Thaïlande	9338	9990	15537	17555	19478
Poland/Pologne	2594	1262	17857	22500	36151
Algeria/Algérie	9145	13225	19985	7863	6885
Australia/Australie	9221	10077	11784	15917	6731
Turkey/Turquie	7086	6743	13602	15811	16852
Morocco/Maroc	8423	10096	11904	12646	15859
Greece/Grèce	13378	11385	10931	9869	9879
Hong Kong	15763	7722	8047	13536	18678
Finland/Finlande	10014	7529	9078	11089	13291
Chile/Chili	5919	8034	8456	10090	14244
Former USSR/Anc. URSS	28268	x25449			
Nigeria/Nigéria	x1419	1596	x11511	x11709	x1837
Indonesia/Indonésie	8444	7001	7300	9866	16249
Hungary/Hongrie	x8087	6766	x7017	x9861	x11604
Myanmar	4415	5709	x10897	x5480	x12917
Portugal	8406	8111	8234	5141	8452
China/Chine	1828	2868	9502	8706	12959
Tunisia/Tunisie	8814	6795	8008	5851	8813

COUNTRIES–PAYS	EXPORTS – EXPORTATIONS				
	1990	1991	1992	1993	1994
Totale	2029646	1951443	2264458	2534978	3246784
Afrique	x11017	x14616	x15647	x18486	x7330
Afrique du Nord	1153	1682	886	835	4017
Amériques	198759	204956	209505	306209	292830
ALAI	82933	72007	74154	84432	94101
MCAC	798	1124	736	x3966	x6816
Asie	804415	769507	950392	1069639	1549047
Moyen–Orient	11983	7630	12479	88348	172042
Europe	973707	921866	1036544	1054131	1293648
CEE	934261	878233	982412	1006874	1239925
AELE	37019	41231	50714	44312	50550
Océanie	x22310	x28169	30994	x50423	x39209
Malaysia/Malaisie	426648	392899	515254	546067	830126
Germany/Allemagne	328623	298811	348851	331857	380222
Netherlands/Pays–Bas	260402	252896	303762	359367	414355
Singapore/Singapour	224000	233743	281535	236651	214197
USA/Etats–Unis d'Amer	98296	102223	99935	180371	143516
Indonesia/Indonésie	81443	80809	84371	136550	240291
Brazil/Brésil	67744	62681	64196	65137	73848
Belgium–Luxembourg	57048	50714	55819	63125	69393
Italy/Italie	52390	53009	59512	44476	56482
United Kingdom	55041	57322	46112	45493	85505
Denmark/Danemark	57332	47360	52222	44141	59395
Sweden/Suède	53774	49796	41111	42953	70883
Norway,SVD,JM	34706	37281	46243	39913	46737
France,Monac	38901	39751	40371	40515	52480
Turkey/Turquie	9310	5598	11014	87284	82432
Canada	16317	29284	34364	37219	47846
New Zealand	19496	25717	26807	27076	31471
Japan/Japon	22877	19128	18481	17059	18622
India/Inde	6366	13109	10951	11182	26542
Philippines	12600	9903	10677	10543	14451
Finland/Finlande	11696	9174	10134	10664	15484
Australia/Australie	2811	2441	4172	23341	7686
Austria/Autriche	4127	6539	11146	11914	x15973
Spain/Espagne	10654	9646	9836	9473	17042
Poland/Pologne	3500	2826	9771	11133	10533
Cote d'Ivoire	x1379	x7874	x7448	x7149	
China/Chine	5265	5270	7135	8043	8967
Hong Kong	10797	4610	5817	9572	12672
Argentina/Argentine	3595	3791	6001	8155	9620
Czech Republic				13790	20480
Czechoslovakia		x6021	x7037		
Switz.Liecht	2314	3950	4471	4399	3813
Mexico/Mexique	3253	2358	2372	5087	3354
Hungary/Hongrie	x1212	x1753	x1943	x5243	x4864
Kenya	5645	668	2374	4978	
Thailand/Thaïlande	687	1432	2060	4024	7978
So. Africa Customs Un	928	1641	1864	2137	
Venezuela	433	371	251	4576	758
Un. Rep. of Tanzania	x288	x1188	x1707	x921	x904
Slovakia				x3474	x3291
Greece/Grèce	1074	863	1857	716	739
Romania/Roumanie		358	1529	1516	2291
Korea, Republic of	703	662	1325	1339	2296
Croatia/Croatie			1769	1500	x1644
Portugal	2011	1081	655	1435	1430
Ireland/Irlande	1188	1271	1025	746	543
Chile/Chili	730	941	1105	880	2199
Yugoslavia SFR	2387	x2387			
Honduras	599	526	229	1523	399
Egypt/Egypte	514	963	548	517	2628

(VALUE AS % OF TOTAL)(VALEUR EN % DU TOTAL)

	1985	1986	1987	1988	1989	1990	1991	1992	1993	1994
Africa	6.7	7.3	x5.2	x7.1	x5.5	x5.6	x6.4	x6.4	x9.1	x7.6
Northern Africa	4.8	4.0	x2.7	4.2	x3.2	x2.7	x3.2	x3.1	x4.6	x3.6
Americas	5.2	x6.7	6.0	5.5	6.2	7.4	8.9	8.5	10.9	10.4
LAIA	1.5	1.7	1.3	1.6	1.7	2.1	2.3	3.1	4.0	3.7
CACM	0.1	0.2	0.2	0.2	0.3	0.2	0.2	0.3	x0.4	0.4
Asia	34.6	36.3	40.8	x34.8	38.5	35.9	32.8	33.3	x31.3	x28.4
Middle East	2.8	13.7	19.7	x8.8	18.1	16.3	x2.9	x3.7	x5.1	x7.2
Europe	48.0	45.2	42.4	46.2	45.4	47.8	48.9	49.6	45.2	49.7
EEC	43.7	40.7	38.1	42.1	41.4	45.9	47.5	48.0	43.9	48.3
EFTA	3.8	4.0	3.7	3.5	3.5	1.2	1.1	1.1	1.0	0.9
Oceania	2.3	x1.5	x0.9	x0.7	x0.6	x0.7	x0.8	x0.8	x1.0	x0.7
Singapore/Singapour	25.2	14.5	12.0	14.7	11.6	9.4	10.8	13.0	12.8	7.7
Germany/Allemagne	10.9	9.4	8.7	9.7	9.8	10.6	12.2	13.1	10.3	10.9
Netherlands/Pays–Bas	6.4	5.7	5.4	5.3	4.9	5.6	5.8	6.0	8.4	8.9
France,Monac	5.7	5.3	5.0	5.9	6.3	7.6	7.1	6.9	6.0	6.0
United Kingdom	5.6	4.9	5.1	6.3	5.6	6.2	5.5	5.6	3.8	6.0
Belgium–Luxembourg	4.1	3.6	3.2	3.7	3.6	3.9	4.7	4.5	4.1	4.8
Bangladesh	0.1	0.3	0.2	x2.0	x1.2		7.5	5.0	x0.8	x0.5
USA/Etats–Unis d'Amer	1.4	1.9	1.8	2.2	2.7	3.5	4.7	3.8	4.1	4.1
Japan/Japon	2.7	2.2	2.5	2.6	2.8	3.1	4.0	3.0	2.9	2.9
Spain/Espagne	0.3	0.5	0.9	1.0	1.1	1.4	2.6	3.0	3.0	3.4

	1985	1986	1987	1988	1989	1990	1991	1992	1993	1994
Afrique	0.2	x0.2	x0.2	x0.3	x0.3	x0.5	x0.8	x0.7	x0.7	x0.2
Afrique du Nord	0.0	0.0	0.0	0.0	0.1	0.1	0.1	0.0	0.0	0.1
Amériques	6.1	6.6	7.2	7.8	8.9	9.7	10.5	9.2	12.1	9.0
ALAI	2.2	2.4	2.1	2.4	4.1	4.1	3.7	3.3	3.3	2.9
MCAC	0.0	0.0	x0.0	0.1	0.1	0.0	0.1	0.0	x0.2	x0.2
Asie	27.3	30.3	36.3	40.5	40.1	39.6	39.4	41.9	42.2	47.7
Moyen–Orient	1.1	1.0	0.6	0.9	0.6	0.6	0.4	0.6	3.5	5.3
Europe	64.8	61.8	53.6	47.6	48.3	48.0	47.2	45.8	41.6	39.8
CEE	58.0	55.4	48.3	43.2	43.3	46.0	45.0	43.4	39.7	38.2
AELE	6.5	6.2	5.1	4.3	4.9	1.8	2.1	2.2	1.7	1.6
Océanie	0.6	x0.6	x0.4	x1.3	1.2	x1.1	x1.4	1.4	x2.0	x1.2
Malaysia/Malaisie	6.3	5.4	16.5	21.6	20.9	21.0	20.1	22.8	21.5	25.6
Germany/Allemagne	20.0	20.1	15.7	15.4	15.4	16.2	15.3	15.4	13.1	11.7
Netherlands/Pays–Bas	16.6	15.2	14.5	12.4	12.4	12.8	13.0	13.4	14.2	12.8
Singapore/Singapour	12.4	18.1	12.7	11.2	13.9	11.0	12.0	12.4	9.3	6.6
USA/Etats–Unis d'Amer	3.6	3.9	4.8	4.9	4.3	4.8	5.2	4.4	7.1	4.4
Indonesia/Indonésie	4.0	2.4	3.2	4.0	2.1	4.0	4.1	3.7	5.4	7.4
Brazil/Brésil	1.2	1.7	1.6	1.8	3.5	3.3	3.2	2.8	2.6	2.3
Belgium–Luxembourg	3.4	3.0	2.8	2.7	2.6	2.8	2.6	2.5	2.5	2.1
Italy/Italie	2.7	2.4	2.7	2.4	2.5	2.6	2.7	2.6	1.8	1.7
United Kingdom	3.8	3.8	3.5	2.4	2.5	2.7	2.9	2.0	1.8	2.6

TRADE BY COMMODITY IN THOUSAND U.S. DOLLARS – COMMERCE PAR PRODUIT EN MILLIERS DE DOLLARS E.U

COUNTRIES–PAYS	IMPORTS – IMPORTATIONS 1990	1991	1992	1993	1994
Total	13759602	12547803	11665691	11097443	14064282
Africa	x180467	168453	x160616	x129940	x170611
Northern Africa	43200	40209	x45886	36587	54893
Americas	1934359	1812716	1818303	1973036	2379410
LAIA	477933	654615	639058	688555	891479
CACM	18927	20128	17497	x20640	x22777
Asia	3403077	3262472	2823230	3269726	4338672
Middle East	212036	x274139	264518	x222058	x240087
Europe	8006117	7028975	6592230	5370741	6745886
EEC	7641920	6714566	6299162	5138395	6438530
EFTA	236409	220092	215763	190170	215964
Oceania	x38621	x37151	x48164	x108632	x77923
Belgium–Luxembourg	1795360	1683414	1606488	1393621	1641941
Germany/Allemagne	1624180	1479244	1260278	942040	1073434
USA/Etats–Unis d'Amer	1145774	913187	951166	1018050	1121449
France,Monac	1147872	859124	816394	665661	830570
Korea, Republic of	1182671	1081546	602363	655104	747715
Netherlands/Pays–Bas	854311	776569	746748	504147	765003
United Kingdom	549256	582927	567305	394926	638551
Italy/Italie	661725	514848	540922	434751	517847
Japan/Japon	636381	538049	402527	461179	516272
China/Chine	162939	287885	305196	331694	471145
Thailand/Thaïlande	275975	286644	296921	335735	510845
Mexico/Mexique	135301	256624	275230	302073	406644
Spain/Espagne	307400	256980	269581	261890	347757
India/Inde	131463	122709	177869	341016	587776
Canada	264853	203597	186142	217009	305394
Indonesia/Indonésie	238162	166132	185550	252565	455218
Sweden/Suède	208005	186622	158021	165604	195498
Hong Kong	177270	163854	151438	178311	250295
Malaysia/Malaisie	106385	96205	166186	177919	195415
Colombia/Colombie	106352	116015	126599	139978	188847
Singapore/Singapour	120529	109055	123738	142614	166169
Turkey/Turquie	94961	101451	123271	132662	155766
Brazil/Brésil	87761	125540	108336	117018	132343
Switz.Liecht	137805	119691	108368	93388	94252
Norway,SVD,JM	97932	99714	106741	96007	120865
Austria/Autriche	174265	115387	97810	83010	75575
Finland/Finlande	141276	87400	84857	118500	159906
Poland/Pologne	38682	56446	77069	95356	170249
Greece/Grèce	82940	84263	59836	75051	72234
Saudi Arabia	68928	99197	76998	x39799	x42182
Israel/Israël	65360	60320	67272	72833	91441
Portugal	61070	55950	60568	65568	86335
So. Africa Customs Un	88369	67205	57984	56581	66735
Hungary/Hongrie	x30567	66650	x57825	x53409	x52909
Venezuela	68214	59184	56399	47542	43766
Philippines	66140	53568	51529	56524	64174
Australia/Australie	26442	23829	33528	94397	63381
Argentina/Argentine	47325	62528	40908	43121	75966
Romania/Roumanie	52921	37963	37682	24113	34150
Yugoslavia SFR	125647	x93001			
Iran (Islamic Rp. of)		x37130	x32527	x9684	x10087
Czechoslovakia	21543	x33625	x37378		
Nigeria/Nigéria	x17999	28520	x24191	x11035	x13655
Croatia/Croatie			30834	25890	x57353
Ireland/Irlande	17481	16588	14826	18363	19307
Chile/Chili	15477	15777	14668	17039	19753
Denmark/Danemark	16778	15251	15528	15263	14573
Pakistan	11323	13582	13087	19165	20110
Morocco/Maroc	16001	13983	12988	12370	17019
Slovakia				x37097	x49951

COUNTRIES–PAYS	EXPORTS – EXPORTATIONS 1990	1991	1992	1993	1994
Totale	16073568	14999997	14524686	12200355	16960413
Afrique	379291	223513	x82964	x123119	x136741
Afrique du Nord	373555	212389	x74982	x107575	x127225
Amériques	3549498	3337526	3094443	3421429	3988464
ALAI	524299	425519	416439	499371	479675
MCAC	55	275	71	x1317	x793
Asie	2101186	2371124	2781735	x2530614	x3610387
Moyen–Orient	564977	786299	860072	x419755	x444154
Europe	9624006	8603956	8293412	5845258	8913680
CEE	9377390	8381522	8123851	5656945	8685386
AELE	186845	168804	145966	158557	205699
Océanie	17309	x22243	x12497	x16836	x8526
France,Monac	3499707	3260814	3241691	664355	3074226
USA/Etats–Unis d'Amer	2233208	2269576	2130490	2396312	2887646
Netherlands/Pays–Bas	2600953	2014306	1713448	1517743	1660091
Germany/Allemagne	1230719	1115717	1083579	1050989	1113824
United Kingdom	741503	978234	985207	1119068	1135488
Japan/Japon	854589	917693	984621	1088411	1482034
Saudi Arabia	365295	691853	781775	x299785	x309999
Canada	787593	641620	546342	523714	614149
Korea, Republic of	288934	318889	569283	641237	965668
Belgium–Luxembourg	308296	289060	430826	589200	884206
Italy/Italie	427407	264498	263026	311475	320115
Mexico/Mexique	118515	187642	186149	241078	153932
Spain/Espagne	252401	217005	196162	179993	185682
Brazil/Brésil	272769	166074	162614	210781	253218
Norway,SVD,JM	168297	145845	124547	141133	184862
Portugal	205523	123143	120436	124298	168433
Singapore/Singapour	150247	130565	112038	111386	300100
Libyan Arab Jamahiriya	363335	197810	x55559	x95293	x96873
Hungary/Hongrie	x146224	x97482	x111735	x89623	x75400
Israel/Israël	96751	87124	91928	96412	128299
Russian Federation			x119826	x146297	x242058
China/Chine	79017	64275	68722	65149	111087
Czechoslovakia		x101651	x78936		
Former USSR/Anc. URSS	4609	x159375			
Argentina/Argentine	115702	63006	59738	32785	56226
Turkey/Turquie	87990	46715	37980	32741	50322
Sweden/Suède	41305	46018	37112	32538	55822
Hong Kong	24614	37561	39204	38195	48368
Qatar	53994	21275	33254	40306	x20068
Czech Republic				90964	141400
India/Inde	31634	21807	27717	37206	61950
Greece/Grèce	16479	20493	20479	39032	28672
Bulgaria/Bulgarie	x160795	x36150	x25639	x13755	x11823
Poland/Pologne	45463	32431	22291	18196	18274
Ukraine			x13644	x50744	x25760
Switz.Liecht	18549	22960	21418	17424	20838
Australia/Australie	17218	22018	12186	15791	7377
Yugoslavia SFR	58609	x48959			
Finland/Finlande	26965	28075	13352	6524	34133
Algeria/Algérie	7896	14012	16906	10999	28541
Bahrain/Bahreïn	x11863	x24625	x5148	x10075	x12431
Slovakia				x38692	x47434
Croatia/Croatie			11484	27033	x21405
Austria/Autriche	22923	12589	12177	12036	x19638
Romania/Roumanie	20058	7940	16290	11502	8203
Indonesia/Indonésie	5082	1141	10561	23626	40743
So. Africa Customs Un	4566	7510	6893	8803	
Ireland/Irlande	1046	8943	3813	7256	2332
Venezuela	11738	3835	5983	8810	6742
Iran (Islamic Rp. of)				x15586	x29930

(VALUE AS % OF TOTAL)(VALEUR EN % DU TOTAL)

	1985	1986	1987	1988	1989	1990	1991	1992	1993	1994
Africa	1.3	x1.6	x1.4	x1.4	x1.3	x1.3	1.3	x1.4	x1.2	x1.2
Northern Africa	0.4	0.4	0.3	0.3	0.4	0.3	0.3	x0.4	0.3	0.4
Americas	26.1	20.2	16.1	16.0	13.3	14.1	14.4	15.5	17.7	16.9
LAIA	6.0	5.5	4.7	5.2	4.6	3.5	5.2	5.5	6.2	6.3
CACM	0.5	0.3	x0.1	0.1	0.1	0.1	0.2	0.1	x0.2	x0.2
Asia	14.5	17.7	x23.2	x27.1	23.8	24.7	26.0	24.2	29.5	30.8
Middle East	1.8	x1.9	x1.6	x1.4	1.6	1.5	x2.2	2.3	x2.0	x1.7
Europe	56.6	58.5	53.1	50.7	57.8	58.2	56.0	56.5	48.4	48.0
EEC	51.2	53.2	47.5	44.8	51.6	55.5	53.5	54.0	46.3	45.8
EFTA	4.0	4.1	4.3	4.6	5.3	1.7	1.8	1.8	1.7	1.5
Oceania	0.8	x1.0	x1.0	0.3	x0.4	x0.3	x0.3	x0.4	x1.0	x0.5
Belgium–Luxembourg	9.8	9.7	9.1	10.5	12.2	13.0	13.4	13.8	12.6	11.7
Germany/Allemagne	10.9	12.1	10.4	8.7	10.8	11.8	11.8	10.8	8.5	7.6
USA/Etats–Unis d'Amer	18.2	12.9	9.8	9.4	7.3	8.3	7.3	8.2	9.2	8.0
France,Monac	6.6	6.9	6.5	6.2	6.7	8.3	6.8	7.0	6.0	5.9
Korea, Republic of	2.9	4.0	4.8	7.4	8.5	8.6	8.6	5.2	5.9	5.3
Netherlands/Pays–Bas	7.9	7.6	6.7	5.3	6.2	6.2	6.2	6.4	4.5	5.4
United Kingdom	5.3	5.2	4.0	4.0	3.9	4.0	4.6	4.9	3.6	4.5
Italy/Italie	5.6	5.8	4.5	4.0	4.9	4.8	4.1	4.6	3.9	3.7
Japan/Japon	4.8	5.4	4.9	5.2	4.9	4.6	4.3	3.5	4.2	3.7
China/Chine			1.2	2.0	1.7	1.2	2.3	2.6	3.0	3.3

	1985	1986	1987	1988	1989	1990	1991	1992	1993	1994
Afrique	0.6	0.5	1.2	1.6	1.7	2.3	1.5	x0.5	x1.0	x0.8
Afrique du Nord	0.5	0.4	1.1	1.5	1.6	2.3	1.4	x0.5	x0.9	x0.8
Amériques	25.4	23.0	21.3	22.5	23.4	22.1	22.2	21.3	28.0	23.5
ALAI	4.0	2.0	2.2	2.7	2.5	3.3	2.8	2.9	4.1	2.8
MCAC	0.0	0.0	x0.0	0.0	x0.0	0.0	0.0	0.0	x0.0	x0.0
Asie	7.5	x8.7	x10.7	11.0	11.8	13.1	15.8	19.1	x20.7	x21.3
Moyen–Orient	1.4	x2.5	x4.1	4.0	3.2	3.5	5.2	5.9	x3.4	x2.6
Europe	64.5	66.4	60.9	59.1	60.2	59.9	57.4	57.1	47.9	52.6
CEE	61.8	63.8	58.3	56.7	58.0	58.3	55.9	55.9	46.4	51.2
AELE	2.1	2.1	2.2	2.1	1.7	1.2	1.1	1.0	1.3	1.2
Océanie	0.2	0.2	x0.5	x0.1	x0.1	0.1	x0.1	x0.1	x0.1	x0.1
France,Monac	19.6	24.0	21.5	19.5	20.3	21.8	21.7	22.3	5.4	18.1
USA/Etats–Unis d'Amer	16.5	16.5	14.7	14.6	15.6	13.9	15.1	14.7	19.6	17.0
Netherlands/Pays–Bas	15.6	15.7	15.2	16.2	15.4	16.2	13.4	11.8	12.4	9.8
Germany/Allemagne	10.4	9.2	7.8	8.4	8.1	7.7	7.4	7.5	8.6	6.6
United Kingdom	6.8	6.8	6.8	5.3	5.7	4.6	6.5	6.8	9.2	6.7
Japan/Japon	3.3	3.6	3.7	3.9	5.8	5.3	6.1	6.8	8.9	8.7
Saudi Arabia	1.3	x2.1	x3.4	3.2	2.3	2.3	4.6	5.4	x2.5	x1.8
Canada	4.9	4.5	4.4	5.2	5.2	4.9	4.3	3.8	4.3	3.6
Korea, Republic of	0.7	0.9	0.7	0.9	0.8	1.8	2.1	3.9	5.3	5.7
Belgium–Luxembourg	2.8	2.4	1.7	1.6	2.1	1.9	1.9	3.0	4.8	5.2

TRADE BY COMMODITY IN THOUSAND U.S. DOLLARS – COMMERCE PAR PRODUIT EN MILLIERS DE DOLLARS E.U

COUNTRIES–PAYS	IMPORTS – IMPORTATIONS 1990	1991	1992	1993	1994
Total	8689104	9069095	8481900	8224253	11867642
Africa	x145521	160098	x155622	x122362	x146134
Northern Africa	42325	40074	50184	27759	32534
Americas	1608589	1692350	1492440	1599481	2642739
LAIA	655657	753228	517162	585435	1049462
CACM	15505	15193	27935	x14832	x21142
Asia	2257597	2854879	2427876	2455247	3319606
Middle East	121322	x158283	x126725	x119107	x140891
Europe	4467022	4155085	4193354	3797364	5442219
EEC	4185061	3919296	3925060	3575499	5140371
EFTA	227536	208108	226481	181295	272635
Oceania	x60071	x60579	x69948	x70614	x97574
Japan/Japon	799764	1002622	839637	821233	1112040
USA/Etats–Unis d'Amer	794152	791750	805179	842935	1391906
Germany/Allemagne	682632	694241	741519	618098	880461
France,Monac	605427	585319	577780	502828	768765
Italy/Italie	554164	567823	535297	471310	697580
United Kingdom	663169	531392	529713	505157	672205
Netherlands/Pays–Bas	569124	470041	486213	491903	694488
Korea, Republic of	430863	521147	396625	452299	660670
Belgium–Luxembourg	445793	417881	416871	379067	523964
Brazil/Brésil	372359	418532	185114	285612	659955
China/Chine	158970	334669	275403	263406	307730
Spain/Espagne	244038	257869	257393	220791	331019
Switz.Liecht	226435	207242	225735	180534	230336
Indonesia/Indonésie	152535	159419	154540	150525	223971
Singapore/Singapour	115722	150201	130679	135938	185861
Thailand/Thaïlande	98754	123583	121369	135999	186069
Canada	120130	114753	124039	140527	159889
Mexico/Mexique	97333	118626	121647	106707	187475
Sweden/Suède	106604	99201	103527	117502	177971
Hong Kong	72131	103474	98028	81548	109992
Russian Federation			x129074	x123623	x83694
Turkey/Turquie	89722	93669	81999	76819	99012
Denmark/Danemark	70745	75377	75477	65440	88242
Malaysia/Malaisie	63232	81516	69200	62872	80089
India/Inde	101158	71670	62275	67538	123648
Austria/Autriche	81253	66800	63604	70308	91741
So. Africa Customs Un	64607	68421	67295	55606	82527
Venezuela	46577	64982	60239	51698	35975
Australia/Australie	47281	49063	57050	56634	80328
Argentina/Argentine	46919	53490	50811	44545	52963
Philippines	41163	45296	46462	48741	51015
Finland/Finlande	66847	53866	40852	45222	84114
Israel/Israël	49039	42134	47190	48806	59249
Colombia/Colombie	38136	39831	45468	40713	54882
Portugal	46872	45764	41481	32580	53605
Poland/Pologne	17333	20555	45548	51883	87047
Pakistan	26473	34977	33524	37452	41596
Ireland/Irlande	28027	31600	31655	30779	44250
Iran (Islamic Rp. of)		x40257	x21266	x20247	x15143
Romania/Roumanie	6461	15453	27866	37772	31799
Chile/Chili	20463	26836	28367	25154	26094
Greece/Grèce	20366	22122	23678	24514	31966
Hungary/Hongrie	x22216	29953	x21053	x18717	x16424
Egypt/Egypte	23510	19128	24845	12160	10181
Czechoslovakia	50453	x23039	x30596		
Nigeria/Nigéria	x13116	25465	x12239	x14268	x8089
Bulgaria/Bulgarie	x43741	x12130	17446	x16727	x12509
Former USSR/Anc. URSS		x44874			
Slovenia/Slovénia			19876	18755	20780
New Zealand	11282	10606	11525	12763	14779

COUNTRIES–PAYS	EXPORTS – EXPORTATIONS 1990	1991	1992	1993	1994
Totale	8105923	7584695	7138112	7799595	10752799
Afrique	143847	136324	x157448	x167656	x312702
Afrique du Nord	86948	87978	x106309	x96796	x250973
Amériques	2073638	2199819	1879811	1808961	2847489
ALAI	327368	371240	333141	352226	604635
MCAC	11409	10572	16037	x17108	x26234
Asie	1568459	1338544	1489581	x1904843	x2649915
Moyen–Orient	498495	x83783	x117359	x539995	x870423
Europe	3856276	3413484	3374523	3591020	4418245
CEE	3731932	3289333	3243641	3458502	4247977
AELE	111373	106631	118894	123150	149939
Océanie	x44030	x107673	x69475	x99572	x256723
Germany/Allemagne	1632978	1536314	1519657	1296625	1751179
USA/Etats–Unis d'Amer	1293860	1261683	1094131	1045134	1461527
Japan/Japon	390707	448736	519288	547379	666462
France,Monac	372727	366917	402662	710047	499142
United Kingdom	667129	421634	400869	374450	420719
Canada	395359	480641	366906	322767	515609
Netherlands/Pays–Bas	310769	300204	226695	368310	585503
Italy/Italie	224263	213937	221533	190474	214696
Saudi Arabia	433236	9348	73541	x490242	x774329
Belgium–Luxembourg	137342	125311	146898	212095	347644
Malaysia/Malaisie	105771	133359	173175	171181	286045
Sweden/Suède	159203	151666	155241	133430	173732
China/Chine	159962	149180	141245	138350	208075
Singapore/Singapour	131945	158787	133620	129824	161949
Brazil/Brésil	103950	103424	137535	153516	181178
Russian Federation			x148389	x178374	x375057
Switz.Liecht	101611	96818	109624	114553	141263
Mexico/Mexique	89207	126266	85980	80352	80026
Spain/Espagne	123370	97849	81255	83198	126781
Israel/Israël	79893	82154	80689	99068	104580
New Zealand	40674	103390	64449	83517	241340
Libyan Arab Jamahiriya	76441	74347	x91217	x82895	x228852
Poland/Pologne	84616	101668	74142	61620	87305
Hong Kong	63121	82731	74411	56025	70242
Finland/Finlande	70560	61956	70026	73413	102759
Chile/Chili	71444	80180	59310	63153	188645
Former USSR/Anc. URSS	225887	x192561			
Korea, Republic of	21330	46826	71079	61090	74160
So. Africa Customs Un	46144	42305	41182	62041	42440
Trinidad and Tobago	39324	61378	43879	39663	196456
Indonesia/Indonésie	12745	32832	54802	44364	78817
Thailand/Thaïlande	20586	37032	48201	43279	29308
Bahrain/Bahreïn	x48293	x52116	x34821	x38938	x70960
Philippines	52958	44348	38558	35570	38428
Argentina/Argentine	44476	46215	36112	32521	41722
Ukraine			x21957	x83235	x77908
Czech Republic				101822	56240
India/Inde	23953	34405	31229	30090	50844
Czechoslovakia		x41668	x50020		
Bulgaria/Bulgarie	x71866	x24650	x10896	x12941	x20557
Romania/Roumanie	4225	14286	14747	14002	68653
Hungary/Hongrie	x22024	x13318	x16869	x10835	x7711
Cuba	x3469	x9968	x14201	x7471	x718
Algeria/Algérie	7315	10993	9665	8798	15509
Norway,SVD,JM	9762	9813	9271	8597	8676
Costa Rica	9838	7537	11038	x8993	x15056
Turkey/Turquie	16106	17306	8459	1640	6078
Slovakia				x25816	x27240
Australia/Australie	2713	4030	4777	15772	13550
Denmark/Danemark	7405	7069	8408	7284	7498

(VALUE AS % OF TOTAL)(VALEUR EN % DU TOTAL)

	1985	1986	1987	1988	1989	1990	1991	1992	1993	1994
Africa	2.0	x2.1	x1.7	x1.8	x1.8	x1.6	1.8	x1.8	x1.5	x1.2
Northern Africa	0.5	0.4	0.4	0.4	0.6	0.5	0.4	0.6	0.3	0.3
Americas	21.9	20.3	16.1	16.8	15.5	18.5	18.7	17.6	19.5	22.3
LAIA	6.4	5.5	4.8	4.5	4.7	7.5	8.3	6.1	7.1	8.8
CACM	0.3	0.2	0.2	0.1	0.1	0.2	0.2	0.3	x0.2	x0.2
Asia	21.6	22.2	x25.0	x29.0	28.8	26.0	31.5	28.7	29.9	28.0
Middle East	1.3	x1.5	x1.5	x1.3	x1.7	1.4	x1.7	x1.5	x1.4	x1.2
Europe	51.8	52.8	50.2	47.0	49.3	51.4	45.8	49.4	46.2	45.9
EEC	44.0	44.7	43.2	40.7	43.2	48.2	43.2	46.3	43.5	43.3
EFTA	6.4	6.7	6.0	5.3	5.3	2.6	2.3	2.7	2.2	2.3
Oceania	0.9	0.7	0.7	0.6	0.6	x0.7	x0.7	x0.8	x0.8	x0.8
Japan/Japon	10.9	10.9	8.5	9.6	9.8	9.2	11.1	9.9	10.0	9.4
USA/Etats–Unis d'Amer	13.8	12.9	9.6	10.7	9.1	9.1	8.7	9.5	10.2	11.7
Germany/Allemagne	9.9	9.7	8.4	6.9	7.6	7.9	7.7	8.7	7.5	7.4
France,Monac	5.9	6.1	6.5	5.9	6.1	7.0	6.5	6.8	6.1	6.5
Italy/Italie	6.2	6.1	6.2	5.9	6.1	6.4	6.3	6.3	5.7	5.9
United Kingdom	4.6	5.1	5.2	6.4	6.6	7.6	5.9	6.2	6.1	5.7
Netherlands/Pays–Bas	6.5	6.2	6.1	5.1	6.3	6.5	5.2	5.7	6.0	5.9
Korea, Republic of	2.6	2.8	3.1	4.7	6.0	5.0	5.7	4.7	5.5	5.6
Belgium–Luxembourg	3.3	3.7	3.4	3.7	3.9	5.1	4.6	4.9	4.6	4.4
Brazil/Brésil	1.1	1.1	1.0	1.0	1.6	4.3	4.6	2.2	3.5	5.6

	1985	1986	1987	1988	1989	1990	1991	1992	1993	1994
Afrique	2.0	1.5	x1.7	x1.9	x1.9	1.8	1.8	x2.2	x2.2	x2.9
Afrique du Nord	1.5	1.1	1.2	1.3	1.0	1.1	1.2	x1.5	x1.2	x2.3
Amériques	27.7	23.4	20.6	20.4	25.3	25.5	29.0	26.4	23.2	26.5
ALAI	5.6	4.5	2.8	3.1	4.1	4.0	4.9	4.7	4.5	5.6
MCAC	0.2	0.2	0.0	0.0	0.0	0.1	0.1	0.2	x0.2	x0.2
Asie	12.5	x16.8	x16.8	20.0	20.2	19.3	17.6	20.9	x24.4	x24.7
Moyen–Orient	3.4	x6.7	x5.6	8.9	7.9	6.1	x1.1	x1.6	x6.9	x8.1
Europe	52.2	52.1	51.7	44.8	45.6	47.6	45.0	47.3	46.0	41.1
CEE	48.5	47.8	47.5	41.1	42.0	46.0	43.4	45.4	44.3	39.5
AELE	3.5	4.3	4.1	3.5	3.4	1.4	1.4	1.7	1.6	1.4
Océanie	0.8	x0.7	x0.6	0.7	0.6	x0.5	x1.4	x1.0	x1.3	x2.4
Germany/Allemagne	21.4	22.4	20.9	17.6	18.5	20.1	20.3	21.3	16.6	16.3
USA/Etats–Unis d'Amer	13.0	13.1	12.7	11.9	15.6	16.0	16.6	15.3	13.4	13.6
Japan/Japon	4.5	4.9	4.8	4.1	4.7	4.8	5.9	7.3	7.0	6.2
France,Monac	3.6	3.6	3.8	3.4	3.6	4.6	4.8	5.6	9.1	4.6
United Kingdom	6.6	5.6	5.0	8.1	7.2	8.2	5.6	5.6	4.8	3.9
Canada	7.7	4.8	3.9	4.6	5.0	4.9	6.3	5.1	4.1	4.8
Netherlands/Pays–Bas	7.9	7.1	6.2	4.0	4.2	3.8	4.0	3.2	4.7	5.4
Italy/Italie	3.2	3.0	5.8	2.6	2.8	2.8	2.8	3.1	2.4	2.0
Saudi Arabia	3.4	x5.4	x4.8	7.4	6.9	5.3	0.1	1.0	x6.3	x7.2
Belgium–Luxembourg	1.8	2.0	1.7	1.7	2.0	1.7	1.7	2.1	2.7	3.2

TRADE BY COMMODITY IN THOUSAND U.S. DOLLARS – COMMERCE PAR PRODUIT EN MILLIERS DE DOLLARS E.U

COUNTRIES–PAYS	IMPORTS – IMPORTATIONS				
	1990	1991	1992	1993	1994
Total	10660250	11599579	12206283	11606653	13765030
Africa	287112	283513	x271587	x253925	x268310
Northern Africa	117216	107044	116075	90220	100351
Americas	1991748	2218719	2601779	2458940	2652606
LAIA	545021	644756	673670	737977	849288
CACM	24278	25143	27934	x27186	x27889
Asia	2514053	2914121	2865940	3103132	3683472
Middle East	205968	x243591	x251428	x261955	x271380
Europe	5541008	5870162	6193278	5449489	6788362
EEC	5099093	5508875	5809710	5106681	6343630
EFTA	316403	307927	306973	287965	394402
Oceania	x137996	x131906	x135605	x173216	x179819
USA/Etats–Unis d'Amer	1091136	1227642	1532854	1325855	1353289
Germany/Allemagne	1126762	1160062	1209508	950388	1109932
France,Monac	824939	807906	830781	672654	897537
Italy/Italie	779423	740961	769128	664198	858814
United Kingdom	205005	701237	747571	701661	870268
Netherlands/Pays–Bas	647934	606060	634652	644499	803562
Belgium–Luxembourg	492024	480918	603228	608072	738479
Japan/Japon	430458	481249	424118	436861	473774
Korea, Republic of	479706	449484	410678	427427	512657
China/Chine	336323	499116	387146	366889	442737
Spain/Espagne	416168	407171	404157	331898	438694
Canada	295890	303779	318142	311362	337077
Switz.Liecht	315412	307170	306080	287319	332157
Thailand/Thaïlande	229981	249583	289331	346014	434288
Indonesia/Indonésie	179086	222626	282179	326774	350037
Singapore/Singapour	117845	168064	189405	234681	246566
Mexico/Mexique	129962	154439	181801	191701	220147
Hong Kong	116829	181236	168332	166372	265882
Brazil/Brésil	147592	146751	137816	180166	209840
Turkey/Turquie	150147	151560	147635	161894	178168
Ireland/Irlande	93464	130970	120223	119771	128078
Pakistan	94479	117274	122753	121529	135769
So. Africa Customs Un	123163	126566	112948	117987	135617
Australia/Australie	109278	102844	104947	140502	139925
Sweden/Suède	136077	129488	116502	101074	118432
Colombia/Colombie	69427	97781	101829	110104	126270
Argentina/Argentine	90699	96755	104461	106408	134747
Malaysia/Malaisie	81307	90959	97825	104762	142135
Austria/Autriche	105090	90648	103906	90380	121448
Philippines	66483	71677	81115	86736	94654
India/Inde	81038	54267	72371	109462	197180
Venezuela	45443	70267	73068	68558	63513
Portugal	77355	72251	75982	56348	63529
Finland/Finlande	74804	70842	64311	64599	85705
Denmark/Danemark	62091	59008	75662	50797	55054
Israel/Israël	54106	53351	57686	65599	76594
Greece/Grèce	57955	51353	54100	50341	54097
Iran (Islamic Rp. of)		x48489	x54901	x32700	x13456
Hungary/Hongrie	x41777	49100	x37674	x41149	x33589
Egypt/Egypte	56820	48977	43425	30596	35111
Chile/Chili	22812	29009	31600	33821	34076
Poland/Pologne	12838	10982	39884	41849	62204
New Zealand	28045	28396	29925	31774	34036
Former USSR/Anc. URSS	17620	x74464			
Algeria/Algérie	22938	19688	31321	21465	17556
Romania/Roumanie	8904	12596	26062	30848	21392
Cayman Is/Is Caïmans	x200	x113	x28802	x37316	x61016
Morocco/Maroc	22620	20974	20552	21030	27981
Peru/Pérou	13697	17783	17479	19840	25670
Russian Federation			x37360	x16945	x12441

COUNTRIES–PAYS	EXPORTS – EXPORTATIONS				
	1990	1991	1992	1993	1994
Totale	10352938	10360509	11695283	11760761	12956052
Afrique	9342	x11198	x9612	x11670	x995
Afrique du Nord	663	1110	922	633	185
Amériques	x2794416	2538899	x3478468	x3114043	2819195
ALAI	412927	501891	547470	525901	608322
MCAC	1349	1506	988	x428	x368
Asie	1671836	2014932	2291051	2501774	3127097
Moyen–Orient	37607	96011	22956	22808	x16712
Europe	5759837	5608678	5768102	6007388	6823403
CEE	5410792	5254937	5374697	5674099	6412248
AELE	319190	332771	373002	323103	387199
Océanie	x7218	x12732	x5858	x4012	x3393
USA/Etats–Unis d'Amer	1842723	1924350	1820582	1795487	2042031
Germany/Allemagne	1783903	1602526	1608632	1400671	1744546
Japan/Japon	1137821	1250852	1418944	1473836	1797370
United Kingdom	1155057	1170454	1083797	947536	1146325
Belgium–Luxembourg	577174	618612	790458	890760	1148199
Bahamas	x438279		x981017	x684680	x44455
France,Monac	394750	383956	374905	870832	534238
Netherlands/Pays–Bas	480771	462835	467836	568398	732726
Mexico/Mexique	260819	322022	351501	352037	423655
Italy/Italie	357650	330709	340635	308122	353668
Switz.Liecht	306167	316122	348392	310684	368956
Korea, Republic of	123175	186598	245656	271979	301238
Austria/Autriche	195865	184074	212091	219990	x215656
China/Chine	142208	149049	201264	255860	332296
Spain/Espagne	215750	261535	176113	154743	180629
Ireland/Irlande	134959	111255	153238	169333	172028
Hong Kong	70743	119086	126749	143570	220859
Canada	97134	108540	127816	106582	123401
Brazil/Brésil	75491	107502	123995	102708	107354
Singapore/Singapour	62832	87809	107340	129922	156416
Sweden/Suède	81056	94960	115197	105423	131049
Israel/Israël	35135	45337	51968	54278	70559
Czechoslovakia		x74750	x52638		
Russian Federation			x43962	x70835	x72096
Hungary/Hongrie	x37569	x32879	x40428	x28623	x35422
Argentina/Argentine	41314	36576	32929	30241	38445
Malaysia/Malaisie	6758	17074	32519	46838	61611
India/Inde	11637	18869	28964	43986	83312
Indonesia/Indonésie	21005	22228	30145	35783	72358
Saudi Arabia	57	78476	504	x257	x890
Turkey/Turquie	35739	16779	21993	21163	11793
Colombia/Colombie	13971	16528	18855	18734	17913
Norway,SVD,JM	13023	16649	24610	12413	18242
Czech Republic				53154	74818
Denmark/Danemark	5592	3925	28463	14545	14089
Poland/Pologne	14940	12625	21486	10932	32396
Portugal	13361	15388	11307	11754	13992
Finland/Finlande	14678	14469	11828	11528	24783
Venezuela	13148	10983	12214	13886	12798
Romania/Roumanie	2755	6702	14996	15194	28489
Former USSR/Anc. URSS	7985	x35895			
Ukraine			x8441	x21179	x12353
So. Africa Customs Un	7961	9685	7957	10248	
Thailand/Thaïlande	14022	15846	7589	4430	5940
Bhutan/Bhoutan		x2675	x9579	x14654	x478
Bulgaria/Bulgarie	x37618	x10116	x9972	x5371	x4340
Slovenia/Slovénia			14029	7452	21420
Yugoslavia SFR	29786	x19585			
Australia/Australie	5149	9808	4137	2118	2677
Chile/Chili	3901	4029	3577	4649	5276

(VALUE AS % OF TOTAL)(VALEUR EN % DU TOTAL)

	1985	1986	1987	1988	1989	1990	1991	1992	1993	1994
Africa	3.1	3.3	x2.6	x2.8	x2.5	2.7	2.5	x2.2	x2.2	x2.0
Northern Africa	1.2	1.2	1.0	1.1	1.0	1.1	0.9	1.0	0.8	0.7
Americas	17.0	16.5	13.9	15.4	18.7	18.7	19.1	21.4	21.2	19.3
LAIA	6.4	6.2	5.3	5.3	5.2	5.1	5.6	5.5	6.4	6.2
CACM	0.4	0.3	x0.3	0.2	0.2	0.2	0.2	0.2	x0.2	x0.2
Asia	21.7	22.3	x28.1	x29.3	24.4	23.5	25.1	23.4	26.7	26.8
Middle East	1.8	x2.8	x2.9	x2.1	x2.0	1.9	x2.1	x2.1	x2.3	x2.0
Europe	55.4	55.5	50.6	48.0	50.2	52.0	50.6	50.7	47.0	49.3
EEC	47.0	47.4	43.4	40.5	42.7	47.8	47.5	47.6	44.0	46.1
EFTA	6.7	6.7	5.9	6.3	6.4	3.0	2.7	2.5	2.5	2.9
Oceania	1.4	x1.2	x1.4	x1.7	x1.8	x1.3	x1.1	x1.1	x1.5	x1.3
USA/Etats–Unis d'Amer	6.1	6.3	5.5	7.1	10.3	10.2	10.6	12.6	11.4	9.8
Germany/Allemagne	9.1	9.3	8.8	8.5	9.3	10.6	10.0	9.9	8.2	8.1
France,Monac	7.1	7.2	6.5	6.8	6.9	7.7	7.0	6.8	5.8	6.5
Italy/Italie	6.1	6.2	5.6	5.8	6.3	7.3	6.4	6.3	5.7	6.2
United Kingdom	6.6	6.1	6.1	2.1	1.8	1.9	6.0	6.1	6.0	6.3
Netherlands/Pays–Bas	6.3	6.2	5.3	5.1	5.5	6.1	5.2	5.2	5.6	5.8
Belgium–Luxembourg	3.5	3.7	3.2	3.5	4.0	4.6	4.1	4.9	5.2	5.4
Japan/Japon	4.3	4.3	3.9	4.4	4.2	4.0	4.1	3.5	3.8	3.4
Korea, Republic of	6.6	6.2	5.0	4.5	5.6	4.5	3.9	3.4	3.7	3.7
China/Chine			3.5	3.9	3.3	3.2	4.3	3.2	3.2	3.2

	1985	1986	1987	1988	1989	1990	1991	1992	1993	1994
Afrique	0.1	x0.1	x0.2	x0.1	x0.1	0.1	x0.1	x0.1	x0.1	x0.0
Afrique du Nord	0.0	x0.0	x0.0	x0.0	0.0	0.0	0.0	0.0	0.0	0.0
Amériques	24.2	23.4	21.5	24.8	x31.8	x27.0	24.5	x29.8	x26.5	21.7
ALAI	5.4	4.1	4.2	5.3	4.3	4.0	4.8	4.7	4.5	4.7
MCAC	0.0	x0.0	x0.0	0.0	0.0	0.0	0.0	0.0	x0.0	x0.0
Asie	9.8	11.5	x13.5	14.9	14.2	16.1	19.4	19.6	21.3	24.1
Moyen–Orient	0.4	0.6	0.4	0.4	0.4	0.4	0.9	0.2	0.2	x0.1
Europe	64.9	64.0	61.3	56.7	52.3	55.6	54.1	49.3	51.1	52.7
CEE	59.3	57.3	54.9	50.6	46.7	52.3	50.7	46.0	48.2	49.5
AELE	5.4	6.4	6.2	5.8	5.3	3.1	3.2	3.2	2.7	3.0
Océanie	0.1	x0.1	x0.0	x0.0	x0.0	x0.1	x0.1	x0.0	x0.0	x0.0
USA/Etats–Unis d'Amer	18.3	18.6	16.6	18.6	19.7	17.8	18.6	15.6	15.3	15.8
Germany/Allemagne	20.0	20.9	18.6	17.3	15.2	17.2	15.5	13.8	11.9	13.5
Japan/Japon	7.7	8.7	8.6	9.5	9.9	11.0	12.1	12.1	12.5	13.9
United Kingdom	13.7	12.6	11.1	10.6	10.1	11.2	11.3	9.3	8.1	8.8
Belgium–Luxembourg	1.5	1.7	1.6	4.4	4.4	5.6	6.0	6.8	7.6	8.9
Bahamas		x0.2	x0.1	x0.1	x7.0	x4.2		x8.4	x5.8	x0.3
France,Monac	3.5	4.0	3.5	3.5	3.2	3.8	3.7	3.2	7.4	4.1
Netherlands/Pays–Bas	6.5	7.5	7.4	4.8	4.4	4.6	4.5	4.0	4.8	5.7
Mexico/Mexique	3.4	2.5	2.7	3.1	2.7	2.5	3.1	3.0	3.0	3.3
Italy/Italie	8.1	3.8	5.9	3.4	3.1	3.5	3.2	2.9	2.6	2.7

TRADE BY COMMODITY IN THOUSAND U.S. DOLLARS – COMMERCE PAR PRODUIT EN MILLIERS DE DOLLARS E.U

COUNTRIES–PAYS	IMPORTS – IMPORTATIONS					COUNTRIES–PAYS	EXPORTS – EXPORTATIONS				
	1990	1991	1992	1993	1994		1990	1991	1992	1993	1994
Total	18039434	19069819	20939951	20895330	23926583	Totale	17333568	18172270	19923530	20139474	22441539
Africa	x313563	x322933	x354945	x345326	x410827	Afrique	x12482	14805	x24647	x37346	x5934
Northern Africa	57859	59514	x62587	70785	100768	Afrique du Nord	1907	4860	x5329	x4735	x5098
Americas	4002394	4499757	4963789	5043596	5629548	Amériques	3015186	3281520	3689937	3433206	3869936
LAIA	1069674	1244032	1355377	1472508	1644151	ALAI	257647	282528	328934	304179	341784
CACM	20292	19227	22130	x31986	x27541	MCAC	262	298	441	x214	x686
Asia	3397846	3808969	4119199	4332730	4924637	Asie	2456517	2763169	2991349	3084287	3776877
Middle East	282836	x374999	x402733	x391697	x375691	Moyen–Orient	69731	70033	40541	x29437	x44657
Europe	9794936	9729792	10969651	10545720	12300721	Europe	11601825	11794325	12949382	13324796	14488258
EEC	8690864	8826486	10002922	9638595	11336276	CEE	9483348	9826812	10762269	11082610	11962949
EFTA	909815	818506	854309	809227	889691	AELE	2082131	1945190	2174557	2227713	2516745
Oceania	x247538	x270522	x331866	x358428	x402979	Océanie	x3271	x3276	x3524	x4443	x4534
USA/Etats–Unis d'Amer	2346480	2684362	2967842	2941102	3234406	Germany/Allemagne	3273035	3343747	3530433	3211909	3588705
Germany/Allemagne	2055391	2084189	2237716	2151606	2802770	USA/Etats–Unis d'Amer	2634397	2926153	3228016	2996362	3400919
France, Monac	1615577	1605538	1886196	1552524	1760793	United Kingdom	2074732	2059362	2347663	2092450	2142734
Japan/Japon	1292504	1426848	1447265	1568532	1797409	Switz.Liecht	1911421	1763560	1951964	2055843	2321761
Italy/Italie	1475132	1406249	1542885	1370540	1692538	Japan/Japon	1554954	1609666	1671652	1691430	1922451
United Kingdom	1068758	1220473	1434908	1472234	1685368	France, Monac	880197	1003244	986034	1657197	1177093
Netherlands/Pays–Bas	611853	612008	833100	1040266	1135827	Italy/Italie	774669	879401	933947	954664	1043376
Switz.Liecht	866807	774152	802524	759296	825028	Netherlands/Pays–Bas	789050	821965	1000490	858023	1027643
Belgium–Luxembourg	578981	583927	622429	781495	765133	Ireland/Irlande	493746	632239	874938	1066399	1393026
Korea, Republic of	492360	547901	566728	598793	647297	Belgium–Luxembourg	596836	561193	585107	769286	1014141
Canada	536770	522153	542947	567248	681212	Korea, Republic of	197166	233836	272492	305168	370199
Spain/Espagne	518067	522239	553999	495110	581147	China/Chine	127350	151401	229287	239632	389697
Brazil/Brésil	428836	471085	448674	549473	644862	Norway, SVD, JM	170710	181629	222588	171853	194978
Mexico/Mexique	295697	333587	386248	385403	410290	Hong Kong	112395	171808	201500	195979	329242
China/Chine	217185	284472	322391	284252	366500	Brazil/Brésil	149846	173760	210252	173254	186667
Australia/Australie	217553	241576	298717	323880	357065	Singapore/Singapour	126032	148441	159530	156210	189427
Turkey/Turquie	210530	237238	259939	251736	242047	Spain/Espagne	142104	151986	151370	149535	236324
Hong Kong	139360	208057	259596	235890	377068	Sweden/Suède	135201	129038	141451	133242	151657
So. Africa Customs Un	174815	177361	193295	191965	234327	India/Inde	96314	132124	124399	133269	188991
Indonesia/Indonésie	177782	165835	175385	211647	245062	Hungary/Hongrie	x84228	x92463	x131002	x116256	x122231
Argentina/Argentine	111364	145919	199772	206234	251388	Austria/Autriche	192817	127006	106307	97073	x96791
Ireland/Irlande	140030	155449	203577	185766	252892	Indonesia/Indonésie	41964	69272	107317	134432	138930
Singapore/Singapour	155623	173345	179000	172914	184207	Israel/Israël	89582	103494	100750	106499	109580
Portugal	152370	165855	177055	151896	160432	Canada	101476	72313	82169	90639	99164
Thailand/Thaïlande	136018	134616	171757	184777	201165	Thailand/Thaïlande	28531	56227	64324	71449	79488
Austria/Autriche	149510	150737	156101	127552	142507	Mexico/Mexique	59844	51077	61541	79286	95624
Israel/Israël	119250	110510	117603	143211	149433	Finland/Finlande	91367	80942	62026	41032	40994
Colombia/Colombie	86838	109449	116881	135019	143559	Czechoslovakia		x89082	x72063		
India/Inde	131018	102381	138944	116920	186824	Argentina/Argentine	36370	41917	45537	37718	47479
Pakistan	89736	94868	111805	110154	81499	Russian Federation			x54136	x45031	x43187
Hungary/Hongrie	x130442	106751	x80556	x95993	x69109	Denmark/Danemark	31627	30770	31411	35658	36462
Greece/Grèce	86753	90543	98789	93347	96913	Bahamas	x21027		x49572	x37005	x11748
Denmark/Danemark	81162	86972	100410	83190	99063	Saudi Arabia	48588	47089	16799	x14793	x13507
Venezuela	62447	90690	89979	83054	65065	Former USSR/Anc. URSS	18156	x76208			
Former USSR/Anc. URSS	17079	x243648				Bulgaria/Bulgarie	x98361	x31160	x15077	x22423	x19653
Sweden/Suède	79872	77770	84293	76418	89210	Czech Republic				61911	74442
Malaysia/Malaisie	51873	56693	76717	88107	100841	Romania/Roumanie	9441	15257	21326	23157	38237
Iran (Islamic Rp. of)		x84266	x71618	x64421	x46860	Turkey/Turquie	18956	22669	22545	12845	29371
Viet Nam	x55808	x65964	x43444	x92918	x58522	Poland/Pologne	4302	8721	22915	17830	29666
Finland/Finlande	77406	64538	71463	56650	71683	So. Africa Customs Un	9811	9340	10907	16196	
Philippines	36455	46587	57769	66690	80234	Malaysia/Malaisie	5530	9341	11272	11167	6489
Norway, SVD, JM	40889	42596	50102	48198	61873	Portugal	7780	5621	9701	14368	11639
Chile/Chili	30358	38496	45187	44847	47209	Yugoslavia SFR	35982	x22022			
Poland/Pologne	8610	16625	48695	62597	84917	Croatia/Croatie			7313	11416	x6250
Nigeria/Nigéria	x29140	26840	x56514	x39477	x22768	Colombia/Colombie	6072	9462	3593	5436	4933
Russian Federation			x67998	x35968	x33255	Latvia/Lettonie			x7449	x7873	633
Czechoslovakia	52333	x54372	x36489			Slovakia				x13820	x11378
New Zealand	28873	26707	30168	32167	43429	Togo			x7982	x5618	
Yugoslavia SFR	191336	x82149				Peru/Pérou	3130	4123	2918	4569	4092
Peru/Pérou	19267	21247	29280	30642	35949	Niger	x115	x34	x60		x91

(VALUE AS % OF TOTAL)(VALEUR EN % DU TOTAL)

	1985	1986	1987	1988	1989	1990	1991	1992	1993	1994		1985	1986	1987	1988	1989	1990	1991	1992	1993	1994
Africa	1.8	x2.3	x2.1	x1.8	x1.8	x1.8	x1.7	x1.7	x1.6	x1.7	Afrique	0.1	x0.0	x0.0	x0.0	x0.1	x0.1	0.1	x0.2	x0.2	x0.0
Northern Africa	0.5	0.6	0.4	0.4	0.3	0.3	0.3	x0.3	0.3	0.4	Afrique du Nord	0.0	x0.0	x0.0	x0.0	0.0	0.0	0.0	x0.0	x0.0	x0.0
Americas	24.6	22.1	19.7	17.3	22.5	22.2	23.6	23.7	24.1	23.6	Amériques	15.4	14.0	13.4	12.2	17.5	17.4	18.1	18.5	17.0	17.2
LAIA	8.0	7.6	6.6	5.4	6.2	5.9	6.5	6.5	7.0	6.9	ALAI	2.0	1.4	1.2	1.4	1.5	1.5	1.6	1.7	1.5	1.5
CACM	0.6	0.2	x0.3	0.1	0.1	0.1	0.1	0.1	x0.2	x0.1	MCAC	0.0	0.0	0.0	0.0	0.0	0.0	0.0	0.0	x0.0	x0.0
Asia	13.7	14.4	x18.9	x19.2	18.9	18.8	20.0	19.7	20.7	20.5	Asie	11.1	12.1	x14.0	x13.0	14.1	14.2	15.2	15.0	15.3	16.9
Middle East	1.9	x2.0	x2.2	x1.8	x1.7	1.6	x2.0	x1.9	x1.9	x1.6	Moyen–Orient	0.0	x0.1	x0.3	0.3	0.5	0.4	0.4	0.2	x0.1	x0.2
Europe	57.5	58.9	55.0	57.2	52.9	54.3	51.0	52.4	50.5	51.4	Europe	72.9	73.2	68.2	71.2	66.1	66.9	64.9	65.0	66.2	64.6
EEC	49.5	51.2	47.7	49.4	46.0	48.2	46.3	47.8	46.1	47.4	CEE	60.5	60.2	56.6	56.7	53.1	54.7	54.1	54.0	55.0	53.3
EFTA	6.6	6.7	6.2	6.6	6.1	5.0	4.3	4.1	3.9	3.7	AELE	12.3	12.9	11.4	14.3	12.8	12.0	10.7	10.9	11.1	11.2
Oceania	1.7	x1.5	x1.5	1.9	x1.7	x1.4	x1.4	x1.6	x1.7	x1.7	Océanie		x0.0	x0.0	x0.0	x0.0	x0.0	x0.0	x0.0	x0.0	x0.0
USA/Etats–Unis d'Amer	11.2	9.9	9.3	8.3	13.0	13.0	14.1	14.2	14.1	13.5	Germany/Allemagne	21.6	23.4	22.6	21.6	19.2	18.9	18.4	17.7	15.9	16.0
Germany/Allemagne	13.4	13.8	13.5	12.7	12.2	11.4	10.9	10.7	10.3	11.7	USA/Etats–Unis d'Amer	12.9	11.9	11.6	10.2	15.4	15.2	16.1	16.2	14.9	15.2
France, Monac	7.3	7.5	7.1	7.7	7.8	9.0	8.4	9.0	7.4	7.4	United Kingdom	15.1	13.4	12.6	11.7	11.2	12.0	11.3	11.8	10.4	9.5
Japan/Japon	5.0	5.4	5.8	5.3	7.5	7.2	7.5	6.9	7.5	7.5	Switz.Liecht	9.3	9.8	8.3	11.0	9.8	11.0	9.7	9.8	10.2	10.3
Italy/Italie	7.3	7.6	6.4	7.9	7.4	8.2	7.4	7.4	6.6	7.1	Japan/Japon	8.7	9.1	8.8	7.3	9.1	9.0	8.9	8.4	8.4	8.6
United Kingdom	8.1	7.3	7.2	6.6	5.6	5.9	6.4	6.9	7.0	7.0	France, Monac	4.8	3.8	4.1	4.6	4.6	5.1	5.5	4.9	8.2	5.2
Netherlands/Pays–Bas	4.3	4.5	3.9	3.5	3.4	3.4	3.2	4.0	5.0	4.7	Italy/Italie	4.7	4.9	4.8	4.6	4.0	4.5	4.8	4.7	4.7	4.6
Switz.Liecht	4.7	4.7	4.2	4.6	4.2	4.8	4.1	3.8	3.6	3.4	Netherlands/Pays–Bas	6.3	6.9	6.1	4.4	4.3	4.6	4.5	5.0	4.3	4.6
Belgium–Luxembourg	2.4	3.0	2.5	3.1	3.1	3.2	3.1	3.0	3.7	3.2	Ireland/Irlande	1.5	0.8	0.6	2.3	2.8	2.8	3.5	4.4	5.3	6.2
Korea, Republic of	2.5	2.5	2.4	2.8	2.9	2.7	2.9	2.7	2.9	2.7	Belgium–Luxembourg	3.1	3.2	2.6	3.6	3.2	3.4	3.1	2.9	3.8	4.5

TRADE BY COMMODITY IN THOUSAND U.S. DOLLARS – COMMERCE PAR PRODUIT EN MILLIERS DE DOLLARS E.U

COUNTRIES–PAYS	IMPORTS – IMPORTATIONS				
	1990	1991	1992	1993	1994
Total	14418767	15031275	16301987	15779105	17503274
Africa	x229302	239466	x229327	x233586	x253871
Northern Africa	109218	100020	98107	97717	100035
Americas	2835770	3328937	3686668	3972297	4528215
LAIA	1001626	1128948	1138436	1263758	1497716
CACM	35541	36522	38170	x41356	x43511
Asia	2882232	3360261	3453464	3552376	3887622
Middle East	180613	x232030	x269072	x276615	x246638
Europe	8035510	7599471	8513911	7554039	8314074
EEC	7456179	7059473	7921765	7005705	7710449
EFTA	473651	481302	524309	498186	553943
Oceania	x231431	x217002	x278828	x319945	x363540
USA/Etats–Unis d'Amer	1505743	1857651	2183306	2286799	2555126
Germany/Allemagne	1334963	1460701	1605316	960464	1123027
Italy/Italie	1355993	1265049	1437222	1158468	1220426
Japan/Japon	993108	1126782	1217966	1417765	1543252
United Kingdom	1657472	1123255	1155592	1033755	820501
France, Monac	1073192	1002972	1129282	1112942	1404702
Spain/Espagne	733538	810733	922072	762111	867795
Korea, Republic of	501610	617331	604501	555326	631721
Belgium–Luxembourg	412856	442674	530772	680128	763282
Switz.Liecht	453639	464535	507344	484324	537211
Netherlands/Pays–Bas	361812	393120	442352	504591	552887
Brazil/Brésil	315922	322396	354329	433111	608979
China/Chine	206985	368036	331342	233578	268225
Canada	247574	273794	289710	331355	399732
Mexico/Mexique	223933	271953	295919	288971	299262
Australia/Australie	203699	194944	254565	292756	317793
Argentina/Argentine	137375	212630	181658	219598	266951
Sweden/Suède	77253	73209	207152	295081	396783
Thailand/Thaïlande	133624	163125	174767	181859	189192
Ireland/Irlande	146250	169049	156509	182625	202653
Singapore/Singapour	162259	156626	157598	189758	201089
Hong Kong	128758	223184	152297	118253	147601
Turkey/Turquie	137239	127194	135620	182886	163159
Indonesia/Indonésie	128455	126663	135897	149376	208079
Colombia/Colombie	143389	104690	107811	137870	148442
Portugal	96629	92686	102292	87013	105906
So. Africa Customs Un	79364	91458	92129	96457	113969
Venezuela	62025	98656	87774	88263	70747
India/Inde	170900	73352	105014	78905	106765
Austria/Autriche	79434	99765	81807	73573	83721
Malaysia/Malaisie	68755	65363	76281	87471	97342
Iran (Islamic Rp. of)		x63878	x79315	x60667	x48002
Greece/Grèce	51252	48936	66774	81240	90922
Hungary/Hongrie	x67794	87238	x50032	x57280	x41268
Israel/Israël	47650	48823	60802	64167	66022
Egypt/Egypte	66070	59614	57205	53573	54290
Philippines	69531	54607	57468	56120	59568
Pakistan	40346	51656	50296	55273	55561
Denmark/Danemark	45200	47774	54017	44191	42324
Former USSR/Anc. URSS	5007	x132384			
Chile/Chili	34407	43067	40572	40478	44783
Finland/Finlande	30336	29548	30605	29522	35520
Russian Federation			x66219	x23174	x13803
Peru/Pérou	36257	36438	26805	20543	21487
Poland/Pologne	11739	21901	32684	28025	41677
Saudi Arabia	26699	24906	39211	x17602	x19569
Morocco/Maroc	26474	24337	26836	24195	25736
Korea Dem People's Rp	x7465	x9880	x23239	x38029	x22948
New Zealand	26459	21291	23038	25144	43090
Ukraine			x15601	x51766	x3706

COUNTRIES–PAYS	EXPORTS – EXPORTATIONS				
	1990	1991	1992	1993	1994
Totale	11863525	12997946	14268273	14471648	17035429
Afrique	24297	x32408	x27528	x22563	x4360
Afrique du Nord	1060	1563	189	395	60
Amériques	1397018	1692082	1852105	1923962	2130828
ALAI	126428	160453	146119	153409	156887
MCAC	78	145	131	x633	x709
Asie	2345919	2918483	3113075	3013988	3147200
Moyen–Orient	32643	15654	10837	x8195	x17476
Europe	7833592	8117757	9040653	9283619	11506249
CEE	6631297	6987350	7785523	8017813	10035279
AELE	1155192	1102568	1221317	1228398	1395236
Océanie	x5381	x10429	x7599	x15015	x19859
Germany/Allemagne	1650037	1837148	2013815	1674883	2081668
USA/Etats–Unis d'Amer	1235727	1497989	1654787	1714711	1911352
Japan/Japon	1188507	1398311	1532711	1409595	1508961
Ireland/Irlande	924591	1066121	1338240	1434653	1943301
Belgium–Luxembourg	1182560	1174972	1102583	1308981	1494851
Switz.Liecht	1154009	1101840	1220588	1228105	1394574
United Kingdom	1065849	1028590	1087851	1023665	1651674
Singapore/Singapour	541741	751668	875738	867732	755888
France, Monac	596055	617751	778843	1094218	1156946
Italy/Italie	412384	357736	486444	443183	487464
Netherlands/Pays–Bas	300850	342550	411002	438574	516110
Spain/Espagne	296054	310839	330179	318494	336519
China/Chine	249540	299226	270630	274798	363754
Hong Kong	130460	216079	146694	120843	140392
Israel/Israël	101601	107152	118174	154912	150594
Austria/Autriche	83749	113094	112182	114136	x113885
Korea, Republic of	72302	83709	106046	113924	123138
Poland/Pologne	98558	89121	94373	75585	77360
Hungary/Hongrie	x85139	x63636	x96152	x82877	x75292
Brazil/Brésil	58374	78297	76470	74950	95759
Sweden/Suède	73487	84434	59014	64300	77549
Denmark/Danemark	28938	25546	36399	70184	112112
Russian Federation			x43309	x73235	x107974
India/Inde	23535	37778	32381	45636	68576
Canada	22629	33199	34386	36517	46380
Mexico/Mexique	25976	31387	35324	33449	34627
Argentina/Argentine	21944	27056	18311	31249	16158
So. Africa Customs Un	22957	29200	26744	20433	
Finland/Finlande	16083	27444	28318	19766	28838
Czechoslovakia		x37109	x27969		
Colombia/Colombie	15698	18742	11547	9389	6764
Czech Republic				37980	50898
Slovenia/Slovénia			14467	17866	49460
Bahamas	x10755		x16276	x15595	x7135
Australia/Australie	4975	9911	7214	13693	19743
Bulgaria/Bulgarie	x53649	x15616	x6716	x6653	x9467
Yugoslavia SFR	46927	x27408			
Belarus/Bélarus			x15323	x11522	x19011
Croatia/Croatie			12149	13289	x11495
Thailand/Thaïlande	1973	5023	9750	9878	10094
Saudi Arabia	25385	12107	6526	x2401	x3381
Former USSR/Anc. URSS	9343	x19414			
Portugal	523	1013	430	12555	33509
Indonesia/Indonésie	1337	1846	7723	3393	3072
Turkey/Turquie	6339	3434	4285	4724	13004
Yugoslavia/Yougoslavie			x7066	x5256	x14163
Slovakia				x8918	x13669
Latvia/Lettonie			x5204	x3669	2957
Ukraine			x2789	x5874	x2124
Chile/Chili	1060	1353	2448	2452	1695

(VALUE AS % OF TOTAL)(VALEUR EN % DU TOTAL)

	1985	1986	1987	1988	1989	1990	1991	1992	1993	1994
Africa	1.8	x1.9	x1.8	x2.1	x1.6	x1.6	1.6	x1.4	x1.5	x1.5
Northern Africa	0.7	0.6	0.6	0.8	0.7	0.8	0.7	0.6	0.6	0.6
Americas	20.3	20.0	18.1	18.1	21.4	19.7	22.2	22.6	25.2	25.9
LAIA	10.3	10.0	9.3	9.5	7.4	6.9	7.5	7.0	8.0	8.6
CACM	0.0	0.3	x0.4	0.3	0.3	0.2	0.2	0.2	x0.3	x0.2
Asia	19.0	19.4	x22.4	x26.6	20.3	20.0	22.3	21.1	22.5	22.2
Middle East	0.8	x1.5	x1.6	x1.6	x1.4	1.3	x1.5	x1.7	x1.8	x1.4
Europe	55.6	56.0	52.5	48.9	53.0	55.7	50.6	52.2	47.9	47.5
EEC	48.5	49.3	46.4	43.8	47.8	51.7	47.0	48.6	44.4	44.1
EFTA	5.8	5.8	5.0	4.3	4.5	3.3	3.2	3.2	3.2	3.2
Oceania	3.1	x2.4	x2.3	2.2	x2.0	x1.6	x1.4	x1.7	x2.0	x2.1
USA/Etats–Unis d'Amer	7.1	6.7	5.6	6.4	11.7	10.4	12.4	13.4	14.5	14.6
Germany/Allemagne	8.5	8.2	7.6	6.3	6.7	9.3	9.7	9.8	6.1	6.4
Italy/Italie	9.7	10.3	9.5	7.8	9.4	9.4	8.4	8.8	7.3	7.0
Japan/Japon	8.0	8.3	8.6	10.4	7.9	6.9	7.5	7.5	9.0	8.8
United Kingdom	7.1	6.6	6.5	10.7	11.8	11.5	7.5	7.1	6.6	4.7
France, Monac	8.5	8.9	8.4	7.1	7.0	7.4	6.7	6.9	7.1	8.0
Spain/Espagne	3.5	3.9	3.9	3.3	4.8	5.1	5.4	5.7	4.8	5.0
Korea, Republic of	3.7	3.4	3.4	3.5	3.3	3.5	4.1	3.7	3.5	3.6
Belgium–Luxembourg	3.0	3.5	3.2	2.6	2.5	2.9	2.9	3.3	4.3	4.4
Switz.Liecht	4.1	4.1	3.4	3.1	3.2	3.1	3.1	3.1	3.1	3.1

	1985	1986	1987	1988	1989	1990	1991	1992	1993	1994
Afrique	0.3	x0.2	x0.2	x0.2	x0.2	0.2	x0.2	x0.2	x0.1	x0.0
Afrique du Nord	0.0	x0.0	0.0	0.0	0.0	0.0	0.0	0.0	0.0	0.0
Amériques	5.0	x5.1	x5.0	x6.3	x12.6	11.8	13.0	12.9	13.3	12.5
ALAI	1.0	1.2	1.1	1.5	1.5	1.1	1.2	1.0	1.1	0.9
MCAC		x0.0	0.0	0.0	0.0	0.0	0.0	0.0	x0.0	x0.0
Asie	15.1	15.9	18.3	22.4	19.6	19.8	22.5	21.8	20.8	18.4
Moyen–Orient	0.1	x0.2	x0.2	x0.3	0.4	0.3	0.1	0.1	x0.1	x0.1
Europe	79.1	78.4	73.9	67.8	65.5	66.0	62.5	63.4	64.2	67.5
CEE	64.1	62.9	59.5	56.5	54.0	55.9	53.8	54.6	55.4	58.9
AELE	14.4	15.0	13.9	10.8	11.2	9.7	8.5	8.6	8.5	8.2
Océanie		x0.0			x0.0	x0.0	x0.1	x0.1	x0.1	x0.1
Germany/Allemagne	16.6	16.0	16.3	14.8	14.1	13.9	14.1	14.1	11.6	12.2
USA/Etats–Unis d'Amer	3.2	2.6	2.7	4.2	10.4	10.4	11.5	11.6	11.8	11.2
Japan/Japon	10.5	11.1	11.5	14.6	10.7	10.0	10.8	10.7	9.7	8.9
Ireland/Irlande	9.2	7.8	6.2	5.4	6.3	7.8	8.2	9.4	9.9	11.4
Belgium–Luxembourg	7.8	7.6	7.5	10.3	9.8	10.0	9.0	7.7	9.0	8.8
Switz.Liecht	12.6	13.1	12.3	9.4	9.9	9.7	8.5	8.6	8.5	8.2
United Kingdom	8.0	8.3	8.6	10.7	8.6	9.0	7.9	7.6	7.1	9.7
Singapore/Singapour	2.1	2.3	2.3	2.9	4.0	4.6	5.8	6.1	6.0	4.4
France, Monac	5.2	5.5	5.2	5.3	5.0	5.0	4.8	5.5	7.6	6.8
Italy/Italie	6.1	6.1	4.6	3.7	3.7	3.5	2.8	3.4	3.1	2.9

TRADE BY COMMODITY IN THOUSAND U.S. DOLLARS – COMMERCE PAR PRODUIT EN MILLIERS DE DOLLARS E.U

IMPORTS – IMPORTATIONS

COUNTRIES–PAYS	1990	1991	1992	1993	1994
Total	7882586	8349226	8844885	8446659	9636295
Africa	x116069	147680	x134903	x127616	x137732
Northern Africa	36924	43732	41334	44966	55677
Americas	1440548	1623003	1949569	2009256	2477671
LAIA	418354	485230	510670	535775	640212
CACM	21166	21185	21187	x19472	x22457
Asia	1536867	1626592	1620155	1595340	1906734
Middle East	123638	x136846	x144971	x114359	x124362
Europe	4616445	4728481	4952387	4457850	4847787
EEC	4113265	4249940	4457945	3993236	4347043
EFTA	456728	455148	466272	439219	474802
Oceania	x82861	x97183	x86927	x119587	x117326
USA/Etats–Unis d'Amer	815865	950240	1256849	1260039	1580699
Germany/Allemagne	1094024	1159103	1224011	959051	823973
Belgium–Luxembourg	571440	595437	629214	490221	572626
France, Monac	484393	501250	503682	520177	572589
United Kingdom	482199	469247	485145	438488	557041
Italy/Italie	445646	476301	481666	433196	511306
Netherlands/Pays–Bas	427354	406667	430615	510061	523476
Switz.Liecht	419985	414577	435363	388475	415863
Japan/Japon	353808	413214	404762	388340	387569
Spain/Espagne	258911	269416	279009	242234	270855
Korea, Republic of	262105	246658	231025	243081	306502
Mexico/Mexique	181212	210920	235966	228241	270714
India/Inde	178997	131258	165595	169224	179861
Canada	128376	138979	139630	176098	219801
Hong Kong	170671	203304	95123	87589	115825
Singapore/Singapour	77846	94455	130963	108393	203878
Indonesia/Indonésie	94680	105928	107015	116553	127360
Brazil/Brésil	99169	102468	97041	129980	151634
China/Chine	48454	109797	111434	88350	126785
Finland/Finlande	50650	65633	97730	94810	113418
Australia/Australie	64058	78242	70166	103299	95553
Thailand/Thaïlande	51664	52345	75975	99180	133358
Sweden/Suède	66268	75733	72262	74737	83105
Ireland/Irlande	54443	60748	74334	57768	111559
Denmark/Danemark	47683	47632	60592	61734	80226
Turkey/Turquie	59958	56376	51522	58965	51988
Argentina/Argentine	32424	43010	55531	59877	84978
Austria/Autriche	67335	55156	50362	47896	61944
So. Africa Customs Un	42247	55199	49318	45071	53295
Venezuela	38482	50327	46844	33821	32288
Israel/Israël	37852	37049	44233	48294	53520
Colombia/Colombie	37432	41702	38713	44928	53052
Portugal	38262	42463	42758	36142	36929
Norway, SVD, JM	36042	39816	30289	50153	58285
Malaysia/Malaisie	29879	31352	33470	41676	50164
Poland/Pologne	9308	8112	39441	52693	64124
Philippines	31447	30516	33631	28597	34964
Hungary/Hongrie	x33407	32462	x25027	x25878	x22159
Pakistan	16390	18511	28765	35021	39673
Greece/Grèce	24656	25155	26564	26721	27996
Iran (Islamic Rp. of)		x18479	x35583	x19223	x21270
Saudi Arabia	26484	30045	22462	x10404	x14958
Egypt/Egypte	14396	16595	19573	20179	31303
Nigeria/Nigéria	x13478	20903	x21593	x11847	x9285
Romania/Roumanie	10295	30636	14483	6938	10251
New Zealand	16732	16929	14581	14842	20140
Jordan/Jordanie	10737	14702	20334	10018	16941
Chile/Chili	9591	12518	15679	14940	15743
Czech Republic				40883	44677
Czechoslovakia	20768	x17828	x18242		

EXPORTS – EXPORTATIONS

COUNTRIES–PAYS	1990	1991	1992	1993	1994
Totale	6990991	7242707	7639504	7734668	8825664
Afrique	x51908	x60241	x44106	x39065	x1269
Afrique du Nord	740	390	141	829	480
Amériques	1476930	1459215	1676595	1784105	1879017
ALAI	90593	213782	250541	248553	252199
MCAC	2080	1740	1953	1766	1580
Asie	999140	1123642	1099965	x1245290	x1844383
Moyen–Orient	133600	98811	55131	x124868	x444834
Europe	4328808	4514657	4740751	4556193	4993753
CEE	4074158	4270801	4474236	4262112	4659974
AELE	247089	239363	263978	289169	332172
Océanie	x15227	x15257	x13062	x12174	x13249
Germany/Allemagne	1476245	1472945	1504567	1221278	1446478
USA/Etats–Unis d'Amer	1298992	1172991	1225828	1255855	1375181
France, Monac	537916	563353	593638	672130	562520
Netherlands/Pays–Bas	586158	611103	575494	568935	592608
Japan/Japon	520387	567427	578553	584786	663132
United Kingdom	294529	470846	588572	577070	560642
Denmark/Danemark	282702	325888	428969	423731	475844
Belgium–Luxembourg	296481	286048	296763	342681	412784
Switz.Liecht	230068	221574	246864	268578	304888
Italy/Italie	203681	183859	184412	198795	218630
Canada	78031	70295	197919	275590	248609
Venezuela	285	93132	126400	120811	104774
China/Chine	80195	98043	110768	130382	196051
Spain/Espagne	167461	164384	112008	57842	118267
Hong Kong	102248	142119	69632	70169	92420
Saudi Arabia	130524	95845	53088	x122496	x440867
Finland/Finlande	109057	75742	71353	75195	105852
Brazil/Brésil	63255	65449	70990	81759	68743
India/Inde	44889	60958	75395	73771	103724
Korea, Republic of	22106	53078	88108	68547	57869
Singapore/Singapour	47634	39874	53211	77414	149937
Israel/Israël	40022	50373	51465	55647	62127
Ireland/Irlande	41817	48212	47808	53059	62638
So. Africa Customs Un	49398	57784	41527	36502	
Austria/Autriche	27456	31673	36314	39398	x53837
Mexico/Mexique	19876	33775	34040	30751	50137
Sweden/Suède	43333	32233	28210	25820	32859
Norway, SVD, JM	17021	17789	17114	20591	27284
Russian Federation			x19734	x33266	x33580
Argentina/Argentine	5527	19605	17148	13756	25412
Malaysia/Malaisie	1859	1724	2165	43256	66933
Hungary/Hongrie	x15786	x14925	x15661	x16403	x12018
Czechoslovakia		x22345	x20028		
Slovakia				x35524	x31887
Poland/Pologne	21933	7235	12304	15686	23001
Australia/Australie	9259	10081	9530	7977	10030
Romania/Roumanie	10355	4430	10935	8720	7564
Bulgaria/Bulgarie	x60788	x7838	x5878	x6866	x4317
Thailand/Thaïlande	3276	4517	4836	4832	5695
Czech Republic				12954	15205
Greece/Grèce	6475	3415	4426	5093	14192
Former USSR/Anc. URSS	2519	x12570			
New Zealand	5922	4959	3521	3600	3148
Korea Dem People's Rp	x264	x4523	x3330	x3463	x252
Indonesia/Indonésie	1829	1485	6639	1972	676
Sri Lanka	56	42	73	4902	81
Guatemala	1585	1631	1672	1527	1405
Yugoslavia SFR	6307	x4151			
Turkey/Turquie	2612	1919	1264	879	2742
Portugal	849	1098	1702	1084	2823

(VALUE AS % OF TOTAL)(VALEUR EN % DU TOTAL)

Imports

	1985	1986	1987	1988	1989	1990	1991	1992	1993	1994
Africa	2.3	2.3	x2.0	x1.9	x1.8	x1.4	1.8	x1.6	x1.5	x1.5
Northern Africa	1.0	0.8	0.7	0.7	0.5	0.5	0.5	0.5	0.5	0.6
Americas	20.4	18.6	16.6	16.0	18.0	18.3	19.4	22.1	23.8	25.7
LAIA	5.9	6.5	6.5	6.0	5.3	5.3	5.8	5.8	6.3	6.6
CACM	0.1	0.6	x0.5	0.3	0.3	0.3	0.3	0.2	x0.2	x0.2
Asia	18.6	18.4	x20.4	x21.8	18.8	19.5	19.5	18.3	18.9	19.8
Middle East	1.0	x1.7	x1.3	x1.3	x1.2	1.6	x1.6	x1.6	x1.4	x1.3
Europe	55.0	57.3	55.7	55.9	58.0	58.6	56.6	56.0	52.8	50.3
EEC	45.7	48.2	47.4	47.6	50.0	52.2	50.9	50.4	47.3	45.1
EFTA	8.7	8.6	7.8	7.6	7.6	5.8	5.5	5.3	5.2	4.9
Oceania	1.7	x1.3	x1.3	x1.2	x1.2	x1.0	x1.1	x1.0	x1.4	x1.2
USA/Etats–Unis d'Amer	12.4	9.1	7.7	7.6	9.7	10.4	11.4	14.2	14.9	16.4
Germany/Allemagne	8.6	8.9	8.9	9.8	11.9	13.9	13.9	13.8	11.4	8.6
Belgium–Luxembourg	6.7	7.4	6.1	6.5	6.2	7.2	7.1	7.1	5.8	5.9
France, Monac	5.6	5.9	6.4	5.9	5.8	6.1	6.0	5.7	6.2	5.9
United Kingdom	5.5	6.1	6.2	6.5	7.0	6.1	5.6	5.5	5.2	5.8
Italy/Italie	5.6	5.8	5.7	5.7	5.5	5.7	5.7	5.4	5.1	5.3
Netherlands/Pays–Bas	5.6	5.9	5.6	5.4	5.8	5.4	4.9	4.9	6.0	5.4
Switz.Liecht	5.1	5.5	4.7	4.9	4.7	5.3	5.0	4.9	4.6	4.3
Japan/Japon	5.2	5.3	5.2	5.4	5.2	4.5	4.9	4.6	4.6	4.0
Spain/Espagne	2.5	3.0	3.2	3.2	3.1	3.3	3.2	3.2	2.9	2.8

Exports

	1985	1986	1987	1988	1989	1990	1991	1992	1993	1994
Afrique	0.6	x0.8	x0.6	x0.7	x0.5	x0.7	x0.8	x0.5	x0.5	x0.0
Afrique du Nord	0.0	x0.0	x0.0	0.0	0.0	0.0	0.0	0.0	0.0	0.0
Amériques	28.8	26.1	25.8	28.1	23.1	21.1	20.2	21.9	23.1	21.3
ALAI	1.4	1.6	1.3	2.0	1.7	1.3	3.0	3.3	3.2	2.9
MCAC	0.0	0.0	0.0	0.0	0.0	0.0	0.0	0.0	0.0	0.0
Asie	8.8	9.3	x11.8	x12.8	13.7	14.3	15.5	14.4	x16.1	x20.9
Moyen–Orient	0.7	x0.2	x0.3	0.4	1.0	1.9	1.4	0.7	x1.6	x5.0
Europe	60.8	62.5	59.2	55.8	60.1	61.9	62.3	62.1	58.9	56.6
CEE	56.4	57.2	53.9	50.2	54.5	58.3	59.0	58.6	55.1	52.8
AELE	4.3	5.2	5.2	5.5	5.5	3.5	3.3	3.5	3.7	3.8
Océanie	0.1	x0.1	x0.2	x0.1	0.2	x0.2	x0.2	x0.2	x0.1	x0.1
Germany/Allemagne	18.2	19.2	17.6	18.8	20.6	21.1	20.3	19.7	15.8	16.4
USA/Etats–Unis d'Amer	21.4	18.6	18.4	20.5	20.4	18.6	16.2	16.0	16.2	15.6
France, Monac	5.4	4.9	4.7	5.4	7.3	7.7	7.8	7.8	8.7	6.4
Netherlands/Pays–Bas	12.4	13.3	12.5	8.0	8.3	8.4	8.4	7.5	7.4	6.7
Japan/Japon	6.3	6.9	7.2	7.9	7.8	7.4	7.8	7.6	7.6	7.5
United Kingdom	4.8	4.9	5.3	3.6	3.6	4.2	6.5	7.7	7.5	6.4
Denmark/Danemark	5.0	5.6	5.1	5.0	3.8	4.0	4.5	5.6	5.5	5.4
Belgium–Luxembourg	3.3	3.4	2.4	3.0	3.7	4.2	3.9	3.9	4.4	4.7
Switz.Liecht	2.8	3.6	3.5	3.4	3.1	3.3	3.1	3.2	3.5	3.5
Italy/Italie	4.8	2.9	3.0	2.6	2.8	2.9	2.5	2.4	2.6	2.5

TRADE BY COMMODITY IN THOUSAND U.S. DOLLARS – COMMERCE PAR PRODUIT EN MILLIERS DE DOLLARS E.U

COUNTRIES–PAYS	IMPORTS – IMPORTATIONS 1990	1991	1992	1993	1994
Total	12219944	12692297	12510384	11487065	13313747
Africa	x552417	561940	x433817	x422402	x406640
Northern Africa	258455	229702	169904	203693	201157
Americas	2730627	2699252	2715903	2589788	3250930
LAIA	589853	625290	654684	562230	656032
CACM	44413	47807	50394	x37495	x42353
Asia	3083127	3832518	3652281	3255272	3765508
Middle East	442555	x601983	x488256	x437499	x369351
Europe	5283896	5088149	5375713	4694400	5497909
EEC	4888064	4793450	5075462	4424707	5207167
EFTA	236773	210363	207063	208568	233955
Oceania	x124268	x118580	x135076	x256992	x155780
USA/Etats–Unis d'Amer	1583356	1546466	1530612	1581549	2118973
Germany/Allemagne	954085	921112	1016789	821020	969942
Japan/Japon	731890	802291	755907	790123	902352
France,Monac	756863	731548	799084	701096	812305
India/Inde	438086	805031	841960	451449	703960
United Kingdom	468286	633981	663277	553953	669257
Italy/Italie	570780	502367	510035	444749	521026
Netherlands/Pays–Bas	484745	439409	472067	428108	466306
Korea, Republic of	370896	420081	397683	436913	501434
Belgium–Luxembourg	432623	390000	438915	417325	493830
Canada	252622	294717	296748	304902	360081
Spain/Espagne	279980	279717	286990	251087	323723
Indonesia/Indonésie	270712	291726	235835	184986	235575
Turkey/Turquie	247661	220833	181356	235589	173860
Sweden/Suède	193842	216571	195730	183800	234149
Austria/Autriche	202410	183006	193579	164122	204240
Mexico/Mexique	131645	157850	188968	176226	181133
Brazil/Brésil	199653	177665	173880	161761	236259
Hong Kong	164435	170427	170292	160014	195598
Malaysia/Malaisie	155209	163653	147356	178894	238072
Singapore/Singapour	121515	136847	153562	160528	154638
Finland/Finlande	185866	163460	143566	126070	173335
Denmark/Danemark	163537	138001	139530	122219	128484
Australia/Australie	72314	74361	89485	217994	112540
Switz.Liecht	132889	116523	118919	109431	121966
Thailand/Thaïlande	98249	99049	107632	120269	126819
Saudi Arabia	85570	142252	114592	x53730	x64218
China/Chine	79283	89939	103619	108172	111775
Venezuela	105042	128149	97217	59330	39018
Philippines	88875	100643	87039	82810	86827
Norway,SVD,JM	99940	89576	83971	95815	109001
Iran (Islamic Rp. of)		x121889	x91780	x52227	x13762
Ireland/Irlande	83975	80441	89869	87785	79556
Morocco/Maroc	81996	85134	63045	81090	82872
So. Africa Customs Un	82343	82424	65023	67769	73640
Former USSR/Anc. URSS	102133	x201558			
Greece/Grèce	46853	55633	56766	71119	70402
Portugal	64219	58205	69265	52254	60613
Nigeria/Nigéria	x53578	73708	x64786	x35540	x22956
Jamaica/Jamaïque	74806	66331	x77187	x29266	x16683
Tunisia/Tunisie	51228	51327	49389	57081	57366
Israel/Israël	46887	48186	53996	55010	63002
Poland/Pologne	33523	34864	56219	49107	59504
Argentina/Argentine	30463	38733	51024	49548	62907
Chile/Chili	47193	49695	44434	36283	46078
Colombia/Colombie	43497	35003	51432	39562	53239
Czechoslovakia	140944	x57398	x61482		
Jordan/Jordanie	38119	56826	28997	26358	43221
Suriname/Suriname	63134	53150	39181	x19048	x10191
Hungary/Hongrie	x40118	52164	x30407	x27344	x23389

COUNTRIES–PAYS	EXPORTS – EXPORTATIONS 1990	1991	1992	1993	1994
Totale	12708119	12515709	11920767	10309398	12240149
Afrique	795285	932345	x975001	864384	1092195
Afrique du Nord	522978	655576	618371	614182	699823
Amériques	2903884	2919844	2717089	2440704	2729912
ALAI	634111	549845	535284	476677	541157
MCAC	5298	4910	2504	x1925	x2451
Asie	2038989	2166005	2332570	x2164941	x2587772
Moyen–Orient	493409	x449247	x483678	x231611	x300038
Europe	5870344	5528677	5503271	4476991	5391372
CEE	5579113	5309609	5272961	4186214	5145494
AELE	207973	183604	192633	192527	210249
Océanie	x95950	x145794	x126175	x130441	x139699
Germany/Allemagne	1687326	1656502	1657680	1408043	1639175
USA/Etats–Unis d'Amer	1427159	1558520	1399340	1236067	1289875
France,Monac	1349330	1229101	1235553	687821	1099884
Japan/Japon	711796	764986	782630	828623	939929
Belgium–Luxembourg	641078	626696	670590	622564	717645
Canada	658600	617975	618364	571197	657794
China/Chine	359376	412054	496468	535774	689635
Netherlands/Pays–Bas	549484	560741	489795	382768	490783
United Kingdom	505696	479895	492988	455593	484251
Morocco/Maroc	348333	427390	401239	350659	471651
Russian Federation			x412090	x501212	x564329
Saudi Arabia	328440	287021	335521	x104146	x103418
Italy/Italie	271820	264994	244522	195598	228239
Mexico/Mexique	251015	213560	227973	185850	211409
So. Africa Customs Un	186836	198352	235217	181664	379186
Former USSR/Anc. URSS	630239	x588956			
Ukraine			x148348	x417979	x298075
Trinidad and Tobago	171687	181360	157491	149006	231674
Brazil/Brésil	185462	169218	155301	152698	172742
Norway,SVD,JM	165902	148981	156783	160044	176143
Tunisia/Tunisie	140540	170771	164219	121450	167102
Spain/Espagne	218174	180905	131403	102870	120397
Australia/Australie	93895	140146	120890	128741	136106
Austria/Autriche	155913	129055	132032	113810	x118739
Hong Kong	115204	112604	121554	117022	139972
Israel/Israël	111157	112327	113424	106586	114884
Korea, Republic of	75230	82448	79003	99756	115478
Singapore/Singapour	60711	92342	82073	77981	92450
Senegal/Sénégal	73405	64049	x113161	56558	x1357
Finland/Finlande	43692	56052	90826	78519	102290
Chile/Chili	81456	73988	74113	58850	67281
Poland/Pologne	121643	74290	68388	63495	101018
Algeria/Algérie	16448	31508	31430	112772	27587
Sweden/Suède	86411	54895	49882	47745	65617
Hungary/Hongrie	x57374	x36557	x50336	x40522	x61915
Iran (Islamic Rp. of)		x46324	x63489	x17336	x19560
Czechoslovakia		x60983	x65033		
Bahrain/Bahreïn	x57578	x64497	x29484	x31786	x46899
Argentina/Argentine	67155	47038	33915	25725	25179
Indonesia/Indonésie	27358	30964	37922	36963	57043
Switz.Liecht	42072	34623	35850	32483	34106
Bulgaria/Bulgarie	x133994	x35074	x42233	x22592	x22136
Ireland/Irlande	28362	28613	34656	26677	23751
Croatia/Croatie			11179	77676	x11334
Qatar	23320	28959	23552	27670	x28935
India/Inde	20739	26409	28283	24072	29035
Portugal	19146	23725	25696	28158	32891
Philippines	37769	40624	18744	15034	12727
Kazakstan			x37859	x35999	x34660
Romania/Roumanie	28982	20592	34519	17115	24690

(VALUE AS % OF TOTAL)(VALEUR EN % DU TOTAL)

	1985	1986	1987	1988	1989	1990	1991	1992	1993	1994
Africa	3.9	x4.3	x3.8	x3.7	x3.5	x4.5	4.4	x3.4	x3.7	x3.1
Northern Africa	1.7	1.8	1.6	1.6	1.7	2.1	1.8	1.4	1.8	1.5
Americas	23.3	22.5	20.2	22.1	21.8	22.3	21.3	21.7	22.5	24.4
LAIA	3.9	4.9	5.1	4.9	4.5	4.8	4.9	5.2	4.9	4.9
CACM	0.2	0.3	0.3	0.3	0.4	0.4	0.4	0.4	x0.3	x0.3
Asia	23.3	23.3	23.7	26.6	25.5	25.3	30.2	29.2	28.4	28.3
Middle East	4.1	3.8	3.7	x4.2	x3.9	3.6	x4.7	x3.9	x3.8	x2.8
Europe	45.1	45.4	44.6	41.3	43.2	43.2	40.1	43.0	40.9	41.3
EEC	37.6	38.4	37.9	34.1	35.8	40.0	37.8	40.6	38.5	39.1
EFTA	6.2	5.9	5.6	5.9	6.1	1.9	1.7	1.7	1.8	1.8
Oceania	1.2	1.1	1.6	1.0	x1.1	x1.0	x1.0	x1.1	x2.2	x1.1
USA/Etats–Unis d'Amer	16.4	14.5	12.4	13.4	12.8	13.0	12.2	12.2	13.8	15.9
Germany/Allemagne	6.9	7.5	6.7	6.8	6.8	7.8	7.3	8.1	7.1	7.3
Japan/Japon	5.7	5.5	5.1	5.6	6.4	6.0	6.3	6.0	6.9	6.8
France,Monac	5.0	5.0	4.9	5.0	5.3	6.2	5.8	6.4	6.1	6.1
India/Inde	4.5	5.0	2.7	4.2	3.6	3.6	6.3	6.7	3.9	5.3
United Kingdom	5.0	5.2	6.1	3.7	3.6	3.8	5.0	5.3	4.8	5.0
Italy/Italie	3.9	4.2	4.2	3.9	4.3	4.7	4.0	4.1	3.9	3.9
Netherlands/Pays–Bas	4.0	3.7	3.7	3.4	3.6	4.0	3.5	3.8	3.7	3.5
Korea, Republic of	1.8	1.9	2.0	2.1	2.6	3.0	3.3	3.2	3.8	3.8
Belgium–Luxembourg	2.9	3.4	3.1	2.7	3.4	3.5	3.1	3.5	3.6	3.7

	1985	1986	1987	1988	1989	1990	1991	1992	1993	1994
Afrique	7.3	8.9	8.1	8.6	5.4	6.3	7.5	x8.2	8.4	8.9
Afrique du Nord	5.6	5.6	5.4	6.1	2.9	4.1	5.2	5.2	6.0	5.7
Amériques	24.6	19.7	18.6	20.4	24.4	22.8	23.3	22.8	23.6	22.3
ALAI	4.6	3.2	3.5	4.0	4.7	5.0	4.4	4.5	4.6	4.4
MCAC	0.0	0.0	x0.0	0.0	0.0	0.0	0.0	0.0	x0.0	x0.0
Asie	10.0	x10.0	x14.4	15.5	15.1	16.1	17.3	19.6	x21.0	x21.1
Moyen–Orient	2.4	x2.1	x3.0	x3.9	x3.4	3.9	x3.6	x4.1	x2.2	x2.5
Europe	51.3	54.0	50.1	45.6	46.7	46.2	44.2	46.2	43.4	44.0
CEE	45.4	48.3	44.9	41.1	41.9	43.9	42.4	44.2	40.6	42.0
AELE	5.0	4.9	4.3	3.8	3.9	1.6	1.5	1.6	1.9	1.7
Océanie	0.4	x0.3	x0.3	0.4	x0.5	x0.8	x1.2	x1.0	x1.3	x1.1
Germany/Allemagne	13.4	15.0	14.1	12.5	12.4	13.3	13.2	13.9	13.7	13.4
USA/Etats–Unis d'Amer	11.7	8.6	8.7	9.9	13.0	11.2	12.5	11.7	12.0	10.5
France,Monac	9.2	10.7	10.3	9.7	10.0	10.6	9.8	10.4	6.7	9.0
Japan/Japon	4.5	5.0	5.2	5.1	5.3	5.6	6.1	6.6	8.0	7.7
Belgium–Luxembourg	3.3	4.0	3.7	4.7	5.0	5.0	5.0	5.6	6.0	5.9
Canada	6.1	5.8	5.1	5.1	5.3	5.2	4.9	5.2	5.5	5.4
China/Chine			2.6	2.9	2.7	2.8	3.3	4.2	5.2	5.6
Netherlands/Pays–Bas	6.0	5.3	5.2	3.9	3.9	4.3	4.5	4.1	3.7	4.0
United Kingdom	4.2	3.9	4.1	3.7	3.7	4.0	3.8	4.1	4.4	4.0
Morocco/Maroc	3.9	4.1	4.3	4.6	1.4	2.7	3.4	3.4	3.4	3.9

TRADE BY COMMODITY IN THOUSAND U.S. DOLLARS – COMMERCE PAR PRODUIT EN MILLIERS DE DOLLARS E.U

COUNTRIES–PAYS	IMPORTS – IMPORTATIONS 1990	1991	1992	1993	1994
Total	9562772	9411685	9971062	9426405	10240533
Africa	x486225	480574	x437689	x443601	x383774
Northern Africa	189694	177532	179312	189489	174809
Americas	1834968	1885621	1981045	2086477	2276333
LAIA	598135	708963	750117	764789	788576
CACM	40018	42032	51729	x54192	x56331
Asia	2161273	2318221	2475518	x2579576	2750252
Middle East	363131	x450252	x500165	x484009	x350793
Europe	4478811	4224098	4680198	3785696	4402551
EEC	4131303	3936215	4342884	3494335	4110224
EFTA	245354	238019	231732	206171	233538
Oceania	273799	x230205	x202063	x235257	x200850
USA/Etats–Unis d'Amer	836940	821189	858219	946506	1074678
Germany/Allemagne	717116	776975	862740	523014	733713
France, Monac	603742	618425	768922	694782	774554
Japan/Japon	436525	489506	436971	456150	540633
United Kingdom	705445	428207	422332	380810	432550
Netherlands/Pays–Bas	461070	446637	452022	332336	340500
Italy/Italie	418513	401551	433496	376011	467386
Belgium–Luxembourg	334815	396998	436268	359660	425330
Hong Kong	271130	282936	298210	312313	364052
Korea, Republic of	221300	258026	268113	279681	321663
Canada	284056	240628	250561	248677	296018
Spain/Espagne	196130	225512	260804	210289	244973
Indonesia/Indonésie	182140	155860	195578	202909	210547
Mexico/Mexique	128083	146846	195493	183827	236143
Australia/Australie	190626	152169	128984	165241	130954
Brazil/Brésil	147580	163857	134772	147133	168795
Switz.Liecht	147531	146808	143818	130037	147383
Sweden/Suède	144717	137675	153077	123975	159764
Thailand/Thaïlande	121681	121865	142139	148798	159067
Malaysia/Malaisie	99806	120377	136522	146544	166231
Venezuela	101204	141133	118295	137329	65766
China/Chine	133181	116478	124041	143561	175677
Iran (Islamic Rp. of)		x124878	x108867	x117751	x45466
Denmark/Danemark	119078	110023	124210	104615	106664
So. Africa Customs Un	135588	124128	108655	105842	99456
Turkey/Turquie	123703	100527	112463	118778	104158
Singapore/Singapour	101715	101072	111346	117716	144909
Austria/Autriche	116802	105920	112808	103915	114405
Finland/Finlande	108111	79660	99359	93922	115368
Philippines	79332	80594	95789	88807	103296
Saudi Arabia	96956	99038	101819	x57211	x48404
Argentina/Argentine	58544	79797	90742	78073	85788
Portugal	80587	81174	90295	73800	77109
Norway, SVD, JM	92912	86786	84018	72904	82301
Chile/Chili	57504	70350	77452	73065	71362
Greece/Grèce	74120	76711	73018	67711	61551
Hungary/Hongrie	x66442	79615	x51162	x60473	x43268
New Zealand	66633	66130	59322	59311	60177
Algeria/Algérie	40089	48014	57736	60785	51927
Colombia/Colombie	40832	37383	59415	67371	71721
Egypt/Egypte	69937	63224	47223	51143	53974
Ireland/Irlande	51058	50745	53534	49494	56356
Israel/Israël	47135	47417	54179	51839	62184
Czechoslovakia	64748	x78433	x71136		
Kuwait/ Koweït	36717	16545	50493	56420	60040
Morocco/Maroc	41873	40443	40872	38904	38589
Nigeria/Nigéria	x26440	41465	x37159	x32482	x18998
Bahrain/Bahreïn	x22294	x24037	x39287	x44827	x7917
Poland/Pologne	21805	24575	41010	40970	49293
Pakistan	30384	34693	34424	33492	32465

COUNTRIES–PAYS	EXPORTS – EXPORTATIONS 1990	1991	1992	1993	1994
Totale	8312219	8079951	8615298	9772540	9315504
Afrique	187626	196790	315799	307748	x378408
Afrique du Nord	93342	60528	69936	57945	63396
Amériques	1900517	2005132	2121613	2224075	2414847
ALAI	267050	286538	323286	399279	456128
MCAC	3772	2735	2988	x2981	x3852
Asie	1283876	1332508	1416965	1443702	1677727
Moyen–Orient	124565	125097	143359	115724	127384
Europe	4289519	4112930	4420464	5523430	4501281
CEE	3949361	3949970	4069084	5193341	4156788
AELE	284550	126338	291311	284759	301351
Océanie	x34681	x32986	x26826	x27640	x65970
Germany/Allemagne	1470979	1493471	1481854	2483328	1457331
USA/Etats–Unis d'Amer	1317579	1401547	1471933	1443094	1535043
United Kingdom	644643	648656	656251	702366	656451
Belgium–Luxembourg	461532	448713	483622	497023	535271
China/Chine	326204	384986	417355	424800	566913
Japan/Japon	390283	370245	375110	384765	415836
Canada	306215	309158	316193	370074	414274
Netherlands/Pays–Bas	335779	341958	366912	267892	315257
France, Monac	173090	169493	227372	558385	349365
Spain/Espagne	236354	203715	217421	200977	212996
So. Africa Customs Un	89721	130628	242237	244441	284087
Italy/Italie	237082	257461	227228	127390	164249
Israel/Israël	176924	177093	155097	182978	165126
Sweden/Suède	184550	175699	175243	147872	195699
Switz.Liecht	124906	126338	148354	149018	174517
Mexico/Mexique	107752	119098	125469	135056	157606
Poland/Pologne	128975	134174	117161	99162	111306
Austria/Autriche	109255	109280	102098	92307	x111227
Turkey/Turquie	95871	94851	112105	93901	107179
Hong Kong	96327	92258	91412	97261	119123
Norway, SVD, JM	159635		142957	135678	126572
Chile/Chili	66492	71262	88877	110011	126468
Finland/Finlande	53364	62470	80447	77183	119246
Korea, Republic of	62585	65240	72311	76211	107739
Russian Federation			x86313	x108025	x90400
Tunisia/Tunisie	70170	59275	65836	56116	55887
Singapore/Singapour	46071	56761	53556	65145	84553
Bulgaria/Bulgarie	x235336	x60117	x79995	x32392	x44689
Brazil/Brésil	35687	34837	43225	75695	48442
Romania/Roumanie	49986	39176	51713	42847	48837
India/Inde	38650	32545	45421	42037	44002
Former USSR/Anc. URSS	124054	x97370			
Slovenia/Slovénia			45819	35419	37662
Argentina/Argentine	26310	25135	21113	34028	70807
Czechoslovakia		x40227	x36246		
Australia/Australie	33337	30513	21036	20440	57992
Venezuela	15533	20219	23558	22713	25927
Ireland/Irlande	22867	20093	23315	19691	18263
Thailand/Thaïlande	9223	13504	20148	22662	16921
Jordan/Jordanie	21258	19286	20645	13536	13382
Hungary/Hongrie	x27207	x19607	x21484	x9985	x12768
Denmark/Danemark	15390	12938	21254	11234	15730
Ukraine			x9740	x33725	x23835
Czech Republic				41612	42757
Yugoslavia SFR	55158	x36514			
Colombia/Colombie	4233	6402	10180	9474	12607
Malaysia/Malaisie	5081	4777	7860	8949	9509
Slovakia				x19364	x16595
Uruguay	4769	5032	5306	5843	6615
Saudi Arabia	797	8053	3228	x4385	x2319

(VALUE AS % OF TOTAL)(VALEUR EN % DU TOTAL)

	1985	1986	1987	1988	1989	1990	1991	1992	1993	1994
Africa	5.7	6.0	x4.9	x4.6	x4.1	x5.1	5.1	x4.4	x4.7	x3.8
Northern Africa	1.9	1.9	1.9	1.9	1.6	2.0	1.9	1.8	2.0	1.7
Americas	21.1	20.1	18.5	17.4	19.4	19.2	20.1	19.8	22.2	22.2
LAIA	7.1	6.2	6.0	5.6	6.2	6.3	7.5	7.5	8.1	7.7
CACM	0.1	0.7	0.5	0.4	0.4	0.4	0.4	0.5	x0.6	x0.6
Asia	22.7	22.5	24.4	x24.9	24.3	22.6	24.6	24.8	x27.4	26.9
Middle East	3.0	x4.1	x4.7	x4.6	x4.0	3.8	x4.8	x5.0	x5.1	x3.4
Europe	44.8	45.6	44.2	46.0	45.1	46.8	44.9	46.9	40.2	43.0
EEC	36.6	37.6	36.5	38.6	37.8	43.2	41.8	43.6	37.1	40.1
EFTA	6.9	6.8	6.5	6.3	6.0	2.6	2.5	2.3	2.2	2.3
Oceania	2.7	2.7	2.7	2.8	x3.1	2.9	x2.4	x2.0	x2.5	x2.0
USA/Etats–Unis d'Amer	9.5	8.9	8.4	8.2	8.9	8.8	8.7	8.6	10.0	10.5
Germany/Allemagne	6.4	6.3	6.0	5.9	6.0	7.5	8.3	8.7	5.5	7.2
France, Monac	5.1	5.4	5.4	5.3	5.4	6.3	6.6	7.7	7.4	7.6
Japan/Japon	4.6	4.2	3.8	4.4	4.9	4.6	5.2	4.4	4.8	5.3
United Kingdom	4.9	4.9	4.6	7.2	7.0	7.4	4.5	4.2	4.0	4.2
Netherlands/Pays–Bas	5.4	5.3	4.9	4.6	4.2	4.8	4.7	4.5	3.5	3.3
Italy/Italie	3.9	4.3	4.4	4.3	4.3	4.4	4.3	4.3	4.0	4.6
Belgium–Luxembourg	2.8	2.8	2.7	2.9	2.8	3.5	4.2	4.4	3.8	4.2
Hong Kong	3.4	3.1	3.2	2.9	3.0	2.8	3.0	3.0	3.3	3.6
Korea, Republic of	1.5	1.6	1.7	2.1	2.3	2.3	2.7	2.7	3.0	3.1

	1985	1986	1987	1988	1989	1990	1991	1992	1993	1994
Afrique	1.2	1.4	1.7	1.8	x2.4	2.3	2.4	3.7	3.1	x4.0
Afrique du Nord	0.6	0.6	0.7	1.0	1.2	1.1	0.7	0.8	0.6	0.7
Amériques	26.7	25.9	22.8	23.3	22.9	22.8	24.8	24.7	22.8	25.9
ALAI	2.2	2.1	2.2	2.5	3.0	3.2	3.5	3.8	4.1	4.9
MCAC	0.0	0.0	x0.0	0.0	0.0	0.0	0.0	0.0	x0.0	x0.0
Asie	11.1	11.6	14.8	14.9	15.4	15.4	16.5	16.5	14.8	18.0
Moyen–Orient	0.9	1.1	1.7	1.7	1.4	1.5	1.5	1.7	1.2	1.4
Europe	56.5	56.4	48.2	47.0	49.9	51.6	50.9	51.3	56.5	48.3
CEE	48.9	48.1	41.0	40.0	42.4	47.5	48.9	47.2	53.1	44.6
AELE	6.9	7.5	6.4	6.4	6.8	3.4	1.6	3.4	2.9	3.2
Océanie	0.2	x0.2	x0.2	x0.3	0.3	x0.4	x0.4	x0.3	x0.3	x0.7
Germany/Allemagne	16.9	18.7	16.3	15.3	16.6	17.7	18.5	17.2	25.4	15.6
USA/Etats–Unis d'Amer	21.1	19.9	17.2	17.8	16.7	15.9	17.3	17.1	14.8	16.5
United Kingdom	6.9	7.0	6.1	6.4	6.6	7.8	8.0	7.6	7.2	7.0
Belgium–Luxembourg	2.2	2.4	1.6	5.1	5.2	5.6	5.6	5.6	5.1	5.7
China/Chine			3.2	3.4	3.9	3.9	4.8	4.8	4.3	6.1
Japan/Japon	5.0	5.2	4.7	4.5	4.8	4.7	4.6	4.4	3.9	4.5
Canada	3.4	3.8	3.2	2.9	3.0	3.7	3.8	3.7	3.8	4.4
Netherlands/Pays–Bas	7.0	7.2	5.9	3.4	3.5	4.0	4.2	4.3	2.7	3.4
France, Monac	3.0	2.9	2.3	2.1	1.9	2.1	2.1	2.6	5.7	3.8
Spain/Espagne	2.1	2.2	2.1	1.9	2.1	2.8	2.5	2.5	2.1	2.3

TRADE BY COMMODITY IN THOUSAND U.S. DOLLARS – COMMERCE PAR PRODUIT EN MILLIERS DE DOLLARS E.U

COUNTRIES–PAYS	IMPORTS – IMPORTATIONS				
	1990	1991	1992	1993	1994
Total	5341058	5611844	5600931	5015703	5576906
Africa	x16749	x16384	x21872	x12815	x14267
Northern Africa	x7238	x6340	x9932	2949	3256
Americas	x1169136	1246488	1249177	1147469	1373461
LAIA	13709	20405	47388	54085	27991
CACM	590	392	724	x415	x377
Asia	1350127	1541825	1680035	1595999	1720636
Middle East	10741	x13941	x22914	x18986	x13101
Europe	2773752	2762844	2607362	?230810	2445378
EEC	2737610	2733569	2577744	2201119	2416898
EFTA	28437	25806	24345	24841	24349
Oceania	x12385	x23501	x11424	x13296	x11476
Japan/Japon	1284248	1382234	1497988	1386810	1446857
USA/Etats–Unis d'Amer	1044429	1158014	1096045	1008171	1206376
France,Monac	774261	738699	662495	685484	607074
Germany/Allemagne	777217	541315	681091	637933	730901
United Kingdom	609383	763715	587678	235896	540425
Spain/Espagne	146455	187589	155969	237253	203360
Sweden/Suède	187400	247394	193710	127902	115020
Netherlands/Pays–Bas	114959	120085	155822	141312	85027
Korea, Republic of	18751	104214	119818	153590	211278
Canada	102562	62201	101563	81494	135924
Italy/Italie	60181	66395	68073	52848	55440
Belgium–Luxembourg	23801	27872	33640	36396	37490
Mexico/Mexique	3358	8980	30384	36454	8137
Switz.Liecht	21104	19773	18827	18874	17243
Austria/Autriche	19627	17284	19719	18218	17273
Russian Federation			x27944	x22591	x18662
Australia/Australie	10499	21820	10147	11867	10251
Singapore/Singapour	12534	13203	11998	5826	5638
Brazil/Brésil	7620	6725	11524	11321	11848
So. Africa Customs Un	6928	8647	10120	8200	8917
Denmark/Danemark	5468	5556	6101	10902	7124
Israel/Israël	5417	6090	7629	8041	6277
Iran (Islamic Rp. of)		x3459	x8860	x7327	x2002
Bulgaria/Bulgarie	x2828	x363	12511	x4613	x479
Malaysia/Malaisie	3896	4906	5928	6437	6934
Hong Kong	7652	6662	6067	4427	7552
Czechoslovakia	2396	x2874	x13748		
Finland/Finlande	10426	6279	5419	4780	4678
Norway,SVD,JM	6777	5500	5248	5715	6784
Turkey/Turquie	4265	4345	5528	5752	6323
China/Chine	2696	3053	4070	5499	16542
Greece/Grèce	3642	4182	2095	6091	6418
Saudi Arabia	4327	3910	5688	x1946	x1892
Former USSR/Anc. URSS		x11367			
Portugal	2924	3186	3803	3599	4474
Sudan/Soudan	x1782	x3455	x7064		
Ireland/Irlande	1866	4018	2130	2505	2194
Hungary/Hongrie	x5460	3546	x2365	x2117	x2531
Argentina/Argentine	487	2308	2530	3087	4447
Poland/Pologne	1665	1953	2204	3095	3344
Cuba	x3699	x2308	x2137	x1682	x1088
Slovenia/Slovénia			2368	2341	2850
Czech Republic				4317	4089
Viet Nam	x124	x3520	x76	x569	x106
New Zealand	1842	1569	1204	1321	1165
Thailand/Thaïlande	431	930	863	1894	1197
Pakistan	1597	899	875	1671	969
Lithuania/Lituanie			2886	x487	16102
Yugoslavia SFR	7643	x3345			
Croatia/Croatie			1585	1531	x792

COUNTRIES–PAYS	EXPORTS – EXPORTATIONS				
	1990	1991	1992	1993	1994
Totale	5058400	5560218	5715971	4756919	4339633
Afrique	x273440	x243116	x517199	x403705	x157003
Afrique du Nord	1375	9932	8641	424	46
Amériques	1502036	1535231	1800504	1600608	1799382
ALAI	2887	3525	2078	5683	2344
MCAC	2	2			
Asie	201111	172329	180232	x296876	x226141
Moyen–Orient	359	2579	484	327	x318
Europe	3078604	3203306	3214344	2451776	2152735
CEE	3057321	3179843	3194622	2439507	2141475
AELE	21106	22166	19704	12264	11239
Océanie	200	4386	524	x638	x1122
France,Monac	1589055	1678429	1613009	1283501	1058723
USA/Etats–Unis d'Amer	1141479	1175477	1384556	1205638	1322816
United Kingdom	552721	633140	931096	628995	556272
Canada	357565	356150	413848	389254	474205
Russian Federation			x573722	x557281	x746102
Niger	x216615	x207268	x375976	x323597	x85656
Germany/Allemagne	448410	475856	226052	198464	174079
Netherlands/Pays–Bas	354368	265733	307247	225082	237901
China/Chine	156859	116037	128520	180006	92900
Former USSR/Anc. URSS		x399383			
So. Africa Customs Un	68	160	98145	55176	42573
Sweden/Suède	45459	47728	42409	24116	18856
Belgium–Luxembourg	29166	33848	37564	39938	46839
Japan/Japon	28299	34068	31218	30988	34514
Gabon	x39264	x25529	x31700	x22578	x28449
Italy/Italie	16850	27152	19208	17837	16921
Switz.Liecht	17710	20261	18419	10975	10169
Mongolia/Mongolie		x80			
Austria/Autriche	9207	8068	9360	10446	x10557
Kazakstan				x26120	x43935
Egypt/Egypte	1375	9878	8641	424	22
Malaysia/Malaisie	9479	10264	6585	528	105
Hong Kong	4555	5810	6469	3108	4933
Spain/Espagne	5193	4236	3267	4105	16618
Finland/Finlande	4209	3158	3236	3295	3166
Uzbekistan/Ouzbékistan			x2573	x7044	x16314
Singapore/Singapour	871	2170	2632	3082	2487
Denmark/Danemark	1781	1885	1286	3174	1160
Argentina/Argentine	1604	2401	1487	2421	1947
Australia/Australie	166	4326	472	622	1117
Norway,SVD,JM	3395	1905	1285	1289	1070
Benin/Bénin			x2730	x1742	
Estonia/Estonie			x1035	x2747	x8388
Venezuela	5	3	4	3058	9
Hungary/Hongrie	x1099	x738	x951	x1053	x1113
Poland/Pologne	525	636	981	1058	1174
Saudi Arabia	5	2503	39		
Ireland/Irlande	874	597	873	553	363
Israel/Israël	344	273	796	829	1678
Korea Dem People's Rp		x271	x290	x1311	x629
Brazil/Brésil	1199	1024	505	114	72
Czechoslovakia		x773	x871		
Korea, Republic of	243	381	451	633	781
Yugoslavia SFR	169	x1295			
Belarus/Bélarus			x32	x738	x66
Czech Republic				760	857
India/Inde	99	342	77	223	13063
Jordan/Jordanie		8	398	177	238
Bulgaria/Bulgarie	x4	x147	x251	x48	x52
Slovakia				x351	x37

(VALUE AS % OF TOTAL)(VALEUR EN % DU TOTAL)

	1985	1986	1987	1988	1989	1990	1991	1992	1993	1994
Africa	0.2	0.2	x0.2	x0.1	x0.2	x0.3	x0.3	x0.4	x0.3	x0.3
Northern Africa	0.0	0.0	0.0	0.0	0.1	x0.1	x0.1	x0.2	0.1	0.1
Americas	25.4	23.3	15.6	17.8	18.3	x21.9	22.2	22.3	22.9	24.7
LAIA	0.2	0.2	0.2	0.2	0.2	0.3	0.4	0.8	1.1	0.5
CACM		0.0	x0.0	0.0	0.0	0.0	0.0	0.0	x0.0	x0.0
Asia	18.0	x16.4	x16.9	x18.8	21.7	25.2	27.4	30.0	31.8	30.9
Middle East	0.1	x0.1	x0.1	x0.2	x0.2	0.2	x0.2	x0.4	x0.4	x0.2
Europe	56.1	59.8	61.1	56.2	55.3	51.9	49.2	46.6	44.5	43.8
EEC	51.6	56.4	56.8	52.1	50.0	51.3	48.7	46.0	43.9	43.3
EFTA	4.5	3.3	4.2	4.1	5.2	0.5	0.5	0.4	0.5	0.4
Oceania	0.2	x0.2	0.2	x0.2	0.2	x0.2	x0.4	x0.2	x0.3	x0.2
Japan/Japon	17.1	15.3	16.0	17.7	20.7	24.0	24.6	26.7	27.6	25.9
USA/Etats–Unis d'Amer	24.8	22.7	15.0	16.5	16.4	19.6	20.6	19.6	20.1	21.6
France,Monac	16.3	19.1	17.6	17.5	14.6	14.5	13.2	11.8	13.7	10.9
Germany/Allemagne	17.7	17.4	17.4	17.1	14.7	14.6	9.6	12.2	12.7	13.1
United Kingdom	8.2	10.1	8.8	7.4	9.0	11.4	13.6	10.5	4.7	9.7
Spain/Espagne	1.8	3.6	5.0	3.2	3.1	2.7	3.3	2.8	4.7	3.6
Sweden/Suède	4.0	2.6	3.5	3.2	4.4	3.5	4.4	3.5	2.6	2.1
Netherlands/Pays–Bas	2.1	1.7	2.3	2.0	2.4	2.2	2.1	2.8	2.8	1.5
Korea, Republic of	0.5	0.5	0.1	0.2	0.3	0.4	1.9	2.1	3.1	3.8
Canada	0.4	0.4	0.3	0.9	1.6	1.9	1.1	1.8	1.6	2.4

	1985	1986	1987	1988	1989	1990	1991	1992	1993	1994
Afrique		x5.1	x5.8	x6.3	x4.5	x5.4	x4.4	x9.0	x8.5	x3.6
Afrique du Nord	0.0	0.0	x0.0	x0.0	x0.0	0.0	0.2	0.2	0.0	0.0
Amériques	40.2	32.8	x21.5	20.4	32.1	29.7	27.6	31.5	33.6	41.5
ALAI	0.0	0.2	0.0	0.1	0.1	0.1	0.1	0.0	0.1	0.1
MCAC		0.0	x0.0	x0.0	x0.0	0.0	0.0		0.0	
Asie	0.5	0.2	1.3	2.5	3.1	4.0	3.1	3.2	x6.3	x5.2
Moyen–Orient	0.0	0.0	x0.0	x0.0	x0.0	0.0	0.0	0.0	0.0	x0.0
Europe	59.2	61.9	55.7	51.4	48.7	60.9	57.6	56.2	51.5	49.6
CEE	58.1	60.5	54.0	49.9	46.5	60.4	57.2	55.9	51.3	49.3
AELE	1.1	1.3	1.6	1.5	2.2	0.4	0.4	0.3	0.3	0.3
Océanie							0.1		x0.0	x0.0
France,Monac	33.5	30.3	27.5	25.9	21.1	31.4	30.2	28.2	27.0	24.4
USA/Etats–Unis d'Amer	30.3	23.7	14.9	12.4	23.8	22.6	21.1	24.2	25.3	30.5
United Kingdom	13.4	17.3	13.7	13.6	11.6	10.9	11.4	16.3	13.2	12.8
Canada	9.9	8.8	6.6	7.9	8.3	7.1	6.4	7.2	8.2	10.9
Russian Federation								x10.0	x11.7	x17.2
Niger		x3.9	x4.8	x5.1	x3.5	x4.3	x3.7	x6.6	x6.8	x2.0
Germany/Allemagne	4.0	5.5	5.6	3.9	7.0	8.9	8.6	4.0	4.2	4.0
Netherlands/Pays–Bas	4.5	5.8	5.4	4.8	4.4	7.0	4.8	5.4	4.7	5.5
China/Chine			0.9	1.7	2.2	3.1	2.1	2.2	3.8	2.1
Former USSR/Anc. URSS			x15.6	x19.4	x11.5		x7.2			

TRADE BY COMMODITY IN THOUSAND U.S. DOLLARS – COMMERCE PAR PRODUIT EN MILLIERS DE DOLLARS E.U

COUNTRIES–PAYS	IMPORTS – IMPORTATIONS				
	1990	1991	1992	1993	1994
Total	8009882	7891774	8587739	8577303	9246216
Africa	x323269	x313626	x357218	x307179	x305198
Northern Africa	85328	89142	101922	89148	89049
Americas	1201478	1318778	1501784	1617581	1705835
LAIA	328463	374989	437317	495926	523506
CACM	19078	21364	26547	x23260	x28759
Asia	2116428	2316524	2452323	2638906	2624109
Middle East	x321168	x324474	x368777	x372057	x315540
Europe	3887529	3688076	4027385	3748542	4331321
EEC	3274406	3142651	3438269	3108329	3613793
EFTA	535410	484817	528842	595262	668762
Oceania	x95408	x102223	x121795	x132613	x138327
USA/Etats–Unis d'Amer	682516	758650	857472	902385	954110
Italy/Italie	689023	641354	655415	571577	663406
Hong Kong	461644	561753	543226	519301	498422
France,Monac	524487	482288	531650	542852	607584
Germany/Allemagne	497324	489161	541466	499901	536102
Switz.Liecht	483553	439146	470030	527449	581666
United Kingdom	453341	422738	494453	323398	459328
Japan/Japon	354996	351206	333142	321606	343051
Korea, Republic of	295788	338804	309808	329388	348815
Netherlands/Pays–Bas	200300	225926	249347	235078	300112
Turkey/Turquie	200685	181161	236016	247733	228084
Belgium–Luxembourg	187003	194079	214834	251386	284651
Spain/Espagne	227229	224963	228093	174994	206288
Indonesia/Indonésie	152793	168765	185881	210946	213470
Canada	155578	153203	169282	185801	188175
Thailand/Thaïlande	133535	128954	161187	170507	164771
China/Chine	69049	110510	147810	196222	206181
Portugal	128014	122001	141116	104657	106974
Mexico/Mexique	75803	87627	111355	121172	135322
Singapore/Singapour	61425	63079	111867	142308	150414
Brazil/Brésil	88368	75182	84702	129581	124337
Australia/Australie	74052	83108	95759	102614	106538
Denmark/Danemark	72444	71815	78746	121970	132032
Austria/Autriche	89664	84824	97907	84805	90407
So. Africa Customs Un	82859	84326	85786	93466	99960
Iran (Islamic Rp. of)	x82761	x105057	x84280	x69296	x34016
Malaysia/Malaisie	63091	74731	79043	81008	98930
Pakistan	55813	60667	72818	84475	80304
Sweden/Suède	71433	61281	64029	68176	92044
Nigeria/Nigéria	x60855	49767	x85528	x57128	x41056
Finland/Finlande	63999	56597	64289	64075	74816
Colombia/Colombie	46985	42827	54325	72106	65384
Norway,SVD,JM	48887	43141	57389	66816	85718
Greece/Grèce	51712	45488	51045	47231	41683
Philippines	31454	33252	41855	59990	54719
Argentina/Argentine	23338	43979	49371	41453	47500
Chile/Chili	30019	34616	44698	52804	59017
Egypt/Egypte	38083	39600	43177	36653	37482
Israel/Israël	33646	36297	41213	36103	36967
Venezuela	18770	34379	39322	30259	24008
Hungary/Hongrie	x39017	24939	x32436	x30598	x25865
Poland/Pologne	15835	17151	33291	36477	46984
Morocco/Maroc	25168	28713	27695	24186	23902
New Zealand	17804	18462	25203	28720	31041
Ireland/Irlande	18434	20136	25881	18228	18365
Czechoslovakia	35900	x30735	x31404		
Peru/Pérou	15866	19112	18508	21343	29017
Yugoslavia SFR	76349	x58767			
India/Inde	16952	13713	18753	24200	42443
Former USSR/Anc. URSS	183948	x50902			

COUNTRIES–PAYS	EXPORTS – EXPORTATIONS				
	1990	1991	1992	1993	1994
Totale	7765038	7907999	8614792	8558721	9383437
Afrique	11108	12402	11191	x11247	x2523
Afrique du Nord	2520	5297	5418	3906	1499
Amériques	468946	448294	548113	563415	648332
ALAI	59579	74393	137155	95346	110531
MCAC	861	726	838	x1090	x1083
Asie	1492455	1738447	1921452	1975075	2191717
Moyen–Orient	10387	4628	11294	x1991	x3533
Europe	5723525	5615103	6054700	5915124	6446977
CEE	4231399	4243474	4547940	4343801	4807665
AELE	1491911	1370217	1504153	1569482	1637779
Océanie	x5849	x6887	x9452	x18338	x14036
Germany/Allemagne	2288246	2243579	2402720	2173858	2336228
Switz.Liecht	1489010	1368670	1502657	1567764	1635872
United Kingdom	808230	812134	834525	779944	776198
Japan/Japon	529504	626253	651833	650425	668369
France,Monac	419237	422514	457471	509150	612323
Hong Kong	337469	431324	443085	444708	430883
USA/Etats–Unis d'Amer	394535	356689	392530	445500	514225
India/Inde	178809	221582	279070	289770	352128
China/Chine	234762	219247	237332	245429	351174
Belgium–Luxembourg	189805	197740	202597	245387	312078
Netherlands/Pays–Bas	139855	165445	184117	161026	230744
Italy/Italie	149712	159049	175522	154179	173254
Korea, Republic of	110506	126471	144443	154335	174985
Spain/Espagne	118336	125136	141675	128301	130145
Denmark/Danemark	72667	73615	91041	135378	163493
Singapore/Singapour	39297	51734	82883	114462	127479
Brazil/Brésil	12794	15361	81048	32352	39882
Czechoslovakia		x54001	x48564		
Thailand/Thaïlande	15733	24924	34102	35815	37811
Indonesia/Indonésie	30624	28954	30537	32599	36184
Argentina/Argentine	26791	29136	27905	32436	33420
Mexico/Mexique	14927	24155	22681	24895	30708
Greece/Grèce	19920	17298	23540	19775	22307
Czech Republic				56995	60627
Poland/Pologne	19534	21583	16440	13814	14438
Austria/Autriche	13029	13603	17342	16528	x14594
Canada	11898	13650	14833	18322	18878
Australia/Australie	4433	5129	6503	10968	13275
Sweden/Suède	5989	5435	7961	9025	21449
Finland/Finlande	3846	4547	7233	9014	12006
Russian Federation			x8783	x7862	x8608
So. Africa Customs Un	4835	5993	4391	5567	
Egypt/Egypte	2122	4966	4940	3329	910
Saudi Arabia	532	1547	7631	x159	x377
Panama	1667	2645	2613	2997	3396
Uruguay	3446	2866	2042	2493	1970
Former USSR/Anc. URSS	27942	x7201			
Malaysia/Malaisie	2522	1543	3435	2079	2980
Wake Island/Ile de Wak	x6	x28	x12		x16
Venezuela	1142	1450	2106	1821	2447
Ireland/Irlande	1246	2515	1303	1391	1494
Turkey/Turquie	5707	900	3064	1027	1839
Norway,SVD,JM	2899	1546	1495	1718	1907
Ukraine			x1662	x2535	x3153
New Zealand	491	699	2050	1330	707
Bulgaria/Bulgarie	x3226	x578	x2419	x818	x184
Hungary/Hongrie	x1117	x999	x1105	x1460	x2562
Romania/Roumanie	3417	1888	741	587	635
Colombia/Colombie	358	957	1064	1015	1486
Korea Dem People's Rp	x1461	x766	x958	x1199	x577

(VALUE AS % OF TOTAL)(VALEUR EN % DU TOTAL)

	1985	1986	1987	1988	1989	1990	1991	1992	1993	1994
Africa	4.6	x4.8	x4.3	x4.4	x3.9	x4.0	x4.0	x4.2	x3.6	x3.3
Northern Africa	1.5	1.1	1.2	1.2	1.1	1.1	1.1	1.2	1.0	1.0
Americas	19.1	17.8	16.2	14.4	14.7	15.0	16.8	17.5	18.9	18.5
LAIA	5.1	4.2	3.8	3.7	4.0	4.1	4.8	5.1	5.8	5.7
CACM	0.4	x0.3	0.3	0.2	0.3	0.2	0.3	0.3	x0.3	x0.3
Asia	22.1	23.1	x24.2	x26.0	24.7	26.5	29.3	28.6	30.8	28.4
Middle East	1.9	x2.5	x2.7	x2.6	x2.8	x4.0	x4.1	x4.3	x4.3	x3.4
Europe	47.7	48.3	46.1	46.6	48.7	48.5	46.7	46.9	43.7	46.8
EEC	36.3	37.3	35.8	36.0	38.3	40.9	39.8	40.0	36.2	39.1
EFTA	9.8	9.7	9.1	9.4	9.5	6.7	6.1	6.2	6.9	7.2
Oceania	1.6	x1.4	x1.2	x1.2	x1.4	x1.1	x1.3	x1.4	x1.5	x1.5
USA/Etats–Unis d'Amer	10.8	10.4	9.8	8.3	8.1	8.5	9.6	10.0	10.5	10.3
Italy/Italie	7.6	7.7	7.5	7.5	8.2	8.6	8.1	7.6	6.7	7.2
Hong Kong	4.7	5.6	4.7	5.1	5.9	5.8	7.1	6.3	6.1	5.4
France,Monac	5.9	6.0	5.7	5.9	6.1	6.5	6.1	6.2	6.3	6.6
Germany/Allemagne	5.8	5.4	5.4	5.3	5.4	6.2	6.2	6.3	5.8	5.8
Switz.Liecht	6.6	6.5	6.0	6.3	6.2	6.0	5.6	5.5	6.1	6.3
United Kingdom	5.3	5.6	5.1	5.2	5.5	5.7	5.4	5.8	3.8	5.0
Japan/Japon	5.0	4.5	4.5	4.6	4.6	4.4	4.5	3.9	3.7	3.7
Korea, Republic of	3.2	3.4	3.0	3.1	3.6	3.7	4.3	3.6	3.8	3.8
Netherlands/Pays–Bas	2.4	2.5	2.3	2.3	2.5	2.5	2.9	2.9	2.7	3.2

	1985	1986	1987	1988	1989	1990	1991	1992	1993	1994
Afrique	0.1	0.1	x0.1	x0.2	0.2	0.2	0.2	0.2	x0.2	x0.0
Afrique du Nord	0.0	0.0	0.0	0.0	0.0	0.0	0.1	0.1	0.0	0.0
Amériques	4.7	4.5	4.6	4.6	5.3	6.0	5.7	6.3	6.6	6.9
ALAI	0.3	0.3	0.4	0.5	0.6	0.8	0.9	1.6	1.1	1.2
MCAC	0.0	0.0	0.0	0.0	0.0	0.0	0.0	0.0	x0.0	x0.0
Asie	14.3	15.7	17.0	17.8	19.1	19.2	22.0	22.3	23.1	23.3
Moyen–Orient	0.3	0.0	0.1	0.2	0.2	0.1	0.1	0.1	x0.0	x0.0
Europe	77.2	75.8	73.7	73.4	73.8	73.7	71.0	70.3	69.1	68.7
CEE	56.2	52.9	50.9	53.3	53.8	54.5	53.7	52.8	50.8	51.2
AELE	20.9	22.9	22.7	20.1	19.9	19.2	17.3	17.5	18.3	17.5
Océanie		x0.0	x0.1	x0.1	x0.0	x0.1	x0.1	x0.1	x0.2	x0.1
Germany/Allemagne	32.4	34.7	33.3	30.2	30.2	29.5	28.4	27.9	25.4	24.9
Switz.Liecht	20.7	22.6	22.4	19.8	19.6	19.2	17.3	17.4	18.3	17.4
United Kingdom	10.9	10.8	10.4	9.8	9.8	10.4	10.3	9.7	9.1	8.3
Japan/Japon	7.4	7.2	6.9	6.6	7.3	6.8	7.9	7.6	7.6	7.1
France,Monac	0.5	0.6	0.6	5.6	5.6	5.4	5.3	5.3	5.9	6.5
Hong Kong	3.4	3.9	3.7	4.0	4.2	4.3	5.5	5.1	5.2	4.6
USA/Etats–Unis d'Amer	4.3	4.1	4.0	3.8	4.6	5.1	4.5	4.6	5.2	5.5
India/Inde	1.0	1.5	1.9	1.9	2.6	2.3	2.8	3.2	3.4	3.8
China/Chine	1.2	1.7	1.9	1.8	2.5	3.0	2.8	2.8	2.9	3.7
Belgium–Luxembourg	1.5	1.6	1.7	2.1	2.3	2.4	2.5	2.4	2.9	3.3

TRADE BY COMMODITY IN THOUSAND U.S. DOLLARS – COMMERCE PAR PRODUIT EN MILLIERS DE DOLLARS E.U

COUNTRIES–PAYS	IMPORTS – IMPORTATIONS					COUNTRIES–PAYS	EXPORTS – EXPORTATIONS				
	1990	1991	1992	1993	1994		1990	1991	1992	1993	1994
Total	743855	763585	857348	756847	807071	Totale	579427	642290	703976	688059	727861
Africa	x34348	45359	x32438	x30250	x28695	Afrique	x48094	x47586	x48431	x44233	x24593
Northern Africa	12673	12137	12677	11731	11647	Afrique du Nord	x316	425	x443	415	793
Americas	84035	135554	166439	154329	146117	Amériques	122206	142875	152122	158866	174450
LAIA	42153	54449	76612	59638	60194	ALAI	100846	117431	122950	129106	141404
CACM	7529	8154	7610	x9997	x7923	MCAC	362	392	933	x1695	x1265
Asia	233617	258235	316151	292282	297133	Asie	47176	70900	96294	114074	100495
Middle East	x19526	x21298	x17744	x15498	x13370	Moyen–Orient	6227	9816	6334	5430	5880
Europe	289794	290150	307091	243247	293899	Europe	353543	374070	398596	359993	418366
EEC	272983	275965	291522	232049	279986	CEE	340623	361714	387401	350178	410348
EFTA	8691	7838	7441	5980	7026	AELE	10527	10281	6780	5022	3982
Oceania	x13306	x16571	x22449	x22479	x25458	Océanie	5390	5017	6512	x8535	x8420
Italy/Italie	106093	102428	100839	73335	89259	Germany/Allemagne	142112	146424	153634	136474	152896
USA/Etats–Unis d'Amer	26380	62276	73584	73484	66994	Italy/Italie	53653	59437	66359	64404	80942
Japan/Japon	49139	58599	58531	51931	54710	Spain/Espagne	42508	50121	55661	41537	45217
Korea, Republic of	47729	53970	57816	53448	53497	Argentina/Argentine	40298	43518	41665	45564	45038
Hong Kong	17259	22049	54722	48083	51335	United Kingdom	41610	40776	43071	39739	42595
Germany/Allemagne	31128	36772	33993	30993	31425	France,Monac	35565	36974	38697	38165	42082
United Kingdom	25706	24489	32676	23542	27050	Hong Kong	15728	21582	37925	37853	41118
France,Monac	21614	21131	24774	20652	23337	So. Africa Customs Un	33743	33887	33635	29761	
Spain/Espagne	22190	20862	21655	23588	32697	Brazil/Brésil	21702	21883	29133	35146	36858
India/Inde	20511	15764	18583	27369	30229	Mexico/Mexique	15768	30081	29632	21919	23582
Mexico/Mexique	11042	17604	25450	18303	17873	USA/Etats–Unis d'Amer	20096	24401	27302	27370	30870
Bangladesh	21776	20317	27614	x7851	x8347	Japan/Japon	9755	12924	17245	17942	10615
Pakistan	17351	18966	17402	18377	20061	Netherlands/Pays–Bas	15499	16462	15866	14563	27206
Netherlands/Pays–Bas	17194	19845	19619	12175	19821	Thailand/Thaïlande	379	7206	10874	14764	4078
Portugal	13313	14377	17788	13649	15225	Peru/Pérou	9978	9296	10340	9952	16657
Australia/Australie	9598	11583	15864	16098	18931	China/Chine	4109	5576	6398	11720	9011
Indonesia/Indonésie	12225	10377	14697	16939	15312	Switz.Liecht	9757	10194	6644	4866	3790
Singapore/Singapour	2880	11461	11949	17446	9462	Turkey/Turquie	6033	9082	6191	4905	5600
Nigeria/Nigéria	x3887	19020	x8086	x5893	x7052	Kenya	4148	5396	6081	6895	x11027
China/Chine	1800	3534	12986	14364	19024	Indonesia/Indonésie	4195	4828	3567	8911	9199
Thailand/Thaïlande	8741	8137	10115	10977	11123	Australia/Australie	5314	3862	5358	6899	6672
Belgium–Luxembourg	6385	7047	6839	7299	8621	Singapore/Singapour	1026	1578	5406	8442	11216
Brazil/Brésil	5997	6807	6346	7872	7882	Denmark/Danemark	2607	2771	4412	6260	9820
Canada	5169	6791	6065	7776	7025	India/Inde	4252	3744	4292	4033	4758
Greece/Grèce	6026	5623	7100	6363	5758	Paraguay	5349	4681	3905	3408	5607
Austria/Autriche	6267	5733	7118	5851	6661	Belgium–Luxembourg	2383	2672	3817	4552	4479
Venezuela	2890	7298	7159	3810	2659	Ireland/Irlande	2703	4173	4086	2741	3582
Denmark/Danemark	4389	5445	6035	5878	8415	Zimbabwe	4283	2884	3752	3858	x5743
New Zealand	3369	4663	6235	6101	6135	Chile/Chili	937	952	2147	5827	6871
Ireland/Irlande	6530	6268	7496	2420	4300	Un. Rep. of Tanzania	x1136	x2122	x3360	x3179	x4033
Iran (Islamic Rp. of)	x6305	x8553	x4290	x3200	x581	Ecuador/Equateur	1474	2931	2365	2385	x2653
Chile/Chili	3617	5014	4830	6009	4246	Uruguay	969	2001	2151	2897	2849
Ecuador/Equateur	1825	1690	12937	1170	x1598	Slovenia/Slovénia			3199	3547	3702
Colombia/Colombie	5880	4041	5532	6057	5544	Nepal/Népal	504	2531	2387	960	x138
Turkey/Turquie	4721	4579	4860	5705	5683	Russian Federation			x1035	x2924	x1163
Morocco/Maroc	3980	4590	6424	4109	3793	New Zealand	76	1155	1154	1596	1733
Argentina/Argentine	2011	3372	5456	5701	9508	Colombia/Colombie	403	580	1223	1838	1232
Poland/Pologne	1331	851	5207	6806	7223	Austria/Autriche	1100	1066	839	594	x436
Switz.Liecht	6285	5102	4262	3133	4185	Korea, Republic of	158	324	622	1541	1647
Philippines	3154	4089	5052	2933	3089	Ethiopia/Ethiopie	3275	1876	327	71	x2570
So. Africa Customs Un	3318	3576	4372	3783	5073	Canada	898	588	881	638	703
Saudi Arabia	2244	4599	4636	x2149	x2698	Yugoslavia SFR	2291	x1910			
Uruguay	3895	3680	3471	3599	3775	Sweden/Suède	725	555	714	554	707
Peru/Pérou	2979	3058	3088	4264	3516	Costa Rica	141	71	371	x1342	x1040
Finland/Finlande	3905	3526	3102	3730	4202	Hungary/Hongrie	x514	x617	x504	x655	x236
Egypt/Egypte	2747	3592	3139	3426	3934	Bolivia/Bolivie	3876	1486			38
Guatemala	1943	2285	2627	4732	2873	Yugoslavia/Yougoslavie			x894	x458	x227
Former USSR/Anc. URSS	64737	x9352				Kazakstan				x1167	x1162
Malaysia/Malaisie	1836	2441	3653	2371	3389	Czechoslovakia		x443	x717		
Costa Rica	3172	3281	2621	x2150	x2133	Mozambique	x870	x821	x283		

(VALUE AS % OF TOTAL)(VALEUR EN % DU TOTAL)

	1985	1986	1987	1988	1989	1990	1991	1992	1993	1994
Africa	4.9	4.8	4.3	x5.2	x4.0	x4.6	6.0	x3.8	x4.0	x3.5
Northern Africa	2.0	1.8	2.2	2.2	1.8	1.7	1.6	1.5	1.6	1.4
Americas	23.7	17.6	17.2	19.1	14.1	11.3	17.7	19.4	20.4	18.1
LAIA	12.5	7.6	7.6	8.6	5.1	5.7	7.1	8.9	7.9	7.5
CACM	2.0	1.3	1.1	1.2	1.4	1.0	1.1	0.9	x1.3	x1.0
Asia	26.1	28.6	29.9	31.6	30.6	31.4	33.8	36.9	38.7	36.8
Middle East	1.1	x1.4	x1.3	x1.2	x2.2	x2.6	x2.8	x2.1	x2.0	x1.7
Europe	38.2	41.3	38.6	36.7	39.8	39.0	38.0	35.8	32.1	36.4
EEC	33.3	36.5	34.0	32.3	36.0	36.7	36.1	34.0	30.7	34.7
EFTA	3.3	3.4	3.3	3.2	2.9	1.2	1.0	0.9	0.8	0.9
Oceania	1.8	x2.0	1.7	x1.9	x2.1	x1.7	x2.1	x2.6	x2.9	x3.1
Italy/Italie	13.3	14.0	12.5	11.7	13.9	14.3	13.4	11.8	9.7	11.1
USA/Etats–Unis d'Amer	6.8	6.1	6.1	7.8	5.9	3.5	8.2	8.6	9.7	8.3
Japan/Japon	6.0	5.9	4.9	4.5	5.9	6.6	7.7	6.8	6.9	6.8
Korea, Republic of	4.0	5.7	6.2	7.0	7.4	6.4	7.1	6.7	7.1	6.6
Hong Kong	3.3	3.7	4.7	2.7	2.6	2.3	2.9	6.4	6.4	6.4
Germany/Allemagne	3.2	3.8	3.8	3.8	3.9	4.2	4.8	4.0	4.1	3.9
United Kingdom	2.5	2.9	3.1	3.1	2.8	3.5	3.2	3.8	3.1	3.4
France,Monac	3.5	3.2	3.1	3.2	3.2	2.9	2.8	2.9	2.7	2.9
Spain/Espagne	2.4	3.1	2.8	2.4	3.2	3.0	2.7	2.5	3.1	4.1
India/Inde	5.8	4.9	3.4	2.5	2.5	2.8	2.1	2.2	3.6	3.7

	1985	1986	1987	1988	1989	1990	1991	1992	1993	1994
Afrique	10.7	10.2	x9.7	x8.8	x8.8	x8.3	x7.4	x6.9	x6.4	x3.4
Afrique du Nord	0.2	0.6	0.1	x0.2	0.3	x0.1	0.1	x0.1	0.1	0.1
Amériques	28.0	23.2	21.6	23.1	23.8	21.1	22.3	21.6	23.1	23.9
ALAI	26.4	21.7	19.9	20.9	19.8	17.4	18.3	17.5	18.8	19.4
MCAC	0.1	x0.0	x0.0	0.1	0.1	0.1	0.1	0.1	x0.2	x0.2
Asie	6.2	7.3	7.8	6.6	8.4	8.2	11.0	13.7	16.5	13.8
Moyen–Orient	0.1	x0.1	x0.3	x0.2	1.2	1.1	1.5	0.9	0.8	0.8
Europe	54.7	59.1	58.2	59.0	57.8	61.0	58.2	56.6	52.3	57.5
CEE	53.1	57.6	56.2	56.2	55.5	58.8	56.3	55.0	50.9	56.4
AELE	1.3	1.1	1.6	2.4	1.9	1.8	1.6	1.0	0.7	0.5
Océanie	0.3	x0.4	x0.6	0.5	x0.4	0.9	0.8	0.9	x1.2	x1.2
Germany/Allemagne	25.1	29.2	26.4	25.9	25.1	24.5	22.8	21.8	19.8	21.0
Italy/Italie	8.2	8.4	9.6	9.6	7.9	9.3	9.3	9.4	9.4	11.1
Spain/Espagne	4.3	4.1	4.8	4.9	6.5	7.3	7.8	7.9	6.0	6.2
Argentina/Argentine	12.9	10.7	9.1	7.9	7.7	7.0	6.8	5.9	6.6	6.2
United Kingdom	4.5	4.8	5.2	5.8	5.6	7.2	6.3	6.1	5.8	5.9
France,Monac	7.8	7.4	6.4	5.9	5.7	6.1	5.8	5.5	5.5	5.8
Hong Kong	2.0	2.9	3.1	2.8	2.6	2.7	3.4	5.4	5.5	5.6
So. Africa Customs Un	7.1	6.8	6.0	5.7	5.7	5.8	5.3	4.8	4.3	
Brazil/Brésil	6.7	5.0	4.3	4.5	3.9	3.7	3.4	4.1	5.1	5.1
Mexico/Mexique	3.2	2.4	2.5	4.8	4.4	2.7	4.7	4.2	3.2	3.2

TRADE BY COMMODITY IN THOUSAND U.S. DOLLARS – COMMERCE PAR PRODUIT EN MILLIERS DE DOLLARS E.U

IMPORTS – IMPORTATIONS

COUNTRIES–PAYS	1990	1991	1992	1993	1994
Total	12001397	11805875	13235267	12776330	14742219
Africa	x405694	440886	x459167	x451418	x478652
Northern Africa	208222	221235	x221317	x230508	x241424
Americas	1480492	1594981	1931995	2140656	2552023
LAIA	357804	389635	571782	644578	812161
CACM	31039	34860	44826	x55101	x56546
Asia	2331387	2395983	2851120	3129999	3681708
Middle East	x474079	x424888	x511116	x522275	x476149
Europe	6688328	6652013	7421642	6363641	7226289
EEC	6051735	6069320	6746071	5791776	6581879
EFTA	479442	461526	497896	451965	502754
Oceania	x152182	x149791	x171392	x178146	x209540
Germany/Allemagne	1033906	1117100	1284747	1023962	1132032
France,Monac	988990	973321	1053453	855797	1008573
USA/Etats–Unis d'Amer	581277	631797	730380	772259	897002
United Kingdom	645069	617341	682763	696540	707592
Italy/Italie	657941	651988	703711	632762	749822
Belgium–Luxembourg	553182	566816	636189	533968	568523
Netherlands/Pays–Bas	606053	571200	627275	479139	583487
Canada	371306	420472	467618	564559	674963
Hong Kong	246101	295087	399725	417511	512685
Spain/Espagne	300794	321039	384550	334680	418164
Austria/Autriche	296551	305285	342416	334147	386447
China/Chine	172858	230481	331592	375335	476958
Japan/Japon	296057	300484	298161	332405	391249
Switz.Liecht	327765	304478	328227	297461	335368
Korea, Republic of	249069	273203	277798	307803	404598
Sweden/Suède	310261	290059	295279	256299	294196
Thailand/Thaïlande	191764	202268	258622	271307	312083
Singapore/Singapour	195417	192472	194292	246784	304668
Denmark/Danemark	177969	186588	209762	176838	195073
Mexico/Mexique	64934	91003	212401	225139	296301
Turkey/Turquie	136619	122704	164354	178830	157556
Greece/Grèce	151914	146379	166655	146951	149139
Norway,SVD,JM	141447	144669	157873	144321	157360
Portugal	127225	137455	164298	135322	159354
Malaysia/Malaisie	91195	116327	154366	162058	207535
Indonesia/Indonésie	119010	116833	141446	166901	201955
Poland/Pologne	24137	72572	122046	170487	221080
Russian Federation			x223822	x119637	x148774
Finland/Finlande	122052	104717	111691	104820	135968
Former USSR/Anc. URSS	635545	x302944			
Brazil/Brésil	107408	85843	96295	119154	157676
Australia/Australie	90667	89186	103632	105925	124218
Saudi Arabia	91938	82096	100436	x107345	x116625
Hungary/Hongrie	x86603	71262	x87036	x93430	x88838
Israel/Israël	65875	70799	89891	89005	102280
Ireland/Irlande	79828	80032	83282	80551	93508
Argentina/Argentine	40355	58951	79415	101128	128604
Iran (Islamic Rp. of)	x76933	x85520	x88545	x56805	x23975
Egypt/Egypte	82383	63393	71350	70124	82628
Nigeria/Nigéria	x48436	74666	x72944	x52706	x38024
Libyan Arab Jamahiriya	42555	68817	x54193	x65226	x53074
Philippines	60148	50003	57330	77125	90608
Czechoslovakia	64368	x68655	x115385		
So. Africa Customs Un	45716	48334	57289	63447	76406
Venezuela	36300	46248	49292	48138	31027
Colombia/Colombie	40446	33735	48247	52265	68270
United Arab Emirates	44824	36587	39646	x52581	x59263
Chile/Chili	30808	33760	43321	48798	53466
New Zealand	36713	33455	38430	48630	64015
Czech Republic				120119	150804

EXPORTS – EXPORTATIONS

COUNTRIES–PAYS	1990	1991	1992	1993	1994
Totale	11637614	11693229	13362867	13166327	15422745
Afrique	53003	39408	36228	43710	22661
Afrique du Nord	31564	16463	7641	12332	21343
Amériques	1491187	1588772	1815539	1945290	2297848
ALAI	146634	135438	161748	187570	237058
MCAC	9040	11220	16220	x14630	x15857
Asie	1338660	1466070	1772652	2025342	2564147
Moyen–Orient	54695	41803	53550	x72615	x83532
Europe	8517860	8420660	9460498	8805412	10152194
CEE	8096120	8066484	8958167	8328156	9616341
AELE	353266	344838	384435	379014	449446
Océanie	188237	143233	218718	x235738	x264316
Germany/Allemagne	2736152	2758169	3073147	2760420	3180247
USA/Etats–Unis d'Amer	1153428	1246505	1430140	1516328	1759993
United Kingdom	1241241	1255353	1373176	1259369	1402410
Netherlands/Pays–Bas	908998	851860	956980	866179	973852
France,Monac	832659	854976	930832	870755	972204
Japan/Japon	684518	758324	873123	934286	1113834
Belgium–Luxembourg	797644	770110	843649	841696	1057967
Italy/Italie	467346	483957	548040	543839	642841
Spain/Espagne	203578	249569	329686	348157	431163
Switz.Liecht	244460	246829	282695	290893	343472
Hong Kong	146863	188018	261088	304688	373129
Singapore/Singapour	175030	179691	221855	246691	327564
Denmark/Danemark	201234	200374	239504	182818	190145
Sweden/Suède	181069	188725	217932	204768	263156
Finland/Finlande	272801	207901	184555	197491	249794
Canada	163168	178052	193604	212191	274025
Australia/Australie	178250	131507	204651	221676	250927
Austria/Autriche	175127	163986	169038	175023	x162684
China/Chine	126753	110568	109253	114279	177006
Korea, Republic of	50151	81077	110688	115835	166194
Norway,SVD,JM	108778	97975	101725	88103	105968
Mexico/Mexique	74890	78701	90906	98234	126821
Malaysia/Malaisie	26187	33951	63003	87514	124731
Slovenia/Slovénia			90262	76739	78986
Thailand/Thaïlande	14150	20800	38016	105660	146910
Brazil/Brésil	20760	25646	34859	51767	56399
Portugal	26313	30857	37847	29568	34350
Greece/Grèce	27761	26931	27299	23539	21611
Ireland/Irlande	23962	23481	26482	24534	33916
So. Africa Customs Un	12798	17249	24072	25933	
Czech Republic				63452	66663
India/Inde	50351	32657	15987	14734	24247
Saudi Arabia	10896	13855	17306	x18926	x26627
Turkey/Turquie	10286	11162	15551	22707	26261
Poland/Pologne	12043	4296	25113	18192	31741
New Zealand	8311	10488	12689	12631	11986
Croatia/Croatie			19664	14485	x5046
United Arab Emirates	16012	7457	10381	x14889	x16216
Czechoslovakia		x13108	x18692		
Indonesia/Indonésie	1074	2651	13522	12634	10528
Uruguay	28316	12473	10159	5922	9625
Israel/Israël	6348	8641	7227	8374	9640
Argentina/Argentine	3260	4432	7147	10907	17138
Hungary/Hongrie	x8018	x6731	x7465	x7648	x7419
Venezuela	11866	5761	7527	8496	8816
Colombia/Colombie	4020	4727	7097	7771	13507
Guatemala	3876	4980	7163	6165	6369
Jordan/Jordanie	5967	5096	4260	8350	6246
Slovakia				x17508	x13719
Egypt/Egypte	4802	8907	3030	5052	4260

(VALUE AS % OF TOTAL)(VALEUR EN % DU TOTAL)

	1985	1986	1987	1988	1989	1990	1991	1992	1993	1994
Africa	4.7	x3.8	x3.6	x3.5	x3.0	x3.4	3.7	x3.4	x3.5	x3.2
Northern Africa	2.9	2.0	1.8	1.7	1.6	1.7	1.9	x1.7	x1.8	x1.6
Americas	14.9	13.9	13.1	11.3	12.5	12.3	13.5	14.6	16.8	17.3
LAIA	3.0	3.1	3.3	3.2	3.4	3.0	3.3	4.3	5.0	5.5
CACM	0.5	0.4	0.3	0.3	0.3	0.3	0.3	0.3	x0.4	x0.4
Asia	17.3	16.0	x18.0	x18.6	17.6	19.4	20.2	21.5	24.5	24.9
Middle East	4.8	x4.5	x3.7	x3.3	x3.3	x4.0	x3.6	x3.9	x4.1	x3.2
Europe	53.6	56.4	53.7	54.1	55.4	55.7	56.3	56.1	49.8	49.0
EEC	42.3	45.1	42.9	43.8	45.2	50.4	51.4	51.0	45.3	44.6
EFTA	9.6	10.0	9.4	9.1	9.0	4.0	3.9	3.8	3.5	3.4
Oceania	1.6	x1.5	x1.3	x1.3	x1.3	x1.3	x1.2	x1.3	x1.4	x1.4
Germany/Allemagne	7.4	8.0	7.3	7.3	7.7	8.6	9.5	9.7	8.0	7.7
France,Monac	7.1	7.8	7.3	7.3	7.3	8.2	8.2	8.0	6.7	6.8
USA/Etats–Unis d'Amer	6.0	5.6	5.1	4.2	4.8	4.8	5.4	5.5	6.0	6.1
United Kingdom	4.5	4.5	4.3	5.0	5.1	5.4	5.2	5.2	5.5	4.8
Italy/Italie	4.5	4.9	4.8	4.7	5.0	5.5	5.5	5.3	5.0	5.1
Belgium–Luxembourg	3.8	3.9	3.9	4.1	4.2	4.6	4.8	4.8	4.2	3.9
Netherlands/Pays–Bas	4.9	5.1	4.9	4.8	4.6	5.0	4.8	4.7	3.8	4.0
Canada	4.5	3.6	3.3	2.9	3.1	3.1	3.6	3.5	4.4	4.6
Hong Kong	1.7	1.6	1.6	1.8	1.8	2.1	2.5	3.0	3.3	3.5
Spain/Espagne	1.1	1.5	1.6	1.8	2.0	2.5	2.7	2.9	2.6	2.8

	1985	1986	1987	1988	1989	1990	1991	1992	1993	1994
Afrique	0.2	0.2	x0.2	x0.2	0.4	0.4	0.3	0.3	0.3	0.1
Afrique du Nord	0.0	x0.0	0.0	0.1	0.2	0.3	0.1	0.1	0.1	0.1
Amériques	9.5	7.1	7.2	7.2	9.7	12.8	13.6	13.6	14.7	14.9
ALAI	1.2	0.8	1.2	1.3	1.4	1.3	1.2	1.2	1.4	1.5
MCAC	0.1	0.0	0.1	0.1	0.1	0.1	0.1	0.1	x0.1	x0.1
Asie	10.2	9.0	x10.1	11.6	11.3	11.5	12.6	13.3	15.4	16.6
Moyen–Orient	0.8	x0.4	x0.7	0.8	x0.6	0.5	0.4	0.4	x0.6	x0.5
Europe	77.8	81.9	79.8	78.0	76.0	73.2	72.0	70.8	66.9	65.8
CEE	69.0	71.2	69.5	68.1	66.9	69.6	69.0	67.0	63.3	62.4
AELE	8.0	9.8	9.6	9.2	8.4	3.0	2.9	2.9	2.9	2.9
Océanie	0.4	0.3	0.3	x0.9	1.7	1.6	1.2	1.6	x1.8	x1.7
Germany/Allemagne	23.2	24.5	24.3	23.5	22.6	23.5	23.6	23.0	21.0	20.6
USA/Etats–Unis d'Amer	6.8	5.2	4.9	4.8	7.2	9.9	10.7	10.7	11.5	11.4
United Kingdom	10.8	9.5	9.8	10.0	9.8	10.7	10.7	10.3	9.6	9.1
Netherlands/Pays–Bas	8.4	8.8	8.6	8.2	7.4	7.8	7.3	7.2	6.6	6.3
France,Monac	8.4	8.2	7.5	7.1	7.2	7.2	7.3	7.0	6.6	6.3
Japan/Japon	6.4	5.8	5.4	5.9	5.9	5.9	6.5	6.5	7.1	7.2
Belgium–Luxembourg	6.1	6.5	6.4	6.4	6.4	6.9	6.6	6.3	6.4	6.9
Italy/Italie	4.1	4.5	3.5	3.5	3.9	4.0	4.1	4.1	4.1	4.2
Spain/Espagne	1.5	1.4	1.6	1.5	1.7	1.7	2.1	2.5	2.6	2.8
Switz.Liecht	2.8	3.0	2.9	2.9	1.9	2.1	2.1	2.1	2.2	2.2

TRADE BY COMMODITY IN THOUSAND U.S. DOLLARS – COMMERCE PAR PRODUIT EN MILLIERS DE DOLLARS E.U

COUNTRIES–PAYS	IMPORTS – IMPORTATIONS 1990	1991	1992	1993	1994
Total	40707884	43416733	50500244	52079205	59103698
Africa	x1965712	x1884922	x2491910	x2354379	x2638274
Northern Africa	783538	706585	x1028919	x931691	x1200996
Americas	5269075	6294220	7603206	8573608	9929200
LAIA	1146262	1495123	1634395	2087984	2756959
CACM	223395	266596	334559	x333108	x357009
Asia	7596763	8465548	9953362	x10591190	x11373054
Middle East	1750239	x1879367	x2121968	x2346541	x2139065
Europe	20290984	23235081	27980486	27542000	31795323
EEC	18523848	21292431	25402310	24632312	28628482
EFTA	1463419	1692865	2159182	2426601	2785277
Oceania	1007855	x1050623	x1287348	x1331540	x1508796
Germany/Allemagne	3396452	4226912	4697786	4221727	5253081
USA/Etats–Unis d'Amer	2539952	3092086	3860723	4198335	4755058
Japan/Japon	2835796	3114112	3672884	3930433	4221960
France, Monac	2646049	3084597	3613578	3587518	4203249
Italy/Italie	2817263	3029695	3721776	3227656	3262451
United Kingdóm	2064220	2422256	2929270	3200098	3430385
Belgium–Luxembourg	1509749	1767455	2112217	2151668	2572013
Netherlands/Pays–Bas	1447321	1540705	2003843	2137660	2804965
Switz.Liecht	1068564	1228701	1648428	1945295	2273779
Spain/Espagne	975703	1172603	1564463	1532783	1846328
Canada	860288	1010655	1293426	1477375	1605200
Austria/Autriche	940322	1014271	1195460	1228777	1341013
Hong Kong	605585	805582	979020	862358	1021829
Sweden/Suède	747577	805130	960166	879205	1004426
Australia/Australie	704945	727671	934708	946906	1100940
Saudi Arabia	640398	622966	845064	x758169	x748163
Denmark/Danemark	493373	551958	666486	605576	726254
Poland/Pologne	162597	435776	513728	654079	737935
Former USSR/Anc. URSS	3880752	x1598950			
Greece/Grèce	343420	387016	511022	588061	644558
Ireland/Irlande	425175	503605	538229	442137	571097
China/Chine	417494	520372	475995	416124	402973
Norway,SVD,JM	364480	432658	473960	446569	474472
Finland/Finlande	416273	445117	453508	411205	482470
Mexico/Mexique	270445	346270	421850	533903	676041
Brazil/Brésil	366958	425829	381827	494356	734005
Korea, Republic of	280447	352662	407688	470112	546411
Portugal	300950	341109	434508	418240	486195
Russian Federation			x628452	x557509	x797459
Iran (Islamic Rp. of)	386000	x393823	x317193	x412281	x222382
So. Africa Customs Un	284279	319202	384127	359007	444290
Algeria/Algérie	340306	217287	442632	366734	509755
Turkey/Turquie	254357	288834	320087	394893	357074
Singapore/Singapour	199784	219181	270997	434557	523993
Hungary/Hongrie	x175917	227243	x316403	x375867	x366660
Thailand/Thaïlande	210285	238667	313814	326862	383193
New Zealand	241505	258646	279467	305406	334359
Argentina/Argentine	96114	182540	274658	356371	495061
India/Inde	258098	227729	313791	257839	298471
Israel/Israël	179117	201609	273459	315723	347039
Malaysia/Malaisie	167713	193618	263332	231955	271765
Pakistan	182928	207286	217844	235310	243117
Philippines	153407	148048	176406	206510	269405
Indonesia/Indonésie	137139	138586	181264	187942	190606
Egypt/Egypte	143386	155494	164897	156493	181409
Tunisia/Tunisie	124540	136400	149468	129516	144171
Venezuela	77269	116685	142832	152411	144053
Ukraine			x19680	x387380	x93174
Nigeria/Nigéria	79191	71106	x170905	x133679	x106361
United Arab Emirates	97646	99349	120879	x142038	x155947

COUNTRIES–PAYS	EXPORTS – EXPORTATIONS 1990	1991	1992	1993	1994
Totale	37753465	41270331	49856862	51661476	58776522
Afrique	99889	85330	126610	128742	92276
Afrique du Nord	39020	42958	62292	64590	81299
Amériques	x5242758	x5563653	x6712124	x7056574	x7668331
ALAI	243050	350575	472264	537903	684352
MCAC	97959	113882	132667	x121078	x140236
Asie	3195478	3756537	4365696	4848781	5670921
Moyen–Orient	211618	155604	171350	253687	278129
Europe	28157593	30893439	37805275	38364736	44081338
CEE	23169963	25993728	31526973	32120689	37308566
AELE	4495060	4799255	5874636	5856026	6384572
Océanie	x257139	x331994	x403049	x481359	x559381
Germany/Allemagne	5861194	6575126	7461155	7599870	8722710
Switz.Liecht	4359698	4658190	5685607	5661952	6194008
USA/Etats–Unis d'Amer	4176948	4679015	5446222	5841792	6184490
United Kingdom	4040354	4515065	5254374	5476915	6009642
France, Monac	3665154	3955696	4828672	4964743	5414831
Belgium–Luxembourg	1632882	1911686	2549663	2720307	3336087
Italy/Italie	1516920	1629241	2472144	2491494	2759299
Sweden/Suède	1311681	1724648	2116048	2177766	2469896
Netherlands/Pays–Bas	1377061	1513097	1826222	1875981	2780660
Denmark/Danemark	1159996	1200325	1517467	1378666	1615297
Ireland/Irlande	960305	1150583	1531653	1392442	1811732
Japan/Japon	878501	1089475	1366526	1472559	1547862
China/Chine	642747	773787	895143	905057	1185298
Austria/Autriche	695775	781188	894899	890345	x973320
Spain/Espagne	632511	736992	781453	837071	1058907
Hong Kong	483312	659800	792151	738260	833011
India/Inde	452812	483471	431241	482878	585763
Australia/Australie	221666	287217	352155	433836	511430
Canada	256529	254340	386756	394972	503437
Singapore/Singapour	209422	220652	247473	371137	494366
Poland/Pologne	163254	322468	119619	206627	200111
Mexico/Mexique	89034	128346	219344	235693	298035
Norway,SVD,JM	134746	140838	188578	193347	189994
Korea, Republic of	115355	139229	171390	181244	218501
Slovenia/Slovénia			215437	234691	283071
Finland/Finlande	155790	139368	146907	155635	192109
Hungary/Hongrie	x144536	x134160	x156603	x147786	x140593
Israel/Israël	76164	95745	118994	187910	276378
Bulgaria/Bulgarie	x271359	x74446	94040	171054	93112
Brazil/Brésil	77989	99710	111031	110810	132806
Portugal	94934	89443	106185	85784	92595
Bahamas	x40528	926			x33194
Jordan/Jordanie	61962	63470	88422	120142	138903
Croatia/Croatie			127410	99664	x74174
Thailand/Thaïlande	27056	35719	58011	126842	86868
Argentina/Argentine	34300	57299	61093	87531	111923
Guatemala	53482	61857	63388	59258	64685
Greece/Grèce	64800	70663	40126	73671	71482
Turkey/Turquie	74200	53498	48237	76369	78090
Malaysia/Malaisie	37343	43779	47054	50822	68079
New Zealand	34506	43669	49682	42733	46549
Czech Republic				128241	148410
Czechoslovakia		x68428	x59449		
Cuba	x356732	x100438	x6099	x19007	x100606
Bermuda/Bermudes	48774	39652	75822	x1685	x1680
Russian Federation			x33001	x81653	x93459
Slovakia				x104323	x88679
Costa Rica	28517	35984	39577	x25792	x39308
So. Africa Customs Un	43897	25836	37670	35914	
Yugoslavia SFR	483233	x89644			

(VALUE AS % OF TOTAL)(VALEUR EN % DU TOTAL)

	1985	1986	1987	1988	1989	1990	1991	1992	1993	1994
Africa	6.1	x6.6	x5.9	x5.2	x5.5	x4.8	x4.3	x5.0	x4.5	x4.5
Northern Africa	2.9	2.7	2.4	2.1	2.5	1.9	1.6	x2.0	x1.8	x2.0
Americas	18.4	16.0	15.5	15.6	12.5	13.0	14.4	15.0	16.5	16.8
LAIA	3.8	3.2	3.2	2.6	2.7	2.8	3.4	3.2	4.0	4.7
CACM	1.4	1.1	x0.9	0.7	0.7	0.5	0.6	0.7	x0.6	x0.6
Asia	18.7	19.3	19.2	x20.6	19.5	18.7	19.5	19.7	x20.4	x19.2
Middle East	4.2	x5.6	4.8	x4.8	x4.4	4.3	x4.3	x4.2	x4.5	x3.6
Europe	45.3	45.8	46.8	46.7	49.1	49.8	53.5	55.4	52.9	53.8
EEC	36.7	37.1	37.8	38.2	40.7	45.5	49.0	50.3	47.3	48.4
EFTA	8.0	8.2	8.5	8.0	7.9	3.6	3.9	4.3	4.7	4.7
Oceania	2.1	1.9	x2.0	2.2	x2.3	2.5	x2.4	x2.5	x2.6	x2.5
Germany/Allemagne	7.4	7.5	7.5	7.2	7.5	8.3	9.7	9.3	8.1	8.9
USA/Etats–Unis d'Amer	9.4	8.4	8.3	9.3	6.0	6.2	7.1	7.6	8.1	8.0
Japan/Japon	7.1	7.0	7.0	7.7	7.7	7.0	7.2	7.3	7.5	7.1
France, Monac	4.3	4.3	4.5	4.9	5.6	6.5	7.1	7.2	6.9	7.1
Italy/Italie	5.3	5.4	5.3	5.8	6.1	6.9	7.0	7.4	6.2	5.5
United Kingdom	4.2	4.0	4.3	4.5	4.9	5.1	5.6	5.8	6.1	5.8
Belgium–Luxembourg	3.0	2.9	3.0	2.9	3.3	3.7	4.1	4.2	4.1	4.4
Netherlands/Pays–Bas	3.2	3.3	3.4	3.2	3.2	3.6	3.5	4.0	4.1	4.7
Switz.Liecht	2.7	2.9	2.9	2.6	2.3	2.6	2.8	3.3	3.7	3.8
Spain/Espagne	1.3	1.5	1.7	1.8	2.1	2.4	2.7	3.1	2.9	3.1

	1985	1986	1987	1988	1989	1990	1991	1992	1993	1994
Afrique	0.4	0.3	x0.3	x0.2	0.2	0.2	0.2	0.3	0.3	0.2
Afrique du Nord	0.1	0.1	0.1	0.1	0.1	0.1	0.1	0.1	0.1	0.1
Amériques	18.7	16.3	14.1	15.0	x13.6	x13.8	x13.5	x13.5	x13.7	x13.1
ALAI	0.9	0.6	0.7	0.6	0.7	0.6	0.8	0.9	1.0	1.2
MCAC	0.5	0.4	0.3	0.4	0.3	0.3	0.3	0.3	x0.2	x0.2
Asie	7.3	6.7	7.1	7.7	8.8	8.4	9.1	8.8	9.4	9.6
Moyen–Orient	0.4	0.4	0.4	0.4	0.9	0.6	0.4	0.3	0.5	0.5
Europe	68.3	71.4	70.9	71.1	73.2	74.6	74.9	75.8	74.3	75.0
CEE	53.9	55.4	54.8	55.2	56.1	61.4	63.0	63.2	62.2	63.5
AELE	13.3	15.1	15.3	15.1	15.5	11.9	11.6	11.8	11.3	10.9
Océanie	0.6	x0.5	x0.6	x0.6	x0.7	x0.7	x0.8	x0.8	x0.9	x0.9
Germany/Allemagne	13.3	14.5	14.5	14.7	14.4	15.5	15.9	15.0	14.7	14.8
Switz.Liecht	9.0	10.4	10.8	10.3	10.2	11.5	11.3	11.4	11.0	10.5
USA/Etats–Unis d'Amer	16.0	14.4	12.2	13.2	11.3	11.1	11.3	10.9	11.3	10.5
United Kingdom	10.4	9.9	9.5	9.7	10.0	10.7	10.9	10.5	10.6	10.2
France, Monac	8.7	8.8	8.5	8.2	8.9	9.7	9.6	9.7	9.6	9.2
Belgium–Luxembourg	3.7	3.9	3.9	3.8	3.9	4.3	4.6	5.1	5.3	5.7
Italy/Italie	4.8	4.6	4.2	4.0	3.8	4.0	3.9	5.0	4.8	4.7
Sweden/Suède	2.3	2.5	2.5	2.8	3.2	3.5	4.2	4.2	4.2	4.2
Netherlands/Pays–Bas	3.4	3.6	3.8	3.8	3.3	3.6	3.7	3.7	3.6	4.7
Denmark/Danemark	2.5	2.7	2.8	2.7	2.7	3.1	2.9	3.0	2.7	2.7

TRADE BY COMMODITY IN THOUSAND U.S. DOLLARS – COMMERCE PAR PRODUIT EN MILLIERS DE DOLLARS E.U

COUNTRIES–PAYS	IMPORTS – IMPORTATIONS 1990	1991	1992	1993	1994
Total	3882792	4042173	4300117	4196916	4837700
Africa	x179201	207810	x193954	x193597	x208846
Northern Africa	53846	47764	44278	47993	55171
Americas	572143	607988	697157	772242	837922
LAIA	158487	182479	207543	256786	278190
CACM	25879	26491	32865	x38153	x37938
Asia	881602	1027399	1005842	1128643	1307315
Middle East	x99483	x130019	x127058	x173050	x174301
Europe	1964763	2024288	2257128	1944563	2311733
EEC	1793953	1858589	2067543	1796767	2101621
EFTA	141142	141298	158726	127809	184008
Oceania	x41959	x48750	x45751	x56864	x51318
Germany/Allemagne	336993	366714	377538	320333	382302
France,Monac	358195	343322	385775	323975	397039
USA/Etats–Unis d'Amer	291958	295451	342502	335230	366243
United Kingdom	298083	295479	331466	301112	338951
Japan/Japon	239136	282440	271167	298748	341137
Italy/Italie	166037	191296	230209	218231	243802
Netherlands/Pays–Bas	160038	181669	202417	177439	196617
Spain/Espagne	127734	140856	163089	142617	176258
Hong Kong	109222	128212	146076	141625	156797
Korea, Republic of	100363	115126	101937	98190	122647
Switz.Liecht	105647	96980	107999	103923	118666
Indonesia/Indonésie	77953	94402	82883	100065	130420
Canada	70149	77153	84878	112504	125591
Belgium–Luxembourg	90279	87154	100932	84837	92459
Ireland/Irlande	93890	88788	92697	62872	78605
Thailand/Thaïlande	47195	55337	56412	67378	88760
So. Africa Customs Un	53903	55883	57673	55008	64987
Mexico/Mexique	37264	44788	57483	63849	73901
Philippines	43957	44516	47561	62016	69692
Singapore/Singapour	40815	43996	49142	52548	64868
Nigeria/Nigéria	x32712	51955	x48261	x45377	x35757
Austria/Autriche	39529	41794	47080	39691	47050
Venezuela	26652	34508	43735	39903	31428
Norway,SVD,JM	34852	43279	49799	23149	64534
Turkey/Turquie	31808	30734	34200	49478	58528
Malaysia/Malaisie	28468	31016	34767	36781	47845
Poland/Pologne	8016	17875	36659	41937	53899
Australia/Australie	25136	29268	25627	37560	28962
Denmark/Danemark	25092	28546	32115	30538	35725
Portugal	35065	31618	33290	25768	31533
Brazil/Brésil	30533	26247	18372	45978	36642
Greece/Grèce	25587	24509	30309	28975	30773
Saudi Arabia	12271	21480	25102	x36631	x42792
Israel/Israël	20890	22781	26337	27236	30505
Chile/Chili	18590	21028	25411	26201	29391
Sweden/Suède	22494	22826	24878	24047	30715
Former USSR/Anc. URSS	152681	x70460			
Colombia/Colombie	15728	16667	20477	27927	37235
China/Chine	15247	20760	21970	20381	20451
Hungary/Hongrie	x25699	13774	x23768	x25191	x20759
India/Inde	28962	29833	11712	14096	17536
Russian Federation			x36538	x18315	x21111
Argentina/Argentine	6658	11929	16201	20346	29371
Egypt/Egypte	24143	19497	13581	13299	15689
Iran (Islamic Rp. of)		x13937	x17239	x15191	x8655
Finland/Finlande	14936	14018	15746	16331	19792
Guatemala	11376	12664	15965	17124	15425
Czechoslovakia	21369	x17320	x25324		
Syrian Arab Republic	12100	x21030	6008	x15085	x16537
United Arab Emirates	7923	11314	12777	x16631	x17451

COUNTRIES–PAYS	EXPORTS – EXPORTATIONS 1990	1991	1992	1993	1994
Totale	3741270	3853708	4101592	4214110	4759787
Afrique	x48715	x43995	x54075	49770	x46905
Afrique du Nord	22207	22418	30024	27187	29326
Amériques	649881	672722	700010	842121	967745
ALAI	109049	112430	133259	147362	163185
MCAC	3373	3099	2976	5545	2444
Asie	512221	557014	502184	547214	650488
Moyen–Orient	17633	8479	10566	x11328	x12265
Europe	2461113	2531532	2800195	2719160	3050619
CEE	1990194	2056134	2275164	2195058	2426665
AELE	465504	470700	507744	512979	611717
Océanie	x15766	x23099	x23403	x24313	x31032
USA/Etats–Unis d'Amer	515314	540369	541684	661032	764113
France,Monac	527386	527294	544932	513996	574377
Switz.Liecht	464379	468619	506624	512393	611066
Germany/Allemagne	383100	422791	466595	447230	518669
United Kingdom	320628	364562	401219	367006	441077
Ireland/Irlande	291482	270800	313452	301905	320021
Netherlands/Pays–Bas	254171	250599	289198	335360	307968
Hong Kong	122346	125770	135106	136578	141224
Japan/Japon	114608	124263	121825	140221	170294
China/Chine	99715	88740	91343	93580	117145
Italy/Italie	69678	69907	75524	72814	77625
Spain/Espagne	46267	53634	65684	65739	78172
Indonesia/Indonésie	60205	100627	28453	34813	41629
Brazil/Brésil	43527	44524	54878	61623	70217
Belgium–Luxembourg	53007	50950	63934	39957	48369
Singapore/Singapour	23221	28652	41566	51714	71042
India/Inde	42294	51274	29696	32321	44202
Argentina/Argentine	22689	25062	29190	31465	35382
Austria/Autriche	20116	20166	25831	21816	x23113
Mexico/Mexique	16835	16785	21634	28397	26708
Australia/Australie	14354	21473	21377	23017	29506
Bulgaria/Bulgarie	x28739	x11799	x13720	x23417	x5621
Thailand/Thaïlande	11413	13517	18081	16026	14024
Morocco/Maroc	13158	14616	16046	16096	16077
Canada	10469	10140	14285	21597	27230
Denmark/Danemark	11018	12213	13626	15232	17484
Israel/Israël	5935	4976	12788	16447	22823
Paraguay	16793	14644	12051	6578	8468
Sweden/Suède	7721	8944	10801	10209	14236
Egypt/Egypte	5425	4554	10430	7781	10028
Slovenia/Slovénia			12714	8103	10361
Turkey/Turquie	8000	5864	6411	6714	7568
Peru/Pérou	4627	5186	4474	6057	7112
So. Africa Customs Un	4481	4583	5847	5077	
Comoros/Comores	x6981	x5577	x5109	3342	x7516
Russian Federation			x6262	x7619	x5321
Viet Nam	x2670	x2450	x5664	x4489	x5015
Colombia/Colombie	1416	2571	3938	4745	7425
Madagascar	3635	3390	3426	3980	6476
Guatemala	2227	2726	2414	5126	1913
Tunisia/Tunisie	3603	3240	3532	3309	3213
Cote d'Ivoire	x3636	x3119	x3454	x2546	x1972
Sri Lanka	3002	2786	2824	2839	3606
Venezuela	438	581	2897	3989	4173
Reunion/Réunion	2915	1621	2297	3400	655
Haiti/Haïti	x2770	x1580	x2976	x2516	x4253
Former USSR/Anc. URSS	x18729	x7007			
Korea Dem People's Rp	x6421	x3193	x1190	x2375	x1148
Hungary/Hongrie	x2207	x2147	x2584	x1904	x2043
Greece/Grèce	2223	2250	1861	2254	3651

(VALUE AS % OF TOTAL)(VALEUR EN % DU TOTAL)

	1985	1986	1987	1988	1989	1990	1991	1992	1993	1994
Africa	4.0	x4.7	x4.4	x4.4	x4.1	x4.6	5.2	x4.5	x4.6	x4.3
Northern Africa	1.5	1.4	1.1	1.1	1.3	1.4	1.2	1.0	1.1	1.1
Americas	23.5	22.0	19.1	19.1	15.8	14.7	15.0	16.2	18.4	17.4
LAIA	6.8	5.9	5.2	4.8	4.9	4.1	4.5	4.8	6.1	5.8
CACM	0.1	0.6	0.6	0.5	0.6	0.7	0.7	0.8	x0.9	x0.8
Asia	18.4	20.0	x21.9	x21.9	23.8	22.7	25.5	23.4	26.9	27.0
Middle East	1.9	x3.5	x3.9	x3.1	x3.8	x2.6	x3.2	x3.0	x4.1	x3.6
Europe	47.9	46.7	45.5	46.3	48.3	50.6	50.1	52.5	46.3	47.8
EEC	42.0	41.1	40.0	40.5	42.8	46.2	46.0	48.1	42.8	43.4
EFTA	5.1	4.9	4.7	5.1	4.9	3.6	3.5	3.7	3.0	3.8
Oceania	1.7	x1.8	x1.4	x1.2	x1.2	x1.0	x1.2	x1.1	x1.3	x1.1
Germany/Allemagne	7.5	7.6	7.5	7.9	7.7	8.7	9.1	8.8	7.6	7.9
France,Monac	9.0	8.8	7.8	8.3	9.0	9.2	8.5	9.0	7.7	8.2
USA/Etats–Unis d'Amer	14.2	12.5	11.0	11.3	7.6	7.5	7.3	8.0	8.0	7.6
United Kingdom	7.8	6.7	6.3	6.5	7.1	7.7	7.3	7.7	7.2	7.0
Japan/Japon	5.1	4.7	4.4	4.6	6.5	6.2	7.0	6.3	7.1	7.1
Italy/Italie	3.8	4.3	4.4	4.1	4.1	4.3	4.7	5.4	5.2	5.0
Netherlands/Pays–Bas	3.5	3.3	3.2	3.3	3.5	4.1	4.5	4.7	4.2	4.1
Spain/Espagne	2.7	3.0	2.9	2.9	3.0	3.3	3.5	3.8	3.4	3.6
Hong Kong	2.6	2.4	2.9	3.2	3.4	2.8	3.2	3.4	3.4	3.2
Korea, Republic of	2.0	2.1	1.9	2.2	2.4	2.6	2.8	2.4	2.3	2.5

	1985	1986	1987	1988	1989	1990	1991	1992	1993	1994
Afrique	2.3	2.2	x2.2	x2.0	x1.8	x1.3	x1.1	x1.3	1.2	x1.0
Afrique du Nord	1.5	1.3	0.9	0.6	0.7	0.6	0.6	0.7	0.6	0.6
Amériques	20.2	17.4	15.4	15.6	16.6	17.4	17.5	17.1	20.0	20.3
ALAI	3.9	2.9	2.6	2.7	2.6	2.9	2.9	3.2	3.5	3.4
MCAC	0.1	0.1	0.1	0.2	0.1	0.1	0.1	0.1	0.1	0.1
Asie	9.7	10.2	13.9	14.8	14.5	13.7	14.5	12.3	13.0	13.7
Moyen–Orient	0.6	0.7	x1.0	0.5	0.5	0.5	0.2	0.3	x0.3	x0.3
Europe	67.3	69.8	65.3	64.1	64.3	65.8	65.7	68.3	64.5	64.1
CEE	53.8	55.1	51.3	51.1	52.0	53.2	53.4	55.5	52.1	51.0
AELE	13.1	14.5	13.9	12.9	12.2	12.4	12.2	12.4	12.2	12.9
Océanie	0.4	x0.3	x0.5	x0.4	x0.3	x0.4	x0.6	x0.5	x0.6	x0.6
USA/Etats–Unis d'Amer	15.7	13.6	12.1	12.1	13.0	13.8	14.0	13.2	15.7	16.1
France,Monac	16.9	17.6	16.4	15.2	14.5	14.1	13.7	13.3	12.2	12.1
Switz.Liecht	12.4	13.7	13.1	12.1	11.4	12.4	12.2	12.4	12.2	12.8
Germany/Allemagne	7.7	8.9	8.6	9.4	9.7	10.2	11.0	11.4	10.6	10.9
United Kingdom	11.1	10.3	9.6	9.5	9.2	8.6	9.5	9.8	8.7	9.3
Ireland/Irlande	5.5	5.5	4.6	5.1	6.5	7.8	7.0	7.6	7.2	6.7
Netherlands/Pays–Bas	7.6	8.0	7.3	7.1	7.0	6.8	6.5	7.1	8.0	6.5
Hong Kong	2.9	2.6	3.0	3.6	3.6	3.3	3.3	3.3	3.2	3.0
Japan/Japon	2.6	2.6	2.7	3.0	3.2	3.1	3.2	3.0	3.3	3.6
China/Chine			3.1	3.3	3.5	2.7	2.3	2.2	2.2	2.5

TRADE BY COMMODITY IN THOUSAND U.S. DOLLARS – COMMERCE PAR PRODUIT EN MILLIERS DE DOLLARS E.U

COUNTRIES–PAYS	IMPORTS – IMPORTATIONS 1990	1991	1992	1993	1994
Total	10475960	10443961	12145970	12446255	14358200
Africa	x193590	x136565	x250148	x223873	x223461
Northern Africa	36759	20151	x39958	x33938	x47517
Americas	1436290	1660529	x2074781	x2288995	x2584803
LAIA	127986	215788	325893	418815	572752
CACM	25467	31511	43492	x54079	x66751
Asia	1719315	1829861	2206925	x2524454	x2997733
Middle East	591961	x568181	706226	x776126	x776175
Europe	5300382	6022625	6971990	6689162	7755881
EEC	4758361	5426075	6291034	6016149	6906814
EFTA	451976	496015	548602	550582	687249
Oceania	x252009	x261788	x303930	x323091	x374605
Germany/Allemagne	910405	1103080	1240773	1146652	1258471
USA/Etats–Unis d'Amer	825422	887087	1113498	1179858	1250303
United Kingdom	647700	697549	819350	836269	925836
Italy/Italie	692783	749841	826070	709831	801552
France,Monac	530358	598486	725245	704554	966519
Belgium–Luxembourg	416740	455745	501465	542591	560153
Netherlands/Pays–Bas	421950	470592	522038	471851	513335
Japan/Japon	356221	429781	436604	493049	623506
Canada	262157	329129	388391	433980	512713
Switz.Liecht	326076	362396	396992	388567	499213
Spain/Espagne	214288	331736	416479	373187	473818
Hong Kong	261567	278694	334779	415099	538889
Singapore/Singapour	216241	264498	351696	388191	464243
Austria/Autriche	219093	236583	273904	284648	335086
Saudi Arabia	240454	244701	251931	x219365	x237217
Sweden/Suède	196128	202879	226158	240370	258471
Australia/Australie	160451	167954	197993	211853	248732
Mexico/Mexique	74712	123868	197201	227072	277818
Denmark/Danemark	120316	148039	203114	193745	219986
United Arab Emirates	144053	121532	165071	x234255	x237689
Portugal	87795	115127	160915	144206	155409
Norway,SVD,JM	113786	119747	137907	149674	175409
Russian Federation			x197260	x204996	x385767
Ireland/Irlande	110196	117998	140508	133589	163843
Greece/Grèce	79996	99302	134706	148626	172443
Poland/Pologne	27799	112241	140080	127655	135715
Malaysia/Malaisie	94695	104723	124818	127685	158499
Former USSR/Anc. URSS	1387514	x313295			
Finland/Finlande	110612	99117	100310	86030	101891
Korea, Republic of	47281	64131	71002	105787	155776
Hungary/Hongrie	x35409	41522	x85298	x110368	x110758
Kuwait/ Koweït	43519	26250	79227	78804	86089
Andorra/Andorre	x53521	x56531	x58298	x58587	x54744
New Zealand	47950	51137	58300	62983	79817
Bahrain/Bahreïn	x48796	x49080	x53632	x68044	x18699
Nigeria/Nigéria	x54855	8139	x83112	x57803	x39482
Bahamas	34549	39556	x47037	x37948	x26679
Czechoslovakia	36395	x41889	x81224		
Thailand/Thaïlande	25166	29348	38647	50210	55093
Israel/Israël	34270	34161	39789	44082	63115
Oman	29445	30770	36151	36629	39769
Ukraine			x9311	x77114	x33680
Lebanon/Liban	x25755	x34593	x24008	x25154	x54111
Chile/Chili	10404	18993	25424	33512	38156
Argentina/Argentine	2711	9644	25660	40828	61012
Czech Republic				70240	86478
Panama	21906	21667	22474	24068	26830
Turkey/Turquie	14149	14713	21360	31899	25186
Reunion/Réunion	18294	19147	24289	23087	23279
Cyprus/Chypre	16503	17776	25052	21415	27804

COUNTRIES–PAYS	EXPORTS – EXPORTATIONS 1990	1991	1992	1993	1994
Totale	10295771	10901551	12755226	13260528	15735586
Afrique	86368	96338	62102	64970	36396
Afrique du Nord	63732	64449	31412	35114	34655
Amériques	1109664	1387113	1618030	1945117	2360243
ALAI	47037	54684	107897	171470	225693
MCAC	20625	24920	28754	28724	x38997
Asie	1408429	1020433	1055054	1177638	1395261
Moyen–Orient	580746	154240	66224	x92607	x116163
Europe	7505710	8288991	9876044	9860282	11676672
CEE	7135725	7870497	9348937	9283105	11014651
AELE	335014	403909	469010	526024	604873
Océanie	68149	x80007	x107607	x122273	x154742
France,Monac	3345791	3554169	4243042	4125366	4836197
United Kingdom	1073933	1236246	1391157	1372801	1766601
Germany/Allemagne	986251	1125549	1446048	1365727	1659757
USA/Etats–Unis d'Amer	901098	1133851	1298622	1503669	1808330
Belgium–Luxembourg	453117	497653	538640	641914	657427
Italy/Italie	406614	417136	501758	501504	643283
Switz.Liecht	328171	394154	458026	517732	595037
Ireland/Irlande	191684	281506	343813	372038	423074
Netherlands/Pays–Bas	227260	256489	295486	305811	380376
Japan/Japon	183372	211143	255352	288032	306866
Spain/Espagne	157298	173986	209007	229598	291646
Singapore/Singapour	82348	127858	191953	233009	302465
Hong Kong	159540	175086	183238	189185	232157
Canada	102822	115936	160059	216902	265131
Denmark/Danemark	95578	101287	123075	116294	97260
China/Chine	148902	74470	89400	121917	105529
Sweden/Suède	66870	81829	98312	92670	110444
Austria/Autriche	49518	63931	93632	84226	x69871
India/Inde	112215	94483	57399	68637	89084
Australia/Australie	38403	44187	54797	64482	94504
Indonesia/Indonésie	49380	52264	77067	29333	36146
Thailand/Thaïlande	17781	52308	39218	47241	61947
New Zealand	28040	34300	44828	50803	56631
Malaysia/Malaisie	32196	35582	42113	41008	48355
Syrian Arab Republic	494744	97493	2959	x619	x310
Brazil/Brésil	13076	15684	25854	44507	38350
Mexico/Mexique	5284	13266	28134	42294	53445
Greece/Grèce	29120	34196	23413	25761	23095
Finland/Finlande	37645	28562	26144	27353	32586
Korea, Republic of	18150	18566	25298	30847	44612
Slovenia/Slovénia			37023	32376	44585
Argentina/Argentine	817	3148	23274	36791	71797
So. Africa Customs Un	10426	16754	24276	18522	
Chile/Chili	4619	12637	19669	27210	28044
Guatemala	14093	16524	19161	19463	25574
Portugal	14651	17563	15409	22043	23034
Egypt/Egypte	40339	34480	10422	9544	11886
Poland/Pologne	32309	17071	19390	17621	30850
Cyprus/Chypre	14151	15082	17085	16328	19929
United Arab Emirates	37127	1569	8571	x36233	x49834
Israel/Israël	13392	9710	12626	21050	28759
Tunisia/Tunisie	10381	14374	10784	16131	14733
Bahamas	19775	30186	x3984	x5769	x852
Saudi Arabia	7924	13918	12052	x10855	x17509
Malta/Malte	4922	11522	13256	10502	x10191
Czech Republic				33910	40228
Norway,SVD,JM	6823	9744	10974	8282	9834
Morocco/Maroc	13009	14683	9436	4447	5279
Bulgaria/Bulgarie		x2341	2388	20663	26337
Venezuela	20406	7122	5441	8551	10958

(VALUE AS % OF TOTAL)(VALEUR EN % DU TOTAL)

	1985	1986	1987	1988	1989	1990	1991	1992	1993	1994
Africa	1.3	x2.1	x1.8	x1.8	x1.7	x1.8	x1.3	x2.1	x1.8	x1.5
Northern Africa	0.4	0.2	0.2	0.3	0.4	0.4	0.2	x0.3	x0.3	x0.3
Americas	16.4	14.5	x13.1	x13.6	14.3	13.7	15.9	x17.1	x18.4	x18.0
LAIA	0.8	0.6	0.5	0.5	0.9	1.2	2.1	2.7	3.4	4.0
CACM	0.6	0.4	0.3	0.4	0.3	0.2	0.3	0.4	x0.4	x0.5
Asia	17.7	x16.5	x15.8	16.9	x16.8	16.4	17.5	18.1	x20.3	x20.9
Middle East	8.3	x7.7	x6.4	6.5	x6.5	5.7	x5.4	5.8	x6.2	x5.4
Europe	50.9	53.5	54.2	52.6	51.2	50.6	57.7	57.4	53.7	54.0
EEC	41.3	43.0	43.7	42.6	41.7	45.4	52.0	51.8	48.3	48.1
EFTA	9.5	9.9	9.8	9.3	8.9	4.3	4.7	4.5	4.4	4.8
Oceania	2.4	x2.2	x2.3	x2.3	x2.5	x2.4	x2.5	x2.5	x2.6	x2.6
Germany/Allemagne	8.1	8.6	8.6	8.1	7.9	8.7	10.6	10.2	9.2	8.8
USA/Etats–Unis d'Amer	10.3	9.1	8.3	8.3	8.6	7.9	8.5	9.2	9.5	8.7
United Kingdom	6.9	6.7	6.4	6.4	6.1	6.2	6.7	6.7	6.7	6.4
Italy/Italie	5.6	6.1	6.4	6.5	6.0	6.6	7.2	6.8	5.7	5.6
France,Monac	4.6	4.7	4.6	4.7	4.7	5.1	5.7	6.0	5.7	6.7
Belgium–Luxembourg	4.3	4.2	4.2	3.8	3.6	4.0	4.4	4.1	4.4	3.9
Netherlands/Pays–Bas	3.7	4.1	4.4	3.9	3.9	4.0	4.5	4.3	3.8	3.6
Japan/Japon	2.5	2.6	2.7	3.0	3.3	3.4	4.1	3.6	4.0	4.3
Canada	2.7	2.4	2.0	2.2	2.4	2.5	3.2	3.2	3.5	3.6
Switz.Liecht	3.2	3.4	3.3	3.3	3.1	3.1	3.5	3.3	3.1	3.5

	1985	1986	1987	1988	1989	1990	1991	1992	1993	1994
Afrique	0.8	0.5	x0.5	0.8	0.8	0.8	0.9	0.5	0.5	0.2
Afrique du Nord	0.3	0.1	0.2	0.6	0.5	0.6	0.6	0.2	0.3	0.2
Amériques	10.1	8.2	7.8	8.6	10.9	10.8	12.8	12.6	14.7	15.0
ALAI	0.5	0.4	0.4	0.4	0.6	0.5	0.5	0.8	1.3	1.4
MCAC	0.4	0.3	0.3	0.4	0.3	0.2	0.2	0.2	0.2	x0.2
Asie	8.4	10.0	x10.6	11.8	11.7	13.7	9.3	8.3	8.8	8.8
Moyen–Orient	1.6	3.7	x3.0	3.1	3.8	5.6	1.4	0.5	x0.7	x0.7
Europe	78.4	79.3	77.8	76.0	73.6	72.9	76.0	77.4	74.4	74.2
CEE	72.8	73.5	72.5	70.5	68.1	69.3	72.2	73.3	70.0	70.0
AELE	4.9	5.3	4.9	4.9	4.6	3.3	3.7	3.7	4.0	3.8
Océanie	0.8	x0.7	x0.7	0.8	x0.8	0.6	x0.7	x0.9	x1.0	x1.0
France,Monac	34.1	34.1	33.6	33.1	32.6	32.5	32.6	33.3	31.1	30.7
United Kingdom	12.5	11.9	11.6	11.7	10.1	10.4	11.3	10.9	10.4	11.2
Germany/Allemagne	9.8	10.7	10.5	10.1	9.6	9.6	10.3	11.3	10.3	10.5
USA/Etats–Unis d'Amer	8.1	6.4	6.0	6.5	8.5	8.8	10.4	10.2	11.3	11.5
Belgium–Luxembourg	4.7	4.5	4.9	4.3	4.1	4.4	4.6	4.2	4.8	4.2
Italy/Italie	3.7	3.8	3.8	3.4	3.8	3.9	3.8	3.9	3.8	4.1
Switz.Liecht	2.9	3.3	3.1	3.3	3.0	3.2	3.6	3.6	3.9	3.8
Ireland/Irlande	1.7	1.8	1.7	1.4	1.6	1.9	2.6	2.7	2.8	2.7
Netherlands/Pays–Bas	2.1	2.4	2.4	2.3	2.1	2.2	2.4	2.3	2.3	2.4
Japan/Japon	2.0	2.1	2.1	2.1	1.9	1.8	1.9	2.0	2.2	2.0

TRADE BY COMMODITY IN THOUSAND U.S. DOLLARS – COMMERCE PAR PRODUIT EN MILLIERS DE DOLLARS E.U

COUNTRIES–PAYS	IMPORTS – IMPORTATIONS 1990	1991	1992	1993	1994
Total	6891363	7178697	8094781	7966996	9048743
Africa	x340909	x232663	x298297	x301665	x324246
Northern Africa	120977	61418	x61397	x78522	x101392
Americas	757328	896858	1038573	x1208192	x1433218
LAIA	144582	183714	254785	319657	417853
CACM	34018	40206	57804	x60293	x72494
Asia	1141020	1275507	1398042	x1551010	x1705043
Middle East	x281918	x289438	x333359	x391862	x323698
Europe	4039866	4166869	4886211	4386053	5017590
EEC	3633413	3807411	4457499	4002999	4593645
EFTA	284168	284885	305287	279855	303351
Oceania	x132775	x133954	x159163	x157535	x185358
France,Monac	650689	652539	740403	617523	733770
Germany/Allemagne	539569	602772	693253	575634	754683
United Kingdom	402196	416909	506476	462961	511750
Belgium–Luxembourg	395093	410827	474902	448976	520023
Netherlands/Pays–Bas	336917	335365	409682	457356	529833
Italy/Italie	315299	339399	385857	347046	373017
USA/Etats–Unis d'Amer	263109	286430	315460	356180	446864
Canada	189119	234865	293083	338988	363790
Sweden/Suède	194977	194051	235644	220347	220738
Switz.Liecht	174605	180902	193529	172555	180847
Austria/Autriche	168911	169333	188304	186903	198452
Spain/Espagne	137182	162589	208121	170232	204076
Hong Kong	132566	154705	178833	174787	209166
Japan/Japon	129765	152319	145004	173313	222289
Ireland/Irlande	111208	126908	151262	112318	122455
Korea, Republic of	106064	126136	116069	125932	149190
Denmark/Danemark	120603	117307	129744	117819	124469
Poland/Pologne	4635	69323	161314	125648	127006
China/Chine	63422	103805	117245	122837	163442
Portugal	81984	91180	125021	111727	114602
Greece/Grèce	77226	99059	108386	90244	95559
Norway,SVD,JM	101687	95086	102594	98957	114050
Singapore/Singapour	85404	82310	95644	108371	114752
Former USSR/Anc. URSS	354762	x277258			
Finland/Finlande	101558	89172	100444	83911	90218
Thailand/Thaïlande	67229	75432	88963	97867	109634
Mexico/Mexique	36741	44573	86176	118798	138064
Australia/Australie	67132	67434	84908	85036	110683
Malaysia/Malaisie	52364	64750	78568	80531	90192
Saudi Arabia	61819	60733	68657	x67876	x63762
Hungary/Hongrie	x38068	46754	x70838	x77543	x70194
Turkey/Turquie	38151	56418	68758	59566	50640
Israel/Israël	55939	49158	57003	57541	66568
Indonesia/Indonésie	36131	40970	50300	60117	78173
Russian Federation			x65652	x71889	x91574
United Arab Emirates	44984	27590	29223	x80348	x70381
Argentina/Argentine	22162	28599	45648	55717	85369
Brazil/Brésil	27844	33127	34567	44537	58757
So. Africa Customs Un	36423	34007	39481	36828	42830
Iran (Islamic Rp. of)		x29878	x34091	x39575	x14602
New Zealand	30633	29015	34250	39458	42968
Nigeria/Nigéria	x39538	7800	x49882	x38964	x21436
Czechoslovakia	26295	x32090	x59555		
Kuwait/ Koweït	19018	15778	35105	39745	44940
Czech Republic				74703	77294
Reunion/Réunion	24182	21480	26487	25214	24074
Yugoslavia/Yougoslavie			x49205	x23721	
Chile/Chili	15989	21100	21879	22395	27025
Cuba	x12757	x34957	x7458	x22605	x21629
India/Inde	21280	22090	20951	20826	33573

COUNTRIES–PAYS	EXPORTS – EXPORTATIONS 1990	1991	1992	1993	1994
Totale	6990357	7202568	8245197	8201419	9273043
Afrique	65081	63338	49331	60196	35453
Afrique du Nord	17617	22993	10056	12474	29690
Amériques	851827	1062373	1217906	1385095	1574342
ALAI	86297	119657	152538	188450	233753
MCAC	23329	27882	40307	45889	56478
Asie	987261	985891	1070688	1105973	1292476
Moyen–Orient	202576	158789	224717	x189038	x197763
Europe	5000933	5021630	5801056	5461593	6115746
CEE	4728220	4783898	5500782	5192366	5855289
AELE	234803	226521	245812	224630	231581
Océanie	43425	45912	55238	x65883	90004
Germany/Allemagne	1497278	1508784	1595874	1466609	1595887
USA/Etats–Unis d'Amer	605979	756242	869599	977481	1071776
France,Monac	669657	745445	914396	787929	875804
United Kingdom	684912	692803	787023	741614	772613
Belgium–Luxembourg	526455	528739	632787	673605	754354
Netherlands/Pays–Bas	489188	498404	559760	547476	658132
Italy/Italie	299895	280233	385085	390908	512836
Japan/Japon	281440	302269	330596	325108	358718
Switz.Liecht	181373	172781	184712	173386	177197
Spain/Espagne	156181	139877	167445	171953	254539
Canada	102104	125438	128210	143564	184715
Denmark/Danemark	111646	105576	121889	131428	149766
Sweden/Suède	118060	114651	113139	94555	109869
Hong Kong	80465	90298	107886	108789	138163
Austria/Autriche	69094	74108	98553	83808	x60455
Malaysia/Malaisie	42985	54242	90760	109894	127138
Singapore/Singapour	101384	73560	77248	83258	111239
Mexico/Mexique	35155	65916	76989	81259	105746
Turkey/Turquie	105328	59962	81402	78554	101634
Indonesia/Indonésie	40641	60397	55794	68520	74623
China/Chine	70640	56591	55982	67539	69705
India/Inde	85312	111242	18298	50491	52872
Norway,SVD,JM	53420	53733	61067	51239	54377
Saudi Arabia	43248	52043	53533	x26174	x34548
Jordan/Jordanie	20726	19712	51709	52002	38266
Ireland/Irlande	35876	37923	45740	37098	38946
Korea, Republic of	45875	31946	41612	43018	82724
Australia/Australie	29057	30001	34253	42651	47982
Brazil/Brésil	9235	16948	28160	46502	53077
Finland/Finlande	37811	31503	29576	23275	25167
Czech Republic				81150	103820
Portugal	24870	16649	35624	19379	24598
So. Africa Customs Un	14377	16054	21056	20420	
New Zealand	12843	14459	19723	22018	40479
Thailand/Thaïlande	14381	14413	18731	21173	33444
Philippines	8877	15789	20092	16750	20311
Guatemala	11243	13092	16328	22297	25317
Slovenia/Slovénia			30021	20488	23652
Israel/Israël	9180	13633	18711	18061	21948
Greece/Grèce	6995	8900	13892	22731	22323
Argentina/Argentine	6451	9301	14589	19313	22919
Czechoslovakia		x5695	x33061		
Croatia/Croatie			17825	18584	x2982
Kenya	5485	10153	9174	16123	x3025
El Salvador	6907	6688	11574	15730	22047
Trinidad and Tobago	8002	10221	10588	12779	13963
Oman	6330	8922	10319	11416	6066
Venezuela	19980	7327	8472	13291	11725
Egypt/Egypte	10592	16875	7748	4206	11918
Peru/Pérou	5459	6319	9556	10649	13295

(VALUE AS % OF TOTAL)(VALEUR EN % DU TOTAL)

	1985	1986	1987	1988	1989	1990	1991	1992	1993	1994
Africa	5.7	x7.1	x6.8	x4.4	x3.9	x4.9	x3.3	x3.7	x3.8	x3.6
Northern Africa	3.1	3.2	3.2	1.2	0.9	1.8	0.9	x0.8	x1.0	x1.1
Americas	14.5	13.5	10.9	11.9	10.9	11.0	12.5	12.8	x15.1	x15.9
LAIA	2.6	2.3	1.8	1.9	2.2	2.1	2.6	3.1	4.0	4.6
CACM	0.9	0.6	0.6	0.6	0.5	0.5	0.6	0.7	x0.8	x0.8
Asia	16.7	x16.5	x17.9	x17.8	x16.5	16.6	17.8	17.3	x19.5	x18.9
Middle East	4.4	x5.1	x5.5	x4.0	x4.6	x4.1	x4.0	x4.1	x4.9	x3.6
Europe	58.9	58.9	59.3	61.1	59.1	58.6	58.0	60.4	55.1	55.5
EEC	47.6	47.4	48.5	50.2	48.2	52.7	53.0	55.1	50.2	50.8
EFTA	9.9	10.4	9.8	9.8	9.8	4.1	4.0	3.8	3.5	3.4
Oceania	2.5	x2.5	x2.1	1.8	x2.0	x1.9	x1.8	x2.0	x2.0	x2.1
France,Monac	9.3	9.0	9.1	9.1	8.9	9.4	9.1	9.1	7.8	8.1
Germany/Allemagne	6.2	6.4	6.6	6.6	6.1	7.8	8.4	8.6	7.2	8.3
United Kingdom	6.0	5.6	6.1	6.7	5.9	5.8	5.8	6.3	5.8	5.7
Belgium–Luxembourg	5.6	5.5	5.4	5.7	5.6	5.7	5.7	5.9	5.6	5.7
Netherlands/Pays–Bas	5.3	5.4	5.4	5.1	4.7	4.9	4.7	5.1	5.7	5.9
Italy/Italie	4.1	3.8	4.5	4.7	4.5	4.6	4.7	4.8	4.4	4.1
USA/Etats–Unis d'Amer	6.4	6.2	4.6	5.1	3.5	3.8	4.0	3.9	4.5	4.9
Canada	2.6	2.2	2.1	2.4	2.6	2.7	3.3	3.6	4.3	4.0
Sweden/Suède	2.3	2.6	2.4	2.7	2.7	2.8	2.7	2.9	2.8	2.4
Switz.Liecht	2.3	2.3	2.2	2.2	2.1	2.5	2.5	2.4	2.2	2.0

	1985	1986	1987	1988	1989	1990	1991	1992	1993	1994
Afrique	0.6	0.9	1.2	0.6	1.3	0.9	0.9	0.6	0.7	0.4
Afrique du Nord	0.0	0.1	0.5	0.2	0.8	0.3	0.3	0.1	0.2	0.3
Amériques	13.6	11.7	10.3	10.7	10.0	12.2	14.7	14.8	16.9	16.9
ALAI	1.2	1.1	0.8	1.0	1.2	1.2	1.7	1.9	2.3	2.5
MCAC	0.6	0.4	0.4	0.4	0.3	0.3	0.4	0.5	0.6	0.6
Asie	10.8	10.4	x11.1	11.9	14.7	14.2	13.7	12.9	13.5	13.9
Moyen–Orient	2.1	x2.2	x2.4	1.7	3.8	2.9	2.2	2.7	x2.3	x2.1
Europe	73.3	75.3	74.8	73.9	72.5	71.5	69.7	70.4	66.6	66.0
CEE	66.0	67.4	67.0	66.7	60.8	67.6	66.4	66.7	63.3	63.1
AELE	6.6	7.2	7.3	6.9	6.4	3.4	3.1	3.0	2.7	2.5
Océanie	0.6	0.5	0.5	x0.7	0.5	0.6	0.6	0.7	x0.8	1.0
Germany/Allemagne	21.4	23.2	23.8	24.1	20.4	21.4	20.9	19.4	17.9	17.2
USA/Etats–Unis d'Amer	9.7	8.3	7.7	7.4	6.8	8.7	10.5	10.5	11.9	11.6
France,Monac	8.8	8.5	7.6	7.8	8.1	9.6	10.3	11.1	9.6	9.4
United Kingdom	11.7	11.1	10.4	10.2	8.7	9.8	9.6	9.5	9.0	8.3
Belgium–Luxembourg	6.9	7.5	8.1	7.4	6.9	7.5	7.3	7.7	8.2	8.1
Netherlands/Pays–Bas	6.6	7.5	7.1	6.9	5.9	7.0	6.9	6.8	6.7	7.1
Italy/Italie	3.5	2.8	2.7	2.8	3.5	4.3	3.9	4.7	4.8	5.5
Japan/Japon	4.9	4.5	3.9	4.2	3.9	4.0	4.2	4.0	4.0	3.9
Switz.Liecht	3.4	3.7	3.6	3.0	2.4	2.6	2.4	2.2	2.1	1.9
Spain/Espagne	1.8	1.5	1.8	1.6	1.7	2.2	1.9	2.0	2.1	2.7

TRADE BY COMMODITY IN THOUSAND U.S. DOLLARS – COMMERCE PAR PRODUIT EN MILLIERS DE DOLLARS E.U

COUNTRIES–PAYS	IMPORTS – IMPORTATIONS 1990	1991	1992	1993	1994
Total	14126863	14883294	15021943	12788950	14585288
Africa	x493382	x551103	x487714	x598712	x493642
Northern Africa	161030	159588	x130483	x142274	x168754
Americas	2380499	2374389	2582640	2918046	3464282
LAIA	830954	883821	1078354	1175564	1492495
CACM	120645	163801	140971	x130785	x180275
Asia	5695390	6820076	6660723	4886657	5291402
Middle East	458752	x666046	x626405	x617243	x372982
Europe	5161117	4765032	4873584	3915327	4727057
EEC	4889251	4565588	4616970	3689284	4524416
EFTA	182609	183884	177348	161005	165654
Oceania	x266619	x283661	x297242	x362632	x459150
China/Chine	2603133	3229489	2995390	1469733	1925516
USA/Etats–Unis d'Amer	1139695	1068356	1092533	1312044	1481556
France,Monac	1243038	989927	1045874	723845	911670
Germany/Allemagne	837695	836337	929403	724578	761445
India/Inde	628775	648652	780497	631687	763928
Brazil/Brésil	381153	440328	510996	583147	712671
Thailand/Thaïlande	430804	404220	494818	539764	536918
Italy/Italie	421065	487925	469169	360331	543729
United Kingdom	509240	499845	453366	344921	485378
Japan/Japon	394838	431885	404308	417639	474556
Belgium–Luxembourg	414024	356328	350857	454606	417382
Viet Nam	x196524	x478616	x285828	x172483	x226643
Spain/Espagne	324875	357559	339481	217058	322848
Turkey/Turquie	247850	264828	238437	309487	168611
Pakistan	241788	279173	237205	258413	170867
Australia/Australie	205270	219792	207484	254814	323145
Malaysia/Malaisie	216647	199162	217420	246063	270847
Netherlands/Pays–Bas	235986	216267	248678	197657	254689
Ireland/Irlande	266097	236726	228606	178814	192319
Canada	183379	184152	186816	213788	203368
Denmark/Danemark	235440	176593	200385	149023	180239
Iran (Islamic Rp. of)		x165876	x167568	x165246	x108309
Philippines	152277	163019	170660	147462	199762
Colombia/Colombie	153468	120605	141781	110062	159432
Sweden/Suède	171367	136141	106386	118076	164654
Korea, Republic of	97475	118447	120929	114302	104945
Chile/Chili	96325	122178	116275	102008	122236
Norway,SVD,JM	97890	102743	100779	97250	104175
Indonesia/Indonésie	96449	57492	141791	99937	75111
Mexico/Mexique	17495	34689	77358	164529	220286
Greece/Grèce	45908	99076	77644	80299	99861
Syrian Arab Republic	46453	x79971	78562	x62254	x34312
Saudi Arabia	125437	108921	80317	x28733	x13420
New Zealand	43832	45997	69998	92406	111859
Switz.Liecht	80419	75202	71515	60957	58157
Austria/Autriche	74347	71605	67803	59594	67059
Malawi	49597	65673	58518	61442	x25127
Argentina/Argentine	26903	40346	67988	73132	123096
Nigeria/Nigéria	x46916	31398	x51032	x90164	x75331
Sri Lanka	64704	59291	49232	63710	64805
Morocco/Maroc	47246	63065	50498	48267	67473
Guatemala	46095	64369	54850	38687	66512
Portugal	54921	56508	56080	42408	67477
Kenya	18459	45857	46950	58484	x43747
So. Africa Customs Un	28566	45956	51147	45849	42209
Venezuela	48616	38995	66176	26128	11692
Poland/Pologne	15927	18688	58020	51608	65285
Finland/Finlande	55248	44748	43236	38075	55668
Costa Rica	31249	33622	34557	x29471	x32458
Zambia/Zambie	x36217	x19890	x35494	x36583	x30534

COUNTRIES–PAYS	EXPORTS – EXPORTATIONS 1990	1991	1992	1993	1994
Totale	13932682	x13947446	11619358	9533557	11731456
Afrique	830919	818995	x775134	x757555	x778885
Afrique du Nord	713722	701568	649792	597944	x660920
Amériques	4315388	4695237	3964159	3357202	4573100
ALAI	225766	253819	208414	174151	199906
MCAC	8325	10462	14180	x12987	x22131
Asie	1438309	1639421	x1745591	x1511013	x1780264
Moyen–Orient	454581	473740	443625	x452710	x632676
Europe	4246969	4279013	4383428	3406267	3908083
CEE	3785851	3799506	3887423	2984784	3500239
AELE	389823	376134	329443	311652	330579
Océanie	20679	x29397	x16851	x16102	x24441
USA/Etats–Unis d'Amer	2586174	2993722	2389945	1823271	2706303
Canada	1421248	1358324	1287687	1276857	1563275
Russian Federation			x1891900	x1326174	x1293452
Germany/Allemagne	628695	877780	1001207	752502	996420
Netherlands/Pays–Bas	984028	936271	926462	698471	848163
Belgium–Luxembourg	758295	671068	653040	502418	634546
Former USSR/Anc. URSS	1478883	x1700728			
Norway,SVD,JM	385164	370212	323566	306620	325612
Morocco/Maroc	411146	381292	286455	311274	271989
France,Monac	299951	318360	331591	286067	282576
Ukraine			x199033	x688635	x385347
Israel/Israël	253858	253475	296311	238124	288120
Tunisia/Tunisie	259449	239612	236441	183360	229783
Indonesia/Indonésie	192819	297174	183730	151831	178286
Bulgaria/Bulgarie	x918663	x332777	165096	92572	140586
Korea, Republic of	188558	167926	183687	196870	224299
Romania/Roumanie	111163	144293	211215	168253	208163
United Kingdom	197359	182411	194185	120667	131719
Spain/Espagne	222603	179012	192873	111736	138766
Saudi Arabia	101967	137998	145055	x121628	x203426
Poland/Pologne	114029	102908	172550	108605	173607
Italy/Italie	199952	116851	153447	101221	45259
Austria/Autriche	129946	130606	119960	103784	x111684
Japan/Japon	100572	118813	108309	103440	97234
Jordan/Jordanie	119474	126997	106747	82551	127857
Qatar	88534	105575	103949	92424	x99655
Philippines	71932	115862	88211	85455	101250
Finland/Finlande	75565	102273	81874	73654	83856
Sweden/Suède	102295	113196	78406	62568	74007
Belarus/Bélarus			x139761	x111465	x169096
Czechoslovakia		x113906	x133360		
Mexico/Mexique	111399	116066	78660	51949	111690
Malaysia/Malaisie	57212	79816	86152	73018	76895
Kazakstan			x194513	x42179	x14814
Libyan Arab Jamahiriya	25383	59067	x77099	x83536	x104682
So. Africa Customs Un	51077	58672	71651	79671	79518
Croatia/Croatie			123069	77240	x75597
Denmark/Danemark	77631	60819	54984	78282	70264
Trinidad and Tobago	59392	67030	59986	59225	58960
Lithuania/Lituanie			49284	x114691	90825
Ireland/Irlande	55387	60540	34976	48900	53622
Venezuela	42938	56127	43946	38614	2998
Brazil/Brésil	38167	48583	39025	45927	36372
Hungary/Hongrie	x156184	x76719	x39718	x14897	x14962
Greece/Grèce	33538	32247	44380	33505	17086
Turkey/Turquie	71167	54621	38158	16832	31974
Kuwait/ Koweït	47994	4437	34416	69944	94503
Bangladesh	14777	44685	12884	46287	x40287
Yugoslavia SFR	71290	x103370			
China/Chine	25318	24736	27692	45817	64911

(VALUE AS % OF TOTAL)(VALEUR EN % DU TOTAL)

	1985	1986	1987	1988	1989	1990	1991	1992	1993	1994
Africa	5.2	4.9	x4.0	x3.5	x4.3	x3.5	x3.7	x3.2	x4.7	x3.4
Northern Africa	1.8	1.8	1.3	1.4	1.3	1.1	1.1	x0.9	x1.1	x1.2
Americas	20.9	21.7	19.6	18.7	18.5	16.9	15.9	17.2	22.8	23.8
LAIA	6.8	7.5	7.3	6.6	6.4	5.9	5.9	7.2	9.2	10.2
CACM	1.1	0.8	1.5	1.1	1.2	0.9	1.1	0.9	x1.0	x1.2
Asia	35.5	26.7	30.2	38.3	38.9	40.4	45.8	44.4	38.3	36.2
Middle East	3.0	x4.6	x5.5	x5.3	x4.6	3.2	x4.5	x4.2	x4.8	x2.6
Europe	32.0	39.8	39.4	33.7	34.8	36.5	32.0	32.4	30.6	32.4
EEC	27.0	34.3	34.7	29.4	30.8	34.6	30.7	30.7	28.8	31.0
EFTA	3.4	4.2	3.8	3.4	3.1	1.3	1.2	1.2	1.3	1.1
Oceania	1.7	1.3	x1.4	x1.3	1.8	x1.9	x1.9	x1.9	x2.8	x3.2
China/Chine	12.8	7.3	12.3	16.9	16.9	18.4	21.7	19.9	11.5	13.2
USA/Etats–Unis d'Amer	9.8	9.6	7.6	8.0	8.1	8.1	7.2	7.3	10.3	10.2
France,Monac	7.1	8.4	8.8	7.4	8.2	8.8	6.7	7.0	5.7	6.3
Germany/Allemagne	4.4	5.9	6.1	5.0	4.8	5.9	5.6	6.2	5.7	5.2
India/Inde	8.1	4.5	1.3	2.4	5.4	4.5	4.4	5.2	4.9	5.2
Brazil/Brésil	2.5	3.4	3.3	2.7	2.4	2.7	3.0	3.4	4.6	4.9
Thailand/Thaïlande	1.7	1.9	1.6	2.2	2.8	3.0	2.7	3.3	4.2	3.7
Italy/Italie	2.4	3.2	3.4	3.1	3.1	3.0	3.3	3.1	2.8	3.7
United Kingdom	2.6	3.2	3.1	2.6	3.2	3.6	3.4	3.0	2.7	3.3
Japan/Japon	2.4	2.6	3.0	3.0	2.9	2.8	2.9	2.7	3.3	3.3

	1985	1986	1987	1988	1989	1990	1991	1992	1993	1994
Afrique	4.6	4.3	3.7	4.8	5.6	6.0	5.9	x6.7	x7.9	x6.7
Afrique du Nord	3.9	3.9	3.2	4.0	4.8	5.1	5.0	5.6	6.3	x5.6
Amériques	35.0	31.1	25.0	25.7	30.6	31.0	33.7	34.2	35.2	39.0
ALAI	1.0	0.6	0.6	0.7	1.0	1.6	1.8	1.8	1.8	1.7
MCAC	0.1	0.1	0.0	0.0	0.1	0.1	0.1	0.1	x0.1	x0.2
Asie	11.2	12.8	x9.4	10.9	11.6	10.3	11.8	x15.0	x15.9	x15.2
Moyen–Orient	3.1	x4.6	x3.6	x4.7	x4.4	3.3	3.4	3.8	x4.7	x5.4
Europe	37.3	38.2	29.9	26.5	29.3	30.5	30.7	37.7	35.7	33.3
CEE	30.4	31.3	24.7	22.0	24.2	27.2	27.2	33.5	31.3	29.8
AELE	5.7	5.8	4.3	3.8	4.4	2.8	2.7	2.8	3.3	2.8
Océanie	0.1	x0.1	x0.1	x0.1	x0.1	0.1	x0.2	x0.1	x0.1	x0.2
USA/Etats–Unis d'Amer	22.9	20.7	16.9	15.8	20.2	18.6	21.5	20.6	19.1	23.1
Canada	10.1	9.0	7.2	8.6	8.8	10.2	9.7	11.1	13.4	13.3
Russian Federation								x16.3	x13.9	x11.0
Germany/Allemagne	5.7	6.4	5.1	4.3	4.0	4.5	6.3	8.6	7.9	8.5
Netherlands/Pays–Bas	7.3	7.7	5.9	5.3	6.0	7.1	6.7	8.0	7.3	7.2
Belgium–Luxembourg	5.9	6.6	4.9	4.0	4.7	5.4	4.8	5.6	5.3	5.4
Former USSR/Anc. URSS	9.7	12.0	8.4	8.4	9.8	10.6	x12.2			
Norway,SVD,JM	2.5	2.5	2.0	1.8	2.3	2.8	2.7	2.8	3.2	2.8
Morocco/Maroc	1.3	1.1	0.8	2.0	2.2	3.0	2.7	2.5	3.3	2.3
France,Monac	2.4	2.3	1.9	1.7	1.8	2.2	2.3	2.9	3.0	2.4

TRADE BY COMMODITY IN THOUSAND U.S. DOLLARS – COMMERCE PAR PRODUIT EN MILLIERS DE DOLLARS E.U

COUNTRIES–PAYS	IMPORTS – IMPORTATIONS 1990	1991	1992	1993	1994
Total	1043660	1165845	1243814	1152120	1033615
Africa	x73866	x67197	x88005	x87074	x75564
Northern Africa	8780	8958	x22222	x26873	x20757
Americas	227005	264097	325240	332970	x325477
LAIA	28405	32908	38818	42248	43763
CACM	1623	1801	2975	2873	x2884
Asia	270949	345981	280984	x280074	x238547
Middle East	x59992	90408	x43863	x55089	x38742
Europe	423545	453225	504469	414902	347046
EEC	350808	398109	419467	345356	302225
EFTA	69512	52414	57095	39829	38967
Oceania	x28109	x30311	x37906	x24559	x32387
USA/Etats–Unis d'Amer	151812	175748	214270	211103	198554
Germany/Allemagne	104166	121904	142910	114939	78650
Hong Kong	91993	107093	112029	99623	89429
Canada	34634	43251	58264	66559	69319
Italy/Italie	38335	62061	52006	36975	34575
Japan/Japon	47999	49068	45300	50301	42333
United Kingdom	42007	47231	45565	42697	41636
France,Monac	34430	34118	37552	35321	33489
Saudi Arabia	18373	64137	6711	x17854	x11650
Netherlands/Pays–Bas	22745	22526	34785	21346	18199
Sweden/Suède	33256	27375	28018	22450	27477
Switz.Liecht	45602	26977	30130	17903	17635
Norway,SVD,JM	22542	23539	25118	20111	19634
Australia/Australie	19697	23679	28363	16422	20935
Indonesia/Indonésie	10651	30291	18702	12726	14457
Singapore/Singapour	23295	22461	21685	17406	15931
Belgium–Luxembourg	12191	21310	15430	17686	11921
Austria/Autriche	22391	18443	20632	15158	16745
Nigeria/Nigéria	x13621	17258	x22606	x11896	x7016
Mexico/Mexique	10282	11089	15075	11612	9729
Zimbabwe	16557	8193	8474	13855	x12676
Spain/Espagne	7155	8961	10955	7473	8519
Libyan Arab Jamahiriya	2957	4505	x9803	x11556	x14948
Malaysia/Malaisie	9007	8336	8968	8465	10770
Korea, Republic of	3498	2978	12646	9777	3178
Denmark/Danemark	7759	8915	8413	7362	7642
Finland/Finlande	9434	9079	8728	6359	9018
Portugal	6928	6628	7002	7499	7001
Argentina/Argentine	1146	3135	6312	10652	10674
Thailand/Thaïlande	3885	9135	4098	6681	6662
Greece/Grèce	4473	6880	5173	7687	5144
Algeria/Algérie	928	618	7453	10513	902
So. Africa Customs Un	4702	4975	5492	7677	12080
Venezuela	4154	5457	4915	5976	6214
Iran (Islamic Rp. of)		x2132	x9071	x4809	x3274
United Arab Emirates	2476	1786	2489	x11463	x7480
Turkey/Turquie	5010	6152	4579	4895	6324
Zambia/Zambie	x8170	x5809	x5233	x3195	x2961
New Zealand	3448	4120	5205	4183	5990
Korea Dem People's Rp	x8080	x10890	x994	x160	
Ghana	x2459	1798	5096	x4738	x6197
Yemen/Yémen	2421	4966	3241	x2108	x934
Philippines	3879	5227	1791	3255	3410
Bahrain/Bahreïn	x21282	x1964	x3232	x4752	x1118
Colombia/Colombie	4105	2455	2565	3797	4707
Un. Rep. of Tanzania	x651	x2789	x4766	x1207	x542
Mongolia/Mongolie		x15	x203	x8194	x13
Brazil/Brésil	1802	2393	2943	2498	2698
Croatia/Croatie			3709	4113	x2754
Ireland/Irlande	5537	2677	2298	2404	2211

COUNTRIES–PAYS	EXPORTS – EXPORTATIONS 1990	1991	1992	1993	1994
Totale	1425789	1033881	1123487	1104317	1079905
Afrique	26989	22353	25793	24387	8398
Afrique du Nord	2603	1673	3147	6819	8261
Amériques	198541	244187	300479	346146	328489
ALAI	9638	12181	15460	22096	23660
MCAC	359	463	912	x555	x1461
Asie	360325	320503	334685	306528	323133
Moyen–Orient	2099	1731	3376	x4445	x1399
Europe	833281	432014	439493	389825	368858
CEE	784080	385844	402650	355951	340705
AELE	38194	35423	23031	24101	22752
Océanie	1933	2225	8544	14069	x20569
USA/Etats–Unis d'Amer	149123	161495	194532	238852	240410
China/Chine	211282	156110	148936	130605	154999
Hong Kong	109148	131722	139214	132703	134835
Germany/Allemagne	116437	111809	124138	103167	101486
United Kingdom	468734	97419	91146	73965	62170
Canada	39223	70006	89397	84510	62353
France,Monac	68439	58805	62276	66819	59766
Sweden/Suède	34270	36466	40471	28208	34053
Belgium–Luxembourg	28861	24142	19118	20823	22886
Norway,SVD,JM	28175	30039	17947	14042	17980
So. Africa Customs Un	23667	20475	22418	16831	
Spain/Espagne	19094	15576	17082	15986	13213
Italy/Italie	17507	13062	16743	13326	12623
Austria/Autriche	15260	14259	15521	13198	x12344
Singapore/Singapour	12877	7149	13730	11538	12935
Netherlands/Pays–Bas	9136	5633	8624	9414	9983
Korea, Republic of	6433	4602	9793	7684	2459
Australia/Australie	960	1452	7127	12582	18468
Switz.Liecht	10019	5378	5084	10057	4772
Japan/Japon	6041	5266	5939	4512	3405
Finland/Finlande	4307	4444	4197	6203	7365
Brazil/Brésil	2472	2707	5689	5873	6732
Czechoslovakia		x6805	x7239		
Philippines	4767	4715	3485	4781	5378
Czech Republic				12717	15533
Chile/Chili	2163	3379	2596	5707	4311
Slovenia/Slovénia			5834	5736	4403
Russian Federation			x3179	x7789	x5062
Yugoslavia SFR	10908	x10726			
Hungary/Hongrie	x2398	x2217	x3852	x4422	x3839
India/Inde	2420	3210	3395	3550	4016
Mexico/Mexique	80	224	3220	6124	6938
Peru/Pérou	3221	3181	1692	2680	3571
Poland/Pologne			3149	3849	5923
Malaysia/Malaisie	2779	2514	2468	1917	606
Macau/Macao	1643	1822	1785	1859	1838
Tunisia/Tunisie	611	9	1016	4194	4763
Denmark/Danemark	1006	1398	1445	1921	2051
Greece/Grèce	558	1725	947	2040	2021
Morocco/Maroc	1958	440	1499	2140	3491
Thailand/Thaïlande	424	1275	1224	1414	564
Argentina/Argentine	1141	1198	1340	1282	1475
United Arab Emirates	1723	174	102	x3392	x784
New Zealand	841	751	1389	1487	2080
Saudi Arabia	298	762	2289	x286	x53
Portugal	353	1020	894	586	742
Former USSR/Anc. URSS		x1943			
Colombia/Colombie	382	851	674	382	617
Korea Dem People's Rp	x254	x194	x540	x1087	x94
Slovakia				x1766	x2000

(VALUE AS % OF TOTAL)(VALEUR EN % DU TOTAL)

	1985	1986	1987	1988	1989	1990	1991	1992	1993	1994
Africa	6.7	x4.9	x7.1	x6.4	x4.7	x7.1	x5.7	x7.0	x7.6	x7.3
Northern Africa	1.0	0.5	0.9	1.1	1.1	0.8	0.8	x1.8	x2.3	x2.0
Americas	24.3	18.5	x17.3	x17.4	22.0	21.8	22.7	26.1	28.9	x31.5
LAIA	4.8	3.3	2.4	2.3	3.6	2.7	2.8	3.1	3.7	4.2
CACM	0.4	0.6	x0.6	0.2	0.4	0.2	0.2	0.2	0.2	x0.3
Asia	22.6	x32.1	19.7	x29.3	x28.9	26.0	29.7	22.6	x24.3	x23.1
Middle East	2.6	x14.7	x2.4	x13.1	x9.8	x5.7	7.8	x3.5	x4.8	x3.7
Europe	41.5	41.9	45.6	37.3	37.3	40.6	38.9	40.6	36.0	33.6
EEC	31.4	31.7	28.5	26.1	26.5	33.6	34.1	33.7	30.0	29.2
EFTA	8.4	9.0	10.7	10.7	10.4	6.7	4.5	4.6	3.5	3.8
Oceania	3.7	1.8	x2.2	2.8	x2.9	x2.7	x2.6	x3.0	x2.1	x3.1
USA/Etats–Unis d'Amer	15.7	12.2	11.0	11.3	13.2	14.5	15.1	17.2	18.3	19.2
Germany/Allemagne	6.8	7.7	7.2	6.2	6.7	10.0	10.5	11.5	10.0	7.6
Hong Kong	9.0	7.7	7.5	6.6	8.8	8.8	9.2	9.0	8.6	8.7
Canada	2.8	1.5	2.1	2.2	3.5	3.3	3.7	4.7	5.8	6.7
Italy/Italie	3.3	3.6	2.9	3.0	3.0	3.7	5.3	4.2	3.2	3.3
Japan/Japon	3.2	3.5	4.7	3.2	3.6	4.6	4.2	3.6	4.4	4.1
United Kingdom	3.8	3.4	3.8	3.4	3.5	4.0	4.1	3.7	3.7	4.0
France,Monac	2.9	1.9	1.8	1.9	2.8	3.3	2.9	3.0	3.1	3.2
Saudi Arabia	0.5	0.3	0.1	0.2	0.3	1.8	5.5	0.5	x1.5	x1.1
Netherlands/Pays–Bas	5.0	3.9	3.0	2.1	1.4	2.2	1.9	2.8	1.9	1.8

	1985	1986	1987	1988	1989	1990	1991	1992	1993	1994
Afrique	1.7	x1.7	x1.4	x1.3	x1.3	1.9	2.2	2.3	2.2	0.8
Afrique du Nord	0.1	0.0	0.1	x0.0	0.1	0.2	0.2	0.3	0.6	0.8
Amériques	12.1	x12.0	x9.8	8.8	11.6	13.9	23.6	26.8	31.4	30.4
ALAI	1.3	1.0	0.7	0.7	0.8	0.7	1.2	1.4	2.0	2.2
MCAC	0.1	0.0	0.0	0.0	0.0	0.0	0.0	0.1	x0.1	x0.1
Asie	18.0	18.0	21.8	28.6	x27.7	25.2	31.0	29.8	27.7	29.9
Moyen–Orient	0.1	0.1	0.2	0.1	x0.1	0.1	0.2	0.3	x0.4	x0.1
Europe	64.8	65.3	52.3	56.6	54.9	58.4	41.8	39.1	35.3	34.2
CEE	35.1	35.7	27.5	48.3	47.8	55.0	37.3	35.8	32.2	31.5
AELE	6.9	7.2	6.4	6.7	6.2	2.7	3.4	2.0	2.2	2.1
Océanie	0.5	0.3	0.3	0.2	0.1	0.1	0.2	0.8	1.3	x1.9
USA/Etats–Unis d'Amer	10.7	7.5	6.6	6.4	8.8	10.5	15.6	17.3	21.6	22.3
China/Chine	8.3	9.0	13.2	20.2	17.2	14.8	15.1	13.3	11.8	14.4
Hong Kong	7.1	7.1	6.3	5.6	7.6	7.7	12.7	12.4	12.0	12.5
Germany/Allemagne	6.7	6.7	6.1	5.7	6.5	8.2	10.8	11.0	9.3	9.4
United Kingdom	6.2	5.8	5.4	29.4	29.2	32.9	9.4	8.1	6.7	5.8
Canada		x3.4	x2.3	1.7	2.0	2.8	6.8	8.0	7.7	5.8
France,Monac	5.0	6.0	4.6	3.0	3.5	4.8	5.7	5.5	6.1	5.5
Sweden/Suède	2.6	2.6	2.1	2.2	2.4	2.4	3.5	3.6	2.6	3.2
Belgium–Luxembourg	3.0	2.7	1.3	1.8	1.5	2.0	2.3	1.7	1.9	2.1
Norway,SVD,JM	1.8	1.5	1.7	2.3	2.0	2.0	2.9	1.6	1.3	1.7

TRADE BY COMMODITY IN THOUSAND U.S. DOLLARS – COMMERCE PAR PRODUIT EN MILLIERS DE DOLLARS E.U

IMPORTS – IMPORTATIONS

COUNTRIES–PAYS	1990	1991	1992	1993	1994
Total	17503394	17775067	18854390	18078860	21764210
Africa	x461166	479139	x456758	x435798	x473470
Northern Africa	196994	225958	182811	160595	x191567
Americas	1900044	2075378	2395389	2787803	3447199
LAIA	474704	598725	734162	873392	1083921
CACM	34368	36700	43645	x43962	x42688
Asia	3531195	3771528	4007122	4664376	5575053
Middle East	x711967	x457343	x474913	x458821	x394696
Europe	11054317	10716142	11491863	9563101	11646170
EEC	10367336	10105506	10831671	8987315	10960443
EFTA	517289	485005	518937	470234	557082
Oceania	x274023	x252544	x270974	x336790	x284258
Germany/Allemagne	2512204	2546108	2765343	2222478	2490790
France,Monac	1595172	1545035	1676393	1392614	1616116
Italy/Italie	1414906	1338618	1408337	1134625	1388347
United Kingdom	1272737	1173300	1262038	1005934	1306035
USA/Etats–Unis d'Amer	772841	782113	898127	1062087	1367602
Belgium–Luxembourg	781441	803584	859700	753755	1047882
Netherlands/Pays–Bas	797586	793493	847967	759399	1022702
Canada	582090	612250	668141	760292	890671
Japan/Japon	604028	694289	660189	660602	686288
Hong Kong	398249	523366	560208	637880	832856
Korea, Republic of	403338	487865	512001	595469	720292
China/Chine	351123	410669	453258	625332	807903
Spain/Espagne	533605	530508	542562	405291	536819
Austria/Autriche	389754	385976	417262	375131	456269
Switz.Liecht	414080	386862	411337	370695	439316
Singapore/Singapour	301537	341187	354511	442685	541175
Sweden/Suède	319426	290859	293310	264060	339421
Malaysia/Malaisie	177290	211317	259433	341396	463426
Mexico/Mexique	123242	162996	265132	312896	415668
Denmark/Danemark	250789	246671	266725	205161	228976
Thailand/Thaïlande	149404	175460	225664	274942	319650
Australia/Australie	212468	191623	201365	256558	195368
Indonesia/Indonésie	159261	165038	187165	264184	325628
Brazil/Brésil	147319	168320	160237	229171	275455
Turkey/Turquie	139599	133747	162641	189119	162238
So. Africa Customs Un	154329	154255	145981	166917	173100
Finland/Finlande	192334	142296	146292	144690	180775
Iran (Islamic Rp. of)	x236286	x170415	x155194	x98962	x41294
Israel/Israël	115243	114721	132483	131446	148118
Portugal	120614	117621	125431	108040	116037
Ireland/Irlande	103686	106661	123289	114407	135005
Former USSR/Anc. URSS		x297508			
Norway,SVD,JM	98792	93182	102668	95310	112102
Argentina/Argentine	44175	80414	97058	112611	152369
Greece/Grèce	83083	84777	97024	101730	95267
Egypt/Egypte	64943	71547	75714	68558	62227
Poland/Pologne	38573	46904	65838	92304	122689
Russian Federation			x122150	x77663	x51355
New Zealand	53293	52741	61701	73108	82173
Saudi Arabia	95167	58349	56846	x65863	x70757
Philippines	42872	60601	46452	69271	92032
Hungary/Hongrie	x56629	47077	x58077	x70083	x68763
Chile/Chili	33137	44145	54847	60096	60836
Venezuela	25300	50548	56640	48306	37027
India/Inde	50215	40885	48716	55243	119963
Pakistan	37208	38751	48826	57120	64802
Czechoslovakia	77146	x64511	x73960		
United Arab Emirates	175863	41517	43171	x48863	x52741
Nigeria/Nigéria	x34706	24204	x59936	x37377	x30162
Slovenia/Slovénia			59510	61337	80021

EXPORTS – EXPORTATIONS

COUNTRIES–PAYS	1990	1991	1992	1993	1994
Totale	16070130	16382699	17471254	17492391	20605207
Afrique	35796	49664	16197	15833	x2672
Afrique du Nord	23341	33325	2310	1586	1468
Amériques	2639834	3042241	3247108	3486265	4192940
ALAI	196733	189550	207097	221767	322610
MCAC	2552	2636	4500	x4385	x4633
Asie	2280675	2437662	2652691	3210337	4144609
Moyen–Orient	171619	66510	67817	50351	x57355
Europe	10944757	10741499	11429822	10649960	12114245
CEE	10334354	10160517	10801774	10089531	11447455
AELE	573456	560116	592561	524225	632054
Océanie	x47516	x43683	x53729	x51921	x59479
Germany/Allemagne	3777385	3710481	3970953	3480731	4226808
USA/Etats–Unis d'Amer	2310568	2698674	2851538	3032173	3560941
Netherlands/Pays–Bas	2252180	2204836	2262718	2046347	2152127
Belgium–Luxembourg	1493916	1512097	1677948	1366967	1787671
Japan/Japon	1236503	1325378	1453469	1678812	2041343
Italy/Italie	862722	830873	859425	879478	1071729
United Kingdom	876592	824186	813244	812211	967752
France,Monac	474545	468318	554227	887044	473602
Korea, Republic of	328179	359417	451126	578234	764752
Switz.Liecht	442034	440541	465800	415262	493241
Hong Kong	215839	296302	297016	370751	507736
Singapore/Singapour	195273	243611	224906	303703	393321
Spain/Espagne	182200	198856	222295	238585	311196
Austria/Autriche	187965	196171	208558	194555	x219363
Canada	129624	151008	183388	227331	304264
Norway,SVD,JM	131399	119561	126645	108795	138720
Sweden/Suède	95451	89268	95360	90349	112676
Mexico/Mexique	56172	72460	69719	68728	132390
Brazil/Brésil	55197	49242	61267	63666	95004
Denmark/Danemark	53247	60063	60275	45064	48033
Turkey/Turquie	49307	55403	53010	42741	41462
Israel/Israël	56386	52142	50870	45547	56328
Colombia/Colombie	18079	31672	41226	45201	48070
Australia/Australie	33981	33597	43443	39940	44194
Thailand/Thaïlande	9348	18844	17193	50171	88385
Indonesia/Indonésie	20607	22488	20758	39729	26316
Poland/Pologne	18398	22953	28985	25937	33905
China/Chine	14940	18653	23403	28371	79149
Finland/Finlande	35600	23229	22859	21679	37208
Ireland/Irlande	27142	27047	36261	3855	14438
Malaysia/Malaisie	12498	15496	21476	28789	46572
India/Inde	8958	11210	18351	27175	70702
Argentina/Argentine	18524	14351	15013	15801	15376
Venezuela	42187	15156	10943	17478	19487
Czechoslovakia		x22138	x21390		
Slovenia/Slovénia			19470	21708	28129
Portugal	10008	9688	12770	15466	16149
So. Africa Customs Un	6710	11025	10985	11869	
New Zealand	10111	10050	10142	11076	15069
Libyan Arab Jamahiriya	21800	27286	x39	x68	
Hungary/Hongrie	x10635	x6502	x9696	x9343	x8089
Slovakia				x22427	x21677
Croatia/Croatie			10474	10595	x5210
Saudi Arabia	37258	8698	7516	x4762	x7443
Russian Federation			x5700	x14596	x10143
Yugoslavia SFR	36453	x20046			
Uruguay	5062	4472	6499	8462	9097
Greece/Grèce	5401	5403	4881	7198	8703
Czech Republic				16517	22706
Bulgaria/Bulgarie	x21280	x6841	x6004	x2789	x1567

(VALUE AS % OF TOTAL)(VALEUR EN % DU TOTAL)

Imports

	1985	1986	1987	1988	1989	1990	1991	1992	1993	1994
Africa	3.1	3.3	x2.7	x3.0	x2.8	x2.7	2.7	x2.4	x2.4	x2.2
Northern Africa	1.4	1.4	1.0	1.2	1.2	1.1	1.3	1.0	0.9	x0.9
Americas	15.3	13.1	10.7	10.6	10.5	10.8	11.6	12.7	15.4	15.9
LAIA	3.6	2.8	2.6	2.8	2.7	2.7	3.4	3.9	4.8	5.0
CACM		0.3	0.2	0.2	0.2	0.2	0.2	0.2	x0.2	x0.2
Asia	13.6	13.6	x16.5	x20.3	18.5	20.2	21.3	21.2	25.8	25.6
Middle East	3.1	x3.1	x2.6	x2.6	x1.9	x4.1	x2.6	x2.5	x2.5	x1.8
Europe	64.8	67.4	62.0	58.7	60.4	63.2	60.3	61.0	52.9	53.5
EEC	54.8	57.3	52.7	50.1	52.3	59.2	56.9	57.4	49.7	50.4
EFTA	8.9	9.3	8.5	7.7	7.3	3.0	2.7	2.8	2.6	2.6
Oceania	2.4	x2.0	x1.9	x1.6	x1.7	x1.5	x1.4	x1.4	x1.8	x1.3
Germany/Allemagne	13.2	14.1	12.4	11.8	12.4	14.4	14.3	14.7	12.3	11.4
France,Monac	8.1	8.7	7.9	7.2	8.1	9.1	8.7	8.9	7.7	7.4
Italy/Italie	6.5	7.1	6.7	7.0	7.2	8.1	7.5	7.5	6.3	6.4
United Kingdom	7.6	7.2	7.0	6.8	6.6	7.3	6.6	6.7	5.6	6.0
USA/Etats–Unis d'Amer	5.6	4.8	3.8	4.5	3.9	4.4	4.4	4.8	5.9	6.3
Belgium–Luxembourg	4.4	4.4	4.0	3.6	3.8	4.5	4.5	4.6	4.2	4.8
Netherlands/Pays–Bas	4.8	4.7	4.2	3.9	4.0	4.6	4.5	4.5	4.2	4.7
Canada	5.9	4.8	3.8	3.0	3.5	3.3	3.4	3.5	4.2	4.1
Japan/Japon	3.5	3.1	3.0	3.3	3.5	3.5	3.9	3.5	3.7	3.2
Hong Kong	1.3	1.4	1.4	2.2	2.5	2.3	2.9	3.0	3.5	3.8

Exports

	1985	1986	1987	1988	1989	1990	1991	1992	1993	1994
Afrique	0.1	x0.1	x0.1	x0.0	x0.0	0.2	0.3	0.1	0.1	x0.0
Afrique du Nord	0.0	0.0	0.0	0.0	0.0	0.1	0.2	0.0	0.0	0.0
Amériques	10.5	8.4	8.5	12.1	16.0	16.4	18.6	18.6	19.9	20.4
ALAI	0.9	0.6	0.7	1.1	1.3	1.2	1.2	1.2	1.3	1.6
MCAC		0.0	0.0	0.0	0.0	0.0	0.0	0.0	x0.0	x0.0
Asie	11.0	11.0	x12.0	x15.4	14.0	14.1	14.9	15.2	18.4	20.1
Moyen–Orient	0.5	0.5	x0.6	0.7	0.8	1.1	0.4	0.4	0.3	x0.3
Europe	78.0	80.1	76.9	69.6	68.5	68.1	65.6	65.4	60.9	58.8
CEE	70.9	72.8	69.9	62.9	62.7	64.3	62.0	61.8	57.7	55.6
AELE	6.7	7.1	6.8	6.6	5.5	3.6	3.4	3.4	3.0	3.1
Océanie	0.2	x0.2	x0.2	x0.3	x0.3	x0.3	x0.3	x0.3	x0.3	x0.3
Germany/Allemagne	24.7	25.7	24.5	24.2	23.1	23.5	22.6	22.7	19.9	20.5
USA/Etats–Unis d'Amer	9.4	7.7	7.7	10.3	13.8	14.4	16.5	16.3	17.3	17.3
Netherlands/Pays–Bas	14.7	15.4	13.9	13.6	13.5	14.0	13.5	13.0	11.7	10.4
Belgium–Luxembourg	7.4	8.0	7.7	7.8	8.5	9.3	9.2	9.6	7.8	8.7
Japan/Japon	8.0	8.3	7.6	8.2	7.9	7.7	8.1	8.3	9.6	9.9
Italy/Italie	5.6	5.6	5.3	5.0	5.3	5.4	5.1	4.9	5.0	5.2
United Kingdom	6.7	6.2	6.1	5.7	5.5	5.5	5.0	4.7	4.6	4.7
France,Monac	7.4	7.3	8.1	2.9	3.0	3.0	2.9	3.2	5.1	2.3
Korea, Republic of	1.2	1.0	1.0	1.7	1.9	2.0	2.2	2.6	3.3	3.7
Switz.Liecht	3.1	3.4	3.2	3.5	2.5	2.8	2.7	2.7	2.4	2.4

TRADE BY COMMODITY IN THOUSAND U.S. DOLLARS – COMMERCE PAR PRODUIT EN MILLIERS DE DOLLARS E.U

COUNTRIES–PAYS	IMPORTS – IMPORTATIONS				
	1990	1991	1992	1993	1994
Total	48512341	49907651	52280088	48094992	58233910
Africa	x1220065	1426213	x1345531	x1286482	x1378371
Northern Africa	537621	646229	592478	599681	697543
Americas	5451939	5868512	6764123	7661423	9273880
LAIA	1287453	1679222	2082981	2419380	2896913
CACM	187442	180475	216627	x227740	x257924
Asia	10061951	11809535	13904550	13886842	16632307
Middle East	x1430639	x1364006	x1524196	x1465407	x1244055
Europe	30229226	29142935	29063886	23744363	29235435
EEC	28394334	27529599	27370610	22257872	27538077
EFTA	1530290	1392358	1386510	1270567	1446769
Oceania	x608316	x607089	x628430	x721348	x715174
Germany/Allemagne	5895024	6016003	6049475	4723145	5606439
France,Monac	4268045	4050871	4111915	3394431	4070477
Italy/Italie	3690761	3611218	3560647	2985984	3759106
United Kingdom	3937950	3641439	3522499	2398699	3669895
China/Chine	1090414	1896816	3669239	3607249	4527931
Hong Kong	2035345	2698864	3087127	3002330	4008138
USA/Etats–Unis d'Amer	2521042	2529031	2869107	3251665	3977105
Belgium–Luxembourg	2348031	2265744	2237119	2211652	2469427
Netherlands/Pays–Bas	2366941	2320938	2330613	1821084	2268538
Canada	1270595	1285663	1427696	1604261	1930959
Spain/Espagne	1297601	1338022	1339088	1075317	1348402
Switz.Liecht	1165201	1049861	1039951	969658	1099876
Austria/Autriche	935548	905159	929917	825316	973974
Sweden/Suède	1084577	977321	892619	768855	963714
Mexico/Mexique	513368	618051	905480	1057617	1281303
Japan/Japon	785049	877272	724758	777715	926649
Denmark/Danemark	840895	805665	790192	650249	742902
Singapore/Singapour	710751	740630	676411	715014	868676
Malaysia/Malaisie	566311	677560	686263	727845	748852
Korea, Republic of	671995	718591	651536	714030	801887
Indonesia/Indonésie	732892	702962	726307	648019	754156
Thailand/Thaïlande	592651	555651	657678	646744	891427
India/Inde	535434	519017	402225	360825	456709
Finland/Finlande	589625	459008	426649	391631	484783
Australia/Australie	379860	389049	385522	471679	410731
Greece/Grèce	413452	427897	432855	374360	401845
Turkey/Turquie	294078	311730	366006	434000	435874
Portugal	351683	356506	404019	322265	388592
Iran (Islamic Rp. of)	x534243	x319718	x365487	x355161	x111641
Ireland/Irlande	374201	353808	343004	314882	389983
Philippines	300546	296077	324749	373697	482211
Saudi Arabia	168337	371466	353967	x228245	x231580
Norway,SVD,JM	341362	318831	326795	283481	326820
Israel/Israël	251159	276101	300894	297722	314914
So. Africa Customs Un	227614	258137	246898	250897	266962
Brazil/Brésil	162924	209652	220567	315181	360868
Egypt/Egypte	228356	264528	232783	241695	288270
Argentina/Argentine	83189	181543	234322	295188	337577
Former USSR/Anc. URSS	450954	x653032			
Poland/Pologne	84450	107213	236440	305104	448125
New Zealand	198004	184550	208314	225737	278760
Nigeria/Nigéria	x134899	196034	x213537	x159940	x98928
Chile/Chili	134435	162202	192803	205059	247533
Russian Federation			x354959	x187292	x134191
Pakistan	144035	147054	191491	196140	201483
Venezuela	72207	160882	150925	140515	97484
Colombia/Colombie	128984	116149	153347	173909	202517
Hungary/Hongrie	x126894	146625	x139410	x148607	x150245
Viet Nam	x71257	x138699	x128630	x122809	x169785
Morocco/Maroc	124867	120085	120871	111855	147082

COUNTRIES–PAYS	EXPORTS – EXPORTATIONS				
	1990	1991	1992	1993	1994
Totale	47502262	49792453	51101563	48368540	58798864
Afrique	x112838	x153042	x211371	x151748	x151210
Afrique du Nord	9916	15603	x40455	x30899	x38051
Amériques	7584241	8518895	8373856	8757610	10371434
ALAI	957455	935004	1065052	1093345	1306471
MCAC	18028	20240	26049	x24724	x37485
Asie	7397326	8709388	9860911	10378899	12900140
Moyen–Orient	1258982	1138085	978804	x940200	x1064799
Europe	31380371	31364488	31557453	27977912	34167948
CEE	30141913	30197739	30233589	26762062	32820024
AELE	1033954	1005123	1069727	1026395	1128403
Océanie	x113402	x155569	x150090	x161437	x182326
Germany/Allemagne	9089237	8946841	9110552	7375792	8880534
USA/Etats–Unis d'Amer	5430668	6261173	5885288	6119507	7118288
France,Monac	4728356	4580799	4568344	3659505	5105499
Belgium–Luxembourg	4162425	4135153	4127881	4289445	5066896
Netherlands/Pays–Bas	4151837	3924878	3849672	3475207	4281884
Japan/Japon	2675579	2829888	3155646	3295163	3912890
Hong Kong	1507144	2198705	2656650	2771199	3535215
United Kingdom	2225058	2532390	2531077	2327720	2714856
Italy/Italie	2067010	2414101	2393186	2233369	2746608
Korea, Republic of	623440	995757	1567674	1676003	2147133
Canada	1172667	1299534	1394153	1510712	1898049
Austria/Autriche	963092	1001697	946101	841076	x893991
Sweden/Suède	911433	882918	869048	813659	931297
Spain/Espagne	826993	790679	819240	805582	1066059
Singapore/Singapour	677199	836070	716877	764204	876729
Saudi Arabia	945935	885710	708403	x670712	x844547
Switz.Liecht	560787	571369	662332	668071	741395
Brazil/Brésil	382175	405046	414191	494949	533479
Norway,SVD,JM	472919	433489	407138	358072	386653
Finland/Finlande	439436	404596	401487	380981	471187
Hungary/Hongrie	x367765	x314729	x446233	x355797	x364733
Mexico/Mexique	265684	259547	374833	322764	380813
Denmark/Danemark	290018	290697	299686	253472	266674
Thailand/Thaïlande	124335	195918	198055	246697	328149
Czechoslovakia		x329019	x261884		
Israel/Israël	184967	183374	171738	179759	218448
Portugal	197303	177598	170780	157319	227447
China/Chine	201212	149861	158953	171908	322964
Australia/Australie	98322	137279	125571	134046	144585
Qatar	156748	128066	146762	119550	x59865
So. Africa Customs Un	89284	121439	153282	100979	107529
Malaysia/Malaisie	45186	59009	110175	178587	258981
Poland/Pologne	139082	120736	129719	82265	72032
Colombia/Colombie	68090	102731	102029	118438	158905
Croatia/Croatie			170462	146008	x173784
Turkey/Turquie	99628	92081	97932	111695	118895
Argentina/Argentine	132876	104532	104857	76337	118141
Ireland/Irlande	62196	75272	75930	104957	116269
Czech Republic				226524	259572
Russian Federation			x65585	x138379	x188754
Indonesia/Indonésie	45062	56436	57693	71752	95864
Slovakia				x174347	x185529
Yugoslavia SFR	200244	x157554			
Greece/Grèce	27519	40119	70604	43978	50823
Romania/Roumanie	68658	38426	59116	48237	99555
Bulgaria/Bulgarie	x107620	x35014	x48970	x53457	x44165
Venezuela	81677	33600	37809	48944	83048
Philippines	20303	24251	32964	29453	28245
New Zealand	14872	17742	23324	26405	36659
India/Inde	18021	15690	23483	27682	88148

(VALUE AS % OF TOTAL)(VALEUR EN % DU TOTAL)

	1985	1986	1987	1988	1989	1990	1991	1992	1993	1994
Africa	3.2	x3.6	x3.1	x3.0	x2.8	x2.5	2.8	x2.6	x2.7	x2.4
Northern Africa	2.0	1.8	1.5	1.4	1.4	1.1	1.3	1.1	1.2	1.2
Americas	10.8	11.6	10.0	9.9	11.6	11.2	11.7	12.9	15.9	15.9
LAIA	2.6	3.9	3.2	3.1	3.0	2.7	3.4	4.0	5.0	5.0
CACM		0.4	0.5	0.5	0.4	0.4	0.4	0.4	x0.5	x0.4
Asia	18.6	17.8	20.3	25.1	20.5	20.7	23.7	26.6	28.8	28.5
Middle East	2.0	x2.6	x2.6	x2.0	x1.9	x2.9	x2.7	x2.9	x3.0	x2.1
Europe	63.6	63.7	62.2	57.9	60.5	62.3	58.4	55.6	49.4	50.2
EEC	54.3	54.0	52.9	49.6	52.2	58.5	55.2	52.4	46.3	47.3
EFTA	9.4	9.3	8.8	7.7	7.8	3.2	2.8	2.7	2.6	2.5
Oceania	2.0	x1.6	x1.6	x1.2	x1.4	x1.3	x1.2	x1.2	x1.5	x1.2
Germany/Allemagne	11.4	11.3	10.9	10.2	10.6	12.2	12.1	11.6	9.8	9.6
France,Monac	7.9	8.0	8.0	7.2	7.5	8.8	8.1	7.9	7.1	7.0
Italy/Italie	7.2	6.9	7.0	6.4	6.9	7.6	7.2	6.8	6.2	6.5
United Kingdom	7.6	7.4	7.7	7.7	7.6	8.1	7.3	6.7	5.0	6.3
China/Chine	4.4	3.3	3.5	6.8	3.7	2.2	3.8	7.0	7.5	7.8
Hong Kong	2.4	2.4	3.3	4.8	4.1	4.2	5.4	5.9	6.2	6.9
USA/Etats–Unis d'Amer	5.2	4.4	3.7	3.5	5.0	5.2	5.1	5.5	6.8	6.8
Belgium–Luxembourg	4.4	4.2	4.0	3.9	4.3	4.8	4.5	4.3	4.6	4.2
Netherlands/Pays–Bas	4.5	4.6	4.4	4.1	4.4	4.9	4.7	4.5	3.8	3.9
Canada	2.7	2.3	2.1	2.5	2.8	2.6	2.6	2.7	3.3	3.3

	1985	1986	1987	1988	1989	1990	1991	1992	1993	1994
Afrique	0.3	x0.2	x0.2	x0.2	x0.3	x0.2	x0.3	x0.4	x0.3	x0.3
Afrique du Nord	0.1	x0.1	x0.0	x0.1	x0.1	0.0	0.0	x0.1	x0.1	x0.1
Amériques	14.1	13.3	13.0	14.2	15.5	16.0	17.1	16.3	18.1	17.6
ALAI	2.1	1.8	2.0	2.4	2.2	2.0	1.9	2.1	2.3	2.2
MCAC		0.1	0.0	0.0	0.0	0.0	0.0	0.1	x0.1	x0.1
Asie	12.4	x12.9	x15.7	x17.7	15.2	15.6	17.5	19.3	21.5	21.9
Moyen–Orient	0.8	x1.8	x2.6	3.0	3.2	2.7	2.3	1.9	x1.9	x1.8
Europe	71.6	72.2	67.2	63.7	66.1	66.1	63.0	61.8	57.8	58.1
CEE	64.7	64.9	60.1	56.9	59.2	63.5	60.6	59.2	55.3	55.8
AELE	6.9	6.9	6.6	6.3	6.5	2.2	2.0	2.1	2.1	1.9
Océanie	0.5	x0.3	x0.2	x0.3	x0.2	x0.2	x0.3	x0.3	x0.3	x0.3
Germany/Allemagne	18.8	19.8	18.4	17.5	17.8	19.1	18.0	17.8	15.2	15.1
USA/Etats–Unis d'Amer	10.0	9.3	8.9	9.1	11.0	11.4	12.6	11.5	12.7	12.1
France,Monac	9.2	9.1	8.1	8.0	9.3	10.0	9.2	8.9	7.6	8.7
Belgium–Luxembourg	9.1	8.7	8.2	7.7	8.1	8.8	8.3	8.1	8.9	8.6
Netherlands/Pays–Bas	9.2	8.9	8.4	8.0	8.0	8.7	7.9	7.5	7.2	7.3
Japan/Japon	7.5	7.3	6.4	5.6	5.5	5.6	5.7	6.2	6.8	6.7
Hong Kong	0.9	1.0	1.6	2.9	2.8	3.2	4.4	5.2	5.7	6.0
United Kingdom	4.8	4.5	4.1	3.8	4.0	4.7	5.1	5.0	4.8	4.6
Italy/Italie	6.1	6.4	5.9	5.0	5.0	4.4	4.8	4.7	4.6	4.7
Korea, Republic of	1.1	1.0	0.9	1.0	1.2	1.3	2.0	3.1	3.5	3.7

TRADE BY COMMODITY IN THOUSAND U.S. DOLLARS – COMMERCE PAR PRODUIT EN MILLIERS DE DOLLARS E.U

COUNTRIES–PAYS	IMPORTS – IMPORTATIONS 1990	1991	1992	1993	1994
Total	2181935	2251261	2351572	2157381	2383035
Africa	85968	82536	80546	x74089	x65347
Northern Africa	42850	40191	45888	36246	34143
Americas	402152	468402	453940	474752	490930
LAIA	155645	212120	181745	191322	204963
CACM	17860	18057	19160	x16420	x15268
Asia	441359	420275	467146	506165	513979
Middle East	x69397	x44333	x66252	x85929	x68901
Europe	1170827	1187140	1278719	1010949	1206130
EEC	1100376	1127848	1207634	952252	1140103
EFTA	55238	52578	55590	47019	53058
Oceania	x52233	x48944	x54249	x53870	x58295
Germany/Allemagne	223693	245237	249046	192946	238346
Italy/Italie	169126	164455	169839	143744	167053
France,Monac	169542	157634	168377	142943	165952
USA/Etats–Unis d'Amer	123916	125379	139109	153964	159752
Belgium–Luxembourg	105771	135535	143867	118590	117595
United Kingdom	133146	130366	143800	70258	118800
Canada	84454	101731	104855	103546	101104
Netherlands/Pays–Bas	64811	73667	96978	94635	120850
Spain/Espagne	96380	84503	89135	58134	68654
Korea, Republic of	60177	67546	71394	73579	74918
China/Chine	49510	58525	61630	75189	63805
Mexico/Mexique	38587	69941	52066	54911	62798
Japan/Japon	65958	55856	60521	56141	73796
Hong Kong	43534	43864	51257	42896	44336
Indonesia/Indonésie	36067	41621	44128	48400	50239
Australia/Australie	41169	39881	44614	43716	48755
Switz.Liecht	43542	38114	38009	33229	38545
Argentina/Argentine	26014	39260	33123	32260	37304
Austria/Autriche	35558	34573	34763	31841	35389
Singapore/Singapour	36893	36384	30261	30412	32599
Sweden/Suède	28898	27964	29683	22798	27441
Colombia/Colombie	30156	23115	29191	26370	24443
Thailand/Thaïlande	20087	21910	26558	29857	34189
Venezuela	13803	29019	22256	23260	26556
So. Africa Customs Un	26950	24579	23472	24209	23915
Ireland/Irlande	13079	17281	18657	24680	21634
Algeria/Algérie	21541	18818	24375	17343	13590
Turkey/Turquie	18410	14763	19972	23662	21667
Brazil/Brésil	16896	20040	15604	22156	26450
Denmark/Danemark	17657	18516	21075	14876	19432
Portugal	17274	16873	18715	14176	15276
Norway,SVD,JM	11199	14193	17282	13547	14229
Malaysia/Malaisie	9588	12360	12426	14168	18371
Greece/Grèce	13800	12175	13345	12219	11601
Kuwait/ Koweït	5742	2836	12617	20128	15458
Philippines	14726	8895	11610	14942	13840
Chile/Chili	8106	10024	12086	10918	9677
Iran (Islamic Rp. of)	x17852	x7680	x8157	x15946	x6832
Finland/Finlande	11640	9068	10353	10414	12079
Poland/Pologne	5911	6647	9081	13501	23273
Israel/Israël	7462	7790	9022	10305	10925
New Zealand	9469	7770	8420	9238	8263
Former USSR/Anc. URSS	7001				
Pakistan	6685	8071	7236	7785	6774
India/Inde	7299	5896	8553	7772	12255
Peru/Pérou	7668	6114	6065	9605	7296
Egypt/Egypte	6705	7060	7753	6156	6112
Uruguay	10937	7246	6654	5417	4994
Morocco/Maroc	6101	5986	6388	5146	6045
Saudi Arabia	7111	3974	4035	x9446	x9409

COUNTRIES–PAYS	EXPORTS – EXPORTATIONS 1990	1991	1992	1993	1994
Totale	1778544	1593072	1658776	1947113	2012630
Afrique	2890	3146	1820	2523	x502
Afrique du Nord	948	1054	628	969	205
Amériques	624340	645243	683725	708790	791905
ALAI	53524	62148	70919	76782	75130
MCAC	1559	2099	2561	x2401	x2197
Asie	209782	217448	214016	213485	222808
Moyen–Orient	7293	3975	8968	x14579	x14229
Europe	926762	712509	740927	995092	968658
CEE	909828	700717	729216	984756	956977
AELE	9515	8441	9605	9250	10525
Océanie	x1532	x791	831	x999	1999
USA/Etats–Unis d'Amer	562518	565823	593447	614384	704036
Germany/Allemagne	141654	128341	145851	346469	395059
Japan/Japon	145400	147187	148175	146593	149082
Italy/Italie	112369	138981	114288	95103	82351
Belgium–Luxembourg	115336	110866	133022	96360	106172
Sweden/Suède	56018	64780	68087	71478	81424
Netherlands/Pays–Bas	57561	60455	58060	69814	75016
Ireland/Irlande	46149	54647	65287	57301	65727
France,Monac	11877	14205	12227	122400	9359
Finland/Finlande	52722	51895	45244	41953	57785
Spain/Espagne	33596	45609	50144	40923	46491
Brazil/Brésil	21667	29823	32593	35490	33616
United Kingdom	275809	24201	29607	36213	29646
Mexico/Mexique	23002	23167	29920	31695	31551
Hong Kong	26176	28127	25064	23336	22303
Singapore/Singapour	16140	22135	19546	15466	19780
Canada	6553	15120	16736	15152	10067
Switz.Liecht	8939	7949	9305	8858	10069
China/Chine	5618	10251	6911	8646	9686
Hungary/Hongrie	x10803	x5567	x8481	x6885	x7048
Colombia/Colombie	6718	7768	6708	6222	6836
Czechoslovakia		x7650	x8226		
Austria/Autriche	4147	4160	5228	4562	x5817
Slovakia				x13062	x7880
Turkey/Turquie	3246	2782	5162	4531	3343
Kuwait/ Koweït	2583	588	3486	5206	6733
India/Inde	1297	1947	1943	1879	3716
Czech Republic				5727	10772
Korea, Republic of	1489	1983	1613	1320	2388
Denmark/Danemark	2016	1650	1432	1758	1427
El Salvador	803	1004	1445	1637	937
So. Africa Customs Un	1745	1827	941	922	
Russian Federation			x1585	x1649	x641
Yugoslavia SFR	6825	x3157			
Venezuela	811	503	1064	1565	295
United Arab Emirates	102	349	160	x2129	x1317
Saudi Arabia	598	x109		x2362	x2128
Argentina/Argentine	504	355	402	1435	2411
Australia/Australie	1273	609	704	773	1606
Tunisia/Tunisie	897	1002	404	622	165
Israel/Israël	1401	1394	200	424	94
Malaysia/Malaisie	126	247	1135	526	729
Costa Rica	267	618	565	x450	x767
Yugoslavia/Yougoslavie			x1274	x261	
Guatemala	488	473	532	296	492
Portugal	325	668	470	143	443
Norway,SVD,JM	576	492	299	391	456
Greece/Grèce	248	258	269	281	261
Poland/Pologne	915	95	560	31	804
Bulgaria/Bulgarie	x468	x95	x131	x376	x241

(VALUE AS % OF TOTAL)(VALEUR EN % DU TOTAL)

	1985	1986	1987	1988	1989	1990	1991	1992	1993	1994
Africa	5.2	5.4	x3.7	x4.5	x3.5	3.9	3.7	3.4	x3.4	x2.7
Northern Africa	2.3	2.4	1.3	1.9	1.6	2.0	1.8	2.0	1.7	1.4
Americas	22.5	20.2	17.8	20.6	19.6	18.4	20.8	19.3	22.0	20.6
LAIA	9.3	8.2	7.7	9.2	7.9	7.1	9.4	7.7	8.9	8.6
CACM	0.8	0.7	0.6	0.7	1.0	0.8	0.8	0.8	x0.8	x0.6
Asia	13.4	13.9	x16.8	x18.0	19.4	20.3	18.6	19.9	23.5	21.6
Middle East	1.7	x2.9	x2.9	x2.7	x3.2	x3.2	x2.0	x2.8	x4.0	x2.9
Europe	54.9	57.0	56.1	52.2	52.4	53.7	52.7	54.4	46.9	50.6
EEC	47.4	48.9	47.7	45.5	45.7	50.4	50.1	51.4	44.1	47.8
EFTA	6.4	7.0	7.2	5.8	5.9	2.5	2.3	2.4	2.2	2.2
Oceania	3.6	x3.0	x3.0	x2.6	x2.8	x2.4	x2.2	x2.4	x2.5	x2.5
Germany/Allemagne	8.4	8.3	7.9	8.1	6.2	10.3	10.9	10.6	8.9	10.0
Italy/Italie	9.0	9.1	8.6	8.3	8.7	7.8	7.3	7.2	6.7	7.0
France,Monac	7.4	7.3	7.1	7.1	7.8	7.8	7.0	7.2	6.6	7.0
USA/Etats–Unis d'Amer	7.9	6.3	5.1	6.3	6.4	5.7	5.6	5.9	7.1	6.7
Belgium–Luxembourg	4.4	4.2	3.7	4.1	4.5	4.8	6.0	6.1	5.5	4.9
United Kingdom	5.3	5.4	5.4	5.6	6.0	6.1	5.8	6.1	3.3	5.0
Canada	3.6	3.4	3.2	3.7	3.6	3.9	4.5	4.5	4.8	4.2
Netherlands/Pays–Bas	3.4	3.6	3.7	3.2	2.8	3.0	3.3	4.1	4.4	5.1
Spain/Espagne	2.1	2.9	2.7	2.9	3.6	4.4	3.8	3.8	2.7	2.9
Korea, Republic of	1.8	1.7	1.8	2.0	2.9	2.8	3.0	3.0	3.4	3.1

	1985	1986	1987	1988	1989	1990	1991	1992	1993	1994
Afrique		x0.1	x0.1	x0.3	x0.3	0.2	0.2	0.2	0.1	x0.0
Afrique du Nord	0.0	x0.0	x0.0	0.1	x0.0	0.1	0.1	0.0	0.0	0.0
Amériques	27.2	26.6	27.3	30.5	32.9	35.1	40.5	41.2	36.4	39.4
ALAI	2.0	2.3	2.8	3.9	3.2	3.0	3.9	4.3	3.9	3.7
MCAC	0.1	0.1	0.1	0.1	0.1	0.1	0.1	0.2	x0.1	x0.1
Asie	9.1	9.0	x8.8	9.8	11.0	11.8	13.6	12.9	11.0	11.1
Moyen–Orient	0.1	x0.2	x0.3	0.4	0.6	0.4	0.2	0.5	x0.7	x0.7
Europe	63.4	64.1	62.6	58.4	54.9	52.1	44.7	44.7	51.1	48.1
CEE	57.4	57.1	55.8	52.7	48.6	51.2	44.0	44.0	50.6	47.5
AELE	5.3	6.4	6.3	5.0	5.7	0.5	0.5	0.6	0.5	0.5
Océanie		x0.0	x0.1	x0.0	x0.1	x0.1	x0.0	0.1	x0.0	0.1
USA/Etats–Unis d'Amer	19.2	18.6	18.4	25.4	28.4	31.6	35.5	35.8	31.6	35.0
Germany/Allemagne	18.6	19.8	19.4	16.4	7.6	8.0	8.1	8.8	17.8	19.6
Japan/Japon	7.8	7.1	6.0	6.2	7.2	8.2	9.2	8.9	7.5	7.4
Italy/Italie	8.6	5.5	5.2	6.2	6.1	6.3	8.7	6.9	4.9	4.1
Belgium–Luxembourg	4.5	5.3	4.8	5.0	6.5	6.5	7.0	8.0	4.9	5.3
Sweden/Suède	1.7	2.3	2.4	2.5	2.8	3.1	4.1	4.1	3.7	4.0
Netherlands/Pays–Bas	5.3	5.5	5.6	2.9	3.3	3.2	3.8	3.5	3.6	3.7
Ireland/Irlande	0.2	0.2	0.3	1.9	2.4	2.6	3.4	3.9	2.9	3.3
France,Monac	2.1	1.9	1.9	0.8	0.7	0.7	0.9	0.7	6.3	0.5
Finland/Finlande	2.2	2.4	2.5	1.8	2.2	3.0	3.3	2.7	2.2	2.9

TRADE BY COMMODITY IN THOUSAND U.S. DOLLARS – COMMERCE PAR PRODUIT EN MILLIERS DE DOLLARS E.U

COUNTRIES–PAYS	IMPORTS – IMPORTATIONS				
	1990	1991	1992	1993	1994
Total	607832	525897	567613	540447	568258
Africa	x17793	28744	x14311	x15895	x10785
Northern Africa	7558	7121	6441	x7916	2896
Americas	152495	135064	190281	190043	200485
LAIA	32449	36376	71705	77170	77669
CACM	10896	13806	15485	3443	x724
Asia	207816	146247	147611	146222	139710
Middle East	97186	20208	20845	x19849	x18269
Europe	204626	198237	201307	169262	196213
EEC	184929	184820	187811	158000	177877
EFTA	15149	12198	11356	9606	16779
Oceania	14428	13860	x12526	x14521	x16749
USA/Etats–Unis d'Amer	64913	69281	89291	92240	104230
Germany/Allemagne	45345	50348	51925	39427	45714
Japan/Japon	28327	34635	37973	40258	38899
Mexico/Mexique	9196	8028	44813	52802	50651
Korea, Republic of	24458	30435	30576	31751	32163
United Kingdom	30041	27282	30643	26884	22541
France, Monac	22668	21659	26255	25228	29372
Italy/Italie	21925	20101	19004	14689	16238
Indonesia/Indonésie	13171	13501	17748	20714	15238
Canada	11814	10143	12100	15327	15404
Netherlands/Pays–Bas	13347	12481	13299	11133	18767
Australia/Australie	11437	12324	10981	13136	15066
Spain/Espagne	14688	13921	13281	8272	9981
Denmark/Danemark	12634	12689	12017	10071	9606
Turkey/Turquie	12228	11792	8758	8302	6249
Argentina/Argentine	6039	10177	10409	6874	8188
Hong Kong	9254	10312	7973	6143	4619
Switz.Liecht	8312	7326	7764	6732	9699
Belgium–Luxembourg	6676	6070	6798	8076	10896
Brazil/Brésil	5592	6609	6034	8066	9175
China/Chine	7469	12027	4986	2306	2672
Singapore/Singapour	6302	5835	7043	6079	6336
Thailand/Thaïlande	4556	4897	5766	6154	5892
Nigeria/Nigéria	x1493	12638	x1594	x2239	x1450
Austria/Autriche	4207	6715	4570	3638	3130
Malaysia/Malaisie	6190	4210	4222	3662	4447
Sweden/Suède	6161	6374	3347	2329	3536
Nicaragua	1473	4926	4627	2357	5
Pakistan	4212	4265	4606	2836	2123
So. Africa Customs Un	4753	5409	3659	2499	2425
Egypt/Egypte	3849	3223	3467	4632	1732
Norway, SVD, JM	6728	4807	3542	2716	6698
Israel/Israël	3214	3152	3654	3265	3778
United Arab Emirates	1004	2183	1830	x5580	x5931
Saudi Arabia	73024	3050	4076	x2427	x4831
Colombia/Colombie	4878	3151	2792	3529	4139
Honduras	4396	3675	4548	63	117
Venezuela	3153	3507	2643	1998	1646
Ireland/Irlande	2505	2622	1401	3692	3235
Portugal	2507	2338	2367	1454	1087
Chile/Chili	1450	1680	2182	1995	2150
Syrian Arab Republic	2937	x1504	3298	x817	x143
Finland/Finlande	1455	1349	2128	2056	2600
Guatemala	1690	1932	2933	67	139
Costa Rica	2109	2132	1826	x400	x300
Morocco/Maroc	1998	1548	1722	873	515
Uruguay	865	1665	1770	448	419
Iran (Islamic Rp. of)	x1620	x834	x1551	x1152	x548
Hungary/Hongrie	x1275	2200	x419	x761	x469
El Salvador	1228	1143	1551	556	163

COUNTRIES–PAYS	EXPORTS – EXPORTATIONS				
	1990	1991	1992	1993	1994
Totale	361253	300715	378315	436388	429667
Afrique	5792	x2619	x3809	x2927	x70
Afrique du Nord	4702	1567	1497	1229	31
Amériques	67738	64371	114049	134130	125695
ALAI	8259	2169	21800	28372	16513
MCAC	986	1019	1719	x122	x122
Asie	92114	100299	78174	77140	80019
Moyen–Orient	x10678	x879	x726	x2574	x1270
Europe	192185	130081	177658	216127	216810
CEE	188233	124677	172814	209972	210337
AELE	3950	5364	4771	6015	6461
Océanie	1252	x2842	4157	x5346	x5843
USA/Etats–Unis d'Amer	50541	55419	83721	99201	103063
Sweden/Suède	39572	43445	66153	61272	60591
France, Monac	38975	37087	45303	60534	53377
China/Chine	43159	53208	35603	31242	37358
Japan/Japon	24792	31178	28875	30406	31937
Germany/Allemagne	12202	12714	12253	24891	28296
Mexico/Mexique	68	58	19734	26048	13580
Austria/Autriche	11397	8892	14951	15901	x17745
Italy/Italie	12630	13354	11131	14474	15241
Hong Kong	9827	10091	8020	6830	4283
United Kingdom	63115			22013	18178
Canada	7053	5661	6710	6331	5932
Denmark/Danemark	1066	751	14422	727	754
Switz.Liecht	3672	5183	4515	5450	5889
Belgium–Luxembourg	5015	4573	4335	4216	4596
Australia/Australie	1230	2812	4139	5199	5825
Singapore/Singapour	2253	2786	1690	2607	2176
Chile/Chili	1188	1786	2002	2151	2848
Netherlands/Pays–Bas	2921	1812	1777	2293	7646
Korea, Republic of	852	1297	1694	1689	1491
Egypt/Egypte	4660	1563	1491	1228	
Spain/Espagne	1148	1103	1428	1726	2786
Ireland/Irlande	74	893	1043	1901	1072
India/Inde	280	600	1179	1125	1021
So. Africa Customs Un	388	426	1426	354	
Costa Rica	322	751	1252	x30	x75
Lebanon/Liban	x126	x747	x618	x663	x708
Cote d'Ivoire	x633	x557	x618	x595	
Saudi Arabia	8344	x23		x1543	x77
Norway, SVD, JM	278	182	256	565	572
Nigeria/Nigéria			x257	x729	x32
Malaysia/Malaisie	32	119	165	367	143
Guatemala	529	156	330		1
Slovakia				x481	x967
Argentina/Argentine	6637	258	37	114	39
United Arab Emirates	x2172			x360	x294
Nicaragua	6	98	108	64	
Indonesia/Indonésie	32	79	156	16	14
Czechoslovakia		x140	x103		
Bulgaria/Bulgarie	x82	x25	x171	x30	x35
Former USSR/Anc. URSS	x1929	x220			
Thailand/Thaïlande	8	12	32	152	14
Slovenia/Slovénia			66	120	3
Panama	110	50	96	37	1
Jordan/Jordanie	18	72	100	3	143
Estonia/Estonie			x32	x133	x99
Czech Republic				163	207
Hungary/Hongrie		x16	x108	x22	x13
Wake Island/Ile de Wak				x125	
Bangladesh	126			112	x13

(VALUE AS % OF TOTAL)(VALEUR EN % DU TOTAL)

	1985	1986	1987	1988	1989	1990	1991	1992	1993	1994
Africa	3.7	3.8	x2.9	x3.9	3.9	x2.9	5.4	x2.5	x3.0	x1.9
Northern Africa	1.0	0.8	0.6	1.0	1.4	1.2	1.4	1.1	x1.5	0.5
Americas	24.8	13.5	12.8	15.1	23.0	25.1	25.7	33.6	35.2	35.3
LAIA	2.0	2.3	2.3	4.8	5.0	5.3	6.9	12.6	14.3	13.7
CACM	13.9	0.7	x0.5	1.6	1.9	1.8	2.6	2.7	0.6	x0.1
Asia	23.0	26.2	22.0	35.8	35.7	34.2	27.8	26.0	27.1	24.6
Middle East	7.8	7.7	4.7	10.6	14.0	16.0	3.8	3.7	x3.7	x3.2
Europe	42.0	50.7	50.3	24.4	27.4	33.7	37.7	35.5	31.3	34.5
EEC	35.3	42.7	43.3	20.6	22.5	30.4	35.1	33.1	29.2	31.3
EFTA	5.8	6.9	6.0	2.5	3.5	2.5	2.3	2.0	1.8	3.0
Oceania	2.1	x1.7	x2.0	3.0	2.3	2.4	2.6	x2.2	x2.7	x3.0
USA/Etats–Unis d'Amer	1.2	1.3	1.2	2.7	8.1	10.7	13.2	15.7	17.1	18.3
Germany/Allemagne	7.9	9.7	9.8	5.2	2.7	7.5	9.6	9.1	7.3	8.0
Japan/Japon	3.5	4.6	4.8	4.4	4.5	4.7	6.6	6.7	7.4	6.8
Mexico/Mexique	0.5	0.4	0.4	0.7	1.3	1.5	1.5	7.9	9.8	8.9
Korea, Republic of	1.7	2.3	1.9	2.0	3.6	4.0	5.8	5.4	5.9	5.7
United Kingdom	4.7	5.4	6.1	4.3	4.1	4.9	5.2	5.4	5.0	4.0
France, Monac	4.5	5.2	5.2	1.2	2.8	3.7	4.1	4.6	4.7	5.2
Italy/Italie	5.2	6.6	6.6	2.3	3.5	3.6	3.8	3.3	2.7	2.9
Indonesia/Indonésie	1.0	1.3	1.1	2.7	1.9	2.2	2.6	3.1	3.8	2.7
Canada	6.3	6.8	6.5	1.3	1.6	1.9	1.9	2.1	2.8	2.7

	1985	1986	1987	1988	1989	1990	1991	1992	1993	1994
Afrique	0.2	x0.4	0.3	3.8	x1.3	1.6	x0.8	x1.0	x0.7	x0.0
Afrique du Nord		x0.0	0.1	0.8	0.3	1.3	0.5	0.4	0.3	0.0
Amériques	29.7	26.1	20.6	46.3	19.5	18.7	21.4	30.1	30.8	29.3
ALAI	2.0	1.9	1.4	2.7	2.0	2.3	0.7	5.8	6.5	3.8
MCAC	1.3	0.1	0.0	0.2	0.1	0.3	0.3	0.5	x0.0	x0.0
Asie	4.2	x5.6	x8.6	x13.3	24.5	25.5	33.4	20.6	17.7	18.7
Moyen–Orient	0.7	x1.1	x2.6	x4.8	x8.1	x3.0	x0.3	x0.2	x0.6	x0.3
Europe	63.0	65.3	66.8	31.0	53.7	53.2	43.3	47.0	49.5	50.5
CEE	56.2	57.8	57.2	24.5	41.9	52.1	41.5	45.7	48.1	49.0
AELE	6.7	7.3	9.2	6.5	11.7	1.1	1.8	1.3	1.4	1.5
Océanie	0.7	x0.8	1.0	x0.1	0.1	0.3	x0.9	1.1	x1.2	x1.4
USA/Etats–Unis d'Amer	26.4	23.4	18.4	42.5	15.5	14.0	18.4	22.1	22.7	24.0
Sweden/Suède	5.1	5.8	5.5	5.0	9.1	11.0	14.4	17.5	14.0	14.1
France, Monac	7.3	7.6	7.1	3.5	8.2	10.8	12.3	12.0	13.9	12.4
China/Chine			1.0	2.6	7.7	11.9	17.7	9.4	7.2	8.7
Japan/Japon	2.7	3.7	3.3	2.0	4.7	6.9	10.4	7.6	7.0	7.4
Germany/Allemagne	10.6	11.3	11.8	2.6	2.4	3.4	4.2	3.2	5.7	6.6
Mexico/Mexique	0.1	0.1	0.1	0.2	0.0	0.0	0.0	5.2	6.0	3.2
Austria/Autriche	0.3	0.5	0.6	1.2	1.9	3.2	3.0	4.0	3.6	x4.1
Italy/Italie	3.0	2.7	2.5	2.3	4.2	3.5	4.4	2.9	3.3	3.5
Hong Kong	0.2	0.4	0.3	0.7	2.7	2.7	3.4	2.1	1.6	1.0

TRADE BY COMMODITY IN THOUSAND U.S. DOLLARS – COMMERCE PAR PRODUIT EN MILLIERS DE DOLLARS E.U

COUNTRIES–PAYS	IMPORTS – IMPORTATIONS				
	1990	1991	1992	1993	1994
Total	8319920	7842218	7594868	7169496	7935004
Africa	x484811	x479921	x497641	x460071	x505298
Northern Africa	x176274	155637	x188575	x165698	x167373
Americas	x1246014	1223512	1362591	x1448137	x1701808
LAIA	346461	408027	460798	522833	694944
CACM	128205	138619	169235	x154190	x162596
Asia	x1442355	x1488059	x1385218	x1417479	x1434265
Middle East	x570950	x550084	x359290	x454546	x346470
Europe	3987702	4010712	3982921	3395371	3780672
EEC	3840397	3867435	3809631	3217833	3608087
EFTA	112188	110045	117484	117468	124070
Oceania	x89339	x95265	x110214	x118400	x143607
France, Monac	1285799	1199546	1220365	940249	1132733
Germany/Allemagne	580783	700465	645253	376386	391544
United Kingdom	309297	329648	324955	370855	366432
Italy/Italie	290208	275625	318206	334335	378920
Canada	292781	275719	300686	325434	420257
Netherlands/Pays–Bas	314324	280813	311504	256361	270523
USA/Etats–Unis d'Amer	217929	201230	262794	294948	274899
Belgium–Luxembourg	241099	264933	210986	248299	288307
Iran (Islamic Rp. of)	x323277	x318096	x112935	x212370	x116993
Spain/Espagne	200281	206470	200606	180096	220340
Japan/Japon	187674	186336	190919	189815	238963
China/Chine	177775	191490	203651	122355	137210
Denmark/Danemark	177661	168837	148204	113428	111242
Thailand/Thaïlande	130538	110146	129401	120554	127596
Former USSR/Anc. URSS	688721	x323982			
Russian Federation			x212566	x111252	x131509
Greece/Grèce	101042	101774	108598	108090	109872
Argentina/Argentine	68051	73573	98414	118435	154166
Ukraine			x50098	x224460	x49116
Hong Kong	63588	80801	104663	82647	85594
Saudi Arabia	88509	104350	85958	x72595	x63371
Switz.Liecht	81599	81461	84648	85114	91723
Austria/Autriche	76393	82492	76556	81261	80437
Mexico/Mexique	45773	59302	73043	104326	156884
Sweden/Suède	85434	79185	86207	63756	83417
Pakistan	61410	85354	69654	68792	64212
Poland/Pologne	16814	44488	69828	89778	121298
Turkey/Turquie	60919	58953	69591	74093	55141
Chile/Chili	50700	56237	71043	69604	65981
So. Africa Customs Un	44974	52798	66298	77522	84494
Egypt/Egypte	56252	56455	61783	67637	48265
Singapore/Singapour	50980	72458	59699	50057	52253
Hungary/Hongrie	x45885	45361	x57821	x77075	x77309
Portugal	73255	71951	58790	48905	66060
Cuba	x125274	x85008	x50783	x41224	x34400
Romania/Roumanie	108605	67553	49359	58106	47820
Ireland/Irlande	51865	58555	53659	56679	65820
Australia/Australie	43503	46862	58850	62042	87363
Costa Rica	43508	50307	63299	x51167	x58185
Brazil/Brésil	41606	45237	61003	45662	86742
Ecuador/Equateur	38352	55333	39040	44932	x51562
Finland/Finlande	52958	47140	45742	39134	42439
Malaysia/Malaisie	36527	39151	42545	43904	50556
Guatemala	36677	36359	49893	37153	40734
Colombia/Colombie	42268	41369	33600	41435	46956
New Zealand	30186	32677	36284	41751	43562
Korea, Republic of	19473	29300	37368	40854	46197
Honduras	23687	28676	37134	40898	33924
Morocco/Maroc	41134	39255	37266	30017	42894
Bulgaria/Bulgarie	x99989	x22529	41036	30690	25966

COUNTRIES–PAYS	EXPORTS – EXPORTATIONS				
	1990	1991	1992	1993	1994
Totale	7346208	7253907	7332731	7112749	8778556
Afrique	x69779	x76149	x90337	x104469	x89250
Afrique du Nord	9530	12631	10947	8326	4826
Amériques	1412115	1301209	1378264	1440519	1562966
ALAI	197871	197303	234658	262106	297243
MCAC	18653	20085	27727	x27713	x35076
Asie	612185	747827	760092	699232	887581
Moyen–Orient	16253	30299	43965	34732	61363
Europe	5095806	5051427	4990736	4731749	6070270
CEE	4505869	4440650	4381649	4206071	5504439
AELE	580394	598389	572956	502090	549417
Océanie	25079	x38164	55935	x63449	x93603
Germany/Allemagne	1530506	1451489	1451712	1279344	1567244
France, Monac	1033936	1082093	1094294	1074134	1336325
USA/Etats–Unis d'Amer	1157244	1050809	1069838	1093736	1162816
United Kingdom	979703	940201	919786	953385	970338
Switz.Liecht	571273	593721	567488	496854	543879
Netherlands/Pays–Bas	426754	387574	392004	376176	488481
Japan/Japon	255347	296072	274610	275415	289909
Italy/Italie	204008	204369	166539	157694	220480
Belgium–Luxembourg	169313	164219	135510	149853	698873
China/Chine	68452	92171	88998	88045	152733
Austria/Autriche	57955	92537	91056	75409	x52677
Colombia/Colombie	46776	68769	87898	96397	101523
Hong Kong	65771	81995	96653	68567	91235
Brazil/Brésil	61221	63746	68470	89889	102183
India/Inde	57619	81813	69045	58738	84162
Singapore/Singapour	33904	52838	67905	61666	59230
So. Africa Customs Un	28453	40048	62711	74162	82302
Spain/Espagne	44827	50932	50195	57176	65954
Israel/Israël	44309	47296	56155	52485	68252
Australia/Australie	21001	33043	51494	54932	60931
Canada	22058	23501	34509	48118	62352
Argentina/Argentine	38526	24027	36169	26749	42100
Sweden/Suède	21605	23016	34291	29457	27439
Malaysia/Malaisie	25835	25698	29613	29331	37591
Mexico/Mexique	14372	19985	20946	21386	22754
Turkey/Turquie	4052	12450	20125	22528	16402
Hungary/Hongrie	x11845	x12805	x18624	x20232	x17927
Denmark/Danemark	15494	17633	13317	15249	16372
Jordan/Jordanie	3765	12253	17647	7964	38294
Cote d'Ivoire	x22692	x14818	x11670	x11241	
Indonesia/Indonésie	25520	15100	12167	8357	10698
Thailand/Thaïlande	8565	15171	10544	9398	14145
Finland/Finlande	7605	9877	11401	13304	16623
Bulgaria/Bulgarie	x34247	x6412	12429	13559	17310
Croatia/Croatie			17991	13840	x4985
Ireland/Irlande	6679	7725	8727	14276	25450
Guatemala	8704	7862	8782	12739	17159
Venezuela	8636	7981	7909	13224	15475
Poland/Pologne	7062	7948	8466	9069	7325
Slovenia/Slovénia			15403	8928	11033
Korea, Republic of	7395	6962	7742	7432	13241
Costa Rica	5063	6360	9830	x5304	x9669
Russian Federation			x9885	x11271	x8557
Barbados/Barbade	6868	7199	6814	5824	x1633
Uruguay	22716	6760	6141	6748	4223
El Salvador	3958	4696	6956	7770	6536
Czech Republic				19008	21756
Egypt/Egypte	4309	9427	6416	2114	2234
New Zealand	3995	4980	4357	8350	32640
Portugal	4420	4847	8047	3429	9358

(VALUE AS % OF TOTAL)(VALEUR EN % DU TOTAL)

	1985	1986	1987	1988	1989	1990	1991	1992	1993	1994
Africa	7.0	x8.9	x7.8	x8.2	x6.4	x5.8	x6.1	x6.6	x6.4	x6.4
Northern Africa	3.2	x3.4	3.0	3.8	x2.5	x2.1	2.0	x2.5	x2.3	x2.1
Americas	22.9	19.5	17.8	18.8	15.5	x14.9	15.6	17.9	x20.2	x21.5
LAIA	4.6	4.5	4.2	4.0	4.5	4.2	5.2	6.1	7.3	8.8
CACM	2.5	2.3	x2.2	1.8	1.8	1.5	1.8	2.2	x2.2	x2.0
Asia	15.0	13.8	x15.6	x16.0	x16.0	x17.3	x19.0	x18.2	x19.8	x18.0
Middle East	3.3	x4.0	x5.3	x4.2	x4.5	x6.9	x7.0	x4.7	x6.3	x4.4
Europe	38.2	40.0	39.7	40.3	47.2	47.9	51.1	52.4	47.4	47.6
EEC	34.2	35.7	35.6	36.3	43.1	46.2	49.3	50.2	44.9	45.5
EFTA	3.4	3.9	3.7	3.6	3.9	1.3	1.4	1.5	1.6	1.6
Oceania	0.9	x0.9	x0.9	x0.8	x1.3	x1.1	x1.2	x1.5	x1.6	x1.8
France, Monac	9.8	10.7	10.5	11.2	14.2	15.5	15.3	16.1	13.1	14.3
Germany/Allemagne	4.7	5.1	5.0	4.8	5.5	7.0	8.9	8.5	5.2	4.9
United Kingdom	4.5	3.7	3.4	3.8	4.3	3.7	4.2	4.3	5.2	4.6
Italy/Italie	2.7	3.0	3.7	3.1	3.5	3.5	3.5	4.2	4.7	4.8
Canada	4.1	3.2	2.4	2.7	4.0	3.5	3.5	4.0	4.5	5.3
Netherlands/Pays–Bas	2.9	2.8	2.9	2.6	3.4	3.8	3.6	4.1	3.6	3.4
USA/Etats–Unis d'Amer	8.7	6.9	6.3	8.1	2.8	2.6	2.6	3.5	4.1	3.5
Belgium–Luxembourg	1.9	2.3	2.5	2.8	2.7	2.9	3.4	2.8	3.5	3.6
Iran (Islamic Rp. of)		x0.8	x2.0	x1.1	x1.4	x3.9	x4.1	x1.5	x3.0	x1.5
Spain/Espagne	1.3	1.6	1.7	1.9	2.3	2.4	2.6	2.6	2.5	2.8

	1985	1986	1987	1988	1989	1990	1991	1992	1993	1994
Afrique	0.8	0.5	x0.6	x0.5	x0.8	x1.0	x1.1	x1.3	x1.4	x1.0
Afrique du Nord	0.0	0.0	0.0	0.0	0.1	0.1	0.2	0.1	0.1	0.1
Amériques	28.9	27.1	25.0	25.6	21.1	19.3	17.9	18.8	20.3	17.8
ALAI	1.6	1.7	2.3	2.1	3.3	2.7	2.7	3.2	3.7	3.4
MCAC	0.4	0.4	0.3	0.3	0.2	0.3	0.3	0.4	x0.4	x0.4
Asie	7.2	6.2	7.4	8.9	9.0	8.4	10.3	10.4	9.8	10.1
Moyen–Orient	0.2	x0.1	0.2	0.2	0.1	0.2	0.4	0.6	0.5	0.7
Europe	61.9	64.8	63.0	60.5	66.1	69.4	69.6	68.1	66.5	69.1
CEE	52.9	56.0	53.3	51.8	56.7	61.3	61.2	59.8	59.1	62.7
AELE	8.8	8.7	9.6	8.6	9.4	7.9	8.2	7.8	7.1	6.3
Océanie	0.3	x0.2	0.4	0.6	x0.5	0.3	x0.5	0.8	x0.9	x1.1
Germany/Allemagne	18.1	20.3	17.3	16.5	18.8	20.8	20.0	19.8	18.0	17.9
France, Monac	9.8	10.2	9.9	9.9	11.8	14.1	14.9	14.9	15.1	15.2
USA/Etats–Unis d'Amer	26.2	24.4	21.8	22.6	17.1	15.8	14.5	14.6	15.4	13.2
United Kingdom	13.6	12.1	13.2	12.7	13.2	13.3	13.0	12.5	13.4	11.1
Switz.Liecht	8.0	7.9	8.6	7.6	8.0	7.8	8.2	7.7	7.0	6.2
Netherlands/Pays–Bas	5.4	5.8	5.4	5.6	5.8	5.8	5.3	5.3	5.3	5.6
Japan/Japon	3.6	3.0	3.2	3.7	4.0	3.5	4.1	3.7	3.9	3.3
Italy/Italie	2.7	3.6	3.5	2.8	2.8	2.8	2.8	2.3	2.2	2.5
Belgium–Luxembourg	1.3	1.8	1.8	1.7	2.0	2.3	2.3	1.8	2.1	8.0
China/Chine	0.2	0.2	0.8	0.8	0.9	0.9	1.3	1.2	1.2	1.7

TRADE BY COMMODITY IN THOUSAND U.S. DOLLARS – COMMERCE PAR PRODUIT EN MILLIERS DE DOLLARS E.U

COUNTRIES–PAYS	IMPORTS – IMPORTATIONS 1990	1991	1992	1993	1994
Total	5367801	5752684	6534816	6311584	7097952
Africa	x116256	x129443	x129284	x125411	x150153
Northern Africa	39094	41470	x46839	46012	47687
Americas	1034692	1025257	1274361	1281894	1450071
LAIA	134396	173277	258345	284135	327902
CACM	11998	12441	16692	x19347	x21807
Asia	1053436	1193160	1371392	1477334	1680475
Middle East	x126802	x130680	x140480	x142609	x107382
Europe	2987951	3188118	3568560	3216219	3563332
EEC	2802286	3013461	3373539	3040600	3370796
EFTA	148439	150543	153797	145724	160249
Oceania	x69234	x68539	x80600	x84392	x98641
USA/Etats–Unis d'Amer	711764	660270	796028	762688	865538
Germany/Allemagne	605898	689751	793259	611272	703619
Japan/Japon	403149	445776	474517	490396	530202
United Kingdom	391226	400576	437122	427324	446117
France,Monac	390917	382609	433485	380791	447360
Italy/Italie	298962	348235	383759	338000	355860
Netherlands/Pays–Bas	280728	300822	331827	344422	348385
Belgium–Luxembourg	191189	201595	223679	224896	253532
Spain/Espagne	149244	156648	187238	164843	196348
Canada	142470	148354	172951	185588	200824
Korea, Republic of	137116	152268	165820	166504	201777
Hong Kong	114819	135890	138979	150879	173251
Mexico/Mexique	79260	89615	142266	151912	175671
Ireland/Irlande	85890	124354	128624	129624	120123
China/Chine	49719	76640	135547	164515	204362
Sweden/Suède	113423	127361	131647	107856	129623
Switz.Liecht	104436	108812	108711	104901	116256
Denmark/Danemark	79892	81232	90922	83367	87454
Finland/Finlande	81702	72331	78026	82660	111251
Indonesia/Indonésie	51220	65341	80327	78759	120035
Austria/Autriche	61407	57056	69281	68523	82988
Australia/Australie	49162	46680	55661	58053	69115
Singapore/Singapour	39918	45714	53797	58220	74307
Malaysia/Malaisie	30615	36698	50366	64892	76503
Thailand/Thaïlande	31632	35095	49962	63698	80874
Poland/Pologne	8795	23407	58478	58525	78745
So. Africa Customs Un	37695	37358	44337	45083	68668
Norway,SVD,JM	41188	38908	42342	38348	41428
Saudi Arabia	39251	46575	45081	x27225	x29013
Greece/Grèce	34138	34257	42368	40728	45070
Portugal	37671	36634	42301	36294	43066
Israel/Israël	25936	27366	34524	33758	39924
Turkey/Turquie	22392	22661	24819	32018	28941
Hungary/Hongrie	x21656	25972	x24309	x27566	x24761
Former USSR/Anc. URSS	35627	x74248			
Iran (Islamic Rp. of)	x18902	x18852	x21991	x33249	x2488
Philippines	23423	22430	21944	28030	34459
Brazil/Brésil	15119	18187	20921	27932	35376
Argentina/Argentine	4302	12641	24436	28708	31724
Venezuela	7513	16370	22602	18589	17588
Chile/Chili	12674	14903	19675	22113	21543
New Zealand	13914	15916	18692	20338	23915
Russian Federation			x37624	x14142	x18715
United Arab Emirates	11464	14025	17309	x14372	x14973
Nigeria/Nigéria	x7490	20572	x10480	x4667	x3072
Czechoslovakia	19125	x16143	x16725		
Algeria/Algérie	5637	5105	9535	15108	9566
Egypt/Egypte	10813	9848	10770	9043	11262
Panama	11070	8979	9900	10322	10896
Colombia/Colombie	5175	5145	9536	11675	16840

COUNTRIES–PAYS	EXPORTS – EXPORTATIONS 1990	1991	1992	1993	1994
Totale	4702144	5050793	5610027	5478396	6133448
Afrique	x12914	x16166	15240	14985	x6069
Afrique du Nord	1925	4351	5439	5434	4963
Amériques	575312	681596	747466	782521	932271
ALAI	86792	110882	130733	138609	159946
MCAC	4570	4657	5601	x5473	x6456
Asie	433766	502239	591072	641092	803160
Moyen–Orient	7759	6334	7809	x7885	x10587
Europe	3240948	3311820	3797870	3531532	3871882
CEE	3093682	3152234	3641295	3433989	3749885
AELE	145184	157943	142488	89103	114306
Océanie	325736	x318508	x328248	x402780	x434316
Germany/Allemagne	757999	778890	870164	825991	909892
Netherlands/Pays–Bas	693919	708820	756627	775104	807634
France,Monac	608774	636835	759824	687757	743917
USA/Etats–Unis d'Amer	423947	501686	531432	551448	675664
New Zealand	295539	293583	288900	310688	387991
Ireland/Irlande	229963	205651	286368	269635	244782
Belgium–Luxembourg	212362	197051	243349	216854	254037
Japan/Japon	163689	183248	205360	225304	250340
United Kingdom	161993	167369	203072	154036	215358
Denmark/Danemark	145509	153822	178358	159505	159821
Italy/Italie	118815	132758	151042	157250	177804
Thailand/Thaïlande	106620	138977	159526	138995	203987
Switz.Liecht	135536	149233	135971	81541	107112
Sweden/Suède	95767	100125	111565	108952	130030
Hong Kong	81018	93681	99865	109190	125394
Poland/Pologne	65016	140780	74639	45179	30885
Canada	57041	61394	76605	84042	88454
Brazil/Brésil	37759	48928	58056	62666	73144
Australia/Australie	30153	22220	39275	91934	46215
Russian Federation			x63475	x60674	x94754
Spain/Espagne	32029	36895	41757	38662	48896
Singapore/Singapour	21885	24550	30878	33776	50114
Korea, Republic of	15855	20718	27513	40653	54100
China/Chine	18086	17593	28772	37090	65350
Hungary/Hongrie	x23963	x19208	x30199	x31828	x27383
Argentina/Argentine	18968	23221	24272	24865	25399
Austria/Autriche	21039	19910	25030	26755	x34669
Ukraine			x17078	x43596	x34512
Colombia/Colombie	12505	15893	16905	17550	17480
Mexico/Mexique	5188	9433	17295	20342	28663
Lithuania/Lituanie			22	x39167	34077
Czechoslovakia		x21394	x16611		
Former USSR/Anc. URSS	8380	x35032			
Indonesia/Indonésie	2567	2406	7165	23360	9670
Finland/Finlande	10135	10867	8429	8215	13521
Malaysia/Malaisie	5656	7090	9878	9339	16711
Uruguay	8507	8983	8604	6183	5788
So. Africa Customs Un	8110	8837	7571	6934	
Belarus/Bélarus			x12413	x10673	x12160
Norway,SVD,JM	9514	8515	6494	7561	7195
Slovenia/Slovénia			11189	5827	6666
Czech Republic				15774	14778
Bulgaria/Bulgarie	x12581	x3634	x7728	x2060	x481
India/Inde	1264	3162	4626	4298	5361
Slovakia				x10138	x9173
Jordan/Jordanie	2829	3233	3927	2731	2501
Guatemala	2173	2188	3223	3533	3938
Pakistan	2088	1929	3530	3318	4146
Latvia/Lettonie			x3418	x3779	6082
Greece/Grèce	1902	1324	2968	2841	3509

(VALUE AS % OF TOTAL)(VALEUR EN % DU TOTAL)

	1985	1986	1987	1988	1989	1990	1991	1992	1993	1994
Africa	2.9	x3.0	x2.5	x2.1	x2.1	x2.2	x2.2	x2.0	x2.0	x2.1
Northern Africa	1.3	0.9	0.8	0.6	0.7	0.7	0.7	x0.7	0.7	0.7
Americas	24.8	21.3	19.8	17.4	20.2	19.3	17.9	19.5	20.3	20.4
LAIA	3.6	2.9	2.6	2.5	2.3	2.5	3.0	4.0	4.5	4.6
CACM	0.8	0.3	0.3	0.2	0.2	0.2	0.2	0.3	x0.3	x0.3
Asia	15.8	16.9	x19.6	x19.2	18.5	19.6	20.7	21.0	23.4	23.6
Middle East	2.2	x2.5	x2.2	x1.9	x1.8	x2.4	x2.3	x2.1	x2.3	x1.5
Europe	53.0	55.0	54.0	57.6	55.4	55.7	55.4	54.6	51.0	50.2
EEC	44.8	47.0	46.1	49.9	47.8	52.2	52.4	51.6	48.2	47.5
EFTA	7.2	7.4	7.1	7.0	7.1	2.8	2.6	2.4	2.3	2.3
Oceania	1.5	x1.4	x1.3	x1.3	x1.3	x1.3	x1.2	x1.2	x1.3	x1.4
USA/Etats–Unis d'Amer	16.6	14.1	13.2	11.3	14.3	13.3	11.5	12.2	12.1	12.2
Germany/Allemagne	8.8	9.1	8.5	9.6	9.1	11.3	12.0	12.1	9.7	9.9
Japan/Japon	7.8	7.5	7.3	8.2	8.0	7.5	7.7	7.3	7.8	7.5
United Kingdom	7.4	7.5	7.6	7.4	7.1	7.3	7.0	6.7	6.8	6.3
France,Monac	5.8	6.0	6.0	6.4	6.6	7.3	6.7	6.6	6.0	6.3
Italy/Italie	5.0	5.1	5.6	7.0	5.5	5.6	6.1	5.9	5.4	5.0
Netherlands/Pays–Bas	4.6	4.7	4.5	4.6	4.8	5.2	5.2	5.1	5.5	4.9
Belgium–Luxembourg	3.4	3.5	3.6	3.7	3.2	3.6	3.5	3.4	3.6	3.6
Spain/Espagne	1.8	2.2	2.5	3.1	2.8	2.8	2.7	2.9	2.6	2.8
Canada	3.2	2.9	2.8	2.9	2.7	2.7	2.6	2.6	2.9	2.8

	1985	1986	1987	1988	1989	1990	1991	1992	1993	1994
Afrique	0.3	x0.3	x0.2	x0.1	x0.1	x0.3	x0.3	0.2	0.2	x0.1
Afrique du Nord	0.0	0.0	0.0	0.0	0.0	0.0	0.1	0.1	0.1	0.1
Amériques	14.0	13.4	12.6	11.5	11.3	12.2	13.4	13.3	14.3	15.2
ALAI	2.3	2.2	2.5	1.8	1.9	1.8	2.2	2.3	2.5	2.6
MCAC	0.3	0.1	0.1	0.2	0.1	0.1	0.1	0.1	x0.1	x0.1
Asie	5.5	5.9	x7.6	x8.6	8.8	9.2	10.0	10.5	11.7	13.1
Moyen–Orient	0.1	x0.1	x0.3	0.2	0.2	0.2	0.1	0.1	x0.1	x0.2
Europe	68.0	69.1	67.9	67.7	69.3	68.9	65.6	67.7	64.5	63.1
CEE	62.9	63.6	62.2	62.2	63.6	65.8	62.4	64.9	62.7	61.1
AELE	5.0	5.5	5.7	5.4	5.6	3.1	3.1	2.5	1.6	1.9
Océanie	9.7	x8.9	x7.2	x6.9	x6.9	6.9	x6.4	x5.8	x7.3	x7.1
Germany/Allemagne	14.5	15.7	14.7	15.3	15.7	16.1	15.4	15.5	15.1	14.8
Netherlands/Pays–Bas	12.2	13.0	12.4	12.0	12.9	14.8	14.0	13.5	14.1	13.2
France,Monac	12.3	12.1	11.8	13.3	13.2	12.9	12.6	13.5	12.6	12.1
USA/Etats–Unis d'Amer	10.2	9.5	8.6	8.6	8.3	9.0	9.9	9.5	10.1	11.0
New Zealand	7.7	7.0	5.3	5.9	6.0	6.3	5.8	5.1	5.7	6.3
Ireland/Irlande	5.4	4.3	4.9	5.2	5.0	4.9	4.1	5.1	4.9	4.0
Belgium–Luxembourg	6.8	6.8	6.4	4.4	4.3	4.5	3.9	4.3	4.0	4.1
Japan/Japon	3.5	3.7	3.3	3.3	3.8	3.5	3.6	3.7	4.1	4.1
United Kingdom	3.3	3.4	3.5	3.2	3.1	3.4	3.3	3.6	2.8	3.5
Denmark/Danemark	2.9	2.6	3.2	3.4	3.7	3.1	3.0	3.2	2.9	2.6

TRADE BY COMMODITY IN THOUSAND U.S. DOLLARS – COMMERCE PAR PRODUIT EN MILLIERS DE DOLLARS E.U

COUNTRIES–PAYS	IMPORTS – IMPORTATIONS 1990	1991	1992	1993	1994
Total	24001399	25240722	27804927	26889847	29620011
Africa	x907291	913370	x1066146	x1032494	x977285
Northern Africa	356675	333283	x371347	x435015	x366762
Americas	2966329	3310782	3885045	4450862	4957974
LAIA	907920	1058230	1302166	1451890	1651453
CACM	44591	45970	61929	x58937	x63434
Asia	6520927	7008350	7967608	8373154	9020794
Middle East	x966808	x1006037	x1078697	x1164972	x1032234
Europe	12377710	12909801	13979360	11985720	13534981
EEC	11411591	12004501	12943587	11114202	12603052
EFTA	713534	729044	793305	692243	784881
Oceania	x481023	x446430	x474858	x528625	x513152
Germany/Allemagne	2178049	2396229	2572912	2047420	2378797
France,Monac	1795523	1801566	1979657	1707335	1980592
Italy/Italie	1568387	1785494	1994817	1545829	1715946
Singapore/Singapour	1569044	1414563	1790849	1799783	1683093
Japan/Japon	1366755	1614595	1557527	1511343	1676529
USA/Etats–Unis d'Amer	1051116	1178131	1459260	1776481	2009304
United Kingdom	1336319	1380369	1425051	1287057	1346621
Belgium–Luxembourg	1067466	1111165	1168238	1016499	1116540
Netherlands/Pays–Bas	961029	970014	1063454	947257	1167161
Korea, Republic of	793371	943585	936667	1005806	1220654
Canada	771983	857658	897166	1001017	1085534
Spain/Espagne	736670	789792	862701	724931	828580
Switz.Liecht	511086	511327	567949	478989	556592
Hong Kong	293877	346067	532410	578320	699253
China/Chine	246101	343058	475819	553253	696587
Austria/Autriche	429920	433883	446330	439425	461478
Sweden/Suède	399502	413585	422770	414898	466585
Mexico/Mexique	232757	267863	387801	472975	556337
Australia/Australie	369946	344038	367982	410957	396414
Indonesia/Indonésie	279993	332910	348597	425979	482555
Thailand/Thaïlande	214481	243031	310809	367435	436886
Iran (Islamic Rp. of)	x216821	x286535	x302648	x325848	x177411
So. Africa Customs Un	243134	254913	287004	286209	307240
Saudi Arabia	211933	277239	264651	x268170	x310894
Malaysia/Malaisie	219826	212918	285793	260445	333898
Denmark/Danemark	218490	220764	236356	204663	232567
Finland/Finlande	244769	209842	206581	213960	243304
Brazil/Brésil	190761	183875	197982	246146	299482
Norway,SVD,JM	193724	208067	215383	204290	218603
Turkey/Turquie	195744	199254	210626	212343	202891
Venezuela	132442	196380	210524	186700	178603
Portugal	188585	193280	225643	166965	184109
Israel/Israël	164403	163491	186001	197298	215340
Greece/Grèce	152268	159128	179666	188256	164830
Argentina/Argentine	114750	150173	185085	189818	201432
Ireland/Irlande	134614	139393	159410	209706	315942
Russian Federation			x263086	x168584	x172204
India/Inde	139742	110378	170441	146191	167346
Nigeria/Nigéria	x92944	135700	x143368	x116432	x70918
Philippines	112384	108352	109565	139214	162902
Egypt/Egypte	121324	111050	123658	120447	102506
Hungary/Hongrie	x112690	129742	x111841	x110498	x107086
Poland/Pologne	29063	49451	127726	160850	207678
Colombia/Colombie	79272	78964	97791	124732	144449
Former USSR/Anc. URSS	191883	x298279			
Pakistan	70483	83959	100546	112951	106008
Chile/Chili	74052	86290	95129	105969	122894
New Zealand	87124	84507	84183	99725	100201
Algeria/Algérie	63816	57556	65748	107403	95066
Libyan Arab Jamahiriya	68709	59797	x70976	x97934	x50059

COUNTRIES–PAYS	EXPORTS – EXPORTATIONS 1990	1991	1992	1993	1994
Totale	21369290	22679665	24872662	25193560	28536531
Afrique	69646	73328	x70784	x71234	x17986
Afrique du Nord	20492	20127	15124	16984	13763
Amériques	4207999	4813960	5278285	5752474	6213498
ALAI	275823	294747	331437	336737	364316
MCAC	6011	7566	8470	8397	x8853
Asie	2777921	2930057	3533630	4287289	5195497
Moyen–Orient	75981	55106	63429	x55597	x60287
Europe	14137997	14722690	15783261	14861916	16845000
CEE	13399536	13990686	14962833	14076002	15917219
AELE	655261	677020	753529	742076	901342
Océanie	x55659	x65870	x73857	x98883	x122182
Germany/Allemagne	4686656	4623758	4828274	4510815	4998707
USA/Etats–Unis d'Amer	3707048	4264463	4623802	5054368	5506401
United Kingdom	1999057	2343352	2395916	2102555	2513685
France,Monac	1825503	1899588	2197841	2144430	2361683
Japan/Japon	1331879	1488599	1655089	1906276	2479813
Netherlands/Pays–Bas	1370390	1397335	1451914	1434751	1608518
Belgium–Luxembourg	1323864	1429228	1383621	1381446	1606620
Italy/Italie	959528	997692	1213308	1198833	1339956
Switz.Liecht	526691	538995	575473	576514	695613
Singapore/Singapour	476987	440957	518053	723920	640390
Hong Kong	260039	291191	445243	516641	590116
Israel/Israël	263616	223658	246311	450729	416092
Sweden/Suède	285225	301158	307887	289986	341668
Canada	204419	233019	304869	331640	316724
Spain/Espagne	186409	215126	263180	235034	272104
Austria/Autriche	204223	207574	230128	212610	x215764
China/Chine	153836	173083	240270	230248	323969
Denmark/Danemark	180509	183415	270672	180838	214706
Norway,SVD,JM	128563	137764	177685	165253	205181
Portugal	180882	177703	161654	103364	117740
Korea, Republic of	92706	109221	146338	174493	231425
Mexico/Mexique	102383	111919	122581	122871	124215
Finland/Finlande	83331	104383	107041	116407	132238
Ireland/Irlande	88116	85645	111805	129543	154826
Brazil/Brésil	105615	97783	102613	115092	120856
Australia/Australie	42184	53580	61602	84811	100897
Malaysia/Malaisie	37963	43231	65667	80248	255476
So. Africa Customs Un	42723	42092	48746	46306	
Venezuela	30014	38490	45441	39675	41468
Argentina/Argentine	26951	33407	47641	42191	52053
Greece/Grèce	25725	24611	39591	35391	39001
Poland/Pologne	6191	6323	69940	18538	23673
Thailand/Thaïlande	20224	24876	30059	38090	50677
Philippines	23624	25763	29891	28948	32434
India/Inde	17130	17694	30382	31905	57587
Russian Federation			x35975	x34054	x36859
Czechoslovakia		x35747	x30628		
Indonesia/Indonésie	10598	16923	18916	30167	39893
Saudi Arabia	18923	24463	28699	x5721	x7172
Yugoslavia SFR	82864	x54471			
Turkey/Turquie	16906	15416	17594	19282	18071
Sri Lanka	12095	13322	16018	15673	14582
Croatia/Croatie			26779	17665	x4234
Slovenia/Slovénia			21549	20316	19865
Hungary/Hongrie	x10724	x8265	x15094	x18138	x15931
Egypt/Egypte	17718	14395	11029	14831	11275
Czech Republic				39708	34234
New Zealand	10948	11983	11332	12975	20847
Slovakia				x33047	x39956
United Arab Emirates	29956	4432	6003	x20490	x24373

(VALUE AS % OF TOTAL)(VALEUR EN % DU TOTAL)

	1985	1986	1987	1988	1989	1990	1991	1992	1993	1994
Africa	4.4	x5.2	x4.4	x4.5	x3.6	x3.8	3.6	x3.8	x3.9	x3.3
Northern Africa	2.0	2.4	1.8	1.9	1.6	1.5	1.3	x1.3	x1.6	x1.2
Americas	15.4	13.7	12.4	12.1	12.3	12.4	13.2	14.0	16.5	16.7
LAIA	6.7	5.2	4.5	4.3	4.0	3.8	4.2	4.7	5.4	5.6
CACM	0.3	0.2	x0.3	0.2	0.2	0.2	0.2	0.2	x0.2	x0.2
Asia	20.1	19.5	x21.5	x22.8	24.7	27.2	27.7	28.7	31.2	30.5
Middle East	3.6	x4.3	x4.0	x4.0	x3.1	x4.0	x4.0	x3.9	x4.3	x3.5
Europe	54.4	56.9	55.5	54.3	53.1	51.6	51.1	50.3	44.6	45.7
EEC	45.7	47.9	46.6	45.8	44.9	47.5	47.6	46.6	41.3	42.5
EFTA	7.3	7.7	7.5	7.2	7.2	3.0	2.9	2.9	2.6	2.6
Oceania	2.5	x2.1	x1.8	x2.0	x2.0	x2.0	x1.8	x1.7	x2.0	x1.8
Germany/Allemagne	9.7	10.1	9.5	8.7	8.5	9.1	9.5	9.3	7.6	8.0
France,Monac	6.7	7.0	6.9	7.2	7.2	7.5	7.1	7.1	6.3	6.7
Italy/Italie	6.3	6.9	6.8	6.7	6.4	6.5	7.1	7.2	5.7	5.8
Singapore/Singapour	1.7	1.4	1.3	1.6	5.3	6.5	5.6	6.4	6.7	5.7
Japan/Japon	6.2	6.0	5.2	5.5	5.8	5.7	6.4	5.6	5.6	5.7
USA/Etats–Unis d'Amer	3.5	3.4	3.5	3.6	3.9	4.4	4.7	5.2	6.6	6.8
United Kingdom	5.5	5.3	5.5	5.6	5.4	5.6	5.5	5.1	4.8	4.5
Belgium–Luxembourg	4.1	4.4	4.3	4.0	4.0	4.4	4.4	4.2	3.8	3.8
Netherlands/Pays–Bas	4.3	4.1	3.8	4.0	3.9	4.0	3.8	3.8	3.5	3.9
Korea, Republic of	2.0	2.2	2.3	2.6	3.1	3.3	3.7	3.4	3.7	4.1

	1985	1986	1987	1988	1989	1990	1991	1992	1993	1994
Afrique	0.2	x0.2	x0.1	x0.2	x0.3	0.3	0.3	x0.3	x0.3	x0.1
Afrique du Nord	0.0	x0.0	x0.0	0.0	0.1	0.1	0.1	0.1	0.1	0.0
Amériques	20.7	18.2	17.2	17.9	18.6	19.7	21.2	21.2	22.9	21.8
ALAI	1.8	1.2	1.2	1.5	1.3	1.3	1.3	1.3	1.3	1.3
MCAC	0.0	0.0	0.0	0.0	0.0	0.0	0.0	0.0	0.0	x0.0
Asie	11.8	11.0	12.2	13.0	13.7	13.0	12.9	14.2	17.1	18.2
Moyen–Orient	0.4	0.3	x0.3	x0.4	x0.3	0.4	0.2	0.3	x0.2	x0.2
Europe	66.0	69.2	68.1	66.6	66.1	66.2	64.9	63.5	59.0	59.0
CEE	60.8	63.5	62.3	60.8	60.4	62.7	61.7	60.2	55.9	55.8
AELE	5.0	5.6	5.6	5.5	5.3	3.1	3.0	3.0	2.9	3.2
Océanie	0.2	0.2	x0.3	0.2	x0.2	x0.2	x0.3	x0.3	x0.4	x0.4
Germany/Allemagne	20.1	22.4	22.5	22.3	21.6	21.9	20.4	19.4	17.9	17.5
USA/Etats–Unis d'Amer	17.1	15.1	14.3	15.3	16.1	17.3	18.8	18.6	20.1	19.3
United Kingdom	9.8	10.0	9.7	8.4	8.5	9.4	10.3	9.6	8.3	8.8
France,Monac	8.5	8.8	8.6	8.5	8.4	8.5	8.4	8.8	8.5	8.3
Japan/Japon	5.5	5.8	6.1	6.6	6.4	6.2	6.6	6.7	7.6	8.7
Netherlands/Pays–Bas	6.6	7.0	6.5	6.6	6.6	6.4	6.2	5.8	5.7	5.6
Belgium–Luxembourg	5.5	5.8	5.5	5.4	5.6	6.2	6.3	5.6	5.5	5.6
Italy/Italie	3.9	3.6	3.7	4.1	4.3	4.5	4.4	4.9	4.8	4.7
Switz.Liecht	1.9	2.3	2.3	2.3	2.3	2.5	2.4	2.3	2.3	2.4
Singapore/Singapour	1.4	1.3	1.3	1.4	2.4	2.2	1.9	2.1	2.9	2.2

TRADE BY COMMODITY IN THOUSAND U.S. DOLLARS – COMMERCE PAR PRODUIT EN MILLIERS DE DOLLARS E.U

COUNTRIES–PAYS	IMPORTS – IMPORTATIONS 1990	1991	1992	1993	1994	COUNTRIES–PAYS	EXPORTS – EXPORTATIONS 1990	1991	1992	1993	1994
Total	10305426	9043480	10072584	10478301	12987637	Totale	9294917	8810946	9734104	10529564	12800322
Africa	179568	161443	173543	149411	205745	Afrique	x134476	133586	x145734	x218947	x395343
Northern Africa	87115	93064	97011	83510	102776	Afrique du Nord	19649	19232	x22771	x25259	66713
Americas	1264655	1135565	1281950	1490704	x1680899	Amériques	1863869	1783039	1867987	2129536	2339055
LAIA	254119	295278	369291	453383	442202	ALAI	1022816	1031527	1084839	1277450	1535736
CACM	7085	2579	4294	x10288	x18249	MCAC	5776	4279	5919	x10897	x19887
Asia	2387976	2840862	3907992	4727758	5543695	Asie	2249508	2362789	2864771	3345481	4316866
Middle East	153050	144963	153077	190744	194458	Moyen–Orient	29603	x14179	x16139	x65081	x107443
Europe	5344919	4382445	4332399	3654349	4987050	Europe	4739562	4188608	4454604	4374161	5202123
EEC	4960843	4044905	4083724	3484448	4730011	CEE	4593469	4076838	4284634	4201606	5023462
EFTA	136082	104156	108259	98510	107219	AELE	54138	46391	55884	61239	66551
Oceania	103464	x92684	95929	x92301	x113541	Océanie	x233469	x235463	x279378	x321588	x358681
Hong Kong	683564	895856	1162684	1483097	1786452	Italy/Italie	2091495	1868626	1986596	2107575	2661775
Italy/Italie	1429972	1052195	1044011	974912	1616881	Hong Kong	465036	605012	805832	1041364	1231428
China/Chine	188439	359749	1081601	1465010	1762839	Korea, Republic of	304255	502762	760177	970692	1302482
Germany/Allemagne	916611	812176	844854	684792	762562	USA/Etats–Unis d'Amer	774073	702839	731901	795369	719748
USA/Etats–Unis d'Amer	720858	603692	667945	778476	897910	Germany/Allemagne	690979	682917	717275	617382	685468
France,Monac	686706	579876	574835	456600	543596	Argentina/Argentine	475203	499674	457408	598760	733416
Korea, Republic of	599834	548132	481645	468657	576863	Brazil/Brésil	287561	305613	385606	401252	457322
Portugal	399683	350876	384282	333689	418805	France,Monac	443810	383757	356078	308706	356653
Spain/Espagne	407437	382498	384657	300054	487076	United Kingdom	423916	343202	350842	335290	373643
United Kingdom	357739	266944	262273	250817	286974	India/Inde	447104	295752	311498	269396	382399
Indonesia/Indonésie	95550	184879	261534	318355	346449	Pakistan	300769	252867	235871	216484	248512
Thailand/Thaïlande	158041	180166	239859	243961	272953	Spain/Espagne	227273	197771	224899	256009	309386
Japan/Japon	250275	211534	192090	175610	201988	Japan/Japon	255113	228155	219046	220437	220442
Canada	238018	191866	185318	189348	217091	Netherlands/Pays–Bas	230688	197703	203910	172845	187934
Brazil/Brésil	179379	182538	158538	197027	184001	Australia/Australie	129798	130946	169298	202303	220232
Netherlands/Pays–Bas	229009	186390	187839	136504	179270	Austria/Autriche	197611	156556	171874	145975	x135864
Hungary/Hongrie	x148508	120908	x148709	x151470	x142434	Thailand/Thaïlande	86922	105465	137203	169026	227568
Turkey/Turquie	109159	104320	113948	152213	157119	Bangladesh	89401	109516	128635	143271	x165950
Austria/Autriche	147061	123930	128043	104080	120090	China/Chine	128210	109691	119459	124817	277953
Belgium–Luxembourg	138217	113865	114573	104039	137865	New Zealand	103450	104205	109909	118942	138137
Mexico/Mexique	33523	37814	99428	139740	160922	Uruguay	120624	112254	107554	100441	122732
Singapore/Singapour	79873	85793	86148	82846	108565	Belgium–Luxembourg	107437	81153	77704	81473	102955
Australia/Australie	89039	81168	85371	81785	100125	So. Africa Customs Un	56309	55505	64373	77441	119969
Switz.Liecht	105500	77731	79179	74945	76395	Indonesia/Indonésie	63549	46430	61052	44840	46948
Former USSR/Anc. URSS	790135	x221195				Sweden/Suède	51963	45414	48417	49505	53541
Yugoslavia SFR	229451	x216008				Slovenia/Slovénia			74908	60976	68514
Philippines	31943	79534	61958	71725	68088	Singapore/Singapour	33268	35190	38865	49522	75341
India/Inde	69724	57244	67700	81394	71859	Poland/Pologne	9743	22500	49508	50206	57222
Tunisia/Tunisie	45417	42887	66249	56561	73750	Mexico/Mexique	28028	30464	44572	46015	73586
So. Africa Customs Un	75532	56022	55332	50861	90545	Paraguay	26973	27181	36143	50407	60531
Romania/Roumanie		4329	54670	78423	121985	Colombia/Colombie	34209	32030	33009	46943	53999
Dominican Republic	x35788	x36084	x46835	x53629	x100538	Denmark/Danemark	33513	32992	40398	34390	34673
Sweden/Suède	57649	48446	42591	40129	46632	Canada	49567	34311	35845	34064	43514
Greece/Grèce	53856	39399	41257	38201	48067	Portugal	23506	26494	38904	30767	38363
Malaysia/Malaisie	19183	30804	39928	44373	62697	Russian Federation			x35566	x58485	x130534
Poland/Pologne	17822	31025	5223	78135	98522	Nigeria/Nigéria	x17499	8897	x15174	x66451	x123340
Denmark/Danemark	46763	42707	39234	30537	36924	Hungary/Hongrie	x39925	x27643	x31283	x26957	x34506
Russian Federation			x70709	x25411	x40920	Norway,SVD,JM	25483	23328	28727	30604	33990
Czechoslovakia	19679	x30794	x57758			Switz.Liecht	27874	22457	26709	30163	32542
Finland/Finlande	79035	36454	28443	22572	37389	Kenya	20666	25350	24402	27508	x52546
Uruguay	21757	31271	29880	25315	28250	Greece/Grèce	27159	22611	27386	25286	22510
Yugoslavia/Yougoslavie			x76768	x2150		Finland/Finlande	25343	21222	21798	22462	25906
Norway,SVD,JM	29697	25613	28482	23111	30338	Yugoslavia SFR	91814	x64195			
Israel/Israël	21127	20670	25164	28435	26796	Yugoslavia/Yougoslavie			x21870	x30684	x9748
Morocco/Maroc	29332	29395	25764	18888	21002	Czechoslovakia		x16137	x34680		
Chile/Chili	8384	20111	26971	25206	19712	Ireland/Irlande	18773	16417	18554	13941	34790
Slovenia/Slovénia			34236	36910	46009	Venezuela	27480	9627	8710	18735	19049
Venezuela	3170	16062	26860	24138	14695	Ukraine			x5075	x31652	x37557
Colombia/Colombie	6570	5012	22760	33708	18396	Saudi Arabia	20240			x36445	x60568
Cyprus/Chypre	25483	19522	22740	13299	15444	Former USSR/Anc. URSS		x34588			

(VALUE AS % OF TOTAL)(VALEUR EN % DU TOTAL)

	1985	1986	1987	1988	1989	1990	1991	1992	1993	1994
Africa	1.5	1.4	1.2	1.6	1.6	1.7	1.8	1.7	1.4	1.6
Northern Africa	0.9	0.8	0.6	0.7	0.7	0.8	1.0	1.0	0.8	0.8
Americas	15.1	15.0	14.3	15.4	16.3	12.3	12.6	12.8	14.2	x13.0
LAIA	2.6	3.7	3.1	2.8	3.9	2.5	3.3	3.7	4.3	3.4
CACM	0.1	0.1	x0.1	0.0	0.0	0.1	0.0	0.0	x0.1	x0.1
Asia	14.1	15.0	19.5	21.2	21.6	23.1	31.4	38.8	45.1	42.7
Middle East	0.7	x1.0	1.4	x1.0	1.1	1.5	1.6	1.5	1.8	1.5
Europe	61.4	62.0	54.9	51.6	51.1	51.9	48.5	43.0	34.9	38.4
EEC	53.6	54.1	48.7	45.8	44.6	48.1	44.7	40.5	33.3	36.4
EFTA	6.1	6.2	4.9	4.2	4.1	1.3	1.2	1.1	0.9	0.8
Oceania	1.5	x1.5	x1.4	x1.4	1.2	1.0	x1.0	0.9	x0.9	x0.9
Hong Kong	3.3	3.9	4.6	5.6	6.5	6.6	9.9	11.5	14.2	13.8
Italy/Italie	12.8	12.6	11.9	12.4	13.1	13.9	11.6	10.4	9.3	12.4
China/Chine			1.8	1.8	1.8	1.8	4.0	10.7	14.0	13.6
Germany/Allemagne	12.9	13.2	11.4	9.8	8.3	8.9	9.0	8.4	6.5	5.9
USA/Etats–Unis d'Amer	9.8	8.4	8.2	9.3	8.8	7.0	6.7	6.6	7.4	6.9
France,Monac	8.4	8.3	6.7	6.1	6.2	6.7	6.4	5.7	4.4	4.2
Korea, Republic of	6.9	6.9	6.2	6.5	6.8	5.8	6.1	4.8	4.5	4.4
Portugal	2.0	2.5	2.7	3.1	2.9	3.9	3.9	3.8	3.2	3.2
Spain/Espagne	2.3	2.4	2.7	3.1	3.5	4.0	4.2	3.8	2.9	3.8
United Kingdom	5.3	4.9	4.5	4.0	3.5	3.5	3.0	2.6	2.4	2.2

	1985	1986	1987	1988	1989	1990	1991	1992	1993	1994
Afrique	0.9	x1.5	x1.9	x2.9	x2.0	x1.4	1.5	x1.5	x2.0	x3.1
Afrique du Nord	0.0	x0.0	x0.1	x0.1	x0.1	0.2	0.2	x0.2	x0.2	0.5
Amériques	19.0	17.7	16.1	18.5	18.5	20.1	20.3	19.2	20.2	18.3
ALAI	11.3	10.4	9.6	11.4	9.9	11.0	11.7	11.1	12.1	12.0
MCAC	0.2	0.1	0.1	0.1	0.1	0.1	0.0	0.1	x0.1	x0.2
Asie	22.3	22.2	25.5	x25.2	23.0	24.2	26.8	29.5	31.8	33.7
Moyen–Orient	0.1	x0.1	x0.2	0.4	0.4	0.3	x0.2	x0.2	x0.6	x0.8
Europe	55.2	56.0	52.6	49.6	52.9	51.0	47.5	45.8	41.5	40.6
CEE	50.2	50.8	47.8	45.3	48.5	49.4	46.3	44.0	39.9	39.2
AELE	4.3	4.8	4.2	3.6	3.5	0.6	0.5	0.6	0.6	0.5
Océanie	2.5	x2.5	x2.8	x2.7	x2.6	x2.5	x2.7	x2.9	x3.1	x2.8
Italy/Italie	20.9	21.5	20.4	19.8	22.3	22.5	21.2	20.4	20.0	20.8
Hong Kong	1.7	2.2	2.9	3.7	4.5	5.0	6.9	8.3	9.9	9.6
Korea, Republic of	0.3	0.5	1.1	1.5	2.4	3.3	5.7	7.8	9.2	10.2
USA/Etats–Unis d'Amer	6.6	6.1	5.7	6.3	7.8	8.3	8.0	7.5	7.6	5.6
Germany/Allemagne	7.6	8.0	6.9	6.8	7.0	7.4	7.8	7.4	5.9	5.4
Argentina/Argentine	6.3	6.4	5.0	4.6	4.4	5.1	5.7	4.7	5.7	5.7
Brazil/Brésil	3.2	2.1	2.6	4.5	2.9	3.1	3.5	4.0	3.8	3.6
France,Monac	5.5	5.1	5.4	4.9	5.1	4.8	4.4	3.7	2.9	2.8
United Kingdom	4.7	4.7	4.9	4.3	4.4	4.6	3.9	3.6	3.2	2.9
India/Inde	7.7	7.1	6.5	5.8	5.6	4.8	3.4	3.2	2.6	3.0

TRADE BY COMMODITY IN THOUSAND U.S. DOLLARS – COMMERCE PAR PRODUIT EN MILLIERS DE DOLLARS E.U

COUNTRIES–PAYS	IMPORTS – IMPORTATIONS 1990	1991	1992	1993	1994
Total	3252868	3763683	4339916	4533435	4978188
Africa	x85258	x107691	x101316	x91548	x98343
Northern Africa	46774	67439	x54605	x50077	x59476
Americas	x703967	x697921	879225	923576	x1062437
LAIA	28880	25772	141331	123484	157816
CACM	3041	3314	3139	x5341	x5145
Asia	684028	899316	1140695	1356729	1367214
Middle East	x36706	x26893	x30718	x45299	x35557
Europe	1644493	1794713	1994979	1936424	2147179
EEC	1519577	1623504	1718766	1686271	1957607
EFTA	81210	74216	81114	76193	88245
Oceania	x45630	x42064	x33241	x40196	x46706
USA/Etats–Unis d'Amer	598976	596461	661420	713522	803651
Germany/Allemagne	505003	545083	549583	481111	504102
China/Chine	167105	263792	367780	359519	307399
Hong Kong	144886	209846	298447	426548	384352
Italy/Italie	175975	248461	316925	355956	490802
France,Monac	256296	257221	232470	211383	234563
United Kingdom	137238	134687	141375	192318	208781
Japan/Japon	103742	125639	147772	167656	208900
Austria/Autriche	114026	102292	109298	118246	137202
Indonesia/Indonésie	59918	87552	93638	108936	121683
Portugal	74679	79381	100424	95582	122363
Korea, Republic of	82181	77025	86300	110655	142147
Croatia/Croatie			129333	136913	x52728
Hungary/Hongrie	x51371	57029	x91339	x78547	x73285
Switz.Liecht	68768	62255	67686	64669	74458
Mexico/Mexique	6786	7184	104999	79445	115709
Netherlands/Pays–Bas	56562	63026	69888	57825	61846
Denmark/Danemark	49124	51940	57531	51169	56759
Former USSR/Anc. URSS		x131780			
Canada	42251	37678	42588	51208	50746
Sweden/Suède	40138	43216	40510	34011	34721
Belgium–Luxembourg	43737	40628	41353	31808	33108
Thailand/Thaïlande	23012	30973	37486	36413	44673
Yugoslavia SFR	39397	x92028			
Australia/Australie	29112	30131	23516	30670	36314
Spain/Espagne	25897	25817	27251	26426	32315
Russian Federation			x55082	x23206	x45619
Philippines	12646	23401	20212	27413	26466
Czechoslovakia	11686	x23337	x46339		
Libyan Arab Jamahiriya	17949	35260	x17878	x16131	x15378
Dominican Republic	x14449	x19424	x17835	x16893	x32435
Tunisia/Tunisie	11467	14015	19195	20201	24504
India/Inde	13529	12732	16540	21787	21999
So. Africa Customs Un	13441	16397	17198	16424	15649
Slovenia/Slovénia			21373	28248	31998
Israel/Israël	11897	12842	17082	16999	16616
Romania/Roumanie		1172	19356	25522	45742
Finland/Finlande	24712	16031	13680	13161	21845
Singapore/Singapour	10889	11687	12075	16741	19890
Turkey/Turquie	8982	9083	11255	19516	9866
Yugoslavia/Yougoslavie			x38218	x618	
Bulgaria/Bulgarie	x12046	x7418	19857	x10078	x27358
Norway,SVD,JM	11690	11127	12583	10806	12960
Morocco/Maroc	9851	11492	10499	8483	10038
Brazil/Brésil	17225	9614	8760	11587	13040
Greece/Grèce	8408	8366	9976	11452	12816
Poland/Pologne		11	7357	20589	27327
New Zealand	14039	9379	7566	8105	7971
Panama	5242	7121	7240	8505	5889
Slovakia				x22656	x28166

COUNTRIES–PAYS	EXPORTS – EXPORTATIONS 1990	1991	1992	1993	1994
Totale	2868393	3192464	3735944	4023923	4740901
Afrique	77767	86391	116839	90131	98807
Afrique du Nord	75092	83368	112068	82221	95687
Amériques	x443975	x466702	543602	636634	x679394
ALAI	192423	204375	257509	325283	357400
MCAC	4783	3034	4546	x4462	x6531
Asie	965652	1042637	1227586	1403886	1694597
Moyen–Orient	11250	x7007	6143	x5702	7440
Europe	1283917	1451386	1592151	1513114	1748675
CEE	1228971	1298619	1414338	1360054	1578104
AELE	18591	17010	18501	20748	26557
Océanie	9345	11989	12739	16863	17145
Italy/Italie	452150	470769	554984	597388	731362
India/Inde	385238	355139	311643	271401	301987
Hong Kong	151729	209881	314511	394899	388736
Germany/Allemagne	267466	282216	295305	262096	274966
USA/Etats–Unis d'Amer	176695	197338	225057	246407	263568
Korea, Republic of	155023	166766	160199	192105	236125
Thailand/Thaïlande	160566	159386	164891	172020	188680
China/Chine	33055	56425	169427	244186	445139
Portugal	110029	120954	133591	131248	146075
Hungary/Hongrie	x83106	x84834	x127656	x114237	x112062
France,Monac	95567	111232	103314	84299	101249
United Kingdom	74043	79642	90219	76709	97081
Brazil/Brésil	80741	74894	72768	97349	96801
Tunisia/Tunisie	50200	59071	91310	64534	81961
Spain/Espagne	88841	75320	63479	62956	82616
Argentina/Argentine	30635	44633	45586	107898	122201
Austria/Autriche	42208	59139	65871	61118	x46945
Mexico/Mexique	19806	19404	72868	72557	85673
Croatia/Croatie			76354	77626	x79374
Colombia/Colombie	36931	48235	54003	38398	40058
Albania/Albanie	x2115	x18482	x25506	x71926	x40043
Yugoslavia SFR	14619	x114615			
Dominican Republic	x43265	x39549	x35866	x36736	x24860
Japan/Japon	23946	28603	34983	40023	36564
Poland/Pologne		35	24744	72439	73047
Netherlands/Pays–Bas	32863	34118	38567	24067	26329
Belgium–Luxembourg	30655	32323	31718	29003	29891
Romania/Roumanie		8107	15112	51495	125365
Malta/Malte	21641	21095	26394	24901	x25402
Indonesia/Indonésie	8504	13229	23786	33641	40343
Canada	21357	20378	20330	23496	26806
Pakistan	13002	18107	17515	23778	20519
Slovenia/Slovénia			31819	26951	28347
Czechoslovakia		x13446	x42881		
Switz.Liecht	17623	16067	17881	20098	24772
Morocco/Maroc	18080	18479	14888	11741	11367
Denmark/Danemark	10371	8154	12496	9345	13122
Czech Republic				26861	28983
Uruguay	20619	14046	8775	3900	3237
Finland/Finlande	11807	9259	7647	6917	8393
Yugoslavia/Yougoslavie				x56	x12
Sweden/Suède	7100	7225	8895	6737	10780
Bulgaria/Bulgarie	x20	x6533	x7110	x9003	x26144
Australia/Australie	3135	4037	6577	10396	6123
Malaysia/Malaisie	8503	6112	6414	7439	9121
Philippines	6077	9054	5045	3336	1686
Slovakia				x17333	x28305
Egypt/Egypte	5947	5311	5837	5929	2330
Singapore/Singapour	3708	6646	4695	4798	6648
Ireland/Irlande	4101	5502	5966	4663	5742

(VALUE AS % OF TOTAL)(VALEUR EN % DU TOTAL)

	1985	1986	1987	1988	1989	1990	1991	1992	1993	1994
Africa	3.6	x3.2	x2.2	x2.3	x2.4	x2.6	x2.8	x2.3	x2.1	x2.0
Northern Africa	2.5	1.9	1.3	1.3	1.4	1.4	1.8	x1.3	x1.1	x1.2
Americas	37.1	x32.4	x22.7	x24.0	x21.9	x21.6	x18.5	20.2	20.4	x21.4
LAIA	2.6	0.3	0.4	0.4	0.5	0.9	0.7	3.3	2.7	3.2
CACM	0.6	0.3	x0.2	0.1	0.1	0.1	0.1	0.1	x0.1	x0.1
Asia	5.7	x6.5	x7.4	x9.7	14.4	21.1	23.9	26.3	30.0	27.4
Middle East	0.9	x1.2	x0.7	x0.8	x0.9	x1.1	x0.7	x0.7	x1.0	x0.7
Europe	50.8	55.8	45.5	45.4	46.6	50.6	47.7	46.0	42.7	43.1
EEC	42.2	46.6	38.0	37.8	38.7	46.7	43.1	39.6	37.2	39.3
EFTA	8.1	8.7	6.8	7.0	7.0	2.5	2.0	1.9	1.7	1.8
Oceania	2.1	x1.6	x1.0	x1.3	1.6	x1.4	x1.1	x0.7	x0.9	x0.9
USA/Etats–Unis d'Amer	30.6	26.1	18.9	20.1	18.3	18.4	15.8	15.2	15.7	16.1
Germany/Allemagne	14.8	17.2	13.8	12.7	13.2	15.5	14.5	12.7	10.6	10.1
China/Chine			0.9	1.5	3.1	5.1	7.0	8.5	7.9	6.2
Hong Kong	0.9	1.0	1.1	2.0	3.9	4.5	5.6	6.9	9.4	7.7
Italy/Italie	1.4	1.8	1.7	2.3	3.5	5.4	6.6	7.3	7.9	9.9
France,Monac	9.4	10.5	7.7	7.1	7.2	7.9	6.8	5.4	4.7	4.7
United Kingdom	3.2	3.1	2.9	3.5	3.2	4.2	3.6	3.3	4.2	4.2
Japan/Japon	1.7	1.7	1.7	2.1	2.6	3.2	3.3	3.4	3.7	4.2
Austria/Autriche	3.1	3.3	2.8	2.9	2.9	3.5	2.7	2.5	2.6	2.8
Indonesia/Indonésie	0.1	0.1	0.1	0.3	0.8	1.8	2.3	2.2	2.4	2.4

	1985	1986	1987	1988	1989	1990	1991	1992	1993	1994
Afrique	2.0	2.8	2.0	x2.4	2.4	2.7	2.7	3.2	2.2	x3.4
Afrique du Nord	1.9	2.6	1.9	1.8	2.4	2.6	2.6	3.0	2.0	1.9
Amériques	20.8	x18.0	x16.4	x16.9	16.4	x15.5	x14.6	14.6	15.8	x14.3
ALAI	8.4	6.9	6.9	6.9	7.4	6.7	6.4	6.9	8.1	7.5
MCAC	0.5	0.3	0.2	0.2	0.2	0.2	0.1	0.1	x0.1	x0.1
Asie	27.5	26.2	x31.7	x35.8	33.0	33.7	32.7	32.8	34.9	35.7
Moyen–Orient	0.6	0.1	0.2	0.4	0.4	0.4	x0.2	0.2	x0.1	0.1
Europe	48.8	52.2	46.5	41.7	44.9	44.8	45.5	42.6	37.6	36.9
CEE	43.9	46.2	41.5	37.7	40.8	42.8	40.7	37.9	33.8	33.3
AELE	3.3	4.5	3.6	2.8	2.8	0.6	0.5	0.5	0.5	0.5
Océanie	0.3	x0.3	0.4	0.3	0.4	0.4	0.4	0.3	0.4	0.3
Italy/Italie	17.1	16.7	14.7	12.0	14.8	15.8	14.7	14.9	14.8	15.4
India/Inde	15.7	13.5	12.5	12.9	13.9	13.4	11.1	8.3	6.7	6.3
Hong Kong	1.1	1.5	1.7	2.7	5.2	5.3	6.6	8.4	9.8	8.1
Germany/Allemagne	8.1	9.6	8.9	9.0	8.9	9.3	8.8	7.9	6.5	5.7
USA/Etats–Unis d'Amer	9.4	7.9	6.8	7.1	7.2	6.2	6.2	6.0	6.1	5.5
Korea, Republic of	3.4	4.1	3.9	4.8	5.3	5.4	5.2	4.3	4.8	5.0
Thailand/Thaïlande	2.5	3.3	3.7	3.9	5.2	5.6	5.0	4.4	4.3	3.8
China/Chine	1.9	1.6	0.3	0.6	0.9	1.2	1.8	4.5	6.1	9.4
Portugal	2.6	3.5	3.2	3.7	3.7	3.8	3.8	3.6	3.3	2.9
Hungary/Hongrie			x1.3	x1.2	x1.6	x2.9	x2.7	x3.4	x2.8	x2.3

TRADE BY COMMODITY IN THOUSAND U.S. DOLLARS – COMMERCE PAR PRODUIT EN MILLIERS DE DOLLARS E.U

COUNTRIES–PAYS	IMPORTS – IMPORTATIONS 1990	1991	1992	1993	1994
Total	1007575	1005962	1149949	998257	1198780
Africa	1703	1352	1586	2502	934
Northern Africa	1141	1104	1459	2321	727
Americas	x42018	x31920	x37481	38206	55288
LAIA	2677	1611	2731	3041	7928
CACM			6	x3	x13
Asia	297182	299883	404331	532118	643689
Middle East	6760	4966	11076	x15284	17423
Europe	637657	652602	686582	402849	464238
EEC	600364	621183	663121	390358	447309
EFTA	26183	19985	16617	7801	8697
Oceania	4735	5219	x5142	x6271	x8251
Greece/Grèce	192151	206229	207216	134047	148283
Italy/Italie	197728	192706	195340	83814	106024
Korea, Republic of	87054	131217	127362	212956	279754
Hong Kong	132756	106312	124118	127469	139014
Germany/Allemagne	65279	76657	103277	71481	70803
China/Chine	18196	18879	88910	107161	132695
Spain/Espagne	32880	48766	44492	18209	19380
United Kingdom	37005	26900	31260	22022	29879
France,Monac	25745	22994	24718	19751	19239
Japan/Japon	38336	23829	23432	19817	22580
USA/Etats–Unis d'Amer	23150	19049	22454	25432	32475
Macau/Macao	7469	7357	11678	24104	27127
Switz.Liecht	23929	17630	14900	6414	7118
Austria/Autriche	10646	9427	13110	9782	10217
Canada	13562	10419	11436	9219	14386
Netherlands/Pays–Bas	9769	10256	10157	8470	13726
Turkey/Turquie	6196	3375	8238	11761	15679
Denmark/Danemark	4558	3747	8368	8155	7990
Thailand/Thaïlande	1600	2101	7224	10030	10091
Portugal	4979	6589	8339	3164	2410
Belgium–Luxembourg	5133	5279	7560	4172	8494
Russian Federation			x8998	x7075	x11920
Hungary/Hongrie	x10283	4009	x6030	x4718	x6620
Sweden/Suède	7119	6095	5147	3436	4674
Lithuania/Lituanie				x13060	1722
Finland/Finlande	6880	5395	4084	3391	5910
Australia/Australie	2802	3463	3536	4119	4867
Yugoslavia SFR	9360	x9790			
Viet Nam		x1281	x551	x7111	x4831
Czechoslovakia	5293	x2479	x6379		
Malaysia/Malaisie	472	1329	3560	2412	3099
Former USSR/Anc. URSS		x6017			
Norway,SVD,JM	2183	2110	1690	1373	1517
Czech Republic				5075	7702
Malta/Malte	1707	1538	2021	1503	x1349
New Zealand	1873	1716	1273	2046	3310
United Arab Emirates	327	771	1883	x2310	x1032
Korea Dem People's Rp	x2730	x403	x2248	x1796	x186
Poland/Pologne	1391	962	272	3039	4920
Tunisia/Tunisie	798	843	1094	2200	469
Yugoslavia/Yougoslavie			x3316	x78	
Israel/Israël	1499	847	1457	654	271
Mexico/Mexique	364	328	878	1636	3242
Bulgaria/Bulgarie	x7028	x1231	817	x741	x3192
India/Inde	16	35	703	1784	5167
Romania/Roumanie		288	1270	842	950
Ukraine			x1833	x497	x1274
Slovenia/Slovénia			806	1486	1715
Croatia/Croatie			608	1528	x4850
Brazil/Brésil	1723	366	828	817	3509

COUNTRIES–PAYS	EXPORTS – EXPORTATIONS 1990	1991	1992	1993	1994
Totale	1062640	1047484	1119551	931580	1114134
Afrique	1753	x1152	x1178	1792	x198
Afrique du Nord	12	14	x80	210	x131
Amériques	100148	80140	75218	65002	93135
ALAI	20717	20455	22703	21580	39952
MCAC					x4
Asie	178592	185186	264032	258931	278895
Moyen–Orient	760	257	1941	3293	2557
Europe	749859	741390	735821	549000	680705
CEE	714051	712507	713856	533775	658511
AELE	30331	23824	18885	12679	17054
Océanie	x16983	x22865	27979	x35052	x34332
Spain/Espagne	217740	211919	223040	191688	233883
Germany/Allemagne	152287	163664	152395	105032	134913
Hong Kong	114657	117971	144079	129081	117921
China/Chine	21483	26353	72926	85217	100584
United Kingdom	86536	61644	60884	52203	65729
France,Monac	69457	76690	63950	31311	33910
Greece/Grèce	46351	59314	74157	33478	32109
Italy/Italie	56217	54530	51897	42355	53065
USA/Etats–Unis d'Amer	66077	49823	43100	33715	39605
Macau/Macao	29132	28663	32276	31729	27935
Finland/Finlande	20754	23698	26118	25883	34308
Belgium–Luxembourg	26979	25518	24414	18370	25759
New Zealand	10410	12436	15381	21404	19135
Argentina/Argentine	9174	9993	13824	14864	20738
Iceland/Islande	16501	14280	13794	9205	12009
Australia/Australie	6556	10403	12597	13648	15190
Canada	12765	9765	9347	9692	13103
Portugal	8076	8202	10546	9698	15288
Denmark/Danemark	8229	8776	7910	10127	12523
Netherlands/Pays–Bas	7493	8024	7672	7478	8713
Russian Federation			x9244	x11151	x12635
Hungary/Hongrie	x3400	x6029	x7952	x5446	x2278
Korea, Republic of	4599	5438	6617	4759	14819
Brazil/Brésil	4572	5245	4966	2900	3931
Switz.Liecht	11422	7140	3615	2092	2532
Poland/Pologne	154	257	2267	10099	17151
Japan/Japon	6495	5698	4568	2220	5547
Uruguay	5516	4533	3547	3258	13241
Austria/Autriche	5156	3568	4132	3278	x3499
Ireland/Irlande	5131	3730	3985	1006	2044
Sweden/Suède	3646	3230	2756	1869	2770
Czechoslovakia		x3035	x4720		
Former USSR/Anc. URSS	9839	x7290			
Turkey/Turquie	60	242	1903	3248	2283
Norway,SVD,JM	2409	2404	1476	1382	2512
Yugoslavia SFR	5356	x4931			
Slovenia/Slovénia			1990	1874	3431
Ukraine			x435	x3182	x1043
So. Africa Customs Un	1506	1084	963	1347	
Slovakia				x2852	x2948
Czech Republic				2414	3291
Korea Dem People's Rp	x191	x210	x159	x1394	x7191
Latvia/Lettonie			x100	x1596	7899
Lithuania/Lituanie				x1620	2423
Albania/Albanie	x14	x25	x126	x850	x306
Yugoslavia/Yougoslavie			x864		
Israel/Israël	598	334	237	232	225
Colombia/Colombie	1202	530	79	171	100
Estonia/Estonie			x27	x504	x75
Malaysia/Malaisie	142	122	95	303	174

(VALUE AS % OF TOTAL)(VALEUR EN % DU TOTAL)

	1985	1986	1987	1988	1989	1990	1991	1992	1993	1994
Africa	0.2	0.2	0.3	0.3	0.2	0.1	0.1	0.1	0.2	0.1
Northern Africa	0.1	0.1	0.1	0.2	0.2	0.1	0.1	0.1	0.2	0.1
Americas	5.7	x4.2	x3.1	x3.1	x4.5	x4.1	x3.1	x3.2	3.9	4.6
LAIA	0.3	0.2	0.2	x0.1	0.2	0.3	0.2	0.2	0.3	0.7
CACM	0.0	x0.0	x0.0	x0.0	0.0	0.0	0.0	0.0	x0.0	x0.0
Asia	20.6	16.4	17.9	20.6	23.6	29.5	29.9	35.2	53.4	53.7
Middle East	0.3	0.2	0.3	0.3	0.5	0.7	0.5	1.0	x1.5	1.5
Europe	72.1	78.2	77.6	74.1	69.5	63.3	64.9	59.7	40.4	38.7
EEC	65.5	71.8	71.5	68.3	63.6	59.6	61.8	57.7	39.1	37.3
EFTA	6.0	6.0	5.7	5.6	4.9	2.6	2.0	1.4	0.8	0.7
Oceania	0.5	x0.3	x0.2	x0.3	x0.3	0.5	0.5	x0.4	x0.6	x0.7
Greece/Grèce	20.6	23.5	22.6	19.3	21.1	19.1	20.5	18.0	13.4	12.4
Italy/Italie	18.0	19.5	22.0	22.7	21.8	19.6	19.2	17.0	8.4	8.8
Korea, Republic of	3.8	2.5	2.3	2.8	5.3	8.6	13.0	11.1	21.3	23.3
Hong Kong	13.0	11.0	9.7	10.7	12.1	13.2	10.6	10.8	12.8	11.6
Germany/Allemagne	10.1	11.0	10.0	9.3	6.6	6.5	7.6	9.0	7.2	5.9
China/Chine			1.8	2.4	1.8	1.8	1.9	7.7	10.7	11.1
Spain/Espagne	1.4	3.2	2.8	3.6	3.5	3.3	4.8	3.9	1.8	1.6
United Kingdom	5.3	4.5	5.1	5.2	4.3	3.7	2.7	2.7	2.2	2.5
France,Monac	3.5	3.5	3.1	2.7	2.2	2.6	2.3	2.1	2.0	1.6
Japan/Japon	2.9	2.4	2.8	3.5	3.2	3.8	2.4	2.0	2.0	1.9

	1985	1986	1987	1988	1989	1990	1991	1992	1993	1994
Afrique	0.1	0.1	x0.2	x0.3	x0.1	0.1	x0.1	x0.1	0.1	x0.0
Afrique du Nord	0.0	0.0	x0.0	x0.0	x0.0	0.0	0.0	x0.0	0.0	x0.0
Amériques	10.0	9.2	9.2	9.9	9.5	9.4	7.7	6.7	7.0	8.3
ALAI	1.0	1.4	1.3	1.1	1.8	1.9	2.0	2.0	2.3	3.6
MCAC	0.0	x0.0	x0.0	x0.0	x0.0			0.0	0.0	x0.0
Asie	3.8	5.1	7.9	10.2	13.7	16.8	17.7	23.6	27.8	25.0
Moyen–Orient	0.0	x0.0	x0.0	0.0	0.0	0.1	0.0	0.2	0.4	0.2
Europe	84.7	84.1	80.2	76.6	73.9	70.6	70.8	65.7	58.9	61.1
CEE	76.8	77.8	74.3	70.3	67.7	67.2	68.0	63.8	57.3	59.1
AELE	7.2	5.9	5.6	5.7	5.7	2.9	2.3	1.7	1.4	1.5
Océanie	0.8	x0.7	x0.7	x1.1	x1.1	x1.6	x2.2	2.5	x3.8	x3.1
Spain/Espagne	14.9	18.4	19.7	18.5	17.9	20.5	20.2	19.9	20.6	21.0
Germany/Allemagne	23.1	20.7	18.8	18.7	15.9	14.3	15.6	13.6	11.3	12.1
Hong Kong	2.5	3.6	3.9	6.1	8.0	10.8	11.3	12.9	13.9	10.6
China/Chine			2.2	2.3	1.8	2.0	2.5	6.5	9.1	9.0
United Kingdom	12.4	12.4	11.0	11.0	9.9	8.1	5.9	5.4	5.6	5.9
France,Monac	6.0	6.3	7.1	6.1	6.7	6.5	7.3	5.7	3.4	3.0
Greece/Grèce	5.0	7.5	6.9	4.9	5.2	4.4	5.7	6.6	3.6	2.9
Italy/Italie	5.5	4.9	4.0	4.1	4.6	5.3	5.2	4.6	4.5	4.8
USA/Etats–Unis d'Amer	6.9	5.8	6.0	7.6	6.5	6.2	4.8	3.8	3.6	3.6
Macau/Macao	0.2	0.2	0.2	0.3	2.7	2.7	2.7	2.9	3.4	2.5

TRADE BY COMMODITY IN THOUSAND U.S. DOLLARS – COMMERCE PAR PRODUIT EN MILLIERS DE DOLLARS E.U

COUNTRIES–PAYS	IMPORTS – IMPORTATIONS 1990	1991	1992	1993	1994
Total	4098972	4254482	4726174	4530414	5068348
Africa	x145905	129231	x142324	x159874	x128777
Northern Africa	69369	61857	x67320	87733	x63506
Americas	766251	802886	910293	1061317	1255093
LAIA	129741	149057	208297	252553	302945
CACM	10700	10211	11761	x17577	x13639
Asia	494956	621294	739317	x763537	774534
Middle East	96357	x125510	x141062	x136000	x106185
Europe	2535268	2517415	2768290	2336961	2680077
EEC	2346296	2358405	2597947	2185672	2510780
EFTA	149043	138320	139119	127698	140565
Oceania	x104672	x91379	x95591	x102884	x114359
Germany/Allemagne	552539	589551	686835	555412	582840
USA/Etats–Unis d'Amer	321621	338541	357256	408618	519606
France,Monac	348660	334013	367120	302082	363312
Canada	271694	278617	307486	362778	399679
Netherlands/Pays–Bas	241071	280346	297206	200849	229837
United Kingdom	255614	242238	263387	248176	293980
Italy/Italie	188014	186618	194188	160767	187957
Belgium–Luxembourg	169329	163405	174481	148499	179799
Spain/Espagne	133400	143329	171109	159518	206546
Austria/Autriche	100346	101697	111434	105209	121217
Sweden/Suède	125055	108894	109082	95543	122542
Mexico/Mexique	40458	56370	100059	109887	147046
Switz.Liecht	93049	85073	85919	81585	91944
Hong Kong	57333	69490	87180	93806	104912
Korea, Republic of	62340	100697	75031	71030	90470
Japan/Japon	65345	78050	84002	82155	90089
Singapore/Singapour	72630	70426	78920	86393	94797
Australia/Australie	70510	67423	73718	76564	87161
China/Chine	9559	18768	79367	84852	93521
Denmark/Danemark	57238	52657	56796	51218	57563
Portugal	51195	50425	51157	53700	49057
Norway,SVD,JM	52201	49397	49698	42978	45355
Saudi Arabia	33855	48002	48240	x35010	x32027
Ireland/Irlande	32740	39410	44664	42140	43608
Finland/Finlande	63078	42238	44300	36670	48284
Thailand/Thaïlande	20840	25592	35221	45272	47888
Brazil/Brésil	25593	26336	32860	46778	64462
Indonesia/Indonésie	27229	26376	35931	27007	34510
Malaysia/Malaisie	21218	22499	30174	35007	30927
So. Africa Customs Un	24004	25315	27218	26751	29712
Israel/Israël	21675	22885	28655	27561	26802
Greece/Grèce	28017	23582	26188	25887	24237
Iran (Islamic Rp. of)		x27329	x26551	x19856	
Turkey/Turquie	15489	17122	25142	31227	22658
Egypt/Egypte	17453	15911	19910	34503	19316
Nepal/Népal	359	23354	23695	21612	x136
Poland/Pologne	2657	6416	20980	36227	40979
Argentina/Argentine	5305	11614	19614	28768	26871
Chile/Chili	15758	16531	19911	20614	21755
Former USSR/Anc. URSS		x51258			
New Zealand	17566	14628	17064	18536	21909
Algeria/Algérie	20001	12804	12709	23025	13716
Nigeria/Nigéria	x16965	9986	x15635	x17428	x7207
Hungary/Hongrie	x17767	13678	x12488	x16773	x21784
Czechoslovakia	6892	x13678	x26495		
Philippines	12573	10707	12443	15794	17896
United Arab Emirates	12780	8711	11853	x17708	x15861
India/Inde	12456	10072	11689	15677	15333
Tunisia/Tunisie	13254	13276	11413	10592	9927
Venezuela	7675	11435	12870	10524	8936

COUNTRIES–PAYS	EXPORTS – EXPORTATIONS 1990	1991	1992	1993	1994
Totale	3993386	4071278	4527464	4542065	5279322
Afrique	7950	9073	x8792	x8160	x4360
Afrique du Nord	2976	3621	3776	2466	3203
Amériques	582351	596536	677372	787688	934200
ALAI	33710	38488	54658	82858	103276
MCAC	4795	3250	4093	3892	x2871
Asie	639569	695009	785960	918584	1089863
Moyen–Orient	12424	10727	17236	15580	19912
Europe	2707148	2713642	2996885	2759329	3179022
CEE	2615301	2657382	2896698	2699898	3104117
AELE	46113	42973	45822	40971	52551
Océanie	x8841	8054	10258	x11159	x14686
Germany/Allemagne	734246	755967	859132	742584	850668
USA/Etats–Unis d'Amer	458001	460358	505684	560632	653190
Italy/Italie	468466	447006	482545	460872	538388
Japan/Japon	370191	372736	405359	500105	565204
France,Monac	313775	316753	345788	376358	430355
United Kingdom	285849	290097	296019	332678	341603
Belgium–Luxembourg	228776	230736	262620	250543	255892
Malaysia/Malaisie	121972	161706	166301	163075	192434
Netherlands/Pays–Bas	110281	153106	167189	112144	185173
Austria/Autriche	135174	132872	138629	119527	x135587
Canada	85094	92899	112223	139377	174466
Spain/Espagne	99604	100816	107822	125282	144911
Sweden/Suède	114152	105329	105444	90430	110646
Ireland/Irlande	74911	77552	81702	45472	49631
Hong Kong	22695	34215	47782	55911	70196
Switz.Liecht	37822	37481	39702	35222	46160
Korea, Republic of	27193	32667	35246	39640	45840
Denmark/Danemark	39597	34952	36011	30533	44801
Thailand/Thaïlande	20908	25428	29174	39673	47695
China/Chine	13351	14996	35176	32851	61846
Singapore/Singapour	23099	20929	23518	31953	45452
Brazil/Brésil	9602	16305	17957	23553	25004
Mexico/Mexique	4590	5557	14833	33703	47572
Turkey/Turquie	10409	9480	16609	14417	17892
Israel/Israël	15389	12600	13698	12757	14842
Czechoslovakia		x17438	x20829		
Croatia/Croatie			33869	1008	x1526
Uruguay	7569	8295	11801	14556	20199
Hungary/Hongrie	x12924	x10580	x15275	x7638	x6516
Slovenia/Slovénia			15854	14472	18388
India/Inde	6339	3550	5969	13279	7355
Poland/Pologne	8028	7213	4962	9068	11871
Slovakia				x20593	x17144
Finland/Finlande	5862	5665	6116	7916	9685
Norway,SVD,JM	8129	5357	5951	5690	6303
Australia/Australie	5081	4374	6386	6000	8517
Indonesia/Indonésie	1253	2452	3917	10178	15127
Portugal	3525	5836	6364	4230	5710
Russian Federation			x5530	x10621	x8358
Bulgaria/Bulgarie	x20106	x6022	x5495	x3906	x3109
Argentina/Argentine	7712	4314	5046	4839	4844
Czech Republic				14192	16030
Yugoslavia SFR	45504	x13252			
New Zealand	3652	3538	3795	4917	6116
So. Africa Customs Un	3697	4302	3552	4244	
Romania/Roumanie	3454	4084	1544	1747	2506
Tunisia/Tunisie	2145	2738	2393	1823	2116
Venezuela	1523	1139	2118	2132	1831
Yugoslavia/Yougoslavie				x797	x498
Chile/Chili	429	1076	1408	2133	1867

(VALUE AS % OF TOTAL)(VALEUR EN % DU TOTAL)

	1985	1986	1987	1988	1989	1990	1991	1992	1993	1994
Africa	5.6	x5.2	x3.9	x3.5	x3.2	x3.6	3.0	x3.0	x3.5	x2.6
Northern Africa	3.2	2.5	1.8	1.6	1.4	1.7	1.5	x1.4	1.9	x1.3
Americas	15.9	x12.0	x9.7	13.0	18.0	18.7	18.9	19.3	23.4	24.7
LAIA	4.5	3.1	2.9	2.8	3.1	3.2	3.5	4.4	5.6	6.0
CACM	1.0	0.4	x0.4	0.3	0.3	0.3	0.2	0.2	x0.4	x0.3
Asia	12.0	11.0	x12.1	x11.2	11.1	12.1	14.6	15.7	x16.8	15.3
Middle East	2.9	x3.1	x2.4	x1.9	x2.0	2.4	x3.0	x3.0	x3.0	x2.1
Europe	62.4	68.2	64.6	63.2	59.4	61.9	59.2	58.6	51.6	52.9
EEC	50.5	55.3	52.2	52.0	49.1	57.2	55.4	55.0	48.2	49.5
EFTA	10.6	11.7	11.2	10.2	9.2	3.6	3.3	2.9	2.8	2.8
Oceania	3.2	x2.9	x2.8	x2.5	x2.6	x2.5	x2.1	x2.0	x2.3	x2.3
Germany/Allemagne	12.0	13.8	12.4	11.3	10.5	13.5	13.9	14.5	12.3	11.5
USA/Etats–Unis d'Amer	6.1	3.8	2.6	3.0	7.5	7.8	8.0	7.6	9.0	10.3
France,Monac	7.7	7.8	7.7	7.6	7.2	8.5	7.9	7.8	6.7	7.2
Canada	3.6	3.1	2.7	6.3	6.6	6.6	6.5	6.5	8.0	7.9
Netherlands/Pays–Bas	4.9	5.6	5.3	5.3	5.2	5.9	6.6	6.3	4.4	4.5
United Kingdom	5.7	6.1	6.0	7.5	6.0	6.2	5.7	5.6	5.5	5.8
Italy/Italie	3.5	4.1	4.1	3.9	3.9	4.6	4.4	4.1	3.5	3.7
Belgium–Luxembourg	4.6	4.4	3.3	3.8	3.8	4.1	3.8	3.7	3.3	3.5
Spain/Espagne	1.3	1.7	1.9	2.0	2.5	3.3	3.4	3.6	3.5	4.1
Austria/Autriche	2.2	2.4	2.3	2.2	2.0	2.4	2.4	2.4	2.3	2.4

	1985	1986	1987	1988	1989	1990	1991	1992	1993	1994
Afrique	0.2	x0.3	0.1	x0.1	x0.2	0.2	0.2	x0.2	x0.2	x0.1
Afrique du Nord	0.0	0.0	0.0	0.0	0.0	0.1	0.1	0.1	0.1	0.1
Amériques	12.4	x9.6	9.5	10.5	12.9	14.6	14.7	14.9	17.3	17.7
ALAI	0.6	0.6	0.6	0.8	0.9	0.8	0.9	1.2	1.8	2.0
MCAC	0.2	0.1	0.1	0.2	0.2	0.1	0.1	0.1	0.1	x0.1
Asie	11.0	10.4	x10.8	14.1	15.3	16.1	17.1	17.4	20.2	20.7
Moyen–Orient	0.3	0.2	x0.3	0.3	0.3	0.3	0.3	0.4	0.3	0.4
Europe	75.3	78.5	76.4	72.1	69.5	67.8	66.7	66.2	60.8	60.2
CEE	65.9	68.9	66.8	63.0	61.3	65.5	65.3	64.0	59.4	58.8
AELE	8.1	8.5	8.5	7.6	7.0	1.2	1.1	1.0	0.9	1.0
Océanie	0.2	x0.3	x0.2	x0.2	0.2	x0.2	0.2	0.2	x0.2	x0.3
Germany/Allemagne	18.0	18.9	17.9	17.7	17.4	18.4	18.6	19.0	16.3	16.1
USA/Etats–Unis d'Amer	5.9	5.4	6.3	6.5	7.9	11.5	11.3	11.2	12.3	12.4
Italy/Italie	12.7	13.3	12.8	11.9	11.4	11.7	11.0	10.7	10.1	10.2
Japan/Japon	6.6	6.3	5.2	8.0	9.2	9.3	9.2	9.0	11.0	10.7
France,Monac	8.3	10.1	9.8	7.8	7.4	7.9	7.8	7.6	8.3	8.2
United Kingdom	8.2	6.7	6.5	7.1	6.3	7.2	7.1	6.5	7.3	6.5
Belgium–Luxembourg	4.8	5.1	5.2	4.6	5.7	5.7	5.7	5.8	5.5	4.8
Malaysia/Malaisie	1.4	1.3	1.6	2.0	2.6	3.1	4.0	3.7	3.6	3.6
Netherlands/Pays–Bas	2.2	2.6	2.7	2.5	2.3	2.8	3.8	3.7	2.5	3.5
Austria/Autriche	3.4	3.6	3.6	3.4	3.0	3.4	3.3	3.1	2.6	x2.6

TRADE BY COMMODITY IN THOUSAND U.S. DOLLARS – COMMERCE PAR PRODUIT EN MILLIERS DE DOLLARS E.U

COUNTRIES–PAYS	IMPORTS – IMPORTATIONS				
	1990	1991	1992	1993	1994
Total	16216006	16534549	18519407	17313343	18912890
Africa	x873164	x611536	x689301	x696001	x703751
Northern Africa	490585	248281	x239635	x277644	x295575
Americas	x4156512	4003190	4342190	4751365	5331470
LAIA	360872	543565	652106	732489	947173
CACM	67393	67290	87878	x94436	x92407
Asia	x2133773	x2551781	x2773678	x2633305	x2483621
Middle East	822367	x1321099	x1266490	x1019942	x872974
Europe	8491219	8788153	10091957	8505327	9607147
EEC	7968476	8268062	9484286	7974921	9023454
EFTA	459762	472340	518602	463092	499363
Oceania	x428490	x447596	x446593	x503439	x571187
USA/Etats–Unis d'Amer	2762772	2451998	2659359	2902985	3218015
Germany/Allemagne	1916787	2174043	2538076	1966983	2164369
United Kingdom	1042740	1027466	1194699	1077547	1153870
France, Monac	997605	979628	1127994	937598	1076812
Italy/Italie	924983	987524	1062277	900756	1071067
Netherlands/Pays–Bas	715336	766839	900558	780167	906250
Canada	737899	772913	784662	860080	929148
Belgium–Luxembourg	622939	632801	716143	615284	712227
Japan/Japon	543519	586603	596086	577334	625699
Spain/Espagne	449132	452106	549730	493891	605156
Saudi Arabia	365309	439354	381650	x335492	x325597
Australia/Australie	334700	336543	355573	375969	456982
Sweden/Suède	383429	362470	363102	288625	353318
Austria/Autriche	248410	282337	371832	351695	342826
Switz.Liecht	306638	314661	355044	307696	324458
Iran (Islamic Rp. of)		x397548	x312396	x80207	x35813
Mexico/Mexique	145079	228457	271665	264668	329871
United Arab Emirates	116533	152410	171246	x192306	x186154
Denmark/Danemark	184120	172261	178201	150812	174150
Singapore/Singapour	105910	119583	157024	176129	193532
Portugal	126880	132835	181133	135794	148771
Norway, SVD, JM	144668	147714	154587	147302	166437
Hong Kong	93711	123971	157804	147389	213553
Afghanistan	x209422	x59548	x165631	x195962	x49151
Greece/Grèce	115624	119510	117511	134256	130465
Algeria/Algérie	308892	89119	89481	119295	92262
Argentina/Argentine	16920	80846	117899	94948	115025
Finland/Finlande	167715	107730	96592	75471	107048
So. Africa Customs Un	70304	77398	88063	82680	96547
Turkey/Turquie	97996	78642	69373	87804	46259
Chile/Chili	58818	61671	72360	92709	95938
Nigeria/Nigéria	x68898	70422	x88121	x65624	x29237
Ireland/Irlande	72777	70514	86439	66040	77124
Egypt/Egypte	91952	79658	66749	70639	81515
Israel/Israël	44921	52325	59500	68328	63213
Kuwait/Koweït	38797	34405	58464	75114	58103
New Zealand	52779	45898	54924	65425	70088
Philippines	36123	29293	52373	72401	81850
Oman	32259	46569	60209	46390	36764
Korea, Republic of	33409	39729	48914	52779	63068
Hungary/Hongrie	x36096	38061	x39654	x58811	x47255
Libyan Arab Jamahiriya	60694	40251	x41815	x53234	x80736
Venezuela	12283	38560	46831	45259	30477
Syrian Arab Republic	10413	x31903	46348	x50993	x45780
China/Chine	23958	30570	44581	50206	28484
Pakistan	34707	35800	40434	45874	48643
Russian Federation			x63566	x56946	x61933
Colombia/Colombie	15665	20232	31323	67180	81662
Brazil/Brésil	38545	30259	27091	58927	131029
Cuba	x111508	x45022	x30979	x31611	x14853

COUNTRIES–PAYS	EXPORTS – EXPORTATIONS				
	1990	1991	1992	1993	1994
Totale	15375828	15762340	17798791	16935134	18719932
Afrique	59481	56648	70782	77741	52040
Afrique du Nord	27560	18091	25484	24279	45448
Amériques	2214870	2421991	2774807	3001930	3329106
ALAI	372103	377904	508673	605894	712651
MCAC	26367	26814	28774	x20497	x27342
Asie	4071929	4141111	4778178	4792420	5277074
Moyen–Orient	139465	172610	216049	x243546	273171
Europe	8786580	8869212	9825452	8665093	9581202
CEE	8498731	8645104	9589990	8493493	9407639
AELE	102536	92609	55928	42057	41678
Océanie	54078	x60542	x69003	x83773	x89273
Japan/Japon	2470741	2449347	2559117	2423615	2602032
France, Monac	2175978	2258532	2470721	2158742	2365608
Germany/Allemagne	1772392	1771974	1927895	1610579	1744130
USA/Etats–Unis d'Amer	1163681	1295235	1430990	1486271	1646299
United Kingdom	1018721	991862	1123231	969577	1112697
Korea, Republic of	872850	897033	1053285	1132027	1232922
Italy/Italie	818169	881611	961518	863099	988030
Spain/Espagne	832626	804528	916340	894183	1057959
Canada	643484	712204	798104	884259	936680
Netherlands/Pays–Bas	605078	653262	700597	699688	712445
Belgium–Luxembourg	596247	602166	709997	578253	627012
Brazil/Brésil	239843	278519	377013	424436	465442
Austria/Autriche	308914	315359	366349	324254	x298282
India/Inde	104184	88508	202692	204591	237520
Turkey/Turquie	52080	136149	173535	169222	200840
China/Chine	106371	116903	161516	199449	258730
Thailand/Thaïlande	89466	104095	140949	165593	192310
Sweden/Suède	101708	102601	130984	131064	151743
Ireland/Irlande	72501	86060	116613	94160	103491
Singapore/Singapour	73559	74444	103077	104519	104414
Slovenia/Slovénia			130474	114813	125257
Indonesia/Indonésie	65669	58355	95829	82511	103435
Israel/Israël	62046	64630	75179	68766	79862
Czechoslovakia		x83085	x120721		
Finland/Finlande	58369	59116	64249	69491	92050
Hungary/Hongrie	x93836	x58483	x75405	x53794	x58924
Hong Kong	36108	51205	74927	58387	73297
Portugal	74258	65189	49308	47622	93124
Poland/Pologne	36347	47673	47427	66130	104679
Malaysia/Malaisie	21099	33184	56212	62981	62685
Yugoslavia SFR	184599	x131081			
Australia/Australie	33560	33932	45221	51614	55774
Chile/Chili	25785	31674	37509	45498	50712
Denmark/Danemark	46891	40951	35998	35944	39012
So. Africa Customs Un	17426	30387	36595	44287	
Switz.Liecht	45048	32401	42982	32814	30027
Czech Republic				91394	115918
Mexico/Mexique	24075	15525	32717	42410	65405
Norway, SVD, JM	57487	60208	12915	9238	11648
New Zealand	18461	26399	21874	26685	33221
Russian Federation			x25087	x46315	x30278
Slovakia				x70243	x77222
Argentina/Argentine	41829	20848	16718	31052	56274
Sri Lanka	14692	10855	20676	25177	37530
Venezuela	7937	5854	17299	33422	42280
Yugoslavia/Yougoslavie				x7295	x3072
Bahrain/Bahreïn	x6853	x12025	x16103	x19397	x19627
Greece/Grèce	16797	11810	16189	16839	22056
Colombia/Colombie	15302	13917	15501	15203	17142
Bulgaria/Bulgarie	x14209	x4325	24445	12855	10859

(VALUE AS % OF TOTAL)(VALEUR EN % DU TOTAL)

	1985	1986	1987	1988	1989	1990	1991	1992	1993	1994
Africa	5.4	x5.4	x4.3	x4.3	x4.1	x5.4	x3.7	x3.7	x4.0	x3.7
Northern Africa	2.7	2.4	1.3	1.7	1.9	3.0	1.5	x1.3	x1.6	x1.6
Americas	34.9	27.4	25.6	24.7	26.7	x25.6	24.2	23.4	27.4	28.2
LAIA	2.1	1.4	1.4	1.5	1.7	2.2	3.3	3.5	4.2	5.0
CACM	0.8	0.6	x0.6	0.4	0.4	0.4	0.4	0.5	x0.5	x0.5
Asia	9.8	x13.4	x12.4	x13.6	x13.5	x13.1	x15.5	x14.9	x15.2	x13.1
Middle East	5.7	x7.5	x6.3	x6.6	x6.4	5.1	x8.0	x6.8	x5.9	x4.6
Europe	46.1	50.5	52.9	52.5	50.8	52.4	53.2	54.5	49.1	50.8
EEC	37.5	41.7	44.1	44.3	43.0	49.1	50.0	51.2	46.1	47.7
EFTA	7.7	8.4	8.5	7.8	7.4	2.8	2.9	2.8	2.7	2.6
Oceania	2.9	x2.2	x2.3	2.7	x2.8	x2.7	x2.7	x2.4	x2.9	x3.0
USA/Etats–Unis d'Amer	25.9	20.7	19.0	17.5	18.8	17.0	14.8	14.4	16.8	17.0
Germany/Allemagne	9.9	11.4	11.2	10.9	10.4	11.8	13.1	13.7	11.4	11.4
United Kingdom	5.6	5.5	5.7	6.2	5.7	6.4	6.2	6.5	6.2	6.1
France, Monac	5.0	5.9	6.3	5.9	5.4	6.2	5.9	6.1	5.4	5.7
Italy/Italie	4.1	4.6	5.0	5.0	5.1	5.7	6.0	5.7	5.2	5.7
Netherlands/Pays–Bas	3.1	3.5	3.6	3.7	3.6	4.4	4.6	4.9	4.5	4.8
Canada	4.5	3.3	3.5	4.3	4.8	4.6	4.7	4.2	5.0	4.9
Belgium–Luxembourg	2.6	2.9	3.1	3.4	3.3	3.8	3.8	3.9	3.6	3.8
Japan/Japon	1.5	2.3	2.6	3.1	3.5	3.4	3.5	3.2	3.3	3.3
Spain/Espagne	0.6	0.8	1.6	1.9	2.3	2.8	2.7	3.0	2.9	3.2

	1985	1986	1987	1988	1989	1990	1991	1992	1993	1994
Afrique	0.2	0.2	0.3	0.3	0.3	0.4	0.4	0.4	0.5	0.3
Afrique du Nord	0.0	0.1	0.1	0.1	0.1	0.2	0.1	0.1	0.1	0.2
Amériques	14.5	12.1	11.6	10.4	11.3	14.5	15.3	15.6	17.7	17.8
ALAI	3.1	2.2	2.3	2.6	2.7	2.4	2.4	2.9	3.6	3.8
MCAC	0.2	0.2	0.2	0.2	0.2	0.2	0.2	0.2	x0.1	x0.1
Asie	28.4	25.7	x25.1	x27.1	27.6	26.5	26.2	26.8	28.3	28.2
Moyen–Orient	0.6	0.5	x0.8	1.1	x1.0	0.9	1.1	1.2	x1.4	1.5
Europe	55.7	60.7	58.7	57.8	57.6	57.1	56.3	55.2	51.2	51.2
CEE	51.0	55.5	53.7	53.0	53.0	55.3	54.8	53.9	50.2	50.3
AELE	3.6	4.1	3.9	3.8	3.6	0.7	0.6	0.3	0.2	0.2
Océanie	0.1	0.1	x0.3	x0.4	x0.3	0.3	x0.4	x0.4	x0.5	x0.5
Japan/Japon	19.9	17.4	14.6	15.8	17.5	16.1	15.5	14.4	14.3	13.9
France, Monac	14.4	15.7	14.6	13.9	13.7	14.2	14.3	13.9	12.7	12.6
Germany/Allemagne	10.3	12.2	11.9	11.6	11.5	11.5	11.2	10.8	9.5	9.3
USA/Etats–Unis d'Amer	4.5	3.4	4.3	5.6	6.1	7.6	8.2	8.0	8.8	8.8
United Kingdom	5.5	6.1	6.1	5.8	6.1	6.6	6.3	6.3	5.7	5.9
Korea, Republic of	5.7	5.5	5.2	5.6	5.4	5.7	5.7	5.9	6.7	6.6
Italy/Italie	5.5	5.7	5.6	5.3	5.3	5.3	5.6	5.4	5.1	5.3
Spain/Espagne	4.3	4.1	4.6	5.2	5.1	5.4	5.1	5.1	5.3	5.7
Canada	6.7	6.3	4.8	1.9	2.2	4.2	4.5	4.5	5.2	5.0
Netherlands/Pays–Bas	2.8	3.2	3.2	3.3	3.4	3.9	4.1	3.9	4.1	3.8

TRADE BY COMMODITY IN THOUSAND U.S. DOLLARS – COMMERCE PAR PRODUIT EN MILLIERS DE DOLLARS E.U

COUNTRIES–PAYS	IMPORTS – IMPORTATIONS 1990	1991	1992	1993	1994
Total	5400124	5753565	6542857	6579254	7655133
Africa	x251810	248587	x251616	x255912	x255519
Northern Africa	116044	115057	110925	119030	115831
Americas	1264702	1401042	1708958	1964710	2406380
LAIA	228293	277752	392180	466785	570712
CACM	13464	14290	18415	x20077	x18682
Asia	806744	955817	1088164	1163566	1280178
Middle East	x115596	x170370	x187716	x182322	x154222
Europe	2790420	2813584	3200034	2822577	3292668
EEC	2584411	2625704	3002710	2633491	3084445
EFTA	157605	165371	159819	154031	173215
Oceania	x194038	x179451	x180149	x194630	x228516
USA/Etats–Unis d'Amer	682413	741095	919413	1056868	1299040
Germany/Allemagne	709603	770593	908210	695164	817842
France,Monac	359726	363792	412231	339998	406958
Canada	290046	313554	333192	380674	486361
United Kingdom	281280	278615	303698	361353	411397
Netherlands/Pays–Bas	207087	210633	245286	176883	193343
Italy/Italie	182161	177434	211198	203558	226728
Spain/Espagne	159161	174670	204413	195130	251756
Belgium–Luxembourg	174198	163241	182193	191101	218075
Mexico/Mexique	71393	96844	180257	210487	271954
Japan/Japon	135493	153523	165605	167585	190511
Sweden/Suède	166406	153463	171706	150570	189385
Singapore/Singapour	110347	134852	149807	167553	162775
Austria/Autriche	137455	139810	158054	142295	160577
Australia/Australie	142273	143494	144055	149348	183396
Korea, Republic of	90519	104831	112972	100077	117603
Thailand/Thaïlande	69294	78784	107728	129726	166470
Switz.Liecht	107108	104207	106783	103331	116146
Malaysia/Malaisie	52109	66887	77195	81851	103316
Hong Kong	50192	58853	69843	84064	91759
Brazil/Brésil	59085	62701	66335	77830	127184
So. Africa Customs Un	62724	60681	67722	63307	74807
Denmark/Danemark	57329	58199	61784	53104	61343
Turkey/Turquie	36810	45462	55562	65213	46283
Norway,SVD,JM	45957	56176	48180	46153	52566
China/Chine	16483	27015	48635	62976	88500
Iran (Islamic Rp. of)		x53267	x52334	x30737	x18896
Finland/Finlande	60789	44843	47417	40321	53372
Indonesia/Indonésie	41974	39872	42878	46807	50525
Portugal	37108	40068	47194	37134	44129
Argentina/Argentine	13264	25518	44020	52361	65108
Poland/Pologne	17458	27482	40353	53882	67414
Venezuela	22311	32116	37213	35376	25617
Saudi Arabia	28622	38102	35686	x30316	x30511
India/Inde	36781	33492	35710	33636	42069
Egypt/Egypte	32560	36254	33495	25112	24867
Hungary/Hongrie	x26182	29907	x29438	x33906	x35667
Israel/Israël	23413	25888	32554	34122	38488
Ireland/Irlande	31354	30609	30942	29903	33737
Algeria/Algérie	34443	24096	28164	37957	34851
New Zealand	24696	23280	28196	32081	35851
Chile/Chili	22683	21214	24803	34179	24104
Philippines	19469	21984	25020	28696	31119
Former USSR/Anc. URSS		x75448			
Morocco/Maroc	22845	23434	21260	27625	25869
Tunisia/Tunisie	19949	19395	22314	18717	18763
Greece/Grèce	20754	19733	18383	16979	15804
Russian Federation			x30820	x21466	x21447
Cuba	x25555	x21939	x13106	x14655	x6935
United Arab Emirates	10857	10633	13175	x22141	x25361

COUNTRIES–PAYS	EXPORTS – EXPORTATIONS 1990	1991	1992	1993	1994
Totale	4777911	5094562	5752145	5952491	6946281
Afrique	10125	11604	13630	14040	x5319
Afrique du Nord	1520	3249	3778	2277	3935
Amériques	734399	833783	961551	1076167	x1292730
ALAI	50850	59730	79284	92270	103674
MCAC	17604	18680	25549	x13681	x27533
Asie	1106281	1294333	1445906	1673056	1978688
Moyen–Orient	9798	12189	13354	x15653	x24937
Europe	2818189	2873562	3217056	3039935	3508601
CEE	2626228	2717613	3033183	2863388	3324182
AELE	121081	116957	128077	125045	139744
Océanie	x18876	x18971	x27884	x30336	x36617
Germany/Allemagne	888320	937382	1065555	1033668	1137956
Japan/Japon	714101	819603	945153	1080063	1284783
USA/Etats–Unis d'Amer	502600	585991	624668	692718	812008
France,Monac	463218	445220	499624	450615	592855
Italy/Italie	394873	398601	443160	421779	465688
United Kingdom	261169	292001	297588	280528	319418
Canada	162639	168915	231508	276492	348525
Netherlands/Pays–Bas	183252	180945	197732	172568	200886
Belgium–Luxembourg	152327	147641	176998	187548	235878
Spain/Espagne	93950	115814	136528	114649	161169
Switz.Liecht	105775	101539	111628	108060	118043
Austria/Autriche	98532	98664	103453	101236	x91016
Korea, Republic of	87706	92404	88442	107968	112411
China/Chine	73819	104630	78697	83756	101783
Thailand/Thaïlande	57047	68663	79833	96183	113501
Singapore/Singapour	54734	65130	73518	85967	116364
Malaysia/Malaisie	41284	59358	69227	85286	91915
Brazil/Brésil	34933	41582	47339	56767	59904
Ireland/Irlande	28131	36709	51873	39814	44059
Hong Kong	23178	28903	36413	49905	57129
Malta/Malte	23801	23635	28425	26028	x23819
Denmark/Danemark	23497	25158	24352	23866	29161
India/Inde	21875	17242	25606	24323	28761
Hungary/Hongrie	x20830	x16931	x22007	x20097	x19912
Australia/Australie	12977	14284	20679	21703	27904
Finland/Finlande	22491	20089	18795	17202	24148
Mexico/Mexique	9591	9305	20677	24611	33008
Costa Rica	16530	17403	24258	x11996	x26636
Czechoslovakia		x23686	x26284		
Norway,SVD,JM	15273	15391	16406	16928	21616
Greece/Grèce	12438	14869	13145	15620	17675
Bulgaria/Bulgarie	x58623	x13705	x16477	x12280	
Poland/Pologne	5150	4970	19086	17007	23938
Slovakia				x40469	x33247
Sri Lanka	6436	7539	11063	14319	14740
Indonesia/Indonésie	5220	7700	9939	13450	16378
Turkey/Turquie	7213	8527	10009	9842	12294
Czech Republic				26336	37053
Slovenia/Slovénia			11839	13608	11520
So. Africa Customs Un	5425	6738	7993	8717	
Israel/Israël	7514	6831	7336	7312	8454
New Zealand	5658	4600	6978	8046	8605
Croatia/Croatie			9413	9156	x7035
Argentina/Argentine	3968	5155	6400	5742	5754
Yugoslavia SFR	47072	x15243			
Portugal	3981	4471	4379	4294	4275
Philippines	2294	2918	3400	4570	5736
Saudi Arabia	1293	2355	2190	x4110	x9003
Yugoslavia/Yougoslavie			x5848	x1232	x539
Russian Federation			x3210	x3722	x3389

(VALUE AS % OF TOTAL)(VALEUR EN % DU TOTAL)

	1985	1986	1987	1988	1989	1990	1991	1992	1993	1994
Africa	5.3	6.0	x5.0	x4.8	x4.0	x4.7	4.4	x3.8	x3.9	x3.4
Northern Africa	3.0	3.2	2.4	2.4	1.9	2.1	2.0	1.7	1.8	1.5
Americas	27.0	23.9	22.0	23.7	21.4	23.4	24.3	26.1	29.8	31.4
LAIA	5.2	4.1	3.7	3.6	3.6	4.2	4.8	6.0	7.1	7.5
CACM	0.4	0.4	0.3	0.3	0.3	0.2	0.2	0.3	x0.3	x0.2
Asia	14.1	14.5	x12.3	x12.7	16.8	14.9	16.6	16.6	17.7	16.7
Middle East	4.1	x4.7	x2.5	x2.0	x2.2	x2.1	x3.0	x2.9	x2.8	x2.0
Europe	48.7	51.3	50.6	49.2	49.1	51.7	48.9	48.9	42.9	43.0
EEC	39.5	41.8	41.3	40.2	40.3	47.9	45.6	45.9	40.0	40.3
EFTA	8.1	8.6	8.5	8.2	8.2	2.9	2.9	2.4	2.3	2.3
Oceania	3.4	x2.8	x2.8	x2.8	x3.4	x3.6	x3.1	x2.7	x3.0	x3.0
USA/Etats–Unis d'Amer	16.9	15.7	14.8	14.2	11.6	12.6	12.9	14.1	16.1	17.0
Germany/Allemagne	10.3	11.5	11.2	10.7	10.6	13.1	13.4	13.9	10.6	10.7
France,Monac	5.8	6.2	6.3	5.8	5.8	6.7	6.3	6.3	5.2	5.3
Canada	3.9	3.1	2.6	4.9	5.3	5.4	5.4	5.1	5.8	6.4
United Kingdom	4.7	4.4	4.6	4.8	4.5	5.2	4.8	4.6	5.5	5.4
Netherlands/Pays–Bas	2.9	3.4	3.2	3.1	3.2	3.8	3.7	3.7	2.7	2.5
Italy/Italie	3.4	3.4	3.2	3.1	3.1	3.4	3.1	3.2	3.1	3.0
Spain/Espagne	1.7	2.0	2.1	2.0	2.3	2.9	3.0	3.1	3.0	3.3
Belgium–Luxembourg	2.2	2.3	2.2	2.6	2.6	3.2	2.8	2.8	2.9	2.8
Mexico/Mexique	1.8	0.9	0.9	1.0	1.2	1.3	1.7	2.8	3.2	3.6

	1985	1986	1987	1988	1989	1990	1991	1992	1993	1994
Afrique	0.2	x0.2	x0.3	x0.1	x0.2	0.2	0.2	0.2	0.2	x0.1
Afrique du Nord	0.0	0.0	0.1	0.0	0.0	0.0	0.1	0.1	0.0	0.1
Amériques	24.2	20.6	19.7	23.3	12.3	15.3	16.3	16.7	18.1	x18.6
ALAI	1.0	0.7	0.6	0.7	1.1	1.1	1.2	1.4	1.6	1.5
MCAC	0.3	0.2	0.3	0.2	0.3	0.4	0.4	0.4	x0.2	x0.4
Asie	15.5	14.0	x19.2	x23.2	23.5	23.2	25.4	25.2	28.1	28.5
Moyen–Orient	0.6	0.6	0.3	0.2	0.2	0.2	0.2	0.2	x0.3	x0.4
Europe	58.6	63.8	58.4	51.2	61.4	59.0	56.4	55.9	51.1	50.5
CEE	49.1	53.6	49.4	42.8	51.8	55.0	53.3	52.7	48.1	47.9
AELE	7.5	8.2	7.5	x6.9	x8.0	2.5	2.3	2.2	2.1	2.0
Océanie	0.2	x0.2	x0.3	x0.3	x0.5	x0.4	x0.4	x0.5	x0.5	x0.5
Germany/Allemagne	16.6	18.5	17.5	15.0	18.0	18.6	18.4	18.5	17.4	16.4
Japan/Japon	9.5	8.4	7.5	12.0	15.7	14.9	16.1	16.4	18.1	18.5
USA/Etats–Unis d'Amer	21.9	18.6	17.9	19.8	8.1	10.5	11.5	10.9	11.6	11.7
France,Monac	7.7	8.4	7.3	7.7	9.1	9.7	8.7	8.7	7.6	8.5
Italy/Italie	6.4	6.9	6.7	6.1	8.0	8.3	7.8	7.7	7.1	6.7
United Kingdom	5.7	5.4	4.6	4.6	5.2	5.5	5.7	5.2	4.7	4.6
Canada	1.0	0.9	0.8	2.5	2.9	3.4	3.3	4.0	4.6	5.0
Netherlands/Pays–Bas	2.6	3.2	3.0	2.9	3.5	3.8	3.6	3.4	2.9	2.9
Belgium–Luxembourg	2.4	2.7	2.7	2.4	3.1	3.2	2.9	3.1	3.2	3.4
Spain/Espagne	1.2	1.4	1.4	1.0	1.5	2.0	2.3	2.4	1.9	2.3

TRADE BY COMMODITY IN THOUSAND U.S. DOLLARS – COMMERCE PAR PRODUIT EN MILLIERS DE DOLLARS E.U

COUNTRIES–PAYS	IMPORTS – IMPORTATIONS 1990	1991	1992	1993	1994
Total	794399	772252	837369	726978	750643
Africa	x13069	x14041	x16821	x10936	x15752
Northern Africa	888	1214	x768	789	1117
Americas	x104085	x115611	x135394	x132779	x131740
LAIA	10226	13743	21240	21801	24648
CACM	193	141	220	x375	x531
Asia	40232	37639	41943	x41698	44457
Middle East	x3726	x4134	x5981	x5383	x4111
Europe	567654	554971	602601	488640	497875
EEC	524933	517058	564317	456583	464519
EFTA	36120	33531	33343	28299	29123
Oceania	x25976	x32057	x31772	x35503	x39749
France,Monac	202871	195516	200158	149740	166268
Germany/Allemagne	103645	108105	134610	130533	110553
USA/Etats–Unis d'Amer	71083	83058	90434	89971	87895
Italy/Italie	58402	58192	60224	40914	49550
Spain/Espagne	41450	47427	50520	33944	35413
Australia/Australie	21569	27606	26175	30290	34058
Switz.Liecht	31685	29363	29084	25252	25625
United Kingdom	32526	25849	25245	19456	20231
Austria/Autriche	19827	21193	24068	22702	22877
Japan/Japon	19869	17111	17857	17769	20805
Portugal	12705	12936	16579	15522	13537
Canada	14675	13014	14719	14778	12583
Netherlands/Pays–Bas	13273	11840	14850	14950	14245
Belgium–Luxembourg	11347	12057	12508	11643	11240
So. Africa Customs Un	10802	11255	13993	8853	12434
Chile/Chili	4917	6525	9662	9376	8616
Sweden/Suède	10932	7785	8020	5376	6811
Denmark/Danemark	6238	6083	6740	5234	5419
Greece/Grèce	4991	5251	6922	4090	5082
New Zealand	4169	4231	5417	4994	5438
Hong Kong	5258	4831	3982	4345	4484
Bulgaria/Bulgarie	x26621	x5488	2531	x4370	x5677
Hungary/Hongrie	x4578	3556	x3130	x4817	x4438
Norway,SVD,JM	3998	3775	3918	2806	3318
Mexico/Mexique	1622	2341	4147	3679	4189
China/Chine	1844	1314	3634	3948	3489
Argentina/Argentine	519	1360	3448	4044	7117
Finland/Finlande	5737	3934	3038	1865	2634
Russian Federation			x6605	x606	x1092
Korea, Republic of	1130	1625	2264	2507	3068
Czechoslovakia	7761	x3857	x2025		
Bahamas	82	87	x3841	x1652	x309
Israel/Israël	1573	1742	1901	1841	1919
Brazil/Brésil	1304	1358	1323	2149	2404
Saudi Arabia	513	1528	1612	x1367	x839
Slovenia/Slovénia			2192	2139	2693
Singapore/Singapour	3247	1276	1503	1435	1384
Venezuela	697	1276	1476	1286	936
Yugoslavia SFR	5980	x3880			
Romania/Roumanie	3247	897	1110	1750	2118
Former USSR/Anc. URSS		x3493			
Thailand/Thaïlande	913	1108	1126	1096	1303
Czech Republic				3206	3680
Cyprus/Chypre	918	811	1232	987	1040
Cuba	x2990	x2533	x128	x12	x49
Turkey/Turquie	966	652	987	965	868
Jamaica/Jamaïque	181	89	x749	x1602	x1028
Ireland/Irlande	987	892	835	615	661
Malaysia/Malaisie	721	919	681	577	668
Slovakia				x2149	x1705

COUNTRIES–PAYS	EXPORTS – EXPORTATIONS 1990	1991	1992	1993	1994
Totale	779549	770709	856444	763455	816109
Afrique	21558	15621	15483	15000	11947
Afrique du Nord	21402	15514	15153	14333	11946
Amériques	26592	27466	32594	31531	36349
ALAI	879	1138	1709	1760	2733
MCAC			15	x81	58
Asie	9602	9265	9144	8134	9098
Moyen–Orient	170	14	71	x128	x114
Europe	716337	712986	793633	702733	751821
CEE	705095	701049	782130	691577	740398
AELE	11088	11905	11087	11032	11358
Océanie	x5443	5037	5548	x4916	5669
Portugal	516689	517665	572175	504973	544081
Spain/Espagne	86979	84603	97890	88660	89198
Germany/Allemagne	36419	37369	40769	36214	33896
USA/Etats–Unis d'Amer	23350	23993	29972	28828	32578
Italy/Italie	21927	20313	24478	23009	25447
France,Monac	24233	20820	22108	16562	17391
Switz.Liecht	11057	11831	10999	11009	11324
Morocco/Maroc	14605	10252	9769	8481	7778
Netherlands/Pays–Bas	4988	7789	10971	8363	15811
United Kingdom	5970	5827	6784	4787	4000
Algeria/Algérie	5131	3852	3885	4480	3327
China/Chine	4351	4890	4076	3250	3521
New Zealand	4430	3993	3862	3829	4197
Hong Kong	3617	3130	3076	3172	3548
Belgium–Luxembourg	2039	2708	1407	2661	2974
Sweden/Suède	3750	1999	2577	2068	2362
Austria/Autriche	1399	1410	2101	2413	x3310
Tunisia/Tunisie	1666	1410	1498	1363	833
Canada	2333	2307	882	833	975
Australia/Australie	838	1043	1686	1056	1472
Japan/Japon	468	719	802	650	794
Denmark/Danemark	493	371	571	917	1355
Brazil/Brésil	309	215	787	695	1086
Colombia/Colombie	178	596	509	319	217
Singapore/Singapour	554	275	656	475	513
So. Africa Customs Un	132	106	328	647	
Czech Republic				1006	704
Ireland/Irlande	34	26	24	535	41
Finland/Finlande	103	129	150	245	302
India/Inde	156	137	220	165	151
Chile/Chili	50	105	82	259	448
Mexico/Mexique	53	66	140	238	708
Slovenia/Slovénia			260	71	50
Argentina/Argentine	64	106	96	124	82
Greece/Grèce	73	21	127	172	228
Korea, Republic of	73	30	101	138	177
Norway,SVD,JM	31	73	89	24	33
Malaysia/Malaisie	195	49	31	71	138
Bulgaria/Bulgarie		x75		x75	x91
Czechoslovakia		x120	x28		
Turkey/Turquie	119	14	65	68	18
Poland/Pologne	14	103		37	204
Venezuela	213	26	62	50	132
Peru/Pérou	12	23	33	76	59
Indonesia/Indonésie			46	66	53
Croatia/Croatie			39	49	x9
Yugoslavia/Yougoslavie			x75		x5
Barbados/Barbade	2	26	12	28	
Guatemala			15	49	42
Hungary/Hongrie	x1	x25	x13	x6	

(VALUE AS % OF TOTAL)(VALEUR EN % DU TOTAL)

	1985	1986	1987	1988	1989	1990	1991	1992	1993	1994
Africa	1.8	2.1	x1.6	x1.8	x1.7	x1.7	x1.9	x2.0	x1.5	x2.1
Northern Africa	0.1	0.1	0.1	0.1	0.2	0.1	0.2	x0.1	0.1	0.1
Americas	15.6	x12.8	x12.3	12.1	13.4	x13.1	x14.9	x16.2	x18.3	x17.6
LAIA	2.0	1.9	1.2	1.3	1.5	1.3	1.8	2.5	3.0	3.3
CACM	0.1	0.0	0.0	0.0	0.0	0.0	0.0	0.0	x0.1	x0.1
Asia	5.9	6.2	x4.9	x5.5	5.7	5.1	4.8	5.0	x5.7	5.9
Middle East	0.6	x0.8	x0.5	x0.4	x0.4	x0.5	x0.5	x0.7	x0.7	x0.5
Europe	70.5	74.3	70.7	68.7	67.9	71.5	71.9	72.0	67.2	66.3
EEC	59.5	62.7	59.5	58.6	58.5	66.1	67.0	67.4	62.8	61.9
EFTA	10.2	10.7	10.4	9.4	8.8	4.5	4.3	4.0	3.9	3.9
Oceania	5.3	x4.2	x3.8	x4.7	x4.5	x3.2	x4.1	x3.8	x4.9	x5.3
France,Monac	23.3	24.3	21.8	20.9	20.6	25.5	25.3	23.9	20.6	22.2
Germany/Allemagne	11.2	11.8	11.3	11.3	12.6	13.0	14.0	16.1	18.0	14.7
USA/Etats–Unis d'Amer	10.8	8.5	8.1	8.2	9.1	8.9	10.8	10.8	12.4	11.7
Italy/Italie	6.4	6.0	6.3	6.5	6.4	7.4	7.5	7.2	5.6	6.6
Spain/Espagne	1.3	2.0	2.6	3.9	4.2	5.2	6.1	6.0	4.7	4.7
Australia/Australie	4.3	3.3	3.1	4.2	3.9	2.7	3.6	3.1	4.2	4.5
Switz.Liecht	3.8	4.0	4.0	3.7	3.0	4.0	3.8	3.5	3.5	3.4
United Kingdom	6.2	6.1	5.3	4.8	4.2	4.1	3.3	3.0	2.7	2.7
Austria/Autriche	2.2	2.4	2.4	2.3	2.4	2.5	2.7	2.9	3.1	3.0
Japan/Japon	3.0	3.4	2.6	2.9	3.5	2.5	2.2	2.1	2.4	2.8

	1985	1986	1987	1988	1989	1990	1991	1992	1993	1994
Afrique	2.5	2.8	2.5	2.6	3.2	2.7	2.0	1.8	2.0	1.5
Afrique du Nord	2.5	2.8	2.5	2.5	3.2	2.7	2.0	1.8	1.9	1.5
Amériques	2.2	1.8	1.4	2.2	2.7	3.4	3.6	3.8	4.1	4.4
ALAI	0.5	0.4	0.2	0.4	0.1	0.1	0.1	0.2	0.2	0.3
MCAC	0.0	0.0	0.0			0.0		0.0	x0.0	0.0
Asie	0.8	0.8	x1.7	2.0	1.3	1.3	1.2	1.1	1.1	1.1
Moyen–Orient	0.0	0.0	x0.0	0.1	0.0	0.0	0.0	0.0	x0.0	x0.0
Europe	93.2	93.5	93.5	92.3	91.9	91.9	92.5	92.7	92.0	92.1
CEE	89.5	89.6	90.1	89.1	89.3	90.4	91.0	91.3	90.6	90.7
AELE	3.6	3.9	3.4	3.1	2.7	1.4	1.5	1.3	1.4	1.4
Océanie	1.3	1.1	x0.8	0.9	x0.7	x0.7	0.7	0.6	x0.6	0.7
Portugal	64.3	65.4	67.0	66.4	66.2	66.3	67.2	66.8	66.1	66.7
Spain/Espagne	11.4	11.0	10.7	10.1	10.4	11.2	11.0	11.4	11.6	10.9
Germany/Allemagne	3.9	4.3	4.0	4.5	4.4	4.7	4.8	4.8	4.7	4.2
USA/Etats–Unis d'Amer	1.7	1.2	1.1	1.6	2.4	3.0	3.1	3.5	3.8	4.0
Italy/Italie	1.6	1.4	1.7	1.6	2.4	2.8	2.6	2.9	3.0	3.1
France,Monac	2.8	2.3	2.3	2.4	2.5	3.1	2.7	2.6	2.2	2.1
Switz.Liecht	0.4	0.6	0.6	0.7	0.9	1.4	1.5	1.3	1.4	1.4
Morocco/Maroc	2.0	2.2	2.0	1.7	2.1	1.9	1.3	1.1	1.1	1.0
Netherlands/Pays–Bas	0.3	0.4	0.4	0.4	0.5	0.6	1.0	1.3	1.1	1.9
United Kingdom	1.6	1.1	0.8	0.9	0.7	0.8	0.8	0.8	0.6	0.5

TRADE BY COMMODITY IN THOUSAND U.S. DOLLARS – COMMERCE PAR PRODUIT EN MILLIERS DE DOLLARS E.U

COUNTRIES–PAYS	IMPORTS – IMPORTATIONS				
	1990	1991	1992	1993	1994
Total	10062337	9733630	10575195	12071824	13046086
Africa	189749	188567	184894	325603	256638
Northern Africa	133322	137821	130466	265634	191854
Americas	1361613	1250608	1740822	2113170	x2421433
LAIA	66285	105876	238150	252815	260425
CACM	7422	7249	12378	x13366	x15413
Asia	3244494	3338623	3488368	5077753	5216802
Middle East	x427172	432744	505797	x492819	x460138
Europe	5115098	4820745	5033775	4375243	4944583
EEC	4706031	4475834	4679141	4051429	4569616
EFTA	355025	303045	282552	259748	311780
Oceania	x73402	x69857	x68611	x74259	x79445
Japan/Japon	1198872	1192047	1188862	2242323	2217165
USA/Etats–Unis d'Amer	1055349	915081	1276279	1595613	1879701
Germany/Allemagne	1143913	1261434	1312186	1125403	1265442
United Kingdom	1018674	798204	826584	798041	833697
China/Chine	536672	588784	731080	860746	914135
Netherlands/Pays–Bas	568023	539849	580716	518437	556495
Korea, Republic of	358238	467091	454392	682721	666908
France, Monac	516560	473093	471810	381511	416027
Italy/Italie	360722	347352	397795	309530	399897
Hong Kong	377405	342111	304767	406875	539004
Belgium–Luxembourg	269033	273794	271500	268597	282327
Singapore/Singapour	177115	195508	177342	247524	205283
Saudi Arabia	179940	208779	225193	x171734	x140812
Switz.Liecht	254053	211193	191066	181736	224051
Denmark/Danemark	218022	199175	206738	171143	206637
Canada	147801	145431	150531	177358	187506
Sweden/Suède	219158	172779	149566	115354	162041
Austria/Autriche	129595	134138	149197	145271	173961
Mexico/Mexique	38513	70215	154194	178525	166911
Spain/Espagne	114966	130437	154318	105280	138460
United Arab Emirates	76389	77533	100141	x118933	x137156
Egypt/Egypte	75257	91635	75063	74024	111572
Norway,SVD,JM	82935	71121	80043	69258	79271
Algeria/Algérie	28363	14340	19644	156264	48201
Australia/Australie	47785	48078	50786	53174	60017
Ireland/Irlande	58946	53221	55200	39906	49109
Greece/Grèce	38401	37646	44522	30090	31094
Portugal	18086	25129	38893	30103	34696
Kuwait/ Koweït	24323	13507	33601	46750	49726
Thailand/Thaïlande	20212	24406	35367	27655	36364
Jordan/Jordanie	16710	19638	29269	28076	25847
Israel/Israël	12241	19225	21916	24684	50415
Oman	18601	22382	22431	18063	15216
Finland/Finlande	31933	29583	20116	12764	19731
Slovenia/Slovénia			31253	30986	38784
So. Africa Customs Un	18841	18691	18450	20040	24891
Poland/Pologne	3787	9884	17923	29353	42867
Argentina/Argentine	2973	8884	18405	28026	35900
Bahrain/Bahreïn	x15425	x13842	x16686	x18352	x11049
Venezuela	3866	12500	19975	15355	12249
Malaysia/Malaisie	8910	12032	14054	21177	34150
Yemen/Yémen	x19406	2903	x18543	x22596	x8633
Libyan Arab Jamahiriya	13997	18283	x10882	x13709	x11885
Hungary/Hongrie	x7834	15353	x12676	x14384	x16369
Iceland/Islande	18037	20731	11443	8755	8458
Qatar	7890	9572	13318	17159	x7249
Turkey/Turquie	10924	10334	10793	18829	17563
Lebanon/Liban	x12729	x19757	x8186	x10793	x24929
Iran (Islamic Rp. of)		x22589	x11307	x3642	x1971
Indonesia/Indonésie	4088	5646	15872	15811	17258

COUNTRIES–PAYS	EXPORTS – EXPORTATIONS				
	1990	1991	1992	1993	1994
Totale	9530188	9274523	10452326	12511780	13371717
Afrique	x244930	x215661	x257940	x257093	x223444
Afrique du Nord	16084	14291	17221	23104	24011
Amériques	1382852	1281714	1670075	2111914	2449798
ALAI	195714	197227	257307	432441	506673
MCAC	10622	10950	14028	x16068	x17777
Asie	3866375	4123407	4868724	6683089	6526177
Moyen–Orient	36392	8170	9219	x17853	x24576
Europe	3641936	3348959	3450627	3197407	3833509
CEE	3392683	3136002	3197549	2984452	3598243
AELE	168360	160920	177643	156886	165043
Océanie	35199	40131	43231	79449	x105263
Indonesia/Indonésie	2785114	3027404	3499859	4585381	4123920
Malaysia/Malaisie	393223	494654	758063	1364293	1563244
USA/Etats–Unis d'Amer	699433	664683	748960	799493	805110
Germany/Allemagne	727964	675810	697487	626236	753009
Canada	474242	406135	646365	860984	1100512
Belgium–Luxembourg	516296	535765	541620	469914	524464
Finland/Finlande	575513	409837	381706	420947	528905
France, Monac	374417	383800	418354	382679	464106
Austria/Autriche	416431	384804	391156	347640	x429605
Singapore/Singapour	202799	227743	227674	252642	210399
Brazil/Brésil	135753	142914	193086	341361	391308
Italy/Italie	224092	201349	215266	214988	257106
Hong Kong	218495	182133	177664	218167	364904
Switz.Liecht	127310	121007	138100	126603	124523
Portugal	135624	123746	109858	72953	98704
Spain/Espagne	88111	98129	93235	110399	123750
Netherlands/Pays–Bas	79852	86213	97914	114815	144528
Denmark/Danemark	79544	76164	77871	72094	75702
Cote d'Ivoire	x78154	x61946	x82279	x69742	x68672
Russian Federation			x85170	x112548	x160301
So. Africa Customs Un	60297	57052	66054	72975	18633
Poland/Pologne	54313	78176	59821	55420	94323
United Kingdom	61421	57734	75697	56315	85603
Sweden/Suède	75807	64205	57501	55280	72145
New Zealand	27820	33631	35335	54272	90475
Philippines	77243	53295	39905	24787	18900
Norway,SVD,JM	41049	39909	39543	30283	40512
Former USSR/Anc. URSS	236446	x108564			
China/Chine	15031	20793	36652	50453	51583
Korea, Republic of	38500	30127	38034	39467	39477
Latvia/Lettonie			x10543	x90229	34535
Greece/Grèce	26242	29120	31261	31631	31360
Japan/Japon	31886	31892	30348	27380	29149
Czechoslovakia		x38619	x46079		
Cameroon/Cameroun	26171	30321	x28003	x21213	x22922
Romania/Roumanie	25903	19380	22149	27548	28413
Slovenia/Slovénia			38333	29637	36097
Thailand/Thaïlande	18947	14718	16686	31654	34447
India/Inde	9004	9933	10470	41362	32978
Congo	23669	x23683	x19978	x18009	x22254
Chile/Chili	8875	13682	16659	22271	24250
Yugoslavia SFR	80867	x52024			
Hungary/Hongrie	x12365	x10230	x20621	x19455	x23049
Ecuador/Equateur	10047	11845	15399	22643	x25268
Croatia/Croatie			22734	22487	x28813
Israel/Israël	21383	15880	15872	12417	11540
Ghana	x14176	3103	17958	x22122	x36166
Gabon	x18212	x14964	x15027	x12918	x14908
Czech Republic				41958	54009
Morocco/Maroc	12637	8775	13728	19046	20074

(VALUE AS % OF TOTAL)(VALEUR EN % DU TOTAL)

	1985	1986	1987	1988	1989	1990	1991	1992	1993	1994
Africa	3.3	3.1	1.9	2.1	2.1	1.9	1.9	1.8	2.7	2.0
Northern Africa	2.7	2.4	1.3	1.7	1.5	1.3	1.4	1.2	2.2	1.5
Americas	25.9	23.0	19.4	16.7	15.0	13.6	12.9	16.5	17.5	x18.5
LAIA	0.8	0.5	0.4	0.5	0.5	0.7	1.1	2.3	2.1	2.0
CACM	0.1	0.1	0.1	0.1	0.1	0.1	0.1	0.1	x0.1	x0.1
Asia	12.7	x12.6	x25.3	x28.8	30.4	32.2	34.3	32.9	42.1	40.0
Middle East	4.8	x4.5	x3.2	4.7	x4.0	x4.2	4.4	4.8	x4.1	x3.5
Europe	55.0	58.6	50.5	50.0	50.5	50.8	49.5	47.6	36.2	37.9
EEC	47.3	50.5	43.3	43.3	43.2	46.8	46.0	44.2	33.6	35.0
EFTA	7.1	7.6	6.8	6.3	6.8	3.5	3.1	2.7	2.2	2.4
Oceania	1.7	x1.3	x1.1	x0.9	x1.0	x0.7	x0.7	x0.6	x0.6	x0.6
Japan/Japon	2.5	3.3	7.5	7.9	13.3	11.9	12.2	11.2	18.6	17.0
USA/Etats–Unis d'Amer	21.3	18.4	15.5	13.5	11.7	10.5	9.4	12.1	13.2	14.4
Germany/Allemagne	9.7	11.4	9.5	8.6	9.3	11.4	13.0	12.4	9.3	9.7
United Kingdom	14.0	13.4	11.7	12.8	11.1	10.1	8.2	7.8	6.6	6.4
China/Chine			6.6	6.5	4.8	5.3	6.0	6.9	7.1	7.0
Netherlands/Pays–Bas	5.7	6.3	5.2	5.1	5.1	5.6	5.5	5.5	4.3	4.3
Korea, Republic of	0.7	0.6	0.5	1.9	2.7	3.6	4.8	4.3	5.7	5.1
France, Monac	5.0	5.7	4.8	4.6	4.5	5.1	4.9	4.5	3.2	3.2
Italy/Italie	3.1	3.1	3.0	3.1	3.1	3.6	3.6	3.8	2.6	3.1
Hong Kong	2.3	2.2	2.8	2.8	3.0	3.8	3.5	2.9	3.4	4.1

	1985	1986	1987	1988	1989	1990	1991	1992	1993	1994
Afrique	1.5	x1.6	x1.8	x2.3	x2.3	x2.5	x2.3	x2.4	x2.1	x1.6
Afrique du Nord	0.1	0.1	0.1	0.1	0.2	0.2	0.2	0.2	0.2	0.2
Amériques	15.1	14.5	12.4	14.4	14.6	14.5	13.8	15.9	16.9	18.4
ALAI	3.3	3.7	3.2	3.9	3.2	2.1	2.1	2.5	3.5	3.8
MCAC	0.2	0.1	0.1	0.1	0.1	0.1	0.1	0.1	x0.1	x0.1
Asie	33.8	30.5	37.6	38.5	36.3	40.6	44.4	46.5	53.4	48.8
Moyen–Orient	1.7	0.6	x0.5	0.5	x0.3	0.4	0.1	0.1	x0.1	x0.2
Europe	44.4	47.4	41.5	39.3	42.0	38.2	36.1	33.0	25.6	28.7
CEE	32.5	34.9	30.3	28.7	30.8	35.6	33.8	30.6	23.9	26.9
AELE	10.6	11.5	10.1	9.9	10.6	1.8	1.7	1.7	1.3	1.2
Océanie	1.1	0.9	0.8	0.4	0.4	0.3	0.4	0.4	0.6	x0.7
Indonesia/Indonésie	20.1	19.3	22.6	23.8	26.1	29.2	32.6	33.5	36.6	30.8
Malaysia/Malaisie	2.6	3.0	3.6	3.1	3.4	4.1	5.3	7.3	10.9	11.7
USA/Etats–Unis d'Amer	4.5	5.5	5.2	6.0	6.3	7.3	7.2	7.2	6.4	6.0
Germany/Allemagne	7.4	8.2	7.1	7.0	7.3	7.6	7.3	6.7	5.0	5.6
Canada	7.0	5.2	3.9	4.3	4.9	5.0	4.4	6.2	6.9	8.2
Belgium–Luxembourg	4.6	5.2	4.6	4.4	4.8	5.4	5.8	5.2	3.8	3.9
Finland/Finlande	5.2	5.6	4.9	4.6	4.9	6.0	4.4	3.7	3.4	4.0
France, Monac	3.3	3.3	2.8	2.7	3.3	3.9	4.1	4.0	3.1	3.5
Austria/Autriche	2.5	3.1	2.8	3.0	3.2	4.4	4.1	3.7	2.8	x3.2
Singapore/Singapour	4.3	3.2	3.0	3.4	2.7	2.1	2.5	2.2	2.0	1.6

TRADE BY COMMODITY IN THOUSAND U.S. DOLLARS – COMMERCE PAR PRODUIT EN MILLIERS DE DOLLARS E.U

IMPORTS – IMPORTATIONS

COUNTRIES–PAYS	1990	1991	1992	1993	1994
Total	7585572	8547051	9411078	8835935	10640733
Africa	x112563	x98079	x155014	x143631	x226169
Northern Africa	41160	29114	x64448	x49265	x114368
Americas	x1519226	x1531398	x1856174	x2043885	x2399954
LAIA	39929	75053	162617	172074	315348
CACM	2630	3728	6488	x9636	x10303
Asia	950835	1367145	1340146	x1385061	x1721007
Middle East	x116108	194944	x238100	x148388	x143096
Europe	4802967	5152732	5875523	5037842	6046714
EEC	4192612	4605754	5330153	4575926	5462444
EFTA	582320	519650	492442	410338	489813
Oceania	x110654	x112754	x110116	x118187	x136715
Germany/Allemagne	1192072	1560977	2141689	1897129	2408140
USA/Etats–Unis d'Amer	1125321	1107555	1324884	1477329	1670760
Japan/Japon	523436	599393	589097	672573	851880
United Kingdom	596210	559926	530074	480866	562394
France, Monac	500372	512521	517563	440313	497742
Netherlands/Pays–Bas	320388	342763	399104	378416	449092
Belgium–Luxembourg	355638	354806	395867	324576	362183
Switz.Liecht	455022	390136	347316	279925	347374
Austria/Autriche	257424	274408	305281	310280	371425
Italy/Italie	223288	280030	322267	237616	250517
Canada	224691	220707	251175	271944	296038
Spain/Espagne	174211	226514	235202	145436	162228
Hong Kong	135488	151318	198345	213202	263104
Russian Federation			x241705	x261286	x231364
Sweden/Suède	236588	190347	156762	104723	106109
Norway, SVD, JM	118830	119483	129127	119417	130292
Saudi Arabia	37448	126285	135635	x47590	x51731
Israel/Israël	21219	219358	41516	24000	28286
Mexico/Mexique	23503	53941	117006	113465	219036
Denmark/Danemark	76192	76987	104557	91486	119984
Former USSR/Anc. URSS	37154	x245070			
Korea, Republic of	36140	64079	80045	97765	134522
Australia/Australie	75047	75012	76691	76075	98765
China/Chine	25677	34733	60811	78737	99204
Portugal	32108	45259	65700	56034	46885
Ireland/Irlande	60456	59065	60817	37834	47363
Finland/Finlande	127493	76924	47473	32952	41701
Singapore/Singapour	33483	36390	41739	59712	81369
Greece/Grèce	40172	45227	47799	38266	36682
Hungary/Hongrie	x19999	22038	x27052	x34753	x32076
Libyan Arab Jamahiriya	20605	15128	x33699	x29294	x24595
United Arab Emirates	10089	8536	8323	x46246	x31074
Indonesia/Indonésie	10632	18451	16787	17259	22966
Guadeloupe	16564	21894	13511	13029	12314
Reunion/Réunion	10318	12299	19687	14561	15819
Poland/Pologne	160	2347	23262	20846	26145
Ukraine			x4234	x41609	x14898
So. Africa Customs Un	13761	14465	15341	14252	16884
Martinique	10319	13735	13836	13253	15298
Malaysia/Malaisie	16181	9734	13055	16020	14772
Iran (Islamic Rp. of)		x12874	x19595	x6077	x4171
Nigeria/Nigéria	x5458	673	x21634	x15126	x3468
Iceland/Islande	8468	10031	15999	10996	12147
Yugoslavia/Yougoslavie			x19475	x15038	x3715
New Zealand	14771	11179	10965	12185	16104
Greenland/Groenland	9529	11489	11388	11152	x5493
Thailand/Thaïlande	4899	17193	7438	9265	12547
Venezuela	1434	3939	16180	11880	5759
Turkey/Turquie	8078	9894	11697	10354	9882
Czechoslovakia	15534	x11702	x19332		

EXPORTS – EXPORTATIONS

COUNTRIES–PAYS	1990	1991	1992	1993	1994
Totale	7449809	8163235	9152131	9203482	11110812
Afrique	x53953	x69443	x66102	x88838	x110059
Afrique du Nord	9050	7783	7615	13590	10969
Amériques	1219708	1389001	1614412	1828777	2177557
ALAI	135898	145771	270449	370230	467913
MCAC	19612	18591	25762	x22287	x30095
Asie	1247431	1511254	1719382	2006403	2533751
Moyen–Orient	33760	52881	51154	x38100	x50493
Europe	4718253	4735663	5171865	4669930	5541493
CEE	4253207	4343313	4654388	4141748	4984033
AELE	283033	279512	263343	303332	298043
Océanie	x31344	x35534	x80924	x44962	x50121
USA/Etats–Unis d'Amer	600237	748694	788925	873051	989183
Germany/Allemagne	756667	760757	787789	618990	628975
Canada	456508	466783	521323	552347	679521
Italy/Italie	497304	502270	509338	428626	522104
France, Monac	429880	471470	508931	458661	545486
Denmark/Danemark	398207	422758	489535	444106	557076
Netherlands/Pays–Bas	374175	421737	499416	433371	540782
China/Chine	253781	343282	457035	491976	650298
Sweden/Suède	441462	414697	421951	450306	621857
Belgium–Luxembourg	362284	377743	384760	371483	391997
Indonesia/Indonésie	274084	25/016	326056	544244	708405
Austria/Autriche	290343	294565	342365	322469	x362018
United Kingdom	221489	238294	226011	167237	218474
Hong Kong	129322	159564	217635	253484	289431
Finland/Finlande	229245	183383	175229	250983	359043
Poland/Pologne	23255	191413	195526	220348	311278
Norway, SVD, JM	205990	196683	166493	200135	185660
Thailand/Thaïlande	130301	145616	164407	190869	225093
Malaysia/Malaisie	97138	124073	151821	173005	203103
Spain/Espagne	138977	136735	191905	116005	159459
Philippines	115614	177182	112714	100715	126972
Slovenia/Slovénia			192804	191125	231260
Brazil/Brésil	64634	79720	101410	147329	201563
Mexico/Mexique	22212	27612	121249	156929	167521
Czechoslovakia		x107250	x191279		
Switz.Liecht	76985	82735	96833	103175	110222
Japan/Japon	57762	79936	94494	71330	78132
Hungary/Hongrie	x90904	x77827	x85182	x58725	x69974
Portugal	81993	82457	77978	59398	64970
Czech Republic				211293	239876
Singapore/Singapour	65004	80668	71985	57725	73817
Korea, Republic of	57644	57536	40831	39314	75292
So. Africa Customs Un	26270	40105	38780	54110	72713
Yugoslavia SFR	180504	x111107			
Australia/Australie	20112	22039	60763	26256	28663
Chile/Chili	28202	19967	28794	42846	54935
Ireland/Irlande	28363	34500	35405	15397	5318
Turkey/Turquie	12664	17344	23206	27405	38548
Croatia/Croatie			35748	29966	x25946
Romania/Roumanie	34154	18891	16941	23608	26421
Sri Lanka	8727	19224	13943	17401	21586
New Zealand	9415	12476	19508	18225	20730
Saudi Arabia	6075	27673	17650	x1785	x4873
Russian Federation			x16986	x26875	x15443
Slovakia				x41271	x44428
Bulgaria/Bulgarie	x25949	x12272	x10288	x8926	x5501
Honduras	6603	8867	11458	8859	10591
Yugoslavia/Yougoslavie			x23539	x878	x275
Costa Rica	9388	6287	9109	x7458	x13596
Viet Nam	x3146	x4408	x7324	x10961	x15898

(VALUE AS % OF TOTAL)(VALEUR EN % DU TOTAL)

	1985	1986	1987	1988	1989	1990	1991	1992	1993	1994
Africa	2.1	x1.7	x1.4	x2.0	x1.8	x1.5	x1.2	x1.7	x1.7	x2.2
Northern Africa	1.6	0.9	0.4	x0.5	x0.6	0.5	0.3	x0.7	x0.6	x1.1
Americas	33.4	x29.6	x27.3	x23.2	x21.8	x20.0	x17.9	x19.7	x23.1	x22.6
LAIA	0.7	0.3	0.3	0.4	0.5	0.5	0.9	1.7	1.9	3.0
CACM	0.0	0.0	x0.0	0.0	0.0	0.0	0.0	0.1	x0.1	x0.1
Asia	11.0	x10.4	x10.3	x11.6	x12.5	12.6	16.0	14.2	x15.7	x16.2
Middle East	4.4	x3.8	x2.2	x2.0	x1.7	x1.5	2.3	x2.5	x1.7	x1.3
Europe	51.0	56.0	58.8	60.6	60.9	63.3	60.3	62.4	57.0	56.8
EEC	38.2	41.4	43.3	45.7	46.2	55.3	53.9	56.6	51.8	51.3
EFTA	12.6	14.3	15.2	14.5	14.5	7.7	6.1	5.2	4.6	4.6
Oceania	1.7	x1.4	x1.2	x1.5	x1.7	x1.5	x1.3	x1.1	x1.3	x1.3
Germany/Allemagne	10.3	11.2	11.8	11.5	11.6	15.7	18.3	22.8	21.5	22.6
USA/Etats–Unis d'Amer	28.1	24.7	22.5	18.7	16.7	14.8	13.0	14.1	16.7	15.7
Japan/Japon	4.0	4.2	5.3	6.6	7.5	6.9	7.0	6.3	7.6	8.0
United Kingdom	6.4	6.6	7.0	7.8	7.5	7.9	6.6	5.6	5.4	5.3
France, Monac	5.5	6.0	6.2	6.8	6.1	6.6	6.0	5.5	5.0	4.7
Netherlands/Pays–Bas	3.3	3.7	3.8	4.0	3.7	4.2	4.0	4.2	4.3	4.2
Belgium–Luxembourg	3.2	3.7	3.7	3.8	3.8	4.7	4.2	4.2	3.7	3.4
Switz.Liecht	4.5	5.2	5.7	5.7	5.7	6.0	4.6	3.7	3.2	3.3
Austria/Autriche	2.3	2.7	2.9	2.8	2.7	3.4	3.2	3.2	3.5	3.5
Italy/Italie	2.0	2.0	2.1	2.4	2.6	2.9	3.3	3.4	2.7	2.4

	1985	1986	1987	1988	1989	1990	1991	1992	1993	1994
Afrique	0.5	x0.7	x0.6	x0.5	x0.6	x0.8	x0.9	x0.7	x1.0	x1.0
Afrique du Nord	0.0	0.0	0.1	0.0	0.1	0.1	0.1	0.1	0.1	0.1
Amériques	22.0	17.6	13.8	12.8	16.9	16.4	17.0	17.6	19.9	19.6
ALAI	4.3	1.8	1.8	1.8	2.0	1.8	1.8	3.0	4.0	4.2
MCAC	0.3	0.3	0.2	0.2	0.3	0.3	0.2	0.3	x0.2	x0.3
Asie	9.6	7.6	x20.0	x19.8	13.4	16.8	18.5	18.7	21.8	22.8
Moyen–Orient	2.0	0.5	x0.5	0.5	0.4	0.5	0.6	0.6	x0.4	x0.5
Europe	62.3	68.8	59.2	61.1	66.5	63.3	58.0	56.5	50.7	49.9
CEE	47.4	50.8	43.7	47.0	50.7	57.1	53.2	50.9	45.0	44.9
AELE	13.2	16.6	14.4	12.5	14.0	3.8	3.4	2.9	3.3	2.7
Océanie	0.4	x0.3	0.2	0.4	x0.4	x0.4	x0.4	x0.9	x0.5	x0.4
USA/Etats–Unis d'Amer	6.2	5.9	4.5	4.3	7.5	8.1	9.2	8.6	9.5	8.9
Germany/Allemagne	8.6	9.4	8.2	8.1	9.5	10.2	9.3	8.6	6.7	5.7
Canada	11.1	9.5	7.2	6.4	7.1	6.1	5.7	5.7	6.0	6.1
Italy/Italie	5.8	5.9	4.8	6.3	6.9	6.7	6.2	5.6	4.7	4.7
France, Monac	4.2	3.9	3.4	4.4	4.8	5.8	5.8	5.6	5.0	4.9
Denmark/Danemark	4.8	5.0	4.6	4.4	4.4	5.3	5.2	5.3	4.8	5.0
Netherlands/Pays–Bas	2.7	3.1	2.6	3.5	4.1	5.0	5.2	5.5	4.7	4.9
China/Chine			1.4	1.9	2.7	3.4	4.2	5.0	5.3	5.9
Sweden/Suède	7.1	7.7	6.5	6.1	5.9	5.9	5.1	4.6	4.9	5.6
Belgium–Luxembourg	2.5	3.0	2.7	3.8	4.1	4.9	4.6	4.2	4.0	3.5

TRADE BY COMMODITY IN THOUSAND U.S. DOLLARS – COMMERCE PAR PRODUIT EN MILLIERS DE DOLLARS E.U

COUNTRIES–PAYS	IMPORTS – IMPORTATIONS 1990	1991	1992	1993	1994
Total	53009149	53010094	54248393	49781827	56655613
Africa	x1186412	1340900	x1379073	x1255721	x1399333
Northern Africa	582311	626194	634700	578923	623805
Americas	10981563	10949467	11146831	12084011	13109197
LAIA	989302	1452508	1768016	2044597	2588666
CACM	248775	263285	319335	x318055	x320408
Asia	6967833	7769672	8473932	8829805	10217660
Middle East	x1353582	x1411301	x1360515	x1398038	x1207510
Europe	31622856	31222538	31424270	25664900	29677941
EEC	29975015	29678769	29767180	24196767	28063291
EFTA	1405119	1369491	1353827	1188356	1354771
Oceania	x1114598	x1029648	x1151807	x1088280	x1230586
USA/Etats–Unis d'Amer	8282029	7722552	7564532	8174821	8466329
Germany/Allemagne	6907870	7182940	7053269	5299825	5981876
United Kingdom	6053310	5711883	5613023	4994312	5432607
France,Monac	4642548	4362314	4411948	3519356	4123950
Netherlands/Pays–Bas	2658104	2682263	2661083	2122618	2417391
Italy/Italie	2556585	2448361	2619578	2021074	2624314
Belgium–Luxembourg	2075104	2090111	2016111	1810131	2158976
Spain/Espagne	1603319	1731208	1805471	1428455	1809756
Hong Kong	1278481	1474305	1624590	1592576	1997648
Canada	1159623	1230226	1224604	1275526	1424173
Japan/Japon	1038546	1085830	1093802	1308960	1515264
China/Chine	592161	804647	1267705	1246271	1634096
Denmark/Danemark	946498	942445	953636	773504	894067
Switz.Liecht	986337	941082	912933	805354	925948
Australia/Australie	858182	808542	860632	850124	962142
Austria/Autriche	681128	689837	734865	637885	751401
Malaysia/Malaisie	481827	585889	635184	625032	753363
Mexico/Mexique	267171	374044	601097	687077	877221
Singapore/Singapour	510850	545490	522786	521353	681564
Korea, Republic of	352015	460539	485033	509180	591109
Sweden/Suède	500062	471212	464955	364596	474932
Ireland/Irlande	423888	420189	428691	348039	393367
Greece/Grèce	367014	391017	386803	377535	412621
Norway,SVD,JM	382909	391583	406196	353876	396702
Thailand/Thaïlande	271788	316677	366909	422646	452024
Portugal	329674	357431	417214	314526	350096
Iran (Islamic Rp. of)	x381228	x446862	x365942	x211072	x120599
Saudi Arabia	286688	336922	324303	x266596	x297206
So. Africa Customs Un	292821	298547	307663	305331	361551
Israel/Israël	264478	267847	327253	306936	384622
Turkey/Turquie	193354	234443	232517	413943	246823
Egypt/Egypte	267617	308516	288951	264122	261785
Argentina/Argentine	47305	164237	289901	351590	410841
Brazil/Brésil	243009	299752	213544	276653	388193
Hungary/Hongrie	x160572	178926	x221057	x240206	x227605
Poland/Pologne	39772	100028	218271	287936	399827
Finland/Finlande	229913	197558	200535	184910	237938
New Zealand	180488	164389	225233	187786	217938
India/Inde	237820	185187	179981	204515	218388
Colombia/Colombie	121274	148590	158588	198458	239836
Indonesia/Indonésie	147336	168019	158583	168310	194169
Philippines	134298	156577	151474	178168	244968
Venezuela	100435	148138	166901	158285	123750
Chile/Chili	81232	121322	153431	154103	186795
Pakistan	129809	145278	149192	126800	115887
Costa Rica	114297	112265	133748	x111019	x118510
Nigeria/Nigéria		107263	x135370	x97864	x90468
Morocco/Maroc	99143	110566	120139	107946	117218
Algeria/Algérie	115656	109200	112599	105828	143496
Former USSR/Anc. URSS	729785	x310199			

COUNTRIES–PAYS	EXPORTS – EXPORTATIONS 1990	1991	1992	1993	1994
Totale	50582150	50802867	51489733	47162657	54988342
Afrique	274869	x283955	x285577	x283537	x268399
Afrique du Nord	8596	8446	8223	7837	11924
Amériques	12422031	13223263	13249452	13266805	14558902
ALAI	1000896	997909	1057343	1100676	1361361
MCAC	11337	11056	14910	16534	20351
Asie	2948726	3320518	3584233	3595171	4490693
Moyen–Orient	59112	53247	63632	x66819	126001
Europe	33780142	32971328	33492561	29084824	34616103
CEE	31764979	31095731	31562864	27367933	32913059
AELE	1797486	1745377	1649949	1515114	1449735
Océanie	x390651	x435751	x440484	x462569	x452388
Canada	7541892	7693822	7426644	7435188	7723197
Finland/Finlande	6799861	6283418	6076301	5629308	6689108
Sweden/Suède	5866611	5832301	5714988	4634060	5339773
Germany/Allemagne	5739584	5460852	5664736	4796142	6059871
USA/Etats–Unis d'Amer	3851688	4512921	4745362	4702237	5443967
France,Monac	2948632	3015371	3250391	2833555	3555631
United Kingdom	2148331	2212347	2325046	2041494	2216076
Netherlands/Pays–Bas	2212180	2138632	2172454	1646619	2139636
Austria/Autriche	2041557	2052151	2068787	1746771	x2091412
Italy/Italie	1523843	1577009	1643626	1586135	1815031
Japan/Japon	1539755	1640747	1611385	1333943	1470867
Belgium–Luxembourg	1352868	1329323	1222023	1122952	1384564
Norway,SVD,JM	1025297	997213	870306	832159	638132
Brazil/Brésil	670430	699959	763797	803531	968945
Switz.Liecht	772175	748152	779602	682955	811602
Hong Kong	419045	612528	754782	817751	1004087
Spain/Espagne	571147	571916	716467	637199	775103
Korea, Republic of	311121	302443	376190	416874	633750
Portugal	218633	281884	349456	400350	495750
Indonesia/Indonésie	122683	219642	277955	404229	486173
New Zealand	277591	293848	286595	295488	332134
So. Africa Customs Un	254937	263187	267314	259288	248549
Singapore/Singapour	209231	229496	204355	240492	309214
Denmark/Danemark	213712	207100	200388	170686	217753
Russian Federation			x165214	x320190	x314821
China/Chine	143866	143099	131685	138570	166576
Australia/Australie	96772	127229	134132	142804	118748
Czechoslovakia		x166262	x197220		
Slovenia/Slovénia			203661	157671	214316
Poland/Pologne	77974	90381	120075	123579	174336
Ireland/Irlande	98816	100235	119679	90083	100352
Chile/Chili	85927	96504	83878	115972	150329
Mexico/Mexique	91158	99668	91930	64353	88602
Malaysia/Malaisie	88916	66199	89872	96460	137781
Former USSR/Anc. URSS	471031	x201070			
Czech Republic				146381	175424
Hungary/Hongrie	x57966	x46047	x58485	x34526	x58055
Yugoslavia SFR	217005	x129166			
Venezuela	47235	35882	42056	39531	53296
Slovakia				x113740	x144814
Greece/Grèce	29024	33012	38522	32581	32999
Turkey/Turquie	33419	33325	37739	29662	81813
Bulgaria/Bulgarie	x89913	x28763	x28691	x25930	x12591
Thailand/Thaïlande	19324	16003	26611	36104	74989
Colombia/Colombie	13579	14397	29380	33808	41190
Croatia/Croatie			41016	35702	x35242
Argentina/Argentine	79618	32538	20052	23008	35425
Romania/Roumanie	38846	26129	22498	25519	36531
India/Inde	10676	14125	23950	23804	55427
American Samoa	x15977	x12120	x19207	x23230	

(VALUE AS % OF TOTAL)(VALEUR EN % DU TOTAL)

	1985	1986	1987	1988	1989	1990	1991	1992	1993	1994
Africa	3.7	x2.7	x2.5	x2.7	x2.5	x2.3	2.6	x2.6	x2.5	x2.4
Northern Africa	1.7	1.2	1.1	1.2	1.2	1.1	1.2	1.2	1.2	1.1
Americas	29.4	25.4	23.3	22.6	22.9	20.7	20.7	20.5	24.3	23.2
LAIA	2.7	2.3	2.2	2.0	2.0	1.9	2.7	3.3	4.1	4.6
CACM	0.6	0.5	0.5	0.5	0.6	0.5	0.5	0.6	x0.6	x0.6
Asia	12.0	12.3	x13.3	x13.4	12.9	13.2	14.7	15.6	17.7	18.1
Middle East	1.6	x2.0	x2.2	x2.3	x2.1	x2.6	x2.7	x2.5	x2.8	x2.1
Europe	50.0	55.1	56.2	56.6	56.8	59.7	58.9	57.9	51.6	52.4
EEC	45.2	49.7	50.8	51.4	51.7	56.5	56.0	54.9	48.6	49.5
EFTA	4.4	5.0	5.0	4.8	4.8	2.7	2.6	2.5	2.4	2.4
Oceania	2.7	x2.2	x2.2	x2.3	x2.4	x2.1	x1.9	x2.1	x2.2	x2.2
USA/Etats–Unis d'Amer	23.0	19.6	17.9	17.2	17.2	15.6	14.6	13.9	16.4	14.9
Germany/Allemagne	10.0	11.5	11.4	11.2	11.0	13.0	13.6	13.0	10.6	10.6
United Kingdom	11.1	10.9	11.6	12.6	12.1	11.4	10.8	10.3	10.0	9.6
France,Monac	6.7	7.6	7.6	7.8	7.8	8.8	8.2	8.1	7.1	7.3
Netherlands/Pays–Bas	4.2	4.8	4.6	4.6	4.5	5.0	5.1	4.9	4.3	4.3
Italy/Italie	3.5	3.9	4.2	3.9	4.3	4.8	4.6	4.8	4.1	4.6
Belgium–Luxembourg	3.2	3.6	3.6	3.6	3.5	3.9	3.9	3.7	3.6	3.8
Spain/Espagne	1.1	1.5	1.7	2.1	2.4	3.0	3.3	3.3	2.9	3.2
Hong Kong	1.8	1.9	2.1	2.3	2.3	2.4	2.8	3.0	3.2	3.5
Canada	2.4	2.2	2.0	2.3	2.4	2.2	2.3	2.3	2.6	2.5

	1985	1986	1987	1988	1989	1990	1991	1992	1993	1994
Afrique	0.4	x0.5	x0.6	x0.5	x0.4	0.5	x0.5	x0.5	x0.6	x0.5
Afrique du Nord	0.0	0.0	0.0	0.0	0.0	0.0	0.0	0.0	0.0	0.0
Amériques	24.3	21.5	19.9	20.0	20.1	24.5	26.0	25.7	28.1	26.4
ALAI	1.3	1.3	1.2	1.7	1.7	2.0	2.0	2.1	2.3	2.5
MCAC	0.0	0.0	0.0	0.0	0.0	0.0	0.0	0.0	0.0	0.0
Asie	4.2	4.3	4.6	x4.7	4.3	5.9	6.5	6.9	7.6	8.2
Moyen–Orient	0.0	x0.1	x0.1	0.1	0.1	0.1	0.1	0.1	x0.1	0.2
Europe	69.2	71.5	71.9	72.1	73.0	66.8	64.9	65.0	61.7	63.0
CEE	44.0	46.0	46.4	46.6	47.5	62.8	61.2	61.3	58.0	59.9
AELE	24.8	25.2	25.1	25.1	25.1	3.6	3.4	3.2	3.2	2.6
Océanie	0.3	x0.5	x0.4	x0.5	x0.5	x0.7	x0.8	x0.8	x1.0	x0.8
Canada	16.9	14.5	13.2	12.9	12.5	14.9	15.1	14.4	15.8	14.0
Finland/Finlande	10.7	10.3	10.4	10.3	10.4	13.4	12.4	11.8	11.9	12.2
Sweden/Suède	9.1	9.6	9.5	9.4	9.1	11.6	11.5	11.1	9.8	9.7
Germany/Allemagne	8.0	8.6	8.7	8.7	8.9	11.3	10.7	11.0	10.2	11.0
USA/Etats–Unis d'Amer	6.0	5.7	5.4	5.4	5.9	7.6	8.9	9.2	10.0	9.9
France,Monac	3.6	3.8	3.9	3.9	4.2	5.8	5.9	6.3	6.0	6.5
United Kingdom	2.4	2.4	2.5	2.7	2.8	4.2	4.4	4.5	4.3	4.0
Netherlands/Pays–Bas	2.7	3.1	3.2	3.2	3.1	4.4	4.2	4.2	3.5	3.9
Austria/Autriche	2.4	2.5	2.6	2.9	2.9	4.0	4.0	4.0	3.7	x3.8
Italy/Italie	2.3	2.4	2.3	2.3	2.4	3.0	3.1	3.2	3.4	3.3

TRADE BY COMMODITY IN THOUSAND U.S. DOLLARS – COMMERCE PAR PRODUIT EN MILLIERS DE DOLLARS E.U

COUNTRIES–PAYS	IMPORTS – IMPORTATIONS 1990	1991	1992	1993	1994
Total	13842793	14415192	16504293	15423174	17150410
Africa	x585174	x382794	x419924	x428035	x368818
Northern Africa	138615	145697	x155301	x153037	x119361
Americas	1906596	2141984	2930082	3210960	3906432
LAIA	347400	492193	1045405	1130138	1472255
CACM	52984	60606	84187	x94277	x110372
Asia	1685461	1794041	2141703	2258529	2499926
Middle East	x440690	394961	x458017	x375803	x382342
Europe	8983915	9476913	10337312	8711187	9500948
EEC	8077717	8523992	9263721	7747901	8462723
EFTA	827817	838166	892816	816480	875522
Oceania	x247940	x299611	x319526	x322956	x333432
Germany/Allemagne	1258114	1507624	1618208	1259795	1408507
France,Monac	1306643	1345571	1498841	1268067	1449561
Netherlands/Pays–Bas	1173410	1224759	1356678	1074930	1177729
United Kingdom	1231440	1243439	1228857	1009635	1041463
USA/Etats–Unis d'Amer	783008	781952	918517	1028833	1261361
Belgium–Luxembourg	790469	797615	888771	808327	871691
Canada	477361	571879	649685	733996	827268
Mexico/Mexique	229649	303925	800982	827775	1103713
Switz.Liecht	483908	489732	522490	497321	528094
Hong Kong	348793	386894	490587	541649	615814
Austria/Autriche	336146	355278	398825	394915	451484
Denmark/Danemark	355776	357812	384437	338187	356726
Italy/Italie	414868	366196	390631	307641	346996
Sweden/Suède	337645	341560	370322	333107	356559
Spain/Espagne	262274	322302	386988	315554	326290
Norway,SVD,JM	318629	320240	341318	293733	320313
Ireland/Irlande	247163	275034	322180	225570	242738
China/Chine	152623	163873	297425	308112	342213
Singapore/Singapour	197386	223765	247517	296687	259791
Australia/Australie	148016	161668	186643	187336	201030
Japan/Japon	119158	141061	143422	169594	219691
Portugal	93069	127706	163832	146870	148737
Greece/Grèce	128559	128470	118160	151918	149094
Finland/Finlande	142141	130627	136993	113384	135147
Poland/Pologne	20230	69517	136580	168938	199661
Hungary/Hongrie	x71188	78393	x118641	x152029	x144170
Saudi Arabia	122153	124503	141066	x78053	x92040
Malaysia/Malaisie	69711	86860	93719	111810	149579
Korea, Republic of	90691	107194	95654	79184	84462
Thailand/Thaïlande	43353	58131	77516	88146	113871
Argentina/Argentine	14697	41261	68986	99254	113653
United Arab Emirates	79455	72402	74832	x55105	x56317
New Zealand	44439	66684	62308	69947	84541
Libyan Arab Jamahiriya	70281	69512	x52992	x47021	x40208
Indonesia/Indonésie	52981	54699	50147	60214	59653
Israel/Israël	41389	44741	47240	46877	64252
Russian Federation			x87178	x50194	x123608
Turkey/Turquie	21786	38778	34470	52705	62540
So. Africa Customs Un	39460	41054	42958	41722	44051
Kuwait/ Koweït	29637	21381	48687	52528	54212
Brazil/Brésil	34713	39950	40456	36202	45546
Chile/Chili	27017	38716	39390	38443	46832
Reunion/Réunion	32195	30654	42353	42464	40839
Philippines	23309	34573	32232	44986	61559
Former USSR/Anc. URSS	231229	x109873			
Venezuela	8825	24153	35949	48135	35355
Slovenia/Slovénia			51093	45209	48943
Czechoslovakia	16298	x24631	x70462		
Algeria/Algérie	15309	13341	38599	42156	14139
Oman	27234	28423	26655	32733	32267

COUNTRIES–PAYS	EXPORTS – EXPORTATIONS 1990	1991	1992	1993	1994
Totale	13061434	13992169	16122560	15840177	17340376
Afrique	68158	81048	86211	86385	26459
Afrique du Nord	20997	28201	35168	32557	21637
Amériques	1804073	2175581	2807568	3156934	3479771
ALAI	171964	166824	549107	633070	509113
MCAC	38777	50047	68985	x76886	x93257
Asie	1604754	1767842	2071103	2355058	2686096
Moyen–Orient	175928	147761	123739	x136573	x157583
Europe	9480211	9831120	10976092	9956062	10809724
CEE	9084585	9451469	10450675	9500641	10352328
AELE	291698	311353	343960	309238	351144
Océanie	64745	x74470	76426	x91889	113205
Germany/Allemagne	3059994	3181510	3427453	3090237	3248523
USA/Etats–Unis d'Amer	1317081	1653842	1789826	1982051	2277392
France,Monac	1165982	1211352	1413172	1246554	1340966
Netherlands/Pays–Bas	866065	934703	1018721	860292	1017059
Italy/Italie	715843	782768	901796	867912	1002332
Belgium–Luxembourg	743894	781791	856318	843642	873189
United Kingdom	622918	675708	729508	696878	791576
Japan/Japon	471060	539591	585392	673951	674777
Austria/Autriche	482044	518719	571879	553214	x533182
Sweden/Suède	480165	478503	552971	478640	530153
Hong Kong	398236	415146	498934	536745	612884
Canada	221007	266239	361188	421804	553731
Mexico/Mexique	60468	52774	418704	422197	290899
China/Chine	149949	178457	304674	363528	444829
Spain/Espagne	263471	289447	290626	245979	313664
Denmark/Danemark	167228	192027	271293	270359	267131
Switz.Liecht	220353	231227	257922	229587	265000
Finland/Finlande	360879	236486	235384	229697	307855
Korea, Republic of	134686	134119	137400	155966	198428
Singapore/Singapour	105768	118061	130513	140072	159424
Malaysia/Malaisie	65797	90593	114201	129548	150879
Norway,SVD,JM	70051	79112	85100	78523	84716
Ireland/Irlande	81033	88497	92102	53476	58532
Indonesia/Indonésie	37581	52950	63632	90288	109001
Slovenia/Slovénia			103058	88801	88149
Saudi Arabia	74423	74267	55160	x50825	x62428
Portugal	52483	61157	65861	39423	42671
Brazil/Brésil	22656	33692	40493	90943	71457
Australia/Australie	44083	49820	46674	53226	67161
Thailand/Thaïlande	28727	39583	46322	52741	92719
So. Africa Customs Un	27887	35384	42668	31189	
Poland/Pologne	13034	16170	46838	43069	66396
Croatia/Croatie			53761	44701	x16036
Colombia/Colombie	16883	21639	31675	42015	43063
El Salvador	17749	16165	31289	43280	43929
New Zealand	17535	19722	26167	34060	42603
Israel/Israël	17824	24329	29964	25262	30007
Chile/Chili	12249	22747	28193	25479	34150
Hungary/Hongrie	x13289	x11977	x21603	x40555	x44564
Turkey/Turquie	26825	27083	22611	21034	27222
Greece/Grèce	22144	18361	23593	24338	25493
Philippines	13251	16478	20624	29032	28745
Czechoslovakia		x29453	x33786		
Yugoslavia SFR	98132	x63010			
Costa Rica	13772	19197	25888	x17134	x25702
Tunisia/Tunisie	9146	17276	20431	21038	13896
Argentina/Argentine	45772	23476	10775	22665	33557
Slovakia				x54599	x48444
Czech Republic				51342	62523
United Arab Emirates	33115	11023	12198	x20605	x20959

(VALUE AS % OF TOTAL)(VALEUR EN % DU TOTAL)

	1985	1986	1987	1988	1989	1990	1991	1992	1993	1994
Africa	3.4	x3.8	x3.3	x4.1	x3.8	x4.2	x2.7	x2.6	x2.8	x2.2
Northern Africa	1.7	1.3	1.1	0.9	0.9	1.0	1.0	x0.9	x1.0	x0.7
Americas	18.6	15.4	x14.2	15.5	15.0	13.8	14.9	17.8	20.8	22.8
LAIA	2.6	1.1	1.4	1.7	2.1	2.5	3.4	6.3	7.3	8.6
CACM	0.7	0.5	0.4	0.6	0.4	0.4	0.4	0.5	x0.6	x0.6
Asia	10.3	x10.1	x10.5	x11.8	11.6	12.2	12.5	13.0	14.6	14.6
Middle East	3.7	x4.1	x3.5	x3.5	x3.2	x3.2	2.7	x2.8	x2.4	x2.2
Europe	61.6	64.4	65.5	62.8	63.9	64.9	65.7	62.6	56.5	55.4
EEC	51.9	53.8	54.6	51.6	52.6	58.4	59.1	56.1	50.2	49.3
EFTA	9.4	10.3	10.5	10.9	11.0	6.0	5.8	5.4	5.3	5.1
Oceania	1.7	x1.8	x1.8	x1.5	x2.0	x1.8	x2.1	x1.9	x2.1	x2.0
Germany/Allemagne	8.3	8.9	9.0	7.6	7.9	9.1	10.5	9.8	8.2	8.2
France,Monac	9.0	9.5	9.2	8.9	9.0	9.4	9.3	9.1	8.2	8.5
Netherlands/Pays–Bas	7.8	8.3	8.3	7.9	7.6	8.5	8.5	8.2	7.0	6.9
United Kingdom	8.6	8.2	8.3	7.8	8.1	8.9	8.6	7.4	6.5	6.1
USA/Etats–Unis d'Amer	10.4	9.1	8.1	8.5	7.4	5.7	5.4	5.6	6.7	7.4
Belgium–Luxembourg	5.6	5.8	5.8	5.3	5.2	5.7	5.5	5.4	5.2	5.1
Canada	3.3	2.8	2.5	3.1	3.4	3.4	4.0	3.9	4.8	4.8
Mexico/Mexique	1.6	0.3	0.7	1.0	1.4	1.7	2.1	4.9	5.4	6.4
Switz.Liecht	2.9	3.2	3.3	3.3	3.3	3.5	3.4	3.2	3.2	3.1
Hong Kong	1.9	1.9	2.0	1.9	2.4	2.5	2.7	3.0	3.5	3.6

	1985	1986	1987	1988	1989	1990	1991	1992	1993	1994
Afrique	0.4	0.4	0.4	x0.4	0.5	0.5	0.6	0.6	0.5	0.2
Afrique du Nord	0.1	0.1	0.1	0.1	0.1	0.2	0.2	0.2	0.2	0.1
Amériques	13.8	11.1	10.8	12.6	12.4	13.8	15.5	17.4	20.0	20.0
ALAI	2.3	1.5	1.6	2.1	1.5	1.3	1.2	3.4	4.0	2.9
MCAC	0.5	0.2	0.2	0.3	0.3	0.3	0.4	0.4	x0.5	x0.5
Asie	7.4	7.3	x10.5	x12.4	11.9	12.2	12.6	12.8	14.9	15.5
Moyen–Orient	0.9	x0.8	x1.2	1.6	x1.5	1.3	1.1	0.8	x0.9	x0.9
Europe	77.6	80.5	76.4	72.6	74.3	72.6	70.3	68.1	62.9	62.3
CEE	61.5	64.0	61.3	59.9	61.9	69.6	67.5	64.8	60.0	59.7
AELE	15.3	15.9	14.5	12.0	11.8	2.2	2.2	2.1	2.0	2.0
Océanie	0.4	0.3	0.3	x0.4	0.5	0.5	x0.5	0.5	x0.6	0.6
Germany/Allemagne	17.2	18.4	18.0	18.5	20.3	23.4	22.7	21.3	19.5	18.7
USA/Etats–Unis d'Amer	9.0	7.1	6.9	8.5	8.7	10.1	11.8	11.1	12.5	13.1
France,Monac	8.7	8.7	8.4	8.0	8.2	8.9	8.7	8.8	7.9	7.7
Netherlands/Pays–Bas	5.7	6.3	5.9	5.9	5.6	6.6	6.7	6.3	5.4	5.9
Italy/Italie	3.2	3.6	3.6	4.0	4.6	5.5	5.6	5.6	5.5	5.8
Belgium–Luxembourg	5.3	5.8	5.4	5.5	5.6	5.7	5.6	5.3	5.3	5.0
United Kingdom	4.5	4.1	4.1	4.3	4.1	4.8	4.8	4.5	4.4	4.6
Japan/Japon	2.9	2.7	2.6	3.1	3.4	3.6	3.9	3.6	4.3	3.9
Austria/Autriche	4.1	4.1	3.9	3.0	3.2	3.7	3.7	3.5	3.5	x3.1
Sweden/Suède	4.5	5.0	4.8	3.9	3.7	3.7	3.4	3.4	3.0	3.1

TRADE BY COMMODITY IN THOUSAND U.S. DOLLARS – COMMERCE PAR PRODUIT EN MILLIERS DE DOLLARS E.U

COUNTRIES–PAYS	IMPORTS – IMPORTATIONS 1990	1991	1992	1993	1994
Total	25549255	25914771	28124016	24961857	29525249
Africa	817802	770796	754211	702125	764939
Northern Africa	518434	463897	455033	389567	457392
Americas	1559179	1831880	2139847	2518932	2824345
LAIA	301015	426427	566578	697863	725016
CACM	45926	46337	54859	x55417	x51471
Asia	7278695	8841966	10113075	9538458	11382129
Middle East	x857304	x1122825	x1124594	x1138134	x988999
Europe	14376192	13540371	14313839	11310585	13504181
EEC	13604019	12922840	13605107	10763851	12907455
EFTA	539577	470144	486381	395593	434491
Oceania	x435331	x487988	x482739	x478263	x554944
Hong Kong	2165608	2583032	2714603	2454748	3125074
Germany/Allemagne	2691311	2644420	2655052	1941602	2112567
Italy/Italie	2477358	2207080	2270845	1822235	2567103
France,Monac	2071284	1914372	2112360	1711094	1874280
United Kingdom	1595721	1600751	1727271	1396439	1635490
China/Chine	593209	746395	1903669	1719224	2140610
Japan/Japon	1200579	1471684	1298946	1103087	1486090
Belgium–Luxembourg	1377043	1329892	1315390	1140151	1432794
Korea, Republic of	743062	1021365	1029521	1068768	1456032
USA/Etats–Unis d'Amer	731935	870126	1001367	1202702	1404406
Netherlands/Pays–Bas	775187	742578	770097	692457	774313
Spain/Espagne	492973	548572	624806	453173	671483
Portugal	508906	506017	585257	409307	484095
Canada	422880	438073	456315	501042	551068
Austria/Autriche	537781	472996	496690	411652	446456
Australia/Australie	357007	409157	402680	398875	464547
Turkey/Turquie	327843	294818	367345	515706	464460
Switz.Liecht	463979	395769	409988	327944	359495
Iran (Islamic Rp. of)	x147830	x487257	x367362	x144511	x58319
Indonesia/Indonésie	328233	268868	310997	280109	279608
Malaysia/Malaisie	168400	232077	283920	246575	327495
Denmark/Danemark	290251	275621	283071	195081	234925
Greece/Grèce	255626	217813	286838	197954	205677
Israel/Israël	179667	207574	234824	237973	246219
Singapore/Singapour	189814	206502	184652	211643	229882
Thailand/Thaïlande	201638	188522	198779	189734	208957
Ireland/Irlande	179670	181970	201406	159408	168440
Syrian Arab Republic	106423	x139292	157160	x207211	x155618
Brazil/Brésil	120263	153578	128871	215496	211527
Sweden/Suède	196920	171654	172525	136599	175458
Macau/Macao	122086	115711	147093	113899	133178
Mauritius/Maurice	100132	111804	119630	145052	127686
Mexico/Mexique	64029	72765	140499	157641	178617
Bangladesh		127389	x138718	x219580	x192203
Egypt/Egypte	124020	108877	114644	114456	133458
Tunisia/Tunisie	120239	111656	117951	99339	107746
Philippines	80943	112331	106259	110284	122252
Morocco/Maroc	109477	118745	115761	93994	110192
Finland/Finlande	153987	109103	103499	96698	124375
Pakistan	101264	105336	93688	73865	53625
Hungary/Hongrie	x102385	94498	x81215	x81694	x87132
So. Africa Customs Un	96991	79667	81447	87286	105306
Saudi Arabia	75181	77788	77225	x84843	x116519
Sri Lanka	40713	73585	80135	83927	95074
Poland/Pologne	38490	42896	69849	124833	161918
India/Inde	146455	60900	69110	104977	159670
Argentina/Argentine	17233	61400	89549	80857	87297
Algeria/Algérie	131052	81735	82634	60538	81248
New Zealand	69423	70979	70316	70800	82292
Norway,SVD,JM	71746	71142	72764	64172	71536

COUNTRIES–PAYS	EXPORTS – EXPORTATIONS 1990	1991	1992	1993	1994
Totale	23087523	23746031	25294256	23067215	27699385
Afrique	677608	611016	553016	480608	680316
Afrique du Nord	464364	375527	321565	279749	474499
Amériques	2355415	2403876	2547705	2281749	2640585
ALAI	826727	795277	1005771	853451	996254
MCAC	37900	33262	39039	x34104	x40044
Asie	7212327	8469878	9134550	8983754	11546704
Moyen–Orient	534571	557440	459464	377761	634785
Europe	12560344	11950306	12670453	10703960	12227399
CEE	11526194	11079361	11708458	9921582	11404102
AELE	882453	784155	807785	655192	679350
Océanie	x64921	x71310	x71022	x230191	x115269
Germany/Allemagne	3379539	3292092	3532768	2800030	3215891
Italy/Italie	2106805	2030787	2167706	2008129	2222872
Hong Kong	1533587	1745338	1938865	1959071	2370215
France,Monac	1543735	1444052	1575407	1264360	1551341
China/Chine	1007971	1274326	1345294	1335390	1778054
United Kingdom	1365137	1323486	1347910	1069183	1248257
Pakistan	1002891	1169832	1275875	1200305	1424135
USA/Etats–Unis d'Amer	1292856	1311828	1224738	1069934	1252714
Japan/Japon	1161656	1227988	1233950	1093893	1126965
Belgium–Luxembourg	1151946	1102435	1107775	1081704	1206014
Korea, Republic of	867563	976284	1046534	947994	1059350
Switz.Liecht	847747	749988	772019	620630	645251
India/Inde	360320	541151	651337	655611	1051163
Spain/Espagne	475741	447897	487089	482133	622314
Turkey/Turquie	492898	470035	435642	347151	597698
Austria/Autriche	452815	407085	443582	370312	x410506
Brazil/Brésil	347519	335964	380538	250419	304604
Indonesia/Indonésie	109482	203678	344136	389953	678760
Thailand/Thaïlande	215284	264637	291334	322775	507862
Canada	196566	262033	276508	323048	350105
Egypt/Egypte	391483	310430	249293	221384	387085
Greece/Grèce	285103	276398	274420	221893	204550
Netherlands/Pays–Bas	241207	223306	216197	208014	233206
Ireland/Irlande	173907	193814	217507	143865	164496
Singapore/Singapour	153984	171704	146316	228464	274365
Mexico/Mexique	159369	168579	172483	182753	190872
Malaysia/Malaisie	98289	116790	148528	224906	328432
So. Africa Customs Un	162645	170201	169766	125589	123122
Uruguay	9847	10092	215905	173006	183305
Portugal	131073	141401	143074	103557	124660
Denmark/Danemark	131547	118040	122405	104848	128641
Argentina/Argentine	121296	107355	94006	114894	140783
Peru/Pérou	129555	119827	88240	65369	88907
Australia/Australie	14575	19518	28752	191517	71814
Czechoslovakia		x103540	x134266		
Israel/Israël	66733	75771	79093	69475	72680
Macau/Macao	41768	67258	75998	70921	70492
Slovakia				x177239	x205716
Morocco/Maroc	66361	58694	62975	44833	55505
Sweden/Suède	61828	55278	49889	38576	36146
Hungary/Hongrie	x67145	x39432	x59123	x44828	x57505
Slovenia/Slovénia			77464	61241	80005
Romania/Roumanie	31847	18964	57397	62152	62066
New Zealand	49925	47553	41426	37618	42851
Poland/Pologne	42875	22208	48399	41390	61933
Russian Federation			x44122	x63172	x109941
Norway,SVD,JM	33312	32633	34606	33513	32826
Bangladesh	41450	34669	32725	29918	x65878
Syrian Arab Republic	20778	x68407	10093	x2264	x4685
Colombia/Colombie	27845	24479	23936	31552	33960

(VALUE AS % OF TOTAL)(VALEUR EN % DU TOTAL)

	1985	1986	1987	1988	1989	1990	1991	1992	1993	1994
Africa	4.3	3.8	2.8	3.1	2.4	3.2	3.0	2.7	2.8	2.6
Northern Africa	2.9	2.4	1.8	2.1	1.5	2.0	1.8	1.6	1.6	1.5
Americas	7.2	x7.1	x6.3	5.7	6.7	6.1	7.0	7.6	10.1	9.5
LAIA	0.9	0.8	0.7	0.8	1.0	1.2	1.6	2.0	2.8	2.5
CACM	0.4	0.2	x0.3	0.2	0.2	0.2	0.2	0.2	x0.2	x0.2
Asia	23.4	23.9	27.5	29.7	30.5	28.5	34.1	35.7	38.2	38.6
Middle East	2.0	x3.6	x2.3	x2.5	x2.6	x3.4	x4.3	x4.0	x4.6	x3.3
Europe	58.8	59.1	54.8	53.5	53.5	56.3	52.2	51.1	45.3	45.7
EEC	51.5	52.1	48.6	47.6	47.6	53.2	49.9	48.6	43.1	43.7
EFTA	6.6	6.4	5.6	5.3	5.2	2.1	1.8	1.7	1.6	1.5
Oceania	2.5	x2.4	x2.1	x2.0	x2.1	x1.7	x1.9	x1.7	x1.9	x1.9
Hong Kong	9.1	9.0	8.9	8.0	9.2	8.5	10.0	9.7	9.8	10.6
Germany/Allemagne	11.4	11.3	10.1	9.4	9.5	10.5	10.2	9.5	7.8	7.2
Italy/Italie	8.3	8.4	8.6	8.8	9.2	9.7	8.5	8.1	7.3	8.7
France,Monac	6.6	6.9	6.4	6.3	6.8	8.1	7.4	7.5	6.9	6.3
United Kingdom	7.3	6.8	6.2	6.5	5.9	6.2	6.2	6.2	5.6	5.5
China/Chine			2.3	3.3	3.6	2.3	2.9	6.8	6.9	7.3
Japan/Japon	5.9	4.2	5.1	6.1	5.6	4.7	5.7	4.6	4.4	5.0
Belgium–Luxembourg	5.5	5.5	4.9	4.8	4.7	5.4	5.1	4.7	4.6	4.9
Korea, Republic of	1.6	2.0	2.9	2.8	3.0	2.9	3.9	3.7	4.3	4.9
USA/Etats–Unis d'Amer	3.6	3.7	3.0	2.5	3.2	2.9	3.4	3.6	4.8	4.8

	1985	1986	1987	1988	1989	1990	1991	1992	1993	1994
Afrique	3.0	2.3	2.6	4.1	3.2	2.9	2.6	2.2	2.0	2.4
Afrique du Nord	1.8	1.8	2.2	1.8	2.4	2.0	1.6	1.3	1.2	1.7
Amériques	9.7	7.8	7.6	7.8	9.6	10.3	10.1	10.0	9.9	9.5
ALAI	4.4	3.6	4.0	3.2	3.6	3.6	3.3	4.0	3.7	3.6
MCAC	0.2	0.1	0.1	0.1	0.1	0.2	0.1	0.2	x0.1	x0.1
Asie	27.6	28.1	x33.8	x33.6	31.9	31.2	35.7	36.1	38.9	41.7
Moyen–Orient	3.5	3.6	3.2	2.8	2.4	2.3	2.3	1.8	1.6	2.3
Europe	58.5	60.5	54.1	52.8	53.7	54.4	50.3	50.1	46.4	44.1
CEE	51.8	53.6	48.1	46.7	47.0	49.9	46.7	46.3	43.0	41.2
AELE	5.9	6.3	5.3	5.4	5.7	3.8	3.3	3.2	2.8	2.5
Océanie	0.9	x0.9	x0.8	x0.4	x0.3	x0.3	x0.3	x0.3	x1.0	x0.4
Germany/Allemagne	13.1	14.1	12.6	13.2	14.0	14.6	13.9	14.0	12.1	11.6
Italy/Italie	8.7	9.3	9.6	7.9	8.4	9.1	8.6	8.6	8.7	8.0
Hong Kong	5.5	5.5	5.2	5.5	7.2	6.6	7.4	7.7	8.5	8.6
France,Monac	8.2	7.9	6.7	6.3	6.9	6.7	6.1	6.2	5.5	5.6
China/Chine	2.1	2.7	5.8	5.2	5.5	4.4	5.4	5.3	5.8	6.4
United Kingdom	5.1	4.9	4.3	4.6	5.3	5.9	5.6	5.3	4.6	4.5
Pakistan	1.9	2.2	2.7	2.4	3.2	4.3	4.9	5.0	5.2	5.1
USA/Etats–Unis d'Amer	4.5	3.5	3.1	3.9	5.0	5.6	5.5	4.8	4.6	4.5
Japan/Japon	7.3	7.1	5.1	4.9	5.2	5.0	5.2	4.9	4.7	4.1
Belgium–Luxembourg	4.8	5.0	4.4	4.4	4.8	5.0	4.6	4.4	4.7	4.4

TRADE BY COMMODITY IN THOUSAND U.S. DOLLARS – COMMERCE PAR PRODUIT EN MILLIERS DE DOLLARS E.U

COUNTRIES–PAYS	IMPORTS – IMPORTATIONS 1990	1991	1992	1993	1994
Total	17420402	18080967	15967367	16539078	17727860
Africa	x948065	x1073364	x1242703	x1352599	x1293585
Northern Africa	459358	481893	565914	601983	646498
Americas	x1691230	1935327	2387651	x2570192	x2566328
LAIA	126036	225518	411157	487704	509928
CACM	28729	34444	47873	x55287	x75342
Asia	6737411	8073364	5764187	x6396480	7197294
Middle East	x307493	x365130	x430487	x640573	x658391
Europe	6893546	6365851	5946686	5318219	5703592
EEC	6471624	5901145	5569605	4685301	5303347
EFTA	250888	223742	219860	198847	218168
Oceania	x312488	x318516	x346301	x313175	x334758
China/Chine	2988909	3716527	1011137	1019133	1288464
Hong Kong	1475604	1750240	1958580	1934569	2272957
USA/Etats–Unis d'Amer	1177542	1341779	1562077	1631006	1570071
Germany/Allemagne	1129754	1126522	1058041	901028	1024019
United Kingdom	1071034	926347	910017	855037	887390
Italy/Italie	1103370	945414	832955	624065	832250
France,Monac	1020761	862702	816163	664580	761864
Japan/Japon	496924	497362	439380	404127	558504
Tunisia/Tunisie	328719	341066	420286	441837	478024
Belgium–Luxembourg	418017	394268	356937	409120	436379
Netherlands/Pays–Bas	433218	418848	389805	297106	325980
Singapore/Singapour	333519	321894	326770	294215	279491
Canada	263569	256563	266290	289273	293603
Korea, Republic of	162375	238177	310405	260689	318980
Malaysia/Malaisie	194697	213653	267832	256347	258463
Portugal	284099	258194	275958	201327	238329
Australia/Australie	207217	208110	222350	201175	223169
Spain/Espagne	201191	215690	224267	155476	183744
Austria/Autriche	240169	210770	206742	177140	181741
Sri Lanka	103145	141438	207089	239934	256739
Thailand/Thaïlande	131817	172953	190116	202279	210208
Philippines	98200	235064	117026	151598	166005
United Arab Emirates	63816	107158	133011	x238874	x199976
Mexico/Mexique	43193	59757	187052	224664	227915
Macau/Macao	159155	165815	161757	143792	156992
Switz.Liecht	174776	146462	141217	127177	136203
Sweden/Suède	150333	149077	144255	113327	129698
Greece/Grèce	147058	149427	134391	115338	115213
Bangladesh		11926	22172	x358062	x416042
Croatia/Croatie			21237	346199	x64054
Indonesia/Indonésie	77731	90673	114532	121759	110918
Hungary/Hongrie	x74774	111882	x104190	x100334	x93835
Morocco/Maroc	100360	109380	97438	98520	112378
Poland/Pologne	61238	14546	30543	258623	322793
Denmark/Danemark	104668	101341	99921	84162	89791
Mauritius/Maurice	86028	85200	87617	111928	116252
Turkey/Turquie	74680	60878	69155	127590	185844
Saudi Arabia	25374	61121	65253	x114829	x110186
Norway,SVD,JM	71764	72059	74887	68173	78491
Yugoslavia SFR	133683	x208248			
Benin/Bénin	x56887	x59695	x57860	x77772	x31142
Finland/Finlande	96354	72689	59701	48496	59223
Argentina/Argentine	3096	46148	64371	64613	60243
Ireland/Irlande	71597	69858	60453	39099	37726
Nigeria/Nigéria	x34192	5264	x76885	x87160	x48063
Chile/Chili	27668	50565	58357	58339	44507
So. Africa Customs Un	52382	62290	53299	47538	54642
Romania/Roumanie	17887	33418	53397	69661	102977
Mongolia/Mongolie	x52146	x2123	x13755	x140317	x4747
Un. Rep. of Tanzania	x4068	x123178	x19847	x12114	x17331

COUNTRIES–PAYS	EXPORTS – EXPORTATIONS 1990	1991	1992	1993	1994
Totale	15559059	15992708	16693588	16350561	18424077
Afrique	x309161	x316449	x265164	x316131	x332217
Afrique du Nord	172379	164755	133068	168740	194830
Amériques	900912	954215	1053838	1117982	1300984
ALAI	319920	333540	381358	392141	453298
MCAC	16879	21612	22563	15510	21330
Asie	6858375	7839966	8537034	8728657	9943786
Moyen–Orient	230159	x262737	216708	x284813	x456642
Europe	6966400	6514345	6600817	5899030	6546431
CEE	6458389	6098658	6175339	5534032	6162515
AELE	459783	383772	377153	314689	334268
Océanie	18715	x22482	28776	x35527	x43577
Hong Kong	1781320	2043409	2320501	2429379	2617576
China/Chine	1822670	2018633	2064417	2248452	2711262
Germany/Allemagne	1781072	1624695	1577042	1396930	1524624
Italy/Italie	1055152	1017455	1096084	1044161	1278420
France,Monac	1088937	1011903	1045137	910550	1054508
Japan/Japon	877956	986848	1036750	890883	850331
Pakistan	605457	747419	866737	837990	964200
India/Inde	571350	622741	688974	683279	913253
USA/Etats–Unis d'Amer	526627	563791	598621	647614	739980
Belgium–Luxembourg	552661	519676	493484	513773	589205
Netherlands/Pays–Bas	532534	507273	521903	397753	392482
United Kingdom	454738	438910	440156	396202	419167
Korea, Republic of	342048	387885	383505	392133	469581
Indonesia/Indonésie	202028	264741	411063	342414	318415
Switz.Liecht	437593	364242	356812	295779	310841
Austria/Autriche	350464	330048	344701	272488	x223384
Spain/Espagne	188811	209805	211472	221826	263824
Brazil/Brésil	135809	163894	221242	209160	207519
Thailand/Thaïlande	141600	163708	190623	201063	229214
Turkey/Turquie	186049	173863	195088	184442	341022
Singapore/Singapour	122862	157229	150863	154010	160791
Portugal	138552	134484	154329	136158	155789
Malaysia/Malaisie	84570	94797	113036	121547	134669
Czechoslovakia		x149184	x132830		
Egypt/Egypte	83492	108761	73261	82842	121337
Ireland/Irlande	90438	82807	70641	74456	70361
Greece/Grèce	71699	78592	67684	56405	67671
Denmark/Danemark	74369	67034	68120	52684	48182
Sweden/Suède	57697	57504	64518	43111	53785
Russian Federation			x56983	x89666	x108184
Tunisia/Tunisie	53049	40588	48480	57261	52564
Colombia/Colombie	39489	51396	46764	47301	54442
Czech Republic				144488	158396
Mexico/Mexique	51747	49516	43239	49420	72322
Canada	32591	31949	48242	61044	83216
Former USSR/Anc. URSS	323756	x115244			
Cote d'Ivoire	x44391	x41239	x36121	x35869	x31378
Macau/Macao	37634	36432	36437	31927	33767
Syrian Arab Republic	26594	x73965	10015		
Israel/Israël	24086	26782	23071	31721	23681
Argentina/Argentine	30482	22426	25191	32019	51054
Hungary/Hongrie	x35497	x25413	x25924	x27399	x28555
Poland/Pologne	41086	25835	22545	18807	19528
Peru/Pérou	39182	25765	18131	22581	26872
Bulgaria/Bulgarie	x70342	x16576	12714	32810	18600
Australia/Australie	12696	14182	20629	27249	35384
Norway,SVD,JM	22133	19522	20339	18910	23427
So. Africa Customs Un	21147	18410	19012	19729	
Finland/Finlande	21249	18456	20068	17534	21111
Mauritius/Maurice	16039	14478	17738	23284	26166

(VALUE AS % OF TOTAL)(VALEUR EN % DU TOTAL)

	1985	1986	1987	1988	1989	1990	1991	1992	1993	1994
Africa	3.7	x5.6	x5.0	x4.8	x4.5	x5.4	x5.9	x7.7	x8.2	x7.3
Northern Africa	1.6	1.8	1.6	1.7	1.9	2.6	2.7	3.5	3.6	3.6
Americas	15.2	13.8	11.6	10.0	x10.7	x9.7	10.7	15.0	x15.5	x14.5
LAIA	0.6	0.5	0.4	0.6	0.8	0.7	1.2	2.6	2.9	2.9
CACM	0.2	0.2	0.2	0.2	0.2	0.2	0.2	0.3	x0.3	x0.4
Asia	21.3	21.4	34.8	38.0	40.0	38.7	44.7	36.1	x38.6	40.6
Middle East	1.0	x1.6	x1.4	x1.5	x2.1	x1.8	x2.0	x2.7	x3.9	x3.7
Europe	49.6	49.4	40.0	37.9	37.7	39.6	35.2	37.2	32.2	32.2
EEC	42.4	42.6	34.7	33.2	33.0	37.1	32.6	34.9	28.3	29.9
EFTA	5.7	5.6	4.2	3.8	3.8	1.4	1.2	1.4	1.2	1.2
Oceania	3.8	x3.1	x2.6	x2.6	x2.4	x1.8	x1.7	x2.1	x1.9	x1.9
China/Chine			14.0	15.3	15.4	17.2	20.6	6.3	6.2	7.3
Hong Kong	9.4	9.5	9.1	8.7	9.6	8.5	9.7	12.3	11.7	12.8
USA/Etats–Unis d'Amer	11.2	10.4	9.0	6.8	7.3	6.8	7.4	9.8	9.9	8.9
Germany/Allemagne	7.0	7.4	5.7	5.2	5.3	6.5	6.2	6.6	5.4	5.8
United Kingdom	8.2	6.7	6.3	6.9	6.0	6.1	5.1	5.7	5.2	5.0
Italy/Italie	7.6	8.0	6.6	5.6	5.7	6.3	5.2	5.2	3.8	4.7
France,Monac	7.1	7.3	5.6	5.2	5.3	5.9	4.8	5.1	4.0	4.3
Japan/Japon	3.5	3.0	2.4	3.3	3.8	2.9	2.8	2.8	2.4	3.2
Tunisia/Tunisie	0.8	1.1	1.0	1.1	1.3	1.9	1.9	2.6	2.7	2.7
Belgium–Luxembourg	2.5	2.6	2.0	2.0	2.1	2.4	2.2	2.2	2.5	2.5

	1985	1986	1987	1988	1989	1990	1991	1992	1993	1994
Afrique	2.4	x2.2	x2.3	x2.2	x1.7	x2.0	x2.0	x1.6	x1.9	x1.8
Afrique du Nord	1.2	1.1	1.2	1.2	1.0	1.1	1.0	0.8	1.0	1.1
Amériques	5.6	5.6	4.7	4.4	5.4	5.8	5.9	6.3	6.8	7.1
ALAI	2.9	2.4	2.3	1.9	2.3	2.1	2.1	2.3	2.4	2.5
MCAC	0.1	0.0	0.1	0.1	0.1	0.1	0.1	0.1	0.1	0.1
Asie	43.7	43.0	46.9	46.3	46.3	44.1	49.0	51.1	53.3	53.9
Moyen–Orient	2.0	2.0	1.7	1.5	1.7	1.5	x1.6	1.3	x1.7	x2.5
Europe	45.3	46.1	41.0	41.5	41.9	44.8	40.7	39.5	36.1	35.5
CEE	38.1	38.9	34.9	35.5	36.6	41.5	38.1	37.0	33.8	33.4
AELE	6.4	6.5	5.6	5.5	5.1	3.0	2.4	2.3	1.9	1.8
Océanie	0.1	0.1	0.1	0.1	0.1	0.1	x0.1	0.1	x0.2	x0.2
Hong Kong	9.2	10.0	11.7	11.2	12.5	11.4	12.8	13.9	14.9	14.2
China/Chine	11.4	12.2	12.3	12.2	13.1	11.7	12.6	12.4	13.8	14.7
Germany/Allemagne	11.6	11.7	10.4	10.5	10.4	11.4	10.2	9.4	8.5	8.3
Italy/Italie	4.8	5.4	5.0	5.4	5.6	6.8	6.4	6.6	6.4	6.9
France,Monac	6.2	6.2	5.7	5.9	6.2	7.0	6.3	6.3	5.6	5.7
Japan/Japon	8.1	7.0	6.0	5.9	5.6	5.6	6.2	6.2	5.4	4.6
Pakistan	3.7	3.0	3.3	3.3	3.6	3.9	4.7	5.2	5.1	5.2
India/Inde	4.0	3.3	3.5	3.5	3.6	3.7	3.9	4.1	4.2	5.0
USA/Etats–Unis d'Amer	2.5	2.9	2.2	2.2	2.8	3.4	3.5	3.6	4.0	4.0
Belgium–Luxembourg	3.4	3.4	3.0	2.8	3.1	3.6	3.2	3.0	3.1	3.2

TRADE BY COMMODITY IN THOUSAND U.S. DOLLARS – COMMERCE PAR PRODUIT EN MILLIERS DE DOLLARS E.U

COUNTRIES–PAYS	IMPORTS – IMPORTATIONS					COUNTRIES–PAYS	EXPORTS – EXPORTATIONS				
	1990	1991	1992	1993	1994		1990	1991	1992	1993	1994
Total	21591582	23619854	26782838	25353921	28235071	Totale	22020872	23396469	26271844	25259748	28528829
Africa	x757467	x903024	x876031	x818455	x860185	Afrique	86767	79225	82280	83547	67764
Northern Africa	320012	363973	402869	x381216	427377	Afrique du Nord	68485	57678	52449	49364	54740
Americas	2049588	2379288	2927543	3200882	3473733	Amériques	883682	947620	1148511	1245154	1359712
LAIA	401566	638978	1052663	1235427	1452254	ALAI	76259	91525	184346	204099	238918
CACM	48556	48738	64109	x57907	x62297	MCAC	20641	24081	37021	38812	x39589
Asia	8632509	10230108	12574972	x12724881	x14408993	Asie	10960432	12633818	14568565	14834109	17318904
Middle East	1904638	1913941	2342851	x2536400	x2573434	Moyen–Orient	744751	x241235	289229	x352071	439843
Europe	9372256	9249770	9355414	7102258	7817759	Europe	9904541	9527935	10201156	8834747	9538009
EEC	8906673	8522821	8850436	6759486	7345688	CEE	9517832	9229094	9873308	8545691	9240679
EFTA	324406	265029	262990	238858	266525	AELE	293784	244678	242820	215640	231643
Oceania	x406048	x386963	x416656	x414464	x477510	Océanie	x24835	x29405	33506	x40774	x51688
Hong Kong	3039402	3630214	3951102	3773857	4430345	Korea, Republic of	3103623	3728582	4187344	4724746	5781680
China/Chine	833506	1196737	2397358	2566625	3146424	Germany/Allemagne	3129667	3082793	3232373	2781554	2775960
Germany/Allemagne	1856449	1838040	1866603	1444077	1525648	Japan/Japon	2347492	2610479	2849368	2696225	2621859
United Kingdom	1722991	1599841	1630797	1436535	1505455	Hong Kong	1854716	2328349	2645402	2512004	2815647
USA/Etats–Unis d'Amer	1028066	1162385	1262457	1326346	1359850	Italy/Italie	2094666	2061032	2265625	1962107	2260590
France,Monac	1207333	1083649	1146269	824491	954284	China/Chine	1094887	1297617	1355674	1291993	2148477
United Arab Emirates	648213	818552	1024580	x1139384	x1164560	France,Monac	1325177	1262539	1375202	1076212	1250341
Italy/Italie	872280	770327	763795	560127	691110	Indonesia/Indonésie	543493	782312	1366694	1205276	1115689
Singapore/Singapour	551098	632050	690426	647136	661444	Belgium–Luxembourg	1057530	1028966	1037357	997493	1013868
Netherlands/Pays–Bas	701650	654651	680694	505668	509972	USA/Etats–Unis d'Amer	701193	743413	825456	894257	937688
Saudi Arabia	665315	571629	620592	x629176	x643269	Pakistan	277898	383971	474409	536883	652874
Korea, Republic of	445939	517658	554042	594104	843856	Thailand/Thaïlande	334725	420081	462907	491648	501475
Mexico/Mexique	213860	298943	627537	737038	829502	Singapore/Singapour	348156	421820	457972	473954	539704
Spain/Espagne	458439	558064	574996	346033	468820	United Kingdom	408574	382512	438370	400003	512609
Belgium–Luxembourg	484358	475437	487165	403556	435070	Netherlands/Pays–Bas	404673	385482	437781	390332	418182
Portugal	440337	456496	518008	337373	343879	Spain/Espagne	259116	275772	290001	266275	339644
Canada	442431	420775	421121	458519	465074	Austria/Autriche	359985	286058	292133	253752	x241212
Greece/Grèce	365038	369022	442172	314863	299348	India/Inde	155792	201801	221700	252041	354566
Thailand/Thaïlande	236725	285393	375610	426563	418753	Switz.Liecht	280934	233254	230157	201807	213718
Japan/Japon	340443	365314	412128	291280	374648	Portugal	196977	186968	210973	172573	170185
Malaysia/Malaisie	251094	277388	312101	278055	304530	Turkey/Turquie	131006	124163	190847	246285	326586
Australia/Australie	287713	275389	286770	284308	336193	Malaysia/Malaisie	97407	142320	162141	179568	212312
Tunisia/Tunisie	186876	208132	265867	252524	284666	Canada	80527	82631	97812	103638	138513
So. Africa Customs Un	225054	283921	230329	202526	186198	Denmark/Danemark	79590	88151	103711	76613	78173
Sri Lanka	150541	205273	240591	255050	320519	Sweden/Suède	82140	80955	90759	77325	88923
Austria/Autriche	274157	243779	231667	192587	201968	Mexico/Mexique	11922	15609	97424	104735	150213
Poland/Pologne	8622	78457	74097	486841	553065	Ireland/Irlande	80283	71332	62759	56202	52471
Indonesia/Indonésie	120835	187155	226384	223201	237752	Czechoslovakia		x89964	x98113		
Hungary/Hongrie	x175607	171248	x225782	x210692	x187225	Cyprus/Chypre	33474	42357	44610	28241	42999
Switz.Liecht	258772	203987	202789	184378	201416	Bulgaria/Bulgarie	x45560	x12531	53731	48465	x22927
Philippines	150453	268429	148799	140625	157960	Israel/Israël	28074	35782	37028	39992	42788
Denmark/Danemark	144937	157387	189414	143614	131365	Slovenia/Slovénia			57704	51885	47713
Viet Nam	x68759	x105151	x133314	x195819	x162793	Syrian Arab Republic	341419	x59277	36168	x2352	x2402
Yugoslavia SFR	91798	x422367				Brazil/Brésil	18655	24255	32744	38762	28684
Afghanistan	x227858	x165628	x122122	x113375	x27816	Morocco/Maroc	32965	35385	29080	28980	26325
Turkey/Turquie	65601	82732	123069	189355	223396	Australia/Australie	21496	25038	27999	35688	46412
Romania/Roumanie	1052	8637	163640	214991	268249	Hungary/Hongrie	x40777	x27908	x33904	x24461	x26501
Israel/Israël	96357	104115	129070	146378	156542	Czech Republic				86272	92368
Sweden/Suède	149258	130572	125537	99315	110683	Poland/Pologne	13846	13352	37876	27408	24575
Argentina/Argentine	10643	74601	142701	128564	121546	Finland/Finlande	28954	24735	22167	18125	21841
Korea Dem People's Rp	x86440	x79806	x141957	x80589	x46543	Korea Dem People's Rp	x13694	x12868	x27529	x23417	x18892
Russian Federation			x166464	x132076	x118756	United Arab Emirates	197695		192	x57898	x49015
Cyprus/Chypre	100348	103123	106070	73977	86197	Yugoslavia SFR	90687	x52318			
Chile/Chili	53026	83183	100008	99864	92662	Tunisia/Tunisie	18151	14657	17704	17671	26386
Finland/Finlande	132693	101918	95534	76125	89748	Chile/Chili	9559	15700	18623	15686	15288
Macau/Macao	96919	92483	90508	85743	98835	Russian Federation			x20353	x26208	x27432
Kuwait/Koweït	101415	19488	124267	117799	109924	Colombia/Colombie	8442	13004	12559	19458	16941
Ireland/Irlande	96753	83636	97785	75123	78338	Greece/Grèce	10488	11787	14096	17124	16680
New Zealand	84846	76164	83239	85311	94249	El Salvador	6823	8904	15825	16670	15048
Bangladesh		x175581	x253670	x240597	x270520	Romania/Roumanie	3083	11735	11209	15482	12539

(VALUE AS % OF TOTAL)(VALEUR EN % DU TOTAL)

	1985	1986	1987	1988	1989	1990	1991	1992	1993	1994		1985	1986	1987	1988	1989	1990	1991	1992	1993	1994
Africa	2.4	x3.6	x3.6	x3.6	x3.0	x3.5	x3.8	x3.3	x3.2	x3.1	Afrique	0.4	0.3	0.3	0.2	0.3	0.4	0.3	0.3	0.4	0.2
Northern Africa	1.1	1.2	1.1	1.4	1.3	1.5	1.6	1.5	x1.5	1.5	Afrique du Nord	0.3	0.3	0.2	0.2	0.3	0.3	0.2	0.2	0.2	0.2
Americas	15.6	13.6	10.9	10.6	10.0	9.5	10.2	11.0	12.6	12.3	Amériques	5.5	4.7	4.3	4.6	4.3	4.0	4.0	4.4	5.0	4.8
LAIA	1.5	1.2	1.2	1.6	1.6	1.9	2.7	4.0	4.9	5.1	ALAI	0.5	0.4	0.4	0.4	0.5	0.3	0.4	0.7	0.8	0.8
CACM	0.5	0.3	0.3	0.2	0.3	0.2	0.2	0.2	x0.2	x0.2	MCAC	0.2	0.1	0.1	0.1	0.1	0.1	0.1	0.1	0.2	x0.1
Asia	35.7	x35.8	x38.2	39.5	x37.6	40.0	42.9	46.4	x50.2	x51.1	Asie	51.0	49.2	x54.0	x52.6	49.4	49.8	54.0	55.5	58.7	60.7
Middle East	11.1	x10.3	x9.6	10.1	x8.8	8.8	8.2	8.8	x10.0	x9.1	Moyen–Orient	2.1	0.8	x1.5	2.6	3.5	3.4	x1.0	1.1	x1.4	1.5
Europe	43.3	44.5	41.1	41.2	41.1	43.4	39.5	35.3	28.0	27.7	Europe	42.7	45.4	39.5	40.9	44.7	45.0	40.7	38.8	35.0	33.4
EEC	37.4	38.7	35.9	36.6	36.7	41.3	36.4	33.4	26.7	26.0	CEE	38.9	41.4	36.1	37.4	40.9	43.2	39.4	37.6	33.8	32.4
EFTA	4.7	5.0	4.3	4.1	3.8	1.5	1.1	1.0	0.9	0.9	AELE	3.1	3.5	2.9	2.9	3.2	1.3	1.0	0.9	0.9	0.8
Oceania	3.0	x2.3	x2.0	x1.9	x1.9	x1.9	x1.7	x1.6	x1.7	x1.7	Océanie	0.1	x0.1	0.1	x0.1	x0.1	x0.1	x0.1	0.1	x0.2	x0.2
Hong Kong	12.3	11.7	12.0	12.2	12.3	14.1	15.5	14.9	14.9	15.7	Korea, Republic of	11.2	12.5	12.4	12.4	13.6	14.1	15.9	15.9	18.7	20.3
China/Chine			3.5	3.7	3.6	3.9	5.1	9.0	10.1	11.1	Germany/Allemagne	11.0	12.6	11.1	11.9	13.2	14.2	13.2	12.3	11.0	9.7
Germany/Allemagne	7.0	7.4	6.4	7.1	7.4	8.6	7.8	7.0	5.7	5.4	Japan/Japon	22.0	19.6	14.7	12.4	11.8	10.7	11.2	10.8	10.7	9.2
United Kingdom	9.8	9.3	8.8	8.8	7.6	8.0	6.8	6.1	5.7	5.3	Hong Kong	6.3	6.6	6.9	7.1	7.9	8.4	10.0	10.1	9.9	9.9
USA/Etats–Unis d'Amer	8.8	7.9	5.9	5.8	5.2	4.8	5.0	4.8	5.2	4.8	Italy/Italie	10.9	10.7	9.0	9.1	9.7	9.5	8.8	8.6	7.8	7.9
France,Monac	5.8	5.9	5.4	5.1	5.1	5.6	4.6	4.3	3.3	3.4	China/Chine	3.9	4.3	5.2	4.8	5.4	5.0	5.5	5.2	5.1	7.5
United Arab Emirates	3.7	2.8	x2.6	3.2	x2.8	3.0	3.5	3.9	x4.5	x4.1	France,Monac	4.5	4.9	4.3	4.8	5.7	6.0	5.4	5.2	4.3	4.4
Italy/Italie	2.9	2.9	3.0	3.3	3.7	4.0	3.3	2.9	2.2	2.4	Indonesia/Indonésie	0.9	0.8	0.9	1.6	1.9	2.5	3.3	5.2	4.8	3.9
Singapore/Singapour	3.7	3.1	3.3	2.7	2.4	2.6	2.7	2.6	2.6	2.3	Belgium–Luxembourg	4.3	4.7	4.3	4.2	4.3	4.8	4.4	3.9	3.9	3.6
Netherlands/Pays–Bas	3.0	3.2	3.0	2.9	2.8	3.2	2.8	2.6	2.0	1.8	USA/Etats–Unis d'Amer	4.4	3.8	3.4	3.6	3.2	3.2	3.2	3.1	3.5	3.3

TRADE BY COMMODITY IN THOUSAND U.S. DOLLARS – COMMERCE PAR PRODUIT EN MILLIERS DE DOLLARS E.U

COUNTRIES–PAYS	IMPORTS – IMPORTATIONS 1990	1991	1992	1993	1994
Total	8765843	8057898	8438305	7946209	8973474
Africa	131880	x145184	x126992	x124329	x176735
Northern Africa	37021	x66625	57660	51901	60642
Americas	963161	1005465	1058199	x1130262	x1161125
LAIA	83231	109034	147383	178473	179055
CACM	4451	4117	3760	x43373	x37876
Asia	2855592	2852631	3044278	3042643	3495238
Middle East	x175720	x144266	x210353	x224067	x258688
Europe	3674974	3728706	3833663	3094518	3539934
EEC	3408543	3285971	3524756	2886081	3236203
EFTA	195319	167448	173004	148692	158948
Oceania	x109010	x107145	x116215	x110584	x125622
Germany/Allemagne	1178370	1157013	1255715	1066447	1149301
Hong Kong	950574	994985	906171	966772	1095943
USA/Etats–Unis d'Amer	675912	706136	694799	689190	721574
Japan/Japon	861165	748431	689796	599825	681821
France,Monac	482667	455145	474127	361591	395167
Korea, Republic of	398807	423552	420012	400208	407786
China/Chine	246881	269949	451472	482016	625082
Italy/Italie	424441	388402	414542	312869	382030
United Kingdom	301033	245425	280970	290220	364835
Canada	170670	162743	181313	182968	177662
Spain/Espagne	158753	183424	194766	120312	140872
Netherlands/Pays–Bas	148981	153992	179210	146555	154771
Portugal	132822	152694	179580	140554	152386
Belgium–Luxembourg	169127	163235	165940	121189	133960
Switz.Liecht	175287	148937	154016	132258	139258
Austria/Autriche	148048	140502	137876	126962	129028
Hungary/Hongrie	x92107	85617	x129838	x136662	x107031
Greece/Grèce	106321	102561	107160	77368	79092
Australia/Australie	85448	85268	88325	85552	98586
Yugoslavia SFR	55790	x249809			
Singapore/Singapour	64978	58714	60895	73708	100417
Poland/Pologne	1674	3913	8912	155391	187854
Sweden/Suède	58958	50642	49918	46384	62722
Romania/Roumanie	2195	8136	53400	79339	100302
United Arab Emirates	27720	32343	36936	x62834	x58926
Korea Dem People's Rp	x29138	x28614	x54677	x41337	x27276
Denmark/Danemark	37243	42446	41846	35821	41090
Mexico/Mexique	25996	32882	42766	42750	52180
Thailand/Thaïlande	19591	26448	39555	46767	60221
Bangladesh		32244	51250	x26567	x32369
Saudi Arabia	30903	19821	24456	x54665	x55741
Ukraine			x18422	x78824	x47508
Turkey/Turquie	22804	21070	30117	42400	46017
Tunisia/Tunisie	17109	24444	33151	35439	40347
Malaysia/Malaisie	16465	26426	32032	33695	63355
Yugoslavia/Yougoslavie			x84970	x6237	x335
Former USSR/Anc. URSS	836942	x83853			
Iran (Islamic Rp. of)	x53778	x24019	x55227	x2739	x25371
So. Africa Customs Un	20997	26662	23279	30255	66817
Russian Federation			x54106	x25530	x43767
Brazil/Brésil	24969	21188	19129	38747	44779
Czechoslovakia	7448	x25408	x52693		
Indonesia/Indonésie	16468	14702	29177	29462	33844
Finland/Finlande	32728	25983	26127	21033	27375
Israel/Israël	13657	17495	25601	28465	19672
Venezuela	5747	17515	29325	20756	6346
Mauritius/Maurice	38602	17441	21318	25590	23899
New Zealand	18893	17858	23015	22233	22833
Slovakia				x60412	x51456
Ireland/Irlande	29052	24507	16979	18775	23574

COUNTRIES–PAYS	EXPORTS – EXPORTATIONS 1990	1991	1992	1993	1994
Totale	8466374	8492708	8976355	8618262	9822794
Afrique	21864	31568	x6335	6459	x3309
Afrique du Nord	18652	27980	1152	2556	2442
Amériques	279692	318042	353142	380454	427607
ALAI	113942	134282	126432	124146	135922
MCAC	181	101	34	1430	2099
Asie	2693140	2900716	2908726	2894841	3401652
Moyen–Orient	17222	x20495	28309	38113	50343
Europe	5170315	5064474	5547282	5130092	5767478
CEE	4963200	4889319	5368215	4980363	5621976
AELE	188943	161234	156665	118549	119298
Océanie	x9705	x10304	x9949	x13089	x12500
Italy/Italie	2406116	2461470	2698890	2467694	2775257
Germany/Allemagne	862762	900563	1037217	945624	1077793
China/Chine	997775	896301	836096	734220	1140961
Hong Kong	671154	770990	771137	880677	929423
United Kingdom	564575	474982	509553	498208	524677
Korea, Republic of	372866	484733	493259	497178	476545
France,Monac	516408	455815	509372	503550	580696
Japan/Japon	262088	282534	337643	361160	422425
India/Inde	195150	208768	203845	170967	203507
USA/Etats–Unis d'Amer	132998	144661	181862	206798	230724
Belgium–Luxembourg	184112	170215	151054	117298	144820
Bangladesh	96045	151571	154132	125889	x67437
Switz.Liecht	184475	156865	153186	115248	114535
Netherlands/Pays–Bas	132299	131575	146284	145611	163908
Austria/Autriche	92252	87584	97663	92356	x97457
Spain/Espagne	66719	67474	73309	81161	84738
Poland/Pologne	75156	65456	49880	48675	62700
Uruguay	46641	50768	52903	53805	51939
Sweden/Suède	46208	43138	44264	43756	55886
Canada	32334	38954	44034	47878	58637
Czechoslovakia		x47614	x54640		
Ireland/Irlande	35549	38029	29515	30570	40137
Czech Republic				95474	108812
Singapore/Singapour	26939	34398	27604	31950	58538
Denmark/Danemark	25927	30734	34980	20833	24749
Peru/Pérou	31099	44220	24933	15808	20522
Turkey/Turquie	14238	15576	27014	32498	42577
Portugal	24135	22353	27060	25278	38429
Thailand/Thaïlande	23175	20453	25369	23323	20640
Brazil/Brésil	14180	15399	18398	19535	22879
Bulgaria/Bulgarie	x19504	x4642	22929	20452	x7028
Lithuania/Lituanie			32169	x7193	29076
Chile/Chili	4320	8019	11117	14495	13591
Romania/Roumanie	19751	10670	12066	9357	11972
Slovenia/Slovénia			12950	17631	15005
Hungary/Hongrie	x21827	x14008	x8788	x7050	x7962
Mexico/Mexique	8620	6995	9870	12319	14412
Macau/Macao	9689	9059	9703	6948	6387
Russian Federation			x8183	x16704	x17837
Former USSR/Anc. URSS	149362	x22246			
Indonesia/Indonésie	9875	8927	7943	5083	4323
Australia/Australie	5885	6956	6564	8175	7561
Israel/Israël	6005	3804	6525	9434	11148
Algeria/Algérie	12365	19418	0	9	
Finland/Finlande	4618	4333	7823	7059	9898
Croatia/Croatie			4838	9228	x8687
Yugoslavia SFR	17986	x13659			
Slovakia				x12280	x11770
So. Africa Customs Un	2826	3254	4515	3114	
New Zealand	3613	3029	3287	4406	4860

(VALUE AS % OF TOTAL)(VALEUR EN % DU TOTAL)

	1985	1986	1987	1988	1989	1990	1991	1992	1993	1994
Africa	1.4	1.5	2.0	x1.2	x1.2	1.5	x1.8	x1.5	x1.6	x1.9
Northern Africa	0.7	0.6	0.5	0.4	0.3	0.4	x0.8	0.7	0.7	0.7
Americas	19.4	16.4	14.2	x12.7	12.0	11.0	12.5	12.6	x14.2	x12.9
LAIA	0.9	0.7	0.8	0.9	0.9	0.9	1.4	1.7	2.2	2.0
CACM	0.0	0.0	x0.0	0.0	0.1	0.1	0.1	0.0	x0.5	x0.4
Asia	25.1	26.8	30.0	34.3	35.3	32.6	35.4	36.1	38.3	38.9
Middle East	2.4	x3.2	x3.1	x2.1	x2.3	x2.0	x1.8	x2.5	x2.8	x2.9
Europe	43.4	46.2	44.0	42.7	41.0	41.9	46.3	45.4	38.9	39.4
EEC	36.9	39.2	37.3	36.8	35.7	38.9	40.8	41.8	36.3	36.1
EFTA	5.7	6.0	5.6	5.0	4.6	2.2	2.1	2.1	1.9	1.8
Oceania	1.5	x1.4	x1.3	x1.4	x1.4	x1.3	x1.3	x1.4	x1.4	x1.4
Germany/Allemagne	12.5	13.3	13.0	12.4	11.5	13.4	14.4	14.9	13.4	12.8
Hong Kong	10.4	10.4	10.5	12.1	11.9	10.8	12.3	10.7	12.2	12.2
USA/Etats–Unis d'Amer	14.6	12.1	10.6	9.2	8.4	7.7	8.8	8.2	8.7	8.0
Japan/Japon	9.0	9.3	9.1	10.5	11.5	9.8	9.3	8.2	7.5	7.6
France,Monac	5.7	5.9	4.9	4.7	5.0	5.5	5.6	5.6	4.6	4.4
Korea, Republic of	1.9	2.2	2.5	3.9	5.0	4.5	5.3	5.0	5.0	4.5
China/Chine			1.9	2.4	2.2	2.8	3.4	5.4	6.1	7.0
Italy/Italie	3.6	3.7	3.7	4.9	5.5	4.8	4.8	4.9	3.9	4.3
United Kingdom	4.6	4.3	4.1	4.1	3.4	3.4	3.0	3.3	3.7	4.1
Canada	3.9	3.4	2.5	2.3	2.2	1.9	2.0	2.1	2.3	2.0

	1985	1986	1987	1988	1989	1990	1991	1992	1993	1994
Afrique	0.1	0.1	0.1	0.1	0.1	0.2	0.3	x0.1		x0.0
Afrique du Nord	0.0	0.0	0.0	0.1	0.1	0.2	0.3	0.0	0.0	0.0
Amériques	3.3	3.2	3.1	3.3	3.6	3.4	3.8	3.9	4.5	4.3
ALAI	1.3	1.2	1.0	1.3	1.5	1.3	1.6	1.4	1.4	1.4
MCAC	0.0	0.0	x0.0	0.0	0.0	0.0	0.0	0.0	0.0	0.0
Asie	29.6	27.8	31.1	33.5	33.7	31.8	34.2	32.4	33.6	34.6
Moyen–Orient	0.9	0.2	0.4	0.3	0.3	0.2	x0.2	0.3	0.4	0.5
Europe	60.8	61.8	57.8	56.2	58.1	61.1	59.6	61.8	59.5	58.7
CEE	56.0	56.7	53.4	52.2	53.9	58.6	57.6	59.8	57.8	57.2
AELE	4.3	4.7	4.0	3.5	3.6	2.2	1.9	1.7	1.4	1.2
Océanie	0.2	x0.3	x0.2	x0.1	x0.1	x0.1	x0.1	x0.1	x0.1	x0.1
Italy/Italie	26.4	27.1	25.3	24.4	25.8	28.4	29.0	30.1	28.6	28.3
Germany/Allemagne	7.8	8.7	8.5	8.6	8.6	10.2	10.6	11.6	11.0	11.0
China/Chine	8.1	9.0	10.7	12.5	12.4	11.8	10.6	9.3	8.5	11.6
Hong Kong	3.6	4.2	5.3	7.3	8.5	7.9	9.1	8.6	10.2	9.5
United Kingdom	8.4	7.4	7.0	7.2	7.0	6.7	5.6	5.7	5.8	5.3
Korea, Republic of	3.8	3.8	4.2	4.8	4.9	4.4	5.7	5.5	5.8	4.9
France,Monac	6.0	6.2	5.9	5.7	5.9	6.1	5.4	5.7	5.8	5.9
Japan/Japon	4.2	4.0	3.4	3.0	3.2	3.1	3.3	3.8	4.2	4.3
India/Inde	4.1	3.2	3.3	2.7	2.7	2.3	2.5	2.3	2.0	2.1
USA/Etats–Unis d'Amer	1.4	1.4	1.4	1.7	1.8	1.6	1.7	2.0	2.4	2.3

TRADE BY COMMODITY IN THOUSAND U.S. DOLLARS – COMMERCE PAR PRODUIT EN MILLIERS DE DOLLARS E.U

COUNTRIES–PAYS	IMPORTS – IMPORTATIONS				
	1990	1991	1992	1993	1994
Total	5604368	6735694	7592040	7564798	8864256
Africa	189951	184745	x168613	x169305	x177624
Northern Africa	79488	77937	67102	62556	64057
Americas	x357196	x453918	x539207	x664146	x810710
LAIA	29625	54597	75846	83099	105184
CACM	9616	10005	10396	x31979	x30490
Asia	2538825	3306609	4139704	4385039	5133164
Middle East	x71284	152414	220109	x198863	x255774
Europe	2336838	2516963	2447880	1962900	2278892
EEC	2198454	2303168	2286494	1838952	2122368
EFTA	98710	104793	106062	96183	109962
Oceania	x104734	x108531	x139368	x133420	x181421
Hong Kong	1052462	1348465	1574338	1648214	2107080
Germany/Allemagne	550839	581903	552848	417574	459344
China/Chine	114853	172928	598844	689126	820773
France, Monac	454636	468724	476593	385369	433161
Singapore/Singapour	309876	328973	336891	324384	283766
USA/Etats–Unis d'Amer	153674	194195	229568	302757	353053
Malaysia/Malaisie	183462	225480	240282	204015	232268
Macau/Macao	203932	219554	214577	207125	236191
Italy/Italie	196018	225689	208199	160606	231991
United Kingdom	203468	186289	198737	202999	232276
Philippines	139936	220051	159502	175943	197120
Thailand/Thaïlande	114702	124237	158264	174869	186369
Austria/Autriche	144246	156737	155913	135832	142846
Belgium–Luxembourg	142908	152020	147360	135598	160038
Canada	125606	130883	135158	157834	194570
Netherlands/Pays–Bas	155090	162062	155831	103390	110737
Indonesia/Indonésie	71048	105106	147409	156308	160803
Sri Lanka	71406	111250	130507	163400	195811
Bangladesh		54479	87755	157620	x100254
Portugal	76948	90905	105383	86994	100468
Switz.Liecht	85769	94123	94584	85398	98952
Japan/Japon	76121	93890	85684	83518	131761
Spain/Espagne	79214	88007	93775	53678	71976
Saudi Arabia	2183	75370	113517	x35556	x32716
Hungary/Hongrie	x50064	76575	x72846	x73410	x73382
Greece/Grèce	80386	78554	76214	50497	58103
Australia/Australie	55834	61572	64114	62195	74864
Israel/Israël	46765	52335	65031	69804	80305
United Arab Emirates	25607	28691	39019	x83393	x85124
Poland/Pologne	1449	19371	25889	103980	135150
Tunisia/Tunisie	52619	46535	47641	37598	37826
Mauritius/Maurice	41422	32562	40384	48754	48191
So. Africa Customs Un	30897	41478	33784	31856	38340
Ireland/Irlande	36614	36233	33247	34392	34429
Yugoslavia SFR	29152	x101223			
Sweden/Suède	32181	33429	35796	31499	31572
Dominican Republic	x13757	x30892	x35857	x33430	x71558
Mexico/Mexique	13926	21194	35703	42507	45991
Korea, Republic of	24831	27777	29185	30329	38512
Russian Federation			x45075	x36069	x43690
New Zealand	29410	27943	26500	26154	34946
Denmark/Danemark	20811	22855	27101	23982	33767
Korea Dem People's Rp	x16261	x22376	x27768	x18145	x10872
Viet Nam	x4544	x16715	x20150	x31296	x37112
Jamaica/Jamaïque	5140	4075	x31587	x29091	x26842
Turkey/Turquie	6830	9318	19692	33796	90588
Guam			x25987	x32195	x44612
Finland/Finlande	25096	19760	19495	16542	21660
Cyprus/Chypre	16351	16539	22960	13380	15118
Czechoslovakia	3924	x13596	x38885		

COUNTRIES–PAYS	EXPORTS – EXPORTATIONS				
	1990	1991	1992	1993	1994
Totale	5549953	6459251	7111388	7134369	8410668
Afrique	21615	33269	20829	22559	8612
Afrique du Nord	2358	3910	3767	4253	2963
Amériques	273173	352421	415291	420875	465381
ALAI	32911	30284	41590	43191	47256
MCAC	3583	4578	7369	4609	2079
Asie	2505040	3238577	3728183	3927233	4811098
Moyen–Orient	195190	218654	113926	67859	144250
Europe	2701256	2786308	2876607	2652270	3015088
CEE	2561848	2654321	2740734	2524038	2874532
AELE	118705	120619	118471	110368	124083
Océanie	x13199	x16254	x17627	x22774	x30723
Hong Kong	1020995	1284955	1519051	1551877	1781807
Germany/Allemagne	847579	889547	930763	783974	858974
Korea, Republic of	336072	520010	681448	839958	1121534
Italy/Italie	526432	541468	553391	571556	652544
China/Chine	318977	418363	499177	543660	745158
Japan/Japon	292253	370399	415212	388088	399526
USA/Etats–Unis d'Amer	221754	296388	330842	324191	346156
France, Monac	273516	277844	286277	281449	368968
Austria/Autriche	209420	228962	252607	228832	x204409
United Kingdom	218355	203725	187843	196105	249794
Singapore/Singapour	130928	183347	164908	194751	198476
Belgium–Luxembourg	143707	143186	135138	120437	129577
Switz.Liecht	111424	113465	110623	102283	114328
Spain/Espagne	105622	109413	110298	97719	122828
Netherlands/Pays–Bas	104993	108197	111775	94728	105517
Malaysia/Malaisie	66258	85742	107584	96050	110666
Turkey/Turquie	49584	66002	71898	63098	140588
Pakistan	26803	34582	66132	91030	92080
Denmark/Danemark	46177	53042	67789	63853	73996
Syrian Arab Republic	141719	141367	31845		
India/Inde	71629	54524	62231	50019	72924
Canada	14807	20962	35262	48679	69178
Greece/Grèce	24762	29228	33235	25721	25796
Sweden/Suède	27554	26958	29921	27083	34695
Indonesia/Indonésie	16247	19612	32090	30927	35509
Poland/Pologne	13844	2427	22630	38877	39607
Macau/Macao	17021	22853	17963	19134	22794
Portugal	17235	21399	23245	13998	23379
So. Africa Customs Un	14356	27246	13741	11600	
Finland/Finlande	13829	18750	14947	13764	20037
Israel/Israël	5592	12091	18399	15286	13591
Philippines	1541	6192	13950	18717	43706
Czech Republic				38242	29118
Czechoslovakia		x17948	x18567		
New Zealand	6623	10882	11316	10969	10098
Brazil/Brésil	4961	5889	15159	10916	10000
Thailand/Thaïlande	2835	4568	9901	12665	21562
Mexico/Mexique	2749	6559	8474	8575	12462
Norway, SVD, JM	6639	7106	7844	8071	9755
Australia/Australie	6043	4884	5309	11072	19027
Hungary/Hongrie	x7099	x8711	x6370	x5739	x6394
Argentina/Argentine	15732	7003	5630	7824	8326
Cyprus/Chypre	3510	8357	6915	2242	1271
Malta/Malte	6056	5647	4100	2744	x3619
Slovenia/Slovénia			7712	4717	5853
Colombia/Colombie	1176	3133	3519	5631	5583
Peru/Pérou	3841	4002	4545	3113	1844
Ireland/Irlande	2664	2601	3505	4819	4018
Guatemala	2842	3636	4352	1342	511
Yugoslavia/Yougoslavie			x2406	x5677	x171

(VALUE AS % OF TOTAL)(VALEUR EN % DU TOTAL)

	1985	1986	1987	1988	1989	1990	1991	1992	1993	1994
Africa	2.6	2.7	2.9	3.5	3.1	3.4	2.7	x2.2	x2.2	x2.0
Northern Africa	1.4	1.6	1.6	1.8	1.6	1.4	1.2	0.9	0.8	0.7
Americas	7.2	x7.7	x6.2	x6.0	x6.4	x6.4	x6.7	x7.1	x8.8	x9.2
LAIA	0.7	0.4	0.4	0.5	0.5	0.5	0.8	1.0	1.1	1.2
CACM	0.5	0.2	0.2	0.2	0.1	0.2	0.1	0.1	x0.4	x0.3
Asia	27.8	33.5	37.8	41.3	43.9	45.3	49.1	54.5	57.9	57.9
Middle East	0.6	x1.2	x0.9	x0.9	x1.5	x1.3	2.3	2.9	x2.6	x2.9
Europe	58.8	53.2	46.6	43.6	37.5	41.7	37.4	32.2	25.9	25.7
EEC	48.9	44.6	39.1	36.8	31.8	39.2	34.2	30.1	24.3	23.9
EFTA	8.8	7.9	6.8	6.0	4.8	1.8	1.6	1.4	1.3	1.2
Oceania	3.1	x2.6	x2.0	x2.1	x2.2	x1.8	x1.6	x1.8	x1.8	x2.0
Hong Kong	9.8	11.2	13.2	15.0	16.7	18.8	20.0	20.7	21.8	23.8
Germany/Allemagne	10.5	10.0	9.2	8.2	7.1	9.8	8.6	7.3	5.5	5.2
China/Chine			1.9	2.0	2.2	2.0	2.6	7.9	9.1	9.3
France, Monac	12.1	10.9	8.8	8.2	7.0	8.1	7.0	6.3	5.1	4.9
Singapore/Singapour	4.9	5.8	6.2	6.1	6.2	5.5	4.9	4.4	4.3	3.2
USA/Etats–Unis d'Amer	1.9	2.2	2.1	1.9	2.6	2.7	2.9	3.0	4.0	4.0
Malaysia/Malaisie	2.0	2.4	2.6	2.7	3.1	3.3	3.3	3.2	2.7	2.6
Macau/Macao	4.4	4.3	3.8	4.3	4.0	3.6	3.3	2.8	2.7	2.7
Italy/Italie	2.3	2.2	2.6	2.8	2.6	3.5	3.4	2.7	2.1	2.6
United Kingdom	5.0	4.0	3.1	3.7	3.3	3.6	2.8	2.6	2.7	2.6

	1985	1986	1987	1988	1989	1990	1991	1992	1993	1994
Afrique	0.1	x0.2	x0.2	x0.1	x0.2	0.4	0.5	0.3	0.4	0.1
Afrique du Nord	0.0	0.0	0.0	x0.0	0.1	0.0	0.1	0.1	0.1	0.0
Amériques	3.1	2.4	1.7	1.8	3.9	5.0	5.4	5.8	5.9	5.5
ALAI	0.4	0.6	0.6	0.5	0.9	0.6	0.5	0.6	0.6	0.6
MCAC	0.1	0.1	0.1	0.1	0.1	0.1	0.1	0.1	0.1	0.0
Asie	27.5	27.7	x43.4	x47.2	45.8	45.2	50.1	52.4	55.1	57.2
Moyen–Orient	2.8	x0.3	0.7	1.4	3.5	3.5	3.4	1.6	1.0	1.7
Europe	67.1	67.6	51.0	47.5	48.5	48.7	43.1	40.5	37.2	35.8
CEE	58.6	59.0	44.7	41.2	42.0	46.2	41.1	38.5	35.4	34.2
AELE	7.9	8.1	6.1	5.8	6.0	2.1	1.9	1.7	1.5	1.5
Océanie	0.1	x0.2	x0.2	x0.3	x0.3	x0.2	x0.2	x0.2	x0.3	x0.3
Hong Kong	9.4	13.5	13.8	14.1	19.1	18.4	19.9	21.4	21.8	21.2
Germany/Allemagne	17.9	19.5	14.9	13.7	14.3	15.3	13.8	13.1	11.0	10.2
Korea, Republic of	0.4	1.2	2.0	2.9	4.7	6.1	8.1	9.6	11.8	13.3
Italy/Italie	13.8	14.0	9.9	8.2	8.0	9.5	8.4	7.8	8.0	7.8
China/Chine			2.5	4.5	6.5	5.7	6.5	7.0	7.6	8.9
Japan/Japon	12.6	10.0	6.8	5.3	5.7	5.3	5.7	5.8	5.4	4.8
USA/Etats–Unis d'Amer	2.4	1.5	0.9	1.1	2.7	4.0	4.6	4.7	4.5	4.1
France, Monac	5.6	5.3	4.4	4.1	4.3	4.9	4.3	4.0	3.9	4.4
Austria/Autriche	3.4	3.6	2.7	2.9	3.1	3.8	3.5	3.6	3.2	x2.4
United Kingdom	5.0	4.3	3.4	3.5	3.5	3.9	3.2	2.6	2.7	3.0

TRADE BY COMMODITY IN THOUSAND U.S. DOLLARS – COMMERCE PAR PRODUIT EN MILLIERS DE DOLLARS E.U

COUNTRIES–PAYS	IMPORTS – IMPORTATIONS				
	1990	1991	1992	1993	1994
Total	2765977	2924674	3379002	3221852	3631247
Africa	x98730	97151	x153153	x160602	x153956
Northern Africa	43976	47726	61938	56565	59292
Americas	313077	353017	493531	552339	662701
LAIA	43657	65523	170726	191702	242961
CACM	5557	6087	7077	x13878	x14213
Asia	710233	903112	1199074	1263558	x1422441
Middle East	92030	102073	157604	x161472	x154250
Europe	1447938	1432506	1422290	1100621	1226726
EEC	1360926	1332348	1327344	1016001	1132078
EFTA	63664	61248	67534	63913	68838
Oceania	x60297	x59607	x56784	x57800	x63075
Hong Kong	239956	307041	355545	360214	423875
Germany/Allemagne	284299	290835	272108	237872	233963
USA/Etats–Unis d'Amer	188993	209474	235407	264720	306595
Italy/Italie	279537	252456	235892	147389	173123
China/Chine	56442	89856	228161	232906	283164
United Kingdom	187940	175317	185468	137647	166918
France,Monac	164913	148709	152639	121118	144398
Japan/Japon	118627	109002	104849	92667	102592
Mexico/Mexique	24841	33881	122207	130287	174148
Austria/Autriche	86789	86917	92348	84455	85363
Spain/Espagne	60085	73378	80114	46502	60294
Netherlands/Pays–Bas	67829	66903	64849	49088	55734
Portugal	53798	61017	69651	49198	47193
Saudi Arabia	45415	43253	73413	x61321	x53485
Singapore/Singapour	47362	51636	55573	56054	65627
Belgium–Luxembourg	59540	57901	55826	45904	55697
Switz.Liecht	49577	48307	52597	49497	53449
Canada	50250	46382	50333	51082	55543
United Arab Emirates	20940	34395	49891	x60238	x60112
Australia/Australie	47997	46280	43492	44359	47594
Korea, Republic of	29651	32181	43930	49935	55772
Tunisia/Tunisie	33620	36705	45671	41961	45400
Philippines	17047	57742	26849	32441	33088
Hungary/Hongrie	x22057	51126	x28707	x34140	x29018
Thailand/Thaïlande	19805	25109	39361	43138	50646
Indonesia/Indonésie	22782	27294	37259	42303	43839
Greece/Grèce	30007	38997	39708	27481	28221
Sweden/Suède	31654	31730	31967	26492	31131
Nigeria/Nigéria	x14361	3295	x39770	x45531	x37341
Sri Lanka	8711	18562	26526	36997	51637
Malaysia/Malaisie	18739	22059	26152	25331	27562
Denmark/Danemark	18304	20002	23295	20394	24668
Bangladesh		x19882	x39258	56558	x35125
Israel/Israël	16971	14174	18953	20658	32150
Argentina/Argentine	2714	10029	21462	19441	19987
So. Africa Customs Un	10376	15770	13511	16078	20123
Ireland/Irlande	22739	16739	13493	12976	13768
Mauritius/Maurice	12840	12892	12795	14227	12881
Norway,SVD,JM	12898	11910	13765	13393	14294
Viet Nam	x3802	x5324	x10921	x19668	x22143
Poland/Pologne	907	4616	1869	28177	38705
Macau/Macao	8450	9962	10364	10893	12588
Finland/Finlande	13492	11448	9986	9486	11607
Yugoslavia SFR	14735	x30882			
Turkey/Turquie	6180	7190	10971	12707	11337
Dominican Republic	x4571	x5704	x9650	x9224	x22902
Romania/Roumanie	4652	1011	9062	14083	19810
Colombia/Colombie	5511	4900	6142	12273	13341
Malta/Malte	8234	7711	8005	7468	x3334
New Zealand	6996	7184	7109	8546	9458

COUNTRIES–PAYS	EXPORTS – EXPORTATIONS				
	1990	1991	1992	1993	1994
Totale	2762208	2997535	3441386	3260820	3369301
Afrique	21310	22356	20270	21501	11121
Afrique du Nord	16773	18252	12682	13762	10395
Amériques	212331	260018	297666	326719	390063
ALAI	15053	20307	46080	58055	69934
MCAC	1648	1768	2023	x3836	x4220
Asie	855725	1081365	1437509	1448933	1383123
Moyen–Orient	24468	x31158	24694	33236	45561
Europe	1650134	1610693	1665410	1440362	1556952
CEE	1409387	1393962	1457175	1256344	1356384
AELE	239216	215433	205643	180241	196660
Océanie	4495	x4105	x6854	x6139	7861
France,Monac	421757	415467	444955	350182	389585
Indonesia/Indonésie	201860	278554	395784	331309	60126
Hong Kong	194154	236325	323747	346582	395742
Germany/Allemagne	293407	300602	318485	282954	306482
Korea, Republic of	156996	199577	245218	269031	298010
USA/Etats–Unis d'Amer	183085	225101	233713	245167	291118
Austria/Autriche	230792	216951	223726	202083	x148567
Switz.Liecht	238294	214733	204602	179420	195530
Japan/Japon	119067	158628	202140	219386	233926
Italy/Italie	104954	100681	107104	125820	158985
United Kingdom	108645	111757	110464	86157	107117
China/Chine	45712	60491	108367	97051	181440
Netherlands/Pays–Bas	84182	78857	73497	61516	72389
Belgium–Luxembourg	64450	63085	71050	58942	66299
Thailand/Thaïlande	22871	36008	50135	56711	60507
Spain/Espagne	46327	46612	46458	38053	43899
India/Inde	14455	25442	33766	33700	30804
Turkey/Turquie	11574	16890	21162	31420	43333
Singapore/Singapour	10626	16658	20559	24951	33257
Mexico/Mexique	2604	4359	25016	32341	35942
Ireland/Irlande	17389	19195	17961	12803	14982
Philippines	3293	21348	12762	12667	12299
Canada	11203	11234	12191	16104	21238
Portugal	10489	12394	11991	8969	11576
Sweden/Suède	10086	10263	11096	9030	12280
Brazil/Brésil	4925	6884	9663	11226	17605
Morocco/Maroc	5546	8154	7833	8708	6133
Finland/Finlande	7088	7056	7691	6394	9282
Pakistan	4014	5204	6268	8894	12337
Colombia/Colombie	4874	5664	6693	7503	6596
Greece/Grèce	4733	5460	6919	7447	7774
Czechoslovakia		x9326	x8965		
So. Africa Customs Un	3803	3506	6999	7038	
Malaysia/Malaisie	2891	4583	6634	6317	8180
Denmark/Danemark	5083	5578	5779	5993	7167
Syrian Arab Republic	7319	x13387	2724	x105	x118
Poland/Pologne	9611	7628	2239	3966	4731
Tunisia/Tunisie	4487	4045	4344	3074	3373
Czech Republic				11027	12922
New Zealand	2285	2237	3646	3236	4395
Viet Nam	50900	x1808	x3357	x3707	x3443
Egypt/Egypte	6735	6053	497	1971	889
Australia/Australie	1984	1658	2847	2683	3327
Macau/Macao	2314	2654	1654	2566	3301
Chile/Chili	467	738	1438	3066	4306
Uruguay	1045	1240	1825	2136	2843
Haiti/Haïti	x1176	x1412	x1777	x1719	x1315
Lithuania/Lituanie			4572	x154	1387
Slovenia/Slovénia			1698	2758	3186
Guatemala	1188	1185	1014	1464	883

(VALUE AS % OF TOTAL)(VALEUR EN % DU TOTAL)

	1985	1986	1987	1988	1989	1990	1991	1992	1993	1994
Africa	3.0	x3.8	x3.6	x4.3	x3.1	x3.6	3.3	x4.6	x5.0	x4.3
Northern Africa	1.6	1.2	0.9	1.3	1.2	1.6	1.6	1.9	1.8	1.6
Americas	15.7	x13.5	x12.8	x10.9	x11.7	11.3	12.1	14.8	17.1	18.3
LAIA	2.5	0.7	0.7	1.0	1.3	1.6	2.3	5.1	6.0	6.7
CACM	0.5	0.3	0.2	0.2	0.2	0.2	0.2	0.2	x0.4	x0.4
Asia	24.9	23.6	23.3	24.2	26.4	25.7	30.4	34.7	39.2	x39.2
Middle East	9.3	x7.4	x4.7	3.9	x4.8	3.3	3.5	4.7	x5.0	x4.2
Europe	48.5	51.6	52.9	52.7	49.9	52.3	49.3	42.6	34.2	33.8
EEC	40.3	43.1	44.3	44.8	43.1	49.2	45.9	39.7	31.5	31.2
EFTA	7.4	7.9	7.8	7.2	6.3	2.3	2.1	2.0	2.0	1.9
Oceania	2.8	x2.3	x2.2	x2.3	x2.3	x2.2	x2.0	x1.7	x1.8	x1.8
Hong Kong	6.5	6.3	6.8	6.8	7.7	8.7	10.6	10.6	11.2	11.7
Germany/Allemagne	8.8	10.1	10.2	9.8	9.1	10.3	10.0	8.1	7.4	6.4
USA/Etats–Unis d'Amer	7.5	7.0	7.2	6.3	6.9	6.8	7.2	7.0	8.2	8.4
Italy/Italie	7.0	7.5	8.3	9.3	9.1	10.1	8.7	7.1	4.6	4.8
China/Chine			1.8	1.9	2.2	2.0	3.1	6.8	7.2	7.8
United Kingdom	6.7	6.5	6.5	6.2	6.0	6.8	6.0	5.6	4.3	4.6
France,Monac	5.8	6.1	5.7	5.6	5.4	6.0	5.1	4.6	3.8	4.0
Japan/Japon	4.1	4.4	4.2	4.8	4.9	4.3	3.8	3.1	2.9	2.8
Mexico/Mexique	1.7	0.2	0.2	0.3	0.7	0.9	1.2	3.7	4.0	4.8
Austria/Autriche	3.0	3.3	3.3	2.9	2.6	3.1	3.0	2.8	2.6	2.4

	1985	1986	1987	1988	1989	1990	1991	1992	1993	1994
Afrique	0.5	0.4	0.3	0.5	0.5	0.7	0.7	0.6	0.6	0.3
Afrique du Nord	0.4	0.2	0.2	0.4	0.4	0.6	0.6	0.4	0.4	0.3
Amériques	6.6	6.6	6.4	7.4	7.0	7.7	8.7	8.6	10.0	11.6
ALAI	0.6	0.4	0.4	0.5	0.6	0.5	0.7	1.3	1.8	2.1
MCAC	0.1	0.0	0.0	0.1	0.0	0.1	0.1	0.1	x0.1	x0.1
Asie	31.3	30.7	x26.1	x27.2	28.2	30.9	36.1	41.8	44.5	41.1
Moyen–Orient	0.6	0.2	0.3	0.8	1.1	0.9	x1.0	0.7	1.0	1.4
Europe	59.8	60.8	62.7	61.0	62.6	59.7	53.7	48.4	44.2	46.2
CEE	40.1	41.5	43.9	44.8	47.0	51.0	46.5	42.3	38.5	40.3
AELE	19.6	19.2	18.8	16.1	15.6	8.7	7.2	6.0	5.5	5.8
Océanie	0.2	0.1	0.2	x0.2	0.2	0.2	x0.1	x0.2	x0.2	0.2
France,Monac	10.3	10.9	11.4	12.2	13.4	15.3	13.9	12.9	10.7	11.6
Indonesia/Indonésie	0.5	1.2	1.0	1.2	3.3	7.3	9.3	11.5	10.2	1.8
Hong Kong	4.3	4.3	5.6	5.6	7.1	7.0	7.9	9.4	10.6	11.7
Germany/Allemagne	7.2	8.0	8.9	9.6	10.4	10.6	10.0	9.3	8.7	9.1
Korea, Republic of	6.2	5.5	5.7	5.7	5.9	5.7	6.7	7.1	8.3	8.8
USA/Etats–Unis d'Amer	5.7	6.0	5.7	6.5	5.9	6.6	7.5	6.8	7.5	8.6
Austria/Autriche	9.0	8.8	9.0	7.5	7.3	8.4	7.2	6.5	6.2	x4.4
Switz.Liecht	9.9	9.7	9.1	7.8	7.6	8.6	7.2	5.9	5.5	5.8
Japan/Japon	5.4	4.0	4.2	4.2	4.4	4.3	5.3	5.9	6.7	6.9
Italy/Italie	2.8	2.5	2.8	3.3	3.6	3.8	3.4	3.1	3.9	4.7

TRADE BY COMMODITY IN THOUSAND U.S. DOLLARS – COMMERCE PAR PRODUIT EN MILLIERS DE DOLLARS E.U

COUNTRIES–PAYS	IMPORTS – IMPORTATIONS 1990	1991	1992	1993	1994
Total	10827922	11603347	12973990	12519481	14003933
Africa	x383768	x451674	x407850	x409487	x413744
Northern Africa	168867	193904	193779	x189691	x194479
Americas	1403133	1509928	1853851	2174285	2483132
LAIA	214060	289793	499377	663401	809991
CACM	25122	24446	29068	x42668	x45494
Asia	2927508	3413310	4120662	4211736	4639729
Middle East	x383672	x362809	x417875	x386376	x345617
Europe	5676683	5723985	6128091	5102344	5730243
EEC	5261333	5276982	5687738	4735871	5302913
EFTA	303539	294380	304805	278209	303537
Oceania	x217862	x211632	x215972	x238040	x258278
Germany/Allemagne	1060607	1153268	1289758	1024097	1154822
Hong Kong	775273	925915	1022134	1061592	1156277
China/Chine	502866	680810	1099755	1018855	1146639
France,Monac	890171	875860	946347	817793	863657
USA/Etats–Unis d'Amer	727959	757077	828409	914998	1021275
United Kingdom	644959	611361	660796	645512	680085
Italy/Italie	536968	535374	548825	434619	504606
Canada	341034	359610	433692	490940	534010
Netherlands/Pays–Bas	420953	400933	426582	351610	362023
Belgium–Luxembourg	327383	344958	404277	318256	393952
Japan/Japon	340666	346759	349840	346589	408153
Spain/Espagne	315223	337771	361681	278814	341809
Korea, Republic of	184117	227776	232856	223159	259454
Indonesia/Indonésie	131056	171311	215027	253261	290356
Sweden/Suède	242895	227711	223793	186670	214647
Mexico/Mexique	49095	80023	196124	316023	415948
Austria/Autriche	198444	191849	209850	182739	202955
Thailand/Thaïlande	164627	165830	193258	204656	199069
Switz.Liecht	183880	180318	191354	175293	192510
Portugal	141047	156792	173616	137707	173567
Iran (Islamic Rp. of)	x157267	x156063	x176054	x107572	x77816
Australia/Australie	130735	128032	134160	152146	169141
Finland/Finlande	184977	148194	141447	121685	152441
Singapore/Singapour	104154	110992	125468	151881	173874
Denmark/Danemark	131112	132614	136899	105886	118054
Norway,SVD,JM	108241	100705	99562	88589	95652
Greece/Grèce	105322	100209	102577	86061	92477
Malaysia/Malaisie	77654	92018	96696	97534	121163
Philippines	53627	95064	86472	98787	111704
So. Africa Customs Un	78080	81216	88212	91134	89724
Russian Federation			x177589	x74685	x84788
Chile/Chili	67088	67963	86115	95487	84213
Poland/Pologne	32928	37737	44711	158048	231640
Turkey/Turquie	56416	60479	79096	87953	87101
Hungary/Hongrie	x64086	71633	x72047	x80356	x78459
Israel/Israël	59123	63604	72993	66259	73720
Saudi Arabia	58084	66063	53617	x77300	x71603
New Zealand	67620	61953	63548	67400	75059
Viet Nam	x30831	x34495	x56075	x98034	x100039
Brazil/Brésil	41666	50349	60814	76202	93257
Tunisia/Tunisie	44392	48462	58736	62473	61838
Ireland/Irlande	61271	60087	61290	44424	47818
Morocco/Maroc	46953	56735	59058	46159	51866
Sri Lanka	29345	41063	48414	52921	75068
Yugoslavia SFR	97068	x136730			
Egypt/Egypte	49686	50028	43358	37949	39357
Former USSR/Anc. URSS	12775	x127517			
Argentina/Argentine	7409	21366	46773	55044	71805
India/Inde	29520	26596	33504	51470	68746
United Arab Emirates	24166	21666	34495	x49336	x43431

COUNTRIES–PAYS	EXPORTS – EXPORTATIONS 1990	1991	1992	1993	1994
Totale	10736589	11289960	12649473	12484557	13963967
Afrique	x41671	x46248	x55271	x51536	x41650
Afrique du Nord	16349	19768	24216	19964	23634
Amériques	1415761	1571504	1774515	1915865	2150620
ALAI	159947	189299	232288	265014	308652
MCAC	9028	10073	12031	x12278	x12787
Asie	2375600	2768547	3215918	3590979	4046350
Moyen–Orient	98675	72155	80247	89411	84174
Europe	6796156	6775893	7455055	6720751	7509457
CEE	6398015	6399000	7028584	6343374	7093448
AELE	358097	352180	367550	327207	362044
Océanie	47237	x53241	59661	x67483	x72686
Germany/Allemagne	1923234	1970881	2186125	1838337	2027704
USA/Etats–Unis d'Amer	1035474	1164718	1310701	1403164	1563488
Italy/Italie	843928	816170	916722	930961	1074950
Japan/Japon	692706	790052	889242	966909	1031976
Hong Kong	614408	770683	838701	903624	972848
Belgium–Luxembourg	761572	765395	860360	805289	924884
Korea, Republic of	545965	638022	811266	923808	1114178
France,Monac	719255	709665	773206	718743	726019
United Kingdom	672758	643943	676504	615318	691430
Netherlands/Pays–Bas	536365	533503	546863	490951	564374
Switz.Liecht	289504	277701	295150	271074	297181
Sweden/Suède	225987	227499	251216	198273	231073
Canada	200924	200157	212005	227040	254591
Spain/Espagne	134754	152786	188825	182104	225565
Austria/Autriche	171558	159641	170851	163990	x161518
China/Chine	105746	128073	151400	183808	288458
Portugal	140708	139381	167873	148609	153078
Finland/Finlande	108757	116465	121594	106538	143386
Brazil/Brésil	76008	94358	105520	112666	149276
Denmark/Danemark	91129	89436	98816	83748	96892
Indonesia/Indonésie	73361	80275	75543	96295	91483
Turkey/Turquie	90461	67961	74396	82937	77029
Thailand/Thaïlande	49169	58658	71869	93564	146674
Israel/Israël	52134	61541	69889	67813	72573
Norway,SVD,JM	65196	72519	69893	53477	61865
Singapore/Singapour	50467	53426	62615	68457	81750
Ireland/Irlande	59715	66636	60632	53349	64450
Mexico/Mexique	37580	38714	53258	64359	67532
Australia/Australie	37031	44456	50925	58615	63355
Bangladesh	8796	26308	39469	48925	x13154
Colombia/Colombie	25809	34032	39057	38258	40136
India/Inde	16858	21594	35834	43237	49562
Pakistan	26181	29474	29211	39163	34771
Czech Republic				91060	95347
Czechoslovakia		x40561	x41598		
Hungary/Hongrie	x29925	x21602	x31288	x25906	x23627
Slovenia/Slovénia			37979	35124	36589
Malaysia/Malaisie	7947	11007	16445	28785	32395
Philippines	24509	17763	19317	17585	18229
So. Africa Customs Un	11625	10842	15029	16067	
Argentina/Argentine	8229	10101	11978	16245	16400
Tunisia/Tunisie	7656	11637	13326	12865	11320
Poland/Pologne	4554	5035	13047	12700	17420
Un. Rep. of Tanzania	x2785	x10412	x10992	x7063	x12732
New Zealand	9983	7945	8651	8540	8963
Venezuela	3376	3253	7620	13947	18047
Greece/Grèce	8096	7398	8997	7165	8126
Croatia/Croatie			12651	10149	x11598
Yugoslavia SFR	37197	x21910			
Morocco/Maroc	6951	5705	7891	3424	5266

(VALUE AS % OF TOTAL)(VALEUR EN % DU TOTAL)

	1985	1986	1987	1988	1989	1990	1991	1992	1993	1994
Africa	3.8	x3.8	x3.8	x4.1	x3.3	x3.5	x3.9	x3.2	x3.2	x2.9
Northern Africa	2.0	1.5	1.6	1.8	1.5	1.6	1.7	1.5	x1.5	x1.4
Americas	21.0	x18.5	x15.7	x14.7	13.3	13.0	13.0	14.3	17.3	17.7
LAIA	2.3	2.0	1.8	1.8	1.9	2.0	2.5	3.8	5.3	5.8
CACM	0.5	0.3	x0.3	0.2	0.3	0.2	0.2	0.2	x0.3	x0.3
Asia	14.7	15.1	18.6	22.4	26.0	27.0	29.4	31.8	33.6	33.1
Middle East	2.0	x2.7	x2.0	x2.1	x2.8	x3.5	x3.1	x3.2	x3.1	x2.5
Europe	56.4	58.7	56.4	53.7	52.7	52.4	49.3	47.2	40.8	40.9
EEC	46.0	48.1	46.3	44.4	43.8	48.6	45.5	43.8	37.8	37.9
EFTA	9.4	9.8	9.3	8.4	8.0	2.8	2.5	2.3	2.2	2.2
Oceania	3.0	x2.6	x2.4	x2.2	x2.2	x2.0	x1.8	x1.6	x1.9	x1.8
Germany/Allemagne	9.1	9.4	8.7	8.5	8.4	9.8	9.9	9.9	8.2	8.2
Hong Kong	4.3	4.0	4.5	5.8	7.2	7.2	8.0	7.9	8.5	8.3
China/Chine			2.8	3.4	4.8	4.6	5.9	8.5	8.1	8.2
France,Monac	8.3	8.8	8.2	7.9	7.5	8.2	7.5	7.3	6.5	6.2
USA/Etats–Unis d'Amer	10.6	9.2	8.2	8.0	6.7	6.7	6.5	6.4	7.3	7.3
United Kingdom	6.5	6.2	6.0	6.0	5.8	6.0	5.3	5.1	5.2	4.9
Italy/Italie	4.4	4.8	4.9	4.5	4.6	5.0	4.6	4.2	3.5	3.6
Canada	6.8	5.3	4.2	3.6	3.5	3.1	3.1	3.3	3.9	3.8
Netherlands/Pays–Bas	3.9	4.2	4.0	3.5	3.4	3.9	3.5	3.3	2.8	2.6
Belgium–Luxembourg	2.8	3.0	2.9	2.9	2.8	3.0	3.0	3.1	2.5	2.8

	1985	1986	1987	1988	1989	1990	1991	1992	1993	1994
Afrique	0.3	0.4	0.3	0.2	0.3	x0.4	x0.4	x0.4	x0.4	x0.3
Afrique du Nord	0.0	0.1	0.1	0.1	0.1	0.2	0.2	0.2	0.2	0.2
Amériques	14.3	12.8	10.8	12.0	12.1	13.2	13.9	14.0	15.4	15.4
ALAI	2.1	1.7	1.3	1.4	1.8	1.5	1.7	1.8	2.1	2.2
MCAC	0.1	0.1	0.1	0.1	0.1	0.1	0.1	0.1	x0.1	x0.1
Asie	16.0	14.5	x20.7	x24.5	22.9	22.1	24.5	25.4	28.8	29.0
Moyen–Orient	0.3	0.2	x0.2	0.2	1.0	0.9	0.6	0.6	0.7	0.6
Europe	68.0	70.9	65.2	60.2	63.1	63.3	60.0	58.9	53.8	53.8
CEE	58.4	60.9	56.0	52.3	55.2	59.6	56.7	55.6	50.8	50.8
AELE	9.2	9.6	8.9	7.5	7.6	3.3	3.1	2.9	2.6	2.6
Océanie	0.4	x0.3	0.3	x0.3	0.4	0.4	x0.5	0.5	x0.5	x0.5
Germany/Allemagne	17.9	19.3	17.3	15.5	16.2	17.9	17.5	17.3	14.7	14.5
USA/Etats–Unis d'Amer	10.9	9.8	8.1	8.5	8.5	9.6	10.3	10.4	11.2	11.2
Italy/Italie	8.3	8.3	7.3	6.7	7.2	7.9	7.2	7.2	7.5	7.7
Japan/Japon	7.2	6.6	6.0	6.5	6.8	6.5	7.0	7.0	7.7	7.4
Hong Kong	3.8	3.0	3.7	4.8	6.2	5.7	6.8	6.6	7.2	7.0
Belgium–Luxembourg	7.0	7.3	6.4	6.3	6.9	7.1	6.8	6.8	6.5	6.6
Korea, Republic of	2.7	3.2	3.2	4.7	5.4	5.1	5.7	6.4	7.4	8.0
France,Monac	5.5	6.0	5.6	5.5	5.9	6.7	6.3	6.1	5.8	5.2
United Kingdom	5.6	5.4	5.5	5.4	5.7	6.3	5.7	5.3	4.9	5.0
Netherlands/Pays–Bas	5.2	5.6	5.5	4.9	5.0	5.0	4.7	4.3	3.9	4.0

TRADE BY COMMODITY IN THOUSAND U.S. DOLLARS – COMMERCE PAR PRODUIT EN MILLIERS DE DOLLARS E.U

IMPORTS – IMPORTATIONS

COUNTRIES–PAYS	1990	1991	1992	1993	1994
Total	8990007	9497590	10159494	10032377	11132660
Africa	x204506	x268706	x263306	x231665	x234738
Northern Africa	x62876	x76624	x77536	x61540	x69869
Americas	x1820542	1950086	2221324	2481623	x2828344
LAIA	81715	120840	223732	292424	289610
CACM	11054	11149	16219	x15622	x16223
Asia	1613153	1816758	2090715	x2230113	x2558459
Middle East	x453079	x485789	540716	x603731	x472151
Europe	4532872	4971973	5259388	4710589	5119656
EEC	4144229	4598512	4852837	4328823	4706159
EFTA	336917	339837	352566	333487	365636
Oceania	x238691	x251386	x259173	x269503	x260452
USA/Etats-Unis d'Amer	1405902	1461848	1643767	1810554	2126954
Germany/Allemagne	1041441	1356827	1376427	1335349	1435496
France,Monac	616901	632557	699455	612841	693098
Japan/Japon	441429	494279	613729	721425	1102326
Hong Kong	402068	480850	580654	563527	608871
United Kingdom	467753	479110	531749	521681	533657
Netherlands/Pays-Bas	423150	424430	454981	387106	446153
Italy/Italie	365108	435216	460442	343856	343225
Belgium-Luxembourg	306400	320660	323494	287663	306441
Canada	249082	276148	262014	280952	308352
Saudi Arabia	204004	235004	228177	x259365	x196558
Switz.Liecht	223410	228817	232577	223937	246790
Spain/Espagne	193914	232112	256915	174306	208834
Sweden/Suède	208405	193153	203281	160147	182835
Australia/Australie	171783	173314	186420	187595	179022
Austria/Autriche	162533	174111	186714	179882	209484
United Arab Emirates	91307	97991	119663	x173143	x146563
Russian Federation			x196283	x137831	x154724
Singapore/Singapour	88848	104211	111050	109072	114967
Norway,SVD,JM	106556	103354	112938	103559	112365
Denmark/Danemark	96165	93237	107975	104255	113045
Mexico/Mexique	37890	39896	100312	153143	128102
Greece/Grèce	74480	73667	70526	75366	72498
Ireland/Irlande	69195	76115	77433	63862	69181
Former USSR/Anc. URSS	439144	x180551			
Finland/Finlande	93801	74439	60207	43184	55315
China/Chine	57592	79976	32062	30340	38949
New Zealand	38592	47625	45199	48731	60005
Libyan Arab Jamahiriya	18915	38741	x42099	x35854	x34738
Portugal	24984	32880	43238	39324	36896
Argentina/Argentine	1595	18046	42482	51549	63529
Korea, Republic of	23826	36468	35063	36749	48213
Kuwait/Koweït	17693	18998	46401	36568	27910
Iran (Islamic Rp. of)	x26429	x45414	x26324	x29673	x6970
So. Africa Customs Un	23123	36239	36909	27205	28178
Ukraine			x4720	x88737	x33729
Malaysia/Malaisie	24707	26358	30815	27772	34115
Venezuela	16657	19017	35809	29135	17384
Hungary/Hongrie	x20644	20211	x25050	x33811	x30957
Chile/Chili	11814	20511	24602	29621	31203
Israel/Israël	19892	16917	21219	26241	32697
Un. Rep. of Tanzania	x6414	x42654	x9150	x4664	x9421
Syrian Arab Republic	10282	x10239	26723	x12141	x20692
Poland/Pologne	22805	11478	8917	28134	57993
Qatar	8848	11406	18014	17991	x3971
Indonesia/Indonésie	14162	16226	16760	14238	7226
Cuba	x12617	x13593	x9994	x13234	x11392
Cyprus/Chypre	10720	13756	12736	9821	8625
Bahrain/Bahreïn	x9189	x9371	x11726	x13565	x7582
Thailand/Thaïlande	7388	8812	11673	13801	16228

EXPORTS – EXPORTATIONS

COUNTRIES–PAYS	1990	1991	1992	1993	1994
Totale	8372704	9060744	10094365	9888435	10871730
Afrique	109850	123063	120330	142361	125915
Afrique du Nord	63028	76961	73167	97769	99858
Amériques	692576	807504	1218928	1269275	1272213
ALAI	263007	294691	694202	714080	654341
MCAC	15250	13502	17365	20255	24021
Asie	3866098	4319597	4858838	4904255	5569382
Moyen-Orient	312804	x450479	381774	368515	419924
Europe	3370654	3436990	3573774	3221750	3471250
CEE	3205221	3262537	3390214	3034590	3267536
AELE	89726	95594	96446	90468	106974
Océanie	37618	x48611	x48254	59588	65323
China/Chine	1375655	1421732	1695098	1741523	2186445
Pakistan	481211	603816	661576	631243	612487
Portugal	636676	630798	680895	565572	609504
Hong Kong	463078	535221	615101	623034	647444
Germany/Allemagne	589907	632767	627717	495364	532007
USA/Etats-Unis d'Amer	360716	433396	451592	477289	502984
India/Inde	340669	331463	405505	424500	543239
Korea, Republic of	325746	340802	338370	344388	353629
Belgium-Luxembourg	372874	361818	344493	311642	328694
Turkey/Turquie	262189	305549	340065	312329	372467
France,Monac	267047	280802	309619	306354	298459
United Kingdom	273342	273505	303565	279955	313274
Italy/Italie	274501	277943	258962	269092	334727
Mexico/Mexique	23278	29252	392290	353988	334119
Netherlands/Pays-Bas	226090	248416	265299	259592	269036
Brazil/Brésil	191769	213715	246413	283645	247990
Spain/Espagne	165466	166861	188503	175627	202470
Indonesia/Indonésie	78337	104618	184841	206313	175062
Thailand/Thaïlande	124309	154624	167915	168466	170864
Austria/Autriche	99664	92371	102739	97665	x99980
Bangladesh	109970	87830	80924	84374	x96910
Poland/Pologne	51839	83436	61426	107123	155689
Greece/Grèce	71437	82005	81322	77491	55849
Denmark/Danemark	81691	77616	82715	78377	86819
Switz.Liecht	72523	74612	75593	76713	88421
Israel/Israël	63825	68293	74550	74696	89659
Hungary/Hongrie	x78379	x69797	x79782	x65435	x59555
Japan/Japon	54356	59473	76057	69929	69510
Sweden/Suède	74007	70992	71556	60061	78800
Czechoslovakia		x87244	x94967		
Canada	39395	51314	43657	46222	58513
Ireland/Irlande	46971	44944	49698	36946	35094
Egypt/Egypte	33329	38799	38254	51258	64740
Syrian Arab Republic	6936	x106380	7472	x7489	x6111
Colombia/Colombie	23433	35695	37237	48201	47970
Philippines	35265	44329	34323	28605	30814
Australia/Australie	26239	35051	31363	36394	41771
Slovenia/Slovénia			46905	48472	49253
Singapore/Singapour	37137	30736	30689	30525	42004
Malaysia/Malaisie	21047	26518	31803	30311	29015
Sri Lanka	13565	20679	34261	30790	44337
Czech Republic				81717	84735
Yugoslavia SFR	75448	x78494			
Viet Nam		x15533	x22312	x31780	x48417
Finland/Finlande	25527	21679	23132	20853	22822
Romania/Roumanie	42214	32199	17177	16036	24874
Morocco/Maroc	13912	18886	21154	21629	12296
Norway,SVD,JM	15925	19448	19863	13149	17664
New Zealand	9930	11902	15682	19798	18583
Bulgaria/Bulgarie	x92011	x27253	x17296		x17493

(VALUE AS % OF TOTAL)(VALEUR EN % DU TOTAL)

Imports

	1985	1986	1987	1988	1989	1990	1991	1992	1993	1994
Africa	3.1	x3.4	x2.7	x3.0	x2.4	x2.3	x2.8	x2.6	x2.3	x2.2
Northern Africa	1.5	x0.7	x0.6	0.9	x0.7	x0.7	x0.8	x0.8	x0.6	x0.6
Americas	26.2	x25.3	x22.5	x20.9	20.2	x20.2	20.5	21.9	24.7	x25.4
LAIA	1.3	0.5	0.5	0.7	0.9	0.9	1.3	2.2	2.9	2.6
CACM	0.2	0.2	x0.2	0.1	0.1	0.1	0.1	0.2	x0.2	x0.1
Asia	18.0	16.4	x17.5	18.4	x20.3	17.9	19.1	20.5	x22.3	x23.0
Middle East	8.3	x6.9	x6.3	x6.0	x5.5	x5.0	x5.1	5.3	x6.0	x4.2
Europe	43.5	46.8	49.1	48.8	48.8	50.4	52.3	51.8	47.0	46.0
EEC	35.9	38.3	40.1	40.4	40.6	46.1	48.4	47.8	43.1	42.3
EFTA	7.5	8.3	8.8	8.2	8.0	3.7	3.6	3.5	3.3	3.3
Oceania	3.5	x2.8	x2.7	x3.1	x3.1	x2.6	x2.6	x2.6	x2.7	x2.3
USA/Etats-Unis d'Amer	20.5	20.1	17.6	16.1	15.2	15.6	15.4	16.2	18.0	19.1
Germany/Allemagne	7.6	8.6	9.2	9.3	9.2	11.6	14.3	13.5	13.3	12.9
France,Monac	6.1	7.0	6.5	6.3	6.3	6.9	6.7	6.9	6.1	6.2
Japan/Japon	2.6	3.0	3.5	4.7	5.8	4.9	5.2	6.0	7.2	9.9
Hong Kong	3.8	3.9	4.3	4.1	4.6	4.5	5.1	5.7	5.6	5.5
United Kingdom	5.6	5.2	5.1	5.4	5.1	5.2	5.0	5.2	5.2	4.8
Netherlands/Pays-Bas	4.2	4.4	4.7	4.3	4.1	4.7	4.5	4.5	3.9	4.0
Italy/Italie	2.6	2.8	3.3	3.6	3.8	4.1	4.6	4.5	3.4	3.1
Belgium-Luxembourg	2.8	2.9	2.9	2.9	3.0	3.4	3.4	3.2	2.9	2.8
Canada	3.3	3.2	2.6	2.7	2.9	2.8	2.9	2.6	2.8	2.8

Exports

	1985	1986	1987	1988	1989	1990	1991	1992	1993	1994
Afrique	0.7	0.7	0.5	1.0	1.0	1.3	1.4	1.2	1.4	1.2
Afrique du Nord	0.3	0.4	0.3	0.5	0.6	0.8	0.8	0.7	1.0	0.9
Amériques	12.3	10.1	8.0	8.5	8.1	8.3	8.9	12.1	12.8	11.7
ALAI	5.5	3.3	2.7	3.2	3.4	3.1	3.3	6.9	7.2	6.0
MCAC	0.3	0.2	0.2	0.2	0.2	0.2	0.1	0.2	0.2	0.2
Asie	36.7	34.4	45.7	47.1	47.2	46.2	47.7	48.1	49.6	51.3
Moyen-Orient	3.6	3.6	3.5	3.4	3.4	3.7	x5.0	3.8	3.7	3.9
Europe	45.5	50.1	38.8	36.8	38.6	40.3	37.9	35.4	32.6	31.9
CEE	40.2	44.5	34.5	32.7	34.6	38.3	36.0	33.6	30.7	30.1
AELE	3.7	4.2	3.3	3.2	3.1	1.1	1.1	1.0	0.9	1.0
Océanie	0.6	x0.7	0.4	x0.4	0.5	0.4	x0.5	x0.5	0.6	0.6
China/Chine	2.0	1.8	13.2	15.4	17.2	16.4	15.7	16.8	17.6	20.1
Pakistan	5.5	6.5	4.8	4.9	5.5	5.7	6.7	6.6	6.4	5.6
Portugal	6.7	7.3	5.9	6.0	6.7	7.6	7.0	6.7	5.7	5.6
Hong Kong	5.9	6.5	5.3	5.1	5.7	5.5	5.9	6.1	6.3	6.0
Germany/Allemagne	6.7	8.2	6.3	6.3	6.7	7.0	7.0	6.2	5.0	4.9
USA/Etats-Unis d'Amer	5.6	5.3	4.2	4.4	3.9	4.3	4.8	4.5	4.8	4.6
India/Inde	5.3	4.0	2.9	3.0	3.8	4.1	3.7	4.0	4.3	5.0
Korea, Republic of	4.9	4.4	4.1	4.3	4.3	3.9	3.8	3.4	3.5	3.3
Belgium-Luxembourg	4.2	4.8	3.7	3.7	4.2	4.5	4.0	3.4	3.2	3.0
Turkey/Turquie	3.4	3.2	2.9	2.9	2.9	3.1	3.4	3.4	3.2	3.4

TRADE BY COMMODITY IN THOUSAND U.S. DOLLARS – COMMERCE PAR PRODUIT EN MILLIERS DE DOLLARS E.U

COUNTRIES–PAYS	IMPORTS – IMPORTATIONS 1990	1991	1992	1993	1994
Total	8725022	8775348	9219051	7836335	8219006
Africa	x57736	x46922	x57899	x52746	x62676
Northern Africa	11983	7307	x13167	x13611	x19793
Americas	1023681	1105632	1259379	1249242	1381761
LAIA	53698	84988	134595	166011	189833
CACM	3000	2339	4256	x5298	x5501
Asia	1237688	1336063	1466931	x1419579	x1496573
Middle East	393081	493115	555761	x496358	x388009
Europe	5926827	5998427	6226209	4855090	4993905
EEC	5464434	5594187	5808901	4472919	4589367
EFTA	444538	387309	391825	356546	374239
Oceania	x137199	x118691	x117102	x117563	x142904
Germany/Allemagne	1917809	2088762	2248451	1785340	1761292
United Kingdom	857163	811159	849166	643994	705216
USA/Etats–Unis d'Amer	660843	644278	780001	743161	824614
France,Monac	739585	682839	685409	504966	500878
Japan/Japon	503324	506840	533469	540352	673501
Netherlands/Pays–Bas	490991	508511	516009	340155	310244
Canada	272838	344677	315204	312326	338991
Belgium–Luxembourg	322185	340774	337787	238951	287242
Switz.Liecht	344865	301618	303831	284006	297271
Italy/Italie	272684	293461	280150	247262	278955
Saudi Arabia	205658	272782	266614	x206512	x168554
Austria/Autriche	208817	214854	224269	218427	218068
Sweden/Suède	222952	196004	180843	140125	148638
Hong Kong	116849	110272	118478	113098	130914
Spain/Espagne	103853	124887	126913	81982	93511
Singapore/Singapour	88470	85853	111134	95739	105307
Australia/Australie	100387	86861	86680	85904	107602
Denmark/Danemark	88505	88703	96598	67694	74180
United Arab Emirates	85913	75209	76927	x92868	x70958
Ireland/Irlande	87354	83985	91673	63538	68761
Norway,SVD,JM	94473	80314	83238	68354	72578
Mexico/Mexique	35261	55349	80025	94846	95408
Greece/Grèce	60790	70816	79842	71323	69489
Kuwait/Koweït	27461	61267	88955	62297	65298
Russian Federation			x53744	x157062	x311571
Korea, Republic of	53700	54185	51959	42139	53086
Portugal	31922	40395	52835	40012	38700
Poland/Pologne	4975	45561	38138	37222	38787
Finland/Finlande	59823	49038	38956	29151	34193
Former USSR/Anc. URSS	278486	x98510			
Iran (Islamic Rp. of)	x5821	x8815	x37826	x46714	x11621
China/Chine	31766	23227	28094	31622	33926
Hungary/Hongrie	x13638	14792	x25939	x35477	x29201
New Zealand	28643	23082	23160	24856	30512
Israel/Israël	10321	16723	19608	29297	28006
Malaysia/Malaisie	16808	17713	21835	24952	27784
Bahrain/Bahreïn	x11471	x15491	x18625	x18593	x8650
Qatar	14677	14644	18327	18205	x9727
So. Africa Customs Un	15732	16482	17617	16154	18530
Chile/Chili	8137	9766	15529	18412	21666
Argentina/Argentine	756	6443	16328	20176	25588
Oman	8796	12547	12487	15686	14975
Czech Republic				35688	40304
Ukraine			x5395	x24612	x15662
Cyprus/Chypre	10540	9146	12041	8471	8910
Lebanon/Liban	x5644	x13788	x7576	x7998	x15326
Czechoslovakia	7300	x6004	x17444		
Indonesia/Indonésie	3784	5576	6243	8478	10914
Romania/Roumanie	2528	2895	6467	10177	7632
Turkey/Turquie	7120	5165	6225	8065	5469

COUNTRIES–PAYS	EXPORTS – EXPORTATIONS 1990	1991	1992	1993	1994
Totale	8591687	9169841	9735004	8431188	9008977
Afrique	111437	90390	94304	92727	82986
Afrique du Nord	96598	75733	79400	80195	81434
Amériques	741552	893217	932146	959314	978133
ALAI	55725	56997	78077	86764	89227
MCAC	774	982	859	x953	x986
Asie	2557518	3098331	3549103	x2818386	x3099950
Moyen–Orient	920399	1384073	1432707	x823676	x1028364
Europe	4980985	4907606	5026215	4417423	4699541
CEE	4811642	4805095	4895098	4306860	4603105
AELE	108516	98172	117405	103726	93296
Océanie	x76172	x64124	x64664	x64432	x83153
Belgium–Luxembourg	2226941	2278446	2348700	2273690	2419439
Iran (Islamic Rp. of)	509100	1125268	1133303	x496046	x736752
USA/Etats–Unis d'Amer	605990	756165	765916	769722	752622
India/Inde	453678	523142	630202	604498	610866
China/Chine	450055	498578	625244	631237	762267
Germany/Allemagne	678282	649409	612253	459893	447729
Netherlands/Pays–Bas	650498	652168	632571	435763	481323
United Kingdom	416789	383200	389714	335766	380362
France,Monac	229432	257548	312623	279283	321076
Turkey/Turquie	202416	189032	262442	292021	253398
Pakistan	236456	224655	209396	160225	191508
Nepal/Népal	80724	98880	166935	196638	x199278
Denmark/Danemark	173980	144887	150573	122848	124500
Austria/Autriche	107701	112452	114800	100211	x89372
Switz.Liecht	106629	96424	115875	103210	92637
Italy/Italie	101390	100347	107636	101691	116455
Canada	78222	78409	86231	101300	134506
Hong Kong	90497	87609	84569	83839	86407
Afghanistan	x78056	x63038	x96226	x90409	x14258
Ireland/Irlande	54811	53794	58463	54209	66511
Mexico/Mexique	44241	40753	57411	62027	66174
Spain/Espagne	62062	56595	57663	42362	52773
Indonesia/Indonésie	29375	49351	51530	48663	36504
Morocco/Maroc	55325	43160	36698	39194	38649
New Zealand	48201	38859	40153	37550	48581
Portugal	39689	37003	36002	31573	36770
Greece/Grèce	22273	40522	32322	31424	27855
Sweden/Suède	40781	33995	36735	33393	32564
Korea, Republic of	32894	38405	33540	24006	27705
Japan/Japon	46323	33233	32818	26073	21009
Egypt/Egypte	30819	24954	26831	30628	34101
Australia/Australie	27680	24807	23429	26430	34060
Saudi Arabia	12226	44083	21254	x8075	x13499
Israel/Israël	22725	27299	24651	17460	23062
Singapore/Singapour	22103	20661	23536	24669	25512
Thailand/Thaïlande	17426	18127	20093	27051	28863
Hungary/Hongrie	x26875	x20326	x17993	x13764	x13180
Turkmenistan/Turkménistn			x34173	x11881	x3101
Azerbaijan			x35040	x8660	x4675
Romania/Roumanie	23284	13596	15851	11537	11291
Brazil/Brésil	5230	8811	12831	18245	18186
Czechoslovakia		x22522	x16295		
So. Africa Customs Un	13194	13511	13736	11058	
Poland/Pologne	17550	12424	11106	10820	12444
Former USSR/Anc. URSS	17575	x33322			
Tunisia/Tunisie	10072	6952	15821	10076	8382
Czech Republic				27352	19148
Malaysia/Malaisie	2640	6517	8775	9946	11249
Philippines	8688	9146	8001	8067	9117
Syrian Arab Republic	9676	x16401	3131	x3003	x1580

(VALUE AS % OF TOTAL)(VALEUR EN % DU TOTAL)

	1985	1986	1987	1988	1989	1990	1991	1992	1993	1994
Africa	0.3	x0.5	x0.6	x0.5	x0.6	x0.7	x0.5	x0.6	x0.7	x0.7
Northern Africa	0.1	0.1	0.1	0.1	0.2	0.1	0.1	x0.1	x0.2	x0.2
Americas	17.4	14.8	x13.2	11.8	12.3	11.7	12.6	13.7	16.0	16.9
LAIA	0.2	0.2	0.2	0.3	0.5	0.6	1.0	1.5	2.1	2.3
CACM	0.1	0.0	x0.0	0.0	0.0	0.0	0.0	0.0	x0.1	x0.1
Asia	14.7	13.2	x13.1	15.9	15.3	14.2	15.3	15.9	x18.1	x18.2
Middle East	8.9	x7.2	x5.5	6.4	x5.2	4.5	5.6	6.0	x6.3	x4.7
Europe	60.1	64.3	66.6	65.8	66.5	67.9	68.4	67.5	62.0	60.8
EEC	49.7	52.9	55.0	55.1	56.2	62.6	63.7	63.0	57.1	55.8
EFTA	10.3	11.3	11.5	10.5	10.2	5.1	4.4	4.3	4.5	4.6
Oceania	2.3	x1.8	x1.5	x1.6	x1.8	x1.6	x1.4	x1.3	x1.5	x1.8
Germany/Allemagne	16.9	18.6	19.1	18.5	19.0	22.0	23.8	24.4	22.8	21.4
United Kingdom	9.0	8.8	9.0	9.7	9.5	9.8	9.2	9.2	8.2	8.6
USA/Etats–Unis d'Amer	14.7	12.6	11.0	8.7	8.4	7.6	7.3	8.5	9.5	10.0
France,Monac	6.6	7.4	7.6	7.6	7.8	8.5	7.8	7.4	6.4	6.1
Japan/Japon	2.8	3.3	4.6	6.1	6.5	5.8	5.8	5.8	6.9	8.2
Netherlands/Pays–Bas	4.9	5.3	5.3	5.3	5.2	5.6	5.8	5.6	4.3	3.8
Canada	2.0	1.6	1.5	2.4	3.0	3.1	3.9	3.4	4.0	4.1
Belgium–Luxembourg	2.5	2.5	2.9	3.2	3.3	3.7	3.9	3.7	3.0	3.5
Switz.Liecht	4.1	4.5	4.4	4.0	3.7	4.0	3.4	3.3	3.6	3.6
Italy/Italie	2.6	2.6	2.8	2.7	2.6	3.1	3.3	3.0	3.2	3.4

	1985	1986	1987	1988	1989	1990	1991	1992	1993	1994
Afrique	1.4	1.3	1.3	1.2	1.3	1.3	0.9	0.9	1.1	0.9
Afrique du Nord	1.3	1.2	1.2	1.2	1.2	1.1	0.8	0.8	1.0	0.9
Amériques	7.6	6.2	5.7	7.1	7.9	8.7	9.7	9.6	11.3	10.8
ALAI	0.4	0.2	0.3	0.7	0.8	0.6	0.6	0.8	1.0	1.0
MCAC	0.0	0.0	0.0	0.0	0.0	0.0	0.0	0.0	x0.0	x0.0
Asie	24.8	30.6	x32.1	31.3	30.0	29.8	33.8	36.5	x33.4	x34.4
Moyen–Orient	3.7	9.7	10.1	7.9	7.7	10.7	15.1	14.7	x9.8	x11.4
Europe	61.6	58.2	55.4	55.1	57.9	58.0	53.5	51.6	52.4	52.2
CEE	57.4	54.3	51.9	51.6	54.4	56.0	52.4	50.3	51.1	51.1
AELE	3.5	3.5	3.1	3.0	2.9	1.3	1.1	1.2	1.2	1.0
Océanie	1.6	x1.2	1.0	x1.0	x0.9	x0.9	x0.7	x0.7	x0.8	x0.9
Belgium–Luxembourg	24.7	23.6	22.2	22.8	24.8	25.9	24.8	24.1	27.0	26.9
Iran (Islamic Rp. of)		6.8	7.1	4.2	4.7	5.9	12.3	11.6	x5.9	x8.2
USA/Etats–Unis d'Amer	5.4	4.4	4.0	5.4	6.0	7.1	8.2	7.9	9.1	8.4
India/Inde	6.0	5.3	5.6	5.6	6.2	5.3	5.7	6.5	7.2	6.8
China/Chine	4.9	4.2	5.0	6.0	6.7	5.2	5.4	6.4	7.5	8.5
Germany/Allemagne	7.5	7.6	7.6	7.6	8.1	7.9	7.1	6.3	5.5	5.0
Netherlands/Pays–Bas	8.9	8.5	8.2	7.4	7.3	7.6	7.1	6.5	5.2	5.3
United Kingdom	6.1	5.1	4.8	4.7	4.8	4.9	4.2	4.0	4.0	4.2
France,Monac	1.9	1.6	1.6	1.8	2.1	2.7	2.8	3.2	3.3	3.6
Turkey/Turquie	2.3	1.6	1.8	1.9	2.3	2.4	2.1	2.7	3.5	2.8

TRADE BY COMMODITY IN THOUSAND U.S. DOLLARS – COMMERCE PAR PRODUIT EN MILLIERS DE DOLLARS E.U

COUNTRIES–PAYS	IMPORTS – IMPORTATIONS 1990	1991	1992	1993	1994
Total	8692803	8567116	8959895	7586631	8911022
Africa	x564490	x565825	x630679	x504520	x507134
Northern Africa	200084	164332	x198646	x152569	x206087
Americas	x1615230	x1312718	x1190944	x1271992	x1609878
LAIA	37785	49650	96067	144214	186543
CACM	4344	5007	8444	x16202	29175
Asia	2371060	2875357	2831361	x2557618	x3188334
Middle East	384107	340815	512785	x659951	x740574
Europe	3580006	3654521	4133628	3066570	3372091
EEC	3302897	3395714	3860476	2828627	3108644
EFTA	231337	217746	199631	179839	211396
Oceania	x107730	x109378	x91678	x85878	x103336
Germany/Allemagne	856868	1028189	1378329	1080566	1176147
USA/Etats–Unis d'Amer	1280667	996785	824689	873155	1141456
Japan/Japon	755926	842834	751279	657184	749079
Netherlands/Pays–Bas	514080	490887	522921	347571	418992
France,Monac	424809	441908	514856	333068	371782
Korea, Republic of	258207	518019	387387	115461	177714
United Kingdom	464406	352976	293082	202234	233695
Hong Kong	261345	247464	275250	295375	383116
Italy/Italie	209695	231269	274286	181315	169973
Spain/Espagne	229746	269612	257180	157960	141665
Belgium–Luxembourg	242264	230177	249472	203500	200194
Singapore/Singapour	156725	195187	237610	242918	296889
Saudi Arabia	138979	176529	228819	x235055	x279112
Thailand/Thaïlande	152876	375757	175468	11168	16474
Switz.Liecht	207314	195123	175192	152667	179923
Austria/Autriche	101763	110280	131282	138674	178254
Canada	151048	127155	115379	116984	119555
Israel/Israël	62629	108336	128336	121739	154379
Nigeria/Nigéria	61381	112963	x92003	x91062	x26767
Algeria/Algérie	81382	97419	98650	82754	119325
Malaysia/Malaisie	28278	51925	86768	111609	101994
Sweden/Suède	91541	81309	74252	55752	61878
Kuwait/Koweït	88170	8845	58781	132171	152969
China/Chine	38112	26131	48030	103068	139837
Denmark/Danemark	56656	55876	64909	48644	59899
United Arab Emirates	34927	27845	41904	x95521	x117245
Sri Lanka	35994	41214	53170	58440	68954
Ireland/Irlande	56092	56048	54063	36979	44330
Philippines	56417	15990	82452	42914	37357
Australia/Australie	63982	55895	38543	37291	58720
Ghana	x12854	7419	86767	x22324	x40528
Mauritius/Maurice	30725	35596	37469	43205	40035
Mexico/Mexique	14547	21212	39098	49877	53508
Oman	10154	23095	32083	40416	34710
Turkey/Turquie	49113	30678	31889	29885	19151
Libyan Arab Jamahiriya	71990	24303	x27676	x29307	x30080
Poland/Pologne	3902	12961	30481	36325	43877
Reunion/Réunion	24560	26183	30799	22062	27633
Finland/Finlande	37958	31319	23968	23711	29974
Morocco/Maroc	19320	23525	37619	16707	12869
Yemen/Yémen	x11741	8689	x45702	x16110	x15296
Qatar	8625	13590	18938	36606	x10262
Cameroon/Cameroun	24413	40756	x13601	x14520	x28256
Macau/Macao	19531	19599	24019	24075	26728
Norway,SVD,JM	21930	19671	21470	24596	29115
Lebanon/Liban	x13299	x20593	x13459	x26388	x63115
Sudan/Soudan	x9002	x12121	x30506	x17407	x23284
Hungary/Hongrie	x10455	15764	x21825	x20980	x23999
Brunei Darussalam	28665	33377	x13057	x11731	x33336
So. Africa Customs Un	15903	18261	21183	18098	19915

COUNTRIES–PAYS	EXPORTS – EXPORTATIONS 1990	1991	1992	1993	1994
Totale	7473619	7624404	8275868	7938902	9139030
Afrique	x217658	x174888	153343	152117	x170333
Afrique du Nord	99856	56167	77380	49846	53316
Amériques	657848	664921	694961	809860	871973
ALAI	268112	266579	280419	342126	373953
MCAC	7393	5762	7870	x5759	x6559
Asie	1610968	1809881	1951939	2053279	2472328
Moyen–Orient	334372	317071	322757	x301168	x391212
Europe	4671867	4613080	5034679	4427803	5059052
CEE	4578231	4534010	4907714	4322982	4934211
AELE	37417	39521	43727	52719	62349
Océanie	21716	28904	x39964	x38688	x37045
Italy/Italie	1885383	1869235	1904848	1693103	1910711
China/Chine	375838	596800	477099	369690	533321
Belgium–Luxembourg	444142	438164	520975	479430	525136
Spain/Espagne	459220	450940	493472	462903	587898
France,Monac	437673	429301	445150	380187	447829
Japan/Japon	210256	279875	441843	478677	544436
Germany/Allemagne	409620	388027	436002	333012	373562
Korea, Republic of	318054	317514	303549	358204	339128
Greece/Grèce	274685	274916	352449	319559	362057
Canada	227042	217569	224418	258827	286234
Portugal	176784	180088	204927	157729	173683
USA/Etats–Unis d'Amer	133161	154409	165362	175977	179884
Turkey/Turquie	114240	149072	184453	137588	202535
Netherlands/Pays–Bas	157726	146283	158577	132064	133901
United Kingdom	137241	146054	138088	132928	144601
India/Inde	42092	65332	111269	172032	230450
Poland/Pologne	49435	71135	112680	151300	196351
Czechoslovakia		x118562	x189577		
Mexico/Mexique	108227	102849	92516	88804	91274
Denmark/Danemark	57440	85362	99308	79631	89700
Brazil/Brésil	26197	36146	80635	125477	132727
Indonesia/Indonésie	100350	48130	114220	77183	46339
Hong Kong	45390	39946	66331	95229	144172
Romania/Roumanie	65628	67937	68248	64019	64023
Tunisia/Tunisie	69499	51157	67057	40806	39501
Austria/Autriche	50773	48010	55793	53326	x56444
Venezuela	72023	59229	40731	51696	69328
Colombia/Colombie	41663	49978	47129	49995	53137
So. Africa Customs Un	26509	43408	48478	53892	66579
Saudi Arabia	58582	77092	43701	x14523	x15111
Czech Republic				131520	138122
Jordan/Jordanie	37767	39488	36281	29387	43870
Singapore/Singapour	36508	31782	38101	33834	46902
Sweden/Suède	21003	23940	35954	40498	49023
Thailand/Thaïlande	4865	4196	7376	88506	117499
Ireland/Irlande	46562	33441	32549	26911	34339
Slovakia				x86681	x96468
Norway,SVD,JM	24590	24936	25175	33318	40939
Malaysia/Malaisie	63961	48757	17634	16234	33689
United Arab Emirates	45349	6637	6881	x68250	x61256
Finland/Finlande	19850	20120	29624	31702	45326
Korea Dem People's Rp	x50199	x34737	x12698	x32903	x19558
Croatia/Croatie			45499	34689	x40177
Kenya	9506	12863	15895	32484	x38744
Australia/Australie	10411	13963	23161	20794	21554
Russian Federation			x22543	x34797	x26240
Switz.Liecht	12826	14580	18550	19401	21281
Syrian Arab Republic	26128	x12794	17301	x19965	x20939
Hungary/Hongrie	x22780	x13820	x16603	x17285	x17101
New Zealand	8937	13537	16213	17114	15231

(VALUE AS % OF TOTAL)(VALEUR EN % DU TOTAL)

	1985	1986	1987	1988	1989	1990	1991	1992	1993	1994
Africa	17.1	14.7	x9.2	x6.2	x5.3	x6.5	x6.6	x7.0	x6.6	x5.7
Northern Africa	13.9	10.0	4.9	3.0	2.4	2.3	1.9	x2.2	x2.0	x2.3
Americas	21.7	22.5	x23.3	x21.9	x20.5	x18.6	x15.3	x13.3	x16.8	x18.1
LAIA	0.6	0.6	0.4	0.5	0.4	0.4	0.6	1.1	1.9	2.1
CACM	0.1	0.1	x0.1	0.0	0.1	0.0	0.1	0.1	x0.2	0.3
Asia	29.8	24.4	23.9	25.0	x25.9	27.3	33.6	31.6	x33.7	x35.7
Middle East	11.9	x8.7	x6.9	6.0	5.1	4.4	4.0	5.7	x8.7	x8.3
Europe	23.3	29.2	34.6	37.2	38.8	41.2	42.7	46.1	40.4	37.8
EEC	19.9	24.7	29.1	32.0	33.4	38.0	39.6	43.1	37.3	34.9
EFTA	3.0	4.2	5.1	4.8	4.9	2.7	2.5	2.2	2.4	2.4
Oceania	0.7	x0.9	x1.0	x1.3	x1.5	x1.2	x1.3	x1.0	x1.2	x1.1
Germany/Allemagne	6.1	7.5	8.5	8.5	8.4	9.9	12.0	15.4	14.2	13.2
USA/Etats–Unis d'Amer	18.6	19.0	19.4	17.7	16.3	14.7	11.6	9.2	11.5	12.8
Japan/Japon	3.6	4.9	7.0	8.8	10.6	8.7	9.8	8.4	8.7	8.4
Netherlands/Pays–Bas	4.4	5.5	6.1	5.9	5.4	5.9	5.7	5.8	4.6	4.7
France,Monac	2.7	3.2	4.0	4.2	4.3	4.9	5.2	5.7	4.4	4.2
Korea, Republic of	0.6	0.2	0.2	0.6	0.7	3.0	6.0	4.3	1.5	2.0
United Kingdom	2.3	2.9	3.6	4.8	5.7	5.3	4.1	3.3	2.7	2.6
Hong Kong	2.7	2.7	3.2	3.7	3.3	3.0	2.9	3.1	3.9	4.3
Italy/Italie	0.6	0.7	1.1	1.8	2.0	2.4	2.7	3.1	2.4	1.9
Spain/Espagne	0.2	0.3	0.7	1.2	1.6	2.6	3.1	2.9	2.1	1.6

	1985	1986	1987	1988	1989	1990	1991	1992	1993	1994
Afrique	1.3	1.3	1.3	1.1	x2.3	x3.0	x2.3	1.9	1.9	x1.8
Afrique du Nord	0.1	0.3	0.5	0.6	1.2	1.3	0.7	0.9	0.6	0.6
Amériques	15.2	12.2	10.2	9.2	9.2	8.8	8.7	8.4	10.2	9.5
ALAI	8.0	5.0	4.4	4.0	4.4	3.6	3.5	3.4	4.3	4.1
MCAC	0.1	0.1	0.1	0.1	0.2	0.1	0.1	0.1	x0.1	x0.1
Asie	19.0	15.7	x18.8	x20.9	21.0	21.5	23.7	23.5	25.8	27.1
Moyen–Orient	3.9	x3.2	x2.5	x3.3	x3.6	4.5	4.2	3.9	x3.8	x4.3
Europe	60.5	66.3	59.6	58.3	62.5	62.5	60.5	60.8	55.8	55.4
CEE	57.7	63.3	57.0	55.9	60.2	61.3	59.5	59.3	54.5	54.0
AELE	1.8	2.1	1.9	1.6	1.6	0.5	0.5	0.5	0.7	0.7
Océanie	0.3	x0.3	x0.2	x0.4	0.3	0.3	0.4	x0.5	x0.5	x0.4
Italy/Italie	21.3	23.8	22.3	23.2	25.5	25.2	24.5	23.0	21.3	20.9
China/Chine	0.1	0.2	1.0	1.1	1.8	5.0	7.8	5.8	4.7	5.8
Belgium–Luxembourg	5.2	6.1	5.7	5.5	5.6	5.9	5.7	6.3	6.0	5.7
Spain/Espagne	7.7	7.4	6.4	6.3	6.2	6.1	5.9	6.0	5.8	6.4
France,Monac	6.0	6.3	5.5	5.1	5.5	5.9	5.6	5.4	4.8	4.9
Japan/Japon	7.4	3.9	2.3	2.3	3.0	2.8	3.7	5.3	6.0	6.0
Germany/Allemagne	4.6	5.9	5.4	5.4	5.6	5.5	5.1	5.3	4.2	4.1
Korea, Republic of	3.9	5.0	5.1	5.6	6.7	4.3	4.2	3.7	4.5	3.7
Greece/Grèce	5.3	5.0	3.8	2.8	3.6	3.7	3.6	4.3	4.0	4.0
Canada	5.0	5.0	3.9	3.5	2.7	3.0	2.9	2.7	3.3	3.1

TRADE BY COMMODITY IN THOUSAND U.S. DOLLARS – COMMERCE PAR PRODUIT EN MILLIERS DE DOLLARS E.U

COUNTRIES–PAYS	IMPORTS – IMPORTATIONS				
	1990	1991	1992	1993	1994
Total	7662873	7487678	8248879	7375504	8343879
Africa	x332412	353751	x345429	x302594	x344643
Northern Africa	118110	138327	x135725	x103231	x133578
Americas	1217979	1149182	1239143	1355055	1517611
LAIA	180853	192394	243298	297182	383038
CACM	13188	12798	19955	x28499	x35965
Asia	x1202165	x1180723	x1345249	x1360791	x1470970
Middle East	x430028	x377662	x498772	x456534	x396499
Europe	4394185	4373869	4908449	3865026	4403471
EEC	4053630	4077874	4597933	3595219	4077919
EFTA	266545	238226	229349	211245	243553
Oceania	x193816	x183304	x209414	x195158	x239600
Germany/Allemagne	1081551	1223587	1556411	1183924	1393656
France,Monac	870859	820772	855558	669378	752545
USA/Etats–Unis d'Amer	652379	594201	643806	721406	776556
Belgium–Luxembourg	425914	422127	456682	372326	405158
United Kingdom	324949	293311	298228	228435	272911
Italy/Italie	264859	274866	290251	205985	206592
Austria/Autriche	227912	224859	244620	239675	268611
Canada	256680	242984	234398	223268	225332
Netherlands/Pays–Bas	237437	224762	264560	204631	239730
Switz.Liecht	202139	177256	174349	161341	182180
Singapore/Singapour	141144	153781	169779	182393	226332
Australia/Australie	163847	153638	175314	164365	200221
Hong Kong	135332	140197	158935	175974	207979
Greece/Grèce	149386	143919	169669	144931	146155
Iran (Islamic Rp. of)	x92603	x114158	x172351	x104791	x23063
Sweden/Suède	121213	118178	120513	94757	101084
Mexico/Mexique	78753	88147	99449	112749	149432
Indonesia/Indonésie	86932	97680	94267	94521	102631
Spain/Espagne	98072	98629	103978	75242	74535
Saudi Arabia	93072	74968	95757	x100126	x115330
Korea, Republic of	104750	105066	88543	72200	73894
So. Africa Customs Un	91705	79799	81177	77495	84225
Poland/Pologne	9210	61915	73356	99126	130313
Portugal	72591	77638	84448	63120	72988
Japan/Japon	72349	71192	64888	67412	85241
Finland/Finlande	91967	71721	64640	54647	66866
Israel/Israël	37069	51624	67077	72273	85191
Turkey/Turquie	68947	52785	49113	59304	57360
China/Chine	29642	37026	52132	71551	93711
Hungary/Hongrie	x75909	41818	x55388	x59135	x65578
Norway,SVD,JM	60997	56709	51185	46745	58195
Denmark/Danemark	45750	41453	43454	31977	46065
Libyan Arab Jamahiriya	24496	41245	x37010	x35435	x32534
Ireland/Irlande	41170	42052	44920	26192	31025
Malaysia/Malaisie	35885	28071	43994	36997	50934
Russian Federation			x56757	x51727	x72878
United Arab Emirates	56541	25327	28825	x44123	x50502
Romania/Roumanie	66121	41861	21925	26701	29198
Argentina/Argentine	9661	17235	29108	41356	58205
Algeria/Algérie	33779	29818	34696	21538	43147
Chile/Chili	19048	16522	31854	33589	28682
Venezuela	14788	13600	29747	35318	37962
Egypt/Egypte	28880	36002	25427	16376	24880
Bahrain/Bahreïn	x20961	x30513	x19339	x24663	x13834
Nigeria/Nigéria	x8883	31386	x21675	x20697	x17656
Czech Republic				70405	91648
Former USSR/Anc. URSS	52128	x62901			
Czechoslovakia	31714	x22319	x36668		
New Zealand	19017	18022	20101	20598	25151
Kuwait/Koweït	13731	4963	24167	29554	36559

COUNTRIES–PAYS	EXPORTS – EXPORTATIONS				
	1990	1991	1992	1993	1994
Totale	7391238	7339291	8127342	8000483	9091957
Afrique	x82008	37797	35114	33306	20964
Afrique du Nord	26756	21654	17458	18395	19780
Amériques	578569	600209	649697	714632	752099
ALAI	200401	236538	285524	341260	361230
MCAC	2416	3371	4503	4338	4588
Asie	514723	530406	608761	643274	722205
Moyen–Orient	59667	76566	86260	x112106	x125803
Europe	6148788	6053251	6676393	6346408	7298686
CEE	6049944	5967668	6583246	6248171	7208754
AELE	44729	48944	53936	51128	56438
Océanie	12053	x18079	x24489	x28709	x44217
Italy/Italie	2378306	2365520	2668171	2694108	3130967
Germany/Allemagne	1148461	1064894	1098934	939337	1013751
Spain/Espagne	686420	747620	927670	936000	1190290
France,Monac	576971	551189	570201	523091	594814
USA/Etats–Unis d'Amer	312646	311763	316746	322166	335070
Netherlands/Pays–Bas	280048	279540	317313	288557	308179
Austria/Autriche	323364	308541	295050	253613	x258004
United Kingdom	261753	258279	253798	213635	228008
Japan/Japon	242647	224314	242125	242621	243759
Belgium–Luxembourg	166075	159789	190677	177962	213859
Brazil/Brésil	86331	90838	119913	164038	173149
Portugal	76747	86153	115679	97481	113434
Mexico/Mexique	52187	76577	89433	100446	119486
Turkey/Turquie	38753	63317	70191	90487	99967
China/Chine	65449	72648	70961	64358	88256
Denmark/Danemark	42567	48166	49345	46248	59220
Thailand/Thaïlande	44352	40642	50652	42831	44848
Switz.Liecht	38278	42099	45998	44803	46992
Czechoslovakia		x52341	x79533		
Canada	56852	46579	40557	43609	47697
Sweden/Suède	41141	37567	40594	34763	42743
Malaysia/Malaisie	16191	25994	38432	48364	59990
Czech Republic				110932	136762
Hong Kong	22914	23532	34888	43954	54477
Hungary/Hongrie	x26219	x22379	x28674	x33767	x28400
Ireland/Irlande	27378	29968	28244	16785	20885
Singapore/Singapour	18912	22341	23082	26105	34741
Venezuela	18304	21783	23142	25149	22268
Argentina/Argentine	24250	24086	23032	20356	18506
Slovakia				x66698	x53730
Australia/Australie	11092	16607	22692	26561	42795
Korea, Republic of	21052	20568	16861	21189	21940
Greece/Grèce	29392	21170	17602	15085	18186
So. Africa Customs Un	16130	14488	16460	13186	
India/Inde	6899	6945	16596	15499	21262
Uruguay	10549	11225	14203	13128	10426
Yugoslavia SFR	53916	x36409			
Tunisia/Tunisie	19038	15262	10415	8808	11410
Croatia/Croatie			16396	18053	x11998
Finland/Finlande	11276	9231	9967	11506	16414
Colombia/Colombie	4586	7546	10330	11938	10474
Bulgaria/Bulgarie	x11977	x6611	x10277	x12251	x17355
Poland/Pologne	3605	6268	12991	8861	15769
Indonesia/Indonésie	3368	2596	11768	12300	13626
Yugoslavia/Yougoslavie			x12046	x11853	x6674
Norway,SVD,JM	6437	6834	7936	6303	9446
Slovenia/Slovénia			10097	9603	10236
Sri Lanka	5673	5809	6328	7526	9037
United Arab Emirates	5270	1080	2329	x10252	x13500
Israel/Israël	2528	4483	4009	3663	2158

(VALUE AS % OF TOTAL)(VALEUR EN % DU TOTAL)

	1985	1986	1987	1988	1989	1990	1991	1992	1993	1994
Africa	5.0	5.3	x4.3	x4.7	x3.9	x4.3	4.8	x4.2	x4.2	x4.1
Northern Africa	2.7	2.8	2.1	2.3	1.5	1.5	1.8	x1.6	x1.4	x1.6
Americas	19.3	x18.8	x16.8	16.7	17.1	15.9	15.4	15.0	18.4	18.2
LAIA	2.2	2.0	1.4	2.0	2.1	2.4	2.6	2.9	4.0	4.6
CACM	0.2	0.1	0.2	0.1	0.1	0.2	0.2	0.2	x0.4	x0.4
Asia	20.5	14.5	x12.9	x14.2	x14.0	x15.7	x15.7	x16.3	x18.5	x17.6
Middle East	7.8	x6.3	x4.9	x5.2	x4.9	x5.6	x5.0	x6.0	x6.2	x4.8
Europe	50.6	56.9	55.0	54.5	55.5	57.3	58.4	59.5	52.4	52.8
EEC	41.6	47.0	45.4	45.4	46.4	52.9	54.5	55.7	48.7	48.9
EFTA	8.3	9.3	8.9	8.5	8.4	3.5	3.2	2.8	2.9	2.9
Oceania	2.5	x2.4	x2.5	x2.5	x3.2	x2.5	x2.5	x2.6	x2.6	x2.9
Germany/Allemagne	10.7	12.3	11.2	11.0	11.4	14.1	16.3	18.9	16.1	16.7
France,Monac	10.4	11.6	11.1	10.5	10.4	11.4	11.0	10.4	9.1	9.0
USA/Etats–Unis d'Amer	11.7	10.9	9.7	8.9	9.5	8.5	7.9	7.8	9.8	9.3
Belgium–Luxembourg	4.3	4.7	4.6	4.7	4.8	5.6	5.6	5.5	5.0	4.9
United Kingdom	3.2	3.5	3.7	4.4	4.5	4.2	3.9	3.6	3.1	3.3
Italy/Italie	2.9	3.2	3.3	3.0	2.9	3.5	3.7	3.5	2.8	2.5
Austria/Autriche	2.6	2.9	2.7	2.6	2.5	3.0	3.0	3.0	3.2	3.2
Canada	4.3	3.8	3.9	4.3	4.1	3.3	3.2	2.8	3.0	2.7
Netherlands/Pays–Bas	2.4	2.8	2.7	2.8	2.8	3.1	3.0	3.2	2.8	2.9
Switz.Liecht	2.4	2.8	2.6	2.5	2.5	2.6	2.4	2.1	2.2	2.2

	1985	1986	1987	1988	1989	1990	1991	1992	1993	1994
Afrique	0.3	0.3	0.3	0.4	0.5	x1.1	0.5	0.4	0.5	0.2
Afrique du Nord	0.0	0.1	0.1	0.2	0.3	0.4	0.3	0.2	0.2	0.2
Amériques	7.5	5.9	6.3	7.1	7.9	7.8	8.2	8.0	9.0	8.3
ALAI	2.5	2.1	2.2	2.6	3.4	2.7	3.2	3.5	4.3	4.0
MCAC	0.0	0.0	0.0	0.1	0.0	0.0	0.0	0.1	0.1	0.1
Asie	8.8	8.0	x7.4	x7.8	7.9	6.9	7.2	7.5	8.1	7.9
Moyen–Orient	0.5	x0.2	x0.5	0.5	x0.7	0.8	1.0	1.1	x1.4	x1.4
Europe	77.9	80.6	79.2	78.9	81.4	83.2	82.5	82.1	79.3	80.3
CEE	71.3	74.0	72.9	72.7	75.4	81.9	81.3	81.0	78.1	79.3
AELE	5.6	5.9	5.7	5.3	5.1	0.6	0.7	0.7	0.6	0.6
Océanie	0.1	x0.1	x0.1	x0.3	x0.2	0.2	x0.2	x0.3	x0.3	x0.5
Italy/Italie	26.7	27.6	28.0	28.4	29.9	32.2	32.2	32.8	33.7	34.4
Germany/Allemagne	15.8	17.2	15.9	15.2	15.1	15.5	14.5	13.5	11.7	11.1
Spain/Espagne	5.6	5.4	6.0	7.1	8.0	9.3	10.2	11.4	11.7	13.1
France,Monac	7.4	7.2	7.2	6.9	7.0	7.8	7.5	7.0	6.5	6.5
USA/Etats–Unis d'Amer	4.4	3.2	3.3	3.6	3.7	4.2	4.2	3.9	4.0	3.7
Netherlands/Pays–Bas	3.1	3.5	3.2	3.4	3.4	3.8	3.8	3.9	3.6	3.4
Austria/Autriche	4.2	4.3	4.3	4.0	3.9	4.4	4.2	3.6	3.2	x2.8
United Kingdom	4.0	3.8	3.5	3.2	3.1	3.5	3.5	3.1	2.7	2.5
Japan/Japon	6.7	6.3	4.2	3.8	3.8	3.3	3.1	3.0	3.0	2.7
Belgium–Luxembourg	1.8	2.1	1.9	1.9	2.0	2.2	2.2	2.3	2.2	2.4

TRADE BY COMMODITY IN THOUSAND U.S. DOLLARS – COMMERCE PAR PRODUIT EN MILLIERS DE DOLLARS E.U

COUNTRIES–PAYS	IMPORTS – IMPORTATIONS				
	1990	1991	1992	1993	1994
Total	9588788	8112157	8848808	8155673	10406425
Africa	x167110	172770	x199018	x203086	x1298677
Northern Africa	66961	69570	x82355	x80435	x82309
Americas	1289244	1315440	1541725	1701961	2062476
LAIA	210974	231968	310201	331380	401290
CACM	14458	14331	17176	x21871	x23732
Asia	1124951	x1277750	1455601	x1577509	1731298
Middle East	x206061	x283489	x311781	x279084	x227600
Europe	5083744	4949059	5337196	4309819	4893161
EEC	4646362	4574593	4945285	3942799	4481012
EFTA	369108	320562	318485	308333	346285
Oceania	x152594	x145581	x157666	x166982	x191235
Germany/Allemagne	1000234	1117922	1330772	1063441	1211732
USA/Etats–Unis d'Amer	739230	760402	872144	1003124	1239314
France,Monac	754768	723944	757761	576439	677893
United Kingdom	539650	452724	466376	391265	437762
Italy/Italie	445788	442923	457383	383191	437537
Belgium–Luxembourg	387562	399655	444991	341742	395196
Netherlands/Pays–Bas	407895	402070	433797	331382	362338
Canada	266501	260316	278653	299615	344571
Switz.Liecht	275179	236202	236066	224211	255703
Austria/Autriche	208253	210623	230480	221761	252434
Sweden/Suède	328121	259325	231873	160199	179011
Spain/Espagne	225640	237102	233005	165903	177713
Japan/Japon	214794	209388	209629	202658	234302
Korea, Republic of	141700	149012	165905	171497	204215
Singapore/Singapour	117538	120378	134650	142052	170731
Thailand/Thaïlande	82272	99633	114680	158084	159916
Malaysia/Malaisie	53930	98734	120015	152774	181940
Australia/Australie	116282	112280	125501	129240	149154
Mexico/Mexique	68520	79452	115581	132366	170454
Iran (Islamic Rp. of)	x61724	x123137	x118125	x77389	x37501
Hong Kong	74178	73044	108445	126110	151710
Denmark/Danemark	78548	83600	89647	77438	89290
Norway,SVD,JM	90725	80849	79008	80688	87187
Finland/Finlande	115640	85129	84588	69989	81598
Portugal	59718	64948	75332	64101	60122
Ireland/Irlande	64621	63887	74933	59726	79708
Indonesia/Indonésie	52370	53825	62770	73282	90232
Turkey/Turquie	59005	54953	63384	69564	59742
China/Chine	38454	39225	57517	90699	104856
Brazil/Brésil	54032	50492	64535	67526	82933
Israel/Israël	40828	57857	58745	54105	60001
Saudi Arabia	29015	47326	63940	x53082	x48783
So. Africa Customs Un	45668	43451	49381	54232	1160446
Poland/Pologne	39211	45942	45040	49997	65706
Hungary/Hongrie	x48107	43408	x38654	x44139	x41418
Russian Federation			x68085	x50108	x60401
Former USSR/Anc. URSS	1546106	x110372			
Argentina/Argentine	28751	33256	36616	35895	49858
Greece/Grèce	29924	30737	34348	36221	38678
India/Inde	31034	26991	36441	33588	40322
Venezuela	18648	27639	38668	27985	22343
Chile/Chili	17375	18900	25161	31406	30746
New Zealand	26657	23616	23028	28342	32498
Algeria/Algérie	20823	23193	22672	28759	30487
Czechoslovakia	33868	x21031	x50363		
Nigeria/Nigéria	x6180	15230	x20961	x26261	x10642
United Arab Emirates	15173	13239	18039	x30152	x30658
Egypt/Egypte	17772	20893	19682	18461	17508
Slovenia/Slovénia			28080	27389	30798
Philippines	11973	15070	17856	21331	26356

COUNTRIES–PAYS	EXPORTS – EXPORTATIONS				
	1990	1991	1992	1993	1994
Totale	8212429	8299376	9173573	8935793	10267686
Afrique	18845	25458	37313	34637	x15467
Afrique du Nord	6489	9104	13054	14195	11854
Amériques	1060637	1120869	1300310	1439247	1693432
ALAI	90883	102516	169180	219588	258195
MCAC	1278	1486	2130	x4147	x3099
Asie	1358171	1457386	1730224	1893964	2255908
Moyen–Orient	21436	14621	21294	x18947	x23953
Europe	5653297	5599087	5947936	5375550	6056070
CEE	5280900	5265063	5559927	5055005	5707615
AELE	310997	280777	294076	238551	271128
Océanie	x21373	27685	x32541	x37945	x51619
Germany/Allemagne	1675301	1717889	1749476	1530398	1695624
Japan/Japon	1037934	1091305	1249791	1300298	1519184
USA/Etats–Unis d'Amer	739952	788258	905010	927292	1084478
France,Monac	627814	596142	661043	594600	699159
United Kingdom	587128	571844	583927	575983	684275
Italy/Italie	522149	531272	540070	494924	623239
Belgium–Luxembourg	463714	458631	480060	468680	558889
Austria/Autriche	411866	390898	428255	379376	x363995
Netherlands/Pays–Bas	343612	347601	380829	303184	325860
Denmark/Danemark	251335	260459	296611	236688	226796
Canada	226230	226148	222551	285260	343478
Spain/Espagne	153458	158087	183066	213611	199532
Switz.Liecht	184032	178561	194152	180740	206539
Sweden/Suède	117683	103651	115313	110145	152983
China/Chine	56480	70824	113493	137671	158375
Malaysia/Malaisie	44987	66198	89846	115941	171940
Norway,SVD,JM	125513	101037	98548	56508	62979
Mexico/Mexique	27914	34937	81108	111525	138980
Finland/Finlande	62373	55305	63388	73138	92474
Brazil/Brésil	47586	48129	60603	81161	88157
Korea, Republic of	61132	57743	61029	68309	88788
Hong Kong	31240	28356	58848	89515	93455
Thailand/Thaïlande	29619	36006	41154	54432	67964
Slovenia/Slovénia			67477	61402	63175
Ireland/Irlande	35231	37497	38314	36616	34395
Singapore/Singapour	27371	35419	31306	37291	48248
Australia/Australie	19004	24182	29061	34208	47475
Czechoslovakia		x28553	x54128		
Portugal	24189	26795	29133	26080	27831
Poland/Pologne	13281	18760	19250	28715	42019
Czech Republic				64704	91846
Indonesia/Indonésie	6913	12647	16627	23004	31618
Yugoslavia SFR	60242	x52196			
So. Africa Customs Un	9764	13068	20996	17978	
Hungary/Hongrie	x12410	x10382	x20053	x17782	x20871
Israel/Israël	11724	12699	13604	16892	16298
India/Inde	15432	15153	12652	13494	16567
Bulgaria/Bulgarie	x2069	x1660	27371	8693	10940
Pakistan	8935	11213	10235	11480	10812
Greece/Grèce	4885	8829	10444	11583	22565
Croatia/Croatie			13656	11651	x10371
Slovakia				x24976	x27592
Turkey/Turquie	5845	5982	8664	10180	13378
Russian Federation			x9194	x11651	x4583
Saudi Arabia	4644	6242	9180	x5019	x4453
Venezuela	4253	4235	9851	6317	6897
Tunisia/Tunisie	1622	3604	6660	7900	4297
Romania/Roumanie	4459	3295	4111	9557	1888
Morocco/Maroc	4669	5309	5716	4959	7191
Yugoslavia/Yougoslavie			x11198	x4579	x1237

(VALUE AS % OF TOTAL)(VALEUR EN % DU TOTAL)

	1985	1986	1987	1988	1989	1990	1991	1992	1993	1994
Africa	8.7	4.6	x2.5	x2.3	x2.1	x1.8	2.1	x2.3	x2.5	x12.5
Northern Africa	7.5	3.1	1.0	0.9	0.8	0.7	0.9	x0.9	x1.0	x0.8
Americas	19.4	x18.5	x16.3	15.8	15.5	13.5	16.2	17.4	20.9	19.8
LAIA	3.6	2.8	2.9	2.5	2.8	2.2	2.9	3.5	4.1	3.9
CACM	0.3	0.2	0.2	0.2	0.2	0.2	0.2	0.2	x0.3	x0.2
Asia	13.0	11.8	x12.5	x13.7	11.7	11.8	x15.8	16.4	x19.3	16.6
Middle East	4.1	x3.7	x2.8	x2.6	x2.1	x2.1	x3.5	x3.5	x3.4	x2.2
Europe	53.0	58.8	60.2	58.6	58.2	53.0	61.0	60.3	52.8	47.0
EEC	42.7	47.5	48.3	47.1	47.1	48.5	56.4	55.9	48.3	43.1
EFTA	9.4	10.5	10.9	10.6	10.3	3.8	4.0	3.6	3.8	3.3
Oceania	2.0	x1.9	x1.9	x1.8	x1.9	x1.6	x1.8	x1.8	x2.0	x1.8
Germany/Allemagne	10.3	11.3	11.2	10.2	9.9	10.4	13.8	15.0	13.0	11.6
USA/Etats–Unis d'Amer	12.3	11.8	9.8	9.7	8.6	7.7	9.4	9.9	12.3	11.9
France,Monac	7.0	8.1	8.4	8.4	8.1	7.9	8.9	8.6	7.1	6.5
United Kingdom	5.1	5.0	5.3	5.8	5.8	5.6	5.6	5.3	4.8	4.2
Italy/Italie	4.2	4.3	4.5	4.1	4.3	4.6	5.5	5.2	4.7	4.2
Belgium–Luxembourg	3.5	4.1	4.0	4.0	3.9	4.0	4.9	5.0	4.2	3.8
Netherlands/Pays–Bas	3.8	4.9	4.9	4.7	4.4	4.3	5.0	4.9	4.1	3.5
Canada	2.7	2.5	2.4	2.8	3.1	2.8	3.2	3.1	3.7	3.3
Switz.Liecht	2.5	2.9	3.1	2.8	2.8	2.9	2.9	2.7	2.7	2.5
Austria/Autriche	1.8	2.0	2.0	2.0	2.0	2.2	2.6	2.6	2.7	2.4

	1985	1986	1987	1988	1989	1990	1991	1992	1993	1994
Afrique	0.1	0.2	0.2	x0.2	x0.2	0.2	0.3	0.4	0.4	x0.2
Afrique du Nord	0.0	0.0	0.0	0.1	0.1	0.1	0.1	0.1	0.2	0.1
Amériques	16.7	12.9	11.8	12.8	11.8	13.0	13.5	14.2	16.1	16.5
ALAI	1.2	0.8	0.9	1.0	1.2	1.1	1.2	1.8	2.5	2.5
MCAC	0.0	0.0	0.0	0.0	0.0	0.0	0.0	0.0	x0.0	x0.0
Asie	12.4	12.5	x14.1	x16.0	15.9	16.6	17.6	18.9	21.2	22.0
Moyen–Orient	0.6	x0.2	x0.3	0.4	x0.3	0.3	0.2	0.2	x0.2	x0.2
Europe	65.6	68.7	68.5	66.2	68.5	68.8	67.5	64.8	60.2	59.0
CEE	55.3	57.8	58.0	56.5	58.3	64.3	63.4	60.6	56.6	55.6
AELE	9.5	10.2	9.9	9.1	9.6	3.8	3.4	3.2	2.7	2.6
Océanie	0.3	x0.2	x0.2	x0.3	x0.3	x0.3	0.3	x0.4	x0.4	x0.5
Germany/Allemagne	17.5	19.7	19.8	18.5	19.1	20.4	20.7	19.1	17.1	16.5
Japan/Japon	9.7	10.4	10.6	11.9	12.1	12.6	13.1	13.6	14.6	14.8
USA/Etats–Unis d'Amer	11.8	8.7	8.3	8.6	7.9	9.0	9.5	9.9	10.4	10.6
France,Monac	7.0	6.8	6.9	6.6	7.0	7.6	7.2	7.2	6.7	6.8
United Kingdom	6.1	5.8	5.9	6.2	6.4	7.1	6.9	6.4	6.4	6.7
Italy/Italie	6.6	6.0	5.8	5.6	6.0	6.4	6.4	5.9	5.5	6.1
Belgium–Luxembourg	4.3	4.9	4.7	4.6	4.8	5.6	5.5	5.2	5.2	5.4
Austria/Autriche	4.7	4.8	4.5	4.2	4.3	5.0	4.7	4.7	4.2	x3.5
Netherlands/Pays–Bas	3.0	3.6	3.9	3.9	3.7	4.2	4.2	4.2	3.4	3.2
Denmark/Danemark	1.6	1.6	1.8	2.1	2.4	3.1	3.1	3.2	2.6	2.2

TRADE BY COMMODITY IN THOUSAND U.S. DOLLARS – COMMERCE PAR PRODUIT EN MILLIERS DE DOLLARS E.U

COUNTRIES–PAYS	IMPORTS – IMPORTATIONS				
	1990	1991	1992	1993	1994
Total	9397104	9635472	10592398	10123100	11903698
Africa	x172968	193906	x216551	x214356	x221452
Northern Africa	85336	103570	113079	117787	116462
Americas	1706126	1807809	2050674	2412057	2973994
LAIA	174738	255613	391944	530558	612962
CACM	19389	18656	25759	x26528	x27890
Asia	1641040	1918832	2122298	2381055	2974784
Middle East	x233627	x275445	x352416	x333572	x268665
Europe	5625625	5495779	5884225	4760227	5307604
EEC	5198644	5112145	5478719	4420556	4941542
EFTA	344432	330014	323463	274871	297116
Oceania	x157083	x135307	x139576	x147059	x173033
Germany/Allemagne	1057306	1115674	1319525	966694	1098850
USA/Etats–Unis d'Amer	864549	863831	941450	1090488	1472515
France, Monac	871471	838700	888919	768592	842845
United Kingdom	768867	720964	732157	638350	647863
Canada	588847	621099	648556	724015	819878
Italy/Italie	612135	599169	584955	506751	581070
Netherlands/Pays–Bas	501502	459003	490028	375427	451540
Japan/Japon	448152	464198	429224	422531	532565
Belgium–Luxembourg	330436	322630	355376	282000	307517
Spain/Espagne	272588	290811	288702	198916	247479
China/Chine	156930	220968	253461	287461	393412
Korea, Republic of	205917	248366	230714	269544	401333
Hong Kong	184371	194515	234198	290270	363743
Switz.Liecht	233179	216526	211114	195296	213431
Sweden/Suède	230634	214645	213534	161608	190451
Austria/Autriche	166476	167727	186251	186289	196782
Mexico/Mexique	53911	91452	182124	236254	266166
Singapore/Singapour	105705	127230	141621	184538	271106
Malaysia/Malaisie	42983	90678	160374	182234	287883
Denmark/Danemark	115263	116144	126217	108795	128391
Thailand/Thaïlande	64351	93182	99672	132869	166839
Saudi Arabia	70652	98194	99035	x86638	x86887
Norway, SVD, JM	105011	105404	102538	74261	78506
Australia/Australie	103781	83764	90437	95639	105404
Portugal	61438	70905	77987	62787	62603
Greece/Grèce	55533	60103	76441	66324	58947
Ireland/Irlande	73422	65475	72035	53304	65939
Brazil/Brésil	43953	54370	61222	74892	93183
Iran (Islamic Rp. of)	x33368	x51074	x94276	x43689	x15891
Turkey/Turquie	37665	44940	54582	84042	39423
Finland/Finlande	81573	70196	66592	44718	61264
Poland/Pologne	2985	9878	84706	83820	114081
Indonesia/Indonésie	42855	54045	41017	70158	58107
Israel/Israël	29969	36600	45811	47177	46336
New Zealand	42490	42481	39961	43492	56099
Hungary/Hongrie	x28367	33159	x45457	x44301	x38310
India/Inde	50965	34417	45582	37494	66827
Chile/Chili	18505	22315	33727	50592	50422
Argentina/Argentine	7720	16401	31925	57777	76160
Algeria/Algérie	22856	24910	37038	43733	37847
United Arab Emirates	36623	27849	31251	x41893	x44476
So. Africa Customs Un	31995	31476	34865	34218	44493
Egypt/Egypte	25668	33926	30968	34225	30070
Russian Federation			x55665	x22355	x35500
Venezuela	12702	18458	22834	28415	19973
Slovenia/Slovénia			32904	31243	38140
Morocco/Maroc	19018	22648	21994	18769	25383
Peru/Pérou	10203	15587	17368	24180	30808
Philippines	25580	17489	18112	18195	28217
Colombia/Colombie	8389	9053	16985	27428	33822

COUNTRIES–PAYS	EXPORTS – EXPORTATIONS				
	1990	1991	1992	1993	1994
Totale	9287696	9646100	10590787	10488034	12324317
Afrique	52527	46482	50362	52056	x10320
Afrique du Nord	5268	6895	3674	2693	4915
Amériques	1557120	1733683	1973398	2253256	2549101
ALAI	143011	198951	317576	365407	428995
MCAC	590	753	873	x1448	x1520
Asie	1597278	1829716	2009003	2210752	2966008
Moyen–Orient	115869	110280	112421	97204	122882
Europe	5880038	5754471	6194747	5598550	6417504
CEE	5720974	5611929	6027792	5452983	6248044
AELE	115437	119829	146008	127637	144002
Océanie	x74420	x73457	x89682	x90755	103809
Germany/Allemagne	1528900	1490959	1536126	1312752	1533679
USA/Etats–Unis d'Amer	1153917	1273757	1369074	1541880	1717384
Japan/Japon	961388	1110851	1204230	1280784	1755454
Belgium–Luxembourg	1263292	1137462	1202344	1110637	1275569
France, Monac	729575	733050	780336	773090	846607
Italy/Italie	649992	651621	688174	649123	739088
United Kingdom	436573	453908	503851	423176	525359
Netherlands/Pays–Bas	346856	351268	374789	355017	385223
Canada	259003	259611	284533	343936	399378
Spain/Espagne	175924	189396	239016	211328	274118
Sweden/Suède	177569	201604	214895	175204	196135
Mexico/Mexique	78956	119168	216601	244109	303594
Hong Kong	129967	135143	161602	212687	272931
Finland/Finlande	148134	144721	166189	173362	191155
China/Chine	135837	173559	157084	149568	202097
Singapore/Singapour	64112	70283	100523	149544	182158
Denmark/Danemark	78412	83703	120956	110794	117710
Switz.Liecht	79003	86149	100616	97697	102219
Korea, Republic of	92879	97741	92583	90281	101470
Austria/Autriche	88170	85793	98040	92051	x82996
Thailand/Thaïlande	21899	44939	91352	112655	131602
Turkey/Turquie	84370	84357	85620	64280	88753
Australia/Australie	58042	61720	77925	78197	88024
Hungary/Hongrie	x30418	x45566	x85023	x71739	x62923
Czechoslovakia		x90860	x103052		
Ireland/Irlande	64950	64112	79785	48379	53764
Poland/Pologne	31889	34598	53578	46303	50385
Brazil/Brésil	29277	34186	45594	54416	57779
So. Africa Customs Un	42899	36640	42565	42877	
Czech Republic				118937	116667
Norway, SVD, JM	36434	33679	45392	29940	41783
Indonesia/Indonésie	33776	31734	30656	46166	55587
Malaysia/Malaisie	21661	22381	23769	35095	65670
Romania/Roumanie	17833	15278	27040	22542	22899
Philippines	10067	21174	19966	18987	22521
Venezuela	4743	12471	18747	28069	31359
Argentina/Argentine	16598	17841	17732	21871	16801
Portugal	25303	20439	20691	13847	23689
Russian Federation			x16373	x27367	x20894
Saudi Arabia	12459	16952	12775	x5995	x4959
New Zealand	15267	11593	11674	12374	15600
Colombia/Colombie	8865	9477	11089	11225	12821
Slovenia/Slovénia			13043	13587	20022
Kuwait/Koweït	6626	1119	8339	16521	20032
Yugoslavia SFR	43490	x22601			
India/Inde	4555	4840	5713	10736	22559
Slovakia				x20584	x19935
Israel/Israël	4121	5670	5831	5030	29247
Former USSR/Anc. URSS	13554	x14453			
Ukraine			x2746	x7993	x6472

(VALUE AS % OF TOTAL)(VALEUR EN % DU TOTAL)

	1985	1986	1987	1988	1989	1990	1991	1992	1993	1994
Africa	3.4	3.3	x2.2	x2.3	x1.8	x1.8	2.0	x2.0	x2.1	x1.9
Northern Africa	2.0	1.8	1.1	1.2	1.1	0.9	1.1	1.1	1.2	1.0
Americas	24.2	19.6	17.7	18.5	x19.3	18.2	18.8	19.3	23.8	25.0
LAIA	2.6	1.9	1.9	1.7	1.7	1.9	2.7	3.7	5.2	5.1
CACM	0.3	0.3	0.3	0.2	0.2	0.2	0.2	0.2	x0.3	x0.2
Asia	16.0	15.1	x16.8	x18.9	18.1	17.5	19.9	20.1	23.5	25.0
Middle East	3.0	x3.5	x2.8	x2.2	x2.0	x2.5	x2.9	x3.3	x3.3	x2.3
Europe	53.1	59.0	59.9	57.0	57.7	59.9	57.0	55.6	47.0	44.6
EEC	44.0	48.8	49.7	48.1	48.9	55.3	53.1	51.7	43.7	41.5
EFTA	8.2	9.5	9.4	8.1	7.9	3.7	3.4	3.1	2.7	2.5
Oceania	2.5	x2.1	x1.9	x1.7	x1.9	x1.7	x1.4	x1.3	x1.5	x1.5
Germany/Allemagne	8.9	10.1	9.6	8.9	9.1	11.3	11.6	12.5	9.5	9.2
USA/Etats–Unis d'Amer	15.0	12.5	11.3	9.9	9.8	9.2	9.0	8.9	10.8	12.4
France, Monac	7.5	8.7	8.5	7.6	8.3	9.3	8.7	8.4	7.6	7.1
United Kingdom	6.9	6.7	7.7	7.9	7.5	8.2	7.5	6.9	6.3	5.4
Canada	5.7	4.3	3.5	6.3	6.7	6.3	6.4	6.1	7.2	6.9
Italy/Italie	4.6	5.3	5.4	5.9	5.8	6.5	6.2	5.5	5.0	4.9
Netherlands/Pays–Bas	4.5	5.0	5.1	4.9	4.9	5.3	4.8	4.6	3.7	3.8
Japan/Japon	3.3	3.1	2.9	3.7	4.5	4.8	4.8	4.1	4.2	4.5
Belgium–Luxembourg	2.5	2.9	3.0	3.4	3.4	3.5	3.3	3.4	2.8	2.6
Spain/Espagne	1.4	1.6	2.0	2.1	2.5	2.9	3.0	2.7	2.0	2.1

	1985	1986	1987	1988	1989	1990	1991	1992	1993	1994
Afrique	0.6	x0.6	0.6	0.5	x0.6	0.6	0.5	0.5	0.5	x0.1
Afrique du Nord	0.0	0.0	0.1	0.1	0.1	0.1	0.1	0.0	0.0	0.0
Amériques	15.8	x15.6	x14.1	14.0	15.0	16.8	18.0	18.6	21.5	20.7
ALAI	3.3	2.1	2.3	2.2	2.0	1.5	2.1	3.0	3.5	3.5
MCAC	0.0	0.0	0.0	0.0	0.0	0.0	0.0	0.0	x0.0	x0.0
Asie	17.7	15.1	x15.8	x19.1	17.7	17.2	19.0	18.9	21.1	24.1
Moyen–Orient	1.4	1.1	1.2	1.3	1.1	1.2	1.1	1.1	0.9	1.0
Europe	62.5	65.3	62.5	59.5	63.5	63.3	59.7	58.5	53.4	52.1
CEE	56.9	59.6	56.4	54.0	57.9	61.6	58.2	56.9	52.0	50.7
AELE	5.4	5.4	5.6	5.1	5.1	1.2	1.2	1.4	1.2	1.2
Océanie	0.5	x0.5	x0.4	x0.5	x0.5	x0.8	x0.8	x0.8	x0.9	0.8
Germany/Allemagne	15.2	16.8	15.1	15.0	15.1	16.5	15.5	14.5	12.5	12.4
USA/Etats–Unis d'Amer	12.5	9.4	8.4	8.7	10.3	12.4	13.2	12.9	14.7	13.9
Japan/Japon	11.7	10.3	9.1	10.9	10.1	10.4	11.5	11.4	12.2	14.2
Belgium–Luxembourg	11.8	12.8	12.6	11.7	12.8	13.6	11.8	11.4	10.6	10.4
France, Monac	7.5	7.2	6.9	6.8	6.8	7.9	7.6	7.4	7.4	6.9
Italy/Italie	6.5	6.7	6.5	6.0	6.3	7.0	6.8	6.5	6.2	6.0
United Kingdom	5.4	4.8	4.1	3.6	5.5	4.7	4.7	4.8	4.0	4.3
Netherlands/Pays–Bas	3.2	3.8	3.6	3.3	3.7	3.7	3.6	3.5	3.4	3.1
Canada		x4.1	x3.5	3.0	2.8	2.8	2.7	2.7	3.3	3.2
Spain/Espagne	1.4	1.6	1.5	1.9	1.8	1.9	2.0	2.3	2.0	2.2

TRADE BY COMMODITY IN THOUSAND U.S. DOLLARS – COMMERCE PAR PRODUIT EN MILLIERS DE DOLLARS E.U

COUNTRIES–PAYS	IMPORTS – IMPORTATIONS				
	1990	1991	1992	1993	1994
Total	6918779	7291988	7788217	7244489	8028803
Africa	x221680	x216712	x211629	x211784	x208757
Northern Africa	77793	59668	x66119	x70674	x80215
Americas	1494357	1565189	1731361	x1735088	x1944658
LAIA	137903	185795	242261	262737	322421
CACM	35169	41446	53483	x62421	x55578
Asia	x1077753	x1127835	1349027	x1441094	x1557209
Middle East	x258061	x278274	x353468	x360522	x309503
Europe	3852068	4088225	4252451	3596779	4028275
EEC	3508598	3771662	3902652	3257721	3650235
EFTA	291563	283855	288865	286388	324913
Oceania	x141848	x133194	x152025	x138381	x160912
USA/Etats–Unis d'Amer	967181	973811	1058556	1073796	1210582
Germany/Allemagne	729170	913032	877419	686634	735319
France,Monac	703183	696031	711964	646632	708911
Italy/Italie	373370	396957	418681	314934	372018
United Kingdom	379299	369334	388484	332268	384752
Belgium–Luxembourg	269134	293402	333651	316312	346928
Netherlands/Pays–Bas	271991	285701	294675	222037	293216
Canada	243071	262323	271844	253949	268525
Switz.Liecht	243025	237450	237164	239562	274027
Japan/Japon	261677	252931	228447	224430	291153
Spain/Espagne	214720	243452	261034	184675	230586
Hong Kong	134918	162550	240302	235731	241753
Singapore/Singapour	111958	122769	142563	168435	205034
Austria/Autriche	119607	130113	143364	137467	158900
Sweden/Suède	137103	128781	138731	111799	118626
Australia/Australie	104621	99768	112260	105095	118863
Korea, Republic of	89700	87521	90956	108528	143569
Mexico/Mexique	48255	63384	95976	103538	112133
Greece/Grèce	75368	76855	91309	88891	86294
Saudi Arabia	70865	70485	89782	x87489	x84530
Denmark/Danemark	78304	81555	80037	67787	71004
Portugal	63260	67263	78901	67836	59115
United Arab Emirates	44068	46063	69540	x95874	x77221
Iran (Islamic Rp. of)	x49268	x62532	x66722	x53266	x12983
So. Africa Customs Un	48892	56683	54145	52936	48099
Ireland/Irlande	50051	52397	50453	50601	49978
Israel/Israël	39434	43506	53430	51926	73511
Malaysia/Malaisie	38415	37515	52334	53310	58254
Poland/Pologne	9878	60810	34227	32439	35434
Norway,SVD,JM	42828	40250	45565	41615	45414
China/Chine	12235	17319	43391	63178	64148
Thailand/Thaïlande	26329	29516	44067	35550	45835
Finland/Finlande	44037	36788	33951	29850	34586
Afghanistan	x30818	x30664	x22676	x36504	x12060
Hungary/Hongrie	x17288	14651	x26926	x40961	x38454
Argentina/Argentine	2508	17435	31029	30238	37588
Brazil/Brésil	39038	30930	18756	28958	.52955
Chile/Chili	19170	19427	26638	29836	22735
New Zealand	28414	24767	25754	22814	30375
Turkey/Turquie	14381	20238	20055	22637	17558
Former USSR/Anc. URSS	65911	x61558			
Venezuela	7380	15738	24349	17974	10799
Oman	10144	15637	15473	20242	23305
Slovenia/Slovénia			28498	22676	22826
Indonesia/Indonésie	14713	14853	14756	21013	25640
Russian Federation			x17954	x32605	x44299
Philippines	13936	13466	14971	19854	22579
Lebanon/Liban	x11966	x20716	x13759	x13063	x21761
Jordan/Jordanie	10785	12043	17032	14625	20054
Algeria/Algérie	11613	16552	9615	16516	14571

COUNTRIES–PAYS	EXPORTS – EXPORTATIONS				
	1990	1991	1992	1993	1994
Totale	6517956	7146071	7507839	7229593	8123359
Afrique	27182	39809	30770	42284	27281
Afrique du Nord	9586	14770	15064	19487	25743
Amériques	716449	797150	875319	903250	1010903
ALAI	244802	278787	305951	314046	325151
MCAC	16729	21766	26916	x33537	x38830
Asie	669049	801722	962203	998776	1089908
Moyen–Orient	133240	127898	148070	135400	146288
Europe	4845984	4918500	5194997	4736752	5352531
CEE	4625172	4702619	4922773	4479500	5052640
AELE	160944	161913	170220	172150	214230
Océanie	x14378	x14651	x15198	x16695	x21670
France,Monac	1384574	1403105	1489811	1394457	1542642
Germany/Allemagne	1014263	999635	1058225	937421	1022621
Italy/Italie	673838	677494	663735	597814	691503
USA/Etats–Unis d'Amer	380489	433098	481100	486426	532476
Austria/Autriche	349104	343991	399507	351217	x504393
United Kingdom	287519	329528	296741	262646	282033
Belgium–Luxembourg	259655	231533	277489	320559	313511
Mexico/Mexique	162377	195058	207830	186856	188386
Japan/Japon	145967	182406	194928	204429	207104
Netherlands/Pays–Bas	178796	200428	217185	122032	87017
Spain/Espagne	134472	161376	159569	169215	221568
Czechoslovakia		x240601	x244440		
Switz.Liecht	152316	149298	155982	160639	197958
Poland/Pologne	85135	228418	92940	99521	131216
Portugal	113012	128356	140912	138915	158933
China/Chine	67336	91740	119798	126016	173737
Turkey/Turquie	109043	103597	117153	114612	117901
Hong Kong	64593	81524	117194	132840	139711
Indonesia/Indonésie	68037	92827	107339	112587	101309
Czech Republic				301908	350226
Singapore/Singapour	64732	77478	102559	109320	116645
Ireland/Irlande	87737	95967	82662	72944	89480
Sweden/Suède	85775	79394	73533	66176	83715
Canada	59673	46198	48937	56531	97832
Brazil/Brésil	27924	36226	46743	67132	50584
Korea, Republic of	37582	44525	50535	49085	57190
Hungary/Hongrie	x52045	x51007	x50623	x42009	x37356
Malaysia/Malaisie	30601	37517	47200	51170	60391
Thailand/Thaïlande	29885	38717	39985	42481	43196
Denmark/Danemark	39375	36459	45925	31388	34624
Romania/Roumanie	34490	35411	32405	36955	46943
Slovenia/Slovénia			43068	46262	48983
Croatia/Croatie			42840	31495	x32644
India/Inde	15184	17117	25449	26335	34400
Yugoslavia SFR	59699	x53745			
Argentina/Argentine	31474	18289	13661	18890	21309
Guatemala	4614	10222	15127	22422	26641
Colombia/Colombie	5656	12401	18921	13919	13240
Slovakia				x39357	x40588
Norway,SVD,JM	8625	12614	14233	11510	16272
Saudi Arabia	4979	17473	14147	x3880	x7306
Australia/Australie	11360	11700	11405	11968	17121
So. Africa Customs Un	8073	11448	9886	13689	
Venezuela	9122	9496	10218	14827	33024
Costa Rica	12011	11479	11735	x10629	x11902
Bulgaria/Bulgarie	x38417	x12741	x8499	x9517	x13663
Finland/Finlande	12861	10892	9907	7822	10699
Egypt/Egypte	5192	11594	8345	8324	17140
Trinidad and Tobago	6118	7080	8951	8889	11374
Kuwait/ Koweït	6875	379	9645	11155	11401

(VALUE AS % OF TOTAL)(VALEUR EN % DU TOTAL)

	1985	1986	1987	1988	1989	1990	1991	1992	1993	1994
Africa	3.9	x3.7	x3.5	x3.3	x2.7	x3.2	x3.0	x2.7	x2.9	x2.6
Northern Africa	1.9	1.2	x1.1	x1.0	x0.9	1.1	0.8	x0.8	x1.0	x1.0
Americas	29.3	x27.0	x24.4	x22.8	22.9	21.6	21.5	22.2	x23.9	x24.2
LAIA	1.4	1.3	1.5	1.2	1.8	2.0	2.5	3.1	3.6	4.0
CACM	1.0	0.7	0.5	0.6	0.5	0.5	0.6	0.7	x0.9	x0.7
Asia	12.8	x13.7	x14.3	x16.0	x16.0	x15.6	x15.5	17.3	x19.9	x19.4
Middle East	4.6	x4.9	x4.2	x4.4	x4.0	x3.7	x3.8	x4.5	x5.0	x3.9
Europe	49.1	51.2	52.7	52.7	53.6	55.7	56.1	54.6	49.6	50.2
EEC	41.9	43.1	44.6	44.8	45.4	50.7	51.7	50.1	45.0	45.5
EFTA	7.0	7.7	7.8	7.6	7.7	4.2	3.9	3.7	4.0	4.0
Oceania	3.0	x2.5	x2.1	x2.3	x2.5	x2.0	x1.8	x2.0	x1.9	x2.0
USA/Etats–Unis d'Amer	20.6	18.9	16.8	16.1	15.5	14.0	13.4	13.6	14.8	15.1
Germany/Allemagne	7.7	8.1	8.6	8.5	8.5	10.5	12.5	11.3	9.5	9.2
France,Monac	7.1	7.5	7.9	8.2	8.8	10.2	9.5	9.1	8.9	8.8
Italy/Italie	4.3	4.5	5.0	4.9	5.1	5.4	5.4	5.4	4.3	4.6
United Kingdom	7.7	6.4	5.5	6.1	5.8	5.5	5.1	5.0	4.6	4.8
Belgium–Luxembourg	3.4	3.7	3.6	3.5	3.4	3.9	4.0	4.3	4.4	4.3
Netherlands/Pays–Bas	3.9	4.3	4.3	3.9	3.6	3.9	3.9	3.8	3.1	3.7
Canada	5.1	4.0	3.4	3.3	3.5	3.5	3.6	3.5	3.5	3.3
Switz.Liecht	2.6	3.1	3.2	3.2	3.1	3.5	3.3	3.0	3.3	3.4
Japan/Japon	2.1	2.2	2.8	3.2	3.7	3.8	3.5	2.9	3.1	3.6

	1985	1986	1987	1988	1989	1990	1991	1992	1993	1994
Afrique	0.2	0.2	0.4	0.5	0.5	0.4	0.6	0.4	0.6	0.3
Afrique du Nord	0.0	0.1	0.0	0.2	0.3	0.1	0.2	0.2	0.3	0.3
Amériques	10.7	x9.1	8.9	7.7	9.4	11.0	11.1	11.7	12.5	12.5
ALAI	2.6	2.0	2.6	2.5	3.2	3.8	3.9	4.1	4.3	4.0
MCAC	0.5	0.5	0.4	0.4	0.3	0.3	0.3	0.4	x0.5	x0.5
Asie	8.2	8.2	x10.5	x11.6	9.4	10.3	11.2	12.8	13.8	13.4
Moyen–Orient	1.7	1.8	1.6	1.7	1.8	2.0	1.8	2.0	1.9	1.8
Europe	75.7	77.7	70.6	71.0	74.0	74.3	68.8	69.2	65.5	65.9
CEE	66.5	67.6	61.4	62.7	65.1	71.0	65.8	65.6	62.0	62.2
AELE	8.0	9.1	8.4	7.6	8.1	2.5	2.3	2.3	2.4	2.6
Océanie	0.3	x0.3	0.2	0.2	0.2	x0.2	x0.2	x0.2	x0.2	x0.3
France,Monac	20.8	19.6	18.3	18.3	19.4	21.2	19.6	19.8	19.3	19.0
Germany/Allemagne	14.3	15.9	14.3	15.3	14.9	15.6	14.0	14.1	13.0	12.6
Italy/Italie	8.8	9.1	7.9	8.2	9.2	10.3	9.5	8.8	8.3	8.5
USA/Etats–Unis d'Amer	5.3	4.0	3.6	3.6	4.5	5.8	6.1	6.4	6.7	6.6
Austria/Autriche	4.8	5.5	5.1	4.5	4.7	5.4	4.8	5.3	4.9	x6.2
United Kingdom	4.9	4.6	4.2	4.3	4.0	4.4	4.6	4.0	3.6	3.5
Belgium–Luxembourg	3.2	3.2	3.3	3.4	3.5	4.0	3.2	3.7	4.4	3.9
Mexico/Mexique	1.7	1.0	1.5	1.7	2.1	2.5	2.7	2.8	2.6	2.3
Japan/Japon	3.0	2.9	2.5	2.3	2.4	2.2	2.6	2.6	2.8	2.5
Netherlands/Pays–Bas	2.1	2.4	2.2	2.3	2.5	2.7	2.8	2.9	1.7	1.1

TRADE BY COMMODITY IN THOUSAND U.S. DOLLARS – COMMERCE PAR PRODUIT EN MILLIERS DE DOLLARS E.U

COUNTRIES–PAYS	IMPORTS – IMPORTATIONS 1990	1991	1992	1993	1994
Total	4751489	4978067	5343221	5062080	5482260
Africa	x36021	x45347	x57652	x51646	x55876
Northern Africa	5174	7532	x12721	x10340	x13642
Americas	x1556269	1605476	x1783426	x1848978	x2014669
LAIA	44038	62282	83545	105910	122100
CACM	2522	3136	5036	x6134	x7532
Asia	695100	762825	907993	x956204	x1044482
Middle East	x97567	x102715	x156697	x139910	x137848
Europe	2225113	2403381	2458659	2053782	2196739
EEC	2023094	2217532	2276863	1888432	2024725
EFTA	165665	169060	163516	146319	152204
Oceania	x120129	x119373	x120450	x112166	x124172
USA/Etats–Unis d'Amer	1318524	1339858	1508909	1548691	1686546
Germany/Allemagne	418950	505891	485764	426769	441042
Hong Kong	239724	317731	416708	440623	474011
Italy/Italie	304015	344887	362909	273583	253798
France, Monac	290044	295051	310432	256854	296970
United Kingdom	223961	226394	232743	204265	278080
Japan/Japon	208266	196877	187787	193982	257044
Netherlands/Pays–Bas	171456	166717	173547	183706	168029
Canada	155219	166511	154665	152404	158026
Spain/Espagne	108357	156959	184116	104366	124576
Belgium–Luxembourg	137953	143925	142349	118520	129771
Switz.Liecht	110609	111092	103073	95288	98037
Sweden/Suède	113415	105142	103039	80919	88758
Australia/Australie	97018	94378	97853	88524	99410
Austria/Autriche	87019	86973	85638	77926	83122
Singapore/Singapour	54967	49434	51484	63857	56259
Norway, SVD, JM	52390	54357	56832	48302	51231
Portugal	34228	46956	54844	44734	33197
Denmark/Danemark	43868	45875	45775	37563	43701
United Arab Emirates	21381	32571	44829	x38616	x27892
Greece/Grèce	30647	33716	38639	39069	37175
Mexico/Mexique	27347	32611	34525	40897	51455
Ireland/Irlande	33775	37482	38300	26397	29366
Saudi Arabia	24134	18874	33439	x38270	x41957
Korea, Republic of	35967	35125	24700	26902	35106
Israel/Israël	20058	18757	24689	26897	30899
So. Africa Customs Un	15216	18536	23929	20192	12158
Iran (Islamic Rp. of)	x4813	x13232	x27896	x16758	x5500
Finland/Finlande	25406	21564	18768	13762	17140
New Zealand	17393	19738	16442	17348	19083
Russian Federation			x23123	x26736	x24859
Argentina/Argentine	1880	6874	17880	23556	21456
Malaysia/Malaisie	13663	12659	14627	12175	13165
Chile/Chili	4065	6163	9708	11615	12936
Cyprus/Chypre	8100	7648	11490	7907	8536
Lebanon/Liban	x8428	x9634	x8021	x7958	x24501
Venezuela	3996	5992	8721	9249	5480
Bulgaria/Bulgarie	x1005	x1113	875	20469	27020
China/Chine	2670	2415	8876	10496	9709
Poland/Pologne	1988	18440	938	1169	2618
Afghanistan	x5395	x3968	x5332	x9110	x2720
Bahamas	4244	3750	x6907	x7513	x2818
Turkey/Turquie	10519	4917	5240	7076	4519
Kuwait/ Koweït	5153	2027	7564	6000	7813
Former USSR/Anc. URSS	93950	x15509			
Morocco/Maroc	2301	4029	5681	5356	4762
Oman	4220	4886	5258	4910	5165
Nigeria/Nigéria	x1709	6394	x4353	x3966	x4001
Bahrain/Bahreïn	x4629	x4570	x4542	x5563	x4266
Malta/Malte	3915	4721	4831	3814	x3002

COUNTRIES–PAYS	EXPORTS – EXPORTATIONS 1990	1991	1992	1993	1994
Totale	4162541	4500222	4818218	4481752	5163886
Afrique	8519	10806	12674	13764	x17555
Afrique du Nord	6383	8047	9902	9916	12989
Amériques	159961	205095	229276	231987	234870
ALAI	63432	93819	99000	96214	97983
MCAC	194	171	248	484	x1533
Asie	1513768	1738776	1982628	1931082	2344649
Moyen–Orient	12678	7525	10284	x11037	x14035
Europe	2372012	2380926	2432160	2135118	2365054
CEE	2333284	2351002	2397295	2103754	2334084
AELE	20443	18701	19252	17477	19031
Océanie	x4436	x6616	x4243	x3673	x6912
China/Chine	406977	523721	594719	562803	981656
Germany/Allemagne	556260	578023	573753	482732	437105
United Kingdom	516784	527215	525052	453558	532369
Japan/Japon	529160	525338	503548	418762	329304
Hong Kong	273752	357710	495157	528588	557256
Italy/Italie	348756	318303	327235	303294	374183
Portugal	225129	244848	266481	230906	282587
France, Monac	184939	185623	206422	175584	201154
Belgium–Luxembourg	115009	127462	119903	99260	109257
USA/Etats–Unis d'Amer	86671	101950	118773	124701	120962
Thailand/Thaïlande	68124	87565	111364	146016	172206
Netherlands/Pays–Bas	102328	106741	113156	121471	150341
Spain/Espagne	123888	120288	112339	107010	118494
Denmark/Danemark	72890	60732	64718	58097	53654
Poland/Pologne	24441	81361	46858	54028	64526
Korea, Republic of	102594	79857	55838	39723	34410
Malaysia/Malaisie	35190	43792	50794	57897	64685
Indonesia/Indonésie	17726	26631	56066	44065	53062
Brazil/Brésil	32202	38217	40034	46366	42634
Philippines	25676	33118	40107	47564	51451
Hungary/Hongrie	x31021	x25779	x36689	x32741	x32627
Mexico/Mexique	10073	14116	40839	30532	36040
Sri Lanka	9060	16984	24060	27035	29609
Czechoslovakia		x27757	x34802		
Austria/Autriche	21659	19642	21102	18928	x17921
Sweden/Suède	23304	20627	20636	17012	21106
Greece/Grèce	15580	18744	23709	14666	13179
Singapore/Singapour	17217	19630	16130	15750	13265
Bulgaria/Bulgarie	x6601	x1943	23233	20803	26844
Colombia/Colombie	6643	30543	6193	7940	7990
Romania/Roumanie	12764	12399	13597	17099	22425
Ireland/Irlande	15253	13483	14578	14932	16229
Viet Nam	x3589	x8454	x12666	x21585	x30346
Czech Republic				39513	46805
Switz.Liecht	13924	12885	12934	12405	12646
Canada	8599	8139	9528	9726	12468
Finland/Finlande	11432	9196	8212	6304	6504
Norway, SVD, JM	6505	5811	6312	5071	6384
Tunisia/Tunisie	4036	3566	6387	5841	7285
Turkey/Turquie	6171	4266	6522	4738	6523
Bangladesh		3029	4798	5708	x9172
Australia/Australie	3309	5352	3465	2704	5694
Yugoslavia SFR	18228	x11065			
Uruguay	2528	3082	3355	3460	2841
Slovenia/Slovénia			5137	4421	3106
Croatia/Croatie			5015	4527	x5091
Russian Federation			x4190	x3451	x2933
Peru/Pérou	1707	2181	2721	2549	2956
Morocco/Maroc	1259	1947	2391	2895	3299
Chile/Chili	7320	2353	3025	1791	1992

(VALUE AS % OF TOTAL)(VALEUR EN % DU TOTAL)

	1985	1986	1987	1988	1989	1990	1991	1992	1993	1994
Africa	0.9	x0.6	x0.8	x0.9	x0.8	x0.7	x0.9	x1.0	x1.0	x1.0
Northern Africa	0.3	0.1	x0.1	x0.1	0.2	0.1	0.2	x0.2	x0.2	x0.2
Americas	49.0	x43.4	x40.8	x38.1	36.2	x32.7	32.3	x33.3	x36.5	x36.7
LAIA	0.3	0.3	0.3	0.5	0.8	0.9	1.3	1.6	2.1	2.2
CACM	0.1	0.1	0.1	0.1	0.1	0.1	0.1	0.1	x0.1	x0.1
Asia	8.0	x9.8	9.6	11.3	12.5	14.6	15.3	17.0	x18.9	x19.1
Middle East	2.0	x2.3	x2.0	1.8	x1.7	x2.1	x2.1	x2.9	x2.8	x2.5
Europe	36.8	41.5	44.4	45.1	45.7	46.8	48.3	46.0	40.6	40.1
EEC	29.5	33.2	35.7	37.0	37.6	42.6	44.5	42.6	37.3	36.9
EFTA	6.9	7.8	8.2	7.5	7.3	3.5	3.4	3.1	2.9	2.8
Oceania	3.3	x2.4	x2.1	x2.4	x2.6	x2.5	x2.4	x2.2	x2.2	x2.3
USA/Etats–Unis d'Amer	42.9	37.2	35.7	33.2	31.0	27.7	26.9	28.2	30.6	30.8
Germany/Allemagne	6.2	6.6	7.4	7.6	7.5	8.8	10.2	9.1	8.4	8.0
Hong Kong	2.7	3.1	3.6	4.2	4.8	5.0	6.4	7.8	8.7	8.6
Italy/Italie	4.2	4.3	4.9	5.4	5.4	6.4	6.9	6.8	5.4	4.6
France, Monac	4.4	5.2	5.3	5.5	5.5	6.1	5.9	5.8	5.1	5.4
United Kingdom	3.5	4.3	4.3	4.8	5.0	4.7	4.5	4.4	4.0	5.1
Japan/Japon	1.4	1.7	2.0	2.6	3.4	4.4	4.0	3.5	3.8	4.7
Netherlands/Pays–Bas	2.4	2.9	3.0	2.9	2.9	3.6	3.3	3.2	3.6	3.1
Canada	5.1	4.9	3.8	3.6	3.7	3.3	3.3	2.9	3.0	2.9
Spain/Espagne	0.8	1.1	1.3	1.6	2.1	2.3	3.2	3.4	2.1	2.3

	1985	1986	1987	1988	1989	1990	1991	1992	1993	1994
Afrique	0.1	0.1	x0.2	0.1	0.3	0.2	0.2	0.2	0.3	x0.3
Afrique du Nord	0.0	0.0	0.1	0.1	0.2	0.2	0.2	0.2	0.2	0.3
Amériques	3.2	2.8	2.5	3.0	3.8	3.9	4.5	4.8	5.2	4.6
ALAI	1.6	1.3	1.1	1.3	1.7	1.5	2.1	2.1	2.1	1.9
MCAC	0.0	0.0	0.0	0.0	0.0	0.0	0.0	0.0	0.0	x0.0
Asie	40.2	37.9	x44.7	x43.8	37.1	36.3	38.6	41.2	43.1	45.4
Moyen–Orient	1.4	0.4	x0.4	0.3	x0.3	0.3	0.2	0.2	x0.2	x0.3
Europe	54.6	57.2	45.0	45.6	54.3	57.0	52.9	50.5	47.6	45.8
CEE	52.0	54.5	42.8	43.6	52.1	56.1	52.2	49.8	46.9	45.2
AELE	2.1	2.2	1.9	1.7	1.8	0.5	0.4	0.4	0.4	0.4
Océanie	0.1	x0.1	0.1	x0.1	x0.1	x0.1	x0.1	x0.1	x0.1	x0.1
China/Chine	5.0	6.0	5.0	5.7	7.9	9.8	11.6	12.3	12.6	19.0
Germany/Allemagne	13.9	15.4	11.6	11.4	13.0	13.4	12.8	11.9	10.8	8.5
United Kingdom	12.8	11.4	8.7	9.6	11.5	12.4	11.7	10.9	10.1	10.3
Japan/Japon	25.4	22.3	14.4	12.7	14.4	12.7	11.7	10.5	9.3	6.4
Hong Kong	3.4	4.0	4.0	4.7	6.5	6.6	7.9	10.3	11.8	10.8
Italy/Italie	8.3	9.2	7.3	6.8	8.1	8.4	7.1	6.8	6.8	7.2
Portugal	2.7	3.2	3.1	3.3	4.4	5.4	5.4	5.5	5.2	5.5
France, Monac	3.9	4.0	3.0	3.1	4.0	4.4	4.1	4.3	3.9	3.9
Belgium–Luxembourg	2.0	2.2	2.0	2.1	2.5	2.8	2.8	2.5	2.2	2.1
USA/Etats–Unis d'Amer	1.6	1.3	1.2	1.6	2.0	2.1	2.3	2.5	2.8	2.3

TRADE BY COMMODITY IN THOUSAND U.S. DOLLARS – COMMERCE PAR PRODUIT EN MILLIERS DE DOLLARS E.U

COUNTRIES–PAYS	IMPORTS – IMPORTATIONS 1990	1991	1992	1993	1994
Total	33797649	32361169	32320226	36552123	38319153
Africa	x186324	129983	x127378	x428528	x487083
Northern Africa	15463	6858	6100	3491	5733
Americas	x4838245	x4842978	x5003885	x5952707	x6670298
LAIA	8161	6658	9978	14491	24084
CACM	203	253	106	x233	x524
Asia	12231061	12101856	12168108	13521355	14215952
Middle East	x102356	x140329	x143504	x248001	x212924
Europe	16398058	15149138	14886149	16533734	16815107
EEC	13281670	12387034	12068232	13711152	14316618
EFTA	3108017	2753891	2812755	2813941	2493633
Oceania	x135051	x132520	x120953	x104199	x123511
Belgium–Luxembourg	7894721	7499700	7426616	8320666	9004683
USA/Etats–Unis d'Amer	4630832	4639121	4803853	5762359	6448865
United Kingdom	3743991	3484838	3263730	4079005	3994884
Israel/Israël	3096747	2738825	3124238	3578259	4152397
Switz.Liecht	3103052	2748909	2808160	2809614	2488683
Japan/Japon	3378660	2821075	2438765	2635735	3058062
India/Inde	2059442	1967199	2732814	2635784	1633441
Hong Kong	1936281	2026380	2364299	2767129	3338577
Thailand/Thaïlande	1090685	1826033	622035	799324	883189
Germany/Allemagne	577361	565160	524396	457091	472850
France, Monac	477232	363771	394738	452985	383353
Singapore/Singapour	149436	226542	216729	186740	261106
Italy/Italie	239303	220231	214557	191624	217162
China/Chine	175107	99875	217373	255034	260378
So. Africa Customs Un	137994	94727	81197	374677	432617
Canada	191201	173469	171694	155229	181737
Malaysia/Malaisie	95703	112853	140617	133823	170904
Australia/Australie	121517	118725	107965	90048	105064
Sri Lanka	74310	70451	78932	124698	133477
Netherlands/Pays–Bas	151889	94836	103406	44656	52753
Portugal	73165	58592	51536	66329	86216
Bahrain/Bahreïn	x34308	x46363	x65767	x34279	x16218
Korea, Republic of	52967	47129	42514	52474	57840
United Arab Emirates	20081	23682	38076	x79253	x84367
Spain/Espagne	49364	43316	33898	37765	31996
Saudi Arabia	3612	3233	4362	x96159	x57289
Lebanon/Liban	x34913	x53840	x21909	x19681	x38218
Mauritius/Maurice	24036	24335	22536	30474	27466
Austria/Autriche	30346	19862	24997	27338	34300
Korea Dem People's Rp	x6160	x9134	x24095	x37965	x24700
Niger		x8			
Sweden/Suède	23325	16974	12936	14463	18638
Viet Nam	x7116	x12678	x12106	x14403	x13571
Bermuda/Bermudes	x5525	x17849	x12393	x8772	x100
New Zealand	12249	10176	11752	12377	15874
Ukraine			x88	x30372	x22966
Cyprus/Chypre	4285	9398	10066	10426	x12317
Georgia/Géorgie				x29495	
Denmark/Danemark	7158	8067	8673	8153	6538
Mexico/Mexique	3624	3972	8002	11566	14198
Brunei Darussalam	10	36	x8123	x13389	x5268
Finland/Finlande	9149	7296	4520	4194	5417
Tunisia/Tunisie	14167	6316	4691	2583	4801
Norway,SVD,JM	4780	4857	4390	4173	4828
Sierra Leone	x2873	x80	x3865	x4924	x807
Greece/Grèce	2705	2603	1600	4037	4954
Russian Federation			x1351	x6833	x19321
Lithuania/Lituanie			4966	x2961	0
Czechoslovakia	505	x273	x7608		
Malta/Malte	5281	4580	2797	353	x1829

COUNTRIES–PAYS	EXPORTS – EXPORTATIONS 1990	1991	1992	1993	1994
Totale	27576685	27190697	29176888	31918042	37113375
Afrique	x739006	x847934	x3104827	x4383616	x4323473
Afrique du Nord	18284	6707	3854	2941	4249
Amériques	2108091	2061611	1964776	2511573	x2914457
ALAI	245290	273192	262804	532642	561993
MCAC		640		x128	x899
Asie	9278327	8757183	9646114	10888535	12713109
Moyen–Orient	x86098	x75421	x65197	x120080	x95327
Europe	15163417	14484438	14136670	13739283	16744264
CEE	12135313	11850586	11608058	10920136	14378963
AELE	3023818	2628843	2527026	2812926	2355348
Océanie	x271042	x355874	x320736	x353983	x381894
Belgium–Luxembourg	7653433	7646962	7711464	8510219	9369771
Israel/Israël	3573280	3395177	3730032	4113847	4967557
India/Inde	2710044	2460479	3119648	3667587	4060449
United Kingdom	3574261	3378355	3004832	1603068	4272160
Switz.Liecht	3022946	2628576	2526704	2812634	2355055
USA/Etats–Unis d'Amer	1802031	1740559	1637204	1850762	2189286
So. Africa Customs Un	7890	6054	2082489	2914002	2703961
Hong Kong	1237993	1157258	1056581	1167106	1350352
Thailand/Thaïlande	879378	940126	843715	949135	1059928
Russian Federation			x683201	x741305	x869480
Germany/Allemagne	397884	365429	389720	330869	318415
Colombia/Colombie	112917	144496	180061	404090	426705
Australia/Australie	197958	261018	235603	231774	259050
Congo	x93705	x143524	x268633	x274627	x234873
Former USSR/Anc. URSS		x676577			
France, Monac	206293	171731	194546	207954	165003
Japan/Japon	175473	171972	196254	196963	234918
Zaire/Zaïre	x139626	x221548	x119182	x162114	x167294
Sri Lanka	162431	121599	161134	209507	225996
China/Chine	208289	139031	175668	149669	385727
Liberia/Libéria	x65510	x74604	x128108	x184922	x321650
Cote d'Ivoire	x108817	x107092	x118147	x108608	x72997
Singapore/Singapour	90702	133425	99769	70274	66198
French Polynesia	x68302	x85203	x79463	x119087	x111239
Brazil/Brésil	117250	107111	61706	103775	106369
Central African Rep.	x70011	x81081	x91435	x99133	x54336
Malaysia/Malaisie	72637	77840	83349	81612	90971
Ghana	x119399	1932	1997	x227715	x332277
Portugal	79390	85996	71257	72109	81835
Sierra Leone	13013	x65289	x83423	x50098	x104268
Guinea/Guinée	x39869	x38381	x49459	x97272	x82484
Netherlands/Pays–Bas	118838	80522	71593	25998	19206
Ireland/Irlande	9226	20719	73556	70765	70811
Sweden/Suède	58877	54887	43565	39586	36673
Mali		x47345	x50248	x37060	x14362
Bahrain/Bahreïn	x34842	x41885	x43994	x45699	x15015
Angola				x122529	x107230
Canada	55051	34386	51328	35746	41050
Austria/Autriche	23162	29460	30997	30933	x22967
Myanmar	12859	8047	17381	x62134	x60783
Mauritius/Maurice	24913	26490	22476	27803	25468
Gambia/Gambie	x2		x44600	x28505	x15301
Korea, Republic of	29778	26236	24987	21358	18201
Lebanon/Liban	x24145	x30095	x12109	x24942	x38166
Bermuda/Bermudes			x249	x63475	x29
Venezuela	13102	19720	18883	19790	23832
Indonesia/Indonésie	14083	16065	24208	18053	20903
Zambia/Zambie	x11335	x17420	x13429	x20254	x17873
Korea Dem People's Rp	x6663	x13489	x13996	x19844	x8697
Italy/Italie	9179	11985	11555	23354	16239

(VALUE AS % OF TOTAL)(VALEUR EN % DU TOTAL)

	1985	1986	1987	1988	1989	1990	1991	1992	1993	1994
Africa	0.4	x0.6	0.5	0.6	0.6	x0.5	0.4	x0.4	x1.1	x1.2
Northern Africa	0.1	0.1	0.1	0.1	0.1	0.0	0.0	0.0	0.0	0.0
Americas	26.3	x22.7	x18.6	x17.9	x16.5	x14.3	x15.0	x15.5	x16.3	x17.4
LAIA	0.1	0.0	0.0	0.0	0.0	0.0	0.0	0.0	0.0	0.1
CACM	0.0	0.0	0.0	x0.0	0.0	0.0	0.0	0.0	x0.0	x0.0
Asia	26.2	28.7	32.9	34.6	36.0	36.2	37.4	37.6	37.0	37.1
Middle East	0.1	x0.2	x0.4	x0.2	x0.3	x0.3	x0.4	x0.4	x0.7	x0.6
Europe	46.8	47.8	47.6	46.5	46.5	48.5	46.8	46.0	45.2	43.9
EEC	37.8	38.2	37.9	37.5	37.4	39.3	38.3	37.3	37.5	37.4
EFTA	9.0	9.5	9.6	9.0	9.0	9.2	8.5	8.7	7.7	6.5
Oceania	0.3	x0.3	x0.3	x0.3	x0.4	x0.4	x0.4	x0.4	x0.3	x0.3
Belgium–Luxembourg	19.6	20.3	21.1	20.4	22.3	23.4	23.2	22.9	22.8	23.5
USA/Etats–Unis d'Amer	25.2	21.8	17.9	17.2	15.7	13.7	14.3	14.8	15.8	16.8
United Kingdom	12.6	13.5	12.1	12.8	10.5	11.1	10.8	10.1	11.2	10.4
Israel/Israël	9.0	9.4	9.5	9.9	9.3	9.2	8.5	9.7	9.8	10.8
Switz.Liecht	8.7	9.3	9.4	8.8	8.9	9.2	8.5	8.7	7.7	6.5
Japan/Japon	5.2	6.5	8.2	9.2	9.0	10.0	8.7	7.5	7.2	8.0
India/Inde	6.3	6.2	6.9	7.5	8.1	6.1	6.1	8.4	7.2	4.3
Hong Kong	4.3	5.0	5.5	5.8	5.8	5.7	6.3	7.3	7.6	8.7
Thailand/Thaïlande	0.6	0.8	1.2	1.0	2.2	3.2	5.6	1.9	2.2	2.3
Germany/Allemagne	1.6	1.7	1.8	1.5	1.7	1.7	1.7	1.6	1.3	1.2

	1985	1986	1987	1988	1989	1990	1991	1992	1993	1994
Afrique	8.9	x10.9	x9.9	x9.2	x3.4	x2.7	x3.1	x10.6	x13.7	x11.7
Afrique du Nord	0.0	0.0	0.0	0.0	0.1	0.1	0.0	0.0	0.0	0.0
Amériques	6.4	x6.8	x8.3	x6.7	x7.7	7.6	7.6	6.7	7.9	x7.8
ALAI	0.5	0.6	0.7	0.7	0.8	0.9	1.0	0.9	1.7	1.5
MCAC	0.0	x0.0	x0.0	x0.0	x0.0	0.0	0.0	0.0	x0.0	x0.0
Asie	28.2	28.1	26.1	28.2	31.1	33.7	32.2	33.1	34.1	34.2
Moyen–Orient	0.0	x0.4	x0.4	x0.2	x0.4	x0.3	x0.3	x0.2	x0.4	x0.3
Europe	55.9	53.6	47.0	48.2	52.3	55.0	53.3	48.5	43.0	45.1
CEE	45.4	43.6	38.2	39.4	42.5	44.0	43.6	39.8	34.2	38.7
AELE	10.5	10.0	8.7	8.8	9.7	11.0	9.7	8.7	8.8	6.3
Océanie	0.5	x0.4	x0.6	0.6	x0.9	x1.0	x1.3	x1.1	x1.1	x1.0
Belgium–Luxembourg	27.1	24.9	22.3	23.3	26.9	27.8	28.1	26.4	26.7	25.2
Israel/Israël	12.3	11.9	10.7	10.9	11.6	13.0	12.5	12.8	12.9	13.4
India/Inde	9.8	9.8	8.9	10.9	11.2	9.8	9.0	10.7	11.5	10.9
United Kingdom	14.2	15.4	13.1	13.5	12.7	13.0	12.4	10.3	5.0	11.5
Switz.Liecht	10.1	9.7	8.5	8.5	9.5	11.0	9.7	8.7	8.8	6.3
USA/Etats–Unis d'Amer	5.6	5.6	5.0	5.4	5.7	6.5	6.4	5.6	5.8	5.9
So. Africa Customs Un	8.4	8.1	6.9	6.0	0.0	0.0	0.0	7.1	9.1	7.3
Hong Kong	2.5	2.2	2.0	2.5	3.4	4.5	4.3	3.6	3.7	3.6
Thailand/Thaïlande	2.0	2.0	2.1	2.0	2.4	3.2	3.5	2.9	3.0	2.9
Russian Federation								x2.3	x2.3	x2.3

TRADE BY COMMODITY IN THOUSAND U.S. DOLLARS – COMMERCE PAR PRODUIT EN MILLIERS DE DOLLARS E.U

IMPORTS – IMPORTATIONS

COUNTRIES–PAYS	1990	1991	1992	1993	1994
Total	8237560	7706413	6946870	7178850	8912763
Africa	91772	187393	x71878	66001	323020
Northern Africa	69046	118122	48361	47427	75630
Americas	1458348	1393784	1342909	1455403	1842751
LAIA	184386	145682	134690	142119	212764
CACM	921	1629	993	1334	1919
Asia	2658792	2741994	2253826	2721455	2695696
Middle East	x188609	x223821	x233449	x234420	x203751
Europe	3730046	3252531	3168067	2746428	3836373
EEC	3634672	3197698	3092589	2681864	3773683
EFTA	50331	45522	43903	35934	40338
Oceania	x40589	x37369	x40033	x52157	x62700
Japan/Japon	1457423	1551642	1054560	1198614	1258936
USA/Etats–Unis d'Amer	1127528	1096185	1061559	1155263	1453066
Germany/Allemagne	981973	911867	847306	615599	946389
Italy/Italie	586388	514160	537195	459071	678334
Korea, Republic of	366843	400891	447021	592464	692359
France,Monac	588033	528830	483746	312250	439037
United Kingdom	336007	276463	280318	309082	400047
Belgium–Luxembourg	294393	271798	285253	235222	320151
Spain/Espagne	268033	253452	218869	189546	290764
Canada	135878	143246	137111	153861	169241
Sweden/Suède	188421	136971	138236	132666	195835
Turkey/Turquie	107274	110572	127809	156704	154797
Finland/Finlande	145538	113950	133784	131391	183507
Bangladesh		97131	98783	105908	x5680
Netherlands/Pays–Bas	65171	53325	47673	194061	179671
Indonesia/Indonésie	81375	76144	88330	102425	115142
China/Chine	202197	57743	33853	165059	78221
India/Inde	121671	93006	75070	39690	81410
Iran (Islamic Rp. of)	x54301	x74306	x67679	x46443	x17297
Mexico/Mexique	56828	51976	62281	72383	124103
Austria/Autriche	93234	63343	59174	54978	79969
Malaysia/Malaisie	43800	46074	63950	64826	84190
Hong Kong	51250	65126	37722	36866	23844
Thailand/Thaïlande	35291	28573	45391	50390	68324
Egypt/Egypte	34297	50053	30636	28845	62480
Australia/Australie	32638	29476	34285	45475	55558
Korea Dem People's Rp	x40909	x33866	x26652	x46434	x14250
Switz.Liecht	42029	32822	33984	27555	28006
Poland/Pologne	87519	34068	27872	32209	35555
Singapore/Singapour	25911	33664	23189	33929	23357
Brazil/Brésil	30359	36998	25524	18197	25971
Denmark/Danemark	29865	28383	23705	21518	27322
Romania/Roumanie	69374	15757	22686	26288	31722
Czech Republic				63719	71947
Saudi Arabia	7870	24676	19735	x18759	x18094
Pacific Isld (Tr Terr.)	x43	x43			
Libyan Arab Jamahiriya	22890	54823	x2556	x4064	x4428
Venezuela	69317	26936	16000	14453	13782
Portugal	21985	18918	20925	13447	17924
Nigeria/Nigéria	x1498	47026	x1156	x1684	x757
Pakistan	21405	16750	12111	18558	15650
Greece/Grèce	30022	21783	12740	10418	11817
Hungary/Hongrie	x23660	28951	x7013	x5944	x5384
Philippines	15048	11817	7190	21142	21463
So. Africa Customs Un	16806	12864	14884	12086	244826
Argentina/Argentine	9317	12417	11721	11123	14440
Colombia/Colombie	10932	10090	10877	9693	12107
Norway,SVD,JM	8224	12439	9840	8329	12288
Slovenia/Slovénia			18359	12249	15564
Algeria/Algérie	7522	8687	6472	11093	4540

EXPORTS – EXPORTATIONS

COUNTRIES–PAYS	1990	1991	1992	1993	1994
Totale	7056473	x6011279	4762243	4785844	6626580
Afrique	251443	215873	231834	202760	x952324
Afrique du Nord	51187	44373	40081	31725	30202
Amériques	1678846	1470124	1258192	1322285	x1555017
ALAI	1120506	970365	935754	888711	1044203
MCAC	9	39	28	33	x100
Asie	766394	890447	x1003745	1106514	1553165
Moyen–Orient	67545	x91419	58621	50749	61133
Europe	2630852	2240215	1902056	1714036	2012727
CEE	1796847	1546687	1390361	1190983	1448626
AELE	669789	585779	403645	405064	470992
Océanie	319194	294391	261609	264296	x344189
Brazil/Brésil	800160	673339	671981	625664	735558
China/Chine	342297	440027	413983	496865	758112
Norway,SVD,JM	625580	553066	372686	367819	429225
Russian Federation			x540044	x738301	x989774
France,Monac	480146	425296	370352	291898	354254
Germany/Allemagne	432254	331861	316891	246331	230671
Ukraine			x133669	x646985	x348667
Former USSR/Anc. URSS	1284139	x772803			
New Caledonia	268809	254206	215458	212389	x280329
Sweden/Suède	202068	193434	203540	172108	223297
USA/Etats–Unis d'Amer	152764	158619	180482	165251	182894
United Kingdom	185225	171748	150584	108005	122159
Dominican Republic	249050	220812	x28803	133750	x153484
Colombia/Colombie	160732	143490	126632	102010	118859
India/Inde	42399	72678	99931	171226	188646
Zimbabwe	154415	115427	116634	102083	x113715
Belgium–Luxembourg	144064	110082	85254	90569	148216
Kazakstan			x163450	x102962	x72223
Canada	131935	87403	82916	94195	109164
Austria/Autriche	119118	100566	90096	73049	x92218
Venezuela	65055	74020	75335	104819	114614
Japan/Japon	49508	52053	82321	96336	253726
Malaysia/Malaisie	98675	69879	71761	78482	97905
Italy/Italie	90819	83840	78108	57115	55400
So. Africa Customs Un	44595	54808	74036	64264	806340
Turkey/Turquie	66141	71697	51306	50081	60666
Finland/Finlande	51176	59607	51996	38560	52086
Hong Kong	53286	71870	39414	38607	28584
Australia/Australie	48064	40021	45697	51092	63390
Mexico/Mexique	50102	45432	36816	36378	33465
Czechoslovakia		x61080	x54819		
Yugoslavia SFR	164216	x107749			
Spain/Espagne	60564	50408	33238	23660	48710
Indonesia/Indonésie	48511	38983	39082	29047	34681
Netherlands/Pays–Bas	8099	7326	3668	84288	103827
Iceland/Islande	41626	30285	28842	34895	38525
Poland/Pologne	77869	32077	25970	26414	25369
Yugoslavia/Yougoslavie			x39404	x39343	x5444
Albania/Albanie	x8709	x18949	x13861	x45345	x12273
Latvia/Lettonie			x5062	67296	8
Slovakia				x65073	x92868
Algeria/Algérie	33971	28957	15321	14815	13843
Chile/Chili	26474	23541	16978	14659	28484
Korea Dem People's Rp	x13613	x25707	x17863	x10345	x11997
Egypt/Egypte	17195	15376	22574	14650	16357
Croatia/Croatie			40056	12362	x25708
Dominica/Dominique		x16439	x14733	x16912	x42045
Trinidad and Tobago	24154	16438	13724	15097	22714
Slovenia/Slovénia			28360	16329	19927
Philippines	33637	12881	5023	10615	10867

(VALUE AS % OF TOTAL)(VALEUR EN % DU TOTAL)

Imports

	1985	1986	1987	1988	1989	1990	1991	1992	1993	1994
Africa	1.3	x1.2	x0.9	0.8	0.9	1.1	2.5	x1.0	1.0	3.6
Northern Africa	0.9	0.5	0.4	0.5	0.6	0.8	1.5	0.7	0.7	0.8
Americas	16.7	17.6	15.7	17.7	16.8	17.7	18.1	19.2	20.2	20.7
LAIA	1.6	1.2	1.5	1.4	1.8	2.2	1.9	1.9	2.0	2.4
CACM	0.0	0.0	x0.0	0.0	0.0	0.0	0.0	0.0	0.0	0.0
Asia	21.1	21.9	x27.0	x30.1	28.7	32.3	35.6	32.1	37.9	30.3
Middle East	2.4	x1.9	x2.1	x1.5	x2.0	x2.3	x2.9	x3.3	x3.3	x2.3
Europe	54.4	52.9	47.8	46.7	50.2	45.3	42.2	45.2	38.3	43.0
EEC	47.7	46.7	41.8	41.0	44.2	44.1	41.5	44.1	37.4	42.3
EFTA	6.1	5.6	5.6	5.4	5.6	0.6	0.6	0.6	0.5	0.5
Oceania	0.6	x0.6	x0.6	0.5	x0.6	x0.5	x0.5	x0.5	x0.7	x0.7
Japan/Japon	14.0	14.1	13.6	18.1	16.7	17.7	20.1	15.0	16.7	14.1
USA/Etats–Unis d'Amer	13.1	14.3	12.1	14.4	12.7	13.7	14.2	15.1	16.1	16.3
Germany/Allemagne	15.7	14.4	12.3	12.6	13.7	11.9	11.8	12.1	8.6	10.6
Italy/Italie	6.2	6.9	6.1	6.2	6.7	7.1	6.7	7.7	6.4	7.6
Korea, Republic of	1.0	1.8	2.4	2.6	4.3	4.5	5.2	6.4	8.3	7.8
France,Monac	9.6	8.2	7.0	5.8	6.8	7.1	6.9	6.9	4.3	4.9
United Kingdom	4.6	4.7	4.6	4.3	4.3	4.1	3.6	4.0	4.3	4.5
Belgium–Luxembourg	3.0	3.1	2.8	3.1	3.5	3.6	3.5	4.1	3.3	3.6
Spain/Espagne	1.8	2.8	2.5	2.5	2.5	3.3	3.3	3.1	2.6	3.3
Canada	1.8	1.9	1.9	1.8	1.9	1.6	1.9	2.0	2.1	1.9

Exports

	1985	1986	1987	1988	1989	1990	1991	1992	1993	1994
Afrique	13.3	13.3	x13.9	x5.6	x3.9	3.5	3.6	4.9	4.2	x14.4
Afrique du Nord	0.2	0.2	0.2	0.3	0.3	0.7	0.7	0.8	0.7	0.5
Amériques	23.1	16.7	15.2	20.7	23.3	23.8	24.5	26.4	27.6	x23.5
ALAI	15.3	11.5	10.2	12.8	14.1	15.9	16.1	19.6	18.6	15.8
MCAC	0.0	0.0	0.0	x0.0	x0.0	0.0	0.0	0.0	0.0	x0.0
Asie	7.1	6.4	9.1	14.3	8.6	10.9	14.8	x21.0	23.1	23.5
Moyen–Orient	0.8	0.8	0.8	1.1	x0.9	1.0	x1.5	1.2	1.1	0.9
Europe	44.4	42.9	39.9	37.9	41.4	37.3	37.3	39.9	35.8	30.4
CEE	28.7	28.4	25.5	21.8	25.4	25.5	25.7	29.2	24.9	21.9
AELE	13.7	13.0	12.7	13.3	13.9	9.5	9.7	8.5	8.5	7.1
Océanie	0.3	x2.9	2.8	4.5	5.7	4.5	4.9	5.5	5.6	x5.2
Brazil/Brésil	11.1	9.1	7.5	9.1	9.7	11.3	11.2	14.1	13.1	11.1
China/Chine			4.1	8.2	3.0	4.9	7.3	8.7	10.4	11.4
Norway,SVD,JM	7.8	7.1	7.1	7.3	7.9	8.9	9.2	7.8	7.7	6.5
Russian Federation								x11.3	x15.4	x14.9
France,Monac	7.3	8.6	7.5	4.9	6.2	6.8	7.1	7.8	6.1	5.3
Germany/Allemagne	6.4	5.7	5.7	5.2	5.4	6.1	5.5	6.7	5.1	3.5
Ukraine								x2.8	x13.5	x5.3
Former USSR/Anc. URSS	11.7	17.5	17.3	14.9	15.3	18.2	x12.9			
New Caledonia		x2.3	2.1	4.0	5.2	3.8	4.2	4.5	4.4	x4.2
Sweden/Suède	3.0	2.8	2.7	2.5	2.7	2.9	3.2	4.3	3.6	3.4

TRADE BY COMMODITY IN THOUSAND U.S. DOLLARS – COMMERCE PAR PRODUIT EN MILLIERS DE DOLLARS E.U

COUNTRIES–PAYS	IMPORTS – IMPORTATIONS 1990	1991	1992	1993	1994
Total	18483636	18594323	17708453	19608746	22278199
Africa	415256	425546	x362425	x417768	x460411
Northern Africa	301287	240479	243770	280008	340966
Americas	2294506	2353088	2672609	3165722	5533760
LAIA	353443	638668	717201	562429	825695
CACM	54089	48900	86984	x74552	x61600
Asia	x6354184	7269587	6600875	9948126	8163491
Middle East	x1330149	x1048348	x983462	x1291824	x710317
Europe	9243587	8291684	7924007	5804339	7781624
EEC	8785771	8057545	7629836	5544915	7514403
EFTA	272206	218708	232163	193375	218518
Oceania	x91381	x157311	x79049	x100358	x91709
USA/Etats–Unis d'Amer	1636010	1486925	1669964	2205993	3962810
Italy/Italie	1964746	1638331	1776122	1189203	1684255
Germany/Allemagne	1789700	1911376	1663046	980436	1365759
China/Chine	104181	69497	779436	3481362	1648777
Korea, Republic of	1331318	1850655	1170962	1134215	1614089
Japan/Japon	1358230	1781765	1078762	1034460	894547
France,Monac	1283559	1134029	1100247	907388	1303925
Thailand/Thaïlande	732344	827457	949037	907485	1164390
Belgium–Luxembourg	1206392	1110594	818179	663495	935574
United Kingdom	750527	603025	678037	676560	569860
Malaysia/Malaisie	300174	408777	400096	546820	544324
Iran (Islamic Rp. of)	x898967	x621114	x489382	x239334	x34217
Turkey/Turquie	224321	292212	309576	730701	424612
Spain/Espagne	394894	404185	482700	303974	382252
Philippines	228634	291907	367038	446979	439679
Mexico/Mexique	167722	358349	375282	297023	468005
Indonesia/Indonésie	315290	326800	209000	372358	382747
Greece/Grèce	462086	357025	228571	142198	160332
Netherlands/Pays–Bas	227707	220302	203987	187183	275067
Singapore/Singapour	171191	222231	155637	215935	155199
India/Inde	235874	141483	242186	209806	311162
Canada	221203	138168	156126	284708	639806
Argentina/Argentine	31824	105350	212330	98368	163705
Israel/Israël	136466	174598	119771	120746	129666
Sweden/Suède	154556	140652	130074	130662	340930
Portugal	159048	131203	156947	109552	158387
Austria/Autriche	155440	136765	153049	86930	119102
Finland/Finlande	132326	163542	108819	78059	94386
Morocco/Maroc	134618	131830	101846	104966	124597
Norway,SVD,JM	139803	112528	115051	98382	101844
Switz.Liecht	130758	104957	116278	94414	116072
Australia/Australie	75980	149528	72105	92484	85724
Denmark/Danemark	95146	96671	117950	78425	111991
Saudi Arabia	94620	9905	20165	x199809	x156811
Jordan/Jordanie	53546	61697	77265	64219	58878
Hong Kong	36932	37837	49319	115223	100531
Egypt/Egypte	59908	59772	54604	63883	x98459
Ecuador/Equateur	66545	83111	24899	63837	x57691
Kenya	62493	62399	42211	62877	x64078
Nigeria/Nigéria	x8651	79210	x27743	x20512	x14138
Guatemala	20809	25332	46692	41254	30650
Chile/Chili	24313	30795	35926	28543	30535
Romania/Roumanie	54145	18195	28981	42466	75117
Algeria/Algérie	2673	9738	25957	53504	44502
Korea Dem People's Rp	x11568	x35396	x35865	x14454	x3804
United Arab Emirates	1096	34827	33957	x16808	x8977
Colombia/Colombie	8704	12821	27581	45004	69331
Hungary/Hongrie	x2336	53614	x11863	x18676	x13461
Libyan Arab Jamahiriya	78798	14013	x33073	x33343	x47248
Tunisia/Tunisie	25121	24970	27350	23667	26080

COUNTRIES–PAYS	EXPORTS – EXPORTATIONS 1990	1991	1992	1993	1994
Totale	17355691	18509170	16858932	17617881	19043802
Afrique	497493	491687	x536256	x509991	x814172
Afrique du Nord	11226	7044	x58388	x88028	x104144
Amériques	2703076	3713936	2950473	3049557	2883176
ALAI	1638344	2107796	2021917	2233234	2171591
MCAC	94	78	85	x677	1170
Asie	2831645	3003591	3301348	4029378	4046509
Moyen–Orient	385425	302023	482588	x630732	x756201
Europe	9965967	9171313	8614324	8698161	9628031
CEE	9878664	9089396	8552896	8651994	9597741
AELE	13668	21978	26906	27325	17686
Océanie	x360727	x407938	418990	x502303	x609999
Germany/Allemagne	2538692	2327505	2225848	2198209	2325156
Belgium–Luxembourg	2498212	2244854	1896286	1703486	2171138
Brazil/Brésil	1302762	1734243	1652469	1743235	1566927
France,Monac	1479478	1386294	1320434	1380240	1507781
Japan/Japon	1087595	1103737	1013556	1477003	1553225
Korea, Republic of	923612	1097126	1177902	1246374	1119027
Russian Federation			x964567	x1997653	x2144019
United Kingdom	980682	925089	882930	832794	903576
Italy/Italie	576105	466540	502936	855307	662406
Netherlands/Pays–Bas	696753	529510	578563	667642	861140
USA/Etats–Unis d'Amer	571551	949186	431021	323296	305177
Canada	482049	654590	489630	475154	398790
So. Africa Customs Un	428748	426610	431967	388560	696548
Turkey/Turquie	383267	299309	450440	491594	599750
Australia/Australie	309885	311908	335373	427830	532543
Finland/Finlande	311079	414779	334873	244861	231570
Sweden/Suède	291000	332248	342153	295453	373849
Poland/Pologne	298457	372765	352522	238287	304662
Ukraine			x82461	x833544	x584946
Former USSR/Anc. URSS		x753937			
Spain/Espagne	167261	222413	248654	275825	321238
Mexico/Mexique	133876	124970	168696	275949	336233
Czechoslovakia		x232384	x306623		
China/Chine	128849	205226	204472	63434	197110
Bulgaria/Bulgarie	x503296	x202732	x140397	x120871	x174975
Venezuela	120030	99225	143343	175108	252812
Korea Dem People's Rp	x129099	x85049	x112545	x184785	x71563
Hungary/Hongrie	x178886	x116605	x148372	x79832	x103716
Indonesia/Indonésie	96897	139411	108077	78539	128582
Austria/Autriche	148112	98295	108266	117812	x154297
Greece/Grèce	183598	128622	98082	63356	73288
New Zealand	49716	95593	83458	70026	75670
India/Inde	31636	27198	61641	125192	81420
Romania/Roumanie	34	40859	88205	75184	104048
Slovakia				x170644	x226049
Iran (Islamic Rp. of)			x28821	x131616	x152374
Argentina/Argentine	53048	104644	17929	23302	7277
Czech Republic				143673	148463
Malaysia/Malaisie	6426	5519	55514	64361	16371
Singapore/Singapour	16103	28927	39023	48412	21985
Zimbabwe	46776	43565	38408	24463	x11550
Chile/Chili	26694	30157	32733	12534	7177
Libyan Arab Jamahiriya			x21721	x47625	x71864
Algeria/Algérie	7782	4989	26712	28741	29996
Yugoslavia SFR	73533	x59897			
Hong Kong	811	586	16439	41833	27934
Kazakstan			x10725	x37087	x48767
Switz.Liecht	7715	13243	13908	11588	7075
Norway,SVD,JM	5953	6833	12879	15737	10595
Republic of Moldova			x1907	x29765	858

(VALUE AS % OF TOTAL)(VALEUR EN % DU TOTAL)

	1985	1986	1987	1988	1989	1990	1991	1992	1993	1994
Africa	3.2	2.3	x1.7	1.8	x2.0	2.2	2.3	x2.0	x2.1	x2.1
Northern Africa	2.2	1.5	1.0	1.1	1.2	1.6	1.3	1.4	1.4	1.5
Americas	11.2	11.6	11.3	12.4	13.9	12.4	12.6	15.1	16.1	24.9
LAIA	3.0	3.7	3.0	3.1	2.6	1.9	3.4	4.1	2.9	3.7
CACM	0.4	0.5	0.3	0.3	0.3	0.3	0.3	0.5	x0.4	x0.3
Asia	30.2	26.7	x29.2	x31.9	32.2	x34.4	39.1	37.3	50.7	36.6
Middle East	7.4	x5.3	x6.1	x4.3	x4.1	x7.2	x5.6	x5.6	x6.6	x3.2
Europe	54.4	58.9	54.8	51.5	49.9	50.0	44.6	44.7	29.6	34.9
EEC	49.4	54.3	50.6	47.8	46.0	47.5	43.3	43.1	28.3	33.7
EFTA	2.6	2.5	2.7	2.8	3.0	1.5	1.2	1.3	1.0	1.0
Oceania	0.1	0.1	0.8	1.1	0.8	x0.5	x0.8	x0.4	x0.5	x0.4
USA/Etats–Unis d'Amer	7.2	6.3	6.4	6.2	9.0	8.9	8.0	9.4	11.3	17.8
Italy/Italie	10.0	11.7	11.1	11.4	11.8	10.6	8.8	10.0	6.1	7.6
Germany/Allemagne	9.7	10.0	10.0	9.1	8.7	9.7	10.3	9.4	5.0	6.1
China/Chine	5.2	3.9	0.8	0.3	0.3	0.6	0.4	4.4	17.8	7.4
Korea, Republic of	5.7	6.1	6.3	5.3	7.0	7.2	10.0	6.6	5.8	7.2
Japan/Japon	5.4	5.6	7.1	9.3	8.6	7.3	9.6	6.1	5.3	4.0
France,Monac	9.4	9.4	8.2	7.0	6.1	6.9	6.1	6.2	4.6	5.9
Thailand/Thaïlande	2.0	1.3	2.3	2.9	3.7	4.0	4.5	5.4	4.6	5.2
Belgium–Luxembourg	4.8	5.2	5.9	6.6	5.3	6.5	6.0	4.6	3.4	4.2
United Kingdom	5.1	5.7	5.4	4.6	3.9	4.1	3.2	3.8	3.5	2.6

	1985	1986	1987	1988	1989	1990	1991	1992	1993	1994
Afrique	1.7	x2.3	x1.7	x0.9	x2.2	2.9	2.7	x3.2	x2.9	x4.3
Afrique du Nord	0.2	0.2	0.2	0.3	0.1	0.1	0.0	x0.3	x0.5	x0.5
Amériques	8.4	7.6	6.6	10.1	18.8	15.6	20.1	17.5	17.3	15.1
ALAI	7.7	6.7	5.9	7.9	11.6	9.4	11.4	12.0	12.7	11.4
MCAC	0.0	0.0	x0.0	0.0	x0.0	0.0	0.0	0.0	x0.0	0.0
Asie	18.5	18.0	16.0	x20.2	17.3	16.3	16.3	19.6	22.9	21.3
Moyen–Orient	2.0	2.1	1.5	2.0	2.0	2.2	1.6	2.9	x3.6	x4.0
Europe	67.8	69.0	59.5	55.9	50.9	57.4	49.6	51.1	49.4	50.6
CEE	62.5	64.5	54.7	51.9	47.2	56.9	49.1	50.7	49.1	50.4
AELE	5.0	4.2	4.0	3.6	3.4	0.1	0.1	0.2	0.2	0.1
Océanie	1.8	1.3	x0.8	0.5	x0.7	x2.1	x2.2	2.5	x2.8	x3.2
Germany/Allemagne	18.4	18.5	16.6	14.3	13.1	14.6	12.6	13.2	12.5	12.2
Belgium–Luxembourg	10.1	11.5	10.0	12.4	10.1	14.4	12.1	11.2	9.7	11.4
Brazil/Brésil	5.4	4.9	5.1	7.1	10.2	7.5	9.4	9.8	9.9	8.2
France,Monac	11.5	12.1	10.2	8.4	7.5	8.5	7.5	7.8	7.8	7.9
Japan/Japon	11.7	10.7	8.1	8.9	7.6	6.3	6.0	6.0	8.4	8.2
Korea, Republic of	4.6	4.5	4.3	6.3	5.7	5.3	5.9	7.0	7.1	5.9
Russian Federation								x5.7	x11.3	x11.3
United Kingdom	4.1	5.0	5.5	5.5	5.1	5.7	5.0	5.2	4.7	4.7
Italy/Italie	4.0	4.3	2.1	1.9	2.5	3.3	2.5	3.0	4.9	3.5
Netherlands/Pays–Bas	6.2	6.5	4.9	4.3	3.6	4.0	2.9	3.4	3.8	4.5

TRADE BY COMMODITY IN THOUSAND U.S. DOLLARS – COMMERCE PAR PRODUIT EN MILLIERS DE DOLLARS E.U

COUNTRIES–PAYS	IMPORTS – IMPORTATIONS				
	1990	1991	1992	1993	1994
Total	19959746	18077059	18044012	21464515	23082395
Africa	1025093	930974	x831000	x782091	x947020
Northern Africa	708534	583646	575450	562108	725932
Americas	2407176	2341462	2627073	2995966	3572885
LAIA	311471	509717	696138	633370	712136
CACM	51857	51886	73986	75146	81305
Asia	x4844058	5151882	5015558	9504701	8887839
Middle East	x1304614	x1277261	x1201177	x1249990	x1116714
Europe	11176749	9349081	9270278	7693100	9224596
EEC	10336943	8710370	8618200	7119927	8605970
EFTA	731620	581849	533623	458114	516085
Oceania	x161030	x139045	x132144	x188517	x176185
Germany/Allemagne	3041811	2577699	2723721	2191183	2601143
China/Chine	367744	103975	572065	4543983	3432965
USA/Etats–Unis d'Amer	1536806	1316496	1440029	1783194	2168694
France,Monac	1728307	1387147	1310466	1068151	1296289
Italy/Italie	1094203	883580	897904	647455	795348
Netherlands/Pays–Bas	953587	819224	801152	653408	778332
Korea, Republic of	588712	1027424	591381	468113	702010
Thailand/Thaïlande	687257	624288	759173	697068	790290
United Kingdom	809671	667545	635129	622411	735853
Hong Kong	509509	555539	452932	891651	913466
Belgium–Luxembourg	661551	596097	603515	592594	666329
Singapore/Singapour	321615	411176	413081	491585	557119
Switz.Liecht	560503	420457	357892	323220	370905
Spain/Espagne	452007	447223	380170	222955	327122
Iran (Islamic Rp. of)	x470848	x596165	x372891	x78082	x22848
Canada	393467	349006	306551	382968	485571
Japan/Japon	356263	443136	257493	281118	200534
Mexico/Mexique	141486	260245	379907	293347	324912
Austria/Autriche	367043	302857	285920	253924	294331
Algeria/Algérie	298184	255763	313166	254047	418180
Sweden/Suède	348795	248503	243954	245310	336768
Malaysia/Malaisie	170523	226821	206470	249245	308505
Saudi Arabia	104803	184891	232512	x245463	x254986
Denmark/Danemark	256423	214251	245985	165853	226591
Portugal	193187	230337	194130	146860	191224
Turkey/Turquie	164325	184297	131326	166220	104094
Norway,SVD,JM	162139	151043	166712	127076	137591
Greece/Grèce	135512	147066	114092	160993	145923
United Arab Emirates	185788	67556	73679	x279609	x322750
Indonesia/Indonésie	152168	120723	128355	158651	205140
Israel/Israël	78150	117658	133815	152828	184598
Finland/Finlande	186456	103674	98262	89104	126931
Morocco/Maroc	53903	85276	96776	85819	72589
Egypt/Egypte	173810	91432	54466	89445	132235
Chile/Chili	39053	61041	82197	86559	59834
Ireland/Irlande	108388	85167	83800	59725	83786
Nigeria/Nigéria	105621	149030	x49813	x22788	x22013
Tunisia/Tunisie	81131	63955	73842	76480	37947
Australia/Australie	68277	60586	57830	74177	91288
Philippines	74074	58330	61674	71807	111575
Venezuela	28668	78677	63266	40512	33178
Oman	38234	54798	51799	61141	52423
India/Inde	71127	58249	54421	51201	96043
Kuwait/ Koweït	55416	7693	56052	97279	130987
Yemen/Yémen	x46838	5455	x74954	x79454	x48879
Syrian Arab Republic	41479	55667	55172	x47068	x27277
Hungary/Hongrie	x23346	65300	x41757	x48545	x44314
Colombia/Colombie	27598	21591	45031	78025	96777
Jordan/Jordanie	14389	13628	51105	78354	58326
Libyan Arab Jamahiriya	93119	79643	x29445	x31471	x42366

COUNTRIES–PAYS	EXPORTS – EXPORTATIONS				
	1990	1991	1992	1993	1994
Totale	19392186	18086213	18310459	20621858	21262200
Afrique	x417108	x432786	x542602	x552270	x348643
Afrique du Nord	28903	16449	x87581	x95559	x111487
Amériques	2062518	1975397	1990070	2320004	2361571
ALAI	907432	732784	757954	941015	883728
MCAC	9951	8771	15710	18270	20832
Asie	3593397	3620218	4087983	5588767	5068853
Moyen–Orient	1053683	938841	957267	1516533	1418863
Europe	12284369	10794428	10699471	10435902	11891731
CEE	11632441	10326430	10229395	9966038	11440266
AELE	406601	389980	386436	398594	378952
Océanie	x59334	x113634	x115749	x124876	x125353
Germany/Allemagne	2272224	2158345	2144575	1859951	2185288
Japan/Japon	1430905	1476733	1498191	2042995	1807568
Italy/Italie	1817208	1519918	1589499	1743689	1816087
France,Monac	1635984	1419206	1472459	1355641	1531227
United Kingdom	1420627	1377928	1332662	1313809	1581299
Belgium–Luxembourg	1535459	1354123	1232259	1151298	1385546
Spain/Espagne	970417	892266	814826	983779	1075072
Turkey/Turquie	739621	732718	730330	1135334	1284574
Brazil/Brésil	572521	550495	621787	713405	613846
USA/Etats–Unis d'Amer	551886	682310	549626	606525	652662
Korea, Republic of	381032	359111	669815	673962	668951
Sweden/Suède	702069	573976	575385	500921	683626
Canada	440373	411622	528572	629464	662919
Russian Federation			x143996	x1158092	x1149577
So. Africa Customs Un	358198	375694	436887	419043	225332
Poland/Pologne	359513	448293	270050	462253	436471
Netherlands/Pays–Bas	385640	345374	343527	317121	380692
Austria/Autriche	496758	359289	351592	294542	x363472
China/Chine	335249	482654	330466	104200	225951
Ukraine			x61052	x760941	x570361
Switz.Liecht	267756	257140	269109	277211	262605
Czechoslovakia		x391270	x349463		
Hong Kong	64048	68744	132394	437448	398354
Romania/Roumanie	192496	130038	181040	323761	268567
Czech Republic				621396	615323
Qatar	178994	137721	176339	203165	x19921
India/Inde	60358	92759	201133	202874	167374
Finland/Finlande	139756	118365	132469	137568	166776
Singapore/Singapour	124762	93594	133389	153847	176629
Norway,SVD,JM	138845	132840	117327	121383	116346
Trinidad and Tobago	113031	110045	130189	122345	137245
Australia/Australie	53125	96314	107787	109997	113890
Ireland/Irlande	135267	101374	95810	113005	106863
Indonesia/Indonésie	51768	67206	76997	140674	60291
Denmark/Danemark	87186	75344	88379	82631	89813
Venezuela	139842	80674	67327	93925	97076
Hungary/Hongrie	x150134	x64600	x55183	x89749	x60761
Malaysia/Malaisie	64396	33314	66947	103743	94755
Mexico/Mexique	79482	51983	32161	78347	81201
Egypt/Egypte	7151	10510	57996	69195	68731
Portugal	30605	22385	40559	73128	60136
Bulgaria/Bulgarie	x125626	x32880	x16978	x78310	x70562
Iran (Islamic Rp. of)		x305	x6343	x113030	x52772
Slovenia/Slovénia			59446	51874	65537
Saudi Arabia	105141	53786	19065	x10575	x15198
Former USSR/Anc. URSS	12908	x80465			
Yugoslavia SFR	245077	x77958			
Argentina/Argentine	107763	27683	17664	32423	52574
United Arab Emirates	21485	9996	12090	x44374	x40371
Greece/Grèce	3227	8521	15394	38955	14369

(VALUE AS % OF TOTAL)(VALEUR EN % DU TOTAL)

	1985	1986	1987	1988	1989	1990	1991	1992	1993	1994
Africa	9.1	8.0	4.6	4.3	5.4	5.2	5.2	x4.6	x3.7	x4.1
Northern Africa	8.2	6.5	3.4	3.2	4.1	3.5	3.2	3.2	2.6	3.1
Americas	22.4	x17.5	x15.9	x16.8	14.8	12.1	12.9	14.6	14.0	15.5
LAIA	2.0	1.2	1.3	1.4	1.4	1.6	2.8	3.9	3.0	3.1
CACM	0.2	0.2	0.2	0.3	0.3	0.3	0.3	0.4	0.4	0.4
Asia	19.2	x19.4	x26.7	x25.7	21.9	x24.3	28.5	27.8	44.3	38.5
Middle East	5.9	x7.1	x5.4	x5.9	x6.2	x6.5	x7.1	x6.7	x5.8	x4.8
Europe	46.7	52.9	47.6	48.6	53.8	56.0	51.7	51.4	35.8	40.0
EEC	39.4	44.7	40.1	41.5	45.8	51.8	48.2	47.8	33.2	37.3
EFTA	6.4	7.3	6.9	6.6	7.5	3.7	3.2	3.0	2.1	2.2
Oceania	1.1	x1.0	x0.9	x1.0	x1.0	x0.8	x0.7	x0.7	x0.8	x0.7
Germany/Allemagne	12.4	13.9	11.8	11.8	13.2	15.2	14.3	15.1	10.2	11.3
China/Chine	2.4	3.4	10.1	4.6	3.9	1.8	0.6	3.2	21.2	14.9
USA/Etats–Unis d'Amer	17.7	13.5	12.0	12.1	10.3	7.7	7.3	8.0	8.3	9.4
France,Monac	6.9	7.9	7.1	7.3	7.6	8.7	7.7	7.3	5.0	5.6
Italy/Italie	3.5	4.3	4.4	4.4	4.8	5.5	4.9	5.0	3.0	3.4
Netherlands/Pays–Bas	4.0	4.7	3.8	4.1	4.2	4.8	4.5	4.4	3.0	3.4
Korea, Republic of	1.7	1.3	1.5	1.8	1.5	2.9	5.7	3.3	2.2	3.0
Thailand/Thaïlande	0.9	0.7	0.8	1.5	2.1	3.4	3.5	4.2	3.2	3.4
United Kingdom	3.3	3.3	3.3	4.0	4.1	4.1	3.7	3.5	2.9	3.2
Hong Kong	3.7	3.0	2.3	2.8	2.5	2.6	3.1	2.5	4.2	4.0

	1985	1986	1987	1988	1989	1990	1991	1992	1993	1994
Afrique	1.3	2.2	x1.8	x0.3	x1.6	x2.1	x2.4	x3.0	x2.6	x1.7
Afrique du Nord	0.0	0.0	0.0	x0.1	0.1	0.1	0.1	x0.5	x0.5	x0.5
Amériques	10.9	x9.6	x8.3	8.8	9.9	10.6	10.9	10.9	11.3	11.1
ALAI	6.7	3.8	3.2	4.5	4.7	4.7	4.1	4.1	4.6	4.2
MCAC	0.0	0.0	x0.0	0.0	0.1	0.1	0.0	0.1	0.1	0.1
Asie	24.7	22.5	x19.6	x19.6	18.1	18.5	20.0	22.3	27.1	23.8
Moyen–Orient	3.1	x3.1	x3.5	x4.0	3.7	5.4	5.2	5.2	7.4	6.7
Europe	58.6	60.7	58.7	58.9	62.9	63.3	59.7	58.4	50.6	55.9
CEE	50.1	51.3	49.5	49.8	53.8	60.0	57.1	55.9	48.3	53.8
AELE	7.4	8.3	8.1	7.9	8.2	2.1	2.2	2.1	1.9	1.8
Océanie	0.4	x0.4	x0.3	x0.3	0.2	x0.3	x0.6	x0.6	x0.6	x0.6
Germany/Allemagne	9.1	10.2	9.9	10.1	10.7	11.7	11.9	11.7	9.0	10.3
Japan/Japon	16.7	14.4	10.9	9.8	9.1	7.4	8.2	8.2	9.9	8.5
Italy/Italie	6.3	6.5	6.5	7.1	8.7	9.4	8.4	8.7	8.5	8.5
France,Monac	7.3	7.3	7.1	7.3	8.2	8.4	7.8	8.0	6.6	7.2
United Kingdom	4.3	4.6	5.0	5.1	5.5	7.3	7.6	7.3	6.4	7.4
Belgium–Luxembourg	6.5	7.5	6.8	6.8	7.1	7.9	7.5	6.7	5.6	6.5
Spain/Espagne	8.3	5.6	4.8	4.6	4.5	5.0	4.9	4.5	4.8	5.1
Turkey/Turquie	2.8	2.3	2.1	2.8	2.4	3.8	4.1	4.0	5.5	6.0
Brazil/Brésil	3.4	2.2	1.8	3.0	2.9	3.0	3.0	3.4	3.5	2.9
USA/Etats–Unis d'Amer	1.0	0.8	1.0	1.1	2.0	2.8	3.8	3.0	2.9	3.1

TRADE BY COMMODITY IN THOUSAND U.S. DOLLARS – COMMERCE PAR PRODUIT EN MILLIERS DE DOLLARS E.U

COUNTRIES–PAYS	IMPORTS – IMPORTATIONS				
	1990	1991	1992	1993	1994
Total	36510187	36633266	38036080	35796233	40688861
Africa	x1084326	970462	x1130734	x1106289	x824033
Northern Africa	577440	469684	510463	510577	416297
Americas	5948857	5804911	6650756	6117137	8061948
LAIA	1148603	1368542	1709624	1560070	1709557
CACM	105848	100645	138768	x127796	x161162
Asia	9453030	10534858	11144498	13163952	12610206
Middle East	x2055310	x2263813	x2128137	x1951947	x1110347
Europe	19110556	17878358	18281369	14252099	18042342
EEC	17533989	16611684	16953294	13201046	16826266
EFTA	1205206	1035817	1016384	841598	1000671
Oceania	x403208	x404588	x435771	x471002	x458145
Germany/Allemagne	4148631	4314588	4440490	3054830	3813783
USA/Etats–Unis d'Amer	3713908	3382552	3903917	3447438	5061246
France,Monac	2788126	2465087	2597414	2026532	2624333
China/Chine	1444300	1317316	1997306	3315300	2684930
Italy/Italie	2364853	2066615	2160410	1638919	2302025
United Kingdom	1936020	1854044	1825576	1609457	1819307
Thailand/Thaïlande	1074745	1301136	1327496	1456200	1377652
Netherlands/Pays–Bas	1434962	1373715	1371540	1098663	1477178
Japan/Japon	997057	1272659	1004123	1146839	1218881
Hong Kong	528253	757780	1148558	1355726	1474820
Belgium–Luxembourg	1056801	1015870	1073823	914807	1154391
Spain/Espagne	1013038	906232	897284	761394	941305
Iran (Islamic Rp. of)	x909742	x1087361	x781887	x499417	x119743
Canada	805483	789216	740418	829668	962500
Malaysia/Malaisie	578176	726227	665172	799642	933946
Korea, Republic of	630364	829679	734389	608433	1025456
Switz.Liecht	842336	732524	691512	594057	689656
Singapore/Singapour	623908	642665	621196	731822	775142
Mexico/Mexique	470898	566673	720377	638836	760724
Turkey/Turquie	584314	468871	583811	775548	434796
Denmark/Danemark	665243	616097	704751	483903	632019
Sweden/Suède	750833	597761	635115	516466	700438
Austria/Autriche	471304	442376	488484	407181	532935
Indonesia/Indonésie	367056	406033	376844	532073	586746
Saudi Arabia	221033	453992	456914	x312818	x250539
Norway,SVD,JM	351987	292169	315533	239044	301735
India/Inde	432936	280457	294273	240479	456096
Portugal	284227	285989	305905	203951	250621
Former USSR/Anc. URSS	1822	x795203			
Philippines	250843	208430	254057	272297	290366
Australia/Australie	208599	194196	214375	275557	262867
Greece/Grèce	203149	325900	130025	183455	182290
Russian Federation			x489658	x141871	x66502
Israel/Israël	185147	201864	196986	212640	194230
Colombia/Colombie	189077	166824	201590	232849	252913
Pakistan	148498	178355	205819	202077	182033
Finland/Finlande	252408	199162	191603	191700	258500
Argentina/Argentine	62048	143067	224484	159653	166081
Egypt/Egypte	166706	154607	138009	156378	103468
Nigeria/Nigéria	41438	91808	x186918	x164820	x97250
Poland/Pologne	94538	77283	148928	195825	258838
Venezuela	51695	146258	164738	91955	68389
Ireland/Irlande	164395	148248	130875	109788	137142
Chile/Chili	92317	101224	125341	136600	136534
Brazil/Brésil	158397	110011	110500	136287	115476
Algeria/Algérie	113785	87136	125136	142183	102255
So. Africa Customs Un	104226	108034	126269	105865	
Morocco/Maroc	131104	103973	118177	90745	91512
New Zealand	101021	96314	99043	111830	146353
Hungary/Hongrie	x87816	95202	x72432	x104338	x87669

COUNTRIES–PAYS	EXPORTS – EXPORTATIONS				
	1990	1991	1992	1993	1994
Totale	37112769	36443934	38062945	35774367	40581748
Afrique	x521530	x514479	x627306	x580102	x567085
Afrique du Nord	88707	49115	x89724	x74254	x67894
Amériques	2882427	3068788	3400515	3295026	3458854
ALAI	1335974	1337611	1407739	1368261	1449302
MCAC	12937	15264	19577	x16326	x27904
Asie	8890411	9491331	10490211	11314996	11739212
Moyen–Orient	138096	63246	37904	x44004	x64998
Europe	23140626	22052185	22193243	18974575	22908782
CEE	22695200	21682532	21783673	18611420	22548544
AELE	275879	277467	292505	238190	259694
Océanie	350635	372910	x412648	x347695	345492
Japan/Japon	6389336	6833178	7147035	7144740	7598273
Germany/Allemagne	6054291	5612120	5698031	4792627	5617483
Belgium–Luxembourg	4339011	3817124	3588308	2963262	3533695
France,Monac	3399771	3317202	3350147	2706780	3192537
Korea, Republic of	1612547	1713485	2078872	2269046	2142451
United Kingdom	1610048	1593288	1702856	1451102	1743867
Sweden/Suède	1391046	1366288	1374259	1318757	1777014
Netherlands/Pays–Bas	1467440	1388702	1460618	1129607	1528749
Italy/Italie	1252168	1220352	1247475	1271420	1553150
USA/Etats–Unis d'Amer	1050528	1195129	1219215	1140630	1143480
Spain/Espagne	1050301	1221670	1049619	994501	1161787
Austria/Autriche	1116775	967611	1012326	934728	x1046241
Brazil/Brésil	653250	864753	926377	867519	934215
Hong Kong	256329	429225	827970	1072171	1167745
Finland/Finlande	620394	709981	785566	769165	989456
Canada	474381	516183	729112	766185	834569
So. Africa Customs Un	395322	428015	507155	447440	472629
Australia/Australie	248952	298335	317395	283308	290425
Russian Federation			x232641	x599384	x878804
Czechoslovakia		x368101	x441125		
Mexico/Mexique	208523	186682	258907	244325	247836
Denmark/Danemark	207757	211846	222769	146492	188419
Romania/Roumanie	317376	171210	147027	250877	307449
Greece/Grèce	115991	197849	226722	83329	145955
Venezuela	181135	177918	146129	173510	142686
Singapore/Singapour	110321	139367	134255	169492	226461
Ukraine			x71563	x369398	x298424
Switz.Liecht	139839	148765	153559	133703	144076
Slovakia				x434296	x479989
Norway,SVD,JM	136041	128691	138935	104487	115618
Bulgaria/Bulgarie	x492433	x95378	136783	123824	223030
China/Chine	162796	146112	70231	84655	115537
Hungary/Hongrie	x118780	x79108	x114827	x87093	x143197
Poland/Pologne	102105	88054	98521	89757	177706
Czech Republic				275806	230952
India/Inde	42056	52622	56765	165695	147638
Argentina/Argentine	276032	83989	61981	70298	115016
New Zealand	98715	73163	68859	62474	53214
Korea Dem People's Rp	x89216	x35712	x10901	x114365	x41686
Portugal	61950	51234	58568	46983	66137
Former USSR/Anc. URSS	117610	x140920			
Kazakstan			x28396	x107595	x88018
Indonesia/Indonésie	30592	27464	34266	40454	56686
Yugoslavia SFR	169217	x91745			
Turkey/Turquie	122649	46309	23511	19479	42099
Slovenia/Slovénia			43957	41444	65266
Malaysia/Malaisie	20429	21828	30287	32672	32770
Yugoslavia/Yougoslavie			x48011	x30870	x10226
Kenya	9176	11967	20752	44120	x13802
Tunisia/Tunisie	12724	25501	27977	10475	22903

(VALUE AS % OF TOTAL)(VALEUR EN % DU TOTAL)

	1985	1986	1987	1988	1989	1990	1991	1992	1993	1994
Africa	3.4	x3.2	x3.1	x2.8	x2.6	x3.0	2.7	x2.9	x3.1	x2.0
Northern Africa	1.9	1.6	1.4	1.4	1.2	1.6	1.3	1.3	1.4	1.0
Americas	29.5	23.7	21.9	18.5	15.6	16.3	15.9	17.5	17.0	19.8
LAIA	2.8	2.4	3.1	2.8	2.9	3.1	3.7	4.5	4.4	4.2
CACM	0.1	0.3	0.4	0.3	0.3	0.3	0.3	0.4	x0.4	x0.4
Asia	25.7	25.9	28.8	x29.9	29.8	25.9	28.7	29.3	36.8	31.0
Middle East	2.7	x3.9	x3.4	x4.0	x3.5	x5.6	x6.2	x5.6	x5.5	x2.7
Europe	38.7	44.8	43.0	46.0	48.9	52.3	48.8	48.1	39.8	44.3
EEC	31.8	37.1	36.1	38.6	41.0	48.0	45.3	44.6	36.9	41.4
EFTA	5.9	6.7	6.1	6.5	6.8	3.3	2.8	2.7	2.4	2.5
Oceania	1.7	x1.5	x1.3	x0.9	x1.4	x1.1	x1.1	x1.1	x1.3	x1.1
Germany/Allemagne	7.7	9.3	8.3	9.2	9.3	11.4	11.8	11.7	8.5	9.4
USA/Etats–Unis d'Amer	23.2	18.3	15.9	12.7	9.9	10.2	9.2	10.3	9.6	12.4
France,Monac	4.9	5.5	5.5	5.8	6.3	7.6	6.7	6.8	5.7	6.4
China/Chine	7.9	7.6	7.7	6.6	9.6	4.0	3.6	5.3	9.3	6.6
Italy/Italie	3.7	4.5	4.8	4.6	5.6	6.5	5.6	5.7	4.6	5.7
United Kingdom	3.7	3.8	3.9	4.7	4.8	5.3	5.1	4.8	4.5	4.5
Thailand/Thaïlande	1.5	1.6	1.9	2.4	2.6	2.9	3.6	3.5	4.1	3.4
Netherlands/Pays–Bas	2.5	2.9	2.8	3.3	3.5	3.9	3.7	3.6	3.1	3.6
Japan/Japon	1.8	1.9	2.3	2.7	2.9	2.7	3.5	2.6	3.2	3.0
Hong Kong	0.9	1.1	1.3	1.5	1.6	1.4	2.1	3.0	3.8	3.6

	1985	1986	1987	1988	1989	1990	1991	1992	1993	1994
Afrique	1.8	x1.7	x1.4	x0.2	x0.9	x1.4	x1.4	x1.6	x1.7	x1.4
Afrique du Nord	0.0	0.1	0.1	0.1	0.1	0.2	0.1	x0.2	x0.2	x0.2
Amériques	8.1	7.6	7.0	8.3	7.7	7.8	8.4	8.9	9.2	8.5
ALAI	3.9	3.6	3.0	4.9	3.8	3.6	3.7	3.7	3.8	3.6
MCAC	0.0	0.0	0.0	0.1	0.0	0.0	0.0	0.1	x0.0	x0.1
Asie	29.1	26.7	x25.8	x25.2	24.5	23.9	26.1	27.6	31.7	28.9
Moyen–Orient	0.7	0.4	0.4	0.8	0.5	0.4	0.2	0.1	x0.1	x0.2
Europe	58.2	61.1	57.2	59.0	61.9	62.4	60.5	58.3	53.0	56.5
CEE	50.3	52.6	48.8	50.7	53.6	61.2	59.5	57.2	52.0	55.6
AELE	7.7	8.3	7.9	8.0	8.1	0.7	0.8	0.8	0.7	0.6
Océanie	0.9	x0.8	x0.6	x0.7	x0.8	0.9	1.0	x1.1	x1.0	0.8
Japan/Japon	25.4	23.1	21.2	19.4	19.3	17.2	18.7	18.8	20.0	18.7
Germany/Allemagne	12.6	12.6	11.9	13.7	14.8	16.3	15.4	15.0	13.4	13.8
Belgium–Luxembourg	9.2	9.9	9.6	9.7	10.6	11.7	10.5	9.4	8.3	8.7
France,Monac	7.8	8.3	7.4	8.0	8.0	9.2	9.1	8.8	7.6	7.9
Korea, Republic of	2.6	2.6	2.6	2.5	3.1	4.3	4.7	5.5	6.3	5.3
United Kingdom	3.0	3.3	3.5	3.4	3.5	4.3	4.4	4.5	4.1	4.3
Sweden/Suède	2.8	2.8	2.8	3.4	3.5	3.7	3.7	3.6	3.7	4.4
Netherlands/Pays–Bas	3.3	3.7	3.3	3.0	3.2	4.0	3.8	3.8	3.2	3.8
Italy/Italie	3.8	3.4	3.2	2.7	2.8	3.4	3.3	3.3	3.6	3.8
USA/Etats–Unis d'Amer	1.3	1.3	1.3	2.2	2.6	2.8	3.3	3.2	3.2	2.8

TRADE BY COMMODITY IN THOUSAND U.S. DOLLARS – COMMERCE PAR PRODUIT EN MILLIERS DE DOLLARS E.U

COUNTRIES–PAYS	IMPORTS – IMPORTATIONS				
	1990	1991	1992	1993	1994
Total	938280	998789	1011720	x950353	1026258
Africa	x122928	86883	x76125	x51717	x34025
Northern Africa	99856	67042	58401	29763	16181
Americas	276967	232269	244981	213745	273696
LAIA	102566	79843	94055	64561	60079
CACM	870	262	521	x661	x671
Asia	x159696	x277935	x252617	x305498	308832
Middle East	x79328	x127356	x106685	x126456	48653
Europe	325931	371035	407782	332303	371900
EEC	261796	312809	334661	263999	307068
EFTA	58744	55011	70342	63197	54095
Oceania	9222	x4564	x2474	x3903	x6129
USA/Etats–Unis d'Amer	115630	115115	120675	107919	171082
Germany/Allemagne	23152	75138	86804	66290	88962
Iran (Islamic Rp. of)	x67928	x52830	x57771	x91041	x2222
Sweden/Suède	22061	30613	50741	62450	65273
Switz.Liecht	51729	45523	46780	45565	43439
China/Chine	7131	7991	42803	78841	162529
Mexico/Mexique	52220	31148	36909	39396	27200
Canada	52259	35241	27399	38103	40073
Saudi Arabia	2384	66272	31389	x2090	x1010
India/Inde	17101	49503	27441	12118	3947
Netherlands/Pays–Bas	40918	38074	35452	12909	14809
France,Monac	38061	32828	35447	12988	14060
Algeria/Algérie	40979	25685	25920	28370	3621
Brazil/Brésil	17612	31405	27685	10362	13601
Indonesia/Indonésie	8321	24475	14656	27423	8862
Italy/Italie	37296	25594	21764	15915	17651
Turkey/Turquie	6831	7137	16018	31314	42948
Norway,SVD,JM	6861	9440	23549	17626	10640
Belgium–Luxembourg	9674	14489	11805	24039	33056
Romania/Roumanie	28449	20487	18982	10633	12276
Egypt/Egypte	36547	30155	18909	486	3940
Finland/Finlande	7587	19031	16032	13183	17189
Portugal	12404	13497	16812	14435	10370
United Kingdom	13764	16355	18242	9490	9950
Spain/Espagne	31554	25540	10374	4451	6220
Malaysia/Malaisie	11407	14650	11364	11756	13938
Venezuela	2694	7899	20850	8667	1418
Israel/Israël	3218	11087	10806	4526	2436
Denmark/Danemark	8859	10145	9019	6847	10440
Greece/Grèce	6500	4386	9828	8214	4232
Korea, Republic of	5909	7303	7151	7229	13945
Morocco/Maroc	9705	9196	11360	197	661
Japan/Japon	7165	7106	6067	5072	7792
Singapore/Singapour	5531	6185	3360	8073	15603
Ireland/Irlande	5080	2578	6781	7494	8163
Hong Kong	3951	9273	3242	3968	3918
Austria/Autriche	4888	4542	5560	5295	6694
Bulgaria/Bulgarie	x6115	x1251	2451	x9864	x1669
Slovakia				x13321	x9850
Pakistan	4306	714	7139	5099	5597
Chile/Chili	4322	5187	3855	3327	7950
Korea Dem People's Rp	x1873	x4294	x2009	x3595	x162
Sri Lanka	863	3291	2621	3757	3616
Poland/Pologne	3561	1937	3071	4211	3050
Nigeria/Nigéria	x5520	634	x6928	x1221	x3024
Guinea/Guinée	x752	x1993	x1740	x3855	x987
Thailand/Thaïlande	2255	2682	3537	946	11065
Mauritania/Mauritanie	x2419	x3331	x1268	x2060	x2457
Australia/Australie	1114	3053	1361	2163	4322
Senegal/Sénégal	1380	1131	x1876	x3311	x71

COUNTRIES–PAYS	EXPORTS – EXPORTATIONS				
	1990	1991	1992	1993	1994
Totale	880076	921847	944687	941178	x944747
Afrique	x22381	5608	11847	x5120	x738
Afrique du Nord	114	1595	1665	133	x228
Amériques	133230	109384	116774	141279	119093
ALAI	11199	12633	28519	5535	6754
MCAC		85	219	87	807
Asie	141311	123593	136468	190465	175188
Moyen–Orient	429	13916	13505	x72	x216
Europe	548854	587893	611077	546998	x551650
CEE	543625	572823	590851	539605	x546570
AELE	3687	3502	16913	6051	4795
Océanie	5767	x5702	6303	7939	6247
Austria/Autriche	123506	152185	192821	166825	x165305
Japan/Japon	111176	84916	90890	122816	135629
Germany/Allemagne	91346	91188	85248	92117	95558
France,Monac	87618	78047	94145	88772	87975
United Kingdom	99860	99264	75967	82190	77270
Belgium–Luxembourg	78800	80519	81151	49940	38690
Canada	64976	51470	53626	80377	60785
USA/Etats–Unis d'Amer	57036	45192	34351	55278	50742
Poland/Pologne	21991	51737	51788	30892	62606
Italy/Italie	22331	32226	27712	27400	23328
Korea, Republic of	18032	15407	17604	27487	19996
China/Chine	5052	4921	10201	29765	10416
Russian Federation			x27536	x14881	x39077
Spain/Espagne	5655	9700	15813	15564	40525
Ukraine			x8612	x29098	x41515
Argentina/Argentine	10328	8199	26392	1355	104
Netherlands/Pays–Bas	17883	16153	7903	7318	5751
Saudi Arabia	288	13876	13411		x7
Switz.Liecht	3191	3109	15701	5001	4427
Sweden/Suède	11157	9519	7165	7047	9624
Former USSR/Anc. URSS		x23116			
Australia/Australie	5767	5676	6216	7779	6239
Czech Republic				17043	24709
So. Africa Customs Un	20818	2875	9536	4265	
Czechoslovakia		x8372	x6002		
Yugoslavia SFR	1542	x11568			
Brazil/Brésil	741	4155	1731	2144	2186
Romania/Roumanie		4415	3052	507	610
Singapore/Singapour	2862	2214	1429	3546	5420
India/Inde	511	1021	182	3161	928
Portugal	2991	2012	1007	286	56
Finland/Finlande	949	945	968	1210	1813
Hong Kong	1029	805	831	1453	281
Yugoslavia/Yougoslavie			x2914	x128	x58
Hungary/Hongrie	x2704	x1339	x1146	x406	x3612
Norway,SVD,JM	496	393	1213	1051	368
Egypt/Egypte	106	1398	1154	101	129
Zimbabwe	878	1013	511	560	x193
Mexico/Mexique	116	147	381	1534	4291
Denmark/Danemark	1295	706	553	681	566
Malaysia/Malaisie	49	147	804	560	1487
Kazakstan			x444	x1031	x362
Croatia/Croatie			294	1143	x150
Bulgaria/Bulgarie	x3828	x689	x233		
Tunisia/Tunisie	8	197	493	32	1
Ireland/Irlande	150	285	397	15	
Latvia/Lettonie				x575	1759
Venezuela	4	99	9	465	173
Mongolia/Mongolie			x295	x258	x15
Slovakia				x527	x276

(VALUE AS % OF TOTAL)(VALEUR EN % DU TOTAL)

	1985	1986	1987	1988	1989	1990	1991	1992	1993	1994
Africa	14.9	x13.8	x12.5	x7.1	x10.8	x13.1	8.7	x7.6	x5.4	x3.3
Northern Africa	12.3	8.5	7.5	3.4	7.3	10.6	6.7	5.8	3.1	1.6
Americas	47.0	35.0	19.6	27.3	27.8	29.5	23.3	24.2	22.5	26.7
LAIA	14.6	10.8	7.6	9.9	9.1	10.9	8.0	9.3	6.8	5.9
CACM	0.5	0.1	0.0	0.0	0.0	0.1	0.0	0.1	x0.1	x0.1
Asia	10.5	x16.3	29.8	25.2	14.1	x17.0	x27.8	x25.0	x32.1	30.1
Middle East	1.9	x3.8	x4.6	x6.9	x3.6	x8.5	x12.8	x10.5	x13.3	4.7
Europe	24.7	32.3	22.2	26.9	32.5	34.7	37.1	40.3	35.0	36.2
EEC	14.8	21.0	14.0	17.2	22.2	27.9	31.3	33.1	27.8	29.9
EFTA	6.1	9.7	7.5	9.3	9.4	6.3	5.5	7.0	6.6	5.3
Oceania	1.0	1.1	0.6	0.2	0.5	1.0	x0.5	x0.2	x0.4	x0.6
USA/Etats–Unis d'Amer	25.3	16.2	8.2	12.0	11.7	12.3	11.5	11.9	11.4	16.7
Germany/Allemagne	0.9	1.3	0.8	1.3	2.2	2.5	7.5	8.6	7.0	8.7
Iran (Islamic Rp. of)		x0.8	x2.4	x1.3	x1.1	x7.2	x5.3	x5.7	x9.6	x0.2
Sweden/Suède	0.6	1.0	1.1	1.2	2.0	2.4	3.1	5.0	6.6	6.4
Switz.Liecht	3.4	5.7	4.8	5.9	5.2	5.5	4.6	4.6	4.8	4.2
China/Chine			6.1	2.4	0.3	0.8	0.8	4.2	8.3	15.8
Mexico/Mexique	11.1	6.1	4.9	4.5	4.9	5.6	3.1	3.6	4.1	2.7
Canada	6.4	7.5	3.7	5.1	5.5	5.6	3.5	2.7	4.0	3.9
Saudi Arabia	0.4	0.2	x0.0	0.1	0.1	0.3	6.6	3.1	x0.2	x0.1
India/Inde	1.3	3.1	10.9	8.0	4.7	1.8	5.0	2.7	1.3	0.4

	1985	1986	1987	1988	1989	1990	1991	1992	1993	1994
Afrique	1.4	1.0	1.6	0.3	x1.2	x2.6	0.6	1.2	x0.6	x0.1
Afrique du Nord			x0.0	x0.0	x0.0	0.0	0.2	0.2	0.0	x0.0
Amériques	8.5	x8.8	x10.8	10.6	9.1	15.2	11.9	12.3	15.0	12.6
ALAI	0.1	0.5	x0.1	0.5	0.2	1.3	1.4	3.0	0.6	0.7
MCAC	0.0	x0.0	x0.0	0.0	x0.0	0.0	0.0	0.0	0.0	0.1
Asie	23.7	20.1	15.3	13.5	12.8	16.0	13.4	14.4	20.2	18.6
Moyen–Orient	0.0	0.2	x0.0	x0.0	x0.1	0.0	1.5	1.4	x0.0	x0.0
Europe	61.3	63.9	61.7	60.6	57.7	62.4	63.8	64.7	58.1	x58.4
CEE	49.8	54.7	48.4	49.1	48.0	61.8	62.1	62.5	57.3	x57.9
AELE	10.7	8.2	10.3	10.7	9.2	0.4	0.4	1.8	0.6	0.5
Océanie	0.6	0.1	0.9	0.3	0.3	0.7	x0.6	0.7	0.8	0.7
Austria/Autriche	8.8	6.6	8.3	8.5	7.6	14.0	16.5	20.4	17.7	x17.5
Japan/Japon	21.3	16.6	11.7	10.3	9.7	12.6	9.2	9.6	13.0	14.4
Germany/Allemagne	14.0	12.3	8.6	9.9	9.1	10.4	9.9	9.0	9.8	10.1
France,Monac	10.0	14.3	7.1	6.5	8.2	10.0	8.5	10.0	9.4	9.3
United Kingdom	7.5	8.3	10.7	9.9	8.7	11.3	10.8	8.0	8.7	8.2
Belgium–Luxembourg	5.8	9.6	6.8	6.8	7.4	9.0	8.7	8.6	5.3	4.1
Canada	4.0	4.3	7.7	5.6	4.1	7.4	5.6	5.7	8.5	6.4
USA/Etats–Unis d'Amer	4.3	3.8	3.0	4.5	4.8	6.5	4.9	3.6	5.9	5.4
Poland/Pologne	3.2	3.8	2.4	3.8	4.3	2.5	5.6	5.5	3.3	6.6
Italy/Italie	1.2	1.5	1.1	3.2	4.3	2.5	3.5	2.9	2.9	2.5

TRADE BY COMMODITY IN THOUSAND U.S. DOLLARS – COMMERCE PAR PRODUIT EN MILLIERS DE DOLLARS E.U

COUNTRIES–PAYS	IMPORTS – IMPORTATIONS 1990	1991	1992	1993	1994
Total	3121709	2903330	3200136	3049540	3632027
Africa	226647	157957	x228179	x230506	x308609
Northern Africa	174745	105986	x174196	x176260	x268804
Americas	x593394	539755	609287	698505	787945
LAIA	56025	70668	90820	112531	118791
CACM	7472	8964	9624	x9443	x11376
Asia	500367	x577139	611028	755990	861977
Middle East	x115782	x151774	x135081	x110443	x105530
Europe	1652807	1503243	1608964	1236946	1543215
EEC	1499691	1380776	1470343	1123245	1418172
EFTA	125998	101691	104941	86189	100780
Oceania	x46449	x44560	x49901	x54159	x62074
USA/Etats-Unis d'Amer	415616	378331	419225	479545	551375
Germany/Allemagne	420744	416825	442721	332853	428035
France,Monac	319607	285840	290612	239453	286423
Netherlands/Pays-Bas	143893	131516	133405	71741	92128
Italy/Italie	120252	98058	103279	82709	107034
Libyan Arab Jamahiriya	128416	55435	x90479	x134267	x242342
United Kingdom	95599	92499	104244	83389	96112
Japan/Japon	69454	85315	75113	87374	126950
Hong Kong	56537	64425	69119	113151	115284
Switz.Liecht	105853	82214	83179	71394	86002
China/Chine	28457	23263	73988	134475	192916
Canada	74298	64842	71726	80868	87795
Belgium-Luxembourg	85084	75940	81572	57949	82209
Spain/Espagne	65769	66733	74034	50942	69396
Austria/Autriche	55493	50302	58940	52333	62365
Iran (Islamic Rp. of)	x36858	x79988	x53656	x25063	x15101
Singapore/Singapour	43438	44875	47056	58779	61955
Mexico/Mexique	28507	31679	49506	64986	71019
Thailand/Thaïlande	41224	42105	39984	52375	54504
Sweden/Suède	41894	38652	46136	39356	53867
Denmark/Danemark	46178	39068	44713	29237	45291
Indonesia/Indonésie	28392	33364	37172	32871	39745
Korea, Republic of	26434	33799	30851	37128	46440
Portugal	28524	30985	34594	29375	35813
Malaysia/Malaisie	21621	31942	28451	33148	36042
Australia/Australie	25835	27499	29549	32053	34639
Czechoslovakia	5557	x36479	x50890		
Algeria/Algérie	16883	18009	45096	20516	5166
Ireland/Irlande	27794	21957	23624	20547	23640
So. Africa Customs Un	20477	19170	22087	23621	
Philippines	15275	13580	14942	35583	14370
Morocco/Maroc	17305	19860	26292	10255	12215
Syrian Arab Republic	10447	x24749	15700	x15485	x10744
Poland/Pologne	11934	14950	16591	23314	32715
Israel/Israël	18930	18290	18892	17301	19079
Norway,SVD,JM	19725	18842	21129	14314	14323
Greece/Grèce	23649	16908	16134	17066	16617
United Arab Emirates	15020	12885	17750	x18302	x18140
Finland/Finlande	25210	15493	16337	16296	19244
India/Inde	19070	16936	16113	14371	20389
New Zealand	17146	13529	16406	17319	22415
Hungary/Hongrie	x23384	15929	x15159	x14819	x11119
Turkey/Turquie	13393	10972	9933	15649	15821
Saudi Arabia	16218	8657	11362	x13077	x18378
Argentina/Argentine	4153	7547	9645	10388	13110
Brazil/Brésil	8328	11584	8295	7495	7880
Bulgaria/Bulgarie	x40160	x4839	8229	x13228	x1782
Slovenia/Slovénia			13174	11305	13878
Sri Lanka	6759	6201	7122	9204	8697
Egypt/Egypte	8999	7899	5654	5839	6083

COUNTRIES–PAYS	EXPORTS – EXPORTATIONS 1990	1991	1992	1993	1994
Totale	3096878	2885213	3031732	2953914	3443771
Afrique	79289	72271	64223	63465	35684
Afrique du Nord	44775	31249	23782	21927	34108
Amériques	261480	x277322	301733	359998	402087
ALAI	45676	47406	49999	64367	67654
MCAC	2557	3196	3746	2448	x2810
Asie	560419	594342	617321	709227	835110
Moyen-Orient	15093	22359	15607	x13823	x14097
Europe	2115004	1832460	1892553	1667782	1989849
CEE	2007572	1775866	1830544	1616275	1929726
AELE	53021	50339	53216	45558	54192
Océanie	14175	x17456	21023	x26056	x34684
Belgium-Luxembourg	501721	458326	477411	417501	492251
Germany/Allemagne	392841	331067	342727	259964	303272
Italy/Italie	318909	292668	269850	277548	316032
Japan/Japon	265396	246737	277441	302900	359983
France,Monac	239966	203585	225188	183031	220214
United Kingdom	192650	176453	172774	176915	193830
Sweden/Suède	167571	152969	154264	143310	187651
Korea, Republic of	130017	140372	131206	156718	200926
Canada	115071	108705	131095	155298	177226
USA/Etats-Unis d'Amer	97682	108640	111044	130186	150074
China/Chine	80650	106792	89424	89205	92932
Spain/Espagne	65620	57328	66789	70356	94376
Austria/Autriche	69128	54983	61198	44216	x62841
Switz.Liecht	44877	45143	48436	41175	47904
Hong Kong	24973	29905	33533	52174	55042
So. Africa Customs Un	31805	37758	36833	36020	
Czechoslovakia		x53537	x55330		
Poland/Pologne	10295	9111	60666	34965	36658
India/Inde	24524	25654	30843	30980	35356
Brazil/Brésil	19612	26030	26590	33421	33772
Netherlands/Pays-Bas	26653	22798	29105	23946	31910
Czech Republic				51653	61543
Malaysia/Malaisie	4286	3950	17584	26855	40335
Australia/Australie	10147	11401	14661	18499	27719
Romania/Roumanie	12218	9362	11564	22401	25070
Egypt/Egypte	25512	9279	15919	15064	29827
Venezuela	8779	10823	10272	12367	11479
Turkey/Turquie	11686	11330	12376	8152	8230
Singapore/Singapour	8721	10391	8597	12319	16683
Thailand/Thaïlande	5036	7141	8613	13521	12251
Russian Federation			x7261	x19476	x25859
Ukraine			x6205	x19879	x29595
Greece/Grèce	6569	9175	10998	5362	6939
Cuba		x9200	x5229	x7113	x2875
New Zealand	4017	6023	6344	7511	6939
Finland/Finlande	9439	6821	6076	5704	7956
Libyan Arab Jamahiriya	15906	16037			
Mexico/Mexique	3503	4869	4970	5676	5755
Portugal	7846	4471	7487	2966	5697
Slovakia				x14522	x17169
Norway,SVD,JM	8139	5196	4780	4383	6288
Saudi Arabia	2157	9126	2307	x2759	x3721
Tunisia/Tunisie	2750	5320	4426	4243	2944
Hungary/Hongrie	x8839	x6495	x4600	x1612	x1675
Slovenia/Slovénia			6650	5500	5748
Ireland/Irlande	6895	3622	4536	3626	4928
Argentina/Argentine	12078	2544	2984	6255	4518
Indonesia/Indonésie	721	644	1802	8935	6789
Former USSR/Anc. URSS		x10079			
Bulgaria/Bulgarie	x31681	x2774	x2634	x2231	x4242

(VALUE AS % OF TOTAL)(VALEUR EN % DU TOTAL)

	1985	1986	1987	1988	1989	1990	1991	1992	1993	1994
Africa	4.5	6.3	5.0	5.3	6.0	7.3	5.5	x7.1	x7.6	x8.5
Northern Africa	2.6	4.7	3.6	3.9	4.4	5.6	3.7	x5.4	x5.8	x7.4
Americas	30.9	x25.9	x22.7	x23.2	22.1	x19.0	18.6	19.0	22.9	21.7
LAIA	1.9	2.0	1.6	1.6	1.9	1.8	2.4	2.8	3.7	3.3
CACM	1.3	1.0	0.6	0.2	0.3	0.2	0.3	0.3	x0.3	x0.3
Asia	15.0	16.1	x16.9	x16.2	x15.3	16.0	x19.9	19.1	24.8	23.7
Middle East	3.1	x4.2	x4.0	x3.3	x2.9	x3.7	x5.2	x4.2	x3.6	x2.9
Europe	45.9	48.9	49.7	49.5	51.1	52.9	51.8	50.3	40.6	42.5
EEC	37.7	40.4	41.4	41.9	43.0	48.0	47.6	45.9	36.8	39.0
EFTA	6.7	7.4	7.3	6.7	7.1	4.0	3.5	3.3	2.8	2.8
Oceania	2.2	x1.5	x1.5	1.3	x1.5	x1.5	x1.5	x1.5	x1.8	x1.7
USA/Etats-Unis d'Amer	24.6	19.3	17.0	16.6	15.9	13.3	13.0	13.1	15.7	15.2
Germany/Allemagne	11.0	12.3	12.0	11.8	12.1	13.5	14.4	13.8	10.9	11.8
France,Monac	7.1	8.0	8.6	8.5	8.5	10.2	9.8	9.1	7.9	7.9
Netherlands/Pays-Bas	3.7	3.8	3.7	3.9	4.0	4.6	4.5	4.2	2.4	2.5
Italy/Italie	3.2	3.2	3.3	3.6	3.9	3.9	3.4	3.2	2.7	2.9
Libyan Arab Jamahiriya	0.4	2.7	1.8	2.3	3.3	4.1	1.9	x2.8	x4.4	x6.7
United Kingdom	2.7	2.7	3.0	3.1	2.9	3.1	3.2	3.3	2.7	2.6
Japan/Japon	0.7	1.0	1.3	2.1	2.1	2.2	2.9	2.3	2.9	3.5
Hong Kong	1.2	1.5	1.8	2.1	2.2	1.8	2.2	2.2	3.7	3.2
Switz.Liecht	2.5	3.1	3.0	2.8	3.0	3.4	2.8	2.6	2.3	2.4

	1985	1986	1987	1988	1989	1990	1991	1992	1993	1994
Afrique	1.2	x1.1	x0.9	0.5	1.7	2.5	2.5	2.1	2.1	1.0
Afrique du Nord	0.0	0.0	0.0	0.2	0.6	1.4	1.1	0.8	0.7	1.0
Amériques	10.8	10.2	9.1	8.9	8.2	8.5	x9.6	10.0	12.2	11.7
ALAI	1.7	1.3	1.4	1.6	1.6	1.5	1.6	1.6	2.2	2.0
MCAC	0.1	0.1	x0.1	0.1	0.1	0.1	0.1	0.1	0.1	x0.1
Asie	19.9	19.1	19.0	18.2	18.2	18.1	20.6	20.4	24.1	24.3
Moyen-Orient	1.3	x0.3	x0.3	0.6	0.7	0.5	0.8	0.5	x0.5	x0.4
Europe	64.4	66.5	65.0	67.2	66.7	68.3	63.5	62.4	56.5	57.8
CEE	53.5	55.8	54.2	57.5	57.0	64.8	61.6	60.4	54.7	56.0
AELE	9.8	10.1	10.1	9.1	9.1	1.7	1.7	1.8	1.5	1.6
Océanie	0.6	0.4	0.5	x0.4	0.3	0.5	x0.6	0.7	x0.9	x1.0
Belgium-Luxembourg	8.0	8.8	8.1	15.4	14.5	16.2	15.9	15.7	14.1	14.3
Germany/Allemagne	12.7	13.7	12.7	11.4	11.4	12.7	11.5	11.3	8.8	8.8
Italy/Italie	5.6	6.4	7.1	6.9	7.2	10.3	10.1	8.9	9.4	9.2
Japan/Japon	14.2	13.2	11.1	9.2	9.3	8.6	8.6	9.2	10.3	10.5
France,Monac	9.2	9.2	8.2	7.4	7.5	7.7	7.1	7.4	6.2	6.4
United Kingdom	4.9	4.5	4.9	5.1	5.0	6.2	6.1	5.7	6.0	5.6
Sweden/Suède	5.9	6.0	5.8	5.6	5.4	5.4	5.3	5.1	4.9	5.4
Korea, Republic of	2.5	3.4	3.7	3.8	3.9	4.2	4.9	4.3	5.3	5.8
Canada	6.2	6.0	5.1	4.5	4.2	3.7	3.8	4.3	5.3	5.1
USA/Etats-Unis d'Amer	2.7	2.8	2.3	2.7	2.3	3.2	3.8	3.7	4.4	4.4

TRADE BY COMMODITY IN THOUSAND U.S. DOLLARS – COMMERCE PAR PRODUIT EN MILLIERS DE DOLLARS E.U

COUNTRIES–PAYS	IMPORTS – IMPORTATIONS 1990	1991	1992	1993	1994
Total	20293638	21127932	19706998	16750078	18956793
Africa	x853763	x1043170	x1351400	x1081755	x1285897
Northern Africa	360778	524146	x741755	x660825	x910421
Americas	3700201	4096101	3080547	3360070	3820446
LAIA	743148	949637	924388	892996	899762
CACM	42389	28739	45121	39335	x45480
Asia	x4995231	x5793698	x6120816	x5382151	x5569170
Middle East	x1729872	x1838947	x2222760	x1582034	x1151984
Europe	8738044	8574855	8670210	6333431	7602302
EEC	7907534	7807539	7705894	5422149	6600225
EFTA	729891	709059	862708	837935	912972
Oceania	x244573	x302535	x217957	x236427	x270672
USA/Etats–Unis d'Amer	2135439	2295260	1428218	1728710	2060855
Germany/Allemagne	1634716	1699447	1867312	1375163	1623896
China/Chine	619300	1027248	972375	998455	1271599
France,Monac	1084404	1000653	938881	701413	853211
United Kingdom	843141	1119157	885317	601524	738734
Netherlands/Pays–Bas	1200927	1039583	900647	616538	683873
Italy/Italie	740451	783128	803396	437643	502600
Iran (Islamic Rp. of)	x469031	x648162	x626108	x580303	x108677
Canada	609505	646300	518343	583993	707523
Singapore/Singapour	505934	621415	581589	496922	525274
Norway,SVD,JM	392929	377504	519722	598515	603572
Indonesia/Indonésie	340735	413677	611499	386322	317392
Belgium–Luxembourg	539867	504648	543822	339643	409216
Saudi Arabia	368302	513458	670207	x177619	x121125
Russian Federation			x519563	x608439	x506742
Former USSR/Anc. URSS	1423262	x1088904			
Malaysia/Malaisie	315245	369395	352066	341211	459139
Mexico/Mexique	166822	249627	379976	383880	305693
Korea, Republic of	330703	428680	281155	277242	391999
Austria/Autriche	343237	314462	339129	290336	346519
Sweden/Suède	423373	335692	331739	261683	348346
Japan/Japon	312576	328686	278336	278859	321192
Switz.Liecht	326927	320651	331116	231894	301208
Denmark/Danemark	301070	288881	316319	254682	289365
Spain/Espagne	362069	328384	308424	222803	333653
Venezuela	176553	429110	213405	124764	165433
Algeria/Algérie	105053	198919	271256	224832	325331
Hong Kong	172413	197830	233824	229991	231337
Nigeria/Nigéria	x102368	184807	x293619	x173251	x106890
India/Inde	260414	158478	151746	221149	184259
Australia/Australie	167738	168289	151861	183650	202573
Tunisia/Tunisie	39256	58254	236001	180472	72782
United Arab Emirates	186797	109800	125402	x216977	x357505
Kuwait/ Koweït	68549	35869	237186	152964	56703
Finland/Finlande	208667	152481	149465	123357	173273
Thailand/Thaïlande	99201	116421	132525	159919	249403
Libyan Arab Jamahiriya	117416	144301	x115938	x146781	x199167
Syrian Arab Republic	104230	x162810	115051	x116908	x117861
Turkey/Turquie	141428	126611	119963	118968	132895
Oman	93464	114097	97441	77480	68998
So. Africa Customs Un	137605	104889	103383	77115	79794
Portugal	90133	101378	115249	67995	173459
Colombia/Colombie	127373	68178	90332	101295	98957
Greece/Grèce	56259	58978	119237	71823	54931
Egypt/Egypte	62217	83069	81624	78359	135530
Poland/Pologne	63007	42249	90278	100940	103346
Ireland/Irlande	79220	80666	86956	57545	69150
Hungary/Hongrie	x56793	87172	x57680	x70937	x60253
Pakistan	41713	54421	49861	94231	92776
Israel/Israël	50662	59129	59302	61534	65978

COUNTRIES–PAYS	EXPORTS – EXPORTATIONS 1990	1991	1992	1993	1994
Totale	19005407	20549575	19065518	16890542	18901148
Afrique	x145204	x149518	x144984	x130714	167752
Afrique du Nord	32962	32532	x38148	x19928	80307
Amériques	2215764	2795445	2470485	2372293	2781012
ALAI	847434	978438	776596	758178	856691
MCAC	8983	10565	12669	x12370	x15815
Asie	4636217	5359922	4659162	4985009	4934202
Moyen–Orient	266782	172548	144947	x157040	x196909
Europe	11531492	11821356	11307106	8949385	10481134
CEE	10949638	11285891	10685837	8475039	9964983
AELE	446789	461836	516999	396323	449210
Océanie	x32895	30795	x43813	x53569	x85273
Japan/Japon	3184268	3821491	3236328	3312569	3152719
Germany/Allemagne	3344701	3450258	3042603	2284794	2872897
Italy/Italie	1797483	1932498	1989059	1779363	2091127
France,Monac	1657720	1606101	1708027	1282691	1550074
USA/Etats–Unis d'Amer	1015654	1323549	1333617	1181781	1419577
United Kingdom	946108	977322	958893	697524	807980
Netherlands/Pays–Bas	608159	866533	680810	442277	487246
Korea, Republic of	535933	537668	472316	554640	525009
Sweden/Suède	654771	563942	526434	436134	571259
Austria/Autriche	653968	551395	519254	436875	x375411
Spain/Espagne	422669	465107	376232	409238	432379
Canada	343108	480671	345553	419335	487174
Belgium–Luxembourg	427996	454655	449241	296594	300615
Switz.Liecht	370209	387065	434899	324362	367901
Argentina/Argentine	300748	398280	298735	290907	273386
Mexico/Mexique	243609	280812	204398	235040	332169
Brazil/Brésil	217893	261004	235895	192644	211172
Singapore/Singapour	166359	233961	197726	207582	252798
China/Chine	198369	204506	202831	189789	253685
Denmark/Danemark	149165	188619	195711	177226	204296
Finland/Finlande	172379	146256	172830	184135	232999
Thailand/Thaïlande	113834	145932	132918	185876	206935
Turkey/Turquie	166251	147505	111444	116480	153693
Czechoslovakia		x149457	x195318		
Malaysia/Malaisie	25244	84960	105419	146043	114233
So. Africa Customs Un	95629	96853	94079	91370	85350
Hong Kong	59945	59507	81525	94356	88835
Norway,SVD,JM	76503	74762	82089	71933	81303
Romania/Roumanie	89582	80928	74466	59176	72710
Poland/Pologne	35877	55331	86587	57980	85296
Czech Republic				179208	187492
India/Inde	40497	46584	48630	71559	77406
Hungary/Hongrie	x74023	x46980	x59613	x38014	x40938
Greece/Grèce	88559	56596	44685	27895	16719
Russian Federation			x42676	x70982	x77424
Croatia/Croatie			52650	46343	x33610
Australia/Australie	23221	23300	33315	40017	68520
Venezuela	79306	31334	28653	24357	19824
Yugoslavia SFR	134785	x73222			
Philippines	14936	24288	7522	27687	24035
Slovakia				x54735	x56562
Slovenia/Slovénia			33508	21176	26301
Saudi Arabia	66129	17538	18179	x10638	x15713
Ukraine			x8815	x37191	x27310
Bulgaria/Bulgarie	x59304	x15909	x14743	x10455	x8759
Former USSR/Anc. URSS	150656	x36061			
Indonesia/Indonésie	7947	14577	8913	12179	21568
Portugal	16782	13413	12980	8992	13947
Israel/Israël	16999	9206	13630	11233	10272
Ireland/Irlande	9044	13059	9077	11301	8034

(VALUE AS % OF TOTAL)(VALEUR EN % DU TOTAL)

	1985	1986	1987	1988	1989	1990	1991	1992	1993	1994
Africa	4.0	4.6	x4.3	x3.8	x3.7	x4.2	x4.9	x6.8	x6.5	x6.8
Northern Africa	2.3	2.4	1.6	1.7	1.7	1.8	2.5	x3.8	x3.9	x4.8
Americas	26.1	16.3	15.7	18.7	17.0	18.2	19.4	15.7	20.1	20.1
LAIA	3.5	2.2	2.0	2.1	2.7	3.7	4.5	4.7	5.3	4.7
CACM	0.1	0.2	x0.2	0.1	0.2	0.2	0.1	0.2	0.2	x0.2
Asia	25.9	24.0	x19.3	x22.1	x23.7	x24.6	x27.4	x31.0	x32.1	x29.3
Middle East	9.5	x9.1	x6.1	x6.9	x7.2	x8.5	x8.7	x11.3	x9.4	x6.1
Europe	28.2	33.5	37.3	35.0	38.8	43.1	40.6	44.0	37.8	40.1
EEC	22.0	26.1	29.0	27.9	31.1	39.0	37.0	39.1	32.4	34.8
EFTA	5.5	6.8	7.7	6.7	7.1	3.6	3.4	4.4	5.0	4.8
Oceania	1.2	x1.1	x1.1	1.2	1.3	x1.2	x1.4	x1.1	x1.4	x1.4
USA/Etats–Unis d'Amer	18.6	11.2	10.5	12.4	10.5	10.5	10.9	7.2	10.3	10.9
Germany/Allemagne	4.2	5.5	6.0	5.7	6.3	8.1	8.0	9.5	8.2	8.6
China/Chine	7.3	6.7	4.6	5.2	5.3	3.1	4.9	4.9	6.0	6.7
France,Monac	2.7	3.2	4.1	3.9	4.2	5.3	4.7	4.8	4.2	4.5
United Kingdom	2.4	2.5	2.7	3.3	3.7	4.2	5.3	4.5	3.6	3.9
Netherlands/Pays–Bas	3.7	4.0	3.8	3.8	3.9	5.9	4.9	4.6	3.7	3.6
Italy/Italie	1.8	2.2	2.6	2.4	3.2	3.6	3.7	4.1	2.6	2.7
Iran (Islamic Rp. of)		x0.9	x0.8	x1.1	x0.7	x2.3	x3.1	x3.2	x3.5	x0.6
Canada	3.0	2.0	2.3	3.3	2.8	3.0	3.1	2.6	3.5	3.7
Singapore/Singapour	1.4	1.1	1.1	1.5	2.0	2.5	2.9	3.0	3.0	2.8

	1985	1986	1987	1988	1989	1990	1991	1992	1993	1994
Afrique	0.4	0.6	0.5	0.2	x0.6	x0.8	x0.8	x0.8	x0.7	0.9
Afrique du Nord	0.0	0.1	0.1	0.1	0.1	0.2	0.2	x0.2	x0.1	0.4
Amériques	8.7	7.0	7.9	9.0	10.8	11.6	13.6	13.0	14.1	14.7
ALAI	3.1	2.6	3.0	3.7	4.3	4.5	4.8	4.1	4.5	4.5
MCAC	0.1	0.0	0.0	0.0	0.0	0.0	0.1	0.1	x0.1	x0.1
Asie	32.7	28.4	x25.3	x28.6	24.1	24.4	26.0	24.4	29.5	26.1
Moyen–Orient	1.0	0.9	x0.9	0.8	1.4	1.4	0.8	0.8	x0.9	x1.0
Europe	54.6	59.8	59.7	56.6	61.1	60.7	57.5	59.3	53.0	55.5
CEE	47.6	51.4	50.4	47.4	51.2	57.6	54.9	56.0	50.2	52.7
AELE	6.6	8.0	8.7	8.6	9.3	2.4	2.2	2.7	2.3	2.4
Océanie	0.2	x0.2	0.3	x0.1	x0.1	x0.2	0.1	x0.2	x0.3	x0.4
Japan/Japon	26.9	23.4	18.4	21.1	16.9	16.8	18.6	17.0	19.6	16.7
Germany/Allemagne	16.5	19.0	17.6	16.5	16.7	17.6	16.8	16.0	13.5	15.2
Italy/Italie	8.4	9.3	9.6	7.8	8.2	9.5	9.4	10.4	10.5	11.1
France,Monac	6.9	6.6	5.9	5.7	7.4	8.7	7.8	9.0	7.6	8.2
USA/Etats–Unis d'Amer	3.6	2.8	2.9	3.3	4.4	5.3	6.4	7.0	7.0	7.5
United Kingdom	3.1	3.2	4.0	3.6	4.3	5.0	4.8	5.0	4.1	4.3
Netherlands/Pays–Bas	2.1	2.4	2.3	2.4	2.6	3.2	4.2	3.6	2.6	2.6
Korea, Republic of	2.9	2.4	2.8	3.0	2.8	2.8	2.6	2.5	3.3	2.8
Sweden/Suède	2.3	2.9	2.9	3.0	3.2	3.4	2.7	2.8	2.6	3.0
Austria/Autriche	2.3	2.5	2.8	3.0	3.3	3.4	2.7	2.7	2.6	x2.0

TRADE BY COMMODITY IN THOUSAND U.S. DOLLARS – COMMERCE PAR PRODUIT EN MILLIERS DE DOLLARS E.U

IMPORTS – IMPORTATIONS

COUNTRIES–PAYS	1990	1991	1992	1993	1994
Total	1940893	1915210	2140805	1957884	2215484
Africa	x90072	x43918	x54713	x42106	x55130
Northern Africa	57397	8038	x21334	x15009	x25868
Americas	343820	340541	424209	443897	503203
LAIA	65860	82403	163108	144088	155347
CACM	4834	5500	8319	4001	5005
Asia	x280065	358768	412856	x440806	483405
Middle East	x50519	x28831	x44343	x49186	x40670
Europe	1170176	1111889	1188867	936987	1081688
EEC	1077986	1032477	1117760	868132	1001476
EFTA	79710	67745	57726	58049	63808
Oceania	x20355	x26286	x32983	x26092	x37556
Germany/Allemagne	281282	294370	341469	218658	270057
USA/Etats-Unis d'Amer	173932	161092	170753	197499	235179
France,Monac	175408	170402	171887	146470	184228
United Kingdom	134728	108975	117676	125770	95068
Italy/Italie	99086	102909	116229	106334	118048
Belgium–Luxembourg	108411	99917	101609	63498	77578
Mexico/Mexique	32529	44326	114893	86977	95546
Netherlands/Pays-Bas	89540	79341	75735	48275	56173
Japan/Japon	53113	74036	66541	62622	72063
Canada	82926	69527	59865	71659	94391
Indonesia/Indonésie	36540	74069	63084	57053	28314
Singapore/Singapour	49581	56991	57640	51386	52218
Malaysia/Malaisie	25298	36483	44535	64839	75408
Austria/Autriche	40211	40659	42030	40114	50598
Korea, Republic of	19923	36918	34923	36551	79669
Sweden/Suède	45853	34805	33510	31164	44150
Switz.Liecht	47460	38433	30707	29551	33622
China/Chine	3087	2751	37546	49969	62973
Norway,SVD,JM	31929	29091	26788	28299	30055
Spain/Espagne	25409	27378	32995	20089	24774
Denmark/Danemark	27204	25686	25299	22937	27113
Thailand/Thaïlande	15575	19346	21107	19001	30777
Finland/Finlande	20203	17791	21828	15482	22283
Ireland/Irlande	17023	16369	20482	15226	17395
Iran (Islamic Rp. of)	x19325	x17070	x19163	x14617	x7437
Chile/Chili	13493	13777	17584	13844	13224
Guyana	x6612	x10771	x13052	x19213	x3742
Slovakia				x35438	x23680
Hong Kong	6317	8640	11378	11260	10902
Papua New Guinea	4368	x9537	x12116	x8218	x10749
Australia/Australie	10538	8800	10890	9701	13732
Venezuela	4864	8064	9811	9601	10941
India/Inde	7325	8549	10388	8137	12118
Nigeria/Nigéria	x6990	12449	x11223	x2866	x2872
Portugal	8391	8271	10763	5979	6502
New Zealand	3715	6144	8267	6809	11323
Hungary/Hongrie	x7605	6293	x6769	x8153	x7805
Brazil/Brésil	6206	6197	5067	9480	9422
Turkey/Turquie	4650	3837	8479	7967	5886
Greece/Grèce	5237	5603	6247	8137	7510
Poland/Pologne	8281	4603	5781	8902	11621
Algeria/Algérie			11181	5731	10053
Syrian Arab Republic	8492	x2230	10127	x3573	x1515
Former USSR/Anc. URSS		x14739			
Israel/Israël	3526	4432	5991	4131	5405
Mongolia/Mongolie	x103	x25	x1661		x14
Peru/Pérou	1937	1726	4974	7116	7138
Argentina/Argentine	165	496	4135	6172	7387
Ghana	x3786	2220	3020	x5540	x8426
Bulgaria/Bulgarie	x3297	x1034	328	x9237	x980

EXPORTS – EXPORTATIONS

COUNTRIES–PAYS	1990	1991	1992	1993	1994
Totale	2442248	2507871	2524669	2370219	2819997
Afrique	27196	7426	4011	4789	x2047
Afrique du Nord	8465	37	184	791	1278
Amériques	310589	471175	369697	387385	432176
ALAI	67214	124247	66309	51187	62426
MCAC	778	835	1618	1570	x672
Asie	284580	310850	353073	380398	549695
Moyen-Orient	5468	5660	7558	8512	12207
Europe	1740707	1610929	1646716	1375455	1540172
CEE	1592484	1539234	1566214	1308319	1459379
AELE	67588	59900	61444	51776	65611
Océanie	x28647	x35000	x35156	x34885	47154
France,Monac	353965	353919	354566	312742	355958
USA/Etats-Unis d'Amer	211173	314781	270407	305335	329299
Germany/Allemagne	383468	321583	307257	253812	268056
Italy/Italie	168143	190905	220295	195582	236376
United Kingdom	160028	167262	171675	167285	175159
Korea, Republic of	124236	139884	102302	92264	107416
Belgium–Luxembourg	117618	107534	108052	96066	114566
China/Chine	20781	31951	122955	144899	213388
Netherlands/Pays-Bas	92580	92233	86311	59415	60165
Spain/Espagne	80709	77550	82502	63082	77309
Denmark/Danemark	79392	70405	64780	46235	63621
Austria/Autriche	64373	62457	65077	52425	x33793
Mexico/Mexique	37385	96307	42786	21323	26330
Poland/Pologne	30404	30335	60625	65899	94665
Japan/Japon	57398	49823	41787	44573	54249
Portugal	40814	43133	45413	23828	32845
Norway,SVD,JM	42762	35869	39353	32587	45326
India/Inde	41506	32673	32417	33766	76536
Canada	30562	31212	31182	29157	39403
Czech Republic				89467	118362
Australia/Australie	22364	27622	30488	28473	38893
Finland/Finlande	30901	27129	24225	24257	25158
Switz.Liecht	24826	24030	22090	19190	20283
Brazil/Brésil	20226	18069	13580	17780	22067
Czechoslovakia		x15522	x32092		
Israel/Israël	16350	20686	13263	11349	14185
Sweden/Suède	16231	16566	15268	10012	14262
Singapore/Singapour	6569	14027	10507	14275	26178
Malaysia/Malaisie	4377	7104	10471	12739	22105
Hungary/Hongrie	x9614	x7706	x10956	x10499	x8491
Ireland/Irlande	3214	6303	18639	1556	788
Slovenia/Slovénia			11893	9547	11017
Romania/Roumanie	216	7252	6530	6780	9843
Turkey/Turquie	4210	5382	5810	7631	10911
New Zealand	5663	7059	4660	6403	8258
Russian Federation			x5927	x10191	x11533
Peru/Pérou	4541	4483	6007	3912	4359
Bulgaria/Bulgarie	x6739	x2923	x5530	x3556	x5913
Yugoslavia SFR	80130	x11698			
So. Africa Customs Un	17239	5907	3437	2317	
Hong Kong	2135	2482	4823	4285	4743
Thailand/Thaïlande	2927	2443	1987	6745	9740
Slovakia				x10806	x11350
Philippines	510	2729	2240	4412	4245
Croatia/Croatie			4520	4850	x3594
Former USSR/Anc. URSS		x8502			
Greece/Grèce	1049	2255	2154	2022	1323
Chile/Chili	1664	2122	431	3247	5530
Argentina/Argentine	1680	1354	1160	2767	1915
Lithuania/Lituanie				x5145	5455

(VALUE AS % OF TOTAL)(VALEUR EN % DU TOTAL)

Imports

	1985	1986	1987	1988	1989	1990	1991	1992	1993	1994
Africa	12.0	x10.9	x7.3	x6.3	x5.4	x4.6	x2.3	x2.6	x2.1	x2.5
Northern Africa	11.5	9.6	5.7	4.7	3.9	3.0	0.4	x1.0	x0.8	x1.2
Americas	21.8	18.6	x14.0	x11.6	17.8	17.7	17.7	19.8	22.6	22.7
LAIA	1.5	2.2	1.0	1.6	2.5	3.4	4.3	7.6	7.4	7.0
CACM	0.2	x0.0	x0.2	0.3	0.3	0.2	0.3	0.4	0.2	0.2
Asia	8.7	x9.5	x10.4	x18.5	x13.4	x14.4	18.7	19.3	x22.5	21.8
Middle East	1.8	x3.1	x2.6	x10.3	x4.7	x2.6	x1.5	x2.1	x2.5	x1.8
Europe	48.7	53.4	45.4	48.4	53.9	60.3	58.1	55.5	47.9	48.8
EEC	39.7	43.8	37.4	40.1	45.2	55.5	53.9	52.2	44.3	45.2
EFTA	7.9	8.8	7.4	7.1	7.8	4.1	3.5	2.7	3.0	2.9
Oceania	1.4	1.1	0.9	1.3	1.2	x1.0	x1.4	x1.5	x1.3	x1.7
Germany/Allemagne	6.8	8.7	7.8	8.6	10.4	14.5	15.4	16.0	11.2	12.2
USA/Etats-Unis d'Amer	8.9	5.1	2.8	2.2	9.5	9.0	8.4	8.0	10.1	10.6
France,Monac	7.8	8.6	7.2	7.5	7.8	9.0	8.9	8.0	7.5	8.3
United Kingdom	4.3	4.3	3.6	5.5	6.6	6.9	5.7	5.5	6.4	4.3
Italy/Italie	2.4	2.6	2.7	3.3	3.9	5.1	5.4	5.4	5.4	5.3
Belgium–Luxembourg	6.9	7.2	5.7	4.9	5.1	5.6	5.2	4.7	3.2	3.5
Mexico/Mexique		0.3	0.3	1.1	1.7	1.7	2.3	5.4	4.4	4.3
Netherlands/Pays-Bas	4.4	4.8	3.9	3.4	3.7	4.6	4.1	3.5	2.5	2.5
Japan/Japon	0.4	0.5	0.4	1.9	2.5	2.7	3.9	3.1	3.2	3.3
Canada	11.1	10.8	9.6	6.6	4.7	4.3	3.6	2.8	3.7	4.3

Exports

	1985	1986	1987	1988	1989	1990	1991	1992	1993	1994
Afrique	1.0	x0.2	x0.2	1.0	1.1	1.1	0.3	0.1	0.2	x0.1
Afrique du Nord	0.0	0.0	0.0	0.0	0.0	0.3	0.0	0.0	0.0	0.0
Amériques	28.4	20.5	20.7	8.2	15.4	12.7	18.8	14.6	16.3	15.4
ALAI	4.8	0.6	3.9	2.2	2.8	2.8	5.0	2.6	2.2	2.2
MCAC	0.0	0.0	0.0	0.0	0.0	0.0	0.0	0.1	0.1	x0.0
Asie	8.5	8.8	7.2	10.7	10.6	11.6	12.4	14.0	16.1	19.5
Moyen-Orient	0.0	0.0	0.0	x0.3	0.2	0.2	0.2	0.3	0.4	0.4
Europe	55.3	62.4	51.5	64.5	67.3	71.3	64.2	65.2	58.0	54.6
CEE	49.1	55.1	45.2	50.6	54.1	65.2	61.4	62.0	55.2	51.8
AELE	5.4	6.4	5.5	4.8	6.3	2.8	2.4	2.4	2.2	2.3
Océanie	0.6	1.1	0.9	1.0	x1.1	x1.1	x1.4	x1.4	x1.5	1.7
France,Monac	7.2	8.8	7.5	9.9	11.4	14.5	14.1	14.0	13.2	12.6
USA/Etats-Unis d'Amer	7.7	6.6	6.1	4.1	11.2	8.6	12.6	10.7	12.9	11.7
Germany/Allemagne	18.4	20.9	16.8	12.8	13.5	15.7	12.8	12.2	10.7	9.5
Italy/Italie	4.5	4.5	3.5	5.4	5.9	6.9	7.6	8.7	8.3	8.4
United Kingdom	5.5	5.3	3.8	6.4	5.7	6.6	6.7	6.8	7.1	6.2
Korea, Republic of	2.5	2.8	2.8	5.1	6.0	5.1	5.6	4.1	3.9	3.8
Belgium–Luxembourg	1.5	1.7	1.5	3.5	3.8	4.8	4.3	4.3	4.1	4.1
China/Chine			0.3	0.5	0.5	0.9	1.3	4.9	6.1	7.6
Netherlands/Pays-Bas	2.0	2.5	2.2	2.8	3.0	3.8	3.7	3.4	2.5	2.1
Spain/Espagne	1.7	2.0	1.7	2.8	2.8	3.3	3.1	3.3	2.7	2.7

TRADE BY COMMODITY IN THOUSAND U.S. DOLLARS – COMMERCE PAR PRODUIT EN MILLIERS DE DOLLARS E.U

COUNTRIES–PAYS	IMPORTS – IMPORTATIONS 1990	1991	1992	1993	1994
Total	8508827	7900347	6737743	6367445	7531507
Africa	x11658	x10296	13993	28832	x23688
Northern Africa	6228	5589	8324	14303	7996
Americas	2523105	2159329	2037018	1815056	2053402
LAIA	61505	36783	43113	51572	77611
CACM	152	102	123	x106	x98
Asia	2320396	2168870	1769166	x1970560	x2474266
Middle East	252090	184645	231704	x179380	x172431
Europe	3567209	3495835	2838167	2479172	2885642
EEC	3127261	2818297	2547933	1893454	2413010
EFTA	436808	672150	285308	582108	466720
Oceania	x46493	x53604	x62672	x55072	x78838
USA/Etats–Unis d'Amer	2326759	2027209	1880917	1653422	1817288
Japan/Japon	1735625	1665994	1135749	1236901	1554784
United Kingdom	1101438	955398	847568	648020	699073
Germany/Allemagne	844305	699022	671273	435827	588663
Switz.Liecht	420072	658392	267990	562394	442604
France,Monac	371604	339903	286843	286147	345266
Italy/Italie	289908	335308	341243	203782	280812
Singapore/Singapour	173848	91757	171693	280501	159908
United Arab Emirates	235257	165746	216287	x156156	x92740
Belgium–Luxembourg	181493	156579	165362	136225	191462
Spain/Espagne	151322	182207	85076	50157	115131
Canada	132449	94039	111957	108860	157636
Hong Kong	48322	91009	74594	99986	99203
Korea, Republic of	51104	82661	73030	73990	115850
Australia/Australie	45037	52348	61286	52925	76880
Netherlands/Pays–Bas	47018	39677	41849	32575	43751
Brazil/Brésil	57892	30782	32718	41404	54282
Thailand/Thaïlande	14328	17786	38357	44545	50142
Sweden/Suède	41053	32538	33840	33105	34789
Austria/Autriche	28463	29195	23851	20755	34648
Norway,SVD,JM	16439	13491	17082	19524	23913
Portugal	16607	13428	16576	12264	13849
Denmark/Danemark	20035	14257	14366	12021	15920
Israel/Israël	12035	10531	13504	15668	21091
China/Chine	19956	11687	13940	14002	16449
Greece/Grèce	15529	10123	10560	10844	12659
India/Inde	6495	6237	7491	10918	246204
Russian Federation			x20679	x761	x1394
So. Africa Customs Un	3288	2807	4483	12028	8145
Finland/Finlande	11107	6010	5681	6834	10728
Malaysia/Malaisie	4150	4500	4948	7619	12865
Hungary/Hongrie	x5413	5035	x9084	x2553	x1712
Iran (Islamic Rp. of)		x8060	x7500	x852	x917
Saudi Arabia	1403	3679	1602	x10240	x66727
Ukraine			x14	x14854	x15594
Algeria/Algérie	1573	1968	2441	9899	872
Ireland/Irlande	7380	4652	3847	4898	26260
Mexico/Mexique	2076	2167	5484	4451	9596
Oman	573	501	781	8045	6438
Turkey/Turquie	10746	4189	2619	1965	2570
Czechoslovakia	16567	x3865	x4491		
Bulgaria/Bulgarie	x5783	x2004	486	x5180	x706
Colombia/Colombie	97	2380	1419	2925	5780
Egypt/Egypte	3169	1807	3085	1642	4028
Cyprus/Chypre	3472	2124	2507	1687	2436
Slovakia				x6114	x3561
Yugoslavia SFR	2742	x5020			
Slovenia/Slovénia			2603	2037	2791
New Zealand	1302	1180	1351	1995	1922
Morocco/Maroc	164	1000	1456	1361	1079

COUNTRIES–PAYS	EXPORTS – EXPORTATIONS 1990	1991	1992	1993	1994
Totale	5262565	x6182032	4477485	4137813	5064184
Afrique	33744	x38151	x248045	30997	x35261
Afrique du Nord	23291	22681	14147	19579	28374
Amériques	1141825	1091909	1094441	1165995	1397707
ALAI	454507	328294	385556	379008	494658
MCAC	1400	614	143	10089	x82
Asie	270349	133794	222346	x308999	x440526
Moyen–Orient	101859	x1100	x134	x9123	x7561
Europe	3603975	3327980	2769573	2475459	2946137
CEE	3069225	2747611	2168884	2000153	2212548
AELE	529461	575431	599433	468091	732158
Océanie	60024	49308	47456	53156	x66665
United Kingdom	1558610	1303828	883252	827218	839388
USA/Etats–Unis d'Amer	421514	598286	537312	589017	665343
Russian Federation			x793727	x865504	x1180983
Switz.Liecht	498348	546434	558269	430003	674494
Germany/Allemagne	598494	555576	487189	460187	496023
Former USSR/Anc. URSS		x1412318			
Belgium–Luxembourg	337642	316423	331611	255675	336654
France,Monac	319109	285628	189442	186795	276856
Mexico/Mexique	301018	233399	208249	187957	214824
Canada	260919	160601	169213	187634	218738
Poland/Pologne	108332	122730	91577	96045	166242
Japan/Japon	79510	70909	131050	100206	134631
Spain/Espagne	54820	80402	97110	100126	79217
So. Africa Customs Un	8351	6750	230367	9165	
Italy/Italie	79835	102615	73524	63983	59561
Chile/Chili	91761	59630	91265	82076	114499
Peru/Pérou	590	790	76264	74081	100154
Sweden/Suède	53230	41416	37103	43640	52181
Australia/Australie	42912	34713	36417	42886	42349
Netherlands/Pays–Bas	34746	33648	36677	41505	54959
Norway,SVD,JM	31112	28997	41165	38088	57664
Kazakstan				x107992	x102119
Singapore/Singapour	24112	18535	30105	34806	98610
Hong Kong	18924	27201	23458	25730	29125
Morocco/Maroc	23289	22681	14145	19556	28348
Austria/Autriche	17992	13974	20159	12345	x10671
Bolivia/Bolivie	54277	27543	5387	12921	14662
Papua New Guinea	14652	13945	10580	8481	x23060
Korea, Republic of	7835	3841	12030	9687	22349
Colombia/Colombie	5003	2479		15392	45774
Denmark/Danemark	7025	6310	5456	3563	3408
Indonesia/Indonésie	6	26	8708	4806	3449
Brazil/Brésil	59	3572	3457	5777	3878
China/Chine	23510	4705	3172	3753	15972
Finland/Finlande	4495	3366	3226	3675	2663
Nicaragua				9993	
Malaysia/Malaisie	734	476	2886	6393	13433
United Arab Emirates	98694	17		x8908	x6280
Korea Dem People's Rp	x7854	x4500	x3254	x257	x77
Belarus/Bélarus			x6008	x930	x457
Ireland/Irlande	1842	2859	2526	48	502
Thailand/Thaïlande	359	666	797	3608	2117
Yugoslavia SFR	5289	x4938			
Zambia/Zambie	x1268	x1476	x1448	x2008	x3201
Czech Republic				4877	2890
Dominican Republic	3468	2748	1661	201	x18874
Czechoslovakia		x2707	x1849		
Portugal	1276	1458	1589	1378	361
Hungary/Hongrie	x1028	x2630	x1489	x304	x1673
India/Inde	793	336	2302	1498	279

(VALUE AS % OF TOTAL)(VALEUR EN % DU TOTAL)

	1985	1986	1987	1988	1989	1990	1991	1992	1993	1994
Africa	0.3	x0.2	0.3	x0.1	x0.2	x0.1	x0.1	0.2	0.5	x0.3
Northern Africa	0.1	0.1	0.2	0.1	0.1	0.1	0.1	0.1	0.2	0.1
Americas	44.1	40.0	27.7	29.7	30.6	29.7	27.4	30.3	28.5	27.2
LAIA	0.9	1.4	0.9	0.8	1.5	0.7	0.5	0.6	0.8	1.0
CACM	0.0	0.0	x0.0	0.0	0.0	0.0	0.0	0.0	x0.0	x0.0
Asia	16.5	17.0	x24.6	x29.2	x26.9	27.2	27.4	26.3	x31.0	x32.8
Middle East	0.4	0.5	x0.3	0.7	x1.7	3.0	2.3	3.4	x2.8	x2.3
Europe	38.8	42.7	46.1	39.4	40.1	41.9	44.2	42.1	38.9	38.3
EEC	31.7	34.7	34.6	33.8	33.2	36.8	35.7	37.8	29.7	32.0
EFTA	6.9	7.9	11.5	5.5	6.9	5.1	8.5	4.2	9.1	6.2
Oceania	0.3	x0.3	x0.4	0.8	x1.1	x0.5	x0.7	x0.9	x0.9	x1.0
USA/Etats–Unis d'Amer	40.7	37.5	26.0	26.1	27.4	27.3	25.7	27.9	26.0	24.1
Japan/Japon	15.3	15.3	21.9	24.8	21.2	20.4	21.1	16.9	19.4	20.6
United Kingdom	8.0	9.7	8.3	9.6	9.1	12.9	12.1	12.6	10.2	9.3
Germany/Allemagne	10.1	10.6	11.6	11.2	12.0	9.9	8.8	10.0	6.8	7.8
Switz.Liecht	4.8	6.1	9.4	3.8	5.4	4.9	8.3	4.0	8.8	5.9
France,Monac	4.3	4.4	3.9	4.1	4.1	4.4	4.3	4.3	4.5	4.6
Italy/Italie	2.0	2.8	3.7	2.8	2.4	3.4	4.2	5.1	3.2	3.7
Singapore/Singapour	0.1	0.3	0.5	0.8	1.3	2.0	1.2	2.5	4.4	2.1
United Arab Emirates	0.2	0.3	x0.1	0.5	x1.5	2.8	2.1	3.2	x2.5	x1.2
Belgium–Luxembourg	3.8	3.1	2.8	2.4	1.8	2.1	2.0	2.5	2.1	2.5

	1985	1986	1987	1988	1989	1990	1991	1992	1993	1994
Afrique	0.9	x0.9	x0.6	0.9	x0.7	0.7	x0.6	x5.5	0.7	x0.7
Afrique du Nord	0.4	0.2	0.3	0.3	0.3	0.4	0.4	0.3	0.5	0.6
Amériques	33.9	27.5	16.6	16.7	19.0	21.7	17.7	24.5	28.2	27.6
ALAI	16.7	14.1	9.0	6.7	7.9	8.6	5.3	8.6	9.2	9.8
MCAC	0.1	0.0	0.0	0.1	0.1	0.0	0.0	0.0	0.2	x0.0
Asie	2.0	1.9	x2.4	x4.2	x2.7	5.1	2.2	4.9	x7.4	x8.7
Moyen–Orient	0.0	0.3	x0.1	0.4	x0.2	1.9	x0.0	x0.0	x0.2	x0.1
Europe	58.3	65.4	42.7	42.7	46.6	68.5	53.8	61.9	59.8	58.2
CEE	47.6	55.3	33.4	29.6	36.6	58.3	44.4	48.4	48.3	43.7
AELE	10.0	9.6	9.1	12.8	9.8	10.1	9.3	13.4	11.3	14.5
Océanie	1.3	x2.6	0.8	x0.4	0.5	1.2	0.8	1.0	1.3	x1.3
United Kingdom	17.1	26.7	14.2	12.0	15.1	29.6	21.1	19.7	20.0	16.6
USA/Etats–Unis d'Amer	7.4	6.1	5.3	5.8	6.3	8.0	9.7	12.0	14.2	13.1
Russian Federation								x17.7	x20.9	x23.3
Switz.Liecht	7.6	7.1	6.7	11.1	7.9	9.5	8.8	12.5	10.4	13.3
Germany/Allemagne	8.8	8.6	7.4	6.8	8.5	11.4	9.0	10.9	11.1	9.8
Former USSR/Anc. URSS			x31.0	x30.8	x28.0		x22.8			
Belgium–Luxembourg	9.4	9.4	4.1	4.5	5.7	6.4	5.1	7.4	6.2	6.6
France,Monac	5.8	4.9	3.5	2.7	3.6	6.1	4.6	4.2	4.5	5.5
Mexico/Mexique	8.5	8.4	5.6	4.5	5.4	5.7	3.8	4.7	4.5	4.2
Canada	9.7	7.1	2.3	3.9	4.6	5.0	2.6	3.8	4.5	4.3

TRADE BY COMMODITY IN THOUSAND U.S. DOLLARS – COMMERCE PAR PRODUIT EN MILLIERS DE DOLLARS E.U

IMPORTS – IMPORTATIONS

COUNTRIES–PAYS	1990	1991	1992	1993	1994
Total	22592969	21254303	22202814	19877961	23603605
Africa	305986	259900	260147	x245831	x268997
Northern Africa	240943	210964	199803	188725	201073
Americas	2598357	2561371	2891925	2952837	3746666
LAIA	439189	618188	835744	776689	906530
CACM	20865	24343	24664	x22811	x28230
Asia	5562439	5895277	6681531	6596300	7425093
Middle East	517443	x538858	x601311	x404918	x476532
Europe	13660431	12228697	11991071	9674457	11684631
EEC	13015585	11731866	11452359	9202763	11121581
EFTA	560608	463530	454177	401883	486468
Oceania	x139793	x129291	x132061	x151004	x199179
Germany/Allemagne	2981102	2977743	2921480	2105924	2833809
France, Monac	2312194	2030466	2026345	1522755	1879533
USA/Etats–Unis d'Amer	1803387	1612238	1676942	1785844	2360877
Italy/Italie	2078721	1806918	1860424	1405630	1758275
Japan/Japon	1929117	1802257	1105849	1044151	1108335
United Kingdom	1471555	1231518	1184257	1359048	1193484
Belgium–Luxembourg	1491308	1213512	1083169	815302	994626
China/Chine	242297	437056	1275328	1211555	889655
Hong Kong	481516	629529	808952	867569	926618
Korea, Republic of	626490	710007	691425	751214	1052613
Singapore/Singapour	443319	485950	673395	643589	793838
Spain/Espagne	559259	622926	610118	409247	510717
Malaysia/Malaisie	297286	373901	443776	507063	669734
Netherlands/Pays–Bas	501595	447658	438503	359115	418482
Thailand/Thaïlande	330118	333935	369027	405656	578689
Austria/Autriche	403321	374332	382871	342011	420938
Switz.Liecht	455594	373103	370452	338884	399825
Canada	281115	270880	317862	335184	421038
Sweden/Suède	386763	326936	290033	258364	319314
India/Inde	315513	181216	286472	280858	373506
Mexico/Mexique	90568	148058	282770	284158	341457
Brazil/Brésil	183810	222821	234661	211850	255241
Indonesia/Indonésie	180262	194587	188722	191645	234610
Saudi Arabia	191987	193813	261324	x92476	x120844
Greece/Grèce	202358	168920	143359	192706	187670
Portugal	165384	159919	164456	116080	152430
Turkey/Turquie	207910	172569	124798	132380	166458
Denmark/Danemark	155612	148009	146831	125087	158996
Finland/Finlande	203574	134535	112417	114262	198865
Israel/Israël	106249	105118	116129	124659	141704
Argentina/Argentine	33193	82730	132064	107857	125590
Australia/Australie	80724	82575	83482	94804	133888
Ireland/Irlande	102839	88475	88097	77230	94443
Venezuela	49708	87854	86876	62189	54030
Norway, SVD, JM	103378	88477	81863	61408	85044
Hungary/Hongrie	x20926	54028	x66757	x71055	x57869
Colombia/Colombie	57518	49652	64748	72148	88372
Iran (Islamic Rp. of)		x89425	x76138	x18714	x5844
Algeria/Algérie	82584	76958	57892	37750	50491
Czechoslovakia	129731	x56989	x112582		
Philippines	41612	33499	50702	73108	99399
Morocco/Maroc	62441	50099	52246	49056	46613
New Zealand	56055	43383	44536	53410	60787
Egypt/Egypte	45175	49328	40102	51254	51186
United Arab Emirates	37947	27651	51659	x57370	x77801
Pakistan	30060	30135	31024	38077	33194
Tunisia/Tunisie	36885	26134	38915	34183	31759
Czech Republic				98957	108892
Slovenia/Slovénia			38634	36670	43544
So. Africa Customs Un	24597	21901	26385	24994	38325

EXPORTS – EXPORTATIONS

COUNTRIES–PAYS	1990	1991	1992	1993	1994
Totale	21566862	21476167	21491238	20892411	22960792
Afrique	x1353875	x1578131	x1329698	x1341446	x616690
Afrique du Nord	14562	6193	9375	1540	2017
Amériques	6827916	6484155	6604970	6158491	6962066
ALAI	4630856	4115713	4388968	3989534	4554026
MCAC	1306	2269	2402	1604	x897
Asie	2510551	2621542	3323637	3666789	4215286
Moyen–Orient	x284857	x194405	x225120	x252267	x260122
Europe	9488521	8651032	8535604	8205724	9375321
CEE	8921915	8184662	8168029	7838985	8976199
AELE	318996	285823	287567	234178	291425
Océanie	x516121	x554509	x609885	x556734	x656107
Chile/Chili	3504603	2901684	3032433	2646062	3160453
Germany/Allemagne	2590428	2397427	2516205	2726158	2730016
Belgium–Luxembourg	1829408	1532771	1440711	1298504	1454495
Japan/Japon	1146144	1194253	1361503	1498492	1632838
USA/Etats–Unis d'Amer	1225752	1336658	1184320	1208946	1287122
France, Monac	1286702	1213405	1202249	1013559	1311514
Canada	956398	1022317	1027609	958074	1118896
Zambia/Zambie	x514335	x935769	x863224	x1002550	x576173
Poland/Pologne	684511	700855	745218	663341	794143
Peru/Pérou	684042	697003	689171	649861	771675
Italy/Italie	740188	664093	641368	600283	857018
Russian Federation			x839775	x925699	x1240194
United Kingdom	629713	588719	560427	545145	762427
Australia/Australie	482096	517825	570706	514265	601922
Hong Kong	177679	292584	471342	526528	585614
Sweden/Suède	504707	460279	439649	384688	451362
Mexico/Mexique	256360	290243	406812	474830	446371
Finland/Finlande	417925	363034	398727	350596	392536
Spain/Espagne	225154	340377	310244	328983	379642
Singapore/Singapour	195952	242120	324926	336188	436090
So. Africa Customs Un	331730	329364	303236	250791	
Austria/Autriche	293530	269447	274390	242143	x261546
Former USSR/Anc. URSS		x734332			
Philippines	283900	227113	222116	273268	286267
Netherlands/Pays–Bas	271030	231281	237474	234527	261897
Brazil/Brésil	165485	217771	252067	206251	155299
Korea, Republic of	158788	188906	241370	243607	318309
Switz.Liecht	189243	175331	177449	144998	177157
China/Chine	125620	128279	158873	140763	218541
Bulgaria/Bulgarie	x101712	x71772	204912	137781	177875
Zaire/Zaïre	x452593	x267133	x97146	x43083	x14033
Malaysia/Malaisie	63179	54404	100484	176530	224743
Norway, SVD, JM	129750	110489	110111	89148	114254
Turkey/Turquie	122965	103535	85134	91351	88009
Greece/Grèce	73018	69624	93756	94475	92999
Kazakstan			x92599	x142700	x149767
Yugoslavia SFR	247404	x180388			
Iran (Islamic Rp. of)	x77076	x34785	x83557	x43494	x12373
Hungary/Hongrie	x60725	x38763	x63416	x43688	x43119
Saudi Arabia	47582	26815	25704	x71498	x95388
Yugoslavia/Yougoslavie			x47317	x65873	x58925
New Zealand	33618	33116	35522	42396	53945
Oman	33445	28180	28454	42340	54453
Ukraine			x56247	x38598	x22225
Czechoslovakia		x34846	x59525		
Indonesia/Indonésie	43595	47328	24148	20290	38028
Un. Rep. of Tanzania	x5946	x23240	x38636	x23694	x11475
Denmark/Danemark	27826	26864	29871	11086	13431
Slovakia				x61618	x60892
Zimbabwe	28008	15787	16612	16074	x12182

(VALUE AS % OF TOTAL)(VALEUR EN % DU TOTAL)

Imports

	1985	1986	1987	1988	1989	1990	1991	1992	1993	1994
Africa	1.5	1.3	1.3	1.2	1.0	1.3	1.2	1.2	x1.2	x1.2
Northern Africa	1.2	1.0	0.9	0.9	0.8	1.1	1.0	0.9	0.9	0.9
Americas	15.9	17.8	16.5	15.2	13.4	11.5	12.1	13.0	14.9	15.9
LAIA	3.0	3.2	3.4	2.6	2.2	1.9	2.9	3.8	3.9	3.8
CACM	0.1	0.1	0.1	0.1	0.1	0.1	0.1	0.1	x0.1	x0.1
Asia	19.1	17.1	x21.3	x23.7	21.7	24.6	27.8	30.1	33.2	31.5
Middle East	1.5	x2.9	x2.5	x2.0	x1.8	2.3	x2.5	x2.7	x2.0	x2.0
Europe	62.5	62.8	57.6	56.9	61.3	60.5	57.5	54.0	48.7	49.5
EEC	54.3	54.7	50.2	50.1	54.3	57.6	55.2	51.6	46.3	47.1
EFTA	7.0	7.4	6.8	6.3	6.6	2.5	2.2	2.0	2.0	2.1
Oceania	0.7	x0.6	x0.6	x0.5	x0.6	x0.6	x0.6	x0.6	x0.7	x0.8
Germany/Allemagne	13.0	12.7	10.6	10.5	11.4	13.2	14.0	13.2	10.6	12.0
France, Monac	8.6	8.5	8.4	8.9	9.7	10.2	9.6	9.1	7.7	8.0
USA/Etats–Unis d'Amer	11.5	13.0	11.5	10.9	9.5	8.0	7.6	7.6	9.0	10.0
Italy/Italie	7.9	8.0	8.0	8.1	8.8	9.2	8.5	8.4	7.1	7.4
Japan/Japon	5.7	4.2	4.9	6.2	7.2	8.5	8.5	5.0	5.3	4.7
United Kingdom	7.0	6.9	6.6	6.6	6.6	6.5	5.8	5.3	6.8	5.1
Belgium–Luxembourg	7.5	7.6	6.1	5.7	6.8	6.6	5.7	4.9	4.1	4.2
China/Chine	4.6	2.2	1.5	1.4	1.4	1.1	2.1	5.7	6.1	3.8
Hong Kong	1.4	1.7	2.1	2.2	1.9	2.1	3.0	3.6	4.4	3.9
Korea, Republic of	1.2	2.1	2.2	2.8	2.4	2.8	3.3	3.1	3.8	4.5

Exports

	1985	1986	1987	1988	1989	1990	1991	1992	1993	1994
Afrique	7.5	x11.9	x10.0	x8.6	x11.2	x6.2	x7.3	x6.2	x6.4	x2.7
Afrique du Nord	0.0	0.0	x0.0	0.0	0.0	0.1	0.0	0.0	0.0	0.0
Amériques	25.7	21.0	21.5	24.4	24.4	31.6	30.2	30.7	29.5	30.3
ALAI	17.0	13.5	14.2	16.5	16.3	21.5	19.2	20.4	19.1	19.8
MCAC	0.0	0.0	0.0	0.0	0.0	0.0	0.0	0.0	0.0	x0.0
Asie	10.2	11.5	x12.2	x14.3	11.1	11.7	12.2	15.5	17.5	18.3
Moyen–Orient	0.7	x1.1	x1.0	x1.2	1.1	x1.3	x0.9	x1.0	x1.2	x1.1
Europe	51.3	51.0	47.2	43.1	43.1	44.0	40.3	39.7	39.3	40.8
CEE	43.6	43.2	39.2	35.9	36.3	41.4	38.1	38.0	37.5	39.1
AELE	7.0	7.1	6.9	6.3	5.9	1.5	1.3	1.3	1.1	1.3
Océanie	1.5	x1.3	x1.4	x1.6	x1.9	x2.4	x2.6	x2.8	x2.7	x2.9
Chile/Chili	13.2	12.3	11.8	12.9	12.8	16.2	13.5	14.1	12.7	13.8
Germany/Allemagne	13.4	14.0	12.8	10.9	10.5	12.0	11.2	11.7	13.0	11.9
Belgium–Luxembourg	8.8	8.7	7.9	7.4	8.3	8.5	7.1	6.7	6.2	6.3
Japan/Japon	6.2	6.9	6.4	5.4	4.8	5.3	5.6	6.3	7.2	7.1
USA/Etats–Unis d'Amer	3.5	2.5	2.7	3.6	3.8	5.7	6.2	5.5	5.8	5.6
France, Monac	5.5	5.4	4.8	4.7	5.2	6.0	5.7	5.6	4.9	5.7
Canada	5.2	5.1	4.6	4.3	4.3	4.4	4.8	4.8	4.6	4.9
Zambia/Zambie	4.8	5.6	5.0	3.9	x4.9	x2.4	x4.4	x4.0	x4.8	x2.5
Poland/Pologne	3.7	3.2	3.0	2.7	2.3	3.2	3.3	3.5	3.2	3.5
Peru/Pérou	2.9	0.6	1.1	1.8	1.4	3.2	3.2	3.2	3.1	3.4

TRADE BY COMMODITY IN THOUSAND U.S. DOLLARS – COMMERCE PAR PRODUIT EN MILLIERS DE DOLLARS E.U

COUNTRIES–PAYS	IMPORTS – IMPORTATIONS 1990	1991	1992	1993	1994
Total	4339581	4155942	3327095	2958540	3615981
Africa	x19522	12605	15205	x8085	17317
Northern Africa	7133	4020	6537	2100	10229
Americas	1295761	1275056	936418	852157	926727
LAIA	79261	85125	75805	62468	79396
CACM	453	356	373	x367	x432
Asia	785876	957234	886933	676124	796235
Middle East	x21329	x22618	x22841	x45280	x19966
Europe	2132876	1859784	1448636	1381701	1829577
EEC	2063826	1813911	1394221	1335408	1771310
EFTA	50794	41672	42519	30018	36822
Oceania	x17933	x17411	x16410	x12992	x14989
USA/Etats–Unis d'Amer	1123471	1070057	805046	693863	744842
Germany/Allemagne	659562	553638	402442	357909	450883
Japan/Japon	500699	554871	305179	286813	388084
France,Monac	412843	342341	292647	244040	301173
United Kingdom	296760	239105	190710	156021	210652
Italy/Italie	203437	241901	162331	181269	254471
Hong Kong	43629	78795	242168	82973	67289
Sweden/Suède	139999	119566	96986	112835	139504
Korea, Republic of	95096	154331	65414	86792	127811
Canada	89674	118419	53662	94378	101453
Belgium–Luxembourg	93101	75979	73283	84251	143249
Spain/Espagne	120761	99206	63299	62320	115700
China/Chine	7511	39122	83591	45957	26293
India/Inde	43196	31406	54918	44113	73266
Finland/Finlande	31058	49254	27577	33841	51266
Netherlands/Pays–Bas	33951	30581	31769	47527	42516
Brazil/Brésil	33948	40767	35401	29235	40254
Switz.Liecht	43322	37131	38293	25978	31565
Austria/Autriche	41080	32474	28290	34223	34911
Singapore/Singapour	23760	23334	26976	24648	35501
Mexico/Mexique	29834	25153	23572	20299	24419
Malaysia/Malaisie	10266	12996	16745	18492	23212
Viet Nam	x85	x2089	x35336	x7885	x36
Ireland/Irlande	18778	17713	14619	12971	18454
Australia/Australie	16305	15889	14976	11611	13690
Thailand/Thaïlande	12412	10170	12066	12232	14009
Israel/Israël	10822	14069	10079	10191	11789
United Arab Emirates	436	281	606	x30253	x5800
Turkey/Turquie	11630	10088	8151	9725	7957
Slovenia/Slovénia			8921	15027	20453
Romania/Roumanie	44270	7023	11389	5069	5186
Hungary/Hongrie	x6363	5945	x4955	x8302	x7679
Argentina/Argentine	5301	7710	7049	3899	4441
So. Africa Customs Un	9144	5615	7539	5027	5765
Iran (Islamic Rp. of)		x4144	x10762	x2401	x1781
Former USSR/Anc. URSS		x16012			
Denmark/Danemark	5739	5646	5101	4268	4692
Norway,SVD,JM	7456	4527	4218	4032	5237
Pakistan	4450	5203	3667	2865	3268
Venezuela	4739	6004	3627	2038	3014
Indonesia/Indonésie	3465	3413	4392	3813	3004
Portugal	4398	3936	3641	2949	2623
Colombia/Colombie	2690	2834	2710	3094	3190
Czech Republic				8502	8579
Saudi Arabia	2028	3251	2614	x2464	x3462
Czechoslovakia	31482	x4360	x3719		
Chile/Chili	1450	1682	2792	2951	2820
Poland/Pologne			2585	4086	8076
Korea Dem People's Rp	x7557	x2243	x1715	x2471	x741
Greece/Grèce	2360	2570	1525	984	1216

COUNTRIES–PAYS	EXPORTS – EXPORTATIONS 1990	1991	1992	1993	1994
Totale	2968352	x3560960	2782486	2460389	2610660
Afrique	202969	212854	163127	97798	x105784
Afrique du Nord	27	163	90		
Amériques	x980614	886188	1091396	885381	856696
ALAI	16904	22279	26853	26796	34417
MCAC					
Asie	148687	174150	255591	151883	286456
Moyen–Orient	x660	x86	x414	x1037	x637
Europe	1600404	1417024	1262432	1173418	1353898
CEE	1039378	918960	858242	832494	918905
AELE	560993	495920	399792	331668	422034
Océanie	x3449	x1958	x903	x141657	4116
Canada	688922	626359	849660	647644	600956
Norway,SVD,JM	542345	481724	386201	320352	408374
United Kingdom	365305	348025	293708	261675	282531
Former USSR/Anc. URSS		x850699			
Germany/Allemagne	320119	278897	289481	273108	277592
Russian Federation			x315155	x475244	x601004
USA/Etats–Unis d'Amer	239791	237021	213180	210003	220973
France,Monac	143878	120234	118074	119171	115110
Hong Kong	27277	46321	161207	64187	46479
So. Africa Customs Un	102435	123659	90874	47371	
Japan/Japon	80420	94883	68438	58040	79344
Zimbabwe	100246	88150	71172	49752	x104463
Finland/Finlande	93687	57516	72194	67619	77109
Australia/Australie	2892	1419	661	141023	4113
Sweden/Suède	42841	32867	27727	24874	42066
Brazil/Brésil	16785	22133	25972	26201	33404
Italy/Italie	26267	41225	17701	14857	25996
Singapore/Singapour	21950	21919	11549	17992	28422
Belgium–Luxembourg	12809	12854	12287	21864	56669
Netherlands/Pays–Bas	8917	5697	7917	25963	20970
Switz.Liecht	18648	14196	13591	11316	13659
Austria/Autriche	12087	10063	10709	12567	x12209
Ireland/Irlande	11158	10180	7059	7016	7136
Estonia/Estonie			x2421	x12950	x7373
Lithuania/Lituanie			1021	x9623	1097
Korea, Republic of	11440	6883	2315	966	12632
Albania/Albanie	x9940	x8661	x1199	x140	x64
Slovenia/Slovénia			423	8026	12921
Czechoslovakia		x2693	x5224		
Czech Republic				7481	1484
India/Inde	112	1296	5804	286	70
Spain/Espagne	2214	1287	1305	3534	1460
Latvia/Lettonie			x4078	x1580	7
China/Chine	2975	272	2606	2599	116006
Hungary/Hongrie	x7839	x2927	x1530	x887	x1955
Belarus/Bélarus			x933	x3883	x254
Bulgaria/Bulgarie	x13918	x3805	x432	x30	x46
Yugoslavia/Yougoslavie			x3696	x17	
Azerbaijan				x3427	
Ukraine			x2228	x1168	x266
Kazakstan			x1605	x1299	x223
Cuba	x34969	x515	x1645	x382	x141
Yugoslavia SFR	11	x2047			
Zambia/Zambie	x20	x771	x777	x490	x1084
Poland/Pologne			591	844	90
Tajikistan/Tadjikistan				x1376	x895
Israel/Israël	1468	212	1002	3	53
Mexico/Mexique	75	118	789	272	681
Korea Dem People's Rp	x1871	x885	x229		
Philippines	480	886	160		17

(VALUE AS % OF TOTAL)(VALEUR EN % DU TOTAL)

	1985	1986	1987	1988	1989	1990	1991	1992	1993	1994
Africa	0.6	0.5	0.6	x0.5	x0.2	x0.4	0.3	0.4	x0.3	0.5
Northern Africa	0.3	0.2	0.3	0.1	0.1	0.2	0.1	0.2	0.1	0.3
Americas	33.2	31.7	28.9	28.6	28.8	29.9	30.7	28.1	28.8	25.6
LAIA	1.6	1.9	1.6	1.6	2.1	1.8	2.0	2.3	2.1	2.2
CACM	0.0	0.0	0.0	0.0	0.0	0.0	0.0	0.0	x0.0	x0.0
Asia	14.3	15.9	x19.5	21.2	18.6	18.1	23.0	26.7	22.8	22.1
Middle East	0.3	0.5	x0.7	x0.4	x0.6	x0.5	x0.5	x0.7	x1.5	x0.6
Europe	51.5	51.1	49.6	48.6	50.1	49.1	44.8	43.5	46.7	50.6
EEC	43.0	43.8	43.8	42.1	43.9	47.6	43.6	41.9	45.1	49.0
EFTA	7.4	6.3	5.1	5.9	5.9	1.2	1.0	1.3	1.0	1.0
Oceania	0.5	x0.7	x0.7	0.3	x0.4	x0.4	x0.4	x0.5	x0.4	x0.4
USA/Etats–Unis d'Amer	29.2	27.2	25.1	25.9	25.3	25.9	25.7	24.2	23.5	20.6
Germany/Allemagne	13.3	14.1	14.8	14.2	14.3	15.2	13.3	12.1	12.1	12.5
Japan/Japon	8.3	8.3	10.7	10.2	10.3	11.5	13.4	9.2	9.7	10.7
France,Monac	7.1	7.7	8.4	7.3	7.6	9.5	8.2	8.8	8.2	8.3
United Kingdom	6.9	6.2	6.4	5.1	5.5	6.8	5.8	5.7	5.3	5.8
Italy/Italie	5.7	6.1	5.3	5.0	4.9	4.7	5.8	4.9	6.1	7.0
Hong Kong	1.4	1.8	1.3	1.8	1.5	1.0	1.9	7.3	2.8	1.9
Sweden/Suède	3.5	2.7	2.5	3.5	3.5	3.2	2.9	2.9	3.8	3.9
Korea, Republic of	1.3	1.9	1.6	1.5	2.2	2.2	3.7	2.0	2.9	3.5
Canada	2.3	2.5	2.1	1.0	1.5	2.1	2.8	1.6	3.2	2.8

	1985	1986	1987	1988	1989	1990	1991	1992	1993	1994
Afrique	8.1	9.8	6.7	7.0	x5.9	6.9	6.0	5.9	3.9	x4.1
Afrique du Nord		0.0	x0.0	0.0	0.0	0.0	0.0	0.0		
Amériques	34.2	x27.8	22.8	x6.6	x6.3	x33.0	24.8	39.2	36.0	32.8
ALAI	0.1	x0.1	0.0	x0.2	0.2	0.6	0.6	1.0	1.1	1.3
MCAC	0.0	x0.0	x0.0		x0.0			0.0		0.0
Asie	7.4	4.5	4.5	4.8	4.8	5.1	4.9	9.2	6.2	10.9
Moyen–Orient	0.0	x0.0	x0.0	0.0	x0.0	x0.0	x0.0	x0.0	x0.0	x0.0
Europe	44.5	47.4	34.6	40.3	36.2	53.9	39.8	45.4	47.7	51.9
CEE	29.1	32.2	22.6	23.6	20.2	35.0	25.8	30.8	33.8	35.2
AELE	15.3	15.3	12.0	16.7	16.0	18.9	13.9	14.4	13.5	16.2
Océanie	5.8	x10.5	3.9	0.2		x0.1	x0.0	x0.0	x5.7	0.2
Canada	23.7	22.6	18.7	2.5	1.8	23.2	17.6	30.5	26.3	23.0
Norway,SVD,JM	9.3	9.4	7.6	12.1	12.7	18.3	13.5	13.9	13.0	15.6
United Kingdom	9.2	10.6	7.3	8.9	7.0	12.3	9.8	10.6	10.6	10.8
Former USSR/Anc. URSS			x26.7	x40.8	x46.2		x23.9			
Germany/Allemagne	9.2	10.4	7.1	6.2	6.1	10.8	7.8	10.4	11.1	10.6
Russian Federation								x11.3	x19.3	x23.0
USA/Etats–Unis d'Amer	10.3	5.1	4.1	3.8	4.3	8.1	6.7	7.7	8.5	8.5
France,Monac	3.9	4.6	3.1	3.0	2.4	4.8	3.4	4.2	4.8	4.4
Hong Kong	1.3	1.5	1.1	1.4	1.5	0.9	1.3	5.8	2.6	1.8
So. Africa Customs Un	5.2	7.0	4.6	3.1	2.7	3.5	3.5	3.3	1.9	

TRADE BY COMMODITY IN THOUSAND U.S. DOLLARS – COMMERCE PAR PRODUIT EN MILLIERS DE DOLLARS E.U

COUNTRIES–PAYS	IMPORTS – IMPORTATIONS				
	1990	1991	1992	1993	1994
Total	29260902	27879642	27880670	25710639	33216610
Africa	x314985	x334083	x375723	x392205	x428570
Northern Africa	138150	133486	166232	180563	229709
Americas	4575027	4047288	4444593	5294723	7445829
LAIA	492197	563005	820924	879051	1058738
CACM	42865	39613	50733	x65799	x60943
Asia	8102145	8438394	7744591	7689847	9250451
Middle East	648138	x778957	x684401	x606936	x606492
Europe	15732049	14613836	14836896	11715575	15339905
EEC	14744320	13814996	13948446	10955478	14212506
EFTA	883928	722827	742000	634962	983721
Oceania	x167597	x159958	x201922	x209811	x243101
Japan/Japon	4771349	4598399	3607991	3451450	3937797
Germany/Allemagne	3767532	3871474	4019741	2683612	3674704
USA/Etats–Unis d'Amer	2927501	2475662	2607008	3358720	5067479
France, Monac	2532209	2271460	2170121	1530772	1920472
United Kingdom	1776879	1540945	1694232	1788569	1725664
Italy/Italie	1799185	1646412	1594809	1224599	1723886
Belgium–Luxembourg	1313413	1215411	1123835	893648	1099552
Korea, Republic of	902940	976405	968895	1102484	1459419
Netherlands/Pays–Bas	1134093	1008781	1044797	894325	1209297
Canada	1045693	901468	905816	941359	1196802
Austria/Autriche	606635	557837	643350	521289	833424
Switz.Liecht	597717	479303	493997	425527	568418
China/Chine	281685	282310	586314	492531	588395
Mexico/Mexique	240370	273713	461406	498015	611701
Spain/Espagne	377182	429289	419945	372573	463146
Hong Kong	280823	349361	429145	388786	519512
Sweden/Suède	481260	424737	392597	341588	582810
Thailand/Thaïlande	310104	349054	332235	385070	461756
Singapore/Singapour	260141	303976	333480	362816	457216
Denmark/Danemark	316588	282698	250301	215515	287879
Malaysia/Malaisie	180844	222886	232253	262004	384860
Norway, SVD, JM	278321	235741	241458	203027	407927
Saudi Arabia	242607	263651	228977	x160884	x194797
Indonesia/Indonésie	111338	199498	161476	198347	254284
Portugal	191472	182404	190011	138469	188786
Turkey/Turquie	214288	146971	149759	209571	169276
Ireland/Irlande	169567	160330	160066	142179	170373
Israel/Israël	139631	138359	135037	129942	164163
Finland/Finlande	192420	127286	127194	117119	190508
Australia/Australie	92934	97567	124659	127502	141781
Iran (Islamic Rp. of)		x177773	x100104	x37254	x24510
Greece/Grèce	85887	95930	117447	91222	142004
Poland/Pologne	61740	56027	90499	137837	165055
Philippines	78989	85421	96868	88091	106732
Venezuela	53653	80589	94915	77484	60655
Brazil/Brésil	76752	70874	67956	89923	125080
Colombia/Colombie	54011	55561	78136	79028	91394
Hungary/Hongrie	x16908	104379	x43290	x58660	x82308
New Zealand	66152	53804	68046	73263	91653
So. Africa Customs Un	53781	64086	56938	64750	67934
India/Inde	58817	41740	29985	76633	171101
Algeria/Algérie	52514	39353	54222	52194	46326
Chile/Chili	32436	34650	50484	55190	57535
Pakistan	34149	31866	60713	41462	45590
United Arab Emirates	51106	33756	42335	x53497	x64175
Czech Republic				123345	164116
Slovenia/Slovénia			59795	60933	90605
Egypt/Egypte	16439	18596	41792	48258	102328
Morocco/Maroc	32069	37337	33301	35662	38880
Nigeria/Nigéria	x18768	42141	x33212	x25925	x21691

COUNTRIES–PAYS	EXPORTS – EXPORTATIONS				
	1990	1991	1992	1993	1994
Totale	28506467	27624300	26715872	24869468	29585807
Afrique	x619948	383596	x371055	x446870	x575633
Afrique du Nord	216957	158199	193417	147762	178039
Amériques	7661906	7751715	7294486	7038558	8486794
ALAI	2206444	2019804	1914323	1790367	2121072
MCAC	22816	19684	28347	x28076	x32877
Asie	x2612071	x2568614	x2853798	x3101834	x3635029
Moyen–Orient	x911208	x847266	x898627	x1131334	x943093
Europe	15001468	13690913	14007624	11990423	14285509
CEE	11641740	10883475	11289288	9767110	11572224
AELE	2767623	2471158	2307637	2031853	2469751
Océanie	x2043560	x1871962	x1733380	x1808986	x1951610
Germany/Allemagne	3387326	3189100	3385564	2751257	3132483
USA/Etats–Unis d'Amer	2868055	3135148	2675640	2328177	2797139
Canada	2560315	2573992	2629375	2849983	3491390
France, Monac	1688662	1586069	1718102	1480223	1682910
Norway, SVD, JM	1900513	1684170	1547026	1394579	1718620
Australia/Australie	1610288	1484126	1389303	1466511	1556172
Netherlands/Pays–Bas	1469661	1300530	1270234	1114827	1371255
Brazil/Brésil	1039097	1111935	1114501	1068513	1189743
Russian Federation			x1076209	x2138907	x3372683
Belgium–Luxembourg	1272478	1150070	1098848	952131	1126185
United Kingdom	1047195	977274	1068062	907742	1151387
Italy/Italie	774538	755369	806327	789055	910690
Japan/Japon	760532	719621	686552	746151	913507
Venezuela	909704	728230	655095	555058	734374
Switz.Liecht	702911	648375	620583	515169	595939
Austria/Autriche	655084	612904	603387	483036	x592867
Bahrain/Bahreïn	x482670	x389531	x460156	x758785	x460286
Spain/Espagne	380668	419820	410452	446817	592889
New Zealand	432479	387675	342498	341344	395277
Sweden/Suède	394527	372410	350711	311660	398910
Former USSR/Anc. URSS		x959516			
United Arab Emirates	301947	365603	327869	x255544	x311671
Greece/Grèce	279243	286706	311933	269490	313123
Hong Kong	165200	188715	272602	255246	348950
Indonesia/Indonésie	223738	176114	196554	170732	235770
Hungary/Hongrie	x261391	x156482	x213432	x170997	x227666
Egypt/Egypte	212170	155064	188146	140558	167287
India/Inde	85558	122109	184966	115354	144137
China/Chine	144605	159606	127146	125686	242108
Korea, Republic of	94263	109874	140503	153490	283314
Argentina/Argentine	241703	161779	114664	127270	160914
Iceland/Islande	164199	138614	140027	122105	155192
Singapore/Singapour	82776	110878	122162	145639	213675
Denmark/Danemark	148814	116383	134273	112467	132568
Romania/Roumanie	215212	118749	130042	101649	154234
Yugoslavia SFR	581314	x328408			
Ghana	x201719	65722	45050	x179378	x315671
Cameroon/Cameroun	139657	108673	x87115	x71737	x78787
Slovenia/Slovénia			140894	122916	157962
Croatia/Croatie			186786	37985	x45469
Finland/Finlande	84250	59838	71639	81994	104528
Malaysia/Malaisie	46155	52688	59910	63388	115401
Israel/Israël	65982	57311	58921	51867	71894
Turkey/Turquie	106256	55661	58928	53282	77390
Poland/Pologne	53972	48530	41049	61988	72016
Ukraine			x36019	x103597	x75973
Czechoslovakia		x69412	x67190		
So. Africa Customs Un	57414	47457	41545	37361	
Ireland/Irlande	25899	34386	38708	48427	37262
Tajikistan/Tadjikistan			x20982	x73637	x89699

(VALUE AS % OF TOTAL)(VALEUR EN % DU TOTAL)

	1985	1986	1987	1988	1989	1990	1991	1992	1993	1994
Africa	1.4	x1.5	x1.3	x0.9	x0.9	x1.1	x1.2	x1.3	x1.6	x1.3
Northern Africa	0.7	0.7	0.6	0.4	0.4	0.5	0.5	0.6	0.7	0.7
Americas	20.3	21.7	18.5	16.5	15.9	15.7	14.5	15.9	20.6	22.5
LAIA	2.3	1.6	1.6	1.3	1.3	1.7	2.0	2.9	3.4	3.2
CACM	0.2	0.1	0.2	0.2	0.1	0.1	0.1	0.2	x0.3	x0.2
Asia	26.6	20.8	x26.8	x30.4	28.1	27.7	30.3	27.8	29.9	27.8
Middle East	1.9	x2.2	x2.4	x2.5	x1.8	2.2	x2.8	x2.5	x2.4	x1.8
Europe	49.2	53.8	49.8	48.9	52.4	53.8	52.4	53.2	45.6	46.2
EEC	42.2	46.0	42.8	42.1	45.2	50.4	49.6	50.0	42.6	42.8
EFTA	6.4	7.3	6.6	6.5	7.0	3.0	2.6	2.7	2.5	3.0
Oceania	0.4	x0.4	x0.4	x0.4	x0.5	x0.5	x0.5	x0.7	x0.8	x0.7
Japan/Japon	13.1	9.8	12.5	16.6	16.3	16.3	16.5	12.9	13.4	11.9
Germany/Allemagne	11.0	11.9	10.6	10.3	12.0	12.9	13.9	14.4	10.4	11.1
USA/Etats–Unis d'Amer	14.6	16.9	13.7	11.6	10.4	10.0	8.9	9.4	13.1	15.3
France, Monac	7.0	8.0	7.1	7.0	7.4	8.7	8.1	7.8	6.0	5.8
United Kingdom	5.3	5.3	5.3	5.3	5.6	6.1	5.5	6.1	7.0	5.2
Italy/Italie	4.8	5.1	5.1	5.2	5.7	6.1	5.9	5.7	4.8	5.2
Belgium–Luxembourg	4.2	4.3	4.0	4.2	4.2	4.5	4.4	4.0	3.5	3.3
Korea, Republic of	1.8	1.9	2.1	2.8	3.0	3.1	3.5	3.5	4.3	4.4
Netherlands/Pays–Bas	3.2	3.6	3.3	3.2	3.2	3.9	3.6	3.7	3.5	3.6
Canada	3.0	2.7	2.7	3.2	3.7	3.6	3.2	3.2	3.7	3.6

	1985	1986	1987	1988	1989	1990	1991	1992	1993	1994
Afrique	2.0	x3.2	x2.8	x2.6	x2.4	x2.2	1.4	x1.4	x1.8	x1.9
Afrique du Nord	1.1	0.8	0.8	0.9	0.8	0.8	0.6	0.7	0.6	0.6
Amériques	26.3	22.0	21.0	24.0	24.6	26.8	28.1	27.3	28.3	28.7
ALAI	10.1	6.3	6.3	7.4	6.9	7.7	7.3	7.2	7.2	7.2
MCAC	0.1	0.1	0.0	0.1	0.1	0.1	0.1	0.1	x0.1	x0.1
Asie	10.1	x9.7	x9.4	x10.2	x8.3	x9.2	x9.3	x10.7	x12.5	x12.3
Moyen–Orient	1.5	x3.0	x2.6	x2.7	x2.7	x3.2	x3.1	x3.4	x4.5	x3.2
Europe	54.7	58.8	52.3	48.2	49.4	52.6	49.6	52.4	48.2	48.3
CEE	39.3	43.0	37.4	34.1	35.4	40.8	39.4	42.3	39.3	39.1
AELE	12.7	13.8	12.8	12.2	12.5	9.7	8.9	8.6	8.2	8.3
Océanie	6.9	6.4	x6.8	x7.5	x7.7	x7.2	x6.8	x6.5	x7.3	x6.6
Germany/Allemagne	11.7	13.4	11.5	10.2	10.4	11.9	11.5	12.7	11.1	10.6
USA/Etats–Unis d'Amer	6.6	5.2	5.6	6.9	8.7	10.1	11.3	10.0	9.4	9.5
Canada	9.3	10.2	8.9	9.4	8.9	9.0	9.3	9.8	11.5	11.8
France, Monac	5.6	6.2	5.4	4.8	4.9	5.9	5.7	6.4	6.0	5.7
Norway, SVD, JM	6.4	6.6	6.5	6.4	6.6	6.7	6.1	5.8	5.6	5.8
Australia/Australie	5.1	4.9	5.2	5.9	6.2	5.6	5.4	5.2	5.9	5.3
Netherlands/Pays–Bas	4.6	5.3	4.6	4.1	4.4	5.2	4.7	4.8	4.5	4.6
Brazil/Brésil	1.7	2.9	3.2	4.2	3.3	3.6	4.0	4.2	4.3	4.0
Russian Federation								x4.0	x8.6	x11.4
Belgium–Luxembourg	4.0	4.4	4.0	3.9	4.2	4.5	4.2	4.1	3.8	3.8

TRADE BY COMMODITY IN THOUSAND U.S. DOLLARS – COMMERCE PAR PRODUIT EN MILLIERS DE DOLLARS E.U

COUNTRIES–PAYS	IMPORTS – IMPORTATIONS 1990	1991	1992	1993	1994
Total	1374922	1087245	1119974	932941	1118618
Africa	30122	38879	30559	x18397	x17705
Northern Africa	26837	33618	26396	x13111	12700
Americas	x128950	110687	151485	145015	197069
LAIA	12874	22108	24703	42251	43848
CACM	1071	845	1455	x1930	x1188
Asia	402378	346015	370759	322987	362542
Middle East	x27709	x34611	x36429	x31536	22718
Europe	782153	566908	546810	423525	515170
EEC	756253	553165	528417	410957	500081
EFTA	16943	11590	10857	6970	10079
Oceania	x4105	x2891	3948	x2621	5137
United Kingdom	225083	171972	161245	164649	162635
USA/Etats–Unis d'Amer	96281	76450	115466	91322	144749
Germany/Allemagne	135260	113907	100999	60298	93102
Korea, Republic of	100916	97671	94693	54625	79094
Malaysia/Malaisie	40669	45152	73754	81108	70330
Japan/Japon	90353	80060	53672	35138	46265
Italy/Italie	113108	58793	56073	37268	41377
Netherlands/Pays–Bas	47484	38361	36414	23521	33335
France, Monac	60952	34776	34815	23431	41296
Belgium–Luxembourg	43367	33138	28418	23594	24253
Austria/Autriche	39290	31372	28937	20844	28901
Indonesia/Indonésie	16354	17323	25151	29800	39231
Thailand/Thaïlande	13995	19446	21927	25830	29942
Spain/Espagne	13747	15468	32685	18960	25108
Singapore/Singapour	41713	14369	28162	22127	20295
Portugal	21746	17204	18461	10238	13644
Turkey/Turquie	12644	12682	11471	16024	16602
Brazil/Brésil	917	9867	5670	22508	25269
Iran (Islamic Rp. of)		x11036	x16500	x10468	
India/Inde	35157	15174	6164	10988	19808
Denmark/Danemark	11948	9885	11465	9481	11934
Algeria/Algérie	9367	13981	7969	5598	4913
Egypt/Egypte	10721	10554	11545	3129	3511
Ireland/Irlande	8372	8845	7154	6456	10700
Philippines	4446	6551	6626	6518	7889
Switz.Liecht	9582	8906	6491	4176	5595
Venezuela	6256	6321	6298	6553	4387
Canada	10966	6473	6122	6061	4563
Hungary/Hongrie	x712	9453	x3186	x4794	x5856
Finland/Finlande	13854	8751	5462	2909	4903
Greece/Grèce	16958	7948	3809	5225	3893
Pakistan	4322	4292	4748	5873	5219
Poland/Pologne	2775	4909	3949	4519	6209
Czechoslovakia	13037	x5059	x6308		
China/Chine	2470	1546	5577	3974	7225
Hong Kong	16039	1858	6205	2521	5286
Viet Nam	x547	x1837	x2934	x5728	x4007
Mexico/Mexique	527	710	5511	3973	3361
United Arab Emirates	5194	6415	2452	x842	x1289
Norway, SVD, JM	7176	2562	4261	2699	4379
Sweden/Suède	5085	2746	2480	4084	5001
Slovenia/Slovénia			4654	3678	3801
Tunisia/Tunisie	3599	3056	3504	1565	2634
Colombia/Colombie	1931	1742	2720	3505	2512
Israel/Israël	3766	2458	2581	2056	2193
Libyan Arab Jamahiriya	1210	3748	x1129	x1998	x103
Chile/Chili	1711	1866	2119	1873	2418
Romania/Roumanie	10451	1669	2306	1802	142
Czech Republic				5490	6178
Cuba	x3453	x1856	x1700	x1665	x1443

COUNTRIES–PAYS	EXPORTS – EXPORTATIONS 1990	1991	1992	1993	1994
Totale	1276067	1074873	1077358	913393	1110939
Afrique	52075	40341	33615	29135	28902
Afrique du Nord	49925	32603	29522	24543	28267
Amériques	327655	244765	257953	198537	223454
ALAI	158059	89261	101155	80069	79148
MCAC	1381	134	453	x76	x140
Asie	112740	x94699	x131792	144002	198690
Moyen–Orient	x3770	x1124	x1648	x2879	x3931
Europe	506235	405406	372519	322351	412200
CEE	487661	393912	363783	309886	402024
AELE	2113	1333	1529	1888	2147
Océanie	x246909	237044	247032	x194323	x206797
Australia/Australie	245726	236337	244767	192428	203432
United Kingdom	133420	96735	89425	88094	94603
Canada	94228	72001	100899	74577	103442
Germany/Allemagne	97392	79763	67489	64175	80377
USA/Etats–Unis d'Amer	73811	83165	55288	43706	40355
Belgium–Luxembourg	75246	59139	62583	52762	83726
Mexico/Mexique	98559	52447	60958	47472	33728
France, Monac	58466	52355	58684	36264	54588
Singapore/Singapour	25258	29854	25045	61250	38321
Sweden/Suède	45311	40324	39496	28524	33708
China/Chine	31925	11644	54114	39166	108818
Peru/Pérou	48303	33309	37487	30139	40487
Morocco/Maroc	48147	31580	28918	24008	28029
Italy/Italie	13610	23073	15397	13642	22347
Korea Dem People's Rp	x11174	x27090	x12350	x2163	x6013
Bulgaria/Bulgarie	x24620	x10291	18397	12440	23737
Netherlands/Pays–Bas	23457	19407	12765	7711	8262
Ireland/Irlande	16773	15146	10345	11016	16018
Indonesia/Indonésie	13238	11117	12371	8510	8686
Former USSR/Anc. URSS		x30359			
Poland/Pologne	5287	5893	8024	6292	10648
Korea, Republic of	3280	3708	5086	10652	10469
Japan/Japon	4228	4174	6365	8384	5559
So. Africa Customs Un	1928	6288	3841	4329	
Russian Federation			x7792	x4386	x5504
Spain/Espagne	17187	4965	2854	3239	3549
Yugoslavia SFR	16461	x10161			
Romania/Roumanie		4040	3254	1960	1134
Slovenia/Slovénia			4159	3605	3853
Kazakstan			x3591	x4106	x4015
Hong Kong	14507	1644	4347	1334	3001
Malaysia/Malaisie	2233	1834	2460	2719	5709
Austria/Autriche	4802	1838	2671	1769	x3061
Czechoslovakia		x1986	x3972		
Czech Republic				3764	4374
New Zealand	1181	707	2264	661	3332
Switz.Liecht	1549	692	1189	1713	1910
India/Inde	768	934	1682	437	2570
Yugoslavia/Yougoslavie			x2576	x444	x209
Brazil/Brésil	4532	1471	848	477	64
United Arab Emirates	1546	573	382	x1725	x2400
Greece/Grèce	51	196	274	1527	124
Denmark/Danemark	1357	630	853	500	817
Israel/Israël	1861	657	836	429	1032
Venezuela	2376	1240	226	407	3702
Myanmar	x360	757	x583	x311	x390
Azerbaijan			x696	x848	
Portugal	437	283	725	536	762
Sudan/Soudan	x852	x326	x604	x459	
Hungary/Hongrie	x179	x49	x799	x538	x772

(VALUE AS % OF TOTAL)(VALEUR EN % DU TOTAL)

	1985	1986	1987	1988	1989	1990	1991	1992	1993	1994
Africa	3.5	3.2	2.7	2.9	2.2	2.2	3.5	2.7	x1.9	x1.6
Northern Africa	2.6	2.5	2.4	2.4	1.8	2.0	3.1	2.4	x1.4	1.1
Americas	10.4	x11.2	x16.6	x12.5	10.1	x9.4	10.2	13.6	15.5	17.6
LAIA	2.0	1.3	2.0	1.2	1.0	0.9	2.0	2.2	4.5	3.9
CACM	0.1	0.2	0.1	0.1	0.1	0.1	0.1	0.1	x0.2	x0.1
Asia	19.2	19.5	x21.2	x25.3	27.1	29.2	31.8	33.1	34.6	32.4
Middle East	1.8	x2.6	x2.3	x4.5	x2.1	x2.0	x3.2	x3.3	x3.4	2.0
Europe	66.2	65.7	55.3	55.1	57.9	56.9	52.1	48.8	45.4	46.1
EEC	59.1	57.9	49.8	49.5	52.4	55.0	50.9	47.2	44.0	44.7
EFTA	6.4	7.0	5.1	4.9	5.1	1.2	1.1	1.0	0.7	0.9
Oceania	0.4	x0.4	x0.4	0.3	0.3	x0.3	x0.2	0.3	x0.3	0.4
United Kingdom	20.5	17.4	17.4	18.1	18.1	16.4	15.8	14.4	17.6	14.5
USA/Etats–Unis d'Amer	7.9	8.5	12.8	9.4	7.8	7.0	7.0	10.3	9.8	12.9
Germany/Allemagne	9.8	10.2	6.8	7.0	9.1	9.8	10.5	9.0	6.5	8.3
Korea, Republic of	2.9	3.4	5.3	5.7	6.6	7.3	9.0	8.5	5.9	7.1
Malaysia/Malaisie	1.4	1.1	1.2	1.5	2.1	3.0	4.2	6.6	8.7	6.3
Japan/Japon	6.9	5.2	3.2	4.6	5.6	6.6	7.4	4.8	3.8	4.1
Italy/Italie	7.3	9.1	6.8	6.8	6.8	8.2	5.4	5.0	4.0	3.7
Netherlands/Pays–Bas	4.0	3.7	3.3	3.0	3.1	3.5	3.5	3.3	2.5	3.0
France, Monac	3.4	3.3	3.8	3.8	3.9	4.4	3.2	3.1	2.5	3.7
Belgium–Luxembourg	4.4	4.9	3.9	3.3	3.7	3.2	3.0	2.5	2.5	2.2

	1985	1986	1987	1988	1989	1990	1991	1992	1993	1994
Afrique	4.0	3.6	3.0	4.0	4.0	4.1	3.8	3.2	3.2	2.6
Afrique du Nord	2.9	3.3	2.7	3.2	3.7	3.9	3.0	2.7	2.7	2.5
Amériques	18.0	19.1	15.2	20.0	21.9	25.7	22.7	23.9	21.7	20.1
ALAI	8.6	8.8	6.7	6.8	9.5	12.4	8.3	9.4	8.8	7.1
MCAC	0.0	0.0	x0.0	0.5	0.4	0.1	0.0	0.0	x0.0	x0.0
Asie	2.6	3.8	x7.2	x6.7	x3.3	8.9	x8.8	x12.3	15.8	17.9
Moyen–Orient	0.0	x0.0	x0.2	x0.2	x0.2	x0.3	x0.1	x0.2	x0.3	x0.4
Europe	50.3	48.2	42.8	40.7	43.9	39.7	37.7	34.6	35.3	37.1
CEE	44.7	42.7	37.5	35.5	38.7	38.2	36.6	33.8	33.9	36.2
AELE	4.4	4.6	4.1	4.5	3.7	0.2	0.1	0.1	0.2	0.2
Océanie	25.2	25.2	26.7	x22.3	19.9	x19.3	22.1	22.9	x21.2	x18.6
Australia/Australie	25.1	25.2	26.7	22.3	19.9	19.3	22.0	22.7	21.1	18.3
United Kingdom	10.3	10.5	8.7	7.7	8.9	10.5	9.0	8.3	9.6	8.5
Canada	6.6	8.2	7.2	11.4	8.4	7.4	6.7	9.4	8.2	9.3
Germany/Allemagne	11.2	11.2	8.6	8.5	8.2	7.6	7.4	6.3	7.0	7.2
USA/Etats–Unis d'Amer	2.8	2.0	1.1	1.2	3.5	5.8	7.7	5.1	4.8	3.6
Belgium–Luxembourg	8.1	7.2	5.9	5.3	6.5	5.9	5.5	5.8	5.8	7.5
Mexico/Mexique	5.4	5.9	4.5	4.8	5.4	7.7	4.9	5.7	5.2	3.0
France, Monac	3.9	4.1	5.2	4.3	5.3	4.6	4.9	5.4	4.0	4.9
Singapore/Singapour	0.1	0.6	0.7	1.6	0.8	2.0	2.8	2.3	6.7	3.4
Sweden/Suède	4.0	4.3	3.8	3.9	3.2	3.6	3.8	3.7	3.1	3.0

TRADE BY COMMODITY IN THOUSAND U.S. DOLLARS – COMMERCE PAR PRODUIT EN MILLIERS DE DOLLARS E.U

COUNTRIES–PAYS	IMPORTS – IMPORTATIONS				
	1990	1991	1992	1993	1994
Total	4016298	3003529	3680510	3355536	3504310
Africa	x91108	69805	x68042	x70413	x35234
Northern Africa	45327	33870	29380	28619	20478
Americas	1177025	779661	1013171	886477	933669
LAIA	87570	82510	101626	94063	83208
CACM	17017	11586	13782	x12961	x14207
Asia	940512	768381	881474	872815	949002
Middle East	68196	x66400	x86216	x62739	x56430
Europe	1630101	1281652	1600903	1397717	1504495
EEC	1541036	1225555	1522780	1333885	1438077
EFTA	67868	49147	48146	44095	48519
Oceania	x43540	x28093	x37647	x31593	x29470
USA/Etats–Unis d'Amer	1039670	668248	879404	759458	811238
Germany/Allemagne	493077	433299	502642	376090	424852
Belgium–Luxembourg	110470	103912	236020	210412	172663
France,Monac	228037	167004	206172	167421	221900
Japan/Japon	256961	193655	157058	104244	78707
United Kingdom	214643	147186	160224	142363	139739
Italy/Italie	172704	122987	142021	113352	127605
Hong Kong	116832	118759	119106	124534	126685
Singapore/Singapour	65423	51914	105749	136627	174888
Indonesia/Indonésie	94330	75377	95040	90586	105119
Netherlands/Pays–Bas	64145	46634	54730	137945	144362
Austria/Autriche	45599	47282	69051	62545	73634
Malaysia/Malaisie	44405	43576	57773	47552	51270
Philippines	50187	43632	52815	46148	50198
China/Chine	6896	16467	59541	61211	80272
Sweden/Suède	72465	46374	44268	43164	46123
Switz.Liecht	63801	46375	45110	40085	44217
Korea, Republic of	41879	29430	33964	47792	73835
India/Inde	120848	43815	30055	25882	34371
Turkey/Turquie	45836	26526	39913	29404	25820
Denmark/Danemark	38850	29885	35792	23140	26080
Czechoslovakia	88500	x35939	x48379		
New Zealand	39099	25702	31343	23188	24104
Portugal	35201	28717	30669	19843	20000
Thailand/Thaïlande	11191	18763	21925	34070	41070
Venezuela	23386	22699	27740	22738	17839
Pakistan	30456	24514	16590	23174	14734
Colombia/Colombie	18979	19510	21687	20787	17055
Greece/Grèce	40115	23642	17855	18518	18906
Spain/Espagne	19596	23268	16633	15188	17527
Saudi Arabia	17232	18827	19612	x12953	x12319
Bangladesh		16069	16365	18261	x23539
Hungary/Hongrie	x5408	22670	x12727	x14619	x10035
Slovakia				x49373	x11942
Israel/Israël	17711	15226	17913	15702	16154
Canada	27186	14314	15003	17031	21073
Brazil/Brésil	21570	14744	15738	14554	13456
Iran (Islamic Rp. of)		x14745	x18733	x10293	x4488
Viet Nam	x6026	x5328	x6666	x26671	x12604
Slovenia/Slovénia			20964	16366	15728
Nigeria/Nigéria	x9621	13801	x10807	x12117	x3030
Egypt/Egypte	13862	10224	11329	12762	5646
Kenya	11329	5911	9133	16364	x4254
Mexico/Mexique	3667	4852	11515	12808	12832
Russian Federation			x7719	x19724	x24909
Chile/Chili	8965	7135	10418	9469	9214
Morocco/Maroc	10284	7338	7356	7793	8576
Romania/Roumanie	26766	5704	9516	6790	2522
Czech Republic				20836	22614
Argentina/Argentine	2755	5415	6481	7923	6470

COUNTRIES–PAYS	EXPORTS – EXPORTATIONS				
	1990	1991	1992	1993	1994
Totale	4240954	3226478	3830655	3454414	3567748
Afrique	x64232	x38463	x29752	x29610	x15150
Afrique du Nord	28618	14366	11138	6995	6883
Amériques	1158648	1007110	1018614	896514	944331
ALAI	351492	318376	307856	327449	322796
MCAC	20025	6447	772	79	317
Asie	x482311	x333325	x476364	x512765	625733
Moyen–Orient	x1351	x1344	1320	x552	x2352
Europe	1960851	1485302	1825425	1565162	1565034
CEE	1703683	1320024	1645300	1387462	1393711
AELE	201848	146544	154085	139073	141854
Océanie	295164	x268602	350350	x283133	x281477
Canada	736666	641596	671543	528616	573598
Belgium–Luxembourg	373019	308805	325584	362375	342009
Australia/Australie	295036	268423	350238	282745	280867
France,Monac	230966	184838	283737	256781	232281
Germany/Allemagne	244184	200073	278600	208625	209555
Spain/Espagne	194861	146166	253022	180985	158652
Netherlands/Pays–Bas	283922	197788	213216	155101	207458
Finland/Finlande	218199	169245	165895	136539	137862
Norway,SVD,JM	199651	145527	152921	138150	140638
Peru/Pérou	129981	149394	145516	130451	141247
China/Chine	30896	15056	98306	179262	251139
Mexico/Mexique	146224	98189	56519	122124	114149
Hong Kong	88246	78468	86150	105642	110982
Korea Dem People's Rp	x172304	x140665	x73252	x42337	x19003
Poland/Pologne	52337	33664	72242	113928	84909
Brazil/Brésil	53637	55000	94606	68538	57488
Russian Federation			x75464	x133848	x121792
Korea, Republic of	87285	34108	75279	51500	91127
United Kingdom	48916	55455	54417	48393	58983
Japan/Japon	45927	37444	56904	51402	52541
Bulgaria/Bulgarie	x226900	x37482	55142	50313	46266
Italy/Italie	94655	51574	58095	28980	36147
USA/Etats–Unis d'Amer	50388	40446	38051	40063	47415
Kazakstan			x53934	x45245	x38675
Singapore/Singapour	38544	19867	21779	20176	37078
Slovenia/Slovénia			14805	15076	17052
Argentina/Argentine	21116	15278	9723	4813	9510
Algeria/Algérie	27927	13952	10627	4826	5891
So. Africa Customs Un	5461	10712	7963	7393	
Zambia/Zambie	x6281	x6455	x4685	x9968	x7129
Former USSR/Anc. URSS		x19610			
Yugoslavia SFR	55319	x18689			
Uzbekistan/Ouzbékistan			x4067	x9815	x9568
Austria/Autriche	10226	3163	4935	4605	x5657
Zaire/Zaïre	x23379	x6206	x4614	x1807	x762
Yugoslavia/Yougoslavie			x10320	x1612	x736
Thailand/Thaïlande	16432	5669	1127	1504	3197
Ukraine			x783	x6773	x6697
Portugal	854	820	4345	1722	534
Honduras	19662	6237	552	7	11
India/Inde	118	21	1948	2336	7231
Venezuela	534	426	1463	1407	237
Czechoslovakia		x1303	x1918		
Switz.Liecht	2198	1017	1128	923	1196
Sweden/Suède	1746	713	1533	721	919
Greece/Grèce	525	554	574	1511	315
Un. Rep. of Tanzania	x67	x322	x651	x1257	x51
Morocco/Maroc	74	103	54	1879	14
Hungary/Hongrie	x46	x1511	x287	x147	x302
Saudi Arabia	492	837	1079		

(VALUE AS % OF TOTAL)(VALEUR EN % DU TOTAL)

	1985	1986	1987	1988	1989	1990	1991	1992	1993	1994
Africa	2.7	2.6	x2.3	x1.9	x2.1	x2.2	2.3	x1.9	x2.1	x1.0
Northern Africa	1.1	1.2	1.1	0.8	0.8	1.1	1.1	0.8	0.9	0.6
Americas	30.0	32.7	31.1	30.5	29.7	29.3	25.9	27.5	26.4	26.7
LAIA	3.1	3.1	4.3	2.6	2.1	2.2	2.7	2.8	2.8	2.4
CACM	0.6	0.6	0.5	0.4	0.4	0.4	0.4	0.4	x0.4	x0.4
Asia	28.2	24.7	x25.9	x24.0	21.8	23.4	25.6	24.0	26.0	27.1
Middle East	1.9	x2.1	x2.3	x1.5	x1.6	1.7	x2.2	x2.3	x1.9	x1.6
Europe	37.9	38.9	32.9	36.3	38.0	40.6	42.7	43.5	41.7	42.9
EEC	32.5	33.8	29.2	31.9	33.7	38.4	40.8	41.4	39.8	41.0
EFTA	3.7	4.3	3.5	3.8	3.8	1.7	1.6	1.3	1.3	1.4
Oceania	1.1	x1.0	x0.8	0.8	1.0	x1.0	x0.9	x1.0	x0.9	x0.8
USA/Etats–Unis d'Amer	26.0	28.2	25.5	26.6	26.7	25.9	22.2	23.9	22.6	23.1
Germany/Allemagne	8.9	10.0	8.2	9.3	9.6	12.3	14.4	13.7	11.2	12.1
Belgium–Luxembourg	3.1	3.1	2.4	2.5	2.5	2.8	3.5	6.4	6.3	4.9
France,Monac	4.4	5.1	4.6	5.0	4.9	5.7	5.6	5.6	5.0	6.3
Japan/Japon	3.1	4.4	4.2	4.6	5.9	6.4	6.4	4.3	3.1	2.2
United Kingdom	6.2	4.9	4.6	5.4	5.4	5.3	4.9	4.4	4.2	4.0
Italy/Italie	3.8	3.5	3.3	2.9	4.0	4.3	4.1	3.9	3.4	3.6
Hong Kong	1.5	3.1	3.2	2.3	2.0	2.9	4.0	3.2	3.7	3.6
Singapore/Singapour	0.5	0.6	1.0	1.7	2.2	1.6	1.7	2.9	4.1	5.0
Indonesia/Indonésie	2.4	2.2	2.1	1.8	1.7	2.3	2.5	2.6	2.7	3.0

	1985	1986	1987	1988	1989	1990	1991	1992	1993	1994
Afrique	1.6	x2.8	x1.7	x2.9	x2.1	x1.5	x1.2	x0.8	x0.8	x0.4
Afrique du Nord	0.5	1.2	0.1	0.8	0.7	0.7	0.4	0.3	0.2	0.2
Amériques	32.6	26.1	23.6	26.1	27.3	27.4	31.2	26.6	26.0	26.5
ALAI	9.1	8.4	7.3	6.4	7.8	8.3	9.9	8.0	9.5	9.0
MCAC	0.0	0.0	0.0	0.4	0.7	0.5	0.2	0.0	0.0	0.0
Asie	3.0	6.9	x12.5	x11.7	x9.9	x11.4	x10.4	x12.4	x14.8	17.6
Moyen–Orient	0.1	0.4	0.1	0.2	x0.0	x0.0	x0.0	0.0	x0.0	x0.1
Europe	53.2	53.3	50.1	46.8	47.6	46.2	46.0	47.7	45.3	43.9
CEE	42.5	42.3	39.3	37.4	38.0	40.2	40.9	43.0	40.2	39.1
AELE	9.2	9.1	9.0	8.4	9.0	4.8	4.5	4.0	4.0	4.0
Océanie	8.3	x9.7	x7.4	7.4	x6.7	7.0	x8.3	9.1	x8.2	x7.9
Canada	22.8	17.2	15.8	18.7	17.7	17.4	19.9	17.5	15.3	16.1
Belgium–Luxembourg	9.2	9.5	9.2	8.2	8.5	8.8	9.6	8.5	10.5	9.6
Australia/Australie	8.3	9.6	7.4	7.4	6.7	7.0	8.3	9.1	8.2	7.9
France,Monac	4.8	5.1	4.9	4.6	5.0	5.4	5.7	7.4	7.4	6.5
Germany/Allemagne	6.7	6.5	6.0	5.6	5.5	5.8	6.2	7.3	6.0	5.9
Spain/Espagne	5.0	3.8	3.7	5.2	5.2	4.6	4.5	6.6	5.2	4.4
Netherlands/Pays–Bas	7.8	7.9	7.1	6.8	6.3	6.7	6.1	5.6	4.5	5.8
Finland/Finlande	5.6	5.3	4.7	4.3	4.8	5.1	5.2	4.3	4.0	3.9
Norway,SVD,JM	3.3	3.5	4.0	3.9	4.0	4.7	4.5	4.0	4.0	3.9
Peru/Pérou	5.4	4.8	4.0	3.0	3.6	3.1	4.6	3.8	3.8	4.0

TRADE BY COMMODITY IN THOUSAND U.S. DOLLARS – COMMERCE PAR PRODUIT EN MILLIERS DE DOLLARS E.U

COUNTRIES–PAYS	IMPORTS – IMPORTATIONS 1990	1991	1992	1993	1994
Total	1210181	1060454	1195045	1159500	1191090
Africa	x13563	13302	x20735	x17961	x18151
Northern Africa	7285	3370	4757	8480	x3675
Americas	324164	261550	279100	264392	282650
LAIA	17585	21556	22847	22823	29018
CACM	968	426	496	x1028	x1414
Asia	397697	410203	451788	454279	438478
Middle East	18900	19534	11663	x13094	x14693
Europe	431023	356239	417138	390358	424161
EEC	406116	342974	403382	378503	413235
EFTA	15544	11133	10418	9183	8771
Oceania	x8594	x6128	7830	11177	11399
USA/Etats–Unis d'Amer	263084	207360	228828	212346	221391
Japan/Japon	222316	211590	183719	155743	160180
Germany/Allemagne	151777	126258	144887	106923	118367
Hong Kong	44561	50653	94995	106420	87313
United Kingdom	46152	45686	66502	98211	82960
France,Monac	62453	53938	57253	47212	55661
Korea, Republic of	39723	38754	46974	49856	61505
Italy/Italie	54067	36623	39947	36765	39189
Singapore/Singapour	32272	36949	41186	29168	22555
Malaysia/Malaisie	10739	22989	25149	29852	28233
Russian Federation			x20662	x56966	x29308
Canada	27986	21210	23666	25910	28332
Netherlands/Pays–Bas	20015	16428	25810	27241	46473
Spain/Espagne	22260	21019	22108	24864	28732
Belgium–Luxembourg	18755	18358	21114	14143	14713
India/Inde	13493	8401	11459	15928	24694
China/Chine	2463	3691	11861	15926	29298
Viet Nam	x284	x264	x3756	x19393	x529
Austria/Autriche	7163	7055	7910	7640	7310
Philippines	5918	7511	9361	3689	3549
So. Africa Customs Un	703	4075	9039	6836	12338
Switz.Liecht	10028	7004	6485	5404	5359
Mexico/Mexique	3975	6039	6814	5950	11179
Turkey/Turquie	10476	7222	5802	5258	5157
Ukraine			x558	x17644	x5461
Hungary/Hongrie	x6592	3932	x5678	x7478	x3162
Australia/Australie	6288	4205	5846	6644	6883
Argentina/Argentine	3178	4582	5748	6089	7056
Portugal	5228	5045	6602	4264	5696
Poland/Pologne	7010	4626	6217	4925	5828
Sweden/Suède	6492	4035	3994	4510	5354
Bangladesh		1527	4585	5957	x1556
Norway,SVD,JM	5439	4072	3899	3751	3376
Venezuela	2463	4213	4143	3281	2072
Romania/Roumanie	6689	2887	4382	3697	3201
Chile/Chili	2038	3216	3071	2822	3048
Greece/Grèce	5714	4403	2565	2072	2857
Colombia/Colombie	3755	2576	2254	2922	2930
Saudi Arabia	2279	2075	3856	x1533	x2671
Nigeria/Nigéria	x2499	4108	x1235	x574	x193
Korea Dem People's Rp	x2167	x1639	x1606	x2390	x552
Jamaica/Jamaïque	6525	5603	x21	x4	x23
Algeria/Algérie	1369	622	913	3932	357
Israel/Israël	1361	1449	1404	2471	1619
Fiji/Fidji	565	860	927	3448	3591
Iran (Islamic Rp. of)		x1870	x750	x2438	x909
Egypt/Egypte	2363	895	1288	2701	1333
Finland/Finlande	2270	1559	1550	1667	1894
Barbados/Barbade	2727	3174	1188	290	x8
United Arab Emirates	3842	2465	294	x1820	x4731

COUNTRIES–PAYS	EXPORTS – EXPORTATIONS 1990	1991	1992	1993	1994
Totale	1446828	1235676	1452343	1211608	1230342
Afrique	8252	10830	6122	x4688	x1311
Afrique du Nord	480	190	107	79	198
Amériques	363369	284680	314754	288550	276264
ALAI	295195	191452	211603	210734	201753
MCAC	21	33	27	x90	x244
Asie	918293	827866	1017362	811687	841479
Moyen–Orient	447	791	219	x1852	x2470
Europe	154859	103983	110395	102688	106625
CEE	151823	102291	107015	101110	104922
AELE	2843	1060	2406	876	1362
Océanie	1903	6294	x3348	2898	3960
Malaysia/Malaisie	340834	256618	293478	198527	204440
Singapore/Singapour	196412	202166	207987	166861	176381
China/Chine	86113	109135	157989	187519	207147
Indonesia/Indonésie	173220	149269	163278	90571	118366
Brazil/Brésil	174408	104745	122487	111382	90898
Bolivia/Bolivie	83728	80324	87549	96004	110032
USA/Etats–Unis d'Amer	64383	88922	98774	71540	66418
Hong Kong	34180	43237	99157	101414	72863
Thailand/Thaïlande	73589	34365	42408	17935	15016
Belgium–Luxembourg	24114	20587	37423	36545	32121
Viet Nam	x7172	x21754	x32943	x30957	x21233
Germany/Allemagne	30515	25406	29209	25030	22099
United Kingdom	55291	30086	15149	14265	17405
Netherlands/Pays–Bas	25961	18226	15163	13069	16131
Philippines		4052	10117	7463	5906
Russian Federation			x2455	x15779	x38555
Canada	3760	4225	4297	6169	7792
Zimbabwe	4856	5885	3802	2804	x485
Australia/Australie	1840	6179	3233	2741	3895
Japan/Japon	3717	3406	3776	4290	9043
Mexico/Mexique	22296	6094	1458	3178	252
France,Monac	3202	2008	2450	2140	6771
Italy/Italie	5947	2536	1777	2015	5736
So. Africa Customs Un	2588	3753	1574	863	
Korea, Republic of	1173	2101	1513	1331	4441
India/Inde	914	858	3134	822	2538
Sweden/Suède	1762	1470	1723	1265	1534
Spain/Espagne	3071	790	1263	2097	1859
Switz.Liecht	2103	984	2295	838	1192
Austria/Autriche	1062	793	953	1677	x843
Ireland/Irlande	128	155	346	2647	187
Lithuania/Lituanie			324	x2590	67
United Arab Emirates	417	725	130	x1517	x2399
Myanmar	x398		x1069	x998	x1541
Rwanda		x994	x533	x463	x30
Former USSR/Anc. URSS		x1818			
Croatia/Croatie			825	565	x302
Portugal	428	52	1299	34	57
Georgia/Géorgie			x37	x646	
Belarus/Bélarus			x64	x606	x844
Czech Republic				625	363
Yugoslavia SFR	14	x564			
Nigeria/Nigéria	241	5	x52	x446	x416
Denmark/Danemark	238	161	163	121	77
Azerbaijan				x374	
Tunisia/Tunisie	166	190	100	79	64
Peru/Pérou	324	252	11	81	216
New Zealand	63	91	96	145	63
Hungary/Hongrie		x6	x218	x77	x114
Albania/Albanie	x131			x246	

(VALUE AS % OF TOTAL)(VALEUR EN % DU TOTAL)

	1985	1986	1987	1988	1989	1990	1991	1992	1993	1994
Africa	1.1	0.8	0.7	0.9	x1.6	x1.2	1.3	x1.8	x1.6	x1.5
Northern Africa	0.9	0.6	0.4	0.6	0.7	0.6	0.3	0.4	0.7	x0.3
Americas	30.5	24.9	24.6	x26.8	27.4	26.8	24.7	23.3	22.8	23.8
LAIA	1.8	2.1	1.9	1.8	1.5	1.5	2.0	1.9	2.0	2.4
CACM	0.1	0.1	0.1	0.0	0.0	0.1	0.0	0.0	x0.1	x0.1
Asia	28.3	31.4	x31.2	x30.6	31.1	32.9	38.7	37.8	39.1	36.8
Middle East	1.1	x1.7	x1.1	x1.0	1.1	1.6	1.8	1.0	x1.1	x1.2
Europe	37.6	40.1	28.5	29.0	33.1	35.6	33.6	34.9	33.7	35.6
EEC	34.1	36.1	25.9	26.3	30.4	33.6	32.3	33.8	32.6	34.7
EFTA	2.3	2.8	2.0	1.8	2.0	1.3	1.0	0.9	0.8	0.7
Oceania	0.5	0.8	0.8	1.0	0.8	x0.7	x0.6	0.7	1.0	1.0
USA/Etats–Unis d'Amer	25.6	20.1	20.4	21.9	21.9	21.7	19.6	19.1	18.3	18.6
Japan/Japon	20.6	16.4	16.4	16.6	19.2	18.4	20.0	15.4	13.4	13.4
Germany/Allemagne	13.3	11.3	10.0	10.3	11.2	12.5	11.9	12.1	9.2	9.9
Hong Kong	2.6	1.8	1.8	2.6	3.8	3.7	4.8	7.9	9.2	7.3
United Kingdom	4.7	4.5	2.6	2.1	3.8	3.8	4.3	5.6	8.5	7.0
France,Monac	5.5	9.4	4.2	4.2	4.8	5.2	5.1	4.8	4.1	4.7
Korea, Republic of	1.1	1.9	2.2	2.3	2.8	3.3	3.7	3.9	4.3	5.2
Italy/Italie	4.0	3.5	3.5	3.4	3.8	4.5	3.5	3.3	3.2	3.3
Singapore/Singapour	0.7	6.9	5.0	2.6	1.6	2.7	3.5	3.4	2.5	1.9
Malaysia/Malaisie	0.3	0.3	0.4	0.4	0.4	0.9	2.2	2.1	2.6	2.4

	1985	1986	1987	1988	1989	1990	1991	1992	1993	1994
Afrique	1.0	1.2	x1.0	0.7	x0.5	0.6	0.9	0.4	x0.4	x0.1
Afrique du Nord		0.0			x0.0	0.0	0.0	0.0	0.0	0.0
Amériques	18.4	17.4	14.4	21.5	24.1	25.1	23.0	21.7	23.8	22.4
ALAI	16.5	14.5	12.3	19.1	21.0	20.4	15.5	14.6	17.4	16.4
MCAC	0.0	0.0	0.0	0.0	0.0	0.0	0.0	0.0	x0.0	x0.0
Asie	69.3	64.4	68.9	62.9	63.3	63.5	67.0	70.1	67.0	68.4
Moyen–Orient	0.1	x0.1	x0.1	0.0	x0.0	0.0	0.1	0.0	x0.2	x0.2
Europe	11.1	16.8	15.5	14.6	9.6	10.7	8.4	7.6	8.5	8.7
CEE	10.9	16.5	15.2	14.1	8.8	10.5	8.3	7.4	8.3	8.5
AELE	0.3	0.3	0.3	0.5	0.7	0.2	0.1	0.2	0.1	0.1
Océanie	0.2	x0.2	x0.1	x0.2	x0.2	0.1	0.5	x0.2	0.2	0.3
Malaysia/Malaisie	30.9	20.3	25.2	23.4	23.5	23.6	20.8	20.2	16.4	16.6
Singapore/Singapour	11.0	17.5	13.9	12.9	11.8	13.6	16.4	14.3	13.8	14.3
China/Chine	3.4	3.5	9.2	6.4	5.5	6.0	8.8	10.9	15.5	16.8
Indonesia/Indonésie	10.8	11.8	11.6	12.0	13.5	12.0	12.1	11.2	7.5	9.6
Brazil/Brésil	10.3	9.8	10.8	15.7	15.3	12.1	8.5	8.4	9.2	7.4
Bolivia/Bolivie	6.1	4.5	1.0	2.9	4.5	5.8	6.5	6.0	7.9	8.9
USA/Etats–Unis d'Amer	1.9	2.8	2.0	2.0	2.9	4.4	7.2	6.8	5.9	5.4
Hong Kong	3.0	1.3	1.3	1.5	3.1	2.4	3.5	6.8	8.4	5.9
Thailand/Thaïlande	9.9	9.4	6.8	6.0	5.3	5.1	2.8	2.9	1.5	1.2
Belgium–Luxembourg	1.0	1.6	1.5	2.5	1.7	1.7	1.7	2.6	3.0	2.6

TRADE BY COMMODITY IN THOUSAND U.S. DOLLARS – COMMERCE PAR PRODUIT EN MILLIERS DE DOLLARS E.U

COUNTRIES–PAYS	IMPORTS – IMPORTATIONS 1990	1991	1992	1993	1994
Total	1962641	1973912	2339596	1966406	2800538
Africa	x10340	x8682	x14247	x7987	x14095
Northern Africa	1027	917	6536	1008	1970
Americas	531165	589518	614064	573847	787159
LAIA	40150	41324	43357	45069	52840
CACM	368	359	1803	239	971
Asia	399451	x567353	670589	529645	799099
Middle East	x14502	x17274	x18563	x19223	x10918
Europe	953482	764755	990533	820869	1157117
EEC	903562	728259	941098	769766	1082848
EFTA	43817	34710	44050	46851	67829
Oceania	23012	x22204	x21155	x22714	x26722
USA/Etats-Unis d'Amer	410254	448356	475293	466232	650301
Japan/Japon	257761	355604	384901	309463	497021
Germany/Allemagne	293558	231365	285799	200713	274381
United Kingdom	222028	184079	255789	242877	289876
France,Monac	119231	103861	134934	89850	159354
Hong Kong	41404	58138	131874	72096	102504
Canada	79252	98693	93070	61716	81827
Italy/Italie	55714	48422	67126	56723	78628
Korea, Republic of	29599	38602	50920	59635	96173
Netherlands/Pays-Bas	48923	23737	34964	55342	76884
Austria/Autriche	41170	38557	40457	31940	51834
Sweden/Suède	40138	32270	45832	30915	56684
Belgium-Luxembourg	47439	34696	39038	28266	47085
Switz.Liecht	31009	26039	29170	24252	30408
Brazil/Brésil	24822	26039	21648	23382	30085
China/Chine	15737	23761	22587	17131	21187
Australia/Australie	21493	20671	19789	21028	25019
Spain/Espagne	21413	19682	21795	17323	25939
India/Inde	22040	16988	20974	20058	31393
Norway,SVD,JM	12801	8626	14720	22303	36931
Korea Dem People's Rp	x1213	x30085	x3090	x375	x1201
Mexico/Mexique	5789	6749	12379	12650	14211
Singapore/Singapour	3948	7996	9708	7496	9630
Israel/Israël	4411	10125	6367	4732	8886
Czechoslovakia	8679	x1457	x18274		
So. Africa Customs Un	7497	6082	4994	6084	11396
Iran (Islamic Rp. of)		x3319	x3894	x8538	x773
Malaysia/Malaisie	3397	2617	3335	9750	9082
Greece/Grèce	4064	3727	3915	5926	6999
Viet Nam	x3		x10484	x2142	x478
Romania/Roumanie	12188	7288	3319	1921	2459
Poland/Pologne	6329	5550	2162	3788	5224
Argentina/Argentine	2903	3651	3952	3761	3660
Bahrain/Bahreïn	x5092	x4223	x2996	x3908	x1281
Russian Federation			x1809	x9060	x37791
United Arab Emirates	5931	4838	4140	x1835	x1906
Hungary/Hongrie	x3699	5156	x2987	x1512	x1045
Turkey/Turquie	1870	2466	2959	4032	5275
Denmark/Danemark	2927	1967	3687	2526	3724
Venezuela	4830	2502	2804	2852	2387
Slovenia/Slovénia			4473	3193	5797
Finland/Finlande	2697	1716	3135	2717	5390
Ireland/Irlande	2322	2424	2050	2971	3641
Indonesia/Indonésie	2551	1663	3203	2457	4533
Egypt/Egypte	799	462	5953	343	656
Thailand/Thaïlande	1563	1802	1765	2920	4801
Saudi Arabia	444	1913	3807	x306	x607
Portugal	1935	1756	2577	1679	2428
New Zealand	1440	1235	1289	1546	1681
Bulgaria/Bulgarie	x10935	x748	2267	x764	x1025

COUNTRIES–PAYS	EXPORTS – EXPORTATIONS 1990	1991	1992	1993	1994
Totale	1737656	1821931	1931873	1556290	2312571
Afrique	x144461	x234919	x262475	x212943	x257513
Afrique du Nord	1360	695	139	128	168
Amériques	504500	536906	484866	404411	536639
ALAI	22147	31907	28171	20632	32243
MCAC	514	276	26	85	x9
Asie	320762	264939	343429	315001	523509
Moyen-Orient	1110	740	390	x1516	x1808
Europe	751478	679840	808116	614334	976146
CEE	563026	516941	618293	473762	740361
AELE	174063	155046	185727	137158	234235
Océanie	x6577	4761	x3327	x3176	x2359
USA/Etats-Unis d'Amer	344766	302835	272173	211937	257225
Canada	137074	201880	183670	171688	246936
France,Monac	195998	185233	196891	83340	180546
Norway,SVD,JM	164046	147391	177251	131867	228215
Germany/Allemagne	130747	126429	145905	128697	176043
China/Chine	151639	131914	128305	134479	270611
United Kingdom	87566	87806	112279	115562	156493
Zambia/Zambie	x24327	x79298	x129146	x106460	x158601
Russian Federation			x111511	x193812	x288028
Japan/Japon	109181	72592	84165	79228	97600
Hong Kong	39013	39822	98954	66856	89142
So. Africa Customs Un	59620	64196	67386	62727	64011
Zaire/Zaïre	x57692	x85112	x55953	x33732	x27315
Netherlands/Pays-Bas	39831	29463	38520	51113	62144
Finland/Finlande	15758	20804	45244	40725	77010
Former USSR/Anc. URSS		x86355			
Ukraine			x13395	x50078	x35661
Austria/Autriche	31247	21595	21157	14774	x27598
Belgium-Luxembourg	27930	18473	17073	14987	21832
Sweden/Suède	9267	8263	24826	8523	9925
Italy/Italie	21272	14545	12070	6935	10768
Czechoslovakia		x5776	x21959		
Switz.Liecht	10017	7655	8452	5289	6014
Kazakstan			x13176	x6551	x12324
Bolivia/Bolivie	2399	5053	8141	6432	8389
Korea, Republic of	10759	7744	6202	4710	8289
Brazil/Brésil	2300	8284	6667	3560	5293
Chile/Chili	883	8819	5796	1878	2868
Zimbabwe	678	3324	4566	4791	x760
Peru/Pérou	6881	5140	3291	4135	7531
Mexico/Mexique	9397	4168	3850	4154	7831
Australia/Australie	4956	4759	3223	2911	2258
Estonia/Estonie			x3343	x6894	x4107
Thailand/Thaïlande	1774	2065	2671	5343	15762
Singapore/Singapour	1946	2519	4311	3207	6347
Hungary/Hongrie	x2241	x2528	x3805	x3609	x1961
Philippines	1987	5242	1628	2501	3904
Un. Rep. of Tanzania	x461	x728	x4238	x4335	x5624
Poland/Pologne	5586	4129	3119	941	2645
Yugoslavia SFR	14361	x7843			
Denmark/Danemark	864	501	795	5655	15738
Lithuania/Lituanie				x6426	745
Spain/Espagne	1777	2948	1866	1233	1219
Yugoslavia/Yougoslavie			x3706	x1053	x480
Latvia/Lettonie			x3925	x287	571
Kyrgyzstan/Kirghizistan			x110	x4084	x12903
Korea Dem People's Rp	x1251	x1270	x1051	x1088	x175
Azerbaijan				x3208	
Portugal	250	188	1145	896	540
Kenya	269	921	989	204	

(VALUE AS % OF TOTAL)(VALEUR EN % DU TOTAL)

	1985	1986	1987	1988	1989	1990	1991	1992	1993	1994
Africa	0.8	x1.3	x1.4	x0.8	x0.5	x0.5	x0.4	x0.6	x0.4	x0.5
Northern Africa	0.1	0.2	0.1	0.0	0.1	0.1	0.0	0.3	0.1	0.1
Americas	31.6	25.0	26.2	26.4	25.4	27.0	29.9	26.3	29.1	28.1
LAIA	3.7	3.6	2.7	2.0	2.6	2.0	2.1	1.9	2.3	1.9
CACM		0.1	0.0	0.0	0.0	0.0	0.0	0.1	0.0	0.0
Asia	15.3	15.9	21.6	21.2	18.6	20.4	x28.7	28.6	27.0	28.6
Middle East	0.3	0.6	x0.3	x0.4	x0.5	x0.7	x0.9	x0.8	x1.0	x0.4
Europe	51.1	54.9	47.3	47.6	51.1	48.6	38.7	42.3	41.7	41.3
EEC	45.1	48.0	41.0	41.0	44.4	46.0	36.9	40.2	39.1	38.7
EFTA	5.7	6.6	6.0	6.4	6.6	2.2	1.8	1.9	2.4	2.4
Oceania	0.8	x1.3	x1.0	1.3	1.4	1.2	x1.1	x0.9	x1.1	x1.0
USA/Etats-Unis d'Amer	25.9	19.7	22.1	21.2	19.2	20.9	22.7	20.3	23.7	23.2
Japan/Japon	10.8	10.7	11.2	14.1	12.7	13.1	18.0	16.5	15.7	17.7
Germany/Allemagne	18.0	19.5	15.3	13.3	14.2	15.0	11.7	12.2	10.2	9.8
United Kingdom	8.1	9.2	7.9	9.1	9.9	11.3	9.3	10.9	12.4	10.4
France,Monac	6.6	5.4	5.4	5.5	6.4	6.1	5.3	5.8	4.6	5.7
Hong Kong	1.4	1.7	2.1	2.1	1.8	2.1	2.9	5.6	3.7	3.7
Canada	2.0	1.6	1.2	2.9	3.4	4.0	5.0	4.0	3.1	2.9
Italy/Italie	2.4	2.4	2.0	2.4	2.6	2.8	2.5	2.9	2.9	2.8
Korea, Republic of	0.4	0.9	3.4	1.0	1.0	1.5	2.0	2.2	3.0	3.4
Netherlands/Pays-Bas	2.9	3.5	2.6	2.0	2.4	2.5	1.2	1.5	2.8	2.7

	1985	1986	1987	1988	1989	1990	1991	1992	1993	1994
Afrique	10.1	x14.5	x15.2	x9.8	x10.9	x8.3	x12.9	x13.6	x13.7	x11.2
Afrique du Nord	0.0	0.0	0.1	0.0	0.0	0.1	0.0	0.0	0.0	0.0
Amériques	23.3	22.5	21.1	21.5	21.9	29.0	29.5	25.1	25.9	23.2
ALAI	1.7	1.2	2.2	2.5	1.5	1.3	1.8	1.5	1.3	1.4
MCAC		0.0	0.0	0.0	x0.1	0.0	0.0	0.0	0.0	x0.0
Asie	11.1	11.5	17.2	18.5	16.9	18.4	14.5	17.8	20.2	22.6
Moyen-Orient	0.1	x0.1	x0.2	0.1	0.1	0.1	0.0	0.0	x0.1	x0.1
Europe	55.3	51.3	43.4	42.7	42.7	43.2	37.3	41.8	39.5	42.2
CEE	32.1	28.8	25.0	28.6	29.4	32.4	28.4	32.0	30.4	32.0
AELE	22.4	21.7	17.2	13.3	12.4	10.0	8.5	9.6	8.8	10.1
Océanie	0.2	0.1	x0.4	1.2	0.6	x0.4	0.3	x0.2	x0.2	x0.1
USA/Etats-Unis d'Amer	21.3	21.0	18.6	14.6	16.2	19.8	16.6	14.1	13.6	11.1
Canada	0.3	0.3	0.3	4.5	4.0	7.9	11.1	9.5	11.0	10.7
France,Monac	6.5	5.8	5.4	8.3	8.7	11.3	10.2	10.2	5.4	7.8
Norway,SVD,JM	15.3	16.1	13.6	8.9	8.7	9.4	8.1	9.2	8.5	9.9
Germany/Allemagne	7.8	7.4	6.5	6.2	7.0	7.5	6.9	7.6	8.3	7.6
China/Chine	3.8	5.2	11.3	10.3	8.4	8.7	7.2	6.6	8.6	11.7
United Kingdom	4.9	4.7	5.1	4.6	4.5	5.0	4.8	5.8	7.4	6.8
Zambia/Zambie		x3.4	x2.8	x2.4	x2.3	x1.4	x4.4	x6.7	x6.8	x6.9
Russian Federation								x5.8	x12.5	x12.5
Japan/Japon	4.5	4.1	3.0	4.3	5.1	6.3	4.0	4.4	5.1	4.2

TRADE BY COMMODITY IN THOUSAND U.S. DOLLARS – COMMERCE PAR PRODUIT EN MILLIERS DE DOLLARS E.U

COUNTRIES–PAYS	IMPORTS – IMPORTATIONS 1990	1991	1992	1993	1994
Total	8583039	9693698	10075223	8074292	9164614
Africa	x565334	x552921	x453920	x443937	x367389
Northern Africa	260986	274256	x158724	x182043	x174556
Americas	x664027	653879	x709341	x741730	x892145
LAIA	83036	122799	219647	236789	282169
CACM	8588	16104	22001	x16694	x30535
Asia	1406746	x1870394	x2149146	x2230150	x2541968
Middle East	x380157	x627100	x812719	x620526	x477405
Europe	5578176	6212459	6368019	4325335	5023969
EEC	4865944	5277014	5714480	3777243	4106175
EFTA	673557	897368	613431	508380	861098
Oceania	x101814	x89469	x199013	x82839	x77412
Germany/Allemagne	1098106	1422982	1870980	1419451	1498224
France,Monac	823920	829398	791358	480779	548130
Netherlands/Pays–Bas	598600	638476	673143	342076	384743
Belgium–Luxembourg	551919	556339	583338	324012	388996
United Kingdom	557092	508919	404397	250279	260518
Switz.Liecht	469103	424015	380332	336882	381261
Austria/Autriche	257691	270960	312521	317392	352691
Iran (Islamic Rp. of)		x308883	x345020	x235891	x70283
Japan/Japon	276358	306535	278618	287679	365007
Norway,SVD,JM	195528	462509	224426	163209	472360
Spain/Espagne	223116	317438	307616	123741	104854
Indonesia/Indonésie	119639	187932	284913	207485	189093
Singapore/Singapour	98117	170557	184121	234326	184896
USA/Etats–Unis d'Amer	225927	189276	171713	222014	288041
Italy/Italie	156700	182832	215982	106555	104289
Denmark/Danemark	150981	170194	173779	132638	142766
Canada	139707	150950	142614	139013	152288
Saudi Arabia	122039	130011	182710	x107803	x118147
Hong Kong	126441	137268	130064	132200	351204
Sweden/Suède	186438	155138	135078	96358	108420
China/Chine	144310	80590	76345	173373	261913
Mexico/Mexique	21075	69039	134679	121556	145667
Russian Federation			x157945	x137519	x216167
Philippines	16727	30700	39926	215511	205094
Libyan Arab Jamahiriya	129920	109128	x64486	x83624	x60671
Korea, Republic of	57869	75710	84753	52570	103162
Malaysia/Malaisie	45267	82315	66381	63052	118872
Former USSR/Anc. URSS	141658	x205495			
United Arab Emirates	55826	29319	81163	x89035	x101782
Portugal	52330	51960	82685	60974	65802
Poland/Pologne	20226	52925	65254	61714	84507
Ireland/Irlande	72878	66492	63812	48107	50669
Nigeria/Nigéria	x40120	15982	x82715	x74329	x19017
Hungary/Hongrie	x34585	23302	x59318	x84657	x60895
Turkey/Turquie	29648	64804	55199	44778	50569
Thailand/Thaïlande	27973	68743	56724	35364	49805
Finland/Finlande	91385	67664	55418	34171	45171
Egypt/Egypte	67660	96750	33478	25067	34516
Australia/Australie	24662	22759	95413	29517	26634
Greece/Grèce	44785	38221	44375	40712	50902
Algeria/Algérie	40330	37195	41388	42792	63167
Czechoslovakia	24699	x25370	x64092		
Israel/Israël	17584	20064	26829	35685	43702
Cameroon/Cameroun	27647	68613	x7022	x4997	x9572
French Guiana	39191	30732	25967	13337	23165
Ukraine			x19563	x48293	x14570
Martinique	30521	26704	20927	17656	22268
Bahrain/Bahreïn	x11946	x24184	x19576	x21376	x8052
Oman	11876	20106	15747	29144	15072
Guadeloupe	28744	25792	20031	18105	20832

COUNTRIES–PAYS	EXPORTS – EXPORTATIONS 1990	1991	1992	1993	1994
Totale	9117629	9963698	10762312	10203000	9884373
Afrique	57079	60187	x75404	67104	x63146
Afrique du Nord	9647	10759	11230	11559	x8695
Amériques	620161	630968	724787	764400	921762
ALAI	74263	58012	114031	100352	135608
MCAC	944	998	1113	5513	7876
Asie	1016669	1197295	1511114	2163680	1760610
Moyen–Orient	105209	66470	91728	x101707	x134402
Europe	7114961	7645365	7964898	6684935	6501287
CEE	6722439	7300934	7548081	6248166	6178107
AELE	276771	299306	371651	387391	259585
Océanie	87562	x162556	x163444	x131124	x171033
Germany/Allemagne	1834102	1915364	1894341	1459306	1523189
Netherlands/Pays–Bas	891159	1403046	1199173	981869	714504
France,Monac	814165	847209	1026521	622207	693352
Italy/Italie	712550	707804	737034	693225	744794
Belgium–Luxembourg	619958	634875	691538	512467	515061
Korea, Republic of	255569	255495	473184	1026154	534669
United Kingdom	516034	527149	501091	507108	546474
USA/Etats–Unis d'Amer	384093	441424	471158	491189	545135
Austria/Autriche	365043	426109	469202	459807	x447323
Japan/Japon	271789	395660	391860	398785	361230
Denmark/Danemark	320874	358833	408684	333506	342635
Switz.Liecht	200702	215191	270650	225722	208842
Sweden/Suède	234769	208831	213562	170705	222534
Spain/Espagne	176643	109014	205066	257175	140693
China/Chine	60944	115847	162718	167612	224574
Poland/Pologne	136583	126741	133071	164479	226506
Canada	150215	121306	129207	159820	227128
Finland/Finlande	153377	95116	133028	175945	195723
Australia/Australie	74970	143429	145559	114287	144112
Norway,SVD,JM	76022	84115	100997	161662	50739
Singapore/Singapour	114741	116745	108465	93397	86919
Thailand/Thaïlande	87079	97277	84644	75901	112455
Hungary/Hongrie	x37775	x35863	x75591	x69693	x68219
Czechoslovakia		x66119	x91615		
Malaysia/Malaisie	34590	47566	46372	48068	64498
Hong Kong	35636	34460	42092	65291	86570
So. Africa Customs Un	33491	37588	52375	46804	50503
Ireland/Irlande	55255	41131	37270	43335	47786
India/Inde	15275	17337	42345	56814	51489
Brazil/Brésil	20091	20916	32371	41407	58793
Indonesia/Indonésie	24224	25935	28692	37028	44149
Czech Republic				91206	120301
Mexico/Mexique	21833	19151	45438	26314	37586
Israel/Israël	5918	14168	30187	41726	49612
Saudi Arabia	28124	28687	38716	x12467	x18549
Turkey/Turquie	12116	19561	20521	33026	43134
Portugal	20526	20324	24086	15776	24995
Slovenia/Slovénia			29094	29429	40908
Philippines	3645	5398	3683	48518	6775
Venezuela	14356	8920	22284	24708	20729
Russian Federation			x29659	x25244	x33797
New Zealand	11999	18333	17344	16124	26060
Yugoslavia SFR	114327	x44543			
Romania/Roumanie	13692	8020	12607	21878	12425
United Arab Emirates	29025	8533	9681	x21843	x31445
Slovakia				x39937	x37004
Greece/Grèce	7305	5449	7487	15736	19044
Jordan/Jordanie	10458	2769	9350	15502	17789
Croatia/Croatie			8508	13481	x19902
Bulgaria/Bulgarie	x23781	x8278	x8929	x4549	x2008

(VALUE AS % OF TOTAL)(VALEUR EN % DU TOTAL)

	1985	1986	1987	1988	1989	1990	1991	1992	1993	1994
Africa	19.3	x12.9	x8.8	x7.0	x5.6	x6.6	x5.7	x4.5	x5.5	x4.0
Northern Africa	13.3	6.8	4.2	2.8	2.5	3.0	2.8	x1.6	x2.3	x1.9
Americas	12.7	x12.6	x9.1	8.6	8.1	x7.8	6.7	x7.0	x9.2	x9.7
LAIA	1.5	1.3	1.1	0.9	0.7	1.0	1.3	2.2	2.9	3.1
CACM	0.4	0.1	x0.1	0.1	0.1	0.1	0.2	0.2	x0.2	x0.3
Asia	26.5	x21.2	x19.5	x19.9	x19.1	16.4	x19.3	x21.3	x27.6	x27.8
Middle East	13.9	x13.3	x7.9	x7.5	x6.7	x4.4	x6.5	x8.1	x7.7	x5.2
Europe	40.1	50.4	58.8	59.9	62.5	65.0	64.1	63.2	53.6	54.8
EEC	29.9	37.7	43.1	44.0	49.3	56.7	54.4	56.7	46.8	44.8
EFTA	9.7	12.1	15.1	15.3	12.7	7.8	9.3	6.1	6.3	9.4
Oceania	0.5	x1.0	x1.1	x1.0	x1.5	x1.2	x0.9	x2.0	x1.0	x0.9
Germany/Allemagne	6.8	9.4	10.4	10.4	11.1	12.8	14.7	18.6	17.6	16.3
France,Monac	4.7	6.5	7.3	7.5	8.5	9.6	8.6	7.9	6.0	6.0
Netherlands/Pays–Bas	4.5	5.6	6.3	5.9	6.1	7.0	6.6	6.7	4.2	4.2
Belgium–Luxembourg	3.3	3.6	4.1	4.5	5.0	6.4	5.7	5.8	4.0	4.2
United Kingdom	4.1	4.7	5.7	6.0	7.0	6.5	5.2	4.0	3.1	2.8
Switz.Liecht	3.0	3.9	4.7	5.0	5.1	5.5	4.4	3.8	4.2	4.2
Austria/Autriche	1.6	2.0	2.4	2.4	2.5	3.0	2.8	3.1	3.9	3.8
Iran (Islamic Rp. of)		x0.8	x1.0	x1.0	x0.5		x3.2	x3.4	x2.9	x0.8
Japan/Japon	0.3	0.5	0.8	1.7	2.6	3.2	3.2	2.8	3.6	4.0
Norway,SVD,JM	3.2	4.0	5.5	5.4	2.1	2.3	4.8	2.2	2.0	5.2

	1985	1986	1987	1988	1989	1990	1991	1992	1993	1994
Afrique	0.5	0.2	x0.2	0.1	x0.3	0.7	0.6	x0.7	0.7	x0.6
Afrique du Nord	0.0	x0.0	0.0	0.0	0.1	0.1	0.1	0.1	0.1	x0.1
Amériques	9.9	8.1	8.2	8.5	7.0	6.8	6.3	6.8	7.5	9.3
ALAI	0.8	0.5	0.6	0.8	0.8	0.8	0.6	1.1	1.0	1.4
MCAC	0.0	0.0	0.0	0.0	0.0	0.0	0.0	0.0	0.1	0.1
Asie	21.9	18.5	12.7	12.8	12.5	11.1	12.0	14.0	21.2	17.9
Moyen–Orient	1.2	x0.7	x1.1	x1.2	x1.2	1.2	0.7	0.9	x1.0	x1.4
Europe	65.1	69.9	72.3	71.6	75.0	78.0	76.7	74.0	65.5	65.8
CEE	54.5	57.8	60.3	60.3	63.6	73.7	73.3	70.1	61.2	62.5
AELE	8.9	10.0	10.9	10.2	9.9	3.0	3.0	3.5	3.8	2.6
Océanie	0.4	x0.4	0.4	0.6	x0.7	1.0	x1.6	x1.5	x1.3	x1.7
Germany/Allemagne	11.4	14.0	14.8	16.7	17.5	20.1	19.2	17.6	14.3	15.4
Netherlands/Pays–Bas	5.6	6.5	8.7	8.0	8.5	9.8	14.1	11.1	9.6	7.2
France,Monac	7.9	6.8	6.6	6.5	6.8	8.9	8.5	9.5	6.1	7.0
Italy/Italie	7.6	9.3	8.2	7.7	8.3	7.8	7.1	6.8	6.8	7.5
Belgium–Luxembourg	4.2	4.6	5.2	5.2	5.9	6.8	6.4	6.4	5.0	5.2
Korea, Republic of	10.9	6.6	4.5	4.8	4.1	2.8	2.6	4.4	10.1	5.4
United Kingdom	7.1	5.6	5.0	4.5	4.6	5.7	5.3	4.7	5.0	5.5
USA/Etats–Unis d'Amer	4.9	3.2	3.3	4.4	3.9	4.2	4.4	4.4	4.8	5.5
Austria/Autriche	2.2	2.6	2.6	2.9	3.1	4.0	4.3	4.4	4.5	x4.5
Japan/Japon	8.1	9.5	5.4	4.1	3.7	3.0	4.0	3.6	3.9	3.7

TRADE BY COMMODITY IN THOUSAND U.S. DOLLARS – COMMERCE PAR PRODUIT EN MILLIERS DE DOLLARS E.U

COUNTRIES–PAYS	IMPORTS – IMPORTATIONS 1990	1991	1992	1993	1994
Total	4497606	5085678	5590541	4974466	5247888
Africa	x236960	x244669	x233507	x253755	x199178
Northern Africa	135320	133954	x102796	x100770	x109103
Americas	635546	695178	883225	918606	1032408
LAIA	115981	145602	252717	285825	378964
CACM	20383	21969	38496	x38880	x41327
Asia	613137	x796045	998116	x1111792	x1039833
Middle East	x155187	x269422	x329414	x306430	x208421
Europe	2851777	3126152	3244592	2435719	2717634
EEC	2646079	2927541	3040031	2247903	2495235
EFTA	178378	169365	165603	149194	173714
Oceania	x90390	x106740	x96929	x77322	x77662
Germany/Allemagne	425279	601805	638839	421472	444676
Netherlands/Pays–Bas	489478	534439	583142	370852	427325
France,Monac	372561	362083	386367	305591	365377
United Kingdom	279471	313445	324542	311581	313715
USA/Etats–Unis d'Amer	273232	254234	286011	296173	342383
Belgium–Luxembourg	319759	305020	297704	229908	261502
Canada	155290	198728	242186	230499	200321
Austria/Autriche	133258	144733	152335	127742	146301
Spain/Espagne	125625	135814	144226	101386	110598
Denmark/Danemark	98194	126475	117537	100350	115045
Switz.Liecht	114685	103977	103338	96179	108300
Italy/Italie	108337	123385	105369	69864	73475
Iran (Islamic Rp. of)		x105917	x84272	x100315	x24083
China/Chine	42165	44222	83568	155852	168947
Mexico/Mexique	48539	52937	107566	105926	109086
Indonesia/Indonésie	40895	56533	105658	82014	55394
Japan/Japon	51388	68187	67769	91312	103966
Singapore/Singapour	60393	73060	76633	69672	78930
Malaysia/Malaisie	48806	61954	72767	83699	43363
Sweden/Suède	79760	78625	73749	59496	62897
Korea, Republic of	72517	69199	74729	67532	101277
Ireland/Irlande	77444	71737	70888	54880	58495
Hong Kong	45187	43901	69838	81328	67960
Norway,SVD,JM	57646	58197	56880	48133	59263
Greece/Grèce	56300	52713	61719	41503	35730
Libyan Arab Jamahiriya	53275	51634	x54382	x35928	x27300
Thailand/Thaïlande	23391	36227	44001	57636	75862
Portugal	46605	49150	57309	30813	49922
Argentina/Argentine	12686	16880	44557	61562	88521
Poland/Pologne	4441	25298	49242	45149	52891
Australia/Australie	30494	37120	41750	37964	37080
Turkey/Turquie	11603	30648	43331	35040	18786
Hungary/Hongrie	x20150	33441	x35930	x39138	x36477
Chile/Chili	25044	29621	31752	43328	52974
Nigeria/Nigéria	x8488	14824	x32679	x51217	x7645
Saudi Arabia	22545	34891	40548	x19078	x21614
Syrian Arab Republic	10407	x10660	52028	x24136	x17280
United Arab Emirates	30484	22758	23822	x31977	x30340
Finland/Finlande	34008	28118	26304	22465	30178
Israel/Israël	19915	21426	26621	26565	28951
Oman	13343	18499	20142	27222	25691
New Zealand	24497	27901	19180	9145	9238
Russian Federation			x25126	x30666	x38850
Algeria/Algérie	34872	28222	4994	22262	46747
Egypt/Egypte	18031	29538	14557	10192	9526
Morocco/Maroc	19459	17004	19041	17175	12293
Czech Republic				50368	57479
Philippines	14547	19745	13881	16676	26959
Gabon	x2339	x15588	x17008	x17589	x2265
Czechoslovakia	14975	x7932	x39892		

COUNTRIES–PAYS	EXPORTS – EXPORTATIONS 1990	1991	1992	1993	1994
Totale	4783464	5247420	5628508	5067204	5560581
Afrique	39112	51966	34137	46007	x11570
Afrique du Nord	2833	4400	6490	5645	8639
Amériques	613837	762657	946608	979364	1014528
ALAI	90254	99095	141584	161923	147941
MCAC	10776	11857	12714	x9938	x14174
Asie	462904	516426	551054	650924	728514
Moyen–Orient	88088	63143	50567	x66271	x64808
Europe	3555404	3751867	3902553	3164265	3576265
CEE	3400612	3622036	3755974	3028467	3448944
AELE	130082	112238	110203	108710	103859
Océanie	53721	67621	x53823	x49806	x61289
Germany/Allemagne	902755	924212	1024931	796261	895277
USA/Etats–Unis d'Amer	411877	520509	658563	648978	654390
United Kingdom	459341	543005	515174	337484	398943
France,Monac	419793	468226	508381	398374	488574
Italy/Italie	361989	421472	426294	419998	451459
Belgium–Luxembourg	412323	409992	420663	312869	309274
Netherlands/Pays–Bas	243301	270247	267294	242951	312295
Canada	86884	113727	119037	137647	178737
Austria/Autriche	119080	113393	134177	107288	x113808
Sweden/Suède	128434	136605	116642	96127	108862
Spain/Espagne	109133	107975	112843	116426	158583
Korea, Republic of	50006	69358	110638	123256	149703
Japan/Japon	99593	99498	97596	89473	92620
Hong Kong	50539	80077	87541	105199	109213
Denmark/Danemark	123669	90539	87672	75628	75025
Switz.Liecht	87112	71607	75269	77804	80116
Singapore/Singapour	42322	60292	50364	56140	68852
Poland/Pologne	15318	33058	66644	58820	53991
Brazil/Brésil	19075	31370	46774	70246	55378
Portugal	38855	40360	51713	54723	56149
Mexico/Mexique	30374	36092	55562	48575	53865
Thailand/Thaïlande	29829	37006	42038	50972	59577
Australia/Australie	42472	55167	40342	29996	39944
China/Chine	23067	28635	41903	52841	69237
Norway,SVD,JM	42968	40573	34934	30901	23743
Malaysia/Malaisie	29486	32780	29354	35470	46746
Finland/Finlande	33026	29381	30791	31971	36779
Greece/Grèce	20428	32328	30317	25412	26887
Hungary/Hongrie	x26137	x26215	x35486	x20652	x20506
Indonesia/Indonésie	9624	16683	23650	39305	41277
Ireland/Irlande	28481	34299	29083	12958	17030
Saudi Arabia	55547	37960	21449	x15428	x15022
So. Africa Customs Un	24838	17578	22565	24361	
Czech Republic				58756	63129
Czechoslovakia		x23756	x32956		
Venezuela	22469	10204	15738	19714	14006
United Arab Emirates	8260	6073	11043	x26249	x28584
India/Inde	19373	14000	10401	17626	13607
New Zealand	8137	9730	11680	18142	20488
Russian Federation			x23570	x9757	x14814
Slovenia/Slovénia			18753	13083	16658
Turkey/Turquie	9640	8091	11354	9959	14578
Slovakia				x22869	x21842
Argentina/Argentine	5157	8563	6970	6465	9712
Costa Rica	6534	7747	8982	x4668	x7817
Croatia/Croatie			11507	9440	x5104
Ecuador/Equateur	5010	4901	7222	8363	x4158
Senegal/Sénégal	4879	7935	x8	10919	
Romania/Roumanie		2281	3588	12079	8048
Yugoslavia SFR	24386	x17389			

(VALUE AS % OF TOTAL)(VALEUR EN % DU TOTAL)

	1985	1986	1987	1988	1989	1990	1991	1992	1993	1994
Africa	7.5	x7.2	x4.8	x4.2	x4.8	x5.3	x4.9	x4.2	x5.1	x3.8
Northern Africa	4.4	3.6	2.0	2.0	2.9	3.0	2.6	x1.8	x2.0	x2.1
Americas	19.6	x16.2	x14.5	13.6	14.4	14.1	13.7	15.8	18.5	19.6
LAIA	2.1	1.4	2.1	1.8	2.2	2.6	2.9	4.5	5.7	7.2
CACM	0.2	0.5	0.7	0.4	0.5	0.5	0.4	0.7	x0.8	x0.8
Asia	15.8	x14.0	x13.1	x15.6	x15.6	13.6	x15.7	17.9	x22.4	x19.8
Middle East	6.0	x6.7	x4.0	x4.4	x5.0	x3.5	x5.3	x5.9	x6.2	x4.0
Europe	54.4	59.6	59.7	57.7	56.5	63.4	61.5	58.0	49.0	51.8
EEC	46.3	50.6	50.6	49.1	48.1	58.8	57.6	54.4	45.2	47.5
EFTA	7.6	8.7	8.7	8.1	7.8	4.0	3.3	3.0	3.0	3.3
Oceania	1.5	x1.5	x1.5	x1.5	x2.1	x2.0	x2.1	x1.7	x1.5	x1.5
Germany/Allemagne	6.9	7.1	6.8	6.8	6.9	9.5	11.8	11.4	8.5	8.5
Netherlands/Pays–Bas	10.2	10.5	10.4	9.4	9.2	10.9	10.5	10.4	7.5	8.1
France,Monac	6.0	6.7	6.6	6.4	6.8	8.3	7.1	6.9	6.1	7.0
United Kingdom	5.7	6.4	7.2	7.3	6.5	6.2	6.2	5.8	6.3	6.0
USA/Etats–Unis d'Amer	10.3	7.5	6.6	7.2	6.7	6.1	5.0	5.1	6.0	6.5
Belgium–Luxembourg	4.6	5.0	4.8	5.2	5.2	7.1	6.0	5.3	4.6	5.0
Canada	5.2	4.4	3.4	2.9	3.5	3.5	3.9	4.3	4.6	3.8
Austria/Autriche	2.0	2.2	2.2	2.2	2.3	3.0	2.8	2.7	2.6	2.8
Spain/Espagne	1.1	1.7	2.2	2.0	2.2	2.8	2.7	2.6	2.0	2.1
Denmark/Danemark	2.2	2.5	2.3	2.0	1.8	2.2	2.5	2.1	2.0	2.2

	1985	1986	1987	1988	1989	1990	1991	1992	1993	1994
Afrique	0.4	x0.8	0.7	x0.1	0.7	0.8	1.0	0.6	0.9	x0.2
Afrique du Nord	0.0	x0.1	x0.0	0.0	0.1	0.1	0.1	0.1	0.1	0.2
Amériques	15.0	12.4	11.8	13.2	12.8	12.8	14.5	16.8	19.3	18.3
ALAI	3.3	1.7	2.1	1.8	2.0	1.9	1.9	2.5	3.2	2.7
MCAC	0.1	0.2	0.3	0.2	0.2	0.2	0.2	0.2	x0.2	x0.3
Asie	12.1	10.5	x9.5	10.9	11.4	9.6	9.9	9.8	12.8	13.1
Moyen–Orient	1.6	0.9	x1.6	1.8	x2.5	1.8	1.2	0.9	x1.3	x1.2
Europe	71.5	75.1	73.4	70.7	72.7	74.3	71.5	69.3	62.4	64.3
CEE	62.6	65.6	64.1	62.1	64.1	71.1	69.0	66.7	59.8	62.0
AELE	8.1	8.7	8.6	7.9	7.9	2.7	2.1	2.0	2.1	1.9
Océanie	0.5	0.4	0.4	x1.1	x1.0	1.2	1.3	x0.9	x0.9	x1.1
Germany/Allemagne	14.8	16.8	16.9	16.7	18.1	18.9	17.6	18.2	15.7	16.1
USA/Etats–Unis d'Amer	9.3	8.1	7.2	8.3	7.8	8.6	9.9	11.7	12.8	11.8
United Kingdom	8.1	8.1	8.2	7.8	7.4	9.6	10.3	9.2	6.7	7.2
France,Monac	8.6	8.6	7.6	7.7	7.8	8.8	8.9	9.0	7.9	8.8
Italy/Italie	7.1	7.4	7.1	6.7	7.3	7.6	8.0	7.6	8.3	8.1
Belgium–Luxembourg	8.5	8.9	9.3	8.6	7.8	8.6	7.8	7.5	6.2	5.6
Netherlands/Pays–Bas	4.8	4.8	4.6	4.5	4.5	5.1	5.2	4.7	4.8	5.6
Canada	2.0	2.1	1.9	2.7	2.6	1.8	2.2	2.1	2.7	3.2
Austria/Autriche	2.1	2.2	2.2	1.9	2.0	2.5	2.2	2.4	2.1	x2.0
Sweden/Suède	2.2	2.7	2.4	2.4	2.4	2.7	2.6	2.1	1.9	2.0

TRADE BY COMMODITY IN THOUSAND U.S. DOLLARS – COMMERCE PAR PRODUIT EN MILLIERS DE DOLLARS E.U

COUNTRIES–PAYS	IMPORTS – IMPORTATIONS				
	1990	1991	1992	1993	1994
Total	3803793	3612830	3819475	3502317	3812597
Africa	x232831	x208206	x216720	x201625	x203161
Northern Africa	80785	80646	x94898	x86114	x81311
Americas	x994337	886650	951889	x980172	x1025217
LAIA	104503	158202	161771	152730	175847
CACM	9734	12224	12554	x20547	x19383
Asia	500963	589842	x720506	x693857	x733291
Middle East	x100602	x192494	x221786	x126181	x129805
Europe	1900968	1758976	1827091	1471611	1717341
EEC	1748349	1622462	1688940	1356758	1570038
EFTA	104570	104008	94062	83647	109137
Oceania	x57725	x48943	x52461	x60867	x55025
USA/Etats–Unis d'Amer	663058	532493	584936	599006	610678
Germany/Allemagne	302519	321905	387101	331323	366710
France, Monac	325330	289543	289334	224835	264926
United Kingdom	234988	211029	209847	192182	192261
Canada	134946	125254	135743	157401	167941
Belgium–Luxembourg	146841	134129	152671	122396	161038
Netherlands/Pays–Bas	157791	135671	136828	94519	114496
Italy/Italie	144306	129981	131563	89948	90392
Austria/Autriche	93800	95329	92316	81857	106881
Singapore/Singapour	66217	73216	79580	86929	88423
Korea, Republic of	29399	54915	66928	76892	82392
Spain/Espagne	91471	71809	75067	51489	71501
Mexico/Mexique	34153	68927	66778	60541	72872
Sweden/Suède	84029	73661	65338	49336	60432
Hong Kong	46200	39673	44634	67507	56482
Norway, SVD, JM	47882	56647	51405	43468	60204
China/Chine	62652	23315	42490	78301	82254
Japan/Japon	40212	47816	48739	44550	51694
Turkey/Turquie	22872	62765	52256	21729	19672
Saudi Arabia	24293	46420	62325	x25196	x51259
Denmark/Danemark	38418	41725	49063	35053	42411
Iran (Islamic Rp. of)		x38978	x55164	x23843	x8885
Indonesia/Indonésie	24843	24400	43168	40854	55960
Switz.Liecht	48968	38042	34188	32673	40580
Thailand/Thaïlande	28899	30574	38114	35251	47607
So. Africa Customs Un	42636	29218	37667	36837	41374
Poland/Pologne	22462	52709	21640	24706	26516
Israel/Israël	14896	28567	29204	34306	29840
Malaysia/Malaisie	28638	28801	31416	31620	39712
Australia/Australie	29717	23701	26607	35766	31026
Portugal	27945	31901	29109	24402	29527
Algeria/Algérie	29315	31189	26357	26145	13596
Ireland/Irlande	31165	34109	27947	18429	25040
Finland/Finlande	42119	25467	23265	21488	25568
Morocco/Maroc	13239	27579	26177	13131	11304
Greece/Grèce	27628	26202	19490	19500	18857
Nigeria/Nigéria	x21830	12926	x24252	x21610	x13102
Philippines	12568	16110	21821	18807	19081
Libyan Arab Jamahiriya	15608	6882	x20400	x29032	x13933
United Arab Emirates	11870	16634	16280	x21910	x21368
Venezuela	9761	12905	18882	15376	12459
Argentina/Argentine	6767	7082	16745	21133	20716
Hungary/Hongrie	x19432	14405	x14611	x15499	x12931
Viet Nam	x1647	x983	x20946	x21346	x8364
Slovenia/Slovénia			23735	18734	19770
Colombia/Colombie	8981	19279	8937	12624	14056
Russian Federation			x14738	x25591	x18617
Chile/Chili	15422	10456	11966	13610	18496
Former USSR/Anc. URSS	24404	x35132			
Brazil/Brésil	10807	12222	11697	10608	12244

COUNTRIES–PAYS	EXPORTS – EXPORTATIONS				
	1990	1991	1992	1993	1994
Totale	3525026	3388854	3573701	3366581	3655350
Afrique	35878	x43610	46936	59539	x14945
Afrique du Nord	6168	6515	14728	19681	x11655
Amériques	441717	424389	459993	511582	531264
ALAI	167478	134579	135886	147812	160804
MCAC	3890	4013	5068	6545	5374
Asie	727134	742081	856585	875430	927677
Moyen–Orient	x72249	66382	80622	x57967	x73323
Europe	2135159	2062190	2101865	1771538	2058614
CEE	2030921	1979504	2014927	1703576	1985780
AELE	68153	70607	70299	56465	63016
Océanie	x17163	20220	x15934	x17936	x21754
Germany/Allemagne	570496	531558	556698	408600	467117
Italy/Italie	324987	322009	347975	304023	308289
Japan/Japon	288594	292494	326702	323849	326172
Belgium–Luxembourg	269032	271304	255547	234691	278344
USA/Etats–Unis d'Amer	201292	226957	251794	275858	287634
France, Monac	236722	242108	266749	225839	276952
Korea, Republic of	213204	198912	213865	209759	220594
United Kingdom	177896	180093	169095	136792	172815
Spain/Espagne	133399	127880	122110	134745	131930
Netherlands/Pays–Bas	132825	127315	135064	119454	165088
China/Chine	70482	93892	99326	127955	147002
Austria/Autriche	91522	79381	72891	55615	x50549
Canada	64587	50678	64343	78453	74570
Brazil/Brésil	56375	50878	60872	64148	62149
Turkey/Turquie	43150	39936	48153	41363	37690
Norway, SVD, JM	40358	43265	38611	27773	29453
Mexico/Mexique	40810	30677	34959	35452	48305
Poland/Pologne	49792	26899	32174	32329	27211
So. Africa Customs Un	21864	28610	26381	33393	
Switz.Liecht	27743	27247	31598	28599	33441
Venezuela	28024	31942	26335	28874	30515
Ireland/Irlande	27449	34225	25994	25645	27057
India/Inde	16518	18305	43651	20242	23818
Hong Kong	18550	17748	17097	42389	26767
Malaysia/Malaisie	6705	12571	25729	37053	40321
Sweden/Suède	24616	26962	23339	21943	58891
Singapore/Singapour	23731	25167	24281	22117	32558
Hungary/Hongrie	x31820	x23166	x16423	x9854	x7120
Czechoslovakia		x17534	x28976		
Saudi Arabia	6846	17520	22875	x4406	x23976
Slovakia				x42381	x32822
Egypt/Egypte	4842	5053	13592	18844	6707
Thailand/Thaïlande	4603	6332	9528	21159	18281
Portugal	13257	12794	15218	8043	14110
Denmark/Danemark	11326	11023	10827	12408	13790
Romania/Roumanie	20893	12623	9082	10565	6287
Australia/Australie	9366	11244	9504	11401	13923
Czech Republic				30155	25883
Russian Federation			x9619	x19372	x10987
Finland/Finlande	11729	7906	9843	11053	17380
Argentina/Argentine	17488	7849	4030	9712	8029
New Zealand	6104	8790	6306	6398	7671
Bahrain/Bahreïn	x12520	x3054	x5242	x7215	x3164
Bulgaria/Bulgarie	x5664	x4424	x5662	x5274	x1773
Indonesia/Indonésie	2215	2860	6180	4821	5489
Colombia/Colombie	2235	5645	4136	3739	5036
Greece/Grèce	5516	4798	3577	4727	3469
Israel/Israël	4530	3994	4894	4213	9494
Zimbabwe	4632	4008	3902	4181	x2964
Former USSR/Anc. URSS	56043	x11648			

(VALUE AS % OF TOTAL)(VALEUR EN % DU TOTAL)

	1985	1986	1987	1988	1989	1990	1991	1992	1993	1994
Africa	6.1	x6.1	x4.9	x4.8	x4.8	x6.1	x5.8	x5.7	x5.8	x5.3
Northern Africa	3.7	2.5	1.6	1.5	1.6	2.1	2.2	x2.5	x2.5	x2.1
Americas	34.2	x31.8	x28.1	30.5	29.9	x26.2	24.5	25.0	x28.0	x26.9
LAIA	2.8	2.7	3.0	3.1	2.4	2.7	4.4	4.2	4.4	4.6
CACM	0.6	0.4	x0.4	0.3	0.3	0.3	0.3	0.3	x0.6	x0.5
Asia	12.4	x9.9	13.3	12.4	12.2	13.1	16.3	x18.8	x19.9	x19.2
Middle East	6.0	x4.4	x3.0	x2.7	x2.3	x2.6	x5.3	x5.8	x3.6	x3.4
Europe	41.2	46.8	46.2	47.3	48.0	50.0	48.7	47.8	42.0	45.0
EEC	32.7	37.5	37.3	38.3	39.3	46.0	44.9	44.2	38.7	41.2
EFTA	7.2	8.1	7.8	7.7	7.5	2.7	2.9	2.5	2.4	2.9
Oceania	1.7	x1.9	x1.8	x1.4	x1.8	x1.5	x1.4	x1.4	x1.7	x1.4
USA/Etats–Unis d'Amer	27.1	24.3	20.3	22.1	21.7	17.4	14.7	15.3	17.1	16.0
Germany/Allemagne	5.7	7.0	6.4	6.3	6.4	8.0	8.9	10.1	9.5	9.6
France, Monac	5.8	6.9	6.8	7.3	7.0	8.6	8.0	7.6	6.4	6.9
United Kingdom	4.9	5.5	5.4	6.0	6.4	6.2	5.8	5.5	5.5	5.0
Canada	2.8	2.6	2.3	3.5	3.9	3.5	3.5	3.6	4.5	4.4
Belgium–Luxembourg	2.4	2.8	2.6	2.8	3.1	3.9	3.7	4.0	3.5	4.2
Netherlands/Pays–Bas	3.7	4.3	3.9	4.0	3.7	4.1	3.8	3.6	2.7	3.0
Italy/Italie	2.6	2.9	3.3	3.0	3.3	3.8	3.6	3.4	2.6	2.4
Austria/Autriche	1.7	2.1	1.9	2.1	2.0	2.5	2.6	2.4	2.3	2.8
Singapore/Singapour	1.0	0.9	0.9	1.0	1.4	1.7	2.0	2.1	2.5	2.3

	1985	1986	1987	1988	1989	1990	1991	1992	1993	1994
Afrique	1.0	x0.8	x0.7	x0.1	x0.6	1.0	x1.2	1.3	1.8	x0.4
Afrique du Nord	0.1	0.0	0.0	0.0	0.0	0.2	0.2	0.4	0.6	x0.3
Amériques	11.4	11.7	13.2	10.0	11.8	12.5	12.5	12.8	15.2	14.5
ALAI	2.6	2.8	3.4	3.9	5.4	4.8	4.0	3.8	4.4	4.4
MCAC	0.1	0.1	x0.2	0.2	0.1	0.1	0.1	0.1	0.2	0.1
Asie	25.1	21.1	19.5	21.1	21.5	20.6	21.8	24.0	26.0	25.4
Moyen–Orient	1.0	x1.1	x0.7	x0.8	x1.4	x2.0	2.0	2.3	x1.7	x2.0
Europe	58.2	61.9	58.0	59.7	58.1	60.6	60.9	58.8	52.6	56.3
CEE	51.6	55.8	52.9	54.3	52.5	57.6	58.4	56.4	50.6	54.3
AELE	5.2	5.1	4.4	4.3	4.6	1.9	2.1	2.0	1.7	1.7
Océanie	0.4	0.4	0.3	0.4	0.4	x0.4	0.6	x0.4	x0.5	x0.6
Germany/Allemagne	12.8	15.6	14.9	15.5	14.9	16.2	15.7	15.6	12.1	12.8
Italy/Italie	7.8	8.6	8.6	9.5	9.2	9.2	9.5	9.7	9.0	8.4
Japan/Japon	14.5	12.1	8.6	8.3	9.3	8.2	8.6	9.1	9.6	8.9
Belgium–Luxembourg	7.6	8.4	7.9	7.8	6.8	7.6	8.0	7.2	7.0	7.6
USA/Etats–Unis d'Amer	2.7	2.8	2.6	3.3	4.3	5.7	6.7	7.0	8.2	7.9
France, Monac	6.7	6.7	6.4	6.4	6.8	6.7	7.1	7.5	6.7	7.6
Korea, Republic of	8.1	6.4	6.2	7.2	6.7	6.0	5.9	6.0	6.2	6.0
United Kingdom	4.6	4.4	4.4	4.3	4.3	5.0	5.3	4.7	4.1	4.7
Spain/Espagne	4.0	3.9	3.1	3.6	3.1	3.8	3.8	3.4	4.0	3.6
Netherlands/Pays–Bas	2.6	3.0	2.9	2.7	3.0	3.8	3.8	3.8	3.5	4.5

TRADE BY COMMODITY IN THOUSAND U.S. DOLLARS – COMMERCE PAR PRODUIT EN MILLIERS DE DOLLARS E.U

COUNTRIES–PAYS	IMPORTS – IMPORTATIONS				
	1990	1991	1992	1993	1994
Total	7299185	7073797	7839054	7773181	9121869
Africa	x193436	x185785	x190320	x190639	x177473
Northern Africa	79992	82942	80276	85097	69156
Americas	2283751	2145544	2563956	2836917	3328754
LAIA	185966	229588	454511	502892	608164
CACM	13981	15312	19756	x19065	x18986
Asia	893726	1107788	1241014	1345839	1535021
Middle East	151529	x206731	x262336	x223874	x165528
Europe	3717417	3433816	3624882	3139673	3780047
EEC	3379551	3154489	3319465	2862656	3467115
EFTA	309222	260813	264421	247160	279442
Oceania	x166647	x152039	x164417	x172900	x197629
USA/Etats-Unis d'Amer	1555938	1411560	1576568	1760507	2080437
Germany/Allemagne	796336	822221	894417	702262	849683
France,Monac	541104	488867	500288	450041	532615
Canada	467597	440358	470856	521593	587032
United Kingdom	442905	391034	409203	415570	469530
Netherlands/Pays-Bas	308517	271581	282465	202361	255728
Mexico/Mexique	74296	105489	289651	324462	396678
Belgium-Luxembourg	270509	236792	251351	228456	261233
Thailand/Thaïlande	135543	159590	181250	254341	305642
Austria/Autriche	174861	170939	198584	179557	217733
Sweden/Suède	232929	193639	182178	165760	216631
Switz.Liecht	225257	183039	184108	173107	198406
Spain/Espagne	151119	164699	185309	173555	235402
Singapore/Singapour	146801	154530	160399	185022	212329
Italy/Italie	190875	184290	175616	136129	173900
Japan/Japon	134091	163974	155243	152749	181462
Australia/Australie	125711	118676	127466	136430	158450
Malaysia/Malaisie	76030	96454	113056	128098	185838
Korea, Republic of	66608	104132	89484	67628	80879
Hong Kong	59103	68675	78586	102393	115921
Denmark/Danemark	78706	74706	81699	74492	91261
Norway,SVD,JM	78260	71351	74572	69024	76064
Turkey/Turquie	40306	44682	66217	74609	46803
Saudi Arabia	47616	63321	76201	x40406	x38093
China/Chine	11673	13490	72049	92592	123284
Brazil/Brésil	51644	51389	50474	57036	75115
Finland/Finlande	94308	55796	49381	46329	67099
So. Africa Customs Un	46680	46216	50821	51918	60480
Iran (Islamic Rp. of)		x50655	x58658	x39158	x8537
Indonesia/Indonésie	38771	42701	44106	49285	51941
Portugal	36594	38384	45082	32184	38056
Israel/Israël	26363	36533	38785	38508	36351
Ireland/Irlande	39723	41173	38252	33848	38935
Argentina/Argentine	7609	14174	33718	41336	50694
Algeria/Algérie	24774	22164	26120	35314	19647
Greece/Grèce	21065	20367	25640	22112	19309
Venezuela	12358	21387	23811	19075	17118
United Arab Emirates	20121	17870	18940	x27095	x30357
New Zealand	21295	18056	19998	22278	27902
Philippines	12313	26327	14074	19230	24523
Hungary/Hongrie	x14272	16584	x17241	x23900	x25883
Egypt/Egypte	17908	18419	17883	18641	18425
Chile/Chili	16783	13887	18132	22866	22377
Poland/Pologne	6109	9319	17206	26507	37639
Tunisia/Tunisie	13460	14593	14343	11476	11163
Morocco/Maroc	12622	13508	13388	10537	10111
India/Inde	12502	9070	13538	11654	21338
Syrian Arab Republic	12719	x10818	11813	x8312	x7507
Slovenia/Slovénia			15466	13893	19251
Nigeria/Nigéria	x7493	8820	x10654	x9547	x5697

COUNTRIES–PAYS	EXPORTS – EXPORTATIONS				
	1990	1991	1992	1993	1994
Totale	6104575	5781401	6186732	6061608	7295852
Afrique	103386	119129	x16138	26675	x5704
Afrique du Nord	5038	6271	2131	10651	3383
Amériques	948602	943908	1051439	1155503	1394045
ALAI	60594	56865	82298	101739	101405
MCAC	2393	3104	3560	3813	x4143
Asie	1426441	1372196	1509549	1683883	2100359
Moyen-Orient	28942	17566	18102	x24899	x24299
Europe	3519653	3242535	3470488	3042544	3622377
CEE	2989785	2784797	2979853	2604128	3109149
AELE	495458	443482	466807	422735	496168
Océanie	x29148	26714	x30706	x30551	x39265
Germany/Allemagne	1096041	1048369	1142819	950205	1116891
Japan/Japon	784824	754088	799143	918478	1149160
USA/Etats-Unis d'Amer	624865	652522	708829	748881	942853
Italy/Italie	596429	545214	575049	515304	599793
Switz.Liecht	483607	432356	454572	410637	485154
France,Monac	345692	313380	337825	299297	359474
Canada	258696	229864	255293	298877	344438
China/Chine	206038	203791	236279	226797	307333
United Kingdom	226394	214173	226718	225568	290295
Korea, Republic of	183064	152762	173665	199644	218814
Netherlands/Pays-Bas	176758	162229	167853	134479	181272
Spain/Espagne	130319	121294	119486	112497	137662
Sweden/Suède	122337	116619	121603	97972	126643
Belgium-Luxembourg	120705	106362	105034	108204	116959
Austria/Autriche	92787	83438	89448	79608	x75482
Hong Kong	61743	62357	67425	82747	83775
Singapore/Singapour	62197	64078	59602	64277	111575
Malaysia/Malaisie	30476	37946	50450	64525	86469
Denmark/Danemark	45658	41204	53394	48934	60079
So. Africa Customs Un	95691	109961	11282	12309	
Poland/Pologne	30220	33335	41530	41759	53228
Brazil/Brésil	24018	27440	36761	42153	44677
India/Inde	19171	22028	37608	41313	41563
Thailand/Thaïlande	19134	24391	30117	31700	42952
Mexico/Mexique	21277	15223	29519	34154	32285
Australia/Australie	22033	20251	23607	22750	31694
Czechoslovakia		x22964	x36463		
Ireland/Irlande	18828	17801	22166	13575	14443
Indonesia/Indonésie	10284	9634	15493	16267	18454
Turkey/Turquie	18046	11652	13059	14021	11435
Czech Republic				36422	42039
Norway,SVD,JM	11851	11124	12218	12090	11000
Hungary/Hongrie	x14856	x10109	x15237	x8884	x9126
Finland/Finlande	12534	8817	10150	10791	15933
Slovenia/Slovénia			14411	10264	13212
Bulgaria/Bulgarie	x20055	x3061	x8854	x11768	x6631
Colombia/Colombie	3229	6879	7843	8851	10033
Russian Federation			x4438	x17902	x8407
Israel/Israël	6554	6462	7593	8162	10543
Sri Lanka	7926	8084	10825	1978	256
New Zealand	6321	5966	6540	7388	6914
Romania/Roumanie	5219	2851	5976	9530	11579
Portugal	4429	4977	6840	6470	12184
Yugoslavia SFR	34201	x14189			
Argentina/Argentine	3928	2696	2438	8855	4777
Slovakia				x13952	x11497
Ukraine			x3587	x9787	x5264
Chile/Chili	3819	3277	4392	4795	5636
Algeria/Algérie	1152	2691	46	6614	1066
Philippines	2448	6271	1044	616	2717

(VALUE AS % OF TOTAL)(VALEUR EN % DU TOTAL)

	1985	1986	1987	1988	1989	1990	1991	1992	1993	1994
Africa	3.2	3.6	x2.9	x2.7	x2.4	x2.6	x2.7	x2.4	x2.5	x2.0
Northern Africa	1.8	1.8	1.2	1.1	0.9	1.1	1.2	1.0	1.1	0.8
Americas	41.4	x35.7	x34.0	34.3	32.4	31.3	30.4	32.7	36.5	36.4
LAIA	3.0	2.2	2.1	2.3	2.2	2.5	3.2	5.8	6.5	6.7
CACM	0.3	0.3	0.3	0.2	0.2	0.2	0.2	0.3	x0.2	x0.2
Asia	10.1	9.0	x9.2	10.4	10.7	12.2	15.6	15.9	17.4	16.8
Middle East	3.1	x2.9	x2.3	x2.1	x1.8	2.1	x2.9	x3.3	x2.9	x1.8
Europe	42.8	49.3	50.5	49.1	50.6	50.9	48.5	46.2	40.4	41.4
EEC	34.0	39.0	39.8	39.3	40.6	46.3	44.6	42.3	36.8	38.0
EFTA	8.5	10.0	10.4	9.6	9.7	4.2	3.7	3.4	3.2	3.1
Oceania	2.3	x2.1	x2.1	x2.1	x2.4	x2.3	x2.1	x2.1	x2.2	x2.1
USA/Etats-Unis d'Amer	30.2	25.9	25.3	23.8	22.2	21.3	20.0	20.1	22.6	22.8
Germany/Allemagne	7.4	8.9	8.6	8.1	9.0	10.9	11.6	11.4	9.0	9.3
France,Monac	5.5	6.2	6.5	6.5	6.6	7.4	6.9	6.4	5.8	5.8
Canada	7.4	6.2	5.4	7.4	7.1	6.4	6.2	6.0	6.7	6.4
United Kingdom	5.2	5.1	5.4	5.8	5.9	6.1	5.5	5.2	5.3	5.1
Netherlands/Pays-Bas	3.3	4.3	4.1	4.0	3.8	4.2	3.8	3.6	2.6	2.8
Mexico/Mexique	1.5	0.6	0.6	0.8	0.9	1.0	1.5	3.7	4.2	4.3
Belgium-Luxembourg	2.6	2.9	2.9	3.2	3.1	3.7	3.3	3.2	2.9	2.9
Thailand/Thaïlande	0.4	0.3	0.5	0.9	1.3	1.9	2.3	2.3	3.3	3.4
Austria/Autriche	1.7	2.0	2.1	1.9	1.9	2.4	2.4	2.5	2.3	2.4

	1985	1986	1987	1988	1989	1990	1991	1992	1993	1994
Afrique	0.3	0.4	0.3	0.1	x1.0	1.7	2.1	x0.3	0.4	x0.1
Afrique du Nord	0.0	0.0	0.0	0.1	0.0	0.1	0.1	0.0	0.2	0.0
Amériques	14.5	12.7	10.0	11.2	12.6	15.6	16.4	17.0	19.1	19.1
ALAI	0.7	0.6	0.7	0.7	0.9	1.0	1.0	1.3	1.7	1.4
MCAC	0.0	0.1	x0.1	0.0	0.0	0.0	0.1	0.1	0.1	x0.1
Asie	25.5	21.8	x30.3	x33.1	24.9	23.4	23.8	24.4	27.8	28.8
Moyen-Orient	0.8	0.5	x0.5	0.5	x0.5	0.5	0.3	0.3	x0.4	x0.3
Europe	58.3	63.9	56.4	53.2	59.4	57.7	56.1	56.1	50.2	49.6
CEE	45.9	50.4	44.6	42.1	47.4	49.0	48.2	48.2	43.0	42.6
AELE	10.9	12.4	11.1	10.4	11.2	8.1	7.7	7.5	7.0	6.8
Océanie	0.4	x0.5	0.4	x0.4	x0.5	x0.5	0.5	x0.5	x0.5	x0.5
Germany/Allemagne	16.0	18.8	16.6	15.6	17.5	18.0	18.1	18.5	15.7	15.3
Japan/Japon	18.5	14.8	11.0	12.7	13.6	12.9	13.0	12.9	15.2	15.8
USA/Etats-Unis d'Amer	7.6	6.6	5.3	5.3	6.7	10.2	11.3	11.5	12.4	12.9
Italy/Italie	9.9	10.6	9.2	8.6	9.7	9.8	9.4	9.3	8.5	8.2
Switz.Liecht	7.1	8.3	7.5	7.1	7.5	7.9	7.5	7.3	6.8	6.6
France,Monac	5.0	5.2	4.7	4.5	5.5	5.7	5.4	5.5	4.9	4.9
Canada	6.0	5.5	4.0	5.1	4.9	4.2	4.0	4.1	4.9	4.7
China/Chine			3.0	3.2	3.7	3.4	3.5	3.8	3.7	4.2
United Kingdom	3.7	3.6	3.3	3.2	3.5	3.7	3.7	3.7	3.7	4.0
Korea, Republic of	3.9	4.2	3.8	3.4	3.5	3.0	2.6	2.8	3.3	3.0

TRADE BY COMMODITY IN THOUSAND U.S. DOLLARS – COMMERCE PAR PRODUIT EN MILLIERS DE DOLLARS E.U

COUNTRIES–PAYS	IMPORTS – IMPORTATIONS 1990	1991	1992	1993	1994
Total	12593645	12922281	13506321	12450720	14021240
Africa	x485330	x439792	x455158	x408995	x421003
Northern Africa	181971	147328	x156265	x147817	x141011
Americas	2685711	3048018	3043495	3525959	3865176
LAIA	428596	583926	678401	734655	831471
CACM	31468	28739	40736	x43135	x41807
Asia	1875290	2218870	2371840	x2436187	2686607
Middle East	x240242	x420953	x511148	x434051	x323205
Europe	6802863	6693540	7151330	5574742	6490158
EEC	6203272	6167411	6615518	5082500	5934369
EFTA	509877	477408	469547	427143	488465
Oceania	x307220	x275500	x289688	x302572	x333530
USA/Etats-Unis d'Amer	1552016	1779613	1622628	1976332	2150776
Germany/Allemagne	1552166	1688506	1655196	1256876	1485427
France,Monac	854406	813672	918536	655287	754137
United Kingdom	768044	721114	747845	665364	750468
Canada	564485	566459	630251	705062	770112
Italy/Italie	626802	603664	668482	505536	597309
Netherlands/Pays-Bas	536468	509163	536224	459309	558606
Belgium-Luxembourg	380086	422251	521025	311847	351417
Japan/Japon	365096	381424	346702	333608	378897
Spain/Espagne	305474	336304	423518	252453	335099
Sweden/Suède	402158	333583	365807	301392	345169
Switz.Liecht	380569	340015	334281	305210	352054
Mexico/Mexique	191217	265554	328635	332161	373262
Austria/Autriche	265753	273773	296342	265962	295878
Singapore/Singapour	231424	258131	271949	295301	347075
Korea, Republic of	226813	253657	263183	279669	323398
Hong Kong	166237	202829	240916	307989	330527
Australia/Australie	231406	206620	217577	226975	252700
Thailand/Thaïlande	164313	167746	188128	214996	271528
Malaysia/Malaisie	116318	138856	188237	184853	205491
Iran (Islamic Rp. of)		x166080	x176394	x119089	x34505
Denmark/Danemark	142846	137891	151024	122578	144711
Norway,SVD,JM	122530	129043	127257	115357	129827
So. Africa Customs Un	107253	115274	119107	98330	115240
Indonesia/Indonésie	113309	131347	92719	87381	105303
Brazil/Brésil	88826	113220	88124	82237	84850
Portugal	87707	94275	100763	82049	75900
Finland/Finlande	147102	94951	84653	79699	108292
China/Chine	54595	72456	82993	95393	143370
Saudi Arabia	66678	74755	97707	x77350	x67044
Ireland/Irlande	75666	79658	82031	65173	74824
United Arab Emirates	46953	57237	95075	x64614	x82153
Hungary/Hongrie	x63981	64402	x67965	x72964	x58827
Israel/Israël	60576	61820	64340	68596	76263
Turkey/Turquie	46141	49679	51378	89057	58238
Venezuela	34925	59551	67197	60072	47138
Greece/Grèce	58593	58607	64072	58974	57132
Argentina/Argentine	15828	35268	64740	77821	120243
Chile/Chili	41500	42480	52626	62208	60899
Algeria/Algérie	80290	45313	46042	52911	51752
India/Inde	44119	38633	48206	50241	64337
New Zealand	45321	41306	44075	50327	58646
Poland/Pologne	23003	32610	38163	44456	59983
Russian Federation			x62425	x52432	x66536
Czechoslovakia	70844	x39418	x73543		
Egypt/Egypte	35169	28950	33581	32076	26633
Colombia/Colombie	16516	17435	25710	50134	67890
Nigeria/Nigéria	x31055	15434	x41366	x35324	x21496
Former USSR/Anc. URSS	179379	x84720			
Morocco/Maroc	24543	27056	27860	18202	19552

COUNTRIES–PAYS	EXPORTS – EXPORTATIONS 1990	1991	1992	1993	1994
Totale	11809070	11894763	12630582	11727533	13334868
Afrique	x47935	44946	x62133	x50305	x9803
Afrique du Nord	4315	3907	4805	2431	x5953
Amériques	1473468	1559640	1687304	1871251	2097369
ALAI	132294	166509	183305	219926	241583
MCAC	3893	3978	5654	6208	6414
Asie	2248018	2653425	2886517	3110490	3568094
Moyen-Orient	23306	13153	14473	x24241	x20878
Europe	7750985	7476220	7842884	6507484	7459746
CEE	7044205	6781247	7106983	5827207	6691307
AELE	630034	645222	671912	614906	706829
Océanie	48248	x50480	x57405	x66722	x77126
Germany/Allemagne	2635383	2525688	2767924	2146977	2523344
Japan/Japon	1240087	1557468	1624595	1683681	1867332
USA/Etats-Unis d'Amer	1151320	1194514	1316031	1431090	1601816
Sweden/Suède	844767	798953	772433	632811	756506
Italy/Italie	657286	654005	664681	564053	637307
Switz.Liecht	606385	623430	648131	595248	682271
United Kingdom	635611	638792	672426	554961	662842
France,Monac	586931	560557	601066	510345	566148
Netherlands/Pays-Bas	507941	499504	473337	417394	453204
China/Chine	348501	373371	448406	495602	635415
Austria/Autriche	371666	336155	356783	332886	x314427
Spain/Espagne	322829	310755	300851	234015	301975
Hong Kong	175139	198435	240921	286697	286852
Belgium-Luxembourg	230651	228289	265235	226507	248242
Canada	181264	189848	175311	188054	209626
Israel/Israël	148362	159227	159445	179726	215535
Singapore/Singapour	111613	139776	148541	154318	213345
Korea, Republic of	86554	89699	107934	130846	181212
India/Inde	71250	68671	91295	91314	90407
Ireland/Irlande	75375	71696	80599	74162	79528
Brazil/Brésil	57280	61148	71433	88043	110255
Denmark/Danemark	70345	69786	73286	48961	58982
Mexico/Mexique	28660	50310	56727	55072	73806
So. Africa Customs Un	36993	34035	50912	40941	
Argentina/Argentine	33169	36678	32931	53326	32657
Portugal	38162	37453	44243	37713	42046
Australia/Australie	28695	30665	34307	39642	49737
Finland/Finlande	47458	33301	28234	27694	36896
Slovenia/Slovénia			39640	46064	46073
Poland/Pologne	53115	38306	22002	24449	32882
Thailand/Thaïlande	9626	17421	18625	32839	25281
Czechoslovakia		x28178	x40445		
New Zealand	18108	18045	21483	26568	27035
Norway,SVD,JM	23642	21791	23736	19656	24468
Malaysia/Malaisie	10579	16405	18694	23905	23187
Hungary/Hongrie	x14292	x16684	x19795	x19427	x18457
Czech Republic				48544	49660
Yugoslavia SFR	74161	x47164			
Greece/Grèce	19568	16080	5883	18726	9859
Colombia/Colombie	5585	10783	9765	13757	16845
Turkey/Turquie	5907	6467	9211	10165	10956
Bulgaria/Bulgarie	x12881	x3741	x7664	x12900	x6832
French Guiana	341	365	1997	21764	32148
Venezuela	6129	6302	10161	5756	4273
Russian Federation			x8548	x13249	x11046
Romania/Roumanie	9086	9503	3675	7833	8289
Yugoslavia/Yougoslavie			x11489	x3674	x1070
Croatia/Croatie			8295	6144	x3862
Former USSR/Anc. URSS	138870	x12754			
Sri Lanka	5797	6258	5788	447	176

(VALUE AS % OF TOTAL)(VALEUR EN % DU TOTAL)

	1985	1986	1987	1988	1989	1990	1991	1992	1993	1994
Africa	5.4	x5.2	x4.2	x4.1	x3.7	x3.9	x3.4	x3.4	x3.3	x3.0
Northern Africa	2.3	1.8	1.3	1.4	1.4	1.4	1.1	x1.2	x1.2	x1.0
Americas	25.5	x22.6	x20.9	21.0	22.7	21.3	23.6	22.6	28.3	27.5
LAIA	3.9	3.6	3.1	3.2	3.4	3.4	4.5	5.0	5.9	5.9
CACM	0.4	0.4	x0.4	0.3	0.3	0.2	0.2	0.3	x0.3	x0.3
Asia	13.4	x13.5	x13.2	x14.8	x14.2	14.9	17.1	17.5	x19.5	19.1
Middle East	3.0	x3.4	x3.1	x3.2	x2.8	x1.9	x3.3	x3.8	x3.5	x2.3
Europe	49.8	52.6	52.6	51.6	52.1	54.0	51.8	52.9	44.8	46.3
EEC	40.1	42.2	42.3	42.2	42.6	49.3	47.7	49.0	40.8	42.3
EFTA	8.8	9.6	9.6	8.8	9.0	4.0	3.7	3.5	3.4	3.5
Oceania	3.0	x2.6	x3.0	x2.5	x2.8	x2.4	x2.1	x2.1	x2.4	x2.4
USA/Etats-Unis d'Amer	15.1	12.9	12.3	11.7	13.1	12.3	13.8	12.0	15.9	15.3
Germany/Allemagne	9.1	10.1	9.9	9.4	9.9	12.3	13.1	12.3	10.1	10.6
France,Monac	5.8	6.3	6.3	6.5	6.1	6.8	6.3	6.8	5.3	5.4
United Kingdom	6.0	5.2	5.3	5.7	5.6	6.1	5.6	5.5	5.3	5.4
Canada	5.6	4.3	4.0	5.3	5.2	4.5	4.4	4.7	5.7	5.5
Italy/Italie	3.9	4.2	4.4	4.3	4.7	5.0	4.7	4.9	4.1	4.3
Netherlands/Pays-Bas	4.0	4.2	4.2	4.2	3.8	4.3	3.9	4.0	3.7	4.0
Belgium-Luxembourg	2.8	2.9	2.5	2.5	2.6	3.0	3.3	3.9	2.5	2.5
Japan/Japon	2.0	1.9	1.9	2.3	2.6	2.9	3.0	2.6	2.7	2.7
Spain/Espagne	1.0	1.2	1.5	1.9	1.9	2.4	2.6	3.1	2.0	2.4

	1985	1986	1987	1988	1989	1990	1991	1992	1993	1994
Afrique	0.4	x0.4	x0.4	x0.3	x0.6	x0.4	0.4	x0.5	x0.4	x0.1
Afrique du Nord	0.0	0.0	x0.0	0.0	0.0	0.0	0.0	0.0	0.0	x0.0
Amériques	13.5	9.9	8.4	9.2	10.7	12.5	13.1	13.4	15.9	15.7
ALAI	1.2	0.9	0.8	1.0	1.1	1.1	1.4	1.5	1.9	1.8
MCAC	0.0	0.1	0.0	0.0	0.0	0.0	0.0	0.0	0.1	0.0
Asie	16.0	16.1	x22.1	x22.9	19.2	19.1	22.3	22.8	26.5	26.7
Moyen-Orient	0.6	0.4	0.7	0.2	x0.2	0.2	0.1	0.1	x0.2	x0.2
Europe	67.0	70.1	63.1	62.1	66.1	65.6	62.9	62.1	55.5	55.9
CEE	51.7	53.7	48.6	48.0	51.0	59.7	57.0	56.3	49.7	50.2
AELE	14.3	15.4	13.6	13.5	14.5	5.3	5.4	5.3	5.2	5.3
Océanie	0.4	x0.3	x0.3	x0.3	0.4	0.4	x0.4	x0.4	x0.6	x0.6
Germany/Allemagne	18.4	20.0	18.2	17.9	19.0	22.3	21.2	21.9	18.3	18.9
Japan/Japon	10.8	11.5	9.3	10.3	11.1	10.5	13.1	12.9	14.4	14.0
USA/Etats-Unis d'Amer	10.8	7.7	6.6	6.9	8.1	9.7	10.0	10.4	12.2	12.0
Sweden/Suède	7.0	7.2	6.4	6.2	6.7	7.2	6.7	6.1	5.4	5.7
Italy/Italie	4.3	4.9	4.7	4.0	4.4	5.6	5.5	5.3	4.8	4.8
Switz.Liecht	4.4	4.9	4.5	4.5	4.6	5.1	5.2	5.1	5.1	5.1
United Kingdom	5.8	4.8	4.6	4.6	4.7	5.4	5.4	5.3	4.7	5.0
France,Monac	4.8	5.0	4.3	4.1	4.3	5.0	4.7	4.8	4.4	4.2
Netherlands/Pays-Bas	3.2	3.5	3.2	3.5	3.9	4.3	4.2	3.7	3.6	3.4
China/Chine	0.3	0.3	2.3	2.5	3.0	3.0	3.1	3.6	4.2	4.8

TRADE BY COMMODITY IN THOUSAND U.S. DOLLARS – COMMERCE PAR PRODUIT EN MILLIERS DE DOLLARS E.U

COUNTRIES–PAYS	IMPORTS – IMPORTATIONS					COUNTRIES–PAYS	EXPORTS – EXPORTATIONS				
	1990	1991	1992	1993	1994		1990	1991	1992	1993	1994
Total	2872783	3118895	3379763	3347004	3733012	Totale	2599941	2784574	3033332	3048070	3478546
Africa	x72519	x75517	x81685	x78185	x81875	Afrique	16346	9953	12700	12042	15718
Northern Africa	18765	18791	x18752	x20878	x22891	Afrique du Nord	14063	7082	9607	8192	14422
Americas	663381	754606	868981	911071	1041536	Amériques	290720	285177	360693	421639	505974
LAIA	69412	94135	140845	156367	206455	ALAI	91706	102562	142534	163437	162523
CACM	10008	10969	15545	x14837	x16018	MCAC	2598	3283	3013	2808	3635
Asia	467764	548334	612030	x662444	x724253	Asie	1027229	1201344	1300373	1329544	1474332
Middle East	x103017	x112974	x148529	x150769	x133700	Moyen–Orient	17610	x4372	x5654	x10965	x8442
Europe	1415632	1590702	1687970	1557035	1717706	Europe	1232308	1260181	1335677	1252207	1446363
EEC	1301433	1486469	1577726	1455627	1601216	CEE	1107592	1125338	1192707	1125945	1299351
EFTA	91329	92255	96084	87562	95622	AELE	123374	133978	139454	124852	143955
Oceania	x87245	x94336	x101482	x95933	x113000	Océanie	10801	x8202	x10023	x10550	12465
USA/Etats–Unis d'Amer	463452	515052	571842	600359	649955	Germany/Allemagne	489175	519137	568294	531091	619418
Germany/Allemagne	315244	409254	417090	370573	402007	Hong Kong	254939	309892	341609	391617	430241
France,Monac	200108	217231	242002	244814	242133	Japan/Japon	302523	335530	347920	295615	264072
Hong Kong	130087	166930	203884	243580	268763	Korea, Republic of	241194	264529	255885	222210	252007
United Kingdom	183073	178275	196385	201617	236561	China/Chine	118923	170669	214048	252150	321005
Italy/Italie	154322	184135	189182	160608	183667	USA/Etats–Unis d'Amer	190318	172337	207954	250088	329094
Canada	101873	115557	123211	121773	150519	United Kingdom	176535	178231	185096	166387	192224
Japan/Japon	121662	128761	116681	111322	138308	Italy/Italie	133560	133519	132126	124329	149211
Spain/Espagne	79333	112171	120854	101107	122954	Switz.Liecht	118650	130815	136045	122629	141189
Netherlands/Pays–Bas	88957	94241	97711	96740	103113	France,Monac	127201	110485	113979	125860	140955
Australia/Australie	67763	75022	81513	74461	89549	Brazil/Brésil	69029	83886	100073	109797	100980
Switz.Liecht	66199	65370	66869	62002	65999	Spain/Espagne	40906	41386	41347	36792	32755
Belgium–Luxembourg	65606	63482	65173	65213	68092	Netherlands/Pays–Bas	34852	34764	37358	36716	39863
Austria/Autriche	53890	52010	57540	47264	54833	Singapore/Singapour	35013	34365	35970	30837	38002
United Arab Emirates	36517	37507	44540	x56024	x55725	Portugal	30707	30351	33512	28388	30151
Sweden/Suède	47562	48258	46965	40948	44478	Indonesia/Indonésie	8707	21314	29821	37129	38521
Singapore/Singapour	34211	43166	44701	43131	48098	Thailand/Thaïlande	10383	15508	22503	27342	49700
Mexico/Mexique	25006	30152	44923	49290	65520	Finland/Finlande	16393	15643	18386	15161	20335
Denmark/Danemark	29138	36869	44107	38865	49473	Pakistan	8964	14544	13954	16987	16769
Saudi Arabia	26067	31747	40434	x34177	x30233	Mexico/Mexique	7693	4043	18767	21703	28483
Greece/Grèce	24838	31017	32455	30606	31488	Sweden/Suède	16656	14475	16187	13689	15383
Argentina/Argentine	7169	20843	33964	28289	44794	India/Inde	15912	11447	12464	19912	29252
Portugal	22602	26033	29740	26644	22799	Greece/Grèce	13667	16637	14317	10952	7766
So. Africa Customs Un	22571	28032	29188	23702	22909	Belgium–Luxembourg	9830	13350	13685	12955	13452
Norway,SVD,JM	22994	24272	26958	23802	27557	Israel/Israël	8071	11313	11278	13865	14389
Korea, Republic of	18794	22791	23469	25164	28774	Argentina/Argentine	6042	6241	10718	12424	12014
Ireland/Irlande	18804	18690	22634	18433	23539	Austria/Autriche	8705	7479	8586	8094	x5605
Israel/Israël	13476	16974	16900	19844	22878	Australia/Australie	9242	6665	8150	8854	10547
Chile/Chili	11800	14607	15840	20061	18950	Ireland/Irlande	5457	5815	5958	9261	17104
Finland/Finlande	17957	14804	15885	12197	16078	Colombia/Colombie	4639	4493	7654	7609	8397
China/Chine	9551	12699	12488	16457	20211	Venezuela	4074	2945	4196	11156	11309
Malaysia/Malaisie	9676	11400	15888	13517	15713	Canada	3569	5019	6363	4821	9112
New Zealand	12716	12483	13457	14415	16895	Egypt/Egypte	9224	3916	6417	5637	11124
Venezuela	4939	8528	14332	15331	9823	Poland/Pologne	10743	8714	3509	3380	5792
Iran (Islamic Rp. of)		x7908	x15952	x13163	x2847	Denmark/Danemark	3913	4029	3876	6270	15128
Poland/Pologne	3833	12922	9913	11647	17443	Czech Republic				13889	14112
Hungary/Hongrie	x5373	14317	x6299	x12756	x13761	Czechoslovakia		x7232	x6371		
Turkey/Turquie	7002	8055	10749	12831	8251	Malaysia/Malaisie	809	2677	4234	5025	3932
Thailand/Thaïlande	7360	8484	10127	12566	14859	Philippines	1948	2818	2989	3772	2958
Brazil/Brésil	6183	3287	9049	13617	26446	Turkey/Turquie	9271	2658	3023	3664	3803
Russian Federation			x10029	x15311	x20517	Guatemala	2575	3186	2983	2727	3228
Nigeria/Nigéria	x6596	2229	x8616	x9043	x6370	Norway,SVD,JM	4724	3162	3407	2222	2758
Cyprus/Chypre	4765	5367	7856	5226	5747	So. Africa Customs Un	1328	2472	2599	3168	
Morocco/Maroc	6451	5836	5974	5407	5311	Morocco/Maroc	2705	2231	2548	1817	824
Lebanon/Liban	x5564	x6924	x4991	x5116	x6736	Russian Federation			x2922	x2694	x843
Former USSR/Anc. URSS	137859	x16884				New Zealand	1481	1310	1698	1518	1885
Peru/Pérou	3162	4496	6019	5200	8383	United Arab Emirates	5683			x4361	x2737
Uruguay	3982	3982	5127	5714	5660	Bulgaria/Bulgarie	x1216	x549	x2213	x1427	x566
Colombia/Colombie	1728	1796	3646	9344	10352	Hungary/Hongrie	x398	x955	x1173	x1167	x943
Costa Rica	4823	4677	5499	x3765	x3927	Slovenia/Slovénia			1883	622	848

(VALUE AS % OF TOTAL)(VALEUR EN % DU TOTAL)

	1985	1986	1987	1988	1989	1990	1991	1992	1993	1994		1985	1986	1987	1988	1989	1990	1991	1992	1993	1994
Africa	2.8	x2.6	x2.5	x2.9	x2.6	x2.5	x2.4	x2.5	x2.3	x2.2	Afrique	0.1	0.1	0.2	0.3	0.5	0.7	0.4	0.4	0.4	0.5
Northern Africa	0.9	0.7	0.5	0.7	0.8	0.7	0.6	x0.6	x0.6	x0.6	Afrique du Nord	0.0	0.1	0.1	0.3	0.3	0.5	0.3	0.3	0.3	0.4
Americas	36.1	31.7	28.1	28.3	25.7	23.1	24.2	25.7	27.2	27.9	Amériques	7.1	6.8	5.4	7.1	10.5	11.2	10.3	11.9	13.9	14.5
LAIA	2.8	2.1	1.8	1.9	2.3	2.4	3.0	4.2	4.7	5.5	ALAI	2.6	2.5	1.9	2.8	4.7	3.5	3.7	4.7	5.4	4.7
CACM	0.6	0.5	0.5	0.5	0.5	0.3	0.4	0.5	x0.4	x0.4	MCAC	0.0	0.0	0.0	0.1	0.1	0.1	0.1	0.1	0.1	0.1
Asia	12.9	x14.7	x14.3	x15.2	x15.4	16.3	17.6	18.2	x19.8	x19.4	Asie	39.2	36.0	x42.5	x46.6	41.4	39.5	43.2	42.8	43.7	42.4
Middle East	4.3	x4.7	x4.2	x3.8	x3.1	x3.6	x3.6	x4.4	x4.5	x3.6	Moyen–Orient	1.4	0.4	0.4	0.4	x0.4	0.7	x0.2	x0.2	x0.4	x0.2
Europe	41.8	45.1	48.9	46.9	47.2	49.3	51.0	49.9	46.5	46.0	Europe	51.4	54.9	49.6	43.6	45.9	47.4	45.3	44.0	41.1	41.6
EEC	34.6	37.2	40.6	39.5	39.8	45.3	47.7	46.7	43.5	42.9	CEE	44.9	47.9	43.3	38.1	39.9	42.6	40.4	39.3	36.9	37.4
EFTA	6.9	7.3	7.6	6.9	6.8	3.2	3.0	2.8	2.6	2.6	AELE	6.4	7.0	6.3	5.5	5.8	4.7	4.8	4.6	4.1	4.1
Oceania	4.2	x3.8	x3.4	x3.4	x3.7	x3.0	x3.0	x3.0	x2.9	x3.1	Océanie	0.5	0.3	0.5	x0.6	x0.6	0.4	x0.3	x0.3	x0.3	0.4
USA/Etats–Unis d'Amer	28.7	25.4	22.3	22.2	18.5	16.1	16.5	16.9	17.9	17.4	Germany/Allemagne	18.7	20.9	19.2	17.1	17.6	18.8	18.6	18.7	17.4	17.8
Germany/Allemagne	8.3	9.0	9.2	8.9	9.6	11.0	13.1	12.3	11.1	10.8	Hong Kong	5.6	5.7	5.4	7.7	10.1	9.8	11.1	11.3	12.8	12.4
France,Monac	5.1	6.0	6.5	6.2	6.2	7.0	7.0	7.2	7.3	6.5	Japan/Japon	21.8	18.6	13.7	13.4	13.2	11.6	12.0	11.5	9.7	7.6
Hong Kong	2.3	2.5	2.5	3.3	4.1	4.5	5.4	6.0	7.3	7.2	Korea, Republic of	8.2	9.3	9.3	11.1	10.6	9.3	9.5	8.4	7.3	7.2
United Kingdom	5.1	4.8	5.6	5.9	5.7	6.4	5.7	5.8	6.0	6.3	China/Chine			3.5	3.8	4.2	4.6	6.1	7.1	8.3	9.2
Italy/Italie	3.6	3.9	4.8	4.6	4.7	5.4	5.9	5.6	4.8	4.9	USA/Etats–Unis d'Amer	4.1	3.9	3.1	3.9	5.3	7.3	6.2	6.9	8.2	9.5
Canada	3.3	2.9	2.7	3.1	3.7	3.5	3.7	3.6	3.6	4.0	United Kingdom	6.7	5.5	5.0	5.2	6.0	6.8	6.4	6.1	5.5	5.5
Japan/Japon	3.2	3.8	4.1	4.4	4.3	4.2	4.1	3.5	3.3	3.7	Italy/Italie	4.7	5.2	4.7	4.3	4.8	5.1	4.8	4.4	4.1	4.3
Spain/Espagne	1.0	1.3	1.7	1.9	2.2	2.8	3.6	3.6	3.0	3.3	Switz.Liecht	4.2	4.6	4.4	3.8	3.9	4.6	4.7	4.5	4.0	4.1
Netherlands/Pays–Bas	3.2	3.5	3.4	3.1	2.9	3.1	3.0	2.9	2.9	2.8	France,Monac	4.9	5.0	4.9	5.3	4.9	4.9	4.0	3.8	4.1	4.1

TRADE BY COMMODITY IN THOUSAND U.S. DOLLARS – COMMERCE PAR PRODUIT EN MILLIERS DE DOLLARS E.U

COUNTRIES–PAYS	IMPORTS – IMPORTATIONS				
	1990	1991	1992	1993	1994
Total	6580526	7469647	8282017	7844822	8594846
Africa	x208246	x222151	x273050	x238707	x242573
Northern Africa	78524	87031	x115902	x78807	x96393
Americas	1620556	1790063	2080165	2273086	x2549577
LAIA	77851	124396	204895	271907	309017
CACM	16908	18710	27326	x34178	x38031
Asia	1178219	1316905	1490378	x1572220	x1760904
Middle East	408976	406696	518810	x451330	x421825
Europe	3361386	3837458	4171692	3408730	3668390
EEC	3063738	3511806	3853875	3083497	3310007
EFTA	242865	255312	266560	272375	301945
Oceania	x151490	x148604	x151297	x147313	x170363
USA/Etats–Unis d'Amer	1215701	1295904	1470855	1581692	1810562
Germany/Allemagne	666699	935126	1006378	891293	901725
France,Monac	477815	481088	517955	430784	459308
United Kingdom	365988	381525	423398	370064	419431
Hong Kong	256092	316360	363634	407323	457691
Italy/Italie	268892	322497	394437	184291	192331
Japan/Japon	218219	272645	279956	339569	443979
Canada	226679	264960	291142	306223	303237
Netherlands/Pays–Bas	258329	263863	297137	241104	275123
Spain/Espagne	216465	274170	320872	190278	224539
Belgium–Luxembourg	243829	262880	273070	233679	257513
Saudi Arabia	209489	215937	231371	x152974	x156625
Switz.Liecht	174851	185343	190602	210916	232956
Austria/Autriche	163081	174976	183038	176387	201696
Australia/Australie	99406	102552	103376	98661	118454
Sweden/Suède	107773	105861	99241	81719	83636
Mexico/Mexique	39215	60011	91094	93697	119074
Greece/Grèce	68216	74567	82194	77726	71162
Singapore/Singapour	81667	69870	74823	86324	104668
Portugal	46422	60060	82408	68565	68010
Denmark/Danemark	66761	69772	74616	61991	70730
Korea, Republic of	66218	67567	69174	67141	82741
Norway,SVD,JM	62592	63663	70301	57333	64666
Kuwait/ Koweït	27751	22417	77577	75819	66299
United Arab Emirates	52014	48404	56307	x63012	x68261
Ireland/Irlande	61339	60524	59360	46169	50899
China/Chine	35692	36882	47910	63750	55890
Hungary/Hongrie	x21450	40065	x47233	x57610	x47160
Poland/Pologne	11381	35145	35746	68463	71612
Finland/Finlande	52129	44895	39773	29447	33904
Israel/Israël	28952	30552	37412	45041	52687
Argentina/Argentine	1005	9816	37698	59867	64403
Nigeria/Nigéria	x21467	28618	x37781	x39882	x27329
Malaysia/Malaisie	26267	34683	34177	34636	41874
So. Africa Customs Un	24652	28890	34778	35797	33656
Algeria/Algérie	13533	15986	55332	21371	17468
Russian Federation			x43707	x36268	x63069
Turkey/Turquie	25800	23989	26155	28064	15351
New Zealand	28255	24470	24104	26765	33069
Chile/Chili	12578	13952	27357	32518	28351
Libyan Arab Jamahiriya	27747	29571	x19435	x18887	x29845
Former USSR/Anc. URSS		x66382			
Lebanon/Liban	x12985	x24245	x16481	x19968	x37542
Indonesia/Indonésie	16652	17384	19443	21736	20062
Cyprus/Chypre	16986	16275	23665	17685	17041
Yugoslavia SFR	41193	x55827			
Jordan/Jordanie	9617	10127	21246	22094	19357
Venezuela	5288	11394	16813	18472	13627
Czech Republic				46440	49928
Tunisia/Tunisie	13581	14649	15646	13769	17826

COUNTRIES–PAYS	EXPORTS – EXPORTATIONS				
	1990	1991	1992	1993	1994
Totale	5653999	6343806	7206669	7248632	8072783
Afrique	45971	53327	48283	60227	x34050
Afrique du Nord	26210	32657	25052	21736	25264
Amériques	574807	777142	966747	1053232	1198578
ALAI	114010	231094	350571	402188	477219
MCAC	3636	5610	7147	x8551	x10477
Asie	1408235	1669523	2060707	2273028	2609644
Moyen–Orient	67049	78853	138930	97395	102402
Europe	3399922	3676721	3934887	3628088	3999127
CEE	3188148	3439026	3625751	3285615	3678877
AELE	153020	178645	203665	265054	266166
Océanie	x30507	x35271	x26597	x33592	47147
Italy/Italie	1017935	1179363	1217139	1142897	1313453
Germany/Allemagne	643327	662648	662293	568246	585539
Hong Kong	427224	546952	644554	672846	730115
France,Monac	444567	490227	529905	462813	520708
USA/Etats–Unis d'Amer	361706	450398	509263	505458	531470
Korea, Republic of	383849	411137	392534	464226	488363
China/Chine	140262	169095	339232	412890	587150
Japan/Japon	215839	218032	213794	216024	242160
Spain/Espagne	194261	194216	222933	199088	216417
Netherlands/Pays–Bas	183715	200777	208332	191589	239545
Mexico/Mexique	40635	133584	228046	238739	307426
Belgium–Luxembourg	170003	181917	199858	203218	211880
United Kingdom	194281	178987	193489	170750	194362
Switz.Liecht	113556	141292	161475	225115	224353
Canada	87961	84344	93712	120516	174800
Indonesia/Indonésie	43397	69108	89636	136191	125874
Thailand/Thaïlande	40446	58812	87907	107301	133234
Brazil/Brésil	44734	56981	79908	116107	119635
Sweden/Suède	85959	82032	84469	70755	78620
Austria/Autriche	65617	66546	84225	82552	x88935
Denmark/Danemark	67071	69013	81044	71421	76342
Turkey/Turquie	38156	49549	100974	62807	73643
India/Inde	37428	48783	72993	78582	98661
Portugal	56409	67392	67625	61553	74991
Hungary/Hongrie	x24292	x29939	x58858	x52944	x42877
Poland/Pologne	59865	40965	39568	38488	45436
Slovenia/Slovénic			64786	47409	35064
Norway,SVD,JM	34534	32434	36559	35085	37616
Singapore/Singapour	27076	31898	32653	29356	39991
Greece/Grèce	17696	24044	31959	29923	34356
Czechoslovakia		x35296	x42485		
Czech Republic				73090	66285
Malaysia/Malaisie	12300	17648	25356	29790	33756
Ireland/Irlande	27572	25268	25714	16079	23483
Romania/Roumanie	25618	12562	23217	20802	16143
Australia/Australie	17856	17746	18144	20555	27703
Colombia/Colombie	9487	16550	16928	20816	19924
Yugoslavia SFR	51261	x51525			
Finland/Finlande	19557	16417	16768	14730	20247
Egypt/Egypte	15563	15038	12619	13125	13517
So. Africa Customs Un	8866	9223	12760	12043	
Philippines	1200	6548	12047	15194	16183
Zimbabwe	5514	5079	6027	19618	x5894
New Zealand	12172	8766	7966	12615	19165
Venezuela	9083	8079	9023	9505	8814
Saudi Arabia	6128	11362	12615	x2244	x2354
Yugoslavia/Yougoslavie			x21331	x1922	x330
Malta/Malte	7175	7277	7556	6978	x7130
Croatia/Croatie			11503	10160	x7361
Jordan/Jordanie	5288	5320	5686	9685	4716

(VALUE AS % OF TOTAL)(VALEUR EN % DU TOTAL)

	1985	1986	1987	1988	1989	1990	1991	1992	1993	1994
Africa	3.7	x4.2	x3.5	x3.3	x3.2	x3.2	x3.0	x3.3	x3.1	x2.8
Northern Africa	2.1	2.1	1.3	1.3	1.3	1.2	1.2	x1.4	x1.0	x1.1
Americas	30.1	x26.9	x25.5	25.4	25.4	24.6	24.0	25.1	29.0	x29.7
LAIA	0.7	0.5	0.6	0.8	1.3	1.2	1.7	2.5	3.5	3.6
CACM	0.5	0.3	0.3	0.3	0.3	0.3	0.3	0.3	x0.4	x0.4
Asia	17.2	x15.9	15.7	17.3	17.2	17.9	17.7	18.0	x20.0	x20.5
Middle East	8.2	x7.4	x6.2	x6.8	x6.3	6.2	5.4	6.3	x5.8	x4.9
Europe	43.8	48.6	49.6	47.7	48.0	51.1	51.4	50.4	43.5	42.7
EEC	37.1	40.9	41.4	39.8	40.0	46.6	47.0	46.5	39.3	38.5
EFTA	6.4	7.1	7.5	7.4	7.4	3.7	3.4	3.2	3.5	3.5
Oceania	3.3	x2.6	x2.3	x2.3	x2.6	x2.3	x2.0	x1.8	x1.9	x2.0
USA/Etats–Unis d'Amer	24.2	21.6	20.2	19.7	19.0	18.5	17.3	17.8	20.2	21.1
Germany/Allemagne	7.3	8.0	8.5	8.3	8.5	10.1	12.5	12.2	11.4	10.5
France,Monac	6.7	7.6	7.8	6.8	6.4	7.3	6.4	6.3	5.5	5.3
United Kingdom	6.4	6.4	5.6	5.9	5.5	5.6	5.1	5.1	4.7	4.9
Hong Kong	2.6	2.5	2.7	3.2	3.3	3.9	4.2	4.4	5.2	5.3
Italy/Italie	2.7	2.6	2.7	3.3	3.4	4.1	4.3	4.8	2.3	2.2
Japan/Japon	2.6	2.2	3.0	3.4	3.8	3.3	3.7	3.4	4.3	5.2
Canada	3.5	3.2	3.2	3.4	3.7	3.4	3.5	3.5	3.9	3.5
Netherlands/Pays–Bas	3.8	4.5	4.1	3.5	3.4	3.9	3.5	3.6	3.1	3.2
Spain/Espagne	1.1	1.7	2.0	2.1	2.6	3.3	3.7	3.9	2.4	2.6

	1985	1986	1987	1988	1989	1990	1991	1992	1993	1994
Afrique	0.7	0.8	0.6	0.5	0.7	0.9	0.8	0.7	0.9	x0.4
Afrique du Nord	0.3	0.4	0.3	0.4	0.6	0.5	0.5	0.3	0.3	0.3
Amériques	10.2	8.5	7.9	8.0	9.3	10.2	12.2	13.4	14.5	14.8
ALAI	1.2	1.2	1.3	1.4	2.0	2.0	3.6	4.9	5.5	5.9
MCAC	0.1	0.1	0.1	0.1	0.1	0.1	0.1	0.1	x0.1	x0.1
Asie	23.3	20.9	x31.3	x33.9	26.7	24.9	26.3	28.6	31.3	32.3
Moyen–Orient	1.2	1.3	x1.4	1.7	1.2	1.2	1.2	1.9	1.3	1.3
Europe	61.4	65.8	53.4	50.9	58.9	60.1	58.0	54.6	50.1	49.5
CEE	55.0	59.2	47.7	45.1	52.8	56.4	54.2	50.3	45.3	45.6
AELE	5.2	5.7	4.8	4.9	5.2	2.7	2.8	2.8	3.7	3.3
Océanie	1.3	x1.0	0.6	0.5	x0.6	x0.5	x0.5	x0.4	x0.5	0.6
Italy/Italie	16.1	16.3	14.2	14.5	17.3	18.0	18.6	16.9	15.8	16.3
Germany/Allemagne	14.4	17.2	12.0	9.3	10.8	11.4	10.4	9.2	7.8	7.3
Hong Kong	5.4	5.1	5.3	6.3	8.1	7.6	8.6	8.9	9.3	9.0
France,Monac	7.4	7.7	6.3	5.9	7.1	7.9	7.7	7.4	6.4	6.5
USA/Etats–Unis d'Amer	7.5	5.7	5.3	5.3	5.8	6.4	7.1	7.1	7.0	6.6
Korea, Republic of	6.1	6.5	6.6	7.9	8.1	6.8	6.5	5.4	6.4	6.0
China/Chine	0.9	0.9	1.7	1.9	2.4	2.5	2.7	4.7	5.7	7.3
Japan/Japon	8.0	5.7	4.0	3.8	3.8	3.8	3.4	3.0	3.0	3.0
Spain/Espagne	3.4	3.0	2.5	2.5	3.1	3.4	3.1	3.1	2.7	2.7
Netherlands/Pays–Bas	2.7	3.5	2.8	2.8	3.0	3.2	3.2	2.9	2.6	3.0

TRADE BY COMMODITY IN THOUSAND U.S. DOLLARS – COMMERCE PAR PRODUIT EN MILLIERS DE DOLLARS E.U

COUNTRIES–PAYS	IMPORTS – IMPORTATIONS 1990	1991	1992	1993	1994
Total	24138351	25094915	29022472	27593417	31816973
Africa	x765248	x751674	x794806	x735284	x762669
Northern Africa	306169	329380	x345708	x305242	x324242
Americas	5515780	5455798	7227045	8127188	9557154
LAIA	587042	697953	2005917	2328785	2753420
CACM	44630	48169	64559	x75734	x82472
Asia	3632801	4446752	5364945	5781508	6584381
Middle East	x562585	x794972	x971450	x904792	x822779
Europe	13421272	13614896	14703114	11839884	13640369
EEC	12375694	12623514	13584511	10873933	12495736
EFTA	932456	872509	914409	814464	963407
Oceania	x500858	x491351	x526393	x592545	x678245
USA/Etats–Unis d'Amer	3398775	3279325	3652459	4008007	4705060
Germany/Allemagne	2417732	2790049	3108421	2474276	2859852
France,Monac	2118620	2014949	2113920	1734426	2021760
United Kingdom	1699751	1684381	1749214	1506467	1566882
Canada	1230046	1210280	1322621	1548934	1839554
Mexico/Mexique	313347	370133	1596661	1776572	2125348
Netherlands/Pays–Bas	1192608	1192223	1268410	860157	1016815
Belgium–Luxembourg	1028797	1018094	1094913	858661	972386
Italy/Italie	986884	982420	1017704	766079	874155
Japan/Japon	654345	739069	726972	737039	867381
Hong Kong	445358	568117	735379	859609	962494
Austria/Autriche	656961	675813	739642	681823	799195
Spain/Espagne	584708	665493	745618	593306	752752
Switz.Liecht	634170	588666	591378	541305	599900
Sweden/Suède	653774	590745	589588	508474	612188
Singapore/Singapour	427804	473263	499921	559648	654004
China/Chine	179103	255105	460972	587264	686198
Thailand/Thaïlande	247038	323349	430910	542036	741872
Malaysia/Malaisie	294634	362869	413337	462665	536959
Australia/Australie	356808	356606	387136	458720	536283
Korea, Republic of	320399	385900	382919	393390	516037
Denmark/Danemark	305645	309724	332230	281965	332761
Norway,SVD,JM	275252	259071	301002	254040	343399
Saudi Arabia	176376	234220	268539	x214657	x208967
Ireland/Irlande	201077	203195	274015	158811	179843
Portugal	155486	176002	204179	142486	158416
Israel/Israël	129992	168399	177393	175953	230479
Iran (Islamic Rp. of)		x166802	x198754	x153100	x41014
Finland/Finlande	244496	181694	180633	152264	201731
Greece/Grèce	129155	138731	166025	154738	146997
Indonesia/Indonésie	98948	122778	168843	143523	173772
So. Africa Customs Un	157671	136213	144558	141253	152976
Turkey/Turquie	98202	108852	134113	168126	174024
United Arab Emirates	110306	112746	138209	x154642	x171817
Brazil/Brésil	104814	100275	86143	148099	166605
Hungary/Hongrie	x82467	70253	x119096	x134333	x134984
Poland/Pologne	20234	48831	98976	136293	189063
New Zealand	88525	81316	83793	87776	102947
Egypt/Egypte	43870	89706	88398	72467	91645
Venezuela	40077	65630	91255	91622	69173
Argentina/Argentine	23623	48076	86157	109640	156604
Philippines	60770	72587	71331	81259	95578
India/Inde	90256	63293	79158	72091	85372
Morocco/Maroc	66389	74310	70958	51358	54799
Myanmar	x4463	4994	86246	94663	x5966
Nigeria/Nigéria	x53788	32799	x77673	x72571	x39458
Chile/Chili	45496	44484	56122	81877	82495
Czechoslovakia	41137	x49808	x132161		
Algeria/Algérie	93403	69429	55358	56579	53358
Tunisia/Tunisie	55260	50328	66969	60203	64784

COUNTRIES–PAYS	EXPORTS – EXPORTATIONS 1990	1991	1992	1993	1994
Totale	22794454	23664263	27109179	26349348	29890786
Afrique	98992	109562	102124	121275	116415
Afrique du Nord	39833	52050	48461	65749	103828
Amériques	3671653	3908038	4508370	5301659	6145690
ALAI	316443	391915	814373	1073530	1102573
MCAC	5157	6333	8360	x9691	x9398
Asie	3530160	3936740	5163560	5723287	6098014
Moyen–Orient	59520	74275	88553	x93022	x133717
Europe	15114968	15245672	16829750	14599909	16742350
CEE	14195763	14390672	15875509	13772577	15803668
AELE	802064	769704	797310	691018	773964
Océanie	x121232	x146767	137072	x165827	x204014
Germany/Allemagne	4584352	4554871	5052229	4346985	4952281
USA/Etats–Unis d'Amer	2534303	2781351	2931298	3301529	3939490
Italy/Italie	2502118	2570049	2903584	2650076	3092028
France,Monac	1700223	1781492	1928433	1678234	1835495
Japan/Japon	1552733	1636066	1786837	1916867	2128139
United Kingdom	1290715	1277961	1303254	1060505	1339221
Austria/Autriche	901537	928449	1040139	961034	x942812
Netherlands/Pays–Bas	875289	891394	999595	828709	945162
Hong Kong	511881	663994	842432	989031	1066211
Canada	810072	720611	748054	909490	1073442
China/Chine	469071	548377	756241	839638	1162278
Switz.Liecht	657660	643939	653034	581324	650932
Belgium–Luxembourg	632212	645289	658879	571878	618915
Mexico/Mexique	152910	228662	649274	837168	847895
Spain/Espagne	494249	521453	610152	546020	669811
Sweden/Suède	474513	459405	487152	414384	535507
Kazakstan			565524	608295	
Denmark/Danemark	300356	308907	328554	299347	332100
Korea, Republic of	264545	271316	284733	316510	377553
Singapore/Singapour	249844	272539	269318	319671	443772
Ireland/Irlande	184490	195640	261505	153858	177667
India/Inde	146401	129497	181726	147230	148027
Portugal	114876	129115	164469	133944	178324
Malaysia/Malaisie	76935	102092	126078	194774	252093
Norway,SVD,JM	142039	123746	142305	107953	121428
Thailand/Thaïlande	82750	110836	113588	135545	188954
Australia/Australie	84814	104669	91468	119511	145141
Finland/Finlande	121255	105356	109049	96386	150807
Poland/Pologne	102334	81057	101445	112295	199159
Israel/Israël	89139	94619	102812	91184	100827
Brazil/Brésil	59009	68250	86236	124743	143108
Hungary/Hongrie	x78107	x81527	x104792	x87304	x94040
Czechoslovakia		x84715	x135090		
Slovenia/Slovénia			106246	100058	122402
Czech Republic				156025	213382
Saudi Arabia	10765	45982	47081	x38569	x65241
New Zealand	35179	39424	40778	45528	57944
Tunisia/Tunisie	29757	39413	30802	53259	66951
So. Africa Customs Un	41523	38554	39433	40346	2294
Russian Federation			x45447	x36688	x39791
Indonesia/Indonésie	10321	10840	24938	45110	53316
Greece/Grèce	19280	20993	28513	31216	33538
Yugoslavia SFR	113268	x79703			
Turkey/Turquie	20808	18843	25076	30340	41991
Argentina/Argentine	20123	19795	16193	32963	26614
Venezuela	28092	18630	24433	25290	21337
Slovakia				x59294	x55708
Peru/Pérou	32352	25781	6249	19167	18948
Bulgaria/Bulgarie	x30585	x16870	x18521	x14043	x5546
Colombia/Colombie	9134	15516	18149	14998	19315

(VALUE AS % OF TOTAL)(VALEUR EN % DU TOTAL)

	1985	1986	1987	1988	1989	1990	1991	1992	1993	1994
Africa	3.7	x3.8	x3.2	x3.3	x2.9	x3.2	x3.0	x2.7	x2.7	x2.4
Northern Africa	1.8	1.5	1.2	1.1	1.1	1.3	1.3	x1.2	x1.1	x1.0
Americas	31.8	x27.4	x26.1	26.2	24.1	22.9	21.8	24.9	29.4	30.1
LAIA	3.6	1.8	2.0	2.0	1.9	2.4	2.8	6.9	8.4	8.7
CACM	0.5	0.3	x0.3	0.2	0.2	0.2	0.2	0.2	x0.3	x0.3
Asia	13.7	x13.2	x13.2	x14.0	14.0	15.0	17.7	18.5	20.9	20.7
Middle East	3.5	x3.8	x3.0	x2.9	x2.5	x2.3	x3.2	x3.3	x3.3	x2.6
Europe	47.5	52.7	53.2	52.3	54.9	55.6	54.3	50.7	42.9	42.9
EEC	37.6	41.7	42.4	42.5	45.0	51.3	50.3	46.8	39.4	39.3
EFTA	9.4	10.6	10.4	9.4	9.5	3.9	3.5	3.2	3.0	3.0
Oceania	2.1	x2.0	x1.9	x2.0	x2.5	x2.0	x1.9	x1.8	x2.2	x2.1
USA/Etats–Unis d'Amer	20.2	18.3	17.5	17.6	15.3	14.1	13.1	12.6	14.5	14.8
Germany/Allemagne	6.9	7.9	7.8	7.5	8.1	10.0	11.1	10.7	9.0	9.0
France,Monac	6.3	6.8	7.2	7.3	7.7	8.8	8.0	7.3	6.3	6.4
United Kingdom	5.3	5.4	5.6	6.3	6.4	7.0	6.7	6.0	5.5	4.9
Canada	6.8	5.6	5.2	5.6	5.7	5.1	4.8	4.6	5.6	5.8
Mexico/Mexique	2.2	0.5	0.8	0.8	0.9	1.3	1.5	5.5	6.4	6.7
Netherlands/Pays–Bas	3.8	4.4	4.4	4.2	4.4	4.9	4.8	4.4	3.1	3.2
Belgium–Luxembourg	3.3	3.6	3.5	3.8	4.0	4.3	4.1	3.8	3.1	3.1
Italy/Italie	2.9	3.3	3.3	3.4	3.8	4.1	3.9	3.5	2.8	2.7
Japan/Japon	2.3	2.2	2.3	2.3	2.6	2.7	2.9	2.5	2.7	2.7

	1985	1986	1987	1988	1989	1990	1991	1992	1993	1994
Afrique	0.3	x0.4	x0.3	0.3	0.4	0.5	0.5	0.3	0.5	0.4
Afrique du Nord	0.0	0.1	0.1	0.1	0.1	0.2	0.2	0.2	0.2	0.3
Amériques	15.3	11.5	11.1	14.1	16.2	16.1	16.5	16.7	20.1	20.6
ALAI	1.9	1.0	1.0	1.4	2.0	1.4	1.7	3.0	4.1	3.7
MCAC	0.1	0.0	0.0	0.0	0.0	0.0	0.0	0.0	x0.0	x0.0
Asie	17.1	17.2	x20.8	x19.1	14.9	15.5	16.6	19.1	21.7	20.4
Moyen–Orient	0.6	0.3	x0.3	0.3	x0.2	0.3	0.3	0.3	x0.4	x0.4
Europe	66.1	69.6	65.7	64.4	66.6	66.3	64.4	62.1	55.4	56.0
CEE	56.0	59.1	55.5	54.7	56.8	62.3	60.8	58.6	52.3	52.9
AELE	9.3	9.9	9.7	9.3	9.2	3.5	3.3	2.9	2.6	2.6
Océanie	0.7	x0.6	0.6	x0.6	x0.7	x0.5	x0.6	0.5	x0.6	x0.7
Germany/Allemagne	17.4	19.7	18.8	19.1	19.1	20.1	19.2	18.6	16.5	16.6
USA/Etats–Unis d'Amer	10.3	8.0	7.7	8.7	10.1	11.1	11.8	10.8	12.5	13.2
Italy/Italie	8.8	9.4	9.1	9.0	10.0	11.0	10.9	10.7	10.1	10.3
France,Monac	7.6	7.9	6.9	6.2	6.8	7.5	7.5	7.1	6.4	6.1
Japan/Japon	7.6	7.1	5.6	6.5	7.0	6.8	6.9	6.6	7.3	7.1
United Kingdom	6.1	5.2	4.8	4.6	4.8	5.7	5.4	4.8	4.0	4.5
Austria/Autriche	3.2	3.6	3.5	3.5	3.5	4.0	3.9	3.8	3.6	x3.2
Netherlands/Pays–Bas	3.0	3.4	3.3	3.3	3.5	3.8	3.8	3.7	3.1	3.2
Hong Kong	1.9	1.9	1.8	2.1	2.2	2.2	2.8	3.1	3.8	3.6
Canada	2.9	2.5	2.3	3.9	4.1	3.6	3.0	2.8	3.5	3.6

TRADE BY COMMODITY IN THOUSAND U.S. DOLLARS – COMMERCE PAR PRODUIT EN MILLIERS DE DOLLARS E.U

IMPORTS – IMPORTATIONS

COUNTRIES–PAYS	1990	1991	1992	1993	1994
Total	x2527933	1966120	2176061	2708771	2213727
Africa	207429	121435	x160086	463714	x154088
Northern Africa	132910	33054	101048	421432	x82961
Americas	x323281	401250	317907	461276	456223
LAIA	126285	85083	151992	256903	280929
CACM	7025	7361	11630	x7242	x5333
Asia	x1459516	x943150	x1138065	x1329362	x1132678
Middle East	x640475	x240351	x328756	x251015	x172666
Europe	421721	401022	491534	347057	369513
EEC	330652	349769	426129	293263	337939
EFTA	16966	28153	53605	39492	24829
Oceania	x9473	x9295	x5191	x7039	x8041
China/Chine	416022	176704	140044	333049	331912
Iran (Islamic Rp. of)	x404396	x166871	x174745	x126668	x21198
Indonesia/Indonésie	46664	80056	184374	174919	173358
USA/Etats-Unis d'Amer	122314	139129	86268	136663	111034
Korea, Republic of	44769	75675	183308	91401	75222
Morocco/Maroc	32943	5669	72809	262121	19446
Mexico/Mexique	27772	34410	87025	138256	28165
Thailand/Thaïlande	55944	68654	79310	69275	53484
Bangladesh				186707	x13658
Saudi Arabia	36472	38749	105088	x31556	x98572
Canada	30674	83497	43790	44094	41743
Germany/Allemagne	39326	54996	53571	53744	47693
Singapore/Singapour	50044	70752	47465	41567	59011
United Kingdom	30550	55808	37580	50958	46547
Algeria/Algérie	68076	14028	11499	117825	16912
Malaysia/Malaisie	5512	61561	54439	26700	29254
Netherlands/Pays-Bas	22651	48080	78950	11353	18525
Israel/Israël	34401	55405	29800	22691	19686
France, Monac	38144	29874	43451	33016	45874
Hong Kong	82218	32379	38703	34057	108509
Belgium–Luxembourg	25829	31909	62058	11020	10189
Switz.Liecht	11813	24011	42779	36246	20751
Philippines	35438	18974	20237	59293	21552
Russian Federation			x35845	x59821	x25283
Chile/Chili	64120	13606	6592	50353	207854
Sweden/Suède	13877	16715	30421	21613	17307
Spain/Espagne	12921	14733	21274	32143	41874
Italy/Italie	21327	25604	27114	14580	10096
Poland/Pologne	13507	16724	23266	26870	38081
Turkey/Turquie	22836	16041	10693	34769	5473
Venezuela	3909	7125	27280	22125	13949
Finland/Finlande	17613	13672	30621	6967	11456
Czechoslovakia	37747	x23291	x27122		
Denmark/Danemark	24377	27878	11863	10466	9387
Bahamas		47172	x1475	x614	x392
So. Africa Customs Un	48511	30554	14168	4142	4319
India/Inde	5753	25422	6712	13301	4238
Reunion/Réunion	229	36005	5390	2394	26925
Pakistan	24904	18515	13730	6985	45777
Qatar	666	3369	4773	27690	x6094
Former USSR/Anc. URSS	3589	x35606			
Egypt/Egypte	14810	6410	7515	20607	13885
Nigeria/Nigéria	x2914	3287	x14124	x15825	x8947
Czech Republic				32270	22068
Greece/Grèce	62387	7349	6914	17454	57282
Ireland/Irlande	6659	11903	7273	10503	6214
Colombia/Colombie	501	5517	9970	13327	2789
Hungary/Hongrie	x9172	11402	x5970	x10506	x8557
Austria/Autriche	5448	6970	8873	11294	7965
Brazil/Brésil	21782	9398	10602	6858	7414

EXPORTS – EXPORTATIONS

COUNTRIES–PAYS	1990	1991	1992	1993	1994
Totale	2007745	2154075	2233960	2507914	2587429
Afrique	6090	11618	x11362	7691	x435
Afrique du Nord	13	89	220	1500	144
Amériques	455681	431105	412792	585184	572613
ALAI	49161	35603	28629	45967	54597
MCAC	21	16	5	95	x28
Asie	454345	523244	556385	x551894	x755483
Moyen-Orient	1852	2012	12763	x28149	x28806
Europe	1023832	985673	1178982	1209353	1156606
CEE	988211	957721	1151839	1177979	1137233
AELE	27402	25045	21889	26407	15942
Océanie	4578	9318	8932	24966	x13119
Japan/Japon	377679	439511	434772	423156	612058
USA/Etats-Unis d'Amer	277272	298439	305743	414502	415355
Germany/Allemagne	169980	255024	226453	215769	174614
France, Monac	106457	134063	204757	209152	244894
United Kingdom	154125	94881	98787	131616	182366
Belgium–Luxembourg	66520	83504	120741	99663	45103
Canada	129104	96873	78288	124202	102232
Finland/Finlande	67709	91043	79296	107702	100438
Italy/Italie	116728	38226	86025	123812	72077
Spain/Espagne	79999	43619	87513	94270	104281
Denmark/Danemark	41482	53457	73689	64565	68695
Austria/Autriche	34428	48778	75058	49259	x39658
Netherlands/Pays-Bas	73840	58057	52073	53566	69555
Former USSR/Anc. URSS	8609	x147251			
Sweden/Suède	75385	51543	44209	27346	34148
Russian Federation			x54293	x46642	x27847
China/Chine	4659	18163	36036	26506	17459
Romania/Roumanie	3003	16403	25317	28356	27796
Hong Kong	14717	15663	19172	28845	27168
Czech Republic				62389	26540
Switz.Liecht	26553	23134	16148	22321	13435
Poland/Pologne	28542	9089	28382	16993	24510
Colombia/Colombie	14993	9590	16686	20996	19920
Korea, Republic of	29003	8668	20732	17573	31618
Australia/Australie	4029	7404	7131	23247	11940
Saudi Arabia	176	1305	11212	x22886	x24664
India/Inde	11622	14871	11365	6726	10775
Singapore/Singapour	6052	9736	10510	11551	10841
Mexico/Mexique	10985	14845	5155	6672	17961
Brazil/Brésil	9615	5693	4850	16000	14200
Czechoslovakia		x15194	x7656		
So. Africa Customs Ur	5622	11297	5869	5396	
Slovakia				x18639	x6612
Malaysia/Malaisie	5495	5166	6342	6143	7855
Norway, SVD, JM	848	1911	5741	4086	2507
Philippines	316	6445	2770	2052	4196
Hungary/Hongrie	x7505	x4932	x4087	x1970	x3622
Portugal	640	4889	2155	814	720
Croatia/Croatie			3353	4258	x1481
New Zealand	369	1890	867	1680	888
Argentina/Argentine	1589	1690	1177	1530	537
Venezuela	11978	3587	317	238	426
Turkey/Turquie	780	458	923	2103	3114
Indonesia/Indonésie	2479	1609	771	754	1501
Niger			x3068		
Yugoslavia SFR	8152	x2906			
Thailand/Thaïlande	343	1216	858	183	1742
Cyprus/Chypre	91	45	409	1543	50
Slovenia/Slovénia			1351	413	1744
Zimbabwe	199	7	1484	120	

(VALUE AS % OF TOTAL)(VALEUR EN % DU TOTAL)

Imports

	1985	1986	1987	1988	1989	1990	1991	1992	1993	1994
Africa	17.7	x8.2	x8.4	x10.5	12.3	8.2	6.2	x7.4	17.2	x7.0
Northern Africa	5.7	2.3	2.2	5.2	8.5	5.3	1.7	4.6	15.6	x3.7
Americas	17.9	13.6	15.0	19.3	x18.2	x12.8	20.4	14.6	17.1	20.6
LAIA	9.4	6.1	6.7	10.5	5.3	5.0	4.3	7.0	9.5	12.7
CACM	0.6	0.4	x0.5	0.4	0.3	0.3	0.4	0.5	x0.3	x0.2
Asia	34.4	x50.1	x38.7	x44.5	39.6	x57.7	x48.0	x52.3	x49.1	x51.1
Middle East	12.6	x28.7	x6.5	11.5	x8.6	x25.3	x12.2	x15.1	x9.3	x7.8
Europe	23.5	21.8	23.6	15.5	23.2	16.7	20.4	22.6	12.8	16.7
EEC	9.4	10.1	11.7	11.8	15.5	13.1	17.8	19.6	10.8	15.3
EFTA	9.0	10.6	10.8	2.8	4.8	0.7	1.4	2.5	1.5	1.1
Oceania	0.7	x0.7	x0.4	0.3	0.4	x0.3	x0.5	x0.3	x0.3	x0.3
China/Chine			12.8	9.0	13.2	16.5	9.0	6.4	12.3	15.0
Iran (Islamic Rp. of)		x2.6	x1.8	x0.9	x1.8	x16.0	x8.5	x8.0	x4.7	x1.0
Indonesia/Indonésie	4.4	2.5	3.8	3.3	2.6	1.8	4.1	8.5	6.5	7.8
USA/Etats-Unis d'Amer	5.6	4.4	6.0	5.6	7.8	4.8	7.1	4.0	5.0	5.0
Korea, Republic of	3.1	3.1	2.9	1.5	2.1	1.8	3.8	8.4	3.4	3.4
Morocco/Maroc	0.5	0.2	0.2	0.1	0.2	1.3	0.3	3.3	9.7	0.9
Mexico/Mexique	6.2	1.9	1.4	2.8	0.9	1.1	1.8	4.0	5.1	1.3
Thailand/Thaïlande	1.2	1.2	1.5	3.5	3.0	2.2	3.5	3.6	2.6	2.4
Bangladesh	0.1	0.7	0.4	x0.1	x0.1				6.9	x0.6
Saudi Arabia	0.7	2.2	0.2	0.2	0.5	1.4	2.0	4.8	x1.2	x4.5

Exports

	1985	1986	1987	1988	1989	1990	1991	1992	1993	1994
Afrique	0.2	x0.2	x0.1	0.1	x0.4	0.3	0.5	x0.5	0.3	x0.0
Afrique du Nord	0.0	x0.0	x0.0	0.0	x0.0	0.0	0.0	0.0	0.1	0.0
Amériques	16.6	12.7	15.0	20.7	25.3	22.7	20.1	18.5	23.4	22.1
ALAI	0.6	0.3	0.6	1.1	1.9	2.4	1.7	1.3	1.8	2.1
MCAC	0.0	x0.0	0.0	x0.0	0.0	0.0	0.0	0.0	0.0	x0.0
Asie	37.0	34.8	x27.3	x15.9	16.1	22.6	24.3	24.9	x22.0	x29.2
Moyen-Orient	0.2	x0.1	x0.0	0.1	0.1	0.1	0.1	0.6	x1.1	x1.1
Europe	43.3	49.6	50.9	49.4	52.8	51.0	45.8	52.8	48.2	44.7
CEE	36.1	41.7	42.5	38.3	42.4	49.2	44.5	51.6	47.0	44.0
AELE	6.7	7.6	8.0	10.8	10.1	1.4	1.2	1.0	1.1	0.6
Océanie	0.1	0.1	0.1	0.1	0.1	0.2	0.4	0.4	1.0	x0.5
Japan/Japon	32.4	32.0	24.8	12.5	12.0	18.8	20.4	19.5	16.9	23.7
USA/Etats-Unis d'Amer	13.4	9.6	9.7	14.1	17.0	13.8	13.9	13.7	16.5	16.1
Germany/Allemagne	8.6	12.3	12.4	10.0	12.3	8.5	11.8	10.1	8.6	6.7
France, Monac	5.8	4.8	4.5	3.3	5.1	5.3	6.2	9.2	8.3	9.5
United Kingdom	8.4	8.4	7.8	6.0	7.0	7.7	4.4	4.4	5.2	7.0
Belgium–Luxembourg	1.4	1.4	1.5	1.8	1.4	3.3	3.9	5.4	4.0	1.7
Canada	2.5	2.8	4.6	5.5	6.4	6.4	4.5	3.5	5.0	4.0
Finland/Finlande	2.4	2.3	2.3	3.3	3.9	3.4	4.2	3.5	4.3	3.9
Italy/Italie	2.2	3.3	4.0	2.1	2.7	5.8	1.8	3.9	4.9	2.8
Spain/Espagne	0.8	0.7	0.6	0.8	1.4	4.0	2.0	3.9	3.8	4.0

TRADE BY COMMODITY IN THOUSAND U.S. DOLLARS – COMMERCE PAR PRODUIT EN MILLIERS DE DOLLARS E.U

COUNTRIES–PAYS	IMPORTS – IMPORTATIONS 1990	1991	1992	1993	1994
Total	x2023690	1979081	2195447	x2178168	3209984
Africa	x68194	x85319	x97344	x117235	x82609
Northern Africa	12829	x24848	x20981	58467	x46380
Americas	299017	272858	298936	348506	837741
LAIA	74262	66681	144538	149192	591620
CACM	603	881	638	x7431	9524
Asia	x944197	969099	1052751	x1183697	1603725
Middle East	x554776	x187560	x133926	x345415	x176510
Europe	506834	609834	708678	476924	592738
EEC	450658	542350	660123	427642	525072
EFTA	40297	40189	41043	45636	58482
Oceania	x14372	x20462	x14175	x16378	x61752
Indonesia/Indonésie	21256	84325	366916	342815	334311
Korea, Republic of	55314	116198	211741	139665	83431
Germany/Allemagne	103505	113657	137777	149293	159161
USA/Etats–Unis d'Amer	183670	133550	109767	139597	177334
Iran (Islamic Rp. of)	x369279	x82252	x70162	x219535	x29576
United Kingdom	47005	84620	125033	69775	87508
Mexico/Mexique	31255	28604	95852	97544	32858
China/Chine	105534	110387	36109	72225	211438
Turkey/Turquie	147073	95541	22457	63095	19605
Philippines	12231	8241	65863	92231	367178
France, Monac	40739	46684	60029	47272	52622
Singapore/Singapour	31833	75190	24333	43945	87628
Israel/Israël	944	48727	35550	54724	20728
Hong Kong	27728	123372	9563	3200	4132
Italy/Italie	39165	42767	64765	26288	28048
India/Inde	40413	43308	64067	17023	31490
So. Africa Customs Un	47454	51876	54958	13524	9308
Netherlands/Pays–Bas	22973	41566	63598	12194	26344
Switz.Liecht	34245	37665	36040	42296	56364
Spain/Espagne	21287	39802	32219	38119	44455
Malaysia/Malaisie	6393	72757	25580	10043	31256
Canada	23664	34954	27817	41984	41321
Pakistan	65666	40003	48519	15756	71101
Denmark/Danemark	57088	58256	20352	17092	13274
Belgium–Luxembourg	39109	30156	54724	7709	11169
Finland/Finlande	20528	16145	53030	16392	12538
Austria/Autriche	18995	40580	20051	15889	31900
Japan/Japon	5958	33672	16858	16172	141131
United Arab Emirates	2756	581	30208	x16431	x20352
Australia/Australie	8379	19189	12391	14749	58522
Algeria/Algérie	11430	6625	6330	32008	16179
Saudi Arabia	15234	4535	5143	x34974	x60216
Portugal	12540	10023	17024	15894	5171
Nigeria/Nigéria	x641	963	x6367	x33807	x6934
Venezuela	8244	16216	15697	8975	8780
Argentina/Argentine	1752	4937	6333	23539	21769
Colombia/Colombie	3788	5756	16650	11355	27380
Thailand/Thaïlande	11768	7740	12854	12591	30682
Sweden/Suède	12299	14642	8909	7821	33578
Poland/Pologne	3831	5270	9593	15101	17786
Brazil/Brésil	27325	9660	8695	5811	431242
Malta/Malte	5407	20824	442	1687	x346
Russian Federation			x8219	x14531	x13037
Sudan/Soudan	x164	x17189	x1029	x364	x217
Libyan Arab Jamahiriya	507	15	x8237	x7972	x10825
Aruba	1479	15469	x527	x55	x1350
Morocco/Maroc	369	229	4010	11623	843
Bangladesh				x13389	x6876
Hungary/Hongrie	x1229	3548	x2518	x7256	x1822
Brunei Darussalam	4075	8691	x538	x2006	x4003

COUNTRIES–PAYS	EXPORTS – EXPORTATIONS 1990	1991	1992	1993	1994
Totale	x2354133	2071097	2135438	2256695	2502796
Afrique	x5695	x685	x6480	x2821	x3766
Afrique du Nord	x103	1	x5296	x514	x3232
Amériques	171022	404339	x361245	508126	x596962
ALAI	2748	3129	3561	13898	5864
MCAC		2	8	10	2
Asie	401964	449205	584680	581999	713699
Moyen–Orient	x2009	x514	x1004	x727	x1833
Europe	999331	1072965	1107861	1101284	1114844
CEE	890347	937107	970628	942031	981415
AELE	107587	131618	129251	148551	130774
Océanie	x6671	2060	1092	2440	x4404
Japan/Japon	366505	377618	553130	542187	636589
Germany/Allemagne	304522	395766	418708	385094	380162
USA/Etats–Unis d'Amer	155858	388915	340438	458123	554616
United Kingdom	213489	158109	140490	122660	218761
Switz.Liecht	107154	131567	128258	148046	129837
France, Monac	127576	137479	134801	105248	182088
Italy/Italie	92713	84404	91953	198085	90247
Austria/Autriche	41293	39692	48035	49328	x48706
Belgium–Luxembourg	18153	43763	47048	11693	8589
Sweden/Suède	30625	32019	31927	30334	18109
Netherlands/Pays–Bas	44612	29781	41017	21195	26738
Czechoslovakia		x64088	x15264		
Former USSR/Anc. URSS	x744874	x71785			
Poland/Pologne	4022	1291	50280	11458	12432
Canada	11897	11062	15966	35179	28117
Russian Federation			x18721	x27549	x46854
Malaysia/Malaisie	13830	34519	1856	6011	20568
Singapore/Singapour	9435	16189	9284	14701	36673
Korea, Republic of	4617	11803	12852	8184	14107
Czech Republic				28473	25663
Hungary/Hongrie	x5687	x4676	x8272	x12349	x17121
Spain/Espagne	7980	4448	7153	11891	5119
Portugal	3090	4899	5965	4340	94
Croatia/Croatie			4402	10289	x2009
Mexico/Mexique	1492	2360	3260	7934	1860
China/Chine	2357	5612	3594	1921	766
Ireland/Irlande	4473	5248	2741	1175	588
India/Inde	142	264	1468	6225	452
Romania/Roumanie	5633		263	6034	13405
Libyan Arab Jamahiriya			x5213	x236	x3228
Yugoslavia SFR	1396	x4240			
Australia/Australie	1414	1893	927	875	3947
So. Africa Customs Un	4638	146	1149	2059	
Colombia/Colombie	962	44	8	3140	261
Hong Kong	2042	1009	1282	846	2245
Slovenia/Slovénia			2422	411	633
Finland/Finlande	1123	1064	433	815	411
Brazil/Brésil	179	394	183	1353	2212
Slovakia				x1712	x322
Jamaica/Jamaïque	13	841	x737		x152
Norway,SVD,JM	433	51	992	506	937
Papua New Guinea	0	11	69	1387	x6
Peru/Pérou		1	1	1444	20
Guadeloupe	118	233	121	582	1062
Saudi Arabia	18	194	641	x55	x1361
Yugoslavia/Yougoslavie			x869		x10
Indonesia/Indonésie	120	575	96	166	172
Denmark/Danemark	626	339	323	128	614
Philippines		788			
Ukraine				x750	x607

(VALUE AS % OF TOTAL)(VALEUR EN % DU TOTAL)

	1985	1986	1987	1988	1989	1990	1991	1992	1993	1994
Africa	9.2	6.1	x3.8	x6.2	x7.3	x3.3	x4.3	x4.4	x5.4	x2.6
Northern Africa	2.8	1.5	0.4	0.9	2.7	0.6	x1.3	x1.0	2.7	x1.4
Americas	35.8	x40.9	x29.5	x22.8	18.0	14.7	13.8	13.6	16.0	26.1
LAIA	16.1	11.4	5.3	7.2	3.8	3.7	3.4	6.6	6.8	18.4
CACM	0.1	0.1	x0.7	0.2	0.1	0.0	0.0	0.0	x0.3	0.3
Asia	22.8	x27.1	x33.2	x33.9	x34.1	x46.6	49.0	48.0	x54.4	49.9
Middle East	2.0	x12.9	x11.1	x6.8	x6.7	x27.4	x9.5	x6.1	x15.9	x5.5
Europe	28.5	21.6	17.2	20.5	26.3	25.0	30.8	32.3	21.9	18.5
EEC	21.3	17.7	14.4	17.0	21.2	22.3	27.4	30.1	19.6	16.4
EFTA	6.3	2.8	2.0	2.9	4.3	2.0	2.0	1.9	2.1	1.8
Oceania	1.4	2.1	1.0	0.4	0.7	x0.7	x1.0	x0.6	x0.7	x1.9
Indonesia/Indonésie	3.7	1.6	8.2	4.3	1.7	1.1	4.3	16.7	15.7	10.4
Korea, Republic of	0.3	0.9	0.5	0.7	1.4	2.7	5.9	9.6	6.4	2.6
Germany/Allemagne	2.5	3.3	3.7	3.8	4.0	5.1	5.7	6.3	6.9	5.0
USA/Etats–Unis d'Amer	13.6	11.2	6.7	7.6	9.9	9.1	6.7	5.0	6.4	5.5
Iran (Islamic Rp. of)		x3.6	x4.9	x1.7	x1.6	x18.2	x4.2	x3.2	x10.1	x0.9
United Kingdom	1.7	1.6	1.4	2.4	2.5	2.3	4.3	5.7	3.2	2.7
Mexico/Mexique	3.0	2.9	3.3	1.6	1.9	1.5	1.4	4.4	4.5	1.0
China/Chine			1.6	6.6	7.3	5.2	5.6	1.6	3.3	6.6
Turkey/Turquie	0.5	3.6	4.4	2.1	3.0	7.3	4.8	1.0	2.9	0.6
Philippines	0.2	0.1	0.0	0.1	1.7	0.6	0.4	3.0	4.2	11.4

	1985	1986	1987	1988	1989	1990	1991	1992	1993	1994
Afrique		x0.1	x0.1	x0.4	x0.2	x0.2	x0.0	x0.3	x0.1	x0.2
Afrique du Nord		x0.1	x0.1	x0.1	x0.1	x0.0	0.0	x0.2	x0.0	x0.1
Amériques	19.8	12.5	x11.0	11.9	x16.5	7.2	19.5	x16.9	22.6	x23.9
ALAI	0.4	0.1	x0.1	0.4	x0.2	0.1	0.2	0.2	0.6	0.2
MCAC			x0.0	x0.0			0.0	0.0	0.0	0.0
Asie	17.8	x21.6	x20.8	15.4	x15.9	17.1	21.6	27.4	25.8	28.5
Moyen–Orient	0.0	x0.3	x0.1	x0.0	x0.4	x0.1	x0.0	x0.0	x0.0	x0.1
Europe	50.2	50.9	48.0	45.8	58.9	42.5	51.8	51.9	48.8	44.5
CEE	40.1	42.0	37.9	34.9	47.1	37.8	45.2	45.5	41.7	39.2
AELE	9.9	8.7	10.0	10.8	11.6	4.6	6.4	6.1	6.6	5.2
Océanie		x0.0	x0.0		0.2	x0.3	0.1		0.1	x0.2
Japan/Japon	17.2	20.7	19.9	14.6	13.3	15.6	18.2	25.9	24.0	25.4
Germany/Allemagne	19.8	19.0	19.1	18.4	17.4	12.9	19.1	19.6	17.1	15.2
USA/Etats–Unis d'Amer	18.4	11.4	9.9	10.4	15.4	6.6	18.8	15.9	20.3	22.2
United Kingdom	7.4	9.7	3.8	4.0	5.4	9.1	7.6	6.6	5.4	8.7
Switz.Liecht	7.8	5.8	6.0	8.1	8.1	4.6	6.4	6.0	6.6	5.2
France, Monac	4.5	3.9	4.0	2.7	10.6	5.4	6.6	6.3	4.7	7.3
Italy/Italie	3.4	3.8	3.1	2.9	6.1	3.9	4.1	4.3	8.8	3.6
Austria/Autriche	0.8	1.0	2.7	1.4	2.1	1.8	1.9	2.2	2.2	x1.9
Belgium–Luxembourg	0.3	0.7	0.4	1.0	1.2	0.8	2.1	2.2	0.5	0.3
Sweden/Suède	1.2	1.8	1.4	1.1	1.3	1.3	1.5	1.5	1.3	0.7

TRADE BY COMMODITY IN THOUSAND U.S. DOLLARS – COMMERCE PAR PRODUIT EN MILLIERS DE DOLLARS E.U

IMPORTS – IMPORTATIONS

COUNTRIES–PAYS	1990	1991	1992	1993	1994
Total	34633237	33016499	36533097	36867140	43473354
Africa	x979765	x841886	x910011	x830954	x865140
Northern Africa	468374	361289	x317818	304832	318116
Americas	12215754	11460192	12921177	15092155	17908020
LAIA	978823	1138944	1566441	1694358	2086640
CACM	37618	43110	48506	x52666	x52891
Asia	x5934528	5389288	5688817	6029551	6825897
Middle East	x2383199	x1354944	x1393041	x1090998	x753710
Europe	14359262	14345102	16152658	13884550	16552820
EEC	13787968	13733233	15586184	13473809	16047287
EFTA	341757	355726	347334	288591	344658
Oceania	x625356	x535928	x602539	x682943	x849148
USA/Etats–Unis d'Amer	7285878	6531874	7281400	8567626	10392347
Canada	3701160	3545372	3827490	4608042	5192795
Germany/Allemagne	3434538	3793042	4376827	2991477	3611455
United Kingdom	2107898	1817974	2063456	2035690	2078980
France, Monac	1857924	1889018	2151499	1772281	2151579
Spain/Espagne	1546135	1604477	1783618	2161657	2612438
Italy/Italie	1192041	1154561	1167353	925529	1050011
Belgium–Luxembourg	939944	842404	1098565	1027501	1522396
Austria/Autriche	646213	729305	867734	753420	859412
Korea, Republic of	439817	604538	640623	748360	1047639
Singapore/Singapour	680554	596910	641527	713157	820821
Netherlands/Pays–Bas	705882	678398	704942	567626	626613
China/Chine	223894	413933	686639	803512	688509
Mexico/Mexique	269510	346599	570717	590696	834850
Australia/Australie	523084	429561	491602	560977	685630
Thailand/Thaïlande	598684	498484	426182	506633	582124
Sweden/Suède	474598	429780	449238	432386	599496
Iran (Islamic Rp. of)	x1599388	x650757	x412584	x186408	x64648
Malaysia/Malaisie	348757	372627	487384	384173	422534
Indonesia/Indonésie	413369	409061	349245	439069	717805
Japan/Japon	316326	287431	372047	475952	464688
Hong Kong	180251	277219	354316	411514	659562
Brazil/Brésil	255337	231800	318228	380177	491420
Turkey/Turquie	254731	260728	305059	358596	207265
Saudi Arabia	169042	248788	414992	x249565	x195225
So. Africa Customs Un	220372	250256	279817	231329	259889
Denmark/Danemark	228906	231418	261133	242526	234288
Portugal	200601	200459	275585	250209	347428
Argentina/Argentine	58908	116689	256489	298875	359689
Norway, SVD, JM	175025	188150	189011	161103	183018
Finland/Finlande	249900	195207	191934	140883	183509
Venezuela	125732	188163	149385	109848	80045
Switz.Liecht	158242	159051	150942	120612	154996
Philippines	87253	90515	124962	195703	293269
Greece/Grèce	125442	111012	121405	108816	85988
Poland/Pologne	27742	67078	98669	166062	243238
United Arab Emirates	115804	79353	86395	x143059	x150533
Algeria/Algérie	211821	121041	87132	90823	106807
Russian Federation			x166465	x115609	x80733
Former USSR/Anc. URSS	312953	x256548			
Nigeria/Nigéria	x85820	30971	x97336	x118813	x68477
Yugoslavia SFR	216022	x239641			
Bangladesh		203113		x33716	x39306
India/Inde	74971	60424	86903	81120	121692
Colombia/Colombie	75399	65807	62467	83031	92244
Hungary/Hongrie	x41588	51210	x70948	x85817	x117273
New Zealand	61361	60569	66498	69334	86105
Egypt/Egypte	81750	61487	61728	72434	66115
Ireland/Irlande	77944	56177	72896	63808	83693
Chile/Chili	59575	50431	71094	71144	62827

EXPORTS – EXPORTATIONS

COUNTRIES–PAYS	1990	1991	1992	1993	1994
Totale	36646239	36693100	40338854	40434620	47474784
Afrique	55100	60381	63756	60801	x17002
Afrique du Nord	19272	16714	12841	12365	13169
Amériques	9987905	9663609	10527593	11853265	13500892
ALAI	2346889	2215295	2364289	2625204	3392848
MCAC	130	288	90	x126	x493
Asie	7325590	7740310	9072575	10957146	13397896
Moyen–Orient	61710	40792	65217	x74357	x113134
Europe	18391080	18704819	20185294	17006030	19780373
CEE	17988372	18359418	19807184	16659432	19433161
AELE	268903	267451	291888	292307	302709
Océanie	257124	x318421	x303252	x301190	x334626
Japan/Japon	6400016	6707636	7794900	9557057	11657153
USA/Etats–Unis d'Amer	5755107	6020567	6655145	7401543	8263842
Germany/Allemagne	5885461	6357720	6526894	5201905	5943856
France, Monac	3106813	2953382	3533970	2705815	3283138
United Kingdom	2761881	2837672	2911097	2635204	3033315
Austria/Autriche	1876144	1856169	2258692	1883158	x1909763
Canada	1881589	1414841	1502327	1819896	1837280
Mexico/Mexique	1394361	1310122	1504616	1653492	2368859
Italy/Italie	1268822	1270650	1408241	1337151	1602597
Spain/Espagne	837481	925156	944484	749018	929701
Sweden/Suède	874388	801229	826371	772008	1227907
Brazil/Brésil	890186	810952	758431	793513	853972
Netherlands/Pays–Bas	399667	434895	420071	387218	429588
Singapore/Singapour	314995	350103	393983	439564	436053
Australia/Australie	243519	314059	297515	294033	328175
Belgium–Luxembourg	227186	221835	226525	339921	431787
Denmark/Danemark	265432	275404	294858	161321	120352
Finland/Finlande	241058	227199	242615	214277	194507
Hong Kong	106056	149596	207754	290269	445023
Switz.Liecht	170190	154637	182607	180757	172423
Malaysia/Malaisie	94369	130234	183725	160237	174779
Portugal	178466	124015	144295	197626	221052
Korea, Republic of	131833	130531	142673	129809	214349
Argentina/Argentine	54051	84065	88785	163938	148838
Norway, SVD, JM	98673	112745	109278	111538	130282
India/Inde	93000	92986	103624	112686	106957
China/Chine	69714	69557	113382	109171	150630
Poland/Pologne	84936	87359	96704	81459	88075
Hungary/Hongrie	x20720	x8220	x34292	x106969	x274769
Turkey/Turquie	42650	34584	56463	47844	83991
Thailand/Thaïlande	24601	30423	45004	60608	67362
So. Africa Customs Un	30712	41199	47414	42999	
Russian Federation			x62658	x54505	x42318
Greece/Grèce	45668	52032	35182	27756	40947
Ireland/Irlande	19351	21505	33887	47054	64651
Slovenia/Slovénia			53389	39986	28317
Czechoslovakia		x47425	x41434		
Yugoslavia SFR	132408	x76612			
Former USSR/Anc. URSS	472898	x55923			
Czech Republic				49119	62381
Israel/Israël	10775	12210	9860	8002	11486
Indonesia/Indonésie	7707	8793	8964	11159	13607
Yugoslavia/Yougoslavie			x17887	x5383	x2733
Tunisia/Tunisie	10166	8451	7711	5301	7678
Croatia/Croatie			11099	7401	x11735
Morocco/Maroc	8105	6381	4576	6593	4982
Romania/Roumanie	15193	4060	7214	5818	6866
Colombia/Colombie	4061	4882	4901	6019	12666
New Zealand	4137	3129	5288	5765	5984
Bulgaria/Bulgarie	x15248	x2132	x6294	x4238	x3940

(VALUE AS % OF TOTAL)(VALEUR EN % DU TOTAL)

Imports

	1985	1986	1987	1988	1989	1990	1991	1992	1993	1994
Africa	2.7	x3.1	x2.9	x3.1	x2.8	x2.8	x2.6	x2.5	x2.2	x2.0
Northern Africa	1.7	1.5	1.1	1.2	1.1	1.4	1.1	x0.9	0.8	0.7
Americas	49.7	44.2	40.0	40.8	40.1	35.2	34.7	35.4	40.9	41.1
LAIA	4.2	3.4	3.3	3.2	2.5	2.8	3.4	4.3	4.6	4.8
CACM	0.2	0.2	x0.2	0.2	0.2	0.1	0.1	0.1	x0.1	x0.1
Asia	9.9	10.2	x11.0	x11.3	11.7	x17.1	16.4	15.6	16.4	15.7
Middle East	2.7	x3.6	x3.2	x2.5	x2.3	x6.9	x4.1	x3.8	x3.0	x1.7
Europe	34.7	39.3	41.9	40.8	41.9	41.5	43.4	44.2	37.7	38.1
EEC	30.1	34.4	36.8	35.8	36.9	39.8	41.6	42.7	36.5	36.9
EFTA	3.9	4.2	4.4	4.4	4.4	1.0	1.1	1.0	0.8	0.8
Oceania	2.1	x2.1	x2.2	2.0	x2.0	x1.8	x1.6	x1.6	x1.8	x2.0
USA/Etats–Unis d'Amer	28.1	25.2	24.2	25.1	25.0	21.0	19.8	19.9	23.2	23.9
Canada	16.7	14.8	11.8	12.0	11.7	10.7	10.7	10.5	12.5	11.9
Germany/Allemagne	6.4	7.7	7.8	8.3	8.7	9.9	11.5	12.0	8.1	8.3
United Kingdom	4.0	4.9	5.5	5.7	6.0	6.1	5.5	5.6	5.5	4.8
France, Monac	3.6	4.1	4.5	4.6	5.2	5.4	5.7	5.9	4.8	4.9
Spain/Espagne	2.1	2.8	3.6	4.4	4.0	4.5	4.9	4.9	5.9	6.0
Italy/Italie	3.3	3.2	3.1	3.1	3.2	3.4	3.5	3.2	2.5	2.4
Belgium–Luxembourg	4.6	5.3	5.7	3.1	2.7	2.7	2.6	3.0	2.8	3.5
Austria/Autriche	1.0	1.2	1.2	1.3	1.4	1.9	2.2	2.4	2.0	2.0
Korea, Republic of	1.5	1.2	1.3	1.4	1.2	1.3	1.8	1.8	2.0	2.4

Exports

	1985	1986	1987	1988	1989	1990	1991	1992	1993	1994
Afrique	0.1	x0.2	x0.2	x0.0	x0.1	0.2	0.2	0.1	0.1	x0.0
Afrique du Nord	0.0	0.0	0.0	0.0	0.0	0.1	0.0	0.0	0.0	0.0
Amériques	38.9	29.5	28.6	28.4	26.6	27.2	26.4	26.1	29.3	28.5
ALAI	8.8	5.3	7.4	6.9	6.9	6.4	6.0	5.9	6.5	7.1
MCAC	0.0	x0.0	x0.0	x0.0	x0.0	0.0	0.0	0.0	x0.0	x0.0
Asie	16.5	18.4	19.8	19.4	20.7	20.0	21.1	22.4	27.1	28.2
Moyen–Orient	0.3	0.1	0.2	0.2	0.2	0.2	0.1	0.2	x0.2	x0.2
Europe	41.1	48.1	47.4	48.8	49.7	50.2	51.0	50.0	42.1	41.7
CEE	35.0	40.5	39.8	41.5	42.0	49.1	50.0	49.1	41.2	40.9
AELE	5.7	7.2	7.2	6.9	7.4	0.7	0.7	0.7	0.7	0.6
Océanie	0.6	0.5	x0.7	0.7	0.6	0.7	x0.9	x0.8	x0.7	x0.7
Japan/Japon	14.7	16.8	17.4	17.0	18.2	17.5	18.3	19.3	23.6	24.6
USA/Etats–Unis d'Amer	22.0	17.9	15.6	15.5	13.9	15.7	16.4	16.5	18.3	17.4
Germany/Allemagne	12.6	15.7	15.4	15.1	13.6	16.1	17.3	16.2	12.9	12.5
France, Monac	5.5	5.9	5.8	7.2	7.6	8.5	8.0	8.8	6.7	6.9
United Kingdom	5.4	4.8	4.5	6.0	6.3	7.5	7.7	7.2	6.5	6.4
Austria/Autriche	2.6	3.7	3.7	3.6	4.1	5.1	5.1	5.6	4.7	x4.0
Canada	8.0	6.3	5.6	6.0	5.8	5.1	3.9	3.7	4.5	3.9
Mexico/Mexique	5.4	2.9	5.1	4.3	4.2	3.8	3.6	3.7	4.1	5.0
Italy/Italie	2.7	3.3	3.4	2.9	3.1	3.5	3.5	3.5	3.3	3.4
Spain/Espagne	1.2	1.5	1.5	1.6	1.9	2.3	2.5	2.3	1.9	2.0

TRADE BY COMMODITY IN THOUSAND U.S. DOLLARS – COMMERCE PAR PRODUIT EN MILLIERS DE DOLLARS E.U

COUNTRIES–PAYS	IMPORTS – IMPORTATIONS				
	1990	1991	1992	1993	1994
Total	22060145	22498653	24770483	25443922	25175282
Africa	x230245	x323362	x300920	x561297	x577786
Northern Africa	71325	113326	x144505	x375514	x383569
Americas	6432655	6792309	7820822	7235101	x7040565
LAIA	402231	485898	591582	435435	325463
CACM	923	4414	5189	x4363	x18608
Asia	x3779694	x3557465	4220152	x5813823	x5270676
Middle East	x962078	x717550	x626198	x1792022	x1142451
Europe	11168612	11485435	12142959	11423941	11861777
EEC	10869717	11177155	11873097	11124236	11470638
EFTA	264443	264157	259805	282564	370333
Oceania	x274730	x300680	x259994	x309737	x272527
USA/Etats–Unis d'Amer	5083385	5348326	6178643	5765333	5809182
United Kingdom	3359836	3225717	3190196	3364627	2917636
France, Monac	2640872	3111142	3374107	3109193	3412598
Germany/Allemagne	1561192	1586467	1671068	1775962	2353082
Netherlands/Pays–Bas	1120930	1262458	1286988	1109706	919813
Japan/Japon	1157492	1053654	1025027	1159492	1162586
Canada	891447	910874	999594	948421	814776
Korea, Republic of	546259	411239	1047133	751770	772296
Singapore/Singapour	471505	668860	731151	792594	657754
Italy/Italie	550459	609758	701244	462458	493976
Iran (Islamic Rp. of)	x593681	x469124	x272211	x774797	x75151
Sweden/Suède	363579	341966	374336	289238	235395
Belgium–Luxembourg	289488	215947	404042	278109	276181
Ireland/Irlande	343173	310012	280728	212435	214194
Spain/Espagne	288551	241502	281180	273042	311127
Malaysia/Malaisie	33653	156009	160948	349301	530629
Australia/Australie	191385	252044	190469	201219	186141
Saudi Arabia	22854	29404	36132	x522600	x484394
United Arab Emirates	46365	64533	182046	x318023	x180588
Indonesia/Indonésie	58573	124493	158877	263229	138810
Venezuela	51634	118087	196322	143354	44124
Switz.Liecht	128774	142919	129974	182692	204114
Mexico/Mexique	106441	160308	164897	124540	129223
Brazil/Brésil	216088	174551	121678	99405	93810
China/Chine	77618	111088	154925	118211	117974
Greece/Grèce	158487	110344	132991	103458	110151
Norway, SVD, JM	126547	112041	125860	94976	157586
Israel/Israël	106892	88298	120223	115747	108941
So. Africa Customs Un	87879	122483	82228	100864	95210
India/Inde	64263	77521	31576	132536	142822
Tunisia/Tunisie	23497	33468	52917	133114	16508
Libyan Arab Jamahiriya	18577	18331	x36460	x135146	x84024
New Zealand	77882	40424	56670	89973	77617
Turkey/Turquie	49800	27432	63352	93677	76107
Philippines	52515	11367	37715	126897	40708
Hong Kong	35871	50868	42857	77564	254179
Austria/Autriche	42789	34229	66818	64370	75520
Denmark/Danemark	56258	57721	35833	39420	37857
Algeria/Algérie	17250	24934	32170	56721	196214
Russian Federation			x78345	x34061	x51768
Qatar	15928	81905	12444	15587	x24259
Finland/Finlande	57005	40280	42108	21630	97420
Morocco/Maroc	6648	29356	18796	46436	80667
Thailand/Thaïlande	10428	11882	26870	46630	26066
Portugal	37100	29613	31459	20588	15688
Pakistan	19896	54766	18649	4648	35246
Nigeria/Nigéria	x22951	6771	x45956	x21137	x16585
Argentina/Argentine	9009	16026	34677	22249	22067
Colombia/Colombie	8410	9692	36827	18847	16718
Sri Lanka	4711	15857	11930	30766	62702

COUNTRIES–PAYS	EXPORTS – EXPORTATIONS				
	1990	1991	1992	1993	1994
Totale	22377122	23485504	25476644	24646851	25339141
Afrique	x16716	x25813	x23352	x78429	x54449
Afrique du Nord	x4988	x4206	x5318	25896	x8583
Amériques	9118617	9659100	9745136	10031091	10239101
ALAI	88962	139902	155600	283553	524416
MCAC	3	3	14	749	
Asie	985247	926445	1496756	x1721677	x1816610
Moyen–Orient	x11621	x20293	x43359	x216180	x201623
Europe	12085593	12701237	14099450	12646231	13061562
CEE	11733258	12260114	13628841	12149270	12534129
AELE	337495	400351	449169	468299	517450
Océanie	x105052	x104525	85565	x57885	x65182
USA/Etats–Unis d'Amer	7731149	8223226	8373151	8387262	8517434
United Kingdom	5178605	4762661	5365786	4914831	4581133
France, Monac	2627359	3105648	3401939	3087186	3324553
Germany/Allemagne	1716674	1879322	2101128	1757298	2200197
Canada	1282559	1291792	1213383	1355213	1187387
Italy/Italie	546300	730224	867187	810263	853301
Netherlands/Pays–Bas	724344	798516	896811	675435	742306
Japan/Japon	322265	437289	635133	551922	671944
Korea, Republic of	380910	145344	436803	520841	541896
Switz.Liecht	239949	293487	363188	366073	417668
Sweden/Suède	287078	293592	342108	302237	275273
Belgium–Luxembourg	232398	265605	309628	337667	270664
Singapore/Singapour	116025	186305	234300	229581	222003
Ireland/Irlande	277760	285554	176319	98383	110856
Mexico/Mexique	75751	125450	145912	189187	302636
Norway, SVD, JM	97546	106865	85981	102226	99781
Australia/Australie	93658	89285	74594	43760	35379
Spain/Espagne	59701	66724	62980	74360	73325
Israel/Israël	79702	77383	67296	55066	70542
Saudi Arabia	440	295	843	x132302	x96287
Austria/Autriche	25313	26842	47857	45236	x35663
Hong Kong	51326	31769	26991	44161	40633
Brazil/Brésil	11118	8925	4623	65942	198208
Malta/Malte	12148	35914	16997	14362	x2125
China/Chine	5131	7658	21084	29268	20376
United Arab Emirates	329			x56236	x64273
Portugal	26649	14859	27777	12707	16916
Former USSR/Anc. URSS	x45921	x55120			
Poland/Pologne	605	4256	10413	37899	20304
Denmark/Danemark	7618	12083	16594	21840	32342
Russian Federation			x25330	x24450	x37472
Malaysia/Malaisie	12864	8399	15619	24314	7701
Iran (Islamic Rp. of)		x11782	x21266	x8296	x2198
New Zealand	11218	14944	10950	13437	29445
Hungary/Hongrie	x9406	x6819	x7986	x21774	x11086
So. Africa Customs Un	1460	3471	5713	22566	
Colombia/Colombie	5	4162	325	25812	17914
Greece/Grèce	18068	13178	9076	5790	7536
Tunisia/Tunisie	233	2260	293	24596	1542
Slovakia				x23435	x2926
India/Inde	585	2038	2964	18184	5810
Czech Republic				16943	26664
Brunei Darussalam			x4672	x10994	x10420
Croatia/Croatie			2449	13158	x7075
Thailand/Thaïlande	92	899	6458	8070	7661
Finland/Finlande	5391	5304	3651	6037	10062
Lebanon/Liban	x32	x3730	x5737	x4960	x1124
Bulgaria/Bulgarie	x3524	x328	x3650	x9693	x40318
Bahrain/Bahreïn	x3174	x3208	x4782	x5620	x1884
Ethiopia/Ethiopie				x10715	x14823

(VALUE AS % OF TOTAL)(VALEUR EN % DU TOTAL)

	1985	1986	1987	1988	1989	1990	1991	1992	1993	1994
Africa	0.8	x1.5	x1.8	x1.5	x1.1	x1.0	x1.4	x1.2	x2.2	x2.3
Northern Africa	0.6	1.0	1.2	0.7	0.3	0.3	0.5	x0.6	x1.5	x1.5
Americas	32.6	31.7	x26.5	x27.3	29.6	29.2	30.2	31.6	28.4	x28.0
LAIA	2.6	2.6	x3.2	x3.3	2.2	1.8	2.2	2.4	1.7	1.3
CACM	0.0	0.0	0.0	0.0	0.0	0.0	0.0	0.0	x0.0	x0.1
Asia	14.6	x14.2	x18.3	x16.4	x14.5	x17.1	x15.8	17.0	x22.8	x21.0
Middle East	1.1	x2.4	x5.6	x2.3	x1.7	x4.4	x3.2	x2.5	x7.0	x4.5
Europe	51.1	51.4	48.9	52.1	52.5	50.6	51.0	49.0	44.9	47.1
EEC	47.6	47.5	45.6	49.0	48.8	49.3	49.7	47.9	43.7	45.6
EFTA	3.2	3.5	2.9	2.8	3.3	1.2	1.2	1.0	1.1	1.5
Oceania	1.0	x1.1	x1.1	1.4	x1.4	x1.2	x1.3	x1.1	x1.2	x1.0
USA/Etats–Unis d'Amer	27.8	27.4	22.0	19.5	22.4	23.0	23.8	24.9	22.7	23.1
United Kingdom	17.0	16.7	15.7	18.4	16.8	15.2	14.3	12.9	13.2	11.6
France, Monac	11.0	10.3	10.6	10.8	8.7	12.0	13.8	13.6	12.2	13.6
Germany/Allemagne	7.3	6.9	6.9	6.1	6.6	7.1	7.1	6.7	7.0	9.3
Netherlands/Pays–Bas	4.2	4.8	4.1	4.9	7.1	5.1	5.6	5.2	4.4	3.7
Japan/Japon	8.2	6.6	6.6	6.3	5.8	5.2	4.7	4.1	4.6	4.6
Canada	2.0	1.4	1.3	4.2	4.8	4.0	4.0	4.0	3.7	3.2
Korea, Republic of	1.4	1.1	1.1	2.0	2.1	2.5	1.8	4.2	3.0	3.1
Singapore/Singapour	0.8	1.5	1.9	1.8	1.6	2.1	3.0	3.0	3.1	2.6
Italy/Italie	3.5	3.1	2.8	2.7	2.7	2.5	2.7	2.8	1.8	2.0

	1985	1986	1987	1988	1989	1990	1991	1992	1993	1994
Afrique		x0.6	x0.4	x0.5	x0.2	x0.1	x0.1	x0.1	x0.3	x0.2
Afrique du Nord		x0.3	x0.2	x0.1	x0.1	x0.0	x0.0	x0.0	0.1	x0.0
Amériques	46.3	x42.0	x40.2	x42.4	x45.2	40.8	41.1	38.2	40.7	40.4
ALAI	0.4	x0.1	x0.3	x0.4	x0.3	0.4	0.6	0.6	1.2	2.1
MCAC		x0.0	x0.0	x0.0	x0.0	0.0	0.0	0.0	0.0	
Asie	2.7	x4.9	x4.6	x4.4	x4.5	4.4	4.0	5.9	x7.0	x7.1
Moyen–Orient	0.1	x1.6	x1.2	x0.9	x0.4	x0.1	x0.1	x0.2	x0.9	x0.8
Europe	50.7	52.3	53.9	51.5	49.5	54.0	54.1	55.3	51.3	51.5
CEE	47.5	49.4	50.4	48.0	46.4	52.4	52.2	53.5	49.3	49.5
AELE	3.0	2.7	3.3	3.4	3.1	1.5	1.7	1.8	1.9	2.0
Océanie		x0.0	x0.1	0.3	x0.3	x0.5	x0.4	0.3	x0.2	x0.3
USA/Etats–Unis d'Amer	38.7	34.6	33.6	36.6	38.7	34.5	35.0	32.9	34.0	33.6
United Kingdom	22.1	22.1	21.7	22.4	23.2	23.1	20.3	21.1	19.9	18.1
France, Monac	8.5	9.3	9.4	8.1	4.7	11.7	13.2	13.4	12.5	13.1
Germany/Allemagne	7.3	6.9	8.5	7.3	7.4	7.7	8.0	8.2	7.1	8.7
Canada	7.2	7.1	6.3	5.4	6.1	5.7	5.5	4.8	5.5	4.7
Italy/Italie	3.3	4.8	4.8	3.1	3.0	2.4	3.1	3.4	3.3	3.4
Netherlands/Pays–Bas	2.3	2.9	2.3	2.7	4.1	3.2	3.4	3.5	2.7	2.9
Japan/Japon	1.4	1.4	1.2	1.5	1.8	1.4	1.9	2.5	2.2	2.7
Korea, Republic of	0.7	0.6	0.6	1.0	1.4	1.7	0.6	1.7	2.1	2.1
Switz.Liecht	1.5	1.0	1.2	1.3	1.3	1.1	1.2	1.4	1.5	1.6

TRADE BY COMMODITY IN THOUSAND U.S. DOLLARS – COMMERCE PAR PRODUIT EN MILLIERS DE DOLLARS E.U

COUNTRIES–PAYS	IMPORTS – IMPORTATIONS 1990	1991	1992	1993	1994
Total	16040372	16409416	18876783	19490887	22025171
Africa	x532613	x535632	x597257	x655561	x596019
Northern Africa	234109	220351	x227443	x291143	x233047
Americas	3273132	3469522	4163233	4761232	5476688
LAIA	535782	557936	1055997	1381581	1460850
CACM	52097	73515	123544	133630	x122220
Asia	x5551503	5950070	7100254	8097673	9270066
Middle East	x1423229	x1157763	x1030824	x980069	x748385
Europe	5830867	5860429	6567926	5452400	6134678
EEC	5293469	5354611	6028592	4941716	5606543
EFTA	489403	470140	483176	447112	471274
Oceania	x342540	x332000	x295837	x366039	x359887
USA/Etats–Unis d'Amer	1982418	2109103	2331452	2620106	3103325
Germany/Allemagne	1351433	1428645	1592093	1325180	1632562
Singapore/Singapour	609487	757491	878278	1179368	1291690
China/Chine	396246	490129	1146809	1155894	1728456
Hong Kong	543012	660241	768899	1012538	1269871
France,Monac	740985	702561	762517	671817	760572
United Kingdom	580565	603119	832465	685463	668456
Thailand/Thaïlande	779406	601494	528933	967306	750083
Italy/Italie	642312	674987	710184	531496	585766
Japan/Japon	511552	557611	609136	670446	870347
Korea, Republic of	431592	507415	620962	590442	646150
Canada	552201	585390	546225	526946	684349
Iran (Islamic Rp. of)	x804102	x552151	x512415	x388938	x68481
Indonesia/Indonésie	171667	400133	600496	370342	367745
Netherlands/Pays–Bas	413556	428897	456533	311269	337922
Mexico/Mexique	132084	185294	418155	560670	641539
Malaysia/Malaisie	163046	292921	380531	426212	768693
Switz.Liecht	382111	334224	354659	312813	350748
Spain/Espagne	286278	300999	351395	278078	337383
Belgium–Luxembourg	295389	307032	306741	221545	240254
Australia/Australie	288617	276245	244479	305752	294167
Sweden/Suède	266448	252122	252447	235895	282814
Austria/Autriche	237064	240047	245964	237613	268643
Philippines	107008	95527	147516	339558	162602
Saudi Arabia	128758	209799	167644	x149455	x165262
Denmark/Danemark	163760	158835	160034	134896	181936
Venezuela	45229	99228	166067	158694	160182
Turkey/Turquie	98664	142171	129787	132741	124223
Norway,SVD,JM	101015	127466	121847	126413	116898
Pakistan	66162	153357	106711	103700	133645
Colombia/Colombie	31198	62679	150428	148210	116035
Nigeria/Nigéria	x50125	85734	x106874	x140076	x66115
Finland/Finlande	110546	81275	124899	89290	125541
Brazil/Brésil	113526	86427	89680	107145	124110
Argentina/Argentine	20689	27188	79183	164829	233487
So. Africa Customs Un	94885	89557	87731	79935	93792
Portugal	75589	70394	105450	67902	58579
Greece/Grèce	71419	49526	77237	92198	52762
Oman	30606	102526	55977	60003	48360
Chile/Chili	83893	50023	51045	115093	103691
India/Inde	106290	80174	64149	71761	220514
United Arab Emirates	54685	57278	55126	x92765	x111775
Egypt/Egypte	34077	59286	63039	81320	67308
Russian Federation			x112735	x88600	x73661
Israel/Israël	52812	52538	69992	64234	114255
Former USSR/Anc. URSS	347052	x168812			
Algeria/Algérie	105338	54276	60076	52350	59988
Ireland/Irlande	58124	56172	50633	59075	73354
Bangladesh	100230	67922	45002	52239	x21400
Peru/Pérou	67129	20249	51416	83346	46755

COUNTRIES–PAYS	EXPORTS – EXPORTATIONS 1990	1991	1992	1993	1994
Totale	13450394	14622341	17102887	18129387	20633852
Afrique	18112	19000	x20870	x26005	x9620
Afrique du Nord	4415	6247	x4913	4591	3000
Amériques	2096400	2596073	3414291	3744457	4066288
ALAI	137651	179164	623114	804533	958648
MCAC	986	1439	2823	x413	x756
Asie	3574473	4189456	5089421	6054330	7086281
Moyen–Orient	29042	30558	26864	x56605	x49153
Europe	7266872	7423591	8228581	7941917	9031683
CEE	6653937	6816670	7524001	7259932	8267819
AELE	462941	523170	554690	547438	617546
Océanie	28775	x38561	x53143	x55151	x53832
Japan/Japon	2157889	2451582	2745021	2935863	3335095
Germany/Allemagne	2341784	2429042	2558288	2348448	2668412
USA/Etats–Unis d'Amer	1665610	2091710	2447504	2612613	2677779
France,Monac	1184961	1212306	1332688	1235359	1395961
United Kingdom	931602	969672	1052813	1019114	1102721
Italy/Italie	763464	768628	872593	791461	905569
Hong Kong	507878	623012	737178	957011	1117194
Singapore/Singapour	344077	414745	465697	679864	900006
China/Chine	185893	255923	558647	712892	778361
Switz.Liecht	441451	480331	518596	524326	586316
Mexico/Mexique	26823	42899	478142	633802	742795
Canada	286259	318960	335737	320576	424084
Denmark/Danemark	200280	244567	307881	290635	417399
Finland/Finlande	173853	170569	237217	432429	507414
Austria/Autriche	236029	217229	260404	281694	x299814
Sweden/Suède	232759	225747	229449	220104	301406
Netherlands/Pays–Bas	177089	205474	237097	225847	224571
Spain/Espagne	183304	165278	204422	186095	260028
Malaysia/Malaisie	25902	91307	175558	268793	333108
Belgium–Luxembourg	191634	161926	164685	178768	128979
Korea, Republic of	170165	161340	164912	163139	191819
Thailand/Thaïlande	85770	116465	143610	189527	306411
Brazil/Brésil	95220	121131	126860	154698	194150
Slovenia/Slovénia			107653	106491	126458
Czechoslovakia		x117632	x87638		
Poland/Pologne	59312	54272	79438	53743	59357
Hungary/Hongrie	x36292	x48144	x65753	x69727	x92274
Australia/Australie	25664	34950	51033	52908	52074
Czech Republic				110656	141385
Russian Federation			x61729	x43448	x56587
Norway,SVD,JM	21486	42839	36092	23110	31202
Ireland/Irlande	19779	27903	41208	31802	31098
Israel/Israël	42827	17928	22457	49338	12156
Bulgaria/Bulgarie	x105121	x26024	x39438	x23272	x17731
Romania/Roumanie	46377	29228	23857	31359	32481
Yugoslavia SFR	149174	x83079			
Former USSR/Anc. URSS	165120	x80151			
India/Inde	20023	16782	33917	22541	23969
Portugal	16334	16185	16590	15281	19328
Croatia/Croatie			22209	18542	x15309
So. Africa Customs Un	9610	6559	12855	15607	
Turkey/Turquie	10095	11465	10834	11989	17420
Saudi Arabia	5473	5391	5258	x21183	x17094
Ukraine			x7097	x23815	x6584
Indonesia/Indonésie	1291	4498	7344	14995	32780
Yugoslavia/Yougoslavie			x19371	x4014	x1503
Argentina/Argentine	8112	8133	5646	4745	8141
Slovakia				x18411	x42909
Greece/Grèce	940	2021	8665	2895	5119
United Arab Emirates	4409			x10234	x6960

(VALUE AS % OF TOTAL)(VALEUR EN % DU TOTAL)

	1985	1986	1987	1988	1989	1990	1991	1992	1993	1994
Africa	7.8	x6.5	x4.6	x4.3	x3.1	x3.3	x3.2	x3.2	x3.4	x2.7
Northern Africa	3.0	2.2	1.7	1.9	1.2	1.5	1.3	x1.2	x1.5	x1.1
Americas	28.8	23.7	20.0	21.6	23.0	20.4	21.1	22.0	24.4	24.9
LAIA	7.7	5.3	3.8	3.9	3.7	3.3	3.4	5.6	7.1	6.6
CACM	0.5	0.4	0.4	0.3	0.4	0.3	0.4	0.7	0.7	x0.6
Asia	20.3	22.0	x24.3	29.4	29.5	x34.6	36.2	37.6	41.6	42.1
Middle East	5.2	x6.8	x5.4	x4.8	x3.3	x8.9	x7.1	x5.5	x5.0	x3.4
Europe	36.6	40.8	42.2	37.7	38.6	36.4	35.7	34.8	28.0	27.9
EEC	28.9	32.1	33.6	30.4	31.4	33.0	32.6	31.9	25.4	25.5
EFTA	6.9	8.0	7.9	6.9	6.9	3.1	2.9	2.6	2.3	2.1
Oceania	2.5	x2.6	x2.4	1.6	x1.8	x2.2	x2.0	x1.5	x1.9	x1.6
USA/Etats–Unis d'Amer	15.1	13.5	12.3	12.8	13.9	12.4	12.9	12.4	13.4	14.1
Germany/Allemagne	6.9	7.8	8.2	7.2	7.8	8.4	8.7	8.4	6.8	7.4
Singapore/Singapour	2.1	2.3	3.0	3.5	3.6	3.8	4.6	4.7	6.1	5.9
China/Chine			1.6	4.2	5.7	2.5	3.0	6.1	5.9	7.8
Hong Kong	1.6	2.1	2.6	3.3	3.9	3.4	4.0	4.1	5.2	5.8
France,Monac	4.0	4.6	4.9	4.0	4.2	4.6	4.3	4.0	3.4	3.5
United Kingdom	3.6	3.4	3.9	3.9	3.8	3.6	3.7	4.4	3.5	3.0
Thailand/Thaïlande	0.1	0.1	0.6	1.0	1.8	4.9	3.7	2.8	5.0	3.4
Italy/Italie	3.6	3.8	4.1	3.9	4.1	4.0	4.1	3.8	2.7	2.7
Japan/Japon	2.5	2.2	2.2	2.7	3.2	3.2	3.4	3.2	3.4	4.0

	1985	1986	1987	1988	1989	1990	1991	1992	1993	1994
Afrique		x0.2	x0.1	x0.1	x0.1	0.2	0.1	x0.1	x0.2	x0.0
Afrique du Nord	0.0	x0.0	x0.0	x0.0	x0.0	0.0	0.0	x0.0	0.0	0.0
Amériques	17.0	11.9	10.7	12.6	x14.8	15.6	17.8	20.0	20.7	19.7
ALAI	2.9	0.7	0.8	0.8	1.0	1.0	1.2	3.6	4.4	4.6
MCAC	0.0	0.0	0.0	0.0	x0.0	0.0	0.0	0.0	x0.0	x0.0
Asie	22.0	21.9	x24.3	x26.9	26.6	26.6	28.7	29.8	33.4	34.3
Moyen–Orient	0.3	x0.3	x0.5	0.3	x0.2	0.2	0.2	0.2	x0.3	x0.2
Europe	50.5	55.3	52.0	47.6	49.9	54.0	50.8	48.1	43.8	43.8
CEE	41.7	46.1	42.6	39.3	41.4	49.5	46.6	44.0	40.0	40.1
AELE	6.6	7.2	7.8	7.4	7.6	3.4	3.6	3.2	3.0	3.0
Océanie	0.1	x0.1	x0.1	0.1	0.2	0.2	x0.3	x0.3	x0.3	x0.3
Japan/Japon	17.0	17.1	14.5	15.3	16.2	16.0	16.8	16.1	16.2	16.2
Germany/Allemagne	13.3	15.8	14.8	14.2	14.8	17.4	16.6	15.0	13.0	12.9
USA/Etats–Unis d'Amer	12.8	10.0	8.7	10.1	12.0	12.4	14.3	14.3	14.4	13.0
France,Monac	7.1	7.8	7.5	6.5	7.2	8.8	8.3	7.8	6.8	6.8
United Kingdom	6.9	7.9	6.3	6.1	5.6	6.9	6.6	6.2	5.6	5.3
Italy/Italie	4.3	4.8	4.7	4.2	5.0	5.7	5.3	5.1	4.4	4.4
Hong Kong	1.9	2.0	2.6	3.3	4.1	3.8	4.3	4.3	5.3	5.4
Singapore/Singapour	1.4	1.5	1.7	2.1	2.7	2.6	2.8	2.7	3.8	4.4
China/Chine			0.7	1.1	1.1	1.4	1.8	3.3	3.9	3.8
Switz.Liecht	2.7	3.1	3.6	3.5	3.2	3.3	3.3	3.0	2.9	2.8

TRADE BY COMMODITY IN THOUSAND U.S. DOLLARS – COMMERCE PAR PRODUIT EN MILLIERS DE DOLLARS E.U

IMPORTS – IMPORTATIONS

COUNTRIES–PAYS	1990	1991	1992	1993	1994
Total	4106875	3613204	3737046	3108237	3353792
Africa	x41279	x73309	x73613	x78763	x47970
Northern Africa	8784	x18726	8230	44844	x11228
Americas	481893	448919	471954	611264	760813
LAIA	96520	121118	111812	188749	225403
CACM	37566	3707	22859	x8349	x8352
Asia	x1012991	819853	768033	550235	640867
Middle East	x177728	x118238	x152175	x124481	x133555
Europe	2117515	2116472	2300623	1689424	1772456
EEC	1855730	1940347	2036010	1479092	1587224
EFTA	225435	166751	224843	182807	178072
Oceania	x48115	x42051	x56285	x57978	x76253
France, Monac	754733	910247	931012	446684	630059
Germany/Allemagne	221501	255686	290909	340271	224432
USA/Etats–Unis d'Amer	184863	189143	213006	259844	352464
China/Chine	510395	345767	143050	36825	86667
Switz.Liecht	192870	139260	196041	156396	149513
Sweden/Suède	151369	140295	143142	159732	134935
Korea, Republic of	94307	118899	78199	171163	143083
Japan/Japon	113593	124010	119303	111758	141529
Canada	103528	106171	106624	128551	154620
United Kingdom	147010	123195	111877	101543	112497
Finland/Finlande	128069	111149	96942	69654	71979
Spain/Espagne	92731	101253	79989	84995	79797
Netherlands/Pays–Bas	95102	85974	94989	53073	41879
Austria/Autriche	75031	71320	84460	67244	83438
Belgium–Luxembourg	97377	54556	88053	57786	80467
Italy/Italie	62526	51640	58020	63934	75366
Bangladesh			170961	x1555	x128
Australia/Australie	42486	34675	42993	45094	60303
Iran (Islamic Rp. of)	x115154	x37391	x52492	x12309	x3362
Kuwait/Koweït	17387	4344	26076	70685	86624
Saudi Arabia	7077	49103	42673	x6170	x8674
So. Africa Customs Un	19323	36362	42984	16815	21117
Brazil/Brésil	22397	24831	15694	48736	55796
Venezuela	7568	16503	29665	36681	38216
Norway, SVD, JM	28808	25230	27818	24914	27371
Mexico/Mexique	7149	18924	20321	30611	56062
Czech Republic				64850	15810
Czechoslovakia	83937	x21075	x43079		
Turkey/Turquie	21624	23140	17402	22250	11948
Hong Kong	10107	11693	24566	21467	22545
Indonesia/Indonésie	19938	10534	18266	26432	19983
Denmark/Danemark	13767	13703	18773	20552	34798
Poland/Pologne	31655	25604	9079	16714	16599
Slovenia/Slovénia			20428	23616	4716
Egypt/Egypte	4159	7685	1940	32928	1476
Portugal	6960	13147	22500	5650	4552
Chile/Chili	26224	9643	12183	16925	15533
Malaysia/Malaisie	5377	22236	7971	7948	15525
Former USSR/Anc. URSS	x244288	x37286			
Hungary/Hongrie	x12001	23962	x5036	x6493	x4700
Pakistan	18107	26447	7574	1377	16008
India/Inde	24169	13308	12371	9419	16842
Russian Federation			x11132	x21004	x17239
Singapore/Singapour	13565	8384	9770	10693	16315
Thailand/Thaïlande	4022	6701	11117	9853	11644
Paraguay	130	1776	8291	16979	26159
Bolivia/Bolivie	1810	23941	1039	1304	1252
Ireland/Irlande	8222	6712	12758	5771	9470
Colombia/Colombie	9516	6450	11943	6755	4990
New Zealand	4755	5855	8629	9035	11721

EXPORTS – EXPORTATIONS

COUNTRIES–PAYS	1990	1991	1992	1993	1994
Totale	x4839590	2995646	3034537	3105850	3001109
Afrique	3501	x3858	x1862	x6421	1844
Afrique du Nord	614	656	227	x3117	x392
Amériques	354094	410337	466736	547078	556599
ALAI	11206	20326	66679	55270	39411
MCAC	.	2		x406	x230
Asie	286623	369195	332455	401864	483277
Moyen–Orient	x1335	10301	1466	x5973	x3384
Europe	2298678	1922361	2183359	2084741	1903333
CEE	2173737	1784254	2057587	1957635	1791790
AELE	108909	133647	114096	115967	103631
Océanie	x4378	x6226	14073	x9817	x8273
Germany/Allemagne	776804	897585	921887	897642	878591
USA/Etats–Unis d'Amer	300129	345097	332388	401544	441086
France, Monac	648125	282242	393213	371524	293162
Japan/Japon	264177	332122	276922	353645	435765
Sweden/Suède	210187	199685	263176	187670	181381
United Kingdom	157856	139865	150383	150992	133027
Switz.Liecht	93192	117402	92376	97405	81143
Austria/Autriche	77799	66229	87512	78439	x41742
Italy/Italie	85211	62139	79718	69393	90054
Canada	40711	43651	62590	89572	75787
Netherlands/Pays–Bas	65057	62550	63950	51224	33432
Poland/Pologne	156781	154335	5587	6164	6471
Belgium–Luxembourg	40393	15004	25787	63508	30431
Spain/Espagne	76275	23985	29166	48305	59833
Mexico/Mexique	1536	7675	51430	35953	17707
Russian Federation			x31353	x60816	x54373
Czechoslovakia		x64052	x15083		
Norway, SVD, JM	15690	16193	21711	18558	22450
Former USSR/Anc. URSS	x1710251	x56105			
Finland/Finlande	18716	17035	15354	15931	19800
China/Chine	3594	8223	23010	9669	12812
Denmark/Danemark	13405	13583	15257	11745	17151
Brazil/Brésil	6191	8936	11172	15340	15884
Czech Republic				35024	22251
Australia/Australie	3947	5305	13223	9306	7856
Ireland/Irlande	2702	2629	9171	9707	11377
Hong Kong	3442	4071	10205	6929	6130
Slovenia/Slovénia			10106	6611	6888
Singapore/Singapour	3961	4692	4720	7266	6939
Hungary/Hongrie	x6433	x4770	x7670	x3479	x10429
Korea, Republic of	4411	4303	5621	5718	8499
Bulgaria/Bulgarie	x16511	x3716	x6530	x3744	x3326
Israel/Israël	3555	2226	2800	5195	3431
Argentina/Argentine	2588	2948	3392	2138	4286
India/Inde	848	254	2708	5359	569
Kuwait/Koweït	33	5720	653	911	152
Slovakia				x6612	x4382
Portugal	1183	1683	2966	1429	1567
Saudi Arabia	538	3759	341	x1472	x320
Yugoslavia/Yougoslavie			x728	x4255	x37
Netherlands Antilles	467	825	3908	x145	x5
So. Africa Customs Un	2544	2480	941	1449	
Malaysia/Malaisie	1097	2167	635	1119	4492
Yugoslavia SFR	16008	x3554			
Korea Dem People's Rp	x3		x3219	x218	x13
Libyan Arab Jamahiriya			x3	x2859	x42
Romania/Roumanie		536	1027	906	925
United Arab Emirates	282			x2268	x1826
Colombia/Colombie	5	284	410	1519	1148
Ukraine			x454	x991	x420

(VALUE AS % OF TOTAL)(VALEUR EN % DU TOTAL)

Imports

	1985	1986	1987	1988	1989	1990	1991	1992	1993	1994
Africa	4.0	3.5	x1.8	x1.9	x1.5	x1.0	x2.0	x2.0	x2.5	x1.4
Northern Africa	1.7	1.0	0.4	0.2	0.3	0.2	x0.5	0.2	1.4	x0.3
Americas	10.8	12.3	8.5	15.0	14.4	11.7	12.5	12.7	19.7	22.7
LAIA	3.1	6.7	4.3	7.8	2.4	2.4	3.4	3.0	6.1	6.7
CACM	0.0	0.2	x0.0	0.0	0.1	0.9	0.1	0.6	x0.3	x0.2
Asia	12.7	12.8	x16.1	x12.8	9.6	x24.7	22.7	20.5	17.7	19.1
Middle East	2.6	x4.4	7.4	4.2	3.1	x4.3	x3.3	x4.1	x4.0	x4.0
Europe	58.0	60.8	48.6	37.7	54.5	51.6	58.6	61.6	54.4	52.8
EEC	44.5	46.3	36.9	23.7	42.5	45.2	53.7	54.5	47.6	47.3
EFTA	12.0	13.8	11.3	12.3	11.5	5.5	4.6	6.0	5.9	5.3
Oceania	2.0	x2.0	x2.0	x1.0	x1.1	x1.2	x1.1	x1.5	x1.8	x2.2
France, Monac	21.1	22.5	18.7	1.8	18.3	18.4	25.2	24.9	14.4	18.8
Germany/Allemagne	3.1	3.6	2.8	5.3	4.4	5.4	7.1	7.8	10.9	6.7
USA/Etats–Unis d'Amer	6.0	4.4	3.4	5.4	4.7	4.5	5.2	5.7	8.4	10.5
China/Chine			0.2	0.5	0.4	12.4	9.6	3.8	1.2	2.6
Switz.Liecht	4.0	4.4	4.5	4.4	3.0	4.7	3.9	5.2	5.0	4.5
Sweden/Suède	3.4	3.5	3.1	3.4	3.6	3.7	3.9	3.8	5.1	4.0
Korea, Republic of	5.4	5.1	3.3	1.9	1.8	2.3	3.3	2.1	5.5	4.3
Japan/Japon	1.3	1.1	1.1	1.6	1.8	2.8	3.4	3.2	3.6	4.2
Canada	1.3	0.8	0.6	1.6	2.0	2.5	2.9	2.9	4.1	4.6
United Kingdom	2.1	2.0	2.1	2.6	3.5	3.6	3.4	3.0	3.3	3.4

Exports

	1985	1986	1987	1988	1989	1990	1991	1992	1993	1994
Afrique		x0.0	x0.0	x0.1	x0.0	0.1	x0.1	x0.0	x0.2	0.1
Afrique du Nord	0.0	x0.0	x0.0	x0.1	x0.0	0.0	0.0	0.0	x0.1	x0.0
Amériques	12.5	13.3	7.8	9.6	7.7	7.3	13.7	15.4	17.6	18.5
ALAI	0.2	0.4	0.5	0.6	0.3	0.2	0.7	2.2	1.8	1.3
MCAC		x0.0	0.0	x0.0		0.0	0.0	0.0	x0.0	x0.0
Asie	6.0	6.6	4.8	x5.7	7.7	5.9	12.4	10.9	13.0	16.1
Moyen–Orient	0.0	x0.2	x0.2	x0.1	x0.0	x0.0	0.3	0.0	x0.2	x0.1
Europe	68.6	66.7	46.8	36.0	57.6	47.5	64.2	72.0	67.1	63.4
CEE	57.8	53.9	39.0	27.1	47.8	44.9	59.6	67.8	63.0	59.7
AELE	8.4	10.4	7.0	8.1	9.5	2.3	4.5	3.8	3.7	3.5
Océanie	0.1	x0.1	x0.1	x0.1	x0.1	x0.1	x0.2	0.4	x0.3	x0.3
Germany/Allemagne	21.8	29.2	20.4	11.8	25.7	16.1	30.0	30.4	28.9	29.3
USA/Etats–Unis d'Amer	12.0	12.4	7.1	8.0	5.9	6.2	11.5	11.0	12.9	14.7
France, Monac	6.0	7.5	6.5	2.7	7.7	13.4	9.4	13.0	12.0	9.8
Japan/Japon	3.0	4.4	2.2	4.4	6.7	5.5	11.1	9.1	11.4	14.5
Sweden/Suède	4.5	4.2	2.2	3.9	3.9	4.3	6.7	8.7	6.0	6.0
United Kingdom	3.0	3.5	2.5	3.0	3.3	3.3	4.7	5.0	4.9	4.4
Switz.Liecht	2.3	3.2	2.7	2.4	3.1	1.9	3.9	3.0	3.1	2.7
Austria/Autriche	1.1	2.3	1.4	1.2	1.9	1.6	2.2	2.9	2.5	x1.4
Italy/Italie	1.5	2.4	1.1	1.2	1.4	1.8	2.1	2.6	2.2	3.0
Canada	0.2	0.3	0.2	1.1	1.4	0.8	1.5	2.1	2.9	2.5

TRADE BY COMMODITY IN THOUSAND U.S. DOLLARS – COMMERCE PAR PRODUIT EN MILLIERS DE DOLLARS E.U

COUNTRIES–PAYS	IMPORTS – IMPORTATIONS 1990	1991	1992	1993	1994
Total	10232155	8182278	8057588	7626392	8625214
Africa	x291420	x311682	x246092	x229277	x242678
Northern Africa	x146194	155550	x119169	x106204	x105565
Americas	1913948	1606544	1680698	2092584	2317530
LAIA	219335	261754	286577	394118	494773
CACM	19210	23256	28210	x34789	x33330
Asia	802389	x816584	x1070718	x1026919	x935686
Middle East	x200450	x248934	x345187	x321564	x147407
Europe	4868347	4448183	4676724	3782916	4424213
EEC	4522308	4148563	4388738	3510200	4092211
EFTA	299015	266726	256011	239663	288997
Oceania	x200080	x121825	x168552	x225775	x295135
France, Monac	1026882	873639	933113	792276	1009964
Germany/Allemagne	711325	890023	969070	696335	798678
USA/Etats–Unis d'Amer	930225	670432	674747	806193	897165
Canada	682188	597420	635022	817350	851324
United Kingdom	562346	478143	523671	544992	560489
Netherlands/Pays–Bas	354673	320388	371314	245053	298621
Belgium–Luxembourg	283057	248085	305436	242368	279173
Former USSR/Anc. URSS	1726562	x703603			
Italy/Italie	273929	249835	256553	191711	192146
Spain/Espagne	255243	248622	218203	172944	194053
Korea, Republic of	206218	188029	218178	190994	160391
Austria/Autriche	208410	191006	191698	162897	187856
Japan/Japon	140815	154686	157329	153466	140760
Switz.Liecht	185841	154797	144203	144999	176522
Denmark/Danemark	202902	156618	153244	108876	148564
Sweden/Suède	207522	142854	151584	119705	161819
Iran (Islamic Rp. of)		x107407	x162399	x139116	x13424
Australia/Australie	156240	90848	129979	173078	226657
Russian Federation			x208555	x171992	x149581
Mexico/Mexique	104289	109297	101673	151469	188296
Ukraine			x150995	x201369	x52292
China/Chine	101756	72109	127981	128396	134900
Ireland/Irlande	124426	105731	113602	88936	109828
Norway, SVD, JM	106879	104382	105695	89980	107037
Saudi Arabia	78245	83225	105032	x79978	x54520
Greece/Grèce	61450	70787	88627	64280	55319
Finland/Finlande	169281	109353	54617	35853	48642
Portugal	80862	63479	58004	43976	47056
Argentina/Argentine	16241	29226	51326	73770	129091
Poland/Pologne	51647	46684	55423	48232	77994
Hungary/Hongrie	x95452	51172	x39150	x48661	x83740
So. Africa Customs Un	40443	33731	37512	51077	72720
Czechoslovakia	152049	x36531	x83864		
Chile/Chili	21356	26588	41223	38824	40782
New Zealand	36646	24634	32196	46117	58953
Turkey/Turquie	34879	25997	24097	45101	22312
Tunisia/Tunisie	12515	25435	34364	30217	18128
Malaysia/Malaisie	15157	26708	33585	24469	28986
Thailand/Thaïlande	21885	26116	30198	28147	29959
Czech Republic				83830	107603
Indonesia/Indonésie	31564	22149	22371	36868	37794
Algeria/Algérie	34369	47289	13107	19290	8523
Romania/Roumanie	64252	26195	16970	35198	88075
Israel/Israël	20687	17447	34649	25137	28816
Libyan Arab Jamahiriya	37780	39928	x14999	x21355	x11824
Brazil/Brésil	9082	21209	20798	22833	49445
Singapore/Singapour	18812	16144	20522	27482	33665
Morocco/Maroc	24210	23199	20498	18634	36279
Ecuador/Equateur	9088	9621	10867	35046	x13313
Venezuela	9086	15496	22004	13506	10045

COUNTRIES–PAYS	EXPORTS – EXPORTATIONS 1990	1991	1992	1993	1994
Totale	9209798	8147004	8379728	7893833	9059327
Afrique	27344	21486	19225	15378	x5458
Afrique du Nord	2864	7200	4712	3246	4490
Amériques	2175139	1935295	2107398	2509063	2716850
ALAI	115183	95320	115206	176051	222991
MCAC	2589	2777	3370	x3215	x3626
Asie	381527	409456	443461	396555	392873
Moyen–Orient	7431	8948	11233	9833	10674
Europe	5754443	5502028	5598428	4715042	5660767
CEE	5521455	5326607	5409103	4553724	5469297
AELE	193917	159248	168648	144698	175050
Océanie	x82520	x65697	x83697	x101254	x94642
USA/Etats–Unis d'Amer	1569626	1505518	1662295	1917081	2048824
Germany/Allemagne	1493081	1801863	1626022	1347011	1524590
Italy/Italie	789304	700041	769423	762805	910112
France, Monac	671412	596751	642986	525448	595047
Netherlands/Pays–Bas	513052	459266	513763	471032	499206
Belgium–Luxembourg	499884	404193	415186	306644	438392
Denmark/Danemark	405907	369958	399209	312929	442011
Canada	486460	329227	324186	411169	440822
United Kingdom	435564	386861	364141	261889	318259
Japan/Japon	285118	298352	322706	270403	249865
Sweden/Suède	338720	262660	292697	238447	338322
Austria/Autriche	173068	166683	179552	165540	x186528
Norway, SVD, JM	141840	115635	111501	91786	127007
Spain/Espagne	76193	80676	101150	69664	93573
Brazil/Brésil	72663	63372	74433	93234	126181
Hungary/Hongrie	x88459	x72075	x62544	x56254	x70481
Finland/Finlande	82962	56991	52007	48285	68760
Australia/Australie	50565	42781	51783	60328	49564
Switz.Liecht	52077	43056	57028	52912	48015
Mexico/Mexique	15328	21342	28111	68636	80641
Ireland/Irlande	36532	30108	38332	33373	42371
New Zealand	31817	22858	31750	40304	45030
Israel/Israël	25880	25445	32163	32640	41980
Poland/Pologne	51321	38201	22204	23474	34573
Russian Federation			x55581	x15854	x9904
Czechoslovakia		x38733	x31782		
China/Chine	15893	16506	19933	26203	30318
Korea, Republic of	10405	27261	20211	14729	16130
Czech Republic				60165	63260
Former USSR/Anc. URSS	556474	x41261			
Singapore/Singapour	9022	9906	9653	14857	13797
Hong Kong	8292	6419	11894	13704	12194
So. Africa Customs Un	16338	8826	12575	8773	
Portugal	4711	9157	12597	6602	9926
Romania/Roumanie	20386	18561	4028	5569	11631
Argentina/Argentine	7336	6482	8246	10627	9973
Turkey/Turquie	3518	7712	7913	7885	8702
Slovenia/Slovénia			10993	10122	13916
India/Inde	12910	7447	7179	5865	7524
Yugoslavia SFR	38953	x16128			
Ukraine			x10467	x5021	x2859
Thailand/Thaïlande	4506	5667	3609	4978	5620
Bulgaria/Bulgarie	x19355	x3280	x5999	x2500	x1721
Croatia/Croatie			5429	3712	x1973
Slovakia				x8166	x7008
Costa Rica	2372	2414	3117	x2546	x2260
Tunisia/Tunisie	1153	2008	2851	2951	2238
Greece/Grèce	1051	1387	2038	4053	2200
Colombia/Colombie	2500	2920	2428	1837	2962
Malaysia/Malaisie	1561	2040	1481	2654	2985

(VALUE AS % OF TOTAL)(VALEUR EN % DU TOTAL)

	1985	1986	1987	1988	1989	1990	1991	1992	1993	1994
Africa	4.6	x5.3	x3.6	x3.6	x3.3	x2.9	x3.8	x3.1	x3.0	x2.8
Northern Africa	2.2	2.5	1.9	1.4	1.1	x1.4	1.9	x1.5	x1.4	x1.2
Americas	23.3	19.8	x18.9	17.7	19.8	18.7	19.6	20.9	27.5	26.9
LAIA	4.4	2.7	1.9	2.6	2.0	2.1	3.2	3.6	5.2	5.7
CACM	0.4	0.3	x0.7	0.3	0.2	0.2	0.3	0.4	x0.5	x0.4
Asia	4.6	x4.8	5.8	x6.2	x6.5	7.9	x10.0	x13.3	x13.4	x10.9
Middle East	2.3	x2.4	x1.6	x1.6	x1.8	x2.0	x3.0	x4.3	x4.2	x1.7
Europe	36.0	38.9	38.6	42.3	46.4	47.6	54.4	58.0	49.6	51.3
EEC	29.8	32.4	32.4	35.7	38.9	44.2	50.7	54.5	46.0	47.4
EFTA	5.7	6.1	6.0	6.4	7.2	2.9	3.3	3.2	3.1	3.4
Oceania	2.5	x1.2	x1.0	1.6	2.1	x2.0	x1.5	x2.1	x3.0	x3.4
France, Monac	7.3	8.1	8.5	9.9	10.1	10.0	10.7	11.6	10.4	11.7
Germany/Allemagne	3.5	4.0	4.2	4.2	5.0	7.0	10.9	12.0	9.1	9.3
USA/Etats–Unis d'Amer	9.6	8.6	8.9	8.8	9.1	9.1	8.2	8.4	10.6	10.4
Canada	8.3	7.6	6.9	5.6	6.8	6.7	7.3	7.9	10.7	9.9
United Kingdom	5.5	5.1	4.4	5.0	5.5	5.5	5.8	6.5	7.1	6.5
Netherlands/Pays–Bas	2.2	2.6	2.6	2.7	2.9	3.5	3.9	4.6	3.2	3.5
Belgium–Luxembourg	1.5	1.8	2.0	2.3	2.4	2.8	3.0	3.8	3.2	3.2
Former USSR/Anc. URSS	21.9	23.2	21.3	19.2	16.5	16.9	x8.6			
Italy/Italie	1.7	1.8	2.0	2.3	2.5	2.7	3.1	3.2	2.5	2.2
Spain/Espagne	1.1	1.5	1.8	1.9	2.3	2.5	3.0	2.7	2.3	2.2

	1985	1986	1987	1988	1989	1990	1991	1992	1993	1994
Afrique	0.2	0.3	0.2	0.2	x0.3	0.3	0.3	0.3	0.2	x0.1
Afrique du Nord	0.0	0.1	0.0	0.1	x0.0	0.0	0.1	0.1	0.0	0.0
Amériques	23.1	18.2	15.7	16.4	23.6	23.6	23.7	25.1	31.8	30.0
ALAI	1.2	1.0	0.8	1.0	1.4	1.3	1.2	1.4	2.2	2.5
MCAC	0.0	0.0	0.0	0.0	0.0	0.0	0.0	0.0	x0.0	x0.0
Asie	6.3	5.7	x5.7	x4.5	4.2	4.2	5.1	5.3	5.0	4.3
Moyen–Orient	0.3	0.2	0.3	0.2	0.1	0.1	0.1	0.1	0.1	0.1
Europe	57.9	60.8	50.0	50.8	61.2	62.5	67.5	66.8	59.7	62.5
CEE	51.5	53.4	44.0	44.5	53.9	60.0	65.4	64.5	57.7	60.4
AELE	6.1	7.1	5.8	5.9	7.2	2.1	2.0	2.0	1.8	1.9
Océanie	1.0	x0.8	x0.7	x0.8	0.9	x0.9	x0.8	x1.0	x1.3	x1.0
USA/Etats–Unis d'Amer	16.6	12.7	10.5	11.2	15.9	17.0	18.5	19.8	24.3	22.6
Germany/Allemagne	15.6	16.8	13.1	12.8	15.5	16.2	22.1	19.4	17.1	16.8
Italy/Italie	7.1	7.0	6.0	6.4	8.5	8.6	8.6	9.2	9.7	10.0
France, Monac	6.2	5.9	4.7	5.0	6.3	7.3	7.3	7.7	6.7	6.6
Netherlands/Pays–Bas	4.5	4.8	4.1	4.1	4.8	5.6	5.6	6.1	6.0	5.5
Belgium–Luxembourg	4.5	4.5	4.2	4.3	5.1	5.4	5.0	5.0	3.9	4.8
Denmark/Danemark	4.0	4.1	3.0	3.2	3.3	4.4	4.5	4.8	4.0	4.9
Canada	5.3	4.4	4.2	4.0	6.3	5.3	4.0	3.9	5.2	4.9
United Kingdom	4.3	4.0	3.7	3.7	4.2	4.7	4.7	4.3	3.3	3.5
Japan/Japon	5.3	5.0	4.5	3.3	3.1	3.1	3.7	3.9	3.4	2.8

TRADE BY COMMODITY IN THOUSAND U.S. DOLLARS – COMMERCE PAR PRODUIT EN MILLIERS DE DOLLARS E.U

COUNTRIES–PAYS	IMPORTS – IMPORTATIONS 1990	1991	1992	1993	1994
Total	6854909	5984604	6210529	5550470	7043833
Africa	x368126	x371574	x330969	x288409	x375230
Northern Africa	185702	236101	x183963	x119827	x103726
Americas	2240753	1878699	2071234	2056256	x2670922
LAIA	223939	241188	279348	211075	281045
CACM	65425	76630	121319	x31165	x35086
Asia	742578	x915286	x1038574	x828959	x814640
Middle East	113372	x386491	x428034	x191925	x114514
Europe	3137642	2560478	2566527	2086466	2783264
EEC	2882894	2384933	2386416	1907501	2534593
EFTA	197751	163122	141024	143957	203137
Oceania	x249740	x108355	x151961	x224105	x320248
USA/Etats–Unis d'Amer	1555167	1171881	1265671	1327788	1829853
France, Monac	682360	547067	480814	417673	596112
Canada	367500	345296	369196	450066	473484
Germany/Allemagne	318757	394488	427317	312405	309975
United Kingdom	298811	230525	240738	347435	391945
Spain/Espagne	193054	212970	178216	134622	254510
Netherlands/Pays–Bas	198698	161237	215064	92730	154051
Thailand/Thaïlande	245138	149736	140299	164723	211690
Iran (Islamic Rp. of)		x174061	x214419	x45378	x11410
Austria/Autriche	133801	129878	142847	132356	139898
Japan/Japon	163849	122891	114281	124545	158430
Italy/Italie	132204	110121	129782	90861	126162
Australia/Australie	198263	65325	100525	144993	222291
Belgium–Luxembourg	141977	93629	120847	90989	139963
Saudi Arabia	44955	141797	122673	x40666	x23626
Portugal	132996	107697	93031	64336	69656
Switz.Liecht	107425	87530	82310	84195	106018
Denmark/Danemark	138332	97060	78823	49652	93750
Korea, Republic of	57457	71017	81845	69479	72399
Greece/Grèce	93875	84752	99188	35594	31896
Sweden/Suède	133838	72155	68995	43245	83007
Mexico/Mexique	83234	83563	69978	28297	52120
Finland/Finlande	209616	87846	47857	43394	69481
Norway,SVD,JM	85928	68414	53475	55398	93425
China/Chine	13629	15859	77862	80835	51015
Ireland/Irlande	74574	55510	62898	52211	74188
Tunisia/Tunisie	24849	42781	66568	59236	26999
Pakistan	30745	40823	59720	43569	37255
So. Africa Customs Un	67495	36784	33400	70934	129587
New Zealand	44454	25223	40484	65843	80370
Guatemala	38158	49713	71460	8455	10730
Venezuela	20234	53118	53208	15431	3531
Korea Dem People's Rp	x35135	x33621	x41566	x33962	x23272
Russian Federation			x41345	x58160	x82088
Algeria/Algérie	40957	86828	11327	1028	342
Chile/Chili	13401	24075	42994	32112	29898
Morocco/Maroc	29844	54410	19813	13935	. 51175
Former USSR/Anc. URSS	39023	x83882			
Argentina/Argentine	10819	15400	34894	32844	55708
Libyan Arab Jamahiriya	34969	16026	x42460	x21267	x9973
Malaysia/Malaisie	24388	22776	24320	28342	27698
Israel/Israël	11783	26933	20421	23869	32972
Syrian Arab Republic	16522	22494	23416	x21161	x21773
Sudan/Soudan	x15046	x18476	x34230	x14154	x5677
Zimbabwe	11909	17919	30220	16819	x40784
Kuwait/ Koweït	4033	17052	25036	15543	11970
Colombia/Colombie	27984	13189	21310	21388	27137
Uruguay	17599	17770	19263	13019	16236
United Arab Emirates	26716	10131	9405	x30126	x18556
Hungary/Hongrie	x21354	25314	x7397	x16675	x23762

COUNTRIES–PAYS	EXPORTS – EXPORTATIONS 1990	1991	1992	1993	1994
Totale	7503725	5834101	5723772	5481771	6711131
Afrique	8970	11265	x30617	x20910	x6110
Afrique du Nord	2104	2591	x24614	x13623	x5316
Amériques	1227059	1207432	1243309	1346216	1621945
ALAI	57201	49505	82011	72346	124457
MCAC	37	194	6	x502	638
Asie	626727	596366	x733947	787506	1015646
Moyen–Orient	15955	7222	6788	x5638	5077
Europe	4640235	3668178	3520224	3162533	3881753
CEE	4509073	3604666	3481923	3141269	3860954
AELE	20586	17137	18839	17172	18498
Océanie	4310	5059	8482	x7924	x5839
Germany/Allemagne	1497309	1247640	1164278	967881	1278304
USA/Etats–Unis d'Amer	960771	1026096	1018469	1046929	1164088
United Kingdom	1373184	959119	996172	943140	1165149
Italy/Italie	800642	768348	658622	668770	725100
Japan/Japon	558326	535350	628673	690081	916289
France, Monac	349799	271429	282947	250958	340003
Canada	208278	130213	142462	218305	327179
Czechoslovakia		x164861	x110275		
Belgium–Luxembourg	184156	109988	111920	47816	42548
Finland/Finlande	112111	86286	83766	89692	142200
Austria/Autriche	96057	79604	75758	72460	x73036
Russian Federation			x117844	x87496	x65445
Brazil/Brésil	42238	46495	73240	51893	62138
Romania/Roumanie	58270	52740	45333	38462	26020
Netherlands/Pays–Bas	39638	35945	47245	43312	36686
China/Chine	40083	41529	37017	47172	41438
Former USSR/Anc. URSS	905324	x104250			
Poland/Pologne	29911	20852	27415	26296	55940
Czech Republic				68164	85503
Belarus/Bélarus			x34521	x29409	x35828
Sweden/Suède	19214	16746	22944	16772	21247
Denmark/Danemark	15919	15110	15668	17552	21227
Yugoslavia SFR	110320	x46329			
Switz.Liecht	18058	15231	15277	15338	16626
Libyan Arab Jamahiriya			x24559	x13394	x4822
Kazakstan			x25228	x5654	
Spain/Espagne	13026	6051	10840	10895	11340
Singapore/Singapour	4585	5487	4812	9556	4346
Ireland/Irlande	6906	6157	6982	5494	
Slovakia				x16365	x11250
Turkmenistan/Turkménistn			x13788	x1909	x713
Australia/Australie	2637	2884	5958	5924	3196
Korea, Republic of	1882	1540	1306	11332	21383
So. Africa Customs Un	2707	4681	4929	4445	
Mexico/Mexique	13922	1519	1725	9728	43279
India/Inde	2673	1867	5321	5742	12117
Croatia/Croatie			10397	2138	x1271
Thailand/Thaïlande	1163	1519	4461	5349	7110
Bulgaria/Bulgarie	x710	x1808	x2291	x5262	x363
Portugal	754	2210	3700	2844	3799
Ukraine			x3292	x5334	x3806
Yugoslavia/Yougoslavie			x7636	x900	x257
Saudi Arabia	9789	3817	3484	x696	
Norway,SVD,JM	2527	1764	3562	1526	1873
Kuwait/ Koweït	615	1823	2551	2313	3963
Peru/Pérou		8	5320	1286	114
Colombia/Colombie		78	49	6107	13046
Lithuania/Lituanie			46	x5434	3765
Anguilla	x4	x127	x5	x5276	x5276
Greece/Grèce	359	31	1082	3683	314

(VALUE AS % OF TOTAL)(VALEUR EN % DU TOTAL)

	1985	1986	1987	1988	1989	1990	1991	1992	1993	1994
Africa	4.8	x6.7	x5.0	x7.6	x4.8	x5.4	x6.2	x5.3	x5.2	x5.3
Northern Africa	2.7	3.0	1.8	2.1	1.2	2.7	3.9	x3.0	x2.2	x1.5
Americas	39.0	37.4	35.0	32.3	32.1	32.6	31.4	33.3	37.0	x37.9
LAIA	3.4	5.0	4.3	4.6	3.8	3.3	4.0	4.5	3.8	4.0
CACM	0.7	0.5	x0.5	0.7	0.5	1.0	1.3	2.0	x0.6	x0.5
Asia	7.6	x9.1	x7.7	x8.5	x8.9	10.9	x15.3	x16.8	x15.0	x11.5
Middle East	2.5	x4.8	x2.5	x2.3	x2.1	1.7	x6.5	x6.9	x3.5	x1.6
Europe	41.7	42.6	45.0	44.3	47.7	45.8	42.8	41.3	37.6	39.5
EEC	32.0	32.8	35.2	34.8	37.3	42.1	39.9	38.4	34.4	36.0
EFTA	8.9	9.0	9.1	8.8	9.5	2.9	2.7	2.3	2.6	2.9
Oceania	5.7	x1.9	x1.6	2.6	x3.9	x3.6	x1.8	x2.5	x4.0	x4.5
USA/Etats–Unis d'Amer	20.0	19.7	19.6	19.1	19.6	22.7	19.6	20.4	23.9	26.0
France, Monac	7.6	7.8	8.6	8.8	9.0	10.0	9.1	7.7	7.5	8.5
Canada	11.5	9.1	8.0	5.6	6.4	5.4	5.8	5.9	8.1	6.7
Germany/Allemagne	2.1	2.6	2.9	2.6	2.6	4.7	6.6	6.9	5.6	4.4
United Kingdom	4.3	3.4	3.9	4.5	4.4	4.4	3.9	3.9	6.3	5.6
Spain/Espagne	1.1	1.9	2.6	3.0	3.4	2.8	3.6	2.9	2.4	3.6
Netherlands/Pays–Bas	2.6	3.3	2.9	2.3	2.4	2.9	2.7	3.5	1.7	2.2
Thailand/Thaïlande	1.0	0.7	1.1	1.7	2.4	3.6	2.5	2.3	3.0	3.0
Iran (Islamic Rp. of)		x1.2	x0.7	x0.1	x0.6		x2.9	x3.5	x0.8	x0.2
Austria/Autriche	1.3	1.4	1.7	1.6	1.5	2.0	2.2	2.3	2.4	2.0

	1985	1986	1987	1988	1989	1990	1991	1992	1993	1994
Afrique		0.2	0.1	0.2	x0.1	0.1	0.2	x0.5	x0.4	x0.1
Afrique du Nord		x0.0	0.0	0.2	x0.1	0.0	0.0	x0.4	x0.2	x0.1
Amériques	19.5	15.6	14.4	19.3	20.3	16.4	20.7	21.7	24.6	24.1
ALAI	1.7	1.9	2.3	3.4	2.3	0.8	0.8	1.4	1.3	1.9
MCAC		x0.0	x0.0	x0.0	x0.0	0.0	0.0	0.0	x0.0	0.0
Asie	15.4	x15.3	15.0	10.2	8.8	8.3	10.2	x12.8	14.4	15.1
Moyen–Orient	0.7	x0.1	x0.0	0.2	0.2	0.2	0.1	0.1	x0.1	0.1
Europe	50.8	50.8	51.1	51.8	52.7	61.8	62.9	61.5	57.7	57.8
CEE	46.5	46.1	46.8	47.6	49.0	60.1	61.8	60.8	57.3	57.5
AELE	2.9	3.1	3.0	3.1	2.9	0.3	0.3	0.3	0.3	0.3
Océanie		x0.0	x0.1	0.1	0.1	0.1	0.1	0.1	x0.1	x0.1
Germany/Allemagne	15.8	15.3	14.3	14.3	15.6	20.0	21.4	20.3	17.7	19.0
USA/Etats–Unis d'Amer	15.1	11.8	10.3	12.5	13.8	12.8	17.6	17.8	19.1	17.3
United Kingdom	11.2	11.3	12.9	13.9	13.8	18.3	16.4	17.4	17.2	17.4
Italy/Italie	10.3	10.3	9.9	10.1	11.0	10.7	13.2	11.5	12.2	10.8
Japan/Japon	14.5	15.1	14.3	9.5	8.3	7.4	9.2	11.0	12.6	13.7
France, Monac	4.8	4.4	4.6	4.1	3.9	4.7	4.7	4.9	4.6	5.1
Canada	2.7	1.9	1.7	3.4	4.0	2.8	2.2	2.5	4.0	4.9
Czechoslovakia	3.1	3.6	3.2	3.3	x1.7		x2.8	x1.9		
Belgium–Luxembourg	0.8	1.1	1.3	1.7	1.4	2.5	1.9	2.0	0.9	0.6
Finland/Finlande	1.3	1.5	1.3	1.4	1.3	1.5	1.5	1.5	1.6	2.1

TRADE BY COMMODITY IN THOUSAND U.S. DOLLARS – COMMERCE PAR PRODUIT EN MILLIERS DE DOLLARS E.U

COUNTRIES–PAYS	IMPORTS – IMPORTATIONS 1990	1991	1992	1993	1994
Total	19237159	16416043	17049048	15861742	18054493
Africa	x1291910	x1034992	x1190622	x991232	x1238312
Northern Africa	519627	373120	x382378	x313704	x316527
Americas	3655276	2844826	3228350	3807273	5627853
LAIA	695089	892172	1180120	1142465	1542926
CACM	36951	33599	46987	x46503	x70959
Asia	4254256	x5430123	x5520371	x5837798	x5156574
Middle East	1043967	x2148948	x2183899	x1925731	x1069019
Europe	7158687	5980933	6093327	4241769	4900072
EEC	6489179	5352927	5556573	3776681	4326359
EFTA	566728	573582	500539	417448	493441
Oceania	x608664	x448428	x823209	x654836	x857410
Germany/Allemagne	1324903	1286059	1777089	952980	915234
USA/Etats-Unis d'Amer	1785975	1018032	1251585	1705115	2649655
Iran (Islamic Rp. of)		x992840	x793783	x386352	x76677
Canada	935438	697790	617938	793806	1220872
Singapore/Singapour	634322	709146	667089	720025	754679
United Kingdom	775806	623759	642171	573645	733170
France, Monac	901708	677498	643514	501416	628434
China/Chine	416190	364786	528936	783442	501559
Italy/Italie	633293	607634	572063	295030	320305
Australia/Australie	454304	315780	618360	458383	649910
Mexico/Mexique	239174	406741	491651	382512	525943
Indonesia/Indonésie	409718	437063	346190	410201	520883
Netherlands/Pays-Bas	404617	388833	432870	362001	414423
Thailand/Thaïlande	340682	343395	332332	414608	601334
Spain/Espagne	857035	609559	304737	155412	229090
Norway, SVD, JM	259482	356840	338933	290869	318529
Korea, Republic of	361669	387692	339832	233808	238928
Malaysia/Malaisie	399579	396651	273935	265420	345355
Russian Federation			x385999	x522726	x357677
Hong Kong	106196	123778	341261	424915	277180
Saudi Arabia	80067	290920	254637	x247777	x172158
Belgium–Luxembourg	318845	277313	280240	230519	291691
United Arab Emirates	197533	182516	222765	x363201	x302750
Austria/Autriche	260617	235609	260563	211747	262261
Nigeria/Nigéria	x125000	160224	x290791	x224169	x171266
Oman	138574	205995	156969	197861	173326
Kuwait/Koweït	60457	147776	273111	134598	85779
Former USSR/Anc. URSS	1903509	x478513			
Chile/Chili	144385	103684	178445	195774	202827
Portugal	200410	176818	193448	106327	108269
Turkey/Turquie	129273	152087	130658	182620	81859
Switz.Liecht	292777	197680	150958	116631	167023
Israel/Israël	64873	171983	116569	153934	171516
So. Africa Customs Un	177175	136092	160072	114822	159407
Denmark/Danemark	204542	107054	132699	130588	128034
Venezuela	74076	139259	158908	71216	53919
Japan/Japon	229892	140646	105471	99375	136912
Greece/Grèce	75371	83508	137546	108425	67272
Sweden/Suède	263996	155105	93625	78619	104220
Qatar	248608	85005	139300	65956	x19167
Colombia/Colombie	70116	45501	120472	109643	167824
New Zealand	51890	44730	132003	83493	126120
Libyan Arab Jamahiriya	146945	98106	x72666	x65892	x76652
Poland/Pologne	83078	77663	46318	111566	50006
Brazil/Brésil	31811	57711	82974	83178	72120
Pakistan	18141	34989	88929	96914	83960
Jordan/Jordanie	26064	24113	71055	120193	20983
Morocco/Maroc	65060	73296	94486	43992	27967
Algeria/Algérie	165116	76070	78300	57047	58357
Papua New Guinea	74146	x66245	x57228	x82934	x50821

COUNTRIES–PAYS	EXPORTS – EXPORTATIONS 1990	1991	1992	1993	1994
Totale	19491995	18037217	18661645	18126784	21089420
Afrique	x60035	134000	x55976	x59406	x17229
Afrique du Nord	14212	8527	x6049	x1635	6061
Amériques	5193012	6182747	6117241	6076787	6874801
ALAI	256023	229148	323657	344584	565142
MCAC	92	244	257	x444	x665
Asie	3515014	3278216	4032504	4570841	5071469
Moyen-Orient	167880	66738	67363	x125425	x168384
Europe	9017565	7923360	8111462	7133214	8838413
CEE	8788413	7750202	7928535	6977306	8676439
AELE	175524	163034	171001	140337	148081
Océanie	88263	122846	156317	123988	x99243
USA/Etats-Unis d'Amer	4498278	5582530	5532974	5407903	5953843
Japan/Japon	2694504	2410036	2922609	3219792	3534168
Germany/Allemagne	1903839	1653499	1611138	1474712	1659639
United Kingdom	1609920	1516798	1570177	1287731	1530200
France, Monac	1395429	1183029	1234527	1005221	1270505
Sweden/Suède	1007936	928083	935565	847095	1093212
Belgium–Luxembourg	1104816	851452	856401	749970	1252309
Italy/Italie	729992	680531	682193	685301	809831
Singapore/Singapour	385777	460205	453982	511264	587347
Netherlands/Pays-Bas	314821	324200	356212	284618	338883
Canada	434582	365539	254636	318010	348491
Austria/Autriche	291973	281785	307567	303359	x329106
Brazil/Brésil	189115	179672	248403	252465	458346
Hong Kong	48789	72634	236036	266489	131626
Finland/Finlande	280707	174762	198007	195454	215680
Korea, Republic of	78819	101143	135946	240739	429960
Russian Federation			x149301	x232194	x44562
Australia/Australie	63121	102076	113406	100307	87091
Romania/Roumanie	222524	181844	67179	24816	28715
Norway, SVD, JM	104423	94323	89991	77197	84279
Poland/Pologne	277342	122465	54547	64090	88273
Malaysia/Malaisie	45597	64051	71516	77116	90519
Spain/Espagne	58145	70161	81504	60993	76895
Switz.Liecht	70966	68637	80721	63060	63624
Denmark/Danemark	64999	60427	65287	58688	67466
China/Chine	57744	64972	43156	51557	63645
Mexico/Mexique	54881	34902	50271	46114	51977
So. Africa Customs Un	18854	29012	43307	35716	841
Czechoslovakia		x52983	x38972		
Cameroon/Cameroun	12398	82191	x642	x598	x226
Oman	12366	26029	19126	23342	25534
Papua New Guinea	18306	14558	36223	16245	x1813
Ireland/Irlande	15445	16708	20252	14992	14974
Hungary/Hongrie	x44288	x11493	x18424	x21414	x18051
United Arab Emirates	80552		3	x50372	x69176
Indonesia/Indonésie	7134	790	37205	5414	7830
Kazakstan			x15621	x25876	x4836
Kuwait/Koweït	3423	5787	12646	22991	28102
Thailand/Thaïlande	1020	5493	15846	18756	19501
Pakistan	9815	15884	11265	8805	4003
Saudi Arabia	28755	15468	13306	x2238	x1810
Czech Republic				30537	31862
India/Inde	5503	6849	11757	8793	11989
Colombia/Colombie	11	7015	2961	15914	27860
Jordan/Jordanie	9718	7313	6640	9027	12751
Qatar	18119	165	11310	8674	
Portugal	8123	6867	8866	4344	4886
Former USSR/Anc. URSS	1028952	x18831			
New Zealand	6450	5418	6058	6382	9514
Slovakia				x17387	x17476

(VALUE AS % OF TOTAL)(VALEUR EN % DU TOTAL)

	1985	1986	1987	1988	1989	1990	1991	1992	1993	1994
Africa	6.0	x7.3	x6.3	x5.5	x5.7	x6.7	x6.3	x6.9	x6.2	x6.9
Northern Africa	3.8	3.2	1.4	1.7	2.0	2.7	2.3	x2.2	x2.0	x1.8
Americas	28.8	24.5	23.1	24.3	20.7	19.0	17.4	19.0	24.0	31.1
LAIA	3.5	2.7	2.4	3.0	3.0	3.6	5.4	6.9	7.2	8.5
CACM	0.4	0.1	x0.2	0.1	0.3	0.2	0.2	0.3	x0.3	x0.4
Asia	20.0	x16.8	x16.0	17.3	18.4	22.1	x33.1	x32.4	x36.8	x28.6
Middle East	8.2	x8.3	x5.8	x4.6	x4.5	5.4	x13.1	x12.8	x12.1	x5.9
Europe	28.0	30.2	33.7	33.4	35.9	37.2	36.4	35.7	26.7	27.1
EEC	21.4	22.8	26.4	27.0	29.0	33.7	32.6	32.6	23.8	24.0
EFTA	5.3	6.5	6.7	6.0	6.3	2.9	3.5	2.9	2.6	2.7
Oceania	4.0	x2.9	2.4	2.6	3.8	x3.1	x2.7	x4.8	x4.1	x4.8
Germany/Allemagne	3.4	3.6	3.7	3.2	3.6	6.9	7.8	10.4	6.0	5.1
USA/Etats-Unis d'Amer	15.6	14.5	13.8	13.9	9.9	9.3	6.2	7.3	10.7	14.7
Iran (Islamic Rp. of)		x0.7	x0.7	x0.6	x0.4		x6.0	x4.7	x2.4	x0.4
Canada	8.0	6.2	6.2	6.3	5.8	4.9	4.3	3.6	5.0	6.8
Singapore/Singapour	2.2	1.4	1.2	1.9	2.4	3.3	4.3	3.9	4.5	4.2
United Kingdom	4.0	3.6	4.2	4.9	4.8	4.0	3.8	3.8	3.6	4.1
France, Monac	3.0	3.6	4.5	4.8	4.9	4.7	4.1	3.8	3.2	3.5
China/Chine			2.4	1.8	2.0	2.2	2.2	3.1	4.9	2.8
Italy/Italie	2.3	2.6	3.5	2.7	2.9	3.3	3.7	3.4	1.9	1.8
Australia/Australie	3.3	2.1	1.7	1.8	2.8	2.4	1.9	3.6	2.9	3.6

	1985	1986	1987	1988	1989	1990	1991	1992	1993	1994
Afrique	0.3	x0.4	x0.3	x0.4	x0.4	x0.3	0.8	x0.3	x0.3	x0.1
Afrique du Nord	0.1	x0.0	x0.0	0.1	0.1	0.1	0.0	x0.0	x0.0	0.0
Amériques	31.2	x24.9	19.7	22.7	23.8	26.6	34.3	32.8	33.5	32.6
ALAI	0.6	0.4	0.8	0.9	1.5	1.3	1.3	1.7	1.9	2.7
MCAC	0.0	x0.0	0.0	x0.0	x0.0	0.0	0.0	0.0	x0.0	x0.0
Asie	17.3	16.1	x14.9	16.6	16.3	18.0	18.2	21.6	25.3	24.1
Moyen-Orient	1.1	0.8	x0.7	0.9	x0.7	0.9	0.4	0.4	x0.7	x0.8
Europe	40.8	46.1	48.3	44.9	46.6	46.3	43.9	43.5	39.4	41.9
CEE	33.8	38.2	40.1	37.2	38.5	45.1	43.0	42.5	38.5	41.1
AELE	6.2	7.0	7.5	7.4	7.6	0.9	0.9	0.9	0.8	0.7
Océanie	0.2	0.2	0.4	0.3	0.4	0.5	0.7	0.8	0.7	x0.5
USA/Etats-Unis d'Amer	26.9	20.6	15.7	19.2	20.0	23.1	31.0	29.6	29.8	28.2
Japan/Japon	13.1	13.2	12.1	13.0	13.0	13.8	13.4	15.7	17.8	16.8
Germany/Allemagne	9.3	10.8	11.2	8.7	9.1	9.8	9.2	8.6	8.1	7.9
United Kingdom	6.5	6.2	6.6	6.0	6.5	8.3	8.4	8.4	7.1	7.3
France, Monac	5.2	6.7	6.6	6.3	6.0	7.2	6.6	6.6	5.5	6.0
Sweden/Suède	3.0	3.4	3.8	4.5	4.5	5.2	5.1	5.0	4.7	5.2
Belgium–Luxembourg	3.1	3.5	4.1	4.5	5.1	5.7	4.7	4.6	4.1	5.9
Italy/Italie	2.5	3.0	2.8	2.8	3.0	3.7	3.8	3.7	3.8	3.8
Singapore/Singapour	1.7	1.1	1.1	1.4	1.5	2.0	2.6	2.4	2.8	2.8
Netherlands/Pays-Bas	1.3	1.4	1.4	1.6	1.5	1.6	1.8	1.9	1.6	1.6

TRADE BY COMMODITY IN THOUSAND U.S. DOLLARS – COMMERCE PAR PRODUIT EN MILLIERS DE DOLLARS E.U

IMPORTS – IMPORTATIONS

COUNTRIES–PAYS	1990	1991	1992	1993	1994
Total	23752250	20608144	23230641	22919416	22160992
Africa	x1080147	951111	x1040222	x823966	x818876
Northern Africa	543129	507279	530647	386450	390221
Americas	3883139	3531860	4202097	4503592	4804198
LAIA	1303575	1265919	1464335	1394890	1577357
CACM	52441	51973	78701	x86135	x79257
Asia	7882891	9069766	11558769	12583319	10759988
Middle East	1049564	x1233351	x1935446	x1908103	x1178387
Europe	6805854	5704202	5740029	4294679	4933295
EEC	6214170	5287936	5316338	3922983	4551916
EFTA	415444	320459	319358	284994	277733
Oceania	x198070	x179294	x191115	x222678	x279407
China/Chine	1204129	1552378	3280638	4475203	3352382
USA/Etats–Unis d'Amer	2178236	1932969	2387110	2715062	2763606
Indonesia/Indonésie	1241105	1654779	913542	815077	836924
Korea, Republic of	1040388	1080922	1056106	1006179	1315724
Hong Kong	648284	824159	1086941	1145868	893437
Germany/Allemagne	997040	969333	991175	770412	827943
Italy/Italie	1182805	977161	943962	709010	926960
Turkey/Turquie	873409	621282	824082	1111228	685160
Pakistan	303072	598858	782249	690169	305000
France,Monac	875985	734371	760663	514787	572866
Thailand/Thaïlande	633977	703606	637495	567192	544308
Iran (Islamic Rp. of)		x459095	x862497	x532475	x128712
United Kingdom	645782	588485	643690	540485	578320
Japan/Japon	605598	541042	533725	432858	467576
Mexico/Mexique	458164	405753	508793	384997	527394
Belgium–Luxembourg	518104	450784	454289	336699	438074
Brazil/Brésil	434350	377093	279729	372414	556999
India/Inde	311192	158017	357068	460996	670864
Spain/Espagne	439566	392575	358611	221057	307363
Portugal	493806	333116	325094	198872	212648
Malaysia/Malaisie	261716	248465	322382	265227	276849
Switz.Liecht	378081	282932	280975	253637	238845
Russian Federation			x297495	x410973	x167973
Former USSR/Anc. URSS	2842493	x690946			
Canada	291067	221290	213146	252332	301471
Netherlands/Pays–Bas	292768	227220	218409	173170	161196
Singapore/Singapour	233262	180954	195992	212372	218165
So. Africa Customs Un	274255	180146	212817	178832	228081
Argentina/Argentine	59115	137065	239091	184631	165969
Austria/Autriche	240969	205392	189223	136382	144597
Egypt/Egypte	137828	168836	182582	159885	124601
Australia/Australie	161330	151083	155305	188816	237720
Greece/Grèce	208765	155633	183837	135516	126532
Poland/Pologne	119758	128866	116479	134261	171803
Colombia/Colombie	95038	80974	120775	171966	103015
Tunisia/Tunisie	140628	142176	132699	95209	87889
Morocco/Maroc	189788	152682	135103	80088	83709
Philippines	117218	90651	121601	110533	162689
Israel/Israël	77109	77397	111849	122066	115144
Nigeria/Nigéria	x53342	93758	x127019	x89777	x39204
Czechoslovakia	246987	x112672	x187119		
Romania/Roumanie	138604	86763	88220	81654	100548
Hungary/Hongrie	x103196	82544	x74827	x77709	x72272
Chile/Chili	61818	60117	88186	76099	55634
Venezuela	38632	64422	86645	56751	28553
Sweden/Suède	93841	75348	68540	59765	77721
Syrian Arab Republic	32703	x21694	64707	x113827	x184354
Sri Lanka	24415	46515	77316	75685	58784
Denmark/Danemark	73938	67968	78310	50001	64427
Saudi Arabia	35667	53065	78249	x42705	x62247

EXPORTS – EXPORTATIONS

COUNTRIES–PAYS	1990	1991	1992	1993	1994
Totale	21435519	19734904	22015406	21407420	21092335
Afrique	14027	14540	26186	23419	x10713
Afrique du Nord	4810	3342	9248	9121	5864
Amériques	1294057	1314084	1303729	1307116	1394234
ALAI	133914	162641	148732	162595	157536
MCAC	369	924	2086	x870	x1924
Asie	5503457	6195582	7144897	7191856	6762423
Moyen–Orient	21313	22593	24094	x33005	x40955
Europe	13868710	11946488	13327841	12650310	12700137
CEE	11596344	10144242	11408577	10924605	10898293
AELE	2238347	1786474	1894098	1709573	1781516
Océanie	x18592	x23173	x23731	x28447	x24857
Germany/Allemagne	5713997	5040611	5847477	5811178	5633353
Japan/Japon	4068699	4563150	5074379	4891706	4510556
Italy/Italie	2695815	2323762	2620833	2546449	2522174
Switz.Liecht	2221445	1772207	1884629	1704349	1772072
USA/Etats–Unis d'Amer	1107095	1098720	1098630	1094131	1184905
Hong Kong	643737	796422	1135642	1221442	967534
France,Monac	875354	745787	863161	748132	863187
United Kingdom	760185	677329	707524	637956	657155
Korea, Republic of	269789	333126	396661	462884	612844
Belgium–Luxembourg	319507	302319	327871	261500	289131
China/Chine	214575	219767	266070	307210	304131
Spain/Espagne	289793	253167	234952	207883	224489
Netherlands/Pays–Bas	323731	252167	247042	193928	200547
Sweden/Suède	226475	198153	184170	168827	192385
Austria/Autriche	199283	162753	174623	184625	x137967
Singapore/Singapour	140277	141138	117795	138427	157166
Brazil/Brésil	106522	124929	118451	129110	121603
Czechoslovakia		x159497	x122370		
Denmark/Danemark	101951	88741	102842	78412	82826
India/Inde	99941	75392	65693	58266	73526
Portugal	44139	51360	52456	49854	51732
Canada	51881	51311	52292	47460	47044
Czech Republic				139548	139029
Poland/Pologne	56505	33441	39261	29888	31215
Thailand/Thaïlande	9916	13697	21753	34937	41358
Mexico/Mexique	16498	17809	22126	23242	20560
Turkey/Turquie	8165	15630	17697	23011	29165
Finland/Finlande	20275	20162	20054	13036	13560
Australia/Australie	11235	17482	12776	15888	18128
Greece/Grèce	9009	11744	13014	14476	17710
Hungary/Hongrie	x29274	x13435	x11461	x14091	x14721
Malaysia/Malaisie	7996	8089	12147	18718	20357
Ireland/Irlande	16793	16149	12559	8350	12077
Russian Federation			x15312	x19294	x18458
So. Africa Customs Un	5216	7929	11977	8466	
Norway,SVD,JM	15986	13628	9336	5077	9428
New Zealand	5863	5409	10187	10669	6495
Slovenia/Slovénia			13706	10495	12788
Former USSR/Anc. URSS	570603	x21658			
Romania/Roumanie	20473	6405	6664	5083	3782
Israel/Israël	11933	4912	7591	5509	11910
Argentina/Argentine	6209	6282	4257	4768	6075
Yugoslavia SFR	31133	x14381			
Indonesia/Indonésie	4132	1876	6174	4251	4139
Colombia/Colombie	1917	9059	1031	1475	2243
Korea Dem People's Rp	x3970	x8048	x1816	x1634	x1009
Macau/Macao	3058	2081	4358	4643	4481
Slovakia				x8779	x9914
Former GDR	x39450	x4364	x4364		
Bulgaria/Bulgarie	x18671	x2144	x4684	x1889	x943

(VALUE AS % OF TOTAL)(VALEUR EN % DU TOTAL)

Imports

	1985	1986	1987	1988	1989	1990	1991	1992	1993	1994
Africa	5.9	x5.1	x3.9	x4.6	x4.3	x4.6	4.6	x4.5	x3.6	x3.7
Northern Africa	3.3	2.2	1.7	1.8	2.0	2.3	2.5	2.3	1.7	1.8
Americas	22.3	21.7	17.9	18.4	17.3	16.4	17.2	18.1	19.6	21.6
LAIA	5.7	5.7	5.0	5.6	5.3	5.5	6.1	6.3	6.1	7.1
CACM	0.4	0.4	0.4	0.2	0.3	0.2	0.3	0.3	x0.4	x0.4
Asia	18.3	19.5	x30.1	x29.3	31.3	33.2	44.0	49.8	54.9	48.5
Middle East	3.8	x5.0	x3.0	x2.6	x2.7	4.4	x6.0	x8.3	x8.3	x5.3
Europe	35.4	37.2	31.4	30.1	28.6	28.7	27.7	24.7	18.7	22.3
EEC	29.0	31.3	26.9	26.2	24.6	26.2	25.7	22.9	17.1	20.5
EFTA	4.4	4.3	3.5	3.2	3.1	1.7	1.6	1.4	1.2	1.3
Oceania	2.1	x1.5	x1.0	1.0	1.3	x0.8	x0.8	x0.8	x0.9	x1.2
China/Chine			6.8	6.5	8.8	5.1	7.5	14.1	19.5	15.1
USA/Etats–Unis d'Amer	13.4	12.7	10.4	10.1	9.8	9.2	9.4	10.3	11.8	12.5
Indonesia/Indonésie	1.2	1.3	1.0	1.3	2.6	5.2	8.0	3.9	3.6	3.8
Korea, Republic of	2.4	2.5	4.1	3.4	3.9	4.4	5.2	4.5	4.4	5.9
Hong Kong	3.1	3.0	3.1	3.1	3.1	2.7	4.0	4.7	5.0	4.0
Germany/Allemagne	4.8	5.0	4.0	3.7	3.8	4.2	4.7	4.3	3.4	3.7
Italy/Italie	5.2	5.9	5.3	5.1	4.6	5.0	4.7	4.1	3.1	4.2
Turkey/Turquie	2.9	2.9	2.0	1.7	1.9	3.7	3.0	3.5	4.8	3.1
Pakistan	0.9	1.1	0.8	1.2	1.2	1.3	2.9	3.4	3.0	1.4
France,Monac	4.3	4.5	3.7	3.5	3.3	3.7	3.6	3.3	2.2	2.6

Exports

	1985	1986	1987	1988	1989	1990	1991	1992	1993	1994
Afrique	0.1	x0.1	x0.0	x0.0	x0.1			0.2	0.1	x0.1
Afrique du Nord	0.0	0.0	0.0	0.0	x0.1	0.0	0.0	0.0	0.0	0.0
Amériques	6.9	5.5	4.9	5.2	6.7	6.0	6.6	5.9	6.1	6.6
ALAI	0.7	0.5	0.5	0.5	0.6	0.6	0.8	0.7	0.8	0.7
MCAC	0.0	x0.0	0.0	x0.0	0.0	0.0	0.0	0.0	x0.0	x0.0
Asie	20.1	18.8	x23.8	x25.1	25.4	25.6	31.3	32.5	33.6	32.0
Moyen–Orient	0.9	0.2	2.0	0.5	x0.1	0.1	0.1	0.1	x0.2	x0.2
Europe	62.3	66.6	60.9	59.9	63.6	64.7	60.5	60.5	59.1	60.2
CEE	48.7	52.4	48.3	47.8	51.5	54.1	51.4	51.8	51.0	51.7
AELE	13.2	13.9	12.3	12.0	11.9	10.4	9.1	8.6	8.0	8.4
Océanie	0.1	x0.1	x0.1	x0.1	x0.1	x0.1	x0.1	x0.1	x0.1	x0.1
Germany/Allemagne	23.9	26.1	23.6	23.8	24.8	26.7	25.5	26.6	27.1	26.7
Japan/Japon	15.5	15.5	14.9	15.7	18.8	19.0	23.1	23.0	22.9	21.4
Italy/Italie	10.2	10.8	10.6	11.0	12.6	12.6	11.8	11.9	11.9	12.0
Switz.Liecht	10.7	11.5	10.1	10.2	10.0	10.4	9.0	8.6	8.0	8.4
USA/Etats–Unis d'Amer	5.3	4.4	3.8	4.4	5.7	5.2	5.6	5.0	5.1	5.6
Hong Kong	2.3	1.8	2.5	3.1	3.4	3.0	4.0	5.2	5.7	4.6
France,Monac	3.2	3.5	3.3	3.5	3.8	4.1	3.8	3.9	3.5	4.1
United Kingdom	3.6	3.3	2.9	3.3	3.4	3.5	3.4	3.2	3.0	3.1
Korea, Republic of	0.3	0.3	0.4	0.7	1.1	1.3	1.7	1.8	2.2	2.9
Belgium–Luxembourg	2.2	2.6	2.5	1.3	1.5	1.5	1.5	1.5	1.2	1.4

TRADE BY COMMODITY IN THOUSAND U.S. DOLLARS – COMMERCE PAR PRODUIT EN MILLIERS DE DOLLARS E.U

COUNTRIES–PAYS	IMPORTS – IMPORTATIONS 1990	1991	1992	1993	1994
Total	7228694	6924198	5815557	5455166	5648757
Africa	146364	127858	x118907	x106988	x178734
Northern Africa	35321	31783	50181	33931	35654
Americas	1691218	1147647	1123641	1200746	1392596
LAIA	458406	265015	300913	328174	345583
CACM	11802	9458	14548	x15811	x8418
Asia	1155338	1658910	1426234	1912778	x1743910
Middle East	58993	x114605	x162783	x94901	x242629
Europe	3542415	3518110	2937442	1911990	2016287
EEC	3295080	3295713	2628946	1748825	1839264
EFTA	209622	200248	274666	142685	149150
Oceania	x108612	x111264	x73462	x130883	x137627
USA/Etats–Unis d'Amer	783544	619142	579338	656232	807319
Germany/Allemagne	637832	673937	558428	343717	432300
France,Monac	629590	671050	495816	239738	240806
Indonesia/Indonésie	199033	408547	253302	547796	388718
United Kingdom	263872	276997	282862	324660	232033
Italy/Italie	367976	333924	265713	178723	180051
China/Chine	77318	172709	230535	325282	366071
Korea, Republic of	174462	280503	190922	246881	170590
Canada	414258	231206	215275	176224	217231
Thailand/Thaïlande	138361	187424	122286	245173	75754
Netherlands/Pays–Bas	164456	253077	176041	121784	131278
Belgium–Luxembourg	157551	292392	170611	80048	101002
Japan/Japon	247726	187003	142772	126249	102201
Sweden/Suède	296149	169718	143854	142222	148070
Spain/Espagne	176242	186007	154816	83408	80365
Austria/Autriche	186472	131087	124866	98122	132151
Switz.Liecht	125703	122212	136682	94703	100296
Malaysia/Malaisie	92138	139657	114718	60781	69553
Mexico/Mexique	124487	79749	115263	102093	127328
Norway,SVD,JM	83644	77546	137449	47546	48004
Finland/Finlande	175090	108540	92759	53548	76944
Hong Kong	36011	51579	76035	102802	102530
Australia/Australie	64832	85916	52537	90705	113520
Former USSR/Anc. URSS	254847	x222909			
Singapore/Singapour	44896	55222	48260	85079	53591
Portugal	138377	112589	48513	27070	18464
Brazil/Brésil	82722	73768	62586	45412	70168
Denmark/Danemark	57682	48774	79228	24244	24186
So. Africa Customs Un	66926	59088	40286	41893	117258
Russian Federation			x86423	x48905	x52603
Iran (Islamic Rp. of)		x27298	x82825	x23576	x95066
Chile/Chili	164234	51935	28101	46787	34533
Poland/Pologne	41052	29250	36761	55361	62999
Turkey/Turquie	31798	60130	32364	25009	21498
Czechoslovakia	196088	x51922	x59139		
Hungary/Hongrie	x16623	41189	x28213	x23538	x24764
Argentina/Argentine	6859	9398	29677	47430	49084
Venezuela	25836	15942	30211	39933	25037
New Zealand	42427	22534	19504	38512	23106
Slovakia				x75989	x36938
Saudi Arabia	7686	15699	29292	x21688	x88880
Colombia/Colombie	43572	14623	21445	29229	24928
Israel/Israël	17799	22136	17995	24190	30076
Greece/Grèce	18797	18947	21080	23752	22341
Philippines	19454	11320	18827	20387	61063
India/Inde	20105	8207	23028	10837	34596
Ireland/Irlande	24993	18674	14359	7789	19271
Pakistan	5203	10141	16345	10611	8230
Morocco/Maroc	8093	13470	13712	9174	14675
Tunisia/Tunisie	7982	4502	20342	9873	4495

COUNTRIES–PAYS	EXPORTS – EXPORTATIONS 1990	1991	1992	1993	1994
Totale	6689257	6717793	5636526	5223197	5511636
Afrique	3370	x2710	4104	x6372	x844
Afrique du Nord	261	467	354	843	x449
Amériques	846788	916261	793190	901767	890552
ALAI	73661	89561	68525	102944	71639
MCAC	21	83	59	x264	x235
Asie	497816	667815	482478	542143	548167
Moyen–Orient	1942	792	1649	x2145	x2965
Europe	5307524	5006032	4292518	3741848	4040583
CEE	4737441	4455453	3772121	3297973	3542797
AELE	567267	548730	517305	441092	494055
Océanie	x11759	x15437	x11711	x13890	x13811
Germany/Allemagne	1625275	1730268	1465189	1118230	1291244
USA/Etats–Unis d'Amer	590696	627130	578599	643277	627647
Italy/Italie	523101	551361	464295	456034	480736
Switz.Liecht	508426	487589	467577	393727	456256
Sweden/Suède	513345	500652	407955	303589	347735
Finland/Finlande	834005	361551	358422	487995	526736
Japan/Japon	417104	543514	327622	333381	343073
United Kingdom	341455	458148	322075	283730	265902
France,Monac	300779	276214	245276	221656	250893
Austria/Autriche	281133	217690	208389	184157	x120043
Canada	179694	197032	143902	153331	190212
Spain/Espagne	133951	121413	105168	101384	90985
Netherlands/Pays–Bas	92615	123806	91378	67841	78517
Hong Kong	29125	53259	84711	109632	100989
Brazil/Brésil	65382	75293	51833	80058	57365
Norway,SVD,JM	58836	61141	49457	46233	35526
Belgium–Luxembourg	44188	46631	51021	35157	34189
Denmark/Danemark	28548	50522	32963	27436	47517
Korea, Republic of	13979	27030	24095	37746	31314
Romania/Roumanie	3780	31816	35650	134	240
Former USSR/Anc. URSS		x66812			
Singapore/Singapour	15711	19090	15623	15292	25493
China/Chine	9507	11285	14362	19443	16713
Ireland/Irlande	15212	12766	14408	8010	4405
Australia/Australie	9758	11933	8256	10080	10102
Mexico/Mexique	2874	4031	9952	14147	5875
Argentina/Argentine	2753	8375	4225	5231	5087
Poland/Pologne	6028	1277	9111	6685	4875
India/Inde	3812	3704	5590	5088	6779
Malaysia/Malaisie	3321	3890	3797	6555	4586
Czechoslovakia		x7427	x4718		
New Zealand	1978	2815	3361	3763	3686
So. Africa Customs Un	2831	1869	3672	4037	
Portugal	2137	2596	4048	1841	2641
Russian Federation			x2406	x6079	x5449
Czech Republic				6783	8172
Hungary/Hongrie	x1934	x2141	x2328	x1688	x2633
Thailand/Thaïlande	315	1118	1844	2456	3797
Pakistan	638	3265	988	344	959
Greece/Grèce	1698	1835	1533	914	1255
Colombia/Colombie	172	1390	1092	1760	1422
Israel/Israël	1258	289	518	2996	7805
Indonesia/Indonésie	3	159	754	2483	2205
Slovenia/Slovénia			2085	1240	2927
Netherlands Antilles	2408	1891	1191	x6	x98
Turkey/Turquie	1158	293	1520	1078	1538
Philippines	948	292	489	1784	917
Korea Dem People's Rp	x38	x27	x253	x1732	x126
Bahamas			x415	x1367	x237
Venezuela	2421	250	917	555	544

(VALUE AS % OF TOTAL)(VALEUR EN % DU TOTAL)

	1985	1986	1987	1988	1989	1990	1991	1992	1993	1994
Africa	1.9	x2.0	x1.9	x2.0	x2.1	2.0	1.9	x2.1	x2.0	x3.2
Northern Africa	0.6	0.8	0.7	0.6	0.5	0.5	0.5	0.9	0.6	0.6
Americas	28.2	x25.8	x18.6	x23.2	26.4	23.4	16.6	19.4	22.1	24.6
LAIA	4.1	2.7	2.3	3.0	3.3	6.3	3.8	5.2	6.0	6.1
CACM	0.3	0.3	0.2	0.1	0.1	0.2	0.1	0.3	x0.3	x0.1
Asia	14.9	11.9	x14.9	x14.9	14.1	16.0	23.9	24.6	35.1	x30.8
Middle East	1.2	x1.7	x0.8	x1.0	x0.8	0.8	x1.7	x2.8	x1.7	x4.3
Europe	48.3	51.3	56.0	50.5	49.9	49.0	50.8	50.5	35.0	35.7
EEC	36.7	39.3	41.9	39.8	39.2	45.6	47.6	45.2	32.1	32.6
EFTA	11.2	11.2	13.5	10.0	10.4	2.9	2.9	4.7	2.6	2.6
Oceania	2.6	x2.9	x2.1	x2.3	2.2	x1.5	x1.6	x1.2	x2.4	x2.4
USA/Etats–Unis d'Amer	15.1	14.6	10.3	12.2	14.4	10.8	8.9	10.0	12.0	14.3
Germany/Allemagne	7.5	8.2	7.1	7.3	7.2	8.8	9.7	9.6	6.3	7.7
France,Monac	4.8	5.7	6.9	5.9	5.3	8.7	9.7	8.5	4.4	4.3
Indonesia/Indonésie	0.6	0.6	3.8	1.5	2.3	2.8	5.9	4.4	10.0	6.9
United Kingdom	5.8	4.1	4.2	6.7	6.0	3.7	4.0	4.9	6.0	4.1
Italy/Italie	2.9	3.5	4.2	3.6	3.8	5.1	4.8	4.6	3.3	3.2
China/Chine			2.0	1.4	1.2	1.1	2.5	4.0	6.0	6.5
Korea, Republic of	1.5	0.8	1.1	1.7	3.0	2.4	4.1	3.3	4.5	3.0
Canada	8.5	7.0	5.3	7.0	8.4	5.7	3.3	3.7	3.2	3.8
Thailand/Thaïlande	0.6	1.1	0.2	0.5	1.0	1.9	2.7	2.1	4.5	1.3

	1985	1986	1987	1988	1989	1990	1991	1992	1993	1994
Afrique		x0.0	x0.0	x0.1	x0.0		x0.0	0.1	x0.1	x0.0
Afrique du Nord	0.0	x0.0	x0.0	x0.0	x0.0	0.0	0.0	0.0	0.0	x0.0
Amériques	16.3	11.4	9.7	11.7	12.6	12.6	13.7	14.1	17.3	16.1
ALAI	2.3	1.4	1.2	1.8	2.6	1.1	1.3	1.2	2.0	1.3
MCAC	0.0	x0.0	0.0	0.0	x0.0	0.0	0.0	0.0	x0.0	x0.0
Asie	7.5	6.8	x7.5	x7.1	6.0	7.5	9.9	8.5	10.3	10.0
Moyen–Orient	0.0	x0.0	x0.0	0.0	x0.0	0.0	0.0	0.0	x0.0	x0.1
Europe	76.0	81.6	81.6	79.9	79.5	79.3	74.5	76.2	71.6	73.3
CEE	55.9	60.1	58.5	56.7	55.3	70.8	66.3	66.9	63.1	64.3
AELE	20.1	21.5	23.1	23.2	24.2	8.5	8.2	9.2	8.4	9.0
Océanie	0.1	0.1	0.1	0.1	x0.3	x0.2	x0.2	x0.2	x0.3	x0.3
Germany/Allemagne	22.2	25.4	23.3	20.3	19.1	24.3	25.8	26.0	21.4	23.4
USA/Etats–Unis d'Amer	8.5	7.3	6.6	7.5	7.4	8.8	9.3	10.3	12.3	11.4
Italy/Italie	6.9	8.1	7.1	7.0	6.7	7.8	8.2	8.2	8.7	8.7
Switz.Liecht	6.0	6.8	6.9	6.3	5.6	7.6	7.3	8.3	7.5	8.3
Sweden/Suède	5.0	5.5	5.4	5.7	5.9	7.7	7.5	7.2	5.8	6.3
Finland/Finlande	6.0	5.3	7.9	7.8	9.6	12.5	5.4	6.4	9.3	9.6
Japan/Japon	6.5	6.0	5.7	4.8	4.9	6.2	8.1	5.8	6.4	6.2
United Kingdom	5.2	4.4	4.5	4.8	4.6	5.1	6.8	5.7	5.4	4.8
France,Monac	4.1	4.4	4.3	4.5	3.5	4.5	4.1	4.4	4.2	4.6
Austria/Autriche	2.4	3.2	2.1	2.6	2.2	4.2	3.2	3.7	3.5	x2.2

TRADE BY COMMODITY IN THOUSAND U.S. DOLLARS – COMMERCE PAR PRODUIT EN MILLIERS DE DOLLARS E.U

COUNTRIES–PAYS	IMPORTS – IMPORTATIONS 1990	1991	1992	1993	1994
Total	11180377	10777028	10858718	10224515	11210977
Africa	x269506	299925	x338779	x362714	x403570
Northern Africa	72854	58780	81754	80902	83318
Americas	2174711	2184048	2378710	2499808	2859466
LAIA	505706	557915	720520	705590	859217
CACM	16209	16364	28807	x70060	x30918
Asia	1915296	1997223	2408020	2841952	3018747
Middle East	163435	x185397	x367622	x430883	x248159
Europe	6100966	5636021	5338631	4012185	4220682
EEC	5694023	5242487	4996662	3704696	3844625
EFTA	351122	351692	302437	270196	318240
Oceania	x189696	x342919	x166329	x248319	x400527
USA/Etats–Unis d'Amer	1229728	1248468	1274297	1391992	1587915
Germany/Allemagne	743853	890419	952425	673851	693772
United Kingdom	1076711	830101	778925	730697	804464
France,Monac	1038157	854146	691350	450731	533855
Italy/Italie	642610	601114	554324	358748	360236
China/Chine	119553	148966	409953	737352	662684
Netherlands/Pays–Bas	448634	455736	454932	342616	329968
Korea, Republic of	392834	383708	320060	327773	544777
Japan/Japon	398886	406288	313284	273019	282547
Spain/Espagne	435854	434988	343388	184959	189827
Canada	379880	324086	326470	304758	338067
Belgium–Luxembourg	365861	298873	294529	259986	300801
Hong Kong	145535	183508	295322	305430	300794
Switz.Liecht	292781	280189	248354	202684	224971
Mexico/Mexique	159981	184166	251109	211475	238971
Austria/Autriche	213762	242162	215810	184971	163852
Australia/Australie	125278	308178	131628	192262	290323
So. Africa Customs Un	117871	165895	176408	211521	246081
Sweden/Suède	242532	145214	254748	137227	164535
Brazil/Brésil	228418	215157	167175	135431	291672
Singapore/Singapour	127323	145522	149157	161401	167187
Malaysia/Malaisie	131470	132900	139505	154614	177238
Indonesia/Indonésie	179546	164606	91848	139593	156859
Denmark/Danemark	127307	146674	120268	107690	117911
Thailand/Thaïlande	107330	106924	129137	115364	167991
Turkey/Turquie	89773	70287	91648	183551	80485
Russian Federation			x154598	x152556	x116414
Portugal	117213	118519	108983	69622	47937
Finland/Finlande	118214	91802	99841	90075	44771
Iran (Islamic Rp. of)		x43112	x138833	x92215	x38432
Argentina/Argentine	7762	28430	98443	145285	129830
Ireland/Irlande	73406	78082	77018	50847	43776
Poland/Pologne	14167	52015	65731	70381	115748
Former USSR/Anc. URSS	361490	x185408			
Israel/Israël	36813	61710	62511	59951	105001
Norway,SVD,JM	55342	67398	50962	65019	90989
Greece/Grèce	49910	54657	50121	62676	48920
Chile/Chili	17359	42725	64813	51597	44714
Venezuela	53612	32605	62330	49854	17897
Czechoslovakia	65800	x37550	x101892		
Hungary/Hongrie	x35899	26636	x39355	x66345	x41005
Colombia/Colombie	21055	22613	35166	68966	69485
Saudi Arabia	24035	25829	37109	x52807	x52319
New Zealand	59586	31126	30265	52069	105944
India/Inde	57950	24953	29068	48081	84647
United Arab Emirates	22304	13616	35369	x31043	x24491
Czech Republic				77191	98788
Egypt/Egypte	17964	15091	23227	32495	26265
Nigeria/Nigéria	x16429	17645	x26772	x25756	x16931
Pakistan	15234	17963	25057	19052	24818

COUNTRIES–PAYS	EXPORTS – EXPORTATIONS 1990	1991	1992	1993	1994
Totale	11105311	10441077	11443607	10557688	11418968
Afrique	x6262	x5884	x8129	x8340	x2329
Afrique du Nord	112	82	1453	1059	656
Amériques	1323572	1324374	1329232	1366332	1383633
ALAI	21905	30644	42636	41436	40428
MCAC	81	100	50	x122	501
Asie	1317205	1513290	1964042	2018219	2244164
Moyen–Orient	2888	4450	4541	x7181	x6798
Europe	8301095	7502146	8068329	7061677	7679735
CEE	7266454	6547616	7012651	6169779	6652780
AELE	1026174	950946	1048215	887584	1019631
Océanie	x34706	x38973	x41729	x55839	x50133
Germany/Allemagne	4062608	3553881	3887254	3375500	3418153
Japan/Japon	1123354	1291762	1301493	1231219	1402263
USA/Etats–Unis d'Amer	1242040	1235838	1205836	1230794	1232107
Switz.Liecht	1012651	939014	1036612	874521	1004476
United Kingdom	921692	872815	900569	781798	863621
Italy/Italie	580965	543155	580538	531183	604933
France,Monac	522779	494526	495474	380410	513837
Netherlands/Pays–Bas	442658	415752	412198	349444	379316
Israel/Israël	2667	2222	304340	376315	411297
Austria/Autriche	158970	155857	193260	185122	x163970
Hong Kong	69943	82295	185224	246127	228426
Belgium–Luxembourg	140109	130158	150754	216593	316295
Denmark/Danemark	136406	120452	125670	114969	125587
Sweden/Suède	171978	128121	127375	102021	112713
Canada	59036	56803	78485	93531	109953
Spain/Espagne	66588	71508	78830	61310	80189
Singapore/Singapour	61496	64376	58875	73479	95452
Australia/Australie	26444	29377	34346	45969	44332
China/Chine	10968	11170	59201	18836	22544
Ireland/Irlande	32104	33623	24222	29178	25672
Korea, Republic of	15917	20728	25962	35178	43353
Czechoslovakia		x41184	x21833		
Portugal	15262	16808	18532	21000	29609
India/Inde	21927	27071	12809	9957	13781
Mexico/Mexique	4266	9571	20747	16482	14237
Brazil/Brésil	9556	13031	14677	17911	19484
Finland/Finlande	13567	9637	15697	18342	14616
Czech Republic				38349	46502
Norway,SVD,JM	13481	11752	11567	12894	14786
Malaysia/Malaisie	5546	5667	7607	14471	9690
New Zealand	7240	8450	6393	5817	5658
So. Africa Customs Un	4693	4826	5737	6384	
Hungary/Hongrie	x7589	x5491	x3420	x3360	x4741
Argentina/Argentine	6971	6914	2350	2901	2816
Poland/Pologne	1282	3153	5297	1792	3347
Thailand/Thaïlande	1786	2169	2559	3179	8297
Malta/Malte	3358	516	5416	1177	x5863
Greece/Grèce	680	1234	2278	2908	4268
Former USSR/Anc. URSS	27417	x6062			
Turkey/Turquie	694	3340	782	1288	3257
American Samoa	x948	x701	x792	x3552	x94
Chile/Chili	214	229	3671	719	710
Russian Federation			x2655	x1071	x2100
Croatia/Croatie			1350	2359	x507
United Arab Emirates	1028			x3706	x433
Venezuela	569	397	404	2684	1217
Cyprus/Chypre	211	424	2184	341	392
Yugoslavia SFR	4535	x2885			
Bulgaria/Bulgarie	x2523	x219	x1186	x995	x355
Slovakia				x2370	x3134

(VALUE AS % OF TOTAL)(VALEUR EN % DU TOTAL)

	1985	1986	1987	1988	1989	1990	1991	1992	1993	1994
Africa	3.2	x2.6	x1.8	x1.8	x1.7	x2.5	2.7	x3.1	x3.6	x3.6
Northern Africa	1.4	1.2	0.6	0.3	0.5	0.7	0.5	0.8	0.8	0.7
Americas	30.5	27.3	22.4	19.4	20.3	19.5	20.3	21.9	24.5	25.5
LAIA	3.5	3.0	2.8	2.8	2.8	4.5	5.2	6.6	6.9	7.7
CACM	0.3	0.2	0.3	0.2	0.2	0.1	0.2	0.3	x0.7	x0.3
Asia	10.8	10.2	x12.6	x13.7	13.2	17.1	18.5	22.2	27.8	27.0
Middle East	1.3	x1.4	x1.1	x1.2	x1.1	1.5	x1.7	x3.4	x4.2	x2.2
Europe	47.0	51.5	54.8	57.2	57.4	54.6	52.3	49.2	39.2	37.6
EEC	38.7	42.5	45.7	49.0	49.6	50.9	48.6	46.0	36.2	34.3
EFTA	7.7	8.5	8.7	7.8	7.5	3.1	3.3	2.8	2.6	2.8
Oceania	3.8	x3.9	x2.8	x2.9	x2.6	x1.7	x3.1	x1.5	x2.4	x3.5
USA/Etats–Unis d'Amer	20.4	18.7	14.7	12.0	12.8	11.0	11.6	11.7	13.6	14.2
Germany/Allemagne	5.2	5.7	4.8	5.6	5.5	6.7	8.3	8.8	6.6	6.2
United Kingdom	9.6	8.8	10.0	12.8	12.3	9.6	7.7	7.2	7.1	7.2
France,Monac	5.6	6.5	7.1	6.9	8.8	9.3	7.9	6.4	4.4	4.8
Italy/Italie	3.7	4.3	5.2	5.7	5.2	5.7	5.6	5.1	3.5	3.2
China/Chine			1.6	1.1	0.9	1.1	1.4	3.8	7.2	5.9
Netherlands/Pays–Bas	3.9	4.1	5.0	4.6	3.3	4.0	4.2	4.2	3.4	2.9
Korea, Republic of	1.3	1.1	1.9	2.4	2.9	3.5	3.6	2.9	3.2	4.9
Japan/Japon	2.4	2.6	2.4	2.8	2.9	3.6	3.8	2.9	2.7	2.5
Spain/Espagne	1.7	2.0	3.1	3.2	3.8	3.9	4.0	3.2	1.8	1.7

	1985	1986	1987	1988	1989	1990	1991	1992	1993	1994
Afrique	0.1	x0.3	x0.1	x0.0	x0.0	x0.0	x0.0	x0.1	x0.1	x0.0
Afrique du Nord	0.0	x0.0	x0.0	x0.0	x0.0	0.0	0.0	0.0	0.0	0.0
Amériques	13.1	x10.2	9.7	10.4	10.7	11.9	12.7	11.6	12.9	12.2
ALAI	0.1	0.1	0.1	0.1	0.1	0.2	0.3	0.4	0.4	0.4
MCAC	0.0	x0.0	0.0	x0.0	x0.0	0.0	0.0	0.0	x0.0	0.0
Asie	12.3	11.9	x9.7	x10.8	12.1	11.8	14.5	17.1	19.1	19.7
Moyen–Orient	0.0	x0.0	x0.1	0.0	x0.0	0.0	0.0	0.0	x0.1	x0.1
Europe	71.7	75.2	73.2	71.9	75.3	74.7	71.9	70.5	66.9	67.3
CEE	61.4	64.4	62.9	60.3	64.1	65.4	62.7	61.3	58.4	58.3
AELE	10.3	10.8	10.3	11.6	11.2	9.2	9.1	9.2	8.4	8.9
Océanie	0.1	x0.1	x0.1	x0.3	x0.3	x0.3	x0.4	x0.4	x0.5	x0.4
Germany/Allemagne	34.7	37.8	37.5	31.9	36.4	36.6	34.0	34.0	32.0	29.9
Japan/Japon	10.8	10.8	8.2	9.1	10.4	10.1	12.4	11.4	11.7	12.3
USA/Etats–Unis d'Amer	11.8	9.2	8.9	9.6	9.8	11.2	11.8	10.5	11.7	10.8
Switz.Liecht	7.5	8.0	7.4	8.3	8.1	9.1	9.0	9.1	8.3	8.8
United Kingdom	10.6	9.8	9.1	8.3	8.2	8.3	8.4	7.9	7.4	7.6
Italy/Italie	4.9	5.0	4.0	4.5	5.2	5.2	5.2	5.1	5.0	5.3
France,Monac	4.0	4.0	3.6	4.3	4.8	4.7	4.7	4.3	3.6	4.5
Netherlands/Pays–Bas	1.9	2.4	2.9	4.3	3.1	4.0	4.0	3.6	3.3	3.3
Israel/Israël	0.0	0.0	0.0	0.0	0.0	0.0	0.0	2.7	3.6	3.6
Austria/Autriche	0.6	0.7	0.7	1.1	1.2	1.4	1.5	1.7	1.8	x1.4

TRADE BY COMMODITY IN THOUSAND U.S. DOLLARS – COMMERCE PAR PRODUIT EN MILLIERS DE DOLLARS E.U

COUNTRIES–PAYS	IMPORTS – IMPORTATIONS 1990	1991	1992	1993	1994
Total	6776899	5293236	5475693	5209350	5224369
Africa	x325575	x296989	x349911	x292522	x280831
Northern Africa	160574	132516	x139920	x110053	97104
Americas	813530	860387	996401	1006947	x1078520
LAIA	202397	257342	351315	373366	415244
CACM	18678	21655	30089	x57209	x38134
Asia	957964	951830	1227241	x1627631	x1653975
Middle East	x103876	x177963	x188497	x249435	x225903
Europe	2158256	2272915	2385134	1773663	1740208
EEC	1946375	2071771	2214649	1616935	1543258
EFTA	172098	151764	136827	132193	156167
Oceania	x91039	x63986	x76853	x95630	x101369
USA/Etats–Unis d'Amer	387961	382102	426752	399912	430928
Germany/Allemagne	293716	384776	433601	282748	248089
China/Chine	253449	193320	247760	592078	567575
United Kingdom	328488	307555	336189	266956	230252
France, Monac	283240	278788	312873	212486	223939
Poland/Pologne	143772	287918	193579	155627	155913
Belgium–Luxembourg	177701	168962	180194	137863	137867
Netherlands/Pays–Bas	152421	164465	182138	120163	129961
Italy/Italie	133237	161022	167201	131608	116450
Russian Federation			x240956	x183773	x215461
Spain/Espagne	141879	166721	147648	103552	102548
Former USSR/Anc. URSS	1963310	x402558			
Canada	147220	121725	134684	124704	129313
Japan/Japon	111551	98624	128594	96395	95187
Korea, Republic of	115421	109262	98773	113003	119606
Thailand/Thaïlande	80999	57665	110402	144110	94929
Indonesia/Indonésie	65232	100884	117566	84486	102235
Mexico/Mexique	74905	97949	109290	91908	127135
Iran (Islamic Rp. of)		x91800	x72537	x96692	x25207
Austria/Autriche	83840	82922	82691	74920	72701
Denmark/Danemark	69967	73684	92441	66644	62264
Switz.Liecht	84462	82254	74166	67097	82024
Greece/Grèce	64758	66129	77096	63525	62011
Czechoslovakia	60186	x74091	x129894		
Sweden/Suède	71118	67930	63158	64104	64871
Malaysia/Malaisie	52840	52362	67271	67915	63152
Norway, SVD, JM	80340	59744	56113	58123	66091
Australia/Australie	69899	44640	55472	63490	70124
Ireland/Irlande	49612	57893	57060	35365	34680
Argentina/Argentine	7378	17064	50915	76371	71510
So. Africa Customs Un	30833	44355	45786	54148	53518
Hungary/Hongrie	x57731	40674	x53951	x45637	x51836
Turkey/Turquie	40080	38180	42871	54981	53297
Singapore/Singapour	28357	43504	50010	40364	51075
Portugal	41405	42386	51726	35732	36164
Philippines	32212	17836	74966	35162	68468
Ukraine			x26894	x98566	x24331
Hong Kong	27598	29035	48098	45709	50021
Brazil/Brésil	30753	32540	54558	34795	44122
Romania/Roumanie	16842	18071	40194	63344	55455
Venezuela	19152	26077	41452	40965	36469
Finland/Finlande	54992	48538	30631	21269	21461
Algeria/Algérie	58131	29150	39415	28996	22606
Czech Republic				95797	72594
Nigeria/Nigéria	x17160	19005	x36599	x34636	x19732
Chile/Chili	15514	18525	25786	39089	28277
Israel/Israël	23275	19172	29019	30446	45763
Tunisia/Tunisie	26098	33519	26452	14877	16374
Morocco/Maroc	27167	25967	21976	26402	25441
Saudi Arabia	18846	16450	17915	x38160	x44027

COUNTRIES–PAYS	EXPORTS – EXPORTATIONS 1990	1991	1992	1993	1994
Totale	5236568	5108412	5519092	5088305	5444162
Afrique	9830	13059	x18667	x20086	x1805
Afrique du Nord	539	1216	x1334	x1833	x921
Amériques	529572	592487	684140	708560	744268
ALAI	38270	37465	64952	69071	75341
MCAC	424	337	603	x653	x1008
Asie	271386	287119	354438	418845	425338
Moyen–Orient	7179	x16500	20131	27953	34871
Europe	4080702	4097874	4353411	3798121	4119888
CEE	3638271	3683376	3936877	3415193	3735076
AELE	393732	372224	400674	362498	378831
Océanie	x46338	x50462	59115	x75854	x75122
Germany/Allemagne	890976	1104772	1154458	983633	1072945
Italy/Italie	877048	803332	778132	779663	855139
USA/Etats–Unis d'Amer	463857	523584	582903	599609	618598
Netherlands/Pays–Bas	558399	561875	587081	448782	559924
Switz.Liecht	364092	340131	366861	331197	346851
Denmark/Danemark	271436	260698	331376	292565	285078
France, Monac	254246	286684	324522	270586	270147
United Kingdom	359708	266360	299736	218123	257964
Japan/Japon	157622	157852	170095	185543	182356
Austria/Autriche	156723	150582	158548	120499	x133811
Spain/Espagne	87593	90658	111530	102374	113186
Belgium–Luxembourg	79082	71189	84716	102558	66809
Sweden/Suède	57890	59898	65060	60648	76204
Australia/Australie	34527	41686	49747	61468	65558
Hong Kong	13979	14780	40667	54370	51291
Canada	24589	29658	32111	37818	47648
Singapore/Singapour	24375	31460	26014	34610	32445
Brazil/Brésil	13816	16931	32952	38553	35869
Norway, SVD, JM	26027	28616	30842	28785	28966
Poland/Pologne	50023	24056	24248	23217	30837
China/Chine	16705	20431	24391	24839	31694
Malaysia/Malaisie	12583	12981	22082	25910	26569
Turkey/Turquie	3535	12057	15259	22951	28183
India/Inde	19866	10649	15289	15297	22128
Czechoslovakia		x25933	x15148		
Yugoslavia SFR	48291	x40552			
Mexico/Mexique	11326	10006	16029	13874	25517
Thailand/Thaïlande	5698	7488	11925	20136	10114
Finland/Finlande	26748	9778	15722	13447	15260
So. Africa Customs Un	4892	7415	13610	12896	
Korea, Republic of	7090	6122	10984	15563	23801
Ireland/Irlande	11540	8273	12758	8747	16033
New Zealand	11467	8592	8107	13024	9478
Czech Republic				26796	31063
Israel/Israël	3253	6936	9410	9179	3436
Slovenia/Slovénia			10006	8970	4526
Portugal	3742	6285	6653	5969	6569
Hungary/Hongrie	x13239	x4518	x6934	x6813	x9656
Argentina/Argentine	8915	5964	5925	5664	5808
Greece/Grèce	3009	2861	6584	7599	6007
Colombia/Colombie	2725	3384	6040	7351	4729
Romania/Roumanie	2034	6611	1851	1391	1638
Iceland/Islande	3613	3477	2970	2516	3015
Croatia/Croatie			4777	3815	x245
Bulgaria/Bulgarie	x18322	x2466	x776	x5227	x1609
Yugoslavia/Yougoslavie			x912	x7045	x580
Russian Federation			x3809	x3841	x2969
Chile/Chili	847	491	3046	2705	2332
Indonesia/Indonésie	2298	1038	2329	1506	2333
Lebanon/Liban	x1001	x1184	x1649	x1335	x2390

(VALUE AS % OF TOTAL)(VALEUR EN % DU TOTAL)

	1985	1986	1987	1988	1989	1990	1991	1992	1993	1994
Africa	6.2	x7.9	x5.1	x5.9	x4.6	x4.8	x5.6	x6.4	x5.6	x5.4
Northern Africa	2.7	2.8	1.8	1.2	1.8	2.4	2.5	x2.6	x2.1	1.9
Americas	19.1	17.1	14.6	13.3	13.6	12.0	16.2	18.2	19.4	x20.6
LAIA	4.5	3.2	3.1	3.3	2.7	3.0	4.9	6.4	7.2	7.9
CACM	0.6	0.4	x0.4	0.5	0.4	0.3	0.4	0.5	x1.1	x0.7
Asia	10.9	x10.5	15.8	x15.5	15.0	14.1	18.0	22.4	x31.2	x31.7
Middle East	2.9	x3.5	x2.0	x2.1	x1.6	x1.5	x3.4	x3.4	x4.8	x4.3
Europe	31.6	34.2	34.7	35.1	35.4	31.8	42.9	43.6	34.0	33.3
EEC	24.3	26.1	26.5	28.7	29.3	28.7	39.1	40.4	31.0	29.5
EFTA	6.3	7.4	7.5	5.9	5.6	2.5	2.9	2.5	2.5	3.0
Oceania	1.9	x1.7	x1.5	1.4	x1.2	x1.3	x1.2	x1.4	x1.9	x1.9
USA/Etats–Unis d'Amer	9.2	8.6	6.7	6.4	5.8	5.7	7.2	7.8	7.7	8.2
Germany/Allemagne	2.7	2.9	3.0	3.6	4.1	4.3	7.3	7.9	5.4	4.7
China/Chine			6.4	4.8	5.3	3.7	3.7	4.5	11.4	10.9
United Kingdom	4.5	4.6	3.8	5.6	5.3	4.8	5.8	6.1	5.1	4.4
France, Monac	3.5	3.9	4.1	3.8	4.3	4.2	5.3	5.7	4.1	4.3
Poland/Pologne	1.5	2.5	2.2	2.2	2.6	2.1	5.4	3.5	3.0	3.0
Belgium–Luxembourg	1.7	1.7	2.1	2.3	2.8	2.6	3.2	3.3	2.6	2.6
Netherlands/Pays–Bas	2.4	2.5	2.5	2.5	2.3	2.2	3.1	3.3	2.3	2.5
Italy/Italie	1.9	1.8	1.8	2.2	1.8	2.0	3.0	3.1	2.5	2.2
Russian Federation								x4.4	x3.5	x4.1

	1985	1986	1987	1988	1989	1990	1991	1992	1993	1994
Afrique	0.1	x0.2	x0.1	x0.3	x0.2	0.2	0.2	x0.3	x0.4	x0.0
Afrique du Nord	0.0	x0.0	0.0	0.0	x0.0	0.0	0.0	x0.0	x0.0	x0.0
Amériques	11.9	x9.6	x8.7	10.0	11.4	10.1	11.6	12.4	13.9	13.6
ALAI	0.6	0.4	0.5	0.5	0.6	0.7	0.7	1.2	1.4	1.4
MCAC	0.0	0.0	0.0	x0.0	0.0	0.0	0.0	0.0	x0.0	x0.0
Asie	5.6	4.7	x4.0	x5.3	5.8	5.2	5.6	6.5	8.2	7.8
Moyen–Orient	0.1	x0.1	x0.2	x0.1	x0.2	0.1	x0.3	0.4	0.5	0.6
Europe	69.2	72.9	68.8	66.6	73.9	77.9	80.2	78.9	74.6	75.7
CEE	54.1	56.0	53.4	56.3	62.1	69.5	72.1	71.3	67.1	68.6
AELE	13.2	15.4	14.2	9.4	10.3	7.5	7.3	7.3	7.1	7.0
Océanie	0.6	0.5	0.7	0.8	0.9	x0.9	x1.0	1.0	x1.5	x1.4
Germany/Allemagne	13.0	15.1	14.9	17.3	17.8	17.0	21.6	20.9	19.3	19.7
Italy/Italie	10.3	10.1	8.9	10.3	12.8	16.7	15.7	14.1	15.3	15.7
USA/Etats–Unis d'Amer	9.9	7.9	7.4	8.7	9.9	8.9	10.2	10.6	11.8	11.4
Netherlands/Pays–Bas	7.2	7.1	6.9	9.0	9.7	10.7	11.0	10.6	8.8	10.3
Switz.Liecht	4.0	5.2	4.2	5.7	5.8	7.0	6.7	6.6	6.5	6.4
Denmark/Danemark	3.4	3.9	2.9	4.2	5.6	5.2	5.1	6.0	5.7	5.2
France, Monac	3.7	3.4	3.9	4.0	4.4	4.9	5.6	5.9	5.3	5.0
United Kingdom	5.4	4.5	4.2	5.2	5.1	6.9	5.2	5.4	4.3	4.7
Japan/Japon	3.6	3.1	2.1	2.6	3.5	3.0	3.1	3.1	3.6	3.3
Austria/Autriche	7.4	8.3	8.4	2.0	2.5	3.0	2.9	2.9	2.4	x2.5

TRADE BY COMMODITY IN THOUSAND U.S. DOLLARS – COMMERCE PAR PRODUIT EN MILLIERS DE DOLLARS E.U

COUNTRIES–PAYS	IMPORTS – IMPORTATIONS				
	1990	1991	1992	1993	1994
Total	42328408	41672884	41183514	41563686	47820855
Africa	x1197808	1465214	x1469326	x1322483	x1340709
Northern Africa	563408	577532	x704686	x635555	x515632
Americas	6959791	6957838	7767541	8636778	10286153
LAIA	1490415	1769471	2566911	2638412	3099686
CACM	62877	42921	69131	x86435	x77768
Asia	12094521	14882506	14545257	18654412	22178231
Middle East	x909870	x1340633	x1984994	x2487328	x1736559
Europe	15820096	15592671	15761887	11205588	12162831
EEC	14512835	14400636	14599862	10144102	11016462
EFTA	1059527	983069	963702	887134	910234
Oceania	x678050	x539979	x524287	x645184	x711048
China/Chine	3749698	4685596	3358967	6035279	7103665
USA/Etats–Unis d'Amer	3885536	3722157	3880397	4368017	5418431
Germany/Allemagne	2552357	3145564	3186095	2228451	2386252
Korea, Republic of	1817244	2112234	1889088	2190947	3301714
France,Monac	2323295	2315218	2173683	1458746	1633783
United Kingdom	2092104	1775722	2007287	1432095	1518934
Malaysia/Malaisie	905858	1239260	1419769	1549191	2113882
Canada	1274631	1243134	1075805	1393761	1548422
Italy/Italie	1240702	1258887	1324692	942044	947837
Japan/Japon	1111338	1142602	1130042	1129138	1257571
Singapore/Singapour	866558	956325	988476	1373904	1780414
Belgium–Luxembourg	1163054	1221756	1167653	670377	723427
Thailand/Thaïlande	723674	1101453	953870	915854	1392507
Spain/Espagne	1216654	1166859	1126130	636972	665017
Iran (Islamic Rp. of)		x619130	x1052995	x1098868	x424044
Mexico/Mexique	617865	700039	1038075	976685	1463568
Netherlands/Pays–Bas	1078937	963195	1093069	640396	759504
Indonesia/Indonésie	734019	855357	898602	726698	952700
Hong Kong	375922	467484	770779	924783	844401
Austria/Autriche	704707	702071	735995	644073	721863
Switz.Liecht	785473	696986	653029	621194	625390
Russian Federation			x1016437	x717992	x788476
Former USSR/Anc. URSS	4377112	x1621410			
Turkey/Turquie	390976	431729	407007	624178	507508
Venezuela	186381	341815	594009	489435	103465
Sweden/Suède	657342	491372	472562	409986	496232
Australia/Australie	553762	416638	407587	482742	543898
Portugal	356827	358591	383230	283103	229910
Brazil/Brésil	252102	304979	337727	381950	623440
Philippines	326732	275550	278944	374297	472446
Denmark/Danemark	334043	320407	304296	213238	248136
Norway,SVD,JM	266463	273532	302654	256834	276954
Israel/Israël	136115	206937	267731	340343	364473
So. Africa Customs Un	238309	279723	241524	250046	391559
Czechoslovakia	383662	x243385	x478850		
Ireland/Irlande	203390	212959	235251	250136	253426
Poland/Pologne		86066	282151	283612	381721
Finland/Finlande	391080	267624	204202	174815	291739
India/Inde	243146	167841	206321	237271	335026
Hungary/Hongrie	x257333	133270	x231435	x219884	x169203
Saudi Arabia	132284	99772	181168	x292407	x280708
Pakistan	71791	186558	232786	135054	174978
Greece/Grèce	198344	200410	185719	159669	140401
Chile/Chili	178677	134222	159401	242558	228814
Argentina/Argentine	32573	95047	184878	251282	319476
Algeria/Algérie	228308	207848	189062	95479	89241
Egypt/Egypte	115596	103252	133996	218279	137812
Nigeria/Nigéria	x77799	104497	x198245	x149647	x102905
Morocco/Maroc	83537	114382	193940	123569	116509
Ukraine			x69286	x356454	x84631

COUNTRIES–PAYS	EXPORTS – EXPORTATIONS				
	1990	1991	1992	1993	1994
Totale	37944586	38755078	39733486	40032710	46561215
Afrique	76474	109433	122766	x116597	x114666
Afrique du Nord	14918	20649	32232	15081	9123
Amériques	5315057	5714697	5877793	6738135	8130266
ALAI	124620	177522	247107	246148	233225
MCAC	386	651	630	x1699	x2123
Asie	7134437	8857953	8154178	10178109	12385836
Moyen–Orient	33612	23220	40448	x87595	x82134
Europe	24044268	23683489	25154099	22517600	25380602
CEE	22155804	21917757	23347042	20863405	23443294
AELE	1800368	1729326	1743332	1595530	1879783
Océanie	x173793	x194934	189071	x237607	x280149
Germany/Allemagne	8462630	8072792	8601122	7424743	8235590
Japan/Japon	4619751	5585611	5752080	6710850	8527624
Italy/Italie	5459011	5612198	5844592	5737252	6445730
USA/Etats–Unis d'Amer	4588165	4916099	4942250	5698831	6882980
France,Monac	1732481	1707906	1931320	1619520	1903291
United Kingdom	1628861	1647219	1813371	1480322	1634416
Switz.Liecht	1681116	1602636	1611203	1494571	1777235
Austria/Autriche	1106662	1104639	1225177	1139705	x1132087
Netherlands/Pays–Bas	927041	1027861	1047311	909808	1063226
Hong Kong	419397	530576	825097	1012845	860858
Sweden/Suède	835056	809981	804042	679999	819117
China/Chine	1114825	1667732	196948	268738	310057
Canada	595365	615808	678834	784029	1004246
Belgium–Luxembourg	659182	619473	600707	562484	616777
Israel/Israël	192293	207041	415060	877819	899927
Denmark/Danemark	466752	472991	533329	454710	478923
Singapore/Singapour	331529	405369	439203	525012	861128
Finland/Finlande	490120	403473	390613	390266	560558
Spain/Espagne	286717	338898	422398	360584	392449
Korea, Republic of	249600	263685	285338	391904	550654
Australia/Australie	138885	159617	164327	213242	244856
Norway,SVD,JM	118903	126407	131917	100812	102406
Brazil/Brésil	45246	65420	93915	115514	95451
Malaysia/Malaisie	54801	66624	82004	114357	129226
Mexico/Mexique	43757	58798	110563	79997	86714
So. Africa Customs Un	50138	74236	83824	91188	99490
Russian Federation			x77843	x147358	x26326
Ireland/Irlande	55897	53215	75554	57651	113690
Thailand/Thaïlande	26444	32407	42124	83967	62974
India/Inde	69380	51039	53005	46731	64367
Hungary/Hongrie	x47726	x48247	x57420	x37274	x43909
Poland/Pologne		5378	48797	70741	77986
Czechoslovakia		x61290	x57261		
Portugal	33511	35755	45503	27356	32092
Romania/Roumanie	8416	17642	47169	25048	16648
Czech Republic				85281	107316
Slovenia/Slovénia			41276	42132	44929
Turkey/Turquie	14210	13505	26584	30571	34613
New Zealand	29163	24953	19904	23010	34425
Argentina/Argentine	23710	21698	18977	18588	16892
Algeria/Algérie	12092	18335	28054	11122	4204
Former USSR/Anc. URSS	1043920	x49577			
Greece/Grèce	11809	11281	12003	19007	15347
Bulgaria/Bulgarie	x65040	x10350	x17042	x13909	x7999
Saudi Arabia	4483	2261	1954	x34337	x24138
Venezuela	6313	18252	8911	8189	5150
Yugoslavia SFR	87074	x34634			
Indonesia/Indonésie	1418	4858	5160	17191	15273
Croatia/Croatie			15184	11013	x5277
Philippines	6232	12738	4344	5598	6713

(VALUE AS % OF TOTAL)(VALEUR EN % DU TOTAL)

	1985	1986	1987	1988	1989	1990	1991	1992	1993	1994
Africa	5.1	x4.4	x3.1	x3.5	x2.6	x2.9	3.5	x3.6	x3.2	x2.8
Northern Africa	3.1	2.2	1.2	1.1	1.0	1.3	1.4	x1.7	x1.5	x1.1
Americas	23.6	23.3	20.0	20.1	18.3	16.5	16.7	18.8	20.8	21.5
LAIA	4.0	3.5	3.2	3.6	3.5	3.5	4.2	6.2	6.3	6.5
CACM	0.2	0.2	x0.2	0.1	0.1	0.1	0.1	0.2	x0.2	x0.2
Asia	20.2	20.9	24.5	26.5	28.0	28.5	35.7	35.3	44.8	46.4
Middle East	2.4	x3.7	x2.1	x2.3	x1.8	x2.1	x3.2	x4.8	x6.0	x3.6
Europe	35.3	36.8	36.1	33.7	35.7	37.4	37.4	38.3	27.0	25.4
EEC	28.0	29.4	29.0	27.4	29.3	34.3	34.6	35.5	24.4	23.0
EFTA	6.4	6.7	6.5	5.7	5.8	2.5	2.4	2.3	2.1	1.9
Oceania	2.2	x2.1	x1.5	1.5	1.6	x1.6	x1.3	x1.3	x1.6	x1.5
China/Chine			8.6	8.0	9.4	8.9	11.2	8.2	14.5	14.9
USA/Etats–Unis d'Amer	14.1	13.6	11.8	12.5	10.6	9.2	8.9	9.4	10.5	11.3
Germany/Allemagne	5.3	5.6	5.0	4.3	4.9	6.0	7.5	7.7	5.4	5.0
Korea, Republic of	3.3	3.5	3.2	3.5	4.9	4.3	5.1	4.6	5.3	6.9
France,Monac	4.1	4.6	4.2	4.3	4.8	5.5	5.6	5.3	3.5	3.4
United Kingdom	5.2	4.7	5.0	4.6	4.8	4.9	4.3	4.9	3.4	3.2
Malaysia/Malaisie	1.6	0.9	0.8	1.3	1.8	2.1	3.0	3.4	3.7	4.4
Canada	4.8	5.0	4.2	3.6	3.2	3.0	3.0	2.6	3.4	3.2
Italy/Italie	2.2	2.4	2.4	2.4	2.4	2.9	3.0	3.2	2.3	2.0
Japan/Japon	2.1	1.8	1.7	1.9	2.2	2.6	2.7	2.7	2.7	2.6

	1985	1986	1987	1988	1989	1990	1991	1992	1993	1994
Afrique	0.1	x0.1	x0.1	x0.2	x0.2	0.2	0.3	0.3	x0.3	x0.2
Afrique du Nord	0.0	x0.0	x0.0	0.0	x0.0	0.0	0.1	0.1	0.0	0.0
Amériques	17.8	14.4	13.0	14.5	14.4	14.0	14.8	14.7	16.8	17.4
ALAI	0.4	0.3	0.3	0.3	0.3	0.3	0.5	0.6	0.6	0.5
MCAC	0.0	0.0	0.0	0.0	0.0	0.0	0.0	0.0	x0.0	x0.0
Asie	14.6	14.0	x16.2	x20.4	20.7	18.8	22.8	20.5	25.5	26.6
Moyen–Orient	0.3	x0.1	x0.2	0.1	x0.1	0.1	0.1	0.1	x0.2	x0.2
Europe	58.4	64.8	62.6	57.9	60.3	63.4	61.1	63.3	56.2	54.5
CEE	49.3	54.9	52.7	48.5	50.7	58.4	56.6	58.8	52.1	50.3
AELE	8.9	9.6	9.6	9.2	9.3	4.7	4.5	4.4	4.0	4.0
Océanie	0.2	x0.3	x0.3	x0.4	0.4	x0.4	x0.5	0.5	x0.6	x0.6
Germany/Allemagne	19.3	22.8	21.3	19.8	19.4	22.3	20.8	21.6	18.5	17.7
Japan/Japon	11.7	11.7	11.7	12.6	14.3	12.2	14.4	14.5	16.8	18.3
Italy/Italie	9.8	11.7	11.7	11.1	12.7	14.4	14.5	14.7	14.3	13.8
USA/Etats–Unis d'Amer	15.7	12.5	10.9	12.4	12.3	12.1	12.7	12.4	14.2	14.8
France,Monac	3.8	4.1	3.7	3.5	3.9	4.6	4.4	4.9	4.0	4.1
United Kingdom	6.0	5.7	5.1	3.9	3.9	4.3	4.3	4.6	3.7	3.5
Switz.Liecht	3.8	4.4	4.6	3.7	3.6	4.4	4.1	4.1	3.7	3.8
Austria/Autriche	1.3	1.3	1.4	2.3	2.4	2.9	2.9	3.1	2.8	x2.4
Netherlands/Pays–Bas	2.6	2.5	2.6	2.1	2.1	2.4	2.7	2.6	2.3	2.3
Hong Kong	1.1	0.9	1.0	1.4	1.5	1.1	1.4	2.1	2.5	1.8

TRADE BY COMMODITY IN THOUSAND U.S. DOLLARS – COMMERCE PAR PRODUIT EN MILLIERS DE DOLLARS E.U

COUNTRIES–PAYS	IMPORTS – IMPORTATIONS					COUNTRIES–PAYS	EXPORTS – EXPORTATIONS				
	1990	1991	1992	1993	1994		1990	1991	1992	1993	1994
Total	26471298	23515194	21550656	18365758	20916300	Totale	24200764	22374167	20989375	18646756	20783851
Africa	524800	428398	x402448	x352021	x338170	Afrique	19547	23048	x12016	x13125	x3244
Northern Africa	273762	191132	188438	164876	x134055	Afrique du Nord	472	1391	1227	784	1237
Americas	4490819	4357265	4406939	4605757	5886551	Amériques	2234164	2271910	2632672	2795077	3373945
LAIA	766001	893559	1311719	1089971	1109032	ALAI	106754	132055	139434	147492	122153
CACM	16533	19054	27874	x19956	x23447	MCAC	1406	1074	1053	x1166	x1762
Asia	4640920	5520525	6080734	6761407	7259635	Asie	5175090	5239698	4828491	5239924	6108944
Middle East	x499434	x900296	x1057651	x982870	x531986	Moyen–Orient	26026	19057	22291	x18841	x24617
Europe	11998376	10938236	9933106	6020549	6698719	Europe	15514608	14107663	13067524	10212517	10893946
EEC	10957319	10128623	9281868	5533918	6164454	CEE	12608337	11909905	11175964	8673235	9024803
EFTA	889625	701042	570474	425222	464576	AELE	2511169	2140214	1839551	1494220	1835313
Oceania	x243795	x184028	x165156	x193160	x274578	Océanie	x43109	x49168	x52921	x55633	x75021
USA/Etats–Unis d'Amer	3010434	2873292	2552326	2908923	3744597	Germany/Allemagne	5747022	5785854	5431275	4095140	4249482
Germany/Allemagne	2793597	2957609	2454942	1313930	1377241	Japan/Japon	4317206	4363761	3849009	4056200	4707231
France, Monac	2049723	1756154	1582654	864210	1011761	USA/Etats–Unis d'Amer	1902741	1903980	2260936	2383032	2987049
China/Chine	543973	604321	1004912	2079811	2218117	Italy/Italie	2206058	2082467	1966656	1689098	1689205
Korea, Republic of	935444	1045248	1078307	788965	1102669	Switz.Liecht	2492050	2130935	1832005	1486753	1822213
United Kingdom	1356363	1152585	1007850	703859	804158	United Kingdom	1181921	1011405	843457	716165	824282
Italy/Italie	1222325	1130081	964238	741128	892447	France, Monac	790521	729529	778022	508949	590869
Japan/Japon	793495	788514	670876	464408	460345	Belgium–Luxembourg	650849	545930	488382	367840	351377
Mexico/Mexique	340391	360819	831029	602909	542078	Austria/Autriche	477805	410711	417143	337587	x260089
Iran (Islamic Rp. of)		x572435	x702668	x517730	x153450	Spain/Espagne	542125	456015	399954	286198	313235
Belgium–Luxembourg	711556	689129	711728	335762	356126	Sweden/Suède	425733	345562	316201	288263	303466
Former USSR/Anc. URSS	3441410	x1645998				Hong Kong	152913	189298	290946	430800	405051
Canada	652020	515159	481023	559433	968573	Netherlands/Pays–Bas	323451	294898	300247	215534	228684
Malaysia/Malaisie	329201	468797	518309	537740	715782	Canada	222368	233110	230578	261118	261530
Austria/Autriche	500991	528586	601658	374385	364308	China/Chine	250317	230039	226675	242432	275302
Switz.Liecht	805814	613151	488947	363507	387781	Singapore/Singapour	163509	190512	181189	208422	290883
Spain/Espagne	649240	524332	675655	251107	296054	Czechoslovakia		x276192	x162479		
Thailand/Thaïlande	393007	521093	435623	477179	548442	Korea, Republic of	108767	118068	123285	123818	199079
Netherlands/Pays–Bas	543285	499156	547945	269466	269955	Denmark/Danemark	117401	124320	115394	67350	75617
Singapore/Singapour	351843	374765	392149	394268	460438	Brazil/Brésil	44579	80327	86555	96150	74917
Russian Federation			x695587	x370334	x398394	Bulgaria/Bulgarie	x261767	x83159	x65349	x40769	x27915
Hong Kong	181660	209821	308957	432552	414151	Romania/Roumanie	121424	97498	55676	28857	25094
Sweden/Suède	443832	328263	261334	201027	342203	Finland/Finlande	82711	63252	55151	56710	86145
Indonesia/Indonésie	224874	284915	250096	244776	319007	Poland/Pologne	96955	53832	63422	46633	45508
Brazil/Brésil	262000	281384	212816	201836	274800	Czech Republic				158324	175922
Turkey/Turquie	131282	223582	177196	264703	160280	Russian Federation			x63996	x91249	x86186
Portugal	152293	148639	146636	206359	103841	Australia/Australie	32466	36312	43503	42997	63879
Australia/Australie	214077	157535	140899	159103	218232	Hungary/Hongrie	x75005	x54678	x45356	x22683	x20027
India/Inde	231191	148345	155149	119369	182756	Thailand/Thaïlande	30865	38415	36610	43839	69087
Denmark/Danemark	190287	177785	144117	99414	128577	India/Inde	52767	40745	39427	37549	40952
Czechoslovakia	262494	x135070	x259385			Former USSR/Anc. URSS	560690	x113904			
So. Africa Customs Un	151152	130591	120053	102796	116327	Mexico/Mexique	22227	29605	39404	32647	32728
Poland/Pologne	294165	132708	116014	84378	112025	Ireland/Irlande	31324	31411	36722	19759	22548
Hungary/Hongrie	x110005	77101	x149041	x99356	x102125	Israel/Israël	38217	27154	30150	28898	39211
Argentina/Argentine	37687	112163	84705	99880	131278	Malaysia/Malaisie	11275	14189	20010	36906	44576
Israel/Israël	63264	96445	80764	85768	113051	Yugoslavia SFR	391678	x56499			
Saudi Arabia	21150	62813	97416	x89147	x90346	Portugal	26192	22458	19065	14769	24893
Algeria/Algérie	175579	97180	84519	60242	23328	Turkey/Turquie	20005	15163	16286	12992	17580
Norway, SVD, JM	82295	85172	79565	60639	75291	Slovenia/Slovénia			20196	21331	22091
Finland/Finlande	219765	107023	62919	54020	98941	Argentina/Argentine	34734	18266	8755	11076	6715
Venezuela	46148	63474	84441	57849	28112	So. Africa Customs Un	16633	17902	8716	9175	
Ukraine			x32497	x172029	x68991	Croatia/Croatie			19550	14451	x9072
Ireland/Irlande	73375	68891	60539	69766	73012	Slovakia				x33193	x34277
Greece/Grèce	50689	60390	59651	49485	45831	New Zealand	9718	12374	8624	11697	10899
Philippines	38690	30266	48567	76935	68404	Greece/Grèce	5181	6050	8296	9873	4910
Chile/Chili	27317	29535	40680	57143	43190	Norway, SVD, JM	19071	9222	7540	7369	13099
Romania/Roumanie	133984	56788	22145	39193	22813	Ukraine			x5060	x14755	x5997
Czech Republic				116829	153251	Yugoslavia/Yougoslavie			x9992	x2224	x1103
Yugoslavia SFR	140655	x98400				Venezuela	4124	1481	2444	4293	1648
Egypt/Egypte	30238	29656	28168	36869	42723	Philippines	1815	4284	744	2088	4238

(VALUE AS % OF TOTAL)(VALEUR EN % DU TOTAL)

	1985	1986	1987	1988	1989	1990	1991	1992	1993	1994		1985	1986	1987	1988	1989	1990	1991	1992	1993	1994
Africa	2.3	x1.8	x1.4	x1.5	x1.7	2.0	1.9	x1.9	x2.0	x1.7	Afrique	0.1	x0.1	x0.0	x0.0	x0.0	0.1	0.1	x0.0	x0.0	x0.0
Northern Africa	1.4	1.0	0.7	0.6	0.7	1.0	0.8	0.9	0.9	x0.6	Afrique du Nord	0.0	0.0	x0.0	0.0	x0.0	0.0	0.0	0.0	0.0	0.0
Americas	28.2	24.2	18.6	17.6	19.2	16.9	18.5	20.5	25.1	28.1	Amériques	10.5	8.8	7.6	7.8	9.8	9.3	10.2	12.6	15.0	16.2
LAIA	3.3	2.2	2.5	3.1	3.0	2.9	3.8	6.1	5.9	5.3	ALAI	0.4	0.3	0.3	0.4	0.4	0.4	0.6	0.7	0.8	0.6
CACM	0.1	0.1	0.1	0.1	0.1	0.1	0.1	0.1	x0.1	x0.1	MCAC	0.0	x0.0	x0.0	0.0	0.0	0.0	0.0	0.0	x0.0	x0.0
Asia	12.8	12.3	x14.5	x17.2	16.3	17.5	23.5	28.2	36.8	34.7	Asie	24.4	23.4	x21.7	x22.4	23.0	21.4	23.4	23.0	28.1	29.4
Middle East	1.3	x1.8	x2.3	x3.5	x2.0	x1.9	x3.8	x4.9	x5.4	x2.5	Moyen–Orient	0.1	0.1	x0.1	0.1	0.1	0.1	0.1	0.1	x0.1	x0.1
Europe	34.6	39.3	38.8	37.8	40.9	45.3	46.5	46.1	32.8	32.0	Europe	56.8	60.1	56.3	56.7	60.0	64.1	63.1	62.3	54.8	52.4
EEC	27.0	31.0	30.6	30.4	33.5	41.4	43.1	43.1	30.1	29.5	CEE	43.2	45.6	42.9	43.2	46.5	52.1	53.2	53.2	46.5	43.4
EFTA	6.4	7.4	7.1	6.6	6.8	3.4	3.0	2.6	2.3	2.2	AELE	12.5	13.4	12.4	12.2	12.1	10.4	9.6	8.8	8.0	8.8
Oceania	1.9	x1.5	1.2	1.0	x1.0	x0.9	x0.7	x0.7	x1.0	x1.3	Océanie	0.1	x0.1	x0.1	x0.1	x0.1	x0.2	x0.2	x0.2	x0.3	x0.4
USA/Etats–Unis d'Amer	19.8	17.4	12.5	11.1	13.1	11.4	12.2	11.8	15.8	17.9	Germany/Allemagne	20.5	23.1	21.8	21.0	22.2	23.7	25.9	25.9	22.0	20.4
Germany/Allemagne	6.7	8.1	7.6	6.9	7.8	10.6	12.6	11.4	7.2	6.6	Japan/Japon	21.2	21.5	17.4	17.0	19.6	17.8	19.5	18.3	21.8	22.6
France, Monac	4.1	4.9	4.8	5.2	5.8	7.7	7.5	7.3	4.7	4.8	USA/Etats–Unis d'Amer	8.5	7.0	6.5	6.7	8.2	7.9	8.5	10.8	12.8	14.4
China/Chine	1.2	2.2	2.4	2.4	2.2	2.1	2.6	4.7	11.3	10.6	Italy/Italie	7.5	7.5	7.1	7.2	8.3	9.1	9.3	9.4	9.1	8.1
Korea, Republic of	2.1	2.3	2.6	2.7	3.5	3.5	4.4	5.0	4.3	5.3	Switz.Liecht	9.3	10.2	9.4	9.2	8.8	10.3	9.5	8.7	8.0	8.8
United Kingdom	4.5	4.7	3.6	4.4	4.9	5.1	4.9	4.7	3.8	3.8	United Kingdom	4.5	3.8	3.9	4.5	4.1	4.9	4.5	4.0	3.8	4.0
Italy/Italie	2.2	2.6	3.5	3.6	4.0	4.6	4.8	4.5	4.0	4.3	France, Monac	2.8	2.9	2.5	2.6	2.8	3.3	3.3	3.7	2.7	2.8
Japan/Japon	2.3	2.0	1.6	2.0	2.5	3.0	3.4	3.1	2.5	2.2	Belgium–Luxembourg	1.6	2.1	1.8	1.8	2.3	2.7	2.4	2.3	2.0	1.7
Mexico/Mexique	1.8	0.9	0.8	1.2	1.3	1.3	1.5	3.9	3.3	2.6	Austria/Autriche	1.2	1.5	1.3	1.3	1.5	2.0	1.8	2.0	1.8	x1.3
Iran (Islamic Rp. of)		x0.6	x1.4	x1.6	x0.7		x2.4	x3.3	x2.8	x0.7	Spain/Espagne	1.6	1.3	1.4	1.4	1.7	2.2	2.0	1.9	1.5	1.5

TRADE BY COMMODITY IN THOUSAND U.S. DOLLARS – COMMERCE PAR PRODUIT EN MILLIERS DE DOLLARS E.U

COUNTRIES–PAYS	IMPORTS – IMPORTATIONS 1990	1991	1992	1993	1994
Total	7527455	7498435	7224444	6128163	7822495
Africa	x203351	164924	x189924	x197902	x378078
Northern Africa	62630	64050	x73077	x71474	x62647
Americas	1309256	1345743	1215600	1509804	1896113
LAIA	317085	340520	350588	459551	722069
CACM	5142	4740	4260	x8744	x8703
Asia	1393926	x2209156	2476352	2317126	3038373
Middle East	x139706	x420028	x446036	x326157	x361892
Europe	2814000	3068100	3053256	1846645	2185931
EEC	2619090	2883108	2908415	1719382	2046274
EFTA	141140	149362	111216	102226	119397
Oceania	x71594	x95756	x98754	x74614	x117164
USA/Etats–Unis d'Amer	705671	765488	635929	808860	909238
Germany/Allemagne	509821	591748	597516	397854	394881
Korea, Republic of	335658	576520	483024	365435	638239
China/Chine	247422	325930	402914	418325	784709
France, Monac	389829	391236	407537	246736	270730
Belgium–Luxembourg	293685	369374	422560	181059	253113
United Kingdom	389097	341234	375518	196691	270757
Italy/Italie	251701	402461	262092	158345	181631
Spain/Espagne	193262	211407	308567	179679	178309
Iran (Islamic Rp. of)		x266998	x281430	x149641	x128296
Thailand/Thaïlande	69167	125532	132934	413083	306141
Canada	236387	208979	209874	220833	243284
Malaysia/Malaisie	97972	147934	255361	170423	238007
Mexico/Mexique	92713	152327	180399	219443	395717
Indonesia/Indonésie	97216	136283	252523	121446	117646
Netherlands/Pays–Bas	172234	151863	166108	97591	175130
Japan/Japon	123963	138325	121543	119156	149422
Hong Kong	79547	87207	111813	152636	135827
Former USSR/Anc. URSS	1235695	x336368			
Singapore/Singapour	96214	112607	99252	98861	132194
Sweden/Suède	113715	135279	88428	57281	97533
Austria/Autriche	113517	101425	89919	76713	90564
Switz.Liecht	102361	113221	71189	72603	74291
Turkey/Turquie	59324	93113	71426	84099	157027
Ukraine			x27101	x217902	x47168
Poland/Pologne	165220	108306	88300	38012	74658
Australia/Australie	59253	84201	86017	57676	96848
Brazil/Brésil	45930	67985	53881	104469	142575
So. Africa Customs Un	100650	67947	76590	77546	282528
Russian Federation			x114766	x45187	x52786
Venezuela	92369	71526	49098	33291	20634
India/Inde	44233	27636	56445	45004	66106
Saudi Arabia	18179	32046	51439	x44787	x29180
Finland/Finlande	57078	52750	37098	28746	43419
Denmark/Danemark	43286	41961	46916	28496	34726
Portugal	46314	37389	42233	33764	26131
Czechoslovakia	88146	x48742	x56324		
Norway,SVD,JM	32901	30059	37379	28341	42479
Greece/Grèce	27818	33467	38780	23325	15906
Algeria/Algérie	29822	33990	33596	20573	18899
Hungary/Hongrie	x33181	33874	x28971	x21827	x22269
Bulgaria/Bulgarie	x171434	x71815	5493	x5206	x5147
Philippines	25551	28136	24310	27396	23564
Chile/Chili	33646	12553	20546	37740	74952
Argentina/Argentine	16960	16140	24912	29324	45774
Israel/Israël	14684	26794	20324	19711	28414
Ireland/Irlande	17735	21514	25142	13102	13443
Mongolia/Mongolie	x28	x37907	x11267	x4776	x58
Slovakia				x52434	x26060
United Arab Emirates	10727	13652	16016	x22256	x20358

COUNTRIES–PAYS	EXPORTS – EXPORTATIONS 1990	1991	1992	1993	1994
Totale	6850211	6945729	6773860	6372389	7353443
Afrique	3651	6033	6985	x4963	x847
Afrique du Nord	355	510	x338	x182	203
Amériques	947861	911121	899307	1007454	1181626
ALAI	31914	33235	47457	70831	46479
MCAC	12	3	26	x998	x2429
Asie	1032150	1421775	1305525	1383851	1911867
Moyen–Orient	4828	3181	4399	x6083	x6993
Europe	4226434	4446029	4471736	3853591	4153513
CEE	3755801	3993386	4006927	3461514	3741307
AELE	423576	429508	438140	368184	389801
Océanie	17890	x16092	18767	14114	x11890
Germany/Allemagne	1285732	1468203	1457589	1194649	1221700
Japan/Japon	819406	1170458	1012003	1028442	1435663
USA/Etats–Unis d'Amer	807505	762093	742969	819135	934985
Italy/Italie	685301	760543	709859	653698	757108
France, Monac	337748	390468	419962	459624	360279
Switz.Liecht	409488	413307	421516	352622	371287
United Kingdom	403896	398377	353765	253587	343240
Sweden/Suède	252733	225116	246578	224551	279420
Austria/Autriche	200200	211686	228858	199199	x173146
Belgium–Luxembourg	197138	191096	226544	162171	165408
Hong Kong	89919	94638	122710	179567	172643
Netherlands/Pays–Bas	154848	148188	141310	98288	124824
Canada	107139	114186	108233	115721	196605
Spain/Espagne	101288	84338	102881	132089	189913
Korea, Republic of	51026	55355	68646	48002	130103
Finland/Finlande	70481	49166	52916	38860	66926
Denmark/Danemark	52593	50267	50657	33679	39260
Singapore/Singapour	31085	39278	29746	42323	72488
China/Chine	11147	32868	33475	44168	46523
Romania/Roumanie	47973	36944	18814	25481	15939
Brazil/Brésil	17408	19544	30671	30525	29335
Poland/Pologne	55173	41104	16870	8172	12143
Czech Republic				55719	47416
Mexico/Mexique	10755	9278	12268	30698	11369
Norway,SVD,JM	14085	15996	16616	15563	18515
Hungary/Hongrie	x14013	x15284	x13967	x12070	x9434
Slovenia/Slovénia			20978	18106	20556
Australia/Australie	16758	13720	12454	12169	10304
Czechoslovakia		x22225	x15485		
Malaysia/Malaisie	7914	8774	10835	9370	20611
India/Inde	5493	6025	9938	9341	11071
Ireland/Irlande	10190	11562	10625	3036	15663
Former USSR/Anc. URSS	490758	x24975			
Thailand/Thaïlande	3647	5573	9105	10060	10493
Yugoslavia SFR	44572	x22676			
Russian Federation			x14458	x7161	x9300
Lithuania/Lituanie			16304	x722	7886
So. Africa Customs Un	2635	4639	6053	3642	
Portugal	2495	3294	3559	6763	3025
Ukraine			x3402	x10184	x4258
Argentina/Argentine	3240	2985	2899	7066	3269
Bulgaria/Bulgarie	x8931	x3200	x5478	x2821	x3364
Israel/Israël	6392	4279	2936	3130	2608
New Zealand	896	2120	5871	1666	1532
Turkey/Turquie	691	1040	1815	3049	3952
Croatia/Croatie			2758	2349	x1270
Greece/Grèce	1147	1070	1824	1318	1395
Slovakia				x4142	x5403
Yugoslavia/Yougoslavie			x2607	x1403	x357
Saudi Arabia	1449	1545	1102	x123	x275

(VALUE AS % OF TOTAL)(VALEUR EN % DU TOTAL)

	1985	1986	1987	1988	1989	1990	1991	1992	1993	1994
Africa	3.0	3.2	x1.5	x1.5	x2.1	x2.7	2.2	x2.7	x3.3	x4.8
Northern Africa	1.7	1.5	0.8	0.6	0.7	0.8	0.9	x1.0	x1.2	x0.8
Americas	27.6	21.8	17.1	18.1	19.3	17.4	18.0	16.8	24.6	24.2
LAIA	5.2	4.9	4.2	4.1	5.1	4.2	4.5	4.9	7.5	9.2
CACM	0.3	0.0	x0.1	0.0	0.1	0.1	0.1	0.1	x0.1	x0.1
Asia	11.6	12.9	19.0	24.8	22.0	18.5	x29.5	34.3	37.8	38.9
Middle East	2.0	x2.5	x1.8	x1.9	x2.0	x1.9	x5.6	x6.2	x5.3	x4.6
Europe	33.1	32.1	30.3	29.0	33.5	37.4	40.9	42.3	30.1	27.9
EEC	26.6	25.6	24.1	24.1	27.9	34.8	38.4	40.3	28.1	26.2
EFTA	5.0	4.8	4.9	4.1	4.8	1.9	2.0	1.5	1.7	1.5
Oceania	2.7	x2.9	x1.7	x1.0	1.0	x0.9	x1.2	x1.3	x1.2	x1.5
USA/Etats–Unis d'Amer	16.4	10.1	8.1	9.8	9.5	9.4	10.2	8.8	13.2	11.6
Germany/Allemagne	5.2	5.4	4.5	4.0	4.5	6.8	7.9	8.3	6.5	5.0
Korea, Republic of	3.1	5.4	3.3	4.2	7.0	4.5	7.7	6.7	6.0	8.2
China/Chine			7.1	10.5	5.9	3.3	4.3	5.6	6.8	10.0
France, Monac	3.7	3.4	3.2	3.3	3.8	5.2	5.2	5.6	4.0	3.5
Belgium–Luxembourg	3.1	2.6	2.9	2.7	3.1	3.9	4.9	5.8	3.0	3.2
United Kingdom	4.4	3.3	3.0	4.5	4.6	5.2	4.6	5.2	3.2	3.5
Italy/Italie	2.5	2.3	2.5	2.1	2.6	3.3	5.4	3.6	2.6	2.3
Spain/Espagne	1.2	1.3	1.6	1.8	2.8	2.6	2.8	4.3	2.9	2.3
Iran (Islamic Rp. of)		x0.8	x0.6	x0.6	x0.6		x3.6	x3.9	x2.4	x1.6

	1985	1986	1987	1988	1989	1990	1991	1992	1993	1994
Afrique		x0.0	x0.0	x0.0	x0.0		0.1	0.1	x0.1	x0.0
Afrique du Nord	0.0	x0.0	x0.0	x0.0	x0.0	0.0	0.0	x0.0	x0.0	0.0
Amériques	11.8	10.6	9.6	10.1	12.7	13.9	13.1	13.3	15.8	16.1
ALAI	0.7	0.3	0.5	0.3	0.4	0.5	0.5	0.7	1.1	0.6
MCAC	0.0	x0.0	x0.0	0.0	x0.0	0.0	0.0	0.0	x0.0	x0.0
Asie	18.3	18.3	x16.3	x18.3	18.9	15.1	20.5	19.3	21.7	26.0
Moyen–Orient	0.1	x0.1	x0.1	0.1	0.1	0.1	0.0	0.1	x0.1	x0.1
Europe	50.7	53.8	56.6	55.9	57.0	61.7	64.0	66.0	60.5	56.5
CEE	40.5	43.5	46.1	44.5	44.7	54.8	57.5	59.2	54.3	50.9
AELE	9.7	9.8	10.1	11.1	11.9	6.2	6.2	6.5	5.8	5.3
Océanie	0.2	x0.2	0.2	x0.1	x0.2	0.3	x0.2	0.3	0.2	x0.2
Germany/Allemagne	13.2	15.8	16.2	14.7	16.1	18.8	21.1	21.5	18.7	16.6
Japan/Japon	16.3	16.8	14.0	14.9	16.2	12.0	16.9	14.9	16.1	19.5
USA/Etats–Unis d'Amer	10.3	9.7	8.4	8.8	11.4	11.8	11.0	11.0	12.9	12.7
Italy/Italie	6.6	7.4	8.8	7.6	8.0	10.0	10.9	10.5	10.3	10.3
France, Monac	4.7	3.9	3.5	5.5	4.0	4.9	5.6	6.2	7.2	4.9
Switz.Liecht	3.3	4.0	4.6	4.9	5.3	6.0	6.0	6.2	5.5	5.0
United Kingdom	4.4	5.5	6.9	5.9	4.5	5.9	5.7	5.2	4.0	4.7
Sweden/Suède	2.9	2.7	2.6	3.1	3.2	3.7	3.2	3.6	3.5	3.8
Austria/Autriche	2.7	2.1	2.2	2.3	2.4	2.9	3.0	3.4	3.1	x2.4
Belgium–Luxembourg	2.0	2.0	1.9	1.6	2.0	2.9	2.8	3.3	2.5	2.2

TRADE BY COMMODITY IN THOUSAND U.S. DOLLARS – COMMERCE PAR PRODUIT EN MILLIERS DE DOLLARS E.U

COUNTRIES–PAYS	IMPORTS – IMPORTATIONS 1990	1991	1992	1993	1994
Total	23018237	25152179	28319376	26686955	29960720
Africa	x1256346	x940128	x1098790	x1141653	x1049979
Northern Africa	557683	413654	x477538	x534256	x534649
Americas	4433240	4236612	4831133	5290891	6334031
LAIA	907314	924689	1348450	1674567	2018209
CACM	55442	64028	89152	x67762	x73867
Asia	5433222	8044742	9943849	x10391889	11792823
Middle East	864789	x1786996	x2516184	x2384805	x1864416
Europe	9937953	10357246	11244956	8696064	9431109
EEC	9071094	9561982	10430965	7978433	8583558
EFTA	688032	654921	669739	585947	671273
Oceania	x352605	x377282	x358675	x421667	x558423
Germany/Allemagne	1632681	1970328	2245859	1750686	1791781
USA/Etats–Unis d'Amer	1878934	1769521	1965501	2013059	2485462
France,Monac	1348990	1435468	1422235	1082620	1222396
Canada	1248335	1207928	1241441	1266835	1493068
Hong Kong	533245	832641	1433250	1445436	1721715
United Kingdom	1137991	1186310	1216756	1034232	1139771
Korea, Republic of	983246	1120876	1085723	794815	1337234
China/Chine	520979	553044	803316	1352572	1854958
Spain/Espagne	831609	913385	1077331	652019	677102
Japan/Japon	588601	800314	862998	810919	846968
Italy/Italie	821666	826349	939790	670693	720632
Iran (Islamic Rp. of)		x651567	x818934	x769320	x278822
Belgium–Luxembourg	748150	734048	843302	599184	641864
Singapore/Singapour	430562	597479	764540	809931	1007297
Thailand/Thaïlande	363361	787785	572357	774092	862455
Indonesia/Indonésie	456762	579218	748886	655961	643078
Netherlands/Pays–Bas	653683	693064	758323	527289	580164
Saudi Arabia	210981	505270	810410	x473629	x460840
Malaysia/Malaisie	241898	523290	559546	687122	737600
Mexico/Mexique	318143	399587	568562	601741	674433
Switz.Liecht	471944	457809	466167	419076	472546
Austria/Autriche	402697	428603	441771	421113	444707
Sweden/Suède	417443	339222	333102	297915	386186
Portugal	271163	300500	351567	230291	205173
Australia/Australie	256657	285350	268660	319959	429937
Russian Federation			x475802	x316062	x378089
Turkey/Turquie	207742	209273	255254	315197	265633
Greece/Grèce	248609	212404	250143	253649	253131
So. Africa Customs Un	389241	232363	245345	236794	236190
Former USSR/Anc. URSS	689823	x713660			
United Arab Emirates	165113	147720	175324	x372326	x402343
Venezuela	181449	127847	239848	315248	398133
Poland/Pologne	124085	130695	268766	218618	260223
Algeria/Algérie	259560	145756	190099	251352	158177
Denmark/Danemark	185688	188768	206317	178292	191367
Norway,SVD,JM	206594	188073	190896	157587	186033
Ireland/Irlande	146300	149736	180049	153266	152755
Finland/Finlande	224423	183796	164420	127182	176528
Czechoslovakia	163380	x152482	x315267		
Chile/Chili	152577	112951	157156	173358	147209
Hungary/Hongrie	x146222	127023	x164264	x143249	x141510
Kuwait/ Koweït	81009	56290	175132	186896	160629
Argentina/Argentine	29534	65557	126102	189139	314963
Israel/Israël	98241	100756	118808	156134	192953
Brazil/Brésil	111249	95893	121321	148360	227570
Nigeria/Nigéria	x51571	33386	x130081	x163034	x68745
Philippines	86319	71032	86128	124131	164600
India/Inde	79664	74364	85039	81414	116159
Libyan Arab Jamahiriya	93236	81299	x72130	x69636	x76696
Pakistan	35024	62435	90931	63843	120508

COUNTRIES–PAYS	EXPORTS – EXPORTATIONS 1990	1991	1992	1993	1994
Totale	23198767	24768574	27775673	27125177	30600724
Afrique	41522	50517	44172	x35690	x8228
Afrique du Nord	23236	15050	13921	7027	5525
Amériques	4311600	4465133	5163281	5488173	6158656
ALAI	274855	256987	478127	515183	667953
MCAC	5237	10229	16520	4765	5632
Asie	4230462	5597444	7272859	7709086	8898545
Moyen–Orient	95268	100442	116119	x95943	x146040
Europe	14160007	14388197	15052222	13547966	15104063
CEE	13237819	13590321	14241540	12794629	14272990
AELE	843584	774588	761115	715642	786778
Océanie	97173	135190	x125026	x178819	x254172
Japan/Japon	3010108	3762210	4481754	4372827	4668831
USA/Etats–Unis d'Amer	3658598	3832205	4244678	4486562	4970435
Germany/Allemagne	3652483	3973539	3982567	3336573	3654941
Italy/Italie	2634597	2731683	2868235	2843533	3089095
France,Monac	1822176	1899475	1976293	1692991	2013919
United Kingdom	1165508	1140792	1166326	1079157	1154577
Hong Kong	212060	369920	800783	958113	1085482
Denmark/Danemark	709338	635695	795152	687764	794063
Sweden/Suède	768152	718587	728754	631615	734348
Switz.Liecht	730203	681910	661351	644081	692292
Netherlands/Pays–Bas	611556	637931	700189	635183	694713
Belgium–Luxembourg	462075	532670	669697	606005	697417
Malaysia/Malaisie	222983	431616	538792	655788	821601
Singapore/Singapour	260788	360549	463243	534577	636518
Canada	366148	362477	419832	474850	504866
Austria/Autriche	433432	429667	423619	396952	x458542
Spain/Espagne	374306	359693	397974	380337	427071
Korea, Republic of	162861	199547	354245	472725	564686
Thailand/Thaïlande	88654	214279	326661	377837	595558
Mexico/Mexique	67756	97709	334540	317604	449015
Ireland/Irlande	229030	247791	237226	210720	238871
Finland/Finlande	275895	183657	158463	183520	199753
Australia/Australie	70470	97405	88709	135452	181791
Brazil/Brésil	116317	92714	83792	136793	146719
Portugal	90966	87154	119220	89748	90970
Israel/Israël	108597	82103	87233	104879	140888
Norway,SVD,JM	113305	92615	99642	71174	94472
China/Chine	37855	34966	55379	74947	163765
Saudi Arabia	34741	61701	64351	x27101	x32859
New Zealand	26247	37428	35135	42351	71462
Argentina/Argentine	30154	30218	32778	36078	36786
Hungary/Hongrie	x25629	x24529	x36367	x31049	x26171
So. Africa Customs Un	15506	31177	27943	25556	
Poland/Pologne	85890	39118	17487	25795	39017
Czechoslovakia		x31103	x33768		
Turkey/Turquie	6236	15963	25191	23252	57532
Czech Republic				63947	77376
India/Inde	19432	17535	18242	24543	28093
Slovenia/Slovénia			31294	26261	35398
Greece/Grèce	8079	11762	17823	20531	24708
Russian Federation			x18343	x29045	x26890
Bulgaria/Bulgarie	x74158	x7547	x22689	x11459	x3202
Venezuela	56823	20085	5194	5091	8600
Macau/Macao	810	7754	12209	9217	4421
Chile/Chili	1754	9860	10292	8556	17524
Colombia/Colombie	1878	6188	11203	8702	7414
United Arab Emirates	26708	2701	1741	x21300	x17277
Former USSR/Anc. URSS	66649	x25584			
Philippines	6505	7718	7941	8987	8638
Yugoslavia SFR	77285	x22321			

(VALUE AS % OF TOTAL)(VALEUR EN % DU TOTAL)

	1985	1986	1987	1988	1989	1990	1991	1992	1993	1994
Africa	6.2	x6.4	x4.4	x3.6	x4.6	x5.5	x3.7	x3.9	x4.3	x3.5
Northern Africa	3.6	3.4	1.6	1.3	1.7	2.4	1.6	x1.7	x2.0	x1.8
Americas	19.7	x18.4	x16.8	18.7	20.0	19.3	16.8	17.0	19.8	21.2
LAIA	4.2	3.2	3.1	3.6	3.5	3.9	3.7	4.8	6.3	6.7
CACM	0.4	0.2	x0.4	0.3	0.3	0.2	0.3	0.3	x0.3	x0.2
Asia	25.5	x23.1	x25.1	x27.7	25.5	23.6	32.0	35.1	x38.9	39.4
Middle East	9.3	x9.0	x6.1	x5.6	x5.3	3.8	x7.1	x8.9	x8.9	x6.2
Europe	40.8	44.0	43.5	40.1	41.1	43.2	41.2	39.7	32.6	31.5
EEC	32.7	35.3	35.0	32.8	33.7	39.4	38.0	36.8	29.9	28.6
EFTA	7.3	8.0	7.9	6.7	6.5	3.0	2.6	2.4	2.2	2.2
Oceania	1.7	x1.5	x1.4	x1.4	x1.5	x1.6	x1.5	x1.3	x1.5	x1.9
Germany/Allemagne	6.3	6.8	6.3	5.5	5.6	7.1	7.8	7.9	6.6	6.0
USA/Etats–Unis d'Amer	9.5	9.1	8.6	8.1	9.0	8.2	7.0	6.9	7.5	8.3
France,Monac	5.4	5.7	5.6	5.1	5.1	5.9	5.7	5.0	4.1	4.1
Canada	4.9	3.8	3.4	5.9	6.3	5.4	4.8	4.4	4.7	5.0
Hong Kong	2.4	2.1	2.0	3.7	2.9	2.3	3.3	5.1	5.4	5.7
United Kingdom	5.2	4.8	4.6	4.9	4.8	4.9	4.7	4.3	3.9	3.8
Korea, Republic of	2.7	3.6	3.5	3.0	4.1	4.3	4.5	3.8	3.0	4.5
China/Chine			3.2	3.7	3.3	2.3	2.2	2.8	5.1	6.2
Spain/Espagne	1.3	2.1	2.9	2.8	2.9	3.6	3.6	3.8	2.4	2.3
Japan/Japon	2.3	2.2	2.0	2.4	2.6	2.6	3.2	3.0	3.0	2.8

	1985	1986	1987	1988	1989	1990	1991	1992	1993	1994
Afrique		x0.0	0.1	x0.0	x0.2	0.2	0.2	0.2	x0.1	x0.0
Afrique du Nord	0.0	0.0	0.0	0.0	0.1	0.1	0.1	0.1	0.0	0.0
Amériques	18.6	15.5	14.8	15.8	17.9	18.5	18.0	18.6	20.2	20.1
ALAI	1.0	0.9	1.0	0.9	1.2	1.2	1.0	1.7	1.9	2.2
MCAC	0.0	0.0	0.0	0.0	0.0	0.0	0.0	0.1	0.0	0.0
Asie	20.0	19.2	x19.1	21.6	20.5	18.2	22.6	26.1	28.4	29.1
Moyen–Orient	0.3	0.3	x0.3	0.5	x0.5	0.4	0.4	0.4	x0.4	x0.5
Europe	58.3	62.6	61.0	57.4	58.5	61.0	58.1	54.2	49.9	49.4
CEE	50.0	53.3	52.5	48.5	50.1	57.1	54.9	51.3	47.2	46.6
AELE	7.6	8.5	8.1	8.5	8.2	3.6	3.1	2.7	2.6	2.6
Océanie	0.3	x0.2	x0.3	x0.4	x0.5	0.4	0.5	x0.4	x0.7	x0.8
Japan/Japon	16.7	15.8	14.2	14.2	14.3	13.0	15.2	16.1	16.1	15.3
USA/Etats–Unis d'Amer	16.4	13.4	12.6	13.7	15.4	15.8	15.5	15.3	16.5	16.2
Germany/Allemagne	14.3	16.4	15.5	14.1	13.7	15.7	16.0	14.3	12.3	11.9
Italy/Italie	10.1	10.9	11.5	9.5	10.4	11.4	11.0	10.3	10.5	10.1
France,Monac	7.3	7.3	7.1	6.4	7.1	7.9	7.7	7.1	6.2	6.6
United Kingdom	4.5	4.0	4.2	4.5	4.2	5.0	4.6	4.2	4.0	3.8
Hong Kong	1.2	0.8	0.9	1.8	1.4	0.9	1.5	2.9	3.5	3.5
Denmark/Danemark	2.8	2.9	2.7	2.5	2.8	3.1	2.6	2.9	2.5	2.6
Sweden/Suède	2.7	2.8	2.7	3.0	2.8	3.3	2.9	2.6	2.3	2.4
Switz.Liecht	2.2	2.8	2.7	2.8	2.6	3.1	2.8	2.4	2.4	2.3

TRADE BY COMMODITY IN THOUSAND U.S. DOLLARS – COMMERCE PAR PRODUIT EN MILLIERS DE DOLLARS E.U

COUNTRIES–PAYS	IMPORTS – IMPORTATIONS 1990	1991	1992	1993	1994
Total	11889271	12255366	13613284	12947276	14696351
Africa	x642064	x621078	x616920	x643974	x658440
Northern Africa	308265	316596	x308465	x315201	x330850
Americas	2508610	2623976	2893672	3228112	3602683
LAIA	517660	633967	720299	838963	848998
CACM	26138	26115	35357	x33851	x39449
Asia	2017175	x2706813	x3139438	x3033666	x3400480
Middle East	374137	x836930	x1064305	x854365	x719364
Europe	5790487	5790615	6536280	5556649	6477163
EEC	5329204	5404925	6120662	5191470	6083032
EFTA	370504	332930	355706	313565	332231
Oceania	x225122	x201411	x220328	x227227	x286282
USA/Etats–Unis d'Amer	1259903	1261146	1433167	1585520	1857880
Germany/Allemagne	986124	1113235	1337918	994486	1128959
France,Monac	988737	999462	1146924	956767	1139320
United Kingdom	658391	668217	737772	875467	973411
Italy/Italie	627954	641901	705993	562021	700536
Canada	572609	590848	610572	677972	774302
Korea, Republic of	455756	598547	496362	481504	617371
Spain/Espagne	364063	370824	430978	340518	389377
Netherlands/Pays–Bas	395577	398562	437521	300204	368977
Iran (Islamic Rp. of)		x309053	x373532	x218726	x125474
Sweden/Suède	325693	289579	281589	262572	331421
Austria/Autriche	248020	249247	299174	271771	336404
Belgium–Luxembourg	293263	274630	288816	242914	289291
Saudi Arabia	100347	251554	338545	x201034	x173674
Singapore/Singapour	211310	226323	268553	269759	364456
Mexico/Mexique	153533	189182	266432	296717	262419
Japan/Japon	269047	239262	225710	209945	255626
Indonesia/Indonésie	130636	190809	264145	216123	210402
Thailand/Thaïlande	129810	156182	217625	270100	339316
Switz.Liecht	229307	204777	202648	182642	198148
Australia/Australie	169088	154468	166741	172973	219243
Malaysia/Malaisie	81287	122370	155881	148523	133288
China/Chine	93902	94311	135789	192689	301904
Norway,SVD,JM	134139	121678	146616	125688	127081
Denmark/Danemark	118210	112750	129839	128944	147340
Turkey/Turquie	91427	114356	121740	129633	102000
Venezuela	74902	140162	117944	106270	83521
Russian Federation			x159729	x199661	x133861
So. Africa Customs Un	108677	98504	111486	108378	123265
Brazil/Brésil	93751	93309	82241	118158	141222
Hong Kong	76207	74723	95044	122218	138467
Finland/Finlande	122057	93345	98439	83519	109261
Libyan Arab Jamahiriya	65106	95239	x86436	x92395	x101505
United Arab Emirates	75463	55640	74810	x136714	x148980
Algeria/Algérie	97107	91067	80518	92486	83538
Argentina/Argentine	29692	54097	93138	103093	124280
Portugal	81635	85842	100009	61230	56143
Hungary/Hongrie	x68767	60020	x66501	x68258	x64167
Israel/Israël	47374	50609	62415	69329	71799
Greece/Grèce	61859	54223	65842	60194	54614
Chile/Chili	62033	48723	60236	66933	69331
Nigeria/Nigéria	x37437	41645	x54868	x77768	x52994
Ireland/Irlande	57620	53107	59849	50862	57978
Egypt/Egypte	60997	53517	53906	55717	61962
Former USSR/Anc. URSS	520166	x161282			
Poland/Pologne	21936	28782	61596	70118	77402
India/Inde	66822	41536	56522	53820	75027
Philippines	34626	35725	35732	60479	66846
Colombia/Colombie	34121	35899	31976	53411	77321
New Zealand	40339	33607	37362	41193	52956

COUNTRIES–PAYS	EXPORTS – EXPORTATIONS 1990	1991	1992	1993	1994
Totale	11401396	11790246	13016447	12853251	14652231
Afrique	x22904	21935	x33202	x34324	x6107
Afrique du Nord	1914	2748	7545	4328	x2381
Amériques	1848996	2104279	2263747	2551356	2801782
ALAI	121926	140973	182583	256450	311449
MCAC	30	131	220	x164	x244
Asie	1697225	1857717	2131132	2375807	2666811
Moyen–Orient	35331	26707	37238	x42219	x56343
Europe	7629000	7655704	8445279	7707880	8962522
CEE	7258374	7273659	8048231	7357077	8596568
AELE	317918	350152	359550	318837	344169
Océanie	x49042	60159	x61170	x63794	x80990
Germany/Allemagne	3048230	3107949	3541468	3171015	3716329
USA/Etats–Unis d'Amer	1563213	1801027	1889838	2085551	2267276
Japan/Japon	1435251	1595292	1784757	1968776	2146058
Italy/Italie	924127	963251	1017860	998730	1118759
France,Monac	795274	775910	848193	863996	1064105
United Kingdom	742930	710294	779918	715674	845383
Netherlands/Pays–Bas	356629	376236	408263	320958	362527
Sweden/Suède	415171	366429	391304	322614	392197
Denmark/Danemark	294180	320711	350612	318495	375620
Switz.Liecht	239028	248400	251578	222543	252326
Austria/Autriche	205727	194340	209451	199063	x171205
Spain/Espagne	190659	195282	229638	168361	222980
Canada	161632	160835	189857	207937	221380
Belgium–Luxembourg	118669	113023	119338	138343	157318
Brazil/Brésil	80308	91948	117572	152972	216016
Norway,SVD,JM	78885	101746	107971	96294	91841
Singapore/Singapour	84229	78462	99209	107214	164335
Ireland/Irlande	71861	67172	74849	71064	88049
Finland/Finlande	81792	72066	62709	60250	74182
Korea, Republic of	47722	48418	58381	63419	81458
Australia/Australie	42353	51771	53248	57392	73476
Hong Kong	28827	32103	46248	60124	72292
Mexico/Mexique	17378	21366	33204	72301	59904
China/Chine	21183	25950	36719	63731	81396
India/Inde	25889	23511	32308	32701	30381
So. Africa Customs Un	16746	16547	22439	26184	
Argentina/Argentine	12777	17632	18106	19870	22705
Czech Republic				55113	54679
Hungary/Hongrie	x13703	x13888	x21158	x18537	x36913
Czechoslovakia		x30289	x22727		
Turkey/Turquie	10472	12320	18119	19107	24198
Romania/Roumanie	7995	11345	13515	17675	8392
Poland/Pologne	3399	16586	11971	11948	17465
Malaysia/Malaisie	8505	10498	13730	13305	15204
Malta/Malte	9629	12508	11131	13794	x692
Thailand/Thaïlande	4761	8548	12337	12755	14783
Bulgaria/Bulgarie	x50072	x8569	12016	8741	7987
Cyprus/Chypre	8664	8422	8787	7377	6030
Slovenia/Slovénia			13496	9894	16165
Russian Federation			x7425	x12304	x8557
New Zealand	6118	7112	6827	5366	7081
Yugoslavia SFR	42976	x19228			
Portugal	6729	6586	7613	3499	4092
Greece/Grèce	6351	4364	7016	5015	3822
Croatia/Croatie			9178	6007	x3106
Indonesia/Indonésie	688	3197	6621	4454	1986
Colombia/Colombie	1625	4651	4538	4935	6050
Peru/Pérou	3909	3852	3610	3317	3469
Former USSR/Anc. URSS	68674	x9346			
Saudi Arabia	2660	2287	1395	x4408	x7850

(VALUE AS % OF TOTAL)(VALEUR EN % DU TOTAL)

	1985	1986	1987	1988	1989	1990	1991	1992	1993	1994
Africa	8.2	x6.8	x5.3	x5.7	x5.5	x5.4	x5.1	x4.5	x4.9	x4.4
Northern Africa	5.1	3.2	2.2	2.5	2.3	2.6	2.6	x2.3	x2.4	x2.3
Americas	23.8	21.1	19.1	21.5	21.8	21.1	21.4	21.2	25.0	24.5
LAIA	6.1	5.3	4.5	4.3	4.1	4.4	5.2	5.3	6.5	5.8
CACM	0.3	0.3	x0.4	0.3	0.3	0.2	0.2	0.3	x0.3	x0.3
Asia	18.0	x18.8	x17.9	x17.1	16.2	17.0	x22.1	x23.0	x23.5	x23.1
Middle East	6.3	x8.9	x6.2	x5.0	x4.1	3.1	x6.8	x7.8	x6.6	x4.9
Europe	42.3	46.0	48.5	47.1	48.4	48.7	47.2	48.0	42.9	44.1
EEC	33.3	36.5	38.5	38.2	39.8	44.8	44.1	45.0	40.1	41.4
EFTA	7.8	8.6	9.0	8.0	7.8	3.1	2.7	2.6	2.4	2.3
Oceania	2.1	x1.8	x1.8	x1.9	2.1	x1.9	x1.6	x1.6	x1.8	x2.0
USA/Etats–Unis d'Amer	11.9	11.1	10.5	11.6	11.5	10.6	10.3	10.5	12.2	12.6
Germany/Allemagne	5.7	6.5	6.7	6.4	6.9	8.3	9.1	9.8	7.7	7.7
France,Monac	5.8	6.3	6.9	7.0	7.5	8.3	8.2	8.4	7.4	7.8
United Kingdom	4.8	4.6	4.6	5.0	5.2	5.5	5.5	5.4	6.8	6.6
Italy/Italie	3.8	4.5	4.9	4.8	5.0	5.3	5.2	5.2	4.3	4.8
Canada	4.8	3.7	3.1	4.6	5.1	4.8	4.8	4.5	5.2	5.3
Korea, Republic of	2.2	2.0	2.5	2.5	2.7	3.8	4.9	3.6	3.7	4.2
Spain/Espagne	1.4	1.8	2.3	2.7	2.5	3.1	3.0	3.2	2.6	2.6
Netherlands/Pays–Bas	2.7	3.0	3.0	2.7	2.8	3.3	3.3	3.2	2.3	2.5
Iran (Islamic Rp. of)		x1.1	x1.1	x0.8	x0.5		x2.5	x2.7	x1.7	x0.9

	1985	1986	1987	1988	1989	1990	1991	1992	1993	1994
Afrique	0.2	x0.1	x0.1	x0.1	x0.1	x0.2	0.1	x0.3	x0.3	x0.0
Afrique du Nord	0.0	x0.0	x0.0	x0.0	x0.0	0.0	0.0	0.1	0.0	x0.0
Amériques	19.4	15.1	13.7	14.1	16.1	16.2	17.8	17.4	19.8	19.1
ALAI	0.9	0.9	0.9	1.0	1.0	1.1	1.2	1.4	2.0	2.1
MCAC	0.0	x0.0	0.0	x0.0	x0.0	0.0	0.0	0.0	x0.0	x0.0
Asie	11.1	10.4	x10.3	x14.3	15.3	14.9	15.7	16.4	18.5	18.2
Moyen–Orient	0.5	x0.4	x0.5	0.4	x0.2	0.3	0.2	0.3	x0.3	x0.4
Europe	63.6	68.2	69.1	65.8	65.6	66.9	64.9	64.9	60.0	61.2
CEE	55.4	59.6	60.0	57.1	57.2	63.7	61.7	61.8	57.2	58.7
AELE	7.4	8.0	8.3	7.9	7.8	2.8	3.0	2.8	2.5	2.3
Océanie	0.3	x0.3	x0.3	x0.4	x0.4	x0.4	0.5	x0.5	x0.5	x0.5
Germany/Allemagne	21.4	24.8	25.7	24.6	25.2	26.7	26.4	27.2	24.7	25.4
USA/Etats–Unis d'Amer	17.4	13.2	12.0	11.8	13.6	13.7	15.3	14.5	16.2	15.5
Japan/Japon	9.2	8.6	7.8	12.0	12.4	12.6	13.5	13.7	15.3	14.6
Italy/Italie	7.7	7.8	8.3	7.4	7.3	8.1	8.2	7.8	7.8	7.6
France,Monac	6.9	6.6	6.2	5.8	5.7	7.0	6.6	6.5	6.7	7.3
United Kingdom	7.0	7.0	5.6	6.0	6.0	6.5	6.0	6.0	5.6	5.8
Netherlands/Pays–Bas	2.4	2.9	3.1	2.8	2.6	3.1	3.2	3.1	2.5	2.5
Sweden/Suède	2.9	3.2	3.1	3.1	3.2	3.6	3.1	3.0	2.5	2.7
Denmark/Danemark	2.2	2.6	2.5	2.5	2.2	2.6	2.7	2.7	2.5	2.6
Switz.Liecht	1.7	2.1	2.1	2.0	2.0	2.1	2.1	1.9	1.7	1.7

TRADE BY COMMODITY IN THOUSAND U.S. DOLLARS – COMMERCE PAR PRODUIT EN MILLIERS DE DOLLARS E.U

COUNTRIES–PAYS	IMPORTS – IMPORTATIONS 1990	1991	1992	1993	1994
Total	19854483	21803723	23897260	23228600	26496951
Africa	x859889	x761855	x794704	x932951	x925644
Northern Africa	411047	345758	x351590	464399	x453275
Americas	4859267	5048962	5515946	6002545	7236981
LAIA	915973	1096995	1498507	1654872	1926795
CACM	32741	39720	50859	x54447	x53027
Asia	3582362	4886473	5879686	x6359601	x7142713
Middle East	425758	x1018759	x1224395	x1221289	x1105918
Europe	9613938	9942841	10746091	8764064	9846034
EEC	8834323	9241925	10020143	8066015	9062431
EFTA	626389	600462	605738	585755	594531
Oceania	x483330	x591059	x485748	x545809	x657037
USA/Etats–Unis d'Amer	2725887	2671796	2708734	2941932	3704613
Germany/Allemagne	1888835	2105826	2363341	1854915	1938204
France,Monac	1351233	1418539	1509090	1240437	1417469
Canada	1006512	1083481	1146830	1243737	1441383
United Kingdom	1096981	1136110	1220729	1094784	1241883
Italy/Italie	915376	977458	1012594	780165	912412
Korea, Republic of	696355	825565	739890	710048	956480
Japan/Japon	551124	646698	658433	693214	754955
Netherlands/Pays–Bas	645893	716418	734776	526173	667137
Spain/Espagne	637423	686332	743698	513640	588082
Mexico/Mexique	287189	368118	661199	712742	918402
Belgium–Luxembourg	614792	579947	594035	532417	570675
Hong Kong	163589	294622	572479	644144	706163
China/Chine	280190	301932	502875	636398	884541
Singapore/Singapour	358612	410643	483061	535187	672084
Australia/Australie	395184	495670	404520	457166	539934
Malaysia/Malaisie	232143	378172	447726	523998	514466
Iran (Islamic Rp. of)		x448804	x483186	x371890	x200912
Sweden/Suède	490368	443230	460972	386401	487605
Austria/Autriche	339186	365424	423736	384150	438556
Indonesia/Indonésie	231543	340417	423468	393437	375879
Thailand/Thaïlande	264874	317132	362926	460919	549420
Switz.Liecht	403404	379347	383118	358012	368674
Saudi Arabia	126717	222239	314758	x268785	x319626
Denmark/Danemark	263550	258777	302308	229685	276630
Venezuela	152604	278514	219905	209501	93966
Norway,SVD,JM	215377	211624	215334	220763	217875
So. Africa Customs Un	178178	178879	193944	185257	214652
Finland/Finlande	216669	172067	208373	173104	191515
Turkey/Turquie	140627	152340	186405	209154	188085
Portugal	173046	179802	203597	139882	129796
Poland/Pologne	42101	92349	184136	217326	264178
Brazil/Brésil	175852	137890	151888	176303	241403
Algeria/Algérie	194808	128899	116199	219151	125187
Argentina/Argentine	57684	100803	165160	194370	270330
Russian Federation			x245083	x200696	x219836
Israel/Israël	113740	119473	144678	169420	200287
Chile/Chili	110464	83796	130096	152200	136376
Greece/Grèce	111860	114045	133077	117757	105971
United Arab Emirates	58678	68808	74781	x199408	x205273
Hungary/Hongrie	x96303	95781	x99366	x104165	x95504
Ireland/Irlande	89112	87950	109816	92506	96494
Former USSR/Anc. URSS	76712	x271447			
Nigeria/Nigéria	x51783	51907	x85428	x124176	x51420
India/Inde	97002	66278	88102	98711	122243
Egypt/Egypte	79197	74256	73932	83165	122018
Philippines	62719	58400	72382	99366	127312
Colombia/Colombie	54830	50101	65240	103066	145229
Czechoslovakia	69629	x64149	x132665		
Czech Republic				190707	210862

COUNTRIES–PAYS	EXPORTS – EXPORTATIONS 1990	1991	1992	1993	1994
Totale	19697160	20798551	23135365	23120124	26404034
Afrique	44977	52474	x100100	x110762	x21953
Afrique du Nord	13654	9008	x17166	4775	5470
Amériques	3831850	4400420	4890361	5283248	6085147
ALAI	329576	373063	607786	725502	964908
MCAC	1187	1306	1335	x1428	x1837
Asie	3740911	4181178	5053121	5534766	6407425
Moyen–Orient	30724	27913	x36095	x56786	x70564
Europe	11861829	12002986	12925749	11964434	13617416
CEE	11076553	11177459	12087310	11204718	12769023
AELE	735606	788361	806645	722962	784246
Océanie	x51611	x49316	x62309	x93607	x120762
Germany/Allemagne	3869157	3976446	4299681	3824210	4295046
USA/Etats–Unis d'Amer	3131475	3691392	3906735	4151755	4655303
Japan/Japon	2841579	3048565	3492450	3786377	4230798
Italy/Italie	1674354	1771105	1856834	1871908	2077883
United Kingdom	1570291	1551456	1477909	1380649	1632409
France,Monac	1356903	1321178	1493691	1342487	1609137
Switz.Liecht	668818	716425	729811	657803	708909
Netherlands/Pays–Bas	537575	569634	659806	515429	538381
Belgium–Luxembourg	396462	405611	591371	688163	755036
Singapore/Singapour	402278	494323	532428	513837	680712
Sweden/Suède	500690	437005	444848	399124	441473
Austria/Autriche	366951	368953	386033	352985	x444880
Canada	365226	330358	372038	401711	457699
Brazil/Brésil	274180	297134	340911	412232	443568
Denmark/Danemark	315621	312453	379238	345257	353918
Hong Kong	138608	187569	383278	463139	496419
Spain/Espagne	289742	321704	333327	305123	388872
Korea, Republic of	100118	149670	212394	254237	277759
Mexico/Mexique	28016	47968	241038	270332	490545
Malaysia/Malaisie	65678	89648	102742	117033	189538
Thailand/Thaïlande	57393	70940	104611	125737	169204
Finland/Finlande	123324	75683	93609	95570	128442
China/Chine	26525	28013	94599	113081	156155
So. Africa Customs Un	27042	36612	80361	102225	13698
Norway,SVD,JM	66788	71843	76830	65026	75318
Ireland/Irlande	61328	52785	53859	69611	84952
Australia/Australie	38659	35964	46950	73053	100465
Israel/Israël	41441	48667	46109	51979	58423
Poland/Pologne	26850	36515	36276	27688	41276
India/Inde	28335	23843	28444	24535	31135
Hungary/Hongrie	x16365	x22214	x29748	x24589	x40025
Argentina/Argentine	20282	17574	16918	32707	20229
Czech Republic				61248	56119
Czechoslovakia		x30968	x24015		
Turkey/Turquie	17009	18648	15812	17697	25132
Slovenia/Slovénia			18101	28150	58119
New Zealand	11990	12840	13521	18386	20070
Yugoslavia SFR	49184	x36436			
Indonesia/Indonésie	4509	5340	11585	19389	36656
Saudi Arabia	3641	3287	4689	x26901	x31532
Portugal	11733	10309	13406	9329	14467
Russian Federation			x11861	x19170	x26567
Bulgaria/Bulgarie	x13173	x3936	x10509	x5451	x1481
Former USSR/Anc. URSS	90578	x16837			
Venezuela	5946	5726	5207	4296	3200
Algeria/Algérie	7178	3661	10200	159	36
Yugoslavia/Yougoslavie			x9373	x2830	x356
Lithuania/Lituanie			10430	x1582	18111
Greece/Grèce	2339	3054	3698	4875	4128
Philippines	2212	4210	3408	3841	6747

(VALUE AS % OF TOTAL)(VALEUR EN % DU TOTAL)

	1985	1986	1987	1988	1989	1990	1991	1992	1993	1994
Africa	4.9	x5.0	x4.1	x4.0	x4.3	x4.3	x3.5	x3.3	x4.0	x3.5
Northern Africa	2.7	2.5	1.6	1.8	1.9	2.1	1.6	x1.5	2.0	x1.7
Americas	30.4	25.4	23.4	24.5	24.8	24.5	23.1	23.0	25.8	27.3
LAIA	6.6	4.9	4.7	4.1	4.1	4.6	5.0	6.3	7.1	7.3
CACM	0.1	0.2	x0.2	0.2	0.2	0.2	0.2	0.2	x0.2	x0.2
Asia	15.2	x16.4	x17.9	x20.9	19.5	18.0	22.4	24.6	x27.4	x27.0
Middle East	3.4	x5.3	x3.7	x3.6	x2.8	2.1	x4.7	x5.1	x5.3	x4.2
Europe	44.8	49.0	48.1	44.8	46.2	48.4	45.6	45.0	37.7	37.2
EEC	35.5	38.8	38.3	36.6	37.8	44.5	42.4	41.9	34.7	34.2
EFTA	8.2	9.0	8.8	7.4	7.5	3.2	2.8	2.5	2.5	2.2
Oceania	3.0	x2.7	x2.9	2.4	x2.6	x2.4	x2.7	x2.1	x2.4	x2.5
USA/Etats–Unis d'Amer	19.4	16.8	15.5	14.4	14.4	13.7	12.3	11.3	12.7	14.0
Germany/Allemagne	6.8	8.0	7.7	7.2	7.5	9.5	9.7	9.9	8.0	7.3
France,Monac	5.3	5.8	5.7	5.7	5.8	6.8	6.5	6.3	5.3	5.3
Canada	3.7	2.9	2.6	5.3	5.6	5.1	5.0	4.8	5.4	5.4
United Kingdom	5.5	5.0	4.8	4.8	4.8	5.5	5.2	5.1	4.7	4.7
Italy/Italie	3.4	3.9	4.1	4.0	4.3	4.6	4.5	4.2	3.4	3.4
Korea, Republic of	2.1	2.4	2.7	2.8	3.2	3.5	3.8	3.1	3.1	3.6
Japan/Japon	2.3	1.9	1.9	2.1	2.4	2.8	3.0	2.8	3.0	2.8
Netherlands/Pays–Bas	2.8	3.3	3.1	2.8	2.8	3.3	3.3	3.1	2.3	2.5
Spain/Espagne	1.6	2.0	2.3	2.5	2.7	3.2	3.1	3.1	2.2	2.2

	1985	1986	1987	1988	1989	1990	1991	1992	1993	1994
Afrique	0.1	x0.2	x0.1	x0.2	x0.2	0.2	0.3	x0.4	x0.4	x0.1
Afrique du Nord	0.0	x0.0	x0.0	0.1	0.1	0.1	0.0	x0.1	0.0	0.0
Amériques	17.1	13.2	12.9	15.7	18.1	19.5	21.1	21.1	22.9	23.1
ALAI	1.4	1.3	1.5	1.7	1.8	1.7	1.8	2.6	3.1	3.7
MCAC	0.0	0.0	0.0	0.0	0.0	0.0	0.0	0.0	x0.0	x0.0
Asie	17.1	16.1	x18.6	x23.9	21.8	19.0	20.1	21.8	23.9	24.2
Moyen–Orient	0.4	0.3	x0.4	0.2	0.2	0.2	0.1	x0.2	x0.2	x0.3
Europe	63.7	68.9	65.6	58.0	58.3	60.2	57.7	55.9	51.7	51.6
CEE	55.0	59.3	56.6	50.1	50.4	56.2	53.7	52.2	48.5	48.4
AELE	8.1	9.1	8.6	7.6	7.7	3.7	3.8	3.5	3.1	3.0
Océanie	0.2	x0.2	x0.2	x0.2	x0.3	x0.3	x0.2	x0.3	x0.4	x0.5
Germany/Allemagne	18.2	21.2	19.9	17.1	17.4	19.6	19.1	18.6	16.5	16.3
USA/Etats–Unis d'Amer	15.2	11.5	11.2	12.1	14.2	15.9	17.7	16.9	18.0	17.6
Japan/Japon	13.8	13.1	11.8	16.4	16.6	14.4	14.7	15.1	16.4	16.0
Italy/Italie	7.8	8.1	8.3	7.8	8.2	8.5	8.5	8.0	8.1	7.9
United Kingdom	8.9	8.4	7.8	7.4	7.1	8.0	7.5	6.4	6.0	6.2
France,Monac	7.7	7.8	7.1	6.0	5.8	6.9	6.4	6.5	5.8	6.1
Switz.Liecht	3.1	3.8	3.4	3.1	2.9	3.4	3.4	3.2	2.8	2.7
Netherlands/Pays–Bas	2.2	2.7	2.6	2.2	2.2	2.7	2.7	2.9	2.2	2.0
Belgium–Luxembourg	1.9	2.3	2.1	1.8	1.9	2.0	2.0	2.6	3.0	2.9
Singapore/Singapour	1.6	1.6	1.6	1.9	2.2	2.0	2.4	2.3	2.2	2.6

TRADE BY COMMODITY IN THOUSAND U.S. DOLLARS – COMMERCE PAR PRODUIT EN MILLIERS DE DOLLARS E.U

COUNTRIES–PAYS	IMPORTS – IMPORTATIONS 1990	1991	1992	1993	1994
Total	24741584	23659549	24245811	21850931	25980351
Africa	x923897	x882635	x970895	x875954	x897274
Northern Africa	371325	297042	x320403	x324991	x319928
Americas	4826096	4277619	4468861	4991304	6244030
LAIA	591336	753192	1028024	1098718	1340516
CACM	22975	25420	35342	x48439	x58167
Asia	3799459	5245559	5798103	x6408184	7859593
Middle East	425475	x989719	x1186645	x1235146	x938204
Europe	11715782	11964427	12134330	8732072	9952694
EEC	10715314	11056440	11284972	7988736	9091821
EFTA	914365	808528	751254	655967	748461
Oceania	x478015	x400589	x416729	x412672	x572927
USA/Etats-Unis d'Amer	2877645	2354493	2398075	2800310	3607295
Germany/Allemagne	1557658	2447218	2663208	1921276	2006313
France,Monac	2006487	1809239	1806186	1201446	1432572
United Kingdom	1634681	1343964	1466670	1200793	1389866
Canada	1123234	967255	849113	884172	1078526
Netherlands/Pays-Bas	923681	974331	976972	623304	845492
Belgium–Luxembourg	950655	951535	923291	699297	815282
Italy/Italie	816740	890414	910240	548304	600286
Korea, Republic of	596964	742329	702773	647786	903053
Spain/Espagne	780711	833191	770322	398354	419895
China/Chine	280454	345366	547564	902770	1233744
Singapore/Singapour	403707	596446	577992	567949	1038796
Hong Kong	412804	391826	489391	673477	812445
Indonesia/Indonésie	313519	532691	459206	495256	498696
Austria/Autriche	474193	502065	507120	439710	512728
Switz.Liecht	636638	538470	476108	429319	465428
Malaysia/Malaisie	300907	402373	457384	507106	621183
Thailand/Thaïlande	285177	422175	456004	428443	544153
Mexico/Mexique	260890	301479	514534	433491	491220
Sweden/Suède	615917	461838	417449	337754	411870
Iran (Islamic Rp. of)		x357674	x446433	x308825	x82990
Japan/Japon	330258	348074	358692	317473	377687
Australia/Australie	374166	278202	285006	300788	420899
Russian Federation			x383782	x387380	x347452
Norway,SVD,JM	261808	251200	258572	214333	270846
Saudi Arabia	105960	162725	200102	x271680	x225988
Denmark/Danemark	215895	223637	229495	173101	206417
Former USSR/Anc. URSS	2284035	x593797			
Portugal	181301	200282	211747	162869	133585
Turkey/Turquie	137164	148742	174342	206351	164677
Finland/Finlande	326968	211310	163767	125583	155680
United Arab Emirates	98354	114029	143373	x231341	x247872
Israel/Israël	102646	150731	149217	141686	181859
So. Africa Customs Un	129007	130007	153564	139344	162221
Chile/Chili	137381	96651	133938	190488	187360
Venezuela	52087	180380	124803	102460	60044
Algeria/Algérie	181795	119043	124770	98374	74780
India/Inde	116635	95436	115314	131260	163209
Poland/Pologne	54612	56870	124976	127756	160291
Pakistan	59675	79233	121555	105929	139215
Greece/Grèce	98316	97262	117391	89930	74492
Ireland/Irlande	132111	110154	121115	67015	87342
Philippines	96775	80105	88574	129287	165694
Hungary/Hongrie	x105456	67898	x129633	x89067	x86612
Czechoslovakia	191689	x105729	x164749		
Nigeria/Nigéria	x42354	39663	x112723	x110236	x50939
Argentina/Argentine	17210	35083	86703	116087	225082
Brazil/Brésil	51634	62996	63333	103114	131973
New Zealand	71211	60579	75126	68305	94205
Morocco/Maroc	59332	52132	53366	78364	86840

COUNTRIES–PAYS	EXPORTS – EXPORTATIONS 1990	1991	1992	1993	1994
Totale	24314989	23461199	24205522	23199230	27009141
Afrique	64459	77442	62396	x76550	x64409
Afrique du Nord	9456	7456	10886	x7115	7675
Amériques	3808396	3926776	4172721	4471723	5191851
ALAI	216435	211555	268085	293011	313362
MCAC	193	245	295	x364	x466
Asie	3959102	4339038	4491665	4933727	6341686
Moyen-Orient	55125	31591	48552	x58822	x83465
Europe	15053150	14558331	14825188	13066257	14854077
CEE	14253901	13811474	13986044	12350332	14046639
AELE	652940	689876	738151	641592	727908
Océanie	100059	123954	153980	x175741	x200618
Germany/Allemagne	4787528	4639169	4709621	3865201	4198267
USA/Etats-Unis d'Amer	3089050	3270263	3393168	3516485	4048977
Japan/Japon	3034897	3286324	3247147	3480223	4167346
France,Monac	1849127	1884449	1849867	1526969	1710926
United Kingdom	1642513	1586199	1472200	1269931	1555109
Italy/Italie	1489500	1413380	1459639	1312480	1604275
Sweden/Suède	992769	984203	958247	828399	1072567
Netherlands/Pays-Bas	952303	911161	934622	823847	1016289
Austria/Autriche	618879	660030	713097	658906	x673485
Belgium–Luxembourg	483548	453600	497765	706112	707916
Canada	497287	438030	506085	639891	824628
Switz.Liecht	474016	496775	554711	512828	571727
Finland/Finlande	648142	483306	496797	467672	588364
Korea, Republic of	366536	393388	456745	470529	678905
Denmark/Danemark	388206	374475	396480	422924	416140
Spain/Espagne	284628	308252	391342	362593	387635
China/Chine	134364	195744	244724	258982	300519
Singapore/Singapour	171533	202700	213721	234482	542160
Hong Kong	115553	137714	176357	271524	370245
Norway,SVD,JM	178281	192874	183196	128723	155358
Bulgaria/Bulgarie	x825073	x114899	x187213	x154140	x31933
Australia/Australie	64577	94736	124095	143685	165265
Mexico/Mexique	122335	100289	135006	119201	154567
Brazil/Brésil	80057	80140	100858	122883	116179
Poland/Pologne	93457	72984	88935	87434	96655
Ireland/Irlande	87869	73551	71755	79784	81080
Hungary/Hongrie	x45503	x73277	x88327	x57002	x67350
Czechoslovakia		x97910	x113611		
So. Africa Customs Un	45394	36933	44579	62217	43319
Malaysia/Malaisie	29175	32552	41991	58340	70651
Slovenia/Slovénia			71718	47448	58689
Czech Republic				112614	112062
New Zealand	31685	26656	24309	30825	34536
Argentina/Argentine	9898	21481	22709	35079	19068
Portugal	26144	28855	27188	20301	26531
Thailand/Thaïlande	13859	17992	20527	37277	66633
Romania/Roumanie	49111	40183	18999	14293	10190
Turkey/Turquie	14031	14574	21039	20104	29382
Yugoslavia SFR	145980	x55620			
India/Inde	22144	13657	20660	18542	17732
Slovakia				x49694	x38271
Indonesia/Indonésie	5338	6525	8256	32903	24566
Russian Federation			x25538	x18903	x18914
Former USSR/Anc. URSS	289310	x33857			
Yugoslavia/Yougoslavie			x13476	x12296	x4068
Ukraine			x10171	x15557	x7436
Cameroon/Cameroun	2954	23616	x59	x339	x46
Croatia/Croatie			13626	10248	x13321
Greece/Grèce	2678	10780	7424	5213	8053
Kuwait/Koweït	7153	2866	9588	7699	4826

(VALUE AS % OF TOTAL)(VALEUR EN % DU TOTAL)

	1985	1986	1987	1988	1989	1990	1991	1992	1993	1994
Africa	4.9	x4.7	x3.2	x3.5	x3.5	x3.7	x3.7	x4.0	x4.0	x3.4
Northern Africa	3.2	2.3	1.4	1.1	1.1	1.5	1.3	x1.3	x1.5	x1.2
Americas	23.3	x21.8	x19.4	18.9	21.7	19.5	18.0	18.4	22.9	24.0
LAIA	3.3	2.4	2.2	2.3	2.4	2.4	3.2	4.2	5.0	5.2
CACM	0.2	0.1	x0.1	0.1	0.1	0.1	0.1	0.1	x0.2	x0.2
Asia	14.2	11.6	x13.6	x13.4	13.5	15.3	22.2	23.9	x29.3	30.3
Middle East	3.7	x4.0	x2.8	x2.6	x2.4	1.7	x4.2	x4.9	x5.7	x3.6
Europe	38.0	41.1	42.9	46.1	46.2	47.4	50.6	50.0	40.0	38.3
EEC	29.2	31.9	33.1	37.0	37.7	43.3	46.7	46.5	36.6	35.0
EFTA	8.0	8.6	9.2	8.6	8.1	3.7	3.4	3.1	3.0	2.9
Oceania	2.2	x2.0	x1.6	x1.8	x2.1	x1.9	x1.7	x1.7	x1.9	x2.2
USA/Etats-Unis d'Amer	14.3	13.6	11.5	10.0	13.3	11.6	10.0	9.9	12.8	13.9
Germany/Allemagne	4.0	4.4	4.7	5.2	5.5	6.3	10.3	11.0	8.8	7.7
France,Monac	5.1	5.8	6.1	6.8	6.8	8.1	7.6	7.4	5.5	5.5
United Kingdom	5.6	5.6	5.3	6.8	6.7	6.6	5.7	6.0	5.5	5.3
Canada	5.1	4.8	4.6	5.9	5.1	4.5	4.1	3.5	4.0	4.2
Netherlands/Pays-Bas	3.0	3.3	3.2	3.3	3.2	3.7	4.1	4.0	2.9	3.3
Belgium–Luxembourg	2.5	2.7	2.7	2.9	3.1	3.8	4.0	3.8	3.2	3.1
Italy/Italie	1.7	2.1	2.2	2.7	2.7	3.3	3.8	3.8	2.5	2.3
Korea, Republic of	1.9	1.7	1.3	1.4	1.9	2.4	3.1	2.9	3.0	3.5
Spain/Espagne	1.0	1.3	1.8	2.3	2.6	3.2	3.5	3.2	1.8	1.6

	1985	1986	1987	1988	1989	1990	1991	1992	1993	1994
Afrique	0.1	x0.2	x0.2	x0.2	x0.2	0.3	0.4	0.3	x0.4	x0.3
Afrique du Nord	0.0	0.0	x0.0	0.1	0.0	0.0	0.0	0.0	x0.0	0.0
Amériques	16.2	12.1	10.5	11.1	14.1	15.6	16.7	17.2	19.3	19.2
ALAI	0.6	0.4	0.4	0.6	1.0	0.9	0.9	1.1	1.3	1.2
MCAC	0.0	0.0	x0.0	x0.0	x0.0	0.0	0.0	0.0	x0.0	x0.0
Asie	18.7	17.9	x15.5	x16.4	16.6	16.3	18.5	18.5	21.3	23.4
Moyen-Orient	0.6	x0.5	x0.4	0.3	0.3	0.2	0.1	0.2	x0.3	x0.3
Europe	61.6	65.8	59.1	59.3	59.6	61.9	62.1	61.2	56.3	55.0
CEE	48.6	52.1	46.7	48.3	48.8	58.6	58.9	57.8	53.2	52.0
AELE	12.3	13.2	12.0	10.0	10.1	2.7	2.9	3.0	2.8	2.7
Océanie	0.3	x0.3	x0.3	0.4	x0.4	0.4	0.5	0.6	x0.8	x0.7
Germany/Allemagne	15.5	17.6	15.7	17.0	16.8	19.7	19.8	19.5	16.7	15.5
USA/Etats-Unis d'Amer	11.7	8.8	7.5	8.2	11.0	12.7	13.9	14.0	15.2	15.0
Japan/Japon	15.5	15.3	11.8	12.2	12.8	12.5	14.0	13.4	15.0	15.4
France,Monac	6.7	6.1	5.0	5.6	5.9	7.6	8.0	7.6	6.6	6.3
United Kingdom	6.6	6.9	5.7	6.1	5.7	6.8	6.8	6.1	5.5	5.8
Italy/Italie	4.4	4.9	4.6	4.6	4.9	6.1	6.0	6.0	5.7	5.9
Sweden/Suède	4.8	5.0	4.6	3.8	3.8	4.1	4.2	4.0	3.6	4.0
Netherlands/Pays-Bas	2.6	2.6	2.5	3.1	3.3	3.9	3.9	3.9	3.6	3.8
Austria/Autriche	1.7	1.9	1.8	1.9	1.9	2.5	2.8	2.9	2.8	x2.5
Belgium–Luxembourg	1.3	1.5	1.3	1.7	1.7	2.0	1.9	2.1	3.0	2.6

TRADE BY COMMODITY IN THOUSAND U.S. DOLLARS – COMMERCE PAR PRODUIT EN MILLIERS DE DOLLARS E.U

COUNTRIES–PAYS	IMPORTS – IMPORTATIONS 1990	1991	1992	1993	1994
Total	15348844	16128296	17038158	16106590	17932287
Africa	x572774	x505173	x544380	x604081	x580546
Northern Africa	202218	199198	x212528	246682	x187505
Americas	3018749	3197436	3711249	4058434	4810682
LAIA	509622	724321	1129623	1285366	1653659
CACM	45306	42262	59619	x63011	x60899
Asia	2269338	2663120	2952029	x3271697	3731419
Middle East	312409	x648004	x697545	x634836	x540409
Europe	8606999	8726892	8793682	7074330	7682541
EEC	7840997	7967261	8038834	6400566	6970503
EFTA	615692	625963	617037	573571	598904
Oceania	x360450	x338533	x377038	x442176	x483095
USA/Etats–Unis d'Amer	1691616	1713459	1823551	1974941	2257179
France,Monac	1505008	1478085	1438050	1177920	1237762
Germany/Allemagne	1297342	1479216	1500350	1110277	1216149
United Kingdom	1097487	946416	1009670	947163	1025836
Canada	683143	620385	619519	646718	754917
Italy/Italie	609709	645158	624792	536426	581468
Spain/Espagne	658610	720663	650001	420085	406689
Netherlands/Pays–Bas	571654	625403	663739	430918	496678
Belgium–Luxembourg	493891	548289	610273	471550	596146
Mexico/Mexique	233035	342679	538289	574275	716406
Japan/Japon	541516	443788	437075	418357	480202
Switz.Liecht	445934	428909	422413	404794	420324
Austria/Autriche	433103	433671	425698	375817	445603
Korea, Republic of	425014	422505	397783	376934	411539
China/Chine	136010	152992	314202	570880	660101
Sweden/Suède	351713	333088	326059	304492	317603
Australia/Australie	282342	265016	298746	353560	374087
Hong Kong	125095	136291	207762	247629	275316
Thailand/Thaïlande	133753	203010	164952	213202	268939
Denmark/Danemark	177213	182926	194754	172105	161551
Poland/Pologne	37628	127686	226631	190758	208840
Norway,SVD,JM	162176	188582	185723	162215	171224
Iran (Islamic Rp. of)		x171093	x229476	x133956	x50051
Singapore/Singapour	143945	150816	175169	202727	257953
Portugal	188419	175392	202765	147944	132394
Malaysia/Malaisie	126861	156553	177319	192142	232064
Turkey/Turquie	125017	155360	179109	190641	180339
So. Africa Customs Un	138055	144561	144608	157489	185336
Indonesia/Indonésie	126098	152431	142081	144859	162908
Finland/Finlande	237356	180080	152102	107070	147258
Brazil/Brésil	75762	128440	144018	155115	263426
Saudi Arabia	101700	135000	140614	x150591	x133607
Argentina/Argentine	25879	47699	147732	201023	288363
Greece/Grèce	122053	119547	139782	123502	122129
Czechoslovakia	166116	x115034	x244638		
Hungary/Hongrie	x119090	104335	x117369	x128785	x131123
Russian Federation			x191266	x145712	x180794
Former USSR/Anc. URSS	27942	x309599			
Ireland/Irlande	97441	99327	100799	75298	83238
Chile/Chili	46740	59750	87110	97964	102516
Israel/Israël	55912	68493	80877	83270	112965
Algeria/Algérie	45238	62440	65180	104841	54965
Venezuela	32430	56537	87504	70193	45501
New Zealand	65502	57839	61994	70826	87667
Philippines	53707	45505	68456	68221	86150
Czech Republic				179780	175602
Colombia/Colombie	33061	31215	38785	76154	103670
Romania/Roumanie	2669	17131	52754	71154	61343
Kuwait/ Koweït	5540	103010	19984	11936	16360
Morocco/Maroc	47667	43974	39385	45230	36093

COUNTRIES–PAYS	EXPORTS – EXPORTATIONS 1990	1991	1992	1993	1994
Totale	15604984	15999657	16836469	16386989	18474668
Afrique	26070	30885	36127	x32386	x3856
Afrique du Nord	2007	4745	2144	2999	1568
Amériques	2369682	2533242	2732682	2864836	3232836
ALAI	113372	136283	284372	273354	279729
MCAC	926	945	1610	x1573	x2718
Asie	1505877	1800259	1879666	2085057	2318147
Moyen–Orient	7136	80572	15528	x16076	x23639
Europe	11563182	11528884	12065437	11233993	12751587
CEE	10659712	10676045	11122443	10368508	11736115
AELE	866735	840721	912104	842903	987547
Océanie	x49335	x58651	x62645	x71522	x85006
Germany/Allemagne	4501213	4540503	4737349	4327168	4798761
Italy/Italie	2130355	2237254	2328144	2423736	2785722
USA/Etats–Unis d'Amer	2055078	2202694	2244696	2350151	2671636
Japan/Japon	1163488	1347213	1404239	1504215	1501019
Switz.Liecht	813330	791535	848594	769446	906022
United Kingdom	752782	765138	790650	749239	884894
Sweden/Suède	892854	826133	754959	674309	913195
France,Monac	690252	668139	717558	622685	647355
Netherlands/Pays–Bas	501864	509180	528613	438310	494982
Denmark/Danemark	389234	372384	394933	324006	310233
Austria/Autriche	275845	259212	259640	213992	x185893
Belgium–Luxembourg	190165	186299	253081	264973	337153
Spain/Espagne	174263	193366	230434	232322	264682
Canada	199122	192185	200675	238626	277365
Hong Kong	110542	131072	192165	247786	285021
Brazil/Brésil	60752	81129	128344	145018	137821
Singapore/Singapour	77329	97743	80423	106306	149688
Mexico/Mexique	16917	17357	114320	77742	88021
Finland/Finlande	100724	61288	79736	60517	71763
Norway,SVD,JM	49919	44383	58401	67755	72216
Israel/Israël	40204	49498	49500	52260	54721
Korea, Republic of	41717	41204	47913	50122	136881
Australia/Australie	38864	41028	44462	53464	60284
China/Chine	14297	14171	37823	48084	66590
Argentina/Argentine	27812	29104	30597	38372	41409
Ireland/Irlande	44704	36421	25497	16777	22856
Kuwait/ Koweït	217	71345	4723	124	118
So. Africa Customs Un	17744	19340	23793	26777	
Malaysia/Malaisie	9811	13150	16760	21330	32048
New Zealand	9705	12927	17917	17575	24558
Hungary/Hongrie	x11614	x12774	x16627	x15655	x17537
Czech Republic				43278	38564
India/Inde	12378	10853	15739	16553	25964
Czechoslovakia		x17916	x21667		
Slovenia/Slovénia			22519	14960	20632
Thailand/Thaïlande	6436	10524	13039	13441	26948
Portugal	9343	11920	12790	10287	8387
Bulgaria/Bulgarie	x57087	x4398	x10569	x15671	x2049
Greece/Grèce	6006	8701	9061	10187	10237
Poland/Pologne	6262	4989	9472	11644	15957
Colombia/Colombie	4458	6638	7607	7398	6365
Iceland/Islande	3486	4804	5109	5702	9308
Turkey/Turquie	2068	2442	5435	7143	13677
Yugoslavia SFR	36115	x11752			
Russian Federation			x6273	x4654	x4361
Indonesia/Indonésie	1259	2224	3515	4293	7731
Saudi Arabia	1537	4097	2459	x2509	x2373
Kenya	1124	142	8404	259	x245
Slovakia				x7870	x5099
Croatia/Croatie			4164	3088	x3606

(VALUE AS % OF TOTAL)(VALEUR EN % DU TOTAL)

	1985	1986	1987	1988	1989	1990	1991	1992	1993	1994
Africa	5.3	7.0	x5.1	x3.9	x4.0	x3.7	x3.1	x3.1	x3.8	x3.2
Northern Africa	1.8	2.2	1.4	1.4	1.2	1.3	1.2	x1.2	1.5	x1.0
Americas	23.8	21.8	x18.9	18.6	21.3	19.7	19.9	21.7	25.2	26.8
LAIA	3.5	3.0	2.4	2.6	3.1	3.3	4.5	6.6	8.0	9.2
CACM	0.3	0.3	x0.3	0.3	0.3	0.3	0.3	0.3	x0.4	x0.3
Asia	9.6	x9.1	x11.6	x12.6	13.9	14.8	16.5	17.3	x20.3	20.8
Middle East	2.5	x3.0	x2.5	x2.4	x2.2	2.0	x4.0	x4.1	x3.9	x3.0
Europe	42.2	44.2	45.4	46.5	54.2	56.1	54.1	51.6	43.9	42.8
EEC	33.7	34.9	35.8	37.8	44.3	51.1	49.4	47.2	39.7	38.9
EFTA	7.8	8.5	8.7	8.1	9.3	4.0	3.9	3.6	3.6	3.3
Oceania	3.0	x2.5	x2.1	2.2	x2.7	x2.4	x2.1	x2.2	x2.7	x2.7
USA/Etats–Unis d'Amer	14.3	13.2	11.7	11.1	12.1	11.0	10.6	10.7	12.3	12.6
France,Monac	6.5	7.0	7.2	7.7	8.7	9.8	9.2	8.4	7.3	6.9
Germany/Allemagne	5.3	5.4	5.4	5.5	6.6	8.5	9.2	8.8	6.9	6.8
United Kingdom	6.0	5.5	5.2	5.8	6.8	7.2	5.9	5.9	5.9	5.7
Canada	5.2	4.6	3.7	4.3	5.1	4.5	3.8	3.6	4.0	4.2
Italy/Italie	2.5	2.6	2.7	2.9	3.5	4.0	4.0	3.7	3.3	3.2
Spain/Espagne	1.4	1.6	2.3	2.5	3.5	4.3	4.5	3.8	2.6	2.3
Netherlands/Pays–Bas	3.0	3.0	3.1	3.2	3.4	3.7	3.9	3.9	2.7	2.8
Belgium–Luxembourg	2.0	2.3	2.2	2.5	2.9	3.2	3.4	3.6	2.9	3.3
Mexico/Mexique	1.3	0.8	0.6	0.7	1.2	1.5	2.1	3.2	3.6	4.0

	1985	1986	1987	1988	1989	1990	1991	1992	1993	1994
Afrique	0.1	x0.1	x0.1	0.2	0.1	0.2	0.2	0.2	x0.2	x0.0
Afrique du Nord	0.0	x0.0	x0.0	0.0	0.0	0.0	0.0	0.0	0.0	0.0
Amériques	13.4	11.0	10.1	11.4	14.6	15.1	15.9	16.2	17.5	17.5
ALAI	0.6	0.6	0.5	0.6	0.9	0.7	0.9	1.7	1.7	1.5
MCAC	0.0	0.0	0.0	0.0	0.0	0.0	0.0	0.0	x0.0	x0.0
Asie	8.5	7.8	x8.3	x9.7	10.0	9.6	11.2	11.1	12.7	12.5
Moyen–Orient	0.0	x0.0	x0.1	0.0	x0.1	0.0	0.5	0.1	x0.1	x0.1
Europe	60.2	64.4	61.3	60.7	72.7	74.1	72.1	71.7	68.6	69.0
CEE	49.9	53.8	50.8	50.7	60.9	68.3	66.7	66.1	63.3	63.5
AELE	10.1	10.4	10.2	9.8	11.6	5.6	5.3	5.4	5.1	5.3
Océanie	0.2	x0.2	x0.2	0.2	x0.3	x0.3	x0.3	x0.4	x0.4	x0.5
Germany/Allemagne	21.5	24.1	22.5	21.9	26.1	28.8	28.4	28.1	26.4	26.0
Italy/Italie	9.1	10.1	9.7	9.4	11.5	13.7	14.0	13.8	14.8	15.1
USA/Etats–Unis d'Amer	11.3	8.9	8.4	9.7	12.4	13.2	13.8	13.3	14.3	14.5
Japan/Japon	7.3	6.7	5.7	6.6	8.0	7.5	8.4	8.3	9.2	8.1
Switz.Liecht	3.8	4.2	4.2	3.9	4.3	5.2	4.9	5.0	4.7	4.9
United Kingdom	4.4	4.2	3.8	4.3	4.8	4.8	4.8	4.7	4.6	4.8
Sweden/Suède	4.8	4.6	4.4	4.3	5.2	5.7	5.2	4.5	4.1	4.9
France,Monac	3.0	3.0	2.8	3.1	3.9	4.4	4.2	4.3	3.8	3.5
Netherlands/Pays–Bas	2.0	2.3	2.3	2.4	2.7	3.2	3.2	3.1	2.7	2.7
Denmark/Danemark	2.1	2.3	2.1	2.0	2.4	2.5	2.3	2.3	2.0	1.7

TRADE BY COMMODITY IN THOUSAND U.S. DOLLARS – COMMERCE PAR PRODUIT EN MILLIERS DE DOLLARS E.U

COUNTRIES–PAYS	IMPORTS – IMPORTATIONS 1990	1991	1992	1993	1994
Total	39144492	40819269	43639704	41470075	47578714
Africa	x1716950	1776131	x1547430	x1567703	x1614166
Northern Africa	831288	781762	x696622	719271	x763315
Americas	8577887	9213751	10169876	11157072	13788330
LAIA	1962852	2234855	2611155	2695629	2980703
CACM	64249	64510	84602	x73846	x74173
Asia	7308689	8973698	10133530	x10718442	11244984
Middle East	1365133	x2231906	x2663931	x2494715	x1568373
Europe	19450194	19107725	20392123	16291711	19056899
EEC	17849117	17756889	18981107	15000142	17639426
EFTA	1299069	1177429	1208650	1129519	1241455
Oceania	x845190	x778233	x789339	x882874	x1010741
USA/Etats–Unis d'Amer	4603703	4940261	5452336	6119310	8071462
Germany/Allemagne	3955053	4384861	4748117	3601751	4210525
France,Monac	2634390	2585424	2679038	2141293	2568095
United Kingdom	2328471	2285698	2454728	2164601	2367984
Canada	1707635	1729160	1828001	2103345	2506093
Italy/Italie	1931761	1852269	1938875	1500426	1858106
Netherlands/Pays–Bas	1438354	1439427	1595154	1050301	1116408
Korea, Republic of	1057916	1288345	1268682	1255079	1549708
Singapore/Singapour	1020415	1141395	1188696	1266891	1513300
Belgium–Luxembourg	1276717	1184831	1298786	931388	1193812
Japan/Japon	1081635	1170862	1118694	1075855	1191755
Austria/Autriche	1018769	1027744	1121125	981289	1131804
Mexico/Mexique	659135	830539	1145310	1146705	1271183
Iran (Islamic Rp. of)		x844058	x840616	x1051888	x215992
Spain/Espagne	957159	939200	966921	745527	859450
China/Chine	420227	515353	852311	1164773	1339304
Sweden/Suède	993764	861621	844317	774709	1078381
Switz.Liecht	904883	792908	781524	707864	797129
Saudi Arabia	739032	694817	991690	x408781	x367731
Australia/Australie	705262	656951	657570	746293	845504
Malaysia/Malaisie	415729	557942	635094	738656	936494
Thailand/Thaïlande	450862	501634	611687	709221	893094
Hong Kong	392137	420749	536876	667186	749588
Brazil/Brésil	543924	488579	470778	488595	598755
So. Africa Customs Un	476158	429302	464389	432646	504613
Indonesia/Indonésie	278741	348332	444778	442390	501996
Turkey/Turquie	329821	365839	417392	439125	371636
Norway,SVD,JM	374735	364072	408803	405902	426809
Denmark/Danemark	390372	382874	420511	351518	415392
Venezuela	243451	362117	337717	276331	215894
India/Inde	388968	282853	325707	298068	383906
Finland/Finlande	396269	279872	297738	286257	376915
Israel/Israël	163603	203296	217538	218117	234414
Argentina/Argentine	97687	157838	229859	246783	336827
Egypt/Egypte	184962	184934	203687	227615	238672
Portugal	210025	216833	243673	153591	156664
Russian Federation			x334716	x276449	x208781
Former USSR/Anc. URSS	555095	x602352			
United Arab Emirates	128790	111469	148835	x324459	x353236
Algeria/Algérie	244455	183836	190272	207943	242896
Greece/Grèce	187041	176502	199619	169815	158950
Nigeria/Nigéria	x69470	255608	x120984	x164525	x87414
Chile/Chili	168063	152733	176498	200174	198733
Poland/Pologne	74892	55391	193162	232265	297679
Hungary/Hongrie	x160803	126739	x161087	x192297	x172585
Ireland/Irlande	130973	139733	172503	147675	146940
Libyan Arab Jamahiriya	214612	226878	x94151	x93294	x106929
Colombia/Colombie	120520	98483	110164	148039	174229
Philippines	88303	97216	98307	139601	143512
Czechoslovakia	147942	x118417	x204552		

COUNTRIES–PAYS	EXPORTS – EXPORTATIONS 1990	1991	1992	1993	1994
Totale	36618283	37093949	40618954	40416923	46365694
Afrique	60428	69563	x85737	x86444	x88658
Afrique du Nord	7596	12682	16662	21716	22781
Amériques	4623356	4966289	5632349	6479876	8340065
ALAI	480675	495562	713670	942500	1194590
MCAC	1837	2429	3214	x3147	x3807
Asie	7349881	8016279	8835198	10239104	11809010
Moyen–Orient	54275	x35725	44277	x75225	x86441
Europe	23730491	23392763	25423347	22826677	25311140
CEE	22361909	22201536	24217542	21709037	24068504
AELE	1120327	1086545	1094645	1026260	1143861
Océanie	114621	x123510	x151539	x162549	x199047
Germany/Allemagne	8737925	8368843	9404190	8486426	9073053
Japan/Japon	5090409	5696571	6170338	6907254	8156829
Italy/Italie	3589171	3989162	4338238	3885864	4374167
USA/Etats–Unis d'Amer	3308748	3502200	3867143	4322117	4966047
France,Monac	2725833	2670238	2900962	2593349	2963467
United Kingdom	2390591	2336035	2442377	2140194	2404392
Canada	825933	962169	1045269	1207192	2169731
Switz.Liecht	1049097	1006213	1009370	950446	1065581
Netherlands/Pays–Bas	893496	844043	945070	727759	791870
Austria/Autriche	834590	782260	838754	767013	x823882
Sweden/Suède	848118	768689	792284	675617	952372
Singapore/Singapour	598755	659895	727043	840963	1061847
Spain/Espagne	628898	745476	680688	793479	749057
Belgium–Luxembourg	717991	711747	765685	698986	832477
Denmark/Danemark	481621	504278	595179	492600	539868
Hong Kong	375134	395949	492928	565243	611704
Mexico/Mexique	211701	197635	425798	548864	777168
Thailand/Thaïlande	245847	276201	280923	613977	370433
China/Chine	301745	285451	373412	419071	537484
Korea, Republic of	269991	303799	356431	404216	459811
Israel/Israël	340737	266480	273995	249768	291778
Brazil/Brésil	201190	217323	212934	272142	308943
Portugal	182333	189074	216963	180615	205412
Finland/Finlande	249952	200450	192462	192781	259977
Australia/Australie	94339	101602	130508	130562	164730
Poland/Pologne	204375	126829	111657	104175	130130
Romania/Roumanie	142678	103117	98633	113543	119816
Hungary/Hongrie	x119677	x89493	x109905	x96089	x94514
Czechoslovakia		x124786	x121265		
Norway,SVD,JM	71181	80311	85257	75653	78267
Ireland/Irlande	73208	81782	92243	62132	85073
Argentina/Argentine	40272	58160	52966	91728	73732
Malaysia/Malaisie	27958	34944	52054	87497	135383
So. Africa Customs Un	44315	52001	63626	57969	60207
Czech Republic				148168	156472
Slovenia/Slovénia			62003	59078	74076
Bulgaria/Bulgarie	x52141	x15231	x46175	x54711	x20267
Slovakia				x105509	x96493
India/Inde	24102	27925	33898	40781	52988
Yugoslavia SFR	244300	x100824			
Russian Federation			x41934	x52538	x70085
Turkey/Turquie	18178	18661	26326	27427	46164
New Zealand	18460	20524	20145	23346	33405
Former USSR/Anc. URSS	186837	x62638			
Indonesia/Indonésie	8228	12158	15015	19309	27108
Saudi Arabia	14295	5738	7254	x22722	x19346
Greece/Grèce	8102	9378	12448	12221	13437
Yugoslavia/Yougoslavie			x27531	x5256	x1717
Tunisia/Tunisie	4245	6739	9446	16126	18374
Croatia/Croatie			15174	13944	x13066

(VALUE AS % OF TOTAL)(VALEUR EN % DU TOTAL)

	1985	1986	1987	1988	1989	1990	1991	1992	1993	1994
Africa	5.7	5.6	x4.7	x4.6	x4.1	x4.4	4.4	x3.6	x3.7	x3.4
Northern Africa	3.0	3.0	2.4	2.3	1.9	2.1	1.9	x1.6	1.7	x1.6
Americas	22.9	20.5	19.2	21.0	22.6	21.9	22.5	23.3	26.9	28.9
LAIA	6.6	5.7	5.2	4.9	4.8	5.0	5.5	6.0	6.5	6.3
CACM	0.2	0.2	0.2	0.2	0.2	0.2	0.2	0.2	x0.2	x0.2
Asia	19.0	17.8	x18.3	x19.4	18.1	18.7	22.0	23.3	x25.8	23.6
Middle East	6.0	x6.1	x5.0	x4.9	x3.6	3.5	x5.5	x6.1	x6.0	x3.3
Europe	47.2	50.9	50.8	47.9	49.0	49.7	46.8	46.7	39.3	40.1
EEC	37.5	40.5	40.5	38.8	40.0	45.6	43.5	43.5	36.2	37.1
EFTA	8.5	9.3	9.3	8.3	8.3	3.3	2.9	2.8	2.7	2.6
Oceania	2.5	x2.2	x2.1	2.1	2.3	x2.2	x1.9	x1.8	x2.2	x2.2
USA/Etats–Unis d'Amer	11.7	11.1	10.5	10.8	12.3	11.8	12.1	12.5	14.8	17.0
Germany/Allemagne	7.6	8.7	8.5	7.9	8.4	10.1	10.7	10.9	8.7	8.8
France,Monac	5.6	5.9	5.9	5.7	5.8	6.7	6.3	6.1	5.2	5.4
United Kingdom	5.7	5.4	5.4	5.6	5.8	5.9	5.6	5.6	5.2	5.0
Canada	3.7	3.1	2.8	4.7	4.9	4.4	4.2	4.2	5.1	5.3
Italy/Italie	3.7	4.2	4.3	4.3	4.4	4.9	4.5	4.4	3.6	3.9
Netherlands/Pays–Bas	3.3	3.6	3.6	3.3	3.2	3.7	3.5	3.7	2.5	2.3
Korea, Republic of	2.1	2.1	2.3	2.3	2.6	2.7	3.2	2.9	3.0	3.3
Singapore/Singapour	2.0	1.8	1.9	2.2	2.5	2.6	2.8	2.7	3.1	3.2
Belgium–Luxembourg	2.4	2.5	2.5	2.7	2.7	3.3	2.9	3.0	2.2	2.5

	1985	1986	1987	1988	1989	1990	1991	1992	1993	1994
Afrique	0.1	x0.1	x0.1	x0.4	x0.1	0.1	0.1	x0.3	x0.2	x0.2
Afrique du Nord	0.0	x0.0	x0.0	0.0	0.0	0.0	0.0	0.0	0.1	0.0
Amériques	12.9	x10.1	9.5	10.0	11.6	12.6	13.4	13.9	16.1	18.0
ALAI	1.1	0.6	0.8	0.9	1.1	1.3	1.3	1.8	2.3	2.6
MCAC	0.0	0.0	0.0	0.0	0.0	0.0	0.0	0.0	x0.0	x0.0
Asie	17.5	16.6	x18.1	x21.8	21.2	20.0	21.6	21.8	25.3	25.4
Moyen–Orient	0.9	x0.3	0.6	0.3	x0.2	0.1	x0.1	0.1	x0.2	x0.2
Europe	66.4	70.0	67.1	63.3	63.7	64.8	63.1	62.6	56.5	54.6
CEE	56.7	59.9	57.5	55.0	55.4	61.1	59.9	59.6	53.7	51.9
AELE	8.4	9.0	8.7	7.6	7.4	3.1	2.9	2.7	2.5	2.5
Océanie	0.3	x0.2	x0.3	x0.3	x0.3	0.3	x0.3	x0.4	x0.4	x0.4
Germany/Allemagne	21.1	23.3	22.7	21.8	21.9	23.9	22.6	23.2	21.0	19.6
Japan/Japon	13.0	13.0	12.3	14.5	15.0	13.9	15.4	15.2	17.1	17.6
Italy/Italie	8.9	9.2	9.2	8.7	9.0	9.8	10.8	10.7	9.6	9.4
USA/Etats–Unis d'Amer	9.7	7.5	7.1	6.6	8.1	9.0	9.4	9.5	10.7	10.7
France,Monac	7.5	7.8	7.1	6.7	6.8	7.4	7.2	7.1	6.4	6.4
United Kingdom	6.7	6.0	5.7	6.0	5.9	6.5	6.3	6.0	5.3	5.2
Canada	2.1	1.8	1.6	2.4	2.4	2.3	2.6	2.6	3.0	4.7
Switz.Liecht	2.9	3.1	3.1	2.7	2.5	2.9	2.7	2.5	2.4	2.3
Netherlands/Pays–Bas	2.3	2.8	2.6	2.2	2.1	2.4	2.3	2.3	1.8	1.7
Austria/Autriche	2.1	2.3	2.1	1.9	1.9	2.3	2.1	2.1	1.9	x1.8

TRADE BY COMMODITY IN THOUSAND U.S. DOLLARS – COMMERCE PAR PRODUIT EN MILLIERS DE DOLLARS E.U

COUNTRIES–PAYS	IMPORTS – IMPORTATIONS 1990	1991	1992	1993	1994
Total	12265270	12876253	13272300	13039562	14564117
Africa	x251661	x260243	x249124	x257868	x266899
Northern Africa	74970	63214	77383	70437	72958
Americas	3563920	3518740	4103605	4523185	5215108
LAIA	282209	428847	554391	613704	760770
CACM	13554	12360	18294	x27172	x32161
Asia	1413872	1828527	1866089	2141383	2521541
Middle East	170115	x353667	x343517	x265630	x216019
Europe	6501724	6681235	6551332	5568108	5979326
EEC	6140336	6366233	6212520	5241699	5630871
EFTA	312695	284126	305223	276092	317468
Oceania	x301786	x266185	x284321	x302520	x354996
USA/Etats–Unis d'Amer	2753122	2596841	2994563	3374394	3939315
Germany/Allemagne	1277285	1534811	1445763	1182539	1266862
Netherlands/Pays–Bas	825867	948388	905291	962311	1061856
France,Monac	981225	985700	982758	807572	843710
United Kingdom	813760	728318	774543	758839	772473
Italy/Italie	663867	672989	674109	474444	489863
Hong Kong	341715	439799	580891	652158	781794
Canada	458065	424634	491681	467255	436201
Spain/Espagne	538713	548344	493980	307361	297187
Singapore/Singapour	207067	265380	263222	398605	459653
Mexico/Mexique	141005	202527	249079	261012	321368
Australia/Australie	236022	210422	222283	235586	281810
Japan/Japon	211798	227109	185182	213559	315765
Switz.Liecht	220417	190443	209731	184537	208329
Belgium–Luxembourg	180820	199567	204626	150162	168796
Sweden/Suède	230365	181681	176964	134514	178125
Austria/Autriche	169238	169240	164155	146819	196304
Korea, Republic of	117787	128896	120931	181798	198600
Denmark/Danemark	144397	109228	129845	114932	112813
China/Chine	115162	133395	85341	94103	108005
Portugal	95749	95404	112520	80864	86903
So. Africa Customs Un	89649	113422	83450	91672	116595
Thailand/Thaïlande	64443	83051	82155	105108	145512
Norway,SVD,JM	88302	87912	91000	88247	105557
Argentina/Argentine	14297	44666	85992	95986	134080
Iran (Islamic Rp. of)		x88695	x76699	x44051	x19068
Turkey/Turquie	63531	75921	61114	66252	42977
Saudi Arabia	22213	75311	73874	x50941	x49539
Russian Federation			x84491	x115231	x145925
Hungary/Hongrie	x38322	77506	x53117	x56260	x35487
Finland/Finlande	128259	77686	58404	49222	81160
Greece/Grèce	47852	77289	57156	50113	50132
Malaysia/Malaisie	51097	56197	61631	62458	87305
Venezuela	22062	46423	61781	65139	36890
United Arab Emirates	41998	57152	61425	x53620	x52523
Poland/Pologne	11317	41938	69636	60093	65588
Brazil/Brésil	40965	52089	53595	60734	113512
New Zealand	55135	45448	51630	56049	61779
Indonesia/Indonésie	61324	57033	40048	40624	39363
Former USSR/Anc. URSS	34121	x121859			
Chile/Chili	19278	28856	36956	43480	38873
Czechoslovakia	102335	x39485	x62670		
Israel/Israël	23572	25467	33863	37335	47588
Ireland/Irlande	42939	37588	32406	22009	24686
Colombia/Colombie	21970	20219	17308	46117	62535
Philippines	20209	20083	24647	34409	40599
Nigeria/Nigéria	x22860	17414	x24551	x35003	x12626
Romania/Roumanie	18894	33109	21092	20944	18508
Czech Republic				70705	71797
Egypt/Egypte	22590	24634	24327	20242	24345

COUNTRIES–PAYS	EXPORTS – EXPORTATIONS 1990	1991	1992	1993	1994
Totale	11724850	11827043	12156568	12061446	13741917
Afrique	9626	x10705	11031	x19266	x4524
Afrique du Nord	2695	3858	3610	9356	1070
Amériques	1150629	1247028	1369851	1380042	1466334
ALAI	137794	175000	247302	347089	444761
MCAC	22	8	43	136	x74
Asie	5293023	5650565	5832168	6244092	7094119
Moyen–Orient	12874	3642	5795	x12922	x15829
Europe	4756910	4841989	4893746	4345998	5120163
CEE	4631531	4714362	4775395	4231683	4992333
AELE	111088	114518	112758	112166	127252
Océanie	17751	x18362	x17940	x17773	x20805
Japan/Japon	3877496	4015179	3892662	3830429	3908797
Netherlands/Pays–Bas	1117533	1157120	1223605	1114192	1555771
Germany/Allemagne	1338110	1175556	1215263	951785	1028437
USA/Etats–Unis d'Amer	899819	982243	1052082	957681	950964
United Kingdom	922171	990172	1005155	947974	1054823
Hong Kong	620379	690012	770058	893990	1200996
France,Monac	523444	643102	636075	561079	627429
Singapore/Singapour	335766	360655	387278	480689	522209
Italy/Italie	354100	412744	375180	327928	297101
China/Chine	161111	184705	252072	318197	553651
Thailand/Thaïlande	42353	117874	215884	321470	415092
Mexico/Mexique	85553	125845	201914	300201	387716
Malaysia/Malaisie	71793	119331	142927	208911	217005
Korea, Republic of	131750	123743	133135	149723	182952
Sweden/Suède	149587	131983	130518	98409	125055
Switz.Liecht	93890	101151	97820	94141	100281
Canada	72451	55296	69004	74505	69705
Belgium–Luxembourg	37052	39557	47308	107055	135261
Spain/Espagne	50538	59022	47096	41146	77429
Brazil/Brésil	51103	48301	42066	39188	43618
Austria/Autriche	41359	44821	44516	28438	x34451
Denmark/Danemark	76283	38934	30575	32263	28111
Bulgaria/Bulgarie	x68256	x16748	x18476	x17115	x5153
Norway,SVD,JM	17197	13365	14926	18025	26971
Australia/Australie	13950	15085	13878	14858	17844
Indonesia/Indonésie	134	4350	13260	20554	67463
Finland/Finlande	7671	9891	8597	13724	18947
Suriname/Suriname	38935	32087	7	x2	
Czech Republic				31568	23759
India/Inde	9485	11203	7021	3197	5959
Romania/Roumanie	3176	19089	111	54	201
Israel/Israël	15761	11050	5343	1304	1802
Ireland/Irlande	8445	7020	6630	3752	4799
Czechoslovakia		x11125	x5232		
So. Africa Customs Un	5482	5008	5376	5664	
Egypt/Egypte	1429	3107	2884	8971	508
Hungary/Hongrie	x3910	x6585	x4509	x3423	x2729
Yugoslavia SFR	13970	x12369			
Portugal	4435	3887	3708	3206	3875
Macau/Macao	1000	6790	3001	851	1311
New Zealand	3538	2811	3862	2717	2823
Argentina/Argentine	786	562	2652	5894	11641
Poland/Pologne	4174	3568	3257	1516	3836
Turkey/Turquie	764	1439	2234	4121	2769
United Arab Emirates	7833		4	x5982	x10162
Korea Dem People's Rp	x12361	x998	x3067	x1277	x539
Russian Federation			x4169	x936	x1327
Yugoslavia/Yougoslavie			x3222	x72	x28
Mali		x45	x114	x2884	x789
Malta/Malte	101	468	986	1568	x37

(VALUE AS % OF TOTAL)(VALEUR EN % DU TOTAL)

	1985	1986	1987	1988	1989	1990	1991	1992	1993	1994
Africa	2.2	x2.1	x2.2	x2.2	x1.9	x2.0	x2.0	x1.8	x2.0	x1.8
Northern Africa	1.1	0.7	0.5	0.5	0.5	0.6	0.5	0.6	0.5	0.5
Americas	39.7	38.2	33.0	32.0	32.6	29.1	27.4	31.0	34.7	35.8
LAIA	1.9	2.1	2.2	2.0	2.2	2.3	3.3	4.2	4.7	5.2
CACM	0.5	0.2	0.2	0.2	0.1	0.1	0.1	0.1	x0.2	x0.2
Asia	10.9	7.4	9.5	11.0	10.5	11.5	14.2	14.1	16.4	17.3
Middle East	1.0	x1.2	x1.0	x1.0	x1.1	1.4	x2.7	x2.6	x2.0	x1.5
Europe	41.9	48.1	50.6	50.1	50.7	53.0	51.9	49.4	42.7	41.1
EEC	36.0	41.0	43.3	42.9	43.7	50.1	49.4	46.8	40.2	38.7
EFTA	5.7	6.8	7.0	6.9	6.6	2.5	2.2	2.3	2.1	2.2
Oceania	3.7	x2.9	x3.1	x3.0	x3.1	x2.5	x2.1	x2.2	x2.3	x2.5
USA/Etats–Unis d'Amer	32.9	31.6	26.6	25.5	25.8	22.4	20.2	22.6	25.9	27.0
Germany/Allemagne	7.9	8.3	8.4	8.1	8.5	10.4	11.9	10.9	9.1	8.7
Netherlands/Pays–Bas	2.6	3.6	3.5	3.9	5.2	6.7	7.4	6.8	7.4	7.3
France,Monac	6.0	7.3	7.7	7.2	7.1	8.0	7.7	7.4	6.2	5.8
United Kingdom	7.1	7.2	7.2	7.2	6.5	6.6	5.7	5.8	5.8	5.3
Italy/Italie	4.5	5.0	5.7	4.9	4.8	5.4	5.2	5.1	3.6	3.4
Hong Kong	2.7	1.5	2.2	2.4	2.5	2.8	3.4	4.4	5.0	5.4
Canada	3.8	3.7	3.6	4.0	4.0	3.7	3.3	3.7	3.6	3.0
Spain/Espagne	1.7	2.5	3.1	3.6	3.7	4.4	4.3	3.7	2.4	2.0
Singapore/Singapour	1.2	1.0	0.9	1.2	1.3	1.7	2.1	2.0	3.1	3.2

	1985	1986	1987	1988	1989	1990	1991	1992	1993	1994
Afrique		x0.0	x0.0	x0.0	x0.0		x0.0		x0.1	x0.0
Afrique du Nord	0.0	x0.0	x0.0	x0.0	x0.0	0.0	0.0	0.0	0.1	0.0
Amériques	8.6	6.2	6.5	7.9	9.4	9.8	10.6	11.2	11.5	10.6
ALAI	1.1	0.8	0.8	1.2	1.2	1.2	1.5	2.0	2.9	3.2
MCAC	0.0	x0.0	x0.0	x0.0	0.0	0.0	0.0	0.0	0.0	x0.0
Asie	60.4	57.3	x51.8	x49.9	48.1	45.1	47.7	48.0	51.8	51.7
Moyen–Orient	0.0	x0.1	x0.0	0.1	x0.1	0.1	0.0	0.0	x0.1	x0.1
Europe	30.2	35.9	36.5	37.4	40.2	40.6	40.9	40.3	36.0	37.3
CEE	27.4	32.6	33.6	34.7	37.6	39.5	39.9	39.3	35.1	36.3
AELE	2.6	3.2	2.8	2.6	2.5	0.9	1.0	0.9	0.9	0.9
Océanie		x0.1	x0.1	x0.2	0.1	0.1	x0.2	x0.1	x0.1	x0.2
Japan/Japon	54.8	52.0	40.2	35.6	36.1	33.1	33.9	32.0	31.8	28.4
Netherlands/Pays–Bas	5.5	6.5	6.8	6.6	8.0	9.5	9.8	10.1	9.2	11.3
Germany/Allemagne	9.4	11.2	11.1	10.1	11.2	11.4	9.9	10.0	7.9	7.5
USA/Etats–Unis d'Amer	7.2	5.1	5.5	6.1	7.2	7.7	8.3	8.7	7.9	6.9
United Kingdom	4.6	5.5	6.5	8.3	7.8	7.9	8.4	8.3	7.9	7.7
Hong Kong	3.3	3.1	3.7	4.5	5.5	5.3	5.8	6.3	7.4	8.7
France,Monac	2.3	3.3	3.3	3.4	4.2	4.5	5.4	5.2	4.7	4.6
Singapore/Singapour	1.6	1.2	1.5	2.1	2.9	2.9	3.0	3.2	4.0	3.8
Italy/Italie	2.6	2.7	2.6	2.7	3.0	3.0	3.5	3.1	2.7	2.2
China/Chine			1.0	1.3	1.3	1.4	1.6	2.1	2.6	4.0

TRADE BY COMMODITY IN THOUSAND U.S. DOLLARS – COMMERCE PAR PRODUIT EN MILLIERS DE DOLLARS E.U

COUNTRIES–PAYS	IMPORTS – IMPORTATIONS				
	1990	1991	1992	1993	1994
Total	74312771	79648681	88781887	96788470	110844593
Africa	x764263	x790065	x935661	x1009399	x1157781
Northern Africa	197600	173436	209915	241896	247951
Americas	20268716	23928531	29256211	34251958	39184077
LAIA	1105082	1692289	2216489	2901437	3601172
CACM	49640	49678	76456	x79039	x88757
Asia	8471664	9517745	10754718	13415083	17704940
Middle East	562248	x775455	x902244	x986752	x745116
Europe	41411929	42372965	45145664	44878539	48975715
EEC	38699368	39836555	42481389	42232859	45983401
EFTA	2520283	2402622	2468998	2444900	2802506
Oceania	x1848238	x1711604	x1837343	x1984012	x2515431
USA/Etats–Unis d'Amer	15757248	18418315	22924675	26929341	30614507
Germany/Allemagne	8919579	10408743	11588867	10249967	10760909
United Kingdom	7518748	7580478	8245111	10461205	9813298
France, Monac	6087834	5831925	6419542	5742422	6415730
Netherlands/Pays–Bas	3893539	3837111	4218545	4840620	5961739
Canada	3221071	3625411	3891945	4207965	4701004
Japan/Japon	2949567	3072125	3225788	3972418	5472042
Italy/Italie	3526319	3570033	3544635	2728532	2912919
Singapore/Singapour	1748885	1906978	2185440	3449338	5083399
Spain/Espagne	2177889	2117543	1897754	1434728	1611110
Switz.Liecht	1873281	1771945	1821694	1821803	2118047
Australia/Australie	1544284	1413765	1563926	1684091	2093242
Sweden/Suède	1504051	1442049	1424755	1396681	1715378
Belgium–Luxembourg	1514613	1438190	1415986	1402955	1701278
Hong Kong	831133	992063	1565294	1636721	2089217
Korea, Republic of	1022782	1239912	1044894	1185081	1602692
Austria/Autriche	989675	1081359	1039622	916864	1083822
Mexico/Mexique	455234	741232	931572	1084777	1305161
Denmark/Danemark	722352	812971	898553	942212	1096923
Ireland/Irlande	572120	488040	543560	1062675	1691901
Norway, SVD, JM	620993	603122	618418	597826	648126
Finland/Finlande	709746	537278	542111	511258	671630
China/Chine	365536	397273	468885	697404	831545
So. Africa Customs Un	363978	411682	470177	521189	627476
Portugal	399125	492128	514705	368713	361247
Brazil/Brésil	189344	240014	383547	540012	744680
Israel/Israël	291556	358705	350760	376638	420074
Poland/Pologne	76728	337570	330407	407570	416233
Turkey/Turquie	348264	334721	344751	392350	276233
Argentina/Argentine	68657	202760	319553	482350	670504
Thailand/Thaïlande	167430	230305	337188	375740	509073
Russian Federation			x442549	x397369	x575641
New Zealand	279037	268720	251789	273537	388273
Malaysia/Malaisie	181581	230263	235188	312132	414063
Venezuela	129707	187700	193388	219584	123256
Greece/Grèce	163778	198708	187642	174028	185519
Hungary/Hongrie	x122905	186735	x161721	x200401	x189532
Former USSR/Anc. URSS	x850626	x533393			
Chile/Chili	100334	126661	170674	198987	237059
Czechoslovakia	353099	x189054	x287569		
Czech Republic				464541	531072
Saudi Arabia	69528	151953	145768	x149967	x111593
Iran (Islamic Rp. of)		x119216	x179573	x137092	x57591
Colombia/Colombie	84002	84725	89772	210584	295556
Indonesia/Indonésie	149774	125026	101052	115856	94171
Philippines	51752	59113	172166	96906	115021
United Arab Emirates	46698	39203	52214	x148971	x144466
India/Inde	59920	47925	72092	84282	127159
Slovenia/Slovénia			83539	100267	101276
Morocco/Maroc	54160	49578	60319	56665	62285

COUNTRIES–PAYS	EXPORTS – EXPORTATIONS				
	1990	1991	1992	1993	1994
Totale	67027504	69234850	76558445	84407123	97797274
Afrique	x17674	x25479	x26877	x28084	x11823
Afrique du Nord	1175	6164	2092	2289	2350
Amériques	17161127	18241457	19591017	20417330	23498377
ALAI	503548	606249	604546	962857	1384522
MCAC	45	69	122	x466	x1423
Asie	22843046	25439874	30789573	35334718	40108159
Moyen–Orient	x43783	x36132	x40088	x101542	x75773
Europe	25465616	25213944	25910411	28274289	33721230
CEE	24898899	24677884	25367958	27716911	33149427
AELE	551998	529104	532716	535937	554980
Océanie	x178925	x247093	x181322	x243565	x330435
USA/Etats–Unis d'Amer	15681682	16480390	17623624	18027349	20427266
Japan/Japon	12172184	13430956	15849001	16860334	15975296
Singapore/Singapour	6828181	7541996	9743098	11951310	14656769
United Kingdom	6839462	6634956	6694232	7267973	8562835
Germany/Allemagne	5320793	5449056	5195664	5196381	5676561
France, Monac	2785128	3114144	3682984	3335460	3882496
Netherlands/Pays–Bas	2261778	2582416	2864092	4267436	5586607
Korea, Republic of	1969685	2090794	2130988	2584738	2799829
Italy/Italie	2196630	1953203	2058154	2087385	2169741
Ireland/Irlande	2505761	1762352	1717060	2615042	3641784
Canada	968584	1149342	1341506	1408193	1643586
Hong Kong	945801	1122478	1259635	1176379	1323460
Spain/Espagne	710638	912899	816291	661443	836318
Belgium–Luxembourg	613007	599473	572985	803707	1016702
Thailand/Thaïlande	357866	515592	508943	948266	2114428
Sweden/Suède	885731	768508	617857	402109	344580
Mexico/Mexique	351516	391891	440612	826060	1243315
Finland/Finlande	239983	266631	480795	551028	721637
China/Chine	96705	142587	301086	558646	987379
Switz.Liecht	303884	299360	319781	368001	353541
Israel/Israël	250698	248451	335185	349112	336882
Denmark/Danemark	226011	270434	293744	294041	497955
Austria/Autriche	293630	316985	332726	194940	x179163
Malaysia/Malaisie	30754	78207	287406	448399	1460149
Norway, SVD, JM	248002	229608	212787	167748	201364
Australia/Australie	151777	192674	161150	218845	303984
Philippines	61561	166580	174862	187949	179232
Brazil/Brésil	52800	105562	85736	85507	93615
Indonesia/Indonésie	306	21866	104242	89017	96213
Argentina/Argentine	95247	103145	67454	42867	39123
India/Inde	59349	31848	33798	59497	83308
Portugal	17537	40404	33049	27787	25758
New Zealand	25900	44177	18391	21313	25516
Poland/Pologne	177959	51229	13900	8479	17500
Hungary/Hongrie	x5386	x6825	x18851	x38934	x33853
So. Africa Customs Un	11571	15634	17031	19885	
Czech Republic				50343	67668
Saudi Arabia	1900	2184	8427	x35987	x36479
United Arab Emirates	8805			x41701	x24724
Korea Dem People's Rp	x21521	x10595	x10853	x16850	x16032
Bahrain/Bahreïn	x8461	x11982	x9939	x11536	x1493
Turkey/Turquie	18519	14151	12388	3530	5332
Bahamas	x72	728	x16033	x12332	x455
Greece/Grèce	2586	6199	8325	12181	7291
Malta/Malte	820	1425	2843	16213	x11395
Romania/Roumanie	5770	19	13585	872	1345
Czechoslovakia		x3780	x9050		
Bulgaria/Bulgarie	x48270	x1522	x3649	x5310	x2449
Cyprus/Chypre	2354	3984	3478	1603	1312
American Samoa	x35			x38	x45

(VALUE AS % OF TOTAL)(VALEUR EN % DU TOTAL)

	1985	1986	1987	1988	1989	1990	1991	1992	1993	1994
Africa	1.7	x1.7	x1.3	x1.5	x1.0	x1.0	x1.0	x1.0	x1.0	x1.1
Northern Africa	0.3	0.3	0.2	0.2	0.3	0.3	0.2	0.2	0.2	0.2
Americas	24.2	23.7	22.4	21.2	27.3	27.2	30.1	32.9	35.4	35.4
LAIA	2.8	1.8	1.7	1.6	1.4	1.5	2.1	2.5	3.0	3.2
CACM		x0.1	0.1	0.1	0.1	0.1	0.1	0.1	x0.1	x0.1
Asia	9.7	8.9	x9.7	x11.0	10.5	11.4	11.9	12.1	13.9	16.0
Middle East	0.9	x1.1	x1.0	0.8	x1.0	0.8	x1.0	x1.0	x1.0	x0.7
Europe	59.5	61.0	59.8	59.3	54.8	55.7	53.2	50.9	46.4	44.2
EEC	51.1	52.1	51.2	50.9	47.2	52.1	50.0	47.8	43.6	41.5
EFTA	8.1	8.6	8.4	8.1	7.4	3.4	3.0	2.8	2.5	2.5
Oceania	3.7	x3.3	x2.8	2.6	x2.7	x2.5	x2.1	x2.0	x2.0	x2.2
USA/Etats–Unis d'Amer	14.2	15.7	14.8	14.3	20.9	21.2	23.1	25.8	27.8	27.6
Germany/Allemagne	10.2	11.2	10.5	10.2	10.1	12.0	13.1	13.1	10.6	9.7
United Kingdom	11.7	10.5	10.8	10.5	9.9	10.1	9.5	9.3	10.8	8.9
France, Monac	8.2	8.7	8.4	8.2	7.6	8.2	7.3	7.2	5.9	5.8
Netherlands/Pays–Bas	4.3	4.8	4.5	5.4	4.5	5.2	4.8	4.8	5.0	5.4
Canada	7.2	5.9	5.5	5.1	4.8	4.3	4.6	4.4	4.3	4.2
Japan/Japon	3.5	3.1	2.8	3.5	3.8	4.0	3.9	3.6	4.1	4.9
Italy/Italie	5.4	5.3	5.4	5.4	4.4	4.7	4.5	4.0	2.8	2.6
Singapore/Singapour	1.1	0.9	1.0	1.4	1.7	2.4	2.4	2.5	3.6	4.6
Spain/Espagne	2.3	2.4	2.5	2.8	2.6	2.9	2.7	2.1	1.5	1.5

	1985	1986	1987	1988	1989	1990	1991	1992	1993	1994
Afrique	0.1	x0.1	x0.0	x0.0	x0.0	x0.0	x0.0	x0.0	x0.0	x0.0
Afrique du Nord	0.0	x0.0	x0.0	x0.0	0.0	0.0	0.0	0.0	0.0	0.0
Amériques	33.7	27.7	23.8	22.7	25.7	25.6	26.4	25.6	24.2	24.1
ALAI	1.3	0.8	0.8	1.0	1.0	0.8	0.9	0.8	1.1	1.4
MCAC		x0.0	x0.0	x0.0	x0.0	0.0	0.0	0.0	x0.0	x0.0
Asie	22.9	28.6	x33.0	x36.6	32.9	34.0	36.8	40.2	41.9	41.0
Moyen–Orient	0.0	x0.0	x0.1	x0.0	x0.0	x0.1	x0.1	x0.1	x0.1	x0.1
Europe	42.1	42.4	37.8	36.1	39.7	38.0	36.4	33.8	33.5	34.5
CEE	38.6	38.9	35.0	33.5	37.0	37.1	35.6	33.1	32.8	33.9
AELE	3.5	3.4	2.9	2.6	2.8	0.8	0.8	0.7	0.6	0.6
Océanie	0.1	x0.1	x0.3	x0.2	x0.2	x0.3	x0.3	x0.2	x0.3	x0.3
USA/Etats–Unis d'Amer	27.3	22.9	19.2	19.8	23.1	23.4	23.8	23.0	21.4	20.9
Japan/Japon	17.1	21.3	19.3	19.4	18.6	18.2	19.4	20.7	20.0	16.3
Singapore/Singapour	3.1	4.0	4.9	6.3	8.0	10.2	10.9	12.7	14.2	15.0
United Kingdom	6.6	5.6	6.1	9.2	10.8	10.2	9.6	8.7	8.6	8.8
Germany/Allemagne	9.5	10.3	8.7	7.4	7.8	7.9	7.9	6.8	6.2	5.8
France, Monac	4.0	5.3	4.9	4.1	4.2	4.2	4.5	4.8	4.0	4.0
Netherlands/Pays–Bas	3.0	3.1	2.6	2.8	3.0	3.4	3.7	3.7	5.1	5.7
Korea, Republic of	1.5	2.1	2.3	3.2	3.3	2.9	3.0	2.8	3.1	2.9
Italy/Italie	4.5	4.0	3.1	3.1	3.4	3.3	2.8	2.7	2.5	2.2
Ireland/Irlande	5.1	5.1	4.6	3.1	3.6	3.7	2.5	2.2	3.1	3.7

TRADE BY COMMODITY IN THOUSAND U.S. DOLLARS – COMMERCE PAR PRODUIT EN MILLIERS DE DOLLARS E.U

COUNTRIES–PAYS	IMPORTS – IMPORTATIONS 1990	1991	1992	1993	1994
Total	50102148	49863871	56729554	57591898	70560200
Africa	x389954	x451571	x452670	x513769	x639948
Northern Africa	70945	78425	96641	89851	94129
Americas	11480234	12176146	14569903	17517059	22634289
LAIA	903652	678286	1302045	1554059	1391555
CACM	23440	23050	36799	x51197	x65347
Asia	8748369	10233424	12625393	13666679	17573967
Middle East	350463	421815	585924	x429501	x381938
Europe	24689765	25439048	27473360	24032521	27615858
EEC	23527943	24300724	26276138	22787235	26162951
EFTA	1075707	1071651	1131800	1135486	1358744
Oceania	x1047333	x1172555	x1280344	x1374326	x1661726
USA/Etats–Unis d'Amer	8988397	9642149	11150248	13654555	18450929
United Kingdom	5422413	5093069	5704316	4933652	5476129
Germany/Allemagne	4693933	5005580	5262114	4698569	5587014
Netherlands/Pays–Bas	3259613	3221129	3328387	2885671	3340690
Singapore/Singapour	2396028	2535688	3149152	3683693	4382758
France,Monac	2956977	3020567	3163529	2707659	3536226
Japan/Japon	2171211	2415599	2720544	2799046	3570636
Hong Kong	1104817	1623396	2236469	2483202	3400770
Canada	1491465	1761889	2001527	2173976	2630013
Italy/Italie	1552801	1797756	2104217	1886788	1971130
Ireland/Irlande	1335865	1357166	1670577	1529475	1577566
Spain/Espagne	873753	1281504	1305871	1161022	1209467
Thailand/Thaïlande	882528	987781	1200459	1269437	1730898
Australia/Australie	917859	1022569	1109243	1191272	1437193
Malaysia/Malaisie	453482	742169	925263	1001917	1420583
Sweden/Suède	938029	894677	908248	688879	753791
Belgium–Luxembourg	832250	836721	973372	564607	645806
Switz.Liecht	729334	717322	731858	752243	917899
Austria/Autriche	605020	715329	701546	619994	698887
China/Chine	290886	437364	694583	801474	1133328
Mexico/Mexique	523808	262019	695717	907698	657878
Korea, Republic of	672292	593094	569550	633680	813742
Denmark/Danemark	546748	569450	599182	555593	652177
Norway,SVD,JM	337173	343440	390689	374473	431625
Brazil/Brésil	239044	223170	310601	340549	377169
So. Africa Customs Un	243768	297141	254683	315313	415632
Finland/Finlande	291211	247839	249859	276549	443149
Israel/Israël	121312	147262	171547	206920	275988
Portugal	147637	171581	181225	144836	152845
Philippines	59940	161025	181309	149327	186303
Saudi Arabia	162995	172667	206274	x75894	x85873
New Zealand	111390	121996	141307	149689	185074
Hungary/Hongrie	x65676	91522	x104402	x168156	x109394
Greece/Grèce	71691	88355	123694	133940	118074
India/Inde	176457	98321	105128	111165	143327
Turkey/Turquie	58756	83501	101686	129160	79157
Argentina/Argentine	37111	61895	132330	88064	122819
Russian Federation			x112287	x158708	x311590
Czechoslovakia	51914	x67398	x152249		
Poland/Pologne	34537	93808	11170	110001	111971
United Arab Emirates	61139	45479	76006	x51435	x68794
Venezuela	39599	48878	58459	60509	34968
Kuwait/ Koweït	17165	35201	66181	51586	62434
Chile/Chili	24707	33494	48844	61250	74989
Egypt/Egypte	31170	39569	53585	42258	41317
Iran (Islamic Rp. of)		x30278	x58013	x43977	x10098
Indonesia/Indonésie	34880	33393	40192	44247	42937
Former USSR/Anc. URSS	3487115	x113430			
Czech Republic				105202	110885
Oman	28305	24411	32061	38178	35006

COUNTRIES–PAYS	EXPORTS – EXPORTATIONS 1990	1991	1992	1993	1994
Totale	47990882	52422767	57918065	59618091	72425196
Afrique	x28351	x29657	x36473	x39784	x14960
Afrique du Nord	831	667	1815	x2032	1963
Amériques	13070016	14294460	15046759	15021008	17726163
ALAI	210579	389435	722419	550699	767376
MCAC	8	53	24	x2759	x6853
Asie	15440892	18094121	22378016	26519383	34417754
Moyen–Orient	12533	x9902	x13692	x26856	x29823
Europe	18664146	19513258	19885769	17405354	19392882
CEE	18353837	19179725	19547133	17104065	19019598
AELE	304673	330376	332819	286252	344441
Océanie	x347232	x456198	x517853	x586893	x810504
USA/Etats–Unis d'Amer	11184828	11998162	12307501	12362910	14017934
Japan/Japon	8764223	9541682	10826678	12422203	15286091
United Kingdom	3588454	4002154	3916157	3694862	4635490
Hong Kong	1952271	2548198	3464703	3876422	4550185
Netherlands/Pays–Bas	3296247	3217561	3418775	2794046	3002344
Singapore/Singapour	2041282	2313865	2836695	4079027	7370905
Germany/Allemagne	3133275	3180612	3230127	2596246	3113838
Ireland/Irlande	2066027	2241971	2722197	2662060	2346950
France,Monac	2506744	2509442	2450796	1967556	2255489
Canada	1667404	1901853	2009103	2093540	2918171
Malaysia/Malaisie	573890	1183640	1944416	2659104	3365643
Italy/Italie	1857013	1947437	1678029	1759623	1898416
Thailand/Thaïlande	1162178	1320846	1685023	1552804	1594177
Korea, Republic of	600163	678435	826895	739870	624424
China/Chine	117332	196860	579630	769816	1123379
Australia/Australie	322433	428727	488468	561162	783785
Belgium–Luxembourg	584088	573368	566376	336123	430264
Sweden/Suède	423470	434235	458220	308790	363334
Mexico/Mexique	123309	242394	529836	391963	651800
Spain/Espagne	262226	334707	376207	323397	298779
Austria/Autriche	267246	332218	346809	297414	x172845
Denmark/Danemark	198018	280419	285981	271332	349981
Switz.Liecht	218896	244565	255081	213154	245873
Israel/Israël	154408	99587	95426	240252	186511
Brazil/Brésil	67840	117769	148147	123225	80178
Norway,SVD,JM	84980	85401	77551	73029	98485
Philippines	7072	163354	19083	27004	53698
Finland/Finlande	91299	71226	56075	72738	128075
India/Inde	43001	22815	35634	52931	67258
Argentina/Argentine	17702	26857	42220	32813	32192
Portugal	76640	49010	33911	13881	13802
So. Africa Customs Un	25678	26543	31956	32966	
New Zealand	23165	25437	27786	24849	25847
Indonesia/Indonésie	323	1233	22138	47084	136209
Hungary/Hongrie	x9498	x14463	x25630	x19012	x23346
Sri Lanka	2036	5212	15347	18699	18693
Czechoslovakia		x9414	x19982		
Greece/Grèce	3029	5305	7470	5998	9991
Czech Republic				17848	24103
Malta/Malte	163	885	2717	9214	x18180
Macau/Macao	5435	3892	6070	2789	6959
United Arab Emirates	4364		10	x10004	x11370
Bulgaria/Bulgarie	x101828	x1380	x6139	x1767	x2073
Saudi Arabia	2391	2114	2936	x3728	x5158
Korea Dem People's Rp	x3063	x2745	x2099	x3610	x2524
Poland/Pologne	7450	4188	190	3941	8048
Slovenia/Slovénia			2204	5241	9370
Iran (Islamic Rp. of)		x1052	x4690	x1522	x1170
Russian Federation			x4320	x2163	x3412
Bahrain/Bahreïn	x1539	x2026	x1183	x2865	x2604

(VALUE AS % OF TOTAL)(VALEUR EN % DU TOTAL)

	1985	1986	1987	1988	1989	1990	1991	1992	1993	1994
Africa	0.6	x0.8	x0.8	x0.9	x0.8	x0.8	x0.9	x0.7	x0.8	x0.9
Northern Africa	0.1	0.2	0.2	0.1	0.1	0.1	0.2	0.2	0.2	0.1
Americas	30.7	30.2	30.9	31.0	24.2	22.9	24.4	25.7	30.4	32.1
LAIA	2.1	1.3	1.7	1.4	1.1	1.8	1.4	2.3	2.7	2.0
CACM		0.0	0.0	0.0	0.0	0.0	0.0	0.1	x0.1	x0.1
Asia	9.0	8.8	11.4	14.1	15.4	17.5	20.5	22.3	23.7	25.0
Middle East	0.7	x0.7	x0.6	0.7	x0.6	0.7	0.8	1.0	x0.7	x0.5
Europe	51.1	50.2	47.3	45.9	50.7	49.3	51.0	48.4	41.7	39.1
EEC	45.6	44.3	42.0	40.8	45.1	47.0	48.7	46.3	39.6	37.1
EFTA	5.2	5.6	5.1	5.0	5.5	2.1	2.1	2.0	2.0	1.9
Oceania	1.7	x1.5	x1.7	1.8	x2.2	x2.1	x2.4	x2.3	x2.4	x2.4
USA/Etats–Unis d'Amer	24.3	24.9	25.4	26.2	19.7	17.9	19.3	19.7	23.7	26.1
United Kingdom	8.6	8.2	8.1	9.3	10.6	10.8	10.2	10.1	8.6	7.8
Germany/Allemagne	9.4	9.5	8.9	7.7	9.2	9.4	10.0	9.3	8.2	7.9
Netherlands/Pays–Bas	5.9	5.5	5.1	5.1	5.6	6.5	6.5	5.9	5.0	4.7
Singapore/Singapour	2.1	2.0	2.7	3.0	4.0	4.8	5.1	5.6	6.4	6.2
France,Monac	5.7	6.1	6.0	5.6	5.6	5.9	6.1	5.6	4.7	5.0
Japan/Japon	2.3	1.9	2.0	2.4	3.6	4.3	4.8	4.8	4.9	5.1
Hong Kong	2.0	1.6	1.7	2.2	2.3	2.2	3.3	3.9	4.3	4.8
Canada	4.2	3.7	3.6	3.3	3.2	3.0	3.5	3.5	3.8	3.7
Italy/Italie	3.5	3.3	3.3	3.3	3.0	3.1	3.6	3.7	3.3	2.8

	1985	1986	1987	1988	1989	1990	1991	1992	1993	1994
Afrique	0.1	x0.1	x0.0	x0.0	x0.0	x0.1	x0.1	x0.1	x0.1	x0.0
Afrique du Nord	0.0	x0.0	x0.0	x0.0	x0.0	0.0	0.0	0.0	x0.0	0.0
Amériques	37.7	32.7	30.2	32.9	29.4	27.3	27.3	26.0	25.1	24.5
ALAI	0.9	0.2	0.2	0.3	0.7	0.4	0.7	1.2	0.9	1.1
MCAC		x0.0	x0.0	x0.0	x0.0	0.0	0.0	0.0	x0.0	x0.0
Asie	17.7	20.1	x25.3	x30.3	31.0	32.2	34.5	38.7	44.4	47.6
Moyen–Orient	0.0	x0.1	x0.1	x0.0	x0.0	0.0	x0.0	x0.0	x0.0	x0.0
Europe	44.2	46.7	43.0	35.3	38.3	38.9	37.2	34.3	29.2	26.8
CEE	41.7	44.0	40.7	33.2	36.0	38.2	36.6	33.7	28.7	26.3
AELE	2.5	2.7	2.3	2.2	2.2	0.6	0.6	0.6	0.5	0.5
Océanie	0.2	x0.2	x0.6	0.5	x0.6	x0.7	x0.9	x0.9	x1.0	x1.1
USA/Etats–Unis d'Amer	36.7	32.4	29.8	29.5	25.3	23.3	22.9	21.2	20.7	19.4
Japan/Japon	9.9	13.0	14.3	17.0	19.6	18.3	18.2	18.7	20.8	21.1
United Kingdom	12.9	11.5	11.1	7.4	6.2	7.5	7.6	6.8	6.2	6.4
Hong Kong	4.0	2.9	2.8	3.1	3.7	4.1	4.9	6.0	6.5	6.3
Netherlands/Pays–Bas	5.0	5.9	5.1	4.7	5.9	6.9	6.1	5.9	4.7	4.1
Singapore/Singapour	2.0	2.3	2.5	3.5	3.8	4.3	4.4	4.9	6.8	10.2
Germany/Allemagne	7.8	9.1	7.6	5.7	6.1	6.5	6.1	5.6	4.4	4.3
Ireland/Irlande	2.6	3.0	3.3	3.8	4.5	4.3	4.3	4.7	4.5	3.2
France,Monac	6.3	6.3	6.2	5.0	5.2	5.2	4.8	4.2	3.3	3.1
Canada	0.0	0.0	0.0	3.1	3.5	3.5	3.6	3.5	3.5	4.0

TRADE BY COMMODITY IN THOUSAND U.S. DOLLARS – COMMERCE PAR PRODUIT EN MILLIERS DE DOLLARS E.U

COUNTRIES–PAYS	IMPORTS – IMPORTATIONS 1990	1991	1992	1993	1994
Total	17225624	18095214	15416757	15749124	17829928
Africa	x136936	x114094	x182200	x233367	x207867
Northern Africa	18187	22531	x47576	94639	91726
Americas	3032060	3061304	3864021	3977077	4954855
LAIA	391576	496774	815660	759845	893220
CACM	12986	13576	24510	x24583	x30878
Asia	2483359	3280454	3750949	x4832371	x6130284
Middle East	356786	x560403	x657606	x805539	x722378
Europe	10828524	10709946	7267522	6280562	6212141
EEC	10054803	10183948	6905172	5954974	5821618
EFTA	500140	464067	330997	294525	349489
Oceania	x136544	x141731	x113943	x276580	x160368
USA/Etats–Unis d'Amer	2293017	2179553	2639577	2799725	3632449
Germany/Allemagne	2846765	3066332	1886248	1774238	1668175
Hong Kong	854438	1109603	1646256	1903982	2467871
France, Monac	1265931	1420444	907602	815678	831589
Italy/Italie	1509613	1458331	908921	588087	594118
Singapore/Singapour	646320	880091	627420	877056	1002530
United Kingdom	1113148	929665	659950	642047	522131
Netherlands/Pays–Bas	911382	839678	577449	564143	508487
Spain/Espagne	593874	680398	671013	372530	434594
Japan/Japon	167115	299576	392637	631922	1007871
Canada	277018	324276	333420	347972	347689
Mexico/Mexique	225569	261360	371213	308069	323583
Belgium–Luxembourg	361260	346588	286343	235666	214284
United Arab Emirates	138445	177918	197528	x417498	x455438
Sweden/Suède	367068	346707	235305	200224	276994
Switz.Liecht	384175	341672	217549	200999	232302
Austria/Autriche	299677	313301	194227	188913	203323
Portugal	255414	279299	206165	180848	154903
Poland/Pologne	159502	404551	59328	45403	46367
Saudi Arabia	108970	141043	156465	x190421	x136723
Denmark/Danemark	177914	192258	139889	145604	158587
Russian Federation			x144616	x270340	x651267
Greece/Grèce	153017	113024	112069	149320	140055
Argentina/Argentine	1716	48918	186938	128873	122281
China/Chine	139934	118174	58376	179796	330905
Iran (Islamic Rp. of)		x99328	x133962	x74045	x11401
Norway, SVD, JM	108131	112204	103205	86233	107471
Australia/Australie	73900	60427	31394	191620	51470
Chile/Chili	44401	62904	97708	109622	105246
Finland/Finlande	139659	131423	65122	45395	59425
Thailand/Thaïlande	64702	66272	93124	75479	99725
Israel/Israël	58786	69209	80564	81627	86021
New Zealand	54919	71867	74233	73994	96394
Former USSR/Anc. URSS	224829	x196056			
Paraguay	49660	56901	53171	64103	101660
Ireland/Irlande	60081	66502	54867	52282	54953
Romania/Roumanie	34860	93178	56270	7882	6263
Hungary/Hongrie	x40683	57546	x37103	x28986	x39054
Venezuela	28320	25822	41687	40074	24888
Nigeria/Nigéria	x31096	10422	x44409	x41824	x20486
Kuwait/ Koweït	14760	18865	39053	30154	32487
Cyprus/Chypre	25480	24066	28719	33710	28523
Oman	9547	21164	42202	17732	14228
Bulgaria/Bulgarie	x54365	x11921	47607	x20601	13646
So. Africa Customs Un	21945	28679	19908	29154	25329
Ukraine			x12323	x61083	x13402
Malaysia/Malaisie	15830	20110	19070	32975	37643
Korea Dem People's Rp	x14335	x19687	x27619	x22971	x5951
Viet Nam	x21449	x6448	x21548	x42180	x129389
Macau/Macao	10389	22563	24689	21135	15087

COUNTRIES–PAYS	EXPORTS – EXPORTATIONS 1990	1991	1992	1993	1994
Totale	16056354	16547383	16389660	16753200	20371815
Afrique	x14250	11489	x9132	x17024	x17698
Afrique du Nord	7501	8736	3930	3159	5763
Amériques	681979	746671	2166775	2557855	3655711
ALAI	34098	32117	1337933	1777045	2703236
MCAC	18	154	32	x380	x201
Asie	7218134	8157409	8980038	9364608	11180153
Moyen–Orient	279643	277458	222192	183316	203194
Europe	7555688	7553491	5206314	4760525	5421247
CEE	7482016	7483878	5141884	4693586	5345665
AELE	32576	26544	17622	13836	16472
Océanie	x6367	x8777	x5134	x6320	x6808
Japan/Japon	2071337	2187811	2402216	2239626	2449809
Korea, Republic of	1506998	1632984	1536527	1462755	1698219
Singapore/Singapour	1332047	1389874	1310689	1340385	1653476
Germany/Allemagne	2199246	1988606	1002218	828085	965615
United Kingdom	1117305	1463229	997931	968339	1217130
Mexico/Mexique	1066	1273	1335994	1774014	2678290
Hong Kong	628238	776014	1088675	1240169	1553743
Malaysia/Malaisie	523395	716648	850877	1236145	1738437
France, Monac	809449	962806	823777	732798	690181
USA/Etats–Unis d'Amer	588914	681907	775927	749924	881834
China/Chine	556192	624627	719517	761348	711449
Thailand/Thaïlande	253803	466220	669986	720443	881493
Austria/Autriche	1004916	912737	371749	408804	x477329
Belgium–Luxembourg	723951	613707	475372	444588	522933
Spain/Espagne	305617	428007	443414	414584	472673
Italy/Italie	498471	401183	440398	425899	462310
Netherlands/Pays–Bas	337656	282842	245110	177162	172462
Turkey/Turquie	197473	243679	190778	135919	152952
Finland/Finlande	207667	151627	123099	139589	159329
Denmark/Danemark	111301	112243	98038	88300	96062
Indonesia/Indonésie	6352	11173	115627	114217	183166
Sweden/Suède	88519	81647	57350	51890	92185
Portugal	70525	78592	57640	9406	14010
Canada	56690	29729	46995	28514	68299
Malta/Malte	31205	33439	31037	39728	x24697
India/Inde	9740	17780	21581	18437	27674
Korea Dem People's Rp	x38534	x26745	x21397	x6475	x3462
Philippines	7634	15751	16620	17656	35609
Hungary/Hongrie	x52454	x30335	x11806	x6613	x25102
Cyprus/Chypre	16945	11953	12889	22990	18834
Switz.Liecht	26502	20850	12378	9612	7833
Brazil/Brésil	31998	30112	270	937	548
Oman	2372	10016	12405	5386	5232
Ukraine			x11407	x16249	x6578
Slovenia/Slovénia			13319	13198	34174
Slovakia				x26452	x27769
Russian Federation			x15291	x10635	x6373
Former USSR/Anc. URSS	517174	x21750			
Israel/Israël	119	213	1097	17623	32099
Norway, SVD, JM	6073	5687	5228	4224	8636
Macau/Macao	1136	10339	2220	2311	1390
Australia/Australie	4827	4401	4211	4774	5858
Lithuania/Lituanie			12236	x504	26959
Ireland/Irlande	7083	6341	4797	1593	541
United Arab Emirates	53566			x12649	x19619
Republic of Moldova			x8952	x3641	13499
Poland/Pologne	6177	8707	1463	896	22821
Romania/Roumanie	453	1732	2037	6670	10448
Malawi	x2041	5	x1550	x8360	x9198
Yugoslavia SFR	9799	x9540			

(VALUE AS % OF TOTAL)(VALEUR EN % DU TOTAL)

	1985	1986	1987	1988	1989	1990	1991	1992	1993	1994
Africa	1.1	x1.5	x1.6	x1.1	x1.0	x0.8	x0.7	x1.2	x1.5	x1.1
Northern Africa	0.6	0.4	0.7	0.6	0.4	0.1	0.1	x0.3	0.6	0.5
Americas	32.2	33.4	25.8	17.5	23.3	17.6	16.9	25.1	25.3	27.8
LAIA	1.2	1.3	1.6	2.8	2.4	2.3	2.7	5.3	4.8	5.0
CACM		0.2	0.1	0.1	0.1	0.1	0.1	0.2	x0.2	x0.2
Asia	28.6	15.4	15.7	x17.5	x14.8	14.4	18.1	24.4	x30.7	x34.3
Middle East	3.9	x3.6	x3.2	x2.8	x2.3	2.1	x3.1	x4.3	x5.1	x4.1
Europe	35.1	47.0	53.5	60.7	57.8	62.9	59.2	47.1	39.9	34.8
EEC	30.4	39.2	44.6	51.7	49.1	58.4	56.3	44.8	37.8	32.7
EFTA	4.2	x7.1	x7.9	8.6	7.6	2.9	2.6	2.1	1.9	2.0
Oceania	1.2	x1.1	x1.3	x0.4	x0.8	x0.7	x0.8	x0.8	x1.8	x0.9
USA/Etats–Unis d'Amer	26.5	27.6	20.5	12.3	18.0	13.3	12.0	17.1	17.8	20.4
Germany/Allemagne	5.4	7.7	9.9	10.6	10.1	16.5	16.9	12.2	11.3	9.4
Hong Kong	4.5	2.9	4.0	5.0	4.2	5.0	6.1	10.7	12.1	13.8
France, Monac	3.4	5.9	6.8	8.3	6.8	7.3	7.8	5.9	5.2	4.7
Italy/Italie	6.3	7.3	7.8	8.3	7.7	8.8	8.1	5.9	3.7	3.3
Singapore/Singapour	2.4	2.5	2.8	2.7	2.5	3.8	4.9	4.1	5.6	5.6
United Kingdom	4.7	5.4	5.1	6.7	6.8	6.5	5.1	4.3	4.1	2.9
Netherlands/Pays–Bas	3.5	4.2	4.9	6.1	4.4	5.3	4.6	3.7	3.6	2.9
Spain/Espagne	0.3	0.7	1.0	1.8	3.4	3.4	3.8	4.4	2.4	2.4
Japan/Japon	0.1	0.2	0.8	1.0	1.8	1.0	1.7	2.5	4.0	5.7

	1985	1986	1987	1988	1989	1990	1991	1992	1993	1994
Afrique		x0.1	x0.1	x0.1	0.1	x0.1	0.1	x0.0	x0.1	x0.1
Afrique du Nord	0.0	0.1	0.1	0.1	0.1	0.0	0.1	0.0	0.0	0.0
Amériques	5.8	x5.2	x4.3	x5.5	x5.6	4.2	4.5	13.2	15.2	18.0
ALAI	1.3	0.5	0.4	0.2	0.4	0.2	0.2	8.2	10.6	13.3
MCAC		x0.0	x0.0	x0.0	x0.0	0.0	0.0	0.0	x0.0	x0.0
Asie	61.8	48.8	x50.4	47.0	42.6	45.0	49.3	54.8	55.9	54.9
Moyen–Orient	0.3	x0.3	x0.3	0.7	0.8	1.7	1.7	1.4	1.1	1.0
Europe	30.3	42.7	40.8	43.0	48.0	47.1	45.6	31.8	28.4	26.6
CEE	25.5	35.8	34.2	35.9	40.6	46.6	45.2	31.4	28.0	26.2
AELE	4.3	6.5	6.2	6.9	7.2	0.2	0.2	0.1	0.1	0.1
Océanie					x0.0	x0.0	x0.1	x0.0	x0.0	x0.0
Japan/Japon	43.1	27.1	17.2	14.1	13.1	12.9	13.2	14.7	13.4	12.0
Korea, Republic of	9.1	11.4	12.6	11.3	10.7	9.4	9.9	9.4	8.7	8.3
Singapore/Singapour	4.7	6.0	6.5	7.1	7.7	8.3	8.4	8.0	8.0	8.1
Germany/Allemagne	9.8	13.7	10.0	11.4	14.4	13.7	12.0	6.1	4.9	4.7
United Kingdom	2.5	3.2	3.8	4.2	5.3	7.0	8.8	6.1	5.8	6.0
Mexico/Mexique	0.9	0.0	0.0	0.0	0.2	0.0	0.0	8.2	10.6	13.1
Hong Kong	3.7	2.8	3.7	4.9	4.0	3.9	4.7	6.6	7.4	7.6
Malaysia/Malaisie	0.8	1.2	1.6	1.4	2.6	3.3	4.3	5.2	7.4	8.5
France, Monac	0.6	1.4	2.3	2.3	3.3	5.0	5.8	5.0	4.4	3.4
USA/Etats–Unis d'Amer	3.8	3.9	3.3	4.5	4.2	3.7	4.1	4.7	4.5	4.3

TRADE BY COMMODITY IN THOUSAND U.S. DOLLARS – COMMERCE PAR PRODUIT EN MILLIERS DE DOLLARS E.U

COUNTRIES–PAYS	IMPORTS – IMPORTATIONS					COUNTRIES–PAYS	EXPORTS – EXPORTATIONS				
	1990	1991	1992	1993	1994		1990	1991	1992	1993	1994
Total	14485383	15807987	16129993	17267033	20845991	Totale	12915972	14320937	15617025	16953809	19872544
Africa	x171447	202648	x197917	x181923	x155411	Afrique	x2861	x3205	x6281	x4680	x2737
Northern Africa	14910	12884	x23080	x40705	x26346	Afrique du Nord	65	x58	140	173	630
Americas	4644668	5448171	6038252	6315709	7764621	Amériques	765056	785499	1722279	1749510	1915741
LAIA	271244	554096	727345	719728	930129	ALAI	320783	290339	1235118	1204157	1257521
CACM	25706	23353	34430	19446	22805	MCAC	36	93	31	x41	314
Asia	3779609	4280914	4107225	4951686	6486366	Asie	10483280	11961655	12056222	13059793	15495985
Middle East	278250	333322	363865	x497736	x485733	Moyen–Orient	53831	23455	14238	x26667	x29964
Europe	5388804	5494304	5417833	5405455	5953824	Europe	1575508	1554386	1822691	2122766	2417188
EEC	5094553	5228106	5184749	5185542	5687044	CEE	1559975	1542754	1807172	2113744	2408194
EFTA	213514	240956	213116	196039	234937	AELE	13774	11165	14963	8652	8670
Oceania	x230439	x190289	x279561	x283855	x372174	Océanie	x5416	x4836	x5807	x7410	x10444
USA/Etats–Unis d'Amer	3836177	4275366	4681032	4897681	6053281	Japan/Japon	2473742	3117454	2901090	2718124	2327153
Hong Kong	1640066	2008731	2146581	2470910	3330198	Hong Kong	2118982	2518470	2609708	3110418	4041711
Germany/Allemagne	1502357	1543846	1537617	1447377	1493245	Singapore/Singapour	1575854	1708442	1744590	1879374	2302044
Singapore/Singapour	627351	715485	836596	1112476	1446360	Malaysia/Malaisie	1099432	1463186	1743508	2090076	2842793
United Kingdom	802721	745250	790041	828952	880918	China/Chine	1428421	1568687	1484204	1610028	2305340
France, Monac	715173	709901	686483	723930	809288	Korea, Republic of	1377336	1230282	1183969	1125993	1092393
Canada	469059	546027	547029	628869	699867	Mexico/Mexique	3635	15062	917261	865995	909112
Italy/Italie	461922	533002	527876	385487	471547	USA/Etats–Unis d'Amer	381224	457251	466890	518711	640395
Netherlands/Pays–Bas	424363	474804	432547	502898	506721	Germany/Allemagne	497954	465075	474848	373632	389612
Japan/Japon	294371	329510	419133	457421	655161	Brazil/Brésil	313423	274398	317061	336191	339083
Spain/Espagne	352912	435997	394048	342841	417733	Netherlands/Pays–Bas	234509	248630	252540	345075	388114
Belgium–Luxembourg	241297	232897	251406	374172	414671	Portugal	157412	151172	295101	333265	415684
Mexico/Mexique	126879	215518	313850	252961	354798	France, Monac	221513	218498	255236	240044	295214
China/Chine	684381	637388	40351	84441	134457	Belgium–Luxembourg	154170	156435	181879	366401	392410
Australia/Australie	184760	144775	226220	231545	297452	United Kingdom	121981	111153	139615	265929	315996
United Arab Emirates	103982	150222	172383	x276376	x296529	Israel/Israël	246242	177620	139112	165433	148792
Argentina/Argentine	3091	144565	204055	220879	214190	Indonesia/Indonésie	37357	76583	156867	238670	268880
Switz.Liecht	168747	191953	158978	144022	164312	Austria/Autriche	81643	83131	88995	58340	x42986
Sweden/Suède	158879	148938	151749	125908	197110	Denmark/Danemark	31383	53558	52716	61462	87826
Austria/Autriche	177060	139329	122083	127212	134422	Philippines	28473	43936	53707	69307	120949
Portugal	78747	97247	115321	104923	89147	Canada	61890	36560	19151	25381	16508
Saudi Arabia	108015	92933	74209	x107953	x101760	Thailand/Thaïlande	30377	25158	16666	10025	6249
Malaysia/Malaisie	95638	89170	95886	88289	99965	Italy/Italie	9048	14196	20512	16494	16351
Denmark/Danemark	55849	59974	71258	96976	128100	Spain/Espagne	18981	15345	14482	18662	16869
Nigeria/Nigéria	x65961	90035	x75811	x43384	x19291	Sweden/Suède	14569	10607	14054	16927	31123
Chile/Chili	35170	61406	72903	73772	74109	Finland/Finlande	14700	13401	10262	15054	14675
Thailand/Thaïlande	52668	49935	69887	75788	111504	Switz.Liecht	10557	9019	10323	5254	6785
Poland/Pologne	29616	75972	43728	57867	41993	Cyprus/Chypre	7803	5469	7273	8952	8762
Israel/Israël	30359	40435	54563	59047	76085	Turkey/Turquie	21359	12668	4645	3825	3327
Norway, SVD, JM	41887	45412	51191	49795	67495	Australia/Australie	4601	4308	4396	6289	9832
Brazil/Brésil	25425	44560	45266	52007	111352	Korea Dem People's Rp	x8703	x5898	x4443	x4071	x1886
So. Africa Customs Un	42131	53944	42088	41898	44397	United Arab Emirates	18533			x11088	x14049
Paraguay	63708	57997	29619	42978	72964	Macau/Macao	619	286	842	9735	6785
Greece/Grèce	28349	29089	34157	65028	60783	Poland/Pologne	29711	7043	1850	1921	2394
Finland/Finlande	65901	52051	43954	30981	52292	Norway, SVD, JM	3217	2146	4640	3398	1884
New Zealand	38864	34867	41961	40229	62492	Ireland/Irlande	1953	1253	6623	843	595
Korea, Republic of	41472	39248	24643	26916	46787	So. Africa Customs Un	899	1686	1572	2816	
Russian Federation			x32376	x52000	x78556	Hungary/Hongrie	x327	x1099	x969	x3556	x24709
Ireland/Irlande	29024	25782	26207	28856	31067	India/Inde	2017	2146	1822	1289	433
Panama	19699	22204	23673	25831	28300	Kuwait/Koweït	3348	810	1279	1648	2222
Iran (Islamic Rp. of)		x13515	x32062	x25128	x9831	Czech Republic				3383	3006
Former USSR/Anc. URSS	x145192	x69111				Former USSR/Anc. URSS	50617	x2711			
Venezuela	9518	15384	22606	27495	16060	Greece/Grèce	105	247	309	1615	738
Kuwait/Koweït	11376	9239	23528	21104	22891	Cote d'Ivoire	x4	x86	x1062	x963	x15
Macau/Macao	993	2048	13397	35990	29742	New Zealand	484	411	1266	419	323
Hungary/Hongrie	x13862	24302	x11919	x14072	x11580	Senegal/Sénégal			x1799		x153
Czech Republic				40997	47676	Russian Federation			x717	x1078	x471
Cyprus/Chypre	10994	11462	11615	15243	11948	Saudi Arabia	493	916	271	x314	x404
Lebanon/Liban	x18869	x23335	x8528	x4005	x5210	Colombia/Colombie		265	497	725	445
Peru/Pérou	1899	6451	11263	16590	42549	Argentina/Argentine	47	285	64	1076	8536

(VALUE AS % OF TOTAL)(VALEUR EN % DU TOTAL)

	1985	1986	1987	1988	1989	1990	1991	1992	1993	1994		1985	1986	1987	1988	1989	1990	1991	1992	1993	1994
Africa	0.8	x1.1	x1.0	x1.2	x0.9	x1.2	1.2	x1.3	x1.0	x0.7	Afrique		x0.0	x0.0	x0.0	x0.1	x0.0	x0.0	x0.0	x0.0	x0.0
Northern Africa	0.2	0.1	0.1	0.1	0.1	0.1	0.1	x0.1	x0.2	x0.1	Afrique du Nord	0.0	x0.0	x0.0	0.0	x0.0	0.0	x0.0	0.0	0.0	0.0
Americas	55.2	45.1	x41.2	42.4	37.1	32.0	34.5	37.4	36.6	37.3	Amériques	11.3	8.6	7.1	7.3	6.7	5.9	5.4	11.0	10.3	9.6
LAIA	2.4	1.4	x1.1	1.9	1.7	1.9	3.5	4.5	4.2	4.5	ALAI	6.1	4.1	3.7	3.4	3.4	2.5	2.0	7.9	7.1	6.3
CACM		0.1	0.2	0.2	0.2	0.2	0.1	0.2	0.1	0.1	MCAC		0.0	x0.0	x0.0	x0.0	0.0	0.0	0.0	x0.0	0.0
Asia	11.0	14.2	18.5	21.0	24.7	26.1	27.0	25.4	28.7	31.1	Asie	73.9	72.4	x77.5	79.6	80.3	81.2	83.5	77.2	77.0	78.0
Middle East	2.7	x3.1	x2.0	2.0	x1.9	1.9	2.1	2.3	x2.9	x2.3	Moyen–Orient	0.2	0.3	x0.2	0.5	0.4	0.4	0.2	0.1	x0.2	x0.2
Europe	30.6	37.6	36.5	32.6	34.1	37.2	34.8	33.6	31.3	28.6	Europe	14.1	18.3	14.4	12.2	12.3	12.2	10.9	11.7	12.5	12.2
EEC	25.3	31.3	30.7	28.5	29.9	35.2	33.1	32.1	30.0	27.3	CEE	12.1	16.4	13.3	11.2	11.2	12.1	10.8	11.6	12.5	12.1
EFTA	5.2	5.9	5.5	3.8	3.8	1.5	1.5	1.3	1.1	1.1	AELE	2.0	1.8	1.1	1.0	1.1	0.1	0.1	0.1	0.1	0.0
Oceania	2.2	x1.6	x1.6	x1.7	x1.8	x1.5	x1.2	x1.8	x1.7	x1.8	Océanie		x0.0		x0.0	x0.0	x0.0	x0.0	x0.0	x0.0	x0.1
USA/Etats–Unis d'Amer	46.9	38.9	36.4	36.4	31.1	26.5	27.0	29.0	28.4	29.0	Japan/Japon	44.5	39.7	25.1	19.8	19.3	19.2	21.8	18.6	16.0	11.7
Hong Kong	3.7	4.5	5.6	6.2	9.2	11.3	12.7	13.3	14.3	16.0	Hong Kong	9.0	9.7	10.8	11.3	14.4	16.4	17.6	16.7	18.3	20.3
Germany/Allemagne	6.8	8.3	7.8	6.8	7.5	10.4	9.8	9.5	8.4	7.2	Singapore/Singapour	8.3	8.3	9.1	11.4	12.9	12.2	11.9	11.2	11.1	11.6
Singapore/Singapour	2.6	3.1	3.0	3.8	3.9	4.3	4.5	5.2	6.4	6.9	Malaysia/Malaisie	3.0	3.7	4.3	5.4	8.2	8.5	10.2	11.2	12.3	14.3
United Kingdom	6.0	6.8	6.4	6.0	6.1	5.5	4.7	4.9	4.8	4.2	China/Chine			6.1	7.8	10.2	11.1	11.0	9.5	9.5	11.6
France, Monac	3.1	4.1	4.0	3.8	4.0	4.9	4.5	4.3	4.2	3.9	Korea, Republic of	8.4	10.2	12.2	12.7	11.7	10.7	8.6	7.6	6.6	5.5
Canada	5.6	4.4	3.2	3.8	4.0	3.2	3.5	3.4	3.6	3.4	Mexico/Mexique	3.6	0.0	0.0	0.0	0.1	0.0	0.1	5.9	5.1	4.6
Italy/Italie	2.0	2.3	2.8	2.7	2.7	3.2	3.4	3.3	2.2	2.3	USA/Etats–Unis d'Amer	3.7	3.1	2.6	2.8	2.2	3.0	3.2	3.0	3.1	3.2
Netherlands/Pays–Bas	1.7	2.5	2.5	2.2	2.3	2.9	3.0	2.7	2.9	2.4	Germany/Allemagne	3.9	4.9	4.2	3.8	3.7	3.9	3.2	3.0	2.2	2.0
Japan/Japon	0.6	1.1	1.7	2.5	3.1	2.0	2.1	2.6	2.6	3.1	Brazil/Brésil	2.5	4.0	3.7	3.4	3.3	2.4	1.9	2.0	2.0	1.7

TRADE BY COMMODITY IN THOUSAND U.S. DOLLARS – COMMERCE PAR PRODUIT EN MILLIERS DE DOLLARS E.U

COUNTRIES–PAYS	IMPORTS – IMPORTATIONS				
	1990	1991	1992	1993	1994
Total	14359299	14739005	18349035	18384384	20567679
Africa	x131547	144851	x166028	x139922	x137943
Northern Africa	23769	28162	x28303	x24770	x29013
Americas	5648550	5936627	7142244	7178438	8017032
LAIA	430590	435945	659672	833927	1102266
CACM	3354	5083	9166	x11143	x11235
Asia	3039309	3507454	4066726	4839786	6033037
Middle East	331063	456832	361599	x496117	x598710
Europe	4515915	4280550	6541831	5842559	5936606
EEC	4201261	4055713	6248076	5582935	5656379
EFTA	193322	181861	271734	240360	257164
Oceania	x334501	x313036	x320736	x277734	x323113
USA/Etats–Unis d'Amer	4758086	4954313	5889764	5775638	6352338
Hong Kong	1146081	1297531	1746006	1538930	2193885
Germany/Allemagne	1040060	1161092	1657507	1468198	1492813
Singapore/Singapour	933000	981417	938126	1665865	1685872
United Kingdom	754817	670677	1010893	981851	1000211
France,Monac	580569	529393	955714	795811	836104
Canada	418022	502566	542148	525693	516840
Italy/Italie	431374	396472	657749	473235	481227
Netherlands/Pays–Bas	393350	364203	586054	531410	522086
Mexico/Mexique	146466	190086	322304	563147	821811
Spain/Espagne	325064	323543	423619	283832	301278
Belgium–Luxembourg	208050	175724	258517	422581	341128
Japan/Japon	172918	220065	265828	321071	530912
Australia/Australie	272813	259331	258928	214442	254672
China/Chine	53336	87553	215045	339091	379213
United Arab Emirates	159909	192243	127099	x308148	x423678
Korea, Republic of	188307	179697	194430	178615	213067
Switz.Liecht	152577	134834	195155	169976	184960
Sweden/Suède	112699	112375	163182	163505	176698
Saudi Arabia	101319	155491	130743	x91501	x85566
Denmark/Danemark	90993	83370	134178	148107	177003
Austria/Autriche	82511	77120	129715	102531	110919
Portugal	73192	68312	139826	88391	74303
Poland/Pologne	122781	221669	34056	29058	33065
Russian Federation			x116791	x161120	x234516
Thailand/Thaïlande	69015	62534	81760	84729	107593
Malaysia/Malaisie	45283	60310	73019	79292	145900
Former USSR/Anc. URSS	338910	x207669			
Norway,SVD,JM	38299	43727	72657	66697	68800
Brazil/Brésil	85185	56804	52731	60089	77635
Argentina/Argentine	1165	26622	65391	73219	56535
Macau/Macao	3906	69762	63621	28780	8620
So. Africa Customs Un	48422	53743	48934	45542	47265
Paraguay	137631	91760	24133	30104	39813
Finland/Finlande	44457	37634	58350	43055	57010
New Zealand	51214	43263	47644	47315	53571
Uruguay	11672	10773	108226	12593	10883
Hungary/Hongrie	x67114	83047	x20976	x22175	x25830
Israel/Israël	50179	43717	44374	33385	35756
Ireland/Irlande	41860	35594	43061	36514	41423
Chile/Chili	31228	33552	39466	32681	30681
Nigeria/Nigéria	x25093	28323	x33368	x34831	x18950
Greece/Grèce	22267	20204	29712	43913	44175
Venezuela	10617	15532	29654	33797	16315
Iran (Islamic Rp. of)		x24807	x18326	x18739	x10385
Oman	9208	14930	21879	22154	16169
Kuwait/ Koweït	15969	13661	22808	17805	20760
Philippines	2542	12008	21080	16296	22477
Turkey/Turquie	13275	18933	14583	13312	9111
Romania/Roumanie	12666	20924	20499	3426	3795

COUNTRIES–PAYS	EXPORTS – EXPORTATIONS				
	1990	1991	1992	1993	1994
Totale	15912604	15854694	17812510	17948683	21063019
Afrique	x4937	x3766	x4044	x4857	x3707
Afrique du Nord	181	397	x259	192	x1328
Amériques	578125	x622552	841130	991483	1189017
ALAI	4301	3791	139340	250389	358594
MCAC	1	4	3	x771	x288
Asie	13349632	13397639	13520103	13774056	16348170
Moyen–Orient	103004	18912	12570	x35513	x29216
Europe	1953990	1808431	3411899	3130583	x3468500
CEE	1857171	1727685	3323328	3064414	x3398761
AELE	96357	80338	88276	65431	69132
Océanie	x15683	x9398	8859	x8166	x10456
Japan/Japon	9139645	8686840	7865429	6737320	6482543
Korea, Republic of	1407974	1544356	1479384	1581845	1756715
Singapore/Singapour	1109322	1135784	1365798	1740997	2347267
Malaysia/Malaisie	422775	735455	1036123	1574579	2302390
Hong Kong	753805	764510	892795	972526	1357843
Germany/Allemagne	378314	342274	1086338	809587	892206
USA/Etats–Unis d'Amer	543198	602424	682118	705773	796055
United Kingdom	533308	469462	550009	565404	704375
Thailand/Thaïlande	268787	355427	420884	341130	593503
France,Monac	271466	302711	455819	318459	367986
Austria/Autriche	145752	111975	499446	456066	x558348
Belgium–Luxembourg	238456	183170	240376	423212	343726
China/Chine	116622	116108	326094	395229	790214
Netherlands/Pays–Bas	159551	177026	288128	284323	290472
Indonesia/Indonésie	1951	6112	76879	353199	620398
Mexico/Mexique	2756	2986	138181	247257	354205
Switz.Liecht	83830	69128	76467	56382	59760
Spain/Espagne	16759	27414	58025	90961	106923
Denmark/Danemark	31922	25936	52191	45608	48556
Portugal	36376	45764	36800	13568	19240
Italy/Italie	29386	24151	31549	34344	24278
Philippines	124	14533	26456	25551	24790
Canada	29221	14152	18415	31259	31501
Hungary/Hongrie	x674	x1425	x20638	x29771	x34209
Sweden/Suède	8980	7983	12974	11739	28314
Norway,SVD,JM	12522	11210	11810	9049	9371
United Arab Emirates	83159			x24101	x13542
Korea Dem People's Rp	x14958	x11585	x9395	x2049	x22974
Finland/Finlande	1762	5014	8285	7551	9588
Australia/Australie	12699	7505	5924	5498	7513
Cyprus/Chypre	10685	5857	4049	3457	3798
Oman	2849	3531	4278	3443	4272
Ireland/Irlande	4620	4562	3117	2893	4143
Israel/Israël	2766	1542	3648	4485	11822
Macau/Macao	471	2447	2842	3898	1351
Poland/Pologne	9063	3839	1826	1534	1649
Czech Republic				7017	6601
Czechoslovakia		x3945	x2863		
New Zealand	2375	1420	2855	2315	2600
India/Inde	4889	3595	1233	1526	5872
So. Africa Customs Un	1676	1960	1876	2029	
Kuwait/ Koweït	3858	3167	1155	1438	2038
Saudi Arabia	1470	2061	1551	x1356	x4918
Brunei Darussalam	95	107	x64	x4034	x189
Russian Federation			x816	x2891	x1611
Former USSR/Anc. URSS		x3440			
Turkey/Turquie	301	1231	847	807	84
Iran (Islamic Rp. of)		x2099	x20	x91	x48
Brazil/Brésil	321	150	132	1722	2306
Saint Lucia/St. Lucie	4	44	x2	x1431	

(VALUE AS % OF TOTAL)(VALEUR EN % DU TOTAL)

	1985	1986	1987	1988	1989	1990	1991	1992	1993	1994
Africa	0.6	x0.7	x0.8	x0.9	x0.7	x0.9	1.0	x0.9	x0.7	x0.6
Northern Africa	0.3	0.2	0.2	0.2	0.2	0.2	0.2	x0.2	x0.1	x0.1
Americas	55.6	51.2	40.5	42.0	42.8	39.3	40.3	39.0	39.1	39.0
LAIA	1.1	1.0	1.0	1.7	2.9	3.0	3.0	3.6	4.5	5.4
CACM	0.0	0.0	0.0	0.0	0.0	0.0	0.0	0.0	x0.1	x0.1
Asia	10.4	8.5	x11.6	18.5	19.4	21.2	23.8	22.2	26.3	29.4
Middle East	2.0	x1.6	x1.9	2.2	x2.3	2.3	3.1	2.0	x2.7	x2.9
Europe	30.9	37.1	43.7	34.3	31.8	31.4	29.0	35.7	31.8	28.9
EEC	27.3	32.6	38.0	30.8	28.1	29.3	27.5	34.1	30.4	27.5
EFTA	3.5	4.4	5.4	3.2	3.0	1.3	1.2	1.5	1.3	1.3
Oceania	2.1	x2.0	x2.0	x2.2	x2.8	x2.4	x2.2	x1.8	x1.5	x1.6
USA/Etats–Unis d'Amer	51.2	47.1	37.1	37.3	36.0	33.1	33.6	32.1	31.4	30.9
Hong Kong	2.9	2.3	3.0	6.5	7.2	8.0	8.8	9.5	8.4	10.7
Germany/Allemagne	6.8	7.4	8.8	7.7	7.1	7.2	7.9	9.0	8.0	7.3
Singapore/Singapour	2.0	2.2	2.8	4.1	5.0	6.5	6.7	5.1	9.1	8.2
United Kingdom	6.9	6.1	6.9	5.8	5.4	5.3	4.6	5.5	5.3	4.9
France,Monac	3.3	4.7	5.4	4.3	3.5	4.0	3.6	5.2	4.3	4.1
Canada	3.2	3.0	2.2	2.9	3.7	2.9	3.4	3.0	2.9	2.5
Italy/Italie	1.9	3.2	4.4	3.2	2.8	3.0	2.7	3.6	2.6	2.3
Netherlands/Pays–Bas	2.7	3.3	3.4	2.0	2.4	2.7	2.5	3.2	2.9	2.5
Mexico/Mexique	0.3	0.0	0.3	0.7	1.1	1.0	1.3	1.8	3.1	4.0

	1985	1986	1987	1988	1989	1990	1991	1992	1993	1994
Afrique	0.1	x0.0	x0.0	x0.0	x0.0	x0.0	x0.0	x0.0	x0.0	x0.0
Afrique du Nord	0.0	x0.0	x0.0	x0.0	x0.0	0.0	0.0	x0.0	0.0	x0.0
Amériques	3.0	x2.4	x2.6	x3.3	x3.8	3.6	x3.9	4.7	5.5	5.6
ALAI	0.0	0.0	0.0	0.0	0.0	0.0	0.0	0.8	1.4	1.7
MCAC	0.0	x0.0	x0.0	x0.0	x0.0	0.0	0.0	0.0	x0.0	x0.0
Asie	82.8	80.1	x77.0	x83.8	83.8	83.9	84.5	75.9	76.8	77.6
Moyen–Orient	0.2	0.2	x0.2	0.3	x0.2	0.6	0.1	0.1	x0.2	x0.1
Europe	13.6	17.0	19.5	12.3	12.0	12.3	11.4	19.2	17.4	x16.5
CEE	11.8	14.8	16.7	11.1	10.7	11.7	10.9	18.7	17.1	x16.1
AELE	1.8	2.2	2.8	1.2	1.3	0.6	0.5	0.5	0.4	0.3
Océanie		x0.0	x0.1	x0.1	x0.1	x0.1	x0.1		x0.0	x0.0
Japan/Japon	75.8	70.8	58.9	58.8	59.5	57.4	54.8	44.2	37.5	30.8
Korea, Republic of	3.0	5.2	8.3	11.4	10.8	8.8	9.7	8.3	8.8	8.3
Singapore/Singapour	1.5	1.5	2.5	4.4	5.7	7.0	7.2	7.7	9.7	11.1
Malaysia/Malaisie	0.1	0.1	0.3	0.9	1.8	2.7	4.6	5.8	8.8	10.9
Hong Kong	2.2	2.2	2.4	3.0	4.1	4.7	4.8	5.0	5.4	6.4
Germany/Allemagne	5.5	7.0	7.8	4.2	2.9	2.4	2.2	6.1	4.5	4.2
USA/Etats–Unis d'Amer	3.0	2.3	2.5	3.0	3.4	3.4	3.8	3.8	3.9	3.8
United Kingdom	2.0	2.1	2.6	2.7	2.8	3.4	3.0	3.1	3.2	3.3
Thailand/Thaïlande	0.0	0.0	0.0	0.1	1.0	1.7	2.2	2.4	1.9	2.8
France,Monac	0.4	0.4	0.5	0.8	1.1	1.7	1.9	2.6	1.8	1.7

TRADE BY COMMODITY IN THOUSAND U.S. DOLLARS – COMMERCE PAR PRODUIT EN MILLIERS DE DOLLARS E.U

COUNTRIES–PAYS	IMPORTS – IMPORTATIONS 1990	1991	1992	1993	1994
Total	55076633	62743789	69318291	76618347	93949786
Africa	x1302158	1416913	x1565534	x1531641	x2092977
Northern Africa	514391	558936	667792	x546449	x632658
Americas	16181860	17149611	19551224	21719479	26204059
LAIA	2134849	2426028	3967459	4563217	5999778
CACM	62656	63836	102628	x198941	x211563
Asia	14038894	18322298	21545513	28191818	35118231
Middle East	994247	x2326880	x2640517	x2408260	x2470873
Europe	21854271	23551461	24222187	22429301	27224264
EEC	20316909	21954374	22575380	20914396	25361410
EFTA	1306229	1333009	1405325	1301254	1588227
Oceania	x1115210	x1159098	x1221110	x1335428	x1686260
USA/Etats–Unis d'Amer	11840095	12482964	13073497	14324135	17030469
Germany/Allemagne	4376856	5298175	5638934	5265307	6321147
Hong Kong	2702747	3318210	4232676	6153285	7616551
United Kingdom	3545809	3575780	3800878	4107733	5178539
China/Chine	1662187	1938016	3083508	4850379	5960875
Singapore/Singapour	2344187	2789499	3004179	3963416	4973456
France,Monac	2527911	2577598	2614833	2335868	2804959
Japan/Japon	1981542	2338148	2272405	2820203	4019057
Canada	1807407	1882238	2130222	2358127	2642736
Malaysia/Malaisie	1088828	1883108	1761512	2284821	2955090
Italy/Italie	2060501	2289336	2024549	1536288	2024393
Netherlands/Pays–Bas	1690588	1816030	1913388	1505890	1578141
Mexico/Mexique	884052	995569	1886384	1967730	2452623
Spain/Espagne	1638663	1625733	1543951	1200074	1409331
Korea, Republic of	1092765	1245882	1376703	1645041	2220992
Thailand/Thaïlande	807117	886355	1058800	1271990	1796124
Belgium–Luxembourg	907516	976773	1021151	1042548	1160122
Sweden/Suède	1039541	1019857	1009727	938601	1362340
Australia/Australie	770047	833481	922450	1054432	1328469
Austria/Autriche	803445	858414	939211	876186	1001806
Iran (Islamic Rp. of)		x859252	x1241120	x563337	x230801
Switz.Liecht	891787	905778	869967	747710	899286
Indonesia/Indonésie	463158	605448	841864	979476	741157
Argentina/Argentine	117026	271493	647494	728117	1102049
Brazil/Brésil	414945	421198	441977	749407	1113765
Denmark/Danemark	446141	503443	527709	550028	726197
Saudi Arabia	225150	536406	416583	x472498	x455357
Norway,SVD,JM	387719	393004	501680	529426	651856
Portugal	324205	406400	579729	401997	429564
Philippines	258160	376621	410094	572818	824637
Russian Federation			x571543	x643210	x1001823
Poland/Pologne	70486	325460	399682	451528	425338
Finland/Finlande	502359	452144	374999	331230	515736
Turkey/Turquie	357439	409476	309336	407374	513525
Hungary/Hongrie	x164967	238317	x394577	x417171	x471646
So. Africa Customs Un	252392	300194	344001	390728	748376
Ireland/Irlande	279900	335729	325065	348103	399215
Greece/Grèce	173474	218961	261256	474543	449920
Venezuela	113914	133962	398324	332400	226717
United Arab Emirates	163121	195662	213451	x418006	x604416
Israel/Israël	164451	214997	242347	357686	482984
New Zealand	294505	255458	219760	218778	276458
Colombia/Colombie	203296	180889	195135	277874	546489
Chile/Chili	192116	174220	182992	258216	216671
Pakistan	170824	132847	202514	252885	156973
India/Inde	170253	101912	167625	169019	249920
Egypt/Egypte	115809	94621	153386	179661	150209
Morocco/Maroc	116201	171906	154505	84464	137205
Former USSR/Anc. URSS	37295	x407601			
Czechoslovakia	142858	x105653	x299032		

COUNTRIES–PAYS	EXPORTS – EXPORTATIONS 1990	1991	1992	1993	1994
Totale	56080469	61845771	68766109	76963770	96167307
Afrique	62169	x72565	x87708	x143324	x104625
Afrique du Nord	21052	24634	24293	35186	34363
Amériques	10047047	10845580	13757154	16219448	19851175
ALAI	150666	179515	1509279	1796406	2430507
MCAC	679	434	536	x3464	x2706
Asie	25728789	30036552	32283453	37082436	45540898
Moyen–Orient	49984	52169	x65473	x115161	x117569
Europe	19808478	20415290	22064287	22820355	29759436
CEE	18899987	19619633	21112715	21910610	28732244
AELE	824201	770404	826127	812485	969265
Océanie	x247836	x253466	x309725	x343698	x504630
Japan/Japon	15161015	17816893	17636892	17801146	18823780
USA/Etats–Unis d'Amer	8387870	9154851	10402377	12262435	14810293
Germany/Allemagne	4195008	4862860	5454665	5297519	6863511
Hong Kong	3305458	3695406	4291380	5970110	7432796
United Kingdom	3033829	3156150	3329219	3527997	4962409
Singapore/Singapour	2337521	2593537	2885775	3941237	6081662
France,Monac	2765951	2780120	2865004	2690277	3328715
Sweden/Suède	2418183	2444002	2582576	2801265	4196738
Korea, Republic of	1981036	2072408	2336606	2922316	3687009
Canada	1494572	1497616	1829139	2139764	2577991
Malaysia/Malaisie	1164024	1492840	1735009	2212128	3158829
Netherlands/Pays–Bas	1537510	1408402	1489096	1439799	1547384
Italy/Italie	1383549	1351636	1334315	1369104	1447935
China/Chine	522096	697064	1350368	1755082	2936782
Belgium–Luxembourg	993714	1057405	1105115	1347654	1639107
Mexico/Mexique	43756	113324	1441751	1719531	2334196
Thailand/Thaïlande	504025	706741	821117	916257	1231826
Finland/Finlande	875980	566819	747477	1056566	1796916
Israel/Israël	413001	444072	550353	718738	1005145
Denmark/Danemark	631055	545725	593368	565210	711678
Spain/Espagne	272215	376332	558648	736096	918884
Switz.Liecht	551173	487393	500180	512280	609949
Austria/Autriche	393192	507218	509206	482947	x487930
Ireland/Irlande	287256	431377	393077	446994	675975
Philippines	190719	314068	311728	393501	499851
Norway,SVD,JM	272851	283009	325752	300165	359243
Australia/Australie	207733	209192	257188	280107	415151
Indonesia/Indonésie	59511	111811	249283	257491	400009
Hungary/Hongrie	x51014	x101408	x183467	x223363	x239542
Portugal	88645	100615	109556	77445	100288
Brazil/Brésil	95763	55935	54627	56880	67294
Greece/Grèce	23346	30415	41394	71737	54774
New Zealand	36781	37492	45348	60674	85268
So. Africa Customs Un	21588	27956	48583	64139	47101
Slovenia/Slovénia			68759	42931	49541
Poland/Pologne	62813	40937	31765	30789	54234
Croatia/Croatie			45673	48785	x2719
Turkey/Turquie	19297	23262	24792	44299	42981
Saudi Arabia	5967	5025	4528		
Tunisia/Tunisie	17781	20744	19071	31234	33213
India/Inde	14438	14228	18396	26989	35712
Czechoslovakia		x35046	x17429		
Korea Dem People's Rp	x17308	x6887	x14309	x30395	x111020
Czech Republic				51144	68104
Bulgaria/Bulgarie	x31206	x6421	x23310	x15134	x3729
Cyprus/Chypre	9936	13286	17424	13522	10053
Russian Federation			x25198	x11834	x16584
Mali	2752	x10701	x3768	x21220	x5270
Slovakia				x30338	x37470
Former USSR/Anc. URSS		x30206			

(VALUE AS % OF TOTAL)(VALEUR EN % DU TOTAL)

	1985	1986	1987	1988	1989	1990	1991	1992	1993	1994
Africa	3.3	x3.5	x2.9	x2.6	x2.2	x2.4	2.3	x2.3	x2.0	x2.2
Northern Africa	1.4	1.2	0.9	0.8	0.8	0.9	0.9	1.0	x0.7	x0.7
Americas	43.6	38.9	32.8	30.1	30.9	29.4	27.3	28.2	28.4	27.9
LAIA	3.1	3.4	3.4	3.1	3.1	3.9	3.9	5.7	6.0	6.4
CACM	0.1	0.2	0.3	0.1	0.1	0.1	0.1	0.1	x0.3	x0.2
Asia	17.5	x18.7	x23.6	x25.1	24.0	25.5	29.2	31.1	36.7	37.4
Middle East	3.5	x5.3	x3.7	x3.3	x2.6	1.8	x3.7	x3.8	x3.1	x2.6
Europe	31.7	35.0	37.1	39.0	39.9	39.7	37.5	34.9	29.3	29.0
EEC	25.9	28.4	30.6	32.4	33.4	36.9	35.0	32.6	27.3	27.0
EFTA	5.7	6.4	6.4	6.3	6.3	2.4	2.1	2.0	1.7	1.7
Oceania	3.0	x2.9	x2.3	x2.1	x2.2	x2.0	x1.8	x1.7	x1.8	x1.8
USA/Etats–Unis d'Amer	35.4	30.5	25.0	23.0	23.4	21.5	19.9	18.9	18.7	18.1
Germany/Allemagne	5.4	6.2	6.8	6.8	6.7	7.9	8.4	8.1	6.9	6.7
Hong Kong	3.0	2.8	3.4	3.8	4.4	4.9	5.3	6.1	8.0	8.1
United Kingdom	5.3	5.6	6.2	6.9	7.0	6.4	5.7	5.5	5.4	5.5
China/Chine			3.1	3.2	2.8	3.0	3.1	4.4	6.3	6.3
Singapore/Singapour	2.0	2.1	2.4	3.1	3.5	4.3	4.4	4.3	5.2	5.3
France,Monac	2.7	2.8	3.3	3.6	3.9	4.6	4.1	3.8	3.0	3.0
Japan/Japon	1.9	2.0	2.2	2.8	3.4	3.6	3.7	3.3	3.7	4.3
Canada	4.4	4.0	3.4	3.4	3.5	3.3	3.0	3.1	3.1	2.8
Malaysia/Malaisie	1.5	1.1	1.0	1.2	1.6	2.0	3.0	2.5	3.0	3.1

	1985	1986	1987	1988	1989	1990	1991	1992	1993	1994
Afrique		x0.1	x0.0	x0.0	x0.0	0.1	x0.1	x0.2	x0.2	x0.1
Afrique du Nord	0.0	x0.0	0.0	0.0	0.0	0.0	0.0	0.0	0.0	0.0
Amériques	20.6	x17.1	14.4	x14.4	x16.8	17.9	17.5	20.0	21.1	20.7
ALAI	0.3	0.4	0.3	0.3	0.3	0.3	0.3	2.2	2.3	2.5
MCAC	0.0	0.0	x0.0	0.0	0.0	0.0	0.0	0.0	x0.0	x0.0
Asie	37.9	40.8	x45.6	x48.7	45.0	45.9	48.5	46.9	48.2	47.4
Moyen–Orient	0.1	x0.1	x0.2	x0.1	x0.1	0.1	0.1	x0.1	x0.3	x0.2
Europe	40.1	40.9	37.4	34.5	36.7	35.3	33.0	32.1	29.6	30.9
CEE	32.5	33.2	30.6	27.7	29.3	33.7	31.7	30.7	28.4	29.9
AELE	7.2	7.4	6.6	6.6	7.3	1.5	1.2	1.2	1.1	1.0
Océanie	0.2	x0.1	x0.2	x0.2	x0.4	x0.4	x0.4	x0.4	x0.4	x0.5
Japan/Japon	28.2	31.4	29.1	30.1	28.4	27.0	28.8	25.6	23.1	19.6
USA/Etats–Unis d'Amer	15.0	12.8	11.0	11.9	14.0	15.0	14.8	15.1	15.9	15.4
Germany/Allemagne	7.6	8.3	8.5	7.1	6.9	7.5	7.9	7.9	6.9	7.1
Hong Kong	3.9	3.7	3.9	4.8	5.5	5.9	6.0	6.2	7.7	7.7
United Kingdom	4.8	4.5	4.0	4.1	4.7	5.4	5.1	4.8	4.6	5.2
Singapore/Singapour	1.8	1.5	2.3	3.2	3.7	4.2	4.2	4.2	5.1	6.3
France,Monac	5.4	5.0	4.8	4.0	4.1	4.9	4.5	4.2	3.5	3.5
Sweden/Suède	4.7	4.1	3.3	3.8	4.1	4.3	4.0	3.8	3.6	4.4
Korea, Republic of	2.0	2.6	3.2	3.2	3.4	3.5	3.4	3.4	3.8	3.8
Canada	5.3	3.7	3.1	2.3	2.5	2.7	2.4	2.7	2.8	2.7

TRADE BY COMMODITY IN THOUSAND U.S. DOLLARS – COMMERCE PAR PRODUIT EN MILLIERS DE DOLLARS E.U

COUNTRIES–PAYS	IMPORTS – IMPORTATIONS 1990	1991	1992	1993	1994
Total	11047185	11992949	13371511	14694752	17639564
Africa	x355114	335754	x354438	x364025	x392258
Northern Africa	187436	145880	x173121	167525	x188858
Americas	2514550	2667555	3352012	3921806	4523604
LAIA	391490	378723	728191	854849	1100390
CACM				x26765	x42036
Asia	3117222	3975998	4502237	5595449	6985130
Middle East	x348750	x419565	x529931	x618280	x474856
Europe	4524868	4707833	4867155	4480765	5337523
EEC	4171335	4356627	4467801	4102884	4941115
EFTA	326203	325663	361493	339830	359585
Oceania	x258689	x179581	x175545	x161413	x188476
USA/Etats–Unis d'Amer	1701810	1862132	2208994	2555237	2814847
Germany/Allemagne	952167	1068201	1104232	1028723	1234121
Hong Kong	616979	818425	1009602	1258082	1546044
Japan/Japon	571437	722514	678310	788220	1008970
Singapore/Singapour	535580	673778	647902	775473	1134594
France,Monac	634266	683356	681013	625027	730963
United Kingdom	672795	635478	647113	663469	794699
Canada	352845	375070	366451	438651	502247
Malaysia/Malaisie	183615	300727	342561	475023	694018
China/Chine	203843	224175	392799	457056	700705
Mexico/Mexique	113303	120906	400982	486834	612970
Italy/Italie	306799	320800	331666	324261	428556
Netherlands/Pays–Bas	331324	319011	327110	252172	275330
Korea, Republic of	245508	258684	268992	360254	417386
Austria/Autriche	253060	269261	249348	224020	283443
Switz.Liecht	247258	241932	257442	239727	262623
Thailand/Thaïlande	142417	197661	217502	306262	372996
Spain/Espagne	224952	268915	256444	184685	201141
Belgium–Luxembourg	226002	235681	256098	192051	201015
Sweden/Suède	239426	228501	223287	211508	278566
Iran (Islamic Rp. of)	x138451	x162977	x211314	x264656	x45151
Indonesia/Indonésie	76655	128880	175685	240238	218504
Brazil/Brésil	102450	117708	125086	140972	195177
Australia/Australie	109274	104363	115924	117152	150792
Saudi Arabia	69293	79722	112563	x123822	x121285
Denmark/Danemark	90410	80402	102349	103241	123949
Portugal	70661	85157	112245	88544	96097
Finland/Finlande	103272	83020	95085	101689	148232
Norway,SVD,JM	74920	77344	98269	96683	92140
Philippines	46795	60646	93941	100538	100440
Turkey/Turquie	69300	73184	52207	74516	69869
Ireland/Irlande	47551	58452	61649	78543	111606
Israel/Israël	47082	54311	62004	79005	114303
So. Africa Customs Un	64306	57333	64543	64322	81677
Algeria/Algérie	72596	44442	75617	57286	51847
United Arab Emirates	38733	20964	57899	x86026	x83384
Argentina/Argentine	18362	28891	57478	75425	121942
Venezuela	48537	42428	63489	46244	47787
Hungary/Hongrie	x29997	20480	x47398	x46809	x51003
Pakistan	29124	64473	20753	29364	34630
Nigeria/Nigéria	x13089	32082	x22995	x42320	x25974
New Zealand	132168	33280	34469	27377	28332
Egypt/Egypte	53076	30116	26065	33041	22538
Chile/Chili	44361	20911	23577	40565	46630
Tunisia/Tunisie	22412	22711	29224	31956	36947
India/Inde	34536	21767	29421	30133	44183
Libyan Arab Jamahiriya	21404	30639	x28779	x18443	x48836
Poland/Pologne	10357	13311	16170	44888	75235
Colombia/Colombie	31189	25846	21037	26908	27157
Bahrain/Bahreïn	x1800	x29497	x33998	x9505	x22533

COUNTRIES–PAYS	EXPORTS – EXPORTATIONS 1990	1991	1992	1993	1994
Totale	10440259	11161630	12964000	14213136	17041404
Afrique	35510	42017	44253	51296	37118
Afrique du Nord	26413	31972	32027	28121	33546
Amériques	1454636	1527822	2348510	2735125	3182808
ALAI	89459	98119	758735	866897	951620
MCAC				x5214	x8361
Asie	3498892	4320709	4834501	5940985	7412766
Moyen–Orient	34163	36495	53404	x83562	x103538
Europe	5116772	5067944	5563965	5302128	6160623
CEE	4728665	4660613	5093249	4835335	5685298
AELE	322721	362697	417544	401407	419793
Océanie	x34420	x32625	x45622	x64440	x85589
Japan/Japon	1494296	1802652	1822150	2016714	2203091
Germany/Allemagne	1695562	1579911	1649063	1485592	1737872
USA/Etats–Unis d'Amer	1132000	1195581	1288673	1538382	1873897
Hong Kong	797900	942680	1159669	1432444	1765669
France,Monac	587157	691643	767838	766702	845829
Mexico/Mexique	53644	50556	667585	765533	819437
Singapore/Singapour	332943	489107	413261	534098	818712
China/Chine	141631	177819	448100	681697	1087040
United Kingdom	412088	392559	480020	434638	516785
Korea, Republic of	355762	391785	377670	406157	442625
Malaysia/Malaisie	249560	331592	367002	455155	489578
Italy/Italie	300689	335876	355333	380567	536609
Switz.Liecht	245339	285899	357577	330440	344608
Netherlands/Pays–Bas	305995	284185	313156	278036	333981
Sweden/Suède	346676	294162	298392	259140	329555
Canada	218910	227128	293998	319405	336008
Austria/Autriche	297489	270906	285130	277801	x204600
Belgium–Luxembourg	229135	240043	276942	252932	274799
Finland/Finlande	199808	214382	216144	257355	357690
Thailand/Thaïlande	32141	78058	112784	221345	336390
Denmark/Danemark	120675	119074	129044	132241	169418
Spain/Espagne	88897	90519	142695	112734	139530
Portugal	78504	81903	110561	108641	120473
Norway,SVD,JM	77362	76775	59964	70964	75180
Ireland/Irlande	59112	57334	56714	75598	104165
Brazil/Brésil	20474	30389	75351	78219	117215
Hungary/Hongrie	x25071	x36781	x53691	x39193	x66433
Turkey/Turquie	26339	29633	46990	52275	70744
Australia/Australie	29576	27279	38852	45889	57847
Tunisia/Tunisie	24397	29599	30915	26517	32670
Poland/Pologne	47161	54344	12316	14128	32882
Bulgaria/Bulgarie	x54243	x18182	x32397	x17537	x4157
Indonesia/Indonésie	7738	12001	21389	32908	46075
Israel/Israël	19282	21880	20016	22024	24390
Philippines	22321	21765	17888	22594	31920
Czechoslovakia		x31853	x20271		
Croatia/Croatie			24205	25569	x26940
India/Inde	6012	11764	14932	23059	34195
Yugoslavia SFR	62083	x40773			
So. Africa Customs Un	7090	7284	9447	20356	
Slovenia/Slovénia			14765	21561	23545
Greece/Grèce	6781	8020	12214	13359	13993
Argentina/Argentine	6804	8566	8315	12354	6450
Czech Republic				27090	30930
Russian Federation			x10582	x16128	x32967
Saudi Arabia	1233	1174	2110	x22850	x26051
Romania/Roumanie	17226	8294	8194	8694	18043
Ukraine			x5102	x19986	x6596
Yugoslavia/Yougoslavie			x11359	x10805	x206
New Zealand	3982	5247	6597	10157	23866

(VALUE AS % OF TOTAL)(VALEUR EN % DU TOTAL)

	1985	1986	1987	1988	1989	1990	1991	1992	1993	1994
Africa	4.0	x4.4	x3.4	x3.4	x3.0	x3.2	2.8	x2.7	x2.4	x2.3
Northern Africa	2.6	1.9	1.5	1.4	1.3	1.7	1.2	x1.3	1.1	x1.1
Americas	33.7	29.7	27.5	29.2	23.6	22.8	22.3	25.1	26.7	25.6
LAIA	3.7	5.8	3.7	3.4	3.7	3.5	3.2	5.4	5.8	6.2
CACM		x0.2	x0.2	x0.2	x0.3				x0.2	x0.2
Asia	22.9	25.1	x26.8	x26.1	27.5	28.2	33.2	33.6	38.1	39.6
Middle East	4.3	x5.9	x4.9	x2.8	x2.5	x3.2	x3.5	x4.0	x4.2	x2.7
Europe	34.4	35.6	36.3	36.1	41.5	41.0	39.3	36.4	30.5	30.3
EEC	28.9	28.5	29.1	29.2	33.7	37.8	36.3	33.4	27.9	28.0
EFTA	5.5	x6.8	x6.9	6.7	7.6	3.0	2.7	2.7	2.3	2.0
Oceania	1.8	x1.4	x1.4	x1.4	x1.4	x2.4	x1.4	x1.3	x1.1	x1.1
USA/Etats–Unis d'Amer	26.8	20.8	21.3	23.0	16.3	15.4	15.5	16.5	17.4	16.0
Germany/Allemagne	6.4	6.6	6.7	6.4	7.4	8.6	8.9	8.3	7.0	7.0
Hong Kong	3.1	3.3	3.8	4.7	5.5	5.6	6.8	7.6	8.6	8.8
Japan/Japon	3.3	2.8	3.0	3.8	5.0	5.2	6.0	5.1	5.4	5.7
Singapore/Singapour	3.5	3.6	3.8	4.4	4.7	4.8	5.6	4.8	5.3	6.4
France,Monac	3.1	3.7	4.0	4.4	5.0	5.7	5.7	5.1	4.3	4.1
United Kingdom	4.9	4.4	4.6	4.7	5.6	6.1	5.3	4.8	4.5	4.5
Canada	2.9	1.9	1.7	2.2	2.7	3.2	3.1	2.7	3.0	2.8
Malaysia/Malaisie	1.4	0.9	1.1	1.0	1.5	1.7	2.5	2.6	3.2	3.9
China/Chine			1.6	1.5	2.4	1.8	1.9	2.9	3.1	4.0

	1985	1986	1987	1988	1989	1990	1991	1992	1993	1994
Afrique	0.2	x0.2	x0.2	x0.3	x0.2	0.4	0.4	0.4	0.3	0.2
Afrique du Nord	0.2	0.1	0.1	0.1	0.2	0.3	0.3	0.2	0.2	0.2
Amériques	11.1	9.9	x7.0	x8.3	x12.8	13.9	13.6	18.1	19.3	18.7
ALAI	0.5	1.5	0.4	0.7	0.8	0.9	0.9	5.9	6.1	5.6
MCAC		x0.0	x0.0	x0.0	x0.0				x0.0	x0.0
Asie	34.2	31.9	x37.4	x40.9	35.2	33.5	38.7	37.3	41.8	43.5
Moyen–Orient	0.1	x0.1	x0.1	x0.1	x0.3	0.3	0.3	0.4	x0.6	x0.6
Europe	51.6	54.5	50.6	46.8	48.2	49.0	45.4	42.9	37.3	36.2
CEE	41.2	42.3	38.8	36.4	38.2	45.3	41.8	39.3	34.0	33.4
AELE	10.4	11.3	11.2	9.7	9.3	3.1	3.2	3.2	2.8	2.5
Océanie	0.1	x0.1	x0.2	x0.2	x0.2	x0.3	x0.3	x0.4	x0.5	x0.5
Japan/Japon	20.7	19.0	16.3	16.3	16.1	14.3	16.2	14.1	14.2	12.9
Germany/Allemagne	14.9	15.7	13.5	13.0	13.6	16.2	14.2	12.7	10.5	10.2
USA/Etats–Unis d'Amer	8.0	6.2	4.8	5.4	10.0	10.8	10.7	9.9	10.8	11.0
Hong Kong	5.9	5.5	5.9	7.2	8.2	7.6	8.4	8.9	10.1	10.4
France,Monac	5.4	5.0	4.8	4.1	4.4	5.6	6.2	5.9	5.4	5.0
Mexico/Mexique		1.1	0.1	0.2	0.3	0.5	0.5	5.1	5.4	4.8
Singapore/Singapour	2.2	2.3	2.4	2.9	2.9	3.2	4.4	3.2	3.8	4.8
China/Chine			0.2	0.4	0.9	1.4	1.6	3.5	4.8	6.4
United Kingdom	4.1	3.5	3.2	3.4	3.4	3.9	3.5	3.7	3.1	3.0
Korea, Republic of	3.4	3.0	3.1	3.6	3,7	3.4	3.5	2.9	2.9	2.6

TRADE BY COMMODITY IN THOUSAND U.S. DOLLARS – COMMERCE PAR PRODUIT EN MILLIERS DE DOLLARS E.U

COUNTRIES–PAYS	IMPORTS – IMPORTATIONS				
	1990	1991	1992	1993	1994
Total	36894481	38753782	42986039	43927234	52252020
Africa	x1104158	x967155	x1126131	x1226084	x1313163
Northern Africa	534043	436503	x525295	x561770	x648012
Americas	9910498	9911549	11015013	12372370	14971796
LAIA	1019310	1139107	2597542	2915538	3763384
CACM	37088	37767	55219	x63767	x70696
Asia	7809385	9538992	11469069	13125179	16156984
Middle East	x1206769	x1398079	x1850414	x1749486	x1502939
Europe	16716033	17199012	18275941	15923747	18297381
EEC	15365661	15888396	16894580	14697578	16898432
EFTA	1202279	1170460	1203633	1089720	1211106
Oceania	x608046	x554507	x604530	x649611	x764333
USA/Etats-Unis d'Amer	6099147	6273966	6215359	7163592	8474942
Germany/Allemagne	3329550	3775935	3729676	3269044	3826446
United Kingdom	2299370	2211032	2468451	2431528	2559385
France,Monac	2176632	2404480	2441779	2082439	2164768
Canada	2481910	2247544	1940389	2040094	2417601
Italy/Italie	1949458	1860568	2002616	1627808	1937278
Singapore/Singapour	1319837	1528356	1696599	2144025	2911947
Malaysia/Malaisie	845027	1241344	1499915	1768939	2567377
Hong Kong	938382	1181486	1406432	1686014	2010618
Mexico/Mexique	338921	438712	1791101	1976846	2470758
Japan/Japon	1013349	1124072	1047295	1139593	1219596
Korea, Republic of	918589	1027666	983988	1076686	1319816
Netherlands/Pays-Bas	1027522	1053274	1136698	879068	1041186
Spain/Espagne	835210	925757	977197	759231	1001652
Belgium-Luxembourg	879078	855917	951853	825066	939787
Switz.Liecht	884850	840703	859466	790717	890199
China/Chine	258854	364209	882387	1111672	1519922
Thailand/Thaïlande	441801	655756	749948	907840	1274956
Austria/Autriche	669307	691996	737661	686906	809912
Sweden/Suède	757871	694860	718322	684066	864548
Iran (Islamic Rp. of)	x414970	x533139	x690570	x644579	x192094
Ireland/Irlande	455366	482768	675195	510556	579965
Indonesia/Indonésie	229231	283202	550634	571241	557170
Australia/Australie	455504	401506	434232	489738	601421
Saudi Arabia	292420	280725	453606	x357101	x413968
Israel/Israël	212500	273119	312624	395171	513723
Portugal	278640	311416	348424	296130	375336
Norway,SVD,JM	302159	311823	329858	285350	309891
Brazil/Brésil	332679	274654	284324	324077	622172
So. Africa Customs Un	269320	281808	295511	294901	343526
Turkey/Turquie	255348	301963	266478	295472	267127
Denmark/Danemark	288748	272987	294206	255675	293325
Finland/Finlande	318437	239945	281582	273842	389892
Philippines	119161	223437	190588	277986	303474
United Arab Emirates	95838	83223	179264	x207372	x275734
Hungary/Hongrie	x112808	111060	x154079	x191067	x207031
Argentina/Argentine	49834	81939	154414	192504	227042
Venezuela	78728	126714	154228	143712	110421
Egypt/Egypte	107766	114932	145767	134560	139513
India/Inde	159724	100390	158848	131142	172386
Algeria/Algérie	181782	102744	122658	164039	217261
Greece/Grèce	100471	107462	130920	116217	114950
Russian Federation			x192493	x121242	x153225
Czechoslovakia	93221	x82991	x222047		
Former USSR/Anc. URSS	320561	x303475			
Poland/Pologne	23942	26373	91350	179051	239977
Tunisia/Tunisie	86281	92838	102715	98050	115335
Chile/Chili	109117	76426	84737	113125	124821
Libyan Arab Jamahiriya	101889	60717	x95380	x96524	x107857
New Zealand	83144	78648	81925	91285	119733

COUNTRIES–PAYS	EXPORTS – EXPORTATIONS				
	1990	1991	1992	1993	1994
Totale	34971339	37447894	41015486	42389237	51542056
Afrique	121197	117160	114290	113348	85305
Afrique du Nord	71160	88764	76301	67433	80028
Amériques	x7515825	x7394121	7892449	8571472	10862389
ALAI	167280	163206	1444854	1689282	2366057
MCAC	14768	16634	20985	x24414	x43874
Asie	8078938	9606985	11063091	13446232	17343043
Moyen-Orient	45873	29525	53821	x100297	x98603
Europe	18852796	19997016	21503388	19724287	22579471
CEE	17111370	18270400	19629141	17980177	20631890
AELE	1576971	1635647	1711067	1582995	1800551
Océanie	x117318	x141032	x182285	x217348	x266781
Germany/Allemagne	7223933	8001420	8324717	7581280	8593155
Japan/Japon	5411622	6310751	6820030	8010940	9729235
USA/Etats-Unis d'Amer	5724259	5484711	5394629	5882377	7235841
France,Monac	3162510	3265020	3714763	3307361	3906868
United Kingdom	1754830	1838605	1945946	1783324	2093326
Switz.Liecht	1490639	1552377	1619511	1501198	1698848
Italy/Italie	1335818	1398299	1517160	1330684	1496157
Canada	1551501	1675902	978313	918274	1030147
Hong Kong	796606	925844	1105465	1458571	1760092
Singapore/Singapour	773470	895521	989605	1218149	2079550
Mexico/Mexique	31465	34987	1301425	1465697	1988462
Netherlands/Pays-Bas	760484	853443	919580	855123	975786
Austria/Autriche	603774	640410	694492	716685	x661231
Malaysia/Malaisie	321199	487187	575347	771302	887203
Belgium-Luxembourg	551736	514790	582584	636512	684081
Sweden/Suède	569485	525968	529020	497282	651287
China/Chine	164456	249876	534668	725232	1053068
Spain/Espagne	348370	390297	486490	451429	567686
Korea, Republic of	307243	364713	399800	469565	662015
Ireland/Irlande	268698	312859	399417	325701	369661
Thailand/Thaïlande	84600	132242	309267	385030	630839
Denmark/Danemark	191930	177614	184277	190913	230037
Finland/Finlande	168092	157128	146879	163254	226073
Portugal	143648	172658	158790	111243	146066
Australia/Australie	93248	113008	142335	180992	213876
Brazil/Brésil	93127	97076	113630	136172	151468
Israel/Israël	118508	107126	120941	115010	189862
Norway,SVD,JM	86255	83242	91520	81778	101695
Poland/Pologne	91224	46994	88786	88438	107909
Hungary/Hongrie	x43945	x39697	x74531	x81801	x118568
Tunisia/Tunisie	60866	71410	64005	55786	70023
India/Inde	31299	43293	50823	60552	63971
Philippines	15569	45645	43872	56788	93960
Slovenia/Slovénia			63228	64513	76126
Malta/Malte	29841	34450	43824	40066	x26936
Indonesia/Indonésie	402	1789	44575	61019	62397
Czechoslovakia		x47518	x58885		
So. Africa Customs Un	45904	24960	34291	42457	
Argentina/Argentine	15133	17831	12976	69114	204419
New Zealand	22647	27142	31151	32157	51668
Croatia/Croatie			38225	45799	x39899
Czech Republic				83399	112494
Greece/Grèce	27700	21528	25027	29387	30477
Dominican Republic	x24937	x26202	x27703	x20959	x141607
Turkey/Turquie	13652	12883	33381	28237	44154
Bulgaria/Bulgarie	x67331	x19890	x26338	x15396	x6939
Costa Rica	14582	16408	20753	x24109	x43498
Yugoslavia SFR	133086	x55190			
Romania/Roumanie	45177	19151	9406	12569	25306
Barbados/Barbade	14251	11179	11833	13664	x16767

(VALUE AS % OF TOTAL)(VALEUR EN % DU TOTAL)

	1985	1986	1987	1988	1989	1990	1991	1992	1993	1994
Africa	4.7	x4.5	x3.6	x3.1	x3.0	x3.0	x2.5	x2.6	x2.8	x2.6
Northern Africa	2.9	2.0	1.6	1.2	1.3	1.4	1.1	x1.2	x1.3	x1.2
Americas	24.1	20.6	19.7	23.2	24.8	26.9	25.6	25.7	28.2	28.6
LAIA	5.8	3.5	3.1	2.9	2.8	2.8	2.9	6.0	6.6	7.2
CACM	0.2	0.1	x0.2	0.1	0.1	0.1	0.1	0.1	x0.1	x0.1
Asia	20.0	x23.3	x24.5	x24.0	20.2	21.1	24.6	26.7	29.9	30.9
Middle East	4.4	x6.6	x4.3	x3.8	x2.7	x3.3	x3.6	x4.3	x4.0	x2.9
Europe	47.3	48.1	47.3	45.2	47.5	45.3	44.4	42.5	36.3	35.0
EEC	38.4	39.1	38.5	37.1	39.4	41.6	41.0	39.3	33.5	32.3
EFTA	8.2	8.5	8.2	7.6	7.8	3.3	3.0	2.8	2.5	2.3
Oceania	2.0	x1.8	x1.8	x1.7	x1.8	x1.7	x1.4	x1.4	x1.5	x1.5
USA/Etats-Unis d'Amer	15.3	14.0	14.1	14.6	16.1	16.5	16.2	14.5	16.3	16.2
Germany/Allemagne	8.2	8.6	8.3	7.6	8.2	9.0	9.7	8.7	7.4	7.3
United Kingdom	6.6	6.1	6.2	6.0	6.3	6.2	5.7	5.7	5.5	4.9
France,Monac	5.5	5.7	5.6	5.2	5.3	5.9	6.2	5.7	4.7	4.1
Canada	2.4	2.1	1.7	4.9	5.1	6.7	5.8	4.5	4.6	4.6
Italy/Italie	4.0	4.3	4.5	4.8	4.9	5.3	4.8	4.7	3.7	3.7
Singapore/Singapour	2.9	3.0	3.5	4.4	3.6	3.6	3.9	3.9	4.9	5.6
Malaysia/Malaisie	1.5	0.9	1.1	1.2	1.7	2.3	3.2	3.5	4.0	4.9
Hong Kong	1.8	1.8	2.0	2.4	2.7	2.5	3.0	3.3	3.8	3.8
Mexico/Mexique	3.1	0.7	0.6	0.7	0.8	0.9	1.1	4.2	4.5	4.7

	1985	1986	1987	1988	1989	1990	1991	1992	1993	1994
Afrique	0.2	0.3	0.3	0.3	0.3	0.3	0.3	0.3	0.3	0.2
Afrique du Nord	0.1	0.1	0.2	0.2	0.2	0.2	0.2	0.2	0.2	0.2
Amériques	18.3	x14.1	x13.5	x15.6	x17.0	x21.5	x19.7	19.2	20.2	21.0
ALAI	2.1	0.3	0.4	0.4	0.5	0.5	0.4	3.5	4.0	4.6
MCAC	0.0	0.0	0.0	0.0	0.0	0.0	0.0	0.1	x0.1	x0.1
Asie	24.2	25.1	x25.1	x27.7	25.4	23.1	25.6	27.0	31.8	33.6
Moyen-Orient	0.2	x0.1	x0.2	0.2	x0.1	0.1	0.1	0.1	x0.2	x0.2
Europe	56.2	59.4	57.8	53.5	55.4	53.9	53.4	52.4	46.5	43.8
CEE	47.2	49.5	48.0	44.8	46.9	48.9	48.8	47.9	42.4	40.0
AELE	8.2	9.2	9.2	8.2	8.0	4.5	4.4	4.2	3.7	3.5
Océanie	0.2	x0.2	x0.2	x0.3	x0.3	x0.3	x0.4	x0.4	x0.5	x0.5
Germany/Allemagne	19.3	21.0	20.9	19.2	20.2	20.7	21.4	20.3	17.9	16.7
Japan/Japon	14.8	16.1	15.8	17.0	17.5	15.5	16.9	16.6	18.9	18.9
USA/Etats-Unis d'Amer	14.9	12.6	12.0	12.9	14.3	16.4	14.6	13.2	13.9	14.0
France,Monac	8.6	9.1	8.4	7.8	8.2	9.0	8.7	9.1	7.8	7.6
United Kingdom	5.6	5.2	5.1	4.9	4.9	5.0	4.9	4.7	4.2	4.1
Switz.Liecht	4.3	4.9	4.8	4.2	4.1	4.3	4.1	3.9	3.5	3.3
Italy/Italie	3.7	3.6	3.6	3.4	3.9	3.8	3.7	3.7	3.1	2.9
Canada	1.1	0.8	0.7	2.0	4.1	4.4	4.5	2.4	2.2	2.0
Hong Kong	1.2	1.3	1.6	2.0	2.5	2.3	2.5	2.7	3.4	3.4
Singapore/Singapour	4.6	3.6	2.8	3.1	2.4	2.2	2.4	2.4	2.9	4.0

TRADE BY COMMODITY IN THOUSAND U.S. DOLLARS – COMMERCE PAR PRODUIT EN MILLIERS DE DOLLARS E.U

COUNTRIES–PAYS	IMPORTS – IMPORTATIONS				
	1990	1991	1992	1993	1994
Total	15266413	16326682	19649208	20526483	23719115
Africa	x530867	511510	x616704	x644557	x607965
Northern Africa	269116	277186	371404	388801	369128
Americas	4236107	4283686	6254107	7217673	8708384
LAIA	313565	387821	1821043	2119507	2429920
CACM	22256	21238	26001	x44165	x56153
Asia	3301054	4012720	4541228	x5241028	5506869
Middle East	x792293	x914910	x988974	x1055100	x666003
Europe	6434261	6801284	7650218	6696787	8060651
EEC	6040171	6418192	7197039	6292974	7586629
EFTA	325361	311039	312948	288006	314932
Oceania	x254759	x340588	x262335	x307402	x332808
USA/Etats–Unis d'Amer	2980432	2944956	3456268	3969394	4970411
Germany/Allemagne	1644259	1983272	2407430	1971823	2421548
Mexico/Mexique	124696	185562	1497944	1707963	1961582
France, Monac	839230	885812	944435	893342	1071869
Canada	754048	785508	846878	991532	1157582
United Kingdom	813735	830124	897822	875502	1042836
Hong Kong	583054	606427	682228	799560	901576
Singapore/Singapour	417401	519924	581649	639058	720966
Japan/Japon	360926	488330	543068	568568	680197
Belgium–Luxembourg	398571	412882	438235	417836	570696
Netherlands/Pays–Bas	441364	416387	459018	368172	419817
China/Chine	217873	236945	371056	566660	640111
Iran (Islamic Rp. of)	x275003	x439989	x338015	x394427	x73463
Malaysia/Malaisie	225840	320332	353332	430222	488550
Spain/Espagne	316206	355925	395608	330200	433939
Austria/Autriche	281981	315242	346004	272143	303609
Sweden/Suède	343436	317698	316656	284121	346383
Italy/Italie	350959	300602	336468	265401	307043
Thailand/Thaïlande	177118	206962	256113	313226	371680
Portugal	214880	212837	235350	208543	252466
Switz.Liecht	215245	196280	188636	173326	194960
Australia/Australie	165131	170710	178609	206296	236278
Saudi Arabia	166894	140797	210692	x186329	x126936
Korea, Republic of	119793	178354	141146	203456	228216
Philippines	109413	155913	156588	179034	243063
Indonesia/Indonésie	93037	113974	171008	185483	220501
Turkey/Turquie	103762	113031	166336	127960	98929
Hungary/Hongrie	x47893	89990	x138119	x168476	x174371
Denmark/Danemark	127446	124738	147514	114770	120487
Ireland/Irlande	123614	123383	126771	109830	106401
Norway, SVD, JM	101811	103045	114806	107112	111806
Finland/Finlande	113144	108194	110493	101113	150157
Egypt/Egypte	66962	67191	91839	138142	132186
United Arab Emirates	94036	67758	77171	x131650	x136383
Pakistan	42045	85818	109293	64569	40376
Argentina/Argentine	13081	30697	84621	142986	138500
Algeria/Algérie	54267	46199	98141	81202	73326
Russian Federation			x97857	x115324	x67830
Israel/Israël	50604	71055	72352	69706	78783
Tunisia/Tunisie	42849	58694	82190	70703	66283
Brazil/Brésil	64518	64251	60192	74204	97306
Former USSR/Anc. URSS	349721	x190827			
New Zealand	32577	103669	34599	37332	45009
Poland/Pologne	31501	33830	58623	76194	85914
So. Africa Customs Un	53528	44803	54086	66713	78499
Libyan Arab Jamahiriya	68031	58239	x42250	x52261	x41378
Slovenia/Slovénia			81493	71184	94989
Greece/Grèce	31346	31096	35234	80178	39376
Venezuela	16938	30265	39825	71900	58508
Czechoslovakia	22433	x34508	x103311		

COUNTRIES–PAYS	EXPORTS – EXPORTATIONS				
	1990	1991	1992	1993	1994
Totale	13226866	14083185	18294498	19525400	22020110
Afrique	121307	131470	197568	185852	187375
Afrique du Nord	84446	110811	172345	157959	181862
Amériques	2713438	2986823	5329453	6508108	7152240
ALAI	310061	286165	2211662	2927633	3129031
MCAC	10821	10484	10917	x13090	x16979
Asie	2776681	3227674	4178805	4741913	5465672
Moyen–Orient	197804	213840	312127	x282195	x312654
Europe	7152201	7262369	8027478	7450182	8432127
CEE	6603400	6849468	7599419	7017019	7976473
AELE	291553	294092	307057	316785	362415
Océanie	87902	x96834	x90093	x117940	x172264
USA/Etats–Unis d'Amer	2098033	2449005	2838325	3263408	3643022
Germany/Allemagne	1788046	1863340	2035488	1796808	2049615
Mexico/Mexique	154192	164603	2077421	2778354	2999618
Japan/Japon	1294812	1411122	1561324	1834152	1878678
France, Monac	800633	850151	991702	893976	989956
Italy/Italie	598317	652973	732528	803337	770460
United Kingdom	816255	700808	647333	638726	755304
Spain/Espagne	320157	433902	586149	482360	615534
Portugal	314864	372366	518248	570196	716144
Hong Kong	291439	356299	467802	619760	753152
Austria/Autriche	438831	478927	518889	420850	x447739
Belgium–Luxembourg	487887	508411	512150	390828	466214
Korea, Republic of	160307	281151	355606	394823	360076
Thailand/Thaïlande	190948	203444	281659	426464	477780
China/Chine	100472	136155	442394	282341	390907
Netherlands/Pays–Bas	207183	267907	259640	315927	353746
Canada	280929	233739	262487	296526	340390
Sweden/Suède	270365	265976	258299	244977	355498
Philippines	158255	183295	268070	310041	450817
Switz.Liecht	212721	223501	240012	257524	290564
Ireland/Irlande	277001	243877	256911	213605	157544
Singapore/Singapour	178825	209497	200402	286197	429862
Malaysia/Malaisie	113363	150815	200904	211427	271615
Turkey/Turquie	103378	134392	216355	201810	218434
Hungary/Hongrie	x65131	x110649	x211163	x212345	x241249
Poland/Pologne	141923	166810	124978	144215	156468
Finland/Finlande	157378	98698	120923	104759	140463
Tunisia/Tunisie	58603	65250	117366	103702	119936
Brazil/Brésil	93513	71098	100106	112089	78779
Greece/Grèce	63546	42343	92014	74660	89209
Denmark/Danemark	62720	69571	69144	66010	69048
Australia/Australie	44649	66178	56530	78569	85185
Norway, SVD, JM	78812	70538	66973	59252	71848
Czechoslovakia		x58698	x103337		
Morocco/Maroc	23528	36602	48165	51180	59826
Saudi Arabia	41759	53095	51290	x18224	x36990
Yugoslavia SFR	254798	x116230			
Croatia/Croatie			57235	43343	x45798
India/Inde	51690	39067	32516	25223	51166
New Zealand	42680	29642	28525	33130	38848
Czech Republic				84635	78952
Israel/Israël	27431	23887	26455	26460	39172
Indonesia/Indonésie	6260	13997	21791	33405	44841
Bulgaria/Bulgarie	x27230	x11144	x29383	x24055	x14004
Russian Federation			x23622	x40553	x50619
United Arab Emirates	14973	12394	17746	x23517	x18619
So. Africa Customs Un	24547	13133	15942	19662	
Slovakia				x46501	x64119
Yugoslavia/Yougoslavie			x39737	x722	x592
Venezuela	26700	16815	8630	11987	11473

(VALUE AS % OF TOTAL)(VALEUR EN % DU TOTAL)

	1985	1986	1987	1988	1989	1990	1991	1992	1993	1994
Africa	5.7	x5.4	x4.2	x3.7	x2.9	x3.5	3.2	x3.2	x3.1	x2.5
Northern Africa	3.7	2.8	2.1	1.8	1.5	1.8	1.7	1.9	1.9	1.6
Americas	30.7	x27.9	27.7	30.9	30.4	27.8	26.2	31.8	35.2	36.7
LAIA	4.2	2.3	2.4	2.2	2.1	2.1	2.4	9.3	10.3	10.2
CACM	0.2	0.2	x0.2	0.1	0.1	0.1	0.1	0.1	x0.2	x0.2
Asia	19.6	x20.4	x20.6	x19.1	18.9	21.6	24.6	23.1	x25.5	23.2
Middle East	7.5	x9.0	x6.3	x5.0	x3.8	x5.2	x5.6	x5.0	x5.1	x2.8
Europe	36.7	39.6	40.4	40.2	42.4	42.1	41.7	38.9	32.6	34.0
EEC	29.8	31.9	32.9	33.2	35.5	39.6	39.3	36.6	30.7	32.0
EFTA	6.1	7.0	6.9	6.5	6.4	2.1	1.9	1.6	1.4	1.3
Oceania	1.5	x1.6	x1.4	x1.5	x1.7	x1.7	x2.1	x1.4	x1.5	x1.4
USA/Etats–Unis d'Amer	23.3	22.2	22.5	22.2	21.4	19.5	18.0	17.6	19.3	21.0
Germany/Allemagne	6.4	7.2	8.3	8.3	8.8	10.8	12.1	12.3	9.6	10.2
Mexico/Mexique	2.6	0.3	0.8	0.8	0.8	0.8	1.1	7.6	8.3	8.3
France, Monac	4.7	5.0	4.9	4.7	5.1	5.5	5.4	4.8	4.4	4.5
Canada	2.1	1.7	1.7	5.6	5.9	4.9	4.8	4.3	4.8	4.9
United Kingdom	5.0	4.9	4.9	5.4	5.6	5.3	5.1	4.6	4.3	4.4
Hong Kong	2.2	2.2	2.4	2.9	3.5	3.8	3.7	3.5	3.9	3.8
Singapore/Singapour	2.8	2.6	2.2	2.5	2.6	2.7	3.2	3.0	3.1	3.0
Japan/Japon	1.0	1.0	1.1	1.3	1.7	2.4	3.0	2.8	2.8	2.9
Belgium–Luxembourg	2.1	2.3	2.1	2.4	2.5	2.6	2.5	2.2	2.0	2.4

	1985	1986	1987	1988	1989	1990	1991	1992	1993	1994
Afrique	0.3	0.4	0.4	0.4	0.5	0.9	0.9	1.1	1.0	0.9
Afrique du Nord	0.2	0.2	0.3	0.3	0.3	0.6	0.8	0.9	0.8	0.8
Amériques	22.0	17.8	17.6	19.9	22.8	20.5	21.2	29.1	33.3	32.5
ALAI	4.3	1.4	2.2	2.6	3.8	2.3	2.0	12.1	15.0	14.2
MCAC	0.1	0.1	0.1	0.1	0.1	0.1	0.1	0.1	x0.1	x0.1
Asie	19.0	19.6	x23.7	x26.0	20.3	21.0	22.9	22.9	24.3	24.8
Moyen–Orient	0.8	x1.5	x2.5	1.5	x1.2	1.5	1.5	1.7	x1.4	x1.4
Europe	56.2	59.8	52.4	48.5	52.8	54.1	51.6	43.9	38.2	38.3
CEE	45.4	48.2	42.0	39.7	42.8	49.9	48.6	41.5	35.9	36.2
AELE	7.6	8.9	8.2	7.0	7.9	2.2	2.1	1.7	1.6	1.6
Océanie	0.3	x0.3	x0.3	0.3	0.5	0.7	x0.7	x0.5	x0.6	x0.8
USA/Etats–Unis d'Amer	15.6	14.3	13.9	14.6	16.1	15.9	17.4	15.5	16.7	16.5
Germany/Allemagne	11.8	13.6	11.8	11.5	12.1	13.5	13.2	11.1	9.2	9.3
Mexico/Mexique	2.8	0.3	1.3	1.7	2.5	1.2	1.2	11.4	14.2	13.6
Japan/Japon	14.5	13.5	9.7	9.8	10.4	9.8	10.0	8.5	9.4	8.5
France, Monac	7.7	6.7	5.5	5.0	5.6	6.1	6.0	5.4	4.6	4.5
Italy/Italie	4.2	5.0	4.3	3.7	4.0	4.5	4.6	4.0	4.1	3.5
United Kingdom	6.7	5.2	4.2	4.3	4.5	6.2	5.0	3.5	3.3	3.4
Spain/Espagne	1.7	1.9	1.9	1.5	1.6	2.4	3.1	3.2	2.5	2.8
Portugal	0.9	1.2	1.4	1.0	1.7	2.4	2.6	2.8	2.9	3.3
Hong Kong	0.9	1.0	1.2	1.7	2.0	2.2	2.5	2.6	3.2	3.4

TRADE BY COMMODITY IN THOUSAND U.S. DOLLARS – COMMERCE PAR PRODUIT EN MILLIERS DE DOLLARS E.U

COUNTRIES–PAYS	IMPORTS – IMPORTATIONS				
	1990	1991	1992	1993	1994
Total	x8103657	7930493	8658240	8541639	8950739
Africa	x137833	133408	x166739	x193318	x192322
Northern Africa	39784	26865	x62308	x69889	75967
Americas	2316913	2557461	2674185	2819221	2734027
LAIA	234804	326572	365802	435245	486299
CACM	15189	2781	7044	x18884	x26283
Asia	x1287764	1413623	1647501	x1817935	2056297
Middle East	x240991	x245830	x293740	x295469	x236917
Europe	3070220	3287754	3786712	3266194	3454783
EEC	2838430	3056146	3549747	3037173	3202684
EFTA	173772	186773	210309	188126	212140
Oceania	x157903	x162828	x166218	x195018	x239253
USA/Etats–Unis d'Amer	1719390	1933327	2009592	2062427	1917033
Germany/Allemagne	627327	744675	893350	726839	743739
France, Monac	514434	518964	578498	532428	627266
Japan/Japon	369806	374272	415357	516171	647514
Netherlands/Pays–Bas	363511	354923	438501	409496	403103
United Kingdom	315395	330583	381782	334957	321168
Italy/Italie	323303	349345	379541	290400	299047
Canada	286005	273739	268347	283151	278257
China/Chine	191066	237889	254499	258287	226386
Spain/Espagne	191048	208300	197757	162766	173030
Hong Kong	91393	143338	212344	201007	192274
Korea, Republic of	139770	187832	157546	197956	319674
Belgium–Luxembourg	140822	139417	185807	153044	167607
Australia/Australie	135415	144212	145502	165395	211939
Austria/Autriche	110960	128377	165877	143255	156575
Switz.Liecht	124236	127623	152622	133755	163198
Mexico/Mexique	72782	115271	114900	158109	194940
Brazil/Brésil	110156	118955	116712	144039	116113
Russian Federation			x163774	x184600	x345526
Sweden/Suède	95474	102673	132707	107329	116892
Iran (Islamic Rp. of)	x122446	x114864	x132821	x83989	x20523
Former USSR/Anc. URSS	x965775	x231837			
Poland/Pologne	23720	59578	73598	91938	64701
So. Africa Customs Un	60957	71636	62141	67900	68340
Saudi Arabia	22603	47705	53488	x85244	x52010
India/Inde	68659	44360	78220	58223	94429
Norway,SVD,JM	47495	56604	55468	51323	46573
Thailand/Thaïlande	34954	43529	45527	66512	83377
Denmark/Danemark	39111	42739	53493	55183	64726
Turkey/Turquie	57439	47286	44251	55831	55073
Finland/Finlande	52151	52471	39390	42264	49011
Singapore/Singapour	33746	36070	38773	58917	62522
Argentina/Argentine	6521	36403	51377	38109	69935
Hungary/Hongrie	x35836	31572	x45055	x48734	x38336
Greece/Grèce	27056	38619	42937	38296	32324
Czechoslovakia	8777	x39172	x73234		
Portugal	25375	33121	37735	30834	36371
Indonesia/Indonésie	23506	23965	40307	37317	26098
Malaysia/Malaisie	21770	22520	34043	34988	36472
Israel/Israël	18396	20627	28059	38893	57165
Ukraine			x10037	x76465	x42052
Chile/Chili	10842	16132	30336	25429	31725
Kuwait/ Koweït	9226	7661	25731	23814	27045
Czech Republic				56116	100314
Venezuela	8378	13667	18401	21302	7784
Pakistan	15239	13458	19181	20045	17230
New Zealand	12215	11529	11214	23780	22851
Libyan Arab Jamahiriya	1383	2194	x17489	x25318	x8698
Ireland/Irlande	12463	11940	22370	10083	11825
Yugoslavia SFR	56549	x42938			

COUNTRIES–PAYS	EXPORTS – EXPORTATIONS				
	1990	1991	1992	1993	1994
Totale	7872128	8986667	9766992	10017128	10785842
Afrique	x2593	x3631	x3542	x5611	x1317
Afrique du Nord	x273	170	x211	x232	605
Amériques	1999167	2388184	2624148	2786437	3084305
ALAI	5871	8752	51115	58412	61753
MCAC	12	8		x139	x140
Asie	1704774	1994104	2085607	2137851	2114556
Moyen–Orient	1337	x1371	x2327	x5164	x5031
Europe	4104941	4562053	4999875	5024103	5516116
CEE	3925484	4381157	4825993	4852687	5333825
AELE	175822	177698	173216	170633	181408
Océanie	x13598	x19234	x25466	x36539	x48286
USA/Etats–Unis d'Amer	1951517	2327606	2512972	2660026	2958179
Germany/Allemagne	1709864	1807067	2149918	2059382	2224286
Japan/Japon	1467164	1705429	1725505	1744399	1688580
Netherlands/Pays–Bas	546882	719703	629619	860083	963487
France, Monac	401277	498363	538283	586750	725598
United Kingdom	436543	491733	535398	420392	351585
Italy/Italie	156145	181184	220941	189837	230844
Sweden/Suède	185094	175575	197363	185705	204733
Finland/Finlande	134448	148229	142910	145293	182162
Hong Kong	82826	112334	161584	153389	129184
Denmark/Danemark	134225	135691	152022	128213	154683
Switz.Liecht	139788	143475	136854	130732	134832
Belgium–Luxembourg	103315	105730	117338	124126	118990
Israel/Israël	80127	94047	112525	134900	157365
Austria/Autriche	61669	62936	65378	62288	x54432
Spain/Espagne	41368	46718	54130	78827	117376
Canada	41174	50558	59425	66916	62431
Norway,SVD,JM	36034	34210	36362	39901	46564
Mexico/Mexique	3250	4217	40008	50669	53666
Korea, Republic of	19699	22186	31805	40208	55579
Singapore/Singapour	24622	29159	27154	37103	42930
Australia/Australie	11745	18027	23190	34358	46443
China/Chine	18885	20492	10781	10875	24353
Hungary/Hongrie	x13231	x6175	x12406	x13692	x6840
Ireland/Irlande	11086	4742	15538	6409	
Poland/Pologne	18397	5413	11963	5236	4871
India/Inde	5200	4480	7262	6403	6868
Brazil/Brésil	763	1392	8755	4462	4974
So. Africa Customs Un	1836	2848	2873	4444	
Portugal	1871	2048	4776	3025	3525
Malaysia/Malaisie	3253	3551	3500	2323	2390
Russian Federation			x4024	x3141	x2419
Greece/Grèce	1505	1247	2380	2358	2124
Argentina/Argentine	1686	2332	1450	2153	1982
Czechoslovakia		x3873	x2031		
Czech Republic				5672	5918
New Zealand	1710	1110	1984	1741	1743
Thailand/Thaïlande	862	481	1358	2477	1507
Former USSR/Anc. URSS	x7919	x3187			
Yugoslavia SFR	3477	x3170			
Bulgaria/Bulgarie	x1378	x413	x1371	x442	x116
Turkey/Turquie	220	547	688	652	2039
Colombia/Colombie	38	469	477	739	732
Cuba	x68	x737	x380	x504	x106
Iran (Islamic Rp. of)		x173	x815	x589	x140
Kuwait/ Koweït	439	207	214	972	498
Slovakia				x1372	x3182
Saudi Arabia	113	x8		x1337	x870
Korea Dem People's Rp	x668	x137	x576	x284	x92
Estonia/Estonie			x79	x823	x406

(VALUE AS % OF TOTAL)(VALEUR EN % DU TOTAL)

	1985	1986	1987	1988	1989	1990	1991	1992	1993	1994
Africa	2.4	2.3	x2.2	x2.1	x1.7	x1.7	1.7	x1.9	x2.3	x2.2
Northern Africa	0.9	0.7	0.5	0.6	0.6	0.5	0.3	x0.7	x0.8	0.8
Americas	39.9	x38.1	x31.9	34.6	31.1	28.5	32.2	30.9	33.0	30.5
LAIA	2.8	3.9	3.5	3.7	3.6	2.9	4.1	4.2	5.1	5.4
CACM	0.2	0.4	0.2	0.1	0.0	0.2	0.0	0.1	x0.2	x0.3
Asia	13.4	13.6	x17.1	x16.8	15.7	x15.9	17.8	19.0	x21.3	23.0
Middle East	2.3	x3.0	x2.5	x2.1	x2.2	x3.0	x3.1	x3.4	x3.5	x2.6
Europe	39.4	42.0	39.2	37.7	41.7	37.9	41.5	43.7	38.2	38.6
EEC	32.9	35.0	32.1	31.5	35.3	35.0	38.5	41.0	35.6	35.8
EFTA	5.7	5.9	5.9	5.7	6.0	2.1	2.4	2.4	2.2	2.4
Oceania	2.7	x2.2	x1.8	x1.8	x2.2	x1.9	x2.1	x1.9	x2.3	x2.6
USA/Etats–Unis d'Amer	31.9	28.2	23.6	26.0	22.6	21.2	24.4	23.2	24.1	21.4
Germany/Allemagne	8.9	9.3	7.9	7.0	7.4	7.7	9.4	10.3	8.5	8.3
France, Monac	4.9	5.7	5.2	5.0	6.2	6.3	6.5	6.7	6.2	7.0
Japan/Japon	4.5	4.8	5.4	5.3	4.8	4.6	4.7	4.8	6.0	7.2
Netherlands/Pays–Bas	4.1	4.9	4.6	3.7	4.1	4.5	4.5	5.1	4.8	4.5
United Kingdom	4.0	3.7	3.3	3.8	4.2	3.9	4.2	4.4	3.9	3.6
Italy/Italie	3.1	3.4	3.3	3.7	3.9	4.0	4.4	4.4	3.4	3.3
Canada	4.7	4.1	3.3	4.3	4.2	3.5	3.5	3.1	3.3	3.1
China/Chine			3.3	3.0	2.7	2.4	3.0	2.9	3.0	2.5
Spain/Espagne	1.3	1.3	1.5	1.8	2.5	2.4	2.6	2.3	1.9	1.9

	1985	1986	1987	1988	1989	1990	1991	1992	1993	1994
Afrique		x0.0	x0.0	x0.0	x0.0	x0.0	x0.0	x0.0	x0.0	x0.0
Afrique du Nord	0.0	x0.0	x0.0	x0.0	x0.0	x0.0	0.0	x0.0	x0.0	0.0
Amériques	29.7	x25.9	x26.0	30.4	24.6	25.4	26.6	26.8	27.8	28.6
ALAI	0.1	0.1	0.1	0.1	0.1	0.1	0.1	0.5	0.6	0.6
MCAC		0.0	x0.0	x0.0	x0.0	0.0	0.0	0.0	x0.0	x0.0
Asie	19.8	17.9	16.8	17.7	20.5	21.7	22.2	21.3	21.4	19.6
Moyen–Orient	0.0	x0.0	x0.0	x0.0	x0.0	0.0	x0.0	x0.0	x0.1	x0.0
Europe	49.0	54.9	53.9	48.9	53.4	52.1	50.8	51.2	50.2	51.1
CEE	43.1	48.9	48.2	43.4	47.1	49.9	48.8	49.4	48.4	49.5
AELE	5.6	5.8	5.5	5.3	6.3	2.2	2.0	1.8	1.7	1.7
Océanie	0.2	x0.2	x0.3	0.3	x0.2	x0.2	x0.2	x0.3	x0.4	x0.4
USA/Etats–Unis d'Amer	29.0	25.4	25.4	29.5	23.8	24.8	25.9	25.7	26.6	27.4
Germany/Allemagne	17.8	20.6	21.2	19.7	21.5	21.7	20.1	22.0	20.6	20.6
Japan/Japon	16.0	15.0	14.2	15.1	17.6	18.6	19.0	17.7	17.4	15.7
Netherlands/Pays–Bas	8.4	8.8	8.1	6.4	6.8	6.9	8.0	6.4	8.6	8.9
France, Monac	3.4	5.3	4.5	4.3	4.2	5.1	5.5	5.5	5.9	6.7
United Kingdom	3.9	3.8	4.1	4.3	4.5	5.5	5.5	5.5	4.2	3.3
Italy/Italie	1.7	2.0	2.0	1.8	1.8	2.0	2.0	2.3	1.9	2.1
Sweden/Suède	2.7	2.7	2.1	1.9	2.2	2.4	2.0	2.0	1.9	1.9
Finland/Finlande	0.7	0.7	0.9	1.4	1.7	1.7	1.6	1.5	1.5	1.7
Hong Kong	0.6	0.5	0.6	0.6	0.8	1.1	1.3	1.7	1.5	1.2

TRADE BY COMMODITY IN THOUSAND U.S. DOLLARS – COMMERCE PAR PRODUIT EN MILLIERS DE DOLLARS E.U

COUNTRIES–PAYS	IMPORTS – IMPORTATIONS 1990	1991	1992	1993	1994
Total	22111150	24099999	26680978	25904898	28215113
Africa	x395497	x412717	x435500	x454512	x455724
Northern Africa	130436	113041	x117510	x142650	x156031
Americas	4391119	4892938	5876783	6432129	7013879
LAIA	373100	645287	984752	1184461	1300239
CACM	24903	25627	36627	x97427	x104445
Asia	3122214	3603623	4423958	x5086442	x5724307
Middle East	780518	x802050	x1065635	x1166067	x1010051
Europe	13342314	14164088	15021727	12789990	13917549
EEC	12335999	13236123	14067750	11907583	12890784
EFTA	811543	810193	818957	768286	859616
Oceania	x428939	x432870	x420758	x553521	x473595
USA/Etats-Unis d'Amer	3114466	3232921	3740674	4007863	4380610
Germany/Allemagne	2446728	2895544	3184138	2747819	3131997
France,Monac	2211932	2160542	2258909	1941894	2072430
Hong Kong	1056977	1354336	1706265	1984689	2224494
United Kingdom	1628761	1679834	1694044	1547102	1576722
Netherlands/Pays-Bas	1097845	1192165	1233338	1135116	1212153
Spain/Espagne	810655	971515	1161981	784127	826484
Canada	719736	828472	951328	989375	1036860
Belgium-Luxembourg	762860	814503	906768	809821	826311
Italy/Italie	785771	893724	956588	677424	736731
Austria/Autriche	583067	611957	644661	616926	672199
Japan/Japon	449734	533896	541010	608143	828206
Switz.Liecht	533991	529396	531054	515997	570659
Sweden/Suède	583862	605952	541504	402923	448622
Mexico/Mexique	198170	306568	396526	401227	441468
Denmark/Danemark	329142	309966	349885	304869	372307
Greece/Grèce	286234	305842	327295	326256	341887
Australia/Australie	284142	280313	256382	396764	317439
Portugal	246306	286631	353270	277734	279836
Singapore/Singapour	215071	235214	263763	326960	434930
Norway,SVD,JM	262166	263246	271380	238846	274671
Saudi Arabia	289301	188912	225382	x324054	x327204
Ireland/Irlande	223125	256902	248457	178392	185346
United Arab Emirates	168305	177949	207235	x279630	x278149
Argentina/Argentine	16079	85026	241998	312895	311472
Finland/Finlande	339711	251045	206912	157180	207758
China/Chine	93087	100564	188323	247123	267728
Israel/Israël	138344	153020	175561	182129	198434
Iran (Islamic Rp. of)	x83804	x116240	x218953	x151481	x30062
Russian Federation			x220519	x224323	x312243
So. Africa Customs Un	116354	137757	143404	139583	144501
Poland/Pologne	63692	147039	125554	134242	170615
Korea, Republic of	101757	121488	116989	131117	187977
Turkey/Turquie	80717	97056	104672	147954	87949
Thailand/Thaïlande	103810	96279	110591	121769	143488
Hungary/Hongrie	x103730	90144	x124355	x113157	x105260
New Zealand	89550	96323	103072	103348	125218
Malaysia/Malaisie	58279	73776	92756	124316	161987
Kuwait/Koweït	41784	66936	107899	89359	80725
Former USSR/Anc. URSS	90828	x257086			
Chile/Chili	42262	50924	84695	105467	118195
Czechoslovakia	86642	x61003	x165512		
Venezuela	17737	59124	73564	74624	46086
Czech Republic				199351	215467
Brazil/Brésil	30630	44364	48128	83913	116704
Uruguay	27029	33245	35484	87435	60647
Bulgaria/Bulgarie	x75187	x21521	53588	x50405	x65412
Cyprus/Chypre	33657	34165	53159	35103	39119
Indonesia/Indonésie	30502	44632	35448	27384	34325
Algeria/Algérie	11583	11954	34267	57237	24063

COUNTRIES–PAYS	EXPORTS – EXPORTATIONS 1990	1991	1992	1993	1994
Totale	21031398	22741829	25647231	25523453	28259865
Afrique	33557	41442	53280	42268	x39317
Afrique du Nord	20907	25304	32935	18000	31570
Amériques	1928619	2274055	2882001	3345212	3501193
ALAI	200276	274636	629286	816140	805197
MCAC	3982	594	966	x42107	x63025
Asie	4695370	5646082	6850466	7620559	8441333
Moyen-Orient	132951	97765	116067	148596	184679
Europe	13674199	14228042	15379742	13942741	15692242
CEE	12958242	13648323	14625231	13251332	14958114
AELE	352238	334950	345938	343349	353991
Océanie	x96923	x119063	x133166	x161865	x216481
Germany/Allemagne	4254640	4349574	4586185	3860677	4102623
Italy/Italie	3347448	3609284	3837870	3624484	4296865
Hong Kong	1518788	1873921	2152286	2464353	2696925
USA/Etats-Unis d'Amer	1599505	1873186	2096533	2290695	2384774
France,Monac	1463148	1613578	1824624	1681913	1849945
Japan/Japon	1178103	1310476	1413551	1340306	1153029
Korea, Republic of	839757	1029709	1096935	1217733	1487616
China/Chine	318434	467488	1030247	1274314	1566018
United Kingdom	786923	810985	875078	780411	951946
Netherlands/Pays-Bas	649947	697145	672756	716115	736316
Spain/Espagne	517460	587137	675423	606859	736877
Sweden/Suède	460718	464776	523523	505835	606475
Austria/Autriche	410662	432221	464749	413572	x445295
Singapore/Singapour	333985	373510	424310	439150	521597
Thailand/Thaïlande	268524	350543	409505	451750	520824
Denmark/Danemark	428167	396833	419493	382065	413320
Mexico/Mexique	83823	137581	446261	565118	601287
Switz.Liecht	274438	267861	274325	281101	284737
Ireland/Irlande	239794	277662	289448	231703	274575
Belgium-Luxembourg	201302	188692	207156	224622	255577
Slovenia/Slovénia			327885	291146	342328
Canada	118220	117802	147570	186300	243540
Brazil/Brésil	96130	103503	141255	199831	145725
Malaysia/Malaisie	54042	89625	131954	174734	198985
Portugal	107997	124359	153453	113886	144224
Hungary/Hongrie	x108349	x88158	x127547	x105734	x113908
Turkey/Turquie	48368	61931	93557	117513	152580
Poland/Pologne	69727	82177	92253	82484	87704
Yugoslavia SFR	361539	x242305			
New Zealand	56726	61571	78662	92519	129109
Finland/Finlande	73548	76187	68951	67218	85037
Norway,SVD,JM	77760	67079	71609	62249	69254
Australia/Australie	39584	56419	54224	67830	86402
Czechoslovakia		x92101	x76007		
Russian Federation			x86749	x65303	x40644
Former USSR/Anc. URSS	312815	x130465			
Slovakia				x122568	x79003
Greece/Grèce	16022	19423	26523	41973	59039
Latvia/Lettonie			x3721	80864	1061
Yugoslavia/Yougoslavie			x59908	x21290	x10796
Bulgaria/Bulgarie	x38100	x16676	x41230	x20378	x5585
Czech Republic				69144	72943
Philippines	13445	16229	26710	23480	32309
Colombia/Colombie	5702	13320	19967	21329	23057
Indonesia/Indonésie	1947	5924	8298	37343	34938
So. Africa Customs Un	8800	13180	16177	20444	
Belarus/Bélarus			x27837	x19558	x11658
India/Inde	8621	11179	19778	15290	19517
Israel/Israël	21461	14526	13241	17185	18960
Romania/Roumanie	14352	22833	10851	10395	9959

(VALUE AS % OF TOTAL)(VALEUR EN % DU TOTAL)

	1985	1986	1987	1988	1989	1990	1991	1992	1993	1994
Africa	2.3	x2.0	x1.8	x2.4	x1.4	x1.8	x1.7	x1.6	x1.7	x1.6
Northern Africa	1.2	0.8	0.6	0.7	0.5	0.6	0.5	x0.4	x0.6	x0.6
Americas	29.1	25.9	22.1	20.8	22.0	19.8	20.4	22.0	24.8	24.9
LAIA	1.0	0.8	1.0	1.4	1.6	1.7	2.7	3.7	4.6	4.6
CACM	0.2	0.2	0.2	0.1	0.1	0.1	0.1	0.1	x0.4	x0.4
Asia	13.5	11.6	x13.1	x14.3	13.4	14.2	15.0	16.6	x19.7	x20.2
Middle East	4.4	x4.2	x3.5	3.5	x3.0	3.5	x3.3	x4.0	x4.5	x3.6
Europe	50.1	56.9	59.2	58.7	59.4	60.3	58.8	56.3	49.4	49.3
EEC	41.2	46.6	48.5	48.5	49.2	55.8	54.9	52.7	46.0	45.7
EFTA	8.6	9.9	10.2	9.8	9.8	3.7	3.4	3.1	3.0	3.0
Oceania	3.2	x2.4	x2.1	x1.9	x2.3	x1.9	x1.8	x1.5	x2.1	x1.7
USA/Etats-Unis d'Amer	22.1	19.3	16.3	15.4	15.7	14.1	13.4	14.0	15.5	15.5
Germany/Allemagne	6.9	7.7	8.6	8.5	8.6	11.2	12.0	11.9	10.6	11.1
France,Monac	7.3	8.9	9.7	9.3	9.2	10.0	9.0	8.5	7.5	7.3
Hong Kong	3.1	2.1	3.0	3.6	4.3	4.8	5.6	6.4	7.7	7.9
United Kingdom	10.1	10.0	8.9	8.9	7.8	7.4	7.0	6.3	6.0	5.6
Netherlands/Pays-Bas	3.3	4.0	4.3	4.1	4.2	5.0	4.9	4.6	4.4	4.3
Spain/Espagne	0.6	1.0	1.4	2.0	2.8	3.7	4.0	4.4	3.0	2.9
Canada	5.2	4.8	3.9	3.3	3.7	3.3	3.4	3.6	3.8	3.7
Belgium-Luxembourg	2.4	2.8	2.9	2.9	3.0	3.5	3.4	3.4	3.1	2.9
Italy/Italie	2.3	2.6	2.7	3.0	3.3	3.6	3.7	3.6	2.6	2.6

	1985	1986	1987	1988	1989	1990	1991	1992	1993	1994
Afrique			x0.0	x0.1	x0.0	0.1	0.2	0.2	0.2	x0.1
Afrique du Nord	0.0	0.0	0.0	0.1	0.0	0.1	0.1	0.1	0.1	0.1
Amériques	7.5	6.1	6.3	7.3	9.0	9.2	10.0	11.2	13.1	12.4
ALAI	1.0	0.6	0.7	0.7	0.9	1.0	1.2	2.5	3.2	2.8
MCAC	0.1	0.0	0.0	0.0	0.0	0.0	0.0	0.0	x0.2	x0.2
Asie	33.2	27.5	x27.9	x29.4	25.4	22.3	24.8	26.7	29.8	29.8
Moyen-Orient	0.3	x0.2	x0.3	0.5	0.5	0.6	0.4	0.5	0.6	0.7
Europe	55.7	62.4	58.3	56.5	62.1	65.0	62.6	60.0	54.6	55.5
CEE	48.4	54.4	51.1	49.7	55.2	61.6	60.0	57.0	51.9	52.9
AELE	6.0	7.0	6.1	5.5	5.7	1.7	1.5	1.3	1.3	1.3
Océanie	0.5	x0.4	x0.5	x0.5	x0.4	x0.5	x0.5	x0.5	x0.6	x0.8
Germany/Allemagne	15.1	18.0	16.8	16.1	18.2	20.2	19.1	17.9	15.1	14.5
Italy/Italie	13.2	14.2	13.3	13.2	14.8	15.9	15.9	15.0	14.2	15.2
Hong Kong	7.8	5.9	6.2	6.7	7.6	7.2	8.2	8.4	9.7	9.5
USA/Etats-Unis d'Amer	5.7	4.4	4.6	5.9	7.3	7.6	8.2	8.2	9.0	8.4
France,Monac	5.5	6.1	5.4	5.2	6.1	7.0	7.1	7.1	6.6	6.5
Japan/Japon	19.4	14.5	10.0	8.2	6.9	5.6	5.8	5.5	5.3	4.1
Korea, Republic of	3.2	4.7	5.6	6.6	5.9	4.0	4.5	4.3	4.8	5.3
China/Chine	0.1	0.2	0.4	0.7	1.0	1.5	2.1	4.0	5.0	5.5
United Kingdom	2.4	2.2	2.7	3.2	3.4	3.7	3.6	3.4	3.1	3.4
Netherlands/Pays-Bas	2.7	2.9	2.7	2.6	2.7	3.1	3.1	2.6	2.8	2.6

TRADE BY COMMODITY IN THOUSAND U.S. DOLLARS – COMMERCE PAR PRODUIT EN MILLIERS DE DOLLARS E.U

COUNTRIES–PAYS	IMPORTS – IMPORTATIONS 1990	1991	1992	1993	1994
Total	60657919	67843512	78202525	93178858	125092498
Africa	328026	363925	x366384	x313555	x393034
Northern Africa	182645	175191	175283	103498	110195
Americas	16283667	17820560	22624303	27532307	36508994
LAIA	776762	842857	2607971	3164156	4273901
CACM	12417	8838	10305	x9150	x10204
Asia	23420950	28757930	32742427	40965391	57406895
Middle East	x458524	x549557	x581539	x479390	x330787
Europe	19760284	20278080	21796091	23382393	29588523
EEC	18779816	19276856	20634797	22231231	28049879
EFTA	488274	468750	499384	561395	758374
Oceania	x287351	x292232	x359352	x528293	x738164
USA/Etats–Unis d'Amer	13139051	14086389	16644248	20813672	27631714
Singapore/Singapour	4488977	5226969	6221522	9073772	14637576
Hong Kong	3704918	4520222	5633480	7153644	8863059
Malaysia/Malaisie	3812400	4534651	5375672	7122482	10798598
Korea, Republic of	4559680	5302160	6011505	5649676	6982537
Germany/Allemagne	4351706	4728158	5107787	5017292	7205976
United Kingdom	4014414	4139572	4556529	5356792	5565889
Japan/Japon	3310374	3911148	3988253	5286400	7306195
Canada	2332830	2859800	3344011	3527791	4577434
Italy/Italie	3103673	3069499	3363684	2763830	3681988
France,Monac	2897462	2955583	2926953	3158752	3761921
Thailand/Thaïlande	1312645	1588637	1899456	2460707	3487027
China/Chine	746565	1032367	1733597	2128099	2917573
Mexico/Mexique	167040	197790	1898092	2249892	3117986
Netherlands/Pays–Bas	844913	1024350	1129824	1668369	1980211
Philippines	399102	1440748	548131	670962	929123
Ireland/Irlande	481971	491539	560631	928122	1299505
Austria/Autriche	760184	662216	573341	627785	860082
Spain/Espagne	610185	620312	596565	563261	663224
Malta/Malte	399974	485894	616686	553434	x718639
Sweden/Suède	472999	437969	521277	689813	905649
Belgium–Luxembourg	490751	450051	443589	498945	703315
Brazil/Brésil	489773	450032	380608	561095	807348
Turkey/Turquie	360630	434163	412101	398414	258252
Finland/Finlande	308278	260837	391824	568624	889735
Switz.Liecht	376675	356394	364468	425456	580793
Australia/Australie	262813	265590	326329	481013	678648
Israel/Israël	198473	248330	292772	392419	502010
Indonesia/Indonésie	155559	173698	189912	300507	327900
India/Inde	251274	201333	240684	211621	269270
Argentina/Argentine	61989	124209	252993	255859	250453
Portugal	220318	222080	210996	143679	238029
Denmark/Danemark	165048	150414	193012	201427	251825
So. Africa Customs Un	124973	140404	165576	183960	256048
Norway,SVD,JM	109691	110571	133228	134362	175601
Poland/Pologne	47623	54270	142517	167478	174769
Hungary/Hongrie	x75271	69755	x84077	x132624	x111371
Iran (Islamic Rp. of)	x74187	x94078	x135747	x25725	x17952
Morocco/Maroc	109193	97916	64769	6513	8150
Greece/Grèce	57915	64276	58786	44541	42529
Former USSR/Anc. URSS	x213116	x151275			
Algeria/Algérie	28640	32827	42056	38392	32944
Russian Federation			x59458	x47133	x57547
Venezuela	13720	30558	33482	39930	28486
Tunisia/Tunisie	26858	25542	32327	38169	47368
Czechoslovakia	71334	x27874	x60310		
New Zealand	20292	19978	26229	39071	53425
Czech Republic				76395	93828
Romania/Roumanie	55716	18855	17607	38829	41642
Saudi Arabia	12468	13005	19796	x31597	x14815

COUNTRIES–PAYS	EXPORTS – EXPORTATIONS 1990	1991	1992	1993	1994
Totale	61212199	68536864	78114522	93477285	126743163
Afrique	114883	139613	x131561	x83681	x52269
Afrique du Nord	110809	131492	100780	38084	38171
Amériques	15393337	16977952	19653722	22560748	29355079
ALAI	127658	142891	845249	762740	1011888
MCAC	1465	3257	843	x1317	x769
Asie	30907605	36444867	42182692	51655225	72398594
Moyen–Orient	2452	x3965	3040	x7293	x10849
Europe	14557019	14868602	16024438	18974581	24671761
CEE	13844905	14055847	14991542	18059838	23550855
AELE	242044	257867	278428	306546	347818
Océanie	x21999	x30287	x32726	x51297	x65925
Japan/Japon	13347449	14859971	17479622	21956377	29263502
USA/Etats–Unis d'Amer	13990618	15134034	16781584	20077905	26452135
Korea, Republic of	5363900	6630536	7762913	8078346	11847982
Malaysia/Malaisie	4321419	4738864	5648042	7289254	9498894
Singapore/Singapour	3674584	4586711	5447811	6852586	12044376
Germany/Allemagne	3977813	4112482	4034527	4092180	5913344
United Kingdom	3105463	3122178	3742932	4952228	6272163
Hong Kong	2561546	2598269	3155322	4105819	5176121
France,Monac	2420096	2470414	2607933	2974165	3738546
Canada	1271001	1691118	2012222	1709729	1886476
Italy/Italie	1476145	1610475	1836439	1781140	2221851
Netherlands/Pays–Bas	1192593	1198419	1283944	2439905	2819924
Thailand/Thaïlande	900991	1121951	1332565	1709216	2240650
Philippines	398738	1375127	593478	805605	1100297
Malta/Malte	438205	544663	743457	595756	x758784
Austria/Autriche	658923	556821	463212	511552	x673474
Mexico/Mexique	46658	44996	744022	671103	918274
Israel/Israël	143141	242014	335319	385467	407271
Ireland/Irlande	263719	259630	290716	395183	736738
China/Chine	127610	184036	310543	359850	614374
Switz.Liecht	231413	245180	262158	285747	320719
Belgium–Luxembourg	146749	170985	146022	324984	423940
Sweden/Suède	183611	163772	165206	175657	269849
Spain/Espagne	132743	131756	145466	180720	262989
Portugal	183651	152771	167849	74931	18384
Brazil/Brésil	79234	96640	98868	89269	92165
Morocco/Maroc	110134	130271	99059	36671	36056
Denmark/Danemark	44856	58052	64442	96967	108186
Indonesia/Indonésie	18315	40592	60935	48985	107321
Finland/Finlande	56476	45957	41384	56426	87500
Poland/Pologne	28553	9261	41759	86382	112277
Australia/Australie	20186	26651	29459	50498	63614
India/Inde	38865	50354	23393	25287	34447
Czechoslovakia		x40863	x26847		
Mali		x1910	x25543	x39070	x8967
Korea Dem People's Rp	x6986	x11852	x25898	x27060	x45350
Norway,SVD,JM	10631	12686	16270	20799	27100
Russian Federation			x12390	x29807	x44183
Czech Republic				38519	52934
Hungary/Hongrie	x6828	x4289	x14337	x14749	x18314
Lithuania/Lituanie			25426	x2011	41897
Barbados/Barbade	215	4711	6896	7900	x324
Former USSR/Anc. URSS	x144654	x15624			
Ukraine			x3325	x11806	x5365
Slovenia/Slovénia			7336	7077	11499
So. Africa Customs Un	3205	5145	3099	5527	
Yugoslavia SFR	31739	x10028			
Bulgaria/Bulgarie	x11968	x1917	x4262	x2512	x1947
Slovakia				x7703	x11643
Greece/Grèce	2056	2121	1468	3800	3968

(VALUE AS % OF TOTAL)(VALEUR EN % DU TOTAL)

	1985	1986	1987	1988	1989	1990	1991	1992	1993	1994
Africa	0.5	x0.6	x0.4	x0.5	0.6	0.5	0.5	x0.5	x0.3	x0.3
Northern Africa	0.2	0.2	0.1	0.1	0.3	0.3	0.3	0.2	0.1	0.1
Americas	32.7	29.1	25.1	24.7	28.5	26.8	26.3	29.0	29.5	29.1
LAIA	3.1	2.3	1.5	1.2	1.3	1.3	1.2	3.3	3.4	3.4
CACM	0.0	0.0	0.0	0.0	0.0	0.0	0.0	0.0	x0.0	x0.0
Asia	28.5	31.5	x37.7	x40.0	36.1	38.6	42.4	41.9	44.0	45.8
Middle East	0.6	x0.7	x0.4	x0.4	0.4	x0.8	x0.8	x0.7	x0.5	x0.3
Europe	37.0	37.4	33.6	32.2	32.9	32.6	29.9	27.9	25.1	23.7
EEC	32.3	33.0	29.6	28.4	29.1	31.0	28.4	26.4	23.9	22.4
EFTA	4.3	4.1	3.6	3.4	3.2	0.8	0.7	0.6	0.6	0.6
Oceania	0.6	x0.6	x0.5	x0.5	x0.5	x0.5	x0.4	x0.5	x0.6	x0.6
USA/Etats–Unis d'Amer	25.3	23.0	20.3	20.5	23.2	21.7	20.8	21.3	22.3	22.1
Singapore/Singapour	6.2	7.1	6.8	7.0	6.8	7.4	7.7	8.0	9.7	11.7
Hong Kong	4.8	5.2	5.5	6.2	6.1	6.1	6.7	7.2	7.7	7.1
Malaysia/Malaisie	6.3	6.4	5.6	4.8	5.6	6.3	6.7	6.9	7.6	8.6
Korea, Republic of	4.5	5.8	6.2	6.3	7.1	7.5	7.8	7.7	6.1	5.6
Germany/Allemagne	8.5	8.9	7.3	6.6	6.8	7.2	7.0	6.5	5.4	5.8
United Kingdom	7.0	6.4	6.1	5.8	6.2	6.6	6.1	5.8	5.7	4.4
Japan/Japon	4.1	4.2	3.7	4.0	5.0	5.5	5.8	5.1	5.7	5.8
Canada	3.8	3.4	3.2	3.0	3.9	3.8	4.2	4.3	3.8	3.7
Italy/Italie	3.8	4.1	4.3	4.4	4.7	5.1	4.5	4.3	3.0	2.9

	1985	1986	1987	1988	1989	1990	1991	1992	1993	1994
Afrique		x0.0	x0.0	x0.0	0.1	0.2	0.2	x0.2	x0.1	x0.0
Afrique du Nord	0.0	0.0	x0.0	x0.0	0.1	0.2	0.2	0.1	0.0	0.0
Amériques	27.8	25.1	21.6	20.6	23.9	25.1	24.7	25.2	24.1	23.2
ALAI	1.4	0.3	0.2	0.2	0.2	0.2	0.2	1.1	0.8	0.8
MCAC	0.0	x0.0	x0.0	x0.0	0.0	0.0	0.0	0.0	x0.0	x0.0
Asie	45.2	47.5	50.8	52.6	52.3	50.5	53.1	54.0	55.3	57.1
Moyen–Orient	0.0	x0.0	x0.0	x0.0	x0.0	0.0	x0.0	0.0	x0.0	x0.0
Europe	26.1	26.5	24.8	24.5	22.8	23.8	21.7	20.5	20.3	19.5
CEE	24.2	24.3	22.4	21.8	20.6	22.6	20.5	19.2	19.3	18.6
AELE	1.6	1.9	2.1	2.3	1.6	0.4	0.4	0.4	0.3	0.3
Océanie		x0.0	x0.0	x0.0	x0.0	x0.0	x0.0	x0.0	x0.1	x0.1
Japan/Japon	20.8	22.7	21.1	22.6	24.7	21.8	21.7	22.4	23.5	23.1
USA/Etats–Unis d'Amer	23.2	22.4	19.7	19.0	21.7	22.9	22.1	21.5	21.5	20.9
Korea, Republic of	5.0	5.8	6.1	7.1	8.2	8.8	9.7	9.9	8.6	9.3
Malaysia/Malaisie	8.0	8.0	7.0	6.1	6.6	7.1	6.9	7.2	7.8	7.5
Singapore/Singapour	6.0	6.0	6.0	5.8	5.8	6.0	6.7	7.0	7.3	9.5
Germany/Allemagne	6.3	6.4	5.9	6.3	6.2	6.5	6.0	5.2	4.4	4.7
United Kingdom	5.7	5.1	4.3	4.2	4.5	5.1	4.6	4.8	5.3	4.9
Hong Kong	3.9	3.5	3.8	4.5	4.4	4.2	3.8	4.0	4.4	4.1
France,Monac	4.3	4.5	4.6	4.1	3.4	4.0	3.6	3.3	3.2	2.9
Canada	2.5	2.0	1.7	1.4	2.0	2.1	2.5	2.6	1.8	1.5

TRADE BY COMMODITY IN THOUSAND U.S. DOLLARS – COMMERCE PAR PRODUIT EN MILLIERS DE DOLLARS E.U

COUNTRIES–PAYS	IMPORTS – IMPORTATIONS				
	1990	1991	1992	1993	1994
Total	39214505	41893969	46939186	48933678	59293478
Africa	x929121	x852957	x907536	x940933	x1123811
Northern Africa	341154	309739	x327136	344785	x368486
Americas	9533159	9657578	11863139	13591935	15755873
LAIA	1340084	1510290	2641022	3245764	3487576
CACM	58901	63995	83991	x93289	x103757
Asia	7412908	8888029	10564533	12137513	15392767
Middle East	x1004811	x1143524	x1373867	x1395371	x1173162
Europe	19771764	20899739	22082933	20619025	25139316
EEC	18378221	19595869	20728381	19366094	23756452
EFTA	1189978	1155781	1182013	1113862	1213470
Oceania	x766929	x781926	x886434	x919389	x1081189
USA/Etats–Unis d'Amer	6036342	5941482	6853189	7745252	9255070
Germany/Allemagne	4615191	5405372	5555206	4986290	6603855
United Kingdom	2599366	2700702	2986435	3394041	4032693
France,Monac	2679214	2763512	2903443	2667390	3114389
Canada	1852989	1941041	2093623	2330510	2673344
Hong Kong	1199157	1641873	2008423	2353919	2667212
Italy/Italie	1830133	1887540	2006840	1693587	2100985
Netherlands/Pays–Bas	1609168	1587688	1676382	1441505	1677706
Japan/Japon	1439914	1550422	1444587	1510339	2186802
Mexico/Mexique	543390	605790	1623268	2004172	1973772
Singapore/Singapour	981915	1117044	1263045	1640181	2512913
Spain/Espagne	1233141	1406852	1459056	1125179	1331528
Belgium–Luxembourg	1034721	1074901	1110566	1072009	1269630
China/Chine	338728	436044	1062806	1172962	1429844
Malaysia/Malaisie	519657	743800	839815	1065330	1590724
Korea, Republic of	663028	773303	806600	938682	1267236
Sweden/Suède	865483	800173	813487	814797	1070366
Thailand/Thaïlande	456569	617162	691543	860669	1139670
Switz.Liecht	738522	720145	720943	697664	765110
Austria/Autriche	655095	664384	725540	719480	816056
Australia/Australie	576147	606400	689289	714119	878892
Norway,SVD,JM	405932	392723	414207	380802	408383
Brazil/Brésil	323500	308280	329929	409261	531501
Denmark/Danemark	333259	340531	366282	332891	376308
Turkey/Turquie	252886	291428	302745	405329	335901
Indonesia/Indonésie	215674	256033	343435	347332	373675
Saudi Arabia	249554	300177	341387	x291225	x267444
Iran (Islamic Rp. of)	x235139	x265196	x354300	x288538	x75513
Portugal	248252	276281	328846	286461	313203
Finland/Finlande	323109	263025	287363	304107	482803
Ireland/Irlande	148486	204589	267668	309692	351910
Argentina/Argentine	74286	153962	244823	315171	385409
So. Africa Customs Un	237809	236420	232541	243172	397738
Israel/Israël	165434	195500	236399	248790	298139
Greece/Grèce	203604	220317	241268	218665	215019
Russian Federation			x350269	x246919	x262891
Poland/Pologne	46405	97065	202038	246372	285607
Venezuela	145092	183917	159954	157772	127017
India/Inde	190247	118376	164653	165089	189879
Hungary/Hongrie	x107927	117014	x147794	x179225	x176943
United Arab Emirates	120550	110112	131191	x199649	x214342
Former USSR/Anc. URSS	332830	x438082			
Philippines	63336	101344	103328	159856	187161
Chile/Chili	80788	106193	115025	132565	143346
New Zealand	118397	104947	115116	124859	151235
Czechoslovakia	138752	x97899	x210446		
Nigeria/Nigéria	x58488	68534	x85500	x98566	x60807
Algeria/Algérie	83076	55087	73432	102469	91394
Egypt/Egypte	78778	75674	72069	79951	86303
Tunisia/Tunisie	68781	61205	80225	63031	76665

COUNTRIES–PAYS	EXPORTS – EXPORTATIONS				
	1990	1991	1992	1993	1994
Totale	36610293	39214491	45227160	49616636	60879563
Afrique	77743	86739	89200	77092	44570
Afrique du Nord	29535	33572	43400	28618	39211
Amériques	5906192	6835758	8863671	10301787	11941689
ALAI	386692	422976	1885215	2364887	2916603
MCAC	19707	22480	26597	x25274	x33193
Asie	10649551	12219175	14146204	17612873	23364114
Moyen–Orient	88983	46672	36427	x80059	x85493
Europe	19341914	19558205	21403611	20703541	24523746
CEE	17783323	18164899	19838322	19220776	22827149
AELE	1356394	1300001	1351699	1303772	1514129
Océanie	x110350	x127741	x147370	x170719	x271524
Japan/Japon	7388587	8187771	9004412	10183463	12185226
Germany/Allemagne	6426859	6607436	7411896	6906792	8180738
USA/Etats–Unis d'Amer	5032843	5959443	6418286	7332395	8223372
United Kingdom	2722658	2710010	2825365	2813046	3695875
France,Monac	2240466	2309003	2551577	2491033	2877068
Italy/Italie	1680221	1722284	1872980	1730516	2040667
Hong Kong	951426	1279889	1717410	2088867	2272004
Netherlands/Pays–Bas	1465991	1440906	1577247	1633706	1700167
Belgium–Luxembourg	1213835	1256727	1316872	1313365	1561992
Mexico/Mexique	190299	190081	1613118	2008824	2518105
Switz.Liecht	1286438	1228876	1273886	1219762	1414222
Korea, Republic of	612397	632494	688388	1733913	3258467
Singapore/Singapour	643736	802902	895585	1118481	1927922
China/Chine	347491	442829	837990	1099652	1700936
Spain/Espagne	669351	687900	769060	738587	895774
Canada	451336	416312	521147	560018	694715
Austria/Autriche	422003	450167	494218	506644	x480549
Sweden/Suède	415330	446538	462822	406772	557420
Malaysia/Malaisie	181933	258004	306175	366432	585441
Thailand/Thaïlande	127067	190751	255216	477639	705741
Brazil/Brésil	141992	172182	207063	262120	284796
Hungary/Hongrie	x178137	x160439	x213184	x245543	x316135
Indonesia/Indonésie	64738	123907	181903	225973	317844
Denmark/Danemark	145751	156236	165902	181810	202887
Ireland/Irlande	88683	100863	105835	213211	271081
Poland/Pologne	95292	72760	170478	173838	199984
Portugal	135104	134675	146920	128201	149617
Finland/Finlande	141507	122240	121440	143298	203325
Australia/Australie	80194	98732	114692	131884	225581
Israel/Israël	97464	104920	115302	106546	128250
Slovenia/Slovénia			158148	147824	161625
India/Inde	99367	113284	60719	72505	88384
Czech Republic				232462	140045
Norway,SVD,JM	69310	70721	77362	83524	99205
Bulgaria/Bulgarie	x122005	x39681	x92042	x53536	x29426
Czechoslovakia		x70319	x84530		
So. Africa Customs Un	26691	35061	39700	40162	
New Zealand	29086	27179	30978	36263	44192
Russian Federation			x52693	x40719	x52789
Yugoslavia SFR	201316	x91494			
Tunisia/Tunisie	23594	23010	31777	22693	32178
Turkey/Turquie	19911	29586	15937	30461	37047
Philippines	33351	19176	23751	30789	47333
Argentina/Argentine	18172	20334	19229	32047	38607
Colombia/Colombie	8433	14130	15243	21178	26324
Greece/Grèce	15254	19602	16189	13795	9988
Chile/Chili	6458	10950	12306	17839	15256
Romania/Roumanie	9745	8717	14583	16319	20259
Costa Rica	11687	12200	13362	x13041	x20440
Croatia/Croatie			25105	13416	x11535

(VALUE AS % OF TOTAL)(VALEUR EN % DU TOTAL)

	1985	1986	1987	1988	1989	1990	1991	1992	1993	1994
Africa	3.1	x3.0	x2.7	x2.6	x2.3	x2.4	x2.1	x1.9	x1.9	x1.9
Northern Africa	1.6	1.2	0.9	0.9	0.9	0.9	0.7	x0.7	0.7	x0.6
Americas	30.9	28.4	25.9	26.5	25.6	24.3	23.0	25.3	27.8	26.6
LAIA	4.4	3.3	2.9	3.0	2.7	3.4	3.6	5.6	6.6	5.9
CACM	0.3	0.2	x0.2	0.2	0.2	0.2	0.2	0.2	x0.2	x0.2
Asia	13.9	13.8	x16.3	x17.9	17.4	18.9	21.2	22.5	24.8	26.0
Middle East	2.7	x2.9	x2.6	x2.3	x2.1	x2.6	x2.7	x2.9	x2.9	x2.0
Europe	46.8	49.7	49.4	47.7	49.9	50.4	49.9	47.0	42.1	42.4
EEC	38.2	40.9	40.8	40.2	42.1	46.9	46.8	44.2	39.6	40.1
EFTA	7.8	8.2	8.0	7.1	7.3	3.0	2.8	2.5	2.3	2.0
Oceania	2.3	x1.9	x1.9	x1.9	x2.2	x2.0	x1.9	x1.9	x1.9	x1.8
USA/Etats–Unis d'Amer	20.2	19.4	18.1	17.7	16.9	15.4	14.2	14.6	15.8	15.6
Germany/Allemagne	8.3	9.2	8.9	8.8	9.7	11.8	12.9	11.8	10.2	11.1
United Kingdom	5.7	5.5	5.7	6.1	6.2	6.6	6.4	6.4	6.9	6.8
France,Monac	5.9	6.5	6.4	6.0	6.2	6.8	6.6	6.2	5.5	5.3
Canada	5.6	4.7	4.1	5.2	5.2	4.7	4.6	4.5	4.8	4.5
Hong Kong	1.8	2.0	2.2	2.6	2.9	3.1	3.9	4.3	4.8	4.5
Italy/Italie	3.8	4.1	4.3	4.3	4.3	4.7	4.5	4.3	3.5	3.5
Netherlands/Pays–Bas	4.0	4.2	4.2	3.9	3.8	4.1	3.8	3.6	2.9	2.8
Japan/Japon	3.3	2.5	2.5	2.9	3.5	3.7	3.7	3.1	3.1	3.7
Mexico/Mexique	1.9	1.1	0.6	0.8	0.9	1.4	1.4	3.5	4.1	3.3

	1985	1986	1987	1988	1989	1990	1991	1992	1993	1994
Afrique	0.2	0.3	0.2	x0.2	0.2	0.2	0.2	0.2	0.2	0.1
Afrique du Nord	0.0	0.0	0.0	0.1	0.1	0.1	0.1	0.1	0.1	0.1
Amériques	18.7	14.4	13.1	14.6	15.9	16.2	17.5	19.6	20.8	19.6
ALAI	1.8	0.7	0.7	0.8	1.0	1.1	1.1	4.2	4.8	4.8
MCAC	0.1	0.1	0.0	0.0	0.1	0.1	0.1	0.1	x0.1	x0.1
Asie	26.3	27.1	x29.8	x31.6	29.7	29.0	31.1	31.3	35.5	38.4
Moyen–Orient	0.3	0.2	x0.2	0.2	x0.1	0.2	0.1	0.1	x0.2	x0.1
Europe	53.2	56.8	52.7	49.7	51.9	52.8	49.9	47.3	41.7	40.3
CEE	45.8	48.9	45.7	43.5	45.5	48.6	46.3	43.9	38.7	37.5
AELE	6.2	6.9	6.3	5.6	5.8	3.7	3.3	3.0	2.6	2.5
Océanie	0.2	x0.2	x0.4	x0.3	x0.3	x0.3	x0.3	x0.3	x0.3	x0.4
Japan/Japon	20.6	21.2	19.1	19.4	21.1	20.2	20.9	19.9	20.5	20.0
Germany/Allemagne	15.1	17.6	16.2	15.1	16.5	17.6	16.8	16.4	13.9	13.4
USA/Etats–Unis d'Amer	15.9	12.9	11.6	12.5	13.4	13.7	15.2	14.2	14.8	13.5
United Kingdom	7.4	7.1	7.1	7.1	7.1	7.4	6.9	6.2	5.7	6.1
France,Monac	6.9	6.6	5.8	5.3	5.4	6.1	5.9	5.6	5.0	4.7
Italy/Italie	4.0	4.1	4.0	3.8	4.3	4.6	4.4	4.1	3.5	3.4
Hong Kong	1.5	1.5	1.6	2.0	2.6	2.6	3.3	3.8	4.2	3.7
Netherlands/Pays–Bas	4.6	5.3	5.0	4.7	4.3	4.0	3.7	3.5	3.3	2.8
Belgium–Luxembourg	2.9	2.9	2.7	2.7	2.9	3.3	3.2	2.9	2.6	2.6
Mexico/Mexique	1.1	0.1	0.3	0.3	0.4	0.5	0.5	3.6	4.0	4.1

TRADE BY COMMODITY IN THOUSAND U.S. DOLLARS – COMMERCE PAR PRODUIT EN MILLIERS DE DOLLARS E.U

IMPORTS – IMPORTATIONS

COUNTRIES–PAYS	1990	1991	1992	1993	1994
Total	165555111	173187582	190693976	181512272	201154544
Africa	x2508344	x2606135	x2371509	x2648260	x2704150
Northern Africa	546414	476633	x505417	x598164	x727689
Americas	58912787	60620164	63112583	68866229	80973583
LAIA	1051064	1956389	3994677	4763592	6870943
CACM	359738	356014	700625	x447360	x422816
Asia	13269417	14506039	18568234	x22133837	x21879356
Middle East	3578493	x5033523	x6347783	x6216232	x4803707
Europe	86684496	91439574	101994515	82757694	89979532
EEC	80734697	85773637	96454170	77913170	83813279
EFTA	5211745	4847759	5018013	4091057	5306652
Oceania	x2643223	x2449337	x2957315	x3204653	x3956437
USA/Etats–Unis d'Amer	47616320	47357531	47816703	53454937	62648606
Germany/Allemagne	17086946	23927697	23776032	17299003	18112628
Italy/Italie	12511456	13478040	16824005	9977561	10728267
France,Monac	12539694	11614645	13528025	11595918	12637371
United Kingdom	13093715	9723545	11668009	13043211	13808177
Canada	9271480	10297169	9834903	9358762	10090369
Belgium–Luxembourg	5888655	6559782	6260174	5839817	6807031
Spain/Espagne	4455403	4553765	6685874	5314808	5353010
Japan/Japon	6188686	5179673	4996726	5052065	6951325
Netherlands/Pays–Bas	4447160	5073911	5017152	4900933	5248413
Switz.Liecht	4512418	4270038	4244616	3446788	4191706
Austria/Autriche	3490607	3834615	4297851	3388306	3670438
Hong Kong	462870	760812	2131138	3714455	3044275
Australia/Australie	1706756	1732820	2145143	2309978	2801924
Saudi Arabia	1440612	1954650	2200031	x1778440	x1510526
Portugal	1395089	1619500	2409775	1881475	1865742
Greece/Grèce	1065059	1532153	2029938	1600195	962242
Sweden/Suède	2137491	1733392	1814788	1195949	1724370
China/Chine	311147	579861	1392694	2130720	1637553
Thailand/Thaïlande	397275	472309	935491	1501809	1535065
Israel/Israël	497567	682465	1049169	1003857	1257751
Denmark/Danemark	751508	802653	939263	856370	1468439
Venezuela	179076	453343	1112887	972528	512293
United Arab Emirates	585638	478733	705049	x1202444	x1033885
Malaysia/Malaisie	792844	917934	649313	770496	1077297
Kuwait/ Koweït	280220	821657	915022	560783	557835
So. Africa Customs Un	857556	737879	617563	927260	932169
Iran (Islamic Rp. of)		x573280	x766885	x544580	x230012
Ireland/Irlande	694896	579970	666340	615301	777458
Argentina/Argentine	11738	202206	791783	844534	1394468
Hungary/Hongrie	x320858	397992	x621393	x806298	x599088
Norway,SVD,JM	642947	493766	710075	592788	1063310
New Zealand	710074	517326	585230	683321	961240
Finland/Finlande	1177018	739968	536944	404323	649691
Oman	289573	378077	599703	632760	500877
Russian Federation			x662933	x822005	x830780
Poland/Pologne	93963	620152	320274	441269	376073
Turkey/Turquie	567698	258591	364688	734229	222011
Chile/Chili	208706	282301	527268	480697	442680
Brazil/Brésil	12542	121274	281351	710203	1522254
Mexico/Mexique	250926	293165	377043	393865	1346757
Philippines	182772	232810	292384	402398	540534
Nigeria/Nigéria	239836	358749	x262844	x272254	x138913
Colombia/Colombie	167108	115171	155158	510368	572658
Pakistan	173165	157596	201855	412961	174292
Yugoslavia SFR	611211	x684630			
Slovenia/Slovénia			191046	458545	431697
Czechoslovakia	64570	x122370	x524789		
Indonesia/Indonésie	356724	238100	169710	190652	85736
Qatar	135720	143274	211922	222237	x126879

EXPORTS – EXPORTATIONS

COUNTRIES–PAYS	1990	1991	1992	1993	1994
Totale	168504986	172305828	191112046	184856121	205571968
Afrique	x121841	x98774	x185490	x174696	x147421
Afrique du Nord	562	283	3673	x1381	x3785
Amériques	27888916	30622481	33999144	39243682	46507285
ALAI	3062209	4049297	4325750	5372949	6436260
MCAC	82	186	145	x866	x1136
Asie	43905032	47721017	52721005	54171916	51724983
Moyen–Orient	432806	391297	582242	x876826	x899823
Europe	94533438	91990769	102999733	89472195	105477330
CEE	93979844	91454512	102194250	88989619	104818910
AELE	155305	188754	212664	155641	137353
Océanie	x346391	x349720	x355526	x424233	x368349
Japan/Japon	41347654	44712595	48572489	47129690	44920662
Germany/Allemagne	41168678	36028957	43053181	35458589	42138784
Canada	14008319	14443872	14963893	19038560	23400509
Belgium–Luxembourg	13627860	13399313	14149290	14214186	16916114
USA/Etats–Unis d'Amer	10810813	12123164	14699105	14824306	16661996
France,Monac	13400099	13357568	14515742	12299040	13788094
Spain/Espagne	7454566	9586543	10816406	9883098	12270245
United Kingdom	5917458	7210084	7468024	6530277	7675195
Italy/Italie	6042286	5875047	5007879	4627711	5897328
Mexico/Mexique	2614144	3628069	3368308	4242481	5238426
Sweden/Suède	3190638	2940872	3429301	2986522	3407107
Korea, Republic of	1849004	2123890	2534117	3883985	4470416
Netherlands/Pays–Bas	1558009	1457551	1529139	1322026	1474521
Hong Kong	121876	238100	748893	1871222	1092303
Austria/Autriche	583021	500601	793446	892287	x543166
Brazil/Brésil	417303	338394	761477	597585	533979
Finland/Finlande	509272	590103	716395	245298	372145
Russian Federation			x818611	x555065	x343227
Australia/Australie	335848	340594	343879	405366	361140
Portugal	326633	238886	420797	335967	228589
Czechoslovakia		x497500	x425479		
Oman	82684	150139	339344	401329	417992
Former USSR/Anc. URSS	1431130	x862827			
Poland/Pologne	101077	39847	260411	553163	523728
Slovenia/Slovénia			447726	315308	513525
Czech Republic				599262	602483
Denmark/Danemark	167807	200671	231391	141791	96140
Switz.Liecht	150286	180075	197811	145626	128826
So. Africa Customs Un	83925	76970	158415	144097	133008
Malaysia/Malaisie	76259	83832	131152	157884	120366
Romania/Roumanie	140982	100474	112776	146532	104114
Argentina/Argentine	17693	59704	100463	185457	180897
Yugoslavia SFR	385131	x344418			
Saudi Arabia	94631	113210	68414	x74848	x58344
United Arab Emirates	148296			x250452	x266476
India/Inde	22648	66023	84502	89684	144693
Venezuela	3851	5705	38039	151017	205027
Turkey/Turquie	40392	57105	73036	48918	70801
Ireland/Irlande	30311	60981	58385	37871	
Yugoslavia/Yougoslavie			x133535	x2825	x584
Uruguay	7568	10872	22992	84658	166803
Thailand/Thaïlande	31680	68512	18061	30398	15379
China/Chine	7747	14309	25472	67797	20104
Kuwait/ Koweït	22048	17055	33390	44530	42363
Chile/Chili	1527	4962	24638	45630	29286
Hungary/Hongrie	x3743	x6191	x34777	x28288	x33657
Qatar	18922	26524	24357	13486	x575
Korea Dem People's Rp	x3571	x13374	x10047	x29620	x4974
Ecuador/Equateur	95	726	5548	42816	x64744
Jordan/Jordanie	7536	11084	20543	8554	13707

(VALUE AS % OF TOTAL)(VALEUR EN % DU TOTAL)

Imports

	1985	1986	1987	1988	1989	1990	1991	1992	1993	1994
Africa	1.1	x1.4	x1.4	x1.7	x1.5	x1.5	x1.5	x1.2	x1.4	x1.4
Northern Africa	0.4	0.3	0.2	0.4	0.3	0.3	0.3	x0.3	x0.3	x0.4
Americas	57.6	52.3	46.5	41.6	38.6	35.6	35.0	33.1	37.9	40.3
LAIA	0.9	0.9	0.8	0.8	0.6	0.6	1.1	2.1	2.6	3.4
CACM	0.1	x0.1	x0.2	x0.1	0.2	0.2	0.2	0.4	x0.2	x0.2
Asia	4.0	4.1	x5.5	x7.4	x7.1	8.0	8.4	9.8	x12.2	x10.9
Middle East	1.3	x1.7	x1.8	x2.0	x2.0	2.2	x2.9	x3.3	x3.4	x2.4
Europe	35.5	40.7	45.2	47.7	50.4	52.4	52.8	53.5	45.6	44.7
EEC	29.8	33.9	37.8	40.1	42.9	48.8	49.5	50.6	42.9	41.7
EFTA	5.5	6.6	7.1	7.3	7.3	3.1	2.8	2.6	2.3	2.6
Oceania	1.6	x1.4	x1.2	x1.3	x2.0	x1.6	x1.4	x1.5	x1.7	x2.0
USA/Etats–Unis d'Amer	46.6	42.9	38.0	33.5	30.6	28.8	27.3	25.1	29.4	31.1
Germany/Allemagne	5.2	6.7	7.5	7.2	7.3	10.3	13.8	12.5	9.5	9.0
Italy/Italie	4.4	4.5	5.6	5.7	6.5	7.6	7.8	8.8	5.5	5.3
France,Monac	4.5	4.9	5.7	5.8	6.7	7.6	6.7	7.1	6.4	6.3
United Kingdom	6.4	6.4	6.3	8.2	8.3	7.9	5.6	6.1	7.2	6.9
Canada	9.5	8.0	7.2	6.9	6.8	5.6	5.9	5.2	5.2	5.0
Belgium–Luxembourg	2.1	2.5	2.8	2.8	3.0	3.6	3.8	3.3	3.2	3.4
Spain/Espagne	0.5	0.8	1.6	2.3	2.5	2.7	2.6	3.5	2.9	2.7
Japan/Japon	0.6	1.0	1.5	2.1	2.7	3.7	3.0	2.6	2.8	3.5
Netherlands/Pays–Bas	2.1	2.8	2.9	2.2	2.4	2.7	2.9	2.6	2.7	2.6

Exports

	1985	1986	1987	1988	1989	1990	1991	1992	1993	1994
Afrique		x0.1	x0.0	x0.0	x0.0	x0.0	x0.0	x0.1	x0.1	x0.1
Afrique du Nord	0.0	x0.0	x0.0	x0.0	x0.0	0.0	0.0	0.0	x0.0	x0.0
Amériques	21.8	17.9	14.6	17.3	17.3	16.5	17.8	17.8	21.2	22.6
ALAI	0.8	0.6	0.8	1.0	1.4	1.8	2.4	2.3	2.9	3.1
MCAC	0.0	x0.0	x0.0	x0.0	x0.0	0.0	0.0	0.0	x0.0	x0.0
Asie	30.5	30.8	29.6	29.8	27.8	26.0	27.6	27.6	29.3	25.2
Moyen–Orient	0.2	0.1	x0.1	0.2	x0.2	0.3	0.2	0.3	x0.5	x0.4
Europe	46.8	50.1	54.3	51.6	53.5	56.1	53.4	53.9	48.4	51.3
CEE	43.7	47.0	51.1	48.7	50.9	55.8	53.1	53.5	48.1	51.0
AELE	2.9	2.9	3.0	2.6	2.5	0.1	0.1	0.1	0.1	0.1
Océanie	0.1	x0.1	x0.1	x0.1	x0.1	x0.2	x0.2	x0.2	x0.2	x0.2
Japan/Japon	29.6	29.4	27.2	27.0	26.1	24.5	25.9	25.4	25.5	21.9
Germany/Allemagne	22.3	23.8	25.3	23.2	23.8	24.4	20.9	22.5	19.2	20.5
Canada	13.8	11.5	8.2	9.9	9.1	8.3	8.4	7.8	10.3	11.4
Belgium–Luxembourg	5.7	6.6	7.3	6.8	6.9	8.1	7.8	7.4	7.7	8.2
USA/Etats–Unis d'Amer	7.2	5.8	5.6	6.4	6.8	6.4	7.0	7.7	8.0	8.1
France,Monac	5.9	6.2	6.5	6.8	7.2	8.0	7.8	7.6	6.7	6.7
Spain/Espagne	2.5	2.6	2.8	3.0	3.5	4.4	5.6	5.7	5.3	6.0
United Kingdom	2.0	1.8	2.5	2.5	2.9	3.5	4.2	3.9	3.5	3.7
Italy/Italie	1.9	2.5	2.8	2.8	3.2	3.6	3.4	2.6	2.5	2.9
Mexico/Mexique	0.1	0.3	0.0	0.4	0.9	1.6	2.1	1.8	2.3	2.5

TRADE BY COMMODITY IN THOUSAND U.S. DOLLARS – COMMERCE PAR PRODUIT EN MILLIERS DE DOLLARS E.U

COUNTRIES–PAYS	IMPORTS – IMPORTATIONS 1990	1991	1992	1993	1994
Total	36261150	36546420	40261215	36549640	41317103
Africa	x1786494	x1537555	x1881265	x1745131	x1999253
Northern Africa	534441	427615	x504695	x360660	x472638
Americas	11912356	12336104	13876819	14747771	15739740
LAIA	667003	1081920	1725404	1897686	2607347
CACM	27478	4875	3954	343978	362747
Asia	3824138	x5818787	x6822457	x7775456	x7319682
Middle East	1144299	x2535336	x2954375	x3136601	x2272016
Europe	16597767	15213618	15818882	10261831	13853616
EEC	15328600	14291577	14932984	9444505	12623263
EFTA	1143030	810840	758593	684142	957317
Oceania	x1334018	x1032153	x1207440	x1346404	x1779396
USA/Etats–Unis d'Amer	8741867	8526190	9878002	10020362	9673192
Germany/Allemagne	2521452	3911153	3682045	2158217	2639403
Canada	2187756	2448569	2014162	2243908	2813808
France,Monac	2717034	2489625	2256418	1444060	2409120
Italy/Italie	1924635	1807761	1759324	820712	1081844
Netherlands/Pays–Bas	1063049	1179054	1267475	783076	966798
Saudi Arabia	610675	923837	804367	x1367527	x937289
Belgium–Luxembourg	983772	1108306	932256	553806	619960
China/Chine	346759	376940	898208	1275005	1226720
Australia/Australie	988036	677946	893714	906930	1336366
United Kingdom	1528605	37450	1177065	1242792	1774255
Singapore/Singapour	661203	642301	783035	1005030	979237
Spain/Espagne	1066312	1022371	907296	384985	535964
Iran (Islamic Rp. of)		x931271	x887731	x370677	x68356
Austria/Autriche	763151	670150	759222	577106	663805
Portugal	565939	498259	706851	478977	620346
Denmark/Danemark	422329	486598	512268	363684	482897
Switz.Liecht	744326	495378	406419	336109	482208
Israel/Israël	181905	375541	351521	454025	588359
So. Africa Customs Un	391034	356770	368934	450570	563631
Chile/Chili	184490	225395	441610	428082	445103
Greece/Grèce	355523	353330	450420	258149	159521
Hong Kong	159883	217760	300913	439154	549119
Norway,SVD,JM	368629	277215	328489	333234	462901
Venezuela	106623	226681	392996	298150	168021
United Arab Emirates	172736	137676	215240	x383355	x369844
Sweden/Suède	534314	310095	206368	148860	267249
Turkey/Turquie	89908	117591	149293	398422	140972
Pakistan	135896	179111	217934	261778	114561
Korea, Republic of	209443	362554	193602	94716	133602
Thailand/Thaïlande	162070	228703	266573	149862	158964
Malaysia/Malaisie	242596	276928	182789	178626	253123
Russian Federation			x265921	x361304	x362632
Kuwait/ Koweït	52081	172075	270066	150623	152423
Mexico/Mexique	112802	158084	232104	162748	201961
Japan/Japon	179426	197555	149756	158307	237892
Finland/Finlande	604986	246082	152662	104166	199972
New Zealand	175780	132308	158448	206164	262222
Hungary/Hongrie	x67862	73133	x180761	x240271	x235505
Poland/Pologne	33445	157970	135468	188434	129424
Philippines	57423	112829	158367	191567	194245
Ireland/Irlande	277498	171342	163314	125916	202130
Argentina/Argentine	7857	37445	157115	264650	558680
Indonesia/Indonésie	182128	125118	144707	128134	239126
Brazil/Brésil	19725	86885	74903	202128	327977
Ecuador/Equateur	57640	100534	131668	130261	x214435
Syrian Arab Republic	8893	x36805	190361	x129411	x169018
Morocco/Maroc	108159	118814	133589	78541	102301
Nigeria/Nigéria	40382	60847	x117507	x138933	x79245
Zimbabwe	62605	149469	74554	56009	x61120

COUNTRIES–PAYS	EXPORTS – EXPORTATIONS 1990	1991	1992	1993	1994
Totale	38074260	39090830	41454565	37313955	41471036
Afrique	93508	81979	x86387	x75283	x111186
Afrique du Nord	10212	11105	x8445	x4377	x4734
Amériques	9884073	10985049	12684629	13184539	13471789
ALAI	495538	612777	1219145	1375136	1858181
MCAC	265	30	119	616	x537
Asie	8977072	9277036	10699052	10993909	11734619
Moyen–Orient	206541	122334	110939	x168583	x263975
Europe	17690175	18261418	17674949	12639664	15760180
CEE	17407765	17925349	17366437	12381144	15438206
AELE	241702	239461	259531	225692	287417
Océanie	41563	53635	43515	61698	x67211
Japan/Japon	8502105	8733588	9939187	9664115	9976244
Canada	6218810	6175993	7717915	7812921	7011676
Germany/Allemagne	5608498	5159095	5151080	3619405	4642561
USA/Etats–Unis d'Amer	3162535	4192232	3743053	3991094	4598984
Italy/Italie	1858268	2079707	1835930	1440211	2030404
France,Monac	1944934	2029630	1937708	1309250	1790255
Sweden/Suède	1876366	2099260	1782889	1217181	1429911
United Kingdom	1365767	1660601	1792659	1510580	1153983
Belgium–Luxembourg	1459109	1652075	1507163	1001898	1381443
Spain/Espagne	1094784	764907	921607	723351	1147516
Netherlands/Pays–Bas	1000468	1035497	835235	511857	777802
Austria/Autriche	574607	764075	874969	595577	x435014
Brazil/Brésil	455133	414465	600740	496327	617650
Mexico/Mexique	25211	168848	586839	669549	853853
Portugal	367700	395874	411214	199568	370881
Russian Federation			x434450	x428871	x105873
Hong Kong	63226	101283	210974	388142	560001
Korea, Republic of	40227	126736	142055	334423	507755
Switz.Liecht	156579	192181	189293	174564	214135
Singapore/Singapour	80697	94972	160173	218497	194845
Finland/Finlande	94456	110672	143868	139236	191260
Czechoslovakia		x191209	x169335		
Denmark/Danemark	131897	137110	130972	79027	80920
Czech Republic				261192	207296
So. Africa Customs Un	46628	53566	66280	57777	87326
Norway,SVD,JM	85123	47270	70061	50522	72997
Romania/Roumanie	20529	111928	19189	29540	24163
China/Chine	29075	30336	53896	64566	78810
Australia/Australie	28926	39949	36372	54096	63514
Saudi Arabia	106011	65417	45351	x15265	x54061
Argentina/Argentine	12715	5248	12244	98455	206958
Former USSR/Anc. URSS	1193719	x104534			
Ireland/Irlande	29841	35649	39118	25339	
Thailand/Thaïlande	13401	3769	15494	79146	78735
India/Inde	10899	40128	29390	26117	39745
Poland/Pologne	26221	8071	50320	33428	68404
Yugoslavia SFR	37624	x84027			
Kuwait/ Koweït	26568	10961	22110	34547	36377
Venezuela	1006	2122	6022	57797	96210
United Arab Emirates	30796			x62813	x102038
Chile/Chili	534	12477	8356	27616	47165
Qatar	8805	17485	20990	5525	x718
Slovenia/Slovénia			19747	17435	17465
Jordan/Jordanie	8029	14696	6176	14116	11946
Hungary/Hongrie	x18861	x12502	x15751	x5248	x5364
Malaysia/Malaisie	4551	7100	8413	12536	7060
Gibraltar	x1378	x12017	x3988	x11905	x7714
Slovakia				x25209	x19188
Israel/Israël	14359	8788	11690	4444	13814
Colombia/Colombie	314	9353	3982	9764	20119

(VALUE AS % OF TOTAL)(VALEUR EN % DU TOTAL)

	1985	1986	1987	1988	1989	1990	1991	1992	1993	1994
Africa	5.1	x5.9	x4.9	x5.7	x5.4	x4.9	x4.2	x4.7	x4.7	x4.9
Northern Africa	3.1	1.9	1.2	1.3	x1.2	1.5	1.2	x1.3	x1.0	x1.1
Americas	46.9	43.2	39.1	33.3	33.5	32.8	33.7	34.4	40.4	38.1
LAIA	1.7	1.7	1.9	2.1	1.7	1.8	3.0	4.3	5.2	6.3
CACM	0.4	0.4	x0.4	1.2	0.0	0.1	0.0	0.0	0.9	0.9
Asia	15.3	x11.4	x10.0	x10.0	8.7	10.5	x16.0	x16.9	x21.3	x17.7
Middle East	5.6	x4.7	x4.6	x4.1	x3.0	3.2	x6.9	x7.3	x8.6	x5.5
Europe	26.9	34.4	39.5	43.8	45.1	45.8	41.6	39.3	28.1	33.5
EEC	20.8	26.9	31.5	35.8	37.4	42.3	39.1	37.1	25.8	30.6
EFTA	5.7	7.1	7.7	7.6	7.4	3.2	2.2	1.9	1.9	2.3
Oceania	5.1	x3.0	x2.4	x3.1	x4.1	x3.7	x2.8	x3.0	x3.6	x4.3
USA/Etats–Unis d'Amer	34.6	31.7	27.1	22.3	24.7	24.1	23.3	24.5	27.4	23.4
Germany/Allemagne	2.2	3.0	3.4	3.8	4.1	7.0	10.7	9.1	5.9	6.4
Canada	8.9	8.3	8.4	6.5	5.9	6.0	6.7	5.0	6.1	6.8
France,Monac	4.1	5.2	6.1	6.3	6.5	7.5	6.8	5.6	4.0	5.8
Italy/Italie	2.6	3.5	4.4	4.9	4.8	5.3	4.9	4.4	2.2	2.6
Netherlands/Pays–Bas	1.7	2.4	2.8	2.4	2.4	2.9	3.2	3.1	2.1	2.3
Saudi Arabia	3.4	1.4	1.5	1.8	1.3	1.7	2.5	2.0	x3.7	x2.3
Belgium–Luxembourg	1.3	2.0	2.1	2.3	2.4	2.7	3.0	2.3	1.5	1.5
China/Chine	5.6	4.1	1.7	1.2	1.0	1.0	1.0	2.2	3.5	3.0
Australia/Australie	4.3	2.2	1.7	2.3	3.1	2.7	1.9	2.2	2.5	3.2

	1985	1986	1987	1988	1989	1990	1991	1992	1993	1994
Afrique	0.1	x0.0	0.1	0.3	0.2	0.2	0.2	x0.2	x0.2	x0.3
Afrique du Nord	0.0	x0.0	0.0	0.0	0.0	0.0	0.0	x0.0	x0.0	x0.0
Amériques	28.6	22.8	27.3	25.5	25.7	25.9	28.1	30.6	35.3	32.5
ALAI	1.6	1.2	5.4	3.9	2.1	1.3	1.6	2.9	3.7	4.5
MCAC		x0.0	x0.0	x0.0	x0.0	0.0	0.0	0.0	0.0	x0.0
Asie	33.6	x32.4	25.3	24.5	23.5	23.6	23.8	25.8	29.5	28.3
Moyen–Orient	0.7	x0.2	x0.3	0.6	0.5	0.5	0.3	0.3	x0.5	x0.6
Europe	32.2	38.6	39.4	43.0	46.8	46.5	46.7	42.6	33.9	38.0
CEE	26.8	32.2	32.9	36.2	39.6	45.7	45.9	41.9	33.2	37.2
AELE	5.3	6.2	6.5	6.7	7.1	0.6	0.6	0.6	0.6	0.7
Océanie	0.1	x0.0	x0.1	x0.1	0.1	0.1	0.1	0.1	0.2	x0.2
Japan/Japon	31.8	31.8	24.6	23.4	22.4	22.3	22.3	24.0	25.9	24.1
Canada	18.0	13.9	14.0	14.1	15.0	16.3	15.8	18.6	20.9	16.9
Germany/Allemagne	9.4	11.5	12.0	12.3	13.4	14.7	13.2	12.4	9.7	11.2
USA/Etats–Unis d'Amer	9.0	7.7	7.8	7.5	8.6	8.3	10.7	9.0	10.7	11.1
Italy/Italie	3.0	3.4	3.5	3.4	3.7	4.9	5.3	4.4	3.9	4.9
France,Monac	3.6	3.9	3.4	3.6	4.2	5.1	5.2	4.7	3.5	4.3
Sweden/Suède	3.8	4.6	5.0	4.9	5.2	4.9	5.4	4.3	3.3	3.4
United Kingdom	1.9	1.7	1.9	2.1	4.2	3.6	4.2	4.3	4.0	2.8
Belgium–Luxembourg	1.9	3.0	2.6	3.6	3.9	3.8	4.2	3.6	2.7	3.3
Spain/Espagne	1.0	1.1	1.3	2.2	2.2	2.9	2.0	2.2	1.9	2.8

TRADE BY COMMODITY IN THOUSAND U.S. DOLLARS – COMMERCE PAR PRODUIT EN MILLIERS DE DOLLARS E.U

COUNTRIES–PAYS	IMPORTS – IMPORTATIONS 1990	1991	1992	1993	1994
Total	7787004	7577466	8858600	8254037	11328264
Africa	x630271	x487471	x555041	x513719	x570064
Northern Africa	219027	132310	x187770	x156999	212019
Americas	1403030	1309784	2032945	2745305	4055881
LAIA	275553	290143	793568	827141	942638
CACM	8109			x85565	x99011
Asia	719985	x1182943	x1617582	x1807258	x2377198
Middle East	244132	x597405	x883546	x708875	x735234
Europe	3912665	4148025	4258362	2791318	3844072
EEC	3604308	3897517	3964325	2535420	3517472
EFTA	243376	222981	255139	184481	206656
Oceania	x101534	x85453	x92098	x149887	x218612
France, Monac	989367	1068599	1106021	626798	1001833
USA/Etats–Unis d'Amer	655016	598735	637434	953076	1771187
Germany/Allemagne	294001	581332	665111	420894	638074
Canada	373185	305573	444656	719233	1066935
Belgium–Luxembourg	452387	583415	342009	352029	430861
Italy/Italie	447233	353600	395051	233914	322831
Netherlands/Pays–Bas	317765	358914	353409	157692	156650
Spain/Espagne	309539	314666	290117	114614	170724
Iran (Islamic Rp. of)		x261143	x388960	x42641	x1346
Hong Kong	81825	140109	245770	271524	549442
United Kingdom	209264	132225	213746	244945	355481
Austria/Autriche	173395	157515	220009	194088	219744
Saudi Arabia	109732	106065	107836	x265399	x334371
Mexico/Mexique	56084	61601	240503	176897	160231
China/Chine	65218	80536	121696	195007	550489
Switz.Liecht	136064	130449	126819	108106	133577
Pakistan	31902	47349	75905	237502	13767
Chile/Chili	59027	79607	123457	139888	141854
Peru/Pérou	43030	41365	189625	104349	131002
Russian Federation			x137027	x160229	x203460
Norway, SVD, JM	103449	88223	121006	73784	70530
Colombia/Colombie	60069	15512	55570	205934	104099
Turkey/Turquie	40869	85271	96770	88534	39043
So. Africa Customs Un	205174	104684	78796	74627	105177
Czechoslovakia	16962	x65060	x168314		
Sweden/Suède	111832	100482	81155	51244	54315
Panama	30694	56512	78492	93046	101343
Portugal	97016	89341	108423	28711	28189
Greece/Grèce	88148	82697	96574	43882	33015
Australia/Australie	76849	50342	63503	99642	161887
Poland/Pologne	25863	81596	45379	68517	66819
Syrian Arab Republic	11543	x16296	99447	x74064	x49690
Nigeria/Nigéria		45952	x59922	x72583	x20608
Venezuela	15412	16507	92227	62753	17911
United Arab Emirates	22335	25507	34994	x100145	x143194
Algeria/Algérie	69953	46822	62020	41007	48235
Singapore/Singapour	40225	32462	45297	71766	55131
Ukraine			x23810	x125110	x41899
Kuwait/Koweït	21506	53353	38242	48715	42584
Egypt/Egypte	57942	26479	48546	54547	97937
Malaysia/Malaisie	30429	47129	45731	36358	34603
Denmark/Danemark	34578	35432	49844	42117	53167
Israel/Israël	25855	35458	34129	50033	77139
Hungary/Hongrie	x22417	38444	x43159	x36873	x37790
Sri Lanka	21583	52515	37903	16030	36404
Bulgaria/Bulgarie	x33407	x42364	27064	x35291	x36292
Romania/Roumanie	15624	36999	14695	48803	29804
Former USSR/Anc. URSS	903528	x98531			
Uzbekistan/Ouzbékistan			x6933	x88230	x55648
Ireland/Irlande	60269	33034	40767	20764	49085

COUNTRIES–PAYS	EXPORTS – EXPORTATIONS 1990	1991	1992	1993	1994
Totale	6706609	7736052	9315027	9045889	12073497
Afrique	14585	22073	x13552	x23028	x3311
Afrique du Nord	2758	6308	1974	x5406	x1970
Amériques	1222982	1299854	1883026	2463166	3478812
ALAI	93177	147560	323800	421044	398226
MCAC				x123	x787
Asie	818250	1190186	1989660	2156056	2662859
Moyen–Orient	40935	52575	92016	x170520	x334665
Europe	4504704	5114080	5331813	4308972	5857867
CEE	4431545	5077347	5233784	4207681	5797558
AELE	35529	28072	57476	49933	37965
Océanie	x4859	2109	6590	x7808	x11819
Germany/Allemagne	1393974	1504153	1864489	1695159	2281475
Japan/Japon	667792	981566	1570344	1536922	1563667
Belgium–Luxembourg	767298	972597	847495	875394	999466
USA/Etats–Unis d'Amer	568641	613769	945580	1125237	1357538
Netherlands/Pays–Bas	1071249	1048565	943622	558451	865097
Canada	560110	538092	611601	915708	1720465
France, Monac	471760	648966	629455	416609	839433
Italy/Italie	324280	330682	426121	139994	108591
Brazil/Brésil	75098	133765	297021	382587	327469
Spain/Espagne	71032	142108	181621	199776	344662
Korea, Republic of	21545	50891	160836	256072	279057
United Kingdom	97336	137001	88451	55398	78612
Hong Kong	28766	42330	72496	130222	389749
Austria/Autriche	56788	63373	75020	80169	x71655
Finland/Finlande	47816	56715	66571	71295	88222
Sweden/Suède	78359	101145	36490	42355	66164
Turkey/Turquie	20394	26211	49991	89317	119006
Hungary/Hongrie	x101553	x69975	x59046	x27775	x8930
India/Inde	36928	43011	58618	20335	45580
Denmark/Danemark	22722	32960	40916	40190	26245
Switz.Liecht	28714	21422	45623	44443	36220
Portugal	25440	34161	25785	25428	24315
Slovenia/Slovénia			35205	38600	14709
Singapore/Singapour	8263	10231	21948	27402	36497
Czech Republic				49731	41483
Oman	707	4260	17700	17381	43289
Russian Federation			x15713	x23533	x16712
So. Africa Customs Un	3994	11475	9718	13080	
United Arab Emirates	509			x27248	x91900
Venezuela	531	3134	6552	16917	27469
Mexico/Mexique	6792	4091	11258	9942	17720
Czechoslovakia		x12397	x12810		
China/Chine	9259	6999	8109	9941	8526
Norway, SVD, JM	6815	6650	11853	5490	1745
Latvia/Lettonie			x741	x21799	31517
Poland/Pologne	4592	2228	13605	6373	6958
Former USSR/Anc. URSS	31838	x21842			
Kuwait/Koweït	2257	6025	4520	10317	15397
Jordan/Jordanie	375	2139	3684	14518	29648
Saudi Arabia	13244	7466	3904	x4834	x16550
Yugoslavia/Yougoslavie			x4598	x10110	x4786
Australia/Australie	4603	1663	6198	6670	11483
Iran (Islamic Rp. of)		x2700	x8378	x2509	x2881
Greece/Grèce	402	1619	4734	5573	3619
Argentina/Argentine	9494	4163	4304	1993	9364
Chile/Chili	467	1519	2684	5352	6955
Ireland/Irlande	3088	3303	3013	1889	
Yugoslavia SFR	37347	x7851			
Algeria/Algérie	2051	5563	709		
Romania/Roumanie	2923	642	2723	2435	751

(VALUE AS % OF TOTAL)(VALEUR EN % DU TOTAL)

	1985	1986	1987	1988	1989	1990	1991	1992	1993	1994
Africa	8.0	x9.1	x7.6	x6.1	x6.6	x8.1	x6.5	x6.3	x6.2	x5.0
Northern Africa	3.5	2.1	1.3	1.4	1.7	2.8	1.7	x2.1	x1.9	1.9
Americas	16.1	17.3	18.9	18.6	16.6	18.0	17.3	22.9	33.3	35.8
LAIA	4.3	3.6	4.0	3.1	2.4	3.5	3.8	9.0	10.0	8.3
CACM	0.3	1.3	x1.4	x0.3	x0.2	0.1			x1.0	x0.9
Asia	35.7	x7.9	x7.8	21.9	20.7	9.3	x15.6	x18.3	x21.9	x21.0
Middle East	24.2	x3.5	x2.8	16.2	16.1	3.1	x7.9	x10.0	x8.6	x6.5
Europe	27.3	46.4	47.6	39.8	43.4	50.2	54.7	48.1	33.8	33.9
EEC	22.6	38.9	40.4	34.1	38.0	46.3	51.4	44.8	30.7	31.1
EFTA	3.8	6.2	6.4	5.3	5.0	3.1	2.9	2.9	2.2	1.8
Oceania	1.6	x1.8	x1.1	x1.0	x1.1	x1.3	x1.1	x1.0	x1.8	x2.0
France, Monac	6.4	11.8	11.9	9.3	10.6	12.7	14.1	12.5	7.6	8.8
USA/Etats–Unis d'Amer	9.4	9.8	11.6	7.8	7.5	8.4	7.9	7.2	11.5	15.6
Germany/Allemagne	1.2	1.9	2.1	1.4	1.7	3.8	7.7	7.5	5.1	5.6
Canada	0.0	0.0	0.1	6.0	4.8	4.8	4.0	5.0	8.7	9.4
Belgium–Luxembourg	1.4	3.2	4.4	3.1	4.6	5.8	7.7	3.9	4.3	3.8
Italy/Italie	1.9	3.9	3.5	3.5	4.2	5.7	4.7	4.5	2.8	2.8
Netherlands/Pays–Bas	1.9	3.2	3.2	2.7	2.7	4.1	4.7	4.0	1.9	1.4
Spain/Espagne	0.7	2.1	4.2	4.8	4.2	4.0	4.2	3.3	1.4	1.5
Iran (Islamic Rp. of)		x0.0	x0.0	x0.0	x0.0		x3.4	x4.4	x0.5	x0.0
Hong Kong	1.4	0.4	0.8	1.4	0.9	1.1	1.8	2.8	3.3	4.9

	1985	1986	1987	1988	1989	1990	1991	1992	1993	1994
Afrique	0.1	x0.1	x0.1	0.1	0.5	0.3	0.2	x0.1	x0.2	x0.0
Afrique du Nord	0.0	x0.0	0.1	0.1	0.3	0.0	0.1	0.0	x0.1	x0.0
Amériques	10.4	10.7	15.0	28.8	23.0	18.2	16.8	20.2	27.3	28.8
ALAI	1.8	1.2	1.6	5.3	4.1	1.4	1.9	3.5	4.7	3.3
MCAC	0.0	x0.0	x0.0	x0.0	x0.0				x0.0	x0.0
Asie	28.8	12.8	12.0	13.8	12.1	12.2	15.4	21.4	23.8	22.1
Moyen–Orient	3.7	x1.1	x0.5	1.4	1.4	0.6	0.7	1.0	x1.9	x2.8
Europe	58.1	72.4	69.2	53.8	60.8	67.2	66.1	57.2	47.6	48.5
CEE	53.8	66.7	65.2	50.4	57.7	66.1	65.6	56.2	46.5	48.0
AELE	2.8	3.6	3.3	2.6	2.4	0.5	0.4	0.6	0.6	0.3
Océanie		x0.0	x0.1	x0.2	x0.1	x0.1		0.1	x0.1	x0.1
Germany/Allemagne	23.1	26.4	25.1	19.5	21.8	20.8	19.4	20.0	18.7	18.9
Japan/Japon	22.0	10.6	10.3	10.8	9.5	10.0	12.7	16.9	17.0	13.0
Belgium–Luxembourg	4.7	7.2	9.7	7.1	8.9	11.4	12.6	9.1	9.7	8.3
USA/Etats–Unis d'Amer	5.6	6.5	10.3	7.6	6.7	8.5	7.9	10.2	12.4	11.2
Netherlands/Pays–Bas	9.8	14.9	14.9	11.6	13.8	16.0	13.6	10.1	6.2	7.2
Canada	3.0	3.0	3.0	16.0	12.3	8.4	7.0	6.6	10.1	14.2
France, Monac	5.0	6.7	5.2	4.9	5.4	7.0	8.4	6.8	4.6	7.0
Italy/Italie	5.5	6.2	4.8	3.2	3.5	4.8	4.3	4.6	1.5	0.9
Brazil/Brésil	1.6	1.0	1.5	2.1	1.5	1.1	1.7	3.2	4.2	2.7
Spain/Espagne	0.8	0.7	0.8	0.6	0.6	1.1	1.8	1.9	2.2	2.9

TRADE BY COMMODITY IN THOUSAND U.S. DOLLARS – COMMERCE PAR PRODUIT EN MILLIERS DE DOLLARS E.U

COUNTRIES–PAYS	IMPORTS – IMPORTATIONS 1990	1991	1992	1993	1994
Total	80599315	78142822	89551757	89599517	96556250
Africa	x1931660	x1647527	x1907982	x1861810	x2321434
Northern Africa	818296	578568	x584482	x555276	x687149
Americas	30643440	26742826	36488145	41034293	38898126
LAIA	3986109	1729954	9042077	9941240	4233034
CACM	64784	64153	81143	x106777	x110021
Asia	10226659	12237699	x9234391	x9605690	10749566
Middle East	1616475	x2746590	x3320628	x2441374	x1715686
Europe	34703994	36119407	40437686	35139425	42200837
EEC	33528492	34744133	39111419	34155936	41076924
EFTA	768137	752545	810863	716181	771744
Oceania	963123	x805539	x890660	x1129637	x1387153
USA/Etats–Unis d'Amer	16604051	15264501	16729192	18650207	20707598
Canada	9742850	9457764	10417945	12129745	13614798
Germany/Allemagne	7260876	8590591	9776769	8233266	10654583
United Kingdom	6737682	6457130	7499504	7283119	7573272
Mexico/Mexique	3029536	511211	6991639	7480483	1441450
France, Monac	4223043	4221956	4735608	3841517	4586820
Spain/Espagne	2791339	3058565	3646445	3739087	4836986
Belgium–Luxembourg	3249492	3175288	3480968	3525140	4335915
Italy/Italie	2434816	2545012	2625621	1750589	1994892
China/Chine	3485268	4686835	908771	999755	740153
Netherlands/Pays–Bas	2055942	1908673	2017194	1408931	1907691
Sweden/Suède	1503967	1429335	1482657	1282089	1716744
Thailand/Thaïlande	1567661	1110160	1036454	1545208	1973512
Austria/Autriche	816032	978710	1177367	1047973	1263692
Portugal	1025840	1069275	1198116	886712	825309
Iran (Islamic Rp. of)		x1251220	x1248466	x556004	x141405
Japan/Japon	776949	933323	1053957	1046475	1136821
Australia/Australie	784348	672783	785352	989466	1244018
Korea, Republic of	484005	625717	674879	774346	1118234
So. Africa Customs Un	448878	537686	683253	674491	1001929
Indonesia/Indonésie	660730	695707	479814	701969	1532541
Argentina/Argentine	145025	259904	720059	876185	968052
Brazil/Brésil	387525	421746	539126	828827	1163583
Singapore/Singapour	592443	488663	547547	637356	759285
Turkey/Turquie	358645	393887	571397	694113	424884
Saudi Arabia	661644	532189	691904	x418716	x385510
Switz.Liecht	506241	503151	529246	455339	451922
Finland/Finlande	643898	558470	604337	323683	474121
Hong Kong	219942	310536	523366	539279	719410
Greece/Grèce	329632	304970	378825	391213	365193
Denmark/Danemark	280320	297364	330896	314302	375327
Venezuela	93378	189577	406983	283203	90652
Norway,SVD,JM	249408	234721	267134	249589	308932
Yugoslavia SFR	383185	x597776			
Nigeria/Nigéria	242025	193096	x173158	x211717	x127652
Poland/Pologne	120122	106148	162739	263293	360790
India/Inde	240466	146855	185886	183468	244108
United Arab Emirates	209982	154156	177869	x176142	x198103
Israel/Israël	139860	145114	175851	181649	172450
Libyan Arab Jamahiriya	227127	185317	x162599	x144025	x173793
Hungary/Hongrie	x106658	85785	x186519	x206085	x258754
Malaysia/Malaisie	125216	139604	138298	172382	230781
Ireland/Irlande	175612	148795	157111	128315	166379
Oman	95357	111675	148153	159209	158990
Kuwait/Koweït	92668	80589	174216	162302	154120
Chile/Chili	99327	110607	143908	160866	154045
Egypt/Egypte	175242	115606	144150	154391	228101
Slovenia/Slovénia			219552	188807	234997
Philippines	192091	72448	91248	187323	202905
Algeria/Algérie	233160	121880	106023	102094	129619

COUNTRIES–PAYS	EXPORTS – EXPORTATIONS 1990	1991	1992	1993	1994
Totale	84174074	84126043	91016998	89852120	104046929
Afrique	169443	x244982	324911	327947	279254
Afrique du Nord	48852	53199	48196	33393	38243
Amériques	22422400	21648051	26258055	30503509	34006006
ALAI	1239610	1411118	2994206	3797959	4391950
MCAC	1129	715	518	x884	4647
Asie	15683695	17003413	14386448	17558085	20909247
Moyen–Orient	210390	129674	181108	239932	281757
Europe	43471789	44454634	49367563	40543086	47880790
CEE	42728146	43801292	48600881	39893113	47201844
AELE	424633	456059	519737	424288	535956
Océanie	x221906	x268585	x282364	x293054	x323195
Germany/Allemagne	16822292	17344248	19437731	16195065	17576079
USA/Etats–Unis d'Amer	14981853	14799129	17037526	19710968	22106129
Japan/Japon	11288466	11652923	12900313	15326026	18118393
France, Monac	8023071	8124911	9393866	7929908	9293339
Canada	6194344	5432640	6219808	6989782	7500234
United Kingdom	5160483	5472562	5640450	3636566	4547046
Italy/Italie	4132138	4138261	4463661	3878585	4429020
Spain/Espagne	2282082	2465060	2831807	2284558	3005309
Sweden/Suède	2132867	2009654	1967275	1850709	3053006
Belgium–Luxembourg	1901752	1857259	2054073	1697412	2041326
China/Chine	3432438	4348081	125963	177723	250528
Mexico/Mexique	416801	498120	1602837	2013789	2328756
Netherlands/Pays–Bas	937992	952432	1117944	931757	1236578
Brazil/Brésil	593900	665709	1011527	1239536	1423802
Austria/Autriche	680958	765128	933109	802999	x1234613
Hong Kong	82802	129573	339021	621570	553372
Korea, Republic of	246602	270968	310265	385061	500839
Denmark/Danemark	253339	262941	314052	306311	372047
Switz.Liecht	219788	262127	308435	237586	285194
Argentina/Argentine	132501	143274	231873	369747	456722
Portugal	221362	242336	281841	216175	238882
Australia/Australie	186652	238636	243747	249150	278362
So. Africa Customs Un	104102	170352	271324	288797	236631
Singapore/Singapour	204473	213805	195609	241933	287536
Norway,SVD,JM	204844	193925	211282	186694	250740
Hungary/Hongrie	x186271	x121146	x174343	x191254	x232488
India/Inde	120483	133730	157361	185162	251370
Finland/Finlande	120363	102536	99214	101957	159780
Slovenia/Slovénia			158084	126456	117622
Thailand/Thaïlande	34975	43237	49978	183115	382894
Turkey/Turquie	61182	56652	86442	90664	116800
Czechoslovakia		x133507	x96424		
Venezuela	64300	57298	71968	92245	85485
Poland/Pologne	209319	96506	63170	47941	62751
Yugoslavia SFR	318763	x196945			
Czech Republic				178995	215361
Philippines	20849	27146	54155	96232	165692
Oman	32326	41171	53081	82716	94508
Ireland/Irlande	54488	57055	58916	48512	
Russian Federation			x73561	x88470	x55175
Slovakia				x159396	x112740
Romania/Roumanie	240116	34992	47256	29113	19956
Former USSR/Anc. URSS	1404273	x109289			
New Zealand	33462	29409	38215	40690	44134
Chile/Chili	15428	23382	38941	45762	54970
Malaysia/Malaisie	18476	17863	25473	45937	63779
Croatia/Croatie			30571	50638	x11510
Morocco/Maroc	25122	26376	23168	17067	18322
Yugoslavia/Yougoslavie			x56608	x8493	x3587
Indonesia/Indonésie	6474	13217	22450	24880	34353

(VALUE AS % OF TOTAL)(VALEUR EN % DU TOTAL)

	1985	1986	1987	1988	1989	1990	1991	1992	1993	1994
Africa	3.4	x2.8	x2.5	x2.7	x2.2	x2.4	x2.1	x2.2	x2.1	x2.4
Northern Africa	1.8	1.3	1.1	1.0	0.8	1.0	0.7	x0.7	x0.6	x0.7
Americas	51.7	44.7	39.3	40.6	38.8	38.0	34.2	40.7	45.8	40.2
LAIA	3.2	2.3	3.0	3.0	1.8	4.9	2.2	10.1	11.1	4.4
CACM	0.2	0.1	x0.1	0.1	0.1	0.1	0.1	0.1	x0.1	x0.1
Asia	6.1	x7.1	x9.6	x11.2	11.2	12.7	15.7	x10.3	x10.8	11.2
Middle East	2.1	x2.7	x2.4	x2.8	x2.2	2.0	x3.5	x3.7	x2.7	x1.8
Europe	33.6	40.0	42.7	39.4	42.1	43.1	46.2	45.2	39.2	43.7
EEC	29.6	35.4	38.0	34.7	37.2	41.6	44.5	43.7	38.1	42.5
EFTA	3.6	4.2	4.3	4.3	4.4	1.0	1.0	0.9	0.8	0.8
Oceania	1.2	x1.1	x0.9	1.0	1.4	1.2	x1.1	x1.0	x1.3	x1.4
USA/Etats–Unis d'Amer	23.7	22.4	20.5	22.5	22.8	20.6	19.5	18.7	20.8	21.4
Canada	24.0	19.3	15.3	14.6	13.6	12.1	12.1	11.6	13.5	14.1
Germany/Allemagne	4.8	5.7	5.9	6.8	7.4	9.0	11.0	10.9	9.2	11.0
United Kingdom	4.8	5.4	6.1	6.9	7.6	8.4	8.3	8.4	8.1	7.8
Mexico/Mexique	1.6	0.5	1.5	1.5	0.5	3.8	0.7	7.8	8.3	1.5
France, Monac	3.5	4.1	4.4	4.6	4.7	5.2	5.4	5.3	4.3	4.8
Spain/Espagne	1.7	2.2	2.7	2.8	3.2	3.5	3.9	4.1	4.2	5.0
Belgium–Luxembourg	7.5	8.8	9.2	3.5	3.5	4.0	4.1	3.9	3.9	4.5
Italy/Italie	2.0	2.2	2.4	2.7	2.9	3.0	3.3	2.9	2.0	2.1
China/Chine	0.7	0.6	2.7	3.4	3.7	4.3	6.0	1.0	1.1	0.8

	1985	1986	1987	1988	1989	1990	1991	1992	1993	1994
Afrique	0.1	0.2	0.1	0.2	x0.2	0.2	x0.3	0.4	0.3	0.2
Afrique du Nord	0.0	0.0	0.1	0.1	0.1	0.1	0.1	0.1	0.0	0.0
Amériques	41.1	32.0	27.7	27.5	26.6	26.7	25.7	28.9	33.9	32.7
ALAI	1.7	1.3	1.5	1.6	1.7	1.5	1.7	3.3	4.2	4.2
MCAC	0.0	0.0	0.0	0.0	0.0	0.0	0.0	0.0	x0.0	0.0
Asie	12.9	16.3	x18.8	16.8	18.5	18.6	20.2	15.8	19.6	20.1
Moyen–Orient	0.2	0.1	x0.2	0.2	0.2	0.2	0.2	0.2	0.3	0.3
Europe	42.2	47.5	47.4	49.9	51.3	51.6	52.8	54.2	45.1	46.0
CEE	38.4	43.2	43.3	45.5	47.0	50.8	52.1	53.4	44.4	45.4
AELE	3.3	3.8	3.8	4.1	3.9	0.5	0.5	0.6	0.5	0.5
Océanie	0.2	x0.2	x0.3	x0.2	x0.3	x0.3	x0.3	x0.3	x0.3	x0.3
Germany/Allemagne	14.5	16.8	16.7	18.4	18.7	20.0	20.6	21.4	18.0	16.9
USA/Etats–Unis d'Amer	24.3	18.0	15.7	17.3	16.1	17.8	17.6	18.7	21.9	21.2
Japan/Japon	12.0	15.5	15.4	12.6	13.9	13.4	13.9	14.2	17.1	17.4
France, Monac	7.3	8.6	8.9	7.9	8.0	9.5	9.7	10.3	8.8	8.9
Canada	15.0	12.7	10.5	8.6	8.8	7.4	6.5	6.8	7.8	7.2
United Kingdom	5.8	5.6	5.3	5.4	5.6	6.1	6.5	6.2	4.0	4.4
Italy/Italie	3.8	4.1	4.0	4.4	4.9	4.9	4.9	4.9	4.3	4.3
Spain/Espagne	1.5	1.8	1.8	2.2	2.5	2.7	2.9	3.1	2.5	2.9
Sweden/Suède	2.3	2.5	2.5	2.8	2.6	2.5	2.4	2.2	2.1	2.9
Belgium–Luxembourg	1.7	1.9	1.9	2.1	2.2	2.3	2.2	2.3	1.9	2.0

TRADE BY COMMODITY IN THOUSAND U.S. DOLLARS – COMMERCE PAR PRODUIT EN MILLIERS DE DOLLARS E.U

COUNTRIES–PAYS	IMPORTS – IMPORTATIONS 1990	1991	1992	1993	1994
Total	9823803	11471184	13345993	14596360	15138447
Africa	x179727	x220155	x315653	x310747	x255067
Northern Africa	44072	51835	52076	44727	45644
Americas	1867921	x2184571	2699076	2999622	3089883
LAIA	175896	329806	620584	720564	758107
CACM	29415	32230	48233	x49933	x45377
Asia	1560638	2262182	2835200	4061520	4625774
Middle East	85145	x237496	x227875	x179060	x120275
Europe	5797499	6520060	7205422	6840544	6726712
EEC	5324320	6052880	6731036	6399023	6253509
EFTA	430557	430662	441960	412285	439219
Oceania	x210174	x216345	x209351	x251725	x294284
Germany/Allemagne	1230849	1576238	1825056	1874047	1796523
USA/Etats–Unis d'Amer	1300112	1456206	1671549	1882820	1937777
France,Monac	914845	1042587	1091799	1048513	1006039
Hong Kong	341810	635657	1023632	1440637	1634067
Italy/Italie	578273	679956	817407	698987	676265
Netherlands/Pays–Bas	463335	547276	575660	621585	591880
United Kingdom	642291	564163	562427	573974	597923
Spain/Espagne	487645	521135	671225	455231	380739
Japan/Japon	223181	298416	309596	385948	496297
Switz.Liecht	342659	333223	338624	317072	321985
China/Chine	64433	163704	169495	552745	586975
Belgium–Luxembourg	227866	282351	286548	310658	315681
Canada	245543	247385	266246	265398	273686
Singapore/Singapour	182178	150831	259171	345698	274402
Austria/Autriche	215960	243058	257732	245974	309863
Indonesia/Indonésie	177567	217284	208094	270297	403476
Argentina/Argentine	10395	99942	269745	268500	225825
Thailand/Thaïlande	132242	164635	192339	246205	289380
Australia/Australie	164533	162788	165859	196892	238483
Sweden/Suède	149234	162974	164339	128793	152612
Portugal	73714	111644	167685	152757	120481
Mexico/Mexique	75183	97114	164692	136929	152815
Malaysia/Malaisie	66896	93754	133211	164269	149673
Greece/Grèce	114507	107405	121175	118869	112468
Denmark/Danemark	104442	103707	100641	104571	119542
Norway,SVD,JM	84825	93641	99805	92599	114630
Iran (Islamic Rp. of)		x116221	x85660	x38973	x24141
Brazil/Brésil	24216	36789	44341	136109	194623
Philippines	45311	38648	57729	89638	112559
Turkey/Turquie	28629	47083	50994	74290	31677
Finland/Finlande	85951	74167	54143	37759	49065
Pakistan	42386	50787	54478	58984	47573
Cuba	x27132	x79459	x47973	x31684	x7419
Nigeria/Nigéria		30790	x45876	x63296	x30156
Korea, Republic of	42296	45790	46988	44766	63198
So. Africa Customs Un	24866	37987	38273	42514	44906
Viet Nam	x22922	x8120	x13920	x92934	x126238
New Zealand	36960	37817	36776	38955	41041
Sri Lanka	45993	41962	31108	33676	40896
Ireland/Irlande	35408	36219	35198	27305	24427
Venezuela	9243	17175	36654	37787	14207
Burkina Faso	x20154		x49088	x30696	x6042
Hungary/Hongrie	x21556	29444	x23416	x26804	x25684
Chile/Chili	11012	17802	26170	35316	31265
Israel/Israël	17710	20494	27347	30611	40315
United Arab Emirates	18410	22199	26537	x19187	x20570
Colombia/Colombie	25366	26654	16564	23463	27781
Saudi Arabia	18824	23466	27717	x12990	x12013
Poland/Pologne	12055	14256	23479	21920	52296
Peru/Pérou	3610	9496	24927	23986	36021

COUNTRIES–PAYS	EXPORTS – EXPORTATIONS 1990	1991	1992	1993	1994
Totale	8547624	9990205	11899653	13705514	13736556
Afrique	13659	x8074	x10670	x10208	x4330
Afrique du Nord	2173	1987	x4613	3603	2870
Amériques	599275	836786	954133	986438	946355
ALAI	37235	32329	110619	103021	81425
MCAC	1075	1222	1083	1060	2003
Asie	4683120	5958906	7472119	9306734	8975011
Moyen–Orient	9536	2602	x4757	x11442	x12059
Europe	3101780	3074070	3381514	3295705	3687834
CEE	2990106	2967184	3258708	3188547	3573498
AELE	84710	81872	91072	83154	88337
Océanie	x9152	x9297	x14318	x20388	x19567
Japan/Japon	3612086	4342488	5135602	6056872	5509562
Italy/Italie	1051435	1008905	1138121	1234931	1553455
Hong Kong	312029	569424	834213	1211170	1223239
USA/Etats–Unis d'Amer	526159	759804	803419	838740	817838
China/Chine	214261	440418	559272	596153	740534
Germany/Allemagne	568400	545350	507721	406978	428691
France,Monac	545062	522152	544755	392492	449167
Netherlands/Pays–Bas	237564	283335	329750	432580	350828
Singapore/Singapour	231604	240754	324142	426945	399220
United Kingdom	184634	195382	218632	209936	238555
India/inde	114945	145104	211077	227831	229373
Spain/Espagne	67494	70356	175159	203267	219273
Indonesia/Indonésie	24560	41067	110136	252350	243229
Thailand/Thaïlande	49843	56363	110430	205604	289670
Belgium–Luxembourg	126223	134540	118662	89935	91403
Korea, Republic of	82099	66269	70504	139823	161868
Malaysia/Malaisie	21295	36043	90356	130935	132677
Switz.Liecht	63274	62612	68479	64289	64268
Austria/Autriche	74229	62746	60757	64952	x73989
Sweden/Suède	60019	56919	61716	54223	61470
Brazil/Brésil	23395	20072	58912	51137	34461
Denmark/Danemark	32264	37792	44626	41868	39802
Portugal	26640	34224	43817	43197	55079
Canada	32806	39875	33687	41626	43708
Czechoslovakia		x61357	x43268		
Mexico/Mexique	5405	5110	40173	36984	31820
Norway,SVD,JM	21436	19259	22592	18863	24069
Czech Republic				57851	61050
Poland/Pologne	17613	22960	9938	12638	30432
Slovenia/Slovénia			22672	22576	24661
Russian Federation			x12152	x27933	x15121
Viet Nam	x43	x122	x6813	x31212	x12247
Australia/Australie	6517	6971	10232	15464	12844
Latvia/Lettonie			x874	x29128	2661
Philippines	6268	11417	4896	8472	12708
Yugoslavia SFR	26935	x24687			
Lithuania/Lituanie			12417	x12201	9218
Hungary/Hongrie	x1429	x6709	x9727	x6143	x3532
Finland/Finlande	8549	7881	6210	7598	9248
Ireland/Irlande	7262	6548	6356	2328	
Chile/Chili	1316	2258	5269	7390	6333
Argentina/Argentine	1907	2845	4520	5067	6450
So. Africa Customs Un	3314	2838	4585	4191	
New Zealand	2498	1959	3867	4331	6040
Turkey/Turquie	1534	1278	2502	6257	7697
Israel/Israël	2800	2857	3878	2683	4069
Macau/Macao	915	3051	3317	2711	2825
Former USSR/Anc. URSS	73787	x8988			
Ukraine			x1995	x6195	x1814
Greece/Grèce	297	1019	2426	4264	2537

(VALUE AS % OF TOTAL)(VALEUR EN % DU TOTAL)

	1985	1986	1987	1988	1989	1990	1991	1992	1993	1994
Africa	3.5	x3.9	x3.3	x3.4	x2.2	x1.9	x1.9	x2.4	x2.1	x1.7
Northern Africa	1.6	1.1	0.6	0.7	0.5	0.4	0.5	0.4	0.3	0.3
Americas	42.2	x36.5	x27.0	23.7	23.1	19.0	x19.1	20.2	20.5	20.4
LAIA	1.2	1.4	1.5	2.1	1.9	1.8	2.9	4.6	4.9	5.0
CACM	0.4	0.3	0.4	0.4	0.3	0.3	0.3	0.4	x0.3	x0.3
Asia	10.6	10.6	x14.4	x18.8	15.9	15.9	19.7	21.2	27.9	30.5
Middle East	1.2	x1.5	x1.0	x1.3	x0.7	0.9	x2.1	x1.7	x1.2	x0.8
Europe	37.2	43.4	49.0	47.9	53.0	59.0	56.8	54.0	46.9	44.4
EEC	30.0	34.4	38.3	40.0	45.3	54.2	52.8	50.4	43.8	41.3
EFTA	7.1	8.8	10.5	7.6	7.5	4.4	3.8	3.3	2.8	2.9
Oceania	3.6	x2.6	x2.6	x2.8	x2.9	x2.2	x1.8	x1.6	x1.7	x1.9
Germany/Allemagne	6.9	8.1	9.2	9.2	10.4	12.5	13.7	13.7	12.8	11.9
USA/Etats–Unis d'Amer	35.0	29.8	21.4	17.8	17.5	13.2	12.7	12.5	12.9	12.8
France,Monac	4.8	6.2	7.3	7.8	8.7	9.3	9.1	8.2	7.2	6.6
Hong Kong	1.4	1.0	1.5	3.3	2.7	3.5	5.5	7.7	9.9	10.8
Italy/Italie	2.9	3.7	3.7	3.3	4.4	5.9	5.9	6.1	4.8	4.5
Netherlands/Pays–Bas	2.9	3.0	3.4	3.3	3.5	4.7	4.8	4.3	4.3	3.9
United Kingdom	4.3	4.2	4.6	5.4	5.9	6.5	4.9	4.2	3.9	3.9
Spain/Espagne	0.8	1.2	2.0	2.7	3.8	5.0	4.5	5.0	3.1	2.5
Japan/Japon	0.7	1.0	1.7	2.4	2.5	2.3	2.6	2.3	2.6	3.3
Switz.Liecht	2.8	4.0	5.7	2.9	2.8	3.5	2.9	2.5	2.2	2.1

	1985	1986	1987	1988	1989	1990	1991	1992	1993	1994
Afrique		x0.1	x0.1	x0.1	x0.2	0.1	x0.1	x0.1	x0.0	x0.0
Afrique du Nord	0.0	0.0	0.0	0.0	0.0	0.0	0.0	x0.0	0.0	0.0
Amériques	2.5	x2.7	3.1	5.0	5.9	7.0	8.4	8.0	7.2	6.9
ALAI	0.2	0.1	0.2	0.5	0.6	0.4	0.3	0.9	0.8	0.6
MCAC	0.0	0.0	0.0	0.0	x0.0	0.0	0.0	0.0	0.0	0.0
Asie	65.4	62.0	x62.8	x61.0	56.0	54.8	59.7	62.8	67.9	65.3
Moyen–Orient	0.2	0.1	x0.1	0.1	x0.1	0.1	0.0	x0.0	x0.1	x0.1
Europe	27.3	30.4	28.6	28.1	34.8	36.3	30.8	28.4	24.0	26.8
CEE	24.2	27.2	25.5	25.8	32.2	35.0	29.7	27.4	23.3	26.0
AELE	2.9	3.0	2.8	2.1	2.3	1.0	0.8	0.8	0.6	0.6
Océanie		x0.0	x0.2	x0.3	x0.2	x0.1	x0.1	x0.1	x0.1	x0.1
Japan/Japon	61.6	58.5	44.9	40.1	44.9	42.3	43.5	43.2	44.2	40.1
Italy/Italie	7.4	9.2	8.7	9.5	11.8	12.3	10.1	9.6	9.0	11.3
Hong Kong	1.2	0.8	1.2	3.0	3.0	3.7	5.7	7.0	8.8	8.9
USA/Etats–Unis d'Amer	2.0	2.3	2.5	3.8	4.7	6.2	7.6	6.8	6.1	6.0
China/Chine	0.4	0.3	1.2	1.4	2.2	2.5	4.4	4.7	4.3	5.4
Germany/Allemagne	5.2	6.1	5.2	4.8	6.5	6.6	5.5	4.3	3.0	3.1
France,Monac	4.4	4.6	4.4	4.6	5.8	6.4	5.2	4.6	2.9	3.3
Netherlands/Pays–Bas	1.6	1.5	1.6	1.6	2.3	2.8	2.8	2.8	3.2	2.6
Singapore/Singapour	0.3	0.3	0.5	0.8	1.9	2.7	2.4	2.7	3.1	2.9
United Kingdom	1.7	1.8	1.7	1.8	1.8	2.2	2.0	1.8	1.5	1.7

TRADE BY COMMODITY IN THOUSAND U.S. DOLLARS – COMMERCE PAR PRODUIT EN MILLIERS DE DOLLARS E.U

COUNTRIES–PAYS	IMPORTS – IMPORTATIONS				
	1990	1991	1992	1993	1994
Total	4969170	5617915	5658520	4654539	5373997
Africa	x153566	x163160	x172010	x170500	x184196
Northern Africa	67272	77683	x80748	x69759	x61727
Americas	652198	708837	913447	1016390	x1247095
LAIA	92433	92052	166693	193490	223403
CACM	9640	11258	14062	x16846	x13330
Asia	399484	x576590	x593706	x730066	x702856
Middle East	59440	x196351	x177692	x189617	x152954
Europe	3535406	3839836	3694355	2489759	2969971
EEC	3242224	3582858	3446697	2248960	2659627
EFTA	269395	236132	219427	199452	246403
Oceania	x59930	x50312	x54763	x77497	x88979
Germany/Allemagne	595835	1083866	969671	498197	530873
Netherlands/Pays-Bas	546174	545085	562205	344706	413820
France,Monac	475252	461840	439341	337292	388541
Canada	299486	316475	86787	416294	482239
USA/Etats-Unis d'Amer	213332	249917	319478	362531	471371
Belgium–Luxembourg	326820	351021	331518	209828	254209
United Kingdom	242343	213153	220655	224531	293168
Austria/Autriche	158643	183278	189319	156928	199331
Switz.Liecht	182164	156768	137174	127515	149770
Spain/Espagne	172369	155305	163812	89216	103791
Denmark/Danemark	144021	138041	139423	111235	124915
Hong Kong	100110	122987	123274	118872	157332
Italy/Italie	130667	132108	138545	90768	104766
Sweden/Suède	220520	148267	119544	77806	113678
Mexico/Mexique	68130	55102	99654	106337	112801
Iran (Islamic Rp. of)		x112778	x76427	x33181	x3581
Norway,SVD,JM	82814	73177	77666	68809	93253
Japan/Japon	74241	67950	70461	79037	128921
China/Chine	10734	14030	27730	132628	32427
Portugal	58545	60225	70345	35010	33235
Hungary/Hongrie	x23709	35187	x78807	x48317	x51320
Former USSR/Anc. URSS	62305	x146192			
Singapore/Singapour	37566	41162	49355	50502	55859
Saudi Arabia	17338	41631	38525	x56037	x56139
Czechoslovakia	23332	x24134	x98637		
Poland/Pologne	14874	43982	35107	39818	47787
Russian Federation			x65090	x52499	x47947
Australia/Australie	37694	27537	33641	48442	55392
Ireland/Irlande	48507	42218	40915	22319	30243
Israel/Israël	30960	32438	35031	32985	41079
Finland/Finlande	94524	42936	26307	26180	48547
Libyan Arab Jamahiriya	20851	31874	x36981	x19896	x19764
Greece/Grèce	28003	25515	35096	24946	20511
Algeria/Algérie	20280	19766	26971	31167	15178
Korea, Republic of	19128	24136	26892	23977	32511
Ukraine			x7515	x66426	x12856
Malaysia/Malaisie	19883	27162	24124	18486	27868
United Arab Emirates	9547	11126	15232	x39081	x33148
Indonesia/Indonésie	13676	16228	27890	19200	13881
Chile/Chili	10404	15263	22101	24413	21299
Bulgaria/Bulgarie	x37250	x28554	13027	x11278	x11257
Thailand/Thaïlande	14334	16450	12009	15510	26032
Czech Republic				33163	47108
So. Africa Customs Un	9010	11967	9557	11015	14005
Venezuela	1431	5482	14173	12676	4798
Argentina/Argentine	541	1811	10999	19494	45946
Oman	6137	10688	6381	13864	25273
Turkey/Turquie	9180	4634	6582	18924	11749
Slovenia/Slovénia			11010	16878	19398
Nigeria/Nigéria		3986	x11780	x11954	x7134

COUNTRIES–PAYS	EXPORTS – EXPORTATIONS				
	1990	1991	1992	1993	1994
Totale	6541962	7025184	7599245	6221307	7247523
Afrique	114359	158809	153861	180526	x158294
Afrique du Nord	14613	4666	2626	6362	2806
Amériques	555894	725530	905330	935966	1103163
ALAI	27900	24483	128951	167667	229962
MCAC	247	328	686	505	x1047
Asie	1680727	1606680	2116858	1584207	1961109
Moyen–Orient	15896	16732	33130	65235	105264
Europe	3995663	4256580	4162069	3258103	3735078
CEE	3829335	4137609	4030558	3152840	3644122
AELE	69381	59424	52585	43432	47842
Océanie	x12595	x14946	x14213	x17898	x21780
Germany/Allemagne	1439587	1437288	1525554	1258181	1380112
Korea, Republic of	1103712	975050	1158183	725692	711741
USA/Etats-Unis d'Amer	474225	645149	717149	687525	762324
France,Monac	569532	704243	614822	425722	484931
United Kingdom	333210	437156	404226	311645	434477
Netherlands/Pays-Bas	321996	372964	360989	266203	302255
China/Chine	121571	245618	388219	324690	692192
Italy/Italie	269717	314847	314521	266451	320587
Belgium–Luxembourg	327656	347710	308896	234669	284798
Japan/Japon	213101	137012	253138	194696	205695
Austria/Autriche	138465	160296	163176	122328	x122470
So. Africa Customs Un	93577	146013	136076	163685	153575
Thailand/Thaïlande	91604	126125	137200	134235	89835
Denmark/Danemark	142350	144592	133482	106230	110773
Poland/Pologne	83365	111351	68878	77028	101631
Mexico/Mexique	17822	11566	108273	110683	162958
Sweden/Suède	86356	83225	68575	54389	64568
Hungary/Hongrie	x32825	x46230	x86523	x61252	x67859
Canada	51250	51083	55030	77564	100875
Finland/Finlande	86528	54335	55064	51987	80565
Spain/Espagne	75442	57113	56607	36248	52126
Russian Federation			x11384	x125508	x13957
Czechoslovakia		x68882	x67870		
Slovenia/Slovénia			62009	53288	41552
Singapore/Singapour	19853	28779	33975	31796	48269
Norway,SVD,JM	44221	37468	29585	21483	31596
Indonesia/Indonésie	61	2516	39336	34464	18506
Turkey/Turquie	2406	3375	18538	48523	84310
India/Inde	37787	19868	31052	18879	5947
Brazil/Brésil	4408	5489	14744	47236	55362
Switz.Liecht	25158	21956	22995	21949	16246
Czech Republic				62509	57053
Yugoslavia SFR	96739	x59482			
Malaysia/Malaisie	5814	7553	13349	33945	59557
Hong Kong	9822	14545	17214	13817	12503
Romania/Roumanie	3334	14632	11559	11439	14486
Israel/Israël	32576	22802	9131	4575	9689
Ireland/Irlande	21881	13036	11416	11164	
Australia/Australie	8665	10578	10177	13223	14184
Latvia/Lettonie			x888	x23467	1179
Albania/Albanie		x6399	x6418	x9679	x3485
Portugal	8449	8223	8722	3928	3766
Slovakia				x20330	x22217
Yugoslavia/Yougoslavie			x14822	x1006	x234
Former USSR/Anc. URSS	39408	x13464			
Greece/Grèce	8163	2578	4508	3695	2693
Philippines	27511	8819	1666	235	397
New Zealand	3486	3356	3392	3936	7501
Ghana		1320	9310		
Saudi Arabia	4497	3927	4855	x1447	x1074

(VALUE AS % OF TOTAL)(VALEUR EN % DU TOTAL)

	1985	1986	1987	1988	1989	1990	1991	1992	1993	1994
Africa	6.5	x7.2	x4.1	x3.7	x3.8	x3.1	x2.9	x3.1	x3.6	x3.5
Northern Africa	4.0	2.9	1.1	1.0	x1.7	1.4	1.4	x1.4	x1.5	x1.1
Americas	15.1	x8.9	x10.1	11.3	x13.9	13.1	12.6	16.2	21.8	x23.2
LAIA	6.3	0.6	2.4	2.0	1.3	1.9	1.6	2.9	4.2	4.2
CACM	0.4	0.4	x0.2	0.2	0.2	0.2	0.2	0.2	x0.4	x0.2
Asia	8.9	x6.6	x7.0	x7.8	8.1	8.0	x10.3	x10.5	x15.7	x13.1
Middle East	5.1	x4.2	x2.7	x1.7	x1.5	1.2	x3.5	x3.1	x4.1	x2.8
Europe	62.5	70.7	71.1	69.2	68.2	71.1	68.3	65.3	53.5	55.3
EEC	47.6	53.6	55.3	54.6	54.4	65.2	63.8	60.9	48.3	49.5
EFTA	14.5	16.8	15.6	14.4	13.6	5.4	4.2	3.9	4.3	4.6
Oceania	1.5	x1.5	x0.9	x0.9	x1.1	x1.2	x0.9	x1.0	x1.6	x1.6
Germany/Allemagne	7.8	8.6	8.6	7.5	7.7	12.0	19.3	17.1	10.7	9.9
Netherlands/Pays-Bas	8.1	9.8	9.5	9.7	8.9	11.0	9.7	9.9	7.4	7.7
France,Monac	7.9	8.7	9.4	8.9	8.1	9.6	8.2	7.8	7.2	7.2
Canada	2.9	2.5	2.8	5.4	6.1	6.0	5.6	6.8	8.9	9.0
USA/Etats-Unis d'Amer	4.5	3.1	2.9	2.7	4.8	4.3	4.4	5.6	7.8	8.8
Belgium–Luxembourg	4.2	5.3	5.5	5.6	5.6	6.6	6.2	5.9	4.5	4.7
United Kingdom	5.8	4.8	4.4	5.1	5.3	4.9	3.8	3.9	4.8	5.5
Austria/Autriche	2.5	2.7	2.8	2.8	2.6	3.2	3.3	3.3	3.4	3.7
Switz.Liecht	3.5	4.0	3.8	3.4	3.1	3.7	2.8	2.4	2.7	2.8
Spain/Espagne	0.7	1.4	2.3	2.7	3.2	3.5	2.8	2.9	1.9	1.9

	1985	1986	1987	1988	1989	1990	1991	1992	1993	1994
Afrique	0.7	0.8	x0.7	x0.8	x1.1	1.7	2.3	2.0	2.9	x2.2
Afrique du Nord	0.1	0.1	x0.0	0.1	0.1	0.2	0.1	0.0	0.1	0.0
Amériques	5.4	x5.2	x5.4	6.4	7.6	8.5	10.3	12.0	15.0	15.2
ALAI	0.7	0.6	0.7	0.7	0.5	0.4	0.3	1.7	2.7	3.2
MCAC	0.0	0.0	x0.0	0.0	0.0	0.0	0.0	0.0	0.0	x0.0
Asie	23.1	16.1	18.4	24.5	27.6	25.7	22.9	27.9	25.5	27.1
Moyen–Orient	0.6	x0.5	x0.6	0.5	0.3	0.2	0.2	0.4	1.0	1.5
Europe	66.7	73.5	68.8	62.7	60.8	61.1	60.6	54.8	52.4	51.5
CEE	57.6	63.9	59.4	55.5	54.3	58.5	58.9	53.0	50.7	50.3
AELE	6.9	8.1	7.7	5.9	5.4	1.1	0.8	0.7	0.7	0.7
Océanie	0.2	x0.1	x0.1	x0.2	x0.3	x0.2	x0.2	x0.2	x0.3	x0.3
Germany/Allemagne	21.4	26.3	25.6	22.7	22.2	22.0	20.5	20.1	20.2	19.0
Korea, Republic of	10.5	8.8	11.8	16.3	18.7	16.9	13.9	15.2	11.7	9.8
USA/Etats-Unis d'Amer	3.8	3.6	3.7	4.1	5.8	7.2	9.2	9.4	11.1	10.5
France,Monac	10.2	9.4	7.9	7.5	7.1	8.7	10.0	8.1	6.8	6.7
United Kingdom	3.7	3.9	4.3	4.8	4.7	5.1	6.2	5.3	5.0	6.0
Netherlands/Pays-Bas	3.1	4.0	3.8	4.0	4.1	4.9	5.3	4.8	4.3	4.2
China/Chine			0.2	0.5	1.1	1.9	3.5	5.1	5.2	9.6
Italy/Italie	5.4	4.4	3.3	3.7	3.7	4.1	4.5	4.1	4.3	4.4
Belgium–Luxembourg	4.3	4.6	4.4	4.3	4.6	5.0	4.9	4.1	3.8	3.9
Japan/Japon	11.4	6.0	3.2	4.6	4.8	3.3	2.0	3.3	3.1	2.8

TRADE BY COMMODITY IN THOUSAND U.S. DOLLARS – COMMERCE PAR PRODUIT EN MILLIERS DE DOLLARS E.U

COUNTRIES–PAYS	IMPORTS – IMPORTATIONS 1990	1991	1992	1993	1994
Total	5600336	x5066396	4822519	5301435	7374732
Africa	x313022	x317507	x362069	x237697	x184488
Northern Africa	126368	137166	162718	72567	87957
Americas	1054778	921243	987443	1065211	1676857
LAIA	176806	175729	157159	211931	314540
CACM	3083	1335	1828	x1685	x1038
Asia	706282	x650718	x995968	x1191718	x987211
Middle East	27292	x217973	x317318	x362757	x206418
Europe	1231185	1856939	2370295	2568819	4201032
EEC	1061570	1692108	2179611	2358196	4021945
EFTA	134730	147505	174275	189229	163870
Oceania	x25744	x31700	x33991	x44144	x83158
USA/Etats–Unis d'Amer	644720	562252	647101	638459	1046051
Russian Federation			x1184577	x339774	x304690
Former USSR/Anc. URSS	1967685	x1157249			
Germany/Allemagne	142233	395741	374783	352001	469959
Netherlands/Pays–Bas	201439	187468	378568	431828	304408
France, Monac	88192	185948	255317	518948	1278130
United Kingdom	128150	159847	257404	384970	1105117
Iran (Islamic Rp. of)		x204033	x281808	x232726	x91887
Canada	206138	174679	170927	206863	308419
Belgium–Luxembourg	94971	132191	142455	215844	245260
Spain/Espagne	73862	156008	239814	73175	83078
Austria/Autriche	65208	91067	203468	121623	159165
Switz.Liecht	109154	114931	136324	142371	99676
Italy/Italie	72918	127515	134568	77210	68153
Japan/Japon	43781	61900	92372	106443	124268
Mexico/Mexique	117887	117428	76016	57159	163454
Korea, Republic of	64980	42675	81527	125377	172800
China/Chine	321824	75672	59146	85199	104137
Indonesia/Indonésie	30030	16446	82679	118863	56055
Sweden/Suède	64084	88909	51869	58549	80592
Hong Kong	27382	33162	54276	74557	48675
Turkey/Turquie	19656	7608	23715	122105	104885
Thailand/Thaïlande	22648	28397	24261	97455	10042
Denmark/Danemark	39675	35067	58041	43143	32119
India/Inde	76087	56943	47067	30488	15662
Norway, SVD, JM	25569	32399	37921	46840	64181
Poland/Pologne	39054	75986	23765	15182	37961
Portugal	16418	32021	42028	39764	73846
Un. Rep. of Tanzania	x80894	x64243	x32331	x14911	x7491
Pakistan	12479	38361	43216	27938	17118
Morocco/Maroc	22706	48046	48636	7114	3520
Egypt/Egypte	56569	34961	38253	24846	20574
Sri Lanka	13493	28760	25712	42281	1549
Mozambique	x11546	x6205	x58492	x27899	x4270
Colombia/Colombie	5948	1219	27759	62855	37519
Greece/Grèce	5937	63578	15107	12776	15249
Australia/Australie	20607	24532	29153	36299	80480
Israel/Israël	4114	4946	45519	38407	14745
Tunisia/Tunisie	6845	32201	49716	5996	2997
Malaysia/Malaisie	29655	13547	56465	12819	47335
Romania/Roumanie	36671	7284	8145	64053	21067
Venezuela	21333	5553	23148	50734	68421
Belarus/Bélarus			x54391	x24222	x6995
Brazil/Brésil	9512	43272	18088	8769	13439
Finland/Finlande	61319	31382	19820	18732	46429
Algeria/Algérie	33971	9761	20224	32463	54842
Ukraine			x9579	x45633	x21463
Zambia/Zambie	x9696	x8314	x8832	x37271	x9565
Hungary/Hongrie	x15496	11142	x6589	x32530	x121000
Czechoslovakia	80358	x19892	x27415		

COUNTRIES–PAYS	EXPORTS – EXPORTATIONS 1990	1991	1992	1993	1994
Totale	4615781	4870873	5961461	5661973	7829900
Afrique	53107	40174	33539	x30793	x1897
Afrique du Nord	3063	134	529	25	1050
Amériques	1172210	1042066	1108745	1200911	1710598
ALAI	81571	53006	85436	76199	52373
MCAC		177	12	45	12
Asie	274334	152552	265198	255328	277459
Moyen–Orient	415	1296	35	x1780	2902
Europe	1938782	3128554	4174782	3844080	5502962
CEE	1806120	3017489	4068421	3600399	5268785
AELE	109519	108690	102709	239581	231689
Océanie	x14487	x16273	12954	x21900	x22450
Germany/Allemagne	642421	1702459	1975222	1525326	2088413
France, Monac	231693	412083	710472	553150	1233202
USA/Etats–Unis d'Amer	497861	529919	552742	541236	705015
Canada	592740	458881	470429	583077	953012
Italy/Italie	128930	155717	376623	378786	295502
Austria/Autriche	187978	199033	294227	337082	x280485
Belgium–Luxembourg	109516	114497	142531	316268	292501
United Kingdom	157064	183503	155793	193444	643163
Japan/Japon	185953	105165	162369	187897	205557
Switz.Liecht	106849	106687	98066	237587	228949
Romania/Roumanie	197081	159804	117918	82017	39937
Czechoslovakia		x147151	x159649		
Sweden/Suède	74554	61412	97455	130980	98519
Spain/Espagne	47452	51396	153418	63698	245702
Netherlands/Pays–Bas	62262	53191	62889	56604	52386
Poland/Pologne	202898	55474	57916	51866	38046
Brazil/Brésil	59714	37542	60831	42565	29037
Denmark/Danemark	1490	33007	88074	14132	5094
Korea, Republic of	58914	11878	77336	12333	19627
Former USSR/Anc. URSS	668666	x99376			
Russian Federation			x58705	x40337	x40157
Czech Republic				96711	136446
So. Africa Customs Un	33018	34996	26394	25042	
Finland/Finlande	157344	43567	9507	25696	26669
Slovakia				x65245	x73965
China/Chine	14548	10117	15265	36994	22297
Hungary/Hongrie	x6303	x25394	x23051	x12326	x25554
Mexico/Mexique	19479	10901	15404	30832	21071
Australia/Australie	14288	13949	12123	21435	22131
Ukraine			x10188	x32960	x15358
Latvia/Lettonie			x2209	22146	35607
India/Inde	6790	5718	6579	9712	20276
Zimbabwe	16234	4439	5749	4689	x474
Argentina/Argentine	2264	2129	8759	2628	1855
Indonesia/Indonésie	8	13058	88	34	16
Bulgaria/Bulgarie	x17647	x3764	x7419	x794	x585
Portugal	3195	5368	807	2609	5478
Norway, SVD, JM	2670	2004	4643	1994	2740
Singapore/Singapour	1809	4134	1424	2564	3618
Slovenia/Slovénia			1554	3640	1853
Hong Kong	713	501	1168	2293	783
Greece/Grèce	228	1810	553	1432	1672
New Zealand	197	2269	666	166	313
Ireland/Irlande	1993	445	849	1192	
Yugoslavia SFR	23143	x2280			
Turkey/Turquie	83	1296	18	782	2834
Colombia/Colombie	1	2004		63	53
Malaysia/Malaisie	1118	180	481	894	660
Lithuania/Lituanie				x1402	4366
Yugoslavia/Yougoslavie			x1140	x23	x29

(VALUE AS % OF TOTAL)(VALEUR EN % DU TOTAL)

	1985	1986	1987	1988	1989	1990	1991	1992	1993	1994
Africa	8.6	x8.1	x5.7	x4.5	x3.3	x5.6	x6.3	x7.6	x4.5	x2.5
Northern Africa	6.5	3.4	1.8	2.1	x1.2	2.3	2.7	3.4	1.4	1.2
Americas	23.6	22.3	16.7	13.8	19.0	18.8	18.1	20.5	20.0	22.8
LAIA	7.1	5.0	1.8	2.7	1.4	3.2	3.5	3.3	4.0	4.3
CACM	0.0	0.0	0.1	0.1	0.0	0.1	0.0	0.0	x0.0	x0.0
Asia	9.8	x7.8	15.4	x17.8	16.1	12.7	x12.8	x20.7	x22.4	x13.4
Middle East	2.7	x2.3	x0.6	x1.6	x1.7	0.5	x4.3	x6.6	x6.8	x2.8
Europe	15.3	16.5	16.1	17.2	18.0	22.0	36.7	49.2	48.5	57.0
EEC	10.7	11.6	11.2	12.2	13.2	19.0	33.4	45.2	44.5	54.5
EFTA	3.0	3.6	3.7	4.1	4.1	2.4	2.9	3.6	3.6	2.2
Oceania	0.5	0.6	0.7	0.8	x0.8	x0.4	x0.6	x0.7	x0.8	x1.1
USA/Etats–Unis d'Amer	9.6	10.5	10.0	7.3	12.8	11.5	11.1	13.4	12.0	14.2
Russian Federation								x24.6	x6.4	x4.1
Former USSR/Anc. URSS	35.4	39.2	35.9	35.3	36.7	35.1	x22.8			
Germany/Allemagne	1.5	1.4	1.6	1.2	1.5	2.5	7.8	7.8	6.6	6.4
Netherlands/Pays–Bas	1.8	2.0	1.3	1.8	2.3	3.6	3.7	7.8	8.1	4.1
France, Monac	0.9	1.1	1.1	1.0	1.0	1.6	3.7	5.3	9.8	17.3
United Kingdom	0.7	1.1	0.9	1.5	1.9	2.3	3.2	5.3	7.3	15.0
Iran (Islamic Rp. of)		x0.4	x0.1	x1.2	x1.0		x4.0	x5.8	x4.4	x1.2
Canada	5.8	5.9	4.3	3.3	3.4	3.7	3.4	3.5	3.9	4.2
Belgium–Luxembourg	0.8	0.8	0.9	0.7	0.9	1.7	2.6	3.0	4.1	3.3

	1985	1986	1987	1988	1989	1990	1991	1992	1993	1994
Afrique	0.4	0.5	x0.4	0.5	0.5	1.1	0.8	0.5	x0.5	x0.0
Afrique du Nord	0.1	0.1	0.0	0.1	0.4	0.1	0.0	0.0	0.0	0.0
Amériques	20.8	24.1	13.9	10.1	22.3	25.4	21.4	18.6	21.3	21.9
ALAI	1.0	0.6	0.5	1.0	0.9	1.8	1.1	1.4	1.3	0.7
MCAC	0.0	x0.0	x0.0	x0.0	x0.0		0.0	0.0	0.0	0.0
Asie	9.5	6.7	11.4	7.5	4.8	5.9	3.2	4.4	4.5	3.5
Moyen–Orient	0.0	x0.0	x0.0	0.0	0.0	0.0	0.0	0.0	x0.0	0.0
Europe	38.2	38.8	35.6	37.8	42.9	42.0	64.2	70.0	67.9	70.3
CEE	35.2	34.0	29.7	29.0	31.9	39.1	61.9	68.2	63.6	67.3
AELE	2.4	4.0	5.4	8.5	10.2	2.4	2.2	1.7	4.2	3.0
Océanie	0.2	0.1	0.2	0.6	0.2	x0.3	x0.3	0.2	x0.4	x0.3
Germany/Allemagne	12.7	9.7	8.4	9.2	12.8	13.9	35.0	33.1	26.9	26.7
France, Monac	12.1	13.0	11.4	8.2	4.5	5.0	8.5	11.9	9.8	15.7
USA/Etats–Unis d'Amer	14.5	13.9	6.5	5.2	9.4	10.8	10.9	9.3	9.6	9.0
Canada	5.4	9.6	6.8	3.9	12.1	12.8	9.4	7.9	10.3	12.2
Italy/Italie	3.7	2.3	1.8	0.8	1.4	2.8	3.2	6.3	6.7	3.8
Austria/Autriche	0.2	0.3	0.3	3.1	4.0	4.1	4.1	4.9	6.0	x3.6
Belgium–Luxembourg	0.9	1.1	0.5	0.6	1.0	2.4	2.4	2.4	5.6	3.7
United Kingdom	3.9	3.6	3.0	2.4	2.1	3.4	3.8	2.6	3.4	8.2
Japan/Japon	8.3	5.3	9.8	6.2	3.3	4.0	2.2	2.7	3.3	2.6
Switz.Liecht	1.4	1.1	1.9	1.7	1.7	2.3	2.2	1.6	4.2	2.9

TRADE BY COMMODITY IN THOUSAND U.S. DOLLARS – COMMERCE PAR PRODUIT EN MILLIERS DE DOLLARS E.U

COUNTRIES–PAYS	IMPORTS – IMPORTATIONS 1990	1991	1992	1993	1994
Total	56822129	66934481	68077633	58186497	60491312
Africa	x1341066	x1236646	x1208163	x1069466	x1288065
Northern Africa	496726	x169591	240835	x251296	384855
Americas	9376263	10804469	11352209	9309372	x10625002
LAIA	829231	768055	1314605	1136696	1794966
CACM	4497	4516	6904	x67005	x189758
Asia	12566394	14037812	19236226	x19556154	x19772899
Middle East	2956791	3347265	5825008	x4523840	x2685756
Europe	29458562	37658890	33659806	26874272	26945093
EEC	27665129	35624959	31992150	25615614	25960387
EFTA	1596618	1960445	1551171	940860	922997
Oceania	x2491636	x2502234	x2052172	x1024983	x1571655
Germany/Allemagne	9652548	13737648	12940641	10159371	9428623
USA/Etats-Unis d'Amer	6428417	7463588	7471974	6383505	6818233
United Kingdom	4437560	5439208	5279863	4821059	5223626
France,Monac	3828192	5348294	4727672	3729757	4398085
Japan/Japon	3261322	3286543	3307848	3209000	3891304
Italy/Italie	2440825	3200784	2887508	1863483	1969733
Saudi Arabia	1949778	2336688	3883697	x1002305	x783053
Canada	1957632	2393241	2338101	1561594	1438299
Korea, Republic of	1068219	1797645	1964640	1846426	2207478
China/Chine	868547	1221076	2033539	2269764	3397005
Spain/Espagne	2036199	2399234	1536880	1042473	1268734
Netherlands/Pays-Bas	1651305	1550445	1849318	1320878	1709062
Singapore/Singapour	986795	1377249	1527798	1755411	1625755
Australia/Australie	1871752	2218406	1422410	661193	980948
Malaysia/Malaisie	995345	1042719	1477712	1698413	2060624
Switz.Liecht	650100	1499850	958297	594992	602142
Belgium–Luxembourg	906918	1217987	737498	1091023	341847
Turkey/Turquie	271835	301411	674011	1404863	802382
Hong Kong	573256	581227	673133	789522	472934
Thailand/Thaïlande	620784	50665	988135	827180	904103
Sweden/Suède	974401	639771	649113	553403	340645
So. Africa Customs Un	173472	595982	440640	437118	362757
Norway,SVD,JM	820510	422092	582702	338396	311669
Denmark/Danemark	620285	847644	325062	151419	179812
Mexico/Mexique	386503	350461	564113	366602	640026
Philippines	305643	237312	281826	622082	140695
India/Inde	289675	64853	137861	935137	732674
United Arab Emirates	205640	102714	357237	x636177	x243898
Indonesia/Indonésie	362311	506879	187550	332523	230192
Bahrain/Bahreïn	x305069	x289237	x293321	x335279	x213427
New Zealand	468755	232022	460656	215063	444635
Ireland/Irlande	299221	358256	267012	241611	184887
Brazil/Brésil	320440	310215	355363	125852	212344
Austria/Autriche	222693	272688	348781	135045	213806
Greece/Grèce	109906	322991	165738	266751	115975
Kuwait/Koweït	127	1466	165856	552743	212595
Iran (Islamic Rp. of)		x175156	x142537	x339387	x247140
Israel/Israël	182353	195493	151037	296859	503836
Hungary/Hongrie	x4951	272284	x115380	x210780	x41867
Pakistan	17342	246890	100918	242600	136988
Finland/Finlande	368820	247986	121757	184118	217177
Russian Federation			x477141	x51885	x438179
Colombia/Colombie	77348	43555	131385	317470	524101
Argentina/Argentine	12139	14484	182479	208980	329338
Brunei Darussalam	27725	37541	x196879	x163253	x264906
Czechoslovakia	1162	x126935	x262166		
Jordan/Jordanie	142762	94164	135260	122473	92068
Cote d'Ivoire	x2369	x80685	x165753	x86390	x8222
Morocco/Maroc	112643	68645	91433	104452	249619
Portugal	116256	42024	155307	55223	368373

COUNTRIES–PAYS	EXPORTS – EXPORTATIONS 1990	1991	1992	1993	1994
Totale	64549266	80026282	81416531	70281671	69923765
Afrique	59630	x70594	x91871	x92256	x91397
Afrique du Nord	4733	x5236	x2002	7242	x283
Amériques	33987425	39237469	39531038	34605601	33537957
ALAI	671120	454722	509720	564412	708064
MCAC	38	47	192	x177	x41830
Asie	1915630	2194594	2920653	3310256	4384005
Moyen–Orient	150248	x117470	x116702	x349430	x482848
Europe	26611215	37460879	38209825	31539179	31216695
CEE	26078988	37020626	37532210	31139438	30808029
AELE	468734	401151	651453	379900	300749
Océanie	436154	582265	563719	531849	476429
USA/Etats–Unis d'Amer	30548962	35482816	36594327	31856291	30431247
France,Monac	6864584	10188015	11021228	9819492	11079016
Germany/Allemagne	7902167	10454544	10657848	8563975	8441042
United Kingdom	3600406	8921985	7815003	5917773	5646891
Canada	2719753	3285824	2360349	2152525	2286992
Italy/Italie	2934660	2667939	2922545	1855235	1999820
Netherlands/Pays–Bas	1887784	1726860	2240820	2652025	1191793
Spain/Espagne	1042286	1166901	1049544	1104462	1351925
Malaysia/Malaisie	265497	481135	706050	873082	1556036
Belgium–Luxembourg	576976	783250	692984	518726	273097
Japan/Japon	444197	538473	616915	601989	661716
Sweden/Suède	613722	593110	517970	365184	431960
Russian Federation			x848155	x614810	x234492
Switz.Liecht	288212	347386	517279	264958	234955
Australia/Australie	291617	344229	372966	408635	388637
Brazil/Brésil	554106	375770	357783	299715	309846
Israel/Israël	292617	316774	294145	340870	355902
Singapore/Singapour	430769	331975	347228	251734	233097
Denmark/Danemark	469219	313457	382647	133576	213691
Korea, Republic of	188139	248536	269168	286364	224811
China/Chine	14309	27728	368567	180764	191678
Former USSR/Anc. URSS	1442800	x375442			
New Zealand	103038	135299	132007	97147	50417
Mexico/Mexique	72330	56443	118564	136177	241155
Thailand/Thaïlande	185	3941	77787	225444	488502
Norway,SVD,JM	169524	53752	134148	114899	39258
Ireland/Irlande	55922	91043	91663	98548	
Hong Kong	61554	53157	89467	77014	69199
Saudi Arabia	15289	12716	24809	x176520	x173065
Austria/Autriche	51569	60597	62102	49107	x48085
Papua New Guinea	21203	96387	38811	22215	x835
Czech Republic				147862	153020
Poland/Pologne	66342	64200	42430	30307	29480
So. Africa Customs Un	30710	34534	45082	45269	
Portugal	37445	33105	50612	33046	83622
Jordan/Jordanie	61929	25179	40241	48131	71955
Oman	35851	44949	20932	45158	43482
Colombia/Colombie	314	8927	5546	96311	137726
Indonesia/Indonésie	14384	8527	13573	54648	65451
Bahrain/Bahreïn	x15672	x22028	x16398	x20701	x5753
Czechoslovakia		x20415	x35581		
Bangladesh				x53488	x36520
Argentina/Argentine	16329	10749	17004	22705	2501
Malta/Malte	9066	10157	18514	14211	x75365
Romania/Roumanie	28825	17319	8036	14440	26818
United Arab Emirates	4287			x39238	x26625
Greece/Grèce	8353	9615	13570	14910	16792
Finland/Finlande	33840	10151	13673	13377	30294
India/Inde	8105	19678	10432	5657	7999
Netherlands Antilles	2335	2323	31746	x187	x512

(VALUE AS % OF TOTAL)(VALEUR EN % DU TOTAL)

	1985	1986	1987	1988	1989	1990	1991	1992	1993	1994
Africa	2.1	2.6	x2.6	x1.9	x1.9	x2.4	x1.9	x1.7	x1.9	x2.1
Northern Africa	0.5	0.5	0.3	0.2	x0.3	0.9	x0.3	0.4	x0.4	0.6
Americas	26.2	26.9	26.4	25.5	19.4	16.5	16.1	16.7	16.0	x17.5
LAIA	1.5	1.8	3.1	1.6	1.3	1.5	1.1	1.9	2.0	3.0
CACM	0.0	0.0	x0.0	0.0	0.0	0.0	0.0	0.0	x0.1	x0.3
Asia	21.7	21.5	21.2	20.8	21.1	22.2	21.0	28.3	x33.6	x32.7
Middle East	5.3	x6.3	x3.2	x4.0	x5.9	5.2	5.0	8.6	x7.8	x4.4
Europe	48.2	44.8	45.9	48.0	51.8	51.8	56.3	49.4	46.2	44.5
EEC	43.4	39.0	40.2	42.8	47.0	48.7	53.2	47.0	44.0	42.9
EFTA	4.1	5.5	5.2	4.9	4.7	2.8	2.9	2.3	1.6	1.5
Oceania	1.8	x3.9	x3.3	3.2	x4.9	x4.4	x3.8	x3.0	x1.8	x2.6
Germany/Allemagne	17.4	15.5	17.8	16.1	18.1	17.0	20.5	19.0	17.5	15.6
USA/Etats–Unis d'Amer	17.3	18.2	17.2	15.2	12.9	11.3	11.2	11.0	11.0	11.3
United Kingdom	10.0	6.7	3.8	7.1	6.8	7.8	8.1	7.8	8.3	8.6
France,Monac	2.8	3.9	4.6	7.3	5.8	6.7	8.0	6.9	6.4	7.3
Japan/Japon	7.2	7.3	6.7	5.6	3.8	5.7	4.9	4.9	5.5	6.4
Italy/Italie	4.7	4.1	4.3	3.3	3.7	4.3	4.8	4.2	3.2	3.3
Saudi Arabia	3.2	3.7	1.9	1.3	3.1	3.4	3.5	5.7	x1.7	x1.3
Canada	7.2	6.4	5.5	8.4	4.7	3.4	3.6	3.4	2.7	2.4
Korea, Republic of	1.8	2.3	1.9	4.0	2.7	1.9	2.7	2.9	3.2	3.6
China/Chine			2.7	1.1	1.4	1.5	1.8	3.0	3.9	5.6

	1985	1986	1987	1988	1989	1990	1991	1992	1993	1994
Afrique	0.1	x0.2	x0.1	x0.1	x0.1		x0.0	x0.2	x0.2	x0.1
Afrique du Nord	0.0	x0.0	x0.0	x0.0	x0.1	0.0	x0.0	x0.0	0.0	x0.0
Amériques	53.5	53.7	56.5	51.5	49.5	52.6	49.0	48.5	49.2	48.0
ALAI	0.7	0.9	1.2	0.9	1.6	1.0	0.6	0.6	0.8	1.0
MCAC	0.0	0.0	x0.0	x0.0	x0.0	0.0	0.0	0.0	x0.0	x0.1
Asie	4.5	3.6	2.9	2.8	3.5	2.9	2.8	3.6	4.7	6.3
Moyen–Orient	0.4	x0.6	x0.4	x0.4	x0.3	0.2	x0.1	x0.1	x0.5	x0.7
Europe	38.4	37.6	35.1	40.9	42.9	41.2	46.8	46.9	44.9	44.6
CEE	37.0	36.0	33.0	39.0	41.4	40.4	46.3	46.1	44.3	44.1
AELE	1.3	1.6	2.0	1.9	1.4	0.7	0.5	0.8	0.5	0.4
Océanie	0.2	0.3	0.7	0.7	x0.7	0.7	0.7	0.7	0.7	0.7
USA/Etats–Unis d'Amer	48.4	47.6	50.9	46.7	44.2	47.3	44.3	44.9	45.3	43.5
France,Monac	8.1	7.1	8.7	10.5	11.6	10.6	12.7	13.5	14.0	15.8
Germany/Allemagne	11.2	8.8	10.1	11.7	13.3	12.2	13.1	13.1	12.2	12.1
United Kingdom	10.4	12.6	6.5	7.8	6.7	5.6	11.1	9.6	8.4	8.1
Canada	4.2	5.1	4.4	3.8	3.6	4.2	4.1	2.9	3.1	3.3
Italy/Italie	3.6	3.2	3.3	3.5	3.3	4.5	3.3	3.6	2.6	2.9
Netherlands/Pays–Bas	1.5	2.0	1.6	2.2	2.5	2.9	2.2	2.8	3.8	1.7
Spain/Espagne	0.4	0.4	0.5	1.5	1.6	1.6	1.5	1.3	1.6	1.9
Malaysia/Malaisie	0.2	0.2	0.1	0.2	0.4	0.4	0.6	0.9	1.2	2.2
Belgium–Luxembourg	0.8	0.7	0.8	0.6	1.0	0.9	1.0	0.9	0.7	0.4

TRADE BY COMMODITY IN THOUSAND U.S. DOLLARS – COMMERCE PAR PRODUIT EN MILLIERS DE DOLLARS E.U

COUNTRIES–PAYS	IMPORTS – IMPORTATIONS 1990	1991	1992	1993	1994
Total	20091379	15631599	x16182845	x17735520	x22037928
Africa	x707003	x732914	x651234	x709634	x5361382
Northern Africa	219178	130148	x112330	98148	120844
Americas	x1492305	x1294487	x3419472	x4550101	x3644724
LAIA	371550	243604	440645	608631	505869
CACM	12569	10711	5687	x7450	18679
Asia	4527891	4170020	5078257	5053970	8066021
Middle East	400883	x370548	415273	x635162	x644763
Europe	9946637	7958007	6581000	6587561	4672495
EEC	6922529	5590009	5052547	4681437	3132550
EFTA	2939455	2281913	1474915	1866981	1184660
Oceania	x401144	x497465	x440014	x815502	x280203
Norway,SVD,JM	2833501	2174242	1277098	1780050	1060550
Bahamas	9824	8065	x2002626	x2309003	x1172042
Singapore/Singapour	919850	862187	1236450	1299427	1227931
Greece/Grèce	527061	882091	819670	1485953	585463
Germany/Allemagne	513816	841173	632361	727606	492246
France,Monac	563748	577705	835517	567502	320417
Malaysia/Malaisie	502560	759924	722538	325381	1328956
Korea, Republic of	747143	211717	840275	718796	1467464
China/Chine	489455	337900	451907	843076	1346466
USA/Etats–Unis d'Amer	342457	256422	327344	987876	821072
Denmark/Danemark	665532	587769	365472	444457	558457
Italy/Italie	504555	576635	485841	332266	83325
Indonesia/Indonésie	481387	558068	486611	326652	514398
Sweden/Suède	595445	750060	393625	152889	341628
United Kingdom	2654014	539743	461413	101855	91505
Former USSR/Anc. URSS	2882388	x955433			
Australia/Australie	250654	334482	33233	555653	86730
Japan/Japon	398260	445662	267307	193150	197288
Liberia/Libéria	x250666	x262465	x280743	x290447	x5053112
Finland/Finlande	213371	214273	228103	361469	40779
Russian Federation			x410688	x332380	x116605
Turkey/Turquie	176032	197193	199527	337533	279408
Netherlands/Pays–Bas	218709	217874	313383	181859	142332
Spain/Espagne	226262	219770	291857	173532	192203
Canada	228160	187231	182980	154270	162198
Thailand/Thaïlande	107206	113271	137182	118799	242637
Venezuela	65328	27213	155246	180718	212504
Hong Kong	61070	70187	113854	178971	136066
Israel/Israël	115124	179066	126964	34874	14098
Bermuda/Bermudes	x48065	x133718	x73116	x94829	x281617
Nigeria/Nigéria	x46125	87247	x113017	x84132	x9275
Guadeloupe	85443	135958	86316	40350	39464
Belgium–Luxembourg	80301	82380	88832	84630	149716
Wallis and Futuna Is	x19	x18464	x229788	x115	x4379
India/Inde	266317	55354	109469	81153	72011
Argentina/Argentine	64433	38776	91429	104243	64610
New Zealand	79174	95858	103993	25820	51242
Switz.Liecht	80730	76795	78972	61225	65470
Morocco/Maroc	187862	108998	32363	69643	20716
Brazil/Brésil	9737	13106	23688	164051	19424
Chile/Chili	92300	65150	53530	76889	94245
Martinique	137904	70139	61870	52912	32392
Iceland/Islande	25224	30876	118845	25706	58640
Gabon	x3077	x55217	x45148	x74541	x5502
Iran (Islamic Rp. of)		x47221	x29931	x94893	x83405
Cayman Is/Is Caïmans	x4981	x2925	x97560	x71143	x237774
Ukraine			x40151	x117385	x5348
Portugal	118990	52984	77360	27185	85946
Bangladesh		38152	47113	70656	x45347
Philippines	3890	6415	26311	110607	668016

COUNTRIES–PAYS	EXPORTS – EXPORTATIONS 1990	1991	1992	1993	1994
Totale	27085280	25154713	30036685	30496238	32078161
Afrique	x301294	x292960	x266216	x287985	x266294
Afrique du Nord	14636	10484	x18466	54963	3150
Amériques	1663460	1616057	x2489685	x2616046	x2537055
ALAI	205747	282852	258905	354882	574554
MCAC	1964	1069	850	x1083	x1479
Asie	9551538	12405696	14165048	15728962	18584728
Moyen–Orient	103370	113203	187119	x127878	x102891
Europe	14452640	9866858	12198023	10716275	9424095
CEE	12113590	7422969	9362557	8896949	7616343
AELE	1835213	2277376	2300008	1615008	1357609
Océanie	174056	221890	315582	x366221	x296709
Japan/Japon	5566130	6722390	7946474	10187698	11615332
Korea, Republic of	2800572	4129112	4112777	4060623	4944844
Germany/Allemagne	1913655	2068200	2605957	2281379	1762319
Norway,SVD,JM	1813510	2258189	2272618	1582256	1322928
USA/Etats–Unis d'Amer	1298944	1174872	1465453	996199	1240890
France,Monac	992741	945404	1531204	922707	721974
Spain/Espagne	866202	885474	1084497	1121062	581459
Denmark/Danemark	763361	680825	1137640	977418	1035867
Italy/Italie	538319	569907	483097	903195	722358
Finland/Finlande	815532	590357	526262	728942	519600
Netherlands/Pays–Bas	535537	624771	691435	454975	642448
Singapore/Singapour	380443	322909	641880	745468	867880
Sweden/Suède	338999	237674	425487	873966	721434
Bahamas	x15203	2481	x541930	x945124	x218882
Poland/Pologne	217497	352566	459613	645971	786584
United Kingdom	5076278	559073	516669	367811	758503
Malaysia/Malaisie	319488	556461	531675	170226	282839
China/Chine	223251	309447	480532	241560	552191
Australia/Australie	142002	185421	287099	313401	206242
Brazil/Brésil	73970	178633	202785	223565	411922
Croatia/Croatie			440560	162342	x282773
Canada	121323	113671	174668	257017	344127
Liberia/Libéria	x222535	x226288	x147496	x142712	x228004
Portugal	94267	48717	155159	129710	38502
Russian Federation			x155414	x154203	x82625
Turkey/Turquie	64818	91879	136823	74780	53779
Romania/Roumanie	42411	95267	106173	49101	126787
Indonesia/Indonésie	57173	95445	54671	98768	68386
Belgium–Luxembourg	61434	62725	83307	55896	60835
Former USSR/Anc. URSS	418993	x197010			
So. Africa Customs Un	35242	16483	92527	79271	15371
Austria/Autriche	56390	78316	58993	17569	x22670
Bulgaria/Bulgarie	x248416	x82078	31659	28554	21734
Korea Dem People's Rp	x177	x33	x110680	x10250	x170
Thailand/Thaïlande	6631	64736	32216	17094	77515
Yugoslavia SFR	427834	x113821			
Greece/Grèce	13796	28365	36477	43596	28374
United Arab Emirates	10617	19312	38767	x46756	x33473
Hong Kong	27341	30279	28982	41349	36907
Argentina/Argentine	25359	32468	22511	30183	46853
New Zealand	28437	32725	25247	26908	88254
Colombia/Colombie	329	22565	114	53174	53740
Faeroe Islds/Is Féroé	26898	23434	39924	12338	7791
Ukraine			x45471	x29861	x51672
Morocco/Maroc	8985	4378	12204	53070	751
Mexico/Mexique	78370	34792	13008	21526	9067
Ireland/Irlande	27807	23889	26373	18723	
Israel/Israël	25410	30263	14026	17817	18210
Yugoslavia/Yougoslavie			x36352	x16278	x32502
Switz.Liecht	11475	16173	18245	13447	12818

(VALUE AS % OF TOTAL)(VALEUR EN % DU TOTAL)

	1985	1986	1987	1988	1989	1990	1991	1992	1993	1994
Africa	2.1	x5.9	x3.2	x2.3	x3.7	x3.5	x4.7	x4.0	x4.0	x24.4
Northern Africa	0.7	2.2	0.9	0.8	1.1	1.1	0.8	x0.7	0.6	0.5
Americas	9.0	x13.1	x11.5	9.7	x7.3	x7.4	x8.2	x21.2	x25.6	x16.6
LAIA	3.5	3.0	3.1	1.7	1.3	1.8	1.6	2.7	3.4	2.3
CACM	0.1	0.0	x0.1	0.1	0.1	0.1	0.1	0.0	x0.0	0.1
Asia	44.9	23.0	x19.5	x16.9	16.3	22.6	26.7	31.3	28.5	36.6
Middle East	2.5	x1.7	x1.0	x1.3	x1.5	2.0	x2.4	2.6	x3.6	x2.9
Europe	21.9	30.7	44.4	50.5	55.3	49.5	50.9	40.7	37.1	21.2
EEC	14.9	20.8	31.7	30.7	30.0	34.5	35.8	31.2	26.4	14.2
EFTA	6.5	9.0	11.4	18.9	24.9	14.6	14.6	9.1	10.5	5.4
Oceania	1.0	x2.0	x2.0	x1.5	x3.6	x2.0	x3.2	x2.7	x4.6	x1.2
Norway,SVD,JM	4.1	5.4	6.9	13.8	19.2	14.1	13.9	7.9	10.0	4.8
Bahamas	0.0	0.1	0.1	0.1	0.1	0.0	0.1	x12.4	x13.0	x5.3
Singapore/Singapour	3.1	4.9	3.9	4.0	3.5	4.6	5.5	7.6	7.3	5.6
Greece/Grèce	4.2	4.7	4.1	4.2	4.0	2.6	5.6	5.1	8.4	2.7
Germany/Allemagne	2.5	1.5	2.3	1.6	1.4	2.6	5.4	3.9	4.1	2.2
France,Monac	1.7	1.4	1.9	2.4	1.4	2.8	3.7	5.2	3.2	1.5
Malaysia/Malaisie	2.5	2.2	1.4	0.9	1.3	2.5	4.9	4.5	1.8	6.0
Korea, Republic of	26.1	4.3	3.0	1.3	2.0	3.7	1.4	5.2	4.1	6.7
China/Chine	4.0	2.4	1.7	1.5	2.1	2.4	2.2	2.8	4.8	6.1
USA/Etats–Unis d'Amer	3.8	4.6	4.8	4.5	3.0	1.7	1.6	2.0	5.6	3.7

	1985	1986	1987	1988	1989	1990	1991	1992	1993	1994
Afrique	0.1	x0.8	x0.7	x0.8	x1.3	x1.1	x1.2	x0.9	x1.0	x0.8
Afrique du Nord	0.1	0.2	x0.0	0.0	0.2	0.1	0.0	x0.1	0.2	0.0
Amériques	4.6	5.1	x7.5	x8.6	x10.3	6.1	6.4	x8.3	x8.6	x7.9
ALAI	1.6	1.5	1.3	0.4	0.5	0.8	1.1	0.9	1.2	1.8
MCAC	0.0	x0.0	x0.0	x0.0	x0.1	0.0	0.0	0.0	x0.0	x0.0
Asie	55.0	40.8	31.1	30.4	30.2	35.2	49.3	47.2	51.6	58.0
Moyen–Orient	0.4	0.2	x0.2	x0.1	x0.1	0.4	0.5	0.6	x0.4	x0.3
Europe	37.6	48.9	56.4	55.4	54.0	53.4	39.2	40.6	35.1	29.4
CEE	20.8	28.0	41.8	42.1	41.6	44.7	29.5	31.2	29.2	23.7
AELE	12.8	17.9	12.8	10.9	10.0	6.8	9.1	7.7	5.3	4.2
Océanie	0.2	x0.2	x0.3	0.6	x0.9	0.6	0.9	1.0	x1.2	x0.9
Japan/Japon	28.5	27.3	20.7	17.3	18.8	20.6	26.7	26.5	33.4	36.2
Korea, Republic of	24.2	10.2	5.4	7.7	7.6	10.3	16.4	13.7	13.3	15.4
Germany/Allemagne	3.0	4.3	6.6	4.7	4.3	7.1	8.2	8.7	7.5	5.5
Norway,SVD,JM	6.1	8.9	7.7	4.3	4.4	6.7	9.0	7.6	5.2	4.1
USA/Etats–Unis d'Amer	2.7	3.2	3.4	4.7	4.3	4.8	4.7	4.9	3.3	3.9
France,Monac	2.1	4.2	3.2	3.0	3.6	3.7	3.8	5.1	3.0	2.3
Spain/Espagne	2.0	1.7	1.4	1.7	1.9	3.2	3.5	3.6	3.7	1.8
Denmark/Danemark	2.4	2.3	2.3	3.2	2.5	2.8	2.7	3.8	3.2	3.2
Italy/Italie	1.3	1.3	1.4	1.5	1.9	2.0	2.3	1.6	3.0	2.3
Finland/Finlande	4.3	5.2	2.7	4.6	3.9	3.0	2.3	1.8	2.4	1.6

TRADE BY COMMODITY IN THOUSAND U.S. DOLLARS – COMMERCE PAR PRODUIT EN MILLIERS DE DOLLARS E.U

COUNTRIES–PAYS	IMPORTS – IMPORTATIONS				
	1990	1991	1992	1993	1994
Total	9599938	10593885	12058351	11615060	13086657
Africa	x197474	x182578	x199725	x219642	x234076
Northern Africa	70072	67660	x65843	x69924	x84849
Americas	x1777642	1865745	2218924	2551757	x2991615
LAIA	76540	114990	175394	217567	288259
CACM	13602	14320	18435	x23271	x29900
Asia	1382410	1572428	1812712	x2174283	x2365698
Middle East	345473	x413407	510296	x543253	x509589
Europe	5941396	6658674	7450240	6200774	6940721
EEC	5408684	6136486	6894302	5718029	6360874
EFTA	480971	477320	489300	426260	488493
Oceania	x145226	x153132	x159390	x157939	x196303
Germany/Allemagne	1335623	1931222	2218985	1780647	1973338
USA/Etats–Unis d'Amer	1268343	1295120	1540654	1798271	2103201
France,Monac	781798	803120	818341	695379	765984
Hong Kong	385406	534434	589740	811592	893388
Netherlands/Pays–Bas	580344	607353	684229	562508	632890
United Kingdom	621332	599787	651960	562978	648353
Belgium–Luxembourg	381484	423236	507423	472427	510161
Canada	321730	356267	411296	446689	486053
Italy/Italie	348726	386554	455442	369963	429070
Spain/Espagne	303606	349680	428604	311886	321453
Austria/Autriche	302988	321990	372154	354351	404441
Switz.Liecht	329231	317885	329687	290145	333245
Sweden/Suède	264005	229856	238730	195867	217742
Japan/Japon	216787	192557	184584	190962	244905
Saudi Arabia	119575	118389	162512	x171391	x161278
Norway,SVD,JM	140678	145625	146545	126069	145670
Singapore/Singapour	102888	109289	135508	163608	184837
Denmark/Danemark	120110	122362	144004	117375	141582
Australia/Australie	102061	108591	116357	118016	144748
China/Chine	58983	67479	107906	152096	166576
Greece/Grèce	103814	90628	100847	93459	95173
United Arab Emirates	90586	72872	96683	x103818	x117810
Ireland/Irlande	90480	102201	100578	67742	71803
Mexico/Mexique	38012	54890	95311	118359	142554
Portugal	62944	81489	98440	74110	71246
Korea, Republic of	107724	84384	73077	69266	63925
Finland/Finlande	111430	87009	74565	59336	77637
Poland/Pologne	1528	12438	67498	89313	114935
Russian Federation			x76857	x91921	x175058
Turkey/Turquie	37954	41818	46363	68184	43374
Hungary/Hongrie	x19075	28772	x56560	x70335	x72084
Malaysia/Malaisie	25970	36123	48235	50910	52877
Iran (Islamic Rp. of)		x47249	x42064	x35260	x8272
Israel/Israël	27805	28875	37116	39596	42787
Kuwait/Koweït	20752	13330	41906	36096	47687
Thailand/Thaïlande	17455	26531	29280	33902	47571
Czech Republic				81257	105157
Romania/Roumanie	4788	28399	37271	10099	14976
Cyprus/Chypre	20545	20345	30313	24617	23738
Nigeria/Nigéria	x13168	12638	x23321	x36733	x26238
New Zealand	25023	22319	22628	27189	36892
Czechoslovakia	33725	x19179	x51314		
So. Africa Customs Un	19946	23337	24697	22213	26324
Former USSR/Anc. URSS	80141	x69090			
Oman	16780	19304	24403	21607	27641
Indonesia/Indonésie	22235	19576	26541	18336	33176
Chile/Chili	12062	11720	20974	25433	27370
Argentina/Argentine	1892	7701	21995	27931	46181
Libyan Arab Jamahiriya	25732	20155	x14472	x19617	x27818
Tunisia/Tunisie	13956	14752	19483	18387	20110

COUNTRIES–PAYS	EXPORTS – EXPORTATIONS				
	1990	1991	1992	1993	1994
Totale	8460510	9327358	10931561	10951279	12440476
Afrique	x35870	39135	39970	45339	30255
Afrique du Nord	19276	27348	26652	30381	28020
Amériques	697526	805653	1036020	1349305	1467988
ALAI	105167	108776	223608	431330	421386
MCAC	8630	8518	12465	x13283	x19883
Asie	1065409	1355904	1740512	2232438	2626157
Moyen–Orient	67743	74672	90265	x95762	x113327
Europe	6538728	6969393	7904745	7018528	7967015
CEE	6214343	6648642	7520961	6681443	7587141
AELE	269975	281235	303058	276657	318657
Océanie	x18358	x22343	20510	x24545	x26036
Germany/Allemagne	1653424	1696249	1954305	1611587	1773755
Italy/Italie	1410373	1536030	1705937	1651658	1921770
France,Monac	768979	841759	956400	858626	958926
Hong Kong	513691	683019	774874	1025302	1098262
USA/Etats–Unis d'Amer	508422	605269	709757	775147	848954
Belgium–Luxembourg	414178	483161	576052	532808	598718
Netherlands/Pays–Bas	422999	474435	530656	436734	494997
Austria/Autriche	343369	403173	454073	371235	x390465
China/Chine	127527	184962	414963	574390	820142
United Kingdom	361604	354081	379355	325279	356281
Spain/Espagne	239282	243045	274491	262465	331019
Sweden/Suède	221596	212782	222189	189434	239200
Switz.Liecht	178502	201473	218630	204121	239801
Mexico/Mexique	48297	67781	178643	372089	344209
Japan/Japon	145607	160972	178691	193469	172819
Denmark/Danemark	151832	168555	194598	164999	181677
Finland/Finlande	122608	111224	132044	158005	220260
Canada	72903	81156	87430	125261	172638
Norway,SVD,JM	91472	79751	84394	72483	78746
Thailand/Thaïlande	40040	59876	76246	98106	123739
Turkey/Turquie	44054	60682	70920	71048	84691
Korea, Republic of	80354	66152	63435	71362	97866
Portugal	53726	62478	69409	62303	64023
Hungary/Hongrie	x34365	x38427	x56695	x67075	x78789
Ireland/Irlande	43441	54842	59137	39114	34178
Singapore/Singapour	32998	35838	43342	49997	69458
Czechoslovakia		x59552	x68517		
Czech Republic				107068	111553
Indonesia/Indonésie	13181	34223	28198	31474	28813
Malaysia/Malaisie	15023	19324	29045	40409	44590
Slovenia/Slovénia			39015	34274	40635
Poland/Pologne	4563	5641	31162	34257	52084
Australia/Australie	14007	16803	14843	17505	18689
Slovakia				x45926	x41082
Romania/Roumanie	27767	11068	15416	18819	35913
Philippines	4917	12037	12952	15302	17967
Yugoslavia SFR	53734	x39222			
Brazil/Brésil	21873	9009	12292	16759	23842
Greece/Grèce	6898	6794	12314	17195	21872
Croatia/Croatie			20152	15955	x16495
India/Inde	11641	10095	9959	14895	17614
Morocco/Maroc	8635	10930	11291	11837	12057
So. Africa Customs Un	7677	8839	11791	12992	
Macau/Macao	7964	8526	10246	14035	12900
Bulgaria/Bulgarie	x19334	x7009	17325	7707	x3455
Colombia/Colombie	7291	8295	9588	13728	15688
Egypt/Egypte	4771	9826	8756	12396	10411
Venezuela	6416	8190	7513	8454	13440
Chile/Chili	8275	3917	6201	8705	10944
Argentina/Argentine	8585	7804	4789	5447	4529

(VALUE AS % OF TOTAL)(VALEUR EN % DU TOTAL)

	1985	1986	1987	1988	1989	1990	1991	1992	1993	1994
Africa	3.5	x3.0	x2.6	x2.4	x2.2	x2.0	x1.7	x1.7	x1.9	x1.8
Northern Africa	2.0	1.2	0.8	0.8	0.8	0.7	0.6	x0.5	x0.6	x0.6
Americas	20.4	x20.4	x19.1	17.0	19.4	x18.6	17.6	18.4	21.9	x22.9
LAIA	0.9	0.6	0.5	0.5	0.6	0.8	1.1	1.5	1.9	2.2
CACM	0.3	0.2	x0.3	0.2	0.2	0.1	0.1	0.2	x0.2	x0.2
Asia	18.5	14.3	12.7	13.7	13.4	14.4	14.9	15.0	x18.7	x18.1
Middle East	11.9	8.1	5.4	4.8	x3.9	3.6	x3.9	4.2	x4.7	x3.9
Europe	52.5	57.8	61.2	62.8	61.6	61.9	62.9	61.8	53.4	53.0
EEC	43.3	47.6	50.4	51.3	50.5	56.3	57.9	57.2	49.2	48.6
EFTA	8.8	9.8	10.3	11.1	10.7	5.0	4.5	4.1	3.7	3.7
Oceania	1.8	x1.4	x1.3	x1.6	x1.6	x1.5	x1.4	x1.4	x1.4	x1.5
Germany/Allemagne	9.9	10.8	11.2	11.5	11.7	13.9	18.2	18.4	15.3	15.1
USA/Etats–Unis d'Amer	14.0	14.4	13.6	11.8	14.1	13.2	12.2	12.8	15.5	16.1
France,Monac	6.9	7.7	8.0	8.4	7.9	8.1	7.6	6.8	6.0	5.9
Hong Kong	2.2	2.0	2.3	2.6	3.3	4.0	5.0	4.9	7.0	6.8
Netherlands/Pays–Bas	4.4	4.8	5.6	5.8	5.4	6.0	5.7	5.7	4.8	4.8
United Kingdom	6.3	6.6	6.7	6.9	6.4	6.5	5.7	5.4	4.8	5.0
Belgium–Luxembourg	3.0	3.3	3.4	3.7	3.5	4.0	4.0	4.2	4.1	3.9
Canada	4.4	3.7	3.7	3.6	3.6	3.4	3.4	3.4	3.8	3.7
Italy/Italie	4.2	4.6	5.0	3.6	3.4	3.6	3.6	3.8	3.2	3.3
Spain/Espagne	1.1	1.7	1.9	2.2	2.7	3.2	3.3	3.6	2.7	2.5

	1985	1986	1987	1988	1989	1990	1991	1992	1993	1994
Afrique	0.2	0.2	0.2	0.3	0.4	x0.4	0.4	0.4	0.4	0.2
Afrique du Nord	0.1	0.1	0.1	0.2	0.3	0.2	0.3	0.2	0.3	0.2
Amériques	11.5	9.1	7.7	7.1	8.3	8.3	8.7	9.5	12.3	11.8
ALAI	2.4	1.5	1.3	1.4	1.6	1.2	1.2	2.0	3.9	3.4
MCAC	0.2	0.1	0.1	0.1	0.1	0.1	0.1	0.1	x0.1	x0.2
Asie	10.3	9.6	x17.5	x18.1	12.0	12.6	14.6	16.0	20.4	21.1
Moyen–Orient	0.6	0.6	0.7	0.7	x0.7	0.8	0.8	0.8	x0.9	x0.9
Europe	74.4	77.8	69.7	70.2	77.2	77.3	74.7	72.3	64.1	64.0
CEE	63.7	66.4	60.1	60.6	66.7	73.5	71.3	68.8	61.0	61.0
AELE	9.6	10.7	9.0	9.0	9.8	3.2	3.0	2.8	2.5	2.6
Océanie	0.2	x0.2	x0.2	x0.2	x0.2	x0.2	x0.2	0.2	x0.2	x0.2
Germany/Allemagne	13.9	15.3	15.4	16.1	17.9	19.5	18.2	17.9	14.7	14.3
Italy/Italie	14.9	15.4	13.7	13.9	15.9	16.7	16.5	15.6	15.1	15.4
France,Monac	8.7	9.3	8.0	7.7	8.2	9.1	9.0	8.7	7.8	7.7
Hong Kong	5.0	4.4	4.1	4.3	5.3	6.1	7.3	7.1	9.4	8.8
USA/Etats–Unis d'Amer	6.1	5.0	4.3	4.5	5.5	6.0	6.5	6.5	7.1	6.8
Belgium–Luxembourg	4.4	4.8	4.1	4.0	4.4	4.9	5.2	5.3	4.9	4.8
Netherlands/Pays–Bas	3.5	3.9	3.8	3.9	4.1	5.0	5.1	4.9	4.0	4.0
Austria/Autriche	3.4	4.0	3.2	3.1	3.6	4.1	4.3	4.2	3.4	x3.1
China/Chine	0.5	0.5	0.9	1.0	1.4	1.5	2.0	3.8	5.2	6.6
United Kingdom	5.0	4.1	3.4	3.4	3.8	4.3	3.8	3.5	3.0	2.9

TRADE BY COMMODITY IN THOUSAND U.S. DOLLARS – COMMERCE PAR PRODUIT EN MILLIERS DE DOLLARS E.U

COUNTRIES–PAYS	IMPORTS – IMPORTATIONS 1990	1991	1992	1993	1994
Total	31668576	32785237	35909365	32922107	38188601
Africa	x363951	x308272	x367390	x398291	x398704
Northern Africa	110469	75496	x119247	x138679	x121656
Americas	7096634	7269237	8423630	9574462	11420538
LAIA	187804	281881	541919	675732	939109
CACM	8987	11607	24807	x35344	x47788
Asia	3225521	3714513	4181341	x4583224	x5772602
Middle East	618017	804100	1021068	x974024	x911061
Europe	19393380	20528438	22089212	17439137	19560564
EEC	17093472	18278185	19794860	15398117	17233190
EFTA	2177091	2118819	2111676	1860973	2081188
Oceania	x364178	x348551	x377368	x373172	x454218
USA/Etats–Unis d'Amer	5509280	5443595	6085658	6905130	8290294
Germany/Allemagne	4323244	5460285	6333110	5006546	5579823
France,Monac	3463245	3289686	3261655	2474347	2737365
Netherlands/Pays–Bas	1875125	1967959	2147864	1454382	1611151
United Kingdom	2032458	1829772	1917127	1614420	1726927
Japan/Japon	1484515	1686029	1740901	1933460	2676587
Belgium–Luxembourg	1499027	1595595	1793787	1340174	1546087
Canada	1116036	1287540	1546235	1740037	1907868
Switz.Liecht	1637176	1585190	1560569	1385519	1544371
Austria/Autriche	963292	1030245	1135491	1100054	1244947
Sweden/Suède	822590	860208	816754	616600	763687
Hong Kong	494708	566976	678160	790979	966805
Italy/Italie	590039	650544	705953	537306	582299
Spain/Espagne	560005	609302	669185	436087	506807
Norway,SVD,JM	506999	493983	514652	446612	506150
Saudi Arabia	289552	349675	422029	x408444	x383785
Mexico/Mexique	150243	213168	398769	445553	612787
Denmark/Danemark	287869	299789	301488	293911	358963
Australia/Australie	262620	255853	271584	279700	345753
Russian Federation			x286727	x450524	x794971
Singapore/Singapour	165904	203326	234964	287200	370363
Portugal	126646	168607	226731	175226	164188
Finland/Finlande	272423	226471	176512	114119	162107
Kuwait/ Koweït	44612	153570	210004	144949	120821
Hungary/Hongrie	x70930	76851	x172358	x182111	x176119
Ireland/Irlande	159603	159618	162992	102812	112808
United Arab Emirates	126278	107847	141495	x172145	x183713
Greece/Grèce	117907	130106	146209	132132	136031
Former USSR/Anc. URSS	1046624	x406661			
Korea, Republic of	129278	136832	106766	132375	203574
Israel/Israël	93109	102592	110059	131324	193018
Poland/Pologne	5200	67741	132788	117030	121959
China/Chine	72348	49208	90684	99615	119122
Libyan Arab Jamahiriya	72447	41747	x77518	x97700	x72257
Czechoslovakia	49310	x48557	x141542		
Ukraine			x14515	x175503	x84563
Malaysia/Malaisie	43684	57429	60487	63449	78651
Reunion/Réunion	63879	60318	64724	52707	59464
Czech Republic				157403	173729
So. Africa Customs Un	37491	41423	50733	48534	59935
Argentina/Argentine	4572	12235	51802	76105	115241
Turkey/Turquie	29667	32097	46660	61263	42956
Guadeloupe	54961	48170	46732	38342	41125
Slovenia/Slovénia			64445	67531	82703
New Zealand	55843	43218	41780	45673	63400
Martinique	40639	44417	43651	38870	40398
Iceland/Islande	32915	39646	36455	28843	30667
Oman	30160	29504	31942	40199	36311
Iran (Islamic Rp. of)		x23010	x44970	x28072	x6477
Qatar	29936	24128	37641	30253	x21112

COUNTRIES–PAYS	EXPORTS – EXPORTATIONS 1990	1991	1992	1993	1994
Totale	28282499	29778524	33069778	32858841	37920556
Afrique	128383	132778	127774	140562	x254200
Afrique du Nord	67888	52022	36848	28718	23090
Amériques	3419898	3929702	5090337	6042860	7188090
ALAI	139087	205345	684623	996252	1228626
MCAC	18816	17592	21818	x32934	x39349
Asie	2666731	3192025	3900920	4872393	5976069
Moyen–Orient	84861	122145	106333	x115036	x126499
Europe	20953773	21233540	22600292	20224122	22475477
CEE	19527265	19984397	21184035	18902574	21100243
AELE	807278	853843	875697	798146	849239
Océanie	x68543	x69011	x76040	x98758	x116161
Italy/Italie	5592659	5621231	5947289	5797352	6735357
Germany/Allemagne	4856558	4884700	4877598	4090292	4323718
USA/Etats–Unis d'Amer	1933290	2515679	2982721	3308637	3728791
France,Monac	1758793	1768618	1935439	1648593	1807696
Denmark/Danemark	1392246	1539873	1723465	1598916	1786350
Belgium–Luxembourg	1368530	1439805	1566300	1409315	1498678
Canada	1310016	1172741	1388858	1694675	2174523
United Kingdom	1006571	1055190	1152532	916165	1095696
Netherlands/Pays–Bas	1007079	1051005	1124068	877153	878434
Sweden/Suède	903457	931327	996981	849575	1013946
China/Chine	321615	464889	825344	1082512	1495573
Switz.Liecht	634656	682554	690148	629334	646499
Austria/Autriche	578639	619578	708941	650647	x663219
Spain/Espagne	591828	586239	613841	552528	727028
Japan/Japon	474495	525268	519528	582888	582202
Indonesia/Indonésie	286269	385019	490503	676146	784440
Thailand/Thaïlande	309628	412234	485824	593966	706728
Hong Kong	276694	340690	431872	569198	709444
Poland/Pologne	199260	351383	403762	580978	894779
Malaysia/Malaisie	171520	269308	393782	566264	768466
Mexico/Mexique	45952	86642	481460	659019	851299
Romania/Roumanie	356016	396634	356681	379175	397480
Singapore/Singapour	191213	211812	225026	234255	240837
Slovenia/Slovénia			308553	321489	374096
Portugal	151213	179736	214343	190355	211871
Finland/Finlande	201285	184679	179427	217176	328046
Philippines	189460	178639	181176	203271	240153
Korea, Republic of	227703	218401	169850	164818	203468
Norway,SVD,JM	172558	171217	185523	168784	202637
Hungary/Hongrie	x139176	x145494	x200296	x159928	x162218
Czechoslovakia		x185616	x280074		
Brazil/Brésil	45204	65365	138535	260101	286903
Yugoslavia SFR	606200	x386613			
Ireland/Irlande	109348	114088	127788	75182	
Croatia/Croatie			109423	148076	x122831
So. Africa Customs Un	45826	63123	74658	82511	208291
Czech Republic				194908	288717
Slovakia				x136737	x126289
Israel/Israël	48669	41733	45142	48080	38448
Russian Federation			x64473	x66595	x49450
Australia/Australie	35630	34205	36678	54171	61215
New Zealand	30155	31901	36346	42389	52746
Yugoslavia/Yougoslavie			x94148	x15794	x4922
Former USSR/Anc. URSS	85896	x101316			
Turkey/Turquie	21131	20712	31527	47440	55608
Bulgaria/Bulgarie	x120527	x38281	32103	24954	40911
Chile/Chili	15959	25074	27338	35383	40378
Egypt/Egypte	58728	41156	23221	19231	14963
Saudi Arabia	11728	47797	26020	x8176	x6933
Greece/Grèce	8577	7848	16025	29326	30203

(VALUE AS % OF TOTAL)(VALEUR EN % DU TOTAL)

	1985	1986	1987	1988	1989	1990	1991	1992	1993	1994
Africa	1.1	x1.3	x1.2	x1.1	x1.0	x1.1	x0.9	x1.0	x1.2	x1.1
Northern Africa	0.7	0.4	0.4	0.4	0.3	0.3	0.2	x0.3	x0.4	x0.3
Americas	30.8	28.3	x25.7	24.1	24.2	22.4	22.1	23.5	29.1	29.9
LAIA	0.2	0.1	0.3	0.4	0.5	0.6	0.9	1.5	2.1	2.5
CACM	0.0	0.0	0.0	0.1	0.0	0.0	0.0	0.1	x0.1	x0.1
Asia	11.9	9.2	8.5	9.5	9.9	10.2	11.4	11.7	x13.9	x15.1
Middle East	6.6	4.5	3.0	2.5	x2.3	2.0	2.5	2.8	x3.0	x2.4
Europe	49.9	55.2	59.2	59.8	60.0	61.2	62.6	61.5	53.0	51.2
EEC	39.1	42.9	45.9	47.0	47.6	54.0	55.8	55.1	46.8	45.1
EFTA	10.7	12.1	13.0	12.6	12.2	6.9	6.5	5.9	5.7	5.4
Oceania	1.4	x1.2	x1.1	x1.1	x1.3	x1.1	x1.1	x1.1	x1.1	x1.2
USA/Etats–Unis d'Amer	27.7	25.2	22.5	19.8	19.2	17.4	16.6	16.9	21.0	21.7
Germany/Allemagne	9.2	9.9	10.8	10.9	11.3	13.7	16.7	17.6	15.2	14.6
France,Monac	8.5	9.8	10.1	10.1	9.8	10.9	10.0	9.1	7.5	7.2
Netherlands/Pays–Bas	4.5	5.1	5.5	5.4	5.1	5.9	6.0	6.0	4.4	4.2
United Kingdom	6.3	6.4	6.4	6.8	6.6	6.4	5.6	5.3	4.9	4.5
Japan/Japon	2.4	2.4	3.0	4.1	4.6	4.7	5.1	4.8	5.9	7.0
Belgium–Luxembourg	2.9	3.4	3.6	3.8	4.0	4.7	4.9	5.0	4.1	4.0
Canada	2.2	2.1	2.0	3.0	3.5	3.5	3.9	4.3	5.3	5.0
Switz.Liecht	3.8	4.4	4.9	4.9	4.7	5.2	4.8	4.3	4.2	4.0
Austria/Autriche	2.2	2.4	2.6	2.6	2.6	3.0	3.1	3.2	3.3	3.3

	1985	1986	1987	1988	1989	1990	1991	1992	1993	1994
Afrique	0.2	0.3	x0.3	0.2	0.3	0.5	0.4	0.4	0.5	x0.6
Afrique du Nord	0.0	0.0	0.0	0.1	0.1	0.2	0.2	0.1	0.1	0.1
Amériques	11.4	9.1	7.3	8.4	9.9	12.1	13.2	15.4	18.4	19.0
ALAI	0.9	0.6	0.4	0.5	0.6	0.5	0.7	2.1	3.0	3.2
MCAC	0.1	0.1	0.1	0.1	0.1	0.1	0.1	0.1	x0.1	x0.1
Asie	6.8	5.8	x14.5	x15.2	9.4	9.4	10.7	11.8	14.8	15.7
Moyen–Orient	0.6	0.5	0.3	0.3	x0.4	0.3	0.4	0.3	x0.4	x0.3
Europe	77.8	78.8	68.6	67.5	75.1	74.1	71.3	68.3	61.5	59.3
CEE	65.7	67.5	58.6	57.7	64.9	69.0	67.1	64.1	57.5	55.6
AELE	9.0	9.1	8.1	7.9	8.2	2.9	2.9	2.6	2.4	2.2
Océanie	0.4	x0.3	x0.3	x0.2	x0.3	x0.2	x0.2	x0.2	x0.3	x0.3
Italy/Italie	18.4	18.8	16.4	16.4	19.1	19.8	18.9	18.0	17.6	17.8
Germany/Allemagne	15.9	17.6	15.1	14.9	16.5	17.2	16.4	14.7	12.4	11.4
USA/Etats–Unis d'Amer	6.2	4.5	3.8	4.4	5.3	6.8	8.4	9.0	10.1	9.8
France,Monac	5.3	5.3	4.6	4.8	5.6	6.2	5.9	5.9	5.0	4.8
Denmark/Danemark	5.4	5.1	4.3	4.0	4.4	4.9	5.2	5.2	4.9	4.7
Belgium–Luxembourg	4.8	4.9	4.3	4.0	4.4	4.8	4.8	4.7	4.3	4.0
Canada	4.2	3.8	3.0	3.4	3.9	4.6	3.9	4.2	5.2	5.7
United Kingdom	4.0	3.4	2.9	2.8	3.3	3.6	3.5	3.5	2.8	2.9
Netherlands/Pays–Bas	2.8	3.1	2.8	2.8	3.2	3.6	3.5	3.4	2.7	2.3
Sweden/Suède	4.6	4.5	3.7	3.4	3.3	3.2	3.1	3.0	2.6	2.7

TRADE BY COMMODITY IN THOUSAND U.S. DOLLARS – COMMERCE PAR PRODUIT EN MILLIERS DE DOLLARS E.U

COUNTRIES–PAYS	IMPORTS – IMPORTATIONS 1990	1991	1992	1993	1994
Total	10353778	11050309	12366614	12714970	14603419
Africa	x76101	x72286	x107713	x126035	x137950
Northern Africa	9597	8273	x15631	x19051	x14500
Americas	2673110	2859002	3088834	3242150	3735021
LAIA	51262	86360	125935	135810	157831
CACM	2942	3438	4719	x5632	x6474
Asia	3384632	3905045	4655047	5205367	6291831
Middle East	168926	198401	222749	x226461	x245099
Europe	3658349	3934634	4210138	3812878	4044787
EEC	3302062	3586263	3828626	3468856	3655463
EFTA	324359	330712	359414	322138	358676
Oceania	x222277	x225182	x265543	x255425	x318500
USA/Etats–Unis d'Amer	2362567	2492862	2675120	2836282	3290758
Hong Kong	1627079	1966564	2439800	2710526	3209974
Japan/Japon	1313368	1487610	1649958	1901015	2373212
Germany/Allemagne	945596	1149579	1143184	1035072	1057315
France,Monac	627772	616867	675095	599926	677834
United Kingdom	551106	503665	548762	574080	589445
Italy/Italie	239460	279522	344498	280588	307411
Switz.Liecht	258625	262787	288208	255603	289062
Canada	217112	240581	248021	231897	244842
Netherlands/Pays–Bas	197544	215123	236342	232417	224348
Belgium–Luxembourg	195174	207875	225683	210853	220558
Singapore/Singapour	212086	183585	221942	230737	281937
Australia/Australie	163566	171788	200318	184727	229971
Spain/Espagne	103343	169550	201344	142592	149231
Austria/Autriche	132175	137166	139469	136735	143531
Sweden/Suède	127209	118404	114045	86536	98967
Saudi Arabia	81740	98694	98537	x87518	x107861
United Arab Emirates	53037	66468	71660	x81346	x76507
Norway,SVD,JM	61930	63860	67005	63365	66581
Mexico/Mexique	29651	49331	69203	66240	67986
Denmark/Danemark	59243	61739	66066	56769	65551
Portugal	25871	35942	47830	37387	33558
China/Chine	6303	7234	46206	50506	49627
Greece/Grèce	28174	29921	33870	30386	32893
Guam	x28252	x23839	x32456	x37710	x44426
Russian Federation			x34792	x57000	x70903
So. Africa Customs Un	19465	25586	27684	30219	33052
Finland/Finlande	41398	33951	26480	19764	23440
Ireland/Irlande	27998	26959	25957	25750	31383
New Zealand	19740	20095	21557	23704	31426
Argentina/Argentine	1002	12603	21868	26452	31184
Korea, Republic of	14777	15312	16680	25056	42844
Kuwait/Koweït	13855	5623	23039	26029	26943
Malaysia/Malaisie	14372	13989	21192	17696	25849
Hungary/Hongrie	x5839	8024	x16079	x19715	x19691
Nigeria/Nigéria	x7631	5057	x14335	x23958	x19824
Venezuela	5785	7727	15330	14179	9689
Poland/Pologne	1989	14685	7951	14428	19574
Israel/Israël	7482	8363	8780	12947	18380
Thailand/Thaïlande	5476	7717	10959	10364	12604
Libyan Arab Jamahiriya	6921	5871	x8734	x12894	x8014
Chile/Chili	3615	5547	8541	12121	13360
Czech Republic				25859	24658
Andorra/Andorre	x7993	x7611	x7773	x6295	x7742
Former USSR/Anc. URSS	315178	x21484			
Czechoslovakia	9147	x7064	x13509		
Reunion/Réunion	6059	5264	6987	5609	5767
Panama	4834	4871	5445	6623	6277
Slovenia/Slovénia			6825	9499	12214
Philippines	2829	4177	4440	6292	8913

COUNTRIES–PAYS	EXPORTS – EXPORTATIONS 1990	1991	1992	1993	1994
Totale	7618396	8188589	10022293	10440776	12437323
Afrique	44163	44218	46681	46575	40860
Afrique du Nord	31960	31364	35663	33566	32495
Amériques	291122	342583	419583	482822	517820
ALAI	111320	131230	165855	218299	188626
MCAC	4226	4235	7159	7517	x8719
Asie	4239576	4920745	6444539	7007147	8288472
Moyen–Orient	59539	44693	53040	42894	x38874
Europe	2919405	2731348	2987815	2784415	3456795
CEE	2865278	2630622	2866565	2670260	3303965
AELE	45451	85752	103746	99116	137544
Océanie	x8860	x6571	x7582	x9659	x15511
Hong Kong	2090476	2683434	3211050	3562049	4072060
China/Chine	385120	492366	1476635	1726966	2364895
Italy/Italie	1140748	952066	1018547	936388	1243545
Korea, Republic of	1096832	1036063	894739	796333	706179
France,Monac	743049	716209	775199	771203	972330
Germany/Allemagne	346456	359824	382651	315168	353190
Thailand/Thaïlande	234111	266552	306511	354663	418787
USA/Etats–Unis d'Amer	145193	176397	213968	222973	263137
Belgium–Luxembourg	188029	172261	208576	216918	231545
India/Inde	134438	161255	215181	198710	253643
Netherlands/Pays–Bas	126931	139707	166026	137455	141376
United Kingdom	125070	127895	132138	142803	170125
Switz.Liecht	42365	83659	101784	96965	134411
Spain/Espagne	101049	78996	96518	75937	110499
Colombia/Colombie	65088	92014	65997	81773	69097
Mexico/Mexique	15136	16039	71888	104456	91672
Indonesia/Indonésie	20543	36156	62440	81575	69704
Philippines	43176	54743	52754	53736	76077
Japan/Japon	54531	54800	51607	46716	41062
Singapore/Singapour	25906	30893	38318	39336	51018
Hungary/Hongrie	x31974	x29816	x40673	x26016	x23616
Turkey/Turquie	35817	30920	32777	30519	28763
Malaysia/Malaisie	12303	19864	36630	35613	40877
Czechoslovakia		x41568	x45184		
Viet Nam	x59575	x13052	x20625	x43043	x101290
Poland/Pologne	16053	40698	14479	19373	22745
Canada	21897	21464	23274	26457	28544
Morocco/Maroc	16932	16955	19321	18050	16683
Denmark/Danemark	19991	20384	19943	13480	16471
Austria/Autriche	20666	15982	16639	14561	x13105
Portugal	10676	10965	16576	16617	17644
Sweden/Suède	19937	17093	15371	11520	13530
Bulgaria/Bulgarie	x45315	x21065	9074	8336	x17217
Tunisia/Tunisie	13092	12220	13162	12840	11708
Brazil/Brésil	8223	7103	14025	15505	12351
Czech Republic				32449	32036
Ireland/Irlande	12205	11494	11082	9524	9945
Sri Lanka	389	1752	9569	16146	34743
Romania/Roumanie	115	9072	6509	8653	11527
Cyprus/Chypre	11573	8906	8593	5955	3501
Macau/Macao	13437	12511	4978	1165	1638
Argentina/Argentine	5332	6048	3628	7383	7301
Dominican Republic	x3575	x5927	x6044	x4853	x26214
Finland/Finlande	6953	4973	5121	5510	7579
Slovenia/Slovénia			8060	6961	8721
Malta/Malte	2540	4173	4991	5613	x3742
Slovakia				x14374	x10378
Pakistan	2852	3713	5866	4365	3858
So. Africa Customs Un	2085	3123	4444	6074	
Australia/Australie	4512	3361	4030	5367	9446

(VALUE AS % OF TOTAL)(VALEUR EN % DU TOTAL)

	1985	1986	1987	1988	1989	1990	1991	1992	1993	1994
Africa	0.6	x0.9	x0.8	x0.9	x0.8	x0.7	x0.6	x0.8	x1.0	x0.9
Northern Africa	0.2	0.1	0.1	0.1	0.1	0.1	0.1	x0.1	x0.1	x0.1
Americas	40.1	x34.4	x31.7	28.4	27.9	25.8	25.8	24.9	25.5	25.6
LAIA	0.3	0.2	0.2	0.2	0.4	0.5	0.8	1.0	1.1	1.1
CACM	0.0	0.0	0.1	0.0	0.0	0.0	0.0	0.0	x0.0	x0.0
Asia	17.5	19.5	22.6	27.6	30.1	32.7	35.3	37.6	41.0	43.1
Middle East	3.7	3.0	2.2	2.0	x1.7	1.6	1.8	1.8	x1.8	x1.7
Europe	33.4	36.9	37.3	36.0	34.8	35.3	35.6	34.0	30.0	27.7
EEC	27.0	29.9	30.6	29.9	29.1	31.9	32.5	31.0	27.3	25.0
EFTA	6.4	6.9	6.6	6.0	5.6	3.1	3.0	2.9	2.5	2.5
Oceania	2.7	x2.6	x2.5	x2.4	x2.6	x2.2	x2.0	x2.2	x2.0	x2.2
USA/Etats–Unis d'Amer	36.8	31.5	29.1	25.7	24.9	22.8	22.6	21.6	22.3	22.5
Hong Kong	7.2	8.6	10.8	13.2	14.4	15.7	17.8	19.7	21.3	22.0
Japan/Japon	4.7	6.2	7.3	9.5	11.4	12.7	13.5	13.3	15.0	16.3
Germany/Allemagne	7.3	8.2	8.5	8.3	7.8	9.1	10.4	9.2	8.1	7.2
France,Monac	5.3	6.2	6.3	5.8	5.8	6.1	5.6	5.5	4.7	4.6
United Kingdom	5.5	5.5	5.4	5.5	5.3	5.3	4.6	4.4	4.5	4.0
Italy/Italie	1.1	1.3	1.7	2.0	2.1	2.3	2.5	2.8	2.2	2.1
Switz.Liecht	2.4	2.6	2.4	2.4	2.3	2.5	2.4	2.3	2.0	2.0
Canada	2.6	2.3	2.0	2.2	2.2	2.1	2.2	2.0	1.8	1.7
Netherlands/Pays–Bas	1.8	2.1	1.9	1.8	1.7	1.9	1.9	1.9	1.8	1.5

	1985	1986	1987	1988	1989	1990	1991	1992	1993	1994
Afrique	0.6	0.8	0.4	0.4	0.4	0.6	0.5	0.4	0.5	0.3
Afrique du Nord	0.4	0.5	0.3	0.3	0.4	0.4	0.4	0.4	0.3	0.3
Amériques	7.6	6.3	3.1	2.5	3.6	3.8	4.2	4.2	4.6	4.1
ALAI	5.5	4.6	1.9	1.1	1.5	1.5	1.6	1.7	2.1	1.5
MCAC	0.0	0.0	0.0	0.0	0.0	0.1	0.1	0.1	0.1	x0.1
Asie	43.8	43.2	x59.9	x61.0	56.5	55.7	60.1	64.3	67.1	66.6
Moyen–Orient	1.0	x0.9	x0.6	0.6	0.7	0.8	0.5	0.5	0.4	x0.3
Europe	43.0	45.4	30.6	31.2	37.2	38.3	33.4	29.8	26.7	27.8
CEE	40.3	42.9	29.1	30.1	36.0	37.6	32.1	28.6	25.6	26.6
AELE	2.1	2.2	1.4	1.0	1.1	0.6	1.0	1.0	0.9	1.1
Océanie	0.1	x0.1	x0.1	x0.1	x0.1	x0.1	x0.1	x0.1	x0.1	x0.1
Hong Kong	18.4	18.0	15.5	18.7	25.5	27.4	32.8	32.0	34.1	32.7
China/Chine	0.1	0.1	4.1	4.9	6.1	5.1	6.0	14.7	16.5	19.0
Italy/Italie	19.9	20.5	13.4	12.6	14.9	15.0	11.6	10.2	9.0	10.0
Korea, Republic of	18.0	18.6	15.1	15.3	17.1	14.4	12.7	8.9	7.6	5.7
France,Monac	6.4	7.8	6.0	7.3	9.4	9.8	8.7	7.7	7.4	7.8
Germany/Allemagne	5.7	6.0	3.9	3.6	4.2	4.5	4.4	3.8	3.0	2.8
Thailand/Thaïlande	0.6	0.8	1.3	2.0	2.9	3.1	3.3	3.1	3.4	3.4
USA/Etats–Unis d'Amer	1.6	1.1	0.8	1.0	1.7	1.9	2.2	2.1	2.1	2.1
Belgium–Luxembourg	1.4	1.8	1.2	2.1	2.2	2.5	2.1	2.1	2.1	1.9
India/Inde	1.5	1.6	1.4	1.2	1.8	1.8	2.0	2.1	1.9	2.0

TRADE BY COMMODITY IN THOUSAND U.S. DOLLARS – COMMERCE PAR PRODUIT EN MILLIERS DE DOLLARS E.U

COUNTRIES–PAYS	IMPORTS – IMPORTATIONS 1990	1991	1992	1993	1994
Total	20135475	22520110	25033246	24339149	26575029
Africa	x200683	x261027	x319722	x308434	x306363
Northern Africa	99754	147628	x134359	x129726	x117297
Americas	x4747164	x4951827	x5945101	x6466026	x7560960
LAIA	157170	228138	431028	463637	616669
CACM	12509	17429	26284	x87554	x92531
Asia	3268827	3758484	4693663	x5081839	x5498896
Middle East	601540	547684	601862	x559533	x565008
Europe	11607796	12930290	13756617	12136164	12783043
EEC	10711077	12017657	12799932	11231241	11804927
EFTA	815055	844921	822444	789788	866341
Oceania	x132569	x148537	x163899	x179317	x215273
USA/Etats–Unis d'Amer	4000273	4162867	4920552	5333795	6049116
Germany/Allemagne	3448857	4104171	3953141	3620862	3817974
Japan/Japon	1390158	1543783	2028566	2305879	2624027
France, Monac	1716969	1749698	1902962	1655395	1691416
Hong Kong	1113618	1435911	1739087	1856276	1883482
United Kingdom	1207911	1252241	1391888	1229791	1190950
Netherlands/Pays–Bas	1060456	1163083	1192147	976558	1035542
Belgium–Luxembourg	923710	953988	1020745	1050737	916742
Italy/Italie	650034	870534	1147169	964074	1124431
Switz.Liecht	587896	616213	582396	585942	625170
Spain/Espagne	311682	471920	638956	427025	486175
Sweden/Suède	458933	436449	463587	325174	453411
Austria/Autriche	367246	376282	393370	377765	387524
Canada	374992	331290	347024	367410	379605
Russian Federation			x531157	x376051	x303896
Saudi Arabia	270302	256181	261017	x214043	x216596
Mexico/Mexique	103383	132075	276255	292808	423979
Norway, SVD, JM	215642	214261	226363	192764	229659
Denmark/Danemark	177251	214496	217635	198503	248408
United Arab Emirates	205788	183688	195101	x187445	x192864
Singapore/Singapour	100193	125613	138688	148068	167462
Ireland/Irlande	121850	137265	151891	106018	120410
Australia/Australie	98163	108480	122210	138100	165474
Dominican Republic	x64133	x93262	x118119	x126840	x324529
Former USSR/Anc. URSS	x17880	x320255			
Finland/Finlande	130153	118651	104583	87032	115675
Portugal	55286	85024	119184	104595	112444
Greece/Grèce	80740	83855	102673	107711	103827
Tunisia/Tunisie	54368	65546	82942	75031	75485
Hungary/Hongrie	x30607	50126	x61107	x64770	x94363
Libyan Arab Jamahiriya	40856	79007	x43830	x50228	x38912
Kuwait/Koweït	41552	29674	68007	71298	60025
Argentina/Argentine	1549	22450	58482	72497	81808
Korea, Republic of	19786	25726	56542	63393	131424
Poland/Pologne	18212	59024	35279	30607	31384
Venezuela	21637	30392	49217	33054	22707
Croatia/Croatie			58281	47141	x36176
Lebanon/Liban	x25613	x35714	x27141	x24280	x41894
Costa Rica	3004	2354	4033	x76849	x82519
Bangladesh		20529	25335	34256	x1016
Slovenia/Slovénia			36887	38295	39949
So. Africa Customs Un	11691	18928	25356	24449	17588
Ukraine			x14435	x52224	x17188
Chile/Chili	6229	10194	20031	36139	36643
China/Chine	4765	5842	18924	32925	45217
Czechoslovakia	40068	x18099	x39559		
New Zealand	15901	16223	19094	21895	28704
Congo	x1012	x16040	x23183	x15477	x12112
Panama	16177	14428	18051	18380	17538
Reunion/Réunion	15104	15389	18039	15023	15429

COUNTRIES–PAYS	EXPORTS – EXPORTATIONS 1990	1991	1992	1993	1994
Totale	18008298	19877926	23645944	23624730	27164070
Afrique	945921	1111502	1236046	1258027	1335269
Afrique du Nord	836386	963429	1062998	1046993	1152633
Amériques	x989868	x1257719	x1652541	x1991882	x2877804
ALAI	213343	260073	435874	479662	594031
MCAC	21358	26807	26000	x159765	x240875
Asie	8048190	8962084	11476594	11944245	13757548
Moyen–Orient	574392	432888	439000	x497268	x489436
Europe	7282325	7980203	8466711	7316480	7805955
CEE	6856194	7156388	7674214	6639277	7077470
AELE	189677	196778	189454	174557	206888
Océanie	44555	44389	50828	56787	83956
China/Chine	1159154	1610554	3621110	3857613	5464734
Hong Kong	2324822	2739822	2988997	3072667	3066386
Italy/Italie	1919335	1915295	1938087	1893142	2140672
Germany/Allemagne	1287318	1360403	1491606	1172848	1182052
Belgium–Luxembourg	807439	880429	1020370	883101	766637
USA/Etats–Unis d'Amer	577083	743319	921565	1067649	1186665
Thailand/Thaïlande	609050	855409	897001	975261	1053503
Korea, Republic of	1142651	1011780	888209	748451	667220
Portugal	813172	855806	935011	679897	723444
Indonesia/Indonésie	358658	526874	787757	841309	823611
Tunisia/Tunisie	516515	584553	706041	698722	870233
United Kingdom	491865	563792	572910	518484	635082
France, Monac	468401	449537	489431	436158	474503
Netherlands/Pays–Bas	370378	423674	480005	419719	474167
Turkey/Turquie	295311	259941	312409	333852	366779
Morocco/Maroc	276383	305546	286700	259247	254919
Hungary/Hongrie	x188960	x178769	x276590	x241083	x226759
Poland/Pologne	84572	63370	165129	396379	466706
Singapore/Singapour	188239	224500	203334	156887	140996
Mexico/Mexique	15415	25928	253914	290748	386872
Korea Dem People's Rp	x86606	x164177	x194007	x195765	x105682
Sri Lanka	128496	141547	194273	215893	240932
Pakistan	122909	132493	193603	223844	243027
Malaysia/Malaisie	149642	171122	187862	183927	199459
Switz.Liecht	176252	183542	175234	164731	186760
Yugoslavia SFR	125709	x521785			
Macau/Macao	188738	168046	166478	172824	182850
Philippines	118231	275676	99156	110395	129137
Bangladesh	562136	108239	171137	196095	x327259
Croatia/Croatie			230427	244128	x231623
Austria/Autriche	167409	157376	167394	135455	x109509
Canada	57126	99081	146400	172194	219596
Spain/Espagne	97482	110213	150766	140734	163141
Czechoslovakia		x177257	x208998		
Denmark/Danemark	82695	119170	130602	113265	138904
Japan/Japon	109281	110368	101156	127350	95294
Viet Nam	x42980	x87973	x118940	x125898	x213101
Greece/Grèce	94734	117201	116864	95903	90455
Colombia/Colombie	105331	140944	85136	90919	103436
Romania/Roumanie	272816	34553	86454	190293	331466
India/Inde	84983	94044	94860	103593	156827
Malta/Malte	97758	96532	99210	94566	x99091
Mauritius/Maurice	63935	90463	88404	105061	93117
Slovenia/Slovénia			145155	129189	127786
Israel/Israël	64130	73441	95204	85380	95964
Dominican Republic	x80611	x85632	x80154	x73685	x574294
Egypt/Egypte	43430	73122	70170	79794	25816
Finland/Finlande	132734	79987	64302	47169	61540
Ireland/Irlande	72622	68109	65932	54755	58189
Costa Rica	10687	12258	11226	x155077	x236511

(VALUE AS % OF TOTAL)(VALEUR EN % DU TOTAL)

	1985	1986	1987	1988	1989	1990	1991	1992	1993	1994
Africa	1.5	x1.2	x1.3	x1.9	x1.1	x1.0	x1.2	x1.3	x1.3	x1.2
Northern Africa	1.2	0.7	0.8	1.4	0.6	0.5	0.7	x0.5	x0.5	x0.4
Americas	29.9	x24.5	x21.4	x22.1	x23.3	x23.5	x22.0	x23.7	x26.5	x28.5
LAIA	1.4	0.5	0.4	0.5	0.6	0.8	1.0	1.7	1.9	2.3
CACM	0.1	0.0	0.0	0.0	0.0	0.1	0.1	0.1	x0.4	x0.3
Asia	14.2	13.5	12.2	14.6	16.5	16.2	16.7	18.7	x20.8	x20.6
Middle East	6.1	5.1	x3.3	4.0	x3.4	3.0	2.4	2.4	x2.3	x2.1
Europe	52.9	59.1	55.6	52.1	50.1	57.6	57.4	55.0	49.9	48.1
EEC	44.4	49.5	46.7	44.2	42.6	53.2	53.4	51.1	46.1	44.4
EFTA	8.4	9.5	8.8	7.8	7.4	4.0	3.8	3.3	3.2	3.3
Oceania	0.8	x0.7	x0.6	x0.6	x0.6	x0.7	x0.7	x0.7	x0.8	x0.8
USA/Etats–Unis d'Amer	25.6	21.0	18.5	18.9	19.9	19.9	18.5	19.7	21.9	22.8
Germany/Allemagne	13.9	16.2	15.2	14.0	13.5	17.1	18.2	15.8	14.9	14.4
Japan/Japon	4.1	4.4	4.9	5.9	7.5	6.9	6.9	8.1	9.5	9.9
France, Monac	5.8	6.9	6.7	6.4	6.5	8.5	7.8	7.6	6.8	6.4
Hong Kong	3.1	3.5	3.4	3.9	4.9	5.5	6.4	6.9	7.6	7.1
United Kingdom	6.9	6.4	5.7	6.4	5.7	6.0	5.6	5.6	5.1	4.5
Netherlands/Pays–Bas	5.6	6.2	5.7	4.9	4.4	5.3	5.2	4.8	4.0	3.9
Belgium–Luxembourg	3.8	4.3	4.1	3.5	3.3	4.6	4.2	4.1	4.3	3.4
Italy/Italie	2.2	2.5	2.6	2.6	2.7	3.2	3.9	4.6	4.0	4.2
Switz.Liecht	2.7	3.1	2.9	2.6	2.5	2.9	2.7	2.3	2.4	2.4

	1985	1986	1987	1988	1989	1990	1991	1992	1993	1994
Afrique	3.2	4.2	3.6	3.4	4.1	5.2	5.6	5.2	5.3	4.9
Afrique du Nord	2.6	3.4	3.1	3.2	3.8	4.6	4.8	4.5	4.4	4.2
Amériques	5.0	x4.6	x4.1	x4.3	4.9	x5.5	x6.3	x7.0	x8.4	x10.6
ALAI	1.5	0.9	1.0	1.0	1.3	1.2	1.3	1.8	2.0	2.2
MCAC	0.2	x0.2	x0.1	0.1	0.1	0.1	0.1	0.1	x0.7	x0.9
Asie	37.2	33.3	42.3	47.9	47.1	44.7	45.1	48.5	50.6	50.6
Moyen–Orient	2.0	1.8	1.8	2.7	2.3	3.2	2.2	1.9	x2.1	x1.8
Europe	50.3	53.9	43.1	37.8	38.5	40.4	40.1	35.8	31.0	28.7
CEE	43.3	47.2	38.2	33.5	34.7	38.1	36.0	32.5	28.1	26.1
AELE	5.0	5.3	3.8	3.4	3.0	1.1	1.0	0.8	0.7	0.8
Océanie	0.1	0.1	x0.1	0.1	0.3	0.2	0.2	0.2	0.2	0.3
China/Chine			5.7	6.3	7.3	6.4	8.1	15.3	16.3	20.1
Hong Kong	13.2	12.1	11.2	12.0	13.5	12.9	13.8	12.6	13.0	11.3
Italy/Italie	14.0	14.8	11.5	9.2	9.9	10.7	9.6	8.2	8.0	7.9
Germany/Allemagne	5.9	7.3	6.2	6.3	6.7	7.1	6.8	6.3	5.0	4.4
Belgium–Luxembourg	3.9	4.3	3.8	3.3	3.6	4.5	4.4	4.3	3.7	2.8
USA/Etats–Unis d'Amer	1.7	1.7	1.6	2.1	2.8	3.2	3.7	3.9	4.5	4.4
Thailand/Thaïlande	1.3	1.5	1.8	2.4	3.2	3.4	4.3	3.8	4.1	3.9
Korea, Republic of	11.8	10.1	9.2	9.9	9.2	6.3	5.1	3.8	3.2	2.5
Portugal	3.3	4.0	3.6	3.6	4.0	4.5	4.3	4.0	2.9	2.7
Indonesia/Indonésie	1.0	0.9	0.7	1.0	1.5	2.0	2.7	3.3	3.6	3.0

TRADE BY COMMODITY IN THOUSAND U.S. DOLLARS – COMMERCE PAR PRODUIT EN MILLIERS DE DOLLARS E.U

COUNTRIES–PAYS	IMPORTS – IMPORTATIONS 1990	1991	1992	1993	1994
Total	31993559	34818390	38518525	37825578	39898228
Africa	x190236	x216994	x240464	x229775	x241134
Northern Africa	60309	85744	x64670	x66656	x76598
Americas	x9207453	x9482534	x11300983	x12426112	x12857927
LAIA	152465	206336	460145	563752	691962
CACM	9336	13737	15753	x69434	x77378
Asia	4736189	5251410	6471108	7651534	8415864
Middle East	707268	568799	756001	x798342	x817912
Europe	17486449	19142203	20120350	17065330	17896369
EEC	15874989	17572915	18456242	15542172	16332646
EFTA	1525640	1493577	1495930	1368042	1428635
Oceania	x175774	x189443	x211447	x241783	x267919
USA/Etats–Unis d'Amer	8221204	8456423	9955237	10955106	11210125
Germany/Allemagne	6170430	7091956	6941348	6336630	6574650
Hong Kong	1804622	2212828	2702562	3345086	3358780
Japan/Japon	1894131	2105092	2554089	2955426	3526011
France, Monac	1769375	1928800	2148237	1819211	1923572
United Kingdom	1923726	1961798	1963300	1708550	1744846
Netherlands/Pays–Bas	1489005	1537383	1612655	1263015	1386417
Belgium–Luxembourg	1004560	1049719	1146065	961646	989417
Switz.Liecht	1106929	1086153	1061509	1007075	1039103
Italy/Italie	633656	847821	1075017	753946	815574
Austria/Autriche	757628	736221	773660	751039	802512
Sweden/Suède	781034	753279	778892	525547	530650
Canada	636835	634128	688748	669636	646594
Spain/Espagne	383566	543606	782793	490264	518155
Norway, SVD, JM	395503	382955	407734	340400	367794
Denmark/Danemark	287978	376507	387136	332823	405813
Russian Federation			x496413	x450285	x381566
Saudi Arabia	351682	252559	307502	x350287	x351103
Mexico/Mexique	90135	116512	311606	387441	491962
Singapore/Singapour	217208	230279	251312	286786	331278
Ireland/Irlande	254851	272432	307044	183218	188228
Finland/Finlande	227018	223083	208207	147868	179153
Australia/Australie	120191	132223	151635	181107	187631
Portugal	89096	129245	187642	141854	140675
United Arab Emirates	133905	127935	148951	x167481	x161229
Greece/Grèce	103065	121066	144244	126560	132984
Kuwait/ Koweït	92250	62711	164661	131929	140474
Former USSR/Anc. URSS	x13184	x320749			
Poland/Pologne	35056	112644	50037	48156	46237
Hungary/Hongrie	x38712	53033	x59993	x75685	x83455
Korea, Republic of	41044	44624	59659	77074	142484
Dominican Republic	x35651	x42093	x63032	x60647	x117052
Lebanon/Liban	x42653	x56384	x41971	x40534	x81709
Venezuela	27010	32160	52166	45109	29495
New Zealand	40373	41165	41521	45647	58975
Slovenia/Slovénia			61763	62987	62682
Libyan Arab Jamahiriya	30581	54986	x27856	x33747	x34850
Reunion/Réunion	39527	35026	41819	31798	35306
So. Africa Customs Un	28149	35242	35592	35391	34574
Croatia/Croatie			53077	52869	x29403
Israel/Israël	11594	14825	29044	57722	75704
Argentina/Argentine	1256	9568	40841	51087	58914
Tunisia/Tunisie	28396	29663	33793	31461	38995
Jordan/Jordanie	19012	21748	35969	35654	16488
Malaysia/Malaisie	20431	26474	39008	25398	33676
China/Chine	12013	12917	30232	43283	55901
Andorra/Andorre	x21906	x25954	x30863	x22836	x22111
Czechoslovakia	44659	x24376	x48027		
Ukraine			x12149	x59751	x19642
Iceland/Islande	23208	24469	26687	20568	21738

COUNTRIES–PAYS	EXPORTS – EXPORTATIONS 1990	1991	1992	1993	1994
Totale	26818738	30289330	34196349	33590650	37762909
Afrique	461420	483484	593741	596750	678701
Afrique du Nord	354907	388745	486283	470473	597584
Amériques	1014333	x1104737	1507278	x1733313	x2347557
ALAI	408437	363459	589783	668153	813218
MCAC	36872	35763	47882	x70724	x91477
Asie	12423481	14727377	17256105	18374239	20594486
Moyen–Orient	895900	871562	894770	1004849	x1113745
Europe	12145280	12952219	13710872	11157462	12085260
CEE	11899024	12142240	12965857	10472782	11409055
AELE	123862	107810	111852	105029	114972
Océanie	57665	64160	x62161	x61264	87316
Hong Kong	4328225	4840365	5337889	5896216	5765031
China/Chine	2021349	2787340	4743802	5252478	6613213
Germany/Allemagne	2949209	3043536	3279013	2646181	2647767
Italy/Italie	2817850	2773953	2911976	2570499	3081711
France, Monac	2052213	2086100	2282722	1720271	1910174
Korea, Republic of	1300207	1211850	1104784	1059724	1034974
India/Inde	1022857	1032755	1217425	1076736	1409207
Thailand/Thaïlande	813390	1035606	927066	922032	1147782
United Kingdom	802550	886146	973067	806933	958707
Indonesia/Indonésie	479112	683466	915881	1002452	860637
Netherlands/Pays–Bas	798627	839575	849825	674679	766420
Turkey/Turquie	683741	677992	715597	779201	846576
USA/Etats–Unis d'Amer	404001	524618	688676	768566	880393
Belgium–Luxembourg	561235	573011	586595	463279	512700
Portugal	565803	571110	585621	400698	413884
Sri Lanka	235206	291629	469375	505639	557036
Poland/Pologne	158983	258843	233052	738872	867671
Greece/Grèce	336261	366641	446135	373743	290030
Hungary/Hongrie	x312602	x303715	x455693	x409487	x373904
Tunisia/Tunisie	250775	270097	351979	353608	441835
Denmark/Danemark	247640	300277	322131	273076	296536
Philippines	130035	523268	156614	163392	193343
Singapore/Singapour	303601	302027	288918	234448	212218
Austria/Autriche	276785	264233	271913	202142	x155305
Malaysia/Malaisie	218324	236201	245295	216719	210912
Yugoslavia SFR	63484	x652106			
Mexico/Mexique	9334	13738	297520	330204	505139
Pakistan	172285	216916	218021	203372	185029
Colombia/Colombie	221007	247172	175592	198149	181397
Macau/Macao	197353	180517	186693	178527	199794
Romania/Roumanie	5631	142122	94956	243160	398589
Slovenia/Slovénia			224344	238389	237604
Bangladesh		139739	130630	162324	x474937
Croatia/Croatie			184816	236216	x200310
Spain/Espagne	100645	103153	122631	118920	150061
Viet Nam	x73427	x102658	x111421	x120825	x188531
Ireland/Irlande	111915	107616	134210	79772	69066
Morocco/Maroc	85650	96647	112487	97068	89070
Japan/Japon	91412	90160	102264	112009	116165
Sweden/Suède	114779	113569	105948	71457	80745
Switz.Liecht	113212	96859	98891	92588	96926
Czechoslovakia		x115995	x168578		
Finland/Finlande	163173	112983	94069	71132	75948
Canada	59590	66187	85792	117331	139352
Bulgaria/Bulgarie	x209325	x91634	x99718	x73476	x126936
Israel/Israël	64962	81424	90736	88204	105221
Cyprus/Chypre	86651	87538	84682	55725	53167
Dominican Republic	x59360	x70119	x61021	x69932	x371395
Ukraine			x35587	x149963	x145556
Korea Dem People's Rp	x47876	x66037	x60070	x58516	x42963

(VALUE AS % OF TOTAL)(VALEUR EN % DU TOTAL)

	1985	1986	1987	1988	1989	1990	1991	1992	1993	1994
Africa	0.6	x0.7	x1.0	x1.2	x0.6	x0.6	x0.6	x0.6	x0.6	x0.6
Northern Africa	0.4	0.2	0.6	0.8	0.2	0.2	0.2	x0.2	x0.2	x0.2
Americas	41.3	x36.3	x32.5	x30.3	x29.8	x28.8	x27.2	x29.3	x32.8	x32.2
LAIA	0.7	0.3	0.2	0.3	0.4	0.5	0.6	1.2	1.5	1.7
CACM		0.0	0.0	0.0	0.0	0.0	0.0	0.0	x0.2	x0.2
Asia	9.0	9.5	9.8	12.1	14.3	14.8	15.1	16.8	20.3	21.1
Middle East	3.8	3.5	x2.9	2.8	x2.5	2.2	1.6	2.0	x2.1	x2.0
Europe	48.2	52.9	53.1	52.8	52.2	54.7	55.0	52.2	45.1	44.9
EEC	37.9	41.7	42.6	42.9	42.8	49.6	50.5	47.9	41.1	40.9
EFTA	10.2	11.1	10.4	9.8	9.3	4.8	4.3	3.9	3.6	3.6
Oceania	0.6	x0.5	x0.5	x0.5	x0.5	x0.5	x0.5	x0.5	x0.6	x0.7
USA/Etats–Unis d'Amer	37.6	33.0	29.7	27.6	26.9	25.7	24.3	25.8	29.0	28.1
Germany/Allemagne	13.6	15.2	16.0	16.5	16.5	19.3	20.4	18.0	16.8	16.5
Hong Kong	2.5	3.1	3.2	3.6	4.7	5.6	6.4	7.0	8.8	8.4
Japan/Japon	2.0	2.2	2.9	4.8	6.3	5.9	6.0	6.6	7.8	8.8
France, Monac	3.6	4.2	4.5	4.6	4.6	5.5	5.5	5.6	4.8	4.8
United Kingdom	5.0	4.9	4.9	5.1	5.3	6.0	5.6	5.1	4.5	4.4
Netherlands/Pays–Bas	4.4	4.7	4.7	4.5	4.2	4.7	4.4	4.2	3.3	3.5
Belgium–Luxembourg	2.7	2.9	2.9	2.8	2.8	3.1	3.0	3.0	2.5	2.5
Switz.Liecht	3.1	3.4	3.3	3.4	3.3	3.5	3.1	2.8	2.7	2.6
Italy/Italie	1.3	1.5	1.7	1.7	1.8	2.0	2.4	2.8	2.0	2.0

	1985	1986	1987	1988	1989	1990	1991	1992	1993	1994
Afrique	1.3	1.4	1.2	1.2	1.4	1.8	1.6	1.7	1.8	1.8
Afrique du Nord	0.9	0.9	0.8	1.0	1.1	1.3	1.3	1.4	1.4	1.6
Amériques	3.0	x2.9	x2.8	x3.5	3.9	3.8	x3.7	4.4	x5.1	x6.2
ALAI	1.2	0.8	1.0	1.2	1.7	1.5	1.2	1.7	2.0	2.2
MCAC		0.1	0.2	0.2	0.2	0.1	0.1	0.1	x0.2	x0.2
Asie	45.1	42.6	47.9	49.0	49.3	46.3	48.7	50.5	54.7	54.6
Moyen–Orient	3.1	2.7	2.8	3.0	3.3	3.3	2.9	2.6	3.0	x2.9
Europe	49.8	52.4	44.1	42.1	43.0	45.3	42.8	40.1	33.2	32.0
CEE	43.5	46.3	39.5	38.1	39.7	44.4	40.1	37.9	31.2	30.2
AELE	4.4	4.4	3.3	2.9	2.5	0.5	0.4	0.3	0.3	0.3
Océanie		x0.0	x0.1		x0.2	0.2	0.2	x0.2	x0.2	0.3
Hong Kong	18.8	17.2	14.8	15.0	16.9	16.1	16.0	15.6	17.6	15.3
China/Chine			4.8	5.9	7.8	7.5	9.2	13.9	15.6	17.5
Germany/Allemagne	10.5	11.7	9.3	9.6	10.2	11.0	10.0	9.6	7.9	7.0
Italy/Italie	9.0	10.1	8.7	8.5	9.3	10.5	9.2	8.5	7.7	8.2
France, Monac	7.1	7.0	6.3	6.1	6.6	7.7	6.9	6.7	5.1	5.1
Korea, Republic of	7.2	6.8	6.1	6.8	6.3	4.8	4.0	3.2	3.2	2.7
India/Inde	4.5	4.2	3.5	3.1	4.0	3.8	3.4	3.6	3.2	3.7
Thailand/Thaïlande	1.9	2.1	2.9	2.9	3.3	3.0	3.4	2.7	2.7	3.0
United Kingdom	4.0	3.6	3.5	3.0	2.7	3.0	2.9	2.8	2.4	2.5
Indonesia/Indonésie	1.1	1.3	1.1	1.3	1.4	1.8	2.3	2.7	3.0	2.3

TRADE BY COMMODITY IN THOUSAND U.S. DOLLARS – COMMERCE PAR PRODUIT EN MILLIERS DE DOLLARS E.U

COUNTRIES–PAYS	IMPORTS – IMPORTATIONS				
	1990	1991	1992	1993	1994
Total	8290788	9307783	11001263	11617433	12407855
Africa	x90419	x83798	x124440	x148678	x192135
Northern Africa	33734	38476	43370	x59164	81418
Americas	x2568229	x2737195	x3688549	x4150891	x4335382
LAIA	68293	100114	229690	228734	282145
CACM	17264	19043	27007	x52692	x63293
Asia	1529159	1835095	2315914	x2649903	x3026778
Middle East	214944	289090	358701	x353985	x407984
Europe	3925563	4408651	4649850	4389352	4515879
EEC	3650274	4141913	4387019	4143958	4251911
EFTA	205499	216601	218187	200183	219485
Oceania	x78663	x86821	x107670	x124167	x145139
USA/Etats–Unis d'Amer	2172272	2278175	3097906	3536354	3622963
Germany/Allemagne	1327476	1577250	1466708	1354279	1374695
Hong Kong	592212	793316	883911	952960	896590
Japan/Japon	608781	615462	699317	852899	1112959
France,Monac	551865	581836	683179	628303	613166
United Kingdom	516066	523719	567961	658275	651857
Netherlands/Pays–Bas	290317	315363	363909	328869	329139
Italy/Italie	184803	272727	308141	273842	335776
Spain/Espagne	144549	221224	297455	222963	233607
Canada	185278	191559	229261	232924	211025
Belgium–Luxembourg	172795	189700	211470	227323	219713
China/Chine	2154	2805	203358	295057	303526
Switz.Liecht	150280	159139	156637	146624	159177
United Arab Emirates	54854	132443	145168	x151445	x166561
Austria/Autriche	115425	129089	121202	124817	125461
Saudi Arabia	64652	112961	134003	x105046	x130646
Sweden/Suède	140482	118341	123168	90598	104706
Mexico/Mexique	45745	53710	124812	128294	163396
Australia/Australie	57030	67141	83925	100631	114938
Singapore/Singapour	61421	67391	81342	96368	150320
Russian Federation			x105981	x91959	x115827
Dominican Republic	x38775	x52178	x64726	x55715	x103285
Denmark/Danemark	56863	53246	56614	59791	68287
Ireland/Irlande	53955	53262	62037	48544	53078
Hungary/Hongrie	x18285	57302	x41080	x64960	x89667
Norway,SVD,JM	51119	52817	57320	50009	56553
Portugal	25751	32342	43969	45750	47888
Tunisia/Tunisie	30380	32546	37930	48490	70696
Finland/Finlande	45928	41605	39783	36728	41612
Greece/Grèce	24000	32209	41423	43875	52926
Kuwait/Koweït	54713	13877	46893	54632	62375
Argentina/Argentine	822	13798	48652	40180	34572
Jamaica/Jamaïque	34601	64012	x8596	x9898	x13636
Former USSR/Anc. URSS	x5630	x81667			
Poland/Pologne	12284	4563	20981	40264	41612
Venezuela	10576	13825	25994	20906	18106
Korea, Republic of	9759	11191	15259	24564	56073
Malaysia/Malaisie	10487	15122	19752	16076	24208
Chile/Chili	5647	8414	17932	22711	30021
Honduras	11557	12613	17121	13275	7760
New Zealand	10758	11041	14980	16222	21488
Costa Rica	3259	2837	4367	x34185	x48925
Romania/Roumanie	3446	1804	18188	18103	27062
Yugoslavia SFR	49545	x33106			
Korea Dem People's Rp	x5948	x7241	x20199	x5272	x3825
Slovenia/Slovénia			14697	17650	13460
Czechoslovakia	30185	x7207	x23440		
Congo	x262	x4699	x9425	x13361	x12599
Malta/Malte	14178	12635	7173	5687	x3896
Ukraine			x7678	x17675	x12340

COUNTRIES–PAYS	EXPORTS – EXPORTATIONS				
	1990	1991	1992	1993	1994
Totale	7117512	8354418	10003209	10698917	12359847
Afrique	281028	309942	344374	407658	456488
Afrique du Nord	177369	186970	204870	207110	258915
Amériques	x387438	x463354	x606744	x765808	x1035889
ALAI	95241	64172	112548	145270	173885
MCAC	13122	15112	30202	x57324	x89827
Asie	4635101	5596647	6761812	7262186	8370364
Moyen–Orient	256702	275100	290155	x360183	x432214
Europe	1680720	1852786	2102943	1975581	2158920
CEE	1593089	1690260	1934712	1829645	1984399
AELE	44814	46588	53743	44706	41460
Océanie	25684	22764	38620	29682	33124
Hong Kong	1502070	1789991	1847902	1906510	1796590
China/Chine	784314	1034418	1816158	2019284	2357228
Korea, Republic of	623077	633540	581729	565352	517475
India/Inde	424050	435523	523428	522863	724586
USA/Etats–Unis d'Amer	224453	334436	394905	481724	597001
Germany/Allemagne	309615	352430	437373	319117	301301
Italy/Italie	317567	332665	356422	392921	450325
Thailand/Thaïlande	209339	255648	295196	358849	516341
Portugal	288625	270558	299383	256344	285679
Indonesia/Indonésie	150318	176667	272904	312039	313906
United Kingdom	209009	245969	255008	257386	328224
Bangladesh		165920	204563	246601	x619348
Turkey/Turquie	197078	177935	195092	225158	260060
France,Monac	171224	158174	181554	186122	200351
Malaysia/Malaisie	125139	134277	184498	195891	214189
Singapore/Singapour	144192	140971	167872	164599	192120
Pakistan	130732	145948	159084	153893	156077
Netherlands/Pays–Bas	102733	116873	146950	151694	159035
Sri Lanka	74624	84286	138700	165959	165311
Macau/Macao	117773	128642	133368	121892	129689
Mauritius/Maurice	81491	95518	107926	162547	151766
Tunisia/Tunisie	85183	96638	105941	105525	130902
Belgium–Luxembourg	73575	84572	108347	111105	104797
Morocco/Maroc	79453	79282	85315	80569	75708
Philippines	21119	118380	36049	41135	38534
Poland/Pologne	9115	4337	35041	127156	142551
Austria/Autriche	48219	52471	58209	52143	x26078
United Arab Emirates	15836	39418	36995	x65856	x67779
Switz.Liecht	43748	45276	51944	43416	36343
Mexico/Mexique	7850	8213	52189	69327	85155
Japan/Japon	22665	31826	43238	45299	47963
Yugoslavia SFR	38782	x112905			
Spain/Espagne	26300	27581	38659	42928	52259
Brazil/Brésil	22673	30984	31488	35641	46552
Romania/Roumanie	357	23421	25202	48515	60320
Oman	1991	18498	35151	34468	46991
Czechoslovakia		x36955	x41384		
Bulgaria/Bulgarie	x81242	x28116	x25530	x21003	x33569
So. Africa Customs Un	9184	16877	25583	26588	
Colombia/Colombie	42543	18075	20347	29629	29116
Slovenia/Slovénia			35474	32119	28379
Costa Rica	4998	5383	10949	x46511	x80958
Croatia/Croatie			29845	30923	x26586
Viet Nam	x31567	x20688	x16325	x22769	x72579
Canada	6951	9148	22062	27157	26046
Hungary/Hongrie	x11690	x13906	x20662	x22645	x25658
Denmark/Danemark	14489	17640	18349	21096	28863
Ireland/Irlande	15071	14010	17082	19450	21079
Nepal/Népal	6157	7330	25475	17102	x20187
Dominican Republic	x20027	x16624	x16473	x14998	x77444

(VALUE AS % OF TOTAL)(VALEUR EN % DU TOTAL)

	1985	1986	1987	1988	1989	1990	1991	1992	1993	1994
Africa	0.7	x1.5	x1.7	x2.0	x0.9	x1.0	x0.9	x1.2	x1.3	x1.5
Northern Africa	0.5	x0.8	0.7	x0.9	0.3	0.4	0.4	0.4	x0.5	0.7
Americas	49.2	x41.2	x33.9	x32.0	x33.0	x30.9	x29.4	x33.5	x35.7	x34.9
LAIA	1.3	0.6	0.5	0.6	0.8	0.8	1.1	2.1	2.0	2.3
CACM	0.1	0.1	x0.1	0.1	0.2	0.2	0.2	0.2	x0.5	x0.5
Asia	10.1	11.3	11.7	14.5	18.4	18.5	19.8	21.0	x22.8	x24.4
Middle East	2.1	x2.5	x3.0	3.2	x3.5	2.6	3.1	3.3	x3.0	x3.3
Europe	38.0	44.1	41.7	41.6	40.0	47.3	47.4	42.3	37.8	36.4
EEC	32.9	37.8	36.2	36.7	35.3	44.0	44.5	39.9	35.7	34.3
EFTA	5.1	6.3	5.4	4.8	4.5	2.5	2.3	2.0	1.7	1.8
Oceania	0.9	x0.8	x0.6	x0.8	x0.9	x0.9	x0.9	x1.0	x1.1	x1.2
USA/Etats–Unis d'Amer	44.7	36.9	30.0	27.8	28.2	26.2	24.5	28.2	30.4	29.2
Germany/Allemagne	10.8	12.9	12.6	12.0	11.5	16.0	16.9	13.3	11.7	11.1
Hong Kong	3.6	4.1	4.1	4.0	5.4	7.1	8.5	8.0	8.2	7.2
Japan/Japon	3.2	3.6	3.7	6.0	8.2	7.3	6.6	6.4	7.3	9.0
France,Monac	4.5	5.4	5.3	5.6	5.6	6.7	6.3	6.2	5.4	4.9
United Kingdom	6.6	6.6	6.0	7.1	6.3	6.2	5.6	5.2	5.7	5.3
Netherlands/Pays–Bas	2.9	3.3	3.1	2.8	2.8	3.5	3.4	3.3	2.8	2.7
Italy/Italie	1.5	2.1	2.4	2.2	1.9	2.2	2.9	2.8	2.4	2.7
Spain/Espagne	0.3	0.5	0.7	0.9	1.1	1.7	2.4	2.7	1.9	1.9
Canada	2.9	2.7	2.1	2.2	2.1	2.2	2.1	2.1	2.0	1.7

	1985	1986	1987	1988	1989	1990	1991	1992	1993	1994
Afrique	3.0	4.0	3.5	3.3	3.1	3.9	3.7	3.5	3.8	3.7
Afrique du Nord	1.7	2.1	2.0	2.1	2.0	2.5	2.2	2.0	1.9	2.1
Amériques	4.4	x4.3	x3.8	x4.1	x5.6	x5.5	x5.5	x6.1	x7.2	x8.3
ALAI	1.3	0.7	0.7	1.1	1.4	1.3	0.8	1.1	1.4	1.4
MCAC	0.1	0.2	0.1	0.1	0.3	0.2	0.2	0.3	x0.5	x0.7
Asie	68.3	65.5	68.7	68.4	68.7	65.1	67.0	67.6	67.9	67.7
Moyen–Orient	4.4	2.6	3.0	2.8	3.9	3.6	3.3	2.9	x3.4	x3.5
Europe	20.9	22.6	18.3	19.7	20.8	23.6	22.2	21.0	18.5	17.5
CEE	18.0	19.9	15.9	17.5	18.3	22.4	20.2	19.3	17.1	16.1
AELE	1.1	1.4	1.2	1.2	1.2	0.6	0.6	0.5	0.4	0.3
Océanie	0.1	x0.2	x0.1	0.2	0.3	0.3	0.2	0.4	0.3	0.3
Hong Kong	20.7	20.5	17.4	17.6	18.6	21.1	21.4	18.5	17.8	14.5
China/Chine			7.9	8.7	10.1	11.0	12.4	18.2	18.9	19.1
Korea, Republic of	18.3	16.3	12.7	12.2	12.1	8.8	7.6	5.8	5.3	4.2
India/Inde	6.5	6.4	4.6	4.4	5.8	6.0	5.2	5.2	4.9	5.9
USA/Etats–Unis d'Amer	1.6	2.1	1.8	1.8	3.1	3.2	4.0	3.9	4.5	4.8
Germany/Allemagne	2.7	3.4	2.7	3.8	3.8	4.4	4.2	4.4	3.0	2.4
Italy/Italie	3.3	3.9	3.0	3.1	3.5	4.5	4.0	3.6	3.7	3.6
Thailand/Thaïlande	3.1	3.5	3.5	3.4	3.6	2.9	3.1	3.0	3.4	4.2
Portugal	4.1	4.5	3.4	3.3	3.4	4.1	3.2	3.0	2.4	2.3
Indonesia/Indonésie	2.2	3.2	1.2	1.5	1.7	2.1	2.1	2.7	2.9	2.5

TRADE BY COMMODITY IN THOUSAND U.S. DOLLARS – COMMERCE PAR PRODUIT EN MILLIERS DE DOLLARS E.U

COUNTRIES–PAYS	IMPORTS – IMPORTATIONS 1990	1991	1992	1993	1994
Total	26030567	29943842	34674043	33063852	35320573
Africa	x103600	x114520	x134546	x141614	x176483
Northern Africa	34862	39982	x39665	x54957	x73516
Americas	x7755871	x7705814	x9039895	x9220293	x10220958
LAIA	91908	130380	274541	314265	413801
CACM	1703	2005	2971	x49981	x54553
Asia	3992379	5030568	6090658	7190884	8603455
Middle East	x119762	294575	x266708	x399969	x421749
Europe	13662352	16310316	18918677	15961770	15711664
EEC	12393569	14905458	17359376	14533664	14332111
EFTA	1173656	1321473	1458508	1312063	1265383
Oceania	x249175	x294536	x313902	x315621	x364709
USA/Etats–Unis d'Amer	7096983	7092499	8202859	8263645	9128550
Germany/Allemagne	4302629	5665028	6750165	5367276	5082113
Japan/Japon	2002009	2309095	2692882	3196905	4241304
Hong Kong	1507656	1909235	2455971	2820357	3067545
France,Monac	2091223	2217965	2471168	2228355	2337623
United Kingdom	1647991	1841239	2047714	1915360	1772661
Netherlands/Pays–Bas	979687	1171496	1412559	1105832	1051478
Switz.Liecht	859375	985063	1066353	957271	921888
Belgium–Luxembourg	742943	835153	921549	753187	772654
Italy/Italie	418984	602025	765783	638520	692668
Austria/Autriche	523716	621155	700989	623301	641160
Sweden/Suède	522961	559526	653593	485163	479699
Spain/Espagne	274964	413818	560171	406652	451036
Canada	481459	403916	452393	490591	495874
Singapore/Singapour	265752	320808	356180	404276	430057
Norway,SVD,JM	298199	318913	375385	340929	329186
Denmark/Danemark	227946	271392	318399	354549	366891
Russian Federation			x378069	x360549	x320659
Australia/Australie	193584	229216	239472	245110	267663
Ireland/Irlande	212288	221782	238212	206600	210355
Portugal	134591	180040	231318	198328	192874
Finland/Finlande	219202	204084	179986	139272	163241
Saudi Arabia	2374	190111	143829	x173286	x183539
Mexico/Mexique	62957	70926	139924	173544	275003
Greece/Grèce	94445	100753	107771	111268	117658
Former USSR/Anc. URSS	x23807	x312422			
Macau/Macao	10885	82083	94488	70960	68578
United Arab Emirates	46814	25935	37802	x144008	x129141
Hungary/Hongrie	x47305	49302	x66355	x83768	x99730
Korea, Republic of	28529	36993	59545	77114	145655
Poland/Pologne	47702	67006	40010	50304	54744
New Zealand	35607	44857	54394	55538	78129
China/Chine	6585	10153	70294	71582	98017
Argentina/Argentine	730	11143	61677	48781	42317
So. Africa Customs Un	31408	38225	39352	31208	43357
Tunisia/Tunisie	20278	22823	26311	35358	50559
Dominican Republic	x22413	x26697	x30742	x25981	x58104
Venezuela	11391	19757	32224	27466	15422
Ukraine			x28082	x50631	x21616
Slovenia/Slovénia			35836	42182	39971
Lebanon/Liban	x26713	x31736	x26216	x19547	x31722
Bangladesh		24364	17715	29680	x2876
Czechoslovakia	75062	x20835	x50262		
Chile/Chili	7410	12175	22403	28369	32656
Israel/Israël	9212	9980	15809	32399	33303
Croatia/Croatie			17663	37385	x37934
Yugoslavia SFR	67246	x54880			
Malaysia/Malaisie	8404	9066	11246	32621	38820
Oman	13706	14924	17795	17852	16070
Iceland/Islande	16082	17497	16770	13864	14310

COUNTRIES–PAYS	EXPORTS – EXPORTATIONS 1990	1991	1992	1993	1994
Totale	25278671	28136750	30876365	29483719	31470193
Afrique	591342	602682	653983	718783	616248
Afrique du Nord	352734	352296	375231	418763	397771
Amériques	x659318	x807651	x1129415	x1447995	x1937692
ALAI	170764	240512	295631	388934	491816
MCAC	6409	10000	11779	x65333	x95419
Asie	13232072	15358197	16263946	16580149	17619917
Moyen–Orient	1060124	1137108	1593080	1652830	1696119
Europe	10319817	10961141	12264522	10108036	10582283
CEE	10079351	10675543	11953229	9843224	10308867
AELE	124437	132428	125723	104129	124890
Océanie	x48149	72774	x75862	x75388	x108788
Hong Kong	4043366	4825305	5861547	5865968	6153215
Italy/Italie	4020736	4069165	4249124	3585141	3740803
China/Chine	3304512	3983372	2822616	3123163	3908284
Korea, Republic of	1563040	1503618	1438454	1412311	1468393
Turkey/Turquie	825352	1054300	1505893	1492417	1520446
Germany/Allemagne	1019453	1143400	1388564	1005484	995609
Portugal	1075220	1096706	1270700	1012892	998575
France,Monac	824317	974006	1109879	1010087	1039519
United Kingdom	888057	987323	1079058	808525	1045692
Thailand/Thaïlande	542866	703504	781574	749776	726304
Singapore/Singapour	631348	682471	732999	616644	553601
Greece/Grèce	525485	527094	697897	591686	563883
USA/Etats–Unis d'Amer	348997	415386	597357	741115	874037
Indonesia/Indonésie	373886	425287	627892	694793	577983
Netherlands/Pays–Bas	467061	563866	631988	513729	562744
Macau/Macao	424987	439865	513821	443016	507642
Denmark/Danemark	354840	399212	492529	435932	412195
Malaysia/Malaisie	316113	370184	421408	407832	405318
Philippines	220462	367378	275788	304666	314557
Belgium–Luxembourg	261569	286247	317074	285042	302692
India/Inde	293171	236620	312774	325304	338536
Austria/Autriche	227735	241264	284231	241923	x229622
Mauritius/Maurice	203038	206029	225528	240703	204235
Bangladesh		159433	238450	266970	x201501
Morocco/Maroc	156272	168320	186632	210769	221161
Pakistan	128877	165631	174414	192059	183610
Israel/Israël	147094	152493	181238	184780	188957
Spain/Espagne	132601	150039	176505	160537	188277
Sri Lanka	92588	115098	144603	179135	180462
Tunisia/Tunisie	144721	133569	146479	158174	165418
Poland/Pologne	51026	63636	147235	210070	229139
Hungary/Hongrie	x93616	x83702	x142411	x121142	x117456
Canada	57970	73736	113736	154490	200784
Ireland/Irlande	77480	94576	131060	96294	113431
Switz.Liecht	94712	104356	97866	83318	88220
Brazil/Brésil	48076	74343	90619	85381	80652
Romania/Roumanie	114249	55165	63455	84815	97109
Sweden/Suède	88011	80754	70481	47490	59184
Mexico/Mexique	16864	13117	62877	119702	216655
Slovenia/Slovénia			96484	83628	74002
Peru/Pérou	43394	52296	53658	73769	79120
Finland/Finlande	116715	61822	54139	48462	56642
Czechoslovakia		x72252	x91021		
Yugoslavia SFR	112879	x150856			
Egypt/Egypte	51740	50398	41910	48455	10990
Colombia/Colombie	14882	47986	35804	55769	52594
Japan/Japon	43650	40670	48731	44816	39656
Bulgaria/Bulgarie	x160395	x54682	x43274	x34160	x60702
Australia/Australie	26608	37471	39462	44060	65759
Croatia/Croatie			51307	65601	x59292

(VALUE AS % OF TOTAL)(VALEUR EN % DU TOTAL)

	1985	1986	1987	1988	1989	1990	1991	1992	1993	1994
Africa	0.6	x0.4	x0.5	x0.6	x0.4	x0.4	x0.4	x0.4	x0.4	x0.5
Northern Africa	0.3	0.2	0.3	0.4	0.1	0.1	0.1	x0.1	x0.2	x0.2
Americas	32.1	x29.1	x23.4	x21.0	x30.9	x29.8	x25.7	x26.1	x27.9	x28.9
LAIA	0.2	0.1	0.1	0.2	0.3	0.4	0.4	0.8	1.0	1.2
CACM	0.0	x0.0	x0.0	0.0	0.0	0.0	0.0	0.0	x0.2	x0.2
Asia	11.5	12.6	13.2	14.6	15.6	15.3	16.8	17.6	21.8	24.4
Middle East	0.1	x0.5	x0.8	x0.4	x0.5	x0.5	1.0	x0.8	x1.2	x1.2
Europe	53.9	56.2	56.3	57.1	46.1	52.5	54.5	54.6	48.3	44.5
EEC	43.5	45.7	45.6	46.7	38.0	47.6	49.8	50.1	44.0	40.6
EFTA	10.3	10.3	10.5	10.3	8.0	4.5	4.4	4.2	4.0	3.6
Oceania	1.2	x1.1	x1.0	x0.9	x0.9	x1.0	x1.0	x0.9	x0.9	x1.1
USA/Etats–Unis d'Amer	29.0	26.1	21.0	18.3	28.2	27.3	23.7	23.7	25.0	25.8
Germany/Allemagne	16.4	17.1	17.2	16.0	12.5	16.5	18.9	19.5	16.2	14.4
Japan/Japon	5.8	6.0	7.3	8.4	8.6	7.7	7.7	7.8	9.7	12.0
Hong Kong	5.0	5.3	4.4	4.7	5.6	5.8	6.4	7.1	8.5	8.7
France,Monac	6.9	7.6	7.6	7.8	6.8	8.0	7.4	7.1	6.7	6.6
United Kingdom	5.0	5.2	5.1	6.2	5.4	6.3	6.1	5.9	5.8	5.0
Netherlands/Pays–Bas	4.3	4.7	4.4	4.0	3.0	3.8	3.9	4.1	3.3	3.0
Switz.Liecht	3.5	3.5	3.4	3.3	2.7	3.3	3.3	3.1	2.9	2.6
Belgium–Luxembourg	2.6	2.8	2.6	2.9	2.3	2.9	2.8	2.7	2.3	2.2
Italy/Italie	1.1	1.1	1.1	1.5	1.3	1.6	2.0	2.2	1.9	2.0

	1985	1986	1987	1988	1989	1990	1991	1992	1993	1994
Afrique	1.6	1.8	1.7	1.8	1.9	2.4	2.1	2.1	2.4	2.0
Afrique du Nord	0.8	0.9	0.9	0.9	1.1	1.4	1.3	1.2	1.4	1.3
Amériques	1.9	1.6	x1.5	2.1	x2.7	x2.6	x2.8	x3.7	x4.9	x6.1
ALAI	0.7	0.6	0.4	0.6	0.7	0.7	0.9	1.0	1.3	1.6
MCAC	0.0	x0.0	x0.0	0.0	0.0	0.0	0.0	0.0	x0.2	x0.3
Asie	40.3	40.4	x51.5	52.2	54.6	52.4	54.6	52.6	56.3	56.0
Moyen–Orient	1.2	1.9	2.3	2.8	3.8	4.2	4.0	5.2	5.6	5.4
Europe	54.6	54.8	42.3	41.3	38.8	40.8	39.0	39.7	34.3	33.6
CEE	49.3	50.1	39.1	38.4	36.2	39.9	37.9	38.7	33.4	32.8
AELE	3.7	3.4	2.5	2.3	2.1	0.5	0.5	0.4	0.4	0.4
Océanie	0.1	x0.2	x0.1	x0.1	x0.2	x0.2	0.3	x0.3	x0.3	x0.4
Hong Kong	19.8	19.3	14.7	14.5	17.8	16.0	17.1	19.0	19.9	19.6
Italy/Italie	21.9	22.8	16.9	15.8	14.7	15.9	14.5	13.8	12.2	11.9
China/Chine			9.1	9.8	11.5	13.1	14.2	9.1	10.6	12.4
Korea, Republic of	9.6	9.5	8.0	8.5	8.8	6.2	5.3	4.7	4.8	4.7
Turkey/Turquie	1.1	1.6	2.0	2.4	3.0	3.3	3.7	4.9	5.1	4.8
Germany/Allemagne	5.3	5.6	4.4	4.1	3.8	4.0	4.1	4.5	3.4	3.2
Portugal	3.2	3.5	3.4	3.5	3.7	4.3	3.9	4.1	3.4	3.2
France,Monac	3.6	3.5	2.6	3.1	3.0	3.3	3.5	3.6	3.4	3.3
United Kingdom	4.8	4.1	3.2	3.6	3.3	3.5	3.5	3.5	2.7	3.3
Thailand/Thaïlande	1.1	1.1	1.3	1.7	2.2	2.1	2.5	2.5	2.5	2.3

TRADE BY COMMODITY IN THOUSAND U.S. DOLLARS – COMMERCE PAR PRODUIT EN MILLIERS DE DOLLARS E.U

COUNTRIES–PAYS	IMPORTS – IMPORTATIONS				
	1990	1991	1992	1993	1994
Total	13142128	15569497	17779054	18645994	20618648
Africa	x112227	x120327	x172023	x170245	x211626
Northern Africa	38143	40504	x59017	x70149	90219
Americas	x2641003	x3002158	x3815321	x4441459	x5483578
LAIA	98984	137251	302808	361869	469878
CACM	10386	8004	9435	x140327	x153176
Asia	2140298	2836536	3419698	x3938053	x4540280
Middle East	x78710	x224060	203739	x444943	x435879
Europe	7809953	9059337	9916570	9546664	9788940
EEC	7287017	8513549	9344533	9020622	9251045
EFTA	420043	440271	471456	437547	449440
Oceania	x117020	x152375	x186011	x203410	x266074
Germany/Allemagne	2449853	3058660	3157690	3088601	3047690
USA/Etats–Unis d'Amer	2108556	2452805	2926083	3255573	4049770
France, Monac	1199340	1344735	1490655	1388624	1558097
Hong Kong	923687	1225754	1426926	1556260	1757989
Japan/Japon	914206	1108051	1456558	1545806	1847940
United Kingdom	961969	1040760	1173467	1183643	1100988
Netherlands/Pays–Bas	557390	637587	717537	734207	752389
Belgium–Luxembourg	394257	448900	494226	550548	564353
Italy/Italie	331974	404344	482365	502051	508333
Spain/Espagne	254880	355104	468336	350156	393283
Austria/Autriche	302558	319545	346609	353908	383060
Canada	267066	274207	319646	329416	350844
Switz.Liecht	283206	290346	290860	287922	294254
Sweden/Suède	285468	284727	326285	253860	270210
Singapore/Singapour	154664	187762	220987	262989	313601
Denmark/Danemark	172233	217364	232608	220999	230390
United Arab Emirates	14743	94570	115844	x240675	x214522
Hungary/Hongrie	x101399	121882	x146980	x180627	x174737
Norway, SVD, JM	126714	136561	167523	140055	145514
Australia/Australie	76263	100816	126983	153672	196105
Ireland/Irlande	105767	116778	129644	115208	126742
Mexico/Mexique	42261	48996	125373	167345	283419
Portugal	66926	93541	128898	113171	120664
Russian Federation			x184275	x127347	x146086
Jamaica/Jamaïque	13536	18513	x103871	x178597	x222755
Finland/Finlande	130004	110053	100404	85977	102197
Saudi Arabia	15465	74601	46593	x142522	x158009
Greece/Grèce	74397	81451	95810	79666	92648
Poland/Pologne	27446	117376	32332	50023	48066
Dominican Republic	x37359	x40853	x63459	x73086	x128626
Venezuela	23852	29101	58254	51642	35011
Costa Rica	3737	3919	4869	x125926	x136385
Tunisia/Tunisie	35641	35244	41852	48187	67672
Chile/Chili	17879	29933	45132	49401	45284
Former USSR/Anc. URSS	x8738	x117925			
Argentina/Argentine	519	11069	46087	56611	50398
Yugoslavia SFR	92357	x94201			
Slovenia/Slovénia			44081	47532	41414
Korea, Republic of	12089	21698	32542	37287	71160
New Zealand	24818	26348	31706	30562	45261
Czechoslovakia	67564	x21870	x57486		
Lebanon/Liban	x17158	x27353	x13833	x15922	x25251
Israel/Israël	10492	12732	16520	27080	31138
Romania/Roumanie		8663	20004	23490	27042
So. Africa Customs Un	9723	12804	15774	18119	21055
Reunion/Réunion	12031	13022	15650	15289	17518
Ukraine			x12276	x30061	x12832
Slovakia				x41670	x15500
Haiti/Haïti	x10309	x9563	x15148	x15363	x5956
Yugoslavia/Yougoslavie			x27086	x10917	x1084

COUNTRIES–PAYS	EXPORTS – EXPORTATIONS				
	1990	1991	1992	1993	1994
Totale	12536478	15058668	17405102	18410205	20728296
Afrique	436525	433713	463207	512365	581150
Afrique du Nord	187332	190645	231970	248877	340747
Amériques	x903339	x1171320	x1609333	x2204046	x3038256
ALAI	219631	272953	437026	536527	639007
MCAC	9887	6152	4543	x175118	x253556
Asie	6077816	7764888	8956830	9474540	10519556
Moyen–Orient	640626	781692	978324	x1106416	x1134061
Europe	4880003	5375262	5991319	5758153	6076013
CEE	4667903	5008712	5608317	5417003	5738279
AELE	146780	149024	143677	148202	156090
Océanie	32861	39798	x38810	x52190	x54955
Hong Kong	1722689	2182895	2339836	2445441	2659244
China/Chine	859436	1040127	1691012	1810439	2332318
USA/Etats–Unis d'Amer	533587	732459	984455	1243058	1355430
Italy/Italie	879986	900956	928360	1055465	1181876
Turkey/Turquie	560645	646130	832654	879449	946602
Germany/Allemagne	657182	733019	814192	680404	705250
France, Monac	605800	644395	696201	716820	798855
Korea, Republic of	751464	745856	645640	650280	652833
Portugal	611363	633430	758255	638978	636082
Thailand/Thaïlande	434339	589627	573862	620988	682299
Greece/Grèce	517625	482123	588043	531164	466611
Indonesia/Indonésie	237258	321464	420796	468642	425924
United Kingdom	288005	342985	400638	392904	470431
India/Inde	276959	298228	408709	417084	480265
Austria/Autriche	324747	355731	393482	333556	x352015
Netherlands/Pays–Bas	245171	290593	345720	379023	390148
Singapore/Singapour	281488	347514	352029	304717	337623
Bangladesh		211891	292451	352839	x341403
Philippines	148242	396341	226417	181798	173849
Pakistan	142654	172362	198232	257034	320453
Malaysia/Malaisie	138755	179355	220181	224502	243892
Mauritius/Maurice	168530	167548	191672	222168	210440
Belgium–Luxembourg	132872	151656	172301	216715	251926
Ireland/Irlande	148783	173731	175497	171304	166229
Hungary/Hongrie	x106742	x113404	x192337	x205278	x193000
Macau/Macao	158693	169272	172562	162002	169399
Denmark/Danemark	109747	140260	159751	137700	122478
Israel/Israël	131073	131042	154234	148179	165086
Sri Lanka	69753	103289	148653	171041	192319
Switz.Liecht	139346	143670	136925	142242	147086
Tunisia/Tunisie	100397	102901	129282	149238	190093
Brazil/Brésil	81031	102577	124745	148758	116378
Mexico/Mexique	15896	21584	134989	175339	284629
Spain/Espagne	79050	98012	106861	115544	141246
Colombia/Colombie	57057	84239	98762	121653	119632
United Arab Emirates	711	34571	92573	x153301	x126744
Morocco/Maroc	72387	76904	93062	90201	77658
Slovenia/Slovénia			136674	119894	104335
Japan/Japon	62381	63963	88146	103000	89899
Jamaica/Jamaïque	33997	51794	x68503	x115018	x318129
Yugoslavia SFR	51697	x207147			
Peru/Pérou	53912	52417	57461	71303	94945
Dominican Republic	x53503	x51017	x53271	x58474	x383005
Costa Rica	5859	3830	1945	x154362	x224980
Poland/Pologne	29346	48050	42867	66444	91082
Syrian Arab Republic	53266	x72698	28361	x41057	x31457
Czechoslovakia		x64318	x73946		
Sweden/Suède	48351	48110	52894	36231	40375
Romania/Roumanie		28404	18690	48887	82777
Croatia/Croatie			42135	51429	x52933

(VALUE AS % OF TOTAL)(VALEUR EN % DU TOTAL)

	1985	1986	1987	1988	1989	1990	1991	1992	1993	1994
Africa	0.5	x0.7	x1.0	x0.8	x0.8	x0.9	x0.8	x1.0	x0.9	x1.0
Northern Africa	0.2	0.3	0.3	0.3	0.2	0.3	0.3	x0.3	x0.4	0.4
Americas	42.4	x39.6	x36.3	x31.8	x21.2	x20.1	x19.3	x21.5	x23.8	x26.6
LAIA	0.7	0.2	0.2	0.3	0.6	0.8	0.9	1.7	1.9	2.3
CACM	0.2	0.1	0.0	0.1	0.2	0.1	0.1	0.1	x0.8	x0.7
Asia	8.2	8.5	9.4	x13.8	17.2	16.2	18.2	19.2	x21.1	x22.0
Middle East	0.5	x1.0	x0.8	x0.8	x1.2	x0.6	x1.4	1.1	x2.4	x2.1
Europe	47.5	49.3	47.0	47.1	53.8	59.4	58.2	55.8	51.2	47.5
EEC	40.2	41.6	39.8	39.9	45.7	55.4	54.7	52.6	48.4	44.9
EFTA	7.2	7.6	7.1	7.2	7.8	3.2	2.8	2.7	2.3	2.2
Oceania	0.6	x0.6	x0.4	x0.6	x0.8	x0.9	x1.0	x1.1	x1.1	x1.3
Germany/Allemagne	13.6	14.5	13.9	13.5	15.1	18.6	19.6	17.8	16.6	14.8
USA/Etats–Unis d'Amer	38.7	36.5	33.5	29.0	17.3	16.0	15.8	16.5	17.5	19.6
France, Monac	7.0	7.3	6.9	6.6	7.4	9.1	8.6	8.4	7.4	7.6
Hong Kong	3.0	3.5	3.8	4.3	6.5	7.0	7.9	8.0	8.3	8.5
Japan/Japon	3.6	3.3	3.8	7.5	8.2	7.0	7.1	8.2	8.3	9.0
United Kingdom	5.7	5.2	5.1	5.6	6.2	7.3	6.7	6.6	6.3	5.3
Netherlands/Pays–Bas	3.7	3.9	3.7	3.3	3.6	4.2	4.1	4.0	3.9	3.6
Belgium–Luxembourg	2.5	2.7	2.5	2.4	2.6	3.0	2.9	2.8	3.0	2.7
Italy/Italie	1.6	1.6	1.5	1.6	2.0	2.5	2.6	2.7	2.7	2.5
Spain/Espagne	0.2	0.3	0.4	0.8	1.6	1.9	2.3	2.6	1.9	1.9

	1985	1986	1987	1988	1989	1990	1991	1992	1993	1994
Afrique	1.3	1.8	1.7	2.0	2.4	3.5	2.9	2.7	2.8	2.8
Afrique du Nord	1.1	1.3	1.0	1.0	1.2	1.5	1.3	1.3	1.4	1.6
Amériques	6.6	x6.4	x4.9	x5.9	x7.1	x7.2	x7.8	x9.2	x11.9	x14.7
ALAI	1.7	1.3	0.9	1.3	1.8	1.8	1.8	2.5	2.9	3.1
MCAC	0.2	0.1	0.1	0.1	0.1	0.1	0.0	0.0	x1.0	x1.2
Asie	41.2	39.8	x49.6	x51.7	50.5	48.4	51.6	51.5	51.5	50.7
Moyen–Orient	5.3	4.5	4.2	4.8	5.6	5.1	5.2	5.6	x6.0	x5.5
Europe	49.7	50.9	39.4	36.7	37.9	38.9	35.7	34.4	31.3	29.3
CEE	42.5	43.4	34.0	31.8	33.2	37.2	33.3	32.2	29.4	27.7
AELE	5.8	6.1	4.5	4.3	4.0	1.2	1.0	0.8	0.8	0.8
Océanie	0.1	x0.0	x0.0	x0.1	0.2	0.3	0.2	x0.3	x0.3	x0.3
Hong Kong	14.9	14.4	12.2	12.2	14.2	13.7	14.5	13.4	13.3	12.8
China/Chine			5.1	6.1	7.1	6.9	6.9	9.7	9.8	11.3
USA/Etats–Unis d'Amer	3.9	3.3	2.5	2.9	4.0	4.3	4.9	5.7	6.8	6.5
Italy/Italie	8.5	8.9	7.1	6.9	6.7	7.0	6.0	5.3	5.7	5.7
Turkey/Turquie	4.1	3.4	3.4	4.1	4.5	4.5	4.3	4.8	4.8	4.6
Germany/Allemagne	7.1	7.3	5.5	5.2	5.0	5.2	4.9	4.7	3.7	3.4
France, Monac	6.0	5.7	4.3	3.9	4.1	4.8	4.3	4.0	3.9	3.9
Korea, Republic of	10.7	10.5	8.5	8.8	7.8	6.0	5.0	3.7	3.5	3.1
Portugal	3.9	4.1	3.5	3.4	4.0	4.9	4.2	4.4	3.5	3.1
Thailand/Thaïlande	1.1	1.3	1.4	2.2	3.2	3.5	3.9	3.3	3.4	3.3

TRADE BY COMMODITY IN THOUSAND U.S. DOLLARS – COMMERCE PAR PRODUIT EN MILLIERS DE DOLLARS E.U

COUNTRIES–PAYS	IMPORTS – IMPORTATIONS 1990	1991	1992	1993	1994
Total	5096213	5042736	5577681	5498577	6290261
Africa	x70877	x69482	x92515	x92043	x111500
Northern Africa	19033	20513	x27839	x30505	x49856
Americas	x908547	889381	x951263	x1048508	x1223685
LAIA	27604	59798	90876	96615	130489
CACM	3701	4489	6582	x9058	x16251
Asia	1094416	1096439	1309176	x1506754	x1838344
Middle East	178099	143189	186377	x236926	x243709
Europe	2565623	2817602	3068359	2677304	2923367
EEC	2358166	2565860	2828345	2468860	2694778
EFTA	182617	190038	208562	192305	209098
Oceania	x70269	x59050	x63360	x71502	x89761
Germany/Allemagne	718138	887532	968193	813385	881718
USA/Etats-Unis d'Amer	727087	681689	720251	808725	922807
Japan/Japon	489711	475157	550218	652887	864399
France,Monac	458489	420523	451141	401034	452180
Hong Kong	282922	313870	336250	362400	431904
United Kingdom	266201	273351	324086	314934	317383
Netherlands/Pays-Bas	183445	194268	210879	194308	219190
Belgium-Luxembourg	138880	142136	155374	138269	167658
Switz.Liecht	131865	133132	146716	137725	143775
Spain/Espagne	95221	126156	154912	112764	123593
Italy/Italie	111059	127496	139670	108236	116831
Austria/Autriche	106533	103392	112692	109179	116530
Canada	113546	98612	104289	108018	121025
Sweden/Suède	88284	93498	101593	83761	94288
Saudi Arabia	95945	62922	81860	x118143	x120588
United Arab Emirates	48945	52040	68908	x77275	x81635
Singapore/Singapour	64763	59163	64835	67023	83328
Denmark/Danemark	48059	59241	59924	62490	60996
Norway,SVD,JM	45838	51611	57225	50704	60977
Australia/Australie	55798	46229	48687	55089	67427
China/Chine	11632	15363	68657	54354	52013
Portugal	34881	41672	50672	41524	42408
Hungary/Hongrie	x21418	30275	x44822	x39675	x34430
Finland/Finlande	54188	44262	38161	30842	41883
Ireland/Irlande	37144	35002	37730	29948	33682
Mexico/Mexique	13134	20193	38757	38243	60100
Korea, Republic of	13906	15245	21385	45620	68784
Russian Federation			x46675	x33618	x40081
Greece/Grèce	17643	17331	23317	28187	26439
Argentina/Argentine	734	15079	21106	22469	20732
Yugoslavia SFR	20298	x57020			
Poland/Pologne	4464	26990	10463	14506	17854
Malaysia/Malaisie	12503	15028	18723	17102	19527
Tunisia/Tunisie	13740	12998	15005	17204	20946
Former USSR/Anc. URSS	340694	x43923			
Romania/Roumanie	721	904	18377	23845	28937
Un. Rep. of Tanzania	x11722	x9649	x16240	x15284	x14801
Israel/Israël	6686	6178	11228	15500	14059
Chile/Chili	3907	7107	13552	11492	12107
So. Africa Customs Un	10612	10887	9410	6729	5354
Sri Lanka	2532	5189	9443	11734	12002
Venezuela	3696	6999	9367	9913	8269
Philippines	6144	10961	7793	6909	9638
New Zealand	7969	7443	8421	9040	11283
Libyan Arab Jamahiriya	2174	3823	x9280	x10422	x26562
Benin/Bénin	x9711	x8387	x8826	x5658	x1936
Netherlands Antilles	x3154	17073	3368	x692	x1881
Thailand/Thaïlande	5279	6025	6962	7901	9111
Kuwait/Koweït	5455	2781	8730	8234	8702
Dominican Republic	x6083	x6506	x5570	x5765	x11646

COUNTRIES–PAYS	EXPORTS – EXPORTATIONS 1990	1991	1992	1993	1994
Totale	4817433	5200893	5234411	5219959	5972651
Afrique	61458	39984	44818	52663	31810
Afrique du Nord	22558	24762	26335	23558	26459
Amériques	x171580	217576	256998	x279540	x379413
ALAI	16832	41153	43795	42478	59261
MCAC	5939	6880	10419	x10557	x23966
Asie	2123034	2462304	2201210	2361559	2707044
Moyen-Orient	97522	103591	108684	143406	180052
Europe	2411315	2405884	2656001	2430681	2764706
CEE	2322815	2311825	2551068	2336022	2667960
AELE	70410	71745	79707	73150	74975
Océanie	5687	x5721	5216	x6292	x9655
Italy/Italie	1137149	1098490	1204918	1040052	1188918
China/Chine	668153	805263	469931	510741	664851
Korea, Republic of	423020	470525	521508	561131	547469
Hong Kong	353259	383460	393464	411827	466767
Germany/Allemagne	347254	388159	427389	358959	360515
France,Monac	299179	240619	273419	290131	330658
United Kingdom	174017	175680	197801	200863	270804
USA/Etats-Unis d'Amer	123334	139913	171882	189463	240307
Portugal	109398	142555	151706	128569	140804
Japan/Japon	151653	131923	135083	117742	96216
India/Inde	109392	106424	116534	140507	172649
Pakistan	66298	88297	127596	123093	139249
Turkey/Turquie	68527	91482	100983	131284	167403
Thailand/Thaïlande	55234	72193	87849	82115	100591
Netherlands/Pays-Bas	61570	69948	81986	75023	103383
Indonesia/Indonésie	29234	90235	58267	71460	76247
Switz.Liecht	63845	65917	75488	69237	69767
Belgium-Luxembourg	53214	53803	53416	81229	97604
Israel/Israël	51719	56407	63261	54249	63565
Austria/Autriche	52659	53653	52932	46760	x56682
Sri Lanka	21566	27925	43411	47171	58834
Malaysia/Malaisie	29872	30558	33795	42074	47042
Spain/Espagne	38978	34516	36466	31874	39342
Hungary/Hongrie	x23178	x27942	x31821	x36946	x24686
Philippines	9355	48777	7088	15202	26387
Canada	14337	19418	21227	28380	37082
Ireland/Irlande	14651	18210	23943	24459	24820
Sweden/Suède	15479	17182	23911	22096	23141
Singapore/Singapour	14720	16561	19022	22260	38142
Tunisia/Tunisie	14858	16604	18204	21445	23654
Denmark/Danemark	9742	10676	14864	26689	19798
Colombia/Colombie	5160	21920	12779	16600	22544
Czechoslovakia		x21756	x24656		
Mexico/Mexique	3883	10314	20329	13154	21535
Mauritius/Maurice	35075	8349	13137	19123	3999
Slovenia/Slovénia			13083	15236	16491
Macau/Macao	15493	11785	8470	6991	7282
Czech Republic				25654	27357
Poland/Pologne	7861	14435	4602	5625	7422
Yugoslavia SFR	17899	x22137			
Syrian Arab Republic	18311	x10446	5699	x3421	x3634
Finland/Finlande	7669	6481	6248	6165	6908
So. Africa Customs Un	3262	5966	3808	9057	
Morocco/Maroc	7063	7307	7817	1640	1792
Costa Rica	3567	3451	5205	x7853	x21175
Romania/Roumanie	224	270	3839	10456	9590
Viet Nam	x1859	x3088	x3010	x6110	x13155
Norway,SVD,JM	4545	4762	3650	3669	4917
Croatia/Croatie			6529	5211	x4820
Bulgaria/Bulgarie	x2494	x3650	x5161	x2380	x3750

(VALUE AS % OF TOTAL)(VALEUR EN % DU TOTAL)

	1985	1986	1987	1988	1989	1990	1991	1992	1993	1994
Africa	1.3	x2.0	x1.8	x1.8	x1.4	x1.4	x1.4	x1.7	x1.7	x1.8
Northern Africa	0.8	0.7	0.7	1.0	0.7	0.4	0.4	x0.5	x0.6	x0.8
Americas	21.2	x17.4	x15.6	x18.4	x20.5	x17.8	17.7	x17.1	x19.1	x19.5
LAIA	0.8	0.3	0.3	0.4	0.5	0.5	1.2	1.6	1.8	2.1
CACM	0.2	0.2	0.1	0.1	0.1	0.1	0.1	0.1	x0.2	x0.3
Asia	16.4	17.2	17.8	19.6	22.5	21.4	21.7	23.5	x27.4	x29.3
Middle East	4.7	x4.2	x3.7	3.5	x3.2	3.5	2.8	3.3	x4.3	x3.9
Europe	54.2	57.1	56.9	52.8	48.5	50.3	55.9	55.0	48.7	46.5
EEC	44.3	46.8	47.0	44.0	40.5	46.3	50.9	50.7	44.9	42.8
EFTA	9.5	9.6	9.3	8.4	7.6	3.6	3.8	3.7	3.5	3.3
Oceania	1.6	x1.2	x1.3	x1.3	x1.6	x1.4	x1.2	x1.1	x1.3	x1.5
Germany/Allemagne	12.8	13.0	13.1	12.5	11.3	14.1	17.6	17.4	14.8	14.0
USA/Etats-Unis d'Amer	15.9	13.0	11.9	14.5	16.8	14.3	13.5	12.9	14.7	14.7
Japan/Japon	6.2	6.9	7.3	8.5	11.2	9.6	9.4	9.9	11.9	13.7
France,Monac	8.5	9.4	9.4	8.5	7.9	9.0	8.3	8.1	7.3	7.2
Hong Kong	3.7	4.1	4.6	5.1	5.7	5.6	6.2	6.0	6.6	6.9
United Kingdom	5.4	5.8	5.9	6.3	5.8	5.2	5.4	5.8	5.7	5.0
Netherlands/Pays-Bas	3.7	4.0	3.6	3.4	3.1	3.6	3.9	3.8	3.5	3.5
Belgium-Luxembourg	2.9	3.0	3.1	2.7	2.2	2.7	2.8	2.8	2.5	2.7
Switz.Liecht	2.5	2.7	2.6	2.5	2.2	2.6	2.6	2.6	2.5	2.3
Spain/Espagne	0.8	1.0	1.0	1.0	1.6	1.9	2.5	2.8	2.1	2.0

	1985	1986	1987	1988	1989	1990	1991	1992	1993	1994
Afrique	1.3	1.7	1.5	1.5	1.2	1.3	0.8	0.9	1.0	0.5
Afrique du Nord	0.5	0.6	0.5	0.5	0.6	0.5	0.5	0.5	0.5	0.4
Amériques	4.0	x3.7	x2.7	x2.9	x3.3	x3.6	4.2	4.9	x5.4	x6.3
ALAI	0.4	0.4	0.3	0.3	0.3	0.3	0.8	0.8	0.8	1.0
MCAC	0.1	0.1	0.1	0.1	0.1	0.1	0.1	0.2	x0.2	x0.4
Asie	34.2	33.4	41.8	46.0	47.0	44.0	47.3	42.1	45.2	45.3
Moyen-Orient	1.5	2.6	1.0	1.3	1.9	2.0	2.0	2.1	2.7	3.0
Europe	57.6	58.8	47.9	44.5	47.2	50.1	46.3	50.7	46.6	46.3
CEE	52.5	53.9	44.0	41.3	44.4	48.2	44.5	48.7	44.8	44.7
AELE	4.7	4.6	3.6	3.0	2.6	1.5	1.4	1.5	1.4	1.3
Océanie	0.1	x0.1	x0.1	x0.1	0.1	0.1	x0.1	0.1	x0.1	x0.2
Italy/Italie	24.1	24.7	19.8	20.3	22.4	23.6	21.1	23.0	19.9	19.9
China/Chine			10.2	12.2	13.3	13.9	15.5	9.0	9.8	11.1
Korea, Republic of	8.5	8.6	8.5	9.6	11.4	8.8	9.0	10.0	10.7	9.2
Hong Kong	9.1	8.6	7.1	7.2	7.9	7.3	7.4	7.5	7.9	7.8
Germany/Allemagne	8.1	9.1	7.6	5.8	5.9	7.2	7.5	8.2	6.9	6.0
France,Monac	5.9	6.5	5.6	5.1	6.4	6.2	4.6	5.2	5.6	5.5
United Kingdom	5.4	4.4	3.6	3.4	3.4	3.6	3.4	3.8	3.8	4.5
USA/Etats-Unis d'Amer	2.1	2.1	1.7	1.8	2.1	2.6	2.7	3.3	3.6	4.0
Portugal	1.3	1.4	1.3	1.6	1.7	2.3	2.7	2.9	2.5	2.4
Japan/Japon	7.9	6.4	4.4	4.6	4.2	3.1	2.5	2.6	2.3	1.6

TRADE BY COMMODITY IN THOUSAND U.S. DOLLARS – COMMERCE PAR PRODUIT EN MILLIERS DE DOLLARS E.U

COUNTRIES–PAYS	IMPORTS – IMPORTATIONS 1990	1991	1992	1993	1994
Total	11425291	10818423	11520251	11579624	12418187
Africa	x61150	x63443	x83421	x112289	x125679
Northern Africa	17274	20812	x24353	x23640	22367
Americas	x3291002	x3200172	3897143	x4257378	x4484659
LAIA	45152	67458	162469	186117	210696
CACM	4590	3062	6444	x9586	x16340
Asia	2422836	2305134	2440214	2459590	2674907
Middle East	x89237	120408	125450	x126468	x112373
Europe	4657525	4765663	4874087	4503370	4849880
EEC	4196971	4356873	4471763	4162528	4481435
EFTA	424323	371838	348386	295179	328491
Oceania	x137609	x141620	x141005	x143530	x170095
USA/Etats–Unis d'Amer	2845237	2796320	3369754	3679820	3876637
Germany/Allemagne	1579354	1676359	1622480	1619551	1679655
Japan/Japon	1485129	1281958	1247321	1112896	1077893
Hong Kong	688506	709144	810213	925892	1080583
France,Monac	599707	591290	621871	513650	551856
United Kingdom	446655	412066	427772	444764	502209
Italy/Italie	258142	304083	385433	347057	379238
Canada	347327	295047	315136	339442	332882
Russian Federation			x419942	x373404	x286756
Spain/Espagne	187271	269719	315174	191437	187255
Netherlands/Pays–Bas	211024	223215	259965	264737	254926
Switz.Liecht	318692	276564	258309	204836	218568
Belgium–Luxembourg	213690	216986	213981	175533	217924
Sweden/Suède	236369	212739	174516	162716	184660
Austria/Autriche	175178	171204	176455	185759	210361
Australia/Australie	115416	118880	118190	118764	140889
Former USSR/Anc. URSS	735975	x284077			
Denmark/Danemark	99585	99797	84275	82497	101419
Norway,SVD,JM	100334	90212	84818	84902	104882
Mexico/Mexique	20230	34227	105738	115396	127039
Singapore/Singapour	58041	63900	80050	80985	97251
Saudi Arabia	32232	72803	66676	x40303	x34427
Finland/Finlande	82078	60320	48309	41911	60187
Greece/Grèce	37553	41266	51439	55791	70641
Portugal	30233	39677	55807	46722	45511
Ireland/Irlande	40131	38152	34285	30402	35595
Korea, Republic of	26514	29104	26704	36183	84154
China/Chine	10032	12330	37306	41754	49785
United Arab Emirates	23149	18299	22384	x40227	x36648
Hungary/Hongrie	x11110	17225	x25533	x28700	x25098
Thailand/Thaïlande	15029	20677	21364	19498	23423
Israel/Israël	13196	12976	18359	24705	26193
Ukraine			x8972	x45761	x13197
Czechoslovakia	53550	x17669	x34670		
New Zealand	14367	15577	15747	18770	22208
Argentina/Argentine	633	5824	19104	23140	26695
So. Africa Customs Un	12660	15141	14252	16970	20117
Chile/Chili	6580	8412	14000	21724	20807
Poland/Pologne	2386	12821	8943	21852	28987
Malaysia/Malaisie	9138	12618	15081	15135	16172
Tunisia/Tunisie	7891	9369	12744	12371	11282
Indonesia/Indonésie	6534	8615	14243	11540	9564
Andorra/Andorre	x12962	x12400	x12726	x9005	x7523
Dominican Republic	x8177	x10212	x14296	x9579	x21716
Sri Lanka	4913	9472	10440	13716	16108
Slovenia/Slovénia			14432	16078	15271
Kuwait/ Koweït	8058	5064	12264	12551	10480
Romania/Roumanie	5740	2904	9488	16554	14800
Venezuela	3683	7045	9989	8500	6137
Philippines	4162	11525	4846	7022	7235

COUNTRIES–PAYS	EXPORTS – EXPORTATIONS 1990	1991	1992	1993	1994
Totale	9905222	9926326	10909884	11142330	11613352
Afrique	74849	74640	70409	51479	40945
Afrique du Nord	63224	63806	60309	40704	36926
Amériques	683305	782945	920680	993940	x1119254
ALAI	180933	208129	323345	363466	388289
MCAC	3968	4418	4575	x11162	x13075
Asie	6299798	6393470	7165813	7568710	7721397
Moyen–Orient	718573	588704	523296	506214	480940
Europe	2674624	2483603	2566752	2339650	2514270
CEE	2536767	2371387	2471037	2257283	2425777
AELE	61866	54291	41415	36068	34706
Océanie	x41536	x42378	x56079	x59021	x74382
Korea, Republic of	2216149	1956621	1687651	1231876	804280
China/Chine	872272	983617	1570532	1905394	2452848
Hong Kong	1131878	1197631	1300818	1414429	1523613
Italy/Italie	749210	663901	659286	626124	743846
Malaysia/Malaisie	339254	411550	589645	688104	755012
Turkey/Turquie	700119	570547	516586	498333	473916
Germany/Allemagne	477655	472202	520442	429276	449459
USA/Etats–Unis d'Amer	357213	433151	458259	465901	486819
India/Inde	321300	327500	432190	390829	429870
Pakistan	264123	301441	379328	431263	390543
Thailand/Thaïlande	161129	176580	229369	504375	306288
Greece/Grèce	224126	248111	290492	240356	193480
France,Monac	250648	221600	235410	202409	220850
United Kingdom	188952	191113	180871	223685	211849
Netherlands/Pays–Bas	143807	149621	167391	152340	167519
Indonesia/Indonésie	37552	82199	135916	168217	194546
Canada	117967	118892	112797	131700	154040
Mexico/Mexique	19401	22854	145417	187959	202673
Japan/Japon	92061	119249	125746	98962	101722
Belgium–Luxembourg	110494	95825	101738	106000	126699
Spain/Espagne	123600	88692	80006	86850	98949
Philippines	34022	148907	49720	51745	48941
Uruguay	71959	76485	77583	59239	61823
Sweden/Suède	61125	65172	67493	56233	53780
Argentina/Argentine	50052	50882	55216	64852	80723
Austria/Autriche	71469	54771	56150	46913	x50398
Sri Lanka	20616	25940	61654	69426	89159
Hungary/Hongrie	x47087	x38790	x55659	x37598	x36654
Singapore/Singapour	24441	27160	46259	49227	50340
Switz.Liecht	54733	47718	35007	31077	29209
Poland/Pologne	24208	57954	21143	33216	38128
Finland/Finlande	56601	40163	35776	29815	32686
Denmark/Danemark	40051	39637	32826	29588	46172
Morocco/Maroc	45217	40294	34258	20774	18482
New Zealand	28038	25973	30140	29448	42242
Colombia/Colombie	13630	34051	18179	21592	13784
Australia/Australie	11978	15438	25182	29307	31472
Portugal	27147	26602	25720	16494	17487
Czechoslovakia		x30007	x37478		
Tunisia/Tunisie	13540	16894	19535	17186	17375
Brazil/Brésil	11890	12182	19078	22010	20325
Yugoslavia SFR	71366	x53245			
Slovenia/Slovénia			27795	24511	27148
Mongolia/Mongolie	x35651	x21228	x7034	x20305	x1666
Ireland/Irlande	11848	13945	17437	11198	12604
Dominican Republic	x14232	x12068	x15237	x14083	x68174
Romania/Roumanie	35903	12361	12220	13633	15389
Czech Republic				38011	45183
Bangladesh	433	1703	7821	19193	x61812
Israel/Israël	17837	9306	6879	7034	4161

(VALUE AS % OF TOTAL)(VALEUR EN % DU TOTAL)

	1985	1986	1987	1988	1989	1990	1991	1992	1993	1994
Africa	0.5	x0.6	x0.5	x0.5	x0.5	x0.5	x0.5	x0.7	x0.9	x1.1
Northern Africa	0.2	0.2	0.1	0.1	0.2	0.2	0.2	x0.2	x0.2	0.2
Americas	36.2	x29.5	x27.1	x31.4	x30.4	x28.8	x29.6	33.8	x36.8	x36.1
LAIA	0.5	0.2	0.2	0.2	0.3	0.4	0.6	1.4	1.6	1.7
CACM	0.1	0.1	x0.1	0.0	0.0	0.0	0.0	0.1	x0.1	x0.1
Asia	10.4	11.7	13.4	16.7	22.0	21.2	21.3	21.2	21.2	21.5
Middle East	0.8	x0.9	x0.9	x0.7	x0.9	x0.8	1.1	1.1	x1.1	x0.9
Europe	45.9	52.1	53.0	45.6	39.7	40.8	44.1	42.3	38.9	39.1
EEC	36.4	41.3	41.9	36.5	32.0	36.7	40.3	38.8	35.9	36.1
EFTA	9.4	10.6	10.9	8.8	7.5	3.7	3.4	3.0	2.5	2.6
Oceania	1.2	x1.0	x0.9	x1.0	x1.2	x1.2	x1.3	x1.3	x1.3	x1.4
USA/Etats–Unis d'Amer	32.8	26.6	24.6	28.3	26.5	24.9	25.8	29.3	31.8	31.2
Germany/Allemagne	15.3	17.9	18.5	14.3	11.1	13.8	15.5	14.1	14.0	13.5
Japan/Japon	6.1	7.0	8.4	10.2	14.4	13.0	11.8	10.8	9.6	8.7
Hong Kong	2.9	3.1	3.4	4.7	5.6	6.0	6.6	7.0	8.0	8.7
France,Monac	4.7	5.5	5.2	5.0	4.6	5.2	5.5	5.4	4.4	4.4
United Kingdom	4.2	3.9	3.7	3.8	3.7	3.9	3.8	3.7	3.8	4.0
Italy/Italie	2.1	2.5	2.6	2.3	2.2	2.3	2.8	3.3	3.0	3.1
Canada	2.7	2.3	2.1	2.6	3.1	3.0	2.7	2.7	2.9	2.7
Russian Federation								x3.6	x3.2	x2.3
Spain/Espagne	0.3	0.4	0.7	1.3	1.4	1.6	2.5	2.7	1.7	1.5

	1985	1986	1987	1988	1989	1990	1991	1992	1993	1994
Afrique	0.9	1.0	0.6	0.7	0.7	0.7	0.7	0.6	0.5	0.4
Afrique du Nord	0.7	0.7	0.6	0.6	0.7	0.6	0.6	0.6	0.4	0.3
Amériques	9.8	9.4	7.4	7.8	7.6	6.9	7.9	8.4	9.0	x9.6
ALAI	2.5	2.2	2.1	2.0	1.9	1.8	2.1	3.0	3.3	3.3
MCAC	0.0	0.1	0.0	0.0	0.0	0.0	0.0	0.0	x0.1	x0.1
Asie	48.2	45.1	56.6	60.5	61.4	63.6	64.4	65.7	68.0	66.5
Moyen–Orient	11.3	6.5	8.5	5.5	6.0	7.3	5.9	4.8	4.5	4.1
Europe	39.5	42.9	32.7	28.8	28.2	27.0	25.0	23.5	21.0	21.6
CEE	33.9	37.8	28.9	25.5	25.1	25.6	23.9	22.6	20.3	20.9
AELE	4.1	4.1	3.0	2.5	2.3	0.6	0.5	0.4	0.3	0.3
Océanie	0.6	x0.5	x0.5	x0.4	x0.4	x0.4	x0.4	x0.5	x0.5	x0.6
Korea, Republic of	18.6	19.7	19.7	21.8	25.2	22.4	19.7	15.5	11.1	6.9
China/Chine			5.2	6.5	7.9	8.8	9.9	14.4	17.1	21.1
Hong Kong	11.2	11.8	10.3	10.2	11.7	11.4	12.1	11.9	12.7	13.1
Italy/Italie	9.0	9.3	7.1	6.7	6.7	7.6	6.7	6.0	5.6	6.4
Malaysia/Malaisie	1.5	1.4	1.3	2.7	3.2	3.4	4.1	5.4	6.2	6.5
Turkey/Turquie	11.2	6.5	8.4	5.4	6.0	7.1	5.7	4.7	4.5	4.1
Germany/Allemagne	7.0	7.5	5.7	4.9	4.7	4.8	4.8	4.8	3.9	3.9
USA/Etats–Unis d'Amer	3.7	3.6	2.7	3.3	3.9	3.6	4.4	4.2	4.2	4.2
India/Inde	0.8	1.1	1.2	1.4	2.5	3.2	3.3	4.0	3.5	3.7
Pakistan	1.5	1.7	1.5	1.5	1.8	2.7	3.0	3.5	3.9	3.4

TRADE BY COMMODITY IN THOUSAND U.S. DOLLARS – COMMERCE PAR PRODUIT EN MILLIERS DE DOLLARS E.U

COUNTRIES–PAYS	IMPORTS – IMPORTATIONS 1990	1991	1992	1993	1994
Total	31582415	32708474	34445627	35630429	38722514
Africa	x321615	x275061	x359398	x414597	x411154
Northern Africa	63084	40818	x34708	x50074	x33203
Americas	10664548	10742287	11501658	12620815	13324515
LAIA	156113	305049	473170	553154	664370
CACM	22723	23512	37869	x40271	x47987
Asia	3802300	5136174	6522815	8016057	9301117
Middle East	486635	575953	614649	x657102	x731063
Europe	13533369	14825122	15375091	13762664	14706047
EEC	12365033	13817048	14166235	12553104	13612799
EFTA	898466	898224	919919	882254	930308
Oceania	x336325	x361080	x425917	x416007	x495027
USA/Etats–Unis d'Amer	9570294	9550326	10153302	11182766	11697379
Germany/Allemagne	4007981	4740469	4721445	4192139	4358245
Hong Kong	1676617	2672882	3804774	4974275	5735248
France,Monac	2058133	2245760	2272009	1998785	2153576
United Kingdom	1981329	1964173	1924590	1763075	1981341
Japan/Japon	1283128	1532154	1701164	1901031	2190943
Netherlands/Pays–Bas	946096	1046438	1074965	958302	999293
Italy/Italie	572534	828757	1000325	773090	987528
Belgium–Luxembourg	759480	810078	839690	707341	758051
Canada	726928	703988	693625	701160	750354
Russian Federation			x1230209	x838725	x1007006
Switz.Liecht	641732	640938	651683	638038	655878
Austria/Autriche	503945	521358	552295	540212	568440
Sweden/Suède	472869	456670	461017	365232	433874
Former USSR/Anc. URSS	2652491	x1105512			
Spain/Espagne	195160	313521	390313	300753	340184
Australia/Australie	257578	275503	336474	327616	382279
Denmark/Danemark	272917	285173	313322	286069	325095
Ireland/Irlande	207753	223691	213071	300226	276497
Saudi Arabia	209410	259512	220329	x243720	x266383
Norway,SVD,JM	242035	240057	251153	230521	259260
Singapore/Singapour	188912	200223	204653	223612	253557
Mexico/Mexique	91113	147864	234270	214024	215652
United Arab Emirates	125347	146903	194969	x216254	x255393
Finland/Finlande	199699	168311	146754	115646	157788
Greece/Grèce	114976	119124	144381	143534	157079
Croatia/Croatie			157219	221892	x62562
Portugal	72162	93525	112058	108699	115809
Argentina/Argentine	3511	44436	110879	128691	141479
Hungary/Hongrie	x63726	73716	x85443	x124289	x179530
So. Africa Customs Un	55854	84240	82152	111513	114023
Poland/Pologne	22467	108508	83626	82017	99554
Ukraine			x45402	x154380	x64559
New Zealand	47300	53917	55319	65498	79755
Kuwait/Koweït	40357	22161	72485	64661	62217
Israel/Israël	34333	34726	49745	68505	96950
Slovenia/Slovénia			62700	53691	49031
Venezuela	16329	25365	43342	47238	19862
Lebanon/Liban	x34734	x45941	x32954	x32717	x62244
Chile/Chili	7988	17802	29947	57746	85962
Korea, Republic of	20511	25147	31696	45945	90021
Panama	43135	32999	31280	33716	36660
Libyan Arab Jamahiriya	52413	32738	x20641	x42303	x25038
Romania/Roumanie	15248	43350	21910	20859	18489
Reunion/Réunion	24889	25599	32905	26600	29269
Brazil/Brésil	20765	36777	13279	34796	84102
Czech Republic				81649	108860
Yugoslavia SFR	237480	x76972			
Czechoslovakia	81659	x19750	x53780		
Andorra/Andorre	x24096	x24778	x24416	x22203	x21307

COUNTRIES–PAYS	EXPORTS – EXPORTATIONS 1990	1991	1992	1993	1994
Totale	26288815	28149351	31512418	33384213	36801311
Afrique	148069	161899	178852	196218	175809
Afrique du Nord	125525	140742	142885	151169	151598
Amériques	1869451	2074687	2436784	2910535	2644027
ALAI	1347937	1471581	1792490	2248159	1850105
MCAC	25375	22661	26266	26895	x34936
Asie	10097358	12347040	14633320	16684253	18662964
Moyen–Orient	102649	x144076	162973	142569	201022
Europe	13549168	12959206	13560050	12805392	14396675
CEE	12679923	12476769	13005982	12233339	13850794
AELE	221504	185348	193529	248095	234383
Océanie	x35655	36509	38000	53318	59846
Italy/Italie	6579796	6236890	6317174	5743107	6465382
Hong Kong	1888290	3104571	4332790	5767781	6554814
China/Chine	1956620	2875470	4084492	5053850	5706857
Korea, Republic of	4164054	3679006	3034392	2128047	1556674
Brazil/Brésil	1106728	1176662	1409065	1859611	1537203
Portugal	1199210	1250357	1479137	1349711	1532211
Indonesia/Indonésie	561208	980975	1300285	1628016	1848348
Spain/Espagne	1445184	1293250	1248971	1214630	1645600
Germany/Allemagne	968646	1168678	1104292	1001723	1082465
Thailand/Thaïlande	743547	881650	955541	1035103	1483562
France,Monac	800191	847592	948607	954233	958576
United Kingdom	464702	527629	562133	551157	664173
USA/Etats–Unis d'Amer	431751	516732	542550	537243	584662
Netherlands/Pays–Bas	329181	371182	452826	499264	488932
Austria/Autriche	415331	338703	389384	362645	x378810
India/Inde	186503	182826	232700	279999	345729
Switz.Liecht	208114	167834	175532	232688	221505
Hungary/Hongrie	x143381	x138563	x203313	x173935	x171123
Mexico/Mexique	74921	99194	208447	197757	150087
Denmark/Danemark	132650	142808	166923	184062	211503
Belgium–Luxembourg	99820	116940	136618	156872	165834
Czechoslovakia		x184284	x214318		
Philippines	78001	134425	116688	142144	175816
Malaysia/Malaisie	96770	106077	119224	115428	116043
Poland/Pologne	168963	107393	103679	109387	121873
Yugoslavia SFR	641276	x293166			
Singapore/Singapour	70999	86944	87408	90693	96060
Slovenia/Slovénia			123364	133551	137207
Croatia/Croatie			109333	147453	x133644
Romania/Roumanie	128389	77654	54822	104255	182537
Turkey/Turquie	32863	58295	82458	93377	158751
Colombia/Colombie	48502	73771	72361	78618	63377
Morocco/Maroc	78644	81633	65816	71758	61560
Japan/Japon	52089	64684	73507	76143	85044
Canada	59655	55679	64731	87796	117151
Bulgaria/Bulgarie	x70806	x31214	87354	73739	98192
Czech Republic				181224	210174
Finland/Finlande	98590	60368	54840	57466	81773
Sweden/Suède	56223	55102	51639	44805	52236
Ireland/Irlande	31197	34424	52279	64036	89499
Viet Nam	x125029	x14314	x27912	x108414	x335849
Tunisia/Tunisie	23808	36233	45217	54802	73898
Chile/Chili	34948	51663	40818	41233	31444
Greece/Grèce	59012	32654	41159	49627	33800
Argentina/Argentine	33073	35811	26271	30778	33654
Pakistan	22478	27172	33627	30441	31685
Slovakia				x89846	x76989
Cyprus/Chypre	33359	34269	29234	22572	18957
Yugoslavia/Yougoslavie			x69848	x13412	x5694
Australia/Australie	15173	19744	20401	32900	30402

(VALUE AS % OF TOTAL)(VALEUR EN % DU TOTAL)

	1985	1986	1987	1988	1989	1990	1991	1992	1993	1994
Africa	0.7	x1.1	x1.2	x1.1	x1.0	x1.0	x0.9	x1.0	x1.2	x1.1
Northern Africa	0.2	0.2	0.3	0.2	0.2	0.2	0.1	x0.1	x0.1	x0.1
Americas	41.7	37.5	35.1	35.6	34.8	33.8	32.9	33.4	35.5	34.4
LAIA	0.2	0.1	0.2	0.3	0.5	0.5	0.9	1.4	1.6	1.7
CACM	0.1	0.1	0.1	0.1	0.1	0.1	0.1	0.1	x0.1	x0.1
Asia	6.6	6.3	7.5	9.5	10.7	12.1	15.7	19.0	22.5	24.0
Middle East	2.1	1.8	1.7	1.6	x1.8	1.5	1.8	1.8	x1.8	x1.9
Europe	39.2	43.2	46.0	44.0	43.2	42.9	45.3	44.6	38.6	38.0
EEC	32.8	36.1	38.5	37.2	36.3	39.2	42.2	41.1	35.2	35.2
EFTA	6.4	7.0	7.3	6.7	6.5	2.8	2.7	2.7	2.5	2.4
Oceania	1.0	1.0	x0.9	x1.1	x1.1	x1.1	x1.1	x1.2	x1.2	x1.3
USA/Etats–Unis d'Amer	38.4	34.3	32.1	32.5	31.2	30.3	29.2	29.5	31.4	30.2
Germany/Allemagne	10.3	11.5	12.4	11.2	11.4	12.7	14.5	13.7	11.8	11.3
Hong Kong	1.4	1.3	1.8	2.6	3.9	5.3	8.2	11.0	14.0	14.8
France,Monac	5.5	6.5	7.0	6.6	6.3	6.5	6.9	6.6	5.6	5.6
United Kingdom	5.4	5.4	5.5	5.9	5.7	6.3	6.0	5.6	4.9	5.1
Japan/Japon	2.5	2.5	3.3	4.3	4.2	4.1	4.7	4.9	5.3	5.7
Netherlands/Pays–Bas	2.6	3.1	3.2	2.9	2.8	3.0	3.2	3.1	2.7	2.6
Italy/Italie	1.4	1.5	1.7	1.8	1.8	1.8	2.5	2.9	2.2	2.6
Belgium–Luxembourg	2.3	2.5	2.6	2.5	2.3	2.4	2.5	2.4	2.0	2.0
Canada	2.3	2.4	2.3	2.3	2.5	2.3	2.2	2.0	2.0	1.9

	1985	1986	1987	1988	1989	1990	1991	1992	1993	1994
Afrique	0.4	0.4	0.3	0.4	0.5	0.5	0.5	0.5	0.5	0.5
Afrique du Nord	0.3	0.3	0.3	0.3	0.4	0.5	0.5	0.5	0.5	0.4
Amériques	9.3	8.2	6.9	7.3	8.4	7.1	7.3	7.7	8.7	7.2
ALAI	7.7	6.6	5.4	5.6	6.7	5.1	5.2	5.7	6.7	5.0
MCAC	0.1	0.1	0.1	0.1	0.1	0.1	0.1	0.1	0.1	x0.1
Asie	18.4	19.4	x36.8	x41.7	33.4	38.4	43.9	46.4	50.0	50.7
Moyen–Orient	0.5	0.4	0.4	0.4	0.5	0.4	x0.5	0.5	0.4	0.5
Europe	65.8	66.1	50.8	46.0	54.7	51.5	46.0	43.0	38.4	39.1
CEE	55.5	57.1	44.9	40.9	48.0	48.2	44.3	41.3	36.6	37.6
AELE	4.8	4.9	3.6	3.0	3.1	0.8	0.7	0.6	0.7	0.6
Océanie	0.1	x0.1	x0.1	x0.1	x0.1	x0.1	0.1	0.1	0.1	0.1
Italy/Italie	30.0	31.2	23.9	21.2	25.1	25.0	22.2	20.0	17.2	17.6
Hong Kong	2.0	2.0	2.2	3.1	5.4	7.2	11.0	13.7	17.3	17.8
China/Chine	1.3	1.5	2.4	3.4	6.0	7.4	10.2	13.0	15.1	15.5
Korea, Republic of	12.3	13.4	12.4	15.5	16.3	15.8	13.1	9.6	6.4	4.2
Brazil/Brésil	7.3	6.2	4.9	5.0	5.8	4.2	4.2	4.5	5.6	4.2
Portugal	2.4	3.2	3.1	3.3	4.2	4.6	4.4	4.7	4.0	4.2
Indonesia/Indonésie	0.1	0.1	0.1	0.3	1.0	2.1	3.5	4.1	4.9	5.0
Spain/Espagne	6.6	6.1	4.9	4.6	5.1	5.5	4.6	4.0	3.6	4.5
Germany/Allemagne	3.8	3.9	3.2	3.0	4.0	3.7	4.2	3.5	3.0	2.9
Thailand/Thaïlande	0.7	0.7	1.0	1.5	2.3	2.8	3.1	3.0	3.1	4.0

TRADE BY COMMODITY IN THOUSAND U.S. DOLLARS – COMMERCE PAR PRODUIT EN MILLIERS DE DOLLARS E.U

COUNTRIES–PAYS	IMPORTS – IMPORTATIONS				
	1990	1991	1992	1993	1994
Total	3708274	4043702	4702324	4953025	5904630
Africa	x34283	x32172	x35253	x43992	x46863
Northern Africa	8346	8161	x9420	x9688	x15549
Americas	926839	965868	1151852	1226589	1459210
LAIA	59174	67470	88371	107970	154058
CACM	1270	1459	1869	x2088	x2871
Asia	816895	969839	1247163	1657465	2149369
Middle East	x64228	x77177	x94671	x159523	x110467
Europe	1838704	1964447	2175894	1915824	2107149
EEC	1658735	1778065	1956282	1710004	1912228
EFTA	164602	174235	206618	193772	182226
Oceania	x59082	x61380	x66512	x74023	x99161
USA/Etats–Unis d'Amer	691509	727118	822315	886052	1045370
Germany/Allemagne	430002	499066	560638	469324	534989
United Kingdom	309152	328948	370888	373530	409396
Japan/Japon	238559	269358	257243	267171	373454
Hong Kong	158407	168175	255829	294582	385476
Singapore/Singapour	91129	115932	195115	400700	625958
France, Monac	209987	223080	253930	217172	228197
Canada	152954	163318	234048	225743	251462
Korea, Republic of	107375	168332	196603	225742	328157
Italy/Italie	174332	179230	186400	144263	159123
Switz.Liecht	118364	128299	149948	143720	122679
Netherlands/Pays–Bas	144272	103981	116312	89202	105598
Sweden/Suède	90436	98806	102469	88861	94921
China/Chine	19201	25796	81993	127503	114543
Spain/Espagne	74044	85223	74666	65626	87571
Belgium–Luxembourg	54370	68471	78408	67123	80232
Austria/Autriche	55013	57056	64656	61094	72642
Australia/Australie	47830	46121	57261	63790	84595
Malaysia/Malaisie	47270	42533	56426	54312	76328
Norway, SVD, JM	44293	45203	55996	49585	58950
Iran (Islamic Rp. of)	x26387	x32533	x45385	x67652	x19968
Israel/Israël	39127	49225	50953	43031	61366
Finland/Finlande	49993	43899	45000	34753	32388
Denmark/Danemark	31946	38351	43324	37764	40289
Mexico/Mexique	13923	20027	38775	41723	71872
Brazil/Brésil	34575	31439	24342	31290	42522
Portugal	18454	20175	30658	22908	26383
Saudi Arabia	7142	11235	12766	x45553	x35313
Turkey/Turquie	18408	20931	21233	24851	36265
Ireland/Irlande	8268	16275	13167	26116	29630
India/Inde	19921	17375	20119	16781	20526
Russian Federation			x36854	x11062	x14448
So. Africa Customs Un	14955	15022	15311	17314	18610
Thailand/Thaïlande	13096	14781	12098	19377	25635
Greece/Grèce	8467	15504	15764	12268	10867
Indonesia/Indonésie	4479	9163	6967	17746	8396
New Zealand	9956	13835	8067	9161	12680
Hungary/Hongrie	x6968	7214	x9605	x11714	x10553
Former USSR/Anc. URSS		x27115			
Argentina/Argentine	736	3271	7960	15754	11164
Poland/Pologne	7534	8373	3929	11812	18988
Philippines	1874	5518	5049	9949	10283
United Arab Emirates	3510	2276	2985	x14323	x9026
Venezuela	4453	5542	6001	6202	3448
Czechoslovakia	10243	x4787	x8623		
Colombia/Colombie	2273	2810	2780	5487	12038
Latvia/Lettonie			x103	10813	1025
Bangladesh				10466	x451
Yugoslavia SFR	12736	x9400			
Slovenia/Slovénia			3683	5603	7042

COUNTRIES–PAYS	EXPORTS – EXPORTATIONS				
	1990	1991	1992	1993	1994
Totale	3826889	4156236	4888514	5046089	6075632
Afrique	x661	x1108	x1802	x1971	x508
Afrique du Nord	29	34	56	23	135
Amériques	826116	951673	1109325	1084015	1258319
ALAI	21998	9937	45303	65843	61192
MCAC	1	1	1	x21	x22
Asie	1337601	1542483	1822463	2173349	2859977
Moyen–Orient	891	x1586	1027	x4548	x3500
Europe	1615710	1605412	1900485	1703443	1865910
CEE	1462468	1453215	1714337	1515485	1682236
AELE	150178	150191	181751	168617	168692
Océanie	x29042	x37196	x45049	x69892	x72380
Japan/Japon	959974	1112067	1131093	1361886	1763087
USA/Etats–Unis d'Amer	770278	904336	979607	934219	1105290
Germany/Allemagne	672192	680726	768270	789227	875740
United Kingdom	288275	317302	434674	316381	328467
Hong Kong	122874	123441	189532	266550	369978
Switz.Liecht	145823	144639	174668	158524	158913
France, Monac	177747	154139	145884	99010	159825
Korea, Republic of	93689	98142	122468	142776	176525
China/Chine	25174	33698	141168	138083	205446
Netherlands/Pays–Bas	127497	113642	110956	65204	95572
Singapore/Singapour	61667	76033	99903	99243	162058
Canada	29543	36180	83313	83908	91633
Italy/Italie	43444	47602	56567	41546	56025
Austria/Autriche	45818	43501	54899	47024	x47622
Malaysia/Malaisie	26968	32229	59206	50207	62455
Australia/Australie	27921	34488	41834	55297	58709
Thailand/Thaïlande	18060	32162	44073	47609	69341
Ireland/Irlande	20172	10985	39592	58537	
Mexico/Mexique	15508	2406	38749	57337	48373
Belgium–Luxembourg	28099	19975	28231	32504	36295
Sweden/Suède	28998	28259	25697	24886	35197
Denmark/Danemark	10661	14749	21064	19302	22568
Israel/Israël	11369	6316	12702	34394	21785
Philippines	1159	9832	11611	16684	18734
Portugal	11960	11365	13015	9116	10934
Russian Federation			x9450	x20292	x26271
Spain/Espagne	6183	8640	8516	8814	11245
Norway, SVD, JM	4355	5551	7082	10093	9779
Slovenia/Slovénia			3368	18928	14820
Macau/Macao	7041	6634	6828	6061	3
Brazil/Brésil	6138	7017	5613	6842	11258
New Zealand	990	2015	3044	14351	13669
India/Inde	8151	9792	2068	3386	3234
Finland/Finlande	1344	2188	6802	3301	2534
Former USSR/Anc. URSS		x10903			
Hungary/Hongrie	x993	x1316	x2840	x3684	x4068
Poland/Pologne	2948	2761	1296	2159	2554
Czechoslovakia		x2750	x3392		
Czech Republic				6096	9050
So. Africa Customs Un	355	783	1332	1570	
Saudi Arabia	8	76	689	x2417	x1370
Bulgaria/Bulgarie	x218	x95	x1289	x994	x1853
Yugoslavia SFR	2982	x1931			
Netherlands Antilles	3713	879	948		
Bahrain/Bahreïn	x47	x501	x39	x1242	x120
Indonesia/Indonésie	514	450	495	720	1599
Belarus/Bélarus			x295	x1231	x937
Venezuela	324	200	527	538	640
Ukraine			x190	x905	x904
Former GDR	x13600	x538	x538		

(VALUE AS % OF TOTAL)(VALEUR EN % DU TOTAL)

	1985	1986	1987	1988	1989	1990	1991	1992	1993	1994
Africa	1.7	x1.6	x1.5	x1.0	x1.1	x0.9	x0.8	x0.7	x0.8	x0.8
Northern Africa	0.8	0.7	0.3	0.3	0.3	0.2	0.2	x0.2	x0.2	x0.3
Americas	32.3	x28.1	x20.6	18.9	25.0	25.0	23.9	24.5	24.7	24.7
LAIA	2.8	2.1	1.4	1.3	1.3	1.6	1.7	1.9	2.2	2.6
CACM	0.1	0.5	0.3	0.0	0.0	0.0	0.0	0.0	x0.0	x0.0
Asia	13.0	16.0	x20.5	x23.2	20.6	22.0	24.0	26.6	33.5	36.4
Middle East	1.3	x1.9	x2.3	x2.5	x1.6	x1.7	x1.9	x2.0	x3.2	x1.9
Europe	50.3	50.9	49.9	50.5	47.7	49.6	48.6	46.3	38.7	35.7
EEC	40.6	39.6	39.0	41.5	38.8	44.7	44.0	41.6	34.5	32.4
EFTA	9.2	10.9	10.4	8.8	8.5	4.4	4.3	4.4	3.9	3.1
Oceania	1.8	x2.7	x1.3	x1.5	x1.3	x1.6	x1.5	x1.4	x1.5	x1.6
USA/Etats–Unis d'Amer	25.5	21.4	16.0	13.8	19.5	18.6	18.0	17.5	17.9	17.7
Germany/Allemagne	11.1	10.6	10.5	11.5	10.3	11.6	12.3	11.9	9.5	9.1
United Kingdom	7.7	7.1	6.0	7.2	7.3	8.3	8.1	7.9	7.5	6.9
Japan/Japon	5.1	4.4	4.2	6.1	6.0	6.4	6.7	5.5	5.4	6.3
Hong Kong	0.8	4.7	4.6	4.6	4.5	4.3	4.2	5.4	5.9	6.5
Singapore/Singapour	0.7	0.8	1.0	1.3	1.8	2.5	2.9	4.1	8.1	10.6
France, Monac	6.8	6.4	7.2	5.8	4.9	5.7	5.5	5.4	4.4	3.9
Canada	3.8	3.3	2.5	3.7	4.0	4.1	4.0	5.0	4.6	4.3
Korea, Republic of	2.0	1.6	2.3	2.4	2.8	2.9	4.2	4.2	4.6	5.6
Italy/Italie	3.1	2.8	3.5	3.7	4.0	4.7	4.4	4.0	2.9	2.7

	1985	1986	1987	1988	1989	1990	1991	1992	1993	1994
Afrique		x0.1	x0.1	x0.1	x0.0	x0.0	x0.0	x0.0	x0.0	x0.0
Afrique du Nord	0.0	x0.1	x0.1	x0.1	x0.0	0.0	0.0	0.0	0.0	0.0
Amériques	18.3	18.8	x13.3	x10.6	22.6	21.6	22.9	22.6	21.5	20.7
ALAI	0.1	0.2	0.1	0.1	0.3	0.6	0.2	0.9	1.3	1.0
MCAC		x0.0	x0.0	x0.0	x0.0	0.0	0.0	0.0	x0.0	x0.0
Asie	31.4	31.5	x31.6	x37.5	35.7	35.0	37.1	37.3	43.1	47.1
Moyen–Orient	0.1	x0.0	x0.1	x0.0	x0.0	0.0	x0.0	0.0	x0.1	x0.1
Europe	49.4	48.6	49.2	46.0	39.0	42.2	38.6	38.9	33.8	30.7
CEE	37.9	37.8	38.7	39.8	33.8	38.2	35.0	35.1	30.0	27.7
AELE	11.5	10.8	10.4	5.8	5.1	3.9	3.6	3.7	3.3	2.8
Océanie		x0.1	x0.2	x0.8	x0.6	x0.8	x0.9	x0.9	x1.4	x1.2
Japan/Japon	25.8	24.5	21.5	26.0	25.7	25.1	26.8	23.1	27.0	29.0
USA/Etats–Unis d'Amer	17.5	18.3	12.7	9.3	21.2	20.1	21.8	20.0	18.5	18.2
Germany/Allemagne	19.8	19.9	20.2	19.1	16.1	17.6	16.4	15.7	15.6	14.4
United Kingdom	7.3	6.3	5.3	7.3	6.7	7.5	7.6	8.9	6.3	5.4
Hong Kong	1.1	2.9	3.0	3.1	3.2	3.2	3.0	3.9	5.3	6.1
Switz.Liecht	9.7	8.5	7.9	3.8	3.3	3.8	3.5	3.6	3.1	2.6
France, Monac	3.4	3.3	4.2	6.3	4.0	4.6	3.7	3.0	2.0	2.6
Korea, Republic of	1.8	2.0	2.2	2.7	3.4	2.4	2.4	2.5	2.8	2.9
China/Chine			0.3	0.3	0.6	0.7	0.8	2.9	2.7	3.4
Netherlands/Pays–Bas	3.3	3.9	4.1	2.5	2.8	3.3	2.7	2.3	1.3	1.6

TRADE BY COMMODITY IN THOUSAND U.S. DOLLARS – COMMERCE PAR PRODUIT EN MILLIERS DE DOLLARS E.U

COUNTRIES–PAYS	IMPORTS – IMPORTATIONS 1990	1991	1992	1993	1994
Total	11742302	11752800	13289863	13339120	14570276
Africa	x333490	x331377	x393757	x388087	x395857
Northern Africa	135116	114259	x153272	x144425	x151811
Americas	x2235163	2583033	2947281	3265591	x3543518
LAIA	282421	399922	523414	587108	650792
CACM	31602	28440	34940	x26103	x29147
Asia	x1810207	x2027545	x2493851	x2695941	x2998178
Middle East	x450243	x525083	x632529	x567441	x415784
Europe	5449981	6114145	6944781	6432641	6972002
EEC	5076429	5750335	6526202	6022435	6520426
EFTA	280203	302735	339404	314173	364178
Oceania	x207524	x242724	x267081	x288837	x346984
USA/Etats–Unis d'Amer	1389115	1604845	1802964	2072150	2199945
Germany/Allemagne	994459	1224705	1456592	1320149	1427502
France,Monac	781774	826590	935763	951214	986618
Japan/Japon	690257	750581	876594	1047617	1280377
Italy/Italie	678066	819310	847092	687393	719491
United Kingdom	581785	645371	732823	741213	764139
Netherlands/Pays–Bas	496468	516755	552011	469671	536902
Canada	419141	443795	482506	481502	510502
Spain/Espagne	409038	444619	488193	430043	448053
Belgium–Luxembourg	332350	371413	429553	429389	539770
Austria/Autriche	178326	202537	250624	241189	263636
Switz.Liecht	190264	202941	231526	216295	244312
Australia/Australie	158241	190321	211499	226744	277462
Sweden/Suède	167237	186765	219645	198374	227780
Ireland/Irlande	137456	148242	192142	158357	167042
Iran (Islamic Rp. of)	x132708	x146762	x195654	x130019	x34152
Korea, Republic of	107400	133305	148055	181568	256537
Turkey/Turquie	120327	129015	147030	172678	127080
Saudi Arabia	104444	163176	158495	x126181	x109512
Mexico/Mexique	67956	106054	165807	174071	197330
Singapore/Singapour	98773	118624	137891	186696	238608
Brazil/Brésil	122592	152961	134206	155056	160019
Hong Kong	91398	107460	159285	163748	207246
Denmark/Danemark	95447	110614	134175	127711	146819
Greece/Grèce	88677	104784	124129	119673	116246
So. Africa Customs Un	98739	104300	123770	114851	131539
China/Chine	50470	67561	135688	130889	128588
Russian Federation			x128495	x168347	x229979
Norway,SVD,JM	85387	94861	100785	91488	114235
Poland/Pologne	45131	81363	88711	110946	101790
Israel/Israël	63280	74107	87070	96784	105717
Portugal	54452	75739	92549	83125	94673
Former USSR/Anc. URSS	1542225	x230881			
Finland/Finlande	80895	72893	70909	64934	81756
Argentina/Argentine	12096	27335	80652	75030	110342
Thailand/Thaïlande	37198	44297	59796	75054	97317
Hungary/Hongrie	x42654	59294	x57637	x54000	x54639
Dominican Republic	x40083	x43223	x50318	x52311	x99549
Egypt/Egypte	39513	36105	54919	54763	57436
India/Inde	52550	36411	59452	48928	70098
New Zealand	35480	39028	39175	44328	53230
Venezuela	18376	35440	46573	38179	26081
Malaysia/Malaisie	25608	36782	40718	42228	52740
Indonesia/Indonésie	27426	40576	26880	39712	24387
Chile/Chili	18342	26915	36583	41380	44691
Czechoslovakia	6921	x32401	x69937		
Pakistan	19202	27373	27105	37104	25127
Colombia/Colombie	16820	18536	17864	53230	59951
Algeria/Algérie	29259	21969	33866	27732	23193
Jordan/Jordanie	12573	15485	33237	27850	28101

COUNTRIES–PAYS	EXPORTS – EXPORTATIONS 1990	1991	1992	1993	1994
Totale	10132936	11138166	12789115	12962519	13703334
Afrique	x22684	15125	21168	22316	x3911
Afrique du Nord	4171	3892	3714	3079	1478
Amériques	x2766149	x3176733	3855440	4055956	x4548258
ALAI	37514	41330	348604	382766	398264
MCAC	253	307	398	x12978	x39017
Asie	1594846	1867708	2180828	2486319	2668777
Moyen–Orient	30013	14990	12463	x19545	x19440
Europe	5616184	5947722	6596459	6240766	6264326
CEE	5246497	5515041	6138366	5817474	5749662
AELE	337201	412141	427585	396617	475130
Océanie	x61127	x87342	x87088	x103641	x129291
USA/Etats–Unis d'Amer	2650266	3055284	3402905	3559998	3860578
Germany/Allemagne	1641175	1801791	1988368	1812209	1830607
Japan/Japon	933232	1088895	1210716	1338328	1352480
United Kingdom	757323	795623	827898	729615	865389
France,Monac	617831	620455	705442	615057	656558
Ireland/Irlande	407444	451386	562711	491950	
Netherlands/Pays–Bas	484388	444926	478190	557029	580234
Italy/Italie	376722	391602	406425	404356	435821
Sweden/Suède	354932	354830	412424	378265	397166
Switz.Liecht	306441	371808	397047	371384	443367
Belgium–Luxembourg	254711	280943	321206	409132	477499
Singapore/Singapour	178278	212678	280077	381479	421316
Mexico/Mexique	11160	12568	313275	333785	353050
Denmark/Danemark	163200	176369	219614	201093	235746
Hong Kong	105710	113245	162926	172725	210743
Malaysia/Malaisie	83071	103627	126419	119223	136196
Pakistan	76897	91723	93465	102038	94051
Israel/Israël	63200	81824	99283	92957	108514
Spain/Espagne	67045	72688	94082	101409	110715
Thailand/Thaïlande	25055	47282	69808	105249	127501
Australia/Australie	46494	64741	59524	75192	95918
China/Chine	29167	39372	64545	88375	115632
Canada	48307	47486	73302	71251	86412
Korea, Republic of	51407	52744	44067	44023	61340
Austria/Autriche	42965	47069	46547	44553	x70173
Finland/Finlande	58557	51558	40935	39675	53424
Norway,SVD,JM	30761	40333	30538	25233	31763
Portugal	18604	24324	31872	30205	31646
New Zealand	14480	21405	26736	28346	33278
Dominican Republic	x27987	x29221	x23330	x23566	x161464
Brazil/Brésil	12676	13742	18966	24372	22523
Malta/Malte	13130	14126	18118	16378	x29547
Hungary/Hongrie	x13672	x13083	x17459	x16004	x18490
Poland/Pologne	14912	14195	16800	14038	44264
So. Africa Customs Un	15662	9880	15448	16781	
India/Inde	15016	12538	10624	14928	17166
Czechoslovakia		x11091	x11756		
Turkey/Turquie	7802	8707	6592	7301	3633
Argentina/Argentine	5210	5489	6269	10775	6321
Colombia/Colombie	3753	4887	4198	6996	8671
Philippines	1730	6843	3117	4774	1275
Costa Rica		10		x12370	x37347
Jordan/Jordanie	1203	3204	3779	4531	8198
Slovakia				x11409	x10780
Czech Republic				11029	13745
Slovenia/Slovénia			4925	5109	7757
Venezuela	3237	2771	3536	3510	3465
Russian Federation			x4642	x4935	x5271
Croatia/Croatie			3905	3436	x1329
Greece/Grèce	1579	1456	2652	2926	4684

(VALUE AS % OF TOTAL)(VALEUR EN % DU TOTAL)

	1985	1986	1987	1988	1989	1990	1991	1992	1993	1994
Africa	3.6	x4.0	x3.3	x3.2	x3.0	x2.8	x2.8	x2.9	x2.9	x2.7
Northern Africa	1.8	1.8	1.2	1.3	1.2	1.2	1.0	x1.2	x1.1	x1.0
Americas	23.2	x21.9	x21.7	19.8	20.4	x19.0	21.9	22.2	24.4	x24.3
LAIA	3.0	2.4	2.3	2.3	2.4	2.4	3.4	3.9	4.4	4.5
CACM	0.4	0.1	x0.3	0.3	0.3	0.3	0.2	0.3	x0.2	x0.2
Asia	16.6	15.2	x12.6	x15.5	x14.6	x15.4	x17.2	x18.8	x20.2	x20.6
Middle East	3.7	x4.1	x3.9	x4.1	x3.2	x3.8	x4.5	x4.8	x4.3	x2.9
Europe	45.7	46.9	50.7	49.7	50.0	46.4	52.0	52.3	48.2	47.9
EEC	38.9	40.1	43.4	42.6	43.1	43.2	48.9	49.1	45.1	44.8
EFTA	6.1	6.2	6.6	6.3	6.2	2.4	2.6	2.6	2.4	2.5
Oceania	2.0	x3.1	x1.8	x1.8	x1.9	x1.7	x2.1	x2.0	x2.1	x2.4
USA/Etats–Unis d'Amer	11.1	11.1	11.4	12.1	12.6	11.8	13.7	13.6	15.5	15.1
Germany/Allemagne	7.3	7.7	8.3	8.5	8.5	8.5	10.4	11.0	9.9	9.8
France,Monac	6.2	6.6	7.6	6.9	6.8	6.7	7.0	7.0	7.1	6.8
Japan/Japon	3.9	3.5	3.7	5.1	5.9	5.9	6.4	6.6	7.9	8.8
Italy/Italie	5.1	5.4	6.1	5.9	5.9	5.8	7.0	6.4	5.2	4.9
United Kingdom	5.7	5.0	5.0	5.0	5.2	5.0	5.5	5.5	5.6	5.2
Netherlands/Pays–Bas	3.1	3.1	3.3	3.6	3.6	4.2	4.4	4.2	3.5	3.7
Canada	8.0	6.6	6.3	4.5	4.2	3.6	3.8	3.6	3.6	3.5
Spain/Espagne	2.4	2.6	2.8	3.0	3.5	3.5	3.8	3.7	3.2	3.1
Belgium–Luxembourg	2.6	2.9	3.0	2.8	2.5	2.8	3.2	3.2	3.2	3.7

	1985	1986	1987	1988	1989	1990	1991	1992	1993	1994
Afrique	0.1	x0.1	x0.1	x0.2	x0.1	x0.3	0.1	0.1	0.1	x0.0
Afrique du Nord	0.0	x0.0	x0.0	0.0	0.0	0.0	0.0	0.0	0.0	0.0
Amériques	21.7	18.6	18.0	x19.9	x28.0	x27.3	x28.6	30.2	31.3	x33.2
ALAI	1.9	0.4	0.5	0.4	0.4	0.4	0.4	2.7	3.0	2.9
MCAC	0.0	0.0	0.0	x0.0	x0.1	0.0	0.0	0.0	x0.1	x0.3
Asie	14.9	14.9	14.6	17.5	15.8	15.7	16.8	17.0	19.1	19.5
Moyen–Orient	0.2	x0.1	x0.0	x0.1	x0.1	0.3	0.1	0.1	x0.2	x0.1
Europe	60.1	63.8	63.3	58.8	54.6	55.4	53.4	51.6	48.1	45.7
CEE	51.7	55.1	54.3	50.3	46.9	51.8	49.5	48.0	44.9	42.0
AELE	7.9	8.3	8.6	8.0	7.3	3.3	3.7	3.3	3.1	3.5
Océanie	0.8	x0.4	x0.7	x0.6	x0.6	x0.6	x0.8	x0.7	x0.8	x0.9
USA/Etats–Unis d'Amer	18.6	17.0	16.4	18.6	26.7	26.2	27.4	26.6	27.5	28.2
Germany/Allemagne	19.3	21.2	18.9	15.8	14.7	16.2	16.2	15.5	14.0	13.4
Japan/Japon	11.0	11.1	10.2	11.3	10.0	9.2	9.8	9.5	10.3	9.9
United Kingdom	8.6	8.2	7.8	7.7	6.7	7.5	7.1	6.5	5.6	6.3
France,Monac	4.5	5.4	6.0	6.0	5.5	6.1	5.6	5.5	4.7	4.8
Ireland/Irlande	4.7	4.5	4.5	4.2	3.9	4.0	4.1	4.4	3.8	
Netherlands/Pays–Bas	2.7	2.9	3.5	3.8	3.9	4.8	4.0	3.7	4.3	4.2
Italy/Italie	3.2	3.6	3.9	3.4	3.5	3.7	3.5	3.2	3.1	3.2
Sweden/Suède	3.2	3.4	3.7	3.6	3.4	3.5	3.2	3.2	2.9	2.9
Switz.Liecht	3.4	3.8	3.8	3.1	2.7	3.0	3.3	3.1	2.9	3.2

TRADE BY COMMODITY IN THOUSAND U.S. DOLLARS – COMMERCE PAR PRODUIT EN MILLIERS DE DOLLARS E.U

COUNTRIES–PAYS	IMPORTS – IMPORTATIONS				
	1990	1991	1992	1993	1994
Total	1360040	1435460	1725448	1877798	2601986
Africa	x64221	80187	x104852	x69640	x83002
Northern Africa	24902	35721	58699	24383	27602
Americas	274856	308212	389957	637123	1205621
LAIA	68776	97066	97293	136508	252855
CACM	3515	4879	5188	x7041	x12977
Asia	x212648	230800	286048	x308301	x347929
Middle East	x39004	x53214	x69249	x62804	x62490
Europe	743896	746110	849855	754001	844526
EEC	685618	689131	786852	692924	777882
EFTA	44363	44959	44755	48669	51471
Oceania	x33087	x29406	x35077	x32947	x39820
USA/Etats–Unis d'Amer	143684	148190	224397	422683	782389
Germany/Allemagne	103791	149198	183204	160006	188213
France,Monac	82592	91582	94206	88531	85468
United Kingdom	85320	70967	76080	91038	62170
Netherlands/Pays–Bas	71999	66764	80815	61640	62122
Sweden/Suède	74268	65602	67969	62564	92035
Spain/Espagne	58173	46300	65238	52740	61435
Belgium–Luxembourg	60218	56152	58922	43923	51280
Italy/Italie	62178	53931	60194	43567	61502
Canada	48945	46080	52543	58904	143033
Mexico/Mexique	20499	43194	38665	69335	144258
Korea, Republic of	35332	43732	43792	39256	45419
Austria/Autriche	29539	29876	37993	40374	54103
Thailand/Thaïlande	25233	21698	23240	44876	48737
Switz.Liecht	26681	26419	25917	24470	25827
Hong Kong	16576	17683	24713	31408	28600
Japan/Japon	18340	20517	22118	28403	29987
Denmark/Danemark	20557	21900	24910	20238	26572
Singapore/Singapour	16416	18033	23477	25361	28015
Australia/Australie	22742	19141	22258	20544	26451
So. Africa Customs Un	17724	18237	22429	21248	21761
Algeria/Algérie	4630	8138	41460	9528	7663
Norway,SVD,JM	16203	17124	17262	23076	24783
Iran (Islamic Rp. of)	x13985	x12820	x17323	x24044	x11023
Argentina/Argentine	2484	6576	15260	20562	30522
China/Chine	2165	4344	16286	21752	22780
Czechoslovakia	11045	x7959	x32817		
Saudi Arabia	7909	13693	12984	x14092	x18598
Colombia/Colombie	7468	14138	13080	12853	14451
Turkey/Turquie	6691	15345	13051	11604	10629
Hungary/Hongrie	x5364	11130	x13420	x12927	x11786
Czech Republic				36249	39747
Malaysia/Malaisie	12134	12773	11484	9307	20167
Brazil/Brésil	18441	13402	8964	10366	25308
Portugal	9509	13528	11909	6187	10703
Finland/Finlande	16790	10904	11214	9131	12434
New Zealand	7828	8104	9815	10806	11316
Greece/Grèce	6131	8422	11108	9050	6071
Poland/Pologne	6614	7077	10075	9889	9213
Egypt/Egypte	8539	9247	7470	6509	9464
Viet Nam	x17412	x4864	x10898	x6992	x8156
Israel/Israël	6433	7497	7688	7377	8214
Indonesia/Indonésie	6251	5899	4946	10739	14075
Philippines	5183	6527	7860	6419	7692
Russian Federation			x7196	x10864	x21586
Venezuela	9016	6312	5721	5774	4232
Pakistan	3957	6201	9519	1916	4574
Chile/Chili	6135	3987	6576	6127	9620
Libyan Arab Jamahiriya	5374	13319	x1155	x1813	x1104
Nigeria/Nigéria	x1138	6305	x2689	x4906	x6456

COUNTRIES–PAYS	EXPORTS – EXPORTATIONS				
	1990	1991	1992	1993	1994
Totale	1359320	1399807	1585400	1733029	2279945
Afrique	x1194	x1841	x1782	x2244	x637
Afrique du Nord	373	39	304	403	403
Amériques	136213	163671	180380	268487	558904
ALAI	12811	16458	26724	39673	52207
MCAC		6		x13	118
Asie	301626	294805	340490	407192	445469
Moyen–Orient	457	x475	x300	x1285	x1417
Europe	887797	905276	1034250	1011484	1236201
CEE	773847	797730	882007	875388	1062237
AELE	87172	82273	92587	79431	102201
Océanie	2499	2645	2311	x3418	x6430
Germany/Allemagne	351543	348319	422845	358676	394848
Japan/Japon	250834	232978	238638	278101	286782
United Kingdom	171360	169916	149373	206004	292463
USA/Etats–Unis d'Amer	102460	129811	126231	185044	363148
France,Monac	82411	101465	105803	101654	130980
Switz.Liecht	85639	81184	90160	74522	99394
Italy/Italie	29791	38459	47659	49460	52766
Hong Kong	24083	29139	44136	62262	62630
Slovenia/Slovénia			51029	54066	71109
Austria/Autriche	32312	31533	35801	37580	x41191
Canada	20526	17085	27258	43605	143257
Netherlands/Pays–Bas	25085	26040	29042	26938	35185
Belgium–Luxembourg	18143	19982	24864	32045	32873
Spain/Espagne	14764	19949	19969	16629	22902
Brazil/Brésil	10748	11452	17890	26471	32789
China/Chine	5158	10870	17618	20557	35016
Sweden/Suède	14790	15581	16478	10494	13577
Denmark/Danemark	18852	13592	12623	13355	10318
Finland/Finlande	10645	9307	11867	11810	15040
Singapore/Singapour	3514	5156	14065	10622	21425
Hungary/Hongrie	x13958	x8818	x12311	x8307	x8229
Yugoslavia SFR	26768	x25128			
Slovakia				x23590	x13823
Korea, Republic of	6876	3359	6740	11882	12100
Israel/Israël	4198	5997	6500	5993	9683
Mexico/Mexique	787	1467	4371	8215	12779
Czechoslovakia		x7148	x5137		
Romania/Roumanie	3812	6320	3630	1580	734
Malaysia/Malaisie	2048	2013	5168	3728	3190
Poland/Pologne	7873	4640	3089	2901	6594
Greece/Grèce	2123	1432	2590	6255	9710
Indonesia/Indonésie	2714	2264	1684	5282	5345
Yugoslavia/Yougoslavie			x6895	x2265	x79
Argentina/Argentine	1052	2328	3568	3102	4512
Portugal	1474	1839	2792	4185	10384
Norway,SVD,JM	1503	1087	2418	4909	2807
Thailand/Thaïlande	1502	2196	1912	3625	5090
Bulgaria/Bulgarie	x3556	x3582	x1953	x1548	x1089
Korea Dem People's Rp			x3433	x3626	x2073
Australia/Australie	1759	2006	1854	2513	5624
So. Africa Customs Un	347	1198	796	1186	
Colombia/Colombie	32	471	392	1749	1021
Lithuania/Lituanie				x2290	8693
Czech Republic				2279	1835
New Zealand	733	612	387	651	802
Croatia/Croatie			997	281	x320
Cote d'Ivoire	x75	x394	x412	x397	
Russian Federation			x662	x531	x442
Turkey/Turquie	270	148	158	751	736
Former USSR/Anc. URSS		x995			

(VALUE AS % OF TOTAL)(VALEUR EN % DU TOTAL)

	1985	1986	1987	1988	1989	1990	1991	1992	1993	1994
Africa	4.9	x5.2	x4.4	x4.8	x5.4	x4.7	5.6	x6.1	x3.7	x3.2
Northern Africa	2.5	2.2	1.8	2.3	2.2	1.8	2.5	3.4	1.3	1.1
Americas	29.4	25.6	24.7	20.9	17.1	20.2	21.4	22.6	33.9	46.4
LAIA	5.3	4.5	3.2	3.1	4.1	5.1	6.8	5.6	7.3	9.7
CACM	0.3	0.4	0.3	0.4	0.4	0.3	0.3	0.3	x0.4	x0.5
Asia	15.9	13.9	13.7	x13.5	13.1	x15.6	16.1	16.6	x16.4	x13.4
Middle East	4.2	x4.4	x2.1	x3.0	x2.2	x2.9	x3.7	x4.0	x3.3	x2.4
Europe	45.6	49.9	50.6	53.7	58.3	54.7	52.0	49.3	40.2	32.5
EEC	35.8	39.0	39.8	42.3	46.7	50.4	48.0	45.6	36.9	29.9
EFTA	8.9	10.2	10.1	10.8	11.0	3.3	3.1	2.6	2.6	2.0
Oceania	2.7	x3.2	x1.7	x2.2	x2.2	x2.4	x2.1	x2.1	x1.8	x1.6
USA/Etats–Unis d'Amer	22.0	19.3	19.5	14.3	8.5	10.6	10.3	13.0	22.5	30.1
Germany/Allemagne	6.3	6.6	6.5	5.5	5.9	7.6	10.4	10.6	8.5	7.2
France,Monac	3.8	3.9	3.9	4.3	4.6	6.1	6.4	5.5	4.7	3.3
United Kingdom	4.5	4.2	4.6	5.4	6.0	6.3	4.9	4.4	4.8	2.4
Netherlands/Pays–Bas	3.8	4.2	4.6	4.4	4.9	5.3	4.7	4.7	3.3	2.4
Sweden/Suède	4.3	4.8	5.3	5.2	5.4	5.5	4.6	3.9	3.3	3.5
Spain/Espagne	2.9	3.4	3.3	2.8	2.9	4.3	3.2	3.8	2.8	2.4
Belgium–Luxembourg	2.3	2.8	2.7	3.9	4.1	4.4	3.9	3.4	2.3	2.0
Italy/Italie	3.3	4.4	4.1	5.5	7.0	4.6	3.8	3.5	2.3	2.4
Canada	1.1	0.7	0.9	2.5	3.2	3.6	3.2	3.0	3.1	5.5

	1985	1986	1987	1988	1989	1990	1991	1992	1993	1994
Afrique	0.1	x0.1	x0.2	0.4	0.1	x0.1	x0.1	x0.2	x0.2	x0.0
Afrique du Nord	0.0	0.0	0.2	0.2	0.1	0.0	0.0	0.0	0.0	0.0
Amériques	11.7	x13.0	x11.2	6.4	9.5	10.0	11.7	11.4	15.5	24.5
ALAI	2.4	2.2	1.9	1.3	1.2	0.9	1.2	1.7	2.3	2.3
MCAC	0.0	x0.0	x0.0	x0.0	x0.0		0.0		x0.0	0.0
Asie	12.7	8.7	x12.7	x24.0	24.4	22.2	21.1	21.5	23.5	19.5
Moyen–Orient	0.0	x0.1	x0.1	x0.0	x0.0	0.0	x0.0	x0.0	x0.1	x0.1
Europe	72.8	75.6	64.9	62.5	61.8	65.3	64.7	65.2	58.4	54.2
CEE	55.9	57.5	50.6	52.5	51.4	56.9	57.0	55.6	50.5	46.6
AELE	14.1	16.1	12.2	8.6	8.9	6.4	5.9	5.8	4.6	4.5
Océanie	0.2	x0.3	x0.2	0.2	x0.3	0.2	0.2	0.1	x0.2	x0.3
Germany/Allemagne	23.7	25.8	22.2	24.7	24.9	25.9	24.9	26.7	20.7	17.3
Japan/Japon	10.8	7.3	6.5	19.2	21.3	18.5	16.6	15.1	16.0	12.6
United Kingdom	9.3	7.7	6.9	10.5	10.1	12.6	12.1	9.4	11.9	12.8
USA/Etats–Unis d'Amer	9.3	6.6	5.7	3.9	6.8	7.5	9.3	8.0	10.7	15.9
France,Monac	9.2	10.5	9.2	6.9	6.1	6.1	7.2	6.7	5.9	5.7
Switz.Liecht	11.0	12.5	8.5	5.4	5.3	6.3	5.8	5.7	4.3	4.4
Italy/Italie	3.3	3.7	2.8	2.5	1.5	2.2	2.7	3.0	2.9	2.3
Hong Kong	0.2	0.1	0.1	0.9	1.3	1.8	2.1	2.8	3.6	2.7
Slovenia/Slovénia								3.2	3.1	3.1
Austria/Autriche	1.7	2.0	2.3	1.8	1.9	2.4	2.3	2.3	2.2	x1.8

TRADE BY COMMODITY IN THOUSAND U.S. DOLLARS – COMMERCE PAR PRODUIT EN MILLIERS DE DOLLARS E.U

COUNTRIES–PAYS	IMPORTS – IMPORTATIONS 1990	1991	1992	1993	1994
Total	39644446	39491165	42244280	40380663	45078802
Africa	x888016	x836419	x942933	x1000696	x1001225
Northern Africa	348183	302417	x344728	x349078	x345938
Americas	7397091	7878313	8818040	9400146	11146020
LAIA	1194346	1488512	1891897	1920667	2273867
CACM	31333	32332	39765	x44272	x45717
Asia	8249000	9070011	9741007	10843378	12347330
Middle East	x904372	x1081553	x1215960	x1354698	x1040114
Europe	20129306	19943462	21163112	17410606	18679385
EEC	18719173	18597172	19751877	16172635	17382360
EFTA	1182145	1194485	1269007	1116920	1145994
Oceania	x836499	x857723	x929682	x939796	x1079040
USA/Etats–Unis d'Amer	4202684	4486718	4992760	5322370	6237375
Germany/Allemagne	3675781	4048214	4387420	3322462	3730132
United Kingdom	3482645	3465012	3493828	3402948	3265976
France, Monac	2748014	2823974	3038049	2487622	2656271
Japan/Japon	2292660	2393175	2187255	2394126	2822753
Italy/Italie	2474643	2397897	2529564	1768760	1942574
Canada	1812849	1704975	1751668	1995637	2462048
Korea, Republic of	1534885	1694184	1732131	2010075	2618715
Netherlands/Pays–Bas	1451438	1384857	1544159	1225959	1296758
Spain/Espagne	1503475	1157324	1214962	972348	1091042
China/Chine	716523	811782	1079195	1288174	1470314
Singapore/Singapour	719677	803211	871446	948272	1164079
Switz.Liecht	874584	853330	881441	762808	792670
Mexico/Mexique	433553	625771	931237	918160	1051871
Sweden/Suède	850837	825441	834578	743763	891741
Australia/Australie	671362	704296	766257	797816	904049
Belgium–Luxembourg	782598	760876	820778	666739	713002
Austria/Autriche	595374	604918	643971	572014	657358
Malaysia/Malaisie	379530	511392	554295	609602	793308
Hong Kong	328829	421283	539770	658516	690630
Iran (Islamic Rp. of)	x324920	x483883	x464414	x385425	x142247
Brazil/Brésil	362725	369134	390623	369071	472796
Norway,SVD,JM	290893	324383	372306	340276	335691
So. Africa Customs Un	296537	311287	337644	373721	381462
Indonesia/Indonésie	278533	319392	342967	351971	322721
Thailand/Thaïlande	259732	317652	329490	358778	523144
India/Inde	363775	249701	346232	280196	278968
Denmark/Danemark	269082	273198	293371	257212	324085
Finland/Finlande	356343	290600	286255	228968	285955
Turkey/Turquie	222271	226201	239485	318634	243222
Portugal	195991	229516	276738	190783	195869
Israel/Israël	189667	210116	224236	249767	267944
Saudi Arabia	127370	176783	224961	x262879	x232534
Ireland/Irlande	201912	192791	206804	185428	190561
Russian Federation			x278563	x290689	x347983
Poland/Pologne	91292	112982	171872	223596	256751
Greece/Grèce	131039	142554	181400	147629	141036
Venezuela	123979	159315	161890	142509	118875
Former USSR/Anc. URSS	1397480	x445389			
Hungary/Hongrie	x139715	132873	x157839	x145766	x140006
Argentina/Argentine	58536	110253	144664	173252	251281
Czechoslovakia	227972	x129339	x264932		
New Zealand	128346	116795	122227	121980	149645
United Arab Emirates	71680	51339	64673	x204498	x223937
Algeria/Algérie	107117	84237	95546	99101	120430
Chile/Chili	78702	76458	90103	106180	134416
Colombia/Colombie	77667	71500	79836	112881	138821
Philippines	59500	55096	65775	114415	119234
Czech Republic				233770	221231
Pakistan	73737	78916	75571	78306	58983

COUNTRIES–PAYS	EXPORTS – EXPORTATIONS 1990	1991	1992	1993	1994
Totale	37195183	38172783	40910781	40382251	44639538
Afrique	x68487	x59726	x68213	x93618	x51251
Afrique du Nord	13266	15883	x14904	25771	14054
Amériques	9889334	10886787	11643811	12424743	13478212
ALAI	148046	168861	412113	521682	619847
MCAC	4845	6303	5033	x531	x1013
Asie	5433345	5989774	6298615	7203168	8568014
Moyen–Orient	x28397	x25644	x40503	x212102	x189657
Europe	21037207	20802923	22532673	20307746	22106656
CEE	18708976	18608634	20231255	18219804	19831244
AELE	2253070	2154819	2234042	2030026	2207540
Océanie	177807	222223	x240538	x212916	x268370
USA/Etats–Unis d'Amer	9032592	9946615	10368932	11045252	11848421
Germany/Allemagne	6677448	6590161	7484608	6601496	7153601
Japan/Japon	3818978	4245706	4476402	4960461	5939437
United Kingdom	4062660	4021518	3994690	3631476	4036057
France, Monac	2516908	2430364	2661090	2368232	2515252
Switz.Liecht	2055194	1947988	1967958	1799394	1928865
Italy/Italie	1305294	1331575	1461013	1385733	1491087
Netherlands/Pays–Bas	1104410	1169041	1327588	1149057	1264779
Sweden/Suède	837983	850393	887013	748691	850234
Canada	687893	749550	832980	846641	976889
Denmark/Danemark	514982	499376	550713	505387	569019
Singapore/Singapour	394427	482389	487966	521947	729451
Hong Kong	321020	360938	477170	568743	583349
Belgium–Luxembourg	428537	438742	478276	475561	539794
Austria/Autriche	438817	409755	451829	444566	x540440
Spain/Espagne	247708	301048	419025	412148	479861
Korea, Republic of	261299	193938	281291	322634	362739
Finland/Finlande	278584	265037	250766	243632	298203
Mexico/Mexique	74927	78675	312149	364869	459574
Norway,SVD,JM	197641	206694	265768	230484	278530
Ireland/Irlande	264895	264504	218255	202904	
Israel/Israël	330304	382196	152187	144988	181904
China/Chine	133927	137381	186409	235040	278963
Australia/Australie	141631	161688	191385	168039	204877
Malaysia/Malaisie	75903	92616	114731	141122	169522
Brazil/Brésil	58948	67471	69745	108737	118681
Poland/Pologne	66332	95990	35650	27698	41037
Thailand/Thaïlande	20396	34356	41764	52416	55929
Saudi Arabia	2957	2613	4999	x118163	x106051
New Zealand	24713	33950	40217	39937	62175
Hungary/Hongrie	x46215	x31438	x43972	x32441	x39716
So. Africa Customs Un	22540	27590	27766	30666	
Portugal	19877	19157	26936	36209	74645
Slovenia/Slovénia			41339	37015	42829
Czechoslovakia		x35686	x34600		
India/Inde	24292	21028	20122	22014	26119
Argentina/Argentine	10764	14057	17738	22899	15953
Russian Federation			x22987	x30276	x33730
Greece/Grèce	10762	17851	19452	14712	18272
Czech Republic				49707	58507
Tunisia/Tunisie	11656	13199	11138	21022	11550
United Arab Emirates	4682			x42361	x38057
Yugoslavia SFR	70390	x36730			
Bahrain/Bahreïn	x7624	x11747	x6445	x18000	x5673
Papua New Guinea	9933	24954	5261	2726	x107
Former USSR/Anc. URSS	375340	x30554			
Turkey/Turquie	4663	4524	13606	8871	13599
Colombia/Colombie	1218	5126	3203	15915	14251
Croatia/Croatie			11995	9413	x16133
Bulgaria/Bulgarie	x34677	x6337	x7809	x6855	x6094

(VALUE AS % OF TOTAL)(VALEUR EN % DU TOTAL)

	1985	1986	1987	1988	1989	1990	1991	1992	1993	1994
Africa	2.5	x2.7	x2.4	x2.4	x2.3	x2.2	x2.1	x2.2	x2.5	x2.2
Northern Africa	1.2	1.1	0.9	0.8	0.8	0.9	0.8	x0.8	x0.9	x0.8
Americas	22.2	x19.3	17.4	18.1	19.4	18.7	20.0	20.9	23.3	24.7
LAIA	3.9	2.6	2.7	2.7	2.8	3.0	3.8	4.5	4.8	5.0
CACM	0.1	0.1	0.1	0.1	0.1	0.1	0.1	0.1	x0.1	x0.1
Asia	16.5	15.6	x19.0	x20.6	20.0	20.8	23.0	23.1	26.8	27.4
Middle East	2.1	x2.8	x2.2	x2.1	x1.9	x2.3	x2.7	x2.9	x3.4	x2.3
Europe	51.1	53.0	52.1	50.2	50.2	50.8	50.5	50.1	43.1	41.4
EEC	42.9	44.0	43.5	42.4	42.8	47.2	47.1	46.8	40.1	38.6
EFTA	7.5	8.3	8.0	7.2	6.9	3.0	3.0	3.0	2.8	2.5
Oceania	2.8	x4.3	x2.1	x2.3	2.3	x2.1	x2.2	x2.2	x2.3	x2.4
USA/Etats–Unis d'Amer	12.5	11.8	10.7	11.0	11.1	10.6	11.4	11.8	13.2	13.8
Germany/Allemagne	8.4	9.4	8.8	8.4	8.5	9.3	10.3	10.4	8.2	8.3
United Kingdom	9.9	8.9	8.4	8.5	8.5	8.8	8.8	8.3	8.4	7.2
France, Monac	6.2	6.3	6.5	6.5	6.3	6.9	7.2	7.2	6.2	5.9
Japan/Japon	5.4	4.6	4.5	5.3	6.0	5.8	6.1	5.2	5.9	6.3
Italy/Italie	4.9	5.2	5.7	5.6	5.7	6.2	6.1	6.0	4.4	4.3
Canada	5.3	4.1	3.4	4.0	4.7	4.6	4.3	4.1	4.9	5.5
Korea, Republic of	2.4	2.8	2.7	3.3	3.8	3.9	4.3	4.1	5.0	5.8
Netherlands/Pays–Bas	3.4	3.8	3.5	3.3	3.5	3.7	3.5	3.7	3.0	2.9
Spain/Espagne	1.9	2.0	2.4	2.3	2.5	3.8	2.9	2.9	2.4	2.4

	1985	1986	1987	1988	1989	1990	1991	1992	1993	1994
Afrique	0.2	x0.2	x0.1	x0.2	x0.2	x0.2	x0.2	x0.2	x0.3	x0.1
Afrique du Nord	0.0	x0.0	x0.0	0.0	0.0	0.0	0.0	x0.0	0.1	0.0
Amériques	31.0	26.2	x23.7	25.0	27.1	26.6	28.5	28.5	30.7	30.2
ALAI	0.6	0.3	0.3	0.2	0.3	0.4	0.4	1.0	1.3	1.4
MCAC	0.0	0.0	0.0	0.0	0.0	0.0	0.0	0.0	x0.0	x0.0
Asie	11.1	12.0	x12.9	x14.3	14.7	14.7	15.7	15.4	17.8	19.2
Moyen–Orient	0.1	x0.3	x0.3	x0.2	x0.2	x0.1	x0.1	x0.1	x0.5	x0.4
Europe	55.7	59.6	59.1	56.4	55.9	56.6	54.5	55.1	50.3	49.5
CEE	46.6	49.2	48.8	47.1	46.6	50.3	48.7	49.5	45.1	44.4
AELE	8.9	10.1	10.0	9.1	9.1	6.1	5.6	5.5	5.0	4.9
Océanie	0.3	x0.3	x0.4	0.4	x0.4	0.4	0.6	x0.6	x0.5	x0.6
USA/Etats–Unis d'Amer	28.0	23.5	21.3	22.9	24.3	24.3	26.1	25.3	27.4	26.5
Germany/Allemagne	15.1	17.7	18.0	17.7	17.2	18.0	17.3	18.3	16.3	16.0
Japan/Japon	8.8	9.5	8.9	10.0	11.0	10.3	11.1	10.9	12.3	13.3
United Kingdom	11.2	11.3	10.6	10.8	10.7	10.9	10.5	9.8	9.0	9.0
France, Monac	7.2	6.0	6.3	6.0	5.8	6.8	6.4	6.5	5.9	5.6
Switz.Liecht	4.8	5.8	5.6	5.1	4.8	5.5	5.1	4.8	4.5	4.3
Italy/Italie	2.9	3.3	3.3	2.9	3.0	3.5	3.5	3.6	3.4	3.3
Netherlands/Pays–Bas	3.2	3.3	3.0	2.6	2.6	3.0	3.1	3.2	2.8	2.8
Sweden/Suède	2.0	2.0	2.0	2.0	2.2	2.3	2.2	2.2	1.9	1.9
Canada	2.4	2.3	2.0	1.9	2.4	1.8	2.0	2.0	2.1	2.2

TRADE BY COMMODITY IN THOUSAND U.S. DOLLARS – COMMERCE PAR PRODUIT EN MILLIERS DE DOLLARS E.U

COUNTRIES–PAYS	IMPORTS – IMPORTATIONS					COUNTRIES–PAYS	EXPORTS – EXPORTATIONS				
	1990	1991	1992	1993	1994		1990	1991	1992	1993	1994
Total	7789987	8488189	9003002	9250149	10516334	Totale	7203808	7855492	8411886	8766234	10013633
Africa	x102910	x80708	x89065	x84011	x82471	Afrique	x6712	x3952	x4733	x4947	x2803
Northern Africa	48345	26456	32943	31918	25435	Afrique du Nord	731	394	189	196	907
Americas	1982969	2233079	2301696	2561826	2980463	Amériques	901022	934652	1143318	1149372	1178121
LAIA	139138	205908	296993	300135	353540	ALAI	20864	30913	79960	81932	70280
CACM	10424	13998	18660	x13114	x13717	MCAC	7	1	15	x2947	x4121
Asia	1862569	2363369	2829014	3140315	3759802	Asie	3973507	4610685	4916527	5339504	6200774
Middle East	184509	x186719	x226634	x204131	x171712	Moyen–Orient	18804	x4736	5229	x10385	x10174
Europe	3586635	3555234	3557168	3220615	3440517	Europe	2218645	2270307	2323204	2242113	2592227
EEC	3339987	3313744	3322676	3022930	3227392	CEE	2061823	2093655	2147409	2089168	2423929
EFTA	219751	223660	219398	179206	192830	AELE	147517	166573	152586	138589	154158
Oceania	x156769	x142864	x148884	x166485	x181175	Océanie	18360	x15194	x15012	x19787	x28277
USA/Etats–Unis d'Amer	1618397	1800347	1782617	2044610	2389399	Japan/Japon	2976713	3268742	2985317	3063378	3592489
Germany/Allemagne	857524	909037	933004	800176	876134	USA/Etats–Unis d'Amer	855450	880290	1029207	1035911	1077382
Hong Kong	502321	725018	917904	961480	1063100	Hong Kong	505674	674382	919160	1028095	1122015
United Kingdom	584711	546135	569486	593618	598779	Germany/Allemagne	895949	861340	880923	822443	835905
France,Monac	523953	507486	489391	464847	476511	United Kingdom	285122	377916	384033	302346	411082
Japan/Japon	319569	440732	511030	503528	654814	China/Chine	66182	83159	338701	402066	486491
Korea, Republic of	261893	289966	232498	383573	606472	Netherlands/Pays–Bas	194383	202064	231151	309619	459306
Italy/Italie	321296	309531	295830	238510	271990	Malaysia/Malaisie	112543	210668	235854	268083	314745
Singapore/Singapour	230837	248264	252330	301456	324634	Italy/Italie	179582	178174	169233	165067	183226
Netherlands/Pays–Bas	250476	253023	256040	228500	272811	Singapore/Singapour	123225	122693	143948	186233	238516
China/Chine	60485	98723	296002	331685	346746	Switz.Liecht	143869	163193	148515	134000	149392
Spain/Espagne	216427	239965	224327	150882	151769	Denmark/Danemark	161415	128552	139233	101281	114358
Malaysia/Malaisie	116586	196583	190301	221530	288475	France,Monac	119348	119093	124173	124680	133876
Canada	182970	179602	180087	185743	204067	Korea, Republic of	77818	91950	95960	115061	150180
Switz.Liecht	174529	175115	171096	133654	143992	Belgium–Luxembourg	97456	89231	72252	129279	163871
Belgium–Luxembourg	153398	131529	140881	162206	172435	Indonesia/Indonésie	33376	50558	73441	155018	117653
Austria/Autriche	121737	134782	137002	115295	120845	Thailand/Thaïlande	33784	53334	80965	85541	99999
Mexico/Mexique	65181	84878	140109	155545	190889	Sweden/Suède	46903	44951	49616	45823	56306
Australia/Australie	123157	117450	122023	129076	142205	Mexico/Mexique	2368	5312	57409	74468	61623
Sweden/Suède	109258	97607	90071	75643	91341	Austria/Autriche	31481	40414	40095	37418	x27166
Saudi Arabia	89330	76849	80443	x38429	x39041	Canada	23116	22635	32562	27151	25151
Thailand/Thaïlande	43276	40126	58569	76998	94357	Israel/Israël	13807	29000	31835	18761	40270
Indonesia/Indonésie	61153	60476	59699	54437	57914	Portugal	23270	24788	25092	17056	16167
Denmark/Danemark	47580	45280	52228	45765	45324	Brazil/Brésil	17629	25092	21849	6248	6553
Portugal	46552	49541	51887	38755	37411	Ireland/Irlande	13937	12597	17107	16032	
Norway,SVD,JM	42565	44229	45318	43197	46552	Australia/Australie	13233	12470	12637	17252	26241
United Arab Emirates	37442	28953	32639	x65042	x74722	Spain/Espagne	10155	11339	11724	14098	15532
Brazil/Brésil	37352	45967	36895	33549	38731	Russian Federation			x13429	x11824	x12795
Argentina/Argentine	4566	27169	51099	37696	43603	Slovenia/Slovénia			10978	13270	13205
Ireland/Irlande	24883	28362	25069	53750	50087	Philippines	1183	14495	143	2827	24638
Israel/Israël	36253	34185	32447	38266	43209	Czechoslovakia		x6089	x7061		
Poland/Pologne	7998	41944	30143	23043	18399	Former USSR/Anc. URSS	66035	x12206			
Iran (Islamic Rp. of)		x25124	x43542	x24503	x3070	Norway,SVD,JM	3648	3380	4071	4589	4766
Finland/Finlande	61777	38703	29211	24619	34240	So. Africa Customs Un	3536	2876	3679	3550	
So. Africa Customs Un	32134	28284	31904	28373	30568	Yugoslavia SFR	9215	x9820			
Greece/Grèce	20415	22763	28248	30362	27715	Macau/Macao	2944	4909	3506	599	443
Philippines	9372	19973	25347	32231	60011	Croatia/Croatie			8848	21	x440
Turkey/Turquie	26408	20612	24118	30187	13665	Finland/Finlande	2437	2194	2356	2934	5509
New Zealand	24815	19915	20715	32236	32474	New Zealand	2307	2531	1892	2189	1923
Hungary/Hongrie	x16473	16040	x16261	x23699	x14368	Czech Republic				6581	7990
Chile/Chili	8240	14263	21075	20269	24904	India/Inde	7276	1633	1756	2201	2395
Venezuela	5814	14583	22455	18311	7591	Cyprus/Chypre	1711	1587	1781	1379	1025
Russian Federation			x21150	x26160	x53295	United Arab Emirates	14482			x3785	x2309
Kuwait/Koweït	7388	8952	19575	17388	18017	Yugoslavia/Yougoslavie			x3024	x675	x179
Czechoslovakia	26624	x11917	x26399			Saudi Arabia	405	1080	1070	x1334	x3081
Former USSR/Anc. URSS	28343	x38211				Costa Rica				x2889	x4111
Morocco/Maroc	12918	10923	11282	8680	6178	Greece/Grèce	378	994	423	1093	1626
Colombia/Colombie	3917	4747	6553	17664	22135	Hungary/Hongrie	x208	x701	x815	x871	x897
India/Inde	12409	5516	8313	9966	16349	Kuwait/ Koweït	877	322	402	1650	883
Egypt/Egypte	10853	4673	7578	9071	7275	Ukraine			x234	x1668	x346

(VALUE AS % OF TOTAL)(VALEUR EN % DU TOTAL)

	1985	1986	1987	1988	1989	1990	1991	1992	1993	1994		1985	1986	1987	1988	1989	1990	1991	1992	1993	1994
Africa	1.7	x1.4	x1.2	x1.5	x1.3	x1.3	x0.9	x1.0	x0.9	x0.8	Afrique		x0.1	x0.0	x0.0	x0.0	x0.0	x0.0	x0.0	x0.0	x0.0
Northern Africa	0.9	0.6	0.4	0.4	0.5	0.6	0.3	0.4	0.3	0.2	Afrique du Nord	0.0	x0.0	x0.0	x0.0	0.0	0.0	0.0	0.0	0.0	0.0
Americas	31.1	31.8	26.0	24.6	27.6	25.4	26.3	25.6	27.7	28.4	Amériques	14.4	x16.1	14.9	12.9	13.4	12.5	11.9	13.6	13.1	11.8
LAIA	1.5	1.3	1.2	1.3	1.6	1.8	2.4	3.3	3.2	3.4	ALAI	0.2	0.2	1.0	1.0	0.9	0.3	0.4	1.0	0.9	0.7
CACM	0.0	0.1	0.2	0.2	0.2	0.1	0.2	0.2	x0.1	x0.1	MCAC	0.0	x0.0	x0.0	x0.0	x0.0	0.0	0.0	0.0	x0.0	x0.0
Asia	20.1	15.5	19.3	22.8	22.6	23.9	27.8	31.4	34.0	35.7	Asie	55.2	51.0	x51.5	x55.3	55.0	55.1	58.7	58.5	61.0	61.9
Middle East	3.6	x3.1	x2.5	2.8	x2.3	2.4	x2.2	x2.5	x2.2	x1.6	Moyen–Orient	0.6	0.4	x0.2	0.5	x0.1	0.3	x0.1	0.1	x0.1	x0.1
Europe	43.2	47.7	49.6	47.8	45.3	46.0	41.9	39.5	34.8	32.7	Europe	29.2	31.3	30.1	28.9	29.9	30.8	28.9	27.6	25.6	25.9
EEC	36.1	40.1	41.7	41.0	39.0	42.9	39.0	36.9	32.7	30.7	CEE	25.2	27.2	26.3	25.5	26.9	28.6	26.7	25.5	23.8	24.2
EFTA	6.9	7.4	7.7	6.5	6.0	2.8	2.6	2.4	1.9	1.8	AELE	3.9	4.1	3.7	3.2	2.9	2.0	2.1	1.8	1.6	1.5
Oceania	3.1	x2.6	x2.3	x1.8	x2.0	x2.0	x1.7	x1.7	x1.8	x1.8	Océanie	0.1	x0.1	x0.3	0.2	x0.2	0.2	x0.2	x0.2	x0.2	x0.3
USA/Etats–Unis d'Amer	25.1	26.1	21.2	19.7	22.6	20.8	21.2	19.8	22.1	22.7	Japan/Japon	45.2	43.2	38.6	39.8	42.7	41.3	41.6	35.5	34.9	35.9
Germany/Allemagne	7.4	8.8	9.8	10.0	9.1	11.0	10.7	10.4	8.7	8.3	USA/Etats–Unis d'Amer	10.8	12.2	10.1	11.4	12.1	11.9	11.2	12.2	11.8	10.8
Hong Kong	5.1	3.6	4.6	5.3	6.0	6.4	8.5	10.2	10.4	10.1	Hong Kong	5.9	4.5	5.4	5.9	7.1	7.0	8.6	10.9	11.7	11.2
United Kingdom	8.2	8.6	8.0	8.3	7.7	7.5	6.4	6.3	6.4	5.7	Germany/Allemagne	11.6	12.6	11.7	11.7	11.9	12.4	11.0	10.5	9.4	8.3
France,Monac	6.1	6.4	7.0	6.5	6.6	6.7	6.0	5.4	5.0	4.5	United Kingdom	3.4	3.5	4.1	3.3	3.9	4.0	4.8	4.6	3.4	4.1
Japan/Japon	4.1	3.2	3.3	3.7	3.8	4.1	5.2	5.7	5.4	6.2	China/Chine	0.0	0.1	0.4	0.4	0.5	0.9	1.1	4.0	4.6	4.9
Korea, Republic of	2.3	1.5	2.3	3.2	4.5	3.4	3.4	2.6	4.1	5.8	Netherlands/Pays–Bas	1.7	1.9	2.1	2.2	2.6	2.7	2.6	2.7	3.5	4.6
Italy/Italie	3.1	3.3	3.6	3.6	3.4	4.1	3.6	3.3	2.6	2.6	Malaysia/Malaisie	0.5	0.5	0.4	0.6	1.1	1.6	2.7	2.8	3.1	3.1
Singapore/Singapour	1.5	1.4	1.5	2.2	2.1	3.0	2.9	2.8	3.3	3.1	Italy/Italie	2.0	2.0	2.0	2.0	2.2	2.5	2.3	2.0	1.9	1.8
Netherlands/Pays–Bas	3.5	3.7	3.4	3.3	2.9	3.2	3.0	2.8	2.5	2.6	Singapore/Singapour	0.5	0.5	0.5	1.0	1.3	1.7	1.6	1.7	2.1	2.4

TRADE BY COMMODITY IN THOUSAND U.S. DOLLARS – COMMERCE PAR PRODUIT EN MILLIERS DE DOLLARS E.U

COUNTRIES–PAYS	IMPORTS – IMPORTATIONS 1990	1991	1992	1993	1994
Total	13526796	13933581	15118573	14524030	15748030
Africa	x244723	260546	x259807	x267233	x289499
Northern Africa	75604	87070	85135	x89865	101523
Americas	2784793	3040691	3410684	3662708	3872701
LAIA	426301	540650	633878	711695	817769
CACM	20926	22890	27702	x30712	x30239
Asia	2294447	2565650	2866210	3135381	3621672
Middle East	226960	x301922	x312352	x345420	x290876
Europe	7680687	7579040	8074141	6899383	7335574
EEC	7220599	7144259	7632853	6503774	6944522
EFTA	410066	396251	395824	357169	355037
Oceania	x318283	x326554	x357241	x384119	x456083
USA/Etats-Unis d'Amer	1837727	1938555	2161268	2313468	2400688
Germany/Allemagne	1537963	1547630	1625719	1415903	1559635
United Kingdom	1206316	1221736	1246321	1226331	1259808
France, Monac	1246786	1179118	1275024	1062417	1137209
Italy/Italie	809698	813552	840355	661497	698949
Netherlands/Pays-Bas	650916	672773	788289	561823	626962
Japan/Japon	501960	529722	555864	650600	738769
Canada	446822	487911	520858	560995	581126
Hong Kong	352155	427887	490546	491679	658912
Singapore/Singapour	331298	355128	443182	498597	603851
Belgium–Luxembourg	470456	441855	498150	355981	375398
Spain/Espagne	382857	398325	426623	337836	348935
Korea, Republic of	291546	327696	368170	400202	468633
Australia/Australie	247908	252721	282660	308200	365423
Switz.Liecht	302410	282170	280766	257574	253788
Sweden/Suède	251555	238012	252929	256439	281920
Mexico/Mexique	149489	175533	229046	245274	279784
Austria/Autriche	206687	205729	216813	201271	211022
Brazil/Brésil	117535	136627	146260	150933	187724
Denmark/Danemark	134609	125303	142536	136117	135274
Thailand/Thaïlande	90799	100966	120781	133946	146426
India/Inde	106558	86841	115331	109390	140619
So. Africa Customs Un	96677	109159	100206	100210	107666
Norway, SVD, JM	100202	106463	107561	92848	93667
Turkey/Turquie	82997	87854	85654	105655	79740
Portugal	88040	88617	103860	80722	76800
Finland/Finlande	118072	96535	91585	82656	101814
Indonesia/Indonésie	66033	77476	81046	105630	131132
China/Chine	89468	80045	89620	93653	100479
Malaysia/Malaisie	70839	81819	84458	88500	100454
Argentina/Argentine	28176	56816	78906	100990	115052
Greece/Grèce	65457	67796	77164	77861	77842
Iran (Islamic Rp. of)		x64281	x87851	x63893	x25019
Israel/Israël	62216	63766	69776	70899	75777
New Zealand	57738	60456	61547	65999	77498
Poland/Pologne	4619	39360	63397	63916	61731
Venezuela	34546	52735	54910	52261	36605
Chile/Chili	33604	46802	51853	56564	59601
United Arab Emirates	60595	52172	37338	x60682	x64012
Saudi Arabia	33265	53091	40187	x54797	x54058
Philippines	41951	41389	45954	56886	66696
Ireland/Irlande	51188	47277	47483	46919	52955
Hungary/Hongrie	x39308	39726	x40498	x44298	x35112
Colombia/Colombie	30278	29473	28090	52941	73806
Egypt/Egypte	27986	34452	31974	30177	35131
Viet Nam	x13401	x33433	x25636	x25949	x22046
Pakistan	22181	24941	26282	26419	27277
Russian Federation			x21241	x48855	x157646
Former USSR/Anc. URSS	74529	x56278			
Nigeria/Nigéria	x15790	8266	x21699	x26037	x17542

COUNTRIES–PAYS	EXPORTS – EXPORTATIONS 1990	1991	1992	1993	1994
Totale	12526586	12990351	13876721	13707077	15306021
Afrique	x6624	7731	7712	7072	x3553
Afrique du Nord	755	919	785	1461	2451
Amériques	2453653	2641423	2672754	2677019	2806534
ALAI	236427	280018	350507	373940	452805
MCAC	92	84	434	x103	x105
Asie	3360658	3601603	3926026	4175355	4736840
Moyen-Orient	46902	8740	11770	x18116	x18252
Europe	6545694	6589159	7087778	6626943	7499541
CEE	6310817	6386252	6861681	6408329	7288209
AELE	229917	199766	214354	207780	204477
Océanie	x124948	x134705	x166028	x201023	237744
Japan/Japon	2785907	3009030	3201532	3328296	3673920
USA/Etats-Unis d'Amer	2054611	2175994	2087557	2063036	2115815
Germany/Allemagne	1661037	1668217	1835732	1716667	1995194
United Kingdom	1381559	1452706	1570093	1389680	1591557
Belgium–Luxembourg	1313040	1269732	1293590	1182416	1293313
France, Monac	818551	853219	910012	856863	904299
Netherlands/Pays-Bas	597169	596463	658397	661467	821104
Singapore/Singapour	262913	281084	323012	377219	492865
Italy/Italie	308286	317869	342502	310097	344936
Hong Kong	199206	219704	266022	323034	412183
Canada	161818	184653	233512	238959	236446
Switz.Liecht	225404	186879	207241	204384	192637
Australia/Australie	121576	131576	163380	198330	234136
Brazil/Brésil	107023	119376	168826	183181	213813
Mexico/Mexique	94637	118783	135099	131982	191817
Spain/Espagne	90407	92561	93729	100925	114162
Sweden/Suède	40694	39824	48398	77099	99154
Austria/Autriche	45164	42060	45775	43330	x35138
Korea, Republic of	31671	30978	43310	49328	55074
Argentina/Argentine	30818	32404	35938	42935	37844
China/Chine	13314	22770	35840	49248	46083
Ireland/Irlande	26242	27086	31521	31255	34453
Denmark/Danemark	23362	19208	21146	19949	37973
Malaysia/Malaisie	6337	10604	11549	14905	16200
Chile/Chili	1743	7424	7476	10688	4410
Hungary/Hongrie	x9922	x8629	x9583	x7013	x6579
Norway, SVD, JM	4495	12886	7096	3393	11838
Thailand/Thaïlande	3527	3049	14506	3357	4982
India/Inde	2376	6249	9398	3352	6142
Finland/Finlande	3225	3653	5700	7915	10559
Macau/Macao	4218	6387	5038	4052	4573
Portugal	1573	2750	2818	7406	3155
Oman	2418	3632	4386	4757	5388
Slovenia/Slovénia			6814	4921	5609
So. Africa Customs Un	2810	2974	4107	4307	
Czech Republic				9389	10961
Cyprus/Chypre	2861	2195	2740	3893	4604
United Arab Emirates	35597	332	266	x5803	x6120
Greece/Grèce	433	831	2269	3259	3212
New Zealand	2609	2209	2120	1824	3025
Croatia/Croatie			4251	1618	x854
Colombia/Colombie	199	451	1897	3520	3341
Jordan/Jordanie	267	916	3011	1134	552
Former GDR	x17160	x2399	x2399		
Israel/Israël	1001	1014	1980	1787	1389
Kenya	989	1236	1351	885	x252
Gibraltar	x10	x12	x37		x15
Czechoslovakia		x1115	x2286		
Mauritius/Maurice	608	2350	838	193	106
Indonesia/Indonésie	2098	714	806	1627	3637

(VALUE AS % OF TOTAL)(VALEUR EN % DU TOTAL)

	1985	1986	1987	1988	1989	1990	1991	1992	1993	1994		1985	1986	1987	1988	1989	1990	1991	1992	1993	1994
Africa	2.2	x2.3	x2.2	x2.3	x2.0	x1.8	1.9	x1.8	x1.8	x1.9	Afrique		x0.1	x0.0	x0.0	x0.0	x0.0				x0.0
Northern Africa	0.9	0.8	0.6	0.8	0.7	0.6	0.6	0.6	x0.6	0.6	Afrique du Nord	0.0	0.0	x0.0	x0.0	x0.0	0.0	0.0	0.0	0.0	0.0
Americas	22.7	21.1	18.7	19.0	21.1	20.6	21.8	22.5	25.2	24.6	Amériques	22.7	20.0	17.5	17.9	19.0	19.6	20.4	19.2	19.5	18.4
LAIA	4.0	3.8	3.3	3.0	3.2	3.2	3.9	4.2	4.9	5.2	ALAI	2.2	1.5	1.8	2.0	2.1	1.9	2.2	2.5	2.7	3.0
CACM	0.2	0.2	x0.2	0.2	0.2	0.2	0.2	0.2	x0.2	x0.2	MCAC	0.0	x0.0	x0.0	0.0	x0.0	0.0	0.0	0.0	x0.0	x0.0
Asia	16.0	15.8	x17.6	18.6	17.0	17.0	18.5	18.9	21.6	23.0	Asie	25.4	26.4	26.2	27.3	27.6	26.8	27.8	28.3	30.5	30.9
Middle East	2.2	x2.6	x2.4	x2.2	x1.9	1.7	x2.2	x2.1	x2.4	x1.8	Moyen-Orient	0.6	0.5	x0.5	0.5	x0.2	0.4	0.1	0.1	x0.1	x0.1
Europe	54.7	56.4	56.7	55.4	55.8	56.8	54.4	53.4	47.5	46.6	Europe	49.9	51.9	52.2	50.8	51.6	52.3	50.7	51.1	48.3	49.0
EEC	47.1	48.3	48.8	48.0	48.8	53.4	51.3	50.5	44.8	44.1	CEE	47.3	49.1	49.4	48.1	49.2	50.4	49.2	49.4	46.8	47.6
EFTA	7.3	7.7	7.5	7.1	6.8	3.0	2.8	2.6	2.5	2.3	AELE	2.6	2.7	2.7	2.7	2.4	1.8	1.5	1.5	1.5	1.3
Oceania	2.9	x2.7	x2.5	x2.5	x2.5	x2.4	x2.3	x2.4	x2.7	x2.9	Océanie	1.5	x1.2	x1.3	x1.4	1.3	x1.0	x1.0	x1.2	x1.5	1.5
USA/Etats-Unis d'Amer	13.8	12.7	11.3	12.3	13.9	13.6	13.9	14.3	15.9	15.2	Japan/Japon	21.6	23.2	22.3	22.8	23.1	22.2	23.2	23.1	24.3	24.0
Germany/Allemagne	11.1	10.7	11.0	10.6	10.2	11.4	11.1	10.8	9.7	9.9	USA/Etats-Unis d'Amer	19.4	17.3	14.5	14.2	15.6	16.4	16.8	15.0	15.1	13.8
United Kingdom	9.4	9.3	9.0	9.1	8.6	8.9	8.8	8.2	8.4	8.0	Germany/Allemagne	10.6	11.4	11.5	12.0	12.3	13.3	12.8	13.2	12.5	13.0
France, Monac	7.5	8.1	8.3	8.2	7.8	9.2	8.5	8.4	7.3	7.2	United Kingdom	10.2	9.9	10.3	10.8	10.8	11.0	11.2	11.3	10.1	10.4
Italy/Italie	5.2	5.0	5.4	5.4	5.4	6.0	5.8	5.6	4.6	4.4	Belgium–Luxembourg	11.0	11.6	11.0	10.3	10.2	10.5	9.8	9.3	8.6	8.4
Netherlands/Pays-Bas	4.1	4.2	3.8	3.7	3.9	4.8	4.8	5.2	3.9	4.0	France, Monac	6.2	5.8	5.9	6.2	6.1	6.5	6.6	6.6	6.3	5.9
Japan/Japon	4.7	4.9	4.4	4.7	4.0	3.7	3.8	3.7	4.5	4.7	Netherlands/Pays-Bas	5.3	6.1	6.8	4.7	5.8	4.8	4.6	4.7	4.8	5.4
Canada	4.4	3.9	3.5	3.3	3.5	3.3	3.5	3.4	3.9	3.7	Singapore/Singapour	0.6	0.5	0.6	1.5	1.9	2.1	2.2	2.3	2.8	3.2
Hong Kong	3.1	2.4	2.7	2.5	2.5	2.6	3.1	3.2	3.4	4.2	Italy/Italie	2.3	2.4	2.3	2.3	2.5	2.5	2.4	2.5	2.3	2.3
Singapore/Singapour	1.1	0.9	1.0	2.1	2.2	2.4	2.5	2.9	3.4	3.8	Hong Kong	2.4	1.7	2.0	1.7	1.8	1.6	1.7	1.9	2.4	2.7

TRADE BY COMMODITY IN THOUSAND U.S. DOLLARS – COMMERCE PAR PRODUIT EN MILLIERS DE DOLLARS E.U

COUNTRIES–PAYS	IMPORTS – IMPORTATIONS 1990	1991	1992	1993	1994
Total	342794	308170	362801	380431	323746
Africa	x6838	x7672	x6149	x5154	x6333
Northern Africa	1438	1321	950	x407	414
Americas	x91612	75058	122422	x145864	94194
LAIA	3727	3511	3859	4432	4530
CACM	207	171	141	x95	x120
Asia	73073	69943	73078	115358	112553
Middle East	3554	x3266	5548	x6836	x7991
Europe	145569	145025	149456	103457	99900
EEC	132201	132561	137340	90800	86030
EFTA	11529	11546	11542	11737	12989
Oceania	x8276	x6947	x6192	x6674	x7743
USA/Etats–Unis d'Amer	71403	60857	107971	131498	77615
France,Monac	40290	47566	53432	42931	37359
Korea, Republic of	29741	26467	33309	72187	67992
Germany/Allemagne	25993	25441	28009	7967	4760
United Kingdom	20452	17955	14148	9512	11039
Spain/Espagne	10056	9739	10658	9559	11673
Thailand/Thaïlande	10743	15518	6112	7272	4956
Japan/Japon	8603	8835	8786	11005	13034
Switz.Liecht	8580	8341	8812	8888	10168
Canada	11930	8533	8093	8282	10273
Australia/Australie	6051	5975	5505	6313	7301
Italy/Italie	6849	4805	6520	5406	2762
Hong Kong	5407	3838	4423	4575	3921
Belgium–Luxembourg	6026	5506	5302	1862	1683
Netherlands/Pays–Bas	5490	5925	4692	1916	2342
Austria/Autriche	3822	3821	3718	3627	4201
Sweden/Suède	4599	3996	3370	3679	4283
Indonesia/Indonésie	4473	3323	3467	3744	4577
So. Africa Customs Un	2923	3074	2750	3221	4058
Israel/Israël	3256	2584	2931	2821	3887
Norway,SVD,JM	2654	2861	2353	2359	2407
Singapore/Singapour	2207	1082	4103	2247	1114
Poland/Pologne	180	452	3515	1246	872
Mexico/Mexique	1784	1446	1604	1745	2140
Ireland/Irlande	2047	2216	1853	671	572
Finland/Finlande	2228	1637	1600	1365	1639
China/Chine	1534	1795	1539	964	1657
Kuwait/ Koweït	1193	670	2079	1506	2208
Portugal	1559	1366	1376	1130	1399
Russian Federation			x3126	x403	x456
Philippines	672	839	886	1767	1066
Denmark/Danemark	1606	1488	1525	403	778
Greece/Grèce	1182	1102	1137	771	1540
United Arab Emirates	214	29	37	x2757	x2805
Hungary/Hongrie	x1120	680	x832	x1102	x537
Malaysia/Malaisie	501	1106	419	733	398
Saudi Arabia	258	430	1574	x247	x471
Iran (Islamic Rp. of)		x465	x660	x1113	x145
Venezuela	620	716	634	788	663
Chile/Chili	445	469	504	523	529
Nigeria/Nigéria	x81	1395	x43	x37	x56
Former USSR/Anc. URSS	11736	x1440			
Turkey/Turquie	921	535	471	424	610
India/Inde	1072	284	544	578	1121
Argentina/Argentine	413	415	561	369	201
Netherlands Antilles	577	545	782	x8	x9
Cyprus/Chypre	315	499	373	343	725
Iceland/Islande	295	344	377	490	414
Czechoslovakia	860	x435	x771		
Martinique	347	367	303	395	422

COUNTRIES–PAYS	EXPORTS – EXPORTATIONS 1990	1991	1992	1993	1994
Totale	334121	301077	366190	370042	308877
Afrique	522	x1249	x1100	x372	x471
Afrique du Nord	49	40	0	1	7
Amériques	72366	66944	113750	142455	86441
ALAI	3555	2329	2254	5875	3457
MCAC	7	8	10	x6	x6
Asie	99261	109742	123489	119095	118334
Moyen–Orient	2013	x471	1764	x1338	x1423
Europe	145733	120059	120364	99712	99128
CEE	144134	118434	119222	97991	97847
AELE	1345	1333	1040	1418	1190
Océanie	x2385	1032	x1945	1401	1941
Canada	24959	28259	74137	98554	39205
Korea, Republic of	38146	57316	61566	62587	74713
United Kingdom	66313	59746	57573	50062	52649
USA/Etats–Unis d'Amer	42963	35619	36884	37538	43628
France,Monac	37141	22660	24472	17023	12999
Israel/Israël	24549	20264	23098	15251	4783
Italy/Italie	14419	16695	18090	17452	20023
Hong Kong	17827	16172	17026	18348	13961
India/Inde	7813	6843	8254	6961	7611
Philippines	3716	4273	6209	6175	7800
Germany/Allemagne	5886	6319	6170	4138	3908
Spain/Espagne	3448	4271	3136	2516	2373
Japan/Japon	1888	2112	2230	4450	3840
Sweden/Suède	2688	2459	2620	1754	1867
Belgium–Luxembourg	3038	1922	2374	2360	2273
Mexico/Mexique	1125	1279	890	4152	1594
Netherlands/Pays–Bas	1067	1490	2808	945	276
Czech Republic				4129	1584
China/Chine	250	665	1794	1537	2921
Australia/Australie	1038	953	1802	1161	1633
Romania/Roumanie	474	38	2300	927	9
Switz.Liecht	1098	1060	784	1268	1072
Hungary/Hongrie	x1516	x338	x1860	x592	x337
Singapore/Singapour	780	929	816	706	404
Argentina/Argentine	333	965	535	735	812
So. Africa Customs Un	270	959	889	185	
Latvia/Lettonie			x3	x2006	31
Denmark/Danemark	570	629	753	528	389
Austria/Autriche	353	571	505	766	x577
Poland/Pologne	714	141	790	910	204
Kuwait/ Koweït	911	166	559	838	760
Russian Federation			x1066	x422	x407
Thailand/Thaïlande	138	417	389	377	608
Mongolia/Mongolie			x11	x1088	
Former USSR/Anc. URSS	9161	x1073			
Brazil/Brésil	50	54	303	572	551
Ireland/Irlande	8601	422	396	68	224
Portugal	148	533	111	125	44
Czechoslovakia		x333	x414		
Saudi Arabia	4	10	650	x38	x114
Norway,SVD,JM	247	273	256	149	119
Cuba	x268	x373	x115	x149	x28
Greece/Grèce	147	397	110	116	26
French Guiana	231	164	196	166	3
Bulgaria/Bulgarie	x1782	x114	x167	x231	x123
Pakistan	159	123	170	155	96
Chile/Chili	2	7	236	175	173
New Zealand	11	36	113	233	304
Colombia/Colombie		12	227	117	264
Finland/Finlande	93	97	103	139	220

(VALUE AS % OF TOTAL)(VALEUR EN % DU TOTAL)

	1985	1986	1987	1988	1989	1990	1991	1992	1993	1994
Africa	6.3	x5.1	x4.4	x3.0	x2.2	x2.0	x2.5	x1.7	x1.3	x2.0
Northern Africa	1.8	1.4	1.2	0.7	0.4	0.4	0.4	0.3	x0.1	0.1
Americas	16.0	18.7	14.8	14.9	28.9	x26.7	24.3	33.8	x38.3	29.0
LAIA	4.7	2.4	1.6	1.2	1.2	1.1	1.1	1.1	1.2	1.4
CACM	0.2	0.3	0.2	0.1	0.1	0.1	0.1	0.0	x0.0	x0.0
Asia	19.2	19.1	x24.9	27.1	22.6	21.4	22.7	20.1	30.3	34.7
Middle East	1.5	x1.8	x2.9	x3.1	x2.4	1.0	x1.1	1.5	x1.8	x2.5
Europe	51.6	49.3	48.2	46.9	39.7	42.5	47.1	41.2	27.2	30.9
EEC	44.5	41.6	40.7	39.8	33.6	38.6	43.0	37.9	23.9	26.6
EFTA	6.2	6.9	7.1	6.7	5.9	3.4	3.7	3.2	3.1	4.0
Oceania	3.4	x3.0	x2.5	x2.1	2.1	x2.4	x2.3	x1.7	x1.8	x2.4
USA/Etats–Unis d'Amer	7.2	12.4	10.6	9.7	24.0	20.8	19.7	29.8	34.6	24.0
France,Monac	7.6	9.2	10.4	10.8	8.2	11.8	15.4	14.7	11.3	11.5
Korea, Republic of	4.4	4.7	6.7	7.4	7.8	8.7	8.6	9.2	19.0	21.0
Germany/Allemagne	7.7	7.3	8.1	7.5	5.9	7.6	8.3	7.7	2.1	1.5
United Kingdom	9.5	8.6	6.4	6.5	7.0	6.0	5.8	3.9	2.5	3.4
Spain/Espagne	6.5	3.6	3.3	3.2	3.1	2.9	3.2	2.9	2.5	3.6
Thailand/Thaïlande	2.2	2.9	2.5	2.7	3.2	3.1	5.0	1.7	1.9	1.5
Japan/Japon	2.8	3.1	4.0	4.7	2.9	2.5	2.9	2.4	2.9	4.0
Switz.Liecht	2.4	2.8	2.5	2.3	2.2	2.5	2.7	2.4	2.3	3.1
Canada	3.0	2.2	1.6	3.1	2.6	3.5	2.8	2.2	2.2	3.2

	1985	1986	1987	1988	1989	1990	1991	1992	1993	1994
Afrique	5.3	x2.5	x0.8	x0.5	x0.5	0.2	x0.4	x0.3	x0.1	x0.2
Afrique du Nord	0.1	x0.1	x0.1	x0.2	x0.2	0.0	0.0	0.0	0.0	0.0
Amériques	24.6	x23.8	x21.5	22.6	21.1	21.6	22.2	31.0	38.5	28.0
ALAI	0.5	0.3	0.4	0.3	0.4	1.1	0.8	0.6	1.6	1.1
MCAC	0.0	x0.0	x0.0	x0.0	x0.0	0.0	0.0	0.0	x0.0	x0.0
Asie	18.7	23.8	26.7	25.0	26.7	29.7	36.4	33.7	32.2	38.3
Moyen–Orient	0.3	x0.6	x1.8	1.1	x1.1	0.6	x0.2	0.5	x0.4	x0.5
Europe	46.8	44.7	44.8	44.8	46.2	43.6	39.9	32.9	26.9	32.1
CEE	44.8	41.9	41.1	42.1	42.8	43.1	39.3	32.6	26.5	31.7
AELE	1.7	2.5	1.8	1.5	1.3	0.4	0.4	0.3	0.4	0.4
Océanie	0.5	x0.5	x0.7	1.0	0.8	x0.7	0.3	x0.5	0.4	0.6
Canada	1.8	5.1	6.6	7.8	8.0	7.5	9.4	20.2	26.6	12.7
Korea, Republic of	4.1	6.4	5.3	6.0	8.4	11.4	19.0	16.8	16.9	24.2
United Kingdom	22.3	20.3	18.6	20.8	21.9	19.8	19.8	15.7	13.5	17.0
USA/Etats–Unis d'Amer	22.1	17.9	14.1	14.3	12.5	12.9	11.8	10.1	10.1	14.1
France,Monac	7.6	8.5	7.8	8.4	8.7	11.1	7.5	6.7	4.6	4.2
Israel/Israël	5.0	6.7	9.2	6.2	3.9	7.3	6.7	6.3	4.1	1.5
Italy/Italie	8.2	7.3	7.9	6.3	5.0	4.3	5.5	4.9	4.7	6.5
Hong Kong	4.1	4.1	4.1	5.2	7.2	5.3	5.4	4.6	5.0	4.5
India/Inde	2.5	2.1	2.1	2.2	2.7	2.3	2.3	2.3	1.9	2.5
Philippines	0.1	0.2	0.3	0.7	1.3	1.1	1.4	1.7	1.7	2.5

TRADE BY COMMODITY IN THOUSAND U.S. DOLLARS – COMMERCE PAR PRODUIT EN MILLIERS DE DOLLARS E.U

COUNTRIES–PAYS	IMPORTS – IMPORTATIONS 1990	1991	1992	1993	1994
Total	4951132	5262624	5842321	5723724	6181225
Africa	x64538	66994	x65407	x76355	x70671
Northern Africa	19795	17160	16212	14823	15712
Americas	1553980	1572330	1773436	1841224	1973746
LAIA	60215	79872	130922	162982	180220
CACM	3885	4386	4633	x4448	x4908
Asia	821635	930921	1081633	1192162	1329735
Middle East	82513	x103172	x125419	x129130	x114925
Europe	2368390	2537750	2757431	2442659	2618567
EEC	2143465	2320809	2521690	2217959	2389669
EFTA	185470	185941	204817	187245	192138
Oceania	x110551	x117850	x120526	x122787	x141290
USA/Etats–Unis d'Amer	1288624	1277403	1411124	1446889	1548928
Germany/Allemagne	528879	635248	715711	621907	639658
France,Monac	286585	310034	331212	314528	360530
Hong Kong	261086	287160	301860	337785	381372
United Kingdom	291194	306066	291517	279616	305934
Japan/Japon	184201	223828	249633	278312	324322
Italy/Italie	218851	236114	253135	202864	200423
Canada	182504	193006	212150	212193	224469
Netherlands/Pays–Bas	157560	165155	194420	161767	206603
Singapore/Singapour	164052	139549	159841	182954	182879
Spain/Espagne	155454	164573	181688	134358	147594
Switz.Liecht	145948	143038	158167	138929	142206
Australia/Australie	90769	99591	102550	103125	115709
Austria/Autriche	95772	95742	108384	95572	98620
Sweden/Suède	100550	98306	101584	90865	99292
Belgium–Luxembourg	92513	90618	99768	86155	92492
Mexico/Mexique	27351	37583	68405	92179	97813
Korea, Republic of	40792	52602	65239	73440	96349
Ireland/Irlande	54143	49429	55790	74606	77155
Denmark/Danemark	53027	54632	58191	49356	48264
Malaysia/Malaisie	33856	43944	56618	48805	60534
Portugal	37152	42432	51759	38976	40154
Norway,SVD,JM	36660	39978	43759	45677	47162
Greece/Grèce	34530	39292	47324	41204	39273
So. Africa Customs Un	35494	40451	39040	41906	42537
Saudi Arabia	30731	39541	42724	x36063	x26506
China/Chine	12066	20618	39703	51740	60948
Finland/Finlande	37253	33168	31210	26185	33676
Israel/Israël	19515	21209	23533	26545	34873
United Arab Emirates	16011	17085	22175	x30791	x34194
Thailand/Thaïlande	7877	9687	18207	25196	33268
New Zealand	16345	14626	14953	16879	22001
Chile/Chili	8306	10882	14535	16924	16973
Iran (Islamic Rp. of)		x8970	x15526	x13897	x3661
Brazil/Brésil	11359	12748	11432	13343	23310
Malta/Malte	15393	12995	11931	12047	x10742
Argentina/Argentine	1271	5601	13586	16480	18863
Hungary/Hongrie	x9531	8767	x12271	x12680	x11677
Poland/Pologne	1056	9668	14775	8865	8734
Cyprus/Chypre	10503	9383	12019	9305	8172
Turkey/Turquie	6787	7716	7858	14166	13839
Venezuela	5408	7054	11038	10378	6641
Indonesia/Indonésie	2070	3161	9557	15459	20509
Andorra/Andorre	x8884	x8850	x8849	x8879	x8292
Kuwait/ Koweït	5270	5657	9905	10809	11353
Bangladesh		12432	12595	x403	x461
Russian Federation			x9252	x13174	x26158
India/Inde	3839	4397	7567	6519	7281
Czechoslovakia	7543	x3474	x14056		
Egypt/Egypte	6320	4877	5710	6458	5842

COUNTRIES–PAYS	EXPORTS – EXPORTATIONS 1990	1991	1992	1993	1994
Totale	4531963	4985067	5506990	5447453	5769702
Afrique	30708	25967	23400	21106	19502
Afrique du Nord	20078	10990	9680	7177	8299
Amériques	481231	550089	606923	633184	701758
ALAI	13347	12150	36133	37470	32734
MCAC	41	18	32	x44	x42
Asie	1629734	1900474	2085236	2207670	2399764
Moyen–Orient	8317	6067	6038	8608	x8106
Europe	2368010	2486758	2762584	2553513	2611594
CEE	2269233	2378910	2617623	2429210	2475177
AELE	61620	62261	84472	75626	80892
Océanie	x14137	14226	x11257	x14343	x17113
Japan/Japon	1099367	1215478	1295127	1285101	1319746
Italy/Italie	580269	615714	731728	676419	782730
Germany/Allemagne	642620	636825	703142	628697	672561
USA/Etats–Unis d'Amer	439721	505769	529194	557625	621108
France,Monac	416334	471563	502562	447656	493197
Hong Kong	243265	276851	322553	393414	446525
Ireland/Irlande	149564	189232	181603	228929	
Korea, Republic of	142677	169371	178153	199708	227511
Austria/Autriche	213532	183746	199044	152121	x192439
United Kingdom	116403	122006	115507	108557	123256
China/Chine	21733	74497	89026	112622	178096
Singapore/Singapour	55503	77917	92050	95779	90434
Switz.Liecht	60533	60819	82231	72748	77111
Netherlands/Pays–Bas	35406	48032	60843	68653	74937
Thailand/Thaïlande	18281	23776	39552	49958	63863
Canada	27650	31580	40808	37641	46739
Malaysia/Malaisie	8285	32557	36322	34114	34957
Malta/Malte	32059	33458	42846	25099	x32469
Sweden/Suède	33951	30882	34445	31135	36632
Belgium–Luxembourg	25433	26895	27121	36373	31102
Spain/Espagne	31030	26678	30922	21795	26439
Denmark/Danemark	14583	16903	19230	16804	28435
Mexico/Mexique	1296	1431	24289	25480	20175
Israel/Israël	18157	13870	16551	11968	10754
Mauritius/Maurice	8352	9215	10884	11539	10670
Australia/Australie	9405	10313	8809	12212	15207
Slovenia/Slovénia			11803	18847	21147
Tunisia/Tunisie	19974	10964	9470	7062	7724
Portugal	7693	8699	9797	8693	8739
Brazil/Brésil	7237	7195	7407	8784	9166
Hungary/Hongrie	x2023	x2551	x10598	x9312	x8699
India/Inde	2788	4344	4342	6026	6539
Yugoslavia SFR	4827	x11894			
Indonesia/Indonésie	2050	2302	2806	6639	9970
Cyprus/Chypre	4049	4086	3581	3298	3422
New Zealand	4089	3866	2326	2044	1862
Yugoslavia/Yougoslavie			x4391	x2511	x1253
Norway,SVD,JM	1086	1442	2233	2872	3780
So. Africa Customs Un	1993	1779	2366	2216	
Philippines	8216	2741	1937	1560	1597
Poland/Pologne	4294	790	2968	2121	3595
Argentina/Argentine	1328	1373	2918	1577	1474
Czechoslovakia		x2605	x2900		
Czech Republic				5216	6594
Finland/Finlande	2118	1177	1259	1763	3134
Jordan/Jordanie	2069	924	690	2103	246
Cameroon/Cameroun	7	3624			
Croatia/Croatie			1221	2180	x580
Greece/Grèce	290	551	421	1614	1578
Latvia/Lettonie			x13	x2512	2301

(VALUE AS % OF TOTAL)(VALEUR EN % DU TOTAL)

	1985	1986	1987	1988	1989	1990	1991	1992	1993	1994
Africa	1.4	1.1	x1.2	x1.3	x1.2	x1.3	1.3	x1.2	x1.3	x1.2
Northern Africa	0.4	0.3	0.3	0.3	0.4	0.4	0.3	0.3	0.3	0.3
Americas	41.1	x37.8	33.4	35.2	33.6	31.4	29.8	30.4	32.2	31.9
LAIA	1.2	1.0	0.9	1.1	1.0	1.2	1.5	2.2	2.8	2.9
CACM	0.1	0.1	x0.1	0.1	0.1	0.1	0.1	0.1	x0.1	x0.1
Asia	11.8	11.0	x13.8	15.4	15.3	16.6	17.7	18.5	20.8	21.5
Middle East	1.4	x1.7	x1.4	x1.7	x1.8	1.7	x2.0	x2.1	x2.3	x1.9
Europe	43.0	47.4	48.7	45.0	46.8	47.8	48.2	47.2	42.7	42.4
EEC	34.9	38.2	39.5	36.9	38.3	43.3	44.1	43.2	38.8	38.7
EFTA	7.6	8.5	8.4	7.5	7.9	3.7	3.5	3.5	3.3	3.1
Oceania	2.4	x2.4	x2.0	x2.1	x2.3	x2.3	x2.3	x2.1	x2.1	x2.3
USA/Etats–Unis d'Amer	35.7	32.3	28.5	30.1	28.1	26.0	24.3	24.2	25.3	25.1
Germany/Allemagne	10.1	11.1	11.5	10.3	9.2	10.7	12.1	12.3	10.9	10.3
France,Monac	4.1	4.5	4.5	4.3	4.6	5.8	5.9	5.7	5.5	5.8
Hong Kong	3.5	3.2	4.0	5.0	5.5	5.3	5.5	5.2	5.9	6.2
United Kingdom	5.9	5.6	5.9	5.6	6.1	5.9	5.8	5.0	4.9	4.9
Japan/Japon	3.5	2.8	3.3	3.2	3.3	3.7	4.3	4.3	4.9	5.2
Italy/Italie	3.3	3.5	3.9	3.6	3.9	4.4	4.5	4.3	3.5	3.2
Canada	4.0	3.9	3.6	3.7	4.0	3.7	3.7	3.6	3.7	3.6
Netherlands/Pays–Bas	2.4	2.8	3.1	2.6	2.8	3.2	3.1	3.3	2.8	3.3
Singapore/Singapour	1.4	1.2	1.4	2.0	2.3	3.3	2.7	2.7	3.2	3.0

	1985	1986	1987	1988	1989	1990	1991	1992	1993	1994
Afrique	0.2	0.2	0.2	0.4	0.5	0.6	0.5	0.4	0.3	0.3
Afrique du Nord	0.0	0.0	0.1	0.3	0.3	0.4	0.2	0.2	0.1	0.1
Amériques	10.3	x9.6	9.5	11.1	9.5	10.6	11.1	11.1	11.6	12.2
ALAI	0.5	0.2	0.2	0.3	0.4	0.3	0.2	0.7	0.7	0.6
MCAC	0.0	0.0	x0.0	x0.0	x0.0	0.0	0.0	0.0	x0.0	x0.0
Asie	37.4	36.4	x39.5	x39.5	36.4	36.0	38.2	37.8	40.5	41.6
Moyen–Orient	0.1	0.1	x0.1	0.2	0.1	0.2	0.1	0.1	0.2	x0.1
Europe	51.2	53.0	49.1	47.6	52.8	52.3	49.9	50.2	46.9	45.3
CEE	44.3	45.7	42.5	40.7	45.8	50.1	47.7	47.5	44.6	42.9
AELE	5.9	6.4	5.8	6.1	6.2	1.4	1.2	1.5	1.4	1.4
Océanie	0.5	x0.6	0.4	x0.3	x0.3	x0.3	0.3	x0.2	x0.3	x0.3
Japan/Japon	27.6	27.4	23.9	22.6	24.9	24.3	24.4	23.5	23.6	22.9
Italy/Italie	8.3	8.7	8.6	8.7	10.5	12.8	12.4	13.3	12.4	13.6
Germany/Allemagne	14.7	15.5	14.5	12.8	13.9	14.2	12.8	12.8	11.5	11.7
USA/Etats–Unis d'Amer	8.9	8.5	8.4	10.0	8.4	9.7	10.1	9.6	10.2	10.8
France,Monac	9.9	10.0	9.3	8.2	8.9	9.2	9.5	9.1	8.2	8.5
Hong Kong	3.9	3.3	3.6	4.3	5.4	5.4	5.6	5.9	7.2	7.7
Ireland/Irlande	2.2	1.8	1.6	2.1	2.7	3.3	3.8	3.3	4.2	
Korea, Republic of	2.6	2.8	3.2	3.3	3.4	3.1	3.4	3.2	3.7	3.9
Austria/Autriche	3.7	4.1	3.6	4.2	4.3	4.7	3.7	3.6	2.8	x3.3
United Kingdom	2.8	2.1	2.1	2.0	2.3	2.6	2.4	2.1	2.0	2.1

TRADE BY COMMODITY IN THOUSAND U.S. DOLLARS – COMMERCE PAR PRODUIT EN MILLIERS DE DOLLARS E.U

COUNTRIES–PAYS	IMPORTS – IMPORTATIONS 1990	1991	1992	1993	1994
Total	14425923	15632049	16701284	17083570	18692221
Africa	x138852	122270	x124959	x125955	x134791
Northern Africa	45549	44051	39114	36268	38729
Americas	2239780	2792532	2855682	3108351	3246780
LAIA	240959	256189	295209	314286	350671
CACM	3755	4502	6862	x5989	x6130
Asia	6963079	7589554	8237244	8829796	9955810
Middle East	522426	616208	720257	x806594	x800679
Europe	4847612	4902654	5243808	4747034	5058284
EEC	4221724	4326155	4600595	4145413	4402112
EFTA	572895	531547	595689	558234	607739
Oceania	x166824	x161300	x187108	x188540	x218916
Hong Kong	3344666	3511143	4057616	4305019	4715086
USA/Etats–Unis d'Amer	1760044	2286531	2330681	2557706	2645647
Japan/Japon	1118024	1180382	1105274	1191711	1438751
Germany/Allemagne	960883	1060719	1120171	1029806	1130411
China/Chine	716820	861041	892072	971031	1033467
Italy/Italie	752423	856752	897853	745941	778052
Singapore/Singapour	644186	605437	654005	750892	920703
United Kingdom	637694	558534	627245	712161	701601
France,Monac	649302	594614	650802	594388	639822
Switz.Liecht	532840	491399	550755	517546	566505
Spain/Espagne	405204	462867	481854	330123	372609
Thailand/Thaïlande	153033	259150	260412	248943	255645
Saudi Arabia	180061	234784	258813	x222016	x222417
Malaysia/Malaisie	196712	226809	234475	227678	277545
United Arab Emirates	143010	162122	192340	x324328	x334427
Korea, Republic of	173711	197957	182379	211394	236208
Canada	156764	172721	163413	177751	181332
Netherlands/Pays–Bas	160678	163897	174131	158978	155932
Austria/Autriche	148882	149310	158035	158359	172610
Belgium–Luxembourg	150468	141610	144885	124823	137888
Australia/Australie	121961	120039	145921	142471	165893
Mexico/Mexique	68275	88614	104599	107662	133450
Sweden/Suède	117345	107698	92042	80417	87964
Portugal	68938	75244	89665	64377	61367
Turkey/Turquie	51629	53317	64256	74101	51916
Brazil/Brésil	93866	63822	46365	77867	86584
Greece/Grèce	56361	54700	64274	58670	64061
Argentina/Argentine	11764	33977	68128	50891	54354
Denmark/Danemark	41830	42438	46104	40987	41998
Norway,SVD,JM	37743	37487	41690	38915	39421
So. Africa Customs Un	43086	37803	37526	36135	47315
Kuwait/ Koweït	34262	20407	48894	42077	43667
Oman	25861	33092	34630	30890	31813
Bahrain/Bahreïn	x19233	x27870	x34902	x32276	x31895
Finland/Finlande	48556	35250	32991	26036	30796
Israel/Israël	22374	24345	28069	31776	40133
Venezuela	10979	19500	28867	25776	15736
Hungary/Hongrie	x19120	16334	x18342	x39010	x24844
Mauritius/Maurice	28715	21662	23002	23231	22945
Korea Dem People's Rp	x5661	x29789	x28275	x7116	x934
Chile/Chili	13809	19997	21717	23141	24107
Ireland/Irlande	23160	22522	20545	20347	27001
Iran (Islamic Rp. of)		x16949	x21630	x20869	x7989
Lebanon/Liban	x33004	x31272	x15051	x12583	x23268
Andorra/Andorre	x22189	x20256	x20670	x15710	x17972
Egypt/Egypte	21418	23328	16557	16070	16324
New Zealand	18986	17727	17836	20075	24635
Qatar	14806	16323	18564	19716	x29876
Philippines	6436	31075	12039	10357	13644
Guam	x16757	x14375	x15985	x20690	x20035

COUNTRIES–PAYS	EXPORTS – EXPORTATIONS 1990	1991	1992	1993	1994
Totale	15374774	15973770	17148754	17339425	19109582
Afrique	50672	42984	41998	37650	38509
Afrique du Nord	16914	15234	14356	10333	13214
Amériques	311298	355080	x419151	x444510	470548
ALAI	20214	24826	47024	52222	56503
MCAC	938	2761	5587	x4993	x384
Asie	7898680	8801447	9351970	9812296	10764666
Moyen–Orient	67480	x37673	x37035	x61863	x62052
Europe	6916326	6693371	7285097	6993192	7782928
CEE	2062069	1954084	2090113	1914672	2138656
AELE	4826818	4721613	5168526	5054165	5623274
Océanie	x21350	x25648	x34716	x34161	x33613
Switz.Liecht	4820864	4714155	5161774	5044740	5614184
Hong Kong	3741375	4029997	4479932	4722663	5193910
Japan/Japon	2292314	2557734	2510090	2403859	2195794
China/Chine	1047388	1127780	1246717	1414254	1741801
Germany/Allemagne	874014	821128	853244	708821	779802
France,Monac	544940	508926	528373	487564	523384
Singapore/Singapour	281386	355912	365012	438095	563354
USA/Etats–Unis d'Amer	278583	313827	318364	348500	371202
Thailand/Thaïlande	185306	284566	325033	274397	375514
Italy/Italie	215116	203466	223516	228573	242258
Korea, Republic of	191821	215721	205985	231910	242232
United Kingdom	177674	152614	224655	238916	329542
Malaysia/Malaisie	76060	103079	106102	139679	225269
Netherlands/Pays–Bas	59835	64944	67433	58275	64235
Spain/Espagne	53722	59721	65098	65572	78955
Belgium–Luxembourg	62216	58733	50778	56703	61765
Brunei Darussalam	219	477	x31838	x69275	x90372
Mexico/Mexique	7078	13424	38237	43226	36958
Australia/Australie	19481	24375	32973	32508	29600
Austria/Autriche	26514	32351	25066	26003	x12996
Indonesia/Indonésie	7846	16933	29093	36036	41538
Mauritius/Maurice	32260	26356	26030	25967	24648
Russian Federation			x29467	x37231	x24964
Philippines	23	62899	364	754	715
Canada	10188	10465	19416	30989	38167
Sweden/Suède	17344	18379	17775	14312	19284
Oman	8906	13888	12830	10858	8190
Tunisia/Tunisie	16198	13830	12646	9529	11721
Former USSR/Anc. URSS	164756	x35912			
Cyprus/Chypre	8396	9490	14129	11788	8017
Denmark/Danemark	10030	11337	12010	11749	10909
Bahamas		35	x27302	x5788	x1740
India/Inde	2384	5832	9517	16710	24420
Portugal	5922	8481	10456	9471	11865
Gibraltar	x9877	x9970	x10832	x6808	x4485
Norway,SVD,JM	5948	7459	6752	9425	9090
United Arab Emirates	28158			x23258	x23017
Brazil/Brésil	8318	8283	5253	5561	4787
Hungary/Hongrie	x2623	x4132	x6513	x6947	x5719
Ireland/Irlande	6264	6067	6254	4889	
Malta/Malte	14756	5456	5843	4711	x6683
Croatia/Croatie			6792	8483	x4148
Lebanon/Liban	x6306	x6368	x4893	x3763	x5083
Finland/Finlande	7752	6978	4667	2811	2756
Czechoslovakia		x7383	x6932		
Costa Rica	912	2711	5553	x4945	x347
Qatar	8544	6012	1129	1464	x2416
Czech Republic				8385	9693
Poland/Pologne	705	6635	886	843	1362
Slovenia/Slovénia			2184	3596	5449

(VALUE AS % OF TOTAL)(VALEUR EN % DU TOTAL)

	1985	1986	1987	1988	1989	1990	1991	1992	1993	1994
Africa	1.2	x1.3	x1.3	x1.1	x1.1	x1.0	0.7	x0.7	x0.7	x0.8
Northern Africa	0.6	0.5	0.4	0.3	0.3	0.3	0.3	0.2	0.2	0.2
Americas	27.2	24.0	x20.7	19.0	11.5	15.5	17.8	17.1	18.2	17.3
LAIA	2.5	2.2	1.4	1.3	1.7	1.7	1.6	1.8	1.8	1.9
CACM	0.0	0.0	0.0	0.0	0.0	0.0	0.0	0.0	x0.0	x0.0
Asia	36.9	37.0	41.4	44.4	49.7	48.3	48.5	49.3	51.7	53.3
Middle East	6.3	x6.5	x5.3	4.2	x4.8	3.6	3.9	4.3	x4.7	x4.3
Europe	32.6	35.8	34.4	33.1	35.6	33.6	31.4	31.4	27.8	27.1
EEC	26.4	29.3	28.6	27.6	29.4	29.3	27.7	27.5	24.3	23.6
EFTA	6.0	6.1	5.5	5.2	5.9	4.0	3.4	3.6	3.3	3.3
Oceania	1.6	x1.5	x1.3	x1.4	x1.5	x1.2	x1.1	x1.1	x1.2	x1.2
Hong Kong	19.0	19.4	18.9	21.2	23.4	23.2	22.5	24.3	25.2	25.2
USA/Etats–Unis d'Amer	22.3	19.5	17.4	15.9	7.7	12.2	14.6	14.0	15.0	14.2
Japan/Japon	4.0	4.1	4.3	5.1	7.5	7.8	7.6	6.6	7.0	7.7
Germany/Allemagne	5.4	6.2	6.2	5.8	6.3	6.7	6.8	6.7	6.0	6.0
China/Chine	0.4	0.2	4.5	5.0	5.3	5.0	5.5	5.3	5.7	5.5
Italy/Italie	4.1	4.7	4.9	4.9	5.2	5.2	5.5	5.4	4.4	4.2
Singapore/Singapour	3.1	2.7	2.8	3.1	3.8	4.5	3.9	3.9	4.4	4.9
United Kingdom	4.8	4.9	4.7	4.8	4.8	4.4	3.6	3.8	4.2	3.8
France,Monac	4.3	5.1	4.7	4.4	4.7	4.5	3.8	3.9	3.5	3.4
Switz.Liecht	3.5	3.5	2.9	2.9	3.4	3.7	3.1	3.3	3.0	3.0

	1985	1986	1987	1988	1989	1990	1991	1992	1993	1994
Afrique	0.2	0.2	0.4	0.4	0.3	0.3	0.3	0.2	0.2	0.2
Afrique du Nord	0.0	0.1	0.1	0.1	0.1	0.1	0.1	0.1	0.1	0.1
Amériques	2.5	x2.1	x1.7	x1.9	x2.1	2.0	2.2	x2.5	x2.6	2.4
ALAI	0.2	0.1	0.1	0.1	0.1	0.1	0.2	0.3	0.3	0.3
MCAC	0.0	x0.0	x0.0	x0.0	0.0	0.0	0.0	0.0	x0.0	x0.0
Asie	54.4	51.5	53.0	54.8	53.7	51.4	55.1	54.5	56.6	56.3
Moyen–Orient	0.4	x0.3	x0.8	x0.4	x0.4	0.4	x0.2	x0.2	x0.4	x0.3
Europe	41.3	44.5	42.7	40.8	42.5	45.0	41.9	42.5	40.3	40.7
CEE	14.5	15.5	14.4	13.7	13.7	13.4	12.2	12.2	11.0	11.2
AELE	26.8	29.0	28.2	27.1	28.7	31.4	29.6	30.1	29.1	29.4
Océanie		x0.0	x0.1	x0.1	x0.1	x0.1	x0.2	x0.2	x0.2	x0.2
Switz.Liecht	26.5	28.7	27.9	26.8	28.4	31.4	29.5	30.1	29.1	29.4
Hong Kong	23.3	22.8	22.1	23.7	25.6	24.3	25.2	26.1	27.2	27.2
Japan/Japon	25.8	23.5	18.9	18.6	16.8	14.9	16.0	14.6	13.9	11.5
China/Chine	0.4	0.7	4.6	5.4	6.1	6.8	7.1	7.3	8.2	9.1
Germany/Allemagne	6.8	7.3	6.6	6.0	6.0	5.7	5.1	5.0	4.1	4.1
France,Monac	3.5	4.0	3.9	3.8	3.6	3.5	3.2	3.1	2.8	2.7
Singapore/Singapour	1.4	1.1	1.0	1.2	1.6	1.8	2.2	2.1	2.5	2.9
USA/Etats–Unis d'Amer	2.0	1.6	1.4	1.6	1.9	1.8	2.0	1.9	2.0	1.9
Thailand/Thaïlande	0.3	0.4	0.3	0.4	0.7	1.2	1.8	1.9	1.6	2.0
Italy/Italie	1.6	1.5	1.3	1.2	1.4	1.4	1.3	1.3	1.3	1.3

TRADE BY COMMODITY IN THOUSAND U.S. DOLLARS – COMMERCE PAR PRODUIT EN MILLIERS DE DOLLARS E.U

COUNTRIES–PAYS	IMPORTS – IMPORTATIONS 1990	1991	1992	1993	1994
Total	18947523	19765346	21620749	19878027	21616968
Africa	x637844	x603685	x657568	x616801	x666682
Northern Africa	146414	x159438	x155777	x137871	125014
Americas	4164350	4411032	5078611	5290128	5831227
LAIA	453904	569968	935407	1062285	1250271
CACM	79622	69354	119035	x59875	x68440
Asia	1860543	1951503	2313046	x2628789	2793322
Middle East	x249447	x257347	x331074	x468751	x354452
Europe	11085444	11490923	12261968	10034979	10870492
EEC	9724519	10100865	10814639	8674224	9371914
EFTA	1294318	1315916	1373310	1297414	1413873
Oceania	x817211	x802652	x831810	x791462	x924001
USA/Etats–Unis d'Amer	1754171	1783668	1965364	2116613	2329043
France,Monac	2013948	2049467	2068658	1477709	1683454
Canada	1670842	1784805	1854528	1854819	1968639
United Kingdom	1668803	1669303	1778220	1498562	1561283
Germany/Allemagne	1348201	1593604	1758701	1292925	1383602
Switz.Liecht	1003172	1008873	1049869	1013517	1121722
Belgium–Luxembourg	988089	994817	1020685	872874	977272
Netherlands/Pays–Bas	845237	869025	952216	717009	779396
Austria/Autriche	738142	735916	802012	758182	842716
Japan/Japon	605341	588520	633703	629669	744154
Australia/Australie	586066	584093	604355	576037	656891
Sweden/Suède	536887	545945	566921	452212	462128
Mexico/Mexique	189713	276272	499602	587319	728953
Spain/Espagne	372145	411746	458519	382055	372828
Italy/Italie	356118	334406	404127	409147	450512
Norway,SVD,JM	277620	291274	307291	269507	278023
Hong Kong	181246	228186	271897	311711	361765
Denmark/Danemark	280378	273833	304171	228795	233172
Singapore/Singapour	210822	234080	247593	269467	296087
Ireland/Irlande	227019	240274	285095	199944	220968
Poland/Pologne	24498	128161	230962	239071	232832
China/Chine	106776	113350	229527	228050	247874
New Zealand	164197	164306	169398	179506	208415
Portugal	114367	143722	175458	167673	162012
So. Africa Customs Un	126562	135815	147925	165583	164178
Finland/Finlande	169584	157663	147361	117090	132469
Korea, Republic of	95241	111946	117808	125779	152369
Malaysia/Malaisie	107752	108239	120304	119604	143688
Brazil/Brésil	102272	108942	80837	96315	134019
Greece/Grèce	65601	81144	92494	100047	110102
Russian Federation			x173384	x97575	x162872
Hungary/Hongrie	x59372	67816	x90398	x97028	x93607
Thailand/Thaïlande	64012	78717	74118	83274	106690
Iran (Islamic Rp. of)	x29941	x64452	x59569	x105295	x11877
Former USSR/Anc. URSS	228099	x212483			
Czechoslovakia	11102	x76551	x131194		
Ecuador/Equateur	14779	14009	117364	68894	x34881
Turkey/Turquie	36958	34457	41940	123012	81783
Saudi Arabia	52469	48248	81118	x69876	x84462
India/Inde	72710	42015	83616	68774	71013
Argentina/Argentine	11396	34751	68065	91016	121496
Venezuela	36691	46894	66744	75228	56750
Philippines	27558	53910	50207	50053	68239
Indonesia/Indonésie	34152	35492	47147	55073	57735
Costa Rica	55421	41601	76415	x18809	x23358
Israel/Israël	42424	40090	44223	47895	51955
Chile/Chili	25866	31557	44261	53188	57089
Morocco/Maroc	37131	41939	47012	37989	42629
Ukraine			x14987	x109392	x32654
Czech Republic				104727	117075

COUNTRIES–PAYS	EXPORTS – EXPORTATIONS 1990	1991	1992	1993	1994
Totale	18586727	19285230	20887758	20120988	21609039
Afrique	43496	49134	41216	67417	40940
Afrique du Nord	17355	15544	16480	15711	20351
Amériques	3949442	4483935	4842923	5300837	5275751
ALAI	235393	333409	415145	511802	496074
MCAC	6654	13714	22278	x18040	x14417
Asie	1578274	1756380	2020239	2145857	2374908
Moyen–Orient	x57192	x46024	x58901	x81727	x64398
Europe	12462620	12734680	13688739	12263809	13518978
CEE	11748366	12069906	12981415	11573936	12807519
AELE	550305	568256	581248	563581	605124
Océanie	x149714	x138748	x166426	x183400	x214143
USA/Etats–Unis d'Amer	3289411	3705036	3899160	4110941	4089269
Germany/Allemagne	3238891	3380707	3692571	3081214	3337786
United Kingdom	2209286	2212676	2359489	2395893	2763378
France,Monac	1616113	1617152	1795722	1474828	1601487
Italy/Italie	1044354	1076466	1068492	1067321	1208130
Netherlands/Pays–Bas	962018	1034759	1134242	816445	863007
Belgium–Luxembourg	918337	937173	1000023	879030	992527
Hong Kong	497362	592285	697132	740478	772700
Spain/Espagne	459842	490150	579256	613375	692041
Switz.Liecht	511390	524806	534844	521575	560097
Japan/Japon	490560	499287	521979	524055	527370
Canada	392197	411780	487298	644687	661338
Austria/Autriche	341102	368828	399055	392903	x354332
Singapore/Singapour	304021	349063	395312	371777	483350
Denmark/Danemark	330483	328186	330864	304629	319345
Sweden/Suède	232606	236086	227651	198251	236867
Finland/Finlande	193367	181956	184607	185384	243244
Ireland/Irlande	134514	140797	154636	111114	151048
Colombia/Colombie	92924	139581	123300	124185	131933
Australia/Australie	117049	112655	126530	140320	177348
Mexico/Mexique	41627	82891	129963	155597	155756
Korea, Republic of	78380	94015	99738	120076	140304
China/Chine	40978	50689	91954	132525	138567
Chile/Chili	20762	39901	60538	69534	79652
Malta/Malte	38809	48444	51837	60106	x14401
Argentina/Argentine	27593	30721	58394	66364	78465
Malaysia/Malaisie	33468	42997	56753	54685	65773
Norway,SVD,JM	38378	42914	45887	40982	44048
Brazil/Brésil	20118	19320	28245	80340	32976
Czechoslovakia		x61918	x64013		
Portugal	42136	39374	34571	31054	22072
Hungary/Hongrie	x34722	x32439	x41865	x30345	x27691
Slovenia/Slovénia			48835	54676	51409
Israel/Israël	28608	33722	32425	32245	33577
Thailand/Thaïlande	13511	18976	24354	42057	89202
New Zealand	31335	22906	25055	27571	33720
Lebanon/Liban	x24444	x24274	x21028	x24859	x22499
Greece/Grèce	25055	25334	20237	22495	22254
India/Inde	19626	18276	22899	24600	31509
Slovakia				x60191	x59441
Czech Republic				46765	56374
Poland/Pologne	6556	9613	17530	19373	35487
Yugoslavia SFR	124133	x45463			
So. Africa Customs Un	13768	13757	11777	17399	
Turkey/Turquie	6420	7863	9994	18649	12660
Jordan/Jordanie	844	615	11053	19149	7405
Guam	x9	x12	x13706	x14177	x2304
Venezuela	29183	13244	7132	7272	4575
Kenya	5763	12971	4280	10384	x645
Honduras	59	5678	10465	8649	3654

(VALUE AS % OF TOTAL)(VALEUR EN % DU TOTAL)

	1985	1986	1987	1988	1989	1990	1991	1992	1993	1994
Africa	3.8	x4.1	x3.5	x3.4	x3.4	x3.4	x3.1	x3.1	x3.1	x3.1
Northern Africa	1.6	1.3	0.8	1.0	0.7	0.8	x0.8	x0.7	x0.7	0.6
Americas	29.4	26.0	22.4	21.6	22.3	22.0	22.4	23.5	26.6	27.0
LAIA	4.1	2.9	2.3	2.0	2.3	2.4	2.9	4.3	5.3	5.8
CACM	0.4	0.3	x0.3	0.2	0.3	0.4	0.4	0.6	x0.3	x0.3
Asia	8.2	8.0	x8.5	x9.5	9.0	9.8	9.9	10.7	x13.2	12.9
Middle East	1.3	x1.8	x1.2	x1.3	x1.3	x1.3	x1.3	x1.5	x2.4	x1.6
Europe	51.9	56.2	59.6	59.5	59.3	58.5	58.1	56.7	50.5	50.3
EEC	40.2	42.8	45.4	46.2	45.6	51.3	51.1	50.0	43.6	43.4
EFTA	11.5	13.1	13.9	13.0	12.7	6.8	6.7	6.4	6.5	6.5
Oceania	5.2	x4.4	x4.0	x4.0	x4.4	x4.4	x4.1	x3.9	x4.0	x4.3
USA/Etats–Unis d'Amer	12.9	12.6	11.1	10.3	9.9	9.3	9.0	9.1	10.6	10.8
France,Monac	8.6	9.5	9.8	9.6	9.3	10.6	10.4	9.6	7.4	7.8
Canada	10.9	8.9	7.6	8.0	8.7	8.8	9.0	8.6	9.3	9.1
United Kingdom	7.5	7.3	7.5	8.7	8.4	8.8	8.4	8.2	7.5	7.2
Germany/Allemagne	5.1	5.4	6.0	6.0	6.0	7.1	8.1	8.1	6.5	6.4
Switz.Liecht	4.3	5.0	5.3	5.0	4.7	5.3	5.1	4.9	5.1	5.2
Belgium–Luxembourg	4.3	4.6	4.9	4.9	4.7	5.2	5.0	4.7	4.4	4.5
Netherlands/Pays–Bas	3.6	4.0	4.1	4.1	3.9	4.5	4.4	4.4	3.6	3.6
Austria/Autriche	2.9	3.3	3.5	3.3	3.3	3.9	3.7	3.7	3.8	3.9
Japan/Japon	2.1	2.0	2.3	2.7	2.9	3.2	3.0	2.9	3.2	3.4

	1985	1986	1987	1988	1989	1990	1991	1992	1993	1994
Afrique	0.2	0.2	0.1	0.3	0.2	0.3	0.3	0.2	0.3	0.2
Afrique du Nord	0.2	0.2	0.1	0.1	0.1	0.1	0.1	0.1	0.1	0.1
Amériques	21.3	18.4	17.2	17.7	21.8	21.2	23.2	23.2	26.3	24.4
ALAI	1.7	1.4	1.4	1.4	1.2	1.3	1.7	2.0	2.5	2.3
MCAC	0.1	0.0	0.0	0.0	0.1	0.0	0.1	0.1	x0.1	x0.1
Asie	8.3	8.3	8.7	9.1	8.5	8.5	9.1	9.7	10.7	11.0
Moyen–Orient	0.4	x0.5	x0.4	x0.3	x0.4	x0.3	x0.2	x0.3	x0.4	x0.3
Europe	67.5	70.7	70.6	69.4	66.9	67.1	66.0	65.5	61.0	62.6
CEE	59.7	62.2	62.4	61.8	59.7	63.2	62.6	62.1	57.5	59.3
AELE	7.0	7.7	7.5	6.9	6.6	3.0	2.9	2.8	2.8	2.8
Océanie	0.9	x0.6	x0.7	x0.8	x0.9	x0.8	x0.7	x0.8	x0.9	x1.0
USA/Etats–Unis d'Amer	15.1	12.6	11.9	13.0	17.4	17.7	19.2	18.7	20.4	18.9
Germany/Allemagne	16.2	18.3	18.4	17.8	17.3	17.4	17.5	17.7	15.3	15.4
United Kingdom	11.9	10.8	11.1	11.3	10.8	11.9	11.5	11.3	11.9	12.8
France,Monac	7.7	8.1	7.9	7.9	7.7	8.7	8.4	8.6	7.3	7.4
Italy/Italie	5.3	5.3	5.3	5.4	5.5	5.6	5.6	5.1	5.3	5.6
Netherlands/Pays–Bas	4.5	4.9	4.8	5.1	4.9	5.2	5.4	5.4	4.1	4.0
Belgium–Luxembourg	4.0	4.5	4.6	4.7	4.5	4.9	4.9	4.8	4.4	4.6
Hong Kong	2.4	2.3	2.4	2.5	2.7	2.7	3.1	3.3	3.7	3.6
Spain/Espagne	3.3	3.0	2.9	2.9	2.3	2.5	2.5	2.8	3.0	3.2
Switz.Liecht	2.8	3.2	2.9	2.7	2.5	2.8	2.7	2.6	2.6	2.6

TRADE BY COMMODITY IN THOUSAND U.S. DOLLARS – COMMERCE PAR PRODUIT EN MILLIERS DE DOLLARS E.U

COUNTRIES–PAYS	IMPORTS – IMPORTATIONS 1990	1991	1992	1993	1994
Total	29425348	31886935	37699074	36543421	42037160
Africa	x581271	x537437	x591702	x653435	x692286
Northern Africa	215294	196835	x208628	x234362	x256386
Americas	5789770	6100597	8506258	9373492	10868372
LAIA	519060	764619	2528941	2877992	3472466
CACM	50061	60538	83534	x112970	x126580
Asia	3850439	4587708	5903807	6833944	8196343
Middle East	x519605	x576816	x733017	x868826	x857655
Europe	18309485	19349096	21289669	18019185	20270565
EEC	16695947	17789938	19623165	16433947	18504795
EFTA	1447614	1403645	1451897	1362864	1546070
Oceania	x645396	x695637	x733995	x780746	x916919
USA/Etats–Unis d'Amer	3849293	3814169	4333418	4763201	5453283
Germany/Allemagne	3357431	4066167	4569573	3724483	4204002
France, Monac	2872520	2921541	3146694	2668677	3026057
United Kingdom	2454354	2411315	2616183	2220354	2463381
Netherlands/Pays–Bas	1927563	1998150	2173959	1652271	1880183
Belgium–Luxembourg	1441850	1502312	1621910	1514803	1654079
Mexico/Mexique	277377	392589	1967610	2150317	2569161
Hong Kong	817143	1054128	1521487	1748111	2100139
Canada	1090485	1181299	1295387	1368530	1530622
Italy/Italie	1095251	1186936	1301622	1032825	1170031
Switz.Liecht	981550	942078	969380	919164	1057198
Japan/Japon	798748	858079	927880	1020592	1277867
Austria/Autriche	736241	776055	864848	836338	937703
Sweden/Suède	778277	736870	743042	630855	720630
Spain/Espagne	444266	577028	772636	660279	798028
Singapore/Singapour	418548	474424	515531	625512	751321
Australia/Australie	470758	501460	525742	579628	670161
China/Chine	188213	268515	561316	643639	759831
Denmark/Danemark	453677	462358	510744	459441	501097
Thailand/Thaïlande	271124	357823	514071	555344	743302
Ireland/Irlande	413175	436283	508760	368282	409803
Norway, SVD, JM	429249	423237	444729	413137	454819
Malaysia/Malaisie	225978	282692	339887	443737	580067
Korea, Republic of	235126	270110	305312	298495	371500
Poland/Pologne	44797	160574	299236	353249	480986
Portugal	201459	234916	296211	247175	254582
Finland/Finlande	342273	285782	268896	220910	273848
Greece/Grèce	177610	194227	228086	197254	211372
Saudi Arabia	155389	142629	167741	x235312	x227878
Argentina/Argentine	23896	72906	181462	241189	294373
Israel/Israël	127922	144267	166705	175748	198972
Hungary/Hongrie	x85198	96702	x165846	x202144	x191883
Turkey/Turquie	98116	124406	140478	174248	134124
United Arab Emirates	72442	99559	121811	x185212	x234124
Russian Federation			x177343	x226399	x340013
New Zealand	113445	119019	130636	142583	173726
Brazil/Brésil	85326	95234	98838	139050	204448
So. Africa Customs Un	89699	103542	107442	115906	125090
Former USSR/Anc. URSS		x278021			
Iran (Islamic Rp. of)	x39006	x67708	x117791	x73114	x27085
Chile/Chili	57479	66909	89768	99645	107332
Indonesia/Indonésie	60197	70380	89417	95356	101486
Philippines	42809	84005	74802	90606	118404
Czechoslovakia	38489	x50445	x152492		
Slovenia/Slovénia			76526	124619	87112
Venezuela	24871	43160	65607	80911	62183
Czech Republic				169256	224246
Tunisia/Tunisie	40961	40693	57254	57187	63636
Morocco/Maroc	42806	46378	52528	49115	54112
Algeria/Algérie	23856	26485	37695	60946	52183

COUNTRIES–PAYS	EXPORTS – EXPORTATIONS 1990	1991	1992	1993	1994
Totale	27274406	29088326	34349781	34360316	39560210
Afrique	59994	75198	79566	108838	x91904
Afrique du Nord	17599	27530	27723	34863	36102
Amériques	3856578	4200600	5579395	6215102	7331518
ALAI	172279	241334	786357	1024740	1091395
MCAC	34028	39136	47829	x53448	x66551
Asie	4333403	4936442	6496738	8066442	9493483
Moyen–Orient	100818	80089	103226	x121350	x158664
Europe	18756619	19566627	21790845	19379375	21911061
CEE	17738284	18560322	20585631	18263363	20639065
AELE	928377	944888	1060980	998817	1147070
Océanie	x145171	x171934	x191603	x210539	x260740
Germany/Allemagne	5215808	5374227	6003034	5217653	5771816
USA/Etats–Unis d'Amer	2903529	3210186	3936027	4190993	4963385
Italy/Italie	2415379	2524438	2761224	2483176	2856373
France, Monac	2033666	2255464	2578842	2421403	2698240
Hong Kong	1357972	1601221	2065991	2332764	2742424
United Kingdom	1737593	1851822	2035941	1617426	1985372
Netherlands/Pays–Bas	1748608	1786680	1935918	1581716	1727193
Belgium–Luxembourg	1519329	1579120	1795150	1703151	1880123
Japan/Japon	934615	1091630	1186191	1298646	1493281
China/Chine	319641	443236	1167281	1429539	2022315
Switz.Liecht	801256	825314	928384	881397	1012237
Canada	724935	692573	791711	926670	1173756
Denmark/Danemark	786948	762102	840540	784128	837897
Sweden/Suède	655468	707038	715095	670552	847282
Austria/Autriche	552218	613628	725631	714093	x740814
Thailand/Thaïlande	220535	284337	357154	1008814	748827
Korea, Republic of	588394	481533	515344	521366	623129
Mexico/Mexique	68123	120741	604487	772060	803404
Spain/Espagne	366842	402684	408655	403692	505621
Singapore/Singapour	311207	359159	365226	410742	587482
Ireland/Irlande	309834	312357	331858	241359	279067
Malaysia/Malaisie	168337	226921	258987	274645	336535
Israel/Israël	180635	189574	240599	274712	334695
Finland/Finlande	236895	215944	223155	213676	261634
Portugal	101486	117474	152035	127614	155142
Norway, SVD, JM	124060	116810	129689	114664	131487
Australia/Australie	90801	110954	117914	119382	158133
India/Inde	49798	52271	72394	192266	217298
Indonesia/Indonésie	44568	66726	103020	130561	141498
Brazil/Brésil	38485	46465	92058	111658	124408
New Zealand	53642	59754	71663	89748	101300
Greece/Grèce	57691	56825	78552	83723	92492
Poland/Pologne	25739	30206	56241	87481	149529
Hungary/Hongrie	x32985	x35378	x59494	x69113	x83297
Czechoslovakia		x52037	x75271		
Czech Republic				125601	153844
Slovenia/Slovénia			61405	57072	67672
So. Africa Customs Un	25835	28474	40327	49226	47146
Philippines	26197	35031	36330	42206	50178
Turkey/Turquie	21630	25584	34105	39640	73351
Croatia/Croatie			53690	42105	x35981
Argentina/Argentine	12561	26117	27592	39258	44522
Colombia/Colombie	9348	16410	23767	41960	50267
Slovakia				x76596	x69065
Costa Rica	18423	19974	21919	x23024	x32237
Venezuela	33233	17736	16786	22974	28885
Saudi Arabia	16295	16971	19505	x14771	x14820
Guatemala	10398	13815	16961	18792	21143
Chile/Chili	4489	8183	15763	25368	28878
Yugoslavia SFR	77888	x48671			

(VALUE AS % OF TOTAL)(VALEUR EN % DU TOTAL)

	1985	1986	1987	1988	1989	1990	1991	1992	1993	1994
Africa	2.1	x2.6	x2.0	x1.8	x1.9	x2.0	x1.7	x1.6	x1.8	x1.6
Northern Africa	1.3	1.0	0.8	0.8	0.8	0.7	0.6	x0.6	x0.6	x0.6
Americas	28.6	x25.0	23.0	20.8	20.2	19.7	19.2	22.5	25.7	25.8
LAIA	2.5	0.9	1.0	1.1	1.4	1.8	2.4	6.7	7.9	8.3
CACM	0.4	0.2	x0.2	0.2	0.2	0.2	0.2	0.2	x0.3	x0.3
Asia	9.6	9.4	10.2	11.2	12.1	13.0	14.3	15.7	18.7	19.5
Middle East	2.6	x2.6	x2.0	x1.8	x1.9	x1.8	x1.8	x1.9	x2.4	x2.0
Europe	56.5	60.2	59.5	60.3	59.9	62.2	60.7	56.5	49.3	48.2
EEC	46.2	49.0	48.5	49.3	49.3	56.7	55.8	52.1	45.0	44.0
EFTA	10.1	10.8	10.6	10.5	10.2	4.9	4.4	3.9	3.7	3.7
Oceania	2.3	x2.1	x1.9	x2.2	x2.4	x2.2	x2.1	x1.9	x2.2	x2.2
USA/Etats–Unis d'Amer	19.4	18.3	16.9	14.7	13.8	13.1	12.0	11.5	13.0	13.0
Germany/Allemagne	8.6	9.2	9.2	9.2	9.3	11.4	12.8	12.1	10.2	10.0
France, Monac	8.1	8.9	8.9	8.6	8.7	9.8	9.2	8.3	7.3	7.2
United Kingdom	7.5	7.4	7.2	7.9	7.8	8.3	7.6	6.9	6.1	5.9
Netherlands/Pays–Bas	6.0	6.4	6.2	5.8	5.7	6.6	6.3	5.8	4.5	4.5
Belgium–Luxembourg	4.1	4.4	4.3	4.2	4.3	4.9	4.7	4.3	4.1	3.9
Mexico/Mexique	1.8	0.2	0.4	0.6	0.8	0.9	1.2	5.2	5.9	6.1
Hong Kong	1.8	1.6	1.8	1.9	2.4	2.8	3.3	4.0	4.8	5.0
Canada	5.3	4.4	3.9	3.9	3.9	3.7	3.7	3.4	3.7	3.6
Italy/Italie	3.0	3.3	3.3	3.4	3.3	3.7	3.7	3.5	2.8	2.8

	1985	1986	1987	1988	1989	1990	1991	1992	1993	1994
Afrique	0.2	x0.2	0.2	x0.2	x0.2	0.2	0.3	0.2	0.3	x0.2
Afrique du Nord	0.0	0.0	0.0	0.0	0.0	0.1	0.1	0.1	0.1	0.1
Amériques	15.3	11.7	9.7	11.0	13.8	14.1	14.4	16.3	18.1	18.5
ALAI	1.8	0.8	0.5	0.5	1.0	0.6	0.8	2.3	3.0	2.8
MCAC	0.3	0.1	0.1	0.1	0.1	0.1	0.1	0.1	x0.2	x0.2
Asie	13.1	12.8	x20.7	x20.5	16.1	15.9	17.0	19.0	23.5	24.0
Moyen–Orient	0.6	0.4	x0.5	0.4	x0.6	0.4	0.3	0.3	x0.4	x0.4
Europe	70.6	74.4	67.6	66.5	68.6	68.8	67.3	63.4	56.4	55.4
CEE	61.7	65.1	59.3	58.0	60.1	65.0	63.8	59.9	53.2	52.2
AELE	8.5	9.1	8.1	8.1	8.2	3.4	3.2	3.1	2.9	2.9
Océanie	0.5	x0.5	x0.5	x0.6	0.6	x0.5	x0.6	x0.6	x0.6	x0.7
Germany/Allemagne	19.2	21.2	19.2	17.9	18.4	19.1	18.5	17.5	15.2	14.6
USA/Etats–Unis d'Amer	11.8	9.6	8.1	7.6	9.8	10.6	11.0	11.5	12.2	12.5
Italy/Italie	8.2	8.5	7.4	8.0	8.3	8.9	8.7	8.0	7.2	7.2
France, Monac	7.1	7.2	6.6	6.2	6.6	7.5	7.8	7.5	7.0	6.8
Hong Kong	4.5	4.5	4.4	4.2	5.1	5.0	5.5	6.0	6.8	6.9
United Kingdom	6.3	5.8	5.5	5.5	5.5	6.4	6.4	5.9	4.7	5.0
Netherlands/Pays–Bas	5.5	6.0	5.5	5.6	5.9	6.4	6.1	5.6	4.6	4.4
Belgium–Luxembourg	4.9	5.3	4.8	4.5	4.9	5.6	5.4	5.2	5.0	4.8
Japan/Japon	4.2	3.8	2.9	3.6	3.8	3.4	3.8	3.5	3.8	3.8
China/Chine			0.4	0.7	1.1	1.2	1.5	3.4	4.2	5.1

TRADE BY COMMODITY IN THOUSAND U.S. DOLLARS – COMMERCE PAR PRODUIT EN MILLIERS DE DOLLARS E.U

COUNTRIES–PAYS	IMPORTS – IMPORTATIONS 1990	1991	1992	1993	1994
Total	28219762	31420929	37355866	38351721	39993801
Africa	x226714	431501	x278589	x241515	x255859
Northern Africa	54055	267637	x72349	56023	72838
Americas	11035664	11085825	13630401	14875665	15664084
LAIA	415304	608309	883934	971575	1322813
CACM	24727	28249	41093	x54965	x60339
Asia	5896490	6867642	7962352	9073576	10235512
Middle East	262090	351817	428560	x497070	x524111
Europe	10155472	12132457	14460179	13119986	12747799
EEC	9362598	11300914	13526035	12252078	11856391
EFTA	667231	728875	790054	744393	773092
Oceania	x496567	x536191	x674221	x641435	x696634
USA/Etats–Unis d'Amer	9493327	9251544	11304517	12307770	12631886
Hong Kong	2257950	2884992	4017092	4582377	5367198
Germany/Allemagne	1984626	2667485	2992887	2694186	2818672
United Kingdom	1677134	1835728	2507923	2539180	2024063
Japan/Japon	1819320	1929494	2157223	2420095	2605587
France,Monac	1670347	1974872	2346111	1985693	1856541
Canada	985837	1093408	1301826	1445780	1537528
Italy/Italie	872242	1086827	1225771	1026540	1027447
Netherlands/Pays–Bas	634194	804955	969009	908210	920414
Spain/Espagne	443643	645412	969622	691536	698412
Belgium–Luxembourg	558437	615433	682209	743710	746162
Switz.Liecht	471460	512077	562111	523116	539512
China/Chine	833029	901735	317824	348312	342249
Australia/Australie	376009	413766	534814	507479	545949
Austria/Autriche	383721	431519	447910	422854	495217
Mexico/Mexique	232143	292168	441651	421077	643786
Sweden/Suède	338406	365490	415354	333853	359213
Singapore/Singapour	243341	260564	339360	392271	419669
Korea, Republic of	184991	221473	324090	406050	446666
Denmark/Danemark	232539	247730	276172	259617	249076
Norway,SVD,JM	181160	200142	214121	206743	219604
Portugal	130537	161617	195065	190633	151441
Argentina/Argentine	19429	98204	194290	195134	224991
Greece/Grèce	106376	140733	161365	182620	225000
Ireland/Irlande	135121	141792	178599	149895	149400
Finland/Finlande	195275	181322	158037	123551	135331
United Arab Emirates	70199	110491	131530	x136122	x170557
Poland/Pologne	31747	144948	106715	111069	121773
Saudi Arabia	66582	94570	102782	x161016	x156769
Malaysia/Malaisie	77429	91051	115492	108258	132095
New Zealand	90831	89658	105907	110351	120849
So. Africa Customs Un	84478	101163	93486	91350	91530
Hungary/Hongrie	x52453	88780	x97314	x91993	x85823
Thailand/Thaïlande	70574	63772	79096	99509	110805
Israel/Israël	60208	65991	75757	91929	110022
Algeria/Algérie	2410	217157	6477	2587	6837
Chile/Chili	32269	51814	70113	90831	·95892
Czechoslovakia	59497	x50230	x117408		
Venezuela	19849	38419	59820	61773	40205
Kuwait/ Koweït	22564	20755	60932	56309	54393
Croatia/Croatie			74788	58437	x48939
Russian Federation			x59106	x73180	x127025
Brazil/Brésil	38283	34693	27833	68981	125688
Turkey/Turquie	31404	35126	39549	52738	41010
Paraguay	42548	45656	27635	36689	56972
Czech Republic				89775	102537
Philippines	15133	23100	23211	39001	53081
Indonesia/Indonésie	19955	24183	26408	31798	35565
Cyprus/Chypre	21157	23883	28724	25962	32587
Egypt/Egypte	26715	24302	26238	26869	29450

COUNTRIES–PAYS	EXPORTS – EXPORTATIONS 1990	1991	1992	1993	1994
Totale	20720878	23430786	28425178	29693361	32900200
Afrique	25612	x28162	38059	33314	x27952
Afrique du Nord	5825	5685	10626	9317	12882
Amériques	2701693	3073058	3943000	4296496	4941111
ALAI	234750	242334	615091	578761	710819
MCAC	2087	2191	3273	x13229	x20897
Asie	10971103	13100872	16498463	17341620	19245736
Moyen–Orient	25899	16190	16461	x25387	x28207
Europe	6641803	6961281	7645336	7679044	8266663
CEE	6246658	6543201	7183640	7175362	7744620
AELE	327004	336046	364550	393341	398718
Océanie	x66157	x72298	x74737	x83779	x110949
Hong Kong	4870826	5906049	8007234	8649705	9702933
China/Chine	1970640	2454457	3487206	4050083	5093089
USA/Etats–Unis d'Amer	2208250	2557550	2984222	3291727	3689598
Japan/Japon	1516066	1957965	2117678	1916447	1583863
Germany/Allemagne	1332836	1413100	1483880	1411437	1496214
Italy/Italie	1070110	1112712	1206668	1203756	1454280
France,Monac	850239	885261	1004022	969741	1061454
Korea, Republic of	1154470	1092901	923043	715364	660805
United Kingdom	872569	868908	917038	832129	1096538
Thailand/Thaïlande	462405	571780	713577	635400	679771
Austria/Autriche	543611	603463	617631	577858	x619705
Netherlands/Pays–Bas	393520	466632	632310	589782	686455
Belgium–Luxembourg	271918	283970	325999	637139	447696
Spain/Espagne	370156	356290	370807	405570	411052
Canada	232528	257417	330679	402056	506630
Malaysia/Malaisie	205540	259074	323890	359745	364019
Singapore/Singapour	265505	302112	303760	298424	327939
Mexico/Mexique	68985	78301	372174	423059	559981
Switz.Liecht	252666	256476	283155	323161	351880
Indonesia/Indonésie	37405	100461	162871	219307	181337
Sweden/Suède	154361	154401	176032	151673	170284
Brazil/Brésil	137083	129992	216124	126123	117296
Ireland/Irlande	133966	132035	163040	137675	
Pakistan	105891	139933	124419	140028	194920
Philippines	67294	119628	119173	137061	165734
Denmark/Danemark	88279	96166	112695	95397	106353
Macau/Macao	187129	115974	102464	83392	95951
Finland/Finlande	96859	89517	94599	96958	124785
Norway,SVD,JM	74327	79569	81382	70149	46836
Australia/Australie	53442	57056	58450	67803	91286
Czechoslovakia		x75545	x90472		
Portugal	52263	54460	59167	47934	52685
Poland/Pologne	29460	50425	49609	51013	67837
Hungary/Hongrie	x34225	x26227	x45249	x58069	x53606
Czech Republic				107544	130651
India/Inde	33866	28104	34793	41374	59627
Malta/Malte	23030	27095	25147	30291	x46466
Sri Lanka	1008	5383	32758	40802	47975
Slovenia/Slovénia			35211	41839	44425
Greece/Grèce	15767	26083	19751	18313	17118
Croatia/Croatie			25557	31076	x26509
Russian Federation			x23193	x32755	x53941
Bulgaria/Bulgarie	x99364	x8073	x33711	x14099	x12026
Yugoslavia SFR	44709	x54582			
Israel/Israël	14293	17215	19999	16317	20359
New Zealand	11810	14527	15680	14388	18374
Colombia/Colombie	5803	15974	9119	9895	9191
Former USSR/Anc. URSS	51378	x29115			
Mauritius/Maurice	8438	7328	10733	10648	9053
So. Africa Customs Un	6308	8706	9162	9075	

(VALUE AS % OF TOTAL)(VALEUR EN % DU TOTAL)

	1985	1986	1987	1988	1989	1990	1991	1992	1993	1994
Africa	1.2	x1.0	x0.9	x0.9	x0.8	x0.8	1.4	x0.8	x0.6	x0.6
Northern Africa	0.5	0.3	0.3	0.2	0.2	0.2	0.9	x0.2	0.1	0.2
Americas	47.5	x42.5	x38.3	36.9	40.8	39.1	35.3	36.4	38.8	39.1
LAIA	1.1	0.7	0.6	0.8	1.2	1.5	1.9	2.4	2.5	3.3
CACM	0.2	0.1	0.1	0.1	0.1	0.1	0.1	0.1	x0.1	x0.2
Asia	11.9	13.4	18.1	19.7	19.3	20.9	21.9	21.3	23.6	25.6
Middle East	1.7	x1.7	x1.2	1.2	x1.0	0.9	1.1	1.1	x1.3	x1.3
Europe	34.9	39.0	38.5	38.3	35.7	36.0	38.6	38.7	34.2	31.9
EEC	28.8	32.2	32.1	31.9	30.2	33.2	36.0	36.2	31.9	29.6
EFTA	5.9	6.5	6.1	6.1	5.3	2.4	2.3	2.1	1.9	1.9
Oceania	2.8	x2.3	x1.9	x1.9	x2.0	x1.8	x1.7	x1.8	x1.7	x1.8
USA/Etats–Unis d'Amer	41.0	36.8	33.5	31.9	35.2	33.6	29.4	30.3	32.1	31.6
Hong Kong	3.8	4.2	5.0	6.0	7.0	8.0	9.2	10.8	11.9	13.4
Germany/Allemagne	6.0	6.8	6.8	6.5	6.0	7.0	8.5	8.0	7.0	7.0
United Kingdom	5.6	5.8	5.8	5.7	5.8	5.9	5.8	6.7	6.6	5.1
Japan/Japon	3.7	4.2	5.2	5.9	6.2	6.4	6.1	5.8	6.3	6.5
France,Monac	5.2	6.0	6.3	6.1	5.6	5.9	6.3	6.3	5.2	4.6
Canada	4.8	4.2	3.7	3.7	3.9	3.5	3.5	3.5	3.8	3.8
Italy/Italie	2.5	2.8	2.9	3.1	2.9	3.1	3.5	3.3	2.7	2.6
Netherlands/Pays–Bas	2.1	2.4	2.3	2.4	2.0	2.2	2.6	2.6	2.4	2.3
Spain/Espagne	0.6	0.7	0.8	1.0	1.2	1.6	2.1	2.6	1.8	1.7

	1985	1986	1987	1988	1989	1990	1991	1992	1993	1994
Afrique	0.2	0.1	x0.1	x0.1	x0.1	0.1	x0.1	0.1	0.1	x0.1
Afrique du Nord	0.1	0.0	0.0	0.0	0.0	0.0	0.0	0.0	0.0	0.0
Amériques	13.3	x9.5	7.9	x8.7	x12.3	13.1	13.1	13.9	14.4	15.1
ALAI	4.2	1.1	1.5	0.7	0.8	1.1	1.0	2.2	1.9	2.2
MCAC	0.0	0.0	0.0	0.0	0.0	0.0	0.0	0.0	x0.0	x0.1
Asie	45.0	45.5	x56.6	x57.4	51.4	53.0	55.9	58.0	58.4	58.5
Moyen–Orient	0.2	0.1	x0.1	0.1	x0.1	0.1	0.1	0.1	x0.1	x0.1
Europe	39.4	42.7	30.5	29.2	33.7	32.1	29.7	26.9	25.9	25.1
CEE	32.2	34.9	25.1	24.1	28.2	30.1	27.9	25.3	24.2	23.5
AELE	6.7	7.4	5.1	4.8	5.2	1.6	1.4	1.3	1.3	1.2
Océanie	0.3	x0.3	x0.3	x0.3	x0.3	x0.3	x0.3	x0.3	x0.3	x0.3
Hong Kong	19.6	20.2	15.6	17.2	22.7	23.5	25.2	28.2	29.1	29.5
China/Chine	1.0	1.6	5.2	6.4	9.1	9.5	10.5	12.3	13.6	15.5
USA/Etats–Unis d'Amer	7.3	6.6	5.1	6.7	10.0	10.7	10.9	10.5	11.1	11.2
Japan/Japon	11.8	9.7	5.8	5.3	6.1	7.3	8.4	7.5	6.5	4.8
Germany/Allemagne	7.0	7.8	5.4	5.0	5.8	6.4	6.0	5.2	4.8	4.5
Italy/Italie	5.8	5.9	4.0	3.7	4.6	5.2	4.7	4.2	4.1	4.4
France,Monac	4.2	4.6	3.1	3.3	3.9	4.1	3.8	3.5	3.3	3.2
Korea, Republic of	7.9	9.5	8.1	7.6	7.4	5.6	4.7	3.2	2.4	2.0
United Kingdom	4.3	4.6	3.7	3.7	4.2	4.2	3.7	3.2	2.8	3.3
Thailand/Thaïlande	0.2	0.3	0.4	0.7	1.8	2.2	2.4	2.5	2.1	2.1

TRADE BY COMMODITY IN THOUSAND U.S. DOLLARS – COMMERCE PAR PRODUIT EN MILLIERS DE DOLLARS E.U

COUNTRIES–PAYS	IMPORTS – IMPORTATIONS 1990	1991	1992	1993	1994
Total	4662283	4874102	5534072	5495266	6148543
Africa	x122323	x124456	x140524	x152915	x149636
Northern Africa	34054	34687	46484	52142	51027
Americas	1137979	1247076	1462609	1596538	1770832
LAIA	127832	182000	298109	328253	365719
CACM	15621	16172	22604	x25812	x27529
Asia	810560	894369	1120455	x1191239	1372401
Middle East	x150717	x171151	x236530	x229150	x191515
Europe	2350369	2398425	2595132	2315679	2592432
EEC	2137130	2203333	2384005	2128832	2383320
EFTA	179107	171769	179082	158651	175987
Oceania	x119307	x123188	x131538	x132288	x148671
USA/Etats–Unis d'Amer	820513	864798	948495	1043510	1162965
Germany/Allemagne	387867	428449	469810	391203	431048
France,Monac	364319	371326	410333	413279	488530
United Kingdom	362435	350546	359138	376128	412414
Hong Kong	190484	201880	295129	316484	370341
Italy/Italie	234694	256880	284785	223170	249703
Netherlands/Pays–Bas	167344	174042	192668	156483	181054
Canada	137329	150709	166577	175740	188390
Singapore/Singapour	149524	150957	152633	168677	213628
Japan/Japon	124679	144996	163134	161957	206122
Spain/Espagne	158789	164092	174653	129314	144510
Mexico/Mexique	62845	86263	158521	167472	185204
Switz.Liecht	137134	130060	132870	114669	122874
Belgium–Luxembourg	107927	109104	115543	105931	108868
Australia/Australie	88889	92531	99131	102362	114163
Sweden/Suède	82378	79753	83760	79300	88665
Austria/Autriche	72619	74357	81908	75850	82781
Korea, Republic of	37997	51740	59047	65595	83818
Denmark/Danemark	51493	52625	58231	48864	55827
Saudi Arabia	44116	49272	61945	x43734	x42991
Malaysia/Malaisie	38528	45659	51496	56729	71449
Portugal	45599	50024	56600	44848	38245
United Arab Emirates	30673	33820	44817	x56971	x60177
Iran (Islamic Rp. of)	x22983	x33994	x47414	x46177	x16298
Thailand/Thaïlande	29551	32451	41863	50387	61638
Norway,SVD,JM	39300	38369	43228	41040	49881
So. Africa Customs Un	34578	38689	40160	41086	41117
Argentina/Argentine	7283	23820	43631	45005	49682
Finland/Finlande	45927	36030	34182	31393	38271
Poland/Pologne	2976	33747	27876	39017	47957
Greece/Grèce	26737	30128	35225	31842	35121
Israel/Israël	25125	27282	30086	32151	38891
Chile/Chili	19512	22089	29485	30681	31884
China/Chine	14263	15282	31111	34695	38782
Hungary/Hongrie	x21877	23730	x27080	x28832	x24015
Ireland/Irlande	29004	25978	27169	21226	28286
Turkey/Turquie	17086	18506	23091	27230	21249
New Zealand	19553	18876	20233	21472	23712
Brazil/Brésil	12214	13402	16210	25021	30807
Kuwait/ Koweït	8837	8278	26453	19513	19900
Indonesia/Indonésie	9696	13903	15946	16271	17878
Egypt/Egypte	5259	10838	15422	15268	13884
Venezuela	5421	9922	15766	14636	11654
Russian Federation			x15066	x24489	x34595
Philippines	7678	9861	11427	16177	22373
India/Inde	8655	8415	14241	14418	21511
Nigeria/Nigéria	x4821	11367	x9787	x11663	x9674
Algeria/Algérie	8038	6850	8264	15790	14018
Morocco/Maroc	7127	8067	9771	9919	8711
Peru/Pérou	3672	6526	9039	10871	15182

COUNTRIES–PAYS	EXPORTS – EXPORTATIONS 1990	1991	1992	1993	1994
Totale	4360784	4501532	5125316	5040133	5629844
Afrique	11112	11271	14188	17247	14376
Afrique du Nord	4175	5291	6950	10136	13381
Amériques	482848	531939	680899	676342	813372
ALAI	45328	56219	159568	161703	219533
MCAC	4040	2497	4021	5787	15473
Asie	1344357	1463923	1744701	1910348	2200164
Moyen–Orient	17028	8051	7829	x13012	x12678
Europe	2479104	2448399	2624754	2375088	2534631
CEE	2306408	2292073	2433682	2219777	2366440
AELE	156783	144640	141050	124462	140938
Océanie	x14110	x13892	x14292	x13743	17188
Japan/Japon	790650	849096	981798	1030498	1128813
Germany/Allemagne	884084	839911	868532	820772	854067
USA/Etats–Unis d'Amer	405424	450720	493530	483985	534195
France,Monac	368386	376001	420635	382143	443521
United Kingdom	309568	317772	339265	273513	324738
Italy/Italie	279565	269913	265552	241217	272154
Hong Kong	168486	178727	239338	266511	315746
China/Chine	85450	103579	166627	185679	242663
Netherlands/Pays–Bas	136815	135253	160235	155404	146415
Switz.Liecht	151626	140763	137463	120329	137781
Austria/Autriche	116324	130408	139408	128694	x116542
Singapore/Singapour	103929	107579	106238	121721	153021
Korea, Republic of	76656	83224	88851	98893	117102
Mexico/Mexique	14050	19086	115614	117500	167566
Malaysia/Malaisie	53722	64059	68859	77987	86259
Sweden/Suède	55329	58668	60845	57182	70335
Ireland/Irlande	51310	49827	49840	42054	1352
Spain/Espagne	38616	43276	53586	43905	51593
Thailand/Thaïlande	24963	33709	38103	39714	46881
Belgium–Luxembourg	32216	35890	34675	37091	40366
Brazil/Brésil	17741	20005	29057	29986	30027
Denmark/Danemark	19534	21185	26402	21877	25467
Indonesia/Indonésie	4256	12699	22260	30015	24559
Canada	25773	20157	21473	22088	29246
India/Inde	5590	8892	11164	29499	46294
Slovenia/Slovénia			20318	19009	20840
Portugal	9409	10154	11409	10993	12880
Czechoslovakia		x15512	x16435		
Croatia/Croatie			24979	6944	x6051
Australia/Australie	10795	10507	10610	9887	12088
Hungary/Hongrie	x10446	x8021	x9872	x7859	x9577
Israel/Israël	9689	8057	8546	7489	15438
Bulgaria/Bulgarie	x15403	x4562	x14028	x5343	x1820
Czech Republic				21510	25780
Poland/Pologne	1432	3649	5297	9473	9583
Colombia/Colombie	4762	8822	4159	5337	5879
Turkey/Turquie	5429	6071	6023	5354	4998
Tunisia/Tunisie	3636	4087	5712	7186	9152
Venezuela	3471	3932	4180	4081	6300
Norway,SVD,JM	5156	3864	3584	4133	3154
Yugoslavia SFR	14270	x11415			
New Zealand	2821	2575	3209	3583	4959
So. Africa Customs Un	2251	2198	3735	3022	
Finland/Finlande	3909	3038	2285	3532	5541
Argentina/Argentine	2650	1917	4007	2816	3872
Kenya	3034	2812	2680	3117	x347
Guatemala	2879	1930	2782	2809	3172
Pakistan	1495	1969	1233	4157	1876
Yugoslavia/Yougoslavie			x4503	x1810	x201
Dominican Republic	x1818	x1707	x1797	x2499	x14452

(VALUE AS % OF TOTAL)(VALEUR EN % DU TOTAL)

	1985	1986	1987	1988	1989	1990	1991	1992	1993	1994
Africa	3.5	x4.2	x3.3	x3.0	x2.6	x2.6	x2.6	x2.5	x2.7	x2.5
Northern Africa	1.4	1.0	0.9	0.8	0.8	0.7	0.7	0.8	0.9	0.8
Americas	23.0	20.8	19.3	19.0	24.7	24.4	25.6	26.4	29.1	28.8
LAIA	3.7	2.7	2.6	2.5	2.8	2.7	3.7	5.4	6.0	5.9
CACM	0.7	0.5	0.5	0.4	0.4	0.3	0.3	0.4	x0.5	x0.4
Asia	15.6	14.6	x15.5	16.9	16.6	17.4	18.3	20.3	x21.6	22.3
Middle East	4.4	x4.0	x3.4	x3.3	x3.4	x3.2	x3.5	x4.3	x4.2	x3.1
Europe	51.2	54.3	54.4	54.0	50.1	50.4	49.2	46.9	42.1	42.2
EEC	42.4	44.7	45.1	45.2	42.0	45.8	45.2	43.1	38.7	38.8
EFTA	8.3	8.9	8.9	8.4	7.7	3.8	3.5	3.2	2.9	2.9
Oceania	3.7	x3.3	x3.2	x3.1	x3.1	x2.5	x2.5	x2.4	x2.5	x2.4
USA/Etats–Unis d'Amer	13.4	12.7	11.6	11.7	17.4	17.6	17.7	17.1	19.0	18.9
Germany/Allemagne	7.3	7.6	7.4	7.3	6.5	8.3	8.8	8.5	7.1	7.0
France,Monac	7.5	8.1	8.0	7.9	7.4	7.8	7.6	7.4	7.5	7.9
United Kingdom	8.0	7.7	8.0	8.3	7.9	7.8	7.2	6.5	6.8	6.7
Hong Kong	3.7	2.7	2.9	3.2	3.8	4.1	4.1	5.3	5.8	6.0
Italy/Italie	5.1	5.1	5.2	5.3	4.8	5.0	5.3	5.1	4.1	4.1
Netherlands/Pays–Bas	3.5	3.8	3.6	3.5	3.2	3.6	3.6	3.5	2.8	2.9
Canada	4.3	3.8	3.4	3.6	3.4	2.9	3.1	3.0	3.2	3.1
Singapore/Singapour	2.3	2.5	2.5	3.0	2.9	3.2	3.1	2.8	3.1	3.5
Japan/Japon	1.8	1.7	2.2	2.7	2.6	2.7	3.0	2.9	2.9	3.4

	1985	1986	1987	1988	1989	1990	1991	1992	1993	1994
Afrique	0.3	0.3	0.3	0.3	x0.2	0.3	0.2	0.3	0.4	0.3
Afrique du Nord	0.1	0.1	0.1	0.1	0.1	0.1	0.1	0.1	0.2	0.2
Amériques	9.6	7.4	6.9	8.0	10.6	11.1	11.9	13.2	13.4	14.4
ALAI	1.8	0.7	0.8	0.9	1.1	1.0	1.2	3.1	3.2	3.9
MCAC	0.2	0.1	0.1	0.1	0.1	0.1	0.1	0.1	0.1	0.3
Asie	29.3	28.7	x31.4	x33.2	31.4	30.9	32.5	34.0	37.9	39.1
Moyen–Orient	0.9	0.5	0.8	0.4	0.3	0.4	0.2	0.2	x0.3	x0.2
Europe	59.0	61.7	56.0	53.6	56.2	56.8	54.4	51.2	47.1	45.0
CEE	49.9	52.0	47.8	45.7	48.9	52.9	50.9	47.5	44.0	42.0
AELE	8.8	9.5	7.9	7.5	7.0	3.6	3.2	2.8	2.5	2.5
Océanie	0.4	x0.2	x0.3	x0.3	0.3	x0.3	x0.3	x0.3	x0.3	0.3
Japan/Japon	21.5	21.6	17.9	18.0	18.4	18.1	18.9	19.2	20.4	20.1
Germany/Allemagne	17.6	19.3	17.7	17.2	18.8	20.3	18.7	16.9	16.3	15.2
USA/Etats–Unis d'Amer	7.3	6.4	5.6	6.2	8.9	9.3	10.0	9.6	9.6	9.5
France,Monac	8.1	8.1	7.7	7.4	7.8	8.4	8.4	8.2	7.6	7.9
United Kingdom	8.5	7.6	7.0	6.1	6.3	7.1	7.1	6.6	5.4	5.8
Italy/Italie	6.8	7.3	6.6	6.0	6.5	6.4	6.0	5.2	4.8	4.8
Hong Kong	3.2	2.5	2.4	3.0	3.9	3.9	4.0	4.7	5.3	5.6
China/Chine	0.8	0.9	1.9	1.8	2.1	2.0	2.3	3.3	3.7	4.3
Netherlands/Pays–Bas	2.2	2.5	2.5	2.7	2.6	3.1	3.0	3.1	3.1	2.6
Switz.Liecht	5.2	5.7	4.5	3.9	3.3	3.5	3.1	2.7	2.4	2.4

TRADE BY COMMODITY IN THOUSAND U.S. DOLLARS – COMMERCE PAR PRODUIT EN MILLIERS DE DOLLARS E.U

COUNTRIES–PAYS	IMPORTS – IMPORTATIONS					COUNTRIES–PAYS	EXPORTS – EXPORTATIONS				
	1990	1991	1992	1993	1994		1990	1991	1992	1993	1994
Total	13887220	8052567	7505415	7182366	7224398	Totale	13984008	8676256	8120529	6506604	7029479
Africa	x21282	x14258	x21871	x27587	x18684	Afrique	x33471	x23448	x21816	x22857	x32618
Northern Africa	259	x727	x480	x243	x1078	Afrique du Nord	549	908	x1324	x1878	x2496
Americas	x2622017	2077163	x2207073	x2766712	x2556507	Amériques	x4243454	2526780	x2031625	x2188970	x1968708
LAIA	8135	17795	25937	21012	33166	ALAI	15263	74291	62811	137782	131799
CACM	1058	1855	1927	x1200	x1700	MCAC	16073	5347	1392	x855	x725
Asia	4311900	1191070	684997	x751005	781689	Asie	361908	245064	233730	x310483	x281418
Middle East	x9002	x11996	x19839	x51515	x30574	Moyen–Orient	x9715	x8070	x15119	x58983	x28788
Europe	6764057	4592996	4472631	3559240	3780367	Europe	9241973	5683587	5735874	3867555	4496849
EEC	5744502	3837231	3754406	3086213	3187669	CEE	7586156	4838769	4699897	2908163	3664983
EFTA	1015500	744744	712042	469601	588132	AELE	1651275	833298	1028862	956697	824685
Oceania	x147251	x84404	x96260	x63523	x76074	Océanie	x69734	x37147	x53313	x27532	x23962
USA/Etats–Unis d'Amer	2308116	1967803	2093737	2662536	2437433	United Kingdom	4033305	2587372	2599521	1817252	1941584
United Kingdom	3469584	2126522	2404005	1718037	1945798	USA/Etats–Unis d'Amer	4074620	2351755	1820608	1912143	1693425
Japan/Japon	4174985	1039865	499416	520658	554813	Switz.Liecht	1614195	811425	1016211	942954	813271
Switz.Liecht	998160	732100	696364	447889	577384	Germany/Allemagne	1540525	914290	749478	324680	479434
Germany/Allemagne	488734	484105	431976	308201	326880	France,Monac	1108279	603926	562110	385970	432025
France,Monac	788709	403238	248619	236554	186760	Netherlands/Pays–Bas	221835	178767	205548	47211	55437
Spain/Espagne	150279	105274	95465	568642	461880	Belgium–Luxembourg	162653	166188	201568	47992	59302
Italy/Italie	208829	226462	222413	49138	40814	Italy/Italie	121749	89704	99316	118401	338902
Netherlands/Pays–Bas	227272	186191	150085	40162	54910	Canada	119296	82562	82198	86744	78833
Belgium–Luxembourg	192216	160690	115547	68528	88251	Hong Kong	93253	70211	87283	92863	105624
Canada	290392	82537	76512	61883	61426	Sweden/Suède	172983	86544	73860	61714	111653
Hong Kong	71255	52515	90886	65657	78496	Denmark/Danemark	88169	78561	72809	49968	57638
Australia/Australie	106538	74113	78788	51143	62207	Spain/Espagne	61748	79709	90082	18988	35515
Korea, Republic of	13354	50231	30859	59284	53833	China/Chine	65684	49836	40800	40799	43299
Austria/Autriche	35675	29986	28861	33631	32651	Former USSR/Anc. URSS		x129617			
Sweden/Suède	109333	41114	13670	36627	14190	Russian Federation			x21810	x99651	x19490
Former USSR/Anc. URSS		x83044				Colombia/Colombie	43	57140	231	59477	100609
Singapore/Singapour	27723	18389	23125	22671	37463	Bahamas	x4610	91	x56648	x44506	x29767
Denmark/Danemark	31015	26164	22855	11577	19994	Australia/Australie	45459	31073	46769	22917	18661
Saudi Arabia	1706	5237	8454	x41009	x4023	Japan/Japon	44322	20791	30528	47862	22715
Norway,SVD,JM	17134	12370	15245	21391	10640	Korea, Republic of	78061	57079	15437	16758	15530
Ireland/Irlande	12416	29272	7314	3561	4676	Austria/Autriche	43763	29813	26882	21083	x146066
Israel/Israël	7074	13713	9299	12071	15199	Brazil/Brésil	3728	49	158	74614	14701
Mexico/Mexique	4389	11012	12860	9203	19407	Czech Republic				69512	208226
So. Africa Customs Un	12078	6853	9835	12524	13293	Peru/Pérou	215	304	55540	221	152
Russian Federation			x18719	x6703	x12475	Israel/Israël	21633	13488	14993	22133	28417
New Zealand	33283	8643	9770	6593	11057	Norway,SVD,JM	36085	20693	11225	12763	10043
Finland/Finlande	25261	11844	5211	4027	3344	Ireland/Irlande	24893	19050	11779	10456	
Bahamas	1497	1465	x2589	x14960	x14441	Hungary/Hongrie	x10751	x16985	x9038	x12614	x10778
Poland/Pologne	415	2102	11248	3657	2067	Lebanon/Liban	x4776	x1504	x1421	x26626	x1972
Czechoslovakia	918	x7076	x6769			Singapore/Singapour	12975	5734	8150	10424	15944
Greece/Grèce	2228	2553	4321	4966	4579	Mexico/Mexique	8351	15643	5717	2935	15546
Hungary/Hongrie	x11733		x4382	x7317	x4140	Poland/Pologne	1079	2055	16291	3200	5485
Brunei Darussalam	185	528	x4163	x6870	x2982	Zimbabwe	5779	5074	7324	8881	x2757
French Polynesia	x3617	x524	x6339	x4634	x1519	So. Africa Customs Un	8652	6697	6206	7635	
Venezuela	1522	4732	3269	3060	2360	Iran (Islamic Rp. of)		x3580	x11864	x2989	x20068
Malta/Malte	2773	3314	4677	2559	x1878	Czechoslovakia		x8716	x8648		
Portugal	2952	3816	4064	2562	2942	Saudi Arabia	96	235	225	x16667	x3066
Ghana	x557	4	130	x9753	x146	Bulgaria/Bulgarie	x17803	x2805	x9855	x2960	x995
Yugoslavia SFR	215	x6411				New Zealand	6252	5176	5425	4030	4462
Colombia/Colombie	55	283	4431	1468	4940	Cuba	x8440	x6528	x2530	x2534	x1070
Cyprus/Chypre	1587	1850	2362	1491	1979	Syrian Arab Republic	19	x1963	4	x9173	x1197
Brazil/Brésil	724	267	678	4729	3054	Gibraltar	x2393	x5169	x3779	x1194	x4135
Iran (Islamic Rp. of)	x927	x891	x2623	x1985	x1365	Greenland/Groenland	2967	3519	3085	3373	x420
Indonesia/Indonésie	1002	335	904	4142	564	Finland/Finlande	3808	2753	3064	2651	4594
China/Chine	412	389	3123	1838	1928	Brunei Darussalam	202		x2979	x4614	x3228
Malaysia/Malaisie	5692	2398	812	1755	2179	Costa Rica	16054	5311	1255	x638	x546
Bermuda/Bermudes	x3565	x792	x1771	x2251	x3372	Un. Rep. of Tanzania	x12178	x6065	x361	x312	x500
Mali		x20	x3211	x1178		Thailand/Thaïlande	4090	2700	2298	1472	1533
Bolivia/Bolivie	18	887	2369	1053	132	Indonesia/Indonésie	1033	2184	1869	1414	1252

(VALUE AS % OF TOTAL)(VALEUR EN % DU TOTAL)

	1985	1986	1987	1988	1989	1990	1991	1992	1993	1994
Africa	0.4	x0.3	x0.4	x0.4	x0.1	x0.2	x0.2	x0.3	x0.4	x0.3
Northern Africa	0.0	x0.0	x0.0	x0.1	x0.0	0.0	x0.0	x0.0	x0.0	x0.0
Americas	54.3	x43.8	x31.8	x25.7	21.0	x18.9	25.8	x29.4	x38.5	x35.4
LAIA	1.8	0.2	0.1	0.2	0.1	0.1	0.2	0.3	0.3	0.5
CACM	0.0	0.0	0.0	x0.0	0.0	0.0	0.0	0.0	x0.0	x0.0
Asia	8.0	9.8	x16.4	21.4	24.3	31.0	14.8	9.1	x10.4	10.8
Middle East	0.8	x0.2	x0.1	x0.1	x0.3	x0.1	x0.1	x0.3	x0.7	x0.4
Europe	35.1	44.2	49.5	48.1	51.4	48.7	57.0	59.6	49.6	52.3
EEC	29.3	35.6	40.7	40.0	42.0	41.4	47.7	50.0	43.0	44.1
EFTA	5.8	8.6	8.8	8.1	9.4	7.3	9.2	9.5	6.5	8.1
Oceania	2.1	x1.9	x1.5	x3.1	x1.5	x1.1	x1.0	x1.3	x0.9	x1.0
USA/Etats–Unis d'Amer	50.2	41.5	29.9	23.9	19.2	16.6	24.4	27.9	37.1	33.7
United Kingdom	18.4	23.0	25.1	24.4	25.8	25.0	26.4	32.0	23.9	26.9
Japan/Japon	5.6	8.2	15.2	20.0	22.7	30.1	12.9	6.7	7.2	7.7
Switz.Liecht	5.1	7.5	7.5	7.0	7.8	7.2	9.1	9.3	6.2	8.0
Germany/Allemagne	3.9	5.0	4.8	4.2	3.6	3.5	6.0	5.8	4.3	4.5
France,Monac	2.4	3.1	3.3	4.0	4.7	5.7	5.0	3.3	3.3	2.6
Spain/Espagne	1.4	0.9	3.0	1.5	2.5	1.1	1.3	1.3	7.9	6.4
Italy/Italie	0.3	0.2	0.4	2.3	1.7	1.5	2.8	3.0	0.7	0.6
Netherlands/Pays–Bas	1.4	1.4	1.5	1.3	1.2	1.6	2.3	2.0	0.6	0.8
Belgium–Luxembourg	0.6	0.8	1.1	1.1	0.8	1.4	2.0	1.5	1.0	1.2

	1985	1986	1987	1988	1989	1990	1991	1992	1993	1994
Afrique	0.3	x0.3	x0.2	x0.4	x0.2	x0.3	x0.3	x0.3	x0.3	x0.5
Afrique du Nord	0.0	x0.0	0.0	x0.0	x0.0	0.0	0.0	x0.0	x0.0	x0.0
Amériques	25.0	x27.6	x26.4	x25.7	x28.4	x30.4	29.2	x25.0	x33.6	x28.0
ALAI	0.6	0.1	x0.1	x0.0	0.1	0.1	0.9	0.8	2.1	1.9
MCAC	0.0	x0.0	x0.0	x0.0	0.0	0.1	0.1	0.0	x0.0	x0.0
Asie	7.4	6.7	5.5	4.4	3.3	2.6	2.8	2.9	x4.8	x4.0
Moyen–Orient	0.0	x0.5	x0.4	x0.2	x0.1	x0.1	x0.1	x0.2	x0.9	x0.4
Europe	66.8	65.0	65.6	67.8	65.2	66.1	65.5	70.6	59.4	64.0
CEE	56.4	54.0	56.3	59.7	52.2	54.2	55.8	57.9	44.7	52.1
AELE	10.4	11.0	9.3	8.1	13.0	11.8	9.6	12.7	14.7	11.7
Océanie	0.4	x0.4	x0.3	x0.3	x0.8	x0.5	x0.4	x0.6	x0.4	x0.3
United Kingdom	32.2	29.6	32.2	25.3	27.5	28.8	29.8	32.0	27.9	27.6
USA/Etats–Unis d'Amer	22.9	25.6	24.7	24.5	27.3	29.1	27.1	22.4	29.4	24.1
Switz.Liecht	9.0	9.8	8.4	7.1	11.9	11.5	9.4	12.5	14.5	11.6
Germany/Allemagne	8.3	7.6	7.1	15.6	12.2	11.0	10.5	9.2	5.0	6.8
France,Monac	7.6	7.2	8.5	8.1	7.1	7.9	7.0	6.9	5.9	6.1
Netherlands/Pays–Bas	2.0	2.3	1.9	1.6	1.6	1.6	2.1	2.5	0.7	0.8
Belgium–Luxembourg	1.5	1.5	1.3	0.9	0.6	1.2	1.9	2.5	0.7	0.8
Italy/Italie	0.9	0.8	1.0	5.8	0.9	0.9	1.0	1.2	1.8	4.8
Canada	1.5	1.5	1.3	0.9	0.8	0.9	1.0	1.0	1.3	1.1
Hong Kong	1.1	0.8	0.8	0.7	0.8	0.7	0.8	1.1	1.4	1.5

TRADE BY COMMODITY IN THOUSAND U.S. DOLLARS – COMMERCE PAR PRODUIT EN MILLIERS DE DOLLARS E.U

COUNTRIES–PAYS	IMPORTS – IMPORTATIONS				
	1990	1991	1992	1993	1994
Total	12110457	12087479	13634115	14755777	16861081
Africa	x63499	x68885	x111807	x97979	x104577
Northern Africa	7814	6272	x32867	x24245	x31814
Americas	x3481423	x3539362	x3924307	x4496182	x5186013
LAIA	45686	71421	102694	130562	173425
CACM	5744	4364	4789	x6188	x8175
Asia	2595473	2647219	3463040	x4043005	x4890139
Middle East	x572747	x608249	x1032259	x1360012	x1366072
Europe	5704232	5575532	5863263	5838062	6395035
EEC	3997419	4021465	4364169	4147465	4707123
EFTA	1676860	1518891	1448223	1635953	1627530
Oceania	x205925	x201715	x220985	x189000	x204812
USA/Etats–Unis d'Amer	3182869	3199974	3538676	4044859	4595902
Switz.Liecht	1615731	1462385	1385344	1570000	1566527
United Kingdom	1273969	1074125	1153165	1384307	1838580
Japan/Japon	1136432	1148444	1054169	987860	1274535
Germany/Allemagne	809718	915179	960527	895336	899983
France,Monac	622712	739915	832161	646826	676389
Hong Kong	588609	591839	766962	832390	885974
United Arab Emirates	245217	309101	385536	x580715	x717170
Spain/Espagne	196046	231214	305579	203301	201703
Italy/Italie	195090	218833	233041	223829	235236
Austria/Autriche	250763	216475	209707	209372	209519
Saudi Arabia	81298	79472	100818	x416593	x275496
Canada	152442	181742	175719	184665	214724
Belgium–Luxembourg	187522	181924	202279	152096	170956
Kuwait/ Koweït	74481	10568	305549	155149	140419
Singapore/Singapour	102928	109045	140418	203631	419565
Netherlands/Pays–Bas	126074	124952	145463	144480	162586
Australia/Australie	148113	138144	151298	125351	146097
Brunei Darussalam	678	215	x140744	x212849	x506951
Sweden/Suède	128410	107461	106948	87112	96392
China/Chine	27111	25152	109862	153427	150250
Lebanon/Liban	x75733	x125150	x69694	x62354	x94132
Israel/Israël	41151	43801	72214	101123	113034
Portugal	39488	55294	77708	74690	64727
Mexico/Mexique	32793	50165	68891	86010	122656
Thailand/Thaïlande	46171	44854	66657	85539	46792
Norway,SVD,JM	57576	52522	58771	62904	57910
Bahrain/Bahreïn	x31545	x16036	x87908	x55789	x62839
Korea, Republic of	44213	40744	43202	61300	60879
Greece/Grèce	37676	37050	38466	44874	54636
Finland/Finlande	56422	47821	31812	25699	34806
Denmark/Danemark	35912	34968	36650	32647	37637
New Zealand	26455	28097	37633	37881	30276
Qatar	3031	22219	30170	46847	x26582
Ireland/Irlande	37616	36254	30665	22898	23973
Malta/Malte	1908	10104	29649	35852	x30391
Oman	41827	28712	26602	18547	28993
Hungary/Hongrie	x21021	15465	x19054	x21287	x21078
Russian Federation			x26795	x26923	x44619
Netherlands Antilles	2628	3886	14216	x32868	x105915
Malaysia/Malaisie	17674	14262	15647	18303	22719
So. Africa Customs Un	12515	13945	12895	16676	11203
Libyan Arab Jamahiriya	37	17	x25140	x17937	x24830
Bahamas	7312	7162	x17433	x18181	x9200
Benin/Bénin	x12216	x14327	x15708	x10516	x6677
Andorra/Andorre	x17900	x13145	x11986	x11467	x9957
Bermuda/Bermudes	x10061	x1954	x10081	x22647	x6062
Slovakia				x33365	x10090
Guam	x6668	x11422	x10233	x10655	x9146
Mauritius/Maurice	6633	11883	10470	9734	10155

COUNTRIES–PAYS	EXPORTS – EXPORTATIONS				
	1990	1991	1992	1993	1994
Totale	13469249	13715626	16191629	17164651	19805480
Afrique	83178	124376	378931	183246	x114027
Afrique du Nord	1235	1425	2181	4995	4753
Amériques	x1113712	x1230122	1383418	x1455724	x1928150
ALAI	144192	164746	222118	334641	631838
MCAC	7423	2331	5143	x30403	x64415
Asie	3883172	4109557	5478112	6015037	7553149
Moyen–Orient	x199987	x100135	x127816	x368710	x505650
Europe	8314751	8117820	8826265	9345569	10059352
CEE	6843843	6633059	7142516	7281620	8032225
AELE	1452445	1458916	1634643	2008327	1973500
Océanie	x66233	x85285	x84592	x79962	x79248
Italy/Italie	3650025	3730640	3975411	4207312	4297512
Switz.Liecht	1445605	1448084	1622357	1992404	1956040
Hong Kong	1118639	1175509	1303132	1406686	1484680
USA/Etats–Unis d'Amer	865761	959111	1039337	940328	954587
United Kingdom	845354	767583	948224	1078533	1527601
Germany/Allemagne	873956	791762	848131	731302	786866
France,Monac	782826	692409	739827	712312	785195
Thailand/Thaïlande	565319	561362	720088	790346	828672
China/Chine	268609	237661	916150	801983	1254779
Malaysia/Malaisie	390938	524032	556763	465281	461229
Israel/Israël	257188	320151	390734	419292	413183
Japan/Japon	364834	349697	368698	338143	352847
Korea, Republic of	311536	334896	339080	337044	338435
India/Inde	179181	282635	315478	336220	446640
Spain/Espagne	194869	172488	181639	153342	202757
Brunei Darussalam	1	2625	x144181	x294788	x329041
Kenya	529	57036	296013	85054	x1905
Austria/Autriche	125379	121562	149206	145506	x140272
Singapore/Singapour	118214	129099	132720	135994	316465
Indonesia/Indonésie	56705	34636	98996	240389	726267
Belgium–Luxembourg	155468	145184	99630	66056	72075
Canada	61690	68056	76109	104454	127388
Peru/Pérou	69071	54528	62585	67540	59456
Mexico/Mexique	20486	47138	53718	60341	83406
Netherlands/Pays–Bas	56570	51387	55961	52030	70940
Lebanon/Liban	x63431	x55738	x47416	x55934	x75655
United Arab Emirates	34461	9846	10984	x122979	x159323
So. Africa Customs Un	54870	38908	45606	51437	62754
Philippines	34144	36585	41626	54786	50510
Ireland/Irlande	42272	45086	47133	36410	39306
Australia/Australie	26368	41585	39742	37353	45088
Brazil/Brésil	36909	38367	40365	39594	40213
New Zealand	29112	29474	39974	38975	32080
Bolivia/Bolivie	42	9	31801	72879	164314
Saudi Arabia	59516	631	542	x103296	x130512
Bahrain/Bahreïn	x15382	x13052	x38466	x40543	x64838
Denmark/Danemark	29619	31918	31899	28191	27747
Malta/Malte	5981	12158	35358	40697	x34511
Mauritius/Maurice	21649	23528	29687	26246	22147
Finland/Finlande	29981	25579	26748	27011	29976
Dominican Republic	x26938	x28060	x21971	x20485	x135172
Chile/Chili	1733	6652	23871	37104	30586
Czech Republic				66511	49736
Portugal	27941	27159	20166	17454	20406
Argentina/Argentine	743	1294	3981	48092	236586
Czechoslovakia		x25560	x27357		
Turkey/Turquie	5849	8402	16658	26917	49292
Greece/Grèce	16775	17948	8199	17601	19562
Norway,SVD,JM	6830	10821	12286	15910	17448
Bahamas	x817	9	x15771	x21473	x2623

(VALUE AS % OF TOTAL)(VALEUR EN % DU TOTAL)

	1985	1986	1987	1988	1989	1990	1991	1992	1993	1994
Africa	1.4	x1.8	x2.1	x1.1	x0.6	x0.5	x0.6	x0.8	x0.7	x0.7
Northern Africa	1.1	1.0	1.1	0.5	0.0	0.1	0.1	x0.2	x0.2	x0.2
Americas	40.8	x38.6	x34.7	x31.8	x30.9	x28.7	x29.3	x28.7	x30.5	x30.7
LAIA	0.2	0.1	0.1	0.2	0.3	0.4	0.6	0.8	0.9	1.0
CACM	0.0	0.0	0.0	0.0	0.0	0.0	0.0	0.0	x0.0	x0.0
Asia	22.4	19.1	x19.8	22.1	x21.3	21.4	21.9	25.4	x27.4	x29.0
Middle East	15.6	10.7	x8.6	8.2	x5.8	x4.7	x5.0	x7.6	x9.2	x8.1
Europe	34.3	39.0	40.7	41.8	44.5	47.1	46.1	43.0	39.6	37.9
EEC	19.7	24.2	26.3	26.7	29.3	33.0	33.3	32.0	28.1	27.9
EFTA	14.6	14.7	14.2	14.9	15.1	13.8	12.6	10.6	11.1	9.7
Oceania	1.1	x1.2	x1.2	x1.8	x1.5	x1.7	x1.7	x1.6	x1.3	x1.2
USA/Etats–Unis d'Amer	37.7	35.2	31.5	28.9	28.3	26.3	26.5	26.0	27.4	27.3
Switz.Liecht	11.5	11.1	10.2	11.1	11.4	13.3	12.1	10.2	10.6	9.3
United Kingdom	6.5	8.1	7.7	8.7	10.3	10.5	8.9	8.5	9.4	10.9
Japan/Japon	2.9	4.6	6.3	7.3	8.5	9.4	9.5	7.7	6.7	7.6
Germany/Allemagne	3.3	4.2	5.1	5.1	5.3	6.7	7.6	7.0	6.1	5.3
France,Monac	3.8	4.3	4.3	4.1	4.8	5.1	6.1	6.1	4.4	4.0
Hong Kong	2.8	2.7	3.3	4.4	4.9	4.9	4.9	5.6	5.6	5.3
United Arab Emirates	1.8	1.3	x2.3	2.3	x2.3	2.0	2.6	2.8	x3.9	x4.3
Spain/Espagne	0.3	0.5	0.6	0.8	0.9	1.6	1.9	2.2	1.4	1.2
Italy/Italie	1.0	1.3	1.5	1.7	1.6	1.6	1.8	1.7	1.5	1.4

	1985	1986	1987	1988	1989	1990	1991	1992	1993	1994
Afrique	0.1	0.3	x0.2	x0.4	x0.5	0.6	0.9	2.4	1.1	x0.6
Afrique du Nord	0.0	x0.0	0.0	0.0	0.0	0.0	0.0	0.0	0.0	0.0
Amériques	5.5	x5.8	x6.5	x7.5	x7.7	x8.3	x9.0	8.6	x8.5	x9.8
ALAI	1.0	0.8	1.0	0.8	1.1	1.1	1.2	1.4	1.9	3.2
MCAC	0.0	0.1	0.1	0.1	0.2	0.1	0.0	0.0	x0.2	x0.3
Asie	19.8	21.8	x28.4	x30.1	28.5	28.8	30.0	33.8	35.0	38.2
Moyen–Orient	0.5	x2.3	x3.5	x2.5	x1.4	x1.5	x0.7	x0.8	x2.1	x2.6
Europe	72.6	70.4	62.8	59.8	62.5	61.7	59.2	54.5	54.4	50.8
CEE	60.6	58.2	53.6	49.3	51.0	50.8	48.4	44.1	42.4	40.6
AELE	11.8	11.9	8.9	10.3	11.3	10.8	10.6	10.1	11.7	10.0
Océanie	0.6	x0.3	x0.3	x0.4	x0.5	x0.5	x0.6	x0.5	x0.4	x0.4
Italy/Italie	36.8	32.2	29.5	27.8	28.3	27.1	27.2	24.6	24.5	21.7
Switz.Liecht	9.4	8.1	7.5	8.9	10.1	10.7	10.6	10.0	11.6	9.9
Hong Kong	6.2	6.4	7.7	8.6	8.6	8.3	8.6	8.0	8.2	7.5
USA/Etats–Unis d'Amer	4.0	4.2	4.5	5.5	5.6	6.4	7.0	6.4	5.5	4.8
United Kingdom	4.8	6.0	7.5	6.0	6.4	6.3	5.6	5.9	6.3	7.7
Germany/Allemagne	6.9	7.0	6.7	6.3	6.4	6.5	5.8	5.2	4.3	4.0
France,Monac	5.0	4.9	4.6	4.5	5.3	5.8	5.0	4.6	4.1	4.0
Thailand/Thaïlande	1.3	2.5	3.5	3.9	4.3	4.2	4.1	4.4	4.6	4.2
China/Chine			1.2	1.2	2.0	2.0	1.7	5.7	4.7	6.3
Malaysia/Malaisie	0.2	0.2	0.6	0.7	1.5	2.9	3.8	3.4	2.7	2.3

TRADE BY COMMODITY IN THOUSAND U.S. DOLLARS – COMMERCE PAR PRODUIT EN MILLIERS DE DOLLARS E.U

COUNTRIES–PAYS	IMPORTS – IMPORTATIONS 1990	1991	1992	1993	1994
Total	19679782	21241204	23225823	23639923	25755141
Africa	x207245	x231699	x222113	x243605	x267115
Northern Africa	42044	35261	x38672	47507	49473
Americas	3919822	4424418	5088592	5732826	6264266
LAIA	370760	512911	769067	946142	1131768
CACM	13122	15011	23807	x21311	x27188
Asia	3231098	3563436	4041971	4739766	5818605
Middle East	254235	320003	x342499	x385478	x330818
Europe	11516225	12123286	13022031	11932134	12344510
EEC	10639282	11243491	12030177	10957804	11302222
EFTA	776927	817239	929350	908951	976301
Oceania	x560661	x581225	x621365	x717536	x799951
USA/Etats–Unis d'Amer	2605760	2860207	3190921	3527529	3696359
Germany/Allemagne	2284356	2706964	2961987	2591892	2806265
United Kingdom	1862316	1785279	2060547	2183891	2063250
France, Monac	1594890	1659285	1717858	1611053	1579865
Netherlands/Pays–Bas	1229955	1279493	1325772	1106066	1111686
Canada	878430	987170	1049719	1183883	1354479
Singapore/Singapour	692715	791351	978785	1010704	1194104
Japan/Japon	765236	782586	831970	1041811	1422226
Italy/Italie	937437	945750	783254	687985	725227
Hong Kong	698586	733580	807463	868259	886776
Belgium–Luxembourg	514465	597355	734621	556987	607459
Switz.Liecht	557559	579351	646048	658963	707112
Spain/Espagne	615153	627719	646323	487020	487832
Australia/Australie	447242	464926	489051	582025	638321
Austria/Autriche	412043	429459	466910	463783	469182
Mexico/Mexique	176592	209300	420028	503603	606092
Sweden/Suède	383122	364271	381747	357997	412862
Korea, Republic of	216867	295783	347628	423904	565193
Denmark/Danemark	229984	260359	322459	264926	295285
Ireland/Irlande	157453	179452	259066	312809	383857
Norway,SVD,JM	207745	221335	266107	235481	254207
China/Chine	170035	171587	229217	250831	282844
Thailand/Thaïlande	140006	141196	150951	269304	502548
Finland/Finlande	226155	194932	130958	107195	138454
Malaysia/Malaisie	91876	108107	124653	195657	252005
Portugal	109582	131113	148643	120434	112955
Argentina/Argentine	20592	87061	128553	137407	151488
So. Africa Customs Un	106448	131686	98733	106517	135728
New Zealand	93662	97108	108297	118210	140978
Israel/Israël	76843	92436	103559	125963	139229
Greece/Grèce	82372	82059	90031	105764	108044
United Arab Emirates	57196	63286	71216	x124334	x130843
Saudi Arabia	68589	108718	72824	x66401	x61884
Brazil/Brésil	70351	82006	56896	101986	132712
Russian Federation			x74052	x134102	x285459
Turkey/Turquie	55476	61458	70690	72653	46371
Poland/Pologne	37938	90434	59436	54250	·61355
Hungary/Hongrie	x52802	46398	x62320	x72293	x61509
Chile/Chili	28618	42391	49786	57331	60836
Czechoslovakia	42048	x40838	x88831		
Former USSR/Anc. URSS	60218	x121379			
Iran (Islamic Rp. of)	x19238	x30399	x48789	x38977	x9418
Venezuela	17208	28603	41981	41337	28861
Czech Republic				88451	96380
India/Inde	25145	26106	29121	32559	60841
Indonesia/Indonésie	23276	22527	25121	36797	37384
Colombia/Colombie	14301	14466	20828	47926	68996
Nigeria/Nigéria	x10765	17253	x23810	x28702	x16678
Paraguay	28307	25960	20296	23414	32370
Philippines	12107	21963	16132	28199	45118

COUNTRIES–PAYS	EXPORTS – EXPORTATIONS 1990	1991	1992	1993	1994
Totale	18906642	20216498	23102060	23707190	26482863
Afrique	x8619	x23947	x10197	x19886	x6314
Afrique du Nord	1821	3439	2050	2383	1741
Amériques	4373541	4810558	5852451	6491627	7256711
ALAI	206287	170634	468831	530586	647435
MCAC	1750	2123	2744	x2474	x3973
Asie	6041314	6356418	6971599	7269544	7748589
Moyen–Orient	66884	46297	68595	x99464	x100930
Europe	8311031	8850619	10052241	9677762	11230907
CEE	8050682	8583244	9740766	9266386	10785855
AELE	255145	263666	302065	407455	438571
Océanie	x65003	x77485	x100043	x101803	x93673
USA/Etats–Unis d'Amer	4006372	4449343	5112012	5664769	6266319
Japan/Japon	3407572	3496703	3668505	3642280	3501814
Germany/Allemagne	2383581	2499911	2482123	2136402	2351829
Ireland/Irlande	1118020	1216044	1665414	1670803	2513809
Netherlands/Pays–Bas	1165737	1247699	1546492	1703334	1581405
United Kingdom	1345114	1392596	1391819	1247962	1575776
Korea, Republic of	1137527	1184644	1103958	1133240	1198588
France, Monac	780378	844636	886440	770741	848389
Hong Kong	760242	768999	851050	871102	783143
Singapore/Singapour	273574	296930	502103	575569	703282
Belgium–Luxembourg	237849	281228	474548	552971	553076
China/Chine	202437	305634	473514	502859	711453
Austria/Autriche	299044	342377	414091	372579	x474320
Mexico/Mexique	171192	142918	423653	448207	570635
Italy/Italie	306991	302493	335485	282485	343727
Switz.Liecht	228190	238504	270007	372243	402774
Canada	155499	185190	265657	291993	333414
Denmark/Danemark	199047	221950	233005	216263	197284
Sweden/Suède	125211	128644	167368	160709	157846
Thailand/Thaïlande	50415	74481	87919	121009	214670
Australia/Australie	59122	71904	93005	93955	84907
Spain/Espagne	59586	69801	92876	95370	119455
Malaysia/Malaisie	55788	56048	64513	117441	208632
Turkey/Turquie	39705	32323	57106	67727	67300
India/Inde	26057	34629	40163	75944	128560
Indonesia/Indonésie	34005	33342	43846	66060	91699
Czech Republic				98710	77144
Macau/Macao	3354	27844	34326	35634	49613
Czechoslovakia		x49352	x48108		
Norway,SVD,JM	26889	25059	31927	34945	35561
Finland/Finlande	12604	18772	28995	30356	41263
Bulgaria/Bulgarie	x32101	x11412	x44315	x11409	x6578
Argentina/Argentine	1410	2487	6087	33595	17176
Brazil/Brésil	4836	6365	11785	23596	19693
Portugal	11235	9795	12784	15658	14289
So. Africa Customs Un	3880	17763	5453	14634	
Hungary/Hongrie	x9573	x8541	x10834	x17798	x10514
Colombia/Colombie	2591	6680	17216	11288	12866
Israel/Israël	8530	9029	12934	11880	12182
Poland/Pologne	7634	13258	7934	9559	44363
Greece/Grèce	6187	7200	9326	10752	13388
Philippines	5346	8803	7007	5564	6560
Korea Dem People's Rp	x5119	x7168	x7573	x6540	x30457
Chile/Chili	3315	5929	4059	10220	21580
Russian Federation			x10019	x10116	x8482
New Zealand	4162	4849	6734	7341	8353
Ukraine			x4081	x13431	x5822
United Arab Emirates	16572	352	1927	x13260	x16743
Saudi Arabia	2107	2688	1929	x8266	x6118
Former USSR/Anc. URSS	26135	x11166			

(VALUE AS % OF TOTAL)(VALEUR EN % DU TOTAL)

	1985	1986	1987	1988	1989	1990	1991	1992	1993	1994
Africa	1.1	x1.0	x1.2	x1.1	x1.0	x1.0	x1.1	x0.9	x1.1	x1.0
Northern Africa	0.4	0.3	0.2	0.2	0.2	0.2	0.2	x0.2	0.2	0.2
Americas	30.1	28.0	23.9	23.7	22.1	19.9	20.8	22.0	24.2	24.3
LAIA	1.8	1.4	1.3	1.3	2.0	1.9	2.4	3.3	4.0	4.4
CACM	0.1	0.1	0.1	0.1	0.1	0.1	0.1	0.1	x0.1	x0.1
Asia	12.3	12.4	x14.1	x15.4	15.6	16.4	16.8	17.4	20.0	22.6
Middle East	1.7	x2.2	x1.6	1.3	x1.4	1.3	1.5	x1.5	x1.6	x1.3
Europe	52.4	54.7	56.8	55.8	57.4	58.5	57.1	56.1	50.5	47.9
EEC	43.9	45.7	47.8	47.2	48.6	54.1	52.9	51.8	46.4	43.9
EFTA	8.2	8.7	8.7	8.3	8.4	3.9	3.8	4.0	3.8	3.8
Oceania	3.1	x2.7	x2.5	x2.6	x2.9	x2.8	x2.7	x2.7	x3.1	x3.1
USA/Etats–Unis d'Amer	26.2	24.9	21.0	17.1	15.0	13.2	13.5	13.7	14.9	14.4
Germany/Allemagne	9.7	9.9	10.2	10.4	10.4	11.6	12.7	12.8	11.0	10.9
United Kingdom	9.9	9.2	9.6	9.6	9.5	9.5	8.4	8.9	9.2	8.0
France, Monac	6.3	7.0	7.4	7.1	7.4	8.1	7.8	7.4	6.8	6.1
Netherlands/Pays–Bas	3.9	4.4	4.8	4.9	5.0	6.2	6.0	5.7	4.7	4.3
Canada	1.7	1.3	1.3	5.0	4.8	4.5	4.6	4.5	5.0	5.3
Singapore/Singapour	2.0	2.3	2.5	3.2	3.5	3.5	3.7	4.2	4.3	4.6
Japan/Japon	3.2	2.9	3.3	4.0	4.3	3.9	3.7	3.6	4.4	5.5
Italy/Italie	3.7	3.8	3.9	3.7	3.9	4.8	4.5	3.4	2.9	2.8
Hong Kong	2.7	2.6	2.3	2.4	3.0	3.5	3.5	3.5	3.7	3.4

	1985	1986	1987	1988	1989	1990	1991	1992	1993	1994
Afrique	0.1	x0.1	x0.0	x0.0	x0.0	x0.0	x0.1	x0.0	x0.1	x0.0
Afrique du Nord	0.0	0.0	0.0	0.0	0.0	0.0	0.0	0.0	0.0	0.0
Amériques	14.7	13.1	13.9	17.4	19.9	23.1	23.8	25.4	27.4	27.4
ALAI	0.7	0.2	0.6	0.8	0.8	1.1	0.8	2.0	2.2	2.4
MCAC	0.0	0.0	0.0	0.0	0.0	0.0	0.0	0.0	x0.0	x0.0
Asie	44.5	43.8	x40.5	38.2	34.5	32.0	31.4	30.1	30.7	29.3
Moyen–Orient	0.2	x0.2	x0.3	0.3	0.3	0.4	0.2	0.3	x0.4	x0.4
Europe	39.7	42.0	41.6	40.8	44.0	44.0	43.8	43.5	40.8	42.4
CEE	37.1	38.9	38.9	38.1	40.9	42.6	42.5	42.2	39.1	40.7
AELE	2.6	3.0	2.7	2.7	3.0	1.3	1.3	1.3	1.7	1.7
Océanie	0.1	x0.2	x0.4	x0.4	x0.4	x0.3	x0.4	x0.4	x0.4	x0.4
USA/Etats–Unis d'Amer	13.7	12.5	13.0	15.9	18.4	21.2	22.0	22.1	23.9	23.7
Japan/Japon	33.9	32.0	27.2	23.5	20.4	18.0	17.3	15.9	15.4	13.2
Germany/Allemagne	12.4	13.5	12.6	11.5	12.6	12.6	12.4	10.7	9.0	8.9
Ireland/Irlande	2.3	2.6	3.2	5.1	6.3	5.9	6.0	7.2	7.0	9.5
Netherlands/Pays–Bas	5.3	5.3	5.3	5.4	5.5	6.2	6.2	6.7	7.2	6.0
United Kingdom	6.5	6.4	6.6	5.9	6.1	7.1	6.9	6.0	5.3	6.0
Korea, Republic of	4.5	6.2	5.9	6.9	6.9	6.0	5.9	4.8	4.8	4.5
France, Monac	4.1	4.5	4.9	4.4	4.2	4.1	4.2	3.8	3.3	3.2
Hong Kong	3.5	3.5	3.0	3.4	3.9	4.0	3.8	3.7	3.7	3.0
Singapore/Singapour	1.4	1.1	1.1	1.0	1.3	1.4	1.5	2.2	2.4	2.7

TRADE BY COMMODITY IN THOUSAND U.S. DOLLARS – COMMERCE PAR PRODUIT EN MILLIERS DE DOLLARS E.U

COUNTRIES–PAYS	IMPORTS – IMPORTATIONS 1990	1991	1992	1993	1994
Total	12296343	13800961	15715270	15726328	17298954
Africa	x226948	x242621	x268251	x302119	x310625
Northern Africa	83029	85889	99624	109485	118260
Americas	2615546	2777446	3269461	3580531	3928946
LAIA	194345	259557	410372	459164	536172
CACM	16493	17962	21905	x29596	x34272
Asia	3266270	3835341	4670242	4767904	5263340
Middle East	x336352	x404265	504804	x442217	x440999
Europe	5714971	6488673	7025438	6467013	7110692
EEC	5169825	5932535	6468507	5933544	6548925
EFTA	465205	472247	482443	473010	479031
Oceania	x250718	x266734	x292434	x303712	x328865
USA/Etats–Unis d'Amer	1975581	2045118	2344612	2562547	2780952
Hong Kong	1168694	1356902	1690182	1760511	1930316
Germany/Allemagne	1233273	1561894	1686780	1510004	1599099
Japan/Japon	951836	1073071	1171096	1237644	1436270
France, Monac	838534	881159	952789	904019	997825
Italy/Italie	492840	615470	672783	586861	659554
United Kingdom	524697	550298	604579	680525	755051
Netherlands/Pays–Bas	490649	547203	600392	523822	609461
Spain/Espagne	349126	422499	477677	382879	414109
Canada	353769	392390	424711	463556	498437
Switz.Liecht	353341	354000	351185	352048	350265
Belgium–Luxembourg	283106	315865	345658	348305	396230
China/Chine	115777	162646	393203	372653	411370
Sweden/Suède	242595	257328	280721	238306	278941
Austria/Autriche	212778	221892	243042	235047	268274
Australia/Australie	194517	211769	232142	245679	262277
Korea, Republic of	159611	190918	208938	198549	246455
Mexico/Mexique	86969	102260	194030	197080	235118
Singapore/Singapour	135666	142909	168168	171225	168584
Saudi Arabia	103152	170762	194296	x106831	x116661
Denmark/Danemark	126563	142245	157251	145039	162321
Greece/Grèce	107935	129639	143252	129767	126513
Portugal	103844	122507	142652	114704	112535
Norway, SVD, JM	105032	110735	123149	113970	121175
United Arab Emirates	71829	71829	95136	x116287	x132015
Finland/Finlande	104459	93352	87759	75346	94763
Turkey/Turquie	56059	61658	77310	90318	80498
Thailand/Thaïlande	59568	63519	74724	84129	97564
Argentina/Argentine	14194	45126	81422	89609	98586
Malaysia/Malaisie	61563	68836	69132	73782	76158
So. Africa Customs Un	55597	63948	66207	73869	81939
Ireland/Irlande	59425	71185	73172	58920	74247
Indonesia/Indonésie	35438	60817	77401	62010	61053
Israel/Israël	48505	51134	65495	73705	77276
Hungary/Hongrie	x34683	60935	x58055	x64190	x61131
Poland/Pologne	19890	7991	51139	105283	129079
Sri Lanka	9804	63112	42397	43554	53979
Tunisia/Tunisie	38359	41529	48321	52889	51369
Philippines	33503	57434	37592	42512	46257
Iran (Islamic Rp. of)	x34353	x39570	x55130	x41927	x19242
New Zealand	36374	36804	40492	43117	48210
Brazil/Brésil	37985	30898	31596	45345	64205
Russian Federation			x53821	x43356	x70262
Chile/Chili	16473	23766	34359	37325	36236
Pakistan	18551	28786	26174	38309	35188
India/Inde	45590	26659	34842	30482	42992
Former USSR/Anc. URSS	69135	x77301			
Romania/Roumanie	3634	14593	23864	33954	44274
Yugoslavia SFR	62257	x66918			
Venezuela	9221	16547	23512	26641	18764

COUNTRIES–PAYS	EXPORTS – EXPORTATIONS 1990	1991	1992	1993	1994
Totale	11186681	11983034	14131516	14373158	16215979
Afrique	42796	47176	x39764	40092	x32437
Afrique du Nord	13595	12944	11632	12413	14071
Amériques	1322795	1561957	1888103	2054165	2270187
ALAI	90183	121907	201065	236061	249342
MCAC	18720	8707	8139	x8056	x11701
Asie	4624846	4930510	6227408	6379471	7529761
Moyen–Orient	161916	27346	30068	x31795	x35726
Europe	4957736	5261736	5787823	5678369	6168173
CEE	4268455	4547796	4980864	4883728	5300261
AELE	651327	680286	762584	752794	827731
Océanie	73552	61834	x70105	x68823	x75856
Hong Kong	1687588	1991804	2437554	2552170	2819094
USA/Etats–Unis d'Amer	1110359	1320059	1550503	1673062	1853098
China/Chine	772825	874624	1603084	1612696	2421850
Germany/Allemagne	1181695	1259285	1377509	1282676	1396951
Japan/Japon	681410	714171	740808	709725	685909
France, Monac	671291	665859	746238	751456	814174
Switz.Liecht	613723	637903	715339	704234	777739
Netherlands/Pays–Bas	478764	533584	625219	575779	639564
Italy/Italie	549368	559344	592362	574082	648739
Korea, Republic of	529130	574817	588072	555933	580428
United Kingdom	429770	474771	487288	523085	645552
Thailand/Thaïlande	209094	242569	263975	310867	302405
Belgium–Luxembourg	208057	236432	261574	314877	325953
Sweden/Suède	233852	247464	256173	243875	282885
Philippines	191687	205105	204198	207434	210719
Denmark/Danemark	160214	178742	223349	194942	217134
Spain/Espagne	113739	131089	129166	124671	139144
Canada	91144	99536	115626	122841	122148
Singapore/Singapour	72952	91846	103964	110358	137286
Ireland/Irlande	77415	83629	98560	114543	3498
Austria/Autriche	88523	91712	95989	99258	x87276
Indonesia/Indonésie	56390	73295	90314	104686	111603
Mexico/Mexique	19675	36035	102867	114687	126611
Brazil/Brésil	38411	48774	61681	74993	70175
Australia/Australie	64562	54716	59547	58463	62718
Portugal	49102	52198	48662	40128	45196
Norway, SVD, JM	37189	41495	44969	45328	45776
Malaysia/Malaisie	26425	39197	43810	45481	53751
Poland/Pologne	92510	43244	35234	45373	54092
Pakistan	25867	28347	35836	42351	43484
Finland/Finlande	21845	27063	28587	28263	36674
India/Inde	22773	18815	26647	36014	39994
Sri Lanka	12664	16253	29791	24529	33949
Hungary/Hongrie	x20874	x20771	x27043	x19946	x19002
Czech Republic				61465	46997
Czechoslovakia		x27461	x31451		
Colombia/Colombie	11587	22729	14187	17121	20960
Croatia/Croatie			24883	28864	x21787
Turkey/Turquie	10195	12001	16885	15259	18883
Romania/Roumanie	12442	15528	15919	12566	9188
So. Africa Customs Un	9720	9944	13063	15120	
Greece/Grèce	4742	6546	10189	16091	17521
Israel/Israël	8314	9648	10042	12983	24303
Yugoslavia SFR	36497	x30536			
Viet Nam	x120476	x8281	x5498	x7723	x15599
Morocco/Maroc	8441	7142	7077	6484	7588
New Zealand	6026	5534	7033	7965	9277
Argentina/Argentine	4115	4069	5857	9235	6588
Slovenia/Slovénia			8754	8640	11209
Macau/Macao	35000	6175	4984	5390	6416

(VALUE AS % OF TOTAL)(VALEUR EN % DU TOTAL)

	1985	1986	1987	1988	1989	1990	1991	1992	1993	1994
Africa	2.0	x2.5	x2.1	x2.0	x1.6	x1.9	x1.8	x1.7	x2.0	x1.8
Northern Africa	1.0	1.1	0.8	0.8	0.6	0.7	0.6	0.6	0.7	0.7
Americas	27.8	x24.6	x23.2	21.7	22.4	21.2	20.2	20.8	22.7	22.8
LAIA	1.9	1.3	1.3	1.3	1.4	1.6	1.9	2.6	2.9	3.1
CACM	0.3	0.2	0.2	0.1	0.1	0.1	0.1	0.1	x0.2	x0.2
Asia	21.9	23.0	23.1	24.1	26.5	26.5	27.7	29.7	30.3	30.4
Middle East	3.9	x4.3	x2.4	x2.7	x3.1	x2.7	x2.9	3.2	x2.8	x2.5
Europe	45.0	46.9	47.8	47.8	45.3	46.5	47.0	44.7	41.1	41.1
EEC	37.3	38.7	39.6	39.6	37.4	42.0	43.0	41.2	37.7	37.9
EFTA	7.2	7.8	7.8	7.7	7.5	3.8	3.4	3.1	3.0	2.8
Oceania	2.4	x2.1	x2.2	x2.1	x2.2	x2.1	x1.9	x1.8	x1.9	x1.9
USA/Etats–Unis d'Amer	21.7	19.0	18.3	16.7	17.2	16.1	14.8	14.9	16.3	16.1
Hong Kong	6.5	6.8	7.6	7.7	8.9	9.5	9.8	10.8	11.2	11.2
Germany/Allemagne	8.6	8.9	9.2	9.3	8.5	10.0	11.3	10.7	9.6	9.2
Japan/Japon	6.7	7.0	7.3	7.6	8.4	7.7	7.8	7.5	7.9	8.3
France, Monac	6.4	6.9	6.7	6.5	6.1	6.8	6.4	6.1	5.7	5.8
Italy/Italie	3.4	3.6	4.0	3.9	3.7	4.0	4.5	4.3	3.7	3.8
United Kingdom	5.4	4.8	4.9	4.8	4.3	4.3	4.0	3.8	4.3	4.4
Netherlands/Pays–Bas	3.5	3.6	3.6	3.7	3.5	4.0	4.0	3.8	3.3	3.5
Spain/Espagne	1.4	1.7	1.9	2.2	2.3	2.8	3.1	3.0	2.4	2.4
Canada	3.5	3.2	2.7	2.9	2.9	2.9	2.8	2.7	2.9	2.9

	1985	1986	1987	1988	1989	1990	1991	1992	1993	1994
Afrique	0.5	0.5	0.4	x0.3	x0.3	0.4	0.4	x0.3	0.3	x0.2
Afrique du Nord	0.1	0.1	0.2	0.1	0.1	0.1	0.1	0.1	0.1	0.1
Amériques	12.2	10.6	8.2	8.4	12.0	11.8	13.0	13.4	14.3	14.0
ALAI	1.2	1.0	0.7	0.9	1.0	0.8	1.0	1.4	1.6	1.5
MCAC	0.1	0.1	0.1	0.1	0.2	0.2	0.1	0.1	x0.1	x0.1
Asie	35.2	34.3	x45.6	x45.9	40.8	41.4	41.1	44.1	44.4	46.5
Moyen–Orient	1.4	1.5	x0.4	1.9	0.3	1.4	0.2	0.2	x0.2	x0.2
Europe	49.4	51.9	42.3	40.6	43.6	44.3	43.9	41.0	39.5	38.0
CEE	40.4	41.8	33.8	32.6	35.3	38.2	38.0	35.2	34.0	32.7
AELE	8.6	9.7	8.1	7.7	8.0	5.8	5.7	5.4	5.2	5.1
Océanie	0.6	x0.7	x0.4	x0.7	x0.6	0.6	0.5	x0.5	x0.5	x0.4
Hong Kong	13.0	13.1	12.0	11.5	15.1	15.1	16.6	17.2	17.8	17.4
USA/Etats–Unis d'Amer	8.6	7.5	5.7	6.5	9.8	9.9	11.0	11.0	11.6	11.4
China/Chine	0.9	1.0	5.8	5.8	7.0	6.9	7.3	11.3	11.2	14.9
Germany/Allemagne	10.4	11.4	9.3	8.9	9.8	10.6	10.5	9.7	8.9	8.6
Japan/Japon	10.8	9.4	6.4	6.0	6.6	6.1	6.0	5.2	4.9	4.2
France, Monac	6.5	6.8	5.3	5.1	5.5	6.0	5.6	5.3	5.2	5.0
Switz.Liecht	4.8	5.7	4.7	4.5	4.7	5.5	5.3	5.1	4.9	4.8
Netherlands/Pays–Bas	4.1	4.3	3.6	3.6	3.9	4.3	4.5	4.4	4.0	3.9
Italy/Italie	5.2	5.2	4.2	4.1	4.5	4.9	4.7	4.2	4.0	4.0
Korea, Republic of	3.7	4.2	3.9	4.4	5.1	4.7	4.8	4.2	3.9	3.6

TRADE BY COMMODITY IN THOUSAND U.S. DOLLARS – COMMERCE PAR PRODUIT EN MILLIERS DE DOLLARS E.U

IMPORTS – IMPORTATIONS

COUNTRIES–PAYS	1990	1991	1992	1993	1994
Total	x8311447	1435998	1110102	534039	635875
Africa	x70466	x70456	72206	50392	x58574
Northern Africa	x338	x146	x277	x192	x235
Americas	108750	111215	108333	91806	94278
LAIA					x165
CACM				x91	x114
Asia	80121	77282	x70861	x30432	x62869
Middle East	x5713	x5241	x3024	x10485	x11018
Europe	1171192	1169015	847462	339198	412421
EEC	1166059	1165351	845061	333337	404829
EFTA					
Oceania	x7033	x4108	x6348	x1958	x3960
United Kingdom	246529	433844	306603	155780	182584
Netherlands/Pays-Bas	246054	189067	162054	17600	24309
France,Monac	124449	143984	129530	33815	48002
Ireland/Irlande	270516	279957			
Sweden/Suède	124586	116544	120870	25711	
Greece/Grèce			124508	97536	139200
Reunion/Réunion	49251	49394	57081	42770	48536
Martinique	36164	38781	49666	30098	38158
Guadeloupe	39589	32623	36489	41850	35364
Singapore/Singapour	24572	22946	17949	17667	23174
Hong Kong	30183	30974	25664		16908
French Guiana	10081	14492	14699	12028	12537
Malaysia/Malaisie	15267	13321	14139		
Bulgaria/Bulgarie	x1751	x911		x17179	x1252
Barbados/Barbade	14799	15683	1275	1080	x801
Un. Rep. of Tanzania	x9262	x11306	x691	x585	x406
Zimbabwe	4475	4901	3728	1367	x1371
Russian Federation			x5119	x4170	x4725
Myanmar			x8061	x211	x299
French Polynesia	x3875	x3103	x3094	x1495	x1004
Iran (Islamic Rp. of)		x2991	x2364	x1917	x709
Spain/Espagne	2017	1794	1408	2888	10708
Brunei Darussalam	2820	3585	x1176	x843	x1489
Djibouti	1		5346	x50	x78
Bahamas		4274	x593	x441	x314
Hungary/Hongrie	x2042		x2386	x2615	x2093
Saudi Arabia				x4621	x4650
United Arab Emirates	x4561			x2959	x2649
Former USSR/Anc. URSS	x6868943	x2850			
St Pierre & Miquelon	x447	x355	x691	x1758	x832
New Caledonia			x2561		x2538
Zambia/Zambie	x1727	x1035	x777	x706	x632
Czechoslovakia		x83	x2434		
Bahrain/Bahreïn	x1014	x1607	x508	x263	x1355
Gibraltar	x1898	x920	x734	x486	x1760
Yugoslavia SFR	x2331	x2059			
Guyana	x1163	x804	x676	x465	x347
Cayman Is/Is Caïmans	2386	1579	x148	x191	x320
Jamaica/Jamaïque			x936	x947	x940
Israel/Israël	352	768	527	416	732
Andorra/Andorre	x905	x685	x675	x323	x514
Gambia/Gambie	x748	x955	x364	x284	x384
Papua New Guinea	2894	x677	x525	x369	x334
Malawi	x995		x699	x572	x345
Falkland Isl (Malvinas)	x1264	x408	x380	x432	x432
Nigeria/Nigéria	x359	390	x40	x716	x444
Gabon	x640	x551	x387	x176	x153
Cote d'Ivoire	x545	x390	x343	x311	x422
Yugoslavia/Yougoslavie			x991		x21
Grenada/Grenade			x537	x396	x306

EXPORTS – EXPORTATIONS

COUNTRIES–PAYS	1990	1991	1992	1993	1994
Totale	x1733213	1216970	1324599	566221	723932
Afrique	x7324	x1974	11841	x1137	x2246
Afrique du Nord	x3	x9	x36	x65	x124
Amériques	x360	x694	x987	x838	x2874
ALAI					x46
MCAC				x10	x20
Asie	132204	165295	144075	23574	124679
Moyen-Orient	x366	x3766	x3223	x3000	x3826
Europe	x1574764	1047781	1164142	538903	591522
CEE	x1573423	1046664	1163102	537775	590286
AELE					
Océanie	x45	x42	x34	x32	x162
United Kingdom	993493	804873	627714	283464	275933
Greece/Grèce			304491	163185	193687
France,Monac	148444	133179	142229	68774	66645
Hong Kong	97902	132452	113759		91959
Netherlands/Pays-Bas	73998	69782	76377	21311	21520
Singapore/Singapour	23778	26741	24620	20346	22630
Ireland/Irlande	35875	35144			
Spain/Espagne	69	583	12225	1027	6808
Djibouti	7	1	9110	x3	x5
Iran (Islamic Rp. of)		x3538	x3135	x2195	x2239
Malaysia/Malaisie	1716	2122	1559		
Gibraltar	x411	x786	x902	x1086	x645
Russian Federation			x2036	x558	x530
Hungary/Hongrie	x327	x306	x1579	x673	x1041
Czechoslovakia		x13	x1876		
Zimbabwe	1162	550	1044	157	x241
Bahamas		336	x534	x388	x173
Nigeria/Nigéria	x1636		x1175	x71	x124
Reunion/Réunion		1075			
Slovakia				x1048	x1092
Myanmar	x8350		x761	x11	x60
Former USSR/Anc. URSS	x16045	x649			
Un. Rep. of Tanzania	x4395	x136	x222	x103	x266
Zambia/Zambie	x20	x110	x112	x142	x153
Bahrain/Bahreïn	x58	x211	x70	x54	x443
Yugoslavia SFR	x921	x316			
United Arab Emirates	x221			x307	x368
Ghana	x20			x286	x405
Bulgaria/Bulgarie	x925	x215	x61	x8	x316
Saudi Arabia				x284	x365
Afghanistan	x11	x95	x113	x41	
Saint Lucia/St. Lucie			x224		x22
Malawi			x54	x134	x213
Martinique	61	46	56	45	47
Bangladesh				x131	x160
Belgium-Luxembourg	103	46	66	14	47
Uganda/Ouganda	16	51		x69	x54
Yugoslavia/Yougoslavie			x119		x1
Syrian Arab Republic		x7		x100	x116
Bermuda/Bermudes				x105	x438
Libyan Arab Jamahiriya			x28	x62	x115
Antigua and Barbuda			x40	x37	x71
Aruba	103	77			x6
Saint-Kitts-Nevis	x1	x6	x28	x37	x45
Cuba		x60	x4	x6	x4
Guyana	x17	x8	x3	x59	x41
Iraq		x6	x9	x50	x152
Korea Dem People's Rp	x33	x44	x12	x5	x5
Montserrat	x79	x55	x5		x19
Andorra/Andorre	x8	x16	x19	x19	x41

(VALUE AS % OF TOTAL)(VALEUR EN % DU TOTAL)

Imports

	1985	1986	1987	1988	1989	1990	1991	1992	1993	1994
Africa	5.6	x4.8	x4.9	x4.4	x4.4	x0.8	x4.9	6.5	9.4	x9.2
Northern Africa	0.1	x0.1	x0.1	x0.3	x0.3	x0.0	x0.0	x0.0	x0.0	x0.0
Americas	3.3	x8.8	x7.0	x13.3	x12.8	1.3	7.7	9.8	17.2	14.8
LAIA		x0.0	x0.0	x0.4	x0.3					x0.0
CACM		x0.0	x0.0	x0.0	x0.0				x0.0	x0.0
Asia	12.3	x11.2	x9.3	x10.5	x10.7	1.0	5.4	x6.3	x5.7	x9.9
Middle East		x0.6	x0.3	x1.9	x1.3	x0.1	x0.4	x0.3	x2.0	x1.7
Europe	78.5	74.1	78.2	x66.4	x67.7	14.1	81.4	76.3	63.5	64.9
EEC	71.8	63.9	66.8	x56.2	x57.3	14.0	81.2	76.1	62.4	63.7
EFTA	6.6	10.2	11.3	x9.7	x10.1					
Oceania	0.2	x1.1	x0.7	x4.0	x3.8	x0.1	x0.3	x0.6	x0.4	x0.6
United Kingdom	40.0	27.7	27.3	14.4	11.3	3.0	30.2	27.6	29.2	28.7
Netherlands/Pays-Bas		x0.2	x0.2	10.9	12.2	3.0	13.2	14.6	3.3	3.8
France,Monac	4.7	5.0	6.1	5.2	7.4	1.5	10.0	11.7	6.3	7.5
Ireland/Irlande	18.7	19.2	19.8	9.9	11.0	3.3	19.5			
Sweden/Suède	6.6	8.9	10.0	5.0	5.6	1.5	8.1	10.9	4.8	
Greece/Grèce		x0.0	x0.0	x0.4	x0.3			11.2	18.3	21.9
Reunion/Réunion	1.2	1.1	1.6	1.1	1.7	0.6	3.4	5.1	8.0	7.6
Martinique	1.1	1.0	0.9	1.0	1.3	0.4	2.7	4.5	5.6	6.0
Guadeloupe	0.4	0.4	0.4	0.4	0.8	0.5	2.3	3.3	7.8	5.6
Singapore/Singapour	2.0	3.1	2.3	1.2	2.7	0.3	1.6	1.6	3.3	3.6

Exports

	1985	1986	1987	1988	1989	1990	1991	1992	1993	1994
Afrique	0.3	x0.4	x0.7	x0.5	x0.5	x0.4	x0.2	0.9	x0.2	x0.3
Afrique du Nord	0.0	x0.0	x0.1	x0.3	x0.3	x0.0	x0.0	x0.0	x0.0	x0.0
Amériques		x4.1	x7.5	x3.6	x3.9	x0.0	x0.1	x0.1	x0.1	x0.4
ALAI		x0.0	x0.1	x0.0	x0.0					x0.0
MCAC		x0.0	x0.0	x0.0	x0.0				x0.0	x0.0
Asie	9.9	x10.2	x21.3	x9.2	x9.3	7.6	13.6	10.9	4.2	17.2
Moyen-Orient	0.1	x0.4	x0.9	x0.3	x0.2	x0.0	x0.3	x0.2	x0.5	x0.5
Europe	89.7	x85.0	x68.7	x83.4	x84.4	x90.9	86.1	87.9	95.2	81.7
CEE	89.7	81.6	x61.2	x78.3	x78.5	x90.8	86.0	87.8	95.0	81.5
AELE		x3.3	x7.4	x5.0	x5.9					
Océanie		x0.3	x0.7	x2.6	x1.6	x0.0	x0.0	x0.0	x0.0	x0.0
United Kingdom	80.9	63.2	x24.2	48.6	44.1	57.3	66.1	47.4	50.1	38.1
Greece/Grèce		x0.1	x0.1	x0.1	x0.1			23.0	28.8	26.8
France,Monac	4.3	4.2	8.0	5.7	7.7	8.6	10.9	10.7	12.1	9.2
Hong Kong	7.0	5.8	12.5	5.0	5.5	5.6	10.9	8.6		12.7
Netherlands/Pays-Bas		x1.1	x2.4	3.8	4.2	4.3	5.7	5.8	3.8	3.0
Singapore/Singapour	2.2	1.5	2.9	1.3	1.1	1.4	2.2	1.9	3.6	3.1
Ireland/Irlande	4.3	3.7	6.6	2.5	1.9	2.1	2.9			
Spain/Espagne		x0.2	0.0	0.0	0.0	0.0	0.0	0.9	0.2	0.9
Djibouti		0.0	x0.0	x0.0	0.0	0.0	0.0	0.7	x0.0	x0.0
Iran (Islamic Rp. of)		x0.2	x0.4	x0.2	x0.1		x0.3	x0.2	x0.4	x0.3

TRADE BY COMMODITY IN THOUSAND U.S. DOLLARS – COMMERCE PAR PRODUIT EN MILLIERS DE DOLLARS E.U

COUNTRIES–PAYS	IMPORTS – IMPORTATIONS 1990	1991	1992	1993	1994
Total	57795148	64079468	64962320	73192709	90475690
Africa	x2678392	4178998	x2664044	x1927766	x2023216
Northern Africa	x25710	x16553	x45304	x20549	x22779
Americas	x19244399	25572606	x21941480	x23100707	34706293
LAIA	159676	6186176	481337	989666	9141791
CACM	302015	362681	310092	x71214	x81777
Asia	9031916	8445088	11518760	13519792	x16288947
Middle East	x456256	x593714	x754985	x1330995	x1804256
Europe	22288180	22015378	24751795	32399558	33240188
EEC	21707476	21428641	23650992	31585605	32408039
EFTA	468695	437376	433534	476478	398518
Oceania	x2817401	x3027195	x3733626	x1881943	x4032987
USA/Etats–Unis d'Amer	15796442	15390461	17282250	18184857	21115300
Germany/Allemagne	6712779	5371063	7546067	16239831	16187039
Belgium–Luxembourg	7068487	6865761	7440473	5855043	6423212
Italy/Italie	4272454	4957950	4576832	4391806	4249829
Canada	2768244	3417684	3456827	3427060	3792190
Japan/Japon	2480154	2651404	3086786	2969722	3507782
Australia/Australie	2679813	2685946	3436066	1747382	3659320
Mexico/Mexique	75	5998524	135736	207446	8249342
So. Africa Customs Un	2268250	2121642	2236804	1619983	1452301
Philippines	2029473	36914	2515991	3009870	4120984
United Kingdom	2173635	2114216	2045785	1359591	1026268
India/Inde	1472682	1555460	1487540	1687924	1905405
Denmark/Danemark	722909	1374020	871217	1199079	1127274
Thailand/Thaïlande	685175	830606	956963	1120512	750283
Ireland/Irlande	311000	296550	627721	1913125	2234045
Singapore/Singapour	594288	707994	707703	885954	1203407
Nigeria/Nigéria	x11299	1677133	x3288	x56436	x45328
China/Chine	283026	215980	590860	712211	735319
Hong Kong	317340	333159	501097	509668	590506
Switz.Liecht	460401	429762	416345	459545	366011
Korea, Republic of	95805	999028	114113	83053	102314
Russian Federation			x825464	x316614	x522033
Iran (Islamic Rp. of)	63000	x333808	x506761	x187003	x317455
Malaysia/Malaisie	35692	161076	197150	650229	813488
Netherlands/Pays–Bas	250945	252357	312826	437009	548506
Colombia/Colombie	55482	53746	187682	581409	652350
Israel/Israël	203932	212244	280470	253282	301916
Former USSR/Anc. URSS	1452780	x745479			
Costa Rica	301930	362627	309725	x71083	x81748
Saudi Arabia	78955	x3	x75	x626045	x742102
Slovenia/Slovénia			274215	256282	239614
Sweden/Suède	154689	142538	164102	153666	132361
Chile/Chili	87967	112413	149923	174346	160627
Oman	173197	96713	116805	179524	127441
Papua New Guinea	8584	x182195	x171376	x9137	x225579
Bulgaria/Bulgarie	x132726	x36884		x268922	x34378
Croatia/Croatie			303392	932	x120543
Un. Rep. of Tanzania	x87503	x158446	x113095	x6888	x18680
Romania/Roumanie	33025	40499	165315	28627	67389
Bahamas	x2		x133456	x100311	x83925
Nepal/Népal		54038	70048	107756	x5851
United Arab Emirates	12760	2979	2401	x214483	x327780
Ukraine			x50756	x130199	x55618
New Caledonia	73156	71344	x20003	62647	x23508
Greenland/Groenland	58429	53048	52127	48123	x3352
Hungary/Hongrie	x85510		x84197	x53593	x58013
Dominican Republic	x39201	x36412	x47832	x47981	x105932
Bahrain/Bahreïn	x66198	x94040	x23956	x9836	x69483
Zimbabwe	43620	54673	46983	23926	x239660
Myanmar	232318	5228	x108740	x8981	x9400

COUNTRIES–PAYS	EXPORTS – EXPORTATIONS 1990	1991	1992	1993	1994
Totale	72575189	72471979	74713431	79134634	80298082
Afrique	x10021516	x9234295	x9606229	x9610590	x102212
Afrique du Nord	x5103	x3476	x22239	x394	x2219
Amériques	19634363	20209374	21229565	x21709707	x24933633
ALAI	554608	622858	520174	479850	684136
MCAC	110340	146033	138930	x16587	x22184
Asie	10399498	8569550	11433998	13737140	15869493
Moyen–Orient	354615	x41881	x65973	x270094	x408801
Europe	21871931	23334686	23707141	31135793	28641316
CEE	21433316	22831748	23275498	30710840	28141102
AELE	412756	386880	373474	403209	457333
Océanie	x8968210	x8545953	x8460757	x2856291	x10604072
USA/Etats–Unis d'Amer	12913146	13591381	14726879	15084508	16675386
So. Africa Customs Un	9716368	9038015	9421218	9523356	
Germany/Allemagne	4389062	6031529	5725004	13073221	10760936
Australia/Australie	8674107	8262217	8210137	2614236	10417280
Canada	5903143	5731102	5719978	6007558	7266841
Japan/Japon	4399750	4873722	5193333	5905301	7316320
Netherlands/Pays–Bas	5009082	4936964	5147717	5013312	6224965
Belgium–Luxembourg	4631481	4918642	5146906	4977374	4460953
Philippines	2564613	1126	3098353	3898218	4707441
Denmark/Danemark	1622668	1849212	1840791	2343209	2605222
United Kingdom	1895811	1782005	2171936	1105276	1253926
Italy/Italie	2017914	1653831	1685563	1383333	1436568
Ireland/Irlande	984012	849197	895290	2041300	
Russian Federation			x1505289	x1485050	x1305223
Singapore/Singapour	569585	724946	784516	1079555	1014334
Hong Kong	426374	494363	758391	846860	792946
Former USSR/Anc. URSS	595752	x1719477			
Spain/Espagne	186220	277738	595574	750756	673461
China/Chine	1160396	723284	405152	358604	324030
Thailand/Thaïlande	272145	339393	337921	553240	310559
Switz.Liecht	400441	377341	363564	393767	448188
India/Inde	357811	278860	355882	362221	430519
Brazil/Brésil	379118	342005	296381	210444	442788
Korea, Republic of	26	840154	299		
Poland/Pologne	690184	713417			
Malaysia/Malaisie	109315	146337	167224	294975	390849
New Zealand	195306	189020	134678	146837	141659
Chile/Chili	113745	147474	153693	155926	183422
Costa Rica	110340	146030	138930	x16579	x22184
Sweden/Suède	389867	259056	19933	6501	
Mexico/Mexique		72999	62208	102909	26082
Romania/Roumanie	98040	73630	80701	62863	67443
Greece/Grèce	182652	193553			x111944
Sri Lanka	74901	55704	51309	59627	59905
Nigeria/Nigéria	x43563	81290	x51945	x22633	x9405
Hungary/Hongrie	x79895	x51898	x75690	x18797	x52203
Saudi Arabia	3			x146051	x150716
New Caledonia	45292	44238	56955	41430	x2590
Czechoslovakia		x1056	x118561		
Myanmar	x35564	38	x112961	x1856	x1771
Yugoslavia SFR	18326	x105392			
United Arab Emirates	126201	10538		x87642	x118880
France,Monac	105534	57594	24912	176	38401
Dominican Republic	66519	41668	x22020	x16471	x120544
Zaire/Zaïre	x22131	x37882	x36417	x4698	x6650
Bahamas	x8		x29026	x46936	x29067
Guam	x23474	x29869	x20680	x15291	x20397
Ukraine			x32305	x30498	x18864
Israel/Israël	14481	15335	20652	23271	23326
Iran (Islamic Rp. of)	198800	x10979	x42058	x4534	x13494

(VALUE AS % OF TOTAL)(VALEUR EN % DU TOTAL)

	1985	1986	1987	1988	1989	1990	1991	1992	1993	1994
Africa	8.1	x8.7	x6.7	x5.2	x4.7	x4.6	6.5	x4.1	x2.6	x2.2
Northern Africa	0.1	x0.6	x0.6	x0.2	x0.5	x0.0	x0.0	x0.1	x0.0	x0.0
Americas	41.6	x35.7	x33.8	x29.5	x34.1	x33.3	40.0	x33.8	x31.5	38.3
LAIA	0.5	x0.9	x1.3	x3.8	x3.1	0.3	9.7	0.7	1.4	10.1
CACM	0.1	x0.2	x0.2	x0.1	x0.7	0.5	0.6	0.5	x0.1	x0.1
Asia	17.7	15.1	21.3	x21.2	16.5	15.6	13.2	17.7	18.5	x18.0
Middle East	1.2	x2.0	4.2	x4.8	x1.9	x0.8	x0.9	x1.2	x1.8	x2.0
Europe	27.3	x35.0	x31.4	36.0	37.4	38.6	34.4	38.1	44.3	36.7
EEC	27.2	x33.0	x30.6	34.9	35.2	37.6	33.4	36.4	43.2	35.8
EFTA	0.0	x1.9	x0.7	x0.9	x1.9	0.8	0.7	0.7	0.7	0.4
Oceania	3.7	x3.7	x3.9	x4.0	x4.0	x4.8	x4.7	x5.8	x2.6	x4.4
USA/Etats–Unis d'Amer	35.7	28.7	26.6	22.0	23.9	27.3	24.0	26.6	24.8	23.3
Germany/Allemagne	15.2	15.6	15.4	12.1	12.3	11.6	8.4	11.6	22.2	17.9
Belgium–Luxembourg	5.2	4.0	3.1	9.5	10.4	12.2	10.7	11.5	8.0	7.1
Italy/Italie	1.1	1.2	1.1	6.7	6.4	7.4	7.7	7.0	6.0	4.7
Canada	5.2	4.3	4.1	2.5	4.8	4.8	5.3	5.3	4.7	4.2
Japan/Japon	6.9	5.0	4.5	4.0	4.1	4.3	4.1	4.8	4.1	3.9
Australia/Australie	3.7	3.3	3.4	3.7	3.2	4.6	4.2	5.3	2.4	4.0
Mexico/Mexique	0.0	0.1	0.2	1.6	1.4	0.0	9.4	0.2	0.3	9.1
So. Africa Customs Un	7.8	7.4	5.5	3.9	3.5	3.9	3.3	3.4	2.2	1.6
Philippines	4.8	3.9	3.8	3.6	3.3	3.5	0.1	3.9	4.1	4.6

	1985	1986	1987	1988	1989	1990	1991	1992	1993	1994
Afrique	28.6	x1.3	x7.7	x17.4	x14.7	x13.8	x12.8	x12.8	x12.1	x0.1
Afrique du Nord	0.0	x0.4	x0.2	x1.6	x1.4	x0.0	x0.0	x0.0	x0.0	x0.0
Amériques	24.9	x29.0	x35.7	x36.3	x39.9	27.0	27.9	28.4	x27.5	x31.0
ALAI	1.1	1.1	0.8	0.6	0.6	0.8	0.9	0.7	0.6	0.9
MCAC	0.1	x0.1	x0.1	x0.0	0.2	0.2	0.2	0.2	x0.0	x0.0
Asie	17.3	20.6	20.7	17.0	11.2	14.3	11.8	15.3	17.4	19.7
Moyen–Orient	0.6	x1.4	x1.1	x0.9	x0.6	0.5	x0.1	x0.1	x0.3	x0.5
Europe	26.2	43.9	31.0	18.3	23.5	30.1	32.2	31.7	39.3	35.7
CEE	26.1	41.9	28.9	17.1	22.1	29.5	31.5	31.2	38.8	35.0
AELE	0.0	x1.9	x2.0	x1.1	x1.4	0.6	0.5	0.5	0.5	0.6
Océanie	2.5	2.3	x2.0	x7.8	x8.2	x12.3	x11.8	x11.4	x3.6	x13.2
USA/Etats–Unis d'Amer	22.7	26.2	33.9	32.1	35.9	17.8	18.8	19.7	19.1	20.8
So. Africa Customs Un	27.8	0.1	x6.4	15.4	13.0	13.4	12.5	12.6	12.0	
Germany/Allemagne	10.9	16.4	12.0	4.6	4.3	6.0	8.3	7.7	16.5	13.4
Australia/Australie	1.8	1.5	1.5	7.5	8.0	12.0	11.4	11.0	3.3	13.0
Canada	1.0	0.9	0.6	3.1	2.9	8.1	7.9	7.7	7.6	9.0
Japan/Japon	5.7	7.3	4.5	5.1	4.8	6.1	6.7	7.0	7.5	9.1
Netherlands/Pays–Bas		x2.1	x1.4	4.7	5.3	6.9	6.8	6.9	6.3	7.8
Belgium–Luxembourg	9.9	15.4	10.3	0.7	5.4	6.4	6.8	6.9	6.3	5.6
Philippines	4.6	4.8	3.5	3.1	2.9	3.5	0.0	4.1	4.9	5.9
Denmark/Danemark	0.3	0.4	0.5	2.0	1.8	2.2	2.6	2.5	3.0	3.2

TRADE BY COMMODITY IN THOUSAND U.S. DOLLARS – COMMERCE PAR PRODUIT EN MILLIERS DE DOLLARS E.U

COUNTRIES–PAYS	IMPORTS – IMPORTATIONS 1990	1991	1992	1993	1994
Total	x5134462	287098	308405	319566	354498
Africa	x1362	x2063	x2786	x2689	3898
Northern Africa	241	277	x1019	233	2107
Americas	66049	64579	66898	66688	x71944
LAIA	2256	2121	4305	2547	3872
CACM	89	62	289	x222	x134
Asia	54249	61730	66693	x91748	x112640
Middle East	6557	6659	12907	x24060	x28723
Europe	153903	152237	162400	151239	158578
EEC	145920	144152	153734	142913	150029
EFTA	7045	7392	7811	7542	7961
Oceania	x10972	x5218	x2154	x3095	x4331
USA/Etats–Unis d'Amer	46396	47135	44051	48134	53813
France,Monac	36989	36113	35880	34425	37552
Italy/Italie	30327	29413	27082	21837	23098
Japan/Japon	21354	24856	22636	24605	27275
Belgium–Luxembourg	18631	16898	20817	20431	23678
Germany/Allemagne	17108	17640	18451	15818	15045
Canada	16125	14622	17344	15291	13291
Hong Kong	13662	14583	11901	16848	22547
Netherlands/Pays–Bas	10960	11213	12559	17219	16327
Spain/Espagne	8982	10104	12484	10154	9240
United Kingdom	10678	9169	10068	8865	8761
Switz.Liecht	6160	6287	6513	6312	6717
United Arab Emirates	933	783	2681	x12910	x17507
Korea, Republic of	1990	3219	4914	7395	9103
Singapore/Singapour	3472	4538	4320	5021	4348
Oman	2312	3898	5523	4318	3076
Sweden/Suède	3247	3386	4446	3681	4786
Australia/Australie	9807	5068	1541	2854	3531
Austria/Autriche	2884	2544	3178	3431	4048
China/Chine	1479	1045	2282	5301	11285
Macau/Macao	1501	2033	3121	3059	2589
Portugal	1407	2304	3451	2060	2945
Denmark/Danemark	1322	1866	2010	2533	1438
Kuwait/Koweït	719	996	2673	2378	2729
Czechoslovakia	2273	x165	x5174		
Israel/Israël	1082	1278	1310	1953	1591
Finland/Finlande	1875	1512	1622	1274	1505
Mexico/Mexique	797	970	1331	1902	2937
So. Africa Customs Un	643	1139	1180	1870	1249
Malaysia/Malaisie	1274	1749	1119	1053	1773
Norway,SVD,JM	873	1061	1220	1182	1174
Qatar	1034	347	1225	1293	x800
Hungary/Hongrie	x341	498	x1392	x825	x781
Greece/Grèce	866	939	620	928	1459
Indonesia/Indonésie	441	423	702	1276	1789
Ireland/Irlande	643	1053	1065	257	147
Poland/Pologne			889	1099	794
Saudi Arabia	779			x1917	x2679
Thailand/Thaïlande	516	707	511	570	1406
Argentina/Argentine	50	308	919	367	488
Ecuador/Equateur	5	5	1504	2	x104
Brazil/Brésil	1344	572	436	88	223
Slovakia				x1008	x202
Czech Republic				946	1315
Jordan/Jordanie	63	80	263	462	479
Pakistan	250	353	314	135	73
Egypt/Egypte	90	149	588	28	1780
Malta/Malte	191	227	293	225	x133
Turkey/Turquie	162	62	179	400	651
Korea Dem People's Rp	x40	x120	x513	x5	

COUNTRIES–PAYS	EXPORTS – EXPORTATIONS 1990	1991	1992	1993	1994
Totale	x410786	274241	303944	298048	316375
Afrique	x77250	x8038	x17617	x21792	x25720
Afrique du Nord	1155	405	x2878	2326	3535
Amériques	x67836	x69881	57196	x62729	x66534
ALAI	3197	4576	4235	4561	4342
MCAC	480	320	743	1970	2172
Asie	74652	66338	74148	81015	89149
Moyen–Orient	17437	18132	15138	x19631	x21829
Europe	105641	108865	126050	101636	104974
CEE	101797	106003	123345	99418	102473
AELE	2307	1821	1845	1887	2200
Océanie	x18601	x11531	x9519	x9293	x11242
Netherlands/Pays–Bas	30842	31091	35839	28374	29410
USA/Etats–Unis d'Amer	28709	31305	26576	28374	27560
Canada	27268	26309	22700	24480	30123
Belgium–Luxembourg	19383	20031	23200	25037	22896
Korea, Republic of	22424	19414	18484	18055	14325
China/Chine	10922	13257	20000	18630	22295
Oman	14430	15423	12923	13004	15721
United Kingdom	14632	14496	15718	10529	15273
France,Monac	9922	10888	13201	14146	13036
Germany/Allemagne	9559	12426	15656	9136	8434
Denmark/Danemark	5694	6345	7924	6370	5991
New Zealand	16394	8994	5034	1670	2471
Hungary/Hongrie	x7789	x4891	x5503	x5049	x5778
Australia/Australie	1546	2176	4233	7113	6982
Hong Kong	3174	2962	3656	6523	9790
Poland/Pologne			3942	5501	3769
Singapore/Singapour	3050	2995	3177	3084	3326
Italy/Italie	2988	2667	3309	2920	3396
Ireland/Irlande	5441	4312	3687	381	490
So. Africa Customs Un	2043	1390	2460	3230	
Mauritius/Maurice	940	2276	1641	2988	4389
Albania/Albanie	x1338	x2177	x2157	x2428	x686
Czechoslovakia		x85	x6327		
Turkey/Turquie	2314	2229	1942	1800	1635
Philippines	659	2132	1842	1836	2861
Czech Republic				5147	4819
Switz.Liecht	1671	1656	1604	1682	1721
Indonesia/Indonésie	2041	1921	1277	1731	3857
Thailand/Thaïlande	949	467	979	3038	3132
United Arab Emirates	285	87	22	x4269	x3173
Egypt/Egypte	1071	221	2172	1928	3059
Togo	14		x2750	x1511	x1828
Colombia/Colombie	759	708	1358	1943	1927
Zimbabwe	259	170	279	3483	x5481
Guyana	x2453	x1756	1450	720	x9
Bangladesh		407	939	2531	x907
Cameroon/Cameroun	528	29	x1851	x1980	x735
Un. Rep. of Tanzania	x69544	x1183	x993	x1650	x2208
Panama	3917	3647	72	101	224
Malaysia/Malaisie	1419	1431	1352	992	1050
Spain/Espagne	562	965	1390	1220	2321
Romania/Roumanie	836	1295	1475	735	1309
Pakistan	968	1447	1119	887	1063
Chile/Chili	1121	636	1289	1073	677
Japan/Japon	836	842	1112	1039	1696
Russian Federation			x1057	x1900	x1605
Myanmar	x10128	7	x2876	x68	x25
Portugal	1088	1200	1495	32	46
Slovakia				x2713	x2262
Israel/Israël	469	659	833	951	1365

(VALUE AS % OF TOTAL)(VALEUR EN % DU TOTAL)

	1985	1986	1987	1988	1989	1990	1991	1992	1993	1994
Africa	0.5	x0.9	x0.3	x0.8	x0.5	x0.0	x0.7	x0.9	x0.9	1.1
Northern Africa	0.4	0.5	x0.1	x0.0	x0.2	0.0	0.1	x0.3	0.1	0.6
Americas	28.6	x27.1	x24.0	23.9	x24.1	1.3	22.5	21.7	20.8	x20.3
LAIA	0.5	x0.8	0.2	0.4	x0.7	0.0	0.7	1.4	0.8	1.1
CACM	0.0	0.0	x0.0	x0.0	0.0	0.0	0.0	0.1	x0.1	x0.0
Asia	27.4	25.3	28.6	19.6	x22.9	1.0	21.5	21.7	x28.7	x31.7
Middle East	1.7	x1.9	x2.7	x2.3	x8.6	0.1	2.3	4.2	x7.5	x8.1
Europe	42.1	43.5	43.3	51.7	47.8	3.0	53.0	52.7	47.3	44.7
EEC	36.4	38.5	37.8	46.6	43.4	2.8	50.2	49.8	44.7	42.3
EFTA	5.1	4.7	5.1	4.8	4.2	0.1	2.6	2.5	2.4	2.2
Oceania	0.6	x0.8	x1.0	x0.6	x2.6	x0.2	x1.8	x0.7	x1.0	x1.2
USA/Etats–Unis d'Amer	20.8	20.8	19.2	19.9	17.2	0.9	16.4	14.3	15.1	15.2
France,Monac	8.2	8.6	8.6	12.6	11.9	0.7	12.6	11.6	10.8	10.6
Italy/Italie	9.7	9.1	8.2	11.0	8.3	0.6	10.2	8.8	6.8	6.5
Japan/Japon	17.6	16.1	15.0	7.3	7.1	0.4	8.7	7.3	7.7	7.7
Belgium–Luxembourg	2.2	2.4	2.4	4.7	4.8	0.4	5.9	6.8	6.4	6.7
Germany/Allemagne	6.7	7.3	6.2	5.7	5.8	0.3	6.1	6.0	4.9	4.2
Canada	6.9	5.2	4.2	3.3	5.8	0.3	5.1	5.6	4.8	3.7
Hong Kong	4.3	3.4	3.3	2.5	3.5	0.3	5.1	3.9	5.3	6.4
Netherlands/Pays–Bas		x1.7	x1.5	2.5	2.8	0.2	3.9	4.1	5.4	4.6
Spain/Espagne	1.4	1.3	3.3	2.3	2.2	0.2	3.5	4.0	3.2	2.6

	1985	1986	1987	1988	1989	1990	1991	1992	1993	1994
Afrique	3.1	x4.5	x12.0	x2.5	x2.8	x18.8	x2.9	x5.8	x7.3	x8.1
Afrique du Nord	1.3	0.4	0.9	0.4	0.5	0.3	0.1	x0.9	0.8	1.1
Amériques	39.9	x34.4	x24.4	17.8	x21.0	x16.5	x25.5	18.8	x21.0	x21.0
ALAI	1.2	1.4	0.9	x1.2	x1.5	0.8	1.7	1.4	1.5	1.4
MCAC	0.8	0.7	0.6	0.6	x1.9	0.1	0.1	0.2	0.7	0.7
Asie	22.7	19.9	x22.1	x18.3	26.1	18.2	24.1	24.4	27.2	28.2
Moyen–Orient	1.0	x0.5	0.5	4.5	x9.5	4.2	6.6	5.0	x6.6	x6.9
Europe	33.0	x40.0	x32.4	29.1	35.1	25.7	39.7	41.5	34.1	33.2
CEE	29.3	x37.4	x30.2	26.9	33.7	24.8	38.7	40.6	33.4	32.4
AELE	3.6	2.6	2.2	1.6	0.9	0.6	0.7	0.6	0.6	0.7
Océanie	0.8	0.9	x1.0	x1.5	x5.5	x4.6	x4.2	x3.1	x3.1	x3.6
Netherlands/Pays–Bas		x8.7	x5.6	7.6	9.9	7.5	11.3	11.8	9.5	9.3
USA/Etats–Unis d'Amer	23.1	16.4	9.4	8.4	11.2	7.0	11.4	8.7	9.5	8.7
Canada	14.1	11.7	11.8	6.8	4.6	6.6	9.6	7.5	8.2	9.5
Belgium–Luxembourg	3.7	3.9	2.9	3.3	5.5	4.7	7.3	7.6	8.4	7.2
Korea, Republic of	9.6	8.6	6.4	4.4	6.6	5.5	7.1	6.1	6.1	4.5
China/Chine			3.8	1.9	3.1	2.7	4.8	6.6	6.3	7.0
Oman	0.0	0.0	x0.0	4.1	7.3	3.5	5.6	4.3	4.4	5.0
United Kingdom	8.8	6.8	6.2	4.4	5.3	3.6	5.3	5.2	3.5	4.8
France,Monac	2.9	3.3	3.1	2.3	3.4	2.4	4.0	4.3	4.7	4.1
Germany/Allemagne	5.2	6.1	3.8	3.0	3.5	2.3	4.5	5.2	3.1	2.7

TRADE BY COMMODITY IN THOUSAND U.S. DOLLARS – COMMERCE PAR PRODUIT EN MILLIERS DE DOLLARS E.U

COUNTRIES–PAYS	IMPORTS – IMPORTATIONS 1990	1991	1992	1993	1994
Total	x3957266	3654838	3923092	x4103357	x5150549
Africa	x139770	21705	x29447	x149649	x96412
Northern Africa	x6752	7220	9684	x10248	16417
Americas	900562	954024	976861	949177	x1019459
LAIA	185301	160658	114743	160128	x194886
CACM	9955	2019	6252	x4795	x5810
Asia	537523	923064	833361	x1497250	x2439048
Middle East	96582	144276	232896	x953535	x1587786
Europe	1767589	1680397	1997666	1426388	1458148
EEC	1591079	1473774	1735512	1241979	1244030
EFTA	175897	205669	260221	181173	210765
Oceania	50760	x69135	x61243	x45581	x115337
United Kingdom	605067	546652	550793	462346	303196
USA/Etats–Unis d'Amer	418925	477390	456000	524347	552181
Canada	283396	309869	392587	255374	258473
Netherlands/Pays–Bas	346401	265082	367003	193653	203311
Korea, Republic of	212881	339633	240370	243256	322612
Saudi Arabia	4164	10663	132859	x609356	x1222876
Finland/Finlande	176103	165818	355937	179765	168400
Japan/Japon	94206	341876	166684	143493	400724
Norway,SVD,JM	136532	168625	227558	152267	178311
Sweden/Suède	173699	156431	130868	102634	154952
Germany/Allemagne	113499	152526	123090	80902	76397
Turkey/Turquie	21102	114231	71582	128660	84027
Colombia/Colombie	130636	105391	55900	127002	39475
Indonesia/Indonésie	23031	60095	105429	80837	39287
United Arab Emirates	59419	759	668	x199950	x108826
Austria/Autriche	24307	42950	82630	72209	184173
Australia/Australie	35179	47502	48935	40173	108470
Denmark/Danemark	18190	43136	53794	33214	17934
Nigeria/Nigéria	x652		x2734	x118961	x58169
Switz.Liecht	39203	36871	32537	28836	32365
Italy/Italie	47928	40861	23914	30926	22929
Spain/Espagne	24035	21591	5873	46170	54651
Mexico/Mexique	4178	19494	30912	11213	94364
Portugal	24213	14117	20220	17011	24139
Thailand/Thaïlande	98120	12749	17479	18996	27928
Malaysia/Malaisie	4731	9435	20414	13851	18427
Venezuela	47650	23763	13681	5455	3027
France,Monac	20338	11937	12789	14068	17563
Bahrain/Bahreïn	x10520	x12116	x18603	x5814	x6269
New Zealand	13441	19642	10951	4034	4803
Brunei Darussalam		1669	x12384	x8625	x20875
Argentina/Argentine	485	3901	9190	7599	5752
Poland/Pologne			7989	10124	7997
Belgium–Luxembourg	11512	6032	6680	5021	15356
Israel/Israël	20	765	7637	8118	
Bulgaria/Bulgarie	x615	x48	5686	x7105	x890
Myanmar			x12387	x5	x159
China/Chine			683	10883	39
Iran (Islamic Rp. of)		x3620	x5095	x1456	x13956
Czechoslovakia	352	x44	x10108		
Hungary/Hongrie	x162	5987	x714	x3065	x1904
Greece/Grèce	5436	5920	1478	2011	889
Bangladesh		888	3619	3921	x1574
Zimbabwe	4036	1123	4238	2989	x1008
Brazil/Brésil	671	4912	1315	1860	1282
Algeria/Algérie	167		5200	2541	5464
Czech Republic				7587	7502
Slovakia				x7392	x3596
Pakistan	309	2007	3755	1329	1768
Philippines	1786	2820	1154	3061	5200

COUNTRIES–PAYS	EXPORTS – EXPORTATIONS 1990	1991	1992	1993	1994
Totale	5354292	4980109	5697064	5280827	5834777
Afrique	x561	x1395	450	4981	x842
Afrique du Nord	242	212	291	4661	282
Amériques	2886273	3130930	3601916	3229149	3967358
ALAI	6882	7688	11084	14217	42403
MCAC	5	377	40	471	111
Asie	x102520	92069	104227	x120512	187361
Moyen–Orient	8169	6354	8792	x15450	x18455
Europe	2290430	1729311	1923674	1866095	1580947
CEE	2134898	1587207	1796947	1710703	1464427
AELE	154351	138320	125222	155170	116023
Océanie	13449	14866	5871	3930	x3268
USA/Etats–Unis d'Amer	2806392	3024168	3379994	2998014	3625877
United Kingdom	1097090	542382	698329	863925	660195
Sweden/Suède	397218	361904	333175	183072	134714
Netherlands/Pays–Bas	247343	259467	197647	117998	150051
Canada	72933	98591	210784	216307	298944
Italy/Italie	118738	135269	188989	98699	123962
Austria/Autriche	49389	80428	174537	143316	x78581
Germany/Allemagne	86720	79327	83809	90349	107559
Norway,SVD,JM	90291	71586	73177	91932	56148
Switz.Liecht	64061	66734	52045	63238	59876
Spain/Espagne	41366	44812	33908	76257	51236
Japan/Japon	39847	37638	44947	43460	83130
France,Monac	25410	20375	19609	65404	89673
Korea, Republic of	14900	41625	27213	33576	57705
Denmark/Danemark	12689	24563	28788	21779	6259
Portugal	26912	21753	22816	22177	24620
Poland/Pologne			38409	19365	44055
Russian Federation			x6702	x36123	x30956
China/Chine			15699	18138	17676
Hungary/Hongrie	x2400	x4351	x12382	x11814	x9838
Belgium–Luxembourg	16311	9103	8659	8453	11321
Australia/Australie	12569	14722	5739	3405	2617
Turkey/Turquie	4973	5881	7709	6931	7755
Ukraine			x10179	x8645	x4466
Czech Republic				18595	25413
Greece/Grèce	12500	3705	1975	12062	19325
Brazil/Brésil	5058	5315	5303	6170	7608
Finland/Finlande	3165	4089	4657	7203	6930
Czechoslovakia		x107	x10073		
Argentina/Argentine	1298	1827	2493	4135	7906
Slovakia				x6355	x4750
Former USSR/Anc. URSS	x55428	x6196			
Mexico/Mexique	389	375	2880	2391	2971
Saudi Arabia	47	408	86	x4827	x5287
Thailand/Thaïlande	841	769	2648	901	1445
Tunisia/Tunisie				4040	15
Indonesia/Indonésie		1784	1801	433	234
Brunei Darussalam			x269	x3729	x154
Yugoslavia SFR	1181	x3783			
United Arab Emirates	2914			x3610	x4884
Israel/Israël	353	1933	35	664	247
Malaysia/Malaisie	713	288	896	1017	6200
Philippines	975	564	657	581	476
Hong Kong	163	204	256	1302	589
Peru/Pérou		38	132	1076	486
Bulgaria/Bulgarie	x2118	x877	x64	x9	x2945
Slovenia/Slovénia			904	15	5
Guatemala	4	350	1	469	2
Morocco/Maroc	225	196	291	312	268
New Zealand	879	131	130	513	644

(VALUE AS % OF TOTAL)(VALEUR EN % DU TOTAL)

	1985	1986	1987	1988	1989	1990	1991	1992	1993	1994
Africa	1.4	x1.4	x2.4	x3.6	x1.4	x3.5	0.6	x0.8	x3.6	x1.9
Northern Africa	0.8	x0.6	x0.3	0.1	0.4	x0.2	0.2	0.2	x0.2	0.3
Americas	18.8	15.0	17.2	24.1	26.3	22.7	26.1	24.9	23.1	x19.8
LAIA	3.7	2.7	4.2	4.7	5.6	4.7	4.4	2.9	3.9	x3.8
CACM	0.0	0.0	x0.0	0.2	0.2	0.3	0.1	0.2	x0.1	x0.1
Asia	8.7	x15.5	x12.6	x14.2	x16.1	13.6	25.3	21.2	x36.5	x47.4
Middle East	0.5	x5.6	x3.1	x4.1	x1.4	2.4	3.9	5.9	x23.2	x30.8
Europe	67.6	65.5	64.0	56.8	54.3	44.7	46.0	50.9	34.8	28.3
EEC	52.6	56.7	51.7	38.7	39.7	40.2	40.3	44.2	30.3	24.2
EFTA	15.0	8.8	12.0	18.1	14.6	4.4	5.6	6.6	4.4	4.1
Oceania	3.5	x2.7	x2.8	1.3	1.8	1.3	x1.9	x1.5	x1.1	x2.2
United Kingdom	11.2	11.9	11.8	14.0	13.2	15.3	15.0	14.0	11.3	5.9
USA/Etats–Unis d'Amer	8.5	7.8	8.4	12.4	12.9	10.6	13.1	11.6	12.8	10.7
Canada	6.5	4.2	4.2	6.8	7.5	7.2	8.5	10.0	6.2	5.0
Netherlands/Pays–Bas		x0.4	x2.2	8.8	10.7	8.8	7.3	9.4	4.7	3.9
Korea, Republic of	0.3	0.7	0.9	3.0	1.9	5.4	9.3	6.1	5.9	6.3
Saudi Arabia	0.2	0.2	0.0	0.1	0.1	0.1	0.3	3.4	x14.9	x23.7
Finland/Finlande	3.0	2.2	3.8	4.9	4.8	4.5	4.5	9.1	4.4	3.3
Japan/Japon	5.2	4.9	4.3	2.8	2.7	2.4	9.4	4.2	3.5	7.8
Norway,SVD,JM	2.2	2.3	3.5	3.6	3.7	3.5	4.6	5.8	3.7	3.5
Sweden/Suède	2.3	2.0	3.4	5.4	5.0	4.4	4.3	3.3	2.5	3.0

	1985	1986	1987	1988	1989	1990	1991	1992	1993	1994
Afrique		x0.0	x0.4	x0.0	x0.2	x0.0	x0.0		0.1	x0.0
Afrique du Nord	0.0	x0.0	x0.0	0.0	0.0	0.0	0.0	0.0	0.1	0.0
Amériques	65.7	45.1	x35.0	x44.1	x43.5	53.9	62.9	63.2	61.2	68.0
ALAI	0.4	0.3	0.2	x0.2	0.2	0.1	0.2	0.2	0.3	0.7
MCAC		x0.0	x0.0	x0.0	x0.0	0.0	0.0	0.0	0.0	0.0
Asie	0.9	x2.7	x2.7	x2.1	x1.4	x2.0	1.9	1.8	x2.2	3.2
Moyen–Orient	0.4	x0.6	x0.4	x0.1	x0.3	0.2	0.1	0.2	x0.3	x0.3
Europe	33.5	x52.1	61.6	52.7	54.4	42.8	34.7	33.8	35.3	27.1
CEE	27.4	x44.4	51.9	34.2	38.6	39.9	31.9	31.5	32.4	25.1
AELE	6.0	7.7	9.7	18.4	15.8	2.9	2.8	2.2	2.9	2.0
Océanie	0.1	x0.1	x0.1	0.3	x0.2	0.3	0.3	0.1	0.1	x0.1
USA/Etats–Unis d'Amer	61.7	42.2	33.4	42.3	41.5	52.4	60.7	59.3	56.8	62.1
United Kingdom	11.8	12.6	36.3	11.8	16.9	20.5	10.9	12.3	16.4	11.3
Sweden/Suède	4.1	6.0	7.5	13.0	12.9	7.4	7.3	5.8	3.5	2.3
Netherlands/Pays–Bas		x11.3	x0.7	3.0	3.3	4.6	5.2	3.5	2.2	2.6
Canada	3.6	2.6	1.4	1.6	1.8	1.4	2.0	3.7	4.1	5.1
Italy/Italie	4.6	7.8	2.3	1.3	1.3	2.2	2.7	3.3	1.9	2.1
Austria/Autriche	0.0	0.1	0.1	0.2	0.4	0.9	1.6	3.1	2.7	x1.3
Germany/Allemagne	1.0	1.1	1.2	1.3	1.2	1.6	1.6	1.5	1.7	1.8
Norway,SVD,JM	0.9	0.9	0.9	1.2	1.6	1.7	1.4	1.3	1.7	1.0
Switz.Liecht	0.7	0.6	1.0	3.9	0.9	1.2	1.3	0.9	1.2	1.0

TRADE BY COMMODITY IN THOUSAND U.S. DOLLARS – COMMERCE PAR PRODUIT EN MILLIERS DE DOLLARS E.U

COUNTRIES–PAYS	IMPORTS – IMPORTATIONS 1990	1991	1992	1993	1994
Total	x290038	204879	183295	x157147	158467
Africa	7868	x1953	x9987	x30264	x6755
Northern Africa	4731	260	x459	x145	x303
Americas	20244	20896	x12433	x10317	x21910
LAIA	7193	7107	928	477	9271
CACM	3711	1710	385	x894	x410
Asia	81627	63040	36968	x30879	x32488
Middle East	185	x469	1752	x1850	x2612
Europe	111652	117513	121448	80954	95718
EEC	110420	111938	120585	80714	94754
EFTA	745	706	403	58	570
Oceania	x7108	x1395	620	x229	x1240
Germany/Allemagne	74193	87618	87233	59173	76358
Ukraine				x58543	
Indonesia/Indonésie	9829	16711	14071	4715	12814
Nigeria/Nigéria			x1062	x24944	x109
United Kingdom	946	4328	12500	5854	7951
Sweden/Suède	18161	4860	10071	4320	2757
Singapore/Singapour	24093	10205	2758	6175	4418
USA/Etats–Unis d'Amer	8034	6521	6997	5451	8522
Malaysia/Malaisie	8129	10683	7308	880	742
Italy/Italie	2863	5875	5281	5127	4634
Hong Kong	7739	8975	3371	2422	2598
Latvia/Lettonie			x13187	x121	
India/Inde	2337	6006	2698	1457	963
Turkmenistan/Turkménistn				x9312	x198
Venezuela	4132	6719	361	17	95
Philippines	28135	6551			22
Austria/Autriche	4844	3606	121	2322	795
Netherlands/Pays–Bas	4985	2496	1589	1002	
Malta/Malte	172	4737	136	19	x84
Sri Lanka	87	1122	1355	1806	2024
Hungary/Hongrie	x82	2	x1732	x2288	x217
Jamaica/Jamaïque		2	x1969	x1850	x1583
Suriname/Suriname	344	3564	2	x175	x196
Spain/Espagne	1290	931	1719	961	405
France,Monac	428	905	1651	1018	498
Zimbabwe	2405	862	936	1620	x897
Russian Federation			x2984	x282	x28
Un. Rep. of Tanzania		x535	x1397	x1301	
Brunei Darussalam	39		x2834	x190	x529
Martinique		1652			45
Japan/Japon	558	615	531	442	191
Bulgaria/Bulgarie		x32	84	x1402	x5
Costa Rica	3629	428	328	x702	x409
Syrian Arab Republic		x7	1438		
Saudi Arabia				x1435	x865
Burkina Faso			x1433		
Mexico/Mexique	75	383	565	416	140
Honduras	4	1150	4	190	
Malawi			x277	x986	x987
Israel/Israël	452	629	118	422	473
French Polynesia	x363	x1012			
Senegal/Sénégal			x969		x9
So. Africa Customs Un		1		965	263
Macau/Macao	37	893	39	30	11
Belgium–Luxembourg	2369	401	231	252	641
Norway,SVD,JM	479	582	135	49	99
Mali			x716		
Cote d'Ivoire			x716		
Nepal/Népal				703	x51
Djibouti	84		681		

COUNTRIES–PAYS	EXPORTS – EXPORTATIONS 1990	1991	1992	1993	1994
Totale	x445917	x145937	225945	181810	144110
Afrique	29956	x7690	x5663	x464	x320
Afrique du Nord				x25	
Amériques	x26228	25062	33880	20352	12123
ALAI	6005	19403	18117	13505	6891
MCAC		8	3653		1
Asie	x20021	x22916	x26148	6230	9183
Moyen–Orient	x631	x540	x3	x55	x222
Europe	85856	81443	159087	153088	119322
CEE	85686	80705	157777	151768	118446
AELE	68		114	567	675
Océanie	x2089	x507	x519	x1010	x878
United Kingdom	5361	11679	92422	87580	74514
Germany/Allemagne	61381	40027	33515	21864	23576
Mexico/Mexique	5880	19341	15877	7066	3850
Austria/Autriche	3885	9523	12569	13598	x6276
Italy/Italie	535	6430	2791	21631	3597
Korea Dem People's Rp	x14815	x16773	x10939	x62	x673
Singapore/Singapour	1524	3150	12303	4102	6819
USA/Etats–Unis d'Amer	7299	2913	9376	4186	3870
France,Monac	1302	3975	8165	2862	4220
Netherlands/Pays–Bas	2442	2651	4997	2755	
Chile/Chili	120	60	2240	5992	3035
Russian Federation			x3541	x4285	x4184
Uganda/Ouganda		x7217			
Cuba	x3395	x1846	x2153	x2104	x1028
Former USSR/Anc. URSS	x277090	x5983			
Belgium–Luxembourg	9487	4637	481	642	1257
Nigeria/Nigéria	x7		x5378	x348	x71
Hong Kong	2933	1876	1073	1045	475
Honduras			3650		
Gibraltar	x16	x603	x936	x681	x101
Portugal	212	362	1376	305	51
Australia/Australie	1587	484	505	931	417
Ireland/Irlande	289	828	936	89	
Hungary/Hongrie	x913	x681	x509	x605	x791
Bulgaria/Bulgarie	x3741	x1604	x25	x21	x373
Macau/Macao			929	688	76
Canada	9529	864	409	295	171
Norway,SVD,JM	63		114	567	673
Malaysia/Malaisie		217	275	63	
Lebanon/Liban	x590	x535			
Finland/Finlande	15	99	185	223	4447
Spain/Espagne	487	215	173	94	59
China/Chine		7	467		87
Uruguay				444	
Andorra/Andorre	x86	x87	x259	x72	x74
Lithuania/Lituanie				x373	
Sweden/Suède	119	111	118	118	355
Liberia/Libéria		x234			
Japan/Japon	3	138	52	36	43
Reunion/Réunion		61	162		
Bahamas			x80	x140	x57
Israel/Israël	67	91	23	59	68
Denmark/Danemark	72	125	40	3	64
Viet Nam		x79	x49	x2	x5
Czechoslovakia		x1	x103		
Angola		101			
So. Africa Customs Un		12	50	25	
Barbados/Barbade				80	
Albania/Albanie	x19	x50	x11	x16	x5
Turks and Caicos Isls			x48	x25	x10

(VALUE AS % OF TOTAL)(VALEUR EN % DU TOTAL)

Imports	1985	1986	1987	1988	1989	1990	1991	1992	1993	1994
Africa	21.7	x0.5	x0.4	1.0	2.5	2.7	x1.0	x5.4	x19.2	x4.3
Northern Africa	0.7	x0.0	x0.1	0.3	1.7	1.6	0.1	x0.3	x0.1	x0.2
Americas	2.8	x18.8	x29.6	x14.0	37.5	7.0	10.2	x6.7	x6.6	x13.8
LAIA	0.2	x2.9	2.7	6.9	32.4	2.5	3.5	0.5	0.3	5.9
CACM	0.1	0.3	0.3	0.3	x0.8	1.3	0.8	0.2	x0.6	x0.3
Asia	14.0	13.7	5.4	26.6	19.6	28.1	30.8	20.2	x19.6	x20.5
Middle East	0.6	x0.5	x0.3	x0.3	0.2	0.1	x0.2	1.0	x1.2	x1.6
Europe	61.3	66.7	64.3	x57.6	x39.5	38.5	57.4	66.3	51.5	60.4
EEC	61.2	58.3	55.6	42.9	26.2	38.1	54.6	65.8	51.4	59.8
EFTA	0.1	x8.2	x8.5	x14.6	x13.2	0.3	0.3	0.2	0.0	0.4
Oceania	0.1	0.2	0.1	0.7	x0.9	x2.4	x0.7	0.4	x0.2	x0.8
Germany/Allemagne	7.9	7.4	9.8	32.3	18.2	25.6	42.8	47.6	37.7	48.2
Ukraine									x37.3	
Indonesia/Indonésie	0.0	0.7	1.7	2.9	3.5	3.4	8.2	7.7	3.0	8.1
Nigeria/Nigéria								x0.6	x15.9	x0.1
United Kingdom	0.7	1.2	1.7	1.5	2.0	0.3	2.1	6.8	3.7	5.0
Sweden/Suède	0.0	0.4	1.2	3.3	2.0	6.3	2.4	5.5	2.7	1.7
Singapore/Singapour	0.2	0.3	1.7	2.0	4.9	8.3	5.0	1.5	3.9	2.8
USA/Etats–Unis d'Amer		x9.0	x22.3	x4.6	3.4	2.8	3.2	3.8	3.5	5.4
Malaysia/Malaisie	0.1	0.0	0.0	0.2	2.5	2.8	5.2	4.0	0.6	0.5
Italy/Italie	0.0	0.3	0.6	1.7	1.1	1.0	2.9	2.9	3.3	2.9

Exports	1985	1986	1987	1988	1989	1990	1991	1992	1993	1994
Afrique		x2.5	x0.9	x93.9	12.0	6.7	x5.3	x2.5	x0.2	x0.2
Afrique du Nord		x0.0	x0.0	x0.0	x0.0				x0.0	
Amériques	1.0	x7.6	x5.2	2.3	22.1	x5.9	17.2	15.0	11.2	8.4
ALAI	0.2	x1.4	x0.4	1.2	17.9	1.3	13.3	8.0	7.4	4.8
MCAC	0.0	x0.0	x0.0	0.0	x0.0		0.0	1.6		0.0
Asie	6.9	8.5	x4.1	x0.7	x13.5	x4.5	x15.7	x11.5	3.5	6.4
Moyen–Orient	0.0	x0.3	x1.0	x0.2	x0.3	x0.1	x0.4	x0.0	x0.0	x0.2
Europe	90.7	x80.9	x87.6	x2.3	x45.3	19.3	55.8	70.4	84.2	82.8
CEE	76.8	37.2	54.2	1.7	36.2	19.2	55.3	69.8	83.5	82.2
AELE	13.9	x43.6	x33.2	x0.5	x9.0	0.0	0.0	0.1	0.3	0.5
Océanie		x0.0	x0.9	x0.1	x0.2	x0.4	x0.3	x0.2	x0.5	x0.6
United Kingdom	6.0	0.3	1.1	0.3	5.2	1.2	8.0	40.9	48.2	51.7
Germany/Allemagne	8.6	4.5	6.2	0.9	19.8	13.8	27.4	14.8	12.0	16.4
Mexico/Mexique		x1.2	x0.4	0.2	4.4	1.3	13.3	7.0	3.9	2.7
Austria/Autriche	12.1	2.4	0.3	0.1	0.7	0.9	6.5	5.6	7.5	x4.4
Italy/Italie	0.1	0.8	0.6	0.0	7.6	0.1	4.4	1.2	11.9	2.5
Korea Dem People's Rp			x0.1	x0.2	x2.5	x3.3	x11.5	x4.8	x0.0	x0.5
Singapore/Singapour	0.7	0.1	0.6	0.1	1.9	0.3	2.2	5.4	2.3	4.7
USA/Etats–Unis d'Amer	0.8	0.8	1.1	0.2	2.8	1.6	2.0	4.1	2.3	2.7
France,Monac	4.2	0.4	0.4	0.0	0.2	0.3	2.7	3.6	1.6	2.9
Netherlands/Pays–Bas		x1.3	x1.0	0.1	0.4	0.5	1.8	2.2	1.5	

971 *GOLD,NON MONETARY NES

OR NON MONETAIRE 971

TRADE BY COMMODITY IN THOUSAND U.S. DOLLARS – COMMERCE PAR PRODUIT EN MILLIERS DE DOLLARS E.U

IMPORTS – IMPORTATIONS

COUNTRIES–PAYS	1990	1991	1992	1993	1994
Total	19891160	20046457	20309199	17792177	21238575
Africa	36398	32984	23782	25107	32092
Northern Africa	24361	22821	6750	8462	15716
Americas	x1734069	x2436515	2553282	3087166	2719090
LAIA	14766	28372	45770	114222	169734
CACM	4712	1773	5009	678	x820
Asia	10183045	9900552	9570130	7160220	10369521
Middle East	1773074	1527467	1673479	x233117	x265764
Europe	7092200	6996223	7325670	6790315	7513264
EEC	6768939	6727098	7161284	6573890	7257581
EFTA	288164	242272	132116	196820	235688
Oceania	x354749	x677340	x816404	x689002	x574100
Italy/Italie	3903729	4172940	4196202	3862685	4173449
Hong Kong	2228512	3628104	3913167	2649700	4051282
Japan/Japon	3575161	2633994	2046690	1953860	2434133
USA/Etats–Unis d'Amer	1082353	1924449	1905507	2016154	1933878
Germany/Allemagne	1360170	1142208	1282897	1428406	1263559
Malaysia/Malaisie	1406906	1369217	700759	973492	1515734
Saudi Arabia	1571730	1391433	1473161	x34929	x3453
Australia/Australie	333471	672180	809414	681505	566660
Canada	572019	455686	583598	940690	604551
France, Monac	638520	553884	608429	497816	670026
Belgium–Luxembourg	343776	337843	466157	248979	182709
Korea, Republic of	258782	274069	362701	396355	713751
Thailand/Thaïlande	241974	180234	220326	285985	390942
Spain/Espagne	216374	246780	273895	129358	221877
Switz.Liecht	259559	229518	119493	178071	217057
India/Inde	506	319	246378	245820	470039
Israel/Israël	126814	153323	150945	167761	167299
Singapore/Singapour	142943	111539	106392	219145	276705
Portugal	77998	92239	128051	125268	127560
Netherlands/Pays–Bas	71781	68070	94052	103210	242708
Oman	73117	80612	93072	80375	137884
Myanmar			x129322	x4572	x6991
Kuwait/ Koweït	71127	5026	60563	52785	30295
Greece/Grèce	33680	27960	31381	43359	41277
Mexico/Mexique	3160	923	10006	84433	150042
Cyprus/Chypre	31045	29524	31428	24276	30106
Austria/Autriche	57557	25000	31507	28609	25363
Bolivia/Bolivie	8868	26202	27006	17600	13938
Sweden/Suède	30230	29590	20878	18014	19373
United Kingdom				59845	252914
United Arab Emirates	4351	14587	8902	x34082	x48501
Malta/Malte	27468	19628	21972	11615	x4732
Norway,SVD,JM	28411	12567	12420	18556	18428
Denmark/Danemark	13665	11371	12572	10529	15094
Ireland/Irlande	11923	9825	8873	10557	12149
Sri Lanka	1233	4609	3043	21242	28554
Dominican Republic	x9458	x11262	x1517	x12920	x4867
Mauritius/Maurice	9865	6034	9263	10119	12068
Romania/Roumanie	1172	56	4727	20418	18404
Panama	4743	13658	9773	409	2718
Finland/Finlande	9536	9388	6392	7256	9524
Brazil/Brésil	2647	647	8288	11973	4968
Tunisia/Tunisie	4926	4253	6653	8321	15575
Libyan Arab Jamahiriya	19340	18252		x1	x1
Jordan/Jordanie	14605	5167	5959	5779	13740
Czech Republic				15948	8454
Zimbabwe	568	3262	6839	4586	
New Zealand	17471	3118	5163	6077	5329
Czechoslovakia	36803	x404	x13215		
Lao People's Dem. Rp.			x8453	x4515	x22327

EXPORTS – EXPORTATIONS

COUNTRIES–PAYS	1990	1991	1992	1993	1994
Totale	x31506914	13384909	14870432	20311948	18662088
Afrique	x202150	x383277	761282	x131656	x120414
Afrique du Nord	140	136	x18181	x7830	x2925
Amériques	5322557	5843406	7337990	12384069	9917989
ALAI	362316	443218	748543	848343	1435290
MCAC	15531	9436	19736	33637	x16855
Asie	1078450	718131	x991438	x1650477	x1891478
Moyen–Orient	175603	27147	55543	x150805	x186486
Europe	1736660	1986443	1726452	2273827	2627151
CEE	1600842	1905160	1645875	2057173	2512963
AELE	108147	71516	74533	213323	107524
Océanie	3015386	3464410	4032149	3853281	x4065499
USA/Etats–Unis d'Amer	3005761	3337011	4092306	9063300	5676508
Australia/Australie	2687581	2841271	3283509	3184947	3478024
Canada	1841218	1965334	2394710	2302020	2592434
Germany/Allemagne	535737	790960	633306	679625	865935
Papua New Guinea	233135	535054	623067	517602	x400669
France, Monac	505524	504965	488704	445393	441822
Belgium–Luxembourg	294022	346316	328278	356364	437227
Former USSR/Anc. URSS	x20144343	x974470			
Chile/Chili	229928	408113	266894	239579	308928
Korea, Republic of	178629	197872	237296	290462	567704
Ghana	x147733	140114	525199	x3783	x1046
Peru/Pérou			400781	209685	340511
Japan/Japon	179869	130097	159201	205641	273778
Indonesia/Indonésie	122146	145205	151515	180238	146315
Russian Federation			x193203	x143504	x432128
Switz.Liecht	98143	60830	62611	200084	87232
Singapore/Singapour	102788	93167	88675	130353	162964
Sweden/Suède	107741	115513	85702	104943	117845
Hong Kong	230504	81309	75156	134802	78337
New Zealand	42310	55988	101469	127791	145103
So. Africa Customs Un	14996	156575	89790	23027	12121
Uzbekistan/Ouzbékistan			x2226	x233812	x170517
Italy/Italie	31030	32881	52625	147900	91374
Venezuela	7072	5921	10380	185274	272411
Philippines	6	1222	34742	162711	212091
Korea Dem People's Rp	x67786	x24985	x76913	x66191	x3390
United Kingdom				149643	92586
Guyana	25200	20400	24600	100413	x139023
Netherlands/Pays–Bas	28146	27338	15488	84982	163942
Mongolia/Mongolie			x67624	x53599	x24581
Mexico/Mexique	97276	17521	42237	54501	82430
United Arab Emirates	141710	4219	23	x104061	x166091
Jordan/Jordanie	1433	18293	52622	30557	13274
Spain/Espagne	25300	32028	9970	48720	163549
Fiji/Fidji	51440	31634	23971	22897	41282
Bolivia/Bolivie	25	35	1874	71612	119088
Ecuador/Equateur	982	249	6175	59384	x36947
Dominican Republic	53600	36818	24343	3894	x22182
Cote d'Ivoire	x1760	x12969	x21880	x24860	x24086
Burkina Faso			x29863	x29633	x16273
Kenya		22698	18397	15113	x16523
Brazil/Brésil	14293	11317	19939	21519	202817
Cuba	x9686	x16028	x12165	x18435	x5162
Finland/Finlande	23812	22524	12248	11590	10663
Nicaragua	14441	8039	8989	28259	3578
Malaysia/Malaisie	8917	9033	11398	24110	23923
Ethiopia/Ethiopie		21348	20185		
Thailand/Thaïlande	1884	5330	16617	17423	34206
Denmark/Danemark	41871	25651	6814	4818	6086
Austria/Autriche	4598	3976	10297	22475	x119996

(VALUE AS % OF TOTAL)(VALEUR EN % DU TOTAL)

	1985	1986	1987	1988	1989	1990	1991	1992	1993	1994
Africa	0.5	0.2	0.5	0.4	0.2	0.2	0.2	0.1	0.1	0.1
Northern Africa	0.5	0.2	0.4	0.4	0.2	0.1	0.1	0.0	0.0	0.1
Americas	33.1	34.2	x18.1	x12.3	x14.6	x8.7	x12.2	12.6	17.3	12.9
LAIA	0.0	0.1	x0.1	0.0	x0.1	0.1	0.1	0.2	0.6	0.8
CACM		0.0	0.0	0.0	0.0	0.0	0.0	0.0	0.0	x0.0
Asia	24.5	36.5	x36.8	x46.8	39.0	51.2	49.4	47.1	40.2	48.8
Middle East	3.1	x0.5	2.2	2.7	7.7	8.9	7.6	8.2	x1.3	x1.3
Europe	41.0	28.3	43.9	39.9	44.5	35.7	34.9	36.1	38.2	35.4
EEC	39.6	27.5	42.9	39.1	43.5	34.0	33.6	35.3	36.9	34.2
EFTA	1.4	0.7	1.0	0.8	1.0	1.4	1.2	0.7	1.1	1.1
Oceania	0.7	x0.5	x0.6	0.5	1.1	x1.8	x3.4	x4.0	x3.9	x2.7
Italy/Italie	21.7	12.6	21.5	18.2	22.5	19.6	20.8	20.7	21.7	19.7
Hong Kong	0.1	0.1	0.3	0.3	0.2	11.2	18.1	19.3	14.9	19.1
Japan/Japon	18.5	34.1	26.0	23.9	22.3	18.0	13.1	10.1	11.0	11.5
USA/Etats–Unis d'Amer	24.6	27.8	12.2	7.2	9.5	5.4	9.6	9.4	11.3	9.1
Germany/Allemagne	7.1	5.7	7.2	7.6	6.9	6.8	5.7	6.3	8.0	5.9
Malaysia/Malaisie	0.8	0.4	0.7	1.8	5.7	7.1	6.8	3.5	5.5	7.1
Saudi Arabia	1.7	0.2	1.4	1.0	5.7	7.9	6.9	7.3	x0.2	x0.0
Australia/Australie	0.6	0.5	0.6	0.5	0.9	1.7	3.4	4.0	3.8	2.7
Canada	8.5	6.2	5.8	5.0	4.7	2.9	2.3	2.9	5.3	2.8
France, Monac	1.8	1.8	2.9	2.6	3.7	3.2	2.8	3.0	2.8	3.2

	1985	1986	1987	1988	1989	1990	1991	1992	1993	1994
Afrique	2.0	x2.2	x2.5	3.5	x2.2	x0.6	x2.9	5.1	x0.6	x0.7
Afrique du Nord		x0.0	x0.0	x0.0	x0.1	0.0	0.0	x0.1	x0.0	x0.0
Amériques	58.3	x72.1	x39.3	x46.2	x38.4	16.9	43.6	49.3	61.0	53.1
ALAI	2.4	x5.1	x5.6	x2.7	x3.9	1.1	3.3	5.0	4.2	7.7
MCAC		x0.1	x0.2	0.1	0.1	0.0	0.1	0.1	0.2	x0.1
Asie	1.7	x3.0	x8.0	x6.3	x6.3	3.4	5.4	x6.7	x8.1	x10.2
Moyen–Orient	0.2	x0.6	x0.9	x1.2	x1.2	0.6	0.2	0.4	x0.7	x1.0
Europe	26.0	15.3	x22.4	x19.8	x24.0	5.5	14.8	11.6	11.2	14.1
CEE	21.5	13.5	x19.2	x18.1	x22.0	5.1	14.2	11.1	10.1	13.5
AELE	4.5	1.7	2.9	1.5	1.9	0.3	0.5	0.5	1.1	0.6
Océanie	12.0	7.4	13.4	14.1	18.0	9.6	25.8	27.2	19.0	x21.8
USA/Etats–Unis d'Amer	24.1	45.5	17.7	31.7	18.7	9.5	24.9	27.5	44.6	30.4
Australia/Australie	8.5	5.2	11.4	12.9	16.7	8.5	21.2	22.1	15.7	18.6
Canada	31.7	20.7	14.4	10.9	14.9	5.8	14.7	16.1	11.3	13.9
Germany/Allemagne	9.1	6.6	4.5	3.9	4.3	1.7	5.9	4.3	3.3	4.6
Papua New Guinea	3.2	1.9	1.5	0.8	0.6	0.7	4.0	4.2	2.5	x2.1
France, Monac	3.8	2.3	3.1	2.4	3.5	1.6	3.8	3.3	2.2	2.4
Belgium–Luxembourg	5.4	1.9	2.3	2.9	4.0	0.9	2.6	2.2	1.8	2.3
Former USSR/Anc. URSS			x14.2	x9.5	x10.8	x63.9	x7.3			
Chile/Chili	1.6	0.8	1.4	1.0	1.4	0.7	3.0	1.8	1.2	1.7
Korea, Republic of	0.0	0.1	0.3	0.4	0.7	0.6	1.5	1.6	1.4	3.0

1994 INTERNATIONAL TRADE STATISTICS YEARBOOK

VOLUME II

SPECIAL TABLES

ANNUAIRE DE STATISTIQUE DU COMMERCE INTERNATIONAL 1994

VOLUME II

TABLEAUX SPECIAUX

Total Imports and Exports by Regions and Countries and Areas
Importations et Exportations Totales par Regions et Pays ou Zones

Imports C.I.F. - Exports F.O.B. - Balance / Importations C.I.F. - Exportations F.O.B. - Balance

Value in million U.S. dollars — Valeur en millions de dollars E.-U.

Country or Area / Pays ou Zone	IMP / EXP / BAL	System	1980	1985	1986	1987	1988	1989	1990	1991	1992	1993	1994
World	IMP		2051532	1996794	2191945	2553221	2906550	3153587	3560228	3536463	3796560	3696317	4222192
Monde	EXP		2006844	1930575	2126153	2490756	2826499	3043286	3436920	3419267	3662205	3625210	4167811
	BAL		-44688	-66219	-65792	-62464	-80051	-110301	-123308	-117196	-134355	-71107	-54381
Developed economies [1,2]	IMP		1406997	1375125	1550499	1840229	2076218	2267507	2585835	2585723	2704717	2520661	2855080
Economies développées [1,2]	EXP		1273676	1281288	1491821	1745970	1990920	2151538	2467420	2491118	2642401	2543105	2861578
	BAL		-133321	-93837	-58677	-94260	-85298	-115969	-118414	-94605	-62317	22444	6498
Developing economies [2]	IMP		484430	455336	459480	519357	623483	687865	778592	858724	995226	1084997	1248226
Eco. en voie de dévelp. [2]	EXP		578014	481705	450822	544005	626692	701107	797047	837902	927490	986630	1178859
	BAL		93584	26369	-8658	24648	3209	13243	18455	-20822	-67736	-98367	-69367
OPEC [3]	IMP		125754	97974	88145	88125	97516	101011	110147	128021	157314	155249	157535
OPEP [3]	EXP		302783	153005	110616	124069	122237	141926	180036	169682	179551	178213	198565
	BAL		177028	55031	22470	35944	24721	40915	69890	41661	22237	22963	41031
LDC [4]	IMP		21585	18037	18737	19005	20902	21071	23475	21995	23474	24157	26399
PMA [4]	EXP		12067	10840	10396	11653	12476	13539	14743	13832	14459	13984	15077
	BAL		-9518	-7198	-8341	-7351	-8425	-7532	-8732	-8163	-9015	-10173	-11322
Other [5]	IMP		160106	166333	181966	193634	206849	198215	195802	92016	96616	90659	118885
Autres [5]	EXP		155154	167582	183510	200781	208886	190640	172453	90247	92314	95476	127373
	BAL		-4952	1249	1544	7147	2038	-7575	-23348	-1768	-4302	4816	8488
Devlpd. Econ.: America	IMP		313947	424448	454036	505296	554997	595229	615676	605871	653774	709578	805651
Eco. dévlpés.: Amérique	EXP		287719	301111	303730	340551	422276	468159	496668	521619	553187	577044	639385
	BAL		-26229	-123337	-150306	-164745	-132721	-127070	-119009	-84252	-100587	-132535	-166267
Canada	IMP	G	62542	80642	85494	92596	112718	119796	123247	124782	129268	139054	155356
Canada	EXP	G	67732	90953	90325	98171	117112	121835	127634	127163	134441	145185	165783
	BAL		5189	10311	4831	5575	4394	2040	4386	2381	5173	6130	10427
United States	IMP	G	256984	352463	382295	424442	459542	492922	516987	508363	553923	603438	689215
Etats-Unis	EXP	G	225566	218815	227158	254122	322427	363812	393592	421730	448163	464773	512521
	BAL		-31418	-133648	-155137	-170320	-137115	-129110	-123395	-86633	-105760	-138665	-176694
Devlpg. Econ.: America	IMP		118067	80181	84768	89207	98731	105571	117647	132699	158230	171788	218803
Eco. evdd. [38]: Amérique	EXP		104927	102967	87882	96557	109813	120676	131257	127864	130802	137303	183925
	BAL		-13140	22785	3114	7350	11082	15105	13609	-4835	-27429	-34485	-34878
LAIA [6]	IMP		85006	53308	56494	62256	71332	75027	85645	103856	127891	140336	185825
ALAI [6]	EXP		80679	85198	69876	80397	93035	102819	112528	111772	115284	121877	167406
	BAL		-4327	31890	13382	18141	21704	27792	26883	7916	-12607	-18459	-18419
Argentina	IMP	S	10541	3814	4724	5818	5322	4203	4077	8275	14872	16651	21527
Argentine	EXP	S	8021	8396	6852	6360	9135	9579	12353	11978	12235	12869	15659
	BAL		-2519	4582	2128	542	3813	5376	8276	3703	-2637	-3782	-5868
Bolivia	IMP	S	665	691	674	766	591	611	687	970	1090	1206	1209
Bolivie	EXP	S	942	623	638	570	600	822	926	849	710	728	1032
	BAL		277	-67	-36	-197	10	211	239	-121	-380	-478	-177
Brazil	IMP	S	24961	14332	15557	16581	16055	19875	22524	22950	23068	27740	35997
Brésil	EXP	S	20132	25639	22349	26224	33494	34383	31414	31620	35793	38597	43558
	BAL		-4829	11307	6792	9643	17439	14508	8890	8670	12725	10857	7561
Chile	IMP	S	5797	3072	3436	4396	5292	7144	7678	8094	10129	11125	11825
Chili	EXP	S	4705	3804	4191	5224	7052	8080	8373	8942	10007	9199	11539
	BAL		-1092	733	755	827	1760	936	695	848	-121	-1927	-286
Colombia	IMP	S	4739	4141	3862	4322	5002	5004	5590	4906	6516	9832	11883
Colombie	EXP	S	3924	3552	5102	4642	5037	5717	6766	7232	6917	7116	8399
	BAL		-814	-589	1240	320	35	712	1176	2326	400	-2716	-3484

See the end of the table for general information and footnotes.

Voir la fin du tableau pour la remarque générale et les notes

SPECIAL TABLE: A **TABLEAU SPECIAL: A**

Total Imports and Exports by Regions and Countries and Areas
Importations et Exportations Totales par Regions et Pays ou Zones

Imports C.I.F. - Exports F.O.B. - Balance / Importations C.I.F. - Exportations F.O.B. - Balance

(Continued / Suite)

Value in million U.S. dollars — Valeur en millions de dollars E.-U.

Country or Area / Pays ou Zone	IMP EXP BAL	system	1980	1985	1986	1987	1988	1989	1990	1991	1992	1993	1994
Ecuador / Equateur	IMP	G	2253	1767	1810	2252	1714	1855	1862	2399	2501	2562	3642
	EXP	G	2481	2905	2172	1928	2192	2354	2714	2852	3007	2904	3717
	BAL		228	1138	361	-324	479	499	853	453	507	342	75
Mexico / Mexique	IMP	G	19431	13762	11918	12761	18954	23633	29993	38184	48138	50147	79375
	EXP	G	15307	21664	16031	20656	20658	22819	26524	27120	27531	30241	60833
	BAL		-4123	7901	4113	7895	1703	-815	-3469	-11064	-20608	-19906	-18542
Paraguay / Paraguay	IMP	S	615	631	832	679	778	819	1352	1212	1424	1698	...
	EXP	S	310	305	275	379	657	1119	959	737	658	694	...
	BAL		-305	-325	-557	-300	-121	301	-393	-475	-766	-1004	...
Peru / Pérou	IMP	S	2500	1835	2909	3562	3348	2749	3470	4195	4861	4901	6794
	EXP	S	3898	2979	2531	2661	2701	3488	3231	3329	3484	3497	4555
	BAL		1399	1144	-378	-901	-647	739	-239	-866	-1377	-1405	-2239
Uruguay / Uruguay	IMP	S	1680	708	870	1142	1157	1203	1343	1637	2045	2326	2773
	EXP	S	1059	909	1088	1189	1405	1599	1693	1605	1703	1645	1913
	BAL		-622	201	218	47	247	396	350	-32	-343	-680	-859
Venezuela[7] / Venezuela[7]	IMP	G	10671	7418	8600	8711	11476	7030	6365	9963	12128	11022	8037
	EXP	G	19919	14438	8660	10577	10113	12867	17586	15518	13247	14397	15525
	BAL		9248	7020	60	1866	-1363	5837	11220	5555	1120	3375	7488
CACM[8] / MCAC[8]	IMP		5996	5087	4773	5478	5719	6116	6360	6795	8525	9273	*9628*
	EXP		4875	3810	4021	3801	3951	4188	4361	4439	4754	5153	*5685*
	BAL		-1121	-1277	-752	-1677	-1768	-1928	-1999	-2356	-3771	-4119	*-3943*
Costa Rica / Costa Rica	IMP	S	1540	1098	1148	1383	1410	1717	1990	1877	2440	2885	3025
	EXP	S	1002	976	1121	1158	1246	1415	1448	1598	1829	2049	2215
	BAL		-539	-122	-27	-224	-164	-303	-541	-279	-611	-835	-810
El Salvador / El Salvador	IMP	S	962	961	935	994	1007	1161	1149	1360	1693	1913	...
	EXP	S	1074	695	755	591	609	496	588	571	610	732	...
	BAL		112	-266	-180	-403	-398	-665	-561	-789	-1083	-1181	...
Guatemala / Guatemala	IMP	S	1598	1175	959	1447	1557	1654	1649	1851	2463	2599	2604
	EXP	S	1520	1057	1044	987	1022	1108	1163	1202	1295	1291	1522
	BAL		-78	-118	85	-460	-535	-546	-486	-649	-1167	-1308	-1083
Honduras / Honduras	IMP	S	1009	888	875	827	940	969	935	955	1037	1130	1056
	EXP	S	830	780	854	791	842	859	831	792	802	814	843
	BAL		-179	-108	-21	-36	-98	-110	-104	-163	-235	-316	-213
Nicaragua / Nicaragua	IMP	G	887	964	857	827	805	615	638	751	892	746	...
	EXP	G	451	302	247	273	233	311	331	275	218	267	...
	BAL		-437	-663	-610	-554	-572	-304	-307	-476	-675	-479	...
Other America / Autres pays d'Amérique	IMP		27064	21786	*23501*	*21473*	*21681*	*24428*	*25643*	*22048*	*21815*	*22179*	*23350*
	EXP		19373	13959	*13985*	*12359*	*12827*	*13669*	*14368*	*11653*	*10764*	*10273*	*10834*
	BAL		-7692	-7828	*-9516*	*-9113*	*-8854*	*-10759*	*-11274*	*-10395*	*-11051*	*-11906*	*-12516*
Antigua and Barbuda / Antigua-Barbuda	IMP	G	105	112	207	222	225	...	...	...	...	...	...
	EXP	G	30	13	20	17	22	...	...	...	...	...	...
	BAL		-75	-99	-188	-205	-203	...	...	...	...	...	...
Aruba / Aruba	IMP	S	.	.	192	236	336	387	536	481	...	...	...
	EXP	S	.	.	24	26	31	23	28	26	...	...	...
	BAL		.	.	-168	-210	-306	-364	-508	-455	...	...	...
Bahamas / Bahamas	IMP	G	7546	3078	3289	3041	2264	3001	2920	1801	...	...	...
	EXP	G	5009	2728	2701	2728	2164	2786	2678	1517	...	...	...
	BAL		-2536	-349	-588	-313	-100	-215	-242	-284	...	...	...

See the end of the table for general information and footnotes.

Voir la fin du tableau pour la remarque générale et les notes

TABLEAU SPECIAL: A

Total Imports and Exports by Regions and Countries and Areas
Importations et Exportations Totales par Regions et Pays ou Zones

Imports C.I.F. - Exports F.O.B. - Balance / Importations C.I.F. - Exportations F.O.B. - Balance

(Continued / Suite)

Value in million U.S. dollars

Valeur en millions de dollars E.-U.

Country or Area / Pays ou Zone	IMP EXP BAL	System	1980	1985	1986	1987	1988	1989	1990	1991	1992	1993	1994
Barbados / Barbade	IMP	G	522	602	587	515	579	673	700	695	521	574	614
	EXP	G	226	347	275	156	176	187	214	205	190	181	181
	BAL		-295	-255	-313	-359	-403	-487	-486	-490	-331	-393	-433
Belize / Belize	IMP	G	150	128	122	143	181	216	211	256	274	281	260
	EXP	G	111	90	93	103	116	125	133	126	141	136	151
	BAL		-39	-38	-29	-40	-65	-91	-78	-130	-134	-144	-109
Bermuda / Bermudes	IMP	G	343	402	492	420	488	535	595	510	562	534	...
	EXP	G	37	23	65	29	31	50	60	55	85	...	...
	BAL		-306	-379	-427	-391	-457	-485	-535	-456	-477	...	...
Cayman Islands / Iles Caïmanes	IMP	S	103	147	161	195	231	259	288	267	...	...	...
	EXP	S	3	2	3	2	2	3	4	3	...	...	...
	BAL		-100	-145	-158	-193	-229	-256	-284	-264	...	...	...
Cuba / Cuba	IMP	S	6505	8758	11139	7584	7579	8124	6745	3690	2185	...	...
	EXP	S	5577	6531	7615	5402	5518	5392	4910	3550	2050	...	...
	BAL		-928	-2227	-3524	-2182	-2061	-2732	-1835	-140	-135	...	...
Dominica / Dominique	IMP	G	48	55	56	66	88	107	118	110	111	...	...
	EXP	G	10	28	43	48	54	45	55	54	56	...	...
	BAL		-38	-27	-12	-18	-33	-62	-63	-55	-55	...	...
Dominican Republic / Rép. dominicaine	IMP	G	1640	1487	1433	1830	1849	2258	2062	1988	2505	2443	2689
	EXP	G	962	735	718	711	890	924	735	658	566	555	565
	BAL		-678	-752	-715	-1119	-959	-1334	-1327	-1330	-1939	-1888	-2124
French Guiana / Guyane française	IMP	S	255	257	295	394	507	568	785	769	669	524	676
	EXP	S	25	38	32	54	51	57	93	70	96	95	136
	BAL		-230	-220	-262	-340	-456	-511	-692	-700	-574	-429	-539
Greenland / Groënland	IMP	G	327	296	360	507	519	399	447	408	457	...	...
	EXP	G	207	174	257	346	391	418	454	341	333	...	...
	BAL		-120	-122	-103	-161	-128	19	6	-67	-124	...	...
Grenada / Grenade	IMP	S	50	69	84	89	92	99	105	121	107	...	...
	EXP	S	17	23	31	32	33	28	27	23	20	...	...
	BAL		-33	-47	-52	-57	-59	-71	-79	-98	-87	...	...
Guadeloupe / Guadeloupe	IMP	S	728	620	762	1038	1243	1251	1650	1644	1509	1393	1539
	EXP	S	107	72	104	93	158	112	118	147	130	128	152
	BAL		-621	-548	-657	-945	-1085	-1139	-1531	-1497	-1380	-1265	-1387
Guyana / Guyana	IMP	S	396	248	240	...	...	258	311	307	443	436	...
	EXP	S	389	166	222	267	230	227	256	251	293	414	459
	BAL		-7	-82	-17	...	...	-30	-55	-55	-150	-22	...
Haiti / Haïti	IMP	G	354	442	360	399	344	291	279	307	293	264	309
	EXP	G	226	168	184	214	179	144	158	133	75	88	77
	BAL		-128	-273	-176	-186	-165	-147	-121	-174	-218	-177	-233
Jamaica / Jamaïque	IMP	G	1171	1111	971	1238	1455	1853	1924	1809	1675	2097	2165
	EXP	G	963	566	589	706	880	998	1158	1097	1048	1069	1193
	BAL		-209	-545	-383	-532	-574	-855	-765	-712	-627	-1028	-972
Martinique / Martinique	IMP	S	843	683	879	1119	1290	1317	1779	1695	1750	1556	1642
	EXP	S	117	162	216	194	196	200	278	216	247	191	218
	BAL		-727	-520	-663	-925	-1093	-1117	-1500	-1479	-1503	-1365	-1424
Montserrat / Montserrat	IMP	S	16	18	...	25	27	37	48	35	34	...	...
	EXP	S	1	3	...	4	2	1	1	1	2	...	...
	BAL		-15	-15	...	-22	-24	-36	-47	-34	-32	...	...

See the end of the table for general information and footnotes.

Voir la fin du tableau pour la remarque générale et les notes

Total Imports and Exports by Regions and Countries and Areas
Importations et Exportations Totales par Regions et Pays ou Zones

Imports C.I.F. - Exports F.O.B. - Balance / Importations C.I.F. - Exportations F.O.B. - Balance

(Continued / Suite)

Value in million U.S. dollars

Valeur en millions de dollars E.-U.

Country or Area / Pays ou Zone	IMP / EXP / BAL	system	1980	1985	1986	1987	1988	1989	1990	1991	1992	1993	1994
Neth. Antilles[9]	IMP	S	5676	2256	1112	1502	1403	1610	2141	2139	1868	1947	...
Antilles néerland[9]	EXP	S	5162	1679	924	1308	1134	1454	1790	1599	1559	1283	...
	BAL		-513	-577	-188	-194	-269	-156	-351	-540	-310	-664	...
Panama[10]	IMP	S	1449	1392	1284	1306	815	965	1489	1695	2019	2187	2404
Panama[10]	EXP	S	353	301	327	336	292	297	321	342	510	508	533
	BAL		-1095	-1091	-957	-970	-523	-668	-1168	-1353	-1509	-1680	-1872
St. Kitts-Nevis	IMP	S	45	51	63	79	93	102	111	...	...	...	...
St. Kitts-Nevis	EXP	S	24	20	25	28	27	29	28	...	...	...	...
	BAL		-21	-31	-38	-52	-66	-74	-83	...	...	...	...
St. Lucia	IMP	S	124	125	155	179	220	274	271	295	313	...	...
St. Lucie	EXP	S	58	57	87	80	116	109	127	110	123	...	...
	BAL		-65	-68	-68	-100	-105	-165	-144	-185	-190	...	...
St. Pierre-Mq.	IMP	S	42	...	...	...	62	84	86	81	76	70	71
St. Pierre-Mq.	EXP	S	6	...	...	...	13	30	26	30	25	1	12
	BAL		-36	...	...	...	-49	-53	-61	-51	-51	-69	-59
St. Vincent-G.	IMP	S	57	79	87	...	...	127	136	140	132	134	135
St. Vincent-G.	EXP	S	15	63	64	...	...	75	83	67	78	58	43
	BAL		-42	-16	-23	...	...	-53	-53	-72	-54	-77	-91
Suriname	IMP	S	518	338	327	294	...	...	472	...	...	...	...
Suriname	EXP	S	501	329	335	306	...	...	472	...	...	...	...
	BAL		-17	-9	7	12	...	...	0	...	...	...	...
Trinidad and Tobago	IMP	S	3178	1538	1350	1219	1128	1221	1262	1663	1429	1448	1133
Trinité-et-Tobago	EXP	S	4077	2147	1386	1462	1413	1578	2080	1985	1850	1612	1872
	BAL		899	609	36	244	285	357	819	322	421	163	739
Devlpd. Econ.: Europe[11]	IMP		898433	769781	916521	1121819	***1262386***	***1382225***	***1654941***	***1662922***	***1733135***	***1481331***	***1671873***
Eco. dévlpés.: Europe[11]	EXP		800863	755136	926898	1114770	***1237350***	***1336772***	***1605727***	***1575537***	***1668578***	***1521092***	***1734205***
	BAL		-97570	-14645	10377	-7049	***-25036***	***-45453***	***-49214***	***-87386***	***-64557***	***39761***	***62332***
EEC[12]	IMP		766307	656090	774650	949128	1071426	1180550	1417826	1444015	1516051	1287517	***1446098***
CEE[12]	EXP		685644	642232	789854	950062	1054476	1143803	1366071	1357206	1444446	1314003	***1493875***
	BAL		-80664	-13858	15204	934	-16950	-36747	-51755	-86809	-71605	26486	***47778***
Belgium/Luxembourg	IMP	S	71863	56211	68729	83550	92453	98596	120325	121060	125153	112255	125616
Belgique/Luxembrg	EXP	S	64653	53762	68960	83308	92149	100095	118328	118355	123564	119530	137271
	BAL		-7209	-2449	231	-242	-304	1499	-1996	-2705	-1589	7275	11655
Denmark[13]	IMP	S	19345	18072	22822	25429	25944	26696	32230	32411	35187	30546	34877
Danemark[13]	EXP	S	16733	16941	21214	25598	27657	28113	35135	36011	41069	37171	41422
	BAL		-2612	-1131	-1608	169	1712	1417	2905	3600	5883	6625	6545
France[14]	IMP	S	134896	108379	129435	158499	177288	190963	233207	230832	238875	200762	230580
France[14]	EXP	S	116035	101709	124863	148402	167813	173073	210169	213441	231913	206240	236047
	BAL		-18861	-6669	-4572	-10096	-9475	-17890	-23038	-17392	-6962	5477	5467
Germany[12,15]	IMP	S	188001	158549	190852	228202	250443	293092	356842	389206	408305	329670	372602
Allemagne[12,15]	EXP	S	192930	184009	243303	294045	323277	365029	422041	402845	430272	365368	414729
	BAL		4929	25460	52451	65844	72834	71937	65200	13639	21967	35698	42126
Greece	IMP	S	10550	10140	11353	13164	12324	16149	19780	21582	23232	22012	...
Grèce	EXP	S	5153	4543	5649	6531	5430	7544	8106	8675	9839	8777	...
	BAL		-5397	-5598	-5704	-6633	-6894	-8605	-11674	-12907	-13393	-13235	...
Ireland	IMP	G	11156	10047	11565	13624	15589	17431	20679	20761	22501	21637	25476
Irlande	EXP	G	8401	10383	12575	15957	18779	20713	23777	24264	28357	28817	34333
	BAL		-2756	336	1010	2333	3190	3282	3098	3502	5856	7180	8858

See the end of the table for general information and footnotes.

Voir la fin du tableau pour la remarque générale et les notes

Total Imports and Exports by Regions and Countries and Areas
Importations et Exportations Totales par Regions et Pays ou Zones

Imports C.I.F. - Exports F.O.B. - Balance / Importations C.I.F. - Exportations F.O.B. - Balance

(Continued / Suite)

Value in million U.S. dollars | Valeur en millions de dollars E.-U.

Country or Area / Pays ou Zone	IMP EXP BAL	system	1980	1985	1986	1987	1988	1989	1990	1991	1992	1993	1994
Italy / Italie	IMP	S	100753	87718	99404	125692	138582	153010	181983	182752	188521	147178	167292
	EXP	S	78114	76741	97631	116413	127886	140623	170385	169536	178164	167772	189263
	BAL		-22640	-10977	-1773	-9279	-10696	-12387	-11598	-13216	-10357	20594	21971
Netherlands / Pays-Bas	IMP	S	76618	65382	75690	91495	99522	104467	126195	127252	134412	121568	130512
	EXP	S	73952	68418	80512	93096	103586	108285	131783	133684	139967	131156	145825
	BAL		-2666	3037	4822	1600	4064	3818	5588	6432	5554	9588	15314
Portugal / Portugal	IMP	S	9312	7655	9648	13966	17941	19205	25358	26405	30348	24320	26665
	EXP	S	4635	5684	7242	9321	10990	12801	16419	16332	18302	15370	17530
	BAL		-4677	-1971	-2407	-4644	-6951	-6404	-8940	-10072	-12046	-8950	-9135
Spain / Espagne	IMP	S	34084	29965	35086	49119	60533	70957	87722	93330	99765	81876	92490
	EXP	S	20719	24249	27231	34199	40340	43463	55646	60197	64342	62872	73285
	BAL		-13366	-5716	-7855	-14920	-20193	-27493	-32075	-33133	-35422	-19004	-19205
United Kingdom[14] / Royaume-Uni[14]	IMP	G	115558	109593	126367	154407	189719	199220	224550	209864	221638	206321	226172
	EXP	G	110149	101414	106975	131210	145482	153299	185326	185306	190542	181559	204009
	BAL		-5409	-8179	-19392	-23197	-44237	-45921	-39224	-24557	-31096	-24761	-22163
EFTA / AELE	IMP		127800	109958	137357	167148	185069	195818	229541	216361	214282	191322	222990
	EXP		111650	109581	132810	159586	177663	187396	224729	216655	222178	205437	238475
	BAL		-16151	-377	-4547	-7561	-7406	-8423	-4813	294	7896	14115	15485
Austria / Autriche	IMP	S	24449	20996	26852	32683	36565	38935	49092	50804	54122	48616	55340
	EXP	S	17493	17247	22529	27175	31062	32485	41138	41126	44377	40200	45031
	BAL		-6957	-3749	-4323	-5508	-5503	-6450	-7954	-9679	-9746	-8416	-10309
Finland / Finlande	IMP	G	15641	13233	15333	18922	21843	24613	27005	21717	20747	18069	23254
	EXP	G	14153	13617	16336	19560	22151	23270	26650	23103	23529	23501	29690
	BAL		-1488	383	1003	638	308	-1343	-355	1387	2782	5432	6436
Iceland / Islande	IMP	S	999	904	1115	1590	1598	1402	1679	1761	1684	1342	1472
	EXP	S	918	816	1099	1374	1424	1386	1591	1549	1528	1400	1623
	BAL		-81	-88	-17	-216	-174	-15	-88	-212	-156	59	151
Norway / Norvège	IMP	G	16928	15560	20307	22641	23223	23680	27219	25576	25916	23892	27280
	EXP	G	18545	19989	18095	21493	22425	27112	34045	34116	35193	31778	34660
	BAL		1617	4429	-2211	-1148	-798	3431	6826	8540	9277	7885	7380
Sweden / Suède	IMP	G	33441	28553	32697	40709	45469	48981	54855	50001	50050	42680	51630
	EXP	G	30908	30467	37267	44509	49890	51607	57512	55229	56149	49864	61299
	BAL		-2533	1913	4571	3800	4421	2626	2656	5227	6099	7184	9669
Switzerland / Suisse	IMP	S	36341	30711	41053	50602	56372	58207	69691	66502	61763	56722	64014
	EXP	S	29632	27446	37484	45474	50712	51536	63793	61532	61403	58694	66172
	BAL		-6709	-3266	-3570	-5128	-5660	-6671	-5898	-4970	-360	1972	2158
Other Developed Europe / A. pays d'Eur. dévlpés	IMP		1253	1115	1351	1832	*2024*	*2002*	*2445*	*2547*	*2801*	*2492*	*2786*
	EXP		659	603	774	983	*1098*	*1223*	*1549*	*1677*	*1954*	*1653*	*1855*
	BAL		-594	-513	-577	-850	*-926*	*-780*	*-896*	*-870*	*-847*	*-840*	*-931*
Faeroe Islands / Iles Féroé	IMP	G	219	248	336	513	478	346	338	303	334	219	...
	EXP	G	188	179	249	345	348	346	418	435	439	327	...
	BAL		-32	-69	-86	-169	-130	0	80	132	105	108	...
Gibraltar / Gibraltar	IMP	G	147	147	164	231	...	...	...	...	...	...	...
	EXP	G	40	62	65	85	...	...	...	...	...	...	...
	BAL		-107	-85	-99	-146	...	...	...	...	...	...	...
Malta / Malte	IMP	G	938	759	887	1140	1353	1480	1961	2114	2349	2166	2406
	EXP	G	483	400	497	605	714	844	1130	1252	1543	1349	1560
	BAL		-455	-359	-391	-535	-639	-636	-831	-862	-806	-817	-846

See the end of the table for general information and footnotes. | Voir la fin du tableau pour la remarque générale et les notes

SPECIAL TABLE: A | **TABLEAU SPECIAL: A**

Total Imports and Exports by Regions and Countries and Areas
Importations et Exportations Totales par Regions et Pays ou Zones

Imports C.I.F. - Exports F.O.B. - Balance / Importations C.I.F. - Exportations F.O.B. - Balance

(Continued / Suite)

Value in million U.S. dollars | Valeur en millions de dollars E.-U.

Country or Area / Pays ou Zone	IMP / EXP / BAL	System	1980	1985	1986	1987	1988	1989	1990	1991	1992	1993	1994
Devlpg. Econ.:[38] Europe[16]	IMP		15064	12164	11750	12603	13154	14802	18890	11804	*15816*	*14107*	*15066*
Eco. evdd. : Europe[16]	EXP		8978	10642	10298	11425	12597	13363	14312	9548	*13819*	*11713*	*12364*
	BAL		-6086	-1522	-1452	-1178	-557	-1438	-4578	-2256	*-1998*	*-2394*	*-2702*
Croatia	IMP	G	.	.	.	.	.	.	.	.	4463	4667	5230
Croatie	EXP	G	.	.	.	.	.	.	.	.	4599	3903	4260
	BAL		.	.	.	.	.	.	.	.	136	-764	-970
Slovenia	IMP	G	.	.	.	.	.	.	.	.	...	6443	7247
Slovénie	EXP	G	.	.	.	.	.	.	.	.	...	6007	6819
	BAL		.	.	.	.	.	.	.	.	...	-436	-427
TFYR Macedonia	IMP	G	.	.	.	.	.	.	.	.	...	1199	...
L'ex-RY Macédoine	EXP	G	.	.	.	.	.	.	.	.	...	1055	...
	BAL		.	.	.	.	.	.	.	.	...	-144	...
Yugoslavia[17]	IMP	S	15064	12164	11750	12603	13154	14802	18890	11804	...	...	...
Yougoslavie[17]	EXP	S	8978	10642	10298	11425	12597	13363	14312	9548	...	...	...
	BAL		-6086	-1522	-1452	-1178	-557	-1438	-4578	-2256	...	...	...
Eastern Europe	IMP		84399	75650	84872	88803	90205	74628	*66244*	44725	51254	54242	*60958*
Europe de l'Est	EXP		78705	80301	86263	92815	98328	81467	*68276*	43973	44543	44462	*50471*
	BAL		-5694	4651	1391	4012	8123	6839	*2033*	-752	-6711	-9780	*-10487*
Bulgaria[7]	IMP	G	9650	13656	15249	16211	16582	14881	12893	3017	5228	4315	4316
Bulgarie[7]	EXP	G	10372	13348	14192	15905	17223	16013	13347	3835	4268	3582	4157
	BAL		722	-308	-1057	-306	640	1132	454	818	-960	-732	-159
Czech Rep[7]	IMP	G	.	.	.	.	.	.	.	.	.	12559	14789
Rép. tchèque[7]	EXP	G	.	.	.	.	.	.	.	.	.	13212	14318
	BAL		.	.	.	.	.	.	.	.	.	653	-471
Fm Czechoslovakia[7,18]	IMP	G	15148	11152	13358	14883	14593	14277	13106	10014	12530	.	.
Tchécsl. (anc.)[7,18]	EXP	G	14891	11510	13227	14723	14894	14440	11882	10878	11656	.	.
	BAL		-257	358	-132	-160	302	162	-1224	863	-874	.	.
Fm German D.R.[7,19]	IMP	G	19082	23433	27414	28786	29647	17778	...	.	.	.	.
Allem R.D., anc.[7,19]	EXP	G	17312	25268	27729	29871	30672	17334	...	.	.	.	.
	BAL		-1770	1835	315	1084	1026	-444	...	.	.	.	.
Hungary	IMP	G	9235	7919	9292	9450	9136	8803	8764	11532	11122	12520	...
Hongrie	EXP	G	8677	8254	8875	9204	9739	9584	9707	10301	10680	8604	...
	BAL		-558	335	-417	-246	603	780	943	-1231	-442	-3916	...
Poland[7]	IMP	G	19089	10799	11208	10844	12240	10085	9528	14261	15913	18834	21383
Pologne[7]	EXP	G	16997	11488	12074	12205	13956	13155	14322	14460	13187	14143	17240
	BAL		-2092	689	866	1361	1716	3070	4794	199	-2726	-4691	-4143
Romania[7]	IMP	S	11855	8401	8082	8311	7641	8436	9115	5600	6147	5683	6291
Roumanie[7]	EXP	S	10045	10173	9761	10491	11391	10486	5870	4124	4372	4536	5997
	BAL		-1810	1772	1679	2179	3750	2050	-3244	-1477	-1775	-1147	-294
Slovakia	IMP	G	.	.	.	.	.	.	.	.	.	6245	6554
Slovaquie	EXP	G	.	.	.	.	.	.	.	.	.	5394	6583
	BAL		.	.	.	.	.	.	.	.	.	-851	30
Former USSR[7,20]	IMP	G	68522	83140	88871	96061	107229	114567	120651	43458	.	.	.
Ancienne URSS[7,20]	EXP	G	76449	87281	97247	107966	110559	109173	104177	46274	.	.	.
	BAL		7927	4141	8375	11905	3330	-5395	-16474	2816	.	.	.
Former USSR-Europe[21]	IMP		.	.	.	.	.	.	.	.	41291	32696	*52925*
Ancienne URSS - Europe[21]	EXP		.	.	.	.	.	.	.	.	47771	51014	*76902*
	BAL		.	.	.	.	.	.	.	.	6480	18318	*23977*

See the end of the table for general information and footnotes. | Voir la fin du tableau pour la remarque générale et les notes

Total Imports and Exports by Regions and Countries and Areas
Importations et Exportations Totales par Regions et Pays ou Zones

Imports C.I.F. - Exports F.O.B. - Balance / Importations C.I.F. - Exportations F.O.B. - Balance

(Continued / Suite)

Value in million U.S. dollars — Valeur en millions de dollars E.-U.

Country or Area / Pays ou Zone	IMP / EXP / BAL	System	1980	1985	1986	1987	1988	1989	1990	1991	1992	1993	1994
Belarus	IMP	G	.	.	.	.	.	.	.	.	1061	747	...
Bélarus	EXP	G	.	.	.	.	.	.	.	.	751	715	...
	BAL		.	.	.	.	.	.	.	.	-310	-32	...
Estonia	IMP	G	.	.	.	.	.	.	.	.	161	927	1672
Estonie	EXP	G	.	.	.	.	.	.	.	.	148	832	1308
	BAL		.	.	.	.	.	.	.	.	-12	-94	-363
Latvia	IMP	G	.	.	.	.	.	.	.	.	843	1088	1241
Lettonie	EXP	G	.	.	.	.	.	.	.	.	896	1179	990
	BAL		.	.	.	.	.	.	.	.	52	91	-252
Lithuania	IMP	G	.	.	.	.	.	.	.	.	125	515	...
Lituanie	EXP	G	.	.	.	.	.	.	.	.	308	700	...
	BAL		.	.	.	.	.	.	.	.	183	185	...
Rep. Moldova	IMP	G	.	.	.	.	.	.	.	.	164	181	...
Rép. de Moldova	EXP	G	.	.	.	.	.	.	.	.	119	174	...
	BAL		.	.	.	.	.	.	.	.	-45	-7	...
Russian Federation	IMP	G	.	.	.	.	.	.	.	.	36984	26807	38650
Féd. de Russie	EXP	G	.	.	.	.	.	.	.	.	42376	44297	63243
	BAL		.	.	.	.	.	.	.	.	5392	17491	24593
Ukraine	IMP	G	.	.	.	.	.	.	.	.	1953	2431	9989
Ukraine	EXP	G	.	.	.	.	.	.	.	.	3173	3116	9708
	BAL		.	.	.	.	.	.	.	.	1220	685	-281
Devlpd. Econ.: Afr/S.Afr.[7,22,23]	IMP	G	18930	10921	12372	14623	17612	17664	17665	17837	18714	19090	22478
Eco. dévlpés.: Afr/A.S.[7,22,23]	EXP	G	24770	15814	17777	20553	20755	21318	22834	22288	22416	23339	24070
	BAL		5840	4893	5405	5930	3144	3655	5169	4451	3702	4249	1592
Devlpg. Econ.: Africa	IMP		74266	*52399*	*55795*	*55085*	*60181*	*61798*	*71325*	*68223*	*73091*	*71989*	*75685*
Eco. evdd.[38]: Afrique	EXP		90337	*59909*	*46701*	*51259*	*50241*	*57834*	*76387*	*71179*	*68785*	*64191*	*70249*
	BAL		16071	*7510*	*-9095*	*-3826*	*-9940*	*-3964*	*5061*	*2956*	*-4305*	*-7798*	*-5436*
North Africa	IMP		31218	26628	29596	27376	31294	*32719*	*38393*	*33245*	*36281*	*36691*	*40035*
Afrique du Nord	EXP		43562	28398	22153	24650	22878	27014	*37929*	*35330*	*32697*	*30934*	*34847*
	BAL		12344	1771	-7443	-2727	-8416	*-5704*	*-464*	*2085*	*-3583*	*-5756*	*-5189*
Algeria	IMP	S	10544	9841	9234	7028	7399	9209	10122	7538	8648	...	...
Algérie	EXP	S	13715	10149	7831	8564	7707	9454	13306	12645	11137	...	...
	BAL		3172	307	-1404	1537	308	245	3184	5107	2489	...	...
Egypt[24]	IMP	S	4860	5495	8680	7596	8657	7434	9202	7754	8357	8213	10224
Egypte[24]	EXP	S	3046	1838	2214	2037	2120	2565	2582	3618	3072	2252	3477
	BAL		-1814	-3657	-6466	-5559	-6537	-4870	-6620	-4135	-5286	-5962	-6746
Libyan Arab Jamah.	IMP	G	6777	4101	4193	4722	5878	5049	5599	5356	...	...	...
J. arabe libyenne	EXP	G	21910	12314	7748	8765	6684	8239	13877	11213	...	...	...
	BAL		15133	8213	3556	4042	806	3190	8278	5857	...	...	...
Morocco	IMP	S	4258	3850	3803	4229	4773	5493	6925	6894	7356	7162	7211
Maroc	EXP	S	2439	2165	2433	2807	3626	3337	4265	4285	3977	3424	4012
	BAL		-1819	-1685	-1370	-1422	-1147	-2156	-2660	-2609	-3379	-3738	-3199
Sudan[25]	IMP	G	1576	757	961	929	1060	...	...	...	...	...	...
Soudan[25]	EXP	G	543	367	333	504	509	671	...	...	...	...	...
	BAL		-1034	-389	-628	-425	-551	...	...	...	...	...	...
Tunisia	IMP	G	3525	2757	2891	3039	3689	4387	5513	5190	6415	6215	6484
Tunisie	EXP	G	2231	1738	1760	2139	2395	2930	3527	3714	4040	3804	4584
	BAL		-1294	-1019	-1131	-900	-1294	-1458	-1985	-1476	-2376	-2411	-1900

See the end of the table for general information and footnotes. — Voir la fin du tableau pour la remarque générale et les notes

Total Imports and Exports by Regions and Countries and Areas
Importations et Exportations Totales par Regions et Pays ou Zones

Imports C.I.F. - Exports F.O.B. - Balance / Importations C.I.F. - Exportations F.O.B. - Balance

(Continued / Suite)

Value in million U.S. dollars — Valeur en millions de dollars E.-U.

Country or Area / Pays ou Zone	IMP / EXP / BAL	System	1980	1985	1986	1987	1988	1989	1990	1991	1992	1993	1994
Other Africa	IMP		43047	25771	26199	27709	28887	29079	32933	34978	36810	35299	35650
Autres pays d'Afrique	EXP		46775	31511	24547	26609	27363	30820	38458	35850	36089	33257	35403
	BAL		3727	5739	-1652	-1099	-1524	1741	5525	872	-721	-2042	-247
CEUCA[26,27]	IMP		2936	2718	3334	3188	2768	2696	2947	2709	2900	2740	2138
UDEAC[26,27]	EXP		4583	3853	2896	2740	3123	4251	5572	5262	5442	5282	4851
	BAL		1647	1136	-438	-449	355	1555	2625	2553	2542	2543	2713
Cameroon[27]	IMP	S	1602	1152	1704	1723	1271	1261	1400	1173	1163	1106	...
Cameroun[27]	EXP	S	1384	722	782	806	924	1273	2002	1834	1840	1901	...
	BAL		-218	-429	-922	-918	-348	12	602	661	678	795	...
Cent. Afr. Rep.[27]	IMP	S	81	113	167	204	141	150	154	179	165	145	...
Rép. centrafr.[27]	EXP	S	115	92	66	130	66	134	120	126	124	130	...
	BAL		35	-21	-101	-74	-75	-16	-34	-53	-42	-15	...
Congo[27]	IMP	S	580	598	597	529	564	517	617	473	686	583	...
Congo[27]	EXP	S	911	1087	777	517	937	1245	975	1029	1183	1069	...
	BAL		331	489	180	-12	373	728	358	556	497	487	...
Gabon[27]	IMP	S	674	855	866	732	791	767	775	884	886	906	...
Gabon[27]	EXP	S	2173	1952	1271	1286	1195	1599	2474	2273	2295	2182	...
	BAL		1499	1097	404	555	404	831	1699	1389	1409	1276	...
ECOWAS[28]	IMP		24351	12498	11158	11481	11394	11249	12687	16740	17634	15928	15361
CEDEAO[28]	EXP		32576	19429	12897	14329	13436	15084	20224	19055	19178	17059	19130
	BAL		8225	6931	1739	2847	2042	3835	7537	2316	1544	1131	3769
Benin	IMP	S	331	343	386	348	326	207	...	...	...	...	...
Bénin	EXP	S	63	152	104	114	71	97	...	...	...	...	...
	BAL		-268	-191	-282	-234	-255	-110	...	...	...	...	...
Burkina Faso	IMP	S	358	333	405	434	454	391	540	536	...	...	...
Burkina Faso	EXP	S	90	70	83	155	142	95	151	105	...	...	...
	BAL		-268	-263	-322	-279	-312	-297	-389	-431	...	...	...
Cape Verde	IMP	S	68	84	107	100	106	112	136	147	180	154	...
Cap-Vert	EXP	S	4	6	4	8	3	7	6	6	5	4	...
	BAL		-64	-78	-103	-92	-103	-105	-130	-140	-175	-150	...
Cote d'Ivoire	IMP	G	2992	1750	2055	2242	2100	2185	2098	...	...	...	...
Côte d'Ivoire	EXP	G	3136	2946	3355	3110	2792	2931	3072	2686	2840	...	...
	BAL		144	1196	1300	868	691	746	975	...	...	...	...
Gambia	IMP	G	165	93	105	127	137	161	200	222	232	...	208
Gambie	EXP	G	31	43	35	40	58	27	40	42	66	...	35
	BAL		-134	-50	-70	-87	-79	-134	-160	-180	-166	...	-173
Ghana	IMP	G	1129	866	1046	1166	904	1277	...	...	2175	...	...
Ghana	EXP	G	1257	623	876	957	1008	1020	...	...	1252	...	...
	BAL		129	-243	-170	-209	104	-257	...	...	-923	...	...
Guinea-Bissau	IMP	S	55	...	...	...	65	79	86	76	181	61	63
Guinée-Bissau	EXP	S	11	...	...	...	16	14	19	20	12	16	33
	BAL		-44	...	...	...	-49	-64	-67	-55	-168	-45	-30
Liberia	IMP	S	535	284	259	308	272	...	...	...	...	...	...
Libéria	EXP	S	600	436	408	382	396	...	...	...	...	...	...
	BAL		66	151	149	75	124	...	...	...	...	...	...
Mali	IMP	S	440	300	444	374	504	340	...	...	...	...	...
Mali	EXP	S	205	124	212	179	214	247	...	...	...	...	...
	BAL		-235	-176	-232	-195	-290	-93	...	...	...	...	...

See the end of the table for general information and footnotes. — Voir la fin du tableau pour la remarque générale et les notes

Total Imports and Exports by Regions and Countries and Areas
Importations et Exportations Totales par Regions et Pays ou Zones

Imports C.I.F. - Exports F.O.B. - Balance / Importations C.I.F. - Exportations F.O.B. - Balance

(Continued / Suite)

Value in million U.S. dollars — Valeur en millions de dollars E.-U.

Country or Area / Pays ou Zone	IMP EXP BAL	System	1980	1985	1986	1987	1988	1989	1990	1991	1992	1993	1994
Mauritania / Mauritanie	IMP	S	286	233	221	235	240	222	...	...	...	...	...
	EXP	S	194	374	349	428	354	437	...	...	...	...	...
	BAL		-92	140	128	193	115	215	...	...	...	...	...
Niger / Niger	IMP	S	594	369	368	311	387	363	389	355	...	...	...
	EXP	S	566	259	317	312	289	244	283	312	...	...	...
	BAL		-28	-110	-52	2	-98	-119	-106	-44	...	...	...
Nigeria / Nigéria	IMP	G	15025	6205	4029	3918	3889	3419	4318	9098	8359	7508	...
	EXP	G	24999	13113	5899	7383	6875	8138	12912	12255	11787	9910	...
	BAL		9974	6908	1870	3464	2986	4719	8593	3158	3428	2402	...
Senegal / Sénégal	IMP	S	1052	812	962	1023	1080	1221	1314	1099	1172	...	...
	EXP	S	477	554	625	606	591	693	762	652	683	...	...
	BAL		-575	-258	-336	-417	-488	-528	-552	-447	-489	...	...
Sierra Leone / Sierra Leone	IMP	G	426	154	132	137	156	182	155	163	156	147	150
	EXP	G	207	130	142	129	106	138	138	145	149	118	116
	BAL		-220	-24	10	-8	-49	-44	-17	-17	-6	-29	-34
Togo / Togo	IMP	S	551	288	312	424	487	472	581	444	395	179	222
	EXP	S	337	190	204	244	242	245	268	253	275	136	162
	BAL		-213	-98	-108	-180	-245	-227	-313	-191	-120	-43	-60
Rest of Africa / Afrique NDA	IMP		15760	10556	11707	13039	*14726*	*15135*	*17299*	*15530*	*16277*	*16632*	*18150*
	EXP		9616	8228	8754	9541	*10805*	*11485*	*12662*	*11533*	*11469*	*10916*	*11421*
	BAL		-6144	-2327	-2953	-3498	*-3921*	*-3649*	*-4637*	*-3997*	*-4808*	*-5716*	*-6729*
Angola / Angola	IMP	S	1341	671	619	443	989	1140	...	...	...	...	...
	EXP	S	1902	2224	1319	2147	2494	2989	3910	3413	3714	...	...
	BAL		561	1553	700	1704	1506	1849	...	...	...	...	...
Burundi / Burundi	IMP	S	168	189	202	206	206	188	235	255	221	196	224
	EXP	S	65	112	154	90	133	78	75	91	73	62	106
	BAL		-103	-76	-49	-116	-73	-110	-161	-164	-148	-134	-117
Chad / Tchad	IMP	S	74	166	212	226	252	235	259	297	243	228	...
	EXP	S	71	62	99	109	159	155	194	194	182	151	...
	BAL		-3	-104	-113	-116	-93	-80	-66	-103	-61	-77	...
Comoros / Comores	IMP	S	30	37	37	52	53	43	52	58	69	...	...
	EXP	S	10	16	20	12	21	18	18	25	22	...	...
	BAL		-21	-21	-17	-40	-31	-25	-34	-33	-46	...	...
Djibouti / Djibouti	IMP	G	213	201	184	205	201	196	215	214	219	...	...
	EXP	G	13	14	20	28	23	25	25	17	16	...	...
	BAL		-201	-187	-164	-177	-178	-172	-190	-197	-203	...	...
Equatorial Guinea / Guinée équatoriale	IMP	S	26	20	52	58	61	55	61	117	92	60	...
	EXP	S	14	17	35	42	49	41	62	83	41	62	...
	BAL		-13	-3	-17	-16	-12	-14	1	-34	-51	3	...
Ethiopia / Ethiopie	IMP	G	721	989	1101	1101	1085	953	1076	472	707	787	1026
	EXP	G	425	334	464	370	421	452	294	189	169	199	343
	BAL		-297	-654	-636	-731	-664	-501	-782	-283	-539	-588	-682
Kenya / Kenya	IMP	G	2119	1436	1613	1755	1975	2148	2124	1799	1828	1711	2120
	EXP	G	1241	958	1200	961	1071	970	1031	1107	1362	1374	1522
	BAL		-878	-479	-414	-795	-903	-1177	-1093	-692	-467	-337	-598
Madagascar / Madagascar	IMP	S	600	402	353	302	383	372	651	435	448	468	434
	EXP	S	402	274	315	333	274	321	319	305	278	261	261
	BAL		-198	-128	-38	31	-109	-50	-332	-130	-170	-207	-173

See the end of the table for general information and footnotes. — Voir la fin du tableau pour la remarque générale et les notes

Total Imports and Exports by Regions and Countries and Areas
Importations et Exportations Totales par Regions et Pays ou Zones

Imports C.I.F. - Exports F.O.B. - Balance / Importations C.I.F. - Exportations F.O.B. - Balance

(Continued / Suite)

Value in million U.S. dollars | Valeur en millions de dollars E.-U.

Country or Area / Pays ou Zone	IMP / EXP / BAL	System	1980	1985	1986	1987	1988	1989	1990	1991	1992	1993	1994
Malawi	IMP	G	439	295	258	295	420	507	575	703	735	545	...
Malawi	EXP	G	295	248	245	277	288	267	417	469	396	319	...
	BAL		-144	-47	-13	-19	-132	-240	-159	-234	-339	-226	...
Mauritius	IMP	G	619	529	684	1013	1289	1326	1618	1558	1624	1919	1897
Maurice	EXP	G	431	440	676	880	997	987	1194	1194	1301	1464	1326
	BAL		-189	-88	-8	-133	-292	-339	-424	-364	-324	-455	-571
Mozambique	IMP	S	800	424	543	642	736	808	878	899	855	955	...
Mozambique	EXP	S	281	77	79	97	103	105	126	162	139	132	...
	BAL		-519	-347	-464	-545	-633	-703	-752	-737	-716	-823	...
Rwanda	IMP	G	243	294	352	357	369	333	290	306	288	...	...
Rwanda	EXP	G	76	98	118	130	101	121	131	93	68	...	...
	BAL		-167	-196	-234	-226	-268	-212	-159	-213	-220	...	...
Réunion	IMP	S	888	841	1137	1464	1662	1732	2160	2129	2315	2057	2365
Réunion	EXP	S	131	97	135	169	158	161	190	150	213	168	171
	BAL		-757	-743	-1003	-1296	-1503	-1571	-1971	-1980	-2102	-1889	-2194
Seychelles	IMP	G	99	99	105	114	159	165	187	172	191	241	203
Seychelles	EXP	G	21	28	18	22	32	34	57	49	48	52	51
	BAL		-78	-71	-87	-92	-127	-131	-130	-123	-144	-189	-152
Somalia	IMP	S	348	112	284	132	...	...	...	...	...	...	...
Somalie	EXP	S	133	91	89	104	...	...	...	...	...	...	...
	BAL		-215	-21	-196	-29	...	...	...	...	...	...	...
U. R. of Tanzania	IMP	G	1240	862	892	904	805	998	1363	1553	1533	1546	1501
R. U. de Tanzanie	EXP	G	580	245	329	282	269	364	331	342	423	455	520
	BAL		-660	-617	-563	-622	-536	-634	-1033	-1211	-1110	-1091	-981
Uganda	IMP	G	293	298	307	848	887	390	293	196	515	...	879
Ouganda	EXP	G	345	387	436	319	274	250	152	200	143	179	410
	BAL		52	89	129	-529	-613	-140	-141	4	-372	...	-469
Zaire	IMP	S	278	792	875	756	763	850	888	711	420	372	382
Zaïre	EXP	S	544	950	1100	975	1120	1254	999	830	427	369	419
	BAL		266	158	225	218	358	404	111	119	7	-4	37
Zambia[6]	IMP	G	1089	714	603	739	839	779	1243	801	908	...	...
Zambie[6]	EXP	G	1307	547	704	873	1178	1344	1414	1128	1095	...	...
	BAL		218	-166	101	133	339	565	171	327	187	...	...
Zimbabwe	IMP	G	1451	1031	1133	1205	1304	1627	1850	2037	2213	...	...
Zimbabwe	EXP	G	1411	1110	1301	1425	1646	1546	1729	1530	1438	...	...
	BAL		-40	79	168	220	342	-81	-121	-506	-775	...	...
Developed economies: Asia	IMP		148871	138926	136419	163233	199071	220304	247819	251145	248312	257951	292442
Eco. développées: Asie	EXP		134014	181736	215985	237615	269743	280922	294829	322281	347824	370787	406909
	BAL		-14857	42811	79565	74382	70671	60618	47010	71136	99512	112836	114467
Israel[29,30]	IMP	S	9682	10136	10813	14348	15018	14347	16790	18658	20253	22624	24242
Israël[29,30]	EXP	S	5538	6260	7154	8454	8198	10738	11576	11921	13119	14825	16884
	BAL		-4144	-3876	-3659	-5894	-6820	-3609	-5214	-6737	-7134	-7799	-7358
Japan	IMP	G	140522	130515	127588	151075	187411	209755	235423	237289	233265	241652	275548
Japon	EXP	G	129810	177202	210813	231351	264903	273983	287648	315163	339911	362286	397373
	BAL		-10712	46687	83225	80276	77492	64227	52225	77873	106646	120635	121825
Devlpg. Econ.: Asia[31]	IMP		273382	307120	303320	358117	*446638*	*500651*	*565518*	*640518*	*742619*	*821972*	*933004*
Eco. evdd.[38]: Asie[31]	EXP		371636	*306300*	*303895*	*382336*	*451080*	*506212*	*572355*	*626260*	*710628*	*769286*	*907905*
	BAL		98254	*-820*	*575*	*24218*	*4443*	*5562*	*6837*	*-14258*	*-31991*	*-52686*	*-25099*

See the end of the table for general information and footnotes. | Voir la fin du tableau pour la remarque générale et les notes

Total Imports and Exports by Regions and Countries and Areas
Importations et Exportations Totales par Regions et Pays ou Zones

Imports C.I.F. - Exports F.O.B. - Balance / Importations C.I.F. - Exportations F.O.B. - Balance

(Continued / Suite)

Value in million U.S. dollars — Valeur en millions de dollars E.-U.

Country or Area / Pays ou Zone	IMP EXP BAL	System	1980	1985	1986	1987	1988	1989	1990	1991	1992	1993	1994
Asia Middle East	IMP		94828	86376	73815	75507	*81699*	*87474*	*98426*	*106980*	*135648*	*140520*	*136122*
Moyen-Orient d'Asie	EXP		208703	*97688*	*75425*	*87019*	*88253*	*100882*	*120055*	*110799*	*122485*	*120124*	*135408*
	BAL		113875	*11312*	*1610*	*11512*	*6553*	*13409*	*21628*	*3820*	*-13163*	*-20396*	*-714*
Non Petroleum Export[32]	IMP		...	...	...	...	...	...	...	...	...	...	...
Petrole N. Compris[32]	EXP		11919	*18780*	*26778*	*25313*	*30205*	*28260*	*59504*	*33500*	*37263*	*29513*	*39140*
	BAL		...	...	...	...	...	...	...	...	...	...	...
Bahrain	IMP	G	3483	3107	2405	2714	2593	3134	3712	4115	4263	3858	3737
Bahreïn	EXP	G	3594	2897	2199	2430	2411	2831	3761	3513	3465	3710	3454
	BAL		111	-210	-206	-284	-182	-302	49	-602	-798	-148	-282
Cyprus	IMP	G	1202	1247	1274	1484	1857	2285	2569	2632	3301	2534	3013
Chypre	EXP	G	533	476	504	621	711	795	948	958	1007	882	960
	BAL		-669	-771	-771	-863	-1146	-1490	-1620	-1674	-2295	-1652	-2053
Iran, Islm. rep. of[33]	IMP	S	12246	11639	9120	9219	8279	...	...	...	30662	...	...
Iran, Rp. Islm d'[33]	EXP	S	14139	13449	6639	...	...	...	...	...	...	...	...
	BAL		1893	1811	-2480	...	...	...	...	...	...	...	...
Iraq	IMP	S	8707	7619	6360	3854	5960	6956	4834	...	...	...	...
Iraq	EXP	S	26278	...	...	...	...	...	...	...	...	...	...
	BAL		17572	...	...	...	...	...	...	...	...	...	...
Jordan	IMP	G	2400	2733	2432	2703	2705	2126	2603	2508	3255	3539	3382
Jordanie	EXP	G	574	791	733	932	1000	1107	1063	1130	1219	1246	1424
	BAL		-1826	-1942	-1699	-1771	-1705	-1019	-1540	-1378	-2035	-2293	-1958
Kuwait	IMP	S	6531	6188	5687	5496	6146	6297	3923	4761	7251	7042	6680
Koweït	EXP	S	19838	10600	7221	8266	7759	11502	6956	1088	6567	10491	11965
	BAL		13307	4412	1535	2770	1613	5205	3033	-3672	-684	3449	5284
Oman	IMP	G	1732	3153	2384	1822	2202	2257	2681	3194	3769	4114	3915
Oman	EXP	G	2387	3938	1834	2491	2476	4068	5508	4871	5428	5299	5545
	BAL		655	785	-550	669	274	1810	2827	1677	1659	1185	1630
Qatar	IMP	S	1429	1139	1099	1134	1267	1326	1695	1720	2015	1891	...
Qatar	EXP	S	5706	3542	...	...	...	2687	3529	3107	3736	3181	...
	BAL		4276	2403	...	...	...	1361	1834	1386	1721	1290	...
Saudi Arabia	IMP	S	30212	23622	19109	20110	21784	21154	24069	29079	33698	28198	23338
Arabe saoudite	EXP	S	109113	27481	20187	23199	24377	28382	44417	47797	50280	42395	...
	BAL		78900	3859	1078	3089	2592	7228	20347	18718	16582	14198	...
Syrian Arab Rep.	IMP	S	4124	3967	2728	2481	2231	2097	2526	3151	3490	4140	5369
Rép. arabe syrienne	EXP	S	2108	1637	1325	1350	1345	3006	4062	3143	3093	3146	3547
	BAL		-2016	-2329	-1404	-1131	-886	908	1536	-8	-397	-993	-1823
Turkey	IMP	S	7910	11344	11105	14158	14335	15792	22302	21047	22872	29174	23270
Turquie	EXP	S	2910	7958	7457	10191	11662	11625	12959	13594	14716	15343	18107
	BAL		-5000	-3386	-3648	-3967	-2673	-4167	-9343	-7453	-8156	-13831	-5163
United Arab Em.	IMP	G	8752	6548	6422	7226	8521	10010	11199	13746	17410	19520	...
Emirats arabes unis	EXP	G	20678	13124	15837	...	...	...	...	...	...	...	...
	BAL		11926	6576	9415	...	...	...	...	...	...	...	...
Yemen[34]	IMP	G	2537	1998	1640	1378	...	...	...	...	...	...	...
Yémen[34]	EXP	G	65	54	37	101	...	...	...	...	...	...	...
	BAL		-2472	-1944	-1604	-1278	...	...	...	...	...	...	...
Other Developing Asia[35]	IMP		178554	220744	229504	282610	364938	*413177*	*467091*	*533538*	*604241*	*678635*	*793214*
A. pays d' Asie evdd.[35,38]	EXP		162933	208612	228470	295317	362827	*405330*	*452300*	*515460*	*583637*	*645230*	*768092*
	BAL		-15621	-12132	-1035	12707	-2111	*-7847*	*-14792*	*-18078*	*-20605*	*-33404*	*-25122*

See the end of the table for general information and footnotes. — Voir la fin du tableau pour la remarque générale et les notes

SPECIAL TABLE: A **TABLEAU SPECIAL: A**

Total Imports and Exports by Regions and Countries and Areas
Importations et Exportations Totales par Regions et Pays ou Zones

Imports C.I.F. - Exports F.O.B. - Balance / Importations C.I.F. - Exportations F.O.B. - Balance

(Continued / Suite)

Value in million U.S. dollars — Valeur en millions de dollars E.-U.

Country or Area / Pays ou Zone	IMP EXP BAL	System	1980	1985	1986	1987	1988	1989	1990	1991	1992	1993	1994
Afghanistan[36]	IMP	G	841	1194	1404	996	900	822	936	616	...	...	...
Afghanistan[36]	EXP	G	670	567	552	512	395	236	235	188	...	...	...
	BAL		-171	-627	-852	-484	-506	-586	-701	-428	...	...	...
Bangladesh	IMP	G	2604	2505	2546	2715	3042	3651	3618	3412	3731	3994	4701
Bangladesh	EXP	G	759	986	880	1067	1291	1305	1671	1689	2098	2278	2650
	BAL		-1845	-1519	-1666	-1648	-1751	-2346	-1946	-1723	-1634	-1716	-2051
Brunei Darussalam	IMP	S	564	615	656	641	744	859	1001	1208	1176	1201	1695
Brunéi Darussalam	EXP	S	4519	2972	1797	1902	1708	1883	2213	2682	2370	2198	2296
	BAL		3955	2357	1141	1261	964	1024	1213	1474	1194	997	602
China	IMP	G	20023	42252	42909	43368	55213	58428	53819	63843	80177	103782	115671
Chine	EXP	G	18120	27349	30940	39492	47466	51952	62423	71892	84571	91665	121014
	BAL		-1903	-14903	-11969	-3876	-7747	-6475	8604	8048	4394	-12118	5343
Hong Kong	IMP	G	22447	29703	35367	48465	63896	72155	82474	100255	123430	138658	161777
Hong-kong	EXP	G	19752	30187	35439	48476	63163	73140	82160	98577	119512	135248	151396
	BAL		-2695	484	72	11	-733	985	-314	-1678	-3918	-3410	-10381
India	IMP	G	14864	15935	15413	16678	19103	20550	23583	20445	23594	22763	26804
Inde	EXP	G	8586	9144	9391	11299	13235	15872	17970	17727	19641	21554	25053
	BAL		-6279	-6791	-6022	-5379	-5869	-4678	-5613	-2718	-3953	-1209	-1751
Indonesia	IMP	S	10834	10262	10718	12891	13249	16360	21837	25869	27280	28086	31985
Indonésie	EXP	S	21909	18590	16075	17135	19465	22160	25674	29543	33861	36825	40054
	BAL		11075	8329	5357	4244	6217	5800	3837	3674	6581	8739	8069
Korea, Republic	IMP	S	22330	31070	31599	41157	51969	61477	69740	81496	81794	83784	102198
Corée, République	EXP	S	17473	30164	34747	47358	60993	62384	64879	71736	76575	82189	95893
	BAL		-4857	-906	3149	6201	9025	907	-4860	-9760	-5219	-1595	-6304
Lao P. Dem. R.	IMP	S	131	131	131	146	162	...	...	...	...	...	...
Rép. dém. po. lao	EXP	S	31	54	60	62	81	...	...	...	...	...	...
	BAL		-100	-77	-71	-84	-81	...	...	...	...	...	...
Macau[37]	IMP	G	543	779	890	1121	1290	1478	1534	1843	1948	1894	2090
Macao[37]	EXP	G	612	906	1046	1397	14[illegible]	1644	1694	1655	1749	1685	1834
	BAL		69	127	156	275	202	166	161	-187	-199	-209	-256
Malaysia	IMP	G	10779	12253	10806	12681	16507	22481	29259	36649	39853	45657	59581
Malaisie	EXP	G	12945	15316	13688	17958	21082	25048	29453	34350	40772	47131	58755
	BAL		2165	3063	2882	5277	4575	2567	194	-2298	918	1474	-826
Maldives	IMP	G	29	53	45	81	90	113	138	161	189	191	222
Maldives	EXP	G	8	23	25	31	40	45	52	54	40	35	46
	BAL		-21	-30	-20	-50	-50	-68	-86	-107	-149	-157	-176
Mongolia	IMP	S	548	1096	1140	1105	1114	963	924	361	418	362	223
Mongolie	EXP	S	403	689	716	718	739	722	661	348	389	361	324
	BAL		-145	-406	-424	-387	-374	-241	-263	-13	-30	-1	102
Myanmar	IMP	G	353	284	304	268	244	191	270	646	651	814	878
Myanmar	EXP	G	472	304	288	219	166	210	325	419	531	586	764
	BAL		119	20	-17	-50	-78	19	55	-227	-120	-228	-114
Nepal	IMP	G	342	455	460	571	679	582	686	765	792	880	...
Népal	EXP	G	80	161	142	151	191	159	209	263	374	391	...
	BAL		-262	-295	-318	-420	-487	-423	-477	-502	-418	-489	...
Pakistan	IMP	G	5350	5891	5377	5829	6620	7119	7356	8461	9365	9481	8829
Pakistan	EXP	G	2618	2740	3379	4178	4527	4779	5523	6464	7273	6672	7294
	BAL		-2732	-3151	-1998	-1652	-2093	-2340	-1833	-1997	-2092	-2808	-1535

See the end of the table for general information and footnotes. Voir la fin du tableau pour la remarque générale et les notes

Total Imports and Exports by Regions and Countries and Areas
Importations et Exportations Totales par Regions et Pays ou Zones

Imports C.I.F. - Exports F.O.B. - Balance / Importations C.I.F. - Exportations F.O.B. - Balance

(Continued / Suite)

Value in million U.S. dollars — Valeur en millions de dollars E.-U.

Country or Area / Pays ou Zone	IMP EXP BAL	System	1980	1985	1986	1987	1988	1989	1990	1991	1992	1993	1994
Philippines / Philippines	IMP	G	8295	5445	5134	6811	8731	10732	13042	12853	15459	17271	...
	EXP	G	5788	4629	4842	5720	7035	7747	8186	8793	9752	12930	...
	BAL		-2507	-816	-293	-1091	-1697	-2985	-4856	-4060	-5707	-4341	...
Singapore / Singapour	IMP	G	24007	26288	25511	32566	43862	49657	60774	66093	72132	85229	102590
	EXP	G	19375	22815	22495	28692	39305	44661	52730	58964	63435	74008	96749
	BAL		-4632	-3473	-3016	-3874	-4558	-4995	-8044	-7129	-8697	-11222	-5841
Sri Lanka / Sri Lanka	IMP	G	2037	1807	1829	2027	2211	2088	2634	3084	3410	3732	4482
	EXP	G	1050	1291	1216	1348	1481	1529	1912	1965	2443	2792	3192
	BAL		-987	-516	-613	-679	-730	-559	-721	-1119	-968	-940	-1290
Thailand / Thaïlande	IMP	G	9214	9242	9181	12994	20285	25770	33065	37569	40686	46077	54388
	EXP	G	6505	7121	8879	11722	15953	20078	23084	28428	32473	36970	45088
	BAL		-2708	-2121	-302	-1272	-4332	-5692	-9981	-9140	-8214	-9107	-9300
Viet Nam / Viet Nam	IMP	G	1314	1857	2155	2455	2757	2566	2752	2338	2541	3924	5000
	EXP	G	339	699	823	854	1038	1946	2404	2087	2581	2985	3600
	BAL		-976	-1159	-1332	-1601	-1719	-620	-348	-251	40	-939	-1400
Former USSR - Asia / Ancienne URSS - Asie	IMP		.	.	.	.	.	.	.	.	*2730*	*2818*	*3668*
	EXP		.	.	.	.	.	.	.	.	*4507*	*3932*	*4405*
	BAL		.	.	.	.	.	.	.	.	*1777*	*1114*	*737*
Armenia / Arménie	IMP	G	.	.	.	.	.	.	.	.	60	85	...
	EXP	G	.	.	.	.	.	.	.	.	12	29	...
	BAL		.	.	.	.	.	.	.	.	-48	-55	...
Azerbaijan / Azerbaïdjan	IMP	G	.	.	.	.	.	.	.	.	333	241	727
	EXP	G	.	.	.	.	.	.	.	.	754	351	625
	BAL		.	.	.	.	.	.	.	.	422	110	-102
Georgia / Géorgie	IMP	G	.	.	.	.	.	.	.	.	...	...	330
	EXP	G	.	.	.	.	.	.	.	.	...	...	209
	BAL		.	.	.	.	.	.	.	.	...	...	-120
Kazakstan / Kazakstan	IMP	G	.	.	.	.	.	.	.	.	469	358	514
	EXP	G	.	.	.	.	.	.	.	.	1398	1271	1095
	BAL		.	.	.	.	.	.	.	.	930	912	581
Kyrgyzstan / Kirghizistan	IMP	G	.	.	.	.	.	.	.	.	70	112	...
	EXP	G	.	.	.	.	.	.	.	.	76	112	...
	BAL		.	.	.	.	.	.	.	.	6	0	...
Tajikistan / Tadjikistan	IMP	G	.	.	.	.	.	.	.	.	...	374	328
	EXP	G	.	.	.	.	.	.	.	.	...	263	356
	BAL		.	.	.	.	.	.	.	.	...	-111	28
Turkmenistan / Turkménistan	IMP	G	.	.	.	.	.	.	.	.	543	501	...
	EXP	G	.	.	.	.	.	.	.	.	1145	1049	...
	BAL		.	.	.	.	.	.	.	.	601	548	...
Uzbekistan / Ouzbékistan	IMP	G	.	.	.	.	.	.	.	.	929	947	1127
	EXP	G	.	.	.	.	.	.	.	.	869	707	1006
	BAL		.	.	.	.	.	.	.	.	-60	-241	-121
Devlpd. Econ.: Oceania / Eco. dévlpés.: Océanie	IMP		26816	31049	31151	35258	42152	52085	49734	47948	50783	52710	62636
	EXP		26310	27491	27432	32481	40796	44367	47362	49393	50396	50842	57010
	BAL		-506	-3558	-3719	-2777	-1356	-7718	-2372	1445	-387	-1868	-5626
Australia / Australie	IMP	G	22399	25900	26109	29321	36101	44944	42024	41651	43808	45478	53415
	EXP	G	21945	22613	22573	26624	33238	37134	39760	41855	42839	42704	47509
	BAL		-454	-3287	-3536	-2697	-2863	-7810	-2264	204	-969	-2773	-5906

See the end of the table for general information and footnotes. — Voir la fin du tableau pour la remarque générale et les notes

SPECIAL TABLE: A **TABLEAU SPECIAL: A**

Total Imports and Exports by Regions and Countries and Areas
Importations et Exportations Totales par Regions et Pays ou Zones

Imports C.I.F. - Exports F.O.B. - Balance / Importations C.I.F. - Exportations F.O.B. - Balance

(Continued / Suite)

Value in million U.S. dollars — Valeur en millions de dollars E.-U.

Country or Area / Pays ou Zone	IMP / EXP / BAL	system	1980	1985	1986	1987	1988	1989	1990	1991	1992	1993	1994
New Zealand	IMP	G	5473	5993	6065	7276	7342	8784	9501	8408	9218	9636	11902
Nouvelle-Zélande	EXP	G	5421	5722	5882	7196	8849	8875	9394	9649	9799	10542	12181
	BAL		-52	-271	-183	-81	1507	91	-107	1241	582	905	280
Devlpg. Econ.: Oceania[38]	IMP		3651	3472	3847	4345	4779	5043	5211	5480	5470	*5140*	*5669*
Eco. evdd.: Océanie	EXP		2135	1887	2046	2429	2960	3022	2737	3050	3456	*4136*	*4416*
	BAL		-1515	-1585	-1801	-1916	-1819	-2022	-2474	-2430	-2014	*-1004*	*-1253*
American Samoa	IMP	S	95	296	313	346	339	378	360	372	418	...	...
Samoa américaines	EXP	S	127	202	254	288	368	308	311	327	318	...	...
	BAL		32	-94	-60	-58	29	-70	-50	-45	-100	...	...
Cook Islands	IMP	S	23	25	26	34	42	44	51	55	59	...	...
Iles Cook	EXP	S	4	3	5	7	4	3	5	5	3	...	...
	BAL		-19	-22	-21	-27	-38	-41	-47	-49	-56	...	...
Fiji	IMP	G	562	442	435	379	461	581	754	652	624	634	825
Fidji	EXP	G	377	236	335	381	372	444	497	450	435	407	546
	BAL		-185	-205	-100	2	-90	-137	-257	-202	-190	-227	-279
French Polynesia	IMP	S	547	549	736	827	808	791	929	915	894	852	881
Polynésie française	EXP	S	30	41	41	83	75	89	111	127	107	148	226
	BAL		-517	-508	-695	-744	-734	-702	-818	-787	-787	-704	-655
Kiribati	IMP	S	21	15	14	18	22	23	27	26	37	...	...
Kiribati	EXP	S	3	4	2	2	5	5	3	3	5	...	...
	BAL		-18	-11	-13	-16	-17	-18	-24	-23	-32	...	...
New Caledonia	IMP	S	457	348	458	626	604	766	883	863	917	849	842
Nouvelle-Calédonie	EXP	S	405	271	191	225	464	675	449	444	409	356	355
	BAL		-52	-78	-268	-401	-139	-91	-434	-420	-507	-493	-487
Papua New Guinea	IMP	G	1176	1008	1068	1262	1593	1546	1271	1615	1521	1299	1528
Pap.-Nouv.-Guinée	EXP	G	1029	928	1031	1241	1452	1300	1177	1460	1926	2584	2637
	BAL		-147	-80	-37	-21	-141	-246	-94	-155	405	1285	1109
Samoa	IMP	G	63	51	47	62	76	75	81	94	110	105	80
Samoa	EXP	G	17	16	11	12	15	13	9	6	6	6	4
	BAL		-45	-35	-37	-50	-61	-63	-72	-88	-104	-98	-76
Solomon Islands	IMP	S	89	83	72	81	98	114	95	110	111	101	...
Iles Salomon	EXP	S	74	70	65	64	81	74	70	83	101	96	...
	BAL		-15	-13	-7	-17	-16	-40	-24	-27	-10	-5	...
Tonga	IMP	G	38	41	41	48	56	54	62	59	63	61	69
Tonga	EXP	G	7	5	6	6	8	9	11	13	12	17	14
	BAL		-30	-36	-35	-42	-48	-45	-50	-46	-50	-44	-55
Vanuatu	IMP	G	73	70	57	70	71	71	96	83	82	76	85
Vanuatu	EXP	G	36	31	17	18	20	22	19	18	24	23	24
	BAL		-37	-39	-40	-52	-51	-49	-77	-64	-58	-53	-61

See the end of the table for general information and footnotes. — Voir la fin du tableau pour la remarque générale et les notes

Total Imports and Exports by Regions and Countries and Areas
Importations et Exportations Totales par Regions et Pays ou Zones

Imports C.I.F. - Exports F.O.B. - Balance / Importations C.I.F. - Exportations F.O.B. - Balance

(continued / suite)

General Note: System: G=General Trade; S=Special Trade.
World imports and exports are the sum of imports and exports of Developed economies, Developing economies and Other. The regional totals for exports and imports have been adjusted to exclude the re-exports of countries or areas comprising each region. Estimates for certain countries or areas not shown separately as well as for those shown separately but for which no data are yet available are included in the regional and world totals. Regional totals containing estimated data are printed in bold italics.
Export and Import values in terms of U.S. dollars for the following countries or areas are derived by United Nations Statistics Division (UNSD) from data published by the International Monetary Fund (IMF) in International Financial Statistics in national currency; the derivation uses external trade conversion factors calculated by UNSD: Antigua and Barbuda, Aruba, Australia, Austria, Bahamas, Bahrain, Bangladesh, Barbados, Belgium/Lux., Belize, Burkina Faso, Burundi, Cameroon, Canada, Cape Verde, Central African Republic, Chad, Comoros, Congo, Cote D'Ivoire, Cyprus, Czech. Republic, Denmark, Djibouti, Dominica, Egypt, France, Gabon, Gambia, Ghana, Greece, Grenada, Guinea Bissau, Guyana, Haiti, Iceland, India, Iran (Islamic Rep. of), Ireland, Italy, Jamaica, Japan, Jordan, Kenya, Rep. of Korea, Kuwait, Liberia, Libyan Arab Jaham., Madagascar, Malawi, Malaysia, Mali, Malta, Mauritania, Mauritius, Morocco, Myanmar, Nepal, Neth. Antilles, New Zealand, Niger, Norway, Oman, Papua N. Guinea, Paraguay, Portugal, Quatar, St. Kitts & Nevis, St. Lucia, St. Vincent & The Grenadines, Samoa, Saudi Arabia, Senegal, Seychelles, Sierra Leone, Singapore, Solomon Islands, Somalia, South Africa, Spain, Sudan, Sweden, Switzerland, Syria, Tanzania, Thailand, Togo, Tonga, Trinidad & Tobago, Tunisia, United Arab Emirates, United Kingdom, Vanuatu and Zimbabwe.
Export and Import values in terms of U.S. dollars for the following countries or areas are as published by the IMF: Afghanistan, Argentina, Bermuda, Bolivia, Brazil, Chile, Colombia, Costa Rica, Dominican Rep., Ecuador, Equatorial Guinea, Guatemala, Honduras, Hong Kong, Indonesia, Israel, Maldives, Mozambique, Nicaragua, Peru, United States, Uruguay.

1 United States, Canada, Developed Economies of Europe, Israel, Japan, Australia, New Zealand and South African Customs Union.
2 This classification is intended for statistical convenience and does not necessarily express a judgement about the stage reached by a particular country in the development process.
3 Algeria, Ecuador, Gabon, Indonesia, Iran (Islamic Rep. of), Iraq, Kuwait, Libyan Arab Jamahiriya, Nigeria, Qatar, Saudi Arabia, United Arab Emirates and Venezuela.
4 The least developed countries are Afghanistan, Angola, Bangladesh, Benin, Bhutan, Burkina Faso, Burundi, Cambodia, Cape Verde, Central African Republic, Chad, Comoros, Djibouti, Equatorial Guinea, Eritrea, Ethiopia, Gambia, Guinea, Guinea-Bissau, Haiti, Kiribati, Lao P.D.R., Lesotho, Liberia, Madagascar, Malawi, Maldives, Mali, Mauritania, Mozambique, Myanmar, Nepal, Niger, Rwanda, Samoa, Sao Tome and Principe, Sierra Leone, Solomon Islands, Somalia, Sudan, Togo, Tuvalu, Uganda, United Republic of Tanzania, Vanuatu, Yemen, Zaire and Zambia.
5 Prior to January 1992 includes Eastern Europe and the former USSR. Beginning January 1992, includes Eastern Europe and the European countries of the former USSR.
6 Latin American Integration Association. Formerly Latin American Free Trade Association.
7 Imports F.O.B.
8 Central American Common Market.
9 Prior to 1986, includes Aruba.
10 Excluding trade of the Free Zone of Colon.
11 Prior to January 1991, includes trade conducted in accordance with the supplementary protocol to the treaty on the basis of relations between the Federal Republic of Germany and the former German Democratic Repulic.
12 Prior to January 1991, excludes trade conducted in accordance with the supplementary protocol to the treaty on the basis of relations between the Federal Republic of Germany and the former German Democratic Republic.
13 Prior to 1983, general trade.
14 Including monetary gold.
15 Data prior to January 1991, pertain to the territorial boundaries of the Federal Republic of Germany prior to 3 October, 1990.
16 Beginning 1992, data refer to Bosnia and Herzegovina, Croatia, Slovenia, TFYR Macedonia, and the Federal Republic of Yugoslavia. Prior to 1992, data refer to the Socialist Federal Republic of Yugoslavia.
17 Beginning January 1992, data refer to the Federal Republic of Yugoslavia. Prior to 1992, data refer to the Socialist Federal Republic of Yugoslavia.
18 Beginning 1985, data are not comparable to those shown for prior periods due to revisions of the koruna to U.S. dollar exchange rate.
19 Beginning 1989, data are not comparable to those shown for prior periods due to revisions of the mark to the U.S. dollar exchange rate.
20 For 1991, data for the former USSR are converted to U.S. dollars using commercial exchange rate of rouble and are not comparable to those shown for prior periods.
21 Excluding inter-trade among countries of the region, except for Estonia, Latvia and Lithuania.
22 Excluding exports of gold bullion and gold coin.
23 The South African Customs Union comprising Botswana, Lesotho, Namibia, South Africa and Swaziland. Trade between the component countries is excluded.
24 Import figures exclude petroleum imported without stated value.
25 Excluding exports of camels to Egypt.
26 Customs and Economic Union of Central Africa.
27 Inter-trade among the members of Customs and Economic Union of Central Africa is excluded.
28 Economic Community of West African States.
29 Imports and exports net of returned goods. The figures also exclude Judea and Samaria and the Gaza area.
30 Excluding military imports.
31 Prior to January 1992, excludes Armenia, Azerbaijan, Georgia, Kazakstan, Kyrgyzstan, Tajikistan, Turkmenistan, and Uzbekistan. Total Developing Asia re-calculated for all periods shown in the table according to the the current composition.
32 Data refer to total exports less petroleum exports of Asia Middle East countries where petroleum, in this case, is the sum of SITC groups 333, 334 and 335.
33 Year ending 20 December of the year stated.
34 Comprises trade of the former Democratic Yemen and former Yemen Arab Republic including any intertrade between them.
35 Includes Peoples Democratic Republic of Korea.
36 Year beginning 21 March of the year stated.
37 Prior to 1981, special trade.

Total Imports and Exports by Regions and Countries and Areas
Importations et Exportations Totales par Regions et Pays ou Zones

Imports C.I.F. - Exports F.O.B. - Balance / Importations C.I.F. - Exportations F.O.B. - Balance

(continued / suite)

Remarque Generale: Systeme: G=Commerce Generale; S=Commerce Special.
Les importations et les exportations totales pour le monde se composent des importations et exportations des Economies développées, des Economies en voie de développement et des Autres. Les totaux régionaux pour importations et exportations ont été ajustés pour exclure les re-exportations des pays ou zones qui comprennent la région. Les totaux régionaux et mondiaux comprennent des estimations pour certains pays ou zones ne figurant pas séparément mais pour lesquels les données ne sont pas encore disponibles. Les totaux régionaux contenant des données estimées sont imprimés en caractéres gras et italique.
Les valeurs en dollars des E.U. des exportations et des impoprtations pour les pays ou zones suivants ont été dérivées par la Division de statistique des Nations Unies (DSNU) des données, exprimées en unités monétaires nationales, que le Fonds Monétaire International publie dans ses Statistiques Financières Internationales; la méthode de dérivation utilisée des facteurs de conversion du commerce extérieur calculés par DSNU: Afrique du Sud, Antigua-et-Barbuda, Antilles Neerl., Arabie saoudite, Aruba, Australie, Autriche, Bahamas, Bahreïn, Bangladesh, Barbade, Belgique/Lux., Belize, Burkina Faso, Burundi, Cameroun, Canada, Cap-Vert, Chypre, Comores, Congo, Côte d'Ivoire, Danemark, Djibouti, Dominique, Egypte, Emirates arabes unis, Espagne, France, Gabon, Gambie, Ghana, Grèce, Grenade, Guinée-Bissau, Guyana, Haïti, Iles Salomon, Inde, Iran (Rep. islamique d'), Irlande, Islande, Italie, Jamah. arabe libyenne, Jamaïque, Japon, Jordanie, Kenya, Koweït, Libéria, Madagascar, Malaisie, Malawi, Mali, Malte, Maroc, Maurice, Mauritanie, Myanmar, Népal, Niger, Norvège, Nouvelle-Zélande, Oman, Papouasie-Nouvelle-Guinée, Paraguay, Portugal, Qatar, Rép. arabe syrienne, Rép. centrafricaine, Rép. de Corée, Rép. tchèque, Rép.-Unie de Tanzanie, Royaume-Uni, St. Kitts et Nevis, St. Lucie, St. Vincent-Grenadines, Samoa, Sénégal, Seychelles, Sierra Leone, Singapour, Somalie, Soudan, Suède, Suisse, Tchad, Thaïlande, Togo, Tonga, Trinité-et-Tobago, Tunisie, Vanuatu et Zimbabwe.
Les valeurs en dollars des E.U. des exportations et des importations pour les pays ou zones suivants sont identiques à celles publiées par le Fonds Monétaire International: Afghanistan, Argentine, Bermudes, Bolivie, Brésil, Chili, Colombie, Costa Rica, Equateur, Etats-Unis d'Amérique, Guatemala, Guinée équatoriale, Honduras, Hong-kong, Indonésie, Israël, Maldives, Mozambique, Nicaragua, Pérou, Rép. dominicaine et Uruguay.

1 Etats-Unis, Canada, pays a économie développés d'Europe, Israël, Japon, Australie, Nouvelle Zélande et l'union douanière de l'Afrique du Sud.

2 Cette classification est utilisée pour plus de commodité dans la présentation des statistiques et n'implique pas nécessairement un jugement quant au stade de développement auquel est parvenu un pays donné.

3 Algérie, Equateur, Gabon, Indonésie, Iran (Rép. islamique d'), Iraq, Koweït, Jamahiriya arabe libyenne, Nigéria, Qatar, Arabie saoudite, Emirates arabes unis et Venezuela.

4 Les pays les moins avancés sont: Afghanistan, Angola, Bangladesh, Bénin, Bhoutan, Burkina Faso, Burundi, Cambodge, Cap Vert, Comores, Djibouti, Eritrea, Ethiopie, Gambie, Guinée, Guinée Bissau, Guinée equatoriale, Haiti, Iles Solomon, Kiribati, Lesotho, Liberia, Madagascar, Malawi, Maldives, Mali, Mauritanie, Mozambique, Myanmar, Népal, Niger, Ouganda, Rép. centrafricaine, Rép. dem. pop. lao, Rép.-Unie de Tanzanie, Rwanda, Samoa, Sao Tomé et Principe, Sierra Léone, Somalie, Soudan, Tchad, Togo, Tuvalu, Vanuatu, Yémen, Zaïre et Zambie.

5 Avant janvier 1992, y compris l'Europe de l'Est et l'ancienne URSS. A partir de janvier 1992 y compris de l'Europe l'Est et les pays européennes de l'anciennce URSS.

6 Association Latino-Américaine d'Intégration. Antérieurement Association Latino-Américaine de Libre-Echange.

7 Importations F.O.B.

8 Marché Commun de l'Amérique Central.

9 Avant 1986, comprend Aruba.

10 Non compris le commerce de la Zone Libre de Colon.

11 Avant janvier 1991, y compris le commerce effectué en accord avec le protocole additionnel au traité définissant la base des relations entre la République Fédérale d'Allemagne et l'ancienne République Démocratique Allemande.

12 Avant janvier 1991, non compris le commerce effectué en accord avec le protocole additionnel au traité définissant la base des relations entre la République Fédérale d'Allemagne et l'ancienne République Démocratique Allemande.

13 Avant 1983, commerce general.

14 Y compris l'or monetaire.

15 Les données relatives à la période précédant janvier 1991 correspondent aux limites territoriales de la Rébublique Fédérale d'Allemagne antérieur au 3 october 1990.

16 A partir de janvier 1992, les données se rapportent à Bosnie-Herzegovine, Croatie, Slovénie, TARY Macédonie, et la République Fédérative de Yougoslavie. Avant 1992, les données se rapportent à la République Fédérative Socialiste de Yougoslavie.

17 A partir de janvier 1992, les données se rapportent à la République Fédérative de Yougoslavie. Avant 1992 les données se rapportent à la République Fédérative Socialiste de Yougoslavie.

18 A partir de l'année 1985 les données ne sont pas comparables aux données des périodes antérieures à cause de révisions de taux de change de koruna au dollar des E.U.

19 A partir de l'année 1989 les données ne sont pas comparables aux données des périodes antérieures à cause de révisions de taux de change de mark au dollar des E.U.

20 Les données de 1991 de l'ancienne URSS sont converties en dollar des E.U. en utilisant le taux de change commercial de rouble et ne sont pas comparables aux données des périodes antérieures.

21 Non compris le commerce avec les autres pays de la région, excepté pour Estonie, Lettonie et Lituanie.

22 Non compris les exportations de lingots et pieces d'or.

23 L'union douaniere de l'afrique meridionale comprend Botswana, Lesotho, Namibie, Afrique du Sud et Swaziland. Non compris le commerce entre ces pays.

24 Non compris le petrole brut dont la valeur a l'importation n'est pas stipulee.

25 Non compris les exportations des chaneaux en Egypte.

26 L'union douanière et économique de l'Afrique centrale.

27 Non compris le commerce entre les pays membres du UDEAC.

28 Communauté économique des états de l'Afrique de l'Ouest.

29 Importations et exportations nets. Ne comprenant pas les marchandises retuournees. Sont egalement exclues les données de la Judee et de Samaria et ainsu que la zone de Gaza.

30 Non compris les importations des economats militaires.

31 Avant janvier 1992 non compris Arménie, Azerbaïdjan, Georgie, Kazakstan, Kirghizistan, Tadjikistan, Turkménistan et Ouzbékistan. Total Asie en voie de développement avait été recalculé pour toutes les périodes données au tableau suivant la composition présente.

Total Imports and Exports by Regions and Countries and Areas
Importations et Exportations Totales par Regions et Pays ou Zones

Imports C.I.F. - Exports F.O.B. - Balance / Importations C.I.F. - Exportations F.O.B. - Balance

(continued / suite)

32 Les données se rapportent aux exportations totales moins les exportations pétrolières de moyen-orient d'Asie. Dans ce cas, le pétrole est la somme des groupes CTCI 333, 334 et 335.

33 Année finissant le 20 Decembre de l'année indiquee.

34 Y compris le commerce de l'ancienne Republique populaire democratique de Yemen, le commerce de l'ancienne republique arabe de Yemen et le commerce entre eux.

35 Y compris les importations et les exportations de la Republique Democratique de Corée.

36 Année commencant le 21 Mars de l' année indiquee.

37 Avant 1981, commerce special.

38 En voie de développement

SPECIAL TABLE: B

World exports by commodity classes and by regions

In million U.S. dollars f.o.b.

Exports to → / ↓ Exports from	Year	World / Monde /1,2,3	Developed economies / Econ. dévelop-pées /2,3,4	Developing economies / Economies en voie de développement /1,3,4: Total	Developing economies /1,3,4: OPEC / OPEP	Eastern Europe and fmr. USSR-Europe / Europe de l'Est et l'anc. URSS-Europe: Total /2,3,7	Eastern Europe and fmr. USSR-Europe: Former USSR-Eur. /10	Developed Economies: Europe: Total /2	Developed Economies: Europe: EEC / CEE /2	Developed Economies: Europe: EFTA / AELE	Developed Economies: South Africa / Afrique du Sud
											Total trade (SITC, Rev. 2 and Rev. 3, 0-9) /6
World /1,2,3	1980	2027619	1336782	500519	128126	140018	60473	879151	747478	129893	13310
	1990	3416432	2445631	777982	110332	155056	73460	1581440	1357824	219303	12676
	1991	3433555	2443256	849681	126210	108344	52538	1581397	1369526	207334	13797
	1992	3703953	2589010	971639	145076	99754	43334	1656370	1440440	211224	14973
	1993	3689745	2495003	1043584	137884	105742	43772	1486386	1287100	194470	15033
Developed economies /2,3,4	1980	1270951	891580	314408	99885	42215	21562	650038	542021	106417	12566
	1990	2445179	1894309	478702	80173	49921	26401	1325757	1129507	192620	11525
	1991	2507026	1901616	526521	92264	56780	27611	1343578	1155722	184035	12075
	1992	2670288	1986604	588766	102995	62774	25590	1403174	1212610	186417	12438
	1993	2574782	1844562	629912	93977	66427	26161	1225278	1051584	169573	12204
Developing economies /1,3,4	1980	601281	400761	153859	22857	19838	12065	188284	174508	13612	743
	1990	788632	482440	263992	27189	27576	19021	193653	178584	14734	1149
	1991	835389	498362	306244	32266	22063	15624	198361	182109	15570	1708
	1992	940790	552201	365848	39969	14752	8414	207497	191109	15909	2502
	1993	1013187	593336	395695	41869	16786	9803	210600	194980	14968	2766
OPEC	1980	326196	234055	69160	3976	1472	182	115783	107649	8081	3
	1990	172056	114320	47453	3002	2775	714	52575	50384	2127	5
	1991	162360	111680	45091	4025	1676	362	50479	47292	3132	3
	1992	169749	115327	49235	6966	2047	455	47961	45887	2037	16
	1993	176248	118978	52328	7313	2195	546	48128	46124	1968	12
Eastern Europe and the former USSR /2,3,7	1980	155386	44442	32252	5384	77966	26846	40829	30950	9865	1
	1990	182621	68883	35288	2971	77559	28037	62032	49733	11949	2
	1991	91140	43278	16916	1680	29501	9304	39458	31695	7729	14
	1992	92875	50205	17025	2112	22227	9330	45699	36722	8898	33
	1993	101777	57105	17977	2038	22529	7808	50509	40537	9929	63
Former USSR /3	1980	76449	24431	19740	1740	32278	.	22672	17260	5413	0
	1990	104177	43065	25520	946	35592	.	38589	32252	6300	0
	1991	46274	...	...	...	...	.	...	...	...	...
	1992	.	.	.	.	.	.	.	.	.	.
	1993	.	.	.	.	.	.	.	.	.	.
Former USSR-Europe /8	1980	.	.	.	.	.	.	.	.	.	.
	1990	.	.	.	.	.	.	.	.	.	.
	1991	.	.	.	.	.	.	.	.	.	.
	1992	48535	26766	9521	865	10211	1736	23874	19254	4594	1
	1993	51395	27612	10138	1026	10355	2194	23037	17275	5755	12
Developed economies-Europe /2	1980	801840	615414	149323	60121	31447	14681	540358	446088	92771	7888
	1990	1578081	1313175	205357	48745	40481	19298	1124815	952251	169210	7911
	1991	1585895	1308421	211067	52775	47113	20183	1133526	969655	160272	7895
	1992	1683664	1377787	232947	58296	53753	19446	1194665	1026346	164446	7729
	1993	1540211	1218141	244057	51913	57056	20112	1031860	880243	147857	7474
European Economic Community /2	1980	689597	527375	132681	54303	23888	10829	462282	384556	76305	7168
	1990	1351043	1122944	179795	43351	30039	13640	962609	820585	138967	7360
	1991	1367722	1125231	185025	46926	38950	17324	975825	839691	132834	7392
	1992	1455380	1186772	205560	52490	44694	16797	1030060	889136	137302	7158
	1993	1328530	1045885	215060	46270	47473	16955	886213	758433	124231	6780
European Free Trade Association	1980	111610	87481	16588	5777	7541	3852	77552	61041	16434	719
	1990	225512	188908	25431	5330	10402	5625	160973	130477	30199	551
	1991	216495	181726	25876	5757	8147	2845	156338	128648	27391	503
	1992	226335	189343	27200	5720	9020	2612	163073	135747	27073	570
	1993	210008	170851	28807	5569	9558	3135	144387	120579	23598	693
Other developed economies	1980	469112	276166	165086	39764	10768	6881	109681	95933	13646	4678
	1990	867098	581133	273345	31428	9440	7103	200941	177257	23411	3613
	1991	921132	593195	315455	39489	9667	7428	210053	186068	23763	4180
	1992	986624	608818	355819	44699	9021	6144	208509	186264	21971	4709
	1993	1034570	626420	385856	42064	9371	6049	193419	171341	21716	4729

For general note and footnotes see end of table.

TABLEAU SPECIAL: B

Exportations mondiales par classes de marchandises et par régions

En millions de dollars E.-U. f.o.b.

Economies développées /2,3,4: Canada	Economies développées: U.S.A. / E.-U.	Economies développées: Japan / Japon	Economies développées: Australia New Zealand / Australie Nouvelle-Zélande	Developing economies / Economies en voie de développement /1,3,4: Africa / Afrique	America / Amerique: Total	America / Amerique: LAIA / ALADI	Asia / Asie: Mid.East / Moyen Orient	Asia / Asie: Other / Autres /9	Oceania / Océanie	← Exportations vers / Année	Exportations en provenance de ↓
Commerce total (CTCI, Rev. 2 et Rev. 3, 0-9) /6											
50753	237607	125386	24138	81953	123134	85316	97427	174596	2949	1980	Monde /1,2,3
110819	491100	192567	44130	79732	136414	90206	102789	433927	4992	1990	
113157	474485	202795	42854	81921	150083	106027	113112	484983	5163	1991	
116348	537372	200522	46892	82410	177529	132592	131725	560376	5352	1992	
124663	593237	209193	48588	78184	190511	143186	131688	625397	5110	1993	
43164	122873	40326	17303	63595	76234	60154	67019	97209	2118	1980	Economies dévelopées /2,3,4
100711	308228	102237	34229	58967	95224	70093	69039	238206	3721	1990	
101350	299509	100473	31542	57476	109527	82713	78738	266711	3747	1991	
104623	320278	97352	34050	61107	129801	100388	89294	295928	4056	1992	
111537	347152	98063	34596	57830	135297	103879	86525	337899	3845	1993	
7359	113313	83253	6729	14194	41837	24455	24234	70225	831	1980	Economies en voie de développement /1,3,4
9804	180214	86708	9744	17337	32523	19300	28998	182003	1269	1990	
11600	173471	100476	11206	22699	36784	22866	31735	212109	1415	1991	
11382	215289	101091	12743	19625	46522	31647	38405	255747	1294	1992	
12715	242738	108792	13884	18591	54139	38620	40476	278077	1250	1993	
4549	57398	53656	2665	3629	23840	12721	9631	30482	9	1980	OPEP
1244	37207	22121	1142	3565	7910	3593	8893	26168	18	1990	
1656	27664	30253	1588	6767	6712	2340	8637	22221	79	1991	
977	34001	30380	1951	3132	8230	5059	9992	27288	47	1992	
1128	36314	31296	2063	3199	9406	6122	10425	28680	43	1993	
230	1421	1807	107	4164	5063	706	6174	7162	0	1980	Europe de l'Est et l'ancienne URSS /2,3,7
303	2658	3622	157	3428	8667	813	4752	13718	2	1990	
207	1505	1846	106	1747	3772	448	2639	6163	1	1991	
343	1805	2079	99	1678	1205	557	4026	8702	3	1992	
411	3348	2338	108	1764	1074	688	4687	9421	15	1993	
46	233	1464	14	1380	3679	130	2210	4574	0	1980	L'ancienne URSS /3
111	1189	3114	62	1515	7406	305	2554	10910	0	1990	
...	...	...	...	...	...	...	...	...	...	1991	
.	.	.	.	.	.	.	.	.	.	1992	
.	.	.	.	.	.	.	.	.	.	1993	
.	.	.	.	.	.	.	.	.	.	1980	L'ancienne URSS-Europe /8
.	.	.	.	.	.	.	.	.	.	1990	
.	.	.	.	.	.	.	.	.	.	1991	
180	910	1746	12	577	613	204	2296	5807	0	1992	
253	2102	2024	12	481	487	224	2878	5990	0	1993	
5777	44042	8181	6129	49626	25478	19374	41359	25147	519	1980	Economies développées-Europe /2
14653	111276	34453	12229	45991	29615	19951	46023	69869	1283	1990	
13981	101419	32719	10454	44179	32364	22440	50607	73134	1111	1991	
13356	109480	31630	11331	45941	37454	26657	56828	83146	1409	1992	
12183	113615	31523	11314	41864	39540	28075	55276	98073	1099	1993	
4953	38619	6672	5309	45716	22214	16875	36698	21653	487	1980	Communauté Economique Européenne /2
11832	95908	28486	10149	42727	25706	16942	40479	58953	1241	1990	
11492	87418	27126	8750	40719	28328	19414	44732	61834	1073	1991	
10890	94519	26351	9375	42726	32891	23365	50810	70860	1380	1992	
9951	98332	26381	9412	38798	35120	24921	49446	83721	1070	1993	
821	5393	1509	819	3870	3260	2498	4653	3493	32	1980	Association Européenne de Libre Echange
2806	15310	5954	2078	3203	3903	3008	5523	10874	42	1990	
2486	13923	5577	1703	3380	4022	3025	5845	11261	38	1991	
2464	14846	5267	1952	3137	4553	3284	5991	12214	29	1992	
2221	15170	5126	1901	2991	4410	3146	5809	14268	29	1993	
37387	78831	32145	11174	13969	50756	40781	25660	72062	1599	1980	Autres economies développées
86059	196953	67784	22000	12976	65609	50142	23016	168337	2438	1990	
87369	198090	67754	21088	13297	77163	60273	28131	193577	2636	1991	
91267	210798	65722	22719	15166	92348	73730	32466	212781	2647	1992	
99353	233536	66540	23282	15965	95757	75804	31250	239827	2746	1993	

Voir la fin du tableau pour la remarque générale et les notes.

SPECIAL TABLE: B

World exports by commodity classes and by regions (continued)

In million U.S. dollars f.o.b.

Exports from ↓ / Exports to →	Year	World / Monde /1,2,3	Developed economies / Econ. dévelop-pées /2,3,4	Developing economies / Economies en voie de développement /1,3,4: Total	Developing economies: OPEC / OPEP	Eastern Europe and fmr. USSR-Europe / Europe de l'Est et l'anc. URSS-Europe: Total /2,3,7	Eastern Europe: Former USSR-Eur. /10	Developed Economies – Europe: Total /2	Europe: EEC / CEE /2	Europe: EFTA / AELE	South Africa / Afrique du Sud
		Total trade (SITC, Rev. 2 and Rev. 3, 0-9) /6 (continued)									
Canada	1980	64935	55286	7601	1869	1776	1317	9447	8565	880	175
	1990	126897	115641	10176	1630	1081	964	12209	10269	1927	143
	1991	126762	114385	10981	1848	1396	1290	11737	10250	1475	109
	1992	134617	122615	10774	1762	1227	1059	11469	9576	1891	118
	1993	144731	134065	10103	1835	563	394	9757	8267	1478	128
United States	1980	216592	128821	82805	17465	3850	1510	65064	57849	7185	2487
	1990	374449	242222	127479	13418	4226	3072	103832	93049	10666	1750
	1991	400984	249153	146869	18587	4673	3500	109122	97514	11524	2131
	1992	424871	252611	166710	21324	5252	3584	107457	97340	10032	2470
	1993	439223	256469	176835	20045	5575	3520	103184	91237	11755	2195
Japan	1980	129807	61602	64619	18482	3585	2778	21436	18120	3264	1809
	1990	286947	170164	113476	13575	3308	2563	62412	53846	8437	1518
	1991	314525	177648	134015	16474	2862	2115	68325	59557	8651	1670
	1992	339651	186080	151727	18995	1844	1128	71584	62952	8488	1757
	1993	360911	188795	169913	17263	2203	1581	64117	56910	7084	2032
Australia, New Zealand	1980	26673	15513	8291	1809	1513	1276	4334	4161	165	126
	1990	47784	29518	16846	2654	715	500	7866	6819	1042	105
	1991	49817	29828	18621	2490	591	505	7210	6315	890	173
	1992	50801	28791	19858	2349	196	82	7483	6762	694	239
	1993	50951	28359	21483	2601	308	231	6717	6197	515	252
Developing economies-Africa	1980	113844	80850	10152	1021	2159	713	47564	45073	2434	17
	1990	73188	60652	10257	1691	1882	985	44845	43734	979	313
	1991	71773	59839	10062	1982	1212	559	44610	42981	1309	293
	1992	69412	57027	10749	2196	922	262	41975	39935	1839	346
	1993	68542	56218	10856	1977	789	217	40737	39332	1185	367
Developing economies-America	1980	102399	65023	28619	3392	6964	5192	25696	23602	2025	161
	1990	134319	94243	30748	4200	6358	4299	32296	29951	2301	337
	1991	131279	90035	34416	4531	4838	4113	30997	29097	1861	346
	1992	154253	108794	43207	4954	937	313	31486	29511	1962	472
	1993	165685	114700	48807	5068	945	471	29167	27168	1955	331
Developing economies-Europe/ 5	1980	8977	3286	1659	851	4033	2489	2807	2385	417	0
	1990	14391	8444	1888	747	4059	2681	7572	6587	978	1
	1991	9548	5601	1247	495	2700	1786	5024	4370	649	0
	1992	13952	8774	4156	296	992	436	8288	7149	1134	2
	1993	12134	8144	2849	189	1010	473	7534	6811	696	3
Developing economies-Middle East	1980	212886	152746	55890	6223	1252	313	84030	77803	6224	0
	1990	113349	59820	43480	6120	4030	2224	30595	28454	2115	51
	1991	104875	59046	39062	6623	3322	1841	28454	25416	3018	59
	1992	111079	64463	40855	9794	2659	790	28220	26320	1860	57
	1993	115375	66487	43040	10251	2947	909	28764	26846	1855	63
Developing economies-Other Asia	1980	161009	96944	57308	11370	5429	3358	27427	24889	2508	565
	1990	450571	257032	177059	14426	11247	8832	77682	69247	8309	445
	1991	514603	281234	220822	18633	9938	7310	88613	79625	8689	1009
	1992	588844	310440	266355	22722	9237	6609	96798	87516	9063	1624
	1993	647363	344599	289258	24370	11096	7733	103712	94174	9241	2002
Former USSR-Asia /9	1980	.	.	.	.	.	.	.	.	.	.
	1990	.	.	.	.	.	.	.	.	.	.
	1991	.	.	.	.	.	.	.	.	.	.
	1992	4453	502	2683	843	377	.	425	366	58	0
	1993	3848	498	2397	759	349	.	394	321	73	0
Developing economies-Oceania	1980	2165	1911	232	0	0	0	760	757	3	0
	1990	2814	2249	560	4	0	0	663	611	52	2
	1991	3311	2607	636	2	53	15	664	621	43	0
	1992	3250	2703	528	7	4	4	729	677	52	0
	1993	4087	3188	886	14	0	0	685	649	37	0

For general note and footnotes see end of table.

Exportations mondiales par classes de marchandises et par régions (suite)

En millions de dollars E.-U. f.o.b.

Economies développées /2,3,4: Canada	Economies développées: U.S.A. E.-U.	Economies développées: Japan Japon	Economies développées: Australia New Zealand Australie Nouvelle-Zélande	Developing economies Economies en voie de développement /1,3,4: Africa Afrique	America Amerique: Total	America Amerique: LAIA ALADI	Asia Asie: Mid.East Moyen Orient	Asia Asie: Other Autres /9	Oceania Océanie	Année	← Exportations vers / Exportations en provenance de ↓
Commerce total (CTCI, Rev. 2 et Rev. 3, 0-9) /6 (suite)											
.	41183	3726	660	932	3288	2396	681	2628	13	1980	Canada
.	95217	7038	909	903	2325	1675	961	5911	27	1990	
.	95501	6243	674	820	2329	1751	1007	6764	21	1991	
.	104056	6198	669	722	2769	2198	840	6408	16	1992	
.	116784	6558	718	682	2856	2296	916	5612	16	1993	
34102	.	20574	4651	6357	38021	31668	10266	27224	184	1980	Etats-Unis
78212	.	46130	9406	6068	52280	41969	10234	58051	289	1990	
79055	.	46111	9181	6562	61326	50671	13719	64523	376	1991	
83217	.	45836	9973	7287	73118	61378	15399	70110	489	1992	
91865	.	46030	9243	6991	75293	62380	15668	78260	404	1993	
2437	31747	.	4065	5958	8537	5923	13114	36480	407	1980	Japon
6726	90893	.	8106	3835	9712	5354	9570	89255	853	1990	
7251	92091	.	7574	3973	12243	6791	11583	105257	784	1991	
7090	96489	.	8158	4648	15053	8936	14201	117071	708	1992	
6328	106353	.	8975	5263	15914	9605	12569	135325	804	1993	
539	2804	6053	1627	611	358	267	1507	4754	991	1980	Australie, Nouvelle-Zélande
765	5503	11880	3365	601	707	610	1891	12319	1263	1990	
738	5218	12994	3449	498	727	583	1475	14440	1448	1991	
799	4685	11883	3657	324	775	659	1500	15833	1422	1992	
1002	4268	12034	4041	589	953	859	1548	16879	1508	1993	
191	30643	2180	51	2349	3546	1575	1841	1518	3	1980	Economies en voie de développement-Afrique
680	13140	1401	58	4991	1037	797	1804	1856	5	1990	
400	12771	1288	47	4941	1085	896	1352	2112	2	1991	
278	12531	1494	61	5187	1218	1100	1630	2206	3	1992	
402	12636	1729	65	5211	1329	1196	1516	2293	8	1993	
2763	30933	4577	167	2295	22152	11524	1593	2128	62	1980	Economies en voie de développement-Amérique
2036	51551	7182	451	1618	20338	13052	2314	6205	30	1990	
2929	47523	7432	437	1696	23317	16037	2201	6978	53	1991	
2358	67158	6527	431	1885	28861	20255	2497	9848	33	1992	
2886	75238	6292	461	1632	34033	24622	2320	10743	42	1993	
28	393	31	12	735	65	36	628	228	2	1980	Economies en voie de développement-Europe /5
62	691	39	66	715	110	47	788	273	2	1990	
41	458	26	44	475	73	31	518	180	1	1991	
43	379	31	22	257	69	35	360	238	1	1992	
39	484	48	23	151	60	28	283	160	1	1993	
2610	20397	43306	2394	3458	12033	9537	11714	27571	111	1980	Economies en voie de développement-Moyen Orient
178	15262	12954	729	2860	3831	1716	12396	23791	3	1990	
806	7266	21377	996	6117	2484	303	11992	18068	58	1991	
538	13054	21305	1187	2260	2690	2586	14126	21499	0	1992	
568	14152	21575	1269	2229	2884	2797	14764	22879	0	1993	
1743	30653	32588	3843	5357	4036	1777	8458	38638	570	1980	Economies en voie de développement-Autres Pays d'Asie
6832	99158	64517	7899	7152	7204	3688	11697	149495	1056	1990	
7409	104981	69707	8872	9468	9822	5597	15669	184323	1119	1991	
8150	121656	71170	10163	10036	13684	7672	19784	221530	1162	1992	
8805	139645	78381	10929	9368	15833	9977	21590	241213	1108	1993	
.	.	.	.	.	.	.	.	.	.	1980	l'ancienne URSS asiatique /9
.	.	.	.	.	.	.	.	.	.	1990	
.	.	.	.	.	.	.	.	.	.	1991	
0	39	38	0	32	119	37	1803	729	0	1992	
0	39	66	0	37	128	40	1525	706	0	1993	
24	296	570	261	0	6	5	0	143	83	1980	Economies en voie de développement-Océanie
16	412	614	542	0	3	1	0	382	174	1990	
15	472	646	811	2	3	2	2	448	181	1991	
16	512	565	881	0	0	0	7	426	94	1992	
15	583	768	1137	0	0	0	2	791	93	1993	

Voir la fin du tableau pour la remarque générale et les notes.

SPECIAL TABLE: B

World exports by commodity classes and by regions (continued)

In million U.S. dollars f.o.b.

Exports to → / ↓ Exports from	Year	World Monde /1,2,3	Developed economies Econ. dévelop-pées /2,3,4	Developing economies Economies en voie de développement /1,3,4 Total	Developing economies OPEC OPEP	Eastern Europe and fmr. USSR-Europe / Europe de l'Est et l'anc. URSS-Europe Total /2,3,7	Eastern Europe and fmr. USSR-Europe Former USSR-Eur. /10	Developed Economies Europe Total /2	Developed Economies Europe EEC CEE /2	Developed Economies Europe EFTA AELE	Developed Economies South Africa Afrique du Sud
		Food, beverages and tobacco (SITC, Rev. 2 and Rev. 3, 0 and 1)									
World /1,2,3	1980	196033	120800	51761	15705	18676	12386	86005	78763	6911	350
	1990	294143	210365	64320	14026	17926	12747	147190	135688	10947	637
	1991	305230	222278	64392	13341	17079	12829	155678	143936	11055	708
	1992	330953	237857	74645	14304	15840	10989	166675	154573	11495	1293
	1993	320103	225414	75021	14401	15467	9960	152009	140598	10885	864
Developed economies /2,3,4	1980	128359	82985	33548	10499	8606	4967	64599	59061	5231	274
	1990	204231	157097	38912	9290	7484	5187	120608	111324	8777	392
	1991	212299	164861	37653	8409	8995	6341	127730	118181	9032	394
	1992	232528	178693	41165	8404	10763	7655	138401	128355	9479	825
	1993	219545	165017	40839	8596	9978	6366	124260	114878	8888	532
Developing economies /1,3,4	1980	62543	35771	16848	5022	8446	6498	19663	18297	1346	76
	1990	80881	49184	23617	4340	7704	5655	23277	21799	1442	245
	1991	86094	53793	25736	4777	6318	5279	24789	23175	1451	312
	1992	90674	54883	32347	5724	3031	1932	24880	23470	1376	462
	1993	93199	56089	33171	5657	3455	2392	24478	23087	1361	328
OPEC	1980	3719	2261	911	284	142	80	1127	1095	31	0
	1990	5329	3549	1511	241	145	81	1542	1511	21	0
	1991	5872	3917	1818	416	136	66	1633	1592	31	0
	1992	6611	4024	2353	585	222	123	1796	1715	74	3
	1993	7043	4198	2510	630	324	222	1841	1762	72	2
Eastern Europe and the former USSR /2,3,7	1980	5131	2043	1365	184	1625	921	1743	1405	334	0
	1990	9032	4083	1790	395	2739	1905	3306	2565	728	0
	1991	6838	3625	1003	154	1766	1209	3159	2580	572	2
	1992	7751	4281	1134	176	2046	1402	3394	2748	640	5
	1993	7360	4309	1010	148	2034	1202	3271	2634	636	4
Former USSR /3	1980	1278	154	963	1	161	.	96	71	24	0
	1990	...	...	...	...	...	.	...	...	...	...
	1991	...	...	...	...	...	.	...	...	...	...
	1992	.	.	.	.	.	.	.	.	.	.
	1993	.	.	.	.	.	.	.	.	.	.
Former USSR-Europe /8	1980	.	.	.	.	.	.	.	.	.	.
	1990	.	.	.	.	.	.	.	.	.	.
	1991	.	.	.	.	.	.	.	.	.	.
	1992	1807	1203	274	26	193	73	593	417	176	0
	1993	1963	1423	294	17	246	111	652	425	227	1
Developed economies-Europe /2	1980	76972	59481	13647	6020	3747	1925	54142	49382	4484	147
	1990	141599	120027	17218	5210	3925	1974	108679	100287	7908	238
	1991	149439	127366	16498	5127	5031	2576	116253	107614	8157	242
	1992	164753	139086	17825	5222	7293	4415	127518	118318	8667	264
	1993	151730	125401	17784	5020	7648	4429	114256	105696	8091	231
European Economic Community /2	1980	72296	56008	12962	5644	3233	1598	51274	47307	3700	138
	1990	132813	112865	16275	5021	3247	1578	102709	95597	6656	234
	1991	140517	119924	15570	4915	4501	2407	110131	102790	6888	238
	1992	155405	131374	16938	5033	6571	4139	120987	113145	7340	259
	1993	142897	118320	16873	4812	6830	4041	108475	101078	6945	225
European Free Trade Association	1980	4489	3295	681	372	514	327	2710	1925	776	9
	1990	8394	6785	932	182	678	396	5624	4369	1227	4
	1991	8490	7031	912	202	529	167	5758	4487	1242	4
	1992	8920	7308	867	176	720	275	6168	4834	1304	5
	1993	8488	6756	893	197	817	387	5482	4334	1131	7
Other developed economies	1980	51387	23504	19900	4480	4859	3042	10457	9679	747	127
	1990	62632	37070	21694	4080	3559	3214	11929	11037	869	154
	1991	62859	37495	21155	3282	3964	3765	11477	10567	875	153
	1992	67775	39607	23340	3182	3469	3240	10883	10037	812	561
	1993	67815	39616	23056	3576	2331	1938	10004	9181	797	300

For general note and footnotes see end of table.

TABLEAU SPECIAL: B

Exportations mondiales par classes de marchandises et par régions (suite)

En millions de dollars E.-U. f.o.b.

Economies développées /2,3,4				Developing economies Economies en voie de développement /1,3,4						← Exportations vers	
Canada	U.S.A. E.-U.	Japan Japon	Australia New Zealand Australie Nouvelle-Zélande	Africa Afrique	America Amerique Total	America Amerique LAIA ALADI	Asia Asie Mid.East Moyen Orient	Asia Asie Other Autres /9	Oceania Océanie	Année	Exportations en provenance de ↓
Produits alimentaires, boisson et tabac (CTCI, Rev. 2 et Rev. 3, 0 et 1)											
3086	17561	12195	1092	11351	11680	8092	11363	15729	600	1980	Monde /1,2,3
6186	26365	27085	2107	11244	12286	7649	13176	25301	734	1990	
6707	26844	29358	2168	10561	12610	8219	12145	27271	767	1991	
6939	28120	31695	2228	11528	14218	9809	13414	33142	773	1992	
7368	29108	32817	2278	11177	15105	10412	13397	33125	741	1993	
2516	6860	7675	652	8703	8469	5934	6871	8570	511	1980	Economies dévelopées /2,3,4
5242	12810	16009	1418	7942	7785	4689	8411	13160	607	1990	
5745	12736	16242	1414	7416	8330	5226	7215	13470	620	1991	
6008	13812	17484	1481	8081	9579	6312	7330	14964	623	1992	
6388	14133	17474	1509	8047	9654	6209	7326	14406	617	1993	
561	10493	4441	436	2503	2815	2138	4289	6865	90	1980	Economies en voie de développement /1,3,4
911	13209	10709	666	2824	3890	2918	4541	11965	127	1990	
931	13890	12919	740	2958	3990	2962	4734	13696	147	1991	
897	14120	13567	734	3257	4566	3467	5898	17748	149	1992	
940	14729	14610	757	2975	5385	4161	5846	18308	123	1993	
11	773	295	54	54	191	160	397	224	0	1980	OPEP
24	1198	734	48	167	224	141	472	628	1	1990	
23	1370	836	54	192	259	127	467	890	2	1991	
33	1268	873	49	200	332	191	809	1003	2	1992	
32	1218	1061	41	232	391	280	813	1067	1	1993	
9	208	79	4	145	397	20	203	294	0	1980	Europe de l'Est et l'ancienne URSS /2,3,7
32	346	367	24	478	612	42	225	175	0	1990	
31	219	198	14	186	290	31	196	105	0	1991	
34	188	644	13	189	74	31	186	430	0	1992	
40	246	733	12	156	66	41	225	412	0	1993	
0	18	37	2	48	349	0	12	259	0	1980	L'ancienne URSS /3
...	...	...	...	...	...	...	...	...	...	1990	
...	...	...	...	...	...	...	...	...	...	1991	
.	.	.	.	.	.	.	.	.	.	1992	
.	.	.	.	.	.	.	.	.	.	1993	
.	.	.	.	.	.	.	.	.	.	1980	L'ancienne URSS-Europe /8
.	.	.	.	.	.	.	.	.	.	1990	
.	.	.	.	.	.	.	.	.	.	1991	
15	35	556	5	38	3	1	15	216	0	1992	
21	91	654	5	30	3	1	18	240	0	1993	
556	3271	959	262	6028	2110	1178	4001	1224	75	1980	Economies développées-Europe /2
1018	5987	3198	560	5629	2656	1283	4857	3061	164	1990	
1032	5574	3393	518	5219	2780	1437	4451	3341	155	1991	
1039	5864	3491	547	5639	3028	1546	4454	3987	158	1992	
999	5689	3320	504	5412	3101	1599	4287	4096	148	1993	
513	2823	877	243	5683	1992	1097	3855	1179	74	1980	Communauté Economique Européenne /2
944	5315	2808	520	5451	2476	1157	4646	2903	163	1990	
953	4899	2883	483	5029	2561	1276	4215	3182	154	1991	
975	5257	3039	514	5489	2837	1417	4237	3776	157	1992	
933	4999	2831	476	5272	2899	1457	4086	3846	147	1993	
43	427	82	19	343	118	81	143	45	1	1980	Association Européenne de Libre Echange
73	653	378	40	177	179	126	203	157	1	1990	
77	644	494	35	187	220	161	225	157	0	1991	
64	578	442	33	147	191	129	203	208	1	1992	
66	675	479	28	137	202	141	188	248	0	1993	
1960	3589	6716	390	2675	6359	4756	2870	7346	436	1980	Autres economies développées
4224	6824	12811	858	2314	5130	3406	3554	10099	443	1990	
4713	7162	12849	896	2198	5550	3788	2765	10129	465	1991	
4969	7948	13992	934	2442	6551	4766	2876	10977	465	1992	
5389	8444	14154	1005	2634	6553	4611	3040	10310	470	1993	

Voir la fin du tableau pour la remarque générale et les notes.

SPECIAL TABLE: B

World exports by commodity classes and by regions (continued)

In million U.S. dollars f.o.b.

Exports to → / ↓ Exports from	Year	World Monde /1,2,3	Developed economies Econ. dévelop-pées /2,3,4	Developing economies Economies en voie de développement /1,3,4 Total	OPEC OPEP	Eastern Europe and fmr. USSR-Europe Europe de l'Est et l'anc. URSS-Europe Total /2,3,7	Former USSR-Eur. /10	Developed Economies: Europe Total /2	EEC CEE /2	EFTA AELE	South Africa Afrique du Sud
		Food, beverages and tobacco (SITC, Rev. 2 and Rev. 3, 0 and 1) (continued)									
Canada	1980	7021	3640	2026	415	1355	1102	1190	1115	74	3
	1990	9945	6801	2273	645	872	839	967	871	93	60
	1991	10476	6856	2414	556	1207	1170	899	817	81	38
	1992	11725	7754	3053	613	918	904	911	816	94	36
	1993	10632	8316	2170	555	146	110	654	594	59	45
United States	1980	30318	14058	12804	2372	2514	975	7598	7069	518	85
	1990	36399	20561	13133	2061	2487	2205	6906	6385	508	75
	1991	36357	20955	12777	1644	2461	2316	6757	6203	526	70
	1992	39928	22683	14563	1716	2433	2245	6581	6074	479	462
	1993	39398	22269	14958	2103	1938	1609	6098	5570	509	227
Japan	1980	1590	519	1069	350	2	1	152	128	21	25
	1990	1612	518	1083	60	10	10	144	136	8	10
	1991	1790	536	1231	44	23	21	152	143	9	10
	1992	1882	554	1296	65	32	27	148	133	14	8
	1993	1973	556	1397	91	20	15	142	125	17	8
Australia, New Zealand	1980	9673	4712	3967	1339	974	964	975	922	47	11
	1990	11214	6281	4728	1314	181	160	1530	1435	90	6
	1991	11124	6545	4303	1037	256	255	1538	1423	111	33
	1992	11763	6770	3863	739	27	24	1727	1595	127	52
	1993	13474	6758	4018	777	126	122	1706	1589	112	18
Developing economies-Africa	1980	9910	7234	1426	616	604	495	5769	5517	247	9
	1990	8274	6360	1581	402	283	213	5162	4983	174	118
	1991	8466	6713	1441	457	248	168	5455	5209	241	130
	1992	8161	6095	1794	544	183	105	4899	4665	229	145
	1993	8312	6252	1809	475	194	119	4982	4711	268	114
Developing economies-America	1980	29064	17698	5126	1309	5625	4482	8945	8112	821	44
	1990	32180	21298	6277	1178	4530	3052	10692	9935	746	115
	1991	32619	22488	6344	1046	3682	3201	11356	10696	643	120
	1992	33425	23138	9502	1270	646	209	11845	11298	539	215
	1993	34832	23383	10497	1361	673	319	11471	10917	547	65
Developing economies-Europe/ 5	1980	1023	517	132	72	375	260	450	387	63	0
	1990	1037	757	100	35	181	87	655	588	65	0
	1991	687	501	66	25	120	58	434	390	43	0
	1992	1316	502	688	18	116	32	456	398	55	0
	1993	1100	510	481	11	109	33	418	371	46	0
Developing economies-Middle East	1980	2696	1090	1260	732	312	144	899	798	101	0
	1990	4848	2344	2004	1083	362	255	1871	1670	190	3
	1991	5282	2540	2261	1322	462	324	1965	1738	222	11
	1992	5827	2420	2961	1623	412	203	1984	1765	213	11
	1993	5982	2639	2904	1662	412	204	2163	1954	202	11
Developing economies-Other Asia	1980	19072	8573	8791	2292	1530	1118	3370	3254	114	22
	1990	33744	17735	13553	1643	2349	2048	4674	4400	266	9
	1991	38171	20806	15509	1927	1806	1528	5328	4892	302	51
	1992	41144	22027	17304	2269	1675	1384	5488	5136	340	91
	1993	42208	22612	17412	2147	2067	1717	5249	4940	298	138
Former USSR-Asia /9	1980	.	.	.	.	.	.	.	.	.	.
	1990	.	.	.	.	.	.	.	.	.	.
	1991	.	.	.	.	.	.	.	.	.	.
	1992	22	5	14	7	3	.	5	4	0	0
	1993	19	4	13	7	2	.	4	4	0	0
Developing economies-Oceania	1980	778	659	114	0	0	0	229	229	0	0
	1990	798	690	103	0	0	0	222	222	0	0
	1991	868	744	114	0	0	0	251	250	1	0
	1992	802	701	97	0	0	0	208	208	0	0
	1993	765	693	67	0	0	0	195	195	0	0

For general note and footnotes see end of table.

Exportations mondiales par classes de marchandises et par régions (suite)

En millions de dollars E.-U. f.o.b.

Economies développées /2,3,4				Developing economies Economies en voie de développement /1,3,4						← Exportations vers	
Canada	U.S.A. E.-U.	Japan Japon	Australia New Zealand Australie Nouvelle-Zélande	Africa Afrique	America Amerique Total	America Amerique LAIA ALADI	Asia Asie Mid.East Moyen Orient	Asia Asie Other Autres /9	Oceania Océanie	Année	Exportations en provenance de ↓
Produits alimentaires, boisson et tabac (CTCI, Rev. 2 et Rev. 3, 0 et 1) (suite)											
.	1731	658	33	325	931	492	166	591	2	1980	Canada
.	4510	1196	63	235	519	311	422	1094	1	1990	
.	4819	1045	53	249	594	406	256	1311	1	1991	
.	5581	1171	52	225	817	657	260	1749	1	1992	
.	6279	1268	49	228	703	543	211	1025	1	1993	
1534	.	4489	131	1746	5188	4127	1260	4371	47	1980	Etats-Unis
3891	.	9162	274	1496	4228	2821	1848	5367	60	1990	
4383	.	9206	311	1473	4571	3129	1652	4978	67	1991	
4656	.	10358	333	1678	5298	3795	1860	5635	70	1992	
5007	.	10265	390	1864	5361	3682	2071	5559	67	1993	
45	258	.	37	177	38	10	213	579	62	1980	Japon
34	282	.	47	19	14	6	49	910	88	1990	
36	290	.	47	20	18	8	39	1056	95	1991	
34	313	.	51	10	23	12	59	1105	96	1992	
30	327	.	49	13	22	9	80	1187	89	1993	
375	1583	1564	187	418	200	126	1225	1799	325	1980	Australie, Nouvelle-Zélande
252	1912	2117	465	434	347	257	1219	2434	294	1990	
253	1945	2296	478	338	345	234	802	2515	302	1991	
263	1913	2325	488	158	390	284	635	2382	298	1992	
334	1690	2504	505	204	445	360	614	2441	313	1993	
25	1123	259	40	670	14	7	421	247	3	1980	Economies en voie de développement-Afrique
53	502	484	21	1044	27	12	268	199	2	1990	
59	484	546	25	922	14	7	256	223	1	1991	
59	436	515	25	1065	17	11	366	315	2	1992	
60	483	573	24	1029	26	19	366	361	2	1993	
370	7383	847	36	851	2545	1976	889	663	3	1980	Economies en voie de développement-Amérique
469	8686	1151	90	582	3484	2675	978	1070	12	1990	
421	8842	1503	117	614	3578	2710	734	1269	15	1991	
352	8925	1571	107	774	4221	3243	977	3462	23	1992	
347	9528	1713	111	739	5070	3980	1053	3595	9	1993	
2	57	4	2	36	15	4	73	8	0	1980	Economies en voie de développement-Europe /5
9	82	3	8	43	2	1	53	2	0	1990	
6	54	2	5	29	1	1	34	2	0	1991	
5	32	3	5	32	3	2	21	3	0	1992	
5	70	10	5	10	3	1	13	3	0	1993	
12	126	41	4	105	7	6	1089	49	0	1980	Economies en voie de développement-Moyen Orient
27	310	98	21	215	40	38	1544	156	0	1990	
28	387	95	22	254	53	49	1641	277	0	1991	
27	245	99	22	295	52	45	2166	430	0	1992	
28	266	127	21	215	45	41	2159	464	0	1993	
128	1563	3238	240	841	230	140	1817	5832	42	1980	Economies en voie de développement-Autres Pays d'Asie
342	3287	8919	465	940	337	191	1697	10493	57	1990	
404	3744	10715	527	1139	344	196	2068	11868	74	1991	
442	4079	11349	526	1091	273	166	2367	13480	86	1992	
485	3974	12158	550	981	241	120	2254	13858	74	1993	
.	.	.	.	.	.	.	.	.	.	1980	l'ancienne URSS asiatique /9
.	.	.	.	.	.	.	.	.	.	1990	
.	.	.	.	.	.	.	.	.	.	1991	
0	0	0	0	1	1	1	12	0	0	1992	
0	0	0	0	1	1	1	11	0	0	1993	
24	241	52	113	0	5	5	0	67	42	1980	Economies en voie de développement-Océanie
11	342	54	62	0	0	0	0	46	56	1990	
13	379	57	44	0	0	0	1	57	57	1991	
12	403	30	48	0	0	0	1	58	38	1992	
14	409	29	46	0	0	0	1	28	39	1993	

Voir la fin du tableau pour la remarque générale et les notes.

SPECIAL TABLE: B

World exports by commodity classes and by regions (continued)

In million U.S. dollars f.o.b.

Exports to → / ↓ Exports from	Year	World Monde /1,2,3	Developed economies Econ. dévelop-pées /2,3,4	Developing economies Economies en voie de développement /1,3,4 Total	OPEC OPEP	Eastern Europe and fmr. USSR-Europe Europe de l'Est et l'anc. URSS-Europe Total /2,3,7	Former USSR-Eur. /10	Developed Economies: Europe Total /2	EEC CEE /2	EFTA AELE	South Africa Afrique du Sud
											Cereals (SITC, Rev. 2 and Rev. 3, 041-045)
World /1,2,3	1980	37331	12197	16833	4080	6762	4398	8257	7823	421	59
	1990	33369	12705	16051	3859	4245	3577	8450	8211	221	125
	1991	30998	12884	13792	2938	4137	3782	8707	8473	212	184
	1992	35643	14201	15418	3195	4675	4255	9330	9081	225	682
	1993	31429	12496	14013	3058	2924	2049	7908	7670	220	355
Developed economies /2,3,4	1980	32016	11831	13389	2814	5257	3069	7965	7561	392	50
	1990	28380	12067	12245	2931	3843	3237	8180	7977	189	112
	1991	25511	11917	9690	2002	3730	3433	8385	8190	179	116
	1992	28880	13016	10314	1793	4215	3869	8948	8743	189	507
	1993	25244	11360	9361	1956	2536	1790	7495	7299	183	262
Developing economies /1,3,4	1980	4987	359	3187	1260	1440	1328	285	259	26	9
	1990	4650	612	3540	926	396	341	251	224	24	13
	1991	5286	951	3987	935	337	280	306	274	27	68
	1992	6618	1168	5078	1398	359	292	372	334	32	175
	1993	6085	1082	4642	1099	352	240	358	319	35	93
OPEC	1980	29	0	29	9	0	0	0	0	0	0
	1990	199	30	124	0	0	0	29	29	0	0
	1991	120	28	92	63	0	0	26	26	0	0
	1992	256	36	220	110	0	0	32	29	1	2
	1993	319	55	264	117	0	0	41	31	8	2
Eastern Europe and the former USSR /2,3,7	1980	329	7	257	5	64	1	7	4	3	0
	1990	339	26	266	2	6	0	20	11	9	0
	1991	200	16	114	2	70	70	15	9	6	0
	1992	145	17	27	4	101	94	10	4	5	0
	1993	100	54	10	3	36	18	54	52	2	0
Former USSR /3	1980	312	0	252	0	61	.	0	0	0	0
	1990	...	...	...	...	...	.	...	...	...	...
	1991	...	...	...	...	...	.	...	...	...	...
	1992	.	.	.	.	.	.	.	.	.	.
	1993	.	.	.	.	.	.	.	.	.	.
Former USSR-Europe /8	1980	.	.	.	.	.	.	.	.	.	.
	1990	.	.	.	.	.	.	.	.	.	.
	1991	.	.	.	.	.	.	.	.	.	.
	1992	9	2	1	1	6	0	2	2	1	0
	1993	61	50	1	1	10	0	50	49	1	0
Developed economies-Europe /2	1980	6939	4541	1378	455	1020	254	4530	4284	242	1
	1990	10551	7307	2074	560	1163	806	7221	7085	128	5
	1991	9842	7663	1455	521	714	532	7512	7410	97	12
	1992	11779	8341	1641	547	1793	1489	8221	8113	100	23
	1993	9820	7010	1451	469	1358	831	6874	6762	101	17
European Economic Community /2	1980	6758	4510	1365	452	882	182	4499	4273	221	1
	1990	10240	7213	1994	549	1026	705	7168	7060	99	5
	1991	9546	7544	1372	512	620	458	7480	7393	82	12
	1992	11474	8254	1571	545	1644	1352	8191	8096	88	23
	1993	9638	6919	1418	469	1299	818	6846	6744	92	17
European Free Trade Association	1980	181	31	12	3	138	72	31	10	21	0
	1990	312	94	80	11	138	101	54	25	29	0
	1991	295	119	83	9	93	73	32	16	15	0
	1992	304	87	69	2	149	138	29	17	12	0
	1993	182	91	33	0	59	13	27	19	9	0
Other developed economies	1980	25077	7290	12011	2359	4238	2815	3435	3277	150	49
	1990	17829	4759	10171	2372	2680	2431	959	891	61	107
	1991	15670	4254	8235	1480	3016	2901	873	780	82	104
	1992	17101	4675	8673	1246	2423	2380	728	629	89	485
	1993	15424	4350	7910	1487	1178	959	622	536	82	245

For general note and footnotes see end of table.

TABLEAU SPECIAL: B

Exportations mondiales par classes de marchandises et par régions (suite)

En millions de dollars E.-U. f.o.b.

conomies éveloppées /2,3,4 Canada	U.S.A. E.-U.	Japan Japon	Australia New Zealand Australie Nouvelle-Zélande	Developing economies Economies en voie de développement /1,3,4 Africa Afrique	America Amerique Total	America Amerique LAIA ALADI	Asia Asie Mid.East Moyen Orient	Asia Asie Other Autres /9	Oceania - Océanie	Année	← Exportations vers / Exportations en provenance de ↓
éréales (CTCI, Rev. 2 et Rev. 3, 041-045)											
134	56	3438	13	3299	4611	3711	2477	6216	74	1980	Monde /1,2,3
157	324	3394	49	3147	3279	2220	3788	5618	47	1990	
123	388	3240	43	2613	3104	2246	2557	5455	38	1991	
183	548	3202	31	3050	3542	2838	2716	6013	20	1992	
185	653	3135	28	2991	3680	2865	2446	4805	17	1993	
134	38	3399	13	2781	3878	3255	1602	4906	71	1980	Economies dévelopées /2,3,4
139	243	3165	35	2509	2301	1603	2636	4588	44	1990	
104	282	2820	27	1945	2122	1464	1536	4028	35	1991	
158	413	2782	16	2279	2422	1812	1354	4191	17	1992	
164	504	2709	15	2397	2364	1675	1298	3241	14	1993	
1	18	39	1	514	587	456	874	1204	3	1980	Economies en voie de développement /1,3,4
15	82	229	13	638	761	617	1123	1012	3	1990	
18	106	419	16	667	885	782	1012	1419	4	1991	
25	133	416	15	769	1120	1025	1352	1807	3	1992	
22	149	426	13	595	1315	1191	1139	1565	3	1993	
0	0	0	0	7	7	5	10	6	0	1980	OPEP
0	0	2	0	39	3	3	59	23	0	1990	
0	0	2	0	3	4	4	20	66	0	1991	
0	0	2	0	46	29	28	60	85	0	1992	
0	9	2	0	60	55	41	63	85	0	1993	
0	0	0	0	4	145	0	1	107	0	1980	Europe de l'Est et l'ancienne URSS /2,3,7
3	0	0	0	0	217	0	29	18	0	1990	
1	0	0	0	0	97	0	9	8	0	1991	
0	3	5	0	2	0	0	10	15	0	1992	
0	0	0	0	0	0	0	9	0	0	1993	
0	0	0	0	0	145	0	0	107	0	1980	L'ancienne URSS /3
...	...	...	...	...	...	...	...	...	...	1990	
...	...	...	...	...	...	...	...	...	...	1991	
.	.	.	.	.	.	.	.	.	.	1992	
.	.	.	.	.	.	.	.	.	.	1993	
.	.	.	.	.	.	.	.	.	.	1980	L'ancienne URSS-Europe /8
.	.	.	.	.	.	.	.	.	.	1990	
.	.	.	.	.	.	.	.	.	.	1991	
0	0	0	0	0	0	0	1	0	0	1992	
0	0	0	0	0	0	0	1	0	0	1993	
0	4	1	0	929	42	6	312	90	0	1980	Economies développées-Europe /2
1	43	2	0	958	117	11	593	335	1	1990	
1	90	5	0	587	119	24	460	273	0	1991	
1	64	19	1	748	138	25	458	251	0	1992	
1	69	19	1	775	160	44	289	196	0	1993	
0	4	1	0	919	42	6	310	90	0	1980	Communauté Economique Européenne /2
1	4	1	0	937	103	11	580	333	1	1990	
1	4	5	0	576	100	21	417	270	0	1991	
1	7	19	1	741	133	25	456	235	0	1992	
1	11	15	1	772	158	44	285	187	0	1993	
0	0	0	0	10	0	0	2	0	0	1980	Association Européenne de Libre Echange
0	40	1	0	21	14	0	12	2	0	1990	
0	86	0	0	10	19	3	43	2	0	1991	
0	57	0	0	6	5	0	3	15	0	1992	
0	58	3	0	3	2	0	5	10	0	1993	
133	34	3398	12	1852	3836	3249	1290	4816	71	1980	Autres economies développées
138	199	3163	35	1552	2184	1592	2043	4253	44	1990	
103	192	2815	26	1359	2003	1440	1076	3756	35	1991	
157	349	2763	15	1531	2284	1787	896	3940	17	1992	
162	435	2690	14	1622	2205	1630	1008	3044	13	1993	

Voir la fin du tableau pour la remarque générale et les notes.

SPECIAL TABLE: B

World exports by commodity classes and by regions (continued)

In million U.S. dollars f.o.b.

Exports to → / ↓ Exports from	Year	World Monde /1,2,3	Developed economies Econ. dévelop-pées /2,3,4	Developing economies Economies en voie de développement /1,3,4 Total	Developing economies OPEC OPEP	Eastern Europe and fmr. USSR-Europe Europe de l'Est et l'anc. URSS-Europe Total /2,3,7	Eastern Europe and fmr. USSR-Europe Former USSR-Eur. /10	Develop[ed] Econom[ies] Europe Total /2	Europe EEC CEE /2	Europe EFTA AELE	South Africa Afrique du Su[d]
		Cereals (SITC, Rev. 2 and Rev. 3, 041-045) (continue[d])									
Canada	1980	3811	924	1537	333	1350	1101	513	504	9	
	1990	3459	821	1810	583	828	803	175	171	4	5
	1991	3890	695	2001	472	1193	1166	142	136	6	3
	1992	4317	913	2510	511	894	894	170	147	23	3
	1993	2698	938	1674	475	86	65	97	89	8	3
United States	1980	17565	6033	8478	1388	2112	938	2902	2753	141	4
	1990	11952	3490	6411	1013	1833	1621	740	677	57	4
	1991	10106	3138	5098	655	1705	1617	706	620	76	4
	1992	11254	3595	5885	668	1527	1485	547	472	65	43
	1993	10736	3329	6087	963	1088	890	515	438	73	20
Japan	1980	243	0	243	60	0	0	0	0	0	
	1990	0	0	0	0	0	0	0	0	0	
	1991	0	0	0	0	0	0	0	0	0	
	1992	0	0	0	0	0	0	0	0	0	
	1993	0	0	0	0	0	0	0	0	0	
Australia, New Zealand	1980	2863	332	1753	578	776	775	20	20	0	
	1990	2195	268	1908	776	18	7	19	19	0	
	1991	1470	258	1094	352	118	118	3	2	0	2
	1992	1432	131	218	66	1	1	8	7	0	2
	1993	1945	56	131	49	4	4	8	7	0	
Developing economies-Africa	1980	278	27	236	95	15	0	22	14	8	
	1990	222	30	188	33	0	0	18	15	3	1
	1991	174	38	127	36	8	0	31	30	1	
	1992	135	18	112	52	5	0	13	13	0	
	1993	139	29	110	40	1	0	20	18	2	
Developing economies-America	1980	1873	184	630	61	1059	1056	157	157	0	
	1990	1621	189	1305	372	118	112	98	90	7	
	1991	1294	292	992	145	6	3	101	93	4	1
	1992	1831	431	1390	188	4	0	169	164	5	10
	1993	1801	291	1469	119	35	27	153	150	3	
Developing economies-Europe/ 5	1980	93	14	10	0	69	35	14	2	12	
	1990	86	12	39	2	35	13	12	10	1	
	1991	55	7	24	2	24	9	7	7	0	
	1992	71	13	48	0	10	3	13	9	1	
	1993	47	6	27	0	14	3	6	5	0	
Developing economies-Middle East	1980	107	3	91	74	13	4	3	1	2	
	1990	208	29	135	17	0	0	29	29	0	
	1991	403	56	242	114	106	106	42	35	7	
	1992	640	63	493	199	84	76	45	40	2	
	1993	344	46	288	130	10	5	38	35	1	
Developing economies-Other Asia	1980	2634	131	2219	1031	285	233	88	84	4	
	1990	2512	352	1872	502	242	216	93	81	12	
	1991	3360	558	2603	638	192	162	126	110	14	3
	1992	3940	643	3035	960	256	213	132	108	23	5
	1993	3754	711	2748	809	292	206	141	111	29	7
Former USSR-Asia /9	1980	.	.	.	.	.	.	.	.	.	
	1990	.	.	.	.	.	.	.	.	.	
	1991	.	.	.	.	.	.	.	.	.	
	1992	1	0	0	0	0	.	0	0	0	[illegible]
	1993	0	0	0	0	0	.	0	0	0	[illegible]
Developing economies-Oceania	1980	2	0	1	0	0	0	0	0	0	[illegible]
	1990	0	0	0	0	0	0	0	0	0	[illegible]
	1991	0	0	0	0	0	0	0	0	0	[illegible]
	1992	0	0	0	0	0	0	0	0	0	[illegible]
	1993	0	0	0	0	0	0	0	0	0	[illegible]

For general note and footnotes see end of table.

TABLEAU SPECIAL: B

Exportations mondiales par classes de marchandises et par régions (suite)

En millions de dollars E.-U. f.o.b.

conomies éveloppées /2,3,4				Developing economies Economies en voie de développement /1,3,4							← Exportations vers
Canada	U.S.A. E.-U.	Japan Japon	Australia New Zealand Australie Nouvelle-Zélande	Africa Afrique	America Amerique Total	America Amerique LAIA ALADI	Asia Asie Mid.East Moyen Orient	Asia Asie Other Autres /9	Oceania Océanie	Année	Exportations en provenance de ↓
éréales (CTCI, Rev. 2 et Rev. 3, 041-045) (suite)											
.	34	353	0	249	610	391	152	516	0	1980	Canada
.	198	389	1	176	258	164	403	972	0	1990	
.	192	327	1	167	394	310	243	1197	0	1991	
.	348	362	3	127	554	501	240	1589	0	1992	
.	435	344	4	181	478	432	192	823	0	1993	
133	.	2751	1	1231	3185	2817	600	3321	5	1980	Etats-Unis
138	.	2391	15	1052	1881	1389	842	2533	7	1990	
103	.	2135	8	1022	1574	1101	519	1970	6	1991	
157	.	2272	7	1342	1701	1258	584	2246	7	1992	
162	.	2275	9	1422	1718	1190	755	2169	6	1993	
0	0	.	0	44	5	5	1	193	0	1980	Japon
0	0	.	0	0	0	0	0	0	0	1990	
0	0	.	0	0	0	0	0	0	0	1991	
0	0	.	0	0	0	0	0	0	0	1992	
0	0	.	0	0	0	0	0	0	0	1993	
0	0	295	11	328	36	36	537	786	66	1980	Australie, Nouvelle-Zélande
0	1	228	19	303	29	29	798	741	36	1990	
0	0	214	18	151	19	19	314	582	29	1991	
0	2	94	5	2	29	29	71	105	10	1992	
0	0	46	2	2	8	8	61	52	7	1993	
0	0	4	0	85	7	6	108	36	0	1980	Economies en voie de développement-Afrique
0	0	0	0	142	4	4	39	2	0	1990	
0	0	0	0	85	2	0	38	1	0	1991	
0	0	0	0	52	0	0	59	0	0	1992	
0	0	0	0	46	1	0	64	0	0	1993	
0	9	7	0	13	448	349	46	123	0	1980	Economies en voie de développement-Amérique
0	12	77	0	28	692	588	405	180	0	1990	
0	14	158	1	45	726	680	130	90	0	1991	
3	31	108	0	131	1013	956	152	95	0	1992	
0	27	94	0	51	1229	1155	124	62	0	1993	
0	0	0	0	9	0	0	0	1	0	1980	Economies en voie de développement-Europe /5
0	0	0	0	8	0	0	30	0	0	1990	
0	0	0	0	6	0	0	18	0	0	1991	
0	0	0	0	20	0	0	3	0	0	1992	
0	0	0	0	5	0	0	0	0	0	1993	
0	0	0	0	37	0	0	55	0	0	1980	Economies en voie de développement-Moyen Orient
0	0	0	0	43	3	3	80	8	0	1990	
0	0	0	0	29	13	11	99	101	0	1991	
0	0	0	0	109	12	8	192	179	0	1992	
0	1	0	0	48	10	9	92	138	0	1993	
1	9	28	1	370	133	100	665	1044	2	1980	Economies en voie de développement-Autres Pays d'Asie
15	69	152	13	416	63	22	568	822	2	1990	
18	91	261	15	502	144	90	728	1226	3	1991	
21	101	307	15	457	96	61	946	1533	3	1992	
22	121	332	13	445	76	27	859	1364	3	1993	
.	.	.	.	.	.	.	.	.	.	1980	l'ancienne URSS asiatique /9
.	.	.	.	.	.	.	.	.	.	1990	
.	.	.	.	.	.	.	.	.	.	1991	
0	0	0	0	0	0	0	0	0	0	1992	
0	0	0	0	0	0	0	0	0	0	1993	
0	0	0	0	0	0	0	0	0	1	1980	Economies en voie de développement-Océanie
0	0	0	0	0	0	0	0	0	0	1990	
0	0	0	0	0	0	0	0	0	0	1991	
0	0	0	0	0	0	0	0	0	0	1992	
0	0	0	0	0	0	0	0	0	0	1993	

Voir la fin du tableau pour la remarque générale et les notes.

SPECIAL TABLE: B

World exports by commodity classes and by regions (continued)

In million U.S. dollars f.o.b.

Exports to → / ↓ Exports from	Year	World Monde /1,2,3	Developed economies Econ. dévelop-pées /2,3,4	Developing economies Economies en voie de développement /1,3,4: Total	Developing economies: OPEC OPEP	Eastern Europe and fmr. USSR-Europe Europe de l'Est et l'anc. URSS-Europe: Total /2,3,7	Eastern Europe and fmr. USSR-Europe: Former USSR-Eur. /10	Europe: Total /2	Europe: EEC CEE /2	Europe: EFTA AELE	South Africa Afrique du Sud
		Crude materials (excluding fuels), oils, fats (SITC, Rev. 2 and Rev. 3, 2 and									
World /1,2,3	1980	136870	93420	29563	4082	9698	3025	59934	54175	5724	57
	1990	174926	124253	41470	4529	8036	3268	80434	72081	8230	42
	1991	163494	114273	42862	4683	5215	2335	73145	65366	7692	39
	1992	167936	115481	47237	5862	4217	1406	73991	65427	8476	49
	1993	162933	107979	47427	5857	3843	1142	64240	56292	7884	48
Developed economies /2,3,4	1980	83700	62198	15065	2567	2686	953	42264	38114	4121	52
	1990	114209	89308	22187	2460	2009	696	60189	53952	6182	29
	1991	107366	82283	22655	2389	1779	762	55601	49490	6052	30
	1992	107770	81973	23442	2555	1778	572	55259	48949	6244	32
	1993	102896	74707	23474	2555	1406	359	45719	40351	5326	32
Developing economies /1,3,4	1980	43589	27643	12205	1369	3400	1727	14965	14101	859	4
	1990	50013	28650	17657	1994	3397	2276	15035	14128	891	13
	1991	49568	28121	19285	2262	2103	1359	14183	13324	832	9
	1992	53014	28948	22568	3170	1216	621	14664	13675	966	17
	1993	52167	27939	22686	3152	1172	608	13780	12720	1037	16
OPEC	1980	5244	3319	1615	82	157	73	1243	1193	50	
	1990	4254	2745	1302	123	111	38	1302	1253	47	
	1991	4806	3153	1535	103	116	41	1427	1305	121	
	1992	5687	3384	2098	176	183	115	1497	1411	86	
	1993	5589	3208	2235	186	134	90	1462	1351	111	
Eastern Europe and the former USSR /2,3,7	1980	9581	3579	2293	146	3612	345	2705	1960	745	
	1990	10705	6294	1626	75	2630	296	5209	4001	1157	
	1991	6561	3869	922	32	1333	215	3361	2553	808	
	1992	7152	4560	1228	137	1223	213	4068	2803	1265	
	1993	7871	5334	1267	150	1265	175	4741	3221	1520	
Former USSR /3	1980	7047	2221	1991	85	2835	.	1381	1089	291	
	1990	...	...	...	...	...	.	...	...	...	.
	1991	...	...	...	...	...	.	...	...	...	.
	1992	.	.	.	.	.	.	.	.	.	
	1993	.	.	.	.	.	.	.	.	.	
Former USSR-Europe /8	1980	.	.	.	.	.	.	.	.	.	
	1990	.	.	.	.	.	.	.	.	.	
	1991	.	.	.	.	.	.	.	.	.	
	1992	4212	2673	748	106	790	21	2218	1398	819	[illegible]
	1993	4890	3287	804	110	799	37	2735	1695	1040	[illegible]
Developed economies-Europe /2	1980	33953	28668	3678	1387	1585	476	27111	23780	3304	23
	1990	53519	46418	5292	982	1274	321	43732	38580	5099	17
	1991	50107	43280	5206	834	1125	302	40678	35668	4956	18
	1992	51171	43965	5332	866	1350	378	41281	36136	5093	16
	1993	44845	37263	5966	960	1143	256	34424	30032	4353	16
European Economic Community /2	1980	24349	20694	2622	931	1011	301	19469	17115	2332	14
	1990	41365	35953	4174	614	865	188	33608	29752	3807	16
	1991	39802	34284	4232	545	924	239	31967	28066	3851	17
	1992	40686	34741	4376	581	1176	346	32317	28301	3968	15
	1993	35460	29221	4908	644	979	219	26741	23335	3369	14
European Free Trade Association	1980	9587	7957	1055	455	574	175	7625	6652	969	8
	1990	12140	10452	1117	367	409	133	10112	8816	1291	[illegible]
	1991	10295	8986	973	287	201	62	8702	7593	1104	[illegible]
	1992	10473	9212	955	285	174	32	8953	7824	1124	[illegible]
	1993	9370	8029	1057	316	164	36	7670	6685	983	1
Other developed economies	1980	49747	33529	11387	1180	1101	477	15154	14334	817	28
	1990	60690	42890	16895	1478	735	375	16458	15372	1083	12
	1991	57259	39003	17449	1555	654	460	14922	13822	1097	12
	1992	56599	38008	18110	1688	428	194	13978	12813	1151	15
	1993	58051	37443	17508	1595	263	104	11294	10320	973	16

For general note and footnotes see end of table.

Exportations mondiales par classes de marchandises et par régions (suite)

En millions de dollars E.-U. f.o.b.

conomies éveloppées /2,3,4				Developing economies Economies en voie de développement /1,3,4						← Exportations vers	
Canada	U.S.A. E.-U.	Japan Japon	Australia New Zealand Australie Nouvelle-Zélande	Africa Afrique	America Amerique Total	America Amerique LAIA ALADI	Asia Asie Mid.East Moyen Orient	Asia Asie Other Autres /9	Oceania Océanie	Année	Exportations en provenance de ↓
atières brutes (sauf combustibles), huiles et graisses (CTCI, Rev. 2 et Rev. 3, 2 et 4)											
2444	10191	19000	1038	3397	4822	3993	2790	15941	61	1980	Monde /1,2,3
3677	14102	23900	1277	4397	6079	4838	3780	25965	81	1990	
3688	12830	22619	1141	3935	6428	5395	3804	27722	104	1991	
3789	14246	21222	1272	4325	6871	5871	5782	29393	97	1992	
3987	15871	21621	1329	4096	7240	6173	6112	29231	115	1993	
2094	6319	10106	685	2264	2999	2519	1402	7753	39	1980	Economies dévelopées /2,3,4
3263	9943	14409	848	2438	3354	2815	2026	13679	57	1990	
3195	8721	13351	744	2244	3754	3203	1869	14241	64	1991	
3239	9541	12459	772	2366	4039	3482	2029	14549	66	1992	
3432	11059	12998	826	2110	4259	3657	2369	14296	65	1993	
343	3837	8064	352	923	1587	1457	1284	7983	23	1980	Economies en voie de développement /1,3,4
411	4113	8467	430	1690	2371	1981	1536	11825	24	1990	
482	4082	8804	397	1557	2482	2143	1798	13252	40	1991	
535	4686	8314	500	1793	2679	2316	3359	14469	32	1992	
532	4780	8096	502	1826	2867	2462	3263	14525	51	1993	
29	636	1410	1	67	42	39	106	1371	0	1980	OPEP
33	640	707	38	190	131	123	168	798	0	1990	
43	660	944	46	136	80	74	290	1008	0	1991	
109	818	853	69	268	111	102	340	1364	0	1992	
59	778	812	59	264	185	169	394	1377	0	1993	
7	34	831	2	210	237	16	103	205	0	1980	Europe de l'Est et l'ancienne URSS /2,3,7
4	46	1024	0	268	354	41	218	460	0	1990	
10	27	464	0	134	193	49	136	228	0	1991	
16	19	449	1	166	153	73	393	374	0	1992	
24	32	527	1	161	113	54	480	410	0	1993	
2	13	823	2	118	227	9	72	157	0	1980	L'ancienne URSS /3
...	...	...	...	...	...	...	...	...	...	1990	
...	...	...	...	...	...	...	...	...	...	1991	
.	.	.	.	.	.	.	.	.	.	1992	
.	.	.	.	.	.	.	.	.	.	1993	
.	.	.	.	.	.	.	.	.	.	1980	L'ancienne URSS-Europe /8
.	.	.	.	.	.	.	.	.	.	1990	
.	.	.	.	.	.	.	.	.	.	1991	
14	10	431	0	46	110	33	273	312	0	1992	
20	22	508	0	48	94	37	319	337	0	1993	
129	737	275	91	1404	308	242	997	575	10	1980	Economies développées-Europe /2
203	1276	710	163	1457	475	347	1077	1743	17	1990	
220	1224	692	136	1295	462	359	1113	1918	14	1991	
241	1298	675	146	1325	512	404	1213	1912	14	1992	
223	1326	827	139	1253	542	436	1467	2344	12	1993	
112	657	188	73	1054	260	205	653	403	10	1980	Communauté Economique Européenne /2
185	1159	594	136	1053	435	314	822	1504	17	1990	
210	1109	602	123	949	420	324	901	1667	14	1991	
227	1189	602	135	977	483	381	992	1659	14	1992	
207	1193	689	127	891	511	412	1206	2042	12	1993	
17	80	87	19	350	48	37	343	172	0	1980	Association Européenne de Libre Echange
18	116	116	26	404	40	34	254	239	0	1990	
10	115	90	12	346	43	35	211	252	0	1991	
13	109	73	10	347	29	23	220	253	0	1992	
16	133	138	12	362	31	23	260	301	0	1993	
1965	5582	9831	593	860	2691	2277	406	7179	29	1980	Autres economies développées
3059	8668	13699	685	981	2879	2468	949	11936	40	1990	
2975	7497	12659	609	950	3291	2844	756	12323	50	1991	
2999	8244	11784	626	1042	3527	3079	816	12637	52	1992	
3209	9732	12170	687	857	3718	3221	902	11952	53	1993	

Voir la fin du tableau pour la remarque générale et les notes.

SPECIAL TABLE: B

World exports by commodity classes and by regions (continued)

In million U.S. dollars f.o.b.

Exports from ↓ / Exports to →	Year	World Monde /1,2,3	Developed economies Econ. dévelop-pées /2,3,4	Developing economies Economies en voie de développement /1,3,4: Total	Developing economies: OPEC OPEP	Eastern Europe and fmr. USSR-Europe Europe de l'Est et l'anc. URSS-Europe: Total /2,3,7	Eastern Europe and fmr. USSR-Europe: Former USSR-Eur. /10	Developed Economies – Europe: Total /2	Europe: EEC CEE /2	Europe: EFTA AELE	South Africa Afrique du Sud
		Crude materials (excluding fuels), oils, fats (SITC, Rev. 2 and Rev. 3, 2 and 4) (continue[d])									
Canada	1980	12577	11188	1136	175	86	43	3632	3402	230	[illegible]
	1990	17697	15839	1784	250	74	36	4429	3884	546	[illegible]
	1991	15521	13762	1728	236	31	20	3939	3358	580	[illegible]
	1992	16032	14309	1680	181	42	7	3589	3113	475	[illegible]
	1993	16727	15183	1511	175	32	7	2856	2443	413	[illegible]
United States	1980	25688	17201	7882	735	430	84	9311	8798	512	[illegible]
	1990	28176	17145	10740	914	288	103	6792	6470	319	[illegible]
	1991	26692	15806	10573	951	311	208	6280	5983	293	[illegible]
	1992	26815	15917	10563	1000	284	165	6662	6356	304	[illegible]
	1993	25855	15419	10273	967	118	64	5591	5349	240	[illegible]
Japan	1980	1580	395	1087	162	97	57	237	220	18	[illegible]
	1990	2044	529	1456	122	58	47	284	259	25	[illegible]
	1991	2087	519	1541	150	27	22	273	254	19	[illegible]
	1992	2300	500	1794	180	6	2	261	243	18	[illegible]
	1993	2297	484	1799	188	14	10	219	200	19	[illegible]
Australia, New Zealand	1980	7717	4474	1262	108	481	292	1716	1685	29	[illegible]
	1990	8501	5884	2341	187	276	189	2391	2358	33	[illegible]
	1991	9036	5716	3081	214	239	211	2078	2022	56	[illegible]
	1992	8838	5409	3384	273	45	16	2102	2014	77	[illegible]
	1993	10767	4641	3285	220	51	20	1424	1360	64	[illegible]
Developing economies-Africa	1980	7424	5713	1011	102	412	58	4834	4670	161	[illegible]
	1990	6285	4416	1505	277	292	87	3728	3576	150	[illegible]
	1991	5890	4288	1360	257	216	40	3623	3469	148	[illegible]
	1992	6081	4274	1523	296	213	4	3558	3353	198	[illegible]
	1993	6097	4253	1540	294	209	2	3541	3300	233	[illegible]
Developing economies-America	1980	11860	8255	2577	476	1003	610	4781	4336	443	[illegible]
	1990	15492	10190	4255	738	1043	685	5797	5398	387	[illegible]
	1991	15328	10043	4683	861	597	410	5528	5155	356	[illegible]
	1992	15072	10199	4684	797	164	46	5597	5136	459	[illegible]
	1993	14786	9514	4988	832	82	44	5035	4496	536	[illegible]
Developing economies-Europe/ 5	1980	685	364	142	28	179	76	353	312	41	[illegible]
	1990	1000	509	159	13	332	244	493	418	74	[illegible]
	1991	661	336	105	8	220	161	326	278	48	[illegible]
	1992	583	390	172	10	20	6	386	341	45	[illegible]
	1993	416	287	115	8	14	2	280	240	39	[illegible]
Developing economies-Middle East	1980	1459	685	487	156	286	75	603	506	97	[illegible]
	1990	2136	947	878	211	215	109	806	720	87	[illegible]
	1991	2225	970	1038	261	212	102	809	694	114	[illegible]
	1992	2409	854	1377	350	145	96	695	615	79	[illegible]
	1993	2452	889	1399	379	139	110	725	652	72	[illegible]
Developing economies-Other Asia	1980	21206	11764	7914	607	1520	908	4117	4002	114	[illegible]
	1990	24056	11795	10616	755	1515	1151	3938	3778	156	[illegible]
	1991	24363	11682	11807	875	859	646	3634	3499	130	[illegible]
	1992	27775	12415	14539	1716	674	469	4155	4000	142	[illegible]
	1993	27089	12024	14294	1638	729	450	3954	3814	128	[illegible]
Former USSR-Asia /9	1980	.	.	.	.	.	.	.	.	.	
	1990	.	.	.	.	.	.	.	.	.	
	1991	.	.	.	.	.	.	.	.	.	
	1992	1991	206	1608	670	67	.	187	178	9	[illegible]
	1993	1808	233	1409	598	166	.	201	178	23	[illegible]
Developing economies-Oceania	1980	955	864	74	0	0	0	278	275	3	[illegible]
	1990	1042	793	244	0	0	0	275	238	37	[illegible]
	1991	1102	802	292	0	0	0	263	228	35	[illegible]
	1992	1094	817	272	1	0	0	273	230	43	[illegible]
	1993	1327	972	349	1	0	0	246	217	28	[illegible]

For general note and footnotes see end of table.

Exportations mondiales par classes de marchandises et par régions (suite)

En millions de dollars E.-U. f.o.b.

conomies éveloppées /2,3,4 Canada	U.S.A. E.-U.	Japan Japon	Australia New Zealand Australie Nouvelle-Zélande	Developing economies Economies en voie de développement /1,3,4 Africa Afrique	America Amerique Total	America Amerique LAIA ALADI	Asia Asie Mid.East Moyen Orient	Asia Asie Other Autres /9	Oceania Océanie	Année	← Exportations vers / Exportations en provenance de ↓
atières brutes (sauf combustibles), huiles et graisses (CTCI, Rev. 2 et Rev. 3, 2 et 4) (suite)											
.	5269	2014	192	217	265	218	41	584	0	1980	Canada
.	7989	3165	187	275	277	258	82	1141	0	1990	
.	6837	2809	108	246	229	210	76	1165	0	1991	
.	7677	2870	117	186	222	205	69	1203	0	1992	
.	9088	3072	124	101	252	244	83	1072	0	1993	
1857	.	5561	214	566	2342	1987	180	4664	10	1980	Etats-Unis
2981	.	6945	226	547	2521	2135	746	6852	14	1990	
2908	.	6163	241	573	2956	2534	554	6441	16	1991	
2923	.	5881	217	604	3210	2785	541	6168	16	1992	
3151	.	6209	237	517	3359	2876	591	5775	15	1993	
40	44	.	38	29	46	35	79	930	1	1980	Japon
32	148	.	40	19	15	13	36	1384	1	1990	
27	154	.	38	22	20	16	43	1454	2	1991	
8	167	.	41	23	23	19	45	1700	2	1992	
9	194	.	40	30	24	20	42	1700	1	1993	
68	258	2254	149	47	33	32	98	997	18	1980	Australie, Nouvelle-Zélande
14	284	2955	222	49	33	32	71	2134	25	1990	
11	285	3111	213	27	52	52	67	2881	31	1991	
48	270	2701	237	38	40	39	102	3171	33	1992	
37	277	2588	271	34	52	52	133	3028	35	1993	
59	336	466	9	249	85	84	106	375	0	1980	Economies en voie de développement-Afrique
57	303	226	21	652	83	79	149	564	0	1990	
61	311	203	10	473	85	74	128	624	1	1991	
70	350	203	11	603	90	87	142	638	1	1992	
69	341	191	16	624	73	73	149	648	0	1993	
144	1772	1503	13	175	1195	1089	376	783	2	1980	Economies en voie de développement-Amérique
222	2198	1857	48	360	1947	1609	423	1481	0	1990	
273	2115	2023	47	354	2017	1728	507	1771	10	1991	
267	2244	1927	51	364	2119	1838	493	1700	0	1992	
291	2307	1755	50	338	2235	1923	517	1874	21	1993	
0	3	5	0	85	1	1	34	22	1	1980	Economies en voie de développement-Europe /5
0	6	3	0	91	6	6	26	36	0	1990	
0	4	2	0	59	4	4	17	25	0	1991	
0	2	1	0	34	0	0	17	4	0	1992	
0	3	1	0	18	0	0	17	2	0	1993	
0	36	45	0	77	1	1	193	182	0	1980	Economies en voie de développement-Moyen Orient
1	53	68	4	112	4	4	299	412	0	1990	
1	44	105	3	159	5	5	452	385	0	1991	
1	49	88	12	220	11	11	549	565	0	1992	
1	59	75	18	227	45	44	573	537	0	1993	
140	1681	5579	219	336	306	282	576	6566	2	1980	Economies en voie de développement-Autres Pays d'Asie
131	1548	5859	296	474	331	284	639	9104	9	1990	
147	1603	6004	272	512	370	332	695	10170	14	1991	
197	2036	5646	337	572	458	380	2153	11313	14	1992	
171	2063	5441	334	619	514	422	2006	11134	13	1993	
.	.	.	.	.	.	.	.	.	.	1980	l'ancienne URSS asiatique /9
.	.	.	.	.	.	.	.	.	.	1990	
.	.	.	.	.	.	.	.	.	.	1991	
0	2	17	0	13	58	21	1410	126	0	1992	
0	5	28	0	22	69	26	1180	137	0	1993	
0	10	466	109	0	0	0	0	57	17	1980	Economies en voie de développement-Océanie
0	5	454	60	0	0	0	0	228	15	1990	
0	5	468	65	0	0	0	0	276	16	1991	
0	6	449	88	0	0	0	5	249	18	1992	
0	7	633	85	0	0	0	1	331	17	1993	

Voir la fin du tableau pour la remarque générale et les notes.

SPECIAL TABLE: B

World exports by commodity classes and by regions (continued)

In million U.S. dollars f.o.b.

Oil seeds and, oleaginous fruit (SITC, Rev. 2 and Rev. 3, 2

Exports from ↓ / Exports to →	Year	World Monde /1,2,3	Developed economies Econ. dévelop-pées /2,3,4	Developing economies Economies en voie de développement /1,3,4: Total	Developing economies: OPEC OPEP	Eastern Europe and fmr. USSR-Europe Europe de l'Est et l'anc. URSS-Europe: Total /2,3,7	Eastern Europe and fmr. USSR-Europe: Former USSR-Eur. /10	Developed economies, Europe: Total /2	Developed economies, Europe: EEC CEE /2	Developed economies, Europe: EFTA AELE
World /1,2,3	1980	9741	7419	1595	136	477	271	5442	5280	161
	1990	10375	8141	1852	200	335	182	5834	5591	231
	1991	10100	7454	2284	232	348	253	5312	5102	194
	1992	10172	7383	2562	230	163	78	5264	5129	134
	1993	9987	7106	2556	282	140	65	4782	4684	96
Developed economies /2,3,4	1980	7623	5993	1228	99	201	56	4273	4155	117
	1990	6856	5604	1083	36	156	61	3804	3730	72
	1991	6799	5185	1387	58	217	176	3466	3391	74
	1992	7131	5286	1686	103	107	52	3589	3513	76
	1993	6848	4920	1817	157	64	23	2983	2941	42
Developing economies /1,3,4	1980	2063	1401	354	30	260	215	1146	1106	39
	1990	3282	2353	751	163	173	120	1857	1738	108
	1991	3096	2101	872	174	119	75	1694	1616	63
	1992	2814	1947	821	128	34	15	1529	1491	37
	1993	2921	2020	708	124	54	39	1635	1601	33
OPEC	1980	123	71	17	1	0	0	65	64	0
	1990	34	22	12	1	0	0	13	11	1
	1991	39	8	30	1	0	0	4	4	0
	1992	50	15	35	3	0	0	9	7	2
	1993	53	15	39	1	0	0	11	10	1
Eastern Europe and the former USSR /2,3,7	1980	54	25	13	6	16	0	23	19	4
	1990	236	184	18	0	6	1	174	123	51
	1991	205	168	25	0	12	2	152	95	58
	1992	227	150	55	0	22	10	146	125	21
	1993	219	166	30	0	22	3	163	142	21
Former USSR /3	1980	2	2	0	0	0	.	0	0	0
	1990	...	...	...	...	...	.	...	...	...
	1991	...	...	...	...	...	.	...	...	...
	1992	.	.	.	.	.	.	.	.	.
	1993	.	.	.	.	.	.	.	.	.
Former USSR-Europe /8	1980	.	.	.	.	.	.	.	.	.
	1990	.	.	.	.	.	.	.	.	.
	1991	.	.	.	.	.	.	.	.	.
	1992	89	62	19	0	8	0	62	59	2
	1993	89	58	23	0	8	0	58	55	3
Developed economies-Europe /2	1980	474	453	9	7	12	3	450	436	14
	1990	2062	2038	14	1	11	0	2027	1998	29
	1991	1717	1690	13	1	14	1	1675	1647	27
	1992	1617	1538	59	12	21	1	1501	1464	37
	1993	1042	949	57	13	35	6	848	814	33
European Economic Community /2	1980	442	424	9	7	9	3	421	409	12
	1990	2031	2016	8	1	7	0	2006	1982	24
	1991	1688	1662	12	1	13	1	1647	1624	23
	1992	1595	1520	58	12	17	1	1483	1452	30
	1993	1013	928	57	13	28	6	826	798	28
European Free Trade Association	1980	32	29	0	0	3	0	29	27	2
	1990	31	21	6	0	4	0	21	16	5
	1991	29	28	0	0	1	0	28	23	5
	1992	22	18	1	0	4	0	18	11	6
	1993	30	22	1	0	7	0	22	16	5
Other developed economies	1980	7149	5540	1218	93	189	53	3823	3719	103
	1990	4794	3567	1070	36	145	61	1777	1732	44
	1991	5082	3495	1374	57	203	175	1791	1744	47
	1992	5513	3749	1627	90	86	51	2089	2050	39
	1993	5805	3971	1760	144	29	17	2136	2126	9

For general note and footnotes see end of table.

Exportations mondiales par classes de marchandises et par régions (suite)

En millions de dollars E.-U. f.o.b.

...onomies ...veloppées /2,3,4: Canada	U.S.A. E.-U.	Japan Japon	Australia New Zealand Australie Nouvelle-Zélande	Developing economies Economies en voie de développement /1,3,4: Africa Afrique	America Amerique: Total	America Amerique: LAIA ALADI	Asia Asie: Mid.East Moyen Orient	Asia Asie: Other Autres /9	Oceania Océanie	Année	← Exportations vers / Exportations en provenance de ↓
...aines et fruits oléagineux (CTCI, Rev. 2 et Rev. 3, 22)											
157	77	1633	20	65	560	518	73	834	4	1980	Monde /1,2,3
149	202	1814	43	94	519	350	76	1120	4	1990	
140	158	1672	44	90	737	605	101	1311	5	1991	
116	151	1667	23	126	932	815	132	1337	3	1992	
163	188	1787	38	114	865	725	123	1439	3	1993	
151	28	1444	15	32	452	416	11	682	0	1980	Economies dévelopées /2,3,4
136	125	1432	23	28	335	261	6	680	3	1990	
106	91	1389	25	22	521	439	8	816	3	1991	
102	79	1374	10	23	730	658	18	896	3	1992	
141	119	1531	25	40	684	593	22	1065	3	1993	
6	49	188	5	27	108	102	62	153	3	1980	Economies en voie de développement /1,3,4
13	69	382	20	66	172	76	71	439	1	1990	
26	64	283	19	68	202	152	93	489	2	1991	
14	71	292	12	100	178	134	96	438	0	1992	
21	69	256	12	73	179	129	80	374	0	1993	
0	0	6	0	0	0	0	1	15	0	1980	OPEP
0	1	8	0	5	4	3	1	2	0	1990	
0	0	2	0	8	5	4	7	10	0	1991	
0	0	3	0	8	7	7	7	11	0	1992	
0	0	3	0	8	22	22	5	4	0	1993	
0	0	2	0	6	0	0	0	0	0	1980	Europe de l'Est et l'ancienne URSS /2,3,7
0	9	0	0	0	13	13	0	0	0	1990	
9	3	0	0	0	14	14	0	7	0	1991	
0	0	0	0	3	23	23	18	3	0	1992	
0	0	0	0	0	3	3	21	0	0	1993	
0	0	2	0	0	0	0	0	0	0	1980	L'ancienne URSS /3
...	...	...	...	...	...	...	...	...	...	1990	
...	...	...	...	...	...	...	...	...	...	1991	
.	.	.	.	.	.	.	.	.	.	1992	
.	.	.	.	.	.	.	.	.	.	1993	
.	.	.	.	.	.	.	.	.	.	1980	L'ancienne URSS-Europe /8
.	.	.	.	.	.	.	.	.	.	1990	
.	.	.	.	.	.	.	.	.	.	1991	
0	0	0	0	0	0	0	17	0	0	1992	
0	0	0	0	0	0	0	21	0	0	1993	
1	1	0	0	6	1	1	1	0	0	1980	Economies développées-Europe /2
4	3	1	1	2	1	1	1	0	0	1990	
7	5	1	0	3	2	1	2	0	0	1991	
10	3	9	0	15	32	32	2	3	0	1992	
12	3	83	1	21	14	14	3	16	0	1993	
1	1	0	0	6	1	1	1	0	0	1980	Communauté Economique Européenne /2
4	3	1	1	2	1	1	1	0	0	1990	
7	5	1	0	3	2	1	2	0	0	1991	
10	3	9	0	14	32	32	2	3	0	1992	
12	3	83	1	21	14	14	3	16	0	1993	
0	0	0	0	0	0	0	0	0	0	1980	Association Européenne de Libre Echange
0	0	0	0	0	0	0	0	0	0	1990	
0	0	0	0	0	0	0	0	0	0	1991	
0	0	0	0	1	0	0	0	0	0	1992	
0	0	0	0	0	0	0	0	0	0	1993	
150	27	1444	15	26	451	415	10	681	0	1980	Autres economies développées
132	121	1431	21	26	333	261	5	680	3	1990	
98	86	1388	25	19	518	438	6	816	3	1991	
91	77	1365	10	8	698	626	16	893	3	1992	
129	116	1449	25	19	669	579	19	1049	3	1993	

Voir la fin du tableau pour la remarque générale et les notes.

SPECIAL TABLE: B

World exports by commodity classes and by regions (continued)

In million U.S. dollars f.o.b.

Exports to → / ↓ Exports from	Year	World Monde /1,2,3	Developed economies Econ. développées /2,3,4	Developing economies Economies en voie de développement /1,3,4 Total	OPEC OPEP	Eastern Europe and fmr. USSR-Europe Europe de l'Est et l'anc. URSS-Europe Total /2,3,7	Former USSR-Eur. /10	Europe Total /2	EEC CEE /2	EFTA AELE	Develop… Economi… South Africa Afrique du Sud
		Oil seeds and, oleaginous fruit (SITC, Rev. 2 and Rev. 3, 22) (continue…									
Canada	1980	553	491	47	9	14	7	159	153	5	
	1990	770	744	26	0	0	0	73	72	2	
	1991	644	617	27	1	0	0	65	63	2	
	1992	604	564	36	1	4	4	68	65	3	
	1993	728	635	87	1	6	3	131	129	2	
United States	1980	6550	5032	1169	83	175	46	3651	3555	96	
	1990	3908	2750	1008	35	145	61	1666	1625	41	
	1991	4313	2804	1305	55	203	175	1684	1641	43	
	1992	4799	3092	1574	90	82	47	1968	1934	34	
	1993	4972	3242	1663	144	23	13	1965	1960	5	
Japan	1980	0	0	0	0	0	0	0	0	0	
	1990	7	0	7	0	0	0	0	0	0	
	1991	8	0	8	0	0	0	0	0	0	
	1992	6	0	6	0	0	0	0	0	0	
	1993	2	0	2	0	0	0	0	0	0	
Australia, New Zealand	1980	8	6	2	1	0	0	2	2	0	
	1990	41	33	8	0	0	0	3	3	0	
	1991	46	30	15	0	0	0	3	3	0	
	1992	44	38	6	0	0	0	5	4	0	
	1993	57	51	5	0	0	0	5	4	0	
Developing economies-Africa	1980	294	178	66	15	13	12	159	151	8	
	1990	194	86	99	28	6	1	69	61	8	
	1991	176	65	99	28	9	1	54	52	2	
	1992	181	73	95	27	8	0	65	61	3	
	1993	196	76	108	29	9	0	58	55	3	
Developing economies-America	1980	1220	894	134	3	193	191	806	783	23	
	1990	2133	1809	292	42	32	0	1565	1463	92	
	1991	1831	1544	262	10	25	0	1404	1334	55	
	1992	1867	1518	344	31	3	0	1324	1296	28	
	1993	1984	1559	273	29	18	17	1401	1373	28	
Developing economies-Europe/ 5	1980	10	9	1	1	1	0	8	5	2	
	1990	7	6	0	0	2	1	6	5	0	
	1991	5	3	0	0	2	1	3	3	0	
	1992	4	3	1	0	0	0	3	2	0	
	1993	1	1	0	0	0	0	1	1	0	
Developing economies-Middle East	1980	13	7	4	2	3	2	5	4	1	
	1990	12	7	5	0	0	0	6	5	0	
	1991	17	7	7	0	3	3	5	5	0	
	1992	18	9	7	0	2	1	8	7	0	
	1993	25	11	13	0	1	1	9	8	0	
Developing economies-Other Asia	1980	442	250	142	9	50	11	134	130	4	
	1990	912	426	352	94	133	118	201	193	7	
	1991	1044	466	499	135	80	70	219	214	5	
	1992	711	321	364	69	21	14	120	115	5	
	1993	682	348	308	67	26	21	153	152	1	
Former USSR-Asia /9	1980	.	.	.	.	.	.	.	.	.	
	1990	.	.	.	.	.	.	.	.	.	
	1991	.	.	.	.	.	.	.	.	.	
	1992	2	2	0	0	0	.	2	2	0	
	1993	1	1	0	0	0	.	1	1	0	
Developing economies-Oceania	1980	84	64	7	0	0	0	34	32	2	
	1990	24	19	3	0	0	0	10	9	1	
	1991	23	17	4	0	0	0	9	8	1	
	1992	33	23	9	0	0	0	9	8	1	
	1993	33	25	7	0	0	0	14	13	1	

For general note and footnotes see end of table.

TABLEAU SPECIAL: B

Exportations mondiales par classes de marchandises et par régions (suite)

En millions de dollars E.-U. f.o.b.

aines et fruits oléagineux (CTCI, Rev. 2 et Rev. 3, 22) (suite)

onomies veloppées /2,3,4				Developing economies / Economies en voie de développement /1,3,4						← Exportations vers	
Canada	U.S.A. / E.-U.	Japan / Japon	Australia New Zealand / Australie Nouvelle-Zélande	Africa / Afrique	America / Amerique: Total	America / Amerique: LAIA / ALADI	Asia / Asie: Mid.East / Moyen Orient	Asia / Asie: Other / Autres /9	Oceania / Océanie	Année	Exportations en provenance de ↓
.	26	306	0	12	9	8	0	26	0	1980	Canada
.	119	551	0	1	1	1	0	23	0	1990	
.	84	468	0	1	1	1	0	25	0	1991	
.	74	418	0	0	12	12	1	23	0	1992	
.	112	391	0	0	54	54	1	31	0	1993	
150	.	1136	12	14	442	408	10	654	0	1980	Etats-Unis
132	.	848	20	11	328	256	4	641	1	1990	
98	.	891	24	5	508	427	6	773	1	1991	
91	.	912	9	2	685	613	14	861	1	1992	
128	.	1009	23	15	615	525	17	1014	1	1993	
0	0	.	0	0	0	0	0	0	0	1980	Japon
0	0	.	0	0	0	0	0	7	0	1990	
0	0	.	0	0	0	0	0	8	0	1991	
0	0	.	0	0	0	0	0	6	0	1992	
0	0	.	0	0	0	0	0	2	0	1993	
0	0	2	3	0	0	0	0	1	0	1980	Australie, Nouvelle-Zélande
0	2	26	1	1	4	4	0	2	1	1990	
0	2	25	1	1	10	10	0	3	2	1991	
0	2	30	1	1	0	0	1	3	2	1992	
1	3	42	1	1	0	0	0	2	2	1993	
3	3	13	0	21	1	1	39	5	0	1980	Economies en voie de développement-Afrique
0	1	7	5	58	0	0	40	1	0	1990	
0	1	7	1	56	0	0	41	1	0	1991	
0	1	7	0	52	0	0	40	2	0	1992	
0	0	7	0	60	0	0	44	1	0	1993	
2	36	42	1	5	107	102	8	14	0	1980	Economies en voie de développement-Amérique
2	57	180	2	3	163	71	1	125	0	1990	
4	48	70	6	4	199	149	6	37	0	1991	
6	54	106	4	43	176	132	9	112	0	1992	
12	51	85	3	10	176	126	5	83	0	1993	
0	1	0	0	0	0	0	1	0	0	1980	Economies en voie de développement-Europe /5
0	0	0	0	0	0	0	0	0	0	1990	
0	0	0	0	0	0	0	0	0	0	1991	
0	0	0	0	0	0	0	0	0	0	1992	
0	0	0	0	0	0	0	0	0	0	1993	
0	0	1	0	0	0	0	3	0	0	1980	Economies en voie de développement-Moyen Orient
0	0	1	0	0	0	0	4	0	0	1990	
0	0	1	0	1	0	0	6	0	0	1991	
0	0	1	0	1	0	0	6	0	0	1992	
0	1	1	0	1	1	1	11	0	0	1993	
1	9	104	1	1	0	0	10	130	0	1980	Economies en voie de développement-Autres Pays d'Asie
11	10	185	13	5	9	5	26	311	0	1990	
21	14	197	12	7	3	3	40	447	2	1991	
8	16	166	8	4	3	2	41	316	0	1992	
10	17	153	8	3	3	3	20	282	0	1993	
.	.	.	.	.	.	.	.	.	.	1980	l'ancienne URSS asiatique /9
.	.	.	.	.	.	.	.	.	.	1990	
.	.	.	.	.	.	.	.	.	.	1991	
0	0	0	0	0	0	0	0	0	0	1992	
0	0	0	0	0	0	0	0	0	0	1993	
0	0	28	2	0	0	0	0	4	3	1980	Economies en voie de développement-Océanie
0	0	8	0	0	0	0	0	2	1	1990	
0	0	8	0	0	0	0	0	4	0	1991	
0	0	12	1	0	0	0	0	8	0	1992	
0	0	10	1	0	0	0	0	7	0	1993	

Voir la fin du tableau pour la remarque générale et les notes.

SPECIAL TABLE: B

World exports by commodity classes and by regions (continued)

In million U.S. dollars f.o.b.

Exports to → / ↓ Exports from	Year	World Monde /1,2,3	Developed economies: Econ. dévelop-pées /2,3,4	Developing economies / Economies en voie de développement /1,3,4: Total	Developing economies: OPEC OPEP	Eastern Europe and fmr. USSR-Europe / Europe de l'Est et l'anc. URSS-Europe: Total /2,3,7	Eastern Europe and fmr. USSR-Europe: Former USSR-Eur. /10	Develop… Econom… – Europe: Total /2	Europe: EEC CEE /2	EFTA AELE	South Africa / Afrique du Sud
Textile fibres (SITC, Rev. 2 and Rev. 3, 2…											
World /1,2,3	1980	18809	9635	6478	711	2364	712	6688	6159	528	12
	1990	24471	13005	9023	1003	2106	770	9337	8663	659	10
	1991	22623	11386	9896	1184	1216	411	7892	7328	560	13
	1992	23148	10975	11215	1864	800	144	7844	7317	509	11
	1993	20631	9116	10447	1647	733	131	6373	5894	474	9
Developed economies /2,3,4	1980	11536	6178	4258	484	828	422	4389	4042	346	12
	1990	15049	9157	5181	602	548	260	6732	6293	436	8
	1991	14519	8319	5567	675	521	272	6004	5561	442	10
	1992	13857	7780	5643	729	330	57	5746	5350	386	8
	1993	11734	6118	5101	619	266	46	4349	4049	298	8
Developing economies /1,3,4	1980	5595	2996	1856	209	716	280	1965	1835	130	
	1990	7606	3187	3382	389	870	499	2026	1911	114	1
	1991	7322	2777	4122	503	413	136	1634	1546	85	2
	1992	8449	2731	5308	1131	356	76	1648	1545	95	2
	1993	7980	2500	5065	1025	330	69	1544	1399	142	1
OPEC	1980	46	37	8	1	0	0	28	25	2	
	1990	107	48	49	5	6	5	40	40	0	
	1991	117	29	81	12	6	5	22	22	0	
	1992	168	33	80	6	54	54	25	25	1	
	1993	176	30	88	4	58	58	23	23	0	
Eastern Europe and the former USSR /2,3,7	1980	1679	461	364	19	820	9	334	283	52	
	1990	1816	661	459	12	687	11	580	458	108	
	1991	782	290	208	6	282	3	253	221	33	
	1992	843	464	264	4	114	11	451	422	28	
	1993	917	498	281	3	137	16	480	446	35	
Former USSR /3	1980	1431	360	346	16	725	.	237	211	26	
	1990	...	...	...	...	...	.	...	...	...	.
	1991	...	...	...	...	...	.	...	...	...	.
	1992	.	.	.	.	.	.	.	.	.	
	1993	.	.	.	.	.	.	.	.	.	
Former USSR-Europe /8	1980	.	.	.	.	.	.	.	.	.	
	1990	.	.	.	.	.	.	.	.	.	
	1991	.	.	.	.	.	.	.	.	.	
	1992	707	392	225	1	90	7	379	359	20	
	1993	692	364	230	1	99	7	350	324	26	
Developed economies-Europe /2	1980	3667	2697	637	141	333	129	2517	2276	240	6
	1990	5931	4493	1048	129	227	55	4119	3740	377	5
	1991	5381	4058	980	123	231	50	3717	3352	363	7
	1992	5486	4136	1007	146	239	37	3782	3453	327	5
	1993	4736	3406	1042	137	196	20	3006	2748	255	5
European Economic Community /2	1980	3221	2408	535	97	277	101	2252	2041	210	4
	1990	5224	4026	984	117	204	46	3684	3344	338	5
	1991	4773	3627	920	112	219	48	3324	2992	331	6
	1992	4930	3752	951	130	225	32	3433	3135	297	5
	1993	4221	3056	977	128	185	16	2729	2500	227	4
European Free Trade Association	1980	446	288	102	44	56	28	265	234	30	1
	1990	706	467	64	11	23	9	435	395	39	
	1991	608	431	60	11	12	2	392	360	32	
	1992	555	383	56	16	14	4	348	318	30	
	1993	513	349	65	9	11	4	276	248	28	
Other developed economies	1980	7868	3481	3621	343	495	294	1872	1766	106	5
	1990	9118	4663	4133	473	321	205	2613	2553	60	2
	1991	9139	4261	4587	552	290	222	2288	2209	79	3
	1992	8371	3644	4636	583	91	20	1965	1896	59	3
	1993	6998	2712	4059	482	70	26	1343	1301	43	2

For general note and footnotes see end of table.

Exportations mondiales par classes de marchandises et par régions (suite)

En millions de dollars E.-U. f.o.b.

conomies éveloppées /2,3,4				Developing economies Economies en voie de développement /1,3,4						← Exportations vers	
Canada	U.S.A. E.-U.	Japan Japon	Australia New Zealand Australie Nouvelle-Zélande	Africa Afrique	America Amerique Total	America Amerique LAIA ALADI	Asia Asie Mid.East Moyen Orient	Asia Asie Other Autres /9	Oceania Océanie	Année	Exportations en provenance de ↓
ibres textiles (CTCI, Rev. 2 et Rev. 3, 26)											
213	330	2128	120	446	429	323	403	4754	6	1980	Monde /1,2,3
181	696	2503	127	907	887	685	547	6366	7	1990	
209	650	2338	114	769	923	774	498	7520	8	1991	
196	741	1904	117	838	1060	856	1852	7347	9	1992	
242	792	1452	115	774	1426	1225	1672	6475	10	1993	
204	166	1168	105	326	234	191	290	3282	4	1980	Economies dévelopées /2,3,4
175	452	1561	102	627	326	271	383	3712	7	1990	
194	403	1489	88	605	384	325	317	4164	8	1991	
179	449	1180	90	635	451	390	375	4105	9	1992	
217	466	882	84	558	766	680	382	3323	10	1993	
9	161	837	15	119	146	131	111	1377	2	1980	Economies en voie de développement /1,3,4
5	233	872	25	276	444	414	140	2481	0	1990	
15	242	818	26	161	487	449	169	3276	0	1991	
17	291	711	28	187	509	434	1411	3166	0	1992	
24	325	554	31	198	574	509	1213	3056	0	1993	
0	8	1	0	3	0	0	4	1	0	1980	OPEP
0	3	4	0	1	17	13	11	19	0	1990	
0	4	2	1	16	2	2	31	28	0	1991	
0	4	2	1	1	4	3	25	48	0	1992	
1	4	1	1	2	4	4	26	53	0	1993	
0	3	123	0	2	50	1	3	94	0	1980	Europe de l'Est et l'ancienne URSS /2,3,7
1	11	70	0	3	117	0	24	174	0	1990	
0	5	31	0	2	52	0	12	81	0	1991	
0	0	13	0	16	100	32	66	76	0	1992	
0	1	16	0	18	85	35	77	96	0	1993	
0	0	123	0	0	49	0	0	86	0	1980	L'ancienne URSS /3
...	...	...	...	...	...	...	...	...	...	1990	
...	...	...	...	...	...	...	...	...	...	1991	
.	.	.	.	.	.	.	.	.	.	1992	
.	.	.	.	.	.	.	.	.	.	1993	
.	.	.	.	.	.	.	.	.	.	1980	L'ancienne URSS-Europe /8
.	.	.	.	.	.	.	.	.	.	1990	
.	.	.	.	.	.	.	.	.	.	1991	
0	0	12	0	11	99	31	49	65	0	1992	
0	0	14	0	12	85	35	62	71	0	1993	
12	57	21	16	190	51	49	146	198	0	1980	Economies développées-Europe /2
15	148	93	33	313	68	63	213	368	0	1990	
16	132	72	27	299	83	80	183	351	1	1991	
17	143	74	37	334	85	82	215	311	1	1992	
17	202	70	32	316	139	132	220	309	0	1993	
12	53	21	14	175	47	44	108	156	0	1980	Communauté Economique Européenne /2
15	122	92	31	304	55	51	196	347	0	1990	
16	101	72	25	294	65	62	171	327	1	1991	
16	116	74	35	329	75	71	202	287	1	1992	
15	144	66	30	311	126	120	208	276	0	1993	
0	4	0	1	15	5	5	38	41	0	1980	Association Européenne de Libre Echange
0	26	1	1	8	13	12	17	21	0	1990	
0	30	1	2	5	18	17	12	24	0	1991	
1	28	0	2	6	11	10	12	24	0	1992	
1	58	4	2	5	13	13	12	33	0	1993	
191	108	1147	89	136	182	142	143	3085	3	1980	Autres economies développées
160	304	1468	69	315	258	208	170	3343	7	1990	
177	271	1416	62	306	301	245	134	3813	7	1991	
162	306	1106	53	301	366	309	160	3794	8	1992	
201	264	812	52	242	627	548	162	3013	9	1993	

Voir la fin du tableau pour la remarque générale et les notes.

SPECIAL TABLE: B

World exports by commodity classes and by regions (continued)

In million U.S. dollars f.o.b.

Exports to → / ↓ Exports from	Year	World Monde /1,2,3	Developed economies Econ. dévelop-pées /2,3,4	Developing economies Economies en voie de développement /1,3,4: Total	Developing economies: OPEC OPEP	Eastern Europe and fmr. USSR-Europe Europe de l'Est et l'anc. URSS-Europe: Total /2,3,7	Eastern Europe and fmr. USSR-Europe: Former USSR-Eur. /10	Develope[d] Economie[s] — Europe: Total /2	Europe: EEC CEE /2	Europe: EFTA AELE	South Africa Afrique du Sud
							Textile fibres (SITC, Rev. 2 and Rev. 3, 26) (continued)				
Canada	1980	71	36	35	9	0	0	5	5	0	0
	1990	202	122	80	4	0	0	8	8	0	1
	1991	190	106	82	3	2	2	6	6	0	1
	1992	224	121	101	5	2	1	3	3	0	0
	1993	185	74	110	5	2	1	2	2	0	0
United States	1980	3929	1503	2372	150	55	5	702	610	92	32
	1990	3899	1585	2270	269	45	2	772	730	41	7
	1991	3698	1380	2280	302	39	4	649	595	54	8
	1992	3106	1025	2026	283	55	8	477	439	38	6
	1993	2671	883	1756	227	32	10	356	331	25	7
Japan	1980	696	87	589	107	20	8	47	38	8	17
	1990	807	154	635	74	18	16	95	83	11	17
	1991	881	165	707	92	9	6	103	94	9	18
	1992	925	161	761	106	3	0	100	89	10	14
	1993	909	156	748	120	4	3	77	66	11	14
Australia, New Zealand	1980	2786	1742	623	76	420	280	1007	1002	5	5
	1990	3663	2372	1034	126	258	187	1361	1356	5	1
	1991	3887	2238	1418	155	230	210	1202	1188	14	3
	1992	3762	2098	1634	186	30	11	1190	1171	10	11
	1993	2993	1442	1362	130	32	14	779	773	6	4
Developing economies-Africa	1980	1299	768	358	10	152	15	590	560	30	0
	1990	1304	597	496	31	156	64	474	458	16	15
	1991	1055	500	476	42	77	16	382	367	15	21
	1992	1087	568	419	42	60	0	461	407	55	12
	1993	1174	599	444	37	59	0	508	411	97	8
Developing economies-America	1980	1771	1100	469	55	202	113	741	717	25	4
	1990	1724	782	800	107	142	110	568	560	8	1
	1991	1700	692	975	144	33	24	467	459	8	0
	1992	1076	475	596	80	2	0	268	265	3	5
	1993	1007	402	602	42	3	1	222	218	4	1
Developing economies-Europe/ 5	1980	60	11	36	8	14	0	11	9	2	0
	1990	112	37	46	5	29	0	33	28	5	0
	1991	71	22	30	4	19	0	19	16	3	0
	1992	79	54	18	1	7	0	53	53	1	0
	1993	16	6	8	0	3	0	6	5	0	0
Developing economies-Middle East	1980	582	252	131	60	199	64	242	183	60	0
	1990	471	269	96	34	101	40	255	241	14	2
	1991	459	218	110	25	129	51	207	191	16	3
	1992	415	177	158	32	76	58	167	164	3	0
	1993	500	210	213	53	74	63	196	183	13	1
Developing economies-Other Asia	1980	1882	865	861	76	149	88	380	367	13	1
	1990	3996	1501	1943	212	443	285	695	624	71	1
	1991	4037	1345	2530	289	156	46	559	514	44	6
	1992	5793	1458	4117	977	211	17	697	657	33	10
	1993	5283	1283	3799	893	192	5	613	583	27	8
Former USSR-Asia /9	1980	.	.	.	.	.	.	.	.	.	.
	1990	.	.	.	.	.	.	.	.	.	.
	1991	.	.	.	.	.	.	.	.	.	.
	1992	1777	184	1433	649	160	.	170	163	8	0
	1993	1607	198	1263	578	146	.	174	164	10	0
Developing economies-Oceania	1980	0	0	0	0	0	0	0	0	0	0
	1990	1	0	1	0	0	0	0	0	0	0
	1991	0	0	0	0	0	0	0	0	0	0
	1992	0	0	0	0	0	0	0	0	0	0
	1993	0	0	0	0	0	0	0	0	0	0

For general note and footnotes see end of table.

Exportations mondiales par classes de marchandises et par régions (suite)

En millions de dollars E.-U. f.o.b.

...onomies ...veloppées /2,3,4				Developing economies / Economies en voie de développement /1,3,4						← Exportations vers	
...anada	U.S.A. E.-U.	Japan Japon	Australia New Zealand Australie Nouvelle-Zélande	Africa Afrique	America Amerique Total	America Amerique LAIA ALADI	Asia Asie Mid.East Moyen Orient	Asia Asie Other Autres /9	Oceania Océanie	Année	Exportations en provenance de ↓
...res textiles (CTCI, Rev. 2 et Rev. 3, 26) (suite)											
.	18	1	12	1	2	2	1	31	0	1980	Canada
.	106	1	6	8	3	3	0	69	0	1990	
.	95	0	3	8	2	1	0	71	0	1991	
.	116	0	1	14	4	3	0	83	0	1992	
.	70	0	1	15	2	2	1	91	0	1993	
180	.	547	33	91	143	112	7	2120	1	1980	Etats-Unis
149	.	631	18	244	230	183	90	1689	0	1990	
167	.	533	18	248	268	215	48	1712	0	1991	
153	.	366	17	234	333	277	45	1414	0	1992	
192	.	307	19	176	599	521	53	927	0	1993	
2	7	.	13	11	20	11	60	499	0	1980	Japon
2	31	.	9	16	5	4	28	586	0	1990	
2	33	.	10	18	7	5	36	646	0	1991	
2	38	.	7	20	7	6	33	700	0	1992	
3	55	.	7	27	6	4	31	683	0	1993	
10	83	599	31	33	18	18	76	433	2	1980	Australie, Nouvelle-Zélande
3	163	797	36	33	14	14	44	917	7	1990	
4	142	847	30	20	22	22	40	1313	7	1991	
2	147	706	28	25	20	20	66	1514	8	1992	
3	132	490	25	17	17	17	69	1249	9	1993	
0	4	167	5	28	0	0	5	252	0	1980	Economies en voie de développement-Afrique
0	1	106	1	192	0	0	6	281	0	1990	
9	1	87	0	83	1	1	3	376	0	1991	
9	1	84	1	79	2	2	4	318	0	1992	
10	1	72	1	73	2	2	4	351	0	1993	
7	117	228	0	8	130	117	37	285	2	1980	Economies en voie de développement-Amérique
1	125	81	0	8	417	393	25	344	0	1990	
1	129	86	0	10	457	426	24	484	0	1991	
2	133	61	0	11	419	384	8	159	0	1992	
1	149	28	0	2	416	396	17	167	0	1993	
0	0	0	0	9	0	0	7	19	0	1980	Economies en voie de développement-Europe /5
0	4	0	0	5	3	3	14	24	0	1990	
0	3	0	0	3	2	2	9	16	0	1991	
0	0	0	0	1	0	0	3	3	0	1992	
0	0	0	0	0	0	0	3	1	0	1993	
0	2	8	0	42	0	0	45	34	0	1980	Economies en voie de développement-Moyen Orient
0	6	5	0	29	1	1	42	12	0	1990	
0	2	3	0	22	0	0	62	17	0	1991	
0	3	5	0	40	4	3	66	44	0	1992	
0	4	9	0	62	38	37	65	44	0	1993	
2	38	434	9	32	15	13	16	788	0	1980	Economies en voie de développement-Autres Pays d'Asie
4	97	680	24	42	23	16	53	1818	0	1990	
5	107	642	26	43	28	20	70	2383	0	1991	
6	155	561	27	56	85	45	1330	2642	0	1992	
13	171	445	30	61	119	75	1125	2493	0	1993	
.	.	.	.	.	.	.	.	.	.	1980	l'ancienne URSS asiatique /9
.	.	.	.	.	.	.	.	.	.	1990	
.	.	.	.	.	.	.	.	.	.	1991	
0	0	14	0	11	55	19	1294	73	0	1992	
0	0	25	0	20	66	25	1091	85	0	1993	
0	0	0	0	0	0	0	0	0	0	1980	Economies en voie de développement-Océanie
0	0	0	0	0	0	0	0	1	0	1990	
0	0	0	0	0	0	0	0	0	0	1991	
0	0	0	0	0	0	0	0	0	0	1992	
0	0	0	0	0	0	0	0	0	0	1993	

Voir la fin du tableau pour la remarque générale et les notes.

SPECIAL TABLE: B

World exports by commodity classes and by regions (continued)

In million U.S. dollars f.o.b.

Crude fertilizers and minerals (SITC, Rev. 2 and Rev. 3, 2

Exports to → / ↓ Exports from	Year	World Monde /1,2,3	Developed economies Econ. dévelop-pées /2,3,4	Developing economies Economies en voie de développement /1,3,4 Total	Developing economies OPEC OPEP	Eastern Europe and fmr. USSR-Europe Europe de l'Est et l'anc. URSS-Europe Total /2,3,7	Eastern Europe and fmr. USSR-Europe Former USSR-Eur. /10	Develop Econom… Europe Total /2	Europe EEC CEE /2	Europe EFTA AELE	South Africa Afrique du Su…
World /1,2,3	1980	11721	7049	2759	373	1465	257	4995	4340	648	1C
	1990	13757	9859	3026	390	720	193	6920	5973	930	7
	1991	12722	9013	3027	375	525	196	6188	5297	870	6
	1992	12307	8447	3240	398	479	150	5883	4971	893	6
	1993	11897	7883	3094	426	408	111	5312	4438	860	6
Developed economies /2,3,4	1980	6497	4619	1265	271	189	8	3446	2969	472	1C
	1990	8201	6514	1435	236	117	27	4769	4023	731	5
	1991	8179	6313	1580	231	135	39	4644	3932	692	4
	1992	7957	6161	1561	226	110	12	4698	3944	736	4
	1993	7610	5609	1391	236	105	8	4168	3429	726	4
Developing economies /1,3,4	1980	3227	1984	754	100	466	197	1151	1079	72	
	1990	3832	2244	1329	151	248	121	1115	1021	92	1
	1991	3548	2106	1263	144	173	111	976	885	90	1
	1992	3786	2061	1512	172	197	105	977	875	101	1
	1993	3739	1983	1577	188	172	91	874	803	69	2
OPEC	1980	189	85	95	12	9	0	25	18	7	
	1990	251	26	214	7	6	3	15	14	1	
	1991	196	36	152	13	8	4	26	12	13	
	1992	391	42	342	29	8	3	22	14	8	
	1993	438	46	387	32	5	1	26	14	12	
Eastern Europe and the former USSR /2,3,7	1980	1997	446	741	2	810	52	397	293	105	
	1990	1724	1101	262	3	355	45	1036	928	108	
	1991	996	595	185	0	217	45	568	480	88	
	1992	564	225	166	0	172	33	207	152	56	
	1993	547	290	126	2	132	12	271	206	65	
Former USSR /3	1980	1487	228	679	1	579	.	179	121	59	
	1990	...	...	...	...	...	.	...	...	...	
	1991	...	...	...	...	...	.	...	...	...	
	1992	.	.	.	.	.	.	.	.	.	
	1993	.	.	.	.	.	.	.	.	.	
Former USSR-Europe /8	1980	.	.	.	.	.	.	.	.	.	
	1990	.	.	.	.	.	.	.	.	.	
	1991	.	.	.	.	.	.	.	.	.	
	1992	155	77	19	0	58	3	62	31	31	
	1993	176	96	22	0	58	5	79	39	40	
Developed economies-Europe /2	1980	3276	2750	400	179	109	7	2562	2142	414	2
	1990	4764	4156	431	118	77	7	3844	3185	644	2
	1991	4686	4056	420	109	91	15	3754	3116	618	2
	1992	4897	4198	475	114	99	7	3914	3282	614	1
	1993	4412	3724	480	125	97	4	3470	2843	614	2
European Economic Community /2	1980	2953	2467	388	174	82	5	2286	1907	374	2
	1990	4093	3574	376	94	52	3	3302	2720	567	2
	1991	4048	3529	369	92	60	3	3264	2691	552	2
	1992	4195	3610	419	101	73	3	3377	2817	543	1
	1993	3774	3194	428	115	73	3	2975	2410	553	1
European Free Trade Association	1980	323	283	13	4	28	2	275	235	40	
	1990	671	581	55	24	25	4	542	465	77	
	1991	638	526	51	16	31	12	490	425	65	
	1992	702	588	56	13	27	3	537	465	71	
	1993	637	530	51	10	24	1	495	433	61	
Other developed economies	1980	3221	1868	865	92	80	1	885	827	57	7
	1990	3436	2359	1004	119	40	20	925	838	87	2
	1991	3493	2258	1160	123	44	24	890	816	74	2
	1992	3059	1963	1086	112	10	5	784	662	122	3
	1993	3199	1886	912	111	8	4	698	586	112	2

For general note and footnotes see end of table.

TABLEAU SPECIAL: B

Exportations mondiales par classes de marchandises et par régions (suite)

En millions de dollars E.-U. f.o.b.

Economies développées /2,3,4				Developing economies Economies en voie de développement /1,3,4							← Exportations vers
Canada	U.S.A. E.-U.	Japan Japon	Australia New Zealand Australie Nouvelle-Zélande	Africa Afrique	America Amerique Total	America Amerique LAIA ALADI	Asia Asie Mid.East Moyen Orient	Asia Asie Other Autres /9	Oceania Océanie	Année	Exportations en provenance de ↓
Engrais et minéraux bruts (CTCI, Rev. 2 et Rev. 3, 27)											
332	719	646	236	408	520	432	261	836	14	1980	Monde /1,2,3
348	1000	1294	167	497	499	400	282	1610	16	1990	
316	973	1292	133	431	533	456	284	1662	23	1991	
320	865	1112	153	486	443	390	349	1835	24	1992	
335	882	1084	151	372	415	363	351	1845	21	1993	
307	328	285	137	296	332	302	129	458	4	1980	Economies dévelopées /2,3,4
291	568	676	107	300	300	266	122	665	6	1990	
264	524	724	65	309	343	302	118	764	8	1991	
267	460	567	77	276	303	267	140	798	9	1992	
284	486	530	63	190	268	233	155	733	7	1993	
25	390	317	98	79	142	117	122	346	10	1980	Economies en voie de développement /1,3,4
58	430	563	60	125	136	108	124	886	10	1990	
52	449	544	67	65	140	121	139	871	15	1991	
53	401	531	77	132	121	108	176	1021	15	1992	
52	393	539	88	133	137	122	159	1100	14	1993	
0	59	0	0	21	3	1	16	56	0	1980	OPEP
0	6	4	1	65	4	3	47	96	0	1990	
0	3	8	0	1	3	2	79	63	0	1991	
0	7	10	1	82	5	3	77	174	0	1992	
0	5	11	1	81	15	14	84	203	0	1993	
0	2	45	2	32	45	14	9	32	0	1980	Europe de l'Est et l'ancienne URSS /2,3,7
0	1	55	0	72	62	26	36	59	0	1990	
0	0	24	0	57	51	33	26	26	0	1991	
0	4	14	0	77	18	15	33	16	0	1992	
0	4	15	0	49	10	9	37	13	0	1993	
0	2	45	2	0	40	9	5	26	0	1980	L'ancienne URSS /3
...	...	...	...	...	...	...	...	...	...	1990	
...	...	...	...	...	...	...	...	...	...	1991	
.	.	.	.	.	.	.	.	.	.	1992	
.	.	.	.	.	.	.	.	.	.	1993	
.	.	.	.	.	.	.	.	.	.	1980	L'ancienne URSS-Europe /8
.	.	.	.	.	.	.	.	.	.	1990	
.	.	.	.	.	.	.	.	.	.	1991	
0	2	13	0	2	0	0	8	9	0	1992	
0	2	15	0	2	0	0	10	10	0	1993	
19	91	39	7	162	33	26	111	58	1	1980	Economies développées-Europe /2
14	130	102	20	125	46	34	82	138	3	1990	
11	115	114	14	105	43	29	83	156	2	1991	
14	127	90	12	111	36	24	104	189	2	1992	
14	106	79	10	102	45	34	117	177	2	1993	
19	90	34	7	160	30	24	108	56	1	1980	Communauté Economique Européenne /2
10	119	85	16	121	33	21	71	123	3	1990	
8	104	96	12	103	34	21	76	131	2	1991	
7	104	73	10	107	30	19	96	160	2	1992	
11	98	60	8	100	40	30	109	152	2	1993	
0	1	4	1	2	2	2	3	2	0	1980	Association Européenne de Libre Echange
4	11	17	3	4	13	13	11	15	0	1990	
3	10	17	2	2	8	7	7	25	0	1991	
7	22	16	3	4	6	5	8	29	0	1992	
3	8	20	1	2	4	4	8	25	0	1993	
288	237	246	129	135	300	275	18	400	2	1980	Autres economies développées
277	438	574	88	175	254	232	40	527	3	1990	
253	409	610	51	204	300	273	35	608	6	1991	
252	333	477	64	165	268	242	36	609	6	1992	
270	380	450	53	88	223	199	38	556	5	1993	

Voir la fin du tableau pour la remarque générale et les notes.

SPECIAL TABLE: B

World exports by commodity classes and by regions (continued)

In million U.S. dollars f.o.b.

Exports to → / ↓ Exports from	Year	World Monde /1,2,3	Developed economies Econ. dévelop-pées /2,3,4	Developing economies Economies en voie de développement /1,3,4 Total	OPEC OPEP	Eastern Europe and fmr. USSR-Europe Europe de l'Est et l'anc. URSS-Europe Total /2,3,7	Former USSR-Eur. /10	Developed Economies: Europe Total /2	EEC CEE /2	EFTA AELE	South Africa Afrique du Sud
Crude fertilizers and minerals (SITC, Rev. 2 and Rev. 3, 27) (continued)											
Canada	1980	1154	747	398	39	9	0	329	315	15	58
	1990	1188	696	471	74	21	18	171	155	16	19
	1991	1091	568	508	60	15	13	130	128	2	12
	1992	827	456	369	44	2	0	82	80	2	13
	1993	636	406	229	32	1	0	52	51	1	6
United States	1980	1410	1010	341	40	58	0	520	488	31	17
	1990	1261	937	323	28	1	0	360	297	64	7
	1991	1385	982	391	40	13	10	392	327	65	8
	1992	1385	978	404	47	3	1	403	308	95	15
	1993	1345	957	383	45	4	3	384	284	100	8
Japan	1980	106	24	76	7	7	1	4	4	0	4
	1990	170	43	124	7	2	2	15	13	2	1
	1991	188	43	143	8	2	2	17	16	1	0
	1992	187	45	141	7	1	1	16	15	1	0
	1993	189	46	142	6	1	1	16	14	1	1
Australia, New Zealand	1980	102	61	41	5	0	0	6	6	0	0
	1990	165	124	40	10	0	0	9	8	1	0
	1991	219	150	69	14	0	0	11	10	1	1
	1992	225	142	83	11	0	0	38	34	5	2
	1993	587	128	65	21	0	0	42	41	2	3
Developing economies-Africa	1980	1385	972	242	22	151	5	879	822	57	2
	1990	1185	762	346	56	76	3	623	580	41	11
	1991	941	635	267	49	39	4	515	467	48	12
	1992	1014	643	310	43	54	3	495	447	47	10
	1993	874	539	282	41	52	1	385	350	35	13
Developing economies-America	1980	511	417	84	10	10	0	71	68	2	1
	1990	600	473	112	13	15	3	111	104	7	2
	1991	603	501	97	11	5	3	106	102	5	2
	1992	519	405	104	13	8	0	99	91	8	1
	1993	499	360	133	12	6	0	83	81	2	2
Developing economies-Europe/ 5	1980	20	7	0	0	12	1	7	7	0	0
	1990	24	19	0	0	5	1	16	15	1	0
	1991	16	12	0	0	4	1	11	10	1	0
	1992	27	10	16	0	1	0	10	9	1	0
	1993	20	7	13	0	0	0	7	6	1	0
Developing economies-Middle East	1980	459	161	228	34	70	8	122	111	11	0
	1990	761	271	447	51	37	10	201	163	39	1
	1991	682	255	392	51	36	19	191	160	31	0
	1992	792	270	500	76	21	2	185	143	42	2
	1993	728	263	452	91	10	1	174	147	27	2
Developing economies-Other Asia	1980	727	330	175	33	222	183	73	72	2	0
	1990	1190	682	391	31	115	104	163	160	3	0
	1991	1210	655	464	33	90	85	153	147	6	0
	1992	1338	684	539	40	113	99	189	185	4	1
	1993	1521	765	654	45	103	89	224	220	4	4
Former USSR-Asia /9	1980	.	.	.	.	.	.	.	.	.	.
	1990	.	.	.	.	.	.	.	.	.	.
	1991	.	.	.	.	.	.	.	.	.	.
	1992	16	0	7	0	9	.	0	0	0	0
	1993	13	0	6	0	7	.	0	0	0	0
Developing economies-Oceania	1980	126	97	25	0	0	0	0	0	0	0
	1990	72	37	32	0	0	0	0	0	0	0
	1991	95	48	43	0	0	0	0	0	0	0
	1992	96	49	43	0	0	0	0	0	0	0
	1993	96	49	43	0	0	0	0	0	0	0

For general note and footnotes see end of table.

TABLEAU SPECIAL: B

Exportations mondiales par classes de marchandises et par régions (suite)

En millions de dollars E.-U. f.o.b.

Economies développées /2,3,4				Developing economies Economies en voie de développement /1,3,4						← Exportations vers	
Canada	U.S.A. E.-U.	Japan Japon	Australia New Zealand Australie Nouvelle-Zélande	Africa Afrique	America Amerique Total	America Amerique LAIA ALADI	Asia Asie Mid.East Moyen Orient	Asia Asie Other Autres /9	Oceania Océanie	Année	Exportations en provenance de ↓
Engrais et minéraux bruts (CTCI, Rev. 2 et Rev. 3, 27) (suite)											
.	231	54	74	97	123	113	3	167	0	1980	Canada
.	386	52	42	136	113	106	28	192	0	1990	
.	345	59	10	156	108	101	18	221	0	1991	
.	277	54	17	122	84	79	7	156	0	1992	
.	287	46	8	50	61	59	6	110	0	1993	
288	.	144	38	36	168	154	12	125	0	1980	Etats-Unis
265	.	280	22	7	136	120	7	172	1	1990	
243	.	313	20	19	177	158	8	186	1	1991	
249	.	282	25	19	169	149	15	200	0	1992	
263	.	272	24	9	148	127	10	215	1	1993	
0	3	.	13	1	3	3	1	70	0	1980	Japon
1	14	.	13	1	0	0	1	122	0	1990	
0	15	.	11	3	0	0	1	139	0	1991	
0	15	.	14	1	1	1	1	137	1	1992	
0	18	.	12	2	0	0	1	138	0	1993	
0	3	48	4	0	2	1	0	37	2	1980	Australie, Nouvelle-Zélande
0	4	107	4	2	0	0	0	36	2	1990	
0	16	117	4	0	3	3	5	56	5	1991	
0	4	93	5	0	6	6	1	70	5	1992	
0	2	75	5	2	1	1	12	47	4	1993	
5	36	49	1	39	63	63	39	63	0	1980	Economies en voie de développement-Afrique
39	47	32	11	90	54	53	29	153	0	1990	
34	41	27	6	45	59	58	19	129	1	1991	
39	67	23	9	106	36	36	24	130	0	1992	
40	62	27	12	105	31	31	21	112	0	1993	
19	289	38	0	2	72	47	2	7	0	1980	Economies en voie de développement-Amérique
13	268	77	2	11	77	51	4	20	0	1990	
10	315	66	1	3	68	51	2	24	0	1991	
8	214	82	0	2	70	57	3	30	0	1992	
5	187	83	0	1	93	78	2	36	0	1993	
0	0	0	0	0	0	0	0	0	0	1980	Economies en voie de développement-Europe /5
0	0	2	0	0	0	0	0	0	0	1990	
0	0	1	0	0	0	0	0	0	0	1991	
0	0	0	0	0	0	0	0	0	0	1992	
0	0	0	0	0	0	0	0	0	0	1993	
0	15	25	0	28	0	0	58	129	0	1980	Economies en voie de développement-Moyen Orient
0	32	33	1	17	1	1	78	323	0	1990	
1	23	36	2	9	4	4	105	255	0	1991	
0	36	39	6	19	7	7	125	333	0	1992	
1	47	22	15	18	7	7	109	308	0	1993	
0	51	198	8	10	7	7	23	132	0	1980	Economies en voie de développement-Autres Pays d'Asie
6	83	420	9	6	4	3	13	365	2	1990	
7	70	413	11	7	9	9	13	433	2	1991	
6	84	387	13	6	9	8	24	497	3	1992	
6	97	406	12	8	6	6	26	613	1	1993	
.	.	.	.	.	.	.	.	.	.	1980	l'ancienne URSS asiatique /9
.	.	.	.	.	.	.	.	.	.	1990	
.	.	.	.	.	.	.	.	.	.	1991	
0	0	0	0	0	0	0	7	0	0	1992	
0	0	0	0	0	0	0	6	0	0	1993	
0	0	8	89	0	0	0	0	15	10	1980	Economies en voie de développement-Océanie
0	0	0	37	0	0	0	0	24	9	1990	
0	0	0	48	0	0	0	0	31	12	1991	
0	0	0	49	0	0	0	0	31	12	1992	
0	0	0	49	0	0	0	0	31	12	1993	

Voir la fin du tableau pour la remarque générale et les notes.

SPECIAL TABLE: B

World exports by commodity classes and by regions (continued)

In million U.S. dollars f.o.b.

Metalliferous ores and metal scrap (SITC, Rev. 2 and Rev. 3, 28)

Exports from ↓ / Exports to →	Year	World Monde /1,2,3	Developed economies: Econ. dévelop-pées /2,3,4	Developing economies / Economies en voie de développement /1,3,4: Total	Developing economies: OPEC OPEP	Eastern Europe and fmr. USSR-Europe / Europe de l'Est et l'anc. URSS-Europe: Total /2,3,7	Eastern Europe and fmr. USSR-Europe: Former USSR-Eur. /10	Developed Economies: Europe: Total /2	Developed Economies: Europe: EEC CEE /2	Developed Economies: Europe: EFTA AELE	Developed Economies: South Africa / Afrique du Sud
World /1,2,3	1980	31716	24202	2932	214	2065	476	14048	12732	1316	92
	1990	36349	26982	6734	548	2428	1131	15816	13843	1971	45
	1991	33548	24851	6947	627	1618	891	14173	12130	2042	29
	1992	32700	23707	7658	672	1272	520	14218	11889	2327	29
	1993	32469	21137	8256	838	996	411	12435	10109	2326	28
Developed economies /2,3,4	1980	18815	14574	1434	75	381	128	9246	8467	779	88
	1990	22306	17992	3978	185	215	51	11393	9940	1452	27
	1991	20233	15852	4115	213	160	34	9988	8457	1530	24
	1992	19016	14459	4259	186	292	116	9376	7829	1545	19
	1993	19540	12579	4716	276	230	102	7941	6591	1350	20
Developing economies /1,3,4	1980	11355	9315	1206	136	744	307	4527	4082	445	4
	1990	12327	8303	2608	363	1342	968	3787	3425	362	18
	1991	12287	8583	2744	413	939	723	3796	3372	424	5
	1992	11930	8290	3130	388	458	296	3915	3422	494	10
	1993	11097	7487	3257	464	286	232	3467	2879	588	9
OPEC	1980	1131	992	86	6	32	0	525	494	31	0
	1990	1467	1129	244	12	30	1	475	442	32	0
	1991	1730	1395	265	15	60	16	516	422	94	0
	1992	1821	1327	401	29	85	56	395	341	54	0
	1993	1546	1106	417	36	22	12	376	303	73	0
Eastern Europe and the former USSR /2,3,7	1980	1546	313	293	4	940	41	275	183	92	0
	1990	1716	688	148	1	871	112	637	478	157	0
	1991	1028	416	88	0	518	134	388	301	88	0
	1992	1754	957	268	98	522	109	926	638	288	0
	1993	1833	1071	282	98	479	77	1027	639	388	0
Former USSR /3	1980	1257	165	250	0	841	.	136	115	21	0
	1990	...	...	...	...	...	.	...	...	...	...
	1991	...	...	...	...	...	.	...	...	...	...
	1992	.	.	.	.	.	.	.	.	.	.
	1993	.	.	.	.	.	.	.	.	.	.
Former USSR-Europe /8	1980	.	.	.	.	.	.	.	.	.	.
	1990	.	.	.	.	.	.	.	.	.	.
	1991	.	.	.	.	.	.	.	.	.	.
	1992	1167	579	211	98	377	1	554	318	236	0
	1993	1186	600	216	96	370	4	567	286	281	0
Developed economies-Europe /2	1980	6260	5909	68	23	282	62	5557	5016	542	76
	1990	8657	7724	750	109	171	39	7340	6504	835	19
	1991	7970	6857	1002	132	105	23	6465	5582	883	18
	1992	7897	6665	1034	112	193	99	6336	5458	877	13
	1993	7592	5882	1549	228	153	88	5478	4742	735	14
European Economic Community /2	1980	5148	4899	46	6	202	54	4627	4218	409	8
	1990	7249	6471	640	43	127	32	6118	5543	575	19
	1991	6721	5736	895	63	83	22	5376	4728	647	17
	1992	6580	5519	893	32	163	91	5204	4562	641	13
	1993	6400	4853	1413	147	126	73	4481	3940	541	14
European Free Trade Association	1980	1107	1005	22	17	80	8	926	793	133	68
	1990	1402	1248	110	66	44	7	1216	956	260	0
	1991	1246	1118	107	69	21	1	1086	850	236	0
	1992	1315	1145	140	80	30	8	1130	894	236	0
	1993	1187	1024	136	80	27	15	993	798	194	0
Other developed economies	1980	12556	8665	1366	51	99	65	3689	3452	237	12
	1990	13649	10268	3228	76	44	12	4053	3436	617	8
	1991	12262	8995	3112	82	56	11	3523	2875	648	6
	1992	11119	7794	3225	74	99	17	3040	2371	668	6
	1993	11948	6698	3167	48	77	14	2463	1849	614	6

For general note and footnotes see end of table.

Exportations mondiales par classes de marchandises et par régions (suite)

En millions de dollars E.-U. f.o.b.

Economies développées /2,3,4				Developing economies Economies en voie de développement /1,3,4						← Exportations vers	
Canada	U.S.A. E.-U.	Japan Japon	Australia New Zealand Australie Nouvelle-Zélande	Africa Afrique	America Amerique Total	America Amerique LAIA ALADI	Asia Asie Mid.East Moyen Orient	Asia Asie Other Autres /9	Oceania Océanie	Année	Exportations en provenance de ↓
Minérais metallifères et dechets dé metaux (CTCI, Rev. 2 et Rev. 3, 28)											
794	2941	6286	36	187	690	656	140	1567	0	1980	Monde /1,2,3
1228	2664	7126	100	317	1016	973	765	4422	0	1990	
1375	2178	7008	82	274	919	867	750	4841	10	1991	
1369	2086	5880	122	326	872	827	862	5490	1	1992	
1351	2028	5200	90	307	889	831	1107	5836	21	1993	
641	1562	3011	21	55	340	329	61	940	0	1980	Economies dévelopées /2,3,4
1012	1563	3954	40	91	424	415	552	2826	0	1990	
1107	1215	3477	35	77	394	382	531	3037	1	1991	
1047	1087	2884	43	181	298	290	499	3231	1	1992	
1049	1107	2423	35	135	315	293	693	3528	0	1993	
153	1365	3251	15	131	342	327	79	602	0	1980	Economies en voie de développement /1,3,4
216	1102	3120	59	226	591	556	186	1548	0	1990	
268	960	3506	47	198	524	486	207	1776	10	1991	
322	996	2968	79	145	570	536	245	2137	0	1992	
299	914	2743	55	168	568	534	299	2179	21	1993	
7	119	340	0	6	13	13	7	56	0	1980	OPEP
9	119	508	17	5	40	40	16	179	0	1990	
8	138	716	17	3	14	13	24	216	0	1991	
68	209	635	20	14	10	9	33	338	0	1992	
15	111	589	14	7	19	18	41	343	0	1993	
1	13	24	0	2	7	0	0	25	0	1980	Europe de l'Est et l'ancienne URSS /2,3,7
0	0	51	0	0	1	1	27	48	0	1990	
0	2	25	0	0	2	0	12	28	0	1991	
0	3	28	0	1	4	1	118	122	0	1992	
3	7	33	0	3	6	4	116	129	0	1993	
0	5	24	0	0	7	0	0	3	0	1980	L'ancienne URSS /3
...	...	...	...	...	...	...	...	...	...	1990	
...	...	...	...	...	...	...	...	...	...	1991	
.	.	.	.	.	.	.	.	.	.	1992	
.	.	.	.	.	.	.	.	.	.	1993	
.	.	.	.	.	.	.	.	.	.	1980	L'ancienne URSS-Europe /8
.	.	.	.	.	.	.	.	.	.	1990	
.	.	.	.	.	.	.	.	.	.	1991	
0	2	23	0	0	4	1	112	93	0	1992	
0	6	27	0	0	3	1	114	97	0	1993	
20	214	35	5	6	10	9	21	23	0	1980	Economies développées-Europe /2
60	145	148	10	51	17	15	168	440	0	1990	
90	160	118	4	50	18	17	296	572	0	1991	
84	123	105	2	57	26	25	286	618	0	1992	
67	171	144	4	51	47	32	505	903	0	1993	
20	206	32	5	5	7	7	11	14	0	1980	Communauté Economique Européenne /2
57	131	137	8	36	17	15	142	378	0	1990	
88	137	112	4	23	16	14	273	523	0	1991	
84	111	103	2	27	24	23	257	546	0	1992	
61	149	141	4	28	46	31	466	834	0	1993	
0	8	3	0	1	3	3	10	9	0	1980	Association Européenne de Libre Echange
3	15	11	3	15	0	0	26	63	0	1990	
2	23	6	0	27	3	3	23	49	0	1991	
0	12	2	0	30	2	2	29	72	0	1992	
5	22	4	0	24	2	2	39	68	0	1993	
621	1348	2977	16	49	331	320	40	916	0	1980	Autres economies développées
952	1417	3806	30	41	408	400	384	2386	0	1990	
1017	1056	3359	30	27	376	365	235	2465	0	1991	
963	964	2779	41	124	272	266	213	2612	1	1992	
982	936	2279	31	84	268	260	188	2625	0	1993	

Voir la fin du tableau pour la remarque générale et les notes.

SPECIAL TABLE: B

World exports by commodity classes and by regions (continued)

In million U.S. dollars f.o.b.

Exports to → / ↓ Exports from	Year	World Monde /1,2,3	Developed economies Econ. dévelop-pées /2,3,4	Developing economies Economies en voie de développement /1,3,4: Total	Developing economies: OPEC OPEP	Eastern Europe and fmr. USSR-Europe Europe de l'Est et l'anc. URSS-Europe: Total /2,3,7	Eastern Europe and fmr. USSR-Europe: Former USSR-Eur. /10	Developed Economies: Europe: Total /2	Developed Economies: Europe: EEC CEE /2	Developed Economies: Europe: EFTA AELE	Developed Economies: South Africa Afrique du Sud
		Metalliferous ores and metal scrap (SITC, Rev. 2 and Rev. 3, 28) (continued)									
Canada	1980	3611	3310	85	2	50	36	1362	1256	106	0
	1990	4116	3769	335	6	11	2	1676	1286	390	5
	1991	3385	3148	235	3	2	0	1605	1152	453	3
	1992	3194	2891	285	1	19	0	1425	1086	339	0
	1993	2650	2426	213	1	11	2	1190	867	323	0
United States	1980	4467	3581	867	45	19	3	1961	1841	120	9
	1990	4943	2848	2085	60	10	10	915	835	81	3
	1991	4039	2270	1743	59	26	10	583	532	51	2
	1992	3421	1998	1399	41	24	12	531	483	48	4
	1993	3257	1840	1411	30	5	5	418	376	42	4
Japan	1980	148	46	79	3	23	23	8	8	0	1
	1990	187	45	142	5	0	0	11	10	1	0
	1991	162	45	118	7	0	0	15	14	1	0
	1992	300	30	270	16	0	0	15	13	1	0
	1993	308	23	285	5	0	0	13	11	2	0
Australia, New Zealand	1980	3555	1714	334	2	6	4	347	335	11	1
	1990	2961	2307	653	4	1	1	641	623	18	0
	1991	3373	2360	1005	13	8	0	587	560	27	0
	1992	3196	2179	1005	14	12	4	602	547	53	2
	1993	4807	1747	1039	9	15	4	389	342	46	1
Developing economies-Africa	1980	2175	1926	115	38	50	3	1516	1482	34	0
	1990	1212	1034	159	75	12	3	830	779	51	11
	1991	1169	988	158	76	15	4	787	729	58	3
	1992	1251	1029	185	76	19	0	817	753	64	2
	1993	1250	1050	183	80	12	0	839	770	69	7
Developing economies-America	1980	5463	4443	613	83	402	179	2275	1926	348	1
	1990	6605	4583	1324	210	698	429	2376	2142	234	1
	1991	6779	4794	1476	253	507	360	2489	2243	246	2
	1992	6495	4797	1539	213	144	40	2593	2245	348	5
	1993	5991	4194	1702	253	41	16	2176	1720	457	1
Developing economies-Europe/ 5	1980	99	27	1	0	71	35	27	17	10	0
	1990	335	77	11	0	247	219	77	57	20	0
	1991	222	51	7	0	164	145	51	38	13	0
	1992	38	21	9	0	8	5	21	15	5	0
	1993	28	15	7	0	5	1	15	12	3	0
Developing economies-Middle East	1980	145	107	30	6	8	1	94	76	18	0
	1990	334	135	112	20	23	8	96	82	13	6
	1991	369	208	135	22	15	5	144	89	55	0
	1992	364	135	190	28	23	18	87	69	18	0
	1993	353	131	187	27	27	25	86	70	16	0
Developing economies-Other Asia	1980	2903	2260	430	9	214	89	437	402	35	3
	1990	3119	1903	851	58	362	309	202	194	8	0
	1991	3014	1993	782	62	239	209	146	127	20	0
	1992	3144	1801	1077	71	264	233	229	211	18	2
	1993	2876	1634	1042	103	201	190	219	202	17	1
Former USSR-Asia /9	1980	.	.	.	.	.	.	.	.	.	.
	1990	.	.	.	.	.	.	.	.	.	.
	1991	.	.	.	.	.	.	.	.	.	.
	1992	97	14	73	7	9	.	11	9	2	0
	1993	88	15	66	7	7	.	10	5	5	0
Developing economies-Oceania	1980	569	552	17	0	0	0	178	178	0	0
	1990	723	570	152	0	0	0	206	170	36	0
	1991	734	549	185	0	0	0	179	146	33	0
	1992	637	507	130	0	0	0	169	128	41	0
	1993	598	462	136	1	0	0	132	105	27	0

For general note and footnotes see end of table.

TABLEAU SPECIAL: B

Exportations mondiales par classes de marchandises et par régions (suite)

En millions de dollars E.-U. f.o.b.

Economies développées /2,3,4				Developing economies · Economies en voie de développement /1,3,4						← Exportations vers	
Canada	U.S.A. E.-U.	Japan Japon	Australia New Zealand Australie Nouvelle-Zélande	Africa Afrique	America Amerique Total	America Amerique LAIA ALADI	Asia Asie Mid.East Moyen Orient	Asia Asie Other Autres /9	Oceania Océanie	Année	Exportations en provenance de ↓
Minérais metallifères et dechets dé metaux (CTCI, Rev. 2 et Rev. 3, 28) (suite)											
.	1225	718	6	2	8	8	1	62	0	1980	Canada
.	1212	868	8	14	55	55	13	251	0	1990	
.	856	676	4	1	35	34	3	192	0	1991	
.	875	587	3	1	24	24	3	256	0	1992	
.	849	387	0	0	34	34	16	163	0	1993	
542	.	1062	6	32	319	309	37	461	0	1980	Etats-Unis
917	.	1007	5	26	344	336	369	1345	0	1990	
992	.	680	11	24	330	319	226	1164	0	1991	
920	.	520	22	10	235	228	196	958	0	1992	
952	.	453	12	10	204	197	158	1039	0	1993	
33	3	.	1	15	1	1	0	63	0	1980	Japon
21	9	.	3	0	1	1	1	140	0	1990	
16	11	.	2	0	0	0	1	117	0	1991	
0	12	.	3	0	0	0	0	269	0	1992	
0	7	.	3	0	0	0	1	284	0	1993	
46	120	1197	3	0	2	2	1	330	0	1980	Australie, Nouvelle-Zélande
3	64	1585	14	0	5	5	1	645	0	1990	
0	70	1690	12	2	8	8	5	987	0	1991	
39	52	1473	11	0	3	3	0	1002	0	1992	
29	35	1283	11	0	22	22	6	1011	0	1993	
45	167	198	0	77	7	7	2	10	0	1980	Economies en voie de développement-Afrique
15	156	21	0	62	5	5	22	55	0	1990	
14	166	18	0	59	5	5	22	55	0	1991	
18	165	27	0	61	2	2	22	83	0	1992	
15	165	25	0	64	2	2	23	78	0	1993	
105	1012	1041	9	53	318	303	57	170	0	1980	Economies en voie de développement-Amérique
189	870	1128	21	127	558	529	98	509	0	1990	
242	691	1360	10	131	511	473	114	704	10	1991	
233	704	1243	19	64	560	527	126	788	0	1992	
258	644	1109	6	89	544	512	140	906	21	1993	
0	0	0	0	0	0	0	1	0	0	1980	Economies en voie de développement-Europe /5
0	0	0	0	0	3	3	0	8	0	1990	
0	0	0	0	0	2	2	0	5	0	1991	
0	0	0	0	0	0	0	0	1	0	1992	
0	0	0	0	4	0	0	0	0	0	1993	
0	4	9	0	0	1	1	11	14	0	1980	Economies en voie de développement-Moyen Orient
0	5	26	3	0	0	0	34	66	0	1990	
0	3	62	0	1	0	0	27	102	0	1991	
0	3	40	5	2	0	0	33	148	0	1992	
0	1	41	3	1	0	0	36	148	0	1993	
3	181	1630	6	1	17	17	8	391	0	1980	Economies en voie de développement-Autres Pays d'Asie
13	70	1590	27	36	25	19	31	757	0	1990	
12	100	1705	29	7	6	6	44	724	0	1991	
71	124	1348	28	18	8	7	64	987	0	1992	
27	102	1263	22	10	21	19	99	911	0	1993	
.	.	.	.	.	.	.	.	.	.	1980	l'ancienne URSS asiatique /9
.	.	.	.	.	.	.	.	.	.	1990	
.	.	.	.	.	.	.	.	.	.	1991	
0	1	2	0	1	2	1	22	49	0	1992	
0	4	2	0	1	2	1	17	46	0	1993	
0	0	373	0	0	0	0	0	17	0	1980	Economies en voie de développement-Océanie
0	0	355	8	0	0	0	0	152	0	1990	
0	0	362	8	0	0	0	0	185	0	1991	
0	1	311	27	0	0	0	0	130	0	1992	
0	1	305	24	0	0	0	0	136	0	1993	

Voir la fin du tableau pour la remarque générale et les notes.

SPECIAL TABLE: B

World exports by commodity classes and by regions (continued)

In million U.S. dollars f.o.b.

Animal and vegetable oils, fats and waxes (SITC, Rev. 2 and Rev. 3, 4)

Exports to → / ↓ Exports from	Year	World Monde /1,2,3	Developed economies Econ. dévelop-pées /2,3,4	Developing economies Economies en voie de développement /1,3,4 Total	Developing economies OPEC OPEP	Eastern Europe and fmr. USSR-Europe Europe de l'Est et l'anc. URSS-Europe Total /2,3,7	Eastern Europe and fmr. USSR-Europe Former USSR-Eur. /10	Developed Economies Europe Total /2	Developed Economies Europe EEC CEE /2	Developed Economies Europe EFTA AELE	Developed Economies South Africa Afrique du Sud
World /1,2,3	1980	11016	5213	5147	1212	557	352	4178	3907	262	53
	1990	13306	6877	5800	927	523	374	5467	5106	310	74
	1991	13728	7379	5930	997	359	220	5893	5614	264	41
	1992	14988	7888	6504	1187	533	331	5907	5606	286	102
	1993	15308	8052	6764	1124	414	201	6052	5714	325	115
Developed economies /2,3,4	1980	6025	2979	2820	737	177	84	2613	2409	196	46
	1990	6921	4504	2184	404	166	72	3795	3571	208	29
	1991	7068	4961	1841	321	212	112	4183	3968	202	17
	1992	7502	5030	1969	328	443	275	4100	3863	223	37
	1993	7295	4935	2028	299	265	111	3941	3682	248	56
Developing economies /1,3,4	1980	4799	2153	2245	466	351	268	1486	1474	11	7
	1990	6088	2230	3533	518	321	299	1532	1492	38	45
	1991	6438	2309	4006	675	121	106	1605	1581	23	23
	1992	7257	2773	4438	857	43	37	1722	1685	36	65
	1993	7302	2592	4614	824	84	72	1587	1543	41	59
OPEC	1980	383	239	104	30	1	0	207	206	1	0
	1990	477	297	164	22	13	13	231	229	0	0
	1991	610	349	260	26	2	2	298	297	0	0
	1992	803	530	270	23	2	2	434	432	2	0
	1993	899	504	380	28	16	15	416	414	2	0
Eastern Europe and the former USSR /2,3,7	1980	193	81	82	8	29	1	79	25	54	0
	1990	297	143	83	5	36	2	140	43	64	0
	1991	222	109	83	1	26	2	105	65	39	0
	1992	230	85	97	1	47	19	85	58	27	0
	1993	711	524	122	1	65	17	524	489	36	0
Former USSR /3	1980	92	20	66	0	7	.	20	10	10	0
	1990	...	...	...	...	...	.	...	...	...	...
	1991	...	...	...	...	...	.	...	...	...	...
	1992	.	.	.	.	.	.	.	.	.	.
	1993	.	.	.	.	.	.	.	.	.	.
Former USSR-Europe /8	1980	.	.	.	.	.	.	.	.	.	.
	1990	.	.	.	.	.	.	.	.	.	.
	1991	.	.	.	.	.	.	.	.	.	.
	1992	56	4	47	0	5	0	4	1	3	0
	1993	497	437	55	0	5	0	437	434	3	0
Developed economies-Europe /2	1980	3515	2331	1056	483	124	48	2199	2003	189	11
	1990	5289	3952	1132	232	138	46	3547	3330	202	17
	1991	5486	4347	879	139	205	106	3926	3718	195	10
	1992	5526	4277	848	140	341	181	3775	3540	221	13
	1993	5146	4139	723	99	234	81	3684	3434	239	25
European Economic Community /2	1980	3239	2139	1002	478	94	47	2017	1858	152	10
	1990	5043	3790	1072	224	114	44	3399	3223	162	16
	1991	5243	4186	814	136	188	102	3782	3611	157	10
	1992	5271	4096	796	132	320	174	3612	3422	176	11
	1993	4884	3946	681	93	207	71	3505	3311	183	25
European Free Trade Association	1980	273	189	54	5	29	1	179	143	36	1
	1990	246	161	60	8	24	2	147	108	39	1
	1991	242	160	65	4	17	4	143	106	37	0
	1992	250	178	51	8	21	7	160	117	43	2
	1993	256	188	41	6	27	10	173	119	54	0
Other developed economies	1980	2510	648	1764	255	53	36	413	406	8	35
	1990	1632	552	1052	173	27	26	247	241	7	12
	1991	1583	614	962	182	6	6	257	250	7	8
	1992	1976	753	1121	188	102	94	325	323	2	24
	1993	2148	796	1305	201	31	30	257	248	9	31

For general note and footnotes see end of table.

TABLEAU SPECIAL: B

Exportations mondiales par classes de marchandises et par régions (suite)

En millions de dollars E.-U. f.o.b.

Economies développées /2,3,4				Developing economies / Economies en voie de développement /1,3,4						← Exportations vers	
Canada	U.S.A. / E.-U.	Japan / Japon	Australia New Zealand / Australie Nouvelle-Zélande	Africa / Afrique	America / Amerique: Total	America / Amerique: LAIA / ALADI	Asia / Asie: Mid.East / Moyen Orient	Asia / Asie: Other / Autres /9	Oceania / Océanie	Année	Exportations en provenance de ↓
Huiles et graisses d'origine animale ou vegetale (CTCI, Rev. 2 et Rev. 3, 4)											
78	518	271	94	1132	811	539	831	2243	16	1980	Monde /1,2,3
109	757	317	127	1134	1041	691	915	2637	20	1990	
120	793	368	134	1232	1099	793	984	2521	22	1991	
131	1102	434	169	1317	1173	883	1117	2779	21	1992	
165	1091	412	182	1294	1256	965	1238	2879	21	1993	
55	82	117	52	900	594	385	391	851	16	1980	Economies dévelopées /2,3,4
87	388	140	43	639	501	329	319	670	15	1990	
98	436	154	48	584	503	338	298	418	15	1991	
111	526	166	54	655	554	371	318	396	13	1992	
147	532	179	52	558	586	428	317	512	13	1993	
23	436	153	42	223	165	153	439	1390	1	1980	Economies en voie de développement /1,3,4
21	369	176	83	489	480	361	591	1965	5	1990	
22	354	214	86	645	567	455	684	2102	7	1991	
21	575	268	115	662	618	511	756	2376	8	1992	
18	558	233	129	728	670	538	841	2360	8	1993	
3	22	7	0	36	3	3	33	33	0	1980	OPEP
8	34	9	15	14	16	15	45	90	0	1990	
10	17	11	13	63	12	12	35	150	0	1991	
11	45	14	26	16	15	14	38	202	0	1992	
8	53	8	18	17	40	33	66	256	0	1993	
0	1	1	0	8	52	0	2	2	0	1980	Europe de l'Est et l'ancienne URSS /2,3,7
1	1	1	0	6	60	1	5	2	0	1990	
0	4	0	0	3	29	0	1	2	0	1991	
0	0	0	0	0	1	0	42	6	0	1992	
0	0	0	0	9	0	0	80	7	0	1993	
0	0	0	0	0	52	0	2	2	0	1980	L'ancienne URSS /3
...	...	...	...	...	...	...	...	...	...	1990	
...	...	...	...	...	...	...	...	...	...	1991	
.	.	.	.	.	.	.	.	.	.	1992	
.	.	.	.	.	.	.	.	.	.	1993	
.	.	.	.	.	.	.	.	.	.	1980	L'ancienne URSS-Europe /8
.	.	.	.	.	.	.	.	.	.	1990	
.	.	.	.	.	.	.	.	.	.	1991	
0	0	0	0	0	0	0	41	6	0	1992	
0	0	0	0	0	0	0	48	7	0	1993	
15	64	9	24	534	56	24	317	85	7	1980	Economies développées-Europe /2
28	275	29	37	434	185	114	209	254	9	1990	
32	280	40	41	350	149	97	165	184	8	1991	
37	329	51	48	334	161	98	187	126	8	1992	
35	288	41	44	267	133	88	130	149	8	1993	
14	59	6	23	513	46	22	313	71	7	1980	Communauté Economique Européenne /2
28	263	29	37	404	177	111	205	242	9	1990	
31	266	40	40	321	140	94	160	165	8	1991	
36	315	50	48	309	154	96	184	113	8	1992	
34	277	40	43	251	126	86	127	139	8	1993	
1	5	3	1	21	9	2	4	14	0	1980	Association Européenne de Libre Echange
1	12	0	0	30	8	3	5	12	0	1990	
1	15	0	0	29	9	3	5	19	0	1991	
0	15	0	0	25	7	2	3	13	0	1992	
1	12	1	1	16	8	2	2	10	0	1993	
40	18	108	29	366	538	361	74	765	8	1980	Autres economies développées
59	112	111	6	205	315	216	110	416	6	1990	
66	156	114	7	235	354	241	133	234	6	1991	
74	197	116	6	321	393	272	131	271	5	1992	
112	244	138	8	291	453	339	187	362	5	1993	

Voir la fin du tableau pour la remarque générale et les notes.

SPECIAL TABLE: B

World exports by commodity classes and by regions (continued)

In million U.S. dollars f.o.b.

Exports to → / ↓ Exports from	Year	World Monde /1,2,3	Developed economies Econ. dévelop-pées /2,3,4	Developing economies Economies en voie de développement /1,3,4: Total	Developing economies: OPEC OPEP	Eastern Europe and fmr. USSR-Europe Europe de l'Est et l'anc. URSS-Europe: Total /2,3,7	Eastern Europe: Former USSR-Eur. /10	Developed Economies: Europe: Total /2	Europe: EEC CEE /2	Europe: EFTA AELE	South Africa Afrique du Sud
Animal and vegetable oils, fats and waxes (SITC, Rev. 2 and Rev. 3, 4) (continued)											
Canada	1980	200	88	112	0	0	0	53	51	2	0
	1990	183	144	38	12	1	0	28	27	0	0
	1991	214	182	32	12	0	0	23	22	1	0
	1992	280	235	45	4	0	0	30	30	0	0
	1993	325	283	41	0	1	0	31	31	0	1
United States	1980	1975	465	1472	229	39	28	290	285	5	24
	1990	1191	306	862	157	23	23	164	163	2	10
	1991	1144	347	791	166	6	5	200	196	4	3
	1992	1447	433	914	177	101	93	277	275	2	4
	1993	1513	427	1058	195	28	27	210	203	8	6
Japan	1980	114	66	41	6	6	0	59	58	0	0
	1990	93	54	35	3	3	3	35	32	4	2
	1991	76	41	35	3	1	1	20	18	2	4
	1992	61	26	36	4	0	0	7	7	0	4
	1993	59	20	38	3	1	1	3	3	0	0
Australia, New Zealand	1980	166	26	133	19	8	8	8	8	0	10
	1990	99	42	57	1	0	0	16	16	1	0
	1991	87	38	49	1	0	0	11	10	1	1
	1992	144	54	90	3	0	0	8	8	0	16
	1993	209	61	131	3	2	2	9	8	1	23
Developing economies-Africa	1980	423	344	30	6	0	0	338	335	1	0
	1990	431	372	58	4	0	0	366	359	6	0
	1991	542	459	83	1	0	0	449	449	0	0
	1992	445	366	79	3	0	0	357	355	2	0
	1993	384	306	77	1	0	0	299	299	0	1
Developing economies-America	1980	1298	446	670	207	182	123	372	366	6	7
	1990	1756	450	1160	298	145	134	282	276	6	44
	1991	1692	363	1313	375	17	16	221	216	4	23
	1992	1667	372	1290	358	4	4	200	196	4	64
	1993	1681	417	1245	336	9	9	205	193	10	53
Developing economies-Europe/ 5	1980	20	10	3	1	8	0	6	4	2	0
	1990	12	6	2	0	3	0	6	5	1	0
	1991	5	3	0	0	2	0	3	3	0	0
	1992	21	4	17	1	0	0	4	4	0	0
	1993	13	4	9	0	0	0	3	3	0	0
Developing economies-Middle East	1980	24	1	21	15	2	0	1	1	0	0
	1990	192	31	107	79	50	50	29	19	10	0
	1991	264	47	192	148	24	23	40	38	2	0
	1992	288	36	232	187	19	17	28	26	2	0
	1993	268	20	225	182	23	20	13	12	2	0
Developing economies-Other Asia	1980	2960	1279	1521	238	160	144	712	710	2	0
	1990	3638	1312	2204	137	123	114	799	783	14	0
	1991	3859	1363	2417	152	78	66	823	807	15	0
	1992	4732	1897	2814	308	20	16	1046	1018	28	1
	1993	4845	1743	3049	305	52	43	973	945	28	6
Former USSR-Asia /9	1980	..	..	..	..	..	..	..	..	..	..
	1990	..	..	..	..	..	..	..	..	..	..
	1991	..	..	..	..	..	..	..	..	..	..
	1992	7	0	7	0	0	..	0	0	0	0
	1993	3	0	3	0	0	..	0	0	0	0
Developing economies-Oceania	1980	73	73	0	0	0	0	58	58	0	0
	1990	59	59	0	0	0	0	51	51	0	0
	1991	76	75	1	0	0	0	68	67	1	0
	1992	105	98	7	1	0	0	88	87	1	0
	1993	111	102	9	0	0	0	93	92	1	0

For general note and footnotes see end of table.

Exportations mondiales par classes de marchandises et par régions (suite)

En millions de dollars E.-U. f.o.b.

Economies développées /2,3,4: Canada	U.S.A. E.-U.	Japan Japon	Australia New Zealand Australie Nouvelle-Zélande	Developing economies / Economies en voie de développement /1,3,4: Africa Afrique	America Amerique: Total	America Amerique: LAIA ALADI	Asia Asie: Mid.East Moyen Orient	Asia Asie: Other Autres /9	Oceania Océanie	Année	← Exportations vers / Exportations en provenance de ↓
Huiles et graisses d'origine animale ou vegetale (CTCI, Rev. 2 et Rev. 3, 4) (suite)											
.	10	21	3	10	10	3	0	92	0	1980	Canada
.	96	20	0	21	11	6	1	6	0	1990	
.	138	20	0	15	4	1	2	10	0	1991	
.	182	23	0	18	13	7	0	13	0	1992	
.	228	24	0	5	9	8	0	27	0	1993	
39	.	82	24	345	525	355	49	540	0	1980	Etats-Unis
58	.	68	4	158	304	209	109	291	0	1990	
64	.	71	5	202	349	240	130	109	0	1991	
73	.	66	4	269	379	265	127	137	0	1992	
110	.	91	5	243	444	331	186	179	0	1993	
0	7	.	0	0	2	2	2	37	0	1980	Japon
1	15	.	0	0	0	0	0	35	0	1990	
2	15	.	0	0	0	0	0	34	0	1991	
1	14	.	0	0	0	0	0	35	0	1992	
1	15	.	0	0	0	0	0	38	0	1993	
0	1	5	1	11	0	0	18	96	7	1980	Australie, Nouvelle-Zélande
0	1	23	2	11	1	1	0	39	6	1990	
0	2	22	2	3	0	0	0	40	6	1991	
0	1	27	2	9	0	0	2	74	4	1992	
0	1	24	3	13	0	0	0	112	5	1993	
0	5	1	0	23	0	0	6	0	0	1980	Economies en voie de développement-Afrique
0	3	1	1	47	0	0	11	1	0	1990	
0	8	1	0	72	0	0	10	0	0	1991	
0	7	2	0	57	10	10	13	0	0	1992	
0	5	2	0	64	0	0	13	0	0	1993	
1	62	3	1	99	156	149	170	224	0	1980	Economies en voie de développement-Amérique
2	87	14	20	162	425	327	245	328	0	1990	
0	71	19	25	170	467	379	307	368	0	1991	
0	72	15	18	150	503	424	292	346	0	1992	
0	113	9	34	170	553	457	282	240	0	1993	
0	0	4	0	0	0	0	3	0	0	1980	Economies en voie de développement-Europe /5
0	0	0	0	2	0	0	0	0	0	1990	
0	0	0	0	0	0	0	0	0	0	1991	
0	0	0	0	1	0	0	4	0	0	1992	
0	0	0	0	0	0	0	1	0	0	1993	
0	0	0	0	3	0	0	18	0	0	1980	Economies en voie de développement-Moyen Orient
0	1	0	0	44	0	0	60	2	0	1990	
0	5	0	0	101	0	0	90	1	0	1991	
0	6	0	0	115	0	0	104	7	0	1992	
0	3	0	0	96	0	0	121	7	0	1993	
23	358	145	35	98	9	4	242	1166	1	1980	Economies en voie de développement-Autres Pays d'Asie
19	273	161	58	234	55	34	275	1634	5	1990	
21	266	194	57	302	100	76	277	1731	7	1991	
20	487	250	91	340	106	78	340	2021	7	1992	
18	434	221	91	397	117	81	422	2105	8	1993	
.	.	.	.	.	.	.	.	.	.	1980	l'ancienne URSS asiatique /9
.	.	.	.	.	.	.	.	.	.	1990	
.	.	.	.	.	.	.	.	.	.	1991	
0	0	0	0	0	0	0	7	0	0	1992	
0	0	0	0	0	0	0	3	0	0	1993	
0	10	0	5	0	0	0	0	0	0	1980	Economies en voie de développement-Océanie
0	4	0	4	0	0	0	0	0	0	1990	
0	4	0	3	0	0	0	0	1	0	1991	
0	4	1	6	0	0	0	4	2	0	1992	
0	4	1	4	0	0	0	1	8	0	1993	

Voir la fin du tableau pour la remarque générale et les notes.

SPECIAL TABLE: B

World exports by commodity classes and by regions (continued)

In million U.S. dollars f.o.b.

Exports from ↓ / Exports to →	Year	World Monde /1,2,3	Developed economies Econ. dévelop-pées /2,3,4	Developing economies Economies en voie de développement /1,3,4: Total	Developing economies: OPEC OPEP	Eastern Europe and fmr. USSR-Europe Europe de l'Est et l'anc. URSS-Europe: Total /2,3,7	Eastern Europe and fmr. USSR-Europe: Former USSR-Eur. /10	Developed Economies: Europe: Total /2	Europe: EEC CEE /2	Europe: EFTA AELE	South Africa Afrique du Sud
		Mineral fuels and related materials (SITC, Rev. 2 and Rev. 3, 3)									
World /1,2,3	1980	492546	358017	89353	5386	16468	563	198892	177681	20916	330
	1990	357484	248673	75558	3207	20218	1393	137403	123711	13256	81
	1991	319796	227017	71299	3772	10533	814	123521	111027	11841	101
	1992	319443	229313	70630	5300	10373	1011	121311	108432	12263	121
	1993	317819	223307	75440	5715	10533	994	113343	100121	12346	123
Developed economies /2,3,4	1980	88092	75040	7208	2273	638	131	58414	50795	7432	108
	1990	105038	88419	11263	1137	875	181	60775	52582	7907	63
	1991	106986	88210	12811	1592	1353	162	62889	54637	7920	84
	1992	104549	86323	13039	1409	1694	191	59678	51438	7871	102
	1993	102263	82197	14373	1600	1546	200	54033	46035	7395	90
Developing economies /1,3,4	1980	364149	262841	76715	3105	1498	15	120669	112442	8122	222
	1990	203999	135588	57080	1868	2866	943	53154	51567	1458	18
	1991	189683	127079	55050	2078	1740	559	49377	47293	1772	17
	1992	189123	126842	55705	3841	1956	200	46115	44219	1698	13
	1993	191108	126031	59081	4068	1992	180	45271	43454	1562	33
OPEC	1980	310181	225176	63070	1859	1137	9	111296	103441	7803	1
	1990	139993	96443	34969	462	2218	463	43805	42921	852	0
	1991	127287	91604	30712	836	1114	145	40545	39348	1155	1
	1992	128324	93515	30239	2627	1448	98	37818	36404	1387	0
	1993	130623	94876	31560	2777	1533	105	37582	36308	1248	2
Eastern Europe and the former USSR /2,3,7	1980	40305	20137	5430	8	14331	417	19809	14444	5363	0
	1990	48447	24666	7215	203	16478	268	23474	19562	3892	0
	1991	23127	11727	3438	101	7440	93	11255	9097	2150	0
	1992	25771	16148	1887	50	6724	620	15518	12776	2694	6
	1993	24449	15079	1986	47	6996	613	14040	10633	3388	0
Former USSR /3	1980	35949	17659	5127	5	13163	.	17363	13024	4339	0
	1990	...	...	...	...	...	.	...	...	...	...
	1991	...	...	...	...	...	.	...	...	...	...
	1992	.	.	.	.	.	.	.	.	.	.
	1993	.	.	.	.	.	.	.	.	.	.
Former USSR-Europe /8	1980	.	.	.	.	.	.	.	.	.	.
	1990	.	.	.	.	.	.	.	.	.	.
	1991	.	.	.	.	.	.	.	.	.	.
	1992	22497	14435	1478	28	6153	457	13826	11768	2040	0
	1993	21183	13014	1723	29	6060	477	11985	9339	2642	0
Developed economies-Europe /2	1980	66761	57733	4407	1915	437	88	55045	47652	7208	48
	1990	69183	62320	2471	615	605	127	54435	46456	7715	35
	1991	69867	61870	2991	882	1138	118	56198	48172	7702	43
	1992	68245	60815	2910	845	1522	147	54438	46358	7725	55
	1993	65205	57075	3826	989	1409	170	50155	42334	7246	33
European Economic Community /2	1980	55498	46579	4345	1904	390	76	43900	37431	6293	48
	1990	50260	43709	2427	608	366	107	37634	32033	5374	35
	1991	50276	42802	2927	871	708	88	38549	32908	5347	43
	1992	47648	40896	2785	821	1017	79	36308	30514	5470	38
	1993	45919	38491	3642	947	940	119	33329	27609	5169	32
European Free Trade Association	1980	11263	11154	62	11	47	12	11146	10221	915	0
	1990	18893	18611	44	7	239	20	16800	14423	2341	0
	1991	19562	19067	64	11	430	30	17648	15264	2355	0
	1992	20544	19919	121	24	504	68	18130	15844	2254	17
	1993	19233	18585	179	43	469	52	16826	14725	2077	1
Other developed economies	1980	21331	17307	2801	358	201	43	3369	3143	224	60
	1990	35855	26099	8793	521	270	54	6340	6127	192	27
	1991	37120	26340	9820	709	215	43	6691	6464	218	40
	1992	36304	25508	10128	564	172	45	5240	5080	147	46
	1993	37058	25122	10547	611	137	30	3878	3701	149	57

For general note and footnotes see end of table.

Exportations mondiales par classes de marchandises et par régions (suite)

En millions de dollars E.-U. f.o.b.

Economies développées /2,3,4: Canada	Economies développées /2,3,4: U.S.A. E.-U.	Economies développées /2,3,4: Japan Japon	Economies développées /2,3,4: Australia New Zealand Australie Nouvelle-Zélande	Developing economies / Economies en voie de développement /1,3,4: Africa Afrique	America Amerique: Total	America Amerique: LAIA ALADI	Asia Asie: Mid.East Moyen Orient	Asia Asie: Other Autres /9	Oceania Océanie	Année	← Exportations vers / Exportations en provenance de ↓
Combustibles minéraux et produits assimiles (CTCI, Rev. 2 et Rev. 3, 3)											
6614	81612	65855	3884	7237	29640	14716	10211	37641	633	1980	Monde /1,2,3
5100	67102	36462	1925	5554	14779	6170	8302	43364	680	1990	
4416	52860	42945	2344	8515	13123	5362	7876	39165	747	1991	
3740	59745	41311	2344	4398	13874	8070	7862	42585	609	1992	
3525	63103	39696	2638	4505	14783	8634	8470	45864	584	1993	
1965	10526	3726	288	2646	1635	1069	1175	1499	125	1980	Economies dévelopées /2,3,4
3914	17108	5791	576	1503	2858	1795	775	5669	287	1990	
2810	15739	5920	489	1620	3260	2191	1429	6014	325	1991	
2740	17583	5512	429	1204	3537	2540	1128	6729	282	1992	
2510	19270	5317	464	1278	3427	2355	1343	7847	295	1993	
4649	71054	61833	3596	4425	26924	13591	8679	34626	508	1980	Economies en voie de développement /1,3,4
1186	49385	30090	1349	3722	10039	4236	6501	35562	393	1990	
1606	36907	36770	1855	6720	9002	3087	5995	32213	422	1991	
955	41884	35500	1915	3100	10233	5433	6068	35123	328	1992	
952	43210	34026	2174	3122	11226	6172	6381	37223	288	1993	
4502	55732	51087	2559	3268	23365	12316	6995	27940	9	1980	OPEP
1053	32610	18226	749	2795	6586	2751	4930	19821	3	1990	
1423	22989	25435	1210	5551	5347	1500	4605	14529	58	1991	
613	28153	25531	1398	2039	6346	3816	4405	16947	0	1992	
740	29578	25539	1436	2052	6846	4200	4626	17495	3	1993	
0	32	296	0	166	1080	57	357	1516	0	1980	Europe de l'Est et l'ancienne URSS /2,3,7
0	610	581	0	329	1882	139	1026	2133	0	1990	
0	214	255	0	174	861	83	452	938	0	1991	
45	279	300	0	94	104	97	667	733	0	1992	
63	623	353	0	105	130	108	746	794	0	1993	
0	20	276	0	161	951	0	343	1469	0	1980	L'ancienne URSS /3
...	...	...	...	...	...	...	...	...	...	1990	
...	...	...	...	...	...	...	...	...	...	1991	
.	.	.	.	.	.	.	.	.	.	1992	
.	.	.	.	.	.	.	.	.	.	1993	
.	.	.	.	.	.	.	.	.	.	1980	L'ancienne URSS-Europe /8
.	.	.	.	.	.	.	.	.	.	1990	
.	.	.	.	.	.	.	.	.	.	1991	
45	263	300	0	85	21	21	563	694	0	1992	
63	612	353	0	89	23	23	701	750	0	1993	
119	2428	32	52	2425	549	96	1034	324	2	1980	Economies développées-Europe /2
1758	5852	62	79	1118	291	137	480	478	5	1990	
1467	3892	54	32	1205	305	168	996	377	5	1991	
1379	4719	75	21	997	326	164	767	695	4	1992	
1276	5429	39	21	1049	499	202	968	1128	4	1993	
118	2422	32	51	2418	546	96	1009	315	2	1980	Communauté Economique Européenne /2
1043	4809	60	79	1114	279	126	473	474	5	1990	
700	3355	53	31	1201	291	168	985	368	5	1991	
580	3855	73	20	987	314	155	753	640	4	1992	
608	4422	37	21	1026	477	184	963	1024	4	1993	
0	6	0	1	7	4	1	25	9	0	1980	Association Européenne de Libre Echange
715	1043	2	0	3	12	11	6	4	0	1990	
767	536	1	1	3	14	0	10	8	0	1991	
799	864	2	0	10	8	4	14	55	0	1992	
668	1007	2	0	23	17	12	5	104	0	1993	
1847	8098	3694	236	221	1086	973	141	1175	123	1980	Autres economies développées
2156	11256	5729	496	385	2567	1658	295	5192	282	1990	
1343	11847	5866	457	415	2955	2023	433	5637	320	1991	
1361	12864	5436	408	206	3211	2376	361	6034	278	1992	
1234	13841	5278	443	230	2928	2153	374	6719	291	1993	

Voir la fin du tableau pour la remarque générale et les notes.

SPECIAL TABLE: B

World exports by commodity classes and by regions (continued)

In million U.S. dollars f.o.b.

Exports to → / ↓ Exports from	Year	World Monde /1,2,3	Developed economies Econ. dévelop-pées /2,3,4	Developing economies Economies en voie de développement /1,3,4: Total	Developing economies: OPEC OPEP	Eastern Europe and fmr. USSR-Europe Europe de l'Est et l'anc. URSS-Europe: Total /2,3,7	Eastern Europe: Former USSR-Eur. /10	Developed Economies: Europe: Total /2	Europe: EEC CEE /2	Europe: EFTA AELE	South Africa Afrique du Sud
		Mineral fuels and related materials (SITC, Rev. 2 and Rev. 3, 3) (continued)									
Canada	1980	9392	9054	338	75	0	0	455	375	80	0
	1990	12670	12169	501	10	0	0	246	203	33	1
	1991	13650	13035	613	6	1	0	402	378	15	0
	1992	14135	13664	470	5	1	0	220	211	9	0
	1993	15192	14601	591	86	0	0	98	85	7	4
United States	1980	8017	6281	1621	207	115	26	2589	2444	142	43
	1990	12175	7757	4278	270	140	29	3839	3724	103	24
	1991	12081	6950	5001	424	131	29	4057	3920	137	29
	1992	11122	5990	5042	238	89	19	3229	3130	100	41
	1993	9736	4860	4784	241	92	5	2235	2155	80	49
Japan	1980	523	89	361	30	73	17	24	24	0	16
	1990	1274	137	1089	19	48	25	22	19	3	3
	1991	1302	140	1122	17	40	14	33	27	6	4
	1992	1595	225	1344	21	25	25	47	42	5	5
	1993	1974	229	1720	17	25	24	54	51	4	4
Australia, New Zealand	1980	2432	1882	481	47	14	0	301	299	2	0
	1990	7011	4316	2235	222	80	0	801	779	22	0
	1991	7626	4657	2460	263	43	0	902	869	33	6
	1992	7912	4514	2917	300	53	0	897	870	27	0
	1993	8413	4233	2993	263	19	0	752	723	30	0
Developing economies-Africa	1980	89589	62726	6517	77	919	0	32861	30879	1935	0
	1990	45490	40624	3811	88	720	205	28057	27445	507	1
	1991	44978	40320	3877	159	294	1	28228	27240	692	0
	1992	41569	36973	3777	122	309	2	25319	24442	698	3
	1993	40304	35765	3868	117	269	0	24266	23555	511	4
Developing economies-America	1980	39899	27913	11437	81	13	12	6907	6444	410	1
	1990	36645	28515	5468	281	281	272	4920	4459	446	10
	1991	30664	23402	5743	137	245	244	3890	3615	275	7
	1992	29781	22292	7118	109	16	15	3540	3397	143	3
	1993	29681	21688	7713	148	13	12	2689	2562	127	12
Developing economies-Europe/ 5	1980	231	188	4	1	40	1	187	154	33	0
	1990	354	292	11	5	51	3	290	191	99	0
	1991	234	194	6	3	34	2	193	127	66	0
	1992	629	226	316	0	84	0	225	202	24	0
	1993	738	339	303	1	96	0	338	315	23	0
Developing economies-Middle East	1980	201461	148081	50033	2711	524	0	80319	74580	5739	0
	1990	85021	46151	32484	1211	1566	261	19330	19024	307	0
	1991	75956	44135	27641	1299	957	145	16363	15737	624	3
	1992	80116	49686	26351	3267	1293	98	16242	15507	735	0
	1993	83547	51999	27670	3483	1393	105	17128	16336	792	0
Developing economies-Other Asia	1980	32938	23911	8716	236	2	1	391	382	6	221
	1990	36474	20007	15291	283	247	203	556	449	99	7
	1991	37835	19028	17768	481	210	166	703	575	115	7
	1992	37013	17665	18129	343	254	85	789	671	98	7
	1993	36019	15761	19189	307	221	62	850	686	109	17
Former USSR-Asia /9	1980	.	.	.	.	.	.	.	.	.	.
	1990	.	.	.	.	.	.	.	.	.	.
	1991	.	.	.	.	.	.	.	.	.	.
	1992	346	142	67	26	137	.	134	101	33	0
	1993	284	100	61	24	123	.	95	59	36	0
Developing economies-Oceania	1980	31	23	8	0	0	0	4	4	0	0
	1990	15	0	15	0	0	0	0	0	0	0
	1991	17	0	15	0	0	0	0	0	0	0
	1992	16	0	15	0	0	0	0	0	0	0
	1993	819	479	339	12	0	0	0	0	0	0

For general note and footnotes see end of table.

TABLEAU SPECIAL: B

Exportations mondiales par classes de marchandises et par régions (suite)

En millions de dollars E.-U. f.o.b.

Economies développées /2,3,4: Canada	Economies développées: U.S.A. E.-U.	Economies développées: Japan Japon	Economies développées: Australia New Zealand Australie Nouvelle-Zélande	Developing economies Economies en voie de développement /1,3,4: Africa Afrique	America Amerique: Total	America Amerique: LAIA ALADI	Asia Asie: Mid.East Moyen Orient	Asia Asie: Other Autres /9	Oceania Océanie	Année	← Exportations vers / Exportations en provenance de ↓
Combustibles minéraux et produits assimiles (CTCI, Rev. 2 et Rev. 3, 3) (suite)											
.	8036	558	5	39	104	95	0	195	0	1980	Canada
.	10647	1275	1	0	106	90	10	385	0	1990	
.	11487	1145	1	22	123	106	13	454	0	1991	
.	12534	906	4	6	121	95	7	336	0	1992	
.	13508	983	7	34	144	126	29	379	5	1993	
1844	.	1741	61	153	889	789	125	388	11	1980	Etats-Unis
2155	.	1455	211	120	2342	1450	202	1530	19	1990	
1324	.	1301	174	139	2603	1691	313	1864	23	1991	
1359	.	1162	149	140	2830	2024	204	1816	17	1992	
1232	.	1135	138	132	2460	1705	174	2010	3	1993	
0	44	.	5	11	90	86	4	255	1	1980	Japon
1	95	.	16	0	20	17	9	1059	0	1990	
0	94	.	8	0	87	85	3	1030	0	1991	
0	167	.	6	1	62	59	5	1277	0	1992	
0	160	.	10	1	32	31	6	1681	0	1993	
3	18	1396	164	18	3	3	12	336	112	1980	Australie, Nouvelle-Zélande
0	488	2743	268	33	99	99	74	1765	258	1990	
19	244	3188	274	43	141	140	104	1880	293	1991	
1	158	3194	248	40	174	174	120	2323	260	1992	
2	166	3008	286	39	253	253	128	2292	281	1993	
93	28608	981	0	870	3346	1394	1190	546	0	1980	Economies en voie de développement-Afrique
536	11629	232	4	1522	836	631	783	248	2	1990	
195	11363	172	1	1668	878	731	430	434	0	1991	
94	11122	147	9	1688	994	910	297	399	0	1992	
214	10878	172	9	1622	1097	993	282	461	3	1993	
1961	17243	1162	3	592	10586	2534	39	133	50	1980	Economies en voie de développement-Amérique
556	21499	1290	9	75	5032	1841	1	346	0	1990	
693	17607	1025	1	89	5243	2023	9	383	16	1991	
442	17467	660	4	153	6216	1939	23	726	0	1992	
288	18018	540	15	133	6894	2439	21	659	6	1993	
0	0	0	0	1	1	0	1	2	0	1980	Economies en voie de développement-Europe /5
0	2	0	0	5	5	0	1	0	0	1990	
0	1	0	0	3	3	0	0	0	0	1991	
0	0	0	0	5	20	0	11	0	0	1992	
0	0	0	0	1	19	0	31	4	0	1993	
2594	20101	42721	2346	2923	12020	9525	7154	26875	111	1980	Economies en voie de développement-Moyen Orient
82	13930	12266	532	1821	3747	1649	5533	20967	1	1990	
707	5983	20215	864	4636	2362	204	5150	15217	58	1991	
419	11664	20389	972	1036	2569	2496	5485	17089	0	1992	
450	12636	20760	1027	1090	2749	2673	5838	17809	0	1993	
0	5100	16957	1240	40	972	138	295	7065	345	1980	Economies en voie de développement-Autres Pays d'Asie
12	2324	16302	803	299	420	115	181	13990	386	1990	
11	1954	15358	988	323	516	129	405	16168	344	1991	
0	1630	14303	929	219	433	88	253	16897	324	1992	
0	1595	12553	728	275	468	67	209	17953	277	1993	
.	.	.	.	.	.	.	.	.	.	1980	l'ancienne URSS asiatique /9
.	.	.	.	.	.	.	.	.	.	1990	
.	.	.	.	.	.	.	.	.	.	1991	
0	8	0	0	3	7	4	44	13	0	1992	
0	5	0	0	3	6	3	41	12	0	1993	
0	1	12	6	0	0	0	0	5	3	1980	Economies en voie de développement-Océanie
0	0	0	0	0	0	0	0	11	4	1990	
0	0	0	0	0	0	0	1	11	4	1991	
0	0	0	0	0	0	0	0	12	3	1992	
0	83	0	395	0	0	0	0	337	2	1993	

Voir la fin du tableau pour la remarque générale et les notes.

SPECIAL TABLE: B

World exports by commodity classes and by regions (continued)

In million U.S. dollars f.o.b.

Exports to → / ↓ Exports from	Year	World Monde /1,2,3	Developed economies / Econ. dévelop-pées /2,3,4	Developing economies / Economies en voie de développement /1,3,4		Eastern Europe and fmr. USSR-Europe / Europe de l'Est et l'anc. URSS-Europe		Developed Economies			
								Europe			South Africa
				Total	OPEC OPEP	Total /2,3,7	Former USSR-Eur. /10	Total /2	EEC CEE /2	EFTA AELE	Afrique du Sud
		Chemicals (SITC, Rev. 2 and Rev. 3, 5)									
World /1,2,3	1980	138523	88854	39068	8892	9593	4425	68974	58192	10681	1413
	1990	300871	208519	76583	11067	12938	7052	157248	135176	21817	1798
	1991	307131	211284	83336	11461	10098	5472	157004	135768	20968	1890
	1992	332922	230254	91772	12617	8571	3055	169563	146836	22453	1993
	1993	328543	220675	95697	12574	9713	3111	156459	134255	21922	1985
Developed economies /2,3,4	1980	122232	82904	32584	7768	5999	2573	65584	55342	10142	1393
	1990	253724	190840	54454	8841	6395	3101	146938	126313	20379	1723
	1991	262246	194949	58440	8896	6795	3248	148440	128328	19860	1785
	1992	281322	211454	61375	9412	6514	2066	159648	138084	21298	1855
	1993	273373	201022	63174	9232	6936	2021	146711	125619	20827	1803
Developing economies /1,3,4	1980	10401	4097	5215	1019	885	602	1756	1638	117	21
	1990	35669	13387	19513	2118	2203	1845	6397	5999	392	74
	1991	38955	13465	23614	2484	1746	1493	5913	5397	500	104
	1992	44343	15221	28213	3105	667	408	6630	6209	413	137
	1993	47358	15888	30474	3235	781	460	6430	5965	449	176
OPEC	1980	1481	877	588	91	6	1	409	408	1	2
	1990	4852	1702	2835	173	39	28	1198	1180	17	0
	1991	4025	1272	2744	409	6	4	776	653	122	1
	1992	4977	1754	3152	709	12	1	1064	994	69	2
	1993	5322	1979	3263	735	25	15	1114	1037	77	2
Eastern Europe and the former USSR /2,3,7	1980	5890	1853	1268	105	2709	1249	1634	1212	421	0
	1990	11477	4292	2616	107	4340	2106	3913	2864	1046	1
	1991	5930	2870	1282	80	1557	731	2651	2043	608	1
	1992	7258	3579	2184	100	1390	581	3286	2543	741	2
	1993	7812	3764	2048	107	1995	630	3318	2671	646	6
Former USSR /3	1980	1704	562	527	22	615	.	438	344	93	0
	1990	...	...	...	...	...	.	...	...	...	...
	1991	...	...	...	...	...	.	...	...	...	...
	1992	.	.	.	.	.	.	.	.	.	.
	1993	.	.	.	.	.	.	.	.	.	.
Former USSR-Europe /8	1980	.	.	.	.	.	.	.	.	.	.
	1990	.	.	.	.	.	.	.	.	.	.
	1991	.	.	.	.	.	.	.	.	.	.
	1992	3141	1473	1250	20	418	67	1334	1016	318	0
	1993	3346	1589	1288	22	469	75	1330	983	347	3
Developed economies-Europe /2	1980	89278	65718	18107	5677	5405	2144	57407	48017	9293	960
	1990	188016	152429	28029	6393	5667	2535	130250	110921	19102	1293
	1991	190770	154187	28543	6209	6107	2689	130996	112095	18653	1318
	1992	206337	167670	30570	6675	6158	1869	141060	120770	20029	1407
	1993	195480	155838	31106	6511	6456	1731	128934	109329	19348	1386
European Economic Community /2	1980	78479	58118	15953	5048	4361	1769	50892	42896	7907	871
	1990	162709	132601	24197	5576	4368	1937	114057	97502	16338	1156
	1991	165051	133867	24612	5439	4965	2270	114460	98250	15971	1160
	1992	178086	144991	26482	5847	4991	1606	122655	105157	17246	1255
	1993	167878	133869	26989	5735	5301	1518	111301	94247	16804	1234
European Free Trade Association	1980	10794	7597	2153	629	1044	375	6512	5119	1386	89
	1990	25290	19813	3828	815	1299	598	16181	13407	2764	137
	1991	25695	20302	3925	765	1142	420	16521	13829	2683	158
	1992	28220	22657	4080	822	1166	263	18385	15594	2783	152
	1993	27574	21948	4110	773	1155	213	17614	15063	2544	152
Other developed economies	1980	32954	17186	14477	2091	594	430	8177	7325	850	432
	1990	65708	38411	26425	2448	729	567	16688	15392	1277	430
	1991	71476	40762	29897	2687	688	558	17444	16233	1207	467
	1992	74985	43784	30805	2738	356	197	18588	17314	1269	448
	1993	77893	45184	32068	2721	480	290	17777	16290	1479	418

For general note and footnotes see end of table.

Exportations mondiales par classes de marchandises et par régions (suite)

En millions de dollars E.-U. f.o.b.

Economies développées /2,3,4: Canada	U.S.A. E.-U.	Japan Japon	Australia New Zealand Australie Nouvelle-Zélande	Developing economies / Economies en voie de développement /1,3,4: Africa Afrique	America Amerique: Total	America Amerique: LAIA ALADI	Asia Asie: Mid.East Moyen Orient	Asia Asie: Other Autres /9	Oceania Océanie	Année	← Exportations vers / Exportations en provenance de ↓
Produits chimiques (CTCI, Rev. 2 et Rev. 3, 5)											
2790	7848	5290	2135	6266	11021	8515	5870	14109	140	1980	Monde /1,2,3
7748	22680	13233	4631	7284	14770	11253	9259	42734	253	1990	
8286	23977	14293	4606	7231	16441	12949	8791	48887	269	1991	
9141	28203	14621	5273	7658	18020	14332	10222	53564	286	1992	
10135	30023	15110	5449	7368	19530	15898	10561	56416	276	1993	
2755	6797	3996	1981	5641	9287	7470	5050	11251	127	1980	Economies dévelopées /2,3,4
7588	18600	10834	4009	6020	11703	9258	7241	27443	206	1990	
8116	19705	11622	4099	5989	13098	10605	6985	30680	221	1991	
8942	23137	11944	4541	6331	14176	11546	7659	31702	235	1992	
9920	24327	12193	4634	6022	15165	12650	7824	32871	224	1993	
29	900	1244	144	477	1439	918	674	2587	12	1980	Economies en voie de développement /1,3,4
151	3879	2252	613	1052	2564	1817	1709	14105	47	1990	
159	4169	2592	502	1122	3160	2292	1616	17638	48	1991	
187	4882	2612	723	1138	3610	2672	2042	20817	49	1992	
206	5370	2845	807	1120	4155	3123	2218	22551	51	1993	
0	29	394	43	26	67	55	114	381	0	1980	OPEP
7	216	119	161	102	239	193	597	1875	1	1990	
8	182	281	23	148	294	219	438	1845	1	1991	
6	266	253	163	104	321	271	778	1934	2	1992	
7	395	282	179	109	346	288	788	2008	3	1993	
6	151	50	9	148	295	128	146	271	0	1980	Europe de l'Est et l'ancienne URSS /2,3,7
9	201	147	9	212	502	178	308	1186	0	1990	
12	104	78	6	121	183	53	190	569	0	1991	
11	184	64	9	189	234	115	521	1045	2	1992	
9	326	72	9	226	210	125	520	994	0	1993	
0	116	5	3	38	135	26	46	113	0	1980	L'ancienne URSS /3
...	...	...	...	...	...	...	...	...	...	1990	
...	...	...	...	...	...	...	...	...	...	1991	
.	.	.	.	.	.	.	.	.	.	1992	
.	.	.	.	.	.	.	.	.	.	1993	
.	.	.	.	.	.	.	.	.	.	1980	L'ancienne URSS-Europe /8
.	.	.	.	.	.	.	.	.	.	1990	
.	.	.	.	.	.	.	.	.	.	1991	
2	116	20	1	97	171	66	303	659	0	1992	
3	227	23	1	102	149	73	335	681	0	1993	
568	3836	1773	866	5107	3665	2822	4151	3994	52	1980	Economies développées-Europe /2
1378	10992	5710	1864	5354	4850	3641	6159	9768	115	1990	
1364	11736	6013	1811	5284	5378	4162	5913	10457	119	1991	
1489	13854	6648	2097	5545	5887	4576	6509	11284	127	1992	
1549	13928	6693	2177	5194	6307	5027	6702	11746	126	1993	
486	3383	1448	762	4710	3094	2376	3615	3544	51	1980	Communauté Economique Européenne /2
1140	9413	4459	1525	4936	3981	2937	5320	8395	114	1990	
1142	9988	4776	1487	4878	4436	3378	5125	8939	118	1991	
1227	11837	5283	1732	5110	4879	3719	5684	9705	126	1992	
1275	11889	5351	1776	4809	5335	4193	5872	10038	123	1993	
82	453	326	104	397	571	445	536	451	1	1980	Association Européenne de Libre Echange
238	1579	1251	339	416	869	704	838	1373	2	1990	
222	1748	1238	324	402	942	784	786	1517	1	1991	
263	2017	1365	365	431	1008	857	822	1578	2	1992	
274	2039	1342	401	382	972	834	829	1706	2	1993	
2187	2961	2222	1115	534	5622	4648	898	7257	75	1980	Autres economies développées
6210	7608	5124	2145	666	6853	5617	1082	17675	90	1990	
6752	7968	5609	2288	705	7720	6443	1072	20224	102	1991	
7453	9283	5296	2444	787	8289	6970	1150	20418	108	1992	
8371	10399	5499	2457	828	8858	7624	1121	21125	99	1993	

Voir la fin du tableau pour la remarque générale et les notes.

SPECIAL TABLE: B

World exports by commodity classes and by regions (continued)

In million U.S. dollars f.o.b.

Exports to → / ↓ Exports from	Year	World Monde /1,2,3	Developed economies Econ. dévelop-pées /2,3,4	Developing economies Economies en voie de développement /1,3,4: Total	Developing economies: OPEC OPEP	Eastern Europe and fmr. USSR-Europe Europe de l'Est et l'anc. URSS-Europe: Total /2,3,7	Eastern Europe and fmr. USSR-Europe: Former USSR-Eur. /10	Develope[d] Economi[es] – Europe: Total /2	Develope[d] Economi[es] – Europe: EEC CEE /2	Develope[d] Economi[es] – Europe: EFTA AELE	Develope[d] Economi[es] – South Africa Afrique du Sud
							Chemicals (SITC, Rev. 2 and Rev. 3, 5) (continue[d])				
Canada	1980	3519	2844	597	46	78	76	633	600	33	17
	1990	6661	5607	1043	114	11	9	596	529	67	11
	1991	6754	5565	1180	112	9	7	483	458	24	7
	1992	7167	6193	954	114	19	11	464	406	57	8
	1993	7464	6557	870	106	37	18	352	331	21	7
United States	1980	20728	11266	9373	1375	89	31	6155	5487	667	300
	1990	38983	23721	14924	1509	339	280	11366	10510	838	311
	1991	42912	25533	16991	1764	387	325	12035	11235	797	341
	1992	43956	26776	17008	1709	172	85	12836	12051	782	312
	1993	45013	27333	17437	1671	243	145	12241	11233	1006	279
Japan	1980	6619	2048	4160	631	412	322	865	759	106	72
	1990	15778	6214	9210	759	354	271	3162	2836	326	69
	1991	17396	6767	10362	738	267	222	3402	3059	342	77
	1992	19078	7764	11190	819	124	89	3865	3482	383	74
	1993	20133	8121	11854	848	158	115	3828	3415	411	78
Australia, New Zealand	1980	669	427	202	24	0	0	70	62	8	6
	1990	1320	830	482	55	6	5	168	161	7	6
	1991	1552	943	603	61	5	4	190	182	8	7
	1992	1664	999	658	74	6	2	220	214	6	10
	1993	1943	1098	745	80	2	1	209	203	6	14
Developing economies-Africa	1980	730	251	411	90	59	37	241	238	3	0
	1990	2689	1311	1241	370	129	105	1271	1254	17	4
	1991	2613	1042	1441	341	117	93	987	977	10	5
	1992	2509	1125	1328	293	41	26	1082	1070	10	7
	1993	2453	1154	1253	288	28	21	1031	1020	10	8
Developing economies-America	1980	2804	1292	1480	158	28	10	485	447	38	14
	1990	6709	3769	2816	278	96	70	1365	1261	103	45
	1991	7242	3837	3320	349	62	57	1340	1217	122	52
	1992	7840	4104	3692	395	7	2	1271	1155	116	43
	1993	8298	4152	4127	413	8	4	1082	948	127	52
Developing economies-Europe/ 5	1980	1010	187	245	135	578	384	172	143	29	0
	1990	1402	597	171	75	634	432	551	464	86	0
	1991	929	396	113	50	420	286	365	308	57	0
	1992	1391	469	708	25	211	104	426	387	39	0
	1993	1223	509	464	25	250	122	458	411	47	0
Developing economies-Middle East	1980	1490	826	629	183	21	17	396	394	2	0
	1990	4880	1294	2660	502	646	624	896	862	34	7
	1991	3796	1012	2280	727	445	413	646	514	131	9
	1992	4366	1422	2744	972	75	37	877	804	72	11
	1993	4537	1484	2790	976	130	67	901	827	72	12
Developing economies-Other Asia	1980	4363	1538	2449	452	198	154	460	415	45	6
	1990	19977	6412	12614	894	698	614	2312	2156	152	18
	1991	24362	7176	16450	1018	702	643	2574	2380	181	38
	1992	28228	8097	19737	1420	333	239	2973	2792	175	76
	1993	30839	8585	21837	1534	365	246	2957	2758	192	104
Former USSR-Asia /9	1980	.	.	.	.	.	.	.	.	.	.
	1990	.	.	.	.	.	.	.	.	.	.
	1991	.	.	.	.	.	.	.	.	.	.
	1992	533	19	470	19	44	.	17	15	2	0
	1993	477	17	420	18	40	.	15	13	2	0
Developing economies-Oceania	1980	3	1	2	0	0	0	1	1	0	0
	1990	13	3	10	0	0	0	1	1	0	0
	1991	13	3	10	0	0	0	1	1	0	0
	1992	8	4	4	0	0	0	1	1	0	0
	1993	8	5	3	0	0	0	1	1	0	0

For general note and footnotes see end of table.

Exportations mondiales par classes de marchandises et par régions (suite)

En millions de dollars E.-U. f.o.b.

Economies développées /2,3,4				Developing economies Economies en voie de développement /1,3,4						← Exportations vers	
					America Amerique		Asia Asie				
Canada	U.S.A. E.-U.	Japan Japon	Australia New Zealand Australie Nouvelle-Zélande	Africa Afrique	Total	LAIA ALADI	Mid.East Moyen Orient	Other Autres /9	Oceania Océanie	Année	Exportations ↓ en provenance de
Produits chimiques (CTCI, Rev. 2 et Rev. 3, 5) (suite)											
.	1983	148	59	20	197	159	21	358	0	1980	Canada
.	4545	278	174	24	155	104	25	836	1	1990	
.	4612	306	152	24	152	102	24	975	1	1991	
.	5264	288	163	37	165	112	24	727	1	1992	
.	5824	240	128	29	171	119	27	640	1	1993	
2126	.	1972	638	413	5118	4223	602	3158	7	1980	Etats-Unis
6050	.	4582	1239	322	6232	5090	695	7622	9	1990	
6590	.	5024	1350	373	7044	5869	691	8820	10	1991	
7285	.	4708	1414	296	7635	6428	758	8263	18	1992	
8202	.	4959	1441	334	8103	6999	738	8232	10	1993	
50	769	.	279	65	263	227	242	3564	14	1980	Japon
109	2479	.	373	68	260	226	260	8604	10	1990	
104	2768	.	389	77	296	253	249	9725	11	1991	
102	3282	.	409	63	325	285	253	10532	11	1992	
105	3681	.	396	63	370	320	220	11188	8	1993	
8	134	80	128	1	6	5	4	137	54	1980	Australie, Nouvelle-Zélande
10	208	141	297	12	12	11	11	376	71	1990	
25	228	159	334	10	19	18	12	480	80	1991	
35	181	175	376	7	30	29	23	521	78	1992	
44	226	186	416	6	32	31	18	611	78	1993	
0	8	2	0	124	36	28	46	195	0	1980	Economies en voie de développement-Afrique
10	20	2	3	404	56	50	315	444	0	1990	
5	36	5	4	429	79	66	313	608	0	1991	
6	15	5	5	410	80	75	257	570	0	1992	
6	96	5	6	428	105	93	280	431	0	1993	
10	598	167	16	45	1334	859	35	59	0	1980	Economies en voie de développement-Amérique
38	2021	239	53	56	2317	1648	45	397	1	1990	
41	2131	227	39	74	2818	2050	30	396	1	1991	
61	2473	203	46	54	3238	2384	54	344	0	1992	
71	2654	239	48	47	3685	2758	83	311	0	1993	
1	10	4	0	85	12	7	127	21	0	1980	Economies en voie de développement-Europe /5
5	32	7	3	71	7	5	45	46	1	1990	
3	21	5	2	47	4	3	30	31	1	1991	
3	31	5	1	30	4	3	33	113	0	1992	
2	39	8	1	25	5	4	34	41	0	1993	
0	3	386	41	29	4	4	261	333	0	1980	Economies en voie de développement-Moyen Orient
1	149	89	150	188	16	16	943	1505	0	1990	
7	89	244	15	170	29	23	835	1236	0	1991	
5	162	205	154	134	19	19	1105	1475	0	1992	
5	178	219	163	110	24	23	1089	1561	0	1993	
18	281	685	87	194	52	20	205	1979	11	1980	Economies en voie de développement-Autres Pays d'Asie
98	1656	1915	403	333	167	97	361	11713	36	1990	
103	1890	2112	442	402	231	150	408	15367	36	1991	
112	2198	2195	516	511	268	190	594	18315	45	1992	
121	2400	2374	588	510	335	245	733	20206	48	1993	
.	.	.	.	.	.	.	.	.	.	1980	l'ancienne URSS asiatique /9
.	.	.	.	.	.	.	.	.	.	1990	
.	.	.	.	.	.	.	.	.	.	1991	
0	1	1	0	2	5	3	32	431	0	1992	
0	1	1	0	3	5	3	26	385	0	1993	
0	0	0	0	0	0	0	0	0	2	1980	Economies en voie de développement-Océanie
0	1	0	1	0	0	0	0	1	9	1990	
0	1	0	1	0	0	0	0	0	10	1991	
0	3	0	1	0	0	0	0	0	4	1992	
0	3	0	0	0	0	0	0	0	3	1993	

Voir la fin du tableau pour la remarque générale et les notes.

SPECIAL TABLE: B

World exports by commodity classes and by regions (continued)

In million U.S. dollars f.o.b.

Exports from ↓ / Exports to →	Year	World Monde /1,2,3	Developed economies Econ. dévelop-pées /2,3,4	Developing economies Economies en voie de développement /1,3,4: Total	Developing economies: OPEC OPEP	Eastern Europe and fmr. USSR-Europe / Europe de l'Est et l'anc. URSS-Europe: Total /2,3,7	Eastern Europe and fmr. USSR-Europe: Former USSR-Eur. /10	Developed Economies – Europe: Total /2	Europe: EEC CEE /2	Europe: EFTA AELE	South Africa Afrique du Sud
		Machinery and transport equipment (SITC, Rev. 2 and Rev. 3, 7)									
World /1,2,3	1980	505644	304673	158711	51386	38897	17683	194841	161220	33259	7515
	1990	1219093	870642	289475	43334	53097	28225	537128	457668	77951	6380
	1991	1260366	889247	330698	54381	35896	17897	553350	478223	73500	7034
	1992	1375276	951920	386245	62282	32759	14422	581516	504904	74810	7008
	1993	1386580	911980	433659	56093	34337	15188	503240	435216	66088	7217
Developed economies /2,3,4	1980	436338	287353	136063	45743	10982	5387	187619	154852	32413	7402
	1990	1021241	777029	220730	36696	19493	10458	502311	427024	73861	6164
	1991	1064443	787039	250388	46928	23407	11357	516038	444877	69617	6603
	1992	1142534	823076	290911	53965	24684	9494	538974	467082	70208	6350
	1993	1112245	759231	320008	47578	26888	10881	455066	391306	62060	6423
Developing economies /1,3,4	1980	30530	14803	14158	3838	1369	852	4990	4635	349	112
	1990	150754	88737	57378	5204	3310	2304	30347	27195	3088	215
	1991	177136	98404	74909	6523	3482	2162	33819	30731	3008	425
	1992	217246	123708	91042	7269	2164	1296	37773	34111	3548	652
	1993	258642	145781	109782	7862	2607	1603	41851	38353	3274	761
OPEC	1980	1538	242	1261	697	1	0	172	165	6	0
	1990	1811	572	1037	546	133	74	289	284	5	0
	1991	2597	895	1481	608	164	58	581	570	10	0
	1992	2778	1207	1442	307	89	65	550	534	16	0
	1993	3747	1569	2151	385	28	18	696	675	21	0
Eastern Europe and the former USSR /2,3,7	1980	38777	2517	8490	1805	26545	11444	2232	1733	497	1
	1990	47100	4877	11367	1434	30293	15464	4470	3448	1001	1
	1991	18788	3804	5401	930	9008	4377	3493	2615	876	6
	1992	15495	5137	4293	1048	5911	3632	4770	3711	1053	7
	1993	15694	6967	3869	652	4841	2704	6323	5557	753	32
Former USSR /3	1980	12227	453	5015	854	6758	.	406	285	122	0
	1990	...	...	...	...	...	.	...	...	...	...
	1991	...	...	...	...	...	.	...	...	...	...
	1992	.	.	.	.	.	.	.	.	.	.
	1993	.	.	.	.	.	.	.	.	.	.
Former USSR-Europe /8	1980	.	.	.	.	.	.	.	.	.	.
	1990	.	.	.	.	.	.	.	.	.	.
	1991	.	.	.	.	.	.	.	.	.	.
	1992	4009	1213	1785	398	970	226	1143	894	249	0
	1993	3353	1024	1528	273	802	321	918	804	114	2
Developed economies-Europe /2	1980	256719	182102	65397	26000	9137	4215	150398	122590	27495	4715
	1990	592273	481620	90789	21224	16970	8825	401359	338563	61529	4137
	1991	599332	480669	95231	25014	20648	9680	406069	348242	56419	4176
	1992	639627	506995	108035	27755	21667	8002	429338	369634	58180	3931
	1993	575795	434016	114168	23636	22777	8618	355241	301946	51853	3715
European Economic Community /2	1980	225301	160088	58230	23618	6913	3107	132374	109379	22701	4383
	1990	517958	422806	79825	19054	12433	6232	353177	300351	51740	3867
	1991	528492	424764	83660	22375	17284	8420	359571	310293	48065	3976
	1992	565369	448496	95866	25332	18076	6844	380630	329277	49969	3711
	1993	507861	383006	100987	21269	19034	7181	313676	267458	44903	3449
European Free Trade Association	1980	31349	21987	7139	2361	2223	1107	17998	13187	4793	333
	1990	73706	58290	10901	2148	4515	2576	47690	37727	9781	270
	1991	70113	55265	11486	2599	3362	1260	45877	37340	8343	200
	1992	73345	57691	12066	2389	3588	1155	47936	39613	8184	219
	1993	67175	50363	13070	2332	3742	1436	40972	33899	6948	265
Other developed economies	1980	179620	105251	70665	19744	1845	1173	37221	32262	4919	2687
	1990	428968	295409	129941	15472	2524	1632	100952	88462	12333	2027
	1991	465111	306370	155157	21914	2759	1677	109969	96635	13198	2427
	1992	502908	316081	182876	26210	3018	1492	109636	97448	12029	2419
	1993	536450	325215	205840	23942	4111	2264	99826	89360	10207	2708

For general note and footnotes see end of table.

Exportations mondiales par classes de marchandises et par régions (suite)

En millions de dollars E.-U. f.o.b.

Economies développées /2,3,4 Canada	U.S.A. E.-U.	Japan Japon	Australia New Zealand Australie Nouvelle-Zélande	Developing economies Economies en voie de développement /1,3,4 Africa Afrique	America Amerique Total	America Amerique LAIA ALADI	Asia Asie Mid.East Moyen Orient	Asia Asie Other Autres /9	Oceania Océanie	Année	← Exportations vers / Exportations en provenance de ↓
Machines et matériél de transport (CTCI, Rev. 2 et Rev. 3, 7)											
22285	62441	7300	8690	30962	39844	31600	34678	48105	756	1980	Monde /1,2,3
56140	211256	35532	20158	30635	54399	38698	35464	161874	1673	1990	
58204	210400	36855	18070	30896	61927	46700	44335	187793	1550	1991	
59136	241505	36362	20234	32098	78591	61156	51914	218193	1911	1992	
63116	271122	39567	21083	29425	83471	65349	50644	264845	1753	1993	
21859	54532	6158	8191	27211	34732	28620	30436	39396	721	1980	Economies dévelopées /2,3,4
53849	166449	26488	17892	26139	45820	34783	30162	112318	1516	1990	
54788	163163	25808	15544	25099	53541	41157	38582	128037	1360	1991	
55712	173919	25109	17169	27120	66425	52336	45478	147359	1710	1992	
58880	190174	25182	17315	25162	68858	53530	43523	177995	1515	1993	
362	7757	1099	475	2196	3334	2668	2464	6123	36	1980	Economies en voie de développement /1,3,4
2245	44552	8991	2222	3176	5398	3613	3825	44653	157	1990	
3387	47030	11014	2500	5107	7082	5375	4823	57508	189	1991	
3389	67331	11221	3037	4418	11783	8661	5410	68689	202	1992	
4187	80508	14354	3736	3671	14341	11591	6169	84997	232	1993	
1	63	6	0	127	48	44	947	138	0	1980	OPEP
5	235	35	8	29	110	72	695	199	4	1990	
18	224	58	14	364	72	56	748	292	5	1991	
13	485	122	36	78	149	121	449	744	22	1992	
40	668	129	35	90	399	372	534	1121	8	1993	
64	152	43	24	1554	1777	312	1778	2586	0	1980	Europe de l'Est et l'ancienne URSS /2,3,7
46	255	54	45	1320	3181	302	1477	4902	0	1990	
29	207	34	27	690	1305	168	930	2248	0	1991	
35	254	32	28	560	383	159	1027	2144	0	1992	
49	440	31	32	592	273	229	952	1853	5	1993	
27	7	9	4	710	1305	87	814	1859	0	1980	L'ancienne URSS /3
...	...	...	...	...	...	...	...	...	...	1990	
...	...	...	...	...	...	...	...	...	...	1991	
.	.	.	.	.	.	.	.	.	.	1992	
.	.	.	.	.	.	.	.	.	.	1993	
.	.	.	.	.	.	.	.	.	.	1980	L'ancienne URSS-Europe /8
.	.	.	.	.	.	.	.	.	.	1990	
.	.	.	.	.	.	.	.	.	.	1991	
9	36	19	4	151	181	49	454	938	0	1992	
12	62	20	4	87	88	55	373	898	0	1993	
2331	18784	2250	2818	20448	12093	9988	17554	11884	196	1980	Economies développées-Europe /2
5633	51086	11750	5648	19805	14544	10280	18807	32661	602	1990	
5864	46715	10976	4371	18647	15785	11161	22447	34411	460	1991	
5469	50510	10047	4780	19110	19275	14118	26207	40014	754	1992	
4399	52313	10569	4802	16864	20172	14460	24887	48941	462	1993	
1930	16380	1855	2439	18708	10451	8746	15630	10512	174	1980	Communauté Economique Européenne /2
4492	44583	10252	4605	18346	12471	8700	16610	27982	586	1990	
4998	40601	9690	3660	16972	13872	9792	19843	29427	451	1991	
4621	44134	8836	3890	17624	16922	12568	23752	34527	746	1992	
3681	46121	9444	3986	15412	17945	13065	22635	42121	454	1993	
400	2403	395	379	1716	1639	1242	1923	1372	23	1980	Association Européenne de Libre Echange
1127	6486	1497	1041	1437	2071	1581	2194	4644	15	1990	
866	6095	1286	711	1644	1902	1369	2591	4954	9	1991	
847	6345	1210	887	1454	2352	1550	2448	5425	9	1992	
708	6155	1119	816	1416	2224	1393	2246	6753	8	1993	
19529	35748	3908	5373	6764	22639	18632	12882	27513	524	1980	Autres economies développées
48216	115363	14738	12244	6333	31276	24503	11354	79657	915	1990	
48924	116448	14832	11172	6452	37756	29996	16135	93626	900	1991	
50243	123409	15062	12389	8009	47149	38218	19271	107346	955	1992	
54481	137860	14614	12513	8298	48686	39070	18636	129054	1053	1993	

Voir la fin du tableau pour la remarque générale et les notes.

SPECIAL TABLE: B

World exports by commodity classes and by regions (continued)

In million U.S. dollars f.o.b.

Exports from ↓ / Exports to →	Year	World / Monde /1,2,3	Developed economies / Econ. dévelop-pées /2,3,4	Developing economies / Economies en voie de développement /1,3,4: Total	Developing economies: OPEC / OPEP	Eastern Europe and fmr. USSR-Europe / Europe de l'Est et l'anc. URSS-Europe: Total /2,3,7	Eastern Europe and fmr. USSR-Europe: Former USSR-Eur. /10	Developed Economies: Europe: Total /2	Developed Economies: Europe: EEC / CEE /2	Developed Economies: Europe: EFTA / AELE	Developed Economies: South Africa / Afrique du Sud
		Machinery and transport equipment (SITC, Rev. 2 and Rev. 3, 7) (continued)									
Canada	1980	16675	14573	1889	840	213	72	887	731	155	56
	1990	47229	44982	2194	327	54	26	2347	2009	337	18
	1991	47411	45187	2147	652	77	42	2634	2383	250	16
	1992	50224	47775	2294	499	155	79	2286	2039	247	23
	1993	57105	54023	2848	574	234	193	2445	2173	271	23
United States	1980	84512	48579	34292	8763	466	269	22285	19739	2540	1334
	1990	172522	114899	56661	6171	661	331	50324	44902	5387	855
	1991	187991	119240	67727	9959	903	436	54145	47867	6250	1145
	1992	200933	118465	80962	12472	1507	674	51194	46024	5140	1054
	1993	208986	117784	88885	11191	2250	1161	46614	42012	4456	1044
Japan	1980	75870	41058	33650	10020	1162	832	13811	11582	2196	1236
	1990	202934	131559	69598	8732	1777	1267	46974	40355	6500	1113
	1991	223087	137750	83606	11142	1731	1179	51808	45101	6599	1217
	1992	243114	144719	97131	13044	1265	710	54245	47612	6506	1282
	1993	259981	147718	110926	11945	1336	861	48586	43185	5291	1585
Australia, New Zealand	1980	1336	676	656	74	1	0	100	87	13	42
	1990	2676	1840	828	133	8	5	410	374	36	21
	1991	3180	2057	1106	122	16	12	490	461	28	26
	1992	3472	2091	1283	155	14	9	506	478	28	28
	1993	4089	2252	1713	181	13	9	533	492	40	30
Developing economies-Africa	1980	239	151	62	15	1	1	141	141	1	0
	1990	1107	563	454	98	84	78	522	512	9	17
	1991	1213	636	489	202	84	65	533	528	3	11
	1992	1179	672	400	136	98	70	608	605	3	16
	1993	1122	671	426	135	19	17	605	598	7	20
Developing economies-America	1980	5214	2018	3193	597	3	1	693	663	29	36
	1990	14192	10886	3250	433	52	42	2029	1920	106	49
	1991	15779	11674	4060	547	41	37	2179	2058	119	69
	1992	31271	24973	6269	676	12	7	2414	2259	155	49
	1993	37545	29528	7954	738	38	26	2091	1929	147	68
Developing economies-Europe/ 5	1980	2546	682	624	291	1240	777	637	594	42	0
	1990	4322	2107	806	341	1409	1012	1965	1769	194	0
	1991	2879	1399	534	225	946	682	1306	1174	129	0
	1992	3419	2285	810	144	322	208	2228	1727	501	0
	1993	2490	1701	512	71	277	196	1643	1466	153	1
Developing economies-Middle East	1980	1694	255	1373	878	1	0	191	182	8	0
	1990	2209	804	1202	856	132	59	747	708	32	6
	1991	3123	1203	1579	922	279	129	1158	1128	28	7
	1992	2928	1172	1534	707	166	95	1111	1063	30	6
	1993	3097	1078	1853	764	127	68	994	916	36	6
Developing economies-Other Asia	1980	20827	11692	8903	2056	124	74	3323	3050	270	75
	1990	128788	74306	51601	3471	1633	1113	25064	22265	2748	141
	1991	153955	83432	68173	4624	2079	1235	28628	25830	2729	338
	1992	178296	94512	81975	5599	1562	912	31370	28417	2859	580
	1993	214281	112717	99016	6154	2146	1296	36472	33398	2931	666
Former USSR-Asia /9	1980	.	.	.	.	.	.	.	.	.	.
	1990	.	.	.	.	.	.	.	.	.	.
	1991	.	.	.	.	.	.	.	.	.	.
	1992	88	3	83	9	2	.	2	1	0	0
	1993	83	2	80	8	1	.	1	1	0	0
Developing economies-Oceania	1980	9	6	3	0	0	0	5	5	0	0
	1990	135	71	64	4	0	0	20	20	0	2
	1991	186	59	74	1	53	15	14	14	0	0
	1992	153	93	54	6	4	4	40	40	1	0
	1993	108	86	22	0	0	0	45	45	0	0

For general note and footnotes see end of table.

Exportations mondiales par classes de marchandises et par régions (suite)

En millions de dollars E.-U. f.o.b.

Economies développées /2,3,4: Canada	Economies développées: U.S.A. E.-U.	Economies développées: Japan Japon	Economies développées: Australia New Zealand Australie Nouvelle-Zélande	Developing economies / Economies en voie de développement /1,3,4: Africa Afrique	America Amerique: Total	America Amerique: LAIA ALADI	Asia Asie: Mid.East Moyen Orient	Asia Asie: Other Autres /9	Oceania Océanie	← Exportations vers / Année	Exportations en provenance de ↓
Machines et matériél de transport (CTCI, Rev. 2 et Rev. 3, 7) (suite)											
.	13387	58	165	204	1048	926	333	282	8	1980	Canada
.	42118	208	271	252	704	541	179	1017	13	1990	
.	42074	222	217	148	654	530	450	866	10	1991	
.	45012	237	189	158	853	693	216	1048	10	1992	
.	50977	282	262	218	967	820	281	1371	7	1993	
18009	.	3786	2452	2320	15928	14046	5427	10295	66	1980	Etats-Unis
42746	.	14302	5220	2718	22488	19892	4769	26410	111	1990	
42872	.	14307	4787	2904	26759	24262	7558	30228	165	1991	
44272	.	14477	5418	3445	33244	30246	8682	35236	251	1992	
49290	.	13951	4528	2960	33761	30247	8880	42994	205	1993	
1500	22008	.	2450	4127	5513	3528	7077	16615	246	1980	Japon
5422	71601	.	6066	3051	7872	3870	6359	51499	608	1990	
5996	72615	.	5535	3093	10162	5075	8069	61645	487	1991	
5919	76376	.	6070	3810	12847	7091	10220	69779	444	1992	
5124	84729	.	6890	4479	13675	7732	9341	82833	578	1993	
15	163	61	294	79	40	29	40	290	205	1980	Australie, Nouvelle-Zélande
25	555	174	655	22	18	14	31	573	183	1990	
31	650	261	599	28	55	26	43	740	238	1991	
29	589	276	661	37	63	57	56	877	249	1992	
33	608	286	759	30	63	57	64	1294	262	1993	
1	8	0	0	53	2	1	6	1	0	1980	Economies en voie de développement-Afrique
2	19	3	1	346	7	7	21	78	0	1990	
56	32	0	0	370	3	2	17	97	0	1991	
26	19	0	0	290	6	0	14	89	0	1992	
29	14	0	0	332	1	0	11	81	0	1993	
67	1022	148	51	427	2555	2252	110	94	6	1980	Economies en voie de développement-Amérique
233	8379	111	77	153	2717	2133	111	256	10	1990	
1054	8021	286	58	197	3473	3037	119	264	4	1991	
797	21403	253	48	182	5566	5043	140	345	7	1992	
1417	25591	288	61	122	7265	6600	141	424	2	1993	
3	36	0	6	325	20	16	148	131	0	1980	Economies en voie de développement-Europe /5
9	97	1	34	354	67	17	300	85	0	1990	
6	64	0	23	238	46	11	198	52	0	1991	
5	42	1	7	99	19	11	157	81	0	1992	
6	43	0	7	61	13	8	87	55	0	1993	
0	57	5	1	149	1	1	1193	29	0	1980	Economies en voie de développement-Moyen Orient
4	38	2	4	88	15	2	1040	46	2	1990	
6	17	2	12	408	9	2	1089	68	0	1991	
6	38	4	3	227	13	3	917	375	0	1992	
5	39	5	20	251	6	4	1003	585	0	1993	
291	6633	945	416	1243	757	398	1007	5867	26	1980	Economies en voie de développement-Autres Pays d'Asie
1993	36011	8874	2069	2235	2592	1455	2353	44154	115	1990	
2265	38881	10725	2378	3892	3550	2322	3400	56988	153	1991	
2552	45809	10963	2949	3620	6179	3604	4181	67752	188	1992	
2729	54815	14059	3615	2903	7055	4979	4928	83840	219	1993	
.	.	.	.	.	.	.	.	.	.	1980	l'ancienne URSS asiatique /9
.	.	.	.	.	.	.	.	.	.	1990	
.	.	.	.	.	.	.	.	.	.	1991	
0	2	0	0	0	6	1	13	64	0	1992	
0	1	0	0	0	6	1	10	64	0	1993	
0	1	0	0	0	0	0	0	0	3	1980	Economies en voie de développement-Océanie
4	8	0	37	0	0	0	0	35	29	1990	
1	15	1	28	2	1	1	1	39	32	1991	
4	19	0	30	0	0	0	0	48	6	1992	
0	7	0	33	0	0	0	0	12	10	1993	

Voir la fin du tableau pour la remarque générale et les notes.

SPECIAL TABLE: B

World exports by commodity classes and by regions (continued)

In million U.S. dollars f.o.b.

Passenger road vehicles and their parts (SITC, Rev. 2, 781.0, 784.1, 785.1, 785.2 and 785.31
(SITC, Rev. 3, 781.2, 784.1, 785.1, 785.2 and 785.31

Exports from ↓ / Exports to →	Year	World Monde /1,2,3	Developed economies Econ. dévelop-pées /2,3,4	Developing economies Economies en voie de développement /1,3,4 Total	OPEC OPEP	Eastern Europe and fmr. USSR-Europe Europe de l'Est et l'anc. URSS-Europe Total /2,3,7	Former USSR-Eur. /10	Develope[d] Economie[s] Europe Total /2	EEC CEE /2	EFTA AELE	South Africa Afrique du Sud
World /1,2,3	1980	65387	54810	9652	4254	860	6	29996	25282	4670	415
	1990	175198	158774	14950	3826	1385	197	90059	77309	12597	166
	1991	179455	159840	17424	5180	2157	348	93673	81550	11968	133
	1992	202199	172510	26741	6967	2892	724	106923	94111	12638	174
	1993	197241	160363	33266	5969	3569	1238	86813	76944	9737	332
Developed economies /2,3,4	1980	63438	54497	8817	4036	69	5	29803	25135	4624	414
	1990	166158	152097	13323	3565	729	150	88257	75680	12429	162
	1991	169167	152228	15144	4806	1787	310	91785	79889	11749	125
	1992	188042	164050	21668	6191	2315	646	103563	91051	12348	167
	1993	178455	150468	24837	5103	3125	1156	83216	73630	9465	316
Developing economies /1,3,4	1980	719	156	553	199	0	0	53	50	3	0
	1990	7484	6130	1245	255	28	9	1268	1151	114	4
	1991	9566	7300	2113	372	129	8	1582	1387	188	9
	1992	12267	7493	4616	715	112	28	2406	2208	188	7
	1993	16596	8513	7913	861	151	61	2252	2046	199	16
OPEC	1980	122	6	115	11	0	0	5	4	1	0
	1990	73	22	44	20	0	0	17	16	1	0
	1991	215	30	180	35	0	0	25	23	2	0
	1992	313	47	252	22	0	0	43	42	1	0
	1993	563	52	510	28	1	0	46	45	1	0
Eastern Europe and the former USSR /2,3,7	1980	1229	156	282	19	791	0	140	97	44	0
	1990	1556	548	382	6	627	38	534	478	54	0
	1991	722	312	167	1	241	29	306	274	32	0
	1992	1890	967	457	61	466	50	955	853	102	0
	1993	2190	1382	515	5	293	21	1345	1268	73	0
Former USSR /3	1980	864	145	245	19	474	.	130	89	41	0
	1990	...	...	...	...	...	.	...	...	...	...
	1991	...	...	...	...	...	.	...	...	...	...
	1992	.	.	.	.	.	.	.	.	.	.
	1993	.	.	.	.	.	.	.	.	.	.
Former USSR-Europe /8	1980	.	.	.	.	.	.	.	.	.	.
	1990	.	.	.	.	.	.	.	.	.	.
	1991	.	.	.	.	.	.	.	.	.	.
	1992	1344	618	327	60	398	5	606	513	93	0
	1993	829	482	215	0	132	6	460	417	43	0
Developed economies-Europe /2	1980	35642	31784	3784	1544	63	5	25524	21765	3724	241
	1990	96949	90788	5582	1328	570	98	74309	64945	9261	135
	1991	94411	87221	5714	1593	1468	210	75927	67187	8644	77
	1992	105478	96555	7063	1580	1850	473	85678	76440	9132	66
	1993	92167	81235	8325	1262	2583	899	68388	60917	7381	118
European Economic Community /2	1980	33872	30198	3617	1489	57	4	24603	21092	3476	240
	1990	92036	86273	5264	1283	489	67	71658	62918	8639	130
	1991	89773	83108	5356	1517	1301	159	73207	64936	8176	74
	1992	99853	91622	6635	1516	1586	337	82432	73586	8740	64
	1993	87442	77374	7794	1204	2251	662	66025	58942	6995	117
European Free Trade Association	1980	1770	1586	166	54	7	2	921	673	247	0
	1990	4905	4507	317	46	81	31	2643	2018	622	6
	1991	4629	4104	358	76	166	51	2710	2242	468	3
	1992	5624	4932	428	65	264	137	3245	2852	392	1
	1993	4724	3860	531	58	332	237	2362	1974	386	0
Other developed economies	1980	27796	22714	5033	2492	6	0	4279	3370	900	174
	1990	69208	61308	7741	2236	159	51	13947	10735	3167	27
	1991	74756	65006	9430	3213	320	100	15858	12701	3104	48
	1992	82564	67495	14605	4611	464	173	17885	14611	3216	102
	1993	86288	69233	16513	3841	542	257	14828	12713	2084	198

For general note and footnotes see end of table.

Exportations mondiales par classes de marchandises et par régions (suite)

En millions de dollars E.-U. f.o.b.

Véhicules rout. et pieces detach. pour transport pass. (CTCI,Rev.2, 781.0, 784.1, 785.1, 785.2 et 785.31)
(CTCI,Rev.3, 781.2, 784.1, 785.1, 785.2 et 785.31)

Economies développées /2,3,4				Developing economies / Economies en voie de développement /1,3,4							← Exportations vers
Canada	U.S.A. / E.-U.	Japan / Japon	Australia New Zealand / Australie Nouvelle-Zélande	Africa / Afrique	America / Amerique: Total	America / Amerique: LAIA / ALADI	Asia / Asie: Mid.East / Moyen Orient	Asia / Asie: Other / Autres /9	Oceania / Océanie	Année	Exportations en provenance de ↓
4473	18338	427	1061	2208	2080	1572	2759	2211	99	1980	Monde /1,2,3
9606	50021	5861	2594	2237	2381	1341	3719	5710	255	1990	
11027	46894	4930	2468	2316	3316	2332	4823	5973	236	1991	
10374	46738	4265	2948	2541	6049	4753	6555	10929	244	1992	
9936	53710	5268	3228	2174	6952	5590	6408	16856	192	1993	
4455	18263	426	1038	2092	1978	1511	2624	1853	97	1980	Economies dévelopées /2,3,4
9219	45766	5762	2469	2102	1882	1100	3469	5078	232	1990	
9935	42537	4799	2342	2093	2605	1791	4483	5081	221	1991	
9769	42548	4123	2803	2315	4395	3295	5861	8555	225	1992	
9009	48835	5046	3006	1921	4743	3590	5425	12051	178	1993	
3	74	1	23	100	74	59	114	263	1	1980	Economies en voie de développement /1,3,4
385	4254	98	114	118	395	238	219	485	22	1990	
1091	4357	132	122	219	669	540	332	832	16	1991	
598	4187	142	143	191	1581	1418	582	2217	19	1992	
918	4869	222	220	251	2121	1921	836	4632	15	1993	
0	0	0	0	57	0	0	57	0	0	1980	OPEP
1	3	0	0	0	3	1	29	10	0	1990	
0	4	0	0	107	6	3	53	13	0	1991	
1	1	2	0	28	44	40	40	139	0	1992	
2	1	3	0	33	194	193	45	238	0	1993	
15	1	0	0	16	28	1	21	96	0	1980	Europe de l'Est et l'ancienne URSS /2,3,7
2	0	0	11	16	104	3	31	148	0	1990	
1	0	0	5	4	42	1	8	59	0	1991	
7	3	0	2	35	73	40	113	157	0	1992	
10	7	0	2	3	88	78	148	172	0	1993	
15	0	0	0	14	26	1	19	71	0	1980	L'ancienne URSS /3
...	...	...	...	...	...	...	...	...	...	1990	
...	...	...	...	...	...	...	...	...	...	1991	
.	.	.	.	.	.	.	.	.	.	1992	
.	.	.	.	.	.	.	.	.	.	1993	
.	.	.	.	.	.	.	.	.	.	1980	L'ancienne URSS-Europe /8
.	.	.	.	.	.	.	.	.	.	1990	
.	.	.	.	.	.	.	.	.	.	1991	
7	2	0	2	30	51	19	104	88	0	1992	
10	6	0	2	0	30	21	70	40	0	1993	
440	4874	346	286	1609	660	530	775	528	40	1980	Economies développées-Europe /2
849	9859	4941	470	1668	631	356	1117	1657	98	1990	
764	5699	4081	334	1532	692	418	1358	1508	79	1991	
765	5884	3251	494	1658	1089	763	1546	2384	88	1992	
508	7433	3829	533	1266	1416	1099	1670	3394	72	1993	
374	4333	337	242	1561	639	512	733	482	40	1980	Communauté Economique Européenne /2
794	8336	4730	408	1631	618	348	1075	1463	98	1990	
719	4591	3906	282	1491	666	397	1270	1354	79	1991	
655	4572	3102	402	1616	1069	746	1470	2138	88	1992	
386	6334	3653	459	1217	1387	1076	1600	3057	72	1993	
66	541	9	43	47	21	18	42	45	0	1980	Association Européenne de Libre Echange
55	1523	211	62	37	14	8	43	194	0	1990	
45	1109	174	52	41	26	21	87	154	0	1991	
110	1312	148	92	42	21	17	76	246	0	1992	
122	1100	176	74	49	29	23	70	336	0	1993	
4015	13389	80	752	484	1318	981	1849	1325	58	1980	Autres economies développées
8370	35907	821	1999	434	1250	744	2351	3421	134	1990	
9170	36837	718	2007	561	1913	1372	3126	3573	141	1991	
9004	36664	872	2310	656	3306	2532	4315	6171	137	1992	
8501	41402	1217	2473	655	3327	2491	3755	8657	106	1993	

Voir la fin du tableau pour la remarque générale et les notes.

SPECIAL TABLE: B

World exports by commodity classes and by regions (continued)

In million U.S. dollars f.o.b.

Passenger road vehicles and their parts (SITC, Rev. 2, 781.0, 784.1, 785.1, 785.2 and 785.31 (SITC, Rev. 3, 781.2, 784.1, 785.1, 785.2 and 785.31) (continued

Exports to → / ↓ Exports from	Year	World Monde /1,2,3	Developed economies Econ. dévelop-pées /2,3,4	Developing economies Economies en voie de développement /1,3,4 Total	Developing economies OPEC OPEP	Eastern Europe and fmr. USSR-Europe Europe de l'Est et l'anc. URSS-Europe Total /2,3,7	Eastern Europe and fmr. USSR-Europe Former USSR-Eur. /10	Developed Economies Europe Total /2	Developed Economies Europe EEC CEE /2	Developed Economies Europe EFTA AELE	Developed Economies South Africa Afrique du Sud
Canada	1980	3968	3631	336	321	0	0	10	6	4	0
	1990	14249	14174	73	47	2	2	65	46	19	0
	1991	14539	14507	30	13	2	1	125	118	7	1
	1992	14991	14902	79	10	10	8	115	112	3	0
	1993	19077	18862	199	13	16	13	162	146	16	0
United States	1980	4537	3741	796	476	0	0	243	164	78	11
	1990	10467	8542	1920	684	6	2	1589	1224	364	4
	1991	11883	9234	2600	1234	48	11	1924	1681	241	5
	1992	14435	9796	4540	1779	100	68	2416	2118	298	5
	1993	14791	9989	4634	1369	168	139	1903	1709	194	6
Japan	1980	19175	15283	3886	1691	6	0	4024	3197	818	162
	1990	44121	38249	5721	1505	151	47	12284	9455	2784	23
	1991	47965	40920	6775	1966	270	88	13803	10896	2856	41
	1992	52639	42459	9827	2821	354	97	15334	12363	2915	95
	1993	51876	40008	11511	2458	357	104	12685	10787	1868	191
Australia, New Zealand	1980	74	59	15	4	0	0	2	2	0	0
	1990	328	320	8	1	0	0	4	3	0	0
	1991	330	324	6	0	0	0	2	1	0	1
	1992	330	319	12	1	0	0	3	3	0	2
	1993	391	358	33	1	0	0	67	62	5	1
Developing economies-Africa	1980	6	3	3	1	0	0	3	3	0	0
	1990	36	6	30	1	0	0	5	5	0	0
	1991	15	5	10	1	0	0	4	4	0	0
	1992	21	8	12	4	0	0	8	8	0	0
	1993	22	9	13	3	0	0	8	8	0	1
Developing economies-America	1980	56	16	40	17	0	0	16	16	0	0
	1990	3173	2821	350	49	2	2	210	210	1	3
	1991	4202	3660	539	71	2	2	66	65	1	3
	1992	4662	3443	1218	121	0	0	100	99	1	1
	1993	5777	4263	1510	139	0	0	70	69	0	1
Developing economies-Europe/ 5	1980	0	0	0	0	0	0	0	0	0	0
	1990	406	329	71	50	6	1	320	318	1	0
	1991	257	219	35	21	3	0	213	211	1	0
	1992	597	567	29	8	1	0	566	565	0	0
	1993	399	360	37	2	2	0	356	355	1	0
Developing economies-Middle East	1980	128	11	115	11	0	0	10	9	1	0
	1990	167	23	129	98	7	1	21	21	0	0
	1991	381	47	325	166	3	1	46	45	1	0
	1992	614	54	544	273	2	1	53	51	2	0
	1993	674	22	649	270	3	2	20	20	0	0
Developing economies-Other Asia	1980	528	126	394	171	0	0	24	22	2	0
	1990	3698	2951	662	57	13	5	712	597	112	1
	1991	4706	3369	1198	113	121	5	1253	1063	184	5
	1992	6370	3421	2810	309	109	28	1679	1485	184	5
	1993	9721	3859	5701	446	145	58	1798	1594	198	15
Former USSR-Asia /9	1980	.	.	.	.	.	.	.	.	.	.
	1990	.	.	.	.	.	.	.	.	.	.
	1991	.	.	.	.	.	.	.	.	.	.
	1992	2	0	1	0	0	.	0	0	0	0
	1993	1	0	1	0	0	.	0	0	0	0
Developing economies-Oceania	1980	1	0	0	0	0	0	0	0	0	0
	1990	4	1	3	0	0	0	0	0	0	0
	1991	6	0	6	0	0	0	0	0	0	0
	1992	3	0	3	0	0	0	0	0	0	0
	1993	3	0	3	0	0	0	0	0	0	0

For general note and footnotes see end of table.

TABLEAU SPECIAL: B

Exportations mondiales par classes de marchandises et par régions (suite)

En millions de dollars E.-U. f.o.b.

Economies développées /2,3,4: Canada	Economies développées: U.S.A. E.-U.	Economies développées: Japan Japon	Economies développées: Australia New Zealand Australie Nouvelle-Zélande	Developing economies Economies en voie de développement /1,3,4: Africa Afrique	America Amerique: Total	America Amerique: LAIA ALADI	Asia Asie: Mid.East Moyen Orient	Asia Asie: Other Autres /9	Oceania Océanie	Année	← Exportations vers / Exportations en provenance de ↓
Vehicules rout. et pieces detach. pour transport pass. (CTCI,Rev.2, 781.0, 784.1, 785.1, 785.2 et 785.31) CTCI,Rev.3, 781.2, 784.1, 785.1, 785.2 et 785.31) (suite)											
.	3620	.	0	1	166	164	169	1	0	1980	Canada
.	14097	10	2	0	3	1	47	22	1	1990	
.	14371	8	1	0	2	0	16	10	1	1991	
.	14782	4	1	1	4	2	13	59	1	1992	
.	18665	33	1	3	18	14	17	161	0	1993	
3379	.	80	20	28	310	248	421	36	2	1980	Etats-Unis
6075	.	789	42	23	454	270	687	749	3	1990	
6517	.	681	38	40	643	475	1173	735	4	1991	
6317	.	864	56	61	1128	889	1452	1889	6	1992	
6726	.	1153	59	54	1043	732	1269	2261	5	1993	
636	9768	.	677	453	838	569	1259	1281	54	1980	Japon
2295	21627	.	1827	392	793	473	1616	2645	128	1990	
2653	22250	.	1875	503	1268	897	1936	2824	134	1991	
2687	21726	.	2097	536	2172	1639	2849	4125	127	1992	
1775	22604	.	2282	550	2259	1739	2469	6123	98	1993	
0	0	0	56	2	4	0	0	7	2	1980	Australie, Nouvelle-Zélande
0	183	4	128	0	0	0	1	5	2	1990	
0	216	13	93	0	0	0	0	4	2	1991	
0	156	2	155	0	0	0	0	9	3	1992	
0	133	27	130	0	0	0	0	29	3	1993	
0	0	0	0	3	0	0	0	0	0	1980	Economies en voie de développement-Afrique
0	0	0	0	30	0	0	0	0	0	1990	
0	0	0	0	9	0	0	0	1	0	1991	
0	0	0	0	12	0	0	0	0	0	1992	
0	0	0	0	13	0	0	0	0	0	1993	
0	0	0	0	0	40	39	0	0	0	1980	Economies en voie de développement-Amérique
12	2593	0	3	8	330	215	0	2	9	1990	
699	2881	9	3	3	526	475	1	7	3	1991	
351	2986	1	3	11	1190	1127	5	7	5	1992	
705	3444	40	3	10	1484	1411	5	10	1	1993	
0	0	0	0	0	0	0	0	0	0	1980	Economies en voie de développement-Europe /5
0	9	0	0	29	1	1	40	0	0	1990	
0	6	0	0	10	1	1	24	0	0	1991	
0	1	0	0	0	3	2	6	1	0	1992	
0	4	0	0	1	1	1	2	0	0	1993	
0	1	0	0	58	0	0	57	0	0	1980	Economies en voie de développement-Moyen Orient
0	0	1	0	5	0	0	119	4	0	1990	
0	0	1	0	120	0	0	190	15	0	1991	
0	1	0	0	54	0	0	307	184	0	1992	
0	1	1	0	64	0	0	316	268	0	1993	
3	73	1	23	39	34	20	57	263	1	1980	Economies en voie de développement-Autres Pays d'Asie
373	1652	97	111	46	64	21	60	477	10	1990	
392	1470	122	119	77	142	64	117	808	10	1991	
247	1199	141	140	114	387	290	264	2026	11	1992	
212	1419	181	217	163	636	510	513	4354	11	1993	
.	.	.	.	.	.	.	.	.	.	1980	l'ancienne URSS asiatique /9
.	.	.	.	.	.	.	.	.	.	1990	
.	.	.	.	.	.	.	.	.	.	1991	
0	0	0	0	0	0	0	0	1	0	1992	
0	0	0	0	0	0	0	0	1	0	1993	
0	0	0	0	0	0	0	0	0	0	1980	Economies en voie de développement-Océanie
0	0	0	0	0	0	0	0	1	3	1990	
0	0	0	0	0	0	0	0	2	3	1991	
0	0	0	0	0	0	0	0	0	3	1992	
0	0	0	0	0	0	0	0	0	3	1993	

Voir la fin du tableau pour la remarque générale et les notes.

SPECIAL TABLE: B

World exports by commodity classes and by regions (continued)

In million U.S. dollars f.o.b.

Exports to → / ↓ Exports from	Year	World Monde /1,2,3	Developed economies Econ. dévelop-pées /2,3,4	Developing economies Economies en voie de développement /1,3,4 Total	Developing economies OPEC OPEP	Eastern Europe and fmr. USSR-Europe Europe de l'Est et l'anc. URSS-Europe Total /2,3,7	Eastern Europe and fmr. USSR-Europe Former USSR-Eur. /10	Develope Economie Europe Total /2	Europe EEC CEE /2	Europe EFTA AELE	South Africa Afrique du Sud
		Other manufactured goods (SITC, Rev. 2 and Rev. 3, 6 and 8									
World /1,2,3	1980	474729	326702	113746	38369	28160	13942	240759	194303	45823	2879
	1990	972570	726974	208525	31640	33263	19263	488952	407914	79702	3075
	1991	992156	729449	235832	35892	24124	11745	490919	414018	75737	3366
	1992	1085293	775109	279216	41543	25214	10485	518319	441760	75325	3746
	1993	1070504	739849	293167	40224	29274	11603	457376	388786	67522	4030
Developed economies /2,3,4	1980	369608	269033	82655	29255	12921	7358	211593	168869	42122	2617
	1990	683293	552718	116356	19592	12583	6100	414191	343006	70123	2622
	1991	687805	545385	127412	21670	13313	5099	412445	345102	66265	2610
	1992	724174	563733	140821	24593	15981	4795	429629	362242	66259	2686
	1993	678744	505614	149679	22126	18343	5593	364037	304881	58190	2727
Developing economies /1,3,4	1980	85246	52734	27583	8443	4115	2311	24687	21984	2678	261
	1990	258902	162269	86671	11535	8053	5966	63931	56614	7242	452
	1991	286539	173308	105912	13992	6627	4746	68697	60955	7662	751
	1992	335243	195956	132968	16592	5569	3931	74982	67889	7000	1051
	1993	358460	214426	136737	17660	6752	4544	76220	69099	7026	1291
OPEC	1980	3832	2022	1689	962	29	18	1492	1303	188	0
	1990	15477	9146	5516	1417	127	29	4339	3155	1165	1
	1991	17094	10360	6560	1601	126	45	5200	3715	1483	1
	1992	20915	11185	9600	2533	93	53	5152	4758	392	5
	1993	23206	12734	10308	2596	151	97	5128	4709	417	0
Eastern Europe and the former USSR /2,3,7	1980	19876	4935	3508	671	11124	4273	4479	3450	1023	0
	1990	30375	11988	5497	514	12626	7197	10830	8294	2337	1
	1991	17812	10757	2509	230	4184	1901	9777	7961	1811	4
	1992	25876	15420	5427	358	3665	1759	13708	11630	2066	9
	1993	33300	19809	6751	437	4178	1465	17119	14807	2306	12
Former USSR /3	1980	4989	308	1451	96	3230	.	286	231	55	0
	1990	...	...	...	...	...	.	...	...	...	...
	1991	...	...	...	...	...	.	...	...	...	...
	1992	.	.	.	.	.	.	.	.	.	.
	1993	.	.	.	.	.	.	.	.	.	.
Former USSR-Europe /8	1980	.	.	.	.	.	.	.	.	.	.
	1990	.	.	.	.	.	.	.	.	.	.
	1991	.	.	.	.	.	.	.	.	.	.
	1992	10297	4939	3258	66	923	187	4039	3399	633	0
	1993	12562	5608	3505	83	910	267	3879	3070	807	0
Developed economies-Europe /2	1980	264145	211403	41665	18164	10904	5772	187446	148197	38668	1642
	1990	508354	437447	58206	13256	11388	5178	375176	308724	65424	1919
	1991	499835	427727	58440	13591	12267	4374	371631	308888	61688	1826
	1992	526670	445907	64250	15472	14968	4195	389307	325994	62210	1813
	1993	472894	386504	67697	13980	16863	4533	328313	272924	54454	1854
European Economic Community /2	1980	220490	176168	36394	16218	7755	3917	156133	124392	31189	1441
	1990	421854	362990	49679	11471	8129	3266	311018	257172	52851	1791
	1991	417914	357026	49966	11690	9787	3461	310123	258871	50229	1697
	1992	441927	373427	55175	13441	12076	3347	325902	273969	50865	1646
	1993	395037	321606	58241	12066	13646	3509	272792	227097	44790	1598
European Free Trade Association	1980	43301	34914	5254	1931	3132	1855	31006	23515	7461	200
	1990	86038	74064	8475	1753	3240	1897	63790	51192	12563	127
	1991	81471	70321	8417	1866	2468	901	61158	49677	11451	130
	1992	84240	72059	9025	1997	2859	817	63041	51678	11327	167
	1993	77390	64501	9407	1889	3193	1003	55187	45503	9654	256
Other developed economies	1980	105463	57630	40990	11091	2017	1585	24147	20672	3453	976
	1990	174938	115270	58151	6336	1196	922	39015	34283	4699	704
	1991	187970	117658	68972	8079	1046	725	40814	36215	4577	784
	1992	197504	117826	76570	9122	1013	600	40322	36248	4048	873
	1993	205850	119110	81982	8147	1480	1061	35724	31957	3736	873

For general note and footnotes see end of table.

TABLEAU SPECIAL: B

Exportations mondiales par classes de marchandises et par régions (suite)

En millions de dollars E.-U. f.o.b.

Economies développées /2,3,4				Developing economies / Economies en voie de développement /1,3,4							← Exportations vers
Canada	U.S.A. E.-U.	Japan Japon	Australia New Zealand Australie Nouvelle-Zélande	Africa Afrique	America Amerique: Total	America Amerique: LAIA ALADI	Asia Asie: Mid.East Moyen Orient	Asia Asie: Other Autres /9	Oceania Océanie	Année	Exportations en provenance de ↓
Articles manufacturés divers (CTCI, Rev. 2 et Rev. 3, 6 et 8)											
10439	51214	12659	6738	19926	23185	16637	28364	38019	660	1980	Monde /1,2,3
28080	137703	51085	12577	19437	29239	18855	29790	122595	1298	1990	
28816	135976	52041	12624	19772	35134	24433	32773	142351	1407	1991	
29973	152069	50845	13656	21312	41646	30121	39360	170724	1371	1992	
32387	169372	55608	13976	20337	46007	33462	39437	181986	1326	1993	
8961	32500	6385	5076	16071	17139	12906	20779	25995	511	1980	Economies dévelopées /2,3,4
23121	74115	25137	8435	14158	20079	14101	18163	58198	808	1990	
23737	69653	23681	8093	14344	23745	17450	19668	65063	874	1991	
24512	71413	21125	8531	15214	27905	21009	23048	70663	851	1992	
26430	76716	20865	8647	14075	29777	22334	21896	80144	827	1993	
1382	18453	6222	1617	3436	5529	3644	6802	11423	149	1980	Economies en voie de développement /1,3,4
4788	63086	25590	4084	4788	8115	4693	10705	62264	488	1990	
4974	65937	28026	4483	5171	10938	6941	12642	76423	533	1991	
5263	79831	29184	5080	5714	13516	9032	15304	96594	519	1992	
5739	91048	34164	5276	5792	15995	11002	16314	97281	490	1993	
6	134	383	8	83	126	107	1070	407	0	1980	OPEP
120	2264	2283	138	243	617	311	1931	2708	10	1990	
140	2190	2651	177	348	655	360	2034	3504	13	1991	
202	2970	2617	235	399	971	558	3119	5088	22	1992	
249	3624	3417	314	417	1238	813	3219	5404	28	1993	
96	261	52	46	419	516	87	783	601	0	1980	Europe de l'Est et l'ancienne URSS /2,3,7
170	502	359	57	490	1044	61	923	2132	2	1990	
106	386	333	48	257	451	42	463	865	0	1991	
198	825	537	46	384	225	79	1008	3466	1	1992	
218	1608	579	53	469	235	125	1227	4562	9	1993	
6	9	4	2	42	301	2	144	248	0	1980	L'ancienne URSS /3
...	...	...	...	...	...	...	...	...	...	1990	
...	...	...	...	...	...	...	...	...	...	1991	
.	.	.	.	.	.	.	.	.	.	1992	
.	.	.	.	.	.	.	.	.	.	1993	
.	.	.	.	.	.	.	.	.	.	1980	L'ancienne URSS-Europe /8
.	.	.	.	.	.	.	.	.	.	1990	
.	.	.	.	.	.	.	.	.	.	1991	
92	403	367	2	83	97	31	475	2583	0	1992	
129	1019	424	2	77	88	33	600	2715	0	1993	
1905	14193	2784	1869	13462	6229	4609	13097	6651	173	1980	Economies développées-Europe /2
4432	35177	12759	3764	12105	6422	3981	13307	21177	369	1990	
3840	31500	11250	3471	11993	7207	4783	13744	21511	349	1991	
3590	32348	10370	3631	12736	7910	5424	16205	23967	343	1992	
3630	34121	9781	3555	11608	8436	5955	15927	28468	341	1993	
1624	12168	2168	1576	12423	5354	3922	11426	5328	165	1980	Communauté Economique Européenne /2
3805	29790	10074	3139	11323	5703	3443	11312	16767	345	1990	
3304	26732	8800	2855	11179	6317	4120	11726	17177	322	1991	
3113	27378	8208	2976	11966	6956	4714	13933	19304	325	1992	
3141	28912	7750	2912	10920	7486	5227	13656	23347	323	1993	
278	2015	616	292	1025	875	687	1669	1323	8	1980	Association Européenne de Libre Echange
626	5365	2685	625	747	715	538	1988	4405	24	1990	
535	4739	2449	615	771	886	663	2014	4328	27	1991	
476	4915	2162	654	731	950	707	2271	4657	18	1992	
488	5148	2031	643	655	949	727	2270	5109	18	1993	
7057	18307	3601	3207	2608	10910	8297	7682	19344	338	1980	Autres economies développées
18689	38938	12378	4671	2053	13658	10119	4855	37021	439	1990	
19897	38153	12431	4622	2351	16538	12667	5924	43552	525	1991	
20922	39066	10755	4900	2478	19995	15585	6842	46697	508	1992	
22800	42595	11085	5093	2467	21340	16379	5969	51676	487	1993	

Voir la fin du tableau pour la remarque générale et les notes.

SPECIAL TABLE: B

World exports by commodity classes and by regions (continued)

In million U.S. dollars f.o.b.

Exports from ↓ / Exports to →	Year	World Monde /1,2,3	Developed economies Econ. dévelop-pées /2,3,4	Developing economies Economies en voie de développement /1,3,4 Total	Developing economies OPEC OPEP	Eastern Europe and fmr. USSR-Europe Europe de l'Est et l'anc. URSS-Europe Total /2,3,7	Eastern Europe and fmr. USSR-Europe Former USSR-Eur. /10	Developed Economies Europe Total /2	Developed Economies Europe EEC CEE /2	Developed Economies Europe EFTA AELE	Developed Economies South Africa Afrique du Sud
		Other manufactured goods (SITC, Rev. 2 and Rev. 3, 6 and 8) (continued)									
Canada	1980	13694	11983	1565	313	41	21	2208	2023	184	25
	1990	24942	23265	1645	259	32	18	2218	2022	196	25
	1991	25253	23144	2067	269	43	24	2566	2336	230	19
	1992	27219	25281	1872	333	65	30	2847	2627	220	21
	1993	29300	27308	1891	322	102	55	2418	2226	189	23
United States	1980	38854	24657	13864	3350	229	123	13801	11682	2113	481
	1990	70956	48373	22356	1932	227	107	19436	17068	2349	331
	1991	78925	51182	27445	3087	296	135	20541	18301	2227	383
	1992	84303	52444	31365	3466	495	288	21408	19207	2187	410
	1993	87239	53051	33542	3191	645	433	19745	17632	2095	406
Japan	1980	42012	16605	23683	7223	1724	1441	5924	5056	852	426
	1990	58727	28470	29349	3793	908	794	10723	9438	1276	295
	1991	63860	28843	34352	4286	665	553	11476	10160	1309	323
	1992	66329	29007	36973	4775	348	236	11786	10468	1307	351
	1993	68442	27971	39856	4072	616	525	10009	8814	1187	324
Australia, New Zealand	1980	3707	2056	1473	190	16	0	837	817	19	24
	1990	6820	4189	2619	325	11	2	810	767	43	18
	1991	7130	4048	3071	404	11	7	690	643	47	27
	1992	7416	3956	3449	442	9	7	817	740	77	45
	1993	7797	3753	3677	407	8	5	604	568	37	70
Developing economies-Africa	1980	5213	4069	711	119	162	122	3039	2952	85	3
	1990	8993	7070	1627	454	374	297	5871	5734	117	103
	1991	8154	6421	1416	544	251	191	5424	5215	200	97
	1992	9128	7082	1877	802	78	55	5843	5656	179	117
	1993	9905	7825	1915	666	70	58	6083	5926	147	153
Developing economies-America	1980	12759	7695	4752	758	292	77	3835	3558	276	31
	1990	27945	18952	8604	1287	354	177	7185	6776	408	61
	1991	28278	17878	10153	1571	205	157	6350	6012	336	64
	1992	35276	23100	11860	1688	93	34	6286	5975	308	64
	1993	38840	25217	13415	1568	130	65	6037	5614	413	66
Developing economies-Europe/ 5	1980	3444	1316	510	322	1618	989	1004	792	209	0
	1990	6230	4143	640	277	1447	900	3583	3126	455	0
	1991	4133	2750	423	184	960	597	2378	2074	303	0
	1992	6568	4880	1440	97	237	84	4546	4076	468	1
	1993	6018	4792	964	73	262	120	4392	4003	387	1
Developing economies-Middle East	1980	3926	1657	2101	1560	108	77	1566	1305	260	0
	1990	14074	8138	4107	2214	1107	916	6855	5394	1454	25
	1991	14016	8764	4166	2040	955	727	7247	5547	1693	27
	1992	15172	8750	5704	2840	566	260	7237	6507	715	27
	1993	15493	8249	6306	2979	746	355	6784	6103	668	30
Developing economies-Other Asia	1980	59564	37682	19484	5682	1935	1045	15021	13155	1847	228
	1990	201197	123598	71599	7302	4771	3675	40302	35459	4800	263
	1991	231456	137089	89659	9652	4256	3073	47166	41981	5122	564
	1992	268614	151733	112013	11165	4594	3497	50864	45477	5321	842
	1993	287737	167939	114076	12374	5544	3946	52728	47262	5404	1040
Former USSR-Asia /9	1980	.	.	.	.	.	.	.	.	.	.
	1990	.	.	.	.	.	.	.	.	.	.
	1991	.	.	.	.	.	.	.	.	.	.
	1992	581	126	425	110	13	.	81	67	14	0
	1993	560	140	404	100	17	.	78	66	12	0
Developing economies-Oceania	1980	340	314	25	0	0	0	223	223	0	0
	1990	464	368	94	0	0	0	133	126	8	0
	1991	502	405	95	0	0	0	133	126	7	0
	1992	486	411	73	0	0	0	207	198	8	0
	1993	467	405	61	0	0	0	197	190	7	0

For general note and footnotes see end of table.

Exportations mondiales par classes de marchandises et par régions (suite)

En millions de dollars E.-U. f.o.b.

Economies développées /2,3,4				Developing economies Economies en voie de développement /1,3,4						← Exportations vers	
Canada	U.S.A. E.-U.	Japan Japon	Australia New Zealand Australie Nouvelle-Zélande	Africa Afrique	America Amerique Total	America Amerique LAIA ALADI	Asia Asie Mid.East Moyen Orient	Asia Asie Other Autres /9	Oceania Océanie	Année	Exportations en provenance de ↓
Articles manufacturés divers (CTCI, Rev. 2 et Rev. 3, 6 et 8) (suite)											
.	9222	288	206	124	722	496	115	598	2	1980	Canada
.	20161	620	188	90	462	308	228	854	7	1990	
.	19782	607	125	115	509	361	180	1255	5	1991	
.	21619	629	125	93	545	414	251	978	2	1992	
.	24051	653	128	55	564	415	276	989	2	1993	
6203	.	2831	1077	894	7599	5758	2006	3285	31	1980	Etats-Unis
17331	.	8910	1689	709	11571	8495	1467	8495	36	1990	
18612	.	9204	1668	951	14285	10868	2293	9814	45	1991	
19806	.	8263	1829	985	17465	13512	2719	10115	49	1992	
21663	.	8615	1919	1045	18819	14307	2571	11026	53	1993	
796	8184	.	1242	1530	2548	2011	5452	14043	75	1980	Japon
1104	14783	.	1497	668	1460	1174	2822	24234	134	1990	
1058	14436	.	1483	754	1577	1290	3133	28702	172	1991	
986	14312	.	1491	731	1681	1393	3572	30843	140	1992	
1007	15063	.	1481	669	1671	1410	2828	34568	114	1993	
25	226	285	657	27	15	10	92	1110	229	1980	Australie, Nouvelle-Zélande
63	546	1551	1199	17	23	21	116	2202	261	1990	
48	508	1519	1254	13	21	19	116	2621	300	1991	
59	551	1118	1361	14	27	25	111	2990	307	1992	
57	515	1055	1447	12	39	37	91	3225	311	1993	
12	535	471	1	372	62	61	70	154	0	1980	Economies en voie de développement-Afrique
21	613	448	5	984	27	16	266	326	0	1990	
23	492	361	6	1046	25	16	207	122	0	1991	
23	535	546	8	1084	30	17	552	192	0	1992	
24	768	784	7	1133	27	17	426	310	2	1993	
206	2825	743	48	204	3888	2788	141	395	1	1980	Economies en voie de développement-Amérique
480	8510	2504	173	391	4776	3118	755	2643	7	1990	
431	8473	2350	183	364	6098	4432	802	2876	7	1991	
372	14269	1906	171	358	7440	5763	811	3248	2	1992	
413	16753	1747	175	250	8804	6864	504	3851	4	1993	
21	258	18	4	203	15	8	245	45	1	1980	Economies en voie de développement-Europe /5
39	468	26	21	150	24	17	362	104	1	1990	
26	311	17	14	99	15	12	239	70	0	1991	
29	270	22	8	55	22	17	122	35	1	1992	
26	328	28	9	35	19	15	102	54	0	1993	
3	58	29	1	173	0	0	1821	102	0	1980	Economies en voie de développement-Moyen Orient
63	739	422	17	425	7	4	2935	678	0	1990	
56	698	674	16	487	24	19	2752	867	0	1991	
80	862	472	21	340	25	12	3807	1495	0	1992	
79	948	339	18	332	15	12	4047	1868	0	1993	
1141	14735	4921	1555	2485	1563	787	4524	10717	132	1980	Economies en voie de développement-Autres Pays d'Asie
4184	52700	22101	3779	2839	3281	1536	6387	58457	444	1990	
4437	55893	24524	4161	3175	4775	2461	8642	72431	489	1991	
4759	63829	26156	4814	3877	5999	3223	10012	91575	493	1992	
5196	72196	31169	5012	4042	7130	4094	11235	91155	464	1993	
.	.	.	.	.	.	.	.	.	.	1980	l'ancienne URSS asiatique /9
.	.	.	.	.	.	.	.	.	.	1990	
.	.	.	.	.	.	.	.	.	.	1991	
0	26	19	0	12	42	9	289	82	0	1992	
0	27	35	0	8	41	7	253	101	0	1993	
0	43	40	8	0	1	1	0	10	14	1980	Economies en voie de développement-Océanie
1	55	88	89	0	1	1	0	57	36	1990	
1	70	99	102	0	1	1	0	57	36	1991	
0	65	82	57	0	0	0	0	50	23	1992	
0	55	97	55	0	0	0	0	42	19	1993	

Voir la fin du tableau pour la remarque générale et les notes.

SPECIAL TABLE: B

World exports by commodity classes and by regions (continued)

In million U.S. dollars f.o.b.

Exports to → / ↓ Exports from	Year	World Monde /1,2,3	Developed economies Econ. dévelop-pées /2,3,4	Developing economies Economies en voie de développement /1,3,4 Total	OPEC OPEP	Eastern Europe and fmr. USSR-Europe Europe de l'Est et l'anc. URSS-Europe Total /2,3,7	Former USSR-Eur. /10	Developed Economies: Europe Total /2	EEC CEE /2	EFTA AELE	South Africa Afrique du Sud
Textile yarn and fabrics (SITC, Rev. 2 and Rev. 3, 65											
World /1,2,3	1980	55748	35472	16734	4670	3177	1622	28264	23580	4549	471
	1990	110426	66380	38819	4425	4556	2364	51313	44657	6500	363
	1991	115864	65764	46230	5414	3503	1240	49599	43620	5830	489
	1992	126401	69397	52674	6658	4048	1089	51864	45819	5891	575
	1993	122063	63025	54087	6808	4678	1181	45028	39716	5177	593
Developed economies /2,3,4	1980	38892	27869	9133	3034	1713	772	23870	19873	3872	423
	1990	65012	50233	12751	1731	1929	488	42458	36825	5498	254
	1991	65132	48771	14182	2069	2079	301	41005	35886	4994	254
	1992	68849	50254	15555	2347	2960	460	42290	37183	4978	226
	1993	62385	43645	15176	2064	3482	575	35497	31108	4281	212
Developing economies /1,3,4	1980	15359	7054	7176	1570	948	553	3922	3386	528	48
	1990	43002	15175	25475	2654	1852	1431	8010	7195	797	109
	1991	49457	16237	31806	3326	1149	833	7947	7238	686	234
	1992	56059	18306	36821	4287	730	477	8846	8036	786	349
	1993	57736	18250	38592	4718	707	437	8553	7782	746	380
OPEC	1980	744	583	160	97	0	0	533	458	74	0
	1990	1916	1065	790	201	50	14	790	734	56	0
	1991	2429	1210	1185	209	33	23	892	837	55	0
	1992	4153	1714	2398	692	27	14	1292	1126	166	1
	1993	4065	1789	2221	681	43	30	1309	1129	180	0
Eastern Europe and the former USSR /2,3,7	1980	1497	548	425	65	515	297	472	320	149	0
	1990	2412	972	593	41	774	446	845	637	205	0
	1991	1275	756	243	19	275	106	647	496	150	1
	1992	1493	837	299	23	357	153	728	600	128	1
	1993	1942	1131	319	26	490	169	978	826	150	1
Former USSR /3	1980	157	35	111	1	11	.	35	28	7	0
	1990	...	...	...	...	...	.	...	...	...	...
	1991	...	...	...	...	...	.	...	...	...	...
	1992	.	.	.	.	.	.	.	.	.	.
	1993	.	.	.	.	.	.	.	.	.	.
Former USSR-Europe /8	1980	.	.	.	.	.	.	.	.	.	.
	1990	.	.	.	.	.	.	.	.	.	.
	1991	.	.	.	.	.	.	.	.	.	.
	1992	314	113	104	0	96	54	100	87	13	0
	1993	405	153	123	0	129	83	127	108	19	0
Developed economies-Europe /2	1980	29265	23949	3880	1452	1404	545	22021	18181	3721	237
	1990	52848	44511	6496	803	1770	363	40050	34573	5349	192
	1991	51619	42747	6786	913	2010	259	38606	33630	4854	187
	1992	54353	44078	7299	1061	2899	431	39939	34961	4852	164
	1993	47996	37423	7085	933	3409	540	33407	29137	4166	148
European Economic Community /2	1980	25885	21161	3457	1286	1235	484	19389	16363	2912	228
	1990	47152	39397	6108	690	1632	322	35308	30783	4399	181
	1991	46384	38131	6381	796	1858	223	34323	30185	4018	177
	1992	48913	39385	6844	913	2671	359	35586	31432	4030	154
	1993	43337	33472	6688	813	3152	449	29761	26206	3453	140
European Free Trade Association	1980	3361	2771	422	166	169	61	2617	1803	809	9
	1990	5677	5096	388	112	139	41	4725	3773	949	11
	1991	5218	4599	405	117	153	36	4266	3429	836	11
	1992	5420	4673	454	148	228	72	4333	3510	822	9
	1993	4645	3937	396	120	257	92	3633	2918	713	8
Other developed economies	1980	9627	3921	5253	1582	309	227	1848	1693	151	186
	1990	12164	5722	6254	928	159	124	2408	2253	149	62
	1991	13513	6024	7395	1156	69	42	2399	2256	140	67
	1992	14496	6176	8256	1286	61	29	2351	2222	126	62
	1993	14388	6222	8091	1131	72	34	2090	1971	116	64

For general note and footnotes see end of table.

TABLEAU SPECIAL: B

Exportations mondiales par classes de marchandises et par régions (suite)

En millions de dollars E.-U. f.o.b.

Economies développées /2,3,4				Developing economies Economies en voie de développement /1,3,4						← Exportations vers	
Canada	U.S.A. E.-U.	Japan Japon	Australia New Zealand Australie Nouvelle-Zélande	Africa Afrique	America Amerique Total	America Amerique LAIA ALADI	Asia Asie Mid.East Moyen Orient	Asia Asie Other Autres /9	Oceania Océanie	Année	Exportations en provenance de ↓
Fils et tissus de matières textiles (CTCI, Rev. 2 et Rev. 3, 65)											
1135	2458	1684	1315	3044	1959	1132	3940	7156	71	1980	Monde /1,2,3
2272	6455	3866	1742	3805	3071	1840	4482	25687	180	1990	
2438	7034	4040	1750	4064	3939	2500	5386	31288	189	1991	
2527	8249	3866	1801	4450	4662	3060	6725	35391	203	1992	
2735	8703	3643	1772	4477	5410	3599	7174	35837	202	1993	
912	1230	545	763	1950	1264	822	2563	2880	31	1980	Economies dévelopées /2,3,4
1653	3079	1590	886	2443	1578	1088	1896	5372	46	1990	
1765	3183	1419	805	2545	1904	1349	2213	6231	56	1991	
1825	3443	1256	808	2745	2179	1617	2569	6986	60	1992	
1981	3678	1076	776	2642	2299	1725	2365	6962	63	1993	
203	1198	1132	534	1044	637	307	1277	4159	39	1980	Economies en voie de développement /1,3,4
593	3312	2261	838	1344	1423	751	2498	19980	134	1990	
649	3799	2611	925	1509	2009	1149	3125	24950	133	1991	
675	4753	2601	977	1693	2471	1440	4049	28295	144	1992	
728	4927	2559	980	1816	3098	1868	4667	28757	138	1993	
1	38	9	2	8	10	9	111	31	0	1980	OPEP
21	111	88	56	16	18	7	233	520	1	1990	
28	112	111	67	67	35	16	244	836	2	1991	
64	157	115	84	71	70	39	779	1474	3	1992	
67	182	129	102	66	107	78	785	1259	3	1993	
20	31	7	18	49	58	3	101	117	0	1980	Europe de l'Est et l'ancienne URSS /2,3,7
27	65	15	18	17	70	1	89	335	0	1990	
24	52	10	20	10	26	2	47	107	0	1991	
27	53	10	16	12	12	3	107	111	0	1992	
26	99	9	16	19	13	6	142	117	0	1993	
0	0	0	0	0	24	0	1	49	0	1980	L'ancienne URSS /3
...	...	...	...	...	...	...	...	...	...	1990	
...	...	...	...	...	...	...	...	...	...	1991	
.	.	.	.	.	.	.	.	.	.	1992	
.	.	.	.	.	.	.	.	.	.	1993	
.	.	.	.	.	.	.	.	.	.	1980	L'ancienne URSS-Europe /8
.	.	.	.	.	.	.	.	.	.	1990	
.	.	.	.	.	.	.	.	.	.	1991	
2	9	2	0	0	1	0	33	68	0	1992	
4	19	3	0	0	1	0	43	78	0	1993	
220	745	408	225	1568	284	200	1224	371	12	1980	Economies développées-Europe /2
380	1995	1309	343	2262	356	255	1112	1349	15	1990	
320	1926	1139	304	2356	464	354	1242	1485	16	1991	
306	2037	1007	293	2565	523	405	1481	1706	14	1992	
284	2120	844	271	2485	544	429	1425	1776	13	1993	
204	689	352	210	1382	260	179	1084	329	11	1980	Communauté Economique Européenne /2
343	1852	1165	315	2184	329	231	1008	1223	14	1990	
292	1788	1014	281	2268	432	324	1137	1349	15	1991	
281	1885	888	269	2460	487	371	1357	1558	14	1992	
261	1971	754	250	2401	511	399	1314	1642	12	1993	
16	55	56	15	185	23	21	140	42	1	1980	Association Européenne de Libre Echange
37	143	144	28	78	27	23	103	126	0	1990	
28	138	125	22	88	32	30	105	135	0	1991	
26	152	119	24	105	36	34	123	148	0	1992	
24	149	90	20	84	34	30	111	133	0	1993	
692	485	137	538	383	981	622	1338	2509	19	1980	Autres economies développées
1273	1083	281	543	181	1223	834	784	4023	32	1990	
1445	1257	280	501	189	1440	995	971	4746	40	1991	
1519	1406	249	516	179	1656	1212	1088	5280	45	1992	
1697	1557	232	505	158	1755	1296	939	5187	51	1993	

Voir la fin du tableau pour la remarque générale et les notes.

SPECIAL TABLE: B

World exports by commodity classes and by regions (continued)

In million U.S. dollars f.o.b.

Exports from ↓ / Exports to →	Year	World Monde /1,2,3	Developed economies Econ. dévelop-pées /2,3,4	Developing economies Economies en voie de développement /1,3,4 Total	OPEC OPEP	Eastern Europe and fmr. USSR-Europe Europe de l'Est et l'anc. URSS-Europe Total /2,3,7	Former USSR-Eur. /10	Developed Economies Europe Total /2	EEC CEE /2	EFTA AELE	South Africa Afrique du Sud
		Textile yarn and fabrics (SITC, Rev. 2 and Rev. 3, 65) (continued)									
Canada	1980	306	244	56	14	6	4	95	81	14	3
	1990	687	586	97	18	3	0	116	104	11	2
	1991	777	668	107	24	2	0	94	86	8	2
	1992	856	759	94	21	3	0	86	81	6	3
	1993	975	902	66	12	6	1	88	82	6	2
United States	1980	3632	2196	1408	347	29	14	1198	1110	86	69
	1990	4922	2948	1946	266	28	10	1228	1160	63	29
	1991	5482	3145	2318	392	19	4	1260	1199	59	33
	1992	5756	3129	2598	428	29	12	1188	1134	52	34
	1993	5879	3207	2630	388	42	19	1088	1035	52	36
Japan	1980	5123	1165	3686	1207	272	209	388	343	44	109
	1990	5859	1681	4053	632	125	113	819	751	67	26
	1991	6524	1669	4811	718	44	37	781	716	65	25
	1992	7078	1685	5368	815	25	17	789	724	62	18
	1993	6717	1505	5190	710	22	13	656	600	54	17
Australia, New Zealand	1980	234	150	82	14	2	0	14	14	1	1
	1990	265	204	60	6	1	0	11	11	0	3
	1991	271	204	66	7	1	0	14	14	0	4
	1992	296	214	82	10	0	0	22	22	0	3
	1993	336	236	97	8	0	0	26	26	0	7
Developing economies-Africa	1980	592	352	127	30	105	81	302	280	22	0
	1990	1201	689	258	83	223	173	603	573	30	27
	1991	1100	683	270	92	120	87	574	541	32	21
	1992	1010	689	268	90	26	15	574	551	22	36
	1993	1022	687	285	94	23	19	565	547	17	29
Developing economies-America	1980	1343	765	507	79	71	2	468	379	88	4
	1990	1962	1318	585	64	58	26	634	584	50	5
	1991	2015	1242	752	60	19	5	565	518	47	4
	1992	2889	1796	1062	112	15	1	572	528	44	5
	1993	2682	1537	1137	101	7	0	378	344	33	6
Developing economies-Europe/ 5	1980	379	111	84	54	184	132	107	83	23	0
	1990	487	323	36	22	127	85	301	270	31	0
	1991	322	215	24	15	83	56	200	180	20	0
	1992	467	323	127	6	16	8	290	267	23	0
	1993	454	348	89	3	17	4	310	295	16	0
Developing economies-Middle East	1980	1117	834	214	153	68	45	793	695	98	0
	1990	2630	1623	488	296	505	471	1446	1344	99	9
	1991	2479	1593	515	263	348	314	1403	1304	95	13
	1992	3018	1968	853	591	138	60	1734	1508	222	13
	1993	3110	1969	944	643	120	53	1704	1454	245	15
Developing economies-Other Asia	1980	11928	4992	6244	1254	520	293	2252	1948	297	44
	1990	36721	11220	24108	2188	940	675	5025	4423	587	68
	1991	43539	12501	30245	2896	579	372	5205	4695	492	196
	1992	48674	13530	34511	3487	536	393	5676	5182	474	295
	1993	50464	13705	36137	3876	540	360	5596	5142	435	330
Former USSR-Asia /9	1980	.	.	.	.	.	.	.	.	.	.
	1990	.	.	.	.	.	.	.	.	.	.
	1991	.	.	.	.	.	.	.	.	.	.
	1992	46	8	34	31	3	.	8	7	1	0
	1993	42	7	34	30	2	.	7	7	0	0
Developing economies-Oceania	1980	0	0	0	0	0	0	0	0	0	0
	1990	2	1	0	0	0	0	0	0	0	0
	1991	2	1	0	0	0	0	0	0	0	0
	1992	1	1	0	0	0	0	0	0	0	0
	1993	4	3	0	0	0	0	0	0	0	0

For general note and footnotes see end of table.

Exportations mondiales par classes de marchandises et par régions (suite)

En millions de dollars E.-U. f.o.b.

Fils et tissus de matières textiles (CTCI, Rev. 2 et Rev. 3, 65) (suite)

Economies développées /2,3,4 — Canada	U.S.A. E.-U.	Japan Japon	Australia New Zealand Australie Nouvelle-Zélande	Developing economies Economies en voie de développement /1,3,4 — Africa Afrique	America Amerique — Total	America Amerique — LAIA ALADI	Asia Asie — Mid.East Moyen Orient	Asia Asie — Other Autres /9	Oceania Océanie	Année	← Exportations vers / Exportations en provenance de ↓
.	93	4	47	5	32	16	7	12	0	1980	Canada
.	426	5	30	3	37	24	7	50	0	1990	
.	527	6	29	7	36	25	12	52	0	1991	
.	628	10	28	4	36	25	18	36	0	1992	
.	771	6	31	2	26	18	11	27	0	1993	
621	.	111	166	150	733	471	209	309	1	1980	Etats-Unis
1195	.	269	168	71	1099	741	211	562	1	1990	
1375	.	264	149	75	1294	881	322	620	2	1991	
1451	.	231	159	63	1514	1103	340	674	3	1992	
1634	.	218	165	59	1602	1175	327	638	3	1993	
61	383	.	222	224	214	133	1109	2127	9	1980	Japon
66	592	.	175	61	68	51	562	3343	17	1990	
57	638	.	164	65	85	63	633	4004	23	1991	
55	654	.	165	51	84	61	720	4488	25	1992	
51	635	.	141	46	98	75	595	4426	24	1993	
7	6	21	100	2	1	1	12	59	9	1980	Australie, Nouvelle-Zélande
4	20	7	160	2	1	1	2	42	13	1990	
4	27	8	147	3	1	1	1	46	14	1991	
4	28	7	149	3	1	1	4	56	17	1992	
5	40	7	152	2	1	1	2	69	23	1993	
10	34	4	1	97	0	0	21	8	0	1980	Economies en voie de développement-Afrique
3	48	4	2	166	1	1	58	18	0	1990	
4	69	4	2	201	1	1	43	13	0	1991	
3	64	5	3	188	1	0	43	22	0	1992	
3	80	4	3	204	2	2	47	20	0	1993	
28	222	23	15	43	438	235	10	14	0	1980	Economies en voie de développement-Amérique
95	498	50	27	35	465	327	26	57	0	1990	
81	524	36	27	22	617	460	33	79	0	1991	
76	1067	46	22	19	827	641	40	175	0	1992	
61	1049	26	14	10	1052	824	23	52	0	1993	
1	3	0	1	28	0	0	49	7	0	1980	Economies en voie de développement-Europe /5
1	19	1	1	6	0	0	26	4	0	1990	
0	13	1	1	4	0	0	17	3	0	1991	
2	31	0	1	1	1	0	7	3	0	1992	
2	35	0	1	2	1	1	5	2	0	1993	
1	38	1	1	10	0	0	182	18	0	1980	Economies en voie de développement-Moyen Orient
21	77	55	6	45	3	2	381	26	0	1990	
17	83	57	8	76	3	2	388	31	0	1991	
48	113	38	4	40	4	3	743	49	0	1992	
52	142	38	3	37	4	2	827	60	0	1993	
163	901	1104	517	866	198	72	1016	4112	39	1980	Economies en voie de développement-Autres Pays d'Asie
473	2671	2150	801	1092	954	421	2006	19875	133	1990	
547	3110	2514	886	1205	1388	687	2645	24824	133	1991	
547	3479	2513	946	1445	1637	795	3215	28046	143	1992	
611	3621	2490	957	1563	2040	1039	3766	28623	137	1993	
.	.	.	.	.	.	.	.	.	.	1980	l'ancienne URSS asiatique /9
.	.	.	.	.	.	.	.	.	.	1990	
.	.	.	.	.	.	.	.	.	.	1991	
0	0	0	0	0	0	0	33	0	0	1992	
0	0	0	0	0	0	0	33	1	0	1993	
0	0	0	0	0	0	0	0	0	0	1980	Economies en voie de développement-Océanie
0	0	0	1	0	0	0	0	0	0	1990	
0	0	0	1	0	0	0	0	0	0	1991	
0	0	0	1	0	0	0	0	0	0	1992	
0	1	0	2	0	0	0	0	0	0	1993	

Voir la fin du tableau pour la remarque générale et les notes.

SPECIAL TABLE: B

World exports by commodity classes and by regions (continued)

In million U.S. dollars f.o.b.

Exports to → / ↓ Exports from	Year	World Monde /1,2,3	Developed economies Econ. dévelop-pées /2,3,4	Developing economies Economies en voie de développement /1,3,4: Total	Developing economies: OPEC OPEP	Eastern Europe and fmr. USSR-Europe Europe de l'Est et l'anc. URSS-Europe: Total /2,3,7	Eastern Europe and fmr. USSR-Europe: Former USSR-Eur. /10	Develope Economie — Europe: Total /2	Europe: EEC CEE /2	Europe: EFTA AELE	South Africa Afrique du Sud
		Iron and steel (SITC, Rev. 2 and Rev. 3, 67									
World /1,2,3	1980	75128	40009	24907	8050	8835	4085	29944	25115	4795	335
	1990	108323	71194	31040	6228	5392	2484	52926	45235	7613	306
	1991	104117	66301	33844	6860	3713	2044	48541	41622	6870	275
	1992	105702	64365	38904	7047	2396	1303	48066	41400	6618	292
	1993	103824	56094	45190	6103	2491	1074	38179	32690	5452	270
Developed economies /2,3,4	1980	64091	36750	20893	6837	5165	3586	28163	23622	4508	328
	1990	81850	59668	19578	4226	2323	1672	47645	40979	6615	269
	1991	80826	56020	22504	4751	2062	1464	44730	38513	6171	236
	1992	79040	54787	22677	4947	1557	886	43925	37712	6171	258
	1993	73867	46923	25333	4009	1590	813	34932	29775	5122	215
Developing economies /1,3,4	1980	5181	2323	2494	946	294	142	856	814	41	7
	1990	17788	8352	8667	1778	430	304	2454	2207	236	38
	1991	18455	7932	10102	2007	400	320	1759	1604	153	39
	1992	19778	7010	12538	1935	211	159	1853	1701	147	33
	1993	22000	6805	14972	1892	200	158	1280	1180	98	53
OPEC	1980	333	108	213	166	12	12	49	49	0	0
	1990	1328	413	896	223	6	4	150	141	0	0
	1991	1079	312	766	157	0	0	67	63	4	0
	1992	1274	241	1032	314	0	0	92	91	1	0
	1993	1468	278	1191	328	0	0	71	70	1	0
Eastern Europe and the former USSR /2,3,7	1980	5855	936	1521	267	3376	356	925	680	245	0
	1990	8686	3174	2795	223	2639	507	2827	2049	761	0
	1991	4837	2348	1237	102	1251	260	2052	1505	547	0
	1992	6884	2568	3689	165	628	257	2289	1987	300	0
	1993	7956	2367	4884	202	701	104	1966	1734	231	1
Former USSR /3	1980	3226	93	721	51	2412	.	93	61	32	0
	1990	...	...	...	...	...	.	...	...	...	...
	1991	...	...	...	...	...	.	...	...	...	...
	1992	.	.	.	.	.	.	.	.	.	.
	1993	.	.	.	.	.	.	.	.	.	.
Former USSR-Europe /8	1980	.	.	.	.	.	.	.	.	.	.
	1990	.	.	.	.	.	.	.	.	.	.
	1991	.	.	.	.	.	.	.	.	.	.
	1992	3999	1141	2658	24	200	16	992	926	67	0
	1993	4018	920	2879	34	220	16	687	621	66	0
Developed economies-Europe /2	1980	41777	29692	8032	3285	4048	2619	26669	22316	4324	189
	1990	61361	51126	8318	2535	1882	1268	45976	39525	6400	192
	1991	58064	47612	8772	2847	1660	1104	43138	37180	5913	163
	1992	56936	46866	8649	2779	1402	749	42588	36650	5897	157
	1993	50710	39315	10194	2312	1180	428	33867	29020	4813	159
European Economic Community /2	1980	36135	25170	7589	3191	3371	2329	22581	19236	3316	162
	1990	52043	43002	7566	2393	1453	982	38735	33766	4922	183
	1991	49343	40108	7897	2670	1330	911	36465	31753	4670	156
	1992	48053	39115	/897	2610	1035	556	35606	31027	4540	150
	1993	42724	32496	9397	2197	825	278	27916	24222	3660	143
European Free Trade Association	1980	5641	4521	443	94	677	291	4088	3079	1008	27
	1990	9317	8124	752	141	429	286	7241	5758	1478	9
	1991	8721	7504	875	177	331	193	6672	5427	1243	7
	1992	8882	7752	751	169	367	194	6981	5623	1357	7
	1993	7985	6819	797	115	355	149	5951	4798	1153	16
Other developed economies	1980	22314	7059	12860	3552	1117	967	1494	1306	184	139
	1990	20489	8542	11260	1692	441	404	1669	1454	215	76
	1991	22762	8408	13732	1904	401	360	1592	1333	258	72
	1992	22104	7921	14028	2169	155	137	1337	1062	273	101
	1993	23157	7608	15139	1697	410	386	1065	756	309	56

For general note and footnotes see end of table.

TABLEAU SPECIAL: B

Exportations mondiales par classes de marchandises et par régions (suite)

En millions de dollars E.-U. f.o.b.

Economies développées /2,3,4 — Canada	U.S.A. E.-U.	Japan Japon	Australia New Zealand Australie Nouvelle-Zélande	Developing economies / Economies en voie de développement /1,3,4 — Africa Afrique	America Amerique — Total	America Amerique — LAIA ALADI	Asia Asie — Mid.East Moyen Orient	Asia Asie — Other Autres /9	Oceania Océanie	Année	← Exportations vers / Exportations en provenance de ↓
Fer et acier (CTCI, Rev. 2 et Rev. 3, 67)											
1119	7105	699	641	3844	4852	4063	5454	9453	79	1980	Monde /1,2,3
2290	10582	4008	758	3300	3812	2733	5499	17201	150	1990	
2192	9561	4500	830	3298	4305	3460	5511	19977	169	1991	
1955	9588	3287	748	3400	4684	3867	6089	24001	129	1992	
2333	10502	3484	833	3077	4266	3428	5465	31838	134	1993	
1068	6219	212	594	3576	4206	3678	4327	8150	75	1980	Economies dévelopées /2,3,4
2127	7912	843	602	2567	2424	2025	3308	10681	113	1990	
2039	7133	936	629	2623	2796	2429	3483	13183	116	1991	
1837	7268	554	560	2744	2899	2515	3770	12830	104	1992	
2168	8028	513	633	2434	2561	2137	3287	16703	105	1993	
48	879	487	47	170	457	365	754	1108	4	1980	Economies en voie de développement /1,3,4
153	2604	2944	156	547	1009	703	1713	5353	37	1990	
148	2380	3403	201	576	1341	1025	1783	6346	53	1991	
105	2244	2582	187	496	1713	1317	1802	8368	25	1992	
151	2305	2811	199	479	1628	1256	1571	11207	22	1993	
0	40	19	0	6	11	9	173	23	0	1980	OPEP
3	130	130	0	73	244	132	379	199	0	1990	
0	125	121	0	55	227	139	237	245	1	1991	
2	104	43	0	48	281	172	384	320	0	1992	
7	177	22	1	59	324	208	402	406	0	1993	
3	7	0	0	98	189	20	372	195	0	1980	Europe de l'Est et l'ancienne URSS /2,3,7
10	65	222	0	186	380	5	477	1167	0	1990	
5	49	161	0	100	168	6	245	447	0	1991	
14	76	151	1	159	71	35	517	2803	0	1992	
15	168	160	1	163	77	34	607	3928	7	1993	
0	0	0	0	1	144	0	93	70	0	1980	L'ancienne URSS /3
...	...	...	...	...	...	...	...	...	...	1990	
...	...	...	...	...	...	...	...	...	...	1991	
.	.	.	.	.	.	.	.	.	.	1992	
.	.	.	.	.	.	.	.	.	.	1993	
.	.	.	.	.	.	.	.	.	.	1980	L'ancienne URSS-Europe /8
.	.	.	.	.	.	.	.	.	.	1990	
.	.	.	.	.	.	.	.	.	.	1991	
7	47	92	0	17	37	9	280	2317	0	1992	
10	111	102	0	17	36	9	337	2482	0	1993	
280	2178	126	106	2590	1452	1245	2231	1210	18	1980	Economies développées-Europe /2
509	3695	342	197	1930	1118	897	2209	2555	28	1990	
416	3094	353	195	1904	1226	1000	2365	2952	25	1991	
397	2992	275	166	2070	1116	902	2342	2774	22	1992	
588	3861	278	211	1848	1076	810	2358	4639	31	1993	
222	1947	47	74	2541	1346	1141	2146	1126	17	1980	Communauté Economique Européenne /2
429	3142	173	138	1859	1032	817	2065	2229	28	1990	
346	2586	176	139	1827	1133	912	2199	2477	25	1991	
336	2513	130	109	1985	1037	830	2201	2404	22	1992	
508	3340	119	138	1785	1010	750	2232	4154	31	1993	
57	231	79	33	49	107	104	85	83	1	1980	Association Européenne de Libre Echange
81	553	169	59	71	86	80	144	326	0	1990	
70	508	177	57	76	93	87	165	475	0	1991	
60	480	146	57	85	78	71	142	369	0	1992	
80	522	159	73	63	65	59	127	484	0	1993	
'789	4041	86	488	985	2753	2433	2096	6940	57	1980	Autres economies développées
1618	4217	501	404	637	1306	1128	1100	8126	84	1990	
1623	4039	583	434	719	1570	1429	1118	10231	92	1991	
1440	4276	279	394	675	1784	1614	1427	10056	82	1992	
1579	4167	234	422	586	1485	1327	929	12064	74	1993	

Voir la fin du tableau pour la remarque générale et les notes.

SPECIAL TABLE: B

World exports by commodity classes and by regions (continued)

In million U.S. dollars f.o.b.

Exports to → / ↓ Exports from	Year	World Monde /1,2,3	Developed economies Econ. développées /2,3,4	Developing economies Economies en voie de développement /1,3,4 Total	OPEC OPEP	Eastern Europe and fmr. USSR-Europe Europe de l'Est et l'anc. URSS-Europe Total /2,3,7	Former USSR-Eur. /10	Developed Economies Europe Total /2	EEC CEE /2	EFTA AELE	South Africa Afrique du Sud
Iron and steel (SITC, Rev. 2 and Rev. 3, 67) (continued)											
Canada	1980	1779	1452	326	55	1	1	154	151	4	2
	1990	2052	1739	305	82	8	8	159	152	7	1
	1991	2311	1707	595	45	8	8	76	69	7	1
	1992	2360	2125	233	19	3	1	104	101	3	1
	1993	2616	2411	203	4	1	1	16	14	1	1
United States	1980	3116	1163	1935	403	18	0	498	457	41	23
	1990	3390	2049	1319	161	21	20	398	362	36	16
	1991	4363	2211	2138	273	14	10	433	387	46	15
	1992	3765	1840	1885	292	40	36	371	322	48	32
	1993	3480	1894	1540	206	45	36	314	275	38	7
Japan	1980	15454	4202	10155	3050	1098	966	767	625	139	110
	1990	12518	3364	8743	1303	411	376	606	459	147	57
	1991	13618	3174	10066	1472	378	342	622	439	183	56
	1992	13346	3007	10230	1718	109	97	629	417	211	66
	1993	14499	2481	11655	1291	363	348	586	320	265	48
Australia, New Zealand	1980	698	218	438	42	0	0	66	66	0	2
	1990	855	382	473	142	0	0	20	19	1	2
	1991	970	412	558	110	0	0	25	24	1	1
	1992	1028	472	556	77	0	0	44	44	0	2
	1993	1099	396	703	98	0	0	18	17	0	1
Developing economies-Africa	1980	274	156	105	40	13	13	130	121	9	0
	1990	563	316	238	39	8	3	227	213	5	15
	1991	465	243	222	44	0	0	161	156	3	16
	1992	587	244	334	81	1	0	171	168	2	11
	1993	612	193	415	79	1	0	111	108	3	23
Developing economies-America	1980	1394	801	554	104	38	10	303	296	8	6
	1990	6370	3064	3207	608	96	73	928	878	50	12
	1991	6603	2835	3717	809	52	47	733	703	30	17
	1992	6374	2400	3943	582	27	14	725	699	25	13
	1993	6651	2396	4219	489	30	26	521	489	31	18
Developing economies-Europe/ 5	1980	229	101	32	16	96	14	70	54	17	0
	1990	843	532	204	66	107	14	467	412	55	0
	1991	556	350	135	43	71	9	309	273	36	0
	1992	474	273	177	15	24	1	224	177	47	0
	1993	366	237	107	6	23	3	188	163	24	0
Developing economies-Middle East	1980	243	22	212	190	1	0	21	20	1	0
	1990	1855	570	1199	547	65	62	368	309	58	4
	1991	1540	299	1162	431	74	68	120	107	12	1
	1992	1822	252	1532	501	36	28	136	112	23	0
	1993	2291	190	2066	569	23	18	78	60	18	0
Developing economies-Other Asia	1980	2835	1038	1588	596	146	106	160	153	7	1
	1990	7912	3679	3765	518	154	152	343	282	61	6
	1991	9048	4016	4814	681	204	196	316	252	63	5
	1992	10256	3613	6514	756	123	116	419	376	42	10
	1993	11835	3578	8131	749	124	110	218	203	15	12
Former USSR-Asia /9	1980	.	.	.	.	.	.	.	.	.	.
	1990	.	.	.	.	.	.	.	.	.	.
	1991	.	.	.	.	.	.	.	.	.	.
	1992	148	50	92	14	4	.	19	15	4	0
	1993	135	42	90	13	3	.	14	11	3	0
Developing economies-Oceania	1980	207	204	2	0	0	0	170	170	0	0
	1990	245	191	54	0	0	0	121	114	8	0
	1991	242	189	53	0	0	0	119	112	7	0
	1992	266	228	38	0	0	0	178	170	8	0
	1993	244	210	34	0	0	0	164	156	7	0

For general note and footnotes see end of table.

TABLEAU SPECIAL: B

Exportations mondiales par classes de marchandises et par régions (suite)

En millions de dollars E.-U. f.o.b.

Economies développées /2,3,4				Developing economies / Economies en voie de développement /1,3,4							← Exportations vers
Canada	U.S.A. / E.-U.	Japan / Japon	Australia New Zealand / Australie Nouvelle-Zélande	Africa / Afrique	America / Amerique: Total	America / Amerique: LAIA / ALADI	Asia / Asie: Mid.East / Moyen Orient	Asia / Asie: Other / Autres /9	Oceania / Océanie	Année	Exportations en provenance de ↓
Fer et acier (CTCI, Rev. 2 et Rev. 3, 67) (suite)											
.	1264	23	10	34	139	113	22	126	0	1980	Canada
.	1563	9	6	36	73	69	67	127	1	1990	
.	1600	16	15	23	48	44	38	485	1	1991	
.	2007	5	7	7	92	88	11	123	0	1992	
.	2385	3	7	9	55	52	1	137	0	1993	
537	.	52	38	171	1218	1089	202	336	3	1980	Etats-Unis
1374	.	212	28	81	815	694	74	345	3	1990	
1403	.	284	45	126	1171	1070	105	734	1	1991	
1280	.	111	28	92	1262	1151	157	371	2	1992	
1428	.	89	36	75	1013	902	71	380	1	1993	
250	2717	.	350	777	1392	1227	1855	6102	10	1980	Japon
173	2249	.	276	251	383	344	809	7269	25	1990	
158	2074	.	262	327	319	293	843	8543	33	1991	
137	1934	.	239	364	305	272	1062	8474	24	1992	
136	1458	.	252	314	323	297	675	10326	18	1993	
2	48	11	90	2	4	2	12	376	43	1980	Australie, Nouvelle-Zélande
18	199	57	86	1	0	0	80	337	55	1990	
14	185	82	105	1	3	3	70	427	56	1991	
22	201	85	118	1	1	1	48	451	55	1992	
15	153	85	126	1	7	7	31	610	54	1993	
0	12	14	0	23	0	0	14	67	0	1980	Economies en voie de développement-Afrique
0	45	27	1	145	2	1	69	22	0	1990	
0	31	33	1	136	2	1	64	20	0	1991	
0	31	30	1	176	5	1	121	31	0	1992	
0	21	38	0	193	3	1	157	61	0	1993	
27	388	73	4	49	374	312	41	90	0	1980	Economies en voie de développement-Amérique
90	1431	567	37	147	931	662	432	1689	0	1990	
80	1360	586	59	170	1229	968	540	1776	0	1991	
48	1209	373	30	154	1610	1247	400	1779	0	1992	
88	1386	351	31	85	1532	1192	213	2390	0	1993	
2	22	7	0	7	0	0	16	9	0	1980	Economies en voie de développement-Europe /5
5	44	14	0	35	1	0	154	13	0	1990	
3	29	9	0	23	0	0	103	9	0	1991	
1	38	8	0	9	0	0	30	7	0	1992	
1	35	12	0	3	0	0	24	15	0	1993	
0	1	0	0	7	0	0	203	1	0	1980	Economies en voie de développement-Moyen Orient
3	96	99	0	168	0	0	721	310	0	1990	
1	84	93	0	126	17	15	577	442	0	1991	
2	73	40	0	57	6	4	710	759	0	1992	
1	78	31	0	82	0	0	767	1217	0	1993	
18	435	381	43	83	83	53	480	939	3	1980	Economies en voie de développement-Autres Pays d'Asie
55	967	2189	117	52	74	38	337	3273	29	1990	
63	855	2634	142	121	92	39	499	4054	47	1991	
53	881	2092	155	102	92	64	540	5758	21	1992	
61	774	2343	167	117	93	64	409	7492	19	1993	
.	.	.	.	.	.	.	.	.	.	1980	l'ancienne URSS asiatique /9
.	.	.	.	.	.	.	.	.	.	1990	
.	.	.	.	.	.	.	.	.	.	1991	
0	23	8	0	3	4	2	39	47	0	1992	
0	21	7	0	3	4	2	32	51	0	1993	
0	21	13	0	0	0	0	0	2	1	1980	Economies en voie de développement-Océanie
1	21	48	0	0	1	1	0	45	8	1990	
1	21	48	0	0	1	1	0	46	6	1991	
0	12	38	0	0	0	0	0	34	4	1992	
0	11	35	0	0	0	0	0	32	2	1993	

Voir la fin du tableau pour la remarque générale et les notes.

SPECIAL TABLE: B

World exports by commodity classes and by regions (continued)

In million U.S. dollars f.o.b.

Non-ferrous metals (SITC, Rev. 2 and Rev. 3, 68)

Exports from ↓ / Exports to →	Year	World / Monde /1,2,3	Developed economies / Econ. dévelop-pées /2,3,4	Developing economies / Economies en voie de développement /1,3,4: Total	Developing economies: OPEC / OPEP	Eastern Europe and fmr. USSR-Europe / Europe de l'Est et l'anc. URSS-Europe: Total /2,3,7	Eastern Europe and fmr. USSR-Europe: Former USSR-Eur. /10	Developed Economies: Europe: Total /2	Developed Economies: Europe: EEC / CEE /2	Developed Economies: Europe: EFTA / AELE	Developed Economies: South Africa / Afrique du Sud
World /1,2,3	1980	49198	40148	6442	1291	1540	549	29517	23912	5591	102
	1990	69963	57220	11595	1564	828	267	37112	32231	4691	82
	1991	64251	51268	12373	1522	503	80	32637	28637	3971	99
	1992	67239	50633	15641	1744	760	99	34007	30033	3949	89
	1993	63288	46185	15729	1709	1068	196	29924	26151	3749	109
Developed economies /2,3,4	1980	35998	30198	4229	1002	726	252	23399	18299	5086	101
	1990	51252	43989	6899	1033	265	71	29611	25353	4229	71
	1991	48190	40369	7439	1052	303	63	26942	23277	3637	92
	1992	45958	37370	8144	1120	384	52	26431	23049	3362	77
	1993	42127	32963	8480	1110	449	54	22764	19586	3158	101
Developing economies /1,3,4	1980	12086	9155	2177	275	538	246	5363	5030	333	1
	1990	16720	11696	4575	493	239	19	6075	5852	221	11
	1991	14701	9708	4847	452	119	11	4616	4468	146	7
	1992	16895	9571	7110	613	68	26	4575	4418	154	12
	1993	16343	9213	6853	591	208	114	4334	4203	127	8
OPEC	1980	1386	1069	254	11	16	5	713	618	96	0
	1990	1986	1268	410	9	0	0	347	346	1	0
	1991	1752	1272	475	25	5	0	287	287	1	0
	1992	1957	1087	867	64	3	0	248	232	15	0
	1993	1439	769	670	62	0	0	176	162	14	0
Eastern Europe and the former USSR /2,3,7	1980	1115	794	36	14	276	51	755	583	172	0
	1990	1991	1535	121	38	324	177	1426	1026	240	0
	1991	1360	1191	87	19	82	6	1080	892	188	0
	1992	4387	3691	387	11	308	21	3001	2567	434	0
	1993	4818	4010	396	7	411	28	2825	2361	464	0
Former USSR /3	1980	1	0	0	0	0	.	0	0	0	0
	1990	...	...	...	...	...	.	...	...	...	...
	1991	...	...	...	...	...	.	...	...	...	...
	1992	.	.	.	.	.	.	.	.	.	.
	1993	.	.	.	.	.	.	.	.	.	.
Former USSR-Europe /8	1980	.	.	.	.	.	.	.	.	.	.
	1990	.	.	.	.	.	.	.	.	.	.
	1991	.	.	.	.	.	.	.	.	.	.
	1992	2964	2546	259	5	160	4	1962	1713	249	0
	1993	3327	2890	277	4	160	3	1790	1475	315	0
Developed economies-Europe /2	1980	23268	20999	1601	581	656	201	19132	14745	4373	69
	1990	32147	29438	2366	731	245	55	26088	22075	3985	56
	1991	29208	26598	2255	610	276	40	23442	20037	3377	69
	1992	29162	26416	2313	591	373	50	23554	20351	3182	44
	1993	26059	22979	2544	614	441	49	20395	17434	2943	48
European Economic Community /2	1980	18681	16845	1311	489	514	157	15464	11735	3716	65
	1990	24664	22306	2092	671	168	40	19956	16942	2987	55
	1991	22502	20202	2003	563	220	28	17983	15398	2559	67
	1992	22600	20234	2006	550	300	40	18180	15700	2459	42
	1993	20453	17717	2284	586	357	39	15838	13559	2262	45
European Free Trade Association	1980	4586	4154	290	92	142	44	3667	3010	657	4
	1990	7472	7121	274	60	77	16	6121	5122	998	2
	1991	6698	6389	252	47	57	12	5451	4632	818	2
	1992	6557	6176	307	41	73	9	5369	4646	722	2
	1993	5603	5259	260	28	83	11	4554	3872	682	3
Other developed economies	1980	12730	9200	2628	421	70	51	4267	3554	713	31
	1990	19105	14551	4534	302	20	16	3523	3278	244	15
	1991	18982	13771	5184	441	26	23	3500	3240	260	23
	1992	16796	10954	5831	530	11	2	2877	2697	180	33
	1993	16069	9984	5936	496	9	4	2369	2153	215	53

For general note and footnotes see end of table.

Exportations mondiales par classes de marchandises et par régions (suite)

En millions de dollars E.-U. f.o.b.

Economies développées /2,3,4				Developing economies Economies en voie de développement /1,3,4						← Exportations vers	
Canada	U.S.A. E.-U.	Japan Japon	Australia New Zealand Australie Nouvelle-Zélande	Africa Afrique	America Amerique Total	America Amerique LAIA ALADI	Asia Asie Mid.East Moyen Orient	Asia Asie Other Autres /9	Oceania Océanie	Année	Exportations en provenance de ↓
Métaux non férreux (CTCI, Rev. 2 et Rev. 3, 68)											
695	6335	3163	192	604	1739	1578	941	2883	10	1980	Monde /1,2,3
1708	9669	7977	422	666	1416	1213	1462	7872	15	1990	
1479	8463	7943	395	621	1635	1464	1260	8732	16	1991	
1521	8044	6273	443	597	2099	1873	1680	11042	16	1992	
1554	8270	5634	438	514	2082	1853	1699	11221	14	1993	
623	4280	1469	182	541	870	743	699	2024	10	1980	Economies dévelopées /2,3,4
1651	7620	4463	335	499	820	721	1011	4444	10	1990	
1447	6803	4520	325	471	865	769	933	5071	13	1991	
1451	5849	2951	370	439	1078	979	897	5623	12	1992	
1467	5654	2362	375	398	1114	1000	947	5902	11	1993	
72	2022	1687	11	62	868	834	226	851	0	1980	Economies en voie de développement /1,3,4
52	2013	3454	85	160	593	491	385	3408	3	1990	
30	1627	3356	67	145	766	693	292	3636	3	1991	
21	1865	3021	68	147	987	885	688	5214	3	1992	
25	1838	2935	62	103	939	841	661	5097	3	1993	
4	20	332	0	1	52	51	15	183	0	1980	OPEP
1	200	719	1	14	100	86	35	258	0	1990	
0	121	863	1	7	101	89	43	324	0	1991	
1	118	718	3	4	135	122	182	546	0	1992	
0	117	473	2	1	168	155	180	322	0	1993	
0	32	6	0	1	2	0	16	8	0	1980	Europe de l'Est et l'ancienne URSS /2,3,7
5	36	61	2	7	2	1	66	19	1	1990	
2	32	67	2	4	3	3	35	26	0	1991	
49	330	301	4	11	35	9	95	205	0	1992	
63	778	337	2	13	30	11	91	222	0	1993	
0	0	0	0	0	0	0	0	0	0	1980	L'ancienne URSS /3
...	...	...	...	...	...	...	...	...	...	1990	
...	...	...	...	...	...	...	...	...	...	1991	
.	.	.	.	.	.	.	.	.	.	1992	
.	.	.	.	.	.	.	.	.	.	1993	
.	.	.	.	.	.	.	.	.	.	1980	L'ancienne URSS-Europe /8
.	.	.	.	.	.	.	.	.	.	1990	
.	.	.	.	.	.	.	.	.	.	1991	
43	286	255	0	3	33	9	37	175	0	1992	
60	740	299	0	3	28	10	46	185	0	1993	
66	1335	263	48	452	246	192	527	291	2	1980	Economies développées-Europe /2
196	1888	930	125	448	211	171	780	809	3	1990	
160	1644	986	137	417	199	156	679	870	5	1991	
117	1617	756	145	383	227	186	642	962	4	1992	
115	1479	619	138	355	216	178	701	1162	3	1993	
41	1014	154	38	401	203	154	420	230	2	1980	Communauté Economique Européenne /2
158	1386	521	89	426	185	152	717	671	3	1990	
130	1224	563	86	396	164	131	634	730	5	1991	
98	1223	424	99	367	183	154	599	775	4	1992	
88	1140	345	97	340	176	148	667	1007	3	1993	
25	320	110	10	51	43	37	106	62	0	1980	Association Européenne de Libre Echange
38	502	409	36	22	26	19	63	138	0	1990	
30	420	423	52	21	34	26	45	140	0	1991	
19	394	332	46	17	44	31	44	187	0	1992	
27	339	275	41	16	40	30	34	154	0	1993	
556	2946	1206	134	89	623	552	172	1733	7	1980	Autres economies développées
1454	5732	3533	210	51	609	550	231	3635	7	1990	
1287	5159	3534	187	54	667	612	254	4200	8	1991	
1334	4232	2195	225	56	850	793	254	4661	9	1992	
1352	4175	1742	237	43	898	823	246	4740	8	1993	

Voir la fin du tableau pour la remarque générale et les notes.

SPECIAL TABLE: B

World exports by commodity classes and by regions (continued)

In million U.S. dollars f.o.b.

Exports to → / ↓ Exports from	Year	World Monde /1,2,3	Developed economies Econ. dévelop-pées /2,3,4	Developing economies Economies en voie de développement /1,3,4: Total	Developing economies: OPEC OPEP	Eastern Europe and fmr. USSR-Europe Europe de l'Est et l'anc. URSS-Europe: Total /2,3,7	Eastern Europe and fmr. USSR-Europe: Former USSR-Eur. /10	Developed Economies: Europe: Total /2	Developed Economies: Europe: EEC CEE /2	Developed Economies: Europe: EFTA AELE	Developed Economies: South Africa Afrique du Sud
		Non-ferrous metals (SITC, Rev. 2 and Rev. 3, 68) (continued)									
Canada	1980	3910	3393	398	60	14	13	859	801	58	1
	1990	5438	5062	376	21	0	0	683	611	72	1
	1991	5303	4933	370	33	0	0	875	774	101	2
	1992	5636	5187	449	27	0	0	1096	994	101	2
	1993	5424	5031	393	41	0	0	992	904	87	2
United States	1980	4939	4001	934	140	3	0	2522	1890	632	18
	1990	5189	3810	1377	105	3	1	827	768	58	3
	1991	5715	3954	1760	203	1	1	892	829	62	10
	1992	4976	3187	1787	212	2	1	830	765	65	6
	1993	4597	2867	1724	173	5	4	778	667	111	6
Japan	1980	1791	822	917	153	52	37	255	234	21	7
	1990	2230	766	1447	82	17	14	156	149	7	7
	1991	2197	546	1628	63	23	23	138	132	6	5
	1992	2399	492	1905	102	1	1	105	98	8	5
	1993	2546	476	2069	91	1	1	100	94	7	2
Australia, New Zealand	1980	1418	928	371	68	0	0	590	590	1	5
	1990	3140	1934	1206	92	0	0	407	397	9	3
	1991	2964	1654	1310	139	0	0	288	285	2	5
	1992	2967	1430	1537	188	0	0	338	337	1	20
	1993	3022	1261	1620	190	0	0	254	252	2	43
Developing economies-Africa	1980	2646	2212	201	16	21	12	1355	1317	38	0
	1990	2130	1895	366	63	9	0	1392	1376	15	10
	1991	1591	1384	187	64	12	0	998	968	31	6
	1992	1784	1509	254	74	3	0	938	914	24	7
	1993	2287	2008	267	92	0	0	1220	1197	24	5
Developing economies-America	1980	4775	3588	1136	46	52	35	2070	2013	57	0
	1990	8195	6900	1222	149	65	2	3534	3390	144	0
	1991	7159	5690	1463	134	3	2	2814	2742	72	0
	1992	7461	5503	1840	165	0	0	2638	2581	57	3
	1993	6920	5108	1735	118	37	0	2447	2395	52	1
Developing economies-Europe/ 5	1980	468	183	34	16	250	46	126	97	29	0
	1990	920	723	52	17	146	6	665	617	48	0
	1991	610	479	34	11	97	4	441	409	32	0
	1992	529	431	78	3	20	2	409	375	34	0
	1993	329	267	55	1	8	1	241	223	18	0
Developing economies-Middle East	1980	626	487	135	79	1	0	461	342	119	0
	1990	1202	448	415	173	12	9	158	150	6	0
	1991	1118	696	404	147	4	3	148	141	6	0
	1992	1457	563	886	218	3	1	175	151	20	0
	1993	1193	398	773	220	5	3	137	113	20	0
Developing economies-Other Asia	1980	3487	2601	671	117	213	153	1302	1212	90	0
	1990	4255	1715	2519	92	7	1	327	319	8	0
	1991	4207	1445	2757	96	3	2	215	209	6	1
	1992	5652	1555	4052	153	42	23	416	397	18	2
	1993	5604	1423	4022	160	158	110	289	275	14	2
Former USSR-Asia /9	1980	.	.	.	.	.	.	.	.	.	.
	1990	.	.	.	.	.	.	.	.	.	.
	1991	.	.	.	.	.	.	.	.	.	.
	1992	323	57	260	43	4	.	46	37	9	0
	1993	306	72	225	40	9	.	45	36	9	0
Developing economies-Oceania	1980	84	84	0	0	0	0	48	48	0	0
	1990	18	16	1	0	0	0	0	0	0	0
	1991	16	15	1	0	0	0	0	0	0	0
	1992	12	11	1	0	0	0	0	0	0	0
	1993	9	9	1	0	0	0	0	0	0	0

For general note and footnotes see end of table.

TABLEAU SPECIAL: B

Exportations mondiales par classes de marchandises et par régions (suite)

En millions de dollars E.-U. f.o.b.

Economies développées /2,3,4: Canada	Economies développées: U.S.A. E.-U.	Economies développées: Japan Japon	Economies développées: Australia New Zealand Australie Nouvelle-Zélande	Developing economies / Economies en voie de développement /1,3,4: Africa Afrique	America Amerique: Total	America Amerique: LAIA ALADI	Asia Asie: Mid.East Moyen Orient	Asia Asie: Other Autres /9	Oceania Océanie	Année	← Exportations vers / Exportations en provenance de ↓
Métaux non férreux (CTCI, Rev. 2 et Rev. 3, 68) (suite)											
.	2324	179	8	25	121	102	12	239	0	1980	Canada
.	3976	355	14	11	23	18	75	268	0	1990	
.	3724	304	2	17	20	17	47	285	0	1991	
.	3778	288	5	14	27	25	45	363	0	1992	
.	3758	258	6	8	41	39	57	286	0	1993	
548	.	846	34	27	471	428	58	374	1	1980	Etats-Unis
1353	.	1571	27	13	536	484	57	771	0	1990	
1216	.	1768	32	23	613	563	128	994	0	1991	
1282	.	1010	34	20	782	728	132	853	0	1992	
1325	.	700	34	13	812	741	122	776	0	1993	
8	531	.	17	21	31	21	76	788	0	1980	Japon
30	540	.	27	6	34	33	44	1362	0	1990	
16	362	.	22	2	21	21	29	1576	0	1991	
38	312	.	25	6	24	23	57	1818	1	1992	
16	324	.	25	5	29	29	48	1986	0	1993	
0	77	181	75	14	0	0	24	327	6	1980	Australie, Nouvelle-Zélande
13	78	1310	123	7	8	8	14	1171	6	1990	
3	49	1194	116	1	4	4	12	1286	7	1991	
4	73	838	157	4	6	6	20	1499	8	1992	
6	41	749	168	1	7	7	18	1586	8	1993	
0	406	452	0	27	61	61	10	53	0	1980	Economies en voie de développement-Afrique
5	81	408	0	61	19	13	45	235	0	1990	
5	61	314	0	74	16	11	27	68	0	1991	
5	61	498	0	94	17	12	28	111	0	1992	
4	62	717	0	66	14	10	29	153	0	1993	
69	876	573	0	6	792	762	3	226	0	1980	Economies en voie de développement-Amérique
30	1600	1717	14	8	563	472	54	580	1	1990	
12	1287	1565	7	17	735	674	25	685	0	1991	
7	1540	1304	6	9	937	859	18	876	0	1992	
5	1518	1128	4	5	886	812	8	835	0	1993	
0	51	5	0	9	5	5	7	12	0	1980	Economies en voie de développement-Europe /5
2	53	1	1	5	4	1	31	12	0	1990	
1	35	0	1	2	3	1	21	8	0	1991	
1	19	1	1	2	1	1	6	3	0	1992	
0	20	0	2	1	2	2	3	3	0	1993	
0	1	26	0	1	0	0	99	34	0	1980	Economies en voie de développement-Moyen Orient
3	54	232	2	69	1	1	210	135	0	1990	
4	47	496	2	39	0	0	167	198	0	1991	
2	24	355	6	11	1	0	387	486	0	1992	
2	24	229	5	7	3	3	401	360	0	1993	
3	669	615	10	18	10	7	106	525	0	1980	Economies en voie de développement-Autres Pays d'Asie
12	225	1097	52	17	6	3	45	2444	3	1990	
8	196	981	43	14	12	7	53	2676	3	1991	
7	221	864	44	31	31	12	249	3738	3	1992	
14	214	860	42	23	33	13	219	3745	2	1993	
.	.	.	.	.	.	.	.	.	.	1980	l'ancienne URSS asiatique /9
.	.	.	.	.	.	.	.	.	.	1990	
.	.	.	.	.	.	.	.	.	.	1991	
0	1	10	0	9	21	6	192	39	0	1992	
0	0	28	0	5	21	5	161	38	0	1993	
0	20	16	0	0	0	0	0	0	0	1980	Economies en voie de développement-Océanie
0	1	0	15	0	0	0	0	1	0	1990	
0	1	0	14	0	0	0	0	1	0	1991	
0	0	0	11	0	0	0	0	1	0	1992	
0	0	0	9	0	0	0	0	1	0	1993	

Voir la fin du tableau pour la remarque générale et les notes.

SPECIAL TABLE: B

World exports by commodity classes and by regions (continued)

In million U.S. dollars f.o.b.

Other manufactured metal products (SITC, Rev. 2 and Rev. 3, 691-695, 699 and 812)

Exports from ↓ / Exports to →	Year	World Monde /1,2,3	Developed economies Econ. dévelop-pées /2,3,4	Developing economies Economies en voie de développement /1,3,4 Total	OPEC OPEP	Eastern Europe and fmr. USSR-Europe Europe de l'Est et l'anc. URSS-Europe Total /2,3,7	Former USSR-Eur. /10	Developed Economies: Europe Total /2	EEC CEE /2	EFTA AELE	South Africa Afrique du Sud
World /1,2,3	1980	37377	22924	12891	6090	1373	482	17489	13931	3504	398
	1990	66057	50983	13519	2766	1429	641	37495	30284	7108	336
	1991	68945	52389	15253	3177	1251	470	38618	31834	6671	308
	1992	74674	55899	17207	3656	1493	407	41195	34582	6509	345
	1993	71429	50366	18872	3287	1977	538	34327	28428	5818	329
Developed economies /2,3,4	1980	33403	21372	10966	5306	912	344	16891	13397	3441	382
	1990	54718	44307	9368	1942	1019	441	35178	28237	6842	308
	1991	56615	45161	10375	2274	1057	360	36098	29561	6428	263
	1992	60703	47758	11556	2637	1351	329	38436	32097	6238	285
	1993	54813	41427	11595	2168	1603	419	31213	25613	5523	253
Developing economies /1,3,4	1980	3262	1357	1770	736	100	43	434	393	41	16
	1990	10477	6222	3983	804	207	125	1888	1686	199	29
	1991	11764	6801	4795	892	139	93	2114	1913	197	45
	1992	13159	7586	5463	1003	74	48	2223	2015	205	59
	1993	15188	8021	7044	1080	98	68	2220	2023	193	76
OPEC	1980	183	28	154	96	0	0	23	23	0	0
	1990	433	118	279	99	7	7	34	33	0	0
	1991	398	110	276	118	8	8	39	38	1	0
	1992	395	110	278	91	6	5	34	33	0	0
	1993	450	127	312	105	10	10	34	34	0	0
Eastern Europe and the former USSR /2,3,7	1980	712	195	155	48	361	95	164	141	23	0
	1990	862	455	167	20	203	75	429	361	67	0
	1991	566	428	83	11	55	17	406	359	46	0
	1992	812	555	188	16	68	30	536	470	65	1
	1993	1428	918	233	40	276	51	894	792	101	1
Former USSR /3	1980	122	7	52	0	64	.	7	6	0	0
	1990	...	...	...	...	...	.	...	...	...	...
	1991	...	...	...	...	...	.	...	...	...	...
	1992	.	.	.	.	.	.	.	.	.	.
	1993	.	.	.	.	.	.	.	.	.	.
Former USSR-Europe /8	1980	.	.	.	.	.	.	.	.	.	.
	1990	.	.	.	.	.	.	.	.	.	.
	1991	.	.	.	.	.	.	.	.	.	.
	1992	206	39	134	0	34	13	38	23	15	0
	1993	252	65	144	0	43	17	63	48	15	0
Developed economies-Europe /2	1980	24592	17132	6635	3683	804	274	15537	12212	3273	254
	1990	42784	36585	5260	1457	923	360	33151	26458	6596	238
	1991	43570	37164	5400	1570	991	314	33962	27651	6204	196
	1992	46746	39456	5972	1854	1285	302	36202	30129	5972	207
	1993	39765	32491	5582	1531	1509	366	29209	23831	5303	182
European Economic Community /2	1980	20723	14075	6115	3430	513	136	12811	10322	2438	225
	1990	35702	30329	4768	1317	590	206	27600	22343	5164	221
	1991	36672	31050	4887	1413	720	234	28504	23419	4983	179
	1992	39422	33045	5392	1689	951	207	30457	25558	4801	187
	1993	33144	26779	5061	1408	1134	243	24150	19778	4298	161
European Free Trade Association	1980	3857	3048	519	252	291	138	2717	1880	834	29
	1990	7072	6249	490	138	333	155	5543	4108	1432	17
	1991	6889	6108	511	155	271	80	5451	4226	1221	17
	1992	7316	6405	578	163	334	95	5740	4565	1171	20
	1993	6614	5706	519	121	375	123	5054	4047	1005	21
Other developed economies	1980	8811	4240	4331	1623	108	70	1354	1186	168	128
	1990	11934	7722	4108	485	95	80	2028	1779	245	70
	1991	13045	7997	4975	704	66	46	2136	1910	224	67
	1992	13957	8302	5584	783	66	27	2234	1968	266	79
	1993	15048	8936	6013	636	93	53	2003	1782	221	71

For general note and footnotes see end of table.

Exportations mondiales par classes de marchandises et par régions (suite)

En millions de dollars E.-U. f.o.b.

Economies développées /2,3,4: Canada	U.S.A. / E.-U.	Japan / Japon	Australia New Zealand / Australie Nouvelle-Zélande	Developing economies / Economies en voie de développement /1,3,4: Africa / Afrique	America / Amerique: Total	America / Amerique: LAIA / ALADI	Asia / Asie: Mid.East / Moyen Orient	Asia / Asie: Other / Autres /9	Oceania / Océanie	Année	← Exportations vers / Exportations en provenance de ↓
Autres produits en metal manufacturés (CTCI, Rev. 2 et Rev. 3, 691-695, 699 et 812)											
1190	2925	341	480	3172	2291	1663	4223	2859	83	1980	Monde /1,2,3
2790	7752	1532	837	2067	2654	1810	2103	6246	167	1990	
2898	7811	1674	827	1914	3146	2371	2508	7265	185	1991	
3070	8291	1678	1033	2001	3603	2818	2899	8205	186	1992	
3464	9378	1670	912	1840	3984	3150	2683	9916	149	1993	
1139	2177	279	407	2885	1995	1463	3615	2174	77	1980	Economies dévelopées /2,3,4
2539	4718	741	599	1685	2140	1532	1404	3754	131	1990	
2612	4583	795	577	1537	2550	1977	1784	4151	145	1991	
2779	4618	788	591	1653	2913	2338	2112	4552	138	1992	
3170	5206	706	627	1458	3129	2538	1838	4826	115	1993	
47	721	62	73	266	273	198	563	661	6	1980	Economies en voie de développement /1,3,4
249	3017	790	238	368	468	273	661	2442	36	1990	
285	3212	878	249	367	574	391	704	3102	39	1991	
290	3661	890	442	332	671	473	755	3541	48	1992	
292	4158	964	285	353	838	604	797	4957	34	1993	
0	4	0	0	23	10	8	104	17	0	1980	OPEP
2	61	21	1	4	59	29	182	34	0	1990	
3	49	17	1	3	53	37	168	50	1	1991	
1	47	26	2	5	80	54	121	68	4	1992	
0	50	34	8	12	92	60	117	87	5	1993	
4	27	0	0	21	22	2	45	23	0	1980	Europe de l'Est et l'ancienne URSS /2,3,7
2	16	0	1	14	46	5	38	51	0	1990	
1	16	0	0	11	22	3	20	12	0	1991	
1	11	1	0	15	19	7	32	111	0	1992	
3	14	0	1	29	17	9	48	133	0	1993	
0	0	0	0	0	17	0	0	9	0	1980	L'ancienne URSS /3
...	...	...	...	...	...	...	...	...	...	1990	
...	...	...	...	...	...	...	...	...	...	1991	
.	.	.	.	.	.	.	.	.	.	1992	
.	.	.	.	.	.	.	.	.	.	1993	
.	.	.	.	.	.	.	.	.	.	1980	L'ancienne URSS-Europe /8
.	.	.	.	.	.	.	.	.	.	1990	
.	.	.	.	.	.	.	.	.	.	1991	
0	0	0	0	2	14	5	13	105	0	1992	
0	0	0	0	2	12	6	16	114	0	1993	
171	809	139	166	2537	831	600	2399	630	22	1980	Economies développées-Europe /2
351	1984	407	283	1562	798	425	1146	1455	51	1990	
325	1824	425	257	1411	930	601	1398	1410	46	1991	
281	1864	422	278	1491	913	614	1671	1661	50	1992	
293	1946	389	273	1259	967	675	1481	1607	43	1993	
133	625	89	141	2395	769	549	2211	545	22	1980	Communauté Economique Européenne /2
271	1577	285	221	1495	750	385	1025	1251	50	1990	
256	1463	296	198	1342	872	555	1279	1185	45	1991	
216	1483	307	216	1435	845	559	1537	1384	49	1992	
232	1557	288	216	1212	906	622	1374	1356	43	1993	
38	183	50	26	141	62	51	187	86	1	1980	Association Européenne de Libre Echange
80	408	122	62	65	49	40	121	204	1	1990	
69	361	129	59	67	58	46	119	226	1	1991	
66	381	115	62	55	67	55	134	277	1	1992	
61	389	101	57	45	61	53	108	250	0	1993	
968	1368	140	241	348	1164	864	1217	1544	55	1980	Autres economies développées
2188	2733	335	315	123	1342	1107	258	2299	80	1990	
2287	2759	370	320	125	1621	1377	386	2740	99	1991	
2497	2754	366	312	162	2000	1723	441	2891	88	1992	
2877	3260	317	354	200	2162	1863	357	3219	72	1993	

Voir la fin du tableau pour la remarque générale et les notes.

SPECIAL TABLE: B

World exports by commodity classes and by regions (continued)

In million U.S. dollars f.o.b.

Exports from ↓ / Exports to →	Year	World Monde /1,2,3	Developed economies Econ. dévelop-pées /2,3,4	Developing economies Economies en voie de développement /1,3,4 Total	Developing economies OPEC OPEP	Eastern Europe and fmr. USSR-Europe Europe de l'Est et l'anc. URSS-Europe Total /2,3,7	Eastern Europe and fmr. USSR-Europe Former USSR-Eur. /10	Developed Economies Europe Total /2	Developed Economies Europe EEC CEE /2	Developed Economies Europe EFTA AELE	Developed Economies South Africa Afrique du Sud
Other manufactured metal products (SITC, Rev. 2 and Rev. 3, 691-695, 699 and 812) (continued)											
Canada	1980	877	718	149	51	10	0	96	87	10	5
	1990	1589	1495	92	14	2	2	104	91	12	8
	1991	1464	1367	94	14	3	2	94	83	11	1
	1992	1532	1447	79	13	6	3	83	73	10	1
	1993	1832	1734	84	12	13	9	95	85	10	1
United States	1980	3943	1986	1944	694	14	8	791	713	78	51
	1990	5477	3675	1793	143	9	3	1118	1008	110	22
	1991	6107	3847	2243	237	18	13	1172	1065	107	23
	1992	6598	4043	2541	268	14	7	1130	1017	112	24
	1993	7107	4273	2804	248	30	19	1067	970	96	23
Japan	1980	3590	1389	2117	863	84	62	423	348	74	65
	1990	4093	2076	1934	278	83	75	615	506	109	35
	1991	4566	2283	2242	339	41	31	668	572	95	37
	1992	4842	2258	2549	387	35	15	783	653	130	48
	1993	5130	2359	2736	316	35	22	608	508	100	39
Australia, New Zealand	1980	216	102	114	14	0	0	16	14	2	5
	1990	354	166	188	43	0	0	24	21	3	1
	1991	473	175	297	104	2	1	29	28	2	2
	1992	458	171	285	110	1	1	27	25	2	2
	1993	439	199	240	50	1	1	34	32	2	2
Developing economies-Africa	1980	49	25	22	5	0	0	24	24	0	0
	1990	153	58	87	34	7	7	45	44	1	8
	1991	188	71	107	58	9	9	60	59	1	8
	1992	172	73	91	47	6	6	61	61	0	8
	1993	207	97	98	46	10	10	78	78	1	9
Developing economies-America	1980	360	117	236	50	7	0	19	16	4	0
	1990	1052	645	404	32	2	2	81	73	8	5
	1991	1193	745	447	44	0	0	83	74	9	3
	1992	1720	1185	528	62	0	0	78	72	6	3
	1993	2095	1409	684	62	1	1	93	88	5	3
Developing economies-Europe/ 5	1980	243	76	84	56	83	37	52	46	6	0
	1990	470	224	140	74	107	57	196	163	32	0
	1991	313	147	95	50	71	38	130	108	21	0
	1992	382	219	139	16	23	10	210	176	34	0
	1993	309	202	84	10	24	13	192	157	34	0
Developing economies-Middle East	1980	210	9	187	135	1	1	7	7	0	0
	1990	512	118	356	237	8	5	98	88	9	0
	1991	469	138	305	212	16	14	113	105	8	1
	1992	479	141	313	239	14	11	124	117	6	0
	1993	499	132	321	246	30	27	114	110	4	2
Developing economies-Other Asia	1980	2400	1130	1241	490	9	5	331	299	31	16
	1990	8283	5173	2993	427	82	55	1468	1317	149	16
	1991	9595	5698	3837	529	43	31	1728	1568	158	34
	1992	10398	5966	4385	639	31	22	1750	1589	159	48
	1993	12074	6180	5855	716	33	17	1744	1591	149	62
Former USSR-Asia /9	1980	.	.	.	.	.	.	.	.	.	.
	1990	.	.	.	.	.	.	.	.	.	.
	1991	.	.	.	.	.	.	.	.	.	.
	1992	5	1	4	1	0	.	0	0	0	0
	1993	3	0	3	0	0	.	0	0	0	0
Developing economies-Oceania	1980	1	1	1	0	0	0	1	1	0	0
	1990	8	4	4	0	0	0	0	0	0	0
	1991	6	2	4	0	0	0	0	0	0	0
	1992	9	3	6	0	0	0	0	0	0	0
	1993	4	2	2	0	0	0	0	0	0	0

For general note and footnotes see end of table.

TABLEAU SPECIAL: B

Exportations mondiales par classes de marchandises et par régions (suite)

En millions de dollars E.-U. f.o.b.

Economies développées /2,3,4				Developing economies Economies en voie de développement /1,3,4						← Exportations vers	
Canada	U.S.A. E.-U.	Japan Japon	Australia New Zealand Australie Nouvelle-Zélande	Africa Afrique	America Amerique Total	America Amerique LAIA ALADI	Asia Asie Mid.East Moyen Orient	Asia Asie Other Autres /9	Oceania Océanie	Année	Exportations en provenance de ↓
Autres produits en metal manufacturés (CTCI, Rev. 2 et Rev. 3, 691-695, 699 et 812) (suite)											
.	589	8	16	27	55	29	38	28	1	1980	Canada
.	1357	9	16	10	26	12	6	46	3	1990	
.	1256	6	8	14	21	8	4	52	3	1991	
.	1347	6	9	8	24	11	6	40	0	1992	
.	1620	7	9	5	24	11	7	47	0	1993	
899	.	127	82	176	953	723	487	319	6	1980	Etats-Unis
2098	.	294	100	36	1149	946	114	487	4	1990	
2187	.	322	96	42	1407	1187	178	610	4	1991	
2417	.	323	108	31	1707	1457	191	606	6	1992	
2761	.	272	110	58	1879	1607	169	691	6	1993	
64	746	.	89	140	151	108	683	1135	7	1980	Japon
71	1258	.	94	49	126	109	131	1609	18	1990	
82	1380	.	112	43	153	143	193	1827	25	1991	
65	1268	.	90	44	251	240	229	2008	16	1992	
95	1501	.	114	54	232	220	160	2282	8	1993	
4	18	5	53	4	3	2	8	59	41	1980	Australie, Nouvelle-Zélande
9	22	13	97	2	2	2	6	123	55	1990	
8	22	18	94	1	2	1	9	218	67	1991	
9	27	15	90	1	5	4	9	204	66	1992	
12	29	15	106	2	11	10	12	158	58	1993	
0	1	0	0	19	0	0	2	0	0	1980	Economies en voie de développement-Afrique
0	3	2	0	73	0	0	10	3	0	1990	
1	1	1	0	94	0	0	9	3	0	1991	
1	2	1	0	76	0	0	12	3	0	1992	
0	0	9	0	77	0	0	12	9	0	1993	
4	90	2	2	14	207	155	13	1	0	1980	Economies en voie de développement-Amérique
15	529	6	9	20	330	200	11	42	1	1990	
28	615	8	7	17	393	272	12	24	1	1991	
27	1041	30	6	8	477	347	18	25	0	1992	
30	1248	27	7	18	623	455	17	26	1	1993	
1	23	0	0	38	1	0	37	8	0	1980	Economies en voie de développement-Europe /5
3	23	0	0	42	3	2	57	38	0	1990	
2	15	0	0	28	3	3	38	26	0	1991	
1	7	0	0	7	1	0	14	8	0	1992	
1	9	0	0	6	0	0	8	8	0	1993	
0	1	0	0	25	0	0	150	12	0	1980	Economies en voie de développement-Moyen Orient
0	18	0	1	20	0	0	318	13	0	1990	
0	21	1	0	12	0	0	272	14	0	1991	
1	14	0	1	21	0	0	274	12	0	1992	
0	14	0	0	18	1	1	280	18	0	1993	
43	606	60	71	170	65	42	360	640	5	1980	Economies en voie de développement-Autres Pays d'Asie
230	2444	782	224	213	135	71	265	2345	33	1990	
254	2560	867	240	215	178	116	372	3033	37	1991	
261	2598	857	434	220	193	125	437	3488	46	1992	
260	2887	927	276	234	214	148	480	4895	32	1993	
.	.	.	.	.	.	.	.	.	.	1980	l'ancienne URSS asiatique /9
.	.	.	.	.	.	.	.	.	.	1990	
.	.	.	.	.	.	.	.	.	.	1991	
0	0	0	0	0	0	0	3	1	0	1992	
0	0	0	0	0	0	0	2	1	0	1993	
0	0	0	0	0	0	0	0	0	1	1980	Economies en voie de développement-Océanie
0	0	0	3	0	0	0	0	1	3	1990	
0	0	0	2	0	0	0	0	2	2	1991	
0	0	1	2	0	0	0	0	5	2	1992	
0	0	1	1	0	0	0	0	1	1	1993	

Voir la fin du tableau pour la remarque générale et les notes.

SPECIAL TABLE: B

World exports by commodity classes and by regions (continued)

In million U.S. dollars f.o.b.

Clothing (SITC, Rev. 2 and Rev. 3, 84)

Exports from ↓ / Exports to →	Year	World Monde /1,2,3	Developed economies Econ. dévelop-pées /2,3,4	Developing economies Economies en voie de développement /1,3,4 Total	Developing economies OPEC OPEP	Eastern Europe and fmr. USSR-Europe Europe de l'Est et l'anc. URSS-Europe Total /2,3,7	Eastern Europe and fmr. USSR-Europe Former USSR-Eur. /10	Developed Economies: Europe Total /2	Developed Economies: Europe EEC CEE /2	Developed Economies: Europe EFTA AELE	Developed Economies: South Africa Afrique du Sud
World /1,2,3	1980	38693	30924	5261	1953	2394	1653	22646	18077	4511	65
	1990	108776	89574	14097	2148	4830	3618	55719	45823	9752	76
	1991	119161	97601	17684	2705	3787	2277	62437	52450	9838	125
	1992	135865	109263	22200	2997	4317	2668	68870	58336	10372	153
	1993	134491	108371	21198	3187	4843	2837	63778	54600	9049	195
Developed economies /2,3,4	1980	19997	17352	2166	718	406	247	15947	12307	3585	26
	1990	45002	40108	4136	446	749	304	34715	27193	7389	23
	1991	47251	41815	4532	477	896	289	36811	29500	7179	30
	1992	52296	45161	5841	670	1287	491	39903	32378	7383	27
	1993	46736	38765	6523	659	1426	562	33241	27077	6051	25
Developing economies /1,3,4	1980	16898	13035	2997	1199	842	473	6227	5385	840	39
	1990	61065	48343	9893	1686	2567	1913	20012	17797	2204	53
	1991	69870	54220	13111	2220	2459	1644	24161	21687	2457	96
	1992	80725	61709	16282	2314	2656	1891	26736	24039	2677	126
	1993	83878	66085	14614	2517	3123	2095	27168	24445	2707	171
OPEC	1980	188	56	131	69	0	0	44	38	6	0
	1990	2125	1637	316	165	22	1	714	664	49	0
	1991	2686	2013	646	307	27	3	1118	1059	58	0
	1992	3772	2830	914	335	26	16	1442	1376	65	1
	1993	3937	2922	964	343	51	31	1375	1311	64	0
Eastern Europe and the former USSR /2,3,7	1980	1799	537	98	37	1146	932	472	385	86	0
	1990	2709	1123	68	16	1514	1402	993	833	159	0
	1991	2041	1566	41	8	433	345	1466	1264	202	0
	1992	2844	2393	77	13	374	286	2230	1919	311	0
	1993	3877	3522	61	11	294	180	3369	3078	291	0
Former USSR /3	1980	29	0	29	0	0	.	0	0	0	0
	1990	...	...	...	...	...	.	...	...	...	...
	1991	...	...	...	...	...	.	...	...	...	...
	1992	.	.	.	.	.	.	.	.	.	.
	1993	.	.	.	.	.	.	.	.	.	.
Former USSR-Europe /8	1980	.	.	.	.	.	.	.	.	.	.
	1990	.	.	.	.	.	.	.	.	.	.
	1991	.	.	.	.	.	.	.	.	.	.
	1992	163	109	11	2	43	39	106	84	22	0
	1993	202	120	16	2	65	59	117	89	28	0
Developed economies-Europe /2	1980	17704	15974	1354	569	373	220	15099	11623	3422	16
	1990	40886	37774	2382	357	721	282	33693	26257	7304	19
	1991	42270	39124	2279	361	858	261	35644	28439	7075	23
	1992	46068	42057	2815	535	1188	403	38638	31214	7283	20
	1993	39621	35293	2958	526	1349	493	32075	25996	5967	20
European Economic Community /2	1980	15438	13942	1319	554	174	50	13123	10514	2556	15
	1990	37889	35088	2309	335	483	118	31148	24554	6462	18
	1991	39458	36541	2217	339	691	202	33179	26712	6337	22
	1992	43207	39482	2740	504	978	317	36174	29438	6596	20
	1993	37217	33160	2885	501	1150	408	30052	24484	5457	20
European Free Trade Association	1980	2066	1849	33	13	184	170	1795	942	853	1
	1990	2817	2525	69	19	223	150	2388	1549	838	1
	1991	2646	2436	54	16	156	48	2321	1586	735	1
	1992	2684	2433	66	21	186	62	2325	1638	686	1
	1993	2251	2002	62	17	187	74	1895	1385	510	1
Other developed economies	1980	2293	1378	812	149	34	27	848	685	163	10
	1990	4116	2334	1754	89	28	22	1021	936	84	4
	1991	4981	2690	2253	116	38	27	1167	1062	104	7
	1992	6228	3104	3026	136	99	87	1265	1164	100	7
	1993	7114	3472	3565	133	77	69	1166	1081	84	4

For general note and footnotes see end of table.

Exportations mondiales par classes de marchandises et par régions (suite)

En millions de dollars E.-U. f.o.b.

Economies développées /2,3,4: Canada	U.S.A. E.-U.	Japan Japon	Australia New Zealand Australie Nouvelle-Zélande	Developing economies Economies en voie de développement /1,3,4: Africa Afrique	America Amerique: Total	America Amerique: LAIA ALADI	Asia Asie: Mid.East Moyen Orient	Asia Asie: Other Autres /9	Oceania Océanie	Année	← Exportations vers / Exportations en provenance de ↓
Vetements (CTCI, Rev. 2 et Rev. 3, 84)											
582	5884	1409	323	1112	1515	745	1560	887	55	1980	Monde /1,2,3
2301	22541	8051	817	1013	2800	941	2190	7463	94	1990	
2196	23268	8595	918	1214	3677	1355	2756	9576	103	1991	
2362	26832	9932	1013	1509	4670	2002	3136	12472	98	1992	
2465	29119	11455	1198	1474	5412	2394	3312	10568	107	1993	
161	757	369	80	582	733	392	547	189	19	1980	Economies dévelopées /2,3,4
606	2620	1903	180	503	1596	572	550	1008	34	1990	
546	2347	1841	185	556	2063	798	589	987	36	1991	
573	2474	1882	210	704	2762	1106	808	1319	34	1992	
614	2560	1967	214	648	3214	1240	817	1585	35	1993	
406	5082	1038	240	515	772	352	985	687	36	1980	Economies en voie de développement /1,3,4
1673	19822	6140	636	498	1202	368	1631	6421	61	1990	
1639	20841	6745	732	653	1611	557	2158	8573	67	1991	
1762	24236	8038	801	801	1905	895	2315	11098	64	1992	
1832	26433	9482	983	812	2196	1153	2486	8948	71	1993	
0	9	1	2	7	1	0	81	43	0	1980	OPEP
52	750	107	14	3	27	9	173	111	2	1990	
49	671	160	15	39	59	7	318	225	3	1991	
52	1047	271	18	60	123	15	378	349	5	1992	
64	1152	306	23	97	106	21	383	371	7	1993	
16	46	1	2	15	10	2	29	11	0	1980	Europe de l'Est et l'ancienne URSS /2,3,7
23	98	8	1	12	2	0	8	34	0	1990	
11	79	9	1	5	3	0	9	16	0	1991	
27	123	12	1	4	3	0	13	55	0	1992	
19	126	6	2	14	1	1	9	34	0	1993	
0	0	0	0	0	0	0	0	6	0	1980	L'ancienne URSS /3
...	...	...	...	...	...	...	...	...	...	1990	
...	...	...	...	...	...	...	...	...	...	1991	
.	.	.	.	.	.	.	.	.	.	1992	
.	.	.	.	.	.	.	.	.	.	1993	
.	.	.	.	.	.	.	.	.	.	1980	L'ancienne URSS-Europe /8
.	.	.	.	.	.	.	.	.	.	1990	
.	.	.	.	.	.	.	.	.	.	1991	
1	2	0	0	0	0	0	2	9	0	1992	
2	2	0	0	0	0	0	2	14	0	1993	
86	449	280	35	530	167	93	442	109	10	1980	Economies développées-Europe /2
362	1982	1588	77	481	230	85	470	733	26	1990	
279	1668	1396	68	536	271	131	489	664	26	1991	
252	1642	1349	72	670	346	199	696	868	25	1992	
226	1586	1198	64	616	341	207	701	1053	25	1993	
76	424	265	32	521	160	88	430	104	9	1980	Communauté Economique Européenne /2
336	1907	1552	74	475	225	82	448	713	26	1990	
262	1604	1363	66	525	263	125	470	649	26	1991	
239	1580	1318	70	658	337	192	671	848	24	1992	
214	1525	1167	62	606	333	201	680	1030	25	1993	
10	25	15	2	8	6	5	11	5	0	1980	Association Européenne de Libre Echange
25	71	36	2	4	5	3	21	20	0	1990	
17	60	32	2	4	7	5	19	15	0	1991	
14	59	32	2	4	10	7	25	19	0	1992	
12	59	31	2	3	8	6	21	20	0	1993	
75	307	89	46	51	566	299	105	79	10	1980	Autres economies développées
244	638	315	104	22	1366	487	80	275	8	1990	
267	679	445	118	20	1792	667	101	323	10	1991	
321	832	533	138	34	2416	907	112	451	9	1992	
388	975	769	150	32	2873	1033	116	533	10	1993	

Voir la fin du tableau pour la remarque générale et les notes.

SPECIAL TABLE: B

World exports by commodity classes and by regions (continued)

In million U.S. dollars f.o.b.

Exports from ↓ / Exports to →	Year	World Monde /1,2,3	Developed economies Econ. dévelop-pées /2,3,4	Developing economies Economies en voie de développement /1,3,4: Total	Developing economies: OPEC OPEP	Eastern Europe and fmr. USSR-Europe Europe de l'Est et l'anc. URSS-Europe: Total /2,3,7	Eastern Europe and fmr. USSR-Europe: Former USSR-Eur. /10	Developed Economies: Europe: Total /2	Developed Economies: Europe: EEC CEE /2	Developed Economies: Europe: EFTA AELE	Developed Economies: South Africa Afrique du Sud
								Clothing (SITC, Rev. 2 and Rev. 3, 84) (continued)			
Canada	1980	211	194	15	3	2	0	111	75	36	0
	1990	328	314	12	3	2	0	23	17	6	0
	1991	404	389	11	4	4	2	37	23	14	0
	1992	527	509	11	4	7	5	31	24	7	0
	1993	662	632	17	4	13	12	30	25	6	0
United States	1980	1219	567	633	87	3	0	413	320	93	4
	1990	2479	972	1500	64	6	3	436	390	45	1
	1991	3215	1232	1956	94	27	19	540	480	59	3
	1992	4093	1427	2610	109	56	51	580	523	56	2
	1993	4808	1680	3078	104	50	47	514	469	45	2
Japan	1980	488	313	146	56	28	27	86	66	20	4
	1990	566	345	203	22	18	18	167	151	15	2
	1991	580	335	239	15	5	5	178	162	16	4
	1992	638	315	320	20	3	3	170	151	18	4
	1993	642	286	355	15	2	2	157	143	14	2
Australia, New Zealand	1980	63	49	13	2	0	0	4	3	0	0
	1990	149	134	15	1	0	0	12	11	2	0
	1991	174	151	22	2	0	0	17	15	2	0
	1992	203	179	23	3	1	1	26	23	3	0
	1993	224	195	28	3	1	1	28	25	3	0
Developing economies-Africa	1980	583	536	29	7	14	10	530	529	1	0
	1990	2702	2595	69	34	34	27	2367	2344	22	10
	1991	2880	2743	89	62	44	38	2529	2506	23	11
	1992	3235	3138	72	32	20	18	2861	2842	19	14
	1993	3375	3263	83	36	12	11	2867	2849	18	8
Developing economies-America	1980	854	499	345	92	9	1	248	208	40	0
	1990	1722	1232	451	30	28	15	261	229	33	0
	1991	1855	1304	521	55	14	13	364	330	34	0
	1992	2700	2265	410	88	3	2	338	306	31	0
	1993	3111	2543	550	160	8	7	318	290	28	0
Developing economies-Europe/ 5	1980	421	113	31	15	278	219	104	69	35	0
	1990	482	324	3	1	155	112	280	264	16	0
	1991	317	214	1	1	102	74	185	175	10	0
	1992	1610	1519	80	0	10	5	1495	1444	50	0
	1993	1715	1632	73	0	9	5	1558	1523	35	0
Developing economies-Middle East	1980	387	146	217	183	23	19	144	128	16	0
	1990	4323	3561	219	157	392	300	3069	2874	195	2
	1991	4404	3794	243	153	359	250	3348	3162	185	2
	1992	5173	4630	305	205	228	94	4022	3795	227	2
	1993	5177	4439	363	193	367	154	3792	3589	204	2
Developing economies-Other Asia	1980	14642	11741	2364	902	517	225	5202	4452	748	39
	1990	51750	40550	9146	1463	1959	1459	14031	12082	1939	41
	1991	60312	46071	12250	1949	1940	1269	17730	15508	2205	83
	1992	67920	50077	15409	1989	2395	1772	18015	15647	2349	110
	1993	70429	54142	13540	2128	2727	1919	18627	16191	2421	160
Former USSR-Asia /9	1980	.	.	.	.	.	.	.	.	.	.
	1990	.	.	.	.	.	.	.	.	.	.
	1991	.	.	.	.	.	.	.	.	.	.
	1992	3	1	2	2	0	.	1	1	0	0
	1993	2	1	1	1	0	.	1	1	0	0
Developing economies-Oceania	1980	12	1	11	0	0	0	0	0	0	0
	1990	86	80	6	0	0	0	4	4	0	0
	1991	102	94	7	0	0	0	5	5	0	0
	1992	87	80	6	0	0	0	5	5	0	0
	1993	72	65	5	0	0	0	4	4	0	0

For general note and footnotes see end of table.

Exportations mondiales par classes de marchandises et par régions (suite)

En millions de dollars E.-U. f.o.b.

Economies développées /2,3,4				Developing economies / Economies en voie de développement /1,3,4							← Exportations vers
Canada	U.S.A. / E.-U.	Japan / Japon	Australia New Zealand / Australie Nouvelle-Zélande	Africa / Afrique	America / Amerique: Total	America / Amerique: LAIA / ALADI	Asia / Asie: Mid.East / Moyen Orient	Asia / Asie: Other / Autres /9	Oceania / Océanie	Année	Exportations en provenance de ↓
Vetements (CTCI, Rev. 2 et Rev. 3, 84) (suite)											
.	74	7	1	2	9	3	1	3	0	1980	Canada
.	281	8	1	0	5	1	2	4	0	1990	
.	340	12	0	0	4	2	3	4	0	1991	
.	469	9	1	0	5	3	3	2	0	1992	
.	591	10	1	0	6	3	4	7	0	1993	
63	.	78	7	20	547	290	38	25	2	1980	Etats-Unis
218	.	297	13	3	1354	480	55	84	1	1990	
246	.	423	14	3	1782	660	79	83	2	1991	
309	.	514	16	5	2401	898	86	112	2	1992	
376	.	750	20	5	2858	1023	87	124	3	1993	
8	206	.	8	29	5	3	63	48	1	1980	Japon
15	154	.	7	3	1	1	22	176	1	1990	
12	134	.	6	2	2	1	16	218	2	1991	
7	127	.	7	3	4	2	19	293	1	1992	
7	113	.	5	2	3	2	15	333	1	1993	
1	11	4	30	0	0	0	2	3	7	1980	Australie, Nouvelle-Zélande
2	29	9	81	0	0	0	1	9	5	1990	
2	26	9	97	0	0	0	1	14	7	1991	
2	28	9	114	0	0	0	2	15	5	1992	
2	34	8	122	0	0	0	2	19	6	1993	
0	6	0	0	27	0	0	2	0	0	1980	Economies en voie de développement-Afrique
11	207	0	1	51	2	0	15	2	0	1990	
9	194	0	0	72	1	0	15	1	0	1991	
11	252	0	0	47	1	0	22	1	0	1992	
12	374	1	0	51	2	0	26	3	2	1993	
10	238	2	2	1	343	192	0	1	0	1980	Economies en voie de développement-Amérique
43	917	10	1	1	446	124	1	2	0	1990	
45	883	11	1	1	516	201	1	2	0	1991	
46	1867	12	1	1	405	308	1	2	0	1992	
45	2166	13	1	0	541	434	2	6	0	1993	
0	8	0	0	19	0	0	11	1	0	1980	Economies en voie de développement-Europe /5
3	40	2	0	0	0	0	2	0	0	1990	
2	26	1	0	0	0	0	1	0	0	1991	
1	22	1	0	1	1	0	1	0	0	1992	
1	72	0	0	1	1	0	0	0	0	1993	
0	1	0	0	45	0	0	171	1	0	1980	Economies en voie de développement-Moyen Orient
28	435	25	1	29	1	0	169	3	0	1990	
29	403	12	1	57	2	0	174	4	0	1991	
22	572	9	1	52	2	1	231	17	0	1992	
19	616	8	1	49	1	1	269	35	0	1993	
395	4828	1036	238	424	429	160	801	678	31	1980	Economies en voie de développement-Autres Pays d'Asie
1587	18200	6103	581	416	753	244	1445	6413	55	1990	
1554	19299	6721	678	522	1091	355	1966	8565	60	1991	
1682	21481	8016	765	700	1495	586	2060	11078	59	1992	
1756	23177	9460	947	712	1651	718	2189	8903	65	1993	
.	.	.	.	.	.	.	.	.	.	1980	l'ancienne URSS asiatique /9
.	.	.	.	.	.	.	.	.	.	1990	
.	.	.	.	.	.	.	.	.	.	1991	
0	0	0	0	0	0	0	2	0	0	1992	
0	0	0	0	0	0	0	1	0	0	1993	
0	0	0	0	0	0	0	0	6	5	1980	Economies en voie de développement-Océanie
1	24	0	52	0	0	0	0	1	5	1990	
0	37	0	52	0	0	0	0	1	6	1991	
0	42	0	34	0	0	0	0	0	5	1992	
0	28	0	33	0	0	0	0	2	4	1993	

Voir la fin du tableau pour la remarque générale et les notes.

SPECIAL TABLE: B

World exports by commodity classes and by regions (continued)

General note

The purpose of this table is to provide data on the network of flows of broad groups of commodities within and between important economic and geographic areas of the world.

The regional analysis in this table is in accordance with that of Special Table A in this issue. For the treatment of data on Germany see the general note on page vi.

Export data in this table are largely comparable to that shown in Special Table A except that Special Table A contains revised data for total exports which are not incorporated into this table if the corresponding revised data at the commodity/destination level are not available. Also, the regional totals shown in Special Table A have been adjusted to exclude the re-exports of countries comprising each region. This adjustment is not made in this table since re-exports are often not available by commodity and by destination.

The commodity classification is in accordance with the United Nations' Standard International Trade Classification (SITC), Revision 2, for 1980 through 1987 except for countries which report trade data only in terms of the SITC, Revised. Beginning 1988 the commodity classification is in accordance with the SITC, Revision 3, except for countries which report trade data only in terms of the SITC, Revision 2, or the SITC, Revised.

The data approximate total exports of all countries and areas of the world with the exception of the inter-trade between China, the Democratic People's Republic of Korea, Mongolia and Viet Nam in 1980 and trade conducted in accordance with the supplementary protocol to the treaty on the basis of relations between the Federal Republic of Germany and the former German Democratic Republic. They are based on official export figures converted, where necessary, to U.S. dollars according to conversion factors published in Table 1 for each country in this volume. Where official figures are not available estimates based on the imports reported by partner countries and on other subsidiary data are used. Some official national data have been adjusted

(a) to approximate the commodity groupings of the SITC and

(b) to approximate calendar years.

The data include special category (confidential) exports, ships' stores and bunkers and exports of minor importance, the destination of which cannot be determined. These data are included in the world totals for each commodity group and in total exports, but are excluded from all regions of destination. Approximately 1 1/2 per cent of total exports are not distributed. All data are generally in accordance with the special trade system.

1/ Excluding the inter-trade between China, the Democratic People's Republic of Korea, Mongolia and Viet Nam in 1980. The figures shown for other years are based on the import statistics of China.

2/ Excluding the trade conducted in accordance with the supplementary protocol to the treaty on the basis of relations between the Federal Republic of Germany (FRG) and the former German Democratic Republic (GDR). Data reported by FRG are as follows:

Value in million United States dollars

	1980	1990
FRG to GDR	2911	13379
FRG from GDR	3073	5129

3/ Exports of the former USSR for which country of destination is not available are included in the totals for the World, the 'Developed economies', the 'Developing economies' and 'Eastern Europe and the former USSR' but are excluded from the regional components of these groupings. For 1991, data for the former USSR are converted to U.S. dollars using the commercial exchange rate of the rouble and are not comparable to those shown for prior periods.

4/ This classification is intended for statistical convenience and does not, necessarily, express a judgement about the stage reached by a particular country in the development process.

5/ Beginning 1992, data refer to the Federal Republic of Yugoslavia, Croatia and Slovenia. Beginning 1993, data refer to the Federal Republic of Yugoslavia, Croatia, Slovenia, Bosnia and Herzegovina, and the former Yugoslav republic of Macedonia. Prior to 1992, data refer to the Socialist Federal Republic of Yugoslavia.

6/ Section 9 of the SITC, which comprises commodities and transactions not classified elsewhere, is included in the total trade but is not shown separately in this table.

7/ Beginning 1992, includes Eastern Europe and the European countries of the former USSR.

8/ Includes Belarus, Estonia, Latvia, Lithuania, Republic of Moldova, the Russian Federation, and Ukraine. Data exclude inter-trade among countries of the former USSR, except for Estonia, Latvia and Lithuania.

9/ Beginning 1992, includes Armenia, Azerbaijan, Georgia, Kazakhstan, Kyrgyzstan, Tajikistan, Turkmenistan, and Uzbekistan. Data for these countries exclude inter-trade among countries of the former USSR, except for Estonia, Latvia and Lithuania.

10/ Prior to 1992, data refer to the former USSR. Beginning 1992, data refer to the European countries of the former USSR, and exclude inter-trade among countries of the former USSR, except for Estonia, Latvia and Lithuania.

Exportations mondiales par classes de marchandises et par régions (suite)

Remarque générale

Le but de ce tableau est de fournir un apercu du courant des marchandises entre les régions importantes économiques et géographiques du monde et de leur commerce intérieur.

L'analyse régionale dans ce tableau est conforme à celle du Tableau Spécial A du présent numéro. Pour le traitement des données de l'Allemagne voir la remarque générale à la page vi.

Les données des exportations dans ce tableau sont en générale comparables aux chiffres qui sont inclus dans le Tableau Spécial A, exceptées que celles du Tableau Spécial A comportent des revisions aux exportations totales qui ne sont pas inclus dans ce tableau si les revisions des données correspondantes au niveau de marchandise/destination ne sont pas disponibles. De plus, les totaux régionaux inclus dans le Tableau Spécial A ont été ajustés pour exclure les re-exportations des pays qui comprennent la région. Cet ajustement n'est pas fait dans ce tableau parce que des re-exportations ne sont pas disponibles fréquemment par marchandise et par destination.

La classification par marchandise utilisée est la Classification type pour le commerce international (CTCI), Revision 2, des Nations Unies, pour les années allant de 1980 à 1987 en dehors des pays qui rapportent exclusivement les données du commerce en accord avec la CTCI, Revisée. A partir de 1988 la classification par marchandise utilisée est en accord avec la CTCI, Revision 3, en dehors des pays qui rapportent exclusivement les données du commerce en accord avec la CTCI, Revision 2, ou la CTCI, Revisée.

Les données approchées des exportations totales de tous pays et régions du monde a l'exclusion des échanges entre la Chine, la République populaire démocratique de Corée, la Mongolie et le Viet Nam en 1980 et le commerce effectué en accord avec le protocole additionnel au traité définissant la base des relations entre la République fédérale d'Allemagne et l'ancienne République démocratique allemande. Elles sont basées sur les chiffres des exportations officielles nationales convertis en dollars E.-U. selon les facteurs de conversion publiés dans le Tableau 1 pour chaque pays dans ce tome. Quand les chiffres officiels ne sont pas disponibles on a recours a des estimations basées sur les importations rapportées par les pays partenaires ou sur d'autres données subsidiaires. Quelques données officielles nationales ont été ajustées

(a) qu'elles correspondent aux groups des marchandises de la CTCI et

(b) qu'elles correspondent aux années civiles.

Les données comprises les exportations de 'special category' (confidentielles), les approvisionnements des navires et combustible de soute et autres exportations de moindre importance dont la destination n'a pu être déterminée. Ces données sont comprises dans les totaux de chaque groupe de marchandise et dans les exportations totales, mais elles ne sont pas comprises dans les régions de destination. Approximativement 1 1/2 pourcent des exportations totales ne sont pas distribuées. En générale, toutes les données correspondent au commerce spécial.

1/ Non compris le commerce entre la Chine, la République populaire démocratique de Corée, la Mongolie et le Viet Nam en 1980. Les chiffres indiqués pour les autres années sont bases sur les statistiques d'importations de la Chine.

2/ Non compris le commerce effectué en accord avec le protocole additionnel au traité définissant la base des relations entre la République fédérale d'Allemagne (RfA) et l'ancienne République démocratique allemande (Rda). Les données fournies par RfA sont les suivantes:

Valeur en millions de dollars des E.-U.

	1980	1990
de RfA vers Rda	2911	13379
de RfA en prov. de Rda	3073	5129

3/ Les exportations en provenance de l'ancienne URSS dont les pays de destination ne sont pas disponibles sont comprises dans les totaux du Monde, des 'Economies développées', des 'Economies en voie de développement' et de 'Europe de l'Est et l'ancienne URSS', mais ils ne sont pas comprises dans chaque partie composant ces régions. Les données relatives à l'année 1991 de l'ancienne URSS sont converties en dollar des E.U. en utilisant le taux de change commercial de rouble et ils ne sont pas comparables aux données des périodes antérieures.

4/ Cette classification est utilisée pour plus de commodité dans la présentation des statistiques et n'implique pas nécessairement un jugement quant au stade de développement auquel est parvenu un pays donné.

5/ A partir de l'année 1992, les données se rapportent à la République fédérative de Yougoslavie, Croatie et Slovénie. A partir de l'année 1993, les données se rapportent à la République fédérative de Yougoslavie, Croatie, Slovénie, Bosnie-Herzégovine et l'ancienne République yougoslave de Macédoine. Avant l'année 1992, les données se rapportent à la République socialiste fédérative de Yougoslavie.

6/ Section 9 de la CTCI, qui représente les articles et transactions non classes ailleurs est comprise dans le commerce total mais n'est pas présentée séparément dans ce tableau.

7/ A partir de janvier 1992, y compris de l'Europe de l'est et les pays européens de l'ancienne URSS.

8/ Y compris Bélarus, Estonie, Lettonie, Lituanie, République de Moldova, Fédération de Russie, et Ukraine. Les données ne comprennent pas le commerce avec les pays de l'ancienne URSS, excepté pour Estonie, Lettonie et Lituanie.

9/ A partir de l'année 1992, y compris Azerbaïdjan, Arménie, Géorgie, Kazakhstan, Kirghizistan, Tadjikistan, Turkménistan, et Ouzbékistan. Les données relatives à ces pays ne comprennent pas le commerce avec les pays de l'ancienne URSS, excepté pour Estonie, Lettonie et Lituanie.

10/ Avant l'année 1992, les données se rapportent à l'ancienne URSS. A partir de l'année 1992, les données se rapportent aux pays européens de l'ancienne URSS, et ils ne comprennent pas le commerce avec les pays de l'ancienne URSS, excepté pour Estonie, Lettonie et Lituanie.

SPECIAL TABLE: C

Growth of world exports by commodity classes and by regions

Annual average rate: in per cent

SITC	Commodity classes	Year	World / Monde /1,2,3	Developed economies / Econ. dévelop-pées /2,3,4	Developing economies / Economies en voie de développement /1,3,4: Total	Developing economies: OPEC / OPEP	Eastern Europe & the former USSR / Europe de l'Est et l'ancienne URSS: Total /2,3,6	Eastern Europe: Former USSR /7	Developed Economies – Europe: Total /2	Europe: EEC / CEE /2	Europe: EFTA / AELE	South Africa / Afrique du Sud
	Origin of exports of major commodity classes											
0-9	Total all commodities /5	1980/93	6.2	7.3	5.4	0.2	-4.1	.	6.7	6.8	6.5	-0.7
		1980/90	7.7	9.8	4.0	-8.7	2.3	4.5	10.2	10.1	10.6	-4.2
		1990/93	2.6	1.7	8.7	0.8	-17.7	.	-0.8	-0.6	-2.3	8.1
		1991/93	3.7	1.3	10.1	4.2	5.7	.	-1.5	-1.4	-1.5	18.1
		1992/93	-0.4	-3.6	7.7	3.8	9.6	5.9	-8.5	-8.7	-7.2	1.4
0&1	Food, live animals, beverages and tobacco	1980/93	5.0	5.5	4.1	6.6	3.7	.	7.0	7.1	6.6	-3.5
		1980/90	6.0	6.9	3.7	5.3	8.4	3.4	9.1	9.1	9.4	1.9
		1990/93	2.9	2.4	4.8	9.7	-6.6	.	2.3	2.5	0.4	-14.9
		1991/93	2.4	1.7	4.0	9.5	3.7	.	0.8	0.8	0.0	-17.5
		1992/93	-3.3	-5.6	2.8	6.5	-5.0	8.6	-7.9	-8.0	-4.8	-9.0
2&4	Crude materials, oils and fats, (fuels excluded)	1980/93	1.8	2.1	1.8	0.6	-1.9	.	2.8	3.8	-0.2	0.6
		1980/90	3.6	4.5	2.0	-2.9	1.6	1.4	6.7	7.9	3.4	10.6
		1990/93	-2.3	-3.4	1.4	9.5	-9.7	.	-5.7	-5.0	-8.3	-19.5
		1991/93	-0.2	-2.1	2.6	7.8	9.5	.	-5.4	-5.6	-4.6	-24.1
		1992/93	-3.0	-4.5	-1.6	-1.7	10.1	16.1	-12.4	-12.8	-10.5	-8.5
3	Mineral fuels, lubricants and related material	1980/93	-4.3	1.5	-6.2	-8.3	-4.9	.	-0.2	-1.9	5.5	6.5
		1980/90	-4.5	2.5	-7.9	-10.7	2.7	3.1	0.5	-1.4	7.7	15.5
		1990/93	-3.8	-0.9	-2.2	-2.3	-20.4	.	-2.0	-3.0	0.6	-14.5
		1991/93	-0.3	-2.2	0.4	1.3	2.8	.	-3.4	-4.4	-0.8	-16.9
		1992/93	-0.5	-2.2	1.0	1.8	-5.1	-5.8	-4.5	-3.6	-6.4	13.1
5	Chemicals	1980/93	9.0	8.4	16.4	13.6	2.9	.	8.2	7.9	9.8	7.0
		1980/90	11.7	11.0	19.3	18.5	10.0	11.8	11.2	11.0	12.9	11.7
		1990/93	3.0	2.5	9.9	3.1	-12.0	.	1.3	1.0	2.9	-3.0
		1991/93	3.4	2.1	10.3	15.0	14.8	.	1.2	0.9	3.6	0.5
		1992/93	-1.3	-2.8	6.8	6.9	7.6	6.5	-5.3	-5.7	-2.3	-9.8
7	Machinery and transport equipment	1980/93	10.6	9.8	23.8	9.3	-8.6	.	8.4	8.5	7.9	12.7
		1980/90	13.4	12.9	25.6	2.4	2.8	3.8	12.7	12.6	13.0	4.1
		1990/93	4.4	2.9	19.7	27.4	-30.7	.	-0.9	-0.7	-3.0	35.4
		1991/93	4.9	2.2	20.8	20.1	-8.6	.	-2.0	-2.0	-2.1	65.8
		1992/93	0.8	-2.7	19.1	34.9	1.3	-16.4	-10.0	-10.2	-8.4	6.9
6&8	Other manufactured goods	1980/93	8.5	6.3	15.4	19.7	5.3	.	6.0	6.0	6.0	4.4
		1980/90	10.8	9.2	17.2	22.1	6.2	5.5	9.8	9.7	10.3	9.1
		1990/93	3.2	-0.2	11.5	14.5	3.1	.	-2.4	-2.2	-3.5	-5.7
		1991/93	3.9	-0.7	11.8	16.5	36.7	.	-2.7	-2.8	-2.5	-3.7
		1992/93	-1.4	-6.3	6.9	11.0	28.7	22.0	-10.2	-10.6	-8.1	7.6
	Destination of exports of major commodity classes											
0-9	Total all commodities /5	1980/93	6.2	6.4	7.6	0.7	-2.8	.	5.4	5.6	4.1	1.2
		1980/90	7.7	9.0	6.5	-2.1	1.5	2.8	8.7	8.9	7.8	-0.7
		1990/93	2.6	0.7	10.3	7.7	-12.0	.	-2.0	-1.8	-3.9	5.8
		1991/93	3.7	1.1	10.8	4.5	-1.2	.	-3.1	-3.1	-3.2	4.4
		1992/93	-0.4	-3.6	7.4	-5.0	6.0	1.0	-10.3	-10.6	-7.9	0.4
0&1	Food, live animals, beverages and tobacco	1980/93	5.0	6.4	3.8	-0.9	-1.9	.	5.9	6.0	4.6	9.5
		1980/90	6.0	8.2	3.2	-1.6	-0.6	0.4	8.0	8.1	6.8	8.9
		1990/93	2.9	2.3	5.3	0.9	-4.8	.	1.1	1.2	-0.2	10.7
		1991/93	2.4	0.7	7.9	3.9	-4.8	.	-1.2	-1.2	-0.8	10.5
		1992/93	-3.3	-5.2	0.5	0.7	-2.4	-9.4	-8.8	-9.0	-5.3	-33.2
2&4	Crude materials, oils and fats, (fuels excluded)	1980/93	1.8	1.5	4.8	3.7	-8.8	.	0.7	0.4	3.3	-1.6
		1980/90	3.6	4.2	5.0	1.5	-2.6	1.1	4.3	4.2	5.3	-4.0
		1990/93	-2.3	-4.6	4.6	8.9	-21.8	.	-7.2	-7.9	-1.4	4.2
		1991/93	-0.2	-2.8	5.2	11.8	-14.2	.	-6.3	-7.2	1.2	10.4
		1992/93	-3.0	-6.5	0.4	-0.1	-8.9	-18.8	-13.2	-14.0	-7.0	-1.6
3	Mineral fuels, lubricants and related material	1980/93	-4.3	-4.6	-1.7	0.6	-4.4	.	-5.5	-5.6	-5.1	-9.4
		1980/90	-4.5	-5.1	-2.4	-7.1	3.0	13.8	-5.1	-5.0	-6.3	-18.2
		1990/93	-3.8	-3.5	-0.1	21.2	-19.5	.	-6.2	-6.8	-2.3	14.9
		1991/93	-0.3	-0.8	2.9	23.1	0.0	.	-4.2	-5.0	2.1	10.4
		1992/93	-0.5	-2.6	6.8	7.8	1.5	-1.7	-6.6	-7.7	0.7	1.7
5	Chemicals	1980/93	9.0	9.5	9.4	3.5	0.1	.	8.5	8.7	7.5	3.5
		1980/90	11.7	13.0	10.1	3.2	4.4	6.9	12.5	12.8	10.7	3.5
		1990/93	3.0	1.9	7.7	4.3	-9.1	.	-0.2	-0.2	0.2	3.4
		1991/93	3.4	2.2	7.2	4.7	-1.9	.	-0.2	-0.6	2.2	2.5
		1992/93	-1.3	-4.2	4.3	-0.3	13.3	1.8	-7.7	-8.6	-2.4	-0.4
7	Machinery and transport equipment	1980/93	10.6	11.6	10.6	0.9	-1.2	.	10.0	10.4	7.1	-0.4
		1980/90	13.4	16.2	9.0	-2.4	4.5	6.9	15.6	16.1	12.9	-2.3
		1990/93	4.4	1.6	14.4	9.0	-13.5	.	-2.1	-1.7	-5.4	4.2
		1991/93	4.9	1.3	14.5	1.6	-2.2	.	-4.6	-4.6	-5.2	1.3
		1992/93	0.8	-4.2	12.3	-9.9	4.8	5.3	-13.5	-13.8	-11.7	3.0
6&8	Other manufactured goods	1980/93	8.5	8.5	9.9	0.5	0.4	.	6.6	7.2	4.0	3.4
		1980/90	10.8	12.1	9.0	-2.7	2.4	4.7	10.7	11.2	8.2	0.9
		1990/93	3.2	0.6	12.0	8.3	-4.2	.	-2.2	-1.6	-5.4	9.4
		1991/93	3.9	0.7	11.5	5.9	10.2	.	-3.5	-3.1	-5.6	9.4
		1992/93	-1.4	-4.5	5.0	-3.2	16.1	10.7	-11.8	-12.0	-10.4	7.6

For general note and footnotes see end of Special Table D.

TABLEAU SPECIAL: C

Croissance des exportations mondiales par catégories de marchandises et par régions

Taux annuel moyen: en pourcentage

Economies développées /2,3,4				Developing economies / Economies en voie de développement /1,3,4						← En provenance ou vers		
Canada	U.S.A. E.-U.	Japan Japon	Australia New Zealand Australie Nouvelle-Zélande	Africa Afrique	America Amerique: Total	America Amerique: LAIA ALADI	Asia Asie: Mid.East Moyen Orient	Asia Asie: Other Autres /8	Oceania Océanie	Année	CTCI:Classes de marchandises ↓	
Provenance des exportations de grandes catégories de marchandises												
8.3	7.3	10.8	6.7	-4.9	4.9	6.2	-5.9	14.9	6.6	1980/93	0-9	Total tous produits /5
10.0	8.1	12.0	8.7	-6.1	4.0	5.1	-8.6	15.8	3.8	1980/90		
4.5	5.5	7.9	2.2	-2.2	7.2	8.7	0.6	12.8	13.2	1990/93		
6.9	4.7	7.1	1.1	-2.3	12.3	14.2	4.9	12.2	11.1	1991/93		
7.5	3.4	6.3	0.3	-1.3	7.4	7.6	3.9	9.9	25.8	1992/93		
4.2	2.7	2.2	3.4	-1.7	1.8	2.9	8.3	8.3	-0.2	1980/93	0&1	Produits alimentaires, boissons et tabacs.
5.1	2.6	0.2	2.1	-2.5	1.5	2.2	8.7	8.5	0.4	1980/90		
2.3	2.7	7.0	6.3	0.2	2.7	4.5	7.3	7.7	-1.4	1990/93		
0.7	4.1	5.0	10.1	-0.9	3.3	4.9	6.4	5.2	-6.1	1991/93		
-9.3	-1.3	4.8	14.5	1.9	4.2	3.7	2.7	2.6	-4.6	1992/93		
2.9	0.1	3.8	3.4	-1.9	2.2	3.1	5.3	2.5	3.3	1980/93	2&4	Matières premières huiles & graisses (combust. exclu.)
5.0	1.3	3.7	1.4	-2.4	3.9	5.3	5.6	1.8	1.3	1980/90		
-1.9	-2.8	4.0	8.2	-1.0	-1.5	-1.9	4.7	4.0	8.4	1990/93		
3.8	-1.6	4.9	9.2	1.7	-1.8	-2.7	5.0	5.4	9.7	1991/93		
4.3	-3.6	-0.1	21.8	0.3	-1.9	-3.4	1.8	-2.5	21.3	1992/93		
4.9	2.0	14.2	13.2	-7.7	-2.9	-2.5	-8.4	0.9	38.7	1980/93	3	Combustibles minéraux et produits
4.4	6.2	13.6	16.3	-9.2	-1.2	-0.6	-11.6	1.5	-9.9	1980/90		
6.2	-7.2	15.7	6.3	-4.0	-6.8	-7.0	-0.6	-0.4	279.4	1990/93		
5.5	-10.2	23.1	5.0	-5.3	-1.6	-1.1	4.9	-2.4	594.1	1991/93		
7.5	-12.5	23.8	6.3	-3.0	-0.3	-1.1	4.3	-2.7	501.8	1992/93		
7.8	8.1	11.8	11.3	12.9	11.5	12.3	11.8	21.6	10.3	1980/93	5	Produits chimiques
9.5	9.4	13.2	10.2	20.5	13.3	14.3	18.5	24.3	23.3	1980/90		
3.9	4.9	8.5	13.8	-3.0	7.3	7.9	-2.4	15.6	-14.9	1990/93		
5.1	2.4	7.6	11.9	-3.1	7.0	8.4	9.3	12.5	-21.6	1991/93		
4.1	2.4	5.5	16.8	-2.2	5.8	5.2	3.9	9.2	0.0	1992/93		
13.1	9.5	13.1	11.8	16.7	21.8	22.2	6.2	26.3	28.2	1980/93	7	Machines et matériels de transports
16.0	10.7	15.1	10.4	24.5	15.4	15.6	3.9	29.7	47.2	1980/90		
6.5	6.6	8.6	15.2	0.4	38.3	39.1	11.9	18.5	-7.2	1990/93		
9.7	5.4	8.0	13.4	-3.8	54.3	54.8	-0.4	18.0	-23.8	1991/93		
13.7	4.0	6.9	17.8	-4.8	20.1	20.4	5.8	20.2	-29.4	1992/93		
7.9	8.4	5.0	7.7	6.6	11.8	12.5	14.7	17.1	3.2	1980/93	6&8	Articles manufacturés divers
8.9	9.0	4.9	9.1	8.1	11.9	12.7	20.0	19.0	4.5	1980/90		
5.5	7.1	5.2	4.6	3.3	11.6	12.0	3.3	12.7	0.2	1990/93		
7.7	5.1	3.5	4.6	10.2	17.2	17.5	5.1	11.5	-3.5	1991/93		
7.6	3.5	3.2	5.1	8.5	10.1	10.3	2.1	7.1	-3.9	1992/93		
Destination des exportations de grandes catégories de marchandises												
9.4	9.6	5.2	7.2	-0.5	4.5	5.3	3.0	13.6	5.6	1980/93	0-9	Total tous produits /5
11.8	10.9	6.3	9.0	-0.4	1.5	0.8	0.8	13.9	7.8	1980/90		
4.0	6.5	2.8	3.2	-0.8	11.7	16.6	8.5	12.9	0.8	1990/93		
4.9	11.8	1.5	6.4	-2.6	12.6	16.1	7.7	13.5	-0.5	1991/93		
7.1	10.3	4.3	3.5	-5.7	7.2	7.9	-0.4	11.4	-4.6	1992/93		
9.1	5.2	10.4	7.6	-0.2	2.6	2.5	1.6	7.7	2.1	1980/93	0&1	Produits alimentaires, boissons et tabacs.
10.4	6.0	12.1	9.8	-0.1	0.7	-0.8	2.1	7.0	2.9	1980/90		
6.0	3.3	6.6	2.6	-0.2	7.1	10.8	0.4	9.3	0.3	1990/93		
4.8	4.1	5.6	2.5	2.8	9.4	12.5	4.8	10.1	-1.7	1991/93		
6.2	3.4	3.4	2.2	-3.2	6.2	6.1	-0.6	-0.2	-4.1	1992/93		
5.0	4.5	1.3	2.5	1.8	4.1	4.4	8.1	6.2	6.5	1980/93	2&4	Matières premières huiles & graisses (combust. exclu.)
6.0	4.7	3.3	3.0	3.8	3.4	2.8	4.4	7.2	4.1	1980/90		
2.7	4.0	-3.3	1.3	-2.5	6.0	8.5	17.3	4.0	12.4	1990/93		
4.0	11.2	-2.2	7.9	1.8	6.1	7.0	26.7	2.7	5.2	1991/93		
5.2	11.4	1.9	4.5	-5.7	5.3	5.1	5.6	-0.6	18.6	1992/93		
-6.1	-2.5	-4.9	-3.8	-4.7	-6.7	-5.2	-1.9	2.0	-0.8	1980/93	3	Combustibles minéraux et produits
-3.6	-2.8	-8.1	-9.5	-3.7	-9.5	-11.7	-2.9	2.0	1.0	1980/90		
-11.6	-2.0	2.9	11.1	-6.8	0.0	11.9	0.7	1.9	-4.9	1990/93		
-10.7	9.3	-3.9	6.1	-27.4	6.1	26.9	3.7	8.2	-11.6	1991/93		
-5.7	5.6	-3.9	12.5	2.1	6.6	7.0	7.7	7.7	-4.1	1992/93		
13.8	14.4	11.1	9.8	1.6	5.9	6.4	6.0	14.9	7.0	1980/93	5	Produits chimiques
15.7	16.4	14.0	11.7	2.2	4.3	4.1	6.7	17.2	8.8	1980/90		
9.4	9.8	4.5	5.6	0.3	9.7	12.2	4.4	9.7	2.8	1990/93		
10.6	11.9	2.8	8.8	0.8	9.0	10.8	9.5	7.4	1.1	1991/93		
10.9	6.4	3.3	3.3	-4.1	8.3	10.9	3.2	5.2	-3.8	1992/93		
11.0	15.8	18.4	9.3	-0.6	7.7	7.5	3.8	18.6	8.8	1980/93	7	Machines et matériels de transports
14.1	19.0	25.4	12.8	-0.2	4.5	2.9	0.3	18.9	12.0	1980/90		
4.0	8.7	3.6	1.5	-1.6	15.3	19.0	12.4	17.8	1.5	1990/93		
4.1	13.5	3.6	8.0	-2.8	16.0	18.2	6.6	18.7	6.3	1991/93		
6.7	12.2	8.8	4.1	-9.0	6.1	6.7	-2.9	21.2	-8.3	1992/93		
12.0	12.7	15.9	7.5	0.1	7.1	7.2	3.3	16.9	7.2	1980/93	6&8	Articles manufacturés divers
15.2	15.2	22.1	9.3	-0.4	3.4	1.8	0.7	18.2	10.1	1980/90		
4.8	7.1	2.8	3.5	1.2	16.2	21.0	9.7	13.9	0.7	1990/93		
5.9	11.5	3.3	5.1	1.0	14.3	16.9	9.5	12.8	-3.0	1991/93		
7.9	11.3	9.3	2.1	-5.4	10.3	10.9	-0.2	6.2	-3.4	1992/93		

Voir la fin du Tableau Spécial D pour la remarque générale et les notes.

SPECIAL TABLE: D

Structure of world exports by commodity classes and by regions

In per cent

SITC	Commodity classes	Year	World Monde /1,2,3	Developed economies Econ. dévelop-pées /2,3,4	Developing economies Economies en voie de développement /1,3,4: Total	Developing economies: OPEC OPEP	Eastern Europe & the former USSR Europe de l'Est et l'ancienne URSS: Total /2,3,6	Eastern Europe & the former USSR: Former USSR /7	Developed Economie[s]: Europe: Total /2	Europe: EEC CEE /2	Europe: EFTA AELE	South Africa Afrique du Sud
	Origin of exports of major commodity classes											
0-9	Total all commodities /5	1980	100.0	62.7	29.7	16.1	7.7	3.8	39.5	34.0	5.5	1.3
		1990	100.0	71.6	23.1	5.0	5.3	3.0	46.2	39.5	6.6	0.6
		1991	100.0	73.0	24.3	4.7	2.7	1.3	46.2	39.8	6.3	0.5
		1992	100.0	72.1	25.4	4.6	2.5	1.3	45.5	39.3	6.1	0.6
		1993	100.0	69.8	27.5	4.8	2.8	1.4	41.7	36.0	5.7	0.6
0&1	Food, live animals, beverages and tobacco	1980	100.0	65.5	31.9	1.9	2.6	0.7	39.3	36.9	2.3	1.1
		1990	100.0	69.4	27.5	1.8	3.1	0.5	48.1	45.2	2.9	0.8
		1991	100.0	69.6	28.2	1.9	2.2	0.2	49.0	46.0	2.8	0.7
		1992	100.0	70.3	27.4	2.0	2.3	0.5	49.8	47.0	2.7	0.5
		1993	100.0	68.6	29.1	2.2	2.3	0.6	47.4	44.6	2.7	0.5
2&4	Crude materials, oils and fats, (fuels excluded)	1980	100.0	61.2	31.8	3.8	7.0	5.1	24.8	17.8	7.0	1.4
		1990	100.0	65.3	28.6	2.4	6.1	4.4	30.6	23.6	6.9	2.2
		1991	100.0	65.7	30.3	2.9	4.0	2.1	30.6	24.3	6.3	2.1
		1992	100.0	64.2	31.6	3.4	4.3	2.5	30.5	24.2	6.2	1.3
		1993	100.0	63.2	32.0	3.4	4.8	3.0	27.5	21.8	5.8	1.2
3	Mineral fuels, lubricants and related material	1980	100.0	17.9	73.9	63.0	8.2	7.3	13.6	11.3	2.3	0.2
		1990	100.0	29.4	57.1	39.2	13.6	12.4	19.4	14.1	5.3	0.7
		1991	100.0	33.5	59.3	39.8	7.2	6.2	21.8	15.7	6.1	0.7
		1992	100.0	32.7	59.2	40.2	8.1	7.0	21.4	14.9	6.4	0.5
		1993	100.0	32.2	60.1	41.1	7.7	6.7	20.5	14.4	6.1	0.5
5	Chemicals	1980	100.0	88.2	7.5	1.1	4.3	1.2	64.4	56.7	7.8	0.4
		1990	100.0	84.3	11.9	1.6	3.8	1.2	62.5	54.1	8.4	0.4
		1991	100.0	85.4	12.7	1.3	1.9	0.5	62.1	53.7	8.4	0.4
		1992	100.0	84.5	13.3	1.5	2.2	0.9	62.0	53.5	8.5	0.4
		1993	100.0	83.2	14.4	1.6	2.4	1.0	59.5	51.1	8.4	0.3
7	Machinery and transport equipment	1980	100.0	86.3	6.0	0.3	7.7	2.4	50.8	44.6	6.2	0.1
		1990	100.0	83.8	12.4	0.1	3.9	1.3	48.6	42.5	6.0	0.1
		1991	100.0	84.5	14.1	0.2	1.5	0.6	47.6	41.9	5.6	0.0
		1992	100.0	83.1	15.8	0.2	1.1	0.3	46.5	41.1	5.3	0.1
		1993	100.0	80.2	18.7	0.3	1.1	0.2	41.5	36.6	4.8	0.1
6&8	Other manufactured goods	1980	100.0	77.9	18.0	0.8	4.2	1.1	55.6	46.4	9.1	0.9
		1990	100.0	70.3	26.6	1.6	3.1	0.7	52.3	43.4	8.8	0.8
		1991	100.0	69.3	28.9	1.7	1.8	0.3	50.4	42.1	8.2	0.7
		1992	100.0	66.7	30.9	1.9	2.4	0.9	48.5	40.7	7.8	0.5
		1993	100.0	63.4	33.5	2.2	3.1	1.2	44.2	36.9	7.2	0.6
	Destination of exports of major commodity classes											
0-9	Total all commodities /5	1980	100.0	65.9	24.7	6.3	6.9	3.0	43.4	36.9	6.4	0.7
		1990	100.0	71.6	22.8	3.2	4.5	2.2	46.3	39.7	6.4	0.4
		1991	100.0	71.2	24.7	3.7	3.2	1.5	46.1	39.9	6.0	0.4
		1992	100.0	69.9	26.2	3.9	2.7	1.2	44.7	38.9	5.7	0.4
		1993	100.0	67.6	28.3	3.7	2.9	1.2	40.3	34.9	5.3	0.4
0&1	Food, live animals, beverages and tobacco	1980	100.0	61.6	26.4	8.0	9.5	6.3	43.9	40.2	3.5	0.2
		1990	100.0	71.5	21.9	4.8	6.1	4.3	50.0	46.1	3.7	0.2
		1991	100.0	72.8	21.1	4.4	5.6	4.2	51.0	47.2	3.6	0.2
		1992	100.0	71.9	22.6	4.3	4.8	3.3	50.4	46.7	3.5	0.4
		1993	100.0	70.4	23.4	4.5	4.8	3.1	47.5	43.9	3.4	0.3
2&4	Crude materials, oils and fats, (fuels excluded)	1980	100.0	68.3	21.6	3.0	7.1	2.2	43.8	39.6	4.2	0.4
		1990	100.0	71.0	23.7	2.6	4.6	1.9	46.0	41.2	4.7	0.2
		1991	100.0	69.9	26.2	2.9	3.2	1.4	44.7	40.0	4.7	0.2
		1992	100.0	68.8	28.1	3.5	2.5	0.8	44.1	39.0	5.0	0.3
		1993	100.0	66.3	29.1	3.6	2.4	0.7	39.4	34.5	4.8	0.3
3	Mineral fuels, lubricants and related material	1980	100.0	72.7	18.1	1.1	3.3	0.1	40.4	36.1	4.2	0.1
		1990	100.0	69.6	21.1	0.9	5.7	0.4	38.4	34.6	3.7	0.0
		1991	100.0	71.0	22.3	1.2	3.3	0.3	38.6	34.7	3.7	0.0
		1992	100.0	71.8	22.1	1.7	3.2	0.3	38.0	33.9	3.8	0.0
		1993	100.0	70.3	23.7	1.8	3.3	0.3	35.7	31.5	3.9	0.0
5	Chemicals	1980	100.0	64.1	28.2	6.4	6.9	3.2	49.8	42.0	7.7	1.0
		1990	100.0	69.3	25.5	3.7	4.3	2.3	52.3	44.9	7.3	0.6
		1991	100.0	68.8	27.1	3.7	3.3	1.8	51.1	44.2	6.8	0.6
		1992	100.0	69.2	27.6	3.8	2.6	0.9	50.9	44.1	6.7	0.6
		1993	100.0	67.2	29.1	3.8	3.0	0.9	47.6	40.9	6.7	0.6
7	Machinery and transport equipment	1980	100.0	60.3	31.4	10.2	7.7	3.5	38.5	31.9	6.6	1.5
		1990	100.0	71.4	23.7	3.6	4.4	2.3	44.1	37.5	6.4	0.5
		1991	100.0	70.6	26.2	4.3	2.8	1.4	43.9	37.9	5.8	0.6
		1992	100.0	69.2	28.1	4.5	2.4	1.0	42.3	36.7	5.4	0.5
		1993	100.0	65.8	31.3	4.0	2.5	1.1	36.3	31.4	4.8	0.5
6&8	Other manufactured goods	1980	100.0	68.8	24.0	8.1	5.9	2.9	50.7	40.9	9.7	0.6
		1990	100.0	74.7	21.4	3.3	3.4	2.0	50.3	41.9	8.2	0.3
		1991	100.0	73.5	23.8	3.6	2.4	1.2	49.5	41.7	7.6	0.3
		1992	100.0	71.4	25.7	3.8	2.3	1.0	47.8	40.7	6.9	0.3
		1993	100.0	69.1	27.4	3.8	2.7	1.1	42.7	36.3	6.3	0.4

For general note and footnotes see end of table.

TABLEAU SPECIAL: D

Structure des exportations mondiales par catégories de marchandises et par régions

En pourcentage

Economies développées /2,3,4				Developing economies / Economies en voie de développement /1,3,4						← En provenance ou vers	
Canada	U.S.A. / E.-U.	Japan / Japon	Australia New Zealand / Australie Nouvelle-Zélande	Africa / Afrique	America / Amerique: Total	America / Amerique: LAIA / ALADI	Asia / Asie: Mid.East / Moyen Orient	Asia / Asie: Other / Autres /8	Oceania / Océanie	Année	CTCI:Classes de marchandises
Provenance des exportations de grandes catégories de marchandises											
3.2	10.7	6.4	1.3	5.6	5.1	3.9	10.5	7.9	0.1	1980	0-9 Total tous produits /5
3.7	11.0	8.4	1.4	2.1	3.9	3.3	3.3	13.2	0.1	1990	
3.7	11.7	9.2	1.5	2.1	3.8	3.2	3.1	15.0	0.1	1991	
3.6	11.5	9.2	1.4	1.9	4.2	3.6	3.0	15.9	0.1	1992	
3.9	11.9	9.8	1.4	1.9	4.5	3.9	3.1	17.5	0.1	1993	
3.6	15.5	0.8	4.9	5.1	14.8	9.9	1.4	9.7	0.4	1980	0&1 Produits alimentaires, boissons et tabacs.
3.4	12.4	0.5	3.8	2.8	10.9	7.7	1.6	11.5	0.3	1990	
3.4	11.9	0.6	3.6	2.8	10.7	7.7	1.7	12.5	0.3	1991	
3.5	12.1	0.6	3.6	2.5	10.1	7.5	1.8	12.4	0.2	1992	
3.3	12.3	0.6	4.2	2.6	10.9	8.1	1.9	13.2	0.2	1993	
9.2	18.8	1.2	5.6	5.4	8.7	7.0	1.1	15.5	0.7	1980	2&4 Matières premières huiles & graisses (combust. exclu.)
10.1	16.1	1.2	4.9	3.6	8.9	7.8	1.2	13.8	0.6	1990	
9.5	16.3	1.3	5.5	3.6	9.4	8.4	1.4	14.9	0.7	1991	
9.5	16.0	1.4	5.3	3.6	9.0	8.0	1.4	16.5	0.7	1992	
10.3	15.9	1.4	6.6	3.7	9.1	8.0	1.5	16.6	0.8	1993	
1.9	1.6	0.1	0.5	18.2	8.1	6.4	40.9	6.7	0.0	1980	3 Combustibles minéraux et produits
3.5	3.4	0.4	2.0	12.7	10.3	8.5	23.8	10.2	0.0	1990	
4.3	3.8	0.4	2.4	14.1	9.6	7.9	23.8	11.8	0.0	1991	
4.4	3.5	0.5	2.5	13.0	9.3	7.8	25.1	11.6	0.0	1992	
4.8	3.1	0.6	2.6	12.7	9.3	7.7	26.3	11.3	0.3	1993	
2.5	15.0	4.8	0.5	0.5	2.0	1.5	1.1	3.1	0.0	1980	5 Produits chimiques
2.2	13.0	5.2	0.4	0.9	2.2	1.8	1.6	6.6	0.0	1990	
2.2	14.0	5.7	0.5	0.9	2.4	1.9	1.2	7.9	0.0	1991	
2.2	13.2	5.7	0.5	0.8	2.4	2.0	1.3	8.5	0.0	1992	
2.3	13.7	6.1	0.6	0.7	2.5	2.1	1.4	9.4	0.0	1993	
3.3	16.7	15.0	0.3	0.0	1.0	1.0	0.3	4.1	0.0	1980	7 Machines et matériels de transports
3.9	14.2	16.6	0.2	0.1	1.2	1.1	0.2	10.6	0.0	1990	
3.8	14.9	17.7	0.3	0.1	1.3	1.2	0.2	12.2	0.0	1991	
3.7	14.6	17.7	0.3	0.1	2.3	2.2	0.2	13.0	0.0	1992	
4.1	15.1	18.7	0.3	0.1	2.7	2.7	0.2	15.5	0.0	1993	
2.9	8.2	8.8	0.8	1.1	2.7	2.4	0.8	12.5	0.1	1980	6&8 Articles manufacturés divers
2.6	7.3	6.0	0.7	0.9	2.9	2.7	1.4	20.7	0.0	1990	
2.5	8.0	6.4	0.7	0.8	2.9	2.7	1.4	23.3	0.1	1991	
2.5	7.8	6.1	0.7	0.8	3.3	3.1	1.4	24.8	0.0	1992	
2.7	8.1	6.4	0.7	0.9	3.6	3.4	1.4	26.9	0.0	1993	
Destination des exportations de grandes catégories de marchandises											
2.5	11.7	6.2	1.2	4.0	6.1	4.2	4.8	8.6	0.1	1980	0-9 Total tous produits /5
3.2	14.4	5.6	1.3	2.3	4.0	2.6	3.0	12.7	0.1	1990	
3.3	13.8	5.9	1.2	2.4	4.4	3.1	3.3	14.1	0.2	1991	
3.1	14.5	5.4	1.3	2.2	4.8	3.6	3.6	15.1	0.1	1992	
3.4	16.1	5.7	1.3	2.1	5.2	3.9	3.6	16.9	0.1	1993	
1.6	9.0	6.2	0.6	5.8	6.0	4.1	5.8	8.0	0.3	1980	0&1 Produits alimentaires, boissons et tabacs.
2.1	9.0	9.2	0.7	3.8	4.2	2.6	4.5	8.6	0.2	1990	
2.2	8.8	9.6	0.7	3.5	4.1	2.7	4.0	8.9	0.3	1991	
2.1	8.5	9.6	0.7	3.5	4.3	3.0	4.1	10.0	0.2	1992	
2.3	9.1	10.2	0.7	3.5	4.7	3.3	4.2	10.3	0.2	1993	
1.8	7.4	13.9	0.8	2.5	3.5	2.9	2.0	11.6	0.0	1980	2&4 Matières premières huiles & graisses (combust. exclu.)
2.1	8.1	13.7	0.7	2.5	3.5	2.8	2.2	14.8	0.0	1990	
2.3	7.8	13.8	0.7	2.4	3.9	3.3	2.3	17.0	0.1	1991	
2.3	8.5	12.6	0.8	2.6	4.1	3.5	3.4	17.5	0.1	1992	
2.4	9.7	13.3	0.8	2.5	4.4	3.8	3.7	17.9	0.1	1993	
1.3	16.6	13.4	0.8	1.5	6.0	3.0	2.1	7.6	0.1	1980	3 Combustibles minéraux et produits
1.4	18.8	10.2	0.5	1.6	4.1	1.7	2.3	12.1	0.2	1990	
1.4	16.5	13.4	0.7	2.7	4.1	1.7	2.5	12.2	0.2	1991	
1.2	18.7	12.9	0.7	1.4	4.3	2.5	2.5	13.3	0.2	1992	
1.1	19.9	12.5	0.8	1.4	4.7	2.7	2.7	14.4	0.2	1993	
2.0	5.7	3.8	1.5	4.5	8.0	6.1	4.2	10.2	0.1	1980	5 Produits chimiques
2.6	7.5	4.4	1.5	2.4	4.9	3.7	3.1	14.2	0.1	1990	
2.7	7.8	4.7	1.5	2.4	5.4	4.2	2.9	15.9	0.1	1991	
2.7	8.5	4.4	1.6	2.3	5.4	4.3	3.1	16.1	0.1	1992	
3.1	9.1	4.6	1.7	2.2	5.9	4.8	3.2	17.2	0.1	1993	
4.4	12.3	1.4	1.7	6.1	7.9	6.2	6.9	9.5	0.1	1980	7 Machines et matériels de transports
4.6	17.3	2.9	1.7	2.5	4.5	3.2	2.9	13.3	0.1	1990	
4.6	16.7	2.9	1.4	2.5	4.9	3.7	3.5	14.9	0.1	1991	
4.3	17.6	2.6	1.5	2.3	5.7	4.4	3.8	15.9	0.1	1992	
4.6	19.5	2.9	1.5	2.1	6.0	4.7	3.6	19.1	0.1	1993	
2.2	10.8	2.7	1.4	4.2	4.9	3.5	6.0	8.0	0.1	1980	6&8 Articles manufacturés divers
2.9	14.2	5.3	1.3	2.0	3.0	1.9	3.1	12.6	0.1	1990	
2.9	13.7	5.2	1.3	2.0	3.5	2.5	3.3	14.3	0.1	1991	
2.8	14.0	4.7	1.3	2.0	3.8	2.8	3.6	15.7	0.1	1992	
3.0	15.8	5.2	1.3	1.9	4.3	3.1	3.7	16.9	0.1	1993	

Voir la fin du tableau pour la remarque générale et les notes.

SPECIAL TABLE: D

Structure of world exports by commodity classes and by regions (continued)

In per cent

Origin or destination → / ↓ SITC Commodity classes	Year	World Monde /1,2,3	Developed economies Econ. dévelop-pées /2,3,4	Developing economies Economies en voie de développement /1,3,4: Total	Developing economies: OPEC OPEP	Eastern Europe & the former USSR Europe de l'Est et l'ancienne URSS: Total /2,3,6	Eastern Europe & the former USSR: Former USSR /7	Develope Economie: Europe: Total /2	Develope Economie: Europe: EEC CEE /2	Develope Economie: Europe: EFTA AELE	Develope Economie: South Africa Afrique du Sud
Commodity composition of the total exports of selected regions											
0-9 Total all commodities /5	1980	100.0	100.0	100.0	100.0	100.0	100.0	100.0	100.0	100.0	100.0
	1990	100.0	100.0	100.0	100.0	100.0	100.0	100.0	100.0	100.0	100.0
	1991	100.0	100.0	100.0	100.0	100.0	100.0	100.0	100.0	100.0	100.0
	1992	100.0	100.0	100.0	100.0	100.0	100.0	100.0	100.0	100.0	100.0
	1993	100.0	100.0	100.0	100.0	100.0	100.0	100.0	100.0	100.0	100.0
0&1 Food, live animals, beverages and tobacco	1980	9.7	10.1	10.4	1.1	3.3	1.7	9.6	10.5	4.0	8.4
	1990	8.6	8.4	10.3	3.1	4.9	1.5	9.0	9.8	3.7	13.0
	1991	8.9	8.5	10.3	3.6	7.5	1.5	9.4	10.3	3.9	13.0
	1992	8.9	8.7	9.6	3.9	8.3	3.7	9.8	10.7	3.9	7.1
	1993	8.7	8.5	9.2	4.0	7.2	3.8	9.9	10.8	4.0	6.3
2&4 Crude materials, oils and fats, (fuels excluded)	1980	6.8	6.6	7.2	1.6	6.2	9.2	4.2	3.5	8.6	7.4
	1990	5.1	4.7	6.3	2.5	5.9	7.4	3.4	3.1	5.4	20.2
	1991	4.8	4.3	5.9	3.0	7.2	7.4	3.2	2.9	4.8	20.2
	1992	4.5	4.0	5.6	3.4	7.7	8.7	3.0	2.8	4.6	9.3
	1993	4.4	4.0	5.1	3.2	7.7	9.5	2.9	2.7	4.5	8.4
3 Mineral fuels, lubricants and related material	1980	24.3	6.9	60.6	95.1	25.9	47.0	8.3	8.0	10.1	3.8
	1990	10.5	4.3	25.9	81.4	26.5	42.6	4.4	3.7	8.4	13.9
	1991	9.3	4.3	22.7	78.4	25.4	42.6	4.4	3.7	9.0	14.0
	1992	8.6	3.9	20.1	75.6	27.7	46.4	4.1	3.3	9.1	6.2
	1993	8.6	4.0	18.9	74.1	24.0	41.2	4.2	3.5	9.2	6.9
5 Chemicals	1980	6.8	9.6	1.7	0.5	3.8	2.2	11.1	11.4	9.7	2.2
	1990	8.8	10.4	4.5	2.8	6.3	3.6	11.9	12.0	11.2	6.5
	1991	8.9	10.5	4.7	2.5	6.5	3.6	12.0	12.1	11.9	6.5
	1992	9.0	10.5	4.7	2.9	7.8	6.5	12.3	12.2	12.5	5.3
	1993	8.9	10.6	4.7	3.0	7.7	6.5	12.7	12.6	13.1	4.7
7 Machinery and transport equipment	1980	24.9	34.3	5.1	0.5	25.0	16.0	32.0	32.7	28.1	2.0
	1990	35.7	41.8	19.1	1.1	25.8	15.2	37.5	38.3	32.7	3.6
	1991	36.7	42.5	21.2	1.6	20.6	15.2	37.8	38.6	32.4	3.6
	1992	37.1	42.8	23.1	1.6	16.7	8.3	38.0	38.8	32.4	6.7
	1993	37.6	43.2	25.5	2.1	15.4	6.5	37.4	38.2	32.0	7.0
6&8 Other manufactured goods	1980	23.4	29.1	14.2	1.2	12.8	6.5	32.9	32.0	38.8	16.3
	1990	28.5	27.9	32.8	9.0	16.6	7.0	32.2	31.2	38.2	40.3
	1991	28.9	27.4	34.3	10.5	19.5	7.0	31.5	30.6	37.6	40.3
	1992	29.3	27.1	35.6	12.3	27.9	21.2	31.3	30.4	37.2	25.2
	1993	29.0	26.4	35.4	13.2	32.7	24.4	30.7	29.7	36.9	26.8
Commodity composition of the world exports to selected regions											
0-9 Total all commodities /5	1980	100.0	100.0	100.0	100.0	100.0	100.0	100.0	100.0	100.0	100.0
	1990	100.0	100.0	100.0	100.0	100.0	100.0	100.0	100.0	100.0	100.0
	1991	100.0	100.0	100.0	100.0	100.0	100.0	100.0	100.0	100.0	100.0
	1992	100.0	100.0	100.0	100.0	100.0	100.0	100.0	100.0	100.0	100.0
	1993	100.0	100.0	100.0	100.0	100.0	100.0	100.0	100.0	100.0	100.0
0&1 Food, live animals, beverages and tobacco	1980	9.7	9.0	10.3	12.3	13.3	20.5	9.8	10.5	5.3	2.6
	1990	8.6	8.6	8.3	12.7	11.6	17.4	9.3	10.0	5.0	5.0
	1991	8.9	9.1	7.6	10.6	15.8	24.4	9.8	10.5	5.3	5.1
	1992	8.9	9.2	7.7	9.9	15.9	25.4	10.1	10.7	5.4	8.6
	1993	8.7	9.0	7.2	10.4	14.6	22.8	10.2	10.9	5.6	5.7
2&4 Crude materials, oils and fats, (fuels excluded)	1980	6.8	7.0	5.9	3.2	6.9	5.0	6.8	7.2	4.4	4.3
	1990	5.1	5.1	5.3	4.1	5.2	4.4	5.1	5.3	3.8	3.4
	1991	4.8	4.7	5.0	3.7	4.8	4.4	4.6	4.8	3.7	2.9
	1992	4.5	4.5	4.9	4.0	4.2	3.2	4.5	4.5	4.0	3.3
	1993	4.4	4.3	4.5	4.2	3.6	2.6	4.3	4.4	4.1	3.2
3 Mineral fuels, lubricants and related material	1980	24.3	26.8	17.9	4.2	11.8	0.9	22.6	23.8	16.1	2.5
	1990	10.5	10.2	9.7	2.9	13.0	1.9	8.7	9.1	6.0	0.6
	1991	9.3	9.3	8.4	3.0	9.7	1.5	7.8	8.1	5.7	0.7
	1992	8.6	8.9	7.3	3.7	10.4	2.3	7.3	7.5	5.8	0.8
	1993	8.6	9.0	7.2	4.1	10.0	2.3	7.6	7.8	6.3	0.8
5 Chemicals	1980	6.8	6.6	7.8	6.9	6.9	7.3	7.8	7.8	8.2	10.6
	1990	8.8	8.5	9.8	10.0	8.3	9.6	9.9	10.0	9.9	14.2
	1991	8.9	8.6	9.8	9.1	9.3	10.4	9.9	9.9	10.1	13.7
	1992	9.0	8.9	9.4	8.7	8.6	7.0	10.2	10.2	10.6	13.3
	1993	8.9	8.8	9.2	9.1	9.2	7.1	10.5	10.4	11.3	13.2
7 Machinery and transport equipment	1980	24.9	22.8	31.7	40.1	27.8	29.2	22.2	21.6	25.6	56.5
	1990	35.7	35.6	37.2	39.3	34.2	38.4	34.0	33.7	35.5	50.3
	1991	36.7	36.4	38.9	43.1	33.1	34.1	35.0	34.9	35.5	51.0
	1992	37.1	36.8	39.8	42.9	32.8	33.3	35.1	35.1	35.4	46.8
	1993	37.6	36.6	41.6	40.7	32.5	34.7	33.9	33.8	34.0	48.0
6&8 Other manufactured goods	1980	23.4	24.4	22.7	29.9	20.1	23.1	27.4	26.0	35.3	21.6
	1990	28.5	29.7	26.8	28.7	21.5	26.2	30.9	30.0	36.3	24.3
	1991	28.9	29.9	27.8	28.4	22.3	22.4	31.0	30.2	36.5	24.4
	1992	29.3	29.9	28.7	28.6	25.3	24.2	31.3	30.7	35.7	25.0
	1993	29.0	29.7	28.1	29.2	27.7	26.5	30.8	30.2	34.7	26.8

For general note and footnotes see end of table.

Structure des exportations mondiales par catégories de marchandises et par régions (suite)

En pourcentage

Economies développées /2,3,4: Canada	U.S.A. / E.-U.	Japan / Japon	Australia New Zealand / Australie Nouvelle-Zélande	Developing economies / Economies en voie de développement /1,3,4: Africa / Afrique	America / Amerique: Total	America / Amerique: LAIA / ALADI	Asia / Asie: Mid.East / Moyen Orient	Asia / Asie: Other / Autres /8	Oceania / Océanie	Année	← En provenance ou vers / CTCI:Classes de marchandises ↓
Composition par marchandises des exportations totales des régions selectionnées											
100.0	100.0	100.0	100.0	100.0	100.0	100.0	100.0	100.0	100.0	1980	0-9 Total tous produits /5
100.0	100.0	100.0	100.0	100.0	100.0	100.0	100.0	100.0	100.0	1990	
100.0	100.0	100.0	100.0	100.0	100.0	100.0	100.0	100.0	100.0	1991	
100.0	100.0	100.0	100.0	100.0	100.0	100.0	100.0	100.0	100.0	1992	
100.0	100.0	100.0	100.0	100.0	100.0	100.0	100.0	100.0	100.0	1993	
10.8	14.0	1.2	36.3	8.7	28.4	24.5	1.3	11.8	35.9	1980	0&1 Produits alimentaires, boissons et tabacs.
7.8	9.7	0.6	23.5	11.3	24.0	20.0	4.3	7.5	28.4	1990	
8.3	9.1	0.6	22.3	11.8	24.8	21.2	5.0	7.4	26.2	1991	
8.7	9.4	0.6	23.2	11.8	21.7	18.5	5.2	7.0	24.7	1992	
7.3	9.0	0.5	26.4	12.1	21.0	17.8	5.2	6.5	18.7	1993	
19.4	11.9	1.2	28.9	6.5	11.6	12.0	0.7	13.2	44.1	1980	2&4 Matières premières huiles & graisses (combust. exclu.)
13.9	7.5	0.7	17.8	8.6	11.5	12.1	1.9	5.3	37.0	1990	
12.2	6.7	0.7	18.1	8.2	11.7	12.3	2.1	4.7	33.3	1991	
11.9	6.3	0.7	17.4	8.8	9.8	9.9	2.2	4.7	33.7	1992	
11.6	5.9	0.6	21.1	8.9	8.9	8.9	2.1	4.2	32.5	1993	
14.5	3.7	0.4	9.1	78.7	39.0	39.9	94.6	20.5	1.4	1980	3 Combustibles minéraux et produits
10.0	3.3	0.4	14.7	62.2	27.3	27.0	75.0	8.1	0.5	1990	
10.8	3.0	0.4	15.3	62.7	23.4	22.6	72.4	7.4	0.5	1991	
10.5	2.6	0.5	15.6	59.9	19.3	18.4	72.1	6.3	0.5	1992	
10.5	2.2	0.5	16.5	58.8	17.9	16.9	72.4	5.6	20.0	1993	
5.4	9.6	5.1	2.5	0.6	2.7	2.7	0.7	2.7	0.1	1980	5 Produits chimiques
5.2	10.4	5.5	2.8	3.7	5.0	4.8	4.3	4.4	0.5	1990	
5.3	10.7	5.5	3.1	3.6	5.5	5.3	3.6	4.7	0.4	1991	
5.3	10.3	5.6	3.3	3.6	5.1	4.8	3.9	4.8	0.2	1992	
5.2	10.2	5.6	3.8	3.6	5.0	4.7	3.9	4.8	0.2	1993	
25.7	39.0	58.4	5.0	0.2	5.1	6.2	0.8	12.9	0.4	1980	7 Machines et matériels de transports
37.2	46.1	70.7	5.6	1.5	10.6	12.1	1.9	28.6	4.8	1990	
37.4	46.9	70.9	6.4	1.7	12.0	13.8	3.0	29.9	5.6	1991	
37.3	47.3	71.6	6.8	1.7	20.3	22.7	2.6	30.3	4.7	1992	
39.5	47.6	72.0	8.0	1.6	22.7	25.4	2.7	33.1	2.6	1993	
21.1	17.9	32.4	13.9	4.6	12.5	14.2	1.8	37.0	15.7	1980	6&8 Articles manufacturés divers
19.7	18.9	20.5	14.3	12.3	20.8	23.1	12.4	44.7	16.5	1990	
19.9	19.7	20.3	14.3	11.4	21.5	23.9	13.4	45.0	15.2	1991	
20.2	19.8	19.5	14.6	13.2	22.9	24.7	13.7	45.6	15.0	1992	
20.2	19.9	19.0	15.3	14.5	23.4	25.3	13.4	44.4	11.4	1993	
Composition par marchandises des exportations mondiales vers régions selectionnées											
100.0	100.0	100.0	100.0	100.0	100.0	100.0	100.0	100.0	100.0	1980	0-9 Total tous produits /5
100.0	100.0	100.0	100.0	100.0	100.0	100.0	100.0	100.0	100.0	1990	
100.0	100.0	100.0	100.0	100.0	100.0	100.0	100.0	100.0	100.0	1991	
100.0	100.0	100.0	100.0	100.0	100.0	100.0	100.0	100.0	100.0	1992	
100.0	100.0	100.0	100.0	100.0	100.0	100.0	100.0	100.0	100.0	1993	
6.1	7.4	9.7	4.5	13.9	9.5	9.5	11.7	9.0	20.3	1980	0&1 Produits alimentaires, boissons et tabacs.
5.6	5.4	14.1	4.8	14.1	9.0	8.5	12.8	5.8	14.7	1990	
5.9	5.7	14.5	5.1	12.9	8.4	7.8	10.7	5.6	14.9	1991	
6.0	5.2	15.8	4.8	14.0	8.0	7.4	10.2	5.9	14.4	1992	
5.9	4.9	15.7	4.7	14.4	7.9	7.3	10.2	5.3	14.5	1993	
4.8	4.3	15.2	4.3	4.1	3.9	4.7	2.9	9.1	2.1	1980	2&4 Matières premières huiles & graisses (combust. exclu.)
3.3	2.9	12.4	2.9	5.5	4.5	5.4	3.7	6.0	1.6	1990	
3.3	2.7	11.2	2.7	4.8	4.3	5.1	3.4	5.7	2.0	1991	
3.3	2.7	10.6	2.7	5.2	3.9	4.4	4.4	5.2	1.8	1992	
3.2	2.7	10.3	2.7	5.2	3.8	4.3	4.7	4.7	2.3	1993	
13.0	34.3	52.5	16.1	8.8	24.1	17.2	10.5	21.6	21.5	1980	3 Combustibles minéraux et produits
4.6	13.7	18.9	4.4	7.0	10.8	6.8	8.1	10.0	13.6	1990	
3.9	11.1	21.2	5.5	10.4	8.7	5.1	7.0	8.1	14.5	1991	
3.2	11.1	20.6	5.0	5.3	7.8	6.1	6.0	7.6	11.4	1992	
2.8	10.6	19.0	5.4	5.8	7.8	6.0	6.5	7.3	11.4	1993	
5.5	3.3	4.2	8.8	7.6	9.0	10.0	6.0	8.1	4.7	1980	5 Produits chimiques
7.0	4.6	6.9	10.5	9.1	10.8	12.5	9.0	9.8	5.1	1990	
7.3	5.1	7.0	10.7	8.8	11.0	12.2	7.8	10.1	5.2	1991	
7.9	5.2	7.3	11.2	9.3	10.2	10.8	7.8	9.6	5.3	1992	
8.1	5.1	7.2	11.2	9.5	10.3	11.1	8.0	9.0	5.4	1993	
43.9	26.3	5.8	36.0	37.8	32.4	37.0	35.6	27.6	25.6	1980	7 Machines et matériels de transports
50.7	43.0	18.5	45.7	38.4	39.9	42.9	34.5	37.3	33.5	1990	
51.4	44.3	18.2	42.2	37.7	41.3	44.0	39.2	38.7	30.0	1991	
50.8	44.9	18.1	43.2	38.9	44.3	46.1	39.4	38.9	35.7	1992	
50.6	45.7	18.9	43.4	37.6	43.8	45.6	38.4	42.4	34.3	1993	
20.6	21.6	10.1	27.9	24.3	18.8	19.5	29.1	21.8	22.4	1980	6&8 Articles manufacturés divers
25.3	28.0	26.5	28.5	24.4	21.4	20.9	29.0	28.3	26.0	1990	
25.5	28.7	25.7	29.5	24.1	23.4	23.0	29.0	29.4	27.3	1991	
25.8	28.3	25.4	29.1	25.9	23.5	22.7	29.9	30.5	25.6	1992	
26.0	28.5	26.6	28.7	25.9	24.1	23.4	29.9	29.0	25.9	1993	

Voir la page suivante pour la remarque générale et les notes.

SPECIAL TABLE: D

Structure of world exports by commodity classes and by regions (continued)
Structure des exportations mondiales par catégories de marchandises et par régions (suite)

General note

The regional analysis in this table and Special Table C is in accordance with Special Table A of this issue.

The figures in this table and table C are derived from the data in Special Table B. For the treatment of data on Germany see the general note on page vi.

The commodity classification is in accordance with the United Nations' Standard International Trade Classification (SITC), Revision 2, for 1980 through 1987 except for countries which report trade data only in terms of the SITC, Revised. Beginning 1988 the commodity classification is in accordance with the SITC, Revision 3, except for countries which report trade data only in terms of the SITC, Revision 2, or the SITC, Revised.

The data approximate total exports of all countries and areas of the world with the exception of the inter-trade between China, the Democratic People's Republic of Korea, Mongolia and Viet Nam in 1980 and trade conducted in accordance with the supplementary protocol to the treaty on the basis of relations between the Federal Republic of Germany and the former German Democratic Republic. They are based on official export figures converted, where necessary, to U.S. dollars according to conversion factors published in Table 1 for each country in this volume. Where official figures are not available estimates based on the imports reported by partner countries and on other subsidiary data are used. Some official national data have been adjusted

(a) to approximate the commodity groupings of the SITC and

(b) to approximate calendar years.

The data include special category (confidential) exports, ships' stores and bunkers and exports of minor importance, the destination of which cannot be determined. These data are included in the world totals for each commodity group and in total exports, but are excluded from all regions of destination. For 'all commodities' approximately 1 1/2 per cent of total exports are not distributed. All data are generally in accordance with the special trade system.

1/ Excluding the inter-trade between China, the Democratic People's Republic of Korea, Mongolia and Viet Nam in 1980. The figures shown for other years are based on the import statistics of China.

2/ Excluding the trade conducted in accordance with the supplementary protocol to the treaty on the basis of relations between the Federal Republic of Germany and former the German Democratic Republic.

3/ Exports of the former USSR for which country of destination is not available are included in the totals for the World, the 'Developed economies', the 'Developing economies' and 'Eastern Europe and the former USSR' but are excluded from the regional components of these groupings.

4/ This classification is intended for statistical convenience and does not, necessarily, express a judgement about the stage reached by a particular country in the development process.

5/ Section 9 of the SITC, which comprises commodities and transactions not classified elsewhere, is included in the total trade but is not shown separately in this table.

6/ Beginning 1992, includes Eastern Europe and the European countries of the former USSR.

7/ Prior to 1992, data refer to the former USSR. Beginning 1992, data refer to the European countries of the former USSR - Belarus Estonia, Latvia, Lithuania, Republic of Moldova, the Russian Federation, and Ukraine.

8/ Beginning 1992, includes Armenia, Azerbaijan, Georgia, Kazakhstan, Kyrgyzstan, Tajikistan, Turkmenistan, and Uzbekistan.

Remarque générale

L'analyse régionale dans ce tableau et le Tableau Spécial C est conforme au Tableau Spécial A de ce numéro.

Les données de ce tableau et le tableau C sont derivées de celles publiées dans le Tableau Spécial B. Pour le traitement des données de l'Allemagne voir la remarque générale à la page vi.

La classification par marchandise utilisée est la Classification type pour le commerce international (CTCI), Revision 2, des Nations Unies, pour les années allant de 1980 à 1987 en dehors des pays qui rapportent exclusivement les données du commerce en accord avec la CTCI, Revisée. A partir de 1988 la classification par marchandise utilisée est en accord avec la CTCI, Revision 3, en dehors des pays qui rapportent exclusivement les données du commerce en accord avec la CTCI, Revision 2, ou la CTCI, Revisée.

Les données approchées des exportations totales de tous pays et régions du monde a l'exclusion des échanges entre la Chine, la République populaire démocratique de Corée, la Mongolie et le Viet Nam en 1980 et le commerce effectué en a ccord avec le protocole additionnel au traité définissant la base des relations entre la République fédérale d'Allemagne et l'ancienne République démocratique allemande. Elles sont basées sur les chiffres des exportations officielles nationales convertis en dollars E.-U. selon les facteurs de conversion publiés dans le Tableau 1 pour chaque pays dans ce tome. Quand les chiffres officiels ne sont pas disponibles on a recours a des estimations basées sur les importations rapportées par les pays partenaires ou sur d'autres données subsidiaires. Quelques données officielles nationales ont été ajustées

(a) qu'elles correspondent aux groups des marchandises de la CTCI et

(b) qu'elles correspondent aux années civiles.

Les données comprises les exportations de 'special category' (confidentielles), les approvisionnements des navires et combustible de soute et autres exportations de moindre importance dont la destination n'a pu être déterminée. Ces données sont comprises dans les totaux de chaque groupe de marchandise et dans les exportations totales, mais elles ne sont pas comprises dans les régions de destination. Pour 'tous produits' approximativement 1 1/2 pourcent des exportations totales ne sont pas distribuées. En générale, toutes les données correspondent au commerce spécial.

1/ Non compris le commerce entre la Chine, la République populaire démocratique de Corée, la Mongolie et le Viet Nam en 1980. Les chiffres indiqués pour les autres années sont bases sur les statistiques d'importations de la Chine.

2/ Non compris le commerce effectué en accord avec le protocole additionnel au traité définissant la base des relations entre la République fédérale d'Allemagne et l'ancienne République démocratique allemande.

3/ Les exportations en provenance de l'ancienne URSS dont les pays de destination ne sont pas disponibles sont comprises dans les totaux du Monde, des 'Economies développées', des 'Economies en voie de développement' et de 'Europe de l'Est et l'ancienne URSS', mais ils ne sont pas comprises dans chaque partie composant ces régions.

4/ Cette classification est utilisée pour plus de commodité dans la présentation des statistiques et n'implique pas nécessairement un jugement quant au stade de développement auquel est parvenu un pays donné.

5/ Section 9 de la CTCI, qui représente les articles et transactions non classes ailleurs est comprise dans le commerce total mais n'est pas présentée séparément dans ce tableau.

6/ A partir de janvier 1992, y compris de l'Europe de l'est et les pays européens de l'ancienne URSS.

7/ Avant l'année 1992, les données se rapportent à l'ancienne URSS. A partir de l'année 1992, les données se rapportent aux pays européens de l'ancienne URSS - Bélarus, Estonie, Lettonie, Lituanie, République de Moldova, Fédération de Russie, et Ukraine.

8/ A partir de l'année 1992, y compris Azerbaïdjan, Arménie, Géorgie, Kazakhstan, Kirghizistan, Tadjikistan, Turkménistan, et Ouzbékistan.

129. Total imports and exports: Index numbers by countries or areas

Imports – Importations
Quantum index
1990 = 100

Country or area	1980	1985	1986	1987	1988	1989	1990	1991	1992	1993	1994
Australia	58	77	74	76	89	108	100	99	107	114	...
Austria	59	69	71	75	82	90	100	101	107	106	119
Bangladesh	...	...	...	...	...	...	...	...	...	...	...
Belgium–Luxembourg	70	73	80	88	88	94	100	104	105	...	...
Bolivia [6]	..	..	..	..	..	..	..	..	..	..	..
Brazil	115	68	92	90	80	92	100	110	...	...	...
Bulgaria	95	127	132	130	137	130	100	83	...	...	...
Canada	61	72	80	89	95	100	100	102	109	120	138
Colombia [6]	..	..	..	..	..	..	..	..	..	..	..
Cyprus [6]	..	..	..	..	..	..	..	..	..	..	..
Czechoslovakia (former) [6]	..	..	..	..	..	..	..	..	..	..	..
Denmark	76	90	96	95	94	94	100	105	109	101	129
Dominica	54	57	63	75	80	93	100	89	...	...	...
Dominican Republic	...	...	...	...	...	...	...	...	...	...	...
Ecuador [6]	..	..	..	..	..	..	..	..	..	..	..
El Salvador [6]	..	..	..	..	..	..	..	..	..	..	..
Ethiopia [6]	..	..	..	..	..	..	..	..	..	..	..
Faeroe Islands	92	112	136	146	146	125	100	100	...	...	...
Fiji [6]	..	..	..	..	..	..	..	..	..	..	..
Finland	73	75	80	86	94	104	100	83	81	78	...
France	71	72	77	82	90	95	100	102	104	97	114
Germany (Fed. Rep.) [7]	64	70	75	79	84	90	100	113	115	104	113
Greece	51	71	72	81	66	89	100	113	119	...	...
Guatemala	89	70	57	88	62	92	100	117	125	133	...
Honduras [6]	..	..	..	..	..	..	..	..	..	..	..
Hong Kong	30	44	49	65	82	90	100	119	145	55	187
Hungary	93	99	102	104	104	105	100	105	98	119	...
Iceland	83	88	95	118	112	100	100	105	97	84	...
India	46	65	85	90	96	97	100	91	120	...	...
Indonesia [6]	..	..	..	..	..	..	..	..	..	..	..
Ireland	63	72	75	80	83	94	100	101	106	112	124
Israel	58	73	86	96	97	92	100	116	130	146	166
Italy	65	72	75	83	88	94	100	104	108	96	...
Japan	57	63	69	75	87	94	100	104	104	107	121
Jordan	85	101	106	110	116	96	100	99	135	148	144
Kenya	127	72	85	89	100	105	100	93	...	...	...
Korea, Republic of	33	51	56	67	77	88	100	117	119	130	158
Liberia [6]	...	...	...	...	...	...	...	...	...	...	...
Malawi [6]	..	..	..	..	..	..	..	..	..	..	..
Malaysia [6]	..	..	..	..	..	..	..	..	..	..	..
Malta [6]	..	..	..	..	..	..	..	..	..	..	..
Mauritius	...	...	...	...	...	...	...	...	...	...	...
Mexico [6]	..	..	..	..	..	..	..	..	..	..	..
Morocco	62	66	66	68	89	87	100	112	128	120	..
Myanmar [6]	..	..	..	..	..	..	..	..	..	..	..
Netherlands	69	77	80	85	90	95	100	104	106	110	118
New Zealand	62	76	75	85	77	93	100	90	100	104	121
Norway [5]	77	94	108	106	95	90	100	102	106	107	...
Pakistan	67	77	75	77	100	105	100	105	122	124	119
Panama [6]	..	..	..	..	..	..	..	..	..	..	..

For general note, see end of table.

Voir la fin du tableau pour la remarque générale.

129. Importations et exportations totales: Indices par pays ou zones

Exports – Exportations
Indice du quantum
1990 = 100

1980	1985	1986	1987	1988	1989	1990	1991	1992	1993	1994	Pays ou zone
64	81	84	94	89	94	100	115	121	128	...	Australie
53	70	71	72	80	90	100	106	111	108	119	Autriche
...	...	...	...	...	...	...	...	...	...	...	Bangladesh
67	77	83	89	90	94	100	104	106	...	...	Belgique–Luxembourg
113	84	94	81	82	94	100	101	99	93	95	Bolivie
61	96	79	92	109	109	100	104	...	...	...	Brésil
94	133	128	130	133	130	100	70	...	...	...	Bulgarie
58	80	84	93	94	96	100	101	110	121	140	Canada
..	..	..	..	..	..	..	..	..	..	..	Colombie [6]
..	..	..	..	..	..	..	..	..	..	..	Chypre [6]
..	..	..	..	..	..	..	..	..	..	..	Tchécoslovaquie (anc.) [6]
65	80	82	83	87	92	100	106	111	108	99	Danemark
27	62	83	96	107	88	100	94	...	...	...	Dominique
99	110	91	111	114	117	100	95	90	93	...	Rép. dominicaine
58	98	105	68	100	98	100	106	108	121	136	Equateur
..	..	..	..	..	..	..	..	..	..	..	El Salvador [6]
104	96	111	104	106	115	100	57	50	...	...	Ethiopie
62	86	86	83	89	102	100	104	...	...	...	Iles Féroé
..	..	..	..	..	..	..	..	..	..	..	Fidji [6]
80	92	93	94	97	97	100	91	99	117	...	Finlande
70	79	78	81	88	95	100	105	108	106	118	France
65	82	83	86	92	99	100	100	102	98	112	Allemagne (Rép.féd.) [7]
74	86	101	103	77	105	100	115	123	...	...	Grèce
92	81	113	90	91	101	100	125	145	136	...	Guatemala
118	115	107	123	109	99	100	88	102	90	79	Honduras
26	43	50	66	84	92	100	117	140	48	176	Hong–kong [4]
74	96	94	97	104	104	100	95	96	84	...	Hongrie
81	86	95	99	98	101	100	92	91	96	...	Islande
76	52	59	71	74	91	100	114	116	...	...	Inde
92	91	98	94	93	102	100	128	117	126	213	Indonésie
44	65	69	79	83	92	100	106	120	132	152	Irlande
62	82	91	101	96	100	100	98	107	121	140	Israël
65	81	82	84	89	97	100	100	104	112	...	Italie
62	88	87	87	91	95	100	102	104	101	103	Japon
40	72	74	88	102	104	100	88	96	104	112	Jordanie
89	81	93	90	95	94	100	108	...	...	...	Kenya
33	60	67	83	93	94	100	110	119	129	146	Corée, République de
...	...	...	...	...	...	...	...	...	...	...	Libéria
..	..	..	..	..	..	..	..	..	..	..	Malawi [6]
65	76	82	86	92	98	100	97	96	86	84	Malaisie
..	..	..	..	..	..	..	..	..	..	..	Malte [6]
...	...	...	...	...	...	...	...	...	...	...	Maurice
		..					..	..	..	..	Mexique [6]
44	66	66	72	82	92	100	108	101	105	...	Maroc
107	100	119	88	59	72	100	96	108	149	137	Myanmar
66	77	80	83	91	95	100	105	108	115	122	Pays–Bas
73	93	91	94	97	95	100	110	113	118	130	Nouvelle–Zélande
54	67	69	78	81	93	100	106	115	121	...	Norvege [5]
51	56	75	82	90	94	100	113	124	112	139	Pakistan
124	97	94	94	79	93	100	95	97	116	...	Panama

For general note, see end of table.

Voir la fin du tableau pour la remarque générale.

SPECIAL TABLE: E

129. Total imports and exports: Index numbers by countries or areas(Continued)

Imports – Importations
Quantum index
1990 = 100

Country or area	1980	1985	1986	1987	1988	1989	1990	1991	1992	1993	1994
Papua New Guinea.[6]	..	..	..	..	..	..	..	..	..	..	..
Peru	...	...	...	...	...	...	...	...	...	...	...
Philippines	66	41	53	64	78	93	100	...	...	...	...
Poland	127	113	118	124	136	138	100	156	...	210	238
Portugal	38	43	52	66	81	88	100	106	119	...	...
Rwanda.[6]	..	..	..	..	..	..	..	..	..	..	..
Seychelles	...	60	64	63	87	97	100	95	107	147	...
Singapore	40	50	54	62	79	87	100	107	114	137	...
Solomon Islands.[6]	..	..	..	..	..	..	..	..	..	..	..
South Africa	132	91	95	95	111	111	100	104	105	109	128
Spain	43	44	52	63	78	91	100	112	121	118	130
Sri Lanka	107	105	120	106	101	95	100	114	125	144	154
Sweden	70	80	83	89	94	100	100	93	95	97	108
Switzerland	68	75	82	88	93	98	100	99	94	93	102
Syrian Arab Republic	133	161	152	114	98	92	100	163	143	...	...
Thailand	38	41	40	49	68	82	100	109	117	131	...
Trinidad and Tobago	124	128	131	103	87	106	100	...	...	...	...
Tunisia	92	77	93	68	85	101	100	107	104	115	...
Turkey	34	68	76	86	86	87	100	96	98	134	105
USSR (former)	63	84	79	78	81	102	100	...	...	...	...
United Kingdom	55	70	75	80	92	100	100	95	101	101	108
United States	54	79	87	90	93	98	100	98	106	117	131
Venezuela.[6]	..	..	..	..	..	..	..	..	..	..	..
Yugoslavia [6]	..	..	..	..	..	..	..	..	..	..	..
Zimbabwe.[6]	..	..	..	..	..	..	..	..	..	..	..

For general note and footnotes, see end of table.

129. Importations et exportations totales: Indices par pays ou zones(suite)

Exports – Exportations
Indice du quantum
1990 = 100

1980	1985	1986	1987	1988	1989	1990	1991	1992	1993	1994	Pays ou zone
..	..	..	..	..	..	..	..	..	..	..	Papouasie–Nvl–Guinée 6
...	...	...	...	...	...	...	...	...	...	...	Pérou
64	60	74	74	84	93	100	...	...	...	...	Philippines
72	77	81	85	92	92	100	103	...	96	114	Pologne
35	56	61	68	74	89	100	101	107	...	...	Portugal
44	67	76	94	72	72	100	87	78	...	...	Rwanda
...	18	17	44	93	102	100	136	126	106	...	Seychelles
34	46	53	62	83	92	100	113	123	145	...	Singapour
74	94	116	85	94	92	100	106	...	...	...	Iles Salomon
92	102	106	98	100	108	100	107	108	109	118	Afrique du Sud
53	76	72	77	85	89	100	111	117	135	160	Espagne
66	83	89	87	84	86	100	104	120	137	184	Sri Lanka
69	90	93	96	99	101	100	98	99	107	114	Suède
71	82	86	86	91	96	100	99	103	104	109	Suisse
54	45	43	46	51	78	100	104	105	...	...	Rép. arabe syrienne
41	59	48	57	72	89	100	119	134	149	...	Thaïlande
88	95	94	92	95	94	100	...	...	...	...	Trinité–et–Tobago
102	82	92	95	96	110	100	110	111	121	...	Tunisie
20	65	71	88	88	95	100	107	110	117	134	Turquie
81	89	98	102	107	113	100	...	...	...	...	URSS (anc.)
67	80	83	87	88	94	100	101	103	103	115	Royaume–Uni
74	63	63	71	84	93	100	106	113	116	126	Etats–Unis 3
..	..	..	..	..	..	..	..	..	..	..	Venezuela 6
..	..	..	..	..	..	..	..	..	..	..	Yougoslavie 6
..	..	..	..	..	..	..	..	..	..	..	Zimbabwe 6

Voir la fin du tableau pour la remarque generale et les notes.

129. Total imports and exports: Index numbers by countries or areas(continued)

Imports – Importations
Unit value index(In national currency)
1990 = 100

Country or area	1980	1985	1986	1987	1988	1989	1990	1991	1992	1993	1994
Australia 2	60	86	94	99	97	96	100	101	106	114	112
Austria	96	113	103	99	100	103	100	100	99	96	94
Bangladesh	43	77	86	95	89	90	100	120	...	...	...
Belgium–Luxembourg	74	112	94	88	94	102	100	98	94	...	...
Bolivia	..	..	..	..	..	..	..	..	..	..	..
Brazil 1	97	90	70	82	89	96	100	93	...	...	...
Bulgaria	...	...	...	...	...	...	...	...	...	...	...
Canada	83	101	101	97	98	98	100	99	103	109	116
Colombia 1	10	30	38	47	60	80	100	121	129	145	157
Cyprus 6	..	..	..	..	..	..	..	..	..	..	..
Czechoslovakia (former) 6	..	..	..	..	..	..	..	..	..	..	..
Denmark	77	111	103	96	97	105	100	100	97	94	107
Dominica	89	79	77	85	92	94	100	104	...	...	...
Dominican Republic	...	...	...	...	...	...	...	...	...	...	...
Ecuador 6	..	..	..	..	..	..	..	..	..	..	..
El Salvador 6	..	..	..	..	..	..	..	..	..	..	..
Ethiopia 6	..	..	..	..	..	..	..	..	..	..	..
Faeroe Islands	73	108	101	116	99	103	100	100	...	...	...
Fiji 6	..	..	..	..	..	..	..	..	..	..	..
Finland	78	105	95	93	95	98	100	102	113	129	...
France	68	111	93	92	95	101	100	99	95	90	94
Germany (Fed.Rep.) 7	97	120	101	95	96	103	100	102	99	93	95
Greece	25	61	68	68	82	92	100	110	118	127	...
Guatemala	109	101	101	100	128	117	100	96	123	119	...
Honduras 6	..	..	..	..	..	..	..	..	..	..	..
Hong Kong	58	83	87	90	94	98	100	102	102	66	104
Hungary	56	73	77	78	81	91	100	146	161	176	...
Iceland	6	44	49	53	63	83	100	103	104	113	...
India	52	65	54	60	69	86	100	122	125	...	...
Indonesia 6	..	..	..	..	..	..	..	..	..	..	..
Ireland	70	104	93	93	99	105	100	102	100	105	109
Israel 1	90	74	74	81	87	93	100	95	95	92	94
Italy	61	111	91	90	94	101	100	99	99	115	...
Japan	164	146	92	85	81	90	100	91	84	74	69
Jordan	59	62	47	48	51	74	100	100	95	96	94
Kenya	29	65	62	63	69	83	100	111	...	...	...
Korea, Republic of 1	97	88	91	88	98	100	100	100	98	92	96
Liberia 6	..	..	..	..	..	..	..	..	..	..	..
Malawi 6	..	..	..	..	..	..	..	..	..	..	..
Malaysia 6	..	..	..	..	..	..	..	..	..	..	..
Malta 6	..	..	..	..	..	..	..	..	..	..	..
Mauritius	54	86	69	72	79	96	100	105	107	118	126
Mexico		...	...	...	...	...	100	100	101	102	...
Morocco 6	...	...	...	...	...	...	...	...	...	...	...
Myanmar 6	..	..	..	..	..	..	..	..	..	..	..
Netherlands	96	122	101	94	94	101	100	100	97	93	92
New Zealand	57	100	97	93	92	99	100	101	108	107	104
Norway 5	69	88	88	91	93	99	100	98	96	97	...
Pakistan	42	73	65	76	78	92	100	107	110	118	138
Panama 6	..	..	..	..	..	..	..	..	..	..	..

For general note, see end of table.

Voir la fin du tableau pour la remarque générale.

129. Importations et exportations totales: Indices par pays our zones(suite)

Exports – Exportations
Indice de la valeur unitaire(En monnaie nationale)
1990 = 100

1980	1985	1986	1987	1988	1989	1990	1991	1992	1993	1994	Pays ou zone
62	79	80	84	94	98	100	91	93	94	92	Australie [2]
92	109	105	103	103	100	100	97	95	91	89	Autriche
58	105	89	83	97	96	100	105	...	...	...	Bangladesh
73	106	96	90	98	106	100	98	97	...	...	Belgique–Luxembourg
176	156	131	104	99	110	100	96	76	64	64	Bolivie
111	87	93	93	102	101	100	96	...	...	...	Brésil [1]
...	...	...	...	...	...	...	...	...	...	...	Bulgarie
88	98	95	94	98	101	100	96	99	104	111	Canada
14	37	57	54	70	73	100	117	118	134	174	Colombie [1]
..	..	..	..	..	..	..	..	..	..	..	Chypre [6]
..	..	..	..	..	..	..	..	..	..	..	Tchécoslovaquie (anc.) [6]
69	102	98	97	96	103	100	101	99	97	89	Danemark
73	81	91	91	99	93	100	105	...	...	...	Dominique
89	91	90	98	90	104	100	95	82	75	...	Rép. dominicaine
165	128	76	86	72	85	100	88	97	75	84	Equateur
64	...	...	...	...	...	100	...	...	...	...	El Salvador
115	110	146	107	111	108	100	97	104	...	...	Ethiopie
68	97	97	103	100	99	100	110	...	...	...	Iles Féroé
..	..	..	..	..	..	..	..	..	..	..	Fidji [6]
65	90	88	89	94	101	100	100	106	113	...	Finlande
63	98	94	93	96	102	100	100	97	94	100	France
84	102	99	96	96	101	100	99	99	94	93	Allemagne (Rép.féd.) [7]
25	57	62	67	80	92	100	110	118	125	...	Grèce
142	109	81	94	96	106	100	79	77	85	...	Guatemala
112	98	127	100	107	105	100	98	77	78	89	Honduras
59	85	87	90	93	98	100	103	104	66	105	Hong–kong [4]
60	71	72	74	79	91	100	131	143	160	...	Hongrie
6	42	51	58	68	85	100	108	104	107	...	Islande
34	60	58	65	78	93	100	111	142	...	...	Inde
157	125	87	88	82	82	100	88	84	77	85	Indonésie
67	104	97	97	104	110	100	99	97	104	105	Irlande
83	72	74	78	89	92	100	100	101	102	100	Israël [1]
50	91	87	88	92	98	100	103	104	115	...	Italie
115	116	98	92	90	97	100	100	100	96	95	Japon
49	58	50	46	53	84	100	111	107	108	113	Jordanie
49	84	90	75	86	92	100	128	...	259	266	Kenya
75	72	76	80	91	100	100	101	99	98	101	Corée, République de [1]
..	..	..	..	..	..	..	..	..	..	..	Libéria [6]
..	..	..	..	..	..	..	..	..	..	..	Malawi [6]
126	103	77	90	99	101	100	102	...	...	...	Malaisie
..	..	..	..	..	..	..	..	..	..	..	Malte [6]
39	63	67	75	80	89	100	106	114	123	129	Maurice
130	...	...	...	...	...	100	92	92	89	...	Mexique
											Maroc [6]
140	132	105	81	93	116	100	102	88	81	84	Myanmar
92	122	103	94	94	100	100	98	95	93	93	Pays–Bas
50	81	79	84	89	101	100	96	104	106	102	Nouvelle–Zélande
80	118	88	85	85	96	100	96	88	88	...	Norvege [5]
51	62	65	79	84	91	100	104	106	116	136	Pakistan
123	106	93	103	93	95	100	101	...	...	...	Panama

For general note, see end of table.

Voir la fin du tableau pour la remarque générale.

129. Total imports and exports: Index numbers by countries or areas(continued)

Imports – Importations
Unit value index(In national currency)
1990 = 100

Country or area	1980	1985	1986	1987	1988	1989	1990	1991	1992	1993	1994
Papua New Guinea	..	..	..	..	..	..	..	..	..	..	..
Peru [6]	..	..	..	..	..	..	..	..	..	..	..
Philippines [6]	..	..	..	..	..	..	..	..	..	..	..
Poland [2]							100	136	...	182	231
Portugal	34	86	79	84	90	97	100	100	95	...	...
Rwanda [6]	..	..	..	..	..	..	..	..	..	..	..
Seychelles	...	118	103	102	100	96	100	97	93	85	...
Singapore	115	105	93	101	101	101	100	97	93	92	...
Solomon Islands [6]	..	..	..	..	..	..	..	..	..	..	..
South Africa	25	57	64	69	81	91	100	105	113	124	136
Spain [2]	63	128	105	101	101	103	100	97	96	101	107
Sri Lanka	33	48	44	53	66	79	100	104	113	123	416
Sweden [2]	64	96	88	91	94	99	100	101	99	112	...
Switzerland	100	105	94	90	93	101	100	100	102	100	95
Syrian Arab Republic	63	69	82	83	102	99	100	101	98	...	...
Thailand	81	102	76	81	89	95	100	104	105	105	...
Trinidad and Tobago	39	50	68	77	86	99	100	...	...	...	...
Tunisia	48	71	70	77	81	89	100	99	94	94	...
Turkey	119	102	86	92	114	95	100	97	95	89	90
USSR (former)	...	...	...	...	...	...	...	...	...	...	...
United Kingdom	64	93	89	91	94	98	100	101	102	111	115
United States	88	87	84	89	94	97	100	100	101	100	102
Venezuela [2]	11	19	23	38	44	83	100	119	140	189	341
Yugoslavia [1, 8]	70	82	74	78	...	...	100	...	...	...	...
Zimbabwe [6]	..	..	..	..	..	..	..	..	..	..	..

For general note and footnotes, see end of table.

129. Importations et exportations totales: Indices par pays our zones

Exports – Exportations
Indice de la valeur unitaire(En monnaie nationale)
1990 = 100

1980	1985	1986	1987	1988	1989	1990	1991	1992	1993	1994	Pays ou zone
..	..	..	..	..	..	..	..	..	..	..	Papouasie–Nvl–Guinée
137	85	69	86	95	104	100	88	87	73	84	Pérou [1]
114	97	83	96	115	112	100	...	...	...	...	Philippines [1]
						100	118	...	191	246	Pologne [2]
28	74	77	86	92	97	100	100	98	...	...	Portugal
118	195	209	111	...	115	100	131	105	...	...	Rwanda
...	169	110	112	112	94	100	88	101	102	...	Seychelles
127	114	98	101	100	100	100	95	88	86	...	Singapour
49	66	59	89	107	108	100	95	...	...	...	Iles Salomon
27	52	61	67	80	96	100	105	111	122	130	Afrique du Sud
51	96	95	97	99	103	100	99	100	104	109	Espagne [2]
35	55	48	60	70	83	100	102	115	127	430	Sri Lanka
57	86	86	88	92	98	100	101	98	108	...	Suède [2]
84	95	92	92	93	99	100	103	103	103	102	Suisse
105	95	70	65	62	77	100	98	68	67	...	Rép. arabe syrienne
79	81	82	88	95	98	100	103	104	105	...	Thaïlande
69	68	66	70	66	84	100	...	...	...	...	Trinité–et–Tobago
53	76	68	78	83	95	100	97	95	96	...	Tunisie
120	84	82	93	119	91	100	99	100	98	95	Turquie
...	...	...	...	...	...	...	...	...	...	...	URSS (anc.)
65	93	86	89	92	97	100	101	103	115	118	Royaume–Uni
78	88	88	90	97	99	100	101	101	101	104	Etats–Unis [3]
12	16	10	19	20	60	100	94	108	127	...	Venezuela [2]
70	74	72	76	...	...	100	...	...	...	...	Yougoslavie [1, 8]
..	..	..	..	..	..	..	..	..	..	..	Zimbabwe [6]

Voir la fin du tableau pour la remarque generale et les notes.

SPECIAL TABLE: E

129. Total imports and exports: Index numbers by countries or areas (continued)

Terms of trade – Termes de l'échange
1990 = 100

Country or area	1980	1985	1986	1987	1988	1989	1990	1991	1992	1993	1994
Australia	103	92	85	85	97	102	100	90	88	82	82
Austria	96	96	102	104	103	97	100	97	96	95	95
Belgium–Luxembourg	99	95	102	102	104	104	100	100	103	...	...
Brazil	114	97	133	113	115	105	100	103	...	...	...
Canada	106	97	94	97	100	103	100	97	96	95	96
Colombia	140	123	150	115	117	91	100	97	91	92	111
Denmark	90	92	95	101	99	98	100	101	102	103	83
Faeroe Islands	93	90	96	89	101	96	100	110	...	...	...
Finland	83	86	93	96	99	103	100	98	94	88	...
France	93	88	101	101	101	101	100	101	102	104	106
Germany (Fed. Rep.)	87	85	98	101	100	98	100	97	100	101	98
Greece	100	93	91	99	98	100	100	100	100	98	...
Hong Kong	102	102	100	100	99	100	100	101	102	100	101
Hungary	107	97	94	95	98	100	100	90	89	91	...
Iceland	100	95	104	109	108	102	100	105	100	95	...
India	65	92	107	108	113	108	100	91	114	...	...
Ireland	96	100	104	104	105	105	100	97	97	99	96
Israel	92	97	100	96	102	99	100	105	106	111	106
Italy	82	82	96	98	98	97	100	104	105	100	...
Japan	70	79	107	108	111	108	100	110	119	130	138
Jordan	83	94	106	96	104	114	100	111	113	113	120
Kenya	169	129	145	119	125	111	100	115	...	...	...
Korea, Republic of	77	82	84	91	93	100	100	101	101	107	105
Mexico	178	...	...	...	...	...	100	92	91	87	...
Netherlands	96	100	102	100	100	99	100	98	98	100	101
New Zealand	88	81	81	90	97	102	100	95	96	99	98
Norway	116	134	100	93	91	97	100	98	92	91	...
Pakistan	121	85	100	104	108	99	100	97	96	98	99
Poland	100	100	100	100	100	114	100	87	...	105	106
Seychelles	...	143	107	110	112	98	100	91	109	120	...
South Africa	108	91	95	97	99	105	100	100	98	98	96
Spain	81	75	90	96	98	100	100	102	104	103	102
Sri Lanka	106	115	109	113	106	105	100	98	102	103	103
Sweden	89	90	98	97	98	99	100	100	99	96	...
Switzerland	84	90	98	102	100	98	100	103	101	103	107
Syrian Arab Republic	167	138	85	78	61	78	100	97	69	...	...
Thailand	98	79	108	109	107	103	100	99	99	100	...
Trinidad and Tobago	177	136	97	91	77	85	100	...	...	...	...
Tunisia	110	107	97	101	102	107	100	98	101	102	...
United Kingdom	102	100	97	98	98	99	100	100	101	104	103
United States	89	101	105	101	103	102	100	101	100	101	102
Venezuela	109	84	43	50	45	72	100	79	77	67	...
Yugoslavia [8]	100	90	97	97	...	...	100	...	...	...	...

General note: These index numbers show the changes in the volume (quantum index) and the average price (unit value index) of total imports and exports. The terms of trade figures are calculated by dividing export unit value indices by the corresponding import unit value indices. The product of the net terms of trade and the quantum index of exports is called the index of the purchasing power of exports. The footnotes to countries appearing in Special Table:A of this volume also apply to the index numbers in this table.

[1] Calculated in terms of U. S. dollars.
[2] Price index numbers; For Australia beginning 1981, for the United States, beginning 1989.
[3] Excludes military exports.
[4] Domestic exports only.
[5] Excluding ships.
[6] Index numbers cannot yet be rebased because of the unavailability of data for **1990.**
[7] Data prior to January 1991 pertain to the territorial boundaries of the Federal Republic of Germany and the former German Democratic Republic prior to 3 October 1990 (See explanatory notes on data pertaining to Germany on page v)
[8] Beginning January 1992, data refer to the Federal Republic of Yugoslavia. Prior to that date, data refer to the Socialist Federal Republic of Yugoslavia.

Importations et exportations totales: Indices par pays ou zones(suite)

Purchasing power of exports – Pouvoir d'achat des exportations

1980 = 100

1980	1985	1986	1987	1988	1989	1990	1991	1992	1993	1994	Pays ou zone
66	75	71	80	86	96	100	104	106	105	...	Australie
51	67	72	75	82	87	100	103	107	103	113	Autriche
66	73	85	91	94	98	100	104	109	...	...	Belgique–Luxembourg
70	93	105	104	125	114	100	107	...	...	...	Brésil
61	78	79	90	94	99	100	98	106	115	134	Canada
..	..	..	..	..	..	..	..	..	..	..	Colombie
59	74	78	84	86	90	100	107	113	111	82	Danemark
58	77	83	74	90	98	100	114	...	...	...	Iles Féroé
66	79	86	90	96	100	100	89	93	103	...	Finlande
65	70	79	82	89	96	100	106	110	110	125	France
57	70	81	87	92	97	100	97	102	99	110	Allemagne (Rép.féd.)
74	80	92	102	75	105	100	115	123	...	...	Grèce
27	44	50	66	83	92	100	118	143	48	178	Hong–kong
79	93	88	92	102	104	100	86	85	76	...	Hongrie
81	82	99	108	106	103	100	97	91	91	...	Islande
49	48	63	77	84	98	100	104	132	...	...	Inde
42	65	72	82	87	97	100	103	116	131	146	Irlande
57	80	91	97	98	99	100	103	113	134	148	Israël
53	66	79	82	87	94	100	104	109	112	...	Italie
43	70	93	94	101	103	100	112	124	131	142	Japon
33	68	78	84	106	119	100	98	108	118	134	Jordanie
150	104	135	107	119	104	100	124	...	...	...	Kenya
25	49	56	76	86	94	100	111	120	138	153	Corée, République de
..	..	..	..	..	.	..	..	..	..	..	Mexique
63	77	82	83	91	94	100	103	106	115	123	Pays–Bas
64	75	74	85	94	97	100	105	108	117	127	Nouvelle–Zélande
63	90	69	73	74	90	100	104	106	110	...	Norvège
62	48	75	85	97	93	100	110	119	110	138	Pakistan
72	77	81	85	92	105	100	90	...	101	121	Pologne
...	26	18	48	104	100	100	124	137	127	...	Seychelles
99	93	101	95	99	113	100	107	106	107	113	Afrique du Sud
43	57	65	74	83	89	100	113	122	139	163	Espagne
70	95	97	98	89	90	100	102	122	141	190	Sri Lanka
61	81	91	93	97	100	100	98	98	103	...	Suède
60	74	84	88	91	94	100	102	104	107	117	Suisse
90	62	37	36	31	61	100	101	72	...	...	Rép. arabe syrienne
40	47	52	62	77	92	100	118	133	149	...	Thaïlande
156	129	91	84	73	80	100	...	...	...	...	Trinité–et–Tobago
112	88	89	96	98	118	100	108	112	123	...	Tunisie
68	80	81	85	86	93	100	101	104	107	118	Royaume–Uni
66	64	66	72	87	95	100	107	113	117	129	Etats–Unis
..	..	..	..	..	..	..	..	..	..	..	Venezuela
..	..	..	..	..	..	..	..	..	..	..	Yougoslavie [8]

Remarque generale: Ces indices indiquent les variations des quantités (indice du quantum) et des prix moyens (indice de la valeur unitaire) des importations ou exportations totales. Les indices des termes de l'échange sont obtenus en divisant les indices de la valeur unitaire à l'exportation par ceux à l'importation. L'indice du pouvoir d'achat des exportations est obtenu en multipliant l'indice des termes de l'échange par l'indice du quantum des exportations. Les notes se rapportant aux pays qui apparaissent dans le Tableau Special:A de ce tome s'appliquent aussi aux indices de ce tableau.

[1] Calculés en dollars des Etats–unis.
[2] Indices des prix; Pour l'Australie à partir de 1981, pour les Etats–unis à partir de 1989.
[3] Non compris les exportations militaires.
[4] Seulement exportations domestiques.
[5] Non compris les navires.
[6] Les indices ne peuvent pas encore être rebasés du fait que les renseignements de 1990 ne sont pas encore disponibles.
[7] Les données relatives à la période précedant janvier 1991 correspondent aux limites territorales de la Republique fédérale d'Allemagne et l'ancienne Republique demoratique allemande antérieur au 3 octobre 1990. (Voir les notes explicatives sur les données concernant l'Allemagne à la page vii).
[8] A partir de janvier 1992, les données se rapportent à la République fédérative de Yougoslavie. Avant cette date les données se rapportent à la République fédérative socialiste de Yugoslavie.

Total exports and imports: index numbers of quantum, unit value and terms of trade by regions
Exportations et importations totales: indices du quantum, de la valeur unitaire et des termes de l'échange par régions

A. Exports - Exportations

1990 = 100

Regions /1	Weight /2 Pondération /2 (%)	1980	1985	1987	1988	1989	1990	1991	1992	1993	1994	Régions /1
		Quantum indices - Indices du quantum /3										
Total	100.0	64	74	82	88	95	100	104	109	114	127	**Totaux**
Developed Economies /4	68.5	66	78	82	88	95	100	102	106	108	118	**Economies Développées /4**
North America	15.7	72	69	77	89	95	100	106	114	119	132	Amérique du Nord
Europe	43.3	64	78	83	88	96	100	101	104	106	115	Europe
EEC	37.2	64	79	83	88	96	100	102	105	107	117	CEE
EFTA	6.0	63	76	82	87	95	100	100	102	104	111	AELE
Africa /5	0.7	58	64	61	62	68	100	100	99	102	112	Afrique /5
Asia	7.3	62	87	88	91	95	100	102	103	102	104	Asie
Oceania	1.5	63	83	89	90	94	100	115	121	125	137	Océanie
Developing Economies /4	31.5	59	63	81	87	94	100	110	120	128	155	**Economies en voie de Développement /4**
Africa		86	73	80	81	86	100	104	102	111	102	Afrique
Asia:		53	56	78	88	93	100	112	124	137	165	Asie:
Asia Middle East		121	64	88	104	104	100	102	103	98	135	Moyen-Orient d'Asie
Other Asia		35	54	75	86	93	100	114	128	142	172	Autres Pays d'Asie
America		66	85	92	87	99	100	107	116	126	151	Amérique
Europe /6		90	100	105	100	104	100	...	...	...	...	Europe /6
		Unit value indices (in U.S. dollars) /7 Indices de la valeur unitaire (en dollars E.-U.) /7										
Total		89	73	85	91	92	100	98	100	95	97	**Totaux**
Developed Economies /4		79	67	86	91	91	100	99	101	95	98	**Economies Développées /4**
North America		81	88	89	96	99	100	99	98	98	98	Amérique du Nord
Europe		78	60	84	88	87	100	97	100	90	92	Europe
EEC		78	60	84	88	87	100	97	100	90	92	CEE
EFTA		79	64	84	86	84	100	97	97	89	93	AELE
Africa /5		92	62	87	90	94	100	99	101	97	95	Afrique /5
Asia		73	70	91	101	101	100	107	114	123	133	Asie
Oceania		90	71	78	95	99	100	91	89	87	89	Océanie
Developing Economies /4		123	96	84	88	92	100	96	97	95	95	**Economies en voie de Développement /4**
Africa		139	107	83	81	87	100	92	92	81	87	Afrique
Asia:		122	95	86	88	93	100	98	99	99	96	Asie:
Asia Middle East		144	127	83	71	81	100	90	94	88	87	Moyen-Orient d'Asie
Other Asia		102	86	87	93	96	100	100	101	101	98	Autres Pays d'Asie
America		121	93	80	96	93	100	91	86	83	92	Amérique
Europe /6		70	74	76	88	90	100	...	...	...	...	Europe /6

For general note and footnotes see end of table

Voir la fin du tableau pour la remarque générale et les notes

Total exports and imports: index numbers of quantum, unit value and terms of trade by regions (continued)
Exportations et importations totales: indices du quantum, de la valeur unitaire et des termes de l'échange par régions (suite)

B. Imports - Importations

1990 = 100

Regions /1	Weight /2 Pondération /2 (%)	1980	1985	1987	1988	1989	1990	1991	1992	1993	1994	Régions /1
		Quantum indices - Indices du quantum /3										
Total	100.0	64	73	84	91	98	100	106	113	114	129	**Totaux**
Developed Economies /4	74.6	64	75	86	92	98	100	104	108	108	119	**Economies Développées** /4
North America	16.7	62	86	97	102	101	100	99	108	119	136	Amérique du Nord
Europe	47.6	65	72	83	89	98	100	106	109	104	112	Europe
EEC	40.8	65	72	83	89	98	100	107	111	105	114	CEE
EFTA	6.8	66	78	90	93	97	100	98	90	90	100	AELE
Africa /5	1.0	124	80	84	100	100	100	99	102	105	126	Afrique /5
Asia	7.9	58	63	76	87	93	100	103	103	108	121	Asie
Oceania	1.4	66	81	79	86	104	100	105	113	108	121	Océanie
Developing Economies /4	25.4	64	66	75	87	95	100	113	130	135	162	**Economies en voie de Développement** /4
Europe /6		114	78	86	78	87	100	...	...	...	...	Europe /6
		Unit value indices (in U.S. dollars) /7 Indices de la valeur unitaire (en dollars E.-U.) /7										
Total		90	76	85	90	91	100	98	99	93	95	**Totaux**
Developed Economies /4		87	73	84	89	91	100	98	99	92	94	**Economies Développées** /4
North America		83	83	85	89	97	100	99	98	97	97	Amérique du Nord
Europe		86	67	84	88	88	100	98	99	89	92	Europe
EEC		86	67	84	88	88	100	98	99	89	92	CEE
EFTA		84	61	85	89	87	100	97	100	92	94	AELE
Africa /5		86	70	91	94	92	100	103	105	99	101	Afrique /5
Asia		104	87	84	91	95	100	98	97	96	97	Asie
Oceania		87	77	89	98	96	100	101	99	98	104	Océanie
Developing Economies /4,8		98	88	88	92	93	100	98	98	95	99	**Economies en voie de Développement** /4,8
Europe /6		70	82	78	89	90	100	...	...	...	...	Europe /6

For general note and footnotes see end of table

Voir la fin du tableau pour la remarque générale et les notes

Total exports and imports: index numbers of quantum, unit value and terms of trade by regions (continued)
Exportations et importations totales: indices du quantum, de la valeur unitaire et des termes de l'échange par régions (suite)

C. Terms of trade /9 - Termes de l'échange /9

1990 = 100

Regions /1	1980	1985	1987	1988	1989	1990	1991	1992	1993	1994	Régions /1
Developed Economies /4	90	91	101	103	100	100	100	102	104	104	**Economies Développées /4**
North America	98	106	105	107	102	100	100	100	101	101	Amérique du Nord
Europe	91	90	100	100	99	100	99	101	101	101	Europe
EEC	91	89	100	100	99	100	99	101	101	101	CEE
EFTA	94	105	100	97	97	100	100	96	97	98	AELE
Africa /5	107	89	95	95	102	100	96	96	98	94	Afrique /5
Asia	71	80	108	111	106	100	109	117	128	136	Asie
Oceania	102	93	88	96	104	100	91	90	88	85	Océanie
Developing Economies /4	125	109	95	96	99	100	98	99	100	96	**Economies en voie de Développement /4**
Europe /6	100	90	98	99	99	100	...	...	...	...	Europe /6

1/ The regional analysis in this table is in accordance with the groupings of countries or areas specified in Special Table A of this issue.

2/ Based on the value of trade, in U.S. dollars, in 1980.

3/ Quantum indices are derived from value data and unit value indices. They are base period weighted.

4/ This classification is intended for statistical convenience and does not, necessarily, express a judgement about the stage reached by a particular country in the development process.

5/ South African Customs Union.

6/ Socialist Federal Republic of Yugoslavia.

7/ Regional aggregates are current period weighted.

8/ Indices, except those for Europe, are based on estimates prepared by the International Monetary Fund.

9/ Unit value index of exports divided by unit value index of imports.

1/ L'analyse régionale dans ce tableau est conforme aux groupes des pays ou zones paraissant dans le Tableau Spécial A.

2/ Calculée d'après la valeur du commerce en 1980, en dollars E.-U.

3/ Les indices du quantum sont calculés à partir des chiffres de la valeur et des indices de la valeur unitaire. Ils sont à coéfficients de pondération correspondant à la période en base.

4/ Cette classification est utilisée pour plus de commodité dans la présentation des statistiques et n'implique pas nécessairement un jugement quant au stade de développement auquel est parvenu un pays donné.

5/ L'Union Douanière d'Afrique Méridionale.

6/ La République socialiste fédérative de Yougoslavie.

7/ Les totaux régionaux sont a coéfficients de pondération correspondant à la période en cours.

8/ Le calcul des indices, sauf ceux pour l'Europe, sont basés sur les estimations preparées par le Fonds monétaire international.

9/ Indice de la valeur unitaire des exportations divisé par l'indice de la valeur unitaire des importations.

SPECIAL TABLE: G

Manufactured goods exports

1990 = 100

Region, country or area	1980	1981	1982	1983	1984	1985	1986	1987	1988	1989	1990	1991	1992	1993	1994
Unit value indices in U.S. dollars - Indices de valeur unitaire en dollars des E.-U.															
Total /1	76	70	70	68	66	66	77	86	93	92	100	100	103	99	...
Developed economies /2	74	69	68	65	63	63	76	85	92	91	100	100	103	97	99
America	72	80	83	84	85	85	86	90	96	99	100	102	100	99	99
Canada	83	87	88	90	91	87	87	90	96	101	100	99	90	88	85
United States /3	69	77	81	83	83	85	88	90	95	98	100	102	103	103	104
Europe /2	74	64	63	59	56	57	72	82	88	87	100	98	101	91	93
EEC /4	74	64	63	60	56	58	72	82	88	87	100	98	101	92	94
Belgium-Luxembourg /5	79	67	63	60	56	58	74	76	89	89	100	97	99	90	93
Denmark	68	62	58	57	54	56	71	85	88	84	100	96	102	92	96
France	77	67	64	61	60	62	73	84	88	86	100	96	100	94	98
Germany /6	73	63	62	60	53	55	73	86	89	87	100	98	103	93	94
Greece	85	79	81	70	66	63	70	78	86	87	100	95	94	...	...
Ireland /7	65	71	48	50	51	63	76	81	88	91	100	95	97	96	89
Italy /5	67	54	58	56	54	54	68	80	85	86	100	99	102	89	86
Netherlands /5	75	65	66	60	57	57	71	83	88	86	100	96	100	92	92
Portugal /7	83	74	63	58	59	60	66	82	88	85	100	101	106	98	84
Spain /7	74	62	63	56	57	55	71	68	83	83	100	95	109	85	86
United Kingdom	76	70	65	61	58	60	70	81	91	88	100	101	102	98	103
EFTA /8	74	67	64	59	56	57	72	84	89	87	100	97	101	87	91
Austria /9	77	67	67	62	58	60	76	90	95	85	100	95	99	90	96
Finland	65	63	61	56	54	54	65	76	85	89	100	95	88	74	82
Iceland /7	82	72	61	62	64	57	66	75	99	103	100	88	86	76	80
Norway	75	69	63	57	59	58	66	78	96	99	100	95	92	80	82
Sweden	76	69	63	57	56	57	71	83	89	90	100	100	101	82	...
Switzerland /5	74	65	64	62	56	55	73	88	88	84	100	98	103	88	99
Other Europe															
Malta	...	...	...	...	...	...	...	...	...	...	...	...	...	...	...
Other developed economies	75	79	74	71	71	70	83	91	101	100	100	107	113	120	129
Australia	92	86	78	76	76	67	67	77	97	102	100	92	86	81	88
Israel	81	77	75	72	70	69	72	76	86	92	100	101	101	102	101
Japan	74	78	73	71	71	70	85	92	102	100	100	108	115	124	134
New Zealand	73	74	72	71	69	66	72	84	107	105	100	94	89	89	98
South Africa	114	94	83	81	70	61	68	84	89	95	100	96	101	100	101
Developing economies /10	87	87	82	77	81	80	79	88	97	98	100	100	103	104	...
Unit value indices in 'SDR' - Indices de valeur unitaire en 'DTS'															
Total /1	79	83	87	86	87	89	89	90	93	98	100	99	99	96	...
Developed economies /2	77	80	84	83	84	85	88	89	93	96	100	99	99	95	94
Developing economies /10	91	100	101	98	107	107	92	92	98	104	100	99	100	101	...

For general note and footnotes see end of table.

Exportations des produits manufacturés

1990 = 100

Unit value indices in national currency - Indices de valeur unitaire en monnaie nationale

1980	1981	1982	1983	1984	1985	1986	1987	1988	1989	1990	1991	1992	1993	1994	Région, pays ou zone
.	.	.	.	.	.	.	.	.	.	.	.	.	.	.	**Totaux**
.	.	.	.	.	.	.	.	.	.	.	.	.	.	.	**Economies développées**
.	.	.	.	.	.	.	.	.	.	.	.	.	.	.	Amérique
83	90	94	96	102	103	104	102	101	102	100	97	94	97	99	Canada
69	77	81	83	83	85	88	90	95	98	100	102	103	103	104	Etats-Unis /3
.	.	.	.	.	.	.	.	.	.	.	.	.	.	.	Europe
.	.	.	.	.	.	.	.	.	.	.	.	.	.	.	CEE
...	...	...	...	...	...	...	...	...	...	...	...	...	...	...	Belgique-Luxembourg /5
62	71	79	84	91	96	94	94	96	100	100	99	100	97	99	Danemark
60	67	77	86	96	102	93	93	96	101	100	99	97	98	100	France
83	88	93	95	96	100	98	96	97	101	100	I 100	100	95	94	Allemagne /6
23	28	34	39	47	55	62	67	77	90	100	110	114	...	...	Grèce
...	...	...	...	...	...	...	...	...	...	...	...	...	...	...	Irlande
...	...	...	...	...	...	...	...	...	...	...	...	...	...	...	Italie /5
82	89	98	94	100	103	96	92	95	101	100	99	97	94	92	Pays-Bas /5
...	...	...	...	...	...	...	...	...	...	...	...	...	...	...	Portugal
...	...	...	...	...	...	...	...	...	...	...	...	...	...	...	Espagne
58	62	66	72	78	83	85	88	91	96	100	102	104	117	120	Royaume-Uni
.	.	.	.	.	.	.	.	.	.	.	.	.	.	.	AELE
88	95	102	100	104	109	103	101	104	99	100	98	96	93	96	Autriche /9
64	71	77	82	86	88	87	88	94	101	100	100	106	112	112	Finlande
...	...	...	...	...	...	...	...	...	...	...	...	...	...	...	Islande
59	63	65	69	77	79	79	84	101	110	100	98	92	92	93	Norvège
55	59	66	74	79	83	85	88	93	98	100	102	100	108	...	Suède
...	...	...	...	...	...	...	...	...	...	...	...	...	...	...	Suisse /5
															Autres pays d'Europe
...	...	...	...	...	...	...	...	...	...	...	...	...	...	...	Malte
.	.	.	.	.	.	.	.	.	.	.	.	.	.	.	Autres économies développées
63	...	...	66	68	75	79	86	96	101	100	92	92	93	94	Australie
...	...	...	...	...	...	...	...	...	...	...	...	...	...	...	Israël
115	118	125	117	116	116	98	93	91	96	100	101	101	95	95	Japon
45	51	58	63	74	80	81	85	97	104	100	97	99	98	99	Nouvelle-Zélande
34	32	34	34	40	52	60	66	78	97	100	103	111	127	139	Afrique du Sud
.	.	.	.	.	.	.	.	.	.	.	.	.	.	.	**Economies en voie de développement**

Voir la fin du tableau pour la remarque générale et les notes.

SPECIAL TABLE: G

Manufactured goods exports (continued)

1990 = 100

Quantum indices - Indices de volume

Region, country or area	1980	1981	1982	1983	1984	1985	1986	1987	1988	1989	1990	1991	1992	1993	1994
Total /1	57	60	59	62	68	71	74	80	87	94	100	105	110	115	...
Developed economies /2	64	67	65	67	73	77	78	82	88	95	100	103	107	108	120
America	68	66	59	58	64	65	66	72	83	90	100	106	114	121	137
Canada	52	54	54	60	72	78	81	85	95	94	100	102	119	136	163
United States	74	71	61	57	61	61	60	68	80	88	100	107	113	117	130
Europe /2	64	66	66	68	74	78	80	84	89	96	100	103	105	106	119
EEC /4	64	66	66	68	73	77	79	84	89	96	100	103	105	105	119
Belgium-Luxembourg	63	63	63	66	69	72	75	89	87	95	100	102	104	112	126
Denmark	65	68	68	74	79	81	82	84	90	93	100	106	114	111	119
France	66	68	66	68	71	72	76	80	87	94	100	107	112	104	116
Germany /6	63	66	68	67	77	81	82	85	91	99	100	102	104	100	111
Greece	69	68	62	74	85	85	101	106	85	106	100	109	127	...	...
Ireland	43	38	62	65	71	65	65	77	85	93	100	108	122	124	151
Italy	65	77	69	74	77	82	83	86	91	97	100	101	103	112	132
Netherlands	64	65	62	69	74	78	83	85	90	95	100	105	106	107	122
Portugal	30	30	37	44	51	54	65	68	75	90	100	101	110	99	130
Spain	50	57	55	59	69	75	66	85	84	94	100	114	109	132	157
United Kingdom	70	65	66	65	70	75	76	82	86	94	100	100	101	95	107
EFTA /8	62	64	65	69	76	80	83	85	90	95	100	99	102	110	117
Austria	51	54	54	57	62	66	70	71	78	90	100	104	109	107	102
Finland	68	72	74	75	82	88	90	94	93	96	100	90	99	117	133
Iceland	82	78	79	111	108	96	102	114	114	108	100	91	94	102	131
Norway	70	70	74	81	81	85	87	91	83	89	100	103	106	105	114
Sweden	66	68	70	77	84	88	91	92	98	100	100	97	98	108	...
Switzerland	62	64	62	64	72	77	81	81	91	96	100	98	100	112	111
Other Europe															
Malta	...	...	...	...	...	...	...	...	...	...	...	...	...	...	...
Other developed economies	61	67	65	71	81	87	86	87	91	95	100	102	104	104	106
Australia	58	57	56	59	63	67	69	82	82	88	100	121	138	162	170
Israel	54	56	54	55	64	72	80	91	94	97	100	98	110	126	146
Japan	61	68	66	72	84	88	87	87	91	96	100	102	103	101	103
New Zealand	68	68	70	72	81	88	86	87	85	92	100	112	120	132	152
South Africa	57	54	61	61	66	85	91	86	91	96	100	109	107	113	95
Developing economies /10	33	36	37	44	49	51	58	71	80	92	100	112	126	144	...

General note

Manufactured goods are here defined to comprise sections 5 through 8 of the Standard International Trade Classification. These sections are: chemicals and related products, manufactured goods classified chiefly by material, machinery and transport equipment and miscellaneous manufactured articles. The economic and geographic groupings in this table are in accordance with those of Special Table A in this issue, although Special Table A includes more detailed geographic sub-groups which make up the groupings 'Other developed economies' and 'Developing economies' of this table. In 1980 the exports of manufactured goods by all 'Developed' and 'Developing' economies accounted for approximately 93 percent of world exports of manufactured goods.

The unit value indices are obtained from national sources, except those of a few countries which the United Nations Statistical Division compiles using their quantity and value figures. For countries that do not compile indices for manufactured goods exports conforming to the above definition, sub-indices are aggregated to approximate an index of SITC sections 5-8. Unit value indices obtained from national indices are rebased, where necessary, so that 1990 = 100. Indices in national currency are converted into U.S. dollars using conversion factors obtained by dividing the weighted average exchange rate of a given currency in the current period by the weighted average exchange rate in the base period. All aggregate unit value indices are current period weighted.

The indices in SDRs are calculated by multiplying the equivalent aggregate indices in U.S. dollars by conversion factors obtained by dividing the SDR/$US exchange rate in the current period by the rate in the base period.

The quantum indices are derived from the value data and the unit value indices. All aggregate quantum indices are base period weighted.

1/ Excludes trade of the countries of Eastern Europe and the former USSR.

2/ Includes the Socialist Federal Republic of Yugoslavia for the years 1970-1979.

3/ Beginning 1989 derived from price indices; national unit value index discontinued.

4/ Excludes Portugal and Spain for the years 1970-1979.

5/ Derived from sub-indices using current weights. Indices for Belgium, beginning 1988, and for Switzerland, beginning 1987, are calculated by the United Nations Statistical Division.

6/ Data prior to January 1991 pertain to the territorial boundaries of the Federal Republic of Germany and the former German Democratic Republic prior to 3 October 1990 (See explanatory notes on data pertaning to Germany on page vi).

7/ Indices are calculated by the United Nations Statistical Division for the years beginning 1981.

8/ Includes Portugal for the years 1970-1979.

9/ Series linked at 1988 by a factor calculated by the United Nations Statistical Division.

10/ Includes the Socialist Federal Republic of Yugoslavia for the years beginning 1980.

Exportations des produits manufacturés (suite)

In thousand million U.S. dollars — En milliards de dollars E.-U.

1970	1980	1981	1982	1983	1984	1985	1986	1987	1988	1989	1990	1991	1992	1993	1994	Région, pays ou zone
								Value - Valeur								
183.41	1049.3	1029.1	982.58	1002.0	1083.4	1138.3	1363.8	1648.7	1927.0	2088.8	2402.3	2514.3	2724.3	2729.0	...	**Totaux** /1
169.14	923.10	900.14	855.43	849.37	906.60	955.64	1159.0	1370.8	1579.5	1688.2	1957.2	2014.9	2146.0	2064.3	2333.7	**Economies développées** /2
39.09	177.98	192.04	177.89	175.05	195.36	199.19	205.06	232.91	286.97	319.63	361.29	389.25	413.80	435.11	489.84	Amérique
9.72	33.89	37.64	38.01	42.47	52.04	53.86	56.19	59.81	72.19	74.46	78.83	79.42	84.61	93.87	108.90	Canada
29.37	144.09	154.40	139.88	132.58	143.32	145.34	148.87	173.11	214.78	245.17	282.46	309.83	329.19	341.24	380.94	Etats-Unis
109.16	605.06	547.29	530.20	519.06	532.42	571.06	734.12	894.89	1011.5	1075.3	1289.1	1290.5	1372.7	1244.1	1423.3	Europe /2
90.35	519.21	467.49	453.19	443.15	453.46	486.97	624.17	762.34	861.55	919.91	1103.0	1112.1	1185.5	1070.8	1226.2	CEE /4
9.61	47.87	40.05	37.41	37.59	37.21	39.75	52.29	64.09	73.83	80.42	95.18	93.84	97.60	95.90	110.83	Belgique-Luxembourg
1.79	9.25	8.90	8.46	8.95	9.00	9.61	12.35	14.92	16.63	16.61	21.14	21.40	24.66	21.65	24.30	Danemark
13.45	83.99	75.50	69.98	68.66	70.48	73.71	92.19	111.69	126.05	134.56	165.29	169.44	184.58	162.83	187.20	France
30.66	166.92	150.82	152.61	146.45	148.63	161.58	217.32	264.48	293.10	309.59	362.01	361.85	387.53	334.59	377.61	Allemagne /6
0.26	2.61	2.39	2.27	2.31	2.51	2.37	3.15	3.69	3.25	4.12	4.45	4.59	5.31	4.82	4.73	Grèce
0.36	4.62	4.54	4.94	5.38	6.04	6.66	8.16	10.26	12.31	13.95	16.50	16.96	19.56	19.60	22.07	Irlande
11.09	65.84	63.26	61.49	62.34	63.06	67.77	86.09	104.04	115.83	125.92	150.63	150.98	158.35	150.13	170.84	Italie
6.78	38.30	34.01	32.86	33.23	33.79	35.54	46.82	56.91	63.55	65.51	80.23	80.89	85.31	79.18	89.86	Pays-Bas
0.60	3.28	2.92	3.06	3.34	3.92	4.32	5.62	7.34	8.72	10.09	13.20	13.39	15.38	12.88	14.48	Portugal
1.32	15.57	14.84	14.89	14.17	16.68	17.57	20.11	24.62	29.90	33.18	42.63	46.08	50.61	47.54	57.53	Espagne
16.34	80.96	70.26	65.22	60.71	62.15	68.08	80.09	100.29	118.37	125.96	151.77	152.62	156.62	141.64	166.70	Royaume-Uni
16.29	85.44	79.43	76.67	75.60	78.63	83.75	109.51	132.01	149.37	154.64	185.03	177.28	185.80	172.14	197.15	AELE /8
2.37	14.92	13.64	13.66	13.48	13.73	15.06	20.17	24.28	27.94	29.07	37.89	37.53	40.66	36.70	37.00	Autriche
1.61	10.31	10.46	10.39	9.70	10.36	10.88	13.57	16.56	18.17	19.77	22.98	19.65	20.05	20.05	25.11	Finlande
0.02	0.20	0.16	0.14	0.20	0.20	0.16	0.20	0.25	0.33	0.32	0.29	0.23	0.23	0.23	0.31	Islande
1.82	7.58	6.87	6.64	6.60	6.77	6.96	8.30	10.08	11.40	12.55	14.22	13.84	13.84	12.05	13.35	Norvège
5.22	24.65	22.96	21.53	21.68	23.22	24.80	31.49	37.54	43.03	43.92	48.90	47.50	48.49	43.13	...	Suède
4.65	27.92	25.34	24.30	23.94	24.34	25.89	35.79	43.30	48.50	49.01	60.76	58.52	62.53	59.98	66.70	Suisse
																Autres pays d'Europe
0.02	0.40	0.37	0.34	0.30	0.33	0.34	0.43	0.54	0.63	0.77	1.00	1.12	1.38	1.21	...	Malte
20.88	140.06	160.81	147.35	155.27	178.82	185.39	219.85	243.03	280.94	293.25	306.87	335.15	359.52	385.08	420.51	Autres économies développées
1.12	4.46	4.12	3.61	3.77	3.94	3.69	3.83	5.23	6.60	7.44	8.28	9.19	9.83	10.85	12.36	Australie
0.56	4.60	4.61	4.26	4.15	4.77	5.26	6.10	7.29	8.44	9.42	10.52	10.47	11.74	13.48	15.50	Israël
18.12	124.50	146.73	134.13	142.08	164.91	170.78	203.36	222.81	257.07	266.59	277.44	304.34	328.52	348.56	381.06	Japon
0.14	1.25	1.28	1.28	1.29	1.43	1.48	1.56	1.85	2.31	2.45	2.54	2.67	2.73	2.98	3.78	Nouvelle-Zélande
0.95	5.24	4.07	4.07	3.98	3.76	4.19	4.99	5.85	6.52	7.35	8.10	...	6.70	9.21	...	Afrique du Sud
14.27	126.16	128.95	127.14	152.58	176.84	182.69	204.80	277.91	346.48	400.60	445.10	499.36	578.22	664.73	...	**Economies en voie de développement** /10

Remarque générale

Les produits manufacturés comprennent les sections 5 à 8 de la Classification type pour le commerce international. Ces sections sont: produits chimiques et produits connexes, articles manufacturés classés principalement d'après la matière première, machines et matérial de transport et articles manufacturés divers. Les groupes économiques et géographiques de ce tableau sont conformes aux groupes des pays ou zones qui paraissent dans le Tableau Spécial A de ce numéro, bien que le Tableau Spécial A comprend plus de détails en ce qui concerne les sous-groupes géographiques lesquels comprennent les groupes des 'Autres économies développées' et 'Economies en voie de développement' de ce tableau. En 1980, les exportations des produits manufacturés par tous les 'Economies développées' et les 'Economies en voie développement' representaient approximativement 93 pourcent de l'ensemble des exportations mondiales des produits manufacturés.

Les indices de la valeur unitaire sont obtenus de sources nationales, a l'exception de quelques pays pour lesquels la Division de Statistiques des Nations Unies calcule ces indices en utilisant les chiffres de la valeur et du volume fournis par ces pays. Pour les pays ne calculant pas leurs indices des exportations des produits manufacturés selon la definition décrite ci-dessus les sous-indices sont agrégés en un indice qui se rapproche les sections 5 à 8 de la CTCI. Les indices qui sont obtenus à partir des indices nationaux sont ramenés, quand nécessaire, à l'année de base 1990 = 100. Les indices en monnaie nationale sont convertis en dollars des E.-U. en les multipliant par un facteur de conversion obtenu en divisant le taux de change courant, moyenne pondérée, d'une monnaie donnée par celui de la période de base. Tous les agrégés des indices de la valeur unitaire sont à coéfficients de pondération correspondant à la période indiquée.

Les indices en DTS sont calculés en multipliant les indices totaux equivalents en dollars E.-U. par un facteur de conversion obtenu en divisant le taux de change courant du DTS/$E-U d'une monnaie donnée par celui de la période de base.

Les indices du quantum sont calculés à partir des chiffres de la valeur et les indices de la valeur unitaire. Tous les agrégés des indices du quantum sont à coéfficients de pondération correspondant à la période en base.

1/ Non compris le commerce des pays de l'Europe de l'Est et l'ancienne URSS.

2/ Y compris la République socialiste fédérative de Yougoslavie pour les années 1970-1979.

3/ A partir de 1989 calculés à partir des indices des prix; l'indice de la valeur unitaire nationale est discontinué.

4/ Non compris le Portugal et l'Espagne pour les années 1970-1979.

5/ Calculés à partir de sous-indices à coéfficients de pondération correspondant à la période en cours. Les indices pour la Belgique, à partir de 1988, et pour la Suisse, à partir de 1987, sont calculés par la Division de Statistique des Nations Unies.

6/ Les Données relatives à la période précédant janvier 1991 correspondent aux limites territoriales de la République féderale d'Allemagne et l'ancienne République democratique allemande antérieur au 3 octobre 1990 (Voir les notes explicatives sur les données concernant l'Allemagne à la page vi).

7/ Les indices sont calculés par la Division de Statistique des Nations Unies pour les années à partir 1981.

8/ Y compris le Portugal pour les années 1970-1979.

9/ Les séries sont enchainées à 1988 par un facteur calculé par la Division de Statistique des Nations Unies.

10/ Y compris la République socialiste fédérative de Yougoslavie pour les années à partir de 1980.

SPECIAL TABLE: H

Fuel imports
Developed economies

1990 = 100

Unit value indices in U.S. dollars - Indices de valeur unitaire en dollars des E.-U.

Region, country or area	1980	1981	1982	1983	1984	1985	1986	1987	1988	1989	1990	1991	1992	1993	1994
Developed economies /1	141	156	146	132	127	123	77	81	72	80	100	92	86	79	74
America	141	159	148	134	131	125	70	82	69	81	100	85	83	77	72
Canada	115	132	128	118	116	113	76	78	72	78	100	86	80	74	68
United States /2	143	160	150	136	133	126	69	82	68	81	100	85	83	78	73
Europe /1	137	151	142	127	122	122	78	80	72	80	100	94	86	78	74
EEC /3	137	152	144	129	123	122	78	80	72	80	100	94	86	78	74
Belgium-Luxembourg /4	132	143	141	128	125	122	83	86	86	81	100	98	89	78	77
Denmark	137	148	138	119	114	118	78	70	72	82	100	96	88	76	76
France	139	153	150	135	128	126	78	80	69	78	100	95	87	79	75
Germany /5	135	154	139	127	118	119	80	81	70	77	100	95	87	77	74
Greece	167	153	177	157	143	147	117	86	89	87	100	114	97	...	...
Ireland /4	133	140	135	124	119	115	77	84	75	82	100	94	88	81	80
Italy /6	125	142	131	119	112	116	70	78	69	80	100	91	84	79	73
Netherlands /6	147	160	144	134	125	122	75	75	71	82	100	92	87	85	72
Portugal /4	143	161	149	126	131	124	74	81	69	78	100	89	81	71	68
Spain /4	149	158	152	136	130	127	75	80	71	80	100	92	82	78	75
United Kingdom	127	141	139	127	123	122	84	87	81	82	100	92	88	78	75
EFTA /7	137	144	133	118	114	112	77	79	71	79	100	94	86	76	73
Austria /8	133	147	132	116	111	115	84	81	73	77	100	96	89	78	69
Finland	143	157	146	123	117	111	81	82	75	84	100	96	87	76	77
Iceland /6	161	155	150	132	111	118	89	93	93	94	100	96	99	89	85
Norway	123	119	109	109	106	104	75	77	70	79	100	92	85	76	82
Sweden	143	150	141	123	120	119	70	77	69	79	100	92	85	75	74
Switzerland	132	134	126	112	105	105	76	78	69	78	100	95	84	77	71
Other Europe															
Malta	...	...	...	...	...	...	...	...	...	...	...	...	...	...	...
Other developed economies	149	164	155	140	131	122	82	84	75	80	100	96	90	85	78
Australia	137	...	141	141	137	127	74	81	71	81	100	88	77	74	73
Israel	164	169	148	134	136	130	69	83	67	82	100	82	80	70	68
Japan	147	163	153	138	131	125	84	83	76	80	100	97	91	86	79
New Zealand	128	155	153	137	122	121	86	83	73	81	100	95	88	84	78
South Africa	...	...	...	...	...	...	...	...	...	...	...	...	...	...	...

For general note and footnotes see end of table.

TABLEAU SPECIAL: H

Importations des produits énergétiques
Pays à économies développées

1990 = 100

Unit value indices in national currency - Indices de valeur unitaire en monnaie nationale

1980	1981	1982	1983	1984	1985	1986	1987	1988	1989	1990	1991	1992	1993	1994	Région, pays ou zone
.	.	.	.	.	.	.	.	.	.	.	.	.	.	.	**Economies développées**
.	.	.	.	.	.	.	.	.	.	.	.	.	.	.	Amérique
116	137	136	127	130	134	91	89	76	80	100	85	82	82	80	Canada
143	160	150	136	133	126	69	82	68	81	100	85	83	78	73	Etats-Unis /2
.	.	.	.	.	.	.	.	.	.	.	.	.	.	.	Europe
.	.	.	.	.	.	.	.	.	.	.	.	.	.	.	CEE
...	...	...	...	...	...	...	...	...	...	...	...	...	...	...	Belgique-Luxembourg
127	172	191	180	192	197	104	78	78	98	100	100	86	80	78	Danemark
109	153	183	189	206	209	99	88	76	92	100	98	85	82	76	France
154	217	211	203	212	217	109	91	76	90	100	I 98	84	80	74	Allemagne /5
45	54	74	87	104	129	104	73	80	89	100	130	118	...	...	Grèce
...	...	...	...	...	...	...	...	...	...	...	...	...	...	...	Irlande
...	...	...	...	...	...	...	...	...	...	...	...	...	...	...	Italie /6
...	...	...	...	...	...	...	...	...	...	...	...	...	...	...	Pays-Bas /6
...	...	...	...	...	...	...	...	...	...	...	...	...	...	...	Portugal
...	...	...	...	...	...	...	...	...	...	...	...	...	...	...	Espagne
97	124	142	150	162	168	101	94	81	89	100	93	89	92	87	Royaume-Uni
.	.	.	.	.	.	.	.	.	.	.	.	.	.	.	AELE
154	208	200	188	198	209	115	91	80	90	100	99	86	80	70	Autriche /8
139	176	183	179	183	179	108	94	83	94	100	101	104	114	104	Finlande
...	...	...	...	...	...	...	...	...	...	...	...	...	...	...	Islande /6
98	109	113	129	139	142	89	82	73	87	100	95	85	86	92	Norvège
102	129	150	159	167	172	85	82	71	86	100	94	83	99	96	Suède
...	...	...	...	...	...	...	...	...	...	...	...	...	...	...	Suisse
															Autres pays d'Europe
...	...	...	...	...	...	...	...	...	...	...	...	...	...	...	Malte
.	.	.	.	.	.	.	.	.	.	.	.	.	.	.	Autres économies développées
93	...	106	120	120	142	85	90	71	80	100	88	83	85	78	Australie
...	...	...	...	...	...	...	...	...	...	...	...	...	...	...	Israël
233	249	263	228	214	209	100	84	67	77	100	91	80	66	56	Japon
78	108	121	123	132	143	97	83	66	81	100	98	98	92	78	Nouvelle-Zélande
...	...	...	...	...	...	...	...	...	...	...	...	...	...	...	Afrique du Sud

Voir la fin du tableau pour la remarque générale et les notes.

Fuel imports (continued)
Developed economies

1990 = 100

Quantum indices - Indices de volume

Region, country or area	1980	1981	1982	1983	1984	1985	1986	1987	1988	1989	1990	1991	1992	1993	1994
Developed economies /1	93	85	79	78	82	80	89	90	91	97	100	103	106	107	112
America	83	77	65	62	67	63	82	82	92	100	100	99	102	110	119
Canada	85	83	59	49	56	56	69	75	79	94	100	92	92	98	104
United States	83	76	65	64	69	64	83	83	94	101	100	100	103	111	120
Europe /1	104	93	90	87	91	91	97	98	91	96	100	106	109	107	110
EEC /3	103	92	89	87	91	90	97	98	91	96	100	107	110	108	110
Belgium-Luxembourg	97	90	87	77	85	79	90	93	80	98	100	108	110	111	116
Denmark	143	129	124	120	120	119	117	130	107	106	100	80	108	91	88
France	115	101	92	86	87	85	93	95	95	97	100	105	106	102	105
Germany /5	109	91	91	90	92	92	96	95	96	92	100	120	123	123	125
Greece	97	83	107	110	120	133	110	136	45	78	100	120	155	...	...
Ireland	93	83	80	75	76	79	95	90	87	88	100	98	99	95	92
Italy	116	114	109	110	110	108	131	117	91	98	100	100	101	92	100
Netherlands	94	82	85	87	89	90	91	104	100	100	100	98	101	99	112
Portugal		55	63	64	63	59	71	70	77	94	100	98	111	111	124
Spain									94	102	100	107	120	107	112
United Kingdom									79	89	100	104	100	105	86
EFTA /7	109	95	90	90	88	91	98	98	91	94	100	99	101	99	109
Austria	90	85	76	73	85	86	87	93	89	91	100	100	99	99	112
Finland	101	89	80	89	84	92	91	103	84	91	100	95	97	95	110
Iceland	64	67	63	62	74	74	75	77	66	79	100	92	87	86	88
Norway	204	163	159	110	114	104	135	133	102	96	100	101	89	89	96
Sweden	114	95	97	98	86	91	100	95	92	96	100	96	103	106	108
Switzerland	98	88	83	93	93	92	101	91	95	94	100	103	106	98	102
Other Europe															
Malta	...	...	...	...	...	...	...	...	...	...	...	...	...	...	...
Other developed economies	83	78	75	74	81	79	79	83	90	96	100	100	104	104	109
Australia	93	...	114	69	70	58	73	75	86	116	100	117	141	163	145
Israel	96	90	94	83	80	78	85	91	104	101	100	118	135	160	155
Japan	83	78	75	75	81	78	78	83	90	95	100	99	102	100	106
New Zealand	133	99	89	97	93	88	85	81	75	90	100	94	94	102	118
South Africa	...	...	...	...	...	...	...	...	...	...	...	...	...	...	...

General note

Fuels are here defined to comprise all the products in section 3 of the Standard International Trade Classification. These products are: coal, coke and briquettes, petroleum, petroleum products and related materials, gas and electric current. The economic and geographic groupings in this table are in accordance with those of Special Table A in this issue, although Special Table A includes more detailed geographic sub-groups which make up the grouping 'Other developed economies' of this table. In 1980 fuel imports by the developed economies amounted to approximately 27 percent of their total imports.

The unit value indices are obtained from national sources, except those of a few countries which the United Nations Statistical Division compiles using their quantity and value figures. For countries that do not compile indices for fuel imports conforming to the above definition, sub-indices are aggregated to approximate an index of SITC section 3. Unit value indices obtained from national indices are rebased, where necessary, so that 1990 = 100. Indices in national currency are converted into U.S. dollars using conversion factors obtained by dividing the weighted average exchange rate of a given currency in the current period by the weighted average exchange rate in the base period. All aggregate unit value indices are current period weighted.

The quantum indices are derived from the value data and the unit value indices. All aggregate quantum indices are base period weighted.

1/ Includes the Socialist Federal Republic of Yugoslavia for the years 1970-1979.

2/ Beginning 1989 derived from price indices; national unit value index discontinued.

3/ Excludes Portugal and Spain for the years 1970-1979.

4/ Indices are calculated by the United Nations Statistical Division for the years beginning 1981.

5/ Data prior to January 1991 pertain to the territorial boundaries of the Federal Republic of Germany and the former German Democratic Republic prior to 3 October 1990 (See explanatory notes on data pertaning to Germany on page vi).

6/ Derived from sub-indices using current weights. Indices for the Netherlands, beginning 1988, and for Switzerland, beginning 1987, are calculated by the United Nations Statistical Division.

7/ Includes Portugal in for the years 1970-1979.

8/ Series linked at 1988 by a factor calculated by the United Nations Statistical Division.

Importations des produits énergétiques (suite)
Pays à économies développées

In thousand million U.S. dollars — En milliards de dollars E.-U.

1970	1980	1981	1982	1983	1984	1985	1986	1987	1988	1989	1990	1991	1992	1993	1994	Région, pays ou zone
								Value - Valeur								
23.71	368.12	366.95	323.35	287.53	290.23	276.12	191.59	206.47	182.15	215.88	278.32	263.29	253.81	236.10	231.64	**Economies développées** /1
3.82	89.41	92.29	72.99	64.26	67.88	60.34	43.59	51.03	48.30	61.44	76.00	64.00	63.99	64.48	65.24	Amérique
0.75	7.16	7.98	5.49	4.19	4.74	4.59	3.79	4.27	4.17	5.35	7.26	5.74	5.33	5.24	5.15	Canada
3.07	82.25	84.32	67.50	60.07	63.14	55.75	39.81	46.76	44.13	56.09	68.74	58.26	58.66	59.24	60.10	Etats-Unis
15.41	199.71	195.55	178.26	156.61	154.47	153.33	106.36	110.88	92.21	106.83	140.52	139.82	132.27	117.46	113.76	Europe /1
12.50	175.99	173.79	159.05	139.57	138.55	137.02	94.40	98.56	81.93	95.03	124.64	125.06	118.52	105.39	101.27	CEE /3
1.03	12.39	12.55	11.92	9.50	10.30	9.32	7.28	7.74	6.65	7.64	9.62	10.17	9.49	8.33	8.60	Belgique-Luxembourg
0.46	4.34	4.23	3.80	3.18	3.02	3.12	2.03	2.01	1.68	1.92	2.20	1.69	2.11	1.53	1.47	Danemark
2.29	35.86	34.82	30.98	25.89	25.06	24.10	16.25	17.05	14.58	16.87	22.33	22.35	20.56	17.86	17.52	France
2.63	41.95	39.84	36.48	32.43	31.21	31.39	21.91	22.01	19.12	20.43	28.51	32.48	30.42	27.15	26.40	Allemagne /5
0.13	2.47	1.94	2.87	2.61	2.63	3.00	1.96	1.79	0.60	1.03	1.52	2.08	2.29	2.42	2.04	Grèce
0.13	1.65	1.56	1.44	1.24	1.20	1.20	0.98	1.01	0.86	0.96	1.33	1.22	1.17	1.03	.98	Irlande
2.10	27.49	30.88	27.25	24.66	23.29	23.92	17.43	17.05	11.73	14.65	18.82	17.08	15.96	13.74	13.64	Italie
1.46	18.50	17.53	16.28	15.42	14.84	14.54	9.01	10.27	9.33	10.85	13.22	11.98	11.56	11.11	10.66	Pays-Bas
0.15	2.25	2.40	2.55	2.22	2.29	1.99	1.44	1.56	1.46	2.01	2.73	2.40	2.46	2.14	2.31	Portugal
0.63	13.14	13.66	12.51	11.69	10.85	10.89	6.72	8.03	6.90	8.46	10.33	10.22	10.15	8.69	8.66	Espagne
2.27	15.96	14.39	12.97	10.73	13.87	13.55	9.39	10.05	9.01	10.21	14.02	13.39	12.35	11.39	8.99	Royaume-Uni
2.14	23.62	21.65	19.10	16.96	15.83	16.22	11.90	12.25	10.22	11.70	15.78	14.65	13.63	11.97	12.40	AELE /7
0.29	3.79	3.93	3.16	2.67	2.96	3.10	2.33	2.36	2.06	2.21	3.15	3.03	2.77	2.45	2.44	Autriche
0.30	4.55	4.37	3.67	3.46	3.11	3.23	2.35	2.68	2.00	2.42	3.17	2.90	2.67	2.30	2.70	Finlande
0.01	0.17	0.17	0.15	0.13	0.13	0.14	0.11	0.12	0.10	0.12	0.16	0.15	0.14	0.12	0.12	Islande
0.28	2.97	2.26	2.04	1.41	1.43	1.27	1.20	1.19	0.84	0.89	1.18	1.10	0.89	0.80	0.92	Norvège
0.75	8.09	7.17	6.74	6.01	5.14	5.41	3.51	3.64	3.14	3.76	4.96	4.41	4.35	3.93	3.94	Suède
0.35	4.07	3.75	3.34	3.28	3.06	3.07	2.42	2.25	2.07	2.30	3.15	3.08	2.81	2.38	2.28	Suisse
																Autres pays d'Europe
0.01	0.10	0.11	0.11	0.09	0.09	0.09	0.05	0.07	0.06	0.10	0.10	0.11	0.11	0.10	...	Malte
4.48	78.99	79.11	72.10	66.65	67.88	62.45	41.64	44.56	41.64	47.61	61.80	59.47	57.55	54.16	52.63	Autres économies développées
0.24	2.76	3.22	3.44	2.10	2.08	1.59	1.15	1.32	1.32	2.03	2.17	2.23	2.37	2.61	2.31	Australie
0.07	2.12	2.05	1.86	1.50	1.46	1.35	0.79	1.03	0.95	1.13	1.35	1.31	1.46	1.51	1.43	Israël
3.91	70.07	72.66	65.73	59.09	60.51	55.90	37.19	39.59	38.91	43.84	57.45	55.19	53.03	49.34	48.15	Japon
0.08	1.24	1.12	0.98	0.97	0.83	0.76	0.53	0.48	0.40	0.53	0.73	0.65	0.60	0.62	0.66	Nouvelle-Zélande
0.18	...	0.07	0.08	...	...	...	...	...	0.06	0.07	0.09	0.10	0.10	0.07	...	Afrique du Sud

Remarque générale

Les produits énergétiques comprennent tous les produits appartenant à la section 3 de la Classification type pour le commerce international. Ces produits sont: houilles, cokes et briquettes, pétrole, produits dérives du pétrole et produits connexes, gaz et énergie électrique. Les groupes économiques et géographiques dans ce tableau sont conformes aux groupes des pays ou zones qui paraissent dans le Tableau Spécial A de ce numéro, bien que le Tableau Spécial A comprend plus de détails en ce qui concerne les sous-groups géographiques lesquels comprennent le groupe des 'Autres économies développées' de ce tableau. En 1980, les importations des produits énergétiques de ces pays representaient approximativement 27 pourcent de leurs importations totales.

Les indices de la valeur unitaire sont obtenus de sources nationales, a l'exception de quelques pays pour lesquels la Division de Statistiques des Nations Unies calculé ces indices en utilisant les chiffres de la valeur et du volume fournis par ces pays. Pour les pays ne calculant pas leurs indices des importations des produits énergétiques selon la definition décrite ci-dessus les sous-indices sont agrégés en un indice qui se rapproche à la section 3 de la CTCI. Les indices qui sont obtenus à partir des indices nationaux sont ramenés, quand nécessaire, à l'année de base 1990 = 100. Les indices en monnaie nationale sont convertis en dollars des E.-U. en les multipliant par un facteur de conversion obtenu en divisant le taux de change courant, moyenne pondérée, d'une monnaie donnée par celui de la période de base. Tous les agrégés des indices de la valeur unitaire sont à coéfficients de pondération correspondant à la période indiquée.

Les indices du quantum sont calculés à partir des chiffres de la valeur et des indices de la valeur unitaire. Tous les agrégés des indices du quantum sont à coéfficients de pondération correspondant à la période en base.

1/ Y compris la République socialiste fédérative de Yougoslavie pour les années 1970-1979.

2/ A partir de 1989 calculés à partir des indices des prix; l'indice de la valeur unitaire nationale est discontinué.

3/ Non compris le Portugal et l'Espagne pour les années 1970-1979.

4/ Les indices sont calculés par la Division de Statistique des Nations Unies pour les années à partir de 1981.

5/ Les données relatives à la période précédant janvier 1991 correspondent aux limites territoriales de la République féderale d'Allemagne et l'ancienne République democratique allemande antérieur au 3 octobre 1990 (Voir les notes explicatives sur les données concernant l'Allemagne à la page vi).

6/ Calculés à partir de sous-indices à coéfficients de pondération correspondant à la période en cours. Les indices pour les Pays-Bas, à partir de 1988, et pour la Suisse, à partir de 1987, sont calculés par la Division de Statistique des Nations Unies.

7/ Y compris le Portugal pour les années 1970-1979.

8/ Les séries sont enchainées à 1988 par un facteur calculé par la Division de Statistique des Nations Unies.

SPECIAL TABLE: I

Some indicators on fuel imports
Developed economies

Region, country or area	1970	1980	1981	1982	1983	1984	1985	1986	1987	1988	1989	1990	1991	1992	1993	1994
Fuel imports as percent of total imports / Importations des produits énergétiques en pourcentage des importations totales																
Developed economies /1	10.0	26.2	27.4	25.7	23.5	21.6	19.9	12.2	11.2	8.7	9.5	10.7	10.0	9.2	9.2	8.0
America	7.2	28.7	27.2	23.6	19.4	16.3	13.8	9.3	10.0	8.5	10.1	12.0	10.2	9.5	8.8	7.8
Canada	5.2	12.1	12.1	10.0	6.8	6.4	6.0	4.7	4.9	3.9	4.7	6.2	4.9	4.3	4.0	3.5
United States	7.2	32.5	30.8	26.5	22.3	18.5	15.4	10.3	11.0	9.6	11.4	13.3	11.4	10.6	9.8	8.7
Europe /1	10.2	22.1	24.5	23.4	21.5	20.9	19.8	11.6	9.9	7.3	7.8	8.5	8.4	7.6	7.8	6.8
EEC /2	10.7	22.7	25.4	24.3	22.3	21.8	20.6	12.1	10.3	7.6	8.1	8.8	8.6	7.8	8.1	7.0
Belgium-Luxembourg	9.1	17.3	20.2	20.6	17.5	18.6	16.6	10.6	9.3	7.2	7.7	8.0	8.4	7.6	7.5	6.8
Denmark	10.4	22.4	24.1	22.6	19.6	18.3	17.3	8.9	7.9	6.4	7.2	7.0	5.3	6.3	5.2	4.3
France	12.0	26.6	28.8	26.8	24.6	24.2	22.4	12.7	10.8	8.2	8.8	9.6	9.7	8.6	8.9	7.7
Germany /3	8.8	22.4	24.3	23.5	21.2	20.4	19.8	11.5	9.6	7.6	7.6	8.3	8.3	7.4	7.9	7.0
Greece	6.9	23.4	22.0	28.7	27.4	27.3	29.5	17.4	13.8	5.0	6.4	7.7	9.6	9.8	10.6	9.8
Ireland	8.1	14.8	14.7	14.8	13.5	12.4	11.9	8.5	7.4	5.5	5.5	6.4	5.9	5.2	4.8	3.9
Italy	14.0	27.6	33.9	31.6	30.7	27.6	26.3	17.0	13.6	8.5	9.6	10.5	9.4	8.5	9.3	8.1
Netherlands	10.9	24.1	26.5	26.0	25.0	23.9	22.3	11.9	11.3	9.3	10.4	10.5	9.5	8.6	9.6	8.2
Portugal	9.2	24.2	24.2	26.5	26.9	28.7	24.6	15.3	11.6	8.2	10.5	10.8	9.1	8.0	8.8	8.7
Spain	13.3	38.5	42.4	39.7	40.1	37.6	36.0	18.9	16.4	11.4	11.8	11.8	11.0	10.2	10.9	9.4
United Kingdom	10.5	13.4	14.1	13.0	10.7	13.1	12.4	7.4	6.5	4.7	5.1	6.2	6.4	5.6	5.4	4.0
EFTA /4	8.5	18.5	19.4	18.1	16.7	15.4	14.9	8.7	7.3	5.5	6.0	6.9	6.8	6.2	6.1	5.5
Austria	8.3	15.5	18.7	16.1	13.8	15.1	14.9	8.6	7.2	5.6	5.7	6.3	6.0	5.1	5.0	4.4
Finland	11.5	29.1	30.8	27.4	26.9	25.0	24.4	15.3	13.5	9.6	9.8	11.7	13.3	12.9	12.8	11.5
Iceland	9.6	16.7	16.5	15.6	16.3	15.8	15.7	9.6	7.4	6.3	8.7	9.8	8.3	8.3	9.2	8.3
Norway	7.7	17.5	14.5	13.2	10.4	10.3	8.7	5.9	5.3	3.6	3.8	4.4	4.3	3.4	3.3	3.4
Sweden	10.6	24.2	24.9	24.5	23.0	19.5	18.9	10.8	9.0	6.8	7.7	9.1	8.9	8.7	9.2	7.6
Switzerland	5.4	11.2	12.2	11.7	11.3	10.3	10.0	5.9	4.5	3.7	3.9	4.5	4.6	4.3	3.9	3.4
Other Europe																
Malta	5.0	10.3	13.5	14.6	12.2	12.9	12.1	6.1	6.4	4.6	6.4	5.1	5.1	4.7	4.7	...
Other developed economies	15.1	41.0	39.3	38.6	41.4	36.0	35.2	23.3	21.3	16.0	16.3	19.4	18.5	17.9	16.3	13.7
Australia	4.9	13.9	13.7	14.5	10.9	9.2	6.9	4.7	4.9	4.0	5.1	5.4	5.5	5.5	5.9	4.5
Israel	5.0	26.5	25.6	22.9	17.4	17.3	16.3	8.2	8.7	7.3	8.5	8.8	7.8	7.7	7.4	7.0
Japan	20.7	49.9	50.7	49.8	46.8	44.3	43.1	29.4	26.5	20.8	20.8	24.5	23.3	22.8	20.5	17.5
New Zealand	6.7	22.5	19.6	16.6	18.1	13.4	12.7	8.7	6.7	5.4	6.0	7.7	7.6	6.5	6.4	5.6
South Africa	...	...	0.3	0.4	...	...	...	...	...	0.3	0.4	0.5	0.5	0.6	0.4	...
Ratio of unit value indices of manufactured goods exports and fuel imports / Quotient des indices de la valeur unitaire des exportations des produits manufacturés et des importations des produits énergétiques (1990 = 100)																
Developed economies /1	226	52	45	46	49	50	52	98	105	128	114	100	108	119	123	134
America	316	51	50	56	63	64	67	124	110	139	122	100	120	121	128	137
Canada	499	72	65	69	76	78	77	115	115	133	128	100	115	114	119	124
United States	287	48	48	54	61	63	67	126	109	139	121	100	121	124	133	143
Europe /1	204	54	43	44	46	46	47	92	103	123	109	100	104	117	117	126
EEC /2	208	54	42	44	46	46	47	92	102	122	109	100	104	118	118	127
Belgium-Luxembourg	210	60	47	44	47	45	47	88	88	104	109	100	98	110	115	121
Denmark	167	49	41	42	47	48	47	91	120	123	103	100	99	116	121	127
France	218	55	44	43	45	46	49	94	105	127	111	100	101	114	120	131
Germany /3	221	54	41	44	47	45	46	91	106	127	112	100	103	119	120	127
Greece	281	51	51	45	44	45	42	60	90	96	100	100	84	97	...	...
Ireland	...	49	51	36	40	43	55	99	97	117	111	100	101	110	118	111
Italy	228	53	37	44	47	48	47	97	103	123	108	100	109	121	112	118
Netherlands	208	51	40	46	44	45	46	94	111	124	105	100	104	115	108	128
Portugal	...	58	45	42	46	45	49	88	101	127	109	100	113	131	139	124
Spain	...	50	39	42	41	44	44	96	85	117	103	100	102	133	108	115
United Kingdom	210	60	50	47	48	48	50	84	93	112	108	100	109	116	127	138
EFTA /4	169	54	46	48	50	50	51	93	106	126	110	100	103	115	111	124
Austria	202	58	46	51	54	52	53	90	111	130	110	100	99	111	115	138
Finland	111	46	40	42	45	47	49	80	93	113	106	100	99	101	98	107
Iceland	164	51	46	42	47	58	49	75	81	106	109	100	91	87	86	94
Norway	167	60	58	58	53	55	56	89	101	138	126	100	103	108	106	101
Sweden	184	53	46	44	47	47	48	101	108	130	114	100	108	120	109	...
Switzerland	175	56	48	51	55	53	53	97	112	127	108	100	103	122	115	140
Other Europe																
Malta	...	...	...	...	...	...	...	...	...	...	...	...	...	...	...	...
Other developed economies	246	51	48	47	51	55	58	101	109	135	125	100	111	125	142	165
Australia	205	67	...	56	54	56	52	91	95	136	126	100	104	111	110	121
Israel	...	50	47	51	54	52	54	105	91	127	112	100	123	127	146	148
Japan	255	50	48	47	51	54	56	101	111	135	126	100	111	126	144	169
New Zealand	173	57	48	48	52	57	56	84	102	147	129	100	100	102	106	127
South Africa	...	...	...	...	...	...	...	...	...	...	...	...	...	...	...	...

TABLEAU SPECIAL: I

Quelques indicateurs sur les importations des produits énergétiques
Pays à économies développées

Fuel imports as percent of total exports
Importations des produits énergétiques en pourcentage des exportations totales

1970	1980	1981	1982	1983	1984	1985	1986	1987	1988	1989	1990	1991	1992	1993	1994	Région, pays ou zone
10.5	29.4	29.6	27.5	24.8	23.5	21.7	13.0	11.9	9.1	10.1	11.4	10.5	9.5	9.2	8.0	**Economies développées** /1
6.5	31.8	30.9	26.5	23.8	22.7	20.5	14.9	15.0	11.1	13.2	15.2	12.1	11.4	11.0	10.1	Amérique
4.6	11.9	11.4	8.0	5.7	5.5	5.3	4.4	4.5	3.7	4.6	5.7	4.5	4.0	3.6	3.1	Canada
7.2	38.0	36.8	32.6	30.7	29.8	27.0	19.3	19.1	13.7	16.1	18.4	14.5	13.8	13.5	12.5	Etats-Unis
11.2	24.9	26.5	25.1	22.5	21.7	20.4	11.5	10.0	7.5	8.1	8.9	8.8	7.9	7.6	6.5	Europe /1
11.1	25.5	27.5	26.1	23.4	22.8	21.2	12.0	10.4	7.8	8.4	9.2	9.1	8.1	7.9	6.7	CEE /2
8.9	19.2	22.6	22.8	18.3	19.9	17.4	10.6	9.3	7.4	7.5	8.1	8.6	7.7	6.9	6.3	Belgique-Luxembourg
13.7	26.4	26.9	25.4	20.4	19.5	18.9	9.9	8.1	6.0	6.9	6.3	4.7	5.3	4.3	3.7	Danemark
12.8	32.2	34.3	33.4	28.4	26.9	24.7	13.6	11.9	9.0	9.8	10.6	10.5	8.9	8.7	7.5	France
7.7	21.8	22.7	20.7	19.2	18.2	17.1	9.0	7.5	5.9	6.0	7.2	8.1	7.1	7.1	6.2	Allemagne /3
20.9	48.0	45.5	66.9	59.1	54.0	66.1	34.7	27.6	11.7	14.0	18.9	24.0	23.3	27.5	22.3	Grèce
12.2	19.5	20.0	17.8	14.4	12.5	11.5	7.8	6.3	4.6	4.6	5.6	5.0	4.1	3.6	3.3	Irlande
15.9	35.4	41.0	37.1	33.9	31.7	30.3	17.8	14.6	9.2	10.4	11.2	10.1	8.9	8.2	7.2	Italie
12.4	25.0	25.5	24.5	23.5	22.5	21.3	11.2	11.1	9.0	10.1	10.1	9.0	8.3	8.5	7.3	Pays-Bas
15.3	48.6	57.5	61.1	48.3	43.9	35.1	20.1	17.1	13.3	15.7	16.7	14.7	13.2	13.9	13.2	Portugal
26.3	63.0	67.1	61.7	59.1	46.5	44.8	24.6	23.5	17.1	19.0	18.6	17.0	15.8	14.3	11.9	Espagne
11.7	13.9	14.0	13.4	11.7	14.7	13.4	8.8	7.7	6.2	6.7	7.6	7.2	6.5	6.6	4.5	Royaume-Uni
10.4	21.2	20.7	19.1	17.0	15.2	15.0	8.9	7.7	5.8	6.2	7.0	6.8	6.0	5.7	5.2	AELE 4/
10.3	21.6	24.8	20.1	17.3	18.8	18.1	10.3	8.7	6.6	6.8	7.5	7.4	6.2	6.1	5.4	Autriche
13.1	32.2	31.2	28.0	27.6	23.0	23.7	14.4	13.3	9.2	10.4	11.9	12.5	11.4	9.8	9.1	Finlande
6.5	18.0	18.8	21.4	17.7	17.9	17.5	9.8	8.5	7.0	8.7	10.3	9.2	9.2	8.9	7.5	Islande
11.6	16.0	12.6	11.6	7.8	7.5	6.8	6.6	5.6	3.8	3.3	3.5	3.2	2.5	2.5	2.7	Norvège
11.0	26.2	25.1	25.2	21.9	17.5	17.8	9.4	8.2	6.3	7.3	8.6	8.0	7.8	7.9	6.4	Suède
6.8	13.7	13.9	12.8	12.8	11.8	11.2	6.4	5.0	4.1	4.5	4.9	5.0	4.3	3.8	3.2	Suisse
																Autres pays d'Europe
27.6	22.3	28.8	31.4	27.0	25.6	22.5	11.6	12.0	8.6	11.3	9.7	9.3	7.8	8.2	...	Malte
16.0	45.7	38.5	39.8	34.1	30.7	27.6	15.9	15.8	12.4	13.5	16.7	14.9	13.5	12.0	10.6	Autres economies développées
5.3	12.9	14.9	16.2	10.8	9.2	7.2	5.3	5.2	4.2	5.7	5.6	5.5	5.7	6.4	5.1	Australie
9.7	38.3	36.2	35.2	29.3	25.1	21.6	11.0	12.2	9.8	10.5	11.2	11.1	11.1	10.2	8.4	Israël
20.2	54.0	47.8	47.3	40.2	35.6	31.8	17.8	17.3	14.7	15.9	20.0	17.5	15.6	13.7	12.2	Japon
7.0	23.6	20.9	18.8	18.6	15.5	13.7	9.3	7.0	4.6	6.1	8.0	6.9	6.4	6.1	5.6	Nouvelle-Zélande
...	...	0.3	0.4	...	...	...	...	...	0.3	0.3	0.4	0.4	0.5	0.3	...	Afrique du Sud

General note

The figures in this table are calculated from those prepared for Special Tables G and H. Total imports and exports used in the calculations are, in general, those published in the United Nations 'Commodity Trade Statistics', Series D.

1/ Includes the Federal Socialist Republic of Yugoslavia for the years 1970-1979.

2/ Excludes Portugal and Spain for the years 1970-1979.

3/ Data prior to January 1991 pertain to the territorial boundaries of the Federal Republic of Germany and the former German Democratic Republic prior to 3 October 1990 (See explanatory notes on data pertaning to Germany on page vi).

4/ Includes Portugal for the years 1970-1979.

Remarque générale

Les chiffres dans ce tableau sont calculés selon les données preparées pour les tableaux spéciaux G et H. Les totales des importations et exportations utilisées dans les calculs sont, en générale, celles publiées dans les documents des Nations Unies intitulés 'Commodity Trade Statistics', Series D.

1/ Y compris la République socialiste fédérative de Yougoslavie pour les années 1970-1979.

2/ Non compris le Portugal et l'Espagne pour les années 1970-1979.

3/ Les données relatives à la période précédant janvier 1991 correspondent aux limites territoriales de la République féderale d'Allemagne et l'ancienne République democratique allemande antérieur au 3 octobre 1990 (Voir les notes explicatives sur les données concernant l'Allemagne à la page vi).

4/ Y compris le Portugal pour les années 1970-1979.

Special Table: J

Export Price Index of Machinery and Transport Equipment for Selected Countries
Indices des Prix des Exportations de Machines et Materiel de Transport pour Certains Pays
1990=100

	1980	1985	1991	1992	1993	1994	
MACHINERY AND TRANSPORT EQUIPMENT	**68**	**67**	**103**	**109**	**110**	**114**	**MACHINES ET MATERIEL DE TRANSPORT**
GERMANY (FED. REP.)	65	49	101	110	106	109	ALLEMAGNE (REP. FED.)
JAPAN	70	71	106	112	119	126	JAPON
SWEDEN	74	57	101	110	88	91	SUEDE
UNITED STATES	66	86	104	106	109	110	ETATS-UNIS
MACHINERY, OTHER THAN ELECTRIC	**68**	**65**	**104**	**111**	**112**	**117**	**MACHINES A L'EXCEPT.DES MACH.ELECTRIQUE**
GERMANY (FED. REP.)	63	47	101	111	107	111	ALLEMAGNE (REP. FED.)
JAPAN	68	66	107	114	126	136	JAPON
SWEDEN	73	54	102	110	87	91	SUEDE
UNITED STATES	71	86	104	107	109	111	ETATS-UNIS
POWER GENERATING MACHINERY, OTHER THAN ELECTRIC	**63**	**69**	**105**	**111**	**115**	**120**	**MACHINES GENERATRICES A L'EXCEPTION DES MACHINES ELECTRIQUES**
GERMANY (FED. REP.)	63	49	100	109	106	111	ALLEMAGNE (REP. FED.)
JAPAN	61	62	109	116	131	141	JAPON
UNITED STATES	63	86	105	109	111	113	ETATS-UNIS
AGRICULTURAL MACHINERY AND IMPLEMENTS	**67**	**67**	**101**	**107**	**107**	**111**	**MACHINES ET APPAREILS AGRICOLES**
GERMANY (FED. REP.)	67	50	100	109	106	111	ALLEMAGNE (REP. FED.)
JAPAN	61	62	101	105	113	118	JAPON
UNITED STATES	69	88	102	105	108	109	ETATS-UNIS
METAL WORKING MACHINERY	**61**	**60**	**102**	**110**	**114**	**119**	**MACHINES POUR LE TRAVAIL DES METAUX**
GERMANY (FED. REP.)	60	46	102	112	109	111	ALLEMAGNE (REP. FED.)
JAPAN	61	69	101	107	122	132	JAPON
UNITED STATES	65	83	106	109	111	111	ETATS-UNIS
TEXTILE AND LEATHER MACHINERY	**65**	**60**	**104**	**111**	**115**	**121**	**MACH.POUR L'INDUSTRIE TEXTILE ET LA PREP. ET LE TRAVAIL DES CUIRS ET PEAUX**
GERMANY (FED. REP.)	64	49	100	108	104	107	ALLEMAGNE (REP. FED.)
JAPAN	66	71	109	116	134	146	JAPON
UNITED STATES	69	81	101	104	105	106	ETATS-UNIS
MACHINES FOR SPECIAL INDUSTRIES	**68**	**68**	**104**	**111**	**114**	**119**	**MACHINES POUR INDUSTRIES SPECIALISEES**
GERMANY (FED. REP.)	65	48	102	113	109	112	ALLEMAGNE (REP. FED.)
JAPAN	70	77	109	117	136	147	JAPON
UNITED STATES	69	87	103	104	107	109	ETATS-UNIS
MACHINERY AND APPLIANCES(OTHER THAN ELECTRICAL)AND MACHINE PARTS,N.E.S.	**65**	**62**	**103**	**111**	**112**	**117**	**MACH.ET APPAR.(A L'EXCEPTION DE L'APPAR ELECT.) ET PIECES DET. POUR MACH. NDA**
GERMANY (FED. REP.)	64	47	101	111	108	111	ALLEMAGNE (REP. FED.)
JAPAN	63	64	105	113	123	132	JAPON
UNITED STATES	66	85	104	107	110	111	ETATS-UNIS
ELECTRICAL MACHINERY, APPARATUS AND APPLIANCES	**78**	**74**	**102**	**106**	**104**	**107**	**MACHINES ET APPAREILS ELECTRIQUES**
GERMANY (FED. REP.)	68	49	101	110	106	109	ALLEMAGNE (REP. FED.)
JAPAN	89	80	102	104	106	110	JAPON
SWEDEN	85	63	97	99	77	79	SUEDE
UNITED STATES	77	90	103	105	104	104	ETATS-UNIS
ELECTRIC POWER MACHINERY AND SWITCHGEAR	**72**	**69**	**102**	**107**	**108**	**110**	**MACH.ELECT.GENERATRICES ET APPAR.POUR LA COUPURE OU LA CON.DES CIRCUITS ELEC.**
GERMANY (FED. REP.)	68	49	101	110	106	109	ALLEMAGNE (REP. FED.)
JAPAN	86	79	103	106	114	117	JAPON
UNITED STATES	69	84	102	103	103	104	ETATS-UNIS
TELECOMMUNICATIONS APPARATUS	**89**	**76**	**104**	**108**	**106**	**109**	**APPAREILS DE TELECOMMUNICATION**
GERMANY (FED. REP.)	95	61	97	103	95	97	ALLEMAGNE (REP. FED.)
JAPAN	91	78	107	111	114	120	JAPON
SWEDEN	94	70	92	92	72	73	SUEDE
UNITED STATES	75	86	107	108	109	107	ETATS-UNIS

FOR GENERAL NOTE SEE END OF TABLE

VOIR LA REMARQUE GENERALE A LA FIN DU TABLEAU

Export Price Index of Machinery and Transport Equipment for Selected Countries(Continued)
Indices des Prix des Exportations de Machines et Materiel de Transport pour Certains Pays(Suite)
1990=100

	1980	1985	1991	1992	1993	1994	
DOMESTIC ELECTRICAL EQUIPMENT	78	65	102	108	107	109	**APPAREILS ELECTRIQUES A USAGE DOMEST.**
GERMANY (FED. REP.)	72	50	100	108	103	104	ALLEMAGNE (REP. FED.)
JAPAN	95	82	106	111	123	123	JAPON
UNITED STATES	71	87	103	105	107	107	ETATS-UNIS
OTHER ELECTRICAL MACHINERY & APPARATUS	82	80	100	103	100	101	**AUTRES MACHINES ET APPAREILS ELECTRIQUE**
GERMANY (FED. REP.)	73	55	101	109	103	105	ALLEMAGNE (REP. FED.)
JAPAN	98	83	98	98	95	99	JAPON
UNITED STATES	81	94	102	104	103	102	ETATS-UNIS
TRANSPORT EQUIPMENT	63	65	103	110	112	116	**MATERIEL DE TRANSPORT**
GERMANY (FED. REP.)	67	50	100	109	104	108	ALLEMAGNE (REP. FED.)
JAPAN	65	68	107	115	123	130	JAPON
SWEDEN	69	58	103	117	96	98	SUEDE
UNITED STATES	56	83	104	106	112	114	ETATS-UNIS
ROAD MOTOR VEHICLES	66	65	102	109	109	115	**VEHICULES AUTOMOBILES ROUTIERS**
GERMANY (FED. REP.)	70	53	99	106	102	106	ALLEMAGNE (REP. FED.)
JAPAN	61	67	105	112	120	131	JAPON
SWEDEN	69	58	103	115	95	96	SUEDE
UNITED STATES	69	90	103	104	105	107	ETATS-UNIS

GENERAL NOTE. THESE INDEXES ARE OF THE LASPEYRES TYPE (BASE WEIGHTED) SHIFTED WHEN NECESSARY SO THAT 1990=100. THEY ARE CONVERTED FROM NATIONAL CURRENCIES INTO U.S. DOLLARS USING CONVERSION FACTORS OBTAINED BY DIVIDING THE CURRENT EXCHANGE RATE OF A GIVEN CURRENCY BY ITS EXCHANGE RATE IN THE BASE PERIOD.
THE TOTALS SHOWN FOR EACH HEADING ARE THE WEIGHTED AVERAGES OF THE INDEXES FOR THE COUNTRIES LISTED WITHIN EACH SPECIFIC HEADING; WEIGHTS BEING THE EXPORTS IN 1990. THE EXPORTS OF THE SELECTED COUNTRIES REPRESENTED IN 1990 BETWEEN 50 AND 60 PERCENT OF THE TOTAL EXPORTS OF ALL HEADINGS SHOWN.
THESE INDEXES, BEING EXPRESSED IN TERMS OF U.S. DOLLARS REFLECT NOT ONLY CHANGES IN PRICES BUT ALSO CHANGES IN THE PARITY BETWEEN NATIONAL CURRENCIES AND THE DOLLAR. THE CATEGORIES OF GOODS ENCOMPASS A BROAD VARIETY OF PRODUCTS; HENCE DIFFERENT TRENDS IN COUNTRY INDEXES OCCUR WITHIN THE SAME HEADING. FOR EXAMPLE, SINCE JAPAN'S EXPORTS OF TRANSPORT EQUIPMENT INCLUDE LARGE VALUES FOR SHIPS. THE TREND OF JAPAN'S INDEX FOR THIS PARTICULAR CATEGORY DEPENDS TO A MUCH GREATER EXTENT UPON THE PRICE OF THESE PRODUCTS AS COMPARED TO OTHER COUNTRIES.

REMARQUE GENERALE. LES INDICES SONT DE TYPE LASPEYRES, LA PERIODE DE BASE ETANT RAMENEE SI NECESSAIRE A L'ANNEE 1990. ILS SONT EXPRIMES EN DOLLARS DES ETATS-UNIS A L'AIDE D'UN FACTEUR DE CONVERSION OBTENU EN DIVISANT POUR UNE MONNAIE DONNEE LE TAUX DE CHANGE DE LA PERIODE COURANTE PAR CELUI DE LA PERIODE DE BASE.
LE TOTAL INDIQUE POUR CHACUNE DES CATEGORIES DE PRODUITS REPRESENTE LA MOYENNE PONDEREE DES INDICES NATIONAUX; LES PONDERATIONS SE RAPPORTANT AUX EXPORTATIONS DE 1990. LES EXPORTATIONS DONT LES INDICES SONT PUBLIES CI-DESSUS ONT REPRESENTE EN 1990 ENTRE 50 ET 60 POUR CENT DES EXPORTATIONS MONDIALES DES DIFFERENTES CATEGORIES DE BIENS D'EQUIPEMENT.
CES INDICES,ETANT EXPRIMES EN DOLLARS,REFLETENT NON SEULEMENT DES MODIFICATIONS DANS LES PRIX MAIS AUSSI LES VARIATIONS DES TAUX DE CHANGE ENTRE LES MONNAIES NATIONALES ET LE DOLLAR. LES CATEGORIES DE BIENS DONT LES INDICES SONT PUBLIES CI-DESSUS INCLUENT UNE GRANDE VARIETE DE PRODUITS CE QUI PEUT SE TRADUIRE, POUR UN MEME TITRE, PAR UNE EVOLUTION DIFFERENTE DES INDICES NATIONAUX. PAR EXEMPLE, LES EXPORTATIONS JAPONAISES DE MATERIEL DE TRANSPORT DEPENDENT LARGEMENT DES EXPORTATIONS DE NAVIRES DONT LA TENDANCE DES PRIX A L'EXPORTATIONS PEUT DIFFERER DE L'EVOLUTION DES PRIX DES AUTRES MATERIELS DE TRANSPORT.

TABLEAU SPECIAL:K

Export price index numbers of primary commodities and non-ferrous base metals
Indices des prix des exportations des matières premières et des métaux non-férreux

1980 = 100

Items	1985	1987	1988	1989	1990	1991	1992	1993	1994	Elements
Primary commodities										Matières premières
Total	85	66	70	72	79	69	68	62	63	Totaux
Developed Economies /1	80	79	90	92	97	92	92	84	86	Economies Développées /1
Developing Economies /1	87	59	61	63	70	59	57	52	52	Economies en Voie de Dév. /1
Food										Produits alimentaires
Total	66	75	87	87	88	85	87	82	87	Totaux
Developed Economies /1	68	79	93	94	98	96	99	90	90	Economies Développées /1
Developing Economies /1	63	66	75	72	69	64	62	64	79	Economies en Voie de Dév. /1
Meat	68	93	101	100	110	106	105	105	106	Viande
Beef	69	99	112	108	115	113	105	102	98	Boeuf
Mutton	63	79	87	86	94	85	91	97	101	Mouton
Pork	68	86	89	97	108	103	106	122	134	Porc
Poultry	66	91	92	87	109	103	109	102	107	Volaille
Bacon	64	79	83	93	105	96	107	91	81	Bacon
Dairy products	73	100	106	101	110	105	110	103	99	Produits laitiers
Milk	88	102	109	104	114	103	107	96	86	Lait
Butter	66	93	100	100	103	103	108	99	101	Beurre
Cheese	65	107	113	103	115	112	123	120	119	Fromage
Eggs	65	88	78	84	97	96	87	84	77	Oeufs
Cereals	70	60	83	89	84	86	92	79	79	Céréales
Wheat	81	65	86	101	82	72	83	81	83	Blé
Rice	66	60	82	81	74	79	75	72	90	Riz
Barley	69	58	75	82	80	71	63	57	55	Orge
Maize	57	54	80	78	92	113	117	85	75	Maïs
Oats	78	56	97	100	76	70	87	80	68	Avoine
Vegetables	61	96	102	95	112	102	108	104	99	Légumes
Potatoes	60	115	112	99	129	120	154	108	73	Pommes de terre
Cassava	52	83	74	63	78	81	83	86	84	Manioc
Beans	69	59	82	117	117	64	66	87	106	Haricots secs
Peas	87	114	154	137	153	156	161	139	137	Pois secs
Tomatoes	54	117	119	92	107	111	98	118	114	Tomates
Onions	45	78	61	68	90	74	84	78	86	Oignons
Beverage crops	85	70	72	62	55	51	47	56	88	Stimulants
Coffee	81	64	67	56	46	42	33	38	81	Café
Cocoa	86	75	67	51	49	44	43	43	53	Cacao
Tea	112	100	112	122	127	128	150	200	206	Thé
Fruits	84	105	112	122	131	142	140	117	126	Fruits
Citrus fruits	83	98	100	100	118	114	110	103	116	Agrumes
Oranges	84	102	103	103	122	114	109	100	115	Oranges
Lemons	78	88	91	92	108	106	102	111	131	Citrons
Grapefruit	81	83	93	88	108	130	123	111	94	Pamplemousses
Other fruits	85	112	125	145	144	170	172	131	137	Autres fruits
Bananas	98	105	130	181	150	147	126	128	115	Bananes
Apples	71	119	121	108	139	194	218	134	159	Pommes
Animal feed	63	85	113	102	87	89	90	88	83	Alimentation animale
Oilseed cake	65	87	114	107	87	88	88	92	85	Tourteaux
Fishmeal	56	76	108	84	88	95	96	73	74	Farine de poisson
Pepper	201	278	208	147	102	77	60	75	113	Poivre
Fish	77	113	119	107	117	122	125	118	119	Poissons
Sugar	15	25	37	46	45	33	33	37	43	Sucre
Wine	78	105	113	124	155	137	134	102	99	Vin
Agricultural non-food										Prod. agr. non-alimentaires
Total	74	86	100	98	100	93	91	84	95	Totaux
Developed Economies /1	75	89	105	105	106	98	94	87	96	Economies Développées /1
Developing Economies /1	73	82	93	88	89	85	85	79	93	Economies en Voie de Dév. /1
Oilseeds, oils and fats	84	69	91	83	78	77	78	81	90	Oléagineux
Groundnuts	70	109	105	103	102	99	97	97	97	Arachides
Soyabeans	76	71	100	89	81	79	78	84	83	Fèves de soya
Linseeds	84	53	93	106	101	62	64	68	70	Graines de lin
Copra	85	69	88	77	51	64	84	66	93	Coprah
Soyabean oil	100	59	83	75	80	78	74	84	107	Huile de soya
Cottonseed oil	115	94	108	107	123	111	112	123	145	Huile de coton
Groundnut oil	107	59	69	91	113	105	72	87	120	Huile d' arachide
Olive oil	79	101	108	108	115	110	106	90	88	Huile d' olive
Palm oil	86	59	75	60	49	58	67	65	90	Huile de palme
Coconut oil	103	63	81	74	48	62	82	64	87	Huile de coprah
Palmkernel oil	82	63	79	69	49	62	84	65	92	Huile de palmiste
Linseed oil	110	69	123	166	169	104	92	90	106	Huile de lin
Sunflower oil	97	57	76	76	77	76	72	86	101	Huile de tournesol
Animal fats	58	59	73	61	64	67	69	67	76	Graisses animales

For general note and footnotes see end of table.

Voir la remarque générale et les notes à la fin du tableau.

Export price index numbers of primary commodities and non-ferrous base metals(continued)
Indices des prix des exportations des matières premières et des métaux non-férreux(suite)

1980 = 100

Items	1985	1987	1988	1989	1990	1991	1992	1993	1994	Elements
Agricultural non-food(continued)										Prod. agr. non-alimentaires(suite)
Forest products	66	94	103	105	114	105	104	91	97	Produits forestiers
Lumber	62	88	100	103	113	106	104	90	95	Bois
Woodpulp	70	91	103	110	113	104	100	86	93	Pâte a papier
Logs	67	107	110	102	116	105	112	101	105	Grumes
Textile fibres	71	81	95	95	95	84	69	63	81	Fibres textiles
Wool	60	82	123	106	95	77	68	57	78	Laine
Cotton	75	79	77	88	93	88	68	65	82	Coton
Jute	140	97	100	101	113	95	80	74	96	Jute
Flax	99	108	116	102	124	92	76	80	110	Lin
Sisal	74	73	75	85	89	84	64	78	85	Sisal
Tobacco	129	110	115	122	125	131	132	128	131	Tabac
Hides and skins	121	174	209	213	192	150	145	156	173	Cuirs et peaux
Natural rubber	53	69	83	66	60	57	60	59	81	Caoutchouc naturel
Minerals										Minéraux
Total	93	59	59	62	71	59	57	51	49	Totaux
Developed Economies /1	106	70	70	74	85	79	76	70	69	Economies Développées /1
Developing Economies /1	92	57	57	59	69	56	54	48	45	Economies en Voie de Dév. /1
Iron ore	84	82	86	98	124	129	127	122	120	Minerai de fer
Chrome ore	93	93	132	189	144	120	108	99	99	Minerai de chrome
Manganese ore	85	78	101	175	243	245	231	164	130	Minerai de manganèse
Fuels	94	58	58	60	70	57	55	49	47	Combustibles
Coal	82	87	90	95	108	103	104	95	97	Charbon
Crude petroleum	91	56	56	59	68	55	53	47	44	Pétrole brut
Natural gas	170	75	68	72	77	83	70	70	67	Gaz naturel
Crude fertilizers	65	60	69	79	78	82	83	73	73	Engrais bruts
Non-ferrous base metals										Métaux non-férreux
Total	71	87	130	124	112	94	89	76	92	Totaux
Developed Economies /1	71	90	137	127	116	98	92	79	96	Economies Développées /1
Developing Economies /1	69	78	114	114	101	86	82	70	84	Economies en Voie de Dév. /1
Copper	64	81	119	131	123	107	104	87	106	Cuivre
Nickel	108	138	284	258	191	173	128	97	117	Nickel
Aluminum	72	93	133	100	93	74	72	66	86	Aluminium
Lead	43	66	73	75	90	62	61	47	61	Plomb
Zinc	94	108	161	216	206	176	183	154	153	Zinc
Tin	68	47	52	61	42	33	36	31	33	Etain
Primary commods excl. crude petroleum										Mat. premières non-compris le pét. brut
Total	77	79	90	90	94	90	89	84	90	Totaux
Developed Economies /1	78	82	94	96	100	97	97	89	91	Economies Développées /1
Developing Economies /1	72	73	81	79	79	76	74	72	85	Economies en Voie de Dév. /1
Minerals excl. crude petroleum										Minéraux non-compris le pét. brut
Total	117	80	80	87	99	101	95	90	89	Totaux
Developed Economies /1	118	81	81	87	98	99	94	89	88	Economies Développées /1
Developing Economies /1	116	76	78	89	102	107	101	94	92	Economies en Voie de Dév. /1

General note

The indexes for primary commodities and non-ferrous base metals and their sub-indexes are weighted averages of price indexes of individual commodities, each of which is based on specific price quotations for representative grades of that commodity in countries that are major traders of the commodity. The weights are determined by the patterns of primary commodities exports in the base year 1980. All indexes are calculated in terms of United States dollars. The indexes are computed using various categories of prices such as export prices f.o.b., import prices c.i.f., wholesale prices, commodity exchange prices, producer's prices and auction prices. For more details and comparable historical series see the United Nations' "Methods Used in Compiling the United Nations Price Indexes for External Trade", Volume 1, Statistical Papers Series M No. 82.

This table does not cover trade of countries of Eastern Europe and the former USSR.

1/ This classification is intended for statistical convenience and does not necessarily express a judgement about the stage reached by a particular country in the development process.

Remarque générale

Les indices des matières premières et des métaux communs non férreux ainsi que les indices de groupes et de sous-groupes représentent les moyennes pondérées des indices des prix individuels, l'indice de chaque marchandise étant fondé sur des cotations déterminées pour des variétés ou qualités représentatives de la marchandise en question dans les pays qui jouent un role important dans le commerce mondial de la dite marchandise. Les coéfficients de pondération sont déterminés par la structure des exportations de produits primaires dans l'année de référence 1980. Tous les indices sont calculés par rapport au dollars des Etats-Unis. Les indices sont calculés à partir de diverses catégories de prix: prix à l'exportation f.a.b., prix à l'importation c.a.f., prix de gros, prix pratiqués par les bourses de marchandises, prix à la production et prix des ventes aux enchères. Pour de plus amples détails et les séries historiques comparables, voir le document du Nations Unies intitulé "Méthodes Utilisées par les Nations Unis pour Etablir les Indices des Prix des Produits de Base Entrant dans le Commerce International", Tome 1, Etudes Statistiques Série M No. 82.

Ce tableau ne concerne pas le commerce des pays de l'Europe de l'Est et de l'ancienne URSS.

1/ Cette classification est utilisée pour plus de commodité dans la présentation des statistiques et n'implique pas nécessairement un jugement quant au stade de développement auquel est parvenu un pays donné.

كيفية الحصول على منشورات الأمم المتحدة

يمكن الحصول على منشورات الأمم المتحدة من المكتبات ودور التوزيع في جميع أنحاء العالم . استعلم عنها من المكتبة التي تتعامل معها أو اكتب إلى : الأمم المتحدة ، قسم البيع في نيويورك أو في جنيف .

如何购取联合国出版物

联合国出版物在全世界各地的书店和经售处均有发售。请向书店询问或写信到纽约或日内瓦的联合国销售组。

HOW TO OBTAIN UNITED NATIONS PUBLICATIONS

United Nations publications may be obtained from bookstores and distributors throughout the world. Consult your bookstore or write to: United Nations, Sales Section, New York or Geneva.

COMMENT SE PROCURER LES PUBLICATIONS DES NATIONS UNIES

Les publications des Nations Unies sont en vente dans les librairies et les agences dépositaires du monde entier. Informez-vous auprès de votre libraire ou adressez-vous à : Nations Unies, Section des ventes, New York ou Genève.

КАК ПОЛУЧИТЬ ИЗДАНИЯ ОРГАНИЗАЦИИ ОБЪЕДИНЕННЫХ НАЦИЙ

Издания Организации Объединенных Наций можно купить в книжных магазинах и агентствах во всех районах мира. Наводите справки об изданиях в вашем книжном магазине или пишите по адресу: Организация Объединенных Наций, Секция по продаже изданий, Нью-Йорк или Женева.

COMO CONSEGUIR PUBLICACIONES DE LAS NACIONES UNIDAS

Las publicaciones de las Naciones Unidas están en venta en librerías y casas distribuidoras en todas partes del mundo. Consulte a su librero o diríjase a: Naciones Unidas, Sección de Ventas, Nueva York o Ginebra.

Litho in United Nations, New York
93860—December 1995—3,650
ISBN 92-1-061164-0

United Nations publication
Sales No. E/F.96.XVII.2, vol. II
ST/ESA/STAT/SER.G/43